KT-177-951

ROGET'S THESAURUS

THE ST. MARTIN'S

ROGET'S THESAURUS

of English Words and Phrases

New Edition Completely Revised and Modernized by
Robert A. Dutch, O.B.E.

ST. MARTIN'S PRESS,
NEW YORK

First Americanized edition of
The Original Roget's Thesaurus
of English Words and Phrases
published in United States by St. Martin's Press 1965

First edition by Peter Mark Roget 1852

New and Enlarged edition by John Lewis Roget 1879

New edition Revised and Enlarged
by Samuel Romilly Roget 1936

Published throughout the world, except the United States,
by Longmans, Green and Co. Ltd.

Library of Congress Catalog Card Number: 64-23442

Manufactured in the United States of America

ISBN — 312-68845-8 — INDEXED

ISBN — 312-68880-6 — PLAIN

CONTENTS

Editor's Preface, 1962 vii

Acknowledgments xix

A Note on Peter Mark Roget xxi

Roget's Preface to the original edition xxv

Roget's Introduction to the original edition xxvii

Roget's Plan of Classification xlv

Tabular Synopsis of Categories xlvii

Instructions lxxvii

Text 1

Index 633

PREFACE

to the Revised Edition 1962

To most people who know it, *Roget's Thesaurus* suggests a collection of synonyms on a grand scale with an index, very useful if you are looking for an alternative expression or are simply at a loss for a word to fit a thought. That the popular idea largely represents Roget's practical aim is clear from his Introduction to the first edition of 1852 (reproduced here on pp. xxvii-xliii); and that this aim was not ill-directed is shown by the scores of reprints, new editions (some unauthorized), imitations and adaptations demanded by generations of users, a demand still continuing after more than a hundred years.

Roget laid his foundations well. This new edition, issued by the same publishers as ushered the first into the world, is indeed somewhat altered in appearance, with a text entirely rewritten and greatly expanded, and an index wholly recompiled, but organically identical with Roget's original. It observes the same principles and stands in the true line of descent from the successive editions brought by Peter Mark Roget himself, and by his son and grandson. For there was nothing haphazard in Roget's design. He set out to make "a collection of words . . . arranged not in alphabetical order, as they are in a Dictionary, but according to the ideas which they express." Words express ideas—the ideas we have of tangible objects as well as of abstractions. Words expressing related ideas may be grouped under general heads; these general heads may be sorted into a system, so that we have a comprehensive classification into which, theoretically, any word in the language may be fitted and related to a context. Such an arrangement imposes the collocation of synonymous expressions in categories and thus attains Roget's object: "The idea being given, to find the word or words by which that idea may be most fitly and aptly expressed."

This is the opposite of a dictionary's function, which is: "The word being given, to find its signification or the idea it is intended to convey." The two functions should not be confused. A thesaurus (in the sense it acquired after Roget used it in the title of his work) does not seek, like a dictionary, to define a word in all its meanings and in one place. Its business is with contexts, not with definitions. It discourses rather than analyzes. It starts with a meaning, not with a word, and sets the words which symbolize some aspect of that meaning in a context, rather like sentences in a book. A valid context exhibits the related aspect of the component words, throwing into relief, by a kind of mutual reflection, those elements of meaning which each individual word can contribute to the governing idea, and suppressing senses which are ambiguous, irrelevant, or incompatible. In itself, the word "lion" holds a variety of associations. When we find it in a context of cats, leopards and tigers, we realize we are dealing with *Felis leo;* in a context of fighters, heroes and knights, it suggests courage; associated with "favorite" and similar words, it presents the idea of a "catch"—a person much sought after. A thesaurus proceeds to register "lion" under the distinct heads of "animal," "courage" and "favorite," and within those heads associates it with as unambiguous a context as possible. Probably most of the complaints of occasional pointlessness in the vocabulary entries of a thesaurus arise because certain words do not appear in the right milieu to display their relevance. Certainly a reader should not have to grope for the meaning, but should be enabled, by a right context, to find immediately the application of a given word to the head under which it stands. But the vocabulary listed under a head is there, not for the purpose of defining words, but of using words to illuminate an idea—as we use them in ordinary speech. Hence the unique advantage of the thesaurus arrangement as a help to the employment of words for their natural purpose—the expression of ideas. A thesaurus is operating on the same lines as a speaker or writer in the process of composition. It images in some measure the working of his brain when, having his idea (corresponding to a thesaurus head), he mentally scans his stock of words (corresponding to the vocabulary of a thesaurus) for the right expression.

It might be objected, on the contrary, that a thesaurus *is* a dictionary, and a clumsy one at that, inasmuch as it attempts to define the meanings inherent in the words chosen as titles for particular heads. We have some hundreds of heads (or thousands, if we include the subheads with which this edition is equipped)—existence, motion, death, life, etc.—and all that the listed vocabulary does (so the argument would run) is to provide words to define those other words—existence, motion and so on—without the precision and economy of a dictionary or the convenience of an alphabetical arrangement. This objection mistakes the function of the words employed in the headings. They are not chosen for themselves but as labels for the general idca treated in the article concerned. They can be changed, so long as the idea remains intact. So far from being *defined*, it is obvious that these titles frequently hold possible meanings which have to be ignored as incommensurate with the idea which is the true definition of the head. When Roget chose "Investment" as a label for the idea of dress, he was not thinking of the investment of money. Some other word might have been selected, and in this edition the same head is labeled "Dressing." In so far as these labels are words and are to be treated as part of the vocabulary, their meaning, as is that of the other words in the list, is to be gathered from the context. Roget's distinction between dictionary and thesaurus is in fact unassailable.

It is Roget's great merit that he devised a system of categories, logically ordered, that is both workable and comprehensive. As edition followed edition, more and more words were drawn in without destroying the framework. In the course of a century of testing, modifications have been made only in matters of detail. The present editor's experience confirms that of his predecessors. Very large extensions of vocabulary have been fitted in, easily and naturally, without slurring the meaning or blunting the point of the inserted words. Details will be more appropriate when the special features of this edition are discussed. How far these categories are "philosophic" (as Roget would say), is a matter for argument. The existing classification having been found so accommodating, the prolonged research necessary for the construction of a fresh one lay outside the scope of this revision.

To construct such a system at all, with no useful guiding precedent, was no mean achievement. Perhaps Roget's happiest inspiration was to utilize methodically the correlation of positive and negative. By setting categories of synonyms and antonyms over against each other he brought into play a wealth of related contexts which otherwise might easily have been overlooked. Moreover, the opposition of two extremes suggested a place for intermediate terms, whether these were, as regards the extremes, neutral (e.g. *Beginning, Middle, End*); or the simple negative of the two opposite positions (*Desire, Indifference, Aversion*); or representing the common standard with which the two opposites are compared (*Insufficiency, Sufficiency, Redundance*). These examples, and the distinctions on which they are based, are taken from Roget's Introduction at p. xxxiv. It is not only the logical neatness which appeals, but also the value of the device as a check on the omission of valid categories of thought for which vocabulary should be supplied. Other arrangements of categories have been tried, notably, in recent years, and most impressively, by the German philologist and classical scholar Franz Dornseiff;[1] others no doubt will be tried in the future. It is difficult to imagine that they will renounce this fruitful expedient, which apparently we owe to Roget him-

[1] *Der Deutsche Wortschatz nach Sachgruppen* (Walter de Gruyter & Co., Berlin. 5th edition 1959). This work has a valuable introduction.

self. Sometimes, perhaps, too fruitful! It would be possible to generate in this way a category which was not only devoid of an exclusive vocabulary of its own (the same could be said of most categories) but which was fully represented, both in idea and verbal content, by some other differently titled category. A few such categories appear to have been noticed in Roget's scheme by successive editors, and have been left to wither away. They have been taken out of this edition.

The point is interesting in its bearing on the validity of categories—a question which goes to the root of the relationship between thought and language. Language behaves like a continuum, coextensive with the thought it symbolizes, and does not easily lend itself to partitioning into self-contained categories. John L. Roget, Peter's son and successor, observes in his preface to the 1879 edition: "Any attempt at a philosophical arrangement under categories of the words of our language must reveal the fact that it is impossible to separate and circumscribe the several groups by absolutely distinct boundary lines." The real trouble, one must suspect, is that apparently no meaning can exist in isolation but each one is an aspect of some other meaning. Probably, every single context in this new edition—it may be, every single word—could be equipped with a cross-reference. The whole network of cross-references is a necessary concession to the nature of language which thus exerts itself to restore the unity of what man, with his artificial categories, has put asunder. Practical convenience alone decides where, in this expanse of words, we erect our dikes and construct our somewhat leaky reservoirs. Since an arbitrary element cannot be excluded from our choice of heads, it would be gratifying if we had an accepted alphabet of ideas under which to list our vocabularies. If, like the Chinese, we had adopted a system of pictograms to write our language, symbolizing words by sense not by sound, we should long ago have been forced to arrange our lexicons by categories of thought, and our dictionaries would, in effect, be thesauruses. What order of words we should have chosen is an interesting speculation. Words, unfortunately, are not like numbers, or we might have found an order of verbal signs as logically compelling as the simple arithmetical series 1, 2, 3. . . . However that may be, a common alphabet of ideas, based on categories equally relevant to the habits of thought and speech of all peoples at all times, would surely show something of the anatomy of language and teach us to differentiate what is conventional in our verbal distinctions from what lies nearer bedrock. We ought to encourage all attempts to build that ultimate, multilingual thesaurus which Roget envisaged with his customary prescience. Equipped at last with a set of truly "philosophic" categories, a philologist might face the perplexing riddle of language and say "I of these will wrest an alphabet, and with still practice learn to know thy meaning."

Such explorations must be left to those more deeply versed in linguistic science. Concerning the present revision of what is purely a thesaurus in English, the following account is rendered.

The vocabulary has been enlarged by some 50,000 entries. These are not all new in the sense that none of them has previously appeared anywhere in the text. The majority are old words in new places. They are not idle repetitions. They are the furniture of new contexts; for our ideas outrun our stock of words, and to express them we must turn over our vocabulary again and again. This accretion of fresh material is fairly evenly spread, and most of the lists have undergone a notable expansion. Deletions were, by comparison, very much fewer and were intended only for the clearance of dead wood. The ax fell mainly on the numerous French and Latin expressions which have not become anglicized, and on the "phrases" (the separate subdivision for which has been suppressed) where these were merely quotations or proverbs and could not with any benefit be transplanted to some other subdivision of the head. Archaisms have not been cleared away wholesale. There are multifarious reasons for consulting a thesaurus, and Samuel Roget observed, in his preface to the 1933 edition, that archaic and even obsolete words may be sought by authors. Of some it may be said that though dead they will not lie down. The time for them to go is when they are not only dead, but buried. No resurrections, however, have been attempted by way of importing extinct material.

The sources of new vocabulary were sought only to a limited extent in printed word-lists in any shape or form, though at the beginning of the revision standard dictionaries were combed through. Abundant inspiration was found in the living word, spoken or written. Sometimes, no interlocutor was necessary. You talked to yourself, and overheard your own idioms. The colloquial idiom was as welcome as the literary, without any censorship of the "speech level," for living usage was the constant criterion. The prolific vitality of American speech furnished many inspirations. It seemed quite unnecessary to mark or isolate these by way of editorial comment. Usage on both sides of the Atlantic shows at the present day a tendency to coalesce and it is no part of the function of this work to supply certificates of origin for what is all equally native. Outright slang, with its transient and shifting vocabulary, so frequently an esoteric jargon, is not specifically drawn on; but many of its terms gain currency in the colloquial idiom, and then, if apt, are welcome. Technical expressions, of which nowadays the general public is increasingly conscious, play their part in non-specialist writings, and it was from this source, on the whole, that technical terms were introduced, as embellishments of an educated vocabulary. It was felt to be less requisite to compile detailed lists of specialized and recondite terms which experts seldom use except for mutual communication and for which interested persons would hardly consult a thesaurus. Space is limited and had to be reserved for more generally useful words. In general the aim has been to provide a full and comprehensive vocabulary, employing words met with at all levels of speech, with no conscious bias towards either literary or colloquial style. In fact, the vocabulary here presented is not only far ampler, but is also fresher and more modern and contemporary than in previous editions. Absolute completeness is unattainable, but the cooperation of readers will be welcome towards remedying what is lacking, so that omissions can be repaired when opportunity arises.

Peter Roget digested his vocabulary under exactly 1000 heads. Later, he himself or subsequent editors inserted others. That they are here reduced to 990 does not imply any significant revaluation of the original scheme, which is as serviceable as ever. The reduction is due to a few heads having been left with only a token vocabulary, or none at all: these have been deleted. More frequently heads expressing the idea of the *agent* have in this edition been transferred to the related general head, except where the idea of agent is of primary importance or has a large vocabulary of its own. This adjustment helps to preserve a parity among the heads as a whole by suppressing some that were essentially subsidiary, and by leaving the heads more uniformly equipped with the full complement of nouns, adjectives and verbs. Occasionally, a single head has been split into two. Those interested in such changes should consult the scheme of classification on pp. vl-iiiil, where they are tabulated.

A modified order of printing has somewhat altered the appearance of the text. In previous editions, the parallel arrangement of contrasted heads in opposite columns was a conspicuous feature, and to many readers doubtless a helpful one. It was, however, liable to involve a somewhat confusing layout of the printed page when, as usually happened, the opposing lists were of unequal length, and when the succession of contrasted heads was interrupted by a correlative head which, having no opposite, was printed the whole width of the page. Moreover, much valuable space was sacrificed in maintaining this pattern. In the present edition, an arrangement in straightforward double column is adopted, numbered sections following in serial order. The contrasted heads are still in juxtaposition and the rearrangement serves the convenience of the user. There is even a gain in logical propriety by according a uniform treatment to all forms of correlation, of which the antithesis of positive and negative is but a special case. The text is no longer divided into chapters corresponding to the major division of Roget's scheme of classification. The numbered sections follow on without interruption.

A conspicuous change will be noticed in the paragraphing of the heads. It was found that with the help of keywords, printed in italics, the vocabulary, within the subdivisions by parts of speech, could be broken up into compact and homogeneous groups to make subheads. This arrangement offers distinct advantages. The keyword, being chosen to denote the tone and general coverage of the subhead, introduces a further element of formal classification. This becomes very useful when the mass of words presented is only very broadly covered by the main heading, and the individual contexts diverge from one another widely in meaning. The subhead, labeled by its keyword, narrows the field of search and within closer limits the inquirer knows what to expect. The same keyword is used in all cross-references and in the index references—occasions when unambiguous information is requisite. With its italic type and prominent position in the text it at once catches the eye. Its part in the referencing apparatus is explained in the Instructions, at p. lxxvii. It is believed that this feature of the revision will justify itself in greater directness, speed and facility of consultation.

Within the subheads, great care has been given to the ordering of vocabulary in context, and to the provision of a multiplicity of cross-references. It is for this that the whole text has been rewritten. The aim of a thesaurus is to suggest words of synonymous meaning. Granted that synonyms are never identical, some words are nevertheless closer in meaning than others. The suggestiveness of a synonymous arrangement is enhanced by bringing such words together. When they are separated by an arbitrary order—e.g. the alphabetical—or haphazardly disordered, something of their force is lost. The mind is jolted to and fro, concentration is impaired, valid connections are overlooked. Where they are knit in a relevant context and juxtaposed in a series of steps with as few gaps in meaning as possible, the mind is led by easy transitions from one nuance to another without distraction. It begins to run on rails and by its own momentum may even elicit an apt word or expression which has escaped record in that part of the text. In such instances the compiler must confess a particular inadequacy in his lists, but may raise a claim for the general effectiveness of his arrangement. Moreover, if the obvious utility of internal cross-references is conceded, the cross-reference should be placed where it is most relevant and demands a context. On such considerations, every word was weighed and its possible relationships examined before it was assigned to its niche. If on the whole the text reads easily, if the rightness of a word in its place is felt, and the suggestiveness of a context acts as a prompt and stimulus, the intended object will have been attained, despite any drawback inherent in the attempt itself. The drawback consists in that quality of words which endows them with several distinct affinities even within a narrow range of context. A context is a great aid to definition, but a definition implies a limitation. The choice of one context for a word eliminates other contexts which might prove as useful. Yet it is impossible to repeat, under the same subhead, all items of vocabulary in all their permutations and combinations of context, in the vain effort to exhaust their affinities. Even if time permitted, space would not. In this dilemma we must accept the fact that words, like atoms, have multiple affinities; they must combine in contexts, as atoms in molecules. Where the molecules are very different, they may appear under different heads. Where, though distinct, they have a family likeness and would in any case appear in the same subhead, a single representative is chosen to stand for the whole proliferating family. This also may be borne in mind. Individual words are not smothered in their context. They may be considered, whenever the reader wishes, in isolation from their neighbors.

The internal cross-references are supplied more liberally than ever before. Lest they be thought excessive, it must be stated that despite their multitude they register only a fraction of the innumerable points of contact within the interlocking network of Roget's system. In their respective places, these references focus the ample resources of the thesaurus on the particular problem in hand. One can hardly be too lavish in setting up signposts where roads are so many and it cannot be foreknown on what route the traveler is bent. In this function, the index is complementary, not a substitute. When once engaged with the text, the inquirer, if he uses the cross-references, will probably be spared the occasion of referring back to the index. Even when not followed up, the reference is not superfluous. The verbal element—the keyword—may be treated as part of the vocabulary.

The sequences of figures appearing under the heading **See**: at the foot of each numbered section are the section numbers of all references quoted in the main head. Most readers will have no occasion for them. They have been consolidated for the benefit of students of language whose theoretical inquiries into the relationships of words may be assisted by such an apparatus. The desirability of an aid of this kind has more than once been expressed.

The subdivision of heads by part of speech has been preserved. Adjectives have been transferred to follow the nouns instead of the verbs. The adverb subdivision sometimes includes expressions which could be called adverbial only by courtesy. Likewise, expressions grammatically adverbial have been admitted among the adjectives, in places where the context seemed propitious. The Phrases (as a separate subdivision) have finally succumbed to the erosion undergone in previous editions.

The Index has been carefully prepared as a necessary aid to finding the right place in the text at which to begin a search. It is by no means a complete alphabetical reference for the whole vocabulary, and it should not be inferred that a word unregistered in the Index is absent from the text. Guidance for its use will be found in the Instructions at p. lxxvii. All that need be said here is that (i) index entries were extracted from a complete set of all the words in the text, and all omissions are deliberate; (ii) every index reference is set out fully with section number, part of speech and keyword. The last particular is important. In previous editions, references were frequently given by section number only and then the inquirer was left with no clue to whether or not the word was recorded in the sense he had in mind. As now recompiled, the Index is free from this obstacle to speedy reference. The keyword—the same as used to introduce a subhead or to define an internal reference—functions similarly in the Index to label a reference and to explain the sense.

Whom does a thesaurus help? It is of prime importance in philological studies and is complementary to dictionary work. Its structure, arrangement and content hold the greatest interest for those concerned with the fundamental symbolism of language. It is an instrument by which a language, viewed as a whole, may be compared with itself at some earlier stage, and with other languages similar and disparate. More particularly, it provides an excellent means to enable workers in the field of machine translation to match the vocabularies of two or more languages. Wherever the concern is not so much with words themselves as with the things that words describe and the way in which people have regarded them, a thesaurus may be called in aid. Also, it generalizes, where a dictionary particularizes. Both a dictionary and a thesaurus take a census of the word-population. The dictionary counts and records individual particulars. It corresponds to the enumeration. A thesaurus more nearly resembles the final reports, where the population is massed in groups, first in this class, then in that, and general conclusions are drawn regarding the state of the nation. The state of the word-population is perhaps not without its relevance in social inquiries.

It is the same method of arrangement that makes a thesaurus so helpful to speakers and writers—to all persons concerned with the expression of ideas. It is the counterpart of the thesaurus we all carry in our memories in which mentally we track down a word. Surely, this characteristic is implied in those criticisms which impugn the merits of all thesauruses: that it is the lazy man's book; that it saves him the trouble of thinking. It would not do this unless it were patterned on our processes of thought and speech. But it is not only the lazy man who has the sense to avail himself of it and so to enhance his faculty of finding words for things.

In the stress of verbal composition we may use a thesaurus as legitimately as a dictionary. Much of our vocabulary is a "recognition" vocabulary. We know a word when we see it which without prompting we should fail to call to mind. We often have this experience when reading a book. Here, then, is a special kind of book in which one may renew that experience at will. It tells you where to look. You are following your line of thought until words begin to fail and thought is embarrassed for want of a verbal mold to give it shape. Then some word—probably a word previously rejected as "not quite near enough"—is turned up in the index, a choice is made from the range of connotations offered in the references under that word, the place is found in the text (the Instructions on pp. lxxvii-xxc explain how this is done), and there, or in some related place to which the internal references point, the right word or expression is met; or a helpful context suggests a better idea—as Dryden observed that the search for a rhyme might sometimes help you to a thought. It may be a problem of changing a word, or of recasting a sentence. It makes no difference, provided the word you think of to look up in the index impinges, however obliquely, on the notion you are entertaining. It might express the exact opposite of your intention. If so, you will find that opposite ideas are juxtaposed in Roget's scheme and you have only to skip to the following or preceding head; or you may stay where you are, and recast your thought in negative form. If you cannot get beyond a word of the vaguest generality—like "greatness" or "motion"—such words are found in the index as freely as the more specific. Indeed, it is the more general words which are most often chosen for the headings of the numbered sections ("Greatness" and "Motion" are examples); and the most general heads afford plenty of references to the more specific which participate in the generalized meaning. Under "Greatness" many kinds of greatness are touched upon, directly or by reference; under "Motion" many kinds of motion. For this reason, the habitual user might do well to acquaint himself with the titles of the headings. Practice will make them familiar, and he will find his facility in using the thesaurus much improved.

Thus every kind of author is served by a thesaurus: original writers struggling with a thought or simply wanting a word (it is no more heinous to forget a word and to consult a thesaurus, than to forget a meaning and look in a dictionary); translators, groping for an equivalent idiom or a corresponding metaphor; copy-writers, précis writers, paraphrasers; the solver of crosswords (it is not cheating to look up a clue in the index); the setter of crosswords—but here the danger is that the solver may be using the same edition! the orator who tells his secretary: "Give me a word, not 'majesty,' suggestive of majesty": the secretary looks up "majesty" and "majestic" in the index; the librettist who must provide a good singable vowel for his vocalist. Reporters in a hurry may consult this book with speed and facility. A more deliberate writer may use it for browsing. I have known a poet who read Roget regularly in order to induce a mood—the heads dealing with sensation and emotion are just right for this. It is good for students of English—native or foreign; in conjunction with a dictionary, it provides beneficial exercises for the enrichment of vocabulary and the distinction of meanings.

Without the capacity for making distinctions, the enrichment may prove a snare. This book does not usurp the function of a dictionary. It keeps to Peter Roget's rule that the words are assumed to be known. It furnishes no labels for "speech level"—for what is scholarly, literary or vulgar, or archaic and obsolete. The occasion and manner of use are left to the reader's tact. It is his responsibility. If he is not sure of a word he should avoid it or make a check in the appropriate work of reference. Otherwise, beware of pitfalls. There was an orator—English was not his native idiom—who on the arrival of a high official had to pronounce an address of welcome expressing the common grief at the death of the reigning monarch and the common joy at the official's condescending visit. He spoke of his two eyes—one dropping tears for the king who had "gone to the bourn from which no traveler turns up"—the other "beaming with happy simpering." "Hail," he went on, "august and up to snuff! Gramercy, gramercy! Single-hearted and monocephalous are we. . . ." It cannot be too firmly stressed that a thesaurus does not displace a dictionary. They are complementary.

R. A. DUTCH

Acknowledgments

Particular thanks are due to Heinz Norden for many detailed suggestions relative to this revision; and to Professor Norman Davis for some valuable comments. With gratitude I acknowledge indebtedness to Margaret Masterman, Director of the Cambridge Language Research Unit, who showed me unsuspected ways of thinking about a thesaurus and its problems.

R. A. D.

A NOTE ON PETER MARK ROGET
1779–1869

Peter Mark Roget was born on Broad Street, Soho, on 18 January 1779. His father, John Roget, a native of Geneva, was pastor of the French Protestant church on Threadneedle Street. His mother, Catharine, was the only surviving sister of Sir Samuel Romilly, the legal reformer whose successful efforts to humanize the English criminal law won him fame and honor. The name is recalled in that of Samuel Romilly Roget, Peter's grandson and third editor of Roget's *Thesaurus*. Descended from Genevan Calvinists on his father's side and from French Huguenots on his mother's, the author of the celebrated *Thesaurus of English Words and Phrases* probably had no English blood in his veins. His Genevan connection stood him in good stead in 1803, when, acting as traveling tutor to the sons of a rich Manchester merchant, he was overtaken in Geneva by the rupture of the Peace of Amiens. He was detained on parole, and only secured his release by pleading the Genevan citizenship of his family.

His father died when Peter was still a child. His mother, from whom he is said to have inherited his systematic habits of thinking, took charge of his education. After a few years in the private school of a Mr. Chauvet—another native of Geneva—at Kensington Square, where he rendered himself proficient in mathematics, he was entered (1793) at Edinburgh University. He took up medicine in 1795 and graduated M.D. at the age of nineteen, having survived the testing experience of an attack of typhus contracted on the wards of the Edinburgh Infirmary.

He opened his professional career with a paper on "The non-prevalence of consumption among butchers, fisherman, etc.," which was published by Dr. Beddoes in his "Essay on the Causes etc. of Pulmonary Consumption." At about the same time he began a correspondence with Davy and with Jeremy Bentham. In 1803, after his return from the continent, having passed a short spell as private physician to the Marquess of Lansdowne, he was appointed Physician to the Manchester Infirmary; and before he transferred himself to London in 1808 he had helped to found the Manchester Medical School and had become a popular lecturer on physiology in the Manchester Philosophic and Literary Society, of which he was vice-president. His migration to London initiated half a century of enormous activity in medical work, scientific research, lecturing and writing.

There is no biography of Roget, but the bare details of his *curriculum vitae* display the intellectual zest of a scholar and the practical zeal of an active social conscience. No doubt he kept himself by his medical practice; and his election, in 1831, as Fellow *speciali gratia* of the Royal College of Physicians is testimony to his professional competence; but the activities we hear of most are not of the profit-making kind. He projected the North London Dispensary and as its first Physician (1810) performed his duties gratuitously for eighteen years. In 1823 he served as Physician of the Millbank Penitentiary—during a dysentery epidemic. In 1828, at the Government's request, he prepared a report on London's water supply. He took an active part in founding the University of London, and was examiner in physiology and comparative anatomy in 1839. He remained a member of the Senate until his death. He was the first Fullerian Professor of Physiology at the Royal Institution and gave many public lectures. The same concern for the public is shown by the type of a good deal of his writing—such as his contributions to the *Encyclopaedia Britannica* (6th and 7th editions), the *Encyclopaedia Metropolitana,* Rees's *Cyclopaedia* and the *Cyclopaedia of Popular Medicine;* most conspicuously in the treatises on electricity, galvanism, magnetism and electromagnetism that he wrote for the Society for the Diffusion of Useful Knowledge, of which he was cofounder. There were articles also in the *Edinburgh Review* and the *Quarterly,* among other periodicals; and papers in the *Annals of Philosophy*. His Bridgewater treatise on *Animal and Vegetable Physiology considered with reference to Natural Theology* was a considerable work, reissued for the third time in 1862.

He was no idle member of the learned societies he supported. He became secretary and vice-president of the Medico-Chirurgical Society, to whose Transactions he contributed many specialist studies. In 1815 the invention of a slide-rule which measured the powers of numbers proved to be his passport to the Fellowship of the Royal Society. Subsequently he became secretary to that Society and for twenty-two years (1827–1849), in addition to his other secretarial duties, edited their Proceedings and prepared for publication the abstracts of the papers.

On retirement from professional practice in 1840, he was much occupied with the construction of a calculating machine, and of a very delicate balance, of which the fulcrum, to avoid friction, was set in a small barrel floating on water. He amused himself—and the readers of the *Illustrated London News*—with the setting of ingenious chess problems; and in 1845 he brought out his "Economic Chessboard," the forerunner of many pocket chessboards.

It was not till 1849, when he was in his seventy-first year, that he resumed work on what is really his greatest invention. After three or four years of incessant labor, as he tells us in his preface, he gave to the world (through the same publishers as have issued successive editions up to the present day) the celebrated *Thesaurus of English Words and Phrases, classified and arranged so as to facilitate the Expression of Ideas and assist in Literary Composition.* Nearly fifty years earlier he had compiled a proto-thesaurus for his own use (he was then teaching in the Manchester Medical School), which employed much the same system of classification. The finished work exemplifies his qualities of systematic thinking, habits of observation, patient industry and sense of the practical. These qualities, and especially the last, ensured its success. In his own lifetime 28 editions were published, and the edition of 1879, brought out by his son John Lewis Roget, embodies his final additions. *Roget's Thesaurus* has since become a familiar title, cherished in all countries to which the English language has spread.

Peter Mark Roget died, at West Malvern, in his ninety-first year, on 12 September 1869. He had married in 1824 and his wife died in 1833 leaving two children, of whom John Lewis Roget (author of *The History of the Old Water Colour Society)* edited the *Thesaurus* after his father's death and bequeathed the same responsibility to his son Samuel Romilly Roget. The edition of 1936 is Samuel Romilly's latest revision.

PREFACE

to The First Edition 1852

It is now nearly fifty years since I first projected a system of verbal classification similar to that on which the present Work is founded. Conceiving that such a compilation might help to supply my own deficiencies, I had, in the year 1805, completed a classed catalog of words on a small scale, but on the same principle, and nearly in the same form, as the Thesaurus now published. I had often during that long interval found this little collection, scanty and imperfect as it was, of much use to me in literary composition, and often contemplated its extension and improvement; but a sense of the magnitude of the task, amidst a multitude of other avocations, deterred me from the attempt. Since my retirement from the duties of Secretary of the Royal Society, however, finding myself possessed of more leisure, and believing that a repertory of which I had myself experienced the advantage might, when amplified, prove useful to others, I resolved to embark on an undertaking which, for the last three or four years, has given me incessant occupation, and has, indeed, imposed upon me an amount of labor very much greater than I had anticipated. Notwithstanding all the pains I have bestowed on its execution, I am fully aware of its numerous deficiencies and imperfections, and of its falling far short of the degree of excellence that might be attained. But, in a Work of this nature, where perfection is placed at so great a distance, I have thought it best to limit my ambition to that moderate share of merit which it may claim in its present form; trusting to the indulgence of those for whose benefit it is intended, and to the candor of critics who, while they find it easy to detect faults, can at the same time duly appreciate difficulties.

P. M. Roget

29 April, 1852

INTRODUCTION

to the original edition 1852

Notes within brackets are by the previous editors. Unbracketed footnoes followed by [*Ed.*] *are by the editor of the* 1962 *edition.*

The present Work is intended to supply, with respect to the English language, a desideratum hitherto unsupplied in any language; namely, a collection of the words it contains and of the idiomatic combinations peculiar to it, arranged, not in alphabetical order as they are in a Dictionary, but according to the *ideas* which they express. The purpose of an ordinary dictionary is simply to explain the meaning of the words; and the problem of which it professes to furnish the solution may be stated thus:—The word being given, to find its signification, or the idea it is intended to convey. The object aimed at in the present undertaking is exactly the converse of this: namely,—The idea being given, to find the word, or words, by which that idea may be most fitly and aptly expressed. For this purpose, the words and phrases of the language are here classed, not according to their sound or their orthography, but strictly according to their *signification.*

The communication of our thoughts by means of language, whether spoken or written, like every other object of mental exertion, constitutes a peculiar art, which, like other arts, cannot be acquired in any perfection but by long and continued practice. Some, indeed, there are more highly gifted than others with a facility of expression, and naturally endowed with the power of eloquence; but to none is it at all times an easy process to embody, in exact and appropriate language, the various trains of ideas that are passing through the mind, or to depict in their true colors and proportions the diversified and nicer shades of feeling which accompany them. To those who are unpracticed in the art of composition, or unused to extempore speaking, these difficulties present themselves in their most formidable aspect. However distinct may be our views, however vivid our conceptions, or however fervent our emotions, we cannot but be often conscious that the phraseology we have at our command is inadequate to do them justice. We seek in vain the words we need, and strive ineffectually to devise forms of expression which shall faithfully portray our thoughts and sentiments. The appropriate terms, notwithstanding our utmost efforts, cannot be conjured up at will. Like "spirits from the vasty deep," they come not when we call; and we are driven to the employment of a set of words and phrases either too general or too limited, too strong or too feeble, which suit not the occasion, which hit not the mark we aim at; and the result of our prolonged exertion is a style at once labored and obscure, vapid and redundant, or vitiated by the still graver faults of affectation or ambiguity.

It is to those who are thus painfully groping their way and struggling with the difficulties of composition that this Work professes to hold out a helping hand. The assistance it gives is that of furnishing on every topic a copious store of words and phrases, adapted to express all the recognizable shades and modifications of the general idea under which those words and phrases are arranged. The inquirer can readily select, out of the ample collection spread out before his eyes in the following pages, those expressions which are best suited to his purpose, and which might not have occurred to him without such assistance. In order to make this selection, he scarcely ever need engage in any critical or elaborate study of the subtle distinction existing between synonymous terms; for if the materials set before him be sufficiently abundant, an instinctive tact will rarely fail to lead him to the proper choice. Even while glancing over the columns of this Work, his eye may chance to light upon a particular term, which may save the cost of a clumsy paraphrase, or spare the labor of a tortuous circumlocution. Some felicitous turn of expression thus introduced will frequently open to the mind of the reader a whole vista of collateral ideas, which could not, without an extended and obtrusive episode, have been unfolded to his view; and often will the judicious insertion of a happy epithet, like a beam of sunshine in a landscape, illumine and adorn the subject which it touches, imparting new grace and giving life and spirit to the picture.

Every workman in the exercise of his art should be provided with proper implements. For the fabrication of complicated and curious pieces of mechanism, the artisan requires a corresponding assortment of various tools and imstruments. For giving proper effect to the fictions of the drama, the actor should have at his disposal a well-furnished wardrobe, supplying the costumes best suited to the personages he is to represent. For the perfect delineation of the beauties of nature, the painter should have within reach of his pencil every variety and combination of hues and tints. Now, the writer, as well as the orator, employs for the accomplishment of his purposes the instrumentality of words; it is in words that he clothes his thoughts; it is by means of words that he depicts his feelings. It is therefore essential to his success that he be provided with a copious vocabulary, and that he possess an entire command of all the resources and appliances of his language. To the acquisition of this power no procedure appears more directly conducive than the study of a methodized system such as that now offered to his use.

The utility of the present Work will be appreciated more especially by those who are engaged in the arduous process of translating into English a work written in another language. Simple as the operation may appear, on a superficial view, of rendering into English each of its sentences, the task of transfusing, with perfect exactness, the sense of the original, preserving at the same time the style and character of its composition, and reflecting with fidelity the mind and the spirit of the author, is a task of extreme difficulty. The cultivation of this useful department of literature was in ancient times strongly recommended both by Cicero and by Quintilian, as essential to the formation of a good writer and accomplished orator. Regarded simply as a mental exercise, the practice of translation is the best training for the attainment of that mastery of language and felicity of diction which are the sources of the highest oratory, and which are requisite for the possession of a graceful and persuasive eloquence. By rendering ourselves the faithful interpreters of the thoughts and feelings of others, we are rewarded with the acquisition of greater readiness and facility in correctly expressing our own; as he who has best learned to execute the orders of a commander becomes himself best qualified to command.

In the earliest periods of civilization, translators were the agents for propagating knowledge from nation to nation, and the value of their labors has been inestimable; but, in the present age, when so many different languages have become the depositories of the vast treasures of literature and of science which have been accumulating for centuries, the utility of accurate translations has greatly increased, and it has become a more important object to attain perfection in the art.

The use of language is not confined to its being the medium through which we communicate our ideas to one another; it fulfills a no-less-important function as an *instrument of thought;* not merely being its vehicle, but giving it wings for flight. Metaphysicians are agreed that scarcely any of our intellectual operations could be carried on to any considerable extent without the agency of words. None but those who are conversant with the philosophy of mental phenomena can be aware of the immense influence that is exercised by language in promoting the development of our ideas, in fixing them in the mind, and in detaining them for steady contemplation. Into every process of reasoning, language enters as an essential element. Words are the instruments by which we form all our abstractions, by which we fashion and embody our ideas, and by which we are enabled to glide along a series of premises and conclusions with a rapidity so great as to leave in the memory no trace of the successive steps of the process; and we remain unconscious how much we owe to this potent auxiliary of the reasoning faculty. It is on this ground, also, that the present Work founds a claim to utility. The review of a catalog of words of analogous signification will often suggest by association other trains of thought, which, presenting the subject under new and varied aspects, will vastly expand the sphere of our mental vision. Amidst the many objects thus brought within the range of our contemplation, some striking similitude or appropriate image, some excursive flight or brilliant conception may flash on the mind, giving point and force to our arguments, awakening a responsive chord in the imagination or sensibility of the reader, and procuring for our reasonings a more ready access both to his understanding and to his heart.

It is of the utmost consequence that strict accuracy should regulate our use of language, and that everyone should acquire the power and the habit of expressing his thoughts with perspicuity and correctness. Few, indeed, can appreciate the real extent and importance of that influence which language has always exercised on human affairs, or can be aware how often these are determined by causes much slighter than are apparent to a superficial observer. False logic, disguised under specious phraseology, too often gains the assent of the unthinking multitude, disseminating far and wide the seeds of prejudice and error. Truisms pass current, and wear the semblance of profound wisdom, when dressed up in the tinsel garb of antithetical phrases, or set off by an imposing pomp of paradox. By a confused jargon of involved and mystical sentences, the imagination is easily inveigled into a transcendental region of clouds, and the understanding beguiled into the belief that it is acquiring knowledge and approaching truth. A misapplied or misapprehended term is sufficient to give rise to fierce and interminable disputes; a misnomer has turned the tide of popular opinion; a verbal sophism has decided a party question; an artful watchword, thrown among combustible materials, has kindled the flame of deadly warfare, and changed the destiny of an empire.

In constructing the following system of classification of the ideas which are expressible by language, my chief aim has been to obtain the greatest amount of practical utility. I have accordingly adopted such principles of arrangement as appeared to me to be the simplest and most natural, and which would not require, for either their comprehension or application, any disciplined acumen, or depth of metaphysical or antiquarian lore. Eschewing all needless refinements and subtleties, I have taken as my guide the more obvious characters of the ideas for which expressions were to be tabulated, arranging them under such classes and categories as reflection and experience had taught me would conduct the inquirer most readily and quickly to the object of his search. Commencing with the ideas expressing abstract relations, I proceeded to those which relate to space and to the phenomena of the material world, and lastly to those in which the mind is concerned, and which comprehend intellect, volition, and feeling; thus establishing six primary Classes of Categories.

1. The first of these classes comprehends ideas derived from the more general and ABSTRACT RELATIONS among things, such as *Existence, Resemblance, Quantity, Order, Number, Time, Power.*

2. The second class refers to SPACE and its various relations, including *Motion,* or change of place.

3. The third class includes all ideas that relate to the MATERIAL WORLD; namely, the *Properties of Matter,* such as *Solidity, Fluidity, Heat, Sound, Light,* and the *Phenomena* they present, as well as the simple *Perceptions* to which they give rise.

4. The fourth class embraces all ideas of phenomena relating to the INTELLECT and its operations; comprising the *Acquisition,* the *Retention,* and the *Communication of Ideas.*

5. The fifth class includes the ideas derived from the exercise of VOLITION; embracing the phenomena and results of our *Voluntary and Active Powers;* such as *Choice, Intention, Utility, Action, Antagonism, Authority, Compact, Property,* &c.

6. The sixth and last class comprehends all ideas derived from the operation of our SENTIENT AND MORAL POWERS; including our *Feelings, Emotions, Passions,* and *Moral and Religious Sentiments.*[1]

The further subdivisions and minuter details will be best understood from an inspection of the Tabular Synopsis of Categories prefixed to the Work, in which are specified the several *topics* or *heads of signification,* under which the words have been

[1] It must necessarily happen in every system of classification framed with this view that ideas and expressions arranged under one class must include also ideas relating to another class; for the operations of the *Intellect* generally involve also those of the *Will,* and *vice versa;* and our *Affections* and *Emotions,* in like manner, generally imply the agency both of the *Intellect* and of the *Will.* All that can be effected, therefore, is to arrange the words according to the principal or dominant idea they convey. *Teaching,* for example, although a Voluntary act, relates primarily to the Communication of Ideas, and is accordingly placed at No. 537, under Class IV Division (II). On the other hand, *Choice, Conduct, Skill,* &c., although implying the cooperation of Voluntary with Intellectual acts, relate principally to the former, and are therefore arranged under Class V.

arranged. By the aid of this table the reader will, with a little practice, readily discover the place which the particular topic he is in search of occupies in the series; and on turning to the page in the body of the Work which contains it, he will find the group of expressions he requires, out of which he may cull those that are most appropriate to his purpose. For the convenience of reference, I have designated each separate group or heading by a particular number; so that if, during the search, any doubt or difficulty should occur, recourse may be had to the copious alphabetical Index of Words at the end of the volume, which will at once indicate the number of the required group.[2]

The object I have proposed to myself in this Work would have been but imperfectly attained if I had confined myself to a mere catalog of words, and had omitted the numerous phrases and forms of expression composed of several words, which are of such frequent use as to entitle them to rank among the constituent parts of the language.[3] Very few of these verbal combinations, so essential to the knowledge of our native tongue, and so profusely abounding in its daily use, are to be met with in ordinary dictionaries. These phrases and forms of expression I have endeavored diligently to collect and to insert in their proper places, under the general ideas that they are designed to convey. Some of these conventional forms, indeed, partake of the nature of proverbial expressions; but actual proverbs, as such, being wholly of a didactic character, do not come within the scope of the present Work; and the reader must therefore not expect to find them here inserted.[4]

For the purpose of exhibiting with greater distinctness the relations between words expressing opposite and correlative ideas, I have, whenever the subject admitted of such an ar-

[2] It often happens that the same word admits of various applications, or may be used in different senses. In consulting the Index the reader will be guided to the number of the heading under which that word, in each particular acceptation, will be found, by means of *supplementary words* printed in Italics; which words, however, are not to be understood as explaining the meaning of the word to which they are annexed, but only as assisting in the required reference. I have also, for shortness' sake, generally omitted words immediately derived from the primary one inserted, which sufficiently represents the whole group of correlative words referable to the same heading. Thus the number affixed to *Beauty* applies to all its derivatives, such as *Beautiful, Beauteous, Beautifulness, Beautifully,* &c., the insertion of which was therefore neeedless.

[3] For example:—To take time by the forelock;—to turn over a new leaf;—to show the white feather;—to have a finger in the pie;—to let the cat out of the bag;—to take care of number one;—to kill two birds with one stone, &c., &c.

[4] See Trench, *On the Lessons in Proverbs.*

rangement, placed them in two parallel columns on the same page, so that each group of expressions may be readily contrasted with those which occupy the adjacent column, and constitute their antithesis.[5] By carrying the eye from the one to the other, the inquirer may often discover forms of expression of which he may avail himself advantageously, to diversify and infuse vigor into his phraseology. Rhetoricians, indeed, are well aware of the power derived from the skillful introduction of antitheses in giving point to an argument, and imparting force and brilliancy to the diction. A too-frequent and indiscreet employment of this figure of rhetoric may, it is true, give rise to a vicious and affected style; but it is unreasonable to condemn indiscriminately the occasional and moderate use of a practice on account of its possible abuse.

The study of correlative terms existing in a particular language may often throw valuable light on the manners and customs of the nations using it. Thus, Hume has drawn important inferences with regard to the state of society among the ancient Romans from certain deficiencies which he remarked in the Latin language.[6]

[5] This arrangement has been modified; see p. xi of the 1962 Preface. [Ed.]

[6] "It is an universal observation," he remarks, "which we may form upon language, that where two related parts of a whole bear any proportion to each other, in numbers, rank, or consideration, there are always correlative terms invented which answer to both the parts, and express their mutual relation. If they bear no proportion to each other, the term is only invented for the less, and marks its distinction from the whole. Thus, *man* and *woman, master* and *servant, father* and *son, prince* and *subject, stranger* and *citizen,* are correlative terms. But the words *seaman, carpenter, smith, tailor,* &c., have no correspondent terms, which express those who are no seamen, no carpenters, &c. Languages differ very much with regard to the particular words where this distinction obtains; and may thence afford very strong inferences concerning the manners and customs of different nations. The military government of the Roman emperors had exalted the soldiery so high that they balanced all the other orders of the state: hence *miles* and *paganus* became relative terms; a thing, till then, unknown to ancient, and still so to modern languages."—"The term for a slave, born and bred in the family, was *verna.* As *servus* was the name of the genus, and *verna* of the species without any correlative, this forms a strong presumption that the latter were by far the least numerous: and from the same principles I infer that if the number of slaves brought by the Romans from foreign countries had not extremely exceeded those which were bred at home, *verna* would have had a correlative, which would have expressed the former species of slaves. But these, it would seem, composed the main body of the ancient slaves, and the latter were but a few exceptions."—HUME, *Essay on the Populousness of Ancient Nations.*

The warlike propensity of the same nation may, in like manner, be inferred from the use of the word *hostis* to denote both a *foreigner* and an *enemy.*

In many cases, two ideas which are completely opposed to each other admit of an intermediate or neutral idea, equidistant from both; all these being expressible by corresponding definite terms. Thus, in the following examples, the words in the first and third columns, which express opposite ideas, admit of the intermediate terms contained in the middle column, having a neutral sense with reference to the former.

Identity	*Difference*	*Contrariety*
Beginning	*Middle*	*End*
Past	*Present*	*Future*

In other cases, the intermediate word is simply the negative to each of two opposite positions; as, for example—

Convexity	*Flatness*	*Concavity*
Desire	*Indifference*	*Aversion*

Sometimes the intermediate word is properly the standard with which each of the extremes is compared; as in the case of

Insufficiency	*Sufficiency*	*Redundance*

for here the middle term, *Sufficiency,* is equally opposed on the one hand to *Insufficiency,* and on the other to *Redundance.*[7]

These forms of correlative expressions would suggest the use of triple, instead of double, columns, for tabulating this threefold order of words; but the practical inconvenience attending such an arrangement would probably overbalance its advantages.

It often happens that the same word has several correlative terms, according to the different relations in which it is considered. Thus, to the word *Giving* are opposed both *Receiving* and *Taking;* the former correlation having reference to the *persons* concerned in the transfer, while the latter relates to the *mode* of transfer. *Old* has for opposite both *New* and *Young,* according as it is applied to *things* or to *living things. Attack* and *Defense* are correlative terms; as are also *Attack* and *Resistance. Resistance,* again, has for its other correlative *Submission. Truth in the abstract* is opposed to *Error;* but the oppo-

[7] [In the following cases, the intermediate word signifies an imperfect degree of each of the qualities set in opposition—

Light	*Dimness*	*Darkness*
Transparency	*Semitransparency*	*Opacity*
Vision	*Dimsightedness*	*Blindness*]

site of *Truth communicated* is *Falsehood. Acquisition* is contrasted both with *Deprivation* and with *Loss. Refusal* is the counterpart both of *Offer* and of *Consent. Disuse* and *Misuse* may either of them be considered as the correlative of *Use. Teaching,* with reference to what is taught, is opposed to *Misteaching;* but with reference to the act itself, its proper reciprocal is *Learning.*

Words contrasted in form do not always bear the same contrast in their meaning. The word *Malefactor,* for example, would, from its derivation, appear to be exactly the opposite of *Benefactor:* but the ideas attached to these two words are far from being directly opposed; for while the latter expresses one who confers a benefit, the former denotes one who has violated the laws.

Independently of the immediate practical uses derivable from the arrangement of words in double columns, many considerations, interesting in a philosophical point of view, are presented by the study of correlative expressions. It will be found, on strict examination, that there seldom exists an exact opposition between two words which may at first sight appear to be the counterparts of one another; for in general, the one will be found to possess in reality more force or extent of meaning than the other with which it is contrasted. The correlative term sometimes assumes the form of a mere negative, although it is really endowed with a considerable positive form. Thus *Disrespect* is not merely the absence of *Respect:* its signification trenches on the opposite idea, namely, *Contempt.* In like manner, *Untruth* is not merely the negative of *Truth;* it involves a degree of *Falsehood. Irreligion,* which is properly *the want of Religion,* is understood as being nearly synonymous with *Impiety.* For these reasons, the reader must not expect that all the words which stand side by side in the two columns shall be the precise correlatives of each other; for the nature of the subject, as well as the imperfections of language, renders it impossible always to preserve such an exactness of correlation.

There exist comparatively few words of a general character to which no correlative term, either of negation or of opposition, can be assigned, and which therefore require no corresponding second column. The correlative idea, especially that which constitutes a sense negative to the primary one, may, indeed, be formed or conceived; but, from its occurring rarely, no word has been framed to represent it; for, in language, as in other matters, the supply fails when there is no probability of a demand. Occasionally we find this deficiency provided for by the contrivance of prefixing the syllable *non;* as, for instance, the negatives of *existence, performance, payment,* &c., are expressed by the compound words *non-existence, non-performance, non-payment,* &c. Functions of a similar kind are performed by the prefixes *dis-*,[8] *anti-*, *contra-*, *mis-*, *in-*, and *un-*.[9] With respect to all these, and especially the last, great latitude is allowed according to the necessities of the case, a latitude which is limited only by the taste and discretion of the writer.

On the other hand, it is hardly possible to find two words having in all respects the same meaning, and being therefore interchangeable; that is, admitting of being employed indiscriminately, the one or the other, in all their applications. The investigation of the distinctions to be drawn between words apparently synonymous forms a separate branch of inquiry, which I have not presumed here to enter upon; for the subject has already occupied the attention of much abler critics than myself, and its complete exhaustion would require the devotion of a whole life. The purpose of this Work, it must be borne in mind, is not to explain the signification of words, but simply to classify and arrange them according to the sense in which they are now used, and which I presume to be already known to the reader. I enter into no inquiry into the changes of meaning they may have undergone in the course of time.[10] I am content to accept them at the value of their present currency, and have no concern with their etymologies, or with the history of their transformations; far less do I venture to thrid the mazes of the vast labyrinth into which I should be led by any attempt at a general discrimination of synonyms. The difficulties I have had to contend with have already been sufficiently great, without this addition to my labors.

The most cursory glance over the pages of a Dictionary will show that a great number of words are used in various senses, sometimes distinguished by slight shades of difference, but often diverging widely from their primary signification, and even, in some cases, bearing to it no perceptible relation. It may even

[8] The words *disannul* and *dissever,* however, have the same meaning as *annul* and *sever; to unloose* is the same as *to loose,* and *inebriety* is synonymous with *ebriety.*

[9] In the case of adjectives, the addition to a substantive of the terminal syllable *less* gives them a negative meaning: as *taste, tasteless; care, careless; hope, hopeless; friend, friendless; fault, faultless;* &c.

[10] Such changes are innumerable: for instance, the words *tyrant, parasite, sophist, churl, knave, villain* anciently conveyed no opprobrious meaning. *Impertinent* merely expressed *irrelative,* and implied neither *rudeness* nor *intrusion,* as it does at present. *Indifferent* originally meant *impartial; extravagant* was simply *digressive;* and *to prevent* was properly *to precede* and *assist.* The old translations of the Scriptures furnish many striking examples of the alterations which time has brought in the signification of words. Much curious information on this subject is contained in Trench's *Lectures on the Study of Words.*

happen that the very same word has two significations quite opposite to one another. This is the case with the verb *to cleave,* which means *to adhere tenaciously,* and also *to separate by a blow. To propugn* sometimes expresses *to attack;* at other times *to defend. To let* is *to hinder,* as well as *to permit. To ravel* means both *to entangle* and *to disentangle. Shameful* and *shameless* are nearly synonymous. *Priceless* may either mean *invaluable* or *of no value. Nervous* is used sometimes for *strong,* at other times for *weak.* The alphabetical Index at the end of this Work sufficiently shows the multiplicity of uses to which, by the elasticity of language, the meaning of words has been stretched, so as to adapt them to a great variety of modified significations in subservience to the nicer shades of thought, which, under peculiarity of circumstances, require corresponding expression. Words thus admitting of different meanings have therefore to be arranged under each of the respective heads corresponding to these various acceptations. There are many words, again, which express ideas compounded of two elementary ideas belonging to different classes. It is therefore necessary to place these words respectively under each of the generic heads to which they relate. The necessity of these repetitions is increased by the circumstance that ideas included under one class are often connected by relations of the same kind as the ideas which belong to another class. Thus we find the same relations of *order* and of *quantity* existing among the ideas of *Time* as among those of *Space.* Sequence in the one is denoted by the same terms as sequence in the other; and the measures of time also express the measures of space. The cause and the effect are often designated by the same word. The word *Sound,* for instance, denotes both the impression made upon the ear by sonorous vibrations, and also the vibrations themselves, which are the cause or source of that impression. *Mixture* is used for the act of mixing, as well as for the product of that operation. *Taste* and *Smell* express both the sensations and the qualities of material bodies giving rise to them. *Thought* is the act of thinking; but the same word denotes also the idea resulting from that act. *Judgment* is the act of deciding, and also the decision come to. *Purchase* is the acquisition of a thing by payment, as well as the thing itself so acquired. *Speech* is both the act of speaking and the words spoken; and so on with regard to an endless multiplicity of words. Mind is essentially distinct from Matter; and yet, in all languages, the attributes of the one are metaphorically transferred to those of the other. Matter, in all its forms, is endowed by the figurative genius of every language with the functions which pertain to intellect; and we perpetually talk of its phenomena and of its powers, as if they resulted from the voluntary influence of one body on another, acting and reacting, impelling and being impelled, controlling and being controlled, as if animated by spontaneous energies and guided by specific intentions. On the other hand, expressions of which the primary signification refers exclusively to the properties and actions of matter are metaphorically applied to the phenomena of thought and volition, and even to the feelings and passions of the soul; and in speaking of a *ray of hope,* a *shade of doubt,* a *flight of fancy,* a *flash of wit,* the *warmth of emotion,* or the *ebullitions of anger,* we are scarcely conscious that we are employing metaphors which have this material origin.

As a general rule, I have deemed it incumbent on me to place words and phrases which appertain more especially to one head, also under the other heads to which they have a relation, whenever it appeared to me that this repetition would suit the convenience of the inquirer, and spare him the trouble of turning to other parts of the work; for I have always preferred to subject myself to the imputation of redundance, rather than incur the reproach of insufficiency.[11] When, however, the divergence of the associated from the primary idea is sufficiently marked, I have contented myself with making a reference to the place where the modified signification will be found.[12] But in order to prevent needless extension, I have, in general, omitted *conjugate words,*[13] which are so obviously derivable from those that are given in the same place that the reader may safely be left to form them for himself. This is the case with adverbs derived from adjectives by the simple addition of the terminal syllable *-ly,* such as *closely, carefully, safely,* &c., from *close, careful, safe,* &c., and also with adjectives or participles immediately derived from the verbs which are already given. In all such cases, an "&c." indicates that reference is understood to

[11] Frequent repetitions of the same series of expressions, accordingly, will be met with under various headings. For example, the word *Relinquishment* with its synonyms occurs as a heading at No. 624, where it applies to *intention,* and also at No. 782, where it refers to *property.* The word *Chance* has two significations, distinct from one another: the one implying the *absence of an assignable cause;* in which case it comes under the category of the relation of Causation, and occupies the No. 156: the other, the *absence of design,* in which latter sense it ranks under the operations of the Will, and has assigned to it the place No. 621. I have, in like manner, distinguished *Sensibility, Pleasure, Pain, Taste,* &c., according as they relate to *Physical* or to *Moral* affections; the former being found at Nos. 375, 377, 378, 390, &c., and the latter at Nos. 822, 827, 828, 850, &c.

[12] See 1962 Preface, p. xiii. [Ed.]

[13] "By *conjugate* or *paronymous* words is meant, correctly speaking, different parts of speech from the same root, which exactly corresponds in point of meaning."—*A Selection of English Synonyms,* edited by Archbishop Whately.

be made to these roots. I have observed the same rule in compiling the Index, retaining only the primary or more simple word, and omitting the conjugate words obviously derived from them. Thus I assume the word *short* as the representative of its immediate derivatives *shortness, shorten, shortening, shortened, shorter, shortly,* which would have had the same references, and which the reader can readily supply.

The same verb is frequently used indiscriminately either in the active or transitive, or in the neuter or intransitive sense. In these cases, I have generally not thought it worth while to increase the bulk of the Work by the needless repetition of that word; for the reader, whom I suppose to understand the use of the words, must also be presumed to be competent to apply them correctly.

There are a multitude of words of a specific character which, although they properly occupy places in the columns of a dictionary, yet, having no relation to general ideas, do not come within the scope of this compilation, and are consequently omitted.[14] The names of objects in Natural History, and technical terms belonging exclusively to Science or to Art, or relating to particular operations, and of which the signification is restricted to those specific objects, come under this category. Exceptions must, however, be made in favor of such words as admit of metaphorical application to general subjects, with which custom has associated them, and of which they may be cited as being typical or illustrative. Thus, the word *Lion* will find a place under the head of *Courage,* of which it is regarded as the type. *Anchor,* being emblematic of *Hope,* is introduced among the words expressing that emotion; and in like manner, *butterfly* and *weathercock,* which are suggestive of fickleness, are included in the category of *Irresolution.*

With regard to the admission of many words and expressions which the classical reader might be disposed to condemn as vulgarisms, or which he, perhaps, might stigmatize as pertaining rather to the slang than to the legitimate language of the day, I would beg to observe, that, having due regard to the uses to which this Work was to be adapted, I did not feel myself justified in excluding them solely on that ground, if they possessed an acknowledged currency in general intercourse. It is obvious that, with respect to degrees of conventionality, I could not have attempted to draw any strict lines of demarcation; and far less could I have presumed to erect any absolute standard

14 [The author did not in all cases rigidly adhere to this rule; and the editors have thought themselves justified both in retaining and in adding some words of the specific character here mentioned, which may be occasionally in request by general writers, although in categories of this nature no attempt at completeness has been made.]

of purity. My object, be it remembered, is not to regulate the use of words, but simply to supply and to suggest such as may be wanted on occasion, leaving the proper selection entirely to the discretion and taste of the employer.[15] If a novelist or a dramatist, for example, proposed to delineate some vulgar personage, he would wish to have the power of putting into the mouth of the speaker expressions that would accord with his character; just as the actor, to revert to a former comparison, who had to personate a peasant, would choose for his attire the most homely garb, and would have just reason to complain if the theatrical wardrobe furnished him with no suitable costume.

Words which have, in process of time, become obsolete, are of course rejected from this collection.[16] On the other hand, I have admitted a considerable number of words and phrases borrowed from other languages, chiefly the French and Latin, some of which may be considered as already naturalized; while others, though avowedly foreign, are frequently employed in English composition, particularly in familiar style, on account of their being peculiarly expressive, and because we have no corresponding words of equal force in our own language.[17] The rapid advances which are being made in scientific knowledge, and consequent improvement in all the arts of life, and the extension of those arts and sciences to so many new purposes and objects, create a continual demand for the formation of new terms to express new agencies, new wants, and new combinations. Such terms, from being at first merely technical, are rendered, by more general use, familiar to the multitude, and having a well-defined acceptation, are eventually incorporated into the language, which they contribute to enlarge and to enrich. *Neologies* of this kind are perfectly legitimate, and highly advantageous; and they necessarily introduce those gradual and progressive changes which every language is destined to

15 [It may be added that the Thesaurus is an aid not only in the choice of appropriate forms of expression, but in the rejection of those which are unfit; and that a vulgar phrase may often furnish a convenient clue to the group of classic synonyms among which it is placed. Moreover, the slang expressions admitted into the work bear but a small proportion to those in constant use by English writers and speakers.]

16 [A few apparently obsolete words have nevertheless found their way into the Thesaurus. In justification of their admission, it may be contended that well-known words, though no longer current, give occasional point by an archaic form of expression, and are of value to the novelist or dramatist who has to depict a bygone age.]

17 All these words and phrases are printed in Italics. [A few of these expressions, although widely used by writers of English, are of a form which is really incorrect or unusual in their own language.]

undergo.[18] Some modern writers, however, have indulged in a habit of arbitrarily fabricating new words and a new-fangled phraseology, without any necessity, and with manifest injury to the purity of the language. This vicious practice, the offspring of indolence or conceit, implies an ignorance or neglect of the riches in which the English language already abounds, and which would have supplied them with words of recognized legitimacy, conveying precisely the same meaning as those they so recklessly coin in the illegal mint of their own fancy.

A work constructed on the plan of classification I have proposed might, if ably executed, be of great value, in tending to limit the fluctuations to which language has always been subject, by establishing an authoritative standard for its regulation. Future historians, philologists, and lexicographers, when investigating the period when new words were introduced, or discussing the import given at the present time to the old, might find their labors lightened by being enabled to appeal to such a standard, instead of having to search for data among the scattered writings of the age. Nor would its utility be confined to a single language; for the principles of its construction are universally applicable to all languages, whether living or dead. On the same plan of classification there might be formed a French, a German, a Latin, or a Greek Thesaurus, possessing, in its respective sphere, the same advantages as those of the English model.[19] Still more useful would be a conjunction of these methodized compilations in two languages, the French and English, for instance; the columns of each being placed in parallel juxtaposition. No means yet devised would so greatly facilitate the acquisition of the one language by those who are acquainted with the other; none would afford such ample assistance to the translator in either language; and none would supply such ready and effectual means of instituting an accurate comparison between them, and of fairly appreciating their respective merits and defects. In a still higher degree would all those advantages be combined and multiplied in a *Polyglot Lexicon* constructed on this system.

[18] Thus, in framing the present classification, I have frequently felt the want of substantive terms corresponding to abstract qualities or ideas denoted by certain adjectives, and have been often tempted to invent words that might express these abstractions; but I have yielded to this temptation only in the four following instances, having framed from the adjectives *irrelative, amorphous, sinistral,* and *gaseous* the abstract nouns *irrelation, amorphism, sinistrality,* and *gaseity*. I have ventured also to introduce the adjective *intersocial* to express the active voluntary relations between man and man.

[19] [This suggestion has been followed, in French, in a *Dictionnaire Idéologique* by T. Robertson (Paris, 1859); and, in German, in a *Deutscher Sprachschatz* by D. Sanders (Hamburg, 1878), and *Deutscher Wortschatz oder Der passende Ausdruck* by A. Schelling (Stuttgart, 1892).]

Metaphysicians engaged in the more profound investigation of the Philosophy of Language will be materially assisted by having the ground thus prepared for them in a previous analysis and classification of our ideas; for such classification of ideas is the true basis on which words, which are their symbols, should be classified.[20] It is by such analysis alone that we can arrive at a clear perception of the relation which these symbols bear to their corresponding ideas, or can obtain a correct knowledge of the elements which enter into the formation of compound ideas, and of the exclusions by which we arrive at the abstractions so perpetually resorted to in the process of reasoning, and in the communication of our thoughts.

Lastly, such analysis alone can determine the principles on

[20] The principle by which I have been guided in framing my verbal classification is the same as that which is employed in the various departments of Natural History. Thus the sectional divisions I have formed correspond to Natural Families in Botany and Zoology, and the filiation of words presents a network analogous to the natural filiation of plants or animals.

The following are the only publications that have come to my knowledge in which any attempt has been made to construct a systematic arrangement of ideas with a view to their expression. The earliest of these, supposed to be at least nine hundred years old, is the AMERA CÓSHA, or *Vocabulary of the Sanscrit Language,* by Amera Sinha, of which an English translation, by the late Henry T. Colebrooke, was printed at Serampoor, in the year 1808. The classification of words is there, as might be expected, exceedingly imperfect and confused, especially in all that relates to abstract ideas or mental operations. This will be apparent from the very title of the first section, which comprehends "*Heaven, Gods, Demons, Fire, Air, Velocity, Eternity, Much*": while *Sin, Virtue, Happiness, Destiny, Cause, Nature, Intellect, Reasoning, Knowledge, Senses, Tastes, Odors, Colors* are all included and jumbled together in the fourth section. A more logical order, however, pervades the sections relating to natural objects, such as *Seas, Earth, Towns, Plants,* and *Animals,* which form separate classes, exhibiting a remarkable effort at analysis at so remote a period of Indian literature.

The well-known work of Bishop Wilkins entitled *An Essay towards a Real Character and a Philosophical Language,* published in 1668, had for its object the formation of a system of symbols which might serve as a universal language. It professed to be founded on a "scheme of analysis of the things or notions to which names were to be assigned"; but notwithstanding the immense labor and ingenuity expended in the construction of this system, it was soon found to be fare too abstruse and recondite for practical application.

In the year 1797, there appeared in Paris an anonymous work, entitled PASIGRAPHIE, *ou Premiers Eléments du nouvel Art-Science d'écrire et d'imprimer une langue de manière à être lu et entendu dans toute autre langue sans traduction,* of which an edition in German was also published. It contains a great number of tabular schemes of categories, all of which appear to be excessively arbitrary and artificial, and extremely difficult of application, as well as of apprehension. [Systems of grouping with relation to ideas are also adopted in an *Analytical Dictionary of the English Language* by David Booth (London, 1835), a *Dictionnaire Analogique de la Langue Française* by P. Boissière (Paris), and a *Dictionnaire Logique de la Langue Française* by L'Abbé Elie Blanc (Paris, 1882).]

which a strictly *Philosophical Language* might be constructed. The probable result of the construction of such a language would be its eventual adoption by every civilized nation; thus realizing that splendid aspiration of philanthropists—the establishment of a Universal Language. However utopian such a project may appear to the present generation, and however abortive may have been the former endeavors of Bishop Wilkins and others to realize it,[21] its accomplishment is surely not beset with greater difficulties than have impeded the progress to many other beneficial objects which in former times appeared to be no less visionary, and which yet were successfully achieved, in later ages, by the continued and persevering exertions of the human intellect. Is there at the present day, then, any ground for despair that at some future stage of that higher civilization to which we trust the world is gradually tending, some new and bolder effort of genius towards the solution of this great problem may be crowned with success, and compass an object of such vast and paramount utility? Nothing, indeed, would conduce more directly to bring about a golden age of union and harmony among the several nations and races of mankind than the removal of that barrier to the interchange of thought and mutual good understanding between man and man which is now interposed by the diversity of their respective languages.

21 "The Languages," observes Horne Tooke, "which are commonly used throughout the world, are much more simple and easy, convenient and philosophical, than Wilkins' scheme for a *real character;* or than any other scheme that has been at any other time imagined or proposed for the purpose.'—"Επεα Πτερόεντα p. 28.

PLAN OF CLASSIFICATION

The numbers in the right-hand column relate to the present edition

Class and Division	*Section*	*Nos.*
I ABSTRACT RELATIONS	**I Existence**	1–8
	II Relation	9–25
	III Quantity	26–59
	IV Order	60–84
	V Number	85–107
	VI Time	108–142
	VII Change	143–155
	VIII Causation	156–182
II SPACE	**I Space in General**	183–194
	II Dimensions	195–242
	III Form	243–264
	IV Motion	265–318
III MATTER	**I Matter in General**	319–323
	II Inorganic Matter	324–357
	III Organic Matter	358–446
IV INTELLECT	**I General**	447–452
Division (I) FORMATION OF IDEAS	**II Precursory Conditions and Operations**	453–465
	III Materials for Reasoning	466–474
	IV Reasoning Processes	475–479
	V Results of Reasoning	480–504
	VI Extension of Thought	505–511
	VII Creative Thought	512–513
Division (II) COMMUNICATION	**I Nature of Ideas Communicated**	514–521

Class and Division	Section	Nos.
OF IDEAS	II **Modes of Communication**	522–546
	III **Means of Communicating Ideas**	547–594
V VOLITION	I **Volition in General**	595–616
Division (I)	II **Prospective Volition**	617–675
INDIVIDUAL	III **Voluntary Action**	676–699
VOLITION	IV **Antagonism**	700–724
	V **Results of Action**	725–732
Division (II)	I **General**	733–755
INTERSOCIAL	II **Special**	756–763
VOLITION	III **Conditional**	764–770
	IV **Possessive Relations**	771–816
VI AFFECTIONS	I **Affections Generally**	817–823
	II **Personal**	824–879
	III **Sympathetic**	880–912
	IV **Moral**	913–964
	V **Religious**	965–990

TABULAR SYNOPSIS OF CATEGORIES

N.B. In the column for heads, the arabic numeral on the left is the number of the head in this edition: that on the right (in brackets) is the corresponding number in the previous edition. Heads with no number on the left do not appear as separate categories in this edition. Heads with no number on the right are new, and do not appear in the previous edition. Where the title of a head has been changed, only the title adopted in this edition is given.

CLASS I. ABSTRACT RELATIONS

Section	*Head*	
I Existence		
1° ABSTRACT	1 Existence	(1)
	2 Non-existence	(2)
2° CONCRETE	3 Substantiality	(3)
	4 Unsubstantiality	(4)
3° FORMAL *internal* *external*	5 Intrinsicality	(5)
	6 Extrinsicality	(6)
4° MODAL *absolute* *relative*	7 State	(7)
	8 Circumstance	(8)
II Relation		
1° ABSOLUTE	9 Relation	(9)
	10 Irrelation	(10)
	11 Consanguinity	(11)
	12 Correlation	(12)

Section	Head	
	13 Identity	(13)
	14 Contrariety	(14)
	15 Difference	(15)
2° CONTINUOUS	16 Uniformity	(16)
	17 Non-uniformity	(16a)
3° PARTIAL	18 Similarity	(17)
	19 Dissimilarity	(18)
	20 Imitation	(19)
	21 Non-imitation	(20)
	(Variation	20a)
	22 Copy	(21)
	23 Prototype	(22)
4° GENERAL	24 Agreement	(23)
	25 Disagreement	(24)

III Quantity

Section	Head	
1° SIMPLE	26 Quantity	(25)
	27 Degree	(26)
2° COMPARATIVE	28 Equality	(27)
	29 Inequality	(28)
	30 Mean	(29)
	31 Compensation	(30)
by comparison with a standard	32 Greatness	(31)
	33 Smallness	(32)
by comparison with an object	34 Superiority	(33)
	35 Inferiority	(34)
changes in quantity	36 Increase	(35)
	37 Decrease	(36)
3° CONJUNCTIVE	38 Addition	(37)
	39 Subduction	(38)
	40 Adjunct	(39)
	41 Remainder	(40)
	42 Decrement	(40a)
	43 Mixture	(41)
	44 Simpleness	(42)
	45 Junction	(43)
	46 Disjunction	(44)
	47 Bond	(45)

Section	Head	
	48 Coherence	(46)
	49 Non-coherence	(47)
	50 Combination	(48)
	51 Decomposition	(49)
4° CONCRETE	52 Whole	(50)
	53 Part	(51)
	54 Completeness	(52)
	55 Incompleteness	(53)
	56 Composition	(54)
	57 Exclusion	(55)
	58 Component	(56)
	59 Extraneousness	(57)

IV Order

Section	Head	
1° GENERAL	60 Order	(58)
	61 Disorder	(59)
	62 Arrangement	(60)
	63 Derangement	(61)
2° CONSECUTIVE	64 Precedence	(62)
	65 Sequence	(63)
	66 Precursor	(64)
	67 Sequel	(65)
	68 Beginning	(66)
	69 End	(67)
	70 Middle	(68)
	71 Continuity	(69)
	72 Discontinuity	(70)
	73 Term	(71)
3° COLLECTIVE	74 Assemblage	(72)
	75 Non-assemblage	(73)
	76 Focus	(74)
4° DISTRIBUTIVE	77 Class	(75)
	78 Inclusion	(76)
	(Exclusion	77)
	79 Generality	(78)
	80 Specialty	(79)
5° CATEGORICAL	81 Rule	(80)
	82 Multiformity	(81)
	83 Conformity	(82)
	84 Unconformity	(83)

Section	*Head*	
V Number		
1° ABSTRACT	85 Number	(84)
	86 Numeration	(85)
	87 List	(86)
2° DETERMINATE	88 Unity	(87)
	89 Accompaniment	(88)
	90 Duality	(89)
	91 Duplication	(90)
	92 Bisection	(91)
	93 Triality	(92)
	94 Triplication	(93)
	95 Trisection	(94)
	96 Quaternity	(95)
	97 Quadruplication	(96)
	98 Quadrisection	(97)
	99 Five and over	(98)
	100 Multisection	(99)
3° INDETERMINATE	101 Plurality	(100)
	102 Fraction	(100a)
	103 Zero	(101)
	104 Multitude	(102)
	105 Fewness	(103)
	106 Repetition	(104)
	107 Infinity	(105)
VI Time		
1° ABSOLUTE	108 Time	(106)
	109 Neverness	(107)
definite	110 Period	(108)
indefinite	111 Course	(109)
	112 { Contingent duration	(108a)
	113 Diuturnity	(110)
	114 Transientness	(111)
	115 Perpetuity	(112)
	116 Instantaneity	(113)
	117 Chronometry	(114)
	118 Anachronism	(115)
2° RELATIVE *to succession*	119 Priority	(116)
	120 Posteriority	(117)
	121 Present time	(118)
	122 Different time	(119)

Section	Head	
	123 Synchronism	(120)
to a period	124 Futurity	(121)
	125 Preterition	(122)
	126 Newness	(123)
	127 Oldness	(124)
	128 Morning	(125)
	129 Evening	(126)
	130 Youth	(127)
	131 Age	(128)
	132 Young person	(129)
	133 Old person	(130)
	134 Adultness	(131)
to an effect or purpose	135 Earliness	(132)
	136 Lateness	(133)
	137 Occasion	(134)
	138 Intempestivity	(135)
3° RECURRENT		
	139 Frequency	(136)
	140 Infrequency	(137)
	141 Periodicity	(138)
	142 Fitfulness	(139)

VII Change

Section	Head	
1° SIMPLE	143 Change	(140)
	144 Permanence	(141)
	145 Cessation	(142)
	146 Continuance	(143)
	147 Conversion	(144)
	148 Reversion	(145)
	149 Revolution	(146)
	150 Substitution	(147)
	151 Interchange	(148)
2° COMPLEX	152 Changeableness	(149)
	153 Stability	(150)
present	154 Eventuality	(151)
future	155 Destiny	(152)

VIII Causation

Section	Head	
1° CONSTANCY OF SEQUENCE	156 Cause	(153)
	157 Effect	(154)
	158 Attribution	(155)
	159 Chance	(156)

Section	Head	
2° CONNECTION BETWEEN CAUSE AND EFFECT	160 Power	(157)
	161 Impotence	(158)
degrees of power	162 Strength	(159)
	163 Weakness	(160)
3° POWER IN OPERATION	164 Production	(161)
	165 Destruction	(162)
	166 Reproduction	(163)
	167 Producer	(164)
	168 Destroyer	(165)
	169 Parentage	(166)
	170 Posterity	(167)
	171 Productiveness	(168)
	172 Unproductiveness	(169)
	173 Agency	(170)
	174 Vigorousness	(171)
	175 Inertness	(172)
	176 Violence	(173)
	177 Moderation	(174)
4° INDIRECT POWER	178 Influence	(175)
	(Absence of influence	175a)
	179 Tendency	(176)
	180 Liability	(177)
5° COMBINATION OF CAUSES	181 Concurrence	(178)
	182 Counteraction	(179)

CLASS II. SPACE

Section	*Head*	
I Space in General		
1° ABSTRACT SPACE	183 Space	(180)
	(Inextension	180a)
definite	184 Region	(181)
limited	185 Place	(182)
2° RELATIVE SPACE	186 Situation	(183)
	187 Location	(184)
	188 Displacement	(185)
3° EXISTENCE IN SPACE	189 Presence	(186)
	190 Absence	(187)
	191 Inhabitant	(188)
	192 Abode	(189)
	193 Contents	(190)
	194 Receptacle	(191)
II Dimensions		
1° GENERAL	195 Size	(192)
	196 Littleness	(193)
	197 Expansion	(194)
	198 Contraction	(195)
	199 Distance	(196)
	200 Nearness	(197)
	201 Interval	(198)
	202 Contiguity	(199)
2° LINEAR	203 Length	(200)
	204 Shortness	(201)
	205 Breadth	(202)
	206 Narrowness	(203)
	207 Layer	(204)
	208 Filament	(205)
	209 Height	(206)
	210 Lowness	(207)
	211 Depth	(208)
	212 Shallowness	(209)
	213 Summit	(210)
	214 Base	(211)
	215 Verticality	(212)
	216 Horizontality	(213)

Section	*Head*	
	217 Pendency	(214)
	218 Support	(215)
	219 Parallelism	(216)
	220 Obliquity	(217)
	221 Inversion	(218)
	222 Crossing	(219)
3° CENTRIC		
general	223 Exteriority	(220)
	224 Interiority	(221)
	225 Centrality	(222)
	226 Covering	(223)
	227 Lining	(224)
	228 Dressing	(225)
	229 Uncovering	(226)
	230 Circumjacence	(227)
	231 Interjacence	(228)
	232 Circumscription	(229)
	233 Outline	(230)
	234 Edge	(231)
	235 Enclosure	(232)
	236 Limit	(233)
special	237 Front	(234)
	238 Rear	(235)
	239 Laterality	(236)
	240 Contraposition	(237)
	241 Dextrality	(238)
	242 Sinistrality	(239)

III Form

Section	*Head*	
1° GENERAL	243 Form	(240)
	244 Amorphism	(241)
	245 Symmetry	(242)
	246 Distortion	(243)
2° SPECIAL	247 Angularity	(244)
	248 Curvature	(245)
	249 Straightness	(246)
	250 Circularity	(247)
	251 Convolution	(248)
	252 Rotundity	(249)
3° SUPERFICIAL	253 Convexity	(250)
		(Flatness 251)
	254 Prominence	
	255 Concavity	(252)
	256 Sharpness	(253)
	257 Bluntness	(254)

Section	Head	
	258 Smoothness	(255)
	259 Roughness	(256)
	260 Notch	(257)
	261 Fold	(258)
	262 Furrow	(259)
	263 Opening	(260)
	264 Closure	(261)
		(Perforator 262)
		(Stopper 263)

IV Motion

Section	Head	
1° GENERAL	265 Motion	(264)
	266 Quiescence	(265)
	267 Land Travel	(266)
	268 Traveler	(268)
	269 Water Travel	(267)
	270 Mariner	(269)
	271 Aeronautics	
	272 Transference	(270)
	273 Carrier	(271)
	274 Vehicle	(272)
	275 Ship	(273)
	276 Aircraft	
2° DEGREES OF MOTION	277 Velocity	(274)
	278 Slowness	(275)
3° CONJOINED WITH FORCE	279 Impulse	(276)
	280 Recoil	(277)
4° WITH REF. TO DIRECTION	281 Direction	(278)
	282 Deviation	(279)
	283 Precession	(280)
	284 Following	(281)
	285 Progression	(282)
	286 Regression	(283)
	287 Propulsion	(284)
	288 Traction	(285)
	289 Approach	(286)
	290 Recession	(287)
	291 Attraction	(288)
	292 Repulsion	(289)
	293 Convergence	(290)
	294 Divergence	(291)
	295 Arrival	(292)
	296 Departure	(293)
	297 Ingress	(294)
	298 Egress	(295)
	299 Reception	(296)
	300 Ejection	(297)
	301 Food	(298)

Section	*Head*	
	302 Excretion	(299)
	303 Insertion	(300)
	304 Extraction	(301)
	305 Passage	(302)
	306 Overstepping	(303)
	307 Shortcoming	(304)
	308 Ascent	(305)
	309 Descent	(306)
	310 Elevation	(307)
	311 Depression	(308)
	312 Leap	(309)
	313 Plunge	(310)
	314 Circuition	(311)
	315 Rotator	(312)
	316 Evolution	(313)
	317 Oscillation	(314)
	318 Agitation	(315)

CLASS III. MATTER

Section	*Head*	
I Matter in General		
	319 Materiality	(316)
	320 Immateriality	(317)
	321 Universe	(318)
	322 Gravity	(319)
	323 Levity	(320)
II Inorganic Matter		
1° SOLIDS	324 Density	(321)
	325 Rarity	(322)
	326 Hardness	(323)
	327 Softness	(324)
	328 Elasticity	(325)
		(Inelasticity 326)
	329 Toughness	(327)
	330 Brittleness	(328)
	331 Structure	(329)
	332 Pulverulence	(330)
	333 Friction	(331)
	334 Lubrication	(332)

Section	Head	
2° FLUIDS		
in general	335 Fluidity	(333)
	336 Gaseity	(334)
	337 Liquefaction	(335)
	338 Vaporization	(336)
specific	339 Water	(337)
	340 Air	(338)
	341 Moisture	(339)
	342 Dryness	(340)
	343 Ocean	(341)
	344 Land	(342)
	345 Gulf	(343)
	346 Lake	
	347 Marsh	(345)
	348 Plain	(344)
	349 Island	(346)
		(Stream 347)
in motion	350 Stream	(348)
	351 Conduit	(350)
	352 Wind	(349)
	353 Air-pipe	(351)
3° IMPERFECT FLUIDS	354 Semiliquidity	(352)
	355 Bubble. Cloud	(353)
	356 Pulpiness	(354)
	357 Unctuousness	(355)
		(oil 356)
		(resin 356a)

III Organic Matter

Section	Head	
1° VITALITY		
general	358 Organization	(357)
	359 Mineral	(358)
	360 Life	(359)
	361 Death	(360)
	362 Killing	(361)
	363 Corpse	(362)
	364 Interment	(363)
special	365 Animality	(364)
	366 Vegetability	(365)
		(Animal 366)
		(Vegetable 367)
	367 Zoology	(368)
	368 Botany	(369)

Section	Head	
	369 Animal husbandry	(370)
	370 Agriculture	(371)
	371 Mankind	(372)
	372 Male	(373)
	373 Female	(374)
2° SENSATION		
general	374 Sensibility	(375)
	375 Insensibility	(376)
	376 Pleasure	(377)
	377 Pain	(378)
special	378 Touch	(379)
	(Sensations of touch 380)	
	(Numbness 381)	
	379 Heat	(382)
	380 Cold	(383)
	381 Calefaction	(384)
	382 Refrigeration	(385)
	383 Furnace	(386)
	384 Refrigerator	(387)
	385 Fuel	(388)
	(Thermometer 389)	
	386 Taste	(390)
	387 Insipidity	(391)
	388 Pungency	(392)
	389 Condiment	(393)
	390 Savoriness	(394)
	391 Unsavoriness	(395)
	392 Sweetness	(396)
	393 Sourness	(397)
	394 Odor	(398)
	395 Inodorousness	(399)
	396 Fragrance	(400)
	397 Fetor	(401)
	398 Sound	(402)
sound in general	399 Silence	(403)
	400 Loudness	(404)
	401 Faintness	(405)
	402 Bang	(406)
	403 Roll	(407)
	404 Resonance	(408)
	405 Non-resonance	(408a)
	406 Sibilation	(409)
	407 Stridor	(410)
	408 Human cry	(411)
	409 Ululation	(412)
musical sounds	410 Melody	(413)
	411 Discord	(414)

Section	Head	
	412 Music	(415)
	413 Musician	(416)
	414 Musical instrument	(417)
perception of sound	415 Hearing	(418)
	416 Deafness	(419)
light in general	417 Light	(420)
	418 Darkness	(421)
	419 Dimness	(422)
	420 Luminary	(423)
	421 Screen	(424)
	422 Transparency	(425)
	423 Opacity	(426)
	424 Semitransparency	(427)
specific light	425 Color	(428)
	426 Achromatism	(429)
	427 Whiteness	(430)
	428 Blackness	(431)
	429 Gray	(432)
	430 Brownness	(433)
	431 Redness	(434)
	432 Greenness	(435)
	433 Yellowness	(436)
	434 Purple	(437)
	435 Blueness	(438)
	436 Orange	(439)
	437 Variegation	(440)
perception of light	438 Vision	(441)
	439 Blindness	(442)
	440 Dimsightedness	(443)
	441 Spectator	(444)
	442 Optical instrument	(445)
	443 Visibility	(446)
	444 Invisibility	(447)
	445 Appearance	(448)
	446 Disappearance	(449)

CLASS IV. INTELLECT

DIVISION (I). FORMATION OF IDEAS

Section		*Head*	
I Intellectual Operations in General			
	447	Intellect	(450)
	448	Non-intellect	(450a)
	449	Thought	(451)
	450	Absence of thought	(452)
	451	Idea	(453)
	452	Topic	(454)
II Precursory Conditions and Operations			
	453	Curiosity	(455)
	454	Incuriosity	(456)
	455	Attention	(457)
	456	Inattention	(458)
	457	Carefulness	(459)
	458	Negligence	(460)
	459	Inquiry	(461)
	460	Answer	(462)
	461	Experiment	(463)
	462	Comparison	(464)
	463	Discrimination	(465)
	464	Indiscrimination	(465a)
	465	Measurement	(466)
III Materials for Reasoning			
	466	Evidence	(467)
	467	Counter-evidence	(468)
	468	Qualification	(469)
degrees of evidence	469	Possibility	(470)
	470	Impossibility	(471)
	471	Probability	(472)

Section	Head	
	472 Improbability	(473)
	473 Certainty	(474)
	474 Uncertainty	(475)
IV Reasoning Processes		
	475 Reasoning	(476)
	476 Intuition	(477)
	477 Sophistry	
	478 Demonstration	(478)
	479 Confutation	(479)
V Results of Reasoning		
	480 Judgment	(480)
	481 Misjudgment	(481)
	482 Overestimation	(482)
	483 Underestimation	(483)
	484 Discovery	(480a)
	485 Belief	(484)
	486 Unbelief	(485)
	487 Credulity	(486)
	(Incredulity	487)
	488 Assent	(488)
	489 Dissent	(489)
	490 Knowledge	(490)
	491 Ignorance	(491)
	492 Scholar	(492)
	493 Ignoramus	(493)
	494 Truth	(494)
	495 Error	(495)
	496 Maxim	(496)
	497 Absurdity	(497)
faculties	498 Intelligence	(498)
	499 Unintelligence	(499)
	500 Sage	(500)
	501 Fool	(501)
	502 Sanity	(502)
	503 Insanity	(503)
	504 Madman	(504)

Section		Head	
VI Extension of Thought			
to the past	505	Memory	(505)
	506	Oblivion	(506)
to the future	507	Expectation	(507)
	508	Inexpectation	(508)
	509	Disappointment	(509)
	510	Foresight	(510)
	511	Prediction	(511)
			(Omen 512)
			(Oracle 513)
VII Creative Thought			
	512	Supposition	(514)
	513	Imagination	(515)

DIVISION (II). COMMUNICATION OF IDEAS

Section		Head	
I Nature of Ideas Communicated			
	514	Meaning	(516)
	515	Unmeaningness	(517)
	516	Intelligibility	(518)
	517	Unintelligibility	(519)
	518	Equivocalness	(520)
	519	Metaphor	(521)
	520	Interpretation	(522)
	521	Misinterpretation	(523)
			(Interpreter 524)
II Modes of Communication			
	522	Manifestation	(525)
	523	Latency	(526)
	524	Information	(527)
	525	Concealment	(528)
	526	Disclosure	(529)
	527	Hiding	(530)
	528	Publication	(531)
	529	News	(532)
	530	Secret	(533)
	531	Messenger	(534)

Section	Head	
	532 Affirmation	(535)
	533 Negation	(536)
	534 Teaching	(537)
	535 Misteaching	(538)
	536 Learning	(539)
	537 Teacher	(540)
	538 Learner	(541)
	539 School	(542)
	540 Veracity	(543)
	541 Falsehood	(544)
	542 Deception	(545)
	543 Untruth	(546)
	544 Dupe	(547)
	545 Deceiver	(548)
	546 Exaggeration	(549)
III Means of Communicating Ideas		
natural	547 Indication	(550)
	548 Record	(551)
	549 Recorder	(553)
	550 Obliteration	(552)
	551 Representation	(554)
	552 Misrepresentation	(555)
	553 Painting	(556)
	554 Sculpture	(557)
	555 Engraving	(558)
	556 Artist	(559)
conventional	557 Language	(560)
	558 Letter	(561)
	559 Word	(562)
	560 Neology	(563)
	561 Nomenclature	(564)
	562 Misnomer	(565)
	563 Phrase	(566)
	564 Grammar	(567)
	565 Solecism	(568)
	566 Style	(569)
qualities of style	567 Perspicuity	(570)
	568 Imperspicuity	(571)
	569 Conciseness	(572)
	570 Diffuseness	(573)
	571 Vigor	(574)
	572 Feebleness	(575)
	573 Plainness	(576)
	574 Ornament	(577)

Section		Head	
	575	Elegance	(578)
	576	Inelegance	(579)
spoken language	577	Voice	(580)
	578	Aphony	(581)
	579	Speech	(582)
	580	Speech defect	(583)
	581	Loquacity	(584)
	582	Taciturnity	(585)
	583	Allocution	(586)
			(Response 587)
	584	Interlocution	(588)
	585	Soliloquy	(589)
written language	586	Writing	(590)
	587	Print	(591)
	588	Correspondence	(592)
	589	Book	(593)
	590	Description	(594)
	591	Dissertation	(595)
	592	Compendium	(596)
	593	Poetry. Prose	(597)
			(Prose 598)
	594	Drama	(599)

CLASS V. VOLITION

DIVISION (I). INDIVIDUAL VOLITION

Section	Head	
I Volition in General		
1° ACTS	595 Will	(600)
	596 Necessity	(601)
	597 Willingness	(602)
	598 Unwillingness	(603)
	599 Resolution	(604)
	600 Perseverance	(604a)
	601 Irresolution	(605)
	602 Obstinacy	(606)
	603 Tergiversation	(607)
	604 Caprice	(608)
	605 Choice	(609)
	606 Absence of choice	(609a)
	607 Rejection	(610)
	608 Predetermination	(611)
	609 Spontaneity	(612)
	610 Habit	(613)
	611 Desuetude	(614)
2° CAUSES	612 Motive	(615)
	(Absence of motive	615a)
	613 Dissuasion	(616)
	614 Pretext	(617)
3° OBJECTS	615 Good	(618)
	616 Evil	(619)
II Prospective Volition		
1° CONCEPTIONAL	617 Intention	(620)
	618 Non-design	(621)
	619 Pursuit	(622)
	620 Avoidance	(623)
	621 Relinquishment	(624)
	622 Business	(625)
	623 Plan	(626)
	624 Way	(627)
	625 Mid-course	(628)

Section	Head	
	626 Circuit	(629)
	627 Requirement	(630)
2° SUBSERVIENCE TO ENDS	628 Instrumentality	(631)
	629 Means	(632)
	630 Tool	(633)
		(Substitute 634)
	631 Materials	(635)
	632 Store	(636)
	633 Provision	(637)
	634 Waste	(638)
	635 Sufficiency	(639)
	636 Insufficiency	(640)
	637 Redundance	(641)
degrees of subservience	638 Importance	(642)
	639 Unimportance	(643)
	640 Utility	(644)
	641 Inutility	(645)
	642 Expedience	(646)
	643 Inexpedience	(647)
	644 Goodness	(648)
	645 Badness	(649)
	646 Perfection	(650)
	647 Imperfection	(651)
	648 Cleanness	(652)
	649 Uncleanness	(653)
	650 Health	(654)
	651 Disease	(655)
	652 Salubrity	(656)
	653 Insalubrity	(657)
	654 Improvement	(658)
	655 Deterioration	(659)
	656 Restoration	(660)
	657 Relapse	(661)
	658 Remedy	(662)
	659 Bane	(663)
contingent subservience	660 Safety	(664)
	661 Danger	(665)
	662 Refuge	(666)
	663 Pitfall	(667)
	664 Warning	(668)
	665 Danger Signal	(669)
	666 Preservation	(670)
	667 Escape	(671)
	668 Deliverance	(672)
3° PRECURSORY MEASURES	669 Preparation	(673)
	670 Non-preparation	(674)
	671 Essay	(675)

Section	*Head*	
	672 Undertaking	(676)
	673 Use	(677)
	674 Non-use	(678)
	675 Misuse	(679)
III Voluntary Action		
1° SIMPLE	676 Action	(680)
	677 Inaction	(681)
	678 Activity	(682)
	679 Inactivity	(683)
	680 Haste	(684)
	681 Leisure	(685)
	682 Exertion	(686)
	683 Repose	(687)
	684 Fatigue	(688)
	685 Refreshment	(689)
	686 Agent	(690)
	687 Workshop	(691)
2° COMPLEX	688 Conduct	(692)
	689 Management	(693)
	690 Director	(694)
	691 Advice	(695)
	692 Council	(696)
	693 Precept	(697)
	694 Skill	(698)
	695 Unskillfulness	(699)
	696 Proficient	(700)
	697 Bungler	(701)
	698 Cunning	(702)
	699 Artlessness	(703)
IV Antagonism		
1° CONDITIONAL	700 Difficulty	(704)
	701 Facility	(705)
2° ACTIVE	702 Hindrance	(706)
	703 Aid	(707)
	704 Opposition	(708)
	705 Opponent	(710)
	706 Cooperation	(709)
	707 Auxiliary	(711)
	708 Party	(712)
	709 Dissension	(713)
	710 Concord	(714)

Section	*Head*	
	711 Defiance	(715)
	712 Attack	(716)
	713 Defense	(717)
	714 Retaliation	(718)
	715 Resistance	(719)
	716 Contention	(720)
	717 Peace	(721)
	718 War	(722)
	719 Pacification	(723)
	720 Mediation	(724)
	721 Submission	(725)
	722 Combatant	(726)
	723 Arms	(727)
	724 Arena	(728)
V Results of Action		
	725 Completion	(729)
	726 Non-completion	(730)
	727 Success	(731)
	728 Failure	(732)
	729 Trophy	(733)
	730 Prosperity	(734)
	731 Adversity	(735)
	732 Mediocrity	(736)

DIVISION (II). INTERSOCIAL VOLITION

Section	*Head*	
I General		
	733 Authority	(737)
	734 Laxity	(738)
	735 Severity	(739)
	736 Lenity	(740)
	737 Command	(741)
	738 Disobedience	(742)
	739 Obedience	(743)
	740 Compulsion	(744)
	741 Master	(745)
	742 Servant	(746)
	743 Badge of Rule	(747)
	744 Freedom	(748)
	745 Subjection	(749)
	746 Liberation	(750)
	747 Restraint	(751)

Section	Head	
	748 Prison	(752)
	749 Keeper	(753)
	750 Prisoner	(754)
	751 Commission	(755)
	752 Abrogation	(756)
	753 Resignation	(757)
	754 Consignee	(758)
	755 Deputy	(759)
II Special		
	756 Permission	(760)
	757 Prohibition	(761)
	758 Consent	(762)
	759 Offer	(763)
	760 Refusal	(764)
	761 Request	(765)
	762 Deprecation	(766)
	763 Petitioner	(767)
III Conditional		
	764 Promise	(768)
	(Release	768a)
	765 Compact	(769)
	766 Conditions	(770)
	767 Security	(771)
	768 Observance	(772)
	769 Non-observance	(773)
	770 Compromise	(774)
IV Possessive Relations		
1° PROPERTY IN GENERAL	771 Acquisition	(775)
	772 Loss	(776)
	773 Possession	(777)
	774 Non-ownership	(777a)
	775 Joint possession	(778)
	776 Possessor	(779)
	777 Property	(780)
	778 Retention	(781)
	779 Non-retention	(782)
2° TRANSFER OF PROPERTY	780 Transfer	(783)
	781 Giving	(784)
	782 Receiving	(785)
	783 Apportionment	(786)
	784 Lending	(787)
	785 Borrowing	(788)

Section	*Head*	
	786 Taking	(789)
	787 Restitution	(790)
	788 Stealing	(791)
	789 Thief	(792)
	790 Booty	(793)
3° INTERCHANGE OF PROPERTY	791 Barter	(794)
	792 Purchase	(795)
	793 Sale	(796)
	794 Merchant	(797)
	795 Merchandise	(798)
	796 Mart	(799)
4° MONETARY RELATIONS	797 Money	(800)
	798 Treasury	(801)
	799 Treasurer	(802)
	800 Wealth	(803)
	801 Poverty	(804)
	802 Credit	(805)
	803 Debt	(806)
	804 Payment	(807)
	805 Non-payment	(808)
	806 Expenditure	(809)
	807 Receipt	(810)
	808 Accounts	(811)
	809 Price	(812)
	810 Discount	(813)
	811 Dearness	(814)
	812 Cheapness	(815)
	813 Liberality	(816)
	814 Economy	(817)
	815 Prodigality	(818)
	816 Parsimony	(819)

CLASS VI. AFFECTIONS

Section	*Head*	
I Affections Generally		
	817 Affections	(820)
	818 Feeling	(821)
	819 Sensibility	(822)
	820 Insensibility	(823)
	821 Excitation	(824)
	822 Excitability	(825)
	823 Inexcitability	(826)
II Personal		
1° PASSIVE	824 Joy	(827)
	825 Suffering	(828)
	826 Pleasurableness	(829)
	827 Painfulness	(830)
	828 Content	(831)
	829 Discontent	(832)
	830 Regret	(833)
	831 Relief	(834)
	832 Aggravation	(835)
	833 Cheerfulness	(836)
	834 Dejection	(837)
	835 Rejoicing	(838)
	836 Lamentation	(839)
	837 Amusement	(840)
	838 Tedium	(841)
	839 Wit	(842)
	840 Dullness	(843)
		(Humorist 844)
2° DISCRIMINATIVE	841 Beauty	(845)
	842 Ugliness	(846)
	843 Beautification	
	844 Ornamentation	(847)
	845 Blemish	(848)
		(Simplicity 849)
	846 Good taste	(850)
	847 Bad taste	(851)
	848 Fashion	(852)
	849 Ridiculousness	(853)
		(Fop 854)
	850 Affectation	(855)
	851 Ridicule	(856)
		(Laughing-stock 857)

Section	*Head*	
3° PROSPECTIVE	852 Hope	(858)
	853 Hopelessness	(859)
	854 Fear	(860)
	855 Courage	(861)
	856 Cowardice	(862)
	857 Rashness	(863)
	858 Caution	(864)
	859 Desire	(865)
	860 Indifference	(866)
	861 Dislike	(867)
	862 Fastidiousness	(868)
	863 Satiety	(869)
4° CONTEMPLATIVE	864 Wonder	(870)
	865 Non-wonder	(871)
		(Prodigy 872)
5° EXTRINSIC	866 Repute	(873)
	867 Disrepute	(874)
	868 Nobility	(875)
	869 Commonalty	(876)
	870 Title	(877)
	871 Pride	(878)
	872 Humility	(879)
	873 Vanity	(880)
	874 Modesty	(881)
	875 Ostentation	(882)
	876 Celebration	(883)
	877 Boasting	(884)
	878 Insolence	(885)
	879 Servility	(886)
		(Blusterer 887)

III Sympathetic

Section	*Head*	
1° SOCIAL	880 Friendship	(888)
	881 Enmity	(889)
		(Friend 890)
		(Enemy 891)
	882 Sociality	(892)
	883 Unsociability	(893)
	884 Courtesy	(894)
	885 Discourtesy	(895)
	886 Congratulation	(896)
	887 Love	(897)
	888 Hatred	(898)
	889 Endearment	(902)
	890 Darling	(899)
	891 Resentment	(900)

Section	*Head*	
	892 Irascibility	(901)
	893 Sullenness	(901a)
	894 Marriage	(903)
	895 Celibacy	(904)
	896 Divorce	(905)
2° DIFFUSIVE	897 Benevolence	(906)
	898 Malevolence	(907)
	899 Malediction	(908)
	900 Threat	(909)
	910 Philanthropy	(910)
	902 Misanthropy	(911)
	903 Benefactor	(912)
	904 Evildoer	(913)
3° SPECIAL	905 Pity	(914)
	906 Pitilessness	(914a)
		(Condolence 915)
4° RETROSPECTIVE	907 Gratitude	(916)
	908 Ingratitude	(917)
	909 Forgiveness	(918)
	910 Revenge	(919)
	911 Jealousy	(920)
	912 Envy	(921)

IV Moral

Section	*Head*	
1° OBLIGATION	913 Right	(922)
	914 Wrong	(923)
	915 Dueness	(924)
	916 Undueness	(925)
	917 Duty	(926)
	918 Dutilessness	(927)
	919 Non-liability	(927a)
2° SENTIMENTS	920 Respect	(928)
	921 Disrespect	(929)
	922 Contempt	(930)
	923 Approbation	(931)
	924 Disapprobation	(932)
	925 Flattery	(933)
	926 Detraction	(934)
		(Flatterer 935)
		(Detractor 936)
	927 Vindication	(937)
	928 Accusation	(938)

Section	Head	
3° CONDITIONS	929 Probity	(939)
	930 Improbity	(940)
		(Knave 941)
	931 Disinterestedness	(942)
	932 Selfishness	(943)
	933 Virtue	(944)
	934 Wickedness	(945)
	935 Innocence	(946)
	936 Guilt	(947)
	937 Good man	(948)
	938 Bad man	(949)
	939 Penitence	(950)
	940 Impenitence	(951)
	941 Atonement	(952)
4° PRACTICE	942 Temperance	(953)
	943 Intemperance	(954)
	944 Sensualism	(954a)
	945 Asceticism	(955)
	946 Fasting	(956)
	947 Gluttony	(957)
	948 Sobriety	(958)
	949 Drunkenness	(959)
	950 Purity	(960)
	951 Impurity	(961)
	952 Libertine	(962)
5° INSTITUTIONS	953 Legality	(963)
	954 Illegality	(964)
	955 Jurisdiction	(965)
	956 Tribunal	(966)
	957 Judge	(967)
	958 Lawyer	(968)
	959 Litigation	(969)
	960 Acquittal	(970)
	961 Condemnation	(971)
	962 Reward	(973)
	963 Punishment	(972)
		(Penalty 974)
	964 Means of punishment	(975)

V Religious

Section	Head	
1° SUPERHUMAN	965 Divineness	(976)
	966 Gods in general	
	967 Pantheon	
	968 Angel	(977)
		(Satan 978)
		(Jupiter 979)

Section	*Head*	
	969 Devil	(980)
	970 Fairy	
	971 Heaven	(981)
	972 Hell	(982)
2° DOCTRINES	973 Religion	(983)
	974 Irreligion	(989)
	975 Revelation	(985)
	(Pseudo-revelation 986)	
	976 Orthodoxy	(983a)
	977 Heterodoxy	(984)
	978 Sectarianism	
3° SENTIMENTS	979 Piety	(987)
	980 Impiety	(988)
4° ACTS	981 Worship	(990)
	982 Idolatry	(991)
	983 Sorcery	(992)
		(Spell 993)
		(Sorcerer 994)
	984 Occultism	
5° INSTITUTIONS	985 Churchdom	(995)
	986 Clergy	(996)
	987 Laity	(997)
	988 Ritual	(998)
	989 Canonicals	(999)
	990 Temple	(1000)

INSTRUCTIONS

INDEX. Having read the preface to this edition, or that part of it beginning "Whom does a thesaurus help?" (p. xv), the reader will understand what kind of words he will be looking up. These words—the main entries—are in roman type and are listed in alphabetical order. When the main entry is a phrase of two or more words, hyphenated or not, its place will still be found in the alphabetical order of consecutive letters, as though it were a single word. When the entry is double, being two distinct words separated by a comma, these are to be regarded as alternatives, either of which may be found in the particular text to which the references point; (s) after an entry means that it may appear in the text in its singular or plural form.

In order to avoid the frequent repetition of references, a word once entered as, say, a noun may not be separately indexed in the form it assumes as a verb or adjective, provided (i) its place in the index, if it were entered, would be very close to that form of the word which is actually indexed; (ii) it occurs only *under the same heads* as that form which *is* indexed; (iii) no difference in meaning is involved, apart from its being a different part of speech. Thus, the verb "admire" is not indexed, while the noun "admiration" has four references. This means that the verb "admire" occurs only in the same four heads, and not elsewhere. On the other hand, the verb "deteriorate" is indexed with four references only; the noun "deterioration" with fourteen. This means that "deteriorate" has four references to heads under which the noun "deterioration" does not occur, and that the other occurrences of the verb "deteriorate" must be looked for among the fourteen heads referenced for the noun "deterioration." The full coverage for the *idea* of deterioration is obtained by combining the references under "deteriorate" and "deterioration," making eighteen in all. This is a typical case, and a safe rule when consulting the index is to include in the same purview adjacent entries, if these register different forms of the same word. Adverbs in -ly are not usually indexed; nor are participial forms in -ed and -ing, except where they have acquired idiomatic senses which differentiate them from the corresponding noun and verb.

The subentries are the references. These comprise three elements—a keyword (in italics), a number, and an abbreviation for part of speech (n. = noun; adj. = adjective; vb. = verb; adv. = adverb). The keyword is not a definition, but gives broadly the sense of the main entry for that particular reference and thus distinguishes it from the other references. It also tells the inquirer that in the head of text corresponding in number, in that subdivision corresponding to the part of speech, there is a subhead denoted by the same italicized keyword. In that subhead he will find the word he has just looked up, associated with words of similar meaning. The number, of course, is the number of the head in which the keyword occurs. The part of speech indicates the particular subdivision of the head to which the subhead appertains. It also removes ambiguity when the meaning of a word depends upon its part of speech. For instance, to understand the word "well," we have to know whether it is being used as a noun, as an adjective, as a verb, or as an adverb.

Condensed references will sometimes be met with. Thus "amputate" occurs with a reference: *cut, sunder* 46 vb. This means that in the head numbered 46, among the verbs, there is a subhead with the keyword *cut,* and another with the keyword *sunder,* and "amputate" is found in both. Another type is exampled under "claim," which has a reference: *desire* 859 n., vb. This means that in the head numbered 859, the keyword *desire* occurs both in the subdivision for nouns and in that for verbs; and the word "claim" (itself both noun and verb) will be found in both places.

To sum up: to find your place in the text, you turn up some suitable word in the index and select the most promising reference, noting the number and the keyword, and the part of speech. You turn to the head bearing the corresponding number. In the subdivision corresponding to the part of speech, you will find the same keyword at the head of a paragraph. In that paragraph you may start your search.

Example (i). Suppose you look up "besetting." It is found with three references, of which perhaps you choose, as closest to your meaning, the one with the keyword *habitual.* This reference is *habitual* 610 adj. You turn to the head of text numbered 610 (it is entitled **Habit**), and note that the subdivision for adjectives (beginning **Adj.**) has three subheads beginning respectively with the italicized keywords *habitual, usual, habituated.* The one you want is, of course, the subhead *habitual.* In this paragraph you find "besetting" in the immediate context of "haunting, clinging, obsessive"; and it is surrounded with other contexts all bearing on the idea of "habitual."

Example (ii). You look up "bungling." It is not in the Index. "Bungle," however, occurs with five references, mainly verbal. You decide that *be clumsy* gives the *idea* you have in mind, though you are not wanting a verb. This reference is "*be clumsy* 695 vb." You turn to the head numbered 695. Under this head, entitled **Unskillfulness,** you have two noun subheads denoted by *unskillfulness* and *bungling,* and three adjectival subheads, viz. *unskillful, unskilled, clumsy*. According as you wish for a noun or an adjective you start looking in the subhead you think most appropriate.

TEXT. The heads are the numbered sections (1–990) which run consecutively through the text and contain the listed vocabulary. The numbers in the top corner of each page are the numbers of those heads whose vocabulary, in whole or in part, is listed on that page. The heads have separate subdivisions (vocabulary permitting) for nouns, adjectives, verbs, adverbs and interjections. Within these subdivisions (interjections excepted) there are paragraphs beginning with a keyword in italics. These are the subheads.

Having reached his subhead, the reader will find in it the word he has looked up, standing by itself, or as the dominant word in a phrase. It will be in a fairly close context, which may offer him immediately what he wants. If not, as he reads through the subhead he will pass in smooth transitions from context to context. To render transitions more distinct, a word or expression is sometimes inserted which is more a pointer to the context than a part of vocabulary. He will frequently encounter cross-references with the same three elements of number, keyword and part of speech as he has found in the index, pointing to other heads. Before following them up, he may wish to expand his field of choice locally. He may begin by looking at some other subhead within the same numbered section. Occasional directions in the text advise him to do so. They occur in the form **See** followed by the keyword in italics. He need not confine himself to the same part of speech, for nouns, adjectives and verbs may often, with little or no variation, be interchanged. This is sometimes suggested in the text by "etc. n.," "etc. adj.," "etc. vb.," which means that fresh vocabulary may be generated from the nouns, adjectives or verbs by modifying them according to the example given. Thus, **206** begins "*Narrowness* etc. adj.," meaning that more nouns may be made by adding -ness to appropriate adjectives. It will be noticed that, among the adjectives listed, "close," "tight" and "strait" may be treated in this way. Many verbal keywords are made by joining the auxiliary verb "be" with an adjective. When the reader meets such a case as "**Vb.** *be short,*—brief etc. adj." (under **204**), it is a hint that other compound expressions like "be brief" can be made by utilizing the adjectival vocabulary. It should not be overlooked that keywords themselves may be treated as part of the vocabulary, and are frequently indexed as such.

Neighboring heads—and not only those that express opposite relationships—frequently have a close bearing on one another. A particular case is when one head expresses a passive or intransitive aspect and another expresses the active aspect of the same idea. **60 Order** represents mainly the notion of a state of order, and **62 Arrangement** that of reduction to order. Similar is the relationship between **230 Circumjacence** (with **233 Outline)** and **232 Circumscription** (with **235 Enclosure**). The inquirer may therefore with good reason first turn to the neighboring heads before striking further afield in following up the internal references; but of course it is the internal references that will offer him the widest range.

Explanatory comment in the text is kept to a minimum and is reserved for the removal of possible ambiguities. Thus, under **Adj.** *broad,* the adj. "wideawake" is explained by (hat); under **N.** *knock,* the entries "cut, drive," and "innings" are both followed by (cricket). In two instances only are these explanatory terms abbreviated: astron. = astronomy; mus. = music.

The titles of the heads are printed in bold type, after the numbers. A head may have more than one such title: e.g. **132 Young person. Young animal. Young plant.** A word or phrase, following a title and printed in roman type, is intended for further definition; e.g. **141 Periodicity**: regularity of recurrence.

PUNCTUATION. In the text, commas are used to separate words; semicolons, roughly, to distinguish contexts; but semicolons no less frequently associate words in subgroups without necessarily exhausting the context. Punctuation is omitted in front of the internal references in order to show that they are part of the context and may even help to sum it up.

ABBREVIATIONS. In the vocabulary, an abbreviation consisting of an initial letter and a period denotes that a preceding word, or that part of it which begins with the same letter, is to be repeated. Thus the context "deck, top d., lower d." is to be read as "deck, top deck, lower deck." Abbreviations for parts of speech occur at the beginnings of the appropriate subdivisions of the head: **N.** = noun; **Adj.** = adjective; **Vb.** = verb; **Adv.** = adverb; **Int.** = interjection. The first four of these abbreviations also occur in the references.

TEXT

For instructions on how to use this text see pages lxxvii-xxc

1 Existence

N. *existence,* esse, being entity; absolute being, absoluteness, givenness; aseity, self-existence; unit of being, monad, Platonic idea, Platonic form; a being, entity, ens; subsistent being, subsistence 360n. *life;* survival, eternity 115n. *perpetuity;* preexistence 119n. *priority;* coexistence, this life 121n. *present time;* existence in space, presence, currency, prevalence 189n. *presence;* entelechy, becoming, evolution 147n. *conversion;* creation 164n. *production;* potentiality 469n. *possibility;* ontology, metaphysics, existentialism, realism 449n. *philosophy.*

reality, realness, actuality, actual existence, entelechy; thatness 80n. *specialty;* positiveness; historicity, factuality, factualness 494n. *truth;* fact, matter of f., positive f., brute f., stubborn f., fait accompli, event 154n. *eventuality;* real thing, not a dream, no joke, no mockery, no kidding; realities, basics, fundamentals, bedrock, brass tacks 638n. *important matter.*

essence, finite existence; nature, real n., quiddity, hypostasis, substance 3n. *substantiality;* constitutive principle, inner being, sum and substance 5n. *intrinsicality;* prime constituent, soul, heart, core, center 224n. *interiority.*

Adj. *existing,* existent, ontic, entitative, outside nothingness, more than potential; existential; essential 5adj. *intrinsic;* absolute, given, self-existing, increate, uncreated; unimagined, unideal; being, in existence, under the sun; preexistent 119adj. *prior;* coexistent 121adj. *present;* subsistent, living, undying, immortal, eternal 115adj. *perpetual;* standing, surviving, extant, undestroyed, indestructible 360adj. *alive;* current, rife, prevalent, in vogue, afloat, on foot 189adj. *ubiquitous;* ontological, metaphysical.

real, essential, quidditative; subsistential, substantive 3adj. *substantial;* actual, positive, factual, historical, grounded, well-g. 494adj. *true;* natural, of nature, physical, of flesh and blood 319adj. *material;* concrete, solid 324adj. *dense.*

Vb. *be,* exist, have being, share in existence; be so and not otherwise; be the case 494vb. *be true;* consist in, inhere in, reside in 5vb. *be intrinsic;* preexist 119vb. *be before;* coexist, coincide 123vb. *synchronize;* subsist 121vb. *be now;* abide, continue 146vb. *go on;* endure, stand 113vb. *last;* vegetate, pass the time, live one's life; be alive, draw breath, see the sun 360vb. *live;* exist in space, be found, be met, stand, lie 186vb. *be situate;* be here, be there, meet one 189vb. *be present;* obtain, prevail, reign, spread, be rife 189vb. *pervade;* take place, come about, occur 154vb. *happen;* hold, hold good 494vb. *be true;* represent, stand for, stand as 13vb. *be identical.*

become, come to be, come into existence, first see the light of day, take flesh 360vb. *be born;* arise, spring up 68vb. *begin;* unfold, develop, grow, take form, take shape 316vb. *evolve;* turn out, change into 147vb. *be turned to.*

Adv. *actually,* really, substantively; essentially, substantially, inherently, intrinsically; ipso facto; in essence, virtually, to all intents and purposes; potentially 469adv. *possibly;* factually, in fact, in point of f. 494adv. *truly.*

See: 3, 5, 13, 68, 80, 113, 115, 119, 121, 123, 146, 147, 154, 164, 186, 189, 224, 316, 319, 324, 360, 449, 469, 494, 638.

2 Non-existence

N. *non-existence,* non-subsistence, inexistence, non-being, nonentity; nonexistence in time 109n. *neverness;* non-existence in space, nullibiety 190n. *absence;* blank, vacuum 190n. *emptiness;* nothing, nil, cipher 103n. *zero;* a nothing, nonentity, thing of naught 4n. *insubstantial thing;* no such thing, no one 190n. *nobody;* nihilism, negativeness 533n. *negation;* negative result 728n. *failure.*

extinction, oblivion, nirvana; no life 361n. *death;* dying out, decay, obsolesence 127n. *oldness;* annihilation, nihilism 165n. *destruction;* abeyance, suspension 752n. *abrogation;* amnesty 506n. *oblivion;* cancellation, rubbing out, sponge, clean slate, tabula rasa 550n. *obliteration.*

Adj. *non-existent,* non-subsistent, inexistent, unexisting, without being; null, minus; nowhere, lost, missing, omitted 190adj. *absent;* negatived, null and void 752adj. *abrogated;* sponged, canceled 550adj. *obliterated.*

unreal, non-actual; without reality, baseless, groundless, unfounded, false 495adj. *erroneous;* visionary, fabulous 513adj. *imaginary;* without substance, without content 4adj. *insubstantial;* unrealized, unmaterialized, unevolved, undeveloped, ungrown 670adj. *immature;* potential, only possible 469adj. *possible;* only supposed 512adj. *suppositional.*

unborn, uncreated, unmade; unbegotten, unconceived; undiscovered, uninvented, unimagined; yet to come, in the womb of time 124adj. *future.*

extinct, died out, vanished, lost and gone forever; no more, dead and gone, defunct 361adj. *dead;* obsolescent, vanishing 361adj. *dying;* obsolete; functus officio, finished, over and done with.

Vb. *not be,* have no existence, have no life; lack reality, exist only in the imagination; be null and void; not happen, never happen, fail to materialize, not come off; be yet unborn

pass away, cease to exist, become extinct, die out, perish from the earth; be no more 361vb. *die;* lose one's life 361vb. *perish;* come to nothing, lapse into nothingness; sink into oblivion 506vb. *be forgotten;* go, fly away, vanish, leave no trace; dematerialize, melt into thin air, sink into the earth 446vb. *disappear;* evaporate 338vb. *vaporize;* melt, dissolve 337vb. *liquefy.*

nullify, reduce to nothing, annihilate, snuff out, blow o.; render null and void, suspend 752vb. *abrogate;* negative 533vb. *negate;* cancel 550vb. *obliterate;* abolish, wipe out 165vb. *destroy.*

Adv. *negatively,* in vacuo; not really, by courtesy only.

See: 4, 103, 109, 124, 127, 165, 190, 337, 338, 361, 446, 469, 495, 506, 512, 513, 533, 550, 670, 728, 752.

3 Substantiality

N. *substantiality,* essentiality 1n. *reality;* substantivity, objectivity; hypostasis, personality, personal existence; corporeity, visibility, tangibility, palpability, concreteness, solidity 319n. *materiality;* ponderability, weight 322n. *gravity;* pithiness, meatiness; stuff, world-s., hyle 319n. *matter;* totality of existence, plenum, world, world of nature 321n. *universe.*

substance, subsistent entity, hypostasis; substratum; thing, something, somebody 319n. *object;* person, creature; body, flesh and blood, living matter 360n. *life;* solid, concretion, corpus 324n. *solid body;* pith, marrow 224n. *interiority:* gist 514n. *meaning.*

Adj. *substantial,* hypostatic, personal 5adj. *intrinsic;* real, objective, natural, of nature, physical 319adj. *material;* concrete, solid, tangible, palpable 324adj. *dense;* considerable 638adj. *important;* bulky 195adj. *large;* heavy 322adj. *weighty;* pithy, meaty, full of substance.

Adv. *substantially,* corporeally, bodily, physically; personally, in person; essentially 5adv. *intrinsically;* largely, mainly, in the main 32adv. *greatly.*

See: 1, 5, 32, 195, 224, 319, 321, 322, 324, 360, 514, 638.

4 Unsubstantiality

N. *insubstantiality,* nothingness 2n. *non-existence;* naught, nothing, nothing at all, not a whit, not a particle, not a scrap 103n. *zero;* no one, not a soul 190n. *nobody;* abstraction, incorporeity, incorporeality 320n. *immateriality;* lack of substance, imponderability, lightness 323n. *levity;* meagerness, tenuity 206n. *thinness;* sparseness 325n. *rarity;* lack of depth, superficiality 212adj. *shallowness;* intangibility, invisibility; inanity, vanity, vacuity, vacancy, void, hollowness 190n. *emptiness;* fatuity 497n. *absurdity;* pointlessness 10n. *irrelevance;* hallucination, self-delusion 542n. *deception;* fantasy 513n. *imagination;* maya, unreality.

insubstantial thing, emblem, token, symbol 547n. *indication;* abstraction, shadow without substance, shadow, shade, dream, vision; ghost, spirit, optical illusion, will-o'-the wisp, ignis fatuus 440n. *visual fallacy;* air, thin a., wind, breath, vapor, mist; bubble, gossamer, snowman 163n. *weak thing;* wisp, straw 639n. *trifle;* vain thing, vanity, vanity of vanities, inanity, fatuity, fool's paradise 499n. *folly;* flight of fancy, figment of the imagination, golden dreams, pipe-dream 413n. *fantasy;* all talk, moonshine, cock-and-bull story; idle talk, gossip, gup, rumor 515n. *empty talk;* tall talk 546n. *exaggeration;* thing of naught, mockery, pretense, chimera, figment, courtesy title; nine days' wonder, flash in the pan, damp squib, blank cartridge; empty voice, vox et praeterea nihil; cry of "wolf," 665n. *false alarm;* figurehead, lay figure, dummy, man of straw; fictitious person, invented character, John Doe and Richard Roe; pomp-

ous ass, stuffed shirt 639n. *nonentity.*
Adj. *insubstantial,* unsubstantial, abstract; inessential, not intrinsic; nonphysical 320adj. *immaterial;* bodiless, bloodless, incorporeal; lightweight 323adj. *light;* light as air, airy, ethereal; thin, tenuous, gauzy, gossamer 422adj. *transparent;* pale 426adj. *colorless;* vaporous, misty 336adj. *gaseous;* fragile 330adj. *brittle;* ghostly, spectral 970adj. *spooky;* fleeting, shadowy, vague 446adj. *disappearing;* vacuous, vacant, hollow, void 190adj. *empty;* vain, inane; honorary, nominal, paper, fictitious; emblematic, symbolic, token 547 adj. *indicating;* without substance, groundless, unfounded; visionary, dreamy, chimerical, fantastical 513 adj. *imaginary;* pointless, senseless, meaningless 515adj. *unmeaning;* blank, characterless, featureless, null; without depth, superficial 212 adj. *shallow.*
Vb. 2vb. *not be;* pass away, nullify.
Adv. *insubstantially,* unreally; nominally, by courtesy; in a vacuum.
See: 2, 10, 103, 163, 190, 206, 212, 320, 323, 325, 330, 336, 413, 422, 426, 440, 446, 497, 499, 513, 515, 542, 546, 547, 639, 665, 970.

5 Intrinsicality

N. *intrinsicality,* inbeing, inexistence, inherence, inhesion, immanence; inwardness, reflexiveness; virtuality, potentiality 160n. *power;* subjectiveness, subjectivity, subjectivism, self-reference; ego, personality 80n. *self.*
essential part, essence, important part, prime ingredient, prime constituent; principle, property, virtue, capacity; quintessence, substance, stuff, quiddity; incarnation, embodiment; life, life-blood, heart's blood, sap; jugular vein, artery; heart, soul, heart and soul; backbone, marrow, pith, fiber; core, kernel; flower; gist, nub, nucleus 638n. *chief thing.*
character, nature, quality; constitution, diathesis, ethos; type, make, stamp, breed; characteristics, complex; cast, color, hue; aspects, features; diagnosis, diagnostics; mark, note.
temperament, temper, humor, disposition, mood, spirit 817n. *affections;* crasis, idiosyncrasy; grain, vein, streak, strain, trait 179n. *tendency;* habit, peculiarity 80n. *specialty.*
heredity, endowment; id, gene, allelomorph, inherited characteristic; inborn capacity; inborn tendency, original sin; ancestry 169n. *genealogy;* telegony, atavism 106n. *recurrence;* traducianism, generationism; Galton's law, Mendelian ratio.
Adj. *intrinsic,* intrinsical, immanent, deep down, deep-seated, deep-rooted; inherent 58adj. *ingredient;* inward, internal 224adj. *interior;* absorbed, inwrought, inwoven, implicit; derived from within, autistic, subjective, introversive, reflexive, inward-looking, introverted; characteristic, personal, indigenous, native; basic, fundamental, radical; a priori, original, primary, elemental, cardinal, normal; essential, substantive; virtual, potential, capable.
genetic, inherited, hereditary, atavistic, heritable, inborn, ingenerate; native, connate, congenital, connatural; incarnate, ingrained, bred in the bone.
characteristic 80adj. *special;* characterizing, qualitative; diagnostic, idiomorphic, proper; ineradicable, settled, incurable, invariable; constant, unchanging.
Vb.. *be intrinsic,* — immanent etc. adj.; inexist, inhere 773n. *belong;* be born like it; inherit, take after, run in the blood; be marked with, be stamped with, be characterized by; involve, mean 523vb. *imply.*
Adv. *intrinsically* etc. adj.; at bottom, fundamentally, essentially, substantially, virtually; in effect, in the main.
See: 58, 80, 106, 160, 179, 224, 523, 638, 773.

6 Extrinsicality

N. *extrinsicality,* objectiveness, objectivity; transcendence 34n. *superiority;* otherness, the other, nonego, not-self 59n. *extraneousness;* externality, outwardness, outer darkness, outer space 223n. *exteriority;* objectification, externalization; projection, extrapolation, extratensivity, extroversion, extrovert; accidence, modality 7n. *state;* accident, contingency, casuality 159n. *chance;* accrual, accessory, acquired characteristic 40n. *adjunct.*
Adj. *extrinsic,* extrinsical 59adj. *extraneous;* transcendent 34adj. *superior;* outward, external, extramural 223adj. *exterior;* outward-looking, extroitive, extroverted; derived from without, acquired, engrafted, inbred, instilled, inculcated; supervenient, accessory, adventitious, adscititious 38adj. *additional;* incidental, acci-

dental, contingent, fortuitous 159adj. *casual;* non-essential, inessential; subsidiary, subordinate 35adj. *inferior.*
Vb. *be extrinsic,* lie without, not belong; transcend 34vb. *be superior;* come from without, supervene 38vb. *accrue.*
make extrinsic, objectify, realize, project, extrapolate 223vb. *externalize;* body forth 551vb. *represent.*
Adv. *extrinsically,* outwardly; from outside.
See: 7, 34, 35, 38, 40, 59, 159, 223, 551.

7 State: absolute condition
N. *state,* modal existence, suchness; estate, lot, walk, walk of life; case, way, plight, pickle 8n. *circumstance;* position, category, status, footing, standing, rank; condition, trim, fettle, fig; habitude, habit, diathesis, complexion 5n. *temperament;* temper, mood 817n. *affections;* state of health, physical condition.
modality, mode, fashion, style; stamp, set, fit, mold 243n. *form;* frame, fabric, bone 331n. *structure;* aspect, phase, light, complexion, guise 445n. *appearance;* tenor 179n. *tendency.*
Adj. *conditionate,* conditional, such; modal, formal 243adj. *formative;* organic 331adj. *structural;* in a state of; in condition, in form, in good f. 694adj. *skillful;* in bad form 695adj. *clumsy.*
Vb. *be in a state of,* be such, be so; be on a footing; stand, lie, labor under; do, fare; possess a state, enjoy a s.
Adv. *conditionally,* it being so, as it is, as things are, as the matter stands, provisionally.
See: 5, 8, 27, 179, 243, 331, 445, 694, 695, 817.

8 Circumstance
N. *circumstance,* circumstances, factors, situation; total situation, personal world, idioverse, life space; environment, milieu 230n. *circumjacence;* context 9n. *relation;* regime, setup 7n. *state;* posture, posture of affairs, look of things, appearances 445n. *appearance;* lay of the land, how the land lies 186n. *bearings;* footing, standing, status, relative position 27n. *degree,* 9n. *relation;* plight, pickle, awkward situation, pass, pinch, corner, hole, jam, dilemma 700n. *predicament.*
juncture, conjuncture, stage, point 154n. *eventuality;* crossroads, crossways, turning point, match point, point of no return; moment, hour, right time, opportunity 137n. *occasion;* critical moment, crucial m., hour of decision, emergency 137n. *crisis.*
Adj. *circumstantial,* given, modal 7adj. *conditionate;* surrounding, environmental, contextual 230adj. *circumjacent;* circumscribing, limiting 232adj. *circumscribed;* provisional, temporary 114adj. *transient;* variable 152adj. *changeful;* dependent on circumstances, contingent, incidental, adventitious 154adj. *eventful;* emergent, critical, crucial; auspicious, favorable 137adj. *opportune;* fitting the circumstances, suitable, seemly 24adj. *agreeing;* appropriate, convenient 642adj. *expedient.*
Adv. *thus,* so, in such wise; like this, in this way; from that angle.
accordingly, and so, according as, depending on; according to circumstances, as the wind blows, as it turns out, as the case may be.
if, if so be, should it so happen, should it be that; in the event of, in the case of, in case; provisionally, provided that 7adv. *conditionally;* supposing, assuming, granting, allowing, taking it that; if not, unless, except, without.
See: 7, 9, 24, 27, 114, 137, 152, 154, 186, 230, 232, 445, 642, 700.

9 Relation
N. *relation,* relatedness, connectedness, "rapport," reference, respect, regard; bearing, direction; concern, concernment, interest, import 638n. *importance;* involvement, implication 5n. *intrinsicality;* appetency 859n. *desire;* relationship, homogeneity, cognation, affinity, affiliation, filiation, kinship 11n. *consanguinity;* classification, classifiability 62n. *arrangement;* belongingness, association, alliance, intimacy 880n. *friendship;* liaison, linkage, connection, link, tie-up, bond of union 47n. *bond;* something in common, common reference, common source, common denominator 775n. *joint possession;* syntax 60n. *order;* context, milieu, environment 8n. *circumstance;* import, intention 514n. *meaning.*
relativeness, relativity, functionality, interconnection, mutual relation, function 12n. *correlation;* same relation, homology, correspondence 13n.

identity, 28n. *equality;* similar relation, analogy 18n. *similarity;* comparability 462n. *comparison;* close relation, apposition, approximation 289n. *approach,* 200n. *nearness,* 202n. *contiguity,* 89n. *accompaniment;* parallel relation, collaterality, registration (printing) 219n. *parallelism,* 245n. *symmetry;* proportionality, perspective, proportion, ratio, scale; causal relation, causality, cause and effect 156n. *cause;* governing relation 178n. *influence;* dependence 745n. *subjection,* 157n. *effect;* subordinate relation 35n. *inferiority;* logical relation (**see** *relevance*); relative position, stage, status, rank 27n. *degree;* serial order 65n. *sequence;* relativism, relationism 449n. *philosophy;* relativist, relationist.

relevance, logical relation, logicality, logical argument 475n. *reasoning;* chain of reasoning, syllogism, sorites 475n. *argumentation;* fitness, suitability, just relation, due proportion 24n. *agreement;* point, application, applicability, appositeness, pertinence, propriety, comparability; case in point, good example, crass e., palmary instance 83n. *example.*

referral, making reference, referment, reference; application, allusion, mention; citation, quotation; frame of reference, object of reference, referent; referendary, referee.

Adj. *relative,* not absolute; relational, referential, respective; relativist, relativistic; referable, referrible; en rapport, related, connected, linked, entwined; bearing upon, concerning, in aid of; of concern, of interest, of import 638adj. *important;* belonging, appertaining, appurtenant 773adj. *possessed;* in common 775adj. *sharing;* mutual, reciprocal, corresponding, answering to 12adj. *correlative;* classifiable, in the same category 62adj. *arranged;* serial, consecutive 65adj. *sequent;* affinitive congenial, affiliated, cognate, kindred 11 adj. *akin;* homologous, analogous, like 18adj. *similar;* comparative, comparable 462adj. *compared;* approximative, approximating, approaching 200adj. *near;* collateral 219adj. *parallel;* proportional, proportionate, varying as, in ratio, to scale; in due proportion, proportionable, commensurate 245adj. *symmetrical;* perspectival, in perspective; contextual, environmental.

relevant, logical, in context; apposite, pertinent, applicable; pointed, to the point, well-directed 475adj. *rational;* proper, appropriate, suitable, fitting 24adj. *apt;* alluding, allusive; quotable, worth mentioning.

Vb. *be related,* have a relation, stand in a r., lie in a perspective; have a reference, refer to, regard, respect, have to do with; bear upon, be a factor 178vb. *influence;* touch, concern, deal with, interest, affect; own a connection 11vb. *be akin;* belong, pertain, appertain; approximate to 289vb. *approach;* answer to, correspond, reciprocate 12vb. *correlate;* have a connection, tie in with; be congruent, register with (printing) 24vb. *accord;* be proportionate, vary as; be relevant, have point, support an analogy, serve as an example; come to the point, get down to brass tacks.

relate, bring into relation, put in perspective; connect with, gear to, gear with; apply, bring to, bear upon; link, connect, entwine, tie up with 45vb. *tie;* frame, provide a background; compare 18vb. *liken;* proportion, symmetrize, parallel; balance 28vb. *equalize;* establish a connection, draw a parallel, find an example 475vb. *reason;* make a reference to, refer to, touch on, allude to, mention; index, supply *or* furnish with references 547vb. *indicate.*

Adv. *relatively,* not absolutely, in a context; in relation, contextually; in its degree, comparatively, in comparison; proportionally, in ratio, to scale, in perspective; conditionally, circumstantially; appropriately 24adv. *pertinently.*

concerning, touching, regarding; as to, as regards, with regard to, with respect to; relating to, with reference to, about, anent, on, under; in connection with; in relation to, bearing on; speaking of, apropos, by the way, by the bye, on the subject of; on the point of, as far as concerns; in the matter of, in re; under the head of; on the part of, on the score of; whereas; forasmuch, inasmuch; concerning which, whereto, whereunder; thereto, thereunder; hereto, hereunder; whereof, thereof, hereof.

See: 5, 8, 11, 12, 13, 18, 24, 27, 28, 35, 45, 47, 60, 62, 65, 83, 89, 156, 157, 178, 200, 202, 219, 245, 289, 449, 462, 475, 514, 547, 638, 745, 773, 775, 800, 859.

10 Irrelation: absence of relation

N. *irrelation,* unrelatedness, absoluteness; independence 744n. *freedom;*

arbitrariness, unilaterality; separateness, insularity, isolation 46n. *separation;* unclassifiability, rootlessness, homelessness; singularity, individuality 80n. *specialty;* lack of connection, inconnection, unconnectedness, no context; inconsequence (**see** *irrelevance*); disconnection, dissociation 46n. *disjunction,* 72n. *discontinuity;* misconnection, wrong association, misdirection, wrong address 495n. *error;* disproportion, asymmetry 246n. *distortion;* incommensurability, disparity 29n. *inequality;* diversity, heterogeneity, multifariousness 15n. *difference,* 17n. *non-uniformity,* 82n. *multiformity;* incongruence 84n. *unconformity;* irreconcilability 14n. *contrariety;* intrusion, intrusiveness, untimeliness 138n. *intempestivity;* no concern, no interest, no business, nobody's b.; square peg in a round hole 25n. *misfit;* exotic, alien element, intruder, cuckoo in the nest 59n. *extraneousness.*

irrelevance, irrelevancy; illogicality, unreason 477n. *sophistry;* pointlessness, inapplicability, bad example, no e.; impertinence, ineptitude; inconsequence, non sequitur; parenthesis, obiter dictum 231n. *interjacence;* diversion, red herring 612n. *incentive;* episode, incidental 154n. *eventuality;* inessential, non-essential 639n. *unimportance.*

Adj. *irrelative,* without relation, unrelated, absolute, self-existing; independent 744adj. *unconfined;* owing nothing to, original 21adj. *unimitated;* irrespective, regardless, non-regarding, unilateral, arbitrary; irrelated, unclassified, unidentified; unclassifiable, rootless, homeless, kinless, birthless, from nowhere; adrift, wandering, astray 282adj. *deviating;* detached, isolated, insular 88adj. *alone;* unconcerned, uninvolved 860adj. *indifferent;* unconnected, without context, misconnected, disconnected, unallied 46adj. *disjoined;* digressive, parenthetic, anecdotal; episodic, incidental 72adj. *discontinuous;* separate, singular, individual 80adj. *special;* private, of no concern, without interest, nothing to do with; inessential 639adj. *trivial;* exotic, foreign, alien, strange outlandish 59adj. *extraneous;* uncongenial, ungermane; intrusive, untimely 138adj. *ill-timed;* inappropriate, inept 25adj. *unapt;* not comparable, incommensurable, disparate 29adj. *unequal;* disproportionate, out of proportion, asymmetrical 246adj. *distorted;* incongruent, discordant 84adj. *unconformable;* irreconcilable 14adj. *contrary;* heterogeneous 17adj. *non-uniform;* multifarious 82adj. *multiform.*

irrelevant, illogical, inapposite, inapplicable, pointless; impertinent, inept, inappropriate 25adj. *disagreeing;* out of order, misapplied, misplaced, misdirected, misaimed, to the wrong address 495adj. *erroneous;* off-target, off the beam, off-center, peripheral; rambling, wandering 570adj. *diffuse;* adrift, beside the point, beside the mark, beside the purpose, foreign to the p., neither here nor there; trivial, inessential 639adj. *unimportant;* inconsequent, inconsequential; parenthetic, obiter; episodic, incidental, ungermane; remote, far-fetched, out-of-the-way, forced, strained; academic, impractical.

Vb. *be unrelated,* have no concern with, have nothing to do w., owe nothing to, disown; have no right to be there, have no place in 190vb. *be absent;* not be one's business, be nobody's b.; not concern, not touch, not interest; be irrelevant, be off the point, avoid the issue, cloud the i., draw a red herring; force, strain; lug in by the heels; ramble, wander, lose the thread 570vb. *be diffuse.*

Adv. *unrelatedly,* irrespective, regardless; without regard, without respect, without reference; irrelevantly, illogically, inappropriately; parenthetically, incidentally, obiter; episodically.

See: 14, 15, 17, 21, 25, 29, 46, 59, 72, 80, 82, 84, 88, 138, 154, 190, 231, 246, 282, 477, 495, 570, 612, 639, 744, 860.

11 Consanguinity: relations of kindred

N. *consanguinity,* relationship, kinship, kindred, blood 169n. *parentage;* filiation, affiliation, apparentation, affinity, propinquity, joking relationship; blood-relationship, agnation, cognation; ancestry, lineage, descent; connection, alliance, family, family connection; ties of family, ties of blood, ties of race, nationality 371n. *nation;* nepotism; atavism.

kinsman, kinswoman, sib; kindred, kith and kin, kinsfolk, relations; near relative, next of kin, distant relation, blood r.; relation by marriage, step-relation; brethren, children, offspring, issue, one's flesh and blood; agnate, cognate, congener, affine; twin, identical t.; brother, sister, uterine brother, blood b., half b., stepbrother; cousin, cousin german, first cousin, second c., cousin once removed; uncle, nunky; aunt, auntie; nephew; niece; father, mother 169n. *parent;* clansman, tribesman, compatriot, fellow.

family, matriarch, patriarch; motherhood, fatherhood, brotherhood, sisterhood, cousinhood; fraternity, sorority, phratry; gens; gotra, one's people; foster son, godson, stepson, adopted s.; godparents, gossip; relations by marriage, in-laws; circle, family c., home c. 882n. *sociality;* hearth and home, household, the old folks at home, homefolks; tribe, horde.

race, stock, stirps, generation, breed, strain, line, side; tribe, phyle, clan, sept; blood group, totem g., ethnic g.; tribalism, nationality, gentility; inbreeding, interbreeding.

Adj. *akin,* sib, kindred, consanguineous, twin-born; matrilinear, out of; patrilinear, by; maternal, paternal; fraternal, brotherly, sisterly, cousinly; avuncular; novercal; related, family, collateral, allied, affined; connatural, congenerous; agnate, cognate, german, uterine; near, related, intimately r. 9adj. *relative;* once removed, twice r.; next-of-kin; step–.

ethnic, racial, tribal, phyletic, clannish, gentile 371adj. *national;* interracial, intertribal; interbred, inbred; Aryan, Hamitic, Semitic; Caucasian, Mongolian, Amerindian, Australasian, Negroid, Negrito.

Vb. *be akin,* share the blood of; claim relationship etc.; own a connection 9vb. *be related;* father, sire, dam 164vb. *generate;* be brother to, be sister to, brother, sister; affiliate, adopt, bring into the family.

See: 9, 164, 169, 371, 882.

12 Correlation: double or reciprocal relation

N. *correlation,* correlativity, corelation, mutual relation, functionality 9n. *relation;* proportionment, proportionality, proportion 245n. *symmetry;* texture, design, pattern, choreography 62n. *arrangement;* network, grid 222n. *network;* correspondence, opposite number 18n. *similarity,* 13n. *identity;* mutuality, interrelation, interconnection; interdependence, mutual dependence; mutualism, mutualist; interaction, interplay, mutual influence; alternation, turn and turn about, see-saw 317n. *oscillation;* reciprocity, reciprocalness, reciprocality, reciprocation 151n. *interchange;* each, each other, one another; give and take 770n. *compromise;* exchange, change, payment in kind 791n. *barter;* lex talionis 714n. *retaliation.*

Adj. *correlative,* reciprocal, commutual, functional 9adj. *relative;* corresponding, correspondent, opposite, answering to, analogous, parallel 18adj. *similar;* proportioned, proportional, proportionate 245adj. *symmetrical;* complementary, complemental, heterosexual; interconnecting, interlocking; mutual, reciprocatory, reciprocating 714adj. *retaliatory;* reacting 280adj. *recoiling;* alternating, alternate, see-saw 317adj. *oscillating;* interlocking, geared, interacting; patterned, woven; interchangeable, exchangeable 151adj. *interchanged;* inter–, intertribal, interracial, international, interstate, interworld; two-way.

Vb. *correlate,* interrelate, interconnect, interlock, interplay, interact; interdepend, mutualize; vary as, be a function of; proportion, symmetrize; correspond, answer to, reflect 18vb. *resemble;* react 280vb. *recoil;* alternate 317vb. *oscillate,* 151vb. *interchange;* reciprocate 714vb. *retaliate;* exchange, counterchange, chop, swop, barter 791vb. *trade;* balance 28vb. *equalize;* set off 31vb. *compensate.*

Adv. *correlatively,* proportionately, as . . . so . . .; mutually, reciprocally, each to each, each other, one another; compensatively, equivalently 28adv. *equally;* interchangeably, in mutual exchange 151adv. *in exchange;* barteringly, in kind 791adv. *in trade;* alternately, by turns, turn and turn about, first one and then the other; contrariwise, vice versa 14adv. *contrarily;* inter, between, shuttlewise 317adv. *to and fro.*

See: 9, 13, 14, 18, 28, 31, 62, 151, 222, 245, 280, 317, 714, 770, 791.

13 Identity

N. *identity,* sameness, oneness, identism 88n. *unity;* the same, no other, the very same, the very one; genuineness 494n. *authenticity;* the real thing, it, absolutely it 21n. *no imitation;* tautology, the very words, ipsissima verba, ditto, quotation

106n. *repetition;* one's very self, oneself, myself 80n. *self;* other self, alter ego, ka, ba, genius, double; oneness with, identification, coincidence, congruence 24n. *agreement;* coalescence, mergence, absorption 299n. *reception;* convertibility, interchangeability, equivalence 28n. *equality;* no difference, distinction, without a d., indistinguishability; same meaning, synonymity, synonymy 514n. *meaning;* same kind, homogeneity, cosubstantiality 16n. *uniformity;* no change, invariability, invariant, constant 153n. *fixture;* counterpart, duplicate 22n. *copy;* fellow, pair, match, twin, Tweedledum and Tweedledee 18n. *analogue;* homonym homophone, homophene, synonym 559n. *word.*

Adj. *identical,* same, self, selfsame, of that ilk; one and the same, one and only 88adj. *one;* coalescent, merging, absorbed; cosubstantial, homoousian; identified with, indistinguishable, interchangeable, convertible, equivalent 28adj. *equal;* homonymous, synonymous, synonymic; coincident, congruent 24adj. *agreeing;* always the same, invariable, invariant, constant, unchanging, unaltered 153adj. *unchangeable;* monotonous 838adj. *tedious;* homgeneous, monolithic 16adj. *uniform;* tautologous, repetitive, repetitional 106adj. *repeated.*

Vb. *be identical,* show no difference, ditto 106vb. *repeat;* coincide, coalesce, merge, be one with, sink one's identity; be congruent, register, agree in all respects 24vb. *accord;* phase 123vb. *synchronize.*
identify, make as one, treat as o., unify; treat as the same, not distinguish, recognize no distinction 464vb. *not discriminate;* homologate, equate, tar with the same brush 28vb. *equalize;* assimilate, match, pair 18vb. *liken;* assert the identity, recognize the i. 561vb. *name,* 80vb. *specify.*

Adv. *identically,* interchangeably, without distinction; in phase, on all fours, in register; ibidem; ditto; in like case, same here.

See: 16, 18, 21, 22, 24, 28, 80, 88, 106, 123, 153, 299, 464, 494, 514, 559, 561, 838.

14 Contrariety

N. *contrariety,* non-identity, non-coincidence, absolute difference, world of d. 15n. *difference;* exclusiveness, mutual e., irreconcilability 10n. *irrelation;* antipathy, repugnance, hostility 888n. *hatred;* adverseness, contrariness, antagonism 704n. *opposition;* antidote 182n. *counteraction;* conflict, clash 279n. *collision;* discord 25n. *disagreement;* contradistinction, contrast, relief, light r., variation, undertone, counterpoint 463n. *discrimination;* contradiction, flat c. 533n. *negation;* contra-indication, counter-symptom 467n. *counter-evidence;* counter-meaning, counter-sense, counter-term, antonym 514n. *meaning;* antinomy, inconsistency, two voices 17n. *non-uniformity;* paradox, ambivalence 518n. *equivocalness;* oppositeness, antithesis, direct opposite, antipodes, antipole, counterpole, opposite pole; other extreme, opposite e., quite the contrary, quite the reverse; other side, opposite s., weather s., weatherboard 240n. *contraposition;* reverse, wrong side 238n. *rear;* inverse 221n. *inversion;* converse, reverse image, mirror, mirror symmetry 417n. *reflection;* opposite direction, headwind, undertow, counterstream 182n. *counteraction.*
polarity, contraries 704n. *opposites;* positive and negative; north and south; east and west; day and night; light and darkness; hot and cold; fire and water; black and white; good and bad; Hyperion to a satyr.

Adj. *contrary,* non-identical, as different as chalk from cheese, anything but 15adj. *different;* contrasting, contrasted, clashing, conflicting, discordant 25adj. *disagreeing;* inconsistent, not uniform 17adj. *non-uniform;* ambivalent, bittersweet, sweet and sour; contradictory, antithetic, adversative 533adj. *negative;* antithetical, diametrically opposite, poles asunder, antipodal, antipodean 240adj. *opposite;* reverse, converse, inverse; antipathetic, repugnant, abhorrent, inimical, hostile 888adj. *hating;* adverse, contrarious, contrariant, untoward, antagonistic 704adj. *opposing;* counteractive, antidotal 182adj. *counteracting;* counter-, anti-.

Vb. *be contrary,* have nothing in common 10vb. *be unrelated,* 15vb. *differ,* 57vb. *exclude;* contrast, stand out 25vb. *disagree;* clash, discord; run counter 240vb. *be opposite;* speak with two voices 518vb. *be equivocal;* contravene, fly in the face of 704vb.

oppose, 738vb. *disobey;* contradict, contra-indicate 533vb. *negate;* counteract 658vb. *remedy;* reverse 752vb. *abrogate;* antithesize, turn the tables 221vb. *invert.*

Adv. *contrarily,* contra, per c., on the other hand, conversely, contrariwise; vice versa, topsy-turvy, upside down; invertedly, inversely; on the contrary, nay rather; otherwise, quite the other way; in contrast, in opposition to; by contraries, by opposites.

See: 10, 15, 17, 25, 57, 182, 221, 238, 240, 279, 417, 463, 467, 514, 518, 532, 533, 658, 704, 738, 752, 888.

15 Difference

N. *difference,* unlikeness 19n. *dissimilarity;* disparity, odds 29n. *inequality;* margin, differential, minus, plus 41n. *remainder;* wide margin 199n. *distance;* narrow margin, approximation 200n. *nearness;* heterogeneity, variety, diverseness, diversity, all sorts and conditions, mixed bag 17n. *non-uniformity;* divergence, departure from 282n. *deviation;* otherness, differentia, distinctness, originality 10n. *irrelation,* 21n. *non-imitation;* discrepancy, incongruity 25n. *disagreement;* incompatibility, antipathy 861n. *dislike;* disharmony, discord, variance 709n. *dissension;* contrast 14n. *contrariety;* opposite, antithesis 240n. *contraposition;* non-conformity 84n. *unconformity;* variation, modification, alteration 143n. *change,* 147n. *conversion.*

differentiation 463n. *discrimination;* specification 80n. *specialty;* contradistinction, distinction, nice d., delicate d., subtle d.; nuance, nicety, shade of difference, fine shade of meaning 514n. *meaning;* distinction without a difference 13n. *identity;* moods and tenses, declension 564n. *grammar.*

variant, differential, different thing, another t., something else, this, that or the other; another story, another version, another pair of shoes, horse of another color; special case 80n. *specialty;* new version, new edition, reissue 589n. *edition.*

Adj. *different,* differing, unlike 19adj. *dissimilar;* original 21adj. *unimitated;* various, variform, diverse, diversified, heterogeneous 17adj. *non-uniform;* multifarious 82adj. *multiform;* assorted, of all sorts, all manner of, divers 43adj. *mixed;* distinct, distinguished, differentiated, discriminated, divided, separated 46adj. *disjoined;* divergent, departing from 282adj. *deviating;* discrepant, discordant, clashing, incongruent, incongruous 25adj. *disagreeing;* disparate 29adj. *unequal;* contrasting, contrasted, far from it, wide apart, poles asunder, anything but 14adj. *contrary;* other, another, not the same, peculiar 80adj. *special;* in a different class 34adj. *superior,* 35adj. *inferior;* somehow different, the same yet not the same, changed, altered 147adj. *converted.*

distinctive, diagnostic 5adj. *characteristic;* differentiating, distinguishing, marking out, differentiating; elative, comparative, superlative, augmentative.

Vb. *differ,* be different etc. adj.; show variety; vary from, diverge f., depart f. 282vb. *deviate;* divaricate, ablude; contrast, clash, jar, conflict 25vb. *disagree;* be at variance 709vb. *quarrel;* modify, vary, make alterations 143vb. *change.*

differentiate, distinguish, mark out, single o., severalize 463adj. *discriminate;* shade, refine, make a distinction, sharpen a d.; particularize 80vb. *specify.*

Adv. *differently,* variously, as modified, after alteration; otherwise, not so, some other way, in a different fashion; in different ways, in many w., multifariously.

See: 5, 10, 13, 14, 17, 19, 21, 25, 29, 34, 35, 36, 41, 43, 46, 80, 82, 84, 143, 147, 199, 200, 240, 282, 463, 514, 564, 589, 709, 861.

16 Uniformity

N. *uniformity,* uniformness, consistency, constancy, steadiness 153n. *stability;* persistence 71n. *continuity,* 146n. *continuance;* order, regularity, method, centralization 60n. *order;* connaturality 18n. *similarity;* homogeneity, homology, monolithic quality; unity, unison, correspondence, accordance 24n. *agreement;* levelness, flushness 258n. *smoothness;* roundness 245n. *symmetry;* sameness, invariability, monotony, level, dead l., even tenor, mixture as before; even pace, rhythm; round, daily r., routine, drill, treadmill 610n. *habit;* monotone, grayness; droning, drone, sing-song, monologue; monolith; pattern, same p., type, stereotype; stamp, common s., same stamp, same mint; set, assortment; suit, flush; standard dress 228n. *uniform;*

assimilation, standardization, mass-production 83n. *conformity;* cliché 106n. *repetition;* regimentation, intolerance, closed shop 740n. *compulsion.*

uniformist, drill sergeant; leveler, egalitarian, eraser of all distinctions; uniformitarian, regimenter.

Adj. *uniform,* all of a piece, one-piece; same all through, monolithic; of one kind, connatural, homogenetic, homologous, of a piece, of a pattern 18adj. *similar;* same, consistent, self-c., constant, steady, stable 153adj. *fixed;* undeviating, unchanging, unvarying, invariable 144adj. *permanent;* rhythmic, measured, even-paced, jog-trot 258adj. *smooth;* undiversified, undifferentiated, unrelieved, unbroken 573adj. *plain;* uncontrasting, without contrast, in uniform, uniformed, liveried; characterless, featureless, faceless, blank; monotonous, droning, sing-song; monotone, drab, gray; repetitive, running through 106adj. *repeated;* standard, normal 83adj. *typical;* patterned, standardized, stereotyped, mass-produced; sorted, assorted, sized; drilled, dressed, aligned, in line; orderly, regular, square, equilateral, circular 245adj. *symmetrical;* straight, level, even, flush, flat 258adj. *smooth.*

Vb. *be uniform,*—homogeneous etc. adj.; follow routine 610vb. *be wont;* sing in unison, sing the same song, chorus 24vb. *accord;* typify 83vb. *conform;* dress, fall in; wear uniform, be in u.

make uniform, stamp, characterize, run through 547vb. *mark;* assimilate, level, level up, level down, tar with the same brush 18vb. *liken;* size, assort; drill, dress, align; standardize, stereotype, pattern; put into uniform; normalize, regularize 83vb. *make conform.*

Adv. *uniformly,* etc. adj.; like clockwork, methodically, habitually, invariably, eternally, endlessly; without exception, in a rut, in a groove.

See: 18, 24, 60, 71, 83, 106, 144, 146, 153, 228, 245, 258, 547, 573, 610, 740.

17 Non-uniformity

N. *non-uniformity,* variability, patchiness 72n. *discontinuity;* unpredictability 152n. *changeableness;* inconstancy, inconsistency, capriciousness 604n. *caprice;* irregularity, no system, no pattern, chaos 61n. *disorder;* untidiness, dishevelment 63n. *derangement;* ruggedness, asymmetry 244n. *amorphism;* raggedness, uneveness, choppiness, jerkiness, 259n. *roughness;* heterogeneity, heteromorphism 15n. *difference;* contrast 14n. *contrariety,* 19n. *dissimilarity;* divarication, divergence 282n. *deviation;* diversity, variety, variousness, multifariousness 82n. *multiformity;* all sorts and conditions, mixed bag, ragbag, lucky dip, odds and ends 43n. *mixture;* patchwork, motley, crazy paving, mosaic; abnormality, exception, special case, sport, new type 84n. *unconformity;* odd man out, lone wolf, rogue elephant 59n. *extraneousness;* uniqueness, nonce word; lack of uniform, mufti; every man in his humor; quot homines tot sententiae; decentralization.

Adj. *non-uniform,* variable, unpredictable, changeable, never the same 152adj. *changeful;* inconstant, inconsistent 604adj. *capricious;* irregular, unsystematic; patternless, unpatterned, shapeless 244adj. *amorphous;* untidy, disheveled, haywire, chaotic 61adj. *orderless;* uneven, bumpy, choppy, jerky 259adj. *rough;* erratic, out of step, out of time, fast, slow, gaining, losing, out of order; contrasting, contrasted 14adj. *contrary;* heterogeneous, various, diverse 15adj. *different,* 19adj. *dissimilar;* multifarious, diversified, of many kinds, of all sorts 82adj. *multiform;* divergent, divaricating 282adj. *deviating;* aberrant, atypical, heterotactous 84adj. *unconformable;* exceptional, unusual, crazy 84adj. *abnormal;* unique, lone 59adj. *extraneous;* out of uniform, in mufti, incorrectly dressed.

Adv. *non-uniformly,* irregularly, erratically, unsystematically; unsmoothly, unevenly, bumpily, jerkily, confusedly, chaotically; all anyhow, all haywire; here, there and everywhere.

See: 14, 15, 19, 43, 59, 61, 63, 72, 82, 84, 152, 244, 259, 282, 604.

18 Similarity

N. *similarity,* resemblance, likeness, similitude; semblance, seeming, appearance, look, form, fashion 445n. *appearance,* 243n. *form;* common feature, point in common, point of resemblance 775n. *participation;* congruity 24n. *agreement;* affinity, kinship 11n. *consanguinity;* homogeneity, homomorphism, connaturality; comparability, analogicalness, analogy, correspondence, parallelism 12n. *correlation;* equivalence, parity 28n. *equality;* proportionality 245n. *symmetry;* no difference 13n. *identity;* general resemblance, family likeness; close resemblance, good likeness, perfect l.; striking likeness, faithful l., photographic l. 553n. *picture;* approximation 200n. *nearness;* partial likeness, distant l., faint resemblance; adumbration, hint; fair comparison, sufficient resemblance, the size of it.

assimilation, likening 462n. *comparison;* reduction to, identification 13n. *identity;* simulation, camouflage, disguise 20n. *imitation;* portrayal 590n. *description;* portraiture 551n. *representation;* alliteration, assonance, homoeoteleuton, rhyme 106n. *repetition;* pun, equivoque, paronomasia 518n. *equivocalness;* homonymy, homophony.

analogue, congener, the like, such like, likes of; type, good example, perfect e. 83n. *example;* correlate, correlative 12n. *correlative;* simile, parallel; equivalent 150n. *substitute;* brother, sister, twin; match, fellow, mate, companion, pendant; pair, sister-ship; double, ringer; complement, counterpart, other half; alter ego, other self, genius, ka, ba; likeness, reflection, shadow, the very picture 551n. *image;* another edition of, spit of, dead spit, living image, chip off the old block; twins, two peas, couple, two of a kind, Arcades ambo, birds of a feather; reproduction, copy 22n. *duplicate.*

Adj. *similar,* resembling, like, much l.; alike, ridiculously a., twin, matching, like as two peas, cast in the same mold; of a piece 16adj. *uniform;* similative, analogical; analogous, parallel, equivalent 28adj. *equal;* corresponding, bracketed with; consubstantial, homogeneous, connatural, congeneric, ejusdem generis; cognate 11adj. *akin;* close, approximate 200adj. *near;* typical, representative 551n. *representing;* reproducing, reflecting; much the same, something like, such like, such as, quasi; rhyming, alliteral, assonant 106adj. *repeated;* punning 518adj. *equivocal.*

lifelike, realistic, photographic, exact, faithful, natural, typical; good of one, true to life, true to nature, true to type; clearly seen, vivid, eidetic, eidotropic 443adj. *well-seen.*

simulating 20adj. *imitative;* seeming, deceptive, camouflaged 542adj. *deceiving;* mock, pseudo 542adj. *spurious;* making a show of 875adj. *showy;* synthetic, artificial, ersatz 150adj. *substituted.*

Vb. *resemble,* be similar to, pass for; mirror, reflect 20vb. *imitate;* seem, seem like, sound l., look as if; look like, take after, have the look of; savor of, smack of; compare with, approximate to, come near to 289vb. *approach;* match, correspond to, answer to 9vb. *relate;* register, match 24vb. *agree;* be bracketed; assonate, rhyme; run in pairs; typify 551vb. *represent.*

liken, assimilate to, approximate, bring near; reduce to 13vb. *identify;* match, twin, bracket with 28vb. *equalize;* make a simile of; connaturalize; portray 20vb. *imitate;* alliterate, rhyme 10vb. *repeat;* pun 518vb. *be equivocal.*

Adv. *similarly,* as, like, as if, quasi, so to speak, as it were; just as, in a way; as in a mirror.

See: 9, 10, 11, 12, 13, 16, 20, 22, 24, 28, 83, 106, 150, 200, 243, 245, 289, 443, 445, 462, 518, 542, 544, 551, 553, 590, 775, 875.

19 Dissimilarity

N. *dissimilarity,* dissimilitude, unlikeness; incomparability 10n. *irrelation;* disparity 29n. *inequality;* diversity, divergence 15n. *difference;* variation, variance, variety 17n. *non-uniformity,* 82n. *multiformity;* contrast 14n. *contrariety;* little in common, nothing in c., no match, not a pair 25n. *disagreement;* novelty, originality, uniqueness 21n. *non-imitation;* dissemblance, dissimilation, camouflage, makeup 525n. *concealment,* 527n. *disguise;* caricature, bad likeness, false copy 552n. *misrepresentation;* foreign body, alien element 59n. *intruder.*

Adj. *dissimilar,* unlike, diverse 15adj. *different;* various 82adj. *multiform;* disparate 29adj. *unequal;* unalike, not comparable 10adj. *irrelative;* far above 34adj. *superior;* far below 35adj. *inferior;* unrelated, unmatched, unpaired 25adj. *mismatched,* 17adj. *non-uniform;* unique, without a second, one and only, original 21adj. *unimitated;* incongruent 25adj. *disagreeing;* untypical, atypical, exotic 84adj. *unconformable;* unprecedented, new and strange, novel 126n. *new;* a far cry from 199adj. *distant;* not true, bad of.

Vb. *be unlike,* etc.adj.; bear no resemblance, have nothing in common 15vb. *differ;* stand out 34vb. *be superior,* 35vb. *be inferior.*

make unlike, discriminate 15vb. *differentiate;* innovate, modify, modulate 143vb. *change,* 147vb. *convert;* caricature 552vb. *misrepresent,* 246vb. *distort;* dissemble 542vb. *deceive;* disguise 525vb. *conceal;* camouflage 18vb. *liken,* 514vb. *fake.*

Adv. *dissimilarly,* discordantly, contrastingly, variously 15adv. *differently.*

See: 10, 14, 15, 17, 18, 21, 25, 29, 34, 35, 59, 82, 84, 126, 143, 147, 199, 246, 525, 527, 541, 544, 552.

20 Imitation

N. *imitation,* copying etc. vb.; sincerest form of flattery; rivalry, emulation, competition 911n. *jealousy;* conventionality, convention, doing as Rome does, traditionalism 83n. *conformity;* want of originality, following, literalism, slavishness, slavish imitation; imitativeness, parrotry (**see** *mimicry*); affectedness 850n. *affectation;* mimesis 551n. *representation;* reflection, mirror, echo, shadow 18n. *assimilation;* quotation, citation, echolalia 106n. *repetition;* paraphrase, translation 520n. *interpretation;* borrowing, cribbing, plagiary, plagiarism, literary theft 788n. *stealing;* forgery, literary f., falsification, counterfeit, fake 541n. *falsehood;* copying, transcribing, transcription, transliteration, tracing 586n. *writing;* duplication, reduplication, multiplication 166n. *reproduction,* 551n. *photography.*

mimicry, mimesis 551n. *representation;* noises off 594 n. *dramaturgy;* mime, pantomime, sign language, gesticulation 547n. *gesture;* ventriloquism 579n. *speech;* portrayal, portraiture 553n. *painting,* 590n. *description;* realism 494n. *accuracy;* mockery, simulacrum, shadow 542n. lesque 851n. *satire;* travesty 552n. *misrepresentation,* 246n. *distortion;* imitativeness, apery, apishness, parrotry 106n. *repetition,* 850n. *affectation;* conjuring, illusionism; simulation, semblance, disguise, camouflage, dissimulation 18n. *similarity,* 19n. *dissimilarity;* pretense, mockery, simulacrum, shadow 542n. *sham,* 4n. *insubstantiality.*

imitator, copycat, ape, sedulous a., monkey; mockingbird, parrot, poll-p., echo; sheep 83n. *conformist,* 284n. *follower;* poseur 850n. *affector;* echoer, yes-man 925n. *flatterer;* mocker, burlesquer, travester 839n. *humorist,* 926n. *detractor;* mime, mimic, impersonator, ventriloquist, conjuror, illusionist 594n. *entertainer;* actor, portrayer, portraitist 556n. *artist;* copyist, scribe, printer, compositor, tracer, copy-typist, transliterator; translator, paraphraser, 520n. *interpreter;* transcriber of life, realist; simulator, hypocrite, 545n. *impostor;* borrower, plagiarist; counterfeiter, forger, faker; duplicator, multiplier, mimeograph, stencil.

Adj. *imitative,* apish, aping, parroting, parrot-like; following; echoing, flattering; posing 850adj. *affected;* disguised, camouflaged; simulating, shamming 541adj. *hypocritical;* pseudo, sham, phony, counterfeit 541n. *false;* ersatz, synthetic 150adj. *substituted;* unoriginal, uninventive, unimaginative, derivative, secondhand, conventional 83adj. *conformable;* paraphrastic, modeled, molded on; copied, slavish, literal; caricatured, parodied, travestied, burlesque; transcribed, transliterated; easy to copy, imitable.

Vb. *imitate,* ape, parrot, flatter, echo, mirror, reflect 18vb. *resemble;* make a show of, pose 850vb. *be affected;* pretend, make-believe, make as if; act, mimic, mime, portray, paint 551vb. *represent;* parody, caricature, burlesque, travesty 851vb. *ridicule;* sham, simulate, put on, play the hypocrite 541vb. *dissemble;* disguise, camouflage 525vb. *conceal;* ventriloquize, conjure 542vb. *deceive.*

copy, draw, counterdraw, trace; copy faithfully, catch, realize; quote, cite, echo, reecho, chorus 106vb. *repeat;* follow copy, compose 587vb. *print;* reprint, duplicate, mimeograph; make copies, replicate, reduplicate, multiply, reel off 166vb. *reproduce;* copy out, transcribe, transliterate, type, type out; paraphrase, translate 520vb. *interpret;* copy from, crib, plagiarize, borrow 788vb. *steal;* counterfeit, forge 541vb. *fake.*

do likewise, do as the Romans do, mold oneself on, pattern oneself on, take as a model, understudy; follow, follow suit, follow my leader, follow in all things; step in the footprints of, follow in the track of, travel in the wake of 65vb. *come after;* do after, say a., echo, reecho, chorus 106vb. *repeat;* follow precedent, follow example, join in the cry, hunt with the hounds, jump on the bandwagon 83vb. *conform;* emulate, rival, compete 911vb. *be jealous;* take a leaf out of another's book, dish the Whigs 34vb. *be superior.*

Adv. *imitatively,* emulously, jealously, in rivalry; like master like man; literally, strictly to the letter, word for word, verbatim, literatim 494adv. *truly;* sic, as per copy.

See: 4, 18, 19, 34, 65, 83, 106, 150, 166, 494, 520, 525, 541, 542, 545, 547, 551, 552, 553, 556, 579, 586, 587, 590, 594, 788, 839, 850, 851, 911, 925, 926.

21 Non-imitation

N. *non-imitation,* creativeness, inventiveness 513n. *imagination;* creation, all my own work 164n. *production;* originality 119n. *priority,* 10n. *irrelation* uniqueness, the one and only 88n. *unity;* inimitability, transcendence 34n. *superiority;* independence, defiance of precedent, line of one's own 744n. *freedom;* precedent, example 23n. *prototype;* new departure 68n. *beginning;* something new, novelty, freshness 126n. *newness;* eccentricity, individuality 84n. *unconformity;* unlikeness 19n. *dissimilarity.*

no imitation, genuineness, sincerity 494n. *authenticity;* real thing, the very thing, genuine article; it, absolutely it 13n. *identity,* 80n. *self;* autograph, holograph, one's own hand, usual signature 586n. *writing.*

Adj. *unimitative,* creative, inventive 513adj. *imaginative;* original, underived, not derivative; prototypal, archetypal; primordial, primary; first, first-hand, first in the field 119adj. *prior;* fresh, novel 126adj. *new;* individual, personal 80adj. *special;* independent 744adj. *free;* eccentric 84adj. *unconformable.*

unimitated, inimitable, transcendent, unmatched, incomparable, out of reach 34adj. *superior;* uncopied, unhackneyed, unplagiarized; unique, one and only 88adj. *one;* authentic, true 494adj. *genuine;* sincere, unadulterated 44adj. *unmixed.*

See: 10, 13, 19, 23, 34, 44, 68, 80, 84, 88, 119, 126, 164, 494, 513, 586, 744.

22 Copy

N. *copy,* exact c., reproduction, replica, facsimile, tracing; apograph, fair copy, transcript, transcription, counterpart 18n. *analogue;* cast, death mask; ectype, stamp, seal, impress, impression, squeeze; mechanical copy, stereotype, electrotype, collotype, lithograph, print, printed matter, pull, proof, revise 587n. *letterpress,* 555n. *engraving;* photograph, photoprint, photostat, positive, negative, contact print 551n. *photography;* "counterfeit presentment," an imitation, dummy, pastiche, pasticcio; forgery, plagiarism, crib 20n. *imitation;* a likeness, resemblance, semblance 18n. *similarity;* study, portrait, drawing 553n. *picture;* icon, image 551n. *representation;* form, model, effigy, sculpture, statue, bronze 554n. *sculpture;* faithful copy, servile imitation, reflex, echo, mirror 106n. *repetition,* 417n. *reflection;* bad copy, apology for, mockery of 552n. *misrepresentation;* malicious copy, distorted image, caricature, cartoon, travesty, parody 851n. *ridicule;* hint, adumbration, shadow; silhouette, outline, sketch, diagram, first copy, draft; metaphrase, paraphrase 520n. *translation.*

duplicate, counterpart, reproduction, cast; carbon copy, carbon; stencil, jellygraph; transfer, rubbing; photograph, photoprint, print, contact p., enlargement, blow-up 551n. *photography;* proof, pull, revise; reprint, straight r., second edition, réchauffé 589n. *book;* model, specimen, show copy 83n. *example.*

See: 18, 20, 83, 106, 417, 520, 551, 552, 553, 554, 555, 587, 589, 851.

23 Prototype

N. *prototype,* archetype, antitype, countertype; type, biotype, common type, everyman 30n. *average;* primitive form, protoplasm 358n. *organism;* original, protoplast, negative; first occurrence, precedent, test case 119n. *priority;* guide, rule, maxim 693n. *precept;* standard, criterion, standard of comparison, frame of reference 12n. *correlation;* ideal 646n. *perfection;* cynosure, mirror 646n. *paragon;* keynote, tuning fork, metronome 465n. *gauge;* module, unit 465n. *meter;* specimen, sample, ensample 83n. *example;* model, subject; exemplar, pattern, paradigm; dummy, mock-up; copybook, copy, printer's c., text, manuscript; blueprint, design, master-plan, scheme 623n. *plan;* rough plan, outline, draft, scantling, sketch.

living model, model, artist's m., poser, sitter, subject; fashion model, mannequin; fugleman, stroke, bandleader, conductor, drum-major, drill master 690n. *leader.*

mold, matrix, mint; plate, shell; frame, wax figure, lay f., tailor's dummy; last; boot-tree; die, stamp, punch, seal, intaglio.

Adj. *prototypal,* exemplary, standard, classic, copybook.

Vb. *be example,* set an e., serve as e., stand as e.; serve as a model, model, sit for, pose.

See: 12, 30, 83, 119, 358, 465, 623, 646, 690, 693.

24 Agreement

N. *agreement,* consentaneity 181n. *concurrence* consentience, consent 488n. *assent;* accord, accordance, chorus, unison 16n. *uniformity;* harmony, syntony, concent 410n. *melody;* consonance, concinnity, concordance, attunement; concert, understanding, mutual understanding, entente, entente cordiale; convention, pact 765n. *compact;* unanimity 488n. *consensus;* consortium 706n. *cooperation;* union 50n. *combination;* peace 710n. *concord.*

conformance 83n. *conformity;* congruence, coincidence 13n. *identity;* consistency 16n. *uniformity;* consequentiality, consequence, logic, logical conclusion 475n. *reasoning;* correspondence, parallelism 18n. *similarity.*

fitness, aptness, qualification, capability 694n. *aptitude;* suitability, sortance, propriety 642n. *expedience;* the right man in the right place, perfect candidate, the very thing, it, the absolute it 13n. *identity;* relevancy, pertinence, admissibility, appositeness, case in point, good example 9n. *relevance;* cognation, commensurability, proportion 9n. *relation;* timeliness, right moment, fit occasion, 137n. *occasion.*

adaptation, conformation, harmonization, synchronization, matching 18n. *assimilation;* reconciliation, reconcilement 719n. *pacification;* coaptation, accommodation, graduation, attunement, adjustment 62n. *arrangement;* compatibility, congeniality, naturalness; fitting, suiting, good fit, perfect f., close f., tight f.; making an agreement, negotiation 770n. *compromise.*

Adj. *agreeing,* right, accordant, in accord, in accordance with; corresponding, correspondent, answering; proportionable, proportional, proportionate, commensurate 12adj. *correlative;* coincident, coinciding, congruent, congruous 28adj. *equal;* squared with, on all fours w., consistent w., conforming 83adj. *conformable;* in conformity, in step, in phase, in tune, synchronized 123adj. *synchronous;* of a piece with, consistent, self-c. 16adj. *uniform;* consonant, concordant, harmonized 410adj. *harmonious;* combining, mixing; suiting, matching 18adj. *similar;* becoming 844adj. *ornamental;* natural, congenial, sympathetic; reconcilable, compatible, coexistent, coexisting, symbiotic; consentaneous, consensual, consentient, agreeable, acquiescent 488adj. *assenting;* concurrent, agreed, all a., at one, in unison, in chorus, unanimous, united; like-minded, of like mind, bipartisan 706adj. *cooperative;* treating, treaty-making, in treaty, negotiating 765adj. *contractual.*

apt, applicable, admissible, germane, appropriate, pertinent, in point, to the point, pointed, well-aimed 9adj. *relevant;* to the purpose, bearing upon 178adj. *influential;* in loco, pat, in place, apropos; right, happy, felicitous, idiomatic 575adj. *elegant;* at home, in one's element; seasonable, opportune 137adj. *timely.*

fit, suitable, sortable, fitting, suited, well-adapted, adaptable, idoneous; capable, qualified, cut out for, deft 694adj. *skillful;* meet, up one's street 642adj. *expedient.*

adjusted, well-a. 60adj. *orderly,* 494adj. *accurate;* timed, synchronized; tuned, strung, pitched, attuned 412adj. *musical;* trimmed, balanced 28adj. *equal;* well-cut, fitting, well-fitting, close-fitting, tight-fitting, tight; made to measure, tailored, snug, comfortable.

Vb. *accord,* be accordant etc. adj.; agree, homologate, concur 488vb. *assent,* 758vb. *consent;* respond, echo, chorus, chime in, ditto 106vb. *repeat;* coincide, register, square with, quadrate w., mesh w., gear w., dovetail 45vb. *join;* fit, fit like a glove, fit to a T; tally, correspond, match, twin 18vb. *resemble;* go with, tone in w., harmonize; comport with, sort w., fadge w., come natural; fit in, belong, feel at home; answer, meet, suit, do 642vb. *be expedient;* fall pat, come apropos, prove timely, fit the occasion, beseem, befit, keep together, march t., run t., hunt t. 706vb.

cooperate; be consistent, be logical, hang t., hold t. 475vb. *be reasonable;* seek accord, treat, negotiate, come to terms 766vb. *make terms;* get on with, hit it off, fraternize, make friends 880vb. *befriend;* sing together, choir 413vb. *sing;* be natural, behave naturally, act one's nature.

adjust, make adjustments 654vb. *rectify;* render accordant etc. adj.; readjust, repair 656vb. *restore;* fit, suit, adapt, accommodate, conform; attune, tune, tune up, pitch, string 410vb. *harmonize;* modulate, tune in; regulate 60vb. *order;* graduate, proportion 12vb. *correlate;* dress, align, size 62vb. *arrange;* balance 28vb. *equalize;* cut, trim 31vb. *compensate;* tailor, make to measure; concert; synchronize.

Adv. *pertinently* etc. adj.; apropos of; in register; in the right context.

See: 9, 12, 13, 16, 18, 28, 31, 45, 50, 60, 62, 83, 106, 123, 137, 178, 181, 410, 412, 413, 475, 488, 494, 575, 642, 654, 656, 694, 706, 710, 719, 758, 765, 766, 770, 844, 880.

25 Disagreement

N. *disagreement,* disaccord; non-agreement, failure to agree, agreement to disagree 489n. *dissent;* dissidence 84n. *unconformity;* divergent opinions, conflict of opinion, controversy, argumentation 475n. *argument;* wrangle, wrangling, bickering 709n. *quarrel;* disunion, disunity, faction 709n. *dissension;* jarring, clash 279n. *collision;* challenge 711n. *defiance,* rupture, breach 718n. *war;* variance, divergence, discrepancy 15n. *difference;* two voices, ambiguity, ambivalence 518n. *equivocalness;* variety 437n. *variegation;* opposition, contradiction, conflict 14n. *contrariety;* dissonance, discordance, disharmony, inharmoniousness, tunelessness 411n. *discord;* non-coincidence, incongruence, incongruity 10n. *irrelation;* disparity 29n. *inequality;* disproportion, asymmetry 246n. *distortion;* unconformability, incompatibility, irreconcilability, hostility 881n. *enmity;* lack of sympathy 861n. *dislike;* interference 702n. *hindrance.*

inaptitude, unfitness, incapacity, incompetence 695n. *unskillfulness;* unfittingness, impropriety 643n. *inexpedience;* inconcinnity 576n. *inelegance;* inapplicability, inadmissibility, irrelevancy 10n. *irrelevance;* intrusiveness, intrusion, interruption, untimeliness 138n. *intempestivity;* inconsistency 17n. *non-uniformity;* maladjustment, incompatibility, unconformability 84n. *unconformity.*

misfit, maladjustment, bad fit; bad match, misalliance, mésalliance 894n. *marriage;* misjoinder; syncretism; oxymoron; paradox; incongruity, false note, jar 411n. *discord;* fish out of water, square peg in a round hole; outsider, foreigner, foreign body 59n. *intruder;* joker, odd man out, sport 84n. *abnormality;* eccentric, oddity 851n. *laughing stock;* ass in a lion's skin 501n. *fool.*

Adj. *disagreeing,* dissenting, unagreed, not unanimous 489adj. *dissenting;* challenging 711adj. *defiant;* at odds, at cross purposes, at variance; at loggerheads, at war 718adj. *warring;* bickering, snapping 709adj. *quarreling;* hostile, antagonistic 881adj. *inimical;* uncongenial, antipathetic, repulsive, nauseating 861adj. *disliked;* contrarious, conflicting, clashing, contradictory 14adj. *contrary;* unnatural, against one's nature; inconsistent 17adj. *non-uniform;* inconsonant, incompatible, irreducible 84adj. *unconformable;* exceptional, outstanding 84adj. *abnormal;* odd, foreign 59adj. *extraneous;* not combining, not mixing; incommensurable 10adj. *irrelative;* disproportionate, disproportioned, out of proportion, unsymmetrical 246adj. *distorted;* inharmonious, grating 411adj. *discordant;* mismatched, misallied, misjoined; ill-matching, ill-matched, ill-assorted, ill-combined; discrepant 15adj. *different;* incongruous 497adj. *absurd.*

unapt, inept, incapable, incompetent 695adj. *unskillful;* unfitted, unsuited, ill-adapted, maladjusted 695adj. *clumsy;* wrong, unfit, unfitting, unsuitable, unbecoming, not for one, improper, inappropriate 643adj. *inexpedient;* impracticable 470adj. *impossible;* ineligible 607adj. *rejected;* intrusive, not wanted, inopportune, unseasonable 138adj. *untimely;* malapropos, inapplicable, inadmissible 10adj. *irrelevant;* unidiomatic 576adj. *inelegant;* out of character, out of keeping; misplaced, out of place, out of joint, out of tune, out of time, out of step, out of phase.

Vb. *disagree* 489vb. *dissent;* differ, dispute 475vb. *argue;* jar, jangle, bicker 709vb. *quarrel;* clash, conflict, collide, contradict 14vb. *be* *contrary;* be discrepant,—unapt etc. adj.; not play, non-cooperate 702vb. *hinder;* have nothing to do with 10 vb. *be unrelated;* come amiss, interfere, intrude, butt in 138vb. *mistime.* *mismatch,* mismate, misjoin; misadapt, misfit, misadjust; miscast; mistime.

Adv. *in defiance of,* in contempt of, despite, in spite of; discordantly etc.adj.

See: 10, 14, 15, 17, 29, 59, 84, 138, 246, 279, 411, 437, 470, 475, 489, 497, 501, 518, 576, 607, 643, 695, 702, 709, 711, 718, 851, 861, 881, 894.

26 Quantity

N. *quantity,* amount, sum 38n. *addition;* total 52n. *whole;* magnitude, amplitude, extent 465n. *measurement;* mass, substance, bulk 195n. *size;* dimension, dimensions, longitude 203n. *length;* width, thickness 205n. *breadth;* altitude 209n. *height;* deepness 211n. *depth;* area, volume, extension 183n. *space;* weight 322n. *gravity,* 323n. *levity;* strength, force, flow, potential, pressure, tension, stress, strain, torque 160n. *energy;* numbers 104n. *multitude;* quotient, fraction, multiple, function, quantic, vector 85n. *number,* 86n. *mathematics,* 101n. *plurality,* 102n. *fraction,* 103n. *zero,* 107n. *infinity;* mean, median 30n. *average.*

finite quantity, limited amount, definite figure; lower limit, upper l., ceiling 236n. *limit;* definite amount, quantum, quotum, quota, quorum; measured quantity, measure, dose, dosage 465n. *measurement;* avoirdupois 322n. *weighment;* ration, whack, take 783n. *portion;* pittance, driblet, cupful, spoonful, thimbleful; capful, bagful, sackful; whole amount, lot, batch, boiling; lock, stock and barrel 52n. *whole;* large amount, masses, heaps 32n. *great quantity;* small amount, bit 33n. *small quantity;* greater amount, more, most, majority 36n. *increase,* 104n. *greater number;* smaller amount, less, not so much 37n. *decrease,* 39n. *subduction,* 105n. *fewness;* stint, piece, task 682n. *labor.*

Adj. *quantitative,* some, certain, any, more or less; quantified, measured.

Vb. *quantify,* express the quantity, allot, rate, ration 783vb. *apportion.*

Adv. *to the amount of;* to the sum of, to the tune of; to such an extent.

See: 30, 32, 33, 36, 37, 38, 39, 52, 85, 86, 101, 102, 103, 104, 105, 107, 160, 183, 195, 203, 205, 209, 211, 236, 322, 323, 465, 682, 783.

27 Degree: relative quantity

N. *degree,* relative quantity, proportion, ratio, scale 12n. *correlation,* 462n. *comparison;* standard, stint 183n. *measure;* amplitude, extent, intensity, frequency, magnitude, size 26n. *quantity;* level, pitch, altitude 209n. *height,* 211n. *depth;* key, register 410n. *musical note;* reach, compass, scope 183n. *range;* rate, tenor, way, speed 265n. *motion;* gradation, graduation, calibration 15n. *differentiation;* differential, shade, nuance; grade, remove, stepping-stone; step, rung, round, tread, stair 308n. *ascent;* point, stage, milestone, turning point, crisis 8n. *juncture;* climax 725n. *completion;* mark, peg, notch, score 547n. *indicator;* bar, line, interval 410n. *notation;* valuation, value 465n. *measurement;* ranking, grading 77n. *classification;* class, kind 77n. *sort;* rank, grade 73n. *serial place;* military rank, lieutenancy, captaincy, majority, colonelcy; hierarchy 733n. *authority;* place, position, situation 187n. *location;* sphere, station, status, standing, footing 8n. *circumstance;* gradualism, gradualness 278n. *slowness.*

Adj. *gradational,* hierarchical, graduated, scalar, calibrated, graded, scaled; gradual, shading off, tapering; fading, fading out.

comparative, relative, proportional, in scale 9adj. *relative;* within the bounds of 236adj. *limited;* measured by.

Vb. *graduate,* rate, class, rank 73vb. *grade;* scale, calibrate; compare, measure.

shade off, taper, die away, pass into, melt into, change gradually, dissolve, fade, fade out; raise by degrees 36vb. *augment;* lower by degrees 37vb. *bate;* whittle down, pare, trim 204vb. *shorten.*

Adv. *by degrees,* gradually, little by little, step by step, drop by drop, bit by bit, inch by inch; by inches, by slow degrees; in some degree, in slight measure; to some extent, just a bit; however little; however much.

See: 8, 9, 12, 15, 26, 36, 37, 73, 77, 86, 183, 187, 204, 209, 211, 236, 265, 278, 308, 410, 452, 462, 547, 725, 733, 783.

28 Equality: sameness of quantity or degree

N. *equality,* same quality, same degree; parity, coequality, coextension, coincidence 24n. *agreement;* symmetry, balance, poise; evenness, level 258n. *smoothness,* 216n. *horizontality;* equability, monotony 16n. *uniformity;* roundness 250n. *circularity;* impartiality 913n. *justice.*

equivalence, likeness 18n. *similarity;* sameness 13n. *identity,* 219n. *parallelism;* interchangeability 151n. *interchange;* equipollence, isotropy, isotropism, isotopism; synonymity, synonym; reciprocation, exchange, fair e. 791n. *barter;* par, quits; equivalent, value, fair v., just price, ransom 809n. *price;* not a pin to choose, six of one and half a dozen of the other, distinction without a difference; level bet, even money; equation.

equilibrium, equipoise, equiponderance, stable equilibrium, balance; even keel, steadiness, uprightness; state of equilibrium, balance of forces, balance of power, balance of trade; deadlock, stalemate 145n. *cessation;* status quo, stable state, equilibration, homeostasis; road-holding ability 153n. *stability;* sea-legs, seat; fin, aileron 153n. *stabilizer;* balance, equilibrant; equilibrist, tight-rope walker, rope-dancer 162n. *athlete.*

equalization, equation, equiparation, equilibration; weighing 322n. *weighment;* coordination, adjustment, readjustment, leveling up, leveling down 656n. *restoration,* 31n. *compensation;* going halves, equal division 92n. *bisection,* 775n. *participation;* reciprocity 12n. *correlation;* tit for tat 714n. *retaliation,* 910n. *revenge;* equalizer, counterpoise 31n. *offset;* equator 92n. *dividing line;* equalization fund; standardizer, bed of Procrustes; return match, second m., second chance.

draw, drawn game, drawn battle, ding-dong; level-pegging; tie, dead heat; no decision, stalemate, deadlock; neck-and-neck race, photo finish; love all, fifteen etc. all, deuce; near thing, narrow margin 200n. *nearness.*

compeer, peer, equal, coequal, match, mate, twin; fellow, brother 18n. *analogue;* equivalent, parallel, opposite number, shadow; rival, corrival, competitor 716n. *contender.*

Adj. *equal,* equi-, iso-, co-; same 13 adj. *identical;* like 18adj. *similar;* neither more nor less, coequal, coordinate, coextensive, coincident, congruent, homologous 24adj. *agreeing,* equiponderant, equipondious; equipollent; equidistant; isoperimetric; isotropic; balanced, in equilibrium, equipendent; homeostatic, steady, stable 153adj. *fixed;* even, level, round, square, flush 258vb. *smooth;* symmetrical, even-sided, equilateral, regular 16adj. *uniform;* equable, unvarying, monotonous, ding-dong 153adj. *unchangeable;* competitive, rival 716adj. *contending;* matched, drawn, tied, parallel, level-pegging, running level, abreast, neck-and-neck; equalized, bracketed; sharing, cosharing; equally divided, half-and-half, fifty-fifty, impartial, democratic 913adj. *just;* on equal terms, on the same footing, on a par, on a level; par, quits.

equivalent, comparable, parallel, interchangeable, synonymous, virtual, convertible; corresponding, reciprocal 12adj. *correlative;* as good as, no better, no worse; tantamount, virtually the same, indistinguishable; much the same, all the s., all one, as broad as it is long 18adj. *similar;* worth, valued at, priced at, standing at 809adj. *priced.*

Vb. *be equal,* equal, countervail, counterpoise, compensate 31vb. *offset;* add nothing, detract n., make no difference, come to the same thing, coincide with, agree w. 24vb. *accord;* be equal to, measure up to, reach, touch; cope with 160vb. *be able;* make the grade, pass muster 635vb. *suffice;* hold one's own, keep up with, keep pace w., run abreast, be level; parallel 219vb. *be parallel;* match, twin 18vb. *resemble;* tie, draw, halve the match; break even; make it all square; leave no remainder; go halves, go shares 775vb. *participate.*

equalize, equiparate, equate 322vb. *weigh;* bracket, match; parallel 462vb. *compare;* balance, strike a b., poise; trim, dress, square, round off, make flush 258vb. *smooth,* 16vb. *make uniform;* fit, accommodate, readjust 24vb. *adjust;* add a make-weight, counterpoise 31vb. *offset;* give points to, handicap 31vb. *compensate;* equilibrate, equilibrize, restore to equilibrium 153vb. *stabilize;* right oneself, ride steady, keep one's balance, hold the road.

Adv. *equally* etc. adj.; pari passu, ceteris paribus; at the same rate; to all intents and purposes, as good as; au pair, on equal terms; in equilibrium; on an even keel.

See: 12, 13, 16, 18, 24, 31, 92, 145, 147, 151, 153, 160, 162, 200, 216, 219, 250, 258, 322, 462, 635, 656, 714, 716, 775, 791, 809, 910, 913.

29 Inequality: difference of degree or quality

N. *inequality,* difference of degree 34n. *superiority,* 35n. *inferiority;* irregularity 17n. *non-uniformity;* variability, patchiness 437n. *variegation;* disproportion, asymmetry 246n. *distortion,* 25n. *disagreement;* oddness, oddity, skewness, lopsidedness 220n. *obliquity;* imparity, disparity 15n. *difference;* unlikeness 19n. *dissimilarity;* disequilibrium, unstable equilibrium, imbalance, unbalance; dizziness, staggers; inclination of balance, tilting of the scales, preponderance, overweight, top-hamper 322n. *gravity;* underweight, short weight, lack of ballast 323n. *levity;* defect, shortcoming, inadequacy 636n. *insufficiency;* odds 17n. *differential;* makeweight, counterpoise 31n. *offset;* grace marks 40n. *extra;* casting vote 605n. *choice;* partiality 481n. *bias,* 914n. *injustice.*

Adj. *unequal,* disparate, incongruent 15adj. *different,* 25adj. *disagreeing,* 19adj. *dissimilar;* unique, unequalled 34adj. *superior,* 644adj. *excellent;* below par 35adj. *inferior;* disproportionate, disproportioned, asymmetrical 246adj. *distorted;* irregular, scalene, lopsided 17adj. *non-uniform;* askew, awry 220adj. *sloping;* odd, uneven 84adj. *uncomformable;* unequable, variable, patchy 437adj. *variegated;* deficient, defective, falling short, inadequate 636adj. *insufficient;* underweight, in ballast 323adj. *light;* overweight 322adj. *heavy;* in disequilibrium, unbalanced, swinging, swaying, rocking 217adj. *pendent;* untrimmed, unballasted, uncounterpoised, uncompensated; overweighted, top-heavy, unwieldy 695 adj. *clumsy;* listing, leaning, canting, heeling 220adj. *oblique;* overbalanced, losing balance, dizzy, toppling, falling 309adj. *descending;* capsizing 221adj. *inverted;* partial, unfair 914adj. *unjust,* 481adj. *biased;* undemocratic 871adj. *proud.*

Vb. *be unequal,* be mismatched 25vb. *disagree;* not balance, not equate, leave a remainder 15vb. *differ;* fall short 35vb. *be inferior;* preponderate, have the advantage, give points to, overtop, outclass, outrank 34vb. *be superior;* outstrip 306vb. *outdo;* be deficient 636vb. *not suffice;* lag 136vb. *be late;* overcompensate, overweigh, tip the scale 322vb. *weigh;* kick the beam, need a makeweight 323vb. *be light;* throw the casting vote; overbalance, capsize 221vb. *be inverted;* list, tilt, lean 220vb. *be oblique;* rock, swing, sway 317vb. *fluctuate;* vary 143vb. *change.*

Adv. *unevenly* etc. adj.

See: 15, 17, 19, 25, 31, 34, 35, 40, 84, 136, 143, 217, 220, 221, 246, 306, 309, 317, 322, 323, 437, 481, 605, 636, 640, 644, 695, 871, 914.

30 Mean

N. *average,* medium, mean, median; intermedium, middle term 73n. *serial place;* balance; happy medium, golden mean 177n. *moderation;* standard product 79n. *generality;* ruck, ordinary run, run of the mill 732n. *mediocrity;* norm 81n. *rule;* the normal 610n. *habit.*

middle point, mediety, halfway 70n. *middle;* middle distance, middle age; middle of the road, mid-way, middle course 625n. *mid-course;* splitting the difference 770n. *compromise;* neutrality 606n. *no choice;* central position 225n. *center.*

middle class, bourgeoisie, bourgeois, black-coat worker, white-collar w., salaried class 732n. *mediocrity.*

common man 869n. *commoner;* everywoman, man-in-the-street, little man, ordinary m., plain m. 79n. *everyman;* typical individual, average specimen 732n. *mediocrity.*

Adj. *median,* mean, average, medial 70adj. *middle,* 225adj. *central;* neither hot nor cold, lukewarm; intermediate, gray; normal, standard, ordinary, commonplace, middling, fifty-fifty, much of a muchness, mediocre; moderate, neutral, middle-of-the-road; middle-class, middle-grade, bourgeois.

Vb. *average out,* average, take the mean, keep to the middle; split the difference, go halfway 770vb. *compromise;* strike a balance, pair off 28vb. *equalize.*

Adv.. *on an average,* in the long run 79adv. *generally;* on the whole, all in all; taking one thing with another, taking all things together; in round numbers.

See: 28, 70, 73, 79, 81, 177, 225, 606, 610, 625, 651, 732, 770, 869.

31 Compensation

N. *compensation,* weighting 28n. *equalization;* rectification, recovery, break-back, come-b. 654n. *amendment;* reaction, neutralization, nullification 182n. *counteraction;* commutation 151n. *interchange,* 150n. *substitution;* redemption, recoupment, recovery; retrieval 771n. *acquisition;* indemnification, reparation 787n. *restitution,* 656n. *restoration;* amends, expiation 941n. *atonement;* recompense, repayment 962n. *reward,* 910n. *revenge,* 714n. *retaliation;* reciprocity, measure for measure 12n. *correlation.*

offset, set-off, allowance, makeweight, balance, casting weight, counterweight, counterpoise, counterbalance, ballast 28n. *equalization;* indemnity, reparations, costs, damages 787n. *restitution;* amends 741n. *atonement;* penance 939n. *penitence;* equivalent, quid pro quo, cover, collateral 150n. *substitute;* counterclaim, cross demand 627n. *requirement;* counter-blow 713n. *defense;* counter-attraction 291n. *attraction;* concession, cession 770n. *compromise;* bribe, hush money, tribute 804n. *payment,* 962n. *reward.*

Adj. *compensatory,* compensating, countervailing, balancing 28adj. *equivalent;* self-correcting, self-canceling; indemnificatory, in damages, restitutory 787adj. *restoring;* amendatory, expiatory 741adj. *atoning;* in the opposite scale, weighed against 462adj. *compared.*

Vb. *compensate,* offer compensation, make amends, make compensation etc. n.; do penance 941vb. *atone;* indemnify, restore, pay back 787vb. *restitute;* make good, make up, make up for, do instead 150vb. *substitute;* add a makeweight, ballast; pay, repay 714vb. *retaliate;* bribe, square 762vb. *reward;* overcompensate, lean over backwards.

set off, offset, allow for; counterpoise, countervail, balance 28vb. *equalize;* neutralize, cancel, nullify 182vb. *counteract;* cover, hedge 858vb. *be cautious;* give and take, concede, cede 770vb. *compromise.*

recoup, recover 656vb. *retrieve;* make up leeway, take up the slack; indemnify oneself, take back, get back 786vb. *take;* make a come-back 656vb. *be restored.*

Adv. *in return,* in consideration, in compensation, in lieu; though, although; at the same time, on the other hand; nevertheless, regardless of; despite, maugre, for all that, notwithstanding; but, still, even so, be that as it may; after all, allowing for; when all is said and done, taking one thing with another; at least, at all events, at any rate.

See: 12, 28, 54, 150, 151, 182, 291, 462, 627, 654, 656, 713, 714, 741, 762, 770, 771, 786, 787, 804, 858, 910, 939, 941, 962.

32 Greatness

N. *greatness,* largeness bigness, girth 195n. *size;* large scale, generous proportions, outsize dimensions, vastness, enormousness, gigantism 195n. *hugeness;* muchness, abundance 635n. *plenty;* amplitude, ampleness, fullness, plenitude, maximum 54n. *completeness;* superabundance, superfluity, more than enough 637n. *redundance;* immoderation 176n. *violence;* exorbitance, excessiveness, excess 546n. *exaggeration;* enormity, immensity, boundlessness 107n. *infinity;* numerosity, numerousness, countlessness 104n. *multitude;* dimensions, magnitude 26n. *quantity,* 27n. *degree;* extension, extent 203n. *length,* 205n. *breadth,* 209n. *height,* 211n. *depth;* expanse, area, volume, capacity 183n. *space;* spaciousness, roominess 183n. *room;* mightiness, might, strength, intensity 160n. *power,* 178n. *influence;* intensification, magnification, multiplication 197n. *expansion;* aggrandizement 36n. *increase;* seriousness 638n. *importance;* eminence 34n. *superiority;* grandeur, grandness 868n. *nobility;* 871n. *pride;* majesty 733n. *authority;* fame, renown 866n. *repute;* noise, din 400n. *loudness.*

great quantity, muchness, galore 635n. *plenty;* crop, harvest, profusion, abundance, productivity 171n. *productiveness;* superfluity, superabundance, flood, spring-tide, spate 637n. *redundance,* 350n. *stream;* expanse, sheet, sea, ocean, world, universe, sight of, world of, power of; much, lot, whole l., fat l., deal, good d., great d.; not a little, not peanuts; too much, more than one bargained for; stock, mint, mine 632n. *store;* quantity, peck, bushel, pints, gallons; lump, heap, mass, stack 74n. *accumulation;* packet, pack, load, full l., cargo, shipload, boatload, trainload, carload, wagonload, truckload, sackload 193n. *contents;* quantities, lots, lashings, oodles, scads, wads, pots, bags; heaps, loads, masses, stacks; oceans, seas, floods, streams; volumes, reams, pages; numbers, not a few, quite a f., crowds, masses, hosts, swarms, multitudes 104n. *multitude;* all, entirety, corpus 52n. *whole.*

main part, almost all, principal part, best p., essential p. 52n. *chief part;* greater part, major p., majority 104n. *greater number;* body, bulk, mass 3n. *substance;* soul 1n. *essence.*

Adj. *great,* greater, main, most, major 34adj. *superior;* maximum, greatest 34adj. *supreme;* grand, big, mickle 195adj. *large;* fair-sized, largish, biggish, pretty big; substantial, considerable, respectable; sizable, of size, large-s., full-s., man-s.; bulky, massy, massive, heavy 322adj. *weighty;* prolonged, lengthy 203adj. *long;* wide, thick 205adj. *broad;* ample, generous, voluminous, capacious 183adj. *spacious;* profound 211adj. *deep;* great in stature, tall, lofty, towering, mountainous, alpine 209adj. *high;* great in strength, Herculean 162adj. *strong;* mighty 160adj. *powerful,* 178adj. *influential;* intense 174adj. *vigorous;* noisy 400adj. *loud;* soaring, mounting, climbing 308adj. *ascending,* 197adj. *expanded;* culminating, at the maximum, at the peak, at the top, at its height, in the zenith, at the limit, at the summit 213adj. *topmost;* great in quantity, plentiful, abundant, overflowing 635adj. *plenteous;* superabundant 637adj. *redundant;* great in number, many, swarming, teeming 104adj. *multitudinous;* great in age, antique, ancient, venerable, immemorial 127adj. *olden,* 131adj. *aged;* great in honor, imperial, august, goodly, precious, of value 644adj. *valuable,* 868adj. *noble;* sublime, exalted 821adj. *impressive;* glorious, worshipful, famed, famous 866adj. *renowned;* grave, solemn, serious 638adj. *important;* excelling, excellent 306adj. *surpassing,* 644adj. *best.*

extensive, ranging, far-flying, far-flung, far-reaching, far-stretching 183adj. *spacious;* widespread, prevalent, epidemic; world-wide, universal, cosmic; mass, indiscriminate, wholesale, whole-hogging, all-embracing, comprehensive 78adj. *inclusive.*

enormous, immense, vast, colossal, giant, gigantic, monumental, massive 195adj. *huge;* record, record-breaking, record-smashing, excelling 306adj. *surpassing.*

prodigious, marvelous, astounding, amazing, astonishing 864adj. *wonderful;* fabulous, incredible, unbelievable, passing belief 486adj. *unbelieved,* 472adj. *improbable,* 470adj. *impossible;* stupendous, terrific, frightful 854adj. *frightening;* breathtaking, overwhelming, out of this world 821adj. *impressive.*

remarkable, signal, noticeable, worth looking at 866adj. *noteworthy;* outstanding, extraordinary, exceptional, uncommon 84adj. *unusual;* eminent, distinguished, marked, of mark 638adj. *notable.*

whopping, whacking, thumping, thundering, rattling, howling, screaming, swingeing; father and mother of; hefty, tall, hulking, strapping, overgrown, clumsy 195adj. *unwieldy.*

flagrant, flaring, glaring, stark-staring; signal, shocking 867adj. *disreputable;* red-hot, white-hot, burning 379adj. *fiery.*

unspeakable, unutterable, indescribable, indefinable, ineffable; beyond expression, past speaking 517adj. *inexpressible.*

exorbitant, harsh, stringent, severe 735adj. *oppressive;* excessive, exceeding, passing, extreme 306adj. *surpassing;* monstrous, outrageous, swingeing, unconscionable; unbearable 827adj. *intolerable;* inordinate, preposterous, extravagant 546adj. *exaggerated;* beyond the limit, going too far, far-going.

consummate, 54adj. *complete;* finished, flawless 646adj. *perfect;* entire, sound 52adj. *whole;* thorough, thorough-paced, thorough-going; whole-hogging, utter, out-and-out, arch, crass, gross, arrant, regular, downright, desperate, unmitigated; far gone.

absolute, the veriest; essential, positive, unequivocal; stark, pure, mere 44adj. *unmixed;* unlimited, unrestricted 107adj. *infinite;* undiminished, unabated, unreduced.

Vb. *be great*—large, etc. adj.; bulk, bulk large, loom, loom up; stretch 183n. *extend;* tower, soar, mount 308vb. *ascend;* scale, transcend 34vb. *be superior;* clear, overtop; exceed, know no bounds, run to extremes, go off the deep end 306vb. *overstep;* enlarge 36vb. *augment;* 197vb. *expand;* swamp, overwhelm 737vb. *defeat.*

Adv. *positively,* verily, veritably, actually, indeed, in fact 494adv. *truly;* seriously, indubitably, in all conscience 473adv. *certainly;* decidedly, absolutely, finally, unequivocally, without

equivocation; directly, specifically, unreservedly; essentially, fundamentally, radically; downright, plumb; flagrantly, blatantly, emphatically.
greatly, much, well; passing, very, right; very much, mighty, ever so; fully, quite, entirely, utterly, without reservation 52adv. *wholly,* 54adv. *completely;* thoroughly, by wholesale; widely, extensively, universally 79adv. *generally;* largely, mainly, mostly, to a large extent; considerably, fairly, pretty, pretty well; a deal, a great d., ever so much, never so m.; increasingly, more than ever, doubly, trebly; specially, particularly; exceptionally; on a large scale, in a big way; vastly, hugely, enormously, gigantically, colossally; heavily, strongly, powerfully, mightily 178adv. *influentially;* actively, strenuously, intensely; closely, narrowly, intensively, zealously, fanatically, hotly, bitterly, fiercely; acutely, sharply, shrewdly, exquisitely; enough, more than e., abundantly, profusely; generously, richly, worthily, magnificently, splendidly, nobly; supremely, preeminently, superlatively; rarely, unusually, wonderfully, strangely; indefinitely, immeasurably, incalculably, infinitely, unspeakably, ineffably; awfully, badly.
extremely, ultra, to extremes, to the limit, without a l., no end of; beyond measure, beyond all bounds; beyond comparison, beyond compare; overly, unduly, improperly, to a fault; out of all proportion, out of all whooping; bitterly, harshly, cruelly, unconscionably, with a vengeance 735adj. *severely;* immoderately, uncontrollably, desperately, madly, frantically, furiously, fanatically, bitterly 176adv. *violently;* exceedingly, excessively, exorbitantly, inordinately, preposterously; foully, abominably, grossly, beastly, monstrously, horribly; confoundedly, deucedly, devilishly, damnably, hellishly; tremendously, terribly, fearfully; finally, irretrievably; unforgivably, mortally.
remarkably, noticeably, markedly, pointedly; sensibly, feelingly; notably, strikingly, signally, emphatically, prominently, glaringly, flagrantly, blatantly; publicly 400adv. *loudly;* eminently, preeminently, egregiously; singularly, peculiarly 79adv. *specially;* curiously, oddly, queerly, strangely, uncommonly, unusually 84adv. *unconformably;* surprisingly, astonishingly, amazingly, incredibly, marvellously, magically 864adv. *wonderfully;* awfully, tremendously, stupendously, fearfully, frighteningly; excitedly, impressively.
painfully, unsparingly, till it hurts; badly, bitterly, hard; seriously, sorely, grievously; sadly, miserably, wretchedly; distressingly, pitiably, piteously, woefully, lamentably; shrewdly, cruelly; savagely; exquisitely, excruciatingly, shockingly, frightfully, dreadfully, terribly, horribly, frighteningly; banefully, poisonously, balefully, mortally.
See: 3, 26, 27, 34, 36, 52, 54, 74, 78, 79, 84, 104, 107, 127, 131, 160, 162, 171, 174, 176, 178, 183, 193, 195, 197, 203, 205, 209, 211, 213, 306, 308, 322, 350, 379, 400, 470, 472, 473, 486, 494, 517, 546, 632, 635, 637, 638, 644, 646, 733, 735, 737, 821, 827, 854, 864, 866, 867, 868, 871.

33 Smallness

N. *smallness,* exiguousness, exiguity, scantiness, moderateness, moderation; small size, diminutiveness, minuteness 196n. *littleness;* brevity 204n. *shortness;* leanness, meagerness 206n. *thinness;* rarefaction 325n. *rarity;* briefness, momentariness 114n. *transientness;* paucity 105n. *fewness;* rareness, sparseness, sparsity 140n. *infrequency;* scarceness, scarcity 636n. *insufficiency,* 307n. *shortcoming;* small means 801n. *poverty;* pettiness, insignificance, meanness 639n. *unimportance,* 35n. *inferiority;* averageness 30n. *average,* 732n. *mediocrity;* no depth 212n. *shallowness;* tenuity 4n. *insubstantiality;* compression, abbreviation, abridgment 198n. *contraction;* diminution 37n. *decrease;* vanishing point, nothingness 2n. *non-existence,* 103n. *zero,* 444n. *invisibility.*
small quantity, modicum, minimum 26n. *finite quantity;* minutiae, trivia; detail, petty detail 80n. *particulars;* nutshell 592n. *compendium;* drop in the bucket, drop in the ocean; homeopathic dose, trifling amount 639n. *trifle;* thimbleful, spoonful, mouthful, capful; trickle, dribble, sprinkling, sprinkle, dash, splash; tinge, tincture, trace, spice, smack, smell, lick; nuance, soupçon, thought, suggestion, shade, shadow, touch, cast; spark, scintilla, gleam, flash; pinch, snatch; snack, sip, bite, mite, morsel, sop; scantling, dole,

iron ration; fragment 53n. *piece;* whit, bit, mite; iota, jot, tittle; ounce, penny-weight, grain, scruple, minim 322n. *weighment;* inch, millimeter 200n. *short distance;* second, moment 116n. *instant;* vanishing point, next to nothing, hardly anything, just enough to swear by; the shadow of a shade 4n. *insubstantial thing.*

small thing, 196n. *miniature;* dot, stop, point, pinpoint; dab, spot, fleck, speck, mote, smut; grain, granule, seed, crumb, groats 332n. *powder;* drop, droplet, driblet, gout; thread, shred, rag, tatter, fritters, fragment 53n. *piece;* cantlet, scrap, flinders, smithereens; flake, snip, snippet, gobbet, small slice, finger; flitters, confetti; chip, clipping, paring, shaving; shiver, sliver, slip; pinprick, snick, prick, nick; hair 208n. *filament.*

small coin, cent, nickel, dime; groat, farthing, half-farthing, nap, mite, widow's m.; sou, centime, doit, stiver, anna, pice, pie, cowrie, bean, cash 797n. *coinage.*

small animal, 196n. *animalcule;* grub, tit, whippet; homunculus, atomy, mite, dwarf, midget, Tom Thumb, minimus, minikin, manikin.

particle, material point, corpuscle; atom, electron, positron, proton, neutron; meson, neutrino, hyperion, mucon; anti-particle, anti-proton, anti-electron; molecule, photon; ion, cation, anion.

Adj. *small,* exiguous, not much, moderate, modest, homeopathic, minimal, infinitesimal; microscopic, ultra-m. 444adj. *invisible;* tiny, weeny, wee, minute, diminutive, miniature 196adj. *little;* smaller 35adj. *lesser;* least, minimum; small-sized, small-framed, small-boned, under-sized 196adj. *dwarfish;* slim, slender, lean, meager, thin 206adj. *narrow;* slight, feeble, puny 163adj. *weak;* delicate, dainty, minikin, fragile 330adj. *brittle;* not heavy, weightless 323adj. *light;* fine, subtle, rarefied 325adj. *rare;* quiet, not loud, soft, low, faint, hushed 401adj. *muted;* not tall, squat 210adj. *low;* not long, brief, skimpy, abbreviated 204adj. *short;* shortened, abridged, cut, compact, compendious, thumbnail 198adj. *contracted;* scanty, scant, scarce 307adj. *deficient;* dribbling, trickling 636adj. *insufficient;* reduced, limited, restricted 747adj. *restrained;* declining, ebbing, at low ebb 37adj. *decreasing;* below par, off peak, below the mark 35adj. *inferior;* less, lesser, least.

inconsiderable, minor, light-weight, trifling, petty, paltry, insignificant 639adj. *unimportant;* not many, soon counted, mighty few 105adj. *few;* inappreciable, unnoticeable 444adj. *invisible;* shadowy, tenuous, evanescent 446adj. *disappearing,* 114adj. *transient;* marginal, negligible 458adj. *neglected;* slight, superficial, cursory 4adj. *insubstantial;* skin-deep 212adj. *shallow;* average, middling, fair, fairish, so-so 30adj. *median;* moderate, modest, humble, tolerable, passable 732adj. *mediocre;* not much of a, no great shakes, beta minus 35adj. *inferior;* no more than, just, only, mere, bare; plain, simple 44adj. *unmixed.*

Vb. *be small,* lie in a nutshell; stay small, not grow, have no size 196vb. *be little;* have no height 210vb. *be low;* have no depth; have no weight 323vb. *be light;* make no sound 401vb. *sound faint;* be less 307vb. *fall short;* get less 37vb. *decrease;* shrink 198vb. *become smaller.*

Adv. *slightly,* exiguously, to a small degree, little; lightly, softly, faintly; superficially, cursorily, grazingly; gradually, imperceptibly, insensibly, invisibly; on a small scale, in a small way, modestly, humbly; fairly, moderately, tolerably, quite; comparatively, relatively, rather, enough, well e.; indifferently, poorly, badly, miserably, wretchedly, dismally; hardly, scarcely, barely, only just; hardly at all, no more than; only, merely, purely, simply; at least, at the very least.

partially, to some degree, in some measure, to a certain extent; somehow, after a fashion, in a manner, some, a little, a bit, just a bit, ever so little, as little as may be; not fully, restrictedly, limitedly, within bounds 55adv. *incompletely;* not wholly, in part 55adv. *partly;* not perfectly 647adv. *imperfectly.*

almost, all but, within an ace of, within an inch of, on the brink of, on the verge of, within sight of, in a fair way to 200adv. *nigh;* near upon, close u., approximately 200adv. *nearly;* just short of, not quite, hardly, scarcely, barely.

about, somewhere, somewhere about, in the region of, thereabouts; on an average, more or less; near enough, a little more, a little less; at a guess, say.

in no way, no ways, no wise, by no

means, not by any manner of means, in no respect, not at all, not in the least, not a bit, not a whit, not a jot, not a shadow, on no account.

See: 2, 4, 26, 30, 35, 37, 44, 53, 55, 80, 103, 105, 114, 116, 140, 163, 196, 198, 200, 204, 206, 208, 210, 212, 307, 322, 323, 325, 332, 401, 444, 446, 458, 592, 631, 636, 639, 647, 732, 747, 797, 801.

34 Superiority

N. *superiority,* superior elevation, higher position; altitude, loftiness, sublimity 209n. *height;* transcendence 32n. *greatness,* 306n. *overstepping;* the tops 213n. *summit;* quality, excellence 644n. *goodness;* ne plus ultra 646n. *perfection;* preferability 605n. *choice;* primacy, pride of place, seniority 64n. *precedence,* 119n. *priority;* eminence, preeminence 866n. *prestige;* higher rank, higher degree 27n. *degree,* 868n. *nobility, aristocracy;* overlordship, paramountcy, supremacy, sovereignty, majesty, imperium 733n. *authority;* domination, predominance, hegemony 178n. *influence;* directorship, leadership 689n. *management;* prepollence, preponderance, prevalence 29n. *inequality;* win, championship 727n. *victory;* prominence 638n. *importance;* one-upmanship 698n. *cunning,* 727n. *success;* excess, surplus 637n. *superfluity;* climax, zenith, culmination 725n. *completion;* maximum, top, peak, crest, crest of the wave; record, high, new h. 213n. *summit.*

vantage, advantage, privilege, prerogative, favor 615n. *benefit;* start, flying s., lead, commanding 1., winning position; odds, points, bisque, pull, edge, bulge; command, upper hand, whip-h.; one up, something in hand, reserves; majority, the big battalions 104n. *greater number;* lion's share, Benjamin's mess; leverage, scope 183n. *room;* vantage ground, coign of vantage.

superior, superior person, superman, wonderman 644n. *exceller;* better man, first choice 890n. *favorite;* high-up, top people, best p. 638n. *bigwig;* one's betters, nobility, aristocracy 868n. *upper class;* overlord, lord's lord, suzerain 741n. *master;* commander, chief, boss, prophet, guide 690n. *leader;* foreman 690n. *manager;* primate, president, chairman, prime minister, primus inter pares 690n. *director;* model 646n. *paragon;* star, top-sawyer 696n. *proficient;* specialist 696n. *expert;* world-beater 644n. *exceller;* winner, prizewinner, prizeman, champion, cup-holder, record-h. 727n. *victor;* prima donna, first lady, head boy; firstborn, elder.

Adj. *superior,* more so; elative, comparative, superlative; major, greater 32adj. *great;* upper, higher, senior, over, super; supernormal, above the average, in a different class 15adj. *different;* better, a cut above 644adj. *excellent;* competitive, more than a match for; one up, ahead, far a., streets a. 64adj. *preceding;* prior, preferable, preferred, favorite 605adj. *chosen;* record, a record for, exceeding, overtopping, vaulting, outmatching 306adj. *surpassing;* on top, winning, victorious 727adj. *successful;* outstanding, marked, distinguished, rare, not like the rest, not as others are, unusual 84adj. *unconformable;* top-level, high-l. 689adj. *directing,* 638adj. *important;* commanding, in authority 733adj. *ruling;* revised, reformed, bettered, all the better for 654adj. *improved;* enlarged, enhanced 197adj. *expanded.*

supreme, arch-, greatest 32adj. *great;* highest, uppermost 213adj. *topmost;* first, chief, foremost 64adj. *preceding;* main, principal, leading, overruling, overriding, cardinal, capital 638adj. *important;* excellent, best; superlative, super, champion, tiptop, first-rate, first-class, A1, front-rank, world-beating 644adj. *best;* facile princeps, on top, top of the class, nulli secundus, second to none, none such; dominant, paramount, preeminent, sovereign, royal, every inch a king; incomparable, unrivaled, unparagoned, matchless, peerless, unparalleled, unequaled 29 adj. *unequal;* unapproached, unapproachable, inimitable 21adj. *unimitated;* unsurpassed 306adj. *surpassing;* without comparison, beyond compare, beyond criticism 646adj. *perfect;* transcendent, transcendental, out of this world.

crowning, capping, culminating 725adj. *completive;* climactic, maximal, maximum; record, record-breaking, best ever 644adj. *best.*

Vb. *be superior,* transcend 10vb. *be unrelated;* rise above, surmount, overtop, tower over, overlook, command 209vb. *be high;* go beyond, outrange, outreach, overpass 306vb. *overstep;* exceed, out-Herod Herod, beat the limit, take the pot, take the cake, take the biscuit; pass, surpass, beat the record, reach a new high; improve on, better, go one b., cap, trump, overtrump; show quality, shine, excel 644vb. *be good;* assert one's superiority, be too much for; steal the show, outshine, eclipse, overshadow, throw into the shade, cut out; put another's nose out of joint, take the shine out of; score off, have the laugh on 851n. *ridicule;* best, outrival, outmatch, outclass, outrank 306vb. *outdo;* outplay, outpoint, outmaneuver, outwit 542vb. *befool;* overtake, leave behind, lap 277vb. *outstrip;* get the better of, worst, sit on, beat, beat hollow, knock into a cocked hat, beat all comers 727vb. *defeat;* rise superior to, rise to the occasion.

predominate, 178vb. *prevail;* preponderate, overbalance, overweigh, tip the scale, turn the s.; change the balance 29vb. *be unequal;* override, sit on 178vb. *prevail;* have the advantage, have the start of, have the whip-hand, have the upper h., have the edge on, have the bulge on; lead, hold the l., be up on, be one up.

come first, stand f., head the list 64vb. *come before;* take precedence, play first fiddle 638vb. *be important;* take the lead, lead the dance, lead the van 237vb. *be in front;* lead, play the l., star 689vb. *direct.*

culminate, come to a head 669vb. *mature;* cap, crown all 213vb. *crown;* rise to a peak; set a new record, reach a new high 725vb. *climax.*

Adv. *beyond,* more, over; over the mark, above the m., above par, over the average; upwards of, in advance of; over and above; at the top of the scale, on the crest, at its height, at the peak, at an advantage.

eminently, egregiously, preeminently, surpassing, prominently, superlatively, supremely; above all, of all things; the most, to crown all, to cap all; par excellence; principally, especially, particularly, peculiarly; a fortiori, even more, all the m.; even, yea; still more, ever more, far and away.

See: 10, 15, 21, 27, 29, 32, 41, 64, 84, 104, 119, 127, 178, 183, 197, 209, 213, 237, 277, 306, 542, 605, 615, 637, 638, 644, 646, 654, 689, 690, 696, 698, 725, 727, 733, 851, 866, 868, 890.

35 Inferiority

N. *inferiority,* minority, inferior numbers 105n. *fewness;* littleness 33n. *smallness;* no record, second best; subordinancy, subordination, dependence 745n. *subjection;* secondariness, supporting role, second fiddle 639n. *unimportance;* lowliness, humbleness 872n. *humility;* second rank, back seat, obscurity 419n. *dimness;* commonness 869n. *commonalty;* disadvantage, handicap 702n. *hindrance;* faultiness, blemish, defect 647n. *imperfection;* deficiency 307n. *shortcoming,* 636n. *insufficiency;* failure 728n. *defeat;* poor quality 645n. *badness,* 812n. *cheapness;* vulgarity 847n. *bad taste;* beggarliness, shabbiness 801n. *poverty;* worsening, decline 655n. *deterioration;* low record, low, minimum, lowest point, nadir, the bottom 214n. *base;* depression, trough 210n. *lowness;* flatness, level, plain 216n. *horizontality;* averageness 732n. *mediocrity.*

inferior, subordinate, subaltern, sub, underling, understrapper, assistant 703n. *aider;* subsidiary 707n. *auxiliary;* agent 755n. *deputy,* 150n. *substitute;* tool, pawn 628n. *instrument;* follower, retainer 742n. *dependent;* menial 742n. *servant;* poor relation 639n. *nonentity;* subject, underdog 742n. *slave;* backbencher, private, other ranks, lower classes 869n. *commonalty;* second, second best, second string, second fiddle, second-rater; bad second, poor s., also-ran; failure, reject 607n. *rejection;* subman, animal; younger, junior.

Adj. *lesser,* less, minor 639adj. *unimportant*; small 33adj. *inconsiderable;* smaller, diminished 37adj. *decreasing;* reduced 198adj. *contracted;* least, smallest, minimal, minimum; lowest, bottommost 214adj. *undermost;* minus 307adj. *deficient.*

inferior, lower, junior, under-, sub-; subordinate, subaltern, understrapping 742adj. *serving;* subject, unfree, dependent, parasitic 745adj. *subjected;* secondary, subsidiary, auxiliary 703adj. *aiding,* 639adj. *unimportant;* second, second-best, second-rate, second-rank 922adj. *contemptible;* humble, lowly, low-level, menial; low-ranking, unclassified; subnormal, substandard, subgrade, C3 607adj. *rejected;* slight, under-weight 323adj. *light;* spoiled, marred, shop-soiled 655adj. *deteriorated;* unsound, defective, patchy, unequal 647adj. *imperfect;* failing 636adj. *insufficient;* shoddy, nasty 645adj. *bad,* 812adj. *cheap,* 847adj. *vulgar;* low, common, low-caste 869adj. *plebeian;* scratch, makeshift 670adj. *un-*

prepared; temporary, provisional 114adj. *ephemeral;* in a lower class, outclassed, outshone, thrown into the shade, worsted, beat 728adj. *defeated;* humiliated 872adj. *humbled;* unworthy, not fit, not fit to hold a candle to, not a patch on.

Vb. *be inferior,* become smaller 37vb. *decrease,* 198vb. *become small;* fall short, come short of, not come up to, fall below 307vb. *fall short;* lag, fall behind; trail 284vb. *follow;* want, lack 636vb. *not suffice;* not make the grade, not pass 728vb. *fail;* bow to 739vb. *obey;* concede the victory; yield, cede, yield the palm, hand it to, knuckle under 721vb. *submit;* play second fiddle, play a supporting role 742vb. *serve;* take a back seat, retire into the shade; hide one's diminished head, slink into obscurity 419vb. *be dim;* lose face, lose caste, lose izzat 867vb. *lose repute;* get worse 655vb. *deteriorate;* slump, sink, sink low, touch depth, reach one's nadir 309vb. *descend.*

Adv. *less,* minus, short of; beneath 210adv. *under;* below average, below par, below the mark; at the bottom, in the lowest place, at low ebb; inferiorly, poorly, basely.

See: 33, 37, 105, 114, 150, 195, 198, 210, 214, 216, 284, 304, 307, 309, 323, 419, 607, 628, 636, 639, 643, 645, 647, 655, 670, 702, 703, 707, 721, 728, 729, 732, 739, 742, 745, 755, 801, 812, 847, 867, 869, 872, 922.

36 Increase

N. *increase,* increment, augmentation, waxing, crescendo; advance, progress 285n. *progression;* growth, build-up, development 164n. *production;* growing pains 536n. *learning;* extension, prolongation, protraction 203n. *lengthening;* widening, broadening; amplification, inflation, dilation 197n. *expansion;* proliferation, swarming 166n. *reproduction;* multiplication, squaring, cubing 86n. *numerical operation;* adding 38n. *addition;* enlargement, magnification, aggrandizement 32n. *greatness;* over-enlargement, excess 546n. *exaggeration;* enhancement, heightening, raising 310n. *elevation;* concentration 324n. *condensation;* recruitment 162n. *strengthening;* intensification, stepping up, doubling, redoubling, trebling 91n. *duplication,* 94n. *triplication;* acceleration, speeding 277n. *spurt;* hotting up, calefaction 381n. *heating;* excitation 174n. *stimulation;* exacerbation 832n. *aggravation;* advancement, rise, uprush, upsurge, ebullition, upward curve, upward trend, anabasis 308n. *ascent,* 654n. *improvement;* flood, tide, rising t., spring t., swell, surge 350n. *wave;* progressiveness, cumulativeness, cumulative effect, synergistic e., snowball 74n. *accumulation;* ascending order 71n. *series.*

increment, augment, bulge; accretion, access, accession, accrual, addition, contribution 40n. *adjunct;* supplement 40n. *extra;* padding, stuffing 303n. *insertion;* percentage, commission, rake-off; interest, gain, net g., profit 771n. *acquisition;* plunder, purchase, prey 790n. *booty;* prize 962n. *reward;* produce, harvest 164n. *product;* take, takings, receipts, proceeds 782n. *receiving.*

Adj. *increasing,* spreading; greater than ever 32adj. *great;* growing, waxing, filling, crescent, on the increase, anabatic; supplementary 38adj. *additional;* ever-increasing, snowballing, cumulative 285adj. *progressive;* augmentative, elative, comparative, intensive; increasable, prolific, fruitful 164adj. *productive;* increased, stretched, aggrandized, swollen, bloated 197adj. *expanded.*

Vb. *grow,* increase, gain, earn interest 771vb. *acquire;* dilate, swell, bulge, wax, fill 197vb. *expand;* fill out, fatten, thicken 205vb. *be broad;* put on weight 322vb. *weigh;* sprout, bud, burgeon, flower, blossom 164vb. *reproduce itself;* breed, spread, swarm, proliferate, multiply 104vb. *be many,* 171vb. *be fruitful;* grow up 669vb. *mature,* 209vb. *be high;* start up, shoot up 68vb. *begin;* run up, climb, mount, rise, gain height 308vb. *ascend;* flare up, shine out 379vb. *be hot,* 417vb. *shine;* gain strength, convalesce, revive, recover 656vb. *be restored,* 162vb. *be strong;* improve 654vb. *get better;* gain ground, advance, get ahead, get on, snowball, accumulate 285vb. *progress;* gain in value, appreciate, rise in price 811vb. *be dear;* exceed, overflow 637vb. *superabound,* 32vb. *be great;* rise to a maximum 34vb. *culminate.*

augment, increase, bump up, double, triple 94vb. *treble,* 97vb. *quadruple;* redouble, square, cube; duplicate 106vb. *repeat;* multiply 164vb. *produce;* grow, breed, raise, rear 369vb. *breed stock,* 370vb. *cultivate,* 669vb. *mature;* enlarge, magnify, distend, inflate, blow up 197vb. *expand;* amplify, develop, build up, fill out, fill in, pad out 54vb. *complete;* condense, concentrate 324vb. *be dense;* implant, infuse 303vb. *insert;* supplement, superadd, repay with interest; import, read into; bring to, contribute to; increase the numbers, make one of, accrue 38vb. *add;* increase the dimensions, prolong, stretch, pull out 203vb. *lengthen;* broaden, widen, thicken, deepen; heighten, enhance, send up 209vb. *make higher;* raise the score, make runs, convert a try, majorize; raise, exalt 310vb. *elevate;* advance, aggrandize 285vb. *promote;* aim higher, raise the sights; speed up 277vb. *accelerate;* intensify, redouble, step up, screw up, stimulate, energize 174vb. *invigorate;* recruit, reinforce, revive 685vb. *refresh,* 656vb. *restore,* 162vb. *strengthen;* overenlarge, glorify 546vb. *exaggerate,* 482vb. *overestimate;* stoke, add fuel to the flame, exacerbate 832vb. *aggravate,* 176vb. *make violent;* maximize, bring to the boil, bring to a head 725vb. *climax.*

Adv. *crescendo,* increasingly etc. adj.; more so, with a vengeance, with knobs on; on the increase, up and up, more and more, always m., all the m.

See: 32, 34, 38, 40, 54, 68, 71, 74, 86, 91, 94, 97, 104, 106, 162, 164, 166, 171, 174, 176, 197, 203, 205, 209, 277, 285, 303, 308, 310, 322, 324, 350, 369, 370, 379, 381, 417, 482, 536, 546, 637, 654, 656, 669, 685, 725, 771, 782, 790, 811, 832, 962

37 Decrease: non-increase

N. *decrease,* getting less, lessening, dwindling, falling off; waning, fading; fade-out, dimming, obscuration, 419n. *dimness;* wane 198n. *contraction,* 206n. *narrowing;* ebb, reflux, retreat, withdrawal 286vb. *regression;* ebb-tide, neap 210n. *lowness;* descending order 71n. *series;* subsidence, sinking, decline, declension, katabasis, downward curve, downward trend, fall, drop, plunge 309n. *descent,* 165n. *ruin;* deflation, recession, slump 655n. *deterioration;* loss of value, depreciation 812n. *cheapness;* loss of reputation 866n. *disrepute;* weakening, enfeeblement 163n. *weakness;* impoverishment 801n. *poverty;* shrinking, diminishing returns; exhaustion 190n. *emptiness;* shortage, shrinkage, evaporation, deliquescence, erosion, decay, crumbling 655n. *dilapidation;* attrition 333n. *friction;* spoilage, leakage, wastage, damage, loss, wear and tear 42n. *decrement;* using up, consumption 634n. *waste;* non-increase, anticlimax 14n. *contrariety;* underproduction 175n. *inertness;* slackness, slackening 679n. *inactivity;* limitation, limit, bound 747n. *restriction;* forfeit, sacrifice 963n. *penalty,* 772n. *loss.*

diminution, making less; subduction, deduction 39n. *subtraction;* exception 57n. *exclusion;* abatement, reduction, restriction 747n. *restraint;* slowing down, deceleration 278n. *slowness;* retrenchment, cut, economization 814n. *economy;* cutting back, pruning, paring, shaving, clipping, docking, curtailment, abridgment, abbreviation 204n. *shortening;* compression, squeeze 198n. *contraction;* abrasion, erosion 333vb. *friction;* melting, dissolution 337vb. *liquefaction;* scattering, dispersal 75n. *dispersion;* weeding, elimination 62n. *sorting,* 300n. *voidance;* extenuation, mitigation, minimization 177n. *moderation;* belittlement, undervaluation 483n. *underestimation,* 926n. *detraction;* demotion, degradation 872n. *humiliation.*

Adj. *decreasing,* dwindling; decrescent, waning, fading, katabatic; deliquescent, melting, evaporating 337adj. *liquefied;* bated, decreased, diminished etc. vb.; unexpanded, unincreased, unstretched; declining, going down, sinking, ebbing; decaying, ruinous 655adj. *dilapidated.*

Vb. *bate,* make less, diminish, decrease, lessen, minify, dequantitate; take away, detract from, deduct 39vb. *subtract;* except 57vb. *exclude;* reduce, step down, scale d., whittle, pare, scrape 206vb. *make thin;* shrink, abridge, abbreviate, boil down 204vb. *shorten;* squeeze, compress, contract 198vb. *make smaller;* limit, bound 747vb. *restrain;* cut down, cut back, retrench 814vb. *economize;* reduce speed, slow down, decelerate 278vb. *retard;* lower, send down 311vb. *depress;* minimize, mitigate, extenuate 177vb. *moderate;* deflate, puncture; belittle, depreciate, undervalue 483vb. *underestimate,* 812vb. *cheapen,* 926vb. *detract;* dwarf, overshadow 34vb. *be superior;* throw into the shadow, darken, obscure 419vb. *bedim;* degrade, demote 872vb. *humiliate;* loosen, ease, relax 701vb. *disencumber;* remit, pardon 909vb. *forgive;* unload, throw overboard 323vb.

lighten; run down, empty, drain, exhaust 300vb. *void;* use up, consume, fritter away 634vb. *waste;* let escape, let evaporate, boil away 338vb. *vaporize;* melt down 337vb. *liquefy;* grind, crumble 332vb. *pulverize;* rub away, abrade, file 333vb. *rub;* gnaw, nibble at, eat away 301vb. *eat;* erode, rust 655vb. *impair;* strip, peel, denude 229vb. *uncover;* pillage, plunder, dispossess 786vb. *deprive,* 801vb. *impoverish;* emasculate, unman 161vb. *disable;* dilute, water 163vb. *weaken,* 43vb. *mix;* thin, thin out, sort o., weed o., depopulate 105vb. *render few;* eliminate, expel 300vb. *eject;* decimate, slaughter, kill off, wipe out 165vb. *destroy,* 361vb. *kill;* reduce to nothing, annihilate 2vb. *nullify;* hush, quiet 399vb. *silence,* 578vb. *make mute;* damp down, cool, extinguish 382vb. *refrigerate;* quell 745vb. *subjugate.*

decrease, grow less, lessen, suffer loss; abate, die down; dwindle, shrink, contract 198vb. *become small;* wane, waste, decay, wear away, consume a., languish 655vb. *deteriorate;* fade, die away, grow dim 419vb. *be dim;* set, hide one's diminished head 867vb. *lose repute;* retreat, withdraw, ebb 286vb. *regress,* 290vb. *recede;* run low, run down, ebb away, drain away, dry up, fail 636vb. *not suffice;* tail off, taper off 206vb. *be narrow,* 293vb. *converge;* subside, sink 313vb. *plunge;* come down, decline, fall, drop, slump, collapse 309vb. *descend;* not grow, stay down, lag 278vb. *decelerate;* melt, deliquesce 337vb. *liquefy;* evaporate 338vb. *vaporize;* thin, thin out, become scarce 325vb. *be rare;* lose numbers 105vb. *be few,* 75vb. *disperse;* die out, become extinct 2vb. *pass away;* lose weight, bant, diet, reduce 323vb. *be light,* 946vb. *starve;* lose one's voice, stop one's noise, pipe down, dry up 578vb. *be mute;* lose, shed, rid oneself; cast off 229vb. *doff;* forfeit, sacrifice 963vb. *be punished.*

Adv. *diminuendo,* decrescendo, decreasingly; less and less, ever l.; in decline, on the wane, at low ebb.

See: 2, 14, 34, 39, 42, 43, 57, 62, 71, 75, 105, 161, 163, 165, 175, 177, 190, 198, 204, 206, 210, 229, 278, 286, 290, 293, 298, 300, 301, 309, 311, 313, 323, 325, 332, 333, 337, 338, 361, 382, 399, 419, 483, 578, 634, 636, 655, 679, 701, 745, 747, 786, 801, 812, 814, 866, 867, 872, 909, 926, 946, 963.

38 Addition

N. *addition,* adding to, annexation, adjection, adjunction, fixture, agglutination 45n. *junction;* imposing, imposition 187n. *location;* superposition, superaddition, superjunction, superfetation; prefixion, anteposition 64n. *precedence;* suffixion, affixture, affixation 65n. *sequence;* supplementation, suppletion 725n. *completion;* contribution, reinforcement 703n. *aid;* accession, accretion, accrual, supervention; interposition, interjection, epenthesis 303n. *insertion,* 78n. *inclusion;* reinforcement 36n. *increase;* increment, supplement, addendum, appendage, appendix 40n. *adjunct;* extra time, overtime 113n. *protraction;* appurtenance 89n. *accompaniment;* summation, adding up, total, toll 86n. *numeration.*

Adj. *additional,* additive; added, included etc. vb.; supervenient, adopted, adscititious, occasional 59adj. *extraneous;* supplementary, supplemental, suppletory 725adj. *completive;* subjunctive; conjunctive 45adj. *conjunct;* subsidiary, auxiliary, contributory 703adj. *aiding;* supernumerary, supererogatory; extra, spare 637adj. *superfluous;* interjected, interposed, epenthetic 303adj. *inserted,* 231adj. *interjacent;* prosthetic 64adj. *preceding.*

Vb. *add,* add up, sum, total, do the addition 86vb. *do sums;* carry over 272vb. *transfer;* add to, annex, append, subjoin; attach, pin to, clip to, tag on, tack on; conjoin, hitch to, yoke to, unite to 45vb. *join, tie;* stick on, glue on, plaster on 48vb. *agglutinate;* add on, preface, prefix, affix, suffix, postfix, infix; introduce 231vb. *intromit;* interpose, interject; read into, import; engraft, let in 303vb. *insert;* bring to, contribute to, make one's contribution, add one's share 36vb. *augment;* swell, extend, expand 197vb. *enlarge;* supplement 54vb. *complete;* lay on, place on, impose, clap on, saddle with, burden w., load w. 187vb. *stow,* 702vb. *hinder;* superadd, superimpose, pile on, heap on; glorify, ornament, add frills, supply the trappings 844vb. *decorate;* plaster, paint over, smear o., coat 226vb. *overlay;* mix with, mix in 43vb. *mix;* take to oneself, annex 786vb. *take;* absorb, take in, include, receive 299vb. *admit.*

accrue, be added 78vb. *be included;* supervene 295vb. *arrive,* 189vb. *be present;* accede, adhere, join 708vb. *join a party;* mix with, combine w.

50vb. *combine;* make an extra, make an addition to, make one more; reinforce, recruit 162vb. *strengthen;* swell the ranks, fill the gap.

Adv. *in addition,* additionally, more, plus, extra; with interest, with a vengeance, with knobs on; and, too, also, item, furthermore, further; likewise, and also, and eke, to boot; else, besides; et cetera; and so on, and so forth, moreover, into the bargain, over and above, including, inclusive of, with, as well as, not to mention, let alone, not forgetting; together with, along w., coupled w., in conjunction w.; conjointly, jointly; even with, despite, for all that.

See: 36, 40, 43, 45, 48, 50, 54, 59, 64, 65, 78, 86, 89, 113, 162, 187, 189, 197, 226, 231, 272, 295, 299, 303, 637, 702, 703, 708, 725, 786, 844.

39 Subduction: non-addition

N. *subtraction,* subduction, deduction, ablation, sublation 86n. *numerical operation;* diminution 37n. *decrease;* abstraction, removal, withdrawal 786n. *taking;* elimination 62n. *sorting;* detrusion, expulsion 300n. *ejection;* clearance 300n. *voidance;* unloading, unpacking 188n. *displacement;* subtrahend, discount 42n. *dec-* sedimentation, abrasion, erosion, detrition 333n. *friction;* retrenchment, curtailment 204n. *shortening;* severance, detruncation, amputation, excision, abscision, recision, circumcision 46n. *disjunction;* castration, mutilation 655n. *impairment;* expurgation, bowdlerization, garbling 648n. *cleansing;* deletion 550n. *obliteration;* minuend 85n. *numerical element;* subtrahend, discount 42n. *decrement;* non-addition, loss of interest.

Adj. *subtracted,* subtractive; mutilated etc. vb.; curtailed, docked, excaudal, acaudal, tailless; beheaded, headless, decapitated; minus, without.

Vb. *subtract,* take away, subduct, deduct, do subtraction; detract from, diminish, decrease 37vb. *bate;* cut 810vb. *discount;* except, take out, keep o., leave o. 57vb. *exclude;* expel 300vb. *eject;* abstract 786vb. *take,* 788vb. *steal;* withdraw, remove; unload, unpack 188vb. *displace;* shift 272vb. *transfer;* empty 300vb. *void;* abrade, scrape, file away, erode 333vb. *rub;* eradicate, uproot, pull up, pull out 304vb. *extract;* pick, pick out, put on one side 605vb. *select;* cross out, blot o., delete, blue-pencil, censor 550n. *obliterate;* expurgate, bowdlerize, garble, mutilate 655vb. *impair;* sever, separate, amputate, excise, abscind; shear, shave off, clip 46vb. *disjoin;* retrench, cut back, cut down, prune, pare, whittle, pollard, lop; decapitate, behead, dock, curtail, detruncate, abridge, abbreviate 204vb. *shorten;* geld, castrate, caponize, spay, emasculate 161vb. *unman;* peel, skin, shuck, strip, divest, denude 229vb. *uncover.*

Adv. *in deduction,* by subtraction etc. n.; less; short of; minus, without, except, excepting, with the exception of, barring, bar, save, exclusive of, save and except, with a reservation.

See: 37, 46, 57, 62, 86, 161, 188, 204, 229, 272, 300, 304, 333, 550, 605, 648, 655, 786, 788 810.

40 Adjunct: thing added

N. *adjunct,* addition, something added, contribution 38n. *addition;* additament, addendum, carry-over; attachment, fixture; annexation; inflection, affix, suffix, prefix, infix, postfix, subscript; preposition, postposition; adjective, adverb 564n. *part of speech;* label, ticket, tab, tag 547n. *indication;* appendage, tail, train, cortege, following 67n. *sequel;* wake, trail 65n. *sequence;* appendix, postscript, envoi, coda, ending 69n. *extremity;* codicil, rider 468n. *qualification;* corollary, complement 725n. *completion;* appurtenance, concomitant, marginalia, footnotes 89n. *accompaniment;* pendant, companion piece, twin, pair, fellow 18n. *analogue;* extension, supplement, prolongation, continuation, second part; annex, wing (of a house), offices, outhouse 164n. *edifice;* offshoot 53n. *branch;* arm 53n. *limb;* extremity 267n. *leg,* 214n. *foot;* increment 37n. *increase;* augment, leaf (of a table); patch, darn, reinforcement 656n. *repair;* piece, strip, length 53n. *part;* padding, stuffing 227n. *lining;* interpolation, interlineation 303n. *insertion;* interlude, intermezzo, episode 231n. *interjacence;* insertion, gusset; flap, fold, lappet, lapel; oddment, accessory, ingredient 58n. *component;* skirt, fringe, border, frill, edging 234n. *edge;* embroidery 844n. *ornamentation;* garnish, garnishing, condiment 389n. *sauce;* frills, trimmings, all that goes with it; trappings 228n. *dress,* 226n.

covering; equipment, furnishing 633n. *provision.*

extra, additive, addendum, something over and above, by-product; percentage, primage, interest, compound i., simple i. 771n. *gain;* refresher, bonus, tip, solatium, something on the side 962n. *reward;* free gift, gratuity, grace marks 781n. *gift;* find, lucky f.; acquisition, accession; oddment, item, odd i.; bye (cricket); supernumerary; reserves, spare parts, spares 633n. *provision;* extra help, reinforcement, ripieno 707n. *auxiliary;* fifth wheel of the coach 641n. *inutility;* luxury, work of supererogation 637n. *superfluity;* extra time, overtime 113n. *protraction.*

See: 18, 37, 38, 53, 58, 65, 67, 69, 89, 113, 164, 214, 226, 227, 228, 231, 234, 267, 303, 389, 468, 547, 564, 633, 637, 641, 656, 707, 725, 771, 781, 844, 962.

41 Remainder: thing remaining

N. *remainder,* residue, residuum; residuals, result, resultant 157n. *effect,* 164n. *product;* margin 15n. *difference;* outstanding, balance, net b. 31n. *offset;* surplus, carry-over 36n. *increment;* overplus, overtrick, excess 637n. *superfluity;* relic, rest, remnant 105n. *fewness;* rump, stump, scrag, end, fag e., butt e. 69n. *extremity;* frustum, torso, trunk 53n. *piece;* fossil, skeleton, bones 363n. *corpse;* husk, empty h.; wreck, wreckage 165n. *ruin;* debris 332n. *powder;* track, trace 548n. *record;* wake, afterglow 65n. *sequence;* all that is left, memories 505n. *remembrance;* remanence, survival 113n. *durability;* vestige, remains.

leavings, leftovers; precipitate, deposit; alluvium, silt 344n. *soil;* sediment; drift, loess, moraine, detritus 272n. *thing transferred;* grounds, lees, heel-taps, dregs; scum, skimmings, dross, scoria, slag, sludge; bilge; dottle; scrapings, shavings, filings, sawdust, crumbs 332n. *powder;* husks, bran, chaff, stubble; peel, peelings; skin, slough, scurf; parings, combings; shorts, trimmings, clippings, cabbage, remnants, strips; scraps, candle-ends, odds and ends, lumber 641n. *rubbish;* rejects 779n. *derelict;* sweepings, scourings, *offscourings;* refuse, waste, sewage 649n. *dirt,* 302n. *excrement.*

survivor, finisher; inheritor, heir, successor 776n. *beneficiary;* widower, widow, relict 896n. *widowed spouse;* orphan 779n. *derelict;* descendant 170n. *posterity.*

Adj. *remaining,* surviving, left, vestigial, resting, resultant; residual; left behind, sedimentary, precipitated 779adj. *not retained;* over, leftover, odd; net, surplus; unspent, unexpended, unexpired, unconsumed; outstanding, carried over; spare, to s., superfluous 637adj. *redundant;* cast-off, pariah, outcast 607adj. *rejected;* orphaned, orphan, widowed.

Vb. *be left,* remain, rest, result, survive.

leave over, leave out 57vb. *exclude;* leave 607vb. *reject.*

See: 15, 31, 36, 53, 57, 65, 69, 105, 113, 157, 164, 165, 170, 272, 302, 332, 344, 363, 505, 548, 607, 637, 641, 645, 649, 776, 779, 896.

42 Decrement: thing deducted

N. *decrement,* deduction, cut 37n. *diminution;* allowance, free a.; rebate 810n. *discount;* reprise, tare, drawback, shortage, defect 307n. *shortcoming,* 636n. *insufficiency;* loss, sacrifice, forfeit 963n. *penalty;* leak, leakage, primage, escape 298n. *egress;* shrinkage 204n. *shortening;* spoilage, wastage; off-take, consumption 634n. *waste;* subtrahend, rake-off 786n. *taking.*

See: 37, 204, 298, 307, 634, 636, 786, 810, 963.

43 Mixture

N. *mixture,* mingling, mixing, stirring; blending, harmonization; concord 24n. *agreement;* admixture 38n. *addition;* commixture, commixion 45n. *junction;* immixture 303n. *insertion;* intermixture, interlarding, interpolation 231n. *interjacence;* interweaving, interlacing 222n. *crossing;* amalgamation, integration 50n. *combination;* merger 706n. *association;* syncretism, eclecticism; fusion, interfusion, alloyage; infusion, suffusion, transfusion, instillation, impregnation 341n. *moistening;* adulteration, watering down, sophistication 655n. *deterioration;* contamination, infection 653n. *insalubrity,* 659n. *poison;* infiltration, penetration, pervasion, permeation 297n. *ingress;* interbreeding, miscegenation, intermarriage 894n. *marriage;* syngamy, allogamy, amphimixis 164n. *propagation;* hybridization, mongrelism, touch of the tar brush; miscibility, solubility 337n. *liquefaction;* crucible, melting-pot; variety 437n. *variegation.*

tincture, something mixed, admixture; ingredient 58n. *component;* strain, streak; sprinkling, infusion; tinge, touch, drop, dash, soupçon 33n. *small quantity;* smack 386n. *taste;* seasoning, spice 389n. *condiment;* color, dye 425n. *hue;* stain, blot 845n. *blemish.*

a mixture, mélange; blend, harmony 710n. *concord;* composition 331n. *texture;* amalgam, fusion, compound, confection 50n. *combination;* cento, pastiche, pasticcio; alloy, bronze, brass, billon, pewter, electrum; magma, paste; culinary compound, sauce, salad, stew, hash, ragout, olla podrida, salmagundi, chowchow, mishmash 301n. *dish;* cocktail, brew, witches' b.; medicinal compound, the mixture, drug 658n. *remedy.*

medley, heterogeneity, complexity 17n. *non-uniformity,* 82n. *multiformity;* motley, patchwork, mosaic 437n. *variegation;* miscellany, miscellanea, old curiosity shop; farrago, gallimaufry, hotch-potch, hash, mash; potpourri; jumble, mess; pie, printer's p.; tangle, entanglement, imbroglio 61n. *confusion;* phantasmagoria, kaleidoscope; clatter 411n. *discord;* omnium gatherum, everybody 74n. *crowd;* Noah's ark 369n. *zoo;* multiracial state; all sorts, odds and ends, paraphernalia, oddments.

hybrid, bigener, cross, cross-breed, mongrel; half-blood, half-breed, half-caste; mestizo, mustee; Eurasian, Cape-colored, mulatto; quadroon, octaroon; sambo, griff, griffin; mule, hinny.

Adj. *mixed,* in the melting pot, mixed up, stirred, well-s.; mixed up in, deep in; blended, harmonized, syncretic, eclectic; fused, alloyed 50adj. *combined;* tempered, adulterated, sophisticated, qualified, watered, weak 163adj. *weakened;* merged, amalgamated 45adj. *conjunct;* composite, half-and-half, fifty-fifty, linsey-woolsey, chryselephantine; complex, complicated, implex, involved 251adj. *convoluted;* tangled, confused, jumbled 63adj. *deranged;* unclassified, unsorted, out of order; heterogeneous 17adj. *non-uniform;* kaleidoscopic, phantasmagoric 82adj. *multiform;* patched, patchy, dappled, motley 437 adj. *variegated;* shot 437adj. *iridescent;* miscellaneous, hotch-potch, medley, promiscuous 464adj. *indiscriminate;* miscible, soluble 337adj. *liquefied;* pervasive, spreading 653adj. *infectious;* hybrid, bigenerous, crossbred, crossed; half-blooded, mongrel; interbred, Eurasian, intermixed, multiracial.

Vb. *mix,* make a mixture, mix up, stir, shake; shuffle, transfuse 272vb. *transpose,* 63vb. *jumble;* knead, pound together, hash, mash 332vb. *pulverize;* brew, compound 56vb. *compose;* fuse, alloy, merge, amalgamate, conjoin 45vb. *join;* blend, harmonize 24vb. *adjust;* mingle, intermingle, intersperse 437n. *variegate;* lace, immix, intermix, interlard, interleave 303vb. *insert;* intertwine, interlace, interweave 222vb. *weave;* tinge, dye 425vb. *color;* imbue, instill, impregnate 303vb. *infuse;* dash, sprinkle, besprinkle 341vb. *moisten;* water, adulterate, sophisticate 163vb. *weaken;* temper, attemper, doctor, medicate 468vb. *qualify;* season, spice 390vb. *appetize;* hybridize, mongrelize, cross, cross-breed 164vb. *generate.*

be mixed, be entangled with, be involved, be mixed up in, be deep in, get into; pervade, permeate, run through, overrun 297vb. *infiltrate;* infect, contaminate; tingle, dye, stain 425vb. *color;* miscegenate, intermarry, interbreed, cross with 164vb. *reproduce itself.*

Adv. *among,* amongst, amid, amidst, with; in the midst of, in the crowd; amongst many, inter alia.

See: 17, 24, 33, 38, 45, 50, 56, 58, 61, 63, 74, 82, 163, 164, 222, 231, 251, 272, 297, 301, 303, 331, 332, 337, 341, 386, 389, 390, 411, 425, 437, 464, 468, 653, 655, 658, 659, 706, 710, 845, 849.

44 Simpleness: freedom from mixture

N. *simpleness* etc. adj.; homogeneity 16n. *uniformity;* purity 648n. *cleanness;* oneness 88n. *unity;* absoluteness, sheerness; fundamentality, bedrock; elementarity, atomicity, indivisibility, insolubility, asexuality; lack of complication, simplicity 516n. *intelligibility,* 537n. *plainness,* 699n. *artlessness;* freedom from mixture, not a trace of, not a hint of 190n. *absence.*

simplification, purification 648n. *cleansing;* reduction 51n. *decomposition;* unification, assimilation 13n. *identity.*

elimination, riddance, clearance 300n. *ejection;* sifting, bolting 62n. *sorting;* expulsion 57n. *exclusion.*

Adj. *simple,* homogeneous, monolithic, of a piece 16adj. *uniform;* absolute, sheer, mere, nothing but;

undifferentiated, asexual; single, unified 88adj. *one;* elemental, atomic, indivisible 52adj. *whole;* primary, irreducible, fundamental, basic 5adj. *intrinsic;* elementary, uncomplicated, unraveled, disentangled, simplified 516adj. *intelligible;* direct, unmediated 249adj. *straight;* unsophisticated, homespun 573adj. *plain,* 699adj. *artless;* single-minded, openhearted, whole-h., sincere, downright, unaffected 540adj. *veracious,* 929n. *honorable;* bare, naked 229adj. *uncovered.*

unmixed, pure and simple, without alloy; clear, pure, clarified, purified, cleansed 648adj. *clean;* wholeblooded, thoroughbred 868adj. *noble;* free from, exempt f., exclusive 57adj. *excluding;* unmingled, unblended, unalloyed, uncompounded, uncombined; undiluted, unadulterated, neat, proof, overproof 162adj. *strong;* unqualified, unmodified; unmedicated, unfortified, unstrengthened; unflavored, unspiced, unseasoned 387adj. *tasteless;* untinged, undyed, uncolored 427adj. *white.*

Vb. *simplify,* unmix, unscramble; render, simple 16vb. *make uniform;* narrow down, factorize, reduce, reduce to its element 51vb. *decompose;* disentangle, unravel 46vb. *disjoin;* unify, make one, unite.

eliminate, sift 62vb. *class;* winnow, bolt, pan; purge 648vb. *purify;* clear; get rid of, weed 57vb. *exclude;* rid 304vb. *extract;* expel 300vb. *eject.*

Adv. *simply* etc. adj.; simply and solely; only, merely, exclusively.

See: 5, 13, 16, 46, 51, 52, 57, 62, 88, 162, 190, 229, 249, 300, 304, 387, 427, 516, 540, 573, 648, 699, 868, 929.

45 Junction

N. *junction,* joining etc. vb.; coming together, meeting, concurrence, conjuction 293n. *convergence;* clash 279n. *collision;* contact 202n. *contiguity,* 378n. *touch;* congress, concourse, forgathering, reunion 74n. *assembly;* confluence, meeting-point, meeting-place 76n. *focus;* concrescence, coalescence, symphysis, fusion, merger 43n. *mixture;* unification, synthesis 50n. *combination;* cohesion, tenacity, inextricability, agglutination 48n. *coherence;* concretion, consolidation, solidification, coagulation 324n. *condensation;* closeness, tightness, compactness, impaction; union, coalition, alliance, symbiosis 706n. *association;* connection, linkage, tie-up, hook-up 47n. *bond;* syngamy, wedlock 894n. *marriage;* interconnection, cross-connection, anastomosis, inosculation; interlocking 222n. *crossing;* communication 305n. *passage;* intercommunication, intercourse, commerce 882n. *sociability;* trade, traffic, exchange 151n. *interchange,* 791n. *trade;* involvement 9n. *relation;* arrival, new a., comer, late-c. 297n. *incomer;* partner, yoke-fellow, sharer 775n. *participator;* accompanist 89n. *concomitant.*

joinder, bringing together 74n. *assemblage;* unification 50n. *combination;* compagination, articulation 56n. *composition,* 331n. *structure;* joining, stringing together, threading t., linking t., concatenation; suture, stitching, knitting, sewing, weaving 222n. *crossing;* tightening, astriction, drawing together, contraction 198n. *compression,* 264n. *closure;* knotting, tying, binding, bandaging, vincture, ligation, alligation; fastening, pinning, infibulation; attaching, attachment, annexing, annexation 38n. *addition;* connecting, earthing; affixture, affixation, suffixment, suffixion, prefixion; fixture, grafting, planting, inosculation 303n. *insertion;* sticking on, agglutination 48n. *coherence;* coupling, accouplement, yoking, pairing, matching 18n. *assimilation,* 462n. *comparison;* bracketing 28n. *equalization;* hyphenization 547n. *punctuation;* joiner, coupler, riveter, welder; comparer, matcher; go-between 231n. *intermediary,* 894n. *matchmaker.*

coition, coitus, copulation, sexual intercourse, intimacy, carnal knowledge; generation 164n. *propagation;* pairing, mating, coupling, couplement; union 894n. *marriage;* enjoyment, consummation; violation, ravishment 951n. *rape.*

joint, joining, juncture, line of j., commissure; crease 261n. *fold;* inner margin, gutter, suture, seam, stitching, stitch 47n. *bond;* weld, weld-joint; splice, splice-joint; miter-joint, miter; dovetail-joint, dovetail and mortise; ball and socket; hasp; latch, catch 218n. *pivot;* hinge-joint, ginglymus, knee, elbow 247n. *angle;* finger, wrist, ankle, knuckle; node; junction, point of j., intersection, crossways 222n. *crossing;* decussation, optic d., chiasm, chiasma, figure X 222n. *cross.*

Adj. *conjunct,* joined etc. vb.; connected, earthed; coupled, matched, paired 28adj. *equal;* conjoined, partnered, participant 775adj. *sharing;* rolled into one, united; joint, allied, incorporated, associated, symbiotic 706adj. *cooperative,* 708adj. *corporate;* betrothed, wedded 894adj. *married;* handfast, holding hands, hand in hand, arm in arm; intimate, involved 5adj. *intrinsic;* coalescent, symphysian 48adj. *cohesive;* composite 50adj. *combined;* put together 74adj. *assembled;* articulated, jointed 331adj. *structural, textural;* stitched, patched; stitched up, sutural.

conjunctive, subjunctive, adjunctive, copulative, adhesive 48adj. *cohesive;* coagulate, astringent 324adj. *solidifying;* coincident 181adj. *concurrent;* coital, venereal.

firm-set, firm, close, fast, secure 153adj. *fixed;* solid, set, solidified 324adj. *dense;* glued, cemented 48adj. *cohesive;* put, pat; planted, rooted, ingrown, impacted; close-printed, close-set, crowded 587adj. *printed;* tight, tight-fitting, wedged, jammed, stuck; inextricable, immovable, unshakable; inseparate, unseverable, insecable; packed, jam-p. 54adj. *full.*

tied, bound, knotted, roped, lashed, belayed; stitched, sewn, gathered; attached, adhering 48adj. *cohesive;* well-tied, tight, taut, tense, fast, secure; intricate, intervolved, tangled, inextricable, indissoluble.

Vb. *join,* conjoin, couple, yoke, hyphenate, harness together, partner; pair, match 18n. *liken,* 462vb. *compare,* 894vb. *marry;* bracket 28vb. *equalize;* put together, lay t., clap t., fit t., piece t., assemble, unite 50vb. *combine;* collect, gather, mobilize, mass 74vb. *bring together;* add to, amass, accumulate 38vb. *add,* 632vb. *store;* associate, ally; merge 43vb. *mix;* embody, reembody, incorporate, consolidate, make one, unify 88vb. *be one, make uniform;* lump together, roll into one 464vb. *not discriminate;* include, embrace 78vb. *comprise;* grip, grapple 778vb. *retain;* make a joint, hinge, articulate, dovetail, mortise, rabbet; fit, set, interlock, engage, gear to; wedge, jam 303vb. *insert;* weld, solder, braze, fuse, cement 48vb. *agglutinate;* draw together, bring ends t., lace, knit, sew, stitch; pin, infibulate, buckle; do up, button up 264vb. *close;* lock, latch; close a gap, seal up; darn, patch, mend, heal over, scab over 656vb. *repair.*

connect, attach, annex (**see** *affix*); tag, clip; thread together, string to., rope t., link t., concatenate; contact 378vb. *touch;* make contact, plug in, earth 202vb. *juxtapose;* interconnect, anastomose, inosculate, open into; link, bridge, span, straddle, bestride 205vb. *be broad;* communicate, intercommunicate, establish communication, hook up with, tie up w. 9vb. *relate;* link closely, entwine.

affix, attach, fix, fasten; fix on, yoke, leash, harness, limber, saddle, bridle, bit; tie up, moor, anchor; tie to, tether, picket; pin on, hang on, hook on, screw on, nail on, shoe; stick on, gum on 48vb. *agglutinate;* suffix, prefix 38vb. *add;* infix, splice, engraft, implant 303vb. *insert;* impact, set, enchase, frame 235vb. *enclose;* drive in, knock in, hammer in 279vb. *strike;* wedge, jam; screw, nail, treenail, rivet, bolt, clamp, clinch; thread, reeve, pass through, weave t.

tie, knot, hitch, bend; lash, belay; knit, cast on, sew, stitch, suture; tack, baste; braid, plait, crochet, twine, twist, intertwine, lace, interlace, interweave 222vb. *weave;* truss, string, rope, strap; lace up, frap, lash up, trice up, brail; tether, picket, moor; pinion, manacle, handcuff; hobble, shackle 747vb. *fetter;* bind, splice, gird, girdle, cinch; bandage, swathe, swaddle, wrap; enfold, embrace, clinch, grip, grapple 235vb. *enclose,* 778vb. *retain.*

tighten, jam, impact; constrict, compress, straiten, narrow; fasten, screw up, make firm, make fast, secure; tauten, draw tight, pull t., lace t.; frap, brace, trice up, brail.

unite with, be joined, linked etc. vb.; join, meet 293vb. *converge;* fit tight, hold t., fit close, adhere, hang together, hold t., stick t. 48vb. *cohere;* interlock, engage, grip, grapple, embrace, entwine, clinch; link up with, hold hands; associate with, mix w. 882vb. *be sociable;* marry 894vb. *wed;* live with, cohabit, bed; lie with, sleep w., have intercourse, have carnal knowledge; consummate marriage, consummate a union; know, enjoy, have, do; board, tumble; deflower, rape, ravish, violate, force 951vb. *debauch;* copulate, couple, mate, pair; mount, tup; cross with, breed w.

Adv. *conjointly,* jointly, in conjunction, in partnership; all together, as one; with, to, on, in.

inseparably, inextricably; securely, firmly, fast, tight.

See: 5, 9, 18, 28, 38, 43, 47, 48, 50, 54,

56, 74, 76, 78, 88, 89, 151, 153, 164, 181, 198, 202, 205, 218, 222, 231, 235, 247, 261, 264, 279, 293, 297, 303, 305, 324, 331, 378, 462, 464, 547, 587, 632, 656, 706, 708, 747, 775, 778, 791, 882, 894, 951.

46 Disjunction

N. *disjunction,* being separated; disconnection, disconnectedness, unthreading, break, ladder, run 72n. *discontinuity;* looseness, incoherence, separability, fissionability 49n. *non-coherence,* 335n. *fluidity;* diffusion, dispersal, scattering 75n. *dispersion;* break-up, disintegration, dissolution, decay 51n. *decomposition,* 655n. *dilapidation;* abstraction, absentmindedness 456n. *abstractedness;* dissociation, withdrawal, disengagement, retirement 621n. *relinquishment,* 753n. *resignation;* surrender, sacrifice 779n. *non-retention,* 37n. *decrease;* moving apart, broadening, widening 294n. *divergence,* 282n. *deviation;* separation 896n. *divorce;* detachment, non-attachment 860n. *indifference,* 606n. *no choice;* neutrality 625n. *mid-course;* isolation, loneliness, quarantine, segregation 883n. *seclusion;* zone, compartment, box, cage 748n. *prison;* insularity 620n. *avoidance;* disunion 709n. *dissension;* dissilience 182n. *counteraction,* 280n. *recoil;* immiscibility, separateness, severalness, severalty 80n. *specialty;* isolationism, separatism 80n. *particularism;* no connection, asyndeton 10n. *irrelation;* distance apart 199n. *farness;* dichotomy 15n. *difference;* interval, space, opening, hole, breach, break, rent, rift, split; fissure, crack, cleft, chasm; cleavage, slit, slot, incision 201n. *gap.*

separation, disjoining, severance, parting, diremption; uncoupling, divorcement 896n. *divorce;* untying, undoing, unthreading, unravelment, laddering; loosening, loosing, freeing 746n. *liberation;* setting apart, sejunction, seposition, segregation 883n. *seclusion;* exception, exemption 57n. *exclusion;* boycott 620n. *avoidance;* expulsion, voidance 300n. *ejection;* picking out, selection 605n. *choice;* putting aside, keeping a. 632n. *storage;* conservation 666n. *preservation;* taking away 39n. *subtraction;* abstraction, deprivation, expropriation 786n. *taking;* detaching, detachment, withdrawal, removal, transfer 188n. *displacement,* 272n. *transference;* denudation, stripping, peeling, plucking 229n. *uncovering;* disjointing, dislocation, luxation; scattering, dispersal 75n. *dispersion;* dissolution, resolution, disintegration 51n. *decomposition;* dissection, analysis, breakdown; disruption, shattering, fragmentation, pulverization, mastication 165n. *destruction;* splitting, fission, nuclear f. 160n. *nucleonics;* breaking, cracking, rupture, fracture 330n. *brittleness;* dividing line, caesura; wall, hedge 231n. *partition;* curtain 421n. *screen;* boundary 236n. *limit.*

scission, section, cleavage, cutting, tearing; division, dichotomy 92n. *bisection;* subdivision, segmentation; partition 783n. *apportionment;* abscission, cutting off, decapitation, curtailment 304n. *shortening,* 37n. *diminution;* elision, syncope 39n. *subtraction;* cutting away, resection, circumcision; cutting open, incision, opening 658n. *surgery;* dissection, discerption; rending, clawing, laceration, dilaceration, divulsion; tearing off, avulsion; nipping, pinching, biting etc. vb.

Adj. *disjunct,* disjoined, divorced; separated, disconnected, unplugged, unstuck; dismounted; broken, interrupted 72adj. *discontinuous;* divided, subdivided, partitioned, bipartite, multipartite; in pieces, quartered, dismembered; severed, cut; torn, rent, riven, cleft, cloven; digitate 201adj. *spaced;* radiating, divergent 282adj. *deviating;* scattered, dispersed, fugitive, uncollected 75adj. *unassembled;* noncohesive, melting, flowing 335n. *fluid;* untied, loosened, loose, free 746adj. *liberated;* unattached, open-ended.

separate, apart, asunder; adrift, lost; unjoined, unfixed, unfastened; unattached, unannexed, unassociated; distinct, discrete, differentiated, separable, distinguishable 15adj. *different;* exempt, excepted 57adj. *excluded;* abstract, abstracted 304adj. *extracted;* immiscible, unassimilable, unassimilated 324adj. *indissoluble;* alien, foreign 59adj. *extraneous,* 84adj. *uncomformable;* external 6adj. *extrinsic,* 223adj. *exterior;* insular, self-sufficient, lonely, isolated 88adj. *alone,* 883adj. *friendless;* shunned, dropped, avoided, boycotted 620adj. *avoiding;* cast-off 607adj. *rejected;* picked out 605adj. *chosen;* abandoned, left 41adj. *remaining;* hostile, opposed, antipathetic 881adj. *inimical,* 14adj. *con-*

trary, 240adj. *opposite;* disjunctive, separative, asyndetic; dichotomous, dividing; selective, diagnostic 15adj. *distinctive.*

severable, separable, detachable; partible, divisible, fissionable, scissile, tearable; dissoluble, dissolvable; distinguishable, not belonging 10adj. *irrelative.*

Vb. *be disjoined,* stand apart, not mix 620vb. *avoid;* go, go away 296vb. *depart;* go apart, go different ways, radiate 294vb. *diverge;* go another way 282vb. *deviate;* separate, part, part company, cut adrift, divorce; split off, hive off; get free, get loose 667vb. *escape;* disengage, unclinch, break away 746vb. *achieve liberty;* cast off, unmoor, let go 779vb. *not retain;* leave, quit, fall away 621vb. *relinquish;* scatter, break it up 75vb. *disperse;* spring apart 280vb. *recoil;* come apart, fall a., break, come to bits, disintegrate 51vb. *decompose;* come undone, unravel, ladder, run; fall off 49vb. *come unstuck;* start, split, crack 263vb. *open;* leak 298vb. *flow out;* melt, run 337vb. *liquefy,* 338vb. *vaporize.*

disjoin, disunite, dissociate, divorce; dispart, part, separate, sunder, sever, dissever; uncouple, dispair; unhitch, disconnect, unplug; cast off (knitting); disengage, ungear, throw out of gear; disjoint, dislocate, wrench; detach, unseat, dismount 49vb. *unstick;* remove, detract, deduct 39vb. *subtract,* 272vb. *transfer;* skin, denude, strip, peel, pluck 229vb. *uncover;* undo, unbutton, unhook, unclasp, unlock, unlatch 263vb. *open;* untie, unknot, cut the knot, disentangle 62vb. *unravel;* loosen, relax, slacken, unstring 177vb. *moderate;* unbind, unchain, unfetter, unloose, loose, free, release 746vb. *liberate;* unharness, unsaddle, unbridle 701vb. *disencumber;* unload, unpack, unbundle 188vb. *displace,* 323vb. *lighten;* expel 300vb. *eject;* dispel, scatter, break up, disband, demobilize 75vb. *disperse;* melt, melt down, evaporate 337vb. *liquefy,* 338vb. *vaporize;* disintegrate 51vb. *decompose;* 332vb. *pulverize,* 165vb. *destroy;* unstitch, unpick.

set apart, put aside 632vb. *store;* conserve 666vb. *preserve;* mark out, tick off, distinguish 15vb. *differentiate,* 463vb. *discriminate;* single out, pick o. 605vb. *select;* except, exempt, leave out 57vb. *exclude;* boycott, send to Coventry 620vb. *avoid;* taboo, black, black-list 757vb. *prohibit;* insulate, isolate, cut off 235vb. *enclose;* zone, compartmentalize, screen off 232vb. *circumscribe;* segregate, sequester, quarantine, maroon 883vb. *seclude;* keep apart, hold a., drive a.; drive a wedge between, estrange, alienate, set against 881vb. *make enemies,* 888vb. *excite hate.*

sunder (**see** *disjoin*); divide, keep apart, flow between, stand b.; subdivide, fragment, chunk, segment, sectionalize, fractionize; reduce, factorize, analyze; dissect, anatomize 51vb. *decompose;* dichotomize, halve 92vb. *bisect;* divide up, split, partition, parcel out 783vb. *apportion;* dismember, disbranch, quarter, carve (**see** *cut*); behead, decapitate, curtail, dock, amputate 204vb. *shorten;* take apart, take to pieces, cannibalize, dismantle, break up, dismount; force open, force apart, wedge a. 263vb. *open;* slit, split, rive; cleave 263vb. *pierce* (**see** *break*).

cut, hew, hack, hackle, slash, gash 655vb. *wound;* prick, stab, knife 263vb. *pierce;* cut through, cleave, rive, saw, chop; cut open, slit 263vb. *open;* cut into, make an incision, incise 555vb. *engrave;* cut deep, cut to the bone, carve, slice; cut round, pare, whittle, chip, trim, bevel, skive; clip, snick, snip; cut short, shave 204vb. *shorten;* cut down, scythe, mow; cut off, abscind, lop, prune, dock, curtail, behead, decapitate, amputate, circumcise (**see** *sunder*); cut up, chop up, quarter, dismember; mince, make mincemeat of 332vb. *pulverize;* bite, bite into, bite through, masticate 301vb. *chew;* scratch, scarify, score, plow 262vb. *groove;* nick 260vb. *notch.*

rend, rive (**see** *sunder*); tear, scratch, claw, scarify, score; gnaw, fret, fray, make ragged; strip, flay, skin, peel, pluck 229vb. *uncover;* rip, slash, slit (**see** *cut*); lacerate, dilacerate, dislimb, dismember; tear piecemeal, tear to pieces, tear to shreds, tear to tatters 165vb. *destroy;* pluck to pieces, divelicate, scamble; mince, grind, crunch, scrunch 301vb. *chew,* 332vb. *pulverize;* explode, blow up, blow to pieces, burst.

break, fracture, rupture, bust; split, burst, blow up, explode; break in pieces, smash, shatter, splinter, shiver 165vb. *demolish;* fragment, comminute, crumble, grind, triturate 332vb. *pulverize;* disintegrate 51vb. *decompose;* break up, dismantle (**see** *sunder*); chip, crack, damage

655vb. *impair;* bend, buckle, warp 246vb. *distort;* break in two, snap, knap; cleave, force apart, wedge a. 263vb. *open.*

Adv. *separately,* severally, singly, one by one, bit by bit, piecemeal, in bits, in pieces, in halves, in twain; discontinuously, unconnectedly, disjointedly, interruptedly.

apart, open, asunder, adrift; off, up, down; to pieces, to bits, to tatters, to shreds; limb from limb.

See: 2, 6, 10, 14, 15, 37, 39, 41, 49, 51, 57, 59, 62, 72, 75, 80, 84, 88, 92, 160, 165, 177, 182, 188, 199, 201, 204, 223, 229, 231, 232, 235, 236, 240, 246, 260, 262, 263, 272, 280, 282, 294, 296, 298, 300, 301, 304, 324, 330, 332, 335, 337, 338, 421, 456, 463, 555, 605, 606, 607, 620, 621, 625, 632, 655, 658, 666, 667, 701, 709, 746, 748, 753, 757, 779, 783, 786, 860, 881, 883, 888, 896.

47 Bond: connecting medium

N. *bond,* connecting medium, vinculum, chain, tie, band, hoop, yoke; bond of union, sympathy, fellow-feeling 905n. *pity;* nexus, connection, link, liaison 9n. *relation;* junction, hinge 45n. *joint;* ramification 53n. *branch;* connective, copula; hyphen, dash, bracket, hook, crotchet 547n. *punctuation;* intermedium, cement (**see** *adhesive*); bondstone, binder; tie-beam, stretcher, girder 218n. *beam;* strut, stay, prop 218n. *supporter;* interconnection, intercommunication, channel, passage, corridor 624n. *way;* stepping-stone 624n. *bridge;* span, arch; isthmus, neck; col, ridge; stair, ladder 308n. *ascent;* life-line; umbilical cord; chord (of an arc).

cable, line, hawser, painter, moorings; guest-rope, guess-warp, tow-line, tow-rope, ripcord, lanyard, communication cord; rope, cord, string, strand, thread 208n. *fiber;* tape, inkle; chain, wire, earth-w.

tackling, tackle, cordage; rigging, running r., standing r., shroud, ratline; sheets, guy, stay; clew line, garnet, halyard, halliard, bowline, lanyard; harness.

ligature, binding, end-paper; ligament, tendon, muscle; tendril, with, withy, osier, bast, raffia 208n. *fiber;* lashing, lasher; string, cord, thread, tape, inkle; band, fillet, ribbon, riband; bandage, roller b., roller, tourniquet 198n. *compressor;* drawstring, thong, latchet, lace, boot-l., tag; braid, plait 222n. *textile;* tie, stock, cravat 228n. *neckwear;* knot, hitch, clinch, bend; Gordian knot, running k., slip k., granny k., reef k., sailor's k.; half-hitch, clove h.; sheepshank, Turk's head.

fastening 45n. *joinder;* fastener, snap f., press f., zip f., zipper; drawstring, ripcord; button, buttonhook, buttonhole, frog; hook and eye; eyelet, eyelet-hole; stud, cufflink; garter, suspender, braces; tiepin, stickpin; brooch, fibula; ouch 844n. *jewelry;* clip, grip, slide, curlers; hairpin, hatpin; skewer, spit, brochette; pin, drawing p., pushp., safety p., toggle p., cotter p., linch p., kingpin; peg, dowel, treenail, trennel; nail, brad, tack, tintack, hobnail, blakey 256n. *sharp point;* holdfast, staple, clamp, batten, cramp, rivet; nut, bolt, screw; buckle, clasp, morse; hasp, hinge 45n. *joint;* catch, safety c., spring c., pawl, click, detent; latch, bolt; lock, lock and key 264n. *closure;* combination lock, yale l.; padlock, handcuffs, bracelets 748n. *fetter;* hank, ring, vervel, terret; hold, bar, post, pile, pale, stake, bollard; cleat, bitt, pawl-b.

coupling, yoke; coupler, draw-bar, draw-head, draw-link, traces; grappling iron, hook, claw; anchor, sheet-a. 662n. *safeguard.*

girdle, band, strap 228n. *belt;* waistband, waist-string, cummerbund, bellyband, girth, roller, cinch, surcingle; cestus, zone; sash, shoulder-belt, bandolier; collar, neckband 228n. *neckwear;* bandeau, fillet, taenia, tiara; hatband; banderole; equator, zodiac.

halter, collar, noose; tether, lead, leash, jess, trash-cord, reins, ribbons; lasso, lariat 250n. *loop;* shackle 748n. *fetter.*

adhesive, glue, fish-glue, bee-glue, lime, birdlime, gum, seccotine, fixative, hair fixer, brilliantine, grease; solder; paste, size, lute, clay, cement, putty, mortar, stucco, plaster, grout 226n. *facing;* wafer, sealing wax; scotch tape; fly-paper 542n. *trap.*

See: 9, 45, 53, 198, 208, 218, 222, 226, 228, 250, 256, 264, 308, 542, 547, 624, 662, 748, 844, 905.

48 Coherence

N. *coherence,* connection, connectedness 71n. *continuity;* chain 71n. *series;* holding together, cohesion, cohesiveness; holding on, tenacity, tenaciousness 778n. *retention;* adherence, adhesion, adhesiveness; cementation, cementing, sticking, soldering, agglutination, conglutination 45n. *junction;* compaction, conglomeration, agglomeration, consolidation, set, 324n. *condensation;* inseparability, indivisibility, union 88n. *unity;* indigestibility 329n. *toughness;* phalanx, serried ranks, unbroken front; monolith, agglomerate, concrete 324n. *solid body;* sticker, burr, leech, limpet, remora, barnacle, parasite; gum, plaster, sticking-p., 47n. *adhesive;* tights, combinations; stickjaw, toffee.

Adj. *cohesive,* coherent, adhesive, adherent; sessile, clinging, tenacious; indigestible 329adj. *tough;* sticky, gummy, gluey, viscous 354adj. *viscid;* compact, well-knit, solid, coagulate, concrete, frozen 324adj. *dense;* shoulder to shoulder, phalanxed, serried; monolithic 16adj. *uniform;* united, infrangible, indivisible, inseparable, inextricable, inseparable; close, tight, fitting, skin-tight, molding.

Vb. *cohere,* hang together, grow together 50vb. *combine;* hold, stick close, hold fast; bunch, close the ranks, stand shoulder to shoulder, rally 74vb. *congregate;* grip, take hold of 778vb. *retain;* hug, clasp, embrace, twine round; close with, clinch; fit, fit tight, mold the figure; adhere, cling, stick; stick to, cleave to, come off on, rub off on; stick on to, freeze on to; stick like a leech, stick like wax, stick like a burr, stick like a limpet, cling like a shadow, hold on like a bulldog, cling like the ivy; cake, coagulate, agglomerate, conglomerate, solidify, consolidate, freeze 324vb. *be dense.*

agglutinate, conglutinate, glue, gum, paste, lute, cement, weld, braze 45vb. *join;* stick to, affix 38vb. *add.*

Adv. *cohesively,* indivisibly, unitedly, solidly, compactly.

See: 16, 38, 45, 47, 50, 71, 74, 88, 324, 329, 354, 778.

49 Non-coherence

N. *non-coherence,* incoherence 72n. *discontinuity;* uncombined state, non-combination, chaos 51n. *decomposition;* scattering 75n. *dispersion;* separability, immiscibility; looseness, bagginess; loosening, relaxation, laxity, freedom 46n. *disjunction;* wateriness, runniness 335n. *fluidity;* slipperiness 258n. *smoothness;* frangibility, rope of sand 330n. *brittleness;* non-adhesion, aloofness; individualist, lone wolf, separatist 84n. *nonconformist.*

Adj. *non-adhesive,* non-adhering, slippery 258adj. *smooth;* not sticky, dry; detached, semidetached 46adj. *separate;* non-cohesive, incoherent, unconsolidated, loose, like grains of sand; unconfined, unpent, free, at large 746adj. *liberated;* loose-knit, relaxed, lax, slack, baggy, flopping, floppy, flapping, flying, streaming; watery, liquid, runny 335adj. *fluid;* open-ended, pendulous, dangling 217adj. *pendent;* uncombined 51adj. *decomposed;* immiscible 59adj. *extraneous;* aloof 620adj. *avoiding.*

Vb. *unstick,* unglue, peel off; detach, unpin; free, loosen, loose, slacken 46vb. *disjoin;* shake off, unseat, dismount; shed, slough 229vb. *doff.*

come unstuck, peel off, melt, thaw, run 337vb. *liquefy;* sit loose to, waver 601vb. *be irresolute;* totter, slip 309vb. *tumble;* dangle, flap 217vb. *hang;* rattle, shake.

See: 46, 51, 59, 72, 75, 84, 217, 229, 258, 309, 330, 335, 337, 601, 620, 746.

50 Combination

N. *combination,* composition, joining together 45n. *joinder;* growing together, coalescence, symphysis 45n. *junction;* fusion, crasis, blending, conflation, synthesis, syncretism 43n. *mixture;* amalgamation, merger, assimilation, digestion, absorption, ingestion 299n. *reception;* uniting, adunation, unification, integration, centralization 88n. *unity;* union, Enosis, Anschluss; incorporation, embodiment, incarnation; synchronization 123n. *synchronism,* 706n. *cooperation;* coagency 181n. *concurrence;* marriage, league, alliance, federation, confederation 706n. *association;* conspiracy, cabal 623n. *plot;* combination of sounds, counterpoint 412n. *music;* chorus 24n. *agreement;* harmony, orchestration 710n. *concord;* aggregation, assembly 74n. *assemblage;* synopsis, conspectus, bird's-eye view 438n. *view;* mosaic, jigsaw.

compound, compound resultant; alloy, amalgam, blend; makeup 56n. *composition.*

Adj. *combined* etc. vb.; united, unified 88adj. *one;* integrated, centralized; incorporate, embodied, incarnate; inbred, ingrained, absorbed 5adj. *intrinsic;* fused, impregnated 43adj. *mixed;* blended, harmonized, adapted 24adj. *adjusted;* connected, yoked, linked, conjugate, conjoint 45adj. *conjunct;* aggregated, congregated 74adj. *assembled;* coalescent, symphysical; synchronized 123vb. *synchronous;* in harmony, in partnership, in league; associated, leagued, allied 706adj. *cooperative;* conspiratorial; coagent 181adj. *concurrent.*

Vb. *combine,* put together, fit t.; compose, make up, intertwine, interweave 222vb. *weave;* harmonize, synchronize 24vb. *accord;* bind, tie 45vb. *join;* unite, unify, centralize; incorporate, absorb, assimilate; merge, amalgamate; blend, compound 43vb. *mix;* fuse, conflate; impregnate, imbue, instill, inoculate 303vb. *infuse;* lump together 38vb. *add;* embody, group, reembody, regroup, rally 74vb. *bring together;* band together, brigade, associate; federate, ally, league with; partner, join hands, team up with 706vb. *cooperate;* fraternize, make friends 880vb. *be friendly;* cement a union, marry 894vb. *wed;* mate, pair, couple 90vb. *pair;* lay heads together, cabal, conspire 623vb. *plot;* coalesce, grow together, run t.; have an affinity, combine with; combine with water, hydrate 339vb. *add water.*

See: 5, 24, 38, 43, 45, 56, 74, 88, 90, 123, 181, 222, 299, 303, 339, 412, 438, 623, 706, 710, 880, 894.

51 Decomposition

N. *decomposition* 46n. *disjunction;* separation, diaeresis; division, partition, compartition; dissection, dismemberment; analysis, breakdown; break-up, factorization, syllabification 44n. *simplification;* parsing 564n. *grammar;* resolution, electrolysis, hydrolysis, photolysis, catalysis; dissolving, dissolution 337n. *liquefaction;* decentralization, relaxation; disintegration 165n. *destruction;* uncombined state, chaos 17n. *non-uniformity.*

decay 655n. *dilapidation;* erosion, wear and tear 37n. *diminution;* disintegration 361n. *death;* corruption, moldering, rotting, putrefaction, mortification, necrosis, gangrene, adipocere 649n. *uncleanness;* rot, rust, mold 659n. *blight;* carrion 363n. *corpse.*

Adj. *decomposed* etc. vb.; resolved, reduced, disintegrated, uncombined, chaotic 46adj. *disjunct;* corrupted, moldering; rotten, bad, off, high, rancid.

Vb. *decompose,* decompound, unmix, unscramble; resolve, reduce, factorize 44vb. *simplify;* separate, separate out, parse, dissect; break down, analyze 46vb. *disjoin;* electrolyze, catalyze; split, fission 46vb. *sunder;* disband, break up 75vb. *disperse;* decentralize, relax 746vb. *liberate;* discompose, disconcert, unsettle, disturb, confuse 63vb. *derange;* render chaotic 61vb. *disorder;* dissolve, melt 337vb. *liquefy;* erode 37vb. *bate;* rot, rust, molder, decay, consume, waste, crumble, wear, perish 655vb. *deteriorate;* corrupt, putrefy, mortify, gangrene 649vb. *make unclean;* disintegrate, go to pieces 165vb. *be destroyed;* slack, slake 339vb. *add water.*

Adv. *analytically,* partitively; on analysis, by a.

See: 17, 37, 44, 46, 61, 63, 75, 165, 337, 339, 361, 363, 564, 649, 655, 659, 746.

52 Whole: principal part

N. *whole,* wholeness, integrality, omneity, fullness 54n. *completeness;* integration, indivisibility, indiscerptibility, integrity, oneness 88n. *unity;* a whole, whole number, integer, integral 88n. *unit;* entirety, ensemble, corpus, complex, four corners of; totality, summation, sum 38n. *addition;* holism, holistic approach, universalization, generalization 79n. *generality;* comprehensiveness, comprehensivity, inclusiveness 78n. *inclusion;* collectivity, world, cosmos 321n. *universe;* idioverse, life space, total situation 7n. *state;* grand view, bird's-eye v., panorama, conspectus, synopsis 438n. *view;* whole course, round, circuit 314n. *circuition.*

all, no omissions, one and all, everybody, everyone; the world, all the w. 74n. *crowd;* the whole, total, aggregate, gross amount, sum, sum total; ensemble, tout e., length and breadth, rough with the smooth; Alpha and Omega, "be all and end all," lock, stock and barrel, hook, line and sinker; unit, family; set, complete s. 71n. *series;* outfit, pack; complete list, inventory 87n. *list;* lot, whole l., the whole caboodle, the whole kit and boodle.

chief part, best part, principal p., major p., essential p. 638n. *chief thing;* ninety-nine per cent, bulk, mass, substance; heap, lump 32n. *great quantity;* tissue, staple; body, torso, trunk, bole, stem, stalk; hull, hulk, skeleton; lion's share, Benjamin's mess; gist, sum and substance, the long and the short; almost all, nearly all; all but a few, majority 104n. *greater number.*

Adj. *whole,* total, universal, holistic; integral, pure, unadulterated 44adj. *unmixed;* entire, ungelded 646adj. *perfect;* grand, gross, full 54adj. *complete;* individual, single, integrated 88adj. *one;* in one piece, seamless; fully restored 656adj. *restored.*

intact, untouched, unaffected; undivided, unsevered, undiminished, unclipped, uncropped, unshorn; undissolved, unabolished, still there; unbroken, undemolished, undestroyed, unbruised, unmangled, unimpaired; uncut, unabridged, unedited, uncensored, unexpurgated 646adj. *undamaged.*

indivisible, impartible 324adj. *indissoluble;* undissolvable, indiscerptible; inseparable 45adj. *conjunct;* monolithic 16adj. *uniform.*

comprehensive, omnibus, all-embracing, full-length 78adj. *inclusive;* holophrastic 557adj. *linguistic;* wholesale, sweeping 32adj. *great;* widespread, epidemic 79adj. *general;* international, world, world-wide, cosmic 79adj. *universal,* 189adj. *ubiquitous.*

Adv. *wholly,* integrally, body and soul, as a whole; entirely, totally, fully, every inch 54adv. *completely;* without deduction, one hundred per cent, in extenso.

on the whole, by and large, altogether, all in all, all things considered, in the long run; substantially, essentially, in substance, in essence; virtually, to all intents and purposes, effectually, in effect; as good as; mainly, in the main 32adv. *greatly;* almost, all but 200adv. *nearly.*

collectively, one and all, all together; comprehensively, and all; in bulk, in the lump, in the mass; in sum, in the aggregate; bodily, en masse, en bloc.

See: 7, 16, 32, 38, 44, 45, 54, 71, 74, 78, 79, 87, 88, 104, 189, 200, 314, 321, 324, 438, 557, 638, 646, 656.

53 Part

N. *part,* not the whole, portion; proportion, certain p.; majority 32n. *main part,* 104n. *greater number;* minority 105n. *fewness,* 33n. *small quantity;* fraction, half, moiety, quarter, tithe, percentage; factor, aliquot, aliquant 85n. *number;* balance, surplus, overplus 41n. *remainder;* quota, contingent; dividend, share, whack 783n. *portion;* item, particular, detail 80n. *particulars;* sentence, paragraph 563n. *phrase;* ingredient, member, constituent, integrant, element 58n. *component;* dissident element, schism, faction 708n. *party;* lap, round 110n. *period;* leg, side 239n. *laterality;* group, subgroup, species, subspecies (**see** *subdivision*); detachment 42n. *decrement;* attachment, fixture, wing 40n. *adjunct;* part of a book, page, leaf, folio, sheet, signature 589vb. *book;* excerpt, extract, passage, quotation, selection 605n. *choice;* text, pericope; geometric part, frustum 41n. *remainder;* segment, sector, section 46n. *scission;* arc 248n. *curve;* hemisphere 252n. *sphere;* part payment, installment, advance, earnest money 804n. *payment;* sample, foretaste 83n. *example;* fragment, cantle, torso, trunk (**see** *piece*).

limb 234n. *edge;* member (**see** *part*); hinderlimb 267n. *leg;* forelimb 271n. *wing;* flipper, fin 269n. *propeller;* arm, forearm, cubit, ulna, brace, hand 378n. *feeler;* elbow, funny bone 247n. *angularity.*

subdivision, segment, sector, section 46n. *scission;* division, compartment; group, subgroup, species, subspecies, family 74n. *group;* classification 62n. *arrangement;* ward, parish, department 184n. *district;* chapter, paragraph, clause, subclause, phrase, verse; fascicle, part, number, issue, installment, book, volume 589n. *edition, reading matter;* canto, fit 593n. *poem.*

branch, subbranch, ramification, offshoot 40n. *adjunct;* bough, limb, spur, twig, tendril, leaf, leaflet; shoot, scion, sucker, slip, sprig, spray 366n. *foliage.*

piece, frustum, torso, trunk 41n. *remainder;* limb, segment, section (**see** *part*); patch, insertion 40n. *adjunct;* length, roll 222n. *textile;* strip, swatch; fragment, unfinished symphony 55n. *incompleteness;* bit, scrap, shred, wisp, rag 33n. *small thing;* frustulum 33n. *particle;* morsel, bite, crust, crumb 33n. *small quantity;* splinter, sliver, chip, snip; cantle, cut, wedge, finger, slice, rasher; gobbet, collop, cutlet, chop, steak; hunk, chunk, lump, mass 195n. *bulk;* clod, turf, divot, sod 344n. *land;* sherd, shard, potsherd, brickbat; flake, scale 207n. *lamina;* dollop, dose, whack, share 783n.

portion; bits and pieces, odds and ends, miscellanea, flotsam and jetsam 43n. *medley;* clippings, shavings, parings, brash, rubble, scree, detritus, moraine, debris 41n. *leavings;* refuse 641n. *rubbish;* shreds, rags, tatters 801n. *poverty;* piece of land, parcel.

Adj. *fragmentary,* broken, brashy, crumbly; in bits, in pieces 46adj. *disjunct;* not whole, limbless, armless, legless, in torso 647adj. *imperfect;* partial, bitty, scrappy 636adj. *insufficient;* half-finished 55adj. *unfinished;* fractional, half, semi, hemi, aliquot; sectional, divided, multifid; departmentalized, compartmentalized, in compartments 46adj. *separate;* shredded, wispy, sliced, minced 33adj. *small.*

brachial, brachiocephalic; membered, brachiate, brachiferous, brachigerous; ulnar, cubital; with branches, branchy.

Vb. *part,* divide, partition, segment, chunk; compartmentalize 46vb. *sunder;* share out 783vb. *apportion;* fragment 46vb. *disjoin.*

Adv. *partly,* in part, scrappily, partially; in a sense 55adv. *incompletely.*

piecemeal, part by part, limb from limb; by installments, by snatches, by inches, by driblets; bit by bit, inch by inch, foot by foot, drop by drop; in detail, in lots.

See: 32, 33, 40, 41, 42, 43, 46, 55, 58, 62, 74, 80, 83, 85, 104, 105, 110, 184, 195, 207, 222, 234, 239, 247, 248, 252, 267, 269, 271, 344, 366, 378, 563, 589, 592, 605, 636, 641, 647, 708, 783, 801, 804.

54 Completeness

N. *completeness,* nothing lacking, nothing to add, entireness, wholeness 52n. *whole;* integration, integrality 88n. *unity;* solidity, solidarity 324n. *density,* 706n. *cooperation;* harmony, balance 710n. *concord;* self-sufficiency 635n. *sufficiency;* entirety, totality 52n. *all;* universality, comprehensivity, comprehensiveness 79n. *generality;* the ideal 646n. *perfection;* ne plus ultra, the limit 236n. *limit;* peak, culmination, crown 213n. *summit;* finish 69n. *end;* last touch 725n. *completion;* fulfillment, consummation 69n. *finality;* whole hog; nothing less than, the utmost 69n. *extremity.*

plenitude, fullness, amplitude, capacity, maximum, one's fill, saturation 635n. *sufficiency;* saturation point 863n. *satiety;* completion, impletion, filling, replenishment, refill; filling up, brimming, over-filling, swamping, drowning; overfulfillment 637n. *redundance;* full house, not a seat empty; complement, full c., full crew, full load; full measure, brimmer, bumper; bellyful, sickener; full size, full length, full extent, full volume; complement, supplement, makeweight 31n. *compensation.*

Adj. *complete,* plenary, full; utter, total; integral, integrated 52adj. *whole;* entire, with all its parts, with nothing missing, with supplement 52adj. *intact,* 646adj. *perfect;* unbroken, undivided, solid 324n. *dense;* self-contained, self-sufficient, self-sufficing 635 adj. *sufficient;* fully furnished 633adj. *provisionary;* comprehensive, omnibus 78adj. *inclusive;* exhaustive, circumstantial, detailed 570adj. *diffuse;* absolute, extreme, radical; thorough, thoroughgoing, whole-hogging, sweeping, wholesale, regular 32adj. *consummate;* unmitigated, downright, plumb, plain 44adj. *unmixed;* crowning, completing, culminating, consummating, supplementary, complementary 725adj. *completive,* 38adj. *additional;* unconfined, unqualified 744 adj. *unconditional.*

full, replete 635adj. *filled;* replenished, refilled, topped up 633adj. *provisionary;* well-filled, well-lined, bulging; brim-full, top-f., brimming, level with, flush; overfull, overflowing, slopping, swamped, drowned; saturated, oozing, leaking 637adj. *redundant;* coming out at the ears, bursting at the seams; crop-full, gorged, full as a tick, sickened with 863adj. *sated;* chock-full, chock-a-block, not an inch to spare; cram-full, crammed, stuffed, packed, full-p., jam-p., packed like sardines, jammed, tight 45adj. *firm-set;* laden, heavy-l., freighted, fraught, full-f., full-charged, full to the hatches; infested, overrun, crawling with, lousy w., stiff w.; full of, rolling in; soaked in, dripping with 341adj. *drenched;* ever-full, inexhaustible 146adj. *unceasing.*

Vb. *be complete,* be integrated, make a whole; reach *or* touch perfection, have everything; culminate, come to a head 725adj. *climax;* reach an end, come to a close, be all over 69vb. *end;* suffice for oneself 635vb. *have enough;* want nothing, lack n. 828vb. *be content;* become complete, fill

out, attain full growth, reach maturity 669vb. *mature;* be filled, fill, fill up, brim, hold no more, run over, slop o., overflow 637vb. *superabound;* gorge, eat *or* drink one's fill 947vb. *gluttonize,* 949vb. *get drunk.*
make complete, complete, integrate, make into a whole 45vb. *join;* make whole 656vb. *restore;* build up, make up, piece together 56vb. *compose;* eke out, supplement, supply, fill a gap 38vb. *add;* make good 31vb. *compensate;* do thoroughly, leave nothing to add, carry out 725vb. *carry through;* overfulfill 637vb. *be superfluous;* put the finishing touch, tie the last thread, cast off 69vb. *terminate.*
fill, fill up, brim, top; soak, saturate 341vb. *drench;* overfill, swamp, drown, overwhelm; top up, replenish 633vb. *provide;* satisfy 635vb. *suffice,* 828vb. *content,* 863vb. *sate*; fill to capacity, cram, pack, stuff, line, bulge out, pack in, pile in, squeeze in, ram in, jam in 303vb. *insert;* load, charge, ram down; lade, freight 187vb. *stow;* fill space, occupy 226vb. *cover;* reach to, extend to 183vb. *extend;* spread over, sprawl o., overrun 189vb. *pervade;* leave no corner, fit tight, be chock-a-block 45vb. *tighten;* fill in, put in, write in, enter 38vb. *add.*

Adv. *completely,* fully, wholly, totally, entirely, utterly, extremely 32 adv. *greatly;* all told, in all, in toto; effectually, virtually, as good as; to all intents, to all intents and purposes; on all accounts, in all respects, every way; quite, all of, altogether; outright, downright; to the heart, to the core, to the marrow; thoroughly, clean, stark, hollow; to one's fill, to the top of one's bent, to the utmost, to the end; out and out, all out, heart and soul, through thick and thin; over head and shoulders, head over heels, neck and crop; to the brim, up to the hilt, up to the neck, up to the ears, up to the eyes; hook, line and sinker; root and branch; down to the ground; with a vengeance, with all the trimmings, and then some; to the last man, to the last breath; without remainder, every whit, every inch; at full length, in extenso; as . . . as can be; as far as possible; to capacity, not an inch to spare.
throughout, all the way, all round, from first to last, from beginning to end, from end to end, from one end to the other, from coast to coast, from Dan to Beersheba, from Land's End to John o' Groats, from Maine to California, from north and south and east and west; fore and aft; from top to bottom, de fond en comble; from top to toe, from head to foot, cap-a-pie; to the bitter end, to the end of the chapter, for good and all.

See: 31, 32, 38, 44, 45, 52, 56, 69, 78, 79, 88, 146, 183, 187, 189, 213, 226, 236, 303, 324, 341, 570, 633, 635, 637, 646, 656, 669, 706, 710, 725, 744, 828, 863, 947, 949.

55 Incompleteness

N. *incompleteness,* defectiveness; unfinished state 647n. *imperfection;* unreadiness 670n. *non-preparation;* underdevelopment, immaturity 670n. *undevelopment;* first beginnings 68n. *debut;* sketch, outline, first draft, rough d. 623n. *plan;* torso, trunk 53n. *piece;* half-measures, sketchiness, scrappiness, a lick and a promise 726n. *non-completion;* perfunctoriness, superficiality, hollowness 4n. *insubstantiality,* 458n. *negligence;* nonfulfillment, deficiency, falling short 307n. *shortcoming,* 636n. *insufficiency;* non-satisfaction, dissatisfaction 829n. *discontent;* mutilation, impairment 655n. *deterioration;* omission, break, gap, missing link 72n. *discontinuity,* 201n. *interval,* 108n. *interim;* semi-, half, quarter; installment, part payment 53n. *part.*
deficit, part wanting, screw loose, missing link, omission, caret 190n. *absence;* defect, shortfall, ullage 42n. *decrement,* 772n. *loss;* default, defalcation 930n. *improbity;* want, lack, need 627n. *requirement.*

Adj. *incomplete,* defective 307adj. *deficient;* short, scant 636adj. *insufficient;* omitting, wanting, lacking, needing, requiring 627adj. *demanding;* short of, shy of; maimed, lame, limping, mangled, marred, mutilated; without, -less; limbless, armless, legless, one-armed, one-legged, one-eyed 163adj. *crippled;* garbled, impaired 655adj. *deteriorated;* cropped, lopped, docked, bobtailed, truncated, shortened 204adj. *short;* blemished, flawed 647adj. *imperfect;* half, semi-, partial, 53adj. *fragmentary;* left unfinished, half-f., neglected 726adj. *uncompleted;* not ready, unready 670adj. *unprepared;* undeveloped, underdeveloped, unripe 670adj. *immature;* raw, crude, rough-hewn 244adj. *amorphous;*

sketchy, scrappy, bitty, hollow, superficial, meager, thin, poor 4adj. *insubstantial;* perfunctory, run-through, half-done, undone 458adj. *neglected;* left, left in the air, left hanging; omitted, missing, lost 190adj. *absent;* interrupted 72adj. *discontinuous;* in default, in arrears, defaulting, defalcating.

unfinished, in progress 285adj. *progressive;* in hand, going on; in embryo, begun 68adj. *beginning;* in preparation, on the stocks.

Vb. *be incomplete,* miss, lack, need 627vb. *require,* 307vb. *fall short;* be wanting 190vb. *be absent;* leave undone 458vb. *neglect;* omit, miss out 57vb. *exclude;* break off, interrupt 72vb. *discontinue;* leave in the air, leave hanging; default, defalcate.

Adv. *incompletely,* partially, by halves, in installments; in arrears, in default.

See: 4, 42, 53, 57, 68, 72, 108, 163, 190, 201, 204, 244, 285, 307, 458, 623, 627, 636, 647, 655, 670, 726, 772, 829, 930.

56 Composition

N. *composition,* constitution, setup, makeup; make, conformation, formation, construction, build-up, build, organization 331n. *structure;* temper, crasis, habit, nature, character, condition 5n. *temperament;* climate, meteorology 340n. *weather;* embodiment, incorporation 78n. *inclusion;* compound 43n. *mixture,* 50n. *combination,* 358n. *organism;* syntax, sentence, period 563n. *phrase;* artistic composition 551n. *art,* 412n. *music,* 553n. *painting,* 554n. *sculpture;* architecture 164n. *edifice;* authorship 586n. *writing,* 593n. *poetry;* dramatic art 594n. *drama;* composing, setting-up, printing, typography 587n. *print;* compilation 74n. *assemblage;* work, construction 164n. *production;* choreography 837n. *dancing;* orchestration, instrumentation, score 412n. *musical piece;* work of art, picture, sculpture, model; literary work 589n. *book,* 593n. *poem,* 591n. *dissertation,* 592n. *anthology;* play 594n. *stage play;* ballet 837n. *dance;* pattern, design 12n. *correlation.*

Adj. *composing,* constituting, making; composed of, made of; containing, having 78adj. *inclusive.*

Vb. *constitute,* compose, be the whole of, form, make; make up, build up to; inhere, belong to, go to the making of, enter into 58vb. *be one of.*

contain, subsume, include 78vb. *comprise;* hold, have, take in, absorb 299vb. *admit;* comprehend, embrace, embody 235vb. *enclose;* involve, imply 5vb. *be intrinsic;* hide 525vb. *conceal.*

compose, compound 43vb. *mix,* 50vb. *combine;* organize, set in order 62vb. *arrange;* synthesize, put together 45vb. *join;* compile, assemble 74vb. *bring together;* compose, set up 587vb. *print;* draft, draw up, indite 586vb. *write;* orchestrate, score 413vb. *compose music;* draw 553vb. *paint;* construct, build, make, fabricate 164vb. *produce;* knit, interweave 222vb. *weave;* pattern, design 12vb. *correlate.*

See: 5, 12, 43, 45, 50, 58, 62, 74, 78, 164, 222, 235, 299, 331, 340, 358, 412, 413, 525, 551, 553, 554, 563, 586, 587, 589, 591, 592, 593, 594, 837.

57 Exclusion

N. *exclusion,* preclusion, preoccupation, preemption; anticipation, forestalling 702n. *hindrance;* possessiveness, monopoly, dog-in-the-manger policy, exclusiveness, closed shop 932n. *selfishness;* non-inclusion, exception; an exception, special case; exception in favor of, exemption, dispensation 746n. *liberation;* leaving out, omission, deliberate o. 607n. *rejection;* non-admission, blackball; no entry, no admission; closed door, lock-out; ban, bar, taboo 757n. *prohibition;* ostracism, boycott 620n. *avoidance;* segregation, seposition, quarantine, color-bar, apartheid, casteism 883n. *seclusion;* intolerance, repression, suppression 481n. *prejudice;* extrusion, expulsion, disbarment, dismissal, deportation, exile, expatriation; removal, elimination, eradication 188n, *displacement;* cancellation, blotting out 550n. *obliteration;* dam, coffer-d., wall, screen partition, pale, curtain, iron c., bamboo c. 235n. *barrier;* great wall of China, Hadrian's wall 713n. *defense;* customs' barrier, tariff, tariff wall 809n. *tax;* place of exile, place of segregation, ghetto, outer darkness 223n. *exteriority.*

Adj. *excluding,* exclusive, exclusory, exemptive; preventive, interdictive, prohibitive 757n. *prohibiting;* preclusive, preemptive; silent about 582adj. *taciturn.*

excluded, barred, excepted etc. vb.; extra-, not included, not admitted; peripheral, hardly in, half in, half out; included out, counted o.; not told, unrecounted, suppressed, stifled; not allowed, disallowed, banned 757adj. *prohibited;* disbarred, struck off 550adj. *obliterated;* shut out, outcaste 607adj. *rejected;* inadmissible, beyond the pale 470adj. *impossible;* foreign 59adj. *extraneous,* 84adj. *unconformable;* removable, exemptile.

Vb. *be excluded,* not belong, stay outside, gain no admission; suffer exile, go into e., 296vb. *depart,* 190vb. *be absent.*

exclude, preclude 470vb. *make impossible;* preoccupy, preempt, forestall 64vb. *come before;* keep out, warn off 747vb. *restrain;* black-ball, deny entry, shut out, shut the door on, spurn 607vb. *reject;* bar, ban, taboo, black, disallow 757vb. *prohibit;* ostracize, cold-shoulder, boycott, outcaste, send to Coventry 620vb. *avoid;* not include, leave out, count o.; exempt, dispense, excuse 746vb. *liberate;* except, make an exception, treat as a special case 19vb. *make unlike;* omit, miss out, pass over, disregard 458vb. *neglect;* lay aside, put a., relegate 46vb. *set apart;* take out, strike o., cancel 550vb. *obliterate;* disbar, strike off, remove, disqualify 188vb. *displace,* 963vb. *punish;* rule out, draw the line; wall off, curtain off, quarantine 232vb. *circumscribe,* 235vb. *enclose;* excommunicate, segregate, sequester 883vb. *seclude;* thrust out, extrude, dismiss, deport, exile, banish, outlaw, expatriate; weed, sift, winnow, bolt 44vb. *eliminate;* sort out, declassify; eradicate, uproot 300vb. *void;* expurgate, garble, censor 648vb. *purify;* deny 533vb. *negate,* 760vb. *refuse;* abandon 621vb. *relinquish.*

Adv. *exclusive of,* excepting, barring, not counting, except, with the exception of, save; bating, short of; let alone, apart from; outside of, extra-.

See: 19, 44, 46, 59, 64, 84, 188, 190, 223, 232, 235, 296, 300, 458, 470, 486, 533, 550, 582, 607, 620, 621, 648, 702, 713, 746, 747, 757, 760, 809, 883, 932, 963.

58 Component

N. *component,* component part, integral p., integrant p., element; link, stitch; word, letter; constituent, part and parcel 53n. *part;* factor, leaven 178n. *influence;* additive, appurtenance, feature 40n. *adjunct;* one of, member, one of us; staff, crew, men, company, complement 686n. *personnel;* ingredient, content 193n. *contents;* works, insides, interior 224n. *interiority;* spare part 40n. *extra;* components, set, outfit 88n. *unit;* complete set, complement.

Adj. *ingredient,* entering into, belonging, proper, native, inherent 5adj. *intrinsic;* component, constituent 56adj. *composing;* built-in, appurtenant 45adj. *conjunct;* admitted, entered, made a member, part of, one of, on the staff; involved, implicated, deep in 43adj. *mixed.*

Vb. *be one of,* make part of, be a member etc. n.; inhere, belong 5vb. *be intrinsic;* enter into, enter into the composition of, become involved with, be implicated in, share 775vb. *participate;* merge in, be merged in 43vb. *be mixed;* belong to, appertain to 9vb. *be related.*

See: 5, 9, 40, 43, 45, 53, 56, 88, 178, 193, 224, 686, 775.

59 Extraneousness

N. *extraneousness,* extraneity, foreignness 6n. *extrinsicality,* 223n. *exteriority;* foreign parts 199n. *farness;* foreign body, foreign substance, alien element, unassimilated e. 84n. *unconformity;* alienism.

foreigner, alien, man from foreign parts, stranger, easterling, sassenach, Southron; continental, tramontane, ultramontanist; non-Greek, barbarian; Celtic fringe; Celestial, Chink; Easterner, Westerner, Southerner, Northerner; Canuck, limejuicer, Africander, Aussie, Malagasy, Monegasque, Muscovite; greaser, dago, wog; paleface, squaw-man; gringo; Martian, Venusian, Saturnian; colonial, creole 188n. *settler;* resident alien, metic, uitlander, expatriate; migrant, emigrant, immigrant, declarant, pommy, hunky, bohunk; refugee, deraciné, displaced person, DP 268n. *wanderer;* foreign population, diaspora, ten lost tribes.

intruder, interloper, cuckoo, squatter; uninvited guest, gate-crasher, stowaway; outsider, novus homo, upstart; not one of us, the stranger in our midst; arrival, new a., new face, newcomer, tenderfoot 297n. *incomer;* invader 712n. *attacker.*

Adj. *extraneous,* of external origin, ulterior, outside 223adj. *exterior,* 6adj. *extrinsic;* interplanetary, interstellar 199adj. *distant;* not indigenous, imported, foreign-made; foreign, alien, peregrine; strange, outlandish, barbarian; oversea, continental, tramontane, ultramontane, Italianate; exotic, hot-house, unacclimatized; gypsy, nomad, wandering 267adj. *traveling;* unassimilated, undigested; indigestible 84adj. *unconformable;* immigrant 297adj. *incoming;* intrusive, interloping, trespassing; infringing, invading 712adj. *attacking;* exceptional 84adj. *unusual;* un-American, un-English 84adj. *abnormal;* not of this world, unnatural, supernatural 983adj. *magical;* inadmissible 57adj. *excluded.*

Adv. *abroad,* in foreign parts, in foreign lands; beyond seas, overseas; from outer space.

See: 6, 57, 84, 188, 199, 223, 267, 268, 297, 712, 983.

60 Order

N. *order,* state of order, orderliness, tidiness, neatness 648n. *cleanness,* 258n. *smoothness;* proportion 245n. *symmetry;* peace, quiet 266n. *quietude;* harmony, music of the spheres 710n. *concord;* good order, economy, system, method, methodicalness, methodology, systematization; fixed order, rule 81n. *regularity,* 16n. *uniformity;* custom, routine 610n. *habit;* strict order, discipline 739n. *obedience;* due order, gradation, subordination, rank, place, position 73n. *serial place;* unbroken order, course, even tenor, progression, series 71n. *continuity;* logical order, serial o., alphabetical o. 65n. *sequence,* 12n. *correlation;* organization, putting in order, disposition, array 62n. *arrangement,* 56n. *composition.*

Adj. *orderly,* harmonious 710adj. *concordant,* 245adj. *symmetrical;* well-behaved, well-drilled, disciplined 739adj. *obedient;* well-regulated, under control, according to rule 81adj. *regular*; ordered, classified, schematic 62adj. *arranged;* methodical, systematic, businesslike; strict, invariable 16adj. *uniform;* routine, steady 610adj. *habitual;* correct, shipshape, trim, neat, tidy, dinky, neat and tidy, neat as a pin; in good trim, in apple-pie order, in perfect o., in its proper place, unconfused 62adj. *arranged;* unruffled, unrumpled 258adj. *smooth;* direct 249adj. *straight;* clear, lucid 516adj. *intelligible.*

Vb. *order,* take order for; dispose 62vb. *arrange;* schematize, systematize, organize 62vb. *regularize;* harmonize, synchronize, regulate 24vb. *adjust;* normalize, standardize 16vb. *make uniform;* keep order, police, control, govern 733vb. *rule,* 737vb. *command.*

be in order, harmonize, synchronize 24vb. *accord;* fall in, range oneself, draw up, line up; fall into place, find one's level; station oneself, take station; take one's place, take one's rank, take one's position 187vb. *place oneself;* keep one's place; rally, rally round 74vb. *congregate;* follow routine 610vb. *be wont.*

Adv. *in order,* strictly, just so, by the book, by the card, according to Cocker, by order, as directed; in turn, in its t., seriatim; gradatim, step by step, by regular steps, by regular gradations, by regular stages, at regular intervals, at stated periods 141adv. *periodically;* orderly, in orderly fashion, methodically, systematically, schematically; all correct, OK.

See: 12, 16, 24, 56, 62, 65, 71, 73, 74, 81, 141, 187, 245, 249, 258, 266, 516, 610, 648, 710, 733, 737, 739.

61 Disorder

N. *disorder,* random order, non-arrangement, non-classification; incoordination, muddle, no plan, no order, no method, no system (**see** *confusion*); chaotic state, chaos, anarchy 734n. *laxity;* irregularity, anomalousness, anomaly 17n. *non-uniformity;* disunion, disaccord, 25n. *disagreement;* irregularity, ectopia; disharmony 411n. *discord;* disorderliness, unruliness, no discipline 738n. *disobedience;* violent behavior, storm, outbreak 176vb. *violence;* nihilism 738n. *sedition;* untidiness, littering, sluttishness, slovenliness, slovenry 649n. *uncleanness;* neglect 458n. *negligence;* discomposure, disarray, dishevelment 63n. *derangement;* dissolution, scattering 75n. *dispersion,* 51n. *decomposition;* upheaval, convulsion 149n. *revolution;* subversion 221n. *overturning;* destruction 165n. *havoc.*

confusion (**see** *disorder*); welter, jumble, hugger-mugger, mix-up, medley, embroilment, imbroglio 43n. *mixture;* wilderness, jungle; chaos, fortuitous concourse of atoms; omnium gatherum, huddle, seething mass, scramble, shambles 74n. *crowd;* muddle, litter, clutter, lumber 641n. *rubbish;* farrago, mess, mass, mash, mishmash, hash, hotchpotch, stock pot, witch's brew, jumble sale, lucky dip; Babel, bedlam, madhouse, confusion worse confounded (**see** *turmoil*).

complexity, complication 700n. *difficulty,* 702n. *hindrance;* implication, involvement, imbroglio, embroilment; intricacy, interlocking, involution, kink 251n. *convolution;* maze, labyrinth; web, spider's w., 222n. *network;* coil, sleave, tangle, twist, tangled skein, ravelment; knot, Gordian k. 47n. *ligature;* wheels within wheels, clockwork, machinery; puzzle 517n. *unintelligibility;* situation, pretty kettle of fish, pretty piece of business, a nice b. 700n. *predicament.*

turmoil, turbulence, tumult, frenzy, ferment, storm, convulsion 176n. *violence;* pandemonium, inferno; hullabaloo, row, riot, uproar 400n. *loudness;* affray, fight, fracas, melee 718n. *battle;* to-do, rumpus, ruction, pudder, pother, trouble, disturbance 318n. *agitation;* whirlwind, tornado, hurricane 352n. *gale;* beargarden, shambles, madhouse, Bedlam; Saturnalia, Donnybrook Fair; roughhouse, rough-and-tumble, free-for-all, spill and pelt, hell broke loose, bull in a china shop; street-fighting, gang warfare 709n. *quarrel;* fat in the fire, devil to pay.

slut, sloven, slattern, draggletail, litterer, litter-lout 649n. *dirty person;* ragamuffin, tatterdemalion 801n. *poor man.*

anarch, anarchist, nihilist; lord of misrule, Mohawk, sons of Belial 738n. *rioter.*

Adj. *orderless,* in disorder, in disarray, disordered, disarranged, disorganized, jumbled, shuffled 63adj. *deranged;* unclassified, ungraded, unsorted; out of order, not in working order, not working 641adj. *useless;* out of joint, out of gear, dislocated 46adj. *disjunct;* out of sorts 651adj. *sick;* irregular, ectopic, in the wrong place, misplaced 188adj. *displaced;* awry, snafu; topsy-turvy, upside down 221adj. *inverted;* wandering, straggling, dispersed 75adj. *unassembled;* random, unarranged, unorganized, uncoordinated, unclassified; unschematic, planless; incoherent, skimble-skamble; irregular, anomalous 17adj. *non-uniform;* unsystematic, unmethodical, desultory, aimless, casual; promiscuous, indiscriminate 463adj. *indiscriminating;* confused, chaotic, in chaos, in a mess, messy 649adj. *dirty;* sloppy, slipshod, kempt, uncombed, disheveled, tumbled, windswept, windblown, tousled, discomposed; littering, untidy, slovenly, sluttish, slatternly, bedraggled, messy 649adj. *dirty;* sloppy, slipshod, slack, informal, careless 456adj. *inattentive.*

complex, intricate, involved, complicated, over-c., over-involved, overcomplicated 251adj. *coiled,* 517adj. *puzzling;* mazy, winding, inextricable 251adj. *labyrinthine;* entangled, balled up, snarled 702adj. *hindered;* knotted 45adj. *tied.*

disorderly, undisciplined, tumultous, rumbustious 738adj. *riotous;* frantic 503adj. *frenzied;* orgiastic, Saturnalian, Bacchic, Dionysiac 949adj. *drunken;* rough, tempestuous, turbulent 176adj. *violent,* 318adj. *agitated;* anarchical, lawless 954adj. *lawbreaking;* wild, harum-scarum, scatterbrained 456adj. *light-minded.*

Vb. *be disordered,* lose all order, fall into disarray, scatter, break up 75vb. *disperse;* get in a mess, fall into confusion, lose cohesion 49vb. *come unstuck;* get out of hand, throw off discipline, riot 738vb. *disobey;* not keep one's place, jump the queue 64vb. *come before;* disorder 63vb. *derange.*

rampage, storm 176vb. *be violent;* rush, mob, break the cordon; roister, roil, riot, 738vb. *revolt;* romp 837vb. *amuse oneself;* play the fool 497vb. *be absurd;* fete, maffick 886vb. *gratulate.*

Adv. *confusedly,* in confusion, in disorder, without order, anyhow; irregularly; by fits and snatches, by fits and starts; chaotically, pell-mell, higgledy-piggledy, helter-skelter, harum-scarum; in turmoil, in a ferment; on the rampage; at sixes and sevens, at cross-purposes; topsy-turvy, upside down 221adv. *inversely;* inextricably.

See: 17, 25, 43, 45, 46, 47, 49, 51, 63, 64, 74, 75, 149, 165, 176, 188, 221, 222, 251, 318, 352, 400, 411, 456, 458, 463, 497, 503, 517, 641, 649, 651, 683, 700, 702, 709, 718, 734, 738, 801, 837, 886, 949, 954.

62 Arrangement: reduction to order

N. *arrangement,* reduction to order; ordering, disposal, disposition, marshaling, arraying, placing 187n. *location;* collocation, grouping 45n. *joinder,* 74n. *assemblage;* division, distribution, allocation, allotment 783n. *apportionment;* method, systematization, organization, reorganization; rationalization 44n. *simplification;*

streamlining 654n. *improvement;* centralization 48n. *coherence;* decentralization 49n. *non-coherence;* administration, staff-work 689n. *management;* planning, making arrangements 623n. *contrivance,* 669n. *preparation;* taxonomy, categorization, classification 561n. *nomenclature;* analysis 51n. *decomposition;* codification, digestion, consolidation; syntax, conjugation 564n. *grammar;* grading, gradation, subordination, graduation, calibration 465n. *measurement,* 71n. *series;* continuation, serialization 71n. *continuity;* timing, synchronization 123n. *synchronism;* formulation, construction 56n. *composition;* result of arrangement, array, system, form 60n. *order;* cosmos 321n. *universe;* organic creature 358n. *organism;* orchestration, score 412n. *music;* layout, pattern, architecture 331n. *structure;* weave 222n. *crossing;* choreography 837n. *dance;* collection, assortment 74n. *accumulation;* schematic arrangement, schematism; register, file 548n. *record;* inventory, catalog, table 87n. *list;* syntagm, code, digest, synopsis 592n. *compendium;* treatise, essay, article 591n. *dissertation,* 589n. *book;* atlas 551n. *map;* scheme 623n. *plan;* composition 770n. *compromise,* 765n. *compact,* 766n. *conditions;* class, group, subgroup 77n. *classification.*

sorting, grading, seeding; reference system, cross-reference 12n. *correlation;* file, filing system, card index, pigeon-hole; sieve, strainer 263n. *porosity;* sorter, sifter.

Adj. *arranged,* disposed, marshaled, arrayed etc. vb.; ordered, schematic, tabulated, tabular; methodical, systematic, organizational; precise, definite, cut and dried; analyzed, classified, assorted; unraveled, disentangled, unscrambled, straightened out; regulated 81n. *regular;* unconfused 60adj. *orderly;* sorted, seeded.

Vb. *arrange,* set, dispose, set up, set out; formulate, form, put into shape, orchestrate, score 56vb. *compose;* form into ranks, rank, range, align, line up, form up; position 187vb. *place;* marshal, array; bring back to order, rally 74vb. *bring together;* place *or* put *or* set in order; fix the order, grade, size, group, space; collocate, thread together 45vb. *connect;* settle, fix, determine, define; allot, allocate, assign, distribute, deal, parcel out 783vb. *apportion;* allot the parts, decide the role, cast 594vb. *dramatize;* improve the order, trim, neaten, tidy, tidy up (**see** *unravel*); arrange for, make arrangements 669vb. *prepare,* 623vb. *plan,* 689vb. *manage.*

regularize, reduce to order, bring order into, straighten out, put to rights 654vb. *rectify,* 24vb. *adjust;* adjust the type, justify 587vb. *print;* regulate, coordinate, phase; organize, systematize, methodize, schematize; standardize, normalize, centralize 16vb. *make uniform.*

class, classify, subsume, group; specify 561vb. *name;* process, process the data; analyze, anatomize, divide; dissect 51vb. *decompose;* rate, rank, grade, evaluate 480vb. *estimate;* sort, sift, seed; sift out, bolt, riddle 44vb. *eliminate;* file, pigeonhole; index, reference, cross-r.; tabulate, alphabeticize; catalog, inventory 87vb. *list;* register 548vb. *record;* codify, digest.

unravel, untangle, disentangle, disembroil, ravel, card, comb out, unweave, uncoil, untwist, untwine 316 vb. *evolve;* iron, press, uncrease, iron out 258vb. *smooth;* unscramble, straighten out, tidy up, clean up, neaten 654vb. *make better;* clear the air, remove misunderstanding, explain 520vb. *interpret.*

See: 12, 16, 24, 44, 45, 48, 49, 51, 56, 60, 71, 74, 77, 81, 87, 123, 187, 222, 258, 263, 316, 321, 331, 358, 412, 465, 480, 520, 548, 551, 561, 564, 587, 589, 591, 592, 594, 623, 654, 669, 689, 765, 766, 770, 783, 837.

63 Derangement

N. *derangement,* subversion of order; shuffling 151n. *interchange;* translocation 272n. *transference;* sabotage, obstruction 702n. *hindrance;* disarrangement, disorganization, discomposure, dishevelment; dislocation 46n. *separation;* displacement, evection (astron.), perturbation (astron.); disturbance, interruption 138n. *intempestivity;* creasing, corrugation 261n. *fold;* madness 503n. *insanity;* upsetting 221n. *inversion;* convulsion 176n. *violence,* 318n. *agitation;* state of disorder 61n. *disorder.*

Adj. *deranged* 61adj. *orderless;* demented 503adj. *insane;* sabotaged 702n. *hindered.*

Vb. *derange,* disarrange, disorder, tumble, put out of gear, throw out of order; disturb, touch 265vb. *move;* meddle, interfere 702vb. *hinder;* mislay, lose 188vb. *misplace;* disorganize, muddle, confound, confuse, convulse, throw into confusion, make havoc, scramble; tamper, spoil, mar, damage, sabotage 655vb. *impair;* force, strain, bend, twist 176vb. *be violent;* unhinge, dislocate, sprain, rick 188vb. *displace;* unseat, dislodge, derail, throw off the rails; unbalance, upset, overturn, capsize 221 vb. *invert,* 149vb. *revolutionize;* unsettle, declassify, detribalize, denationalize; shake, jiggle, toss 318vb. *agitate;* trouble, perturb, discompose, disconcert, ruffle, rattle, flurry, fluster 456vb. *distract;* interrupt, break in on 138vb. *mistime;* misdirect, disorientate, throw one off his bearings 495vb. *mislead,* 655vb. *pervert;* dement, drive mad 503vb. *make mad,* 891vb. *enrage.*

jumble, shuffle 151vb. *interchange,* 272vb. *transpose;* mix up 43vb. *mix;* toss, tumble 318vb. *agitate;* ruffle, dishevel, tousle, fluff; rumple, crumple, crease, crush 261vb. *fold;* untidy, mess, muck up; muddle, huddle, mess up, litter, clutter; scatter, fling about 75vb. *disperse.*

bedevil, confuse, make a mess *or* hash of; confound, complicate, perplex, involve, ravel, ball up, entangle, tangle, embroil; turn topsy-turvy, turn upside down 221vb. *invert;* send haywire.

See: 43, 46, 61, 75, 138, 149, 151, 176, 188, 221, 261, 265, 272, 318, 456, 495, 503, 655, 702, 891.

64 Precedence

N. *precedence,* antecedence, antecedency, going before, coming b., line-jumping 283n. *precession;* anteriority 119n. *priority;* front position, anteposition, prefixion, prothesis 237n. *front;* higher position, pride of place 34n. *superiority;* preference 605n. *choice;* preeminence, excellence 638n. *importance;* captaincy, leadership, hegemony 733n. *authority;* the lead, le pas; leading, guiding, pioneering; precedent 66n. *precursor;* past history 125n. *preterition.*

Adj. *preceding,* etc. vb.; precedent, prodromal; antecedent, foregoing, outgoing; anterior, former, previous, 119adj. *prior;* before-mentioned, above-m.; aforesaid, said; precursory, precursive, prevenient; leading, guiding, pioneering; preliminary, prefatory, introductory; prelusive, prelusory; proemial, preparatory, anacrustic; prepositive, prothetic, prefixed, prepositional 237adj. *fore;* first come, first served.

Vb. *come before,* be first to arrive 283vb. *precede;* go first, run ahead, jump the line; lead, guide, conduct, show the way, point the trail 547vb. *indicate;* forerun, pioneer, clear the way, blaze the trail 484vb. *discover;* head, take the lead, have the pas 237vb. *be in front;* have precedence, take p., outrank 34vb. *be superior;* lead the dance, set the fashion, set the example 178vb. *influence;* open, lead off, kick off 68vb. *begin;* preamble, prelude, preface, prologize; introduce, usher in, ring in 68vb. *auspicate;* have the start, get ahead 119vb. *be before.*

prepose, put in front, lead with, head w.; advance, station, station before, throw out a screen 187vb. *place;* prefix 38vb. *add;* front, face, tip, top 237vb. *be in front;* presuppose 512vb. *suppose,* 475vb. *premise;* preface, prelude 68vb. *initiate.*

Adv. *before,* in advance 283adv. *ahead;* preparatory to, as a preliminary; earlier 119adv. *before* (in time); ante, supra, above 237adv. *in front.*

See: 34, 38, 66, 68, 119, 125, 178, 187, 237, 283, 475, 484, 512, 547, 605, 638, 773.

65 Sequence

N. *sequence,* coming after, subsequence, descent, line, lineage 120n. *posteriority;* going after 284n. *following;* logical sequence, inference 475n. *reasoning;* postposition, suffixion, suffixment 38n. *addition;* 45n. *joinder;* sonship 170n. *posterity;* succession, successorship, Elijah's mantle 780n. *transfer;* series 71n. *continuity;* successiveness, alternation, serialization; continuation, prolongation 113n. *protraction,* 146n. *continuance;* consecution, pursuance 619n. *pursuit;* overtaking 306n. *overstepping,* 727n. *success;* secondariness, subordinacy, subordination, second place, proxime accessit, honorable mention 35n. *inferiority;* last place 238n. *rear;* no priority 639n. *unimportance;* consequence 67n. *sequel,* 157n. *effect;* conclusion 69n. *end.*

Adj. *sequent,* following, succeeding, incoming; ensuing, sequacious; proximate, next 200adj. *near;* posterior, latter, later 120adj. *subsequent;* successive, consecutive 71adj. *continuous;* alternating, amebean, antiphonal 12adj. *correlative;* alternative, every second, every other; postpositive, postpositional 238adj. *back;* consequent, resulting 157adj. *caused.*

Vb. *come after,* have one's turn, come next, ensue 284vb. *follow;* follow close, tread on the heels 200vb. *be near;* succeed, inherit, step into the shoes of, supplant 150vb. *substitute;* alternate, turn and turn about 141vb. *be periodic;* relieve, take over.

place after, suffix, append; subscribe, subjoin 38vb. *add.*

Adv. *after,* following; afterwards 120adv. *subsequently,* 238adv. *behind;* at the end, in relays, in waves, successively; as follows, consequentially 157adj. *consequently;* in the end 69adv. *finally;* next, later; infra, below.

See: 12, 35, 38, 45, 67, 69, 71, 113, 120, 141, 146, 150, 157, 170, 200, 272, 284, 306, 475, 619, 639, 727, 780.

66 Precursor

N. *precursor,* predecessor, ancestor, forebear, patriarch 169n. *parent;* first man, Adam, antediluvian 125n. *antiquity;* eldest, firstborn; protomartyr; discoverer, inventor 461n. *experimenter;* pioneer, voortrekker, pathfinder, explorer 268n. *traveler;* guide, link-boy, voorlooper, bellwether 690n. *leader;* scout, scouter, skirmisher; vanguard, avant-garde, innovator; forerunner, prodrome, van-courier, outrider; herald, harbinger, announcer 531n. *messenger;* dawn, false d.; anticipation, prefigurement, foretaste, preview, premonition, forewarning 664n. *warning,* 511n. *omen;* precedent 83n. *example;* antecedent, prefix, preposition 40n. *adjunct;* eve, vigil, day before 119n. *priority.*

prelude, preliminary, anacrusis, prolusion, preamble, preface, prologue, foreword, avant-propos; headline; proem, opening, exordium, prolegomenon, introduction 68n. *beginning;* lead, heading, frontispiece 237n. *front;* groundwork, foundation 218n. *basis,* 669n. *preparation;* overture, voluntary, ritornello 412n. *musical piece;* premises, presupposition 512n. *supposition.*

Adj. *precursory,* preliminary, exploratory 669n. *preparatory;* prelusive, prelusory, anacrustic; proemial, introductory, prefatory 68adj. *beginning;* inaugural, foundational; precedent, prodromal 64adj. *preceding.*

See: 40, 64, 68, 83, 119, 125, 169, 218, 237, 268, 412, 461, 511, 512, 531, 664, 669, 690.

67 Sequel

N. *sequel,* consequence, result, by-product 157n. *effect;* conclusion 69n. *end;* sequela, after-effect; hangover, morning after 949n. *crapulence;* after-taste; afterglow; aftermath, aftergrowth, after-crop 157n. *growth;* afterbirth, afterburden, placenta, secundines, afterpain 164n. *propagation;* inheritance, legacy, testament, will 777n. *dower;* surprise, afterclap 508n. *inexpectation;* afterthought, second thought, better t., ésprit d'escalier; double-take, second try, aftercast, aftergame; afterpiece, postlude, epilogue, postscript; peroration, envoi, last words, more last w.; follow-through, follow-up 725n. *completion;* continuation, sequel, second part, second volume, next chapter 589n. *book;* tag, tailpiece, heelpiece, colophon, coda 238n. *rear;* appendage, appendix, codicil, supplement 40adj. *adjunct;* suffix, affix, subscript, inflection, enclitic, proclitic 564n. *grammar;* afterpart, tail; line, ponytail 259n. *hair;* after-course, afters, dessert 301n. *dish;* survival, after-life, hereafter 124n. *future state.*

retinue, following, followers 284n. *follower;* suite, train, cortege, rout 71n. *procession;* tail, line, wake 89n. *concomitant;* trailer 274n. *vehicle.*

aftercomer, after-generations, the unborn, descendant 170n. *posterity;* heir, inheritor 776n. *beneficiary;* next man in, successor; replacement, supplanter 150n. *substitute;* relief, reserve 707n. *auxiliary;* fresh blood, new broom 126n. *modernist, upstart;* latecomer, newcomer, new arrival 297n. *incomer;* gleaner 370n. *husbandman;* jackal 742n. *dependent;* last man in, finalist, finisher 41n. *survivor.*

See: 40, 69, 71, 89, 124, 126, 150, 157, 164, 170, 238, 259, 274, 284, 297, 301, 370, 508, 564, 589, 707, 725, 742, 776, 777, 949.

68 Beginning

N. *beginning,* birth, rise (**see** *origin*); infancy, babyhood 130n. *youth;* 126n. *newness;* primitiveness 127n. *oldness;* commencement; onset 295n. *arrival;* incipience, inception, inchoation, foundation, establishment; origination, invention 484n. *discovery;* initiative, demarche; exordium, introduction 66n. *prelude;* end of the beginning, curtain-raiser; alpha, first letter, initial; head, heading, headline, caption 547n. *label;* title-page, prelims; van, front, forefront 237n. *front;* dawn 128n. *morning;* handsel, running in, teething troubles; first blush, first glance, first sight, first impression, first lap, first round, first stage; primer, outline; rudiments, elements, principia, first principles, alphabet, ABC; leading up to 289n. *approach;* outbreak, onset, brunt 712n. *attack;* debutant, starter 538n. *beginner;* precedent 66n. *precursor;* preliminaries 669n. *preparation.*

debut, coming out, inauguration, opening, unveiling; first night, premiere, first appearance, first offense; premier pas, first step, first move, move, gambit; maiden voyage, maiden speech.

start, outset; starting point, point of departure, zero hour, D-day; send-off, setting out, embarkation 296n. *departure;* rising of the curtain; kick-off; fresh start, new beginning, resumption, reopening 148n. *reversion;* new departure, thin end of the wedge, precedent; standing start, flying s.; starter, self-s.

origin, origination, derivation; genesis, birth, nativity; provenance, ancestry 169n. *parentage;* front, fons et origo; rise 156n. *source;* bud, germ, egg, protoplasm; first beginnings, cradle, incunabula 192n. *home.*

entrance 297n. *way in;* inlet 345n. *gulf;* mouth, opening 263n. *orifice;* threshold, vestibule, porch, portico, propylon, gateway 624n. *access;* gate, postern 263n. *doorway;* frontier, border 236n. *limit;* outskirts, skirts, environs, suburbs 230n. *circumjacence;* foothills, outlier; pass, ghat, corridor 289n. *approach,* 305n. *passage.*

Adj. *beginning,* initiatory, initiative, inceptive, inchoative; introductory, prefatory, proemial 66adj. *precursory* inaugural, foundational; elemental, rudimental 156adj. *fundamental;* aboriginal, primeval, 127adj. *primal;* rudimentary, elementary, crude 670adj. *immature;* embryonic, nascent, budding, incipient, inchoate, raw, begun, in preparation 726adj. *uncompleted;* just begun, newly opened, launched.

first, initial, maiden, starting, natal; original 21adj. *unimitated;* unprecedented 126adj. *new;* foremost, front 237adj. *fore;* leading, principal, head, chief 34adj. *supreme.*

Vb. *begin,* make a beginning, commence, inchoate; set in, open, dawn, break out, burst forth, spring up, crop up; arise, rise, take one's r., take one's birth; spring from; come into existence, come into the world 360vb. *be born;* make one's debut, come out; start, enter upon, embark on 296vb. *start out;* start work, clock in; handsel, run in; begin at the beginning, start from scratch, begin ab ovo; resume, begin again, begin de novo, make a fresh start 148vb. *revert;* start afresh, shuffle the cards, reshuffle, resume, recommence, reopen; set to, set about, set to work; attack, wade into, tackle, face, address oneself; go to it 672vb. *undertake.*

initiate, found, launch; originate, invent, think of 484vb. *discover;* usher in, ring in, open the door to, introduce; start, start up, switch on; prompt, promote, set going; raise, set on foot; put to work 622vb. *employ;* handsel, run in; take the initiative, lead, lead off, lead the way, take the lead, pioneer, open up, break new ground 64vb. *come before;* broach, open, raise the subject, ventilate, air; open the ball, break the ice, set the ball rolling; throw the first stone, open fire; take the first step, take the plunge, cross the Rubicon, burn one's boats; apply the match, touch off, spark off, set off.

auspicate, inaugurate, open; institute, install, induct 751vb. *commission;* found, set up, establish 156vb. *cause;* baptize, christen, launch 561vb. *name;* initiate, blood, flesh; lay the foundations, lay the foundation stone, cut the first turf 669vb. *prepare.*

Adv. *initially,* originally, at the beginning, in the b., in the bud, in embryo, in its infancy, from the beginning, from its birth; ab initio, ab ovo; first, firstly, in the first place, imprimis; primarly, first of all, before everything, first and foremost; as a start, for a beginning.

See: 21, 34, 64, 66, 126, 127, 128, 130, 148, 156, 169, 192, 230, 236, 237, 263, 289, 295, 296, 297, 305, 345, 360, 484, 538, 547, 561, 622, 624, 664, 669, 670, 672, 712, 726, 751.

69 End

N. *end,* close, conclusion, consummation, apodosis 725n. *completion;* pay-off, result, end-r. 157n. *effect;* termination, determination, closure, guillotine; finishing stroke, death blow, quietus, coup de grâce; knock-out, stopper, finisher 279n. *knock;* ending, finish, finale, curtain; term, period, stop, halt 145n. *cessation;* final stage, latter end 129n. *evening;* beginning of the end, peroration, last words, swansong, envoi, coda 67n. *sequel;* last stage, last round, last lap, home stretch; last ball, last over; last breath, last gasp, extremities; final examination, finals 459n. *exam.* **See** *finality.*

extremity, final point, omega; ultimate point, extreme, pole; extreme case, ne plus ultra; farthest point, world's end, ultima Thule, where the rainbow ends 199n. *farness;* fringe, verge, brink 234n. *edge;* frontier, boundary 236n. *limit;* terminal point, terminus, terminal 295n. *goal,* 617n. *objective;* dregs, last d.; heel, toe, bottom, nadir 214n. *base;* bottom dollar, last penny 801n. *poverty;* tip, nib, cusp, point, vertex, peak, top 213n. *summit;* tail 67n. *sequel,* 53n. *limb;* shirt-tail, coat-t. 217n. *pendant;* end, head, terminal, butt-end, gable-e., fag-e. 238n. *rear;* tag, epilogue, postscript, appendix 40n. *adjunct;* desinence, inflection, suffix 564n. *grammar.*

finality, bitter end; time, time up; conclusion, end of the matter 54n. *completeness;* drop of the curtain, break-up, wind-up 145n. *cessation;* dissolution 361n. *death;* eschatology, last things, doom, destiny 596n. *fate;* last trump, crack of doom, Götterdämmerung; resurrection day, Day of Judgment, end of the world, end of time, end of all things 124n. *future state.*

Adj. *ending,* final, terminal, last, ultimate; extreme, polar; definitive, conclusive, crowning, completing 725adj. *completive;* conterminate, conterminous, conterminable; ended, at an end; settled, terminated, finalized, decided, set at rest; over, over and done with; off, all off, canceled; played out, finished; penultimate, last but one; antepenultimate, last but two; hindmost, rear 238n. *back;* caudal.

Vb. *end,* come to an end, expire, run out 111vb. *elapse;* close, finish, conclude, be all over; become extinct, die out 361vb. *die,* 2vb. *pass away;* come to a close, draw to a c., have run its course; fade away, peter out; stop, clock out, go home 145vb. *cease.*

terminate, conclude, close, determine, decide, settle; apply the closure, bring to an end, put an end to, put a term to, put a stop to, make an end of, put paid to; finish, achieve, consummate, get through, play out, act o., see it o. 725vb. *carry through;* ring down the curtain, draw stumps, put up the shutters, shut up shop, wind up, close down; switch off, ring off, hang up; stop 145vb. *halt.*

Adv. *finally,* in conclusion, in fine; at last; once for all; to the bitter end, to the last gasp, to the end of the chapter.

See: 2, 40, 53, 54, 67, 124, 129, 145, 157, 199, 213, 214, 217, 234, 236, 238, 279, 295, 361, 459, 564, 596, 617, 725, 801.

70 Middle

N. *middle,* midst, mediety; mean 30n. *average;* medium, middle term; thick, thick of things; heart, body, kernel; nave, hub, navel, umbilicus, omphalos 225n. *center;* nucleus, nucleolus 224n. *interiority;* midweek, midwinter, half-tide, slack water 625n. *mid-course;* bisection, midline, equator, the Line 28n. *equalization;* midrib, midriff, diaphragm 231n. *partition;* half distance, middle d., equidistance, halfway house; mixed economy 43n. *mixture.*

Adj. *middle,* medial, mesial, mean, mid; mediate, middlemost, midmost 225adj. *central;* middling 177adj. *moderate,* 625adj. *neutral;* intermediate, intervocalic 231adj. *interjacent;* equidistant; mediterranean, equatorial.

Adv. *midway,* in the middle, in the thick, midway, halfway; midships.

See: 28, 30, 43, 177, 224, 225, 231, 625.

71 Continuity: uninterrupted sequence

N. *continuity,* continuousness, uninterruptedness, unbrokenness, monotony 16n. *uniformity;* consecution, overlap; immediacy, directness; consecutiveness, successiveness, succession; line, lineage, descent, dynasty; one thing after another, serialization 65n. *sequence;* continuous time, endlessness 115n. *perpetuity;* continuous motion 146n. *continuance;* endless band 315n. *rotation;* repetitiveness, alternation, recurrence 106n. *repetition,* 141n. *periodicity,* 139n. *frequency;* cumulativeness, snowball 36n. *increase;* gradualism, Fabianism 278n. *slowness;* course, run, career, flow, steady f., trend, steady t. 179n. *tendency;* progressiveness 285n. *progression;* circuit, round 314n. *circuition;* daily round, routine, practice, custom 610n. *habit;* track, locus, trail, wake 67n. *sequel;* catenation, concatenation, catena, chain, chain-reaction, chain letter; circle 250n. *circularity.*

series, seriation, gradation 27n. *degree;* succession, run, progression, arithmetic p., geometric p.; ascending order 36n. *increase;* descending order 37n. *decrease;* pedigree, family tree, lineage 169n. *genealogy;* chain, line, string, thread; unbroken line, line of battle, thin red line; rank, file, echelon; array 62n. *arrangement;* row, windrow; colonnade, peristyle, portico; ninepins; ladder, steps, stairs, staircase 308n. *ascent;* range, tier, story 207n. *layer;* keyboard, manual; set, suite, suit (of cards); assortment 77n. *classification;* team, crew, eight, eleven, fifteen 74n. *group;* gamut, scale 410n. *musical note;* stepping stones 624n. *bridge;* cursus honorum; hierarchy.

procession 267n. *marching;* cavalcade 875n. *pageant;* crocodile, queue, tail, cortege, train, suite 67n. *retinue;* caravan, file, single f.; funeral procession, funeral 364n. *obsequies;* ovation, triumph, Lord Mayor's Show 876n. *celebration.*

Adj. *continuous,* continued, run-on 45adj. *conjunct;* consecutive, running, successive, sequential 65adj. *sequent;* serial, serialized; seriate, catenary; progressive, gradual 179adj. *tending;* overlapping, unbroken, uninterrupted, circular; direct, immediate, unmediated; continual, incessant, unremitting, unintermitted, nonstop, constant, perennial, evergreen 115adj. *perpetual;* rhythmic 110adj. *periodic;* repetitive, recurrent, monotonous 106adj. *repeated,* 16adj. *uniform;* linear, lineal, rectilinear 249adj. *straight.*

Vb. *run on,* continue, following in a series; line up, fall in, queue up; succeed, overlap 65adj. *come after;* file, defile, keep single file; circle 626vb. *circuit.*

continuate, run on, extend, prolong 113vb. *spin out,* 203vb. *lengthen;* serialize, arrange in succession, catenate, thread, string 45vb. *connect;* dress, size, grade 27vb. *graduate;* file, tabulate 87vb. *list;* maintain continuity, keep the succession, provide an heir.

Adv. *continuously* etc. adj.; serially, seriatim; successively, in succession, in turn; one after another; at a stretch, handrunning, running; cumulatively, progressively; gradually, step by step, hand over hand; in procession, in file, in single f., in Indian f., in column, in line ahead, nose to tail.

See: 16, 27, 36, 45, 65, 67, 74, 77, 87, 106, 110, 113, 115, 139, 141, 146, 169, 179, 203, 207, 249, 250, 267, 278, 285, 308, 314, 315, 364, 410, 610, 624, 626, 875, 876.

72 Discontinuity: interrupted sequence

N. *discontinuity,* solution of continuity, intermittence; discontinuation, discontinuance 145n. *cessation;* interval, intermission, pause 145n. *lull;* disconnectedness, randomness 61n. *disorder;* unevenness, joltiness, jerkiness 17n. *non-uniformity,* 259n. *roughness;* dotted line; broken ranks; ladder, run 46n. *disjunction;* interruption, intervention, interposition; parenthesis, episode 231n. *interjection;* caesura, division 46n. *separation,* 547n. *punctuation;* break, fracture, flaw, fault, split, crack, cut 201n. *gap;* missing link, lost connection; broken thread, anacoluthon, non sequitur; illogicality, sophism 477n. *sophistry;* patchwork, crazy quilt, crazy paving 437n. *variegation;* incoherence, rhapsody, purple patch 568n. *imperspicuity,* 25n. *misfit;* alternation 141n. *periodicity;* irregularity, ragged volley 142n. *fitfulness.*

Adj. *discontinuous,* unsuccessive, nonrecurrent, unrepeated; discontinued; interrupted, broken, stopping; disconnected 46adj. *disjunct;* discrete 46adj. *separate;* few and far between 140adj. *infrequent;* patchy 437adj. *variegated,* 17adj. *non-uniform;* desultory, intermittent, intermitting 142adj. *fitful;* alternate, alternating 141adj. *periodic;* spasmodic 17adj. *non-uniform;* jerky, jolty, bumpy, uneven 259adj. *rough;* incoherent, anacoluthic 477adj. *illogical;* parenthetic, episodic, not belonging 303adj. *inserted,* 59adj. *extraneous.*

Vb. *be discontinuous,* pause, rest 145vb. *stop;* alternate, intermit.

discontinue, interrupt, intervene, chip in, break, break in upon 231vb. *interfere;* interpose, interject, punctuate 231vb. *put between;* disconnect, break the connection, snap the thread 46vb. *disjoin.*

Adv. *discontinuously,* at intervals, occasionally, infrequently, irregularly, by snatches, by jerks, by skips, by catches, by fits and starts; skippingly, desultorily.
See: 17, 25, 46, 59, 61, 141, 142, 145, 201, 231, 259, 303, 437, 477, 547, 568.

73 Term: serial position
N. *serial place,* term, order, remove 27n. *degree;* rank, ranking, grade, gradation; station, place, position, pitch; status, standing, footing; point, mark, pitch, level, story; step, tread, round, rung; stage, milestone, climacteric, climax 213n. *summit;* bottom rung, nadir 214n. *base.*
Vb. *grade,* rank, rate, place; put one in his place; bring down a peg; stagger, space out 201vb. *space,* 27vb. *graduate.*
have rank, hold r., hold a place, occupy a position, 186vb. *be situate;* fall into place, drop into p., find a niche 187vb. *place oneself.*
See: 27, 186, 187, 201, 213, 214.

74 Assemblage
N. *assemblage,* bringing together, collection 50n. *combination,* 62n. *arrangement;* collocation, juxtaposition 202n. *contiguity;* colligation, contesseration 45n. *joinder;* compilation, corpus, anthology 56n. *composition;* gathering, ingathering, reaping, harvest, vintage 370n. *agriculture,* 771n. *acquisition;* harvest-home 632n. *storage,* 876n. *celebration;* consolidation, concentration; centering, focusing; mobilization, muster, levy, call-up 718n. *war measures;* review, parade, wappenschaw 875n. *pageant;* rally, whipping in, round-up, line-up; herding, shepherding, stock-breeding, cicuration 369n. *animal husbandry;* collectivization, collective, kolkhoz 740n. *compulsion,* 370n. *farm;* party-making, conspiracy, caucus 708n. *party;* noun of assembly; portmanteau word; syntax 564n. *grammar.*
assembly, mutual attraction 291n. *attraction;* getting together, ganging up; forgathering, congregation, concourse, conflux, concurrence 293n. *convergence;* gathering, meeting, mass-m., meet, coven; conventicle, business meeting, board m., convention; gemot, shire-moot, legislature, conclave 692n. *council;* eisteddfod, festival 876n. *celebration;* social gathering, levee, reunion, get-together, conversazione; company, at home, drawing room, salon, party 882n. *sociality;* circle, knitting-bee, spelling-b.; discussion meeting, symposium 584n. *conference.*
group, constellation, galaxy, cluster, star 321n. *star;* bevy, flock, herd; drove, team; pack, kennel; stable, string; nest, aerie; brood, hatch; gaggle, flight, covey; shoal, school; unit, brigade 722n. *formation;* batch, lot, clutch; brace, pair, span, pride of lions 90n. *duality;* leash, four-in-hand 96n. *quaternity;* set, class, genus, species, subspecies 77n. *sort;* breed, tribe, clan, household 11n. *family;* brotherhood, fellowship, college 706n. *association;* movement 708n. *party;* sphere, quarter, circle 524n. *informant;* charmed circle, coterie 644n. *elite;* social group, the classes 868n. *nobility,* 869n. *commonalty;* we-group, in-group, they-group, out-group, they 80n. *self;* age-group, stream 123n. *synchronism;* hand (at cards) set, partially ordered s. 71n. *series.*
band, company, circus; troupe, cast 594n. *actor;* brass band, string b. 413n. *orchestra;* team, string, eleven, eight; knot, bunch; set, coterie, ring; gang, party, work p., fatigue p.; committee, commission 754n. *consignee;* ship's company, crew, complement, man-power, staff 686n. *personnel;* following 67n. *retinue;* meiny; squadron, troop, platoon; unit, regiment, corps 722n. *formation;* squad, posse, posse comitatus; force, body, host 722n. *armed force,* 104n. *multitude;* brotherhood, band of brothers, merry men; Band of Hope; panel 87n. *list;* establishment, cadre 331n. *structure.*
crowd, throng 104n. *multitude;* huddle, swarm, colony, bee-hive, bike, vespiary; small crowd, knot, bunch; the masses, mass, mob, rout 869n. *rabble;* sea of faces, full house, houseful 54n. *completeness;* congestion, press, squash, jam, scrum, rush, crush; rush-hour, crush-h. 680n. *haste;* flood, spate, deluge, stream, streams of 32n. *great quantity;* volley, shower, hail, storm; condensation, populousness, over-population 324n. *density;* infestation, invasion 297n. *ingress;* herd instinct, crowd psychology, mass emotion 818n. *feeling.*
bunch, assortment, lot, mixed l. 43n. *medley;* clump, tuft, wisp, handful;

pencil of rays; bag 194n. *receptacle;* clip, bundle, packet, package, parcel, budget; file, dossier 548n. *record;* bale, roll, bolt, seroon; load, pack, fardel 193n. *contents;* fascine, fagot; fasces; shock, sheaf, stook, truss, heap; swath, gavel, rick, stack, haycock 632n. *storage;* forest, copse 366n. *wood;* bouquet, nosegay, posy; clue, skein, hank.

accumulation, heaping up, acervation, cumulation; agglomeration, conglomeration, conglobation, aggregation; coacervation, coagmentation; massing, amassment; concentration, collectivization; pile-up 279n. *collision;* masonry, mass, pile, pyramid 164n. *edifice,* 209n. *high structure;* congeries, heap; drift, snowdrift; snowball 36n. *increment;* debris, detritus 41n. *leavings;* dustheap, dump, shoot 641n. *rubbish;* cumulus, storm-cloud 355n. *cloud;* store, storage 633n. *provision,* 799n. *treasury;* magazine, armory, quiver 723n. *arsenal;* park, artillery p., car p.; set, lot 71n. *series;* mixed lot, mixed bag 43n. *medley;* kit, stock; range, selection, assortment 795n. *merchandise;* shop-window, display 522n. *exhibit;* museum 632n. *collection;* menagerie, Noah's Ark, aquarium 369n. *zoo;* literary collection 589n. *library;* miscellanea, miscellany, collectanea, compilation 56n. *composition;* symposium, festschrift 591n. *dissertation.*

accumulator, miser 816n. *niggard,* 798n. *treasurer;* connoisseur 492n. *collector;* gatherer, reaper, harvester, picker, gleaner 369n. *husbandman;* convener, assembler; whip, whipper-in; shepherd, sheep dog 369n. *herdsman;* battery 632n. *storage.*

Adj. *assembled,* met, well-met, ill-m.; convened, summoned; mobilized, called-up, banded; collectivized; crowded, packed, huddled, serried 324adj. *dense;* close-printed, tight; populated, over-p., over-crowded, humming with, lousy with, stiff with 54adj. *full;* populous, teeming, swarming, thick on the ground, thick as flies 104adj. *multitudinous;* in a crowd, seething, milling; in formation, ranked, in order 62adj. *arranged.*

Vb. *congregate,* meet, forgather, rendezvous; assemble, reassemble, rejoin; associate, come together, get t., join t., flock t., pig t.; make a crowd, gather, collect, troop, rally, roll up, swell the ranks; resort to, center on, focus on, make for 293vb. *converge;* band, gang up; mass, concentrate, mobilize; conglomerate, huddle, cluster, bunch, crowd, nest; throng, swarm, seethe, mill around; surge, stream, flood 36vb. *grow;* swarm in, infest, invade 297vb. *irrupt.*

bring together, assemble, put together, draw t. 45vb. *join;* draw 291vb. *attract;* gather, collect, rally, muster, call up, mobilize; concentrate, consolidate; collocate, lump together, group, brigade, unite; compile 56vb. *compose;* bring into focus, focus, center; convene, convoke, convocate, hold a meeting; herd, shepherd, get in, whip in, call in, round up, corral 235vb. *enclose;* mass, aggregate, acervate, rake up, dredge up; accumulate, conglomerate, heap, pile, amass; catch, take, rake in, net 771vb. *acquire;* scrape together, save 632vb. *store;* truss, bundle, parcel, package; bunch, bind, colligate, fasciculate 45vb. *tie;* pack, cram, stuff 54vb. *fill;* build up, pile up, pile Pelion on Ossa 310vb. *elevate.*

Adv. *together,* unitedly, as one; collectively, all together, en masse, in a mass, in a body.

See: 11, 32, 36, 41, 43, 45, 50, 54, 56, 62, 67, 71, 77, 80, 87, 90, 96, 104, 123, 164, 193, 194, 202, 209, 235, 279, 291, 293, 297, 310, 321, 324, 331, 355, 366 369, 370, 413, 492, 522, 524, 548, 564, 584, 594, 632, 633, 641, 644, 680, 686, 692, 706, 708, 718, 722, 723, 740, 754, 771, 795, 798, 799, 818, 868, 869, 875, 876, 882.

75 Non-assemblage. Dispersion

N. *dispersion,* scattering, diffraction, break-up 46n. *disjunction;* branching out, fanning o., spread, scatter, radiation 294n. *divergence;* distribution 783n. *apportionment;* delegation, decentralization; disintegration 51n. *decomposition;* evaporation, boiling away 338n. *vaporization,* 337n. *liquefaction;* dissipation 634n. *waste;* circulation, diffusion; dissemination, broadcasting; spraying, sprinkling, spargefaction, circumfusion, interspersion 341n. *moistening;* dispersal, going home; sprawl, sprawling, trailing; disbandment, demobilization; flotsam and jetsam, sea-drift, driftwood 272n. *thing transferred;* disjecta membra; waifs and strays, displaced person; dispersed population, diaspora.

Adj. *unassembled,* dispersed, disbanded, demobilized etc. vb.; scattered, strung out, sporadic, sparse, few and far between 140n. *infrequent;* broadcast, diffused; spreading, widespread, far-flung 183adj. *spacious;* epidemic 79adj. *universal;* spread, dispread, separated 46adj. *separate;* disheveled, streaming, sprawling 61adj. *orderless;* decentralized; branching, radiating, centrifugal 294adj. *divergent;* off-center, adrift, astray; straggling, wandering 267adj. *traveling.*

Vb. *be dispersed,* disperse, scatter, spread, spread out, fan o., thin o., rarefy 325vb. *be rare;* spread fast, spread like wildfire, flood; radiate, branch, branch out 294vb. *diverge;* break up, separate, break ranks, fall out, dismiss 46vb. *be disjointed;* lose coherence, break away 49vb. *come unstuck;* hive off, go on one's own way, go each his own w. 267vb. *wander;* drift away, drift apart; straggle, trail, fall behind 282vb. *stray;* spread over, sprawl over, cover 226vb. *overlie;* explode, blow up, burst, fly apart, fly in all directions 176vb. *be violent;* evaporate, melt 338vb. *vaporize,* 337vb. *liquefy;* disintegrate, dissolve, decay 51vb. *decompose.*

disperse, scatter, diffract; dispread, separate 46vb. *sunder;* thin out, string o.; disseminate, broadcast, sow, strew, strow, bestrew, spread; dissipate, dispel, disintegrate 51vb. *decompose;* scatter to the winds 634vb. *waste;* dispense, deal, deal out, allot 783vb. *apportion;* decentralize; break up, disband, disembody, demobilize, send home 46vb. *disjoin;* draft, draft off, detach 272vb. *send;* diffuse, sprinkle, besprinkle, splash, spray, spatter, bespatter 341vb. *moisten;* circulate, put into circulation, utter; retail 793vb. *sell;* throw into confusion, disorder 63vb. *derange;* rout 727vb. *defeat.*

Adv. *sporadically,* here and there, sparsely, in twos and threes; passim, everywhere, in all quarters.

See: 46, 49, 51, 61, 63, 79, 140, 176, 183, 226, 267, 272, 282, 294, 325, 337, 338, 341, 634, 727, 783, 793.

76 Focus: place of meeting

N. *focus,* corradiation; focal point, point of convergence, town center 293n. *convergence,* 225n. *center;* crossways, crossroads; switchboard, exchange; hub, nub, core, heart, kernel 70n. *middle;* hall, civic center, village hall, village green; campus; market place, agora, forum 796n. *mart;* resort, retreat, haunt, stamping ground, place of resort; club, pub, local 192n. *tavern;* headquarters, depot; rallying point, standard; venue, rendezvous, trysting place 192n. *meeting place;* tryst, assignation; nest, fireside, home ground 192n. *home;* cynosure, center of attraction, honey-pot 291n. *magnet;* place of pilgrimage, mecca, Rome, Zion, promised land 295n. *goal,* 617n. *objective.*

Vb. *focus,* center, corradiate 293vb. *converge;* centralize, concentrate, focus upon; bring to a point, bring to a focus, bring to an issue.

See: 70, 192, 225, 291, 293, 295, 617, 796.

77 Class

N. *classification,* categorization, generification; diagnosis, specification, designation; category, class, predicament, bracket; cadre; head, heading, subhead, section, subsection 53n. *subdivision;* division, branch, department, faculty; pocket, pigeon-hole 194n. *compartment;* province, sphere, range; sex, gender; blood group, age g., stream 74n. *group;* coterie, clique 74n. *band;* persuasion, denomination 978n. *sect.*

sort, order, type, variety, kind; manner, genre, style; character, quality, grade 5n. *character;* mark, brand 547n. *label;* kidney, feather, color; stamp, mold, shape, make 243n. *form;* assortment, kit, set, suit, lot.

breed, strain, blood, family, kin, tribe, clan, sept, line 11n. *race,* 169n. *genealogy;* caste, subcaste, gotra, phylum, genus, species, subspecies; genotype, monotype.

Adj. *generic,* sexual, masculine, feminine, neuter.

classificatory, classificational, taxonomic; sectional, denominational 978adj. *sectarian.*

See: 5, 53, 74, 169, 194, 243, 547, 978.

78 Inclusion

N. *inclusion,* comprising, comprisal; incorporation, embodiment, assimilation, encapsulation; comprehension, admission 299n. *reception;* admissibility, eligibility; membership 775n. *participation;* inclusiveness, inclusivity, coverage, full c. 79n. *generality;* all-roundness, versatility 694n. *skill;* comprehensiveness, no exception, no omission, nothing omitted; set, complete s., complement, package 52n. *whole;* package deal 765n.

compact; constitution 56n. *composition;* capacity, volume, measure 183n. *space,* 465n. *measurement;* accommodation 183n. *room.*

Adj. *inclusive,* including, comprising, counting, containing, having; holding, consisting of 56adj. *composing;* incorporative, incorporating; non-exclusive, accommodating; overall, all-embracing 52adj. *comprehensive;* wholesale, sweeping, without omission, with no exception, total, global, world-wide, universal 52adj. *whole;* synoptical 79adj. *general;* broad-based, wide 205adj. *broad.*

included, admitted, admissible, eligible; component, constituent, making up 56adj. *composing;* inherent 58adj. *ingredient,* 5adj. *intrinsic;* belonging, pertinent 9adj. *relative;* classified with, of the same class 18adj. *similar;* congenerous, congeneric 11adj. *akin;* entered, recorded, on the list 87adj. *listed;* merged 38adj. *additional,* 45adj. *conjunct;* inner 224adj. *interior.*

Vb. *be included,* be contained, be comprised, make one of 58vb. *be one of;* enlist, enroll oneself, swell the ranks, join, obtain membership 708vb. *join a party;* come under, fall u., range u., range with, merge in 43vb. *be mixed;* appertain to, pertain, refer to 9vb. *be related;* come in, go in, enter into 297vb. *enter;* constitute 56vb. *compose;* overlap, inhere, belong 5vb. *be intrinsic.*

comprise, include, consist of, hold, have, count, boast 56vb. *contain;* take, measure 28vb. *be equal;* receive, take in 299vb. *admit;* accommodate, find room for; comprehend, encapsulate 226vb. *cover;* embody, incorporate; embrace, encircle, ensphere, envelop, embox, encase, ensepulcher; enisle, embower 235vb. *enclose;* have everything, exhaust the possibilities 644vb. *be good;* involve, imply.

number with, count w., reckon among, enumerate in; subsume, place under, classify as; put in, arrange in 62vb. *class;* not omit, take into account.

Adv. *including,* inclusively; from A to Z; et cetera.

See: 5, 9, 11, 18, 28, 38, 43, 45, 52, 56, 58, 62, 79, 87, 183, 205, 224, 226, 235, 297, 299, 465, 644, 694, 708, 765, 775.

79 Generality

N. *generality,* universality, general applicability; catholicity, Catholicism 976n. *orthodoxy;* ecumenicity, ecumenicalism; generalization, the universals; macrocosm 321n. *universe,* 52n. *whole;* panorama, synopsis, conspectus, bird's-eye view 438n. *view;* inclusiveness, comprehensivity, something for everybody, open house, dragnet 78n. *inclusion;* currency, prevalence, custom 610n. *habit,* 848n. *fashion;* pervasiveness, rifeness, ubiquity 189n. *presence;* pandemic, epidemic 651n. *disease;* broadness, looseness, imprecision 495n. *inexactness,* 464n. *indiscrimination;* open letter, circular 528n. *publicity;* commonness, ruck, run, general r., run of the mill 30adj. *average;* ordinariness 732n. *mediocrity;* internationalism, cosmopolitanism 901n. *philanthropy;* impersonality; generification 77n. *classification.*

everyman, everywoman; man in the street, little man; common type 30n. *common man;* everybody, everyone, one and all, all and sundry, every mother's son, every man Jack, all hands 52n. *all;* all the world and his wife, Tom, Dick and Harry, the masses 869n. *commonalty;* all sorts, anyone, whosoever, N or M; whatsoever, what have you, what you will 562n. *no name.*

Adj. *general,* generic, typical, representative, standard; encyclopedic, broad-based; collective, all-embracing, pan-; blanket 52adj. *comprehensive;* broad, sweeping, panoramic, synoptic; current, prevalent 189adj. *ubiquitous;* usual, customary 610adj. *habitual;* vague, loose, indefinite 495adj. *inexact;* undetermined, unspecified, undenominational, unsectarian, impersonal 10adj. *irrelative;* common, ordinary, average 30adj. *median;* popular, mass, vulgar 869adj. *plebeian;* for everybody, multipurpose.

universal, catholic, ecumenical, cosmopolitan, international, global, world-wide, nation-w., state-w., widespread 75adj. *unassembled;* pervasive, penetrating, besetting, prevalent, epidemic, pandemic 189adj. *ubiquitous;* every, each, all, all without exception 52adj. *whole.*

Vb. *be general,* cover all cases 78vb. *comprise;* prevail, obtain, be the rule, have currency 610vb. *be wont;* go about, stalk abroad; penetrate 189vb. *pervade.*

generalize, render general etc. adj.; broaden, widen, universalize; spread, broadcast 75vb. *disperse.*

Adv. *generally,* without exception, universally etc. adj.; mainly 52adv. *wholly;* to a man, to the last m.; always, for better for worse; generally speaking, in the long run, by and large 30adv. *on an average;* loosely, vaguely.
See: 10, 30, 52, 75, 77, 78, 189, 321, 438, 464, 495, 528, 562, 610, 651, 732, 848, 869, 901, 976.

80 Specialty
N. *specialty,* specific quality, specificity, personality, uniqueness; singularity; originality, individuality, particularity; personality, makeup 5n. *character;* characteristic, personal c., recessive c., dominant c.; specialty, idiosyncrasy, peculiarity, distinctive feature, mannerism; trait, mark, feature, attribute; sine qua non 89n. *accompaniment;* distinction, point of difference, personal equation, differentiae 15n. *difference;* idiom, peculiar i.; jargon, patter, brogue, patois 560n. *dialect;* technical language, private l. 557n. *language;* variant reading; version, lection 15n. *variant;* exception, isolated instance, special case 84n. *unconformity;* special skill, special study, specialization 694n. *skill.*
particulars, details, minutiae, items, counts, special points, specification; circumstances; the ins and outs of.
particularism, chosen race, Peculiar People; exclusiveness, class consciousness, caste; nationality, nationalism, individualism, private enterprise.
self, ego, id-ego, identity, selfhood, personality; I, myself, number one; we, ourselves; yourself, himself, herself, itself, themselves; we-group, in-g. 74n. *group;* real self, inner s.; outward s.; the other; the absolute; Atman; a person, a character, individual, being 371n. *person.*
Adj. *special,* specific, respective, particular; sui generis, peculiar, singular, unique; individual, idiosyncratic, idiomatic, original 21adj. *unimitated;* native, proper, personal, private, selfish; appropriate 642adj. *expedient;* typical, diagnostic 5adj. *characteristic;* distinctive, uncommon, marked, noteworthy, out of the ordinary 84adj. *unusual;* several 15adj. *different.*
definite, definitive, defining; determinate, quantified; distinct, concrete, express; clear-cut, clean-c., cut and dried; certain, exact, precise 494adj. *accurate;* itemized, detailed, circumstantial; bespoke, made to order, made to measure.
private, intimate, esoteric, personal, exclusive; patented; extraprofessional; off the record, for one's private ear, secret 523adj. *latent.*
Vb. *specify,* be specific, express in figures, enumerate, quantify 86vb. *number;* particularize, itemize, detail, inventorize 87vb. *list;* descend to particulars, enter into detail 570vb. *be diffuse;* define, determine 236vb. *limit,* 463vb. *discriminate;* pinpoint, locate 187vb. *place;* come to the point, explain 520vb. *interpret;* signify, denote 514vb. *mean;* designate, point out 547vb. *indicate;* realize, translate into fact, substantiate 156vb. *cause;* individualize, personalize 15vb. *differentiate;* specialize 455vb. *be attentive,* 536vb. *study.*
Adv. *specially,* especially, in particular, personally, for one's own part; specifically, ad hominem, to order; with respect to.
severally, each, apiece, one by one; respectively, in turn, seriatim; in detail, bit by bit.
namely, that is to say, videlicet, viz., to wit, i.e., e.g.
See: 5, 15, 21, 74, 84, 86, 87, 89, 156, 187, 236, 371, 455, 463, 494, 514, 520, 523, 536, 547, 557, 560, 570, 642, 694.

81 Rule
N. *rule,* norm, formula, canon, code; maxim, principle 693n. *precept;* law, law of nature; firm principle, hard-and-fast rule, settled law; strict law, law of the Medes and Persians; incongruous law, Procrustean law, subsidiary law, by-law; regulation, order, standing o.; party line; guide, precedent, model, pattern 23n. *prototype;* form, standard, keynote 83n. *example.*
regularity, consistency, constancy 16n. *uniformity;* order, natural o., established o., order of things 60n. *order;* normality, normalcy, normal state, natural condition; form, set f., routine, drill, practice, custom 610n. *habit;* fixed ways, rut, groove, streetcar lines; methodicalness, method, system 62n. *arrangement;* convention, parrotry 83n. *conformity.*
Adj. *regular,* constant, steady 141adj. *periodic;* even 258adj. *smooth;* circular, square 646adj. *perfect;* systematized, standardized 16adj. *uniform;* regulated, according to rule,

methodical, systematic 60adj. *orderly;* regulative, normative; normal, unexceptional 83adj. *typical;* customary 610adj. *usual;* conforming, conventional 83adj. *conformable.*

Adv. *by rule,* by the book, by the clock; regularly.

See: 16, 23, 60, 62, 83, 141, 258, 610, 646, 693.

82 Multiformity

N. *multiformity,* omniformity; heterogeneity, variety, diversity 17n. *nonuniformity;* multifariousness, many-sidedness, many-headedness, polymorphism; polypsychism; schizophrenia, split personality 503n. *psychopathy;* metamorphism, metamorphosis; variability, changeability 152n. *changeableness,* 437n. *variegation;* capriciousness 604n. *caprice;* all-rounder; Proteus, Jekyll and Hyde; kaleidoscope.

Adj. *multiform,* polymorphic; multifold, multifid; multifarious, multigenerous; multiplex, multiplicate, manifold, many-headed, many-sided; omniform, omnigenerous, omnifarious; polygenous, metamorphic; protean, versatile, all-round; variform, heterogeneous, motley, mosaic 17adj. *non-uniform;* epicene; indiscriminate, irregular, diversified, many-colored, polychrome 437adj. *variegated;* divers, sundry; all manner of, of every description, of all sorts and kinds 16adj. *different;* variable, changeable 152adj. *changeful;* whimsical 604adj. *capricious;* polypsychical; schizophrenic.

See: 16, 17, 152, 437, 503, 604.

83 Conformity

N. *conformity,* conformation 24n. *conformance;* faithfulness 768n. *observance;* accommodation, adjustment, reconcilement, reconciliation 24adj. *agreement, adaptation;* self-adaptation, pliancy, malleability 327adj. *softness;* acquiescence 721n. *submission;* assimilation, acclimatization, naturalization 147n. *conversion,* 18n. *similarity;* conventionality 850n. *affectation,* 848n. *etiquette;* traditionalism, orthodoxism, orthodoxness 976n. *orthodoxy;* formalism, strictness 735n. *severity;* convention, form 848n. *fashion,* 610n. *practice;* parrotry, parrot cry 106n. *repetition,* 925n. *flattery,* 20n. *imitation;* ordinariness 79n. *generality.*

example, exemplar, type, pattern, model 23n. *prototype;* exemplification, stock example, crass e., locus classicus; case, case in point, instance, palmary i.; illustration, practical demonstration, object lesson; sample, random s., cross section; representative, specimen, specimen page, representative selection; trailer, foretaste 66n. *precursor;* precedent.

conformist, conformer, conventionalist, traditionalist; philistine, Babbitt; formalist, pedant, precisian; copycat; 20n. *imitator,* 925n. *flatterer;* follower, loyalist, orthodoxist 976n. *the orthodox.*

Adj. *conformable,* adaptable, adjustable, consistent with; malleable, pliant 327adj. *flexible;* agreeable, complaisant, accommodating 24adj. *agreeing;* conforming, following, faithful, loyal, true-blue 768adj. *observant;* conventional, traditional 976adj. *orthodox;* slavish, servile 20adj. *imitative,* 925adj. *flattering;* adjusted, adapted, acclimatized 610adj. *habituated;* absorbed, digested, assimilated, naturalized 78adj. *included.*

typical, normal, natural, of daily occurrence, everyday, ordinary, common, common or garden; average 30adj. *median,* 732adj. *mediocre;* true to type; commonplace, prosaic; conventional; habitual 610adj. *usual;* representative, stock, standard; normative, exemplary, illustrative; in point 9adj. *relevant.*

regular, regulated, according to the book, according to rule, technical, shipshape, copybook; correct, sound, proper, canonical 976adj. *orthodox;* precise, scrupulous, point-device 875adj. *formal;* rigid, strict, unbending, uncompromising, Procrustean 735adj. *severe.*

Vb. *conform,* correspond, conform to 24vb. *agree;* trim, rub off the corners, adapt oneself, accommodate o., adjust o., mold o.; fit in, know one's place; pass, pass muster, pass current 635vb. *suffice;* bend, yield, take the shape of 327vb. *soften;* fall into line, toe the l., fall in with 721vb. *submit;* comply with 768vb. *observe;* tally with, chime in with 24vb. *accord;* rubberstamp, say ditto, echo 106vb. *repeat;* take dictation 30vb. *copy;* stick to rule, obey regulations, follow precedent 739vb. *obey;* keep in step, follow the fashion, follow the crowd, do as others do, do as the Romans do; join in the cry, join the majority, jump on the band wagon, emulate; have no will of one's own, drift with the tide, swim with the stream 601vb. *be irresolute;* follow in the steps of, keep to the beaten track, run on streetcar lines, run in a groove, stick in a rut 610vb. *be wont;* support, keep one in countenance 701vb. *patronize,* 925vb. *flatter.*

make conform, conform, assimilate, naturalize 18vb. *liken;* acclimatize 610vb. *habituate;* bring under rule, systematize 62vb. *regularize;* normalize, conventionalize, standardize; put in uniform, dress, drill 16vb. *make uniform;* shape, form, press 243vb. *efform;* stamp, imprint 547vb. *mark;* train, lead 689vb. *direct;* bend, twist, force 740vb. *compel;* accommodate, fit, fit in, square, trim 24vb. *adjust;* rub off the corners 258vb. *smooth.*

exemplify, illustrate, cite, quote, instance; produce an example, give an instance.

Adv. *conformably* etc. adj.; by rule; by the card; agreeably to, in conformity, in line with, in accordance, in keeping with; according to; according to plan; consistently with; as usual, of course, as a matter of c.; for form's sake; for the look of it; for example, for instance.

See: 9, 18, 20, 23, 24, 30, 78, 79, 106, 147, 243, 258, 327, 547, 601, 610, 635, 689, 701, 721, 732, 735, 739, 740, 768, 848, 850, 864, 875, 925, 976.

84 Unconformity

N. *unconformity,* disconformity, inconsistency 25n. *disagreement,* 17adj. *non-uniformity;* contrast, oasis 14n. *contrariety;* exceptionality, strangeness 59n. *extraneousness;* nonconformity, nonconformism, unorthodoxy 977n. *heterodoxy;* dissidence 489n. *dissent,* 769n. *non-observance;* deviationism, Titoism 744n. *independence;* anomalousness, eccentricity, irregularity 282n. *deviation;* informality, unconventionality, angularity, awkwardness 893n. *sullenness;* bizarreness, piquancy, freakishness, oddity; rarity 140n. *infrequency;* infringement, infraction, infraction of rule, violation of law 954n. *illegality;* breach of practice, defiance of custom, departure from usage; replacement 188n. *displacement,* 63n. *derangement;* anomaly, ectopia; monstrosity, wonder, miracle 864n. *prodigy;* exception 57n. *exclusion;* exemption, salvo, saving clause 919n. *non-liability;* special case, isolated instance 80n. *specialty;* individuality, idiosyncrasy, peculiarity, singularity, mannerism; originality, uniqueness 21n. *non-imitation.*

abnormality, aberration 282n. *deviation;* abortion, miscreation, monstrous birth, terata, teratogenesis, monstrosity, monster; sexual abnormality, homosexualism, lesbianism; nymphomania, andromania, necrophilia, sadism, masochism; transvestism; virilism, viraginity, gynandry 372n. *male;* androgyny 373n. *female;* hermaphroditism 161n. *impotence.*

nonconformist, dissident, dissenter 489n. *dissentient,* 977n. *heretic;* sectarian 978n. *sectarist;* deviationist, Titoist 603n. *tergiversator;* non-striker, blackleg, scab 938n. *cad;* unconventionalist, Bohemian; rebel, angry young man; handful, recalcitrant 738n. *revolter;* fanatic 504n. *crank;* outsider, outlaw, criminal 904n. *offender;* pariah 883n. *outcaste;* hermit 883n. *solitary;* gypsy, nomad, tramp 268n. *wanderer;* odd man out, joker, ugly duckling; square peg in a round hole, fish out of water 25n. *misfit;* odd type, black swan, sport, freak, variety, lusus naturae; oddity, original, character, card, queer fish 851n. *laughing stock;* curiosity, rarity, rare example, one in a million; neither fish, flesh, fowl nor good red herring, neither one thing nor the other; hermaphrodite, gynander, androgyn 161n. *eunuch;* homosexual, lesbian, pansy, fairy, queer, pervert; sadist, masochist; mongrel, half-breed, cross-breed, half-blood, mulatto, mestizo, métis; mule 43n. *hybrid.*

rara avis, mythical beast, unicorn, phoenix, griffin, simurgh, wyvern, roc, liver; sphinx, hippogriff, manticore, chimera, centaur, sagittary; minotaur, dragon, hydra; cockatrice, basilisk, salamander; kraken, sea serpent, Loch Ness monster, sea horse, hippocampus; Cerberus, Gorgon, Snark; Cyclops; merman, mermaid, siren, Lorelei.

Adj. *unconformable,* inadjustable 25adj. *unapt;* contrarious, antipathetic 14 adj. *contrary;* unmalleable, stiff 326adj. *rigid,* 602adj. *obstinate;* recalcitrant 711adj. *defiant;* crotchety, prickly, awkward, all edges 604adj. *capricious,* 893adj. *sullen;* arbitrary, a law to oneself 744adj. *independent;* freakish, egregious; original, sui generis, unique, 80adj. *special;* not joining, keeping out, standing o., staying o.; blacklegging 603adj. *tergiversating;* nonconformist, dissident 489adj. *dissenting,* 978adj. *sectarian;* unorthodox, heretical 977adj. *heterodox;* unconverted, non-practicing 769adj. *non-observant;* uncon entional, bohemian, informal, unfashionable; irregular, against the rules, off-side, not done 924adj. *disapproved;* infringing, lawless, criminal 954adj. *illegal;* aberrant, astray, off the beam, off the rails 282adj. *deviating;* misplaced, out of one's element, out of place, ectopic, out of order 188adj. *displaced,* 61adj. *orderless;* incongruous, out of step, out of line, out of tune, out of keeping 25adj. *disagreeing,* 411adj. *discordant;* alien, exotic 59adj. *extraneous;* unidentifiable, unclassifiable, hard to place, nondescript, nameless 491adj. *unknown;* eremetical, solitary, exclusive 883adj. *unsociable;* stray, nomadic, wandering 267adj. *traveling;* amphibious, ambiguous 518adj. *equivocal;* exempted, exempt 919adj. *nonliable.*

unusual, uncustomary, unwonted 611adj. *unaccustomed;* unfamiliar 491adj. *unknown;* new-fangled 126adj. *new;* out of the way, outlandish 59adj. *extraneous;* extraordinary, phenomenal, supernormal; unparalleled, unexampled; singular, unique 80adj. *special,* 140adj. *infrequent;* rare, choice, recherché 644adj. *excellent;* strange, bizarre, curious, odd, queer, rum, rummy; funny, peculiar, fantastic, grotesque 849adj. *ridiculous;* noteworthy, remarkable, surprising, astonishing, miraculous, teratical 864adj. *wonderful;* mysterious, inexplicable, unaccountable 523adj. *occult;* unimaginable, incredible 470adj. *impossible,* 472adj. *improbable;* monstrous, unnatural, preternatural, supernatural; outsize 32adj. *enormous;* outré 546adj. *exaggerated;* shocking, scandalizing 924adj. *disapproved;* unmentionable, indescribable, left undescribed 517adj. *inexpressible.*

abnormal, unnatural, supernatural, preternatural (**see** *unusual*); aberrant, freakish; untypical, atypical, unrepresentative, exceptional; eccentric, anomalous, anomalistic 17adj. *non-uniform;* homosexual, lesbian, queer; epicene, androgynous, gynandrous; mongrel, hybrid 43adj. *mixed;* irregular, heteroclite; unidiomatic, solecistic 565adj. *ungrammatical;* non-standard, substandard, subnormal; supernormal 32adj. *great;* ridiculous 497adj. *absurd;* asymmetrical, deformed, amorphous, shapeless 246adj. *distorted.*

Vb. *be unconformable,* have no business there; infringe a law, infringe a habit, infringe usage, infringe custom; break a law, break a habit, break a usage, break custom; violate a law, violate habit, violate usage, violate custom; put the clock back 117vb. *time;* get round, drive a coach and six through; stretch a point; leave the beaten track, baffle all description, beggar all d.

Adv. *unconformably* etc. adj.; except, unless, save, barring, beside, without, save and except, let alone; however, yet, but.

See: 14, 17, 21, 25, 32, 43, 59, 61, 80, 117, 126, 140, 161, 188, 246, 267, 282, 326, 372, 373, 411, 470, 472, 489, 491, 497, 518, 523, 546, 565, 602, 603, 604, 611, 644, 711, 744, 769, 849, 851, 864, 872, 883, 893, 919, 924, 954, 977, 978.

85 Number

N. *number,* any n., numeric; cardinal number, ordinal n.; round n., indefinite numeral; prime number, odd n., even n., whole n., integer; figurative numbers, pyramidal n., polygonal n.; numeral, numeral adjective; cipher, digit, figure, recurring f., repetend; numerals, Arabic n., Roman n., algorithm; quantity, unknown q., X, symbol; function, variable; surd; expression, algebraism; formula, series.

numerical element, subtrahend; totitive, totient; multiplicand, multiplier, multiplicator; coefficient, multiple, dividend, divisor, aliquant, aliquot part, quotient, factor, submultiple, fraction, proper f., improper f.; mixed number; numerator, denominator; decimal system, decimal, circulating d., recurring d., repetend; common measure, common factor, common denominator; reciprocal, complement; power, root, square r., cube r.; exponent, index, logarithm, antilogarithm; modulus, differential, integral, fluxion, fluent; operator, sign.

ratio, proportion; progression, arithmetic progression, geometric p., harmonic p.; trigonometric ratio, sine, tangent, secant; cosine, cotangent, cosecant; percentage, per cent, per mil, per hour.

numerical result, answer, product, equation; sum, total, aggregate 52n. *whole;* difference, residual 41n. *re-*

mainder; bill, score, tally 38n. *addition.*

Adj. *numerical,* numerary, numeral; arithmetical; cardinal, ordinal; round, whole; even, odd; prime; figurate; positive, negative, surd, radical; divisible, aliquot; multiple; reciprocal, complementary; fractional, decimal; incommensurable; commensurable, proportional; exponential, logarithmic, logometric, differential, fluxional, integral, rational, irrational; real, imaginary.

See: 38, 41, 52.

86 Numeration

N. *numeration,* numbering, enumeration, census, recension, counting, ciphering, figuring, reckoning, dead r.; sum, tale, tally, score, break, runs, points; count, recount; figure-work, summation, calculation, supputation, computation 465n. *measurement;* page-numbering, pagination; algorithm, algorism, decimal system; counting on the fingers, dactylonomy; money-counting, accountancy 808n. *accounts;* counting heads, poll, capitulation; head-count, hand-c.; counting again, recapitulation.

mathematics, arithmetic, algebra, fluxions; differential calculus, integral c., infinitesimal c.; calculus of differences; geometry, trigonometry; graphs, logarithms; rhabdology; Napier's bones.

numerical operation, figure-work, notation; addition, subtraction, multiplication, division, proportion, rule of three, practice, equations, analysis, ancient a., modern a., extraction of roots, reduction, involution, evolution, approximation, interpolation; differentiation, integration, permutation, combination, variation.

statistics, figures, tables, averages; statistical inquiry, poll, Gallup p. 605n. *vote;* census, capitation; roll call, muster, muster-roll, account 87n. *list;* demography, birth rate, death r., vital statistics; price index, cost of living 809n. *price.*

counting instrument, abacus, swanpan, quipu; ready reckoner, multiplication table; logometer, scale measure, tape-m., yardstick 465n. *gauge;* sliding rule, slide r.; tallies, counters, Napier's bones; comptometer, calculating machine, adding m., computing m.; difference engine; cash register, totalizator, tote, calculator; electronic computer, Ernie.

computer, numberer, enumerator, census-taker; abacist; calculator, counter, teller, pollster; mathematician, wrangler; arithmetician, geometrician, algebraist; statistician, statist, bookkeeper 808n. *accountant;* actuary, geometer, geodesist 465n. *surveyor.*

Adj. *numerable,* numberable, countable; calculable, computable, measurable, mensurable 465adj. *metric;* commensurable, commensurate 28 adj. *equal;* proportionable 9adj. *relative;* incommensurable, incommensurate 29adj. *unequal,* 10adj. *irrelative;* eligible, admissible 78adj. *included.*

statistical, expressed in numbers, ciphered, numbered, figured out; mathematical, arithmetic, algebraic; geometric, trigonometric; in ratio, in proportion, percentile.

Vb. *number,* cast, count, tell; score, keep the s., keep the count; tell off, tick off; affix numbers, foliate, paginate; enumerate, census, poll, count heads, count hands, count noses; take the number, take a poll, take a census; muster, call over, call the roll, take roll-call; take stock, inventorize 87vb. *list;* recount, recapitulate, recite, go over 106vb. *repeat;* check, audit, balance, book-keep, keep accounts 808vb. *account;* aggregate, amount to, total, tot up to, come to.

do sums, cast up, carry over, totalize, tot up 38vb. *add;* take away 39vb. *subtract;* multiply 36vb. *augment;* divide 46vb. *sunder;* algebraize, geometrize, square, cube, extract roots; figure, cipher; work out, reduce; compute, calculate, reckon, reckon up 465vb. *measure;* estimate 465vb. *appraise.*

See: 9, 10, 28, 29, 36, 38, 39, 46, 78, 87, 106, 465, 605, 808, 809.

87 List

N. *list,* enumeration, items; list of items, inventory, stock list; table, catalog; portfolio 767n. *security;* statement, tabular s., schedule, manifest, bill of lading; check-list; invoice; numerical list, score; price-list, tariff, bill, account, itemized a. 809n. *price;* registry, cartulary; cadastre, terrier, Domesday Book; file, register, death r., birth r. 548n. *record;* ticket, docket, tally 547n. *label;* ledger, books 808n. *account book;* table of contents, bill of fare, menu, diet-sheet 301n. *eating;* playbill, program, prospectus 759n. *of-*

fer; synopsis, syllabus 592n. *compendium;* roll, electoral r., voting list 605n. *electorate;* muster-roll, check-r., payroll; civil list, army l., navy l., active l., retired l. 686n. *personnel;* statistical list, census l., returns 86n. *numeration;* book-list, reading list, library l. 589n. *reading matter;* bibliography, publisher's catalog, catalogue raisonné 524n. *guide-book;* list of names, rota, roster, panel; waiting list, short l.; string of names, visitors' book; dramatis personae, characters in the play; family tree, pedigree 169n. *genealogy;* scroll, roll of honor, honors' board, martyrology, bead-roll, diptych; black list 928n. *accused person,* 924n. *censure;* sick list 651n. *sick person;* date-list, calendar, engagement book 505n. *reminder;* question-list, questionnaire; alphabetical list, alphabet 60n. *order,* 558n. *letter;* repertory, repertoire.

word list, vocabulary, glossary, lexicon, thesaurus, gradus 559n. *dictionary.*

directory, gazetteer, atlas; almanac, calendar, timetable 117n. *chronology;* army list, navy l., Crockford, Burke's Peerage 524n. *guide-book;* index, card i., thumb i. 547n. *indication.*

Adj. *listed* etc. vb.; entered, cataloged, tabulated, indexed; cadastral.

Vb. *list,* make a l., enumerate; itemize, inventory, catalog, calendar, index, tabulate; file, docket, schedule, enter, book, post 548vb. *register;* enlist, matriculate, enroll, impanel, inscribe; score, keep s., keep count 86vb. *number.*

See: 60, 86, 117, 169, 301, 505, 524, 547, 548, 558, 559, 589, 592, 605, 651, 686, 759, 767, 808, 809, 924, 928.

88 Unity

N. *unity,* oneness, absoluteness 44n. *simpleness;* integrality, integration, wholeness 52n. *whole;* uniqueness, singularity, individuality 80n. *specialty;* univocity 514n. *meaning;* singleness, single state 895n. *celibacy;* isolation, solitude, loneliness 883n. *seclusion;* isolability 46n. *separation;* union, undividedness, indivisibility, solidarity 324n. *density,* 706n. *association,* unification 50n. *combination.*

unit, integer, one, ace, item, piece; individual, point, atom, monad, entity, a being, a person 371n. *person;* single piece, monolith; singleton, monotype, nonce-word; none else, no other, naught beside; single instance, isolated i., only exception; sole survivor 41n. *survivor;* solo, solo performance; single person, bachelor 895n. *celibate;* hermit 883n. *solitary;* monocle; set, outfit, package 58n. *component;* package deal.

Adj. *one,* not plural, singular, sole, single; unique, only, lone, one and only; unrepeated, only-begotten; without a second, first and last; a, an, a certain 562adj. *anonymous;* individual 80adj. *special;* absolute, universal 79adj. *general;* unitary, unific, univocal, unicameral, unilateral; mono-; monocular; monotonous, monolithic 16adj. *uniform;* unified, rolled into one, compact, solid 45adj. *conjunct,* 324n. *dense,* 48adj. *cohesive;* indivisible, insecable, inseverable, indiscerptible, indissoluble, irresolvable.

alone, lonely, homeless, rootless, orphaned, kithless 883adj. *friendless;* lonesome, solitary, lone, eremetical 883adj. *unsociable;* isolable, isolated 46adj. *disjunct;* insular, enisled 199adj. *removed;* single-handed, on one's own; unaccompanied, unescorted, unchaperoned; unpaired, fellowless, azygous; monadic, monatomic; celibate, bachelor 895adj. *unwedded.*

Vb. *be one,* stand alone, stew in one's own juice; unite 50vb. *combine;* isolate 46vb. *set apart.*

Adv. *singly,* one by one, one at a time; once, once only, for the nonce, for this time only, never again, only, solely, simply; alone, on one's own, by oneself, per se; in the singular.

See: 41, 44, 45, 46, 50, 52, 58, 79, 80, 199, 324, 371, 514, 562, 706, 883, 895.

89 Accompaniment

N. *accompaniment,* concomitance, togetherness 71n. *continuity,* 45n. *junction,* 5n. *intrinsicality;* inseparability, sine qua non, permanent attribute; society, associating with, companionship, partnership, consortship, association 706n. *cooperation;* operating with, coefficience, coagency 181n. *concurrence;* coincidence, contemporaneity, simultaneity 123n. *synchronism;* bearing company, fellow-travelling, escort, company, attendance; parallel course 219n. *parallelism;* life with, coexistence.

concomitant, attribute, sine qua non 5n. *essential part;* coefficient, accessory, appendage, appurtenance, fixture 40adj. *adjunct;* epiphenomenon, symptom 547n. *indication*; coincidence 159n. *chance;* context, circumstance 7n. *state;* background, noises off; accompaniment, musical a., obbligato; accompanist 413n. *musician;* entourage, court 742n. *retainer;* attendant, following, suite, cortege, train, tail 67n. *retinue;* rout 71n. *procession;* convoy, escort, guide, cicerone 690n. *leader;* chaperon, squire 660n. *protector,* 749n. *keeper;* cavalier, wooer 887n. *lover;* tracker, dogger 619n. *hunter;* inseparable, shadow, Mary's little lamb 284n. *follower;* consort 894n. *spouse;* comrade, companion, boon c. 880n. *friend;* stable, companion, yoke-fellow, mate, coworker, partner, associate 707n. *colleague;* fellow-traveler 707n. *collaborator;* twin, fellow, pair 18n. *analogue;* satellite, parasite, hanger-on, client, stooge 742n. *dependent;* waiter 742n. *servant;* embroidery, decoration 844n. *ornamentation;* fringe 234n. *edging.*

Adj. *accompanying,* with, concomitant, attendant, background; always with, inseparable, built-in 45adj. *conjunct;* partnering, associated, coupled, paired; hand-in-glove 706adj. *cooperative,* 181n. *concurrent;* obbligato 410adj. *harmonious;* accessory, belonging 78adj. *included,* 58adj. *ingredient;* satellite, satellitic 745adj. *subject;* epiphenomenal, symptomatic 547adj. *indicating;* incidental, coincidental 159adj. *casual;* coexistent, contemporaneous, contemporary, simultaneous.

Vb. *accompany,* be found with, be seen w.; coexist, have a life with; cohabit, live with, stable w., walk w., keep company w., consort w., walk out w.; string along with, row in the same boat; attend, wait on, come to heel, dance attendance on 284vb. *follow;* bear one company, squire, chaperon, protect, keep 660vb. *safeguard;* convoy, escort, guide, conduct, lead, usher 64vb. *come before;* track, dog, shadow 619vb. *pursue;* associate, partner 706vb. *cooperate;* gang up with, chum up w. 880vb. *befriend;* coincide, keep time with 123vb. *synchronize,* 181vb. *concur;* imply 5vb. *be intrinsic;* carry with, bring in its train 156vb. *cause;* be inseparable, follow as night follows day 157vb. *depend;* belong, go with, go together 9vb. *be related.*

Adv. *with,* withal; therewith, herewith 38adv. *in addition;* with others, together with, along w., in company w.; in convoy, hand in hand, arm in arm, side by side; cheek by jowl; jointly, all together, in a body, collectively, inseparably, unitedly.

See: 5, 7, 9, 18, 40, 45, 58, 64, 67, 71, 78, 123, 156, 157, 159, 181, 219, 234, 284, 410, 413, 547, 619, 660, 690, 706, 707, 742, 745, 749, 844, 880, 887, 894.

90 Duality

N. *duality,* dualism; two times, twice; double-sidedness; duplicity; biformity, polarity; dyad, two, deuce, twain, couple, brace, pair, fellows; cheeks, jaws; doublets, twins, Castor and Pollux, Gemini, Siamese twins, identical t., Tweedledum and Tweedledee; yoke, span, conjugation, couplet, distich; double harness, twosome; duel, duet, tandem, bireme, two-seater; Janus; biped; dyarchy.

Adj. *dual,* dualistic; dyadic, binary, binomial; bilateral, bicameral; twin, biparous; conduplicate, duplex 91adj. *double;* paired, coupled etc. vb.; conjugate, both the one and the other; in twos, both; tête-à-tête; double-sided, bipartisan; amphibious; ambidextrous 91adj. *double;* biform, bifront, bifrontal, two-faced; dihedral; di-, bi-.

Vb. *pair,* unite in pairs, couple, match, bracket, yoke; conduplicate, mate; pair off.

See: 91.

91 Duplication

N. *duplication;* doubling 261n. *fold;* gemination, ingemination; reduplication, encore, repeat, repeat performance; iteration, echo 106n. *repetition;* renewal 656n. *restoration;* copy, carbon c., stencil 22n. *duplicate;* repeater.

Adj. *double,* doubled, twice; duplex, bifarious; bicapital, bifold, biform, bivalent; twofold, two-sided, two-headed, two-edged; bifacial, bifrontal, bifronted, double-faced; amphibious, ambidextrous; double-sided; of double meaning 518adj. *equivocal;* of double sex, hermaphrodite; twin, duplicate, ingeminate; second; dual 90adj. *dual.*

Vb. *double,* multiply by two; redouble, square; ingeminate, encore, echo, second 106vb. *repeat;* renew 656vb. *restore;* duplicate, twin; reduplicate, stencil 22vb. *copy.*

Adv. *twice,* once more; over again

106adv. *again;* once and again, as much again, twofold; secondly, in the second place, again; twice as much.

See: 22, 90, 106, 261, 518, 656.

92 Bisection

N. *bisection,* bipartition, dichotomy, subdichotomy; dividing by two, halving etc. vb.; dimidiation; hendiadys; half, moiety, fifty per cent 53n. *part;* hemisphere 252n. *sphere.*

bifurcation, forking, branching, furcation, ramification, divarication 294n. *divergence;* fork, prong 222n. *cross.*

dividing line, diameter, diagonal, equator; parting, suture, seam; dateline; party-wall 231n. *partition.*

Adj. *bisected,* halved etc. vb.; dimidiate, bifid, bipartite, biconjugate, bicuspid; bifurcous, bifurcate, bifurcated; dichotomic, dichotomous; semi-, demi-, hemi-; cloven, cleft 46adj. *disjunct.*

Vb. *bisect,* transect; divide, split, cleave 46vb. *sunder;* cut in two, dimidiate, dichotomize, share, go halves, divide with, go fifty-fifty 783vb. *apportion;* halve, divide by two.

bifurcate, separate, fork; branch off, branch out, ramify, divaricate 294vb. *diverge.*

See: 46, 53, 222, 231, 252, 294, 783.

93 Triality

N. *triality,* trinity, Trimurti; triunity; triplicity 94n. *triplication.*

three, triad, trine; threesome, triumvirate, leash; troika; triplet, trey, trio, ternion, trinomial; trimester, triennium; trefoil, shamrock, triangle, trident, tripod; tricorn, triphthong, triptych, trilogy, trireme, triobol; third power, cube; third person; tertium quid.

Adj. *three,* trinal, triform, trinomial; tertiary, trimetric; three in one, triune, tripartite; three-dimensional, tridimensional; three-sided, triangular, trilateral, leg-of-mutton; three-pointed, trinacrian; three-monthly, trimestrail, quarterly; tri-.

Adv. *in threes,* three by three; three times thrice.

See: 94.

94 Triplication

N. *triplication,* triplicity; trebleness; hat-trick.

Adj. *treble,* triple; trine, tern, ternary; triplex, triplicate, threefold, trilogistic; third, trinal; trihedral; trilateral.

Vb. *treble,* triple, triplicate, cube.

Adv. *trebly,* triply, threefold; three times, thrice; twice and again; in the third place, thirdly.

95 Trisection

N. *trisection,* tripartition, trichotomy; third, third part; tierce.

Adj. *trifid,* trisected; tripartite, trichotomous, trisulcate; tierce, tierced.

Vb. *trisect,* divide into three parts, divide by three; trifurcate.

96 Quaternity

N. *quaternity,* four, tetrad, tetractys; square, tetragon, quadrilateral, quadrangle, quad; quadrature, quarter; tetrastich, tetrapod, tetrameter; tetragrammaton; tetramorph; quaternion, quartet, foursome; four-in-hand, quadriga; quatrefoil; quadruplet, quad; quadruped; quadrennium; quadrilateral; four corners of 52n. *whole.*

Adj. *four,* quaternary, quaternal; quartite; quartic, tetractic, quadratic; quadrate, square, quadrilateral, tetrahedral, four-square; quadrennial, quadrivalent; quadrilateral; quadri-.

See: 52.

97 Quadruplication

N. *quadruplication,* quadruplicity; squaring.

Adj. *fourfold,* quadruplicate, quadruplex; squared; quadrable.

Vb. *quadruple,* quadruplicate, multiply by four; square, biquadrate; quadruplex.

Adv. *four times;* fourthly, in the fourth place.

98 Quadrisection

N. *quadrisection,* quadripartition; quartering etc. vb.; fourth, fourth part; quart, quarter, quartern; farthing, quarto.

Adj. *quartered;* quadrifid, quadripartite.

Vb. *quadrisect,* quarter, divide into four parts, divide by four.

99 Five and over

N. *five and over;* five, cinque, quint, quintuplet; pentad, fiver; quincunx; pentagon; pentameter; Pentateuch,

pentacle; pentapolis; pentarchy.
over five, six, half-a-dozen, sextet, hexad, sixer; hexagon; Hexateuch; hexameter; seven, heptad, week, week of Sundays, sabbatical year; septennium; heptarchy; eight, octave, octet, octad; octagon; nine, three times three; ennead; novena; ten, tenner, decade, decad; tetractys; decury, decemvirate; eleven, hendecasyllable; twelve, dozen; thirteen, baker's dozen, long d.; twenty, a score; double figures.
over twenty, four and twenty, two dozen; twenty-five, pony; forty; two score; fifty, half a hundred, jubilee; sixty, three score; sexagenarian; seventy, three score and ten, septuagenarian; eighty, four score, octogenarian; ninety, nonagenarian.
hundred, century, centenary; hecatomb; hundredweight; centurion; centenarian; centipede; the hundred days; hundred per cent; treble figures.
over one hundred, a gross; thousand, chiliad, grand; millennium; ten thousand, myriad; hundred thousand, plum, lakh; million; ten million, crore, hundred lakhs; thousand million, milliard; billion; million million; trillion, quadrillion, centillion, multimillion; millionaire, billionaire, milliardaire.
Adj. *fifth and over,* five, quinary, quintuple; fifth; senary, sextuple; sixth; seventh; octuple; eighth; ninefold, ninth; tenfold, decimal, denary, decuple, tenth; eleventh; twelfth; duodenary, duodenal; in one's teens; vigesimal, twentieth; centesimal, centuple, centuplicate, centennial, centenary, centenarian, centurial; secular, hundredth; thousandth, millenary; millionth, billionth.
Vb. *centuriate,* centesimate.

100 Multisection
N. *multisection,* quinquesection, decimation, centesimation.
Adj. *multifid,* quinquefid, quinquepartite; quinquarticular; octifid; decimal, tenth, tithe, teind; duodecimal, twelfth; sexagesimal, sexagenary; hundredth, centesimal; millesimal.
Vb. *multisect,* decimate, quinquesect.

101 Plurality
N. *plurality,* the plural; multiplicity, many-sidedness 104n. *multitude;* a number, a certain number; some, one or two, two or three; a few, several; majority 104n. *greater number.*
Adj. *plural,* in the p., not singular; composite, multiple, many-sided; more than one, some, certain; not alone, accompanied, in company 45adj. *conjunct;* upwards of, more, in the majority 104adj. *many.*
Adv. *et cetera.*
See: 45, 104.

102 Fraction: less than one
N. *fraction,* fractional part, fragment 53n. *part,* 783n. *portion;* shred 33n. *small quantity.*
Adj. *fractional,* portional, partial 53adj. *fragmentary,* 33adj. *small.*
See: 33, 53, 783.

103 Zero
N. *zero,* nil, nothing, simply n., next to nothing, infinitely little; naught, nought, nix; no score, love, duck's egg, duck; blank; figure naught, cipher; nullity, nothingness 2n. *non-existence,* 4n. *insubstantiality;* none, nobody, not a soul 190n. *absence;* zero level, nadir.
Adj. *not one,* not any, null, zero; invisible, infinitely little, null 4adj. *insubstantial,* 2adj. *non-existent.*
Adv. *at zero,* from scratch.
See: 2, 4, 190.

104 Multitude
N. *multitude,* numerousness, numerosity, multiplicity; large number, round n., enormous n., multimillion 99n. *over one hundred;* a quantity, clutter, hantle, lots, loads, heaps 32n. *great quantity;* numbers, scores, myriads, millions, lakhs, crores; a sea of, a world of, a sight of; host, array, squadrons, legion, phalanx, battalions 722n. *army;* throng, mob, rout, all the world and his wife 74n. *crowd;* tribe, horde.
certain quantity, peck, bushel, pinch; galaxy, bevy, cloud, flock, flight, covey; shoal, school; flock, herd, drove; swarm, hive, ant-heap, colony 74n. *group;* nest, clutch, litter, farrow, fry 132n. *youngling.*
greater number, weight of numbers, majority, great m., mass, bulk, mainstream 32n. *main part;* multiplication, multiple 101n. *plurality.*
Adj. *many,* several, sundry, divers, various, a thousand and one; quite a few, not a f., considerable, numerous, very many, ever so m., many more; untold, unnumbered, un-

counted 107adj. *infinite;* multinomial; many-headed 82adj. *multiform;* ever-recurring 139adj. *frequent,* 106 adj. *repeated;* much, ample, multiple, multiplied; profuse, in profusion, abundant, superabundant, generous, lavish, overflowing, galore 635adj. *plenteous,* 32adj. *great.*
multitudinous, massed, crowded, thronged, studded with 54adj. *full;* populous, peopled, populated, overp. 324adj. *dense;* multiferous, teeming, crawling, humming, alive with 171adj. *prolific;* thick, thick on the ground, thick as hops, thick as hail; coming thick and fast 139adj. *frequent;* incalculable, innumerable, inexhaustible, countless, endless 107adj. *infinite;* countless as the stars, countless as the sands; as the hairs on one's head; heaven knows how many.
Vb. *be many,*—various etc. adj.; swarm with, crawl w., hum w., bristle w., teem w. 54vb. *fill;* pullulate, multiply 171vb. *be fruitful;* clutter, crowd, throng, swarm, mass, flock, troop 74vb. *congregate;* swarm like ants, swarm like locusts; flood, overflow; swamp, overwhelm 341vb. *drench;* infest, overrun, irrupt 297vb. *infiltrate;* add to the number, swell the ranks 36vb. *augment;* overweigh, outnumber, make a majority 32vb. *be great.*
See: 32, 36, 54, 74, 99, 101, 106, 107, 132, 139, 171, 297, 324, 341, 635, 722.

105 Fewness

N. *fewness,* paucity, underpopulation; exiguity, thinness, sparsity, sparseness, rarity 140n. *infrequency;* stringency 636n. *scarcity;* a few, a handful, maniple; thin house, sparse population; small number, trickle, mere t. 33n. *small quantity;* limited number, too few, no quorum; minority, one or two, two or three, half a dozen, not enough to matter; remnant, sole survivor 41n. *remainder.*
Adj. *few,* weak in numbers, scant, scanty 636adj. *scarce;* thin, thin on the ground, sparse, rare, scattered, few and far between 140adj. *infrequent;* soon counted, to be counted on one's fingers; fewer, reduced, diminished in number, losing n. 37adj. *decreasing;* too few, in a minority, without a quorum.
Vb. *be few,* be weak in numbers, be underpopulated; seldom occur.
render few, reduce, diminish, pare 198vb. *make smaller;* scale down, decimate, thin the ranks; eliminate, weed, thin, sort out 300vb. *eject;* defect, desert; underman, understaff.
Adv. *here and there,* in dribs and drabs, in a trickle; sparsely, rarely, infrequently.
See: 33, 37, 41, 140, 198, 300, 636.

106 Repetition

N. *repetition,* doing again, iteration, reiteration; doubling, ditto, reduplication 20n. *imitation,* 91n. *duplication;* going over, recital, recapitulation; practicing, rehearsal 610n. *practice;* beginning again, renewal, resumption, reprise 68n. *beginning;* saying again, palilogy, anadiplosis, anaphora 566n. *style,* 574n. *ornament;* harping, tautology, tautophony 570n. *diffuseness;* stammering, battology 580n. *speech defect;* a repetition, repeat, repeat performance, encore; replay, return match, revenge; chorus, chant, song, refrain, burden, ritornello, ritornel 412n. *vocal music;* echo, repercussion, reverberation, chime 404n. *resonance;* cliché, quotation, citation, plagiarism; sound-echo, alliteration, assonance, rhyme (**see** *recurrence*); twice-told tale, old story, chestnut 838n. *tedium;* parrot-cry; phonograph record; rehandling, restatement, new edition, reprint, new impression, reissue 589n. *edition;* rifacimento, réchauffé, rehash 656n. *restoration;* repeater, cuckoo, parrot; creature of habit.
recurrence, repetitiveness 139n. *frequency;* cycle, round, rebirth, reincarnation 141n. *regular return;* succession, run, series, serial 71n. *continuity;* recurring decimal, repetend; throw-back, atavism 5n. *heredity;* reappearance, curtain call, curtain; return 295n. *arrival;* rhythm, drumming, hammering 141n. *periodicity;* alliteration, assonance, rhyme 18n. *assimilation* 593n. *prosody;* stale repetition, monotony, ding-dong 16n. *uniformity,* 838n. *tedium;* same old round, mixture as before, busman's holiday, routine 610n. *habit.*
Adj. *repeated,* repetitional, repetitionary; repeatable, quotable 950adj. *pure;* recurrent, recurring, ever-r. 141adj. *periodic;* haunting 505adj. *remembered;* tautological, repetitive, repetitious, harping, iterative; stale, cliché-ridden 572adj. *feeble;* echoing, rhyming, chiming, alliterative, assonant 18adj. *similar;* monotonous, sing-song, ding-dong 16adj. *un-*

iform, 838adj. *tedious;* rhythmic, drumming, hammering; incessant, habitual 139adj. *frequent;* retold, twice-told, said before, quoted, cited; above-mentioned, aforesaid 66adj. *precursory;* plagiarized 20adj. *imitative.*

Vb. *repeat,* do again, iterate, cut and come again; duplicate, reduplicate, redouble 91vb. *double;* multiply 166vb. *reproduce;* reiterate, ingeminate, say again, recapitulate, go over; retell, restate, reword, rephrase; always say, trot out; say one's piece, recite, say over, say after; echo, ditto, parrot, plagiarize 20vb. *copy,* 925vb. *flatter;* quote, cite 505vb. *remember;* go over the same ground, practice, rehearse; play back (a record); begin again, restart, resume 68vb. *begin;* replay, give an encore, reprint, reissue, republish; rehash, renew, revive 656vb. *restore;* belch 300vb. *eruct.*

repeat oneself, reverberate, reecho 404vb. *resound;* drum, beat a tattoo; chant, chorus 16vb. *be uniform;* give an encore; quote oneself, tautologize 570vb. *be diffuse;* battologize 580vb. *stammer;* trot out, plug, labor, harp on, harp on the same string; din into one's ears, go on at, hammer at; recur to, revert to, return to 505vb. *remember;* go back, retrace one's steps 286vb. *regress;* go the same round, commute, be a creature of habit 610vb. *be wont.*

reoccur, recur, return, revert, happen again; reappear, pop up, show up again; never hear the last of; turn up like a bad penny; haunt, obsess 505vb. *be remembered.*

Adv. *repeatedly,* recurrently, frequently 139adv. *often;* again and again, over and over, many times o., times without number, time and again; time after time, day after day, year after year; day by day, year in year out; morning, noon and night.

again, afresh, anew, over again, for the second time, once more; ditto; encore, bis; de novo, da capo; re-.

See: 5, 16, 18, 20, 66, 68, 71, 91, 139, 141, 166, 286, 295, 300, 404, 412, 505, 566, 570, 572, 574, 580, 589, 593, 610, 656, 838, 925, 950.

107 Infinity

N. *infinity,* infinitude, infiniteness, boundlessness, limitlessness, illimitability; eternity 115n. *perpetuity.*

Adj. *infinite,* indefinite; immense, measureless; eternal 115adj. *perpetual;* numberless, countless, sumless, innumerable, immeasurable, illimitable, interminable; incalculable, unfathomable, incomprehensible, unapproachable; inexhaustible, without number, without limit, without end, no end of; without measure, limitless, endless, boundless, teemless; untold, unnumbered 104adj. *many;* unmeasured, unbounded, unlimited.

Adv. *infinitely,* to infinity, ad infinitum; without end, indefinitely; boundlessly, illimitably; immeasurably 32adv. *greatly.*

See: 32, 104, 115.

108 Time

N. *time,* tide; tense 564n. *grammar;* duration, extent 183n. *space;* limited time, season, term, semester, tenancy, tenure; spell, stint; span, space 110n. *period;* a bit, a while; the whole time, the entire period, life, lifetime; stream of time, lapse, course 111n. *course of time;* years, days; whirligig of time, Time's scythe, Time's hourglass, sands of time, ravages of t., noiseless foot of t.; fourth dimension; aorist, indefinite time; past time, past tense, retrospective time 125n. *preterition,* 119n. *priority;* prospective time 124n. *futurity;* contemporaneity 121n. *present time;* recent time 126n. *newness;* antiquity, distant time 127n. *oldness.*

interim, intermediate time, pendency, while; interval, entr'acte, break, playtime, recess, pause 145n. *lull;* interval of leisure 681n. *leisure;* intermission, intermittence, interregnum, interlude, episode 72n. *discontinuity;* close season 145n. *halt;* respite, adjournment 136n. *delay;* midweek 70n. *middle.*

date, day, age, day and a., reign 110n. *era;* vintage, year, regnal y., time of life 117n. *chronology;* birthday, nativity 141n. *anniversary;* day of the week, calends, ides, nones; moment 116n. *instant;* target date, zero hour, D-day; term, fixed day, day of settlement, quarter-day, pay-d.

Adj. *continuing,* permanent 115adj. *perpetual,* 146adj. *unceasing;* on foot, in process of; repetitive, recurrent 106adj. *repeated;* temporal 141adj. *periodic.*

intermediate, interglacial, interlunar, interwar; midweek; intercalary, intercalated, inter-.

dated, calendared; pre-Christian 119adj. *prior;* post-Christian, postwar 120adj. *subsequent.*

Vb. *continue,* endure, drag on 113vb. *last;* roll on, intervene, pass 111vb. *elapse;* take time, take up t., fill t., occupy t. 183vb. *extend;* live through, sustain; stay, remain, abide, outlive, survive 113vb. *outlast;* take its time, wait 136vb. *pend.*

pass time, vegetate, breathe, subsist 360vb. *live;* age, grow old 127vb. *be old;* spend time, consume t., use t., employ t. 678vb. *be busy;* while away t., kill t., summer, winter, week-end 681vb. *have leisure;* waste t. 679vb. *be inactive;* mark time, tide over 136vb. *wait;* take the right time, seize an opportunity 137vb. *profit by;* have one's day, enjoy a spell.

fix the time, calendar, date, put a date to 117vb. *time;* make an engagement.

Adv. *while,* whilst, during, pending; during the time, during the interval; day by day; in the course of; for the time being, meantime, meanwhile; between whiles, in the meantime, in the interim; from day to day, from hour to hour; hourly 139adv. *often;* for a time, for a season; till, until, up to, yet; always, the whole time, all the time 139adv. *perpetually;* all along 54adv. *throughout;* for good 113adv. *for long.*

when, what time; one day, once upon a time, one fine morning; in the days of, in the time of, in the year of.

anno Domini, A.D.; ante Christum A.C.; before Christ, B.C. before the Christian era, B.C.E.; anno urbis conditae, A.U.C.; anno regni, A.R., in the year of his reign.

See: 54, 70, 72, 106, 110, 111, 113, 115, 116, 119, 120, 121, 124, 125, 126, 127, 136, 137, 139, 141, 145, 146, 183, 360, 564, 678, 679, 681.

109 Neverness

N. *neverness,* Greek Calends; Tib's eve; blue moon; dies non; no time, datelessness, eternity 115n. *perpetuity.*

Adv. *never,* not ever, at no time, at no period, on no occasion, not in donkey's years; nevermore, never again; over one's dead body; never before, never in one's born days; without date, sine die; before the beginning of time; out of time.

See: 115.

110 Period

N. *period,* matter of time; long period, long run 113n. *diuturnity;* short period, short run 114n. *transientness;* season; close season 145n. *lull;* time of day, morning, evening; time of year, spring, summer, autumn, winter 128n. *morning,* 129n. *evening;* one's time, fixed t., term; notice, warning, ultimatum 766n. *conditions;* time up 69n. *finality;* measured time, spell, stint, shift, span, stretch, sentence; innings, turn; round, chukker, bout, lap; vigil, watch, nightwatch, dogwatch; length of time, second, minute, hour; particular time, rush-hour, crush-h., pause, interval 108n. *interim;* day, weekd., working d.; week, sennight, octave, novena; fortnight, month, moon, lunation; quarter, trimester; half year, semester; twelve month, year, sidereal y., light y., sabbatical y.; olympiad, lustrum, quinquennium; decade, decennium, the Nineties, the Twenties; indiction; silver wedding, golden w., jubilee, diamond j. 141n. *anniversary;* century, millennium; annus mirabilis; time up to now, one's born days; life, lifetime, life-sentence.

era, time, age, days; epoch, Samvat; cycle, Sothic c., Metonic c.; Platonic year, Great Year, Annus Magnus, yuga, kalpa; geological period, Ice Age, Stone A., Saturnian A.

Adj. *periodic,* seasonal; hourly, horary; annual, biennial, quinquennial, decennial, centennial.

secular, epochal, millennial; Archean, primary, Paleozoic; secondary, Mesozoic; tertiary, Cenozoic; quaternary, recent; Eocene, Miocene, Pliocene, Pleistocene, Neocene; Eolithic, Paleolithic, Mesolithic, Neolithic, Chalcolithic.

Adv. *man and boy,* in a lifetime; by periods, periodically, seasonally; for a term, for the term of one's natural life, for a lifetime.

See: 69, 108, 113, 114, 128, 129, 141, 145, 766.

111 Course: indefinite duration

N. *course of time,* matter of t., progress of t., process of t., sucession of t., lapse of t., flow of t., flux of t., effluxion, stream of time, tide of t., march of t., step of t., flight of t.; duration 108n. *time,* 146n. *continuance;* continuous tense, imperfect t. 564n. *grammar;* indefinite time, infinite t. 113n. *diuturnity.*

Adj. *elapsing,* wearing, passing, rolling 285adj. *progressive,* 146n. *unceasing;* consuming 114 adj. *tran-*

sient; aging, getting older 131adj. *aged.*

Vb. *elapse,* pass, lapse, flow, run, roll, proceed, advance, press on 285vb. *progress;* wear on, drag on, crawl 278vb. *move slowly;* flit, fly, slip, slide, glide 277vb. *move fast;* run its course, expire 69vb. *end;* go by, pass by, slip by 125vb. *be passed;* have one's day, enjoy a spell 108vb. *pass time.*

Adv. *in time,* in due time, in due season; in course of time, in process of t., in the fullness of t., with the years.

See: 69, 108, 113, 114, 125, 131, 146, 277, 278, 285, 564.

112 Contingent Duration

Adv. *during pleasure,* during good behavior; provisionally, precariously, by favor; for the present; so long as it lasts; as *or* so long as.

113 Diuturnity: long duration

N. *diuturnity,* length of time, a long t., unconscionable t., a week of Sundays, years, years on end; a lifetime, life sentence; generations, a century, an age, ages, aeons 115n. *perpetuity;* length of days, cat's nine lives, longevity 131n. *age;* distance of time, corridor of t., antiquity 125n. *preterition.*

durability, lasting quality, endurance, defiance of time; survival, survivance 146n. *continuance;* permanence 153n. *stability;* inveteracy, long standing, good age 127n. *oldness;* long run, long innings.

protraction, prolongation, extension 203n. *lengthening;* dragging out, spinning o., filibustering, stonewalling 702n. *hindrance,* 715n. *resistance;* interminability, wait, long w. 136n. *delay,* 278n. *slowness;* extra time, overtime 38n. *addition;* long spell, long innings, long run.

Adj. *lasting,* abiding, diuturnal 146adj. *continuing;* secular, agelong, lifelong, livelong; longstanding, inveterate, deep-seated, deep-rooted; of long duration, long-term, long-service, marathon 203adj. *long;* too long, unconscionable; durable, perdurable, enduring 162adj. *strong;* longeval, longlived, macrobiotic 131 adj. *aged;* evergreen, sempervirent, unfading, fresh 126adj. *new;* eternal, perennial 115adj. *perpetual;* persistent, chronic 602adj. *obstinate;* intransmutable, intransient, constant, stable, permanent 153adj. *unchangeable.*

protracted, prolonged, lengthened, extended, stretched, spun out, drawn o. 197adj. *expanded;* lingering, delayed, tarrying 278adj. *slow;* long-pending, long-awaited 136adj. *late;* interminable, long-winded, time-wasting 570adj. *prolix.*

Vb. *last,* endure, stand, stay, remain, abide, continue 146vb. *go on;* have roots, brave the years, defy time, never end 115vb. *be eternal;* carry one's years 131vb. *grow old;* wear, wear well 162vb. *be strong.*

outlast, outlive, outwear, outstay, survive; remain 41vb. *be left;* live to fight another day; have nine lives.

spin out, draw o., drag o.; protract, prolong 203vb. *lengthen;* temporize, gain time, procrastinate 136vb. *put off;* talk out, filibuster 702vb. *obstruct.*

drag on, be interminable, never end; drag its slow length along, inch, creep, linger, dawdle 278vb. *move slowly;* tarry, delay, waste time, wait 136vb. *be late.*

Adv. *for long,* long, for a long time, for ages, for years, many a long day; for good, for all time, for better for worse; till blue in the face; till the cows come home.

all along, all day, all day long, the livelong day; all the year round, round the clock, hour by hour, day by day; before and since; ever since.

long ago, long since, in the distant past, long, long ago; in ancient days, in bygone times 125adv. *formerly.*

at last, in the long run, after many days, not before it was time.

See: 41, 115, 122, 125, 126, 127, 131, 136, 146, 153, 162, 197, 203, 278, 570, 602, 702, 715.

114 Transientness

N. *transientness,* transience, transitoriness 4n. *insubstantiality;* ephemerality, impermanence; evanescence 446n. *disappearance;* volatility 338n. *vaporization;* fugacity 277n. *velocity;* caducity, fragility 330n. *brittleness;* mortality, perishability 361n. *death;* frailty 163n. *weakness;* mutability 152n. *changeableness;* capriciousness, fickleness 604n. *caprice;* suddenness 116n. *instantaneity;* temporariness, provisionality; temporary arrangement, acting a., makeshift 150n. *substitute;* interregnum 108n. *interim.*

brief span, briefness, brevity 204n. *shortness;* mortal span, short life and a merry one; summer lightning, meteor-flash, flash in the pan, nine days' wonder; bubble reputation 355n. *bubble;* may fly, snowman, snows of yesteryear, snow in the sun, smoke in the wind; April shower, summer cloud 4n. *insubstantial thing;* milk tooth; short run 110n. *period,* 277n. *spurt;* spasm, moment 116n. *instant.*

Adj. *transient,* time-bound, temporal, impermanent, transitory, fading, passing 4adj. *insubstantial;* fair-weather, summer; cursory, flying, fleeting, fugitive, fugacious 277adj. *speedy;* shifty, slippery, slipping; precarious, volatile; evanescent 446adj. *disappearing;* unsettled, rootless; flickering, mutable, changeable 152adj. *changeful;* fickle, flighty 604adj. *capricious.*

ephermeral, of a day, short-lived, non-durable; perishable, mortal 361adj. *dying;* deciduous, frail 163adj. *weak,* 330adj. *brittle;* impermanent, temporary, acting, provisional, for the time being; doomed, under sentence.

brief, short-term, short-service 204adj. *short;* summary, short and sweet 569adj. *concise;* quick, fleet, brisk 277adj. *speedy;* sudden, momentary, meteoric, like a flash 116adj. *instantaneous;* harried, pressed for time, in a hurry 680adj. *hasty;* at short notice, extemporaneous, off-hand 609adj. *spontaneous.*

Vb. *be transient,*—transitory etc. adj.; not stay, not last; flit, fleet, fly, gallop 277vb. *move fast;* fade, flicker, vanish, evanesce, melt, evaporate 446vb. *disappear;* fade like a dream, flit like a shadow, pass like a summer cloud, burst like a bubble, have no roots 2vb. *pass away.*

Adv. *transiently,* briefly, temporarily, provisionally; for the present, for the moment, for a time, for the time being; instantly 116adv. *instantaneously;* easy come, easy go; here today and gone tomorrow; touch and go.

See: 2, 4, 108, 116, 150, 152, 163, 204, 277, 330, 338, 355, 361, 446, 569, 604, 609, 680.

115 Perpetuity: endless duration

N. *perpetuity,* perennity; endless time, infinite duration 107n. *infinity;* sempiternity, everlastingness; eternity, timelessness; never-endingness, interminability 113n. *diuturnity;* immortality, athanasia, incorruption 146n. *continuance;* perpetuation, immortalization; lasting monument 505n. *reminder.*

Adj. *perpetual,* long-lasting, durable, perdurable 113adj. *lasting;* aeonian, agelong 127adj. *immemorial;* non-stop, constant, continual, ceaseless, incessant 146adj. *unceasing;* flowing, ever-flowing, uninterrupted 71adj. *continuous;* dateless, ageless, unaging, unchanging, immutable 144adj. *permanent;* evergreen, unfading, amaranthine, incorruptible; imperishable, undying, deathless, immortal; unending, never-ending, interminable; indesinent, endless, without end, timeless, eternal, eterne, co-eternal.

Vb. *perpetuate,* make permanent, establish; immortalize, eternalize, eternize.

be eternal,—perpetual etc. adj.; last for ever, endure for e., live for e.; go on for e., have no end, never stop.

Adv. *forever,* in perpetuity, on and on; ever and always, for aye, evermore, ever and ever, for ever and a day; time without end, world without e.; for keeps, for good and all, for better for worse; to the end of time, till doomsday, to the crack of doom; to infinity; unchangeably, constantly, non-stop, as a matter of habit 610adv. *habitually.*

See: 71, 107, 113, 127, 144, 146, 505, 610.

116 Instantaneity: point of time

N. *instantaneity,* instantaneousness, immediateness, immediacy; simultaneity 121n. *present time;* suddenness, abruptness 508n. *inexpectation;* precise time 135n. *punctuality;* momentariness 114n. *transientness.*

instant, moment, point, point of time; second, split s., half a s., tick, trice, jiffy, half a j.; breath; burst, crack; stroke, coup; flash, lightning f.; twinkle, twinkling, the twinkling of an eye; two shakes; the very moment, the very hour, the stroke of.

Adj. *instantaneous,* simultaneous, immediate, instant, sudden, abrupt; flickering, flashing; quick as thought, quick as lightning, with the speed of light, like a flash 277adj. *speedy;* on time, punctual 135adj. *early.*

Adv. *instantaneously,* instantly, instanter, immediately; punctually, without delay, in half a mo, soon; promptly, readily, presto, pronto;

without warning, without notice, abruptly; overnight, all at once, all of a sudden 135adj. *suddenly;* plump, slap, slap-bang, in one's tracks; in the same breath, at the same instant, at a stroke, at one jump, at one swoop; in a trice, in a moment, in a tick, in the twinkling of an eye; at the drop of a hat, on the spot, on the dot; extempore, impromptu, on the spur of the moment, slapdash, off-hand, before you could say Jack Robinson, before you could say knife; like a flash, like a shot, like greased lightning 277adv. *swiftly;* touch and go; no sooner said than done.

See: 114, 121, 135, 274, 277, 508.

117 Chronometry

N. *chronometry,* chronoscopy, horometry, horology; horography, watch-making; calendar-making; timing, dating; time-keeping, watching.

clock time, right time, exact t., correct t., B.B.C. t., true t., astronomer's t., solar t., sidereal t., Greenwich t., mean t., standard t., local t., continental t.; the time now, the hour, time of day, time of night; bedtime; summer time, double summer t., daylight saving.

timekeeper, chronometer, marine c., ship's c.; timepiece, horologe; clock, dial, face; hand, second h., minute h., hour h. 547n. *indicator;* bob, pendulum 317n. *oscillation;* electric clock, pendulum c., grandfather c., calendar c., alarm c., alarum; Big Ben; water-clock, clepsydra; watch, ticker; fob-watch, hunter, repeater; wrist-watch; sundial, gnomon; hour-glass, sand-glass, egg-glass; chronograph, chronoscope, chronopher; time-signal, pip, siren, hooter; gong, bell, five-minute b., minute-b., minute-gun, time-ball; timer, stop-watch, parking-meter, traffic light 305n. *traffic control;* time-fuse, time-switch; metronome, conductor, band-leader 413n. *musician;* watchmaker, clock-maker, horologer.

chronology, dendrochronology; carbon 14; dating, chronogram; date, age, epoch, style 110n. *era;* old style, O.S., new style, Gregorian s.; almanac, Old Moore, calendar, perpetual c., fixed c., Gregorian c., Julian c.; ephemeris, Nautical Almanac; menology, chronicle, annals, fasti, diary, journal, log-book 548n. *record;* date list, time-chart 87n. *list;* timetable 87n. *directory.*

chronologist, chronographer, chronologer, calendar-maker, calendarist, datary, chronogrammatist; chronicler, annalist, diarist 549n. *recorder.*

Adj. *chronological,* chronometrical, horological, timekeeping; chronographic; annalistic, diaristic 548adj. *recording;* calendarial, chronogrammatic, datal, temporal; isochronous, isochronal 123adj. *synchronous;* in time 137adj. *timely.*

Vb. *time,* clock; fix the time, fix the date; match times 123vb. *synchronize;* phase 24vb. *adjust;* adjust the hands, put the clock forward 135vb. *be early;* put the clock back 136vb. *be late,* 84vb. *be unconformable;* wind the clock, set the alarm 669vb. *make ready;* calendar, chronologize, chronicle, diarize 548vb. *record;* date, be dated, bear date; measure time, mark t., beat t., keep t.; count the minutes, watch the clock; clock in 64vb. *begin;* clock out 145vb. *cease;* ring in 68vb. *initiate;* ring out 69vb. *terminate.*

Adv. *o'clock,* a.m., p.m.

See: 14, 24, 68, 69, 84, 87, 110, 123, 135, 136, 137, 305, 317, 413, 547, 548, 549, 669.

118 Anachronism

N. *anachronism,* metachronism, parachronism, prochronism; wrong date, wrong day, chronological error, antichronism; mistiming, previousness, prolepsis 135n. *anticipation;* disregard of time, unpunctuality 136n. *lateness;* neglect of time, oblivion of t. 506n. *oblivion;* untimeliness, wrong moment 138n. *intempestivity.*

Adj. *anachronistic,* misdated, undated; antedated, foredated, prochronous, previous, before time, too early 135adj. *early;* metachronous, post-dated 136adj. *late;* overdue, unpunctual, behind time; slow, losing; fast, gaining; out of due time, out of season, out of date, behind the times, old-fashioned 84adj. *unconformable.*

Vb. *misdate,* mistake the date 138vb. *mistime;* antedate, foredate, anticipate 135vb. *be early;* be overdue, be behind time, postdate 136vb. *be late;* be fast, gain; be slow, lose; be unpunctual, take no note of time.

See: 84, 135, 136, 138, 506.

119 Priority

N. *priority,* antecedence, anteriority, previousness, preoccurrence, preexistence; primogeniture, birthright; eldest, firstborn, son and heir; flying start 64n. *precedence;* leading 283n. *precession;* the past, yesteryear, yesterday 125n. *preterition;* eve, vigil, day before; precedent, antecedent; foretaste, preview, prerelease; aperitif 66n. *precursor.*

Adj. *prior,* pre-, fore; earliest, first, first in the field, precedent 64adj. *preceding;* previous, earlier, anterior, antecedent; prewar, prenatal, predeceased; preexisting, preexistent; elder, eldest, firstborn; former, ci-devant, one-time, whilom, erstwhile, ex-, retired; foregoing, aforementioned, before-mentioned, abovementioned; aforesaid, said; introductory, prefatory, preluding 66adj. *precursory;* premised, given, presupposed 512adj. *supposed.*

Vb. *be before* 135vb. *be early,* come before, go b. 283vb. *precede;* forerun, antecede; preexist.

do before, premise, presuppose 512vb. *suppose;* predecease, prefabricate, prearrange, precontract, preexempt, precondemn, prenotify, preview; be previous, anticipate, forestall, jump the gun, jump the queue; steal a march on, gain the start 277vb. *outstrip;* lead 283vb. *precede,* 64vb. *come before.*

Adv. *before,* pre-, prior to, beforehand; just before, on the eve of; earlier, previously; ultimo, ult.; afore, ere, theretofore, erewhile; aforetime, ere now, before n.; ere then, before t., already, yet; in anticipation, anticipating; precedently, until now.

See: 64, 66, 125, 135, 277, 283, 512.

120 Posteriority

N. *posteriority,* subsequence, supervention; ultimogeniture, succession 65n. *sequence,* 284n. *following;* days to come 124n. *futurity;* line, lineage, descent, successor, descendant 170n. *posterity;* postnatus, cadet; late-comer, new arrival; remainder, reversion, inheritance, post-obit; aftermath, morning after 67n. *sequel.*

Adj. *subsequent,* post-, posterior, following, next, after, later; last in date, puisné, junior, cadet, younger, youngest 130adj. *young;* succeeding, designate, to be 124adj. *future;* postliminious; postnate; postdiluvial, postdiluvian; posthumous, post-obit; postwar, post-Christian; postprandial, after-dinner 65adj. *sequent.*

Vb. *ensue,* supervene, follow after 65vb. *come after;* go after 284vb. *follow,* 157vb. *result;* succeed, step into the shoes of 771vb. *inherit.*

Adv. *subsequently,* later, next time; after, afterwards; at a subsequent period, at a later p.; next, in the sequel, in process of time; thereafter, thereupon, upon which, eftsoons; since, from that time, from that moment; from the start, from the word "go"; after a while, after a time; soon after, close upon; next month, proximo.

See: 65, 67, 124, 130, 157, 170, 284, 771.

121 The Present Time

N. *present time,* contemporaneity, contemporaneousness, topicality 126n. *modernism;* time being, the present, the now; present time, present day, present moment; this hour, this moment, this instant 116n. *instantaneity;* juncture, opportunity, crisis 137n. *occasion;* this time, nonce; the times, modern t., current t., these days; today, twentieth century, now-a-days; this date, current d., even d.; one's age, one's present a., mental a., physical a.; present generation, one's contemporaries 123n. *contemporary.*

Adj. *present,* actual, instant, current, existing, that is; of this date, of today's d., of even d.; topical, contemporary, contemporaneous; present-day, latest, up-to-the-minute, up-to-date 126adj. *modern;* for the occasion, occasional.

Vb. *be now,* exist 1vb. *be;* live in the present, live for the day, live from hand to mouth; be modern 126vb. *modernize;* be one's age, admit one's a., 123vb. *synchronize.*

Adv. *at present,* now, at this time, at this moment; at the present time, contemporaneously, contemporarily; today, now-a-days; at this time of day, even now; already, but now, just now; this time, on the present occasion; for the time being, for the nonce; on the nail, on the spot 116adv. *instantaneously;* on the spur of the moment 609adv. *extempore;* now or never; now as always.

until now, to this day, to the present day, up to now; including today, through; from the start, from the word "go" 113adv. *all along.*

See: 1, 113, 116, 123, 126, 137, 609.

122 Different Time

N. *different time,* other times, better

t.; another time, some other t., not now, not today, any time but this; jam yesterday, and jam tomorrow, but never jam today 124n. *futurity;* parachronism 118n. *anachronism.*

Adj. *non-contemporary,* unmodern 84adj. *unconformable;* behind the times 127adj. *antiquated;* before the times, futuristic 124adj. *future;* metachronous 118adj. *anachronistic.*

Adv. *not now,* ago, earlier, later, then; sometimes, somewhiles; once, once upon a time; one day, one fine morning, one of these days; sometime, somewhen; some time or other, sooner or later; anytime, any old t.; any time now; soon; whenever you will, as soon as you like; otherwhile, otherwhiles.

See: 84, 118, 124, 125, 127.

123 Synchronism

N. *synchronism,* coexistence, coincidence, concomitance 89n. *accompaniment,* 181n. *concurrence;* simultaneity, same time 116n. *instantaneity;* contemporaneity, contemporaneousness, same date, same day 121n. *present time;* coevality, same age, twin birth 28n. *equality;* level-pegging, level time, dead heat 28n. *draw;* synchronization, phasing, syntony, isochronism.

contemporary, coeval, twin 28n. *compeer;* one's contemporaries, one's own generation, one's age group; age-group, stream, class, year 74n. *group.*

Adj. *synchronous,* synchronal, synchronic; contemporary, contemporaneous 121adj. *present,* 126adj. *modern;* simultaneous, coincident, coexistent, coeternal, conterminous, concomitant 24adj. *agreeing,* 89adj. *accompanying;* level, neck and neck 28adj. *equal;* matched in age, coeval, twin, born together, of the same age, of the same year, of the same vintage; synchronized, timed, syntonic, phased, isochronous, on the beat, punctual; met, well-m. 74adj. *assembled.*

Vb. *synchronize,* contemporize, coexist 89vb. *accompany;* encounter, coincide, arrive together 295vb. *meet;* keep time, watch the beat 284vb. *follow;* syntonize, tune, phase 24vb. *adjust;* run neck and neck, run a dead heat, equal another's time, equal the record 28vb. *equal;* pace, keep in step with; take the same time, isochronize; reach the same age; die together.

Adv. *synchronously,* concurrently, at the same time, isochronously, for the same time, along with, pari passu, in time, on the beat, simultaneously, as soon as, just as, at the moment of, in the same breath 116adv. *instantaneously;* while, whilst, concomitantly 89adv. *with.*

See: 24, 28, 74, 89, 116, 121, 126, 181, 284, 295.

124 Futurity: prospective time

N. *futurity,* future tense; womb of time, time to come, days and years to come; morrow 120n. *posteriority;* future, time ahead, prospect, outlook 507n. *expectation;* coming events, fate 154n. *eventuality,* 155n. *destiny;* near future, tomorrow, mañana, next week, next year 121n. *present time,* 200n. *nearness;* advent 289n. *approach;* distant future, remote f., after ages 199n. *distance;* future generations, descendants, heirs, heritage 170n. *posterity;* successorship, shadow cabinet 65n. *sequence,* 669n. *preparation.*

future state, latter end 69n. *finality;* what fate holds in store 155n. *destiny,* 596n. *fate;* doomsday, crack of doom, judgment day, resurrection day 956n. *tribunal;* postexistence, after-life, life to come, hereafter, kingdom come 971n. *heaven;* damnation 972n. *hell;* good time coming, millennium 730n. *prosperity;* rebirth, reincarnation 106n. *repetition.*

looking ahead, anticipation 669n. *preparation;* prospect, prospects, outlook 507n. *expectation;* great expectations, expectances 852n. *hope;* horoscope, foresight 511n. *prediction.*

Adj. *future,* not in the present, to be, to come; about to be, coming, nearing 289n. *approaching;* nigh, near in time, close at hand 200adj. *near;* due, destined, fated, threatening, imminent, overhanging 155adj. *impending;* in the future, ahead, yet to come, waiting, millennial 154adj. *eventual;* prospective, designate, earmarked 605adj. *chosen;* promised, looked for 507adj. *expected,* 471adj. *probable;* predicted, predictable, foreseeable, sure 473adj. *certain;* ready to, rising, getting on for; potential, on, maturing, ripening 469 adj. *possible;* later, ulterior, posterior 120adj. *subsequent.*

Vb. *be to come,* lie ahead, lie in the future, be for tomorrow; be destined, threaten, overhang 155vb. *impend;* near, draw nigh 289vb. *approach;* be imminent, be just round the corner, cast its shadow before, stare one in the face 200vb. *be near;* shall, will.

look ahead, look forward, see it coming, await 507vb. *expect,* 852vb. *hope;* foresee 511 vb. *predict;* anticipate, forestall 135vb. *be early.*

Adv. *prospectively,* eventually, ultimately, later; in fullness of time, in due course, in the long run; tomorrow, soon, sooner or later, some day; hereafter, not today, not yet, on the eve of, on the point of; close upon; about to.

henceforth, in future, from this time forth, from now on; thenceforward.

See: 65, 69, 106, 120, 121, 135, 154, 155, 170, 199, 200, 289, 469, 471, 473, 507, 511, 596, 605, 669, 730, 852, 956, 971, 972.

125 Preterition: retrospective time

N. *preterition* 119n. *priority;* retrospection, looking back 505n. *remembrance;* past tense, historic t., narrative t., preterit, perfect, pluperfect 564n. *grammar;* the past, recent p., only yesterday 126n. *nearness;* distant past, history, antiquity; old story, matter of history 127n. *oldness;* past times, times of yore, days of y., olden days, good old d., bygone d.; auld lang syne, yesterday, yesteryear, former times; ancien régime; Victorian Age, Elizabethan A., Renaissance, Cinquecento, part of history.

antiquity, high a., rust of a., eld; creation, when time began, time immemorial, distance of time, distant t.; remote ages; prehistory, ancient h., medieval h.; geological times, Paleolithic Age, Stone A., prehistoric a., heroic a., mythological a., Vedic A., classical a.; Dark Ages, Middle A. 110n. *era;* the ancients, ancientry; relic, fossil, eolith, microlith 41n. *leavings,* 127n. *archaism;* ruin, ancient monument, megalith, Stonehenge 548n. *monument;* antiquarium, museum 632n. *collection;* ancient lineage, old descent 169n. *genealogy.*

palaetiology, paleontology, paleozoology, paleology, paleography, archaeography; archaeology, digging up the past; antiquarianism; medievalism.

antiquarian, paleontologist, archaeologist; paleologist; antiquary, Dryasdust, Oldbuck 492n. *scholar;* historian, prehistorian; medievalist 549n. *chronicler;* Egyptologist, Assyriologist, Semiticist, Hebraist, Arabist, Sanskritist, classicist 557n. *linguist;* revivalist; archaist, Pre-Raphaelite 556n. *artist.*

Adj. *past,* in the p., historical; ancient, prehistoric, Ogygian 127adj. *olden;* early, primitive, proto-, dawn 127adj. *primal;* recently past 126adj. *new;* wholly past, gone, bygone, lost, irrecoverable, dead and buried 506adj. *forgotten;* passed away, no more, died out, dead as the dodo 2adj. *extinct,* 361adj. *dead;* passé, has-been, obsolete, exploded 647adj. *disused,* 127adj. *antiquated;* over, blown o., done, over and done with, behind one; elapsed, lapsed, expired, run out, ended, finished 69adj. *ending;* unrenewed, unrevived.

former, late, pristine, quondam, erstwhile; whilom, sometime, one-time, ci-devant, ex-; retired, outgoing 753adj. *resigning;* ancestral, ancient, prehistoric 127adj. *immemorial;* not within living memory.

preterit, grammatically past, in the past tense; simple past, past continuous, perfect, imperfect, pluperfect.

foregoing, last, latter, above-mentioned, aforesaid 64adj. *preceding;* recent, overnight 126adj. *new.*

retrospective, looking back, backward-looking; archaizing 505adj. *remembering;* retroactive, going back; with hind-sight 148vb. *reverted.*

Vb. *be past,* have elapsed, have expired; have run its course, have had its day; pass, elapse, blow over, be o., pass off; be a dead letter.

look back, track back, cast the eyes b.; antiquarianize, archaeologize, dig up the past, exhume; put the clock back, go back to the past, archaize, hark back 505vb. *retrospect.*

Adv. *formerly,* aforetime, of old, of yore; erst, whilom, erewhile, time was, ago, in olden times; anciently, long ago, long since; a long while, a long time ago; once upon a time; years ago, ages a.; lately, some time ago, some time since, some time back; yesterday, the day before yesterday; yestreen, yestereve, yesternight; yesterweek, yesteryear; last year, last season, last month, ultimo.

retrospectively; retroactively; historically speaking, ere now, before now, hitherto, heretofore; no longer; from time immemorial; in the memory of man; time out of mind; already, yet; till now, up to this time; from the start, from the word "go" 121adv. *until now;* ex post facto; supra, above 64adv. *before.*

See: 2, 41, 64, 69, 110, 119, 121, 126, 127, 148, 169, 361, 492, 505, 506, 548, 549, 556, 557, 564, 632, 674, 753.

126 Newness

N. *newness,* recency, recent date, recent occurrence, recent past 124n. *preterition,* 121n. *present time;* neonomianism, innovation, neoterism 560n. *neology;* originality 21n. *nonimitation;* novelty, gloss of n.; freshness, dewiness 648n. *clearness;* greenness, immaturity, rawness 130n. *youth;* renovation, renewal, revival 656n. *restoration.*

modernism, modernity, modernness, modernization; up-to-dateness, topicality, contemporaneity 121n. *present time;* the latest, the latest thing, latest fashion; the last word, dernier cri; new look, contemporary style 848n. *fashion.*

modernist, neologist, neoteric, futurist; advanced thinker, avant-garde, neonomian; bright young thing; modern generation.

upstart, novus homo, mushroom, parvenu, nouveau riche 847n. *vulgarian.*

Adj. *new,* recent, of recent date, of recent occurrence; upstart, mushroom; novel, original, unhackneyed, unprecedented, unheard of 68adj. *beginning;* brand-new, fire-n., span-n.; like new, in mint condition, new-looking 648adj. *clean;* green, evergreen, dewy, juicy, sappy 128adj. *vernal*; fresh, fresh as a rose; fresh as a daisy; fresh as paint; virgin, maiden, fledgling; newborn, born yesterday 130adj. *young;* raw, unripe, unfledged 669adj. *immature;* just out, just published, newmade, straight from the factory; untried, untrodden, unbeaten, unexplored 491adj. *unknown;* untested 461adj. *experimental;* unhandselled, unbroken, not broken in, not yet run in; unfleshed, newfleshed, newfledged; budding, prentice.

modern, late, latter-day; contemporary, topical 121adj. *present;* up-to-the-minute, up-to-date; à la mode, abreast of the fashion; ultramodern, advanced, avant-garde, futuristic, untraditional, non-traditional; innovating, neoteric, newfangled, newfashioned 560adj. *neological;* revolutionary, neonomian.

modernized, renewed, renovated, redone, repainted 656n. *restored;* given a new look, brought up to date, reedited; looking like new, freshened up 648adj. *clean.*

Vb. *modernize,* bring up to date, adapt to modern needs; have the new look, go modern, go contemporary; move with the times 285vb. *progress.*

Adv. *newly,* afresh, anew, like new; recently, just now, only yesterday, the other day; not long ago, a short time a.; lately, latterly, of late.

See: 21, 68, 121, 124, 128, 130, 285, 461, 491, 560, 648, 656, 669, 847, 848.

127 Oldness

N. *oldness,* primitiveness, the prime 68n. *beginning;* age, eld, hoary e.; cobwebs of antiquity, dust of ages, ruin, ruins 125n. *antiquity,* 649n. *dirt;* maturity, ripeness, mellowness 669n. *maturation;* decline, rust 51n. *decay;* senility 131n. *age;* eldership, primogeniture 131n. *seniority.*

archaism, antiquities 125n. *antiquity;* thing of the past, relic of the p.; ancien régime; vieux jeu; museum piece, antique, fossil, prehistoric animal; Gothic script, blackletter type; fogy, old-timer, has-been, back number, extinct volcano 728n. *loser.*

tradition, lore, folklore, mythology; inveteracy, custom, prescription, immemorial usage 610n. *habit;* common law, smriti, sunna, hadith; ancient wisdom, the way of our forefathers; word of mouth 579n. *speech.*

Adj. *olden,* old, ancient, antique, of historical interest; venerable, patriarchal; archaic, ancient, old-world; time-worn, ruined; prehistoric, mythological, heroic, Vedic, classic, Byzantine, Dark Age, feudal, medieval, Pre-Raphaelite; elder, senior, eldest, first-born 131adj. *older;* historical 125adj. *past,* 866adj. *renowned.*

primal, prime, primitive, primeval, primordial, primogenous, primordinate, aboriginal 68adj. *beginning;* geological, paleocrystic, Paleozoic, fossil, preglacial, Paleolithic; early, proto-, dawn-, eo-; antemundane, pre-adamite, antediluvian; diluvian, out of the Ark, patriarchal; Cronian, Saturnian, Ogygian.

immemorial, ancestral, traditional, time-honored, prescriptive, customary, used 610adj. *habitual;* venerable 866adj. *worshipful;* inveterate, rooted, established, long-standing 153adj. *fixed;* Ogygian, old as the hills, old as Adam, old as Methuselah, old as history, old as time, hoary with age, age-old 131adj. *aged.* *antiquated,* of other times, archaic, black-letter; last-century, Victorian, prewar 119adj. *prior;* anachronistic, archaizing 125adj. *retrospective;* fossilized, ossified, static 144vb. *permanent;* behind the times, out of date, out of fashion, antediluvian, out of the Ark; conservative, old-fashioned, old-school; passé, outworn, exploded, gone by, gone out, run o. 125adj. *past;* decayed, perished 655adj. *dilapidated;* rusty, moth-eaten, crumbling; mildewed, moss-grown, moldering, rotting, rotten 51adj. *decomposed;* fusty, stale, secondhand; obsolete, over-age, obsolescent; superseded, superannuated, on the shelf; out of use 674adj. *disused;* aging, old, senile 131adj. *aged.*

Vb. *be old,*—antiquated etc. adj.; go back in time, belong to the past, have had its day, have seen its d. 69vb. *end;* age 131vb. *grow old;* fade, wither 655vb. *deteriorate;* molder, stale, fust; rot, rust, perish, decay 51vb. *decompose.*

Adv. *anciently,* since the world was made, since the year one, since the days of Methuselah; anno Domini.

See: 51, 68, 119, 125, 131, 144, 153, 579, 610, 649, 655, 659, 669, 674, 728, 866.

128 Morning. Spring. Summer

N. *morning,* morn, forenoon, a.m.; small hours 135n. *earliness;* matins, prime, tierce, terce; dawn, false d., dawning, morning twilight, cockcrow 66n. *precursor;* sunrise, sun-up, daybreak, dayspring 417n. *light;* peep of day, break of d.; first blush of day, alpenglow; full day, prime of the morning; Aurora, Eos, Usha; daystar, orb of day 321n. *sun.*

noon, high noon, meridian, midday, noonday, noontide; eight bells, twelve o'clock.

spring, springtime, springtide, vernal season, spring s., seed-time, Primavera, Ver; vernal equinox, first point of Aries.

summer 379n. *heat;* summertime, summertide, midsummer, midsummer's day, high summer; Indian summer, St. Luke's s., St. Martin's s.

Adj. *matinal,* matutinal, morning; auroral, dawning, fresh, dewy 135adj. *early;* antemeridian; noon.

vernal, equinoctial, spring; springlike, sappy, juicy, flowering, florescent 130adj. *young.*

summery, summer, estival 379adj. *warm.*

Adv. *at sunrise,* at dawn of day, with the lark; past midnight, in the small hours; a.m.

See: 66, 130, 135, 321, 379, 417.

129 Evening. Autumn. Winter

N. *evening,* eventide, even, eve, dewy e.; evensong, vespers, afternoon, p.m.; matinee (theater); afternoon tea, five o'clock; dog-watches, sunset, sundown, setting sun, going down of the sun; alpenglow; dusk, crepuscule, twilight, gloaming 419n. *half-light;* candlelight, cockshut; close of day, nightfall, dark, blindman's holiday, night-time 418n. *darkness;* bed-time 679n. *sleep;* curfew, last post 136n. *lateness,* 69n. *finality.*

midnight, dead of night, night's high noon; witching time; night-watch, small hours.

autumn, fall, fall of the year, fall of the leaf; harvest, harvest-time; harvest moon, hunter's m.; Indian summer; autumnal equinox; "season of mists and mellow fruitfulness."

winter 380n. *wintriness;* winter-time, winter-tide; midwinter, winter solstice 70n. *middle.*

Adj. *vespertine,* afternoon, postmeridian; evening; dusky, crepuscular 418adj. *dark,* 419n. *dim;* nightly, nocturnal, noctivagant; benighted, late; bed-time.

autumnal, equinoctial.

wintry, winter, brumal, hiemal, winterbound 380adj. *cold.*

Adv. *post meridiem,* late, late at night; at night, by n.; all through the night.

See: 69, 70, 136, 380, 418, 419, 679.

130 Youth

N. *youth,* freshness, juiciness, sappiness 126n. *newness,* 174n. *vigorousness;* young blood, youthfulness, youngness, juvenility, juvenescence; juniority 35n. *inferiority;* incunabula, earliest stage, infancy, babyhood, childhood, childish years, tender age 68n. *beginning;* puppyhood, puppy fat; boyhood, girlhood, youthhood, school-going age; one's teens, teenage, adolescence, pubescence, age of puberty, boyishness, girlishness, awkward age, growing pains; younger generation, rising g. 132n. *young person;* growing boy, minor, ward.

nonage, tender age, immaturity, minority, infancy, pupilage, pucelage, wardship, leading strings, status pupillaris, cradle, nursery, kindergarten.
salad days, school d., student d., undergraduate d.; Flegeljahre, heyday, heyday of the blood, springtime of youth; prime of life, flower of l., seed-time of l.; golden season of l., bloom, florescence.
Adj. *young,* youthful, boyish, girlish; virginal, maidenly, teenage, juvenile, adolescent, pubescent, growing, ripening 136adj. *increasing;* budding, sappy, florescent, flowering 128adj. *vernal;* beardless, unripe, green, callow, awkward, raw, unfledged 670adj. *immature;* of school-going age, under-age, minor, infant, in statu pupillari; younger, minor, junior, puisné, cadet; youngest, minimus; childish 132adj. *infantine;* ever-young, evergreen, unwrinkled, ageless.
See: 35, 68, 126, 128, 132, 136, 174, 670.

131 Age

N. *age,* eld 127n. *oldness;* one's age, time of life, years; middle age, ripe a., riper a.; pensionable age, retiring a., superannuation 753n. *resignation;* old age, hoary old a., gray hairs, white h.; three-score years and ten, four score and upward; senescence, evening of one's days, decline of life, declining years, vale of y.; the sere and yellow leaf, autumn of life, winter of l.; ricketiness, decrepitude, caducity, senility, anility, second childhood, dotage 51n. *decay;* longevity, green old age, ripe old a.; change of life, menopause; critical age, climacteric, grand c. 137n. *occasion.*
seniority, old man's privilege 64n. *precedence;* primogeniture 119n. *priority;* higher rank 34n. *superiority;* eldership, deanship, doyen; elders, presbytery, senate, gerousia 692n. *council.*
gerontology, nostology, gerontotherapy, geriatrics, care of the aged 658n. *therapy.*
Adj. *aged,* old, elderly, matronly; middle-aged, ripe, mature, mellow 669adj. *matured;* overblown, overripe, run to seed; of a certain age, not so young as one was, no chicken; past one's prime, getting old, going gray, graying, white-haired, gray-h., hoary, hoary-headed; aging, senescent, waning, declining, decaying, moribund 361adj. *dying;* wrinkled, lined, marked with crow's feet, rheumy-eyed, toothless, palsied, withered, decrepit, rickety 655adj. *deteriorated;* driveling, doddering, doting, doited, crazy 499adj. *foolish;* senile, anile, failing, with softening of the brain; in years, advanced in y., stricken in y., with one foot in the grave; old as Methuselah, old as Adam; venerable, patriarchal 920adj. *respected;* so many years old, turned of, rising; too old, past it, past the time for; superannuated, effete, passé 127adj. *antiquated;* gerontic, senatorial 733adj. *governmental.*
older, big, major; elder, senior 34adj. *superior;* first-born, eldest, primogenital 119adj. *prior;* eldest, maximum.
Vb. *grow old,* age; show one's years, wrinkle, go gray, turn white; pass three-score years and ten, have one foot in the grave.
See: 34, 51, 64, 73, 119, 127, 137, 361, 499, 655, 658, 669, 692, 733, 793, 920.

132 Young person. Young animal. Young plant

N. *child,* childer, children, nursery; young boy, man child, babe, baby; infant, nursling, suckling, weanling, fosterling; bairn, little one, little tot, little chap, mite, tiny, toddler, bantling; brat, kid, kidlet; papoose, bambino, bacha, pickaninny; little darling, little angel, little monkey; cherub, young innocent, gosling; imp, elf, changeling. **See** *youngling.*
youngster, juvenile, young person, young hopeful, boy, schoolboy, stripling, adolescent; youth, callant, lad, laddie; urchin, nipper, shaver, whipper-snapper; codling, cub, unlicked c.; hobbledehoy, Teddy-boy; minor, master, junior, cadet; midshipman, cabin-boy, powder-monkey; buttons, call-boy, page-b. 742n. *servant;* girl, schoolgirl, lass, lassie, missie, wench, maid, maiden, virgin; chit, chicken, chick, miss, young m., junior m.; teenager, bobbysoxer, flapper, tomboy, hoyden, romp; giglet, minx, baggage; colleen, mademoiselle, damsel, damozel, nymph, nymphet. **See** *youngling.*
youngling, young animal, yearling, lamb, lambkin, ewelamb, kid, calf, heifer, pigling, piglet; fawn, colt, foal, filly; kit, kitten; puppy, pup, whelp, cub; chick, chicken, pullet;

duckling, gosling, cygnet 365n. *animal, bird;* fledgling, nestling, eyas, squab; fry, litter, farrow, clutch, spawn, brood; larva, pupa, nymph; chrysalis, cocoon, tadpole; embryo, fetus 156n. *source.*

young plant, seedling, set; sucker, shoot, sprout, slip; twig, sprig, scion, sapling 366n. *plant.*

Adj. *infantine,* baby, dolly, infantile, babyish, childish, childlike; juvenile, boyish, girlish 130adj. *young;* kittenish, coltish, hoydenish; newborn, newfledged, fledgy, unfledged, unbreeched 126adj. *new;* in the cradle, in arms, in swaddling bands, in long clothes, in leading strings; small, knee-high 196adj. *little.*

See: 126, 130, 156, 196, 365, 366, 742.

133 Old person

N. *old man,* old gentleman; elder, senior, sir 34n. *superior;* oldster, graybeard, gaffer, pantaloon, antiquity; dotard; veteran, old soldier, Chelsea pensioner, old-age p.; old 'un, old hand, dugout; old-stager, old-timer 696n. *expert;* fossil, old fogy 501n. *fool;* grandfather, grandsire, grandpa, patiarch; elders, ancestors, forefathers 169n. *parent;* sexagenarian, octogenarian, nonagenarian, centenarian; Methuselah, pre-adamite, antediluvian; Nestor, Rip van Winkle, Old Parr.

old woman, old lady, grandmother, granny, grandam beldam; no chicken, gammer, crone, carline; old dutch 894n. *spouse;* hag, witch 904n. *hell-hag.*

old couple, Darby and Joan, Philemon and Baucis, the old folks.

See: 34, 169, 501, 696, 894, 904.

134 Adultness

N. *adultness,* adulthood, grown-upness, maturescence; riper years, years of discretion 463n. *discrimination;* legal age, voting a., majority, full age, man's estate; manhood, womanhood, virility 372n. *male,* 373n. *female;* badge of manhood, beard, toga virilis, key of the door; maturity, prime, prime of life, life's high noon; bloom, florescence 669n. *maturation;* meridian of life, floruit.

adult, grown-up, big boy, big girl; man 372n. *male;* woman, matron 373n. *female;* no chicken; youth, jawan, stripling.

Adj. *grown-up,* adult, out of one's teens, in long trousers; major, of age, responsible; mature, full-grown 669adj. *matured;* nubile 894adj. *marriageable;* virile, manly, 372adj. *male;* womanly, matronly 373adj. *female;* blooming, florescent, full-blown, in full bloom, full-fledged; in one's prime 130adj. *young.*

Vb. *come of age,* be grown up, reach man's estate, attain majority, be twenty-one, have the key of the door; grow a beard, put on long trousers, assume the toga virilis; put one's hair up; have sown one's wild oats, settle down, earn one's living.

See: 130, 372, 373, 463, 669, 894.

135 Earliness

N. *earliness,* early hour, prime 128n. *morning;* beginnings, early stage, primitiveness 68n. *beginning;* early riser, early bird; early comer, first arrival 66n. *precursor;* primitive, aborigine, earliest inhabitant 191n. *native.*

punctuality, timeliness 137n. *occasion;* dispatch, promptitude 678n. *activity;* haste 277n. *velocity;* suddenness 113n. *instantaneity.*

anticipation, prevenience, a stitch in time 510n. *foresight,* 669n. *preparation;* prematurity, early maturity, precocity; forestalling 64n. *precedence.*

Adj. *early,* prime, in the small hours; prevenient, previous 119adj. *prior;* timely, in time, on t., in good t., punctual, prompt; forward, advance, in advance; advanced, precocious, rareripe, fresh 126adj. *new;* summary, sudden, immediate 116adj. *instantaneous,* 508adj. *unexpected;* expected soon, next on the list, forthcoming, ready 669adj. *prepared;* impending, imminent, at hand 200adj. *near;* too early, over-early, premature, abortive, misfired 670adj. *immature.*

Vb. *be early,*—premature etc. adj.; be betimes, be beforehand etc. adv.; anticipate, draw on futurity; forestall, get there first 64vb. *come before;* seize the occasion, take time by the forelock; gain the start, steal a march on 306vb. *outdo;* engage, book, preengage, preempt, reserve, pay in advance; secure, order, bespeak; expedite 277vb. *accelerate;* lose no time 680vb. *hasten;* be precocious, ripen early; start too soon, jump the gun; put the clock forward, gain time, gain, go fast.

Adv. *betimes,* early, soon, anon,

rathe; eft, eftsoons; ere long, before long; first thing, at the first opportunity; with time enough, punctually, to the minute, in time, in good time, in due time; time enough.

beforehand, in advance, in anticipation; without waiting, precipitately 680adv. *hastily;* precociously, prematurely, too soon, before one's time.

suddenly, without notice 508adv. *unexpectedly;* without delay, without a pause 116adv. *instantaneously;* at the sight of; before ink was dry; forthwith, incontinent, shortly, directly; at short notice, off-hand, extempore, at the drop of a hat.

See: 64, 66, 68, 113, 116, 119, 128, 137, 191, 200, 277, 306, 508, 510, 669, 670, 678, 680.

136 Lateness

N. *lateness,* late hour, small hours; high time, eleventh hour, last minute; unreadiness, backwardness, slow development 670n. *non-preparation,* 499n. *unintelligence;* opsimathy 536n. *study;* tardiness, lagging, hysteresis 278n. *slowness;* afterthought, delayed reaction, double take 67n. *sequel;* latecomer, last arrival; opsimath 538n. *learner;* slow starter, late riser 278n. *slowcoach;* lieabed, laggard 679n. *idler;* Micawber, Fabius Cunctator; waiter on Providence.

delay, cunctation, Fabian policy, "wait and see" 858n. *caution;* extension, prolongation, gaining time, dragging out, obstruction, filibustering, filibuster 113n. *protraction,* 702n. *hindrance;* deceleration, retardation, check 278n. *slowness;* detention, hold-up 747n. *restraint;* postponement, adjournment, ampliation; prorogation, remand, pause, truce 145n. *lull;* deferment, moratorium, respite, days of grace; suspension, stay, stay of execution; suspension of penalty, reprieve 752n. *abrogation,* 909n. *forgiveness;* putting off, procrastination, mañana 679n. *sluggishness;* dilatoriness, red-tapism, red tape, law's delays, chancery suit; shelving, pigeon-hole, cold storage 679n. *inactivity;* penalty for delay, demurrage, contango 805n. *non-payment.*

Adj. *late,* late in the day, eleventh-hour, last-minute, deathbed; too late, twelfth-hour; overdue, delayed, belated, benighted; behindhand, lagging, after time, behind t.; sluggish, hysteretic; backward, long about it 278adj. *slow;* cunctatious, cunctatory 858adj. *cautious;* unready, unpunctual, never on time; procrastinating, dilatory 679adj. *inactive;* deferred etc. vb.; postliminious; posthumous 120adj. *subsequent.*

Vb. *be late,* sit up late, rise late, keep late hours, burn the midnight oil; lag, lag behind 284vb. *follow;* stay, tarry, take time, be long about it, linger, dawdle, saunter, loiter 278vb. *move slowly;* hang about, hang around, hang back 679vb. *be inactive;* dally, dilly-dally; miss, miss a chance, lose an opportunity, let the moment pass, oversleep 138vb. *lose a chance;* be behindhand, have leeway to make up; put the clock back, not move with the times 125vb. *look back;* be losing, lose stock (clock).

wait 507vb. *await;* bide, stay, bide one's time, take one's t., wait and see, bide the issue, sleep on it, consult one's pillow 677vb. *not act;* stand and wait, stand about, sit a.; be kept waiting, wait impatiently, cool one's heels, dangle, dance attendance.

pend, hang, drag 113vb. *drag on;* hang fire, hang in the balance, tremble in the b. 474vb. *be uncertain;* stand, stand over, lie o., stay put 266vb. *be quiescent.*

put off, defer, prorogue, postpone, adjourn, lay over; keep, reserve, hold over; keep pending, file, pigeonhole; table, lay on the t.; shelve, put in cold storage, keep on ice; remand, send back; suspend, hold in abeyance; respite, reprieve, waive 909vb. *forgive;* procrastinate, protract, delay, retard, hold up, lengthen out, gain time, filibuster 113vb. *spin out;* temporize, tide over; stall, keep one waiting; withhold, deny 760vb. *refuse.*

Adv. *late;* after time, behind t.; late in the day, at sunset, at the eleventh hour, last thing; at length, at last, at long l., ultimately; till all hours; too late, too late for 138adv. *inopportunely.*

tardily, slowly, leisurely, deliberately, at one's leisure.

See: 67, 113, 120, 125, 138, 145, 175, 266, 278, 284, 474, 499, 536, 538, 670, 677, 679, 702, 747, 752, 760, 805, 858, 909.

137 Occasion: timeliness

N. *occasion,* event, welcome e. 154n. *eventuality;* meeting of events, juncture, conjuncture 181n. *concur-*

rence; timeliness, tempestivity, opportuneness, readiness, ripeness; fittingness 24n. *fitness,* 642n. *expedience;* just the time, just the moment; right time, proper t., suitable season; auspicious hour, moment, well-chosen m., well-timed initiative; high time, nick of t., eleventh hour 136n. *lateness;* occasionalism 449n. *philosophy.*

opportunity, given time, borrowed t., time's forelock 759n. *offer;* favorable opportunity, fine o., golden o. 469n. *possibility;* one's chance, lucky moment, luck, piece of l. 159n. *chance;* best chance 605n. *choice;* only chance 606n. *no choice;* opening, room, elbow r., field 183n. *space;* liberty, independence, freedom of choice 744n. *freedom;* convenience, spare time 681n. *leisure;* no let, no hindrance, fair field, clear f., clear stage 159n. *fair chance;* handle, lever, instrument 630n. *tool,* 629n. *means;* stepping-stone 624n. *bridge.*

crisis, critical time, key point, key moment; turning point, psychological moment, crucial m., emergency, extremity, pressure, pinch, push 700n. *predicament;* eleventh hour, last minute 136n. *lateness.*

Adj. *timely,* timeous, in time, within the time limit; on time, to the minute, punctual 135adj. *early;* seasonable, welcome, well-timed; just in time, in the nick of t., at the eleventh hour.

opportune, favorable, providential, heaven-sent, auspicious, propitious; fortunate, lucky, happy 730adj. *prosperous;* for the occasion, fitting 24adj. *apt,* 642adj. *expedient;* as occasion requires, occasional 140adj. *infrequent.*

crucial, critical, key, momentous, decisive 638adj. *important.*

Vb. *profit by,* improve the occasion; seize the chance, take the opportunity, make an opening, create an o.; take time by the forelock, strike while the iron is hot, make hay while the sun shines; spare the time for; cash in on, capitalize.

Adv. *opportunely,* in proper time, in due time, in proper course, in due c., in the fullness of time; in proper season, in due s.; at the right time, all in good time; in the nick of time, just in time, at the eleventh hour, now or never.

incidentally, by the way, by the by; en passant, apropos; parenthetically, by way of parenthesis; while speaking of, while on this subject; extempore, on the spur of the moment, on the spur of the occasion; for this occasion, for the nonce.

See: 24, 135, 136, 140, 154, 159, 181, 183, 449, 469, 605, 606, 624, 629, 630, 638, 642, 681, 700, 730, 744, 759.

138 Intempestivity

N. *intempestivity,* wrong time, unsuitable t., improper t., untimeliness, unseasonableness 643n. *inexpedience;* inopportunity, contretemps; evil hour 731n. *ill fortune;* intrusion, interruption, disturbance 72n. *discontinuity;* mistiming 118n *anachronism.*

Adj. *ill-timed,* mistimed, misjudged, ill-judged, ill-advised 481n. *misjudging;* untimely, intempestive, untoward; interrupting, intrusive; malapropos, inconvenient, unsuited 25 adj. *unapt,* 643adj. *inexpedient;* unseasonable, off-season; unpunctual, not in time 136adj. *late;* premature, too soon for 135 adj. *early;* wise after the event 118adj. *anachronistic.*

inopportune, untoward, inauspicious, unpropitious, unfavorable, ill-omened, ill-starred, unlucky, unhappy 731adj. *unfortunate.*

Vb. *mistime,* time it badly 481vb. *misjudge;* intrude, disturb, break in upon, find engaged.

be engaged, be too busy, be occupied, be not at home; be otherwise engaged, have other fish to fry 678vb. *be busy.*

lose a chance, waste time, miss the bus, miss the boat, miss the train 728vb. *fail;* drop a sitter, bungle 695vb. *be unskillful;* oversleep, lose the opportunity, let the opportunity slip, let the occasion pass 136vb. *be late;* allow to lapse, let slip through one's fingers 458vb. *neglect;* spoil a good chance, stand in one's own light, shut the stable door when the steed is stolen 695vb. *stultify oneself.*

Adv. *inopportunely,* amiss; as ill luck would have it, in an evil hour; the time having gone by, a day after the fair.

See: 25, 72, 118, 135, 136, 458, 481, 643, 678, 695, 728, 731.

139 Frequency

N. *frequency,* rapid succession, rapid fire 71n. *continuity;* oftenness, hourliness, unfailing regularity 141n. *periodicity;* doubling, redoubling 106n. *repetition;* frequenting, haunting, regular visits, assiduous attendance.

Adj. *frequent,* recurrent 106adj. *re-*

peated; common, of common occurrence, not rare 104adj. *many;* thick-coming 104adj. *multitudinous;* incessant, perpetual, continual, non-stop, constant, sustained, steady 146adj. *unceasing;* regular, hourly 141adj. *periodic;* hunting, frequenting, assiduous 610adj. *habitual.*

Vb. *recur* 106vb. *reoccur;* do nothing but; keep, keep on, fire away 146vb. *go on;* frequent, haunt 882vb. *visit;* obsess; plague, pester 827vb. *incommode.*

Adv. *often,* oft, many a time and oft; oft-times, often-t., a thousand t.; frequently, commonly, often to be met with, not once or twice; not seldom, not infrequently, again and again 106adv. *repeatedly;* in quick succession, in rapid succession; regularly, daily, hourly, every day, every hour, every moment; in innumerable cases, in many instances; as often as you like, ad lib, ad libitum.

perpetually, continually, constantly, incessantly, steadily, without ceasing 71adv. *continuously;* at all times, daily and hourly, night and day, day and night, day after day, morning, noon and night; ever and anon.

sometimes, occasionally, every so often, at times, now and then, from time to time, there being times when, often enough; and again 106adv. *again.*

See: 71, 104, 106, 141, 146, 610, 827, 882.

140 Infrequency

N. *infrequency,* infrequence, rareness, rarity 105n. *fewness;* seldomness, uncommonness; intermittence 72n. *discontinuity;* phoenix 84n. *rara avis.*

Adj. *infrequent,* uncommon, sporadic, occasional; intermittent 72adj. *discontinuous;* scarce, rare, rare as a blue diamond 105adj. *few;* almost unheard of, unprecedented 84adj. *unusual;* not to be repeated; single 88adj. *one.*

Adv. *seldom,* once in a way; rarely, scarcely, hardly, only sometimes, only occasionally; not often, infrequently, unoften; scarcely ever, hardly e., once in a blue moon; once, once for all, just this once, once only; like angel's visits, few and far between.

See: 72, 84, 105.

141 Periodicity: regularity of recurrence

N. *periodicity,* regularity, punctuality, regularity of recurrence, rhythm, steadiness, evenness 16n. *uniformity;* timing, phasing, serialization 71n. *continuity;* alternation, in-and-out system (politics); reciprocity 12n. *correlation;* tidal flow, ebb and f., alternating current, wave movement, tidal m. 317n. *fluctuation;* to-and-fro movement, pendulum m., piston m., shuttle m.; shuttle service; pulsation, pulse, beat, rhythm, pendulum, piston, shuttle, swing 317n. *oscillation;* chorus, refrain 106n. *recurrence;* throb 318n. *agitation;* drum-beat 403n. *roll;* tide 350n. *wave;* rate of pulsation, frequency, wave f.; turn, round, circuit, lap, chukker; shift, relay 110n. *period.*

regular return, rota, cycle, circuit, revolution, life cycle, wheel of life 314n. *circuition,* 315n. *rotation;* yearly cycle, seasons 128n. *morning,* 129n. *evening;* synodical period; fixed interval, stated time 110n. *period*; routine, daily round 60n. *order,* 610n. *habit;* catamenia, menses, monthlies, flowers; days of the week, months of the year; week-end, black Monday, quarter-day; leap year; feast, fast, saint's day, red-letter day 876n. *special day.*

anniversary, birthday, jubilee, silver wedding, golden w.; centenary, bicentenary, tercentenary, quater-centenary; Lent, Good Friday, Easter, Christmas, Boxing Day, New Year, Hogmanay; St. George's Day, St. Andrew's D., St. Patrick's D., St. David's D.; King's or Queen's Birthday, Lincoln's B.; Empire Day, Independence D., Republic D.; Fourth of July, 14 Juillet; Durga Poojah, Diwali; Ramadan, Mohurrum.

Adj. *periodic,* periodical, cyclic, circling, revolving 315adj. *rotary;* tidal, undulatory, fluctuating 317adj. *oscillating;* measured, rhythmical, steady, even, regular, constant, punctual, methodical, like clockwork 81adj. *regular;* breathing, pulsating, pulsatory, pulsatile; throbbing, beating 318adj. *agitated;* recurrent, recurring, intermittent, remittent 106 adj. *repeated;* reciprocal, alternate, alternating 12adj. *correlative;* serial, successive, serialized 65adj. *sequent,* 71adj. *continuous.*

seasonal, anniversary; paschal, lenten; at fixed intervals, hourly, daily, nightly, diurnal, semidiurnal, quotidian, tertian, biweekly, weekly, hebdomadal, hebdomadary, fortnightly, monthly; menstrual, catamenial; yearly, annual, biennial, triennial, quadrennial, quinquennial, decennial; bissextile, centennial, secular.

Vb. *be periodic,* recur 106vb. *reoccur;* serialize, recur in regular order, recur in constant succession 60vb. *be in order,* 71vb. *run on,* 65vb. *come after;* turn, revolve, circle 315vb. *rotate;* return, come round again; take its turn, turn and turn about, alternate; be intermittent, intermit; reciprocate 12vb. *correlate;* fluctuate, undulate 317vb. *oscillate;* beat, pulse, pulsate, throb 318vb. *be agitated;* heave, pant 352vb. *breathe;* swing, sway 217vb. *hang;* ply, go and return, commute 610vb. *be wont.*

Adv. *periodically* etc. adj.; regularly, at regular intervals, at stated times; at fixed periods, at established p.; punctually etc. adj.; seasonally, hourly, daily, weekly, monthly, yearly; from day to day, day by day; per diem, per annum; at intervals, intermittently, every now and then, every so often, ever and anon.

by turns; in turn, in rotation, turn and turn about, alternately, every other day, off and on, ride and tie; round and round, to and fro, up and down, from side to side.

See: 12, 16, 60, 65, 71, 72, 81, 106, 110, 128, 129, 217, 314, 315, 317, 318, 350, 352, 403, 610, 876, 998.

142 Fitfulness: irregularity of recurrence

N. *fitfulness,* irregularity, irregularity of recurrence 61n. *disorder;* jerkiness, fits and starts 17n. *non-uniformity,* 318n. *spasm;* remittency 114n. *transience* 72n. *discontinuity;* unsteadiness, inconstancy, variability 152adj. *changeableness,* 143n. *change;* whimiscality, capriciousness, April weather, unpredictability 604n. *caprice;* eccentricity; wobbling, staggering, lurching 318n. *oscillation.*

Adj. *fitful,* periodic, remittent, intermittent 72adj. *discontinuous;* irregular 84adj. *unconformable;* uneven 29adj. *unequal;* occasional 140adj. *infrequent;* unrhythmical, unsteady, fluttering 17adj. *non-uniform;* inconstant, uncertain, unpunctual; variable, veering 152adj. *changeful;* spasmodic, jerky 318adj. *agitated;* wobbling, halting, wavering, flickering, guttering; rambling, rhapsodical, desultory, unsystematic 61adj. *orderless;* erratic, eccentric, moody 604adj. *capricious.*

Adv. *fitfully,* irregularly etc. adj.; unevenly, by fits and starts, now and then 72adv. *discontinuously.*

See: 17, 29, 61, 72, 84, 114, 140, 143, 152, 318, 604.

143 Change: difference at different times

N. *change,* alteration, variation 15n. *difference;* mutation, permutation, modulation, inflection, declension; frequent change, mutability, variability 152n. *changeableness;* partial change, modification, adjustment, process, treatment 468n. *qualification;* total change 147n. *conversion;* sudden change, violent c. 149n. *revolution;* break, break with the past, innovation 126n. *newness;* change for the better, reformation 654n. *improvement;* change for the worse 655n. *deterioration;* change of direction, diversion, shift, turn 282n. *deviation,* 286n. *regression;* change of position, transition, metastasis 305n. *passage;* translation, transposition, metathesis 272n. *transference,* 188n. *displacement,* 151n. *interchange;* alternation, metagenesis, everting, eversion, overthrow 221n. *inversion;* contact action, catalysis, leavening; change of opinion, resilement 603n. *tergiversation.*

transformation, transfiguration, transfigurement; unrecognizability, transmogrification; metamorphosis, geological m., metasomatosis; metabolism, constructive m., anabolism; destructive metabolism, catabolism; transmutation, transubstantiation 147n. *conversion;* transanimation, transmigration, metempsychosis; reincarnation, avatar; transcription (mus.), version, adaptation, translation 520n. *interpretation,* 521n. *misinterpretation.*

alterer, alterant, alterative; converter, transformer; catalytic agent, catalyst, enzyme, ferment, leaven; adapter, modifier, reviser, editor; censor, bowdlerizer; alchemist, chemist; dyer; changer; money-changer; quick-change artist 545n. *conjuror;* magician 983n. *sorcerer;* kaleidoscope 437n. *variegation;* weathercock, renegade 603n. *tergiversator;* improver 654n. *reformer.*

Adj. *changeable,* variable, mutable; fickle 604adj. *capricious;* affected, changed etc. vb.; newfangled 126adj. *new;* transitional, provisional, modifiable, qualifiable; alternative, transmutative; checkered, kaleidoscopic 437adj. *variegated.*

Vb. *change,* be changed, alter 152vb. *vary;* wax and wane 36vb. *increase,* 37vb. *decrease;* change color, change countenance 426vb. *lose color;* change one's tune 603vb. *tergiversate;* vacillate, wobble 474vb. *be uncertain;* blow hot and cold, chop and change 604vb. *be capricious;* turn, shift, veer, back 282vb. *deviate;* change course, tack, jibe 269vb. *navigate;* make a transition, pass to 305vb. *pass;* take a turn, turn the corner 656vb. *revive;* turn over a new leaf, convert 654vb. *get better;* submit to change, come under the influence 83vb. *conform;* move with the times 126vb. *modernize.*

modify, alter, vary, modulate, diversify, shift the scene 437vb. *variegate;* superinduce, superimpose 38vb. *add;* make a change, introduce changes, innovate, bring in new blood 126vb. *modernize;* turn upside down, subvert, evert 149vb. *revolutionize,* 221vb. *invert;* reverse, turn back 148vb. *revert;* make changes, rearrange, reorder, reset 62vb. *arrange;* adapt 24vb. *adjust;* conform 83vb. *make conform;* recast, remold, reshape 243vb. *efform;* process, treat; revise, edit, reedit, correct 654vb. *rectify;* reform 654vb. *improve;* vamp, revamp, patch, darn 656vb. *restore;* change for the worse, deteriorate 655vb. *pervert;* tamper with, fiddle w., mar, spoil 656vb. *impair;* warp, bend, strain, twist, deform 246vb. *distort;* stain, dye, discolor 425vb. *color,* 426vb. *decolorize;* adulterate, denature, doctor, qualify 43vb. *mix,* 163vb. *weaken;* cover, mask, disguise 525vb. *conceal;* change round, shuffle the cards 151vb. *interchange,* 272vb. *transpose;* try a change, spin the wheel 461vb. *experiment;* effect a change, work a c., leaven 156vb. *cause;* affect, turn the scale 178vb. *influence;* transform, transfigure, metamorphose, transmute, transubstantiate, alchemize 147vb. *convert;* metabolize, digest; conjure, juggle 542vb. *deceive.*

Adv. *mutatis mutandis*

See: 15, 24, 36, 37, 38, 43, 62, 83, 126, 147, 149, 151, 152, 156, 163, 178, 188, 221, 243, 246, 269, 272, 282, 286, 305, 425, 426, 437, 461, 468, 474, 520, 521, 525, 542, 545, 603, 604, 654, 655, 656, 983.

144 Permanence: absence of change

N. *permanence,* permanency, no change, status quo; invariability, unchangeability, immutability 153n. *stability;* lasting quality, persistence 600n. *perseverance;* endurance, duration 113n. *durability,* 115n. *perpetuity;* fixity, fixity of purpose, immobility, immovableness 602n. *obstinacy;* firmness, rock, bedrock, foundation, solidity 324n. *density;* sustenance, maintenance, conservation 666n. *preservation,* 146n. *continuance;* law, rule 81n. *regularity;* fixed law, law of the Medes and Persians, written constitution, entrenched clause 153n. *fixture;* standing, long s., inveteracy 127n. *oldness;* tradition, custom, practice 610n. *habit;* fixed attitude, conservatism, bourbonism, die-hardism; routine, fixed r., standing order, standing dish 60n. *order;* unprogressiveness, static condition 266n. *quiescence;* traditionalist, bourbon, conservative, stick-in-the-mud, no-changer, die-hard 602n. *opinionist.*

Adj. *permanent,* enduring, durable 113adj. *lasting;* persisting, persistent, continuing, unfailing, sustained, maintained 146adj. *unceasing,* 115adj. *perpetual;* inveterate, prescriptive, long-standing 127adj. *immemorial;* perpetuated, standing, established, well-e., entrenched, fixed, unchangeable, immutable, unmodifiable, unrepealable 153adj. *vested;* intact, inviolate, undestroyed, unchanged, unsuppressed; living, well-preserved 666adj. *preserved;* unchanging, conservative, bourbon, die-hard 602adj. *obstinate;* unprogressive, stationary, static, immobile 266adj. *quiescent;* unaltered, uninfluenced, unaffected, still the same, recognizable 13adj. *identical.*

Vb. *stay,* come to stay, set in 153vb. *be stable;* abide, bide, endure, subsist, outlive, survive, outlast 113vb. *last;* persist, hold, hold good; hold on, hold it, maintain, sustain, keep up, keep on 146vb. *go on;* rest, remain, tarry, live 192vb. *dwell;* stand fast, dig one's toes in 600vb. *persevere;* stand on, stand pat, take one's position, stand one's ground, hold *or* keep one's ground *or* footing 599vb. *stand firm;* stand still, resist change, stick in the mud 266vb. *be quiescent;* grow moss 127vb. *be old;* remain the same, not change one's spots; allow to stand, let be, let alone, laisser faire, let sleeping dogs lie 756vb. *permit.*

Adv. *as before,* in statu quo, uti possidetis, without a shadow of turning;

at a stand, at a standstill; permanently, for good.

See: 13, 60, 81, 113, 115, 127, 146, 153, 192, 266, 324, 599, 600, 602, 666, 756.

145 Cessation: change from action to rest

N. *cessation,* surcease, desinence; desistance, discontinuance, discontinuation 72n. *discontinuity;* arrest 747n. *restraint;* withdrawal 753n. *resignation,* 621n. *relinquishment.*

stop, halt, stand; dead stop, dead stand; standstill, deadlock, stalemate 28n. *draw;* checkmate 728n. *defeat;* breakdown 728n. *failure;* discontinuance, stoppage, stall; shut-down, closing-d., non-resumption 69n. *end;* hitch, check 702n. *hindrance;* stopping-up, blockage 264n. *closure;* interruption 72n. *discontinuity;* abruption, breaking-off, walk-out 709n. *dissension;* closure of debate, guillotine 399n. *silence;* full stop 547n. *punctuation.*

strike, stopping work 679n. *inactivity,* 715n. *resistance;* general strike, "national holiday," hartal; slow-down, working to rule, meticulosis; stoppage, walk-out, sit-down strike, lightning s.; unofficial strike, mutiny 738n. *disobedience;* lock-out 57n. *exclusion.*

lull, rest, interval (mus.) 410n. *tempo;* pause, remission, recess, break 685n. *refreshment;* holiday, day off, time o. 681n. *leisure;* intermission, interlude, interregnum 108n. *interim;* abeyance, suspense, suspension; close season, respite, moratorium, truce, armistice, cease-fire, standstill 136n. *delay.*

stopping-place, port of call, port, harbor 192n. *stable;* stop, halt, pull-up, whistle-stop, station; bus-stop, request s.; terminus, terminal, air t. 271n. *air travel;* dead end, blind alley, cul-de-sac; billet, destination, the grave 295n. *goal,* 69n. *finality.*

Vb. *cease,* stay, desist, refrain, hold, hold one's hand; stop, halt, stand, rest, surcease, rest on one's oars, repose on one's laurels 683vb. *repose;* have done with, see the last of, end, finish 69vb. *terminate;* interrupt, leave off, knock o.; break o., let up 72vb. *discontinue;* ring off, hang up 578vb. *be mute;* withhold one's labor, cease work, stop w., strike w., down tools, strike, come out 715vb. *resist;* lock out 57vb. *exclude;* pipe down 399vb. *be silent;* come to an end, dry up, peter out, run o., run down 634vb. *waste;* fade out, fade away 446vb. *disappear;* come off, end its run, be taken off; fold up, collapse 728vb. *fail;* die away, blow over, clear up 125vb. *be past;* stand down, withdraw, retire 753vb. *resign;* leave, leave off; give up, give over 621vb. *relinquish;* shut up, shut down, close; shut up shop, put up the shutters, go out of business, wind up; shut off steam, switch off; cease fire 719vb. *make peace;* sound the last post, ring down the curtain, call it a day 266vb. *be quiescent;* go to sleep 679vb. *sleep.*

halt, stop, put a stop to; arrest, check, dam 702vb. *obstruct;* hold up, call off; pull up, cut short, call a halt, interrupt; intervene 747vb. *restrain;* cause a stoppage, call out, stage a strike, bring to a stand, bring to a standstill, freeze 679vb. *make inactive;* checkmate, stalemate, thwart 702vb. *hinder;* check oneself, stop short, drop in one's tracks, stand in one's t.; grind to a halt, seize, seize up, stall, jam, stick, catch; brake, put on the b., pull the check cord 278vb. *retard.*

pause, halt for a moment, stop for breath; hold back, hang fire 278vb. *move slowly;* wait awhile, suspend, intermit, remit, allow an interval 136vb. *wait;* recess, sit down, take breath, relax, rest 683vb. *repose.*

Int. halt! hold! stop! enough! avast! have done! a truce to! soft! desist! refrain! forbear! leave off! shut up! give over! chuck it! drop it! come off it! stow it! cheese it! scram! skedaddle!

See: 28, 57, 69, 72, 108, 125, 136, 192, 264, 266, 271, 278, 295, 399, 410, 446, 547, 578, 621, 634, 679, 681, 683, 685, 702, 709, 715, 719, 728, 738, 747, 753.

146 Continuance in action

N. *continuance,* continualness, continuation 71n. *continuity,* 144n. *permanence,* 179n. *tendency;* extension, prolongation 113n. *protraction;* maintenance, perpetuation 115n. *perpetuity;* sustained action, persistence 600n. *perseverance;* progress 285n. *progression;* uninterrupted course, break, run, unbroken r., not-out score, rally 71n. *series;* recurrence 106n. *repetition.*

Adj. *unceasing,* continuing etc. vb.; continual, steady, sustained, unstopped; non-stop, uninterrupted, unintermitting, unremitting 71adj.

continuous; unvarying, unshifting 81adj. *regular;* unreversed, unrevoked, unvaried 153adj. *fixed;* undying, 115n. *perpetual;* unfailing, ever-running, inexhaustible 635adj. *plenteous;* invariable, inconvertible 153adj. *unchangeable;* batting, not out, still in, in play 113adj. *lasting;* persistent, persisting 600adj. *persevering;* haunting, recurrent 106adj. *repeated;* standing, incessant; obsessive.

Vb. *go on,* keep going, march on, drive on, proceed, advance 285vb. *progress;* run on, never end 115vb. *be eternal;* — and — (e.g. rain and rain, pour and pour); roll on, pursue its course, take its c., trend 179vb. *tend;* endure, stick, hold, abide, rest, remain 143vb. *stay*; obsess, haunt, frequent 139vb. *recur;* keep at it, persist, hold on, carry on, jog on, plod on, plug on, slog on 600vb. *persevere;* sit it out, wait, wait till the end, see the end of, hang on 725vb. *carry through;* be not out, bat all day, carry one's bat; see one's days out, live out one's time 68vb. *end.*

sustain, maintain, uphold, keep on foot 218vb. *support;* follow up, follow through 71vb. *continuate;* keep up, keep alive 666vb. *preserve;* keep on, harp on 106vb. *repeat;* keep it up, prolong, protract 113vb. *spin out,* 115vb. *perpetuate;* keep the pot boiling, keep the ball rolling; prolong the rally, keep the ball in play; not interfere, let be, let alone, let things take their course, laisser faire, let it rip 756vb. *permit.*

Int. carry on! drive on! never say die! not out!

See: 68, 71, 81, 106, 113, 115, 139, 143, 144, 153, 179, 218, 285, 600, 635, 666, 725, 756.

147 Conversion: change to something different

N. *conversion,* converting, turning into, making i.; processing 164n. *production;* reduction, resolution, crystallization; fermentation, ferment, leaven; chemistry, alchemy; mutation, transmutation, transfiguration 143n. *transformation;* bewitchment, enchantment, bedevilment 983n. *sorcery;* progress 285n. *progression,* 157n. *growth;* course, lapse, flux 113n. *course of time;* development 36n. *increase,* 316n. *evolution;* degeneration, perversion 655n. *deterioration;* regeneration, reformation 654n. *improvement;* assimilation, naturalization 78n. *inclusion;* alienization, denaturalization 916n. *loss of right;* brainwashing 178n. *influence;* evangelization, proselytization 534n. *teaching,* 612n. *inducement;* convertibility 469n. *possibility.*

transition, transit 305n. *passage;* movement, shift, translation, transfer 272n. *transference;* transports, ecstasy 818n. *feeling;* life cycle; transmigration; conjugation, declension 564n. *grammar.*

crucible, melting pot, alembic, caldron, alfet, retort, test tube 461n. *testing agent.*

changed person, new man; convert, neophyte, catechumen, proselyte, disciple 538n. *learner;* renegade, deserter, apostate, turncoat 603n. *tergiversator;* pervert, degenerate 938n. *bad man.*

Adj. converted, influenced, affected; turned into, made i. etc. vb.; assimilated, naturalized, reborn, regenerate; proselytized, brainwashed; becoming, transitional; evolving, developing, growing into; transformed, transfigured, bewitched, unrecognizable 15adj. *different;* convertible, impressionable 143adj. *changeable.*

Vb. *be turned to,* be converted into, become, get; come to, turn to, ferment, develop into, evolve i., ripen i. 316vb. *evolve;* fall into, pass i., slide i., shift i., illapse 305vb. *pass;* melt into, merge i. 43vb. *be mixed;* settle into, sink i.; mellow 669vb. *mature;* wax 36vb. *grow;* degenerate 655vb. *deteriorate;* take the impress of, take the shape of, take the nature of, assume the character of; be transformed, not know oneself; suffer a sea change, undergo a secular change 143vb. *change;* enter a phase, enter a stage.

convert, reduce, ferment, leaven; make into, reduce to, resolve into, turn i., conjure i., enchant 983vb. *bewitch;* transmute, alchemize; render, process, make, mold, form, shapen, shape, hew into shape 244vb. *efform;* brainwash 178vb. *influence;* proselytize, evangelize, missionize 534vb. *teach;* regenerate 656vb. *revive;* paganize, dechristianize 655vb. *pervert.*

transform, transfigure; camouflage, disguise 525vb. *conceal;* render 520vb. *translate;* traduce 521vb. *misinterpret;* reshape, deform 246vb. *distort;* change the face of, change out of recognition 149vb. *revolutionize;* reform, make something of

654vb. *make better;* refound, new-model, reorganize, redress 656vb. *restore;* assimilate, absorb, naturalize, americanize, anglicize, europeanize, hellenize, indianize, sinify, orientalize; internationalize; detribalize, denaturalize, alienize 916vb. *disentitle,* 57vb. *exclude.*

Adv. *convertibly,* evolvingly; on the way to, in transit.

See: 15, 36, 43, 57, 78, 113, 143, 149, 157, 164, 178, 244, 246, 272, 275, 285, 305, 316, 461, 469, 520, 521, 525, 534, 538, 564, 603, 612, 654, 655, 656, 669, 818, 916, 938, 983.

148 Reversion

N. *reversion,* reverting, going back, return, regress, retrogression, retrocession, retreat, withdrawal, ebb 286n. *regression;* tracing back, derivation 156n. *source;* return to the past, harking back 126n. *archaism;* atavism, throwback 5n. *heredity;* looking back, retrospection 505n. *remembrance*; retrospective action, retrospectivity, retroaction; reaction 182n. *counteraction,* 31n. *compensation;* repercussion, kick, back-kick, back-fire 280n. *recoil;* revulsion, revulsion of feeling, disenchantment 830n. *regret;* counter-revolution, reversal 149n. *revolution,* 603n. *tergiversation;* volte-face, about turn, U-t., right-about t. 240n. *contraposition;* backsliding, recidivism 657n. *relapse;* reconversion 656n. *restoration;* retroversion, retroflexion, retortion 248n. *curvature,* 246n. *distortion;* chiasmus, chiastic order 221n. *inversion;* giving back, cession, replacement, reinstatement 787n. *restitution;* getting back, recovery, retrieval 771n. *acquisition;* retort, tu quoque 479n. *confutation;* turn, turning point, turn of the tide, calm before the storm 137n. *crisis;* alternation, swing, swing of the pendulum 141n. *periodicity,* 106n. *recurrence,* 317n. *oscillation;* to-and-fro movement, coming and going, commuting; round trip, there and back, out and home; return journey, return ticket; retroversion, retranslation 520n. *translation;* back where one started, status quo; resumption, recommencement 68vb. *start;* taking back, escheat 786n. *taking.*

Adj. *reverted,* reversed, reversionary, retrogressive, recessive, reflexive 286adj. *regressive;* chiastic 221adj. *inverted;* revulsive 280adj. *recoiling;* reactionary, retroactive 125adj. *retrospective;* atavistic 5adj. *genetic;* recovered, disenchanted 656adj. *restored.*

Vb. *revert,* go back, turn b., turn, return, retrace 286vb. *regress;* reverse, face about, turn a. 221vb. *invert;* ebb, retreat, withdraw 290vb. *recede;* kick back, kick 280vb. *recoil;* slip back, slide b., backslide 657vb. *relapse;* hark back, archaize; start again, restart, go back to the beginning, undo, unmake 68vb. *begin;* restore the status quo, revive 656vb. *restore;* derestrict, decontrol, deration 746vb. *liberate;* reconvert, disenchant, remove the spell 656vb. *cure;* take back, recover 656vb. *retrieve;* resume, escheat 771vb. *acquire;* give back, make restitution, reinstate, replace 787vb. *restitute.*

Adv. *reversibly,* back to the beginning, as you were; invertedly, wrong side out.

See: 5, 31, 68, 106, 125, 126, 137, 141, 149, 156, 182, 221, 240, 246, 248, 280, 286, 290, 317, 479, 505, 520, 603, 656, 657, 746, 771, 786, 787, 830.

149 Revolution: sudden or violent change

N. *revolution,* full circle, circuit 315n. *rotation;* radical change, organic c.; tabula rasa, clean slate, clean sweep 550n. *obliteration;* sudden change, catastrophe, peripeteia, surprise, coup d'état 508n. *inexpectation;* transilience, leap, plunge, jerk, start, throe 318n. *spasm;* shift, swing, switch, switch over, landslide; violent change, bouleversement, upset, overthrow, subversion, inversion 221n. *overturning;* convulsion, shake-up, upheaval, eruption, explosion, cataclysm 176n. *outbreak;* avalanche, landslip, crash, debacle 309n. *descent,* 165n. *havoc;* revulsion, counter-revolution 148n. *reversion,* 738n. *revolt;* total change, abolition, nullification 752n. *abrogation, deposal.*

revolutionist, abolitionist, radical, revolutionary, Marxist, red 738n. *revolter;* seditionist 738n. *agitator;* anarchist 168n. *destroyer.*

Adj. *revolutionary* 126adj. *new;* innovating, radical, thoroughgoing, root and branch 54adj. *complete;* cataclysmic, catastrophic, seismic, world-shaking 165adj. *destructive;* seditious, subversive, Marxist, red 738adj. *disobedient;* anarchistic 176adj. *violent;* transilient.

Vb. *revolutionize,* subvert, overturn 221vb. *invert;* switch over 603vb. *ter-*

giversate; uproot, eradicate, make a clean sweep 550vb. *obliterate,* 165vb. *demolish;* break with the past, remodel, new-model, refashion 126vb. *modernize;* change the face of, change beyond recognition 147vb. *transform.*

See: 54, 126, 147, 148, 165, 168, 176, 221, 309, 315, 318, 508, 550, 603, 738, 752.

150 Substitution: change of one thing for another.

N. *substitution,* subrogation, surrogation; by-election 605n. *vote;* commutation, exchange, switch, shuffle 151n. *interchange;* supplanting, supersession, replacement, transfer 272n. *transference;* metonymy 519n. *trope;* vicariousness, devotion, self-d., self-sacrifice 931n. *disinterestedness;* expiation, compensation 941n. *atonement;* compounding, composition.

substitute, sub, badli, succedaneum; proxy, alternate, agent, representative 759n. *deputy;* understudy, stand-in 594n. *actor;* ghost, ghost-writer 589n. *author;* locum tenens, locum 658n. *doctor;* reserve, reservist, twelfth man 707n. *auxiliary;* replacement, remount; relief, successor, supplanter 67n. *aftercomer;* double, ringer, changeling 545n. *imposter;* dummy 4n. *insubstantial thing;* synonym, doublet 559n. *word;* alternative, second best, pis aller, ersatz 35n. *inferiority;* whipping-boy, chopping-block, scapegoat, sin-offering, guilt-o., sacrifice 981n. *oblation;* makeshift, stopgap, jury mast; palimpsest; expedient, temporary e., working arrangement, modus vivendi 770n. *compromise,* 642n. *expedience.*

quid pro quo, equivalent 28n. *compeer;* consideration, purchase money; value, worth 809n. *price;* payment in lieu, composition, scutage, redemption 804n. *payment;* something in exchange, new lamps for old, replacement; change 797n. *money.*

Adj. *substituted,* substitutive, substitutionary, substitutional; vicarious 941adj. *atoning;* substitutable, interchangeable, commutable 28adj. *equivalent;* dummy, imitation, mock, ersatz 35adj. *inferior;* makeshift, stopgap, provisional, temporary 114 adj. *ephemeral.*

Vb. *substitute,* change for, commute; exchange, switch 151vb. *interchange;* take *or* offer in exchange, compound 770vb. *compromise;* make do with, put up w., make a shift w.; put in the place of, replace with; count as, treat as, regard as; replace, step into the shoes of, succeed 65vb. *come after;* supersede, supplant, displace, oust 300vb. *eject;* take the place of, be substitute for, do duty f., count f., stand in f., act f., understudy f. 755vb. *deputize;* act the part of, ghost for; shoulder the blame for, take the rap f., cover up f., compound f.; rob Peter to pay Paul; overprint 550vb. *obliterate.*

Adv. *instead,* in place, in lieu, in the stead, in the room, in the room of; by proxy; alternatively, as an alternative; in default of, for want of better.

See: 4, 28, 34, 35, 65, 67, 114, 151, 272, 300, 519, 545, 550, 559, 589, 594, 605, 642, 658, 707, 755, 759, 770, 804, 809, 931, 941, 981.

151 Interchange: double or mutual change

N. *interchange,* interchangeability, reciprocality; swap, counterchange, exchange 791n. *barter;* commutation, permutation, intermutation; transposal, transposition, mutual transfer; castling (chess), shuffle, shuffling 272n. *transference;* reciprocity, mutuality; interplay, two-way traffic, reciprocation 12n. *correlation;* quid pro quo; rally (tennis), battledore and shuttlecock, give and take; retort, repartee 460n. *rejoinder;* tit for tat, eye for an eye, tooth for a tooth, a Roland for an Oliver 714n. *retaliation;* log-rolling 706n. *cooperation.*

Adj. *interchanged,* switched, exchanged, counterchanged etc. vb.; bartered, swapped; in exchange, au pair; reciprocating, mutual, two-way 12adj. *correlative;* in exchange 714adj. *retaliatory;* inter-, intercurrent, intercontinental, interdepartmental; interchangeable, substitutable, convertible, commutable 28adj. *equivalent.*

Vb. *interchange,* exchange, counterchange; change money, convert; chop, swap, barter 791vb. *trade;* permute, commute; switch, shuffle, castle (chess) 272vb. *transpose;* give and take 770vb. *compromise;* reciprocate 12vb. *correlate;* give as good as one gets 714vb. *retaliate;* bandy words, answer back, return the compliment, rejoin 460vb. *answer;* take in each other's washing, scratch each other's back 706vb. *cooperate.*

Adv. *in exchange,* vice versa, mutatis mutandis; backwards and forwards, to and fro, by turns, turn and turn about, turn about; each in his turn, every one in his turn; in kind; au pair; interchangeably, conversely.

See: 12, 28, 272, 460, 706, 714, 770, 791.

152 Changeableness

N. *changeableness,* changeability, mutability, changefulness 143n. *change;* variability, variety 17n. *non-uniformity,* 437n. *variegation;* inconsistency, inconstancy, irregularity; instability, imbalance, disequilibrium, unstable equilibrium 29n. *inequality;* weak foundation, unsteadiness, rockiness, wobbliness, vertigo, staggers; plasticity, pliancy 327n. *softness;* unfixity, fluidness 335n. *fluidity;* lubricity, slipperiness 258n. *smoothness;* mobility, restlessness, darting, starting, fidgeting, fidget, inquietude, disquiet 318n. *agitation;* fluctuation, alternation 317n. *oscillation;* turning, veering, chopping and changing 142n. *fitfulness;* impermanence, transience, flicker, flash 114n. *transientness;* vacillation, hesitation, wavering, floating vote 601n. *irresolution;* yea and nay 603n. *tergiversation;* fickleness, capriciousness 604n. *caprice;* flightiness, light-mindedness 456n. *inattention;* versatility 694n. *aptitude.*

changeable thing, moon, Proteus, chameleon; variety show, shifting scene, kaleidoscope; wax, clay; mercury, quicksilver 335n. *fluid;* wind, weathercock, vane; eddy; April showers; wheel, whirligig; fortune, wheel of fortune; vicissitude, luck 159n. *chance;* variable, variable quantity 85n. *numerical element;* play of expression, mobile features 445n. *appearance.*

Adj. *changeful,* changing, mutable, alterable, phased 143adj. *changeable;* varying, variable 17adj. *non-uniform;* kaleidoscopic, protean 82adj. *multiform;* quick-change, versatile 694adj. *skillful;* uncertain, unreliable, vacillating, wavering 601adj. *irresolute;* unpredictable, unaccountable 508n. *unexpected;* never the same, unstaid, mercurial 15adj. *different;* wayward, fickle, whimsical 604adj. *capricious;* giddy, dizzy, flighty, wanton, irresponsible 456adj. *lightminded;* shifty, inconstant, unfaithful, disloyal 603adj. *tergiversating.*

unstable, unsteady, unstaid; wavering, wobbling, rocky, tottering, staggery, reeling, rolling; mobile, unquiet, restless, fidgety 318adj. *agitated;* desultory, spasmodic, flickering 142adj. *fitful;* touch and go 114adj. *transient;* shifting, veering, turning, chopping and changing 282adj. *deviating;* whiffling, gusty 352adj. *puffing;* unsettled, unfixed, loose, unattached, floating; erratic, mercurial; rootless, homeless 59adj. *extraneous;* vagrant, rambling, roving, wandering 267adj. *traveling;* vibrating, vibratory, alternating, fluctuating, tidal 317adj. *oscillating;* yielding, impressionable, malleable, alterable, plastic 327adj. *soft;* flowing, running, melting 335adj. *fluid.*

Vb. *vary,* be changeful, show variety 437vb. *variegate;* ring the changes, go through phases, show p., have as many phases as the moon 143vb. *change;* chop and change, change and change about; dodge, double 620vb. *avoid;* shuffle, be shifty 518vb. *be equivocal;* writhe 251vb. *wriggle;* dart, flit, flitter 265vb. *be in motion;* leap, dance, flicker, gutter 417vb. *shine;* twinkle, flash; wave, wave in the wind, flutter, flap 217vb. *hang;* shake, tremble 318vb. *be agitated;* wobble, stagger, rock, reel, sway, swing, vibrate 317vb. *oscillate;* alternate, ebb and flow, wax and wane 317vb. *fluctuate;* veer, tack, yaw 282vb. *deviate,* 269vb. *navigate;* whiffle, puff 352vb. *blow;* vacillate, waver, hesitate, float, drift, change one's mind 601vb. *be irresolute;* hover, hover between two extremes, blow hot and cold, play fast and loose 603vb. *tergiversate;* be inconstant, change one's fancy 604vb. *be capricious.*

Adv. *changeably,* variably; fitfully, off and on, now this now that.

See: 15, 17, 29, 59, 82, 85, 114, 142, 143, 159, 217, 251, 258, 265, 267, 269, 282, 317, 318, 327, 335, 352, 417, 437, 445, 456, 508, 518, 601, 603, 604, 620, 694.

153 Stability

N. *stability,* immutability; unchangeableness, unchangeability; irreversibility, invariability, constancy 16n. *uniformity;* firmness, fixity, rootedness; indelibility 144n. *permanence;* rest, immobility, immovability 266n. *quiesence;* steadiness, stable equilibrium, stable state, homeostasis, balance 28n. *equality;* stabilization, stabiliment; nerve, unshaken n., aplomb 601n. *resolution;* stiffness, inflexibility 326n. *hardness,* 602n. *obstinacy;* solidarity, solidity 324n. *density;* stiffening, ankylosis 326n. *hardening.*

fixture, establishment, firm foundation; foundations, rock, bedrock, pillar, pyramid; invariant, constant; fast dye, fast color; leopard's spots, Ethiopian's skin; law, law of the Medes and Persians, the Twelve Tables, the Ten Commandments, written constitution, entrenched clause, prescriptive right 953n. *legality.*

stabilizer, fin, center-board, keel; counter-weight, ballast 31n. *offset;* stabilimeter.

Adj. *unchangeable,* unsusceptible of change; stiff, inflexible 602adj. *obstinate;* unwavering 599adj. *resolute;* fiducial, predictable, reliable 473adj. *certain;* immutable, intransmutable, incommutable; inconvertible; irresoluble, irreducible, indissoluble; changeless, unchanging, unchanged, unaltered, inalterable, irreversible; unshrinkable, shrinkproof; indeclinable; stereotyped, unvarying, invariable, constant 16adj. *uniform;* steady, undeviating 81adj. *regular;* durable 113adj. *lasting,* 144adj. *permanent;* undying, perennial, indeciduous, evergreen 115adj. *perpetual;* imperishable, indestructible, inextinguishable 660adj. *invulnerable.* **See** *fixed.*

vested, established, well-e., well-founded, entrenched, settled; inveterate, prescriptive; irrevocable, irreversible, reverseless; incontrovertible, indefeasible, of right; valid, confirmed, ratified 473adj. *undisputed,* 488adj. *assented.*

fixed, steadfast, firm, immovable, irremovable; steady, stable, balanced, homeostatic; fast, in grain, ingrained, indelible; ineradicable, rooted, well-r., deep-r.; deep-seated, firm-s., well-based, on a rock; standing pat; tethered, moored, anchored 45adj. *tied;* at rest, at anchor, riding at a.; run aground, stuck fast, stranded, grounded, high and dry; pinned down, transfixed; immobile, like a statue, quiet as a stone 266adj. *still.*

Vb. *be stable,*—fixed etc. adj.; stand, stick fast, hold 599vb. *stand firm;* show aplomb, show self-assurance, not bat an eyelid; weather the storm 113vb. *outlast;* set in, come to stay 144vb. *stay;* settle, settle down 192vb. *dwell;* strike root, take r., strike deep, have long roots.

stabilize, stabilitate, root, entrench, found, establish, stablish, build on a rock 115vb. *perpetuate;* erect, set up, set on its feet 215vb. *render vertical;* float, set afloat; fix, set, stereotype, grave on granite; make valid, validate, confirm, ratify 488vb. *endorse;* retain, stet; bind, make sure, make fast 45vb. *tie;* keep steady, hold the road, retain equilibrium, balance 28vb. *equalize.*

See: 16, 28, 31, 45, 81, 113, 115, 144, 192, 215, 266, 324, 326, 473, 488, 599, 601, 602, 660, 953.

154 Eventuality: present events

N. *eventuality,* incidence, eventuation, realization; event, phenomenon, incidental; fact, matter of f., naked f. 1n. *reality;* case, circumstance, state of affairs 7n. *state;* occurrence, hap, happening, incident, adventure 137n. *occasion;* fortune, accident, casualty, contingency 159n. *chance;* misadventure, mishap 731n. *ill-fortune;* emergency, pass 137n. *crisis;* coincidence 181n. *concurrence;* advent 289n. *approach;* encounter, meeting; transaction, proceeding, affair 676n. *action;* result, product, consequence, issue, outcome, upshot 157n. *effect;* denouement, solution, unraveling 316n. *evolution;* peripeteia, catastrophe 68n. *end.*

affairs, matters, doings, transactions 676n. *deed;* agenda, order of the day; involvement, concern, concerns, interests, irons in the fire, axes to grind 622n. *business;* world, life, situation 8n. *circumstance;* affairs in general, state of affairs; course of events, march of e., stream of e., tide of e. 111n. *course of time;* run of affairs, chapter of accidents, ups and downs of life, vicissitudes 730n. *prosperity,* 731n. *adversity.*

Adj. *eventual,* consequential, resulting, resultant, eventuating, issuing in 157adj. *caused;* circumstantial, contingent.

happening, incidental, accidental, occasional; doing, adoing, current, on foot, afloat, in the wind, on the agenda; on the anvil, in preparation.

eventful, stirring, bustling, busy, full of incidents, crowded with i. 678adj. *active;* momentous, critical 638adj. *important.*

Vb. *happen,* become, come into existence 360vb. *be born;* materialize, be realized, come off 727vb. *succeed;*

take place, occur, come about, come to pass; befall, betide 159vb. *chance;* turn up, pop up, crop up, start up, spring up, arise 295vb. *arrive;* present itself, announce i. 189vb. *be present;* supervene 284vb. *follow;* eventuate, issue, emanate 157vb. *result;* turn out, fall o., work o., pan o.; be on foot, take its course, hold its c., advance 285vb. *progress;* continue 146vb. *go on;* go off, pass o. 125vb. *be past;* fall to one's lot, be one's great chance; be so, prove, prove to be; bring about, occasion 156vb. *cause.*

meet with, incur, encounter 295vb. *meet;* realize, find 484vb. *discover;* experience, pass through, go t.; have been through 490vb. *know,* 818vb. *feel;* have adventures, endure, undergo 825vb. *suffer.*

Adv. *eventually,* ultimately, in the event of, in case; in the course of things, in the natural course of t., in the ordinary course of t.; as things go, as times go; as the world goes, as the world wags; as the cat jumps; as it may turn out, as it may happen.

See: 1, 7, 8, 27, 68, 111, 125, 137, 146, 156, 157, 159, 181, 189, 284, 285, 289, 295, 316, 360, 484, 490, 622, 638, 676, 678, 727, 730, 731, 818, 825.

155 Destiny: future events

N. *destiny,* what's to come, one's stars 596n. *fate;* horoscope, forecast 511n. *prediction;* prospect, outlook 507n. *expectation;* coming events, future plans, intentions 124n. *futurity,* 617n. *intention;* something in store, rod in pickle 900n. *threat;* imminence, impendence, proximity 200n. *nearness,* 289n. *approach;* postexistence, future existence, hereafter 124n. *future state;* next world, afterworld, world to come 971n. *heaven;* foredoom, predestination 596n. *necessity,* 473n. *certainty;* danger 900n. *threat.*

Adj. *impending,* overhanging, hanging over, lowering, hovering, imminent 900adj. *threatening;* preparing, brewing, cooking, stewing 669adj. *preparatory;* destined, predestined, in the stars, on the knees of the gods 596adj. *fated;* predicted, forthcoming, forecast 511adj. *predicting;* inescapable, inevitable, going to be, bound to happen 473adj. *certain;* due, owing 596adj. *necessary;* in the wind, in the cards 471adj. *probable;* on the agenda, intended, decided on 608adj. *predetermined;* in prospect, in view, in the offing, on the horizon, looming on the h., in the distance 443adj. *visible;* in the future, to come, in the womb of time 124adj. *future;* at hand, close 200adj. *near,* 289adj. *approaching;* instant, immediate, about to be, on the point of 116adj. *instantaneous;* pregnant with, heavy w. 511adj. *presageful;* in store, in reserve, in pickle, ready, kept r. 669adj. *prepared;* in embryo 68adj. *beginning.*

Vb. *impend* 124vb. *be to come;* hang over, lie o., hover, lower, loom 900vb. *threaten;* come on, draw nigh 289vb. *approach;* front, face, stare one in the f. 237vb. *be in front;* breathe down one's neck 200vb. *be near;* ripen 669vb. *mature.*

predestine, destine, doom, foredoom, preordain, foreordain 596vb. *necessitate;* foreshadow, adumbrate, presage 511vb. *predict;* have ready, get r., have in store, have in pickle 669vb. *make ready;* plan, intend 608vb. *predetermine.*

Adv. *in the future,* in time, in the long run; all in good time; in the event 154adv. *eventually;* whatever may happen; expectedly 471adv. *probably;* soon, at any moment.

See: 69, 116, 124, 154, 200, 237, 289, 443, 471, 473, 507, 511, 596, 608, 617, 669, 900, 971.

156 Cause: constant antecedent

N. *causation,* causality, cause and effect, ground and consequent; etiology 158n. *attribution;* authorship; origination, originality 21n. *non-imitation;* invention 484n. *discovery;* inspiration 178n. *influence;* generation, evocation, provocation 164n. *production;* impulsion, stimulation, fomentation, encouragement, motivation 612n. *motive;* planting, watering, cultivation 370n. *agriculture;* abetment 706n. *cooperation;* temptation, inciting 612n. *inducement.*

cause, first c., final c., remote c., proximate c., causa causans; vera causa, mover, first m., primum mobile, God 965n. *the Deity;* creator, maker 167n. *producer;* begetter, only b., father 169n. *parent;* causer, effecter, occasioner; author, originator, founder; inventor, agent, leaven; stimulus 174n. *stimulant;* contributor, factor, decisive f., moment, determinant; inspirer, tempter, mainspring 612n. *motivator;* fomentor, aider, abettor; hidden hand, undercurrents 178n. *influence;* planetary influence, stars 155n. *destiny;* fate 596n. *necessity;* force 740n. *compulsion.*

source, fountain, fount, fons et origo 68n. *origin;* head-waters, spring, well-head, fountain-h., well-spring; mine, quarry 632n. *store;* birthplace 192n. *home;* genesis, ancestry, lineage, descent 169n. *parentage;* parent, ancestor, progenitor; loins 164n. *genitalia;* rudiment, element, principle, first p., first thing; germen, germ, seed, sperm; egg, fetus, embryo; chrysalis, cocoon 194n. *receptacle;* bud, stem, stalk, staple, stock, trunk, bole; taproot, root, bulb; radix, radical, etymon, derivation, etymology 557n. *linguistics;* foundation, bedrock 214n. *base;* groundwork, spadework, beginnings 68n. *beginning;* raw material, ore 631n. *materials.*

seedbed, hotbed, nidus 192n. *nest;* cradle, nursery 68n. *origin;* breeding place, incubator, womb 164n. *propagation;* hothouse, conservatory 370n. *garden.*

causal means, appliance 629n. *means;* pivot, hinge, lever, instrument 630n. *tool;* dynamo, generator, battery 160n. *energy;* motor, engine, turbine 630n. *machine;* last straw that breaks the camel's back.

reason why, reason, cause, the why and wherefore; explanation 460n. *answer,* 520n. *interpretation;* excuse 614n. *pretext;* ground, basis, rationale, occasion, causa causans, raison d'être.

Adj. *causal,* causative, formative, factitive, effective, effectual 727adj. *successful;* pivotal, determinant, decisive, final 69adj. *ending;* seminal, germinal 164adj. *productive;* inceptive, embryonic 68adj. *beginning;* suggestive, inspiring 178adj. *influential;* impelling 740adj. *compelling;* answerable, responsible; at the bottom of, original; etiological, explanatory; creative, inventive 21adj. *unimitated.*

fundamental, primary, elemental; foundational, radical, basic; crucial, central 638adj. *important;* original, aboriginal 68adj. *first;* primitive, primordial 127adj. *primal.*

Vb. *cause,* originate, create, make 164vb. *produce;* beget, be the author of 164vb. *generate;* invent 484vb. *discover;* be the reason 158vb. *account for;* underlie, be *or* lie at the bottom of, be answerable, be responsible; institute, found, lay the foundations, inaugurate 68vb. *auspicate;* set up, erect 310vb. *elevate;* launch, set afloat, set afoot, set going, spark off, touch o. 68vb. *start;* open, open up, broach 68vb. *initiate;* seed, sow, plant, water 370vb. *cultivate;* effect, effectuate, bring about, bring off, bring to pass 727vb. *succeed;* procure, provide the means, engineer 623vb. *plan;* bring on, superinduce, precipitate 680vb. *hasten;* bring out, draw o., evoke, elicit 304vb. *extract;* provoke, arouse, awaken 821vb. *excite;* stimulate 174vb. *invigorate;* kindle, inspire, incite, tempt 612vb. *induce;* occasion, give occasion for 612vb. *motivate;* have an effect, show its result, make or mar 178vb. *influence;* be the agent, do the deed 676vb. *do;* determine, decide, give the decision 480vb. *judge;* decide the result, turn the scale, give the casting vote 178vb. *prevail,* 34vb. *predominate.*

conduce, tend to 179vb. *tend;* lead to 64vb. *come before;* contribute to, operate to 703vb. *minister to;* involve, imply 5vb. *be intrinsic;* have the effect, entail, draw down, give rise to, open the door to 68vb. *initiate;* promote, advance, encourage, foster, foment, abet 703vb. *aid.*

Adv. *causally,* because, by reason of, behind the scenes 178vb. *influentially.*

See: 21, 34, 64, 68, 69, 127, 155, 158, 160, 164, 167, 169, 174, 178, 179, 180, 192, 194, 214, 304, 310, 370, 460, 480, 484, 520, 557, 596, 612, 614, 623, 629, 630, 631, 632, 638, 676, 680, 703, 706, 727, 740, 821, 965.

157 Effect: constant sequel

N. *effect,* consequent, consequence 65n. *sequence;* result, resultance; derivation, derivative, precipitate 41n. *remainder;* upshot, outcome, issue, denouement 154n. *eventuality;* final result, termination 69n. *end;* visible effect, mark, print, impress 548n. *trace;* after-effect, aftermath, sequela, legacy, backwash, wake, repercussion 67n. *sequel;* resultant action, response 460n. *answer;* performance 676n. *deed;* reaction 182n. *counteraction;* handiwork 164n. *product;* karma 596n. *fate;* moral effect 178n. *influence.*

growth, outgrowth, development 36n. *increase;* bud, blossom, florescence, fruit; ear, spica, spike; produce, crop, harvest; woolclip; profit 771n. *gain.*

Adj. *caused,* owing to, due to, attributed to; consequential, resulting from, consequent upon 65adj. *sequent;* contingent, depending, dependent on 745adj. *subject;* resultant, derivable, derivative, descended; unoriginal, secondary 20adj. *imitative;* arising, emergent, emanating, developed from, evolved f.; born of, out of, by; ending in, issuing in 154adj. *eventual;* effected, done.

inherited, heritable, hereditary, Mendelian.

Vb. *result,* be the r., come of; follow on, wait on, accrue 284vb. *follow;* be owing to, be due to; owe everything to, borrow from 785vb. *borrow;* have a common origin 9vb. *be related;* take its source, derive from, descend f., originate f., originate in, come from, come out of; issue, proceed, emanate 298vb. *emerge;* begin from, grow f., spring f., arise f.; develop, unfold 316vb. *evolve;* bud, sprout, germinate 36vb. *grow;* show a trace, show an effect, receive an impression, bear the stamp 522vb. *show;* bear the consequences 154vb. *meet with,* 963vb. *be punished;* turn out, pan o., work o., eventuate 154vb. *happen.*

depend, hang upon, hinge on, pivot on, turn on 12vb. *correlate,* 745vb. *be subject.*

Adv. *consequently,* as a consequence, in consequence; because of, as a result, all along of; of course, naturally, necessarily; eventually; it follows that, and so.

See: 9, 12, 20, 36, 41, 65, 67, 69, 154, 164, 178, 182, 284, 298, 316, 460, 522, 548, 596, 676, 745, 771, 785, 963.

158 Attribution: assignment of cause

N. *attribution,* assignment of cause; reference to, imputation, ascription; theory, hypothesis, assumption, conjecture 512n. *supposition;* explanation 520n. *interpretation*; finding reasons, accounting for; etiology, palaetiology 459n. *inquiry;* rationale 156n. *reason why;* apparentation, filiation, affiliation 169n. *parentage;* derivation 156n. *source;* an attribute 89n. *concomitant;* credit, credit title, acknowledgment 915n. *dueness.*

Adj. *attributed* etc. vb.; attributable, assignable, imputable, referable, referrible; assigned to, referred to 9adj. *relative;* credited, imputed, putative 512adj. *supposed;* inferred, inferable, derivable, traceable; owing to, explained by 157adj. *caused.*

Vb. *attribute,* ascribe, impute; say of, assert of, predicate 532vb. *affirm;* accord, grant, allow 781vb. *give;* put down to, set down to; assign to, refer to, point to, trace to, derive from 9vb. *relate;* lay at the door of, filiate, father upon; charge with, charge on, saddle with, saddle on; found upon, ground u.; make responsible, blame for 928vb. *accuse;* bring home to 478vb. *demonstrate;* credit, credit with, acknowledge 915vb. *grant claims.*

account for, explain, say how it happens 520vb. *interpret;* theorize, hypothesize, assume 512vb. *suppose;* infer the cause, derive the reason.

Adv. *hence,* thence, therefore; whence, wherefore; for, since, forasmuch as; on account of, because, owing to, thanks to, on that account, from this cause, from that cause, propter hoc, ergo, thus, so; that's why.

why? wherefore? whence? how? how come? cui bono?

somehow, in some way, in some such way; somehow or other.

See: 9, 89, 156, 157, 169, 459, 478, 512, 520, 532, 781, 915, 928.

159 Chance: no assignable cause

N. *chance,* blind c., fortuity, indeterminacy; randomness; indetermination, fortuitousness; uncertainty principle, upredictability 474n. *uncertainty;* unaccountability, inexplicability 517n. *unintelligibility;* lot, fortune, wheel of f. 596n. *fate;* whatever comes, potluck; good fortune, luck, good l., run of l. 730n. *prosperity;* bad luck, rotten l. 731n. *ill fortune;* hap, hazard, accident, casualty, contingency, coincidence, chapter of accidents 154n. *eventuality;* non-intention, chance hit, lucky shot, fluke 618n. *non-design;* rare chance, chance in a million 140n. *infrequency;* chance meeting, chance encounter 508n. *inexpectation;* chance discovery, serendipity 484n. *discovery.*

equal chance, even c., fifty-fifty 28n. *equality;* toss-up, spin of the coin, heads or tails, throw of the dice, turn of the card; lucky dip, random sample; lottery, raffle, tombola, sweepstake, premium bond, football pool 618n. *gambling;* sortes Virgilianae, sortes Biblicae 511n. *divination.*

fair chance, sporting c., fighting c., gambling c. 469n. *possibility;* good chance, main c., best c., favorable c. 137n. *opportunity;* long odds, odds on, odds 34n. *vantage;* small risk, good bet, the probabilities 471n. *probability.*

calculation of chance, theory of probabilities, doctrine of chance, actuarial calculation, mathematical probability; risk-taking, assurance, insurance, underwriting 672n. *undertaking;* speculation 461n. *experiment;* bookmaking 618n. *gambling.*

Adj. *casual,* fortuitous, chance, haphazard, random, stray 618n. *designless;* adventitious, adventive, accidental, incidental, contingent 154adj. *happening;* non-causal, epiphenomenal, coincidental 89n. *accompanying;* chancy, fluky, dicey, incalculable 474adj. *uncertain.*

causeless, groundless, uncaused, unforeseeable, unpredictable, undetermined, indeterminate 474adj. *uncertain;* unmotivated, unintended, undesigned, unplanned, unmeant 618adj. *unintentional;* unaccountable, inexplicable 517adj. *puzzling.*

Vb. *chance,* hap, turn up, pop up, fall to one's lot, so happen 154vb. *happen;* chance upon, light u., hit u., stumble u., blunder u. 154vb. *meet with,* 484vb. *discover;* risk it, chance it, leave it to chance 618vb. *gamble;* have small chance 472vb. *be unlikely.*

Adv. *by chance,* by accident; accidentally, casually, unintentionally, fortuitously, randomly 618adv. *at random;* perchance, perhaps; for aught one knows 469adv. *possibly;* luckily, as good luck would have it; unluckily, as ill luck would have it; according to chance, as it may be, as it may chance, as it may turn up, as it may happen, as the case may be, whatever happens, in any event; unpredictably 508adv. *unexpectedly;* unaccountably, inexplicably.

See: 28, 34, 89, 137, 140, 154, 461, 469, 471, 472, 474, 484, 508, 511, 517, 596, 618, 672, 730, 731.

160 Power

N. *power,* potency, puissance, mightiness 32n. *greatness;* prepotency, prepollence, prevalence, predominance 34n. *superiority;* omnipotence, almightiness 733n. *authority;* control, sway 733n. *governance*; moral power, ascendancy 178n. *influence;* spiritual power, mana; witchcraft 983n. *sorcery;* staying power, endurance 153n. *stability;* physical power, might, muscle, right arm, right hand 162n. *strength;* dint, might and main, effort, endeavor 682n. *exertion;* force 740n. *compulsion;* stress, strain, shear; weight 322n. *gravity;* weight of numbers 104n. *greater number;* manpower 686n. *personnel;* position of power, vantage ground 34n. *vantage;* validity 494n. *truth;* cogency, emphasis 532n. *affirmation;* extra power, overdrive.

ability, ableness, capability, potentiality, virtuality 469n. *possibility;* competency, efficiency, efficacy, effectuality 694n. *skill;* capacity, faculty, virtue, property 5n. *intrinsicality;* qualification 24n. *fitness;* attribute 89n. *concomitant;* endowment, gift 694n. *aptitude;* compass, reach, grasp 183n. *range;* susceptibility, affectibility 180n. *liability;* trend 179n. *tendency;* empowering, enablement, authorization 756n. *permission.*

energy, liveliness, vigor, dynamism 174n. *vigorousness;* physical energy, chemical e., kinetic e., dynamic e., electrical e., atomic e., nuclear e.; mechanical energy, engine power, horse-power; inertia, vis inertiae 175n. *inertness;* resistance 333n. *friction;* force, field of f.; force of gravity 322n. *gravity;* buoyancy 323n. *levity;* compression, spring 328n. *elasticity;* pressure, head, charge, steam; full pressure, steam up; tension, high t.; motive power, electromotive force; pulling power 288n. *traction;* pushing power, thrust, jet, jet propulsion 287n. *propulsion,* 279n. *impulse;* magnetism 291n. *attraction;* negative magnetism 292n. *repulsion;* suction 299n. *reception;* expulsion 300n. *ejection;* potential function, potential; unit of work, erg, action; foot-pound, poundal.

electricity, active e., static e.; positive electricity, negative e.; voltaic electricity, galvanic e.; atmospheric electricity, free e., induced e.; animal electricity, organic e.; lightning, spark; electrodynamics, electrostatics, electromagnetism; electrification, inductance, capacitance, voltaism, galvanism; electric shock, electric pulse; amperage, electric current, direct c., alternating c.; circuit, short c., closed c., open c.; lightning conductor, live wire; cable, pylon, grid, distributor; generator, dynamo; battery, storage b., dry b., wet b., cell, fuel c.; electric unit, volt, watt, kilowatt, megawatt; resistance, ohm; current, ampere, amp, milliamp; potential, voltage.

nucleonics, electronics, nuclear physics; atomic fission, nuclear f., thermonuclear f.; cyclotron, atom-smasher, betatron, bevatron; cosmotron, high-energy accelerator; atomic pile, reactor, chain-reactor, breeder-r.; moderator, Zeta, zero energy thermonuclear apparatus; mushroom, fall-out, radioactive cloud 659n. *poison,* 417n. *radiation.*

Adj. *powerful,* potent, multipotent 162adj. *strong;* puissant, mighty, overmighty 32adj. *great;* ascendant, rising, in the ascendant 36adj. *increasing;* prepotent, prevalent, prevailing, predominant 178adj. *influential;* almighty, omnipotent, irresistible 34adj. *supreme;* with full powers, empowered, plenipotent 733adj. *authoritative;* competent, capable, able, adequate, equal to, up to 635adj. *sufficient;* omnicompetent, multicompetent 694adj. *expert;* efficacious, effectual, effective 727adj. *successful;* of power, of might, operative, workable, having teeth; in force, valid, unrepealed, unrepealable 153adj. *vested;* cogent, compulsive 740adj. *compelling;* forcible 176adj. *violent;* armipotent, bellicose 718adj. *warlike;* with resources 800adj. *rich;* productive 171adj. *prolific;* virtual, potential 469adj. *possible.*

dynamic, energetic 174adj. *vigorous;* high-potential, high-tension, supercharged; magnetic 291adj. *attracting;* tractive 288adj. *drawing;* propelling 287adj. *propulsive,* 279adj. *impelling;* locomotive, kinetic 265adj. *moving;* powered, engined, driven by; live, electric, electromagnetic, hydroelectric; atomic, electronic, nuclear, thermonuclear, radioactive.

Vb. *be able,*—powerful etc. adj.; can, have it in one's power, have it in one; be capable of, have the virtue, have the property; compass, manage 676vb. *do;* measure up to 635vb. *suffice;* have power, exercise p., control 733vb. *dominate;* force, 740vb. *compel;* gain power, come to p. 178vb. *prevail.*

empower, enable, endow, authorize; endow with power, invest with p.; put teeth into, arm 162vb. *strengthen;* electrify, charge, magnetize; impart engine-power, power, engine.

Adv. *powerfully* etc. adj.; by virtue of, by dint of, with might and man.

See: 5, 24, 32, 34, 36, 89, 104, 153, 162, 171, 174, 176, 178, 179, 180, 183, 265, 279, 287, 288, 291, 292, 299, 300, 322, 323, 328, 333, 417, 469, 494, 532, 635, 659, 676, 682, 686, 694, 718, 727, 733, 740, 800, 983.

161 Impotence

N. *impotence,* lack of power, no authority, power vacuum; invalidity, impuissance 163n. *weakness;* inability, incapacity; incapability, incompetence, inefficiency 728n. *failure,* 695n. *unskillfulness;* ineptitude, unfitness 25n. *inaptitude;* decrepitude 131n. *age;* caducity 114n. *transientness,* invalidation, disqualification 752n. *abrogation;* sterility, sterilization 172n. *unproductivity;* disarmament, demilitarization 719n. *pacification;* demobilization 75n. *dispersion.*

helplessness, defenselessness 661n. *vulnerability;* harmlessness 935n. *innocence;* powerlessness 745n. *subjection;* impotent fury, gnashing of teeth 830n. *regret;* prostration, exhaustion, inanition 684n. *fatigue;* collapse, breakdown 728n. *failure;* unconsciousness, deliquium, faint, swoon, coma; numbness, narcosis 375n. *insensibility;* stroke, syncope, apoplexy, hemiplegia, paraplegia 651n. *disease;* sideration 651n. *paralysis;* cramp, cramps 747n. *restraint;* torpor 677n. *inaction;* atrophy, sweeny, mortification 655n. *deterioration;* palsy, senility, old age 131n. *age;* ataxia, locomotor a.; loss of control, incontinence; mental decay, softening of the brain 503n. *insanity;* mental weakness, imbecility 499n. *unintelligence;* mutism, deaf-mutism 578n. *aphony;* legal incapacity, pupilage, minority 130n. *nonage;* babyhood, infancy 130n. *youth;* invalid 651n. *sick person,* 163n. *weakling.*

eunuch, castrato; no-man; gelding, capon, bullock, steer, neuter; freemartin, hermaphrodite.

ineffectuality, ineffectiveness, futility 497n. *absurdity;* vanity 4n. *insubstantiality;* uselessness 641n. *inutility;* flash in the pan 114n. *transientness;* dead letter, waste paper, scrap of p. 752n. *abrogation;* figurehead, dummy, man of straw 4n. *insubstantial thing;* blank cartridge, vox et praeterea nihil, empty thunder.

Adj. *powerless,* not able, unable; not enabled, unempowered, unauthorized, without authority; nominal, figurehead, constitutional 4adj. *insubstantial;* nugatory, invalid, null and void, of none effect; unconstitutional 954adj. *illegal;* lame and impotent, without a leg to stand on

163adj. *weak;* inoperative, not working, unexercised, unemployed 679adj. *inactive;* suspended, in abeyance, canceled, withdrawn 752adj. *abrogated;* abolished, swept away, gone by the board 165adj. *destroyed;* obsolete, laid on the shelf 127adj. *antiquated;* disabled, disqualified, deposed; unqualified, unfit, unfitted, inept 25adj. *unapt;* unworkable, dud, good for nothing 641adj. *useless;* inadequate 636adj. *insufficient;* ineffective, inefficacious, ineffectual, feeble 728adj. *unsuccessful;* incapable, incompetent, inefficient 695adj. *unskillful;* mechanically powerless, unpowered, unengined; unequipped 670adj. *unprepared.*

defenseless, helpless, without resource, bereaved, bereft 772adj. *losing;* kithless, kinless, orphan, unfriended 883adj. *friendless;* seely, harmless 935adj. *innocent;* barehanded, weaponless, armless, unarmed, disarmed 670adj. *unequipped;* unfortified, exposed, indefensible, untenable, pregnable, vincible 661 adj. *vulnerable.*

impotent, powerless, feeble 163adj. *weak;* emasculated, castrated, caponized, gelded, unsexed, unmanned 163adj. *crippled;* sexless, neuter; sterile, barren, infertile 172adj. *unproductive;* worn out, exhausted, used up, effete; senile, palsied 131adj. *aged;* paralytic, arthritic, stiff 326adj. *hard;* unconscious, comatose, numb, benumbed 375adj. *insensible;* disjointed 61adj. *orderless;* out of joint 46adj. *disjunct;* without self-control, incontinent; done up, dead-beat, foundered 684adj. *fatigued;* prostrated, flat 216adj. *supine;* nerveless, spineless, invertebrate 601adj. *irresolute;* shattered, unhinged, unnerved, demoralized 854adj. *nervous;* hors de combat, out of the running 728adj. *defeated;* helpless, rudderless, drifting 282adj. *deviating;* waterlogged, swamped; on one's beam ends, laid on one's back 728adj. *grounded;* baffled, thwarted, gnashing one's teeth 702 adj. *hindered.*

Vb. *be impotent,*—defenseless etc. adj.; be unable, cannot, not work, not do, not alter things; not help, have no help to offer 641vb. *be useless;* strive in vain, avail nothing, end in smoke, fade out 728vb. *fail;* have no power 745vb. *be subject;* lose power of resistance 721vb. *submit;* feel helpless, shrug, wring one's hands; gnash one's teeth 830vb. *regret;* do nothing, look on, stand by 441vb. *watch;* have a hopeless case, not have a leg to stand on; go by the board 446vb. *disappear;* lose consciousness, faint, swoon, pass out 375vb. *be insensible;* drop, collapse 163vb. *be weak.*

disable, incapacitate, unfit 641vb. *make useless;* disqualify 916vb. *disentitle;* deprive of power, invalidate, decontrol 752vb. *abrogate;* disarm, demilitarize 163vb. *weaken;* neutralize 182vb. *counteract;* undermine, sap, burrow 255vb. *make concave;* exhaust, use up, consume 634vb. *waste;* wind, prostrate, bowl over, knock out 279vb. *strike;* double up, cramp, benumb, paralyze 679vb. *make inactive;* sprain, rick, wrench, twist, dislocate; cripple, lame, maim, hobble, nobble, hamstring, hock, hough 702vb. *hinder,* 655vb. *impair;* stifle, throttle, suffocate, strangle, garrote 362vb. *kill;* muzzle, deaden 399vb. *silence;* spike the guns, draw the teeth, clip the wings, scotch the snake; tie the hands, cramp one's style; sabotage, ratten, put a spoke into one's wheel, throw a spanner *or* monkey-wrench into the works; deflate, take the wind out of one's sails, put out of gear, unhinge, unbrace, unstring 46vb. *disjoin;* put out of action, put out of commission 674vb. *disuse.*

unman, unnerve, enervate, palsy, cowardize 854vb. *frighten;* devitalize 163vb. *weaken;* emasculate, castrate, spay, geld, caponize, effeminate 172vb. *sterilize.*

See: 4, 25, 46, 61, 63, 75, 113, 114, 127, 130, 131, 163, 165, 172, 182, 216, 255, 279, 282, 326, 362, 375, 399, 497, 499, 503, 578, 601, 634, 636, 641, 651, 655, 661, 670, 674, 677, 679, 684, 695, 702, 719, 728, 745, 747, 752, 772, 830, 854, 883, 916, 935, 954.

162 Strength

N. *strength,* might, potency, horsepower, engine-p. 160n. *power;* energy 174n. *vigorousness;* force, physical f., main f. 735n. *brute force;* resilience, spring 328n. *elasticity;* tone, tonicity, tension, temper, capacity to bear, tolerance; iron, steel, adamant 326n. *hardness;* oak, heart of oak 329n. *toughness;* staying power, endurance, grit 600n. *stamina.*

vitality, healthiness 650n. *health;* vigor, liveliness 360n. *life;* animal spirits 833n. *cheerfulness;* virility, red-bloodedness, red blood 855n.

manliness, 372n. *male;* stoutness, sturdiness 599n. *resolution;* aggressiveness 718n. *bellicosity;* physique, muscularity, muscle, biceps, sinews, thews and sinews; bone, marrow, pith, pithiness, beef, brawn 195n. *size;* grip, iron g., vice-like g. 778n. *retention;* titanic strength, strength of Hercules.

athletics 837n. *sport;* athleticism, gymnastics, feats of strength, calisthenics 682n. *exercise;* acrobatics, aerobatics 875n. *ostentation;* agonism, agonistics 716n. *contest;* palaestra 724n. *arena.*

athlete, gymnast, tumbler, acrobat, contortionist, trapeze artist, circus rider, bareback r.; circus animal, performing flea; agonist, Blue, all-rounder, pancratiast 716n. *contender;* wrestler 716n. *wrestling;* heavyweight 722n. *pugilist;* weight-lifter, strong man; champion 644n. *exceller;* he-man 372n. *male;* strong-arm man, bully, bruiser, tough guy 857n. *desperado;* chucker-out, bouncer 300n. *ejector;* amazon, virago 373n. *woman;* matador, picador, toreador 362n. *killer;* Sandow, Milo, Hercules; Samson, Goliath, Antaeus, Atlas, Titan; giant refreshed 195n. *giant;* tower of strength 707n. *auxiliary.*

strengthening etc. vb.; reinforcement 703n. *aid;* stiffening, toughening, tempering 326n. *hardening;* invigoration, tonic effect 174n. *stimulation;* reanimation, refocillation 685n. *refreshment;* revival 656n. *restoration;* emphasis, stress 532n. *affirmation.*

science of forces, dynamics, statics, hydrodynamics, hydrostatics, electrodynamics, electrostatics; thermodynamics; triangle of forces.

Adj. *strong,* lusty, youthful 130adj. *young;* mighty, puissant, potent, armed 160adj. *powerful;* high-powered, high-geared, high-tension; all-powerful, omnipotent, overpowering, overwhelming 34adj. *superior;* incontestable, irresistible, resistless, more than a match for, victorious 727adj. *unbeaten;* sovereign, supreme 733adj. *ruling;* valid, in full force; in full swing 146adj. *unceasing*; in the plenitude of power, undiminished 32adj. *great;* like a giant refreshed 685adj. *refreshed;* in high feather, in fine f., in fine mettle, sound as a roach 650adj. *healthy;* heavy 322adj. *weighty;* strong as; strong-arm; forceful, forcible 735adj. *severe;* urgent, pressing, compulsive 740adj. *compelling;* emphatic, emphasized 532adj. *assertive;* tempered, iron-hard, hard as iron, steely, adamantine 326adj. *hard;* case-hardened, toughened 329adj. *tough;* deep-rooted 45adj. *firm-set;* firm, stable 153adj. *fixed;* thick-ribbed, well-built, stout; strong as a horse, strong as a lion, strong as an ox; strong as brandy, heady, alcoholic 949adj. *intoxicating;* strengthened, reinforced, double-strength; fortified, entrenched, defended, inviolable, unassailable 660adj. *invulnerable;* strong-smelling, odoriferous 394adj. *odorous.*

unyielding, staunch 599adj. *resolute;* stubborn 602adj. *obstinate;* persistent 600adj. *persevering;* unstretchable, inelastic 326adj. *rigid;* shatter-proof, unbreakable, infrangible, solid 324adj. *dense;* impregnable 660adj. *invulnerable;* indomitable, unconquerable, invincible, unbeatable 727adj. *unbeaten;* inextinguishable, unquenchable, unallayed 146adj. *unceasing;* unflagging, tireless, unexhausted 678adj. *industrious;* unweakened, unwithered, unworn, evergreen 113adj. *lasting;* proof, of proof, sound; *waterproof,* weather-proof, rustproof, damp-proof, impermeable, gas-proof, leak p. 264 adj. *sealed off;* fire-proof, bullet-p., bomb-p.

stalwart, stout, sturdy, hardy, rugged, robust 174adj. *vigorous;* of good physique, able-bodied, muscular, muscly, brawny; sinewy, wiry 678adj. *active;* strapping, well-knit, well set-up, broad-shouldered, thickset, burly, beefy, husky, hefty 195adj. *large;* gigantic, colossal, titanic, Herculean 195adj. *huge.*

athletic, gymnastic, acrobatic, agonistic, palaestric 716adj. *contending;* exercised, fit, fighting f., in training, in condition 650adj. *healthy;* amazonian.

manly, masculine 372adj. *male;* unwomanly, amazonian; virile, red-blooded, manful 855adj. *courageous;* in the prime of manhood 134adj. *adult.*

Vb. *be strong,*—mighty etc. adj.; have what it takes; pack a punch; gird up one's loins 669vb. *prepare;* come in force; be stronger, overpower, overmatch, overwhelm 727vb. *overmaster;* get stronger, convalesce, recover, revive 656vb. *be restored,* 685vb. *be refreshed;* get up, freshen (wind), blow hard, blow great guns 352vb. *blow.*

strengthen, confirm, give strength to,

lend force to 36vb. *augment;* underline, stress 532vb. *emphasize;* reinforce, fortify, entrench; stuff 227vb. *line;* buttress, prop, sustain 218vb. *support;* nerve, brace, steel 855vb. *give courage;* stiffen, toughen, temper, case-harden 326vb. *harden;* energize, act like a tonic 174vb. *invigorate;* animate, enliven, quicken 821vb. *excite;* vivify, revivify 656vb. *revive;* recruit, refect 685vb. *refresh;* set one on his legs 656vb. *cure;* set up, build up 310vb. *elevate;* screw up, wind up 45vb. *tighten;* power, engine, motor 160vb. *empower.*

Adv. *strongly,* powerfully etc. adj.; by force etc. n.; by main force, by compulsion, with might and main; in force.

See: 32, 34, 36, 45, 113, 130, 134, 146, 153, 160, 174, 193, 195, 218, 227, 264, 300, 310, 322, 324, 326, 328, 329, 352, 360, 362, 372, 373, 394, 532, 599, 600, 602, 644, 650, 656, 660, 678, 682, 685, 699, 703, 707, 716, 722, 724, 727, 735, 737, 740, 778, 833, 837, 855, 857, 875, 949.

163 Weakness

N. *weakness,* lack of strength, feebleness; helplessness, imbecility 161n. *impotence;* incapacity to bear, intolerance; flimsiness, slightness, lightness 323n. *levity;* wispiness, sleaziness; lack of temper, fragility, frailness 330n. *brittleness;* delicacy, tenderness 327n. *softness;* effeminacy, womanishness; unfirmness, unsteadiness, shakiness, wobbliness, giddiness, disequilibrium 29n. *inequality;* weak foundation, feet of clay, instability 152n. *changeableness;* moral weakness, frailty, infirmity of purpose 601n. *irresolution;* bodily weakness, weakliness, debility, infirmity, decrepitude, caducity, senility 131n. *age;* invalidism, delicate health 651n. *ill-health;* atony, no tone, no toughness, flaccidity, flabbiness, floppiness 335n. *fluidity;* fleshiness, corpulence 195n. *bulk;* weak state, asthenia, adynamy, cachexia; anemia, bloodlessness; loss of strength, enervation, inanition, faintness, langor, torpor, inactivity 679n. *sluggishness;* exhaustion, prostration, collapse 684n. *fatigue;* unconsciousness, swoon 375n. *insensibility;* decline, declension 655n. *deterioration;* weakening, softening, mitigation 177n. *moderation;* relaxation 734n. *laxity;* loosening 46n. *disjunction;* adulteration, watering, dilution 43n. *mixture;* emasculation; invalidation 752n. *abrogation;* effect of weakness, crack, fault 201n. *gap;* flaw 849n. *blemish;* strain, sprain, dislocation 63n. *derangement;* inadequacy 636n. *insufficiency,* 647n. *defect.*

weakling, effeminate, pansy; lightweight 639n. *nonentity;* softling, softy, sissy, milksop, mollycoddle; old woman, invalid, hypochondriac 651n. *sick person;* lame dog, lame duck 731n. *unlucky person;* infant, babe-in-arms, babe 132n. *child;* baby, cry-baby 856n. *coward;* mamma's boy, mother's darling, teacher's pet 890n. *favorite;* doormat, jellyfish, victim 825n. *sufferer;* gull 544n. *dupe.*

weak thing, flimsy article, reed, broken r., thread, rope of sand; sandcastle, mud pie, house built on sand, house of cards, house of bricks, cobweb, gossamer 4n. *insubstantial thing;* matchwood, matchstick, eggshell, paper, tissue p.; glass, china 330n. *brittleness;* water, dishwater, slops, milk and water, thin gruel.

Adj. *weak,* powerless, strengthless, without force, invalid, unconfirmed 161adj. *impotent;* under-strength, under-proof; unfortified, unstrengthened, aidless, helpless 161adj. *defenseless;* harmless, seely 935adj. *innocent;* baby, babyish 132adj. *infantine;* effeminate, pansy, womanish 373adj. *female;* poor, feeble, slight, puny 33adj. *small;* lightweight 323adj. *light;* slightly built, of poor physique 196adj. *little;* thin 206adj. *lean;* feebleminded, imbecile 499adj. *foolish;* sheepish, gutless, weak-willed, half-hearted 601adj. *irresolute;* nerveless, unnerved 854adj. *nervous;* spineless, invertebrate, submissive, yielding 721adj. *submitting;* marrowless, pithless 4adj. *insubstantial;* sapless 342adj. *dry;* bloodless, anemic, pale 426adj. *colorless;* untempered, unhardened, limp, flaccid, flabby, floppy 327adj. *soft;* drooping, sagging, giving 217adj. *pendent;* untaut, unstrung, slack, loose, relaxed 734adj. *lax,* 46adj. *disjunct;* watery, washy, wishy-washy, milk-and-water, insipid 387adj. *tasteless;* low, quiet, faint, hardly heard 401adj. *muted;* palsied, doddering, tottering, decrepit, old 131adj. *aged;* too weak, past it, weak as a child, weak as a baby; weak as water 604adj. *capricious;* rickety, tottery, shaky, wobbly 152adj. *unstable;* torpid 679adj. *inactive,* 266adj. *quiescent;* in its begin-

nings, only beginning, infant 68adj. *beginning,* 126adj. *new,* 130adj. *young.* **See** *flimsy.*
weakened, debilitated, diminished, deflated 37adj. *decreasing;* tapped, drained 190adj. *empty;* wasted, spent, effete, used up, burned out 673adj. *used;* misused, abused; sapped, undermined, disarmed, disabled, laid low 161adj. *defenseless;* stripped, denuded, exposed, bare 229adj. *uncovered;* flagging, failing, exhausted, wearied, weary 684adj. *fatigued;* strained, overstrained 246adj. *distorted;* weather-beaten, worn, broken, crumbling, tumble-down 655adj. *dilapidated;* the worse for wear, not what it was, on its last legs; rotten, rusting, withered, decaying, in decay 51adj. *decomposed;* deactivated, neutralized 175adj. *inert;* diluted, adulterated, watered, watered down 43adj. *mixed.* **See** *crippled.*
weakly, infirm, debile, asthenic, adynamic, delicate, sickly 651adj. *unhealthy;* groggy, rocky; seedy, poorly; pulled down, reduced 206adj. *lean;* languid, languishing; faint, fainting, faintish; sallow, lackluster 426adj. *colorless;* listless, lustless.
crippled, halt, lame, game, limping, hobbling; hamstrung, hobbled, hipshot; knock-kneed; stiff in the joints, arthritic, rheumatic, gouty; legless, armless, handless, eyeless 647adj. *imperfect.*
flimsy, delicate, gossamer, sleazy, wispy, tenuous 4adj. *insubstantial;* frail, tearable, fragile, frangible, friable, shattery 330adj. *brittle;* gimcrack, jerry-built, shoddy 641adj. *useless;* rickety, ramshackle, shaky, tottery, teetering, creaky, crazy, tumble-down 655adj. *dilapidated.*
Vb. *be weak,* grow w., weaken; sicken 651vb. *be ill;* faint, fail, languish, flag 684vb. *be fatigued;* drop, fall 309vb. *tumble;* decline 655vb. *deteriorate;* droop, wilt, fade 131vb. *grow old;* wear thin, crumble; soften 327vb. *soften;* yield, give way, sag, spring, start 263vb. *open;* totter, teeter, sway, reel 317vb. *oscillate;* tremble, shake 318vb. *be agitated;* halt, limp, hirple, go lame 278vb. *move slowly;* have one foot in the grave 127vb. *be old.*
weaken, enfeeble, debilitate, enervate; unnerve, rattle 854vb. *frighten;* relax, slacken, unbrace, loosen 46vb. *disjoin;* shake, soften up 327vb. *soften;* strain, sprain, cripple, lame 161vb. *disable;* cramp 702vb. *obstruct;* effeminate 161vb. *unman;* disarm, take the edge off, obtund 257vb. *blunt;* impoverish, starve; deprive, rob 786vb. *take away;* reduce, extenuate, thin, lessen 37vb. *bate;* dilute, water, water down, adulterate 43vb. *mix;* denature, devitalize; deactionate, neutralize 182vb. *counteract;* reduce in number, decimate 105vb. *render few;* invalidate 752vb. *abrogate;* damage, spoil 655vb. *impair;* dismantle, slight 165vb. *demolish;* sap, undermine, burrow; hurt, injure 655vb. *wound;* sicken, distemper.
See: 4, 29, 33, 37, 43, 46, 51, 63, 68, 105, 126, 127, 130, 131, 132, 152, 161, 165, 175, 177, 182, 184, 190, 195, 196, 201, 203, 206, 217, 229, 246, 257, 263, 266, 278, 309, 317, 318, 323, 327, 330, 335, 342, 373, 375, 387, 401, 426, 437, 499, 544, 601, 604, 636, 637, 639, 641, 647, 651, 655, 673, 679, 684, 702, 721, 731, 734, 752, 786, 825, 849, 854, 856, 890, 935.

164 Production

N. *production,* producing, creation; mental creation, cerebration 449n. *thought;* origination, invention, original work 21n. *non-imitation,* 484n. *discovery;* creative urge, productivity 171n. *productiveness;* effort, endeavor 671n. *essay,* 672n. *undertaking;* artistic effort, composition, authorship 551n. *art,* 553n. *painting,* 554n. *sculpture,* 586n. *writing;* musicianship 413n. *musical skill;* doing, performance, output, outturn, through-put 676n. *action;* execution, accomplishment, achievement 725n. *effectuation;* concoction, brewing 669n. *preparation;* formation, shaping, forming, conformation, workmanship, craftsmanship 243n. *efformation;* organization 331n. *structure,* 62n. *arrangement;* tectonics, engineering, building, edification, architecture; construction, establishment, erection 310n. *elevation;* making, fabrication, manufacture, industry 622vb. *business;* processing, process 147n. *conversion;* machining, assembly; assembly line, production l. 630n. *machine;* industrialization, increased output, mass production, automation; minting 797n. *coinage;* book production, printing, publication 587n. *print,* 589n. *book;* farming, growing 370n. *agriculture;* breeding 369n. *animal husbandry;* development, ribbon-d. 316n. *evolution.*

product, creature, creation, result 157n. *effect;* output, outturn; end-product, by-p.; extract, essence, confection; work of one's hands, handiwork, artifact; manufacture, article, thing 319n. *object;* ware 795n. *merchandise;* earthenware 381n. *pottery;* stoneware, hardware, ironware; production, work, opus, oeuvre, piece 56n. *composition;* chef d'oeuvre, crowning achievement 694n. *masterpiece;* fruit, flower, blossom, berry; produce, yield, harvest, crop, reaping, mowing, vintage 157n. *growth;* interest, increase, return 771n. *gain;* mental product, brainchild, conception 451n. *idea;* figment, fiction 513n. *ideality;* offspring, young, egg, spat, seed 132n. *youngling.*

edifice, piece of architecture, building, structure, fabric, erection, pile, dome, tower, skyscraper 209n. *high structure;* pyramid 548n. *monument;* church 990n. *temple;* mausoleum 364n. *tomb;* habitation, mansion, hall 192n. *house;* college 539n. *school;* fortress 713n. *fort;* sandcastle, mud pie 163n. *weak thing;* stonework, brickwork, bricks and mortar.

propagation 166n. *reproduction;* fertility, fecundity 171n. *productiveness;* proliferation, multiplication 36n. *increase;* breeding, hatching, incubation; copulation 45n. *coition;* generation, procreation, genesis, biogenesis, homogenesis, xenogenesis; parthenogenesis, virgin birth; autogenesis, abiogenesis, spontaneous generation; arrenotoky; thelytoky, gynogenesis; teratogenesis 84n. *abnormality;* fertilization, fecundation, superfecundation; impregnation, insemination, artificial i., pollination; conception, pregnancy, epigenesis, germination, gestation; birth, nativity 68vb. *origin;* growth, development, birthrate 157n. *growth;* fructification, fruition, florescence, efflorescence, flowering 669n. *maturation;* parenthood, motherhood, fatherhood, paternity 169n. *parentage;* genesiology.

obstetrics, midwifery, midders, maternity work; parturition, birth, childbirth, childbed, confinement, lying-in; accouchement, twilight sleep; labor, labor pain, travail, throe, birth-t., birth-pang, pains; delivery, forceps d.; cesarean, cesarean operation; omentum, caul, umbilical cord, placenta, afterbirth; obstetrician, maternity specialist; midwife, dai, accoucheur, accoucheuse 658n. *nurse;* stork, gooseberry bush.

genitalia, loins, womb 156n. *source;* organs of generation, parts, private p., privities; parts of shame, pudenda; intromittent organ, male o., member, penis; testicle, scrotum; vulva, vagina, uterus, ovary, fallopian tubes; seed, pollen; seminal fluid, sperm, spermatozoa; phallus, phallic emblem, lingam; yoni.

Adj. *productive,* creative, inventive; shaping, constructive, architectonic 331adj. *structural;* manufacturing, industrial 243adj. *formative;* genesial, genesiological; philoprogenitive, fertile, proliferating, spawning, teeming 171adj. *prolific;* potent, genial, genetic, germinal, seminal 171adj. *generative;* polliniferous, pollinigerous; pregnant, enceinte; breeding, broody; expecting, carrying, gravid, heavy with, big w., fraught w.; with child, with young, in the family way; parturient, brought to bed of, in the straw, obstetric, obstetrical 658adj. *medical;* puerperal, puerperous; thelytokous, arrenotokous; viviparous, oviparous, autogenous, abiogenetic; parthenogenetic; genital, vulvar, vaginal, phallic, priapic.

produced, made, created, creaturely; artificial, cultivated; manufactured, processed; hand-made, done by hand; untouched by hand, machine-made, mass-produced; multiplied; begotten 360adj. *born;* fathered, sired, dammed; bred, hatched; sown, grown; thought of, invented.

Vb. *produce,* create, originate, make; invent 484vb. *discover;* think up, conceive 513vb. *imagine;* operate 676vb. *do;* frame, form, shape 243vb. *efform;* loom 222vb. *weave;* forge, chisel, carve, sculpt, cast; coin 797vb. *mint;* manufacture, fabricate, prefabricate, process, machine; mass-produce, churn out, multiply; construct, build, upbuild, raise, rear, erect, set up, run up 310vb. *elevate;* put together, assemble, compose 45vb. *join;* mine 304vb. *extract;* establish, found, constitute, institute 68vb. *initiate;* organize, get up 62vb. *arrange;* engineer, contrive 623vb. *plan;* perform, implement, execute, achieve, accomplish 725vb. *carry out;* bring about, yield results, effect 156vb. *cause;* unfold, develop 316vb. *evolve;* breed, hatch, rear 369vb. *breed stock;* sow, grow, farm 370vb. *cultivate;* bring up, educate 534vb. *train.*

reproduce itself, yield, give increase,

flower, seed, sprout, blossom, bud, bloom, be out; burgeon 197vb. *expand;* fruit, bear fruit, fructify 669vb. *mature;* multiply, breed, hatch, teem, spawn, spat, pullulate 104vb. *be many;* carry, bear, bring forth, give birth; ean, yean, farrow, lamb, foal, drop, calve, pup, whelp, kitten, kindle, lay, seed; lie in, be brought to bed of; have offspring, have progeny; come to birth 360vb. *be born.*

generate, evolve, produce; fecundate, cover, impregnate, inseminate, pollinate; copulate 45vb. *unite with;* procreate, progenerate, propagate; beget, get, engender; father, sire; bring into being, bring into the world, usher into the w.; give life to, bring into existence, call into being; breed, hatch, incubate, raise, rear 369vb. *breed stock;* raise from seed, grow 370vb. *cultivate.*

See: 21, 45, 56, 62, 68, 104, 137, 147, 156, 157, 163, 166, 169, 171, 192, 197, 209, 222, 243, 304, 310, 316, 319, 331, 360, 364, 369, 370, 381, 413, 449, 451, 484, 513, 534, 539, 548, 551, 553, 554, 586, 587, 589, 622, 623, 630, 658, 669, 671, 672, 676, 684, 694, 713, 725, 771, 795, 797, 990.

165 Destruction: non-production

N. *destruction,* unmaking, undoing 148n. *reversion;* blotting out 550n. *obliteration;* blowing out, snuffing o., annihilation, nullification 2n. *extinction;* abolition, suppression, supersession 752n. *abrogation;* suffocation, stifling, silencing 599n. *silence;* subversion 221n. *overturning,* 149n. *revolution;* prostration, precipitation, overthrow 311n. *depression;* leveling, razing, flattening 216n. *horizontality;* dissolving, dissolution 51n. *decomposition;* breaking up, tearing down, demolition, demolishment, slighting 655n. *dilapidation,* 46n. *disjunction;* disruption, diruption 46n. *scission;* crushing, grinding, pulverization 322n. *pulverulence;* incineration 381n. *burning;* liquidation, elimination, extirpation, eradication, deracination, uprooting 300n. *ejection;* wiping out, mopping up 725n. *completion;* decimation, mass murder, genocide 362n. *slaughter;* doing in, spifflication; destructiveness, mischief, persecution, iconoclasm, biblioclasm, vandalism, wrecking activities, sabotage 702n. *hindrance;* fire-raising 381n. *incendiarism.*

havoc, scene of destruction, chaos 61n. *confusion, turmoil;* desolation, wilderness, scorched earth 172n. *desert;* carnage, shambles, Belsen 362n. *slaughter-house;* upheaval, cataclysm, inundation, storm 176n. *violence;* devastation, laying waste, ravages; depredation, razzia, raid 788n. *spoliation;* blitz 712n. *bombardment;* holocaust, hecatomb 981n. *oblation;* consumption, reckless expense 634n. *waste.*

ruin, downfall, ruination, perdition, one's undoing; crushing blow, catastrophe 731n. *adversity;* collapse, debacle, landslide 149n. *revolution;* breakdown, break-up, crack-up 728n. *failure;* wreck, shipwreck, wreckage, wrack; sinking, loss, total l.; Waterloo, Caudine Forks, Sedan 728n. *defeat;* knock-out blow, KO 279n. *knock;* beginning of the end, road to ruin 655n. *deterioration;* apocalypse, doom, crack of doom, knell, end 69n. *finality,* 961n. *condemnation;* ruins 127n. *oldness.*

Adj. *destructive,* destroying, internecine, annihilating etc. vb.; root and branch 54adj. *complete;* consuming, ruinous 634adj. *wasteful;* sacrificial, costly 811adj. *dear;* exhausting, crushing 684adj. *fatiguing;* apocalyptic, cataclysmic, overwhelming 176adj. *violent;* raging 176adj. *furious;* merciless 906adj. *pitiless;* mortal, suicidal, cut-throat 362adj. *deadly;* subversive, subversionary 149adj. *revolutionary;* incendiary, mischievous, pernicious 645adj. *harmful,* poisonous 653adj. *toxic.*

destroyed, undone, ruined, fallen; wiped out etc. vb.; crushed, ground; pulped, broken up; suppressed, squashed, quashed 752adj. *abrogated;* lost, foundered, torpedoed, sunk, sunk without trace; done for, kaput, spifflicated; falling, perishing, in ruins 655adj. *dilapidated;* doomed, marked out for destruction; in course of demolition, in the breaker's hands 69adj. *ending.*

Vb. *destroy,* undo, unmake 148vb. *revert;* abolish, annihilate, liquidate, exterminate 2vb. *nullify;* devour, consume, eat up 301vb. *eat;* swallow up, engulf 299vb. *absorb;* swamp, overwhelm, drown 341vb. *drench;* incinerate, burn up, gut 381vb. *burn;* wreck, shipwreck, sink, torpedo, scupper 313vb. *plunge;* end, put an end to 69vb. *terminate;* do for, do in, put down, put away, do away with, make away w., get rid of 362vb. *kill;* poison 362vb. *murder;*

decimate 105vb. *render few;* spare none, leave no survivor 362vb. *slaughter,* 906vb. *be pitiless;* remove, extirpate, eradicate, deracinate, uproot, root up 300vb. *eject;* wipe out, wipe off the map, expunge, efface, erase, delete, blot out, strike out, cancel 550vb. *obliterate;* annul, revoke 752vb. *abrogate;* dispel, scatter, dissipate 75vb. *disperse;* dissolve 337vb. *liquefy;* evaporate 338vb. *vaporize;* disrupt 46vb. *disjoin;* disorganize, confuse, confound 63vb. *derange;* destroy form, deface 244vb. *deform;* destroy an argument 479vb. *confute;* knock out, flatten out; spifflicate; put the kibosh on, make short work of, mop up; dish, cook one's goose, sabotage 702vb. *obstruct;* play hell with, play the deuce with 63vb. *bedevil,* 634vb. *waste;* ruin, be the ruin of, be one's undoing.

demolish, damage, slight 655vb. *impair;* dismantle, break down, knock d., pull d., tear d. 46vb. *disjoin;* level, raze, level to the ground, lay in the dust 216vb. *flatten;* throw down, prostrate, steamroller, bulldoze 311vb. *fell;* blow down, blow away, carry a.; cut down, mow d. 204vb. *shorten,* 362vb. *slaughter;* knock over, kick o.; subvert, overthrow, overturn, overset, upset 221vb. *invert;* sap, sap the very foundations 163vb. *weaken;* undermine, mine, blow up, blow sky-high; bombard, bomb, blitz, blow to pieces 712vb. *fire at;* break up, smash up; smash, shatter, shiver, smash to smithereens 46vb. *break;* pulp, crush, grind 332vb. *pulverize;* crush to pieces, atomize, knock to atoms, grind to bits, make mincemeat of; rend, tear up, rend to pieces, tear to bits, tear to shreds, tear to rags, pull to pieces, pluck to p., pick to p. 46vb. *sunder;* shake to pieces 318vb. *agitate;* beat down, batter, ram 279vb. *strike;* strip, bare, unwall, unroof 229vb. *uncover.*

suppress, quench, blow out, put o., snuff o. 382vb. *extinguish;* nip in the bud, cut short, cut off 72vb. *discontinue;* quell, put down, stamp out, trample out, trample under foot, stamp on, sit on 735vb. *oppress;* squelch, squash 216vb. *flatten;* quash, revoke 752vb. *abrogate;* blanket, stifle, suffocate, burke; keep under, repress, cover 525vb. *conceal;* drown, submerge, sink, scuttle, scupper, torpedo, sink without trace 313vb. *plunge,* 311vb. *depress;* kill, kill out.

lay waste, desolate, devastate, depopulate 300vb. *void;* despoil, depredate, raid 788vb. *rob;* damage, spoil, mar, ruin, ruinate 655vb. *impair;* ravage, deal destruction, run amok, make havoc, make a shambles, fill with carnage 176vb. *be violent;* scorch the earth, sow with salt 172vb. *sterilize;* lay in ruins 311vb. *abase;* lay in ashes 381vb. *burn;* waste with fire and sword 634vb. *waste.*

consume, devour, eat up, lick up, gobble up; swallow up, engulf 299vb. *absorb;* squander, run through, fling to the winds, play ducks and drakes 634vb. *waste;* throw to the dogs, cast before swine 675vb. *misuse.*

be destroyed, go west, go under, be lost 361vb. *perish;* sink, go down 313vb. *plunge;* be all over with, be all up with 69vb. *end;* fall, fall to the ground, totter to its fall, bite the dust 309vb. *tumble;* go on the rocks, break up, split, go to wreck, go to shivers, go to pieces, crumple up; fall into ruin, go to rack and ruin, crumble, crumble to dust 665vb. *deteriorate;* go to the wall, succumb; go to pot, go to the dogs, go to hell.

Adv. *destructively,* crushingly, with crushing effect, with a sledge hammer.

See: 2, 46, 51, 54, 63, 69, 72, 75, 105, 127, 148, 149, 163, 172, 176, 204, 216, 221, 226, 229, 244, 279, 299, 300, 301, 311, 313, 318, 332, 337, 338, 341, 361, 362, 381, 382, 479, 525, 550, 559, 634, 645, 653, 655, 665, 675, 684, 702, 712, 725, 728, 731, 735, 752, 788, 811, 906, 981.

166 Reproduction

N. *reproduction,* procreation, syngenesis, 164n. *production;* remaking, refashioning, reshaping, reconstruction; rediscovery 484n. *discovery;* redoing 106n. *repetition;* reduplication, mass production 171n. *productiveness;* multiplication, duplication, printing 587n. *print;* renovation, renewal 656n. *restoration;* regeneration, revivification, resuscitation, reanimation 656n. *revival;* resurrection, resurgence; reappearance 106n. *recurrence;* atavism 5n. *heredity;* reincarnation, palingenesis, metempsychosis, transmigration of souls 124n. *future state;* new edition, reprint 589n. *edition;* copy 22n. *duplicate;* phoenix, Alcestis.

Adj. *reproductive,* progenitive; reproduced, renewed, renewing; resurrectional, resurrectionary; renascent, resurgent, reappearing; Hydra-headed, phoenix-like.

Vb. *reproduce,* remake, refashion, recoin, reconstruct; rebuild, refound, reestablish, rediscover; duplicate 20vb. *copy,* 106vb. *repeat;* take after, throw back to, inherit 18vb. *resemble,* 148vb. *revert;* renovate, renew 656vb. *restore;* regenerate, revivify, resuscitate, reanimate 656vb. *revive;* reappear, resurge 106vb. *reoccur;* resurrect, stir up the embers; mass-produce, multiply; print off, reel o. 587n. *print;* crop up, spring up like mushrooms, breed 164vb. *reproduce itself,* 104vb. *be many.*

See: 5, 18, 20, 22, 104, 106, 124, 148, 164, 171, 484, 587, 589, 656.

167 Producer

N. *producer,* creator, maker, Nature; originator, inventor, discoverer, mover, instigator 612n. *motivator;* founder, establisher; generator, fertilizer, pollinator; inseminator, donor; begetter 169n. *parent;* creative worker, writer 589n. *author;* composer 413n. *musician;* painter, sculptor 556n. *artist;* deviser, designer 623n. *planner;* constructor, builder, architect, engineer; manufacturer, industrialist 686n. *agent;* executive 676n. *doer;* laborer 686n. *worker;* artificer, craftsman 686n. *artisan;* farmer, grower, planter, cultivator, agriculturist, gardener 370n. *husbandman;* stock-farmer, raiser, cattle-r., sheep farmer 369n. *breeder;* miner, extractor; stage-producer 594n. *stage-manager.*

See: 169, 369, 370, 413, 556, 589, 594, 612, 623, 676, 686.

168 Destroyer

N. *destroyer,* remover, leveler, abolitionist, iconoclast, annihilationist, nihilist, anarchist 149n. *revolutionist;* wrecker, destructionist, arsonist, pyromaniac 381n. *incendiarism;* spoiler, despoiler, ravager, raider 712n. *attacker,* 789n. *robber;* saboteur 702n. *hinderer;* defacer, eraser 550n. *obliteration;* killer, assassin 362n. *murderer;* executioner 963n. *punisher;* barbarian, Hun, Tartar, Vandal; time, hand of t., time's scythe 111n. *course of time;* angel of death 361n. *death;* destructive agency, locust 947n. *glutton;* moth, worm, rust, erosion 51n. *decay;* corrosive, acid, cankerworm, mildew, blight, poison 659n. *bane;* earthquake, fire, flood; instrument of destruction, sword 723n. *weapon;* gunpowder, dynamite, blasting powder 723vb. *explosive;* torpedo 723n. *bomb;* fire-extinguisher 382n. *extinguisher;* sponge, eraser.

See: 51, 111, 149, 361, 362, 381, 382, 550, 659, 702, 712, 723, 789, 947, 973.

169 Parentage

N. *parentage,* paternity, maternity; parenthood, fatherhood, motherhood; loins, womb 156n. *source;* kinship 11n. *consanguinity.*

parent, father, sire, dad, daddy, papa, pop, governor, the old man; head of the family, paterfamilias; genitor, progenitor, procreator, begetter, author of one's existence; grandfather, grandsire, grandad, great-grandfather 133n. *old man;* founder of the family, ancestor, forefather, forebear, patriarch, predecessor 66n. *precursor;* first parents, Adam and Eve 371n. *mankind;* foster-father, stepfather.

genealogy, family tree, lineage 11n. *family;* race history, pedigree, phylogamy, heredity; line, blood-l., blood, strain; blue blood 868n. *nobility;* stock, stem, tribe, house, race, clan, sept 11n. *race;* descent, extraction, birth, ancestry 68n. *origin;* theogony.

maternity, motherhood; mother, dam, mamma, mama, ma, mommy, mom, grandmother, grandam, grandma, gran, granny; materfamilias, matron, matriarch; beldam 133n. *old woman;* foster-mother, stepmother, mother-in-law.

Adj. *parental,* paternal; maternal, matronly; fatherly, fatherlike; motherly, stepmotherly; family, linear, patrilineal, matrilinear; ancestral; hereditary; patriarchal 127adj. *immemorial;* racial, phyletic 11adj. *ethnic.*

See: 11, 66, 68, 127, 133, 156, 371, 818.

170 Posterity

N. *posterity,* progeny, issue, offspring, young, little ones 132n. *child;* breed 11n. *race;* brood, seed, litter, farrow, spawn, spat 132n. *youngling;* fruit of the womb, children, grandchildren 11n. *family;* aftercomers, succession, heirs, inheritance, heritage; rising generation 130n. *youth.*

descendant, son, daughter, pledge;

child, bantling, chip off the old block, infant 132n. *child;* scion, shoot, sprout, sprit 132n. *young plant;* heir, heiress, heir of the body 776n. *beneficiary;* branch, ramification, daughter-house, daughter-nation, colony; graft, offshoot, offset.
sonship, filiation, line, lineage, descent, straight d., male d.; indirect descent, collaterality, ramification; irregular descent, illegitimacy 954n. *bastardy;* succession, heredity, heirship; primogeniture 119n. *priority.*
Adj. *filial,* daughterly; descended, lineal; collateral; primogenital 119n. *prior;* adopted, adoptive; step-; hereditary, inherited, Mendelian.
See: 11, 119, 130, 132, 776, 954.

171 Productiveness

N. *productiveness,* productivity, mass production; booming economy 730n. *prosperity;* overproductivity, superabundance, glut 637n. *redundance;* high birthrate, fecundity, fertility, luxuriance, lushness, exuberance, richness, uberty 635n. *plenty;* productive capacity, biotic potential; procreation, multiplication 164n. *propagation;* fructification 669n. *maturation;* fecundation, superfetation; fertilization, pollination, insemination, artificial i., A.I.D.; inventiveness, resourcefulness 513n. *imagination.*
fertilizer, chemical f., manure, artificial m., fish-m., guano, fish-g., dung, mold, silt, compost 370n. *agriculture;* semen, sperm, seed, roe, soft r., milt, milter; spermatic fluid.
abundance, wealth, riot, foison, harvest 32n. *great quantity;* teeming womb, mother earth, rich soil; hotbed, nursery 68n. *origin;* cornucopia, land flowing with milk and honey; second crop, aftergrowth, aftermath 67n. *sequel;* warren, antheap 104n. *multitude;* mother goddess, Earthmother; milch cow; rabbit.
Adj. *prolific,* fertile, fecund, feracious; teeming, multiparous, spawning 164adj. *productive;* fruitful, fruitbearing, frugiferous, fructiferous; pregnant, heavy with, parturient; exuberant, lush, luxuriant, rich, fat, uberous 635adj. *plenteous;* copious, streaming, pouring; paying 640adj. *profitable;* creative, inventive, resourceful.
generative, procreant, procreative, philoprogenitive, potent; life-giving, spermatic, seminal, germinal; originative, all-creating, omnific; propagable.
Vb. *make fruitful,* make productive etc. adj.; plant, fertilize, water, irrigate, manure, guanize, dung, top-dress 370vb. *cultivate;* impregnate, fecundate, inseminate, spermatize; procreate, produce 164vb. *generate.*
be fruitful,—prolific etc. adj.; conceive, germinate, bud, blossom; bear, give birth, have children; teem, proliferate, pullulate, swarm, multiply, propagate 104vb. *be many;* send up the birthrate; populate.
See: 32, 67, 68, 104, 164, 370, 513, 635, 637, 640, 669, 730.

172 Unproductiveness

N. *unproductivity,* unproductiveness, dearth, famine 636n. *scarcity;* sterility, barrenness, infertility, infecundity; contraception, sterilization 161n. *impotence;* dying race, falling birthrate, slow growth 37vb. *decrease;* virginity 895n. *celibacy;* change of life, menopause; unprofitableness, poor return, losing business 772n. *loss;* unprofitability 641n. *inutility;* stagnation, waste of time, maiden over 641n. *lost labor;* slack market, idleness 679n. *inactivity.*
desert, dryness, aridity 342n. *dryness;* desolation, waste, barren w., unsown w., heath, barren h., wild, wilderness, howling w.; sand, dustbowl; salt flat 347n. *marsh;* icy waste 380n. *ice;* Sahara, Gobi; waste of waters 343n. *ocean;* desert island, solitude 883n. *seclusion.*
Adj. *unproductive,* dried up, exhausted, wasted, sparse, scarce 636adj. *insufficient;* waste, desert, desolate; poor, stony, shallow; unprolific, barren, infertile, sterile; unfruitful, acarpous, infecund, teemless; rootless, seedless, ungerminating; arid, unwatered, unirrigated 342adj. *dry;* fallow, stagnating 674adj. *disused;* unsown, unmanured, unplowed, untilled, uncultivated, unharvested; obtiose 679adj. *inactive;* childless, issueless, without issue; celibate 895adj. *unwedded;* fruitless, unprofitable 641adj. *profitless,* inoperative, null and void, of no effect 161adj. *impotent;* ineffective 728adj. *unsuccessful;* addled, abortive 670adj. *unprepared.*
Vb. *be unproductive,*—unprolific etc. adj.; rust, stagnate, lie fallow 679vb. *be inactive;* cease work 145vb. *cease;* bury one's talent 674vb. *not use;* hang fire, come to

nothing, come to naught 728vb. *fail;* flash in the pan, abort 728vb. *miscarry;* have no issue, lower the birthrate.

sterilize, castrate, geld 161vb. *unman;* sow with salt 165vb. *lay waste;* addle 51vb. *decompose;* disinfect 648vb. *purify.*

See: 37, 51, 145, 161, 165, 342, 343, 347, 380, 636, 641, 648, 670, 674, 679, 728, 772, 883, 895.

173 Agency

N. *agency,* operation, work, working, doing 676n. *action;* job, office 622n. *function;* exercise 673n. *use;* force, strain, stress, play, swing 160n. power; interaction, interworking 178n. *influence;* procuration, procurement 689n. *management;* service 628n. *instrumentality;* effectiveness, efficiency 156n. *causation;* quickening power 174n. *stimulation;* maintenance 218n. *support;* coagency 706n. *cooperation;* homestroke, execution 725n. *effectuation;* process, treatment, handling.

Adj. *operative,* effectual, efficient, efficacious 727adj. *successful;* drastic 735adj. *severe;* executive, operational, functional; acting, working, in action, in operation, in force, in play, in exercise, at work 676adj. *doing,* 673adj. *used;* on foot, on the active list, up and doing 678adj. *active;* live, potent, of power 160adj. *dynamic,* 174adj. *vigorous;* practical, workable, applicable 642adj. *expedient;* serviceable 640adj. *useful;* worked upon, acted u., wrought u.

Vb. *operate,* be in action, be in play, play; act, work, go, run 676vb. *do;* start up, tick over, idle; serve, execute, perform 622vb. *function;* do its job 727vb. *be successful;* take effect 156vb. *cause;* have effect, act upon, bear u., work u., play u. 178vb. *influence;* put forth one's power, strike 678vb. *be active;* maintain, sustain 218vb. *support;* make operate, bring into play, wind up, turn on, switch on, flick *or* flip the switch; actuate, power, drive 265vb. *move;* process, treat; manipulate, handle, wield, brandish 378vb. *touch,* 673vb. *use;* stimulate, excite 174vb. *invigorate.*

See: 156, 160, 174, 178, 218, 265, 378, 622, 628, 640, 642, 673, 676, 678, 689, 706, 725, 727, 735.

174 Vigor: physical energy

N. *vigorousness,* lustiness, energy, vigor, life 678n. *activity;* dynamism, physical energy, dynamic e., pressure, force 160n. *energy;* intensity, high pressure 162n. *strength,* 32n. *greatness;* dash, élan, rush, impetuosity 680n. *haste;* exertion, effort 682n. *labor;* zest, zestfulness 824n. *joy;* liveliness, spirit, vim, fire, mettle, blood 855n. *courage;* ginger, fizz, verve, pep, drive, go; enterprise, initiative 672n. *undertaking;* vehemence 176n. *violence;* aggressiveness, thrust, push, kick, punch 712n. *attack;* grip, bite, teeth, backbone, gristle, spunk 599n. *resolution;* live wire, dynamo, dynamite, quicksilver; rocket, jet; display of energy 277n. *spurt;* show of force, demonstration 854n. *intimidation.*

stimulation, activation, tonic effect; intensification, boost, stepping up, bumping up 36n. *increase;* excitement 821n. *excitation;* stir, bustle, splutter 678n. *activity;* perturbation 318n. *agitation;* ferment, fermentation, leaven; ebullience, ebullition 318n. *commotion;* froth, foam 355n. *bubble;* steam 381n. *heating.*

keenness, acritude, acridity, acrimony, mordancy, causticity, virulence 388n. *pungency;* poignancy, point, edge 256n. *sharpness;* zeal 597n. *willingness.*

stimulant, energizer, activator, booster; stimulus, fillip, shot, shot in the arm; crack of the whip, spur, prick, prod, goad, lash 612n. *incentive;* hormone, restorative, tonic; bracer, pick-me-up, aperitif, appetizer 390n. *savoriness;* seasoning, spice 389n. *sauce;* drink, alcohol 301n. *liquor;* aphrodisiac, philter, love p.; cantharides, Spanish fly; pep talk, rousing cheer 821n. *excitant.*

Adj. *vigorous,* energetic, 678adj. *active;* radioactive 362adj. *deadly;* forcible, forceful 162adj. *strong;* vehement 176adj. *violent;* vivid, vibrant 160n. *dynamic;* high-pressure, intense, strenuous 678adj. *industrious;* enterprising, go-ahead 285adj. *progressive;* aggressive, pushful, thrustful 712adj. *attacking;* keen, alacritous 597adj. *willing;* double-edged, double-shotted, double-distilled, potent 160adj. *powerful;* full of beans, full of punch, full of pep, peppy, zestful, lusty, mettlesome, brisk, live 819adj. *lively;* nippy, snappy; fizzy, heady, racy; tonic, bracing, rousing, invigorating, stimulating 821adj. *exciting;* drastic, stringent, harsh, punishing 735adj. *severe;* intensified, stepped up, gingered up, hepped up, souped up 656adj. *restored;* recruited 685 adj. *refreshed;* thriving, lush 171adj. *prolific;* hearty, full-blooded.

keen, acute, sharp, incisive, trenchant 571n. *forceful;* mordant, biting, pointed, sarcastic 851adj. *derisive;* virulent, corrosive, caustic, escharotic 388adj. *pungent;* acrid, acid, acidulous 393adj. *sour.*

Vb. *be vigorous,* thrive, have zest, enjoy life 650vb. *be healthy;* burst with energy, overflow with e., feel one's oats 162vb. *be strong;* show energy 678vb. *be active;* be up and doing 682vb. *exert oneself;* exert energy, drive, push 279vb. *impel;* bang, slam, wrench, cut right through 176vb. *force;* raise the pressure, get up steam, turn on the s., spurt 277vb. *accelerate;* be thorough, strike home 725vb. *carry through;* strike hard, hammer, dint, dent 279vb. *strike;* show one's power, tell upon, make an impression 178vb. *influence,* 821vb. *impress;* throw one's weight about 678vb. *meddle;* show fight, take the offensive 712vb. *attack.*

invigorate, energize, activate; intensify, double, redouble; wind up, step up, bump up, pep up, ginger up, boost 160vb. *strengthen;* rouse, kindle, inflame, stimulate, enliven, quicken 821vb. *excite;* act like a tonic, hearten, animate 833vb. *cheer;* go to one's head, intoxicate 949vb. *inebriate;* freshen, recruit 685vb. *refresh;* give an edge to 256vb. *sharpen;* force, dung, manure, fertilize 370vb. *cultivate.*

Adv. *vigorously,* forcibly, with telling effect; zestfully, lustily.

See: 32, 36, 160, 162, 171, 176, 178, 256, 277, 279, 285, 301, 318, 355, 362, 370, 381, 388, 389, 390, 393, 571, 597, 599, 612, 650, 656, 658, 672, 678, 680, 682, 685, 712, 725, 735, 819, 821, 824, 833, 851, 854, 855, 949.

175 Inertness

N. *inertness,* inertia 677n. *inaction;* lifelessness, languor, paralysis, torpor, torpidity 375n. *insensibility;* rest, vegetation, stagnation, passivity 266n. *quiescence;* dormancy 523n. *latency;* mental inertness, dullness, sloth 679n. *sluggishness;* immobility 602n. *obstinacy;* impassiveness, stolidity 823n. *inexcitability;* gutlessness 601n. *irresolution;* spent fires, extinct volcano.

Adj. *inert,* unactivated, unaroused, passive, dead 677adj. *non-acting;* lifeless, languid, torpid, numb 375adj. *insensible;* heavy, lumpish, sluggish 278adj. *slow,* 679adj. *inactive;* quiet, vegetating, stagnant 266adj. *quiescent;* slack, low-pressure, untensed 734adj. *lax;* apathetic, neutral 860adj. *indifferent,* 820adj. *impassive;* pacific, unwarlike, unaggressive 717adj. *peaceful,* 823adj. *inexcitable;* uninfluential 161adj. *powerless;* deactivated, unexerted, suspended, in abeyance 752adj. *abrogated;* smoldering, dormant 523adj. *latent.*

Vb. *be inert,* be inactive etc. adj.; slumber 679vb. *sleep;* hang fire, not catch; smolder 523vb. *lurk;* lie, stagnate, vegetate 266vb. *be quiescent.*

Adv. *inactively* etc. adj.; at rest; in suspense, in abeyance, in reserve.

See: 161, 266, 278, 375, 523, 601, 602, 677, 679, 717, 734, 752, 820, 823, 860.

176 Violence

N. *violence,* vehemence, impetuosity 174n. *vigorousness;* destructiveness, vandalism 165n. *destruction;* boisterousness, turbulence, storminess 318n. *commotion;* bluster, uproar, riot, row, rumpus, furore 61n. *turmoil;* roughness, ungentleness, severe handling, extremities 735n. *severity;* force, hammer blows, high hand, coup de main, strong-arm work, outrage, terrorism 735n. *brute force;* barbarity, brutality, savagery, bloodlust 898n. *inhumanity;* malignity, mercilessness 906n. *pitilessness;* exacerbation, exasperation 832n. *aggravation;* brainstorm, hysterics 822n. *excitable state;* fit, throes, paroxysm 318n. *spasm;* shock, clash 279n. *collision;* wrench, twist, dislocation, torture 63n. *derangement,* 246n. *distortion.*

outbreak, outburst, ebullition, effervescence 318n. *agitation;* cataclysm, flood, tidal wave 350n. *wave;* convulsion, earthquake, quake, tremor 149n. *revolution;* eruption, volcano 383n. *furnace;* explosion, blowup, burst, blast 165n. *destruction;* displosion, dissilience 46n. *disjunction;* detonation 400n. *loudness;* rush, onrush, outrush, sortie 712n. *attack;* gush, spurt, jet 350n. *stream;* torrent, rapids 350n. *current.*

storm, turmoil, ferment, war of the elements; weather, dirty w., rough w., inclement w., inclemency; tempest, hurricane 352n. *gale;* thunder,

thunder and lightning, fulguration; rainstorm, cloudburst 350n. *rain;* hailstorm, snowstorm, blizzard 380n. *wintriness;* sandstorm, duststorm 352n. *gale;* magnetic storm; gale force.

violent creature, brute, beast, wild b.; dragon, tiger, wolf, she w., mad dog; demon, devil, hell-hound, hell-cat, fury 938n. *monster;* savage, barbarian, Vandal, iconoclast 168vb. *destroyer;* he-man, cave m. 372n. *male;* man of blood, assassin, executioner, butcher, Herod 362n. *murderer;* berserk, homicidal maniac 504n. *madman;* rough, tough, rowdy; hooligan, bully, terror, holy t. 735n. *tyrant;* thunderer, fire-eater, bravo 877n. *boaster;* fire-brand, incendiary 738n. *agitator;* revolutionary, anarchist, nihilist, terrorist 149n. *revolutionist;* hotspur, madcap 855n. *brave person;* virago, termagant, amazon; spitfire, scold 892n. *shrew;* Erinys, Tisiphone, Megaera, Alecto 891n. *Fury.*

Adj. *violent,* vehement, forcible 162adj. *strong;* acute 256adj. *sharp;* unmitigated; excessive, outrageous, extravagant 32adj. *exorbitant;* rude, ungentle, abrupt, brusque, bluff 885adj. *discourteous;* extreme, severe, tyrannical, heavy-handed 735 adj. *oppressive;* primitive, barbarous, savage, brutal, bloody 898adj. *cruel;* hot-blooded 892adj. *irascible;* aggressive, bellicose 718adj. *warlike;* rampant, charging 712adj. *attacking;* struggling, kicking, thrashing about 61adj. *disorderly;* rough, boisterous, wild, raging, blustery, blustrous, tempestuous, stormy 352adj. *windy;* drenching, torrential 350adj. *rainy;* uproarious, obstreperous 400adj. *loud;* rowdy, turbulent, tumultuous, tumultuary 738adj. *riotous;* incendiary, anarchistic, nihilistic 149adj. *revolutionary;* intemperate, immoderate, unbridled; ungovernable, unruly, uncontrollable 738adj. *disobedient;* unrepressed, unquelled, irrepressible 744adj. *independent;* unextinguished, inextinguishable, quenchless, unquenched 174adj. *vigorous;* ebullient, hot, red-hot, inflamed 381adj. *heated;* inflammatory, scorching, flaming 379adj. *fiery;* eruptive, cataclysmic, overwhelming, volcanic, seismic 165adj. *destructive;* detonating, explosive, bursting; convulsive, spasmodic 318adj. *agitated;* full of violence, disturbed, troublous, stirring 61adj. *orderless.*

furious, boiling, on the boil, towering; infuriate, maddened 891adj. *angry;* impetuous, rampant, gnashing; roaring, howling; headstrong 680adj. *hasty;* desperate 857adj. *rash;* savage, tameless, wild; blustering, threatening, cursing 899adj. *maledicent;* vicious, fierce, ferocious 898 adj. *cruel;* blood-thirsty, ravening, berserk 362adj. *murderous;* waspish, tigerish; frantic, hysterical, in hysterics 503adj. *frenzied.*

Vb. *be violent,* break bounds, run wild, run riot, run amok, tear, rush, rush about, rush headlong, rush head foremost 277vb. *move fast;* surge forward, mob 712vb. *charge;* break the peace, raise a storm, riot, make a riot, kick up a row, kick up a fuss, kick up a dust 61vb. *rampage;* resort to violence, take to arms 718vb. *go to war,* 738vb. *revolt;* see red, go berserk 891vb. *be angry;* storm, rage, roar, bluster, come in like a lion 352vb. *blow;* ferment, foam, fume, run high, boil over 318vb. *effervesce;* burst its banks, flood, overwhelm 350vb. *flow;* explode, go off, blow up, detonate, burst, fly, flash, flare; let fly, let off, fulminate; erupt, break out, fly o., burst o.; struggle, strain, scratch, bite, kick, lash out 715vb. *resist;* savage, maul 655vb. *wound;* bear down, bear hard on, ride roughshod, tyrannize, out-Herod Herod 735vb. *oppress;* spread like wildfire, overrun 297vb. *irrupt,* 165vb. *lay waste.*

force, use f., smash 46vb. *break;* tear, rend 46vb. *sunder;* bruise, crush 332vb. *pulverize;* convulse, blow up 165vb. *demolish;* strain, wrench, pull, dislocate; torture, twist, warp, deform 246vb. *distort;* force open, prize o., pry o., jimmy 263vb. *open;* blow open, burst o.; shock, shake 318vb. *agitate;* do violence to, abuse 675vb. *misuse;* violate, ravish, rape 951vb. *debauch.*

make violent, stir, quicken, stimulate 821vb. *excite;* urge, goad, lash, whip 612vb. *incite;* poke, stoke, stir up, inflame 381vb. *kindle;* add fuel to the flame, blow the embers 381vb. *heat;* foment, exacerbate, exasperate 832vb. *aggravate;* whet 256vb. *sharpen;* irritate, infuriate, lash into fury, fan into f. 891vb. *enrage;* madden 503vb. *make mad.*

Adv. *violently,* forcibly, by storm, by force, by main force, amain; with might and main; tooth and nail, hammer and tongs, vi et armis, at the sword's point, at the point of the bayonet; tyrannously, with a high hand; at one fell swoop, through thick and thin, in desperation, with a vengeance; precipitately, headlong, head foremost, head first; like a bull at a gate, like Gaderene swine.

See: 32, 46, 61, 62, 145, 149, 162, 165, 168, 174, 246, 256, 263, 277, 297, 318, 332, 350, 352, 362, 372, 379, 380, 381, 383, 400, 503, 504, 612, 655, 675, 680, 712, 715, 718, 735, 738, 744, 821, 822, 832, 855, 857, 877, 885, 891, 892, 898, 906, 928, 951.

177 Moderation

N. *moderation,* non-violence, gentleness 736n. *lenity;* harmlessness, innocuousness 935n. *innocence;* moderateness, reasonableness, measure, golden mean 732n. *mediocrity;* temperateness, restraint, self-control 942n. *temperance;* soberness 948n. *sobriety,* 874n. *modesty;* impassivity, mental calmness 823n. *inexcitability;* impartiality, neutrality 625vb. *midcourse;* correction, adjustment, modulation; mutual concession 770n. *compromise;* mitigation 831n. *relief;* relaxation, remission 734n. *laxity;* easing, alleviation, mollification; appeasement, assuagement, détente 719n. *pacification;* tranquilization, sedation; quiet, calm, dead c. 266n. *quietude;* control, check 747n. *restraint.*

moderator, palliative, stopgap, solvent 658n. *remedy;* lenitive, alleviative, demulcent 658n. *balm;* rose water, soothing syrup, milk, oil on troubled waters; calmative, sedative, tranquilizer, nightcap, bromide, barbiturate 679n. *soporific;* anodyne, opiate, poppy, opium, laudanum 375n. *anesthetic;* wet blanket, damper 613n. *dissuasion;* cooler, cold water, cold shower 382n. *extinguisher;* brake 747n. *restraint;* neutralizer; anaphrodisiac 658n. *antidote;* cushion, shock-absorber 327n. *softness;* mollifier, peacemaker, pacificator 720n. *mediator;* controller, restraining hand, rein.

Adj. *moderate,* unextreme, non-violent, reasonable, judicious 480n. *judicial;* tame, gentle, gentle as a lamb, harmless, mild, mild as milk 736adj. *lenient;* milk and water, innocuous 935adj. *innocent,* 163adj. *weak;* measured, restricted, limited 747adj. *restrained;* chastened, subdued, self-controlled, tempered 942adj. *temperate,* 948adj. *sober;* cool, calm 823adj. *inexcitable;* still, quiet, untroubled 266adj. *tranquil;* peaceful, peaceable, pacific 717adj. *peaceful;* leftish, pink, non-extreme 625 adj. *neutral,* 860adj. *indifferent.*

lenitive, unexciting, unirritating, abirritant 658adj. *remedial;* alleviative, assuaging, pain-killing, anodyne, calmative, sedative, hypnotic, narcotic 679adj. *somnific;* smooth 327 adj. *soft;* soothing, bland, demulcent; emollient; oily 334adj. *lubricated;* comforting 685adj. *refreshing;* disarming 719adj. *pacificatory.*

Vb. *be moderate,*—gentle etc. adj.; hold a mean 625vb. *be halfway,* 732vb. *be middling;* keep within bounds, keep within compass 942vb. *be temperate;* sober down, settle 266vb. *be quiescent;* disarm, keep the peace 717vb. *be at peace;* remit, relent 905vb. *show mercy;* show consideration, not press 736vb. *be lenient;* not resist, go quietly, go out like a lamb; shorten sail 278vb. *decelerate.*

moderate, mitigate, temper, attemper, contemper; correct 24vb. *adjust;* tame, check, curb, control, govern, limit, keep within limits 747vb. *restrain;* abate, lessen, diminish, slacken 37vb. *bate;* palliate, extenuate, qualify 163vb. *weaken;* obtund, take the edge off, slake, sheathe the sword 257vb. *blunt;* break the fall, cushion 218vb. *support;* moderate language, tone down, chasten, blue-pencil, euphemize 648vb. *purify;* sober, sober down, dampen, damp, cool, chill, throw cold water on 382vb. *refrigerate,* 613vb. *dissuade;* reduce the temperature, bank down the fires; blanket, smother, subdue, quell 382vb. *extinguish.*

assuage, ease, pour balm, mollify, lenify 327vb. *soften;* alleviate, lighten 831vb. *relieve;* deactivate, take the sting out 182vb. *counteract;* allay, lay, deaden 375vb. *render insensible;* soothe, calm, compose, tranquilize, still, quiet, hush, lull, rock, cradle, rock to sleep 266vb. *bring to rest;* dulcify 392vb. *sweeten;* disarm, appease, smooth over, pour oil on the troubled waters 719vb. *pacify;* assuage one's thirst, slake 301vb. *drink.*

Adv. *moderately,* within bounds, within limits, within compass, within reason; at half speed, under easy sail; so-so, averagely; gingerly, half-heartedly, nervously.

See: 24, 37, 163, 183, 218, 257, 266, 278, 301, 327, 334, 375, 382, 392, 480,

613, 625, 648, 658, 679, 717, 719, 720, 732, 734, 736, 747, 770, 823, 831, 860, 874, 905, 935, 942, 948.

178 Influence

N. *influence,* capability, power, potentiality 160n. *ability;* prevalence, predominance 34n. *superiority;* mightiness, over-mightiness, magnitude 32n. *greatness,* 638n. *importance;* position of influence, vantage ground, footing, hold, grip; leverage, play 744n. *scope;* purchase, fulcrum 218n. *pivot;* physical influence, weight, heft, pressure, gravitation 322n. *gravity;* pull, drag, magnetism 291n. *attraction;* counter-attraction 292n. *repulsion,* 182n. *counteraction;* thrust, drive 287n. *propulsion;* impact 279n. *impulse;* leaven, contagion, infection; atavism, telegony 5n. *heredity;* occult influence, mana, magic, spell 983n. *sorcery;* stars, heavens, destiny 596n. *fate;* fascination, hypnotism, mesmerism; malign influence, curse, ruin 659n. *bane;* emotion, impulse, impression, feeling 817n. *affections;* suasion, persuasion, insinuation, suggestion, impulsion, inspiration 612n. *motive;* personality, leadership, credit, repute 866n. *prestige;* hegemony, ascendancy, domination, tyranny 733n. *authority;* sway, control, dominance, reign 733n. *governance;* factor, contributing f., vital role, leading part 156n. *cause;* indirect influence, patronage, interest, favor, pull, friend at court, wire-pulling; strings, wires, lever 630n. *tool;* secret influence, hidden hand, power behind the throne, Grey Eminence 523n. *latency;* manipulator, wire-puller, mover, maneuverer 612n. *motivator;* man of influence, uncrowned king, big wheel, a host in himself 638n. *bigwig;* powers that be, the Establishment 733n. *government;* atmosphere, climate.

Adj. *influential,* dominant, predominant, prevalent, prevailing 34adj. *supreme;* in power, ruling, regnant, reigning, commanding, listened to, obeyed; recognized, with authority, of a., in a. 733adj. *authoritative;* rising, ascendant, in the ascendant 36adj. *increasing;* strong, potent, mighty, overmighty 32adj. *great,* 160adj. *powerful;* leading, guiding, hegemonical 689adj. *directing;* activating, inspiring, encouraging; active in, busy, meddling 678adj. *active;* contributing, effective 156adj. *causal;* weighty, key, momentous, decisive, world-shattering, earth-shaking 638adj. *important;* telling, moving, emotional 821adj. *impressive;* appealing, attractive 291adj. *attracting;* gripping, fascinating; irresistible, hypnotic, mesmeric 740adj. *compelling;* persuasive, suggestive, insinuating, tempting 612adj. *inducive;* habit-forming; educative, instructive 534adj. *educational;* spreading, catching, contagious 653adj. *infectious;* pervasive 189adj. *ubiquitous.*

Vb. *influence,* have i., command i., have a pull, have drag, carry weight, cut ice, have a hold on, have in one's power; have the ear of, be listened to, be recognized, be obeyed 737vb. *command;* dominate, tower over, bestride; lead by the nose, have under one's thumb, wind round one's little finger, wear the breeches 34vb. *be superior;* exert influence, make oneself felt, assert oneself; pull one's weight, throw one's weight into the scale, weigh in; put pressure on, lobby, pull strings, pull the s. 612vb. *motivate;* make one's voice heard, gain a hearing 455vb. *attract notice;* affect, tell, turn the scale; bear upon, work u., tell u. 821vb. *impress;* urge, prompt, tempt, incite, inspire, work upon, dispose, persuade, prevail upon, convince, carry with one 612vb. *induce;* force 740vb. *compel;* sway, tyrannize; color, prejudice 481vb. *bias;* appeal, allure, fascinate, hypnotize, mesmerize 291vb. *attract;* disgust, put off 292vb. *repel;* make, be the making of 654vb. *make better;* make or mar, change 147vb. *transform;* infect, leaven, color 143vb. *modify;* contaminate, mar 655vb. *impair;* actuate, work 173vb. *operate;* play a part, play a leading p., guide 689vb. *direct;* lead the dance, set the fashion, be the model for 23vb. *be example.*

prevail, establish one's influence, outweigh, overweigh, override, overbear, turn the scale 34vb. *predominate;* overawe, overcome, subdue, subjugate; gain head, gain the upper hand, gain full play, master 727vb. *overmaster;* control, rule, lead 733vb. *dominate;* take a hold on, take a grip on, hold 778vb. *retain;* gain a footing, take root, take hold, strike root in, settle 144vb. *stay;* permeate, run through, color 189vb. *pervade;* catch on, spread, rage, be rife, spread like wildfire.

Adv. *influentially,* to good effect, with telling e.; within one's orbit.

See: 5, 23, 32, 34, 36, 133, 143, 147,

156, 160, 173, 182, 189, 218, 279, 287, 291, 292, 322, 455, 481, 523, 534, 596, 612, 630, 638, 653, 654, 655, 659, 678, 689, 727, 733, 737, 740, 744, 745, 778, 817, 821, 866, 983.

179 Tendency

N. *tendency,* trend, tenor; tempo, set, drift 281n. *direction;* course, stream, main current, main stream, zeitgeist, spirit of the times, spirit of the age; conatus, nisus; affinity 291n. *attraction;* polarity 240n. *contraposition;* aptness 24n. *fitness;* gift, instinct for 694n. *aptitude;* proneness, proclivity, propensity, predisposition, readiness, inclination, penchant, liking, leaning, bias, prejudice; weakness 180n. *liability;* cast, bent, turn, grain; a strain of 43n. *tincture;* vein, humor, mood; tone, quality, nature, characteristic 5n. *temperament;* special gift, idiosyncrasy 80n. *specialty.*

Adj. *tending,* trending, conducive, leading to, pointing to; tendentious, working toward, aiming at 617adj. *intending;* in a fair way to, calculated to 471adj. *probable;* centrifugal 620adj. *avoiding;* subservient 180adj. *liable;* ready to, about to 669adj. *prepared.*

Vb. *tend,* trend, verge, lean, incline; set in, set, set toward, gravitate t. 289vb. *approach;* affect, dispose, carry, bias, bend to, warp, turn 178vb. *influence;* point to, lead to 156vb. *conduce;* bid fair to, be calculated to 471vb. *be likely;* redound to, contribute to 285vb. *promote.*

See: 5, 24, 43, 80, 156, 178, 180, 240, 281, 285, 289, 291, 471, 617, 620, 669, 694.

180 Liability

N. *liability,* liableness, weakness 179n. *trend;* exposure 661n. *vulnerability;* susceptibility, susceptivity, impressibility 374n. *sensibility;* potentiality 469n. *possibility;* likelihood 471n. *probability;* obligation, responsibility, accountability, amenability 917n. *duty.*

Adj. *liable,* apt to 179adj. *tending;* subject to, obnoxious to, the prey of, at the mercy of 745adj. *subject;* open to, exposed to, in danger of 661adj. *vulnerable;* dependent on, contingent 157adj. *caused;* incident to, incidental; possible, on the cards, within the range of 469adj. *possible;* incurring, unexempt from; susceptible 819adj. *impressible;* answerable, responsible, amenable, accountable 917adj. *dutied.*

Vb. *be liable,*—subject to etc. adj.; be responsible, answer for 917vb. *incur a duty;* incur, lay oneself open to, run the chance of, stand the chance of; stand to, stand to gain, stand to lose; expose oneself 661vb. *be in danger;* lie under 745vb. *be subject;* open a door to 156vb. *conduce.*

See: 156, 157, 179, 374, 469, 471, 661, 745, 819, 917.

181 Concurrence: combination of causes

N. *concurrence,* combined operation, joint effort, collaboration, coagency, synergy, synergism 706n. *cooperation;* coincidence, consilience 83n. *conformity;* concord, harmony 24n. *agreement;* compliance 758n. *consent;* concurrent opinion, consensus 488n. *assent;* acquiescence, non-resistance 721n. *submission;* concert, joint planning, collusion, conspiracy 623n. *plot;* league, alliance, partnership 706n. *association;* conjunction, union, liaison 45n. *junction.*

Adj. *concurrent,* concurring etc. vb.; coagent, synergic 706adj. *cooperative;* coincident, concomitant, parallel 89adj. *accompanying;* in alliance, banded together 708adj. *corporate;* of one mind, at one with 488adj. *assenting;* joint, combined 45adj. *conjunct;* conforming 83adj. *conformable;* colluding, conniving, abetting, contributing, involved 703adj. *aiding.*

Vb. *concur,* acquiesce 488vb. *assent;* collude, connive, conspire 623vb. *plot;* agree, harmonize 24vb. *accord;* hang together, pull t. 706vb. *cooperate;* contribute, help, aid, abet, serve 703vb. *minister to;* promote, subserve 156vb. *conduce;* go with, go along w., go hand in hand w., keep pace w., keep abreast of, run parallel to 89vb. *accompany;* unite, stand together 48vb. *cohere.*

Adv. *concurrently,* with one consent, with one accord, in harmony, hand in hand, hand in glove.

See: 24, 45, 48, 83, 89, 156, 488, 623, 703, 706, 708, 721, 758.

182 Counteraction

N. *counteraction,* opposing causes, action and reaction; polarity 240n. *contraposition;* antagonism, antipathy, clash, conflict, mutual c. 14n. *contrariety,* 279n. *collision;* return action, reaction, retroaction, repercussion, back-fire, back-kick, backlash 280n. *recoil;* renitency, recalcitrance, kicking back 715vb. *resistance,* 704n. *opposition;* inertia, vis inertiae, friction, drag, check 702n. *hindrance;* interference, counterpressure, repression, suppression 747vb. *restraint;* intolerance, persecution 735n. *severity;* neutralization, deactivation 177n. *moderation;* nullification, cancellation 165n. *destruction;* cross-current, counter-sea, head-wind 702n. *obstacle;* counterspell, counter-charm, counter-irritant, neutralizer 658n. *antidote;* counter-balance, counterweight 31n. *offset;* counterblast, counter-move 688n. *tactics;* defensive measures, deterrent 713n. *defense;* prevention, preventive, preventative, inhibitor 757n. *prohibition.*

Adj. *counteracting,* counter, counteractive; conflicting 14adj. *contrary;* antipathetic, antagonistic, hostile 881adj. *inimical;* resistant, recalcitrant, renitent 715adj. *resisting;* reactionary, retroactionary 280adj. *recoiling;* frictional, retarding, checking 747adj. *restraining;* preventive, preventative; antidotal, corrective 658adj. *remedial;* balancing, off-setting 31adj. *compensatory.*

Vb. *counteract,* counter, run c., cross, traverse, work against, go a., militate a.; not conduce to 702vb. *hinder;* react 280vb. *recoil;* agitate against, persecute 881vb. *be inimical;* resist, withstand, defend oneself 704vb. *oppose;* antagonize, conflict with 14vb. *be contrary;* clash, jostle 279vb. *collide;* interfere 678vb. *meddle;* countervail, cancel out, counterpoise, overpoise 31vb. *set off;* repress 165vb. *suppress;* undo, cancel 752vb. *abrogate;* neutralize, deactivate, demagnetize, degauss; find a remedy, cure 658vb. *remedy;* recover 656vb. *retrieve;* prevent, inhibit 757vb. *prohibit.*

Adv. *although,* in spite of, despite, notwithstanding; against, contrary to 704adv. *in opposition.*

See: 14, 31, 165, 177, 240, 279, 280, 656, 658, 678, 688, 702, 704, 713, 715, 735, 747, 752, 757, 881.

183 Space: indefinite space

N. *space,* expanse, expansion; extension, spatial e., extent, superficial e., surface, area; volume, cubic content; continuum, stretch 71n. *continuity;* empty space 190n. *emptiness;* depth of space, abyss 211n. *depth;* unlimited space, infinite s. 107n. *infinity;* sky, outer space, interstellar s. 321n. *heavens;* world, wide w., length and breadth of the land; geographical space, terrain, open space, open country; lung, green belt, wide horizons, wide open spaces 348n. *plain;* upland, moorland, campagna, veld, prairie, steppe 348n. *grassland;* outback, back blocks 184n. *region;* wild, wilderness, waste 172n. *desert;* everywhere, ubiquity 189n. *presence.*

measure, proportions, dimension 203n. *length,* 205n. *breadth,* 209n. *height,* 211n. *depth;* area, surface a.; square measure, acreage, acres, rods, poles and perches; square inch, square yard, hectare, hide; volume, cubic content 195n. *size.*

range, reach, carry, compass, coverage; stretch, grasp; radius, latitude, amplitude; sweep, spread, ramification; play, swing 744n. *scope;* sphere, field, arena 184n. *region;* purview, prospect 438n. *view;* perspective, focal distance 199n. *distance;* telescopic range, light-grasp; magnifying power 417n. *optics.*

room, space, accommodation; capacity, internal c., roomage, storage, storage space 632n. *storage;* seating capacity, seating; standing room, breathing r.; margin, free space, clearance, windage; room overhead, headroom, headway; sea room, seaway, leeway; opening, way 263n. *open space;* living space, Lebensraum, development area; elbow room, room to swing a cat in.

Adj. *spatial,* space; spatiotemporal; volumetric, cubic, three-dimensional; flat, superficial, two-dimensional.

spacious 32adj. *extensive;* expansive, roomy; ample, vast, capacious, broad, deep, wide; amplitudinous, voluminous, baggy 195adj. *large;* broad-based 79adj. *general;* far-reaching, widespread, world-wide, global, world 52adj. *whole;* uncircumscribed, boundless, spaceless 107adj. *infinite;* shoreless, trackless, pathless; extending, spreading, branching, ramified.

Vb. *extend,* spread, spread out, range, cover; span, straddle, bestride 226vb. *overlie;* extend to, reach to 202vb. *be contiguous;* branch, ramify.

Adv. *widely,* capaciously, voluminously; extensively, everywhere, wherever; far and near, far and wide, all over, all the world over, throughout the world; under the sun, on the face of the earth, in every quarter, in all quarters, in all lands; from end to end, from pole to pole, from coast to coast, from China to Peru, from Dan to Beersheba, from Land's End to John o' Groats, from Maine to California 54adv. *throughout;* from all the points of the compass; to the four winds, to the uttermost parts of the earth; from here to nowhere, from here to the back of beyond; at every turn, here, there and everywhere, right and left.

See: 32, 52, 54, 71, 79, 107, 172, 184, 189, 190, 195, 199, 203, 205, 209, 211, 226, 263, 321, 348, 417, 438, 632, 744.

184 Region: definite space

N. *region,* locality, parts 185n. *place;* sphere, orb, hemisphere; zone, belt; latitude, parallel, meridian; clime, climate; tract, terrain, country, ground, soil 344n. *land;* geographic unit, island, peninsula, continent, land-mass; sea 343n. *ocean;* compass, circumference, circle, circuit 233n. *outline;* boundaries, bound, shore, confine, march 236n. *limit;* pale, precincts, enclosure, close, enclave, exclave, salient 235n. *enclosure;* corridor 624n. *access;* area, field, theater 724n. *arena;* exclusive area, charmed circle. **See** *territory.*

territory, sphere, zone; beat, pitch, ground; lot, holding, claim 235n. *enclosure;* grounds, park, allodium 777n. *estate;* national boundaries, domain, territorial waters, twelve-mile limit; continental shelf, airspace; possession, dependency, dominion; colony, settlement; motherland, fatherland, homeland 192n. *abode;* commonwealth, republic, kingdom, realm, state, empire 733n. *polity;* principality, duchy, arch-d., grand-d., palatinate; debatable territory, no-man's land, Tom Tiddler's ground 774n. *non-ownership.*

district, purlieus, haunt 187n. *locality;* subregion, quarter, division 53n. *subdivision;* state, province, county, shire, bailiwick, riding, lathe, wapentake, hundred, soke, tithing; diocese, bishopric, archbishopric, parish, ward, constituency; borough, township, urban district, rural d., metropolitan area: village, town, city, conurbation 192n. *abode;* zillah, taluk, canton, volost, department, arrondissement, commune; deme, nome, nomarchy, toparchy; suburb, suburbia, downtown, uptown, West End, East End, City; clubland, theaterland, dockland; Highlands, Lowlands, Wild West; outland, back blocks; hinterland, heartland.

Adj. *regional,* territorial, continental, peninsular, insular; national, state; subdivisional, local, municipal, parochial, provincial, red-brick; suburban, urban, rural, up-country; district, town, country.

See: 53, 185, 187, 192, 233, 235, 236, 343, 344, 624, 724, 733, 774, 777.

185 Place: limited space

N. *place,* emplacement, site, location, position 186n. *situation;* station, substation; quarter, locality 184n. *district;* assigned place, pitch, beat, billet, socket, groove; center, meeting-place 76n. *focus;* birthplace, dwelling p., fireside 192n. *home;* place of residence, address, habitat 187n. *location;* premises, building, mansion 192n. *house;* spot, plot; point, dot, pinpoint; niche, nook, corner, hole, glory h., pigeon-hole, pocket 194n. *compartment;* confine, bound, baseline, crease (cricket) 236n. *limit;* confined place, prison, coffin, grave; precinct, bailey, garth, enclosure, paddock, compound, pen, close, quadrangle, square; yard, area, areaway, backyard, courtyard, court, base-c., fore-c., center c. 235n. *enclosure;* patio, atrium, hall; farmyard, home farm, field 371n. *farm;* walk, sheeprun 369n. *stockfarm;* highways and byways, ins and outs, every nook and corner.

Adv. *somewhere,* some place, wherever it may be, here and there, in various places, passim; locally 200 adv. *nigh.*

See: 76, 184, 186, 187, 192, 194, 235, 236, 369, 371.

186 Situation

N. *situation,* position, setting; time and place, when and where; location, address, whereabouts; point, stage, milestone 27n. *degree;* site, seat, emplacement, habitat, base 185n. *place;* post, station; status, standing, ground, footing 7n. *state;* standpoint, point of view 480n. *estimate;* side, aspect 445n. *appearance;* attitude, posture, pose 688n. *con-*

duct; one's place, place in a book, reference, chapter and verse; topography, chorography, cosmography 321n. *geography;* chart 551n. *map.*

bearings, compass direction, latitude and longitude, declination, right ascension, northing, southing 281n. *direction;* radio-location 187n. *location.*

Adj. *situated,* situate, located at, living at, to be found at; settled, set; stationed, posted; occupying 187adj. *located;* local, topical; topographical, geographic.

Vb. *be situate,* be situated, center on; be found at, have one's address at, have one's seat in; have its center in; be, lie, stand; be stationed, be posted; live, live at 192vb. *dwell;* touch 200vb. *be near.*

Adv. *in place,* in situ, in loco, here, there; in, on, over, under; hereabout, thereabout; whereabout; here and there, passim; in such and such surroundings, in such and such environs; at the sign of.

See: 7, 27, 185, 187, 192, 200, 281, 321, 445, 480, 551, 688.

187 Location

N. *location,* placing, placement, emplacement, collocation, disposition; posting, stationing; finding the place, locating, pinpointing; centering, localization 200n. *nearness;* localization, domestication, naturalization, indenization; settling, colonization, population; settlement, lodgment, establishment, fixation, installation; putting down, deposition, putting back, reposition 62n. *arrangement;* putting in 303n. *insertion;* packing, stowage, loading, lading 632n. *storage.*

locality, quarters, purlieus, environs, environment, surroundings, milieu, neighborhood, parts 184n. *district;* address, street, place of residence, habitat 192n. *abode;* seat, site 185n. *place;* meeting place, venue, haunt 76n. *focus.*

station, seat, site, emplacement, position 186n. *situation;* depot, base, military b., naval b., air b.; colony, settlement; anchorage, roadstead, mooring, mooring mast 662n. *refuge;* cantonment, lines, police l., civil l.; camp, encampment, bivouac, campsite, temporary abode; hostel 192n. *abode;* halting place, lay-by, park, parking place 145n. *stopping place.*

Adj. *located,* placed etc. vb.; positioned, stationed, posted 186adj. *situated;* ensconced, embedded, embosomed 232adj. *circumscribed;* rooted, settled, domesticated 153adj. *fixed;* encamped, camping, lodged 192adj. *residing;* moored, anchored, at anchor 266adj. *quiescent;* vested in, in the hands of, in the possession of 773adj. *possessed;* reposed in, transferred to 780adj. *transferred;* well-placed, favorably situated.

Vb. *place,* collocate, assign a place 62vb. *arrange;* situate, position, site, locate; base, center, localize; narrow down, pinpoint, pin down; find the place, put one's finger on; place right, aim well, hit, hit the mark 281vb. *aim;* put, lay, set, seat; station, post, park; install, ensconce, set up, establish, fix 153vb. *stabilize;* fix in, root, plant, implant, embed, graft 303vb. *insert;* bed, bed down, put to bed, tuck in, tuck up, cradle; accommodate, find a place for, find room for, lodge, house, quarter, billet; quarter upon, billet on; impose, saddle on; moor, tether, picket, anchor 47vb. *tie;* dock, berth 266vb. *bring to rest;* deposit, lay down, put d., set d.; stand, put up, erect 310vb. *elevate;* place with, transfer, bestow, invest 780vb. *convey;* array, deploy.

replace, put back, sheathe, put up (a sword), bring back, reinstate 656vb. *restore;* redeposit, reinvest, replant, reset.

stow, put away, put by; imburse, pocket, pouch, purse; pack, bale, store, lade, freight, put on board 193vb. *load;* fill, squeeze in, cram in 54vb. *make complete.*

place oneself, stand, take one's place, take one's stand, anchor, drop a., cast a., come to a. 266vb. *come to rest;* settle, strike root, take r., gain a footing, entrench, dig in 144vb. *stay;* perch, alight, sit on, sit, squat, park; pitch on, pitch one's tent, encamp, camp, bivouac; stop at, lodge, put up; hive, burrow; ensconce oneself, locate o., establish o., find a home; settle, colonize, populate, people 192vb. *dwell;* endenizen, get naturalized, become a citizen.

See: 47, 54, 62, 76, 144, 145, 153, 184, 185, 186, 192, 200, 232, 266, 281, 303, 310, 632, 656, 662, 773, 780.

188 Displacement

N. *displacement,* dislocation, derailment 83n. *derangement;* misplacement, wrong place, ectopia 84n. *abnormality;* shift, move 265n. *motion;* light-shift, Doppler effect; aberration, aberration of light, perturbation (astron.) 282n. *deviation;* translocation, transposition, transshipment, transfer 272n. *transference;* mutual transfer 151n. *interchange;* relief, supersession 150n. *substitution;* removal, taking away 304n. *extraction;* unloading, unpacking, unshipment, disencumbrance 831n. *relief;* ejectment, expulsion, ablegation 300n. *ejection;* weeding, eradication 300n. *voidance;* exile, banishment 883n. *seclusion;* refugee, displaced person, DP 268n. *wanderer;* fish out of water, square peg in a round hole 25n. *misfit;* unloader, remover, removal man.

Adj. *displaced* etc. vb.; removed, transported 272adj. *transferable;* aberrant 282adj. *deviating;* unplaced, unhoused, unharbored; unestablished, rootless, unsettled; roofless, houseless, homeless; out of a job, out of the picture, out of touch, out in the cold 57adj. *excluded.*

misplaced, ectopic 84adj. *abnormal;* out of one's element, like a fish out of water; out of place, inappropriate 10adj. *irrelevant;* mislaid, lost, missing 190adj. *absent.*

Vb. *displace,* disturb, disorientate, derail, dislocate; dislodge, unseat, unfix, unstick 46vb. *disjoin;* dispel, scatter, send flying 75vb. *disperse;* shift, remove, translate 265vb. *move;* cart away, transport 272vb. *transfer;* alter the position, change round; transpose, translocate 151vb. *interchange;* dispatch, post 272vb. *send;* ablegate, relegate, banish, exile 300vb. *dismiss;* set aside, supersede 150vb. *substitute,* 752vb. *depose;* displant, disnest, eradicate, uproot 300vb. *eject;* discharge, unload, offload, unship, tranship; clear away, rake, sweep, sweep up 648vb. *clean;* take away, take off, cart off; lift, raise, uplift 310vb. *elevate;* draw, draw out, pull o. 304vb. *extract.*

misplace, mislay, lose, lose touch with, lose track of.

See: 10, 25, 46, 57, 63, 75, 83, 84, 150, 151, 190, 265, 268, 272, 282, 300, 304, 310, 648, 752, 831, 883.

189 Presence

N. *presence,* being there, existence, whereness; being everywhere, ubiety, ubiquity, ubiquitariness, omnipresence; permeation, pervasion, diffusion; availability, bird in the hand; physical presence, bodily p., personal p.; attendance, personal a.; residence, occupancy, occupation, lodgement 773n. *possession;* visit, descent, stay; nowness, present moment 121n. *present time;* man on the spot; spectator, bystander 441n. *onlookers.*

Adj. *on the spot,* present, existent, in being 1adj. *existing;* occupying, in occupation; inhabiting, resident, resiant, residentiary, domiciled 192adj. *residing;* attendant, waiting, still there, not gone, hanging on; ready, on tap, available, on the menu, on 669vb. *prepared;* at home, at hand, within reach, on call, on sight; under one's nose, before one's eyes 443adj. *well-seen;* looking on, standing by.

ubiquitous, ubiquitary, omnipresent, permeating, pervading, pervasive, diffused through.

Vb. *be present,* exist, be; take up space, occupy, hold 773vb. *possess;* stand, lie 186vb. *be situate;* look on, stand by, witness 441vb. *watch;* resort to, frequent, haunt, meet one at every turn; stay, sojourn, summer, winter, revisit 882vb. *visit;* attend, assist at, grace the occasion; make one at, make one of, answer one's name, answer the roll call; occur 154vb. *happen;* turn up, present oneself, announce o., send in one's card 295vb. *arrive;* show one's face, put in an appearance, look in on; face, confront; present, introduce, bring in, produce 522vb. *show.*

pervade, permeate, fill 54vb. *make complete;* be diffused through, be disseminated, imbue, impregnate, soak, run through; overrun, swarm over, spread, meet one at every turn 297vb. *infiltrate;* make one's presence felt 178vb. *influence.*

Adv. *here,* there, where, everywhere, all over the place; in situ, in place, in front; aboard, on board, at home; on the spot; in presence of, before, under the eyes of, under the nose of, in the face of; personally, in person, in propria persona.

See: 1, 54, 78, 121, 154, 186, 192, 295, 297, 441, 443, 669, 773, 882.

190 Absence: nullibiety

N. *absence,* non-presence, disappearing trick 446n. *disappearance;* being nowhere, nullibiety, utopia, inexistence 2n. *non-existence;* being elsewhere, alibi; non-residence, living away; leave of absence, furlough; non-attendance, truancy, absenteeism 620n. *avoidance;* absentee,

truant 620n. *avoider;* deprivation 772vb. *loss.*
emptiness, bareness, empty space, void, vacuity, inanity, vacancy; nothing inside, hollowness, shell; vacuum, air-pocket; empties, dead men (empty bottles); blank cartridge, blank paper, clean sheet; virgin territory, no-man's land; waste, desolation 172n. *desert;* vacant lot, building site 183n. *room.*
nobody, no one, nobody present, nobody on earth; not a soul, not a cat, not a living thing; empty house, non-existent audience.
Adj. *absent,* not present, not found, unrepresented; away, not resident; gone from home, on tour, on location; out, not at home; gone, flown, disappeared 446adj. *disappearing;* lacking, minus, to seek, wanting, missing, wanted; truant, absentee 667adj. *escaped;* unavailable, unprocurable, off the menu, off 636adj. *unprovided;* lost, nowhere to be found; inexistent 2adj. *non-existent;* exempt from, spared, exempted; on leave, on furlough; omitted, left out 57adj. *excluded.*
empty, vacant, vacuous, inane; void, devoid, bare; blank, clean; characterless, featureless; without content, hollow; vacant, unoccupied, uninhabited, untenanted, tenantless; unstaffed, crewless, unofficered, unmanned; depopulated; desert, deserted 621adj. *relinquished;* unpeopled, unsettled, uncolonized; god-forsaken, lonely; unhabitable, uninhabitable.
Vb. *be absent,* have no place in, take no part in; absent oneself, spare one's presence; stay away, keep away, keep out of the way, play truant 620vb. *avoid;* be missed, leave a gap; leave empty, evacuate, vacate; empty, exhaust 300vb. *void.*
go away, withdraw, leave, relieve of one's presence 296vb. *depart;* make oneself scarce, slip out, slip away, be off, retreat 296vb. *decamp,* 667vb. *escape;* vanish 446vb. *disappear;* move over, make room, vacate.
Adv. *without,* minus, sans; in default of, for want of; in vacuo.
not here, not there; neither here nor there; elsewhere, somewhere else; nowhere, no place; in one's absence, behind one's back.
See: 2, 57, 172, 183, 296, 300, 446, 620, 621, 636, 667, 772.

191 Inhabitant

N. *dweller,* inhabitant, habitant, denizen, indweller; sojourner, commorant, parasite; mainlander, continental; insular, islander; isthmian; landsman, landlubber; mountaineer, hillman, hillbilly, dalesman, highlander, lowlander, plainsman; forester, woodman, backwoodsman; frontiersman, borderer, marcher; city-dweller, town-d., suburbanite; countryman, rustic, ruralist, villager; peasant 370n. *husbandman;* steppe-dweller, desert-d., tent-d., bedouin; cave-dweller, troglodyte; slum-dweller 801n. *poor man.* **See** *native.*
resident, householder, goodman, family man; housewife, hausfrau, chatelaine, housekeeper; cottager, cotter, cottier, crofter; addressee, occupier, occupant, incumbent, residentiary 776n. *possession;* locum tenens 150n. *substitute;* tenant, renter, lessee, lease-holder; inmate, inpatient; indoor servant 742n. *domestic;* houseman 658n. *doctor;* garrison, crew 686n. *personnel;* lodger, boarder, roomer, paying guest, p.g.; guest, visitor, someone to stay; uninvited guest, cuckoo, squatter 59n. *intruder.*
native, aboriginal, aborigines, autochthones, earliest inhabitants, first-comers 66n. *precursor;* people, tribe 371n. *nation;* local, local inhabitant, tribal; parishioner, townsman, townee, city man, cit, oppidan, cockney, suburbanite, yokel; compatriot, fellow-countryman, fellow-citizen; national, citizen, burgess, burgher, voter; Yankee, Yank, Briton, Britisher; Caledonian, Scottie, Taffy, Paddy; Londoner, Mancunian, Liverpudlian, Aberdonian; New Yorker, Virginian; Canuck 59n. *foreigner;* earth-dweller, terrestrial, tellurian; space-dweller, Martian, Venusian.
settler, pioneer; backsettler 66n. *precursor;* immigrant, colonist, colonial, creole; squatter 59n. *intruder;* planter 370n. *husbandman;* inquiline, metic, resident alien 59n. *foreigner;* Ditcher, Pilgrim Fathers; parasite, parasitic organism.
habitancy, population, urban p., rural p., townspeople, country folk; populace, people, people at large, citizenry, tenantry, yeomanry; villagery, villadom, suburbia; city-full, house-full; household, menage 11n. *family;* settlement, stronghold; colony, plantation, community, village c.
Adj. *native,* vernacular, popular, national, swadeshi; indigenous, autochthonous, aboriginal, enchorial,

terrigenous; earthbound, terrestrial, tellurian; home, home-made; domestic, domiciliary, domesticated; settle, domiciliated, naturalized.
occupied, occupied by, indwelt; garrisoned by, manned, staffed.
See: 11, 59, 66, 150, 370, 371, 658, 686, 742, 776, 801.

192 Abode: place of habitation or resort

N. *abode,* abiding place, habitat, haunt, place to live in, place, province, sphere; habitation, local h., street, house, home; address, house-number, number; where one lives, where one's lot is cast; domicile, residence, residency; town, city, capital, metropolis; headquarters, base 76n. *focus;* temporary abode, hang-out, camp; holiday home, seaside resort, watering place, hill-station; spa, sanatorium 658n. *hospital;* outstation, cantonment, lines, civil l. 187n. *station;* bivouac, encampment, castrametation; rus in urbe, home away from home.
quarters, accommodation, billet, berth; barrack, casemate, casern; bunkhouse, lodging, lodgings, rooms, chambers, diggings, digs, chummery; residential hotel, guest house, boarding h., lodging h., pension, boarding, hostel, dormitory, dorm; sorority house, fraternity h.
dwelling, roof over one's head 226n. *roof;* prehistoric dwelling, lake-d., crannog, broch, brough; tower, keep; cave, hut, kraal, igloo; wigwam, tepee, wickiup, tent, tabernacle 226n. *canopy;* lair, den, hole, tree; hive, bee-h., burrow, warren, earth, set 662n. *shelter;* apiary, aviary 369n. *zoo.*
nest, nidification, nidus; branch 366n. *tree;* aerie, eyrie, perch, roost; covert, gullery, rookery, swannery, hatchery, aviary, apiary, wasp's nest, ant-heap, ant-hill; chrysalis, cocoon 226n. *wrapping;* cradle 68n. *origin.*
home, hearth, fireside, chimney corner, inglenook, rooftree, roof, paternal r., homestead, toft, household; cradle, birthplace, "house where I was born" 68n. *origin;* native land, la patrie, motherland, fatherland, homeland, one's country, God's own country, the Old Country, blighty, Albion; native soil, native ground, native heath, homeground, hometown; haunt, stamping ground; household gods, teraphim, Lares and Penates; Hestia, Vesta.
house, religious house, house of God 990n. *temple;* home, residence, dwelling-house, country h., town h.; dower-house, semi-detached h., thatched h.; Queen Anne house, Georgian h., Regency h., colonial h.; council house, prefab; bungalow, ranchhouse, villa, chalet; seat, place, mansion, hall; chateau, castle, keep, tower; manor house, manor, grange, lodge, priory, abbey; palace, alcazar; palatial residence, dome; steading, farmstead, croft, messuage, toft and croft, hacienda; official residence, White House, Mansion H.; embassy, consulate; building, skyscraper 164n. *edifice;* convent 986n. *monastery.*
small house, bijou residence, flatlet; snuggery, chalet, lodge, cottage, cot; cabin, log c., hut, shebang, adobe; hovel, dump, hole, slum-dwelling; box, shooting b., hunting lodge; shed, shanty, shack, lean-to, penthouse, outhouse; shelter, tent, booth, bothy, stall, shieling; barn, grange 636n. *store;* houseboat, budgerow 275n. *boat;* house on wheels, caravan, trailer, house-t. 274n. *vehicle.* **See** *flat.*
housing, bricks and mortar, built-up area; housing estate, hutments; urbanization, conurbation; city, town, burgh, suburb, satellite town; dormitory area, industrial a., development a.; crescent, terrace, circus, square; block, court, row, mansions, villas, buildings; houses, tenements; slum, condemned building; hamlet, ham, village, thorp, dorp, bustee; villadom, suburbia.
street, high s., avenue 624n. *road;* lane, alley, wynd, by-street, back street, side s., passage, arcade, covered way 624n. *path;* mall, grove, walk, parade, promenade, boulevard; pier, embankment.
flat, service f., mews f., penthouse; apartment, suite, suite of rooms, chambers 194n. *chamber;* maisonette, duplex, walkup; apartment house, block of flats, mews, tenements, rents.
stable, byre, cowshed, cowhouse, shippen; kennel, doghouse, dog-hole; sty, pigpen, fold, sheepfold, sheepcote 235n. *enclosure;* dovecote, pigeoncote, pigeon-hole; stall, cage, coop, hencoop, hutch; stabling, mews, coach-house, garage, hangar; boathouse; marina, dock, dry d., floating d., graving d.; basin, wharf, roads, roadstead, port, interport 662n. *shelter;* berth, lay-by, quay.

jetty, pier, ghat 266n. *resting place.*
inn, hotel, hostelry, hospice, motel, bed and breakfast; doss-house, bunk-h., kip, flophouse; auberge, posada, caravansary, khan; dak bungalow, circuit house, rest-house; restroom, waiting room.
tavern, alehouse, pothouse, mughouse; public house, pub, local, roadhouse; gin palace, gin mill, grog-shop, dram-s., toddy-s.; speakeasy, dive, honky-tonk, shebeen; estaminet, bodega; wine cellar, beer c., beer hall, brauhaus; bar, saloon, taproom.
café, restaurant, self-service r., cafeteria, automat; eating-house, chophouse; beanery, diner, dinette, luncheonette; brasserie, bistro; grillroom, rotisserie; coffee house, espresso café, milk-bar, soda-fountain; lunch-counter, snack-bar, self-service b.; teahouse, teashop, tea-room, refreshment room, buffet, canteen, Naafi; coffee stall; pull-up, carman's rest.
meeting place, conventicle, meeting house 990n. *church;* assembly rooms, pump-room; club, night-c., holiday camp 837n. *place of amusement;* race-course, dog track 724n. *arena;* theater, auditorium, stadium, stand 441n. *onlooker;* gymnasium, drill hall, parade ground 539n. *school;* piazza, quadrangle, quad, campus, village green 76n. *focus;* market, market square, forum, supermarket 796n. *mart.*
pleasance, park, grounds, pleasure g., gardens, walk, mall, green, bowling g., game reserve, national park, parkland, chase 837n. *pleasure ground.*
pavilion, kiosk, rotunda, folly, bower, grotto, solar, solarium 194n. *arbor;* stoa, colonade, arcade, peristyle, cloister; tent, marquee, shamiana 226n. *canopy.*
retreat, sanctuary, refuge, asylum, ark 662n. *shelter;* den, snuggery, sanctum sanctorum, study 194n. *chamber;* cell, hermitage 883n. *seclusion;* cloister 986n. *monastery;* ashram; almshouse, grace and favor house; workhouse, poorhouse; ghetto 748n. *prison;* cache, hole 527n. *hiding-place.*
Adj. *residing,* abiding, dwelling, keeping, living; at home, in residence; residential, fit for habitation; parasitic, autoecious.
urban, towny, oppidan, metropolitan, cosmopolitan, suburban; built-up, citified, urbanized, suburbanized.
provincial, parochial, regional, local, domestic; up-country, countrified, rural, rustic.
architectural, architectonic, edificial; Gothic, classical; cottage-style, bungalow-type; palatial, grand; detached, semi-d.; single-story, double-s.; double-fronted.
Vb. *dwell,* dwell in, inhabit, populate, people 189vb. *be present;* settle, colonize 786vb. *appropriate;* frequent, haunt 882vb. *visit;* take up one's abode, reside, remain, abide, sojourn, live 185vb. *be situate;* take rooms, put up at, stay, keep, lodge, lie, sleep at; have an address, hang out; tenant, occupy, squat 773vb. *possess;* bunk, room, chum with, p.g.; stable, nestle, perch, roost, nest, hive, burrow; camp, encamp, bivouac, pitch, pitch one's tent, make one's quarters 187vb. *place oneself;* tent, tabernacle, shelter 662vb. *seek refuge;* berth, dock, anchor 266vb. *come to rest.*
urbanize, citify, suburbanize, conurbate, town-plan, develop, build up.
See: 68, 76, 164, 185, 187, 189, 194, 226, 235, 266, 274, 275, 366, 369, 441, 527, 539, 624, 636, 658, 662, 724, 748, 773, 786, 796, 837, 882, 883, 986, 990.

193 Contents: things contained
N. *contents,* ingredients, items, components, constituents, parts 58n. *component;* inventory 87n. *list;* furnishings, equipment 633n. *provision;* load, payload, cargo, lading, freight, shipment, cartload, busload, shipload 272n. *thing transferred;* enclosure, inside 224n. *insides;* stuffing, filling, stopping, wadding 227n. *lining;* handful, cupful, quiverful 104n. *certain quantity.*
Vb. *load,* lade, freight, charge, burden 187vb. *stow;* take in, take on board, ship; overburden, break one's back 322vb. *weigh;* pack, pack in, fit in, tuck in 303vb. *insert;* pack tight, squeeze in, cram, stuff 54vb. *fill;* pad, wad 227vb. *line;* hide, conceal 56vb. *contain.*
See: 54, 56, 58, 87, 104, 187, 224, 227, 272, 303, 322, 633.

194 Receptacle
N. *receptacle,* container; tray, in-t., out-t.; recipient, holder; frame 218n. *supporter;* cage 748n. *prison;* folder, wrapper, envelope, cover, file 235n. *enclosure;* net, seine, trawl, beam-t. 222n. *network;* hairnet, snood 228n.

headgear; sheath, chrysalis, cocoon 226n. *wrapping;* capsule, ampul; pod, calyx, boll; inkwell, ink-horn; socket, mortise 255n. *cavity;* groove, slot 262n. *furrow;* hole, cave, cavity 263n. *opening;* bosom, lap 261n. *fold;* slot-machine; pin-cushion; catch-all, trap; well, reservoir, hold 632n. *store;* drain, pool, cess-pool, sump 649n. *sink;* crockery, china-ware, glassware 381n. *pottery.*

bladder, air-bladder, waterwings; balloon, gas-bag; sac, cyst, vesicle, utricle, blister, bubble 253n. *swelling;* udder, bag, teat 253n. *bosom.*

maw, stomach, tummy, breadbasket, little Mary; abdomen, belly, paunch, venter 253n. *swelling;* gizzard, gullet, weasand, crop, craw, jaws, mouth, esophagus 263n. *orifice.*

compartment, cell, cellule, follicle, ventricle; tray, in-t., out-t.; cage, iron lung; cubicle, loculus; driving-seat, cab; sentry-box; box 594n. *theater;* pew, stall, choir-stall, chancel 990n. *church interior;* niche, nook, cranny, recess, bay, oriel, mihrab; pigeon-hole, cubby-h., drawer; shelving, rack 218n. *shelf;* story, floor, mezzanine f., entresol, deck, between-decks, 'tween-d., lazaretto 207n. *layer.*

cabinet, closet, commode, wardrobe, press, chest of drawers, tallboy, highboy; cupboard, corner c., dresser; buffet, sideboard 218n. *stand;* chiffonier, cellaret, dumb waiter; secretary, escritoire, davenport, bureau, desk, writing d.; bookcase; china cabinet.

basket, cran, creel; hamper, luncheon basket; breadbasket, canister; pannier, dosser, dorser; trug, maund, punnet, rush basket, frail; crib, cradle, bassinet, whisket; clothes basket, buckbasket; work-basket, waste-paper b.; wicker-work, basket-work, corbeille; framework, crate, kit 218n. *frame;* gabion 713n. *fortification.*

box, chest, ark; coffer, locker; case, canteen; safe, till, money-box 799n. *treasury;* boot, imperial; coffin, sarcophagus, cist 364n. *tomb;* packing-case, tea-chest; provision box, tuck-box; attaché case, dispatch c., dispatch box; suitcase, expanding s.; trunk, valise, portmanteau, uniform case; sea chest, ditty-box; bandbox, hatbox; ammunition box, canister, caisson 723n. *ammunition;* boxes, luggage, baggage, impedimenta; brake-van, luggage v.

small box, pillbox, snuffbox, tinder-box, matchbox, cigarette-b., cigar-b., pencil-b.; cardboard box, carton, packet, metal box, can, tin, cigarette t., tobacco t., caddy, tea-caddy, canister, casket, pyx, reliquary, shrine; pepper-box, pepper-mill, caster; nest of boxes.

bag, sack; handbag, vanity bag, reticule, tidy; shopping bag, paper b.; cornet, twist; Gladstone bag, carpet-bag, traveling-bag, overnight b., last-minute b.; sleeping-bag, flea-b.; bedding-roll; hold-all, grip-sack, grip, haversack, knapsack, rucksack, kitbag, ditty-bag, duffle b., saddle-bag, nosebag; satchel, sabretache, budget, scrip, bundle, swag.

case, pocket c., étui, housewife, wallet, scrip-case; billfold, note-case, card case, spectacle c., jewel c., compact, vasculum; brief-case, portfolio; scabbard, sheath; pistol case, holster; arrow case, quiver 632n. *store;* penholder; finger-stall.

pocket, waistcoat p., side-p., hip-p., trouser-p., breastpocket; fob, placket; purse, pouch, poke, money-bag; sleeve.

vat, dye-v., butt, water-b., cask, barrel, tun, tub, keg, breaker; wine-cask, puncheon, pipe, hogshead, tierce, firkin, kilderkin, pottle 465n. *metrology;* brewer's vat, hopper, cistern, tank 632n. *store.*

vessel, vase, urn, jar, amphora, ampulla, cruse, crock, pot, water-p.; pipkin, gugglet, pitcher, ewer, jug, toby-jug; gourd calabash 366n. *plant;* carafe, decanter, bottle, water-b.; leather bottle, blackjack, wineskin; wine bottle, demijohn, magnum, jeroboam; flask, hip-f., flagon, nipperkin, vial, phial; cruet; honeypot, jam-jar; gallipot, carboy, bolthead, crucible, retort, receiver, alembic, cucurbit, matrass, cupel, test-tube 463n. *testing agent;* cupping-glass; chamber-pot, potty, jerry, bed-pan, commode, thunder-box 302n. *excretion;* trough, trug; pail, milk-p., milk-can; bucket, wooden b., piggin, skeel; lota, can, watering c.; flowerpot, jardiniere; bin, dust-b., garbage can, trash c., gubbins 649n. *sink;* scuttle, coal-s., perdonium; kibble, tub; bath, hip-b.

caldron 383n. *heater;* alfet; boiler, copper, kettle, posnet, skillet, etna, dixie, pan, saucepan, stewpan, frying-pan, casserole, pyrex dish, mess-tin, mess can; tea urn, teapot, samovar, coffee-pot, percolator, biggin; censer, cassolette; hot-water bottle, warming pan.

cup, egg-c., teacup, coffee-cup; tea-service, tea-set; chalice, goblet, beaker; drinking-cup, loving c.; quaich; horn, drinking-h., tankard, stoup, can, cannikin, pannikin, mug, stein, toby, noggin, rummer, tyg, tass, tassie; tumbler, glass, wine-glass, liqueur g.; cupel.

bowl, basin, hand-b., wash-b., laver, shaving-mug; slop-bowl, mixing-bowl, crater, punchbowl, drinking-bowl, jorum; soup-plate, soup-bowl, porringer, pottinger; manger, trough; colander, vegetable dish, tureen, terrine, sauce-boat, gravy-boat; spittoon, cuspidor; flower-bowl, jardiniere 844n. *ornamentation;* watch-glass, crystal.

plate, salver, tray, paten, patera, patella; platter, trencher, charger, dish, center d., epergne; saucer; pan, scale 322n. *scales;* palette; mortar-board, hod.

ladle, dipper, baler, scoop, cupped hands; spoon, tablespoon, dessert-spoon, teaspoon, eggspoon, soup-spoon; spade, trowel, spatula 274n. *shovel.*

chamber, room, apartment 192n. *flat;* cockpit, cubicle, cab; cabin, stateroom; roundhouse, cuddy; audience chamber, presence c., throne-room; cabinet, closet, study, den, sanctum, adytum 192n. *retreat;* library, studio, atelier, workroom, office 687n. *workshop;* playroom, nursery, schoolroom; drawing room, sitting r., reception r.; living room, lounge, parlor, saloon, salon, boudoir; bedroom, sleeping room, dormitory; dressing room; bathroom, bathhouse; dining room, salle-à-manger, messroom, mess hall, refectory, canteen, grill-room 192n. *café;* gunroom, wardroom, smoking room, billiard r.; bar, tap-room, writing room, scriptorum; cook-house, galley, kitchen; scullery, pantry, larder, still-room; dairy, laundry, offices, out-house; coachhouse, garage 192n. *stable;* store-room, lumber r., glory hole 162n. *storage;* retiring room, cloakroom, lavatory 649n. *latrine.* **See** *compartment.*

lobby, vestibule, foyer, anteroom, waiting room 263n. *doorway;* corridor, passage; veranda, piazza, loggia, balcony, portico, porch, stoa, propylaeum, atrium.

cellar, cellarage, vault, crypt, basement 214n. *base;* coal-hole, bunker 662n. *storage;* dust-hole, dust-bin 649n. *sink;* hold, dungeon 748n. *prison.*

attic, loft, hayloft, cockloft; penthouse, garret, top story 213n. *summit.*

arbor, alcove, bower, grotto, grot, summer-house, gazebo, pergola 192n. *pavilion;* conservatory, greenhouse, glasshouse 370n. *garden.*

Adj. *recipient,* receptive, capacious, voluminous 183adj. *spacious;* containing, hiding, framing, enclosing; pouchy, baggy.

cellular, multicellular, camerated, compartmentalized; locular, multilocular, loculated; marsupial, polygastric, ventricular; abdominal, gastral, ventral, stomachic, ventricose, bellied 253adj. *convex.*

capsular, saccular, sacculated, cystic, siliquose; vascular, vesicular.

See: 162, 192, 207, 214, 218, 222, 226, 228, 235, 253, 255, 261, 262, 263, 274, 302, 322, 364, 366, 370, 381, 383, 463, 465, 594, 632, 649, 662, 687, 713, 723, 748, 799, 844, 990.

195 Size

N. *size,* magnitude, order of m.; proportions, dimensions, measurements 183n. *measure;* extent, expanse, area 183n. *space;* extension 203n. *length,* 209n. *height,* 211n. *depth;* width, amplitude 205n. *breadth;* volume, cubature; girth, circumference 233n. *outline;* bulk, mass, weight 322n. *gravity;* capacity, intake, tunnage, tonnage; measured size, scantling, caliber 465n. *measurement;* real size, true dimensions 494n. *accuracy;* greatest size, maximum 32n. *greatness;* full size, life size 54n. *plenitude;* large size, king s., magnum; largest portion 52n. *chief part;* excessive size, hypertrophy, giantism, gigantism.

hugeness, largeness, bigness, grandiosity 32n. *greatness;* enormity, enormousness, immensity, vastness, giantship; towering proportions, monstrosity, gigantism 209n. *height.*

bulk, mass, weight, heft 322n. *gravity;* lump, block, clod, nugget 324n. *solid body;* bushel, mound, heap 32n. *great quantity;* mountain, pyramid 209n. *high structure;* massiveness, bulkiness; turgidity, obesity, corpulence, fatness, plumpness, chunkiness, fleshiness, meatiness; flesh and blood, full habit, chunky figure, corporation, gorbelly 253n. *swelling;* fat man, tun, tun of flesh, Falstaff.

giant, colossus 209n. *tall creature;* mountain of a man, young giant, lusty infant; ogre, monster; leviathan, behemoth, whale, porpoise, Triton among the minnows; hippopotamus, elephant; mammoth, megatherium, dinosaur; giantry, Gargantua, Brobdingnagian, Goliath, Gog and Magog, Typhon, Antaeus, Briareus, Cyclops, Kraken.

whopper, spanker, thumper, strapper; a mountain of a . . . .

Adj. *large,* of size, big 32adj. *great;* large-size, king-s., jumbo; pretty large, fair-sized, considerable, sizable, good-sized; bulky, massive, massy 322adj. *weighty;* ample, capacious, voluminous, baggy; amplitudinous, comprehensive 205adj. *broad;* extensive 183adj. *spacious;* monumental, towering, mountainous 209adj. *tall;* fine, magnificent, spanking, thumping, thundering, whacking 32adj. *whopping;* man-size, life-s., large as life; well-grown, large-limbed, elephantine; macroscopic, large-scale, megalithic; big for one's age, lusty, healthy 162adj. *strong;* so big, of that order.

huge, immense, enormous, vast, mighty, grandiose, stupendous, monstrous 32adj. *prodigious;* biggest ever, record-size; colossal, gigantic, giant, giant-like, mountainous; Brobdingnagian, titanic, Herculean, Gargantuan; cyclopean, megalithic; outsize, oversize, overlarge 32adj. *exorbitant;* limitless 107adj. *infinite.*

fleshy, meaty, fat, stout, obese, overweight; plump, plumpish, chubby, podgy, pudgy, fubsy; squat, five by five, square, dumpy, chunky; tubby, portly, corpulent, paunchy, pot-bellied, gorbellied 253adj. *convex;* puffy, pursy, bloated, blowsy, bosomy 197adj. *expanded;* round, full, full-faced, chub-f., chubby-f.; round, full, double-chinned, dimpled, dimply, jolly, chopping, goodly, lusty; in condition, in good c., in good case, well-fed, well-grown, strapping, beefy, brawny 162adj. *stalwart;* plump as a dumpling, plump as a partridge, fat as a quail, fat as butter, fat as brawn, fat as bacon, fat as a pig.

unwieldy, hulking, lumbering, gangling, lolloping; hulky, lumpy, lumpish, lubberly; too big, elephantine, overweight; awkward, muscle-bound 695adj. *clumsy.*

Vb. *be large,*—big etc. adj.; become large 197vb. *expand*; have size, loom large, bulk l., bulk, fill space 183vb. *extend;* tower, soar 209vb. *be high.*

See: 32, 33, 37, 52, 53, 54, 68, 107, 162, 183, 197, 198, 203, 206, 209, 211, 233, 253, 322, 324, 332, 444, 465, 494, 695.

196 Littleness

N. *littleness* etc. adj.; small size, miniature quality 33n. *smallness;* lack of height 204n. *shortness;* diminutiveness, dwarfishness, stuntedness; scantiness, paucity, exiguity 105n. *fewness;* meagerness 206n. *thinness;* —kin,—let.

minuteness, point, mathematical p., vanishing p.; pinpoint, pinhead; crystal; monad, atom, electron, molecule; drop, droplet, dust, grain; seed, mustardseed, grass seed, millet s., barleycorn 33n. *small thing, particle;* bubble, button, molehill 639n. *trifle.*

miniature 553n. *picture;* microphotograph, reduction 551n. *photography;* Elzevir edition, duodecimo 589n. *edition;* thumbnail sketch, epitome 592n. *compendium;* model, microcosm; bubble car, minicar 274n. *automobile.*

dwarf, midget, pigmy, elf, atomy, lilliputian, blastie; chit, pigwidgeon, urchin, dapperling, dandiprat, cocksparrow, pipsqueak; manikin, doll, puppet; Tom Thumb, Hop-o'-my-thumb, homunculus; shrimp, runt, miserable specimen.

animalcule, microorganism, microzoon; amoeba, protozoon, bacillus, bacteria, infusoria, anaerobe, microbe, germ, virus, entozoon; mite, tick, nit, maggot, grub, worm; insect, ant, pismire, emmet; midge, gnat, fly, tit, tom-tit; fingerling, small fry, shrimp, sprat, minnow; mouse, titmouse, shrew-mouse; whippet, bantam, runt.

micrology, microscopy, micrography, microphotography; microscope, microspectroscope, micrometer, Vernier scale.

Adj. *little* 33adj. *small;* petite, dainty, dinky, dolly, elfin; diminutive, pigmy, lilliputian; wee, titchy, tiny, teeny, teeny-weeny, itsy-witsy; toy, baby, pocket, pocket-size, pint-size, duodecimo; miniature, model; portable, compact, handy; runty, puny 163adj. *weak;* petty 33adj. *inconsiderable;* one-horse 639adj. *unimportant.*

dwarfish, dwarf, dwarfed, pigmy, undersized, stunted, weazen, wizened, shrunk 198adj. *contracted;* squat, dumpy 204adj. *short;* runty, knee-

high, knee-high to a grasshopper.
exiguous, minimal, slight, scant, scanty, homeopathic 33adj. *small;* thin, meager, scrubby, scraggy 206 adj. *lean;* rudimentary, embryonic 68adj. *beginning;* bitty 53adj. *fragmentary.*
minute, micro-, microscopic, ultramicroscopic, infinitesimal; atomic, molecular, corpuscular; granular 332adj. *powdery;* inappreciable, imperceptible, intangible, impalpable 444adj. *invisible.*
Vb. *be little,*—petite etc. adj.; contract 198vb. *become small;* dwindle 37vb. *decrease;* require small space, take up no room, lie in a nutshell, fit in a small compass, fit on the head of a pin.
Adv. *in small compass,* in a nutshell; on a small scale, in miniature.
See: 33, 37, 53, 68, 105, 163, 204, 206, 274, 332, 444, 551, 553, 589, 592, 639.

197 Expansion
N. *expansion,* increase of size, ascending order, crescendo; enlargement, augmentation, aggrandizement 36n. *increase;* ampliation, amplification, supplementation, reinforcement 38n. *addition;* hypertrophy, giantism, gigantism; overenlargement, hyperbole 546n. *exaggeration;* stretching, stretching oneself, pandiculation; extension, spread, deployment, fanning out 75n. *dispersion;* increment, accretion 40n. *adjunct;* upgrowth, overgrowth, germination, pullulation, development 157n. *growth,* 164n. *production;* overstaffing, Parkinson's law 637n. *superfluity;* extensibility, expansibility, dilatability 328adj. *elasticity.*
dilation, dilatation, distension, diastole; blowing up, inflation, reflation; puffing, puff 352n. *sufflation;* swelling up, turgescence, turgidity, tumescence, intumescence, tumefaction; tympany; puffiness, dropsy, tumor 253n. *swelling.*
Adj. *expanded* etc. vb.; larger, bigger, bigger than before, bigger than ever; expanding 36adj. *increasing;* stuffed, padded out, supplemented; spreading, widespread, deployed; expansive 183adj. *spacious;* fan-shaped, flabelliform 204adj. *broad;* wide open, patulous, gaping 263adj. *open;* tumescent, budding, bursting, florescent, flowering, out 134adj. *adult;* full-blown, full-grown, full-formed 669adj. *matured;* overblown, overgrown, hypertrophied 546adj. *exaggerated;* obese, pursy, puffy, swag-bellied, pot-b., bloated, fat 195adj. *fleshy;* swollen, turgescent, turgid; distended, stretched, tight; tumid, dropsical, varicose, bulbous 250adj. *convex;* bladder-like; ampullaceous, ampullar, pouchy.
Vb. *expand,* greaten, grow larger, increase, wax, grow, snowball 36vb. *grow;* widen, broaden 205vb. *be broad;* spread, fan out, deploy, extend, take open order 75vb. *be dispersed;* spread over, spread like wild-fire, overrun, mantle, straddle 226vb. *cover;* incrassate, thicken; rise, prove (e.g. dough); gather, swell, distend, dilate, fill out; balloon, belly 253vb. *be convex;* get fat, gain flesh, put on weight; split one's breeches, burst at the seams; grow up, spring up, germinate, bud, burgeon, shoot, sprout, open, put forth, burst f., blossom, flower, floresce, blow, bloom, be out 171vb. *be fruitful;* stretch oneself, pandiculate.
enlarge, greaten, aggrandize; make larger, expand; rarefy (by expansion); leaven 310vb. *elevate;* bore, ream; widen, broaden, let out; open, pull out; stretch, extend 203vb. *lengthen;* intensify, heighten, deepen, draw out; amplify, supplement, reinforce 38vb. *add;* develop, build up 36vb. *augment;* distend, inflate, reflate, pump up, blow up, puff, puff up, puff out 352vb. *sufflate;* stuff, pad 227vb. *line;* cram, fill to bursting 54n. *fill;* feed up, fatten, plump up, bloat, pinguefy 301vb. *feed;* enlarge, blow up 551vb. *photograph;* magnify, overenlarge, overdevelop 546vb. *exaggerate;* double, redouble.
See: 36, 38, 40, 54, 75, 134, 157, 163, 164, 171, 183, 195, 203, 204, 205, 226, 227, 250, 253, 263, 301, 310, 328, 352, 546, 551, 637, 669.

198 Contraction
N. *contraction,* reduction, abatement, lessening, deflation 37n. *diminution;* decrease, shrinkage, descending order, diminuendo 42n. *decrement;* curtailment, abbreviation, syncope, elision 204n. *shortening;* state of contraction, contracture; consolidation 324n. *condensation;* freezing 382n. *refrigeration;* pulling together, drawing t. 45n. *joinder,* 264n. *closure*; attenuation, emaciation, tabefaction, consumption, marasmus, withering, atrophy; decline, retreat, recession, slump 655n. *deterioration;*

neck, isthmus, bottleneck, hourglass, wasp-waist 206n. *narrowness;* epitome 592n. *compendium.*

compression, coarctation, pressure, compressure, compaction, squeeze, squeezing, stricture, stenosis, strangulation; constriction, constringency, astriction, astringency; contractility, compressibility.

compressor, squeezer, mangle, roller 258n. *smoother;* tightener, constrictor, astringent; bandage, binder, tourniquet 658n. *surgical dressing;* belt, band, cingle, garter 47n. *girdle;* whalebone, stays, corset 228n. *underwear;* straitjacket, iron boot, bed of Procrustes 964n. *instrument of torture;* bear, python, boa constrictor.

Adj. *contracted,* shrunk, shrunken, smaller 33adj. *small;* waning 37adj. *decreasing;* constricted, strangled, strangulated; unexpanded, deflated, condensed 324adj. *dense;* compact, compacted, compressed; pinched, nipped, tightened, drawn tight 206adj. *narrow,* 264adj. *closed;* compressible, contractile, systaltic; stunted, wizened 196adj. *dwarfish;* tabid, tabescent, marasmic, wasting, consumptive 655adj. *deteriorated.*

compressive, contractional, astringent, binding, constipating.

Vb. *become small,* grow less, lessen, dwindle, wane, ebb, fall away 37vb. *decrease;* wither, waste, decay 51vb. *decompose;* lose weight, lose flesh 323vb. *be light;* contract, shrink, narrow, taper, taper off, draw in 206vb. *be narrow;* condense 324vb. *be dense;* evaporate 338vb. *vaporize;* draw together, close up 264vb. *close;* pucker, purse, corrugate, wrinkle 261vb. *fold;* stop expanding, level off.

make smaller, lessen, reduce 37vb. *bate;* contract, shrink, abridge, take in, cut down to life size, dwarf, bedwarf 204vb. *shorten;* bant, diet, slim, take off weight 323vb. *lighten;* taper, narrow, attenuate, thin, emaciate 206vb. *make thin;* puncture, deflate, degas, rarefy, pump out, exhaust, empty, drain 300vb. *void;* boil down, evaporate 338vb. *vaporize;* coarctate, constrict, constringe, pinch, nip, squeeze, bind, bandage, garter, corset; draw in, draw tight, strain, tauten 45vb. *tighten;* draw together 264vb. *close,* 45vb. *join;* compress, hug, crush, strangle, strangulate; compact, constipate, condense, nucleate 324vb. *be dense;* squeeze in, pack tight, cram 193vb. *load;* cramp, restrict 747vb. *restrain;* limit 232vb. *circumscribe;* chip, whittle, share, shear, clip, trim, shingle, poll, pollard 46vb. *cut;* scrape, file, grind 332vb. *pulverize;* fold up, crumple 261vb. *fold;* roll, press, flatten 258vb. *smooth;* huddle, crowd.

See: 33, 37, 42, 45, 46, 47, 51, 193, 196, 204, 206, 228, 232, 261, 264, 300, 323, 324, 332, 338, 382, 592, 655, 658, 747, 964.

199 Distance

N. *distance,* astronomical d., depths of space 183n. *space;* measured distance, mileage, footage 203n. *length;* focal distance; parallax; longinquity, elongation, greatest e., aphelion, apogee; far distance, horizon, false h., skyline, offing; background 238n. *rear;* periphery, circumference 233n. *outline;* reach, grasp, compass, span, stride, giant's s. 183n. *range;* far cry, long long trail, long run, marathon; drift, dispersion 282n. *deviation.*

farness, far distance, remoteness, aloofness; removal 46n. *separation;* antipodes, pole 240n. *contraposition;* world's end, ultima Thule, Pillars of Hercules; ne plus ultra, back of beyond; Far West, Far East; foreign parts, outlands 59n. *extraneousness;* outpost, out-station 883n. *seclusion;* outskirts 223n. *exteriority;* outer edge, frontier 236n. *limit;* unavailability 190n. *absence.*

Adj. *distant,* distal, peripheral, terminal; far, farther; ulterior; ultimate, furthermost, farthest; long-distance, long-range; yon, yonder; not local, away; off-shore, on the horizon; remote, aloof; hyperborean, antipodean, enisled; out of range, telescopic; lost to sight, lost to view, out of sight 444adj. *invisible;* off-center, wide, wide of the mark.

removed, incontiguous, separated, inaccessible, unapproachable, un-get-at-able, out of touch, out of the way; beyond, over the horizon; overseas, transmarine, transpontine, transoceanic, transatlantic, transpacific, transpolar, transalpine, transpadane, ultramontane; ultramundane, out of this world.

Vb. *be distant,* stretch to, reach to, extend to, spread to, go to, get to, stretch away to, carry to, carry on to 183vb. *extend;* carry, range; outdistance, outrange, outreach 306vb. *outdo;* keep distance, remain at a d., keep off, hold off, stand off, lie off;

keep clear of, stand aloof, stand clear of, keep a safe distance, give a wide berth 620vb. *avoid.*

Adv. *afar,* away, not locally; far, far away, far afield, far off, way o., wide away, way behind, way in front; uptown, downtown; yonder, in the distance, in the offing, on the horizon; at a distance, a great way off, a long way away, a far cry to; at the limit of vision, out of sight; nobody knows where, out of the way; to the ends of the earth, to the back of beyond, to the uttermost end; far and wide 183adv. *widely;* from pole to pole, asunder, apart, abroad, afield; at arm's length.

beyond, further, farther; further on, ahead, in front; clear of, wide of, wide of the mark; below the horizon, hull down; up over, down under, over the border, over the hills and far away.

too far, out of reach, out of range, out of sight, out of hearing, out of earshot, out of the sphere of, out of bounds.

See: 46, 59, 183, 190, 203, 204, 223, 233, 236, 237, 238, 240, 282, 306, 444, 620, 883.

200 Nearness

N. *nearness,* proximity, propinquity, closeness, near distance, foreground 237n. *front;* vicinage, neighborhood 230n. *circumjacence;* brink, verge 234n. *edge;* adjacency 202n. *contiguity;* collision course 293n. *convergence;* approximation 289n. *approach;* centering, localization 187n. *location.*

short distance, no d., shortest d., beeline, short cut; step, short step, walking distance; striking distance, close quarters, close grips; close range, earshot, gunshot, pistol-shot, bowshot, arrowshot, stone's throw, biscuit toss, spitting distance; short span, inch, millimeter, finger's breadth, hair's breadth, hair space 201n. *gap;* close up, near approach; nearest approach, perigee, perihelion; close finish, photo f., near thing 716n. *contest.*

near place, vicinage, neighborhood, purlieus, environs, banlieu, suburbs, confines 187n. *locality;* approaches, borderlands; ringside seat, next door 202n. *contiguity;* second place, proxime accessit 65n. *sequence.*

Adj. *near,* proximate, proximal; very near, approximate; approximating, getting warm, warm 289adj. *approaching;* about to meet 293adj. *convergent;* nearby, wayside, roadside 289adj. *accessible;* not far, hard by, inshore; near at hand, at hand, handy, present 189adj. *on the spot;* near the surface 212adj. *shallow;* home, local, in the neighborhood; close to, next to, neighboring, limitrophe, bordering on, verging on, adjacent, adjoining, jostling, rubbing shoulders 202adj. *contiguous;* fronting, facing 237adj. *fore;* close, intimate, inseparable 45adj. *conjunct;* at close quarters, at close grips; close-run, neck-and-neck, with nothing between, level 716adj. *contending;* near in blood, related 11adj. *akin.*

Vb. *be near,* be around, be about 189vb. *be present;* hang around, hang about; approximate, draw near, get warm 289vb. *approach;* meet 293vb. *converge;* neighbor, stand by, abut, adjoin, border, verge upon 202vb. *be contiguous;* trench upon 306vb. *encroach;* come close, skirt, graze, shave, brush, skim, hedge-hop, hover over; jostle, buzz, get in the way 702vb. *obstruct;* sit on one's tail, follow close, make a good second; come to heel, tread on the heels of 284vb. *follow;* fawn on, spaniel; clasp, cling to, hug, cuddle 889vb. *caress;* huddle, crowd, close up, close the ranks 74vb. *congregate.*

bring near, approach, approximate; move up, place side by side 204vb. *juxtapose.*

Adv. *nigh,* not far, locally; near, hard by, fast by, close to, close up to, close upon; in the way, at close range, at close quarters; within call, within hearing, within earshot, within a stone's throw, only a step, at no great distance, not far from; at one's door, at one's feet, at one's elbow, at one's side, under one's nose; in the presence of, face to face; in juxtaposition, next door, side by side, cheek by jowl, tête-à-tête, arm in arm, beside, alongside, yard-arm to yard-arm; on the circumference, on the periphery, on *or* in the confines of, on the skirts of, in the outskirts, at the threshold; brinking on, verging on, on the brink of, on the verge of, on the tip of one's tongue.

nearly, practically, almost, all but; more or less, near enough, roughly, around, somewhere around; in the region of; about, much a., hereabouts, thereabouts, nearabouts, circa; closely, approximately; hard on, close on; well-nigh, as good as, on the way to; within an ace of, just about to.

See: 11, 45, 65, 74, 187, 189, 201, 202, 204, 212, 230, 234, 237, 284, 289, 293, 306, 702, 716, 889.

201 Interval

N. *interval,* distance between, space, jump; narrow interval, half-space, hair space 200n. *short distance;* interspace, daylight, head, length; metope, demi-m., semi-m. (architecture); clearance, margin, freeboard 183n. *room;* interval of time, interregnum 107n. *interim;* pause, break, truce 145n. *lull;* interruption, incompleteness, jump, leap; musical interval, tone, semitone, third, fourth, fifth 410n. *musical note.*

gap, interstice, mesh 222n. *network;* cavity, hole 263n. *orifice;* pass, defile, gat, ghat, wind-gap 305n. *passage;* ditch, dike, nullah, trench 351n. *drain;* water-jump, ha-ha, sunk fence 235n. *barrier;* ravine, gorge, gully, crevasse, canyon, intervale 255n. *valley;* fatiscence, cleft, crevice, chink, crack, rift, rime, scissure, cut, gash, tear, rent, slit 46n. *scission;* flaw, fault, breach, break, split, fracture, rupture, fissure, chap 46n. *separation;* slot, groove 262n. *furrow;* indentation 260n. *notch;* seam, join 45n. *joint;* leak 298n. *outlet;* abyss, abysm, chasm 211n. *depth;* yawning gulf, void 190n. *emptiness;* inlet, creek, gulch 345n. *gulf.*

Adj. *spaced,* spaced out, intervalled, with an interval, leaded; gappy, gapped; fatiscent, split, cloven, cleft, cracked, rimous, rimose 46adj. *disjunct;* dehiscent, gaping 263adj. *open;* far between; latticed, meshed, reticulated.

Vb. *space,* interval, space out, lead (typography) 46vb. *set apart;* seam, crack, split, start, gape, dehisce 263vb. *open;* win by a head, win by a length; clear, show daylight between; lattice, mesh, reticulate; raft 370vb. *cultivate.*

Adv. *at intervals* 72adv. *discontinuously;* now and then, now and again, every so often, off and on; with an interval, by a head, by a length.

See: 45, 46, 72, 107, 145, 183, 190, 200, 211, 222, 235, 255, 260, 262, 263, 298, 345, 351, 370, 410.

202 Contiguity

N. *contiguity,* juxtaposition, apposition, proximity, close p. 200n. *nearness;* touching 378n. *touch;* no interval 71n. *continuity;* contact, tangency; abuttal, abutment; intercommunication, osculation; meeting, encounter, reencounter 293n. *convergence;* appulse, appulsion, conjunction, syzygy (astron.) 45n. *junction;* close contact, adhesion, cohesion 48n. *coherence;* coexistence, coincidence, concomitance 89n. *accompaniment;* grazing contact, tangent; border, fringe 234n. *edge;* borderland, frontier 236n. *limit;* buffer state 231n. *interjacence.*

Adj. *contiguous,* touching, in contact; osculatory, intercommunicating; tangential, grazing, brushing, abutting, end to end; conterminous, adjacent, with no interval 71adj. *continuous;* adjoining, close to, jostling, rubbing shoulders 200adj. *near.*

Vb. *be contiguous,* overlap 378vb. *touch;* make contact, come in c., brush, rub, skim, scrape, graze, kiss; join, meet 293vb. *converge;* stick, adhere 48vb. *cohere;* lie end to end, abut; abut on, adjoin, reach to, extend to 183vb. *extend;* sit next to, rub shoulders with, crowd, jostle 200vb. *be near;* border with, march w., skirt 234vb. *hem;* coexist, coincide 89vb. *accompany;* osculate, intercommunicate 45vb. *connect;* get in touch, contact.

juxtapose, set side by side, range together, bring into contact, knock persons' heads together.

Adv. *contiguously,* tangentially; in contact, in close c.; next, close; end to end; cheek by jowl; hand in hand, arm in arm; from hand to hand.

See: 45, 48, 71, 89, 183, 200, 231, 234, 236, 293, 378.

203 Length. Longimetry

N. *length,* longitude; extent, extension; reach, long arm; full length, overall l.; stretch, span, mileage, footage 199n. *distance;* perspective 211n. *depth.*

lengthening etc. vb.; prolongation, extension, production, spinning out 113n. *protraction;* stretching, tension, tensure; spreading out, stringing o.

line, bar, rule, tape, strip, stripe, streak; spoke, radius; single file, line ahead 65n. *sequence;* straight line, right l. 249n. *straightness;* bent line 248n. *curvature;* cord, thread 208n. *fiber;* rope 47n. *cable.*

long measure, linear m., measurement of length, longimetry, micrometry 465n. *measurement;* unit of length, finger, hand, hand's breadth, palm, span, cubit; arm's length, fathom; head, length; pace, step; inch, nail, foot, yard, ell; rod, pole, perch; chain, furlong, stade; mile, statute m., sea m., nautical m., knot, German mile, league; millimeter, centimeter, meter, kilometer; kos, verst, parasang; degree of latitude, degree of longitude; microinch, micron, wavelength; astronomical unit, light-year, parsec.

Adj. *long,* lengthy, extensive, longsome, measured in miles; long-drawn 113adj. *protracted;* lengthened, elongated, outstretched, extended, strung out 75adj. *unassembled;* wire-drawn, lank 206adj. *lean;* lanky, long-legged 209adj. *tall;* as long as my arm, as long as today and tomorrow, long as a wet week; interminable, no end to 838adj. *tedious;* polysyllabic; sesquipedalian 570adj. *prolix;* unshortened, unabridged, full-length 54adj. *complete.*

longitudinal, oblong, lineal, linear; one-dimensional.

Vb. *be long,*—lengthy etc. adj.; stretch, outstretch, stretch out; make a long arm; reach, stretch to 183vb. *extend;* drag, trail, drag its slow length along 113vb. *drag on.*

lengthen, stretch, elongate, draw out, wire draw 206vb. *make thin;* pull out, stretch o., spreadeagle; stretch oneself, pandiculate 197vb. *expand;* spread oneself out, sprawl 216vb. *be horizontal;* spread out, string o., deploy 75vb. *disperse;* extend, pay out, uncoil, unfurl, unroll, unfold 316vb. *evolve;* let out, drop the hem; produce, continue; prolong, protract 113vb. *spin out;* drawl 580vb. *stammer.*

look along, view in perspective; have a clear view, see from end to end 438vb. *scan;* enfilade.

Adv. *longwise,* longways, lengthwise; along, endlong; longitudinally, radially, in line ahead, in single file; one in front and one behind, tandem; in a line, in perspective; at full length, end to end, overall; fore and aft; head to foot, head to tail, stem to stern, top to toe, head to heels, from the crown of the head to the sole of the foot.

See: 47, 54, 65, 75, 113, 197, 199, 206, 208, 209, 211, 216, 248, 249, 316, 438, 465, 570, 580, 838.

204 Shortness

N. *shortness* etc. adj.; brevity, briefness; transience 114n. *brief span;* inch, microinch 200n. *short distance;* low stature, dwarfishness, short legs, duck's disease 196n. *littleness;* no height 210n. *lowness;* shortage 41n. *decrement,* 307n. *shortcoming;* scantiness, exiguity 105n. *fewness;* scarceness 636n. *insufficiency;* concision 569n. *conciseness;* short hair, Eton crop, crew cut.

shortening, abridgment, abbreviation, abbreviature, curtailment, cut-back, decurtation, reduction 37n. *diminution;* contraction 198n. *compression;* retrenchment 814n. *economy;* elision, ellipsis, aphaeresis, apocope, syncope.

shortener, cutter, abridger, abstracter 592n. *epitomizer.*

Adj. *short,* brief 114adj., *transient;* not big, dwarfish 196adj. *little;* not tall, squab, squabby, squat, dumpy, stumpy, stocky, thick-set, stub, stubby 195adj. *fleshy;* not high, flat 210n. *low;* flat-nosed, pug, snub, snubby, retroussé, blunt 257adj. *unsharpened;* not long, inch-long; skimpy, scanty, scrimpy, revealing (of dress) 636adj. *insufficient;* foreshortened 246adj. *distorted;* shortened, half-length, abbreviated, abridged, catalectic; cut, curtailed, docked, beheaded, truncated, headless, topless, crownless; shaven, shorn, mown, well-m.; short of speech, sparing of words, terse 569adj. *concise;* elliptic (of style); half-finished 55adj. *unfinished;* epitomized, potted, compact 592adj. *compendious;* compacted, compressed 198adj. *contracted.*

Vb. *be short,*—brief etc. adj.; come short 307vb. *fall short.*

shorten, abridge, abbreviate; pot, epitomize, boil down 592vb. *abstract;* sum up, recapitulate 569vb. *be concise;* compress, contract, telescope 198vb. *make smaller;* reduce, diminish 37vb. *bate;* foreshorten 246vb. *distort;* take in, put a tuck in, raise the hem, turn up, tuck up, kilt; behead, obtruncate, guillotine, ax, chop up, hew 46vb. *cut;* cut short, dock, curtail, truncate; cut back, cut down, pare d., lop, poll, pollard, prune; shear, shave, trim, clip, bob, shingle; taper, narrow down; mow, reap, crop; nip, snub, nip in the bud, frostbite 655vb. *wound;* stunt, check the growth of 278vb. *retard;* scrimp, skimp, scant 636vb. *make insufficient;* retrench 814vb. *economize.*

Adv. *shortly* etc. adj.; in short; compendiously, in brief compass, economically.

See: 37, 41, 46, 55, 105, 114, 195, 196, 198, 200, 210, 246, 257, 278, 307, 569, 592, 636, 655, 814.

205 Breadth. Thickness

N. *breadth,* width, latitude; width across, diameter, radius, semidiameter; gauge, broad g., bore, caliber; broadness, expanse, superficial extent, amplitude 183n. *range;* wideness, fullness, bagginess.

thickness, crassitude, stoutness, corpulence 195n. *size;* dilatation 197n. *dilation.*

Adj. *broad,* wide, expansive, unspanned, ample 183adj. *spacious;* wide-cut, full, baggy; discous, fanlike, flabelliform, umbelliferous; outspread, outstretched; broad-bottomed, broad-based; callipygic, wide-hipped; broad in the beam, beamy, wide as a church door; broad-brimmed, wide-awake (hat); wide-mouthed 263adj. *open;* broad-shouldered, broad-chested 162adj. *stalwart;* non-specific 79adj. *general;* indecent 951adj. *impure.*

thick, stout, dumpy, squat, squab, thickset, tubby, stubby 195adj. *fleshy;* thick-lipped, blubber-l., full-l.; thick-ribbed, stout-timbered 162adj. *strong;* thick as a rope; pyknic, solid 324adj. *dense;* semi-liquid, ropy, to be cut with a knife 354adj. *viscid.*

Vb. *be broad,*—thick etc. adj.; get broad, broaden, widen, fatten thicken; fan out, deploy 197vb. *expand;* straddle, bestride, span 226vb. *overlie.*

Adv. *broadwise,* thick end first.

See: 79, 162, 183, 195, 197, 226, 263, 324, 354, 951.

206 Narrowness. Thinness

N. *narrowness* etc. adj.; narrow interval, closeness, tight squeeze, hair's breadth, finger's b. 200n. *short distance;* lack of breadth, length without b., line, strip, stripe, streak; vein, capillary 208n. *filament;* knife-edge, razor's edge, tightrope, wire; narrow gauge; bottleneck, narrows, strait, euripus 345n. *gulf;* ridge, col, saddle 209n. *high land;* ravine, gully 255n. *valley;* pass, ghat 305n. *passage;* neck, isthmus, land-bridge 624n. *bridge.*

thinness etc. adj.; lack of thickness, exility, tenuity, macilency, emaciation, consumption; scrag, skin and bone, skeleton, anatomy; scarecrow, rake, shadow, spindle-shanks, bare-bones; haggardness, lantern jaws, hatchet face, sunken cheeks; thread, paper, tissue 422vb. *transparency;* shaving, slip, tendril, tapeworm 163n. *weakling.*

narrowing, angustation, coarctation, compression 198n. *contraction;* taper, tapering 293n. *convergence;* neck, isthmus; stricture, constriction, middle c., waistline; middle, waist, wasp-w., hourglass; wasp.

Adj. *narrow,* not wide, narrow-gauge; strait, tight, close, incapacious; compressed, pinched, unexpanded 198adj. *contracted;* not thick, fine, thin 422adj. *transparent;* tight-drawn, spun, fine-s., wire-drawn 203adj. *long;* extenuated, thread-like, capillary 208adj. *fibrous;* taper, tapering 293adj. *convergent;* slight, slight-made, delicate 163adj. *weak;* gracile, slender, slim, svelte, slinky, sylph-like; willowy, arrowy, rangy; long-legged, lanky, gangling; narrow-waisted, wasp-w.; isthmian; bottle-necked.

lean, thin, spare, meager, skinny, bony; cadaverous, fleshless, skin-and-bone, skeletal, bare-boned, raw-b.; haggard, gaunt, lantern-jawed, hatchet-faced; spindly, spindling, spindle-shanked, spidery; undersized, weedy, scrawny, scrub, scraggy, rickety; extenuated, tabid, marcid 51adj. *decomposed;* consumptive, emaciated, wasted, withered, wizened, pinched, peaky 651adj. *sick;* sere, shriveled 131adj. *aged;* starved, starveling 636adj. *underfed;* miserable, herring-gutted; macilent, jejune; wraith-like, worn to a shadow, thin as a rake, thin as a lath, thin as a wafer, thin as a pencil, thin as a whipping-post, without an ounce of flesh to spare.

Vb. *be narrow,*—thin etc. adj.; straiten, narrow, taper 293vb. *converge.*

make thin, contract, compress, pinch, nip 198vb. *make smaller;* make oneself thin, starve, underfeed, bant, reduce, take off weight; improve one's figure, slenderize, slim; draw, wiredraw, spin, spin fine 203vb. *lengthen;* attenuate 325vb. *rarefy.*

See: 51, 131, 163, 198, 200, 203, 208, 209, 255, 293, 305, 325, 345, 422, 624, 651, 946.

207 Layer

N. *layer,* stratum, substratum, underlayer, floor 214n. *base;* outcrop, basset 254n. *projection;* bed, course, master-c., range, row; zone, vein, seam, lode; thickness, ply; story, tier, floor, mezzanine f., entresol, landing; stage, planking, platform 218n. *frame;* deck, top d., lower d., upper d., orlop d., quarter d., bridge 275n. *ship;* film 423n. *opacity;* bloom, dross, scum; patina, coating, coat, top-layer 226n. *covering;* scale, scab, membrane, peel, pellicle, sheath, bark, integument 226n. *skin;* level, water l., table, water t.; atmospheric layer 340n. *atmosphere.*

lamina, sheet, slab, foil, strip; plate-glass, plate, tin-p., sheet-iron, sheet-steel; latten, white l.; plank, board, clapboard; slat, lath, leaf, trencher, table, table-top; tablet, plaque, panel; slab, flag, flagstone, slate, shale; shingle, tile; brick, domino; slide; wafer, shaving, flake, slice, cut, rasher; cardboard, sheet of paper, page, folio; card, playing-c.; discolith, dish.

stratification, stratigraphy; layering, lamination; laminability, flakiness, schistosity, scaliness, squamation; overlapping, overlap; nest of boxes, Chinese b., sandwich; coats of an onion, layer on layer, level upon level 231n. *interjacence.*

Adj. *layered,* lamellar, lamelliform, lemellated; laminated, laminiferous; laminal, laminar, laminary, laminous; laminable, flaky; schistose, schistous, micaceous, slaty, shaly; foliated, foliate, foliaceous, membranous; bedded, stratified, stratiform; zoned, seamed; overlapping, clinker-built; tabular, decked, storied, in stories, in layers; scaly, squamose, squamous, squamiferous; filmy 226adj. *covered.*

Vb. *laminate,* lay, deck, layer, shingle, overlap 226vb. *overlay;* zone, stratify, sandwich; plate, veneer, coat 226vb. *coat;* delaminate, flake off, whittle, skive, pare, peel, strip 229vb. *uncover;* shave, slice.

See: 214, 218, 226, 229, 231, 254, 275, 340, 423.

208 Filament

N. *filament,* capillament, cilium, lash, eyelash, beard, down 299n. *hair;* flock, lock, lock of wool, lock of hair, wisp, curl; list, thrum 234n. *edging;* fibril, funicle, barb, tendril 778n. *nippers;* whisker, antenna, antennule, funiculus 378n. *feeler;* gossamer, cobweb, web 222n. *network;* capillary, vein, venule, veinlet 351n. *conduit;* ramification, branch; wire, element, wick, spill 420n. *torch.*

fiber, natural f., animal f., hair, camel-h., rabbit-h.; angora, goat's hair, mohair, cashmere; llama hair, alpaca, vicuna; wool, merino; mungo, shoddy; silk, real s.; wild silk, tussah, tussore; vegetable fiber, cotton, raw c., cotton wool, silk-cotton; linen, flax, hemp, cannabis; jute, sisal, coir, kapok; harl, hards; tow, oakum; bast, raffia; worsted, sewing-silk; yarn, staple; spun yarn, continuous-filament y.; thread, pack t.; twine, twist, strand, cord, whipcord, string, line, rope, ropework 47n. *cable;* artificial fiber, rayon, nylon 222n. *textile.*

strip, fascia, band, bandage, linen; tape, strap, ribbon, riband; fillet 47n. *girdle;* lath, slat, batten, spline 207n. *lamina;* shaving, wafer; splinter, shiver 53n. *piece;* streak, strake 203n. *line.*

Adj. *fibrous,* fibrillous; woolly, cottony, silky; filamentous, filaceous, filiform; whiskery, downy, fleecy 259adj. *hairy;* wiry, threadlike, funicular; capillary, capilliform; fine-spun, wire-drawn 206adj. *narrow;* stringy, ropy 205adj. *thick;* anguilliform 248adj. *convoluted;* flagelliform, lashlike; lingulate, strap-shaped; antenniform, antennary, antennal.

See: 47, 53, 203, 205, 206, 207, 222, 229, 234, 248, 259, 351, 378, 420, 778.

209 Height

N. *height,* perpendicular length, vertical range, long way to fall; altitude, elevation, ceiling, pitch 213n. *summit;* loftiness, steepness, dizzy height; tallness, stature; eminence, sublimity; sky, stratosphere 340n. *atmosphere.*

high land, height, highlands, heights, steeps, uplands, wold, moor, moorland, downs, rolling country; rising ground, rise, bank, brae, slope, climb; knap, hill, eminence, mount, mountain; fell, scar, tor, Alp, Everest; mountain range, sierra, massif, Alps, Himalayas, Andes, Rockies; ridge, hog's back, col, saddle 624n. *bridge;* spur, foothill, ledge 254n. *projection;* crest, peak, pike, hilltop 213n. *summit;* steepness, precipice, cliff, chalk c., white walls of Old England; crag, scar, bluff, steep, escarpment; chine, clough, barrance 255n. *valley;* summit level, mesa; butte, plateau, tableland, Tibet 216n. *horizontality.*

monticle, knoll, hillock, kopje, hummock, hump, dune, sand-d.; barrow, long b., round b. 364n. *tomb;* mound, heap, spoil-heap 641n. *rubbish;* tell 548n. *monument;* molehill, tussock, pimple 253n. *swelling.*

high structure, column, pillar, turret, tower, "cloud-capped towers"; dome, pile, noble p., skyscraper 164n. *edifice;* steeple, spire, belfry, campanile 990n. *church exterior;* minaret, muezzin's tower; obelisk, Cleopatra's Needle; roof, cupola, dome; colossus 554n. *sculpture;* mausoleum, pyramid 364n. *tomb;* pagoda, gopura 990n. *temple;* ziggurat, Tower of Babel; Eiffel Tower; mast, topmast, topgallant mast; flagstaff, pikestaff; pole, maypole; lamppost, standard; pylon, radio-mast; masthead, truck 213n. *summit;* watch-tower, crow's nest, aerie 438n. *view;* column of smoke, mushroom.

tall creature, giraffe, elephant, mammoth, longlegs, lamppost, beanpole, six-footer, seven-f., grenadier, colossus 195n. *giant;* pine, cedar, cedar of Lebanon, sequoia, California redwood 366n. *tree.*

high water, high tide, flood t., spring t. 350n. *current;* billow, tidal wave, tsunami 350n. *wave;* cataract 350n. *waterfall;* flood, flood level.

altimetry, altimeter, height-finder, hypsometer, barograph 465n. *meter.*

Adj. *high,* high-up, sky-high; eminent, uplifted, exalted, lofty, sublime, supernal 310adj. *elevated;* highest 213adj. *topmost;* perching, hanging (gardens); aerial, airborne, flying; soaring, aspiring 308adj. *ascending;* towering, cloud-capped, cloud-topped, cloud-touching, heaven-kissing; sky-scraping; steep, dizzy, vertiginous; knee-high, breast-h., shoulder-h., high as one's heart; altitudinal, altimetric.

tall, lanky, rangy, long-legged, long-necked, giraffelike; statuesque, colossal, gigantic, monumental 195adj. *huge;* tall as a maypole, tall as a poplar, tall as a steeple.

alpine, subalpine, alpestrine, Andean, Himalayan; mountainous, hilly, moorland, upland, highland; not flat, rolling; monticolous, hill-dwelling; orogenic.

overhanging, hovering; floating over, supernatant; beetling, superimposed, overlying; overshadowing, dominating; incumbent, superincumbent; over one's head, aloft; projecting, prominent 250adj. *salient.*

Vb. *be high,*—tall etc. adj.; tower, soar; surmount, clear, overtop, overlook, dominate, command 34vb. *be superior;* overhang, overshadow 226vb. *cover;* beetle, impend 250vb. *jut;* hover, hang over 217vb. *hang;* culminate, north, south, be in the zenith 725vb. *climax;* mount, bestride, bestraddle; grow taller, add to one's inches; upgrow; rise 308vb. *ascend;* stand on tiptoe, stand on another's shoulders, mount on stilts 310vb. *lift oneself.*

make higher, heighten, build up, raise, hold aloft 310vb. *elevate.*

Adv. *aloft,* up, on high, high up, in the clouds; atop, on top, on the crest; above, overhead, up over; above stairs, upstairs; upwards, skyward, heavenward; straight up, steeply 215adv. *vertically;* on tiptoe, on stilts, on the shoulders of; breast high, up to the teeth, over head and ears; from top to bottom 54adv. *throughout.*

See: 34, 54, 164, 195, 213, 215, 216, 217, 226, 244, 250, 254, 255, 308, 310, 340, 350, 364, 366, 438, 465, 548, 554, 624, 641, 725, 990.

210 Lowness

N. *lowness,* debasement 311n. *depression;* prostration, recumbency 216n. *supination;* non-elevation, no height, sea level, flatness 216n. *horizontality;* levelness, flatland, steppe 348n. *plain;* low elevation, lowlands, molehill, pimple 196n. *littleness;* gentle slope, slight gradient 220n. *acclivity;* subjacency, lower level, foothill 35n. *inferiority;* bottomlands, bottom, hollow, depression 255n. *valley;* sea bottom, sea floor, benthos 343n. *ocean;* subterraneity, depths, cellarage, well, mine 211n. *depth;* floor, foot 214n. *base;* underside, undersurface, underbelly 240n. *contraposition;* nadir, lowest position; low water, low ebb, low tide, ebb t., neap t. 350n. *current.*

Adj. *low,* not high, squat 204adj. *short;* unerect, not upright, crouched, crouching, stooping, bending 220adj. *oblique;* recumbent, laid low, prostrate 216adj. *supine;* low-lying, flat, level with the ground, at sea level 216adj. *horizontal;* subjacent, lower, under, nether 35adj. *inferior;* lowered, debased 311adj. *depressed;* flattened, rounded, blunt

257adj. *unsharpened;* subterranean, subterrene, underground, below the surface, submarine 523adj. *latent,* 211adj. *deep;* underfoot 745adj. *subjected.*

Vb. *be low,*—flat etc. adj.; lie low, lie flat 216vb. *be horizontal;* be beneath, underlie 523vb. *lurk;* slouch, stoop, crouch 311vb. *stoop;* crawl, wallow, grovel 721vb. *knuckle under;* lower, debase, depress 311vb. *abase.*

Adv. *under,* beneath, underneath, neath; below, at the foot of; downwards; adown, down, face-down; underfoot, underground, downstairs, below stairs; at a low ebb; below par.

See: 35, 196, 200, 204, 211, 214, 216, 220, 240, 255, 257, 311, 343, 348, 350, 523, 721, 745.

211 Depth

N. *depth,* deepness etc. adj.; perspective 203n. *length;* vertical range, profundity, lowest depth, lowest point, nadir; deeps, deep water 343n. *ocean;* unknown depths 663n. *pitfall;* depression, bottom 255n. *valley;* hollow, pit, shaft, mine, well 255n. *cavity;* abyss, abysm, chasm, yawning depths 345n. *gulf;* subterraneity, cellarage 194n. *cellar;* cave, hypogeum, bowels of the earth 210n. *lowness;* underworld, bottomless pit 972n. *hell;* fathoming, soundings, sounding machine, sounding rod, sounding line, sound, probe, plummet, lead, sounding l.; diving bell, bathysphere, bathyscaphe; submarine, submariner, frogman 313n. *diver;* depth required, draft, displacement, sinkage; bathymeter, bathymetry 465n. *measurement.*

Adj. *deep,* steep, plunging, profound; abysmal, yawning, cavernous; abyssal, deep-sea; deep-seated, deep-rooted 152adj. *fixed;* unplumbed, bottomless, reachless, soundless, fathomless; unsounded, unfathomed, unsoundable, unfathomable; subjacent, subterranean, underground, subterrene, hypogeal; underwater, undersea, subaqueous, submarine; buried, deep in, immersed, submerged 311adj. *depressed;* sunk, foundered, drowned; deepish, navigable; knee-deep, ankle-d.; deep-bosomed, bathycolpic; deep as a well; infernal, deep as hell; depth-haunting, bathyphilous; depth-measuring, bathymetric.

Vb. *be deep,*—profound etc. adj.; deepen, hollow, dig 255vb. *make concave;* fathom, sound, take soundings, plumb, heave the lead; go deep, plumb the depth, touch bottom, reach one's nadir 210vb. *be low;* sink to the bottom, plunge 313vb. *founder;* gape, yawn.

Adv. *deeply,* profoundly; deep down, beyond one's depth, out of one's depth, deep in, over one's head, over head and ears, up to the eyes.

See: 152, 203, 210, 255, 311, 313, 343, 345, 465, 663, 972.

212 Shallowness

N. *shallowness* etc. adj.; no depth, superficiality 4n. *unsubstantiality;* thin surface 223n. *exteriority;* veneer, thin coat 226n. *skin;* surface injury, scratch, mere s., pinprick, graze 639n. *trifle;* shoal water, shoals, shallows; pond, puddle 346n. *lake;* ripple, catspaw 350n. *wave;* light soil, stony ground 344n. *soil.*

Adj. *shallow,* slight, superficial 4adj. *insubstantial;* surface, skin-deep; near the surface, not deep; ankle-deep, knee-d.; shoal, shoaly, unnavigable; just enough to wet one's feet; light, thin, thinly spread 206adj. *narrow.*

See: 4, 206, 223, 226, 344, 346, 350, 639.

213 Summit

N. *summit,* summity; fountain-head, well-head 156n. *source;* sky, heaven, seventh h.; pole, north p., south p.; highest point, top, peak, crest, apex, pinnacle, crown; maximum height, utmost h., pitch; zenith, meridian, high noon, culmination, apogee; culminating point, crowning p.; acme, ne plus ultra 646n. *perfection;* crest of the wave, top of the tree 730n. *prosperity;* top of the curve, high-water mark 236n. *limit;* climax, turning point, turn of the tide 137n. *crisis;* dividing line, divide, watershed, water-parting, Great Divide 231n. *partition;* coping, coping-stone, capstone, keystone; lintel, pediment, entablature, architrave, epistyle; frieze, zoophorus; tympanum, capital, cornice; battlements, parapet 713n. *fort. vertex,* apex, crown, cap, brow, head; tip, cusp, spike, nib, end 69n. *extremity;* spire, finial 990n. *church exterior;* stairhead, landing 308n. *ascent;* acropolis 713n. *fort;* summit level, hilltop, mountain-top, plateau, tableland 209n. *highland;* tree-top, house-t., roof-t.; gable, gable-end; fastigium, leads, ceiling 226n. *roof;* upper chamber, garret 194n. *attic;* top story; topside, upper deck, quarter d., hurricane d., boat d., bridge 275n. *ship;* topmast, topgallant mast; masthead, crow's nest, truck 209n. *high structure;* upper works, top-hamper.

head, headpiece, pate, poll, sconce; noddle, nob, nut, crumpet, bean; upper story, belfry; brow, dome, forehead; brain, gray matter 498n. *intelligence;* epicranium, pericranium; scalp, crown, double c.; skull, cranium, brainpan 255n. *cavity;* occiput, sinciput; meninx, pia mater, dura m., arachnoid; fontanel; craniology craniognomy, craniognasy, cranioscopy, craniometry.

Adj. *topmost,* top, highest 209adj. *high;* uppermost, overmost 34adj. *supreme;* polar, apical, crowning; capital, head; cephalic, cranial, occipital, sincipital; culminating, zenithal, meridian, meridional; tip-top, super 644adj. *topping.*

Vb. *crown,* cap, head, top, tip, surmount, crest, overtop 34vb. *be high;* culminate, consummate 725vb. *climax;* go up top, take top place 34vb. *be superior.*

Adv. *atop,* on top, at the top, at the top of the tree, at the top of the ladder; on the crest, on the crest of the wave; tip-toe, on tip-toe.

See: 34, 69, 156, 173, 194, 209, 226, 231, 236, 255, 275, 308, 498, 644, 646, 713, 725, 730, 990.

214 Base

N. *base,* foot, toe, skirt 210n. *lowness;* bottom, fundament; lowest point, rock bottom, nadir, low water; footing, foundation 218n. *basis;* root, fundus, fundamental 68n. *origin;* groundwork, substructure, chassis 218n. *frame;* substratum, floor, underlayer, bed, bedrock; ground, earth, foundations; baseline, sill; base-level, basement, ground floor 194n. *cellar;* flooring, pavement, paving-stone, flag 226n. *paving;* carpet, drugget 226n. *floor-cover;* baseboard, wainscot, plinth, dado; keel, keelson; hold, orlop, bilge; sump, drain 649n. *sink.*

foot, feet, tootsies, pedal extremities; forefoot, hindfoot; sole, pad; heel, instep, arch; toe, toe-nail, great toe, hallux; trotter, hoof, cloven h.; paw, pug; claw, talon 778n. *nippers;* ankle, ankle-bone, fetlock, pastern.

Adj. *undermost,* lowermost, nethermost, bottom, rock-b. 210adj. *low;* basic, basal, fundamental; fundal; grounded, on the bottom, touching b.; based on, founded on, grounded on, built on, underlying 218adj. *supporting.*

footed, pedal; hoofed, cloven-h., ungulate, clawed, taloned; soled, heeled, shod, shoed; toed, five-t.; club-footed, hammer-toed 845adj. *blemished.*

Adv. *in the trough,* at the bottom; basically, fundamentally.

See: 68, 194, 210, 218, 226, 649, 778, 845.

215 Verticality

N. *verticality,* the vertical, erectness, uprightness, upright carriage; steepness, sheerness, precipitousness 209n. *height;* perpendicularity, right angle, square; elevation, azimuth circle; vertical line, plumbline, plummet; vertical structure, hoist, upright, pole, wall, palisade; sheer face, precipice, cliff, bluff, steep 209n. *high land;* perpendicular drop, straight d., vertical height, rise.

Adj. *vertical,* upright, erect, standing; perpendicular, rectangular, orthogonal; sheer, abrupt, steep, precipitous 209adj. *high;* straight, plumb; straight up, straight down; upstanding, standing up, on one's feet, on one's legs; bolt upright, stiff as a ramrod, unbowed, head-up; rampant, rearing; on end.

Vb. *be vertical,* stick up, cock up, bristle, stand on end; stand erect, stand upright, hold oneself straight; rise, stand, rise to one's feet, ramp, rear; vacate one's seat 920vb. *show respect;* keep standing, have no seat, sit on one's thumb.

make vertical, erect, rear, raise, pitch 310vb. *elevate;* raise on its legs, upend; stand, set up, stick up, raise up, cock up.

Adv. *vertically* etc. adj.; palewise (heraldry); upright, head-up; on end, up on end, endwise, up; on one's legs, standing, all standing; at right angles, perpendicularly; down, straight-d., plumb.

See: 209, 310, 920.

216 Horizontality

N. *horizontality,* horizontal, horizontal angle, azimuth; horizontalism, horizontalization; horizontal line, ruling, rule; horizontal course, strike; flatness 258n. *smoothness;* level, plane, dead level, dead flat, level plane; sea level, water l., water table; stratum; slab, tablet, table 207n. *layer;* level stretch, steppe 348n. *plain;* flats 347n. *marsh;* platform, ledge 254n. *projection;* terrace, esplanade, estrade; plateau, tableland 209n. *high land;* bowling green, cricket ground, court, baseball diamond, hockey rink, tennis court, croquet lawn 728n. *arena;* billiard table; flatbed; gridiron; pancake; dish, platter 194n. *plate;* spirit-level, T-square 465n. *gauge;* horizon, false h., horizon line 236n. *limit.*

supination, resupination; recumbency, lying down etc. vb.; reclination, decumbence, decumbency, discumbency; prostration; proneness; accumbation.

flattener, iron, flat-i., mangle, press, trouser-p.; rolling pin, roller, garden-r., road-r., steamroller 258n. *smoother.*

Adj. *flat,* horizontal, level, plane, even, flush 258adj. *smooth;* trodden, trodden flat, beaten f.; flat as a pancake, flat as a board, flat as my hand, flat as a fluke, flat as a flounder, flat as a billiard table, flat as a bowling green; unwrinkled, smooth, smooth as glass, calm, calm as a millpond; alluvial.

supine, flat on one's back; prone, face down, prostrate; recumbent, decumbent, procumbent, accumbent; jacent, lying down, couchant; abed, laid out; sprawling, lolling.

Vb. *be horizontal,* lie, lie down, lie flat, lie prostrate, lie on one's back; recline, couch, sprawl, loll 311vb. *sit down;* grovel 311vb. *stoop;* become horizontal, straighten out, level out.

flatten, lay out, roll o., lay down, spread; lay flat, beat f., tread f., stamp down, trample d., squash; make flush, align, level, even, plane 28vb. *equalize;* iron, iron out, roll, mangle 258vb. *smooth;* smooth down, plaster d.; prostrate, knock down, floor, gravel, ground 311vb. *fell.*

Adv. *horizontally,* flat, on one's back; fessewise, fesswise (heraldry).

See: 28, 194, 207, 209, 236, 254, 258, 311, 347, 348, 465, 728.

217 Pendency

N. *pendency,* pensility, pensileness; dependency, dependence; suspension, hanging, danglement, dangle; set, hang.

pendant 18n. *analogue;* hanging ornament, pendicle, dangler, drop, eardrop, earring 844n. *jewelry;* tassel, bobble, tag 844n. *trimming;* hangings, draperies, drapes, curtains, arras, tapestry 226n. *covering;* train, skirt, coat-tail; flap, lappet, tippet 228n. *dress;* queue, pigtail, tail, brush 67n. *sequel,* 259n. *hair;* dewlap, lobe, appendix 40n. *adjunct;* pendule, pendulum, bob, swing, hammock 317n. *oscillation;* chandelier, gasalier, electrolier, ceiling light 420n. *lamp;* icicle, stalactite.

hanger, coat-h., curtain-rod, curtain-ring, runner, ring; hook, tenterhook, staple, peg, knob, nail, yoke, cowlstaff 218n. *supporter;* suspender, braces, suspender-belt 228n. *underwear;* clothesline 47n. *cable;* clotheshorse 218n. *frame;* davit, crane, derrick 310n. *lifter;* spar, mast 218n. *pillar;* gallows, gibbet, crucifix 964n. *pillory;* garter 47n. *halter.*

Adj. *pendent,* hanging, pendulous, pensile; hanging from, dependent, suspended, dangling etc. vb.; hanging the head, nodding, drooping, weeping; lowering, overhanging; beetling 254adj. *salient;* decumbent, open-ended, loose 46adj. *disjunct;* baggy, flowing; floating (in the wind), waving, streaming, rippling; pedunculate, tailed, caudate; penduline.

Vb. *hang,* be pendent, drape, set; hang down, depend, trail, flow; hang on to, swing from; swing, sway, dangle, bob; hang the head, nod, weep, droop, sag, swag, daggle; hang in the wind, stream, wave, float, ripple, flap; hang over, hover; overhang, lower 226vb. *overlie;* suspend, hang up, sling, hook up, hitch, fasten to, append 45n. *join;* curtain 226vb. *cover.*

See: 18, 40, 45, 46, 47, 67, 218, 226, 228, 254, 259, 310, 317, 420, 844, 964.

218 Support

N. *support,* moral s., encouragement 703n. *aid;* uplift, sustenance, sustentation, maintenance, upkeep, nurture 633n. *provision;* subsidy 703n. *subvention;* point d'appui, locus standi, footing, ground, leg to stand on; hold, foothold, handhold, toe-hold 778n. *retention;* life-buoy, life-belt 662n. *safeguard.*

supporter, carriage, carrier; support, mounting, bearing; underframe, chassis; buttress, flying b., arc-boutant; abutment, embankment, wall, retaining w.; underpinning, shore, jack, prop, clothes-p.; flagstaff, jackstaff, sprag, stanchion, rod, bar, transom, steadier, brace, strut; stay, mainstay, guy, shrouds, rigging 47n. *tackling;* sprit, boom, spar, mast, yard, yardarm, fid, cross-tree, outrigger, cathead 254n. *protection;* trunk, stem, stalk, caudex, pedicle, pedicel, peduncle 366n. *plant;* arch, Roman a., Gothic a., Saracenic a., ogive 248n. *curve;* keystone, headstone, corner-stone, springer; cantilever; *pier* (**see** *pillar*); bandage, jockstrap, truss, splint; stiffener, whalebone; stays 228n. *underwear;* suspender, garter, braces, yoke; cowlstaff 217n. *hanger;* rest, headrest, backrest, footrest, stirrup; handrail (**see** *handle*); skid, chock, sprag, wedge 702n. *obstacle;* stang, staff, baton, stick, walking s., cane, alpenstock, bourdon, crutch, crook; leg-support, irons; bracket (**see** *shelf*); trivet, hob (**see** *stand*); arm, back, shoulder, broad shoulders; shoulder-blade, clavicle, collarbone, backbone, spine, neck, cervix; world-bearer, Atlas; helper, patron 707n. *auxiliary.*

handle, holder, penholder, cigarette-holder 195n. *receptacle;* hold, grip, hilt, pommel, haft; knob, door-handle; lug, ear, loop; railing, handrail, rail, poop-r., taffrail, balustrade; shaft, spear-s., oar-s., loom; handlebar, tiller; winder, crank, crank-handle; lever, trigger 630n. *tool.*

basis, foundation, solid f., concrete f.; sleeper; stereobate, substratum 207n. *layer;* ground, groundwork, floor, bed, bedrock, rock bottom 214n. *base;* flooring, pavement 226n. *paving;* terra firma 344n. *land;* perch, footing, foothold.

stand, tripod, trivet, hob; wine-stand, coaster; lampstand, lamppost, standard; anvil, block, bench; table, tea-t., teapoy; dining-table, board; console, console table; sideboard, dresser 194n. *cabinet;* work-table, desk, counter; pedestal, plinth, socle; stylobate, podium; platform, staddle, gantry; emplacement, banquette; firestep; footplate; foot-pace, landing, half-l.; landing-stage, pier; dais, pulpit, stage 539n. *rostrum;* doorstep, threshold 263n. *entrance;* altar-step, predella 990n. *altar;* step, stair, tread, rung, round 308n. *ascent;* stilt 310n. *lifter;* sole, heel 214n. *foot;* shank 267n. *leg*; shoe, boot 228n. *footwear.*

seat, throne, sedes gestatoria, masnad, guddee, woolsack; bank, bench, form, settle, podium; window-seat, rumble s., bucket s., sofa s., box s., box, dickey; pew, choir-stall, misericord 990n. *church interior;* stall, fauteuil 594n. *theater;* chair, armchair, easy c., elbow c., rocking c., basket c., high c., chaise longue; dining chair, triclinium; sofa, settee, divan, couch, ottoman, Chesterfield, sociable, loveseat; stool, footstool, campstool, faldstool; taboret, pouf, mora; prie-dieu, kneeler, cushion; riding seat, saddle, side-s., pack s., flat s., stock s., pillion, spring-seat; howdah, pad; stocks, ducking-stool 964n. *pillory;* electric chair, hot seat 964n. *means of execution;* lap, knees; carpet 226n. *floor-cover.*

bed, cot, crib, cradle, bassinet; marriage bed, bridal b., double b., single b., trundle b., day-b.; couch, tester, four-poster; charpoy, truckle bed, camp-b., pallet, shake-down, bunk; hammock 217n. *pendant;* sickbed, litter, hurdle, stretcher 658n. *hospital;* bedding 226n. *coverlet;* bedstead, bedstock, slats; bier 364n. *funeral.*

cushion, air-c., pillow; bolster, Dutch wife; mattress, spring m.; straw mattress, under-m., palliasse; squab, hassock, kneeler; prayer-mat.

beam, balk, joist, girder, rafter, raft, tie-beam 47n. *bond;* summer, breast-s., summer-beam, summer-tree; cross-beam, transom, cross-bar, traverse, travis, trave; architrave, lintel.

pillar, shaft, pier, pile, pendentive, post, kingpost, stock; jamb, door-j.; newel-post, bannister, balustrade, baluster; mullion; pilaster, column, Doric c., Ionic c., Corinthian c., portico, stoa; caryatid, telamon, Atlantes; spinal column, spine, backbone, vertebrae; neck, cervix.

pivot, fulcrum, fulciment, lever, purchase; hinge 45n. *joint;* pole, axis; axle, axletree, spindle, arbor, pintle 315n. *rotator;* bearing, gudgeon, trunnion; rowlock, thole-pin; centerboard, keel.

shelf, ledge, offset 254n. *projection;* corbel, bracket, console, ancon; retable, niche 194n. *compartment;* sill, window-s., mantlepiece, mantleshelf, rack, cupboard, dresser 194n. *cabinet;* counter, plank, board, table, leaf, slab 207n. *lamina.*

frame, bony f., skeleton, ribs; framework, scaffolding 331n. *structure;* chassis, fuselage, body (of a car), undercarriage; trestle; easel, clotheshorse; cage, trave 235n. *enclosure;* tailor's dummy, farthingale, hoop 228n. *skirt;* picture-frame, window f., sash, window-s. 223n. *outline.*

Adj. *supporting,* sustentative, sustaining; fundamental, basal; columellar, columnar; cervical, spinal; structural, skeletal; framing, holding.

Vb. *support,* sustain, bear, carry, hold, shoulder; uphold, upbear; hold up, bear up, buoy up; prop, shore up, underprop, underpin, jack up 310vb. *elevate;* bolster, bolster up, cushion; reinforce, underset 162vb. *strengthen;* bandage, brace, truss 45vb. *tighten;* steady, stay; cradle, pillow, cup, cup one's chin; nourish, nurture 301vb. *feed;* maintain, keep on foot 804vb. *pay;* back up, give support, lend s., furnish s., afford s., supply s. 703vb. *aid;* frame, set, mount 235vb. *enclose;* give foundations, bottom, ground, found, base, embed 153vb. *stabilize;* stand, endure, stand up to, stand the strain, take the s. 635vb. *suffice.*

be supported, stand on, recline on, lie on, sit on, loll on, repose on, rest on; bear on, press, press on, step on, lean on, abut on; rely on, ground oneself on, be based on; command support, have at one's back, have behind one.

Adv. *astride,* astraddle, piggyback.

See: 45, 47, 153, 162, 194, 195, 207, 214, 217, 223, 226, 228, 235, 248, 254, 263, 267, 301, 308, 310, 315, 331, 344, 366, 539, 594, 630, 633, 635, 658, 662, 702, 703, 707, 708, 778, 804, 964, 990.

219 Parallelism

N. *parallelism,* non-convergence, non-divergence, equidistance, coextension, collimation, concentricity; parallel, correspondence 28n. *equality;* parallel lines, lines of latitude; streetcar lines, rails, railroad tracks; parallelogram, parallelepiped.

Adj. *parallel,* coextensive, collateral, concurrent, concentric; equidistant 28adj. *equal;* corresponding, correspondent 18adj. *similar.*

Vb. *be parallel,* run together, run abreast, lie parallel; correspond, concur; collimate, parallel, draw a p.

Adv. *in parallel,* alongside, collaterally; side by side, abreast.

See: 18, 28.

220 Obliquity

N. *obliquity,* obliqueness, skewness; oblique line, diagonal; oblique figure, rhomboid 247n. *angular figure;* oblique angle, inclination 247n. *angularity;* oblique direction, side-pressure; indirection, indirectness, squint; curvature, camber, bend, springing line, skewback 248n. *curve;* changing direction, crankiness, crookedness, scoliosis, zigzag, chevron; switchback 251n. *meandering;* oblique motion, knight's move, divagation, digression, swerve, lurch, stagger, swag 282n. *deviation;* splay, bias, twist, warp, perversion 246n. *distortion;* leaning, list, tip, cant; slopeness, slope, slant, tilt, rake, rakish angle; sloping face, batter; sloping edge, bevel, bezel; inclined plane, ramp, chute, slide; Tower of Pisa, leaning tower; measurement of inclination 247n. *angular measure.*

acclivity, rise, ascent; ramp, incline, gradient; hill, rising ground 209n. *monticle;* hillside, khud, khudside, bank 239n. *laterality;* declivity, fall, dip, downhill, devexity, shelving beach 309n. *descent;* easy ascent, easy descent, gentle slope, rapid s.; steepness, cliff, precipice 215n. *verticality;* escarpment, scarp, glacis 712n. *fortification;* talus, landslide, scree.

Adj. *oblique,* inclined, abaxial, plagihedral; bevel, bezel; tipsy, tilted, rakish; biased, askew, skew, slant, aslant, ajee; out of the perpendicular, battered, clinal, leaning; recumbent, stooping; cater-cornered, rhomboidal 247adj. *angular;* wry, awry, wonky, skew-whiff, crooked, squinting, cock-eyed, knock-kneed 246adj. *distorted;* diagonal, transverse, transversal, antiparallel; athwart, thwart, cross 222adj. *crossed;* indirect, zigzag, herringbone, bent 248adj. *curved;* stepped, in echelon; divergent, non-parallel 282adj. *deviating.*

sloping, acclivous, uphill 308adj. *ascending;* rising, declivous, downhill, falling, declining, devex 309adj. *descending;* anticlinal, anaclinal, synclinal, cataclinal; steep, abrupt, sheer, precipitous, breakneck 215adj. *vertical;* easy, gentle, rounded.

Vb. *be oblique,*—tilted etc. adj.; incline, lean; tilt, slope, slant, shelve, decline 309vb. *descend;* rise, climb 308vb. *ascend;* cut, cut across, diagonalize, transect 222vb. *cross;* lean, tip, lean over, bank, heel, careen, cant; bend, sag, swag, give; bend over 311vb. *stoop;* walk sideways, edge, sidle, sidestep; look sideways, squint; zigzag; jink, swerve; diverge, converge.

render oblique, incline, lean, slant, slope, cant, tilt, tip, rake; splay 282vb. *deviate;* bend, crook, twist, warp 246vb. *distort;* chamfer, bevel; sway, bias, divert 282vb. *deflect;* curve, camber 248vb. *make curved.*

Adv. *obliquely* etc. adj.; diagonally, crosswise 222adv. *across;* on the cross, on the bias; askew, rakishly, tipsily; aslant, slantwise, on the slant; askance, asquint; edgewise, sidelong, sideways; aslope, off the vertical, off plumb, at an angle, at a rakish a.; on one side, all on one s.; by a side wind.

See: 209, 215, 222, 239, 246, 247, 248, 251, 282, 308, 309, 311, 712.

221 Inversion

N. *inversion,* turning back to front, palindrome, hysteron proteron; turning inside out, eversion; turning backwards, retroversion, reversal 148n. *reversion;* turning inward, introversion, invagination; turning over, pronation, capsizal (**see** *overturning*); turn of the tide, return 286n. *regression;* oppositeness 14n. *contrariety,* 240n. *contraposition;* transposition, transposal, metathesis 151n. *interchange;* inverted order (linguistic), chiasmus, anastrophe, hyperbaton, hypallage 519n. *trope;* confused order, synchysis, spoonerism; interrupted order, tmesis, parenthesis 72n. *discontinuity,* 231n. *interjacence.*

overturning, capsize, capsizal, upset, spill, overset; somersault, somerset, culbut, cartwheel, hand-spring; subversion, undermining 149n. *revolution;* pronation 216n. *supination.*

Adj. *inverted,* inverse, back-to-front; palindromic; upside down, everted, invaginated, inside out, wrong side out; capsized, upside down, bottom up, keel upwards; capsizing, top-heavy; topsy-turvy, head over heels, on one's head; flat, prone 216n. *supine;* reverse, reversed 14adj. *contrary;* antipodean, antipodal 240adj. *opposite;* hyperbatic, chiastic, antithetic.

Vb. *be inverted,* turn round, go r., wheel r., turn about, face a., right about turn 286vb. *turn back;* turn over, heel o., capsize, turn turtle; tilt over 220vb. *be oblique;* go over, topple o. 309vb. *tumble;* stand on one's head; reverse, back, back away, go backwards 286vb. *regress.*

invert, transpose, put the cart before the horse 151vb. *interchange;* reverse, turn the tables; retrovert, turn back; turn down 261vb. *fold;* introvert, invaginate; turn inside out, evaginate; upturn, overturn, tip over, spill, upset, capsize, turn; topsy-turvy.

Adv. *inversely* etc. adj.; vice versa; contrariwise, other way round; arsy-versy, topsy-turvy, head over heels, heels in the air; face down, face downwards.

See: 14, 72, 148, 149, 151, 216, 220, 231, 240, 261, 286, 309, 519.

222 Crossing: intertexture

N. *crossing,* crossing over and under, plain weaving; criss-cross, transversion, transection, intersection; decussation, X-shape; chiasma, quincunx; intertexture, interlacement; intertwinement, arabesque; interdigitation; anastomosis, inosculation; plexure, plexus, braid, wreath, plait 251n. *convolution;* entanglement, intricacy, skein, sleave, cat's cradle 61n. *complexity;* crossway, cross-roads, intersection, road-junction 624n. *road;* level crossing 624n. *railroad;* viaduct, fly-over 624n. *bridge,* 305n. *traffic control.*

cross, crux, rood, crucifix 988n. *ritual object;* pectoral 989n. *vestments;* ansate cross, Lorraine c., Greek c., Maltese c., Celtic c., St. Andrew's C.; saltire 547n. *heraldry;* crosslet, swastika, fylfot, tau; cross-bar, transom 218n. *beam;* scissors, pincers, nutcrackers, forceps 778n. *nippers.*

network, reticulation, meshwork, netting, webbing, matting, wickerwork, mokes, trellis, wattle, raddle; lattice, grating, grid, grill, gridiron; tracery, fretwork, filigree 844n. *ornamental art;* lace, crochet, knitting; web, cobweb; net, fishnet, seine, dragnet, trawl, beam-t. 235n. *enclosure;* plexus, mesh, moke, reticle.

textile, weave, web, loom; woven stuff, piecegoods, dry goods; bolt, roll, length, piece, cloth, stuff, material; broadcloth, fabric, tissue, suiting; jute, burlap, hessian, gunny, sacking, sackcloth; hemp, canvas; linen, lawn, cambric; duck; tapestry, blanketing, toweling, crash; mohair, cashmere; alpaca, vicuna, angora; wool, merino, worsted; frieze, felt; jersey, stockinette, paramatta; homespun, khadi, khaddar, duffle, hodden, kersey, tweed, serge, shalloon, baize; flannel, flannelette, swansdown; swanskin; linenette, cotton, drill, nankeen, muslin, mull, mulmul, nainsook, jaconet; silesia, calico, dowlas, long-cloth, fustian, moleskin, sharkskin, dimity, gingham, voile, madras, percale, rep, seersucker, poplin; chintz, cretonne, holland, silk, foulard, georgette, grosgrain, damask, brocade, samite, satin, sateen, ninon, taffeta, tussah, tussore, sarcenet, shantung, chiffon, surah, pongee; velvet, velveteen, velour; corduroy; tulle, organdy, organza; lace, bullion, chenille, crochet-work, crewel-work artificial fabric, cellulose f., artificial silk, rayon.

weaving, texture, weftage; web, warp, weft, woof; frame, loom, shuttle; weaver, stockinger, knitter; spinning wheel, distaff, whorl; spinner, spinster; spider.

Adj. *crossed,* crossing, cross, criss-cross; quadrivial; diagonal, transverse, cross-eyed, squinting 220adj. *oblique;* decussated, X-shaped, chiastic, quincunxial; cross-legged, cruciform, crucial, forked, furcate, furcular 247adj. *angular;* plexal, plexiform; knotted, matted, balled-up, raveled 61adj. *complex;* pleached, plaited, interlaced, interfretted, interwoven; textile, loomed, woven, hand-woven, tweedy; trellised, latticed, grated, mullioned, barred; streaked, striped.

reticular, reticulated, retiform, webbed, webby; netted, meshed 201adj. *spaced.*

Vb. *cross,* cross over, cross under 305vb. *pass;* intersect, cut, diagonalize 220vb. *be oblique;* decussate, anastomose, inosculate, interdigitate; splice, dovetail, link 45vb. *join;* reticulate, mesh, net, knot; fork, bifurcate 247vb. *angulate.*

weave, loom; pleach, plait, braid; felt, twill, knit, crochet; spin, slub.

enlace, interlace, interlink, interlock, interdigitate, intertwine, intertwist, interweave, enmesh, engage gear; twine, entwine, twist, raddle, wreathe, pleach; mat, ravel, tangle, entangle, dishevel 63vb. *derange.*

Adv. *across,* thwart, transversely; decussatively, crosswise, saltire-wise; with folded arms, arm in arm.

See: 45, 61, 63, 201, 218, 220, 235, 247, 251, 305, 547, 624, 778, 844, 988, 989.

223 Exteriority

N. *exteriority,* the external; outwardness, externality 230n. *circumjacence;* periphery, circumference, sidelines 233n. *outline;* exterior, outward appearance 445n. *mien;* surface, superficies, superstratum, crust, cortex, shell 226n. *skin;* outer side, face, facet, façade 237n. *front;* outside, out of doors, open air; outer space 199n. *distance;* other side 240n. *contraposition;* externalism, regard for externals 982n. *idolatry;* externalization, extroversion, extrovert 6n. *extrinsicality;* extraterritoriality 57n. *exclusion;* foreignness 59n. *extraneousness;* eccentricity 84n. *unconformity;* outsider 84n. *nonconformist.*

Adj. *exterior,* outward, extra-; external 10adj. *irrelative;* roundabout, peripheral 230adj. *circumjacent;* outer, outermost, outlying 199adj. *distant;* outside, outboard; outdoor, extramural; foreign 59adj. *extraneous;* extraterritorial 57adj. *excluding;* extrovert, extra-regarding, outward-looking 6adj. *extrinsic;* centrifugal 620adj. *avoiding;* exogenous; eccentric 282adj. *deviating;* outstanding, egregious 34adj. *superior;* surface, superficial, epidermic, cortical; skin-deep 212adj. *shallow;* frontal, facial 237adj. *fore.*

Vb. *be exterior,* lie beyond, lie outside etc. adv.; frame, enclose 230vb. *surround;* look outward 6vb. *be extrinsic.*

externalize, body forth, objectify 6vb. *make extrinsic;* project, extrapolate; extern 300vb. *eject.*

Adv. *externally,* outwardly, outwards, superficially, on the surface; on the face of it, to the outsider; outside, extra muros; out, out of doors, in the cold, in the sun, in the open, in the open air, al fresco.

See: 6, 10, 34, 57, 59, 84, 199, 212, 226, 230, 233, 237, 240, 282, 300, 445, 620, 982.

224 Interiority

N. *interiority,* interior, inside, indoors; inner surface, undersurface; endoderm 226n. *skin;* sap-wood, heart-w. 366n. *wood;* inmost being, heart's blood, soul; marrow, pith; heart, center, breast, bosom 225n. *centrality;* inland, heartland, hinterland, up-country; pith, marrow 3n. *substance;* subsoil, substratum 214n. *base;* permeation, pervasion 189n. *presence,* 231n. *interjacence;* interspace 201n. *interval;* deepness, cave, pit, penetralia, recesses, innermost r. 211n. *depth;* endogamy 894n. *mar-*

riage; introversion 5n. *intrinsicality;* self-absorption, egoism, egotism, egocentrism 932n. *selfishness;* introvert, egoist 932n. *egotist;* inmate, indweller 191n. *dweller;* internee 750n. *prisoner.*

insides 193n. *contents;* inner man, interior man; internal organs, vitals; heart, ticker; bowels, entrails, guts, pluck, tripe; intestines, colon, rectum; viscera, liver and lights; spleen; milt; abdomen, belly, paunch, underbelly; womb, uterus; stomach, tummy 194n. *maw;* chest, solar plexus; gland; endocrine; cell 358n. *organism;* offal, chitterlings, haslet, kidney, liver.

Adj. *interior,* internal, inward 5adj. *intrinsic;* inside, inner, innermost, midmost 225adj. *central;* inland, upcountry 211adj. *deep;* domestic, home, vernacular; intimate, familiar 490adj. *known;* indoor, intramural, shut in, enclosed; inboard, built-in, inwrought; endemic 192adj. *residing;* deep-seated, ingrown 153adj. *fixed;* intestinal, visceral, alvine; intravenous, subcutaneous; interstitial, endocardial 231adj. *interjacent;* inward-looking, intraregarding, introvert 5adj. *intrinsic;* endo-, endogamous; endogenous.

Vb. *be inside,*—internal etc. adj.; be within etc. adv.; lie within, lie beneath, be at the bottom of; show through 443vb. *be visible.*

enclose, hold 78vb. *comprise;* place within, embed 303vb. *insert;* keep inside, intern 747vb. *imprison;* enfold, embay 235vb. *enclose.*

Adv. *inside,* within, in, deep in, deep down; inly, intimately; deeply, profoundly, at heart; inwardly, herein, therein, wherein; withinside, within doors, indoors, at home, ben, chez, at the sign of.

See: 3, 5, 78, 153, 189, 191, 192, 193, 194, 201, 211, 214, 225, 226, 231, 303, 358, 366, 443, 490, 747, 750, 894, 932.

225 Centrality

N. *centrality,* centricality, centricity; centricalness, middleness 70n. *middle;* centripetence; centralization, focalization, concentration, nucleation 324n. *condensation;* central position, mid p. 231n. *interjacence;* waist-line, center-line, parting 231n. *partition;* Ptolemaic system, Copernican s.

center, dead c.; centroid, center of mass, center of gravity, center of pressure, center of percussion, center of buoyancy, metacenter, epicenter; storm-center, hotbed; heart, core, kernel, nub, hub, nave, nucleus, nucleolus; navel, umbilicus; spine, backbone, chine, midrib; marrow, pith 224n. *interiority;* pole, axis, fulcrum, center-board 218n. *pivot;* center point, mid p. 70n. *middle;* fess point 547n. *heraldry;* eye, pupil; bull's-eye, blank, target 617n. *objective.*

Adj. *central,* centro-, centric, centrical, centroidal; nuclear, nucleal, nucleolar; centermost, midmost 70adj. *middle;* axial, focal, pivotal; mesogastric, umbilical, umbilicate; homocentric, concentric; geocentric; heliocentric; spinal, vertebral; centripetal; metropolitan, chief, head 34adj. *supreme.*

Vb. *centralize,* center, take c.; focus, bring to a f., center upon, concentrate, nucleate, consolidate 324vb. *be dense.*

Adv. *centrally,* at heart, at the core, middle, midst, amongst; in the midst, in the middle.

See: 34, 70, 218, 224, 231, 324, 547, 617.

226 Covering

N. *covering,* obduction, superposition, superimposition, overlaying; overlap, overlapping, imbrication; coating, stratification 207n. *layer;* top layer, top-dressing, mulch, topsoil 344n. *soil;* cover, covercle, lid; gravestone, ledger 364n. *tomb;* flap, shutter, operculum 421n. *screen;* glass, glass front, watch-glass, crystal 422n. *transparency;* cap, top, plug, bung, cork 263n. *stopper;* pledget, dossil, tampon, tompion 658n. *surgical dressing;* carapace, shell, tortoise-shell, snail s., oyster s. 326n. *hardness;* mail, plate, armor p. 713n. *armor;* shield, cowl, cowling, bonnet, hood (of a car); scab 207n. *lamina;* crust, fur 649n. *dirt;* capsule, ferrule, sheath, envelope 194n. *receptacle;* finger-stall, pillow-case, pillow-slip; chair cover, antimacassar; hangings, curtains, window c., drapes, arras, tapestry, wallpaper 217n. *pendant;* mask, gas-m., iron m. 527n. *disguise;* air 340n. *atmosphere.*

roof, cupola 253n. *dome;* mansard roof, pitched r., gable r., flat r.; housetop, rooftop, roof-ridge 213n. *vertex;* leads, slates, slating, tiles, tiling, pantile, shingle, thatch, thatching; eaves 234n. *edge;* ceiling, rafters; deck.

canopy, ciborium, baldachin; tilt, awning, velarium, sun-blind 421n. *screen;* marquee, shamiana, pavilion, tent, bell-tent; tent-cloth, canvas, tarpaulin, mosquito net 222n. *network.*
shade, film 421n. *screen;* hood, eyelid, eyelash; blind, sun-b., venetian b., persiennes, shutters, slats; curtain, veil; umbrella, gamp, bumbershoot, brolly; parasol, sunshade; sun-bonnet, sun-helmet, sola topee 228n. *headgear;* visor, sun-screen; peak (of a cap); dark glasses 442n. *eyeglass.*
wrapping, wrapper, paper, cellophane; bandage, roll 45n. *girdle;* lint, plaster, cast, dressing 658n. *surgical dressing;* book-cover, binding, boards, covers, straw-board, mill-b., dust-jacket 589n. *bookbinding;* jacket, coat 228n. *tunic;* mantle 228n. *cloak;* comforter, scarf, chudder 228n. *shawl;* loincloth 228n. *shirt;* life-belt, Mae West 662n. *safeguard;* cocoon, chrysalis; cerement, shroud, winding sheet, mummy-cloth 364n. *grave clothes.*
skin, outer s., scarf-s., cuticle, epidermis, ectoderm; true skin, cutis, derm, corium, enderm; tegument; integument, peel, bark, crust, rind, coat, cortex; husk, hull, shell, pod, cod, shuck, jacket; pellicle, film; scalp 213n. *head;* scale 207n. *lamina;* pelt, peltry, fleece, fell, fur; leather, hide, rawhide, imitation leather, leatheroid; shagreen, calf, cowhide, morocco, pigskin, crocodile, alligator, elk, kid, sealskin, deerskin, doeskin; lambskin, sheepskin, woolfell, woolskin; rabbit skin; chinchilla; sable, mink, muskrat; vair, ermine, miniver, marten; feathers, coverts 259n. *plumage.*
paving, flooring, floor, parquet; deck, floorboards, duck-b.; pavement, pavé; flags, paving-stone; sett, cobble, cobblestone; tarmac 624n. *road.*
coverlet, bedspread, counterpane, bedding, bed-clothes, bed-sheets; sheet, contour s., quilt, eiderdown, blanket, rug; caparison, housings, trappings; saddlecloth, horsecloth, numdah.
floor-cover, carpet, stair-c., pile c., persian c.; mat, doormat; rug, scatter r., hooked r.; drugget, numdah; linoleum, oilcloth; matting; red carpet 875n. *formality.*
facing, revetment 162n. *strengthening;* veneer, coating, varnish, japan, lacquer, enamel, glaze; encrustation, rough-cast, pebble-dash; stucco, compo, plaster, parget, rendering; wash, whitewash, distemper, stain, polish, smearing, inunction, ointment; impasto, paint 425n. *pigment.*

Adj. *overlying,* overlaying, overarching; overlapping, tegular, imbricated; cloaking etc. vb.
covered, roofed, roofed in, ceiled, wallpapered, carpeted; tented, garaged, under cover, under canvas; under shelter 660n. *safe;* cloaked, cowled, veiled, hooded 525adj. *concealed;* loricated, armor-plated, ironclad; metaled, paved; overbuilt, built over; snow-capped, ice-covered; inundated, flooded; smothered, plastered.
dermal, cutaneous, cortical, cuticular; tegumentary; scaly, squamous; epidermic, epidermoid.

Vb. *cover,* superpose, superimpose; roof, roof in, put the lid on, cap, tip; spread, lay (a table); overlay, smother; lap, wrap, enwrap, enfold 235vb. *enclose;* blanket, mantle, muffle, moble; hood, veil 525vb. *conceal;* case, bind, cover (books); bandage, swathe, wrap round, dress 658vb. *doctor;* sheathe, encapsulate, encase 303vb. *insert;* embox; wall in, wall up; keep under cover, lock up, garage.
overlie, overarch, overhang, overlap; overshadow 419vb. *bedim;* span, bestride, straddle, bestraddle 205vb. *be broad;* overflood, inundate 341vb. *drench;* skim, skim over, crust, scab.
overlay, pave, floor, cement; ceil, roof, dome, overarch, deck; paper, wallpaper 227vb. *line;* overspread, top-dress, mulch; spread, smear, besmear; butter, anoint; powder, dust, sand.
coat, revet, face, do over; grout, rough-cast, encrust, shingle; stucco, plaster, parget, render; veneer, varnish, lacquer, japan, enamel, glaze; paint, whitewash, distemper, stain 425vb. *color;* tar, pitch, pay; daub, bedaub, scumble, overpaint, grease, lay it on thick; gild, plate, silver, besilver; electroplate, silverplate; waterproof, fire-p. 660vb. *safeguard.*

See: 45, 162, 194, 205, 207, 213, 217, 222, 227, 228, 234, 235, 253, 259, 263, 303, 326, 340, 341, 344, 364, 419, 421, 422, 425, 442, 525, 527, 589, 624, 649, 658, 660, 662, 717, 875.

227 Lining

N. *lining,* interlining 231n. *interjacence;* coating, inner c.; stuffing, wadding, padding, bombast; interlining, inlay; backing, facing; doublure 589n. *bookbinding;* upholstery; papering, wallpaper; wainscoting, paneling, wainscot, brattice; metal lining, bushing; brake-lining; packing, pack, dunnage; filling, stopping (dentistry); washer, shim.

Vb. *line,* encrust 226vb. *coat;* interlard, inlay; back, face, paper, wallpaper; upholster, cushion; stuff, pad, wad; fill, pack; bush; fother.

See: 226, 231, 589.

228 Dressing

N. *dressing,* investment, investiture; clothing, covering, dressing up, toilet, toilette; overdressing, foppishness 848n. *fashion;* vesture, dress, garb, attire, trim; garniture, accouterment, caparison, harness, housing, trappings; rigging, rig; rig-out, turnout; tailoring, millinery, mercery.

clothing, wear; raiment, linen; apparel, wearing a.; clothes, garments, weeds, things, doings; gear, vestments, habiliments; wardrobe, outfit, trousseau; layette, baby clothes, swaddling c., baby linen; togs, toggery, duds, traps; old clothes, slops; reach-me-downs, hand-me-downs, rags, tatters; best, best clothes, clean linen, fine raiment; Sunday best, Sunday-go-to-meeting clothes, best bib and tucker; party dress, glad rags; pearlies, ostrich feathers, frippery 844n. *finery;* fancy dress; theatrical properties; change of raiment, new suit; masquerade; woollens, cottons. **See** *dress.*

dress, frock, gown, creation; garment, costume, habit, riding h.; suiting, suit, store s., lounge s., office s., ready-made s., tailormade s., bespoke s.; boiler s., siren s., track s.; three-piece s., two-piece s., two-piece; salwar kameez, sari, dhoti, lungi, sarong; civilian dress, civvies, mufti.

formal dress, correct d., coronation d., regalia, court dress, durbar d., full d.; grande toilette, evening dress, tails, white tie and tails; morning dress; academic dress, cap and gown; mourning, black, weepers, widow's weeds.

uniform, regimentals, accouterment; full dress, undress, mess kit; battle dress, fatigues; khaki, jungle green, field gray, red coat 547n. *livery;* robes, vestments, priestly v., clerical dress 989n. *canonicals;* academicals, cap and gown.

informal dress, undress, mufti, deshabille, dishabille, negligee, boudoir dress, dressing gown, peignoir, bathrobe, wrapper, pajamas, bed-jacket; housecoat, kimono, tea-gown, cocktail dress; tuxedo, dinner jacket, smoking j., shooting coat; slippers, slacks.

robe, robes, sweeping r., trailing garments; baby clothes, long clothes, drapery, drapes 217n. *pendant;* sari; himation; pallium, peplum, peplos; stole, pelisse, domino (**see** *cloak*); sheet, winding s., shroud 364n. *grave clothes.*

tunic, body-coat; coat, cut-away c., swallow-tail c., tail c., frock c.; coatee, jacket, reefer j., single-breasted j., double-breasted j.; dinner jacket, smoking j., tuxedo, monkey jacket, pea-j., pilot j., Eton j., mess j., short j., blazer; Norfolk jacket, shooting coat; parka, wind-breaker; leotard; gym dress, drill d.; tabard, dolman, gambison; jerkin, doublet, jama; paletot, caftan, gaberdine, sanbenito; cassock, soutane; toga, chiton.

vest, waistcoat, bolero; stomacher, jumper, jersey, guernsey, cardigan, spencer, pullover, sweater, banian, singlet, zephyr.

trousers, long t., peg-top t., pants, long p., peg-p., ski-p., frontier p.; trews, breeks, kerseys, overalls, pantaloons, pantalets; bloomers, bag-trousers, petticoat t., salwar; slacks, bags, Cambridge b., Oxford b.; chaparajos, chaps, dungarees, overalls, denims, jeans, blue j., levis, pedal-pushers, sweat pants; drawers, shorts, Bermuda s., half-pants, short p.

breeches, knee b., riding b., jodhpurs; buckskins, unmentionables, inexpressibles; small-clothes, smalls; knickerbockers, knickers; galligaskins, plus fours; toreador pants; rompers, crawlers.

skirt, outer petticoat, kirtle; grass skirt, Hawaiian s., full s., divided s., slit s., hobble s., jupe, crinoline, hoop-skirt, farthingale, pannier, hoop; ballet skirt, tutu; kilt, fillibeg; overskirt, peplum; sporran; bustle, tournure.

apron, pinafore, pinner, jumper, overall; bib, tucker, front, false shirt, dickey; fichu.

loincloth, breechcloth, breechclout, malkoch; loin-guard; diaper, nappy.

bodywear, linen, lingerie; shirt, punjabi, vest, singlet; banian; smock, shift, chemise, slip, petticoat, princess p., waist-p.; blouse, waist, shirtwaist, basque; stomacher, bodice, choli, camisole, chemisette, corsage; corselet.

underwear, undies, dessous, lingerie,

frillies; underclothes, underlinen, undershirt, underbodice, undervest, underskirt, underdrawers, underpants; pants, combinations, woollies; drawers, knickers, bloomers, pettipants; panties, scanties, briefs, step-ins, camiknickers, camibockers; foundation garment, corset, stays, whalebone; two-way stretch, girdle, pantie-girdle; brassiere, bra; braces, suspenders; suspender belt, garter, shoulder-straps.

nightwear, sleeping suit, nightgown, nightshirt, nighty; pajamas, shorties; bedsocks, bed-jacket, nightcap.

beachwear, play-suit, bikini; bathing costume, swim-suit, bathing drawers, bathing-suit, trunks.

overcoat, coat, fur c., fur-lined c., mink c.; top-coat, long-c., greatcoat, uniform coat; trench-coat, surtout, redingote, riding coat; duffle coat, loden c.; waterproof, mackintosh, raincoat; storm-coat, sou'wester, oilskins; slicker, pea-jacket, windcheater, wrap-rascal; spencer, raglan, burberry, benjamin.

cloak, mantle, mantelet, chlamys; military cloak, sagum; capote, cape, talma, poncho, manteau, mantua, pelisse, roquelaure, cardinal, tippet, pelerine; huke, haik, burnoose, yashmak, veil 421n. *screen;* domino 527n. *disguise.*

shawl, mantilla, ascot; stole, chudder; scarf, wrapper, choker; comforter, muffler, plaid; prayer-scarf, tallith.

headgear, head-dress, mantilla; plumes, feathers, ostrich f.; ribbons 844n. *finery;* crown, coronet, tiara 743n. *regalia;* fillet, snood, coif, wimple 47n. *girdle;* headband, kerchief; turban, puggaree; fez, tarboosh; hood, cowl, calash; helmet, Balaclava h., busby, bearskin, shako, kepi, forage cap, side-c., pill-box; casque, morion, steel hat 713n. *armor;* cap, cloth c., skull-c., smoking c., peaked c., riding c., jockey c.; fast-cap, stocking c.; beret, tam-o'-shanter, tam; balmoral, glen-garry; hat, tile, lid, beany; crown, peak, brim; soft hat, homburg, trilby; pork-pie hat, billycock; fedora, felt hat; beaver, castor, coonskin cap; slouch hat, terai h.; stetson, ten-gallon hat, tyrolean h.; broadbrimmed hat, wideawake, petasos; bowler hat, derby, topper, top-hat, tall h., silk h., chimney-pot h.; opera hat, crush h., gibus; straw hat, boater, panama, astrakhan, leghorn; bonnet, sun-bonnet, mobcap, toque, cloche hat, picture h., Dolly Varden h.; three-cornered hat, tricorne; witch's hat, dunce's cap; priest's cap, biretta, cardinal's hat, red h., shovel h. 989n. *canonicals.*

wig, peruke, periwig, full-bottomed w., bagwig, curled wig, tie-w., barrister's w.; false hair, toupee; coiffure 259n. *hair.*

footwear, footgear, buskin, sock; bootee, footlet, bootikin; boot, ammunition b.; top-boot, riding b., jack-b., Russian b., Wellington, Hessian; border boots, high-heel b., thigh-boot, gambado; hipboot, waders; shoe, court s.; wooden shoe, clog, sabot, patten, karam; high heels, peg h., spike h.; brogues, moccasin, sandal, chapli; rope shoe, espadrilles; gumshoe, rubbers, plimsol, sneakers, creepers, loafers; overshoe, galosh; slipper, mule, pump; ballet shoe, toe-slipper; snow-shoe, ski-boot; boot-tree, stretcher; skate, roller s., ice-s., ski 274n. *sled.*

legwear, hosiery; stockings, nylons; tights, fleshings; trunks, hose, gaskins; half-hose, socks, knee-s., golf-s.; leggings, gaiters, cutikins, galligaskins; spatter-dashes, spats; puttees, antigropelos; greaves 713n. *armor;* garter; gambado, waders. **See** *footwear.*

neckwear, ruff, collar, high c., stiff c., soft c.; dog-collar, white choker 989n. *canonicals;* neckband, choker, cravat, stock, tie; neckerchief, neckcloth, bandana; boa, fur, scarf, stole, tallith (**see** *shawl*); necklace 844n. *finery.*

belt, waistband; cummerbund, sash, obi; armlet, armband; bandolier, bellyband, girth 47n. *girdle.*

glove, gauntlet, long gloves; mitten, bootikin; muff, muffetee.

sleeve, arm, armhole; leg-of-mutton sleeve, raglan s.; wristband, cuff.

clothier, outfitter, costumer; tailor, snip, cutter, couturier; dressmaker, sempstress, seamstress, modiste; breeches-maker; shoemaker, bootmaker; cobbler, cordwainer, souter, Crispin 686n. *artisan;* hosier, hatter, milliner, draper, linendraper, haberdasher, mercer; slopshop; valet, tirewoman 742n. *domestic;* dresser, mistress of the wardrobe 594n. *stage hand.*

Adj. *dressed,* clothed, clad, dight; rigged out, invested, garmented, habited, costumed, breeched; uniformed, liveried; shod, gloved, hatted; well-dressed, soigné, en grande toilette, en grande tenue; tailored, tailormade, ready-made; wearable, sartorial.

Vb. *dress,* clothe, breech; array, apparel, garment, dight, garb, tire, attire, habilitate; robe, enrobe, drape, sheet, mantle; accouter, uniform, put in u., equip, rig, rig out, fit o., harness, caparison 669vb. *make ready;* dress up, bedizen, deck, prank, perk, trim 843vb. *primp;* envelop, wrap, lap, enfold, wrap up, fold up, muffle up, roll up in, swaddle, swathe, shroud, sheathe 226vb. *cover.*

wear, put on, assume, don, slip on, slip into, get i., huddle i.; clothe oneself, attire o., get one's clothes on; have on, dress in, carry, sport; dress up 875vb. *be ostentacious;* change one's clothes, change, change into.

See: 47, 217, 226, 259, 274, 364, 421, 527, 547, 549, 594, 669, 686, 713, 742, 743, 843, 844, 848, 875, 989.

229 Uncovering

N. *uncovering,* divestment, undressing etc. vb.; exposure, cult of the nude, nudism, naturism; striptease 594n. *stage show;* undress, dishabille, deshabille 228n. *informal dress;* moulting, shedding, decortication, exfoliation, excoriation, peeling, desquamation; depilation, shaving; denudation, devastation 165n. *havoc.*

bareness, décolleté, décolletage, bare neck, low n., plunging neckline; nudity, nakedness, state of nature, birthday suit, nu intégral, the altogether, the buff, the raw, not a stitch on; baldness, hairlessness, falling hair, alopecia, acomia; tonsure; shaveling, baldpate, baldhead.

stripper, nudist, naturist, ecdysiast, stripteaser; skinner, furrier, flayer, peeler; nude figure, nude.

Adj. *uncovered,* bared; exposed, unveiled, showing 522adj. *manifest;* divested, forcibly d., debagged; stripped, peeled; without one's clothes, unclad, unclothed, undressed, unappareled; décolleté, barenecked, low-n., bare-armed, barebacked, bareback; bare-legged, barefoot, unshod, discalced; hatless, bareheaded, en déshabillé, in one's shirt-sleeves; underclothed, underdressed; bare, naked, nude, raw; in a state of nature, in nature's garb, in nature's buff, au naturel, in one's birthday suit, with nothing on, without a stitch; stark, stark naked, starkers; acomous, leafless; molting, unfeathered, unfledged; poorly dressed, threadbare, out-at-elbows, ragged 801adj. *poor;* drawn, unsheathed 304adj. *extracted.*

hairless, bald, baldheaded, smooth, beardless, shaved, shaven, clean-s., tonsured; bald as a coot, bald as an egg, bald as a billiard ball, bare as the back of one's hand; napless, threadbare; mangy 651adj. *diseased;* thin, thin on top.

Vb. *uncover,* unveil, undrape, unrobe, undress, unclothe; divest, debag; strip, skin, scalp, flay, tear off; pluck, peel, bark, decorticate, excoriate, exfoliate, desquamate; hull, shuck, shell, stone; bone, fillet 300vb. *void;* denude, denudate 165vb. *lay waste;* expose, bare, lay open 526vb. *disclose;* unsheathe, draw (a sword) 304vb. *extract;* unwrap, unfold, unpack; unroof, take the lid off 263vb. *open;* scrape, scrape off, abrade 333vb. *rub.*

doff, uncap, uncover, raise one's hat; take off, strip off, slip off, slip out of, step out of; change, change one's clothes; shed, cast, cast a clout; molt, mew, cast its skin; divest oneself, undress, disrobe, uncase, uncoif, peel, strip; undo, unbutton, unlace, untie 46vb. *disjoin.*

See: 46, 165, 228, 263, 300, 304, 333, 522, 526, 594, 651, 801.

230 Circumjacence

N. *circumjacence,* circumambience, ambience, medium, atmosphere, aura; halo 250n. *loop;* encompassment, containment 235n. *enclosure;* compass, circuit, circumference, periphery, perimeter 233n. *outline;* surrounding, milieu, environment, entourage; background, setting, scene 594n. *stage set;* neighborhood, vicinity 200n. *near place;* outskirts, environs, boulevards, suburbs, faubourgs, banlieues; purlieus, precincts 192n. *street;* outpost, border 236n. *limit;* wall, fortification 235n. *fence;* wrap-around 47n. *girdle.*

Adj. *circumjacent,* circum-; circumambient; circumfluent, ambient, atmospheric; surrounding etc. vb.; framing, circumferential, peripheral; shutting in, claustral; roundabout 314adj. *circuitous;* suburban 200adj. *near.*

Vb. *surround,* lie around, compass, encompass, environ, lap; encircle 314vb. *circle;* girdle, begird, engird, cincture, encincture 235vb. *enclose;* wreathe around, twine a.; embrace, hug 889vb. *caress;* contain, keep in, cloister, shut in, hem in, embay 232vb. *circumscribe;* beset, invest, blockade 712vb. *besiege.*

Adv. *around,* about, on every side, round about, all round; on all sides, right and left; without, outside, in the neighborhood, in the outskirts.

See: 47, 192, 200, 232, 233, 235, 236, 250, 314, 594, 712, 889.

231 Interjacence

N. *interjacence,* intermediacy, interlocation; intervenience, intervention, intercurrence, penetration, interpenetration, permeation, infiltration 189n. *presence;* interdigitation 222n. *crossing;* dovetailing 45n. *junction;* middle position 70n. *middle.*

partition, curtain, iron c., bamboo c. 421n. *screen;* Great Wall of China 713n. *defenses;* wall, party-w., brattice, bulk-head 235n. *fence;* divide, watershed, parting 46n. *separation;* division, cloison, panel 57n. *subdivision;* interface, septum, diaphragm, midriff; field-boundary, balk, ridge, ail; common frontier 236n. *limit.*

intermediary, medium, intermedium, link 47n. *bond;* negotiator, go-between, broker 720n. *mediator;* ghatak, marriage broker 894n. *match-maker;* agent 755n. *deputy;* middleman, retailer 794n. *merchant;* intercessor, pleader, advocate 707n. *patron;* buffer, bumper, fender, cushion 662n. *safeguard;* buffer-state, no man's land, halfway house 70n. *middle.*

interjection, putting between, interposition, sandwiching; interpolation, intercalation, embolism, interlineation, interspersion, intromission 300n. *insertion;* interruption, interference, obtrusion, intrusion, butting in 72n. *discontinuity;* interference, meddling 702n. *hindrance;* thing inserted, episode, parenthesis, obiter dictum 40n. *adjunct;* infix, insert, flyleaf; glide-sound, glide, thematic vowel; wedge, washer, shim.

interjector, interpolator; intruder, interloper 702n. *hinderer.*

Adj. *interjacent,* interposed, sandwiched; episodic, parenthetical, in brackets; intercurrent, intermediary, intervenient, intervening etc. vb.; intercessory, mediating 720n. *mediatory;* intercalary, embolismal 303adj. *inserted;* intrusive 59adj. *extraneous;* inter-, interstitial, intercostal, intermural; interplanetary, interstellar; intermediate, thematic 303adj. *inserted;* median, medium, mean, mediterranean 70adj. *middle;* embosomed, merged 78adj. *included;* partioning, septal.

Vb. *lie between,* come b., stand b.; intervene 625vb. *be halfway;* slide in, interpenetrate, permeate, soak in 189vb. *pervade.*

intromit, let in 299vb. *admit;* introduce, sheathe, invaginate; throw in, foist in, plow in, work in, wedge in, edge in, jam in, force in 303vb. *insert;* ingrain 303vb. *infuse;* splice, dovetail, mortise 45vb. *join;* smuggle in, slide in, worm in, insinuate 297vb. *infiltrate.*

put between, sandwich; cushion 227vb. *line;* interpose, interject; interpolate, intercalate, interline; interleave, interlard, intersperse; interweave, interdigitate 222vb. *enlace;* bracket, put between brackets, parenthesize.

interfere, come between, get b., intercept 702vb. *hinder;* intervene, intercede 720vb. *mediate;* interrupt, obtrude, thrust in, thrust one's nose in, butt in 297vb. *intrude;* invade, trespass 306vb. *encroach;* put one's oar in, put one's clap in; have a finger in the pie 678vb. *meddle.*

Adv. *between,* betwixt, 'twixt, betwixt and between; among, amongst, amid, amidst, mid, midst; in the middle of; in the thick of; sandwich-wise, parenthetically; in the meanwhile, in the meantime 108adv. *while.*

See: 40, 45, 46, 47, 57, 59, 70, 72, 78, 108, 189, 222, 227, 235, 236, 297, 299, 300, 303, 306, 421, 625, 662, 678, 702, 707, 713, 720, 755, 794, 894.

232 Circumscription

N. *circumscription,* enclosing 235n. *enclosure;* drawing round, circle, balloon; ringing round, hedging r., fencing r.; surrounding, framing, girdling, encincture; circumvallation, investment, siege, blockade 712n. *attack;* envelopment, encirclement, containment, confinement, limitation 747n. *restriction;* ring 235n. *fence.*

Adj. *circumscribed* etc. vb.; encircled, encompassed, enveloped; surrounded, begirt; lapped, embosomed, embayed, landlocked; in a ring fence; framed 233adj. *outlined;* boxed, boxed up, encysted; walled in, mewed up, cloistered, immured 747adj. *imprisoned;* invested, beleaguered, besieged; held in, contained, confined 747adj. *restrained;*

limited, restricted, finite.

Vb. *circumscribe,* describe a circle, ring round, encircle, encompass; envelop, close in, cut off, circumvallate, invest, beleaguer, blockade 712vb. *besiege;* hem in, corral; enclose, rail in, hedge in, fence in; box, cage, wall in, immure, cloister 747vb. *imprison;* frame 230vb. *surround;* encase, enfold, enshrine, embosom, embay; edge, border 236vb. *limit;* clasp, clip, embrace 889vb. *caress.*

See: 230, 233, 235, 236, 712, 747, 889.

233 Outline

N. *outline,* circumference, perimeter, periphery; surround, frame, rim 234n. *edge;* ambit, compass, circuit 250n. *circle;* delineation, lines, lineaments, features 445n. *feature;* profile, relief 239n. *laterality;* silhouette 553n. *picture;* sketch, rough s. 623n. *plan;* skeleton, framework 331n. *structure;* tournure, contour, contour line, shape 243n. *form;* isogonic line, coast-l., land l., bounds 236n. *limit;* zone, zodiac, belt, baldric, Sam Browne, girth, girdle, band, cingle, tire, fillet, circlet 250n. *loop;* line drawn round, balloon, circle 232n. *circumscription;* ring, cordon 235n. *barrier;* figure, diagram; trace, tracing.

Adj. *outlined,* framed etc. vb.; in outline, etched; peripheral, perimetric, circumferential.

Vb. *outline,* describe a circle, construct a figure 232vb. *circumscribe;* frame 230vb. *surround;* delineate, draw, silhouette, profile, trace 551vb. *represent;* etch 555vb. *engrave;* map, block out, sketch o., sketch; diagrammatize, not fill in.

See: 230, 232, 234, 235, 236, 239, 243, 250, 331, 445, 551, 553, 555, 623.

234 Edge

N. *edge,* verge, brim; outer edge, fly (of a flag); tip, brink, skirt, fringe, margin, margent 69n. *extremity;* inner edge, hoist (of a flag); confines, bounds, boundary, frontier, border 236n. *limit;* littoral, coast, land-line, beach, strand, seaside, seashore, waterline, water's edge, front, waterf. 344n. *shore;* wharf, quay, dock 192n. *stable;* sideline, side, brim, curb, curbside, wayside, roadside, riverside, bank 239n. *laterality;* hedge, railing 235n. *fence;* felloe, felly, tire 250n. *wheel;* projecting edge, lip, ledge, eave, rim, welt, flange, gunwale 254n. *projection;* raised edge, coaming; horizon, ends of the earth, skyline 199n. *farness.*

threshold, limen; doorstep, door, portal, porch 263n. *doorway;* mouth, jaws, chops, chaps, fauces 194n. *maw.*

edging, frame 233n. *outline;* thrum, list, selvage; hem, hemline, border; skirting, purfling, piping; basque, fringe, frill, flounce, furbelow, valance 844n. *trimming;* exergue; crenation, milling 260n. *notch;* wavy edge, scallop 251n. *coil.*

Adj. *marginal,* liminal, border, skirting, marginated; riverine, coastal; riverside, roadside, wayside; labial, labiated; edged, trimmed, bordered.

Vb. *hem,* edge, border, trim, fringe, purfle; mill, crenelate 260vb. *notch;* bound, confine 236vb. *limit.*

See: 69, 192, 194, 199, 233, 235, 236, 239, 247, 251, 254, 260, 263, 344, 844.

235 Enclosure

N. *enclosure,* inclosure, envelope, case 194n. *receptacle;* wrapper 226n. *wrapping*; girdle, zone, ring, perimeter, circumference, periphery 233n. *outline;* surround, frame, picture-f.; clausure, enceinte, precinct; temenos 990n. *holy place;* reserve 883n. *seclusion;* lot, holding, claim 184n. *territory;* fold, pen, pinfold, infold, sheepfold, shippen, sty 369n. *cattle pen;* stock-yard, croft 370n. *farm;* garth, park 370n. *garden;* compound, yard, pound, paddock, field; parking lot, car-park 192n. *stable;* corral, kraal, stockade, zareba, circumvallation, lines 713n. *defenses;* net, fishnet, seine, trawl 222n. *network;* fishtrap 542n. *trap;* cell, box, cage 748n. *prison.*

fence, ring f., wire f., sunk f., ha-ha, hedge, quickset h., hedgerow, espalier; rails, balustrade, banisters, paling, railing, taffrail; pale, wall, Chinese w.; moat, dike, dyke, ditch, fosse, trench, vallum, curtain 713n. *defenses.*

barrier, wall, brick w.; barricade, cordon, pale; turnstile 702n. *obstacle;* palisade, stockade, zareba 713n. *fort*; portcullis, gate, door, bolt, bar 264n. *closure.*

Vb. *enclose,* inclose, fence in, cordon, cordon off, surround; pen, hem, ring 232vb. *circumscribe;* cloister, immure, cage 747vb. *imprison;* wrap, lap, enwrap, enfold, fold up 261vb. *fold;* fold in one's arms, hug, em-

brace 889vb. *caress;* frame, set, mount, box, embox.
See: 184, 192, 194, 222, 226, 232, 233, 261, 264, 369, 370, 542, 702, 713, 747, 748, 883, 889, 990.

236 Limit

N. *limit,* limitation 747n. *restriction,* 468n. *qualification;* definition, delimitation, demarcation 783n. *apportionment;* limiting factor, upper limit, ceiling, high-water mark 213n. *summit;* lower limit, threshold, low-water mark 214n. *base;* utmost, uttermost, extreme, furthest point, farthest reach, ne plus ultra, pole 69n. *extremity;* ends of the earth, Ultima Thule, Pillars of Hercules, Ocean 199n. *farness;* terminus, terminal, butt 69n. *end;* goal, target, winning-post, touch, touch-line, home, base 617n. *objective;* turning-point 137n. *crisis;* point of no return, Rubicon 599n. *resolution;* limit of endurance, tolerance, capacity, end of one's tether; physical limit, outside edge, perimeter, periphery, circumference 233n. *outline;* tide-mark, seamark 344n. *shore;* landmark, boundary stone, mere s.; milestone 27n. *degree;* curb, curbstone 624n. *road;* bourn, boundary, verge, mere, green belt; frontier, border, marches 234n. *edge;* national frontier, state boundary, three-mile limit; line, demarcation l., date-l., partition-l., isogonic l.; divide, parting 231n. *partition;* horizon, equator, terminator; crease; deadline, time-limit, term 110n. *period;* ultimatum 900n. *threat;* speed limit 278n. *slowness.*
Adj. *limited,* definite, conterminate, conterminable, limitable; finite; limitary, terminal; frontier, border, borderline, bordering, boundary.
Vb. *limit,* bound, border, edge 234vb. *hem;* top 213vb. *crown;* define, confine, condition 468vb. *qualify;* restrict, stint 747vb. *restrain;* encompass, beat the bounds 232vb. *circumscribe;* draw the line, delimit, demarcate, stake out; mere, mark out, chalk o. 547vb. *mark.*
Adv. *thus far,* so far, thus far and no further; between the tide-marks, on the borderline.
See: 27, 69, 110, 137, 199, 213, 214, 231, 232, 233, 234, 243, 278, 344, 468, 547, 599, 617, 624, 747, 783, 900.

237 Front

N. *front,* fore, front, forefront 64n. *precedence;* forepart, forepiece; prefix, frontispiece; forelock 259n. *hair;* forecourt, anteroom, entrance 263n. *doorway;* foreground, proscenium 200n. *nearness;* anteriority 119n. *priority;* anteposition, front rank, fore r., first line, front l.; forward line, center forward; avant garde, vanguard, van, advance guard; spearhead, forlorn hope 712n. *attacker;* outpost, scout; forerunner, pioneer 66n. *precursor.*
face, frontage, façade, facia; face of a coin, obverse, head; right side, outer s.; front view, front elevation; brow, forehead, glabella; chin, mentum; physiognomy, metoposcopy, features, visage, countenance, frontispiece, figurehead, phiz, map, mug, pan, kisser, dial, disk, disc 445n. *feature;* prominent feature, nose, snout, conk 254n. *protuberance.*
prow, prore, nose, beak, rostrum, figurehead; bow, bows; bowsprit; jib, foremast, forecastle, fo'c'sle, forestay, forepeak 275n. *ship.*
Adj. *fore,* forward, front, obverse; frontal, head-on, oncoming, facing 240adj. *opposite;* anterior, prepositional, prosthetic, prefixed 64adj. *preceding.*
Vb. *be in front,* stand in front etc. adv.; front, confront, face, face up to 240vb. *be opposite;* breast, stem, brave; bend forwards, lean f. 220vb. *be oblique;* come to the front, come to the fore, forge ahead, take the lead, head 64vb. *come before.*
Adv. *in front,* before, in advance, in the lead, in the van, vanward; ahead, right a., infra, further on 199adv. *beyond;* far ahead, coastward, landward; before one's face, before one's eyes; face to face, vis à vis; in the foreground, in the forefront; head first, head foremost; feet first, feet foremost.
See: 64, 66, 119, 199, 200, 220, 240, 254, 259, 263, 275, 445, 712.

238 Rear

N. *rear,* rearward, afterpart, back end, tail e., stern 69n. *extremity;* tailpiece, heel, colophon; coda 412n. *musical piece;* tail, brush, scut, pigtail, queue 67n. *sequel;* wake, train 67n. *retinue;* last place, rear rank, back seat 35n. *inferiority;* rearguard 67n. *aftercomer;* subsequence 120n. *posteriority;* background, hinterland, depths, far corner 199n. *distance;* behind, backstage, back side; reverse side, wrong s., verso 240n. *contraposition;* reverse, other side of the medal; backdoor, back entrance, postern 263n. *doorway;* back (of the body), dorsum, chine; backbone, spine, rachis 218n. *supporter;* back of the neck, scruff of the n., nape, scruff, short hairs; back of the head, occiput 213n. *head.*

buttocks, breech, backside, posterior, posteriors, cheek; bottom, seat, sit-me-down; bum, arse, ass; rear, stern, tail; fanny, hips; hindquarters, croup, crupper, haunches, haunch, ham, hunkers, hunkies; rump, loin; dorsal region, lumbar r., lower back, coccyx; fundament, anus.

poop, stern, stern-sheets, afterpart, quarter, counter, rudderpost, rudder, rear-mast, mizzenmast 275n. *ship.*

Adj. *back,* rear, postern; posterior, after, hind, hinder, hindermost, rearmost; mizzen; bent back, backswept 253adj. *convex;* reverse 240adj. *opposite;* placed last 35adj. *inferior;* spinal, rachial, vertebral, retral, dorsal, lumbar, glutal, popliteal; anal; caudal, caudate, caudiform.

Vb. *be behind,* stand b.; back on, back; back up 703vb. *aid;* follow, bring up the rear 65vb. *come after;* lag, trail, drop behind, fall astern 278vb. *move slowly;* tail, shadow, dog 619vb. *pursue;* follow at heel 284vb. *follow;* bend backwards, lean b. 220vb. *be oblique.*

Adv. *rearward,* behind, back of; in the rear, in the ruck; at the back, in the background; behind one's back; after, aftermost, sternmost; aft, abaft, astern, aback; to the rear, hindward, backward, retro; supra, above; on the heels of, at the tail of, at the back of, close behind; overpage, overleaf; back to back.

See: 35, 65, 67, 69, 120, 199, 213, 218, 220, 240, 253, 263, 275, 278, 284, 412, 619, 703.

239 Laterality

N. *laterality,* sidedness; side movement 317n. *oscillation;* sidestep 282n. *deviation;* sideline, side, bank 234n. *edge;* coast 344n. *shore;* siding, side-entrance, side-door; gable, gable-end; broadside; beam; quarter 236n. *poop;* flank, ribs, pleura; wing, fin, hand; cheek, jowl, chops, chaps, gill; temples, side-face, half-face; profile, side elevation; lee, lee-side, leeward; weatherside, windward 281n. *direction;* orientation, east, orient, Levant; west, occidental 281n. *compass point;* off side, on s., near s. 241n. *dextrality,* 242n. *sinistrality.*

Adj. *lateral,* laparo-; side 234adj. *marginal;* sidelong, glancing; parietal, buccal, sideface; costal, pleural, winglike, aliform; flanking, skirting; flanked, sided; many-sided, multilateral, bilateral, trilateral, quadrilateral; collateral 219adj. *parallel;* moving sideways, edging, sidling; eastern, eastward, easterly, orient, oriental, auroral, Levantine, Anatolian; west, western, westerly, westward, occidental, Hesperian 281adj. *directed.*

Vb. *flank,* side, edge, skirt, border 234vb. *hem;* coast, move sideways, passage, sidle; sideslip, sidestep 282vb. *deviate;* extend sideways, deploy, outflank 306vb. *overstep.*

Adv. *sideways,* laterally; askance, asquint; sidelong, broadside on; on one side, abreast, abeam, alongside; aside, beside; by the side of, side by side, cheek by jowl 200adv. *nigh;* to windward, to leeward, alee; coastwise; right and left; on her beam ends.

See: 200, 219, 234, 236, 241, 242, 281, 282, 306, 317, 344.

240 Contraposition

N. *contraposition,* antithesis, opposition, antipodes 14n. *contrariety;* opposite side, other s.; reverse, back 238n. *rear;* polarity, polarization; opposite poles, North and South; cross-current, headwind 704n. *opposition;* reversal, inverse 221n. *inversion.*

Adj. *opposite,* contrapositive, reverse, inverse 221adj. *inverted;* contrary, subcontrary 14adj. *contrary;* facing, fronting, confronting, oncoming 239adj. *fore;* diametrically opposite, antipodal, antipodean; polarized, polar; antarctic, arctic, northern, septentrional, boreal, southern, austral 281adj. *directed.*

Vb. *be opposite* etc. adj.; stand opposite, lie o.; subtend; face, confront 237vb. *be in front;* run counter 182vb. *counteract;* oppose, contrapose.

Adv. *against,* over the way, over against; as poles asunder; facing, face to face, vis à vis; back to back; on the other side, overleaf, overpage, next page; contrariwise, vice versa.

See: 14, 182, 221, 237, 238, 239, 281, 704.

241 Dextrality

N. *dextrality,* right hand, right-handedness; ambidexterity, ambidextrousness 694n. *skill;* right, dexter; offside, starboard; right-hand page, recto; right wing, right-winger.

Adj. *dextral,* right-hand, starboard, offside; right-handed, dexterous, ambidextral, ambidextrous 694adj. *skillful;* dextrorsal, dextrad; dexiotropic, dextrorotatory; right-wing.

Adv. *dextrally,* on the right; right-handedly, ambidextrously; to the right, dextrad, a-starboard.

See: 694.

242 Sinistrality

N. *sinistrality,* left hand, left-handedness; left, sinister, nearside, on s.; larboard, port; left wing, left-winger; levogyration.

Adj. *sinistral,* sinister, sinistrous, left, left-handed, sinistromanual, gauche, gauchipawed 695adj. *clumsy;* offside, nearside, sinistrad, sinistrorse, sinistrorsal; levogyrate; levogyrous.

Adv. *sinistrally,* on the left, a-port, off side; leftwards, sinistrad.

See: 695.

243 Form

N. *form,* substantial f., Platonic f., idea; essence 3n. *substance;* significant form, inner f., inscape; art form 551n. *art,* 593n. *verse form;* word form 557n. *linguistics;* shape, turn, lines, architecture; formation, conformation, configuration, fashion, style, design 331n. *structure;* contour, silhouette, relief, profile, frame, outline; figure, cut, set, trim, build, cut of one's jib, lineament 445n. *feature;* physiognomy 237n. *face;* look, expression, appearance 445n. *mien;* posture, attitude, stance; type, kind, pattern, stamp, cast, mold, blank 23n. *prototype;* format, type-face, typography 587n. *print;* morphology, morphography, isomorphism.

efformation, formation, forming, shaping, creation 164n. *production;* expression, formulation 62n. *arrangement;* designing, patterning; molding 554n. *sculpture;* turning, joinery; etymology, word-formation 557n. *linguistics.*

Adj. *formed* etc. vb.; receiving form, plastic, fictile; sculptured, carved, molded, turned, rounded, squared; shaped, fashioned, fully f., styled, stylized; ready-made, tailored in advance; matured, ready 669adj. *prepared;* solid, concrete 324adj. *dense;* dimensional, two-d., three-d.; isomorphous.

formative, plasmic, informing, normative; giving form, formal; plastic, glyptic, architectural 331adj. *structural.*

Vb. *efform,* inform, form; create, make 164vb. *produce;* shape, fashion, figure, pattern; turn, round, square; cut, tailor; cut out, silhouette 233vb. *outline;* sketch, draw 551vb. *represent;* model, carve, chisel 554vb. *sculpt;* hew, rough-h. 46vb. *cut;* mold, cast, rough-c.; stamp, coin, mint; hammer out, blank o., block o., knock o., punch o.; carpenter, mason; forge, smith, smithy; knead, work, work up into; construct, build, frame 310vb. *elevate;* express, formulate, put into shape, pull into s., lick into s., knock into s.

See: 3, 23, 46, 62, 164, 233, 237, 310, 324, 331, 445, 551, 554, 557, 587, 593, 669.

244 Amorphism: absence of form

N. *amorphism,* informity, unformedness, prime matter; confusion, chaos 61n. *disorder;* amorphousness, lack of shape, mussiness, shapelessness; lack of definition, vagueness, fuzziness; rawness, uncouthness 670n. *undevelopment;* rough diamond, unlicked cub; disfigurement, defacement, mutilation, deformation, deformity 246n. *distortion.*

Adj. *amorphous,* formless, unformed; liquid 335adj. *fluid;* shapeless, featureless, characterless; messy, chaotic 61adj. *orderless;* undefined, ill-defined, lacking definition, vague, fuzzy, blurred 419adj. *shadowy;* unfashioned, unshapen, unformed, unmade; embryonic 68adj. *beginning;* raw, unlicked 670adj. *immature;* unhewn, in the rough 55adj. *incomplete;* rude, inchoate, uncouth, barbarous, Gothic 699adj. *artless;* rugged 259adj. *rough;* unshapely 842 adj. *unsightly;* malformed, misshapen, gnarled 246adj. *deformed.*

Vb. *deform,* deprive of form, unmake, unshape 165vb. *destroy;* dissolve, melt 337vb. *liquefy;* knock out of shape, batter 46vb. *break;* grind, pulp 332vb. *pulverize;* warp, twist 246vb. *distort;* deface, disfigure 842vb. *make ugly;* mutilate, truncate

655vb. *impair;* jumble, disorder 63vb. *derange.*

See: 46, 55, 61, 63, 68, 165, 246, 259, 332, 335, 337, 419, 655, 670, 699, 842.

245 Symmetry: regularity of form

N. *symmetry,* bilateral s., trilateral s., multilateral s., correspondence, proportion 12n. *correlation;* balance 28n. *equilibrium;* regularity, evenness 16n. *uniformity;* arborescence, branching, ramification 219n. *parallelism;* shapeliness, regular features, classic f. 841n. *beauty;* harmony; eurythmy, eurythmic 24n. *agreement;* rhythm 141n. *periodicity;* finish 646n. *perfection.*

Adj. *symmetrical,* balanced 28adj. *equal;* proportioned, well-p. 12adj. *correlative;* rhythmical, harmonious, congruent 24adj. *agreeing;* congruent, coextensive; corresponding 219adj. *parallel;* analogous 18adj. *similar;* smooth, even 16adj. *uniform;* squared, rounded, round, evensided, isosceles, equilateral 81adj. *regular;* crystalline; arborescent, arboriform, dendriform, branching, ramose; formal, classic, comely 841adj. *shapely;* undeformed, well set-up 249adj. *straight;* undistorted, unwarped, unbiased 493adj. *true;* finished, complete in all its parts 54adj. *complete.*

See: 12, 16, 18, 24, 28, 54, 81, 141, 219, 249, 493, 646, 841.

246 Distortion: irregularity of form

N. *distortion,* asymmetry, disproportion, misproportion, want of symmetry 10n. *irrelation;* imbalance, disequilibrium 29n. *inequality;* lopsidedness, crookedness 220n. *obliquity;* anamorphosis, projection, Mercator's p. 551n. *map;* detortion, contortion; thrust, stress, strain, shear, bending moment, twisting m.; bias, warp; buckle, bend, screw, twist 251n. *convolution;* facial distortion, grimace, mop, mow, moue, snarl, rictus 547n. *gesture;* misconstruction 521n. *misinterpretation;* perversion 552n. *misrepresentation;* misdirection 542n. *deception.*

deformity, malformation, malconformation, monstrosity, abortion 84n. *abnormality;* curvature of the spine, kyphosis 248n. *curvature;* teratogeny; clubfoot, talipes, valgus 845n. *blemish;* ugliness, hideosity 842n. *eyesore;* teratology.

Adj. *distorted* etc. vb.; irregular, asymmetric, unsymmetrical, disproportionate 17adj. *non-uniform;* weighted, biased; not true, not straight; anamorphous, grotesque; out of shape, warped 244adj. *amorphous;* buckled, twisted, gnarled 251adj. *convoluted;* wry, awry, askew, crazy, crooked, cock-eyed; on one side 220adj. *oblique;* contortive, grimacing, scowling, snarling.

deformed, ugly 842adj. *unsightly;* misproportioned, ill-proportioned, scalene; defective 647adj. *imperfect;* ill-made, misshapen, misbegotten; rickety, rachitic; crump, hunchbacked, humpbacked, bunchbacked; kyphotic, crook-backed, crooked as a ram's horn; wry-necked; bandy, bandy-legged, bow-legged, bow-kneed; knock-kneed, cow-hocked; pigeon-toed; splay-footed; club-footed, taliped; web-footed; round-shouldered, pigeon-chested; snub-nosed, simous, hare-lipped 845adj. *blemished;* curtailed of one's fair proportions; stumpy 204adj. *short;* haggard, gaunt 206adj. *lean;* bloated 195adj. *fleshy.*

Vb. *distort,* disproportion, weight, bias; contort, screw, twist, knot 251vb. *twine;* bend, warp 251vb. *crinkle;* buckle, crumple; strain, sprain, wrest, torture, rack 63vb. *dislocate;* misshape, botch 244vb. *deform;* batter, knock out of shape; pervert 552vb. *misrepresent;* misconstrue 521vb. *misinterpret;* writhe 251vb. *wriggle;* grimace, make faces, mop and mow 547vb. *gesticulate;* snarl, scowl, frown 893vb. *be sullen.*

See: 10, 17, 29, 63, 84, 195, 204, 206, 220, 244, 248, 251, 521, 542, 547, 551, 552, 647, 842, 845, 893.

247 Angularity

N. *angularity,* angulation, aduncity, hookedness, crotchet, bracket, hook; bend, scythe, sickle, scimitar 248n. *curvature;* chevron, zigzag 220n. *obliquity;* V-shape, elbow, knee, knee-joint; shoulder, withers 253n. *camber;* knuckle, ankle, groin 45n. *joint;* crutch, crotch, fluke 222n. *cross;* fork, bifurcation, crossways, branching 222n. *crossing;* corner, nook, niche, recess, oriel 194n. *compartment;* wedge, arrow-head, broad arrow, cusp 254n. *prominence;* flexure 261n. *fold;* indentation 260n. *notch.*

angle, right a., acute a., obtuse a., salient a., reentrant a., spherical a., trigonometric a., solid a., dihedral a. *angular measure,* goniometry, trigonometry, altimetry; angular elevation, angular distance, angular velocity; second, degree, minute; radian; goniometer, altimeter; clinometer, graphometer; level, theodolite; transit circle; sextant, quadrant; protractor.

angular figure, triangle, isosceles t., equilateral t., scalene t., spherical t., trigon; parallelogram, rectangle, square, quadrangle, quadrature; quadrilateral, lozenge, diamond; rhomb, rhombus, rhomboid; tetragon, polygon, pentagon, hexagon, heptagon, octagon, decagon, decahedron, polyhedron; cube, pyramid, wedge; prism, parallelepiped; Platonic bodies.

Adj. *angular,* aduncous, aduncate, hooked, uncinated, hook-nosed, aquiline, rostrate; falciform, falcated 248adj. *curved;* angled, sharp-a., cornered; crooked, zigzag 220adj. *oblique;* jagged, serrated, crinkled 260adj. *notched;* jointed, geniculated, elbowed; akimbo; knock-kneed; crotched, forked, bifurcate, furcated, furcular, V-shaped.

angulated, triangular, trigonal, trilateral; wedge-shaped, cuneate, cuniform, fusiform; rectangular, right-angled, orthogonal; square, square-shaped, four-square, quadrangular, quadrilateral, four-sided, squared; diamond-shaped, lozenge-s.; multilateral, polygonal, decahedral, polyhedral; cubical, rhomboidal, pyramidal.

Vb. *angulate,* angle, make corners, corner; hook, crook, bend 248vb. *make curved;* wrinkle, fold 251vb. *crinkle;* zigzag 220vb. *be oblique;* fork, bifurcate, divaricate, branch, ramify 294vb. *diverge;* go off at a tangent 282vb. *deviate.*

See: 45, 194, 220, 222, 248, 251, 253, 254, 260, 261, 282, 294.

Thesaurus Dell

248 Curvature

N. *curvature,* curvity, curvation; incurvity, incurvation, inward curve 255n. *concavity;* outward curve 253n. *convexity;* flexure, flexion conflexure, inflection 261n. *fold;* arcuation, sweep, bending; bowing, stooping 311n. *obeisance;* bending down, deflection; turning away, detour 282n. *deviation;* downward bend, devexity 309n. *descent;* recurvature, recurvity, retroflexion 221n. *inversion;* curling, curliness, sinuosity 251n. *convolution;* aduncity 247n. *angularity;* curvature of the spine, kyphosis 246n. *deformity.*

curve, slight c. 253n. *camber;* turn, bend, sharp b., hairpin b., U-turn; bay, bight 345n. *gulf;* figure eight 250n. *loop;* tracery, curl, festoon 251n. *convolution;* bow, Cupid's b., rainbow 250n. *arc;* arch, spring of an a., arcade, vault 253n. *dome;* crescent, lunule, half-moon, horseshoe, meniscus, lens; catenary, parabola, hyperbola, conic section; caustic line, caustic, diacaustic, catacaustic, cardioid, conchoid; arch (of the foot), instep; crane-neck, swan-n.

Adj. *curved,* cambered etc. vb.; flexed, bent, reentrant 220adj. *oblique;* bowed, stooping 311adj. *depressed;* curviform, bowlike, curvilineal, curvilinear; rounded, curvaceous, bosomy, wavy, billowy 251adj. *undulatory;* aquiline, hook-nosed, parrot-beaked 247adj. *angular;* rostrate, beaked, beaklike, bill-shaped; bent back, recurved, recurvous, recurvative; retroussé, turned-up, tip-tilted 221adj. *inverted;* circumflex; arched, archiform, vaulted 253adj. *arcuate;* bow-legged 246adj. *deformed;* down-curving, devex 309adj. *descending;* hooked, falciform, falcated; semicircular 250adj. *circular;* crescentic, luniform, lunular, lunate, semilunar, horned; meniscal, lentiform, lenticular, reniform; cordiform, cordated, cardioidal, heart-shaped, bell-s., pear-s., fig-s.; conchoidal.

Vb. *be curved,*—bent etc. adj.; curve, bend, loop, camber, arch, sweep, sag, swag, give, give in the middle 217vb. *hang;* reenter, recurve, recurvate; curvet 312vb. *leap.*

make curved, bend, crook 247vb. *angulate;* turn, round 250vb. *make round;* bend in, incurvate, inflect; bend, back, recurve, retroflect 221vb. *invert;* bend over, bend down, bow, incline 311vb. *stoop;* turn over 261vb. *fold;* turn away 282vb. *deflect;* arcuate, arch, arch over, concamerate; coil 251vb. *twine;* loop, curl, wave, frizzle 251vb. *crinkle;* loop the loop, make figure eights.

See: 217, 220, 221, 225, 246, 247, 250, 251, 253, 255, 261, 282, 309, 311, 312, 345.

249 Straightness

N. *straightness,* directness, rectilinearity; perpendicularity 215n. *verticality;* inflexibility, rigidity 326n. *hard-*

ness; chord, straight line, right l., direct l., bee-l., air l.; Roman road; straight stretch, straight, reach; short cut 200n. *short distance;* rectitude 929n. *probity.*

Adj. *straight,* direct, even, right, true; in a line, linear; straight-lined, rectilinear, rectilineal; perpendicular 215adj. *vertical;* unbent, unwarped, unturned, undistorted; stiff, inflexible 326adj. *rigid;* uncurled, out of curl; straightened, unfrizzed, dekinked; dead straight, undeviating, unswerving, undeflected, on the beam, straight as an arrow, like a homing pigeon.

Vb. *be straight,*—direct etc. adj.; go straight, ride the beam; steer straight, follow the great circle; have no turning, not incline, not bend, not turn, not deviate, not deviate to either side, turn neither right nor left.

straighten, make straight, set s., set right, put straight 654vb. *rectify;* iron out 216vb. *flatten;* unbend (a bow); dekink, uncurl 258vb. *smooth;* stretch tight; unwrap 62vb. *unravel;* uncoil, unroll, unfurl, unfold 316vb. *evolve.*

Adv. *straight on,* directly, as the crow flies; straight, plumb.

See: 62, 200, 215, 216, 258, 316, 326, 654, 929.

250 Circularity: simple circularity

N. *circularity,* orbicularity, roundness, rondure 252n. *rotundity;* annulation, annularity.

circle, full c., circumference 233n. *outline;* great circle, equator; orb, annulus; rundle, roundel, roundlet; areola; plate, saucer; round, disc, disk, discus; coin, sequin, confetti; hoop, ring, quoit; runner, washer, terret, vervel; eye, iris; eyelet, loophole, keyhole 263n. *orifice;* circular course, circuit, roundabout; fairy ring; zodiac; ring formation, annulation, smoke-ring.

loop, figure eight 251n. *convolution;* ringlet, curl 259n. *hair;* bracelet, armlet, armilla, torque, clasp 844n. *finery;* crown, coronet 743n. *regalia;* corona, aureole, halo; wreath, garland, fillet, chaplet, snood, fascia 228n. *headgear;* collar, necklace, neckband 228n. *neckwear;* band, cordon, sash, girdle, zone, cestos, cincture, waistband, cummerbund 228n. *belt;* baldric, bandolier 47n. *girdle;* lasso, lariat 47n. *halter;* knot, tie.

wheel, truckle, pulley, caster; truck; hub, nave-plate; felloe, felly, tire; rubber tire, tubeless t., inner tube, outer t.; roller 252n. *rotundity.*

arc, semicircle, half-circle, hemicycle, half-moon, crescent, rainbow 248n. *curve;* sector, quadrant, sextant; ellipse, oval, ovule; ellipsoid, cycloid, epicycloid.

orbit, cycle, epicycle, circuit, ecliptic; circulation 314n. *circuition.*

Adj. *round,* rounded, circular, cyclic, discoid; orbicular, ringlike, ringed, annular, annulate, annulose, semicircular, hemicyclic; oval, ovate; elliptic, ovoid, egg-shaped, crescent-s., pear-s. 248adj. *curved;* cycloidal, spherical 252adj. *rotund.*

Vb. *make round* etc. adj.; round, turn.

go round, girdle, encircle 230vb. *surround;* describe a circle 233vb. *outline;* move round, circulate, orbit, go into o. 314adj. *circle.*

See: 47, 228, 233, 248, 251, 252, 259, 263, 314, 743, 844.

251 Convolution: complex circularity

N. *convolution,* involution, circumvolution, intricacy; flexuosity, anfractuosity, sinuosity, sinuousness; tortility, tortuosity, torsion, intorsion; inosculation; reticulation 222n. *network;* twine, crape, twist 208n. *fiber;* ripple 350n. *wave;* wrinkle, corrugation 261n. *fold;* indentation, ragged edge 260n. *notch;* waviness, undulation.

coil, roll, twist; turban, puggaree 228n. *headgear;* spiral, cochlea, helix; screw, screw-thread, worm, corkscrew; spring, wound s., coiled s.; armature; whorl, snailshell, ammonite; verticil, rundle; whirlpool 350n. *eddy,* 315n. *vortex;* tendril, creeper, convolvulus 366n. *plant;* scollop, scallop, scalloped edge 234n. *edging;* kink, curl; ringlet, lovelock 259n. *hair;* scroll, volute, fiddlehead, flourish, curlicue, squiggle 844n. *ornamentation;* Cupid's bow; hairpin.

meandering, meander, winding course, crankiness; winding, windings and turnings, twists and turns, ambages, circumbendibus 282n. *deviation;* labyrinth, maze 530n. *enigma;* switchback, crank, zigzag 220n. *obliquity.*

serpent, snake, eel, worm, wriggler 365n. *reptile.*

Adj. *convoluted,* twisted, contorted, intorted 246adj. *distorted;* tortile, tortive, torsile; cranky, ambagious; winding, twining, anfractuous, sin-

uous, tortuous, flexuous; indented, crumpled, ragged 260adj. *notched;* crumpled, buckled 261adj. *folded.*
labyrinthine, mazy, meandering, serpentine; twisting, turning 314adj. *circuitous.*
snaky, serpentine, serpentiform; eellike, anguilliform, wormlike, vermiform, vermicular; squirming, wriggling, peristaltic, sigmoidal.
undulatory, undulating, rolling, heaving; up-and-down, switchback; wavy, curly, frizzy, kinky, crinkly, woolly, crimped; scolloped, wrinkled, corrugated, indented, ragged 260adj. *notched;* flamboyant.
coiled, spiral, helical, turbinated, cochlear; wormed, turbinate, whorled, verticillate; wound, wound up; coiling, spiraling.
intricate, involved, complicated, raveled, perplexed 61adj. *complex.*
Vb. *twine,* twist, twirl, roll, coil, corkscrew, spire, spiral 315vb. *rotate;* wreathe, entwine 222vb. *enlace;* be convoluted,—twisted etc. adj.; turn and twist, bend 248vb. *be curved.*
crinkle, crimp, frizz, crape, crisp, curl; wave, undulate, ripple, popple; wrinkle, corrugate 261vb. *fold;* indent, scallop, scollop 260vb. *notch;* crumple 246vb. *distort.*
meander, snake, crank, crankle, twist and turn, zigzag, corkscrew. **See** *twine.*
wriggle, writhe, squirm, shimmy, shake; move sinuously, worm, serpentine.
Adv. in and out, round about, crankily.
See: 61, 208, 220, 222, 228, 234, 246, 248, 259, 260, 261, 282, 314, 315, 350, 365, 530, 844.

252 Rotundity

N. *rotundity,* rondure, roundness, orbicularity 250n. *circularity;* sphericity, sphericality, spheroidicity; globularity, globosity, cylindricity, gibbosity, gibbousness 253n. *convexity.*
sphere, globe, spheroid, oblate s., ellipsoid, globoid, geoid; hollow sphere, bladder; balloon, air-b. 276n. *airship;* soap-bubble 355n. *bubble;* ball, football, pelota, wood (bowls), billiard ball, marble, alley, taw; cannon-ball, bullet, shot, pellet; bead, pill, pea, boll, oakapple; spherule, globule, globulite; drop, droplet, dewdrop, ink-drop, blot; vesicle, bulb, onion, knob, pommel 254n. *protuberance;* thread-ball, clew; boulder, rolling stone; hemisphere, hump, mushroom 253n. *dome;* round head, bullet h., turnip h.
cylinder, roll, roly-poly; roller, rolling pin 258n. *smoother;* rod; round, rung; round tower, column; bole, trunk, stalk 218n. *supporter;* pipe, drain-pipe 263n. *tube;* funnel, chimney-pot 263n. *chimney;* round box, pillbox; drum 194n. *vessel.*
cone, conoid; shadow-cone, penumbra 419n. *half-light;* sugarloaf 253n. *dome;* cornet, horn, drinking-h. 194n. *cup;* top, spinning t., peg-t.; pear-shape, bell-s., egg-s.
Adj. *rotund,* orbicular 250adj. *round;* spherical, sphery, spherular; globular, globy, globulous, global; round-headed, bullet-headed; beady, beadlike, globulitic; hemispheric, spheroidal, ovoid, oviform, egg-shaped; cylindrical, columnar, tubular, lumbriciform; conic, conical; conoid, conoidal; bell-shaped, campaniform, campanulate, napiform, pyriform, pear-shaped, egg-s.; heart-shaped, cardiac; fungiform, moniliform; humped, gibbous; onion-shaped; bulbous 253adj. *convex;* pot-bellied 195adj. *fleshy;* sphered, balled.
Vb. *round,* make spherical; form into a sphere, form into a globe etc. n.; sphere, globe, ball; balloon; mushroom; clew, coil up, roll.
See: 194, 195, 218, 250, 253, 254, 258, 263, 276, 355, 419.

253 Convexity

N. *convexity,* convexness; lordosis, arcuation, arching; sphericity 252n. *rotundity;* gibbosity, bulginess, humpiness, bulge, bilge; projection, protrusion, protuberance 254n. *prominence;* excrescency, intumescence, tumescence, tumidity, turgidity 197n. *expansion;* paunchiness 195n. *bulk;* pimpliness, wartiness, wart-hog; double convexity, lenticular form; lens 442n. *optical device.*
swelling, growth, excrescence, knot, nodosity, node, nodule; exostosis, apophysis, condyle, knuckle; edema, emphysema, condylema, sarcoma; bubo, bump, gall, carbuncle, bunion, corn, blain, wart, wen; boil, furuncle, sty, pimple, papule, blister, vesicle; polypus, adenoids, hemorrhoids, piles; proud flesh, wheal; inkdrop, blot 252n. *sphere;* bleb, airbubble, soap-b. 355n. *bubble;* boss, torus, knob, bullion, nub, nubble;

bulb, button, bud; belly, pot-belly, corporation, paunch 195n. *bulk;* billow, swell 350n. *wave;* bulge, bunt.
bosom, bust, breast, breasts, bubs; mamma, mamilla, papilla, nipple, pap, dug, teat, udder; thorax, chest; cuirass, breastplate.
dome, cupola, vault 226n. *roof;* beehive 192n. *nest;* brow, forehead 237n. *face;* skull, cranium, bald head 213n. *head;* hemisphere, arch of heaven; mound, round barrow, long b., hummock, hillock, molehill, tussock, mamelon, sugarloaf 209n. *monticle;* mushroom, umbrella.
camber, gentle curve 248n. *curve;* arch, bow, rainbow; hump, humpback, hunchback; dorsum, back 238n. *rear;* shoulder, withers 218n. *supporter;* calf 267n. *leg;* elbow 247n. *angularity.*

Adj. *convex,* out-bowed, protruding 254adj. *salient;* hemispheric, domelike, 252adj. *rotund;* lentiform, lenticular; gibbous, humpy, lumpy; curvaceous, bosomy, billowy 248adj. *curved;* billowing, bulging, bellying, ballooning; swelling, swollen 197adj. *expanded;* bloated, pot-bellied 195adj. *fleshy;* turgid, tumid, tumescent, tumorous, tuberous; verrucose, warty, papulous, papulose, pimply; wart-shaped, verruciform; blistery, vesicular.
arcuate, cambered, arched, bowed 248adj. *curved;* rounded; hillocky, hummocky, moutonné, mammiform.

Vb. *be convex,* camber, arch, bow; swell, belly, bulge, balloon, mushroom; bag, bunt, pout; convex, emboss, chase, beat out 254vb. *jut.*

See: 192, 194, 195, 197, 209, 213, 218, 226, 237, 247, 248, 252, 254, 267, 350, 355, 442.

254 Prominence

N. *prominence,* eminence 209n. *high land,* 638n. *importance;* solar prominence, solar flare; tongue, tongue of flame.
projection, salient, salient angle 247n. *angle;* outstretched arm, forefinger, index f.; sprit, bowsprit; outrigger; tongue of land, spit, point, mull, promontory, foreland, headland 344n. *land;* peninsula, chersonese 349n. *island;* spur, foothill; jetty, mole, breakwater, groin, pier 662n. *shelter;* outwork 713n. *fortification;* pilaster, buttress 218n. *supporter;* shelf, sill, ledge, soffit, balcony; eaves 226n. *roof;* overhang, forerake, sternrake 220n. *obliquity;* flange, lip 234n. *edge;* tang, tongue; tenon 45n. *joint;* snag, stump, outcrop; cartographic projection 551n. *map.*
protuberance, bump 253n. *swelling;* prominent feature; nose, snout, conk; beak, rostrum; muzzle, proboscis, trunk; antenna 378n. *feeler;* chin, mentum, jaw, brow, beetlebrow 237n. *face;* figurehead 237n. *prow;* horn, antler 256n. *sharp point.*
relievo, relief, basso-relievo, alto-r., mezzo-r., low relief, bas r., high r.; embossment 844vb. *ornamental art;* cameo 554n. *sculpture.*

Adj. *salient,* bold, jutting, prominent, protuberant; emissile, protruding, popping, popping out; overhung, beetle-browed; underhung, undershot; repoussé, embossed, in relief, in high r., in low r.

Vb. *jut,* project, protrude, pout, pop, pop out, start o.; stand out, stick o., poke o., hang o. 443vb. *be visible;* bristle up, cock up 259vb. *roughen;* shoot up, start up, swell up 197vb. *expand;* overhang, hang over, beetle over, impend 217vb. *hang.*

See: 45, 197, 209, 217, 218, 220, 226, 234, 237, 247, 253, 256, 259, 344, 349, 378, 443, 544, 551, 554, 638, 662, 713, 844.

255 Concavity

N. *concavity,* concaveness, incurvation, incurvity 248n. *curvature;* hollowness 190n. *emptiness;* depression, dint, dent; impression, stamp, imprint, footprint 548n. *trace;* intaglio 555n. *engraving;* plowing, furrowing 262n. *furrow;* indentation 260n. *notch;* gap, lacuna 201n. *interval.*
cavity, hollow, niche, recess, corner 194n. *compartment;* hole, den, burrow, warren 192n. *dwelling;* pit, chasm, abyss 211n. *depth;* cave, cavern, antre; grot, grotto, alcove 194n. *arbor;* cul-de-sac, blind alley, impasse 702n. *obstacle;* hollow vessel, cup, saucer, bowl, basin, trough 194n. *vessel;* sewer 649n. *sink;* cell, follicle; sentellum, pore 263n. *orifice;* dimple, pockmark; honeycomb, sponge 263n. *porosity;* funnel, tunnel 263n. *tube;* groove, mortise, socket 262n. *furrow;* tooth-socket, alveolus; antrum, sinus; bay, bight, cove, creek, inlet 345n. *gulf;* channel, alveus, riverbed, wadi, ditch, nullah 351n. *conduit;* hole in the ground, dip, depression, pot-hole, punchbowl, crater; volcano 383n. *furnace.*

valley, vale, dell, dingle, comb, cwm, U-valley, river valley, strath; glen, glade, dip, depression, slade, dene; ravine, gorge, crevasse, barranca, canyon, gully 201n. *gap.*
excavation, dug-out, grave, grave-pit 364n. *tomb;* vertical excavation, shaft, mine, coal m., pit, coal p., colliery, quarry 632n. *store;* gallery, working g., adit, sap, trench, tunnel, burrow, warren 263n. *tunnel;* underground railway, subway; archaeological excavation, dig; cutting, cut.
excavator, miner, coal-m., quarrier; digger, dredger; sapper, burrower, tunneler; grave-digger, fossor.
Adj. *concave,* hollow, cavernous, speluncar; vaulted, arched 248adj. *curved;* hollowed out, scooped o., dug o.; caved in, stove in; depressed, sunk, sunken; spoonlike, saucer-shaped, cupped; capsular, funnel-shaped, infundibular, infundibuliform; bell-shaped, campaniform; cellular, socketed, alveolate, alveolar; full of holes, honeycombed; spongy, spongious, porous 263adj. *perforated.*
Vb. *be concave,* retreat, retire, cave in; cup, incurve.
make concave, depress, press in, punch in, stamp, impress; buckle, dent, dint, stave in; crush, push in, beat in; excavate, hollow, dig, spade, delve, scrape, scratch, scrabble, trench 262vb. *groove;* mine, sap, undermine, burrow, tunnel, bore; honeycomb, perforate 263vb. *pierce;* scoop out, dig o., gouge o., scratch o. 300vb. *eject;* hole, pit, pockmark; indent 260vb. *notch;* sink a shaft, make a hole.
See: 190, 192, 194, 201, 211, 248, 260, 262, 263, 300, 345, 351, 364, 383, 548, 555, 632, 649, 702.

256 Sharpness

N. *sharpness,* acuity, acuteness, acumination, pointedness, sting; serration, saw-edge 260n. *notch;* spinosity, thorniness, prickliness; acridity 388n. *pungency;* suddenness 116n. *instantaneity.*
sharp point, sting, prick, point, cusp 213n. *vertex;* nail, tack, staple 47n. *fastening;* nib, tag, pin, needle, bodkin, skewer, skiver, spit, broach, brochette; lancet, fleam, awl, bradawl, drill, borer, auger 263n. *perforator;* arrow, shaft, bolt, quarrel, arrow-head, barb, sword-point, rapier, lance, pike 723n. *spear;* fishing spear, gaff, harpoon; dagger, poniard, stiletto 723n. *weapon;* spike, caltrop, chevaux-de-frise, barbed wire, barbwire 713n. *defenses;* spur, rowel; gaffle, cockspur; goad, ox-g., ankus 612n. *incentive;* fork, prong, tine, pick, pickax, horn, antler, quill; claw, talon, nails 778n. *nippers;* spire, flèche, steeple; peak, crag, arête 213n. *summit.*
prickle, thorn, brier, bramble, thistle, nettle, cactus; bristle 259n. *hair;* beard, awn, spica, spiculum, spicula; porcupine, hedgehog; spine, needle.
tooth, tusk, tush, fang; brick-tooth, gag-t.; first teeth, milktooth; canine tooth, incisor, grinder, molar, premolar teeth; pearls, ivories; dentition, front teeth, back t., cheek t.; set of teeth, denture, false teeth, artificial t., gold t., plate, bridge; comb, saw, hand-s.; cog, ratchet, sprocket, denticulation 260n. *notch.*
sharp edge, cutting e., edged tool, edge-tool; razor's edge, knife-e., sword-e.; broken glass; cutlery, steel, razor; blade, razor-blade; share, plow-s., colter 370n. *farm tool;* spade, mattock, trowel 274n. *shovel;* scythe, sickle, hook, reaping-h., rip-h., bill-h., pruning-h.; cutter, grass-c., lawn-mower; scissors, barber's s., pinking s., aesculap; shears, clippers, secateurs, surgical knife, scalpel, bistoury, catling; chisel, plane, spokeshave, scraper, draw-knife 258n. *smoother;* knife, bread-k., carver, carving knife, fish k., slicer; penknife, sheath-k., clasp-k., jack-k., bowie-k., shive-k., gully, whittle; machete, dao, dah, kukri, kris, creese, parang, panger; chopper, cleaver, wedge; hatchet, ax, adz; battle-ax, sax; bill, tomahawk; sword, broadsword, falchion, hanger, cutlass, scimitar 723n. *side arms.*
sharpener, knife-s., pencil-s., oilstone, whetstone, grindstone, rubstone; hone, steel, file, strop; emery, emery-paper, sandpaper.
Adj. *sharp,* stinging, keen, acute; edged, cutting; swordlike, ensiform; pointed, unblunted, unbated; sharp-pointed, cusped, cuspidate, mucronate; barbed, spurred; sagittal, arrowy; spiked, spiky, spiny, spinous, thorny, brambly, briery, thistly; needlelike, aciform, acicular, aciculated; aculeiform, prickly, bristly, bristling, bearded 259adj. *hairy;* awned, awning; hastate, spear-like; studded, muricated, snaggy, craggy, jagged 259adj. *rough;* comblike, pectinated 260adj. *notched;* sharp-edged, knife-e., razor-e.; sharp as a

razor, keen as a r., sharp as a needle; sharpened, whetted etc. vb.; set, sharp-set, razor-sharp.

toothed, odontoid; toothy, brick-toothed; tusky, fanged, dental, denticulate; dentiform; cogged, serrated, saw-edged, emarginate 260adj. *notched.*

tapering, acuminate, conical, pyramidal 293adj. *convergent;* horned, cornute, corniculate; spindle-shaped, fusiform, lance-shaped, lanceolate, lanceolar.

Vb. *be sharp,*—stinging etc. adj.; have a point, prick, sting; have an edge, bite 46vb. *cut;* taper, come to a point, end in a point 293vb. *converge.*

sharpen, edge, put an edge on, whet, hone, oilstone, grind, file, strop, set; barb, spur, point, aculeate, acuminate, spiculate; stud.

See: 46, 47, 116, 213, 258, 259, 260, 263, 274, 293, 370, 388, 612, 713, 723, 778.

257 Bluntness

N. *bluntness,* flatness, bluffness; curves, hard c., flat c.; rustiness, dullness; toothlessness, lack of bite; blunt instrument, foil; blunt edge, blade, flat.

Adj. *unsharpened,* unwhetted; blunt, blunted, unpointed, bated (of a sword); rusty, dull, dull-edged; edgeless, pointless; lacking bite, toothless, edentulous, edentate; obtuse, dull-witted 499adj. *unintelligent;* numb, insensitive 375adj. *unfeeling;* blunt-nosed, stub, stubby, snub, square; round, rounded, curving 248adj. *curved;* flat, flattened, bluff; blunting, obtundent.

Vb. *blunt,* make blunt, turn, turn the edge, disedge; take off the point, bate (a foil); obtund, dull, rust; draw the teeth 161vb. *disable;* be blunt, not cut, pull, scrape, tear.

See: 161, 248, 375, 499.

258 Smoothness

N. *smoothness* etc. adj.; glabreity; smooth texture, silkiness; silk, satin, velvet, velure; fleeciness, down, swansdown 327n. *softness;* smooth hair, sleekness; smooth surface, mahogany, marble, glass, ice; flatness, levelness, lawn, plumb wicket, bowling green, billiard table 216n. *horizontality;* pavement, tarmac, asphalt, flags 226n. *paving;* levigation, polish, varnish, gloss, glaze, shine, finish; slipperiness, slip-way, slide; lubricity, oiliness, greasiness 334n. *lubrication;* smooth water, dead w., calm, dead c. 266n. *quiescence.*

smoother, roller, garden r., steam roller, road roller; bulldozer; rolling pin 216n. *flattener;* iron, flat-i., smoothing-i., tailor's goose; mangle, wringer; press, hot-p., trouser-p.; plane, spokeshave, draw-knife 256n. *sharp edge;* sandpaper, emery paper, emery-board; file, nail-f.; burnisher, turpentine and beeswax, powder; polish, varnish, enamel 226n. *facing;* lubricator, grease, oil, grease-gun, oil-can 334n. *lubricant.*

Adj. *smooth,* non-friction, non-adhesive, streamlined; slithery, slippery, skiddy; lubricous, lubric, oily, greasy, buttery, soapy; greased, oiled 334adj. *lubricated;* polished, shiny, varnished, waxed, enameled, lacquered, glazed; soft, suave, bland, soothing 177adj. *lenitive;* smooth-textured, silky, silken, satiny, velvety; downy, woolly, lanate 259adj. *fleecy;* marble, glassy; bald, glabrous; sleek, slick, well-brushed, unruffled; unwrinkled, uncrumpled; plane, rolled, even, unbroken, level, flat, plumb, flush 216adj. *horizontal;* calm, glassy, quiet, 266adj. *still;* rounded 248adj. *curved;* edgeless, blunt 257adj. *unsharpened;* smooth-skinned, barkless; smooth-haired, leiotrichous; smooth as marble, smooth as glass, smooth as ice, smooth as bark, smooth as velvet, smooth as oil, slippery as an eel.

Vb. *smooth,* remove friction, streamline; oil, grease, butter 334vb. *lubricate;* smoothen, plane, planish, even, level; file, rub down 333vb. *rub;* roll, calender, steamroll; press, hot-p., uncrease, iron, mangle 216vb. *flatten;* mow, shave, cut 204vb. *shorten;* smooth over, smooth down 177vb. *assuage;* iron out 62vb. *unravel;* starch, launder 648vb. *clean;* shine, burnish 417vb. *make bright;* levigate, buff, polish, glaze, wax, varnish 226vb. *coat;* pave, macadamize, tarmac 226vb. *overlay.*

go smoothly, glide, float, roll, bowl along, run on rails; slip, slide, skid 265vb. *be in motion;* skate, ski; feel no friction, coast, free-wheel.

See: 62, 177, 204, 216, 226, 248, 256, 257, 259, 265, 266, 327, 333, 334, 417, 648.

259 Roughness

N. *roughness,* asperity, harshness

735n. *severity;* rough treatment 176n. *violence;* salebrosity, broken ground; broken water, choppiness 350n. *wave;* rough air, turbulence 352n. *wind;* shattered surface, brokenness, broken glass; jaggedness, toothiness; serration, saw-edge, deckle-e. 260n. *notch;* ruggedness, cragginess; sierra 209n. *high land;* rough course, uneasy progress; unevenness, joltiness, bumpiness; corrugation, rugosity, ripple, ripple mark, corrugated iron 261n. *fold;* rut 262n. *furrow;* coarseness, coarse grain, knobbliness, nodosity 253n. *convexity;* rough surface, washboard, grater, file, sandpaper, emery paper; rough texture, sackcloth, corduroy; creeping flesh, gooseflesh, horripilation; rough skin, chap, crack; bristliness, hispidity, shagginess; hairiness, villosity; undergrowth, overgrowth 366n. *wood;* stubble, burr, bristle, scrubbing-brush, awn 256n. *prickle.*

hair, head of h., shock of h., matted h.; mop, mane, fleece, shag; bristle, stubble; locks, flowing l.; tresses, curls, ringlet, tight curl; kiss-curl; strand, plait; pigtail, pony-tail; topknot, forelock, elflock, lovelock, scalplock, tika; cowlick, quiff; pompadour, roll; fringe, bang, fuzz, earphones, bun, chignon; false hair, switch, wig, toupee 228n. *headgear;* thin hair, wisp; beard, beaver, goatee, imperial, Vandyke; whiskers, mutton-chops; moustache, mustachio, toothbrush, handlebars; eyebrows, eyelashes, cilia 208n. *filament;* woolliness, fleeciness, downiness, fluffiness; down, pubescence, papus, wool, fur, budge 226n. *skin;* tuft, flock; goat's hair, mohair, cashmere, llama's hair, alpaca, vicuna 208n. *fiber;* pile, nap; shag; velvet, velour, plush 327n. *softness;* floss, fluff, fuzz, thistledown 323n. *levity;* horsehair 227n. *lining.*

plumage, pinion 271n. *wing;* plumosity, feathering; feathers, coverts, wing c.; neck feathers, hackle f., hackle; plume, panache, crest; peacock's feathers, ostrich f., osprey f. 844n. *finery;* quill.

Adj. *rough,* unsmooth, uneven, broken; asperous, salebrous; rippling, choppy, storm-tossed; rutty, rutted, pitted, potholed, poached; bumpy, jolting, bone-breaking; chunky, crisp, rough-cast; lumpy, stony, nodular, nubbly, knobby, studded, muricate; knotted, gnarled, cross-grained, coarse-g., coarse; lined, wrinkled, corrugated, ridged 262adj. *furrowed;* rough-edged, deckle-e. 260adj. *notched;* craggy, cragged, jagged; crankling, crinkled 251adj. *convoluted;* horripilant, creeping; scabrous, scabby; blistered, blebby; ruffled, unkempt, unpolished; unbolted, unsifted; rough-hewn, sketchy 55adj. *incomplete.*

hairy, pilose, villous, crinose, crinite; woolly, fleecy, furry; hirsute, shaggy, shagged, tufty, matted, shock-headed; hispid, bristly, bristling 256adj. *sharp;* setous, setose, setaceous; wispy, filamentous, fimbriated, ciliated, fringed, befringed; bewhiskered, bearded, moustached; unshaven, unshorn; unplucked; curly, frizzy, fuzzy, tight-curled, woolly.

downy, nappy, shaggy; pubescent, tomentose, pappose; velvety, peachy; fluffy, feathery, plumose, plumigerous, fledged.

fleecy, woolly, fluffy; lanate, lanated, lanuginous.

Vb. *be rough,*—hairy etc. adj.; bristle, bristle up 254vb. *jut;* creep (of flesh), horripilate; go against the grain; scratch, catch; jolt, bump, jerk 278vb. *move slowly.*

roughen, rough-cast, rough-hew; knurl, mill, crenate, serrate, indent, engrail 260vb. *notch;* stud, boss; crinkle, crisp, corrugate, wrinkle, ripple, popple 262vb. *groove;* disorder, ruffle, tousle, shag 63vb. *derange;* rumple, crumple 261vb. *fold;* rub up the wrong way, set on edge.

Adv. *on edge,* against the grain; in the rough.

See: 55, 63, 176, 208, 209, 226, 227, 228, 251, 253, 254, 256, 260, 261, 262, 271, 278, 323, 327, 350, 352, 366, 735, 844.

260 Notch

N. *notch,* serration, serrulation, saw-edge, ragged e. 256n. *sharpness;* indentation, deckle-edge; machicolation, crenellation 713n. *fortification;* nick, cut, gash, kerf; crenation, crenature 201n. *gap;* indent, dent, dimple 255n. *concavity;* scollop, scallop, Vandyke (lace), dog-tooth 844n. *pattern;* cog, ratchet, cog-wheel, rachet-w.; saw, hacksaw, circular saw 256n. *tooth;* battlement, embrasure, crenelle.

Adj. *notched,* notchy, jagged, jaggy 256adj. *sharp;* crenate, crenated, crenellated; toothed, dentate, dentated, denticulated; serrated, palmate, emarginated; finely serrated, serrulate; serratodentate.

Vb. *notch,* serrate, tooth, cog; nick, score, scratch, scotch, scarify, bite, slice 46vb. *cut;* crenellate, crenulate, machicolate; indent, scallop, Vandyke; jag, pink, slash; dent, mill, knurl; pinch, snip, crimp 198vb. *make smaller.*
See: 46, 198, 201, 255, 256, 713, 844.

261 Fold

N. *fold,* plicature, plication, flexure, flexion, duplicature, doubling; reverse, hem; lapel, cuff, turn-up, dog's ear; plait, ply, pleat, box-p., accordion p.; tuck, gather, pucker, ruche, ruffle; flounce, frounce; crease, crushed fold; wrinkle, rivel, frown, wrinkles, crow's feet 131n. *age;* crinkle, crankle; crumple, rumple; joint, elbow 247n. *angularity.*
Adj. *folded,* doubled; gathered; creasy, wrinkly, puckery; dog-eared; creased, crumpled, crushed 63adj. *deranged;* turn-down, turn-over.
Vb. *fold,* plicate, double, turn over, roll; crease, pleat; corrugate, furrow, wrinkle 262vb. *groove;* rumple, rimple, crumple 63vb. *derange;* curl, frizzle, frizz 251vb. *crinkle;* ruffle, pucker, cockle up, gather, frounce, ruck, shirr, smock, twill; tuck, tuck up, kilt; hem, cuff; turn up, turn down, turn under, double down; enfold, enwrap, wrap, swathe 235vb. *enclose;* fold up, roll up, furl, reef.
See: 63, 131, 247, 251, 255, 262.

262 Furrow

N. *furrow,* groove, chase, slot, slit, crack, chink, cranny 201n. *gap;* trough, hollow 255n. *cavity;* engraving, sulcus; glyph, triglyph; fluting, goffering, rifling; chamfer, bezel, incision, gash, scratch, score 46vb. *scission;* streak, striate 437n. *striation;* wake, wheel-mark, rut 548n. *trace;* gutter, runnel, kennel, ditch, dike, dyke, trench, dug-out, moat, fosse, channel 351n. *conduit;* ravine 255n. *valley;* furrowed surface, corduroy, whipcord, corrugated iron, washboard, plowed field; ripple, catspaw 350n. *wave.*
Adj. *furrowed,* plowed etc. vb.; fluted, rifled, goffered; striated, sulcated, bisulcous, trisulcate; canalled, canaliculated; channeled, rutty; wrinkled, lined 261adj. *folded;* rippling, wavy 350adj. *flowing.*
Vb. *groove,* slot, flute, chamfer, rifle; chase; gash, scratch, score, incise 46vb. *cut;* claw, tear 655vb. *wound;* striate, streak 437vb. *variegate;* grave, carve, enchase, bite in, etch, cross-hatch 555vb. *engrave;* furrow, plow, channel, rut, wrinkle, line; corrugate, goffer 261vb. *fold.*
See: 46, 201, 255, 261, 350, 351, 437, 548, 555, 655.

263 Opening

N. *opening,* patefaction, throwing open, flinging wide; unstopping, uncorking 229n. *uncovering;* pandiculation, stretching 197n. *expansion;* yawn, yawning, oscitation; oscitancy; dehiscence, hiation, gaping; fatiscence, hiatus, lacuna, space, interval, gat 201n. *gap;* aperture, split, crack, leak 46n. *disjunction;* hole, hollow 255n. *cavity;* placket-hole 194n. *pocket.*
perforation, piercing, tattooing etc. vb.; impalement, puncture, acupuncture, venepuncture; pertusion, appertion, terebration, trephining; boring, bore-hole, bore, caliber; pinhole, eyelet.
porosity, porousness, sponge; sieve, sifter, cribble, riddle, screen 62n. *sorting;* strainer, tea-s., colander; holeyness, honeycomb.
orifice, blind o., aperture, slot; oral cavity, mouth, gob, trap, clap, jaws, muzzle; throat, gullet, weasand, esophagus 194n. *maw;* sucker; mouthpiece, mouthpipe, flue-pipe 353n. *airpipe;* nozzle, spout, vent, venthole, vomitory, blower, blow-hole, air-h., spiracle; nasal cavity, nostril; inlet, outlet; river-mouth, embouchure; small orifice, ostiole; foramen, pore; breathing pores, stomata; hole, crater, pot-hole 255n. *cavity;* touchhole, pin-h., button-h., arm-h., keyh., punch-h.; manhole, pigeon-hole 194n. *compartment;* eye, eye of a needle, eyelet, deadeye; grommet, ring 250n. *loop.*
window, fenestration; shop-window, glass front; casement, embrasure, loophole 713n. *fortification;* bay-window, sash-w., box-w.; lattice, grill; rose window, perpendicular w., decorated w., lancet w. 990n. *church exterior;* oriel, dormer; light, lightwell, fan-light, skylight, transom, companion, window-frame; cabin window, port, porthole; peep-hole, key-hole; hagioscope, squint 990n. *church interior;* car window, windshield, rear window, side w.; window pane 422n. *transparency.*
doorway, archway; threshold 68n. *entrance;* approach, drive, drive-in, en-

try 297n. *way in;* exit, vomitory; passage, corridor, gangway, adit, gallery 624n. *access;* gate, city gates; portal, porch, propylaeum; door, house-d., church-d.; lychgate; back door, postern 238n. *rear;* small door, wicket; scuttle, hatch, hatchway; trapdoor, companion-way; door-jamb, gatepost, lintel; doorstep; door-keeper, ostiary, durwan 264n. *janitor.*

open space 183n. *space;* yard, court 185n. *place;* opening, clearing, glade; panorama, vista 438n. *view;* landscape, champaign 348n. *plain;* alley, aisle, corridor, thoroughfare 305n. *passage;* estuary 345n. *gulf.*

tunnel, boring; subway, underpass, underground, tube; mine, shaft, pit, gallery, adit 255n. *excavation;* bolthole, rabbit-h., fox-h., mouse-h.; funnel 252n. *cone;* sewer 351n. *drain.*

tube, pipe 351n. *conduit;* main, tap, faucet; efflux tube, adjutage; tubule, pipette, cannula; tubing, piping, pipe-line, hose; artery, vein, capillary; colon, gut 224n. *insides;* funnel, fistula.

chimney, factory c., smoke-stack, funnel; smoke-duct, flue; volcano, fumarole, smoke-hole 383n. *furnace.*

opener, key, master-k., skeleton-k., passe-partout; corkscrew, tin-opener, can-o., bottle-o.; aperient, purgative, pull-through; password, open sesame; passport, safe conduct; pass, ticket 756n. *permit.*

perforator, piercer, borer, corer; gimlet, wimble, corkscrew; auger, drill, pneumatic d., road d., dentist's d.; burr, bit, spike b., brace and b.; reamer, rimer; trepan, trephine; probe, lancet, fleam, stylet, trocar; bodkin, needle, hypodermic n.; awl, bradawl 256n. *sharp point;* pin, nail 47n. *fastening;* skewer, spit, broach, stiletto 723n. *weapon;* punch, puncheon, stapler; dibble; digging-stick; pickax, pick, ice-p.

Adj. *open,* patent, exposed to view 522adj. *manifest;* unclosed, unstopped, unshut, ajar; unobstructed, admitting 289adj. *accessible;* wide-open, agape, gaping; yawning, oscitant; open-mouthed, slack-jawed; opening, aperient; blooming, out.

perforated etc. vb.; perforate, drilled, bored; honeycombed, riddled; peppered, shot through; cribriform, foraminous; holey, full of holes; windowed, fenestrated, fenestrate.

porous, permeable, pervious, spongy, percolating, leachy, leaky, leaking.

tubular, tubulous, tubulated, cannular, piped; cylindrical 252adj. *rotund;* funnel-shaped, infundibular; fistulous; vascular, capillary.

Vb. *open,* unclose, unfold, ope; unlock, unlatch; open the door, fling wide the gates 299vb. *admit;* pull out (a drawer); uncover, bare 229vb. *doff;* unstop, uncork; unrip, unseam 46vb. *disjoin;* lay open, throw o. 522vb. *show;* force open, steam o. 176vb. *force;* cut open, rip o., tear o., crack o.; enlarge a hole, ream; dehisce, fly open, split, gape, yawn; burst, explode; crack at the seams, start, leak; space out, interval 201vb. *space;* open out, fan o., deploy 75vb. *be dispersed;* separate, part, hold a.; unclench, open one's hand; bloom, be out.

pierce, empiercc, transpierce, transfix; gore, run through, stick, pink, lance, bayonet, spear 655vb. *wound;* spike, skewer, spit; prick, puncture, tattoo; probe, stab, poke; inject; perforate, hole, riddle, pepper, honeycomb; nail, drive, hammer in 279vb. *strike;* knock holes in, punch, punch full of holes; hull (a ship), scuttle, stave in; tap, drain 304vb. *extract;* bore, drill, wimble; trephine, trepan; burrow, tunnel, mine 255vb. *make concave;* cut through, penetrate 297vb. *enter;* impale.

Adv. *openly* etc. adj.; patently, frankly, unguardedly; on the rooftops; out, out in the open.

See: 46, 47, 62, 68, 75, 176, 183, 185, 194, 197, 201, 224, 229, 238, 250, 252, 255, 256, 264, 279, 289, 297, 299, 304, 305, 345, 348, 351, 353, 383, 422, 438, 522, 624, 655, 713, 723, 990.

264 Closure

N. *closure,* closing, shutting etc. vb.; door in one's face; occlusion, stoppage; contraction, strangulation 198n. *compression;* sealing off, blockade 232n. *circumscription;* investment 235n. *enclosure;* embolism, obstruction, obturation; infarction, constipation, obstipation, strangury; dead-end, cul-de-sac, impasse, blank wall 702n. *obstacle;* blind gut, cecum; imperforation, imperviousness, impermeability.

stopper, stopple, cork, plug, fid, bung, peg, spill, spigot, spike (of a gun); ramrod, rammer, piston; valve, slide v.; wedge, embolus, wad, dossil, pledget, tampon, tampion, wadding, padding, stuffing, stopping 227n. *lining;* gobstopper, stickjaw 301n. *sweetmeat;* gag, muzzle, silencer

748n. *fetter;* obturator, shutter 421n. *screen;* tight bandage, tourniquet 198n. *compressor;* damper, choke, cutout; vent-peg, tap, faucet, stopcock, bibcock; top, lid, cap, cover 226n. *covering;* lock, key, bolt, bar, staple 47n. *fastening;* cordon 235n. *fence;* stopgap 150n. *substitute.*

janitor, doorkeeper, gatekeeper, porter, durwan, ostiary; commissionaire, concierge; sentry, sentinel, watchman 660n. *protector;* warden, guard 749n. *keeper;* jailer, turnkey, Cerberus, Argus 749n. *jailer.*

Adj. *closed,* unopened; shut etc. vb.; operculated, shuttered, bolted, barred; stoppered, obturated; unpierced, imporous, non-porous; imperforate, unholed; impervious, impermeable 324n. *dense;* impenetrable, impassable, unpassable 470adj. *impracticable;* invious, pathless, wayless, untrodden 883adj. *secluded;* cecal, dead end, blank; infarcted, stuffed up, bunged up; strangulated, strangurious 198adj. *contracted;* drawn, drawn together, joined 45adj. *conjoint.*

sealed off, sealed, hermetically s.; cloistered, claustral; close, unventilated, stuffy, muggy; staunch, tight, air-t., gas-t.; proof, water-p., gas-p., air-p., mouse-p. 660adj. *invulnerable.*

Vb. *close,* shut, occlude, seal; clinch, fix, bind, make tight 45vb. *tighten;* put the lid on 226vb. *cover;* batten down the hatches, make all tight; put the door to, clap to, slam, bang (a door); lock, fasten, snap, snap to; fill, stuff, wad, pack, jam 193vb. *load;* plug, fother; bung, cork, stopper, obturate, spike (a gun); button, do up 45vb. *join;* knit, draw the ends together; block, dam, staunch, choke, throttle, strangle, smother, asphyxiate 702vb. *obstruct;* blockade 712vb. *besiege;* enclose, surround, shut in, seal off 232vb. *circumscribe;* trap, bolt, bar, lock in 747vb. *imprison;* shut down, clamp d., batten d., ram d., tamp d., cram d.; put an end to 69vb. *terminate;* come to an end 69vb. *end,* 145vb. *cease.*

See: 45, 47, 69, 145, 150, 193, 198, 226, 227, 232, 235, 301, 324, 421, 470, 660, 702, 712, 747, 748, 749, 883.

265 Motion: successive change of place

N. *motion,* change of position 143n. *change;* movement, going, move, march; speed-rate, speed, air-s., ground-s.; pace, tempo; power of movement, motility, mobility, movableness; kinetic energy, motive power, motivity; proper motion, radial m., angular m.; forward motion, advance, progress, headway 285n. *progression;* backward motion, sternway 286n. *regression,* 290n. *recession;* motion towards 289n. *approach,* 293n. *convergence;* motion away, driftway, declension 294n. *divergence,* 282n. *deviation;* upward motion, rising 308n. *ascent;* downward motion, sinking 309n. *descent,* 313n. *plunge;* motion round, circumnavigation 314n. *circuition;* axial motion 315n. *rotation;* to and fro movement, fluctuation 317n. *oscillation;* irregular motion 318n. *agitation;* stir, bustle, unrest, restlessness 678n. *activity;* rapid motion 277n. *velocity;* slow motion 278n. *slowness;* regular motion 16n. *uniformity,* 71n. *continuity;* recurring movement, rhythm 141n. *periodicity;* motion in front 283n. *precession;* motion after 284n. *following,* 619n. *pursuit;* process 316n. *evolution;* conduction, conductivity 272n. *transference;* current, flow, flux, drift 350n. *stream;* course, career, run; locomotion, traffic, traffic movement, flow of traffic 305n. *passing along;* transit 305n. *passage;* transportation 272n. *transport;* running, walking, footslogging 267n. *pedestrianism;* riding 267n. *equitation;* travel 267n. *land travel,* 269n. *water travel,* 271n. *air travel;* dancing, gliding, sliding, skating, rolling; maneuver, maneuvering 688n. *tactics;* bodily movement, exercise 162n. *athletics;* gesticulation 547n. *gesture;* bowel movement 302n. *cacation;* cinematography, motion picture 445n. *cinema;* laws of motion, kinematics, kinetics, dynamics; kinesiatrics, kinesipathy, kinesitherapy 658n. *therapy.*

gait, walk, port, carriage 688n. *conduct;* tread, tramp, footfall, stamp; pace, step, stride; run, lope; jog-trot, dog-t.; dance-step, hop, skip, jump 312n. *leap;* waddle, shuffle; swagger, proud step, stalk, strut, goose-step 875n. *formality;* march, slow m., quick m., double; trot, piaffer, amble, canter, gallop, hand-g. 267n. *equitation.*

Adj. *moving* etc. vb.; in motion; motive, motory, motor; motile, movable, mobile; progressive, regressive; locomotive, automotive; transitional, shifting 305adj. *passing;* mercurial 152adj. *changeful;* unquiet, restless 678adj. *active;* nomadic 267adj.

traveling; drifting, erratic, runaway 282adj. *deviating;* kinematic, kinematical; kinetic, kinesodic; cinematographic.

Vb. *be in motion,* move, go, hie, gang, wend, trail; gather way 269vb. *navigate;* budge, stir; stir in the wind, flutter, wave, flap 217vb. *hang;* march, tramp 267vb. *walk;* place one's feet, tread; trip, dance 312vb. *leap;* shuffle, waddle 278vb. *move slowly;* toddle, patter; run 277vb. *move fast;* run on wheels, roll, taxi; stream, roll on, drift 350vb. *flow;* paddle 269vb. *row;* skitter, slide, slither, slithe, skate, ski, toboggan, glide 258vb. *go smoothly;* volitate, fly, frisk, flit, flitter, dart, hover; climb 308vb. *ascend;* sink, plunge 309vb. *descend;* cruise, steam, chug, keep going, proceed 146vb. *go on;* make one's way, pick one's w., fight one's w., elbow one's w. 285vb. *progress;* pass through, wade t., pass by 305vb. *pass;* shift, dodge, duck, shift about, jink, tack, maneuver 282vb. *deviate;* hover about, hang a. 136vb. *wait;* remove, move house, change one's address, shift one's quarters; change places 151vb. *interchange;* move over, make room 190vb. *go away;* travel, stray 267vb. *wander;* develop 316vb. *evolve;* motion, gesture 547vb. *gesticulate.*

move, impart motion, put in m.; render movable, set going, power; put on wheels, put skates under; actuate, flick, flip, switch 173vb. *operate;* stir, stir up, jerk, pluck, twitch 318 vb. *agitate;* budge, shift, manhandle, trundle, roll, wheel 188vb. *displace;* push, shove 279vb. *impel;* move on, drive, hustle 680vb. *hasten;* tug, pull 288vb. *draw;* fling, throw 287vb. *propel;* convey, transport 272vb. *transfer;* dispatch 272vb. *send;* mobilize, set on foot 74vb. *bring together;* scatter 75vb. *disperse;* raise, uplift 310vb. *elevate;* throw down, let fall, drop 311vb. *depress;* make a move, maneuver; transpose 151vb. *interchange.*

Adv. *on the move,* under way, on one's w., on the go, on the hop, on the run, on the fly; on the march, on the tramp, on the wing.

See: 16, 71, 74, 75, 136, 141, 143, 146, 151, 152, 162, 173, 188, 190, 217, 227, 258, 267, 269, 271, 272, 277, 278, 279, 282, 283, 284, 285, 286, 287, 288, 289, 290, 293, 294, 302, 305, 308, 309, 310, 311, 312, 313, 314, 315, 316, 317, 318, 350, 445, 547, 619, 658, 678, 680, 688, 875.

266 Quiescence

N. *quiescence,* dying down, running down, subsidence 145n. *cessation;* rest, stillness; deathliness, deadness; stagnation, stagnancy 679n. *inactivity;* pause, truce, standstill 145n. *lull;* stand, stoppage, halt; fix, deadlock, lock; full stop, dead s., dead stand 145n. *stop;* embargo 757n. *prohibition;* immobility, fixity, rigidity, stiffness 326n. *hardness;* steadiness, equilibrium 153n. *stability;* numbness, trance, catalepsy 375n. *insensibility.*

quietude, quiet, quietness, stillness, hush 399n. *silence;* tranquillity, peacefulness, indisturbance 717n. *peace;* rest 683n. *repose;* eternal rest 361n. *death;* sleepiness, slumber 679n. *sleep;* calm, dead c., flat c. 258n. *smoothness;* windlessness, not a breath of air; dead quiet, not a mouse stirring; home-keeping, domesticity; passivity, quietism; quietist 717n. *pacifist;* tranquilizer 177n. *moderator.*

resting place, bivouac 192n. *quarters;* house of rest, roof 192n. *home;* shelter, haven 662n. *refuge;* place of rest, pillow 218n. *bed;* journey's end 295n. *goal;* last rest, grave 364n. *tomb.*

Adj. *quiescent,* quiet, still; asleep 679adj. *sleepy;* resting, at rest, becalmed; at anchor, anchored, moored, docked; at a stand, at a standstill, stopped, idle 679adj. *inactive;* unemployed, out of commission 674adj. *unused;* dormant, unaroused, dying 361adj. *dead;* stagnant, vegetating, unprogressive, static, stationary 175adj. *inert;* sitting, sedentary, chair-borne; on one's back 216adj. *supine;* settled, stay-at-home, home-keeping, home-loving, domesticated 828adj. *content;* untraveled, unadventurous 858adj. *cautious;* unmoved 860adj. *indifferent.*

tranquil, undisturbed, sequestered 883adj. *secluded;* peaceful, restful; unhurried, easy-going 681adj. *leisurely;* unstirring, uneventful, without incident 16adj. *uniform;* calm, windless, airless; unbroken, glassy 258adj. *smooth;* sunny, halcyon 730adj. *palmy;* at ease, easeful, comfortable, relaxed, unstrung, unemphatic 683adj. *reposeful;* unruffled, unwrinkled, unworried, serene 823adj. *inexcitable.*

still, unmoving, unstirring, unbudging; standing, unbubbly, unfrothy, flat 387adj. *tasteless;* immobile, moveless, motionless, gestureless; expressionless, deadpan, poker-faced

820adj. *impassive;* steady, unwinking, unblinking 153adj. *unchangeable;* standing still, rooted, rooted to the ground 153adj. *fixed;* immovable, unable to move, stuck; stiff, frozen 326adj. *rigid;* benumbed, numb, petrified, paralyzed 375adj. *insensible;* quiet, hushed, soundless 399adj. *silent;* stock-still, still as a statue, still as a post, still as death; quiet as a stone, quiet as a mouse.

Vb. *be quiescent* etc. adj.; quiesce, subside, die down 37vb. *decrease;* pipe down 399vb. *be silent;* stand still, lie s., keep quiet; stagnate, vegetate 175vb. *be inert;* stand, mark time 136vb. *wait;* stay put, sit tight, stand pat, remain in situ, not stir, not budge, remain, abide 144vb. *stay;* stand to, lie to, ride at anchor; tarry 145vb. *pause;* rest, sit down, take breath, rest on one's laurels, rest on one's oars, rest and be thankful 683vb. *repose;* retire, go to bed, doss down 679vb. *sleep;* settle, settle down 187vb. *place oneself;* keep within doors, stay at home, not go out 883vb. *be unsocial;* ground, stick fast; catch, jam; stand fast, stand like a post; not stir a step, not stir a peg; be at a stand 145vb. *cease.*

come to rest, stop, hold, stop short, stop in one's tracks, stop dead in one's tracks 145vb. *halt;* pull up, draw up; slow down 278vb. *decelerate;* anchor, cast a., come to an a., alight 295vb. *land;* relax, calm down, rest, pause 683vb. *repose.*

bring to rest, quiet, make q., quieten, quell, hush 399vb. *silence;* full, soothe, calm down 177vb. *assuage;* lull to sleep, cradle, rock; let alone, let well alone, let sleeping dogs lie 620vb. *avoid;* bring to a standstill, bring to, lay to, heave to; brake, put the brake on 278vb. *retard;* stay, immobilize 679vb. *make inactive;* put a stop to, lay an embargo on 757vb. *prohibit.*

Adv. *at a stand,* at a halt; in repose, far from the madding crowd; after life's fitful fever.

Int. stop! stay! halt! whoa! hold! hold hard! hold it! don't move! lay off! avast! basta! bas! pipe down!

See: 16, 37, 136, 144, 145, 153, 175, 177, 187, 192, 216, 218, 258, 278, 295, 326, 361, 364, 375, 387, 388, 399, 620, 662, 674, 679, 681, 683, 717, 730, 757, 820, 823, 828, 858, 860, 883.

267 Land travel

N. *land travel,* travel, traveling, wayfaring; seeing the world, globe-trotting, tourism; ambulation, walking; riding, ride and tie; driving, coaching, motoring, cycling; journey, voyage, trip; course, passage, sweep, reconnaissance, peregrination, pilgrimage, hajj; expedition, safari, trek; hunting expedition, stalk; exploration, gold-rush 484n. *discovery;* business trip, errand 917n. *duty;* pleasure trip, tour, continental t., grand t.; circuit, turn, round trip, round tour 314n. *circuition;* jaunt, hop; ride, joy-r., drive, lift, free l.; excursion, outing, airing, ramble, constitutional, promenade; ambulation, perambulation, walk, heel and toe; stroll, saunter, hike, march, run, jog-trot 265n. *gait;* paddling, wading.

wandering, errantry, wanderlust, nomadism; vagrancy, vagabondage, vagabondism; no fixed address; roving, rambling, pereration, waltzing Matilda; tramping, traipsing, flitting, gadding, gallivanting; migration, emigration 298n. *egress;* immigration 297n. *ingress;* demigration, intermigration; transmigration 305n. *passage.*

pedestrianism, walking, going on foot, footing it, shanks's mare; foot-slogging, heel and toe; stumping, tramping, marching; ambulation, perambulation; circumambulation 314n. *circuition;* walk, promenade, constitutional; stroll, saunter, amble, ramble; hike, tramp, march, walking-tour; run, trot, jog-t., lope; amble, canter, gallop, hand g. 265n. *gait;* paddle, paddling, wading; foot-race, running-r. 716n. *racing;* stalking, stalk 619n. *chase;* walking about, peripateticism; prowling, loitering; sleep-walking, noctambulation, noctambulism, somnambulism 375n. *insensibility;* going on all fours, creeping, crawling, crawl.

marching, campaigning, campaign; maneuvers, marching and countermarching, advance, retreat; march, route-m., night-m.; quick march, slow m., route-m.; cavalcade, procession, parade, march past 875n. *formality;* column, file, cortege, train, caravan.

equitation, equestrianism, horsemanship, manege, dressage 694n. *skill;* show-jumping, steeplechasing 716n. *contest;* horse-racing; riding, bareback r. 162n. *athletics;* haute école, caracole, piaffe, curvet 265n. *gait.*

conveyance, lift; flat feet, legs,

shanks's mare; horseback, mount 273n. *horse;* bicycle, car, bus, train, streetcar, trailer, ambulance 274n. *vehicle;* traffic, wheeled t., motor t., road t. 305n. *passing along.*

leg, foreleg, hindleg; limb, nether l. 53n. *limb;* shank, knee, shin, calf; thigh, ham, hock, hough; popliteal tendons, hamstrings; gluteal muscle, gluteus; legs, pegs, pins, underpinnings 218n. *supporter;* stumps, stilts; stump, wooden leg, artificial l.; bow legs, bandy l. 845n. *blemish;* long legs, spindle shanks 206n. *thinness;* thick legs, piano l.; shank bone, shin bone, tibia.

itinerary, route 624n. *way;* march, course 281n. *direction;* route-map, road m., plan, chart 551n. *map;* guide, Baedeker, Murray, road-book, handbook, timetable, Bradshaw 524n. *guide book;* milestone, fingerpost 547n. *signpost;* halt, stop, stopover, terminus 145n. *stopping place.*

Adj. *traveling* etc. vb.; journeying, itinerant, wayfaring, peregrine; travel-stained, dusty 649adj. *dirty;* traveled, much-t.; touring, globe-trotting, rubbernecking; passing through, stopping over, visiting 305 adj. *passing;* nomadic, nomad, floating, unsettled; mundivagrant, migratory, homeless, rootless, déraciné 59 adj. *extraneous;* footloose, on the road, roving, roaming, rambling, hiking, errant, wandering 282adj. *deviating;* ambulant, strolling, circumforaneous, peripatetic; tramping, vagabond; walking, pedestrian, ambulatory, perambulatory; marching, footslogging; discursive, gadding, flitting, traipsing, gallivanting; automotive, locomotive, self-moving 265adj. *moving;* self-driving, self-driven, self-drive; noctivagrant, somnambular, sleep-walking.

crural, genual, femoral, popliteal, gluteal; legged, bow-l., bandy-l. 845adj. *blemished;* thighed, strong-t., round-t.; well-calved, well-hocked; long-legged, leggy, leggity 209adj. *tall;* spindly, spindle-shanked, calfless 206adj. *lean;* piano-legged, thick-ankled 205adj. *thick.*

Vb. *travel,* fare, journey, peregrinate; tour, see the world, visit, explore 484vb. *discover;* go places, sightsee, rubberneck; pilgrimage, go on a pilgrimage; make a journey, take a j., go on a j.; go on safari, trek, hump bluey; set out, fare forth, pack, bundle, take wing, flit 296vb. *depart;* migrate, emigrate, immigrate, settle 187vb. *place oneself;* go to, hie to, repair to, resort to, betake oneself to 295vb. *arrive,* 882vb. *visit;* go, cruise 265vb. *be in motion;* wend, wend one's way, stir one's stumps, bend one's steps, bend one's course, shape one's c., lay a c., tread a path, pursue a p., follow the road; make one's way, pick one's w., thread one's w., plow one's w.; jog on, trudge on, peg on, wag on, shuffle on, pad on, tramp on, march on, chug on 146vb. *sustain;* course, race, post 277vb. *move fast;* proceed, advance 285vb. *progress;* coast, freewheel, glide, slide, skate, ski, skim, roll along, bowl a., fly a. 258vb. *go smoothly.*

traverse, cross, range, pass through, range t., peragrate, pererrate, perambulate 305vb. *pass;* circumambulate, go round, beat the bounds, fetch a circle 314vb. *circle;* go the rounds, go one's rounds, patrol; scout, reconnoiter 438vb. *scan;* sweep, sweep through; scour, scour the country 297vb. *irrupt.*

wander, nomadize, migrate; rove, roam; knock around, bum, ramble, stroll, saunter, dawdle, walk about, walk aimlessly; gad, traipse, gallivant, gad about, hover, flit about, dart a. 265vb. *be in motion;* prowl, skulk 523vb. *lurk;* straggle, trail 75vb. *be dispersed;* lose the way, wander away 282vb. *stray.*

walk, step, tread, pace, stride; stride out 277vb. *move fast;* strut, stalk, prance 871vb. *be proud;* tread lightly, tiptoe, trip, dance, curvet 312 vb. *leap;* tread heavily, stamp, tramp, goose-step; toddle, patter; stagger, lurch; halt, limp; waddle, straddle; shuffle, dawdle 278vb. *move slowly;* paddle, wade; go on foot, go by shanks's mare, foot it, hoof it, stump, hike, plod, trudge, jog; go, go for a walk, ambulate, perambulate; peripateticize, pace up and down; have a run, take the air, take one's constitutional; march, quick march, double, slow-march; file, file off, defile, march in procession 65vb. *come after;* walk behind 284vb. *follow;* walk in front 283vb. *precede.*

ride, mount, back (horse), take horse; trot, amble, tittup, canter, gallop; prance, curvet, piaffe, caracole, passage; cycle, bicycle, push-bike, motor-cycle; drive, motor, taxi, cab; go by car, go by bus, go by streetcar, go by taxi; go by road, go by subway, go by train; go by air 271vb.

fly; take a lift, cadge a l., thumb a l., hitch-hike.

Adv. *on foot,* on hoof, on horseback, on shanks's mare, on shanks's pony, by the marrowbone stage; en route 272adv. *in transit;* by road, by rail.

Int. come along! get along! get out! git! go away! be off! buzz off! hop it! skedaddle! scram!

See: 53, 59, 75, 145, 146, 162, 187, 205, 206, 209, 218, 258, 265, 271, 273, 274, 277, 278, 281, 282, 285, 295, 296, 297, 298, 305, 312, 314, 375, 438, 484, 523, 524, 547, 551, 619, 624, 649, 694, 716, 845, 871, 875, 882, 917.

268 Traveler

N. *traveler,* itinerant, wayfarer, peregrinator; voyager 270n. *mariner;* space-traveler, space-man 271n. *aeronaut;* pilgrim, palmer, hajji; walker, hiker, trekker; globe-trotter, tourist, rubberneck, sightseer 441n. *spectator;* tripper, excursionist; vacationer, visitor; pioneer, pathfinder, explorer 66n. *precursor;* adventurer, forty-niner; alpinist, mountaineer, cragsman 308n. *climber;* roundsman, hawker 794n. *peddler;* traveling salesman, commercial traveler 793n. *seller;* messenger, errand-boy 531n. *courier;* pursuivant, process-server 955n. *law officer;* daily traveler, commuter, season-ticket holder; Ulysses, Gulliver, Wandering Jew.

wanderer, migrant, bird of passage, visitant 365n. *bird;* floating population, nomad, gypsy, Romany, Bohemian, tzigane, Arab, bedouin, rover, ranger, rambler, straggler; stroller; strolling player, wandering minstrel 594n. *entertainer;* rolling stone, drifter, vagrant, scatterling, vagabond, tramp, swagman, sundowner, hobo, bum, bummer, landloper; loafer, beachcomber 679n. *idler;* ski-bum 162n. *athlete;* emigrant, immigrant, émigré 59n. *foreigner;* refugee, displaced person, DP, stateless person; runaway, fugitive, escapee 620n. *avoider;* déraciné, homeless wanderer, solivagant 883n. *solitary;* waif, stray, street-arab, street-beggar 801n. *poor man;* Wandering Jew, Flying Dutchman; comet 321n. *meteor.*

pedestrian, foot-passenger, walker, hoofer, tramper; pacer; runner, foot-racer; wader, paddler; skater, skier; ambulator, peripatetic; hiker, hitch-h., marcher, footslogger; footman 722n. *infantry;* noctambulist, somnambulist, sleepwalker; prowler, night-walker; footpad 789n. *robber;* toddler.

rider, horse-rider, camel-r., cameleer; elephant-rider, mahout; horseman, horsewoman, equestrian, equestrienne; postilion, post-boy 531n. *courier;* man on horseback, cavalier, knight, chivalry 722n. *cavalry;* hunt, huntsman 619n. *hunter;* jockey, show-jumper 716n. *contender;* trainer, breaker 369n. *breeder;* rough-rider, bronco-buster, cowboy, cow-puncher, gaucho, centaur; cyclist, bicyclist, wheelman, pedal-pusher; circus-rider, trick-rider 162n. *athlete;* motor-cyclist; back-seat driver; passenger, strap hanger, commuter.

driver, drover, teamster, muleteer; mahout, elephant-driver, camel-d., cameleer; charioteer, coachman, whip; postilion, post-boy; carter, wagoner, drayman, truckman; cabman, cabdriver, cabby, hackie, jarvey; voiturier, vetturino, gharry wallah; car-driver, chauffeur, motorist, automobilist; scorcher 277n. *speeder;* joy-rider; L-driver 538n. *beginner;* taxi-driver, taximan; bus-driver, streetcar-d.; lorry-d., truck-d., van-d., tractor-d.; motorman, engine-driver, engineer, shunter; stoker, footplate man; guard, conductor, brakeman; Jehu, Autolycus.

See: 59, 66, 162, 270, 271, 277, 308, 321, 365, 369, 441, 531, 538, 594, 619, 620, 679, 716, 722, 789, 793, 794, 801, 883, 955.

269 Water travel

N. *water travel,* ocean t., sea t., river t., underwater t.; seafaring, sea service, nautical life, life on the ocean wave; navigation, voyaging, sailing, cruising; coasting, gutter-crawling; boating, yachting, rowing (**see** *aquatics*); voyage, navigation, cruise, sail, steam; course, run, passage, crossing; circumnavigation, periplus 314n. *circuition;* marine exploration, submarine e. 484n. *discovery;* sea adventures, naval exploits; sea trip, river t., breath of sea air 685n. *refreshment;* way, headway, steerage way, sternway, seaway 265n. *motion;* leeway, driftway 282n. *deviation;* wake, track, wash, backwash 350n. *eddy;* sea path, ocean track, steamer route, sea lane, approaches 624n. *route;* ship 275n. *ship;* sailor 270n. *mariner.*

navigation, piloting, steering, pilotage, pilotism 689n. *directorship;* plane sailing, plain s., spherical s., great-circle s., parallel s.; compass reading, dead reckoning 465n. *measurement;* pilotship, helmsmanship, seamanship 694n. *skill;* nautical experience, weather eye, sea legs; naval exercises, naval maneuvers, fleet operations, naval tactics, weather gauge 688n. *tactics.*

aquatics, water sports 837n. *sport;* boating, sailing, yachting, cruising; rowing, sculling, canoeing; boat racing, yacht r., speedboat r. 716n. *racing;* water-skiing, aquaplaning, surf-riding; natation, swimming, floating; stroke, breast-s., side-s., crawl; diving, plunging 313n. *plunge;* wading, paddling; bathing costume, swimsuit, bathing trunks, bikini 228n. *beachwear;* bathing machine.

sailing aid, navigational instrument, sextant, quadrant, backstaff 247n. *angular measure;* chronometer, ship's c. 117n. *timekeeper;* log, line, lead, plummet 313n. *diver;* compass, magnetic c., ship's c.; needle, magnetic n., south-pointing instrument; card, compass c.; binnacle; gyrocompass; radar 689n. *directorship;* asdic; helm, wheel, tiller, rudder, steering oar; seamark, buoy, lighthouse, pharos, lightship 547n. *signpost;* chart, Admiralty c., portolano 551n. *map;* nautical almanac, ephemeris 524n. *guide-book.*

propeller, screw, twin screw, blade; paddle-wheel, stern-w., float-board; oar, sweep, paddle, scull; pole, punt-p. 287n. *propellant;* fin, flipper, fish's tail 53n. *limb;* sails, canvas 275n. *sail.*

Adj. *seafaring,* sea, salty, deep-sea; sailorlike, sailorly 270adj. *seamanlike;* nautical, naval 275adj. *marine;* navigational, navigating, sailing, steaming, plying, coasting, ferrying; seagoing, oceangoing; at sea, on the high seas, afloat, waterborne, on board; pitching, tossing, rolling, wallowing; seasick, green; seaworthy, tight, snug; navigable, boatable; deep, broad, smooth.

swimming, natatory, floating, sailing; launched, afloat, buoyant; natatorial, aquatic, like a duck.

Vb. *go to sea,* follow the s., join the navy; become a sailor, get one's sea legs; be in sail, sail before the mast; live on board, live afloat; go sailing, boat, yacht; launch, launch a ship, christen a s. 68vb. *auspicate.*

voyage, sail, go by sea, go by ship, take the sea route; take ship, take a cabin, book one's berth, book a passage; embark, go on board, put to sea, set sail 296vb. *start out;* cross the ocean, cross the sea 267vb. *traverse;* disembark, land 295vb. *arrive;* cruise, visit ports; navigate, steam, ply, run, tramp, ferry; coast, hug the shore; gutter-crawl; roll, pitch, toss, tumble, wallow 317vb. *oscillate.*

navigate, man a ship, work a s., crew; put to sea, set sail; launch, push off, boom off; unmoor, cast off, weigh anchor; raise steam, get up s.; hoist sail, spread canvas; get under way, gather w., make w., carry sail 265vb. *be in motion;* drop the pilot; set a course, make for, head for 281vb. *steer for;* read the chart, go by the card 281vb. *orientate;* pilot, steer, hold the helm, captain 689vb. *direct;* stroke, cox, coxswain; trim the sails, square, square away; change course, veer, jibe, yaw 282vb. *deviate;* put about, wear ship 282vb. *turn round;* run before the wind, scud 277vb. *move fast;* put the helm up, fall to leeward, pay off; put the helm down, luff, bring into the wind; beat to windward, tack, weather; round, double a point, circumnavigate 314vb. *circle;* be taken aback, be caught amidships 700vb. *be in difficulty;* careen, list, heel over 220vb. *be oblique;* turn turtle, capsize, overturn, overset 221vb. *invert;* ride out, ride out the storm, weather the s., keep afloat 667vb. *escape;* run for port 662vb. *seek refuge;* lie to, lay to, heave to 266vb. *bring to rest;* take soundings, heave the lead 465vb. *measure;* tide over 507vb. *await;* tow, haul, warp, kedge, club-haul 288vb. *draw;* ground, run aground, wreck, cast away 165vb. *destroy;* sight land, raise, make a landfall, take on a pilot 289vb. *approach;* make port; cast anchor, drop a.; moor, tie up, dock, disembark 296vb. *land;* cross one's bows, take the wind out of one's sails, outmaneuver, gain the weather gauge 702vb. *obstruct;* foul 279vb. *collide;* back, go astern 286vb. *regress;* surface, break water 298vb. *emerge;* flood the tanks, dive 313vb. *plunge;* shoot, shoot a bridge, shoot the rapids 305vb. *pass.*

row, ply the oar, get the sweeps out; pull, stroke, scull; feather; punt; paddle, canoe; boat; shoot the rapids.

swim, float, sail, ride, ride on an even keel; scud, skim, skitter; surf-ride, surf-board, water-ski, aquaplane; strike out, breast the current, stem the stream; tread water; dive 313vb. *plunge;* bathe, dip, duck; wade, paddle, splash about, get wet 341vb. *be wet.*

Adv. *under way,* all aboard; under sail, under canvas, under steam; before the mast; on deck, on the bridge, on the quarterdeck; at the helm, at the wheel; swimmingly 701adv. *easily.*

See: 53, 68, 117, 165, 200, 221, 228, 247, 265, 266, 267, 270, 275, 277, 279, 281, 282, 287, 288, 289, 295, 296, 298, 305, 313, 314, 317, 341, 350, 465, 484, 507, 524, 547, 551, 624, 662, 667, 685, 688, 689, 694, 700, 701, 702, 716, 837.

270 Mariner

N. *mariner,* sailor, sailor-man, seaman, seafarer, seafaring man; salt, old s., sea dog, shellback; tar, Jack Tar, matelot; no sailor, bad s., landlubber 697n. *bungler;* shipman, skipper, master mariner, master, ship's m.; mate, boatswain, bo'sun; coxswain; able seaman, A.B. 696n. *expert;* deckhand, swabbie, lascar; ship's steward, cabin boy 742n. *servant;* crew, complement, ship's c., men 686n. *personnel;* trawler, whaler, deep-sea fisherman; sea rover, privateer, sea king, Viking, pirate 789n. *robber;* sea scout; argonaut, Jason; Ancient Mariner, Flying Dutchman, Captain Ahab, Gulliver, Old Man of the Sea; sea god, Neptune, Poseidon, Varuna.

navigator, pilot, sailing master, helmsman, steersman, wheelman, man at the wheel, quartermaster; coxswain, cox 690n. *director;* leadsman, lookout man; foretopman, reefer; boatswain, bo'sun's mate; circumnavigator 314n. *circler;* compass, binnacle, gyrocompass 269n. *sailing aid.*

naval man 722n. *navy man;* man-o'-war's man, blue-jacket, gob, rating, petty-officer, midshipman, middy, midshipmite, snotty, lieutenant, sub-l., lieutenant-commander, commander, captain, flag officer, commodore, admiral, vice a., rear a.; Sea Lord; submariner; marine, royal m., jolly; coastguardsman, coast guard 749n. *keeper.*

boatman, waterman, hoveler; rower, rowing man, wet bob; gigsman, gig; galleyman, galley-slave; oar, oarsman, sculler, punter; yachtsman, yachter; canoer, canoeist; ferryman, gondolier; wherryman, bargeman, bargee, lighterman; stevedore, docker, longshoreman.

Adj. *seamanlike,* sailorly, like a sailor 694adj. *expert;* nautical, naval 275adj. *marine.*

See: 269, 275, 314, 686, 690, 694, 696, 697, 722, 742, 749, 789.

271 Aeronautics

N. *aeronautics,* aeromechanics, aerodynamics, aerostatics, aerodonetics; air station, ballooning, balloonry; rocketry 276n. *rocket;* volitation, flight, bird f., natural f.; aerial flight, vertical f., horizontal f., level f.; jet flight, subsonic f., supersonic f. 277n. *velocity;* stratospheric flight, hypersonic f., space f.; aviation, flying, night f., blind f., instrument f.; formation flying 875n. *formality;* stunt flying, aerobatics 875n. *ostentation;* gliding, planing, volplaning, looping the loop; spin, roll, side-slip; volplane, nose-dive, pull-out; crash-dive, crash, prang 309n. *descent;* pancake, crash-landing, forced l.; touch down 295n. *arrival;* take off 296n. *departure.*

air travel, space t.; air transport, airlift 272n. *transport;* air service, airline, airways; airlane, air course, air route 624n. *route;* line of flight 281n. *direction;* air space 184n. *territory;* takeoff, touchdown, landing, three-point l.; landing ground, airstrip, runway, tarmac, airfield, airdrome, airport, heliport; terminal, air-t. 295n. *goal;* hangar 192n. *stable.*

aeronaut, aerostat, balloonist; glider; parachutist; paratrooper 722n. *soldier;* aviator, airman, birdman; astronaut, spaceman, space traveler; air traveler, air passenger 268n. *rider;* air-hostess 742n. *servant;* flier, flying-man, pilot, air-p., jet-p.; air-crew, navigator, observer, bombardier; pilot officer, flying o., flight sergeant, flight-lieutenant, squadron leader, wing commander, group captain, air commodore, air marshal; aircraftman 722n. *air force;* air personnel, ground staff 686n. *personnel;* Icarus, Daedalus.

wing, pinion, feathers, wing-feather, wingspread 259n. *plumage;* backswept wing, Delta-w., variable w.; aileron, flaps; talaria, winged heels.

Adj. *flying,* on the wing; volitant, volant; fluttering, flitting, hovering 265adj. *moving;* winged, alar, pinnate, feathered; aerial 340adj. *airy;* airworthy, airborne, soaring, climbing 308adj. *ascending;* airsick; losing height 309adj. *descending;* grounded 311adj. *depressed;* aeronautical, aviational; aerodynamic, aerostatic; aerobatic.

Vb. *fly,* flight, wing, take the w., be on the w.; wing one's way, wing one's flight, be wafted, cross the sky; soar, rise 308vb. *ascend;* hover, hang over 217vb. *hang;* flutter, volitate 265vb. *be in motion;* taxi, take off, clear, leave the ground, climb, circle 296vb. *depart;* glide, plane 258vb. *go smoothly;* float, drift, drift like a balloon 282n. *deviate;* stunt, spin, roll, side-slip, loop the loop, volplane; hedgehop, skim the rooftops, buzz 200vb. *be near;* stall, dive, nose-d., spiral 313vb. *plunge;* crash, prang, force-land 309vb. *tumble;* pull out, flatten o.; touch down 295vb. *land;* bale out, jump, parachute, hit the silk; keep in flight, stay up, not fall; orbit, go into o. 314vb. *circle.*

Adv. *in flight,* on the wing, on the beam.

See: 184, 192, 200, 217, 258, 259, 265, 268, 272, 276, 277, 281, 282, 295, 296, 308, 309, 311, 313, 314, 340, 686, 722, 742, 875.

272 Transference

N. *transference,* change of place, translocation, transplantation, transshipment, transfer; shifting, shift, drift, continental d. 282n. *deviation;* translation (to a post), posting, cross-p. 751n. *mandate;* transposition, metathesis 151n. *interchange;* removal, remotion, amotion, relegation, deportation, expulsion 300n. *ejection;* unpacking, unloading 188n. *displacement;* exportation, export 791n. *trade;* mutual transfer 791n. *barter;* importation, import 299n. *reception;* transmittal, sending, remittance, dispatch; recalling, recall, revocation, revoke 752n. *abrogation;* extradition 304n. *extraction;* recovery, retrieval 771n. *acquisition;* handing over, delivery, hand-over, take-o., conveyance, transfer of property, donation 780n. *transfer;* committal, trust 751n. *commission;* jail delivery, habeas corpus, release 746n. *liberation;* transition, metastasis; passing over, trajection, ferry, ferriage 305n. *passage;* transmigration, transmigration of souls, metempsychosis; transmission, throughput; transduction, conduction, convection; transfusion, complete t. (of blood), perfusion; decantation; diffusion, dispersal 75n. *dispersion;* communication, contact 378n. *touch;* contagion, infection, contamination 178n. *influence;* literary conversion, transcription, transumption, copying, transliteration 520n. *translation;* felonious removal, asportation, helping oneself 788n. *stealing.*

transport, transportation, vection, vectitation, vecture; conveyance, carriage, water-c., waft, waftage, shipping, shipment; carrying, humping, portage, porterage, haulage, draft 288n. *traction;* carting, cartage, wagonage, drayage, freightage, air freight, airlift; means of transport, rail, road, sea, air; escalator, moving staircase, travolator, moving pavement, vehicle 274n. *conveyor.*

thing transferred, carry-over 40n. *extra;* flotsam, jetsam, driftwood, drift, sea d.; alluvium, detritus, scree, moraine 53n. *piece;* sediment, deposit 649n. *dirt;* pledge, hostage, trust 767n. *security;* gift, legacy, bequest 781n. *gift;* lease, 777n. *property;* cargo, load, payload, freight, consignment, shipment 193n. *contents;* goods, mails; luggage, baggage, impedimenta; person transferred, passenger, rider, commuter 268n. *traveler.*

transferrer, transferor, testator, conveyancer 781n. *giver;* sender, remitter, dispatcher, dispatch clerk, consignor, addresser; shipper, shipping agent, transporter; exporter, importer 794n. *merchant;* conveyor, ferryman 273n. *carrier;* post office, post, express p., mail, postman 531n. *mails;* communicator, transmitter, diffuser; infectious person, vector, carrier (of a disease) 651n. *sick person;* pipe-line, tap 632n. *store;* decanter, siphon.

Adj. *transferable,* conveyable, assignable, negotiable, devisable; transportable, movable, portable, carriageable; roadworthy, airworthy, seaworthy; portative, transmissive, conductive; transmissible, communicable; contagious 653adj. *infectious.*

Vb. *transfer,* hand over, deliver 780vb. *convey;* devise, leave 780vb. *bequeath;* commit, assign, entrust 751vb. *commission;* transmit, hand down, hand on, pass on; make over, turn over, hand to, pass to; pass, pass the buck; export, transport, ship, waft, lift, fly 273vb. *carry;* traject, ferry, set across; put across, put over 524vb. *communicate;* infect, contaminate 178vb. *influence;* conduct, convect; radiate 300vb. *emit;* carry over 38vb. *add;* transfer itself, come off (e.g. wet paint), adhere, stick 48vb. *cohere.*

transpose, shift, move 188vb. *displace;* switch, shunt, shuffle, castle (chess), cross-post 151vb. *interchange;* transfer, post, translate; detach, detail, draft; relegate, deport, expel 300vb. *eject;* drag, pull 288vb. *draw;* push, shove 279vb. *impel;* transfuse, decant, strain off, siphon off, draft off 300vb. *void;* unload, remove 188vb. *displace;* shovel, ladle, spoon out, dip, bail; spade, dig 255vb. *make concave;* transliterate, transdialect 520vb. *translate;* transume, copy, make a c., take a c.

send, have conveyed, remit, transmit, dispatch; ship, rail, truck; direct, consign, address; post, mail; redirect, readdress, post on, forward; send by hand, send by post, send through the mail, dispatch by mail; send for, order, order in, order up 627vb. *require;* send away, detach, detail; send flying 287vb. *propel.*

Adv. *in transit,* en route, on the way; by hand, per manus; by remittance, by transfer; by gift, by will; from hand to hand, from pillar to post.

See: 38, 40, 48, 53, 75, 151, 178, 188, 193, 255, 268, 273, 274, 279, 282, 287, 288, 299, 300, 304, 305, 378, 520, 524, 531, 627, 632, 649, 651, 653, 746, 751, 752, 767, 771, 777, 780, 781, 788, 789, 791, 794.

273 Carrier

N. *carrier,* common c., hauler, carter, wagoner, tranter; shipper, transporter, exporter, importer 272n. *transferrer;* gondolier, ferryman 270n. *boatman;* lorry-driver, truck-d., taxi-d., bus-d., busman, streetcar-driver 268n. *driver;* delivery van, lorry, truck, tractor, freight-train 274n. *vehicle;* cargo vessel, freighter, tramp 275n. *ship;* conductor, lightning c., lightning rod; carriage, undercarriage 218n. *supporter;* carrier bag 194n. *bag;* conveyor belt, escalator, moving staircase, travolator, moving pavement 274n. *conveyor;* skate, ski, snowshoe; germ-carrier, vector.

bearer, litter-b., palkee-b., stretcher-b.; caddie, golf-c.; shield-bearer, cup-bearer 742n. *retainer;* porter, redcap, coolie, hamal; coalheaver, bummaree, stevedore; letter-carrier, carrier pigeon, postman, special messenger, express 531n. *courier.*

beast of burden, jument, pack-horse, pack-mule, sumpter-horse, sumpter-mule; ass, she-a., donkey, moke, Neddy, cuddy, burro; ox, oxen, cattle, plow-c., draft-c.; sledge-dog, husky; reindeer, llama; camel, dromedary, elephant 365n. *animal.*

horse, equine species, quadruped, horseflesh; courser, steed; stallion, gelding, mare, colt, filly, foal; stud-horse, broodmare, stud, stable; roan, gray, bay, chestnut, sorrel, liver-chestnut, black, piebald, skewbald, pinto, paint, dun, palomino, buckskin; dobbin, Rosinante; winged horse, Pegasus.

thoroughbred, blood-horse, bloodstock; Arab, Waler, Hambletonian; Barbary horse, barb; pacer, stepper, high-s., trotter; courser, race-horse, racer, goer, stayer; sprinter, quarter-horse 277n. *speeder;* steeplechaser, hurdler, fencer, jumper, hunter; Morgan, Tennessee Walker.

drafthorse, draught-horse, cart-h., dray-h.; shaft-horse, track-h.; carriage-horse, coach-h., post-h.; plow-h., shire-h., Clydesdale, punch, Suffolk p., Percheron, Belgian; pit-pony.

war-horse, cavalry h., remount; charger, courser, steed 722n. *cavalry;* Bucephalus, Bayard, Copenhagen, Marengo, Rosinante.

saddle-horse, riding-h., cow-pony, cow-cutting horse, roping-h.; mount, hack, roadster; jade, tit, screw, nag; padnag, pad, ambler; mustang, bronco; palfrey, genet; riding mule, alborak.

pony, cob, tit, galloway, garron, shelty; Shetland pony, fell p., Welsh mountain p., Dartmoor p., Exmoor p., New Forest p.

Adj. *bearing,* carrier, shouldering, burdened, freighted, loaded, overloaded, hag-ridden; piggyback.

equine, horsey, horse-faced; roan, gray (**see** *horse*); asinine; mulish.

Vb. *carry,* bear 218vb. *support;* hump, heave, tote; caddie; stoop one's back to, shoulder, bear on one's back, carry on one's shoulders; fetch, bring, reach; fetch and carry, trant; transport, cart, vehicle, truck, rail, railroad; ship, waft, raft; lift, fly 272vb. *transfer;* carry through, carry over, pass o., carry across, traject, ferry; convey, conduct, convoy, escort 89vb. *accompany;* have a rider, be ridden, be mounted; be saddled with, be burdened w., endure 825vb. *suffer;* be loaded with, be fraught 54vb. *be complete.*

See: 54, 89, 194, 218, 268, 270, 272, 274, 275, 365, 531, 722, 742, 825.

274 Vehicle

N. *vehicle,* conveyance, public c.; transport, public t., vehicular traffic, wheeled t., road t.; sedan-chair, palanquin, palankeen, palkee, dooly, dandy; litter, horse-l.; brancard, stretcher, hurdle, crate; ambulance, fire-engine; Black Maria, paddy-wagon; tumbril, dead-cart, hearse; snowplow; Sno-Cat, weasel; tractor, caterpillar t., tracked vehicle; hobbyhorse; roller-coaster, switchback, bumping car.

sled, sledge, sleigh, dog-s., horse-s., deer-s., kibitka, cariole; bob-sleigh, bob-sled, toboggan, luge, coaster, ice-yacht; skate, ice skate, roller s.; snowshoes, skis, runners.

bicycle, velocipede, cycle, pedal-c., bike, push-b., safety-bicycle, safety, lady's bicycle, sit-up-and-beg, tandem; penny-farthing, bone-breaker; monocycle, unicycle, tricycle, quadricycle; motorized bicycle, moped; scooter, motor-s., motorcycle, motorbike; motorcycle combination, side-car; invalid carriage; cycle-ricksha.

pushcart, perambulator, pram, baby-carriage, kiddy-cart, bassinet; Bath-chair, wheel-c., invalid-c.; jinrikisha, ricksha; barrow, wheel-b., hand-b., coster-b.; hand-cart, go-c., golf-c.; trolley, lawn-mower, garden-m., grass-cutter.

cart, ox-c., bullock-c., bail gharry, hackery; horse-and-cart, horse-cart, dog-c., gig; van, furniture-v., removal-v., moving-v., pantechnicon; horse-van, dray, milk-float; farm-cart, haywain, hay-wagon; wain, wagon, covered w., prairie-schooner, Cape-cart; caravan, trailer; limber, gun-carriage; tumbril, dead-cart, dust-c.; bathing machine.

carriage, horse-c., equipage, turn-out, rig; chariot, coach, state c., coach and four; riding-carriage, caroche, landau, landaulet, berlin, victoria, brougham, barouche, phaeton, clarence, sociable, coupé; surrey, buckboard, buggy, wagonette; traveling carriage, dormeuse, chaise, shay, calèche, calash, britska, unicorn; droshky, kibitka, tarantass, araba; racing chariot, quadriga; four-in-hand, drag, tally-ho, brake, char-abanc; two-wheeler, cabriolet, curricle, tilbury, whiskey, whitechapel, vis-à-vis, outside car, jaunting-c., beachwagon; ekka, tonga, hackery; trap, gig, pony-cart, dog-c., governess-c.; cariole, sulky, desobligeant; shandrydan, rattletrap; house on wheels, caravan, trailer, house-t. 192n. *small house.*

war-chariot, scythed c., weapon carrier; gun-carriage, caisson, limber, ammunition wagon; tank, armored car, armor 722n. *cavalry;* jeep, staff car.

stage-coach, stage-wagon, stage, tally-ho, mail-c., mail-phaeton; diligence, post-chaise, omnibus, horse-bus. **See** *bus.*

cab, hackney-carriage, horse-cab, four-wheeler, growler, hansom, fly; fiacre, droshky, thika-gharry; taxi-cab, taxi, jitney, hack; ricksha, jinrikisha, cycle-ricksha.

bus, horse-b., steam-b., motor-b.; omnibus, double-decker, single-d.; autobus, trolley-bus, motor-coach, coach.

streetcar, horse-car, tram, trolley-car, trolley, cable-c.

automobile, horseless carriage, motor-car; motor, auto, car; limousine, landaulet, sedan, saloon, hard-top, open-car, tourer, sports car, racing c.; convertible; coupé, two-seater, two-door, four-door; jeep; roadster, runabout; station wagon, beach-wagon, estate-car, shooting-brake; motor-van, lorry, truck, bowser, tanker; flivver, model-T, tin lizzie; rattletrap, old crock, bus, jalopy; hotrod, souped-up car; autocar, tricar; bubblecar, minicar; motor ambulance; steam-car.

train, railway train, parliamentary t., special t.; boat-t., corridor t.; express train, through t.; stopping train, local t., omnibus t., passenger t., passenger, workmen's t., goods t., freight t., luggage t., milk t., mail t., night t.; Pullman, wagon-lit, sleeping-car, sleeper; club-car, observation c.; restaurant car, dining c., diner; smoker, non-smoker, ladies only; rolling stock, coach, car, carriage, compartment, coupé; caboose; brake-van, guard's van, brake, luggage van; truck, goods t., flat-car, freight c.; cattle-truck, horse-box; hand-car, trolley; bogie; electric train, diesel t., underground t., elevated t.; railway, railroad, railway line, line, track, rails, sleepers, fishplate; electric railway, underground r., underground tube, metro, subway; elevated, monorail, funicular.

locomotive, steam engine, pony e., shunter, tanker; choo-choo, puff-puff, puffer, pufferbelly, Puffing Billy, Rocket; traction engine,

steamroller; steamcar, steam omnibus; diesel, diesel engine.
conveyor, conveyor belt, escalator, moving staircase, travolator, moving pavement.
shovel, spoon, spatula 194n. *ladle;* spade, spud, spaddle, loy, hoe, trowel, hod; pitchfork, hay-fork; knife and fork, chop-sticks.
Adj. *vehicular,* wheeled, on wheels; on rails, on runners, on sleds, on skates; automobile, automotive, locomotive; non-stop, express, through; stopping, omnibus, local.
See: 192, 194, 722.

275 Ship
N. *ship,* vessel, boat, craft; great ship, tall s.; little ship, cockboat, cockleshell; bottom, keel, sail; tub, hull; hulk, prison-ship; Argo, Ark, Noah's Ark; steamer, screw-s. steamship, steamboat, motorship, rotor s.; paddle-boat; stern-wheeler, river-boat, showboat; passenger ship, liner, ocean greyhound, floating palace; channel steamer, ferry, train-f.; deck unit; mail-ship, mail-steamer, packet, steam-p.; dredger, hopper, hopper-barge, mud-hopper; transport, hospital ship; store-ship, tender, escort vessel; pilot vessel; tug, launch; lightship, cable-s.; cog, galleon, dromond, carrack, caravel, carvel, gallivat, grab, junk; underwater craft, submarine, U-boat 722n. *warship;* fireship.
galley, war-g., galley-foist, foist, gallias, galleass, galliot, lymphad; catur; pirate-ship, Viking-s., corsair, penteconter, bireme, trireme, quadrireme, quinquereme.
merchant ship, merchantman, merchant, trader; cog, galleon, argosy, levanter, dromond, carrack, polacre, polacca; caravel, galliot; Indiaman, East I., West I.; cargo-boat, freighter, tramp; coaster, coasting-vessel, chasse-marée, hoy, crumster, bilander, hooker; collier, tanker; banana-boat, tea-clipper; slaver, slave-ship.
fishing-boat, whaler, sealer, trawler, dogger, drifter, dory, fishing smack, herring-fisher, trow, buss, coble.
sailing-ship, sailboat, sailing vessel, sailer; wind-jammer, clipper ship, tall s., full-rigged s., square-rigged s., fore-and-aft-rigged s., schooner-rigged s., lateen-rigged s.; four-masted ship; three-masted s., three-master, bark, barque, barkentine; two-masted ship, brig, hermaphrodite-b., cutter-b., brigantine, schooner, pinnace, snow, grab; frigate, sloop, corvette 722n. *warship;* cutter, ketch, yawl, dandy, lugger; xebec, felucca, tartan, saic, caïque, dhow, gallivat, junk, lorcha, sampan; sailing barge, smack, gabert, hoy, hooker, nobby, bawley; yacht, skiff.
sail, sail-cloth, canvas; square sail, lug-s., lug, lateen-s., fore-and-aft s., leg-of-mutton s., spanker; course, mainsail, main-course, foresail, fore-course; topsail, topgallant s., royal, skysail; jib, staysail, spinnaker, balloon-s., studding-s., stud-s., boom-sail.
boat, skiff, cockle-shell, foldboat, cockboat; lifeboat; ship's boat, long-b., jolly-b., fly-b., bumboat; picket boat, pinnace; cutter, gig, cutter-g., whale-g.; barge, trow, lighter; state-barge, bucentaur, dahabeah; wherry, ferry, ferry-boat, canal-b., hooker, bilander; towboat, tug; launch, motorboat, motor launch, Chris-craft, speedboat, cabin-cruiser, outboard; yacht, pleasure boat; house boat, budgerow 192n. *small house.*
rowboat, rowing boat, galley; eight, racing e.; sculler, shell, funny, randan; eight-oar, four-o., pair-o.; gig-pair; dinghy, flat-bottomed d., rubber d.; outrigger, punt, gondola, coracle, curragh; canoe, double-c., trow; dug-out; piragua, proa, prau, kayak, umiak.
raft, balsa r., float, log, catamaran, jangada.
shipping, craft, forest of masts; argosy, fleet, flotilla, squadron 722n. *navy;* marine, mercantile marine, merchant navy, shipping line.
Adj. *marine,* maritime, naval, nautical, seagoing, oceangoing 269adj. *seafaring;* seaworthy, water-w., weatherly; snug, tight, shipshape; rigged, square-r. (**see** *sailing ship*); clinker-built, cruiser-b., flush-decked.
Adv. *afloat,* aboard, on board ship, on ship-board; under sail, under steam, under canvas.
See: 192, 269, 722.

276 Aircraft
N. *aircraft* 271n. *aeronautics;* aerodyne, flying machine, heavier-than-air m.; aeroplane, airplane, clipper; plane, monoplane, biplane, triplane; hydroplane, sea-plane, flying-boat; passenger plane, freight-plane, mail-p.; warplane, fighter, bomber 722n. *air force;* stratocruiser, jet-plane, jet,

turbo-j., turbo-prop; helicopter, autogiro, rotodyne; flying bedstead; hovercraft, air car; glider, sailplane; flying instruments, controls, joystick, rudder, tail, wings, flaps, aileron; prop 269n. *propeller;* cockpit, catwalk, under-carriage, landing gear; parachute, ejector-seat 300n. *ejector;* flight simulator; airdrome 271n. *air travel.*

airship, aerostat, balloon, gas-b., fire-b., Montgolfier b.; captive balloon, observation b., weather b., blimp; dirigible, zeppelin; kite, box-k.; parachute; magic carpet; balloon-basket, nacelle, car, gondola.

rocket, rocketry, sky-rocket; guided missile, intercontinental ballistic m. 723n. *missile weapon;* doodlebug, V2.

space-ship, flying saucer; satellite, artificial s., sputnik, blip, lunik; communications satellite, radio-mirror, echo balloon; space-station.

Adj. *aviational,* aeronautical, aerodynamic, aerostatic; balloonistic, astronautical, space-flying 271adj. *flying;* airworthy; heavier than air, lighter than air.

See: 269, 271, 300, 722, 723.

277 Velocity

N. *velocity,* pernicity, celerity, rapidity, swiftness, quickness, liveliness; instantaneousness, speed of thought 116n. *instantaneity;* no loss of time, promptness, expedition, dispatch; speed, tempo, rate, pace, bat 265n. *motion;* speed-rate, miles per hour, knots; speed of light, speed of sound, supersonic speed; great speed, lightning s., telegraphic s.; maximum speed, express s., full s., full steam; utmost speed, press of sail, full s., crowded canvas; precipitation, hurry, flurry 680n. *haste;* reckless speed, headlong s. 857n. *rashness;* type of speed, streak, blue s., streak of lightning, flash, lightning f.; flight, swallow f., jet f., supersonic f.; wind, storm, torrent; electricity, telegraph, lightning, greased l.; thought; quicksilver; speed measurement, velocimeter, tachometer, speedometer 465n. *gauge;* wind gauge 340n. *pneumatics;* log, log-line; speed-trap 542n. *trap.*

spurt, acceleration, speed-up, overtaking; burst, burst of speed, burst of energy; thrust, drive, impetus 279n. *impulse;* jump, spring, bound, leap, pounce 312n. *leap;* whiz, swoop, swoosh, zip, uprush, zoom; down rush, dive, power-d.; flying start, rush, dash, scamper, run, sprint, gallop.

speeding, driving, hard d., overdriving; no speed limit, scorching, racing; bowling along, rattling a.; course, race, career, full c.; full speed, full lick, full bat; pace, smart p., strapping p., rattling p., spanking rate; quick march, quick step, double, forced march; post-haste 680n. *haste;* clean pair of heels, quick retreat 667n. *escape;* racecourse, speed-track 716n. *racing.*

speeder, hustler, speed merchant, scorcher, racing-driver, jehu 268n. *driver;* runner, racer; galloper, jockey; courser, racehorse 273n. *thoroughbred;* greyhound, hunting leopard; hare, deer, doe, antelope; flier, bird, eagle, swallow; arrow, arrow from the bow, bullet, cannon-ball 287n. *missile;* jet, rocket; fast sailer, clipper 275n. *ship;* express, express train; express messenger, Ariel, Mercury 531n. *courier;* magic carpet, seven-league boots.

Adj. *speedy,* swift, fast, quick, rapid; dashing, lively, smart, snappy, zippy 174adj. *vigorous;* wasting no time, expeditious, hustling 680adj. *hasty;* prompt 135adj. *early;* immediate 116adj. *instantaneous;* high-geared, high-speed, adapted for speed, streamlined; speeding, racing; running, charging, runaway; flying, whizzing, hurtling, pelting; whirling, tempestuous; breakneck, headlong, precipitate 857adj. *rash;* fleet, fleet of foot, light-footed, nimble-f., quick-f., light of heel; darting, starting, flashing; swift-moving, agile, nimble, slippery, evasive; mercurial, like quicksilver 152adj. *changeful;* winged, eagle-w., like a bird; arrowy, like an arrow; like a flash, like greased lightning, like the wind, quick as lightning, quick as thought, quick as the wind, like a bat out of hell; meteoric, electric, telegraphic, transonic, supersonic, hypersonic.

Vb. *move fast,* move, shift, travel, speed; drive, pelt, streak, flash, flare; scorch, burn the ground, scour the plain, tear up the road; scud, careen; skim, nip, cut; bowl along 258vb. *go smoothly;* sweep along, tear a., rattle a., thunder a., storm a.; tear, rip, zip, rush, dash; fly, wing, whiz, hurtle; zoom, dive; dash off, tear o., dart o., dash on, dash forward; run, lap; trot, double, lope, gallop; bolt, cut and run, scoot, skedaddle, scamper, scurry, skelter, scuttle; show a clean pair of heels 620vb. *run away;* hare, run like a h., run like a rabbit, run like the wind, run like mad; start, dart, dartle, flit; fisk, frisk, whisk; spring, bound, leap, jump, pounce; ride hard, ride and spur, put one's best foot forward, stir one's stumps, step out; hie, hurry, post, haste 680vb. *hasten;* charge, career, go full tilt, go full pelt, go full lick, go full bat, go full steam, go all out; ignore the speed limit.

accelerate, raise the tempo; gather momentum, impart m., spurt, sprint, put on speed, pick up s., whip up s., step on it, step on the gas, open the throttle, open up, crowd canvas; quicken one's speed, mend one's pace, get a move on; set off at a score, get off to a flying start; make up time, make forced marches, make the best of one's way; quicken, step up, give one his head, drive, spur, urge, urge on; clap spurs to, lend wings to, put dynamite under, expedite 680vb. *hasten.*

outstrip, overtake, overhaul, catch up, catch up with; lap, outpace, outrun, outmarch, outsail, outwalk, outdrive 306vb. *outdo;* gain on, distance, outdistance, leave behind, leave standing; make the running, have the legs of, have the heels of, romp home, win the race 34vb. *be superior.*

Adv. *swiftly* etc. adj.; trippingly, apace; posthaste, with speed, at express s., at full s., at full tilt; in full career, in full gallop, with whip and spur, all out, flat out, ventre à terre; helter-skelter, headlong, tantivy, presto, pronto; like a shot, like an arrow, before you could say Jack Robinson; in full sail, under press of sail *or* canvas; on eagle's wings, with giant strides, in seven-league boots; in double-quick time, nineteen to the dozen, as fast as one's legs *or* heels would carry one; in high gear, at the top of one's speed; by leaps and bounds, in geometrical progression; immediately 116adv. *instantaneously.*

See: 34, 116, 135, 152, 174, 258, 265, 268, 273, 275, 279, 286, 287, 312, 340, 465, 531, 542, 620, 667, 680, 682, 716, 857.

278 Slowness

N. *slowness,* slackness, lentor, languor 679n. *sluggishness;* inertia 175n. *inertness;* refusal to be hurried, festina lente, deliberation, tentativeness, gradualism, Fabianism; hesitation 858n. *caution;* reluctance 598n. *unwillingness;* go-slow, go-slow strike, slow-down, meticulosis, working to rule 145n. *strike;* slowing down, deceleration, retardation, drag 333n. *friction;* brake, curb 747n. *restraint;* leisureliness, no hurry, time to spare, leisurely progress, easy stages 681n. *leisure;* slow motion, low gear; slow march, dead m.; slow time, andante; slow pace, foot-p., snail's p., crawl, creep, dawdle; mincing steps, walk, piaffer, amble, jog-trot, dog-t. 265n. *gait;* limping, claudication; standing start, slow s.; lagging, lag, hysteresis 136n. *delay.*

slowcoach, snail, slug, tortoise; stopping train, omnibus t., slow t.; funeral procession, cortege; dawdler, loiterer, lingerer, slow starter, non-starter, laggard, sluggard, lie-abed, sleepy-head, Weary Willie; sloucher 598n. *slacker;* drone 679n. *idler.*

Adj. *slow,* go-slow; slow-paced, andante, low-geared, slow-motion; oozy, trickling; snail-like, tortoise-l., creeping, crawling, dragging; slow-moving 695adj. *clumsy;* limping, halting; taking one's time, tardy, tardigrade, dilatory, lagging, hysteretic 136adj. *late;* long about it, unhurried 681adj. *leisurely;* deliberate 823adj. *patient;* Fabian, cunctative 858adj. *cautious;* groping, tentative 461adj. *experimental;* languid, slack, sluggish 679adj. *lazy;* apathetic, phlegmatic 375adj. *insensible;* gradual, imperceptible, unnoticeable; invisible, stealthy.

Vb. *move slowly,* go slow, amble, crawl, creep, inch, inch along, ease a.; ooze, drip, trickle, dribble 350vb. *flow;* drift 282vb. *deviate;* hang over, hover; shamble, slouch, shuffle, scuff; toddle, waddle, take short steps, mince; plod, trudge, tramp, lumber, stump, stump along; wobble, totter, stagger, lurch; struggle, chug, jolt, bump, creak; halt, limp, hobble, hirple, claudicate, go lame; drag one's steps, flag, falter 684vb. *be fatigued;* trail, lag, fall behind 284vb. *follow;* not get started, not start, hang fire, drag one's feet, drag oneself 598vb. *be loath;* tarry, be long about it, not be hurried, take one's time 136vb. *be late;* laze, slug, idle 679vb. *be inactive;* take it easy, stroll, saunter, dawdle 267vb. *walk;* march in slow time, march in funeral procession; barely move, hardly beat, tick over; grope, feel one's way 461vb. *be tentative;* hesitate 858vb. *be cautious;* speak slowly, drawl 580vb. *stammer.*

decelerate, slow down, slow up, ease up, lose momentum; reduce speed, slacken s., slacken one's pace; smell the ground (of ships); relax, slacken, ease off 145vb. *pause;* lose ground, flag, falter 684vb. *be fatigued.*

retard, check, curb, rein in, throttle down 177vb. *moderate;* reef, shorten sail, take in s., strike s. 269vb. *navigate;* brake, put on the b., put on the drag 747vb. *restrain;* back-pedal, back-water, back-paddle, put the engines astern, reverse 286vb. *regress,* 221vb. *invert;* handicap, clip the wings 702vb. *hinder;* douse, dim, dip, turn down (a wick) 419vb. *bedim.*

Adv. *slowly* etc. adj.; leisurely, lazily, sluggishly; creepingly, creakily, joltily; at half speed, at low s., in low gear, in bottom g.; with mincing steps, at a foot's pace, at a snail's p., at a funeral p.; with clipped wings, slower than molasses; in slow time, piano, adagio, largo, larghetto, lento, andante.

gradatim, gradually etc. adj.; by degrees, by slow d., by inches, little by little, bit by bit, inch by inch, step by step, by easy stages.

See: 136, 145, 175, 221, 265, 267, 269, 282, 284, 286, 333, 350, 375, 419, 461, 580, 598, 679, 681, 684, 695, 702, 747, 823, 858.

279 Impulse

N. *impulse,* impulsion, pressure; impetus, momentum; boost, stir-up 174n. *stimulant;* encouragement 612n. *incentive;* pulsion, drive, thrust, push, shove, heave; batting, on-drive, off-d., straight d. (cricket); throw, fling 287n. *propulsion;* lunge, riposte, kick 712n. *attack;* percussion, beating, tapping, drumming; beat, drum-b. 403n. *roll;* recoilless beat, dead b., thud, douse; arietation, ramming, bulldozing, hammering; butting, butt (**see** *collision*); concussion, shaking, rattling; shock, impact; slam, bang; flick, clip, tap 378n. *touch;* shake, rattle, jolt, jerk, yerk, wrench 318n. *agitation;* pulsation, pulse 318n. *spasm;* overdrive, transmission (mechanics); science of forces, mechanics, dynamics.

collision, head-on c., frontal c.; grazing collision, scrape 333n. *friction;* clash 14n. *contrariety;* cannon, carambole; impact, bump, shock, crash, smash, encounter, meeting; brunt, charge, élan 712n. *attack;* collision course 293n. *convergence;* multiple collision, pile-up 74n. *accumulation.*

hammer, sledge-h., sledge, steam-hammer, trip-h.; hammer-head, peen; hammer-stone, pile-driver, punch, puncher; bat, beetle, maul, mall, mallet; flail; tapper, knocker, door-k.; cosh, blackjack, knuckle-duster, brass knuckle, cudgel, mace, bicycle chain, sandbag 723n. *weapon;* boxing glove; pestle, anvil; hammerer, cudgeler, pummeler, beater, carpet-b.

ram, battering-r., bulldozer; pile-driver, monkey; ramrod; rammer, tamper, tamp, tamping-iron, tamping-bar, stemmer; cue, billiard c., pusher; shover.

knock, dint, dent 255n. *concavity;* rap, tap, clap; dab, pat, fillip, flip, flick; nudge, dig 547n. *gesture;* smack, slap; cuff, clout, clump, buffet, box on the ears; blow, douse; stroke, hit, crack; cut, drive (cricket); thwack, thump, biff, bang; punch, left, right, straight left, uppercut, jab, hook; body-blow, wild b., haymaker, swipe; knock-out blow, shrewd b.; stamp, kick, calcitration; whap, swat; spanking, paddling, trouncing, dusting, licking, leathering, whipping, flogging, beating, hammering, pummeling, rain of blows; hiding 963n. *corporal punishment;* assault, assault and battery 712n. *attack;* exchange of blows, fisticuffs, cut and thrust, hammer and tongs 61n. *turmoil;* innings (cricket).

Adj. *impelling* etc. vb.; impellent, impulsive; dynamic, dynamical, thrustful; impelled etc. vb.

Vb. *impel,* fling, heave, throw 287vb. *propel;* give an impetus, impart momentum; slam, bang 264vb. *close;* press, press in, press up, press down; push, thrust, shove; ram down, tamp; shove off, boom off; boom, punt; hustle, prod, urge, spur 277vb. *accelerate;* fillip, flip, flick; jerk, yerk, shake, rattle, shock, jog, jolt, jostle, justle 318vb. *agitate;* shoulder, elbow, push out of the way, push around 282vb. *deflect;* throw out, run out, expel 300vb. *eject;* frog-march; drive forward, flog on, whip on; goad 612vb. *incite;* drive, start, run, set going, set moving 173vb. *operate;* raise 310vb. *elevate;* plunge, dip, douse 311vb. *depress.*

collide, make impact 378vb. *touch;* appulse 289vb. *approach;* impinge 306vb. *encroach;* come into collision 293vb. *converge;* meet, encounter, clash; cross swords, fence 712vb. *foin;* ram, butt, bunt, batter, dint, dent; batter at, bulldoze; bump into, bump against; graze, graze against 333vb. *rub;* butt against, collide a.; drive into, crash i., run i., run over; clash with, collide w., foul, fall foul of; run one's head against, run into a brick wall, run against, charge a., dash a. 712vb. *charge;* clash against, grate a., bark one's shins, stub one's toe; trip, trip over 309vb. *tumble;* knock together, knock heads t., clash the cymbals, clap one's hands.

strike, smite, hit, land a blow, plant a b.; aim a blow, hit out at; lunge, lunge at, poke at, strike at; hit wildly, swing, flail, beat the air; strike hard, slam, bang, knock; knock down, floor 311vb. *fell;* pat, patter; flip, fillip, tickle; tap, rap, clap; slap, smack, skelp; clump, clout, box the ears of; box, spar, fisticuff 716vb. *fight;* buffet, punch, thump, thwack, whack, wham, rain blows, pummel, trounce, belabor, beat up; pound, batter 332vb. *pulverize;* biff, bash, slosh, sock, slug, cosh, cudgel, club; blackjack, sandbag, hit over the head, crown; concuss, stun, knock out, leave senseless; spank, paddle, thrash, beat, whip, cane 963vb. *flog;* dust, tan, tress, hide, leather, strap, give a hiding 963vb. *punish;* hammer, peen; thresh, scutch, swingle, shingle, flail; flap, squash, swat 216vb. *flatten;* paw, stroke 889vb. *caress;* scratch, maul 655vb. *wound;* run through, bayonet, pink 263vb. *pierce;* tear 46vb. *cut;* throw stones at, stone, pelt, snowball 712vb. *lapidate;* head (a football); bat, strike a ball, swipe, drive, turn, glance, cut, crack, lift (at cricket); smash, volley (tennis).

kick, spurn, boot, knee, calcitrate; trample, tread on, stamp on, kneel on; ride over, ride roughshod; spur, dig in one's heels; heel, punt, dribble, shoot (a football).

See: 14, 46, 61, 74, 173, 174, 212, 216, 255, 263, 264, 277, 282, 287, 289, 293, 300, 306, 309, 310, 311, 318, 332, 333, 378, 403, 547, 612, 655, 712, 716, 723, 889, 962, 963.

280 Recoil

N. *recoil,* revulsion, revulsion of feeling; reaction, retroaction, reflux 148vb. *reversion;* repercussion, reverberation, echo 404n. *resonance;* reflex 417n. *reflection;* kick, kickback, back-lash; ricochet, cannon, carom, carambole; rebound, bounce, spring, springboard 328n. *elasticity;* ducks and drakes; swing-back, swing of the pendulum 317n. *oscillation;* return (at tennis), boomerang; rebuff, repulse, bloody nose, contrecoup 292n. *repulsion;* reactionary, reactionist.

Adj. *recoiling,* rebounding etc. vb.; recalcitrant, repercussive, refluent, revulsive; retroactive, reactionary 148adj. *reverted.*

Vb. *recoil,* react 182vb. *counteract;* shrink, wince, flinch, jib, shy 620vb. *avoid;* recalcitrate, kick back, hit b.; ricochet, cannon, cannon off; uncoil, spring back, fly b., bound b., rebound; return, swing back 148vb. *revert;* repercuss, have repercussions; reverberate, echo 404vb. *resound;* shine again, reflect 417vb. *shine;* return on one's head, boomerang 714vb. *retaliate.*

See: 148, 182, 292, 317, 328, 404, 417, 620, 714.

281 Direction

N. *direction,* bearing, compass reading 186n. *bearings;* lie of the land 186n. *situation;* orientation, collimation, alignment; set, drift 350n. *current;* tenor, trending, bending 179n. *tendency;* aim; course, beam; beeline, air-line, straight shot, line of sight, optical axis 249n. *straightness;* course, tack; line, line of march, track, way, path, road 624n. *route;* steering, steerage; aim, target 295n. *goal;* compass, pelorus 269n. *sailing aid;* collimator, sights 442n. *optical device;* fingerpost 547n. *signpost;* direction-finder, range f. 465n. *gauge.*

compass point, cardinal points, half points, quarter points; quarter, north, east, south, west; magnetic north; rhumb, azimuth, line of collimation.

Adj. *directed* etc. vb.; orientated, directed toward, pointing t., signposted; aimed, well-a., well-directed, well-placed 187adj. *located;* bound for 617adj. *intending;* aligned with 219adj. *parallel;* axial, diagonal 220adj. *oblique;* cross-country, downtown; upwind, downwind; direct, undeviating, unswerving, straightforward, one-way 249adj. *straight;* northern, northerly, southerly, meridional; western, occidental;

eastern, oriental; directive, guiding; directable, under sailing orders.

Vb. *orientate,* orientate oneself, box the compass, take one's bearings, shoot the sun, check one's course, plot one's c. 269vb. *navigate;* find which way the wind blows, see how the land lies; take a direction, have a d., bear; direct oneself, ask the way, inquire the address; direct, show the way, signpost, point out the way 547vb. *indicate;* pinpoint, locate 187vb. *place;* keep on the beam 249vb. *be straight;* face, front 237vb. *be in front.*

steer for, steer, shape a course for, set the helm f., be bound f., head f., run f., stand f., make f., aim f.; make towards, bend one's steps to, go to, go towards, go straight for, go direct f., march f.; march on, align one's march, march on a point; go straight to the point, hold the line, keep on the beam, keep the nose down 249vb. *be straight.*

point to, point out, point, point towards, signpost 547vb. *indicate;* trend, trend towards, incline t., verge, dip, bend 179vb. *tend.*

aim, level, point; take aim, aim at; train one's sights, draw a bead on, level at; collimate, sight, set one's sights; aim well, hit the mark, land, plant 187vb. *place.*

Adv. *toward,* versus, facing; on the way, on the road to, on the high r. to; through, via, by way of; straight, direct, straight forwards; point-blank, straight as an arrow; in a direct line, in a straight line, in a line with, in a line for; directly, full tilt at, as the crow flies; upstream, downstream; upwind, downwind; before the wind, close to the w., near the w.; against the w., in the wind's eye, close-hauled; downtown; in all directions, in all manner of ways, from *or* to the four winds; hither, thither; clockwise, anti-clockwise, counter-clockwise, widdershins; whither, which way?

See: 179, 186, 187, 219, 220, 237, 249, 269, 295, 350, 442, 465, 547, 617, 624.

282 Deviation

N. *deviation,* disorientation, misdirection, wrong course, wrong turning; aberration, aberrancy, deflection, refraction; diversion, digression; departure, declension 220n. *obliquity;* flection, flexion, swerve, bend, obliquation 248n. *curvature;* branching off, divarication 294n. *divergence;* deviousness, detour, bypath, circumbendibus, long way round 626n. *circuit;* exorbitation, short circuit; evagation, vagrancy 267n. *wandering;* fall, lapse 495n. *error;* wandering mind 456n. *abstractedness;* drift, leeway; oblique motion, passaging, crab-walk, sidestep, sideslip; break, leg-b., off-b., googly (cricket); knight's move (chess); zigzag, slalom course; deployment, fanning out 75n. *dispersion.*

Adj. *deviating,* aberrant, non-conformist, abnormal, deviant 84adj. *unconformable;* eccentric, off-center; excursive, out of orbit, exorbitant, extravagant; errant, wandering, rambling, roving, vagrant, loose, foot-l. 267adj. *traveling;* undirected, unguided, random, without rule, erratic 495adj. *inexact;* desultory 72adj. *discontinuous;* abstracted 456adj. *inattentive;* discursive, off the subject 10adj. *irrelevant;* disorientated, without bearings, off-course, off-beam, lost, stray, astray; misdirected, misaimed, ill-a., off-target, off the mark, wide of the m., wide; off the fairway, in the rough (golf); devious, winding, roundabout 314adj. *circuitous;* indirect, crooked, zigzag, zigzagging 220adj. *oblique;* branching, divaricating, once removed, twice r. 294adj. *divergent.*

Vb. *deviate,* tralineate, leave the straight, digress; branch out, divaricate 294vb. *diverge;* turn, filter, turn a corner, swerve; turn out of one's way, go out of one's way, depart from one's course; step aside, make way for; alter course, change direction, yaw, tack; veer, back (wind); trend, bend, curve 248vb. *be curved;* zigzag, twine, twist 251vb. *meander;* swing, wobble 317vb. *oscillate;* steer clear of, sheer off, edge o., ease o., bear o.; sidle, passage; slide, skid, sideslip; break (cricket); glance, fly off at a tangent 220vb. *be oblique;* shy, jib, sidestep 620vb. *avoid.*

turn round, turn about, about turn, wheel, wheel about, face a., face the other way; reverse, reverse direction, return 148vb. *revert;* go back 286vb. *turn back.*

stray, err, ramble, rove, drift, divagate, straggle 267vb. *wander;* go astray, go adrift, miss one's way, lose the w., get lost; lose one's bearings, lose one's sense of direction, take the wrong turning, foul the line 495vb. *blunder;* lose track of, lose the thread 456vb. *be inattentive.*

deflect, bend, crook 220vb. *render*

oblique; warp, screw; put off the scent, misdirect, misaddress 495vb. *mislead;* avert 713vb. *parry;* divert, change the course of, put rudder on; draw aside, push a., pull a.; bias, put screw on (billiards); slice, pull, shank (golf); hook, glance, bowl a break, bowl wide (cricket); shuffle, shift, switch, shunt 151vb. *interchange;* wear ship 269vb. *navigate;* put on one side, side-track, sidestep.

Adv. *astray,* adrift; out; wide of the mark, off the mark; right about; round about; erratically, all manner of ways; indirectly, at one remove, at a tangent, sideways, diagonally 220adv. *obliquely;* sidling, crabwise.

See: 10, 72, 84, 148, 151, 220, 248, 251, 267, 269, 286, 294, 317, 456, 495, 620, 626.

283 Precession: going before

N. *precession* 119n. *priority,* 64n. *precedence;* going before, prevention, line-jumping; leading, heading, flying start; pride of place, head of the table, head of the school, head of the class, head of the river; lead, leading role 34n. *superiority;* pioneer 66n. *precursor;* van, vanguard 237n. *front.*

Adj. *foremost,* first; leading etc. vb.

Vb. *precede,* go before, forerun, herald; usher in, introduce; head, lead, take the van, head the line; go in front, go in advance, clear the way, lead the w., lead the dance, guide, conduct 689vb. *direct;* take the lead, get the lead, get the start, have the start; steal a march, get before, get in front, jump the line; get ahead of, lap 277vb. *outstrip;* be beforehand 135vb. *be early;* take precedence over, have right of way 64vb. *come before.*

Adv. *ahead,* before, in advance, in the van, in front, foremost, headmost; primarily, first of all; elders first.

See: 34, 64, 119, 135, 237, 277, 689.

284 Following: going after

N. *following* 65n. *sequence;* run, suit, thirteen of a suit 71n. *series;* one after another, ODTAA; subsequence 120n. *posteriority;* pursuit, pursuance 619n. *chase;* succession, reversion 780n. *transfer;* last place 238n. *rear.*

follower, attendant, hanger-on, dangler, client 742n. *dependent;* train, tail, wake, cortege, suite, followers 67n. *retinue;* following, party, adherent, supporter 703n. *aider;* satellite, moon, artificial satellite, sputnik, space-station 276n. *spaceship;* trailer, house-t. 274n. *carriage;* tender 275n. *ship.*

Adj. *following,* subsequent 65adj. *sequent.*

Vb. *follow,* come behind, succeed, follow on, follow after, follow close upon, sit on one's tail, follow in the wake of, tread on the heels of, tread in the steps of, follow the footprints of, come to heel 65vb. *come after;* stick like a shadow, bedog, spaniel, tag after, hang on the skirts of, beset; attend, wait on, dance attendance on 742vb. *serve;* dog, shadow, trail, tail, track 619vb. *pursue;* drop behind, fall b., lag, trail, dawdle 278vb. *move slowly;* bring up the rear 238vb. *be behind.*

Adv. *behind;* in the rear 238adv. *rearward;* in the train of, in the wake of 65adv. *after;* later 117adv. *o'clock.*

See: 65, 67, 71, 117, 120, 238, 274, 275, 276, 278, 619, 703, 742, 780.

285 Progression: motion forwards

N. *progression,* arithmetic p., geometric p. 36n. *increase;* ongoing, march, way, course, career; march of time 111n. *course of time;* progress, steady p., forward march 265n. *motion;* sudden progress, stride, leap, jump, leaps and bounds 277n. *spurt;* irreversibility, irresistible progress, majestic p., flood, tide 350n. *current;* gain, ground gained, advance, headway 654n. *improvement;* getting ahead, overtaking 306n. *overstepping;* encroachment 712n. *attack;* next step, development, evolution 308n. *ascent;* mystic progress, purgation, illumination, union 979n. *piety,* 981n. *worship;* furtherance, promotion, advancement, preferment; rise, raise, lift, leg-up 310n. *elevation;* progressiveness, "onward and upward department" 654n. *reformism;* enterprise, go-getting 672n. *undertaking;* achievement 727n. *success;* economic progress 730n. *prosperity;* progressive, improver 654n. *reformer;* go-getter, coming man, upstart 730n. *made man.*

Adj. *progressive,* progressing, enterprising, go-getting, forward-looking, reformist; advancing etc. vb.; profluent, flowing on 265adj. *moving;* unbroken, irreversible; advanced, up-to-date, abreast of the times 126adj. *modern.*

Vb. *progress,* proceed 265vb. *be in*

motion; advance, take a step forward, come on, develop 316vb. *evolve;* show promise 654vb. *improve;* get on, do well 730vb. *prosper;* march on, run on, flow on, pass on, jog on, wag on, rub on, hold on, keep on 146vb. *go on;* move with the times 126vb. *modernize;* maintain progress, never look back, hold one's lead; press on, push on, drive on, push forward, press f., press onwards 680vb. *hasten;* make a good start, make initial progress, make good p., break the back of; gain, gain ground, make headway, make head, make way; make strides, make rapid s., get over the ground, cover g. 277vb. *move fast;* get forward, get a move on, get ahead, shoot a., forge a., advance by leaps and bounds; gain on, distance, outdistance, leave behind 277vb. *outstrip;* gain height, rise, rise higher 308vb. *climb;* reach toward, reach out to, raise the sights; make up leeway, recover lost ground 31vb. *recoup;* gain time, make up t.

promote, further, contribute to, advance 703vb. *aid;* prefer, move up, raise, lift, bounce up, jump up 310vb. *elevate;* bring forward, push, force, develop, grow 36vb. *augment;* step up 277vb. *accelerate;* put ahead, put in front, put forward 64vb. *prepose;* favor, make for, bring on, conduce 156vb. *cause.*

Adv. *forward,* onward, forth, on, ahead, forrard; progressively, by leaps and bounds; on the way, on one's way, under w., en route for, on the road to, on the high r. to 272adv. *in transit;* in progress, in mid p., in sight of.

Int. Forward! Forrad! Forrad on! Advance! Proceed! March! Excelsior!

See: 31, 36, 64, 111, 126, 146, 156, 197, 265, 272, 277, 306, 308, 310, 316, 350, 654, 672, 680, 703, 712, 727, 730, 979, 981.

286 Regression: motion backwards

N. *regression,* regress, infinite r.; reverse direction, retroflexion, retrocession, retrogression, retrogradation, retroaction, backward step 148n. *reversion;* motion from, recess, retreat, withdrawal, retirement, disengagement 290n. *recession;* regurgitation 300n. *voidance;* crab-like motion 220n. *obliquity;* reversing, backing, reining back; falling away, decline, drop, fall, slump 655n. *deterioration.*

return, remigration, homeward journey; home-coming 295n. *arrival;* reentrance, reentry 297n. *ingress;* going back, turn of the tide, reflux, refluence, ebb, regurgitation 350n. *current;* veering, backing; relapse, backsliding, recidivation 603n. *tergiversation;* U-turn, volte-face, about-turn 148n. *reversion;* countermarch, counter-movement, countermotion 182n. *counteraction;* turn, turning point 137n. *crisis;* resilience 328n. *elasticity;* reflex 280n. *recoil;* return to starting point, argument in a circle.

Adj. *regressive,* receding, declining, ebbing; refluent, reflex; retrogressive, retrograde, backward; backward-looking 125adj. *retrospective;* reactionary 280adj. *recoiling;* backing, anticlockwise, counter-clockwise; reverse, reversible 148adj. *reverted;* resilient 328adj. *elastic;* remigrating, returning, homing, homeward-bound.

Vb. *regress,* recede, retrogress, retrograde, retrocede; retreat, sound a r., beat a r.; retire, withdraw, fall back, draw b.; turn away, turn tail 620vb. *run away;* disengage, back out, back down 753vb. *resign;* give way, give ground, lose g.; recede into the distance 446vb. *disappear;* fall behind, fall astern, drop a. 278vb. *move slowly;* reverse, back, go backwards; crawfish, back-water; run back, flow back, regurgitate; not hold, slip back; ebb, slump, fall, drop, decline 309vb. *descend;* bounce back 280vb. *recoil.*

turn back, put b., retrace one's steps; remigrate, go back, home, return 148vb. *revert;* look back, look over one's shoulder, hark back 505vb. *retrospect;* turn one's back, turn on one's heel; veer round, wheel r., about face, execute a volte face 603vb. *tergiversate;* double, double back, counter-march; start back, jib, shy, shrink 620vb. *avoid;* go back, come b., come back again, go home, come h.; come back to where one started, box the compass.

Adv. *backward,* back, astern, in reverse; to the right about; reflexively; back to where one started.

Int. back! hard astern! hands off!

See: 125, 137, 148, 182, 220, 278, 280, 290, 295, 297, 300, 309, 328, 350, 446, 505, 603, 620, 655, 753.

287 Propulsion

N. *propulsion,* jet-p., drive; impulsion, push 279n. *impulse;* projection, jaculation; throwing, tossing, hurling, pelting, slinging, stone-throwing; precipitation; defenestration 300n. *ejection;* cast, throw, chuck, toss, pitch and t.; fling, sling, shy, cock-shy; pot-shot, pot, shot, long s.; shooting, firing, discharge, volley 712n. *bombardment;* bowling, pitching, throw-in, full toss, yorker, lob (cricket); kick, punt, dribble (football); stroke, drive, straight d., on-d., off-d., swipe 279n. *knock;* pull, slice (golf); service, return, rally, volley, kill, smash (tennis); ballistics, gunnery, musketry, sniping, pea-shooting; archery, toxophily; marksmanship 694n. *skill;* gun-shot, bow-s., stone's throw 199n. *distance.*

missile, projectile, shell, rocket, cannon-ball, grape-shot, grape, ball, bullet, shot, small-s.; sling-stone, sling-shot, pellet, brickbat, stone, snowball; arrow, quarrel, bolt, shaft, javelin, dart 723n. *missile weapon;* ball, tennis-b., golf-b., cricket-b., hockey-b., floater; football, leather; bowl, wood, puck, curling-stone; quoit, discus; hammer, caber.

propellant, thrust, driving force, jet, steam 160n. *energy;* thruster, pusher, shover; tail-wind, following w. 352n. *wind;* lever, pedal, bicycle-p.; oar, sweep, paddle; screw, blade, paddle-wheel 269n. *propeller;* coal, petrol, gasoline, gas, oil, diesel o. 385n. *fuel;* gunpowder, guncotton, dynamite, cordite 723n. *explosive;* blunderbuss, shotgun, rifle, sporting r., double-barreled r., repeating r., elephant gun 723n. *fire-arm;* revolver, six-shooter 723n. *pistol;* pop-gun, water-pistol 723n. *toy gun;* blow-pipe, pea-shooter; catapult, mangonel, sling, bow, longbow, crossbow 723n. *missile weapon.*

shooter, gunman, rifleman, musketeer, pistoleer; gunner, gun-layer; archer, bowman, toxophilite, slinger, catapultier 722n. *soldier;* marksman, sharpshooter, sniper, shot, good s., crack s. 696n. *proficient.*

thrower, hurler, caster, pelter, stoner, snowballer; knife-thrower, javelin-t., discus-t., stone-t., slinger; bowler, pitcher, curler; server, striker (tennis); projector.

Adj. *propulsive,* propellant, propelling etc. vb.; expulsive, explosive, propelled etc. vb.; projectile, missile.

Vb. *propel,* jaculate, launch, project; flight, throw, cast, heave, pitch, toss, cant, chuck, shy; bowl, lob, york; hurl, fling, sling, catapult; dart, flick; pelt, stone, shower, snowball 712vb. *lapidate;* precipitate, send flying, send headlong, defenestrate; expel, pitchfork 300vb. *eject;* blow away, puff a.; blow up, fulminate, put dynamite under; serve, return, volley, smash, kill (tennis); bat, slam, slog; sky, loft; drive, on-d., straight-d.; cut, pull, hook, glance (cricket); shank, slice 279vb. *strike;* kick, dribble, punt (football); push, shove, shoulder, ease along 279vb. *impel;* wheel, pedal, roll, bowl, trundle, bowl a hoop 315vb. *rotate;* move on, drive, hustle 265vb. *move;* sweep, sweep up, sweep before one, drive like leaves; put to flight 727vb. *defeat.*

shoot, fire, open fire, fire off; volley, fire a v.; discharge, explode, let off, send off; let fly, shower with arrows, volley and thunder; draw a bead on, pull the trigger; cannonade, bombard 712vb. *fire at;* snipe, pot, pot at; pepper 263vb. *pierce.*

See: 160, 199, 263, 265, 269, 279, 300, 315, 352, 385, 694, 696, 712, 722, 723, 725, 727.

288 Traction

N. *traction,* drawing etc. vb.; pulling back, retractiveness, retraction; retractility, retractability; magnetism 291n. *attraction;* towage, haulage; draft, pull, haul; tug, tow; tow-line, tow-rope; rake, dragnet; drawer, puller, tugger, tower, hauler, haulier; retractor; lugsail, square sail 275n. *sail;* windlass 310n. *lifter;* tug, tugboat 275n. *ship;* tractor, traction, engine 274n. *locomotive;* lodestone 291n. *magnet;* rowing, a strong pull and a long pull and a pull all together; strain, tug of war 716n. *contest;* thing drawn, trailer 274n. *train.*

Adj. *drawing* etc. vb., tractive; pulling back, retractive, retractile, retractable; attractive, magnetic 291adj. *attracting;* tractile, ductile; drawn, horse-d.

Vb. *draw,* pull, haul, hale, trice, warp, kedge 269vb. *navigate;* tug, tow, take in tow; lug, drag, draggle, train, trail, trawl; rake, rake in, rake out; wind in, wind up, lift, heave 310vb. *elevate;* drag down 311vb. *depress;* pull out 304vb. *extract;* wrench, yank 63vb. *derange;* jerk, twitch, pluck, snatch at 318vb. *agitate;* pull toward 291vb. *attract;* pull back, draw b., pull in, draw in, retract.

See: 63, 269, 274, 275, 291, 304, 310, 311, 318, 716.

289 Approach: motion towards

N. *approach,* coming toward, advance 285n. *progression;* near approach, approximation, appulse 200n. *nearness;* access, accession 38n. *addition;* flowing toward, afflux, affluxion 350n. *stream;* meeting, confluence 293n. *convergence;* attack, onset, advent, coming 295n. *arrival,* 189n. *presence;* approach from behind, overtaking, overlapping 619n. *pursuit;* adient behavior, adient response (psychology); advances, overture 759n. *offer;* means of approach, accessibility, approaches 624n. *access.*

Adj. *approaching,* nearing, getting warm etc. vb.; close, approximative 200adj. *near;* meeting 293 adj. *convergent;* confluent, affluent, tributary; overhanging, hovering, closing in, imminent 155adj. *impending;* advancing, coming, oncoming 295adj. *arriving.*

accessible, approachable, get-at-able; within reach, attainable 469adj. *possible;* available, obtainable 189adj. *on the spot;* wayside, roadside, near-by 200adj. *near;* welcoming, inviting 291adj. *attracting,* 882adj. *sociable;* well-paved, metaled, well-laid, smooth 624adj. *communicating.*

Vb. *approach,* approximate, verge on 18vb. *resemble;* appropinquate 200vb. *be near;* come within range 295adj. *arrive;* feel the attraction of, be drawn; come to close quarters, come closer, meet 293vb. *converge;* run down 279vb. *collide;* near, draw n., get n., go n., come n.; move near, run up to, step up to, sidle up to; roll up 74vb. *congregate;* roll in 297vb. *enter;* accost 884vb. *greet;* make up to, make overtures, make passes 889vb. *caress;* lean toward, incline, trend 179vb. *tend;* move toward, walk t., make t., drift t., set t., fall t.; advance 285vb. *progress;* advance upon, bear down on 712vb. *attack;* close, close in, close in on 232vb. *circumscribe;* hover 155vb. *impend;* gain upon, catch up with, overtake 277vb. *outstrip;* follow hard, narrow the gap, breathe down one's neck, tread on one's heels, run one close; be in sight of, make the land, make a landfall 295vb. *land;* hug the coast, hug the shore, hug the land, coast, gutter-crawl 269vb. *navigate;* accede, adhere, join 38vb. *accrue.*

Int. this way! come closer! roll up!

See: 18, 38, 74, 155, 179, 189, 200, 232, 269, 277, 279, 285, 291, 293, 295, 297, 350, 469, 619, 622, 624, 712, 759, 882, 884, 889.

290 Recession: motion from

N. *recession,* retirement, withdrawal, retreat, retrocession 286n. *regression;* leak 298n. *outflow;* emigration, evacuation 296n. *departure;* resignation 621n. *relinquishment;* flight 667n. *escape;* shrinking, flinching 620n. *avoidance;* abient behavior, abient response (psychology) 280n. *recoil.*

Adj. *receding* etc. vb.; retreating 286adj. *regressive.*

Vb. *recede,* retire, withdraw, fall back, draw b., retreat 286vb. *regress;* ebb, subside, shrink, decline 37vb. *decrease;* go, go away, leave, evacuate, emigrate 296vb. *depart;* go outside, go out, pour out 298vb. *emerge;* leak, leak out 298vb. *flow out;* move from, move away, move off, move further, stand off, put space between, widen the gap 199vb. *be distant;* stand aside, make way, veer away, sheer off 282vb. *deviate;* drift away 282vb. *stray;* back away, shrink a., flinch 620vb. *avoid;* flee 620vb. *run away;* get away 667vb. *escape;* go back 282vb. *turn round;* jump back 280vb. *recoil;* come off, come away, come unstuck 46vb. *be disjoined.*

See: 37, 46, 199, 280, 282, 286, 296, 298, 620, 621, 667.

291 Attraction

N. *attraction,* adduction, pull, drag, draw, tug; drawing to, pulling toward; magnetization, magnetism, gravity, force of g.; itch, itch for 859n. *desire;* affinity, sympathy; attractiveness, seductiveness, appeal, allure; allurement, seduction, temptation, lure, bait, decoy, charm, siren song 612n. *inducement;* charmer, temptress, siren, Circe 612n. *motivator;* center of attraction, cynosure 890n. *favorite.*

magnet, bar m.; coil magnet, solenoid; magnetite, magnetized iron, siderite, lodestone; lodestar 520n. *guide;* magnetizer.

Adj. *attracting* etc. vb., attrahent, adducent, adductive, associative, attractive; magnetic, magnetized; seductive, charming 612adj. *inducive;* centripetal.

Vb. *attract,* magnetize, pull, drag, tug 288vb. *draw;* adduct, exercise a pull, draw toward, pull t., drag t., tug t.;

appeal, charm, move, pluck at one's heartstrings 821vb. *impress;* lure, allure, bait 612vb. *tempt;* decoy 542vb. *ensnare.*
See: 285, 520, 542, 612, 821, 859, 890.

292 Repulsion

N. *repulsion,* repellance, repellancy, repellence, repellency; repulsive force, centrifugal f.; repellent quality, repulsiveness 842n. *ugliness;* reflection 280n. *recoil;* driving off, beating o. 713n. *defense;* repulse, rebuff, snub, refusal 607n. *rejection;* brush off, dismissal 300n. *ejection.*
Adj. *repellent,* repelling etc. vb.; repulsive 842adj. *ugly;* off-putting, antipathetic 861adj. *disliked;* abducent, abductive; centrifugal.
Vb. *repel,* retrude, put away; push away, butt a., butt, head 279vb. *impel;* drive away, chase a., retund, repulse, beat off, fend off, block, stonewall 713vb. *parry;* dispel 75vb. *disperse;* turn away, reflect 282vb. *deflect;* be deaf to 760vb. *refuse;* rebuff, snub, brush off, reject one's advances 607vb. *reject;* give one the bird, give the cold shoulder, keep at arm's length, make one keep his distance 883vb. *make unwelcome;* show the door to, shut the door in one's face, send one off with a flea in his ear, send packing, send one about his business, give one his walking papers; boot out, sack 300vb. *dismiss;* prove antipathetic, put off, excite nausea 861vb. *cause dislike.*
See: 75, 279, 280, 282, 300, 607, 713, 760, 842, 861, 883.

293 Convergence

N. *convergence,* mutual approach 289n. *approach;* narrowing gap; collision course 279n. *collision;* concourse, confluence, conflux, meeting 45n. *junction;* congress, concurrence, concentration, resort, assembly 74n. *assemblage;* closing in, pincer movement 232n. *circumscription;* centering, corradiation, focalization 76n. *focus;* narrowing, coming to a point, tapering, taper 206n. *narrowness;* converging line, asymptote, tangent; convergent view, perspective, vanishing point, vanishing line, vanishing plane 438vb. *view.*
Adj. *convergent,* converging etc. vb.; focusing, focused; centripetal, centering; confluent, concurrent 45adj. *conjunctive;* asymptotic, tangential; pointed, tapering, conical, pyramidal; knock-kneed.
Vb. *converge,* come closer, draw in, close in; narrow the gap; fall in with, come together 295vb. *meet;* unite, gather together, get t., roll up 74vb. *congregate;* roll in, pour in, enter in 297vb. *enter;* close with, intercept, head off, close in upon 232vb. *circumscribe;* pinch, nip 198vb. *make smaller;* concentrate, corradiate, focus, bring into f.; align convergently, toe in; center, center on, center in 225vb. *centralize;* taper, come to a point, narrow down 206vb. *be narrow.*
See: 45, 74, 76, 198, 206, 225, 232, 279, 289, 295, 297, 438.

294 Divergence

N. *divergence,* divergency 15n. *difference;* complete divergence, contradiction 14n. *contrariety;* centrifugence, going apart, divarication; moving apart, parting 46n. *separation;* aberration, declination 282n. *deviation;* spread, fanning out, deployment 75n. *dispersion;* parting of the ways, fork, bifurcation, crossroads 222n. *crossing;* radiation, ramification, branching out; rays, spokes.
Adj. *divergent,* diverging etc. vb.; divaricate, separated; radiating, radiant; centrifugal, centrifuge; aberrant 282adj. *deviating.*
Vb. *diverge* 15vb. *differ;* radiate, star; ramify, branch off, branch out; split off, fork, bifurcate; part, part ways, part company 46vb. *be disjoined;* file off, go one's own way; change direction, switch; glance off, fly off, fly off at a tangent 282vb. *deviate;* deploy, fan out, spread, scatter 75vb. *be dispersed;* divaricate, straddle, step wide; spread-eagle; splay, splay apart.
See: 14, 15, 46, 75, 222, 282.

295 Arrival

N. *arrival,* advent, accession 289n. *approach,* 189n. *presence;* onset 68n. *beginning;* coming, reaching, making; landfall, landing, touchdown, docking, mooring 266vb. *quiescence;* debarkation, disembarkation 298n. *egress;* rejoining, meeting, reencounter, encounter 154n. *eventuality;* home-coming, recursion, remigration 286n. *return;* prodigal's return, reception, welcome, aloha 876n. *celebration;* visitor, visitant, new arrival, recent a., homing pigeon 297n. *incomer;* arrival at the winning post, finish, close f., photo f. 716n. *contest;* last lap, home stretch.

goal 617n. *objective;* bourn, terra firma 192n. *home;* journey's end, final point, terminal p. 69n. *end;* stop, stopover, stage, halt 145n. *stopping place;* billet, resting place, landing p.; port, interport, harbor, haven, anchorage, roadstead 662n. *shelter;* dock, dry-d., berth 192n. *stable;* airdrome, airport, heliport, terminal, air-t. 271n. *air travel;* terminus, railway t., railway station, junction, depot, rendezvous 192n. *meeting-place.*

Adj. *arriving* etc. vb.; homing, homeward-bound; terminal; nearing 289adj. *approaching,* 155adj. *impending.*

Vb. *arrive,* come, reach, fetch up at, get there 189vb. *be present;* reach one's destination, make land, sight, raise; make a landfall, make port; dock, berth, tie up, moor, drop anchor 266vb. *come to rest* (**see** *land*); unharness, unhitch, outspan; home, come h., get h., return h. 286vb. *regress;* hit, make, win to, gain, attain; finish the race, breast the tape; reach one's goal, be in at the death 725vb. *carry through;* stand at the door, be on the doorstep, be on the threshold, knock at the door, look for a welcome 297vb. *enter;* burst in 297vb. *irrupt;* make one's appearance, show up, pop up, turn up, roll up, drop in 882vb. *visit;* put in, pull in, stop at, stop over, stop off, break journey, stop 145vb. *pause;* clock in, time one's arrival 135vb. *be early;* arrive at, find 484vb. *discover;* arrive at the top 727vb. *be successful,* 730vb. *prosper;* be brought, be delivered, come to hand.

land, unload, discharge 188vb. *displace;* beach, ground, run aground, touch down, make a landing; step ashore, go a., disembark, debouch, pour out 298vb. *emerge;* surrender one's ticket, detrain, debus, get off the plane; get off, get down, alight, light on, perch 309vb. *descend;* dismount, quit the saddle, set foot to ground.

meet, join, rejoin, see again; receive, greet, welcome, shake hands 882vb. *be sociable;* go to meet, come to m., meet the train, meet the plane, meet the bus, be at the station; keep a date, rendezvous; come upon, encounter, come in contact, run into, meet by chance 154vb. *meet with;* hit, bump into, butt i., knock i., collide with 279vb. *collide;* burst upon, light u., pitch u.; gather, assemble 74vb. *congregate.*

Int. home at last! home again! welcome! greetings! well-met! hello! pleased to meet you!

See: 68, 69, 74, 135, 145, 154, 155, 188, 189, 192, 266, 271, 279, 286, 289, 297, 298, 309, 484, 617, 662, 716, 725, 727, 730, 876, 882.

296 Departure

N. *departure,* leaving, parting, removal, going away; walk-out, exit 298n. *egress;* pulling out, emigration 290n. *recession;* remigration, going back 286n. *return;* migration, exodus, hegira; hop, flight, flit, moonlight f., decampment, elopement, get-away 667n. *escape;* embarkation, going on board 297n. *ingress;* mounting, saddling 267n. *equitation;* setting out, starting out, outset 68n. *start;* takeoff 308n. *ascent;* zero hour, time of departure, moment of leave-taking; point of departure, place of d., port of embarkation, place of e., departure platform; starting-point, starting-post, stake-boat.

valediction, valedictory, funeral oration, epitaph, obituary 364n. *obsequies;* leave-taking, congé, dismissal; goodbye, good night, farewell, adieu; one's adieus, last handshake, waving goodbye; send-off, farewell address, speeches; farewell song, aloha; last post, last words, parting shot; stirrup-cup, doch-an-dorrach, one for the road, nightcap.

Adj. *departing* etc. vb.; valedictory, farewell; parting, leaving, taking l.; outward bound; emigrational.

Vb. *depart,* quit, leave, abandon 621vb. *relinquish;* retire, withdraw 286vb. *turn back;* remove, leave the neighborhood, leave the country, leave home, emigrate, expatriate oneself, absent o. 190vb. *go away;* leave the nest, take wing; take one's leave, take one's departure, take a ticket; be gone, be going, have one for the road; bid farewell, say goodbye, say goodnight, make one's adieus, tear oneself away, receive one's congé, call for one's passport; leave work, cease w. 145vb. *cease;* clock out, go home 298vb. *emerge;* quit the scene, leave the stage, exit, make one's e. 753vb. *resign;* depart this life 361vb. *die.*

decamp, up sticks, strike tents, fold

up one's tent, break camp, break up; march out, pack up, pack off, clear o.; clear out, evacuate; make tracks, walk one's chalks, sling one's hook; be off, beetle o., buzz o., slink o., slope o., push o., shove o.; take wing 271vb. *fly;* vamoose, skedaddle, beat it, hop it, scram, bolt, skip, slip away, cut a., cut, cut and run 277vb. *move fast;* flee, take flight 620vb. *run away;* flit, make a moonlight f., leave no trace 446vb. *disappear;* elope, welsh, abscond, give one the slip 667vb. *escape.*

start out, be off, get going, set out 68vb. *begin;* set forth, sally f., issue f., strike out, march out, debouch 298vb. *emerge;* gird oneself, be ready to start, warm up 669vb. *make ready;* take ship, embark, go on board 297vb. *enter;* hoist the blue peter, unmoor, cast off, weigh anchor, push off, get under way, set sail, spread s., spread canvas, drop the pilot, put out to sea, leave the land behind 269vb. *navigate;* mount, set foot in the stirrup, bit, bridle, harness, saddle 267vb. *ride;* hitch up, inspan, pile in, hop on; enplane, entrain; catch a train, catch a plane, catch a bus; pull out of the station, take off, be on one's way, be in flight, be on the first lap; see off, wave goodbye, speed the parting guest.

See: 68, 145, 190, 267, 269, 271, 277, 286, 290, 297, 298, 308, 361, 364, 446, 620, 621, 667, 669, 753.

297 Ingress: motion into

N. *ingress,* introgression, entry, entrance; reentry, reentrance 286n. *return;* incoming, income 807n. *receipt;* inflow, influx, flood 350n. *stream;* inpouring, inrush; invasion, forced entry, inroad, raid, irruption, incursion 712n. *attack;* illapse, immersion, diffusion, osmose, osmosis; penetration, interpenetration, infiltration, insinuation 231n. *interjacence,* 303n. *insertion;* immigration, expansionism; indrawal, indraft, intake 299n. *reception;* import, importation 272n. *transference;* right of entry, non-restriction, admission, admittance, access, entrée 756n. *permission;* free trade, free imports, free market, free port, open-door policy 791n. *trade,* 744n. *scope;* ticket, pass 756n. *permit.*

way in, way, path 624n. *access;* entrance, entry, door 263n. *doorway;* mouth, opening 263n. *orifice;* intake, inlet 345n. *gulf;* channel 351n. *conduit;* open door, free port 796n. *mart.*

incomer, newcomer, new arrival, new member, new face; new boy 538n. *beginner;* visitant, visitor, caller 882n. *social person;* immigrant, migrant, colonist, settler, uitlander, metic 59n. *foreigner;* stowaway, unwelcome guest 59n. *intruder;* invader, raider 712n. *attacker;* housebreaker, picklock 789n. *thief;* entrant, competitor 716n. *contender;* person admitted, ticket-holder, card-h.; audience, house, gate 441n. *onlookers.*

Adj. *incoming,* ingressive, ingoing, inward, inward bound, homing; intrusive, trespassing; irruptive, invasive 712adj. *attacking;* penetrating, flooding; allowed in, imported.

Vb. *enter,* turn into, go in, come in, move in, drive in, run in, step in, walk in, file in; follow in 65vb. *come after;* set foot in, cross the threshold, darken the doors; let oneself in; unlock the door, turn the key 263vb. *open;* gain admittance, have the entrée, be invited; look in, drop in, blow in, drop in, call 882vb. *visit;* board, get aboard; get in, hop in, jump in, pile in; squeeze into, wedge oneself i., pack oneself i., jam oneself i.; creep in, slip in, edge in, slink in, sneak in, steal in; work one's way into, buy one's way into, work oneself into, insinuate oneself; worm into, bore i. 263vb. *pierce;* bite into, eat i., cut i. 260vb. *notch;* put one's foot in, tread in, fall into, drop i. 309vb. *tumble;* sink into, plunge i., dive i. 313vb. *plunge;* join, enlist in, enroll oneself 58vb. *be one of;* immigrate, settle in 187vb. *place oneself;* let in 299vb. *admit;* put in 303vb. *insert;* enter oneself, enter for 716vb. *contend.*

infiltrate, percolate, seep, soak through, go t., soak into, leak i., drip i.; sink in, penetrate, mix in, interpenetrate, interfuse 43vb. *mix;* taint, infect 655vb. *impair;* filter in, wriggle into, worm one's way i., insinuate oneself i.; look for an entrance, find one's way in.

irrupt, rush in, burst in, charge in, crash in, smash in, break in, storm in 176vb. *force;* flood, overflow, flow in, pour in, flood in 350vb. *flow;* crowd in, throng in, roll in, swarm in, press in 74vb. *congregate;* invade, raid, break through, board, lay aboard, storm, escalade 712vb. *attack.*

intrude, trespass, gate-crash, outstay one's welcome; horn in, barge in, break in upon, burst in u., interrupt 63vb. *derange;* break in, burgle, housebreak, pick the lock 788vb. *steal.*
See: 43, 58, 59, 65, 74, 187, 231, 260, 263, 272, 286, 299, 303, 309, 313, 345, 350, 351, 441, 538, 624, 655, 712, 716, 744, 756, 789, 791, 794, 796, 807, 882.

298 Egress: motion out of
N. *egress,* egression, going out; exit, walk-off; walk-out, exodus, evacuation 296n. *departure;* emigration, expatriation, exile 883n. *seclusion;* emergence, emerging, debouchment; emersion, surfacing; emanation, efflux, issue; evaporation, exhalation 338n. *vaporization;* eruption, proruption, outburst 176n. *outbreak;* breakout 667n. *escape;* outcome, issue 157n. *effect;* off-take, consumption 634n. *waste;* outgo, outgoings, outlay 806n. *expenditure;* export, exportation 272n. *transference;* migrant, emigrant, émigré 59n. *foreigner;* expatriate, colonist 191n. settler; expellee, exile, remittance man.
outflow, effluence, efflux, effluxion, effusion; issue, outpouring, gushing, streaming; exudation, oozing, dribbling, weeping; extravasation, extravasation of blood, bleeding, hemophilia 302n. *hemorrhage;* transudation, perspiration, diaphoresis, sweating, sweat; percolation, distillation; leak, escape, leakage, seepage 634n. *waste;* drain, running sore 772n. *loss;* defluxion, outfall, discharge, disemboguement, drainage, draining 300n. *voidance;* overflow, spill, flood, inundation 350n. *waterfall;* jet, fountain, spring 156n. *source;* gusher, well; streaming eyes, runny nose.
outlet, vent, chute, exhaust; spout, tap; pore, blow-hole, spiracle 263n. *orifice,* 352n. *respiration;* sluice, flood-gate 351n. *conduit;* exhaust, exhaust-pipe, adjutage; spout, drainpipe, gargoyle; exit, way out, path 624n. *access;* out-gate, sally-port 263n. *doorway;* escape, loophole 667n. *means of escape.*
Adj. *outgoing,* outward bound; egressive, emergent, issuing, emanating; oozy, runny, leaky; running, leaking, bleeding; effusive, effused, extravasated; erupting, eruptive, explosive, volcanic 300adj. *expulsive;* spent 806adj. *expended.*
Vb. *emerge,* pop out, project 254vb. *jut;* surface, break water 308vb. *ascend;* emanate, transpire 528vb. *be published;* egress, issue, debouch, sally; issue forth, sally f., come f., go f.; issue out, go o., come o., pass o., walk o., march o. 267vb. *walk;* jump out, bail o. 312vb. *leap;* clear out, evacuate 296vb. *decamp;* emigrate, demigrate 267vb. *travel;* exit, walk off 296vb. *depart;* erupt, break out, break through, burst the bonds 667vb. *escape;* get the boot, get the bird, get the push.
flow out, flood o., pour o., stream o. 350vb. *flow;* gush, spurt, spirt, spout, jet; drain out, run, drip, dribble, trickle, ooze; rise, surge, well, well up, well over, boil o.; overflow, spill, spill over, slop o.; run off, escape, leak, effuse, find vent, vent itself, discharge i., disembogue, debouch; flood, inundate 341vb. *drench;* bleed, weep, effuse, extravasate 300vb. *emit.*
exude, transude, perspire, sweat, steam 379vb. *be hot;* ooze, seep, seep through, run t., leak t.; transcolate, percolate, strain, strain out, filter, filtrate, distill; run, dribble, drip, drop, drivel, drool, slaver, slabber, slobber, salivate, water at the mouth 341vb. *be wet;* transpire, exhale 352vb. *breathe.*
See: 59, 156, 157, 176, 191, 254, 263, 267, 272, 296, 300, 302, 308, 312, 338, 341, 350, 352, 379, 528, 624, 634, 667, 772, 806, 883.

299 Reception
N. *reception,* admission, admittance, entrée, access; calling in, invitation 759n. *offer;* receptivity, acceptance; open arms, welcome, effusive w. 876n. *celebration;* taking in, introception, enlistment, enrollment, naturalization 78n. *inclusion;* initiation, baptism 534n. *teaching;* asylum, sanctuary, shelter 660n. *protection;* bringing in, introduction; importation, import 272n. *transference;* indrawal, indraft; inbreathing, inhalation 352n. *respiration;* sucking, suction; assimilation, digestion, absorption, resorption, resorbence; engulfing, engulfment, swallowing, ingurgitation; ingestion (of food) 301n. *eating;* imbibition, fluid intake 301n. *drinking;* intake, consumption 634n. *waste;* intromission, immission 303n. *insertion;* interjection 231n. *interjacence;* receptibility, admissibility.
Adj. *admitting,* receptive, introceptive; freely admitting, inviting, wel-

coming 289adj. *accessible;* receivable, receptible, admissible, acceptable; absorptive, absorbent; ingestive; digestive, assimilative; introductory, initiatory, baptismal; intromittent.

Vb. *admit,* readmit; receive, accept, naturalize; grant asylum, afford sanctuary, shelter 660vb. *safeguard;* welcome, fling wide the gates; invite, call in 759vb. *offer;* enlist, enroll, take on 622vb. *employ;* give entrance *or* admittance to, pass in, allow in, allow access; give a ticket to, sell tickets; throw open, open the door, open the hatches 263vb. *open;* bring in, import, land 272vb. *transfer;* let in, show in, usher, usher in, introduce 64vb. *come before;* send in 272vb. *send;* initiate, baptize 534vb. *teach;* intromit, infiltrate 303vb. *insert;* take, be given, get 782vb. *receive;* not deny 488vb. *assent;* avow 526vb. *confess.*

absorb, incorporate, engross, assimilate, digest; suck, suck in; soak up, sponge, mop up, blot 342vb. *dry;* resorb, reabsorb; take in, ingest, ingurgitate, imbibe; lap up, swallow, swallow up, engulf, engorge, gulp, gobble 301vb. *eat, drink;* breathe in, inhale 352vb. *breathe;* sniff, snuff, snuff up, sniff up 394vb. *smell;* get the smell of, scent, scent out, smell out 484vb. *detect;* get the taste of 386vb. *taste.*

See: 64, 78, 231, 263, 272, 289, 301, 303, 342, 352, 386, 394, 484, 488, 526, 534, 634, 660, 662, 759, 782, 876.

300 Ejection

N. *ejection,* ejaculation, extrusion, expulsion; precipitation, defenestration 287n. *propulsion;* disbarment, striking off, disqualification 57n. *exclusion;* throwing out, chucking o., drumming o., rogue's march; dismissal, discharge, sack, boot, push, bounce 607n. *rejection;* externment, deportation, extradition; relegation, exile, banishment 883n. *seclusion;* eviction, dislodgment 188n. *displacement;* ejectment, dispossession, deprivation, ouster 786n. *expropriation;* jettison, throwing overboard 779n. *non-retention;* total ejection, clean sweep, elimination 165n. *destruction;* emission, effusion, shedding, spilling; libation 981n. *oblation;* secretion 46n. *separation;* salivation 302n. *excretion;* emissivity, radioactivity 417n. *radiation;* expellee, deportee, refugee 883n. *outcaste.*

ejector, evicter, dispossessor, depriver 786n. *taker;* displacer, supplanter, superseder 150n. *substitute;* expeller, chucker-out, bouncer; expellant, emetic, sickener; aperient 658n. *cathartic;* secretory; salivant, sialagogue; propellant 723n. *explosive;* belcher; volcano 383n. *furnace;* emitter, radiator; ejecting mechanism, ejector-seat 276n. *aircraft;* cuckoo 59n. *intruder.*

voidance, clearance, clearage, drainage; eruption, eruptiveness 176n. *outbreak;* egestion, regurgitation, disgorgement; vomition, vomiting, nausea, vomit; ructation, eructation, gas, wind, burp, belch; breaking wind, crepitation, belching, rumbling, grumbling, collywobbles; blood-letting, cupping, bleeding, venesection, phlebotomy, paracentesis, tapping; elimination, evacuation 302n. *excretion.*

Adj. *expulsive,* expellant, extrusive, explosive; eruptive, effusive; radiating, emitting, emissive; salivant, secretory, salivary; sickening, emetic; cathartic, emetocarthartic; sialagogue, emmenagogic.

vomiting, sick, sickened, nauseated; belching, sea-sick, air-s., car-s., train-s.

Vb. *eject,* expel, send down 963vb. *punish;* strike off, strike off the roll, disbar 57vb. *exclude;* export, send away 272vb. *transfer;* deport, extern, expatriate, exile, banish, transport 883vb. *seclude;* extrude, detrude; throw up, cast up, wash up, wash ashore; spit out, spew o.; put out, push o., turf o., throw o., chuck o., fling o., bounce; kick out, boot o.; bundle out, hustle o.; drum out, play the rogue's march; defenestrate, precipitate 287vb. *propel;* pull out 304vb. *extract;* unearth, root out, weed o., uproot, eradicate, deracinate 165vb. *destroy;* rub out, cross o., erase, eliminate 550vb. *obliterate;* exorcise, rid, get rid of, rid oneself, get shut of; shake off, brush o.; dispossess, expropriate 786vb. *deprive;* out, oust, evict, dislodge, unhouse, turn out, turn adrift, turn out of house and home 188vb. *displace;* hunt out, smoke o. 619vb. *hunt;* jettison, discard, throw away, throw overboard 779vb. *not retain;* blackball 607vb. *reject;* ostracize, cut, cut dead, send to Coventry, give the cold shoulder 883vb. *make unwelcome;* take the place of, supplant, supersede, replace 150vb. *substitute.*

dismiss, discharge, lay off, turn off,

make redundant, drop 674vb. *disuse;* ax, sack, fire, give the sack, give the boot, give the push; turn away, send one about his business, send to the right about, send one away with a flea in his ear, send packing, send to Jericho; see off, shoo o., shoo away 854vb. *frighten;* show the door, give the gate, show out, bow o.; bowl out, run o., catch o., take one's wicket; exorcise, tell to go, order off, order away 757vb. *prohibit.*

void, evacuate, eliminate 302vb. *excrete;* vent, disgorge, discharge; empty, drain; pour out, decant 272vb. *transpose;* drink up, drain to the dregs 301vb. *drink;* drain off, strain off, bail, bail out, pump o., suck o., run o.; run off, siphon o., open the sluices, open the floodgates, turn on the tap 263vb. *open;* draw off, milk, bleed, tap, broach 263vb. *pierce;* cup, let blood, draw b., tap one's claret 304vb. *extract;* clear, sweep away, clear a., sweep off, clear o., clean up, make a clean sweep of 648vb. *clean;* clean out, clear out, curette; unload, unlade, unship, unpack, break bulk, discargo 188vb. *displace;* exenterate, disembowel, eviscerate, gut, clean, bone, fillet 229vb. *uncover;* denazify, disinfest 648vb. *purify;* desolate, depopulate, dispeople, unpeople 105vb. *render few;* empty a fire-arm, fire 287vb. *shoot.*

emit, send out 272vb. *send;* emit rays 417vb. *radiate;* emit a smell, give off, exhale, breathe out, perfume, scent 394vb. *smell;* vapor, fume, smoke, steam, puff 338vb. *vaporize;* spit, spatter, sputter, splutter; effuse, pour, spend, spill, shed, sprinkle; spurt, spurtle, squirt, jet, gush 341vb. *moisten;* extravasate, bleed 341vb. *be wet;* drip, drop, ooze; drivel, dribble, drool, slobber, slaver, salivate 298vb. *exude;* sweat, perspire 379vb. *be hot;* secrete 632vb. *store;* egest, pass 302vb. *excrete;* drop (a foal), lay (an egg) 164vb. *generate;* let out, pass o., give an exit to.

vomit, be sick, bring up, throw up, cast up, disgorge, retch, keck; spew, puke, cat; feel nausea, heave.

eruct, eructate, crepitate, rumble inside; belch, burp, gurk; break wind, blow off, fart; hiccough, hawk, clear the throat, expectorate, spit, gob.

See: 46, 57, 59, 105, 150, 164, 165, 176, 187, 188, 229, 263, 272, 276, 287, 298, 301, 302, 304, 338, 379, 383, 394, 417, 550, 607, 619, 632, 648, 658, 674, 723, 757, 779, 786, 854, 883, 963, 981.

301 Food: eating and drinking

N. *eating* etc. vb.; taking food, ingestion; alimentation, nutrition; food instinct, alimentiveness; feeding, forcible f.; consumption, devouring; swallowing, deglutition; biting, chewing, mastication; manducation, carnal m., literal m., spiritual m. (theology); rumination, digestion; animal feeding, grass f., pasture, pasturing, cropping; eating meals, table, diet, dining, lunching; communal feeding, messing; dining out, regalement 882n. *sociability;* partaking, delicate feeding; tasting, nibbling, pecking, licking, playing with one's food; ingurgitation, guzzling, heavy eating, overeating, overindulgence 944n. *sensualism,* 947n. *gluttony;* appetite, voracity, wolfishness 859n. *hunger;* omnivorousness, pantophagy 464n. *indiscrimination;* eating habits, table manners 610n. *practice;* flesh-eating, carnivorousness, creophagy, hippophagy, ichthyophagy; man-eating, cannibalism; herbivorousness, vegetarianism; edibility, digestibility.

feasting, eating and drinking, ingurgitation, guzzling, swilling; banqueting, epulation; lavish entertainment, regalement; orgy, Roman o., Lucullan banquet, Sardanapalian b., feast, banquet, state-b., bump-supper, spree, beanfeast, beano; picnic, barbecue, cookout, clambake; Christmas dinner, blow-out, spread (**see** *meal*); good table, festal cheer, groaning board; fleshpots, milk and honey 635n. *plenty;* banquet-hall, hall (of a college), dining room, mess r., refectory 192n. *café.*

dieting, dietetics 658n. *therapy;* banting, thinning 206n. *thinness;* reducing 946n. *fasting;* diet, balanced d.; glossop lunch, Oslo breakfast; regimen, regime, course, dietary, diet sheet; meager diet, poor table; vitamins, proteins; carbohydrates, roughage (**see** *food content*); digestive pill, food tablet, vitamin t.; dietician, nutritionist, nutrition expert.

gastronomy, gastronomics, gastrology, palate-tickling, epicureanism, epicurism 944n. *sensualism;* gourmandise, gourmandism, good living, high l. 947n. *gluttony;* dainty palate, refined p. 463n. *discrimination;* epicure, gourmet, Lucullus (**see** *eater*).

cookery, cooking, baking, dressing; domestic science, home economics, catering 633n. *provision;* culinary department, cuisine; baker, cook, chef, cuisinier; cookshop, bakery, rotisserie, restaurant 192n. *café;* kitchen, cook-house, bake-h.; oven 383n. *furnace;* cooking medium, butter, grease, dripping lard; barm 323n. *leaven;* cookery book, cookbook 589n. *textbook;* recipe, receipt 496n. *maxim.*

eater, feeder, consumer, partaker, taster, nibbler, picker, pecker; boarder, messer, messmate; breakfaster, luncher, diner; banqueter, feaster, picnicker; diner-out, dining club 882n. *sociability;* dainty feeder, connoisseur, gourmet, epicure, trencherman, gourmand, bon viveur, epicure, Lucullus, belly-worshiper; smell-feast, parasite 947n. *glutton;* flesh-eater, meat-e., carnivore; man-eater, cannibal, anthropophage, anthropophaginian, anthropophagist; vegetarian, wheat-eater, rice-e., herbivore; hearty eater, hungry e.; wolf, cormorant, vulture, locust 168n. *destroyer;* teeth, jaws, mandibles 256n. *tooth;* mouth, pecker, gullet, stomach, belly, paunch 194n. *maw.*

provisions, stores, commissariat; provender, contents of the larder, foodstuff, tinned *or* canned food, groceries; provisioning, keep, board, entertainment, sustenance 633n. *provision;* commons, sizing, provend, ration, helping 783n. *portion;* buttery, buttery-hatch, pantry, larder, still-room 632n. *storage;* hot-box, meat-safe; ice-box, frigidaire, fridge 384n. *refrigerator.*

provender, animal food, fodder, feed, pasture, pasturage, forage; corn, oats, grain, barley, hay, grass, mast, seed; foodstuffs, dry feed, winter f., cow f., chicken f.; salt-lick.

food, meat, bread, staff of life; aliment, nutriment, liquid n.; alimentation, nutrition; nurture, sustenance, nourishment, food and drink, pabulum, pap; food for the body, food for the mind, food for the spirit; food for the gods, nectar and ambrosia, amrit; one's daily bread, one's bread-and-butter 622n. *vocation;* bread and dripping, bread and cheese, bread and onions; foodstuffs, comestibles, edibles, eatables, eats, victuals, viands, provender; bellytimber, grub, tuck, prog, scoff, tack, hardtack, biscuit, salt pork, dogsbody, pemmican; bad food, carrion, offal; cheer, good c., good food, good table, regular meals, fleshpots, fat of the land; creature comforts, cakes and ale, cates; dainties, tidbits, luxuries 637n. *superfluity;* flavoring, sauce 389n. *condiment.*

food content, vitamins; calories, roughage; mineral salts; calcium, phosphorus, iron, water; protein; fat, oil; carbohydrates, starch, sugar; monosaccharide, simple sugar; glucose, galactose, fructose; disaccharide, double sugar; maltose, malt sugar; lactose, milk sugar.

mouthful, bite, nibble, morsel 33n. *small quantity;* sop, sip, swallow; gobbet, slice, tidbit, sandwich, snack, crust; chocolate, chow, candy, sweet, gobstopper, toffee, stickjaw, chewing gum (**see** *sweatmeat*); cud, quid, something to chew; tablet, pill 658n. *drug.*

meal, refreshment, fare; light meal, snack, sandwich, club-s., grinder, hamburger, hot dog; heavy meal, square m., full m., substantial m.; sit-down meal, repast, collation, regalement, regale, refection, spread, feed, blow, blow-out, bust, beanfeast, beano (**see** *feasting*); picnic, fête champêtre, barbecue, cookout, clambake, wiener roast; junket 837n. *festivity;* chance meal, pot-luck; morning tea, chota hazri; breakfast, elevenses, luncheon, lunch, tiffin; tea, five o'clock, high tea; dinner, supper, fork s., buffet s.; ordinary, table d'hôte; ordered meal, a la carte, order; menu, carte, bill of fare, diet-sheet 87n. *list;* dietary (**see** *dieting*); cover, table, place; help, helping 783n. *portion;* serving, serving up, dishing up; self-service.

dish, cover, course; hors d'oeuvres, eggs, omelet, salad, Russian s., vegetable s., mayonnaise 389n. *sauce;* main dish, side-d., dessert, savory; specialty, specialité de la maison, pièce de résistance, plat du jour; eggs and bacon, liver and b., fish and chips, sausages and mash, bubble and squeak, waffles and creamed chicken, tripe and onions; mixed grill; curry and rice, pilau, pilaf; hotchpotch, haggis, jugged hare, hash, stew, Irish s.; chowder, chop suey, sweet and sour pork; spaghetti, macaroni, risotto, mince, ragout, fricassee, salmi, casserole, goulash; made-up dish, réchauffé.

soup, thin s., thick s., clear s.; broth, brew, potage, consommé; stock, bouillon, bisque, puree; mulligatawny, minestrone, borsch, bouillabaisse, gumbo, skilly.

fish food, fish 365n. *table fish;* freshwater f., saltwater f.; fish cakes, fish pie; fresh fish, smoked f.; fried fish, boiled f., soused f.; kipper, bloater, herring, buckling, sardine, brisling; gurnard; haddock, mackerel, plaice, whitebait, turbot, mullet, carp, salmon, rock s., trout; hilsa, begti, pomfret, mahseer; shellfish, oyster, bivalve; lobster, langouste, crab, shrimp, prawn, scampi, chingri; scallop; mussel, cockle, whelk, winkle; smoked salmon, caviar, fish roe, cod's r., shad roe, soft r., hard r.

meat, flesh; roast, rôti, roast beef of Old England; red meat, beef, mutton, pork, venison; white meat, game 365n. *poultry;* kabob; minced meat, sausage m., force-m., meat extract, meatball; cut, joint, leg, half l., fillet end, shank e.; baron of beef, sirloin; saddle, undercut, shoulder, neck, collar, chuck, skirt, knuckle; aitchbone, scrag end, breast, brisket; shin, loin, flank, ribs, rolled r., topside, silver s.; chop, loin c., chump c., mutton c., lamb c., pork c.; steak, fillet s., rump s., porterhouse s., ham s., hamburger; pork, suckling pig, sucking p., pork pie, ham, bacon, streaky b., boiled b., gammon; fried bacon, rasher; tongue, ox-tongue, lamb's t.; knuckle, oxtail, cow-heel, calf's head; pig's trotters, pig's knuckles, chitterlings, haslet, pig's fry; offal, tripe, giblets, kidney, liver, heart, brain, sweetbread; sausage, banger, pork sausage, liver s., breakfast s., salami; hot dog, wiener, frankfurter, cocktail sausage; grease, lard, bard, dripping; bacon fat, bacon rind.

pudding, hasty p., batter p., Yorkshire p., pease p., Christmas p., plum p., suet p.; duff, plum d., spotted dog, roly-poly, dumpling; sweet, rice pudding, semolina p., tapioca p., sago p., bread-and-butter p.; sweet, trifle, jelly, blancmange, custard; ice, vanilla ice, sundae; fritters, fruit salad, compote; soufflé, mousse, crumble.

sweetmeat, sweets, sugarplum, candy, chocolate, liqueur c., caramel; marzipan, Turkish delight, marshmallows, licorice; toffee, butterscotch, rock, lollipop, lolly, all-day sucker 392n. *sweet;* preserves, compote, jam, jelly, marmalade, cranberry sauce; crystallized fruit, ginger, stone g., chow-chow; sandesh, rashagula, halvah, barfi, jelapi.

fruit, soft f.; stone-fruit, drupe; orange, Jaffa o., navel o., tangerine, mandarin; apple, pippin, medlar; pear, avocado p., alligator p.; peach, apricot; banana, plantain; pineapple, pomegranate; lichi, mangosteen, mango, passion fruit, granadilla, guava, pomelo; grape, muscat, raisin; plum, prune, damson, maraschino cherry; cherry, wild-c., gean; currant, red c., white c., black c.; olive, date, fig; berry, gooseberry, cape-g., tipari; bilberry, dewberry, elderberry, blackberry, strawberry, raspberry, redberry, loganberry, blueberry, whortleberry, cranberry, huckleberry; jackfruit, breadfruit; pawpaw, papaya; melon, watermelon, cantaloupe, honeydew melon, muskmelon, Persian m., casaba m., Spanish m.; nut, coconut, almond, chestnut, walnut; filbert, hazel-nut, Brazil n., peanut, monkey-nut, groundnut, cashew n., Barcelona n., pistachio n.

tuber, root, rhizome; ginger; artichoke, Jerusalem a.; underground fungus, truffle; potato, spud, sweet potato, yam, turnip, swede, nalkal, parsnip, beetroot; carrot; fried potatoes, french-fried p., chips, crisps, mashed p., creamed p., baked p.

vegetable 366n. *plant;* greens, vegetables, garden-stuff; cabbage, red c., pickled c., sauerkraut, slaw, coleslaw, cauliflower, kale, seakale, curly kale, cole, colewort, broccoli, sprouts, brussels s.; beans, haricot b., string b., runner b., scarlet runner; broad beans, lima b., wax b., soybeans; lettuce, cabbage l., cos l.; okra, gumbo, rhubarb, celery, horseradish, spinach, sedge, bamboo shoots; eggplant, aubergine, brinjal; asparagus, sparrowgrass; artichoke, Jerusalem a.; chicory, endive, leek, chive, garlic; onion, spring o., Spanish o., shallot, scallion; squash, summer s., acorn s., zucchini, ladies' fingers; marrow, courgette; cucumber, pumpkin, gourd; tomato, loveapple; pepper, red p., green p., chili, capsicum, paprika, pimento; pea, green p., petits pois, split peas; pulse, lentil, gram; edible fungus, boletus edulis, bolet, mushroom, truffle.

potherb, herb, culinary h., sweet h., marjoram, rosemary, mint, thyme, bay, dill, mace, sage, sorrel, fennel; laxative herb, senna; parsley, cress, watercress; clove, caper, chicory, borage, hops.

cereal, gruel, skilly, brewis, brose; porridge, stirabout, oatmeal; cornflakes, cream of wheat; bread, wheat b., rye b., black b., pumpernickel; loaf, cottage l., currant l., teacake; roll, croissant, rusk; crust; toast, buttered t.; roti, chapati,

luchot; batter-cake, pancake; flapjack, waffle, succotash; crumpet, muffin; corn, maize, grain, wheat, rye, oats, barley, millet; meal, flour, atta; barley-meal, peameal.
pastry, bakemeat, patty, pasty, singhara, turnover, crumble; tart, flan, puff, pie, pie-crust; cake, seed c.; birthday cake, wedding c., layer c.; delicatessen, confectionery; patisserie, gateau; shortbread, gingerbread; biscuit, zwieback, snap, cracker, wafer; barley-cake, bannock; oat-cake, scone; crumpet, muffin, English m.; bun, Bath b.; doughnut, jelly-d., cruller.
milk product, cream, curds, junket, yogurt; whey, cheese, goat's c., cream c., cottage c., Dutch c., Edam, Cheddar, Cheshire, Camembert, Roquefort, Gruyère, Brie, Parmesan; ripe cheese, Gorgonzola, Stilton; toasted cheese, Welsh rabbit.
drinking, imbibing, imbibition, fluid intake; potation; sipping, tasting, wine-tasting 463n. *discrimination;* gulping, swilling, soaking 299n. *reception;* one's cups, bibbing, wine-b.; drinking to excess 949n. *drunkenness;* giving to drink, watering, drenching; libation 981n. *oblation;* drinking time, bever; drinker, bibber, swiller, sipper, quaffer.
potion, something to drink, thirst-quencher; drink, draft, dram, drench; gulp, sop, sup; noggin, stoup, bottle, bowl, glass 194n. *vessel;* glassful, bumper; swig, nip, tot, peg, double p., wallop, snorter, snifter, chaser, long drink, short d.; quick one, short o., short; snort; backhander; nightcap, stirrup-cup, one for the road; health, toast; beverage, posset; mixed drink, concoction, cocktail 43n. *mixture;* decoction, infusion (**see** *liquor*).
soft drink, teetotal d., non-alcoholic beverage, thirst-quencher, water, drinking w., filtered w., eau potable, spring water, fountain; soda water, fizzy-w., soda, soda-fountain, siphon; table-water, mineral w., mineral, barley water; milk, milkshake, frappé, float; ginger beer, ginger pop, ginger ale, cola, Coca-Cola, coke; fizz, pop, lemonade, orangeade; cordial, fruit juice, lime j., orange j., lemon j., grapefruit j., tomato j.; coconut milk, dab-juice; tea, cha, Pekoe, Bohea, Indian tea, China t., green t., Russian t., maté; coffee, Turkish c., white c., cappuccino; chocolate, cocoa; shrub, sherbet, syrup. **See** *milk.*
liquor, liquid 335n. *fluid;* nectar, soma; booze, stimulant; brew, fermented liquor, intoxicating l. (**see** *wine*); alcohol, wood-a., alc; malt-liquor, hops, beer, small b., swipes; draft beer; bottled b.; ale, strong a., nog; stout, lager, bitter, porter, home-brew; cider, perry, mead, Athole brose; wheat-wine, rice-beer, sake, pachwai, marua, mahu; pagla pani, arrack, raki, toddy; distilled liquor, spiritous l., spirits, ardent s., raw s., firewater, hooch; brandy, cognac, eau-de-vie; gin, sloe g., schnapps, mother's ruin, blue r.; whisky, usquebaugh, Scotch whisky, scotch; rye, bourbon; whiskey, Irish w., poteen; rum, grog, hot g., punch, rum p., milk p., eggnog; cordial, spiced wine, negus, posset, hippocras; mulled wine, caudle; flavored wine, cup, claret-c.; mixed drink, shandygaff, stingo, highball, brandy and soda, whiskey and s.; julep, cocktail; aperitif; liqueur.
wine, the grape, juice of the g., blood of the g.; red wine, tawny w., white w., vin rosé; spumante, sparkling wine, still w., sweet w., dry w., medium w., heavy w., light w., vintage w.; vin ordinaire, vin du pays; sherry, sack, port, Madeira; claret, lal shrub; champagne, fizz, bubbly; hock, Rhenish, Burgundy, sparkling B., Bordeaux, Tokay; chianti, retsina; Falernian, Chian.
milk, top of the m., cream; cow's milk, beastings; goat's milk, camel's m., mare's m., koumiss; mother's milk, breast m.; dried m., skimmed m., condensed m., predigested m., pasteurized m.; curdled milk, curds, junket. **See** *milk product.*
Adj. *feeding,* eating, grazing etc. vb.; flesh-eating, meat-e.; carnivorous, creophagous, cannibalistic; omophagic, omophagous; herbivorous, graminivorous, frugivorous, phytovorous; wheat-eating, rice-e., vegetarian; omnivorous 464adj. *indiscriminating;* greedy, wolfish 947adj. *gluttonous;* water-drinking, teetotal, teetotaling, tea-drinking 942adj. *temperate;* liquorish, swilling, bibulous, tippling, drinking 949adj. *drunken;* well-fed, well-nourished; nursed, breast-fed; full up, crammed 863adj. *sated.*
edible, eatable; ritually pure, kosher, esculent, cibarious, comestible; manducable, digestible, predigested; potable, drinkable; milky, lactic; worth eating, palatable, succulent, palate-tickling, dainty, delicious 386adj. *tasty,* 390adj. *savory;* cereal,

wheaten; fermented, spirituous, alcoholic, hard 949adj. *intoxicating;* nonalcoholic, soft.
nourishing, feeding, sustaining; nutritious, nutritive, nutritional; alimentary, cibarious; vitaminous, dietetic; fattening, rich, calorific; wholesome 652adj. *salubrious;* body-building, bone-b.
culinary, dressed, oven-ready, made-up; underdone, red, rare, raw; done, well-d.; over-cooked, burned; roasted etc. vb. (**see** *cook*); gastronomic, epicurean.
mensal, prandial, commensal; messing, dining, lunching; before-dinner, preprandial; after-dinner, postprandial; self-service.

Vb. *eat,* feed, fare, board, mess, keep hall; partake, discuss 386vb. *taste;* take a meal, have a feed, break one's fast, break bread; breakfast, lunch, have tea, dine, sup; dine out, regale, feast, banquet, carouse 837vb. *revel;* eat well, feed full, have a good appetite, do justice to, ply a good knife and fork, be a good trencherman, ask for more; water at the mouth, drool, raven 859vb. *be hungry;* fall to, set to, tuck in, lay in, stuff oneself, fill one's stomach 863vb. *sate;* guzzle, gormandize 947vb. *gluttonize;* go through a meal, take every course, eat up, make a clean plate; lick the platter, lick the plate 165vb. *consume;* swallow, gulp down, snap up, devour, dispatch, bolt, wolf, make short work of; play the parasite, feed on, live on, fatten on, batten on, prey on; nibble, peck, lick, play with one's food, have a poor appetite; nibble at, peck at, sniff at; ingest, digest 299vb. *absorb.*
chew, masticate, manducate, champ, munch, crunch, scrunch; mumble, mouth, worry, gnaw; press with one's teeth, bite; grind 332vb. *pulverize;* tear, rend, chew up 46vb. *cut.*
graze, browse, pasture, crop, feed; ruminate, chew the cud.
drink, imbibe, ingest, suck, absorb; quaff, drink up, drink one's fill, slake one's thirst; lap, sip, sup; wet one's lips, wet one's whistle; draw the cork, crack a bottle; lap up, soak, sponge up, wash down; swill, swig, tipple, tope 949vb. *get drunk;* toss off one's glass, drain one's g., empty the g., empty the bottle; raise one's glass, pledge 876vb. *toast;* take a backhander, have another, wet the other eye, take one for the road; refill one's glass 633vb. *replenish;* give to drink, wine, water, drench; prepare a drink, medicine, posset, caudle; lay in drink, lay down a cellar 633vb. *provide.*
feed, nourish, vitaminize; nurture, sustain, board; victual, cater, purvey 633vb. *provide;* nurse, breast-feed, give suck; pasture, graze, drive to pasture, put out to grass; fatten, fatten up 197vb. *enlarge;* give to eat, fill one's mouth; dine, wine, feast, banquet, have to dinner 882vb. *be hospitable.*
cook, prepare a meal, do to a turn; put in the oven, bake, scallop; roast, spit; broil, grill, griddle, devil, curry; sauté, fry; fry sunny-side up, double-fry (eggs); scramble, poach; boil, parboil; coddle, seethe, simmer, steam; casserole, stew; baste, lard, bard; whip, whisk, stir; draw, gut, bone, fillet; stuff, dress, garnish; sauce, flavor, spice.

See: 33, 43, 46, 87, 165, 168, 192, 194, 197, 206, 256, 299, 323, 332, 335, 365, 366, 383, 384, 386, 389, 390, 392, 463, 464, 496, 589, 610, 622, 632, 633, 635, 637, 652, 658, 783, 837, 859, 863, 876, 882, 942, 944, 946, 947, 949, 981.

302 Excretion

N. *excretion,* discharge, secretion, extrusion 300n. *ejection;* effusion, extravasation, ecchymosis; emanation 298n. *egress;* exhalation, breathing out 352n. *respiration;* exudation, sudation, perspiration, sweating, induced sweat, diaphoresis 298n. *outflow;* cold, catarrh, hay fever, pollinosis; salivation, expectoration, spitting; coughing, cough; urination, micturition, passing.
hemorrhage, bleeding, extravasation of blood, hemophilia 335n. *blood;* monthly discharge, menses, catamenia, flowers, leucorrhea.
cacation, defecation, evacuation, elimination, clearance 300n. *voidance;* movement, motion; regular motion, one's daily functions; frequency, diarrhea, dysentery; copremesis.
excrement, feces, stool, excreta, ordure; hardened feces, coprolith; dung, horse-dung, cow-pat; droppings, guano; piss, urine, water; spittle, spit, sputum, sputa; saliva, slaver, slabber, slobber, froth, foam; rheum, phlegm; slough, cast, exuviae, exuvial; feculence, egesta, ejecta 649n. *dirt.*

Adj. *excretory,* secretory; purgative, eliminant; ejective, diuretic; diaphoretic, sudorific; perspiratory, sudoriparous; fecal, feculent;

rheumy, watery; cast-off, exuvial.

Vb. *excrete,* secrete; pass, move; defecate, ease oneself, stool, go to s.; urinate, piddle, wet; make water, spend a penny; piss, stale; sweat, perspire, steam 379vb. *be hot;* salivate, slobber 298vb. *exude;* water at the mouth 859vb. *be hungry;* foam at the mouth 891vb. *be angry;* cast, slough, shed one's skin 229vb. *doff.*

See: 298, 300, 335, 352, 379, 649, 859, 891.

303 Insertion: forcible ingress

N. *insertion,* intercalation, embolism, interpolation, parenthesis 231n. *interjection;* adding 38n. *addition;* introduction, insinuation 297n. *ingress;* importation 299n. *reception;* infixion, impaction, impactment; planting, transplantation 370n. *agriculture;* inoculation, injection, shot 263n. *perforation;* infusion, enema, clyster; thing inserted, insert, inset; stuffing 227n. *lining.*

immersion, submersion, submergence 311n. *depression;* dip, bath 313n. *plunge;* baptism 988n. *Christian rite;* burial, burial at sea 364n. *interment.*

Adj. *inserted* etc. vb.; added 38adj. *additional;* thematic, intermediate 231adj. *interjacent;* coffined 364adj. *buried.*

Vb. *insert,* intromit, introduce; import 299vb. *admit;* put into, thrust i., intrude; poke into, stick i.; empierce 264vb. *pierce;* ram into, jam i., stuff i., pack i., tuck i., press i., pop i., whip i. 193vb. *load;* pocket, impocket, purse 782vb. *receive;* knock into, hammer i., drive i. 279vb. *impel;* put in, inlay, inset 227vb. *line;* mount, frame 232vb. *circumscribe;* subjoin 38vb. *add;* interject 231vb. *put between;* drop, drop in, put in the slot 311vb. *let fall;* putt, hole out; pot, hole; put in the ground, lay to rest, bury 364vb. *inter;* sheathe, encapsulate, embox, encase 226vb. *cover.*

infuse, drop in, instill, pour in 43vb. *mix;* imbue, imbrue, impregnate; transfuse, decant 272vb. *transpose;* squirt in, inject, poke 263vb. *pierce.*

implant, plant, transplant, plant out 187vb. *place;* graft, engraft, imp, bud; inoculate; embed, bury; infix, wedge in, impact, dovetail 45vb. *join.*

immerse, immerge, merge, bathe, steep, souse, marinate, soak 341vb. *drench;* baptize 988vb. *perform ritual;* duck, dip 313vb. *plunge;* submerge, flood; immerse oneself, bury oneself in, be deep in, plunge in medias res 455vb. *be attentive.*

See: 38, 45, 187, 193, 226, 227, 231, 232, 263, 272, 279, 297, 299, 311, 313, 341, 363, 364, 370, 455, 782, 988.

304 Extraction: forcible egress

N. *extraction,* withdrawal, outing, removal 188n. *displacement;* elimination, eradication 300n. *ejection;* extermination, extirpation, 165n. *destruction;* extrication, unravelment, disengagement, liberation 668n. *deliverance;* evulsion, avulsion, tearing out, ripping o.; cutting out, exsection, embryectomy; expression, squeezing out; exsuction, sucking out; drawing out, pull, tug, wrench 288n. *traction;* digging out, excavation; extractive industry, mining, quarrying; fishery; distillation 338n. *vaporization;* drawing off, tapping, milking; thing extracted, essence, extract.

extractor, gouger; miner, quarrier; wrench, forceps, pincers, pliers, tweezers 778n. *nippers;* corkscrew, screwdriver 263n. *opener;* lever 218n. *pivot;* scoop, spoon 274n. *shovel;* pick, pickax; rake; toothpick 648n. *cleaner;* excavator, dredge, dredger; syringe, siphon; Persian wheel, shadoof, swipe 341n. *irrigator.*

Adj. *extracted* etc. vb.; extractive.

Vb. *extract,* pull 288vb. *draw;* draw out, elicit, educe; unfold 316vb. *evolve;* pull out, take o., get o., pluck; withdraw, exsect, cut out, rip o., tear o., whip o.; excavate, mine, quarry, dig out; dredge, dredge up; expel, lever out, winkle o., smoke o. 300vb. *eject;* extort, wring; express, press out, squeeze o., gouge o.; force out, wring o., wrench o., drag o.; draw off, milk, tap; suck, void; wring from, squeeze f., drag f.; pull up, weed up, dig up, grub up, rake up; remove, eliminate, root up, uproot, pluck up by the roots, eradicate, deracinate, unroot, averruncate 165vb. *destroy;* prune, thin out, deforest 105vb. *render few;* distill 338vb. *vaporize;* extricate, unravel, free 746vb. *liberate;* unwrap, unpack, unload 300vb. *void;* eviscerate, gut, shuck, shell 229vb. *uncover;* pick out 605vb. *select.*

See: 105, 165, 188, 218, 229, 263, 274, 288, 300, 316, 338, 341, 605, 648, 668, 746, 778.

305 Passage: motion through

N. *passage,* transmission 272n.

transference; transduction 272n. *transport;* passing, passing through, traversing; transition, abrupt t., transilience 306n. *overstepping;* transcursion, transit, traverse, crossing, journey, voyage, perambulation, patrol 267n. *land travel;* passage into, penetration, interpenetration, permeation, infiltration; transudation, osmosis, osmose, endosmose 297n. *ingress;* exosmose 298n. *egress;* intercurrence, intervention 231n. *interjacence;* pass, defile, ghat 624n. *access;* stepping-stone, fly-over, underpass 624n. *bridge;* track, route, orbit 624n. *path;* intersection, crossroad 222n. *crossing;* channel 351n. *conduit.*

passing along, thoroughfare; traffic, pedestrian t., wheeled t., vehicular t.; road traffic, ocean t., air t.; traffic movement, flow of traffic, circulation; traffic pattern, walking, crossing, cycling, driving, carrying; loading, unloading; waiting, parking, curb-side p., off-street p.; traffic load, traffic density; traffic conflict, traffic jam, procession, line.

traffic control, traffic engineering; traffic rules, highway code, rule of the road 496n. *maxim;* traffic lane, one-way street, fly-over, underpass; clearway 624n. *road;* diversion, alternative route 282n. *deviation;* street furniture, white line, double white l., traffic lights, roundabout; clover leaf, pedestrian crossing, zebra c., Belisha beacon, refuge, island; car-park, parking place, parking area *or* zone; parking meter, lay-by; traffic police, traffic cop, road patrol; traffic engineer; traffic warden, meter maid, Lapp Lizzie.

Adj. *passing* etc. vb.; transitional, transilient; intercurrent, osmotic, endosmotic.

Vb. *pass,* pass by, leave on one side, skirt, coast 200vb. *be near;* flash by 277vb. *move fast,* 114vb. *be transient;* pass along, join the traffic, keep in the t., circulate, weave; pass through, transit, traverse; shoot through, shoot a bridge, shoot the rapids 269vb. *navigate;* pass out, come out the other side 298vb. *emerge;* go through, soak t., percolate, permeate 189vb. *pervade;* pass and repass, patrol, work over, beat, scour, go over the ground; pass into, penetrate, infiltrate 297vb. *enter;* bore, perforate 263vb. *pierce;* thread, thrid, thread through 45vb. *connect;* enfilade 203vb. *look along;* open a way, force a passage 297vb. *irrupt;* worm one's way, elbow through, muscle t., clear the ground 285vb. *progress;* cross, go across, cross over, make a crossing, reach the other side 295vb. *arrive;* wade across, ford; get through, get past, negotiate; pass in front, cut across, cross one's bows 702vb. *obstruct;* step over, straddle, bestride 205vb. *be broad;* bridge, bridge over 226vb. *cover;* carry over, carry across, traject, transmit 272vb. *transpose;* pass to, hand, reach, pass from hand to hand, hand over 780vb. *convey;* let pass, skip 458vb. *disregard;* pass a test, graduate 727vb. *succeed;* barely pass, scrape through, struggle t.; repass 286vb. *turn back;* pass beyond 306vb. *overstep.*

Adv. *en passant,* by the way.

See: 45, 114, 189, 200, 203, 205, 222, 226, 231, 261, 263, 267, 269, 272, 277, 282, 285, 286, 295, 297, 298, 306, 351, 458, 496, 624, 702, 727, 780.

306 Overstepping: motion beyond

N. *overstepping,* transcursion, transilience, leap-frog 305n. *passage;* transcendence 34n. *superiority;* excursion, extravagation 282n. *deviation;* transgression, trespass 936n. *guilt;* usurpation, encroachment 916n. *arrogation;* infringement, infraction, intrusion 916n. *undueness;* expansionism, greediness 859n. *desire;* over-extension, ribbon development 197n. *expansion;* overfulfillment; excessiveness 637n. *redundance;* overrating 482n. *overestimation;* overdoing it 546n. *exaggeration;* over-indulgence 943n. *intemperance.*

Adj. *surpassing* etc. vb.; one up on 34adj. *superior;* over-extended, overlong, overhigh; too strong, overpowered; excessive 32adj. *exorbitant;* out of bounds, out of reach.

Vb. *overstep,* overpass, overgo, leave behind; go beyond, go too far; exceed, exceed the limit; overrun, override, overshoot, overshoot the mark, aim too high; overlap 226vb. *overlie;* surmount, jump over, leap o., skip o., leap-frog 312vb. *leap;* step over, cross 305vb. *pass;* cross the Rubicon, pass the point of no return; overfill, brim over, spill o. 54vb. *fill;* overfulfill 637vb. *superabound;* overdo 546vb. *exaggerate;* strain, stretch, stretch a point; overbid, overcall one's hand, have one's bluff called, overestimate 482vb. *overrate;* over-indulge 943vb. *be intemperate;* overstay, oversleep 136vb. *be late.*

encroach, break bounds, make inroads 712vb. *attack;* infringe, transgress, trespass 954vb. *be illegal;* poach 788vb. *steal;* squat, usurp 786vb. *appropriate;* barge in, horn in 297vb. *intrude;* overlap, impinge, trench upon, entrench on; eat away, erode 655vb. *impair;* infest, overrun 297vb. *irrupt;* overflow, flood 341vb. *drench.*

outdo, exceed, surpass, outclass; transcend, rise above, mount a., soar a., outsoar, outrange, outrival 34vb. *be superior;* go one better, overcall, overbid, outbid; outwit, overreach 542vb. *befool;* outmaneuver, outflank, gain the weather-gauge; steal a march on; make the running 277vb. *move fast;* outgo, outpace, outwalk, outmarch, outrun, outride, outjump, outsail, outdistance, distance; overhaul, gain upon, overtake, come in front, shoot ahead; lap, leave standing 277vb. *outstrip;* leave behind, race, beat, beat hollow 727vb. *defeat.*

See: 34, 54, 136, 197, 226, 277, 282, 297, 305, 312, 341, 482, 542, 546, 637, 655, 712, 727, 786, 788, 859, 916, 936, 943, 954.

307 Shortcoming

N. *shortcoming,* falling short, inadequacy etc. vb. 636n. *insufficiency;* a minus, deficit, short measure, shortage, shortfall, loss 42vb. *decrement;* leeway, drift 282n. *deviation;* unfinished state 55n. *incompleteness;* non-fulfillment, delinquency, default, defalcation 726n. *non-completion;* labor in vain 641n. *lost labor;* no go 728n. *failure;* fault, defect 647n. *imperfection,* 845n. *blemish;* something missing, want, lack, need 627n. *requirement.*

Adj. *deficient,* short, short of, minus, wanting, lacking, missing; catalectic; underpowered, substandard; half-done, perfunctory 55adj. *incomplete;* out of one's depth, not up to scratch, inadequate 636adj. *insufficient;* failing, running short 636adj. *scarce;* unattained, unreached, tantalizing.

Vb. *fall short,* come s., run s. 636vb. *not suffice;* not stretch, not reach to; lack, want, be without 627vb. *require;* miss, miss the mark; lag 136vb. *be late;* stop short, fall by the way, not stay the course; break down, stick in the mud, get bogged down; fall behind, lose ground, slip back; slump, collapse 286vb. *regress;* fall through, fall to the ground, come to nothing, end in smoke, fizzle out, fail 728vb. *miscarry;* miss stays, lose s.; labor in vain 641n. *waste effort;* tantalize, not come up to expectations 509vb. *disappoint.*

Adv. *behindhand,* in arrears; not enough; below the mark, far from it; to no purpose, in vain.

See: 42, 55, 136, 282, 286, 509, 627, 636, 641, 647, 726, 728, 845.

308 Ascent: motion upwards

N. *ascent,* ascension, upward motion, gaining height; defiance of gravity, levitation; taking off, leaving ground, takeoff 296n. *departure;* flying up, soaring, spiraling, mushrooming; zooming, zoom 271n. *aeronautics;* culmination 213n. *summit;* floating up, surfacing, breaking surface; going up, rising, uprising; rise, uprise, upgrowth; uprush, upsurge 36n. *increase;* updraft, rising air, rising current; sunrise, sun-up, dawn 128n. *morning;* moonrise, star-rise; mounting, climbing, skylarking; hill-climbing, mountaineering, alpinism; ladder-climbing, escalade 712n. *attack;* jump, vault, pole-v., pole-jump 312n. *leap;* bounce 280n. *recoil;* rising ground, hill 209n. *high land;* gradient, slope, ramp 220n. *acclivity;* rising pitch 410n. *musical note;* means of ascent, stairs, steps, flight of stairs, staircase, stairway, landing; ladder, step-l., accommodation l., Jacob's l., companion-way; rope-ladder, ratline; stair, step, tread, rung; lift, ski-l., elevator, escalator 310n. *lifter;* fire escape 667n. *means of escape.*

climber, mountaineer, alpinist, cragsman, Alpine Club; stegophilist; foretopman, steeple-jack; excelsior-figure; rocket, sky-r.; soarer, lark, skylark, laverock; gusher, spouter, geyser, fountain 350n. *stream.*

Adj. *ascending,* rising etc. vb., climbing, scansorial, scandent; rearing, rampant; buoyant, floating 323adj. *light;* supernatant, superfluitant; airborne, gaining height; excelsior; anabatic, in the ascendant; uphill, steep 215n. *vertical;* ladderlike, scalar, scalariform; scalable, climbable.

Vb. *ascend,* rise, uprise, leave the ground; defy gravity, levitate; take off, become airborne, fly up 271vb. *fly;* gain height, mount, soar, spiral, zoom, climb; reach the top, reach the zenith, culminate; float up, bob up, surface, break water; jump up, spring; dance, toss 312vb. *leap;*

bounce 280vb. *recoil;* push up, grow up, upheave; tower, aspire, spire 209vb. *be high;* gush, spurt, spout, jet, play 298vb. *flow out;* get up, start up, stand up, rear, rear up, ramp 215vb. *be vertical;* rise to one's feet, vacate one's seat 920vb. *show respect;* trend upwards, wind u., slope u., steepen 220vb. *be oblique;* take an upturn, improve 654vb. *get better;* go up, blow up, explode.

climb, walk up, struggle up; mount, make *or* work one's way up; go climbing, mountaineer; skylark; clamber, scramble, swarm up, shin up, monkey up, climb hand over fist; surmount, top, breast, scale, scale the heights 209vb. *be high;* go over the top, escalade 712vb. *attack;* go upstairs, mount a ladder; mount (a horse), climb into the saddle.

Adv. *up,* uphill, upstairs; excelsior, ever higher; hand over fist.

See: 36, 128, 209, 213, 215, 220, 271, 280, 296, 298, 310, 312, 323, 350, 410, 654, 667, 712, 920.

309 Descent

N. *descent,* descension, declension; declination 282n. *deviation;* falling, dropping, landing; downward trend, decline, drop, slump 37n. *decrease;* come-down, demotion 872n. *humiliation;* downfall, debacle, collapse 165n. *ruin;* trip, stumble; titubation, lurch, capsize 221n. *overturning;* tumble, cropper, crash, fate of Icarus; downrush, swoop, stoop, pounce; dive, header, belly-flop 313n. *plunge;* nose-dive, power-d. 271n. *aeronautics;* sliding down, glissade; subsidence, landslide, avalanche; downdraft 352n. *wind;* downpour, shower 350n. *rain;* cascade, nappe 350n. *waterfall;* downthrow (geology); declivity, hill, slope, tilt, dip 220n. *acclivity;* precipice, sheer drop 215n. *verticality;* submergence, sinkage 311n. *depression;* boring, tunnelling, burrowing, mining, sapping, undermining 263n. *tunnel;* speleology, pot-holing; descender, faller, tumbler; plunger 313n. *diver;* burrower, miner, sapper 255n. *excavator;* parachutist 271n. *aeronaut;* paratrooper 722n. *soldier;* speleologist, pot-holer.

Adj. *descending* etc. vb.; descendant, declining, declivitous 220adj. *sloping;* labent, decurrent, decursive, swooping; deciduous; tumble-down, falling, titubant, tottering; tilting, nodding to its fall; sinking, foundering; burrowing, sapping; demoted, downcast, down at heart, drooping 311adj. *depressed;* submersible, sinkable.

Vb. *descend,* come down, go d., dip d.; decline, abate, ebb 37vb. *decrease;* go downhill, slump 655vb. *deteriorate;* reach a lower level, fall, drop, sink; soak in, seep down 297vb. *infiltrate;* get lower and lower, reach the depths, touch depth, touch bottom 210vb. *be low;* reach one's nadir 35vb. *be inferior;* sink to the bottom, gravitate, precipitate, settle, set; fall down, fall in, cave in, fall to the ground, collapse; sink in, subside, slip, give way; hang down, prolapse, droop, sag, swag 217vb. *hang;* go under water, draw, have draft; submerge, fill the tanks, dive 313vb. *plunge;* drown 313vb. *founder;* go underground, sink into the earth; dig down, burrow, bore, tunnel, mine, sap, undermine 255vb. *make concave;* drop from the sky, parachute; swoop, stoop, pounce; fly down, flutter d.; lose height, drop down, swing low; touch down, alight, light, perch 295vb. *land;* lower oneself, get down, climb d., step d., get off, fall o., dismount; slide down, glissade, luge, toboggan; fall like rain, shower, pour, cascade, drip, drizzle, patter 350vb. *rain;* take a lower place, come down a peg 872vb. *be humble;* make an obeisance, bow down, dip, duck 311vb. *stoop;* flop, plop.

tumble, fall; tumble down, fall d.; topple, nod to its fall; topple over, overbalance, capsize 221vb. *be inverted;* miss one's footing, slip, slip up, trip, stumble; lose one's balance, titubate, stagger, totter, lurch, tilt 220vb. *be oblique;* rise and fall, pitch, toss, roll; take a header, dive 313vb. *plunge;* take a running jump, precipitate oneself 312vb. *leap;* fall off, take a fall, be thrown, come a cropper, go for a Burton; fall on one's face, fall prostrate, bite the dust, measure one's length; plop, plump, plump down 311vb. *sit down;* slump, sprawl; fall through the air, spiral, spiral down, nose-dive, crash, prang.

Adv. *down,* downwards, adown; downhill, downstairs, downstream; nose-down.

See: 35, 37, 165, 210, 215, 217, 220, 221, 255, 263, 271, 282, 295, 297, 311, 312, 313, 350, 352, 655, 722, 872.

310 Elevation

N. *elevation,* raising etc. vb.; erection, sublevation, upheaval; picking up, lift; uplift, leg-up 703vb. *aid;* sublimation, exaltation; assumption, bodily a.; uprising, uptrend, upswing 308n. *ascent;* defiance of gravity, levitation; an elevation, eminence 209n. *high land,* 254n. *prominence;* height above sea level 209n. *height.*

lifter, erector, builder, steel-erector, spiderman; raiser, lightener, yeast 323n. *leaven;* lever, jack 218n. *pivot;* dredger; crane, derrick, hoist, windlass; winch, capstan, jeer-c.; purchase, rope and pulley, block and tackle, luff-tackle, jeers; dumb waiter, lift, ski-l., elevator; escalator, moving staircase 274n. *conveyor;* hot air, gas, hydrogen, helium; spring, springboard, trampoline.

Adj. *elevated* etc. vb.; exalted, uplifted; erectile, attollent; erected, set up; upright, erect, upstanding, rampant 215adj. *vertical;* mounted, on high; lofty, sublime 209adj. *high.*

Vb. *elevate,* heighten 209vb. *make higher;* puff up, blow up, swell, leaven 197vb. *enlarge;* raise, erect, set up, put up, run up, rear up, build up, build; lift, lift up, raise up, heave up; uplift, upraise; jack up, prop 218vb. *support;* prevent from falling, hold up, bear up, upbear; prevent from sinking, buoy, buoy up; raise aloft, hold a., hold up, wave; hoist, haul up, brail, trice; furl 261vb. *fold;* raise from the ground, pick up, take up; pull up, wind up; weigh, trip (anchor); fish up, drag up, dredge up, dredge 304vb. *extract;* exalt, sublimate; chair, shoulder; put on a pedestal; put on top, mount 313vb. *crown;* jump up, bounce up 285vb. *promote;* give a lift, give a leg-up 703vb. *aid;* throw in the air, throw up, cast up, toss up; sky, loft; send up, shoot up, lob 287vb. *propel;* perk, perk up (one's head); prick up (one's ears); bristle, bristle up.

lift oneself, arise, rise 308vb. *ascend;* stand up, get up, jump up, leap up, spring up, spring to one's feet; pull oneself up; hold oneself up, hold one's head up, draw oneself up to one's full height, stand on tiptoe 215vb. *be vertical.*

Adv. *on,* on stilts, on tiptoe; on one's legs, on one's hind legs; on the shoulders of, on the back of.

See: 197, 209, 215, 218, 254, 261, 274, 285, 287, 304, 308, 313, 323, 703.

311 Depression

N. *depression,* lowering, hauling down etc. vb.; pushing down, detrusion 279n. *impulse;* ducking, sousing 313n. *plunge;* debasement 655n. *deterioration;* demotion, reduction 872n. *humiliation;* subversion 149n. *revolution;* overthrow, prostration 216n. *supination;* overturn, overset, upset 221n. *overturning;* precipitation, defenestration 287n. *propulsion;* keeping under, suppression; a depression, dent, dip, hollow 255n. *cavity;* low pressure 340n. *weather.*

obeisance, reverence, bow, salaam, kowtow, kissing hands 884n. *courtesy;* curtsy, court c., bob, duck, nod 884n. *courteous act;* kneeling, genuflection 920n. *respect.*

Adj. *depressed* etc. vb.; at a low ebb 210adj. *low;* prostrate 216adj. *supine;* sedentary, sitting, sit-down; depressive, detrusive; submersible.

Vb. *depress,* detrude, push down, thrust d. 279vb. *impel;* shut down (a lid) 264vb. *close;* hold down, keep d., hold under 165vb. *suppress;* lower, let down, take d.; lower a flag, dip, half-mast, haul down, strike; deflate, defizz, puncture 198vb. *make smaller;* let drop (**see** *let fall*); pitch, precipitate; defenestrate, fling down, send headlong, drop over the side; sink, scuttle, send to the bottom, drown 309vb. *descend;* duck, souse, douse, dip 313vb. *plunge;* weigh on, press on 322vb. *weigh;* capsize, roll over, tip, tilt 221vb. *invert;* crush, stave in, bash in, dent, hollow 255vb. *make concave.*

let fall, drop, shed; let go 779vb. *not retain;* let slip *or* slide through one's fingers; pour, pour out, decant 300vb. *void;* spill, slop 341vb. *moisten;* sprinkle, shower, scatter, dust; sow, broadcast 75vb. *disperse;* lay down, put d., set d., throw d., fling d. (**see** *fell*); pitch *or* chuck overboard, drop over the side; precipitate, send headlong, defenestrate 287vb. *propel.*

fell, trip, topple, tumble, overthrow; prostrate, lay low, lay one on his back 216vb. *flatten;* knock down, bowl over, floor, drop, down; throw down, cast d., fling d. (**see** *let fall*); pull down, tear d., dash d., raze, slight, level, raze to the ground, pull about one's ears, trample in the dust 165vb. *demolish;* hew down, cut d., lumber 46vb. *cut;* blow down 352vb. *blow;* bring down, undermine; bring down, shoot d., wing 287vb. *shoot.*

abase, debase, lower the standard; water, adulterate 655vb. *deteriorate;* demote, reduce to the ranks, cashier 752vb. *depose;* humble, deflate, puncture, debunk, bate one's pretensions, take down a peg, cut down to size, take the wind out of one's sails, take a rise out of 872vb. *humiliate;* crush, squash 165vb. *suppress;* snub 883vb. *make unwelcome.*

sit down, sit, be seated, sit on the ground, squat, squat on one's hunkers; kneel, recline, couch, stretch oneself out 216vb. *be horizontal;* roost, nest 683vb. *repose;* take a seat, seat oneself, park one's hips; perch, alight 309vb. *descend.*

stoop, bend, bend down, get d.; bend over, bend forward, bend backward; lean forward, lean over backward; cringe, crouch, cower 721vb. *knuckle under;* bow, scrape, arch one's back; duck, bob, curtsy, bob a c. 884vb. *pay respects;* nod, incline one's head 488vb. *assent;* bow down, do reverence, make obeisance, kiss hands, salaam, prostrate oneself, kowtow 920vb. *show respect;* kneel, kneel to, genuflect.

See: 46, 75, 149, 165, 198, 210, 216, 221, 255, 264, 279, 287, 300, 309, 313, 322, 340, 341, 352, 488, 655, 683, 721, 752, 779, 872, 883, 884, 920.

312 Leap

N. *leap,* saltation, skipping, capering, leap-frogging; jump, hop, skip; spring, bound, vault; high jump, long j., running j.; hop, skip and a jump; caper, gambol, frolic; kick, high k.; prance, curvet, caracole, capriole, demivolt, gambado, buck, buckjump; springy step, light tread 265n. *gait;* dance step; dance, reel, jig, Highland fling, cakewalk 837n. *dancing.*

jumper, high-j., pole-vaulter, hurdler, steeplechaser; skipper, hopper, leapfrogger; caperer, prancer; dancer, waltzer, foxtrotter, jiver, hoofer, shuffler; tap-dancer, soft-shoe d.; ballerina, corps de ballet; male dancer, dancing man; dancing girl, nautch girl 594n. *entertainer;* kangaroo, stag, goat, chamois, springbok, jumping-mouse; jerboa, grasshopper, cicada, frog, flea; bucking horse, bucker; jumping cracker, jumping bean; jumping jack, Jack-in-the-box 837n. *plaything.*

Adj. *leaping* etc. vb.; saltatory, saltatorial; skittish, frisky, fresh 819adj. *lively;* skipping, hopping; dancing, choric; bobbing, bucking, bouncing; tossing.

Vb. *leap,* jump, take a running j.; spring, bound, vault, pole-v., hurdle, jump over the sticks, steeplechase, take one's fences; skip, hop, leapfrog, bob, bounce, buck, bob up and down, dab; trip, foot it, tread a measure, stamp, hoof it 837vb. *dance;* caper, cut capers, gambol, frisk, gambado; prance, paw the ground, ramp, rear, backjump, plunge; cavort, curvet, caracole; start, startle, give a jump; jump up, leap up, spring up 308vb. *ascend;* jump over, clear, leap over the moon; flounce, flounder, jerk 318vb. *be agitated;* writhe 251vb. *wriggle.*

Adv. *by leaps and bounds,* on the light fantastic toe, trippingly; at a single bound.

See: 251, 265, 308, 318, 594, 819, 837.

313 Plunge

N. *plunge,* swoop, pounce, stoop 309n. *descent;* nose-dive, power dive 271n. *aeronautics;* dive, header, belly-flop; dip, ducking; immersion, submergence; crashdive; drowning, sinking; gambler's plunge, gamble 618n. *gambling.*

diver, frogman, under-water swimmer; diving bird, merganser 365n. *waterfowl;* submariner; submarine, bathysphere, sinker, diving-bell; plunger, lead, plummet; fathometer 465n. *meter.*

Vb. *plunge,* dip, duck, bathe 341vb. *be wet;* fall in, jump in, plump, plop; dive, make a plunge, take a header; welter, wallow, pitch and toss; souse, douse, immerse, submerse, drown; submerge, flood the tanks, crash-dive 309vb. *descend;* sink, scuttle, send to the bottom, send to Davy Jones's locker 311vb. *depress;* sound, fathom, plumb the depths, heave the lead 465vb. *measure;* plunge into 857vb. *be rash.*

founder, go down 309vb. *descend;* get out of one's depth; drown, settle down, go to the bottom, go down like a stone; sink, sink like lead, sink like a sack of potatoes.

See: 271, 309, 311, 341, 365, 465, 618, 857.

314 Circuition: curvilinear motion

N. *circuition,* circulation, circumambulation, circumnavigation, circling, wheeling, gyre, spiral 315n. *rotation;* turning, cornering, turn, U-turn

286n. *return;* orbit; ambit, compass, lap; circuit, tour, round trip, full circle; helix 251n. *coil;* unwinding 316n. *evolution;* circuitousness, circumbendibus, roundabout way, northwest passage.

circler, girdler, circumambulator; circumnavigator 270n. *mariner*; circuiter 957n. *judge;* circuitor 690n. *manager;* roundsman 794n. *tradesman;* patrol, patrolman 441n. *spectator;* moon, satellite 321n. *planet.*

Adj. *circuitous,* turning etc. vb.; circumforaneous, peripatetic 267adj. *traveling;* circumfluent, circumambient; circumflex 248adj. *curved;* circumnavigable; devious 626adj. *roundabout,* 282adj. *deviating;* orbital.

Vb. *circle,* circulate, go the round, make the round of; compass, circuit, make a c., lap; tour, do the round trip; go round, skirt; circumambulate, circumnavigate, circumaviate; go round the world, put a girdle round the earth; turn, round, double a point, weather a p.; round a corner, corner, turn a c.; revolve, orbit; wheel, spiral, come full circle, box the compass, chase one's tail 315vb. *rotate;* turn round, bend r.; put about, wheel a., face a., turn on one's heel 286vb. *turn back;* draw a circle, describe a circle 232vb. *circumscribe;* curve, wind, twist, wind one's way 251vb. *meander;* make a detour 626vb. *circuit.*

See: 215, 232, 248, 251, 267, 270, 282, 286, 315, 316, 321, 441, 626, 690, 794, 957.

315 Rotation: motion in a continued circle

N. *rotation,* orbital motion, revolving, orbiting; revolution, full circle; gyration, circling, spiraling; circulation, circumfluence; spinning motion, spin, circumrotation, circumgyration, circumvolution, turbination; rolling, volutation 285n. *progression;* spiral, roll, turn, twirl, waltz, pirouette, reel 837n. *dance;* whirlabout, whirl, whirr; dizzy round, rat race 678n. *overactivity;* dizziness, vertigo; turning power, turning tendency, verticity; science of rotatory motion, gyrostatics, trochilics.

vortex, whirl; whirlwind, whirlblast, tornado, cyclone 352n. *gale;* waterspout, whirlpool, swirl, surge, gurge 350n. *eddy;* Maelstrom, Charybdis; smoke-ring 250n. *loop.*

rotator, rotor, spinner; whirl, whirligig, teetotum, yo-yo, top, peg t., spinning t., humming t.; roundabout, merry-go-round; churn, whisk; potter's wheel, lathe, mandrel, circular saw; spinning wheel, charka, spinning jenny, whorl; flywheel, prayer-w., roulette-w., wheel of fortune 250n. *wheel;* gyroscope, gyrostat; turntable; phonograph record; windmill, fan, sail; propeller, prop, screw, air-s.; winder, capstan 310n. *lifter;* swivel, hinge; spit, jack; spindle, axle, axis, shaft 218n. *pivot;* reel, roller, rolling pin 252n. *cylinder;* rolling stone, planet 268n. *wanderer;* Ixion.

Adj. *rotary,* trochilic; rotating, spinning etc. vb.; rotary, rotatory, circumrotatory; gyratory, gyroscopic, gyrostatic; gyral; circling, cyclic; vortical, vorticose, vorticular; cyclonic, turbinated; vertiginous, dizzy.

Vb. *rotate,* revolve, orbit, go into orbit, assume an o. 314vb. *circle;* turn right round, box the compass, chase one's own tail; spin, spin like a top, spin like a teetotum, twirl, pirouette; circumvolve, gyre, gyrate, waltz, wheel; whirl, whir, hum 404vb. *resound;* swirl, eddy 350 vb. *flow*; bowl, trundle, troll, trill; set rolling, roll, roll along; spin with one's fingers, twirl; churn, whisk 43vb. *mix;* turn, crank, wind, reel, spin, yarn; slue, slue round, swing round; roll up, furl 261vb. *fold;* roll itself up, scroll; wallow, welter; mill around.

Adv. *round and round,* in a circle, in circles, clockwise, anticlockwise, counter-clockwise, sunwise, widdershins; head over heels.

See: 43, 218, 250, 252, 261, 268, 285, 310, 314, 350, 352, 404, 678, 837.

316 Evolution: motion in a reverse circle

N. *evolution,* unrolling, unfolding, unfurling; explication, denouement 154n. *eventuality;* counter-spin, eversion 221n. *inversion;* development 157n. *growth;* evolutionism, Darwinism.

Adj. *evolving,* unwinding etc. vb.; evolved etc. vb.; evolutionary, evolutionistic.

Vb. *evolve,* unfold, unfurl, unroll, unwind, uncoil, uncurl, untwist, untwine, explicate, unravel, disentangle 60vb. *order;* evolute, develop, grow into 147vb. *be turned to;* roll back 263vb. *open.*

See: 60, 147, 154, 157, 221, 263.

317 Oscillation: reciprocating motion

N. *oscillation,* libration, nutation, lunar n.; harmonic motion, pendular m., swing of the pendulum; vibration, vibratiuncle, tremor; vibrancy, resonance 141n. *periodicity;* pulsation, throbbing, drumming, pulse, beat, throb; flutter, palpitation 318n. *agitation;* breathing 352n. *respiration;* undulation, wave-motion, frequency, frequency band, wavelength 417n. *radiation;* heat wave, sound w., radio w., sky-w., tidal w., tsunami 350n. *wave;* seismic disturbance, earthquake, ground wave, tremor 176n. *violence;* seismology, seismograph, vibroscope; oscillator, vibrator; pendulum, bob 217n. *pendant.* **See** *fluctuation.*

fluctuation, wave motion (**see** *oscillation*); alternation, reciprocation 12n. *correlation;* to-and-fro movement, coming and going, shuttle service; ups and downs, boom and bust, ebb and flow, flux and reflux, systole and diastole; night and day 14n. *contrariety;* reeling, lurching, rolling, pitching; roll, pitch, lurch, stagger, reel; shake, wag, dance; springboard 328n. *elasticity;* swing, see-saw; rocker, rocking chair, rocking horse; shuttlecock, shuttle; mental fluctuation, wavering, vacillation 601n. *irresolution,* 474n. *dubiety.*

Adj. *oscillating* etc. vb.; oscillatory, undulatory; swaying, libratory; pulsatory, palpitating, vibratory, vibratile; earth-shaking, seismic; pendular, pendulous, dangling; reeling, staggery, groggy; rhythmic, rhythmical 141adj. *periodic.*

Vb. *oscillate,* emit waves 417vb. *radiate;* undulate; vibrate, pulsate, pulse, beat, drum; tick, throb, palpitate; respire, exhale, inhale, pant, heave 352vb. *breathe;* nutate, librate; play, sway, nod; swing, dangle 217vb. *hang;* see-saw, rock; give, swag; hunt, lurch, reel, stagger, tooter, teeter, waddle, wobble, wiggle, waggle, wag; bob, bounce, bob up and down, dance 312vb. *leap;* toss, roll, pitch, tumble, wallow; rattle, chatter, shake; flutter, quiver, shiver 318vb. *be agitated;* flicker 417vb. *shine;* echo 404vb. *resound.* **See** *fluctuate.*

fluctuate, alternate, reciprocate 12vb. *correlate;* ebb and flow, come and go, pass and repass, leap-frog; wamble, slop about inside one; wallow, flounder 313vb. *plunge.*

brandish, wave, wag, waggle, shake, flourish; wave to and fro, shake up and down, flutter.

Adv. *to and fro,* backward and forward, in and out, up and down, side to side, left to right and right to left; zig-zag, see-saw, wibble-wabble; like buckets in a well; shuttlewise.

See: 12, 14, 141, 176, 217, 312, 313, 318, 328, 350, 352, 404, 417, 474, 601.

318 Agitation: irregular motion

N. *agitation,* irregular motion, jerkiness, fits and starts, unsteadiness 152n. *changeableness;* joltiness, bumpiness, broken water, choppiness, pitching, rolling 259n. *roughness;* unsteady beam, flicker, twinkle 417n. *flash;* sudden motion, start, jump 508n. *inexpectation;* shaking, succussion, shake, jig, jiggle; toss 287n. *propulsion;* shock, jar, jolt, jerk, jounce, bounce, bump, rock 279n. *knock;* nudge, dig 547n. *gesture;* vibration, thrill, throb, pulse, pit-a-pat, palpitation, flutter 317n. *oscillation;* shuddering, shudder, shiver, frisson; quiver, quaver, tremor; tremulousness, trembling, palsy (**see** *spasm*); restlessness, feverishness, fever; tossing, turning, jactitation, jactitance; jiving, hopping 678n. *activity,* 837n. *dancing;* itchiness, itch, vellication 378n. *formication;* twitchiness. twitch, grimacing, grimace; mental agitation, perturbation, disquiet 825n. *worry;* trepidation, jumpiness, twitter, flap 854n. *nervousness;* the shakes, jumps, jitters, shivers, fidgets, "the channels," aspen, aspen-leaf.

spasm, ague, rigor, chattering; uncontrollable tremor, palsy; twitch, subsultus; tic, nervous t.; chorea, St. Vitus' dance, the jerks; tarantism; lockjaw, tetanus; cramp, the cramps; throe 377n. *pang;* convulsion, paroxysm, access, orgasm 503n. *frenzy;* staggers, megrims; fit, epilepsy, falling sickness; pulse, throb 317n. *oscillation;* attack, seizure, stroke.

commotion, turmoil, turbulence, tumult, tumultuation; hurly-burly, hubbub, bobbery, brouhaha; fever, rush, rout 680n. *haste;* furore 503n. *frenzy;* fuss, bother 678n. *restlessness;* racket, din 400n. *loudness;* stir, ferment, boiling, fermentation, ebullition, effervescence 355n. *bubble;* ground swell, heavy sea 350n. *wave;* tempest, thunderstorm, magnetic s. 176n. *storm;* whirlpool 315n. *vortex;*

whirlwind 352n. *gale;* disturbance, atmospherics.

Adj. *agitated,* shaken, fluttering, waving, brandished; shaking, successive; troubled, unquiet 819adj. *lively;* feverish, fevered, restless; scratchy, jittery, jumpy, all of a twitter, in a flap, in a flutter 854adj. *nervous;* hopping, leaping, like a cat on hot bricks; breathless, panting; subsultory, twitching, itchy; convulsive, spasmodic, spastic; saltatory, choreic, choreal; giddy-paced 456adj. *light-minded;* doddering, palsied, aguey; shaky, tremulous, a-tremble; thrilling, vibrating 317adj. *oscillating.*

Vb. *be agitated,* ripple, popple, boil 355vb. *bubble;* stir, move, dash; shake, tremble, quiver, quaver, shiver; have an ague, throw a fit; writhe, squirm, itch, twitch 251vb. *wriggle;* jactitate, toss, turn, toss about, thresh a.; kick, plunge 176vb. *be violent;* flounder, flop, wallow, roll, reel, pitch 317vb. *fluctuate;* sway, swag 220vb. *be oblique;* pulse, beat, thrill, vibrate; wag, waggle, wobble, stagger, lurch, dodder, totter, teeter, dither 317vb. *oscillate;* whir, whirl 315vb. *rotate;* jump about, hop, bob, bounce, dance 312vb. *leap;* flicker, twinkle, gutter, sputter, spatter 417vb. *shine;* flap, flutter, twitter, start, jump; throb, pant, palpitate, go pit-a-pat 821vb. *be excited;* bustle, rush, mill around 61vb. *rampage;* ramp, roar 891vb. *be angry.*

agitate, disturb, rumple, ruffle, untidy 63vb. *derange;* discompose, perturb, worry 827vb. *displease;* ripple, puddle, muddy; stir, stir up 43vb. *mix;* whisk, whip, beat, churn 315vb. *rotate;* toss, wallop 287vb. *propel;* shake up, succuss, shake; wag, waggle, wave, flourish 317vb. *brandish;* flutter, fly (a flag); jog, joggle, jiggle, jolt, jounce, nudge, dig; jerk, pluck, twitch, vellicate.

effervesce, froth, spume, foam, foam at the mouth, bubble, bubble up 355vb. *bubble;* boil, boil over, seethe, simmer, sizzle, spit 379vb. *be hot;* ferment, work.

Adv. *jerkily,* pit-a-pat; subsultorily etc. adj.; by fits and starts, with a hop, skip and a jump; spasmodically, convulsively, in convulsions, in fits, in spasms.

See: 43, 61, 63, 152, 176, 220, 251, 259, 279, 287, 312, 315, 317, 350, 352, 355, 377, 378, 379, 400, 417, 456, 503, 508, 547, 678, 819, 821, 825, 827, 837, 854, 891.

319 Materiality

N. *materiality,* materialness, empirical world, world of experience; corporeity, corporeality, corporality, corporalness, bodiliness; material existence, world of nature 3n. *substantiality;* physical being, physical condition 1n. *existence;* plenum 321n. *world;* concreteness, tangibility, palpability, solidity 324n. *density;* weight 322n. gravity, 638n. *importance;* personality, individuality 80n. *specialty;* embodiment, incarnation, reincarnation, metempsychosis; realization, materialization; hylism, positivism, materialism, dialectical m., Marxism; unspirituality, worldliness, sensuality 944n. *sensualism;* materialist, hylicist; realist, somatist, positivist.

matter, brute m., stuff; plenum; hyle, prime matter, prima materia; mass, material, body, frame 331n. *structure;* substance, solid s., corpus; organic matter, flesh, flesh and blood, plasma, protoplasm 358n. *organism;* real world, world of nature, Nature.

object, tangible o., bird in the hand; inanimate object, still life; flesh and blood, real person 371n. *person;* thing, gadget, something, commodity, article, item; sticks and stones 359n. *mineral;* raw material 631n. *materials.*

element, elementary unit, sense datum; principle, first p. 68n. *origin;* the four elements, earth, air, fire, water; unit of being, monad; factor, ingredient 58n. *component;* chemical element, basic substance; physical element, atom, molecule; fundamental particle, subatom, electron, beta particle, negatron, positron, neutron, meson, proton 33n. *particle;* nucleus, nucleon; helium nucleus, alpha particle; neutrino, hyperion; anti-particle, anti-electron; photon; quantum; ion.

physics, physical science, science of matter; science of bodies, somatics, somatology; nuclear physics; applied physics, technology 694n. *skill;* natural philosophy, experimental p. 490n. *science.*

Adj. *material,* hylic; real, natural; massy, solid, concrete, palpable, tangible, ponderable, sensible; weighty 638adj. *important;* somatoscopic, somatic; physical, spatiotemporal; objective, impersonal, neuter; hypostatic 3adj. *substantial;* incarnate, incorporate; coporeal, bodily, fleshly, of flesh and blood, incorporated, reincarnated, realized, materialized;

materialistic, worldly, unspiritual 944n. *sensual.*

Vb. *materialize,* substantialize, hypostatize, corporealize; objectify 223vb. *externalize;* realize, make real, body forth; embody, incorporate; incarnate, personify; substantiate.

See: 1, 3, 33, 58, 68, 80, 223, 321, 322, 324, 331, 358, 359, 371, 490, 631, 638, 694, 944.

320 Immateriality

N. *immateriality,* unreality 4n. *insubstantiality;* incorporeity, incorporeality, dematerialization, disembodiment, inextension, imponderability, intangibility, ghostliness, shadowiness; superficiality 639adj. *unimportance;* immaterialism, idealism, Platonism; spirituality, other worldliness; animism; spiritualism, psychism 984n. *occultism;* other world, world of spirits, astral plane; eternity 115n. *perpetuity;* animist, spiritualist 984n. *occultist;* idealist 449n. *philosopher;* astral body 970n. *ghost.*

subjectivity, personality, selfhood, myself, me, yours truly; ego, id, superego; psyche, higher self, spiritual s. 80n. *self.*

Adj. *immaterial,* immateriate, without mass; incorporeal, incorporal, asomatous; aery, ghostly, shadowy 4adj. *insubstantial;* unextended, imponderable, intangible; superficial 639adj. *unimportant;* bodiless, unembodied, discarnate, disembodied; supernal, extramundane, unearthly, supersensory, psychic, pneumatoscopic, spiritistic, astral 984adj. *psychic;* spiritual, otherwordly 973adj. *religious;* personal, subjective.

Vb. *disembody,* spiritualize, dematerialize, disincarnate.

See: 4, 80, 115, 450, 639, 970, 973, 984, 987.

321 Universe

N. *universe,* omneity 52n. *whole;* world, creation, all c.; sum of things, plenum, matter and anti-matter; cosmos, macrocosm, microcosm; space-time continuum; expanding universe, island u.; anagalactic space, metagalactic s.

world, wide w., four corners of the earth; home of man, sublunary sphere; earth, middle e.; globe, sphere, terrestrial s., terraqueous globe, geoid, terrestrial surface, crust; subcrust, Moho; atlas, world-map 551n. *map;* Old World, New World; earth-shine; geocentric system, Ptolemaic s.; personal world, idioverse, life space, total situation 8n. *circumstance.*

heavens, sky, welkin, empyrean, ether, ethereal sphere; firmament, vault of heaven; night-sky, starlit s., aurora borealis, northern lights, aurora australis; zodiacal light, counterglow, gegenschein.

star, heavenly body, celestial b.; sidereal sphere, starry host, host of heaven; asterism, constellation, Great Bear, Little B., Plow, Dipper, Charles' Wain, Cassiopeia's Chair, Pleiades, Orion, Orion's Belt, Southern Cross; starlight, starshine; population I, population II; main sequence, blue star, white s., yellow s., red s.; double star, binary, spectroscopic b., primary, secondary, component, comes; triple star, quadruple s., multiple s.; variable star, long-period variable, Mirid; short-period variable, Cepheid; pseudo-Cepheid; eclipsing variable, Algolid, Lyrid; irregular variable, secular v.; giant, supergiant, Betelgeuse; subgiant, dwarf, red d., white d., Sirius B; new star, nova, supernova, Tycho's star; pole star, North Star, Polaris, circumpolar star; Star of David, Star of Bethlehem; Milky Way, galactic plane, star cloud; star cluster, globular c., open c., moving c., local c.; galaxy, supergalaxy, island universe; stellar motion, star stream, radial velocity, proper motion.

nebula, galactic n., gaseous n., green n., irregular n., planetary n., invisible n., dark n., interstellar matter; extragalactic nebula, white n., Magellanic n., spiral n.

zodiac, signs of the z., Aries (the Ram), Taurus (the Bull), Gemini (the Twins), Cancer (the Crab), Leo (the Lion), Virgo (the Virgin), Libra (the Balance), Scorpius *or* Scorpio (the Scorpion), Sagittarius (the Archer), Capricorn (the Goat), Aquarius (the Man with the Watering-pot), Pisces (the Fish); ecliptic; house, mansion, lunar m.

planet, major p., minor p., asteroid, planetoid; Mercury; Venus, morning star, evening s.; Mars, red planet; Earth, Jupiter, Saturn, Uranus, Neptune, Pluto; comet, hairy star, wandering s., Halley's comet; planetary orbit, cometary o., parabolic o., hyperbolic o.; ascending node, descending n.

meteor, falling star, shooting s., fire-

ball, meteorite, aerolite, bolide, chondrite; meteoroid; micrometeorite; meteor shower; radiant point.
sun, day-star, orb of day, midnight sun; parhelion, mock sun; sunlight, photosphere, chromosphere; facula, flocculus, sun spot, solar prominence, solar flare, corona; Sol, Helios, Titan, Phoebus; solar system, heliocentric s.
moon, satellite; new moon, old moon in the young moon's arm, waxing moon, waning m., half-m., crescent m., horned m., gibbous m., full m., harvest m., hunter's m.; paraselene, mock moon; man in the moon, lunarian; Luna, Diana, Phoebe, Cynthia, Hecate; moonlight.
satellite, earth s., artificial s., spaceship, space station, sputnik, lunik, arknik; moons of Mars, Phobos, Deimos; moons of Jupiter, Io, Europa, Ganymede, Callisto etc.; moons of Saturn, Mimas, Enceladus, Tethys, Dione, Rhea, Titan, Hyperion, Iapetus, Phoebe; moons of Uranus, Miranda, Ariel, Umbriel, Titania, Oberon; moons of Neptune, Triton, Nereid.
astronomy, star-lore, star-gazing, star-watching, meteor-w.; radio astronomy; astrophysics; stellar photography; selenography, uranography, uranology; astrology, astromancy, horoscope 511n. *divination;* observatory, planetarium; telescope, astronomical t., radio t., refractor, reflector, Newtonian telescope, Cassegrainian t., Gregorian t.; finder, eyepiece; object-glass, optic g., mirror, flat 442n. *telescope;* spectroscope, orrery, eidouranion, astrolabe; astronomer, radio a., astrophysicist; star-gazer, star-watcher; astrologer, astromancer.
uranometry, right ascension, declension, hour angle, hour circle, declination c.; reference c., great c.; celestial pole, galactic p., celestial equator, galactic e.; equinoctial colure, solstitial c., true equinox, vernal e., first point of Aries, autumnal equinox; geocentric latitude *or* longitude, heliocentric latitude *or* longitude, galactic latitude *or* longitude; node, ascending n., descending n.; libration, nutation; precession, precession of the equinox; solstice, lunistice.
cosmography, cosmology, cosmogony, cosmogonist, cosmographer.
geography, orography, oceanography, cosmography, physiography, geodesy, geology; geographer, geodesist, geologist; hydrology, hydrography, hydrogeology.

Adj. *cosmic,* universal, cosmic, cosmologic, cosmogonic, cosmographic; interstellar, intersidereal; galactic, metagalactic.
celestial, heavenly, empyreal, sphery; starry, star-spangled; sidereal, astral, stellar; solar, heliacal, zodiacal; lunary, lunar, selenic, lunate; lunisolar; nebular, nebulous; heliocentric, geocentric, planetocentric; cometary, meteoric, meteorological; uranological, uranometrical; equinoctial, solstitial.
planetary, planetoidal, asteroidal, satellitic, planetocentric; Mercurian, Venusian, Martian, Jovian, Saturnian, Neptunian, Plutonian.
telluric, tellurian, terrestrial, terrene, terraqueous; sublunary, subastral; Old-World, New-World; polar, equatorial; worldwide, world, global, international, universal 183adj. *spacious;* worldly, earthly.
astronomic, astronomical, astrophysical, star-gazing, star-watching; astrological, astromantic; telescopic, spectroscopic.
geographic, geographical, oceanographic, orographical; geologic; geodesic, geodetic, physiographic; hydrogeologic, hydrographic, hydrologic.

Adv. *under the sun,* on the face of the globe, here below, on earth.

See: 8, 52, 183, 276, 442, 511, 551.

322 Gravity

N. *gravity,* gravitation, force of gravity, gravitational pull; weight, weightiness, heaviness, ponderosity; specific gravity; incumbency, pressure, displacement, sinkage, draft; incubus, encumbrance, load, lading, freight; burden, burthen; ballast, makeweight, rider, counterpoise 31n. *offset;* mass, lump 324n. *solid body;* lump of, weight of, mass of; plummet 313n. *diver;* weight, bob, sinker, lead, stone, millstone; geostatics, statics.
weighment, weighing, ponderation; balancing, equipoise 28n. *equalization;* weights, avoirdupois weight, troy w., apothecary's w.; grain, carat, carat-grain, scruple, pennyweight, drachma; ounce, pound, stone, quarter, tod, quintal, hundredweight, ton; gram, kilogram; tola, seer, maund; megaton, kiloton; axle-load, laden weight.
scales, weighing-machine; steelyard,

beam; balance, spring-b.; pan, scale, weight; platform scale, weigh-bridge.

Adj. *weighty,* heavy, ponderous; leaden, heavy as lead; weighing etc. vb.; cumbersome, cumbrous 195adj. *unwieldy;* lumpish, massy, massive 324adj. *dense;* pressing, incumbent, superincumbent 735n. *oppressive;* having weight, weighing, with a weight of; weighted, loaded, charged, burdened; overweighted, overburdened, overloaded; gravitational, gravitative.

Vb. *weigh,* have weight, exert w., gravitate; weigh equal, balance 28vb. *be equal;* counterpoise, counterweigh 31vb. *compensate;* outweigh, overweigh, overbalance 34vb. *predominate;* tip the scale, turn the s., depress the s.; wallow, sink, gravitate, settle 313vb. *founder,* 309vb. *descend;* weigh heavy, be h., lie h.; press, weigh on, weigh one down, hang like a millstone 311vb. *depress;* load, cumber 702vb. *hinder;* try the weight of, take the weight of, put on the scales, lay in the scale 465vb. *measure;* weigh oneself, stand on the scales.

make heavy, weight, hang weights on; charge, burden, overweight, overburden, overload 193vb. *load.*

Adv. *weightily,* heavily, leadenly.

See: 28, 31, 34, 195, 309, 311, 313, 324, 465, 702.

323 Levity

N. *levity,* lightness etc. adj.; thinness, air, ether 325n. *rarity;* buoyance, buoyancy; volatility 338n. *vaporization;* weightlessness, imponderability, imponderableness; defiance of gravity, levitation 308n. *ascent;* feather-weight, feather-down, fluff, thistle-down, cobweb, gossamer; dust, mote, straw 4n. *insubstantial thing;* cork, buoy, bubble; gas, hot air, helium, hydrogen 310n. *lifter.*

leaven, lightener; ferment, enzyme, zymogen, barm, yeast, baking-powder, self-raising flour.

Adj. *light,* underweight 307adj. *deficient;* light-weight, feather-w.; portable, handy 196adj. *little;* light-footed, light-fingered, pussy-foot; non-gravitational, weightless, without weight; imponderous, imponderable, unweighable; sublime, ethereal, airy, gaseous, astatic, volatile, sublimated 325adj. *rare;* uncompressed, doughy, barmy, yeasty, fermenting, zymotic, enzymic; aerated, frothy, foamy, whipped; peptic, digestible 301adj. *edible;* floating, buoyant, unsinkable; feathery, light as air, light as a feather, light as a fairy; lightening, unloading; raising, self-raising, leavening.

Vb. *be light* etc. adj.; defy gravity, levitate, surface, float to the surface, float 308vb. *ascend;* swim; balloon 197vb. *expand;* be outweighed, kick the beam.

lighten, make light, make lighter, reduce weight; ease 701vb. *disencumber;* lighten ship, throw overboard, jettison 300vb. *void;* volatilize, gasify, vaporize 340vb. *aerify;* leaven, work; raise, levitate 310vb. *elevate.*

See: 4, 196, 197, 300, 301, 307, 308, 310, 325, 338, 340, 701.

324 Density

N. *density,* solidity; compactness, solidness, concreteness, thickness, concentration; consistence, spissitude; incompressibility 326n. *hardness;* impenetrability, impermeability, imporosity; indissolubility, indiscerptibility, indivisibility; cohesion, inseparability 48n. *coherence;* relative density, specific gravity; densimeter, hydrometer, aerometer.

condensation, inspissation, constipation; thickening etc. vb.; incrassation, consolidation, concentration; concretion, nucleation; caseation, coagulation; solidation, solidification, consolidation; congealment, gelatination, jellification; glaciation; ossification, petrifaction, fossilization 326n. *hardening;* crystallization; sedimentation, precipitation; condenser, compressor, thickener, gelatin, rennet, pepsin 354n. *thickening.*

solid body, solid; lump, mass 319n. *matter;* knot, block; condensation, nucleus, hard core; conglomerate, concretion; concrete, cement; stone, crystal, hardpan, burl, trap 344n. *rock;* precipitate, deposit, sediment, silt, slag, clay, cake, clod; bone, ossicle; gristle, cartilage 329n. *toughness;* coagulum, curd, clot, blood-c., grume, thrombus; embolus, tophus, calculus; solid mass, phalanx, serried ranks; wall, blank w. 702n. *obstacle.*

Adj. *dense,* thick, crass; close, heavy, stuffy (air); foggy, murky, to be cut with a knife; lumpy, ropy, grumous, clotted, curdled; caked, caky; matted, knotted, tangled 48adj. *cohesive;* coherent, consistent, monolithic; firm, close-textured, knotty, gnarled; substantial, massy, massive 322adj.

weighty; concrete, solid, frozen, solidified etc. vb.; crystallic, crystalline, crystallized; condensed, nuclear, nucleal; costive, constipated; compact, close-packed, firm-p.; thickset, thick-growing, thick, bushy, luxuriant 635adj. *plenteous;* serried, massed, densely arrayed; incompressible, inelastic 326adj. *rigid;* impermeable, impenetrable, impervious, imporous, without holes; indivisible, indiscerptible, infrangible, unbreakable 162adj. *strong.*

indissoluble, undissolvable, insoluble, infusible; undissolved, unliquefied, unmelted, unthawed, hard-frozen; precipitated, sedimentary.

solidifying, binding, constipating; freezing, congealing; styptic, styptical, astringent, hemostatic.

Vb. *be dense,*—solid etc. adj.; become solid, solidify, consolidate; conglomerate, cement 48vb. *cohere;* condense, nucleate, form a core *or* kernel; densen, thicken, inspissate, incrassate; precipitate, deposit; freeze, glaciate 380vb. *be cold;* set, take a set.; gelatinize, jellify, jell; congeal, coagulate, clot, curdle; cake, crust, candy; crystal, crystallize; fossilize, petrify, ossify 326vb. *harden;* compact, compress, contract, squeeze 198vb. *make smaller;* pack, squeeze in, cram, ram down 193vb. *load;* mass, crowd 74vb. *bring together;* bind, constipate; sediment, precipitate, deposit.

See: 48, 74, 162, 193, 198, 319, 322, 326, 329, 344, 354, 380, 635, 702.

325 Rarity

N. *rarity,* low pressure, vacuum, near v. 190n. *emptiness;* subtility, compressibility, sponginess 327n. *softness;* tenuity, fineness 206n. *thinness;* insolidity 4n. *insubstantiality;* lightness 323n. *levity;* incorporeality, ethereality 320n. *immateriality;* airiness, windiness, ether, gas 336n. *gaseity,* 340n. *air;* rarefaction, expansion, dilatation, pressure reduction, attentuation; subtilization, etherealization; seldomness 140n. *infrequency.*

Adj. *rare,* tenuous, thin, fine, subtile, subtle; flimsy, slight 4adj. *insubstantial;* low-pressure, uncompact, uncompressed; compressible, spongy 328adj. *elastic;* rarefied, aerified, aerated 336adj. *gaseous;* void, hollow 190adj. *empty;* ethereal, aery 323adj. *light;* incorporeal 320adj. *immaterial;* wispy, straggly.

Vb. *rarefy,* reduce the pressure, expand, dilate; make a vacuum, pump out, exhaust 300vb. *void;* subtilize, attentuate, refine, thin; dilute, adulterate 163vb. *weaken;* gasify, volatilize 338vb. *vaporize.*

See: 4, 140, 163, 190, 206, 300, 320, 323, 327, 328, 336, 338, 340.

326 Hardness

N. *hardness,* durity; unyielding quality, intractability, renitency, resistance; starchiness, stiffness, rigor, rigidity, inflexibility; inextensibility, inelasticity; firmness, temper; grittiness 329n. *toughness;* callosity, callousness; stoniness, rockiness, cragginess; grit, stone, pebble, boulder, crag; granite, flint, silica, quartz, marble, diamond 344n. *rock;* adamant, metal, duralumin; steel, hard s., iron, wrought i., cast i.; nails, hardware, stoneware; cement, concrete, ferro-c.; brick, baked b.; block, board, heart-wood, duramen; hardwood, teak, oak, heart of o. 366n. *wood;* bone, gristle, cartilage; a callosity, callus, corn, kibe; blain, chilblain; shell, hard s.; hard core, hard center, jawbreaker; brick wall; stiffener, starch, wax; whalebone, corset, splint 218n. *supporter.*

hardening, induration; stiffening, backing; starching; steeling, tempering; vulcanization; petrifaction, lapidification, lapidescence, fossilization; crystallization, vitrification, glaciation; ossification, cornification; sclerosis, scleriasis, hardening of the arteries; toughening 682n. *exercise.*

Adj. *hard,* adamant, adamantine, adamantean; unbreakable, infrangible 162adj. *strong;* fortified, armored, steeled, proof; iron, cast-i.; steel, steely; concrete, ferro-c.; hardboiled 329adj. *tough;* hard as iron, hard as steel, hard as stone, hard as bone, hard as nails; callous, stony, rocky, flinty; gritty; gravelly, pebbly; lithic, granitic; crystalline, vitreous, glassy; horny, corneous; bony, osseous, ossific; cartilaginous, gristly; hardened, indurate, indurated, tempered, case-hardened, calloused; petrified, fossilized, ossified; icy, frozen, hard-f., frozen over 329adj. *tough;* sclerotic.

rigid, stubborn, obdurate 602adj. *obstinate;* intractable, unmalleable, unadaptable; firm, inflexible, unbending 162adj. *unyielding;* incompressible, inextensible, resistant; inelastic, unsprung, springless; unadaptable; starch, starchy, starched; unlimber, muscle-bound 695adj. *clumsy;* tense, taut, tight, tight-strung, firm-packed 45adj. *firm-set;* stiff, stark, stiff as a poker, stiff as a ramrod, stiff as buckram, stiff as a board.

Vb. *harden,* render hard etc. adj.; steel 162vb. *strengthen;* indurate, temper, vulcanize, toughen; hardboil 301vb. *cook;* petrify, fossilize, ossify; calcify, vitrify, crystallize; glaciate, freeze 382vb. *refrigerate;* stiffen, back, starch, wax (a moustache), tauten 45vb. *tighten.*

See: 45, 162, 198, 218, 301, 329, 344, 366, 382, 602, 662, 682, 695.

327 Softness

N. *softness,* tenderness, gentleness; pliableness etc. adj.; compliance 739n. *obedience;* pliancy, pliability, flexibility, plasticity, ductility, tractility; malleability, sequacity, adaptability; suppleness, litheness; springiness, turfiness, springing, suspension 328n. *elasticity;* extendibility, extensibility; impressibility, doughiness 356n. *pulpiness;* sponginess, flaccidity, flabbiness, floppiness; laxity, looseness 335n. *fluidity;* sogginess, squelchiness, marshiness 347n. *marsh;* flocculence, downiness; velvetiness; butter, grease, oil, wax, plasticine, clay, dough, pudding, soap, plastic; padding, wadding, pad 227n. *lining;* cushion, pillow, armchair, feather-bed 376n. *euphoria;* velvet, plush, down, eiderdown, fleece 259n. *hair;* feathers 259n. *plumage;* snowflake 330n. *brittleness;* soft handling, light touch, light rein, velvet glove 736n. *lenity.*

Adj. *soft,* not tough, tender 301adj. *edible;* melting 335adj. *fluidal;* giving, yielding, compressible; springy, sprung 328adj. *elastic;* pneumatic, cushiony, pillowy, padded; impressible, as wax, waxy, doughy, argilaceous; spongy, soggy, mushy, squelchy 347n. *marshy;* medullary, pithy; pulpy, squashy, juicy, mellow, overripe 669n. *matured;* fleecy, flocculent 259adj. *downy;* turfy, mossy, grassy; plushy, velvety, silky 258adj. *smooth;* unstiffened, unstarched, limp; flaccid, flabby, floppy; unstrung, relaxed; gentle, light; soft as butter, soft as wax, soft as soap, soft as down, soft as velvet, soft as silk; tender as a chicken; softening, emollient 177adj. *lenitive.* *flexible,* whippy, bendable; pliant, pliable; ductile, tractile, malleable, moldable, sequacious, adaptable; plastic, thermoplastic; extensile, stretchable 328adj. *elastic;* lithe, supple, lissome, limber, loose-limbed, double-jointed; acrobatic 162adj. *athletic.*

Vb. *soften,* mollify 177vb. *assuage;* render soft, velvet, tenderize; mellow 669vb. *mature;* oil, grease 334vb. *lubricate;* knead, massage, mash, pulp, squash 332vb. *pulverize;* macerate, steep 341vb. *drench;* cushion, pillow, temper 177vb. *moderate;* relax, unstring 46vb. *disjoin;* yield, give, give way, relax, bend; unbend 683vb. *repose;* relent 736vb. *be lenient.*

See: 46, 162, 177, 227, 258, 259, 301, 328, 330, 332, 334, 335, 347, 356, 376, 669, 683, 736, 739.

328 Elasticity

N. *elasticity,* give, stretch; spring, springiness; suspension, knee action; stretchability, tensibility, extensibility; resilience, bounce 280n. *recoil;* renitency, buoyancy, rubber, india-r., elastic, gum e.; caoutchouc, gutta-percha; whalebone, baleen; elastin.

Adj. *elastic,* stretchy, stretchable, tensile, extensile, extensible; springy, bouncy, resilient 280adj. *recoiling;* renitent, buoyant; sprung, well-s.; ductile 327adj. *soft;* systaltic, peristaltic.

Vb. *be elastic*—tensile etc. adj.; bounce, spring, spring back 280vb. *recoil;* stretch, give.

See: 280, 327.

329 Toughness

N. *toughness,* durability, infrangibility 162n. *strength;* stubbornness 602n. *obstinacy;* tenacity, holding quality 778n. *retention;* cohesion 48n. *coherence;* viscidity 354n. *semiliquidity;* leatheriness, inedibility, indigestibility; leather, gristle, cartilage 326n. *hardness.*

Adj. *tough,* durable, resisting; close-woven, strong-fibered 162adj. *strong;* tenacious, retentive, clinging, adhesive, sticky, gummy 48adj. *cohesive;* viscid 354adj. *semi-liquid;* infrangible, unbreakable, untearable, shock-proof; vulcanized, toughened; hard-boiled, overdone; stringy, fibrous; gristly, cartilaginous; rubbery, leathery, coriaceous, tough as whit-leather; indigestible, inedible; non-elastic, inelastic, unsprung, springless 326adj.

rigid; unyielding, stubborn 602adj. *obstinate.*

Vb. *be tough,*—durable etc. adj.; resist fracture, be unbreakable; toughen, tan, case-harden; mercerize, vulcanize, temper, anneal 162vb. *strengthen.*

See: 48, 162, 326, 354, 602, 778.

330 Brittleness

N. *brittleness* etc. adj.; frangibility; friability, friableness, crumbliness 332n. *pulverulence;* fissility 46n. *scission;* laminability, flakiness 207n. *lamina;* fragility, frailty, flimsiness 163n. *weakness;* bubble, eggshell, matchwood, rice-paper, piecrust; shale, slate; glass, china, crockery 381n. *pottery;* pane, window, glass house; house of cards, sandcastle, mud pie 163n. *weak thing.*

Adj. *brittle,* breakable, frangible; fragile, glassy, brittle as glass; papery, like parchment; shattery, shivery, splintery; friable, crumbly 332adj. *powdery;* crisp, crimp, short, like shortbread; flaky, laminable; fissile, splitting; scissile, lacerable, tearable 46adj. *severable;* frail, delicate, flimsy, eggshell 163adj. *weak;* gimcrack, crazy, ill-made 4adj. *insubstantial;* tumble-down 655adj. *dilapidated;* ready to break, ready to burst, explosive.

Vb. *be brittle,*—fragile etc. adj.; fracture 46vb. *break;* crack, snap; star, craze; split, shatter, shiver, fragment; splinter, break short, snap off; burst, fly, explode; give way, fall in, crash 309vb. *tumble;* fall to pieces 655vb. *deteriorate;* wear thin; crumble 332vb. *pulverize;* crumble to dust 131vb. *grow old;* live in a glass house.

Int. fragile! with care!

See: 4, 46, 131, 163, 207, 309, 332, 381, 655.

331 Structure. Texture

N. *structure,* organization, pattern, plan; complex 52n. *whole;* mold, shape, build 243n. *form;* constitution, setup, content, substance 56n. *composition;* construction, make, works, workings; compaction, architecture, tectonics, architectonics; fabric, work, brickwork, stonework, woodwork 631n. *materials;* scaffold, framework, chassis, shell 218n. *frame;* lamination, cleavage 207n. *stratification;* body, carcass, person, physique, anatomy 358n. *organism;* bony structure, skeleton, bone, horn; science of structure, organology, physiology, myology, splanchnology, neurology, angiology, adenology, histology, angiography, adenography 358n. *biology.*

texture, intertexture, contexture, network 222n. *crossing;* tissue, fabric, stuff 222n. *textile;* staple, denier 208n. *fiber;* web, weave, warp and woof, warp and weft 222n. *weaving;* nap, pile 259n. *hair;* granular texture, granulation, grain, grit; fineness of grain 258n. *smoothness;* coarseness of grain 259n. *roughness;* surface 223n. *exteriority;* feel 378n. *touch.*

Adj. *structural,* organic; skeletal; anatomic, astronomical; organismal, organologic; organizational, constructional; tectonic, architectural.

textural, textile, woven 222adj. *crossed;* fine-woven, close-w.; ribbed, twilled; grained, granular; fine-grained, silky, satiny 258adj. *smooth;* coarse-grained, gritty 259adj. *rough;* fine, fine-spun, delicate, subtile, gossamery, filmy; coarse, homespun, hodden, linsey-woolsey.

See: 52, 56, 207, 208, 218, 222, 223, 243, 258, 259, 358, 378, 631.

332 Pulverulence

N. *pulverulence,* powderiness; efflorescence, "flowers" (chemistry), dustiness 649n. *dirt;* sandiness, sabulosity; grittiness; granulation; friability, crumbliness 330n. *brittleness;* pulverization, levigation, trituration; attrition, detrition, attenuation, disintegration, erosion 51n. *decomposition;* grinding, milling, multure; abrasion, filling, limation 333n. *friction;* fragmentation, comminution, contusion 46n. *disjunction;* spreading dust, dusting, powdering, frosting.

powder, face-p. 843n. *cosmetic;* pollen, spore, microspore, sporule; dust, coal-d., soot, ash 649n. *dirt;* smeddum, smitham; flour, atta, farina; grist, meal, bran; sawdust, filings, limature, scobs; powdery deposit, efflorescence, flowers; flocculi, magistery; debris, detritus 41n. *leavings;* sand, grit, gravel; grain, seed, pip, crumb 53n. *piece;* granule, grain of powder 33n. *particle;* flake, snowflake; smoke, column of s., smoke-cloud, dust-c.; fog, smog 355n. *cloud;* dust storm, dust devil 176n. *storm.*

pulverizer, miller, grinder; roller, crusher, masher, atomizer; mill, millstone, muller, quern, quernstone; pestle, pestle and mortar; hand-mill, coffee-m., pepper-m.; grater, cheese-g., nutmeg-g., grindstone, file; abrasive, sandpaper, emery paper; molar, teeth 256n. *tooth;* chopper 256n. *sharp edge;* sledge, sledge-hammer 279n. *hammer;* bulldozer 279n. *ram.*

Adj. *powdery,* pulverulent, scobiform; dusty, dust-covered, sooty, smoky 649adj. *dirty;* sandy, sabulous, arenose, arenarious, arenaceous; farinaceous, branny, floury; granulated, granular; gritty, gravelly; flocculent, furfuraceous, efflorescent; grated, milled, ground, sifted, bolted; crumbling, crumbled; crumbly, friable 330adj. *brittle.*

Vb. *pulverize,* powder, reduce to p., grind to p.; triturate, levigate, granulate; crush, kibble, kevel, mash, comminute, contuse, contund, shatter, fragment, disintegrate 46vb. *break;* grind, mill, mince, beat, bruise, pound, bray; knead; crumble, crumb; crunch, scrunch 301vb. *chew;* chip, flake, grate, scrape, rasp, file, abrade, rub down 333vb. *rub;* weather, wear down, rust, erode 51vb. *decompose.*

See: 33, 41, 46, 51, 53, 176, 256, 279, 301, 330, 333, 355, 649, 843.

333 Friction

N. *friction,* frictional force, drag 278n. *slowness;* frication, confrication, affriction; rubbing etc. vb.; attrition, rubbing against, rubbing together 279n. *collision;* rubbing out, erasure 550n. *obliteration;* abrasion, scraping; limature, filing 332n. *pulverulence;* wearing away, erosion 165 n. *destruction;* scrape, graze, scratch; brushing, rub; polish, levigation; elbow grease; shampoo, massage, facial m., facial 843n. *beautification;* eraser, rubber, rosin; masseur, masseuse, shampooer 843n. *beautician.*

Adj. *rubbing,* frictional, fretting, grating; anatriptic, abrasive; fricative.

Vb. *rub,* friction; rub in 303vb. *insert;* rub against, strike (a match); fret, fray, chafe, gall; graze, scratch, scarify 655vb. *wound;* rub off, abrade; scrape, scrub, scour; brush, rub down, curry, curry-comb 648vb. *clean;* polish, buff, levigate 258vb. *smooth;* rub out, erase 550vb. *obliterate;* gnaw, erode, wear away 165vb. *consume;* rasp, file, grind 332vb. *pulverize;* knead, shampoo, massage; wax, rosin, chalk (one's cue); grate, be rusty, catch, stick; rub gently, stroke 889vb. *caress;* iron 258vb. *smooth.*

See: 165, 258, 278, 279, 303, 332, 550, 648, 655, 843.

334 Lubrication

N. *lubrication,* lubrification; anointment, unction, oiling etc. vb.; lubricity 357n. *unctousness;* non-friction 258n. *smoothness.*

lubricant, graphite, plumbago, black lead; glycerin, wax, grease, cart g. 357n. *oil;* soap, lather 648n. *cleanser;* saliva, spit, spittle, synovia; ointment, salve 658n. *balm;* emollient, lenitive 357n. *unguent;* lubricator, oil-can, grease-gun.

Adj. *lubricated* etc. vb.; smooth-running, well-oiled, well-greased; not rusty, silent.

Vb. *lubricate,* lubricitate, oil, grease, wax, soap, lather; grease leather, liquor; butter 357vb. *pinguefy;* anoint, pour balm.

See: 258, 357, 648, 658.

335 Fluidity

N. *fluidity,* fluidness, liquidity, liquidness; fluxure, fluxility; wateriness, rheuminess 339n. *water;* juiciness, sappiness 356n. *pulpiness;* non-viscosity, non-coagulation, hemophilia; solubility, solubleness, fluxibility, liquidescence 337n. *liquefaction;* gaseous character 336n. *gaseity;* bloodiness, goriness 354n. *semiliquidity;* hydrology, hydrometry, hydrostatics, hydrodynamics; hydraulics, hydrokinetics.

fluid, elastic f. 336n. *gas;* non-elastic fluid, liquid; water, running w. 339n. *water;* drink 301n. *liquor;* milk, whey, ghee, buttermilk; juice, sap, latex; humor, chyle, rheum, mucus, saliva 302n. *excrement;* serum, serosity, lymph, plasma; ichor, pus, sanies; gore (**see** *blood*); sauce, gravy, meat juice, gippo, gruel 301n. *soup;* hydrocele, dropsy 651n. *disease.*

blood, ichor, claret; life-blood 360n. *life;* blood-stream, circulation; red blood 372n. *male;* blue blood 868n. *nobility;* gore, cruor, sanies, grume; clot, blood c., thrombus 324n. *solid body;* hemad, corpuscle, red c., white c., platelet; lymph, plasma, serum, blood s., serosity; serolin; cruorin, hemoglobin, hematoglobulin; hematogenesis, hematosis, sanguification; blood group; blood-count; hematoscopy, hematoscope, hemometer; hematics, hematology.

Adj. *fluidal,* fluidic, fluid 244adj.

amorphous; liquid, liquiform, not solid, not gaseous; not congealing, uncongealed; fluxible, fluxive, apt to flow, unclotted, clear, clarified; soluble, liquescent, melting 337adj. *liquefied;* fluent, running 350adj. *flowing;* runny, rheumy, phlegmy 339adj. *watery;* succulent, juicy, sappy, squashy 327adj. *soft;* plasmatic, lymphatic, serous; sanious, ichorous, gory; pussy, mattery, suppurating 653adj. *toxic;* hydrostatic, hydrodynamic.

sanguineous, hemic, hemal, hemogenic; serous, lymphatic, plasmatic; bloody, sanguinary 431adj. *bloodshot;* gory, sanious, ichorous; bleeding, hemophilic.

See: 244, 301, 302, 324, 327, 336, 337, 339, 350, 354, 356, 360, 372, 431, 651, 653, 868.

336 Gaseity

N. *gaseity,* gaseousness, vaporousness etc. adj.; windiness, flatulence, flatulency 352n. *wind;* aeration, gasification; volatility 338n. *vaporization;* pneumatostatics; aerostatics, aerodynamics 340n. *pneumatics.*

gas, vapor, elastic fluid; ether 340n. *air;* effluvium, exhalation, miasma 298n. *egress;* flatus 352n. *wind;* fume, reek, smoke; steam, water vapor 355n. *cloud;* laughing gas, coal g.; marsh gas, poison g., mustard g. 659n. *poison;* damp, after-d., black d., choke d., fire d.; heavy hydrogen, deuterium; air-bladder, inner tube 194n. *bladder;* balloon, gas-b., air-b. 276n. *airship;* gasworks, gas plant, gasification p. 687n. *workshop;* gasholder, gasometer 632n. *storage;* gasalier 420n. *lamp;* gas-meter, gasoscope 465n. *meter.*

Adj. *gaseous,* gasiform; vaporous, steamy, volatile, evaporable 338adj. *vaporific;* aerial, airy, aeriform, ethereal 340adj. *airy;* gassy, windy, flatulent; effluvial, miasmic 659adj. *baneful;* pneumatic, aerostatic, aerodynamic.

Vb. *gasify,* aerate 340vb. *aerify;* vapor, steam, emit vapor 338vb. *vaporize;* let off steam, blow off s. 300vb. *emit;* turn on the gas; combine with gas, oxygenate, hydrogenate, hydrogenize.

See: 194, 276, 298, 300, 304, 338, 340, 352, 355, 420, 465, 632, 659, 687.

337 Liquefaction

N. *liquefaction,* liquidization; liquescence; solubility, deliquation, liquescency, deliquescence, fluxibility; fluidification 335n. *fluidity;* fusion, colliquation, colliquefaction 43n. *mixture;* lixiviation, dissolution; thaw, melting, unfreezing 381n. *heating;* solvent, dissolvent, flux, diluent, menstruum, alkahest, aqua fortis; liquefier, liquefacient; anticoagulant 658n. *antidote.*

solution, decoction, infusion, apozem; flux, lixivium, lye.

Adj. *liquefied,* molten; runny, liquescent, uncongealed, deliquescent; liquefacient, colliquative, solvent; soluble, dissoluble, liquefiable, fluxible 335adj. *fluidal.*

Vb. *liquefy,* liquidize, render liquid, unclot, clarify 350adj. *make flow;* liquate, dissolve, resolve, deliquesce, run 350n. *flow;* unfreeze, melt, thaw 381vb. *heat;* melt down, fuse, render, clarify; leach, lixiviate; hold in solution; cast, found.

See: 43, 335, 350, 381.

338 Vaporization

N. *vaporization,* atomization; exhalation 355n. *cloud;* gasification, aerification; evaporation, volatilization, distillation, cohobation, sublimation; steaming, fumigation, vaporability, volatility.

vaporizer, evaporater; atomizer, spray, fine s.; retort, still, distillery, vaporimeter, atmometer.

Adj. *vaporific,* volatilized etc. vb.; reeking; vaporing, steaming etc. vb.; vaporous, vapory, vaporish; steamy, gassy, smoky; evaporable, vaporable, vaporizable, volatile.

Vb. *vaporize,* evaporate; render vaporous, render gaseous; aerify 336adj. *gasify;* volatilize, distill, sublime, sublimate, exhale, transpire, emit vapor, blow off steam 300vb. *emit;* smoke, fume, reek, steam; fumigate, spray; make a spray, atomize.

See: 300, 336, 355.

339 Water

N. *water,* H_2O; heavy water, D_2O; hard water, soft w.; drinking water, tap w., mineral w., soda w. 301n. *soft drink;* water vapor, steam 355n. *cloud;* rain water 350n. *rain;* spring water, running w. 350n. *stream;* holy water 988n. *ritual object;* eye-water, tear 836n. *lamentation;* high water, high tide, spring t., neap t., low water 350n. *wave;* standing water, still w. 346n. *lake;* sea water, salt w., brine, briny, blue water 343n. *ocean;* soap and water, bath water, lotion, douche, splash, ablution, balneation, bath 648n. *cleansing;* lavender water, scent 843n. *cosmetic;* diluent, adulteration, dilution 655n. *impairment;* wateriness, damp, wet; watering, spargefaction 341n. *moistening;* water-carrier, bheesty; water-cart, watering-cart, water jug, ewer 194n. *vessel;* tap, standpipe, hydrant 351n. *conduit;* waterer, hose 341n. *irrigator;* hydrometry 341n. *hydrometry.*

Adj. *watery,* aqueous, aquatic, lymphatic; hydro-, hydrated, hydrous; hydrological, hydrographic 321adj. *geographic;* adulterated, diluted 163adj. *weak;* still, non-effervescent; fizzy, effervescent; wet, moist, drenching 341adj. *humid;* balneal 648adj. *cleansing;* hydrotherapeutic 658adj. *medical;* sudorific, hydrotic, hydragogue.

Vb. *add water,* water, water down, adulterate, dilute 163vb. *weaken;* steep, soak, liquor; irrigate, drench 341vb. *moisten;* combine with water, hydrate; slack, slake 51vb. *decompose.*

See: 51, 163, 194, 301, 321, 341, 343, 346, 350, 351, 355, 648, 655, 658, 836, 843, 988.

340 Air

N. *air,* 336n. *gas;* thin air 325n. *rarity;* cushion of air, air-pocket 190n. *emptiness;* blast 352n. *wind;* common air, oxygen, nitrogen, neon, argon, ozone; welkin, blue, blue sky 355n. *cloud;* open air, open, out-of-doors, exposure 183n. *space;* airing 342n. *desiccation;* aeration 338n. *vaporization;* ventilation, fanning 685n. refreshment; air-conditioning, air-cooling 382n. *refrigeration;* ventilator, blower, fan, air-conditioner 384n. *refrigerator;* air-filter 648n. *cleanser.*

atmosphere, aerosphere; Heaviside layer, Kennelly-Heaviside l.; radiation layer, Van Allen belt 207n. *layer;* ionosphere, troposphere, tropopause, stratosphere; isothermal layer.

weather, the elements; fair weather, calm w., halcyon days; windless weather, doldrums; atmospheric pressure, anticyclone, high pressure; cyclone, low pressure; rough weather 176n. *storm;* bad weather, foul w., wet w.; changeable weather, rise and fall of the barometer; meteorology, aeroscopy, aeromancy, weather forecast 511n. *prediction;* isobar, decibar, millibar; glass, mercury, barometer; weather ship; barograph, weather glass, weather gauge; vane, weather-v., weathercock; hygrometer, weather-house; weather prophet, weatherman, meteorologist; climate, climatology, climatography; climatologist.

pneumatics, aerodynamics, aerography, aeroscopy, aerology, barometry, anemometry 352n. *anemology;* aerometer, baroscope, barometer, aneroid b., barograph, barogram; vane, weather-vane, weather-cock.

Adj. *airy,* ethereal 4adj. *insubstantial;* skyey; aerial, aeriform; pneumatic, aeriferous, containing air, aerated; inflated, blown up, flatulent 197adj. *expanded;* effervescent, oxygenated 355adj. *bubbly;* breezy, 352adj. *windy;* well-ventilated, fresh, air-conditioned 382adj. *cooled;* meteorological, weather-wise; atmospheric, baric, barometric; cyclonic, anticyclonic; high-pressure 324n. *dense;* low-pressure 325adj. *rare;* climatic, climatological.

Vb. *aerify,* aerate, oxygenate; air, expose 342vb. *dry;* ventilate, freshen, deodorize 648vb. *clean;* fan, winnow, make a draft 352vb. *blow;* take an airing 352vb. *breathe.*

Adv. *alfresco,* out of doors, in the open air, in the open, under the open sky, in the sun.

See: 4, 176, 183, 190, 197, 207, 324, 325, 336, 338, 342, 352, 355, 382, 384, 511, 648, 685.

341 Moisture

N. *moisture,* humidity, sap, juice 335n. *fluid;* dampness, wetness, moistness; dewiness; dankishness, dankness; sogginess, swampiness, marshiness; saturation, saturation point 863n. *satiety;* leakiness 298n. *outflow;* pluviosity, raininess, showeriness; rainfall, high r., wet weather; damp, dank, wet; spray, spindrift, froth, foam 355n. *bubble;* mist, fog, fog bank 355n. *cloud;* scotch mist, drizzle 350n. *rain;* drip, dew, night-d., morning-d.; drop, rain-d., dew-d., tear-d.; wet eyes, tears 836n. *lamentation;* saliva, salivation, slabber, slobber, spit, spittle 302n. *excrement;* ooze, slime, mud, squelch, fen 347n. *marsh;* soaked object, sop.

moistening, madefaction, humidification; humectation, bedewing, rorification; damping, wetting, drenching, soaking; saturation, deluge 350n. *rain;* spargefaction, sprinkling, sprinkle, asperges, aspersion, ducking, submersion, total immersion 303n. *immersion;* overflow, flood, inundation 350n. *waterfall;* lotion, balneation, wash, bath 648n. *ablution;* baptism 988n. *Christian rite;* infiltration, percolation, leaching; irrigation, watering, spraying, hosing; injection; gargle; hydrotherapy 658n. *therapy.*

irrigator, sprinkler, aspergillum; waterer, watering-cart; watering-pot, watering-can; spray, rose; hose, garden h., syringe, water pistol, squirt, squirt-gun; pump, fire-engine; Persian wheel, shadoof, swipe; cistern, dam, reservoir 632n. *store;* sluice, water pipe 351n. *conduit.*

hygrometry, hydrography, hydrology; hygrometer, udometer, rain-gauge, pluviometer, nilometer; hygroscope, weather-housc.

Adj. *humid,* moistened; moistening, humective, humectant; wet 339adj. *watery;* pluvious, pluvial; drizzling, drizzly 350adj. *rainy;* undried, damp, moist, dripping; dank, muggy, foggy, misty 355adj. *cloudy;* undrained, oozy, muddy, slimy, slushy, squashy, squelchy, fenny 347adj. *marshy;* dewy, fresh, bedewed, roral, roscid, roriferous; juicy, sappy 335adj. *fluidal;* dribbling, drip-dropping, seeping, percolating; wetted, steeped, sprinkled; dabbled; gory, bloody 335adj. *sanguineous.*

drenched, saturated, irriguous, irrigated; soaking, sopping, slopping, streaming, reeking; sodden, soaked, deluged; wet through, wet to the skin, wringing wet; weltering, wallowing, waterlogged, awash, swamped, drowned.

Vb. *be wet,*—moist etc. adj.; be soggy, squelch, suck; slobber, salivate, sweat, perspire 298vb. *exude;* steam, reek 300vb. *emit;* percolate, seep 297vb. *infiltrate;* weep, bleed, stream; ooze, drip, leak 298vb. *flow out;* trickle, drizzle, rain, pour, come down cats and dogs 350n. *rain;* get wet,—drenched etc. adj.; not have a dry thread; dip, duck, dive 313vb. *plunge;* bathe, wash; paddle, wade, ford; wallow, welter.

moisten, humidify, humectate, humect; wet, dampen; dilute, hydrate 339vb. *add water;* lick, lap, wash; splash, swash; spill, slop 311vb. *let fall;* flood, spray, syringe, sprinkle, besprinkle; sparge, asperse, asperge; bedew, bedabble, dabble; baste, affuse 303vb. *infuse;* gargle.

drench, saturate, imbrue, imbue; soak, deluge, wet through, make run with; leach, lixiviate; wash, lave, bathe; sluice, sloosh, rinse 648vb. *clean;* baptize 988vb. *perform ritual;* plunge, dip, duck, submerge, drown 303vb. *immerse;* swamp, whelm, flood, inundate, flood out, waterlog; douse, souse, steep; macerate, steep; pickle, brine 666vb. *preserve.*

irrigate, water, supply w., hose, pump; inundate, flood, overflow, submerge; percolate 297vb. *infiltrate;* syringe, gargle; squirt, inject.

See: 297, 298, 300, 302, 303, 311, 313, 335, 339, 347, 350, 351, 355, 632, 648, 658, 666, 836, 863, 988.

342 Dryness

N. *dryness,* siccity, aridity; need for water, thirst 859n. *hunger;* drought, drouth, low rainfall, rainlessness, desert conditions; sandiness, sands 172n. *desert;* dry climate, sunny South; sun, sunniness 379n. *heat.*

desiccation, exsiccation, arefaction; drying, drying up; airing, evaporation 338n. *vaporization;* draining, drainage; dehydration, dephlegmation; insolation, aprication, sunning 381n. *heating;* bleaching, fading, withering, searing 426n. *achromatism;* blotting, mopping 648n. *cleansing.*

drier, desiccator, evaporator; siccative, sand, blotting paper, blotter, blotting; absorbent, absorbent material; mop, swab, swabber, sponge, towel, toweling 648n. *cleanser;* dehydrator, drying machine, hair-dryer; wringer, mangle 198n. *compressor.*

Adj. *dry,* needing water, thirsty, droughty 859adj. *hungry;* unirrigated, irrigable; arid, rainless, waterless, riverless; sandy, dusty 332adj. *powdery;* bare, brown, grassless; desert, Saharan; anhydrous, dehydrated, desiccated; shriveled, withered, sere, faded 426adj. *colorless;* dried up, sapless, juiceless, mummified, parchment-like; sunned, insolated; aired; sundried, wind-d., bleached; burned, scorched, baked, parched 379adj. *hot;* free from rain, sunny, fine, cloudless, fair; freed from wet, dried out, drained, evaporated; squeezed dry, mangled; protected from wet, waterproofed, waterproof, rainproof, damp-p., watertight, tight, snug, proof; unwetted, unmoistened, dry-footed, dry-shod; out of water, high and dry; dry as a bone, dry as a stick, dry as a biscuit, dry as a mummy; dry as dust 838adj. *tedious;* adapted to drought, xerophilous; non-greasy, non-skid, skid-proof; unsweetened 393adj. *sour.*

Vb. *be dry,*—thirsty etc. adj.; keep dry, wear a mackintosh, hold off the wet, keep watertight; dry up, evaporate 338vb. *vaporize;* become dry, dry off.

dry, dehumidify, desiccate; dehydrate, anhydrate; ditch, drain; wring out, mangle, hang on the clothes line, hang out, peg o., air, evaporate 338vb. *vaporize;* sun, expose to sunlight, insolate, apricate, sun-dry; smoke, kipper, cure; parch, scorch, bake, burn 381vb. *heat;* sere, shrivel, bleach; mummify 666vb. *preserve;* dry up, stop the flow 350vb. *stanch;* blot, blot up, mop, mop up, soak up, sponge 299vb. *absorb;* swab, wipe, wipe up, wipe dry 648vb. *clean.*

See: 172, 198, 299, 332, 338, 350, 379, 381, 393, 426, 648, 666, 838, 859.

343 Ocean

N. *ocean,* sea, blue water, salt w., brine, briny; waters, billows, waves, tide 350n. *wave;* Davy Jones's locker; main, deep, deep sea; high seas, great waters; trackless deep, watery waste, kala pani; herring pond, big drink; sea lane, steamer track; sea floor, sea bottom, ooze, benthos; the seven seas; Atlantic, Pacific, Antarctic Ocean, Red Sea, Yellow S., White S., Sargasso S.; prehistoric sea *or* ocean, Tethys.

sea god, Oceanus, Neptune, Varuna, Triton, Amphitrite, Tethys; old man of the sea, merman.

sea nymph, Oceanid, naiad, Nereid, siren; Calypso, Undine; mermaid; bathing-beauty; water sprite 970n. *fairy.*

oceanography, hydrography, bathymetry; sea survey, Admiralty chart; bathysphere, bathyscaphe, bathymeter; oceanographer, hydrographer.

Adj. *oceanic,* thalassic, pelagic, pelagian; sea, marine, maritime; ocean-going, seagoing, seaworthy 269adj. *seafaring;* submarine, undersea, underwater; benthic, benthonic; hydrographic, bathymetric.

Adv. *at sea,* on the sea, on the high seas; afloat.

See: 269, 350, 970.

344 Land

N. *land,* dry l., terra firma; earth, ground, crust, earth's c. 321n. *world;* continent, mainland; heart-land, hinterland; midland, inland, interior 224n. *interiority;* peninsular, delta, promontory, tongue of land 254n. *projection;* isthmus, neck of land, land-bridge; terrain, heights, highlands 209n. *high land;* lowlands 210n. *lowness;* steppe, fields 348n. *plain;* wilderness 172n. *desert;* oasis, Fertile Crescent; isle 349n. *island;* zone, clime; country, district, tract 184n. *region;* territory, possessions, acres, estate, real e. 777n. *lands;* physical features, stratigraphy, geology 321n. *geography;* landsman, landlubber, continental, mainlander, islander, isthmian 191n. *dweller.*

shore, coast-line 233n. *outline;* coast, rock c., iron-bound c. 234n. *edge;* strand, beach, sands, shingle; sea-beach, seaboard, seashore, seaside; seacliff, seabank; plage, lido, riviera; bank, riverbank, riverside, lea, water-meadow; submerged coast, continental shelf.

soil, glebe, farmland, arable land 370n. *farm;* pasture 348n. *grassland;* deposit, eolian d., moraine, geest, silt, alluvium, alluvion, loess; topsoil, sand, dust, undersoil, subsoil; mold, leaf m., humus; loam, clay, bole, marl; cledge, Fuller's earth; argil, potter's clay, China clay, kaolin 381n. *pottery;* flinty soil, gravel, chalk, limestone; stone, pebble, flint; turf, divot, sod, clod 53n. *piece.*

rock, cliff, scar, crag; stone, boulder; submerged rock, reef, skerry; igneous rock; granite, hypabyssal rock, abyssal r., volcanic r.; lava, lapilli, tuff; volcanic glass, obsidian; sedimentary rock, bedded r., sandstone, shale, limestone, chalk, calcite; metamorphic rock, conglomerate, schist, marble; massive rock; mineral rock.

Adj. *territorial,* landed, praedial, farming, agricultural 370adj. *agrarian;* terrigenous, terrene 321adj. *telluric;* earthy, alluvial, silty; loamy, humic; clayey, marly, chalky; flinty, pebbly, gravelly, stony, lithic, rocky; granitic, marble, metamorphic; slaty, shaly, skerry.

coastal, coasting; littoral, riparian, ripuarian, riverine, riverside, seaside; shore, on-shore.

inland, continental, midland, highland, interior, central.

Adv. *on land,* on dry l., by l., overland, ashore, on shore; between the tide-marks.

See: 53, 172, 184, 191, 209, 210, 224,

233, 234, 254, 321, 348, 349, 370, 381, 777.

345 Gulf: inlet

N. *gulf,* bay, bight, cove, creek, lagoon; natural harbor, road, roadstead; inlet, outlet, bayou; indraft, arm of the sea, fjord; mouth, estuary 263n. *orifice;* firth, frith, kyle; sound, strait, belt, gut, euripus, channel.

See: 263.

346 Lake

N. *lake,* mere, lagoon, land-locked water; loch, lough, linn; fresh-water lake, salt l.; inland sea, Dead Sea; ox-bow lake, bayou; broad, broads; standing water, dead w., sheet of w.; mud flat, wash 347n. *marsh;* pool, tarn, pond, dew-p.; fishpond, fishpool, piscina, aquarium; swimming pool, swimming bath; millpond, millpool, mill-race, milldam; artificial lake, dam, reservoir 632n. *storage;* well, artesian w.; basin, tank, cistern, sump, cesspool, sewer 649n. *sink;* ditch, irrigation d., dike 351n. *drain;* water-hole, puddle, sough, splash, wallow; Irish bridge.

Adj. *lacustrine,* lake-dwelling, landlocked.

See: 347, 351, 632, 649.

347 Marsh

N. *marsh,* marish; marshland, slobland; fen, moorland, moor; everglade, jheel, wash; flat, mud f., salt f., salt-marsh, salt pan, salina; morass, slough, swamp, bog, moss, quagmire, quicksand; bottom, undrained basin, playa; wallow, hogwallow, sough; thaw, slush, squash, mire, mud, ooze; forest swamp, taiga, Serbonian bog; Slough of Despond.

Adj. *marshy,* paludine, paludal; moorish, moory; swampy, boggy, fenny; oozy, quaggy, poachy; squashy, squelchy, spongy 327adj. *soft;* slushy 354adj. *semiliquid;* muddy, miry, slabby 649adj. *dirty;* undrained, waterlogged, uliginous 341adj. *drenched;* growing in swamps, uliginal.

See: 327, 341, 354, 649.

348 Plain

N. *plain,* peneplain; dene, dale, basin, lowlands 255n. *valley;* flats 347n. *marsh;* delta, alluvial plain, landes; sands, desert s., waste, wild 172n. *desert;* tundra, ling t.; ice-plain, ice-field, ice-floe 380n. *ice;* grasslands, steppe, prairie, savanna, pampas, llanos, campos; heath, common, wold, weald; moor, moorland, fell; upland, plateau, tableland, mesa, paramo; bush, veld, High V., Middle V., Low V., Bush V.; range, open country, rolling c., champaign, campagna; fields, green belt, lung, parkland, national park 263n. *open space;* fairway, green 216n. *horizontality;* lowlands, low countries 210n. *lowness.*

grassland, pasture, pasturage, grazing 369n. *animal husbandry;* sheeprun, sheepwalk; field, meadow, water-m., mead, lea; chase, park, grounds; green, greensward, sward, lawn, turf, sod; plot, plat, grass-p. 370n. *garden.*

Adj. *champaign,* campestrian, campestral; flat, open, steppe-like, rolling.

See: 172, 216, 255, 263, 347, 369, 370, 380.

349 Island

N. *island,* isle, islet; river-island, eyot, ait, holm; lagoon-island, atoll, reef, coral r.; cay, key; sandbank, bar; floating island, iceberg; "all-but island," peninsula; island continent; island universe, galaxy 321n. *star;* archipelago; insularity, insulation 883n. *seclusion;* insular, islander, islesman 191n. *dweller.*

Adj. *insular,* circumfluous, sea-girt; islanded, isolated, marooned; isleted, archipelagian, archipelagic.

See: 191, 321, 883.

350 Stream: water in motion

N. *stream,* running water, river, subterranean r.; navigable river, waterway; tributary, branch, feeder, affluent, effluent, distributary; reach; watercourse, streamlet, rivulet, creek, brook, brooklet, bourn, burn, gipsy, beck, rill, rillet, gill, runnel, runlet; fresh, freshet, torrent, mountain t., force; sike, arroyo, wadi; spring, fountain, fount, fountain-head 156n. *source;* jet, spout, gush; gusher, geyser, hot spring, well 632n. *store.*

current, flow, set; flux, defluxion; profluence 285n. *progression;* effluence 298n. *egress;* confluence, corrivation 293n. *convergence;* indraft, inflow 297n. *ingress;* outflow, reflux 286n. *regression;* undercurrent, undertow, cross-current, rip tide 182n. *counteraction;* tide, spring t., neap

t.; tidal flow, tidal current, ebb and flow, tidal rise and fall 317n. *fluctuation;* tideway, bore, eagre; race, tidal r., mill-r., mill-stream; tap, standpipe, hydrant 351n. *conduit;* bloodstream, circulation 314n. *circuition.*
eddy, whirlpool, swirl, maelstrom, Charybdis 315n. *vortex;* surge, gurge, regurgitation, reflux 290n. *recession;* wash, backwash, wake 67n. *sequel.*
waterfall, cataract, catadupe, niagara; cascade, force, overfall, rapids, watershoot, weir, nappe; flush, chute, spillway, sluice; overflow, spill; flood, inundation, cataclysm 341n. *moistening,* 298n. *outflow.*
wave, bow-w.; wash, backwash; ripple, cat's-paw 262n. *furrow;* swell, ground s. 197n. *expansion;* billow, roller, comber, beach-c.; breaker, surf, white horses, white caps; tidal wave, tsunami 176n. *storm;* bore, eagre; rip, overfall; broken water, choppiness 259n. *roughness;* sea, choppy s., cross s., long s., short s., heavy s., angry s.; waviness, undulation.
rain, rainfall 341n. *moisture;* precipitation; drizzle, mizzle; shower, downpour, drencher, soaker, cloudburst; flurry 352n. *gale;* pouring rain, teaming r., drenching r., drowning r.; raininess, wet spell, foul weather; rainy season, the rains, monsoon; predominance of Aquarius, reign of St. Swithin; plash, patter; dropping, dripping etc. vb.; hyetography; rain-gauge 341n. *hygrometry.*

Adj. *flowing* etc. vb.; fluxive, fluid, runny 335adj. *fluidal;* fluent, profluent, affluent, diffluent; streamy, fluvial, fluviatile, tidal; making, running, coursing, racing; streaming; in flood, in spate; flooding, inundatory, cataclysmic; surging, rolling, rippling, purling, eddying; popply, choppy 259adj. *rough;* winding, meandering, meandrous 251adj. *labyrinthine;* oozy, sluggish 278adj. *slow;* pouring, sheeting, dripping, dropping, stillicidous; gushing, spirting, spouting 298adj. *outgoing;* inflowing 297adj. *incoming.*
rainy, showery, drizzly, spitting, spotting; wet 341adj. *humid;* monsoonish.

Vb. *flow,* run, course; set, make; ebb, regurgitate 286vb. *regress;* swirl, eddy 315vb. *rotate;* surge, break, dash, ripple, popple, wrinkle; roll, swell; buck, bounce 312vb. *leap;* gush, rush, spurt, spout, jet, play, squirt, splutter; well, well up, issue 298vb. *emerge;* pour, stream; trickle, dribble 298vb. *exude;* drip, drop 309vb. *descend;* plash, lap, wash, swash, splash 341vb. *moisten;* flow softly, purl, trill, murmur, babble, bubble, burble, gurgle, guggle; flow over, overflow, flood, inundate, deluge 341vb. *drench;* flow into, fall i., drain i., empty i., spill i., leak i., distill i. 297vb. *enter;* open, disembogue, discharge itself 298vb. *flow out;* flow through, leak, percolate 305vb. *pass;* ooze, wind 251vb. *meander.*
rain, shower, stream, pour, pelt; come down, rain hard, pour with rain, rain in torrents, rain cats and dogs, rain pitchforks; sheet, come down in sheets, come down in buckets; patter, drizzle, mizzle, drip, drop, spit, sprinkle; be wet, rain and rain, set in.
make flow, cause to f., make a current, send out a stream; make *or* pass water 302vb. *excrete;* pump 300vb. *eject;* broach, tap, turn on the t., open the cocks, open the sluice gates 263vb. *open;* pour, pour out, spill 311vb. *let fall;* transfuse, decant 272vb. *transpose;* empty, drain out 300vb. *void;* water 341vb. *irrigate;* unclot, clear, clarify, melt 337vb. *liquefy.*
stanch, stop the flow, stem the course 342vb. *dry;* apply a tourniquet, compress 198vb. *make smaller;* stop a leak, plug 264vb. *close;* obstruct the flow, stem, dam, dam up 702vb. *obstruct.*

See: 67, 156, 176, 182, 197, 198, 251, 259, 263, 264, 272, 278, 285, 286, 290, 293, 297, 298, 300, 302, 305, 309, 311, 312, 314, 315, 317, 335, 337, 341, 342, 351, 352, 632, 702.

351 Conduit

N. *conduit,* water channel, tideway, riverbed, alveus; arroyo, wadi; trough, basin, riverbasin 194n. *receptacle;* canyon, ravine, gorge, barranca, gully 255n. *valley;* ditch, dike, nullah; trench, moat, watercourse, canal, channel, gutter, runnel, runner; duct, aqueduct; plumbing, water pipe, main, water m.; pipe, hose-p., hose; standpipe, hydrant, siphon, tap, spout, waterspout, gargoyle, funnel 263n. *tube;* valve, penstock; sluice, weir, lock, floodgate, watergate, spillway; oil-pipe, pipeline, Pluto 272n. *transferrer;* gullet, throat 194n. *maw;* neck (of a bottle);

blood vessel, vein, artery, aorta, jugular vein; veinlet, capillary 208n. *filament.*
drain, kennel, gutter, pantile; gargoyle, waterspout; scupper, overflow, piscina, waste-pipe, drain-p.; ajutage, efflux-tube; covered drain, culvert; open drain, ditch, sewer, sough 649n. *sink;* emunctory, intestine, colon, alimentary canal 224n. *insides;* clyster, catheter, enema-can 302n. *excretion.*
See: 194, 208, 224, 255, 263, 272, 302, 649.

352 Wind: air in motion

N. *wind* 340n. *air;* draft, downdraft, updraft; windiness etc. adj.; blowiness, gustiness, breeziness, squalliness, storminess, weather; flatus; afflatus; blast, blow (**see** *breeze, gale*); current, air-c., cross-c. 350n. *current;* headwind 182n. *counteraction;* tailwind, following wind 287n. *propellant;* air-stream, slip-s.; air pocket; windlessness, calm air 266n. *quietude;* cold draft, cold wind, icy blast; hot wind, sirocco, leveche, khamsin, harmattan, lu, simoom; seasonal wind, monsoon, etesian winds, meltemi; regular wind, prevailing w., trade w., antitrades, Brave West Winds, Roaring Forties; north wind, Boreas, bise, mistral, tramontano; south wind, föhn, chinook; east wind, Eurus, levanter; west wind, Zephyr, Favonius; wind god, Aeolus, cave of Aeolus.
anemology, aerodynamics, anemography 340n. *pneumatics;* wind-rose, Beaufort scale; anemometer, wind-gauge, weather-cock, weather-vane, wind-sock, wind-cone; wind-tunnel.
breeze, zephyr, light air; breath, breath of air, waft, whiff, puff, gust, capful of wind; light breeze, gentle b., stiff b.; sea breeze, cooling b., doctor.
gale, half g., fresh wind, strong w., high w., violent w., howling w.; blow, hard b., blast, gust, flurry, flaw; squall, thick s., black s., white s.; storm-wind, buster, northwester, sou'wester, hurricane; whirlwind, whirlblast; cyclone, tornado, typhoon, simoom 315n. *vortex;* thunderstorm, windstorm, dust-storm, dust-devil, blizzard 176n. *storm;* weather, dirty w., ugly w., stormy w., windy w., stress of w.; gale force.
sufflation, insufflation, perflation; inflation 197n. *dilation;* blowing up, pumping, pumping up; pumping out, exhaustion 300n. *voidance;* pump, air-p., stirrup-p., bicycle-p.; bellows, windbag, bagpipe; blow-pipe; exhaust-pipe, exhaust 298n. *outlet.*
ventilation, airing 340n. *air;* cross-ventilation, draft; fanning, cooling; ventiduct, ventilator; blower, fan, electric f., punkah, pull-p., chowrie, thermantidote, air-conditioner 384n. *refrigerator.*
respiration, breathing, breathing in, breathing out, inhalation, exhalation, expiration, inspiration; stomach wind, windiness, ventosity, eructation, belch; lungs, bellows, iron lung, oxygen tent; windpipe 353n. *airpipe;* sneezing, sternutation 406n. *sibilation;* coughing, cough, whooping c., croup, strangles; sigh, sob, gulp, hiccough, catching of the breath; hard breathing, panting; wheeze, rattle, death r.

Adj. *windy,* airy, exposed, drafty, blowy; ventilated, fresh; blowing, breezy, puffy, gusty, squally; blusterous, blustery, blasty, dirty, foul, stormy, tempestuous, boisterous 176adj. *violent;* windswept, windblown; storm-tossed, storm-bound; flatulent, ventose; fizzy, gassy; aeolian, favonian, boreal, zephyrous; monsoonish, cyclonic.
puffing, huffing; snorting, wheezing; wheezy, asthmatic, stertorous, panting, heaving; breathless 318adj. *agitated;* sniffy, snuffly, sneezy; pulmonic, pulmonary, pulmonate; coughy, chesty.

Vb. *blow,* puff, breeze, blast; freshen, blow hard, blow great guns, blow a hurricane, rage, storm 176vb. *be violent;* howl, roar, bellow 409vb. *ululate;* screech, scream, whistle, pipe, sing in the shrouds 407vb. *shrill;* hum, moan, mutter, sough, sigh 401vb. *sound faint;* stream in the air, wave, flap, shake, flutter 318vb. *agitate;* draw, make a draft, ventilate, fan 382vb. *refrigerate;* blow along, waft 287vb. *propel;* veer, back 282vb. *deviate.*
breathe, respire, breathe in, inhale, draw; breathe out, exhale; aspirate, puff, huff, whiff, whiffle; sniff, sniffle, snuffle, snort; breathe hard, breathe heavily, sough, gasp, pant, heave; wheeze, sneeze, cough 407vb. *rasp;* sigh, sob, gulp, suck one's breath, catch the b., hiccup; belch, burp 300vb. *eruct.*
sufflate, inflate, perflate, dilate; blow up, pump up 197vb. *enlarge;* pump out, exhaust 300vb. *void.*
See: 176, 182, 197, 266, 282, 287, 298,

300, 315, 318, 340, 350, 353, 382, 384, 401, 406, 407, 409.

353 Air-pipe

N. *air-pipe,* air-shaft, air-way; air-passage, wind-way, wind-tunnel; air-tube, blowpipe; pea-shooter 287n. *shooter;* windpipe, trachea, larynx; weasand, bronchia, bronchus; throat, gullet; nose, nostril, spiracle, blow-hole, nozzle, vent, mouthpiece 263n. *orifice;* mouth-pipe, flue-p. 414n. *organ;* gas-main, gas-pipe; tobacco pipe, pipe, briar, hookah 388n. *tobacco;* funnel, smoke-stack, flue, chimney-pot, chimney-stack 263n. *chimney;* ventiduct, air-duct, ventilator; air-hole, smoke-duct 263n. *window;* jalousie, venetian blind, grating.

See: 263, 287, 388, 414.

354 Semiliquidity

N. *semiliquidity,* stodginess, spissitude, crassitude 324n. *density;* mucosity, viscidity; lentor, clamminess, ropiness, colloidality; semiliquid, colloid, emulsion, emulsoid, albumen, mucus, mucilage, phlegm, pituita, clot, grume, gore 324n. *solid body;* pus, matter; juice, sap 356n. *pulpiness;* soup, gumbo, gravy, pudding, cornflour, cream, curds, junket, pap, mush, mash; mud, slush, squash, thaw, ooze, slime, slob; sullage, silt 347n. *marsh;* sediment, grounds 649n. *dirt;* molten lava 381n. *ash.*

thickening, inspissation, incrassation, coagulation, curdling, clotting 324n. *condensation;* gelation, gelefaction; emulsification; thickener, starch, flour, rennet, curdler; gelatin, isinglass, pepsin.

viscidity, glutinosity, glueyness, gumminess, gummosity, stickiness, treacliness, slabbiness, adhesiveness 48n. *cohesion;* glue, gluten, gum, mastic, wax, beeswax 47n. *adhesive;* emulsion, collodion, colloid; glair, size, paste, glaze, slip; treacle, jam, syrup, honey 392n. *sweetness.*

Adj. *semiliquid,* semifluid; stodgy, thick, soupy, lumpy, ropy 324adj. *dense;* unclarified, curdled, clotted, jellied, gelified, gelatinous, pulpy, juicy, sappy, milky, creamy, lactescent, lacteal, lactiferous; starchy, amylaceous; emulsive; colloidal; thawing, half-frozen, half-melted, slushy, waterlogged, muddy, mushy, slabby, squashy, squelchy 347adj. *marshy;* slimy, silty, sedimentary.

See *viscid.*

viscid, lentous, grumous, gummy, adhesive 48adj. *cohesive;* clammy, sticky, tacky; jammy, treacly, syrupy, gluey; glairy, glaireous, glarigenous; mucous, mucoid, mucilaginous, muciferous, muciparous, mucigenous; muculent, phlegmatic, pituitous.

Vb. *thicken,* inspissate, incrassate 324vb. *be dense;* coagulate 48vb. *cohere;* emulsify; collodionize; gelatinize, gelatinify, gel, jell; starch 326n. *harden;* curdle, clot, churn, beat up, mash, pulp 332vb. *pulverize;* muddy, puddle 649vb. *make unclean.*

See: 47, 48, 324, 326, 332, 347, 356, 381, 392, 649.

355 Bubble. Cloud: air and water mixed

N. *bubble,* bubbles, suds, lather, foam, froth; head, top; seafoam, spume, surf, spray, spindrift 341n. *moisture;* yeast, barm 323n. *leaven;* scum 649n. *dirt;* bubbling, boiling, effervescence; fermentation, yeastiness, fizziness, fizz.

cloud, cloudlet, scud, rack; rain-cloud, nimbus; woolpack, cumulus, cirrus, cirrocumulus, stratus, cirrostratus; mackerel sky, mare's tail; dirty sky; vapor, steam 338n. *vaporization;* haze, mist, fog, smog, London special; overcast; cloudiness, film 419n. *dimness;* nebulosity 321n. *nebula;* nephology, nephelognosy.

Adj. *bubbly,* bubbling etc. vb.; effervescent, fizzy, sparkling; foaming, foamy; spumy, spumous, spumose; with a head on, frothy, soapy, lathery; yeasty, up, aerated 323adj. *light;* scummy 649adj. *dirty.*

cloudy, clouded, overcast, overclouded; nubiferous, nubilous, nebulous; cirrose, cirrostratous, cirrocumular; thick, foggy, hazy, misty, brumous 419adj. *dim;* vaporous, steamy, steaming 338adj. *vaporific;* nephological.

Vb. *bubble,* spume, foam, froth, form a head; mantle, scum; ream, cream; boil, fizzle, guggle, gurgle 318vb. *effervesce;* ferment, fizz, sparkle; aerate 340vb. *aerify;* steam 338vb. *vaporize.*

cloud, cloud over, overcast; be cloudy,—misty etc. adj.; becloud, befog, mist up 419vb. *be dim.*

See: 318, 321, 323, 338, 340, 341, 419, 422, 649.

356 Pulpiness

N. *pulpiness,* doughiness, sponginess;

juiciness, sappiness 327n. *softness;* poultice, pulp, pith, paste, porridge; pudding, pap; mush, mash, squash; dough, batter, sponge, fool, mashed potato; rob, jam 354adj. *viscidity;* mousse, guava cheese; grume, gore 354n. *semiliquidity;* papier-mâché, wood-pulp; dental pulp, pulp-canal, pulp-cavity, pulp-chamber; pulper, pulp-digester; pulping, mastication; steeping, maceration, macerator.

Adj. *pulpy,* pulpous, pulped, mashed 354adj. *semiliquid;* mushy, pappy 327adj. *soft;* succulent, juicy, sappy, squashy, ripe, overripe 669adj. *mature;* flabby, dimply 195adj. *fleshy;* doughy, pasty; macerated, steeped 341adj. *drenched;* soggy, spongy 347adj. *marshy.*

See: 195, 327, 341, 347, 354, 669.

357 Unctuousness

N. *unctuousness* etc. adj.; unctuosity, oiliness, greasiness, lubricity, soapiness 334n. *lubrication;* fattiness, pinguescence; anointment, unction.

oil, volatile o., essential o.; lubricating oil, brain o., signal o.; animal oil, whale o., cod-liver o., shark-liver o., halibut-liver o., neat's-foot o.; vegetable oil, olive o., coconut o., linseed o., cottonseed o., colza o., castor o., rape o., groundnut o.; mineral oil, shale o., rock o., crystal o., coal o.; fuel oil, paraffin, kerosine, petroleum, petrol, gasoline, gas 385n. *fuel.*

fat, animal f., adeps, adipocere, grease; blubber, tallow, spermaceti; sebum, cerin, wax; suet, lard, dripping, bacon-fat; glycerin, stearin, oleogine, olein, elain, butyrin; butter, clarified b., ghee; margarine, butterine; cream, Devonshire c., Cornish c.; rich milk, top m.; buttermilk; soap, carbolic s.; washing soap, bath s., scented s., soap flakes 648n. *cleanser.*

unguent, salve, unction, ointment, cerate; liniment, embrocation, lanolin, vaseline; spike oil, spikenard, nard; hair-oil, macassar o., brilliantine; pomade, pomatum; cream, face-cream, hand-c. 843n. *cosmetic.*

resin, resinoid, rosin, colophony, resinate, gum, gum arabic, tragacanth, mastic, myrrh, frankincense, camphor, labdanum; lac, amber, ambergris; pitch, tar, bitumen, asphalt; varnish, copal, megilp, shellac, lacquer, japan; synthetic resin, Bakelite.

Adj. *fatty,* pinguid, pinguescent; fat, adipose 195adj. *fleshy;* sebaceous, cereous, waxy, waxen, cerated; lardaceous, lardy; saponaceous, soapy; butyric, butyraceous, buttery, creamy, milky, rich 390adj. *savory.*

unctuous, unguentary, greasy, oleic, oily, oleaginous; anointed, dripping with oil, basted; slippery, greased, oiled 334adj. *lubricated.*

resinous, resiny, resinic, resiniform, resinaceous, resiniferous; bituminous, pitchy, tarry, asphaltic; myrrhy, masticic, gummic, gummiferous, gummous; varnished, japanned.

Vb. *pinguefy,* fatten; oleaginize, grease, oil 334vb. *lubricate;* baste; butter, butter up; resinify, resin, rosin.

See: 195, 334, 385, 390, 648, 843.

358 Organization

N. *organism,* organic matter, organization; organized world, organized nature, organic n., living n., animized n., living beings; animal and vegetable kingdom, flora and fauna, biota; biotype, living matter, cell, protoplasm, cytoplasm, bioplasm, bioplast, nucleoplasm; cytoblast; idioplasm, germ plasm; chromosome, chromatin; albumen, protein; organic remains, fossil.

biology, microbiology; biognosy, science of life, natural history, nature study; biogeny, phylogeny; organic chemistry, biochemistry, plasmology; anatomy, physiology 331n. *structure;* zoography 367n. *zoology;* phytography 368n. *botany;* animal economy, ecology, bionomics; genetics, biogenetics, eugenics, cacogenics; cytogenics, cytology; embryology, morphology; evolution, natural selection, survival of the fittest, vitalism; Darwinism, Lamarckism, neo-Darwinism; biogenist, naturalist, biologist, zoologist; evolutionist, Darwinist.

Adj. *organic,* organized, organizational; cellular, unicellular, multicellular; plasmic, protoplasmic.

biological, biogenetic; physiological, zoological, paleontological; embryological; vitalistic, evolutionary, Darwinian.

See: 331, 367, 368, 369.

359 Mineral: inorganic matter

N. *mineral,* mineral world, mineral kingdom; inorganic matter, unorganized m., inanimate m., brute m.; metal, noble m., precious m., base m.; mineralogical deposit, coal measures 632n. *store.*

mineralogy, geology, geognosy, geoscopy; mineralogy, lithology, petrology; oryctology, oryctography; metallurgy, metallography; speleology, glaciology.

Adj. *inorganic,* unorganized; inanimate, azoic; mineral, non-animal, non-vegetable; mineralogical; metallurgical.

See: 632.

360 Life

N. *life,* living, being alive, animate existence, being 1n. *existence;* the living, living and breathing world; living being, being, soul, spirit; vegetative soul 366n. *vegetability;* animal soul 365n. *animality;* living soul 371n. *mankind;* gift of life, birth, nativity 68n. *origin;* new birth, revivification 656n. *revival;* life to come 124n. *future state;* immortal life 971n. *heaven;* imparting life, vivification, vitalization, animation; vitality, vital force, beating heart, strong pulse; hold on life, survival, cat's nine lives, longevity 113n. *diuturnity;* animal spirits, liveliness, animation 819n. *sensibility;* wind, breath, breathing 352n. *respiration;* vital air, breath of life, breath of one's nostrils; life-blood, heart's blood 335n. *blood;* vital spark, vital flame; seat of life, heart, artery, jugular vein; vital necessity, nourishment, staff of life 301n. *food;* biological function, parenthood, motherhood, fatherhood 164n. *propagation;* sex, sexual activity 45n. *coition;* living matter, germinal m., protoplasm, bioplasm, tissue, living t.; macromolecule, bioplast; cell, unicellular organism 358n. *organism;* cooperative living, symbiosis 706n. *association;* lifetime, one's born days; capacity for life, viability, viableness 469n. *possibility.*

Adj. *alive,* living, quick, live; breathing, alive and kicking; animated 819adj. *lively;* in life, incarnate, in the flesh; not dead, surviving, in the land of the living, above ground, on this side of the grave; long-lived, tenacious of life 113adj. *lasting;* capable of life, viable; vital, vivifying, Promethean; vivified, enlivened 656adj. *restored;* biotic, symbiotic, biological; protoplasmatic, protoplasmic, protoplastic, bioplastic.

born, born alive; begotten, fathered, sired; mothered, dammed; foaled, dropped; out of, by 11adj. *akin;* spawned, littered; laid, new-l., hatched 164adj. *produced.*

Vb. *live,* be alive, have life; respire, draw breath 352vb. *breathe;* exist, subsist 1n. *be;* live one's life, walk the earth, strut and fret one's hour upon the stage; come to life, come to, liven, liven up, quicken, revive 656vb. *be restored;* not die, be spared, survive 41vb. *be left;* cheat death, have nine lives; live in 191vb. *inhabit.*

be born, come into the world, first see the light 68vb. *begin;* have one's nativity, be incarnated; fetch breath, draw b.; be begotten, be conceived.

vitalize, give birth to, beget, conceive, support life 164vb. *generate;* vivify, vivificate, liven, enliven, breathe life into, bring to life 174vb. *invigorate;* revitalize, put new life into, reanimate 656vb. *revive;* support life, provide a living, keep alive, keep body and soul together, keep the wolf from the door 301vb. *feed.*

See: 1, 11, 41, 45, 64, 68, 113, 124, 164, 174, 191, 301, 335, 352, 358, 365, 366, 371, 469, 656, 706, 819, 971.

361 Death

N. *death,* no life 2n. *extinction;* process of death, dying (**see** *decease*); mortality, perishability, ephemerality 114n. *transientness;* martyrdom; sentence of death, doom, crack of d., knell, death-k.; death blow, quietus 362n. *killing;* mortification, putrefaction 51n. *decay;* the beyond, the great divide, the great adventure; deathliness, rest, eternal r., long sleep 266n. *quietude;* Abraham's bosom 971n. *heaven;* the grave, Sheol 364n. *tomb;* hand of death, jaws of d., shadow of d., shades of d.; lower regions, Stygian darkness; Death, the last summoner, Angel of Death, King of D., King of Terrors, Pluto, Hades; postmortem, autopsy, necropsy, necrotomy 364n. *inquest;* mortuary, dead-house, charnel h., morgue 364n. *cemetery.*

decease, end of life, extinction, end, exit, demise; departure, passing, passing away, passing over; natural death, easy d., quiet end, euthanasia 376n. *euphoria;* release, happy r., welcome end; fatality, fatal casualty; sudden death, violent d., untimely end; death by drowning, watery grave; death on the roads; heart failure, suffocation, asphyxia, apnea; hemorrhage, bleeding to death; fatal disease, killing d. 651n. *disease;*

dying day, last hour; death-bed, death-watch, death scene; last agony, last gasp, last breath, dying b.; swan-song, death-rattle 69n. *finality;* stroke of death, article of d.; extreme unction; passing bell 364n. *obsequies;* knell, death k., death's door.

the dead, forefathers 66n. *precursor;* loved ones, the great majority; the shades, the spirits, ghosts, phantoms 970n. *ghost;* dead corpses 363n. *corpse;* next world 124n. *future state;* world of spirits, underworld, netherworld, halls of death, Hades, Stygian shore, Styx; Elysium, meads of asphodel, happy hunting grounds 971n. *mythic heaven.*

death roll, mortality, death-toll, death-rate; bill of mortality, casualty list; necrology, death register 87n. *list;* death certificate 548n. *record;* martyrology; obituary, death column, death notice; the dead, the fallen, the lost; casualties, the dead and dying.

Adj. *dying* etc. vb.; mortal, ephemeral, perishable 114adj. *transient;* moribund, half-dead, with one foot in the grave, deathlike, deathly; hippocratic, deathly pale; given over, given up, despaired of; slipping, going, going off, slipping away, sinking; sick unto death 651adj. *sick;* on one's death-bed, at death's door; at the last gasp, struggling for breath; on one's last legs, in articulo mortis, at the point of death; sentenced to death, under sentence of death, doomed, fey 961adj. *condemned.*

dead, deceased, demised, no more; passed over, passed away, released, departed, gone; long gone, dead and gone, dead and buried, in the grave, six feet under 364adj. *buried;* born dead, stillborn; lifeless, breathless, still; extinct, inanimate, exanimate, bereft of life; stone dead, cold, stiff; dead as mutton, dead as a doornail, dead as a herring, dead as nits; departed this life, out of this world, called to one's eternal rest, gathered to one's fathers, in Abraham's bosom, numbered with the dead; launched into eternity, behind the veil, on the other side, beyond the grave, beyond mortal ken; gone to Elysium, gone to the happy hunting grounds; defunct, late, lamented, regretted, sainted; martyred, slaughtered, massacred, killed.

Vb. *die* (**see** *perish*); be dead, lie in the grave, be gone, be no more, cease to be, cease to live 2vb. *pass away;* end one's life, decease, demise; go, succumb, expire, stop breathing, give up the ghost, resign one's breath, breathe one's last; drop off, close one's eyes, fall asleep, sleep one's last sleep; pass, pass over, be taken; go 296vb. *depart;* ring down the curtain, shuffle off this mortal coil, pay the debt of nature, go the way of all flesh, go to one's last home, go to one's long account; join the majority, join the choir invisible, join the angels, meet one's Maker, go to glory, reach a better world, awake to life immortal; croak, peg out, go o., snuff o., go west, hop the twig, kick the bucket, turn up one's toes, push up the daisies.

perish, die out, become extinct 2vb. *pass away;* go to the wall 165vb. *be destroyed;* come to dust, turn to d. 51vb. *decompose;* meet one's death, meet one's end, meet one's fate, die with one's boots on; get killed, be killed, fall, lose one's life, be lost; relinquish one's life, lay down one's l., surrender one's l.; become a martyr, make the supreme sacrifice; catch one's death, die untimely, snuff out like a candle, drop dead; die a violent death, break one's neck; bleed to death; drown, go to Davy Jones's locker 313vb. *founder;* suffer execution, die the death, walk the plank, receive one's death warrant; commit suicide 362vb. *kill oneself.*

Adv. *post-obit,* postmortem; in the article of death, in the event of d.

See: 2, 51, 66, 69, 87, 114, 124, 165, 266, 296, 313, 362, 363, 364, 376, 548, 651, 961, 971, 987.

362 Killing: destruction of life

N. *killing* etc. vb., slaying 165n. *destruction;* destruction of life, phthisozoics; taking life, dealing death, trucidation; occision; blood-sports, hunting, shooting 619n. chase; blood-shedding, blood-letting; vivisection; mercy-killing, euthanasia; murder, assassination, bumping off, thuggee (**see** *homicide*); poisoning, drowning, suffocation, strangulation, hanging; ritual killing, immolation, sacrifice; martyrization, martyrdom; crucifixion, execution 963n. *capital punishment;* judicial murder, auto-da-fé, burning alive; dispatch, deathblow, coup de grâce, final stroke, quietus; violent death, fatal accident, fatal casualty, death on the roads, car smash, train s., plane crash.

homicide, manslaughter; murder, cap-

ital m.; assassination, thuggee, burkism; crime passionel 911n. *jealousy;* regicide, tyrannicide, parricide, patricide, matricide, fratricide; aborticide, infanticide, exposure, exposure of infants; genocide (**see** *slaughter*).
suicide, self-slaughter, self-destruction, felo-de-se; self-devotion, suttee, hara-kiri; mass-suicide, race-suicide.
slaughter, bloodshed, high casualties, butchery, carnage, shambles; wholesale murder, blood-bath, massacre, noyade, fusillade, battue, holocaust; pogrom, purge, liquidation, decimation, extermination, annihilation 165n. *destruction;* race-murder, genocide; war, battle 718n. *warfare;* Roman holiday, gladiatorial combat 716n. *duel;* Massacre of the Innocents, Sicilian Vespers, massacre of St. Bartholomew's Day.
slaughter-house, abattoir, knacker's yard, shambles; bull-ring 724n. *arena;* field of battle; battlefield 724n. *battleground;* field of blood, Aceldama; Auschwitz, Belsen, gas-chamber.
killer, slayer, man of blood; mercy-killer 905n. *pity;* soldier 722n. *combatant;* slaughter, butcher, knacker; huntsman 619n. *hunter;* trapper, rat-catcher, exterminator; toreador, picador, matador 162n. *athlete;* executioner, hangman, headsman 963n. *punisher;* homicide (**see** *murderer*); homicidal maniac, head-hunter; beast of prey, man-eater; block, gibbet, ax, guillotine, scaffold 964n. *means of execution;* insecticide, poison, hemlock 659n. *bane.*
murderer, homicide, killer; Cain, assassin, poisoner, strangler, garroter, thug; gangster, gunman; bravo, desperado, cutthroat, high-binder 904n. *ruffian;* parricide, regicide, tyrannicide.

Adj. *deadly,* killing, lethal; fell, mortal, fatal, deathly; involving life, capital; death-bringing, lethiferous, mortiferous, poisonous 653adj. *toxic;* asphyxiant, suffocating, stifling; unhealthy, miasmic 653n. *insalubrious;* inoperable, incurable.
murderous, homicidal, genocidal; suicidal, self-destructive; internecine, slaughterous, death-dealing; sanguinary, sanguinolent, ensanguined, bloody, gory, bloodstained, red-handed; blood-guilty, bloodthirsty, thirsting for blood 898adj. *cruel;* headhunting, man-eating, cannibalistic.

Vb. *kill,* slay, take life, end l., deprive of l.; do in, do for 165vb. *destroy;* cut off, nip in the bud, shorten one's life; put down, put to sleep; hasten one's end, bring down to the grave; drive to death, work to d., put to d., hang, gibbet, turn off, send to the scaffold, behead, guillotine, impale 963vb. *execute;* stone, stone to death 712vb. *lapidate;* make away with, do away w., dispatch, send out of the world, get rid of, send one to his long account, launch into eternity; deal a deathblow, give the coup de grâce, put one out of his misery, give one his quietus; shed blood, saber, spear, put to the sword, lance, bayonet, stab, run through 263vb. *pierce;* shoot down, pistol, blow the brains out 287vb. *shoot;* strangle, wring the neck of, garrote, bowstring; choke, suffocate, smother, overlay, stifle, drown; smite, brain, spill the brains of, pole-ax, sandbag, blackjack 279vb. *strike;* send to the stake, burn alive, roast a. 381vb. *burn;* immolate, sacrifice, offer up; martyr, martyrize; condemn to death, sign the death warrant, ring the knell 961vb. *condemn;* wither, deaden.
slaughter, butcher, pole-ax, cut the throat of, drain the life-blood of; do execution, massacre, slay en masse, smite hip and thigh, put to the sword; decimate, scupper, wipe out; cut to pieces, cut to ribbons, cut down, shoot d., mow d.; steep one's hands in blood, wade in b., give no quarter, spare none 906vb. *be pitiless;* annihilate, exterminate, liquidate, purge, send to the gas-chamber, commit genocide 165vb. *destroy.*
murder, commit m., assassinate, do for, settle, bump off, rub out; take for a ride, make to walk the plank; smother, burke, strangle, poison, gas.
kill oneself, do oneself in, commit suicide, suicide, put an end to one's life; commit hara-kiri, commit suttee; hang oneself, shoot oneself, blow out one's brains, cut one's throat; fall on one's sword, die in the high Roman fashion; put one's head in the oven, gas oneself, take poison; jump overboard, drown oneself; get oneself killed, have a fatal accident 361vb. *perish.*

Adv. *in at the death,* in at the kill.

Int. no quarter! cry havoc!

See: 162, 165, 263, 279, 287, 361, 381, 619, 653, 659, 712, 716, 718, 722, 724, 898, 904, 905, 906, 911, 961, 963, 964.

363 Corpse

N. *corpse,* corse, dead body, body; dead man, murderee, victim; defunct, goner, stiff; cadaver, carcass, skeleton, bones, dry b.; embalmed corpse, mummy; reliquiae, mortal remains, relics, ashes; clay, dust, earth; tenement of clay, mortal coil; carrion, food for worms, food for fishes; organic remains, fossil 125n. *palaetiology;* shade, manes, zombi 970n. *ghost.*

Adj. *cadaverous,* corpselike; deathlike, deathly; stiff, carrion.

See: 125, 970.

364 Interment

N. *interment,* burial, sepulture, entombment; encoffinment, urning, urn burial; disposal of the dead, burial customs, inhumation, cremation, incineration, embalming, mummification; embalmment, myrrh, spices; coffin, kist, shell, casket, urn, cinerary u., funerary u.; sarcophagus, mummy-case; pyre, funeral pile, crematorium; mortuary, charnel-house; bone-urn, ossuary; funeral parlor; sexton, grave-digger; mortician, undertaker, funeral director; embalmer, pollinator.

obsequies, exequies, obit; mourning, weeping and wailing, wake 836n. *lamentation;* last rites, burial service; funeral rites, funeral solemnity, funeral procession, cortege; knell, passing bell; dead march, muffled drum, last post, taps; memorial service, requiem, funeral hymn, Dies Irae, funeral oration, funeral sermon; elegy, dirge 836n. *lament;* inscription, epitaph, necrologue, obituary, lapidary phrases, RIP, hic jacet; sepulchral monument, stele, tombstone, gravestone, headstone, ledger; brass; hatchment; stone cross, war memorial; cenotaph 548n. *monument;* epitaphist, necrologist, obituary-writer; monumental mason.

funeral, hearse, bier, pall, catafalque, coffin; mourner, weeper, keener; mute, pall-bearer, dom; lych-gate (**see** *obsequies*).

grave clothes, cerements, cere cloth, shroud, winding sheet, mummy-wrapping.

cemetery, burial place; God's acre, garden of sleep, garden of remembrance; churchyard, graveyard, boneyard; urn cemetery, catacomb, columbarium; tower of silence; necropolis, city of the dead; valley of dry bones, Golgotha; mortuary, morgue.

tomb, vault, crypt; mummy-chamber; pyramid, mastaba; tower of silence; mausoleum, sepulcher, tope, stupa; grave, narrow house, long home; grave pit, cist, sepulchral c., beehive tomb, shaft t.; barrow, long b., round b., tumulus, cairn, cromlech, dolmen, menhir 548n. *monument;* memorial, cenotaph.

inquest 459n. *inquiry;* necropsy, autopsy, postmortem, postmortem examination; exhumation, disinterment, disentombment.

Adj. *buried,* interred, coffined, urned etc. vb.; laid to rest, in the grave, below ground, under g., six feet under, pushing up the daisies 361adj. *dead.*

funereal, funerary, funebral; somber, sad 428adj. *black;* mourning; elegiac, mortuary, cinerary, crematory, sepulchral; obsequial, obituary; lapidary, epitaphial, epitaphic; necrological, dirgelike 836adj. *lamenting.*

Vb. *inter,* inhume, bury; lay out, prepare for burial, close the eyes; embalm, mummify; coffin, encoffin, kist; urn, inurn, entomb, ensepulcher; lay in the grave, consign to earth, lay to rest, put to bed with a shovel, burn on the pyre, cremate, incinerate 381vb. *burn;* go to a funeral, take the burial service, say prayers for the dead, sing a requiem, sing a dirge; toll the knell, sound the last post, play taps; mourn, keen, hold a wake 836vb. *lament.*

exhume, disinter, unbury; disentomb, untomb, unsepulcher; unearth, dig up.

Adv. *in memoriam,* post-obit, postmortem, beneath the sod.

See: 361, 381, 428, 459, 548, 836.

365 Animality. Animal

N. *animality,* animation, animal life, animal spirits; animal kingdom, fauna, brute creation; physique, flesh, flesh and blood; animalization, zoomorphism, Pan; animal behavior 944n. *sensualism.*

animal, created being, living thing; birds, beasts and fishes; creature, brute, beast, dumb animal, creeping thing; protozoon, metazoon; zoophyte 196n. *animalcule;* mammal, marsupial, batrachian, amphibian, fish, mollusk, crustacean, bird, reptile, worm, insect, arachnid; invertebrate, vertebrate, articulate, biped; quadruped, ass, donkey, moke; mule 273n. *horse, beast of burden;* wild horse, kiang, warragal; zebra, giraffe; carnivore, herbivore, omnivore, man-eater; wild animal, animal ferae naturae, game, beast of prey, beast of the field; pack, wolf-p.; flock, herd; stock, livestock 369n. *stock farm;* tame animal, domestic a., pet; extinct animal, dodo, auk, moa; prehistoric animal, pterodactyl, coelenterate; saurian, ichthyosaurus, plesiosaurus, dinosaur, brontosaur, megatherium; big animal, bruin, bear, grizzly, brown bear, black b., white b., polar b.; elephant, rogue e., tusker; mammoth, mastodon; pachyderm, hippopotamus, rhinoceros; keitloa; fabled animal, unicorn, griffin, abominable snowman, yeti 84n. *rara avis.*

bird, winged thing, fowl, fowls of the air, denizens of the day; young bird, fledgling, squab 132n. *youngling;* avifauna, birdlife; migrant, winter visitor, summer v.; bird of omen, raven, jackdaw, crow, rook, albatross; cagebird; song-bird, humming-b., singing-b., songster, warbler, nightingale, bulbul, lark; thrush, mavis; blackbird, merle, linnet, canary, cuckoo, koel; talking bird, parrot, polly, macaw, myna, parakeet, budgerigar, magpie; dove, turtle-d., ring-d., cushat, culver, pigeon, wood-p., pouter p., homing p., carrier p.; sparrow, wheatear, finch, tit, wren, babbler; woodpecker, yaffle; colored bird, peacock, bird of paradise, golden oriole, scarlet minivet, scarlet tanager, cardinal, bluebird, blue jay, goldfinch, robin; swift, chimney s., swallow, martin; nightbird, owl, night-o., barn-o., screech-o., hoot-o., nightjar, stone-curlew, bat, flying fox; scavenging bird, carrion crow, king-c., drongo, jungle-crow, adjutant bird, vulture, bird of Mars, king vulture, Bengal v., white scavenger; pharaoh's chicken, arctic skua.

bird of prey, lammergeier, eagle, eaglet, erne, golden eagle, sea-e., crested serpent eagle, bird of Jove; gled, kite, pariah k., Brahminy k.; harrier, osprey, buzzard, buzzard-eagle; hawk, sparrow-h., chicken-h., falcon, peregrine f., hobby, merlin, shrike; fishing bird, kingfisher, gannet, cormorant, shag, skua, artic s.; gull, herring g., kittiwake, tern, oyster-catcher; puffin, razorbill, guillemot; petrel, stormy p., shearwater, ocean bird; marsh bird, wading b., stork, crane, demoiselle c., avocet, heron, hern, paddy-bird, spoon-bill, ibis, flamingo.

waterfowl, swan, cob, pen, cygnet; duck, drake, duckling; goose, gander, gosling; teal, whistling t.; ouzel, mallard, widgeon, moorhen, coot, jaçana, diver, grebe, dabchick; merganser, goosander.

flightless bird, ratite, ostrich, emu, cassowary; apteryx, kiwi; moa, dodo, penguin.

table bird, game bird, woodcock, woodpigeon, squab, peacock, peahen, peafowl, grouse, ptarmigan, capercaillie, pheasant, partridge, duck, snipe, snippet; quail, ortolan; turkey, gobbler; guinea-fowl, guinea-hen, goose, chicken.

poultry, hen, biddy, Dame Partlet, cock, cockerel, dunghill cock, rooster, Chanticleer; barndoor fowl, barnyard fowl; chicken, pullet; spring chicken, boiler, broiler, roaster, capon; Orpington, Rhode Island hen, Wyandotte.

cattle, herd, livestock, neat, kine, beeves; bull, cow, calf, heifer, fatling, yearling; maverick; Brahman bull, Apis; ox, oxen, steer, stot, stirk, bullock; beef cattle, highland c., Black Angus, Aberdeen A., Hereford, beef shorthorn, Galloway, Belted G.; dairy cattle, dairy herd, milchcow, Guernsey, Jersey, Alderney, Friesian, Dexter; dual-purpose cattle, Red Poll, shorthorn, Lincoln; buffalo, bison, aurochs, urus, nilgai; yak, musk-ox; goat, billy-g., nanny-g., mountain g., wild g.

sheep, baa-baa, ram, tup, wether, bell-w., ewe, lamb, ewe-l., lambkin; tag, teg; South Down, Hampshire D., Dorset Horn, Cheviot; mountain sheep, Ovis Poli.

pig, swine, boar, wild b., tusker; hog, sow; piglet, pigling, sucking-pig, suckling-p., shoat, porker; Large White, Large Black, Middle White, Wessex Saddleback, Berkshire, Tamworth.

dog, bow-wow, bitch, whelp, puppy-dog, pup, puppy, mutt; cur, hound, tyke; mongrel, pariah dog, pi-d.; coach-dog Dalmatian; watch-dog, house-d., ban-d., police d., bloodhound, mastiff; sheepdog, collie, Welsh c., Newfoundland, Doberman pinscher; bulldog, boxer, bullterrier, wolfhound, Russian wolfhound, borzoi, Afghan hound, Alsatian; Great Dane; St. Bernard; greyhound, courser, running-dog, whippet; pack, hunting p.; game dog, elk-hound, deer-h., stag-h., boar-h., fox-h., otter-h., badger-h., basset-h.; badger-dog, dachshund; lurcher; harrier, beagle, whippet; gun-dog, retriever, golden r., Labrador r., pointer, setter, Irish s.;

spaniel, water s., terrier, smooth-haired t., short-haired t., wire-haired t., wire-haired fox-t., Jones t., sealyham, black-and-tan terrier, long-haired t., rough-haired t., Scottish t., Skye t., Irish t., Kerry blue t., Dandy Dinmont, cairn, Airedale; cocker spaniel, springer s., King Charles s.; show dog, fancy d., toy d., Mexican hairless, Pomeranian; lapdog, chow, Pekingese, pug-dog; Welsh corgie; poodle, French p., miniature p., toy p.; husky, sledge-dog; wild dog, dingo; canine, wolf, prairie w., prairie dog; barking wolf, coyote.

cat, grimalkin, puss, pussy, kitten, kit, kitty-cat, pussy c.; tom, tom-c., gib-c.; mouser; Cheshire cat; tabby cat, Persian c., Siamese c., Angora c., Abyssinian c., Manx c., tortoiseshell c., marmalade c., blue c., black c., cream c.; feline, lion, tiger, leopard, cheetah, panther, puma, jaguar, cougar, red lion, American l.; wild-cat, bobcat, cat-a-mountain, lynx.

deer, cervidae, cervine family; stag, hart, hind, buck, fawn, pricket; red deer, fallow d., roe d., roe, roebuck; musk-deer, reindeer, caribou; hog-deer, Babirusa; gazelle, antelope, springbok, wildebeest, gnu; elk, moose, Cape-elk, eland.

monkey, jacko, rhesus monkey, squirrel m., Midas m., marmoset, tamarin; hanuman, langur; ape, anthropoid a., chimpanzee, jocko, gorilla, baboon, orangutan, mandrill; monkeydom, bandarlog; monkey god, hanuman.

reptile, creeping thing; ophidian, serpent, sea s.; snake, rattlesnake, water s., water moccasin, adder, asp; viper, Russell's v.; copperhead; krait; cobra, king c., hamadryad; cerastes, mamba, anaconda, boa constrictor, python; amphibian, crocodile, alligator, caiman, mugger, gavial; annelid, worm, earthworm; lizard, slow-worm, chameleon, iguana, gecko, tiktiki, salamander, polywog, amphisbaena; basilisk, cockatrice; chelonian, turtle, tortoise, terrapin; malacostracan, crab.

frog, batrachian, bull-frog, croaker, paddock, toad, horned t.; eft, newt, tadpole.

marsupial, kangaroo, wallaby, opossum, wombat, marmose.

rodent, rat, brown r., black r., sewer r., plague r., pack r., bandicoot; mouse, field-m., shrew; mole, hamster, guinea-pig; gopher, marmot, woodchuck; beaver, squirrel, red s., gray s., black s., striped s., chipmunk, hackee; mongoose, raccoon, ichneumon; porcupine.

fly, winged insect; house-fly, bluebottle, horsefly, dragonfly, butterfly, moth; caddis-fly, mayfly, greenfly, blackfly; ladybird; firefly; gadfly, gnat, midge, mosquito, gallinipper, culex, anopheles; bee, honey-b., queen b., worker b., bumble-b., humble-b., drone; wasp, yellow-jacket, hornet; beetle, stag b., flying b., Japanese b., Colorado b., cockroach.

vermin, parasite; insect, chrysalis, cocoon; perfect insect, imago; bug, bedbug, louse, bed-l., flea, nit; maggot, earwig, mite, cheese-m.; weevil, boll-w., curculio; ant, emmet, pismire; red ant, white a., winged a., soldier a., worker a.; termite; pest, garden p., slug, wireworm, caterpillar; woodworm, death-watch beetle; locust, grasshopper, cicada, cicala; cricket, house-c., field-c.; rabbit, bunny, bunny-rabbit, coney; hare, leveret; Reynard, fox, dog-f., vixen; stoat, ferret, weasel, skunk, polecat.

fish, sea f., river f.; marine animal, cetacean, whale, leviathan, delphinoid, grampus; sperm whale, baleen w., bottle-nosed w., narwhal; dolphin, porpoise, seal, sea lion, sea bear, walrus; shark, sharkray, angel fish, monk f., tiddle f.; swordfish, sawfish, starfish, sea urchin, sea horse, jelly-fish, ray fish, stingray; torpedo, numb-fish, cramp-f., cramp-ray; flying fish; goldfish; cephalopod, octopus, calamary, cuttlefish, squid, pen-fish, inkfish, sepia; goby, gudgeon; wrasse, ballan; pike, jack, luce; mollusk, bivalve. **See** *table fish.*

table fish 301n. *fish food;* salmon, grilse; pirling; grayling; trout, bream, roach, dace, perch, bass, carp, rui; tunny, tuna, mackerel, sturgeon, mullet, turbot, halibut, brill, cod, hake, haddock, herring, buckling, shad, dory, plaice, skate, sole, flounder, whiting, smelt, sprat, sardine, whitebait; hilsa, beckti, pomfret; mangofish, mahseer; shellfish, lobster, langouste, homard, crawfish, crayfish, crab; shrimp, prawn, chingree; oyster, bluepoint o.; clam, quahog, cherry-stone clam, little-neck c.; winkle, mussel, cockle, whelk; eel, sea e., conger e., elver, grig.

Adj. *animal,* animalcular, animalculine; beastly, bestial; human, manly, subhuman; therianthropic, theriomorphic, zoomorphic; zoological; mammalian, warm-blooded; primatial, anthropoidal, lemurine; equine, asinine, mulish; cervine; bovine, taurine, ruminant; ovine, sheepish; hircine, goatish; porcine, piggy; ursine; elephantine; rhinocerotic; canine, doggy; lupine, wolfish; feline, catty, tigerish, leonine; tigroid, pantherine; vulpine, vixenish, foxy; avian, birdlike; aquiline, vulturine; passerine, columbine, columbaceous, dovelike; cold-blooded, fishy, piscine, piscatorial, piscatory, molluscan; amphibian, amphibious; batrachian, reptilian, ophidian, snaky, serpentine, viperish, colubrine, colubriform; vermicular, wormy, weevilly; insectile, entomological.

See: 84, 132, 196, 273, 301, 369, 944.

366 Vegetability. Plant

N. *vegetability,* vegetable life, vegetable kingdom; flora, vegetation; flowering, blooming, florescence, frondescence; lushness, rankness, luxuriance 635n. *plenty;* green belt 348n. *plain;* vegetation god, Dionysus, Flora, Pan, Silenus; faun, dryad, hamadryad, woodnymph 967n. *nymph.*

wood, timber, lumber, softwood, hardwood, heart-wood; forest, virgin f., primeval f.; rain-forest; taiga; weald, wold, jungle, bush, heath, scrub, maquis 348n. *grassland;* greenwood, woodland, bocage, copse, coppice, spinney, spinet; thicket, brake, covert; park, chase, game-preserve; frith, shaw, hurst, holt; plantation, arboretum, pinery; orchard, orangery 370n. *garden;* grove, clump, tope, clearing; brushwood, underwood, undergrowth; bushiness, shrubbery, bushes, windbreak, hedge, hedgerow.

forestry, dendrology, silviculture, tree-planting, afforestation, conservation; woodman, forester, forest-guard, verderer; wood-cutter, lumberman, lumberjack; dendrologist.

tree, shrub, sapling, scion, stock; pollard; shoot, sucker, trunk, bole; limb, branch, bough, twig; leguminous tree, coniferous t., greenwood tree, evergreen t., deciduous t., softwood t., hardwood t., ironwood t.; fruit tree, nut t., timber t.; oak, holm o., ilex; teak, sal; mahogany, walnut, ebony; ash, mountain a., rowan; beech, copper b.; birch, silver b., chestnut, horse c.; willow, weeping w.; alder; poplar, Lombardy p., white p., black p., trembling p., aspen; lime, linden; elm, sycamore, plane; cornel, dogwood; pine, white p., fir, Scotch f., silver f., Douglas f., redwood, sequoia, Wellingtonia; cedar, deodar, larch, spruce, Norway s.; maple, Japanese m., sugar m., rock m., striped m., moosewood; silver maple, red m.; cypress, yew, box, holly; myrtle, laurel, bay; casuarina, beef-wood; fig-tree, pipal, banyan; palm, date-p., coconut-p., fan-p., bottle-p.; acacia, flowering tree, Japanese cherry, purple prunus, magnolia, camellia, rhododendron, azalea, ixora, lilac, laburnum, asoka; gul mor *or* gold mohur; mandara, coral-tree, simmul t., silk-cotton t.; gum-tree, eucalyptus, rubber-tree, aloes, lignaloes, agave; bamboo, cane, sugar c.

foliage, foliation, frondescence; leafiness, leafage, umbrage; ramage, limb, branch, bough, twig; spray, sprig; tree-top; leaf, frond, flag; leaflet, foliole; fir-cone, pine-needle; seed-leaf, cotyledon; leaf-stalk, petiole, stalk, stem, tigella, caulicle, radical.

plant, growing thing; sucker, wort, weed; seed, root, bulb; thallophyte, gametophyte, sporophyte; greenery, herb 301n. *potherb, vegetable, tuber;* succulent plant, leguminous p., legume, vetch, pulse, lentil, bean; parasitic plant, ivy, creeper, vine, bine, tendril; cucurbit, calabash, gourd, marrow, melon; thorn, thistle, cactus, euphorbia; spurge; heath, heather, ling; broom, furze, gorse, fern, bracken; moss, bog m., peat m., sphagnum; lichen, fungus, bolet, mushroom, truffle, toadstool, puff-ball, spore; mold, mucor, penicillin; osier, sedge, reed, rush, bullrush; algae, conferva, confervite, seaweed, wrack, sea w., sargasso, gulfweed.

flower, floweret, blossom, bloom, bud, node, burgeon; petal, sepal; calyx, wild flower, garden f., annual, biennial, triennial, perennial; hot-house plant, exotic; flowerbed, seedbed; gardening, horticulture, floriculture.

grass 348n. *grassland;* pasture, pasturage, herbage, verdure, turf, sod, divot; bent, Rhode Island b., esparto grass, Spanish g., spear g., couch g., blue g., Kentucky blue g., Marion blue g., citronella; lawn grass, wild g.; cut grass, hay; graminiferous plant, millet; trefoil, shamrock; clover, four-leaf c.

corn, grain, cereal plant, farinaceous p. 301n. *cereal;* wheat, oats, barley, rye, buckwheat, spelt, emmer; Indian corn, maize, mealies, rice, paddy; Indian millet, sorghum, guinea-corn, durra; straw, stubble; chaff, husk; ground corn, hominy, meal, flour.

Adj. *vegetal,* vegetative, vegetable, botanical; evergreen; deciduous; horticultural, floricultural; floral, flowery, blooming, bloomy; rank, lush, overgrown; weedy, weed-ridden; verdant, verdurous, green; grassy, mossy; turfy, caespitose; turfen, caespititious; gramineous, graminiferous, poaceous, herbaceous, herbal; leguminous, vetchy; fungous, fungoid, fungiform; exogenous, endogenous.

arboreal, arborical, arboreous, dendriform, dendritic, treelike, forestal; arborescent, forested, timbered; woodland, woody, wooded, sylvan, beechy; grovy, bosky; wild, jungly, scrubby; bushy, shrubby, copsy; silvicultural, forested, planted; dendrologous, dendrological.

wooden, wood, xyloid, ligneous, lignous; hard-grained, soft-grained.

Vb. *vegetate,* germinate, sprout, shoot 164vb. *produce;* plant, grow, garden, botanize 370vb. *cultivate;* forest, afforest, reforest.

See: 164, 301, 348, 370, 635, 967.

367 Zoology: the science of animals

N. *zoology,* zoonomy, zoography, zootomy; animal physiology, comparative p., morphology 331n. *structure;* ichthyotomy, anatomy, comparative a.; anthropology, ornithology, bird lore, bird watching, ornithoscopy, ichthyology, herpetology, malacology, helminthology, entomology; oryctology, paleontology; taxidermy.

zoologist, ornithologist, ichthyologist, entomologist, anatomist.

Adj. *zoological* etc. n.

See: 331.

368 Botany: the science of plants

N. *botany,* phytography, phytology, phytonomy; vegetable physiology, plant pathology; herborization, botanization; dendrology 366n. *forestry;* mycology, fungology, algology; botanical garden 370n. *garden;* hortus siccus, herbarium, herbal.

botanist, herbist, herbarist, herbalist, herborist, herbarian.

Adj. *botanical* etc. n.

Vb. *botanize* etc. n.

See: 366, 370.

369 Animal husbandry

N. *animal husbandry,* animal management, training, manege; thremmatology, domestication, breeding, stock-b., rearing, cicuration; taming etc. vb.; zoohygiantics, veterinary science; phthisozoics 362n. *killing;* horse-breeding, cattle-raising, sheep-farming, pig-keeping, chicken-k., bee-k.; stirpiculture, pisciculture, apiculture, sericulture; veterinary surgeon, vet, horse doctor 658n. *doctor;* hostler, groom, stable boy 742n. *servant;* farrier, blacksmith; keeper, gamekeeper, gillie.

stock farm, stud f., stud; dairy farm, cattle f.; fish farm, fishery, hatchery; fish pond, fish tank, piscina, vivarium; duck pond; pig farm, piggery; beehive, hive, apiary; pasture, grazing, sheeprun, sheepwalk; chicken farm, chicken-run, hen-r., free range; hen-battery, deep litter.

cattle pen, byre 192n. *stable;* sheepfold, pinfold 235n. *enclosure;* coop, hencoop, henhouse, cowhouse, cowshed, pigsty; swannery, goosery; aquarium, bird-cage 748n. *prison;* bear-pit, cockpit 724n. *arena;* Noah's Ark.

zoo, zoological gardens, menagerie, circus; aviary, vivarium, terrarium, aquarium.

breeder, stock-b., horse-b.; trainer, animal t., lion-tamer; cattle-farmer, sheep-f., wool-grower, pig-keeper, bee-k., apiarist; fancier, bird-f., pigeon-f.

herdsman, herd, neatherd, cattleherd, cowherd; stockman, cattleman; rancher; cowman, cowkeeper, cowboy, cowpuncher, bronco-buster, gaucho; shepherd, shepherdess; goatherd; goose-girl; milkmaid; fodderer.

Adj. *tamed,* broken, broken in; gentle, docile; domestic, domesticated; reared, raised, bred; pure-bred, thoroughbred, half-bred; stirpicultural.

Vb. *break in,* tame, cicurate; domesticate, acclimatize 610vb. *habituate;* train 534vb. *teach;* back, mount, whip, spur 267vb. *ride;* yoke, harness, hitch, bridle, saddle; cage, corral, round up, ride, herd 747vb. *restrain.*

breed stock, breed, grow, hatch, culture, incubate, nurture, fatten; ranch, farm 370vb. *cultivate;* hive, swarm 104vb. *be many;* rear, raise.

groom, currycomb, rub down, stable, bed down; tend, herd, shepherd; shear, fleece; milk; drench, water, fodder 301vb. *feed.*

See: 104, 192, 235, 267, 301, 362, 370, 534, 610, 658, 724, 742, 747, 748.

370 Agriculture

N. *agriculture,* agronomy, agronomics, rural economy; cultivation, sowing, reaping; growth, harvest, crop, vintage 632n. *store;* husbandry, farming, mixed f., intensive f., contour f.; cattle farming, dairy f. 369n. *animal husbandry;* wheat farming, arable f.; geoponics, hydroponics, tray agriculture, tank farming; spade farming, tillage, tilth, spadework; floriculture, flower-growing; horticulture, gardening; fruit-growing, pomiculture, citriculture; olericulture, kitchen gardening; viticulture, viniculture, wine-growing, vine-dressing; arboriculture, silviculture, afforestation 366n. *forestry;* landscape gardening, landscape architecture; water, dung, manure 171n. *fertilizer;* fodder, winter feed 301n. *provender;* silage, ensilage 632n. *storage.*

farm, home f., grange; arable farm, dairy f., stock f., sheep f., cattle f., ranch, hacienda; model farm; state farm, collective f., kolkhoz, kibbutz; farmland, arable land, plow-l., fallow 344n. *soil;* herbage, pasturage, pasture, fields, meadows 348n. *grassland;* demesne, manor-farm, estate, holding, small-h., croft 777n. *lands;* allotment, kitchen garden; market garden, truck g., hop g.; tea-garden, tea-estate; nursery-garden, nursery; vinery, vineyard; fruit-farm, orchard.

garden, botanical g., flower-g., rose-g., rock g., ornamental g., winter g.; vegetable garden, cabbage patch, kitchen garden, allotment; fruit garden, orchard, orangery; tree garden, arboretum, pinery 366n. *wood;* patch, plot, plat, grass-p., grass, lawn, park 235n. *enclosure;* border, bed, flower-b., knot, parterre 844n. *ornamental art;* seedbed, frame, cold f., cucumber f. 164n. *propagation;* cloche, conservatory, hot-house, greenhouse, glasshouse 383n. *heater;* flowerpot 194n. *vessel.*

husbandman, farmer, farm manager, farm-bailiff, granger; cultivator, planter, tea-p., coffee-p., rubber-p.; agriculturist, tiller of the soil, peasant, ryot, under-r., kulak, muzhik, paysanne; serf, ascriptus glebae; share-cropper, metayer, tenant-farmer; gentleman farmer, yeoman; small-holder, crofter, allotment-holder, lambardar, zamindar; fruit-farmer, orchardist; winegrower, vineyardist; farm hand, plower, sower, reaper, harvester, mower, gleaner; thresher, barnsman; picker, hop-p., vintager; agricultural folk, farming community, peasantry; good farmer, improving landlord 654n. *reformer;* farming type, Boer, Adam, Triptolemus.

gardener, horticulturist, mali, flower-grower; topiarist, landscape gardener; seedsman, nurseryman; market gardener; hop-grower, fruit-g., citriculturist, vine-grower, vine-dresser; forester 366n. *forestry;* planter, digger, delver.

farm tool, plow, plowshare, colter; harrow, chain h., spike h.; spade, hoe, rake, trowel; dibble, digging-stick; hayrake, hay-fork, pitchfork; scythe, sickle, reaping hook, shears, secateur 256n. *sharp edge;* flail, winnowing fan; winepress; cutter, reaper, thresher, binder, baler, combine-harvester; tractor; hay-wagon; byre, cowshed; barn, hayloft, silo 632n. *storage.*

Adj. *agrarian,* peasant, farming; agrestic, georgic, bucolic, pastoral, rustic, Boeotian; agricultural, agronomic, geoponic, praedial, manorial, collective; arable, cultivable; plowed, dug, planted, transplanted.

horticultural, garden, gardening, topiary; cultured, hot-house, exotic, artificial.

Vb. *cultivate,* farm, ranch, garden, grow; till, till the soil, scratch the s.; dig, delve, spade, dibble; seed, sow, broadcast, scatter the seed, set, plant, dibble in, transplant, plant out, bed o.; plow, raft 201vb. *space;* replow, backset; harrow, rake, hoe; weed, prune, top and lop, thin out 204vb. *shorten;* graft, engraft, imp 303vb. *implant;* force, fertilize, dung, manure 174vb. *invigorate;* grass over, sod, rotate the crop; leave fallow 674vb. *not use;* harvest, gather in 632vb. *store;* glean, reap, mow, cut, scythe, cut a swathe; bind, bale, stook, sheaf; flail 332vb. *pulverize;* thresh, winnow, sift, bolt 46vb. *separate;* crop, pluck, pick, gather; tread out the grapes; ensile, ensilate; improve one's land 654vb. *make better;* enclose, fence 235vb. *enclose;* ditch, drain 342vb. *dry;* water 341vb. *irrigate.*

See: 46, 164, 171, 174, 194, 201, 204, 235, 256, 301, 303, 332, 336, 344, 348, 366, 369, 383, 632, 654, 674, 777, 844.

371 Mankind

N. *mankind,* womankind, humankind; humanity, human nature, creaturehood; flesh, mortality; generations of man, peoples of the earth; the world,

everyone, everybody, the living, ourselves; human race, human species, man; tellurian, earthling; human being, Adam, Adamite, lord of creation; civilized man, political animal, civilized world, comity of nations 654n. *civilization;* uncivilized man, savage, backward peoples; zoological man, hominidae, hominid, homo sapiens; oreanthropus, early man, dawn man, Eoanthropus, Plesianthropus, Sinanthropus; Neanderthal man, Peking m., Java m., caveman; ape-man, Australopithecus, pithecanthropus; non-Adamic man; nation, ethnic type 11n. *race.*
anthropology, anthropography, anthroposophy; anthropometry, craniometry, craniology; anthropogenesis, somatology; ethnology, ethnography, folklore, mythology; social anthropology, demography; social science, humanitarianism 901n. *sociology.*
person, individual, human being, everyman, everywoman; creature, fellow c., mortal, body; a being, soul, living s.; God's image; one, somebody, someone, so and so, such a one; party, customer, character, type, element; chap, guy, bloke, fellow, cove, johnny 372n. *male;* personage, figure, person of note, VIP 638n. *bigwig;* star 890n. *favorite;* dramatis personae, all those concerned 686n. *personnel;* unit, head, hand, nose.
social group, society, community 706n. *association;* human family 11n. *family;* primitive society, tribalism; organized society, international s., comity of nations 654n. *civilization;* community at large, people, persons, folk; public, general p., man in the street, you and me; population, populace, citizenry 191n. *native;* stratified society, the classes; the masses, the million, hoi polloi, the herd, the lower orders, working classes 869n. *commonalty.*
nation, nationality, statehood, nationalism, national consciousness; ultranationalism, chauvinism, expansionism, imperialism; civil society, body politic, Leviathan, people, demos; state, city-s., welfare s., civil s., nation s., multiracial s.; realm, commonwealth, commonweal 733n. *polity;* democracy, aristocracy.
Adj. *human,* creaturely, mortal, fleshly; Adamite, Adamitic, Adamitical; earthborn, tellurian; anthropoid, hominal; anthropological, ethnographical, racial 11adj. *ethnic;* societal, societary; cosmopolitan, international.
anthropocentric, personal, individual.
national, state, civic, civil, public, general, communal, tribal, social,
See: 11, 191, 372, 638, 654, 686, 706, 733, 869, 890, 901.

372 Male

N. *male,* male sex, man, he; manliness, masculinity, manhood; androcentricism, male exclusiveness; mannishness, viraginity, gynandry; he-man, cave-m.; gentleman, sir, esquire, master; lord, my l., his lordship; Mr., mister, monsieur, Herr, señor, don, dom, senhor, signor; sahib, sri, srijut, babu, mirza; tovarich, comrade, citoyen; yeoman, wight, swain, fellow, guy, blade, bloke, beau, chap, cove, card, chappie, johnny, buffer; gaffer, goodman; father, grandfather 169n. *parent;* uncle, nephew, brother; boy, man-child 132n. *youngster;* son 170n. *sonship;* husband 894n. *spouse;* groom, bridegroom 894n. *bridesman;* bachelor; Adonis, Adam; stag party, menfolk.
male animal, cock, cockerel, rooster; drake, gander; male swan, cob; buck, stag, hart, staggard, spay, pricket, brocket, fawn; horse, stallion, entire horse, stud h., colt, foal; bull, calf, bull-c., bullock, ox, steer, stot; boar, hog, ram, tup; he-goat, billy g.; dog, dog-fox, tom-cat, gib-c.; gelding, capon, neuter cat.
Adj. *male,* masculine, androcentric; manly, he, virile; mannish, unfeminine, unwomanly; viraginous, gynandrous; manlike, trousered, pipe-smoking; arrhenotokous.
See: 132, 169, 170, 894.

373 Female

N. *female,* feminine gender, she, her, -ess; femineity, feminality, muliebrity; femininity, the eternal feminine; womanhood 134n. *adultness;* womanliness, girlishness; feminism; womanishness, effeminacy, androgyny 163n. *weakness;* gynecology, gyniatrics, gynics; gynogenesis 164n. *propagation.*
womankind, the sex, female s., fair s., gentle s., softer s.; the distaff side, womenfolk, women, matronage; hen party; gyneceum, women's quarters, zenana, purdah, seraglio, harem.
woman, Eve, she; petticoat, skirt; girl, girlie; virgin, maiden; nun, unmarried woman, old maid 895n. *spin-*

ster; coed, undergraduette; bachelor girl, new woman, career w., suffragette; bride, matron, dowager, married woman, wife, squaw 894n. *spouse;* mother, grandmother 169n. *parent;* wench, lass, nymph; lady, burd; filly 132n. *youngster;* grisette, midinette; blonde, brunette, platinum blonde; sweetheart, bird 887n. *loved one;* moll, doll, bit of fluff, broad, mistress, courtesan 952n. *loose woman;* quean, cotquean; shrew, virago, amazon; goddess, Venus, Aphrodite; aunt, niece, sister, daughter.

lady, gentlewoman; dame, madam, ma'am, mistress, Mrs., miss, madame, mademoiselle, Fraulein, Frau; signora, signorina, señora, señorita, srijukta, srimati, memsahib, mem; milady, ladyship, donna; goody, gammer, goodwife.

female animal, hen, duck, goose; pen (female swan); bitch, she-dog; mare, filly; cow, heifer, sow, gilt; ewe, ewe-lamb, gimmer; nanny-goat, she-g.; hind, doe; vixen, she-fox; tigress, lioness, she-bear.

Adj. *female,* gynecic, gynecian, mammiferous; she, feminine, petticoat; girlish, womanly, ladylike, maidenly, matronal, matronly; feminist, feministic; womanish, effeminate, unmanly; feminized, androgynous; thelytokous 164adj. *productive.*

See: 132, 134, 163, 164, 169, 887, 894, 895, 952.

374 Physical sensibility

N. *sensibility,* sensitiveness, tenderness, exposed nerve; soreness, sensitivity, touchiness, sore point; perceptivity, awareness, consciousness 819n. *moral sensibility;* physical sensibility, susceptivity, susceptibility, affectibility, soft spot; passibility, hyperesthesia, allergy; aestheticism, aesthetics; aesthete 846n. *man of taste;* touchy person, sensitive plant, thin skin 892n. *irascibility.*

sense, sensory process, external senses; touch, hearing, taste, smell, sight, sixth sense; sensation, impression 818n. *feeling;* effect, response, reaction, reflex, synesthesia; autosuggestion, autohypnosis, couéism; extrasensory perception, telepathy, thought-transference.

Adj. *sentient,* sensitive, sensitized; sensible, affectible, susceptible, passible; thin-skinned, touchy 892adj. *irascible;* sensuous 818adj. *feeling;* perceptive, aware, conscious 490adj. *knowing;* acute, sharp, keen 377adj. *painful;* tender, raw, sore, exposed; impressionable, alive, alive to, responsive; suggestible, over-impressionable, over-sensitive, hypersensitive, over-quick, high-strung, over-s. 822adj. *excitable;* ticklish, itchy.

striking, keen, sharp, acute, vivid, clear, lively; sudden, sensational 821adj. *impressive.*

Vb. *have feeling,* sense, become aware, awaken, wake up; perceive, realize 490vb. *know;* be sensible of 818vb. *feel;* react, tingle 819vb. *be sensitive;* have one's senses, hear, see, touch, taste; not contain one's feelings, burst, gush, overflow 822vb. *be excitable.*

cause feeling, stir the senses, stir the blood; stir, disturb 318vb. *agitate;* arouse, awaken, excite, strike, make *or* produce an impression 821vb. *impress;* arrest, astonish, cause a sensation 508vb. *surprise;* make sensible, bring home 534vb. *teach;* sharpen, cultivate 174vb. *invigorate;* refine, aestheticize; touch the quick, touch on the raw 377vb. *give pain;* increase sensitivity, sensitize.

Adv. *to the quick,* to the heart, on the raw.

See: 174, 318, 377, 490, 508, 534, 818, 819, 821, 822, 846, 892.

375 Physical insensibility

N. *insensibility,* physical i., impassability, insensitiveness; mental insensibility, impercipience, obtuseness 499n. *unintelligence;* insentience, anesthesia, hysterical anesthesia, la belle indifference; analgesia; narcotization, hypnosis, hypnotism, autohypnosis, autosuggestion; paralysis, palsy; numbness, narcosis; catalepsy, stupor, coma, trance, unconsciousness; narcolepsy, narcotism, sleeping-sickness 651n. *disease;* twilight sleep 679n. *sleep;* Sleeping Beauty, Rip van Winkle; amorality 820n. *moral insensibility.*

anesthetic, dope 658n. *drug;* anesthetic agent, local anesthetic, general a., ether, chloroform, morphia, cocaine, novocaine, chloral; gas, nitrous oxide, laughing gas; narcotic, sleeping tablets, sleeping draft 679n. *soporific;* opium, laudanum, poppy-seed; pain-killer, analgesic 177n. *moderator.*

Adj. *insensible,* insensitive, insentient, insensate; obtuse, dull, stupid 499adj. *unintelligent;* imperceptive, impercipient; unhearing 416adj.

deaf; unseeing 439adj. *blind;* senseless, sense-bereft, unconscious; inert 679adj. *inactive;* stony, stiff, cold, dead 266adj. *quiescent;* numb, benumbed, frozen; paralyzed, paralytic, palsied; doped, dopey, drugged; anesthetized, hypnotized; punch-drunk, dazed, stupefied; tranced, comatose 679adj. *sleepy;* anesthetic, analgesic; hypnotic, mesmeric 679adj. *somnific.*

unfeeling, callous, inured, indurated, hardened, case-h; insensitive, tactless; pachydermatous, thick-skinned; impassible, proof, shock-p.; impersonal 820adj. *impassive.*

Vb. *be insensible,*—insentient etc. adj.; not react 679vb. *be inactive;* have a thick skin 820vb. *be insensitive;* become insensible, harden oneself; indurate, cease to feel.

render insensible, make insensible; obtund 257vb. *blunt;* paralyze, benumb; freeze 382vb. *refrigerate;* deaden, put to sleep, induce s., hypnotize, mesmerize 679vb. *make inactive;* anesthetize, put under gas, chloroform; narcotize, drug, dope; dull, stupefy; stun, concuss, brain, knock out, render unconscious 279vb. *strike;* pall, cloy 863vb. *sate.*

See: 257, 266, 279, 382, 416, 439, 499, 651, 658, 679, 820, 863.

376 Physical Pleasure

N. *pleasure,* material p., physical p., sensual p., sensuous p.; gratification, sensuousness, sensuality, self-indulgence, bodily enjoyment, animal gratification, luxuria, luxuriousness, hedonism 944n. *sensualism;* dissipation, round of pleasure, cup of Circe 943n. *intemperance;* rest 685n. *refreshment;* treat, diversion, entertainment, divertissement 837n. bonne-bouche, titillation, relish *amusement;* feast, regale 301n. *feasting;* good feeding, eutrophy, 386n. *taste;* gusto, zest, keen appreciation; enjoyment, delight, happiness 824n. *joy.*

euphoria, well-being, contentment 828n. *content;* easeful living, gracious l.; ease, heart's-ease; convenience, comfort, coziness, snugness, creature comforts; luxury, luxuries 637n. *superfluity;* lap of luxury, clover, purple and fine linen 800n. *wealth;* feather-bed, bed of down, bed of roses, velvet, cushion, pillow 327n. *softness;* peace, quiet, rest 683n. *repose;* quiet dreams 679n. *sleep;* painlessness, euthanasia.

Adj. *pleasant,* pleasure-giving 826adj. *pleasurable;* pleasing, tickling, titillating; delightful, delightsome; welcome, grateful, gratifying, satisfying 685adj. *refreshing;* genial, congenial, cordial, heartwarming; nice, agreeable, enjoyable 837adj. *amusing;* palatable, delicious 386adj. *tasty;* sugary 392adj. *sweet;* perfumed 396adj. *fragrant;* tuneful 410adj. *melodious;* lovely 841adj. *beautiful.*

comfortable, affording comfort, comfy, homely, snug, cozy, warm, comforting, restful 683adj. *reposeful;* peaceful 266adj. *tranquil;* convenient, easy, painless; easeful, downy 327adj. *soft;* luxurious, de-luxe; enjoying comfort, euphoric, in comfort, at one's ease, slippered; happy, gratified 828adj. *content;* relieved 685adj. *refreshed.*

sensuous, of the senses, appealing to the s.; bodily, physical 319adj. *material;* voluptuous, pleasure-loving, enjoying, epicurean, hedonistic 944adj. *sensual.*

Vb. *enjoy,* relish, like, quite l.; feel pleasure, receive p., experience p. 824vb. *be pleased;* luxuriate in, revel in, riot in, swim in, roll in, wallow in 683vb. *repose;* gloat on, gloat over, get a kick out of; lick one's lips, smack one's l. 386vb. *taste;* apricate; bask, bask in the sunshine 379vb. *be hot;* live on the fat of the land, live comfortably, live in comfort 730vb. *prosper;* give pleasure 826vb. *please.*

Adv. *in comfort* etc. n.; at one's ease; in clover, on velvet, on a bed of roses.

See: 177, 257, 266, 279, 319, 327, 382, 386, 392, 396, 410, 416, 439 499, 637, 651, 679, 683, 685, 730, 800, 824, 826, 828, 837, 841, 863, 944.

377 Physical pain

N. *pain,* physical p., bodily p.; discomfort, malaise, inconvenience; distress, thin time, hell 731vb. *adversity;* sufferance 825n. *suffering;* exhaustion, weariness, strain 684n. *fatigue;* hurt, bruise; cut, gash 655n. *wound;* aching, smarting, heart-ache, dolor, anguish, agony, lancination, slow death, death by inches, torment, torture, cruciation; crucifixion, martyrdom, vivisection; rack, wheel, thumbscrew 964n. *instrument of torture;* painfulness, sore, soreness, tenderness; malaise, discomfort; painful aftermath, hangover 949n. *crapulence;* nightmare, ephialtes 854n. *fear.*

pang, smart, twinge, nip, pinch; throe,

thrill; stitch, cramp, cramps, convulsion 318n. *spasm;* sting, sharp pain, shooting p., darting p., gnawing p.; ache, headache, splitting head, migraine, megrim, hemicrania; tooth-ache, ear-a., belly-a., gripe, colic, collywobbles; neuritis, neuralgia, angina; arthritis, rheumatoid a., rheumatism, fibrositis; sciatica, lumbago, gout.

Adj. *painful,* paining, aching, agonizing, excruciating, exquisite; harrowing, racking, tormenting; poignant 827adj. *distressing;* burning, biting, stabbing, shooting, tingling, smarting, throbbing; sore, raw, tender, exposed; bitter, bitter-sweet 393adj. *sour;* disagreeable, uncomfortable, inconvenient 827adj. *unpleasant.*

pained, hurt, tortured, martyred, agonized etc. vb.; suffering, aching, flinching, wincing, quivering, writhing.

Vb. *give pain,* ache, hurt, pain, sting; inflict pain, excruciate, put to torure, lacerate, torment, twist the arm of, rack, wring 963vb. *torture;* flog, crucify, martyr 963vb. *punish;* vivisect, lancinate, tear, harrow, lacerate 46vb. *cut;* prick, stab 263vb. *pierce;* gripe, nip, pinch, tweak, twinge, shoot, throb; devour, bite, gnaw 301vb. *eat;* grind, grate, jar, set on edge; fret, chafe, gall 333vb. *rub;* irritate 832vb. *aggravate;* put on the rack, break on the wheel; kill by inches, prolong the agony; grate on the ear 411vb. *discord;* inconvenience, annoy, distress 827vb. *incommode.*

feel pain, suffer p., feel the pangs 825vb. *suffer;* agonize, ache, smart, chafe; twitch, wince, flinch, writhe, squirm, creep, shiver, quiver, jactitate 318vb. *be agitated;* tingle, get pins and needles; sit on thorns, have a thin time, be a martyr, go through it 731vb. *have trouble;* shriek, yell, scream, howl, groan 408vb. *cry;* weep 836vb. *lament;* lick one's wounds.

See: 46, 263, 301, 318, 333, 393, 408, 411, 655, 684, 731, 825, 827, 832, 836, 854, 949, 963, 964.

378 Touch: sensation of touch

N. *touch,* taction, tactility, palpability; contrectation, handling, feeling, palpation, manipulation; massage, kneading, squeeze, pressure 333n. *friction;* graze, contact 202n. *contiguity;* stroke, pat; flick, flip, tap 279n. *impulse;* tact, feel 463n. *discrimination;* sense of touch, fine t., precision 494n. *accuracy;* delicacy, artistry 694n. *skill.*

formication, titillation, tickling sensation; creeps, goose-flesh; tingle, tingling, pins-and-needles; scratchiness, itchiness, itch, urtication, urticaria, nettlerash, hives; dhobi's itch, prickly heat 651n. *skin disease;* phthiriasis, pediculosis 649n. *uncleanness.*

feeler, organ of touch, palp, palpus, antenna, whisker; proboscis, tongue; digit, forefinger, thumb (**see** *finger*); green fingers; hand, paw, palm, flipper.

finger, forefinger, index, middle finger, ring f., little f.; thumb, pollex; hallux, great toe 214n. *foot;* five fingers, bunch of fives, "pickers and stealers"; hand, fist 778n. *nippers;* finger-nail, talon.

Adj. *tactual,* tactile; palpal, palpiform; touching, lambent, licking, grazing etc. vb.; touchable, tangible, palpable 324adj. *dense;* light of touch, light-fingered; heavy-handed 695adj. *clumsy.*

handed, with hands; right-handed 241adj. *dextral;* left-handed 242adj. *sinistral;* thumbed, fingered; five-finger; manual, digital.

Vb. *touch,* make contact, graze, scrape, brush, glance; kiss, osculate 202vb. *be contiguous;* impinge, overlap; hit, meet 279vb. *collide;* feel, palp, palpate; finger, thumb, take between finger and thumb, pinch, nip, vellicate, massage 333vb. *rub;* palm, run the hand over, pass the fingers o.; stroke, pat down 258vb. *smooth;* wipe, sweep 648vb. *clean;* touch lightly, tap, pat, flick, flip, tickle, scratch; lick, tongue; paw, clip, fondle 889vb. *caress;* handle, twiddle, tweedle, fiddle with; manipulate, wield, manhandle 173vb. *operate;* touch roughly, bruise, crush 377vb. *give pain;* fumble, grope, grabble, grubble, put out a feeler, throw out a f. 461vb. *be tentative.*

itch, tickle, tingle, creep, have goose-flesh, have the creeps; prick, prickle, titillate, urticate, scratch; thrill, excite, irritate.

See: 173, 202, 214, 241, 242, 258, 279, 324, 333, 377, 461, 463, 494, 648, 649, 651, 694, 695, 778, 889.

379 Heat

N. *heat,* calidity, caloric, phlogiston; radiant heat; convected heat; incalescence, recalescence, decalescence; emission of heat, diathermancy; incandescence, flame, glow, flush, blush; warmth, fervor, ardor; specific heat, blood h., body h.; fever heat, pyrexia, fever, hectic, inflammation 651n. *disease;* high temperature, white heat; ebullition, boiling point, flash p., melting p.; torrid heat, tropical h., sweltering h., swelter, summer heat, high summer, flaming June; dog-days, canicule 128n. *summer;* heat wave, scorcher; hot wind, simoom, sirocco; hot spring, geyser, hot water, steam; insolation 381n. *heating;* sun, solar heat 420n. *luminary.*

fire, devouring element, flames; bonfire, bale-fire, watch-f., beacon f., St. Elmo's f.; death-fire, pyre 364n. *obsequies;* coal fire, gas f., electric f. 383n. *heater;* empyrosis, deflagration, conflagration; wild-fire, forest f., prairie f.; blaze, flame, sheet of f., wall of f.; spark, scintillation, flash, arc 417n. *light;* eruption, volcano 383n. *furnace;* fireworks, pyrotechnics; arson 381n. *incendiarism;* fire worship 981n. *worship;* smell of burning, empyreuma 381n. *burning.*

thermometry, heat measurement, thermometer, differential t., clinical t., Fahrenheit t., centigrade t., Réaumur t.; diathermometer; thermometrograph, thermoscope, pyroscope, thermopile, thermostat, air-conditioner; pyrometer, radio micrometer, calorimeter; thermal unit, British Thermal Unit, BTU, therm, calorie; pyrology, thermology, thermotics, thermodynamics; thermography, thermograph.

Adj. *hot,* heated, superheated, overheated; inflamed, fervent, fervid; flaming, glowing, red-hot, white-h.; diathermic, diathermanous; piping hot, smoking h.; hot as pepper 388adj. *pungent;* calescent, incalescent, recalescent; feverish, febrile, fevered; sweltering, sudorific, sweating, perspiring; on the boil, boiling, ebullient, scalding; tropical, torrid, scorching, grilling, baking, toasting, roasting; scorched, scalded 381adj. *heated;* thirsty, burning, parched 342adj. *dry;* running a temperature, in a fever, in a heat, in a sweat, in a muck s.

fiery, ardent, burning, blazing, flaming, flaring; unquenched, unextinguished; smoking, smoldering; ablaze, afire, on fire, in flames; candescent, incandescent, molten, glowing, aglow; pyrogenic, igneous, pyrogenous; ignited, lit, alight, kindled, enkindled; volcanic, erupting, plutonic.

warm, hypothermal, tepid, lukewarm, unfrozen; temperate, mild, genial, balmy; fair, set f., sunny, sunshiny 417adj. *undimmed;* summery, aestival; tropical, equatorial; canicular, torrid, sultry; stuffy, close; overheated, uncooled, unventilated; oppressive, suffocating, stifling 653adj. *insalubrious;* warm as toast; snug 376adj. *comfortable;* at room temperature, at blood heat.

Vb. *be hot,* be warm, get warm etc. adj.; incalesce, recalesce, incandesce; burn, kindle, catch fire, take f., draw; blaze, flare, flame, flame up, burst into flame; glow, flush; smoke, smolder, reek, fume, let off steam 300vb. *emit;* boil, seethe 318vb. *effervesce;* toast, grill, roast, sizzle, crackle, frizzle, fry, bake 381vb. *burn;* get burned, scorch, boil dry; apricate, bask, sun oneself, sunbathe; get sunburned, tan; swelter, sweat, perspire; melt, thaw 337vb. *liquefy;* thirst, parch 342vb. *be dry;* stifle, pant, gasp for breath, fight for air; be in a fever, have f., run a temperature; keep warm, wrap up.

See: 128, 300, 318, 337, 342, 364, 376, 381, 383, 388, 417, 420, 651, 653, 981.

380 Cold

N. *coldness* etc. adj.; low temperature, drop in t.; cool, coolness, freshness; cold, absolute c., zero temperature, zero; frigidity, gelidity; iciness, frostiness; sensation of cold, chilliness, algidity, algor, rigor, shivering, shivers, chattering of the teeth, goose-flesh, goose pimples, goose-skin, frostbite, chilblains; chill, catching cold; cold climate, high latitude, Siberia, Nova Zembla, north pole, south p.; Arctic, Antarctica.

wintriness, winter, depth of w., hard w.; cold weather, cold front; inclemency, wintry weather, arctic conditions, polar temperature, degrees of frost; snow-storm, hail-s., blizzard; frost, Jack Frost, rime, hoarfrost, white frost, sharp f., hard f.; sleet, hail, silver thaw, freeze.

snow, snowflake, snow-crystal, snowfall, avalanche, snow-drift, snowstorm, flurry of snow; snow-line, snowball, snowman; snow-plow, snow-shoe.

ice, dry i., ice-cube; hailstone, icicle; ice-cap, ice-sheet, ice-field, floe, ice-f., ice-hill, ice-foot, ice-belt, ice-ledge; iceberg, berg, ice-island; ice-drift, ice-stream, glacier, ice-fall, serac; shelf-ice, pack-i.; driven snow, frozen s., névé, frozen sea; ice-work, ice-action, ice-quake; ice-ship, ice-yacht, ice-plow, ice-chamber, ice-box 382n. *refrigeration;* ice-master; ice-craft.

Adj. *cold,* without heat, impervious to heat, adiathermic; cool, temperate; shady, chill, chilly; unheated, unwarmed, unthawed; fresh, raw, keen, bitter, nipping, biting, piercing, aguish; inclement, freezing, frore, ice-cold, bitterly c.; frigid, hiemal, brumal 129adj. *wintry;* winterbound, frosty, frost-bound, snowy, niveous, sleety, icy; glacial, ice-capped, glaciered; boreal, polar, arctic, antarctic, Siberian; like ice, cold as charity, cold as Christmas; isocheimal, isocheimenal.

a-cold, feeling cold, chilly, shivering, chattering, shivery, algid, aguish, aguey; blue, blue with cold; starved with cold, chilled to the bone, frozen, frost-bitten, frost-nipped; cold as a frog, cold as marble, stone-cold, clay-cold, cold as death.

Vb. *be cold* etc. adj.; grow cold, lose heat, drop in temperature; feel cold, chatter, shiver, tremble, shake, quake, quiver, shudder, didder; freeze, starve, perish with cold; catch cold, get a chill; chill 382vb. *refrigerate.*

Adv. *frostily,* frigidly, bitterly, coldly.

See: 129, 382.

381 Calefaction

N. *heating,* superheating, increase of temperature, tepefaction, calefaction, torrefaction; diathermy, diathermancy, transcalency; calorification, calorific value, thermal efficiency; inflammation, warming, aprication, insolation, sunning 342n. *desiccation;* melting, thawing 337n. *liquefaction;* smelting, scorification, cupellation; boiling, ebullition; coction, digestion, cooking 301n. *cookery;* decoction, distillation; anti-freeze mixture.

burning, combustion, incension; inflammation, kindling, ignition, accension; flagration, deflagration, conflagration 379n. *fire;* incineration, calcination, concremation; ustulation, roasting; cremation 364n. *interment;* suttee, self-burning 362n. *suicide;* auto-da-fé, holocaust 981n. *oblation;* cauterization, cautery, branding; scorching, singeing, charring, carbonization; inflammability, combustibility; burner, touch-hole 383n. *furnace;* cauterant, cauterizer, caustic, moxa, vitriol; hot-iron, branding i., brand; match, touch-paper 385n. *lighter;* fire-attendant, fueler, stoker, fireman; burn-mark, burn, brand, singe, scald, sunburn, tan, empyreuma.

incendiarism, arson, fire-raising, pyromania; incendiary, arsonist, fire-raiser, fire-bug, petroleur, petroleuse; firebrand, revolutionary 738n. *agitator.*

warm clothes, furs, woolens, woollies, flannel; parka, wrapper, wrap, muffler, muff; warm 228n. *overcoat;* blanket 226n. *coverlet;* padding, wadding 227n. *lining.*

ash, ashes, volcanic ash, lava, tuff, carbon, soot, smut, lampblack, smoke; product of combustion, clinker, charcoal, ember, cinder, coke, slag, dross, scoria, sullage, oxide, bone-ash.

pottery, ceramics; earthenware, lusterware, glazed w.; majolica, faience, chinaware, porcelain; crockery, china, bone c., Wedgwood c., Worcester c., Derby c., Sèvres c., Delft c., Dresden c.; willow-pattern, terra-cotta, tile, brick, sun-dried b., mud b.; pot, urn 194n. *vessel.*

Adj. *heated,* superheated 379adj. *hot;* centrally heated, winterized; lit, kindled, fired; incendiarized, burned, burned out, burned down, gutted; cooked, roasted, toasted, grilled, baked; réchauffé, hotted up, warmed up; melted, fused, molten; overheated; steamy, smoky; scorched, charred, adust, singed, branded; tanned, sun-t., sunburned; empyreumatic.

heating, warming etc. vb.; calefactive, calorific, caustic, burning; incendiary, inflammatory; diathermal, diathermanous 385adj. *combustible;* anti-freeze.

Vb. *heat,* raise the temperature, warm; provide heating, winterize; keep the cold out, take off the chill; hot up, warm up, stoke up; thaw, thaw out; inflame, chafe, foment 832vb. *aggravate;* overheat, stive, stew, stifle, suffocate; insolate, sun, parch, shrivel, sear 432vb. *dry;* torrefy, toast, bake, grill, fry, roast 301vb. *cook;* melt, defrost, deice 337vb. *liquefy;* smelt, cupel, scorify; fuse, weld, vulcanize; cast, found.

kindle, enkindle, ignite, light, strike a l.; apply the match, apply the torch, set fire to, touch off 385vb. *fire;* re-

kindle, relume; fuel, stoke, feed the flames, fan the fire, add fuel to the f., poke the f., stir the f., blow the f.; make the fire, rub two sticks together. *burn,* burn up, burn out, gut; commit to the flames, consign to the f.; make a bonfire of, send to the stake; fire, incendiarize; cremate, incinerate, burn to ashes; boil dry 342vb. *dry;* carbonize, calcine, oxidize, corrode; coal, char, singe, scorch, tan; cauterize, brand, burn in; scald.
See: 194, 226, 227, 228, 301, 337, 342, 362, 364, 379, 383, 385, 432, 738, 832, 981.

382 Refrigeration
N. *refrigeration,* infrigidation, cooling, reduction of temperature; icing etc. vb.; freezing, freezing up, glaciation, conglaciation, congelation 380n. *ice;* solidification 324n. *condensation;* exposure; ventilation, air-conditioning; deep-freeze 384n. *refrigerator.*
incombustibility, incombustibleness, non-inflammability, fire-resistance; asbestos, amiant, amianthus.
extinguisher, fire-e., fire-annihilator; water, hose, sprinkler, hydrant, standpipe; fire-engine, fire-brigade, fire-station; fireman, fire-fighter.
Adj. *cooled* etc. vb.; ventilated, air-conditioned; frozen, frozen up; ice-capped, glaciered; frosted, iced, glacé; with ice, on the rocks 380adj. *cold;* cooling etc. vb.; frigorific, refrigerative, deep-freeze.
incombustible, unburnable; uninflammable, non-inflammable; fire-resistant, fire-proof, flame-p., burn-p.; asbestic, amiantine; damped, wetted 341 adj. *drenched.*
Vb. *refrigerate,* cool, fan, air-condition, freshen up 685vb. *refresh;* ventilate, air 340vb. *aerify;* reduce the temperature, turn off the heat; keep the heat out, keep the sun off, shade, shadow 421vb. *screen;* frost, freeze, congeal, glaciate; make ice, ice, glacify; ice up, ice over; chill, benumb, starve, petrify, nip, pinch, bite, pierce; chill to the marrow, make one's teeth chatter; expose to the cold, frost-nip, frost-bite.
extinguish, quench, snuff, put out, blow o., snuff o.; choke, stifle 165vb. *suppress;* damp, douse, damp down, bank d.; rake out, stamp o., stub o.; stop burning, go out, burn o., die down.
See: 165, 324, 340, 341, 380, 384, 421, 685.

383 Furnace
N. *furnace,* fiery f.; the stake 964n. *means of execution;* volcano, solfatara, fumarole; touch-hole, gun-barrel; forge, blast-furnace, reverberatory, kiln, lime-k., brick-k.; oast, oast-house; incinerator, destructor; crematory, crematorium; stove, kitchen s., charcoal s., gas s., electric s., primus s., oil s.; oven, gas o., electric o., chula; range, kitchen r., kitchener; cooker, oil c., gas c., electric c., fireless c.; gas-ring, burner, alcohol b., bunsen b.; blow-lamp, oxyacetylene l.; fire, kitchen f., coal f., coke f., wood f. 379n. *fire;* fire-box, fire-place, grate, hearth, ingle; fire-irons, andirons, fire-dog; poker, tongs, shovel; hob, trivet; fireguard, fender; flue 263vb. *chimney.*
heater, radiator, hypocaust, hot-water pipe, boiler, salamander, copper, caldron, kettle, electric k. 194n. *caldron;* brazier, fire-pan, warming p., chafing dish, hot-water bottle; electric blanket, handwarmer, foot-warmer; hot-case, hot-plate; still, retort, alembic, cucurbit, crucible, athanor 461n. *testing agent;* blowpipe, bellows, tuyere, damper; hot baths, thermae, hummum, Turkish bath, calidarium, tepidarium, sudatorium 648n. *ablution;* hotbed, hot-house, conservatory 370n. *garden;* sun-trap, solarium; kitchen, galley, cookhouse, caboose; gridiron, grill, fryingpan, stewpan; toaster, electric t.; flat-iron, electric i. 258n. *smoother;* curling-iron; heating agent, flame, sunlight 381n. *calefaction;* gas, electricity; steam, hot air; wood, coal 385n. *fuel.*
See: 194, 258, 263, 370, 379, 381, 385, 461, 648, 964.

384 Refrigerator
N. *refrigerator,* cooler; ventilator, fan, punkah, air-conditioner; cooling-room, frigidarium; frigidaire, fridge, refrigeratory, refrigerating plant, refrigerating machine, freezer, wine-cooler, ice-pail; coolant, freezing mixture, snow, ice; ice-house, ice-chest, ice-box, ice-pack, ice-bag; ice-cubes, rocks; cold storage, deep-freeze 382n. *refrigeration.*
See: 382.

385 Fuel
N. *fuel,* inflammable material, combustible, food for the flames; firing,

kindling, briquette, fire-ball; wood, brushwood, firewood, fagot, log, yule l.; turf, peat, peat-moss, peat-hag, peat bog; lignite, brown coal, wood c., charcoal; chemical fuel, oil, fuel o., petrol, gasoline, gas, high octane, diesel oil, derv, hidyne; paraffin, kerosine, spirit, methylated s., napalm; gas, natural g., coal g., acetylene.

coal, black diamond, sea coal, steam c., hard c., anthracite, wallsend, cannel coal, bituminous c.; coal dust, culm, slack, nutty s.; coal seam, coal deposit, coal measure, coalfield 632n. *store;* cinders, embers 381n. *ash;* coke, gas-c.; smokeless fuel.

lighter, petrol-l., cigarette l., igniter, light, illuminant, taper, spill, candle 420n. *torch;* coal, ember, brand, fire-b.; firebarrel, fire-ship; wick, fuse, touch-paper, match, slow m.; linstock, portfire 723n. *fire-arm;* cap, detonator; safety-match, friction m., lucifer, vesta, vesuvian, congreve, fusee, locofoco; self-igniting match; flint, steel, tinder, German t., touchwood, punk, spunk, amadou; tinderbox, match-box.

fumigator, incense, joss-stick, sulphur, brimstone.

Adj. *combustible,* burnable, inflammable, explosive; carboniferous, carbonaceous, coal-bearing, coaly.

Vb. *fire,* stoke, feed, fuel, coal, add fuel to the flames; make the fire; rub two sticks together 381vb. *kindle.*

See: 381, 420, 632, 723.

386 Taste

N. *taste,* sapor, sapidity, savor; flavor, flavoring; smack, smatch, tang, twang, after-taste; relish, gust, gusto, zest, appetite 859n. *liking;* tasting, gustation, degustation; palate, velum, tongue, gustatory nerve, taste-buds; tooth, stomach; refinement 846n. *good taste.*

Adj. *tasty,* sapid, saporific, palatable, gustable, well-tasting, appetizing 390adj. *savory;* flavored, doctored, spiced, spicy, racy, rich, strong, full-flavored, full-bodied, generous, vintage; gustatory, gustative.

Vb. *taste,* degust, find palatable, smack the lips, roll on the tongue, lick one's fingers; savor, sample, try; sip, lick, sup, nibble 301vb. *eat;* have a taste, taste of, savor of, smack of, relish of 18vb. *resemble;* taste well, tickle the palate 390vb. *appetize.*

See: 18, 301, 390, 846, 859.

387 Insipidity

N. *insipidity,* vapidity, jejunity, vapidness, jejuneness, flatness, staleness, tastelessness etc. adj.; water, milk and water, pap, cat-lap.

Adj. *tasteless,* without taste, void of taste; jejune, vapid, insipid, watery, milk-and-water; mild, underproof; with water, diluted, adulterated 163adj. *weakened;* wishy-washy, deadish, flat, stale; savorless, gustless, flavorless, unflavored, unspiced; unsavored, untasted; in bad taste 847adj. *vulgar.*

See: 163, 847.

388 Pungency

N. *pungency,* piquancy, poignancy, sting, bite, edge; burning taste, causticity; hot taste, spiciness; sharp taste, acridity, sharpness, acerbity, acidity 393n. *sourness;* roughness, harshness; strong taste, strength, tang, twang, race; bad taste 391adj. *unsavoriness;* salt, brine, ginger, pepper, mustard, curry, chili 389n. *condiment;* niter, saltpeter, ammonia, salammoniac, smelling salts, hartshorn 656n. *restoration;* cordial, pick-me-up, bracer 174n. *stimulant;* dram, nip, tot 301n. *potion;* hemp, ganja 658n. *drug.*

tobacco, baccy, nicotine; the weed, fragrant w., Indian w.; tobacco-leaf, Virginia tobacco, Turkish t., Russian t.; snuff, rappee, maccoboy; plug of tobacco, plug, quid, fid, twist; chewing tobacco, pipe-t., shag; cigar, cheroot, Burma c., segar, Havana; cigarette, fag, gasper, reefer, nail, woodbine; tobacco-pipe, clay-p., dudeen, churchwarden; briar, corncob; meerschaum, hubble-bubble, hookah, nargileh; pipe of peace, calumet; bowl, stem; tobacco juice, tobacco stain; snuff-taker; tobacco-chewer; smoker, pipe-s., cigarette-s., cigar-s.; tobacconist, tobacco shop, cigar store, cigar divan; snuffbox, cigarette-case, cigar-c., cigarette-box, cigar-box; pipe-rack; pipe-cleaner, reamer; tobacco-pouch, tobacco-jar; smoking jacket, smoking cap; smoker, smoking car.

Adj. *pungent,* penetrating, strong; stinging, mordant, biting 256adj. *sharp;* caustic, burning; harsh 259adj. *rough;* bitter, acrid, tart, astringent 393adj. *sour;* heady, overproof, meracious; full-flavored, nutty; strong-flavored, high-tasted, high, gamy, off; high-seasoned, spicy,

spiced, curried; hot, peppery, hot as pepper; smoky.
salty, salt, brackish, briny, salsuginous, saline, pickled, salt as brine, salt as a herring, salt as Lot's wife.
Vb. *be pungent,* sting, bite the tongue, set the teeth on edge, make the eyes water.
season, salt, brine, pickle; flavor, sauce; spice, pepper, devil, curry; smoke, smoke-dry, kipper 666vb. *preserve.*
smoke, use tobacco, indulge, smoke a pipe, draw, suck, inhale; puff, blow smoke-rings; blow smoke, funk; chew, quid; take snuff, take a pinch.
See: 174, 256, 259, 301, 389, 391, 393, 656, 658, 666.

389 Condiment
N. *condiment,* seasoning, flavoring, dressing, relish; caviar; jam, marmalade 392n. *sweet;* pickles, achar; salt, garlic s.; mustard, French m.; pepper, cayenne, chili, chili pepper; capsicum, paprika, pimento, red pepper, green p.; black pepper, peppercorn; curry, curry powder; vegetable curry, meat c.; onion, garlic 301n. *potherb;* spicery, spices, spice, allspice, Jamaica pepper, mace, cinnamon, turmeric, saffron, galingale, ginger, nutmeg, clove, caper, caraway.
sauce, roux; sauce piquante, sauce tartare, tabasco sauce, horseradish s., caper s.; apple sauce, cranberry s., mint s.; tomato sauce, catsup; pepper sauce; chutney, sweet c., mango c., strong c.
Vb. See 388vb. *season.*
See: 301, 388, 392.

390 Savoriness
N. *savoriness,* right taste, tastiness, palatability; raciness, fine flavor, full f., richness; body, bouquet; savory, relish, appetizer; delicacy, dainty, cate, bakemeat, tidbit, bonne-bouche; caviar; cocktail eats, hors d'oeuvre; game, venison, turtle; ambrosia, nectar, amrita; epicure's delight.
Adj. *savory,* nice, good, good to eat, worth eating; flavored, spicy 386adj. *tasty;* well-dressed, well-cooked, done to a turn; tempting, appetizing, gustful; well-tasted, to one's taste, palatable, toothsome, sweet; dainty, lickerish, delicate; delectable, delicious, exquisite, epicurean; ambrosial, nectareous, fit for the gods; luscious, juicy, succulent; creamy, rich, greasy; right-flavored, racy; rare-flavored, full-f., vintage.
Vb. *appetize,* spice 388vb. *season;* be savory, tickle the appetite, tickle the palate, flatter the p.; taste good, taste sweet 392vb. *sweeten;* like, relish, savor, lap up, smack the lips, roll one's tongue, lick one's fingers, water at the mouth 386vb. *taste.*
See: 386, 388, 392.

391 Unsavoriness
N. *unsavoriness* etc. adj.; unpalatability, nasty taste, wrong t.; rankness, rottenness, unwholesomeness 653n. *insalubrity;* roughness, coarseness, plain cooking 573n. *plainness;* amaritude, acerbity, acritude 393n. *sourness;* austerity, prison fare, bread and water, water of affliction, bread of a.; aloes, quassia, rue; bitter pill, gall and wormwood; asafetida, emetic, sickener, poison 659n. *bane.*
Adj. *unsavory,* flat 387adj. *tasteless;* ill-flavored, unpalatable, unappetizing; coarse, raw, undressed, ill-cooked; uneatable, inedible; hard, leathery 329adj. *tough;* sugarless, unsweetened; rough 388adj. *pungent;* bitter, bitter as gall, acrid, acid 393 adj. *sour;* undrinkable, corked; rank, rancid, stinking 397adj. *fetid;* nasty, filthy, offensive, repulsive, disgusting, loathsome 827adj. *unpleasant;* sickening, emetic, nauseous, nauseating 861adj. *disliked;* poisonous 653adj. *toxic.*
Vb. *be unpalatable* etc. adj.; disgust, repel, sicken, nauseate, turn the stomach 861vb. *cause dislike;* poison; lose its savor, pall.
See: 329, 387, 388, 393, 397, 573, 653, 659, 827, 861.

392 Sweetness
N. *sweetness,* dulcitude; sweetening, dulcification, dulcoration; sugariness, saccharinity; charm 826n. *pleasurableness;* sweet smell 396n. *fragrance;* sweet music 410n. *melody;* saccharometer 465n. *gauge.*
sweet, sweetening, honey, honeycomb, honeypot, honeydew; honeysuckle 396n. *fragrance;* saccharine, saccharose, sucrose, glucose, dextrose, fructose, galactose; sugar, cane s., beet s., malt s., milk s.; invert sugar, saccharum; molasses, jaggery; syrup, treacle; sweet drink, julep, nectar, hydromel, mead, metheglin, liqueur, sweet wine; conserve, preserve, con-

densed milk, jam, marmalade, jelly; candy, sugar-c., sugar-plum; icing; sugar-coating; sweets, marzipan, Turkish delight, chocolate, toffee, toffee-apple, fudge, butterscotch, licorice, gum; comfit, bonbon, jujube, caramel, lollipop, rock; confectionery, confection, cake, pastry, tart, puff, pie, pudding; crystallized fruits 301n. *sweetmeat.*

Adj. *sweet,* sweet to the taste, sweetened, honied, honeyed, candied, crystallized; sugared, sugary saccharine, sacchariferous; honey-bearing, melliferous; ambrosial, nectareous, luscious, sweet as honey, sweet as sugar, sweet as a nut 390adj. *savory;* sweet to the ear, mellifluous, dulcet, harmonious 410adj. *melodious;* sweet to the senses 376adj. *pleasant;* sweet to the mind 826adj. *pleasurable.*

Vb. *sweeten,* sugar, candy, crystallize, ice; sugar the pill, coat the p.; dulcify, dulcorate, edulcorate, saccharize; sweeten wine, mull.

See: 301, 376, 390, 396, 410, 465, 826.

393 Sourness

N. *sourness,* acidity, acerbity; tartness, bitterness, vinegariness; sharpness 388n. *pungency;* acetous fermentation, acidosis; acid, argol, tartar; lemon, vinegar; crab, crab-apple; verjuice, alum, bitter aloes, bitters; gall, wormwood, absinthe.

Adj. *sour,* sourish, acid, acidulous, acidulated, subacid, acescent, acetous, acetose, acid-forming, tartaric; acerb, crabbed, tart, bitter; vinegary, sour as vinegar; unripe, green, hard, rough 670adj. *immature;* astringent, styptic; sugarless, unsugared; unsweetened, dry.

Vb. *be sour* etc. adj.; sour, turn, turn sour; acetify, acidify, acidulate; ferment; tartarize; set one's teeth on edge.

See: 388, 670.

394 Odor

N. *odor,* smell, aroma, bouquet; sweet smell, perfume, essence 396n. *fragrance;* bad smell, stink 397n. *fetor;* exhalation, effluvium, emanation; smoke, fume, reek, nidor; breath, whiff; strong smell, odorousness, redolence, graveolence; scent, trail 548n. *trace;* olfaction, sense of smell, act of smelling; olfactory, nostril, nose 254n. *protuberance;* keen-scentedness, flair.

Adj. *odorous,* endowed with scent, odoriferous, smelling; scented, perfumed 396adj. *fragrant;* graveolent, strong, heady, heavy, full-bodied 388adj. *pungent;* smelly, redolent, nidorous, reeking; malodorous, whiffy, niffy 397adj. *fetid;* smelly, reaching one's nostrils; olfactory, quick-scented, sharp-nosed.

Vb. *smell,* have an odor, reach one's nostrils; smell of, breathe of, smell strong of, reek of, reek; give out a smell, exhale; smell out, scent, nose, wind, get wind of 484vb. *detect;* snuff, snuff up, sniff, breathe in, inhale 352vb. *breathe;* make to smell, scent, perfume, incense, fumigate, thurify, cruse.

See: 254, 352, 388, 396, 397, 484, 548.

395 Inodorousness

N. *inodorousness,* odorlessness, scentlessness; absence of smell, want of s.; loss of s.; inability to smell, ansomia; noselessness, lack of flair; deodorant, deodorizer, fumes, incense, pastil, pastille; deodorization, fumigation, ventilation, purification 648n. *cleansing.*

Adj. *odorless,* inodorous, inodorate, scentless, without smell, wanting s.; unscented, unperfumed; deodorized; deodorizing; noseless, without sense of smell, without flair.

Vb. *have no smell,* not smell, want s.; be inodorous, —scentless etc. adj.; deodorize, take away the smell, defumigate; ventilate, clear the air 648vb. *purify;* lose the scent 495vb. *err.*

See: 495, 648.

396 Fragrance

N. *fragrance,* sweet smell, sweet savor, balminess 392n. *sweetness;* odor of sanctity 979n. *piety;* redolence, aroma, bouquet 394n. *odor;* violet, rose; bank of violets, bed of roses; flower-garden, rose-g. 370n. *garden;* buttonhole, boutonniere, nosegay; thurification, fumigation; perfumery, perfumer.

scent, perfume, aromatic p., aromatic gum, balm, myrrh, incense, frankincense; spicery 389n. *condiment;* breath-sweetener, cloves, pastil, pastille; musk, civet, ambergris, camphor, sandal, sandalwood; otto, ottar, attar; lavender, thyme, spearmint, chypre, vanilla, citronella oil; frangipane, bergamot, orris root, woodruff; toilet water, lavender w., rose w., attar of roses, eau-de-cologne; sandalwood paste, patchouli, pomade, hair-oil, face-powder, scented soap 843n. *cosmetic;* scent-bag, lavender-b., sachet, pouncet box; pomander, potpourri, scent-bottle, smelling-b., vinaigrette; joss-stick, censer, thurible, incense-bearer, incense-boat.

Adj. *fragrant,* redolent, aromatic, scented, perfumed; incense-breathing, balmy, ambrosial; sweet-scented, sweet-perfumed; thuriferous, perfumatory, musky, muscadine; spicy, fruity; of roses, fragrant as a rose; laid up in lavender.

Vb. *be fragrant,* smell sweet, smell like a rose, have a perfume, scent, perfume, fumigate, thurify, cense; embalm, lay up in lavender.

See: 370, 389, 392, 394, 843, 979.

397 Fetor

N. *fetor,* fetidity, fetidness, offensiveness; offense to the nose, graveolence, bad smell, bad odor, foul o., malodor; body-odor, BO, armpits; foul breath, halitosis; stink, stench, reek; noxous stench, mephitis; smell of burning, empyreuma; smell of death, taint, corruption, rancidity, putrefaction 51n. *decay;* foulness 649n. *dirt;* mustiness, fustiness, staleness, stale air, frowst; fungus, garlic, asafetida; stoat, skunk, polecat; stinkard, stinker, stink-pot, stink-bomb, bad egg; dung 302n. *excrement;* latrine, sewer 649n. *sink.*

Adj. *fetid,* olid, graveolent, strong-smelling, heavy, strong; reeking, nidorous; ill-smelling, ill-scented, malodorous, not of roses; smelly, whiffy, niffy; stinking, rank, hircine; fruity, gamy, high; bad, gone b., tainted, rancid; suppurating, gangrenous 51adj. *decomposed;* stale, musty, reasty, fusty, frowsty, frowzy, unventilated, stuffy, suffocating; foul, noisome, noxious, sulphurous, mephitic 653adj. *toxic;* acrid 388adj. *pungent;* burning, empyreumatic; nasty, disagreeable, fulsome 827adj. *unpleasant.*

Vb. *stink,* smell, reek; make a smell, funk, fart, blow off; have a bad smell, smell strong, smell offensively; smell bad 51vb. *decompose;* stink in the nostrils, stink to high heaven, make one hold one's nose; smell like a bad egg, smell like a drain; stink like a fen, stink like a pig, stink like a goat, stink like a polecat; overpower with stink, stink out.

See: 51, 302, 388, 649, 653, 827.

398 Sound

N. *sound,* auditory effect, distinctness; audibility, reception 415n. *hearing;* sounding, sonance, sound-making; sterophonic sound; radio noise 417n. *radiation;* sonority, sonorousness 404n. *resonance;* noise, loud sound 400n. *loudness;* low sound, softness 401n. *faintness;* quality of sound, tone, pitch, level, cadence; accent, intonation, twang, timbre 577n. *voice;* tune, strain 410n. *melody,* 412n. *music;* types of sound 402n. *bang,* 403n. *roll,* 404n. *resonance,* 405n. *non-resonance,* 406n. *sibilation,* 407n. *stridor,* 408n. *cry,* 409n. *ululation,* 412n. *discord;* transmission of sound, telephone 531n. *telecommunication;* gramophone 414n. *phonograph;* loudspeaker 415n. *hearing aid;* unit of sound, decibel, sone; sonic barrier, sound b.

acoustics, phonics; catacoustics, cataphonics, diacoustics, diaphonics, phonology, phonography; phonetics; acoustician; phonetician, phoneticist, phonetist, phonographer; audiometer, sonometer.

speech sound, simple sound, phone, syllable, dissyllable, polysyllable; consonant, spirant, liquid, sibilant; dental, nasal, palatal, guttural, velar, labiovelar; fricative; aspirate, rough breathing, smooth b.; stop; click; plosive, semiplosive; sonant; surd; semivowel; glide, glide sound; voiced breath, vowel, front v., middle v., back v.; diphthong, triphthong 577n. *voice;* monophthongization, diphthongization; modified sound, allophone; vowel gradation, ablaut; umlaut; guna, vriddhi; assimilation, dissimilation; samdhi; vocable 559n. *word;* sound symbol, phonogram 558n. *spoken letter,* 586n. *script.*

Adj. *sounding,* soniferous, sonorific; sonic; supersonic; plain, audible, distinct, heard; resounding, sonorous 404adj. *resonant;* stentorian 400adj. *loud;* auditory, acoustic; phonic, phonetic; sonantal, vocal, voweled, voiced, monophthongal, diphthongal; sonant, sonorant; consonantal; spirantal, surd, unvoiced.

Vb. *sound,* produce s., give out s., emit s., make a noise 400vb. *be loud,* 404vb. *resound;* phonetize, phonate.

See: 400, 401, 402, 403, 404, 405, 406, 407, 408, 409, 410, 412, 414, 415, 417, 531, 558, 559, 577, 586.

399 Silence

N. *silence,* soundlessness, inaudibility, not a sound, not a squeak; stillness, hush, lull, rest, peace, quiet 266n. *quiescence;* muteness, speechlessness 578n. *aphony;* solemn silence, awful s., pin-drop s., deathlike s., dead s., perfect s.

Adj. *silent,* still, stilly, hushed, whist; calm, peaceful, quiet 266adj. *quiescent;* soft, faint 401n. *muted;* noiseless, soundless, frictionless, soundproof; aphonic, speechless, tongueless, mute 578n. *voiceless;* unsounded, unuttered, unspoken; solemn, awful, deathlike, silent as the grave.

Vb. *be silent,* not open one's mouth, hold one's tongue 582vb. *be taciturn;* not speak 578vb. *be mute;* be still, make no noise, make not a sound; become silent, relapse into silence, pipe down, lose one's voice.

silence, still, lull, hush, quiet, quieten, make silent; play down, soft-pedal; stifle, muffle, gag, stop, stop someone's mouth, muzzel, put the lid on, put to silence 578vb. *make mute;* drown, drown the noise.

Int. hush! sh! silence! quiet! peace! soft! whist! hold your tongue! keep your mouth shut! shut up! keep your trap shut! dry up! cut the cackle! stow it! be still! mum's the word!

See: 266, 401, 578, 582.

400 Loudness

N. *loudness,* distinctness, audibility 398n. *sound;* noise, loud n., ear-splitting n.; broken *or* shattered silence, knock, knocking; burst of sound, report, loud r., slam, clap, thunderclap, burst, shell b., explosion 402n. *bang;* alarum, alarm, honk, toot, tootle 665n. *danger signal;* prolonged noise, reverberation, plangency, boom, rattle 403n. *roll;* thunder, rattling t., war in heaven 176n. *storm;* dashing, surging, hissing 406n. *sibilation;* fire, gunfire, artillery, blitz 712 n. *bombardment;* stridency, brassiness, shrillness, blast, blare, bray, fanfare, flourish, tucket, flourish of trumpets 407n. *stridor;* trumpet blast, clarion call, view halloo 547n. *call;* sonority, organ notes, clang, clangor 404n. *resonance;* bells, peal, carrillon 412n. *campanology;* diapason, swell, crescendo, fortissimo, full blast, full chorus; vociferation, clamor, outcry, roaring, shouting, screaming, shout, howl, scream, roar 408n. *cry,* 409n. *ululation;* loud laughter, cachinnation 835n. *laughter;* loud breathing, stertorousness 352n. *respiration;* noisiness, din, row, deafening r., racket, clatter, hubbub, hullabaloo, ballyhoo, song and dance, slamming, banging, stamping, chanting, hooting, uproar, tumult, rowdiness, fracas, brawl, pandemonium, hell let loose 61n. *turmoil.*

megaphone, amplifier, loud pedal; loudhailer, loudspeaker, speaker, microphone, mike; ear-trumpet 415n. *hearing aid;* loud instrument, whistle, siren, hooter, horn, klaxon; buzzer, bell alarm, doorknocker; trumpet, brass; stentorian voice, lungs, good l., lungs of brass, iron throat; Stentor, town-crier.

Adj. *loud,* distinct, audible, heard; noisy, full of noise, rackety, uproarious, rowdy, rumbustious, riproaring, obstreperous, tumultuous 61adj. *orderless;* multisonous, many-tongued 411adj. *discordant;* clamorous, clamant, shouting, screaming, bellowing 408adj. *crying;* big-mouthed, loud-m.; sonorous, booming, deep, full, powerful; lusty, full-throated, stentorian, brazen-mouthed, trumpet-tongued; deafening, dinning; piercing, ear-splitting, ear-rending; thundering, thunderous, rattling, crashing; pealing, clangorous, plangent, strepitous; shrill, high-sounding 407adj. *strident;* blatant, blaring, brassy; echoing, resounding 404adj. *resonant;* swelling, crescendo; fortissimo, enough to waken the dead.

Vb. *be loud,*—noisy etc. adj.; break the silence; speak up, give tongue, raise the voice, strain one's v., strain; call, cat-call, caterwaul; skirl, scream, whistle 407vb. *shrill;* vociferate, shout 411vb. *cry;* cachinnate 835vb. *laugh;* roar, bellow, howl 412vb. *ululate;* din, sound, boom, reverberate 404vb. *resound;* rattle, thunder, fulminate, storm; surge, clash 406vb. *hiss;* ring, peal, clang, crash; bray, blare; slam 402vb. *bang;* burst, explode, detonate, go off; knock, knock hard, hammer; deafen, stun; split the ears, rend the ear-drums, ring in the ear; swell, fill the air; rend the skies, make the welkin ring, rattle the windows, awake the echoes, startle the e., awake the dead; raise Cain, kick up a shindy, stamp 61vb. *rampage.*

Adv. *loudly* etc. adj.; noisily, diningly; aloud, at the top of one's voice, lustily; in full cry, full blast,

full chorus; fortissimo, crescendo.
See: 61, 176, 352, 398, 402, 403, 404, 406, 407, 408, 409, 411, 412, 415, 547, 665, 712, 835.

401 Faintness

N. *faintness,* softness, indistinctness, inaudibility; less sound, reduction of s., noise abatement; dull sound, thud, thump, bump 405n. *non-resonance;* whisper, susurration; breath, bated b., under-b., undertone, undersong, undercurrent of sound; murmur, hum, sigh, sough, moan; scratch, squeak, creak, pop; tick, click; tinkle, clink, chink; buzz, whir; purr, purl, plash, swish; rustle, frou-frou; patter, pitter-p., pit-a-pat; soft footfall, pad; soft voice, quiet tone, conversation level.
silencer, noise-queller, mute, damper, sordine, soft pedal; stopper 414n. *mute;* rubber heel, rubber soles; grease, oil 334n. *lubricant.*
Adj. *muted,* distant, faint, inaudible, uncaught; just heard, barely h., half-h.; trembling in the air, dying away; weak, feeble, unemphatic, unstressed, unaccented; soft, low, gentle; purling, rippling; piano, subdued, hushed, stealthy, whispered; dull, dead 405adj. *non-resonant;* muffled, stifled, bated 407adj. *hoarse.*
Vb. *sound faint,* drop one's voice, whisper, breathe, murmur, mutter 578vb. *speak low;* sing low, hum, croon, purr; purl, babble, ripple, plash, lap, gurgle, guggle 350vb. *flow;* tinkle, chime; moan, sigh, sough 352vb. *blow;* rustle, swish; tremble, melt; float on the air, steal on the air, melt on the a., die on the ear; squeak, creak; plop, pop; tick, click; clink, chink; thud, thump 405vb. *sound dead.*
mute, soften, dull, deaden, dampen, soft-pedal; hush, muffle, stifle 399vb. *silence.*
Adv. *faintly,* in a whisper, with bated breath, between the teeth; sotto voce, aside, in an undertone; piano, pianissimo; à la sourdine; inaudibly, distantly, out of earshot.
See: 334, 350, 352, 399, 405, 407, 414, 578.

402 Bang: sudden and violent noise

N. *bang,* report, explosion, detonation, blast, blow-out, back-fire; crash 400n. *loudness;* crepitation, crackling, crackle; smack, crack, snap; slap, clap, tap, rap, rat-tat-tat; knock, slam; plop, plunk; burst, burst of fire, firing, crackle of musketry; volley, round, salvo; shot, pistol-s.; cracker, squib, phataka, bomb, grenade; gun, rifle, shot-gun, pop-g. 723n. *fire-arm.*
Adj. *rapping* etc. vb.
Vb. *crackle,* crepitate; sizzle, fizzle, spit 318vb. *effervesce;* crack, split, click, rattle; snap, clap, rap, tap, slap, smack; plop, plump, plonk, plunk.
bang, slam, clash, crash, boom; explode, blast, detonate; pop, go p.; back-fire; burst, burst on the ear.
See: 318, 400, 723.

403 Roll: repeated and protracted sounds

N. *roll,* rumbling, grumbling; din, rattle, racket, clatter, chatter, clutter; booming, clang, ping, reverberation 404n. *resonance;* drumming, tattoo, devil's t., rub-a-dub, rat-a-tat, pit-a-pat; tantara, peal, carillon 412n. *campanology;* ding-dong, tick-tock, cuckoo 106n. *repetition;* trill, tremolo, vibrato 410n. *musical note;* quaver; hum, whir, buzz; ringing, singing, tinnitus; drumfire, barrage, machine-gun.
Adj. *rolling* etc. vb.; ding-dong, monotonous 106adj. *repeated;* like a bee in a bottle.
Vb. *roll,* drum, tattoo, beat a t.; drum in the ear; roar, din in the ear; grumble, rumble, drone, hum, whir; trill, chime, peal, toll; tick, beat; rattle, chatter, clatter, clack; reverberate, clang, ping, ring, sing, sing in the ear; quaver, shake, tremble, vibrate; patter 401vb. *sound faint.*
See: 106, 401, 404, 410, 412.

404 Resonance

N. *resonance,* vibration 317n. *oscillation;* reverberation, reflection; lingering note, echo 106n. *recurrence;* ringing, ringing in the ear, singing, tinnitus; bell-ringing, tintinnabulation 412n. *campanology;* peal, carillon; sonority, clang, clangor, plangency; brass 400n. *loudness;* peal, blare, bray, flourish, tucket; sounding brass, tinkling cymbal; tinkle, jingle; chink, clink; ping, ring, chime; low note, deep n., grave n., bass n., pedal n. 410n. *musical note;* low voice, basso, basso profondo, bass, baritone, bass-b., contralto.
Adj. *resonant,* vibrant, reverberant,

resounding etc. vb.; echoing, reboant, reboantic; lingering; sonorous, plangent; ringing, tintinnabulary; basso, deep-toned, deep-sounding, deep-mouthed; booming, hollow, sepulchral.

Vb. *resound,* vibrate, reverberate, echo, reecho; whir, buzz; hum, ring in the ear, sing; ping, ring, ding; jingle, jangle, chink, clink, clank, clunk; tink, tinkle; gong, chime, tintinnabulate; tootle, toot, trumpet, blare, bray 400vb. *be loud;* gurgle, guggle, plash, splash.

See: 106, 317, 400, 410, 412.

405 Non-resonance

N. *non-resonance,* non-vibration, dead sound, dull s.; thud, thump, bump; plump, plop, plonk, plunk; cracked bell 411n. *discord;* muffled drums 401n. *faintness;* mute, damper, sordine 401n. *silencer.*

Adj. *non-resonant,* muffled, damped 401adj. *muted;* dead, dull, heavy; cracked 407adj. *hoarse;* soundproof 399adj. *silent.*

Vb. *sound dead,* be non-resonant, not vibrate, arouse no echoes, fall dead on the ear; tink, click, flap; thump, thud, bump, pound; stop the vibrations, damp the reverberations; soft-pedal, muffle, damp, stop, soften, deaden, stifle, silence 401vb. *mute.*

See: 399, 401, 407.

406 Sibilation: hissing sound

N. *sibilation,* sibilance, hissing, hiss; assibilation, sigmatism, sigma, sibilant; sneeze, sternutation; sputter, splutter; surge, splash, plash; rustle, frou-frou 407n. *stridor;* sucking noise, squelch; swish, swoosh, escape of air; hisser, goose, viper, adder, serpent.

Adj. *sibilant,* sibilatory, hissing, sigmatic; wheezy, asthmatic.

Vb. *hiss,* sibilate, sigmate, assibilize, assibilate; sneeze, snort, wheeze, snuffle, whistle; buzz, fizz, fizzle, sizzle, sputter, splutter, spit; seethe, surge, splash, plash, boil, bubble 318vb. *effervesce;* swish, swoosh, whiz; squelch, suck; rustle 407vb. *rasp.*

See: 318, 407.

407 Stridor: harsh sound

N. *stridor,* stridency, discordance, cacophony 411n. *discord;* roughness, raucousness, hoarseness, huskiness; harsh sound, aspirate, guttural; squeakiness, rustiness 333n. *friction;* scrape, scratch, creak, squeak; stridulation, screechiness; shriek, screech, squawk, yawp, yelp 409n. *ululation;* high pitch, shrillness, piping, whistling, wolf whistle; piercing note, high n., acute n., sharp n. 410n. *musical note;* high voice, soprano, falsetto, tenor, counter-tenor; nasality, twang, drone; skirl, brassiness, brass, blare 400n. *loudness;* pipe, fife, piccolo 414n. *flute;* penny trumpet, whistle, penny w.; treble.

Adj. *strident,* stridulent, stridulous; unoiled, grating, rusty, creaky, creaking (**see** *hoarse*); harsh, horrisonous; brassy, brazen, metallic; high, high-pitched, high-toned, acute, shrill, piping; piercing, tinny, ear-splitting 400adj. *loud;* blaring, braying; dry, reedy, squeaky, squawky, scratchy; cracked 405adj. *non-resonant;* sharp, flat, inharmonious, cacophonous 411adj. *discordant.*

hoarse, husky, throaty, guttural, raucous, rough, gruff; rasping, scraping, creaking; grunting, growling; hollow, deep, grum, sepulchral; snoring, stertorous.

Vb. *rasp,* stridulate, grate, crunch, scrunch, grind, saw, scrape, scratch; snore, snort; cough, hawk, clear the throat, choke, gasp, sob, catch the breath; bray, croak, caw, screech 409vb. *ululate;* grunt, speak in the throat, burr, aspirate, gutturalize; crack, break (of the voice); jar, grate on the ear, set the teeth on edge, clash, jangle, twang, twangle, clank, clink 411vb. *discord.*

shrill, stridulate; play the bagpipes, drone, skirl; trumpet, blare 400vb. *be loud;* pipe, flute, wind the horn 413vb. *play music;* whistle, cat-call, caterwaul 408vb. *cry;* scream, squeal, yelp, screech, squawk; buzz, hum, whine 409vb. *ululate;* split the ears, lift the roof; strain, crack one's voice, strain one's vocal chords.

See: 333, 400, 405, 408, 409, 410, 411, 413, 414.

408 Human Cry

N. *cry,* animal cry 409n. *ululation;* human cry, exclamation. ejaculation 577n. *voice;* utterance 579n. *speech;* talk, chat, conversation 584n. *interlocution;* raised voice, vociferation, vociferousness, clamorousness, shouting, outcry, clamor, hullabaloo 400n. *loudness;* yodel, song, chant, chorus 412n. *vocal music;* shout, yell, whoop, bawl; howl, scream, shriek 407vb. *stridor,* 377n. *pain;* halloo, hail 547n. *call;* view halloo, yoiks, hue and cry 619n. *chase;* cheer, hurrah, huzzah 835n. *rejoicing;* cachinnation, laugh, giggle, snigger 835n. *laughter;* hoot, boo 924n. *disapprobation;* plaint, complaint 762n. *deprecation;* plaining, plaintiveness, sob, sigh 836n. *lamentation;* caterwaul, squeal, wail, whine, boo-hoo; grunt, gasp 352n. *respiration;* shouter, bawler, yeller; rooter, cheerer; crier, barker; town-crier, Stentor.

Adj. *crying,* bawling, clamant, clamorous; loud, vocal, vociferous; stentorian, full-throated, full-lunged, lusty; rousing, cheering; fretful, tearful 836adj. *lamenting.*

Vb. *cry,* cry out, exclaim, ejaculate, pipe up 579vb. *speak;* call, call out, hail, halloo 884vb. *greet;* raise a cry, whoop, yoiks; hoot, boo, whistle 924vb. *disapprove;* cheer, hurrah, root (**see** *vociferate*); shout, bawl, hollo, yell; scream, screech, howl, groan 377vb. *feel pain;* cachinnate, snigger, giggle 835vb. *laugh;* caterwaul, squall, boo-hoo, whine, whimper, wail, fret, mewl, pule 836vb. *weep;* yammer, moan, sob, sigh 836vb. *lament;* mutter, grumble 401vb. *sound faint,* 825vb. *be discontented;* gasp, grunt, snort, snore 352vb. *breathe;* squeak, squawk, yap, yawp, bark 409vb. *ululate.*

vociferate, clamor, start shouting, shout, bawl, yell; chant, chorus 413vb. *sing;* cheer, give three times three, hurrah, huzzah, exult 835vb. *rejoice;* cheer for, root; hiss, hoot, boo, bawl out, shout down 924vb. *disapprove;* roar, bellow 409vb. *ululate;* yell, cry out, sing o., thunder o.; raise the voice, give v., strain one's lungs, crack one's throat, make oneself hoarse, shout at the top of one's voice, shout at the top of one's lungs 400vb. *be loud.*

See: 352, 377, 400, 401, 407, 409, 412, 413, 547, 577, 579, 584, 619, 762, 825, 835, 836, 884, 924.

409 Ululation: animal sounds

N. *ululation,* animal noise, howling, belling; barking, baying, latration, buzzing, humming, bombilation, drone; twittering, fritinancy; call, cry, note, wood-note, bird-note, bird-call; squeak, cheep, twitter, tweet-tweet; buzz, hum; croak, cronk, crunk, caw; coo, hiss; quack, squawk, screech, baa, moo, neigh, whinny, hee-haw; cock-a-doodle-doo, cuckoo, tu-whit tu-whoo; meow, bark, yelp, yap, snap, snarl, growl (**see** under vb. *ululate*).

Adj. *ululant,* mugient, remugient, reboant; blatant, latrant; deep-mouthed, full-m.; full-throated 400adj. *loud;* roaring, lowing, cackling etc. vb.

Vb. *ululate,* cry, call; squawk, screech; caterwaul, yawl, howl, wail; roar, bellow; hum, drone, buzz, bombinate, bombilate; spit 406vb. *hiss;* latrate, bark, bay, bay at the moon; yelp, yap, yawp; snap, snarl, gnar, growl, whine; trumpet, bell, troat; bray, neigh, whinny; bleat, baa; low, moo; meow, mew, mewl, purr; quack, cackle, gaggle, guggle; gobble, gabble, cluck, clack, crow; grunt, gruntle, snort; pipe, pule, blatter, chatter, sing, chirp, chirrup, cheep, tweet, twitter, chuckle, churr, whir, coo, caw, croak, crunk; hoot, honk, boom; grate, chirk, crick; stridulate, squeak 407vb. *rasp;* sing like a bird, warble, carol, whistle 413vb. *sing.*

See: 400, 406, 407, 413.

410 Melody: concord

N. *melody,* musicality 412n. *music;* musicalness, melodiousness, musical quality, tonality, euphony, euphonism; harmoniousness, chime, harmony, concent, concord, concert 24n. *agreement;* consonance, assonance, attunement; unison, unisonance, homophony; preparation, resolution (of a discord); harmonics, harmonization, counterpoint, polyphony; faux-bourdon, faburden, thorough bass, ground b., Alberti b.; part, second, chorus; orchestration, instrumentation; phrasing 413n. *musical skill;* phrase, passage, theme, leitmotiv, coda; movement 412n. *musical piece.*

musical note, note, keys, keyboard, manual, pedal point, organ p.; black notes, white n., sharp, flat, natural, tone, semitone, quartertone; keynote, fundamental n.; leading note, tonic, supertonic, submediant, mediant, subdominant, dominant, subtonic; interval, second, third, fourth, fifth, sixth, seventh, octave; diatessaron, diapason; gamut, scale 410n. *key;* chord, broken c., primary c., secondary c., tertiary c., tetrachord, perfect fourth, arpeggio; grace note, grace, crush note, appoggiatura, appoggiato, acciaccatura, mordent, shake, tremolo, trill, cadenza; tone, tonality, register, pitch, concert p., high p., low p.; high note 407n. *stridor;* low note 404n. *resonance;* undertone, overtone, harmonic, upper partial; sustained note, monotone, drone; sennet, flourish 412n. *tune;* bugle-call 547n. *call.*

notation, musical n., tonic solfa, solmization; written music, score; signature, clef, treble c., bass c., tenor c., bar, stave, line, shaft, space, brace; rest, pause, interval; breve, semibreve, minim, crotchet, quaver, semiquaver, demisemiquaver, hemidemisemiquaver.

tempo, time, beat; rhythm 593n. *prosody;* measure, timing; syncopation, syncope; suspension, prolongation, long note, short n., suspended n.; prolonged n.; tempo rubato; rallentando, andante 412adv. *adagio.*

key, signature, clef, modulation, major key, minor k.; scale, gamut, major scale, minor s., diatonic s., chromatic s., harmonic s., enharmonic s., twelve-tone s.; mode, Gregorian m., Greek m., Lydian m., Phrygian m., Ionian m., Aeolian m., Doric m., mixolydian, hypolydian; oriental mode, Indian m., raga, rag.

Adj. *melodious,* melodic, musical, canorous, tuneful, tunable, singable, *muted;* sweet, dulcet, mellifluous; high-fidelity, clear, clear as a bell, ringing, chiming; silvery, silver-toned, silver-tongued; fine-toned, full-t. 404adj. *resonant;* euphonious, euphonic, true, well-pitched.

harmonious, harmonizing, concordant, consonant 24adj. *agreeing;* in pitch; in chorus; assonant, rhyming, matching 18adj. *similar;* symphonic, symphonious, polyphonic; homophonous, unisonant, isotonic, homophonic, monophonic, monotonous, droning.

harmonic, enharmonic, diatonic, chromatic; tonal, atonal, sharp, flat, twelve-toned; keyed, modal, minor, major, Doric, Lydian.

Vb. *harmonize,* concert, have the right pitch, blend, chime 24vb. *accord;* chorus 413vb. *sing;* attune, tune, tune up, pitch, string 24vb. *adjust;* be in key, be in unison, be on the beat; compose, melodize, put to music, symphonize, orchestrate 413vb. *compose music;* modulate, arpeggio, run, shake, trill; resolve a discord, restore harmony.

See: 18, 24, 401, 404, 407, 410, 412, 413, 547, 593.

411 Discord

N. *discord,* conflict of sounds, discordance, dissonance, disharmony 25n. *disagreement;* atonality, consecutive fifths; preparation (of a discord); harshness, hoarseness, cacophony 407n. *stridor;* confused sounds, Babel, Dutch concert, cat's c., sweeper's band, marrowbones and cleavers, caterwauling 400n. *loudness;* row, din, noise, pandemonium, Bedlam, tumult, racket, atmospherics 61n. *turmoil.*

Adj. *discordant,* dissonant, absonant, jangling, discording 25adj. *disagreeing;* conflicting 14adj. *contrary;* jarring, grating, scraping, rasping, harsh, raucous, cacophonous 407adj. *strident;* inharmonious, unharmonized; unmelodious, unmusical, untunable, untuneful, musicless; untuned, cracked; off pitch, off key, out of tune, sharp, flat; atonal, toneless, tuneless, droning, sing-song.

Vb. *discord,* lack harmony 25vb. *disagree;* jangle, jar, grate, clash, crash; saw, scrape 407vb. *rasp;* be harsh, be out of tune; play sharp, play flat; drone, whine; prepare, prepare a discord; render discordant, unstring.

See: 14, 25, 61, 400, 407.

412 Music

N. *music,* harmony; sweet music 410n. *melody;* musicianship 413n. *musical skill;* music-making, playing, minstrelsy, harping; strumming, vamping; writing music, composing, composition; instrumental music, pipe m., military m.; counterpoint, contrapuntal music; classical music., chamber m., organ m., sacred m., folk m., traditional m.; popular music, light m.; descriptive music, program m., modern m., electronic m., musique concrète; phonograph music, tinned m., canned m., recorded m.; dance music, hot m., syncopation; ragtime, jazz, jive, swing, bebop, bop, blues, boogie-woogie, rock'n'roll; written music, the music, score, full s.; performance, concert, orchestral c., choral c., smoking-c., singsong; music festival, eisteddfod; school of music, conservatoire, tin-pan alley.

campanology, bell-ringing, hand-r., mechanical r.; ringing, chiming; peal, full p., muffled p.; touch, chime; method-ringing, change-r., hunting, dodging, making place; hunt, hunt forward, hunt backward, dodge; round, change; method,

Grandsire, Plain Bob, Treble Bob, Stedman; set of bells, carillon, doubles, triples, caters, cinques; minor, major, royal; maximus; bell, Great Tom, Great Paul, Czar Kolokol; treble bell, tenor b. 414n. *gong;* church-bell 547n. *call;* bell-ringer, carilloneur, campanologist.

tune, signature t., hymn t.; refrain; melodic line; air, popular a., aria, solo; melody, strain; peal, chime, carillon; flourish, sennet, tucket; phrase, passage, measure; Lydian airs, siren strains.

musical piece, piece, composition, opus, work, piece of music; record, recording; orchestration, instrumentation; arrangement, adaptation, setting, transcription; voluntary, prelude, overture, intermezzo, finale; accompaniment, incidental music, background m.; romance, rhapsody, extravaganza, impromptu, fantasia, caprice, capriccio, humoresque, divertissement, variations, ricercari; medley, switchback, pasticcio, potpourri; etude, study; suite, fugue, canon, toccata, toccatina, ricercata; sonata, sonatina, symphony; symphonic poem, tone p.; pastorale, scherzo, rondo, jig, reel; passacaglia, chaconne, rigadoon, saraband, galliard, gavotte, minuet, tarantella, siciliano, mazurka, polonaise, schottische, waltz, polka 837n. *dance;* march, bridal m., wedding m., dead m., funeral m., dirge, pibroch, coronach; nocturne, nachtmusik, abendmusik, serenade, berceuse; aubade; introductory phrase, anacrusis; statement, exposition, development, variation; theme, motive, leitmotiv, signature tune; movement; passage, phrase; chord, mordent, cadenza, coda; feminine ending.

vocal music, singing, vocalism, lyricism; part, singing p.; opera, operetta, light opera, comic o., opéra bouffe, musical comedy, musical 594n. *stage play;* choir-singing, oratorio, cantata, chorale; hymn-singing, psalmody, hymnology; descant, chant, plain c., Gregorian c., plainsong; canto fermo, cantus, cantillation, recitative; bel canto, coloratura, bravura; singing practice, solfeggio, solfa, solmization; introit, anthem, canticle, psalm 981n. *hymn;* song, lay, carol, lyric; canzonet, cavatina, lieder, lied, ballad; ditty, chantey, calypso; part song, glee, madrigal, round, catch; stave, verse; chorus, refrain, burden, undersong; choral hymn, antiphony, dithyramb; boat-song, barcarole; lullaby, cradle-song, berceuse; serenade, aubade; bridal hymn, wedding h., epithalamium, prothalamium; love-song, amorous ditty; song, bird-s., bird-call, dawn chorus; dirge, threnody, coronach 836n. *lament;* musical declamation, recitative; words to be sung, libretto; song-book, hymn-book, psalter.

duet, duo, trio, quartet, quintet, sextet, septet, octet; concerto, concerto grosso, solo, monody; ensemble, tutti.

Adj. *musical* 410adj. *melodious;* philharmonic, symphonic; melodic, arioso, cantabile; vocal, singable; operatic, recitative; lyric, melic; choral, dithyrambic; hymnal, psalmodic; harmonized 410adj. *harmonious;* contrapuntal; orchestrated, scored; set, set to music, arranged; instrumental, orchestral, for strings; hot, jazzy, syncopated, swing, swung.

Adv. *adagio,* lento, largo, larghetto, andante, andantino, maestoso, moderato; allegro, allegretto; spiritoso, vivace, veloce, accelerando, presto, prestissimo; piano, mezzo-p., pianissimo, forte, mezzo-f., fortissimo, sforzando, con brio, capriccioso, scherzo, scherzando; legato, sostenuto, staccato; crescendo, diminuendo, rallentando; affettuoso, arioso, cantabile, parlante; obbligato, tremolo, pizzicato, vibrato; rubato.

See: 410, 413, 414, 547, 594, 836, 837, 981.

413 Musician

N. *musician,* artiste, virtuoso, soloist; bravura player 696n. *proficient;* player, executant, performer, concert artist; ripieno 40n. *extra;* bard, minstrel, jongleur, troubadour, trovatore, minnesinger, gleeman; composer, symphonist, contrapuntist; scorer, arranger, harmonist; syncopator, jazzer, swinger, bebopper, bopper, hepcat; music-writer, librettist, song-writer, lyrist, lieder-writer, hymn-w., hymnographer, psalmist; music teacher, music-master, concert-m., kapell-meister, master of the music, band-leader, conductor (**see** *orchestra*); Apollo, Pan, Orpheus, Amphion, Marsyas, Pied Piper; music critic, concert-goer, opera-g.

instrumentalist, player, piano-p., pianist, cembalist, accompanist; keyboard performer, organist, accordionist, concertinist; violinist, fiddler, crowder, scraper; violist, violoncellist, cellist; harper, harpist, lyrist, clairschacher, luter, lutanist, theorbist, guitarist, mandolinist, banjoist; strummer, thrummer; piper, fifer, piccolo-player, flautist, flutist, clarinettist, oboist, bassoonist; saxophonist, horn-player, trumpeter, bugler, corneter, cornetist, clarionist; bell-ringer, carilloneur, campanologist; drummer, drummer-boy, drum-major; timpanist; organ-grinder, hurdy-gurdy man.

orchestra, symphony o., string o., quartet, quintet; strings, brass, wood-wind, percussion, drums; band, string b., German b., jazz b., ragtime b., Pandean b., drum and fife b., brass b., military b., pipe b., percussion b., sweepers' b., skiffle-group; conductor, baton-wielder, maestro, bandmaster; band-leader, leader, first violin; orchestra-player, bandsman; ripieno 40n. *extra.*

vocalist, singer, songster, warbler, caroler, chanter; chantress, chanteuse, songstress; siren, mermaid, Lorelei; melodist, troubadour, gleeman, gleesinger, madrigal singer, minstrel, wandering m., ballad-singer, street-s., carol-s.; serenader, crooner; opera singer, prima donna, diva; cantatrice, coloratura; aria singer, lieder s.; castrato, soprano, mezzo-s., contralto, alto, tenor, counter-t., baritone, bass-b., bass, basso, basso profondo; song-bird, nightingale, philomel, lark, thrush, mavis, blackbird 365n. *bird.*

choir, chorus, waits, carol-singers, glee-club; choir-festival, massed choirs, eisteddfod; chorister, choirboy, choir-man; precentor, cantor, choir-master, choir-leader; the Muses, tuneful Nine.

musical skill, musical ability, musical appreciation; musicianship, bardship, minstrelsy; performance, execution, fingering, touch, expression; virtuosity, bravma 694n. *skill.*

Adj. *musicianly,* fond of music, knowing music, musical; minstrel, Orphean, bardic; vocal, coloratura, lyric, melic, choral; plain-song, Gregorian, melodic 410adj. *melodious;* instrumental, orchestral, symphonic, contrapuntal; songful, warbling, caroling etc. vb.; scored, arranged, composed; in music, to m.

Vb. *be musical,* learn music, teach m., like m., read m., sight-read; have a good ear, have a correct e., have perfect pitch.

compose music, compose, write music, put to music, set to m., score, arrange, transpose, orchestrate, arrange in parts, supply the counterpoint, harmonize, melodize, improvise, extemporize.

play music, play, perform, execute, render, interpret; conduct, wield the baton, beat time, mark the time; syncopate; play the piano, accompany; pedal, vamp, strum; brush the ivories, tickle the i., thump the keyboard; harp, pluck, sweep the strings, strike the lyre, pluck the guitar; thrum, twang, twangle; violin, fiddle, bow, scrape, saw; play the concertina, squeeze the box, grind the organ; wind, wind the horn, blow, bugle, blow the b., sound the horn, sound, trumpet, sound the t., toot, tootle; pipe, flute, whistle; doodle, squeeze the bag; clash the cymbals; drum, tattoo, beat, tap, beat the drum, beat a ruffle 403vb. *roll;* ring, peal the bells, ring a change; toll, knell; tune, string, fret, set to concert pitch; practice, do scales, improvise, extemporize, play a voluntary, prelude; begin playing, strike up.

sing, vocalize, chant, hymn; intone, cantillate, descant; warble, carol, lilt, trill, quaver, shake; croon, hum, whistle, yodel; solfa, solmizate; harmonize, sing seconds; chorus, choir; sing to, serenade; sing the praises, minstrel; chirp, chirrup, twitter, pipe 409vb. *ululate;* purl 401vb. *sound faint.*

See: 40, 365, 401, 403, 409, 410, 694, 696.

414 Musical instruments

N. *musical instrument,* band, music, concert 413n. *orchestra;* strings, brass, wind, wood-wind, percussion, batterie; sounding board, diaphragm, sound box; comb.

harp, stringed instrument, monochord, heptachord, aeolian harp, Jew's h.; clairs chach; lyre, lute, archlute, theorbo; bandore, bandurria; cithara, cittern, zither, gittern, guitar, electric g., mandolin, mandola, harp-lute; banjo, ukelele, uke, balalaika; psaltery, vina, samisen; plectrum, fret.

viol, rebec, violin, Cremona, Stradivarius, fiddle, kit-f., kit, crowd; viola, tenor, violin, viola d'amore, viola da gamba, violoncello, cello, bass-viol, contrabasso, double-bass; polychord; bow, fiddlestick; string, catgut; bridge; resin.

piano, pianoforte, grand piano, concert grand, baby g.; upright piano, cottage p.; virginals, cymbalo, dulcimer, harpsichord, spinet; clavichord, clarichord, manichord; piano-organ, piano-player, player-piano, pianola, electric piano; xylophone, marimba; clavier, keyboard, manual, keys, ivories; loud pedal, soft p., celeste, damper.

organ, pipe-o., church o., Hammond o., electric o., steam o., calliope; reed organ, seraphine, American organ, melodeon, harmonium, harmoniphon; mouth organ, harmonica; accordion, piano-a., concertina; barrel-organ, hurdy-gurdy; humming top; organ-pipe, mouth-p., flue-p., organ-stop, flue-s.; manual, keyboard; organ-loft, organ-blower.

flute, bass f., fife, piccolo, flageolet, recorder; wood-wind, reed instrument, clarinet, tenor c., corno di bassetto, basset horn, bass clarionet; shawm, hautboy, oboe, tenor o., cor anglais; bassoon, double b., contrafagotto; ocarina, sweet potato; pipe, oaten p., oat, reed, straw; bagpipes, musette, Irish bagpipes, union pipes; panpipes, Pandean p., syrinx; whistle, penny w., tin w.; siren, pitch-pipe; siren; mouthpiece.

horn, bugle-h., post-h., hunting h.; bugle, trumpet, clarion; alpenhorn, French horn, flugelhorn, saxhorn, althorn, helicon horn, brass h.; euphonium, ophicleide, serpent, bombardon; saxophone, sax, saxcornet, cornet, cornet à pistons, cornopean; trombone, sackbut, tuba, sax-t., bass-t.; conch shell.

gong, bell, tintinnabulum; treble bell, tenor b.; church-bell, dinner-b., telephone-b.; alarm-bell, fire-b., tocsin 665n. *danger signal;* tintinnabulation, peal, carillon, chimes, bells; knackers, bones, rattle b., clappers, castanets, cymbals; rattle, sistrum; xylophone, marimba; musical glasses, harmonica; tubular bell, glockenspiel; triangle; tuning fork; sounding board; percussion instrument.

drum, big d., bass d., tenor d., side d., kettle d., war d., tom-tom; tabor, tabret, taboret, tambourine, timbrel; tabla, timpanum, timpani; caisse, grosse c.

phonograph, gramophone, victrola; record-player, radiogram, play-back, pick-up; record, recording, disc, platter, long-playing record, long-player; musical box, juke b., nickelodeon; needle, fiber-n.; diaphragm; baffle-board; soundbox, speaker.

mute, damper, sordine, pedal, soft p., celeste 401n. *silencer.*

See: 401, 413, 665.

415 Hearing

N. *hearing,* audition 398n. *acoustics;* sense of hearing, good h.; good ear, nice e., sharp e., acute e., quick e., sensitive e., correct e., musical e., ear for music; audibility, reception, good r.; earshot, carrying distance, range, reach; something to hear, earful.

listening, hearkening 739n. *obedience,* 455n. *attention;* auscultation, aural examination 459n. *inquiry;* listening-in, tuning-in; lip-reading 520n. *interpretation;* eavesdropping, overhearing, phone-tapping 523n. *latency;* sound-recording 548n. *record;* audition, voice-testing 461n. *experiment;* interview, audience, hearing 584n. *conference;* legal hearing 959n. *legal trial.*

listener, auscultator; stethoscopist; hearer, audience, auditorium, auditory; stalls, pit, gallery 441n. *spectator;* audient, disciple, lecture-goer 538n. *learner;* auditor, examiner 459n. *questioner.*

ear, auditory apparatus, auditory nerve, acoustic organ; lug, lobe, auricle, earhole; external ear, pinna; inner ear, internal e.; aural cavity, cochlea, eardrum, tympanum; malleus, incus, stapes; auditory canal, labyrinth; otology; otoscopy.

hearing aid, stethoscope, otoscope, hearing instrument, ear-trumpet, audiphone, auriphone; loud-speaker, loud-hailer, public address system 528n. *publication;* microphone, mike, amplifier 400n. *megaphone;* speaking-tube, blower; telephone, phone, receiver, headphone, earphone, radiophone, walkie-talkie 531n. *telecommunication;* sound-recorder, asdic, sound tape, dictaphone 549n. *recording instrument;* radiogram, gramophone 414n. *phonograph.*

Adj. *auditory,* hearing, auricular, aural, otological, otoscopic, stethoscopic; auditive, acoustic, audile, keen-eared, sharp-e., open-e.; listening, prick-eared, all ears 455adj. *attentive;* within earshot, audible, heard 398adj. *sounding.*

Vb. *hear,* catch; listen, examine by ear, auscultate, put one's ear to; lip-read 520vb. *interpret;* listen in, switch on, tune in, adjust the receiver; prepare to hear, lift the receiver; overhear, eavesdrop; intercept, tap, tap the wires; hearken, give ear, lend e., incline one's e.; give audience, interview, grant an interview 459vb. *interrogate;* hear confession, shrive 526vb. *confess;* be all ears, hang on the lips of 455vb. *be attentive;* strain one's ears, prick up one's e.; catch a sound, pick up a message; be told, hear say 524vb. *be informed.*

be heard, become audible, reach the ear, fill the e., sound in the e., fall on the e. 398vb. *sound;* ring in the e. 400vb. *be loud;* gain a hearing, have audience.

Adv. *in earshot,* in one's hearing, with ears agog.

See: 398, 400, 404, 414, 441, 455, 459, 461, 520, 523, 524, 528, 531, 538, 548, 549, 584, 739, 959.

416 Deafness

N. *deafness,* dull hearing, hardness of hearing; deaf ears, surdity, deaf-mutism; deaf-and-dumb speech, dactylogy; deaf-and-dumb person, deaf-mute, the deaf and dumb; inaudibility 399n. *silence.*

Adj. *deaf,* earless, dull of ear, hard of hearing, stone-deaf, deaf as a post, deaf as an adder, deaf as a beetle; deaf and dumb, deaf-mute; deafened, stunned, unable to hear; deaf to, unhearing, not listening 456adj. *inattentive;* deaf to music, tone-deaf, unmusical; hard to hear 401adj. *muted;* inaudible, out of earshot, out of hearing 399adj. *silent.*

Vb. *be deaf,* not hear, hear nothing, fail to catch; not listen, refuse to hear, shut one's ears, stop one's e., close one's e., plug one's e. 458vb. *disregard;* turn a deaf ear to 760vb. *refuse;* be hard of hearing, use a hearing aid; lip-read, use lip-reading 520vb. *translate;* talk with one's fingers.

deafen, make deaf, stun, split the eardrum, drown one's hearing 400vb. *be loud.*

See: 399, 400, 401, 456, 458, 520, 760.

417 Light

N. *light,* day-l., light of day, noonday, noontide, noon, broad day, sunlight, sun 420n. *luminary;* starlight, moonlight, moonshine, earthshine; half-light, twilight 419n. *dimness;* artificial light, candle-l., fire-l. 420n. *lighting;* illumination, irradiation, splendor, effulgence, refulgence, intensity, brightness, vividness, brilliance; albedo, luminosity, candlepower; incandescence, radiance (**see** *glow*); sheen, shine, gloss, luster (**see** *reflection*); blaze, blaze of light, sheet of l., flood of l.; glare, dazzle, dazzlement; flare, prominence, flame 379n. *fire;* halo, nimbus, glory, gloriole, aura, aureole, corona; variegated light, spectrum, visible s., iridescence, rainbow 437n. *variegation;* coloration, riot of color 425n. *color;* white 427n. *whiteness.*

flash, emication, fulguration, coruscation; lightning, lightning flash, levin; beam, ray, green r., green flash; Bailey's beads; streak, meteor-flash; scintillation, sparkle, spark; glint, glitter, play, play of light; blink, twinkle, twinkling, flicker, flickering, glimmer, glim, gleam, shimmer, shimmering; spangle, tinsel; flashlight, firefly 420n. *glow-worm.*

glow, flush, sunset glow, afterglow, dawn, sunset; steady flame, steady beam; lambency, lambent light, soft l.; aurora, aurora borealis, aurora australis; northern lights; Milky Way, galaxy, zodiacal light, gegenschein; radiance, incandescence 379n. *heat;* luminescence, fluorescence, phosphorescence; ignis fatuus, jack-o'-lantern, friar's lantern, will-o'-the-wisp, St. Elmo's fire 420n. *glow-worm.*

radiation, visible r., invisible r.; radiant heat, radiant energy; actinism, emission; radioactivity, fall-out, mushroom, radioactive cloud; radiation belt, Van Allen layer 340n. *atmosphere;* ray, beam, pencil; searchlight, headlight, stream of light; infrared ray, ultraviolet r., Roentgen rays, X-ray, gamma r., beta r., cosmic r., microwave; light wave, radio w.; long w., sky w., short w.; wavelength, beam width; high frequency; interference; photon; photoelectric cell.

reflection, refractivity, refraction, double r.; dispersion, scattering, interference, polarization; albedo, polish, gloss, sheen, luster; glare, dazzle, blink, ice-b.; reflecting surface, reflector, mirror 442n. *mirror;* mirror-image 551n. *image.*

light contrast, tonality, chiaroscuro, clairobscur; light and shade, black and white, half-tone, mezzotint; highlights.

optics, photics, photometry, actinometry; dioptrics, catoptrics, spectrology, spectroscopy; heliography 551n.

photography; radioscopy, radiometry, radiology; magnification, magnifying power, light-grasp 197n. *expansion.*

Adj. *luminous,* luminiferous, lucific, lucid, lucent; luculent; light, lit, well-lit, flood-l., flooded with light; bright, gay, shining, resplendent. splendent, splendid, brilliant, vivid; colorful 425adj. *colored;* radiant, effulgent, refulgent; dazzling, blinding, glaring, garish; incandescent, flaring, flaming, aflame, aglow, ablaze 379adj. *fiery;* glowing, blushing, auroral, orient 431adj. *red;* luminescent, phosphorescent, noctilucous; soft, lambent, playing; beaming, beamy, beamish; glittery, flashing, glinting, rutilant, meteoric; scintillant, scintillating, sparkling; lustrous, shiny, sheeny, glossy; reflecting, catoptric; refractive, dioptric, anaclastic; optical, photometric.

undimmed, clear, bright, fair, set f.; cloudless, shadowless, unclouded, unshaded; sunny, sunshiny; moonlit, starlit, starry; light as day, bright as noonday, bright as silver; burnished, polished, glassy, gleaming; lucid, pellucid, diaphanous, translucent 422adj. *transparent.*

radiating, radiant, radioactive, reflective, reflecting.

Vb. *shine,* be bright, burn, blaze, flame, flare 379vb. *be hot;* glow, incandesce, phosphoresce; shine full, glare, dazzle, bedazzle, blind; play, dance; flash, fulgurate, coruscate; glisten, glister, blink; glimmer, flicker, twinkle; glitter, shimmer, glance; scintillate, sparkle, spark, make sparks; shine again, reflect; take a shine, come up, gleam.

radiate, beam, shoot, shoot out rays 300vb. *emit;* reflect, refract; be radioactive, bombard; X-ray.

make bright, lighten, dispel the darkness, dawn, rise; clear, clear up, lift, brighten; light, strike a l., ignite, inflame 381vb. *kindle;* light up, switch on; show a light, hang out a l.; shed luster, throw light on; shine upon, flood with light, illuminate, illume, relume; shine within, shine through 443vb. *be visible;* transilluminate, pass light through; polish, burnish, rub up 648vb. *clean.*

See: 197, 300, 340, 379, 381, 419, 420, 422, 425, 427, 431, 437, 443, 452, 551, 648.

418 Darkness

N. *darkness,* dark; black 428n. *blackness;* night, dark n., nightfall, blind man's holiday; dead of night, witching time 129n. *midnight;* pitchy darkness, thick d., total d.; Cimmerian darkness, Egyptian d., Stygian d., Erebus; obscurity, murk, gloom, dusk 421n. *obfuscation;* tenebrosity, umbrageousness, shadiness, shadows 419n. *dimness;* shade, shadow, umbra, penumbra; silhouette, skiagraph, radiograph; skiagraphy; groping, noctivagation; dark place, dark-room; cavern, mine, dungeon, depths.

obscuration, obfuscation, darkening; blackout, brown-o., dim-o., fade-o.; occultation, eclipse, total e. 446n. *disappearance;* extinction of light, lights out; Tenebrae 988n. *ritual act;* sunset, sundown 129n. *evening;* blackening, adumbration, shading, hatching; distribution of shade, chiaroscuro; dark-lantern; dimmer, dipper 382n. *extinguisher;* obscurantist, darkener of counsel.

Adj. *dark,* subfusc, somber, dark-colored, swart, swarthy 428adj. *black;* darksome, obscure, pitch-dark, pitchy, sooty, black as night; cavernous, dark as a tunnel, black as a pit; Cimmerian, Stygian, Tartarean; caliginous, murky; funereal, gloomy, dismal; dingy, lurid; tenebrous, shady, umbrageous 419adj. *shadowy;* all black, silhouetted; shaded, darkened 421adj. *screened;* darkling, benighted; nocturnal, noctivagous, noctivagant; hidden, veiled, secret 523 adj. *occult.*

unlit, unlighted, unilluminated; not shining, aphotic, lightless; beamless, sunless, moonless, starless; eclipsed, overshadowed, overcast 421adj. *screened;* misted, befogged, clouded, beclouded, cloudy 423adj. *opaque;* switched off, extinguished; dipped, dimmed, blacked out; obscured, obfuscated.

Vb. *be dark,* grow d., lower, gather; fade out 419vb. *be dim;* lurk in the shadows 523vb. *lurk;* look black, gloom.

darken, black, brown; black out, brown o., dim o.; lower the light, turn down, turn down the wick; occult, eclipse, mantle 226vb. *cover;* curtain, shutter, veil 421vb. *screen;* obscure, obfuscate, obumbrate; bedarken, begloom, bemist, befog, dim, tone down 419vb. *bedim;* overcast, overcloud, overshadow, cast in the shade, spread gloom; spread a shade, cast a shadow; adumbrate, silhouette 551vb. *represent;* shade, hatch, fill

in; paint over 440vb. *blur;* over-expose, over-develop 428vb. *blacken.*
snuff out, extinguish, quench, put out the light, pinch out, blow o., switch off, dip, douse.
Adv. *darkling,* in the dark, in the shade, in the shadows; at night, by night.
See: 129, 226, 382, 419, 421, 423, 428, 440, 446, 523, 551, 988.

419 Dimness

N. *dimness,* bad seeing, indistinctness, vagueness, fuzziness, blur; loom; faintness, paleness 426n. *achromatism;* grayness 429n. *gray;* dullness, lack of sparkle, rustiness; blue light, red l.; cloudiness, smokiness, fuliginosity 423n. *opacity;* mistiness, fogginess, nebulosity; murk, gloom 418n. *darkness;* fog, mist 355n. *cloud;* shadowiness, shadow, shade, shadow of a shade; specter 970n. *ghost.*
half-light, semidarkness, bad light; waning light, gloaming 129n. *evening;* shades of evening, twilight, dusk, crepuscule, cockshut time; daybreak, break of day, demijour, gray dawn; penumbra, half-shadow, partial eclipse, annular e.
glimmer, flicker 417n. *flash;* "ineffectual fire," noctiluca, firefly 420n. *glow-worm;* candle-light, rush-l., fire-l. 417n. *light;* ember, coal 381n. *ash;* smoky light, farthing candle, dip-c., dip; dark-lantern 420n. *lamp;* moonbeam, moonlight, starlight, earthlight, earthshine.
Adj. *dim,* darkish, darksome; dusky, dusk, twilight, crepuscular; wan, dun, subfusc, gray, pale 426adj. *colorless;* faint, faded, waning; indistinct, blurred, bleary; glassy, dull, lack-luster, leaden; filmy, hazy, foggy, fog-bound, misty, obnubilated, nebulous, nebular 355adj. *cloudy;* thick, smoky, sooty, muddy 423adj. *opaque;* dingy, grimy, rusty, rusted, mildewed, unpolished, unburnished 649adj. *dirty.*
shadowy, umbrageous, shady, shaded, overspread, overshadowed, overcast, overclouded 226vb. *covered;* vague, indistinct, undefined, confused, fuzzy, blurry, looming; deceptive; half-seen, half-glimpsed, withdrawn, half-hidden 444adj. *invisible;* half-lit, partially eclipsed 418adj. *unlit;* dreamlike, ghostly 523adj. *occult;* coming and going 446adj. *disappearing.*
Vb. *be dim,*—faint etc. adj.; be indistinct, loom; grow gray, grizzle, fade, wane, fade out, pale, grow p. 426vb. *lose color;* lour, lower, gloom, darkle; glimmer, flicker, gutter, sputter; lurk in the shade, be lost in the shadows 523vb. *lurk.*
bedim, dim, dip; lower the flame, turn down the wick, turn down, fade out 418vb. *snuff out;* obscure, blur the outline, blear 440vb. *blur;* smirch, smear, besmirch, besmear, sully; rust, mildew, begrime, muddy, dirty 649vb. *make unclean;* smoke, fog, mist, befog, bemist, becloud 423vb. *make opaque;* overshadow, overcast; shade, shadow, veil, veil the brightness 226vb. *cover;* shade in, hatch 418vb. *darken.*
Adv. *dimly,* vaguely, indistinctly etc. adj.; at half-lights.
See: 129, 226, 355, 381, 417, 418, 420, 423, 426, 429, 440, 444, 446, 523, 649, 970.

420 Luminary: source of light

N. *luminary,* illuminant 417n. *light;* naked light, flame 379n. *fire;* flare, gas-f. (**see** *lamp*); source of light, orb of day 321n. *sun;* orb of night 321n. *moon;* starlight 321n. *star;* bright star, first magnitude s., Sirius, Vega, Aldebaran, Betelgeuse, Canopus, Alpha Centauri; evening star, Hesperus, Vesper, Venus; morning star, Phosphorus, Lucifer; shooting-star, fireball 321n. *meteor;* galaxy, Milky Way, zodiacal light, gegenschein, aurora, northern lights 321n. *heavens;* fulguration, lightning, sheet-l., fork-l., summer l., lightning flash, levin; scintilla, spark, sparkle 417n. *flash.*
glow-worm 417n. *glow;* lampyrine, firefly, fire-beetle; noctiluca; fata morgana, ignis fatuus, will-o'-the-wisp, friar's lantern, jack-o'-lantern; fire-ball, St. Elmo's fire, corposant; phophorescent light, corpse-candle, deadlight, death-fire, death-flame; fire-drake, fiery dragon.
torch, brand, coal, ember 381n. *ash;* torchlight, link, flambeau, cresset, match 385n. *lighter;* candle, bougie, tallow candle, wax c., corpse-c.; taper, wax-t.; spill, wick, dip, farthing d., rush, rush-light, night-l., naked l., flare, gas-f., burner, Bunsen b.; torch-bearer, lampadist, link-boy.
lamp, lamplight; lantern, dark-l., lanthorn, glim, bull's-eye; safety lamp, Davy l., miner's l.; oil lamp, hurricane l., duplex l., moderator l., moderator, lampion, Argand; gas lamp,

incandescent l., gas mantle, mantle; electric lamp, torch, flashlight, searchlight, arc light, headlamp, headlight, side-light; anti-dazzle l., fog-lamp; stoplight, tail-light, reflector; bulb, flashbulb, photoflood, electric bulb, filament; vapor light, neon l., neon tube; magic lantern, projector; chandelier, gasalier, luster, electrolier, candelabra, girandole; lamppost, lampstand, sconce, candlestick; link-boy, lamplighter.

lighting, illumination, irradiation; artificial lighting, street-l.; indirect lighting; gas-lighting, electric lighting, neon l., daylight l., fluorescent l.; floodlighting, son et lumière, limelight, spotlight, footlight.

signal light, warning l. 665n. *danger signal;* traffic light, red l., green l., amber l., stoplight, trafficator, blinker; Very light, Bengal l., rocket, star shell, parachute light; flare, beacon, beacon-fire, bale-f.; lighthouse, lightship.

fireworks, illuminations, firework display, pyrotechnics; sky-rocket, Roman candle, catherine wheel, sparkler, fizgig; thunderflash 723n. *explosive;* Greek fire, Bengal light.

Adj. *luminescent,* luminous, self-l., incandescent, shining; lampyrine, lampyrid; phosphoric, phosphorescent, fluorescent, neon; radiant 417adj. *radiating;* colorful 425adj. *colored;* illuminated, well-lit; bright, gay.

Vb. *illuminate,* light up, light 417vb. *shine, make bright.*

See: 321, 379, 381, 385, 417, 425, 665, 723.

421 Screen

N. *screen,* shield 660n. *protection;* covert 662n. *shelter;* bower 194n. *arbor;* glade, umbrage, shady nook 418n. *darkness;* windshield, windscreen, sunshade, parasol; sun helmet, sola topee 226n. *shade;* awning, dust-cover 226n. *canopy;* sunscreen, visor; lamp-shade; eye-shade, blinkers, blinders; eyelid, eyelashes 438n. *eye;* dark glasses, blue spectacles, colored s., sun glasses; frosted lens, smoked glass, frosted g., opaque g., polarized g. 423n. *opacity;* stained glass 437n. *variegation;* filter, sieve 62n. *sorting;* partition, wall, hedge, windbreak 235n. *fence;* iron curtain, bamboo c. 57n. *exclusion;* mask 527n. *disguise;* hood, veil, mantle 228n. *cloak.*

curtain 226n. *shade;* window curtain, bead c.; shade, blind, sunblind, khus khus, tatti, chick; persienne, venetian blind, roller b.; shutter, window s., deadlight.

obfuscation, smoke-screen; fog, mist 341n. *moisture;* pall, cloud, dust, film, scale 423n. *opacity.*

Adj. *screened,* sheltered; sunproof, cool 380adj. *cold;* shady, umbrageous, bowery 419adj. *shadowy;* blindfolded, hooded 439adj. *blind;* screening, impervious, impermeable.

Vb. *screen,* shield, shelter 660vb. *safeguard;* protect 713vb. *defend;* be a blind, cover up for; ward off, fend off 713vb. *parry;* blanket, keep off, keep out 57vb. *exclude;* cover up, veil, hood 226vb. *cover;* mask, hide, occult 525vb. *conceal;* intercept 702vb. *obstruct;* blinker, blindfold 439vb. *blind;* keep out the light, shade, shadow, darken; curtain, curtain off, canopy, draw the curtains, pull down the blind, spread the awning; put up the shutters, close the s. 264vb. *close;* cloud, fog, mist 419vb. *bedim;* smoke, frost, glaze, film 423vb. *make opaque;* filter, sieve, bolt, sort, sort out 62vb. *class.*

See: 57, 62, 194, 226, 235, 264, 341, 380, 418, 419, 423, 437, 438, 439, 525, 660, 662, 702, 713.

422 Transparency

N. *transparency,* transmission of light, transillumination; transparence, translucence, diaphaneity, unobstructed vision; thinness, gauziness; lucidity, pellucidity, limpidity; clearness, clarity; glassiness, vitreosity; hyalescence; transparent medium, hyaline, water, lymph, ice, crystal, mica, glass, sheet-g., plate-g., optical g., magnifying g., lens, eyepiece; pane, window-p., shop-window; watch-glass, crystal; sheer silk, diaphane; gossamer, gauze, lace, chiffon 4n. *insubstantial thing.*

Adj. *transparent,* seen through, transpicuous, diaphanous, revealing, sheer; thin, fine, gauzy, pellucid, translucid; translucent, tralucent; liquid, limpid; crystal, crystalline, hyaline, vitreous, glassy; clear, serene, lucid; crystal-clear, clear as crystal.

Vb. *be transparent,*—transpicuous etc. adj.; transmit light, show through; shine through, transilluminate, pass light through 417vb. *make bright;* render transparent, clarify.

See: 4, 417.

423 Opacity

N. *opacity,* opaqueness; thickness,

solidity 324n. *density;* filminess, frost; turbidity, fuliginosity, muddiness, dirtiness 649n. *dirt;* devitrification; fog, mist, dense fog, smog, pea-souper, London special 355n. *cloud;* film, scale 421n. *screen;* smoke-cloud, smoke-screen 421n. *obfuscation.*

Adj. *opaque,* opacious; impervious, adiactinic, adiathermic; non-transparent, thick, impervious to light, blank, windowless; not clear, clear as mud; unclarified, devitrified; cloudy, filmy, turbid, drumly, muddy, muddied, puddled; foggy, fog-bound; hazy, misty, murky, smoky, sooty, fuliginous 419adj. *dim;* unwashed, uncleaned 649adj. *dirty;* nubilous, nubiferous; vaporous, fumid; coated, frosted, misted, clouded.

Vb. *make opaque,* devitrify; cloud, cloud over, thicken; frost, film, smoke 419vb. *bedim;* obfuscate; scumble, overpaint 226vb. *coat;* be opaque, obstruct the light 421vb. *screen.*

See: 226, 324, 355, 419, 421, 649.

424 Semitransparency

N. *semitransparency,* milkiness, lactescence; pearliness, opalescence; smoked glass, frosted g., colored spectacles, dark glasses; gauze, muslin; horn, mica; tissue, tissue paper.

Adj. *semitransparent,* semipellucid, semiopaque, semidiaphanous, gauzy; translucent, opalescent, opaline, milky, lactescent, pearly; frosted, mat, misty, fumé 419adj. *dim,* 355adj. *cloudy.*

See: 355, 419.

425 Color

N. *color,* natural c., pure c., positive c., neutral c., primitive c., primary c.; three primaries, complementary color, secondary c., tertiary c.; broken color, chromatic dispersion, chromatic aberration; range of color, chromatic scale; prism, spectrum, rainbow 437n. *variegation;* mixture of colors, harmony, discord; coloration 553n. *painting;* local color 590n. *description;* riot of color, splash 437n. *variegation;* heraldic color, tincture, metal, fur 547n. *heraldry.*

chromatics, science of color, chromatoscopy, chromatology, spectrum analysis; chromascope, tintometer; spectroscope, prism.

hue, color quality, chromatism, tone, value, key; brilliance, intensity, warmth, loudness; softness, deadness, dullness; coloration, livery; pigmentation, coloring, complexion, natural color; hue of health, flush, blush, glow; ruddiness 431n. *redness;* sickly hue, pallor 426n. *achromatism;* faded hue, discoloration; tint, shade, cast, grain, dye; tinge, patina; half-tone, half-light, mezzotint.

pigment, coloring matter, rouge, warpaint, peroxide 843n. *cosmetic;* dyestuff, dye, fast d., grain; vegetable dye, madder, cochineal 431n. *red pigment;* indigo 434n. *purple;* woad 435n. *blue;* artificial dye, synthetic d., aniline d.; stain, fixative, mordant; wash, color-wash, whitewash, distemper; paint, medium, oil paints 553n. *art equipment;* oils, water colors, tempera, pastel; palette, paintbox, paints.

Adj. *colored,* in color, painted, toned, tinged, dyed, double-d., tinted etc. vb.; colorific, tinctorial, tingent; fast, unfading, constant; colorful, chromatic, polychromatic; monochromatic 16adj. *uniform;* prismatic, spectroscopic; kaleidoscopic, many-colored, particolored 437adj. *variegated.*

florid, colorful, high-colored, full-c., deep-c., bright-hued; ruddy 431adj. *red;* intense, deep, strong, emphatic; unfaded, vivid, brilliant; warm, glowing, rich, gorgeous; painted, gay, bright; gaudy, garish, showy, flashy; glaring, flaring, flaunting, spectacular; harsh, stark, raw, crude; lurid, loud, screaming, shrieking; clashing, discordant 25adj. *disagreeing.*

soft-hued, soft, quiet, tender, delicate, refined; pearly, creamy 427adj. *whitish;* light, pale, pastel; dull, flat, mat, dead; simple, sober, sad 573adj. *plain;* somber, dark 428adj. *black;* drab, dingy, faded; patinated, weathered, mellow; matching, toning, harmonious 24adj. *agreeing.*

Vb. *color,* lay on the c., daub, scumble 553vb. *paint;* rouge 431vb. *redden,* 843vb. *primp;* pigment, tattoo; dye, dip, imbue, imbrue; grain, woad 435vb. *blue;* tint, touch up; shade, shadow 428vb. *blacken;* tinct, tinge; wash, color-wash, distemper, varnish, japan, lacquer 226vb. *coat;* stain, discolor; come off (e.g. on one's fingers); tan, weather, mellow; illuminate, miniate, emblazon; whitewash, calcimine, silver 427vb. *whiten;* yellow 433vb. *gild;* enamel,

pie 437vb. *variegate.*
See: 16, 24, 25, 226, 426, 427, 428, 431, 433, 434, 435, 437, 547, 553, 573, 590, 843.

426 Achromatism: absence of color

N. *achromatism,* achromaticity, colorlessness; fade, decoloration, discoloration, etiolation, fading, bleaching 427n. *whiteness;* under-exposure 551n. *photography;* pallor, pallidity, paleness; no color, anemia, bloodlessness; pigment deficiency, albinism; neutral tint; monochrome; black and white; albino, blond, platinum b.
bleacher, decolorant, peroxide, bleaching powder, lime; bleachery.
Adj. *colorless,* hueless, toneless, lusterless; uncolored, achromatic, achromatistous; decolored, discolored; bleached, etiolated, under-exposed; faded, fading; unpigmented, albino, light-colored, fair, blond 433adj. *yellow;* glossless, mousy; bloodless, exsanguine, anemic; without color, drained of color, drained of blood; washed out, off-color; pale, pallid 427adj. *white;* ashy, ashen, ashen-hued, livid, tallow-faced, whey-f.; pasty, sallow, sickly 651adj. *unhealthy;* dingy, dull, leaden 429adj. *gray;* blank, glassy, lack-luster; lurid, ghastly, wan 419adj. *dim;* deathly, cadaverous, pale as a corpse, pale as death, pale as ashes 361adj. *dead.*
Vb. *lose color* 419vb. *be dim;* pale, fade, bleach, blanch, turn pale, change countenance 427vb. *whiten;* run, come off.
decolorize, decolor, achromatize, fade, etiolate; blanch, bleach, peroxide 427vb. *whiten;* deprive of color, drain of c., drain, wash out; tone down, deaden, weaken; pale, dim 419vb. *bedim;* dull, tarnish, discolor, stain 649vb. *make unclean.*
See: 361, 419, 427, 429, 433, 551, 649, 651.

427 Whiteness

N. *whiteness,* albescence, albification, albication; etiolation; lack of pigment, leucosis, albinism, leucoderma; whitishness, lactescence, creaminess, pearliness; hoariness, canescence; white light 417n. *light;* white heat 379n. *heat.*
white thing, alabaster, marble; snow, driven s., snow-drift, snowflake; chalk, paper, milk, flour, ivory, lily; silver, white metal, white gold, pewter, platinum; pearl, teeth; white man, paleface, white; albino, albiness.
whiting, white lead, pipeclay; calamine, whitewash, white paint, Chinese white, Spanish w., Paris w., flake w., zinc w.
Adj. *white,* candid, pure, albescent; dazzling, light, bright 417adj. *luminous;* silvered, silvery, silver, argent, argentine; alabaster, marble; chalky, cretaceous; snowy, niveous, snow-capped, snow-covered; hoar, frosty, frosted; foaming, spumy, foam-flecked; soapy, lathery; white hot 379adj. *hot;* white as marble, white as alabaster, white like ivory, white as a statue, white as a lily, white as milk, white as paper, white as a sheet; pure white, lily-white, milk-w., snow-w.; white-skinned, Caucasian; lacking pigment, leucous, albinistic, leucodermatous; whitened, white-washed, bleached 648adj. *clean.*
whitish, pearly, milky, creamy 424adj. *semitransparent;* ivory, eburnated; waxen, sallow, pale; off-white, half-w.; unbleached, ecru; canescent, grizzled 429adj. *gray;* pepper-and-salt 437adj. *mottled;* blond, fair, ash-blond, platinum b., fair-haired, flaxen-h., tow-headed; dusty, white with dust.
Vb. *whiten,* white, pipeclay, white-wash, calcimine, wash 648vb. *clean;* blanch, bleach; etiolate, fade 426vb. *decolorize;* frost, besnow; silver, grizzle.
See: 379, 417, 424, 426, 429, 437, 648.

428 Blackness

N. *blackness,* nigrescence, nigritude 418n. *darkness;* inkiness, lividity, black, sable; melanism, swarthiness, swartness, pigmentation, pigment, dark coloring, touch of the tar brush, color; depth, deep tone; black and white, chiaroscuro 437n. *checker;* blackening, nigrification, infuscation 418n. *obscuration;* denigration 926n. *detraction.*
negro, negress, mammy; nigger, buck n., black, darky, sambo, pickaninny; blackamoor, Ethiopian, man of color, colored man; the colored; negrito, negrillo.
black thing, coal, charcoal, soot, pitch, tar, tar-barrel; ebony, jet, ink, smudge, black eye; blackberry, blackthorn, sloe; crow, raven, blackbird; black clothes, crape, mourning.
black pigment, blacking, lampblack, ivory b., blue-b., nigrosine; ink, writ-

ing-i., drawing-i., India i., printer's i., printing i.; japan, niello; burnt cork.

Adj. *black,* atramentous, sable; jetty, ebon, inky, pitchy 418adj. *dark;* sooty, fuliginous, smoky, smudgy, smutty 649adj. *dirty;* black-haired, black-locked, raven, raven-haired; black-eyed, sloe-e.; dark, brunette; black-skinned, negroid, Ethiopian; pigmented, colored; sad, somber, funereal, mourning 364adj. *funereal;* atrabilious, gloomy 893adj. *sullen;* coal-black, collied; jet-black, sloe-b., pitch-b.; deep, of the deepest dye; black as coal, black as jet, black as a shoe, black as my hat, black as a tar-barrel, black as the ace of spades, black as a tinker's pot; nocturnal, black as night, black as midnight 129adj. *vespertine;* black as November 129adj. *wintry;* black in the face, black as thunder 891adj. *angry.*

blackish, rather black, nigrescent; swarthy, swart, black-a-vised, black-faced, dark, dark-skinned, tanned, sun-t.; colored, pigmented; livid, black and blue; overexposed; low-toned, low in tone 419adj. *dim.*

Vb. *blacken,* black, nigrify, infuscate, ebonize; ink, ink in; dirty, soot, smoke, blot, smutch, smudge, smirch 649vb. *make unclean;* deepen, over-develop 418vb. *darken;* singe, char 381vb. *burn.*

See: 129, 364, 381, 418, 419, 437, 649, 891, 893, 926.

429 Gray

N. *gray,* grayness, canescence, neutral tint, pepper and salt, chiaroscuro, grisaille; gray hairs, hoary head; Payne's gray, field g., oyster, gun-metal, ashes.

Adj. *gray,* neutral, sad, somber, dull, leaden, livid; cool, quiet; canescent, graying, grizzled, grizzly, hoary, hoar; glaucous; light-gray, steely, pearly, silvery; silvered, frosted; powder-gray, smoky; ashen, ashy, ash-colored, cinerary, cinereous; field-gray, steel-g., iron-g.; slate-g., stone-g.; pearl-g., oyster-g.; mouse-g., mousy, mole; dark gray, char-coal-gray; pepper-and-salt, dapple gray, gray-green.

430 Brownness

N. *brownness,* brown, bronze; sun-brown, sun-tan, sun-burn; snuff, to-bacco-leaf; autumn colors, dead leaf; coffee, chocolate, walnut, mahogany, amber, copper; khaki; burnt almond; no blond, brunette.

brown paint, bister, ocher, sepia, Vandyke brown, sienna, burnt s., umber, burnt u.

Adj. *brown,* brownish; browned, adust, singed, charred, toasted; bronzed, tanned, sunburned; dark, brunette; reddish-brown, bay, bayard, dapple, roan, auburn, chestnut, sorrel; nutbrown, hazel; cinnamon; beige, fawn, bronze, buff, khaki; light-brown, ecru; tawny, fuscous, tan, foxy, russet, maroon; coppery, cupreous, yellowish brown, feuille-mort; dark brown, mahogany, puce, chocolate, coffee-colored; rust-colored, snuff-c., liver-c.; brown as a berry, brown as mahogany.

Vb. *embrown,* brown, bronze, tan, sunburn; singe, char, toast 381vb. *burn.*

See: 381.

431 Redness

N. *redness,* flush, hectic f., blush; fire-glow, sunset g. 417n. *glow;* dawn, Aurora 128n. *morning;* rubification, reddening, warmth, rubescence, erubescence; rosiness, ruddiness, bloom, red cheeks, apple c., cherry lips; high color, floridness, full habit, rubicundity; type of red, pink, cyclamen, rose, poppy, geranium, peony, cherry, strawberry, plum, damson, peach; tomato; ruby, garnet, carbuncle, carnelian; coral; rust, iron mold; salmon, lobster; red blood, gore 335n. *blood;* port wine, claret 301n. *wine;* flame 379n. *fire;* cardinal bird, scarlet minivet, redbreast, robin; redskin, red Indian, redman; red-head, gingernob; redcoat 722n. *soldier;* rubric, red ink; red planet, Mars.

red color, red, vermeil, gules; rose-red, poppy-r., coquelicot; Pompeian red, Turkey r., post-office r., mail-box r.; scarlet, vermilion; cardinal red, imperial purple, Tyrian red; magenta, crimson, cramoisie, carmine, kermes; cherry, cerise, claret-red, maroon, puce; murrey, damask; pink, salmon p., couleur de rose, rose du Barry, carnation; flesh pink, flesh tint, flesh color; stammel color; rust, rust-red; Judas-color.

red pigment, red dye, grain, scarlet g., murex, cochineal, carmine; kermes; dragon's blood; cinnabar, vermilion; ruddle, madder; crimson lake, Indian red, Venetian red, rosaniline, solferino; corallin, peonin; red ocher; red lead, minium; red ink; rouge, lipstick 843n. *cosmetic.*

Adj. *red,* rose-r., rosy, roseate; reddish-pink, rubeous, flesh-colored; coral, russet; scarlet, vermilion; tomato-red; crimson, imperial purple; murrey, stammel; ruddy, rubicund, sanguine, florid, blowsy; red-cheeked, apple-c.; sandy, carroty, red-haired, ginger-h., rufous; auburn, titian; rusty, ferrugineous, ferruginous, rubiginous, rust-colored; lateritious, brick-red; warm, hot, fiery, glowing, flushed, fevered, hectic; flushing, erubescent, rubescent; rose-colored, ruby-c., cherry-c., plum-c., peach-c., salmon-c.; wine-colored; wine-dark; tawny, foxy, Judas-colored; lobster-red; red-hot 379adj. *hot;* red as fire, red as blood, red as a turkey-cock, red as a lobster; dyed red, reddened, rouged, carmined, raddled, farded, painted, lipsticked.

bloodshot, bloodstained, blood-red; sanguinary, bloody, gory, incarnadine, ensanguined 335adj. *sanguineous.*

Vb. *redden,* rubify, rubricate, miniate; rouge, raddle 843vb. *primp;* incarnadine, dye red, stain with blood; flush, blush, glow; mantle, color, color up, crimson.

See: 128, 301, 335, 379, 417, 722, 843.

432 Greenness

N. *greenness,* green, verdancy, greenery, greenwood; verdure, viridity, viridescence; olive, myrtle; lime; grass, moss, turf, green leaf 366n. *foliage;* jade, emerald, malachite, beryl, chrysoprase, olivenite, verd-antique, green porphyry, aquamarine, verdigris; patina.

green color, vert, jungle green, leaf g., grass g., Lincoln g.; sea g., channel g., Nile g.; bottle green, forest g., olive g., pea g., sage g., jade g.; celadon, reseda, mignonette.

green pigment, terre verte, celadonite, viridian, verditer, bice, green b., Paris green; chlorophyll, etiolin.

Adj. *green,* viridescent, verdant, emerald; verdurous, grassy, leafy; grass-green, forest-g.; olive, olivaceous, glaucous, virescent, leek-green, porraceous; light green, chlorine; greenish, bilious; lime, chartreuse; dull green, glaucous.

See: 366.

433 Yellowness

N. *yellowness,* yellow color, canary yellow, mustard y.; yellow metal, gold, old g.; yellow flower, crocus, buttercup, primrose, daffodil, saffron, mustard; topaz; light yellow, lemon, honey; biliousness, jaundice, icterus; xanthodermia, xanthoma, xanthochromism, xanthopsia; yellow fever.

yellow pigment, gamboge, cadmium yellow, chrome y., Indian y., lemon y., orpiment, yellow ocher, Claude tint, massicot, aureolin, luteic acid, lutein; weld, luteolin, xanthin.

Adj. *yellow,* gold, golden, aureate, gilt, gilded; fulvous, fulvid, flavous, fallow, sallow, honey-pale; yellowish, icteroid, icteric, bilious, jaundiced, icteritious, xanthic; deep yellow, luteous; light yellow, sandy, flaxen, fair-haired, blond, platinum b., tawny, buff; creamy, cream-colored; citrine, lemon-colored, citron-c., primrose-c., straw-c., sulfur-c., mustard-c., saffron-c., butter-c., butter-faced; yellow as parchment, yellow as a quince, yellow as a guinea, yellow as a crow's foot.

Vb. *gild,* gilt, yellow, jaundice.

434 Purple

N. *purple,* blue and red, bishop's purple; heliotrope, lavender, pansy, violet, Parma v.; gridelin, amethyst; purpure, Tyrian purple, gentian violet; dark purple, mulberry color, lividness 428n. *blackness;* bright purple, mauve.

Adj. *purple,* purply, purplish, violet, violaceous, purple-red; mauve, lavender, lilac, puce, plum-colored; pansy-colored, ianthine; hyacinthine, heliotrope; livid, dark purple, mulberry; black and blue 428adj. *black.*

Vb. *empurple,* purple.

See: 428.

435 Blueness

N. *blueness,* blue, sky, blue s., sea; blue color, azure, cerulean, celeste, perse, watchet, smalt; robin's egg, peacock, hyacinth, bluebell, cornflower, violet, forget-me-not; sapphire, turquoise, lapis lazuli, beryl, aquamarine; bluishness, cyanosis; lividness, lividity; cyanometer.

blue pigment, blue dye, bice, indigo, woad; cyanin; cyanine; saxony blue, saxe b., Prussian b., ultramarine, French blue, Persian b., cobalt, cobalt blue, zaffer, smalt; cerulean, azulene; blue-bag.

Adj. *blue,* azure, azurine, cyanic;

cerulean, skyey, atmospheric; sky-blue, air-force b., watchet-b.; light blue, Cambridge b., pale b., garter-b., powder b., steel b., robin's-egg b.; royal blue, peacock b., pavonian; aquamarine, sea-b., cyan-b., electric b.; ultramarine; deep blue, dark b., Oxford b., midnight b., navy b., navy; hyacinthine, blue-black, black and blue, livid; bluish, perse; cold, steely; cyanosed.

Vb. *blue,* azure; dye blue, woad.

436 Orange

N. *orange,* red and yellow, gold, old g.; or 547n. *heraldry;* sunflower, helianthus, apricot, mandarin, tangerine, ginger, copper, flame; ocher, Mars orange, cadmium, henna, helianthin.

Adj. *orange,* ochreous, cupreous, coppery, ginger; orange-colored, apricot-c., flame-c., copper-c., brass-c.; tenné.

See: 547.

437 Variegation

N. *variegation,* variety, diversification, diversity 15n. *difference;* dancing light, glancing l. 417n. *light;* play of color, shot colors, iridescence, irisation; pavonine, nacre, mother-of-pearl; shot silk, pigeon's neck, gorge-de-pigeon; dichromatism, trichomatism; dichroism, trichomism, tricolor, polychrome, multicolor 425n. *color;* peacock, peacock's tail, butterfly, tortoiseshell, chameleon; Joseph's coat, motley, harlequin, patchwork; mixture of color, medley of c., riot of c.; stained glass, kaleidoscope; rainbow, rainbow effect, band of color, spectrum, prism.

checker, chequer, checkerwork, check, pepper-and-salt; plaid, tartan; chessboard pattern, chess-board, draught-b., checker b.; mosaic, tessellation, tesserae, marquetry, parquetry, crazy-paving 82n. *multiformity.*

striation, striae; line, streak, band, bar, stripe, tricolor; zebra, tiger; streakiness, mackerel sky; crack, craze 330n. *brittleness.*

maculation, dappling, stippling, marbling; spottiness, patchiness 17n. *non-uniformity;* patch, speck, speckle, spots, pockmarks, freckle 845n. *blemish;* maculae, sunspot; leopard, spotted dog.

Adj. *variegated* etc. vb., diversified, daedal; embroidered, worked 844adj. *ornamental;* polychromatic, colorful 425adj. *florid;* bicolor, tricolor; dichroic, dichromatic, dichromic; trichromatic, trichroic; many-hued, many-colored, multicolored, particolored, motley, patched, crazy, of all colors; kaleidoscopic 82adj. *multiform;* rainbow-colored, rainbow, iridal, iridian; prismatic, spectral; plaid, mosaic, tessellated, parquet; paned, paneled.

iridescent, irisated, versicolor, chameleon; nacreous, mother-of-pearl; opalescent, opaline, pearly 424adj. *semitransparent;* shot, shot through with, gorge-de-pigeon, pavonian, moiré, watered, chatoyant, cymophanous.

pied, particolored, black-and-white, pepper-and-salt, grizzled, piebald, skewbald, roan, pinto, checkered, check, dappled, patchy.

mottled, marbled, jaspered, veined; studded, maculose, maculous, spotted, spotty, patchy; speckled, speckledy, freckled; streaky, streaked, striated, lined, barred, banded, striped; brinded, brindled, tabby; pocked, pockmarked, fleabitten 845adj. *blemished;* cloudy, powdered, dusted, dusty.

Vb. *variegate,* diversify, fret; punctuate; checker, check; patch 656vb. *repair;* embroider, work 844vb. *decorate;* braid, quilt; damascene, inlay, tessellate, tile; stud, mottle, speckle, freckle, spangle, spot; sprinkle, powder, dust; tattoo, stipple, dapple; streak, stripe, striate; marble, jasper, vein, cloud 423vb. *make opaque;* stain, blot, maculate, discolor 649vb. *make unclean;* make iridescent, irisate; interchange color, play.

See: 15, 17, 82, 417, 423, 424, 425, 649, 656, 844, 845.

438 Vision

N. *vision,* sight, power of s., light-grasp; eyesight; seeing, visualization 513n. *imagination;* perception, recognition; acuity (of vision), good sight, keen s., sharp s., long s., far s., normal s.; defective vision, short sight 440n. *dim sight;* mental sight, perspicacity 498n. *intelligence;* second sight 984n. *occultism;* type of vision, double vision, stereoscopic v., binocular v., radial v., averted v.; aided vision, magnification; tired vision, winking, blinking; eye-testing, sight-t.; oculist, optician, ophthalmologist 417n. *optics;* dream 440n. *visual fallacy.*

eye, visual organ, organ of vision, eyeball, iris, pupil, white, cornea, retina, optic nerve; optics, orbs, lights, peepers, weepers; saucer eyes, goggle e., bugle e., gooseberry e.; eyelashes, eyelid 421n. *screen;* lashes, sweeping l.; naked eye, unaided e.; clear eye, sharp e., piercing e., penetrating e., gimlet e., X-ray e.; dull eye, glass e. 439n. *blindness;* evil eye 983n. *sorcery;* hawk, eagle, cat, lynx, ferret, Argus; basilisk, cockatrice, Gorgon.

look, regard, glance, side-g., squint; tail *or* corner of the eye; glint, blink; penetrating glance, gaze, steady g.; observation, contemplation, speculation, watch; stare, fixed s.; come-hither look, glad eye, ogle, leer, grimace 889n. *endearment;* wink 524n. *hint;* dirty look, scowl, evil eye; peep, peek, glimpse, rapid g., half an eye; mien 445n. *appearance.*

inspection, ocular i., ocular demonstration; examination, visual e., autopsy 459n. *inquiry;* view, preview 522n. *manifestation;* oversight 689n. *management;* survey, overview; sweep, reconnaissance, reconnoiter, perlustration, tour of inspection; sight-seeing, rubbernecking; look, look-around, look-see, dekko, once-over, coup d'oeil, rapid survey, rapid glance; second glance, double take; review, revision; mental inspection, speculation, introspection 449n. *thought;* conspection, discernment, catching sight, espial, view, first v., first sight; looking round, observation, prying, spying; espionage; peeping, scopophilia, Peeping Tom.

view, full v., eyeful; vista, prospect, outlook, perspective; conspectus, panorama, bird's-eye view, commanding v.; horizon, false h.; line of sight, line of vision; range of view, ken 490n. *knowledge;* field of view, amphitheater 724n. *arena;* scene, setting, stage 594n. *theater;* angle of vision, slant, point of view, viewpoint, standpoint 485n. *opinion;* observation point, look-out, crow's nest, watch-tower; belvedere, gazebo; astrodome, conning tower; observatory, observation balloon; stand, grandstand, stall, ringside seat 441n. *onlookers;* loophole, peephole, hagioscope 263n. *window.*

Adj. *seeing* etc. vb., visual, perceptible, specious 443adj. *visible;* panoramic, perspectual; ocular, ophthalmic; optical; stereoscopic, binocular; orthopic, perspicacious, clear-sighted, sharp-s., sharp-eyed, keen-e., gimlet-e., eagle-e., hawk-e., lynx-e., ferret-e., Argus-e.; far-sighted, sagacious 498adj. *wise;* second-sighted, visionary 513adj. *imaginative.*

Vb. *see,* behold, visualize, use one's eyes; see true, keep in perspective; perceive, discern, distinguish, make out, pick o., recognize, ken 490vb. *know;* take in, see at a glance 498vb. *be wise;* descry, discover 484vb. *detect;* sight, espy, spy, spot, observe 445vb. *notice;* clap eyes on, catch sight of, sight (land), raise; catch a glimpse of, glimpse, have a side-light; view, command a view of, hold in view, have in sight; see with one's own eyes, witness, look on, be a spectator 441vb. *watch;* dream, see visions, see things 513vb. *imagine;* see in the dark, have second sight 510vb. *foresee;* become visible 443vb. *be visible.*

gaze, regard, quiz, gaze at, look, look at; look full in the face; look intently, eye, stare, peer, squinny; stare at, stare hard, goggle, gape, gawk; focus, rivet one's eyes, fix one's gaze; glare, look black 891vb. *be angry;* glance, glance at; take a slant, squint, look askance; wink, blink 524vb. *hint;* give the glad eye, ogle, leer 889vb. *court;* gloat, gloat over 947vb. *gluttonize;* steal a glance, peep, peek, take a peep; direct one's gaze, cock one's eye, cast one's eyes on, bend one's looks on, turn one's eyes on; notice, take n., look upon 455vb. *be attentive;* lift up one's eyes, look up; look down, look round, look in front; look ahead, look before one, look before and after 858vb. *be cautious;* look away 458vb. *disregard;* look at each other, exchange glances.

scan, scrutinize, inspect, examine, take stock of; contemplate, pore, pore over 536vb. *study;* look over, look through; have *or* take a look at, have a dekko; see, go and see, take in, sight-see, rubberneck; pilgrimage, go to see 882vb. *visit;* view, survey, sweep, reconnoiter; scout, spy out the land; peep, peek 453vb. *be curious;* spy, speculate, pry, snoop; observe, keep under observation, watch 457vb. *invigilate;* hold in view, keep in sight; watch out for, look out f. 507vb. *await;* keep watch, look out, keep looking, keep one's eyes skinned *or* peeled; strain one's eyes, peer; squint at, squinny; crane, crane one's neck, stand on tiptoe.

Adv. *at sight,* at first sight, at the first blush, prima facie; in view 443adv. *visibly;* in sight of; with one's eyes open.

Int. look! dekko! view halloo!
See: 263, 417, 421, 439, 440, 441, 443, 445, 449, 453, 455, 457, 458, 459, 484, 485, 490, 498, 507, 510, 513, 522, 524, 536, 594, 689, 724, 858, 882, 889, 891, 947, 983, 984.

439 Blindness

N. *blindness,* lack of vision; benightedness, darkness 491n. *ignorance;* sightlessness, eyelessness, cecity, anopsy, ablepsy; making blind, blinding, excecation; eye-disease, amaurosis, amblyopia, glaucoma, "drop serene," cataract; night blindness, snow b., color b.; dim-sightedness 440n. *dim sight;* blind side, blind spot, blind eye 456n. *inattention;* glass eye, artificial e.; blind man, the blind; sandman 679n. *soporific;* aid for the blind, braille 586n. *script;* white stick.

Adj. *blind,* sightless, eyeless, visionless, dark; unseeing, undiscerning, unperceiving, unnoticing, unobserving 456adj. *inattentive;* blinded, excecate; blindfold, blinkered; in the dark, benighted; cataractal, glaucomatic, amaurotic 440adj. *dim-sighted;* gravel-blind, stone-blind, sand-blind, stark-b.; blind as a mole, blind as a bat, blind as a buzzard, blind as an owl, blind as a beetle.

Vb. *be blind,* not use one's eyes; go blind, lose one's sight, lose one's eyes; not see; lose sight of; grope in the dark, feel one's way 461vb. *be tentative;* lose one's way, walk in darkness 495vb. *err;* have the eyes bandaged, wear blinkers; be blind to 491vb. *not know;* ignore, have a blind spot, not look, shut the eyes to, avert the eyes, turn away the e., look the other way 458vb. *disregard;* not bear the light, blink, wink, squint 440vb. *be dim-sighted.*

blind, render b., deprive of sight; excecate, put one's eyes out, gouge one's eyes o.; dazzle, daze; darken, obscure, eclipse 419vb. *bedim;* screen from sight; blinker, blindfold, bandage 421vb. *screen;* hoodwink, bluff, throw dust in one's eyes 495vb. *mislead.*

See: 419, 421, 440, 456, 458, 461, 491, 495, 586, 679.

440 Dim-sightedness: imperfect vision

N. *dim sight,* weak s., failing s., dim-sightedness, dull-sightedness; near-blindness, purblindness 439n. *blindness;* half-vision, partial v., blurred v., imperfect v., defective v.; weak eyes, eye-strain; amblyopia, half-sight, short s., near s., nearsightedness, myopia; presbyopia, long sight, far s.; double sight, double vision, confusion of v.; astigmatism, teichopsia, cataract, film; glaucoma, iridization; scotoma, dizziness, swimming; color blindness, Daltonism, dichromism, red-green blindness; chromato-pseudoblepsis, chromatodysopia; snow blindness, niphablepsia; day blindness, hemeralopia; night blindness, nyctalopy, nyctalopia, moon blindness, moonblink; lippitude, blearedness; ophthalmia, ophthalmitis; conjunctivitis, pink eye; obliquity of vision, cast; convergent vision, strabismus, strabism, squint, cross-eye; wall-eye, cock-e., swivel-e.; myosis; wink, blink, nictitation, nystagmus; obstructed vision, eye-shade, blinker, blinder, screen, veil, curtain 421n. *screen;* blind side, blind spot 456n. *inattention.*

visual fallacy, anamorphosis 246n. *distortion;* refraction 417n. *reflection;* aberration of light 282n. *deviation;* false light 552n. *misrepresentation;* illusion, optical i., trick of light, trick of the eyesight, phantasmagoria 542n. *sleight;* mirage 542n. *deception;* fata morgana, ignis fatuus, will-o'-the-wisp 420n. *glowworm;* phantasm, phantasma, phantom, specter, specter of the Brocken, wraith, apparition 970n. *ghost;* vision, dream 513n. *fantasy;* distorting mirror, magic m., magic lantern 442n. *optical device.*

Adj. *dim-sighted,* purblind, half-blind, gravel-b., dark; weak-eyed, bespectacled; myopic, short-sighted, near-s.; presbyopic, long-sighted, astigmatic; color-blind, dichromatic; hemeralopic, nyctalopic; dim-eyed, one-e., monocular, monoculous, monoculate; wall-eyed, squinting; strabismal, strabismic, cross-eyed; swivel-eyed, goggle-e., blear-e., moon-e., mope-e., cock-e.; myotic, nystagmic; blinking, dazzled, dazed; blinded, temporarily b. 439adj. *blind;* swimming, dizzy; amaurotic, cataractal, glaucomatic.

Vb. *be dim-sighted,*—myopic etc. adj.; not see well, need spectacles, change one's glasses; have a mist before the eyes, have a film over the e., get something in one's e.; grope, peer, screw up the eyes, squint; blink, bat the eyelid; wink, nictitate, nictate; see double, grow dazzled,

dazzle, swim; grow blurred, dim, fail; see through a glass darkly.
blur, render indistinct, confuse; glare, dazzle, bedazzle, daze 417vb. *shine;* darken, dim, mist, fog, smoke, smudge 419vb. *bedim;* be indistinct, loom 419vb. *be dim.*
See: 246, 282, 417, 419, 420, 421, 439, 442, 456, 513, 542, 552, 970.

441 Spectator

N. *spectator,* beholder, seer; mystic 513n. *visionary;* looker, viewer, observer, watcher; inspector, examiner, scrutator, scrutinizer 690n. *manager;* waiter, attendant 742n. *servant;* witness, eye-w.; passer-by, bystander, onlooker; looker-on, gazer, starer, gaper, goggler, sidewalk superintendent; eyer, ogler, quizzer; sightseer, rubberneck, tourist, globetrotter 268n. *traveler;* star-gazer, astronomer; bird watcher, watchbird; spotter, look-out 484n. *detector;* watchman, night-w., watch, sentinel, sentry 664n. *warner;* patrolman, patrol 314n. *circler;* scout, spy, snoop 459n. *detective;* moviegoer, cinemagoer, theatergoer 594n. *playgoer;* televiewer, television fan; art critic 480n. *estimator;* backseat driver 691n. *adviser.*
onlookers, audience, auditorium, sea of faces; box-office, gate, house, gallery, peanut g., bleachers, grandstand, pit, stalls; crowd, supporters, followers, aficionados, fans 707n. *patron;* viewership.
Vb. *watch,* look on, look at, look in, view 438vb. *see;* witness 189vb. *be present;* follow, follow with the eyes, observe, attend 455vb. *be attentive;* eye, ogle, quiz; gape, gawk, stare; spy, spy out, scout, scout out 438vb. *scan.*
See: 189, 268, 314, 438, 455, 459, 480, 484, 513, 594, 664, 690, 691, 707, 742.

442 Optical Instrument

N. *optical device,* optical instrument; glass, sheet-g., watch-glass, crystal 422n. *transparency;* lens, meniscus, achromatic lens, astigmatic l., bifocal l., telephoto l.; eyepiece, ocular, object-glass; sunglass, burning-glass; optometer, ophthalmoscope, skiascope, retinoscope, amblyoscope; helioscope, coronograph; periscope, teinoscope, omniscope, radar; prism, spectroscope, telespectroscope, diffraction grating, polariscope; multiplying glass, polyscope; kaleidoscope; thaumatrope; stereoscope; stereopticon; photoscope, photometer, lucimeter, actinometer, radiometer, eriometer; projector, megascope, epidiascope, magic lantern 445n. *cinema;* slide, colored s.
eyeglass, spectacles, specs, goggles, giglamps, barnacles; glasses, reading g., distance g., horn-rimmed g.; sunglasses, dark glasses; pince-nez, nippers; bifocal glasses, bifocals; thick glasses, pebble g.; contact lens; lorgnette, monocle, quizzing-glass; magnifying glass, reading g.; spectacle-maker, oculist, optician, ophthalmologist; optometrist, optometry.
telescope, astronomical t., terrestrial t., equatorial t., achromatic t., inverting t., refractor, reflector, Newtonian r., Cassegrainian r., Huyghenian r.; finder, view-f., range-f., 321n. *astronomy;* spy-glass, field-g., night-g.; binoculars, prism b., opera glass.
microscope, photomicroscope, electron microscope, ultramicroscope; microscopy, microphotography, microscopist.
mirror, bronze m., steel m., magic m., distorting m., concave m., flat, speculum; rear-view mirror, traffic m.; glass, hand-mirror, hand-glass, looking-g., pier-g., cheval-g., full-length mirror.
camera, camera lucida, camera obscura, pin-hole camera; hand camera, box c.; stereocamera, telephoto lens, movie-camera, X-ray c.; microphotography 551n. *photography;* plate, wet p., dry p.; film, microfilm, fast film, slow f., panchromatic f.
See: 321, 422, 445, 551.

443 Visibility

N. *visibility,* perceptibility, discernibility, observability; visuality, presence to the eyes 445n. *appearance;* apparency, sight, exposure; distinctness, clearness, clarity, conspicuity, conspicuousness, prominence; eyewitness, ocular proof, ocular evidence, ocular demonstration, object lesson 522n. *manifestation;* scene, field of view 438n. *view;* atmospheric visibility, seeing, good s., bad s., high visibility, low v.; limit of visibility, ceiling, visible distance, eye-range, eye-shot 183n. *range.*
Adj. *visible,* seeable, viewable; perceptible, perceivable, discernible, observable, detectable; noticeable, remarkable; recognizable, unmistakable, palpable; symptomatic 547adj. *indicating;* apparent 445adj. *ap-*

pearing; evident, showing 522adj. *manifest;* exposed, open, naked, outcropping, exposed to view, open to v.; sighted, in view, in full v., before one's eyes, under one's e. 189adj. *on the spot;* visible to the naked eye, macroscopic; telescopic, just visible, at the limit of vision; panoramic, stereoscopic, periscopic.

well-seen, obvious, showing for all to see 522adj. *shown;* plain, clear, clear-cut, as clear as day; definite, well-defined, well-marked; distinct, unblurred, in focus; unclouded, undisguised, uncovered, unhidden; spectacular, conspicuous, pointed, prominent, cynosural; kenspeckle; eye-catching, striking, shining 417adj. *luminous;* glaring, staring; pronounced, in bold relief, in strong r., in high r., in high light; visualized, well-visualized, eidetic, eidotropic; under one's nose, in plain sight, plain as plain, plain as a pikestaff, plain as the way to parish church, plain as the nose on your face.

Vb. *be visible,* become visible, be seen, show, show through, shine t. 422vb. *be transparent;* speak for itself, attract attention, call for notice 455vb. *attract notice;* meet the eye; hit, strike, catch *or* hit the eye, stand out, act as a landmark; come to light, dawn upon; loom, heave in sight, come into view, show its face 445vb. *appear;* pop up, crop up, turn up, show up 295vb. *arrive;* spring up, start up, arise 68vb. *begin;* surface, break s. 308vb. *ascend;* emanate, come out, creep out 298vb. *emerge;* stick out, project 254vb. *jut;* show, materialize, develop; manifest itself, expose i., betray i. 522vb. *be plain;* symptomatize 547vb. *indicate;* come on the stage, make one's entry 297vb. *enter;* come forward, come forth, stand f., advance; fill the eyes, dazzle, glare; shine forth, break through the clouds 417vb. *shine;* have no secrets, live in a glass house; remain visible, stay in sight, float before one's eyes; make visible, expose 522vb. *manifest.*

Adv. *visibly* etc. adj., in sight of, before one's eyes, within eye-shot; on show, on view.

See: 68, 183, 189, 254, 295, 297, 298, 308, 417, 422, 438, 445, 455, 522, 547.

444 Invisibility

N. *invisibility,* non-appearance 190n. *absence;* vanishment, thin air 446n. *disappearance;* imperceptibility, indistinctness, vagueness, indefiniteness; poor visibility, obscurity 419n. *dimness;* remoteness, distance 199n. *farness;* littleness, smallness 196n. *minuteness;* sequestration 883n. *seclusion;* delitescence, submergence 523n. *latency;* disguisement, hiding 525n. *concealment;* mystification, mystery 525n. *secrecy;* smoke screen, mist, fog, veil, curtain, pall 421n. *screen;* blind spot, blind eye 439n. *blindness;* blind corner 663n. *pitfall;* hidden menace 661n. *danger;* impermeability, blank wall 423n. *opacity.*

Adj. *invisible,* imperceptible, unapparent, unnoticeable, indiscernible; indistinguishable, unrecognizable; unseen, unsighted; viewless, sightless, unviewed; unnoticed, unregarded 458adj. *neglected;* out of sight, out of eye-shot 446adj. *disappearing;* not in sight, remote 199adj. *distant;* sequestered 883adj. *secluded;* hidden, lurking, submerged, delitescent 523adj. *latent;* disguised, camouflaged 525adj. *concealed;* shadowy, dark, secret, mysterious 421adj. *screened;* eclipsed, darkened, dark 418adj. *unlit.*

ill-seen, part-s., half-s.; unclear, ill-defined, ill-marked, undefined, indefinite, indistinct 419adj. *dim;* faint, inconspicuous, microscopic 196adj. *minute;* confused, vague, blurred, blurry, out of focus; fuzzy, misty, hazy 424adj. *semitransparent.*

Vb. *be unseen,* lie out of sight; hide, couch, ensconce oneself, lie in ambush 523vb. *lurk;* escape notice, blush unseen 872vb. *be humble;* become invisible, pale, fade, die 419vb. *be dim;* hide one's diminished head 872vb. *be humbled;* move out of sight, be lost to view, vanish 446vb. *disappear;* make invisible, hide away, submerge 525vb. *conceal;* blind, veil 421vb. *screen;* darken, eclipse 419vb. *bedim.*

Adv. *invisibly,* silently 525adv. *stealthily;* behind the scenes; in the dark.

See: 190, 196, 199, 418, 419, 421, 423, 424, 439, 446, 458, 523, 525, 661, 663, 872, 883.

445 Appearance

N. *appearance,* phenomenon, epiphenomenon 89n. *concomitant;* event, happening, occurrence 154n. *eventuality;* apparency, apparition 443n. *visibility;* first appearance, rise, arising 68n. *beginning;* becoming, realization, materialization, embodiment, presence 1n. *existence;* showing, exhibition, display, view, demonstration 522n. *manifestation;* preview, premonstration; shadowing forth 511n. *prediction,* 471n. *probability;* revelation 484n. *discovery;* externals, outside 223n. *exteriority;* appearances, look of things; visual impact, face value, first blush; impression, effect; show, seeming, semblance; side, aspect, guise, color, light, outline, shape, dimension 243n. *form;* set, hang, look; respect, point *or* angle of view 438n. *view;* a manifestation, emanation, theophany; vision 531n. *fantasy;* false appearance, mirage, hallucination, illusion 440n. *visual fallacy;* apparition, phantasm, specter 970n. *ghost;* reflection, image, mirror i. 18n. *similarity;* mental image, after-image.

spectacle, impressiveness, effectiveness, impression, effect; speciousness, meretriciousness, decoration 844n. *ornamentation;* feast for the eyes, eyeful, vision, sight, scene; panorama, bird's-eye view 438n. *view;* display, lavish d., pageantry, pageant, parade, review 875n. *ostentation;* illuminations, son et lumière; pyrotechnics 420n. *fireworks;* presentation, show, exhibition, exposition 522n. *exhibit;* art exhibition 553n. *picture;* visual entertainment, peepshow, raree-s., gallanty s.; phantasmagoria 440n. *visual fallacy;* kaleidoscope 437n. *variegation;* diorama, cyclorama, georama, cosmorama; staging, tableau, transformation scene; set, decor, setting, backcloth, background 594n. *stage set;* revue, extravaganza, pantomime, floor show 594n. *stage show;* television, video (**see** *cinema*); cynosure, landmark, seamark 547n. *signpost.*

cinema, cinematograph, bioscope, biograph, cinema-screen, silver s.; photoplay, motion picture, moving p.; movie-show, film s., cinerama; movies, flickers, flicks, films; celluloid, film, stereoscopic f., three-dimensional f., 3D; silent film, sound f., talkie; cartoon, animated c., newsreel, documentary, short, double feature, trailer, blip, preview; film production, montage, continuity, cutting, scenario; cinema studio, Hollywood; cinema house, picture palace, nickelodeon 594n. *theater;* projector, ciné-camera 442n. *camera.*

mien, look, face; play of feature, expression; countenance, favor; complexion, color, cast; air, demeanor, carriage, port, presence; gesture, posture, behavior 688n. *conduct.*

feature, trait, mark, lineament; lines, cut, shape, fashion, figure 243n. *form;* contour, relief, elevation, profile, silhouette; visage, physiognomy, cut of one's jib, phiz 237n. *face.*

Adj. *appearing,* apparent, phenomenal; seeming, specious, ostensible; deceptive 542adj. *deceiving;* outward, external 223adj. *exterior;* outcropping, showing, on view 443adj. *visible;* open to view, exhibited 552adj. *shown;* impressive, effective, spectacular 875adj. *showy;* decorative, meretricious 844adj. *ornamental;* showing itself, revealed, theophanic 522adj. *manifest;* visionary, dreamlike 513adj. *imaginary.*

Vb. *appear,* show, show through 443vb. *be visible;* seem, look so 18vb. *resemble;* have the look of, wear the look of, present the appearance of, exhibit the form of, assume the guise of, take the shape of; figure in, display oneself, cut a figure 875vb. *be ostentatious;* be on show, be on exhibit; exhibit 522vb. *manifest;* start, rise, arise; dawn, break 68vb. *begin;* eventuate 154vb. *happen;* materialize, pop up 295vb. *arrive;* haunt, walk 970vb. *goblinize.*

Adv. *apparently,* manifestly, distinctly 443adv. *visibly;* ostensibly, seemingly, to all appearances, as it seems, to all seeming, to the eye, at first sight, at the first blush; on the face of it; to the view, in the eyes of; on view, on show, on exhibition.

See: 1, 18, 68, 89, 154, 223, 237, 243, 295, 308, 420, 437, 438, 440, 442, 443, 471, 484 511 513, 522, 542, 547, 553, 594, 688, 844, 875, 970.

446 Disappearance

N. *disappearance,* vanishment; disappearing trick, vanishing t. 542n. *sleight;* flight 667n. *escape;* exit 296n. *departure;* evanescence, evaporation 338n. *vaporization;* dematerialization, dissipation, dissolution 51n. *decomposition;* extinction 2n. *non-existence;* occultation, eclipse 418n. *obscuration;* dissolving views, fade-out; vanishing point, thin air 444n. *invisibility.*

Adj. *disappearing,* vanishing; evanescent 114adj. *transient;* dissipated, dispersed; missing, vanished 190adj. *absent;* lost, lost to sight, lost to view 444adj. *invisible;* gone 2adj. *ex-*

tinct.

Vb. *disappear,* vanish, do the vanishing trick; dematerialize, melt into thin air; evanesce, evaporate 338vb. *vaporize;* dissolve, melt, melt away 337vb. *liquefy;* waste, consume, wear away, wear off, dwindle, dwindle to vanishing point 37vb. *decrease;* fade, fade out, pale 426vb. *lose color;* fade away 114vb. *be transient;* be occulted, suffer *or* undergo an eclipse 419vb. *be dim;* disperse, dissipate, diffuse, scatter 75vb. *be dispersed;* absent oneself, fail to appear, play truant 190vb. *be absent;* go, be gone, depart 296vb. *decamp;* run away, get a. 667vb. *escape;* hide, lie low, be in hiding 523vb. *lurk;* cover one's tracks, leave no trace 525vb. *conceal;* be lost to sight 444vb. *be unseen;* retire from view, seclude oneself 883vb. *seclude;* become extinct, leave not a rack behind 2vb. *pass away;* make disappear, erase, dispel 550vb. *obliterate.*

See: 2, 37, 51, 75, 114, 190, 296, 337, 338, 418, 419, 426, 444, 523, 525, 542, 550, 667 883.

447 Intellect

N. *intellect,* mind, psyche, psychic organism, mentality; understanding, intellection, conception; thinking principle, intellectual faculty, cogitative f.; rationality, reasoning power; reason, discursive r., association of ideas 475n. *reasoning;* philosophy 449n. *thought;* awareness, sense, consciousness, self-c., stream of c. 455n. *attention;* cognizance, noesis, perception, apperception, percipience, insight; extrasensory perception, instinct 476n. *intuition;* flair, judgment 463n. *discrimination;* noology, intellectualism, intellectuality; mental capacity, brains, parts, wits, senses, sense, gray matter 498n. *intelligence;* great intellect, genius; mental evolution, psychogenesis; seat of thought, organ of t., brain, anterior b., cerebrum; hinder brain, little b., cerebellum; medulla oblongata; meninx, pia mater, dura m., arachnoid 213n. *head;* sensorium, sensory 818n. *feeling.*

psychology, science of mind, psychics, metapsychology, metapsychics; parapsychology, abnormal psychology 503n. *psychopathy;* psychosomatics, Freudianism, Freudian psychology, Jungian p., Adlerian p.; Gestalt psychology, Gestalt theory, configurationism, behaviorism; empirical psychology; psychography, psychometry, psychoanalysis; psychopathology, psychiatry, psychotherapy 658n. *therapy;* psychophysiology, psychophysics, psychobiology.

psychologist, psychoanalyst, psychiatrist, psychotherapist, psychopathologist, mental specialist, alienist, mad doctor 658n. *doctor.*

spirit, soul, mind, inner m., inner sense, second s.; heart, heart's core, breast, bosom, inner man 224n. *interiority;* double, ka, ba, genius 80n. *self;* psyche, pneuma, id, ego, superego, self, subliminal s., the unconscious, the subconscious; personality, dual p., multiple p., split p. 503n. *psychopathy;* spiritualism, spiritism, psychomancy, psychic research 984n. *occultism;* spiritualist, occultist.

Adj. *mental,* thinking, endowed with reason, reasoning 475adj. *rational;* cerebral, intellectual, conceptive, noological; noetic, conceptual, abstract; theoretical 512adj. *suppositional;* unconcrete 320adj. *immaterial;* perceptual, percipient, perceptive; cognitive, cognizant 490adj. *knowing;* conscious, self-c., subjective.

psychic, psychical, psychological; subconscious, subliminal; spiritualistic, mediumistic, psychomantic 984adj. *psychic;* spiritual, otherworldly 320adj. *immaterial.*

Vb. *cognize,* perceive, apperceive 490vb. *know;* realize, sense, become aware of, become conscious of; objectify 223vb. *externalize;* note 438vb. *see;* advert, mark 455vb. *notice;* ratiocinate 475vb. *reason;* understand 498vb. *be wise;* conceptualize, intellectualize 449vb. *think;* conceive, invent 484vb. *discover;* ideate 513vb. *imagine;* appreciate 480vb. *estimate.*

See: 80, 213, 223, 224, 320, 438, 449, 455, 463, 475, 480, 490, 498, 503, 512, 513, 658, 818, 948, 984.

448 Non-intellect

N. *non-intellect,* unintellectuality; brute creation 365n. *animality;* vegetation 366n. *vegetability;* inanimate nature, sticks and stones; instinct, brute i. 476n. *intuition;* unreason, vacuity, brainlessness, mindlessness 450n. *incogitance;* brain injury, brain damage, disordered intellect 503n. *insanity.*

Adj. *mindless,* non-intellectual, unintellectual; animal, vegetable; mineral,

inanimate 359adj. *inorganic;* unreasoning 450adj. *unthinking;* instinctive, brute 476adj. *intuitive;* unoriginal, uninventive, unidea'd 20adj. *imitative;* brainless, empty-headed 499adj. *foolish;* moronic, wanting 503adj. *insane.*
See: 20, 359, 365, 366, 450, 476, 499, 503.

449 Thought

N. *thought,* mental process, thinking; mental act, ideation; intellectual exercise, mental e., mental action, mentation, cogitation; cerebration, lucubration, head-work, thinking-cap; brain-work, brain-fag; hard thinking, hard thought, worry, concentrated thought, concentration 455n. *attention;* deep thought, profound t., depth of t., profundity 498n. *wisdom;* abstract thought, imageless t.; thoughts, ideas 451n. *idea;* conception, conceit, workings of the mind, inmost thoughts 513n. *ideality;* flow of thought, current of t., train of t., succession of t.; association of ideas, reason 475n. *reasoning;* brown study, reverie, musing, wandering thoughts 456n. *abstractedness;* thinking out, excogitation (**see** *meditation*); invention, inventiveness 513n. *imagination;* second thoughts, afterthought, reconsideration, esprit d'escalier 67n. *sequel;* retrospection, hindsight 505n. *memory;* mature thought 669n. *preparation;* forethought, prudence 510n. *foresight;* thought transference, telepathy 531n. *telecommunication.*
meditation, thoughtfulness, speculation 459n. *inquiry;* reflection, deep r., brooding, rumination, consideration, pondering; contemplation 438n. *inspection;* introspection, self-thought, self-communing 5n. *intrinsicality;* self-consultation, self-advising, wishful thinking 932n. *selfishness;* religious contemplation, retreat, mysticism 979n. *piety;* deliberation, taking counsel 691n. *advice;* excogitation, thinking out 480n. *judgment;* examination, close study, concentration, application 536n. *study.*
philosophy, ontology, metaphysics; speculation, philosophical thought, abstract t., systematic t.; scientific thought, science, natural s., natural philosophy; philosophic doctrine, philosophic system, philosophic theory 512n. *supposition;* school of philosophy; idealism, subjective i., objective i., conceptualism, transcendentalism; phenomenalism, realism, nominalism, positivism, logical p.; existentialism, voluntarism; holism, holoism; rationalism, humanism, hedonism, eudaemonism; utilitarianism, materialism; probabilism, pragmatism; relativism, relativity; agnosticism, skepticism, Pyrrhonism 486n. *doubt;* eclecticism; atheism 974n. *irreligion;* fatalism 596n. *fate;* Pythagoreanism, Platonism, Aristotelianism; Stoicism, Epicureanism, Cynicism; Neoplatonism, gnostic philosophy, gnosticism; scholasticism, Thomism, Scotism, Averroism; Cartesianism, Berkeleyanism, Kantianism, Hegelianism, neo-H., dialectical materialism, Marxism; Bergsonism; Hindu philosophy, Vedanta, Sankhya, Mimansa, Yoga, Advaita, monism; Dvaita, pluralism; unitarianism 973n. *deism.*
philosopher, thinker, man of thought 492n. *intellectual;* metaphysician, Vedantist (**see** *philosophy*); school of philosophers, pre-Socratics, Eleatics, Peripatetics, Academy, Stoa; Garden of Epicurus, Diogenes' tub.
Adj. *thoughtful,* conceptive, ideative, speculative (**see** *philosophic*); cogitative, deliberative; full of thought, pensive, meditative, contemplative, reflective; self-communing, introspective; ruminant, wrapped in thought, lost in t., deep in t.; absorbed 455adj. *obsessed;* musing, dreaming, dreamy 456adj. *abstracted;* concentrating, concentrated 455adj. *attentive;* studying 536adj. *studious;* thoughtful for others, considerate 901n. *philanthropic;* prudent 510adj. *foreseeing.*
philosophic, metaphysical, ontological, speculative, abstract, systematic, rational, logical.
Vb. *think,* ween, trow 512vb. *suppose;* conceive, form ideas, ideate; fancy 513vb. *imagine;* devote thought to, bestow thought upon, think about, cogitate (**see** *meditate*); employ one's mind, use one's brain, put on one's thinking-cap; concentrate, collect one's thoughts, pull one's wits together 455vb. *be attentive;* bend the mind, apply the m., trouble one's head about, animadvert; lucubrate, cerebrate, mull, work over, hammer at 536vb. *study;* think hard, beat one's brains, cudgel one's b., rack one's b., worry at; think out, think up, excogitate, invent 484vb. *discover;* devise 623vb. *plan;* take into one's head, have an idea, entertain

an i., cherish an i., become obsessed, get a bee in one's bonnet 481vb. *be biased;* bear in mind, be mindful, think on 505vb. *remember.*

meditate, ruminate, chew the cud, chew over, digest, discuss; inquire into 459vb. *inquire;* reflect, contemplate, study; speculate, philosophize; intellectualize 447vb. *cognize;* think about, consider, take into consideration; take stock of, perpend, ponder, weigh 480vb. *estimate;* think over, turn o., revolve, con over, run over in the mind 505vb. *memorize;* bethink oneself, reconsider, review, reexamine, have second thoughts; take counsel, advise with, consult one's pillow, sleep on it 691vb. *consult;* commune with oneself, introspect; brood, brood upon, muse, fall into a brown study; go into retreat.

dawn upon, occur to, flash on the mind, cross the m., float in the m., rise in the m.; suggest itself, present itself to the mind.

cause thought, provoke *or* challenge t., make one think, impress the mind, strike 821vb. *impress;* penetrate, sink in, fasten on the mind, become an idée fixe, obsess 481vb. *bias.*

engross, absorb, preoccupy, monopolize; engross one's thoughts, run in one's head, occupy the mind, fill the m., be uppermost in one's mind, come first in one's thoughts; haunt, obsess 481vb. *bias;* fascinate 983vb. *bewitch.*

Adv. *in mind,* in contemplation, under consideration; taking into consideration, bearing in mind, all things considered; on reflection, on consideration, on second thought; come to think of it.

See: 5, 67, 438, 447, 451, 455, 456, 459, 475, 480, 481, 484, 486, 492, 498, 505, 510, 512, 513, 531, 536, 596, 623, 669, 691, 821, 901, 932, 973, 974, 979, 983.

450 Absence of thought

N. *incogitance,* inability to think 448n. *non-intellect;* blank mind, fallow m. 491n. *ignorance;* vacancy, abstraction 456n. *abstractedness;* inanity, blankness, fatuity, empty head 499n. *unintelligence;* want of thought, thoughtlessness 456n. *inattention;* conditioned reflex, automatism; instinctiveness, instinct 476n. *intuition;* sticks and stones.

Adj. *unthinking,* incogitant, unreflecting, unphilosophic, unintellectual 448adj. *mindless;* incapable of thought, unidea'd, unimaginative, uninventive 20adj. *imitative;* blank, vacant, empty-headed 190adj. *empty;* incogitant, not thinking 456adj. *inattentive;* unoccupied, relaxed; thoughtless, inconsiderate 932adj. *selfish;* irrational 477adj. *illogical;* beef-witted, stolid, stupid, wanting 499adj. *unintelligent;* inanimate, inorganic; animal, vegetable, mineral.

unthought, unthought of, inconceivable, incogitable, unconsidered, undreamed, not to be thought of, not to be dreamed of 470adj. *impossible.*

Vb. *not think,* not reflect; leave the mind fallow *or* unoccupied, leave one's mind uncultivated 491vb. *not know;* be blank, be vacant; not think of, put out of one's mind, dismiss from one's thoughts, laugh off 458vb. *disregard;* dream, indulge in reveries 456vb. *be inattentive;* go by instinct 476vb. *intuit;* think wrongly 481vb. *misjudge.*

See: 20, 190, 448, 456, 458, 470, 476, 477, 481, 491, 499, 932.

451 Idea

N. *idea,* noumenon, notion, a thought; object of thought, abstract idea, concept; mere idea, theory 512n. *supposition;* percept, image, mental i.; Platonic idea, archetype 23n. *prototype;* conception, perception, apprehension 447n. *intellect;* reflection, observation 449n. *thought;* impression, conceit, fancy, fantasy 513n. *imagination;* product of imagination, figment, fiction; associated ideas, complex; invention, brain-creation, brain-child; brain wave, happy thought 484n. *discovery;* wheeze, wrinkle, device 623n. *contrivance;* what one thinks, view, point of v., slant, attitude 485n. *opinion;* principle, leading idea, main idea.

Adj. *ideational,* ideative 449adj. *thoughtful;* notional, ideal 513adj. *imaginary.*

See: 23, 447, 449, 480, 484, 485, 512, 513, 623.

452 Topic

N. *topic,* subject of thought, food for t., mental pabulum; gossip, rumor 529n. *news;* subject matter, subject; contents, chapter, section, head, main h. 53n. *subdivision;* what it is about, argument, plot, theme; text, commonplace, burden, motif; musical topic, statement, leitmotiv 412n. *musical piece;* concern, interest, human i.; matter, affair, situation 8n. *circumstance;* shop 622n. *business;* topic for discussion, business on hand, agenda, order paper 623n. *policy;* item on the agenda, motion 761n. *request;* resolution 480n. *judgment;* problem, headache 459n. *question;* heart of the question, gist, pith; theorem, proposition 512n. *supposition;* thesis, case, point 475n. *argument;* issue, moot point, debatable p., point at issue; field, field of inquiry, field of study 536n. *study.*

Adj. *topical,* thematic; challenging, thought-provoking; mooted, debatable 474adj. *uncertain;* thought about, uppermost in the mind, fit for consideration.

Adv. *in question,* in the mind, on the brain, in one's thoughts; on foot, on the tapis, on the agenda; before the house, under consideration, under discussion, under advisement.

See: 8, 53, 412, 459, 474, 475, 480, 512, 529, 536, 622, 623, 761.

453 Curiosity: desire for knowledge

N. *curiosity,* intellectual c., inquiring mind, thirst *or* itch for knowledge 536n. *study;* morbid curiosity, ghoulishness; prurience, voyeurism, scopophilia; interest, itch, inquisitiveness, curiousness; zeal, meddlesomeness, officiousness 678n. *over-activity;* wanting to know; asking questions, quizzing 459n. *question;* sightseeing, rubbernecking, thirst for travel 267n. *land travel.*

inquisitor, censor, examiner, cross-e., interrogator, questioner, quizzer, enfant terrible 459n. *inquirer;* inquisitive person, pry; busybody, ultracrepidarian 678n. *meddler;* newshound, gossip, quidnunc 529n. *newsmonger;* seeker, searcher, explorer, experimentalist 461n. *experimenter;* sightseer, globe-trotter, rubberneck 441n. *spectator;* window-shopper, snoop, snooper, spy 459n. *detective;* eavesdropper, interceptor, phonetapper 415n. *listener;* "impertinent pry," Paul Pry, Peeping Tom, Actaeon; Nosy Parker, Rosa Dartle.

Adj. *inquisitive,* curious, interested; searching, seeking, avid for knowledge 536adj. *studious;* morbidly curious, ghoulish, prurient; new mongering, hungering for news, agog, all ears 415adj. *auditory;* wanting to know, burning with curiosity, itching, hungry for; over-curious, nosy, snoopy, prying, spying, peeping, peeking; questioning, inquisitorial 459adj. *inquiring;* busy, overbusy, meddlesome, interfering, officious, ultracrepidarian 678adj. *meddling.*

Vb. *be curious,* want to know, only want to know; seek, look for 459vb. *search;* test, research 461vb. *experiment;* feel a concern, be interested, take an interest; show interest, show curiosity, prick up one's ears 455vb. *be attentive;* dig up, nose out, pick up news; peep, peek, spy 438vb. *scan;* snoop, pry 459vb. *inquire;* eavesdrop, tap the line, intercept, listen, listen in 415vb. *hear;* stick one's nose in, be nosy, interfere, act the busybody 678vb. *meddle;* ask questions, quiz, question 459vb. *interrogate;* look, stare, stand and stare, gape, gawk 438vb. *gaze;* rubberneck, sight-see, window-shop.

Int. what news! what's new? what next?

See: 267, 415, 438, 441, 455, 459, 461, 529, 536, 678.

454 Incuriosity

N. *incuriosity,* lack of interest, incuriousness, no questions; uninterest, unconcern, no interest, insouciance 860n. *indifference;* apathy, phlegmatism 820n. *moral insensibility;* adiaphorism, indifferentism; blunted curiosity 863n. *satiety.*

Adj. *incurious,* uninquisitive, unreflecting 450adj. *unthinking;* without interest, uninterested; aloof, distant; unadmiring 865adj. *unastonished;* wearied 838adj. *bored;* unconcerned, uninvolved 860adj. *indifferent;* listless, inert, apathetic 820adj. *impassive.*

Vb. *be incurious,*—indifferent etc. adj.; have no curiosity, not think about, take no interest 456vb. *be inattentive;* feel no concern, couldn't care less, not trouble oneself, not bother with 860vb. *be indifferent;* mind one's own business, go one's own way 820vb. *be insensitive;* see nothing, hear n., look the other way 458vb. *disregard.*

See: 450, 455, 456, 458, 820, 838, 860, 863, 865.

455 Attention

N. *attention,* notice, regard 438n. *look;* perpension, advertence 449n. *thought;* heed, alertness, readiness, attentiveness, observance, mindfulness 457n. *carefulness;* observation, watchfulness, eyes on, watch, guard 457n. *surveillance;* wariness, circumspection 858n. *caution;* contemplation, introspection 449n. *meditation;* intentness, intentiveness, earnestness, seriousness 599n. *resolution;* undivided attention, whole a.; whole mind, concentration, application, studiousness, close study 536n. *study;* examination, scrutiny, check-up, review 438n. *inspection;* close attention, minute a., meticulosity, attention to detail, particularity, minuteness, finicalness, pedantry 494n. *accuracy;* diligent attention, diligence, pains, trouble 678n. *assiduity;* exclusive attention, rapt a.; single-mindedness; absorption, preoccupation, brown study 456n. *inattention;* interest, inquisitive attention 453n. *curiosity;* obsession, monomania 503n. *mania.*

Adj. *attentive,* intent, diligent, assiduous 678adj. *industrious;* heedful, mindful, regardful 457adj. *careful;* alert, ready, on one's toes; open-eyed, waking, wakeful, awake, wide-a.; awake to, alive to, sensing 819adj. *sensitive;* conscious, thinking 449adj. *thoughtful;* observant, sharp-eyed, observing, watching, watchful 457adj. *vigilant;* attending, paying attention, missing nothing; all eyes 438adj. *seeing;* all ears, prick-eared; all attention, undistracted, deep in; serious, earnest; study-bent 536adj. *studious;* close, minute, nice, meticulous, particular, finical, pedantic 494n. *accurate;* on the watch, on the look-out, on the stretch 507adj. *expectant.*

obsessed, interested, over-i., over-curious 453adj. *curious;* single-minded, possessed, engrossed, preoccupied, rapt, suspended, wrapped up in, taken up with; haunted by 854adj. *fearing;* monomaniacal 503adj. *crazed.*

Vb. *be attentive,* attend, give attention, pay a.; look to, heed, pay h., mind 457vb. *be careful;* trouble oneself, care, take trouble *or* pains, bother 682vb. *exert oneself;* advert, listen, prick up one's ears, sit up, sit up and take notice; take seriously, fasten on 638vb. *make important;* give one's attention, give one's mind to, bend the mind to, direct one's thoughts to 449vb. *think;* strain one's attention, miss nothing; watch, be all eyes 438vb. *gaze;* be all ears, drink in, hang on the lips of 415vb. *hear;* focus (one's mind on), rivet one's attention to, concentrate on, fix on; examine, inspect, scrutinize, vet, review, pass under review 438vb. *scan;* overhaul, revise 654vb. *make better;* study closely, pore, mull, read, re-read, digest 536vb. *study;* pay some attention, glance at, look into, dip into, skip, flick over the leaves, turn the pages.

be mindful, keep in mind, bear in m., have in m. 505vb. *remember;* not forget, think of, spare a thought for, regard, look on 438vb. *see;* lend an ear to 415vb. *hear;* take care of, see to 689vb. *manage;* have regard to, have an eye to, keep in sight, keep in view 617vb. *intend;* not lose sight of, keep track of 619vb. *pursue.*

notice, note, take n., register; make note of, mark, advert, recognize; take cognizance of, take into consideration, review, reconsider 449vb. *meditate;* take account of, consider, weigh, perpend 480vb. *judge;* animadvert upon, comment u., remark on, talk about, discuss 584vb. *converse;* mention, just m., mention in passing, touch on 524vb. *hint;* recall, revert to, hark back 106vb. *repeat;* think worthy of attention, deign to notice, condescend to; have time for, spare time f., find time f. 681vb. *have leisure;* acknowledge, salute 884vb. *greet.*

attract notice, draw the attention, hold the a., focus the a., rivet the a., be the cynosure of all eyes, cut a figure 875vb. *be ostentatious;* arouse notice, arrest one's n., strike one's n.; interest; excite attention, invite a., solicit a., claim a., demand a., meet with a.; catch the eye, fall under observation 443vb. *be visible;* make one see, bring under notice 522vb. *show;* bring forward, call one's attention to, indigitate, advertise 528vb. *publish;* lay the finger on, point the finger, point out, point to 547vb. *indicate;* stress, underline 532vb. *emphasize;* occupy, keep guessing 612vb. *tempt;* fascinate, haunt, monopolize, obsess 449vb. *engross;* call soldiers to attention 737vb. *command.*

Int. see! mark! lo! ecce! behold! lo and behold! look! look here! see here! look out! look alive! look to it! soho! hark! oyez! mind! halloo! observe! nota bene, N.B., take notice! warning! take care! watch your step!

See: 106, 415, 438, 443, 449, 453, 456, 457, 480, 494, 503, 505, 507, 522, 524, 528, 532, 536, 547, 584, 599, 612, 617, 619, 638, 654, 678, 681, 682, 689, 737, 819, 854, 858, 875, 884.

456 Inattention

N. *inattention,* inadvertence, inadvertency, forgetfulness 506n. *oblivion;* oversight, aberration; parapraxia 495n. *error;* lack of interest, lack of observation 454n. *incuriosity;* aloofness, detachment, unconcern 860n. *indifference;* non-observance, disregard 458n. *negligence;* inconsideration, heedlessness 857n. *rashness;* want of thought, inconsiderateness 481n. *misjudgment,* 932n. *selfishness;* aimlessness, desultoriness 282n. *deviation;* superficiality, flippancy 212n. *shallowness;* étourderie, dizziness, giddiness, lightmindedness, levity, volatility 604n. *caprice;* deaf ears 416n. *deafness;* blind eyes, blind spot, blind side 439n. *blindness;* absent-mindedness, wandering wits 450n. *incogitance;* Johnny-head-in-air, stargazer, daydreamer.

abstractedness, abstraction, absent-mindedness, wandering attention, absence of mind; wool-gathering, daydreaming, star-gazing, doodling; fit of abstraction, deep musing, reverie, brown study; distraction, preoccupation, divided attention.

Adj. *inattentive,* careless 458adj. *negligent;* off one's guard 508adj. *inexpectant;* unobservant, unnoticing 454adj. *incurious;* unseeing 439adj. *blind;* unhearing 416adj. *deaf;* undiscerning 464adj. *indiscriminating;* unmindful, unheeding, inadvertent, not thinking, unreflecting 450adj. *unthinking;* not concentrating, half asleep, only half awake; listless 860adj. *indifferent;* apathetic 820adj. *impassive;* oblivious 506adj. forgetful; inconsiderate, without consideration, thoughtless, heedless, regardless 857adj. *rash;* off-hands, cursory, superficial, unthorough 212adj. *shallow.*

abstracted, distrait, absent-minded, absent, far away, not there; lost, lost in thought, wrapped in t., rapt, absorbed, in the clouds, star-gazing; bemused, sunk in a brown study, deep in reverie, pensive, dreamy, dreaming, day-d., mooning, wool-gathering; nodding, napping, half-awake, betwixt sleep and waking 679adj. *sleepy.*

distracted, preoccupied, engrossed; otherwise engaged, with divided attention; dazed, dazzled, disconcerted, put out, put out of one's stride, put off, put off one's stroke; rattled, unnerved 854adj. *nervous.*

light-minded, unfixed, unconcentrated, wandering, desultory, trifling; frivolous, flippant, insouciant; airy, volatile, mercurial, bird-witted, flighty, giddy, dizzy, écervelé; scatter-brained, hare-b.; wild, romping, harum-scarum, rantipole; addled, brainsick 503adj. *crazed;* inconstant, to one thing constant never 604adj. *capricious.*

Vb. *be inattentive,* not attend, pay no attention, pay no heed, not listen, hear nothing, see n.; close one's eyes 439vb. *be blind;* stop one's ears 416vb. *be deaf;* not register, not notice, not use one's eyes; not hear the penny drop, not click, not catch; overlook, commit an oversight 495vb. *blunder;* be off one's guard, let slip, be caught out, catch oneself o., catch oneself doing; not remember 506vb. *forget;* dream, drowse, nod 679vb. *sleep;* not concentrate, trifle, play at; be abstracted, moider, moither, wander, let one's thoughts wander, let one's mind w., let one's wits go bird-nesting, go wool-gathering, indulge in reverie, fall into a brown study, muse, be lost in thought, moon, star-gaze; idle, doodle 679vb. *be inactive;* be distracted, digress, lose the thread, fluff one's notes 282vb. *stray;* be disconcerted, be rattled 854vb. *be nervous;* be put off one's stroke, be put out of one's stride 702vb. *hinder* (**see** *distract*); disregard, ignore 458vb. *neglect;* have no time for, think nothing of, think little of 922vb. *hold cheap.*

distract, call away, divert, divert one's attention, draw off one's a.; make forget, put out of one's head, drive out of one's mind; entice, throw, a sop to Cerberus 612vb. *tempt;* confuse, muddle 63vb. *derange;* disturb, interrupt 72vb. *discontinue;* disconcert, upset, perplex, discompose, fluster, bother, flurry, rattle 318vb. *agitate;* put one off his stoke, put one out of his stride 702vb. *obstruct;* daze, dazzle 439vb. *blind;* bewilder, flummox 474vb. *puzzle;* fuddle, addle 503vb. *make mad;* play with, amuse.

escape notice, escape attention, blush unseen, be overlooked 523vb. *lurk;* fall on deaf ears, meet a blind spot, not click; not hold the attention, go in at one ear and out at the other, slip one's memory 506vb. *be forgotten.*

Adv. *inadvertently,* per incuriam, by oversight; rashly, giddily, gaily, lightheartedly.

See: 63, 72, 212, 282, 318, 416, 439, 450, 454, 458, 474, 481, 495, 503, 506,

508, 523, 604, 612, 679, 702, 820, 854, 857, 860, 922, 932.

457 Carefulness

N. *carefulness,* mindfulness, attentiveness, diligence, pains 678n. *assiduity;* heed, care, utmost c. 455n. *attention;* anxiety, solicitude 825n. *worry;* loving care 897n. *benevolence;* tidiness, orderliness, neatness 60n. *order;* attention to detail, thoroughness, meticulousness, minuteness, circumstantiality, particularity; nicety, exactness, exactitude 494n. *accuracy;* over-nicety, pedantry, perfectionism 862n. *fastidiousness;* conscience, scruples, scrupulosity 929n. *probity;* vigilance, wakefulness, watchfulness, alertness, readiness 669n. *preparedness;* circumspection, prudence, wariness 858n. *caution;* forethought 510n. *foresight.*

surveillance, an eye on, eyes on, watching, guarding, watch and ward 660n. *protection;* vigilance, invigilation, inspection; baby-sitting, chaperonage; look-out, weather-eye; vigil, watch, death-w.; guard, sentry-go; eyes of Argus, taskmaster's eye, watchful e., lidless e. 438n. *eye;* chaperon, sentry, sentinel 660n. *protection,* 749n. *keeper.*

Adj. *careful,* thoughtful, considerate, considered, mindful, regardful, heedful 455adj. *attentive;* taking care, painstaking; solicitous, anxious; gingerly, afraid to touch; loving, tender; conscientious, scrupulous, honest 929adj. *honorable;* diligent, assiduous 678adj. *industrious;* thorough, thoroughgoing; meticulous, minute, particular, circumstantial; exact 494adj. *accurate;* pedantic, overcareful, perfectionist 862adj. *fastidious;* nice, tidy, neat, clean 60adj. *orderly;* minding the pennies, thrifty, penurious, miserly 816adj. *parsimonious.*

vigilant, alert, on guard, on the qui vive, on one's toes; watching, watchful, wakeful, wide-awake; observant, sharp-eyed; all eyes, open-eyed, lidless-e., Argus-e., lynx-e. 438adj. *seeing;* prudent, provident, forehanded, far-sighted 510adj. *foreseeing;* surefooted, picking one's steps; circumspect, circumspective, looking before and after 858adj. *cautious.*

Vb. *be careful,* reck, mind, heed 455vb. *be attentive;* take precautions, check, recheck 858vb. *be cautious;* have one's eyes open, have one's wits about one, keep a lookout, look before and after, look right then left, mind one's step, watch one's s.; pick one's steps, feel one's way 461vb. *be tentative;* speak by the card, mind one's Ps and Qs; mind one's business, count one's money, look after the pennies 814vb. *economize;* tidy, keep t. 62vb. *arrange;* take pains, do with care, be meticulous; try, do one's best 682vb. *exert oneself.*

look after, look to, see to, take care of, see to 689vb. *manage;* take charge of, accept responsibility for; care for, mind, tend, keep 660vb. *safeguard;* sit up with, baby-sit; nurse, foster, cherish 889vb. *pet;* regard, tender 920vb. *respect;* keep an eye, keep a sharp eye on, keep tabs on, chaperon, play gooseberry; serve 703vb. *minister to.*

invigilate, stay awake, sit up; keep vigil, watch; stand sentinel; keep watch, keep watch and ward; look out, keep a sharp look-out, watch out for; keep one's weather-eye open, sleep with one eye o., keep one's ear to the ground; mount guard, set watch, post sentries, stand to 660vb. *safeguard.*

Adv. *carefully,* attentively, diligently; studiously, thoroughly; lovingly, tenderly; painfully, anxiously; with care, gingerly.

See: 60, 62, 438, 455, 461, 494, 510, 660, 664, 669, 678, 682, 689, 703, 749, 814, 816, 825, 858, 862, 889, 897, 920, 929.

458 Negligence

N. *negligence,* carelessness 456n. *inattention;* neglectfulness, forgetfulness 506n. *oblivion;* remissness, neglect, oversight, omission; non-observance, default, laches, culpable negligence 918n. *dutilessness;* unwatchfulness, unwariness, unguarded hour, unguarded minute, unpreparedness 670n. *non-preparation;* disregard, non-interference, laissez-faire 620n. *avoidance;* unconcern, insouciance, nonchalance, don't-care attitude 860n. *indifference;* recklessness 857n. *rashness;* procrastination 136n. *delay;* supineness, slackness, laziness 679n. *inactivity;* slovenliness, sluttishness, untidiness 61n. *disorder;* inaccuracy, inexactitude 495n. *inexactness;* off-handedness, casualness, laxness 734n. *laxity;* superficiality 212n. *shallowness;* trifling, scamping, skipping, dodging, botching 695n. *bungling;* scamped work, skimped w., botched job, loose ends 728n. *fail-*

ure; passing over, not mentioning, paraleipsis 582n. *taciturnity;* trifler, slacker, waster 679n. *idler;* procrastinator, shirker; waiter on Providence, Micawber; sloven 61n. *slut.*

Adj. *negligent,* neglectful, careless, unmindful 456adj. *inattentive;* remiss 918adj. *dutiless;* thoughtless 450adj. *unthinking;* oblivious 506adj. *forgetful;* uncaring, insouciant 860adj. *indifferent;* regardless, reckless 857adj. *rash;* heedless 769adj. *nonobservant;* casual, off-hand, unstrict 734adj. *lax;* slapdash, unthorough, perfunctory, superficial; inaccurate 495adj. *inexact;* slack, supine 679adj. *lazy;* procrastinating 136adj. *late;* sluttish, untidy, slovenly 649adj. *dirty;* not looking, unwary, unwatchful, off guard 508adj. *inexpectant;* unguarded, uncircumspect 670adj. *unprepared;* disregarding, ignoring 620adj. *avoiding.*

neglected, uncared for, untended; ill-kept, unkempt 649adj. *dirty;* unprotected, unguarded, unchaperoned; deserted; unattended, left alone 621adj. *relinquished;* lost sight of, unthought of, unheeded, unmissed, unregarded 860adj. *unwanted;* disregarded, ignored, in the cold; unconsidered, overlooked, omitted; unnoticed, unmarked, unremarked, unperceived, unobserved 444adj. *invisible;* shelved, pigeon-holed, put aside 136adj. *late;* unstudied, unexamined, unsifted, unscanned, unweighed, unexplored, unconned 670adj. *unprepared;* undone, half-done, perfunctory 726adj. *uncompleted;* buried, wrapped in a napkin, hid under a bushel 674adj. *unused.*

Vb. *neglect,* omit, pretermit; pass over; forbear (**see** *disregard*); lose sight of, overlook 456vb. *be inattentive;* leave undone, not finish, leave half-done, leave loose ends, do by halves 726vb. *not complete;* botch, bungle 695vb. *be clumsy;* slur, skimp, scamp 204vb. *shorten;* skip over, jump, skim through, not mention, gloss over, slur over 525vb. *conceal;* be unthorough, dabble in, play with, trifle, fribble 837vb. *amuse oneself.*

disregard, ignore, pass over, give the go-by, dodge, shirk, blink, blench 620vb. *avoid;* wink at, connive at, take no notice 734vb. *be lax;* refuse to see, turn a blind eye to, pay no regard to, dismiss 439vb. *be blind;* forbear, forget it, excuse, overlook 909vb. *forgive;* leave out of one's calculations, discount 483vb. *underestimate;* pass by, pass by on the other side 282vb. *deviate;* turn one's back on, slight, cold shoulder, cut, cut dead 885vb. *be rude;* turn a deaf ear to 416vb. *be deaf;* not trouble oneself with, not trouble one's head about, have no time for, laugh off, pooh-pooh, treat as of no account 922vb. *hold cheap;* leave unregarded, leave out in the cold 57vb. *exclude;* leave in the lurch, desert, abandon 621vb. *relinquish.*

be neglectful, doze, drowse, nod 678vb. *sleep;* be off one's guard, omit precautions; be caught napping, oversleep; be caught with one's pants down 508vb. *not expect;* drift, laissez-faire, procrastinate, let slide, let slip, let the grass grow under one's feet; not bother, take it easy, let things rip 679vb. *be inactive;* shelve, pigeon-hole, lay aside, push aside, put a., lay a. 136vb. *put off;* make neglectful, lull, throw off one's guard, put off one's guard, catch napping, catch bending 508vb. *surprise.*

Adv. *negligently,* per incuriam; anyhow; cursorily, perfunctorily.

See: 57, 61, 136, 212, 282, 416, 439, 444, 450, 456, 483, 495, 506, 508, 525, 582, 620, 621, 649, 670, 674, 678, 679, 695, 726, 728, 734, 769, 837, 857, 860, 885, 909, 918, 922.

459 Inquiry

N. *inquiry,* asking, questioning (**see** *interrogation*); challenge (**see** *question*); asking after, asking about, directing oneself, taking information, getting i. 524n. *information;* close inquiry, searching i., strict i., witch-hunt, spy-mania (**see** *search*); inquisition, examination, investigation, visitation; inquest, postmortem, autopsy, audit, trial 959n, *legal trial;* public inquiry, secret i.; commission of inquiry, work party (**see** *inquirer*); statistical inquiry, poll, Gallup p., straw vote 605n. *vote;* probe, test, means t., check-up, check, trial run 461n. *experiment;* review, scrutiny, overview 438n. *inspection;* introspection, self-examination; research, blue-sky r., fundamental r., applied r. 536n. *study;* exploration, reconnaissance, reconnoiter, survey 484n. *discovery;* discussion, ventilation, airing, canvassing, consultation 584n. *conference;* philosophical inquiry, metaphysical i., scientific i. 449n. *philosophy;* prying, nosing 453n. *curiosity.*

interrogation, questioning, interpellation, asking questions, putting q., formulating q.; forensic examination, examination-in-chief; leading question, cross-examination, cross-question; reexamination; quiz, brain trust; interrogatory; catechism; inquisition, third degree, grilling; dialogue, dialectic, question and answer, interlocution; Socratic method, Socratic elenchus, zetetic philosophy; question time, question hour.

question, question mark, interrogation m., note of interrogation 547n. *punctuation;* query, request for information, chad; questions, questionnaire 87n. *list;* question list, question paper, examination p.; interrogatory, interpellation, Parliamentary question; challenge, fair question, plain q.; catch, cross-question; indirect question, feeler, leading question; moot point, knotty p., debating p.; quodlibet, question propounded, point at issue, side-issue, porism; controversy, field of c., contention, bone of c. 475n. *argument;* problem, poser, stumper, headache, unsolved mystery 530n. *enigma.*

exam., examination, oral e., viva voce e., viva; interview, audition 415n. *hearing;* practical examination, written e.; test, mental t., intelligence t.; entrance examination, common entrance, responsions, little go, matriculation, matric., 11-plus examination, school-leaving e., General Certificate of Education, G.C.E., Intermediate, tripos, moderations, mods., Greats, Modern G., finals; doctorate examination, bar e.; advanced level, scholarship l., degree l., pass l., honors l.; catechumen 460n. *respondent;* examinee, entrant, sitter 461n. *testee.*

search, probe, investigation, inquiry; quest, hunt, witch-h., treasure-h. 619n. *pursuit;* house-search, perquisition, domiciliary visit, house-to-house search; search of one's person, frisking; rummaging, turning over; exploration, excavation, archaeological e., digging, dig; speleology, potholing; search-party; search-warrant.

police inquiry, investigation, criminal i., detection 484n. *discovery;* detective work, shadowing, house-watching; grilling, third degree; Criminal Investigation Department, CID, Federal Bureau of Investigation, FBI, Intelligence Branch, IB; secret police, Gestapo, Cheka, Ogpu, NKVD.

secret service, espionage, counter-e., spying, intelligence, MI5; informer, spy, undercover agent, cloak-and-dagger man; spy-ring.

detective, investigator, criminologist; plain-clothes man; inquiry agent, private detective, private eye; hotel detective, store d.; amateur detective; Federal agent, G-man, CID man; tec, sleuth, bloodhound, gumshoe, flat-foot, dick, snooper, snoop, nose, spy 524n. *informer;* Bow-street runner; graphologist, handwriting expert.

inquirer, investigator, prober, indagator; asker (**see** *questioner*); quidnunc 529vb. *newsmonger;* seeker, thinker, seeker for truth, Diogenes and his lantern 449n. *philosopher;* searcher, looker, rummager, search-party; inventor, discoverer; dowser, water-diviner 484n. *detector;* prospector, gold-digger; talent scout; scout, spy, surveyor, reconnoiterer; inspector, visitor 438n. *inspection;* checker, scrutineer, censor 480n. *judge;* examiner, tester, test-pilot, researcher, research worker, analyst, analyzer, dissector, vivisector 461n. *experimenter;* sampler, pollster, canvasser; explorer 268n. *traveler;* bagman, carpet-bagger 794n. *peddle.*

questioner, cross-q., cross-examiner; interrogator, querist, interpellator, interlocutor, interviewer; catechizer 453n. *inquisitor;* quizzer, enfant terrible; riddler, enigmatist; examiner of conscience, confessor 986n. *clergy.*

Adj. *inquiring,* curious, prying, nosy 453adj. *inquisitive;* quizzing, quizzical; interrogatory, interrogative; requisitory, requisitive, examining, catechetical, inquisitional, cross-questioning; elenctic, dialectic, maieutic, heuristic, zetetic; probing, poking, digging; testing, searching, fact-finding, exploratory, empirical, tentative 461adj. *experimental;* analytic, diagnostic.

moot, in question, questionable, debatable; problematic, doubtful 474adj. *uncertain;* knotty, puzzling 700adj. *difficult;* fit for inquiry, proposed, propounded; undetermined, undecided, untried, left open.

Vb. *inquire,* ask, want to know 491vb. *not know;* demand 761vb. *request;* canvass, agitate, air, ventilate, discuss, bring in question, subject to examination 475vb. *argue;* ask for, look for, inquire for, seek, search for, hunt for 619vb. *pursue;* inquire into, probe, delve into, dig i., dig down i., go deep i., sound; investigate, conduct an inquiry, hold an i., institute an i., set up an i., throw open to i., call in Scotland Yard; try, hear 959vb. *try a case;* review, audit, scrutinize, monitor; analyze, dissect, parse, sift, winnow, thresh out; research, study, consider, examine 449vb. *meditate;* check, check on; feel the pulse, take the temperature; follow up an inquiry, pursue an i., get to the bottom of, fathom, see into, X-ray 438vb. *scan;* peer, peep, peek, snoop, spy, pry, peep behind the curtain 453vb. *be curious;* survey, reconnoiter, explore, feel one's way 461vb. *be tentative;* test, try, sample, taste 461vb. *experiment;* introspect, examine oneself, take a look at.

interrogate, ask questions, put q., speer; interpellate, question; cross-question, cross-examine, reexamine; interview, hold a viva; examine, subject to questioning, sound, probe, quiz, catechize, grill, give the third degree; put to the question 963vb. *torture;* pump, pick the brains, suck the b.; move the question, put the q., pop the q.; pose, propose a question, propound a q., raise a q., moot a q., moot.

search, seek, look for; conduct a search, rummage, ransack, comb; scrabble, scour, clean out, turn over, rake o., turn out, rake through, go t., search t., look into every nook and corner; pry into, peer i., peep i., peek i.; overhaul, frisk, go over, search one's pockets, feel in one's p., search for, feel for, grope for, hunt for, fish, go fishing, fish for, dig for; cast about, seek a clue, follow the trail 619vb. *pursue;* probe, explore, go in quest of 461vb. *be tentative;* dig, excavate, archaeologize; prospect, dowse, treasure-hunt, embark on a t.

be questionable,—debatable etc. adj.; be open to question, call for inquiry, challenge an answer, be subject to examination, be open to inquiry, be under investigation.

Adv. *on trial,* under investigation, under inquiry, sub judice; up for inquiry.

in search of, on the track of, cui bono?

inquiringly, interrogatively; why? wherefore? why on earth? why, oh why? how? how come?

See: 87, 268, 415, 438, 449, 453, 460, 461, 474, 475, 480, 484, 491, 524, 525, 530, 536, 547, 561, 584, 605, 619, 622, 700, 761, 794, 959, 963, 986.

460 Answer

N. *answer,* replication, reaction; reply, response, responsion; answer by mail, acknowledgment, return 588n. *correspondence;* official reply, rescript, rescription 496n. *maxim;* returns, results 548n. *record;* echo, antiphon, antiphony, responsal, respond 106n. *repetition;* password, countersign; keyword, open sesame; answering back, back-talk, backchat, repartee; retort, counterblast, riposte 714n. *retaliation;* give and take, question and answer, dialogue 584n. *interlocution;* last word, final answer; Parthian shot; clue, key, right answer, explanation, solution 520n. *interpretation;* enigmatic answer, oracle, Delphic oracle 530n. *enigma.*

rejoinder, counter-statement, reply, rebuttal, plea in rebuttal, rebutter, surrejoinder, surrebutter 479n. *confutation;* defense, speech for the defense, reply; contradiction 533n. *negation,* 467n. *counter-evidence;* countercharge, counter-accusation, tu quoque 928n. *accusation.*

respondent, defendant; answerer, responder, replier, correspondent; examinee 461n. *testee;* candidate, applicant, entrant, sitter 716n. *contender.*

Adj. *answering,* replying etc. vb.; respondent, responsive, echoic 106adj. *repeated;* counter 182adj. *counteracting;* corresponding 588adj. *epistolary;* antiphonic, antiphonal; corresponding to 28adj. *equal;* contradicting 533adj. *negative;* refuting, rebutting; oracular; conclusive, final, Parthian.

Vb. *answer,* give a., return a.; reply, write back, acknowledge, respond, be responsive, echo, reecho 106vb. *repeat;* react, answer back, retort, riposte 714vb. *retaliate;* say in reply, rejoin, rebut, counter 479vb. *confute;* contradict 533vb. *negate;* be respondent, defend, have the right of reply; provide the answer, have the a. 642vb. *be expedient;* answer the question, solve the riddle 520vb. *interpret;* set at rest, decide 480vb. *judge;* satisfy the demand, satisfy 635vb. *suffice;* suit the requirements 642vb. *be expedient;* answer to, correspond to 12vb. *correlate.*

Adv. *in reply,* by way of rejoinder; antiphonally.

See: 12, 28, 106, 182, 461, 467, 479, 480, 496, 520, 530, 533, 548, 584, 588, 635, 642, 714, 716, 928.

461 Experiment

N. *experiment,* practical e., scientific e., controlled e., control e.; experimentalism, experimentation, experimental method, verification, verification by experiment; exploration, probe; analysis, examination 459n. *inquiry;* object lesson, probation, proof 478n. *demonstration;* assay, docimasy 480n. *estimate;* testability; check, test, crucial t., acid t., test case; practical test, trial, trials, try-out, work-out, trial run, practice r., trial canter, trial flight 671n. *essay;* ranging shot; audition, voice-test; ordeal, ordeal by fire, ordeal by water 959n. *legal trial;* pilot scheme, rough sketch, first draft, sketch-book; first steps, teething troubles 68n. *debut.*

empiricism, speculation, guesswork 512n. *conjecture;* tentativeness, tentative method; experience, practice, rule of thumb, trial, trial and error, hit and miss; random shot, shot in the dark, leap in the d., gamble 618n. *gambling;* instinct, light of nature 476n. *intuition;* sampling, random sample, straw vote, Gallup poll; feeler 378n. *touch;* straw to show which way the wind is blowing, kite-flying, trial balloon, ballon d'essai.

experimenter, experimentalist, empiricist, researcher, research worker, analyst, analyzer, vivisector; pollster, assayer, chemist; tester; test-driver, test-pilot; speculator, prospector, sourdough, forty-niner; prober, explorer, adventurer 459n. *inquirer;* dabbler 493n. *sciolist;* gamester 618n. *gambler.*

testing agent, criterion, touchstone; standard, yardstick 465n. *gauge;* control; reagent, litmus paper, crucible, cupel, retort, test-tube; pyx, pyx-chest; alfet 194n. *caldron;* proving ground, wind-tunnel; flight-simulator, road-driving simulator.

testee, examinee 460n. *respondent;* candidate, entrant, sitter 716n. *contender;* subject of experiment, subject, patient; guinea-pig, rabbit, mouse, hamster, monkey.

Adj. *experimental,* analytic, analytical, docimastic, verificatory, probatory, probative, probationary; provisional, tentative 618adj. *speculative;* exploratory 459adj. *inquiring;* empirical, guided by experience; venturesome 671adj. *essaying;* testable, verifiable, in the experimental stage 474adj. *uncertain.*

Vb. *experiment,* experimentalize, make experiments; check, check on, verify; prove, put to the proof, submit to the p., bring to p.; assay, analyze; research; dabble; experiment upon, vivisect, make a guinea-pig of, practice upon; test, put to the t., subject to a t. 459vb. *inquire;* try, try a thing once; try out, give a trial to 671vb. *essay;* try one's strength, test one's muscles; give one a try, try with, send *or* put a man in (cricket); sample 386vb. *taste;* take a random sample, take a straw vote, take a Gallup poll; put to the vote 605vb. *vote;* rehearse, practice 534vb. *train;* be tested, undergo a test, come to the t.

be tentative, be empirical, seek experience, feel one's way, proceed by trial and error, procced by guess and God; feel 378vb. *touch;* probe, grope, fumble; get the feel of 536vb. *learn;* throw out a feeler, fly a kite, feel the pulse, consult the barometer, see how the land lies; fish, fish for, angle for, bob for, cast one's net, trawl, put out a t.; wait and see, see what happens; try it on, see how far one can go; try one's fortune, try one's luck, speculate 618vb. *gamble;* venture; explore, prospect 672vb. *undertake;* probe, sound 459vb. *inquire.*

Adv. *experimentally,* on test, on trial, on approval; empirically, by rule of thumb, by trial and error, by light of nature, by guess and God; on spec.

See: 68, 194, 378, 383, 386, 459, 460, 465, 474, 476, 478, 480, 493, 512, 534, 536, 605, 618, 671, 672, 716, 959.

462 Comparison

N. *comparison,* analogical procedure; comparing, likening; confrontation, collation, juxtaposition, setting side by side 202n. *contiguity;* check 459n. *inquiry;* comparability, points of comparison, analogy, likeness, similitude 18n. *similarity;* identification 13n. *identity;* contrast 15n. *differentiation;* simile, allegory 519n. *metaphor;* standard of comparison, criterion, pattern, model, check-list, control 23n. *prototype;* comparer, collator.

Adj. *compared,* collated; compared with, likened, contrasted; comparative, comparable, analogical; relative, correlative; allegorical, metaphorical 519adj. *figurative.*

Vb. *compare,* collate, confront; set side by side, bring together 202vb. *juxtapose;* draw a comparison, similize 18n. *liken,* 13vb. *identify;* parallel; contrast 15n. *differentiate;* compare and contrast 463vb. *discriminate;* match, pair, balance 28vb. *equalize;* view together, check with 12vb. *correlate;* institute a comparison, draw a parallel; compare to, compare with, criticize; compare notes, match ideas, exchange views.

Adv. *comparatively,* analogically; in comparison, as compared; relatively 12adj. *correlatively.*

See: 12, 13, 15, 18, 23, 28, 202, 459, 463, 519.

463 Discrimination

N. *discrimination,* distinction, diorism 15n. *differentiation;* discernment, discretion, ability to make distinctions, appreciation of differences, discriminating judgment 480n. *judgment;* insight, perception, nice p., acumen, flair 498n. *intelligence;* appreciation, careful a., critique, critical appraisal 480n. *estimate;* sensitivity 494n. *accuracy;* sensibility 819n. *moral sensibility;* delicacy, refinement 846n. *good taste;* tact, feel 378n. *touch;* timing, sense of t., sense of the occasion; diagnosis, diagnostics 520n. *interpretation;* nicety, particularity 862n. *fastidiousness;* fine palate 386n. *taste;* logical nicety, subtlety, hair-splitting, logic-chopping 475n. *reasoning;* sifting, *separation,* sorting out 62n. *sorting;* selection 605n. *choice;* nice difference, shade of d., nuance, fine shade 15n. *difference.*

Adj. *discriminating,* discriminative, selective, dioristic, judicious, discerning, discreet; accurate, sensitive 494adj. *exact;* fine, delicate, nice, particular 862adj. *fastidious;* thoughtful, tactful 513adj. *imaginative;* tasting, appraising, critical 480adj. *judicial;* diagnostic 15adj. *distinctive.*

Vb. *discriminate,* distinguish, diagnose 15vb. *differentiate;* compare and contrast 462vb. *compare;* sort, sort out, sieve, bolt, sift, van, winnow; severalize, separate, separate the sheep from the goats, sort the wheat from the chaff 46vb. *set apart;* pick out 605vb. *select;* exercise discretion, see the difference, make a distinction, make an exception, draw the line 468vb. *qualify;* refine, refine upon, split hairs, chop logic 475vb. *reason;* criticize, appraise, taste 480vb. *estimate;* weigh, consider, make a judgment 480vb. *judge;* discern, have insight; know what's what, know one's way about, know one's stuff, know a hawk from a handsaw 490n. *know;* take into account, give weight to 638vb. *make important;* attribute just value to 913vb. *be just.*

See: 15, 46, 62, 378, 386, 462, 468, 475, 480, 490, 494, 498, 513, 520, 605, 638, 819, 846, 862, 913.

464 Indiscrimination

N. *indiscrimination,* lack of discrimination, promiscuousness, promiscuity, universality 79n. *generality;* lack of judgment, uncriticalness, simplicity; obtuseness 499n. *unintelligence;* indiscretion, want of consideration 857n. *rashness;* imperceptivity 439n. *blindness;* unimaginativeness, tactlessness, insensitiveness, insensibility 820n. *moral insensibility;* tastelessness, unrefinement, vulgarity 847n. *bad taste;* coarseness, inaccuracy 495n. *inexactness;* vagueness, loose terms.

Adj. *indiscriminate,* unsorted 61adj. *orderless;* rolled into one, undistinguished, undifferentiated, same for everybody 16adj. *uniform;* random, unaimed, undirected; confused, undefined, unmeasured 474adj. *uncertain;* promiscuous, haphazard, wholesale, blanket 79adj. *general.*
indiscriminating, unselective, undiscerning, uncritical 499adj. *unintelligent;* imperceptive, obtuse; tactless, insensitive, unimaginative 820adj. *impassive;* unrefined 847adj. *vulgar;* indiscreet, ill-judged 857adj. *rash;* tone-deaf 416adj. *deaf;* color-blind 439adj. *blind;* coarse, inaccurate 495adj. *inexact.*

Vb. *not discriminate,* be indiscriminate, avoid precision, confound opposites, be unselective 606vb. *be neutral;* exercise no discretion 499vb. *be foolish;* make no distinction, see no difference, swallow whole; roll into one, lump everything together, heap t. 74vb. *bring together;* jumble, muddle, confuse, confound 63vb. *derange;* ignore distinctions, obliterate d., average, take an a., smooth out 30vb. *average out.*

See: 16, 30, 61, 63, 74, 79, 416, 439, 495, 499, 606, 820, 847, 857.

465 Measurement

N. *measurement,* admeasurement, quantification; mensuration, surveying, triangulation, cadastral survey;

geodetics, geodesy; metage, assize, weighment; posology, dose, dosage 26n. *finite quantity;* rating, valuation, evaluation; appraisal, appraisement, assessment, appreciation, estimation 480n. *estimate;* calculation, computation, reckoning 86n. *numeration;* gematria 984n. *occultism;* dead reckoning, gauging; checking, check; reading, reading off; metrics, longimetry, micrometry 203n. *long measure;* trigonometry; second, degree, minute, quadrant 247n. *angular measure;* cubature; mecometry; focimetry; focometry; measurement of rhythm, orthometry.

geometry, plane g., planimetry; solid geometry, stereometry; altimetry, hypsometry; Euclidean geometry, non-Euclidean g.; geometer.

metrology, dimensions, length, breadth, height, depth, thickness; weights and measures, metric system; weights 322n. *weighment;* axle-load; linear measure 203n. *long measure;* measure of capacity, volume, cubature, cubic contents 183n. *space;* liquid measure, gill, pint, imperial p., quart, gallon, imperial g.; barrel, pipe, hogshead 194n. *vessel;* liter; apothecaries' fluid measure, minim, dram; dry measure, peck, bushel, quarter; firlot, boll, chalder, chaldron; ephah, homer; unit of energy, ohm, watt 160n. *electricity;* poundal 160n. *energy;* candlepower 417n. *light;* decibel, sone 398n. *sound.*

coordinate, ordinate and abscissa, polar coordinates, latitude and longitude, right ascension and declension, altitude and azimuth.

gauge, measure, scale, graduated s.; time scale 117n. *chronometry;* balance 322n. *scales;* nonius, vernier; footrule, yardstick; pace-stick; yard measure, tape m., steel tape, meter bar; standard, chain, link, pole, rod; lead, log, log-line; fathometer; ruler, slide-rule; straightedge, T-square, set-sq.; dividers, calipers, compass, protractor; sextant, quadrant 247n. *angular measure;* backstaff, Jacob's staff 269n. *sailing aid;* theodolite, planisphere, alidade; astrolabe, armillary sphere 321n. *astronomy;* index, Plimsoll line, Plimsoll mark 547n. *indication;* high-water mark, tide-m., watermark 236n. *limit;* axis, coordinate; milestone 547n. *signpost.*

meter, measuring-instrument; goniometer, planimeter; altimeter 209n. *altimetry;* thermometer 379n. *thermometry;* barometer, anemometer 352n. *anemology;* dynamometer; hygrometer 341n. *hygrometry;* fluviometer, nilometer; gas meter; speed gauge, speedometer, cyclometer, pedometer 277n. *velocity;* time-gauge, metronome, time-switch, parking-meter 117n. *timekeeper;* micrometer, ultramicrometer, tasimeter, Geiger counter; seismograph; geophone.

surveyor, land s., quantity s.; topographer, cartographer, oceanographer, hydrographer, geodesist; geometer.

appraiser, valuer, estimator, assessor, measurer, surveyor 480n. *judge.*

Adj. *metric,* metrical, mensural, dimensional, three-d., four-d.; cubic, volumetric, linear, longimetrical, micrometric; cadastral, topographical; geodetic.

measured, surveyed, mapped, plotted, taped; graduated, calibrated; mensurable, measurable, meterable, assessable, computable, calculable.

Vb. *measure,* mete, mensurate, survey; compute, calculate, count, reckon, quantize 86vb. *number;* quantify, take the dimensions, measure the length and breadth; size, calculate the s.; estimate the average 30vb. *average out;* beat the bounds, pace out, count one's steps; measure one's length 309vb. *tumble;* tape, span; caliper, use the dividers; probe, sound, fathom, plumb 313vb. *plunge;* take soundings, heave the lead, heave the log; pace, check the speed 117vb. *time;* balance 322vb. *weigh.*

gauge, meter, take a reading, read, read off; standardize, fix the standard, set a standard 16vb. *make uniform;* grade, mark off, calibrate 27vb. *graduate;* reduce to scale, draw to s., draw a plan, map 551vb. *represent.*

appraise, gauge, value, cost, rate, set a value on, fix the price of 809vb. *price;* evaluate, estimate, make an e., form an e.; appreciate, assess 480vb. *estimate;* form an opinion 480vb. *judge;* tape, have taped, have the measure of, size up.

mete out, mete, measure out, weigh, weigh out, dole o.; divide, share, share out 775vb. *participate,* 783vb. *apportion.*

See: 16, 26, 27, 30, 86, 117, 160, 183, 194, 203, 209, 220, 236, 247, 269, 277, 309, 313, 321, 322, 341, 352, 379, 398, 417, 480, 547, 551, 775, 783, 809, 984.

466 Evidence

N. *evidence,* facts, data, case-history;

grounds 475n. *reasons;* precognita, premises 475n. *premise;* hearsay, what the soldier said, hearsay evidence 524n. *report;* indirect evidence, collateral e., secondary e.; circumstantial evidence 8n. *circumstance;* constructive evidence 512n. *supposition;* prima facie evidence; intrinsic evidence, internal e., presumptive e., direct e., demonstrative e., final e., conclusive e., proof 478n. *demonstration;* supporting evidence, corroboration; verification, confirmation 473n. *certainty;* rebutting evidence 467n. *counter-evidence;* one-sided evidence, ex parte e.; piece of evidence, fact, relevant f.; document, exhibit, finger-prints 548n. *record;* clue 524n. *hint;* symptom, sign 547n. *indication;* reference, quotation, citation, chapter and verse; one's authorities, documentation; line of evidence, chain of authorities; authority, scripturality, canonicity.

testimony, witness; statement, evidence in chief 524n. *information;* admission, confession 526n. *disclosure;* one's case, plea 614n. *pretext;* word, assertion, allegation 532n. *affirmation;* Bible evidence, evidence on oath; sworn evidence, legal e., deposition, affidavit, attestation 532n. *oath;* State's evidence, Queen's e.; word of mouth, oral evidence, verbal e.; documentary evidence, written e.; evidence to character, compurgation, wager at law 927n. *vindication;* copy of the evidence, case record, dossier 548n. *record;* written contract 765n. *compact;* deed, testament 767n. *security.*

credential, compurgation 927n. *vindication;* testimonial, chit, character, recommendation, references; seal, signature, counter-s., endorsement, docket; voucher, warranty, warrant, certificate, diploma 767n. *security;* ticket, passport, visa 756n. *permit;* authority, scripture.

witness, eye-w. 441n. *spectator;* earwitness 415n. *listener;* indicator, informant, telltale 524n. *informer;* deponent, testifier, swearer, attester, attestant 765n. *signatory;* witness to character, compurgator, oath-helper; sponsor 707n. *patron.*

Adj. *evidential,* evidentiary, offering evidence, testificatory; prima facie 445adj. *appearing;* suggesting, suggestive, significant 514adj. *meaningful;* showing, indicative, symptomatic 547adj. *indicating;* indirect, secondary, circumstantial; first-hand, direct, seen, heard; deducible, verifiable 471adj. *probable;* constructive 512adj. *suppositional;* cumulative, supporting, corroborative, confirmatory; telling, damning 928adj. *accusing;* presumptive, reliable 473adj. *certain;* probative, proving, demonstrative, conclusive, decisive, final 478adj. *demonstrating;* based on, grounded on; founded on fact, factual, documentary, documented 473adj. *positive;* authentic, well-grounded, well-based 494adj. *true;* weighty, authoritative 178adj. *influential;* biblical, scriptural, canonical 976adj. *orthodox;* testified, attested, witnessed; spoken to, sworn to; in evidence, on the record, documented 548adj. *recorded.*

Vb. *evidence,* show, evince, furnish evidence; show signs of, have the makings of 852vb. *give hope;* betoken, bespeak 551vb. *represent;* breathe of, tell of, declare 522vb. *manifest;* lend color to 471vb. *make likely;* tell its own tale, speak for itself, speak volumes; have weight, carry w. 178vb. *influence;* suggest 547vb. *indicate;* argue, involve 523vb. *imply.*

testify, witness; take one's oath, swear, be sworn, speak on oath 532vb. *affirm;* bear witness, take the stand, give evidence, speak to, depose, depone, swear to, vouch for, give one's word; authenticate, certify 473vb. *make certain;* attest, subscribe, countersign, endorse, sign; plead, state one's case 475vb. *argue;* admit, avow, acknowledge 526vb. *confess;* speak to character, compurgate, testimonialize.

corroborate, support, buttress 162vb. *strengthen;* sustain, uphold in evidence 927vb. *vindicate;* bear out, circumstantiate, verify; validate, confirm, ratify, establish, make out, make good 473vb. *make certain;* lead evidence, adduce e.; bring one's witnesses, produce one's w., confront w.; put the evidence, produce the e., document; collect evidence, assemble the facts; concoct evidence, fabricate e. 541vb. *fake;* outswear 467vb. *tell against;* adduce, cite the evidence, quote the e., quote the leading case, quote one's authorities, give the reference, give chapter and verse.

See: 8, 162, 178, 415, 441, 445, 467, 471, 473, 475, 478, 494, 512, 514, 522, 523, 524, 526, 532, 541, 547, 548, 551, 614, 707, 756, 765, 767, 852, 927, 929, 976.

467 Counter-evidence

N. *counter-evidence,* adverse symptom, contra-indication 14n. *contrariety;* answering evidence, opposite e., rebutting e.; evidence against, evidence on the other side, defense, rebuttal 460n. *answer;* refutation, disproof 479n. *confutation;* denial 533n. *negation;* justification 927n. *vindication;* oath against oath, one word against another; counter-oath, counter-protest, tu quoque argument, reverse of the shield; conflicting evidence, contradictory e., negative e.; mitigating evidence 468n. *qualification;* hostile witness, hostile evidence 603n. *tergiversation.*

Adj. *countervailing,* rebutting 460adj. *answering;* canceling out, counteractive 182adj. *counteracting;* cutting both ways, ambiguous 518adj. *equivocal;* converse, opposite, in the opposite scale 14adj. *contrary;* denying, negatory 533adj. *negative;* damaging, telling against, contra-indicating; refutatory, refutative; qualificatory 468adj. *qualifying.*

unattested, unsworn; lacking proof, unproven, not proved 474adj. *uncertain;* unsupported, uncorroborated; disproved 479adj. *confuted;* trumped-up, fabricated 541adj. *false.*

Vb. *tell against,* damage the case; weigh against, countervail; contravene, traverse, run counter, contradict, contraindicate; rebut 479vb. *confute;* oppose, point the other way 14vb. *be contrary;* cancel out 182vb. *counteract;* cut both ways 518vb. *be equivocal;* prove a negative 533vb. *negate;* lead counter-evidence, lead for the other side; tell another story, alter the case; not improve, weaken, damage, spoil; undermine, subvert 165vb. *destroy;* demolish the case, turn the tables, turn the scale, convict of perjury; contradict oneself, turn hostile 603vb. *tergiversate.*

Adv. *conversely,* per contra, on the other hand, on the other side, in rebuttal, in rejoinder.

See: 14, 165, 182, 460, 468, 474, 479, 518, 533, 541, 603, 927.

468 Qualification

N. *qualification,* specification 80n. *specialty;* requisite 627n. *requirement;* leaven, coloring, tinge; modification 143n. *change;* mitigation 177n. *moderation;* condition 766n. *conditions;* limitation 747n. *restriction;* proviso, reservation; exception, salvo, saving clause, escape c., escalator c.; exemption 919n. *non-liability;* demure, objection, but 704n. *opposition;* consideration, discount, abatement, reduction, allowance, grains of a.; extenuating circumstances; redeeming feature 31n. *offset.*

Adj. *qualifying,* qualificative, qualificatory; modifying, altering the case; mitigatory 177adj. *lenitive;* extenuating, palliative, excusing, weakening, coloring, leavening; contingent, provisional 766adj. *conditional;* discounting, abating; saving, excepting, exempting; circumstanced, qualified, not absolute; exceptional, exempted, exempt 919adj. *non-liable.*

Vb. *qualify,* condition, limit, restrict 747vb. *restrain;* color, shade 419vb. *bedim;* leaven, alter 143vb. *modify;* temper, palliate, mitigate 177vb. *moderate;* adulterate 163vb. *weaken;* excuse 927vb. *extenuate;* grant, make allowance for, 810n. *discount;* abate 37vb. *bate;* make exceptions 919vb. *exempt;* introduce new conditions, alter the case; insert a qualifying clause; relax, relax the rigor of 734vb. *be lax;* take exception, object, demur, raise an objection 762vb. *deprecate.*

Adv. *provided,* provided always, with the proviso that, according as, subject to, conditionally, with the understanding; granting, admitting, supposing; allowing for, with grains of allowance, cum grano salis; not absolutely, not invariably; if, if not, unless 8adv. *if;* though, although, even if.

nevertheless, even so, all the same; despite, in spite of; but, yet, still, at all events; whether, whether or no.

See: 8, 31, 37, 80, 143, 163, 177, 419, 627, 704, 734, 747, 762, 766, 810, 919, 927.

469 Possibility

N. *possibility,* potentiality, virtuality; capacity, viability, viableness, workability 160n. *ability;* what is possible, all that is p. 635n. *sufficiency;* what may be 124n. *futurity;* what might be, the might-have-been 125n. *preterition;* the possible, the feasible; what one can do, best one can do, limit of one's endeavor; contingency, a possibility, chance, off-chance 159n. *fair chance;* good chance 137n. *opportunity;* bare possibility, ghost of a chance; likelihood 471n. *probability;* thinkability, credibility 485n. *belief;* practicability, operability 642n. *expedience;* practicableness, feasibility, easiness 701n. *facility;* superability, negotiability; availability, accessability, approachability; compatibility 24n. *agreement;* risk of.

Adj. *possible,* virtual, potential, of power, able, capable, viable; arguable, reasonable; feasible, practicable, negotiable 701adj. *easy;* workable, performable, achievable; doable, operable; attainable, approachable, accessible, obtainable, realizable; superable, surmountable; not too difficult, not impossible, within the bounds of possibility; available, still open, not excluded; conceivable, thinkable, credible, imaginable; practical, compatible with the circumstances 642adj. *expedient;* allowable, permissible, legal 756adj. *permitted;* contingent 124adj. *future;* on the cards, on the dice 471adj. *probable;* only possible, not inevitable, evitable, revocable 620adj. *avoidable;* liable, tending.

Vb. *be possible,*—feasible etc. adj.; may, might, maybe, might be; might have been, could have b., should have b.; admit of, allow 756vb. *permit;* bear, be open to, offer an opportunity for; be a possibility, depend, be contingent, lie within the bounds of possibility.

make possible, enable 160vb. *empower;* allow 756vb. *permit;* clear the path, smoothe the way, remove the obstacles, put in the way of 701vb. *facilitate.*

Adv. *possibly,* potentially, virtually; perhaps, perchance, within reach, within measurable distance; peradventure, may be, haply, mayhap; if possible, if so be; wind and weather permitting, God willing, Deo volente, D.V.

See: 24, 124, 125, 137, 159, 160, 471, 485, 620, 635, 642, 701, 756.

470 Impossibility

N. *impossibility* etc.adj.; unthinkability, no chance, not a chance of, not a Chinaman's chance 853n. *hopelessness;* what cannot be, what can never be; irrevocability, the might-have-been; impasse, deadlock 702n. *obstacle;* infeasibility, impracticability 643n. *inexpedience;* no permission 757n. *prohibition;* unavailability, inaccessibility, unapproachability, sour grapes; insuperability, impossible task, no go, Sisyphean operation 700n. *hard task.*

Adj. *impossible,* not possible; not allowed, ruled out, excluded, against the rules 757adj. *prohibited;* out of the question, hopeless; unnatural, against nature; unreasonable, contrary to reason, self-contradictory 477adj. *illogical;* unscientific; untrue, incompatible with the facts, untrue to fact 495adj. *erroneous;* too improbable, incredible, inconceivable, unthinkable, unimaginable, unheard of 486adj. *unbelieved;* miraculous 864adj. *wonderful;* visionary, idealistic, unrealistic, out of this world 513adj. *imaginary*; irrevocable, beyond recall 830adj. *regretted.*

impracticable, unfeasible, not to be done; unworkable, unviable; unachievable, unrealizable, unsolvable, insoluble, inextricable, too hard 700adj. *difficult;* incurable, inoperable; insuperable, insurmountable, impassable, unbridgeable, unbridged; impervious, unnavigable, unmotorable; unapproachable, inaccessible, unobtainable, unavailable, not to be had, out of reach, beyond one's reach, not within one's grasp; elusive 667adj. *escaped.*

Vb. *be impossible,* — impracticable etc.adj., exceed possibility, defy all possibilities; fly in the face of reason 477vb. *reason ill;* have no chance whatever.

make impossible, rule out, exclude, disallow 757vb. *prohibit;* put out of reach, tantalize, set an impossible task; deny the possibility, eat one's hat if 533vb. *negate.*

try impossibilities, labor in vain 641vb. *waste effort;* have nothing to go upon, grasp at shadows; be in two places at once, square the circle, discover the secret of perpetual motion, discover the philosopher's stone, find the elixir of life, find a needle in a haystack; build castles in the air, weave a rope of sand, skin a flint, gather grapes from thorns, make bricks without straw, catch a weasel asleep, milk a he-goat into a sieve; make cheese from chalk, make a silk purse out of a sow's ear, wash a blackamoor white, change a leopard's spots; extract sunbeams from cucumbers, set the Thames on fire, write on water.

Adv. *impossibly,* nohow.

See: 477, 486, 495, 513, 533, 641, 643, 667, 700, 702, 757, 830, 853, 864.

471 Probability

N. *probability,* likelihood, likeliness,

159n. *chance;* good chance, favorable c., reasonable c., fair c., sporting c. 469n. *possibility;* prospect, excellent p. 511n. *prediction;* fair expectation 507n. *expectation;* well-grounded hope 852n. *hope;* real risk, real danger 661n. *danger;* liability, natural course 179n. *tendency;* presumption, natural p.; presumptive evidence, circumstantial e. 466n. *evidence;* credibility; likely belief 485n. *belief;* plausibility, reasonability, good reason 475n. *reasons;* verisimilitude, color, show of, semblance 445n. *appearance;* theory of probability; probabilism, probabilist.

Adj. *probable,* likely 180adj. *liable;* on the cards, in a fair way; natural, to be expected, foreseeable; presumable, presumptive; reliable, to be acted on 473adj. *certain;* hopeful, promising 507adj. *expected;* in danger of 661adj. *vulnerable;* highly possible 469adj. *possible.*

plausible, specious, colorable; apparent, ostensible 445adj. *appearing;* logical 475adj. *rational;* convincing, persuasive, believable, easy of belief 485adj. *credible;* well-grounded, well-founded 494adj. *true;* ben trovato 24adj. *apt.*

Vb. *be likely,*—probable etc. adj., have a chance, be on the cards, stand a chance, run a good c. 469vb. *be possible;* bid fair, be in danger of; show signs, have the makings of 852vb. *give hope.*

make likely, make probable, probabilize, increase the chances; involve 523vb. *imply;* entail 156vb. *conduce;* put in the way to, promote 703vb. *aid;* lend color to, give a color to 466vb. *evidence.*

assume, presume, take for granted, flatter oneself 485vb. *believe;* conjecture, guess, dare say 512vb. *suppose;* think likely, look for 507vb. *expect;* read the future, see ahead 510vb. *foresee;* rely, count upon 473vb. *be certain;* deduce, infer 475vb. *reason.*

Adv. *probably,* in all probability, in all likelihood, as is to be expected; very likely, most l., ten to one, by all odds; seeming, apparently, prima facie; belike, as likely as not.

See: 24, 156, 159, 179, 180, 445, 466, 469, 473, 475, 485, 494, 507, 510, 511, 512, 523, 661, 703, 852.

472 Improbability

N. *improbability,* unlikelihood, doubt, real d. 474n. *uncertainty;* little chance, chance in a million, off-chance, small c., poor c., bad c., unfavorable c., scarcely a c., scarcely any c., not a ghost of a c., no c. 470n. *impossibility;* long odds, bare possibility; pious hopes, small h., poor prospect 508n. *inexpectation;* rare occurrence, rarity 140n. *infrequency;* implausibility, traveler's tale, fisherman's yarn 541n. *falsehood.*

Adj. *improbable,* unlikely, more than doubtful, dubious 474adj. *uncertain;* contrary to all reasonable expectations, unforeseeable 508adj. *unexpected;* hard to believe, unconvincing, implausible 474adj. *uncertified;* rare 140adj. *infrequent;* unheard of, unimaginable, inconceivable 470adj. *impossible;* incredible, too good to be true 486adj. *unbelieved.*

Vb. *be unlikely,*—improbable, look impossible etc. adj.; have a bare chance, show little hope, offer small chance; be implausible, be hard to believe, lend no color to, strain one's belief 486vb. *cause doubt;* think unlikely, throw doubt on 508vb. *not expect.*

Int. not likely! no fear!

See: 140, 470, 474, 486, 508, 541.

473 Certainty

N. *certainty,* objective c., certitude, certain knowledge 490n. *knowledge;* certainness, assuredness, sureness; certain issue, inevitability, inexorability, irrevocability, necessity 596n. *fate;* inerrancy, freedom from error, infallibilism, infallibility; indubitability, reliability, utter r., unimpeachability 494n. *truth;* certainty of meaning, unambiguity, univocity; no case to answer, incontrovertibility, irrefutability, indisputability, proof 478n. *demonstration;* authentication, ratification, validation; certification, verification, confirmation; attestation 466n. *testimony;* making sure, check 459n. *inquiry;* ascertainment 484n. *discovery;* dead certainty, cert, dead c., sure thing, safe bet, cinch, open-and-shut case; fact, ascertained f., indubitable f., positive f. 3n. *substantiality;* matter of fact, accomplished f., fait accompli 154n. *eventuality;* res judicata, settled decision 480n. *judgment;* gospel, Bible 511n. *oracle;* dogma 976n. *orthodoxy;* dictum, ipse dixit, ex cathedra utterance, axiom 496n. *maxim;* court of final appeal, judgment seat 956n. *tribunal;*

last word, ultimatum 766n. *conditions.*
positiveness, subjective certainty, moral c.; assurance, confidence, conviction, persuasion 485n. *belief;* unshakable opinion, doctrinaire o. 485n. *opinion;* idée fixe, fixity, obsession 481n. *bias;* dogmatism, orthodoxy, hyperorthodoxy, bigotry 602n. *opiniatrety;* infallibility, air of i., self-confidence; pontification, laying down the law.
doctrinaire, self-opinionated person 602n. *opinionist;* dogmatist, infallibilist; bigot, fanatic, zealot; oracle, Sir Oracle, know-all 500n. *wiseacre.*
Adj. *certain,* sure, reliable, solid, unshakable, well-founded, well-grounded 3adj. *substantial;* authoritative, official 494adj. *genuine;* factual, historical 494adj. *true;* ascertained, certified, attested, guaranteed, warranted; tested, tried, foolproof 660adj. *safe;* infallible, unerring, inerrant 540 dj. *veracious;* axiomatic, dogmatic, taken for granted 485adj. *credal;* self-evident, axiomatic, evident, apparent; unequivocal, unambiguous, univocal; unmistakable, clear, clear as day 443adj. *well-seen;* inevitable, unavoidable, ineluctable, irrevocable, inexorable, necessary 596adj. *fated;* bound, bound to be, in the bag; sure as fate, sure as death and taxes 124adj. *future;* sure as a gun, safe as houses 660adj. *invulnerable;* verifiable, testable, demonstrable 478adj. *demonstrated.*
positive, confident, assured, self-assured, certain in one's mind, undoubting, convinced, persuaded, certified, sure 485adj. *believing;* opinionated, self-o.; dogmatizing, pontifical, oracular; dogmatic, doctrinaire 976adj. *orthodox;* obsessed, bigoted, fanatical 481adj. *biased;* unshaken, set, fixed, fixed in one's opinions 153adj. *unchangeable;* clean-cut, clear-c., definite, defined, unambiguous, unequivocal, univocal 516adj. *intelligible;* convincing 485adj. *credible;* classified, in its place 62adj. *arranged;* affirmative, categorical, absolute, unqualified, final, ultimate, conclusive, settled without appeal.
undisputed, beyond doubt, axiomatic, uncontroversial; unquestioned, undoubted, uncontested, indubitable, unquestionable, questionless, incontrovertible, incontestable, unchallengeable, unimpeachable, undeniable, irrefutable, irrefragable, indefeasible.
Vb. *be certain,*—sure etc. adj.; leave no doubt, be clear as day, stand to reason, be axiomatic 475vb. *be reasonable;* be positive, be assured, satisfy oneself, convince o., feel sure, be clear in one's mind, make no doubt, hold for true 485vb. *believe;* understand, know for certain 490vb. *know;* hold to one's opinions, dismiss all doubt; depend on it, rely on, trust in, swear by; gamble on, bet on, go Nap on, put one's shirt on.
dogmatize, pontificate, lay down the law, play the oracle, know all the answers.
make certain, certify, authenticate, ratify, seal, sign 488vb. *endorse;* guarantee, warrant, assure; finalize, settle, decide 480vb. *judge;* remove doubt, persuade 485vb. *convince;* classify 62vb. *arrange;* make sure, ascertain, check, verify, confirm, clinch 466vb. *corroborate;* reassure oneself, take a second look, do a double take; make assurance doubly sure 660vb. *safeguard;* reinsure 858vb. *be cautious;* ensure, make inevitable 596vb. *necessitate.*
Adv. *certainly,* definitely, certes, for sure, to be sure, no doubt, doubtless, of course, as a matter of c., no question; no two ways about it; without fail, sink or swim, rain or shine, come what will.
See: 3, 62, 124, 153, 154, 443, 459, 466, 475, 478, 480, 481, 484, 485, 488, 490, 494, 496, 500, 511, 516, 540, 596, 602, 660, 766, 858, 956, 976.

474 Uncertainty

N. *uncertainty,* unverifiability, incertitude, doubtfulness, dubiousness; ambiguity 518n. *equivocalness;* vagueness, haziness, obscurity 418n. *darkness;* mist, haze, fog 355n. *cloud;* yes and no, indeterminacy, indetermination, borderline case; indefiniteness, roving commission; query, question mark 459n. *question;* open question, anybody's guess; nothing to go on, guesswork 512n. *conjecture;* contingency, double c., doubtful event 159n. *chance;* gamble, toss-up, wager 618n. *gambling;* leap in the dark, bow at a venture, blind bargain, pig in a poke, blind date; something or other, this or that.
dubiety, dubitancy, dubitation 486n. *doubt;* state of doubt, open mind, suspended judgment, open verdict; suspense, waiting 507n. *expectation;* doubt, indecision, hesitancy, vacillation, fluctuation, seesaw, floating

vote 601n. *irresolution;* embarrassment, perplexity, bewilderment, bafflement, nonplus, quandary; dilemma, cleft stick, option of difficulties, Morton's fork 530n. *enigma.*

unreliability, liability to error, fallibility 495n. *error;* insecurity, precariousness, touch and go 661n. *danger;* untrustworthiness, treacherousness; fluidity, unsteadiness, variability, changeability 152n. *changeableness;* unpredictability, unexpectedness 508n. *inexpectation;* fickleness, capriciousness, whimsicality 604n. *caprice;* slipperiness, suppleness 930n. *improbity;* treachery 930n. *perfidy,* 603n. *tergiversation;* lack of security, no guarantee, no collateral, bare word, dicer's oath, scrap of paper, paper guarantee.

Adj. *uncertain,* unsure, doubtful, dubious, not axiomatic; unverifiable (**see** *uncertified*); insecure, chancy, risky 661adj. *unsafe;* treacherous (**see** *unreliable*); subject to chance, casual; occasional, sporadic 140adj. *infrequent;* temporary, provisional 114adj. *transient;* fluid 152adj. *unstable;* contingent, depending on, dependent 766vb. *conditional;* unpredictable, unforeseeable 508adj. *unexpected;* aoristic, indeterminate, undefined, undetermined, unclassified; random 61adj. *orderless;* indecisive, undecided, open, in suspense; in question, under inquiry; moot, open to question, questionable, arguable, debatable, disputable, controvertible, controversial; problematic, hypothetical, speculative 512adj. *suppositional;* undefinable, borderline; ambiguous 518adj. *equivocal;* paradoxical 477adj. *illogical;* oracular, enigmatic, cryptic, obscure 517adj. *puzzling;* vague, hazy, misty, cloudy 419adj. *shadowy;* mysterious, veiled 523adj. *occult;* unsolved, unresolved, unexplained 517adj. *unintelligible;* perplexing, bewildering, embarrassing, confusing.

unreliable, undependable, untrustworthy; slippery 930adj. *dishonest;* treacherous 930adj. *perfidious;* ratting 603adj. *tergiversating;* unsteady, unstable, variable, changeable 152adj. *changeful;* unpredictable, unforeseeable; fickle, whimsical 604adj. *capricious;* fallible, open to error 495adj. *erroneous;* precarious, ticklish, touch and go.

doubting, in doubt, doubtful, dubious, full of doubt; agnostic, skeptical 486adj. *unbelieving;* sitting on the fence, in two minds; in suspense, open-minded; distrustful, mistrustful 858adj. *cautious;* uncertain, unassured, unconfident; hesitant, undecided, wavering 601adj. *irresolute;* unable to say, afraid to say; dazed, baffled, perplexed, bewildered, distracted, distraught 517adj. *puzzled;* nonplussed, stumped, brought to a stand, at one's wits' end, on the horns of a dilemma; lost, disorientated, guessing, abroad, at sea, adrift, drifting, astray, at a loss, at fault, clueless 491adj. *ignorant.*

uncertified, unverified, unchecked; awaiting confirmation, unconfirmed, uncorroborated, unauthenticated, unratified, unsigned, unsealed, unwitnessed, unattested; unwarranted, unguaranteed; unauthoritative, unofficial, apocryphal, unauthentic; unproved, undemonstrated; unascertained, untold, uncounted; untried, untested, in the experimental stage.

Vb. *be uncertain,* be contingent, lie in the lap of the gods; hinge on, be dependent on 157vb. *depend;* be touch and go, tremble in the balance; be open to question, non liquet; be ambiguous 518vb. *be equivocal;* make doubt, have one's doubts 486vb. *doubt;* wait and see, wait on events 508vb. *await;* have a suspicion, suspect, wonder, wonder whether; dither, be in two minds, hover, float, sit on the fence, sway, seesaw, waver, vacillate, falter, pause, hesitate 601vb. *be irresolute;* avoid a decision, boggle, stickle, demur; moider, be in a maze, flounder, drift, be at sea; have nothing to go on, grope, fumble, cast about, beat a., experiment 461vb. *be tentative;* lose the clue, lose the thread, miss one's way, get lost 282vb. *stray;* lose the scent, be at fault, come to a stand; not know which way to turn, be at one's wits' end, have no answer, be in a dilemma, be in a quandary; wouldn't swear, could be wrong.

puzzle, perplex, confuse, daze, bewilder, addle the wits; baffle, nonplus, flummox, stump, gravel 727vb. *defeat;* mystify, keep one guessing; bamboozle 542vb. *befool;* fuzz, fog, fox, throw off the scent 495vb. *mislead;* plunge in doubt, vex with d. 486vb. *cause doubt;* make one think, ask for thought, demand reflection.

Adv. *in suspense,* in a state of uncertainty, on the horns of a dilemma, in a maze, in a daze.

See: 61, 114, 140, 152, 157, 159, 282, 355, 418, 419, 459, 461, 477, 486, 491, 495, 507, 508, 512, 517, 518, 523, 530, 542, 601, 603, 604, 618, 661, 727, 766, 858, 930.

475 Reasoning

N. *reasoning,* ratiocination, force of argument; reason, discursive r.; intuitive reason 476n. *intuition;* sweet reason, reasonableness, rationality; dialectics, art of reasoning, logic; logical process, logical sequence, inference, general i., generalization; distinction 15n. *differentiation;* apriorism, apriority, a priori reasoning, deductive r., deduction; induction, inductive reasoning, a posteriori r., empirical r., Baconian method; rationalism, euhemerism, dialecticism, dialectic 449n. *philosophy;* arithmetic 86n. *mathematics;* plain reason, simple arithmetic.

premise, postulate, postulate of reason, basis or reasoning; universals, five predictables; principle, general p., first p.; lemma, starting-point; assumption, stipulation 512n. *supposition;* axiom, self-evident truth 496n. *maxim;* datum, data; provisional hypothesis, hypothesis ad hoc, one's position.

argumentation, critical examination, analysis 459n. *inquiry;* method of argument, rules of pleading; dialectic, Socratic elenchus, dialogue, logical disputation; logical scheme, synthesis; epagoge, syllogization, sorites, syllogism, elench, prosyllogism, enthymeme, major premise, minor p.; philosopheme, proposition, thesis, theorem, problem; predication, lemma, predicate, philosopheme; dilemma, horn of d., Morton's fork 474n. *uncertainty;* conclusion, logical c., QED 478n. *demonstration;* paradoxical conclusion, paradox 497n. *absurdity;* reductio ad absurdum.

argument, discussion, symposium, dialogue; swapping opinions, give and take, cut and thrust; opposing arguments, disceptation, disputation, controversy, debate 489n. *dissent;* appeal to reason, set *or* formal argument, plea, pleading, special p., thesis, case; reasons, submission; defensive argument, apologetics, defense; aggressive argument, destructive a., polemics, polemic; conciliatory argument 719n. *irenics;* wordy argument, logomachy, war of words, paper war 709n. *quarrel;* propaganda, pamphleteering 534n. *teaching;* controversialism, argumentativeness, ergotism, hair-splitting, logic-chopping; contentiousness, wrangling, jangling 709n. *dissension;* bad argument, sophism 477n. *sophistry;* legal argument, pleadings 959n. *litigation;* argumentum ad hominem, play on the feelings; argumentum ad baculum 740n. *compulsion;* argument by analogy, parity of reasoning; tu quoque argument, same to you.

reasons, basis of argument, grounds; real reasons 156n. *cause;* alleged reason 614n. *pretext;* arguments, pros and cons; case, good c., case to answer; sound argument, strong a., cogent a., conclusive a., unanswerable a. 478n. *demonstration;* point, valid p., point well taken, clincher.

reasoner, theologian 449n. *philosopher;* logician, dialectician, syllogist, syllogizer; rationalist, euhemerist, sophister 477n. *sophist;* casuist; polemic, polemicist, apologist, controversalist, eristic, controvertist; arguer, debater, disputant; proponent, mooter, canvasser; pleader 958n. *lawyer;* wrangler 709n. *quarreler;* argumentative person, sea lawyer, barrack-room l., logomachist, quibbler, pedant; scholastic, schoolman 492n. *intellectual;* mathematician, pure m.

Adj. *rational,* clear-headed, reasoning, reasonable; rationalistic, euhemeristic; ratiocinative, ratiocinatory, logical; cogent, acceptable, admissible, to the point, pointed, well-grounded, well-argued 9adj. *relevant;* sensible, fair 913adj. *just;* dianoëtic, discursory, analytic, synthetic; consistent, systematic, methodological; dialectic, discursive, deductive, inductive, epagogic, maieutic, inferential, a posteriori, a priori, universal; axiomatic 473adj. *certain;* tenable 469adj. *possible.*

arguing, appealing to reason; polemic, irenic, apologetic; controversial, disputatious, eristic, argumentative, logomachic; quibbling 477adj. *sophistical;* disputable, controvertible, debatable, arguable 474adj. *uncertain.*

Vb. *be reasonable* 471vb. *be likely;* stand to reason, follow, hang together, hold water; appeal to reason; listen to reason, be guided by r., obey r., bow to r.; accept the argument, yield to a.; admit, concede, grant, allow 488vb. *assent;* have a case, have logic on one's side.

reason, philosophize 449vb. *think;* syllogize, ratiocinate; rationalize, explain away; apply reason, bring reason to bear, put two and two together; infer, deduce, induct; explain 520vb. *interpret;* chop logic, logomachize.

argue, argufy, bandy arguments, give and take, cut and thrust; hold an argument, hold a symposium; exchange opinions, discuss, canvass; debate, dispute, discept, logomachize; quibble, split hairs, chop logic; indulge in argument, argue the case, argue the point, take a p., stick to one's p.; stress, strain, work an argument to death 532vb. *emphasize;* put one's case, plead; propagandize, pamphleteer 534vb. *teach;* take up the case, defend; attack, polemicize; try conclusion, cross swords, join issue, demur, cavil 489vb. *dissent;* analyze, pull to pieces; out-argue, overwhelm with argument, bludgeon 479vb. *confute;* prove one's case 478vb. *demonstrate;* have words, wrangle 709vb. *bicker;* answer back, make a rejoinder 460vb. *answer;* start an argument, open a discussion; propose, bring up, moot; confer 691vb. *consult.*

premise, posit, postulate, stipulate, lay down, assume, hypothesize 512vb. *suppose;* take for granted, regard as axiomatic, refer to first principles.

Adv. *reasonably,* fairly, rationally, logically; polemically; hypothetically; a priori, a posteriori, a fortiori, how much the more, much less; consequently; for reasons given; in argument, in one's submission.

See: 9, 15, 86, 156, 449, 459, 460, 471, 473, 474, 476, 477, 478, 479, 480, 488, 489, 492, 496, 497, 512, 520, 532, 534, 614, 691, 709, 719, 740, 913, 958, 959.

476 Intuition: absence of reason

N. *intuition,* instinct, automatic reaction, association; light of nature, sixth sense, psi, psi faculty; telepathy; insight, clairvoyance; direct apprehension, unmediated perception, a priori knowledge; divination, dowsing, radiesthesia; inspiration, presentiment, impulse, mere feeling 818n. *feeling;* rule of thumb; hunch, impression, sense, guesswork; untutored intelligence, illogic, feminine reason, feminine logic; self-deception, wishful thinking; unreason 503n. *insanity.*

Adj. *intuitive,* instinctive, impulsive; non-discursive; involuntary 609adj. *spontaneous;* above reason, beyond r., independent of r., unknown to logic, inspirational, inspired, clairvoyant, direct, unmediated.

Vb. *intuit,* know by instinct, have a sixth sense; sense, feel in one's bones, somehow feel; react automatically, react instinctively; go by impressions, rely on intuition, dispense with reason, use feminine logic; guess, have a g., use guesswork, work on a hunch.

Adv. *intuitively,* instinctively, by instinct, by guess and God, by nature's light.

See: 503, 609, 818.

477 Sophistry: false reasoning

N. *sophistry,* affective logic, rationalization; illogicalness, illogic; feminine logic 476n. *intuition;* sophistical reasoning, false r., fallacious r., specious r., vicious r., evasive r.; mental reservation, arrière pensée 525n. *concealment;* equivocation, mystification; word fence, tongue f.; casuistry, jesuitry; subtlety, over-s.; special pleading, hair-splitting, logic-chopping; claptrap, mere words; logomachy, quibbling, quibble, quillet; chicanery, chicane, subterfuge, shuffle, dodge; evasion 614n. *pretext.*

sophism, a sophistry, specious argument, insincere a.; exploded argument, fallacious a.; illogicality, fallacy, paralogism; bad logic, loose thinking; solecism, flaw, logical f., flaw in the argument; begging the question, ignoratio elenchi; circular reasoning, arguing in a circle, petitio principii; unwarranted conclusion, non sequitur, post hoc ergo propter hoc; contradiction in terms, antilogy; ignotum per ignotius; weak case, bad c., false c.; lame and impotent conclusion.

sophist; sophister, sophistical reasoner, casuist, quibbler, equivocator; caviler, devil's advocate; captious critic.

Adj. *sophistical,* specious, plausible, ad captandum; evasive, insincere; hollow, empty; deceptive, illusive, illusory; over-refined, over-subtle, finespun; pettifogging, captious, quibbling; sophisticated, tortuous; casuistical, jesuitical.

illogical, contrary to reason, irrational, unreasonable; unreasoned, arbitrary; paralogistic, fallacious, fallible; contradictory, self-c., inconsistent; incongruous, absonant, absonous; unwarranted, invalid, untenable, unsound; unfounded, ungrounded,

groundless; inconsequent, inconsequential; incorrect, unscientific, false 495adj. *erroneous.*
ill-reasoned, unrigorous, inconclusive; unproved, unsustained; weak, feeble; frivolous, airy, flimsy; loose, woolly, muddled, confused; woolly-headed, muddle-h.; wishful, instinctive.
Vb. *reason ill,* paralogize, mistake one's logic, mistake one's conclusion, argue in a circle, beg the question, not see the wood for the trees; not have a leg to stand on; talk at random, babble, burble 515vb. *mean nothing.*
sophisticate, mislead 535vb. *misteach;* mystify 542vb. *befool;* quibble, cavil, split hairs 475vb. *argue;* equivocate 518vb. *be equivocal;* dodge, shuffle, fence 713vb. *parry;* not come to the point, beat about the bush 570vb. *be diffuse;* evade 667vb. *elude;* varnish, gloss over, whitewash 541vb. *cant;* color 552vb. *misrepresent;* pervert, misapply 675vb. *misuse;* pervert reason, twist the argument, torture logic; prove that white is black, make the worse appear the better cause.
See: 475, 476, 495, 515, 518, 525, 535, 541, 542, 552, 570, 614, 667, 675, 713.

478 Demonstration

N. *demonstration,* logic of facts, documentation 466n. *evidence;* proven fact 494n. *truth;* proof, rigorous p.; comprobation, establishment, apodixis; conclusive proof, final p.; conclusiveness, irrefragability 473n. *certainty;* verification, ascertainment, probation, experimentum crucis 461n. *experiment;* deduction, inference, argument, triumph of a. 475n. *reasoning;* exposition, clarification 522n. *manifestation;* burden of proof, onus.
Adj. *demonstrating,* demonstrative, probative 466adj. *evidential;* deducible, inferential, consequential, following, consectary 9adj. *relevant;* apodictic 532adj. *affirmative;* convincing, proving; conclusive, categorical, decisive, crucial; heuristic 534adj. *educational.*
demonstrated, evident, in evidence 466adj. *evidential;* taken as proved, established, granted, allowed; unconfuted, unrefuted, unanswered; open and shut, unanswerable, undeniable, irrefutable, irrefragable, irresistible, incontrovertible 473adj. *certain;* capable of proof, demonstrable, testable, discoverable.
Vb. *demonstrate,* prove; show, evince 522vb. *manifest;* justify 927vb. *vindicate;* bear out 466vb. *corroborate;* produce the evidence, document, substantiate, establish, verify 466vb. *evidence;* infer, deduce, draw, draw a conclusion 475vb. *reason;* settle the question, set the question at rest, satisfy, reduce to demonstration 473vb. *make certain;* make out, make out a case, prove one's point, clinch an argument, have the best of an a. 485vb. *convince;* avoid confutation, save.
be proved, be demonstrated, prove to be true, emerge, follow, follow of course, stand to reason 475vb. *be reasonable;* stand, hold water, hold good 494vb. *be true.*
Adv. *of course,* provedly, undeniably; as already proved; QED.
See: 9, 461, 466, 473, 475, 485, 494, 522, 532, 534, 927.

479 Confutation

N. *confutation,* refutation, redargution, disproof, invalidation; successful cross-examination, elenchus, exposure; conviction 961n. *condemnation;* rebuttal, rejoinder, crushing *or* effective r., complete answer 460n. *answer;* clincher, finisher, knockdown argument, crowning a.; tu quoque argument, retort, repartee 839n. *witticism;* reductio ad absurdum 851n. *ridicule;* contradiction, denial, denunciation 533n. *negation;* exploded argument, proved fallacy 477n. *sophism.*
Adj. *confuted,* disproved etc. vb.; silenced, exposed, without a leg to stand on; convicted 961adj. *condemned;* convicted on one's showing, condemned out of one's own mouth; disprovable, refutable, confutable; tending to refutation, refutatory, refutative.
Vb. *confute,* refute, redargue, disprove, invalidate; rebut, retort, have an answer, explain away; negative, deny, contradict 533vb. *negate;* give the lie to, force to withdraw; prove the contrary, show the fallacy of; cut the ground from under; confound, silence, reduce to s., stop the mouth, shut up, floor, gravel, nonplus; condemn one out of his own mouth; show up, expose; convict 961vb. *condemn;* convict one of unreason, defeat one's reason; riddle, destroy, explode, demolish; demolish one's arguments; have, have in one's hand, have one on the hip; over-

throw, squash, crush, overwhelm 727vb. *defeat;* riddle the defense, outargue, triumph in argument, have the better of the a., get the better of, score off; parry, avoid the trap; stand, stand up to argument; dismiss, override, sweep aside, brush a.; brook no denial, affirm the contrary 532vb. *affirm.*

be confuted,—refuted etc. adj.; fall to the ground, have not a leg to stand on; exhaust one's arguments; have nothing left to say, have no answer.

Adv. *in rebuttal,* in disproof; on the other hand, per contra.

See: 460, 477, 532, 533, 727, 839, 851, 961.

480 Judgment: conclusion

N. *judgment,* judging (**see** *estimate*); good judgment, discretion 463n. *discrimination;* bad judgment, indiscretion 464n. *indiscrimination;* power of judgment, discretionary judgment, arbitrament 733n. *authority;* arbitration, arbitrage, umpirage; judgment on facts, verdict, finding; penal judgment, sentence 963n. *punishment;* spoken judgment, pronouncement; act of judgment, decision, adjudication, award; order, ruling; order of the court 737n. *decree;* interlocutory decree, decree nisi; decree absolute; judgment in appeal, appellate judgment; irrevocable decision; settled decision, res judicata; final judgment, conclusion, conclusion of the matter, result, upshot; moral 496n. *maxim;* reasoned judgment, ergotism, deduction, inference, corollary, porism 475n. *reasoning;* vox populi, voting, referendum, plebiscite, poll, casting vote 605n. *vote.*

estimate, estimation, view 485n. *opinion;* assessment, valuation, evaluation, calculation 465n, *measurement;* consideration, ponderation; comparing, contrasting 462n. *comparison;* transvaluation 147n. *conversion;* appreciation, appraisal, appraisement; criticism, constructive c. 703n. *aid;* destructive criticism 702n. *hindrance;* critique, crit, review, notice, press n., comment, comments, observations, remarks 591n. *dissertation;* summing up, recapitulation; survey 438n. *inspection;* inspection report 524n. *report;* favorable report 923n. *approbation;* unfavorable report, censure 924n. *dissapprobation;* legal opinion, counsel's o., second o. 691n. *advice.*

estimator, judge, adjudicator; arbitrator, umpire, referee; surveyor, valuer 465n. *appraiser;* inspector, inspecting officer, referendary, reporter, examiner 459n. *inquirer;* counselor 691n. *adviser;* censor, critic, reviewer, commentator 591n. *dissertator;* commentator, observer 520n. *interpreter;* juror, juryman, assessor 957n. *jury;* voter, elector, constituent 605n. *electorate.*

Adj. *judicial,* judicious, judgmatic 463adj. *discriminating;* unbiased, dispassionate 913adj. *just;* juridical, juristic, arbitral; judicatory, decretal; determinative, conclusive; moralizing, moralistic, sententious; expressive of opinion, censorial; censorious 924adj. *disapproving;* critical, appreciative; advisory 691adj. *advising.*

Vb. *judge,* sit in judgment, hold the scales; arbitrate, referee; hear, try, hear the case, try the cause 955vb. *hold court;* uphold an objection, disallow an o.; rule, pronounce; find, find for, find against; decree, award, adjudge, adjudicate; decide, settle, conclude; confirm, make absolute; pass judgment, deliver j.; sentence, pass s., doom 961vb. *condemn;* agree on a verdict, return a v., bring in a v.; consider one's vote 605vb. *vote;* judge well, see straight; deduct, infer 475vb. *reason;* gather, collect; sum up, recapitulate; moralize 534vb. *teach.*

estimate, form an e., make an e., measure, calculate, make 465vb. *gauge;* value, evaluate, appraise; rate, rank; sum up, size up; ween, weet, conjecture, guess 512vb. *suppose;* cast up, take stock 808vb. *account;* consider, weigh, ponder, perpend 449vb. *meditate;* examine, investigate, vet 495vb. *inquire;* express an opinion, pass an o., report on; commentate, comment, criticize, review, do reviewing 591vb. *dissert;* survey, pass under review 438vb. *scan;* censor, censure 924vb. *disapprove.*

Adv. *sub judice,* under trial, under sentence.

See: 147, 438, 449, 459, 462, 463, 464, 465, 475, 485, 496, 512, 520, 524, 534, 591, 605, 691, 702, 703, 733, 737, 808, 913, 923, 924, 955, 957, 961, 963.

481 Misjudgment: prejudice

N. *misjudgment,* miscalculation, misreckoning, miscomputation, misconception, misconjecture, wrong impression 495n. *error;* loose thinking 495n. *inexactness;* bad judgment, poor j. 464n. *indiscrimination;* fallibility, gullibility 499n. *unintelligence;* obliquity of judgment, misconstruction 521n. *misinterpretation;* wrong verdict, bad v., miscarriage of justice 914n. *injustice;* overvaluation 482n. *overestimation;* undervaluation 483n. *underestimation;* autosuggestion, self-deception, wishful thinking 542n. *deception;* fool's paradise 513n. *fantasy;* false dawn, false appearance.

prejudgment, prejudication, foregone conclusion 608n. *predetermination;* preconception, preapprehension, prenotion; parti pris, mind made up; presentiment 476n. *intuition;* something on the brain, preconceived idea; idée fixe, infatuation, obsession, monomania 503n. *mania.*

prejudice, prepossession, predilection; partiality, favoritism 914n. *injustice;* bias, biased judgment, warped j., jaundiced eye; blind spot, blind side, mote in the eye, beam in the e. 439n. *blindness;* one-sidedness, partialism, party spirit 708n. *party;* partisanship, clannishness, cliquism, esprit de corps; sectionalism, parochialism, provincialism, insularity; odium theologicum 978n. *sectarianism;* chauvinism, xenophobia, my country right or wrong; snobbishness, class war, class prejudice, race p.; racialism, racism, Aryanism; color-prejudice, negrophobia; apartheid, segregation 883n. *seclusion;* intolerance, persecution, anti-Semitism 888n. *hatred.*

narrow mind, narrow-mindedness, narrow views, narrow sympathies; cramped ideas, confined i.; insularity, parochialism, provincialism; closed mind, one-track m.; one-sidedness, over-specialization; legalism, pedantry, donnishness, hypercriticism 735n. *severity;* bigotry, fanaticism, odium theologicum 602n. *opiniatrety;* legalist, pedant, stickler; freak 504n. *crank;* faddist 862n. *perfectionist;* zealot, bigot, fanatic 473n. *doctrinaire.*

bias, unbalance, disequilibrium 29n. *inequality;* warp, bent, slant, liability 179n. *tendency;* angle, point of view, private opinion 485n. *opinion;* parti pris, mind made up (**see** *prejudgment*); infatuation, obsession 503n. *mania;* crankiness, whimsicality, fad, craze, whim, hobby, crochet 604n. *caprice.*

Adj. *misjudging,* misconceiving, misinterpreting etc. vb.; miscalculating, in error, out 495adj. *mistaken;* fallible, gullible 499adj. *foolish;* wrong, wrong-headed; unseeing 439adj. *blind;* myopic, purblind, short-sighted 440adj. *dim-sighted;* misguided, superstitious 487adj. *credulous;* subjective, unrealistic, visionary, impractical; crankish, faddy, faddish, crotchety, whimsical, cracked 503adj. *crazed;* besotted, infatuated 887adj. *enamored;* haunted, obsessed, eaten up with.

narrow-minded, narrow, confined, cramped; parochial, provincial, insular; pedantic, donnish 735adj. *severe;* legalistic, literal, literal-minded, unimaginative, matter-of-fact; hypercritical, over-scrupulous, fussy 862adj. *fastidious;* stiff, unbending 602adj. *obstinate;* dictatorial, dogmatic 473adj. *positive;* opinionated, opinionative; self-opinioned, self-conceited 871adj. *proud.*

biased, viewy; warped, twisted, swayed; jaundiced, embittered; prejudiced, closed; snobbish, clannish, cliquish 708adj. *sectional;* partisan, one-sided, party-minded 978adj. *sectarian;* nationalistic, chauvinistic, xenophobic; predisposed, prepossessed, preconceived; prejudging 608adj. *predetermined;* unreasoning, unreasonable 477adj. *illogical;* illiberal, intolerant, persecuting 735adj. *oppressive;* bigoted, fanatic 602adj. *obstinate;* blinded 439adj. *blind;* class-prejudiced, color-p.

Vb. *misjudge,* miscalculate, miscompute, miscount, misestimate 495vb. *blunder;* undervalue, minimize 483vb. *underestimate;* overestimate, overvalue 482vb. *overrate;* guess wrong, misconjecture, misconceive 521vb. *misinterpret;* overreach oneself, overplay one's hand; reckon without one's host, get the wrong sow by the ear 695vb. *stultify oneself;* over-specialize, not see the wood for the trees; not see beyond one's nose 499vb. *be foolish;* fly in the face of facts 477vb. *reason ill.*

prejudge, forejudge, judge beforehand, prejudicate 608vb. *predetermine;* prejudice the issue, precondemn; preconceive, presuppose, presume 475vb. *premise;* rush to conclusions, jump to c., run away with a notion 857vb. *be rash.*

bias, warp, twist, bend; jaundice, prejudice, fill with p.; prepossess, predispose 178vb. *influence;* infatuate, haunt, obsess 449vb. *engross.*

be biased,—prejudiced etc. adj.; be one-sided, see one side only, show favoritism, favor one side 914vb. *do wrong;* lean, favor, take sides, have a down on, be unfair 735vb. *oppress;* pontificate 473vb. *dogmatize;* blind oneself to, have a blind side, have a blind spot 439vb. *be blind.*

See: 29, 178, 179, 439, 440, 449, 464, 473, 475, 476, 477, 482, 483, 485, 487, 495, 499, 503, 504, 513, 521, 542, 602, 604, 608, 695, 708, 735, 857, 862, 871, 883, 887, 888, 914, 978.

482 Overestimation

N. *overestimation,* overestimate, over-enthusiasm, overvaluation 481n. *misjudgment;* over-statement 546n. *exaggeration;* boasting 877n. *boast;* ballyhoo, build-up, crying-up 528n. *advertisement;* overpraise, fine talking, rodomontade, panegyric, bombast, gush, gas, hot air, much cry and little wool 515n. *empty talk;* storm in a teacup, much ado about nothing; megalomania, vanity 871n. *pride;* over-confidence 857n. *rashness;* egotism 932n. *selfishness;* over-optimism, optimistic forecast, optimism; pessimism, defeatism 853n. *hopelessness;* optimist, prisoner of hope 852n. *hope;* pessimist, calamity prophet, Jonah, defeatist; exaggerator, puffer, barker, advertiser 528n. *publicizer.*

Adj. *optimistic,* sanguine, over-sanguine, over-confident; high-pitched, over-p.; enthusiastic, over-enthusiastic, raving.

overrated, overestimated, overvalued, overpraised; puffed, puffed-up, cracked-up, cried-up, overdone 546adj. *exaggerated.*

Vb. *overrate,* overreckon, overestimate; overvalue, overprice 811vb. *overcharge;* rave, idealize, overprize, overpraise, think too much of; make too much of 546vb. *exaggerate;* strain, over-emphasize, overstress, overdo, play up, overstrain, overpitch, inflate, magnify 197vb. *enlarge;* boost, cry up, puff, panegyrize; attach too much importance to, make mountains out of molehills, catch at straws; maximize, make the most of; make the best of, whitewash.

See: 197, 481, 515, 528, 546, 811, 852, 853, 857, 871, 877, 932.

483 Underestimation

N. *underestimation,* underestimate, undervaluation, minimization, minimism; conservative estimate, modest calculation 177n. *moderation;* depreciation 926n. *detraction;* understatement, litotes, meiosis; euphemism 950n. *prudery;* self-depreciation over-modesty 872n. *humility;* false modesty, mock-m., irony 850n. *affectation;* pessimism 853n. *hopelessness;* futilitarian, pessimist, minimizer.

Adj. *depreciating,* depreciative, depreciatory, pejorative, slighting, belittling, pooh-poohing 926adj. *detracting;* underestimating, minimizing, conservative 177adj. *moderate;* modest 872adj. *humble;* pessimistic, despairing 853adj. *hopeless;* mock-modest 850adj. *affected;* glozing, euphemistic 541adj. *hypocritical.*

undervalued, underrated, underpriced, insufficiently appreciated, underpraised, unprized, unappreciated; slighted, pooh-poohed 458adj. *neglected.*

Vb. *underestimate,* underrate, undervalue, underprice; mark down, discount 812vb. *cheapen;* depreciate, underpraise, run down, cry d., disparage 926vb. *detract;* slight, pooh-pooh 922vb. *hold cheap;* misprize, not do justice to, do less than justice 481vb. *misjudge;* understate, spare one's blushes; euphemize, gloze; play down, soft-pedal, slur over; make the least of, minimize, minimalize; deflate, cut down to size, make light of, belittle, make no account of, set no store by, think too little of 922vb. *despise;* set at naught, scorn 851vb. *ridicule.*

See: 177, 458, 481, 541, 812, 850, 851, 853, 872, 922, 926, 950.

484 Discovery

N. *discovery,* finding, rediscovery; invention; exploration, speleology, potholing; detective instinct, nose, flair 619n. *pursuit;* detection, spotting, espial 438n. *inspection;* radiolocation 187n. *location;* dowsing, radiesthesia; ascertainment 473n. *certainty;* exposure, revelation 522n. *manifestation;* illumination, realization, disenchantment; accidental discovery, serendipity; a discovery, an invention, an inspiration; strike, find, trover, treasure-trove; eye-opener 508n. *inexpectation;* solution, explanation 520n. *interpretation;* key, open-sesame 263n. *opener.*

detector, lie-d., sound d., asdic, sonar; radar; finder, telescopic f. 442n. *telescope;* dowser; discoverer, inventor; explorer 268n. *traveler;* archaeologist, speleologist, pot-holer 459n. *inquirer.*

Adj. *discovering,* exploratory 461adj. *experimental;* on the scent, on the track, on the trail, warm, getting w.; near discovery, ripe for detection.

Vb. *discover,* rediscover, invent, explore, find a way 461vb. *experiment;* find out, hit it, have it; strike, hit, hit upon; come upon, happen on, stumble on; meet, encounter 154vb. *meet with;* realize, tumble to, see the truth, see the light, see as it really is, see in its true colors 516vb. *understand;* locate 187vb. *place;* recognize, identify 490vb. *know;* verify, check 473vb. *make certain;* fish up, dig up, unearth, disinter, bring to light 522vb. *manifest;* elicit, worm out, ferret o., smell o.; get wind of 524vb. *be informed.*

detect, expose, show up 522vb. *show;* get at the facts, find a clue, be on the track, be near the truth, be getting warm, see daylight; put one's finger on the spot, hit the nail on the head, saddle the right horse; spot, sight, catch sight of, perceive 438vb. *see;* sense, trace, pick up; see the cloven hoof, smell a rat; nose, scent, wind, scent out; follow, trace, track down 619vb. *hunt;* set a trap for, trap, catch out 542vb. *ensnare;* make an arrest, announce the discovery of.

Int. eureka!

See: 154, 187, 263, 268, 438, 442, 459, 461, 473, 490, 508, 516, 520, 522, 542, 619.

485 Belief

N. *belief,* act of believing, suspension of disbelief; credence, credit; state of belief, assurance, conviction, persuasion; strong feeling, firm impression; confidence, reliance, dependence on, trust, faith; religious belief 973n. *religious faith;* full belief, full assurance, plerophory; ignorance of, doubt 487n. *credulity;* implicit belief, firm b., fixed b. 473n. *certainty;* obsession, blind belief 481n. *prejudice;* instinctive belief 476n. *intuition;* subjective belief, self-persuasion, self-conviction; hope and belief, expectation, sanguine e. 852n. *hope;* public belief, popular b., common b., public opinion; credibility 471n. *probability;* one's credit, one's troth 929n. *probity;* token of credit, pledge.

creed, formulated belief, credo, what one holds, what one believes; dogma, doxy 976n. *orthodoxy;* precepts, principles, tenets, articles; catechism, articles of faith, credenda; rubric, canon, rule 496n. *maxim;* declaration of faith, professed belief, profession, confession, confession of faith 526n. *disclosure;* doctrine, system, school, ism 449n. *philosophy;* study of creeds, symbolics 973n. *theology.*

opinion, one's opinions, one's conviction, one's persuasion; sentiment, mind, view; point of view, viewpoint, stand, position, angle; impression 818n. *feeling;* conception, concept, thought 451n. *idea;* thinking, way of thinking, way of thought, body of opinions, Anschauung 449n. *philosophy;* assumption, presumption, principle 475n. *premise;* theory, hypothesis 512n. *supposition;* surmise, guess 512n. *conjecture;* conclusion 480n. *judgment.*

Adj. *believing,* holding, maintaining, declaring etc. vb.; confident, assured, reliant, unshaken, secure 473adj. *certain;* sure, cocksure 473adj. *positive;* convinced, persuaded, satisfied, converted, sold on; imbued with, penetrated w., obsessed w., possessed; firm in, wedded to; confiding, trustful, trusting, unhesitating, undoubting, unquestioning, unsuspecting, unsuspicious 487adj. *credulous;* conforming, loyal, pious 976adj. *orthodox;* having opinions, viewy, opinionated 481adj. *biased.*

credible, plausible, believable, tenable, reasonable 469adj. *possible;* likely, to be expected 471adj. *probable;* reliable, trustworthy, trusty; fiduciary, fiducial; worthy of credence, deserving belief, commanding b., demanding b., persuasive, convincing, impressive 178adj. *influential;* trusted, believed; held, maintained; accepted, credited, accredited; supposed, putative, hypothetical 512adj. *suppositional.*

credal, taught, doctrinal, dogmatic, confessional; canonical, orthodox, authoritative, accredited, ex cathedra; of faith, accepted on trust; undeniable, absolute, unshakable 473adj. *undisputed.*

Vb. *believe,* be a believer 976vb. *be orthodox;* credit, put faith in, give faith to; hold, hold for true; maintain, declare 532vb. *affirm;* believe religiously, perceive as true, take for gospel, believe for certain, firmly believe; profess, confess, recite the creed; receive, accept, admit, agree 488vb. *assent;* take on trust, take on credit; swallow, swallow whole

487vb. *be credulous;* take for granted, assume 475vb. *premise;* have no doubt, make no d., cast doubt away, know for certain, be sold on, be obsessed with 473vb. *be certain;* rest assured, be easy in one's mind about, be secure in the belief, rest in the b.; have confidence in, confide, trust, rely on, depend on, take one at his word; give one credit for, pin one's faith on, pin one's hopes on; have faith in, believe in, swear by, reckon on, count on, calculate on; be told, understand, know 524vb. *be informed;* come to believe, be converted; realize 484vb. *discover;* take as proven, grant, allow.

opine, think, conceive, fancy, ween, trow; have a hunch, surmise, guess 512vb. *suppose;* suspect, rather s.; be under the impression, have the i. 818vb. *feel;* deem, esteem, apprehend, assume, presume, take it, hold; embrace an opinion, adopt an o., imbibe an o., get hold of an idea, get it into one's head; have views, have a point of view, view as, take as, regard as, account as, consider as, look upon as, set down for, hold for; hold an opinion, cherish an o., foster an o.; express an opinion, hazard an o. 532vb. *affirm;* change one's opinion 603vb. *recant.*

convince, make believe, assure, persuade, satisfy; make realize, bring home to; make confident, restore one's faith; convert, win over, bring o., bring round, wean from; bring to the faith, evangelize, spread the gospel; propagate a belief, propagandize, indoctrinate 534vb. *teach;* cram down one's throat; sell an idea to, put over, put across, possess one's mind with; gain one's confidence, sway one's belief 178vb. *influence;* compel belief, extort b.; obsess, haunt, mesmerize, hypnotize; convince oneself, be sold on.

be believed, be widely b., be received; go down, go down well, be swallowed; produce conviction, carry c.; find credence, pass current, pass for truth, capture belief, take hold of the mind, possess the m., dominate the m.

Adv. *credibly,* believably, supposedly, to the best of one's knowledge and belief; faithfully, on faith, on trust, on authority; on the strength of, on the evidence of, as warranted.

See: 178, 449, 451, 469, 471, 473, 475, 476, 480, 481, 484, 487, 488, 496, 512, 524, 526, 532, 534, 603, 818, 852, 929, 973, 976.

486 Unbelief. Doubt

N. *unbelief,* non-belief, disbelief, incredulity, discredit; disagreement 489n. *dissent;* inability to believe, agnosticism; denial, denial of assent 533n. *negation;* contrary belief, conviction to the contrary 704n. *opposition;* blank unbelief, unfaith, want of faith; infidelity, misbelief, miscreance 977n. *heresy;* atheism, nullifidianism 974n. *irreligion;* derision, scorn, mockery 851n. *ridicule;* change of belief, loss of faith, reversal of opinion, retraction 603n. *recantation;* incredibility, implausibility 472n. *improbability.*

doubt 474n. *dubiety;* half-belief, critical attitude, hesitation, wavering, uncertainty; misdoubt, misgiving, gaingiving, distrust, mistrust; suspiciousness, scrupulosity; settled doubt, thorough d., skepticism, pyrrhonism; reserve, reservation 468n. *qualification;* demur, objection 704n. *opposition;* scruple, qualm, suspicion 854n. *fear;* jealousness 911n. *jealousy.*

unbeliever, no believer, disbeliever; misbeliever, infidel, miscreant 977n. *heretic;* atheist 974n. *irreligionist;* skeptic, pyrrhonist, agnostic; doubter, doubting Thomas; dissenter 489n. *dissentient;* lapsed believer, retractor, recanter 603n. *tergiversator;* denier 533n. *negation;* absolute disbeliever, dissenter from all creeds, nullifidian; scoffer, mocker, scorner 926n. *detractor.*

Adj. *unbelieving,* disbelieving, incredulous, skeptical; misbelieving, miscreant, infidel; unfaithful, lapsed 603adj. *tergiversating;* doubtful, hesitating, wavering 474adj. *doubting;* suspicious, shy, shy of 854adj. *nervous;* over-suspicious 911adj. *jealous;* slow to believe, distrustful, mistrustful; inconvincible, impervious, hard to convince; nullifidian, creedless.

unbelieved, disbelieved, discredited, exploded; distrusted, mistrusted etc. vb.; incredible, unbelievable 470adj. *impossible;* inconceivable, unimaginable, staggering 864adj. *wonderful;* hard to believe, hardly credible; untenable, undeserving of belief, unworthy of credit; open to suspicion, open to doubt, unreliable, suspect, suspicious, questionable, disputable

474adj. *uncertified;* so-called, pretended.

Vb. *disbelieve,* be incredulous, find hard to believe, explain away, discredit, refuse credit, greet with skepticism, withhold assent, disagree 489vb. *dissent;* mock, scoff at 851vb. *ridicule;* deny, deny outright 533vb. *negate;* refuse to admit, ignore; change one's belief, retract, lapse, relapse 603vb. *recant;* believe amiss, misbelieve.

doubt, half believe 474vb. *be uncertain;* demur, object, cavil, question, scruple, boggle, stick at, have reservations 468vb. *qualify;* pause, stop and consider, hesitate, waver 601vb. *be irresolute;* treat with reserve, distrust, suspect, have fears 854vb. *be nervous;* be shy of, shy at; be skeptical, doubt the truth of, take leave to doubt; have questions, have one's doubts, cherish d., cherish scruples; entertain suspicions, smell a rat, scent a fallacy, see the cloven hoof; hold back, not go all the way 598vb. *be loath.*

cause doubt, cast d., raise questions; involve in suspicion, render suspect; discredit 926vb. *defame;* shake, shake one's faith, undermine one's belief; stagger, startle 508vb. *surprise;* pass belief 472vb. *be unlikely;* argue against, deter, tempt 613vb. *dissuade;* impugn, attack 479vb. *confute;* keep one guessing 517vb. *be unintelligible.*

Adv. *incredibly,* unbelievably; in utter disbelief.

doubtfully, hesitatingly, cum grano salis, with a pinch of salt.

See: 7, 468, 470, 472, 474, 479, 489, 508, 517, 533, 598, 601, 603, 613, 704, 851, 854, 864, 911, 926, 974, 977.

487 Credulity

N. *credulity,* credulousness; simplicity, gullibility, cullibility; rash belief, uncritical acceptance 485n. *belief;* will to believe, blind faith, unquestioning belief, gross credulity 612n. *persuasibility;* infatuation, dotage; self-delusion, self-deception, wishful thinking; superstition, blind reasoning 481n. *misjudgment;* one's blind side 456n. *inattention;* bigotry, fanaticism 602n. *opiniatrety;* hyperorthodoxy 83n. *conformity;* credulous person, simpleton, sucker, gull, pigeon 544n. *dupe.*

Adj. *credulous,* believing, persuasible, amenable; hoaxable, easily taken in, easily deceived 544adj. *gullible;* naïve, simple, green; childish, silly, stupid 499adj. *foolish;* over-credulous, over-trustful, over-confident; doting, infatuated; obsessed; superstitious 481adj. *misjudging;* confiding, trustful, unsuspecting.

Vb. *be credulous,* be easily persuaded; think wishfully 477vb. *reason ill;* follow implicitly, believe at the first word, take the first suggestion, fall for, take on trust, take for granted, take for gospel 485vb. *believe;* take the bait, swallow, swallow anything, swallow whole, swallow hook, line and sinker; run away with an idea, run away with a notion, rush to a conclusion; think the moon is made of green cheese, take the shadow for the substance; catch at straws, hope eternally; have no judgment, dote 481vb. *misjudge.*

See: 83, 456, 477, 481, 485, 499, 544, 602, 612.

488 Assent

N. *assent,* yes, yea, amen; hearty assent, welcome; agreement, concurrence 758n. *consent;* acceptance, agreement in principle 597n. *willingness;* acquiescence 721n. *submission;* acknowledgment, recognition, realization; no denial, admission, clean breast, plea of guilty, self-condemnation 939n. *penitence;* confession, avowal 526n. *disclosure;* declaration of faith, profession 532n. *affirmation;* sanction, nod, OK, imprimatur, green light 756n. *permission;* approval 923n. *approbation;* concurrent testimony, accordance, corroboration 466n. *evidence;* confirmation, verification 478n. *demonstration;* validation, ratification; authentication, certification, endorsement, seal, signature, mark, cross; visa, pass 756n. *permit;* stamp, rubber s. 547n. *label;* favor, sympathy 706n. *cooperation;* support 703n. *aid;* assentation 925n. *flattery.*

consensus, consentience, same mind 24n. *agreement;* concordance, harmony 710n. *concord;* unanimity, solid vote, general consent, common c., universal agreement, universal testimony; consentaneity, popular belief, public opinion, vox populi, general voice; chorus, single voice; likemindedness, thinking alike, mutual sympathy, two minds with but a single thought 18n. *similarity;* bipartisanship, interparty agreement; bargain 765n. *compact.*

assenter, follower 83n. *conformist;*

fellow-traveler, cooperator 707n. *collaborator;* assentator, yes-man 925n. *flatterer;* the ayes, consentient voice, willing voter; cheerer, acclaimer 923n. *commender;* upholder, supporter, active s., abettor 703n. *aider;* seconder, assentor 707n. *patron;* ratifier, authenticator; subscriber, endorser 765n. *signatory;* party, consenting p., covenanter; confessor, professor, declarant.

Adj. *assenting,* assentient 758adj. *consenting;* consentient, concurrent, party to 24adj. *agreeing;* fellow-traveling, aiding and abetting, collaborating 706adj. *cooperative;* inclined to assent, assentaneous; likeminded, sympathetic, welcoming 880adj. *friendly;* consentaneous 710adj. *concordant;* unanimous, solid, with one voice, in chorus; acquiescent 597adj. *willing;* delighted 824adj. *pleased;* allowing, granting 756adj. *permitting;* sanctionary, ratificatory; not opposed, conceding.

assented, acquiesced in, voted, carried, carried by acclamation, carried nem con, agreed on all hands; unopposed, unanimous; uncontradicted, unquestioned, uncontested, unchallenged, uncontroverted 473adj. *undisputed;* admitted, granted, conceded 756adj. *permitted;* ratified, confirmed, signed, sealed; uncontroversial, non-party, bipartisan.

Vb. *assent,* concur, agree with 24vb. *agree;* welcome, hail, cheer, acclaim 923vb. *applaud;* agree on all points, accept in toto, go all the way with, have no reservations 473vb. *be certain;* accept, agree in principle, like the idea; not deny, concede, admit, acknowledge, grant, allow 475vb. *be reasonable;* admit the charge, plead guilty, avow 526vb. *confess;* signify assent, nod a., nod, say aye, say yes, agree to, give one's assent, yield a. 758vb. *consent;* sanction 756vb. *permit;* ratify (**see** *endorse*); coincide in opinion, voice the same o., enter into another's o., chime in with, echo, ditto, say amen, say hear hear; say the same, chorus; defer to 920vb. *respect;* be a yes-man, rubber-stamp 925vb. *flatter;* reciprocate, sympathize 880vb. *be friendly;* accede, adhere, side with 708vb. *join a party;* collaborate, go along with, travel w., strike in w. 706vb. *cooperate;* tolerate (**see** *acquiesce*); covenant, agree upon, close with, have a mutual agreement 765vb. *contract.*

acquiesce, not oppose, accept, abide by 739vb. *obey;* tolerate, not mind, put up with, suffer, endure; sign on the dotted line, toe the l. 721vb. *submit;* yield, defer to, withdraw one's objections; let the ayes have it, allow 756vb. *permit;* let it happen, look on 441vb. *watch;* go with the stream, swim with the s., float with the current, join in the chorus, follow the fashion, run with the pack 83vb. *conform.*

endorse, second, support, vote for, give one's vote to 703vb. *patronize;* subscribe to, attest 547vb. *sign;* seal, stamp, rubber-stamp, confirm, ratify, sanction 758vb. *consent;* authenticate 473vb. *make certain;* countersign.

Adv. *consentingly,* willingly, with all one's heart, agreeably; by consent, in full agreement, all the way, on all points.

unanimously, with one accord, with one voice, with one consent, in chorus, to a man, nem con; by show of hands, by acclamation.

Int. amen! amen to that! hear, hear! aye, aye! so be it! good! well! very well! well and good! as you say! you said it! just so! how true! yes indeed! granted! yes!

See: 18, 24, 83, 441, 466, 473, 475, 478, 526, 532, 547, 597, 703, 706, 707, 708, 710, 721, 739, 756, 758, 765, 824, 880, 920, 923, 925, 939.

489 Dissent

N. *dissent,* amicable dissent, agreement to disagree; dissidence, difference, the dissidence of dissent, confirmed opposition 704n. *opposition;* dissentience, no brief for; difference of opinion, diversity of o., cleavage of o., dissentient voice, contrary vote, disagreement, discordance, controversy 709n. *dissension;* party feeling, party spirit, faction 708n. *party;* popular clamor 891n. *anger;* disaffection 829n. *discontent;* disatisfaction, disapproval 924n. *disapprobation;* repudiation 607n. *rejection;* protestantism, nonconformism, schism 978n. *sectarianism;* withdrawal, secession 621n. *relinquishment;* hartal, walk-out 145n. *strike;* reluctance 598n. *unwillingness;* recusancy 738n. *disobedience;* non-compliance 769n. *non-observance;* denial, non-consent 760n. *refusal;* contradiction 533n. *negation;* recantation, retraction 603n. *tergiversation;* dubitation 486n. *doubt;* caviling, demur, objection, demurrer, reservation 468n. *qualification;* protest, expostulation, protestation, hostile demonstration 762n. *deprecation;* challenge 711n. *defiance;* passive resistance, non-cooperation 738n. *sedition.*

dissentient, objector, caviler, critic 926n. *detractor;* interrupter, heckler, obstructor 702n. *hinderer;* dissident, dissenter, protester, recusant, non-juror, protestant 84n. *nonconformist;* sectary, sectarian 978n. *sectarist;* separatist, seceder 978n. *schismatic;* rebel 738n. *revolter;* grouser 829n. *malcontent;* odd man out, minority; splinter-group, cave, faction 708n. *party;* the noes, the opposition 704n. *opposition;* non-cooperator, conscientious objector, non-juror, passive resister 705n. *opponent;* challenger, agitator, firebrand, revolutionary 149n. *revolutionist;* recanter, apostate 603n. *tergiversator.*

Adj. *dissenting,* dissentient, differing, dissident 709adj. *quarreling;* agnostic, skeptical, unconvinced, unconverted 486adj. *unbelieving;* separatist, schismatic 978adj. *sectarian;* non-conformist 84adj. *unconformable;* malcontent, dissatisfied 829adj. *discontented;* recanting, apostate 603adj. *tergiversating;* unassenting, unconsenting, not consenting 760adj. *refusing;* protesting 762adj. *deprecatory;* non-juring, recusant, non-compliant 769adj. *non-observant;* disinclined, loath, reluctant 598adj. *unwilling;* obstructive 702adj. *hindering;* challenging 711adj. *defiant;* resistant 704adj. *opposing;* intolerant, persecuting 735adj. *oppressive.*

unadmitted, unacknowledged, negatived, denied 533adj. *negative;* out of the question, disallowed 757adj. *prohibited.*

Vb. *dissent,* differ, agree to d. 25vb. *disagree;* disagree in opinion, beg to differ, make bold to d., combat an opinion, take one up on 479vb. *confute;* demur, enter a demurrer, object, raise objections, cavil, boggle, scruple 468vb. *qualify;* protest, raise one's voice against, demonstrate a., 762vb. *deprecate;* resist 704vb. *oppose;* challenge 711vb. *defy;* be unwilling, show reluctance 598vb. *be loath;* withhold assent, will otherwise, say no, shake one's head 760vb. *refuse;* shrug one's shoulders 860vb. *be indifferent;* disallow 757vb. *prohibit;* negative, contradict 533vb. *negate;* repudiate, hold no brief for, not defend; have no notion of, never intend to 607vb. *reject;* look askance at, not hold with, revolt at the idea 924vb. *disapprove;* go one's own way, secede, withdraw 621vb. *relinquish;* recant, retract 603vb. *apostatize;* argue, wrangle, bicker 709vb. *quarrel.*

Adv. *no,* on the contrary; at issue with, at variance w.; under protest.

Int. God forbid! not on your life! ask me another! tell that to the marines! never again! not so but far otherwise!

See: 25, 84, 145, 149, 468, 479, 486, 533, 598, 603, 607, 621, 702, 704, 705, 708, 709, 711, 735, 738, 757, 760, 762, 769, 829, 860, 891, 924, 926, 978.

490 Knowledge

N. *knowledge,* ken; knowing, cognition, cognizance, recognition, realization; intellection, apprehension, comprehension, perception, understanding, grasp, mastery 447n. *intellect;* conscience, consciousness, awareness; precognition 510n. *foresight;* illumination, lights, enlightenment, insight 498n. *wisdom;* acquired knowledge, learning, lore (**see** *erudition*); experience, practical e., acquaintance, acquaintanceship, familiarity, intimacy; private knowledge, privity, being in the know, sharing the secret 524n. *information;* public knowledge, notoriety, common knowledge, open secret 528n. *publicity;* complete knowledge, omniscience; partial knowledge, intimation, sidelight, glimpse, glimmering, inkling, suggestion 524n. *hint;* suspicion, scent; sensory knowledge, impression 818n. *feeling;* self-knowledge, introspection; detection, clue 484n. *discovery;* specialism, expert knowledge, know-how, expertise 694n. *skillfulness;* half-knowledge, semi-ignorance, smattering 491n. *sciolism;* knowability, knowableness, cognizability, recognizability 516n. *intelligibility;* science of knowledge, theory of k., epistemology.

erudition, lore, wisdom, scholarship, letters, literature 536n. *learning;* acquired knowledge, general k., practical k., empirical k., experimental k.; academic knowledge, professional k., encyclopedic k., universal k., pansophy; solid learning, deep l., profound learning; small l., superficial l., smattering, dilettantism 491n. *sciolism;* reading, wide r., desultory r.; booklearning, bookishness, bibliomania; pedantry, donnishness; information, precise i., varied i., general i.; mine of information, encyclopedia 589n. *library;* department of learning, faculty 539n. *academy.*

culture, letters 557n. *literature;* the humanities, the arts; education, instruction 534n. *teaching;* liberal education, scientific e., self-e., self-instruction; civilization, cultivation, cultivation of the mind; sophistication, acquirements, acquisitions, attainments, accomplishments, proficiency, mastery.

science, exact s., natural s., etiology, metascience; natural philosophy, experimental p.; scientific knowledge, systematic k., progressive k., accurate k., verified k., body of k., organized k., technology; tree of knowledge, circle of the sciences, ologies and isms.

Adj. *knowing,* all-k., encyclopedic, omniscient 498adj. *wise;* apprehensive, cognizant, cognitive 447adj. *mental;* conscious, aware 455adj. *attentive;* alive to, sensible of 819adj. *sensitive;* experienced, no stranger to, at home with, acquainted, familiar with 610adj. *habituated;* intimate, privy to, sharing the secret, in the know, behind the scenes 524 adj. *informed;* fly, canny, shrewd 498adj. *intelligent;* conversant, practiced, versed in, proficient 694adj. *expert.*

instructed, briefed, primed, made acquainted, informed of 524adj. *informed;* taught, trained, bred to; clerkly, lettered, literate; scribal, literary; schooled, educated, well-e.; learned, book-l., book-wise, bookish; erudite, scholarly; read in, well-read, widely r., deep-r., well-informed, knowledgable; donnish, scholastic, pedantic; highbrow, intellectual, cultured, cultivated, sophisticated; forward in, strong in, well-qualified; professional, specialized 694adj. *expert.*

known, cognized, perceived, seen, heard; ascertained, verified 473adj. *certain;* realized, understood; discovered, explored; noted, celebrated, famous 866adj. *renowned;* no secret, public, notorious 528adj. *well-known;* familiar, intimate, dear; too familiar, hackneyed, trite; proverbial, household, commonplace, corny 610adj. *habitual;* current, prevalent 79adj. *general;* memorized, known by heart, learned off, learned by rote, well-conned, well-scanned 505 adj. *remembered;* knowable, cognizable, cognoscible; teachable, discoverable 516adj. *intelligible.*

Vb. *know,* ken, wot, wot of, ween, wit; have knowledge, be acquainted; apprehend, conceive, catch, grasp, twig, click, have, take 516vb. *understand;* know entirely, possess, comprehend; come to know, realize; get to know, acquaint oneself, familiarize o.; know again, recognize; know the value, appreciate; be conscious of, be aware, have cognizance, be cognizant 447vb. *cognize;* discern 463vb. *discriminate;* perceive 438vb. *see;* examine, study 438vb. *scan;* go over, mull, con 455vb. *be attentive;* know well, know full w., be thoroughly acquainted with, see through, read one like a book, know inside out, know down to the ground; know for a fact 473vb. *be certain;* know of, have knowledge of, know something; be in the know, be in the secret, have the low-down 524vb. *be informed;* know by heart, know by rote 505vb. *memorize;* know backwards, have it pat, have at one's finger tips, be master of, be expert in 694vb. *be expert;* have some knowledge of, smatter 491vb. *not know;* experience, know by e., learn one's lesson 536vb. *learn;* know all the answers, be omniscient; know what's what, know what to do, see one's way, know one's way about 498vb. *be wise.*

be known, become k., come to one's knowledge, be brought to one's notice 455vb. *attract notice;* lie within one's cognizance, be knowable; be public, have no secrets 528vb. *be published.*

Adv. *knowingly,* with knowledge; learnedly, scientifically.

See: 79, 438, 447, 455, 463, 473, 484, 491, 498, 505, 510, 516, 524, 528, 534, 536, 539, 557, 589, 610, 694, 818, 819, 866.

491 Ignorance

N. *ignorance,* unknowing, nescience; lack of news, no word of; unawareness, unconsciousness 375n. *insensibility;* incognizance, non-recognition, non-realization; incomprehension, incapacity, backwardness 499n. *unintelligence;* inappreciation, philistinism 439n. *blindness;* obstacle to knowledge, obscurantism; false knowledge, superstition 495n. *error;* blind ignorance, abysmal i., crass i., pit of i.; lack of knowledge, no science; lack of education, uneducation, no schools; untaught state, blankness, blank mind, tabula rasa; unacquaintance, unfamiliarity, inexperience, lack of experience, greenness, rawness; gaucherie, awkwardness; inexpertness, inexpertise, laymanship 695n. *unskillfulness;* innocence, simplicity, naïvete 699n. *artlessness;* nothing to go on, lack of information, general ignorance, anybody's guess, bewilderment 474n. *uncertainty;* moral ignorance, unwisdom 499n. *folly;* darkness, benightedness, unenlightenment; savagery, heathenism, paganism 982n. *idolatry;* Age of Ignorance, jahiliya; imperfect knowledge, semi-ignorance (**see** *sciolism*); ignorant person, illiterate 493n. *ignoramus;* layman, non-expert 697n. *bungler;* obscurantist; philistine.

unknown thing, obstacle to knowledge; unknown quantity, matter of ignorance; Dark Ages, prehistory 125n. *antiquity;* sealed book, Greek; terra incognita, unknown country, unexplored ground, virgin soil; dark horse, enigma, mystery 530n. *secret;* unidentified body; unknown person, Mr. X., anonymity 562n. *no name.*

sciolism, smattering, a little learning; glimmering, glimpse, half-glimpse 524n. *hint;* vagueness, half-knowledge 495n. *inexactness;* unreal knowledge 495n. *error;* superficiality 212n. *shallowness;* affectation of knowledge, shallow profundity, pedantry, quackery, charlatanism, charlatanry 850n. *affectation;* smatterer 493n. *sciolist.*

Adj. *ignorant,* nescient, unknowing, blank; incognitive, unrealizing; in ignorance, unweeting, unwitting; unaware, unconscious 375adj. *insensible;* unhearing, unseeing; unfamiliar with, unacquainted, a stranger to, not at home with; in the dark (**see** *uninstructed*); reduced to guessing, mystified 474adj. *uncertain;* bewildered, confused, at one's wits' end; clueless, blindfolded 439adj. *blind;* groping, tentative 461adj. *experimental;* lay, amateurish, non-professional, unqualified, inexpert 695adj. *unskillful;* unversed, not conversant, inexperienced, uninitiated, green, raw; innocent of, guiltless 935adj. *innocent;* naïve, simple 669adj. *artless;* knowing no better, gauche, awkward; without the light, unenlightened, benighted; savage, uncivilized; pagan, heathenish 982adj. *idolatrous;* backward, dull, dense, dumb 499adj. *unintelligent;* foolish 499adj. *unwise;* obscurantist, unscientific; dark, superstitious, prescientific 481adj. *misjudging;* old-fashioned, behind the age, behind the times 125adj. *retrospective;* unretentive, forgetting 506adj. *forgetful;* regardless 456adj. *inattentive;* willfully ignorant, indifferent 454adj. *incurious.*

uninstructed, unbriefed, uninformed, unapprized, not told, no wiser, kept in the dark; not rightly informed, misinformed, mistaught, misled, hoodwinked; not fully informed, ill-i., vague, vague about 474adj. *uncertain;* unschooled, untaught, untutored, untrained; unlettered, illiterate, uneducated; unlearned, bookless, without arts, without letters; uncultivated, uncultured, low-brow; inerudite, unscholarly, unbookish, unread, philistine; simple, dull, dense, dumb (**see** *ignorant*).

unknown, unbeknown, untold, unheard; unspoken, unsaid, unuttered; unbeheld, unseen, never seen 444adj. *invisible;* hidden, veiled 525adj. *concealed;* unrecognized 525adj. *disguised;* unapprehended, unrealized, unperceived; unexplained 517adj. *unintelligible;* dark, enigmatic, mysterious 523adj. *occult;* strange, new, unfamiliar, unprecedented; unnamed 562adj. *anonymous;* unidentified, unclassified, uninvestigated; undiscovered, unexplored, uncharted, unplumbed, unfathomed; untried, untested; virgin, novel 126adj. *new;* unknowable, incognizable, undiscoverable; unforeseeable, unpredictable 124adj. *future;* unknown to fame, inconspicuous, obscure, humble 639adj. *unimportant;* lost, missing 190adj. *absent;* out of mind 506adj. *forgotten.*

smattering, sciolistic; unqualified, quack 850adj. *affected;* half-educated, half-learned, half-baked, semiliterate, semieducated; half-instructed, knowing half one's brief; shallow, superficial, dilettante, dabbling, coquetting.

Vb. *not know,* be ignorant, be in the dark, lack information, have nothing to go on; be innocent of, be green, know no better; know not, wist not, cannot say 582vb. *be taciturn;* have no conception, have no notion, have no clue, have no idea, have not the remotest i., can only guess, be reduced to guessing 512vb. *suppose;* know nothing of, be in a state of nescience, wallow in ignorance; not hear 416vb. *be deaf;* have a film over one's eyes, not see 439vb. *be blind;* not know what to make of 474vb. *be uncertain;* not know the first thing about, have everything to learn 695vb. *be unskillful;* not know chalk from cheese 464vb. *not discriminate;* misunderstand 517vb. *not understand;* misconstrue 481vb. *misjudge;* half know, know a little, smatter, dabble in, coquette with; half glimpse, guess, suspect, wonder 486vb. *doubt;* unlearn 506vb. *forget;* lack interest 454vb. *be incurious;* refuse to know, ignore 458vb. *disregard;* make ignorant, unteach 535vb. *misteach;* keep in the dark, mystify 525vb. *keep secret;* profess igorance, shrug one's shoulders 860vb. *be indifferent;* want to know, ask 459vb. *inquire;* grope, fumble 461vb. *be tentative.*

Adv. *ignorantly,* in ignorance, unawares; unconsciously; unlearnedly, amateurishly, unscientifically.

See: 124, 125, 126, 190, 212, 375, 416, 439, 444, 454, 456, 458, 459, 461, 464, 474, 481, 486, 493, 495, 499, 506, 512, 517, 523, 524, 525, 530, 535, 562, 566, 582, 639, 695, 697, 699, 850, 860, 935, 982.

492 Scholar

N. *scholar,* savant, philologist, learned man, man of erudition, man of learning, man of education; don, professor, pedagogue 537n. *teacher;* doctor, clerk, learned c., scribe, pedant, bookworm; philomath, polyhistor, pantologist, encyclopedist; prodigy of learning, mine of information, walking encyclopedia, talking dictionary; student, serious student 538n. *learner;* degree-holder, qualified person, professional, specialist 696n. *proficient;* world of learning, academic circles, clerisy, professoriat.

intellectual, scholastic, schoolman, clerk 449n. *philosopher;* brainworker; mastermind, wise man, brain, genius, prodigy 500n. *sage;* publicist; know-all, brain trust; highbrow, egghead, bluestocking, longhair; intelligentsia, literati, illuminati, philosophe; man of science, scientist; academist, academician, Immortal; patron of learning, Maecenas.

collector, connoisseur, dilettante 846n. *man of taste;* bibliophile, book-collector, bibliomaniac; librarian, curator 749n. *keeper;* antiquary 125n. *antiquarian;* numismatist, philatelist, stamp-collector; collector of words, compiler, lexicographer, glossographer, philologist, etymologist 557n. *linguist.*

See: 125, 449, 500, 537, 538, 557, 696, 749, 846.

493 Ignoramus

N. *ignoramus,* know-nothing, illiterate, no scholar, lowbrow; duffer, wooden spoon, pudding head, numskull 501n. *dunce;* blockhead, goof, goose, moron 501n. *fool;* greenhorn, novice, raw recruit, griffin, lubber 538n. *beginner;* simpleton, babe, innocent 544n. *dupe;* unteachable person, obscurantist.

sciolist, smatterer, half-scholar, pedant 500n. *wiseacre;* dabbler, dilettante; quack, charlatan 545n. *impostor.*

See: 500, 501, 538, 545.

494 Truth

N. *truth,* the very t., verity, sooth, good s.; rightness, intrinsic truth; basic truth, primary premise; consistency, self-c., accordance with fact; honest truth, dinkum, fair d., dinkum oil; plain truth, mere t.; sober truth, stern t.; light of truth, revealed t., gospel t., light, gospel, Bible 975n. *revelation;* nature 321n. *world;* facts of life 1n. *existence;* actuality, historicity 1n. *reality;* factualness, fact, matter of f. 3n. *substantiality;* home-truth, candor, frankness 929n. *probity;* naked truth, unvarnished t., unqualified t., unalloyed t., the t., the whole t. and nothing but the t.; truth-speaking, truthfulness 540n. *veracity;* appearance of truth, verisimilitude 471n. *probability;* study of truth, alethiology.

authenticity, validity, realness, genuineness; real Simon Pure, the real thing, the very t., the article, it 13n. *identity;* no illusion, no fake 21n. *no imitation.*

accuracy, care for truth, attention to fact; verisimilitude, realism, local color, "warts and all"; fine adjustment, sensitivity, fidelity, high f., exactitude, exactness, preciseness, precision, mathematical p., clock-work p.; micrometry 465n. *measurement;* orthology, mot juste, aptness 24n. *adaptation;* meticulousness 455n. *attention;* pedantry, rigidity, rigor, letter of the law 735n. *severity;* literality, literalness 514n. *meaning;* true report, ipsissima verba 540n. *verac-*

ity; chapter and verse, facts, statistics 466n. *evidence.*

Adj. *true,* veritable; correct, right, so; real, tangible 3adj. *substantial;* actual, factual, historical; well-grounded, well-founded; well-argued, well-taken 478adj. *demonstrated;* literal, truthful 540adj. *veracious;* true to the facts, true to scale, true to the letter (**see** *accurate*); categorically true, substantially t.; likely 471adj. *probable;* ascertained 473adj. *certain;* unimpeachable 473adj. *undisputed;* consistent, self-c., logical, reasonable 475adj. *rational;* very likely 471adj. *probable;* natural, true to life, true to nature, undistorted, faithful; realistic, objective; unromantic, unideal, down to earth; candid, honest, unflattering.

genuine, no other, as represented; authentic, valid, guaranteed, official, pukka; sound, solid, reliable, honest 929adj. *trustworthy;* natural, pure, sterling, true as steel, true as touch, simon-pure; true-bred, legitimate; unadulterated, unsophisticated, unvarnished, uncolored, undisguised, undistorted, unexaggerated; in one's own name, autonymous.

accurate, exact, precise, definite, defined; well-adjusted, well-pitched, high-fidelity, dead-on 24adj. *adjusted;* well-aimed, direct, straight, dead-center 281adj. *directed;* unerring, undeviating; constant, regular 16adj. *uniform;* punctual, right, correct, true; never wrong, infallible; close, faithful, representative, photographic; fine, nice, delicate, sensitive; mathematical, scientific, micrometric; micrometer-minded, mathematically exact, scientifically e., religiously e.; scrupulous, punctilious, meticulous, strict, severe 455adj. *attentive;* word for word, literal; literal-minded, rigid, pedantic, just so 862adj. *fastidious.*

Vb. *be true,* be so, be just so, happen, exist 1vb. *be;* hold, hold true, hold good, hold water, stand the test, ring true; conform to fact, prove true, hold together, be consistent; have truth, enshrine a t.; speak truth, omit no detail 540vb. *be truthful;* look true, seem real, come alive, copy nature 551vb. *represent;* square, set, trim 24vb. *adjust;* substantiate 466vb. *corroborate;* prove 478vb. *demonstrate;* get at the truth, hit the nail on the head 484vb. *detect.*

Adv. *truly,* verily, undeniably, really, genuinely, actually, indeed; sic, literally, to the letter, word for word; exactly, accurately, precisely, plumb, right, to an inch, to a hair, to a nicety, to a turn, to a T, just right; in every detail, in all respects.

See: 1, 3, 13, 16, 21, 24, 281, 321, 455, 465, 466, 471, 473, 475, 478, 484, 514, 540, 551, 735, 862, 929, 975.

495 Error

N. *error,* erroneousness, wrongness; silliness 497n. *absurdity;* untruth, unreality, non-objectivity; falsity, unfactualness, non-historicity 2n. *nonexistence;* errancy, deviation from the truth 282n. *deviation;* logical error, fallacy, self-contradiction 477n. *sophism;* credal error, unorthodoxy 977n. *heterodoxy;* mists of error, wrong ideas, exploded i., superstition; liability to error, fallibility 481n. *misjudgment;* subjective error, subjectivity, unrealism, wishful thinking, self-deceit, self-deception; misunderstanding, misconception, misconstruction, cross-purposes 521n. *misinterpretation;* misguidance 535n. *misteaching;* bad memory, paramnesia, forgetfulness 506n. *oblivion;* falseness, untruthfulness 541n. *falsehood;* illusion, hallucination, mirage, trick of sight 440n. *visual fallacy;* false light, false dawn 509n. *disappointment;* mental error, delusion 503n. *insanity;* flattering hope, dream 513n. *fantasy;* false impression, wrong idea (**see** *mistake*); wrong tendency, warped notion, prejudice 481n. *bias.*

inexactness, inexactitude, inaccuracy, imprecision, wildness, non-adjustment; faultiness, systematic error, probable e.; unrigorousness, looseness, laxity, broadness, generalization 79n. *generality;* loose thinking 477n. *sophistry;* negligence 456n. *inattention;* mistiming 118n. *anachronism;* misstatement, misreport, misinformation, bad reporting 552n. *misrepresentation;* misquotation (**see** *mistake*); misuse of language, malapropism 565n. *solecism.*

mistake, bad idea (**see** *error*); miscalculation 481n. *misjudgment;* blunder, botching 695n. *bungling;* wrong impression, mistaken identity, wrong person, wrong address; glaring error, bloomer, boner, clanger, howler, schoolboy h., screamer, gaffe, bull, Irish b. 497n. *absurdity;* loose thread, oversight 456n. *inattention;* mishit, bosh shot, bungle 728n. *fail-*

ure; slip, slip of the pen, lapsus calami, slip of the tongue, lapsus linguae, malapropism 565n. *solecism;* clerical error, typist's e.; typographical error, printer's e., misprint, erratum, corrigendum; inadvertency, trip, stumble; bad tactics, wrong step, faux pas; blot, flaw 845n. *blemish.*

Adj. *erroneous,* erring, wrong; solecistical 565adj. *ungrammatical;* in error (**see** *mistaken*); unfactual, unhistorical, mythological 2adj. *unreal;* aberrant 282adj. *deviating;* wide of the truth, devoid of t. 543adj. *untrue;* unsound, unscientific, unreasoned, ill-reasoned, self-contradictory 477adj. *illogical;* implausible 472adj. *improbable;* unsubstantiated, uncorroborated, unfounded, ungrounded, disproved 479 adj. *confuted;* exploded 924adj. *disapproved;* fallacious, misleading 535adj. *misteaching;* unauthentic, apocryphal, unscriptural, unbiblical; perverted, unorthodox, heretical 977adj. *heterodox;* untruthful, lying 541adj. *false;* ungenuine, mock 542adj. *spurious;* hallucinatory, illusive, delusive, deceptive 542adj. *deceiving;* subjective, unrealistic, wild, fantastical, visionary 513adj. *imaginary;* fallible, liable to error, wrongheaded, perverse, prejudiced 481adj. *biased;* superstitious 491adj. *ignorant.*

mistaken, wrongly taken, mistook, misunderstood, misconceived, misrepresented, perverted; misread, misprinted; miscalculated, misjudged 481adj. *misjudging;* in error, misled, misguided; misinformed, ill-informed, deluded 491adj. *uninstructed;* slipping, blundering 695adj. *clumsy;* straying, wandering 282adj. *deviating;* wide, misaimed, misdirected, off-target; at fault, out, off the scent, off the track, off the beam, on the wrong tack, on the wrong scent, off the rails, at sea 474adj. *uncertain.*

inexact, inaccurate, unstrict; unrigorous, broad, generalized 79adj. *general;* not factual, incorrect, misstated, misreported, garbled; imprecise, erratic, wild, hit or miss; insensitive, clumsy; out, wildly o., maladjusted, ill-adjusted, out of adjustment, out of register; untuned, out of tune, out of gear; unsynchronized, slow, losing, fast, gaining; uncorrected, unrevised, uncompared; faulty, full of faults, flawed, botched, mangled 695adj. *bungled;* misprinted, misread, misinterpreted, mistranslated 521adj. *misinterpreted.*

Vb. *err,* commit an error, fall into e., go wrong, mistake, make a m.; be under error, labor under a misapprehension, bark up the wrong tree; be in the wrong, be mistaken; delude oneself, suffer hallucinations 481vb. *misjudge;* be misled, be misguided; receive a wrong impression, play at cross-purposes, misunderstand, misconceive, misapprehend, get it wrong, get one wrong 517vb. *not understand;* miscalculate, miscount, misreckon 482vb. *overrate,* 483vb. *underestimate;* go astray 282vb. *stray;* gain, be fast 135vb. *be early;* lose, be slow, stop 136vb. *be late.*

blunder, trip, stumble, miss, fault 695vb. *be clumsy;* slip, slip up, drop a brick, commit a faux pas, put one's foot wrong; betray oneself, give oneself away 526vb. *disclose;* blot one's copybook, blot, flaw, bungle 728vb. *fail;* play into one's hands 695vb. *stultify oneself;* misnumber, miscount 481vb. *misjudge;* misread, misquote, misprint, mistake the meaning, mistranslate 521vb. *misinterpret.*

mislead, misdirect, give the wrong address 282vb. *deflect;* misinform, lead into error, pervert, cause to err, involve in error, steep in e., start a heresy 535vb. *misteach;* beguile, befool, lead one a dance, lead one up the garden path 542vb. *deceive;* give a false impression, create a false i., falsify, garble 541vb. *dissemble;* gloze 925vb. *flatter.*

See: 2, 79, 118, 135, 136, 282, 418, 440, 456, 472, 474, 477, 479, 481, 482, 483, 491, 497, 503, 506, 509, 513, 517, 521, 523, 526, 535, 541, 542, 543, 552, 565, 695, 728, 845, 924, 925, 977.

496 Maxim

N. *maxim,* apothegm, gnome, adage, saw, proverb, byword, aphorism; dictum, saying, pithy s., stock s., common s., received s., true s., truth; epigram, mot, word, sentence, brocard 839n. *witticism;* wise maxim, sententious utterance, sage reflection; truism, cliché, commonplace, banality, hackneyed saying, trite remark, glimpse of the obvious, bromide; motto, slogan, catchword; text, sloka, sutra, rule 693n. *precept;* scholium, comment, note, remark, observation 532n. *affirmation;* moral, edifying story, pious fiction 979n. *piety;* phylactery, formulary; book of

proverbs, collection of sayings.
axiom, self-evident truth, truism; principle, postulate, theorem, formula.
Adj. *aphoristic,* gnomic, sententious, proverbial, moralizing 498adj. *wise;* epigrammatic, piquant, pithy, packed with sense 839adj. *witty,* terse, snappy 569adj. *concise;* enigmatic, oracular 517adj. *puzzling;* common, banal, trite, hackneyed, commonplace, stock 610adj. *usual;* axiomatic 693adj. *preceptive;* phylacteric.
Adv. *proverbially,* as the saying goes, as they say; pithily, in a nutshell; aphoristically, epigrammatically, wittily; by way of moral.
See: 498, 517, 532, 569, 610, 639, 693, 839, 979.

497 Absurdity

N. *absurdity,* height of a., absurdness 849n. *ridiculousness;* ineptitude, inconsequence 10n. *irrelevance;* false logic 477n. *sophistry;* foolishness, silliness, silly season 499n. *folly;* senselessness, futility, fatuity, skiamachy 641n. *inutility;* wildness, stultiloquy, stultiloquence; nonsense-verse, amphigory; talking rot, talking through one's hat; rot, rubbish, nonsense, gammon, stuff and nonsense, kibosh, farrago, gibberish, jargon, twaddle 515n. *silly talk;* rhapsody, romance, romancing, fustian, bombast 546n. *exaggeration;* Irish bull, Irishism, Hibernicism, malapropism, howler, screamer 495n. *mistake;* paradox 508n. *inexpectation;* spoonerism, joke 839n. *witticism;* pun, equivoque, play upon words 518n. *equivocalness;* riddle, riddle-me-ree 530n. *enigma;* quibble, verbal q. 477n. *sophism;* anticlimax, bathos, descent from the sublime to the ridiculous; sell, swiz, catch 542n. *trap.*
foolery, antics, fooling about, silliness, asininity, tomfoolery; vagary, whimsy, whimsicality 604n. *whim;* extravagance, extravaganza, silly symphony; escapade, scrape 700n. *predicament;* practical joke, monkey trick, piece of nonsense; drollery, comicality 849n. *ridiculousness;* clowning, buffoonery, burlesque, parody, caricature 851n. *ridicule;* farce, mummery, pretense 850n. *affectation;* exhibition 875n. *ostentation.*
Adj. *absurd,* inept 25adj. *unapt;* ludicrous, laughable, comical, grotesque 849adj. *ridiculous;* silly, asinine 499adj. *foolish;* Pickwickian, nonsensical, senseless 515adj. *unmeaning;* preposterous, without rhyme or reason 477adj. *illogical;* wild, egregious, overdone, extravagant 546adj. *exaggerated;* pretentious 850adj. *affected;* frantic 503adj. *frenzied;* fanciful, fantastic 513adj. *imaginative;* futile, fatuous 641adj. *useless;* paradoxical 508adj. *unexpected;* inconsistent 10adj. *irrelevant;* quibbling 477adj. *sophistical;* punning 518adj. *equivocal;* macaronic 43adj. *mixed.*
Vb. *be absurd,* play the fool, act like a fool, behave like an idiot 499vb. *be foolish;* fool, fool about, play practical jokes; be a laughing-stock 849vb. *be ridiculous;* clown, burlesque, parody, caricature, guy 851vb. *ridicule;* talk like a fool, talk rot, talk through one's hat, jargonize, talk gibberish, gibber 515vb. *mean nothing;* talk wild, rant, rave 503vb. *be insane;* rhapsodize, romance 546vb. *exaggerate.*
See: 10, 25, 43, 107, 477, 495, 499, 503, 508, 513, 515, 518, 530, 542, 546, 604, 641, 700, 839, 849, 850, 851, 875.

498 Intelligence. Wisdom

N. *intelligence,* thinking power, intellectualism 447n. *intellect;* brains, good b., brain, gray matter, head, headpiece, upper story; practical headpiece, nous, wit, mother-w., common sense; lights, understanding, sense, good s., horse s., gumption, know-how; wits, sharp w., ready w., quick thinking, quickness, readiness, esprit; ability, capacity, mental c., mental grasp; mental ratio, caliber, mental c., IQ; high IQ, forwardness, brightness; braininess, cleverness 694n. *aptitude;* mental gifts, giftedness, attainment, brilliance, talent, genius, highest g.; ideas, inspiration, sheer i. 476n. *intuition;* brainwave, bright idea 451n. *idea.*
sagacity, judgment, good j., cool j., discretion, discernment 463n. *discrimination;* perception, perspicacity, clear thought, clear thinking; acumen, sharpness, acuteness, acuity, penetration; practicality, practical mind, shrewdness, long-headedness; level-headedness, balance 502n. *sanity;* prudence, forethought, far-sightedness 510n. *foresight;* subtleness, subtlety, craft, craftiness 698n. *cunning;* vigilance, awareness 457n. *carefulness;* policy, good p., tact, statesmanship 688n. *tactics.*

wisdom, ripe w., wise understanding, sapience; grasp of intellect, profundity of thought 449n. *thought;* depth, depth of mind, breadth of m., reach of m., enlargement of m.; experience, life-long e., digested e., ripe e., fund of e., ripe knowledge 490n. *knowledge;* tolerance, enlarged views; right views, soundness; mental poise, mental balance, ballast, sobriety, objectivity, enlightenment.

Adj. *intelligent,* endowed with brains, brainy, clever, forward, bright; brilliant, scintillating, talented, of genius 694adj. *gifted;* capable, able, practical 694adj. *skillful;* apt, ready, quick, quick on the uptake, acute, sharp, sharp-witted, quick-w., nimble-w.; alive, aware 455adj. *attentive;* astute, shrewd, fly, smart, canny, not born yesterday; too clever by half, over-clever, clever-clever; sagacious, provident, prudent, watchful 457n. *careful;* far-sighted, clear-s., 510adj. *foreseeing;* discerning 463adj. *discriminating;* perspicacious, penetrating, clear-headed, long-h., hard-h., calculating; subtle, crafty, wily, foxy, artful 698adj. *cunning;* politic, statesmanlike.

wise, sage, sapient; thinking, reflecting 449adj. *thoughtful;* reasoning 475adj. *rational;* highbrow, intellectual, profound, deep, oracular; sound, sensible, reasonable 502adj. *sane;* staid, sober 834adj. *serious;* reliable, responsible 929adj. *trustworthy;* experienced, cool, unflattered, undazzled, unperplexed, unbaffled; balanced, level-headed, realistic, objective; judicious, judgmatical, impartial 913adj. *just;* tolerant, fair-minded, enlightened, unbiased, non-partisan; unfanatical, unbigoted, unprejudiced, unprepossessed, unwarped; broad, broad-minded, latitudinarian; tactful, politic, wise in one's generation 689adj. *cunning;* wise as a serpent, wise as an owl, wise as Solomon, wise as Solon; well-advised, well-considered, well-judged, wisely decided 642adj. *expedient.*

Vb. *be wise,*—intelligent etc. adj.; use one's wits, use one's head, use one's intelligence; accumulate experience, have a fund of wisdom 490vb. *know;* have brains, show one's metal, scintillate, shine 644vb. *be good;* have a head on one's shoulders, have one's wits about one, see through a brick wall; see with half an eye, see at a glance; know what's what, know how to live, get around; be realistic, be one's age; show foresight 510vb. *foresee;* be prudent, take care 858vb. *be cautious;* grasp, fathom 516vb. *understand;* discern, see through, penetrate 438vb. *see;* distinguish 463vb. *discriminate;* have sense, listen to reason 475vb. *be reasonable;* plan well, be politic 623vb. *plan;* have tact, be wise in one's generation 698vb. *be cunning;* come to one's senses, repent 939vb. *be penitent.*

See: 438, 447, 449, 451, 455, 457, 463, 475, 476, 490, 502, 510, 516, 623, 642, 644, 688, 694, 698, 834, 858, 913, 929, 939.

499 Unintelligence. Folly

N. *unintelligence,* lack of i., want of intellect 448n. *non-intellect;* poverty of intellect, clouded i. 503n. *insanity;* weakness of i., bovine understanding, lack of brains, upper story to let; feeble-mindedness, low IQ, low mental age, immaturity, infantilism; mental handicap, retarded brain, backwardness; imbecility, idiocy; stupidity, slowness, dullness, obtuseness, thickheadedness, crassness, denseness; blockishness, sottishness, oafishness, owlishness, stolidity, hebetude 820n. *moral insensibility;* one's weak side, poor head, no brain; incapacity, meanest capacity, incompetence 695n. *unskillfulness;* naivety, simplicity, fallibility, gullibility 481n. *misjudgment;* inanity, vacuity, vacuousness, no depth, superficiality 212n. *shallowness;* unreadiness, delayed reaction; impercipience, tactlessness, awkwardness, gaucherie 464n. *indiscrimination.*

folly, foolishness, extravagance, eccentricity 849n. *ridiculousness;* fool's idea, fool's trick, act of folly 497n. *foolery;* nugacity, trifling, levity, frivolity, giddiness 456n. *inattention;* lip-wisdom, unreason, illogic 477n. *sophistry;* unwisdom, desipience, ineptitude; fatuity, fatuousness, pointlessness; silliness, asininity; recklessness, wildness, incaution 857n. *rashness;* blind side, obsession infatuation 481n. *misjudgment;* puerility, boyishness, childishness 130n. *nonage;* second childhood, senility, anility, dotage 131n. *age;* driveling, babbling, maundering; conceit, empty-headedness 873n. *vanity.*

Adj. *unintelligent,* unintellectual, lowbrow; ungifted, untalented, no genius; incompetent 695adj. *clumsy;*

not bright, dull; handicapped, undeveloped, immature; backward, retarded, feeble-minded, moronic, cretinous, imbecile 503adj. *insane;* deficient, wanting, not there, vacant; limited, borné, weak, weak in the upper story; impercipient, unperceptive, slow, slow in the uptake; stupid, obtuse, dense, crass, gross, heavy, sottish, stolid, bovine, Boeotian, blockish, oafish, doltish, owlish; dumb, dim, dim-witted, dull-w., slow-w., thick-w., beef-w., fat-w., half-w.; thick-skulled, addlepated, clod-p., muddle-headed, muddy-h., puzzle-h.; lack-brained, half-b., cracked, barmy 503adj. *crazed;* non-understanding, impenetrable, unteachable, impervious; prosaic, literal, matter-of-fact, unimaginative; muddled, addled, wrong-headed, pig-h. 481adj. *misjudging.*

foolish, silly, idiotic, imbecile, asinine, apish; nonsensical, senseless, insensate, fatuous, futile, inane, insulse 497adj. *absurd;* ludicrous, laughable 849adj. *ridiculous;* like a fool, fallible 544adj. *gullible;* simple, naïve 699adj. *artless;* inexperienced 491adj. *ignorant;* tactless, gauche, awkward; soft, wet, soppy, sawney, goody-goody 935adj. *innocent;* gumptionless, germless; goofy, gawky, sappy, dopey, dizzy, unconscious; childish, babyish, puerile, infantile 132adj. *infantine;* gaga, senile, anile 131adj. *aged;* besotted, fond, doting; amorous, sentimental, spoony 887adj. *enamored;* dazed, fuddled, maudlin 949adj. *drunk;* vaporing, babbling, burbling, driveling, maundering; mindless, witless, brainless (**see** *unintelligent*); shallow, shallow-minded, shallow-headed, superficial, frivolous, anserine, bird-witted, feather-brained, crack-b., rattle-b., scatter-b. 456adj. *light-minded;* fooling, playing the fool, acting the f., misbehaving, desipient, boyish; eccentric, unstable, extravagant, wild; scatty, nutty, dotty, daft 503adj. *crazed.*

unwise, unblessed with wisdom, unenlightened; obscurantist, unscientific 491adj. *ignorant;* unphilosophic, unintellectual; unreasoning, irrational 477adj. *illogical;* indiscreet 464adj. *indiscriminating;* injudicious 481adj. *misjudging;* undiscerning, unseeing, unforeseeing, short-sighted 439adj. *blind;* unteachable, insensate; thoughtless 450adj. *unthinking;* uncalculating, impatient 680adj. *hasty;* incautious, reckless 857adj. *rash;* prejudice, intolerant 481adj. *narrow-minded;* inconsistent, unbalanced, ill-proportioned, penny-wise, pound-foolish; unreasonable, against reason; inept, incongruous, unseemly, improper 643adj. *inexpedient;* ill-advised, ill-judged, miscalculated 495adj. *mistaken.*

Vb. *be foolish,* maunder, dote, drivel, babble, burble, talk through one's hat 515vb. *mean nothing;* go haywire, lose one's wits, take leave of one's senses, go off one's head 503vb. *be insane;* be unintelligent, have no brains, lack b., lack sense; never learn, stay bottom of the class; invite ridicule, look like a fool, look foolish, sit like a block 849vb. *be ridiculous;* make a fool of oneself, play the fool, act the f., act the giddy goat 497vb. *be absurd;* frivol, sow one's wild oats, misbehave 837vb. *amuse oneself;* burn one's fingers 695vb. *stultify oneself;* plunge into error 495vb. *err;* miscalculate 481vb. *misjudge.*

See: 130, 131, 132, 212, 439, 448, 450, 456, 464, 477, 481, 491, 495, 497, 503, 515, 544, 643, 680, 695, 699, 820, 837, 849, 857, 873, 887, 935, 949.

500 Sage

N. *sage,* nobody's fool; wise man, statesman; oracle, elder statesman, counselor, consultant, expert 691n. *adviser;* genius, master-mind; master, mentor, guide, guru, pundit, acharya 537n. *teacher;* rishi, Buddha, seer, prophet 511n. *diviner;* yogi, swami, sannyasi 945n. *ascetic;* leading light, shining l., luminary; master spirit, great soul, mahatma; doctor, thinker 449n. *philosopher;* egghead, long head, highbrow 492n. *intellectual;* wizard 983n. *sorcerer;* magus, magian, Magi, wise men from the East; Solomon, Daniel, second D., Daniel come to judgment, learned judge; Aesop, Nestor, Solon, Seven Sages; Grand Old Man, GOM.

wiseacre, know-all, smart aleck; brain trust; witling, wise fool, wise men of Gotham; wisest fool in Christendom.

See: 449, 492, 511, 537, 691, 945, 983.

501 Fool

N. *fool,* tomfool, Tom o' Bedlam 504n. *madman;* perfect fool, precious f.; ass, donkey, calf; owl, goose, cuckoo, gowk, daw, gull, woodcock, buzzard; mooncalf, idiot, congenital i., born fool, natural, changeling, cretin, moron, imbecile; halfwit, sot, stupid, silly, silly-billy; butt, clown, zany, jester 851n. *laughing-stock;* addle-head, muddle-h., blunderer, incompetent 697n. *bungler;* dizzy, scatterbrains, rattle-head, giddy-h.; trifler 493n. *sciolist;* witling 500n. *wiseacre;* crackpot, eccentric, odd fellow 504n. *crank;* gaffer, old fogy; babbler, burbler, driveler; dotard 133n. *old man.*

ninny, simpleton, simp, Simple Simon; Tom Noddy, charley; tony, gaby, noodle, noddy, nincompoop, moonraker, juggins, muggins, booby, boob, sap, saphead, stiff, big s., stick, poor s., dizzy, dope, gowk, galoot, goof; lubber, greenhorn 538n. *beginner;* wet, drip, milksop, mollycoddle, softy, goody-goody, sawney, soppy; child, babe 935n. *innocent;* butt, mug, flat 544n. *dupe;* gaper, gawker.

dunce, dullard, no conjuror; blockhead, woodenhead, numskull, duffer, dolt, dumbbell; fathead, thick-head, bonehead, beetle-head, pin-h., dunderhead, blunderhead, muttonhead, bullhead, cabbage-head, chucklehead, jolter-head, jobbernowl; lackwit, lackbrain, dizzard, numps; chump, clot, clod, clod-poli, clodpate, clod-hopper, oaf, lout, booby, loon, bumpkin; block, stock, stone; ivory, solid i.

See: 133, 493, 500, 504, 538, 544, 697, 851, 935.

502 Sanity

N. *sanity,* saneness, soundness, soundness of mind; reasonableness; rationality, reasonability, reason; balance, mental b.; mental equilibrium; sobriety, common sense; coherence 516n. *intelligibility;* lucidity, lucid interval, lucid moment; normality, proper mind, senses, sober s.; sound mind, mens sana; mental hygiene, mental health.

Adj. *sane,* normal, not neurotic; of sound mind, sound-minded, mentally sound, all there; in one's senses, compos mentis, in one's right mind, in possession of onc's facultics; rational, reasonable 498adj. *intelligent;* common-sensical, sober, sober-minded; fully conscious, in one's sober senses; coherent 516adj. *intelligible;* lucid, not wandering, clear-headed; undisturbed, balanced; cool, calculating 480adj. *judicial;* sane enough, not certifiable.

Vb. *be sane,* have one's wits, keep one's senses, retain one's reason; be of sound mind, become sane, recover one's mind, come to one's senses, sober down, sober up.

make sane, restore to sanity, bring one to his right mind; sober, bring round.

Adv. *sanely,* soberly, lucidly; reasonably, in a reasonable spirit, like a reasonable man.

See: 480, 498, 516.

503 Insanity

N. *insanity,* brain damage, unsoundness of mind, alienation, lunacy, madness, amentia; mental sickness, mental disease; mental instability, intellectual unbalance; psychopathic condition, abnormal psychology; mental derangement, loss of reason, disorder of r., unsound mind, darkened m., troubled brain, clouded b., disordered reason, reason undermined, deranged intellect, mind overthrown; mental decay, senile d., dotage, softening of the brain 131n. *age;* dementia, senile d., presenile d.; mental deficiency, idiocy, congenital i., imbecility, cretinism, morosis, feeblemindedness 499n. *unintelligence;* derangement, aberration 84n. *abnormality;* obsession, craze, fad 481n. *bias;* fanaticism 481n. *prejudice;* alienism, psychiatry, psychotherapy 658n. *therapy;* mad doctor, alienist, psychiatrist 658n. *doctor.*

psychopathy, certifiability; psychopathic condition, psychosis; neuropathy, neurosis, psychoneurosis, anxiety neurosis, compulsion n.; nerves, nervous disorder; hysteria, shellshock; attack of nerves, nervous breakdown, brainstorm; phobia, claustrophobia, agoraphobia, acrophobia, triskaidekaphobia 854n. *phobia;* the insanities; delusional insanity, paranoia, delusions, hallucinations, lycanthropy; confusion, paraphrenia, catatonia, schizophrenia, split personality, dual p., multiple p.; obsession; frustration; depression, depressed state; manic depression, elation; mania, hypomania; hypochondriasis, hypochrondria, pathoneurosis; hyp, melancholia, blues, blue devils 834n. *melancholy.* **See** *mania.*

mania, hypomania, megalomania, persecution mania, religious m.; pathomania, kleptomania; homicidal mania, suicidal m.; nymphomania, gamomania, bibliomania, monomania.

frenzy, furor, Corybantiasm; rabies, canine madness, hydrophobia; phrenetic condition, paraphronesis, paraphrosyne; ecstasy, delirium, raving; distraction, wandering of the mind 456n. *abstractedness;* incoherence 517n. *unintelligibility;* delirium tremens, dt's, jim-jams 949n. *alcoholism;* epilepsy, fit, paroxysm 318n. *spasm;* brain fever, cerebral f., calenture of the brain; siriasis, sunstroke; vertigo, dizziness, swimming.

eccentricity, craziness, crankiness, faddishness; queerness, oddness, strange behavior; oddity, twist, kink, crank, fad 84n. *abnormality;* a screw loose, a slate l., a tile l., bats in the belfry, rats in the upper story; obsession, monomania, ruling passion, fixed idea 481n. *bias.*

madhouse, mental home, mental hospital, nerve h., hospital for mental diseases; asylum, lunatic a., insane a.; Bedlam, Colney Hatch; boobyhatch, loony-bin, nut-house, bug-h., padded cell 658n. *hospital.*

Adj. *insane,* mad, lunatic, moonstruck, hazy; of unsound mind, not in one's right m., non compos mentis, alienated, bereft of reason, deprived of one's wits, deranged, demented; certifiable, mental; abnormal, psychologically a., mentally sick, mentally ill, diseased in mind, brain-damaged; psychopathic; psychotic; neurasthenic, neurotic, hysterical; paranoiac, paraphrenic, schizophrenic, schizoid; manic, maniacal; catatonic, depressive, manic-d., elated; hypochondriac, hipped, hippy, hippish 834adj. *melancholic;* monomaniac; kleptomaniac; claustrophobic; idiotic, imbecile, moronic, cretinous, defective, subnormal, feebleminded, weak in the head, wanting 499adj. *unintelligent;* raving mad, horn-m., stark staring m., mad as a hatter, mad as a March hare (**see** *frenzied*); in an asylum, declared insane, certified.

crazed, wildered in one's wits, wandering, mazed, moidered 456adj. *abstracted;* not all there, not right in the head; off one's head, round the bend, up the pole; demented, driven mad, maddened, madded (**see** *frenzied*); unhinged, unbalanced, off one's rocker; bedeviled, pixilated, pixy-led, deluded; infatuated, obsessed, eaten up with, possessed; fond, doting 887adj. *enamored;* driveling, in one's second childhood; brainsick, touched in the head, touched, wanting; idiotic, mad-brained, scatter-brained, shatter-b., crack-brained 499adj. *foolish;* crackers, scatty, screwy, nutty, nuts, batty, bats, cuckoo, wacky, fruit-cakey, loco; crazy, daft, daffy, dippy, loony, loopy, potty, dotty; cranky, faddy, eccentric, erratic, funny, queer, odd, peculiar 84adj. *abnormal;* crotchety, whimsical 604adj. *capricious;* dizzy, vertiginous, giddy 456adj. *light-minded.*

frenzied, rabid, maddened, madded; hornmad, furious, foaming at the mouth 891adj. *angry;* haggard, wild, distraught 456adj. *distracted;* possessed, possessed with a devil, bedeviled, bacchic, Corybantic; frantic, phrenic, demented, like one possessed, beside oneself, uncontrollable; berserk, seeing red, running amok 176adj. *violent;* mast, temporarily insane; epileptic, having fits; delirious, seeing things, raving, rambling, wandering, incoherent, lightheaded, fevered, brainsick 651adj. *sick.*

Vb. *be insane,* — mad, — crazed etc. adj.; have bats in the belfry, have a screw loose; dote, drivel 499vb. *be foolish;* ramble, wander; babble, rave; Corybantiate; foam at the mouth; be delirious, see things.

go mad, run m., go off one's head, go off one's rocker, go crackers, become a lunatic, have to be certified; lose one's reason, lose one's wits; go berserk, run amok, see red, foam at the mouth, lose one's head 891vb. *get angry.*

make mad, drive m., send m., drive insane; mad, madden; craze, derange, dement, dementate; send one off his head, send one out of his mind; overthrow one's reason, undermine one's r., turn one's brain; unhinge, unbalance, send one off his rocker; infuriate, make one see red 891vb. *enrage;* infatuate, possess, obsess; go to one's head, turn one's h. 542vb. *befool.*

See: 84, 131, 176, 318, 456, 481, 499, 517, 542, 604, 651, 658, 834, 854, 887, 891, 949.

504 Madman

N. *madman,* lunatic, maddy, mental case; bedlamite, Tom o' Bedlam, candidate for Bedlam; screwball, nut, loon, loony; madcap, mad dog; abnormal character, psychopath, psychopathic personality, unstable p., aggressive p., antisocial p., sociopath; hysteric, neurotic, neuropath;

psychotic; paranoiac; schizoid; manic-depressive; maenad, bacchante, Corybant; raving lunatic, maniac; kleptomaniac, automaniac, pyromaniac, monomaniac, megalomaniac; dipsomaniac 949adj. *drunkard;* dope addict, dope fiend; drug addict, drug fiend; hypochondriac, melancholic 834n. *moper;* idiot, congenital i., natural, cretin, moron, mongolian idiot, idiot savant 501n. *fool.*

crank, crackpot, nut, crackbrain, screwball; eccentric, oddity, odd bird, fogy 851adj. *laughing-stock;* freak, deviationist 84n. *nonconformist;* fad, faddist, fanatic, extremist, lunatic fringe; fanatico, fan, aficionado, balletomane; seer, dreamer 513n. *visionary;* rhapsodist, enthusiast; knight-errant, Don Quixote.

See: 84, 501, 513, 834, 851, 949.

505 Memory

N. *memory,* good m., retentivity, retention; tenacious memory, capacious m., trustworthy m., correct m., exact m., ready m., prompt m.; collective memory, race m., atavism; tablets of memory; Mnemosyne.

remembrance, exercise of memory, recollection, recall; commemoration, rememoration, evocation; rehearsal, recapitulation 106n. *repetition;* memorization, remembering, learning by heart 536n. *learning;* reminiscence, thoughts of the past, reminiscent vein, retrospection, review, retrospect, hindsight; flashback, recurrence; afterthought 67n. *sequel;* regrets 830n. *regret;* memorabilia, memoirs, reminiscences, recollections; history, narration 590n. *narrative;* fame, notoriety, place in history 866n. *famousness;* memoranda, things to be remembered.

reminder, memento, memorial, testimonial, commemoration 876n. *celebration;* token of remembrance, souvenir, keepsake, autograph; relic, monument, trophy, bust, statue 548n. *record;* remembrancer, flapper, keeper of one's conscience, prompter; testifier 466n. *witness;* memorandum, aide-mémoire, note, memorandum book, notebook, diary, engagement d., address book, album, autograph a., photograph a., scrapbook, commonplace-book, prompt b.; leading question, prompt, prompting, suggestion, cue 524n. *hint;* mnemonic, aid to memory.

mnemonics, mnemotechnics, mnemotechny, art of memory, Pelmanism; mnemonic device, memoria technica, artificial memory, electronic brain; mnemonician, mnemonist.

Adj. *remembered,* recollected etc. vb.; retained, retained in the memory, not forgotten, unforgotten; fresh, fresh in one's memory, green in the remembrance, of recent memory; present to the mind, uppermost in one's thoughts; of lasting remembrance, of blessed memory, missed, regretted; memorable, unforgettable, not to be forgotten; haunting, persistent, undying; deep-rooted, deep-seated, indelible, inscribed upon the mind, lodged in one's m., stamped on one's memory, impressed on one's recollection; embalmed in the memory, kept alive in one's mind; got by heart, memorized 490adj. *known.*

remembering, mindful, faithful to the memory, keeping in mind, holding in remembrance; evocative, memorial, commemorative 876adj. *celebrative;* reminiscent, recollecting, anecdotic, anecdotal; unable to forget, haunted, obsessed, plagued; recalling, reminding, mnemonic, prompting, suggesting.

Vb. *remember,* mind, recognize, know again 490vb. *know;* recollect, bethink oneself; not forget, bottle up 666vb. *preserve;* retain, hold in mind, retain the memory of; embalm *or* keep alive in one's thoughts, treasure in one's t., store in one's memories; never forget, be unable to f.; recall, call to mind, think of; reminisce, write one's memoirs; remind oneself, make a note of, keep a memorandum, write it down. **See** *memorize.*

retrospect, recollect, recall, recapture; reflect, review, think back, think back upon, trace b., retrace, hark back, carry one's thoughts back, cast one's mind b.; bring back to memory, summon up, conjure u., rake up the past, dig up the p., dwell on the p., live in the p.; archaize 125adj. *look back;* rip up old wounds, renew old days, recapture old times; make an effort to remember, rack one's brains to r., flog one's memory.

remind, put one in mind, jog one's memory, refresh one's m., renew one's m.; pluck one by the sleeve 455vb. *attract notice;* drop a hint, prompt, suggest 524vb. *hint;* not allow one to forget, abide in the memory, haunt, obsess; not let sleeping dogs lie, fan the embers 821vb. *excite;* turn another's mind back, make one think of, evoke the memory o.; commemorate, raise a memorial, redeem from oblivion, keep the memory green, toast 876vb. *celebrate;* relate, recount, recapitulate 106vb. *repeat;* memorialize, petition 761vb. *request;* write history, narrate 590vb. *describe.*

memorize, commit to memory, get to know, con 490vb. *know;* con over, get by heart, learn by rote 536vb. *learn;* repeat, repeat one's lesson 106vb. *repeat;* fix in one's memory, rivet in one's m., stamp in one's m., grave on the mind, hammer into one's head, drive into one's h.; burden the memory with, stuff the mind w., cram the mind w., load the mind w.

be remembered, stay in the memory, stick in the mind, recur, recur to one's thoughts 106vb. *reoccur;* flash across one's mind, ring a bell, set one's memory working; haunt, dwell in one's thoughts, abide in one's memory, run in one's thoughts, haunt one's t., not leave one's t.; lurk in one's mind, rise from the subconscious, emerge into consciousness; make history, live in h., leave a name 866vb. *have repute.*

Adv. *in memory,* in memory of, to the memory of, in memoriam; by heart, by rote, from memory.

See: 67, 106, 125, 455, 466, 490, 524, 536, 548, 590, 666, 761, 821, 830, 866, 876.

506 Oblivion

N. *oblivion,* forgetfulness, absent-mindedness 456n. *abstractedness;* loss of memory, amnesia, fugue, absence, total blank; hysterical amnesia 503n. *insanity;* misremembrance, paramnesia; insensibility, insensibility of the past, no sense of history; benefits forgot 908n. *ingratitude;* dim memory, hazy recollection; defective memory, failing m., loose m., slippery m., treacherous m.; decay of memory, lapse of m., memory like a sieve; effacement 550n. *obliteration;* Lethe, waters of L., waters of oblivion; good riddance.

amnesty, letting bygones be bygones, obliteration of grievances, burial of g., burial of the hatchet; pardon, free p., absolution 909n. *forgiveness.*

Adj. *forgotten,* clean f., beyond recall; well forgotten, not missed; unremembered, left; disremembered, misremembered etc. vb.; almost remembered, on the tip of one's tongue; gone out of one's head, passed out of recollection, bygone, out of mind, buried, dead and b., sunk in oblivion, amnestied 909adj. *forgiven.*

forgetful, forgetting, oblivious; sunk in oblivion, steeped in Lethe; insensible, unconscious of the past; not historically minded; unable to remember, suffering from amnesia, amnesic; marked by loss of memory, amnemonic; causing loss of memory, amnestic, lethean; unmindful, heedless, mindless 458adj. *negligent;* absent-minded, inclined to forget 456adj. *abstracted;* willing to forget, unresentful 909adj. *forgiving;* unwilling to remember, conveniently forgetting 918adj. *dutiless;* unmindful of favors, ingrate 908adj. *ungrateful.*

Vb. *forget,* clean f., misremember, disremember, have no recollection; drop from one's thoughts, think no more of; wean one's thoughts from, discharge from one's memory, bury in oblivion, consign to o., be oblivious; amnesty, let bygones be bygones, bury the hatchet 909vb. *forgive;* break with the past, unlearn, efface 550vb. *obliterate;* suffer from amnesia, remember nothing; be forgetful, need reminding; lose sight of, leave behind; be absent-minded, fluff one's notes 456vb. *be inattentive;* have a short memory, have a memory like a sieve, let in one ear and out of the other, forget one's own name; almost remember, have on the tip of one's tongue, not call to mind.

be forgotten, slip one's memory, escape one's m., fade from one's mind; sink into oblivion, fall into o., drop out of the news; be overlooked 456vb. *escape notice.*

See: 456, 458, 503, 550, 908, 909, 918.

507 Expectation

N. *expectation,* state of e., expectancy 455n. *attention;* contemplation 617n. *intention;* confident expectation, reliance, confidence, trust 473n. *certainty;* presumption 475n. *premise;* foretaste 135n. *anticipation;* optimism, cheerful expectation 833n. *cheerfulness;* eager expectation, anxious e., sanguine e. 859n. *desire;* ardent expectation, breathless e., 852n. *hope;* waiting, suspense 474n. *uncertainty;* pessimism, dread, apprehension, apprehensiveness 854n. *fear;* anxiety 825n. *worry;* waiting for the end 853n. *hopelessness;* expectance, one's expectations, one's prospects 471n.

probability; reckoning, calculation 480n. *estimate;* prospect, look-out, outlook, forecast 511n. *prediction;* contingency 469n. *possibility;* destiny 596n. *fate;* defeated expectation, frustrated e., tantalization, torment of Tantalus 509n. *disappointment;* expected thing, the usual 610n. *practice.*

Adj. *expectant,* expecting, in expectation, in hourly e.; in suspense, on the waiting list, on the short l.; sure, confident 473adj. *certain;* anticipatory, anticipant, anticipating, banking on; presuming, taking for granted; predicting 511adj. *foreseeing;* unsurprised 865adj. *unastonished;* forewarned, forearmed, ready 669adj. *prepared;* waiting, waiting for, awaiting; on the look-out, on the watch for, standing by, on call 457adj. *vigilant;* tense, keyed up 821adj. *excited;* tantalized, on tenterhooks, on the rack, on the tiptoe of expectation, agape, agog 859adj. *desiring;* optimistic, hopeful, sanguine 852adj. *hoping;* apprehensive, dreading, worried, anxious 854adj. *nervous;* pessimistic, expecting the worst 853adj. *hopeless;* wondering, open-eyed, open-mouthed, curious 453adj. *inquisitive;* expecting a baby, expecting, parturient 164adj. *productive.*

expected, long e.; up to expectation, not surprising 865adj. *unastonishing;* anticipated, presumed, predicted, foreseen, foreseeable 471adj. *probable;* prospective, future, on the horizon 155adj. *impending;* contemplated, intended, in view, in prospect, in one's eye 617adj. *intending;* hoped for, longed for 859adj. *desired;* apprehended, dreaded, feared 854adj. *frightening.*

Vb. *expect,* look for, have in prospect, face the prospect, face; contemplate, have in mind, hold in view, promise oneself 617vb. *intend;* reckon, calculate 480vb. *estimate;* predict, forecast 510vb. *foresee;* see it coming 865vb. *not wonder;* think likely, presume 471vb. *assume;* be confident, rely on, bank on, count upon 473vb. *be certain;* anticipate, forestall 669vb. *prepare oneself;* look out for, watch out f., be waiting f., be ready f. 457vb. *be careful;* stand by, be on call; tarry for (**see** *await*); apprehend, dread 854vb. *fear;* look forward to, hope for 852vb. *hope,* 859vb. *desire;* hope and believe 485vb. *believe.*

await, be on the waiting list; stand waiting, stand and wait, dance attendance 136vb. *wait;* line up, mark time, bide one's t.; stand at attention, stand by, be on call; hold one's breath, be in suspense, open one's mouth for; keep one waiting; have in store for, be in store for, be expected, 155vb. *impend;* tantalize, make one's mouth water, lead one to expect 859vb. *cause desire.*

Adv. *expectantly,* in suspense, with bated breath, on edge, on the anxious seat; on the waiting list.

See: 135, 136, 155, 164, 453, 457, 469, 471, 473, 475, 480, 485, 509, 510, 511, 596, 610, 617, 669, 821, 825, 833, 852, 853, 854, 859, 865.

508 Inexpectation

N. *inexpectation,* non-expectation, no expectation 472n. *improbability;* no hope 853n. *hopelessness;* uninterest, apathy 454n. *incuriosity;* unpreparedness 670n. *non-preparation;* unexpectedness, unforeseen contingency, unusual occurrence; unexpected result, miscalculation 495n. *error;* lack of warning, surprise, surprisal, disconcertment; the unexpected, the unforeseen, surprise packet, jack-in-the-box, afterclap; shock, nasty s., start, jolt, turn; blow, sudden b., staggering b.; bolt from the blue, thunderclap, bombshell; revelation, eye-opener; paradox, reversal, peripeteia 221n *inversion;* astonishment, amazement 864n. *wonder;* anticlimax, descent from the sublime to the ridiculous; false expectation 509n. *disappointment.*

Adj. *unexpected,* unanticipated, unprepared for, unlooked for, unhoped for; unguessed, unpredicted, unforeseen; unforeseeable, unpredictable 472adj. *improbable;* unheralded, unannounced; without warning, surprising; arresting, eye-opening, staggering, amazing 864adj. *wonderful;* shocking, startling 854adj. *frightening;* sudden 116adj. *instantaneous;* like a bombshell, like a bolt from the blue, dropped from the clouds; uncatered for 670adj. *unprepared;* contrary to expectation, against e.; paradoxical 518adj. *equivocal;* out of one's reckoning, out of one's ken, out of one's experience, unprecedented, unexampled 84adj. *unusual;* freakish 84adj. *abnormal;* whimsical 604adj. *capricious;* full of surprises, unaccountable 517adj. *puzzling.*

inexpectant, non-e., unexpecting, unguessing, unsuspecting, off guard, unguarded 456adj. *inattentive;* unaware, uniformed 491adj. *ignorant;* unwarned, unforewarned; surprised, disconcerted, taken by surprise, taken aback, caught napping, caught bending, caught on the hop, on the wrong foot 670adj. *unprepared;* astonished, thunderstruck, dazed, stunned 864adj. *wondering;* startled, jolted, shocked; without expectations, unhopeful 853adj. *hopeless;* apathetic, incurious 860adj. *indifferent.*

Vb. *not expect,* not look for, not contemplate, think unlikely, not foresee 472vb. *be unlikely;* not hope for 853vb. *despair;* be caught out, walk into the trap, fall into the t.; be taken aback, be taken by surprise 670vb. *be unprepared;* get a start, have a jolt, start, jump; have one's eyes opened, receive a revelation; look surprised, stare.

surprise, take by s., spring something on one, spring a mine under; catch, trap, ambush 542vb. *ensnare;* catch unawares, catch napping, catch bending, catch off one's guard; startle, jolt, make one jump, give one a turn; take aback, stagger, stun; take one's breath away, knock one down with a feather, bowl one over, give one an eye-opener; astonish, amaze, astound, dumbfound 864vb. *be wonderful;* shock, electrify 821vb. *impress;* come like a thunderclap; drop from the clouds, pop out of the blue; fall upon, burst u., bounce u., spring u., pounce on; steal upon, creep u.; come up from behind, take one on his blind side.

Adv. *unexpectedly,* suddenly, abruptly 116adv. *instantaneously;* all of a sudden, without warning, without notice, like a thief in the night.

See: 84, 116, 221, 454, 456, 472, 491, 495, 509, 517, 518, 542, 604, 670, 821, 853, 854, 864.

509 Disappointment

N. *disappointment,* sad d., bitter d., regrets 830n. *regret;* continued disappointment, tantalization, frustration, feeling of f., bafflement; blighted hopes, unsatisfied h., betrayed h., hopes unrealized 853n. *hopelessness;* false expectation, vain e., much cry and little wool 482n. *overestimation;* bad news 529n. *news;* not what one expected, disillusionment 829n. *discontent;* miscalculation 481n. *misjudgment;* mirage, false dawn, fool's paradise; blow, setback, balk 702n. *hitch;* non-fulfillment, partial success, near failure 726n. *non-completion;* ad luck, trick of fortune, slip 'twixt the cup and the lip 731n. *ill fortune;* anticlimax 508n. *inexpectation;* comedown, let-d. 872n. *humiliation;* damp squib 728n. *failure.*

Adj. *disappointed,* expecting otherwise 508adj. *inexpectant;* frustrated, thwarted 702adj. *hindered;* baffled, foiled 728adj. *defeated;* disconcerted, crestfallen, out of countenance, humiliated 872adj. *humbled;* disgruntled, soured 829adj. *discontented;* sick with disappointment 853adj. *hopeless;* heartbroken 834adj. *dejected;* ill-served, let down, betrayed; refused, turned away 607adj. *rejected.*

disappointing, unsatisfying, unsatisfactory 636adj. *insufficient;* not up to expectation, less than one's hopes 829adj. *discontenting;* miscarried, abortive 728adj. *unsuccessful;* cheating, deceptive 542adj. *deceiving.*

Vb. *be disappointed,*—unsuccessful etc. adj.; try in vain 728vb. *fail;* have hoped for something better, not realize one's expectations 307vb. *fall short;* expect otherwise, be let down, have hoped better of; find to one's cost 830vb. *regret;* find one a false prophet, listen too often 544vb. *be duped;* laugh on the wrong side of one's face, be crestfallen, look blue, look blank 872vb. *be humbled;* be sick with disappointment, be sick at heart, be hopeless 853vb. *despair.*

disappoint, not come up to expectations 307vb. *fall short;* falsify *or* belie one's expectation; defeat one's hopes, break one's h., dash one's h., crush one's h., blight one's h., deceive one's h., betray one's h.; burst the bubble, disillusion; serve ill, fail one, let down, leave one in the lurch, not come up to scratch; balk, foil, thwart, frustrate 702vb. *hinder;* amaze, dumbfound 508vb. *surprise;* disconcert, humble 872vb. *humiliate;* betray, play one false 930vb. *be dishonest;* play one a trick, jilt, bilk 542vb. *befool;* dash the cup from one's lips, tantalize, leave unsatisfied, discontent, spoil one's pleasure, dissatisfy, disgruntle, sour, embitter with disappointment 829vb. *cause discontent;* refuse, deny, turn away 607vb. *reject.*

Adv. *disappointingly,* tantalizingly, so near and yet so far.

See: 307, 481, 482, 508, 529, 542, 544,

607, 636, 702, 726, 728, 731, 829, 830, 834, 853, 872, 930.

510 Foresight

N. *foresight,* prevision, preview, foreglimpse; anticipation, foretaste; prenotion, precognition, foreknowledge, prescience, second sight, clairvoyance; premonition, presentiment, foreboding, forewarning 511n. *omen;* prognosis, prognostication 511n. *prediction;* foregone conclusion 473n. *certainty;* program, prospectus 623n. *plan;* forethought, long-sightedness 498n. *sagacity;* predeliberation 608n. *predetermination;* prudence, providence 858n. *caution;* intelligent anticipation, readiness, provision 669n. *preparation.*

Adj. *foreseeing,* foresighted, prospective, prognostic, predictive 511adj. *predicting;* clairvoyant, second-sighted, prophetic; prescient, far-sighted, weather-wise, sagacious 498adj. *wise;* looking ahead, provident, prudent 858adj. *cautious;* anticipant, anticipatory 507adj. *expectant.*

Vb. *foresee,* foreglimpse, preview, prophesy, forecast, divine 511vb. *predict;* forewarn 664vb. *warn;* foreknow, see *or* peep *or* pry into the future, read the f., have second sight; have prior information, know in advance 524vb. *be informed;* see ahead, look a., see it coming, scent, scent from afar, feel in one's bones; be beforehand, anticipate, forestall 135vb. *be early;* make provision 669vb. *prepare;* surmise, make a good guess 512vb. *suppose;* forejudge, predeliberate 608vb. *predetermine;* show prudence, plan ahead 623vb. *plan;* look to the future, have an eye to the f., see how the cat jumps, see how the wind blows 124vb. *look ahead;* have an eye on the main chance 498vb. *be wise;* feel one's way, keep a sharp look-out 455vb. *be attentive;* lay up for a rainy day 633vb. *provide;* take precautions, provide against 858vb. *be cautious.*

See: 124, 135, 455, 473, 498, 507, 511, 512, 524, 608, 623, 633, 664, 669, 858.

511 Prediction

N. *prediction,* foretelling, forewarning, prophecy; apocalypse 975n. *revelation;* forecast, weather f.; prognostication, prognosis; presentiment, foreboding 510n. *foresight;* presage, prefiguration, prefigurement; program, prospectus 623n. *plan;* announcement, notice, advance n. 528n. *publication;* warning, preliminary w., warning shot 665n. *danger signal;* prospect 507n. *expectation;* shape of things to come, horoscope, fortune; type 23n. *prototype.*

divination, clairvoyance; augury, auguration, hariolation; mantology, vaticination, soothsaying; astrology, astromancy, horoscopy, casting nativities, genethliacs; fortune-telling, palmistry, chiromancy; crystal-gazing, crystallomancy; sortilege, casting lots; dowsing, radiesthesia 484n. *discovery.*

theomancy, bibliomancy, psychomancy, sciomancy, aeromancy, chaomancy, meteoromancy, austromancy; haruspicy, hieroscopy, hieromancy, ichthyomancy, anthropomancy; pyromancy, tephromancy, sideromancy, capnomancy; myomancy, orniscopy, ornithomancy, alectryomancy, ophiomancy; botanomancy, hydromancy, pegomancy; rhabdomancy; crithomancy, aleuromancy, alphitomancy, halomancy; cleromancy, sortilege, belomancy, axinomancy, coscinomancy; dactyliomancy, geomancy, lithomancy, pessomancy, psephomancy; catoptromancy.

omen, portent, presage, writing on the wall; prognostic, symptom, sign 547n. *indication;* augury, auspice; forewarning, caution 664n. *warning;* harbinger, herald 531n. *messenger;* prefigurement, foretoken, type; ominousness, portentousness, gathering clouds, signs of the times 661n. *danger;* bird of omen, bird of ill omen, owl, raven.

oracle, consultant 500n. *sage;* meteorologist, weather prophet; calamity prophet, Cassandra 664n. *warner;* prophet, prophetess, seer; forecaster, soothsayer; clairvoyant, medium 984 n. *occultist;* Delphic oracle, Pythian o., Python, pythoness, Pythia; sibyl, sibylline leaves, sibylline books, Old Moore; Tiresias, Witch of Endor, sphinx; cards, dice, lot; tripod, crystal, mirror, tea leaves, palm; Bible, sortes Vergilianae.

diviner, water d., dowser 983n. *sorcerer;* tipster 618n. *gambler;* astrologer, caster of nativities; fortune-teller, gipsy, palmist, crystal-gazer, geomancer; augur, augurist, haruspex.

Adj. *predicting* etc.vb.; predictive, foretelling; presentient, clairvoyant 510adj. *foreseeing;* fortune-telling; weather-wise; prophetic, vaticinal, mantic, fatidical, apocalyptic; oracular, sibylline; monitory, premonitory, foreboding 664adj. *cautionary;* heralding, prefiguring 66adj. *precursory.* *presageful,* significant, ominous, portentous, big with fate, pregnant with doom; augurial, auspicial, haruspical, extispicious; auspicious, promising, favorable 730adj. *prosperous;* sinister 731adj. *adverse.*

Vb. *predict,* forecast, make a prediction, prognosticate, make a prognosis; foretell, prophesy, vaticinate, forebode, bode, ominate, augur, spell; foretoken, presage, portend; foreshow, premonstrate, foreshadow, prefigure, shadow forth, precurse, forerun, herald, be harbinger, usher in 64vb. *come before;* point to, betoken, typify, signify 547vb. *indicate;* announce, give notice, notify 528vb. *advertise;* forewarn, give warning 664vb. *warn;* look black, lour, lower, menace 900vb. *threaten;* promise, augur well, bid fair to, give hopes of, hold out hopes, raise expectations, excite e. 852vb. *give hope.*

divine, auspicate, augurate, haruspicate; take the auspices, take the omens; soothsay, vaticinate, hariolate; draw a horoscope, cast a nativity; cast lots 618vb. *gamble;* tell fortunes; read the future, read the signs, read the stars; read the cards, read one's hand.

See: 23, 64, 66, 484, 500, 507, 510, 528, 531, 547, 618, 623, 661, 664, 665, 730, 731, 852, 900, 983, 984.

512 Supposition

N. *supposition,* supposal, notion, the idea of 451n. *idea;* fancy, conceit 513n. *ideality;* pretense, pretending 850n. *affectation;* presumption, assumption, presupposition, postulation, postulate, postulatum 475n. *premise;* condition, stipulation 766n. *conditions;* proposal, proposition 759vb. *offer;* submission 475n. *argument;* hypothesis, working h., theory, theorem 452n. *topic;* thesis, position, stand, attitude, orientation, standpoint 485n. *opinion;* suggestion, loose s., casual s.; suggestiveness 524n. *hint;* basis of supposition, clue, data, datum 466n. *evidence;* suspicion, hunch, inkling (**see** *conjecture*); instinct 476n. *intuition;* association of ideas 449n. *thought;* supposability, conjecturability 469n. *possibility.*

conjecture, unverified supposition, conjecturability, guess, surmise, suspicion; mere notion, bare supposition, vague suspicion, rough guess, crude estimate; shrewd idea 476n. *intuition;* construction, reconstruction; guesswork, guessing, speculation; gamble, shot, shot in the dark 618n. *gambling.*

theorist, hypothesist, theorizer, theoretician; supposer, surmiser, guesser; academic person, critic, armchair c., armchair detective; doctrinarian 473n. *doctrinaire;* speculator, thinker 449n. *philosopher;* backroom boy 623n. *planner;* plunger 618n. *gambler.*

Adj. *suppositional,* supposing etc.vb.; suppositive, notional, conjectural, guessing, propositional, hypothetical, theoretical, armchair, speculative, academic, of academic interest; gratuitous, unverified; suggestive, hinting, allusive, stimulating, thought-provoking.

supposed etc.vb.; assumed, presumed. premised, taken, postulated; proposed, mooted 452adj. *topical;* given, granted, granted for the sake of argument 488adj. *assented;* suppositive, putative, presumptive; pretended, so-called, quasi; not real 2adj. *unreal;* alleged, supposititious, fabled, fancied 543adj. *untrue;* supposable, surmisable, imaginable 513adj. *imaginary.*

Vb. *suppose,* just s., pretend 850vb. *be affected;* fancy, dream 513vb. *imagine;* think, conceive, take into one's head 485vb. *opine;* divine, have a hunch 476vb. *intuit;* surmise, conjecture, hazard a c., guess, give a g., make a g.; suppose so, dare say; persuade oneself 485vb. *believe;* presume, assume, presuppose, presurmise 475vb. *premise;* posit, lay down, assert 532vb. *affirm;* take for granted, take, take it, postulate 475vb. *reason;* speculate, have a theory, hypothesize, theorize 449vb. *meditate;* sketch, draft, outline 623vb. *plan;* rely on supposition 618vb. *gamble.*

propound, propose, mean seriously 759vb. *offer;* put on the agenda, moot, move, propose a motion 761vb. *request;* put a case, submit, make one's submission 475vb. *argue;* put forth, make a suggestion, venture to say, put forward a notion, throw out an idea 691vb. *advise;* suggest, adumbrate, allude 524vb. *hint;* put an idea into one's head, urge 612vb. *motivate.*

Adv. *supposedly,* reputedly, seemingly; on the assumption that, ex hypothesi.

See: 2, 449, 451, 452, 466, 469, 473,

475, 476, 485, 488, 513, 524, 532, 543, 612, 618, 623, 691, 759, 761, 766, 850.

513 Imagination

N. *imagination*, power of i., visual i., vivid i., highly colored i., fertile i., bold i., wild i., fervent i.; imaginativeness, creativeness; originality, inventiveness 21n. *non-imitation;* ingenuity, resourcefulness 694n. *skill;* fancifulness, stretch of the imagination (**see** *ideality*); understanding, insight, empathy, sympathy 819n. *moral sensibility;* poetic imagination, frenzy, poetic f., ecstasy, inspiration, afflatus, divine a.; fancy, the mind's eye, visualization, objectification, image-building, imagery, word painting; artistry, creative work.

ideality, idealization, excogitation, conception 449n. *thought;* concept, image, conceit, fancy, coinage of the brain, brain-creation, notion 451n. *idea;* whim, whimsy, whim-wham, maggot, crimkum-crankum 497n. *absurdity;* vagary 604n. *caprice;* figment, fiction 541n. *falsehood;* work of fiction, story 590n. *novel;* imaginative exercise, flight of fancy, play of f., uncontrolled imagination, romance, extravaganza, rhapsody 546n. *exaggeration;* poetic license 593n. *poetry;* quixotry, knight-errantry, shadow boxing.

fantasy, wildest dreams; vision, dream, bad d., nightmare; bugbear, phantom 970n. *ghost;* shadow, vapor 419n. *dimness;* mirage, fata morgana 440n. *visual fallacy;* delusion, hallucination, chimera 495n. *error;* reverie, brown study 456n. *abstractedness;* trance, somnambulism 375n. *insensibility;* sick fancy, delirium 503n. *frenzy;* subjectivity, autistic distortion, autosuggestion; wishful thinking 477n. *sophistry;* window-shopping, castle-building, make-believe, day-dream, golden d., pipe-d. 859n. *desire*; romanticisc, escapism, idealism, utopianism; Utopia, Erewhon; promised land, El Dorado; Happy Valley, Fortunate Isles, Isles of the Blest; land of Cockaigne, kingdom of Micomicon, Ruritania, Shangri-la, Atlantis; fairyland, wonderland, land of Prester John; cloud-cuckoo land, dream l., dream world, castles in Spain, castle in the air; pie in the sky, good time coming, millennium 124n. *future state;* man in the moon, Flying Dutchman; idle fancy, myth 543n. *fable.*

visionary, seer 511n. *diviner;* dreamer, day-d., mopus, somnambulist; idealist, utopian 901n. *philanthropist;* castle-builder, escapist, ostrich, ostrich-head 620n. *avoider;* romantic, romancer, romanticist, rhapsodist, myth-maker; enthusiast, knight-errant, fool-e., Don Quixote 504n. *crank;* creative worker 556n. *artist.*

Adj. *imaginative*, creative, lively, original, idea'd, inventive, fertile, ingenious; resourceful 694adj. *skillful;* fancy-led, romancing, romantic, high-flying; high-flown, rhapsodical 546 adj. *exaggerated;* poetic, fictional; utopian, idealistic; rhapsodic, enthusiastic; dreaming, tranced; extravagant, fantastical, whimsical, preposterous, impractical 497adj. *absurd;* visionary, other-worldly, quixotic; imaginal, visualizing, eidetic, eidotropic.

imaginary, unreal, unsubstantial 4adj. *insubstantial;* subjective, notional, chimerical, illusory 495adj. *erroneous;* dreamy, visionary, not of this world, ideal; cloudy, vaporous 419 adj. *shadowy;* unhistorical, fictitious, fabulous, fabled, legendary, mythic, mythological 543adj. *untrue;* fanciful, fancy-bred, fancied, imagined, fabricated, hatched; dreamed-up, air-drawn, air-built; hypothetical 512 adj. *suppositional;* pretended, make-believe.

Vb. *imagine*, ideate 449vb. *think;* fancy, dream; excogitate, think of, think up, dream up; make up, devise, invent, originate, create, have an inspiration 609vb. *improvise;* coin, hatch, concoct, fabricate 164vb. *produce;* visualize, envisage, see in the mind's eye 438vb. *see;* conceive, form an image; figure to oneself, picture to o., represent to o.; paint, word-p., conjure up a vision, objectify, realize, capture, recapture 551 vb. *represent;* use one's imagination, give reins to one's i., run riot in imagination 546vb. *exaggerate;* play with one's thoughts, pretend, make-believe, daydream 456vb. *be inattentive;* build utopias, build castles in the air; see visions, dream dreams; idealize, romanticize, fictionalize, rhapsodize 546vb. *exaggerate;* enter into, empathize, sympathize 516vb *understand.*

Adv. *imaginatively*, in imagination, in thought; with imagination; in the mind's eye.

See: 4, 21, 124, 164, 375, 419, 438, 440, 449, 451, 456, 477, 495, 497, 503, 504, 511, 512, 516, 541, 543,

546, 551, 556, 590, 593, 604, 609, 620, 694, 819, 859, 901, 970.

514 Meaning

N. *meaning,* idea conveyed, substance, essence, sum, sum and substance, gist, pith; contents, text, matter, subject m. 452n. *topic;* semantic content, sense, drift, tenor, purport, import, implication, coloring; force, effect; relevance, bearing, scope; meaningfulness, semantic flow, context, running c. (**see** *connotation*); expression, mode of e., diction 566n. *style;* semantics, semasiology 557n. *linguistics.*

connotation, denotation, signification, significance, reference, application; context; original meaning, derivation 156n. *source;* range of meaning, semantic field, comprehension; extended meaning, extension; intention, main meaning, leading sense; specialized meaning, peculiar m., idiom 80n. *specialty;* subsidiary sense, submeaning; received meaning, usage, acceptance, accepted meaning 520n. *interpretation;* single meaning, univocity, unambiguity 516n. *intelligibility;* double meaning, ambiguity 518n. *equivocalness;* same meaning, equivalent meaning, convertible terms, synonym, synonymousness, synonymity, equivalence, tautonymity 13n. *identity;* opposite meaning, antonym, antonymity 14n. *contrariety;* contradictory meaning, countersense; changed meaning, semantic shift; level of meaning, literal meaning, literality, translationese 573n. *plainness;* metaphorical meaning 519 n. *metaphor;* hidden meaning, esoteric sense 523n. *latency;* constructive sense, implied s.; Pickwickian sense, nonsense 497n. *absurdity.*

Adj. *meaningful,* significant, of moment 638adj. *important;* substantial, pithy, full of meaning, replete with m., packed with m., pregnant; meaning etc.vb.; importing, purporting, significative, significatory, indicative 547adj. *indicating;* expressive, suggestive, evocative, allusive, implicit; express, explicit 573adj. *plain;* declaratory 532adj. *affirmative;* interpretative 520adj. *interpretive.*

semantic, semasiological, philological, etymological 557adj. *linguistic;* connotational, connotative; denotational, denotative; literal, verbal 573n. *plain;* metaphorical 519adj. *figurative;* biplanar, on two levels; univocal, unambiguous 516adj. *intelligible;* ambiguous 518adj. *equivocal;* synonymous, homonymous 13adj. *identical;* tantamount, equivalent 18 adj. *similar;* tautologous 106adj. *repeated;* antonymous 14adj. *contrary;* idiomatic 80adj. *special;* paraphrastic 520adj. *interpretive;* obscure 568 adj. *imperspicuous;* clear 567adj. *perspicuous;* implied, constructive 523adj. *latent;* Pickwickian, nonsensical 497adj. *absurd;* meaningless 515adj. *unmeaning.*

Vb. *mean,* have a meaning, bear a sense, mean something; convey a meaning, get across 524vb. *communicate;* typify, symbolize 547vb. *indicate;* signify, denote, connote, stand for 551vb. *represent;* import, purport, intend; point to, add up to, boil down to, spell, involve 523vb. *imply;* convey, express, declare, assert 532vb. *affirm;* bespeak, tell of, speak of, breathe of, speak volumes 466vb. *evidence;* mean to say, be trying to s., drive at, really mean, have in mind, allude to, refer to; be synonymous, have the same meaning 13vb. *be identical;* say it in other words, tautologize 106vb. *repeat;* mean the same thing, agree in meaning, coincide 24vb. *agree;* conflict in meaning, be opposed in m. 25vb. *disagree;* draw a meaning, infer, understand by 516vb. *understand.*

Adv. significantly, meaningly, with meaning, to the effect that; in a sense, in some s.; as meant, as intended, as understood; in the sense that *or* of; according to the book, from the context; literally, verbally; metaphorically, constructively.

See: 13, 14, 18, 24, 25, 80, 106, 156, 452, 466, 497, 515, 516, 518, 519, 520, 523, 524, 532, 547, 551, 557, 566, 567, 568, 573, 638.

515 Unmeaningness

N. *unmeaningness,* meaninglessness, lack of meaning, absence of m., no meaning, no context; no bearing 10 adj. *irrelevance;* non-significance 639n. *unimportance;* amphigory 497 n. *absurdity;* inanity, emptiness, triteness; truism, platitude 496n. *maxim;* unreason, illogicality 477n. *sophistry;* invalidity, dead letter, nullity 161n. *ineffectuality;* illegibility, scribble, scribbling 586vb. *script;* daub 552n. *misrepresentation;* empty sound, meaningless noise, strumming; sounding brass, tinkling cymbal 490n. *loudness;* jargon, rigmarole, rigmarolery, hocus-pocus, galimatias; gibberish, gabble, High Dutch, double D., Greek, Babel 517n. *unintelligibility;* incoherence, raving, delirium 503n. *frenzy;* double-talk, mystification 530n. *enigma;* insincerity 925n. *flattery.*

silly talk, senseless t., nonsense 497n. *absurdity;* stuff, stuff and nonsense, balderdash, gammon, rubbish, rot, tommy-rot; drivel, twaddle, fiddle-faddle, fudge; bosh, tosh, tripe, piffle, bilge, hog-wash, wish-wash.

empty talk, idle speeches, soft nothings, wind, gas, hot air, vaporing, verbiage 570n. *diffuseness;* rant, bombast, fustian, rodomontade 877n. *boasting;* blether, blather, blatherskite, blah-blah, flap-doodle; guff, pi-jaw, claptrap, poppy-cock; humbug 541n. *falsehood;* moonshine, bunkum, bunk, baloney, hooey; flummery, blarney 925n. *flattery;* talk, chatter, prattle, prate, prating, patter, babble, gabble, palaver, jabber, jabber-jabber 584n. *chat;* cliché.

Adj. *unmeaning,* meaningless, without meaning, Pickwickian; amphigoric, nonsense, nonsensical 497adj. *absurd;* senseless, null; unexpressive, unidiomatic 25adj. *unapt;* nonsignificant, insignificant, inane, empty, trivial, trite 639adj. *unimportant;* fatuous, piffling, blithering, bilgy, washy; trashy, trumpery, rubbishy; twaddling, waffling, windy, ranting 546adj. *exaggerated;* incoherent, raving, gibbering 503adj. *frenzied.*

unmeant, unintentional, involuntary, unintended, unimplied, unalluded to; mistranslated 521adj. *misinterpreted;* insincere 925adj. *flattering.*

Vb. *mean nothing,* be unmeaning, have no meaning; scribble, scratch, daub, strum; talk bunkum, talk like an idiot 497vb. *be absurd;* talk, babble, prattle, prate, palaver, gabble, jabber, clack 584vb. *converse;* talk double Dutch, talk Greek, talk gibberish, doubletalk 517vb. *be unintelligible;* rant 546vb. *exaggerate;* rave, drivel, drool, blether, blat, waffle, twaddle; vapor, talk hot air, gas 499vb. *be foolish;* not mean what one says, blarney 925vb. *flatter;* make nonsense of 521vb. *misinterpret;* have no meaning for, pass over one's head 474vb. *puzzle.*

See: 10, 25, 161, 400, 474, 477, 496, 497, 499, 503, 517, 521, 530, 541, 546, 552, 570, 584, 586, 639, 877, 925.

516 Intelligibility

N. *intelligibility,* knowability, cognizability; explicability, teachability, penetrability; apprehensibility, comprehensibility, adaptation to the understanding; readability, legibility, decipherability; clearness, clarity, coherence, limpidity, lucidity 567n. *perspicuity;* precision, unambiguity 473n. *certainty;* simplicity, straightforwardness, plain speaking, plain speech, downright utterance; plain words, plain English, mother tongue; simple eloquence, unadorned style 573n. *plainness;* easiness, paraphrase, simplification 701n. *facility;* amplification, popularization, haute vulgarisation 520n. *interpretation.*

Adj. *intelligible,* understandable, penetrable, realizable, comprehensible, apprehensible; coherent 502adj. *sane;* distinguishable, audible, recognizable, unmistakable; discoverable, cognizable, knowable 490adj. *known;* explicable, teachable; unambiguous, unequivocal 514adj. *meaningful;* explicit, positive 473adj. *certain;* unblurred, distinct, clear-cut, precise 80adj. *definite;* plain-spoken, unevasive, unadorned, downright, forthright 573adj. *plain;* uninvolved, straightforward, simple 701adj. *easy;* obvious, easy to understand, easy to grasp, made easy, adapted to the understanding, clear to the meanest capacity; explained, predigested, simplified, popularized, popular, for the million 520adj. *interpreted;* clear, limpid 422adj. *transparent;* pellucid, lucid 567adj. *perspicuous;* readable, legible, decipherable, well-written, printed, in print; luminous, clear as daylight, clear as noonday, plain as a pikestaff 443adj. *visible.*

expressive, telling, vivid, graphic, highly colored, emphatic, strong, strongly worded 590adj. *descriptive;* illustrative, explicatory 520adj. *interpretive;* amplifying, paraphrasing, popularizing.

Vb. *be intelligible,*—clear,—easy etc. adj.; be realized, come alive, take on depth; be readable, read easily; make sense, add up, speak to the understanding 475vb. *be reasonable;* tell its own tale, speak for itself 466vb. *evidence;* have no secrets, be on the surface 443vb. *be visible;* make understood, clarify, clear up, open one's eyes, elucidate 520vb. *interpret;* make easy, simplify, popularize 701 vb. *facilitate;* recapitulate 106vb. *repeat;* labor the obvious 532vb. *emphasize.*

understand, comprehend, apprehend 490vb. *know;* master 536vb. *learn;* have, hold, retain 505vb. *remember;* have understanding 498vb. *be wise;* see through, penetrate, fathom, get to the bottom of 484vb. *detect;* spot, descry, discern, distinguish, make out, see at a glance, see with half an eye 438vb. *see;* recognize, make no mistake 473vb. *be certain;* grasp, get hold of, seize, seize the meaning, be on to it, cotton on to; get the hang of, take in, register; be with one, follow, savvy; collect, get, catch on, twig; realize, get wise to, tumble to; begin to understand, come to u., have it dawn on one, have one's eyes opened, see it all; be undeceived, be disillusioned 830vb. *regret;* get to know, be told 524vb. *be informed.*

Adv. *intelligibly,* expressively, lucidly, plainly, simply, in plain terms, in clear terms, in simplified vocabulary.

See: 80, 106, 422, 438, 443, 466, 473, 475, 484, 490, 498, 502, 505, 514, 520, 524, 532, 536, 567, 573, 590, 701, 830.

517 Unintelligibility

N. *unintelligibility,* incomprehensibility, inapprehensibility, unaccountability, inconceivability; inexplicability, impenetrability; perplexity, difficulty 474adj. *uncertainty;* obscurity 568adj. *imperspicuity;* ambiguity 518n. *equivocalness;* mystification 515n. *unmeaningness;* incoherence 503n. *insanity;* double Dutch, gibberish; private language, slang; idioglossia 580n. *speech defect;* undecipherability, illegibility, unreadability; scribble, scrawl 586n. *lettering;* inaudibility 401n. *faintness;* Greek, sealed book 530n. *secret;* hard saying, paradox, knotty point, obscure problem, pons asinorum, crux, riddle 530n. *enigma;* mysterious behavior, sphinx-like attitude, baffling demeanor; bad pronunciation 580n. *speech defect;* foreign language, strange idiom 560n. *dialect.*

Adj. *unintelligible,* incomprehensible, inapprehensible, inconceivable, not understandable, not to be understood, inexplicable, unaccountable, not to be accounted for; unknowable, unrecognizable, incognizable, undiscoverable, as Greek to one 491adj. *unknown;* unfathomable, unbridgeable, unsearchable, inscrutable, impenetrable; blank, poker-faced, expressionless 820adj. *impassive;* inaudible 401adj. *muted;* unreadable, illegible, undecipherable; undiscernible 444vb. *invisible;* hidden, arcane 523adj. *occult;* dark, shrouded in mystery; esoteric 80adj. *private;* sphinx-like, enigmatic, oracular (**see** *puzzling*).

puzzling, hard to understand, difficult, hard, crabbed; beyond one, over one's head, recondite, abtruse, elusive; enigmatic, mysterious 523 adj. *occult;* half-understood, nebulous, misty, hazy, dim, obscure 419 adj. *shadowy;* clear as mud, clear as ditch water 568adj. *imperspicuous;* ambiguous 518adj. *equivocal;* of doubtful meaning, oracular; paradoxical 508adj. *unexpected;* unexplained, without a solution, insoluble, unsolvable; unsolved, unresolved 474 adj. *uncertain.*

inexpressible, unspeakable, unmentionable, untranslatable; unpronounceable, unutterable, ineffable; incommunicable, indefinable; profound, deep; mystic, mystical, transcendental.

puzzled, mystified, unable to understand, wondering, out of one's depth, flummoxed, baffled, perplexed, nonplussed 474adj. *uncertain.*

Vb. *be unintelligible,*—puzzling,—inexpressible etc.adj.; be hard, be difficult, present a puzzle, make one's head ache 474vb. *puzzle;* talk in riddles, speak oracles 518vb. *be equivocal;* talk double Dutch, talk gibberish 515vb. *mean nothing;* keep one guessing 486vb. *cause doubt;* perplex, complicate, entangle, confuse 63vb. *bedevil;* be too deep, go over one's head, be beyond one's reach; elude one's grasp, escape one; pass comprehension, baffle understanding; require explanation, have no answer, need an interpreter; write badly, scribble, scrawl.

not understand, not penetrate, find unintelligible, not make out, not know what to make of, make nothing of, make neither head nor tail of, be unable to account for; puzzle over; find too difficult, give up; be out of one's depth 491vb. *not know;* wonder, be at sea 474vb. *be uncertain;* not know what one is about, have no grasp 695vb. *be unskillful;* misunderstand one another, play at cross-purposes 495vb. *blunder;* get one wrong 481vb. *misjudge;* not register 456vb. *be inattentive.*

See: 13, 63, 80, 401, 419, 444, 456, 474, 481, 486, 491, 495, 503, 508, 515, 518, 523, 530, 560, 568, 580, 586, 695, 820.

518 Equivocalness

N. *equivocalness*, two voices 14n. *contrariety;* ambiguity, ambivalence 517n. *unintelligibility;* indefiniteness, vagueness 474adj. *uncertainty;* double meaning, amphiboly, amphibology, ambiloquy 514n. *meaning;* doubletalk 515n. *unmeaningness;* conundrum, riddle, oracle, oracular utterance 530n. *enigma;* mental reservation 525n. *concealment;* prevarication, balancing act; equivocation, white lie 543n. *untruth;* quibble, quibbling 477n. *sophistry;* wordplay, play upon words, paronomasia 574n. *ornament;* pun, calembour, equivoque, double entendre 839n. *witticism;* anagram, paragram, acrostic; synonymy, homonymy, homophone; tautonym.

Adj. *equivocal*, not univocal, ambiguous epicene, ambivalent; double, double-tongued, two-edged; equivocating, prevaricating; vague, evasive, oracular; amphibolous, homonymous; anagrammatic.

Vb. *be equivocal*, cut both ways; play upon words, pun; have two meanings, have a second meaning 514vb. *mean;* speak oracles, equivocate, speak with two voices 14vb. *be contrary;* prevaricate, make a mental reservation 541vb. *dissemble.*

See: 14, 474, 477, 514, 515, 517, 525, 530, 541, 543, 574, 839.

519 Metaphor: figure of speech

N. *metaphor*, mixed m.; tralatition, transference; allusion, application; misapplication, catachresis; extended metaphor, allegorization, allegory; mystical interpretation, anagoge 520n. *interpretation;* apologue, fable, parable 534n. *teaching;* symbolism, non-literality, figurativeness, imagery 513n. *imagination;* simile, likeness 462n. *comparison;* personification, prosopopoeia.

trope, figure, figure of speech, turn of s., flourish; manner of speech, façon de parler; irony, sarcasm 851n. *satire;* rhetorical figure 574n. *ornament;* metonymy, antonomasia, synecdoche, synecdochism, enallage; anaphora, paraleipsis; aposiopesis; litotes 483n. *underestimation;* hyperbole 546n. *exaggeration;* stress, emphasis; euphuism, euphemism 850n. *affectation;* colloquialism 573n. *plainness;* contrast, antithesis 462n. *comparison;* metathesis 221n. *inversion;* paronomasia, word-play 518n. *equivocalness;* asyndeton 46n. *disjunction.*

Adj. *figurative*, metaphorical, tropical, tralatitious, catachrestic; allusive, symbolical, typical, allegorical, anagogic; parabolical; comparative, similitudinous 462adj. *compared;* euphuistic, tortured, euphemistic 850 adj. *affected;* colloquial 573adj. *plain;* hyperbolic 546adj. *exaggerated;* satirical, sarcastic, ironical 851adj. *derisive;* flowery, florid 574 adj. *ornate;* oratorical 574adj. *rhetorical.*

Vb. *figure*, image, embody, personify; typify, symbolize 551vb. *represent;* allegorize, parabolize, fable; prefigure, adumbrate; apply, allude; refer, similitudinize, liken, contrast 462vb. *compare;* employ metaphor, indulge in tropes 574vb. *ornament.*

Adv. *metaphorically*, not literally, tropically, figuratively, in a figure, by allusion; in a way, so to say, in a manner of speaking.

See: 46, 221, 462, 483, 513, 518, 520, 534, 546, 551, 573, 574, 850, 851.

520 Interpretation

N. *interpretation*, definition, explanation, explication, exposition, exegesis, epexegesis; elucidation, light, clarification, illumination; illustration, exemplification 83n. *example;* enucleation, resolution, solution, key, clue, the secret 460n. *answer;* decipherment, decoding, cracking 484n. *discovery;* emendation 654n. *amendment;* application, particular interpretation, twist, turn; construction, construe, reading, lection 514n. *meaning;* euhemerism, demythologization; allegorization 519n. *metaphor;* accepted reading, usual text, vulgate; alternative reading, variant r.; criticism, textual c., higher c., literary c., critique, review 480n. *estimate;* critical power, critic's gift 480n. *judgment;* insight, feeling, sympathy 819n. *moral sensibility.*

commentary, comment, editorial c., Targum; scholium, gloss, footnote; inscription, caption, legend 563n. *phrase;* motto, moral 693n. *precept;* annotation, glossography, notes, marginalia, adversaria; apparatus criticus, critical edition; glossary, lexicon 559n. *dictionary.*

translation, version, rendering, free translation, loose rendering; faithful translation, literal t., construe; key, crib, Bohn; rewording, paraphrase, metaphrase; précis, abridgment, epitome 592n. *compendium;* adaptation, simplification, amplification 516n. *intelligibility;* transliteration, decoding, decipherment; lip-reading.

hermeneutics, exegetics, science of interpretation, translator's art; epigraphy, paleography 557n. *linguistics;* diagnostics, symptomatology, semeiology, semeiotics; phrenology, metoposcopy; prophecy 511n. *divination.*

interpreter, clarifier, explainer, exponent, expounder, expositor, exegete 537n. *teacher;* rationalist, rationalizer, euhemerist, demythologizer; editor 528n. *publicizer;* Masorete, textual critic; emender, emendator; commentator, annotator, note-maker, glossographer, scholiast, glossarist; critic, reviewer 480n. *estimator;* oneirocritic, oneiroscopist, medium 511n. *diviner;* polyglot 557n. *linguist;* translator, paraphraser, paraphrast; solver, cipherer, coder, decoder; lip-reader; epigraphist, paleographer 125 n. *antiquarian;* spokesman, prolocutor, mouthpiece, representative 754n. *delegate;* executant, player, performer 413n. *musician;* poet, novelist, painter, sculptor 556n. *artist.*

guide, precedent 83n. *example;* lamp, light, star; dragoman, courier, man from Cook's, cicerone 690n. *leader;* showman, demonstrator 522n. *exhibitor.*

Adj. *interpretive*, interpretative, constructive; explanatory, explicatory, explicative, elucidatory; expositive, expository; exegetical, hermeneutic; defining, definitive; illuminating, illustrative, exemplary; glossarial, annotative, scholiastic, editorial; lip-reading, translative, paraphrastic, metaphrastic; polyglot; mediumistic; cosignificative, synonymous, equivalent 28 adj. *equal;* literal, strict, word-for-word 494adj. *accurate;* faithful 551 adj. *representing;* free 495adj. *inexact.*

interpreted etc. vb.; explained, defined, expounded, elucidated, clarified; annotated, commented, commentated, edited; translated, rendered, Englished; deciphered, decoded, cracked.

Vb. *interpret*, define, clarify, make clear; explain, unfold, expound, elucidate 516vb. *be intelligible;* illustrate 83vb. *exemplify;* comment; demonstrate 522 vb. *show;* act as guide, show round; comment on, edit, write notes for, annotate, compose a commentary, gloss, gloze, gloze upon; read, spell, spell out; adopt a reading, accept an interpretation, construe, put a construction on, understand by, give a sense to, make sense of, put a meaning on 516vb. *understand;* illuminate, throw light on, enlighten 524vb. *inform;* account for, find the cause, deduce, infer 475vb. *reason;* act as interpreter, be spokesman 551vb. *represent;* typify, symbolize; popularize, simplify 701vb. *facilitate.*

translate, make a version, make a key, make a crib; render, do into, turn i., English; retranslate, rehash, reword, rephrase, paraphrase; abridge, amplify, adapt; transliterate, transcribe; code, put into code; lip-read.

decipher, crack, crack the cipher, decode; find the meaning, read hieroglyphics; read, spell out, puzzle o., make o., work o.; piece together, find the sense of, find the key to; solve, resolve, enucleate, unravel, unriddle, disentangle, read between the lines.

Adv. *in plain words,* plainly, in plain English; by way of explanation, as interpreted; in other words, to wit, namely; to make it plain, to explain.

See: 28, 83, 125, 413, 460, 475, 480, 484, 494, 495, 511, 514, 516, 519, 522, 524, 528, 537, 551, 556, 557, 559, 563, 592, 654, 690, 693, 701, 754, 819.

521 Misinterpretation

N. *misinterpretation*, misunderstanding, misconstruction, misapprehension, wrong end of the stick; cross-purposes 495n. *mistake;* misexposition 535n. *misteaching;* mistranslation, misconstruction, translator's error; wrong interpretation, false construction; twist, turn, misapplication, perversion 246n. *distortion;* strained sense; false reading; false coloring, dark glasses, rose-colored spectacles; garbling, falsification 552 n. *misrepresentation;* over-coloring 546n. *exaggeration;* depreciation 483 n. *underestimation;* parody, travesty 851n. *ridicule;* abuse of language, misapplication, catachresis 565n. *solecism.*

Adj. *misinterpreted* etc. vb., misconstrued, mistranslated; glozed, badly edited; misread, misexpressed.

Vb. *misinterpret*, misunderstand, misapprehend, misconceive 481vb. *misjudge;* get wrong, get one wrong, get hold of the wrong end of the stick; misread, misspell 495vb. *blunder;* misexplain, set in a false light 535vb. *misteach;* mistranslate, misconstrue, put a false sense *or* construction on; give a twist *or* turn, pervert, strain the sense, wrest the meaning, wrench, twist, twist the words 246vb. *distort;*

equivocate, play upon words 518vb. *be equivocal;* add a meaning, read into, write i. 38vb. *add;* leave out, suppress 39vb. *subtract;* misexpress, misquote; falsify, garble, gloze 552vb. *misrepresent;* travesty, parody, caricature, guy 851vb. *ridicule;* overpraise 482vb. *overrate;* underpraise 483vb. *underestimate;* inflate 546vb. *exaggerate;* traduce 926vb. *defame.*

See: 38, 39, 246, 481, 482, 483, 495, 518, 535, 546, 552, 565, 851, 926.

522 Manifestation

N. *manifestation,* revelation, unfolding, discovery, daylight, divulgence 526n. *disclosure;* expression, formulation 532n. *affirmation;* proof, quotation, citation 466n. *evidence;* confrontation 462n. *comparison;* presentation, production, projection, enactment 551n. *representation;* symbolization, typification 547n. *indication;* sign 547n. *signal;* premonstration, preview 438n. *view;* showing, demonstration, exhibition; display, showing off 875n. *ostentation;* proclamation 528n. *publication;* unconcealment, openness, flagrance 528n. *publicity;* candor, plain speaking, plain speech, home-truth 573n. *plainness;* prominence, conspicuousness, relief 443n. *visibility;* apparition, vision, materialization 445n. *appearance;* séance 984n. *occultism;* Shekinah, glory 965n. *theophany;* incarnation, avatar.

exhibit, specimen, sample 83n. *example;* piece of evidence, quotation, citation 466n. *evidence;* showpiece, collector's p., museum p., antique, curio; display, show, dress s., mannequin parade 445n. *spectacle;* scene 438n. *view;* showplace, showroom, showcase, show-card, bill, affiche, placard, billboard 528n. *advertisement;* sign 547n. *label;* shop-window, front w., museum, gallery 632n. *collection;* exhibition, exposition, fair 796n. *mart;* projection 551n. *image.*

exhibitor, advertiser, publicist 528n. *publicizer;* shower, displayer, demonstrator; showman, pageant-maker; producer, impresario 594n. *stage manager;* exhibitionist, peacock 873n. *vain person;* wearer, sporter, flaunter.

Adj. *manifest,* apparent, ostensible 445adj. *appearing;* plain, clear, defined 80adj. *definite;* explained, plain as a pike-staff, clear as noonday 516 adj. *intelligible;* unconcealed, showing 443adj. *visible;* conspicuous, noticeable, notable, prominent, pronounced, striking, salient, in relief, in the foreground, in the limelight 443adj. *well-seen;* open, patent, evident, obvious; gross, crass, palpable; self-evident, autoptical, written all over one, for all to see, unmistakable, recognizable, identifiable, uncontestable 473adj. *certain;* public, famous, notorious 528adj. *well-known;* catching the eye, eye-catching 875adj. *showy;* arrant, glaring, stark-staring, flagrant, loud, on the rooftops.

undisguised, unshaded; spoken, overt, explicit, express, emphatic 532adj. *affirmative;* in the open, public; exoteric; unreserved, open, candid, heart-to-heart, off the record 540adj. *veracious;* frank, downright, forthright, straightforward, outspoken, blunt, plain-spoken 573adj. *plain;* bold, daring 711adj. *defiant;* brazen, shameless, immodest, barefaced 951 adj. *impure;* bare, naked, naked and unashamed 229adj. *uncovered;* flaunting, unconcealed, inconcealable (**see** *manifest*).

shown, manifested etc. vb.; declared, divulged 526adj. *disclosed;* showing, featured, on show, on display, on 443 adj. *visible;* exhibited, shown off; brought forth, produced; adduced, cited, quoted; confronted, brought face to face; worn, sported; unfurled, flaunted, waved, brandished; advertised, publicized 528adj. *published;* expressible, producible, showable.

Vb. *manifest,* reveal, divulge 526vb. *disclose;* evince, give sign, give token, show signs of 466vb. *evidence;* bring to light 484vb. *discover;* explain, make plain, make obvious 520vb. *interpret;* expose, lay bare, unroll, unfurl, unsheathe 229vb. *uncover;* open up, throw open, lay o. 263vb. *open;* elicit, draw forth, drag out 304vb. *extract;* invent, bring forth 164 vb. *produce;* bring out, shadow forth, body f.; incorporate, incarnate, personify 223vb. *externalize;* typify, symbolize, exemplify 547vb. *indicate;* point up, enhance, develop 36vb. *augment;* throw light on, enlighten 420vb. *illuminate;* highlight, spotlight, set in strong relief 532vb. *emphasize;* express, formulate 532vb. *affirm;* bring, bring up, adduce, cite, quote; bring to the fore, place in the foreground 638vb. *make important;* bring to notice, trot out, proclaim, publicize 528vb. *publish;* show for what it is, show up (**see** *show*); solve, elucidate 520vb. *decipher.*

show, make a spectacle, exhibit, display; set out, expose to view, offer to the v., set before one's eyes, dangle; wave, flourish 317vb. *brandish;* sport 228vb. *wear;* flaunt, parade 875vb. *be ostentatious;* make a show of, affect 850vb. *be affected;* present, feature, enact 551vb. *represent;* put on, put on show, stage, release 594vb. *dramatize;* show off, set o., model (garments); put one through his paces; demonstrate 534 vb. *teach;* show round, show over, point out, draw attention, bring to notice 547vb. *indicate;* confront, bring face to face; reflect, image, mirror, hold up the mirror to 20vb. *imitate;* tear off the mask, show up, expose 526 vb. *disclose.*

be plain,—explicit etc. adj.; show one's face, unveil 229vb. *doff;* show one's true colors, fly one's flag, have no secrets, make no mystery, wear one's heart on one's sleeve; show one's mind, speak out, tell to one's face, make no secret of 573vb. *speak plainly;* speak for itself, tell its own story 516vb. *be intelligible;* be obvious, stand to reason, go without saying 478vb. *be proved;* be conspicuous, stand out, stand out a mile 443vb. *be visible;* show up, show up well, hold the stage, hold the limelight, stand in full view 455vb. *attract notice;* loom large, stare one in the face 200vb. *be near;* appear on the horizon, rear its head, transpire, emanate, come to light 445vb. *appear.*

Adv. *manifestly,* plainly, obviously, palpably, grossly, crassly, openly, publicly, for all to see, notoriously, flagrantly, undisguisedly; at first blush, prima facie; externally, on the face of it, superficially; open and above-board, with cards on the table; before all, in public, in open court, under the eye of heaven; in full view, on the stage.

See: 20, 36, 80, 83, 164, 200, 223, 228, 229, 263, 304, 317, 420, 438, 443, 445, 455, 462, 466, 473, 478, 484, 516, 520, 526, 528, 532, 534, 540, 547, 551, 573, 594, 632, 638, 711, 796, 850, 873, 875, 951, 965, 984.

523 Latency

N. *latency,* no signs of, delitescence 525n. *concealment;* insidiousness, treachery 930n. *perfidy;* dormancy, dormant condition, potentiality 469n. *possibility;* esoterism, esotericism, cabala 984n. *occultism;* occultness, mysticism; hidden meaning, occult m., veiled m. 517n. *unintelligibility;* ambiguous advice 511n. *oracle;* symbolism, allegory, anagoge 519n. *metaphor;* implication, adumbration, symbolization; mystery 530n. *secret;* penetralia 224n. *interiority;* dark 418 n. *darkness;* shadowiness 419n. *dimness;* imperceptibility 444n. *invisibility;* more than meets the eye; deceptive appearance, hidden fires, hidden depths; slumbering volcano, sleeping lion 661n. *danger;* dark horse, mystery man, anonymity 562n. *no name;* nigger in the woodpile, snake in the grass 663n. *pitfall;* hidden hand, wire-puller, strings, friend at court, power behind the throne 178n. *influence;* secret influence, lurking disease; unsoundness, something rotten; innuendo, insinuation, suggestion 524n. *hint;* half-spoken word, inexpression, sealed lips 582n. *taciturnity;* undercurrent, undertone, undersong, aside 401n. *faintness;* clandestinity, secret society, cabal, intrigue 623n. *plot;* ambushment 527 n. *ambush;* code, invisible writing, steganography, cryptography.

Adj. *latent,* lurking, skulking, delitescent 525adj. *concealed;* dormant, sleeping 679adj. *inactive;* passive 266 adj. *quiescent;* potential, undeveloped 469adj. *possible;* unguessed, unsuspected, crypto- 491adj. *unknown;* submerged, underlying, subterranean, below the surface 211adj. *deep;* in the background, behind the scenes, backroom, undercover 421adj. *screened;* unmanifested, unseen, unspied, undetected, unexposed 444adj. *invisible;* arcane, obscure 418adj. *dark;* impenetrable, undiscoverable 517adj. *unintelligible;* tucked away, sequestered 883adj. *secluded;* awaiting discovery, undiscovered, unexplored, untracked, untraced, uninvented, unexplained, unsolved.

tacit, unsaid, unspoken, half-spoken, unpronounced, unexpressed, unvoiced, unbreathed; unmentioned, untold of, unsung; undivulged, unproclaimed, undeclared; unwritten, unpublished, unedited; understood, implied, implicit; implicational, suggestive; inferential, allusive, allusory.

occult, mysterious, mystic; symbolic, allegorical, anagogical 519adj. *figurative;* cryptic, esoteric 984adj. *cabalistic;* veiled, muffled, covert; indirect, crooked 220adj. *oblique;* clandestine, secret; insidious, treacherous 930adj. *perfidious;* underhand 525adj. *stealthy;* undiscovered, hush-hush, top-secret; not public, off the record 80adj. *private;* coded, steganographic, cryptographic 525vb. *disguised.*

Vb. *lurk*, hide, be latent, be a stowaway; burrow, stay underground; lie hid, lie in ambush; lie low, lie low and say nothing, lie doggo, make no sign 266vb. *be quiescent;* avoid notice, escape observation 444vb. *be unseen;* evade detection, escape recognition, act behind the scenes, pull the wires, laugh in one's sleeve; creep, slink, tiptoe, walk on tiptoe 525vb. *be stealthy;* underlie, be at the bottom of 156vb. *cause;* smoke, smolder 175vb. *be inert;* leave one's sting behind.

imply, insinuate, whisper, murmur, suggest 524vb. *hint;* understand, infer, leave an inference, allude, be allusive; symbolize, connote, carry a suggestion, involve, spell 514vb. *mean.*

See: 80, 156, 175, 178, 211, 220, 224, 266, 401, 418, 419, 421, 444, 469, 491, 511, 514, 517, 519, 524, 525, 527, 530, 562, 582, 623, 661, 663, 883, 930, 984.

524 Information

N. *information*, communication of knowledge, transmission of k., dissemination, diffusion; mailing list, distribution l. 588n. *correspondence;* chain of authorities, tradition, hearsay; enlightenment, instruction, briefing 534n. *teaching;* thought-transference, intercommunication 531 n. *telecommunication;* sharing of information, communication; telling, narration 590n. *narrative;* notification, announcement, annunciation, intimation, warning, advice, notice, mention, tip, tip-off (**see** *hint*); advertisement 528n. *publicity;* common knowledge, general information, gen; factual information, facts, the goods, documentary 494n. *truth;* inside information, dope, lowdown, private source, confidence 530n. *secret;* earliest information, scoop; stock of information, acquaintance, the know 490n. *knowledge;* recorded information, file, dossier 548n. *record;* piece of information, word, report, intelligence 529n. *news;* a communication, wire, telegram, cable, cablegram, radiogram 529n. *message;* flood of information, spate of news, outpouring; communicativeness, talking 581 n. *loquacity;* unauthorized communication, indiscretion.

report, information called for 459n. *inquiry;* paper, command p., white paper; account, true a., narrative report 590n. *narrative;* statement, state, return 86n. *statistics;* specification, estimates 480n. *estimate;* progress report, confidential r.; information offered, dispatch, bulletin, communiqué, hand-out 529n. *news;* representation, presentation (of one's case), case; memorial, petition 761n. *entreaty;* remonstrance, round-robin 762n. *deprecation;* letters, dispatches 588n. *correspondence.*

hint, gentle h., whisper, aside, subaudition, subauditur 401n. *faintness;* indirect hint, intimation; broad hint, signal, nod, wink, look, nudge, kick, by-play, gesticulation 547n. *gesture;* prompt, cue 505n. *reminder;* suggestion, lead, leading question 547n. *indication;* caution, monition 664n. *warning;* something to go on, tip, tip-off (**see** information); word, passing w., word in the ear, word to the wise, verb. sap. 691n. *advice;* insinuation, innuendo 926n. *calumny;* clue, symptom 520n. *interpretation;* sidelight, glimpse, inkling, adumbration 419n. *glimmer;* suspicion, inference, guess 512n. *conjecture;* good tip, wheeze, dodge, wrinkle 623n. *contrivance.*

informant, teller 590n. *narrator;* spokesman 579n. *speaker;* mouthpiece, representative 754n. *delegate;* announcer, radio a., notifier, advertiser, annunciator 528n. *publicizer;* harbinger, herald 531n. *messenger;* testifier 466n. *witness;* one in the know, authority, source; quarter, channel, circle, grape-vine; go-between, contact 231n. *intermediary;* informed circles, information center; communicator, intelligencer, correspondent, special c., reporter, newshound, commentator, columnist, gossip writer 529n. *newsmonger;* tipper, tipster 691n. *adviser;* guide, topographer; blurter, "big mouth."

informer, common i., delator 928n. *accuser;* spy, snoop, sleuth 459n. *detective;* stool-pigeon, nark, copper's n., snitch, fink, blabber, squealer, squeaker, peacher; approver 603n. *tergiversator;* peek, eavesdropper, tell-tale, tale-bearer, tattler, tattle-tale, gossip 529n. *newsmonger.*

guide-book, travelogue, topography; Baedeker, Murray; handbook, manual, vade mecum; timetable, Bradshaw, A.B.C.; itinerary, route map, chart, plan 551n. *map;* gazetteer; nautical almanac, ephemeris; catalog 87n. *directory;* cicerone, courier 520 n. *guide.*

Adj. *informative*, communicative, newsy, chatty, gossipy; informatory, informational, instructive, instructional, documentary 534adj. *educational;* expressive 532adj. *affirmative;* expository 520adj. *interpretive;* in writing 586adj. *written;* oral, verbal, spoken, nuncupatory, nuncupative 579adj. *speaking;* annunciatory 528 adj. *publishing;* advisory 691adj. *advising;* monitory 664adj. *cautionary;* explicit, clear 80adj. *definite;* candid, plain-spoken 573adj. *plain;* over-communicative, talking, indiscreet 581adj. *loquacious;* hinting, insinuating, suggesting.

informed, well-i., kept i.; posted, primed, briefed, instructed 490adj. *knowing;* told, certified, au courant, in the know, in on, in the picture.

Vb. *inform*, certify, advise, beg to a.; intimate, impart, convey (**see** *communicate*); apprise, acquaint, have one know, give to understand; possess, possess one with the facts, brief, instruct 534vb. *teach;* let one know, put one in the picture; enlighten, open the mind, fill with information 534vb. *educate;* point out, direct one's attention 547vb. *indicate;* insinuate (**see** *hint*); entrust with information, confide, get confidential, mention privately; put one wise, put right, correct, disabuse, unbeguile, undeceive, disillusion; be specific, state, name, signify 80vb. *specify;* mention, refer to, touch on, speak of 579vb. *speak;* gossip, spread rumors; be indiscreet, open one's mouth, blurt out, talk 581vb. *be loquacious;* break the news, reveal 526vb. *disclose;* tell, blab, split, peach, squeal, blow the gaff 526vb. *confess;* rat, turn Queen's evidence, turn State's e., involve an accomplice 603vb. *tergiversate;* tell tales, tell on, report against; inform against, lay an information, delate, denounce 928vb. *accuse.*

communicate, transmit, pass on, pass on information; dispatch news 588 vb. *correspond;* report, cover, make a report, submit a r.; report progress, post, keep posted; get through, get across, put it over; contact, get in touch; convey, bring word, send w., leave w., write 588vb. *correspond;* flash news, flash; send a message, speak, semaphore 547vb. *signal;* wire, telegraph, telephone, ring, ring up, call, dial; disseminate, broadcast, telecast, televise; announce, annunciate, notify, give notice, serve n. 528vb. *advertise;* give out, put out, carry a report, publicize 528vb. *publish;* retail, recount, narrate 590vb. *describe;* commune 584vb. *converse;* swap news, exchange information, pool one's knowledge.

hint, drop a h., adumbrate, suggest, throw out a suggestion, put in one's head; prompt, give the cue 505vb. *remind;* caution 664vb. *warn;* tip off 691vb. *advise;* wink, tip the wink; nudge 547vb. *gesticulate;* insinuate, breathe, whisper, say in one's ear, touch upon, just mention, mention in passing, say by the way, let fall, imply, allude, leave an inference, leave one to gather, intimate.

be informed, have the facts 490vb. *know;* be told, receive information, have it from; keep one's ears open, get to hear of, use one's ears, overhear 415vb. *hear;* get wind of, get scent of 484vb. *discover;* gather, infer, realize 516vb. *understand;* come to know, get a report, get the facts 536vb. *learn;* open one's eyes, awaken to, become alive to 455vb. *be attentive;* ask for information, call for a report 459vb. *inquire;* have information, have the dope, have something to tell; claim to know 532vb. *affirm.*

Adv. *reportedly*, as stated, on information received, by report; in the air, according to rumor, from what one can gather, if one can trust one's ears.

See: 80, 86, 87, 231, 401, 415, 419, 455, 459, 466, 480, 484, 490, 494, 505, 512, 516, 520, 526, 528, 529, 530, 531, 532, 534, 536, 547, 548, 573, 579, 581, 584, 586, 588, 590, 603, 623, 664, 691, 754, 761, 762, 926, 928.

525 Concealment

N. *concealment*, confinement, purdah 883n. *seclusion;* hiding, latitancy 523n. *latency;* covering up, burial 364n. *internment;* occultation 446n. *disappearance;* cache 527n. *hiding-place;* crypt 364n. *tomb;* disguisement, disguise, camouflage 542n. *deception;* masquerade, bal masqué; anonymity, incognito 562n. *no name;* smoke-screen 421n. *screen;* reticence, reserve, closeness, discretion, no word of 582n. *taciturnity;* secret thought, mental reservation, arrière pensée; lack of candor, vagueness, evasion, evasiveness 518n. *equivocalness;* mystification 421n. obfuscation; misinformation 535n. *misteaching;* white lie 543n. *mental dishonesty;* subterfuge 542n. *trickery;* suppression, suppression of the truth 543n. *untruth;* deceitfulness, dissimulation, obreption 541n. *duplicity.*

secrecy, close s. 399n. *silence;* secretness, mystery 530n. *secret;* seal of secrecy, hearing in camera, auricular confession; freemasonry; clandestinity, secretiveness, furtiveness, stealthiness, clandestine behavior; underhand dealing 930n. *improbity;* conspiracy 623n. *plot;* crvptography, steganography, cipher, code 517n. *unintelligibility;* invisible ink, sympathetic i.

Adj. *concealed,* crypto-, hidden; hiding, lost, perdu; esconced, in ambush, lying in wait 523adj. *latent;* confined, incommunicado 747adj. *imprisoned;* mysterious, recondite, arcane 517adj. *unintelligible;* cryptic 523adj. *occult;* private 883adj. *secluded;* privy, confidential, off the record; auricular, secret, top-secret, hush-hush, inviolable, inviolate, unrevealed, irrevealable; undisclosed, untold; unsigned, unnamed 562adj. *anonymous;* covert, covered 364adj. *buried;* hooded, veiled, eclipsed 421 adj. *screened;* stifled, suppressed, clandestine, undercover, underground, subterranean 211adj. *deep.*

disguised, camouflaged; incognito 562 adj. *anonymous;* unrecognized, unrecognizable 491adj. *unknown;* disfigured, deformed 246adj. *distorted;* masked 421adj. *screened;* overpainted 226adj. *covered;* blotted 550adj. *obliterated;* coded, codified, cryptographic, steganographic 517 adj. *unintelligible.*

stealthy, silent, furtive, like a thief; softly treading, feline, catlike, pussyfoot, on tiptoe; prowling, skulking, loitering, lurking; clandestine, hugger-mugger, conspiratorial, cloak-and-dagger; hole-and-corner, backdoor, underhand, surreptitious, obreptitious 930adj. *dishonest.*

reticent, reserved, withdrawn; noncommittal, incommunicative, cagey, evasive; vague, studiously v.; not talking, discreet, silent 582adj. *taciturn;* tight-lipped, poker-faced; close, secretive, buttoned up, close as wax, close as an oyster, clamlike; in one's shell 883adj. *unsociable.*

Vb. *conceal,* hide, hide away, secrete, ensconce, confine, keep in purdah 883vb. *seclude;* stow away, lock up, seal up, bottle up 632vb. *store;* hide underground, bury 364vb. *inter;* put out of sight, sweep under the mat, cover up 226vb. *cover;* varnish, gloss over 226vb. *overlay;* overpaint, blot 550vb. *obliterate;* slur, slur over, not mention 458vb. *disregard;* smother, stifle 165vb. *suppress;* veil, muffle, mask, disguise, camouflage; shroud, becurtain, draw the curtain 421vb. *screen;* shade, obscure, eclipse 418vb. *darken;* befog, becloud, obfuscate 419vb. *bedim;* hide one's identity, assume a mask, masquerade 541vb. *dissemble;* code, encode, use a cipher 517vb. *be unintelligible.*

keep secret, keep it dark, keep snug, keep close, keep under one's hat; look blank, look poker-faced, keep a straight face, be mum, keep one's mouth shut, hold one's tongue, breathe not a word, not utter a syllable, not talk, keep one's counsel, make no sign 582vb. *be taciturn;* be discreet, neither confirm nor deny; keep back, reserve, withhold, let it go no further; hush up, cover up, suppress, sink; keep in the background, keep in the shade; let not one's right hand know what one's left hand does; blindfold, bamboozle, keep in the dark 542vb. *deceive.*

be stealthy, —furtive, —evasive etc. adj.; hugger-mugger, conspire 623vb. *plot;* snoop, sneak, slink, creep; steal along, steal by, steal past; tiptoe, go on t., pussyfoot; prowl, skulk, loiter; be anonymous, stay incognito; wear a mask, assume a disguise 541vb. *dissemble;* lie doggo 523vb. *lurk;* evade, shun, hide from, dodge 620 vb. *avoid;* play hide-and-seek, play bo-peep, hide in holes and corners; leave no address, cover one's tracks, take cover; vanish 446vb. *disappear;* hide from the light, retire from sight, withdraw into seclusion, bury oneself, stay in one's shell 883vb. *be unsocial;* lay an ambush 527vb. *ambush.*

Adv. *secretly,* hugger-mugger, conspiratorially; confidentially, sotto voce, with bated breath; entre nous, between ourselves; aside, to oneself, in petto; in one's sleeve; sub rosa, without beat of drum; not for publication, privately, in camera; behind closed doors, anonymously, incognito, with nobody the wiser.

stealthily, furtively, by stealth, like a thief in the night; in the dark 444 adv. *invisibly;* underhand, by the back-door, in a hole-and-corner way; on the sly, by subterfuge.

See: 165, 211, 226, 246, 364, 399, 418, 419, 421, 444, 446, 458, 491, 517, 518, 523, 527, 530, 535, 541, 542, 543, 550, 562, 582, 585, 620,

623, 632, 747, 883, 930.

526 Disclosure

N. *disclosure,* revealment, revelation. apocalypse; daylight, hard d.; discovery, uncovering; unwelcome discovery, disillusionment 509n. *disappointment;* denouement, catastrophe, peripeteia 154n. *eventuality;* lid off, divulgement, divulgence 528n. *publication;* exposure, showing up 522n. *manifestation;* explanations, clearing the air, showdown; communication leak, indiscretion; bewrayment, betrayal, give-away; cloven hoof, tell-tale sign, blush, self-betrayal; State's evidence, Queen's e. 603n. *tergiversation;* acknowledgment, admission, avowal, confession; auricular confession, confessional 939n. *penitence;* clean breast, whole truth, cards on the table 494n. *truth.*

Adj. *disclosed,* exposed, revealed 522adj. *shown;* showing 443adj. *visible;* confessed, avowed, acknowledged; with the lid off 263adj. *open;* divested 229adj. *uncovered.*

disclosing, uncovering, unclosing, opening; revelatory, apocalyptic, manifesting; revealing 422adj. *transparent;* expository, explicatory, explanatory 520adj. *interpretive;* divulgatory 528adj. *publishing;* communicative 524adj. *informative;* leaky, indiscreet, garrulous 581adj. *loquacious;* tell-tale, indicative 547 adj. *indicating;* bewraying, betraying; confessing, confessional, penitent 939adj. *repentant.*

Vb. *disclose,* reveal, expose, show up 522vb. *manifest;* bare, lay b., strip b., denude 229vb. *doff;* unfold, unroll, unfurl, unpack, unwrap 229vb. *uncover;* unshroud, unscreen, uncurtain, unveil, lift the veil, draw the v., raise the curtain, let in daylight; unseal, break the seal, break the wax, unclose 263vb. *open;* lay open, open up 484vb. *discover;* catch out 484vb. *detect;* bewray, not hide 422vb. *be transparent;* give away, betray; uncloak, unmask, tear off the mask; expose onself, betray o., give oneself away 495vb. *blunder;* declare oneself, lift the mask, drop the m., throw off the m., throw off all disguise; show for what it is, cut down to life size, debunk; disabuse, correct, set right, undeceive, unbeguile, disillusion, open the eyes 524vb. *inform;* take the lid off, unkennel, let the cat out of the bag (**see** divulge).

divulge, be open about, declare, vent, ventilate, air, canvass, publicize 528 vb. *publish;* let on, blurt out, blow the gaff, talk out of turn, spill the beans, let the cat out of the bag; speak of, talk, must tell; utter, breathe 579vb. *speak;* let out, leak 524vb. *communicate;* let drop, let fall 524vb. *hint;* come out with 573vb. *speak plainly;* get it off one's chest, unbosom oneself; confide, let one into the secret, open one's mind, bare one's m.; declare one's intentions, show one's hand, show one's cards, put one's cards on the table; report, tell, tell tales out of school, tell on 928vb. *accuse;* betray the secret, split, peach, squeal, blab 524vb. *inform;* rat 603vb. *tergiversate.*

confess, admit, avow, acknowledge; concede, grant, allow, own 488vb. *assent;* own up, implicate oneself, plead guilty, admit the soft impeachment; come out with, come across with, come clean, tell all, admit everything, speak the truth 540vb. *be truthful;* make a clean breast, unburden one's conscience, go to confession, recount one's sins, be shriven 939vb. *be penitent;* turn State's evidence 603vb. *tergiversate.*

be disclosed, come out, blow up 445 vb. *appear;* come out in evidence, come to light 478vb. *be proved;* show the cloven hoof, show its face, show its colors, stand revealed 522 vb. *be plain;* transpire, become known 490vb. *be known;* leak out, ooze o., creep o. 298vb. *emerge;* peep out, show 443vb. *be visible;* show through 422vb. *be transparent;* come as a revelation, break through the clouds, flash on the mind 449vb. *dawn upon;* give oneself away, there speaks . . . .

See: 154, 229, 263, 298, 422, 443, 445, 449, 478, 484, 488, 490, 494, 495, 509, 520, 522, 524, 528, 540, 547, 573, 579, 581, 603, 928, 939.

527 Hiding. Disguise

N. *hiding-place,* hide, hide-out, hole, hidey-h., funk-h. 662n. *refuge;* lair, den 192n. *retreat;* cache, secret place, abditory, oubliette; crypt, vault 194n. *cellar;* closet, secret drawer, hidden panel, safe place, safe, safe deposit 632n. *storage;* recess, corner, nook, cranny, niche, holes and corners, secret passage, underground p.; cover, underground

662n. *shelter;* backstairs, backroom, adytum, penetralia, inmost recesses 224n. *interiority.*

ambush, ambuscade, ambushment 525n. *concealment;* lurking-place, spider's web 542n. *trap;* catch 663 n. *pitfall;* stalking horse, Trojan h., decoy, stool-pigeon 545n. *imposter;* agent provocateur 633n. *trouble-maker.*

disguise, blind, camouflage, protective coloring 542n. *deception;* dummy, lath painted to look like iron 20n. *imitation;* veneer 226n. *covering;* mask, visor, veil 228n. *cloak;* domino, masquerade dress, fancy d.; cloud, smoke-screen, cover 421n. *screen.*

hider, lurker, skulker, stowaway, nigger in the woodpile; dodger 620n. *avoider;* masker, masquerader; wolf in sheep's clothing 545n. *impostor.*

Vb. *ambush*, set an a., lie in a., lie in wait 523vb. *lurk;* set a trap for 542vb. *ensnare;* assume a disguise, wear a mask; throw out a smoke-screen, obfuscate; waylay.

See: 20, 192, 194, 224, 226, 228, 421, 523, 525, 542, 545, 620, 632, 662, 663.

528 Publication

N. *publication,* spreading abroad, dissemination, divulgation 526n. *disclosure;* promulgation, proclamation; edict, ukase, ban 737vb. *decree;* arrière-ban; call-up, summons; cry, rallying c., call, bugle-c., trumpet-c. 547n. *call;* tucket, sennet, flourish, beat of drum, flourish of trumpets 400n. *loudness;* notification, public notice, official bulletin; announcement, pronouncement, pronunciamento, manifesto, program, platform; publishing, book-trade, bookselling 589n. *book;* broadcasting 531n. *telecommunication;* broadcast, telecast, newscast 529n. *news;* kite-flying 529n. *rumor;* circulation, circular, encyclical.

publicity, publicness, common knowledge 490n. *knowledge;* open discussion, ventilation, canvassing, canvass; openness, flagrancy, blatancy 522n. *manifestation;* cry, open secret, open scandal; notoriety, fame 866n. *famousness;* currency, wide c.; circulation, wide c., country-wide c.; sale, extensive sales; readership, viewership; public relations, propaganda; display, showmanship, salesmanship, window-dressing 875n. *ostentation;* sensationalism, ballyhoo 546n. *exaggeration;* publicization, advertising, press a., radio a., sky-writing; medium of publicity, radio 531n. *telecommunication;* public-address system, loud speaker, loud hailer 415n. *hearing aid;* public comment, journalism, reporting, rapportage, coverage, report, write-up (**see** *the press*); newsreel, newscast, newsletter 529n. *news;* correspondence column, open letter; editorial 591n. *article;* pulpit, platform, hustings, soap-box 539n. *rostrum;* printing press 587n. *print;* letters of fire, letters of gold.

advertisement, public notice, press n., gazette, insertion, ad, small a., want ad, personal column; agony c.; headline, banner, streamer, screamer, spread; puff, blurb, boost, ballyhoo, build-up, limelight, spotlight; bill, affiche, poster, show-card 522n. *exhibit;* billboard, hoarding, placard, sandwich board, display b., notice b., bulletin b.

the press, fourth estate, Fleet Street, newspaper world, news business, the papers; newspaper, newssheet, sheet, paper, rag, tabloid, comic strip; serious press, gutter p., yellow p., tabloid p.; organ, journal, daily paper, daily, morning paper, evening p., Sunday p., illustrated p., picture p.; issue, edition, late e., stop-press e., sports e., extra; magazine section, serial, supplement, trade s.; leaflet, handbill, pamphlet, brochure, broadsheet, squib, open letter, newsletter.

journal, review, magazine, periodical, daily, weekly, monthly, quarterly, half-yearly, annual; gazette, trade organ, house o., trade publication 589n. *reading matter.*

publicizer, canvasser, advertiser, notifier, announcer; herald, trumpet 531 n. *messenger;* proclaimer, crier, town-crier, bellman; barker, booster; bill-sticker, sandwich man; publicist, printer, publisher 589n. *bookman;* reporter, correspondent, gentleman of the press, press representative, cub, newshound, pressman, journalist 589n. *author;* copy-writer, blurb-w., commercial artist, publicity agent, press a., advertising a.; public relations officer, PRO, propagandist, pamphleteer 537n. *preacher.*

Adj. *published,* in print 587adj. *printed;* in circulation, circulating, passing round, current; in the news, public 490adj. *known;* open, exoteric; distributed, circularized, dis-

seminated, broadcast; ventilated, canvassed.
publishing, promulgatory, declaratory, notificatory, annunciative.
well-known, public, celebrated, famous, notorious, crying, flagrant, blatant, glaring, sensational 522adj. *manifest.*
Vb. *publish*, make public, carry a report 524vb. *communicate;* report, cover, write up; write an open letter, drag into the limelight, bring into the open, reveal 526vb. *divulge;* highlight, spotlight 532vb. *emphasize;* radio, broadcast, telecast, televise, relay, diffuse 524vb. *inform;* spread, circulate, distribute, disseminate, circularize; canvass, ventilate, discuss 475vb. *argue;* pamphleteer, propagate 534vb. *teach;* use the press 587vb. *print;* serialize, edit, issue, get out, put o., give o., send forth, give to the world, lay before the public; spread a rumor, fly a kite; rumor, make news of, bruit, noise abroad, spread a.; talk about, retail, pass round, put about, bandy a., hawk a., buzz a. 581vb. *be loquacious;* voice, broach, talk of, speak of, utter, emit 579vb. *speak.*
proclaim, announce, promulgate, notify, gazette; ban, denounce, raise a hue and cry 928vb. *accuse;* pronounce, declare 532vb. *affirm;* make a proclamation, issue a pronouncement, publish a manifesto; celebrate, noise, trumpet, blazon, herald, cry, shout, scream, thunder 400vb. *be loud;* declaim, shout from the housetops, proclaim at the crossroads, warn by beat of drum, announce with a flourish of trumpets, send round the town-crier.
advertise, publicize, canvass, insert a notice, bill, placard, post, stick up a notice, put on the billboards; tell the world, put on the map, put in headlines, headline, splash; put in lights, spotlight, build up; make much of, feature; sell, boost, puff, cry up, write up, glorify 482vb. *overrate;* din, din into one's ears, plug 106vb. *repeat.*
be published, become public, issue, come out; acquire notoriety, hit the headlines; circulate, pass current, pass from mouth to mouth, pass round, go the rounds, get about, spread abroad, spread like wildfire, fly about, buzz a.; find a publisher, see oneself in print, get printed, get into the papers; have a circulation, sell well, go like a best-seller 793vb. *be sold.*
Adv. *publicly*, openly, in open court, with open windows, with open doors; in the limelight.
See: 106, 400, 415, 475, 482, 490, 522, 524, 526, 529, 531, 532, 534, 537, 539, 546, 547, 579, 581, 587, 589, 591, 737, 793, 866, 875, 928.

529 News

N. *news*, good n.; bad news 509n. *disappointment;* tidings, glad t.; gospel, evangel 973n. *religion;* budget of news, packet of n., news-packet, dispatches, diplomatic bag; intelligence, report, dispatch, word, advice; piece of information, something to tell, tidbit, flash 524n. *information;* bulletin, communiqué, hand-out; newspaper report, press notice; fresh news, stirring n., latest n., stop-press n.; sensation, scoop; old news, stale n.; copy, filler; yarn, story, old s., tall s.; broadcast, telecast, newscast, newsreel 528n. *publicity;* news value.
rumor, unverified news, unconfirmed report; flying rumor, fame; hearsay, gossip, gup, talk, talk of the town, tittle-tattle 584n. *chat;* scandal 926n. *calumny;* noise, cry, buzz, bruit; false report, hoax, canard; grapevine; kite-flying.
message, oral m., word of mouth, word, advice, tip 524n. *information;* communication 547n. *signal;* marconigram, wireless message, radiogram, cablegram, cable, telegram, wire, lettergram 531n. *telecommunication;* letter, postcard, letters, dispatches 588n. *correspondence;* ring, phone-call; errand, embassy 751n. *commission.*
newsmonger, quidnunc, gossip, talker 584n. *interlocutor;* tattler, chatterer; scandalmonger 926n. *defamer;* retailer of news, newspeddler; newsman, newshound, news reporter, reporter, sob-sister, special correspondent 589n. *author;* newsboy, news agent, newsvendor.
Adj. *rumored*, talked about, in the news, in the papers; reported, currently r., going about, passing round; rife, afloat, in circulation, in everyone's mouth, on all tongues; full of news, newsy, gossipy, chatty 524adj. *informative.*
Vb. *rumor*, fly a kite; send or dispatch news 588vb. correspond. **See** 524vb. *inform*, 526vb. *disclose*, 528 vb. *publish.*

See: 509, 524, 526, 528, 531, 547, 588, 589, 751, 926, 973.

530 Secret

N. *secret,* dead s., profound s.; secret lore, esotery, esoterism, arcanum, mystery 984n. *occultism;* confidential matter, sealed orders, hush-hush subject, top-secret file; confidential communication, confidence; sphinx, man of mystery, enigmatic personality; Mr. X. 562n. *no name;* dark horse, unknown quantity; unmentionable thing, skeleton in the cupboard; unknown country, terra incognita 491n. *unknown thing;* sealed book, secrets of the prison house.

enigma, mystery, puzzle, Chinese p.; problem, hyperproblem, poser, brain-twister, teaser; hard nut to crack, hard saying, knotty point, vexed question, crux, crux criticorum 700n. *difficulty;* cipher, code, cryptogram, hieroglyphics 517n. *unintelligibility;* word-puzzle, logogriph, anagram, acrostic, crossword; riddle, riddle-me-ree, conundrum, rebus; charade, dumb c.; intricacy, labyrinth, maze, labyrinthine m., Hyrcanian wood 61n. *complexity.*

See: 61, 491, 517, 562, 700, 984.

531 Messenger

N. *messenger,* forerunner 66n. *precursor;* harbinger 511n. *omen;* message-bearer (**see** *courier*); announcer, crier, town-crier, bellman 528n. *publicizer;* ambassador, minister, nuncio, legate, spokesman 754n. *envoy;* apostle, emissary; flag-bearer, parlementaire, herald, trumpet; pursuivant, summoner, process-server 955n. *law-officer;* go-between, contact, contact-man 231n. *intermediary.*

courier, runner, King's messenger, express m., express, dispatch-bearer, dispatch-rider, estafette, mounted courier; postboy, telegraph boy, messenger b., errand b., office-b., corridor girl; call-boy, bell-hop, page, buttons, commissionaire; harkara, peon, chaprassi; carrier pigeon 273n. *carrier;* Iris, Hermes, Mercury, Ariel.

mails, letters 588n. *correspondence;* mail, post, pigeon-p.; surface mail, sea-m., air-m.; mail-train, mail-coach, mail car, mail boat, mail packet, mail plane; mail service, delivery, postal d., special d.; sorter, postman, mailman, dakwallah, letter-carrier; postmaster, postmistress, postmaster general; post office, mail o., GPO, poste restante; postbox, letter box, pillar b.; mailbag, letter-bag, diplomatic bag.

telecommunication, long-distance communication; cable, cablegram, telegram, wire 529n. *message;* signaling, flag-s., semaphore, smoke-signal, beacon, beacon fire 547n. *signal;* wireless, wireless communication, radio c., radio, sound r., television; radio signal, Morse, Morse code; pip; telephone, radio t., walkie-talkie, telegraph, grape-vine t., radio t.; teleprinter; transmitter, radio mast, aerial, antenna; telegraph wire, telegraph pole; receiver, earphone, headphone; microphone, mike, loud-speaker, loud hailer, public-address system; broadcasting, broadcast, simulcast, relay; broadcaster, radio announcer; listener-in; televiewer looker-in.

See: 66, 231, 273, 511, 528, 529, 547, 588, 754, 955.

532 Affirmation

N. *affirmation,* affirmance; proposition, subject and predicate; saying, dictum 496n. *maxim;* predication, statement, truth-claim 512n. *supposition;* sentence, expressed opinion, conclusion 480n. *judgment;* voice, choice, suffrage, ballot 605n. *vote;* expression, formulation; written statement, prepared text; one's position, one's stand; declaration, profession, jactitation; allegation 928n. *accusation;* assertion, unsupported a., ipse dixit, say-so; asseveration, averment, admission; confession, avowal 526n. *disclosure;* corroboration, confirmation, assurance, avouchment, one's word, warrant 466n. *testimony;* insistence, vehemence, peremptoriness 571n. *vigor;* stress, accent, accent on, emphasis, over-statement; palilogy 106n. *repetition;* challenge, provocation 711n. *defiance;* protest 762n. *deprecation;* appeal, representation, adjurement, adjuration 761n. *entreaty;* observation, remark, interjection 579n. *speech;* comment, criticism, positive c., constructive c. 480n. *estimate;* assertiveness, self-assertion, push, thrust, drive 174n. *vigorousness;* pontification, dogmatism 473n. *positiveness.*

oath, Bible o., oath-taking, oath-giving, adjurement, swearing, assertory oath, solemn affirmation, statement on oath, deposition, affidavit 466n. *testimony;* promissory oath, word of a gentleman, pledge, promise, warrant, guarantee 764n. *promise.*

Adj. affirmative, affirming, professing etc. vb.; not negative 473adj. *positive;* predicatory, predicative; declaratory, declarative 526adj. *disclosing;* pronunciative, enunciative 528adj. *publishing;* valid, in force, unretracted, unretractable 473adj. *undisputed;* committed, pledged, guaranteed, promised 764adj. *promissory;* earnest, meaning 617adj. *intending;* solemn, sworn, on oath, formal; affirmable, predictable.

assertive, assertorial, saying, telling; assured, dogmatic, confident, self-assured 473adj. *positive;* pushing, thrustful, trenchant, incisive, pointed, decisive, decided 571adj. *forceful;* distinct 80adj. *definite;* express, peremptory, categorical, absolute, brooking no denial, emphatic, insistent; vehement, thundering 176 adj. *violent;* making no bones, flat, broad, round, blunt, strong, outspoken, strongly worded 573adj. *plain;* pontificial, of faith, unquestionable, ex cathedra 485adj. *credal;* challenging, provocative 711adj. *defiant.*

Vb. *affirm*, state, express, formulate, set down; declare, pronounce, enunciate 528vb. *proclaim;* give expression to, voice 579vb. *speak;* remark, comment, observe, say; state with conviction, be bound, dare be sworn 485vb. *opine;* mean what one says, vow, protest; make a statement, make an assertion, assert, predicate; maintain, stand for, hold, contend 475vb. *argue;* make one's point 478 vb. *demonstrate;* advance, urge 512 vb. *propound;* represent, put one's case, submit; appeal, adjure, claim 761vb. *request;* allege, pretend, asseverate, avouch, aver; bear witness 466vb. *testify;* certify, confirm, warrant, guarantee 466vb. *corroborate;* commit oneself, go as far as; pledge, engage 764vb. *promise;* hold out 759vb. *offer;* profess, avow; admit 526vb. *confess;* abide by, not retreat, not retract 599vb. *stand firm;* challenge 711vb. *defy;* repudiate 533vb. *negate;* speak up, speak out, say outright, assert roundly, put it bluntly, make no bones about 573vb. *speak plainly;* be assertive, brook no denial, shout, shout down; claim to know, say so, lay down, lay down the law, speak ex cathedra, pontificate 473vb. *dogmatize;* have one's say, have the last word.

swear, be sworn, swear an oath, take o., take one's Bible o.; attest, confirm by oath 466vb. *corroborate; swear,* be sworn, swear an oath, take cross one's heart, solemnly affirm, make solemn affirmation 466vb. *testify;* kiss the book, swear on the Bible, swear by all that is holy, take God's name in vain.

emphasize, stress, lay stress on, accent, accentuate, shout; underline, put in italics, italicize, dot the i's and cross the t's; raise one's voice, speak up, roar thunder, fulminate 400vb. *be loud;* bang *or* thump the table; be urgent, be instant, be earnest; insist, positively i. 737vb. *command;* say with emphasis, drive home, impress on, rub in; plug, dwell on, say again and again, reaffirm, reassert, labor 106vb. *repeat;* single out, highlight, enhance, point up 638vb. *make important;* urge, enforce.

Adv. *affirmatively*, positively, without fear of contradiction, ex cathedra; seriously, joking apart, in sober earnest; on oath, on the Bible; in all conscience, upon one's word, upon one's honor 543adv. *truly.*

See: 80, 106, 174, 176, 400, 466, 473, 475, 478, 480, 485, 496, 512, 526, 528, 533, 543, 571, 573, 579, 599, 605, 617, 638, 711, 737, 759, 761, 762, 764, 928.

533 Negation

N. *negation*, negative, nay; denial 760n. *refusal;* refusal of belief, disbelief 486n. *unbelief;* disagreement 489n. *dissent;* contrary assertion, rebuttal, appeal, cross-a. 460n. *rejoinder;* refutation, disproof 479n. *confutation;* emphatic denial, contradiction, flat c., gainsaying; the lie, lie direct, démenti; challenge 711n. *defiance;* demurrer 468n. *qualification;* protest 762n. *deprecation;* repudiation, disclaimer, disavowal, disownment, dissociation, non-association 607n. *rejection;* abnegation, renunciation 621n. *relinquishment;* retractation, palinode, abjuration, abjurement, swearing off 603n. *recantation;* negative attitude, non-corroboration, inability to confirm; refusal of consent, disallowance 757n. *prohibition;* recusancy 769n. *non-observance;* contravention 738n. *disobedience;* cancellation, invalidation, revocation 752n. *abrogation.*

Adj. *negative,* denying, negating, negatory; adversative, contradictory 14adj. *contrary;* contravening 738 adj. *disobedient;* protesting, protestant 762adj. *deprecatory;* recusant, non-juring 769adj. *non-observant;* abrogative, revocatory; abnegatory, renunciatory 753adj. *resigning;* denied, disowned, unfathered.

Vb. *negate,* negative; contravene 738 vb. *disobey;* deny, gainsay, give the lie to, belie, contradict, deny flatly, contradict absolutely, issue a démenti; deny the possibility, eat one's hat if 470vb. *make impossible;* disaffirm, repudiate, disavow, disclaim, disown, leave unfathered 607vb. *reject;* not confirm, refuse to corroborate; not maintain, hold no brief for 860vb. *be indifferent;* deny in part, demur, object 468vb. *qualify;* disagree 489vb. *dissent;* dissociate oneself 704vb. *oppose;* affirm the contrary, controvert, traverse, impugn, question, call in q., refute, rebut, disprove 479vb. *confute;* refuse credence 486vb. *disbelieve;* protest, appeal against 762vb. *deprecate;* challenge, stand up to 711vb. *defy;* thwart 702vb. *obstruct*; say no, shake one's head 760vb. *refuse;* disallow 757vb. *prohibit;* revoke, invalidate 752vb. *abrogate;* abnegate, renounce 621vb. *relinquish;* abjure, forswear, swear off 603vb. *recant;* go back on one's word 603vb. *tergiversate.*

Adv. *nay* 489adv. *no;* negatively.

Int. never! a thousand times no! nothing of the kind! quite the contrary!

See: 14, 460, 468, 470, 479, 486, 489, 603, 607, 621, 702, 704, 711, 738, 752, 753, 757, 760, 762, 769, 860.

534 Teaching

N. *teaching,* pedagogy, paedeutics, hypnopedagogics; private teaching, tutoring; education, schooling, upbringing; tutelage, leading strings; direction, guidance, instruction, edification; spoon-feeding; dictation; tuition, preparation, coaching, tutorial; initiation, introduction; training, discipline, drill, exercitation 682 n. *exercise;* inculcation, catechization, indoctrination, preaching, pulpitry, homiletics; proselytism, propagandism; persuasion, conversion, conviction; conditioning, brainwashing; pamphleteering, propaganda 528 n. *publicity;* Cominform; information center.

education, liberal arts, liberal education, classical e., scientific e., technical e., religious e., denominational e., secular e.; moral education, moral tuition, moral training; technical training, sloyd, technological training, vocational t.; coeducation, progressive e., Froebel e., Froebelism, kindergarten method, Montessori m.; monitorial system; elementary education, primary e., secondary e., university e., advanced e., advanced studies, postgraduate s.; physical education, gymnastics, physical jerks, calisthenics, eurythmics.

curriculum, course of study 536n. *learning*; course, preliminary c.; first lessons, propaedeutics, ABC, the three R's 68n. *beginning;* set books, prescribed text 589n. *textbook;* set task, exercise, homework, prep; trivium, grammar, rhetoric, logic; quadrivium, arithmetic, geometry, astronomy, music; Greats, Modern G. 459n. *exam;* correspondence course, course of lectures, university extension l., classes, evening c., night c., seminar.

lecture, reading, prelection, discourse, disquisition; sermon, preachment, homily, lesson, apologue, parable; discussion-play 594n. *stage play;* readership, lectureship, professorship, chair.

Adj. *educational*, pedagogic, paedeutic, tutorial; scholastic, scholarly, academic; instructional, informational; instructive 524adj. *informative;* educative, didactive, didactic, hortative; doctrinal, normative; edifying, moralizing, homiletic, preachy; primary, secondary etc. n.; cultural, humane, scientific.

Vb. *educate,* edify (**see** *teach*); breed, rear, nurse, nurture, bring up, develop, form, lick into shape; put to school, send to s., have taught; tutor, teach, school; ground, coach, cram, prime 669vb. *prepare;* guide 689vb. *direct;* instruct 524vb. *inform;* enlighten, illumine, enlarge the mind, open the m.; sharpen the wits, open the eyes; fill with new ideas, stuff with knowledge, cram with facts, impress on the memory; knock into the head, inculcate, indoctrinate, imbue, impregnate, infuse, instill, infix, implant, engraft, sow the seeds of; remove falsehood, disabuse, unteach; chasten, sober.

teach, be a teacher, profess, give lessons, teach class, hold classes; lecture, deliver lectures; tutor, impart instruction; dictate, read out; preach, harangue, sermonize; discourse, hold forth; moralize, point a moral; elucidate, expound 520vb. *interpret;* train the mind, indoctrinate, inoculate; pamphleteer, disseminate propaganda, propagandize, proselytize, condition, brainwash 178vb. *influence.*

train, coach 669vb. *prepare;* take on, take in hand, initiate, tame 369vb. *break in;* nurse, foster, inure, put through the mill, put through the grind; drill, exercise, practice, make second nature, familiarize, accustom 610vb. *habituate;* make fit, qualify; house-train, teach manners, teach how to behave 369vb. *groom.*

See: 68, 178, 369, 459, 520, 524, 528, 536, 589, 594, 610, 669, 682, 689.

535 Misteaching

N. *misteaching,* misinstruction, misguidance, misleading, misdirection; quackery, a case of the blind leading the blind; misintelligence, misinformation 552n. *misrepresentation;* mystification 421n. *obfuscation;* allonym, false name 525n. *concealment;* wrong attribution, wrong emendation, miscorrection 495n. *mistake;* obscurantism 490n. *ignorance;* false teaching, bad t., propaganda 541n. *falsehood;* perversion 246n. *distortion;* false logic, illogic 477n. *sophistry;* college of Laputa.

Adj. *misteaching* etc. vb.; unedifying, propagandist; obscurantist 491adj. *ignorant;* mistaught, misled, misdirected 495adj. *mistaken.*

Vb. *misteach,* miseducate, bring up wrong; misinstruct, misinform, miscorrect, misname, misdirect, misguide 495vb. *mislead;* not edify, corrupt, abuse the mind 934vb. *make wicked;* pervert 246vb. *distort;* misdescribe 552vb. *misrepresent;* cry wolf, put on a false scent 542vb. *deceive;* lie 541vb. *be false;* preach to the wise, teach one's grandmother to suck eggs; leave no wiser, keep in ignorance, take advantage of one's ignorance; suppress knowledge, unteach; propagandize, brainwash; explain away.

See: 246, 421, 477, 490, 491, 495, 525, 541, 542, 552, 934.

536 Learning

N. *learning,* lore, wide reading, scholarship, attainments 490n. *erudition;* acquisition of knowledge, acquisition of skill; thirst for knowledge, intellectual curiosity 453n. *curiosity;* pupilage, tutelage, apprenticeship, prenticeship, novitiate, tirocinium, initiation 669n. *preparation;* first steps, teething troubles 68n. *beginning;* docility, teachability 694n. *aptitude,* self-instruction, self-education, self-improvement; culture, cultivation, self-c.; late learning, opsimathy.

study, studying; application, studiousness; cramming, grind, cram, mugging, mulling; studies, course of s., lessons, class, class-work, desk-w.; homework, prep, preparation; revision, refresher course, further reading, further study; perusal, reading, close r., attentive r. 455n. *attention;* research, research work, investigation 459n. *inquiry.*

Adj. *studious,* devoted to studies, academic; partial to reading, bookish, well-read, scholarly, erudite, learned, scholastic 490adj. *knowing;* sedulous, diligent, degree-hungry 678adj. *industrious;* receptive, teachable, docile 597adj. *willing;* self-taught, self-instructed, autodidact; immersed in study, deep in 455adj. *attentive.*

Vb. *learn,* pursue one's education, get oneself taught, go to school, attend college, read, take lessons, sit at the feet of, hear lectures, take a course, take a refresher c.; acquire knowledge, gain information, collect i., glean i., assimilate learning, imbibe, drink in, cram oneself with facts, know one's f. 490vb. *know;* apprentice oneself, learn one's trade, serve an apprenticeship, article oneself 669vb. *prepare oneself;* train, practice, exercise 610vb. *be wont;* get the feel of, master; get by heart, learn by rote 505vb. *memorize;* finish one's education, graduate.

study, prosecute one's studies, apply oneself, burn the midnight oil; do, take up; research into 459vb. *inquire;* study particularly, specialize, major in; swot, cram, grind, mug, mull, get up; revise, go over, brush up; read, peruse, spell, pore, wade through; thumb, browse, skip, turn the leaves, dip into; be studious, be a reading man, mind one's book, pore over; devote oneself to reading, bury oneself in one's books, become a polymath.

Adv. *studiously,* at one's books; under training, in articles.

See: 68, 453, 455, 459, 490, 505, 597, 610, 669, 678, 694.

537 Teacher

N. *teacher*, preceptor, mentor 520n. *guide;* minister 986n. *pastor;* guru, acharya 500n. *sage;* instructor, institutor; tutor, private t., private teacher, munshi; crammer, coach; bear-leader, governor, governess, nurse, dry-nurse, duenna 749n. *keeper;* educationist, pedagogue; pedant 500n. *wiseacre;* dominie, beak, abecedarian; master, schoolmaster, classmaster, housemaster, headmaster, principal; schoolmistress; schoolmarm, dame, schooldame, lady teacher; underteacher, pupil t., usher, monitor; disciplinarian, proctor, prefect; don, fellow; lecturer, expositor, exponent 520n. *interpreter;* prelector, reader, professor, Regius p., faculty member; catechist, catechizer; initiator, mystagogue, coryphaeus; confidant, consultant 691n. *adviser;* teaching staff, faculty, professoriat, senior common room.

trainer, instructor, physical i., gymnastic i., swimming i.; coach, athletic c.; choirmaster; dancing-master; drill-sergeant; disciplinarian, rod, cane-wielder; animal trainer, horse-t., breaker-in, lion-tamer 369n. *breeder.*

preacher, lay p. 986n. *pastor;* pulpiteer, Boanerges, orator 579n. *speaker;* gospeler, evangelist; apostle, missionary, pioneer 660n. *precursor;* seer, prophet, major p., minor p. 511n. *oracle;* pamphleteer, propagandist 528n. *publicizer;* proverbialist 500n. *sage.*

Adj. See 534adj. *educational.*

See: 66, 369, 500, 511, 520, 528, 579, 691, 749, 986.

538 Learner

N. *learner,* disciple, follower, chela; proselyte, convert, catechumen; late learner, opsimath; self-taught person, do-it-yourself fan, autodidact; empiricist 461n. *experimenter;* swotter, mugger, bookworm 492n. *scholar;* alumnus, student, pupil, scholar, schoolboy, schoolgirl, schoolmiss, schoolgoer, day-scholar, day-boy, boarder; schoolfellow, schoolmate, classmate; fellow-student, condisciple.

beginner, young idea, novice, inceptor, debutant; abecedarian, alphabetarian; new boy, fag, tyro, greenhorn, tenderfoot, neophyte; rabbit, amateur 987n. *layman;* recruit, raw r., buck private; initiate, catechumen; colt, trainee, apprentice, 'prentice, articled clerk; probationer, probationer nurse, pupil teacher; first offender; L-driver, examinee 461n. *testee.*

college student, colleger, collegian, seminarist; undergraduate, undergraduette; freshman, frosh, first-year man; sophomore, soph, junior, senior; sophister; man student, woman s., girl s.; commoner, pensioner, sizar, exhibitioner; scholarship-holder, state scholar, Rhodes s.; prize boy, prizeman; passman; honors student, advanced s.; graduate, postgraduate student, fellow; law student, mootman; art student; research worker, researcher, specialist.

class, standard, form, grade, remove, shell, stream; lower form, upper f., sixth f., scholarship class; art class, life c.; seminar.

Adj. *studentlike*, schoolboyish 130 adj. *young;* undergraduate, collegiate, sophomoric; pupilary, discipular; prentice; scholarly 536adj. *studious;* rudimentary, raw, abecedarian; probationary; in leading strings, in statu pupillari.

See: 130, 461, 492, 536, 987.

539 School

N. *academy*, institute, institution, teaching i.; college, seminary, lycée, gymnasium; conservatoire, school of music, school of dancing, dancing school, art s., academy of dramatic art; wrestling school, palestra; school of deportment, finishing school; university, university college; school of philosophy, Academy, Lyceum, Stoa.

school, nursery s., crèche, kindergarten; infant school, dame s.; private school; aided school; preparatory school, prep s., preprep s., preschool; primary school, elementary s., middle s., middle English s.; higher grade school, central s., secondary school, high-s., high English s., secondary modern s., grammar s., comprehensive s.; collegiate school, public s., boarding s., day s.; Board school, L.C.C. s., village s., parish s., county s., state s., night s., continuation s.; convent school, denominational s., church s., Sunday s.; school for the blind, deaf-and-dumb s., school for backward children, school for the educationally subnormal; reformatory, reform school, borstal s., Borstal, remand home; school building, school architecture.

training school, nursery, training

ground, gymnasium 724n. *arena;* crammer; finishing school; training ship, training college, teachers training c., teachers training school, école normale, normal school; law school, medical school, medical college, teaching hospital; military school, military college, staff college; Dartmouth, Sandhurst, Woolwich, Cranwell; West Point, Annapolis.
trade school, vocational s., technical training s.; technical college, technical institute, polytechnic; engineering school, engineering college; research laboratory, research institute; commercial institute, secretarial school, business college.
classroom, schoolroom; study; lecture-room, lecture-hall, auditorium, theater, amphitheater; desk, reading d., class d.; schoolbook, reader, crib, hornbook, abecedary, primer 589n. *textbook;* slate, copybook, exercise book; visual aid.
rostrum, bema, tribune, dais, forum; platform, stage, hustings, soap-box; chair 534n. *lecture;* pulpit, lectern, ambo; leader page, column 528n. *publicity.*
Adj. See 534adj. *educational.*
See: 528, 534, 589, 724.

540 Veracity

N. *veracity*, veraciousness, truthfulness, truth-telling, truth-speaking; nothing but fact, fidelity, fidelity to fact, verisimilitude, realism, exactitude 494n. *accuracy;* openness, frankness, candor 522n. *manifestation;* bona fides, honor bright, no kidding; love of truth, honesty, sincerity 929 n. *probity;* simplicity, ingenuousness 699n. *artlessness;* downrightness, plain speaking, plain dealing 573n. *plainness;* baldness, plain words, home-truth, unvarnished tale, undisguised meaning, unambiguity, true statement, honest truth, sober t. 494n. *truth;* clean breast, true confession, unqualified admission 526vb. *disclosure;* circumstantiality, particularity, full details, nothing omittted 570n. *diffuseness;* truth-speaker, no liar, prophet.
Adj. *veracious,* truthful 494adj. *true;* telling the truth, veridical, not lying, unperjured; as good as one's word, reliable 929adj. *trustworthy;* factual, sticking to fact, ungarbled, undistorted, bald, unembroidered, unvarnished, unexaggerated, scrupulous, exact, just 494adj. *accurate;* full, particular, circumstantial 570adj. *diffuse;* simple, ingenuous 699adj. *artless;* bona fide, meant, intended; unaffected, unpretentious, unfeigned, undissembling, open, above-board 522adj. *undisguised;* candid, unreserved, forthcoming; blunt, free, downright, forthright, plain-speaking, outspoken, straightforward 573adj. *plain;* unambiguous 516adj. *intelligible;* honest, sincere, true-hearted, true-blue, loyal 929adj. *honorable;* truly spoken, fulfilled, proved, verified 478adj. *demonstrated;* infallible, prophetic 511adj. *presageful.*
Vb. *be truthful,* tell the truth, tell no lie, swear true 532vb. *swear;* stick to the facts 494vb. *be true;* speak in earnest, mean it, really mean, honestly m.; not joke, weigh one's words 834vb. *be serious;* speak one's mind, open one's heart, keep nothing back 522vb. *show;* make a clean breast, confess the truth 526 vb. *confess;* drop the mask, appear in one's true colors 526vb. *disclose;* be prophetic 511vb. *predict*; verify one's heart 494adv. *truly;* to tell the *strate.*
Adv. *truthfully,* really and truly, bona fide, sincerely, from the bottom of one's heart 494adv. *truly;* to tell the truth, frankly, candidly, without fear or favor; factually, exactly, just as it happened.
See: 478, 494, 511, 516, 522, 526, 532, 570, 573, 699, 834, 929.

541 Falsehood

N. falsehood, falseness, spuriousness, falsity; treachery, bad faith, Punic f., Judas kiss 930n. *perfidy;* untruthfulness, unveracity, mendacity, deceitfulness; lying, habitual l., pathological l., mythomania; oath-breaking, perjury, false swearing 543n. *untruth;* invention of lies, fabrication, fiction; faking, forgery, falsification 542n. *deception;* imaginativeness, invention 513n. *imagination;* disingenuousness, prevarication, equivocation, evasion, shuffling, fencing 518n. *equivocalness;* economy of truth, suppressio veri, suggestio falsi; jesuitry, jesuitism, casuistry; overstatement 546n. *exaggeration;* perversion 246n. *distortion;* false coloring, misrepresentation 521n. *misinterpretation;* meretriciousness 875n. *ostentation;* humbug, bunkum, baloney, hokum, hooey, gammon, flim-flam, bam 515n. empty talk; cant, eyewash, hogwash (**see** *duplicity*); euphemism, mealy-mouthedness, blarney, soft soap, taffy 925n. *flattery.*

duplicity, false conduct, double life, double-dealing 930n. *improbity;* guile 542n. *trickery;* hollowness, front, façade, outside, show, window-dressing 875n. *ostentation;* pretense, hollow p., bluff, act, fake, counterfeit, imposture 542n. *sham;* hypocrisy, acting, play-a., simulation, dissimulation, dissembling, insincerity, tongue in cheek, cant; lip-homage, mouth-honor, cupboard love; pharisaism, false piety; crocodile tears, show of sympathy; Judas kiss, Cornish hug; fraud, pious f., legal fiction, diplomatic illness; cheat, cheating; put-up job, frame-up 930n. *foul play;* quackery, charlatanry, charlatanism 850n. *pretension;* low cunning, artfulness 698n. *cunning.*

Adj. *false,* not true, truthless, without truth; untruthful, lying, unveracious, imaginative, mendacious 543adj. *untrue;* perfidious, treacherous, forsworn, perjured; sly, artful 698adj. *cunning;* disingenuous, dishonest, uncandid, unfair, ambiguous, evasive, shuffling 518adj. *equivocal;* falsified, garbled; meretricious, embellished, touched up, varnished, painted; overdone 546adj. *exaggerated;* ungenuine, imitated, counterfeit, fake, phony, sham, snide, quack, bogus 542adj. *spurious;* cheating, deceptive, deceitful, fraudulent 542adj. *deceiving;* covinous, collusive, collusory; engineered, rigged, packed.

hypocritical, hollow, empty, insincere, diplomatic, put on, imitated, pretended, seeming, feigned; make-believe, acting, play-a.; double, two-faced, double-hearted, double-tongued, double-handed, treacherous, double-dealing, Machiavellian 930 adj. *perfidious;* sanctimonious, tartuffish, pharisaical; jesuitical, casuistical; plausible, smooth, smooth-tongued, smooth-spoken, oily; mealy-mouthed, euphemistic 850adj. *affected;* canting, gushing 925adj. *flattering.*

Vb. *be false,* — perjured, — forsworn etc. adj.; perjure oneself, bear false witness, swear falsely, swear that black is white; forswear 603vb. *recant;* palter, palter with the truth, economize t.; lie, tell lies, utter a falsehood; tell the tale, swing the lead; strain, strain the truth, tell a tall story 546vb. *exaggerate;* tell a fib, tell a whopper, lie hard, lie like a trooper; invent, make believe, make up, romance 513vb. *imagine;* put a false construction on 521vb. *misinterpret;* garble, falsify, pervert 246vb. *distort;* overstate, understate 552vb. *misrepresent;* misreport, misquote, miscite, misinform, cry wolf 535vb. *misteach;* lull, soothe 925vb. *flatter;* play false, play a double game 930vb. *be dishonest;* break faith, betray 769 vb. *not observe.*

dissemble, dissimulate, disguise 525 vb. *conceal;* simulate, counterfeit 20 vb. *imitate;* put on, assume, affect, dress up, play-act, play a part, go through the motions, make a show of 594vb. *act;* feign, pass off for, sham, pretend, show false colors, sail under false c.; malinger, sham Abraham 542vb. *deceive;* lack candor, hide the truth, say less than the t., keep something back; not give a straight answer, prevaricate, palter, beat about the bush, shuffle, dodge, trim 518vb. *equivocate.*

cant, gloze, euphemize, mince matters, garble; color, varnish, paint, embroider, varnish right and puzzle wrong; gloss over, put a gloss on, clean the outside of the platter; play the hypocrite, act a part, put on an act; say the grapes are sour 850vb. *be affected.*

fake, fabricate, coin, forge, plagiarize, counterfeit 20vb. *imitate;* get up, trump up, frame; manipulate, rig, pack (a jury); spin, weave, cook, cook up, concoct, hatch, invent 623 vb. *plot.*

Adv. *falsely,* slyly, deceitfully, under false pretenses; hypocritically, à la Tartuffe, with a double tongue, mendaciously.

See: 20, 246, 513, 515, 518, 521, 525, 535, 542, 543, 546, 552, 594, 603, 623, 698, 769, 850, 875, 925, 930.

542 Deception

N. *deception,* ingannation, kidding, tongue in cheek; circumvention, outwitting; self-deception, wishful thinking 487n. *credulity;* infatuation 499n. *folly;* fallacy 477n. *sophistry;* illusion, delusion, hallucination, imagination's artful aid 495n. *error;* deceptiveness 523n. *latency* (**see** *trap*); false appearance, mockery, mirage, will-o'-the-wisp 440n. *visual fallacy;* show, outward s., meretriciousness, paint (**see** *sham*); false reputation, feet of clay; hollowness, bubble 4n. *insubstantiality;* falseness, deceit, quackery, imposture, lie 541n. *falsehood;* deceitfulness, guile, craft, artfulness 698n. *cunning;* hypocrisy, insincerity 541n. *duplicity;* treachery, betrayal 930n. *perfidy;* practice, machination, hanky-panky, collusion, covin 623n. *plot;* fraudulence, cozenage, cheating, cheat, diddling, diddle; spoofery, hoax (**see** *trickery*); ventriloquism (**see** *sleight*).

trickery, coggery, gullery, dupery, swindling, skulduggery, shenanigan; jockeyship, sharp practice, chicane, chicanery, legal c., pettifogging; swindle, chouse, ramp, wangle, fiddle, diddle, swizzle, swiz, sell, bite, fraud, cheat; cardsharping, cogging 930n. *foul play;* trick, bag of tricks, tricks of the trade, confidence trick, wile, ruse, shift, dodge, artful d., fetch, reach, blind, dust, feint 698n. *stratagem;* wrinkle 623n. *contrivance;* bait, diversion, tub to a whale; hocus, hoax, bluff, spoof, leg-pull; game, sport, joke, practical j., rag 839n. *witticism;* April fooling, spoofery.

sleight, pass, sleight of hand, quickness of the h., legerdemain, prestidigitation, conjuring, hocus-pocus, illusion, ventriloquism; juggling, jugglery, juggle, googly; thimblerig, three-card trick; magic 983n. *sorcery.*

trap, deathtrap 527n. *ambush;* catch 503n. *enigma;* plant, frame-up 930n. *foul play;* noose, snare, gin, net, spring-n., spring-gun; springe, springle, hook, sniggle, mine; diversion, blind, decoy, decoy duck, kill, bait, lure; baited trap, rat t., mouse t., fly-paper, lime-twig, birdlime; booby-trap, trip-wire, deadfall, pit, keddah 663n. *pitfall;* trapdoor, sliding panel, false bottom 530n. *secret;* fatal gift, poisoned chalice, Trojan horse.

sham, false front 541n. *duplicity;* make-believe, pretense 850n. *affectation;* paint, whitewash, varnish, gloss; white sepulcher, man of straw, wolf in sheep's clothing, lath painted to look like iron; dummy, scarecrow 4n. *insubstantial thing;* imitation, simulacrum, facsimile 22n. *copy;* mockery, hollow m.; counterfeit, forgery, fake; masquerade, mummery, mask, disguise, borrowed plumes, false colors 525n. *concealment;* shoddy, brummagem, jerry-building 641n. *rubbish;* imitation ware, tinsel, paste, ormolu, ormolu varnish, mosaic gold; German silver, britannia metal.

Adj. *deceiving,* deceitful, lying 543 adj. *untrue;* deceptive 523adj. *latent;* hallucinatory, illusive, delusive, elusive, illusory; slippery 258adj. *smooth;* fraudulent, humbugging, cheating, cogging; lulling, soothing 925adj. *flattering;* beguiling, treacherous, insidious 930adj. *perfidious;* trumped-up, framed, colorable 541 adj. *false;* feigned, pretended 541adj. *hypocritical;* juggling, conjuring, prestigious; sleightful, tricky, crafty, wily, guileful, artful 698adj. *cunning;* collusive, covinous; painted, whited, whitewashed, sugared, coated, plated (**see** *spurious*).

spurious, base-born, illegitimate, adulterine 954adj. *bastard;* ungenuine, false, faked, fake; sham, counterfeit; make-believe, mock, ersatz, bogus, phony; pseudo, so-called; not natural, artificial, paste, cultured; shoddy, rubbishy 641adj. *useless;* tinsel, meretricious, flash, catchpenny, pinchbeck, brummagem 812 adj. *cheap;* jerry-built, cardboard 330 adj. *brittle;* adulterated, sophisticated 43adj. *mixed;* underweight 323adj. *light.*

Vb. *deceive,* delude, illude, dazzle; beguile, sugar the pill, gild the p.; let down 509vb. *disappoint;* hoodwink, blinker, blindfold 439vb. *blind;* kid, bluff, bamboozle, hoax, humbug, hornswoggle, gammon; snatch a verdict, throw dust in the eyes, lead up the garden path 495vb. *mislead;* spoof, mystify 535vb. *misteach;* play false, leave in the lurch, betray, double-cross 930vb. *be dishonest;* practice, practice upon, intrigue 623vb. *plot;* circumvent, overreach, outreach, outwit, outmaneuver 306vb. *outdo;* forestall, steal a march on 135vb. *be early;* pull a fast one, be too smart for, outsmart 698vb. *be cunning;* trick, dupe (**see** *befool*); cheat, cozen, sharp, swindle, swizzle, sell, bite, do, do down; diddle, bubble, do out of, bilk, gyp, chouse, pluck, obtain money by false pretenses 788vb. *defraud;* juggle, conjure, make a pass, force a card, palm off, foist o.; fob, fob off with; live on one's wits, try it on, practice chicanery, pettifog; gerrymander, tinker; cog, cog the dice, load the d., mark the cards, pack the c., stack the deck; play the hypocrite, impose upon 541vb. *dissemble;* brazen out, put a good face upon, whitewash 541vb. *cant;* counterfeit 541 vb. *fake.*

befool, fool, make a fool of, make an ass of, make one look silly, fool one to the top of his bent; mock, make game of 851vb. *ridicule;* rag, play tricks on, pull one's leg, have one on, make an April fool of, play a joke on 497vb. *be absurd;* sport with, trifle w., throw over, jilt; take in, have, dupe, cully, victimize, gull, outwit; trick, trap, catch, catch out, take advantage of, practice upon, practice on one's credulity, kid, stuff up, dope; spoof, bamboozle, fake out, string, hocus (**see** *deceive*); cog, cajole, get round, flatter, fawn on, make things pleasant for, lull, soothe 925vb. *flatter;* let down, let in for, leave in the lurch, leave one holding the baby, leave one holding the bag 509vb. *disappoint;* send on a fool's errand, send on a wild-goose chase 495vb. *mislead.*

ensnare, snare, trap, entrap, set a trap for, lay a trap for, lime, lime the twig, entoil, enmesh, entangle, illaqueate, net, benet; trip, trip up, catch, catch out, hook, sniggle; bait, bait the trap, bait the hook, dangle a bait, lure, decoy, entice, inveigle 612vb. *tempt;* divert, throw a tub to a whale; lie in wait, waylay, forelay 527vb. *ambush;* nab, nick, kidnap, crimp, trepan, shanghai 788vb. *steal.*

Adv. *deceptively,* deceitfully; under cover of, in the garb of, disguisedly; over the left.

See: 4, 22, 43, 135, 258, 306, 323, 330, 439, 440, 477, 487, 495, 497, 499, 509, 523, 525, 527, 530, 535, 541, 543, 612, 623, 641, 663, 698, 788, 812, 839, 850, 851, 925, 930, 954, 983.

543 Untruth

N. *untruth,* thing that is not, reverse of the truth 541n. *falsehood;* less than the truth, understatement 483n. *underestimation;* more than the truth, overstatement 546n. *exaggeration;* lie, downright l., shameless l., calm l.; taradiddle, fib, whopper, crammer; false statement, terminological inexactitude; broken word, dicer's oath, lover's o., breach of promise 930n. *perfidy;* perjury, false oath; false evidence, pack of lies, trumped-up story, frame-up 466n. *evidence;* concoction, fiction, fabrication, invention 513n. *ideality* (**see** *fable*); misstatement, misinformation 535n. *misteaching;* misrepresentation, perversion 246n. *distortion;* gloss, varnish, garbling, falsification 521n. *misinterpretation;* lie factory, propaganda machine.

mental dishonesty, disingenuousness, economy of truth, half-truth, partial t., near t., half-lie; white l., pious fraud, mental reservation 468n. *qualification;* suggestio falsi, suppressio veri 525n. *concealment;* show, make-believe; tongue in cheek, pretense, profession, false plea, excuse 614n. *pretext;* evasion, subterfuge, shift, shuffle, ambiguity 518n. *equivocalness;* self-depreciation, irony, back-handed compliment 850n. *affectation;* artificiality, unnaturalness; sham, empty words 541n. *duplicity;* Judas kiss 930n. *perfidy;* mask 527n. *disguise.*

fable, invention, fiction, imaginative exercise 513n. *ideality;* story, tale 590n. *narrative;* tall story, tall order, shaggy-dog story, fishy s., fish s., fisherman's yarn, traveler's tale 546n. *exaggeration;* Canterbury tale, fairy-t., nursery t., märchen, romance, tale, yarn, story, cock-and-bull s., all my eye and Betty Martin 497n. *absurdity;* claptrap, gossip, gup, guff, bazaar rumor, canard 529n. *rumor;* myth, mythology; moonshine, farce, mare's nest, sell, swiz, hum, hoax, humbug, flummery 515n. *empty talk.*

Adj. *untrue,* lying, mendacious 541adj. *false;* trumped-up, framed, cooked, hatched, concocted; far from the truth, nothing less true; mythological, fabulous; unfounded, empty; fictitious, imagined, make-believe, well-imagined, ben trovato; faked, artificial, synthetic, factitious; phony, bogus, soi-disant, so-called; overstated 546adj. *exaggerated;* boasting 877adj. *boastful;* perjured, forsworn 930 adj. *perfidious;* evasive, shuffling, surreptitious 518adj. *equivocal;* ironical 850adj. *affected;* satirical, mocking 851adj. *derisive.*

Vb. *be untrue,* sound u., not ring true 472vb. *be unlikely;* lie, be a liar 541 vb. *be false;* spin a yarn, draw the long bow 546vb. *exaggerate;* make-believe, draw on one's imagination 513vb. *imagine;* be phony, pretend, sham, counterfeit, forge, falsify 541 vb. *dissemble.*

See: 246, 466, 468, 472, 483, 497, 513, 515, 518, 525, 527, 529, 535, 541, 546, 614, 850, 851, 877, 930, 940.

544 Dupe

N. *dupe,* fool, old f., April f. 851n. *laughing-stock;* Simple Simon 501n. *ninny;* credulous fool, one easily taken in, easy prey, victim, sucker, gull, pigeon, jay, cull, cully, mug, flat, dude, greenhorn, innocent 538n. *beginner;* puppet, cat's-paw, pawn 630n. *too;* ignorant masses, admass.

Adj. *gullible* 487adj. *credulous;* duped, taken in, had, done, diddled 542adj.

deceiving; innocent, green, silly 499 adj. *foolish.*

Vb. *be duped*, be had, be done, be taken in; fall for, walk into the trap, rise, nibble, swallow the bait, swallow hook line and sinker; take wooden nickels, buy a gold brick; catch a Tartar 508vb. *not expect.*

See: 487, 499, 501, 508, 538, 542, 630, 851.

545 Deceiver

N. *deceiver*, gay d., seducer 952n. *libertine;* kidder, ragger, leg-puller; dissembler, actor, shammer, hypocrite, canter, whited sepulcher, pharisee, Pecksniff, Tartuffe, Joseph Surface, Mawworm; false friend, fair-weather f., jilt, jilter, shuffler, turncoat, trimmer, rat 603n. *tergiversator;* traitor, Judas, four-flusher, double-crosser 938n. *knave;* serpent, snake in the grass, snake in one's bosom 663n. *trouble-maker;* plotter, intrigant, conspirator 623n. *planner;* counterfeiter, forger, faker, plagiarizer 20n. *imitator.*

liar, confirmed l., pathological l. 541n. *falsehood;* fibster, fibber, story-teller; romancer, fabulist; imaginative person, yarner, yarn-spinner; angler, traveler, mythologist; pseudologist, fabricator, equivocator, palterer; oath-breaker, perjurer, false witness; Ananias, father of lies.

imposter, shammer, malingerer, adventurer, usurper; cuckoo in the nest 59n. *intruder;* ass in the lion's skin, wolf in sheep's clothing; boaster, bluffer, ringer; pretender, quack, quack-salver, mountebank, saltimbanco, medicaster, empiric 850n. *affector;* fake, fraud, humbug; masquerader, mummer 525n. *concealment.*

trickster, hoaxer, spoofer, bamboozler; cheat, cheater, cozener; jockey, horse-coper, carpet-bagger; sharper, card-s., thimblerigger, cogger; shyster, pettifogger; swindler, bilker, diddler, gyp 789n. *defrauder;* slicker, spieler, twister, chiseler, jobber, rogue 938n. *knave;* confidence trickster, confidence man, con-man, magsman 477n. *sophist;* crimp, decoy, stool-pigeon, decoy-duck, agent provocateur; fiddler, manipulator, rigger, fixer; wily bird, fox 698n. *slyboots.*

conjuror, illusionist, prestidigitator, galigali man, juggler, ventriloquist; quick-change artist; magician, necromancer 983n. *sorcerer.*

See: 20, 59, 477, 525, 541, 603, 623, 663, 698, 789, 850, 938, 952, 983.

546 Exaggeration

N. *exaggeration*, over-emphasis, inflation, magnification, enlargement 197 n. *expansion;* optimism 482n. *overestimation;* stretch, strain, straining; extravagance, exaggerated lengths, extremes, immoderation, extremism; excess, excessiveness, violence 943n. *intemperance;* inordinacy, exorbitance, overdoing it, piling Ossa upon Pelion; overacting, histrionics 875n. *ostentation;* sensationalism, ballyhoo, puffery 528n. *publicity;* overstatement, hyperbole, figure of speech 519n. *trope;* adulation 925n. *flattery;* coloring, high c. 574n. *ornament;* embroidery 38n. *addition;* disproportion 246n. *distortion;* caricature, burlesque 851n. *satire;* exacerbation 832 n. *aggravation;* big talk, boast 877n. *boasting;* rant, ranting, tirade, rodomontade, grandiloquence 574n. *magniloquence;* overpraise, excessive loyalty chauvinism 481n. *prejudice;* tall story, yarn, shaggy-dog story, traveler's tale 543n. *fable;* aretalogy, miracle-mongering; men in buckram, flight of fancy, stretch of the imagination 513n. *imagination;* fuss, pother, excitement, storm in a teacup, much ado about nothing 318n. *commotion;* extremist, exaggerator; sensationalist, miracle-monger, aretalogist; Baron Munchausen 545n. *liar.*

Adj. *exaggerated*, magnified, enlarged 197adj. *expanded;* added to, embroidered; strained, over-emphasized, overweighted, overdone, overstated, over-colored, inflated, hyperbolical 574adj. *rhetorical;* overacted, histrionic; bombastic, swelling 877adj. *boastful;* tall, fanciful, high-flying, steep, egregious, preposterous, outrageous 497adj. *absurd;* extravagant, excessive, outré, extremist; violent, immoderate 32adj. *exorbitant;* inordinate 943adj. *intemperate.*

Vb. *exaggerate*, maximize, magnify, expand, inflate 197vb. *enlarge;* over-amplify, over-elaborate; add to, pile up 38vb. *add;* touch up, enhance, heighten, add a flourish, embroider 844vb. *decorate;* lay it on thick, overdo, over-color, over-draw, overcharge, overload; overweight, overstress, over-emphasize 638vb. *make important;* overpraise, puff, oversell, cry up 482vb. *overrate;* make much of, make too much of 925vb. *flatter;* stretch, strain 246vb. *distort;* caricature 851vb. *satirize;* go to all lengths, not know when to stop, protest too much, speak in superlatives, hyperbolize; overact, dramatize, out-Herod

Herod; rant, talk big 877vb. *boast;* run riot, go to extremes, pile Pelion on Ossa; draw the long bow, overshoot the mark 306vb. *overstep;* spin a yarn, draw on the imagination, deal in the marvelous, tell travelers' tales 541vb. *be false;* make mountains out of molehills, make a storm in a teacup; intensify, exacerbate 832vb. *aggravate;* overcompensate, lean over backwards.

See: 32, 38, 197, 246, 306, 318, 481, 482, 497, 513, 519, 528, 541, 543, 545, 574, 638, 832, 844, 851, 875, 877, 925, 943.

547 Indication

N. *indication*, pointing out, drawing attention, showing 522n. *manifestation;* signification, meaning 514n. *connotation;* notification 524n. *information;* symbolization, symbolism 551n. *representation;* symbol, conventional s., x, letter; magic symbol, pentacle 983n. *talisman;* natural symbol, image, type, figure; token, emblem, figurehead (**see** *badge*); something to go by, symptom, sign 466n. *evidence;* tell-tale sign, blush 526n. *disclosure;* nudge, wink 524n. *hint* (**see** *gesture*); straw in the wind, sign of the times 511n. *omen;* clue, scent, whiff 484n. *detector;* noise, footfall 398n. *sound;* interpretation of symptoms, symptomatology, semeiology, semeiotics 520n. *hermeneutics;* pointer, finger, forefinger, index finger (**see** *indicator*); indice, exponent 85n. *number;* guide, index, thumb-i. 87n. *directory;* key 520n. *interpretation;* marker, mark, guide-m.; white mark, blaze; nick, scratch 260n. *notch;* line, score, stroke; note, side-n., underrunner, catchword (**see** *punctuation*); stamp, print, impression; stigma, stigmata; prick, tattooing, tattoomark 263n. *perforation;* mole, scar, birthmark, strawberry mark 845n. *blemish;* legend, caption 590n. *description;* inscription, epitaph; motto, cipher; love-token, favor (**see** *badge*).

identification, naming 561n. *nomenclature;* 77n. *classification;* means of identification, brand, trademark, imprint (**see** *label*); name and address; autograph, signature, hand 586n. *script;* fingerprint, footprint, spoor, track, trail 548n. *trace;* secret sign, password, open sesame, watchword, countersign; diagnostic, markings, stripes, spots, color, coloring, cloven hoof; characteristic, trait, lineament, outline, form, shape 445n. *feature;* personal characteristic, trick, trick of speech, shibboleth; mole, scar, birthmark, strawberry mark 845n. *blemish;* divining rod 484n. *detector;* criterion 461n. *testing agent;* mark, note.

symbology, symbolization, dactylogy; cipher, code 525n. *secrecy;* symbolography, picture-writing, hieroglyphics 586n. *script;* gypsy signs, hobo s., scout s.

gesture, gesticulation, sign-language, semeiology, dactylogy; deaf-and-dumb language; sign 524n. *hint;* pantomime, by-play, dumb-show, charade, dumb c.; demeanor, look in one's eyes, tone of one's voice 445n. *mien;* motion, move; tick, twitch 318n. *spasm;* shrug, shrug of the shoulders; wag of the head, nod, beck, wink, flicker of the eyelash, twinkle, glance, ogle, leer, grimace 438n. *look;* smile, laugh 835n. *laughter;* touch, kick, nudge, jog, dig in the ribs 279n. *knock;* hug, clap on the shoulders; hand-pressure, squeeze of the hand, handshake, grip 778n. *retention;* push, shove 279n. *impulse;* pointing, signal, waving, wave, hand-signal, wave of the hand; raising one's hand, wagging one's forefinger; drumming one's fingers, tapping one's foot, stamp of the foot 822n. *excitable state;* clenching one's teeth, gritting one's t. 599n. *resolution;* gnashing one's teeth, snap, snapping one's jaws 892n. *irascibility;* wringing one's hands, tearing one's hair 836n. *lamentation;* clenched fist 711 n. *defiance;* flag-waving, umbrella w., hat-w. 876n. *celebration;* clap, clapping, hand-c., cheer 923n. *applause;* hiss, hissing, hooting, boo, booing, Bronx cheer 924n. *disapprobation;* frown, scowl, 893n. *sullenness;* pout, moue, pursing of the lips 829n. *discontent.*

signal 529n. *message;* sign, symptom 522n. *manifestation;* flash, rocket, Very light; signaling, railway signal, smoke-s., heliograph, semaphore, telegraph, Morse 531n. *telecommunication;* flash lamp, signal l. 420n. *lamp;* warning light, beacon, beacon fire, bale-f., watch-f. 379n. *fire;* balize, warning signal, red flag, warning light, red l., green l., traffic l., Belisha beacon 420n. *signal light;* alarum, alarm, warning signal, distress s., SOS 664n. *danger signal;* whistle, police w.; siren, hooter, bell, electric b., buzzer, knocker, door-k. 414n. *gong;* door-bell, alarm-b., Inchcape b., Lutine b.; church bells, angelus, carillon, sacring bell; time-signal, pip, minute-gun, dinner-gong, dinner-bell 117n. *chronometry;* passing bell, knell, muffled drum 364n. *obsequies.*

indicator, index, pointer, arrow, needle, compass n., magnetic n.; arm, finger, index-f.; hand, hour-h., minute-h., second-h., clock-h., watch-h. 117n. *timekeeper;* Plimsoll line 465n. *gauge;* traffic indicator, trafficator, semaphore; direction-finder, radar; white line 305n. *traffic control;* weathercock, wind sock, straw in the wind 340n. *weather.*

signpost, direction post, finger-p., hand-p., milestone, milepost, military column, waymark; lighthouse, lightship, buoy 662n. *safeguard;* compass 269n. *sailing aid;* lodestar, guiding s., pole s. 690n. *leader;* North Star, Polaris, Southern Cross 321n. *star;* cynosure, landmark, seamark, Pillars of Hercules; cairn, monument, memorial 505n. *reminder;* tide-mark 236n. *limit;* guide-mark, bench mark.

call, proclamation, ban, hue-and-cry 528n. *publication;* shout, hail; invitation; call to prayer, church-bell, muezzin's cry 981n. *worship;* summons, word, word of command 737n. *command;* bugle, trumpet, bugle-call, reveille, assemble, charge, advance, rally, retreat; lights out, last post; peal, sennet, flourish; drum, drum-beat, drum-roll, tattoo, taps 403n. *roll;* call to arms, Fiery Cross; battle-cry, war-c., rallying c., slogan, catchword, watchword, shibboleth; challenge, countersign; paying calls, round of calls, visiting 882n. *social round;* calling, profession 622n. *vocation.*

badge, token, emblem, symbol, sign, figurehead (**see** *indication*); insignia (**see** *heraldry*); markings, military m., roundel, badge of sovereignty, throne, scepter, orb, crown 743n. *regalia;* mark of authority, badge of of office, wand of o., Black Rod, mace, keys 743n. *badge of rule;* baton, stars, pips, spurs, stripes, epaulet 743n. *badge of rank;* medal, gong, cross, Victoria Cross, George C., Iron C.; order, star, garter, sash, ribbon 729n. *decoration;* badge of merit, laurels, bays, wreath, fillet, chaplet, garland 729n. *trophy;* blue, half-b., cap, oar; badge of loyalty, favor, rosette, primrose, love-knot; badge of mourning, black, crepe, weepers, widow's weeds 228n. *dress.*

livery, dress, national d. 228n. *uniform;* tartan, tie, old school t., blazer; regimental badge, brassard, epaulet, chevron, stripes, pips, wings; flash, hackle, cockade, rosette.

heraldry, armory, blazonry; heraldic register, Roll of Arms; armorial bearings, coat of arms; achievement, funereal a., hatchment; shield, escutcheon; crest, torse, wreath, helmet, crown, coronet, mantling, lambrequin; supporters, motto; compartment, lozenge; ordinary, honorable ordinaries, chief, base, pale, fess, bend, bend sinister, chevron, pile, saltire, cross; subordinaries, orb, inescutcheon, bordure, lozenge, fusil, pall, gyron, flaunches; marshaling, quartering, impaling, dimidiating; differencing, difference; fess point, honor p., nombril p.; charge, beacon, bugle, garb, water-bouget, fetterlock; animal charge, lion, unicorn, griffin, yale, cockatrice, eagle, alerion, falcon, martlet; floral charge, Tudor rose, cinquefoil, trefoil, planta genista; badge, antelope, bear and ragged staff, portcullis; national emblem, rose, thistle, leek, daffodil, shamrock, lilies, fleur-de-lys; device, national d., charkha, eagle, bear, hammer and sickle; swastika, fylfot; skull and crossbones; heraldic tincture, color, gules, azure, vert, sable, purpure, tenné, murray; metal, or, gold, yellow, argent, silver, white; fur, ermine, ermines, erminois, pean, vair, potent; heraldic personnel, College of Arms, herald, Earl Marshal, King of Arms, Garter, Clarenceaux, Norroy and Ulster, Chief Herald of Ireland; Lyon King of Arms; herald, Chester, Somerset, Richmond, York, Windsor, Lancaster; Albany, Marchmont, Rothesay, herald extraordinary, Maltravers, Norfolk, Fitzalan; pursuivant, Bluemantle, Rouge Croix, Rouge Dragon; Carrick, Kintyre; Unicorn.

flag, ensign, white e., blue e.; red ensign, Red Duster; jack, pilot j., merchant j.; colors, ship's c., regimental c., King's Color, Queen's C.; cavalry colors, guidon; standard, banner, gonfalon; banneret, bannerol, banderole, oriflamme; pennant, swallow-tail, triple tail; pendant, broad p., burgee; bunting, Blue Peter, yellow flag; white flag 721n. *submission;* eagle, Roman e.; crescent; tri-color; Union Jack; Stars and Stripes, Old Glory, Star-Spangled Banner; Red Flag; black flag, pirate f., bloody banner, Jolly Roger, Old R., skull and crossbones; parts of a flag, hoist, fly, canton; flagpole, flag-mast, color pike.

label, mark of identification, tattoo-mark, caste-m. (**see** *identification*); ticket, billet, bill, docket, counterfoil, stub, duplicate; tally, tessera, counter, chip; tick, letter, number, check, mark, countermark; tie-label, tab, tag; name-tape, name-plate, name-board, sign-b.; sign, bush, barber's pole, three balls 522n. *exhibit;* plate, brass p., trade sign, trademark, hall-m., cachet; earmark, brand, stigma, broad arrow, mark of Cain; fool's-cap, dunce's c.; seal, signet, sigil, stamp, impress, impression, seal-i.; caption, heading, title, superscription, rubric; imprint, colophon, signation, watermark; bookplate, monomark, name, name and address; card, visiting c., address c.; birth certificate, identification papers; passport, pass 756n. *permit;* endorsement 466n. *credential;* witness, signature, sign-manual, autograph, cipher, mark, cross, initials, monogram, paraph; finger-print, thumb-print, footprint 548n. *trace.*

punctuation, punctuation mark, point, stop, full s., period; comma, virgule, colon, semicolon; inverted commas, quotation marks, apostrophe, quotes; exclamation mark, exclamation point, question mark, note of interrogation, parentheses, brackets, square b., crotchet, crook, brace; hyphen, hyphenation; dash, dot, caret mark, omission m., blank; asterisk, asterism, star; obelus, dagger, squiggle, marginal finger, hand, index; accent, grave a., acute a., circumflex a.; barytone, oxytone, paroxytone, proparoxytone, perispomenon, properispomenon; diaeresis, cedilla, tilde; diacritical mark, vowel point, macron, breve, umlaut; sigla, stroke, mark of abbreviation, paragraph; plus sign, minus s., multiplication s., division s., equals s., decimal point; underlining, sublineation; italics, bold type, heavy t. 587n. *print-type;* capital letter, cap, initial c.

Adj. *indicating*, indicative, indicatory, pointing; significative, connotative, expressive, implicative, suggestive, suggesting 514adj. *meaningful;* figuring, typical, representative, token, symbolic, emblematic, nominal, diagrammatic 551adj. *representing;* telltale, revealing, betraying, bewraying 526adj. *disclosing;* signalizing, symptomatic 466adj. *evidential;* diagnostic, semeiological, symptomatological; characteristic, personal, individual 80adj. *special;* demonstrative, explanatory, exponential 520adj. *interpretive;* ominous, prophetic 511 adj. *presageful;* gesticulatory, pantomimic; signaling, signing, thumbing.

heraldic, emblematic; crested, armorial, blazoned, emblazoned, marshaled, quartered, impaled, dimidiated, differenced; paly, pily, barry, gyronny; dexter, sinister; gules, azure, vert, purpure, sable, tenné, murray, or, argent, ermine; rampant, guardant, reguardant, forcene, couchant, statant, sejant, genuant, passant.

marked etc. vb.; recognized, characterized, known by; scarred, branded, stigmatized, earmarked; denoted, numbered, lettered; referenced, indexed, denotable; indelible.

Vb. *indicate,* point 281vb. *point to;* point out, exhibit 522vb. *show;* describe heraldically, blazon; mark out, blaze; register, read, tell 548vb. *record;* name, identify, classify 80vb. *specify;* index, make an i., reference, supply references, refer; point the way, show the w., guide 689vb. *direct;* signify, denote, connote, suggest, imply, involve, spell, bespeak, argue 514vb. *mean;* symbolize, typify, betoken, stand for, be the sign of 551vb. *represent;* declare 532vb. *affirm;* signalize, highlight 532vb. *emphasize;* evince, show signs of, bear the marks of, bear the stamp of, give evidence of, attest, testify, witness 466vb. *evidence;* intimate 524vb. *hint;* betray, reveal 526vb. *disclose;* inform against 524vb. *inform;* prefigure, forebode, presage 511vb. *predict.*

mark, mark off, mark out, chalk o., flag o., lay o., demarcate, delimit 236vb. *limit;* label, ticket, docket, tag, tab, keep tabs on; earmark, designate; note, annotate, put a mark on, trace upon, line, score, underline, underscore; number, letter, page; tick, tick off; nick 260vb. *notch;* chalk, chalk up; scratch, scribble, cover 586vb. *write;* blot, stain, blacken 649vb. *make unclean;* scar, disfigure 842vb. *make ugly;* punctuate, dot, dash, cross, obelize, asterisk; put one's mark on, leave fingerprints, leave footprints; blaze, brand, burn in; stigmatize, prick, tattoo 263vb. *pierce;* stamp, seal, punch, impress, emboss; imprint, overprint 587vb. *print;* etch 555vb. *engrave;* mark heraldically, crest, emblazon; impale, dimidiate, quarter, difference; marshal, charge.

sign, ratify, countersign 488vb. *en-*

dorse; autograph, write one's signature, write one's name; put one's hand to, subscribe, undersign; initial, paraph; put one's mark, put one's cross; make signation; attest, witness 466vb. *testify*.

gesticulate, pantomime, mime, mimic, suit the action to the word 20vb. *imitate;* wave one's hands, talk with one's h., saw the air; wave, wag, waggle; wave to, hold out one's hand 884vb. *greet;* wave one's hat, stamp 923vb. *applaud;* wave one's arms, semaphore; gesture, motion, sign; point, thumb, beckon, raise one's hand 455vb. *attract notice;* nod, beck, wink, shrug; jog, nudg,e poke, dig in the ribs, clap on the back; look, look volumes, glance, leer, ogle 438 vb. *gaze;* twinkle, smile 835vb. *laugh;* raise one's eyebrows, wag the finger, wag the head 924vb. *disapprove;* wring one's hands, tear one's hair 836vb. *lament;* grit one's teeth, clench one's t. 599vb. *be resolute;* gnash one's teeth 891vb. *be angry;* snap, bite 893vb. *be sullen;* grimace, pout, scowl, frown 829vb. *be discontented;* cock a snook, curl one's lip 922vb. *despise;* shuffle, scrape one's feet, paw the ground; pat, stroke 889vb. *caress*.

signal, make a s., hang out a s., send a s., exchange signals, speak 524vb. *communicate;* tap out a message, semaphore, heliograph; flag, thumb; wave on, wave by, wave through; unfurl the flag, fly the f., break the f., dip the f., dip, half-mast, salute; alert, alarum, sound the alarm, dial the police 665vb. *raise the alarm;* beat the drum, sound the trumpets; fire a warning shot 664vb. *warn*.

Adv. *symbolically*, heraldically; by this token, in token of; in dumb show, in sign language, in pantomime.

See: 20, 77, 80, 85, 87, 117, 228, 236, 260, 263, 269, 279, 281, 305, 318, 321, 340, 364, 379, 398, 403, 414, 420, 438, 445, 455, 461, 465, 466, 484, 488, 505, 511, 514, 520, 522, 524, 525, 526, 528, 529, 531, 532, 548, 551, 555, 561, 581, 586, 587, 590, 599, 622, 649, 662, 664, 665, 689, 690, 711, 721, 729, 737, 743, 756, 778, 822, 829, 835, 836, 842, 845, 876, 882, 884, 889, 891, 892, 893, 922, 923, 924, 981, 983.

548 Record

N. *record*, recording, documentation; historical record, memoir, chronicle, annals, history 590n. *narrative;* biographical record, case history, psychic profile, histogram, psychogram 590n. *biography;* dossier, rogues' gallery; public record, gazette, official journal, Hansard, Congressional Record; official publication, Blue Book, White Paper; recorded material, minutes, transactions, acta; notes, annotations, marginalia, adversaria, jottings, dottings, cuttings, press-c; memorabilia, memorandum 505n. *reminder;* reports, returns, statements 524n. *report;* tally, score-sheet, score-board; evidentiary record, form, document, muniment; voucher, certificate, diploma 466n. *credential;* birth certificate, death c., marriage lines 767n. *title-deed;* copy, spare c., carbon c., 22n. *duplicate;* documentation, records, preserved r., old r., archives, papers, correspondence; record, book, roll, register, registry, cartulary; tablet, table, note-book, minute-b., log-b., log, diary, journal, scrap-book, album; ledger, cash-book, day-b., check-b. 808n. *account-book;* file, index, waiting list 87n. *list;* card, Microcard, microfilm; inscription, legend, caption, heading 547n. *indication;* wall-writing, graffito 586n. *script*.

registration, registry, record-keeping; recording, sound r., tape-r.; inscribing, engraving, epigraphy; enrollment, enlistment; booking, reservation; entering, entry, double-e., book-keeping, accountancy 808n. *accounts;* filing, indexing, docket, docket-stamp.

monument, memorial 505n. *reminder;* mausoleum 364n. *tomb;* statue, bust 551n. *image;* brass, tablet, slab, inscription 364n. *obsequies;* hatchment, funerary, achievement 547n. *heraldry;* pillar, column, memorial arch, obelisk, monolith; ancient monument, archaeological m., cromlech, dolmen, cairn, menhir, gilgal, megalith, barrow, tell 125n. *antiquity;* testimonial, cup, prize, ribbon, decoration 729n. *trophy*.

trace, vestige, relic, remains 41n. *leavings;* footstep, footprint, footmark, hoofmark, pug-mark, tread; spoor, slot; scent, smell, piste; wake, wash, trail, smoke-t., track, sound-t.; furrow, swath, path; fingermark, thumb-impression 547n. *indication;* fingerprint, dabs 466n. *evidence*; mark, stain, scar, cicatrix, scratch, weal, wale, welt 845n. *blemish*.

Adj. *recording* etc. vb., recordative 505adj. *remembering;* annalistic, record-making; self-recording; record-

able; monumental, epigraphic, inscriptional.
recorded, on record, in the file, documented; filed, indexed, entered, booked, registered; down, put d.; in writing 586adj. *written;* in print, in black and white 587adj. *printed;* traceable, vestigial, extant 41adj. *remaining*.
Vb. *record*, tape-record; document, put on record, place on r.; docket, file, index, catalog, store in the archives; inscribe, cut, carve, grave, incise 555vb. *engrave;* take down, set down in black and white, put in a book, commit to writing 586vb. *write;* have printed 587vb. *print;* write down, jot d.; note, mark, make a note of; minute, calendar; chronicle, historify 590vb. *describe*.
register, mark up, chalk up, tick off, score; tabulate, table, enroll, enlist 87vb. *list;* fill in, fill up, enter, post, book; reserve, put on the list, put on the waiting l.; inscribe, enscroll, blazon; log, diarize, journalize 808vb. *account*.
Adv. *on record*, in the file, in the index, on the books.
See: 22, 41, 87, 125, 364, 466, 505, 524, 547, 551, 555, 586, 587, 590, 729, 767, 808, 845.

549 Recorder
N. *recorder*, registrar, record-keeper, archivist, remembrancer; Master of the Rolls, Custos Rotulorum; notary, protonotary; amanuensis, stenographer, scriniary, scribe; secretary, referencer, receptionist; writer, penpusher; clerk, babu; record-clerk, tally-c., filing-c., book-keeper 808n. *accountant;* engraver 555n. *engraving;* draftsman 556n. *artist;* photographer, cameraman, snapshotter 551n. *photography;* filing cabinet, record room, muniment r., Record Office; Recording Angel.
chronicler, saga-man, annalist, diarist, historian, historiographer, biographer, autobiographer 590n. *narrator;* archaeologist, antiquary 125n. *antiquarian;* memorialist 763n. *petitioner;* reporter, pressman, journalist, columnist, gossip-writer, newsman 529n. *newsmonger;* press photographer, candid camera.
recording instrument, recorder, tape-r.; record, disc, long-player 414n. *phonograph;* dictaphone, telautograph, printing telegraph, teleprinter, tape-machine, ticker-tape; cash register; turnstile; seismograph, speedometer 465n. *gauge;* time-recorder, stopwatch 117n. *timekeeper;* hygrometer 341n. *hygrometry;* anemometer 340n. *pneumatics;* camera, photostat; pen, pencil 586n. *stationery*.
See: 117, 125, 340, 341, 414, 465, 529, 551, 555, 556, 586, 590, 763, 808.

550 Obliteration
N. *obliteration*, erasure, rasure, effacement; overprinting, defacement; deletion, blue pencil, censorship; crossing out, cancellation, cancel; circumduction, annulment, cassation 752n. *abrogation;* burial, oblivion 506n. *amnesty;* blot, stain 649n. *dirt;* tabula rasa, clean slate, clean sweep 149n. *revolution;* eraser, duster, sponge, rubber, india-rubber; paint-stripper, abrasive 648n. *cleaning utensil*.
Adj. *obliterated*, wiped out, effaced; out of print, leaving no trace, printless, unrecorded, unregistered, unwritten; intestate.
Vb. *obliterate*, remove the traces, cover, cover up 525vb. *conceal;* overpaint, overprint, deface, make illegible; efface, erase, rase, scratch out, rub o.; abrade 333vb. *rub;* expunge, sponge out, wash o., wipe o.; blot, black out, blot o.; rub off, wipe o., wash o.; take out, cancel, delete, dele; strike out, cross out, ring, score through, draw the pen t., censor, blue-pencil; wipe off the map, bury, cover 364vb. *inter;* sink in oblivion 506vb. *forget;* submerge 165vb. *suppress;* drown 399vb. *silence;* leave no trace 446vb. *disappear;* be effaced 506vb. *be forgotten*.
See: 149, 165, 333, 364, 399, 446, 506, 525, 648, 649, 752.

551 Representation
N. *representation*, acting for, agentship 751n. *commission;* personification, incarnation, embodiment; typifying, typification, symbolization 547n. *indication;* conventional representation, diagram, picture-writing, hieroglyphics 586n. *writing;* presentment, presentation, projection, realization, evocation 522n. *manifestation;* assuming the part of, personation, impersonation; enactment, performance, doing 594n. *acting;* mimesis, mimicry, noises off, charade, dumb show 20n. *imitation;* depiction, characterization 590n. *description;* delineation, graphic d., drawing, illustration, graphic treatment, ico-

nography 553n. *painting;* likeness, similitude 18n. *similarity;* exact likeness, double, facsimile 22n. *duplicate;* trace, tracing, diagraph 233n. *outline;* reflection (**see** *image*); portraiture, portrayal; pictorial equivalent, true picture, striking likeness, speaking l., photographic l., realism 553n. *picture;* bad likeness, indifferent l. 552n. *misrepresentation;* reproduction, lithograph, oleograph, collotype 555n. *printing;* etching 555 n. *engraving;* design, blueprint, draft, rough d., cartoon, sketch, outline 623n. *plan;* slide 422n. *transparency*.

image, very i., exact i. 22n. *duplicate;* eidetic image, clear i.; mental image, after-image 451n. *idea*; projection, reflected image 417n. *reflection;* idol, graven image 982n. *idolatry;* painted image, icon; statuary, statue, colossus; statuette, bust, torso, head 554n. *sculpture;* effigy, figure, figurine; wax figure, waxwork; dummy, tailor's d., lay figure; model, working m.; doll, poupée, golliwog; marionette, fantoccini; puppet, maumet, manikin; snowman, gingerbread man; scarecrow; robot, automation; type, symbol.

art, fine a., graphic a. 553n. *painting;* plastic art 554n. *sculpture;* architecture; modern art, classical a., Renaissance a., Hellenistic a., Greek a., oriental a.; Byzantinism, Romanesque art, Gothic a., baroque a., rococo a.; expressionism, modernism; functional art, commercial a., non-functional a., decorative a. 844n. *ornamental art;* the minor arts, illumination, calligraphy, weaving, tapestry, embroidery, pottery.

photography, radiography, skiagraphy; cinematography 445n. *cinema;* rotograph, photograph, photo, photostat, snapshot, snap, shot; color photo, transparency, slide; print, photo-p., still; exposure, over-e., under-e; reduction, enlargement, blow-up, close-up; plate, film, color f., panchromatic f., fast f.; skiagram, radiograph, X-ray; heliotype, calotype, talbotype, daguerreotype; camera obscura 442n. *camera;* cameraman, cinematographer, photographer, snap-shotter; radiographer.

map, chart, plan, outline, sketch map, relief m., political m., survey m., road m., air m., star m.; Admiralty chart, portulan, portolano; ground plan, ichnography; scenograph, elevation, side-e., projection, Mercator's p., Chad's p.; atlas, world a.; map-making, cartography.

Adj. *representing,* reflecting etc. vb.; representative 590adj. *descriptive;* pictorial, graphic, vivid; emblematic, symbolic; figurative, illustrative, diagrammatic; representational, realistic, naturalistic, impressionist, surrealistic; photographic, photogenic, paintable.

represented, drawn, delineated etc.vb.; fairly drawn, well represented; reflected, imaged; painted, pictured; being drawn, sitting for.

Vb. *represent,* act for 755vb. *deputize;* stand for, symbolize 514vb. *mean;* type, typify, incarnate, embody, personify; act the part of, assume the role of; personate, impersonate, pose as 542vb. *deceive;* pose, model, sit for 23vb. *be example;* present, enact, perform, do 594vb. *dramatize;* project, shadow forth, shadow out, adumbrate, suggest; reflect, image, hold the mirror up to nature; mimic, mime, copy 20vb. *imitate;* depict, characterize 590vb. *describe;* delineate, limn, draw, picture, portray, figure; illustrate, emblazon 553vb. *paint;* hit off, make a likeness, catch a l., catch, realize, register; make an image, carve, cast 554vb. *sculpt;* cut 555vb. *engrave;* mold, shape 243vb. *efform;* take the shape, follow the s., mold upon, fashion u.; design, blueprint, draft, sketch out, chalk o. 623 vb. *plan;* diagrammatize, diagram, make a d., construct a figure, describe a circle 233vb. *outline;* sketch, dash off 609vb. *improvise;* map, chart, survey, plot.

photograph, photo, take a p.; snapshot, snap, take a s.; take, shoot, film; X-ray, radiograph, daguerreotype; expose, develop, enlarge, blow up, reduce.

See: 18, 20, 22, 23, 233, 243, 417, 422, 442, 445, 451, 514, 522, 542, 547, 552, 553, 554, 555, 586, 590, 594, 609, 623, 751, 755, 844, 982.

552 Misrepresentation

N. *misrepresentation*, false light, not a true picture 541n. *falsehood;* unfair picture, bad likeness 914n. *injustice;* travesty, parody 546n. *exaggeration;* caricature, burlesque, guy 851n. *ridicule;* flattering portrait 925n. *flattery;* non-realism, non-representational art 551n. *art;* bad art, daubing, sign-painting; daub, botch; twist, turn, misapplication, anamorphosis, deformation, distorted image, false i., distorting mirror 246n. *distortion;* misreport, misquotation, misinformation 535n. *misteaching;* misexposi-

tion 521n. *misinterpretation.*
Adj. *misrepresented* etc. vb.
Vb. *misrepresent,* misdescribe 535vb. *misteach;* deform 246vb. *distort;* give a twist *or* turn, miscolor, tone down 925vb. *flatter;* over-dramatize 546vb. *exaggerate;* overdraw, caricature, guy, burlesque, parody, travesty; daub, botch, splash; lie about, traduce 926vb. *detract;* lie 541vb. *be false.*
See: 246, 521, 535, 541, 546, 551, 851, 914, 925, 926.

553 Painting

N. *painting,* graphic art, coloring, rubrication, illumination; daubing, finger-painting; washing, tinting, touching up; depicting, drawing, sketching 551n. *representation;* artistry, composition, rectilinear c., design, technique, draftsmanship, brushwork; treatment, tone, values, atmosphere, ambience, local color; monotone, monochrome, polychrome 425n. *color;* black and white, chiaroscuro, grisaille.
art style, style of painting, grand style, grand manner; intimate style, genre (**see** *art subject*); pasticcio, pastiche; iconography, portrait-painting, portraiture, historical painting, landscape p., scene-p., scenography, sign-painting, miniature p.; oil-painting, watercoloring, painting in tempera; fresco painting, mural p., encaustic p., impasto.
school of painting, the primitives, Byzantine school, Renaissance s., Sienese s., Florentine s., Venetian s., Perugian s., Umbrian s., Dutch s., Flemish s., German s., American s.; proto-baroque, mannerism, baroque, rococo, Pre-Raphaelitism, neo-classicism, realism, romanticism, impressionism, post-impressionism, neo-I., cubism, expressionism, pointillism, vorticism, neo-plasticism, functionalism, futurism, surrealism; abstract art; Tachism, action painting; Euston Road, Bloomsbury, Greenwich Village.
art subject, landscape, seascape, skyscape, cloudscape; view, scene, prospect, diorama, panorama, bird's-eye view; interior, still life, nocturne, nude; crucifixion, pietà.
picture, pictorial equivalent 551n. *representation;* easel-picture, cabinet p.; tableau, mosaic, tapestry; painting, pastiche, icon, triptych, diptych; fresco, mural, wall-painting; canvas, daub; drawing, line-d.; sketch, outline, cartoon; oil-painting, watercolor, aquarelle, pastel, black-and-white drawing, pen-and-ink d., pencil d., charcoal d.; cartoon, chad, caricature, silhouette; miniature, vignette, thumb-nail sketch, illuminated initial; old master, masterpiece; study, nocturne, nude, portrait, full-length p., three-quarter length p., half-l. p., kit-cat, head, profile, full-face portrait; print, photoprint 551n. *photography;* rotograph, photogravure, reproduction, photographic r., half-tone; aquatint, woodcut 555n. *engraving;* print, plate; illustration, picture postcard, cigarette card, fag-c., stamp, transfer; picture book, photograph album, illustrated work 589n. *book.*
art equipment, palette, palette knife, paint-brush, paint-box, paint-tube; paints, oils, oil paint, poster p.; watercolors, tempera, distemper, gouache, gesso, varnish 226n. *facing;* ink, crayon, pastel, chalk, charcoal; pen, pencil; canvas, easel, picture-frame; studio, atelier, art museum, picture-gallery; model, sitter, poser, subject; drysaltery 633n. *provision.*
Adj. *painted,* daubed, scumbled, plastered etc. vb.; graphic, pictorial, scenic, picturesque, decorative 844 adj. *ornamental;* pastel, in paint, in oils in watercolors, in tempera 425 adj. *colored;* linear, black-and-white, shaded, stippled; chiaroscuro, grisaille 429adj. *gray;* painterly, paintable 551adj. *representing.*
Vb. *paint,* colorize 425vb. *color;* tint, touch up, daub; dead-color, scumble, put on, paint on; spread a color, drive a c., lay on the c., lay it on thick 226vb. *coat;* splash the color, slap on the c.; paint a picture, portray, do a portrait, draw, sketch, limn, cartoon 551vb. *represent;* miniate, rubricate, illuminate; do in oils, do in watercolors, do in tempera, do in black and white; ink, chalk, crayon, pencil, stencil, shade, stipple; pinxit, delineavit, fecit.
See: 226, 425, 429, 551, 555, 589, 633, 847.

554 Sculpture

N. *sculpture,* plastic art 551n. *representation;* modeling, figuring; carving, stone cutting, wood-carving; molding, ceroplastics, petroglyph, rock-carving, bone-c., shell-c., scrimshaw; statuary; group; statue, colossus; statuette, figurine, bust, torso, head, cast, plaster c., waxwork 551n.

image; ceramics 381n. *pottery;* anaglyph, cameo, intaglio, relief, half-relief, mezzo-relievo 254n. *relievo;* stone, marble, Parian m.; bronze, clay, wax, plasticine; modeling tool, chisel, burin.

Adj. *glyptic,* sculptured, carved; statuary, statuesque, marmoreal; anaglyptic, in relief 254adj. *salient;* ceroplastic; toreutic.

Vb. *sculpt,* sculpture, cut, carve, chisel, chip; model, mold, cast; sculpsit.

See: 254, 381, 551.

555 Engraving

N. *engraving,* etching, line engraving, plate e., steel e., copper e., chalcography; zincography, cerography, glyptography, gem-cutting, gem-engraving; mezzotint, aquatint; wood-engraving, xylography, lignography, woodcut; drypoint; steel plate, copper p., graphotype; stone, block, wood-b.; chisel, graver, burin, bur, bur-chisel, needle, drypoint, etching-p., style.

printing, type-p. 587n. *print;* plate printing, copper-plate p., intaglio p., anastatic p.; lithography, photolithography, photogravure, chromolithography, colorprinting, three-color p., four-color p.; stereotype, autotype, graphotype, heliotype; stamping, impression; die, punch, stamp.

Vb. *engrave,* grave, incise, cut; etch, stipple, scrape; bite, bite in; impress, stamp; lithograph 587vb. *print;* mezzotint, aquatint, incisit, sculpsit, imprimit.

See: 587.

556 Artist

N. *artist,* craftsman 686n. *artisan;* artmaster, designer, draftsman; fashion-artist, dress-designer, couturier; drawer, sketcher, delineator, limner; copyist; caricaturist, cartoonist; illustrator, commercial artist; painter, colorist, luminist, luminarist; dauber, pavement artist, scene-painter, sign-p.; oil-painter, water-color p., aquarellist, pastelist; illuminator, miniaturist; portrait-painter, landscape-p., marine p., genre p., still-life p., fruit-and-flower p.; academician, R.A., old master, modern m.; Pre-Raphaelite, impressionist, fauvist, dadaist, cubist, futurist, vorticist, surrealist, action painter 553n. *school of painting.*

sculptor, carver, statuary, monumental mason, modeler, wax-m., molder, figurist; image-maker, idol-m.

engraver, etcher, aquatinter; lapidary, chaser, gem-engraver, enameler, enamelist; typographer, type-cutter 587n. *printer.*

See: 553, 587, 686.

557 Language

N. *language,* tongue, speech, idiom; spoken language, living l.; patter, lingo, bat 560n. *dialect;* mother tongue, native t., native language; vernacular, common speech, folk s., vulgar dialect; correct speech, idiomatic s., Queen's English; lingua franca, Koine, Hindustani, kitchen H., Swahili, pidgin, pidgin English, Chinook; sign-language, semeiology 547n. *gesticulation;* diplomatic language, international l.; artificial language, Esperanto, Ido, Volapuk; universal language, pasilaly; private language, invented l., idioglossia, idiolalia; official language, Mandarin, Hindi, standard English; written language, officialese, translationese; learned language, dead l., Latin, Greek, Sanskrit, Pali, Pahlevi, Coptic, Ethiopic; confusion of tongues, polyglot medley, Babel, babble 61n. *confusion.*

language type, inflected language, analytical l., agglutinative l., monosyllabic l., tonal l.; language group, family of languages, Aryan, Indo-European, Indo-Germanic, Indo-Aryan, Hamitic, Semitic, Dravidian; Turanian, Ural-Altaic, Finno-Tartar, Finno-Ugrian; Sino-Tibetan, Tibeto-Chinese; Bantu.

linguistics, language study, glossology, glottology, dialectology, philology, comparative p.; comparative grammar 564n. *grammar;* phonetics 577n. *pronunciation;* Grimm's law, Verner's l.; derivation 559n. *etymology;* morphology; semasiology, semantics 514n. *meaning;* onomasiology 561n. *nomenclature;* paleography 125n. *palaetiology;* linguistic distribution, linguistic geography, word-g.; genius of a language, feel of a l., sprachgefühl, sense of idiom; polyglatism, bilingualism.

literature, polite l., written language, belles lettres 589n. *reading matter;* letters, humane scholarship, arts, humanities, litterae humaniores 654n. *civilization;* Muses, literary circles, republic of letters, P.E.N. 589n. *author;* literary history, history of literature; Golden Age, Silver A., Augustan A., Classical A.; compendium of literature 592n. *anthology;* digest, chrestomathy, reader 589n. *textbook.*

linguist, language student, philologist, glottologist; etymologist, lexicographer 559n. *etymology;* semasiologist, onomasiologist, grammarian 564n. *grammar;* phonetician 398n. *acoustics;* student of literature, man of letters, belletrist 492n. *scholar;* humanist, humane scholar, classical s., oriental s.; Hellenist, Latinist, Sanskritist, sinologist, Semiticist, Arabist, Hebraist, Hispanicist; polyglot, bilingual speaker, bilinguist.

Adj. *linguistic*, philological, etymological, grammatical, morphological; lexicographical, onomasiological, semasiological; analytic; agglutinative; monosyllabic; tonal, inflected; holophrastic; correct, pure; written, literary, standard; spoken, living, idiomatic; vulgar, colloquial, vernacular, slangy 560adj. *dialectical;* local, enchorial; current, common, demotic; bilingual, diglot; multilingual, polyglot.

literary, written, polished, polite, humanistic, classical, belletristic; lettered, learned, dead.

See: 61, 125, 398, 492, 514, 547, 559, 560, 561, 564, 577, 589, 592, 654.

558 Letter

N. *letter*, part of the alphabet; sign, character, written c. 586n. *script;* alphabetism, alphabetics, alphabet, ABC, abecedary, criss-cross row; syllabic alphabet, syllabary; Chinese character, ideogram, ideograph; pictogram, cuneiform, hieroglyphic; ogham alphabet, runic a., futhark; Greek alphabet, Roman a., Cyrillic a.; Devanagari, Nagari, Brahui; runic letter, wen; lettering, black letter, Gothic, italic; ampersand; big letter, capital l., cap, majuscule; small letter, minuscule; block letter, uncial; printed letter, letterpress, type, bold t. 587n. *print-type.*

initials, first letter; monogram, cipher; anagram, acrostic.

spoken letter, phone, phoneme 398n. *speech sound;* consonant, spirant, fricative, aspirate; labial, liquid, dental, palatal, cerebral, guttural, mute, surd; sonant, voiced letter; vowel, semivowel, diphthong, triphthong 577n. *voice;* syllable, monosyllable, disyllable, polysyllable; prefix, affix, suffix.

spelling, orthography, cacography; phonography, lexigraphy; anagrammatism, metagrammatism; spelling game, spelling bee.

Adj. *literal*, in letters, lettered; alphabetical, abecedarian; in syllables, syllabic; Cyrillic; runic, oghamic; cuneiform, hieroglyphic 586adj. *written;* Gothic, italic, roman, uncial; large, majuscule, capital, initial; small minuscule; lexigraphical, spelled, orthographic; ciphered, monogrammatic; anacrostic, anagrammatic; phonetic, consonantal, vocalic, voiced 577adj. *vocal.*

Vb. *spell,* spell out, read, syllable; use an alphabet, alphabetize; letter, form letters, uncialize 586vb. *write;* initial 547vb. *sign;* cipher, make a monogram; anagrammatize.

Adv. *alphabetically*, by letters; syllabically, in syllables.

See: 398, 547, 577, 581, 586, 587.

559 Word

N. *word*, Verbum, Logos 965n. *the Deity;* expression, locution 563n. *phrase;* term vocable 561n. *name;* phoneme, syllable 398n. *speech sound;* semanteme 514n. *meaning;* gloss, glossa; isogloss, synonym, tautonym 13n. *identity;* homonym, homophene, homophone, pun 518n. *equivocalness;* antonym 14n. *contrariety;* etymon, root, false r., backformation; derivation, derivative, paronym, doublet; morphological unit, morpheme, stem, inflection, affix, suffix, prefix, infix; part of speech 564n. *grammar*; diminutive, pejorative, intensive; cliché, vogue-word; nonce-word, new word, loan-w., loan-translation, calque 560n. *neology;* rhyming word, assonant 18 n. *similarity;* bad word, nasty w., swear-word 899n. *malediction;* hard word, jawbreaker, long word, polysyllable; short word, monosyllable; many words, verbiage, wordiness, verbosity 570n. *pleonasm;* lexicography, speedwriting 569n. *conciseness.*

dictionary, rhyming d., polyglot d.; lexicon, wordbook, wordstock, wordlist, glossary, vocabulary; thesaurus, gradus; compilation, concordance.

etymology, derivation of words, philology 557n. *linguistics;* morphology; semasiology 514n. *meaning;* phonology, orthoepy 577n. *pronunciation;* onomasiology, terminology 561n. *nomenclature;* lexicology, lexicography; logophile, philologist, ety-

mologist, lexicographer, compiler, dictionarian.
Adj. *verbal*, literal; titular, nominal; etymological, lexical, vocabular; philological, lexicographical, lexigraphical; derivative, conjugate, cognate, paronymous; synonymous, autonymous 514adj. *semantic;* worldly, verbose 570adj. *pleonastic.*
Adv. *verbally*, lexically; verbatim 494 adv. *truly.*
See: 13, 14, 18, 398, 494, 514, 518, 557, 560, 561, 563, 564, 569, 570, 577, 899, 965.

560 Neology

N. *neology*, neologism, neolalia, neoterism 126n. *newness;* coinage, new c., new word, nonce-w., vogue-w., cliché; imported w., loan-w., loan translation, calque 559n. *word;* unfamiliar word, jawbreaker, newfangled expression, slang e.; technical language, jargon, technical term, term of art; barbarism, caconym, hybrid, hyrid expression; corruption, monkish Latin, dog L.; novelese, journalese, officialese, newspeak; affected language, archaism, Lallans 850n. *affectation;* abuse of language, abuse of terms, mis-saying, antiphrasis, malapropism 565n. *solecism;* word-play, spoonerism 839n. *witticism;* paraphrasia, paralalia, idioglossia, idiolalia 580n. *speech defect.*
dialect, idiom, lingo, patois, brogue, vernacular 557n. *language;* cockney, Doric, broad Scots, Lallans; broken English, pidgin E., pidgin, Chinook; Koine, lingua franca, hybrid language; Briticism, anglicism, Americanism, Scotticism, Hibernicism, gallicism, Teutonism, Sinicism; chi-chi, babuism; provincialism, localism, vernacularism; sigmatism, iotacism 580n. *speech defect;* neologist, wordcoiner, neoterist; dialectology 557n. *linguistics.*
slang, vulgarism, colloquialism, byword; jargon, argot, cant, patter; gypsy lingo, Romany; flash tongue, thieves' Latin, peddler's French, St. Giles Greek, rhyming slang; Billingsgate; Wall St. slang; doubletalk, backchat; macaronics, gibberish 515n. *empty talk.*
Adj. *neological*, neoteristic, newfangled, newly coined, not in the dictionary; barbaric, barbarous, unidiomatic, hybrid, corrupt, pidgin; loaned, borrowed, imported, foreign, revived, archaic, obsolete; irregular, solecistic 565adj. *ungrammatical.*
dialectal, vernacular, kailyard; Doric, cockney, broad; provincial, local; homely, colloquial; unliterary, slangy, argotic, canting, cant; jargonistic, journalistic; technical, special.
Vb. *neologize*, coin words, invent vocabulary; talk slang, jargonize, cant; talk cockney, talk Doric, burr.
See: 126, 515, 557, 559, 565, 580, 839, 850.

561 Nomenclature

N. *nomenclature,* naming etc. vb.; calling, nomination, cognomination; giving one's name, eponymy; onomatology, terminology, orismology; dedication, nuncupation, declaration 532n. *affirmation;* description, designation, appellation, denomination; antonomasia 519n. *trope;* addressing, compellation, apostrophe; roll call 583n. *allocution;* christening, naming ceremony, baptism 988n. *Christian rite;* study of place-names, toponymy.
name, nomen, first name, forename, Christian name, prenomen; surname, patronymic, matronymic, cognomen; maiden name, married n.; appellation, moniker; nickname, pet name, by-name, agnomen, kenning; epithet, description; title, handle, style, signature; heading, head, caption 547n. *indication;* designation, appellative; name and address 547n. *label;* term, cant t., special t., technical t., term of art 560n. *neology;* name-child, same name, namesake, synonym, eponym, tautonym, counter-term, antonym; pseudonym 562n. *misnomer;* noun, proper n. 564n. *part of speech;* list of names, onomasticon; placename, local n.
nomenclator, roll-caller, announcer, toastmaster; onomatologist; terminologist; namer, namegiver, eponym, christener, baptizer.
Adj. *named,* called etc. vb.; titled, entitled, christened; known as, alias; so-called, soi-disant; hight, yclept; nominal, titular; named after, eponymous, theophoric; fitly named, what one may fairly call; nameable.
naming, nuncupative, nuncupatory 532adj. *affirmative;* appellative, compellative, terminological, orismological.
Vb. *name*, call, give a name, christen, baptize 988vb. *perform ritual;* give one's name to, eponymize; call by the name of, surname, nickname, dub, clepe; give one his title, sir, bemadam; title, entitle, style, term

80vb. *specify;* distinguish 463vb. *discriminate;* define, characterize 547vb. *label;* call by name, call the roll, call out the names, nomenclate, announce; divulge the name 526vb. *divulge;* blacklist 924vb. *exprobate.*

be named, own *or* bear *or* go by the name of; answer to; sail under the flag of.

Adv. *by name;* namely; terminologically.

See: 50, 80, 463, 519, 526, 532, 547, 560, 562, 564, 583, 924, 988.

562 Misnomer

N. *misnomer*, misnaming, miscalling; malapropism 565n. *solecism;* wrong name, false n., alias, assumed title; nom de guerre, nom de plume, penname; nom de theatre, stage name, pseudonym, allonym; nickname, pet name 561n. *name;* pseudonymity.

no name, anonymity; anonym, certain person, so-and-so, N. or M., sir or madam; Mr. X, Monsieur Tel, A. N. Other; what d'ye call 'em, thingummy-bob; this or that; and co.; some, any, what-have-you.

Adj. *misnamed*, miscalled, mistitled etc. vb.; self-christened, self-styled, soi-disant, would-be, so-called, quasi, pseudonymous.

anonymous, unknown, nameless, without a name; incognito, innominate, unnamed, unsigned; a certain, certain, such; some, any, this or that.

Vb. *misname*, mistake the name of, miscall, misterm, mistitle; nickname, dub 561vb. *name;* misname oneself, assume an alias; conceal one's name, be anonymous; not subscribe, refuse to sign; write under an assumed name, usurp the name.

See: 561, 565.

563 Phrase

N. *phrase*, form of words; clause, sentence, period, paragraph; expression, locution; idiom, idiotism, mannerism 80n. *specialty;* fixed expression, formula, set phrase, set terms; hackneyed expression, well-worn phrase, cliché, commonplace 610n. *habit;* saying, motto, moral, epigram 496n. *maxim;* lapidary phrase, epitaph 364n. *obsequies;* inscription, legend, caption 548n. *record;* phrases, empty p., words, compliments 515n. *empty talk;* terminology 561n. *nomenclature;* phraseology, phrasing, diction, wording, choice of language, choice of expression, turn of e.; well-turned phrase, rounded p. 575n. *elegance;* roundabout phrase, periphrasis, circumlocution 570n. *diffuseness;* paraphrase 520n. *translation;* written phrase, phraseogram, phraseograph 586n. *script;* phrasemonger, phrase-maker, epigraphist, epigrammatist, proverbialist 575n. *stylist.*

Adj. *phraseological*, sentential, periodic, in phrases, in sentences; idiomatic; well-rounded, well-couched.

Vb. *phrase*, word, articulate, syllable; reword, rephrase 520vb. *translate;* express, put in words, clothe in w., find words for, state 532vb. *affirm;* put words together, turn a sentence, round a period 566vb. *show style.*

Adv. *in terms*, in good set t., **in** round t., in set phrases.

See: 80, 364, 496, 515, 520, 532, 548, 561, 566, 570, 575, 586, 610.

564 Grammar

N. *grammar*, comparative g., philology 557n. *linguistics;* grammarianism, grammatical studies, analysis, parsing, construing; praxis, paradigm; accidence, inflection, case; conjugation, mode, voice, tense; number, gender, agreement of g.; accentuation, pointing, vowel p. 547n. *punctuation;* nunation, mimation; guna, vriddhi; umlaut, ablaut, attraction, assimilation, dissimilation; ablative absolute, genitive a., locative a.; syntax, word order, parataxis, asyndeton, ellipsis, apposition; bad grammar 565n. *solecism;* good grammar, grammaticalness, correct style, jus et norma loquendi.

part of speech, substantive, noun, undeclined n., asymptote; common noun, proper n.; adjective; adnoun; verb, irregular v.; adverb, preposition, postposition, copula, conjunction; particle, augment, syllabic a., temporal a.; augmentative, affix, suffix, postfix, infix; inflection, case-ending; formative, morpheme, semanteme; denominative, deverbative; diminutive, intensive.

Adj. *grammatical*, correct; syntactical, inflectional; heteroclite, asymptote; irregular, anomalous; masculine, feminine, neuter; singular, dual, plural; substantial, adjectival, adnominal; verbal, adverbial; participial; prepositional; denominative, deverbal; conjunctive, copulative; elative, comparative, superlative.

Vb. *parse*, analyze, inflect, punctuate, conjugate, decline; construe 520vb.

interpret; know one's grammar.
See: 520, 547, 557, 565.

565 Solecism
N. *solecism,* bad grammar, false g., faulty syntax, false concord, nonsequence of tenses, misconjugation; missaying, antiphrasis; misapplication, catachresis; irregularity, impropriety, barbarism 560n. *neology;* malapropism, cacology, bull, slip, faux pas, slip of the tongue, lapsus linguae 495n. *mistake;* mispronunciation, dropping one's aitches, lisp, lallation, lambdacism 580n. *speech defect;* misspelling, cacography.
Adj. *ungrammatical,* solecistic, solecistical; irregular, abnormal; faulty, improper, incongruous; misapplied, catachrestic.
Vb. *solecize,* ignore grammar, disdain g., violate g., forget one's syntax; break Priscian's head, murder the Queen's English; mispronounce 580 vb. *stammer;* lisp, drop one's aitches; misspell 495vb. *blunder.*
See: 495, 560, 580.

566 Style
N. *style,* fashion, mode, tone, manner, vein, strain 688n. *conduct;* one's own style, personal s., idiosyncrasy, mannerism, trick 80n. *specialty;* mode of expression, diction, parlance, phrasing, phraseology 563n. *phrase;* choice of words, vocabulary, choice v.; literary style, command of language, command of idiom, raciness, power 571n. *vigor;* tact, feeling for words, sprachgefühl, sense of language; literary charm, grace 575n. *elegance;* word magic, word-spinning 579n. *oratory;* weak style 572n. *feebleness;* severe style, vernacular s., kailyard school 573n. *plainness;* elaborate style 574n. *ornament;* clumsy style 576n. *inelegance.*
Adj. *stylistic,* mannered, literary; elegant, ornate, rhetorical, word-spinning; racy, idiomatic; plain, perspicuous, forceful
Vb. *show style,* conform to idiom, care for words, spin w.; style, express, measure one's words 563vb. *phrase.*
See: 80, 563, 571, 572, 573, 574, 575, 576, 579, 688.

567 Perspicuity
N. *perspicuity,* perspicuousness, clearness, clarity, lucidity, limpidity 422 n. *transparency;* limpid style 516n. *intelligibility;* directness 573n. *plainness;* definition, definiteness, exactness 494n. *accuracy.*
Adj. *perspicuous,* lucid, limpid 422 adj. *transparent;* clear, unambiguous 516adj. *intelligible;* explicit, clearcut 80adj. *definite;* exact 494adj. *accurate;* uninvolved, direct 573adj. *plain.*
See: 80, 422, 494, 516, 573.

568 Imperspicuity
N. *imperspicuity,* imperspicuousness, obscurity 517n. *unintelligibility;* cloudiness, fogginess 423n. *opacity;* abstraction, abstruseness; complexity, involved style, cultism, Gongorism 574n. *ornament;* hard words, Johnsonese, Carlylese 700n. *difficulty;* imprecision, impreciseness, vagueness 474n. *uncertainty;* inaccuracy 495n. *inexactness;* ambiguity 518n. *equivocalness;* mysteriousness, oracular style 530n. *enigma;* profundity, deepness 211n. *depth;* overcompression, ellipsis 569n. *conciseness;* cloud of words, verbiage 570n. *diffuseness.*
Adj. *imperspicuous,* unclear, untransparent, cloudy 423adj. *opaque;* obscure 418adj. *dark;* oracular, mysterious, enigmatic 517adj. *unintelligible;* abstruse, profound 211adj. *deep;* allusive, indirect 523adj. *latent;* vague, imprecise, indefinite 474adj. *uncertain;* ambiguous 518 adj. *equivocal;* confused, tangled, involved 61adj. *complex;* harsh, crabbed, stiff 576adj. *inelegant;* hard, full of long words, Johnsonian 700 adj. *difficult.*
See: 61, 211, 418, 423, 474, 495, 517, 518, 523, 530, 569, 570, 574, 576, 700.

569 Conciseness
N. *conciseness,* concision, succinctness, brevity, soul of wit; pithiness, pithy saying 496n. *maxim;* aphorism, epigram 839n. *witticism;* economy of words, verbal economy, no words wasted, few words, terseness, Spartan brevity, laconism; compression, telegraphese; ellipsis, aposiopesis; syncope, abbreviation, contraction 204n. *shortening;* compendiousness, epitome, outline, brief sketch 592n. *compendium;* monostich, Japanese poem; compactness, portmanteau word, telescope w.; clipped speech, monosyllabism 582n. *taciturnity;*

nutshell, the long and the short of it 204n. *shortness.*

Adj. *concise,* brief, not long in telling, short and sweet 204adj. *short;* laconic, monosyllabic, sparing of words 582adj. *taciturn;* irreducible, succinct; to the point, trenchant; curt, brusque 885adj. *ungracious;* compendious, condensed, tight, close, compact; pithy, pregnant, sententious, neat, exact, pointed, aphoristic, epigrammatic, Tacitean; elliptic, telegraphic, contracted, compressed; summary, cut short, abbreviated.

Vb. *be concise,*—brief etc. adj; need few words, not beat about the bush, come to the point, cut a long story short; telescope, compress, condense, contract, abridge, abbreviate 204vb. *shorten;* outline, sketch; summarize, sum up, resume 592vb. *abstract;* allow no words, be short with, cut short, cut off; laconize, spare speech, economize words, waste no w., clip one's w. 582vb. *be taciturn;* express pithily, epigrammatize 839vb. *be witty.*

Adv. *concisely,* pithily, summarily, briefly; without wasting words, in brief, in short, in a word, in one sentence, in a nutshell; to cut a long story short; to sum up.

See: 204, 496, 582, 592, 839, 885.

570 Diffuseness

N. *diffuseness* etc. adj.; profuseness, copiousness, amplitude; amplification, dilation 197n. *expansion;* expatiation, circumstantiality, minuteness; fertility, output, productivity, penny-a-lining, word-spinning 171n. *productiveness;* inspiration, vein, flow, outpouring; abundance, overflow, overflowing words, exuberance, redundancy 637n. *redundance;* richness, rich vocabulary, wealth of terms; polylogy, verbosity, wordiness, verbiage, flatulence, vaporing, cloud of words; fluency, non-stop talking, verbal diarrhea 581n. *loquacity;* long-windedness, prolixity, length, epic l.; repetitiveness, reiteration 106n. *repetition;* twice-told tale 838n. *tedium;* gush, rigmarole, drivel 515n. *empty talk;* effusion, tirade, harangue, sermon, speeches 579n. *oration;* descant, disquisition 591n. *dissertation.*

pleonasm, superfluity, redundancy 637 n. *redundance;* hypercharacterization; perissology; battology, tautology, palilogy 106n. *repetition;* prolixity, macrology; circumlocution, periphrasis, roundabout phrases, periphrases; ambages, beating about the bush 518n. *equivocalness;* padding, expletive; verse-filler 40n. *extra;* episode, excursus, excursion, digression 10n. *irrelevance.*

Adj. *diffuse,* verbose, non-stop 581 adj. *loquacious;* profuse, copious, ample, rich: fertile, abundant 171adj. *prolific;* inspired, in the vein, flowing, fluent; exuberant, overflowing 637adj. *redundant;* expatiating, circumstantial, detailed, minute; gushing, effusive; flatulent, windy, vaporing, frothy; polysyllabic, sesquipedalian, magniloquent 574adj. *ornate.*

prolix, of many words, long-winded, wordy, prosy, prosing; spun out, made to last, long drawn out, long-drawn 113adj. *protracted;* longsome, boring 838adj. *tedious;* lengthy, epic, never-ending 203adj. *long;* spreading, diffusive, discursive, excursive, digressing, episodic; rambling, maundering 282adj. *deviating;* desultory, pointless 10adj. *irrelevant;* indirect, circumlocutory, periphrastic, ambagious, roundabout.

pleonastic, hypercharacterized; redundant, excessive 637adj. *superfluous;* repetitious, repetitional, repetitive, battological 106adj. *repeated;* tautologous, tautological; padded, padded out.

Vb. *be diffuse,* — prolix etc. adj.; dilate, expatiate, amplify, particularize, detail, expand, enlarge upon; descant, discourse at length; repeat, tautologize, battologize 106vb. *repeat oneself;* pad, pad out, swell o., draw o., spin o., protract 203vb. *lengthen;* gush, pour out 350vb. *flow;* let oneself go, rant, harangue, perorate 579vb. *orate;* be in the vain, launch out on; spin a long yarn 838vb. *be tedious;* wander, branch out, digress 282vb. *deviate;* ramble, maunder, drivel, yarn, never end; beat about the bush, not come to the point 518vb. *equivocate.*

Adv. *diffusely,* at large, in extenso, at full length, about it and about.

See: 10, 40, 106, 113, 171, 197, 203, 282, 515, 518, 574, 579, 581, 591, 637, 838.

571 Vigor

N. *vigor* 174n. *vigorousness;* power, strength, vitality, drive, force, forcefulness 160n. *energy;* incisiveness, trenchancy, decision; vim, punch, pep, guts; sparkle, verve, vivacity, liveliness, vividness, raciness; spirit, fire, ardor, glow, warmth, vehemence, enthusiasm, passion 818n. *feeling;* bite, piquancy, poignancy, sharpness, mordancy 388n. *pungency;* strong language, serious l., stress, underlining, emphasis 532n. *affirmation;* palilogia, iteration, reiteration 106n. *repetition;* seriousness, gravity, weight, sententiousness; impressiveness, loftiness, elevation, sublimity, grandeur, grandiloquence, declamation 574n. *magniloquence;* rhetoric 579n. *eloquence.*

Adj. *forceful,* powerful, nervous 162 adj. *strong;* energetic, peppy, with punch 174adj. *vigorous;* racy, idiomatic; bold, dashing, spirited, sparkling, vivacious 819adj. *lively;* warm, glowing, fiery, ardent, enthusiastic, impassioned 818adj. *fervent;* vehement, emphatic, insistent, reiterative, positive 532adj. *affirmative;* slashing, cutting, incisive, trenchant 256adj. *sharp;* pointed, pungent, mordant, salty 839adj. *witty;* grave, sententious, full of point, strongly worded 834adj. *serious;* heavy, meaty, solid; weighty, crushing 740adj. *compelling;* vivid, graphic, effective 551adj. *representing;* flowing, inspired, in the vein 579adj. *eloquent;* high-toned, lofty, grand, sublime 821adj. *impressive.*

Adv. *forcefully,* vigorously, energetically, vehemently; in good set terms, in glowing t.

See: 106, 160, 162, 174, 256, 388, 532, 551, 574, 579, 740, 818, 819, 821, 834, 839.

572 Feebleness

N. *feebleness* 163n. *weakness;* weak style, enervated s.; prosiness, frigidity, ineffectiveness, flatness, staleness, vapidity 387n. *insipidity;* jejunity, poverty, thinness, enervation, flaccidity, lack of force, lack of sparkle; lack of style, baldness 573n. *plainness;* anticlimax.

Adj. *feeble,* weak, thin, flat, vapid, insipid 387adj. *tasteless;* wishy-washy, watery; sloppy, sentimental; meager, jejune, exhausted; colorless, bald 573adj. *plain;* languid, flaccid, nerveless, tame; undramatic, unspirited, uninspired, unelevated, unimpassioned, unemphatic; ineffective, cold, frigid, uninspiring, unexciting; monotonous, prosy, dull, dry, boring 838adj. *tedious;* cliché-ridden, stale, pretentious, flatulent, overambitious; forced, over-emphatic, forcible-feeble; inane, empty; juvenile, childish; careless, slovenly, slipshod, limping; limp, loose, lax, inexact, disconnected, disjointed, rambling, vaporing; bad, poor, trashy 847 adj. *vulgar.*

See: 163, 387, 573, 838, 847.

573 Plainness

N. *plainness,* naturalness, honesty, simplicity, unadorned s. 699n. *artlessness;* austerity, severity, baldness, bareness, starkness; matter-of-factness, plain prose 593n. *prose;* plain words, plain English 516n. *intelligibility;* homespun, household words; rustic flavor, vernacular, common speech, vulgar parlance; idiom, natural i.; unaffectedness 874 n. *modesty;* frankness, coarseness, four-letter word, Anglo-Saxon monosyllable.

Adj. *plain,* simple 699adj. *artless;* austere, severe, disciplined; bald, stark, bare; neat 648adj. *clean;* unadorned, uncolored, unpainted, unvarnished, unembellished; unemphatic, undramatic, unsensational; unassuming, unpretentious 874adj. *modest;* uninflated, chaste, not meretricious 950adj. *pure;* unaffected, honest, unartificial, natural, idiomatic; homely, homey, homespun, vernacular, Saxon; prosaic, sober 834adj. *serious;* dry, stodgy 838adj. *tedious;* humdrum, workaday, everyday, commonplace 610 adj. *usual;* unimaginative, uninspired, unpoetical 593adj. *prosaic.*

Vb. *speak plainly,* call a spade a spade, use the vernacular 516vb. *be intelligible;* chasten one's style, purify one's diction, moderate one's vocabulary; say outright, come to the point, come down to brass tacks.

Adv. *plainly,* simply; prosaically, in prose; in the vernacular, in plain words, in common parlance; directly, point-blank; not to put too fine a point upon it.

See: 483, 516, 593, 610, 648, 699, 834, 838, 874, 950.

574 Ornament

N. *ornament,* embellishment, color, decoration, embroidery, frills 844n. *ornamentation;* floridness, floweriness, flowers of speech, taffeta phrases, word-arabesque 563n. *phrase;* prose run mad, Gongorism, cultism, euphuism; preciosity, preciousness, euphemism, rhetoric, flourish of r., purple patch, syllabub;

figurativeness, figure of speech 519n. *trope;* alliteration, assonance, homoeoteleuton; palilogy, anaphora, epistrophe, symploce; anadiplosis; inversion, anastrophe, hyperbaton; chiasmus, chiastic order; parison; enjambment; metaphor, simile, antithesis.

magniloquence, high tone 579n. *eloquence;* grandiloquence, declamation, orotundity 571n. *vigor;* turgidity, turgescence, flatulence, inflation, swollen diction, swelling utterance; pretentiousness, affectation, pomposity 875n. *ostentation;* talking big 877n. *boasting;* highfalutin, high-sounding words, bombast, rant, fustian, rodomontade 515n. *empty talk;* Johnsonese, long words, sesquipedalian w. 559n. *word;* teratology, tales of marvel 513n. *fantasy.*

phrasemonger, fine writer, word-spinner, euphuist, euphemist 575n. *stylist;* rhetorician, orator 579n. *speaker.*

Adj. *ornate*, beautified 844adj. *ornamented;* rich, florid, flowery; precious, Gongoresque, euphuistic, euphemistic; pretentious 850adj. *affected;* meretricious, flashy, flaming, flamboyant, frothing, frothy 875adj. *showy;* brassy, sonorous, clanging 400adj. *loud;* tropical, alliterative, antithetical 519adj. *figurative;* overloaded, stiff, stilted; pedantic, long-worded, sesquipedalian, Johnsonian.

rhetorical, declamatory, oratorical 579 adj. *eloquent;* resonant, sonorous 400adj. *loud;* mouthy, orotund; high-pitched, high-flown, high-flying, highfalutin; grandiose, stately; bombastic, pompous, fustian; grandiloquent, magniloquent, altiloquent; inflated, tumid, turgid, tumescent, swelling, swollen; antithetical, alliterative, metaphorical, tropical 519adj. *figurative.*

Vb. *ornament*, beautify, grace, adorn, enrich 844vb. *decorate;* charge, overlay, overload; elaborate, load with ornament, grace with all the flowers of speech; euphuize, euphemize; smell of the lamp, over-elaborate.

See: 400, 513, 519, 546, 559, 563, 571, 579, 844, 850, 875, 877.

575 Elegance

N. *elegance*, style, perfect s.; grace, gracefulness 841n. *beauty;* refinement, taste 846n. *good taste;* propriety, restraint, distinction, dignity; clarity 567n. *perspicuity;* Attic quality, purity, simplicity; idiom, natural i. 573n. *plainness;* harmony, euphony, concinnity, balance, proportion 245n. *symmetry;* rhythm, numerosity, ease, flow, smoothness, fluency, readiness, felicity, the right word in the right place; neatness, polish, finish; well-turned period, rounded p.; elaboration, artificiality.

stylist, stylish writer 574n. *phrasemonger;* classical author, classic, Atticist, purist.

Adj. *elegant*, concinnous, concinnate 841adj. *beautiful;* graced, well-g., graceful; stylish, polite, refined 846 adj. *tasteful;* uncommon, distinguished, dignified; not meretricious, chaste 950adj. *pure;* good, correct, idiomatic, sensitive; expressive, clear 567adj. *perspicuous;* simple, natural, unaffected 573adj. *plain;* unlabored, ready, easy, smooth, flowing, fluent, tripping, rhythmic, mellifluous, euphonious; harmonious, balanced, proportioned 245adj. *symmetrical;* neat, felicitous, happy, right, neatly put, well-turned; artistic, wrought, elaborate, artificial; polished, finished, soigné, manicured, chic; restrained, controlled; flawless 646adj. *perfect;* classic, classical, Attic, Ciceronian, Augustan.

Vb. *be elegant*, show taste 846vb. *have taste;* have a good style, write well, have a light touch; elaborate, polish, refine 646vb. *perfect;* manicure, trim 841vb. *beautify;* grace one's style, turn a period, point an antithesis 566vb. *show style.*

See: 245, 567, 573, 646, 841, 846, 950.

576 Inelegance

N. *inelegance*, inconcinnity; clumsiness, roughness, uncouthness 699n. *artlessness;* coarseness, lack of finish, lack of polish 647n. *imperfection;* harshness, cacophony 411n. *discord;* lack of ease, lack of flow, stiffness, stiltedness 326n. *hardness;* unwieldiness, cumbrousness, combrous language, sesquipedalianism, sesquipedality, hard words, jawbreaker; impropriety, barbarism, Gothicism, Saxonism; incorrectness, catachresis, misapplication 565n. *solecism;* mispronunciation 580n. *speech defect;* vulgarism, vulgarity 847n. *bad taste;* mannerism, unnaturalness, artificiality 850n. *affectation;* exhibitionism 875n. *ostentation;* meretriciousness, shoddy, tinsel 542n. *sham;* unrestraint, excess 637n. *superfluity;* turgidity, pomposity 574n. *magniloquence.*

Adj. *inelegant*, inconcinnous, ungraceful, graceless 842adj. *ugly;* faulty, incorrect, unclassical; unfinished, unpolished, unrefined 647adj. *imperfect;* unclear 568adj. *imperspicuous;* coarse, crude, rude, doggerel, uncouth, barbarous, Gothic 699adj. *artless;* impolite, tasteless 847adj. *vulgar;* unchaste, impure, meretricious; unrestrained, immoderate, excessive; turgid, pompous 574adj. *rhetorical;* forced, labored, artificial, unnatural, mannered 850adj. *affected;* ludicrous, grotesque 849adj. *ridiculous;* offensive, repulsive, jarring, grating 861adj. *disliked;* heavy, ponderous, insensitive; rough, harsh, crabbed, uneasy, abrupt; halting, cramped, unready, unfluent; clumsy, awkward, gauche; stiff, stilted 875 adj. *formal.*

See: 326, 411, 542, 565, 568, 574, 580, 637, 647, 699, 842, 847, 849, 850, 861, 875.

577 Voice

N. *voice,* vocal sound 398n. *sound;* speech signal, speaking voice 579n. *speech;* singing voice, musical v., fine v. 412n. *vocal music;* powerful voice, vociferation 400n. *loudness;* tongue, vocal organs, vocal cords *or* chords, vocal bands, lungs, bellows; larynx; artificial larynx, oral vibrator; vocalization, phoneme, vowel, broad v., pure v., diphthong, triphthong, open vowel, closed v., semivowel, voiced consonant, syllable 398n. *speech sound;* articulation, clear a., distinctness; utterance, enunciation, delivery, attack; articulate sound 408n. *cry;* exclamation, ejaculation, gasp; mutter, whisper, stage-w. 401n. *faintness;* tone of voice, accents, timber, pitch, tone, intonation; ventriloquism, gastriloquism.

pronunciation, articulation, elocution, enunciation, inflection, accentuation, stress, emphasis; ictus, arsis, thesis; accent, tonic a., speech a., sentence a.; pure accent, correct a.; native accent, broad a., foreign a.; burr, brogue, trill, roll; aspiration, rough breathing, glottal stop; iotacism, sigmatism, lisping, lallation 580n. *speech defect;* mispronunciation 565n. *solecism.*

Adj. *vocal,* voiced, oral, aloud, out loud; vocalic, vowel-like, sonant; phonetic, enunciative; articulate, distinct, clear; well-spoken, well-sung, in good voice 410adj. *melodious;* pronounced, uttered, spoken, dictated, read out, read aloud; aspirated 407adj. *hoarse;* accented, tonal, accentual, accentuated; open, broad-voweled, closed, close-voweled; guttural, cerebral, palatal, liquid, lingual, nasal, fricative, labial.

Vb. *voice,* pronounce, syllable 579vb. *speak;* mouth, give tongue, give voice, express, utter, enunciate, articulate; labialize, palatalize, vocalize, vowelize; breathe, aspirate, sound one's aitches; trill, roll, burr; stress 532n. *emphasize;* accent, pronounce with stress; raise the voice, lower the v., whisper, stage-w.; exclaim, ejaculate, rap out, blurt o. 408vb. *cry;* chant, warble, carol, hum 413vb. *sing;* shout, vociferate, use one's voice 400vb. *be loud;* mispronounce, lisp, distort one's vowels, swallow one's consonants, speak thick 580vb. *stammer.*

See: 398, 400, 401, 407, 408, 410, 412, 413, 532, 565, 579, 580.

578 Aphony

N. *aphony,* aphonia, voicelessness, no voice, loss of v.; difficulty in speaking, dysphony, disphonia, inarticulation; thick speech, hoarseness, huskiness, raucity; willful silence, obmutescence 399n. *silence;* going dumb, dumbness, mutism, deaf-m.; bad voice, harsh v., unmusical v., tuneless v. 407n. *stridor;* childish treble, falsetto; changing voice, breaking v., cracked v.; sob, sobbing; undertone, low voice, small v., muffled tones, whisper, bated breath 401n. *faintness;* surd, unvoiced consonant; mute, deaf-m., dummy; voiceless speech, sign language, deaf-and-dumb language 547 n. *gesticulation.*

Adj. *voiceless,* aphonic, dysphonic; unvoiced, surd; breathed, whispered, muffled, low-voiced, inaudible 401 adj. *muted;* mute, dumb, deaf and dumb; incapable of utterance, speechless, tongueless, wordless; inarticulate, unvocal, tongue-tied; not speaking, obmutescent, mum, silent 582adj. *taciturn;* silenced, gagged; dry, hollow, sepulchral, breaking, cracked, croaking, hoarse as a raven 407adj. *hoarse;* breathless, out of breath.

Vb. *be mute,* be mum 582vb. *be taciturn;* hold one's tongue 525vb. *keep secret;* bridle one's tongue, check one's speech, dry up, ring off, hang up; lose one's voice, be struck dumb, lose power of speech; talk with one's hands 547vb. *gesticulate;* have difficulty in speaking 580vb. *stammer.*

make mute, strike dumb, dumbfound, take one's breath away, rob one of words; tie one's tongue, stick in one's throat, choke one's utterance; muffle, hush, deaden 401vb. *mute;* shout down, drown one's voice; muzzle, gag, stifle 165vb. *suppress;* put a gag on, stop one's mouth, cut out one's tongue; shut one up, cut one short, hang up on; still, hush, put to silence, put to sleep 399vb. *silence.*

speak low, speak softly, whisper, stage-w. 401vb. *sound faint;* whisper in one's ear 524vb. *hint;* lower one's voice, drop one's v., cover one's mouth, put one's hand before one's m.

Adv. *voicelessly,* in hushed tones, in a whisper, with bated breath; in an undertone, sotto voce, under one's breath, in an aside.

See: 165, 399, 401, 407, 524, 525, 547, 580, 582.

579 Speech

N. *speech,* faculty of s., organ of s., tongue, lips 557n. *language;* oral communication, word of mouth 524n. *report;* spoken word, accents, tones 559n. *word;* verbal intercourse, conference, colloquy, conversation, talk, palaver, prattle, chinwag 584n. *interlocution;* address, apostrophe 583 n. *allocution;* ready speech, fluency, talkativeness, volubility 581n. *loquacity;* prolixity, effusion 570n. *diffuseness;* cultivated speech, elocution, voice production; mode of speech, articulation, utterance, delivery, enunciation, prolation, emission 577n. *pronunciation;* ventriloquism, gastriloquism 542n. *sleight;* speech without words, sign language, eye l. 547n. *gesticulation;* thing said, say, speech, dictum, utterance, remark, observation, comment, interjection 532n. *affirmation;* pretty speeches, compliments 889n. *endearment;* given word, parole 764n. *promise.*

oration, speech, effusion; allowed speech, one's say; public speech, formal s., prepared s., discourse, address, talk; salutatory, welcoming address, illuminated a. 876n. *celebration;* valedictory, farewell address, funeral oration 364n. *obsequies;* final speech, winding-up s., after-dinner s.; prelection, lection, broadcast, travelogue 534n. *lecture;* recitation, recital, reading; set speech, declamation, oratorical display (**see** *eloquence*); pulpit eloquence, pulpitry, sermon, preachment, homily, exhortation; platform eloquence, harangue, tub-thumping, rodomontade, earful, mouthful; hostile eloquence, tirade, diatribe, philippic, invective; monologue 585n. *soliloquy;* written speech, dictation, paper, screed 591n. *dissertation;* parts of a speech, rhetorical divisions, proem, prologue, diegesis, narration, digression, proof, peroration.

oratory, art of speaking, rhetoric, public speaking, forensic oratory, parliamentary o., mob o., tub-thumping; speech-making, speechifying, speechification; declamation, elocution, vaporing, ranting, rant; vituperation, invective.

eloquence, facundity, eloquent tongue, oratorical gifts, gift of gab, fluency, command of words, art of w., word-spinning 566n. *style;* power of speech, power 571n. *vigor;* grandiloquence, orotundity, sublimity 574n. *magniloquence;* elocution, good delivery, impressive diction, burst of eloquence, storm of words, peroration, purple patch, syllabub.

speaker, sayer, utterer; talked, spieler, prattler, gossiper 581n. *chatterer;* conversationalist, colloquist 584n. *interlocutor;* speechifier, speech-maker, speech-writer, rhetor, rhetorician, elocutionist; orator, Public O., oratress, oratrix, public speaker, after-dinner s.; improviser, adlibber; declaimer, ranter, platform orator, stump o., soap-box o., tub-thumper; word-spinner, spellbinder; haranguer, diatribist; lecturer, broadcaster, dissertator, dissertationist; pulpiteer, Boanerges; cushion thumper 534n. *preacher;* spokesman, prolocutor, prologue, presenter, narrator, chorus 594n. *actor;* mouthpiece 754 n. *delegate;* advocate, pleader, mediator 231n. *intermediary;* gabber, patterer, salesman 793n. *seller;* Demosthenes, Cicero; monologuist, so liloquizer 585n. *soliloquist.*

Adj. *speaking,* talking; able to speak, with a tongue in one's head, fluent, outspoken, free-speaking, talkative 581n. *loquacious;* oral 577adj. *vocal;* well-spoken, soft-s., loud-s.; audible, spoken, verbal; elocutionary.

eloquent, spellbinding, silver-tongued, trumpet-t.; elocutionary, oratorical 574n. *rhetorical;* grandiloquent, declamatory, tub-thumping, ranting, word-spinning.

Vb. *speak*, mention, say; utter, articulate, syllable 577vb. *voice;* pronounce, declare, say a mouthful 532 vb. *affirm;* say out, blurt 526vb. *divulge;* whisper, breathe 524n. *hint;* confabulate, talk, put in a word or two, permit oneself to say 584vb. *converse;* emit, give out, give utterance; break silence, open one's mouth *or* lips, pipe up, speak up, raise one's voice; wag one's tongue, give t., rattle on, spiel, gossip, prattle, chatter 581vb. *be loquacious;* patter, jabber, gabble; have one's say, talk one's fill, expatiate 570vb. *be diffuse;* trot out, reel off, recite; read, read aloud, read out, dictate; speak a language, speak with tongues, sling the bat; have a tongue in one's head, speak for oneself; talk with one's hands 547vb. *gesticulate.*

orate, make speeches, speechify, oratorize; declaim, deliver a speech, read a s.; hold forth, spout, be on one's legs; take the floor, rise to speak, mount the tribune, mount the pulpit; preach, preachify, sermonize, homilize, harangue; lecture, discourse, address 534vb. *teach;* invoke, apostrophize 583vb. *speak to;* flourish, perorate, mouth, rant, stump, tub-thump; speak like an angel, spellbind, be eloquent, have the gift of gab; talk to oneself, monologize 585vb. *soliloquize.*

See: 231, 364, 524, 526, 532, 534, 542, 547, 557, 559, 566, 570, 571, 574, 577, 581, 583, 584, 585, 591, 594, 754, 764, 793, 876, 889.

580 Speech defect

N. *speech defect*, aphasia, loss of speech, aphonia 578n. *aphony;* paraphemia, paraphasia, paralalia, aboiement; idioglossia, idiolalia 560n. *neology;* stammering, traulism, stammer, stutter, lambdacism, lallation, lisp; dysphony, impediment in one's speech, hesitation, drawl; indistinctness, inarticulateness, thick speech, plum in one's mouth, cleft palate; burr, brogue 560n. *dialect;* accent, twang, nasal t. 577n. *pronunciation;* affectation, Oxford accent, haw-haw 246n. *distortion.*

Adj. *stammering,* stuttering etc. vb.; balbutient; nasal, adenoidal; indistinct, thick, inarticulate; tongue-tied, aphasic, aphasiac; breathless 578adj. *voiceless.*

Vb. *stammer*, stutter, balbutiate, balbucinate; drawl, hesitate, falter, quaver, hem and haw; mammer, mumble, mutter; lisp, lambdacize, lallate; blabber, snuffle, snort, sputter, splutter; nasalize, speak through the nose, drone; clip one's words, swallow one's w., gabble; blubber, sob; mispronounce 565vb. *solecize.*

See: 246, 560, 565, 577, 578.

581 Loquacity

N. *loquacity*, loquaciousness, garrulity, talkativeness, conversableness, communicativeness; volubility, flowing tongue, flow of words, fluency 570n. *diffuseness;* verbosity, wordiness, prolixity; much speaking, multiloquence, running on, spate of words, logorrhea, verbal diarrhea, inexhaustible vocabulary; gab, gift of g. 579n. *eloquence;* garrulous old age, anecdotage 505n. *remembrance.*

chatter, chattering, gossiping, gabble, gibble-gabble, gab, jabber, palaver, much talk, talkee-talkee, clack, clappers, claver, quack, cackle, babble, prattle; small talk, gossip, tittle-tattle; froth, gush, prate, jaw, gas, hot air 515n. *empty talk.*

chatterer, non-stop talker, rapid speaker; chinwag, rattle, chatterbox; gossip, tattler 529n. *newsmonger;* magpie, parrot, jay; talker, gabber, driveler, haverel, ranter, quacker; preacher, sermonizer; proser, windbag, gas-bag, gasser; conversationalist 584n. *interlocutor.*

Adj. *loquacious*, talkative, garrulous, tongue-wagging, gossiping, tattling; communicative, chatty, gossipy, newsy 524adj. *informative;* gabbing, babbling, gabbling, gassy, windy, prosing, verbose, long-winded, long-tongued 570adj. *prolix;* non-stop, voluble, running on, fluent, glib, ready, effusive, gushing; conversable, conversational 584adj. *conversing.*

Vb. *be loquacious,*—talkative etc. adj.; have a long tongue, chatter, rattle, run on, reel off; gossip, tattle 584vb. *converse;* clack, quack, gabble, jabber, patter, twaddle 515vb. *mean nothing;* talk, jaw, gab, prate, prose, gas, waffle, haver; drone, maunder, drivel; launch out, start talking, shoot; be glib, oil one's tongue; have one's say, talk at length; expatiate, effuse, gush 570vb. *be diffuse;* outtalk, talk down; talk out time, filibuster 113vb. *spin out;* talk oneself hoarse, talk oneself out of breath, talk the hind leg off a donkey, din in the ears; talk shop, bore 838vb. *be tedious;* engage in conversation, buttonhole; must have an audience; not let one get a word in edgeways.

Adv. *loquaciously*, glibly, fluently etc. adj.

See: 113, 505, 515, 524, 529, 570, 571, 579, 584, 838.

582 Taciturnity

N. *taciturnity*, silent habit 399n. *silence;* incommunicativeness, reserve, reticence, guarded utterance 525n. *secrecy;* few words, shortness, brusqueness, curtness, gruffness 885 n. *rudeness;* willful silence, obmutescence 578n. *aphony*; breaking off, aposiopesis; pauciloquy, economy of words, laconism 569n. *conciseness;* no speaker, no orator; no talker, not a gossip, man of few words, laconian; clam, oyster, sauce.

Adj. *taciturn,* mute 399adj. *silent;* sparing of words, saying little, monosyllabic, short, curt, laconic, brusque, gruff 569adj. *concise;* not talking, obmutescent, mum; inconversable, incommunicative; not effusive, withdrawn; reserved, guarded 525adj. *reticent;* close, close-mouthed, close-tongued, tight-lipped; not to be drawn, discreet 858adj. *cautious;* inarticulate, tongue-tied 578adj. *voiceless;* not hearing 416adj. *deaf.*

Vb. be taciturn,—laconic etc. adj.; spare one's words, need few w. 569 vb. *be concise;* not talk, say nothing, have little to say; observe silence, make no answer; not be drawn, refuse comment, neither confirm nor deny; keep one's counsel 525vb. *keep secret;* recommend silence, put one's finger to one's lips; hold one's peace, hold one's tongue, put a bridle on one's t.; fall silent, relapse into s., pipe down, dry up, run out of words 145vb. *cease;* be speechless, lose one's tongue 578vb. *be mute;* waste no words on, save one's breath, not mention, leave out, pass over, omit 458vb. *disregard.*

Int. hush! shut up! mum! chut! no comment!

See: 145, 399, 416, 458, 525, 569, 578, 858, 885.

583 Allocution

N. *allocution,* alloquy, apostrophe; address, lecture, talk, speech 579n. *oration;* feigned dialogue, dialogism 584n. *interlocution;* greeting, salutation, hail; invocation, appeal, interjection, interpellation; buttonholing, word in the ear, aside; hearers, listeners, audience 415n. *listener.*

Adj. *vocative*, salutatory, invocatory.

Vb. *speak to*, speak at; address, talk to, lecture to; turn to, direct one's words at, apostrophize; appeal to, pray to, invoke; sir, bemadam; approach, accost; hail, call to, salute, say good-morning 884vb. *greet;* pass the time of day, parley with 584vb. *converse;* take aside, buttonhole.

See: 415, 579, 584, 884.

584 Interlocution

N. *interlocution*, parley, colloquy, converse, conversation, causerie, talk; dialogue, question and answer; exchange, repartee; confabulation, verbal intercourse, social i. 882n. *sociality;* commerce, communion, intercommunion, communication, intercommunication 524n. *information;* duologue, trialogue, symposium, tête-à-tête.

chat, causerie, chit-chat, talk, small t., table-t., tea-table t.; town talk, village t., gossip 529n. *rumor;* tattle, tittle-tattle 581n. *chatter;* cozy chat, tête-à-tête.

conference, colloquy, conversations, talks, pourparler, parley, pow-wow, palaver; discussion, debate, symposium, seminar; controversy, polemics, logomachy 475n. *argument;* exchange of views, talks across the table, high-level talks, summitry; negotiations, bargaining, treaty-making 765n. *treaty;* conclave, convention, meeting, gathering 74n. *assembly;* reception, conversazione, party, crush 882n. *social gathering;* audience, interview, audition 415n. *hearing;* consultation, putting heads together, huddle, council, war-c., round-table conference, summit 691 n. *advice;* conference room, boardroom, council chamber 692n. *council;* debating hall, lecture h. 539n. *classroom;* durbar, audience-chamber, reception-room; auditorium 441 n. *onlookers.*

interlocutor, collocutor, colloquist, dialogist, symposiast; examiner, interviewer, cross-examiner, interpellant 459n. *inquirer;* answerer 460n. *respondent;* partner in a conversation, addressee, confabulator, conversationalist, talker 581n. *chatterer;* gossip, tattler, tabby 529n. *newsmonger.*

Adj. *conversing*, interlocutory, confabulatory, collocutory, dialogistic;

conversable, conversational; chatty, gossipy 581adj. *loquacious;* newsy, communicative 524adj. *informative;* conferring, in conference; discursive, conferential; consultatory, consultative, advisory 691adj. *advising.*

Vb. *converse,* parley, talk together (**see** *confer*); confabulate, collogue, pass the time of day; partake in a symposium, engage in a duologue; lead one on, draw one out; buttonhole, enter into conversation, carry on a c., join in a c., put in a word, bandy words, exchange w., question, answer; shine in conversation, have a good talk; chat, have a c., have a cozy c., let one's hair down; gossip, tattle 581vb. *be loquacious;* commune with, talk privately, get confidential with, be closeted with; whisper together, talk tête-à-tête, get in a huddle.

confer, talk it over, take counsel, sit in council, hold conclave, meet in the boardroom; hold a council of war, pow-wow, palaver; canvass, discuss, debate 475vb. *argue;* parley, negotiate, hold conversations; advise with, consult w., sit w. 691vb. *consult.*

See: 74, 415, 441, 459, 460, 475, 524, 529, 539, 581, 691, 692, 765, 882.

585 Soliloquy

N. *soliloquy,* soliloquium, monologue, monody; apostrophe; aside.

soliloquist, soliloquizer, monologist, monodist.

Adj. *soliloquizing* etc. vb.; monological.

Vb. *soliloquize,* talk to oneself, say to oneself, say aside, think aloud; apostrophize, pray to, pray aloud; answer one's own questions, be one's own interlocutor; talk to the four walls, address an empty house, have oneself for audience.

586 Writing

N. *writing,* creative w., composition, literary c., literary activities, authorship, journalism, cacoethes scribendi 590n. *description;* output, literary o. 557n. *literature;* a writing, script, copy, writings, works, books 589n. *reading matter;* ink-slinging, inkshed; quill-driving, scrivenership, writership, clerkship, paper-work 548n. *record;* copying, transcribing, transcription, rewriting, overwriting; autography, holography; ways of writing, handwriting, chirography, stylography, cerography; writing small, micrography; longhand, longhand reporting, logography; shorthand writing, shorthand, lexigraphy, polygraphy, brachygraphy, speedwriting, phonography; contraction, phonogram, phraseogram, phraseography; stenography, typewriting, typing 587n. *print;* braille; secret writing, steganography, ciphering, cipher, code 530n. *secret;* picture-writing, ideography; sign-writing, sky-writing 528n. *advertisement;* inscribing, carving, cutting, graving, epigraphy 555n. *engraving;* writing left to right *or* right to left, boustrophedon; study of handwriting, graphology.

lettering, formation of letters, stroke, stroke of the pen, up-stroke, down-s., pothook, pothooks and hangers; line, dot, point; flourish, curlicue, squiggle, scroll 251n. *convolution;* handwriting, hand, fist; calligraphy, pencraft, penmanship; fair hand, clerkly h., copper-plate h., law-h., "fair Roman hand"; cursive hand, running h., flowing h., round h.; script writing, print-w., beacon-w., italic; bad writing, cacography, clumsy hand; botched writing, overwriting; illegible writing, scribble, scrawl, illegible signature 517n. *unintelligibility;* script, letters, characters, alphabet, block letter, uncial; capital, majuscule, initial, small letter, minuscule 558n. *letter;* ogham, runes, futhark; pictogram, ideogram; ideograph; cuneiform, arrowhead; Minoan linear B.; embossed writing, braille; letters of fire, letters of gold.

script, written matter, inscribed page, illuminated address; well-written specimen, calligraph; writing, screed, scrawl, scribble; manuscript, palimpsest, codex 589n. *book;* original, one's own hand, autograph, holograph; signature, sign-manual, initial, cross, mark 547n. *indication;* copy, transcript, transcription, fair copy 22n. *duplicate;* typescript, stencil; printed matter 587n. *letterpress;* letter, epistle, rescript, written reply, rescription 588n. *correspondence;* tablet, table; inscription, epigraph, graffito 548n. *record;* superscription, caption, heading; letters of fire, letters of gold.

stationery, writing materials, pen and paper, pen and ink; ink, writing i., printing i., drawing i., copying i., marking i., indelible i., invisble i.; stylus, reed, quill, pen, quill-p., fountain p., ball-point p.; nib, steel n.; stylograph, stylo; pencil, slate-p., lead-p.; crayon, chalk; papyrus, palm leaves, parchment, vellum, rice paper, foolscap 631n. *paper;* newsprint; writing paper, note-p., wove p., laid p., scented p.; notebook, pad, block, slate, tablet, table; slate, blackboard; stone, brick, rock, wall; inkpot, ink-bottle, ink-horn, inkstand, inkwell; penholder, penwiper, pensharpener, penknife; blotting paper, sand; typewriter, typewriter ribbon, ribbon, stencil; writing room, scriptorium.

penman, calligraphist, calligrapher; cacographer, scribbler, scrawler; inkster, writer, pen-driver, quill-d., scrivener, scribe, clerk 549n. *recorder;* copyist, transcriber; signwriter, sky-w. 528n. *publicizer;* epigrapher, inscriber; subscriber, signer, initialer, signatory; longhand writer, logographer; creative writer, script-w. 589n. *author;* letter-writer 588n. *correspondent;* graphologist, handwriting expert 484n. *detector.*

stenographer, shorthand writer, tachygraph, typewriter, typist, stenotypist.

Adj. *written,* inscribed, inscriptional, epigraphic; in black and white 548 adj. *recorded;* in writing, in longhand, in shorthand; logographic, stenographic; handwritten, manuscript, autograph, holograph; signed, under one's hand; scriptory, penned, penciled, scrawled, scribbled etc. vb.; fairly written, copybook, copperplate, clerkly, literate; cursive, demotic, hieratic, ideographic, hieroglyphic, cuneiform; lettered, alphabetic; runic, Gothic, uncial, roman, italic; perpendicular, upright, sloping, spidery.

Vb. *write,* be literate, use the pen, scribe; form characters, character, engrave, inscribe; letter, block, print; flourish, scroll; write a good hand, calligraph; write a bad hand, write badly, scribble, scrabble, scrawl, blot, erase, interline, overwrite; reduce to writing, put in w., set down, set down in black and white, write down, jot d., note 548vb. *record;* transcribe, copy, copy out, fair-copy, write out, write fair, engross; take down, take dictation, take shorthand, stenotype, typewrite, type, type out; take down longhand, logograph; throw on paper, draft, formulate, redact; compose, concoct, indite; pen, pencil, dash off; write letters 588vb. *correspond;* write one's name, make one's signature, subscribe 547vb. *sign;* take up the pen, put pen to paper, spill ink, stain paper, cover reams; be an author, write books 590vb. *describe,* 591vb. *dissert;* write poetry 593vb. poetize.

See: 22, 251, 484, 517, 528, 530, 547, 548, 549, 555, 557, 558, 587, 588, 589, 590, 591, 593, 631.

587 Print

N. *print,* printing, typing, typewriting 586n. *writing;* typography, printing from type, block printing, plate p., offset process, lithography, photolithography 555n. *engraving;* photocopying, varitype; typesetting, composing, composition, makeup, setting, hand-setting; monotype, linotype, stereotype, electrotype; plate, shell; presswork, make-ready, printing off, running off, machining.

letterpress, lettering, linage, printed matter, print, impression, presswork; copy, pull, proof, first p., galley p., page p., revise; sheet, form, quire, signature; printed page, imposed sheet; caption, heading, colophon, imprint; margin, gutter; dummy, trial copy, proof c.; offprint.

print-type, type, movable t., fixed t., stereotype, plate; type-mold, matrix; type-matter, setting, set type, standing t., broken t., distributed t., pie, printer's p.; upper case, lower c., capitals, caps, initial c.; font, typeface, body f., bastard type, bold type, heavy t., leaded t., Clarendon; roman, italic, Gothic, black letter 558n. *letter;* shoulder, shank, beard, ascender, descender, serif, sans serif; lead, rule, swelled r., en r., em r.; space, hair space, en space, em s.; type bar, slug.

type size, point s., type measure, type scale; excelsior, brilliant, diamond, pearl, agate, ruby, nonpareil, minion, brevier, bourgeois, long primer, small pica, pica, English, Columbian, great primer.

press, printing p., printing works, pressworks, printers; type-foundry; composing room, press r., machining r.; handpress, flatbed, rotary press, linotype, monotype, offset press; quoin, frame, composing stick, case.

printer, book-p., jobbing p., pressman; setter, type-s., compositor, printer's devil, printer's reader, proof r.; typographer, type-cutter.

Adj. *printed,* in print 528adj. *pub-*

lished; set, composed, machined, imposed etc. vb.; in type, in italic, in bold, in roman; typographical; leaded 201adj. *spaced;* close-printed, tight, crowded.

Vb. *print,* stamp; set, compose; align, justify; set up in type, make ready, impose, machine, run off, pull off, strike off, print off; finish printing, distribute the type; lithograph, litho, offset, stereotype; get ready for the press, send to p., see through the p., proofread, correct; have printed, bring out 528vb. *publish.*

See: 201, 528, 555, 558, 586.

588 Correspondence

N. *correspondence,* stream of c., exchange of letters; communication, epistolary c., postal c. 524n. *information;* mailing list, distribution l.; mail, letters, post, postbag, mailbag, budget, diplomatic bag 531n. *mails;* letter, epistle, missive, billet, dispatch, bulletin; love-letter, billet doux, valentine 889n. *endearment;* postcard, picture postcard, card, letter c.; air letter, airgraph, air mail, sea mail; business letter, favor, enclosure; open letter 528n. *publicity;* circular letter, circular, chain letter; official correspondence, dispatch, rescript; demiofficial letter, note, line, chit; answer, acknowledgment; envelope, cover, stamp, seal; letter-box, pillar box.

correspondent, letter-writer, pen-pal, poison pen; recipient, addressee; foreign correspondent, contributor; contact 524n. *informant.*

Adj. *epistolary,* postal, by post; under cover of, enclosed.

Vb. *correspond,* correspond with, exchange letters, maintain *or* keep up a correspondence, keep in touch with 524vb. *communicate;* use the post, write to, send a letter to, drop a line, send a chit; compose dispatches, report 524vb. *inform;* finish one's correspondence, do one's mail; acknowledge, reply, write back, reply by return 460vb. *answer;* circularize 528vb. *publish;* write again, bombard with letters; post off, forward, mail, airmail; stamp, seal, frank, address; open a letter, unstick, unseal 263vb. *open.*

Adv. *by letter,* by mail, through the post.

in correspondence, in touch, in contact; on the phone, on the line.

See: 263, 460, 524, 528, 531, 889.

589 Book

N. *book,* title, volume, tome, roll; codex, manuscript, MS, palimpsest; script, typescript, unpublished work; published work, publication, bestseller, potboiler; unsold book, remainder; work, standard w., classic; major work, monumental w., magnum opus; opuscule, slim volume; chapbook, booklet; illustrated work, picture book 553n. *picture;* magazine, periodical, rag 528n. *journal;* brochure, pamphlet 528n. *the press;* bound book, cased book, hard-back, paperback (**see** *edition*).

reading matter, printed word, written w. 586n. *writing;* script, copy; test, the words, libretto, scenario, "book of the play"; proof, revise, pull 587n. *letterpress;* writings, prose literature 593n. *prose;* poetical literature 593n. *poetry;* classical literature, standard l., serious l., light l. 557n. *literature;* literary subject, fiction, history, biography, travel 590n. *description;* work of fiction 590n. *novel;* biographical work, memoirs, memorabilia 590n. *biography;* addresses, speeches 579n. *oration;* essay, tract, tractate 591n. *dissertation;* piece, occasional pieces, fugitive p. 591n. *article;* miscellanea, marginalia, jottings, thoughts, pensées; poetical works, divan 593n. *poem;* selections, flowers, beauties 592n. *anthology;* early works, juvenilia; posthumous works, remains; complete works, corpus, omnibus volume; periodical, review, magazine, weekly, monthly, quarterly, annual 528n. *journal;* issue, number, back n.; part, installment, serial, sequel, continuation, second part; reader.

textbook, schoolbook, class book, desk b., copybook 539n. *classroom;* abecedary, hornbook; primer, grammar, gradus; text, plain t., annotated t., prescribed t.; selection, chrestomathy, delectus 592n. *anthology;* standard text, handbook, manual, enchiridion, breviary; cookery book, cook-book, recipe b. (**see** *reference book*).

reference book, work of reference, encyclopedia, cyclopedia 490n. *erudition;* lexicon 559n. *dictionary;* biographical dictionary, dictionary of quotations, dictionary of placenames gazetteer, time-table 87n. *directory;* calendar 548n. *record;* guide 524n. *guide-book;* notebook, diary, album 505n. *reminder;* bibliography, publisher's catalog, reading list.

edition, series, set, collection, library; bound edition, library e., de luxe e., best e., prize e., school e., popular e., cheap e., standard e., major e., complete e., collected e., complete works; incunabula, old edition, first e., new e., revised e.; reissue, reprint; illustrated edition, special e., limited e., connoisseur's e., expurgated e.; adaptation, abridgment 592n. *compendium;* duodecimo, sextodecimo, octodecimo, octavo, quarto, folio; book production, layout, preliminary matter, prelims, preface, prefatory note, publisher's n., author's n., bibliographical n.; dedication, invocation, acknowledgments; title, bastard t., half-t.; flyleaf, title page, end-p., colophon; table of contents, table of illustrations; errata, corrigenda, addenda; appendix, supplement, index; heading, page h., folio h., chaper h., section h., headline, running h., footnote; margin, head m., foot m., gutter; folio, page, leaf, recto, verso; sheet, form, signature, quire; chapter, division, part, section; paragraph, clause, passage, excerpt, inset; plate, print, illustration, halftone, line-drawing 553n. *picture.*

bookbinding, binding, casing, rebinding, stripping; folding, gathering, sewing, stitching; case, cover, jacket, dust j. 226n. *wrappings;* boards, paper b., straw-board, cardboard; cloth, limp c., linen, scrim, buckram, leather, pigskin, morocco, vellum, parchment; tooling, blind-t., gold-t., gilding, marbling; bindery, bookbinder.

library, bibliotheca, book-collection, series; national library, state l., public l., branch l., traveling l., mobile l., lending l., circulating l., book club; bookshelf, bookcase, bookrack, book-ends; bookshop, book store, booksellers.

bookman, man of letters, litterateur, literary gent; reader, bookworm 492n. *scholar;* bibliophile, booklover, book-collector, bibliomaniac; bibliographer; librarianship, librarian, library assistant; bookselling, bibliopole, stationer, bookseller, antiquarian b., book-dealer, secondhand b.; publisher, book-p.; editor, redactor; reviewing, book-reviewer, reviewer 480n. *estimator.*

author, authoress, writer, creative w.; literary man, man of letters; fiction-writer, novelist, historian, biographer 590n. *narrator;* essayist, editorialist 591n. *dissertator;* prose-writer; verse-writer 593n. *poet*; playwright, librettist, script writer 594n. *dramatist;* freelance; journalist 528 n. *publicizer;* pressman, reporter, reporterette, sob-sister 529n. *newsmonger;* editor, subeditor, contributor, correspondent, special c., war c., sports c., columnist, gossip-writer, diarist; scribbler, penpusher, hack, Grub Street h., penny-a-liner; ghost, ghost-writer; reviser, Yahwist, Elohist.

Adj. *bibliographical*, bookways, bookwise, in book form; cloth-bound, paper-backed; tooled, marbled, gilt; book-loving, book-selling, book-publishing.

See: 87, 226, 480, 490, 492, 505, 524, 528, 529, 539, 548, 553, 557, 559, 579, 586, 587, 590, 591, 592, 593, 594.

590 Description

N. *description*, account, full a.; statement, exposé, statement of facts, summary 524n. *report;* brief, abstract, inscription, caption, legend 592n. *compendium;* narration, relation, rehearsal, recital (**see** *narrative*); specification, characterization, details, particulars, catalogue raisonnée 87n. *list;* portrayal; delineation, depiction; sketch, character s., profile, prosopography 551 n. *representation*; psychography, psychognosis; psychic profile, case history 548n. *record;* evocation, word-painting, picture, true p., realism, Zolaism; descriptive account, travelogue 524n. *guide-book;* vignette, thumbnail sketch; idyll, eclogue 593n. *poem;* eulogy, satire; obituary, epitaph, lapidary inscription 364n. *obsequies.*

narrative, argument, plot, subplot, scenario; historiography, history, annals, chronicle 548n. *record;* account, imaginary a., fiction; story, tale, fabliau, tradition, legend, legendry, mythology, myth, saga, epic, epos; allegory, parable, apologue, story with a moral; fairy-tale, old wives' t., yarn 543n. *fable;* anecdote, reminiscence, sayings, logia 505n. *remembrance.*

biography, real-life story, human interest; life, curriculum vitae, life story, life and death of; experiences, adventures, fortunes; aretalogy, hagiology, hagiography, martyrology; obituary, necrology; rogues' gallery,

Newgate calendar; personal account, autobiography, confessions, memoirs, memorabilia, memorials 505n. *remembrance*; diary, journals 548n. *record*; personal correspondence, letters 588n. *correspondence*.

novel, fiction, tale; historical novel, fictional biography; novelette, short story; light reading, bedside r. 589n. *reading matter;* romance, love-story, fairy-s., adventure s., Western, science fiction; novel of low life, picaresque novel; crime-story, detective s., 'tecker, whodunit; thriller, shocker, shilling s., penny dreadful, dime novel, horror comic; paperback, pulp magazine; popular novel, best-seller; potboiler, trash 589n. *book*.

narrator, describer, delineator, descriptive writer; reporter, relater; raconteur, anecdotist; yarner, storyteller, fabler, fabulist, mythologist; fiction writer 589n. *author;* romancer, novelist, plot-constructor; biographer, Boswell, Plutarch; aretalogist, hagiographer, martyrologist, autobiographer, memoir-writer, diarist; historian, historiographer, chronicler, annalist, saga-man 549n. *recorder;* Muse of History, Clio.

Adj. *descriptive*, descriptional, graphic, vivid, representational, well-drawn, sharp 551adj. *representing;* true to nature, natural, realistic, real-life, photographic, convincing; picturesque 821adj. *impressive;* impressionistic, suggestive; full, detailed, circumstantial, particular 570 adj. *diffuse;* storied, traditional, legendary, mythological; epic, heroic, aretalogical, romantic; picaresque, sordid; narrative, historical, biographical, autobiographical; factual, documentary 494adj. *accurate;* fictional, imaginative 513adj. *imaginary*.

Vb. *describe*, delineate, draw, picture, depict, paint, 551vb. *represent;* evoke, bring to life, tell vividly, make one see; characterize, particularize, detail, enter into, descend to 80vb. *specify;* sketch, adumbrate 233 vb. *outline;* relate, recount, rehearse, recite, report, give an account 524vb. *communicate;* write, write about 548vb. *record;* write history, historify; narrate, tell, tell a story, yarn, spin a y.; have a plot, construct a p., make a story out of; put into a novel, fictionalize; romance, fable 513vb. *imagine;* review, recapitulate 106vb. *repeat;* reminisce, fight one's battles over again 505 vb. *retrospect*.

See: 87, 106, 233, 364, 494, 505, 513, 524, 543, 548, 549, 551, 570, 588, 589, 592, 593, 821.

591 Dissertation

N. *dissertation,* treatise, pandect, tract, tractate; exposition, summary e., aperçu; theme, thesis 475n. *argument;* disquisition, essay, examination, survey 459n. *inquiry;* discourse, descant, discussion; excursus, memoir, paper, monograph, study; introductory study, prolegomenon; screed, harangue, homily, sermon 534n. *lecture;* commentary, textbook, almagest.

article, signed a., magazine a., syndicated a.; leading article, leader, editorial; essay, causerie; comment, commentary, review, notice, critique, criticism, write-up, write-down.

dissertator, essayist, expositor, tractator, tractarian; pamphleteer, publicist 528n. *publicizer;* editor, leader-writer, editorialist; writer, belletrist, contributor 589n. *author;* reviewer, critic, commentator 520n. *interpreter*.

Adj. *discursive*, discursory, discursive, disquisitional 475adj. *arguing;* expository, critical 520adj. *interpretive*.

Vb. *dissert*, treat, handle, write about, deal with; descant, dissertate, discourse upon 475vb. *argue;* pursue a theme, develop a thesis, descant upon a subject; go into, inquire into, survey; set out, discuss, canvass, ventilate, air one's views; notice, criticize, comment upon, write up, write down; write an essay, produce a treatise, do a paper; annotate, commentate 520vb. *interpret*.

See: 459, 475, 520, 528, 534, 589.

592 Compendium

N. *compendium,* epitome, resumé, summary, brief; contents, heads, analysis; abstract, sum and substance, docket; consolidation, digest, pandect; breviary, textbook; multum in parvo, précis; aperçu, conspectus, synopsis, bird's-eye view, survey; review, recapitulation; draft, minute, note 548n. *record;* sketch, thumbnail s., outline, skeleton; blueprint 623n. *plan;* syllabus, prospectus 87n. *list*; abridgment, abbreviation 204n. *shortening;* contraction, compression 569n. *conciseness*.

anthology, spicilegium, treasury, flowers, beauties, best pieces; selections, delectus, chrestomathy 589n. *textbook;* collection, compilation, collectanea, miscellanea, miscellany; collection of poems, divan; analecta, analects, fugitive pieces; gleanings, chapters, leaves, pages, chips; album, scrap-a., scrap-book, note b., sketch-b., commonplace-b.; anthologist.

epitomizer, abridger, abbreviator, cutter; abstractor, summarizer, potter, précis-writer 204n. *shortener.*

Adj. *compendious,* pithy 569adj. *concise;* analytical, synoptic; abstracted, abridged 204adj. *short;* potted, compacted; analectic, collected, excerpted etc. vb.

Vb. *abstract,* sum up, resume, summarize, epitomize, reduce, abbreviate, abridge 204vb. *shorten;* docket 548vb. *record;* condense, pot, give sum and substance 569vb. *be concise;* consolidate, compile 87vb. *list;* collect 74vb. *bring together;* excerpt, glean, select, anthologize; diagrammatize, sketch, sketch out 233 vb. *outline.*

Adv. *in sum,* in substance, in brief, at a glance, synoptically.

See: 74, 87, 204, 233, 548, 569, 589, 623.

593 Poetry. Prose

N. *poetry,* poesy, balladry, minstrelsy, song; versification (**see** *prosody*); poetic art, poetics; verse, rhyme, numbers; poetic fire, poetic vein, poetic inspiration, numen, afflatus, divine a.; Muses, tuneful Nine, Pierides, Calliope; Parnassus, Helicon, Castalian spring, Pierian s., Hippocrene.

poem, poetic composition; versification, lines, verses, stanzas, strains; narrative verse, heroic poem, epic, mock-e.; dramatic poem, lyric drama, verse-play; Greek tragedy, Greek comedy, satyr play, trilogy, tetralogy 594n. *drama;* lyric verse, melic v., gnomic v.; ode, epode, choric ode, Pindaric o., sapphic o., Horatian o.; palinode; dithyramb; dirge, elegiac poem, elegy; idyll, eclogue; georgic, bucolic poem; occasional poem, prothalamion, epithalamium; song, hymn, chantey, lays 412n. *vocal music;* warsong, marching song; love-song, erotic poem; drinking song, anacreontic; collected poems, divan 592n. *anthology;* canto, fit.

doggerel, lame verse, balladry; jingle, crambo, runes, nursery rhyme; cento, macaronic verse, macaronics, leonine verses, fescennine v., Hudibrastic v., satire, limerick.

verse form, sonnet, sestet, Petrarchan sonnet, Shakespearean s.; ballade, rondeau, virelay, triolet; burden, refrain, envoi; couplet, heroic c., elegiac c.; distich, sloka; triplet, terza rima, quatrain, ghazel; sestina, ottava rima, Spenserian stanza; sapphic verse, alcaic v., Anacreontic v.; hendecasyllables; limping iambics, scazon; blank verse, free v., vers libre; verse, versicle, stanza, stave, laisse, strophe, antistrophe; stichomythia; broken line, half l., hemistich. **See** *prosody.*

prosody, versification, metrics, meter, syllabic m., measure, numbers, scansion; rhyme, rhyme royal, bout rimé; assonance, alliteration, masculine ending, feminine e.; rhythm, sprung r.; prose rhythm; metrical unit, foot, catalectic f., acatalectic f., pada; iamb, trochee, choreus, bacchius, tribrach, amphibrach, amphimacer, cretic, ionic, glyconic, pherecratic; dactyl, anapest; logaoedic verse, dactylo-epitrite; dimeter, trimeter, tetrameter; hexameter, pentameter; senarius, iambic line, iambic trimeter, iambic pentameter, blank verse; couplet, sloka; alexandrine, heroic couplet, elegiac c.; arsis, thesis, ictus, beat, stress, accent, accentuation; elision; enjambment, caesura, diaeresis.

poet, major p., minor p., poet laureate; versemonger, poetaster; prosodist, versifier, metrist, hexametrist, iambist, vers-librist; rhymer, rhymester, rhymist, jingler, board minstrel, balladist, skald, troubadour, minnesinger, meistersinger; epic poet, lyric p., lyrist, bucolic poet, dramatic p., dithyrambist, elegist, elegiac poet, sonneteer, balladmonger; song-writer, librettist; improviser, improvisator; reciter, rhapsode, rhapsodist, jongleur.

prose, not verse, prose rhythm; prosaicism, prosaism, prosiness, prose-writing, everyday language; prosaist, prose-writer 589n. *author.*

Adj. *poetic,* poetical, bardic; songful, tuneful; Castalian, Pierian; heroic, Homeric, Dantesque, Miltonic; mock-heroic, satiric; elegiac, lyrical, dithyrambic, rhapsodic; lyric, Pindaric, sapphic, alcaic, Horatian; bucolic, eclogic, Theocritean, Vergilian; rhyming, jingling etc. vb.; doggerel, macaronic; leonine, fescennine; prosodic, prosodical, metrical, scanning, scanned; iambic, trochaic, spondaic, dactylic, anapestic; in verse, stanzaic; catalectic; Petrarchan, Chaucerian, Shakespearean, Spenserian.

prosaic, unpoetical, unversified; prosy 570adj. *diffuse;* in prose, matter-of-fact 573adj. *plain;* pedestrian.

Vb. *poetize*, sing, tune one's lyre, mount Pegasus; metrify, prosodize, scan; rhyme, jingle; versify, put in verse, put in rhyme; make verses, elegize, compose an epic, write a lyric, write a sonnet, sonneteer; celebrate in verse, berhyme; lampoon, satirize.

write prose, stick to prose, prose.

See: 412, 507, 570, 573, 589, 592, 594.

594 Drama

N. *drama*, traffic of the stage; the drama, the theater, the stage, the play, the scene, the boards, the footlights; theater world, stage w., theaterland; cinema world, silver screen, Hollywood 445n. *cinema;* show business, dramatic entertainment, straight drama, legitimate theater; stock, summer s., repertory, rep; theatricals, amateur t.; masque, charade, dumb c., tableau 551n. *representation;* tragic mask, comic m., buskin, sock, cothurnus; Tragic Muse, Melpomene; Comic Muse, Thalia; Thespis.

dramaturgy, play construction, dramatic form; dramatization, theatricals, dramatics; melodramatics, histrionics; theatricality, staginess; good theater, bad t., good cinema; play-writing, scenario-w., script-w., libretto-w.; play-craft, stage-c., histrionic art, thespian a.; action, movement, plot, subplot, underplot, 590n. *narrative;* characterization 551n. *representation;* production, choragy, revival; casting; rehearsal; dress rehearsal; direction, stage-production, stage-management, showmanship; staging, stage directions; dialogue, soliloquy, stage-whisper, aside; gagging, business; entrance, parodos; exit, exodos (**see** acting); rising of the curtain, prologue, chorus; opening scene, first act, last a., finale, epilogue, curtain; interval, intermission, break; enactment, performance, command p., first p., premiere, first night, gala n., matinee, first house, second h.; encore, curtain-call; successful production, sell-out, hit, smash h., long run.

stage play, play, work; piece, show; libretto, scenario, script, text, playbook, promptbook; masque, mystery, miracle play, morality p., Nativity p., passion p., Oberammergau; drama, Greek d., trilogy, tetralogy; problem play, discussion p.; dramatic representation 551n. *representation;* five-act play, one-act p.; prologue, induction; curtain-raiser, interlude, entr'acte, divertissement, afterpiece, postlude, exode; monodrama; melodrama; tragedy, high t.; comedy, light c., tragicomedy, comédie larmoyante; comedy of manners, Restoration comedy, drawing-room c.; low comedy, farce, slapstick, burlesque, extravaganza 849n. *ridiculousness;* pantomime, harlequinade; musical comedy, musical, light opera, comic o., opera bouffe, grand opera; photoplay, screen-play, Western, horse-opera 445n. *cinema;* radio play, radio drama, soap opera; ballet, dumb show, mime, mimodrama, miming; puppetry, puppet-show, Punch and Judy, marionettes, fantoccini.

stage show 445n. *spectacle;* variety, music hall, vaudeville; review, revue, one-man r., intimate r.; Follies, leg-show, flesh-s., strip-s., non-stop s.; floor-show, cabaret; song and dance, act, turn; star turn, transformation scene, set piece, tableau.

stage set, stagery, set, setting, decor, mise-en-scène, scenery, scene 445n. *spectacle*; drop-scene, drop, backdrop, back-cloth, side-scene, scrim; screen, tormentor, wings, flat; background, foreground, front stage, upstage, downstage, backstage; stage, boards; apron-stage, revolving s.; proscenium, proscenium arch; curtain, fire c., safety c., act-drop; trap, star t., grave t. (**see** *theater*); properties, props, costume, theatrical c.; makeup, grease-paint.

theater, amphitheater, stadium 724n. *arena*; circus, hippodrome; cinema, drive-in c., passion pit; cinema house, picture h., movie h., picture palace 445n. *cinema;* Greek theater, Elizabethan t., open-air t.; showboat, pier, pavilion; theaterhouse, playhouse, house, opera h., music hall, vaudeville theater, puppet t., variety house; night club, bôite de nuit, cabaret; parts of a theater (**see** *stage set*); stage, boards, proscenium, wings, coulisses, flies, tormentor, screen flats; dressing room, green r.; footlights, floats, battens, spotlight, bunch light, limelight; auditorium, orchestra; seating, stalls, orchestra s., fauteuil, front rows; box, stage-b.; pit, parterre; circle, dress c., upper c., mezzanine; gallery, balcony, gods; vestibule, foyer, bar, box-office, stage-door.

acting, personification, mimesis 551n. *representation;* pantomime, miming, taking off 20n. *mimicry;* histrionics, play-acting, stage-a., film-a., character-a.; ham-acting, barnstorming; overacting, staginess, theatricality; repertoire; character, role, creating a r.; starring role, lead, second l.; part, good p., fat p.; supporting part, playing opposite; speaking part, walk-on p.; stock part, ingenue, soubrette, confidante, heavy father, injured husband, merry widow, stage villain; chief part, name p.; hero, heroine; stage fright.

actor, play-a., thespian, Roscius; mimic, mime, pantomimist 20n. *imitator;* mummer, guisard; player, stage p., strolling p., trouper; barnstormer, ham actor; old stager, rep player, character actor; star, star actor, star player, matinee idol 890n. *favorite;* opera singer, prima donna, diva; ballet dancer, ballerina, prima b., danseuse, première coryphée; tragedian, tragedienne; comedian, comedienne, light comedian, low c., comic (**see** *entertainer*); protagonist, deuteragonist, lead, second l., leading man, leading lady, juvenile lead, jeune premier; chorus, gentlemen of the chorus; chorus girl, show g., chorine; understudy, stand-in 150n. *substitute;* mute, figurante, supernumerary, super, extra, general utility; concert-party, pierrot, pierrette; troupe, company, cast, corps de ballet; dramatis personae, characters, cast of c. persons in the play; member of the cast, one of the company; presenter, narrator; chorus, prologue, compère 579n. *speaker.*

entertainer, public e., performer; artiste, artist, quick-change a.; street artist, busker; diseuse, patterer, monologist; minstrel, jongleur; crooner, pop singer; juggler 545n. *conjuror;* contortionist, posture artist, equilibrist, trapezist, tumbler 162n. *athlete;* gladiator 722n. *combatant;* mountebank, fool, coxcomb, cap and bells, pantaloon, harlequin, columbine, pierrot, pierrette, Punch, punchinello, buffoon, clown, merry-andrew, stooge; dancing girl, nautch g., geisha g.

stage-hand, prop-man, stage carpenter, scene-painter, scene-shifter; electrician, machinist; costumier, costume-mistress, wigmaker, makeup man; prompter, call-boy, program-seller, usher, usherette.

stage-manager, producer, director, compère, manager, actor m., business m., press agent; impresario, showman; backer, angel, choragus.

dramatist, dramaturge, dramaturgist; tragic poet, comic p. 593n. *poet;* mimographer; playwright, scenario writer, script-w., lyric-w., librettist; gagman, joke-writer; dramatic critic.

playgoer, theatergoer, operagoer, filmgoer; theater fan, film f., movie f.; ballet fan, balletomane; first-nighter, queuer; stagedoor Johnny; audience, house, packed h., full h., sell-out; stalls, boxes, pit, circle, gallery, balcony; groundling, pittite, galleryite, gallery gods, gods 441n. *spectator;* claque, claqueur; deadhead, free seats; dramatic critic, play-reviewer.

Adj. *dramatic,* dramaturgical; scenic, theatrical, stagy 551adj. *representing;* live, legitimate; thespian, histrionic, mimetic, 20adj. *imitative;* tragic, buskined; thalian, comic, tragicomic; farcical, burlesque, knockabout, slapstick 849adj. *funny;* operatic; melodramatic, sensational 821adj. *exciting;* produced, released, showing, running 522adj. *shown;* dramatized, acted; badly acted, ham, hammy, barnstorming; on the stage, acting, play-a., trouping; cast, cast for; featured, starred, billed; well-cast, all-star; stage-struck, theater-minded, film-m., theater-going.

Vb. *dramatize*, be a dramatist, write plays, write for the stage; make a play of, put in a play; do a play, put on the stage, stage, stagify, produce, direct, stage-manage; rehearse, cut; cast, give a part, assign a role; star, feature, bill; present, put on, release 522vb. *show;* open, open a season; raise *or* ring up the curtain; be produced, come out.

act, go on the stage, tread the boards, troupe; perform, enact, play, play-act, do a play 551n. *represent;* personify, personate, act the role, take the part; mime, pantomime, take off 20vb. *imitate;* create a role, play a part, play lead; play opposite, support; star, steal the show, take the center of the stage, upstage, take all the limelight; ham, barnstorm, overact, overdramatize 546vb. *exaggerate;* rant, roar, out-Herod Herod; underact, throw away; walk on; understudy, stand in 150vb. *substitute;* con one's part, rehearse, speak one's lines, patter, gag; dramatize oneself 875vb. *be ostentatious.*

Adv. *on stage,* off s., up s., down s.; backstage, behind the footlights, in the limelight; dramatically.
See: 20, 150, 162, 441, 445, 522, 545, 546, 551, 579, 590, 593, 722, 724, 821, 849, 875, 890.

595 Will

N. *will,* willing, volition; mere will, nonconative w., velleity; disposition, inclination, mind, preference 597n. *willingness;* conative will, conation, conatus, active will, effort of w. 682n. *exertion;* strength of will, will-power, determination 599n. *resolution;* controlled will, self-control 942 n. *temperance;* intent, purpose 617n. *intention;* decision 608n. *predetermination;* one's will and pleasure 737n. *command;* appetence, appetency 859 n. *desire;* sweet will 932n. *selfishness;* self-will, willfulness 602n. *obstinacy;* whimsicality 604n. *caprice;* free will, self-determination 744n. *independence;* free choice, option, discretion 605n. *choice;* unprompted will, voluntariness, voluntaryism, spontaneousness, spontaneity 597n. *voluntary work;* primacy of will, voluntarism.

Adj. *volitional,* willing, volitive, conative, pertaining to will; unprompted, unasked, unbidden, freewill, spontaneous, original 597adj. *voluntary;* discretional, discretionary, optional 605adj. *choosing;* minded, so m. 617adj. *intending;* self-willed, willful 602adj. *obstinate;* arbitrary, autocratic, dictatorial 735adj. *authoritarian;* independent, self-determined 744adj. *free;* determined 599 adj. *resolute;* decided, prepense, intentional, willed, intended 608adj. *predetermined.*

Vb. *will,* have volition, exercise the will; impose one's will, have one's w., have one's way, have it all one's own w. 737vb. *command;* do what one chooses, please oneself 744vb. *be free;* be so minded, list, see fit, think f. 605vb. *choose;* purpose, determine 617vb. *intend;* wish 859vb. *desire;* have a mind *or* will of one's own, be independent, go one's own way 734vb. *please oneself;* exercise one's discretion, judge for oneself 480vb. *judge;* act on one's own authority, take the responsibility; be self-willed, take the law into one's own hands, take the bit between one's teeth 602vb. *be obstinate;* volunteer, offer, do of one's own accord, do without prompting 597vb. *be willing;* originate 156vb. *cause.*

Adv. *at will,* at pleasure, ad libitum, ad lib, as it seems good; voluntarily, of one's own free will, of one's own accord; spontaneously, out of one's own head, for the heck of it.
See: 156, 480, 597, 599, 602, 604, 605, 608, 617, 682, 735, 737, 744, 859, 932, 942.

596 Necessity

N. *necessity,* hard n., stern n., compelling n.; no alternative, no escape, no option, Hobson's choice 606n. *no choice;* last shift, last resort 700n. *predicament;* inevitability, inevitableness 155n. *destiny;* necessitation, dictation, necessitarianism, determinism, fatalism 608n. *predetermination;* dictation of events, force of circumstances, act of God, fatality 154n. *eventuality;* no freedom 745n. *subjection;* physical necessity, law of nature; force, superior f. 740n. *compulsion;* logical necessity, logic, necessary conclusion, proof 478n. *demonstration;* legal necessity, force of law 953n. *law;* moral necessity, obligation, conscience 917n. *duty;* necessitude, indispensability, a necessity, a necessary, a must 627n. *requirement;* necessitousness, want, lack 801n. *poverty;* involuntariness, reflex action, reflex, conditioned r.; instinct, impulse, blind i. 476n. *intuition.*
fate, inexorable f., lot, inescapable l., karma, kismet; doom, foredoom, predestination, preordination, election 155n. *destiny;* book of fate, God's will, will of Allah, will of heaven, weird; fortune 159n. *chance;* stars, planets, astral influence; the Fates, Parcae, Norns; sisters three, Lachesis, Clotho, Atropos.
fatalist, determinist, predestinarian, necessitarian; pawn, automaton, robot, machine 630n. *tool.*

Adj. *necessary,* indispensable, requisite, unforgoable 627adj. *required;* logically necessary, logical, dictated by reason, unanswerable; demontrable 478adj. *demonstrated;* necessitating, imperative, compulsive 740 adj. *compelling;* overriding, irresistible, resistless 34adj. *superior;* binding 917adj. *obligatory;* with force of law 953adj. *legal;* necessitated, inevitable, unavoidable, inescapable, inexorable, irrevocable 473adj. *certain;* leaving no choice, dictated, imposed, necessitarian, deterministic 606adj. *choiceless.*

involuntary, instinctive 476adj. *intuitive;* unpremeditated, unwilled, unintended 618adj. *unintentional;* unconscious, unthinking, unwitting, blind, impulsive 609adj. *spontaneous;* unassenting 598adj. *unwilling;* conditioned, reflex, controlled, automatic, machinelike, mechanistic, mechanical.

fated, decided by fate, karmic; appointed, destined, predestined, ordained, preordained 608adj. *predetermined;* subject to fate, forechosen, elect 605adj. *chosen;* doomed, foredoomed, prejudged, precondemned 961adj. *condemned;* bound, obliged 745adj. *subject.*

Vb. *be forced*, suffer compulsion, incur the necessity, lie under the n.; admit the necessity, submit to the n. 721vb. *submit;* be fated, bow to fate, dree one's weird; be cornered, be driven into a corner, be pushed to the wall 700vb. *be in difficulty;* know no alternative, have no choice, have no option; be unable to help it, be so constituted; be subject to impulse, be guided by instinct 745vb. *be subject.*

necessitate, dictate, impose, oblige 740vb. *compel*; bind by fate, destine, doom, foredoom, predestinate 155vb. *predestine;* insist, brook no denial; leave no choice, impose the necessity, drive into a corner; demand 627vb. *require.*

Adv. *necessarily*, of necessity, of course, perforce 740adv. *by force;* willy-nilly, nolens volens, bon gré mal grés, coûte que coûte.

See: 34, 154, 155, 473, 476, 478, 598, 605, 606, 608, 609, 618, 627, 630, 700, 721, 740, 745, 801, 917, 953, 961.

597 Willingness

N. *willingness*, voluntariness, volunteering; spontaneousness 609n. *spontaneity;* free choice, option 605n. *choice;* disposition, mind, animus; inclination, leaning, bent, bias, penchant, propensity 179n. *tendency;* facility 694n. *aptitude;* predisposition, readiness, right mood, favorable humor, receptive frame of mind; cordiality, good will 897 n. *benevolence;* acquiescence 488n. *assent;* compliance 758n. *consent;* ready acquiescence, cheerful consent, alacrity, promptness, zeal, earnestness, eagerness, zealousness, ardor, enthusiasm; initiative, forwardness; impatience, over-eagerness, over-zealousness, ardor of the chase 678n. *overactivity;* devotion, self-d., dedication, sacrifice 931n. *disinterestedness;* helpfulness 706n. *cooperation;* loyalty 739n. *obedience;* pliancy, docility, tractability 612n. *persuasibility;* submissiveness 721n. *submission;* obsequiousness 879n. *servility.*

voluntary work, voluntary service 901n. *philanthropy;* honorary employment, unpaid labor, labor of love, self-appointed task; gratuitous effort, work of supererogation 637 n. *superfluity;* freewill offering 781 n. *gift.*

volunteer, unpaid worker, ready w., no shirker, no sloucher 678n. *busy person.*

Adj. *willing*, acquiescent 488adj. *assenting;* compliant, agreeable, content 758adj. *consenting;* in the mood, in the vein, receptive, favorable, favorably minded, inclined, disposed, well-d., predisposed, amenable; gracious, genial, cordial; happy, pleased, glad, charmed, delighted; ready 669adj. *prepared;* ready and willing, prompt, quick 678adj. *active;* forward, anticipating; alacritous, zealous, eager, enthusiastic, dedicated; over-eager, impatient, spoiling for, raring to go; dependable, reliable 768adj. *observant;* earnest, trying, doing one's best 671adj. *essaying;* helpful 706adj. *cooperative;* docile, teachable, suasible, biddable 24adj. *apt;* loyal 739adj. *obedient;* submissive 721adj. *submitting;* obsequious 879adj. *servile;* fain, desirous, dying to 859adj. *desiring;* would-be 852adj. *hoping;* meaning, meaning to 617adj. *intending.*

voluntary, offered, unprompted, unforced, unsought, unasked, unbidden 609adj. *spontaneous;* unsolicited, uncalled for, self-imposed; nonmandatory, discretional, open to choice, optional 605adj. *chosen;* volunteering 759adj. *offering;* gratuitous, free, honorary, unpaid 812 adj. *uncharged.*

Vb. *be willing*, — ready etc. adj.; not mind, have half a mind to; feel like, have a great mind to 595vb. *will;* be fain 859vb. *desire;* mean 617vb. *intend;* agree, acquiesce 488 vb. *assent;* comply 758vb. *consent;* hearken, lend an ear to, give a willing ear, be found willing 739vb. *obey;* try, do one's best 671vb.

essay; show zeal, go out of one's way to, lean over backwards, overcompensate; collaborate 706vb. *cooperate;* anticipate, meet halfway; swallow, jump at, catch at; can't wait, be thrilled at the idea; stomach, make no bones, have no scruple, not hesitate; choose freely 605vb. *choose;* volunteer, sacrifice oneself 759vb. *offer oneself*.

Adv. *willingly,* with a will, readily, cordially, heartily; voluntarily, spontaneously, without asking, before a.; with open arms, with all one's heart, heart and soul, con amore, with a good grace, without demur, nothing loath; gladly, with pleasure.

See: 24, 179, 488, 595, 605, 609, 612, 617, 637, 669, 671, 678, 694, 706, 721, 739, 758, 759, 768, 781, 812, 852, 859, 879, 897, 901, 931.

598 Unwillingness

N. *unwillingness,* disinclination, indisposition, reluctance; disagreement 489n. *dissent;* demur, objection 468 n. *qualification;* protest 762n. *deprecation;* renitence 704n. *opposition;* rejection 760n. *refusal;* unhelpfulness, non-cooperation 702n. *hindrance;* dissociation, non-association, abstention 190n. *absence;* unenthusiasm, lifelessness, want of alacrity, lack of zeal 860n. *indifference;* backwardness 278n. *slowness;* hesitation 858n. *caution;* scruple, qualm of conscience 486n. *doubt;* repugnance 861n. *dislike;* recoil, aversion, averseness, no stomach for, shrinking 620n. *avoidance;* bashfulness 874n. *modesty;* nonobservance 738n. *disobedience;* indocility, refractoriness, fractiousness; sulks, sulkiness 893n. *sullenness;* perfunctoriness, grudging service; undependability, unreliability 474n. *uncertainty;* shelving, postponement, procrastination 136n. *delay;* laziness 679n. *sluggishness;* neglect, remissness 458n. *negligence.*

slacker, forced labor, unwilling servant 278n. *slowcoach;* idle apprentice 679n. *idler.*

Adj. *unwilling,* indisposed, loath, reluctant, averse; not prepared, not minded, not so m., not in the mood 760adj. *refusing;* unconsenting, unreconciled 489adj. *dissenting;* renitent, adverse, opposed, unalterably o., irreconcilable 704adj. *opposing;* demurring, protesting 762adj. *deprecatory;* squeamish, with no stomach for 861adj. *disliking;* full of regrets, regretful, with regret 830adj. *regretting;* hesitant 858adj. *cautious;* shy, bashful 847adj. *modest;* shrinking, shirking 620adj. *avoiding;* unzealous, unenthusiastic, half-hearted; backward, dragging 278adj. *slow;* unhelpful, uncooperative, go-slow 702adj. *hindering;* non-cooperating, fractious, restive, recalcitrant, kicking 738adj. *disobedient;* not trying, perfunctory, unthorough, remiss 458adj. *negligent;* grudging, sulky 893adj. *sullen;* unspontaneous, forced, begrudged.

Vb. *be loath,* — unwilling etc. adj.; not have the heart to, not stomach 861vb. *dislike;* disagree, stickle, stick, boggle 489vb. *dissent;* object, demur, protest, kick 762vb. *deprecate;* resist 704vb. *oppose;* reject 760vb. *refuse;* recoil, turn away, back a., not face, blench, fight shy, duck, jib, shirk 620vb. *avoid;* skimp, scamp 458vb. *neglect;* drag one's feet, look over one's shoulder, hang back, hang fire, go slow, run rusty 278vb. *move slowly;* slack, not try, not pull one's weight 679 vb. *be inactive;* not play, noncooperate, dissociate oneself, abstain 702vb. *obstruct;* grudge, begrudge, make faces, grimace 893vb. *be sullen;* drag oneself, make o.; do with regret, have regrets 830vb. *regret*; tear oneself away 296vb. *depart.*

Adv. *unwillingly,* reluctantly, under protest, under pressure, with a bad grace, in spite of oneself, against one's will, sore against the grain; regretfully, with regret.

See: 136, 190, 278, 296, 458, 468, 474, 486, 489, 620, 679, 702, 704, 738, 760, 762, 830, 858, 860, 861, 874, 893.

599 Resolution

N. *resolution,* sticking point, resoluteness, determination, grim d.; zeal, earnestness, seriousness; resolve, fixed r., mind made up, decision 608n. *predetermination;* drive, vigor 174n. *vigorousness;* energy, frantic e., desperate e., desperation 678n. *activity;* thoroughness 725 n. *completion;* fixity of purpose, concentration, iron will, will-power 595n. *will;* self-control, self-restraint, self-mastery, self-conquest, self-command, self-possession; tenacity 600 n. *perseverence;* aplomb, mettle, daring, dash, élan 712n. *attack;*

guts, pluck, grit, backbone; heroism, moral courage 855n. *courage;* single-mindedness, devotedness, devotion, utter d., self-d., dedication; firm principles, reliability, staunchness, steadiness, constancy, firmness 153n. *stability;* insistence, pressure 740n. *compulsion;* sternness, relentlessness, ruthlessness, inexorability, implacability 906n. *pitilessness;* inflexibility, steeliness 326n. *hardness;* iron, cast i., steel, rock; clenched teeth, hearts of oak, bull-dog breed 600n. *stamina.*

Adj. *resolute*, resolved, made up, determined 597adj. *willing;* desperate, stopping at nothing; serious, earnest, concentrated; intent upon, set u., bent u. 617adj. *intending;* insistent, pressing, urgent, driving, forceful, energetic, heroic 174adj. *vigorous;* zealous, thorough, whole-hogging 455adj. *attentive;* steady, firm, staunch, reliable, constant 153 adj. *unchangeable;* iron-willed, strong-w., strong-minded, unbending, immovable, unyielding, inflexible, uncompromising, intransigent 602adj. *obstinate;* stern, grim, inexorable, implacable, relentless, ruthless, merciless 906adj. *pitiless;* iron, cast-i., steely, tough as steel, hard as iron 326adj. *hard;* undaunted, nothing daunted 855adj. *unfearing;* unshaken, unshakable, unshrinking, unflinching, game, tenacious 600 adj. *persevering;* indomitable 727 adj. *unbeaten;* steeled, armored, proof; self-controlled, self-restrained 942adj. *temperate;* self-possessed, self-reliant, self-confident; purposeful, serious, earnest, whole-hearted, single-minded, devoted, dedicated.

Vb. *be resolute,* — determined etc. adj.; steel oneself, brace o., set one's face, grit *or* clench one's teeth (**see** *stand firm*); make up one's mind, take a resolution, will, resolve, determine, purpose 617vb. *intend;* decide, fix, seal, conclude, finish with 69vb. *terminate;* take on oneself, accept responsibility; know one's own mind, insist, press, urge, not take "no" for an answer 532vb. *emphasize;* cut through, override, put one's foot down, stand no nonsense; stick at nothing, not stop at trifles, go to all lengths, push to extremes; go the whole hog, see it through 725vb. *carry through;* face, face the odds 661vb. *face danger;* outface, dare 711vb. *defy;* endure, go through fire and water 825vb. *suffer;* face the issue, bring to a head, take the bull by the horns; take the plunge, cross the Rubicon, burn one's boats, burn one's bridges, throw away the scabbard, nail one's colors to the mast; be single-hearted, set one's heart on, take up, go in for, take up in earnest, devote *or* dedicate oneself, give oneself to, give up everything for; set to, buckle to, go to it, put one's shoulder to the wheel, put one's heart into, grapple, strain 682vb. *exert oneself.*

stand firm, dig in, dig one's toes in, stand one's ground, stay put, stand pat; not budge, not yield, not compromise; never despair, stand fast, hold f., stick f., hold out 600vb. *persevere;* bear the brunt, have what it takes, fight on, stick it out, grin and bear it, endure 825vb. *suffer;* die hard, die game, die fighting, die with one's boots on; go down with colors flying, nail one's colors to the mast.

Adv. *resolutely*, seriously, earnestly, in good earnest; with firm determination, with fixed resolve; at any price, at all costs, at any hazard; manfully, like a man; come what may, live or die, neck or nothing, once for all.

See: 69, 153, 174, 326, 455, 532, 595, 597, 600, 602, 608, 617, 661, 678, 682, 712, 725, 727, 740, 771, 825, 855, 906, 942.

600 Perserverance

N. *perseverance*, persistence, tenacity, pertinacity, pertinaciousness, stubbornness 602n. *obstinacy;* staunchness, constancy, steadfastness 599n. *resolution;* singlemindedness, singleness of purpose, concentration 455n. *attention;* sedulity, application, tirelessness, indefatigability, assiduousness, industriousness 678n. *assiduity;* doggedness, plodding, hard trying, hard work 682n. *exertion;* endurance, patience 825n. *suffering;* maintenance 146n. *continuance;* ceaselessness 144n. *permanence;* iteration, repeated efforts, unflagging e. 106n. *repetition.*

stamina, staying power, indefatigability 162n. *strength;* grit, backbone, game, pluck, bottom; bull-dog courage, diehard c. 855n. *courage;* hard core, diehard, last ditcher, old guard 602n. *opinionist;* trier, hard t., stayer, willing worker 686 n. *worker.*

Adj. persevering, persistent, tenacious, stubborn 602adj. *obstinate;* game, plucky; hard-trying, patient, plodding, dogged 678adj. *industrious;* strenuous 682adj. *laborious;* steady, unfaltering, unwavering, undrooping, enduring, unflagging, unwearied, untiring, indefatigable; unsleeping, sleepless 457adj. *vigilant;* unfailing, unremitting, unintermittent, constant 146adj. *unceasing;* renewed, iterated, reiterated 106adj. *repeated;* indomitable, unconquerable, unconquered 727adj. *unbeaten;* undaunted, undiscouraged, game to the last, true to the end 599adj. *resolute.*

Vb. *persevere*, persist, keep at it, not take "no" for an answer; not despair, never d., never say die, hope on 852vb. *hope;* endure, have what it takes, come up for more 825vb. *suffer;* try, keep on trying, try and try again 671vb. *essay;* maintain, keep up, follow up 146vb. *sustain;* plod, slog, slog away, peg a., peg at, plug at, hammer at, work at 682vb. *work;* continue, go on, keep on, keep the pot boiling, keep the ball rolling, rally, keep going; not let go, cling, hold fast, maintain one's grip 778vb. *retain;* hang on, stick it out, sit out, see through, wait till the end; be in at the death, stand by the grave of, survive 41vb. *be left;* maintain one's ground, not budge, not stir 602vb. *be obstinate;* stick to one's guns, hold out, hold out to the last, die in the last ditch, die at one's post 599vb. *stand firm;* work till one drops, die in harness; labor unceasingly, spare no pains, move heaven and earth, knock at every door 682vb. *exert oneself;* bring to conclusion, see the end of, complete 725vb. *carry through.*

Adv. *persistently*, perseveringly; through thick and thin, through fire and water, sink or swim 559adv. *resolutely;* repeatedly, unendingly, ceaselessly.

See: 41, 106, 144, 146, 162, 455, 457, 599, 602, 671, 678, 682, 725, 727, 778, 825, 852, 855.

601 Irresolution

N. *irresolution,* infirmity of purpose, faintheartedness, loss of nerve, no grit 856n. *cowardice;* non-perseverance, broken resolve, broken promise 603n. *tergiversation;* unsettlement, indecision, uncertainty, floating vote 474n. *dubiety;* hesitation, overcaution 858n. *caution;* inconstancy, fluctuation, vacillation, blowing hot and cold 152n. *changeableness;* levity, fickleness, whimsicality, irresponsibility 604n. *caprice;* lack of will-power, lack of drive 175n. *inertness;* good nature, easy-goingness, compromise 734n. *laxity;* lack of thoroughness, half-heartedness, half-measures 726n. *non-completion;* lukewarmness, listlessness, apathy 860n. *indifference;* no will of one's own, abulia, weak will 163n. *weakness;* impressibility, suggestibility 612n. *persuasibility;* pliancy, overpliancy 327n. *softness;* obsequiousness 879n. *servility;* submissiveness, slavishness 721n. *submission.*

waverer, wobbler, dodderer, shilly-shallyer; shuttlecock, butterfly, feather 152n. *changeable thing;* ass between two bundles of hay, floating voter; weathercock, chameleon, turncoat 603n. *tergiversator;* faint-heart, compromiser.

Adj. *irresolute*, undecided, indecisive, of two minds, vacillating; unable to make up one's mind, undetermined, unresolved, uncertain 474adj. *doubting;* squeamish, boggling, hesitating 598adj. *unwilling;* gutless, timid, tremulous, faint-hearted, unheroic, faint, nerveless 856adj. *cowardly;* shaken, rattled 854adj. *nervous;* half-hearted, lukewarm 860adj. *indifferent;* wobbling, unstaunch, unsteadfast, infirm, infirm of purpose 474adj. *unreliable;* characterless, featureless 175adj. *inert;* compromising, weak-willed, weak-minded, weak-kneed 163adj. *weak;* suggestible, flexible, pliant 327adj. *soft;* easy-going, good-natured 734adj. *lax;* inconstant, various, variable, temperamental 152adj. *changeful;* whimsical, mercurial, not to be pinned down 604adj. *capricious;* emotional, restless, unfixed, unballasted, without ballast 152adj. *unstable;* irresponsible, giddy, feather-brained, light 456adj. *light-minded;* fidgety, impatient, unpersevering; unthorough, superficial 456 adj. *inattentive;* unfaithful 603adj. *tergiversating.*

Vb. *be irresolute*, — undecided etc. adj.; back away, blink, jib, shy, shirk 620vb. *avoid;* palter, shuffle, shilly-shally 518vb. *equivocate;* fluctuate, vacillate, see-saw, wobble, waver, sway, hover, teeter, dodder, dither 317vb. *oscillate;* blow hot and cold, back and fill, hem and haw, will and will not, be in two minds, turn round in circles, not know what to do, be at one's wits' end 474vb. *be uncertain;* leave in suspense, keep undecided, delay, put off a decision 136vb. *put off;* dally, dilly-dally 136vb. *wait;* debate, balance 475vb. *argue;* hesitate 858vb. *be cautious;* falter, grow weary 684 vb. *be fatigued;* not persevere, give up 621vb. *relinquish;* make a compromise, take half-measures 770vb. *compromise;* yield, give way 721vb. *submit;* change sides, go over 603vb. *apostatize.*

Adv. *irresolutely*, faint-heartedly, hesitantly; from pillar to post; seesaw; between the devil and the deep blue sea.

See: 136, 152, 163, 175, 317, 327, 456, 474, 475, 518, 598, 603, 604, 612, 620, 621, 684, 721, 726, 734, 770, 854, 856, 858, 860, 879.

602 Obstinacy

N. *obstinacy*, unyielding temper; determination, will 599n. *resolution;* grimness, doggedness, tenacity 600 n. *perseverance;* stubbornness, obduracy, obduration; pervicacity, self-will, pig-headedness; inelasticity, inflexibility, woodenness, toughness 326n. *hardness;* no compromise, intransigence; constancy, irreversibility, fixity 153n. *stability;* stiff neck, contumacy 715n. *resistance;* incorrigibility 940n. *impenitence;* indocility, intractability, mulishness, dourness, sulkiness 893n. *sullenness;* perversity, wrongheadedness, bloody-mindedness.

opiniatrety, self-opinion, opiniativeness, opinionatedness 473n. *positiveness;* dogmatism, bigotry, zealotry; rigorism, intolerance, fanaticism 735n. *severity;* ruling passion, infatuation, obsession, monomania, idée fixe 481n. *bias;* blind side 439n. *blindness;* illiberality, obscurantism 491n. *ignorance;* old school, ancien régime.

opinionist, stubborn fellow, mule; stick-in-the-mud, blimp; fanatic, rigorist, stickler, pedant, dogmatist, zealot, bigot, persecutor 481n. *narrow mind;* sticker, stayer; chronic; last-ditcher, die-hard, bitter-ender; fogy 504n. *crank.*

Adj. *obstinate*, stubborn, pervicacious; pig-headed, mulish; unyielding, firm, determined 599adj. *resolute;* dogged, tenacious 600adj. *persevering;* stiff, rigid, inelastic, wooden 326adj. *hard;* inflexible, unbending, stiff-backed; obdurate, hardened, case-h., rock-ribbed; uncompromising, intransigent; unmoved, uninfluenced, immovable 153adj. *unchangeable;* inexorable, unappeasable, implacable, merciless 906adj. *pitiless;* set, wedded, set in one's ways, hidebound, ultraconservative, blimpish 610adj. *habituated;* unteachable, obscurantist, impervious, blind, deaf; opinionated, dogmatic, pedantic 473adj. *positive;* obsessed, bigoted, fanatic 481adj. *biased;* dour, grim 893adj. *sullen;* indocile, hard-mouthed, stiff-necked, contumacious, impenitent (**see** *willful*); perverse, incorrigible, bloody-minded; possessive, dog-in-the-manger; irremovable, irreversible; persistent, incurable, chronic 113adj. *lasting.*

willful, self-willed, forward, wayward, arbitrary; entêté, headstrong, perverse; unruly, jibbing, restive, refractory; irrepressible, ungovernable, unmanageable, intractable, uncontrollable 738adj. *disobedient;* impersuasible, incorrigible, contumacious; cross-grained, crotchety 892 adj. *irascible.*

Vb. *be obstinate*, — stubborn etc. adj.; persist 600vb. *persevere;* brazen it out 940vb. *be impenitent;* stick to one's guns, stand out, not budge, stay put, stand pat 599vb. *stand firm;* insist, brook no denial, not take "no" for an answer; go one's way, want one's own w., must have one's way. 734vb. *please oneself;* opinionate 473vb. *dogmatize;* be wedded to one's own opinions, not change one's mind 473vb. *be certain;* stay in a rut, cling to custom 610vb. *be wont;* not listen, take no advice, take the bit between one's teeth, damn the consequences 857vb. *be rash;* not yield to treatment, become chronic 113vb. *last.*

Adv. *obstinately*, pigheadedly, mulishly, like a mule.

See: 113, 153, 326, 439, 473, 481, 504, 599, 600, 610, 715, 734, 735, 738, 857, 892, 893, 906, 940.

603 Tergiversation

N. *tergiversation*, change of mind, better thoughts; afterthought, second thought 67n. *sequel;* change of purpose, alteration of plan, new resolve; good resolution, break with the past, repentance 939n. *penitence;* revulsion 280n. *recoil;* backsliding, recidivation, recidivism 657

n. *relapse;* change of direction 282n. *deviation;* resilement, reversal, about-face, volte-face, looking back 286n. *return;* versatility, slipperiness, suppleness, unreliability, untrustworthiness 930n. *improbity;* apostasy, recreancy (**see** *recantation*); defection, desertion 918n. *dutilessness;* ratting, going over, treachery 930n. *perfidy;* secession, withdrawal 978n. *schism;* abandonment 621n. *relinquishment;* change of mood, temperament; coquetry 604n. *caprice.*

recantation, palinode, eating one's words, retractation, retraction; resilement, withdrawal; renunciation, abjuration, abjurement, forswearing, swearing off 532n. *oath;* disavowal, disclaimer, denial 533n. *negation;* revocation, revokement, recall 752 n. *abrogation.*

tergiversator, turncoat, turnabout, rat; weathercock 152n. *changeable thing;* time-server, trimmer, Vicar of Bray 518n. *equivocalness;* double-dealer, Janus, two-faced person, Mr. Facing-both-ways 545n. *deceiver;* jilt, flirt, coquette 604n. *caprice;* recanter, recreant, apostate, renegade, runagate, renegado, forswearer; traitor, betrayer 938n. *knave;* medizer, quisling, fifth columnist, collaborationist 707n. *collaborator;* lost leader, deserter, quitter, ratter; tell-tale, peacher, squealer, approver 524n. *informer;* strike-breaker, blackleg, scab; deviationist, secessionist, seceder, schismatic, mugwump 978n. *schismatic;* runaway, bolter, flincher 620 n. *avoider;* recidivist, backslider 904 n. *offender;* convert, proselyte 147n. *changed person.*

Adj. *tergiversating*, trimming etc. vb.; shuffling 518adj. *equivocal;* slippery, supple, versatile, treacherous 930 adj. *perfidious;* double-dealing 541 adj. *hypocritical;* reactionary, going back 286adj. *regressive;* fickle 604 adj. *capricious;* time-serving, time-pleasing 925adj. *flattering;* vacillating 601adj. *irresolute;* apostate, recanting, renegade; recidivist, relapsed; false, unfaithful, disloyal 918adj. *dutiless.*

Vb. *tergiversate*, change one's mind, think again, think better of it, change one's tune 601vb. *be irresolute;* back out, scratch, withdraw 753vb. *resign;* back down, crawl 872 vb. *be humbled;* apologize (**see** *recant*); change front, change round, swerve, tack, wheel about 282vb. *turn round;* turn one's back on 286vb. *turn back;* turn over a new leaf, make good resolutions, repent 939vb. *be penitent;* reform, mend one's ways 654vb. *get better;* fall back, backslide 657vb. *relapse;* trim, shuffle, face both ways, run with the hare and hunt with the hounds 518 vb. *be equivocal;* ditch, jilt, throw over, desert 918vb. *fail in duty;* forsake, abandon, wash one's hands of 621vb. *relinquish;* turn against, play false.

apostatize, turn one's coat, change sides, medize; let down the side, change one's allegiance; switch, switch over, join the opposition, cross over, cross the floor; blackleg, rat; betray, collaborate 930vb. *be dishonest;* be off with the old love, jump on the bandwagon, follow the rising star.

recant, unsay, eat one's words, eat one's hat; eat humble pie, apologize; take back, go back on, recall one's words, resile, withdraw; retract, disavow, disclaim, repudiate, deny 533 vb. *negate;* renounce, renunciate, abjure, forswear, swear off; recall, revoke, rescind 752vb. *abrogate.*

See: 67, 147, 152, 280, 282, 286, 518, 524, 532, 533, 541, 545, 601, 604, 620, 621, 654, 657, 707, 752, 753, 872, 904, 918, 925, 930, 939, 978.

604 Caprice

N. *caprice*, fancy, fantastic notion 513n. *fantasy;* capriciousness, arbitrariness, motivelessness, purposelessness; whimsicality, freakishness, crankiness 497n. *absurdity;* faddishness, faddiness, faddism 481n. *bias;* inconsistency 25n. *disagreement;* fitfulness, changeability, variability, fickleness, unreliability, temperament, levity, giddiness, lightmindedness, irresponsibility 152n. *changeableness;* inconstancy, coquettishness, flirtatiousness; playfulness; temperament, fretfulness, pettishness 892n. *irascibility.*

whim, caprice, whimsy, whimwam, vagary, sweet will, humor, fit, crotchet, bee in the bonnet, maggot, quirk, kink, fad, craze, freak; escapade, prank, boutade, wild-goose chase 497n. *foolery;* coquetry, flirtation.

Adj. *capricious*, motiveless, purposeless; whimsical, fanciful, fantastic; humorsome, temperamental, crotchety, maggoty, fitful; hysterical, mad 503adj. *insane;* freakish, prankish, wanton, wayward, erratic, inconsistent; faddy, faddish, particular 862 adj. *fastidious;* captious, arbitrary, unreasonable; fretful, contrary, uncomfortable 892adj. *irascible;* undisciplined, refractory 602adj. *willful;* uncertain, unpredictable 508adj. *unexpected;* volatile, mercurial, skittish, giddy, frivolous 456adj. *light-minded;* inconsistent, inconstant, variable 152adj. *unstable;* irresponsible, unreliable, fickle 603adj. *tergiversating;* flirtatious, coquettish, playful.

Vb. *be capricious,* — whimsical etc. adj.; show caprice, take it into one's head; pick and choose 862vb. *be fastidious;* chop and change, blow hot and cold 152vb. *vary;* have a bee in one's bonnet, have a maggot in one's brain; be fickle, take up a thing and drop it; vacillate 318vb. *fluctuate;* play pranks, play tricks 497vb. *be absurd;* flirt, coquet 837 vb. *amuse oneself.*

Adv. *capriciously,* fitfully, by fits and starts, now this, now that; as the humor takes one, at one's own sweet will.

See: 25, 152, 318, 456, 481, 497, 503, 508, 513, 602, 603, 837, 862, 892.

605 Choice

N. *choice,* act of choosing, election 463n. *discrimination;* picking and choosing, eclecticism 862n. *fastidiousness;* picking out, selection; co-option, cooptation, adoption; designation, nomination, appointment 751 n. *commission;* right of choice, option, preoption; freedom of choice, discretion, pick; deliberate choice, decision 481n. *judgment;* preference, predilection, inclination, leaning, bias 179n. *tendency;* taste 859n. *liking;* availability 759n. *offer;* range of choice, selection, list, short l.; possible choice, alternative, embarras de choix; difficult choice, option of difficulties, dilemma 474n. *dubiety;* limited choice, no real alternative; only choice, Hobson's choice, nothing for it but 606n. *no choice;* blind choice 464n. *indiscrimination;* better choice, preferability, desirability, greater good, lesser evil 642n. *expediences;* one's preference, favor, fancy, first choice, top seed; thing chosen, selection, pickings, gleanings, excerpts; literary selection 592n. *anthology;* unlucky choice, bad bargain; unfair choice, favoritism 914n. *injustice.*

vote, voice 485n. *opinion;* representation, proportional r., cumulative vote, transferable v., casting v., ballot, secret b., open vote; card vote; vote-counting, show of hands, division, poll, Gallup p., plebiscite, referendum; suffrage, universal s., adult s., manhood s.; franchise, right of representation, votes for women, women's suffrage, suffragettism; parliamentary system, electoral s., ballot-box, vox populi; polling, counting heads, counting noses; election, general e., "democracy's feast"; by-election; indirect election, primary e., primary; polls, voting, electioneering, canvassing, canvass, hustings, candidature; successful election, return.

electorate, voters, balloter, elector, plumper, straw voter, fagot v.; electoral college; quorum; electoral roll, voting list, voter's l.; constituent, constituency; borough, pocket b., rotten b.; polling booth, ballot-box, voting paper; slate, ticket.

Adj. *choosing,* optional, discretional 595adj. *volitional;* exercising choice, showing preference, preferential, favoring 923adj. *approving;* selective, eclectic; cooptative, elective, electoral; voting, present and v.; vote-catching, electioneering, canvassing.

chosen, well-c.; worth choosing, not to be sniffed at; preferable, better 642adj. *expedient;* select, choice, recherché, picked, hand-p. 644adj. *excellent;* sorted, assorted, seeded 62adj. *arranged;* elect, designate; elected, returned; on approval; preferred, special, favorite, fancy, pet; God's own; by appointment.

Vb. *choose,* have a voice, have free will 595vb. *will;* eliminate the alternatives, make one's choice, make one's bed; exercise one's discretion, accept, opt, opt for, take up an option; elect, coopt, adopt, put on the list 923vb. *approve;* would like, favor, fancy, like best; incline, lean, have a bias 179vb. *tend;* prefer, have a preference, like better, have rather; might as well, might do worse; go in for, take up; think fit, think it best to, decide, make up one's mind 480vb. *judge;* come out for, come down f., plump f., come down on one side; take the plunge, cross the Rubicon, burn one's boats 599vb. *be resolute;* range oneself, take sides, side, back, support, embrace, espouse, cast in one's lot with 703vb. *patronize;* take for better or worse 894vb. *wed.*

select, pick, pick out, sort o., seed; pass 923vb. *approve;* nominate, appoint 751vb. *commission;* designate, mark out, mark down 547vb. *mark;* preselect, earmark, reserve 46vb. *set apart;* recommend, put up, propose, second 703vb. *patronize;* excerpt, cull, anthologize 592vb. *abstract;* glean, winnow, sift, bolt 463vb. *discriminate;* draw the line, separate; skim, skim off, cream, pick the best; indulge one's fancy, pick and choose 862vb. *be fastidious.*

vote, have a v., have a voice; have the vote, be enfranchised, be on the electoral roll; poll, go to the polls; cast a vote, register one's v., raise one's hand, divide; vote for, elect, return; electioneer, canvass; accept a candidature, stand 759vb. *offer oneself;* put to the vote, present the alternatives, take a poll; count heads, count noses; hold an election, go to the country, appeal to the electorate.

Adv. *optionally,* at pleasure; by ballot; alternatively, either . . . or; preferably, rather, sooner; by choice, a la carte.

See: 46, 62, 179, 463, 464, 474, 480, 481, 485, 547, 592, 595, 599, 606, 642, 644, 703, 751, 759, 859, 862, 894, 914, 923.

606 Absence of Choice

N. *no choice,* choicelessness, no alternative, dictation 596n. *necessity;* dictated choice, Hobson's c. 740n. *compulsion;* any, the first that comes 464n. *indiscrimination;* no favoritism, impartiality, first come first served 913n. *justice;* no preference, non-committal, neutrality, apathy 860n. *indifference;* moral apathy, amoralism, amorality; no difference, six of one and half a dozen of the other, "a plague on both your houses" 28n. *equality;* indecision, open mind, open-mindedness 474n. *dubiety;* floating vote 601n. *irresolution;* refusal to vote, non-election, abstention 598n. *unwillingness;* no election, spoiled ballot paper; disfranchisement, disqualification, no vote, no voice.

Adj. *choiceless,* without alternative, necessitated 596adj. *necessary;* without a preference, unable to choose, happy either way 625adj. *neutral;* open-minded, open to conviction, unresolved, undecided, undetermined 601adj. *irresolute;* uninterested, apathetic 860adj. *indifferent;* morally neutral, amoral, amoralistic; disinterested, motiveless; without favoritism, impartial 913adj. *just;* not voting, abstaining 598adj. *unwilling;* non-voting, voteless, disfranchised, disqualified; nothing to offer, featureless, characterless 860adj. *unwanted.*

Vb. *be neutral,* take no sides, make no choice, not vote, refuse to v., withhold one's v., abstain; waive, waive one's choice, stand aside 621 vb. *relinquish;* stand between 625vb. *be halfway;* sit on the fence 601vb. *be irresolute;* not care 860vb. *be indifferent.*

have no choice, have no alternative, suffer dictation, have Hobson's choice, take it or leave it, make a virtue of necessity 596vb. *be forced;* have no voice, have no vote; lose one's vote, spoil one's ballot paper.

Adv. *neither,* neither. . . . nor.

See: 28, 464, 474, 596, 598, 601, 621, 625, 740, 860, 913.

607 Rejection

N. *rejection,* non-acceptance, declination, waiver, waiving; non-approval, disapproval 924n. *disapprobation;* abnegation, repudiation, denial 533n. *negation;* apostasy 603n. *recantation;* rebuff, repulse 760n. *refusal;* spurn, kick, more kicks than ha'pence; rejection at the polls, electoral defeat, lost election, hostile vote, forfeiture of deposit 728n. *defeat;* elimination, outcasting 300n. *ejection;* nonconsideration, counting out, exception, exemption 57n. *exclusion;* disuse, discarding, disemployment 674n. *non-use;* discard, reject, wallflower; unpopular cause, lost c.

Adj. rejected etc. vb.; ineligible, unchosen, outvoted 860adj. *unwanted;* unaccepted, returned, sent back, tried and found wanting, declined with thanks 924adj. *disapproved;* kept out, excluded, outcast 57adj. *excluded;* unfit for consideration, not be thought of, out of the question 643adj. *inexpedient;* discharged 674adj. *disused.*

Vb. *reject,* not accept, decline, say no to, rebuff, repulse, spurn, kick 760vb. *refuse;* not approve, not pass, return, send back, return with thanks 924n. *disapprove;* not consider, pass over, ignore 458vb. *disregard;* vote against, not vote, not choose, outvote 489vb. *dissent;* scrap, discard, ditch, throw away, throw aside, lay a., give up 674vb. *disuse;* disallow, revoke 752vb. *abrogate;* set aside, supersede 752vb.

depose; expel, out-caste, thrust out, fling o. 300vb. *eject*; sort out, draw the line 44vb. *eliminate;* except, count out, exempt 57vb. *exclude;* cold-shoulder, turn one's back on 885vb. *be rude;* not want, not cater for 883vb. *make unwelcome;* disclaim, disavow, deny 533vb. *negate;* abnegate, repudiate, apostatize 603 vb. *recant;* scout, scorn, set at naught, disdain, laugh at, mock, deride 851vb. *ridicule;* sniff at, look a gift horse in the mouth 922 vb. *hold cheap.*

See: 57, 300, 458, 489, 533, 603, 643, 674, 728, 752, 760, 851, 860, 883, 885, 922, 924.

608 Predetermination

N. *predetermination*, predestination 596n. *necessity*; appointment, foreordination, preordination 155n. *destiny;* decree 595n. *will;* premeditation, predeliberation, resolve, project 617n. *intention;* prearrangement 669n. *preparation;* work on hand, order of the day, orders, order paper, agenda 622n. *business;* frame-up, put-up job, packed jury 623n. *plot;* parti pris, closed mind 481n. *prejudice;* predisposal, foregone conclusion, ready-made verdict, agreed result.

Adj. *predetermined*, decreed, premeditated etc. vb.; appointed, predestined, foreordained 596n. *fated;* deliberate, willed, aforethought, prepense 617 adj. *intending;* with a motive, designed, studied, calculated; weighed, considered, advised; well-devised, devised, controlled, contrived 623adj. *planned;* put-up, framed, stacked, packed, ready-made, prearranged 669adj. *prepared.*

Vb. *predetermine*, destine, appoint, predispose, foreordain, predestinate 155vb. *predestine;* premeditate, preconceive, resolve beforehand 617vb. *intend;* agree beforehand, preconcert; will the end 595vb. *will;* contrive a result, ensure a r. 156vb. *cause;* contrive, arrange, prearrange 623vb. *plan;* frame, put up, pack a jury, stack the cards 541vb. *fake.*

See: 155, 156, 481, 541, 595, 596, 617, 622, 623, 669.

609 Spontaneity

N. *spontaneity*, unpremeditation; ad hoc measures, improvisation; extemporization, ad-libbing, impromptu 670n. *nonpreparation;* involuntariness, reflex, automatic r.; impulsiveness, impulse, blind i., spurt 476n. *intuition;* inconsideration, spur of the moment; inspiration, sudden thought, hunch, flash 451n. *idea.*

improviser, extemporizer, improvisator, improvisatrice; creature of impulse.

Adj. *spontaneous*, off-hand, ad hoc, improvised, extemporaneous, sudden, snap; makeshift, catch-as-catch-can 670adj. *unprepared;* impromptu, unpremeditated, unmeditated, unrehearsed, indeliberate 618adj. *unintentional;* unprompted, unmotivated, unprovoked; unguarded, incautious 857adj. *rash;* natural, instinctive, involuntary, automatic 476adj. *intuitive;* untaught 699adj. *artless;* impulsive, emotional 818adj. *feeling.*

Vb. *improvise*, not prepare, extemporize, vamp 670vb. *be unprepared;* obey an impulse, act on the spur of the moment; blurt, come out with, say what comes uppermost, flash out with an answer; rise to the occasion.

Adv. *extempore*, extemporaneously, impromptu, ad hoc, on the spur of the moment, off-hand, off the cuff.

See: 451, 476, 618, 670, 699, 818, 857.

610 Habit

N. *habit,* native h. 5n. *character;* habitude, assuetude, force of habit; consuetude, familiarity, second nature; study, occupation; addiction, confirmed habit, daily h., constitutional; knack, trick, instinct, leaning 179n. *tendency;* bad habit, cacoëthes; usage, standard u., long habit, custom, standing c., old c., one's old way; use, wont, user 146n. *continuance;* inveteracy, prescription 113n. *diuturnity;* tradition, law, precedent; way, ways, the old w.; beaten track, streetcar lines, groove, rut; fixed ways, round, daily r., dailiness, regularity 141n. *periodicity;* run, routine, system 60n. *order;* red tape, red-tapeism, beadledom, conventionalism, traditionalism, conservatism, old school 83n. *conformity;* occupational disease.

practice, common p., usual custom, matter of course; conformism, conventionalism, conventionality 83n. *conformity;* institution, ritual, observance 988n. *rite;* religious observance, cultus 981n. *cult;* mode, vogue, craze 848n. *fashion;* convention, protocol, done thing, the usual; form, good f. 848n. *etiquette;* man-

ners, manners and customs; table manners, eating habits; rules and regulations, standing order, rules of business, routine 688n. *conduct;* spit and polish, pipe-clay, bull 60n. *order.*
habituation, assuefaction, training 534n. *teaching;* inurement, seasoning, hardening 669n. *maturation;* naturalization, acclimatization, radication; conditioning, association, reflex, conditioned r., fixation, complex; drill, repetitive job 106n. *repetition.*
habitué, creature of habit, addict, drug a., dope-fiend; routine monger, traditionalist, conventionalist 83n. *conformist;* customer, regular c., client 792n. *purchaser;* frequenter, devotee, fan.

Adj. *habitual,* customary, consuetudinal, familiar 490n. *known;* routine, stereotyped 81adj. *regular;* conventional, traditionary, traditional 976 adj. *orthodox;* inveterate, prescriptive, time-honored, permanent 113 adj. *lasting;* resulting from habit, occupational; haunting, besetting, clinging, obsessive; habit-forming 612adj. *inducive;* fast, ingrained, dyed in the wool; rooted, deep-r., deep-seated, implanted, engrafted 153adj. *fixed;* imbued, dyed, soaked, permeated 341adj. *drenched.* **See** *usual.*
usual, accustomed, wonted, traditional; in character, natural; household, familiar, well-known 490adj. *known;* unoriginal, trite, trodden, beaten, well-worn, hackneyed; banal, commonplace, common, ordinary 79adj. *general;* set, stock 83adj. *typical;* prevalent, widespread, obtaining, current 79adj. *universal;* monthly, daily, everyday, of everyday occurrence 139adj. *frequent;* practiced, done; admitted, acknowledged, received, accepted, accredited, recognized, understood; right, settled, established, professional, official 923 adj. *approved;* de rigueur 740adj. *compelling;* invariable 153adj. *unchangeable;* modish, in the mode 848adj. *fashionable.*
habituated, in the habit of, accustomed to, known to; given to, addicted to; dedicated, devoted to, wedded to; used to, familiar with, conversant w., at home in 490adj. *knowing;* practiced, inured, seasoned, hardened 669adj. *prepared;* broken in, trained, tame 369adj. *tamed;* naturalized, acclimatized.

Vb. *be wont,* love to, be known to, be used to, use to; have the habit of, be a creature of habit; go daily, haunt, frequent; make a habit of, take up, go in for; never vary, observe routine, move in a rut, stick in a groove, tread the beaten track, go on in the jog-trot way, cling to custom; become a habit, catch on, gain upon one, grow on o., take hold of o.; stick, cling, adhere 48 vb. *cohere;* settle, take root, radicate; be the rule, obtain 178vb. *prevail;* come into use, acquire the force of custom, hold good for.
habituate, accustom oneself, get used to, get in the way of, get the knack of, get the feel of, play oneself in, take in one's stride; take to, acquire the habit, learn a h., cultivate a h.; fall into a habit; grow into a habit, catch oneself doing; keep one's hand in, practice 106vb. *repeat;* accustom, inure, season, harden, case-harden 534vb. *train;* domesticate, tame 369 vb. *break in;* sanctify by custom, naturalize, acclimatize; implant, engraft, imbue 534vb. *teach.*

Adv. *habitually,* regularly, with regularity 141adv. *periodically;* customarily, wontedly, occupationally, in the habit of; of course, as usual, according to one's wont; mechanically, automatically, by force of habit; in one's stride.

See: 5, 48, 60, 79, 81, 83, 106, 113, 139, 141, 146, 153, 178, 179, 341, 369, 490, 534, 612, 669, 688, 740, 792, 848, 923, 976, 981, 988.

611 Desuetude

N. *desuetude,* disusage, discontinuance, disuse, inusitation 674n. *nonuse;* rust, decay 655n. *deterioration;* lost habit, lost skill, rustiness, lack of practice 695n. *unskillfulness;* discarded custom, abolition 752n. *abrogation;* forgotten custom 506n. *oblivion,* 550n. *obliteration;* outgrown custom, outgrowing, weaning, ablactation 134n. *adultness;* new custom, originality 21n. *non-imitation;* unwontedness, no such custom, nonprevalence; not the form, not the thing, not protocol, not etiquette, unconventionality 84n. *unconformity;* want of habit, inexperience, unfamiliarity 491n. *ignorance.*

Adj. *unwonted,* not customary, uncurrent, non-prevalent; unused, unpracticed, unobserved, not done; unnecessary, not de rigueur; not in vogue, unfashionable 847adj. *vulgar;* out of fashion, old-fashioned, defunct 125adj. *past;* outgrown, discarded 674adj. *disused;* against custom, unconventional 84adj. *unconformable;* unsanctified by custom, untraditional, unprecedented, unhackneyed, original 21adj. *unimitative.*

unhabituated, unaccustomed, not in the habit of 769adj. *non-observant;* untrained, unbacked, unbroken, not broken in, untamed, undomesticated; uninured, unseasoned, unripe 670 adj. *immature;* unfamiliar, inexperienced, new to, new, raw, fresh, green 491adj. *uninstructed;* disaccustomed, weaned; out of the habit, rusty 695adj. *unskillful.*

Vb. *disaccustom*, wean from, cure of 656vb. *cure;* disaccustom oneself, break a habit, drop a h., lose a h.; wean oneself from, outgrow; throw off, slough, slough off, shed 229vb. *doff.*

be unused, not catch on; try a thing once, not do it again; not be done, offend custom, infringe protocol; lapse, fall into disuse, wear off, wear away 127vb. *be old;* rust 655vb. *deteriorate.*

See: 21, 84, 87, 125, 127, 134, 229, 491, 506, 550, 655, 656, 670, 674, 695, 752, 769, 847.

612 Motive

N. *motive*, cause of action 156n. *cause;* rationale, reason, ground 156 n. *reason why;* motivation, driving force, impulsion, spring, mainspring 156n. *causation;* ideal, principle, guiding star, lodestar, direction 689 n. *directorship;* aspiration 852n. *hope;* ambition 859n. *desire;* calling, call 622n. *vocation;* conscience, dictate of c., honor 917n. *duty;* shame 854n. *fear;* personal reasons, ulterior motive 932n. *selfishness;* impulse, spur of the moment, inspiration 609n. *spontaneity.*

inducement, pressure, instance, urgency, press, insistence; pressure group, lobby, lobbying 178n. *influence;* indirect influence, side-pressure; provocation, urging, incitement, encouragement, incitation, instigation, prompting, inspiration 821 n. *excitation;* countenance, support, abetment 703n. *aid;* solicitation, invitation 761n. *request;* temptation, enticement, allurement, seduction, seductiveness, tantalization, witchery, bewitchment, fascination, charm, attractiveness, magnetism 291n. *attraction;* cajolery, blandishment 925n. *flattery;* coaxing, wheedling 889n. *endearment;* persuasion, persuasiveness, salesmanship, sales talk 579n. *oratory;* pep-talk, trumpet-call, rallying cry 547n. *call;* exhortation, preachment 534n. *lecture;* pleading, advocacy 691n. *advice;* propaganda, advertising 528n. *advertisement;* bribery, palm-greasing 962n. *reward;* castigation 963n. *punishment;* honeyed words, siren song, voice of the tempter, winning ways.

persuasibility, docility, tractability, teachableness 597adj. *willingness;* pliancy, pliability 327n. *softness;* susceptibility, susceptivity, attractability, suggestibility, impressibility, sensitivity, emotionalism 819n. *moral sensibility;* credulousness 487n. *credulity.*

incentive, inducement; stimulus, fillip, flip, tickle, tickler, prod, spur, goad, ankus, whip, riding w., crop, riding c.; rod, big stick, crack of the whip 900n. *threat;* energizer, tonic, provocative, carrot, sop, sop to Cerberus, dram 174n. *stimulant;* charm 983n. *spell;* attraction, lodestone 291 n. *magnet;* lodestar, gleam; will-o'-the-wisp 440n. *visual fallacy;* lure, decoy, decoy duck, bait, golden b., fly, cast 542n. *trap;* profit 771n. *gain;* cash, gold 797n. *money;* pay, salary, perks, pay increase, rise, raise, bonus 804n. *payment;* donation, donative 781n. *gift;* gratification, tip, baksheesh, bribe 962n. *reward;* golden apple, forbidden fruit; tempting offer 759n. *offer.*

motivator, mover, prime m. 156n. *cause;* manipulator, manager, wire-puller 178n. *influence;* maneuverer, tactician, strategist 623n. *planner;* instigator, prompter, suggester, hinter; inspirer, counselor 691n. *adviser;* abettor, aider and abettor 703 n. *aider;* agent provocateur 545n. *deceiver;* tantalizer, tempter, seducer; temptress, vamp, siren, Circe; hypnotizer, hypnotist; persuader, orator, rhetorician 579n. *speaker;* advocate, pleader; coaxer, wheedler, cozener 925n. *flatterer;* vote-catcher, vote-snatcher; patterer, salesman, advertiser, propagandist 528n. *publicizer;* ringleader 690n. *leader;* firebrand, incendiary, seditionist, sedition-monger 738n. *agitator;* lobbyist, lobby, pressure-group.

Adj. *inducive*, protreptic, directive, motive; motivating, wire-pulling, lobbying 178adj. *influential;* inductive, incentive, provocative; energizing, stimulating, tonic, peppy; challenging, encouraging, rousing, incendiary 821adj. *exciting;* prompting, hortatory, insinuating, hinting; teasing, tantilizing; inviting, tempting, alluring, attractive 291adj. *attracting;* fascinating, bewitching 983adj. *sorcerous;* irresistible, hypnotic, mesmeric; habit-forming 610adj. *habitual.*

induced, brought on 157adj. *caused;* inspired, motivated; incited, egged on, tarred on 821adj. *excited;* receptive, tractable, docile 597adj. *willing;* spellbound 983adj. *bewitched;* smitten 887adj. *enamored;* suasible, persuasible 487adj. *credulous.*

Vb. *motivate,* motive, move, actuate, manipulate 173vb. *operate;* work upon, play u., act u., operate u. 178vb. *influence;* weigh, count, be a consideration, sway 178vb. *prevail;* call the tune, override, overbear 34vb. *predominate;* work on the feelings, appeal, challenge, shame into (**see** *incite*); infect, inject with, inoculate, poison; interest, intrigue 821vb. *impress;* charm, fascinate, captivate, hypnotize, spellbind 983 vb. *bewitch;* enamor, turn one's head 887vb. *excite love;* pull 291vb. *attract;* drag 288vb. *draw;* push 279 vb. *impel;* force, enforce 740vb. *compel;* bend, incline, dispose; predispose, prejudice 481vb. *bias;* predestine 608vb. *predetermine;* lead, direct 689n. *manage;* lead astray 495vb. *mislead;* give a lead, ringlead; set the fashion, set an example, set the pace, lead the dance 283vb. *precede.*

incite, energize, lend force to, stimulate 174vb. *invigorate;* sound the trumpet, encourage, keep in countenance 855vb. *give courage;* inspirit, inspire, animate, provoke, rouse, rally 821vb. *excite;* evoke, call forth, challenge; exhort, invite, urge, insist, press, exert pressure, put pressure on, lobby; nag, goad, prod, spur, prick, tickle; whip, lash, flog; tar on, hound on, set on, egg on; drive, hurry, hurry up 680vb. *hasten;* instigate, prompt, put up to; abet, aid and a. 703vb. *aid;* insinuate, suggest 524vb. *hint;* advocate, recommend, counsel 691vb. *advise;* start, kindle 68vb. *initiate.*

induce, bring about 156vb. *cause;* persuade, overpersuade, carry with one 485vb. *convince;* carry one's point, prevail upon, talk into, push i., drive i., bully i., browbeat (**see** *motivate*); bring round, talk round 147vb. *convert;* bring to one's side, bring over, win o., gain o., procure, enlist, engage; talk over, cajole, coax, blandish 889vb. *pet;* conciliate, appease 719vb. *pacify;* entice, seduce (**see** *tempt*).

tempt, try, lead into temptation; entice, dangle before one's eyes, make one's mouth water; tantalize, tease; allure, lure, bait, inveigle 542vb. *ensnare;* tickle, coax, wheedle, blandish, cajole, pat, pat on the back, stroke 889vb. *pet;* pander to, make things easy for, gild the pill, sugar the p. 925vb. *flatter.*

bribe, offer an inducement 759vb. *offer;* suborn, seduce, tamper with, doctor, corrupt; square, buy off, buy over; oil, grease the palm, tickle the p., give a sop to Cerberus; tip, gratify 962vb. *reward.*

be induced, yield, succumb 721vb. *submit;* concede 758vb. *consent;* obey one's conscience, act on principle; come *or* fall under the influence; admit the influence, feel the urge, hear the call; be infected, catch, catch the infection.

See: 34, 68, 147, 156, 173, 174, 178, 279, 283, 288, 291, 327, 440, 481, 485, 487, 495, 524, 528, 534, 542, 545, 547, 579, 597, 608, 609, 610, 622, 623, 680, 689, 690, 691, 703, 719, 721, 738, 740, 758, 759, 761, 771, 781, 797, 804, 819, 821, 852, 854, 855, 859, 887, 889, 900, 917, 925, 932, 962, 963, 983.

613 Dissuasion

N. *dissuasion,* dehortation, contrary advice; caution 664n. *warning;* discouragement 702n. *hindrance;* deterrence 854n. *intimidation;* objection, expostulation, remonstrance, reproof, admonition 762n. *deprecation;* no encouragement, disincentive; deterrent 665n. *danger signal;* contraindication, counter-symptom 14n. *contrariety;* cold water, damper, wet blanket; kill-joy, spoilsport 702n. *hinderer.*

Adj. *dissuasive,* discouraging, chilling, damping; dehortatory, expostulatory 762adj. *deprecatory;* monitory, warning against 664adj. *cautionary.*

Vb. *dissuade,* dehort, persuade against, advise a., argue a., convince to the contrary 479vb. *confute;* caution 664vb. *warn;* wag a forefinger 924vb. *reprove;* expostulate, remonstrate, cry out against, protest a. 762vb. *deprecate;* shake, stagger, give one pause 486vb. *cause doubt;* intimidate 900vb. *threaten;* terrorize, deter, frighten away, daunt, cow 854vb. *frighten;* choke off, head off, steer one away from, turn one aside 282vb. *deflect;* wean away from 611 vb. *disaccustom;* hold one back, keep back, act as a drag 747vb. *restrain;* render averse, disenchant, disillusion, disincline, indispose, disaffect; set against, put off, repel, disgust, fill with distaste 861vb. *cause dislike;* dishearten, discourage, dispirit, depress 834vb. *deject;* throw cold water on, dampen, quench, cool, chill, damp the ardor; take the edge off 257vb. *blunt;* calm, quiet 177vb. *moderate.*

See: 14, 177, 257, 282, 479, 486, 611, 664, 665, 702, 747, 762, 834, 854, 861, 900, 924.

614 Pretext

N. *pretext,* ostensible motive, alleged m.; statement, allegation, profession, claim 532n. *affirmation;* plea, excuse, defense, apology, apologia, justification 927n. *vindication;* let-out, loophole, alibi 667n. *means of escape;* locus standi, leg to stand on, peg to hang something on 218n. *supporter;* shallow pretext, thin excuse, equivocation 518n. *equivocalness;* special pleading, quibble 477n. *sophism;* salvo, proviso 468n. *qualification;* subterfuge 698n. *stratagem;* false plea, pretense, previous engagement, diplomatic illness 543n. *untruth;* blind, dust thrown in the eyes 421n. *obfuscation;* stalking horse, smoke-screen, cloak, cover 421n. *screen;* apology for, simulacrum, makeshift 150n. *substitute;* color, gloss, guise 445n. *appearance;* bluff, sour grapes.

Adj. *ostensible,* alleged, pretended; colorable, specious, plausible; seeming.

excusing, self-e., exculpatory, apologetic, vindicatory, justificatory 927 adj. *vindicating.*

Vb. *plead,* allege, claim, profess 532 vb. *affirm;* pretext, make one's pretext, take the plea of 475vb. *argue;* make excuses, offer an excuse, excuse oneself, defend o. 927vb. *justify;* gloss over, palliate 927vb. *extenuate;* express regret, apologize 830vb. *regret;* shelter under, take shelter u., take hold as a handle for, use as a peg, use as a stalking horse; make capital of 137vb. *profit by;* find a loophole, wriggle out of, ride off on 667vb. *escape;* bluff, say the grapes are sour; varnish 425vb. *color;* blind, throw dust in the eyes 542vb. *befool;* pretend, affect 850vb. *be affected.*

Adv. *ostensibly,* as an excuse, as alleged, as claimed; on the plea of, on the pretext of.

See: 137, 150, 218, 421, 425, 445, 468, 475, 477, 518, 532, 542, 543, 667, 698, 830, 850, 927.

615 Good

N. *good,* one's g., what is good for one; the best, supreme good, summum bonum; public weal, common weal, common good; balance of interest, greater good, lesser evil, the greatest happiness of the greatest number, utilitarianism 642n. *expedience;* weal, well-being, welfare 730n. *prosperity;* riches 800n. *wealth;* luck, good l., fortune, fair *or* good f.; happy days, happy ending 824n. *happiness;* blessing, benison, world of good (**see** *benefit*); well-wishing, benediction 897n. *benevolence.*

benefit, something to one's advantage, advantage, interest, commodity; service, behoof, behalf 640n. *utility;* crop, harvest, return 771n. *acquisition;* profit, increment, unearned i. 771n. *gain;* edification, betterment 654n. *improvement;* boon 781n. *gift;* good turn 897n. *kind act;* favor, blessing, blessing in disguise; godsend, windfall, piece of luck, treasure-trove, find, prize, nuts; good thing, desirable object, the very thing, just the t. 859n. *desired object.*

Adj. *good,* goodly, fine; blessed, beatific 824adj. *happy;* gainful 640adj. *profitable;* advantageous, heaven-sent 644adj. *beneficial;* worthwhile 644adj. *valuable;* helpful 706 adj. *cooperative;* praiseworthy, commendable, recommended 923adj. *approved;* edifying, moral 933adj. *virtuous;* pleasure-giving 826adj. *pleasurable.*

Vb. *benefit,* favor, bless; do good, help, serve, avail, be of service 640 vb. *be useful;* edify, advantage, profit; pay, repay 771vb. *be profitable;* turn out well, be all for the best, come right in the end.

flourish, thrive, do well; rise, rise in the world, be on top of the w., ride high on the hog's back 730vb. *prosper;* arrive 727vb. *succeed;* benefit by, gain by, be the better for, improve 654vb. *get better;* turn to good account, make capital of, cash in on 137vb. *profit by;* make a profit 771vb. *gain;* make money 800 vb. *get rich.*

Adv. *well,* aright, satisfactorily, favorably, profitably, happily, not amiss; to one's advantage, to one's benefit, for the best; in fine style, on the up and up.

See: 137, 640, 644, 654, 706, 727, 730, 771, 781, 800, 824, 826, 859, 897, 923, 933.

616 Evil

N. *evil,* moral e., fault, wickedness, devilment 934n. *vice;* evil conduct, mischievousness, injuriousness, disservice, injury, dirty trick 930n. *foul play;* wrong, injury, outrage 914n. *injustice;* crying evil, shame, abuse; curse, scourge, poison, pest, plague, sore, running s. 659n. *bane;* ill, ills that flesh is heir to, Pandora's box; sad world, vale of tears; bale, trouble, troubles 731n. *adversity;* affliction, bread of a., misery, distress 825n. *suffering;* grief, woe 825n. *sorrow;* unease, malaise, discomfort 825 n. *worry;* nuisance 827n. *annoyance;* hurt, bodily harm, wound, bruise, cut, gash 377n. *pain;* blow, mortal b., buffet, stroke 279n. *knock;* outrageous fortune, slings and arrows, misfortune, calamity, bad luck, ill hap 731n. *ill fortune;* casualty, accident 154n. *eventuality;* fatality 361n. *death;* catastrophe 165n. *ruin;* tragedy, sad ending 655n. *deterioration;* mischief, harm, damage 772n. *loss;* ill effect, bad result, damaged interest, prejudice; disadvantage 35n. *inferiority;* drawback, flaw 647n. *defect;* setback 702n. *hitch;* evil plight 700n. *predicament;* indigence 801n. *poverty;* sense of injury, grievance, complaint, protest 829n. *discontent;* vindictiveness 910n. *revengefulness;* principle of evil 969n. *Satan.*

Adj. *evil,* wicked 934adj. vicious; black, foul, shameful 914adj. *wrong;* bad, too bad, sad, plaguey 645adj. *damnable;* unlucky, inauspicious, sinister 731adj. *adverse;* insidious, injurious, prejudicial, disadvantageous 645adj. *harmful;* troublous, troubled 827adj. *distressing;* fatal, fell, mortal, deathly 362adj. *deadly;* ruinous, disastrous 165adj. *destructive;* catastrophic, calamitous, tragic 731adj. *unfortunate;* all wrong, awry, out of joint, Satanic 969adj. *diabolic.*

Adv. *amiss,* wrong, all wrong, awry; unfortunately, unhappily, unluckily; to one's cost, for one's sins; worse luck!

See: 35, 154, 165, 279, 361, 362, 377, 642, 645, 647, 655, 659, 700, 702, 731, 772, 801, 825, 827, 829, 910, 914, 930, 934, 969.

617 Intention

N. *intention,* intent, intendment; intentionality, deliberateness; calculation, calculated risk 480n. *estimate;* purpose, set p., settled p., determination, predetermination, resolve 599n. *resolution;* animus, mind; guilty mind, mens rea 936n. *guilt;* good intention 897n. *benevolence;* view, prospect, purview; future intention, contemplation 124n. *looking ahead;* constant intention, study, pursuit, occupation 622n. *business;* project, design 623n. *plan;* enterprise 627n. *undertaking;* ambition 859n. *desire;* formulated intention, decision 480n. *judgment;* final decision, ultimatum 766n. *conditions;* proposal, bid, final b. 759n. *offer;* engagement 764n. *promise;* solemn threat 900n. *threat;* final intention, destination 69 n. *end;* teleology, final cause 156n. *causation;* be-all and end-all, raison d'être 156n. *reason why;* trend 179n. *tendency;* drift 514n. *meaning;* tendentiousness 597n. *willingness.*

objective, destination, object, end, end in view, aim; by-end, by-aim, ax to grind; mark, butt, target; target area, bull's-eye 225n. *center;* tape, winning-post 295n. *goal;* quarry, game, prey 619n. *chase;* prize, crown, wreath 729n. *trophy;* dream, aspiration, heart's desire, Promised Land, El Dorado 859n. *desired object.*

Adj. *intending,* intent, studying, serious; hell-bent 599n. *resolute;* intentional, deliberate, voluntary 595adj. *volitional;* out to, out for, all out f.; having in view, purposive, teleological; meaning 514adj. *meaningful;* minded, disposed, inclined 597adj. *willing;* prospective, would-be, aspiring, ambitious 859adj. *desiring.*

intended, for a purpose, tendential, tendentious; deliberate, intentional, studied, designed, purposed, purposeful, aforethought 608adj. *predetermined.*

Vb. *intend,* purpose, propose; have in mind, have in view, contemplate; study, meditate; reckon to, calculate, look for 507vb. *expect;* foresee the necessity of 510vb. *foresee;* mean to, really mean, have every intention 599vb. *be resolute;* have a purpose, harbor a design; resolve, determine, premeditate 608vb. *predetermine;* project, design, plan for 623vb. *plan;* take on oneself, shoulder 672vb. *undertake;* engage 764vb. *promise;* threaten to 900vb. *threaten;* intend for, destine f., destine, doom 155vb. *predestine;* mark down for, earmark 547vb. *mark;* hold for, keep f., reserve f.; intend for oneself (**see** *aim at*); mean by it 514vb. *mean.*

aim at, make one's target, go for, go in for, take up; go after, go all out for, drive at, labor for, study f., strive after 619vb. *pursue;* try for, bid f., make a bid, endeavor 671vb. *essay;* be after, have an eye on, have designs on, promise oneself, propose to oneself, nurse an ambition, aspire to, dream of, think of, talk of 859vb. *desire;* take aim, point at, level at, train one's sights, raise one's s., aim high 281vb. *aim.*

Adv. *purposely,* on purpose, seriously, with one's eyes open, in cold blood, deliberately, pointedly, intentionally; designedly, advisedly, knowingly, wittingly, voluntarily; with malace aforethought; for, for a purpose, in order to; with the intention of, with a view to, with the object of, in pursuance of, pursuant to; as planned, as designed, according to plan, as arranged; to design, to one's own d.

See: 69, 124, 155, 156, 179, 225, 281, 295, 480, 507, 510, 514, 547, 595, 597, 599, 608, 617, 619, 622, 623, 672, 729, 759, 764, 766, 859, 897, 900, 936.

618 Non-design. Gamble

N. *non-design,* indetermination, indeterminacy, unpredictability 159n. *chance;* involuntariness, instinct 609 n. *spontaneity;* coincidence, mere c. 89n. *accompaniment;* accident, casualty, fluke, luck, mere l. 154n. *eventuality;* good luck, windfall; bad luck, mischance 616n. *evil;* lottery, luck of the draw (**see** *gambling*); sortilegy, sortition, drawing lots, casting l., sortes Vergilianae, sortes Biblicae 511n. *divination;* lot, wheel of fortune 596n. *fate;* mascot, amulet, charm, porte-bonheur, swastika 983n. *talisman.*

gambling, taking a chance, risk-taking; plunge, risk, hazard 661n. *danger;* gamble, pot-luck 159n. *chance;* venture, speculation, flutter 461n. *experiment;* shot, random s., shot in the dark, leap in the d., pig in a poke, blind bargain 474n. *uncertainty;* bid, throw; toss of a coin, turn of a card; wager, bet, stake, ante, psychic bid; last throw, desperate bid 857n. *rashness;* dice-box, dice, die, bones, ivories, craps; element of risk, game of chance, play, roulette, rouge et noir 837n. *gambling game;* betting, turf, horse-racing, dog-r. 716n. *racing;* draw, lottery, raffle, tombola, sweepstake, premium bond, football pool; tontine; gambling on the market, futures.

gaming-house, hall, gambling h., betting house, pool room, casino; racecourse, turf; totalizator, tote, pari mutuel.

bourse, exchange, stock e., curb e., bucket shop.

gambler, gamester, player, dicer; better, layer, backer, punter; bookmaker, bookie, tipster; man of enterprise, risk-taker; gentleman of fortune, venturer, adventurer, merchant a., undertaker, entrepreneur 672n. *undertaking;* speculator, piker, plunger, manipulator; bear, bull, stag; experimentalist 461n. *experimenter.*

Adj. *unintentional,* non-intentional, unintended, unmeant, not meant 596 adj. *involuntary;* unpurposed, undesigned, unpremeditated, unrehearsed 609adj. *spontaneous;* accidental, fortuitous, coincidental 159adj. *casual.*

designless, aimless, planless, purposeless; motiveless 159n. *causeless;* promiscuous 464adj. *indiscriminate;* undirected, unguided, random, haphazard 282adj. *deviating;* wandering, footloose 267adj. *traveling;* meaningless, driftless 515adj. *unmeaning.*

speculative, experimental 474vb. *uncertain;* hazardous, risky, chancy, dicey, aleatory; risk-taking, venturesome, adventurous, enterprising.

Vb. *gamble,* game, play; throw, dice, bet, stake, wager, lay; call one's hand, overcall; gamble deep, play high, play for high stakes, double the s.; take bets, make a book; back, punt; cover a bet, cover, hedge 660 vb. *seek safety;* play the market, speculate, have a flutter 461vb. *experiment;* hazard, risk run a r., take risks, buy blind, buy a pig in a poke 857vb. *be rash;* venture, chance it, take one's chance, tempt fortune, try one's luck, trust to chance, spin the wheel, shuffle the cards; cut for aces; raffle, draw, draw lots, cast l., stand the hazard.

Adv. *at random*, by the way, incidentally, haphazardly; unintentionally, unwittingly; chancily, riskily; at a venture, by guess and God, on the off-chance.

See: 89, 154, 159, 267, 282, 461, 464, 474, 511, 515, 596, 609, 615, 616, 660, 661, 672, 716, 837, 857, 983.

619 Pursuit

N. *pursuit*, pursuing, pursuance, hunting, seeking, looking for, quest 459n. *search;* adient behavior, adient response, approach r. 289n. *approach;* persecution, witch-hunt; tracking, trailing, dogging 284n. *following;* trial, prosecution, 959n. *legal trial;* enterprise, adventure 672n. *undertaking;* calling 622n. *vocation;* avocation, profession, hobby, activities, affairs 622n. *business.*

chase, stern-c., hard c., run, run for one's money; steeplechase, paperchase 716n. *racing;* hunt, hunting, hounding, hue and cry, tally-ho, hark; beat, drive, battue, beating; shooting, gunning, hunting and shooting 837n. *sport;* blood sport, fox-hunt, deer-h., lion-h., tiger-h.; elephant-hunt, keddah; boar-hunt, pigsticking; stalking, deer-s; hawking, fowling, falconry; fishing, angling, fly-fishing, trawling; beagling, coursing, ratting, trapping; fishing rod, rod and line, bait, fly; fowling-piece 287n. *shooter;* fish-trap, rat-t. 542n. *trap;* game, quarry, prey, victim 617n. *objective;* catch 771n. *acquisition.*

hunter, quester, seeker, searcher 459 n. *inquirer;* search-party; pursuer, dogger, tracker, trailer, shadow; huntsman, huntress; whip, whipper-in; Nimrod, Diana; sportsman, sportswoman 837n. *player;* gun, shot, good s., marksman 287n. *shooter;* head-hunter 362n. *killer;* fox-hunter, stag-h., lion-h., courser, beagler, coney-catcher, rat-c., ratter, trapper, stalker, deer-s.; bird-catcher, fowler, falconer, hawker; fisher, fisherman, piscator, angler, compleat a.; shrimper; trawler, trawlerman, whaler; field, pack, hounds, cry of h.; hound, fox-h., deer-h., boar-h. 365n. *dog;* hawk 365n. *bird of prey;* beast of prey, man-eater 365n. *animal;* mouser 365n. *cat.*

Adj. *pursuing*, pursuant, seeking, questing 459adj. *inquiring;* in quest of, sent after; chasing, in pursuit, in hot p., in full cry, on the scent, on the trail 284adj. *following;* hunting, shooting; fishing, piscatorial.

Vb. *pursue*, seek, look for, cast about; be gunning for, hunt for, fish for, dig for 459vb. *search;* send after, send for, send out a search party 272vb. *send;* stalk, prowl after, sneak a.; shadow, dog, track, trail, tail, sit on one's t., follow the scent 284vb. *follow;* scent out 484vb. *discover;* witch-hunt, harry, persecute 735vb. *oppress;* chase, give c., hunt, whoop, hollo, hark, hark on, cry on; raise the hunt, raise the hue and cry; run down, ride d., rush at, tilt at, ride full tilt at, charge at 712vb. *charge;* leap at, jump at 312vb. *leap;* snatch at 786vb. *take;* make one's game, make one's quarry 617 vb. *aim at;* set one's course 281vb. *steer for;* be after, make it one's business 617vb. *intend;* pursue one's ends, ride one's hobby 622vb. *busy oneself;* run after, set one's cap at, woo 889vb. *court;* press on 680vb. *hasten;* push one's way, elbow one's w., fight one's w. 285vb. *progress.*

hunt, go hunting, go shooting, go ratting; follow the chase, ride to hounds, pig-stick; fish, angle, fly-fish; trawl; whale; shrimp; net, catch 542vb. *ensnare;* mouse, play cat and m.; stalk, deer-s., fowl, hawk; course, beagle; start game, flush, start, start up; hunt men, head-hunt.

Adv. *pursuant to*, in pursuance of, in quest of, after; in chase, on the trail, on the track.

See: 272, 281, 284, 285, 289, 300, 312, 362, 365, 459, 484, 542, 617, 622, 672, 680, 712, 716, 735, 771, 786, 837, 889, 959.

620 Avoidance

N. *avoidance*, prevention 702n. *hindrance;* abstinence, abstention 942n. *temperance;* forbearance, refraining 177n. *moderation;* refusal 607n. *rejection;* inaction 679n. *inactivity;* passivity 266n. *quiescence;* non-intervention, non-involvement, neutrality 860n. *indifference;* evasiveness 518n. *equivocalness;* evasive action, dodge, jink, sidestep; delaying action, non-cooperation 769 n. *non-observance;* centrifugal force; retreat, withdrawal 286n. *regression;* evasion, slip, flight, elusion, avolation 667n. *escape;* start aside, jib, shy, shrinking 854n. *fear;* shunning, wide berth, safe distance 199n. *distance;* shyness 598n. *unwillingness;*

shirking 458n. *negligence;* skulking 523n. *latency;* abient behavior 280n. *recoil;* defense mechanism, defense reaction 713n. *defense;* repression, suppression 757n. *prohibition;* escapism.

avoider, non-drinker 942n. *abstainer;* dodger, sidestepper, evader, levanter, bilker, welsher 545n. *trickster;* shrinker, quitter 856n. *coward;* slacker, sloucher, scrimshanker 679n. *idler;* skulker 527n. *hider;* truant, deserter 918n. *dutilessness;* apostate, renegade, runagate 603n. *tergiversator;* runaway, fugitive, refugee, displaced person, DP, escapee 667n. *escaper;* escapist 513n. *visionary.*

Adj. *avoiding,* shunning; evasive, elusive, slippery, hard to catch; untamed, wild; shy 874adj. *modest;* blinking, blenching, shrinking, cowering 854adj. *nervous;* backward, non-cooperative, reluctant 598adj. *unwilling;* non-committal, unforthcoming 582adj. *taciturn;* passive, inert 679adj. *inactive;* non-involved, non-committed, uncommitted 625adj. *neutral;* centrifugal; fugitive, hunted, runaway, fly-by-night 667adj. *escaped;* hiding, skulking 523adj. *latent;* repressive, suppressive; defensive, abient.

avoidable, evasible, escapable, preventable; unsought, unattempted.

Vb. *avoid,* not go near, keep off, keep away; by-pass, give one the go-by, look the other way, take the other w., turn aside 294vb. *diverge;* boycott, cold-shoulder 883vb. *make unwelcome;* hold aloof, stand apart, have no hand in, not soil one's fingers, keep one's hands clean, wash one's hands of, shun, eschew, leave, let alone, have nothing to do with; fight shy, back away, draw back 290 vb. *recede;* hold off, stand aloof, keep one's distance, keep a respectful d., give a wide berth, keep out of the way, keep clear, stand c., get out of the way, make way for; forbear, spare; refrain, abstain, forswear, deny oneself, do without, not touch 942vb. *be temperate;* avoid hitting, pull one's punches 177vb. *moderate;* hold back, hang b., not try, not attempt 598vb. *be loath;* shelve, postpone 136vb. *put off;* shirk 458vb. *neglect;* shrink, flinch, start aside, jib, refuse, shy, blink, blench 854vb. *be nervous;* take evasive action, lead one a dance, throw one off the scent, play hide-and-seek; jink, sidestep, dodge, duck, deflect 713vb. *parry;* evade, escape, be spared 667vb. *elude;* skulk, cower, hide 523vb. *lurk;* disown, deny 533 vb. *negate;* repress, suppress 757vb. *prohibit;* make excuses, ride off 614 vb. *plead;* prevent, foil 702vb. *hinder.*

run away, desert, play truant, take French leave 918vb. *fail in duty;* abscond, welsh, flit, levant, elope 667vb. *escape;* absent oneself 190 vb. *be absent;* withdraw, retire, retreat, beat a r., turn tail, turn one's back 282vb. *turn round;* flee; flit, fly, take to light,, run for one's life; be off, make o., slope o., scamper o., bolt, run, cut and run, show a clean pair of heels, take to one's h., make oneself scarce, run for one's life, scoot, scram, skedaddle 277vb. *move fast;* slip the cable, part company, break away 296vb. *decamp;* steal away, sneak off, slink o., shuffle o., creep o.; scuttle, bunk, do a b.

Int. *hands off!* keep off! beware! forbear!

See: 136, 177, 190, 199, 266, 277, 280, 282, 286, 290, 294, 296, 458, 513, 518, 523, 527, 545, 582, 598, 603, 607, 614, 625, 667, 679, 702, 713, 757, 769, 854, 856, 860, 874, 883, 918, 942.

621 Relinquishment

N. *relinquishment,* abandonment; going, leaving, evacuation 296n. *departure;* dereliction, desertion, truancy, defection 918n. *dutilessness;* withdrawal, secession 978n. *schism;* walk-out 145n. *strike;* yielding, giving up, handing over, cession 780n. *transfer;* forgoing, waiver, renunciation 779n. *non-retention;* retirement 753n. *resignation;* disuse 674n. *non-use;* disusage, non-continuance 611 n. *desuetude;* cancellation, annulment 752n. *abrogation;* world well lost 883n. *seclusion.*

Adj. *relinquished,* forsaken, cast-off, marooned, abandoned etc. vb.; waived, forgone 779n. *not retained.*

Vb. *relinquish,* drop, let go, leave hold of, unclench, quit one's hold, loosen one's grip 779vb. *not retain;* surrender, resign, give up, yield; waive, forgo; bate one's pretensions 872vb. *be humble;* cede, hand over, transfer 780vb. *convey;* forfeit 772 vb. *lose;* renounce, swear off, abnegate, recant, change one's mind 603 vb. *tergiversate;* not proceed with, drop *or* give up the idea, forget it 506vb. *forget;* wean oneself 611vb. *disaccustom;* forswear, deny oneself, abstain 620vb. *avoid;* shed, slough, cast off, divest 299vb. *doff;* drop, discard, write off 674vb. *disuse;* lose interest 860vb. *be indifferent;* abdicate, back down, scratch, stand down, withdraw, retire 753vb. *resign;* give in, throw up the sponge, throw up the game, throw in one's hand 721vb. *submit;* leave, quit, move out, vacate, tear oneself away 296vb. *depart;* forsake, abandon, quit one's post, desert 918 vb. *fail in duty;* play truant 190vb. *be absent;* strike work, strike, come out 145vb. *cease;* walk out, secede 978vb. *schismatize;* go over, rat, let down the side 603vb. *apostatize;* throw over, ditch, jilt, break it off, go back on one's word 541vb. *be false;* abandon discussion, waste no more time, pass on to the next, shelve, postpone 136vb. *put off;* annul, cancel 752vb. *abrogate.*

See: 136, 145, 190, 229, 296, 506, 541, 603, 611, 620, 674, 721, 752, 753, 772, 779, 780, 860, 872, 883, 918, 978.

622 Business

N. *business,* affairs, business a., interests, iron in the fire; main business, occupation, concern, care; aim, ambition 617n. *intention;* business on hand, case, agenda; enterprise, undertaking, pursuit 678n. *activity;* routine, business r., office r., round, daily r. 610n. *practice;* business life, daily work, journey w., course of w.; business circles, business world, City; art, industry, commerce, commerce and industry; big business; cottage industry, home i.; industrialism, industrialization, industrial arts, manufacture 164n. *production;* trade, craft, handicraft, mystery 694n. *skill;* guild, business association 706n. *association;* employment, work, avocation (**see** *vocation*); side-interest, hobby, pastime 837n. *amusement;* religious business 981n. *cult.*

vocation, calling, life-work, mission, apostolate 751n. *commission;* life, walk, walk of life, race, career; chosen career, labor of love, self-imposed task 597n. *voluntary work;* livelihood, daily bread, one's bread and butter; profession, métier; craft, trade; line, line of country (**see** *function*); exacting profession, high calling; religious profession, ministry, cure of souls; cloth, veil, habit 985n. *churchdom;* military profession, arms 718n. *war;* naval profession, sea; legal profession 953n. *law;* teaching profession, education 534n. *teaching;* medical profession, medicine, practice; business profession, industry, commerce 791n. *trade;* government service, service, administration 733n. *government;* public service, public life; social service 901n. *sociology.*

job, ploys, activities 678n. *activity;* chores, odd jobs, work, task, set task, exercise 682n. *labor;* duty, charge, commission, mission, errand, quest 751n. *mandate;* employ, service, employment, full e.; hours of work, working day, work-day; occupation, situation, position, berth, incumbency, appointment, post, office; regular employment, full-time job, permanency; temporary job, part-time j.; situation wanted, vacancy; labor office, labor exchange, employment agency, Ministry of Labor.

function, what one has to do; capacity, office, duty; realm, province, sphere; scope, field, terms of reference 183n. *range;* department, line, line of country; role, part; business, job; concern, care, look-out.

Adj. *businesslike,* efficient 694adj. *skillful;* industrious, busy 678adj. *active;* vocational, professional, career; industrial, commercial, financial; occupational, functional; official, governmental; routine, systematic 60adj. *orderly;* work-a-day 610 adj. *habitual;* earning, in employment, employed, self-e.; in hand, on h., on foot 669adj. *preparatory.*

Vb. *employ,* busy, occupy, take up one's time, fill one's t., keep one engaged; give employment, engage, recruit, hire, enlist, appoint, post 751vb. *commission;* entertain, take on the payroll, wage 804vb. *pay;* give a situation to, offer a job to, fill a vacancy, staff with, staff; industrialize.

busy oneself, work, work for 742vb. *serve;* have a profession, be employed, do a job, earn, earn one's living; take on a job, apply for a j., take a situation, accept a s.; be doing, be up and d. 678vb. *be busy;* concern oneself with, make it one's business, touch 678vb. *meddle;* work at, ply; engage in, turn to, turn one's hand to, take up, engage in, go in for; have to do, have on one's hands, have one's hands full, take on oneself, bear the burden, bear the brunt, take on one's shoulders 917vb. *incur a duty;* work with one's hands, work with one's brains; ride one's hobby 837vb. *amuse oneself.*

function, work, go 173vb. *operate;* fill a role, play one's part, carry on; officiate, act, do the offices, discharge the functions, exercise the f., serve as, do duty, perform the duties, do the work of; substitute, stand in for 755vb. *deputize;* hold office, hold a portfolio, hold a place, hold down a job, have a job, serve (**see** *busy oneself*).

do business, transact, negotiate 766vb. *make terms;* ply a trade, ply a craft, exercise a profession, follow a calling, work at a job; have a business, engage in, carry on, drive a trade, carry on a t., keep shop; do business with, deal w., enter into trade relations 791vb. *trade;* transact business, mind one's b., attend to one's b., go about one's b.; labor in one's vocation, earn one's living (**see** *busy oneself*); be an employer, be an industrialist; set up in business, open a shop, put up one's sign.

Adv. *professionally,* in businesslike fashion; in the course of, all in a day's work.

See: 60, 164, 173, 183, 534, 597, 610, 617, 669, 678, 682, 694, 706, 718, 733, 742, 751, 755, 766, 791, 804, 837, 901, 917, 953, 981, 985.

623 Plan

N. *plan,* scheme, design; planning, contrivance; organization, systematization, rationalization, centralization 60n. *order;* program, project, proposal 617n. *intention;* proposition, suggestion, motion, resolution (**see** *policy*); master-plan, five-year p., detailed p., ground-p., blueprint 551n. *map;* sketch, outline, rough scheme, pilot s., draft, first d., memorandum; skeleton, rough cast; model, dummy 23n. *prototype;* proof, revise, proof copy, show c. 22n. *copy;* planning office, back room, headquarters, base of operations.

policy, forethought 510n. *foresight;* statesmanship 498n. *wisdom;* course of action, procedure, strategy 688n. *tactics;* address, approach, attack 624n. *way;* steps, measures 676n. *action;* stroke of policy, coup d'état 676n. *deed;* proposed action, forecast 511n. *prediction;* program, prospectus, platform, plank, ticket, slate; schedule, agenda, order of the day 622n. *business;* line, party l.

contrivance, expedient, resource, recourse, resort, card, trump, card up one's sleeve 629n. *means;* recipe, receipt, nostrum 658n. *remedy;* loophole, way out, alternative, answer 667n. *means of escape;* artifice, device, gimmick, dodge, shift, flag of convenience 698n. *stratagem;* wangle, fiddle 930n. *foul play;* knack, trick 694n. *skill;* stunt, wheeze; inspiration, hit, happy thought, bright idea, right i. 451n. *idea;* notion, invention; tool, weapon, contraption, gadget 628n. *instrument;* ad hoc measure, improvisation 609n. *spontaneity;* makeshift, makedo 150n. *substitute;* feat, tour de force; stroke, master-s., coup 676n. *deed.*

plot, subplot, underplot; deep-laid plot, intrigue; web, web of intrigue, practice; cabal, conspiracy, inside job; frame-up, machination; manipulation, wire-pulling 612n. *motive;* secret influence 523n. *latency;* counterplot, countermine 713n. *defense;* argument 590n. *narrative.*

planner, contriver, engineer, framer, inventor, orginator, hatcher; proposer, promoter, projector; founder, author, builder; designer, schematist, backroom boy, boffin 696n. *expert;* organizer, systematizer; strategist, tactician, maneuverer; statesman, politician, Machiavellian; schemer, ax-grinder; careerist, go-getter 678n. *busy person;* plotter, intriguer, intrigant, spinner, spider; cabal, conspirator; fifth column, fifth columnist.

Adj. *planned,* blueprinted, schematic, worked out, matured 669adj. *prepared;* organized, systematized 60 adj. *orderly;* under consideration, in draft, in proof; strategic, tactical; framed, plotted, engineered.

planning, contriving, resourceful, ingenious 698adj. *cunning;* purposeful, scheming, up to something; involved, deep in; intriguing, plotting, conspiratorial; Machiavellian.

Vb. *plan,* resolve 617vb. *intend;* approach, approach a problem, attack; make a plan, draw up, design, draft, blueprint; frame, shape 243vb. *efform;* revise, recast 654vb. *rectify;* project, plan out, work o., cut o., sketch o., chalk o., strike o., map o., lay o.; program, lay down a plan, lay the foundation; shape a course, mark out a course; organize, systematize; rationalize, schematize, methodize 60vb. *order;* schedule, phase, adjust; invent, think up, hit on, fall on 484vb. *discover;* find a way, tide over; contrive, devise, engineer; hatch, concoct, mature 669 vb. *prepare;* arrange, prearrange 608vb. *predetermine;* calculate, think ahead, look a. 498vb. *be wise;* have a policy, order one's measures, follow a plan, work to a schedule; do everything with a purpose, have an ax to grind, grind one's ax.

plot, scheme, have designs, be up to something; manipulate, pull wires 178vb. *influence;* cabal, intrigue, practice; conspire, concert, concoct, hatch a plot, lay a p., lay a train, dig a pit, undermine, countermine 542vb. *ensnare;* work against, maneuver a.; frame 541vb. *fake*.

See: 22, 23, 60, 87, 150, 178, 243, 451, 484, 498, 510, 511, 523, 541 542, 551, 608, 609, 612, 617, 622, 624, 628, 629, 654, 658, 667, 669, 676, 678, 688, 694, 696, 698, 713, 930.

624 Way

N. *way*, route 267n. *itinerary;* manner, wise, guise; fashion, style 243n. *form;* method, mode, line, approach, address, attack; procedure, process, way of, way of doing things, modus operandi 688n. *tactics;* operation, treatment; modus vivendi, working arrangement 770n. *compromise;* usual way, routine 610n. *practice;* technique, know-how 694n. *skill;* going, gait 265n. *motion;* forward way, progress 285n. *progression;* way of life, behavior 688n. *conduct*. **See** *route*.

access, means of a., right of way, communications; way to, direct approach 289n. *approach;* entrance, door 263n. *doorway;* side-entrance, back-e., tradesman's e.; adit, drive, gangway; porch, hall, hallway, vestibule, lobby, corridor; way through, pass, defile 305n. passage; intersection, junction, crossing; zebra crossing, pedestrian c. 305n. *traffic control;* strait, sound, gut 345n. *gulf;* channel, artery, canal, culvert 351n. *conduit;* lock, stile, turnstile, tollgate; way up, stairs, flight of s., stairway, staircase, step, tread, ladder, step-l., fireman's l. 308n. *ascent*.

bridge, way over; footbridge, overbridge, fly-over; suspension bridge, cantilever b., hump-b.; viaduct, span; railway bridge; bridge of boats, pontoon, floating bridge, bascule-b., Bailey b.; drawbridge; stepping-stone, gangway, gangplank, catwalk, duck-boards; ford, ferry 305n. *passage;* way under, underpass 263n. *tunnel;* bridge-way, culvert, Irish bridge; land-bridge, isthmus, neck.

route, direction, way to, way through, way by, way up, way over, way out; line, course, march, tack, track, beaten t., beat; trajectory, orbit; lane, traffic l., air l., sea-lane., seapath; short cut, by-pass; detour, circumbendibus, roundabout way 626n. *circuit;* line of communication, line of retreat, line of advance.

path, pathway, footpath, sidewalk, pavement, by-path, tow-p., side-p.; bridle-path, ride, horse-track; byway, lane, track, sheep-t., trail, mountain t.; glade, walk, run, drive, carriage-d.; promenade, esplanade, parade, front, seafront, avenue, boulevard, mall 192n. *street;* arcade, colonnade, aisle, cloister, ambulatory; race-track, running t., speed-t. 724n. *arena;* channel, fairway.

road, high-r., highway, Queen's h., highways and by-ways; main road, side-r., approach r., service r., private r., occupation r.; turnpike, pike, national road, route nationale; thoroughfare, through road, trunk r., arterial r., artery, by-pass; motor road, autobahn, autostrada, speed-track, expressway, throughway, parkway; motorway; slipway, acceleration lane; clearway 305n. *traffic control;* crossroad, crossways, junction, intersection, traffic circle, clover leaf; crossing, pedestian c., zebra c.; roadway, carriageway, dual c., twin-track; paved road, pavement, causeway, chaussée 192n. *street;* high street, one-way s., two-way s., side-s.; alley-way, wynd, alley, blind a., cul-de-sac; pavement, sidewalk, trottoir, curb, curbstone; paving, pavé, cobbles, paving-stone, flag, flagstones; macadam, tarmac, asphalt; surface, road-s., skid-proof s.; road-building, traffic engineering.

railroad, railway, line; permanent way, track, lines, railway l., streetcar l.; monorail, funicular, cableway, ropeway, telpher line; overhead railway, elevated r., underground r., subway, tube 274n. *train;* light railway, meter gauge, broad g., standard g.; junction, level crossing, tunnel, cutting; siding, marshaling yard; station, stop, whistle s., platform 145n. *stopping place;* signal, signal box, cabin; rails, points, ties, frog, fishplate.

Adj. *communicating*, granting access; through, main, arterial, trunk; bridged, fly-over; paved, metaled, cobbled; well-paved, well-laid, smooth, skid-proof; signposted, lit, well-lit; trafficky, busy; trodden, beaten.

Adv. *via*, by way of, in transit.

how, in what manner? by what means? on what lines?

See: 145, 192, 243, 263, 265, 267, 274, 285, 289, 305, 308, 345, 351, 610, 626, 688, 694, 724, 770.

625 Mid-course

N. *mid-course*, middle course, middle of the road, via media; balance, golden mean, happy m., mediocrity, aurea mediocritas 30n. *average;* central position, halfway, halfway house, mid-stream 30n. *middle point;* slack water, half tide; direct course, non-deviation, straight line, short cut, bee-line, short circuit 249n. *straightness;* great-circle sailing 269 n. *navigation;* non-committal, neutrality, correctness 177n. *moderation;* lukewarmness, half-measures 601n. *irresolution;* mutual concession 770 n. *compromise.*

moderate, non-extremist, minimalist, Menshevist; middle-of-the-roader, half-and-halfer; neutral, uncommitted person, uncommitted nation; Laodicean.

Adj. *neutral*, impartial, correct 913 adj. *right;* non-committal, uncommitted, unattached; detached 860adj. *indifferent;* moderate, non-extreme, unextreme, middle-of-the-road 225 adj. *central;* sitting on the fence, lukewarm, half-and-half 601adj. *irresolute;* neither one thing nor the other, gray.

undeviating, unswerving, keeping to the middle 225adj. *central;* looking neither to right nor left, direct 249 adj. *straight;* in between, halfway, intermediate 231adj. *interjacent.*

Vb. *be mid-stream*, keep to the middle, steer a middle course, hold straight on, not deviate, not swerve, look neither to right nor to left.

be halfway, go halfway, meet h. 770 vb. *compromise;* be in between, occupy the center, hold the scales, balance 28vb. *equalize;* sit on the fence 474vb. *be uncertain;* trim, equivocate 518vb. *be equivocal.*

See: 28, 30, 177, 225, 231, 249, 269, 474, 518, 601, 770, 860, 913.

626 Circuit

N. *circuit*, roundabout way, longest way, circuitous route, by-pass, detour, loop, loop-line, divagation, digression 282n. *deviation;* ambages 251n. *convolution;* circulation, circumambulation, ambit, orbit, gyre, round, lap 314n. *circuition;* circumference 250n. *circle;* full circle, looping the loop.

Adj. *roundabout*, circuitous, indirect, out of the way; circumlocutory 570 adj. *diffuse;* circulatory, circumambulating; rounding, skirting; encompassing, surrounding 230adj. *circumjacent.*

Vb. *circuit*, round, lap, beat the bounds, go round, make a circuit, loop the loop 314vb. *circle;* make a detour, go out of one's way 282vb. *deviate;* turn, by-pass, short-circuit 620vb. *avoid*; lead one a dance, beat about the bush; divagate, zigzag 294vb. *diverge;* encircle, embrace, encompass 230vb. *surround;* keep to the circumference, skirt, edge round.

Adv. *round about*, round the world, in a roundabout way, circuitously, indirectly, from pillar to post.

See: 230, 250, 251, 282, 294, 314, 570, 620.

627 Requirement

N. *requirement*, requisite, desideratum, want, lack, need 636n. *insufficiency;* defect, shortage 42n. *decrement;* stipulation, prerequisite, first condition, prior conditions 766n. *conditions;* essential, sine qua non, a necessary, a must 596n. *necessity;* needs, necessities, necessaries; indent, order, requisition, shopping list; demand, consumer d., call for, run upon, seller's market 792n. *purchase;* consumption, input, intake 634n. *waste;* balance due, what is owing 803n. *debt;* claim 761n. *request;* ultimatum, imposition, mandate, charge, injunction 737n. *command.*

needfulness, case of need, occasion; necessity for, essentiality, indispensability, desirability; necessitousness, want, pinch, stress 801n. *poverty;* exigence 740n. *compulsion;* urgency 137n. *crisis;* vitalness, matter of life and death 638n. *important matter;* obligation 917n. *duty;* bare minimum, the least one can do, face-saving measures; possible need, encasement.

Adj. *required,* requisite, prerequisite, needful, needed; necessary, essential, vital, indispensable, not to be spared; called for, in request, in demand 859 adj. *desired;* reserved, earmarked, booked; wanted, lacking, missing, desiderated, to seek 190adj. *absent.*

necessitous, in want, in need, pinched, feeling the pinch; lacking, deprived of; needing badly, craving; destitute

801adj. *poor;* starving 636adj. *underfed.*
demanding, crying, crying out for, calling for, imperative, urgent, instant, exigent, pressing, pinching; compulsory 740adj. *compelling.*
Vb. *require,* need, want, lack 636vb. *be unsatisfied;* not have, be without, stand in need of, feel a need, have occasion for; miss, desiderate; need badly, crave 859vb. *desire;* call for, cry out f., shout f., clamor f.; claim, put in a claim for, apply f. 761vb. *request;* find necessary, find indispensable, be unable to do without, must have; consume, take 634 vb. *waste;* create a need, invent a want, render necessary, necessitate, oblige 740vb. *compel;* make demands, raise a demand 737vb. *demand;* stipulate 766vb. *give terms;* order, send an order for, indent, requisition 633vb. *provide;* reserve, book, earmark.
Adv. *in need,* in want; necessarily, sine qua non; of necessity, at a pinch.
See: 42, 137, 596, 633, 634, 636, 638, 737, 740, 761, 766, 792, 803, 859, 917.

628 Instrumentality

N. *instrumentality,* operation 173n. *agency;* occasion 156n. *cause;* result 157n. *effect;* pressure 178n. *influence;* efficacy 160n. *power;* occult power, magic 983n. *sorcery;* services, help, assistance, midwifery 703 n. *aid;* support 706n. *cooperation;* intervention, intermediacy, interference 678n. *activity;* subservience 739n. *obedience;* medium 629n. *means;* use, employment, application, serviceability, handiness 640n. *utility;* use of machinery, instrumentation, mechanization, automation 630n. *machine.*
instrument, hand, organ, sense o.; handmaid, minister, slave, slave of the lamp 742n. *servant;* agent, midwife, medium, help, assistant 703n. *aider;* pawn, piece on the board 837 n. *chessman;* robot 630n. *machine;* cat's-paw, stooge; weapon, implement, appliance, lever 630n. *tool;* magic ring, Aladdin's lamp 983n. *spell;* key, pass-k., skeleton k., latch-k. 263n. *opener;* open sesame, watchword, password, passport, safe-conduct, warrant 756n. *permit;* stepping-stone 624n. *bridge;* channel, high road, highway 624n. *road;* push-button, switch; device, expedient, makeshift, gadget 623n. *contrivance;* card, trump.
Adj. instrumental, working, automatic, push-button 173adj. *operative;* effective, efficient, efficacious, effectual 160adj. *powerful;* telling, weighty 178adj. *influential;* magic 983adj. *magical;* conducive 156adj. *causal;* practical, applied; serviceable, general-purpose, employable, handy 640 adj. *useful;* ready, available 597adj. *willing;* forwarding, promoting, assisting, helpful 703adj. *aiding;* obstetric, maieutic; functional, agential, subservient, ministerial; mediational, intermediate, intervening; mediated by.
Vb. *be instrumental*, work, act 173vb. *operate;* perform 676vb. *do;* minister, serve, work for, subserve, lend oneself (*or* itself) to, pander to 703 vb. *minister to;* help, assist 703vb. *aid;* advance, promote 703vb. *patronize;* have a hand in 775vb. *participate;* be the instrument, be the hand, be a cat's-paw, pull another's chestnuts out of the fire 640 vb. *be useful;* intermediate, interpose, intervene 720vb. *mediate;* use one's influence, pull strings 178vb. *influence;* effect 156vb. *cause;* tend 156vb. *conduce;* achieve 725vb. *carry through.*
Adv. *through*, per, by the hand of, by means of, using the help of.
See: 156, 157, 160, 173, 178, 263, 597, 623, 624, 629, 630, 640, 676, 678, 703, 706, 720, 725, 739, 742, 756, 775, 837, 983.

629 Means

N. *means*, ways and m., wherewithal; power, capacity 160n. *ability;* good hand, card, right c., trump, aces; conveniences, facilities; appliances, tools, tools of the trade, bag of tricks 630n. *tool;* technique, know-how 694n. *skill;* equipment, supplies, stock, munitions, ammunition 633n. *provision;* resources, economic r., natural r., raw material 631n. *materials;* labor resources, pool of labor, manpower 686n. *personnel;* financial resources, sinews of war 800n. *wealth;* liquidity 797n. *money;* capital, working c. 628n. *instrument;* assets, stock-in-trade 777n. *property;* stocks and shares, investments, investment portfolio; revenue, income, receipts, credits 807n. *receipt;* borrowing capacity, line of credit 802n. *credit;* reserves, stand-by, shot in one's locker, card up one's sleeve, two strings to one's bow 662n. *safeguard;* freedom of choice, alternative 605n. *choice;* method, measures, steps 624n. *way;* cure, specific 658n. *remedy;* expedient, device, resort, recourse 623n. *contrivance;* makeshift, ad hoc measure 150n. *substitute;* let-out 667 n. *means of escape;* desperate remedy, last resort, last hope, last throw 618n. *gambling;* method of working, mechanical means 630n. *mechanics.*

Vb. *find means,* provide the wherewithal, supply, find, furnish 633vb. *provide;* equip, fit out 669vb. *make ready;* finance, raise the money, promote, float; have the means, be able, be in a position to 160vb. *be able;* contrive, be resourceful, not be at a loss, find a way 623vb. *plan;* beg, borrow or steal, get by hook or by crook 771vb. *acquire.*

Adv. *by means of,* with, wherewith; by, using, through; with the aid of; by dint of.

See: 150, 160, 605, 618, 623, 624, 628, 630, 631, 633, 658, 662, 667, 669, 686, 694, 771, 777, 797, 800, 802, 807.

630 Tool

N. *tool,* precision t., implement 628n. *instrument;* apparatus, appliance, utensil; weapon, arm 723n. *arms;* device, mechanical d., gadget 623 n. *contrivance;* mechanical aid, inclined plane; screw, turnscrew, screwdriver 263n. *perforator;* wrench, spanner; pliers, tweezers 778n. *nippers;* chisel, wedge, edged tool 256n. *sharp edge;* rope 47n. *cable;* peg, nail 217n. *hanger,* 218n. *support;* leverage, lever, jimmy, crow, crowbar, handspike, jack 218n. *pivot;* grip, lug, helve, haft, shaft, thill, tiller, helm, rudder 218n. *handle;* pulley, sheave, parbuckle 250n. *wheel;* switch, cock, stopcock; gunlock, trigger; pedal, pole, punt-p. 287n. *propulsion;* prehistoric tool, flint; tools of the trade, toolkit, do-it-yourself k., bag of tricks.

machine, mechanical device; machinery, mechanism, works; clockwork, wheelwork, wheels within wheels; spring, mainspring, hairspring; gears, gearing, spur g., bevel g., syncromesh, automatic change; motor, engine, internal combustion e., diesel e., gas e., steam e.; robot, automaton; learning machine, self-organizing system.

mechanics, engineering, telemechanics; servomechanics, cybernetics; automatic control, automation; mechanical power, mechanical advantage; technicology, technology.

equipment, furniture, appointments; gear, tackle 47n. *tackling;* fittings, fixture 40adj. *adjunct;* upholstery, furnishing, soft f.; outfit, kit; trappings, accouterment 228n. *dress;* harness 226n. *covering;* utensils, impedimenta, paraphernalia, chattels 777n. *property;* ware, stock-in-trade 795n. *merchandise.*

machinist, operator, driver, minder, machine-m. 686n. *agent;* engineer, mechanic, fitter; tool-user, craftsman 686n. *artisan.*

Adj. *mechanical,* mechanistic, powered, power-driven; automatic; robot, self-acting 628adj. *instrumental;* machine-minded, tool-using.

See: 40, 47, 217, 218, 226, 228, 250, 256, 263, 287, 623, 628, 686, 723, 777, 778, 795.

631 Materials

N. *materials,* resources 629n. *means;* material, stuff, staple, stock 3n. *substance;* raw material, grist; meat, fodder 301n. *food;* oil 385n. *fuel;* chemical material, fissionable m., uranium, thorium; ore, mineral, metal, pig-iron, ingot; clay, adobe, china clay, potter's c., argil, kaolin, gypsum 344n. *soil;* crockery 381n. *pottery;* plastic, latex, celluloid; rope, cord, fiber glass 208n. *fiber;* leather 226n. *skin;* timber, log, fagot, stick 366n. *wood;* rafter, beam, balk, stretcher, board, plank, planking, lath, stave 207n. *lamina;* cloth, fabric 222n. *textile.*

building material, brick 381n. *pottery;* bricks and mortar, lath and plaster, slate, tile, shingle, stone, marble, rance, ashlar, masonry; compo, composition, cement, concrete, ferroconcrete; paving material, flag, flagstone, cobble; gravel, macadam, tarmac, asphalt.

paper, rag-p., pulp, wood-p., newsprint; calendered paper, art p., drawing p., carbon p., tissue-p.; papier-mâché, cardboard, pasteboard, straw-board, carton; sheet, foolscap, quire, ream; note-paper 586n. *stationery.*

See: 3, 207, 208, 222, 226, 301, 344, 366, 381, 385, 586, 629.

632 Store

N. *store,* mass, heap, load, stack,

stock-pile, build-up 74n. *accumulation;* packet, bundle, budget, bagful 26n. *quantity;* harvest, crop, vintage, mow 771n. *acquisition;* haystack, haycock, rick, hay-r.; stock, stock-in-trade 795n. *merchandise;* assets, capital, holding, investment 777n. *property;* fund, reserve f., reserves, something in hand, backlog; unexpended balance, savings, savings account, nest-egg; deposit, hoard, treasure, honeycomb; buried treasure, cache 527n. *hiding place;* bottom drawer, hope chest, trousseau, two of everything 633n. *provision;* pool, kitty; common fund, common stock, community chest 775n. *joint possession;* quarry, mine, gold-m.; natural deposit, mineral d., coal d.; coal-field, gas-f., oil-f.; coal-mine, colliery, working, shaft; coal-face, seam, stringer, lode; pipe, pipe-vein; vein, rich v.; bonanza, strike 484n. *discovery;* well, oil-w., gusher; fountain, fount 156n. *source;* supply, constant s., stream; tap, pipeline; milch-cow, cornucopia, abundance 635n. *plenty;* repertoire, range (**see** *collection*).

storage, stowage, gathering, garnering 74n. *accumulation;* conservation, ensilage, bottling 666n. *preservation;* safe deposit 660n. *protection;* stabling, warehousing; storage, storage space, shelf-room, space, accommodation 183n. *room;* hold, bunker 194n. *cellar;* store-town, supply base, promptuary, storehouse, storeroom, stockroom; warehouse, goods-shed, go-down; depository, depot, entrepôt; dock, wharf, garage 192n. *stable;* magazine, arsenal, armory, gun-room; treasure-house 799n. *treasury;* exchequer, bank, safe, strongroom, vault, coffer, money-box, money-bag, till, slot-machine; hive, honeycomb; granary, garner, barn, silo, silo pit; reservoir, cistern, tank, gas-holder, gasometer; battery, storage b., dry b., wet b.; garage, gas station, filling s., gasoline pump; dump, sump, drain, cesspool, sewage farm 649n. *sink;* panary, pantry, larder, buttery, still-room 194n. *chamber;* spence, cupboard, shelf 194n. *cabinet;* refrigerator, fridge, deep-freeze; portmanteau, hold-all, packing-case 194n. *box;* container, holder, quiver 194n. *receptacle.*

collection, set, complete s.; archives, file 548n. *record;* folder, bundle, portfolio 74n. *accumulation;* museum, antiquarium 125n. *antiquity;* gallery, art g.; book-collection, library, thesaurus 559n. *dictionary;* menagerie, aquarium 369n. *zoo;* waxworks, exhibition 522n. *exhibit;* repertory, repertoire, bag of tricks.

Adj. stored, hived etc.vb.; in store, in deposit; in hand, held; in reserve, unexpended; banked, funded, invested; available, in stock; spare, supernumerary.

Vb. *store,* stow, pack, bundle 193vb. *load;* roll up, fold up; lay up, stow away, put a.; dump, garage, stable, warehouse; garner, barn; gather, harvest, reap, mow, pick, glean 370n. *cultivate;* stack, heap, pile, amass, accumulate 74vb. *bring together;* stock up, lay in, stockpile, pile up, build up, build up one's stocks 36vb. *augment;* take on, take in, fuel, coal, bunker 633vb. *provide;* fill, fill up, top up, refill, refuel 633 vb. *replenish;* put by, save, keep, hold, file, hang on to, keep by one 778vb. *retain;* bottle, bottle up, pickle 666 vb. *preserve;* leave, set aside, keep back, keep in hand, reserve, put in r.; fund, bank, deposit, invest; hoard, treasure, hive; bury, hide 525 vb. *conceal;* husband, save up, salt away, make a nest-egg, prepare for a rainy day 814vb. *economize;* equip oneself, put in the bottom drawer 669vb. *prepare oneself;* pool, put in the kitty 775vb. *socialize.*

See: 26, 36, 74, 125, 156, 183, 192, 193, 194, 369, 370, 484, 522, 525, 527, 548, 559, 633, 635, 649, 660, 663, 666, 669, 771, 775, 777, 795, 799, 814.

633 Provision

N. *provision,* providing, furnishing, logistics, equipment 669n. *fitting out;* purveyance, catering; service, delivery; self-service; procuring, pandering; feeding, entertainment, bed and board, board and lodging, maintenance; assistance, lending, lend-lease 703n. *subvention;* supply, food s., water s., constant s., feed; commissariat, provisioning, supplies, stores, rations, iron r., emergency r., reserves 632n. *store;* reinforcement, replenishment, refill, filling-up 54n. *plenitude;* food, sizing 301n. *provisions;* provender; help, helping, portion 301n. *meal;* grist, grist to the mill; fuel, fuel to the flame; produce 164n. *product;* increase, return 771n. *gain;* budgeting, budget 808n. *accounts;* possible need, encasement 669n. *preparation.*

provider, donor 781n. *giver;* creditor,

money-lender, uncle 784n. *lender;* wet-nurse, feeder; purser 798n. *treasurer;* steward, butler, pantler, comprador; commissary, quartermaster, storekeeper; supplier, victualler, sutler; provision merchant, drysalter, grocer, green-g. baker, poulterer, fishmonger, butcher, vintner, wine merchant; retailer, middle-man, shopkeeper 794n. *tradesman;* procurer, pander, pimp 952n. *bawd.*

caterer, purveyor, hotelier, hotelkeeper, restaurateur; innkeeper, alewife, landlord, mine host, publican; housekeeper, housewife; cook, chef; pastry-cook, confectioner.

Adj. *provisionary,* commissarial; self-service; sufficing, all-s. 635adj. *sufficient;* supplied, provided, well-found, all found; available, on tap, on the menu, on 189adj. *present.*

Vb. *provide,* afford, offer, lend 781vb. *give;* provision, find, find one in; equip, furnish, arm, man, fit out 669 vb. *make ready;* supply, suppeditate; maintain supply, keep fed with; yield 164vb. *produce;* bring in a supply, lead, pump in, pipeline; cater, purvey; procure, pander, pimp; service, service an order, fill an o. 793vb. *sell;* deliver, make deliveries, deliver the goods; hand out, hand round, serve, serve up, dish up; victual, feed, cook for, board, put up, maintain, keep, clothe; stock, keep a s.; budget, make provision, make due p.; provide for oneself, provision o., take on supplies, stock up, lay in a stock 632vb. *store;* fuel, coal, bunker; gather food, forage, water; tap, draw, draw on, milk 304vb. *extract;* export, import 791vb. *trade.*

replenish, reinforce, recruit, make good, make up; fill up, top up, refill 54vb. *fill;* revictual, restock, refuel, reload.

See: 52, 54, 164, 301, 304, 632, 635, 669, 703, 771, 781, 784, 791, 793, 794, 798, 952.

634 Waste

N. *waste,* wastage 42n. *decrement;* leakage, ebb 298n. *outflow;* inroad, consumption; intake 627n. *requirement;* spending, outlay, expense 806 n. *expenditure;* using up, depletion, exhaustion, drainage 300n. *voidance;* dissipation 75n. *dispersion;* evaporation 338n. *vaporization;* melting 337 n. *liquefaction;* damage 772n. *loss;* wear and tear 655n. *deterioration;* wastefulness, uneconomy, over-lavishness, extravagance, overspending, unnecessary expenditure 815n. *prodigality;* misapplication, useless expenditure, frittering away 675n. *misuse;* mischief, wanton destruction, destructiveness, sabotage 165n. *destruction;* waste product, refuse, exhaust 641n. *rubbish.*

Adj. *wasteful,* extravagant, unnecessary, uneconomic 815adj. *prodigal;* mischievous 165 adj. *destructive.*

wasted, exhausted, depleted, consumed; gone to waste, gone down the sink; fruitless, bootless, profitless 641adj. *useless;* ill-spent, misapplied; of no avail, futile, in vain.

Vb. *waste,* consume, make inroads on, wade into; drink, swallow, devour, eat up 301vb. *eat;* spend, lay out 806vb. *expend;* take, use up, exhaust, deplete, drain, suck dry 300vb. *void;* dissipate, scatter, broadcast 75vb. *disperse;* abuse, overstrain, overwork, overcrop, impoverish, milk, milk dry 675vb. *misuse;* wear out, dilapidate, damage 655vb. *impair;* put to wrong use, misapply, fritter away, cast before swine; make no use of 674vb. *not use;* labor in vain 641vb. *waste effort;* be extravagant, overspend, squander, run through, throw away, pour down the drain, burn the candle at both ends 815vb. *be prodigal;* be careless, slop, spill; be destructive, ruin, destroy, sabotage, play havoc 165vb. *lay waste;* be wasted, wane, decay, suffer loss 37vb. *decrease;* leak, ebb, run low, dry up 298vb. *flow out;* melt, melt away 337vb. *liquefy;* evaporate 338vb. *vaporize;* run out, give o. 636vb. *not suffice;* burn out, burn away, gutter 381vb. *burn;* run to seed 655vb. *deteriorate;* run to waste, go down the drain.

See: 37, 42, 75, 165, 298, 300, 301, 337, 338, 381, 627, 636, 641, 655, 674, 675, 772, 806, 809, 815.

635 Sufficiency

N. *sufficiency,* right amount; right qualities, qualification; right number, quorum; adequacy, enough, pass marks; assets, adequate income, competence, living wage; exact requirement, no surplus; minimum, no less, bare minimum, least one can do; full measure, satisfaction, ample s., contentment, all that could be desired 828n. *content;* acceptability, the possible, all that is p. 469n. *possibility;* fulfillment 725n. *comple-*

tion; repletion, one's fill, bellyful 863n. *satiety.*
plenty, God's p., horn of p., cornucopia 171n. *abundance;* outpouring, showers of, flood, tide, spate, streams 350n. *stream;* lots, lashings, galore 32n. *great quantity;* fullness, copiousness, amplitude 54n. *plenitude;* affluence, riches 800n. *wealth;* fat of the land, luxury, full table, feast, banquet 301n. *feasting;* orgy, riot, profusion 815n. *prodigality;* richness, fat; fertility, productivity, luxuriance, lushness, rankness 171n. *productiveness;* foison, harvest, rich h., bumper crop; rich vein, bonanza, ample store, more where it came from 632n. *store;* more than enough, too much, superabundance 637n. *redundance.*
Adj. *sufficient,* sufficing, all-s. 633 adj. *provisionary;* self-sufficient 54 adj. *complete;* enough, adequate, competent; equal to, a match for 28adj. *equal;* satisfactory, satisfying 828adj. *contenting;* measured, commensurate, up to the mark; just right, not too much, not too little; barely sufficient, no more than enough; usable 673adj. *used;* makeshift, provisional 150adj. *substituted.*
plenteous, plentiful, ample, enough and to spare, more than enough 637adj. *superfluous;* open-handed, generous, lavish 813adj. *liberal;* extravagant 815adj. *prodigal;* wholesale, without stint, unsparing, unmeasured, exhaustless, inexhaustible 32adj. *great;* luxuriant, luxuriating, riotous, lush, rank, fertile, fat 171 adj. *productive;* profuse, abundant, copious, overflowing 637adj. *redundant;* rich, opulent, affluent 800adj. *moneyed.*
filled, well-f., flush 54adj. *full;* chock-full, replete, satiated 863adj. *sated;* satisfied, contented 828adj. *content;* well-provided, well-stocked, well-furnished 633adj. *provisionary;* rich in, teeming, crawling with 104adj. *multitudinous.*
Vb. *suffice*, be enough, do, answer 642vb. *be expedient;* just do, work, serve, serve as a makeshift; qualify, reach, make the grade 727vb. *be successful;* pass, pass muster, wash; measure up to, meet requirements, fill the bill; do all that is possible, rise to the occasion; stand, stand up to, take the strain 218vb. *support;* do the needful 725vb. *carry out;* fill, fill up, saturate 54vb. *complete;* refill 633vb. *replenish;* prove acceptable, satisfy 828vb. *content;* more than satisfy, satiate, give one his bellyful 863vb. *sate;* provide for, make adequate provision 633vb. *provide.*
abound, be plentiful, proliferate, teem, swarm, bristle with, crawl w. 104vb. *be many;* exuberate, riot, luxuriate 171vb. *be fruitful;* flow, shower, snow, pour, stream, sheet 350vb. *rain;* brim, overflow 637vb. *superabound;* roll in, wallow in, swim in 800vb. *be rich.*
have enough, be satisfied 828vb. *be content;* eat one's fill 301vb. *eat;* drink one's fill 301vb. *drink;* be sated, have one's bellyful, be fed up 829vb. *be discontented;* have the means 800vb. *afford.*
Adv. *enough,* sufficiently, amply, to the full, to one's heart's content; ad libitum, ad-lib, on tap, on demand; abundantly, inexhaustibly, interminably.
See: 28, 32, 54, 104, 150, 171, 218, 301, 350, 469, 632, 633, 637, 642, 673, 725, 727, 800, 813, 815, 828, 829, 863.

636 Insufficiency

N. *insufficiency*, not enough; nonsatisfaction 829n. *discontent;* inadequacy, incompetence; minginess, little enough, nothing to spare, less than somewhat 33n. *small quantity;* too few, no quorum 105n. *fewness;* deficiency, imperfection 647n. *defect;* deficit 55n. *incompleteness;* nonfulfillment 726n. *non-completion;* half-measures, tinkering, failure, weakness 307n. *shortcoming;* bankruptcy 805n. *insolvency;* bare subsistence, subsistence level, pittance, dole, mite; stinginess 816n. *parsimony;* short allowance, short commons, iron rations, half r.; austerity, Lenten fare, Spartan f., starvation diet, bread and water 945n. *asceticism;* fast day 946n. *fasting.*
scarcity, scarceness, paucity 140n. *infrequency;* dearth, leanness, seven lean years; drought, famine, starvation; infertility 172n. *unproductiveness;* shortfall 307n. *shortcoming;* power-cut 37n. *decrease;* short supply, seller's market; stint, scantiness, meagerness 801n. *poverty;* lack, want, need 627n. *needfulness;* ebb, low water 212n. *shallowness.*
Adj. *insufficient*, not satisfying, unsatisfactory, disappointing 829adj. *discontenting;* inadequate, not enough, too litttle; too small, cramping 33adj. *small;* deficient, lacking

55adj. *incomplete;* wanting, found w., poor 35adj. *inferior;* incompetent, unequal to, not up to it 695 adj. *unskillful;* weak, thin, watery, unnourishing 4adj. *insubstantial;* niggardly, sparing, mingy 816adj. *parsimonious.*

unprovided; unsupplied, unfurnished, ill-furnished, ill-supplied, unreplenished; vacant, bare 190adj. *empty;* empty-handed 728adj. *unsuccessful;* unsatisfied, unfilled, unsated 829adj. *discontented;* insatiable 859adj. *greedy;* deficient in, starved of; cramped 702adj. *hindered;* undercapitalized, understaffed, undermanned, underofficered; stinted, rationed, skimped; not provided, unavailable, off the menu, off 190adj. *absent.*

underfed, undernourished, under-vitaminized; half-fed, half-starved, on short commons; unfed, famished, starved, famine-stricken, starving 946adj. *fasting;* starveling, spare, scurvy, thin, meager, scrimp, stunted, jejune 206adj. *lean.*

scarce, rare 140adj. *infrequent;* sparse 105adj. *few*; short, in short supply, hard to get, hard to come by, not to be had, unavailable, unprocurable, unobtainable, out of season, out of stock.

Vb. *not suffice*, be insufficient, — inadequate etc.adj.; not meet requirements 647vb. *be imperfect;* want, lack, need, require, leave a gap 627 vb. *require;* fail 509vb. *disappoint;* fall below 35vb. *be inferior;* come short, default 307vb. *fall short;* run out, dry up, take half measures, tinker, paper over the cracks 726vb. *not complete.*

be unsatisfied, ask for more, beg for m., come again, take a second helping, feel hungry 859vb. *be hungry;* feel dissatisfied, increase one's demands 829vb. *be discontented;* spurn an offer, reject with contempt 607vb. *reject;* desiderate, miss, want, feel the lack, stand in need of, feel something is missing 627vb. *require;* be a glutton for, be unable to have enough of 947vb. *gluttonize.*

make insufficient, ask *or* expect too much; overwork, overcrop, impoverish, damage 655vb. *impair;* exhaust, deplete, run down, squander 634vb. *waste;* stint, skimp, scant, ration, put on half rations, put on short commons, put on short allowance 816vb. *be parsimonious;* disinherit, cut off with a shilling 786vb. *deprive;* cramp 747vb. *restrain.*

Adv. *insufficiently*, not enough; in default, failing, for want of.

See: 33, 35, 37, 55, 105, 140, 172, 190, 206, 212, 307, 509, 607, 627, 634, 647, 655, 695, 702, 725, 728, 747, 786, 801, 805, 816, 829, 859, 945, 946, 947.

637 Redundance

N. *redundance*, over-brimming, overspill, overflow, inundation, flood 298 n. *outflow;* abundance, superabundance, exuberance, luxuriance, riot, profusion 635n. *plenty;* richness, bonanza 632n. *store;* upsurge, uprush 36n. *increase;* avalanche, spate 32n. *great quantity;* too many, mob 74n. *crowd;* saturation, saturation point, over-saturation 54n. *plenitude;* excessiveness, nimiety, exorbitance, excess, extremes, too much 546n. *exaggeration;* overdoing it, over-extension, over-expansion, too many irons in the fire 678n. *overactivity;* over-politeness, officiousness; overpraise, over-optimism 482n. *overestimation;* overmeasure, overpayment, overweight; burden, load, overload, last straw 322n. *gravity;* more than is fair, lion's share 32n. *main part;* overindulgence 943n. *intemperance;* overfeeding 947n. *gluttony;* overdrinking 949n. *drunkenness;* overdose, surfeit, engorgement, plethora, congestion 863n. *satiety;* more than enough, bellyful 635n. *satisfaction;* glut, drug on the market (**see** *superfluity*); fat, fattiness.

superfluity, more than is needed, luxury, luxuriousness; luxuries, nonnecessaries, luxury article; overfulfillment, duplication, supererogation, work of s.; something over, bonus, spare cash, money to burn 40n. *extra;* margin, overlap, excess, overplus, surplusage, surplus, balance 41n. *remainder;* superfluousness, excrescence, accessory, parasite 641n. *inutility;* useless word, expletive, verse-filler 570n. *pleonasm;* tautology 570n. *diffuseness;* redundancy, more men than jobs, underemployment, unemployment 679n. *inactivity;* more jobs than men, overemployment 678 n. *activity;* too much of a good thing, glut, drug on the market; surfeit, sickener, overdose 863n. *satiety.*

Adj. *redundant*, too many, one too m. 104adj. *many;* overmuch, excessive 32adj. *exorbitant;* overdone 546adj. *exaggerated;* overflowing, overfull, slopping, running over, brimming, filled to overflowing 54 adj. *full;* flooding, streaming 350adj. *flowing;* saturated, supersaturated 341adj. *drenched;* cloying, satiating 838adj. *tedious;* cloyed, satiated 863 adj. *sated;* replete, gorged, crammed, stuffed, bursting; overcharged, overloaded; congested, plethoric; dropsical, turgid 197adj. *expanded.*

superfluous, supererogatory, supervacaneaus; supernumerary; adscititious, excrescent; needless, unnecessary, unrequired, uncalled for 641 adj. *useless;* excessive, more than one asked for; luxury, luxurious; expletive 570n. *pleonastic;* surplus, extra, over and above 41adj. *remaining;* above one's needs, spare, to spare 38adj. *additional;* de trop, on one's hands, a-begging 860adj. *unwanted;* dispensable, expendable, replaceable 812adj. *cheap.*

Vb. *superabound*, riot, luxuriate 635 vb. *abound;* run riot, overproduce, overpopulate 171vb. *be fruitful;* bristle with, burst w., meet one at every turn, outnumber 104vb. *be many;* overflow, brim over, well o., ooze at every pore, burst at the seams 54vb. *be complete;* stream, flood, inundate, burst its banks, deluge, overwhelm 350vb. *flow;* whelm, engulf 299vb. *absorb;* know no bounds, spread far and wide 306vb. *overstep;* overlap 183vb. *extend;* soak, saturate 341vb. *drench;* stuff, gorge, cram 54vb. *fill;* congest, choke, suffocate; overdose, oversatisfy, glut, cloy, satiate, sicken 863vb. *sate;* overfeed, pamper oneself, overeat, overdrink 943vb. *be intemperate;* overfulfill, oversubscribe, do more than enough; oversell, drug the market; overstock, pile up, overemploy; overdo, pile it on, lay it on thick, lay it on with a trowel 546vb. *exaggerate;* overload, overburden; overcharge, surcharge; lavish, lavish upon 813vb. *be liberal;* be lavish, make a splash 815vb. *be prodigal;* roll in, crawl with, stink of 800vb. *be rich.*

be superfluous, — redundant etc.adj.; go a-begging, remain on one's hands 41vb. *be left;* hang heavy on one's hands 679vb. *be inactive;* do twice over, duplicate; carry coals to Newcastle, gild refined gold, paint the lily, teach one's grandmother to suck eggs; labor the obvious, kill the slain, flog a dead horse 641 vb. *waste effort;* exceed requirements, have no use 641vb. *be useless;* go in for luxuries.

Adv. *redundantly*, over and above, too much, overly, excessively, beyond measure; enough and to spare; in excess of requirements.

See: 32, 36, 38, 40, 41, 54, 74, 104, 171, 183, 197, 298, 299, 306, 322, 341, 350, 482, 546, 570, 632, 635, 641, 678, 679, 800, 812, 813, 815, 838, 860, 863, 943, 947, 949.

638 Importance

N. *importance*, first i., primacy, priority, urgency 64n. *precedence;* paramountcy, supremacy, 34n. *superiority;* essentiality, irreplaceability; import, consequence, significance, weight, weightiness, gravity, seriousness, solemnity; materiality, materialness, substance, pith, moment 3n. *substantiality;* interest, consideration, concern 622n. *business;* notability, memorability, mark, prominence, distinction, eminence 866n. *repute;* influence 866n. *prestige;* size, magnitude 32n. *greatness;* rank, optimacy 868n. *nobility;* value, excellence, merit 644n. *goodness;* use, usefulness 640n. *utility;* stress, emphasis, insistence 532n. *affirmation.*

important matter, vital concern; turning point 137n. *crisis;* breath of one's nostrils, be-all and end-all; grave affair, not peanuts, no joke, no laughing matter, matter of life and death; notable point, memorandum, memoranda, notandum 505 n. *reminder;* big news, great n. 529n. *news;* great doings, exploit 676n. *deed;* red-letter day, great d. 876n. *special day.*

chief thing, what matters, the thing, great t., main t.; issue, supreme i. 452n. *topic;* fundamentals, bedrock, fact 1n. *reality;* essential, sine qua non 627n. *requirement;* priority, first choice 605n. *choice;* gist 514n. *meaning;* substance 5n. *essential part;* best part, cream, salt, pick 644n. *elite;* keynote, cornerstone, mainstay; head and front, spearhead; sum and substance, heart of the matter, heart, core, hard c., kernel, nucleus, nub 225n. *center;* hub 218n. *pivot;* cardinal point, main p., salient p., half the battle 32n. *main part;* chief hope, trump card, main chance.

bigwig, personage, notability, personality, man of mark 866n. *person of repute;* great man, VIP, brass hat; his nibs, big shot, big noise, big bug, big wheel, big man on campus,

BMOC; great card, panjandrum; leading light, master spirit 500n. *sage;* kingpin, key man 696n. *expert;* first fiddle, prima donna, star, catch, great c. 890n. *favorite;* lion, big game; uncrowned king, head, chief, Mr. Big 34n. *superior;* superior person, superman, wonderman, lord of creation; king, lord 868n. *nobility;* summit, top people, establishment 733n. *authority.*

Adj. *important,* weighty, grave, solemn, serious; pregnant, big; of weight, of consideration, of importance, of concern; considerable, worth considering; world-shattering, earth-shaking, seismic 178adj. *influential;* momentous, critical, fateful 137adj. *timely;* chief, capital, cardinal, staple, major, main, paramount 34adj. *supreme;* essential, material, to the point 9adj. *relevant;* pivotal 225n. *central;* basic, fundamental, bedrock, radical, going to the root; primary, prime, foremost, leading; overriding, overruling, uppermost 34adj. *superior;* worth-while, not to be despised, not to be overlooked, not to be sneezed at 644adj. *valuable;* necessary, indispensable, irreplaceable, key 627adj. *required;* helpful 640 adj. *useful;* significant, telling, trenchant 514adj. *meaningful;* pressing, insistent, urgent, high-priority; overdue 136adj. *late;* high-level, top-l., summital 213adj. *topmost;* top-secret 523adj. *latent;* high, grand, noble 32adj. *great.*

notable, of mark, egregious 32adj. *remarkable;* memorable, signal, unforgettable 505adj. *remembered;* first-rate, outstanding, excelling 34 adj. *superior;* ranking, top-rank, top-flight 644adj. *excellent;* big-time, conspicuous, prominent, eminent, distinguished, exalted, august 866 adj. *noteworthy;* dignified, imposing, commanding 821adj. *impressive;* newsworthy, front-page; eventful, stirring, breath-taking, shattering, earth-shaking, seismic, epoch-making.

Vb. *be important,* matter, be a consideration, be an object 612vb. *motivate;* weigh, carry, tell, count 178vb. *influence;* import, signify 514vb. *mean;* concern, interest, affect 9vb. *be related;* have priority, come first 34vb. *predominate;* take the lead 64vb. *come before;* be something, be somebody 920vb. *command respect;* take the limelight, deserve notice, make a stir, create a sensation, cut a figure, cut a dash 455vb. *attract notice.*

make important, give weight to, attach *or* ascribe importance to; seize on, fasten on; bring to the fore, place in the foreground; enhance, highlight; rub in, stress, underline, labor 532vb. *emphasize;* put in capital letters, headline, splash, splosh 528vb. *advertise;* bring to notice, put on the map 528vb. *proclaim;* write in letters of gold 876vb. *celebrate;* magnify 197 vb. *enlarge;* overweight 546vb. *exaggerate;* honor, glorify, exalt 920 vb. *show respect;* take seriously, make a fuss about, make a stir, make much ado; value, esteem, make much of, set store by, think everything of 920vb. *respect;* overestimate 482vb. *overrate.*

Adv. *importantly,* primarily, significantly; materially, largely, in the main, above all, to crown all; par excellence.

See: 1, 3, 5, 9, 32, 34, 64, 136, 137, 178, 197, 213, 218, 225, 452, 455, 482, 500, 505, 514, 523, 528, 529, 532, 546, 605, 612, 622, 627, 640, 644, 676, 696, 733, 821, 866, 868, 876, 890, 920.

639 Unimportance

N. *unimportance,* inconsequence; secondariness 35n. *inferiority;* insignificance 515n. *unmeaningness;* immateriality, inessentiality 4n. *insubstantiality;* vanity, vacancy 190n. *emptiness;* nothingness, nullity 2n. *non-existence;* pettiness 33n. *smallness;* paltriness, meanness 922n. *despisedness;* triviality, nugacity; superficiality 212n. *shallowness;* flippancy, snap of the fingers, frivolity; nominalness, worthlessness 812n. *cheapness;* uselessness 641n. *inutility;* irrelevance, sideshow, red herring 10n. *irrelation.*

trifle, inessential, triviality, technicality; nothing, mere n., no matter, no great m., parish pump; accessory, secondary matter, side-show; nothing in particular, matter of indifference, neither mass nor matins; no great shakes, nothing to speak of, nothing to boast of; smatter; tithe, fraction 53n. *part;* fribble, bagatelle, tinker's damn, straw, rush, chaff, pin, button, row of buttons, feather, dust; cobweb, gossamer 330n. *brittleness;* small item, twopence, small change, small beer, small potatoes; chicken-feed, flea-bite, pap; pinprick, scratch; nothing to it, child's play 701n. *easy thing;* jest, joke, practical j., farce 837n. *amusement;* peccadillo, venial sin; trifles, trivia, minutiae, detail, petty d. 80n. *particulars;* whit, jot, tittle, the least bit, trickle, drop in the ocean 33n. *small quantity;* doit, cent, brass farthing, bawbee 33n. *small coin;* nonsense, fudge, fiddlesticks 497n. *absurdity.*

bauble, toy, rattle 837n. *plaything;* gewgaw, knick-knack, kickshaw, bric-a-brac; novelty, trinket, bibelot; tinsel, trumpery, frippery, trash, gimcrack, stuff; froth, foam 355n. *bubble.*

nonentity, nobody, obscurity; man of straw 4n. *insubstantial thing;* figurehead, cipher, sleeping partner; fribble, trifler, smatterer; mediocrity, light-weight, small beer; tail (of a team) 697n. *bungler;* small fry, small game; other ranks, lower orders 869n. *commonalty;* second fiddle 35n. *inferior;* underling, understrapper 742n. *servant;* pawn, pawn in the game, piece on the board, stooge, puppet 628n. *instrument;* Cinderella 801n. *poor man;* pipsqueak, squit, trash 867n. *object of scorn.*

Adj. *unimportant,* immaterial 4adj. *insubstantial;* ineffectual, uninfluential, inconsequential; insignificant 515adj. *unmeaning;* off the point 10adj. *irrelevant;* inessential, nonessential, not vital; unnecessary, dispensable, expendable; puny 196 adj. *little;* small, petty, trifling, nugatory, flimsy, paltry 33adj. *inconsiderable;* negligible, inappreciable, not worth considering, out of the running; weak, powerless 161 adj. *impotent;* wretched, miserable, pitiful, pitiable, pathetic; poor, mean, sorry, scurvy, scruffy, shabby, vile 645adj. *bad;* obscure, disregarded, overlooked 458adj. *neglected;* of no account, overrated, beneath notice, beneath contempt 922adj. *contemptible;* low-level, of second rank, secondary, minor, by, subsidiary, peripheral 35adj. *inferior.*

trivial, trifling, piffling, piddling, peddling, fiddling, niggling, whiffling; pettifogging, pinpricking; technical; footling, frivolous, puerile, childish 499adj. *foolish;* windy, airy, frothy 4adj. *insubstantial;* superficial 212 adj. *shallow;* slight 33adj. *small;* light-weight 323adj. *light;* not serious, forgivable, venial; twopenny-halfpenny, one-horse, second-rate, third-r.; rubbishy, trumpery, trashy, tawdry, catchpenny, pinchbeck, potboiling, shoddy, gimcrack 645adj. *bad;* two-a-penny 812adj. *cheap;* worthless, valueless 641adj. *useless;* not worth while, not worth a thought, not worth a curse 922adj. *contemptible;* toy, token, nominal, symbolic 547adj. *indicating;* commonplace, ordinary, uneventful 610adj. *usual.*

Vb. *be unimportant,* — valueless etc. adj.; not matter, weigh light upon, have no weight, not weigh, not count, count for nothing, cut no ice, signify little; think unimportant, not overrate, shrug off, snap one's fingers 922vb. *hold cheap;* reduce one's importance, cut down to size 872vb. *humiliate.*

Int. no matter! what matter! never mind! so what!

See: 2, 4, 10, 33, 35, 53, 80, 100, 161, 196, 212, 323, 330, 355, 458, 497, 499, 515, 547, 610, 628, 641, 645, 697, 701, 742, 801, 812, 837, 867, 869, 872, 922.

640 Utility

N. *utility,* use, usefulness; employability, serviceability, handiness 628 n. *instrumentality;* efficacy, efficiency 160n. *ability;* adequacy 635n. *sufficiency;* adaptability, applicability, suitability 642n. *expedience;* readiness, availability 189n. *presence;* service, avail, help, great h., stead 703n. *aid;* value, worth, merit 644n. *goodness;* virtue, function, capacity, potency 160n. *power;* advantage, commodity; profitability, earning capacity, productivity 171n. *productiveness;* profit 771n. *gain;* convenience, benefit, general b., public utility, common weal, public good 615n. *good;* utilitarianism, employment, utilization 673n. *use.*

Adj. *useful,* of use, helpful, of service 703adj. *aiding;* sensible, practical, applied, functional; versatile, multipurpose, all-purpose, of all work; practicable, commodious, convenient 642adj. *expedient;* handy, ready, rough and r.; at hand, available, on tap; serviceable, fit for, good for, disposable, adaptable, applicable; fit for use, ready for u., usable, employable; good, valid, current; subsidiary, subservient 628 adj. *instrumental;* able, competent, efficacious, effective, effectual, efficient 160adj. *powerful;* conducive 179adj. *tending;* adequate 635adj.

sufficient; pragmatic, utilitarian.
profitable, paying, remunerative 771 adj. *gainful;* prolific, fertile 164 adj. *productive;* beneficial, advantageous, to one's advantage, edifying, worth-while 615n. *good;* worth one's salt, worth one's keep, invaluable, priceless 644adj. *valuable*.
Vb. *be useful*, — of use etc.adj.; avail, bestead, stead, stand one in good s.; come in handy, have some use, perform a function; function, work 173vb. *operate;* perform 676 vb. *do;* serve, subserve, serve one's turn, answer one's turn 635vb. *suffice;* suit one's purpose 642vb. *be expedient;* favor one's purpose, help, advance, promote 703vb. *aid;* do service, do yeoman s. 742vb. *serve;* conduce 179vb. *tend;* benefit, profit, advantage 644vb. *do good;* bear fruit 171vb. *be fruitful;* pay, make use of, utilize 673vb. *use;* remunerate, bring grist to the mill 771vb. *be profitable*.
find useful, have a use for, employ, make use of, utilize 673vb. *use*; turn to account, improve on, find one's account in, find one's advantage in, make capital of 137vb. *profit by;* count one's winnings, take one's profit, reap the benefit of 771vb. *gain;* be the better for 654 vb. *get better;* enjoy, enjoy the possession of 773vb. *possess*.
Adv. *usefully*, serviceably; advantageously; pro bono publico; cui bono? to whose advantage?
See: 137, 160, 164, 171, 173, 179, 189, 615, 628, 635, 642, 644, 654, 673, 676, 703, 742, 771, 773.

641 Inutility

N. *inutility*, uselessness; no function, no purpose, superfluousness 637n. *superfluity;* nugacity, futility, inanity, vanity, vanity of vanities 497n. *absurdity;* worthlessness, unemployability; inadequacy 636n. *insufficiency;* inefficiency, ineffectualness, inability 161n. *impotence;* inefficiency, incompetence, ineptitude 695n. *unskillfulness;* unserviceableness, inconvenience, unsuitability, unfitness 643 n. *inexpedience;* inapplicability, unadaptability; unprofitability, no benefit 172n. *unproductivity;* disservice, mischief, damage, detriment 772n. *loss*; unsubservience, recalcitrance 598n. *unwillingness*.
lost labor, wasted l. 728n. *failure;* waste of breath, waste of time; lost trouble, labor in vain, wild-goose chase, fool's errand, sleeveless e.; labor of Sisyphus, Penelope's web; half-measures, tinkering.
rubbish, good riddance, trash, stuff; waste, refuse, lumber, junk, old iron, litter; spoilage, waste paper, mullock; scourings, off-s., sweepings, dregs, lees, dottle, combings, shavings 41n. *leavings;* chaff, husks, bran; scraps, bits, orts, broken meats, crumbs; offal, carrion; dust, muck, debris, slag, dross, scum 649 n. *dirt;* peel, orange-p.; dead wood, stubble, weeds, tares; odds and ends, bits and pieces, rags, old clothes, cast-offs; reject, throw-out; midden, rubbish-heap, dust-h., spoil-h., spoil bank; dust-hole, dump; picked bone, sucked orange, empty bottle, empties, deads; dead letter, caput mortuum; back number 127n. *archaism*.
Adj. *useless*, functionless, purposeless, pointless; futile, nugatory 497 adj. *absurd;* unpractical, impracticable, unworkable, effort-wasting; non-functional 844adj. *ornamental;* otiose, redundant, exerescent 637adj. *superfluous;* expendable, dispensable, unnecessary, unneeded, uncalled for 860adj. *unwanted;* unfit, unapt, inapplicable 643adj. *inexpedient;* fit for nothing, unusable, unemployable, unadaptable; unqualified, inefficient, incompetent 695adj. *unskillful;* unable, ineffective, ineffectual, feckless 161adj. *impotent;* non-functioning, inoperative; uncurrent, invalid 752adj. *abrogated;* unserviceable, out of order, not working, disordered 63adj. *deranged;* broken down, effete, worn out, past work, hors de combat, obsolete, outmoded 127adj. *antiquated;* hopeless, vain, idle (**see** *profitless*).
profitless, loss-making, unprofitable, not worth while, wasteful, not paying, ill-spent 722adj. *losing;* vain, in vain, abortive 728adj. *unsuccessful;* unrewarding, unrewarded, thankless; fruitless, barren, sterile 172adj. *unproductive;* idle 679n. lazy; worthless, good for nothing, valueless, no earthly use; rubbishy, trashy, no good, not worth powder and shot, not worth the paper it is written on 645adj. *bad;* unsalable, dear at any price 811adj. *dear*.
Vb. *be useless*, have no use, waste one's time; achieve no purpose, end in futility; not help 702vb. *hinder;* not work, not function 728vb. *fail;*

refuse to work 677vb. *not act;* fall by the wayside 172vb. *be unproductive;* go a-begging 637vb. *be superfluous.*

make useless, disqualify, unfit, disarm, take the sting out of 161vb. *disable;* castrate 161vb. *unman;* cripple, lame, clip the wings 655vb. *impair;* dismantle, unmount, dismast, unrig, put out of commission, lay up 679vb. *make inactive;* sabotage, throw a spanner in the works, put a spoke in one's wheel 702vb. *obstruct;* disassemble, undo, take to pieces, break up 46vb. *disjoin;* deface, withdraw from currency, render uncurrent 752adj. *abrogate;* devalue 812vb. *cheapen;* make barren, sow with salt 172vb. *sterilize.*

waste effort, labor the obvious; spend one's breath, lose one's labor, labor in vain, sweat for nothing, flog a dead horse, beat the air, lash the waves, cry for the moon; attempt the impossible 470vb. *try impossibilities;* tinker, paper over the cracks, spoil the ship for a ha'p'orth of tar 726vb. *not complete.*

Adv. *uselessly,* to no purpose; helplessly, ineffectually.

See: 41, 46, 63, 127, 161, 172, 470, 497, 598, 636, 637, 643, 645, 649, 655, 677, 679, 695, 702, 726, 728, 752, 772, 811, 812, 844, 860.

642 Expedience

N. *expedience,* expediency, good policy; answer, right a., advisability, desirability, worthwhileness, suitability 640n. *utility;* fitness, propriety 915n. *dueness;* high time, due t., right t., proper t., opportunity 137n. *occasion;* rule of expediency, convenience, pragmatism, utilitarianism, opportunism, time-serving; profit, advantage 615n. *benefit;* facilities, conveniences 629n. *means;* an expedient, pis aller 623n. *contrivance.*

Adj. *expedient,* expediential, advisable, commendable; better to, desirable, worth-while; acceptable 923adj. *approved;* up one's street, suitable 24adj. *fit;* fitting, befitting, seemly, proper 913adj. *right;* owing 915 adj. *due;* in loco, well-timed opportune 137adj. *timely;* politic 498adj. *wise;* advantageous, profitable 640adj. *useful;* convenient, workable, practical, pragmatic, practicable, negotiable; qualified, cut out for; to the purpose, adapted to, applicable; handy, effective, effectual.

Vb. *be expedient,* speak to one's condition, come not amiss, serve the time, suit the occasion, beseem, befit; be to the purpose, expedite one's end, help 703vb. *aid;* forward, advance, promote 640vb. *be useful;* answer, have the desired effect, produce results 156vb. *conduce;* wash, work, do, serve, deliver the goods, fill the bill 635vb. *suffice;* achieve one's aim 727vb. *succeed;* qualify for, fit, be just the thing 24vb. *accord;* profit, advantage, benefit 644vb. *do good.*

Adv. *expediently,* conveniently, fittingly, opportunely; in the right place at the right time.

See: 24, 156, 498, 615, 623, 629, 635, 640, 644, 703, 727, 913, 915, 923.

643 Inexpedience

N. *inexpedience,* inexpediency; no answer, not the a., bad policy, counsel of despair 495n. *error;* inadvisability, undesirability; unsuitability, unfitness 25n. *inaptitude;* impropriety, unfittingness, unseemliness 916n. *undueness;* wrongness 914 n. *wrong;* inopportuneness, untimeliness 138n. *intempestivity;* disqualification, disability, handicap 702 n. *obstacle;* discommodity, inconvenience, disadvantage, detriment; doubtful advantage, mixed blessing, pis aller.

Adj. *inexpedient,* better not, unadvisable, uncommendable, not recommended 924adj. *disapproved;* ill-advised, impolitic 499adj. *unwise;* inappropriate, unfitting, out of place, unseemly 916adj. *undue;* not right, improper, objectionable 914adj. *wrong;* unfit, ineligible, inadmissible, unsuitable, unhappy, inept 25 adj. *unapt;* unseasonable, inopportune, untimely, wrongly timed 138 adj. *ill-timed;* unsatisfactory 636adj. *insufficient;* discommodious, inconvenient; detrimental, disadvantageous, hurtful 645adj. *harmful;* unhealthy, unwholesome 653adj. *insalubrious;* unprofitable 641adj. *useless;* unhelpful 702adj. *hindering;* untoward 731adj. *adverse;* ill-contrived, awkward 695adj. *clumsy;* incommodious, cumbersome, lumbering, hulking 195adj. *unwieldy.*

Vb. *be inexpedient,* — inadvisable etc.adj.; not fit, come amiss, won't do, won't wash, not answer; not help 641vb. *be useless;* bother, discommode, put to inconvenience 827 vb. *incommode;* disadvantage, penalize, hurt 645vb. *harm;* work against 702vb. *obstruct;* embarrass 700vb. *be difficult.*

See: 25, 138, 195, 495, 499, 636, 641, 645, 653, 695, 700, 702, 731, 827, 914, 916, 924.

644 Goodness

N. *goodness,* soundness 650n. *health;* virtuosity 694n. *skill;* quality, good q., classic q., vintage; good points, redeeming feature; merit, desert, title to fame; nothing like, excellence, eminence, supereminence 34 n. *superiority;* virtue, worth, value 809n. *price;* pricelessness, superexcellence 32n. *greatness;* flawlessness 646n. *perfection;* distilled essence, quintessence 1n. *essence;* beneficence 897n. *benevolence;* virtuous character 933n. *virtue.*

elite, chosen few, chosen people, the saints; pick, prime, flower; cream, crême de la crême, salt of the earth, flower of the flock, pick of the bunch, seeded player; crack troops, corps d'élite; top people 638n. *bigwig;* charmed circle, top drawer, upper ten, best people 868n. *nobility;* choice bit, tidbit, prime cut, piece de résistance; plum, prize 729n. *trophy.*

exceller, nonpareil, nonesuch; prodigy, genius; superman, wonderman, wonder, wonder of the world, Stupor Mundi, Admirable Crichton 646 n. *paragon;* grand fellow, one of the best 937n. *good man;* one in a thousand, treasure, perfect t. 890n. *darling;* jewel, pearl, ruby, diamond 844n. *gem;* gem of the first water, pearl of price, gold, pure g., refined g.; chef d'oeuvre, pièce de résistance, collector's piece, museum p. 694n. *masterpiece;* record-smasher, record-breaker, best-seller, best ever; the goods, winner, fizzer, whiz-banger, lalapalooza, humdinger, corker, knockout, hit, smash h.; star, idol 890n. *favorite;* best of its kind, the tops, top-notcher, top seed, first-rater; champion, cock of the walk, cock of the roost, title-holder, world-beater, prizewinner 727n. *victor.*

Adj. *excellent,* eximious; well-done, exemplary, worth imitating; good, good as gold 933adj. *virtuous;* above par, preferable, better 34adj. *superior;* very good, first-rate, super-excellent, alpha plus 306adj. *surpassing;* prime, quality, good q., fine, superfine, most desirable; God's own, superlative; all-star, of the first water, rare, vintage, classic 646adj. *perfect;* choice, select, picked, hand-picked, tested, exquisite, recherché 605adj. *chosen;* exclusive, pure 44 adj. *unmixed;* worthy, meritorious 915adj. *deserving;* admired, admirable, estimable, praiseworthy, creditable 923adj. *approvable;* famous, great; couleur de rose, glorious, dazzling, splendid, magnificent, marvelous, wonderful, terrific, superb.

topping, top-notch, top-hole (**see** *best*); lovely, glorious, heavenly, out of this world; super, wizard, zingy; smashing, stunning, corking, ripping, spiffing; swell, great, grand, famous, dandy, crackerjack, hunky-dory; scrumptious, delicious, juicy, plum 826adj. *pleasurable.*

best, very b., optimum, A1, champion, bonzer, tip-top, top-notch, nothing like; first, first-rate, crack; second to none 34adj. *supreme;* unequaled, unmatched, peerless, matchless, unparalleled, unparagoned; best-ever, record, record-smashing, best-selling 34adj. *crowning;* capital, cardinal 638adj. *important.*

valuable, of value, invaluable, inestimable, priceless, above price, costly, rich 811adj. *of price;* irreplaceable, unique, rare, precious, golden, worth its weight in gold, worth a king's ransom; sterling, gilt-edged, sound, solid.

beneficial, wholesome, healthy, salutary, sound 652adj. *salubrious;* refreshing, edifying, worth-while, advantageous, profitable 640adj. *useful;* favorable, kind, propitious 730adj. *prosperous;* harmless, hurtless, inoffensive, unobnoxious, innocuous 935adj. *innocent.*

not bad, tolerable, passable, standard, up to the mark, in good condition, in fair c., fair, satisfactory 635adj. *sufficient;* nice, decent, pretty good, all right; sound, fresh, unspoiled; unexceptionable, unobjectionable; indifferent, middling, mediocre, ordinary, fifty-fifty, average 30adj. *median.*

Vb. *be good,* — sound etc.adj.; have quality; have merit, deserve well 915vb. *deserve;* qualify, stand the test, pass, pass muster, pass with flying colors 635vb. *suffice;* challenge comparison, vie, rival, equal the best 28vb. *equal;* excel, transcend, overtop, bear away the bell,

take the prize 34vb. *be superior.*
do good, have a good effect, edify; do a world of good 652vb. *be salubrious;* be the making of, make a man of 654vb. *make better;* help 615vb. *benefit;* favor, smile on 730 vb. *prosper;* do a favor, do a good turn, confer an obligation, put in one's debt 897vb. *be benevolent;* not hurt, do no harm, break no bones.
Adv. *aright*, well, rightly, properly, admirably, excellently, famously.
See: 28, 30, 32, 34, 44, 306, 605, 615, 635. 638, 640, 646, 652, 654, 694, 726, 727, 729, 730, 809, 811, 826, 844, 868, 890, 897, 915, 923, 933, 935, 937.

645 Badness
N. *badness*, bad qualities, obnoxiousness, nastiness, beastliness, foulness, grossness, rottenness; demerit, unworthiness, worthlessness; low quality, low standard 35n. *inferiority;* faultiness, flaw 647n. *imperfection;* poor make, shoddiness 641n. *inutility;* clumsiness 695n. *unskillfulness;* rankness, unsoundness, taint, decay, corruption 655n. *deterioration;* disruption, confusion 61n. *disorder;* peccancy, morbidity 651n. *disease;* harmfulness, hurtfulness, balefulness, ill, hurt, harm, injury, detriment, damage, mischief 616n. *evil;* noxiousness, poisonousness, deadliness, virulence 653n. *insalubrity;* poison, blight 659n. *bane;* pestilence 651n. *plague;* contamination, center of infection, plague spot, hotbed 651n. *infection;* affair, scandal 867n. *slur;* abomination, filth 649n. *uncleanness;* sewer 649n. *sink;* bitterness, gall, wormwood 393n. *sourness;* painfulness, sting, ache, pang, thorn in the flesh 377n. *pain;* molestation 827n. *annoyance;* anguish 825n. *suffering;* harshness, tyranny, maltreatment, oppression, persecution, intolerance 735n. *severity;* unkindness, cruelty, malignancy, malignity, spitefulness, spite 898n. *malevolence;* depravity, vice 934n. *wickedness;* sin 936n. *guilt;* bad influence, evil genius; evil spirit 970n. *demon;* ill wind, evil star 731n. *misfortune;* black magic, evil eye, hoodoo, jinx 983n. *sorcery;* curse 899n. *malediction;* snake in the grass 663 n. *trouble-maker;* bad character 904n. *evildoer.*
Adj. *bad*, arrant, vile, base, ill-conditioned; gross, black; utterly bad, irredeemable, as bad as bad can be; bad of its kind, poor, mean, wretched, measly, low-grade, not good enough, execrable, awful 35adj. *inferior;* no good, worthless, shoddy, ropy, punk 641adj. *useless;* unsatisfactory, faulty, flawed 647adj. *imperfect;* bad at, incompetent, inefficient, unskilled, skill-less 695adj. *clumsy;* badly done, mangled, spoiled 695adj. *bungled;* scruffy, filthy 649adj. *dirty;* foul, fulsome, noisome 397adj. *fetid* (**see** *not nice*); gone bad, rank, unfresh, unsound, affected, tainted 655adj. *deteriorated;* corrupt, decaying, decayed, rotten to the core 51adj. *decomposed;* peccant, disordered, infected, envenomed, poisoned, septic 651adj. *diseased;* irremediable, incurable; depraved, vicious, villainous, accursed 934adj. *wicked;* heinous, sinful 936 adj. *guilty;* wrongful, unjust 914adj. *wrong;* sinister 616adj. *evil* (**see** *harmful*); immeritorious, unworthy; shameful, scandalous 867adj. *discreditable;* sad, melancholy, lamentable, deplorable, pitiable, pitiful, woeful, grievous, sore 827adj. *distressing;* unendurable 827adj. *intolerable;* heavy, onerous, burdensome 684adj. *fatiguing;* too bad 827adj. *annoying.*
harmful, hurtful, scatheful; malefic, mischievous, wanton, outrageous 898 adj. *maleficent;* injurious, damaging, detrimental, prejudicial, disadvantageous, disserviceable 643adj. *inexpedient;* deleterious, corrosive, wasting, consuming 165adj. *destructive;* pernicious, fatal 362adj. *deadly;* costly 811adj. *dear;* disastrous, ruinous, calamitous 731adj. *adverse;* denant, unhealthy, unwholesome, noisome, miasmal, infectious 653adj. generative, noxious, malign, malig*insalubrious;* poisonous, venomous 653adj. *toxic;* unsafe, risky 661adj. *dangerous;* sinister, ominous, dire, dreadful, baleful, baneful, accursed 616adj. *evil;* spiteful, malicious, ill-conditioned, mischief-making, puckish, impish 898adj. *unkind;* bloody, bloodthirsty, inhuman 898adj. *cruel;* outrageous, rough, furious 176adj. *violent;* harsh, intolerant, persecuting 735adj. *oppressive.*
not nice, unlikable, obnoxious, poisonous, septic; nasty, beastly, horrid, horrible, ghastly, awful, dreadful, perfectly d.; scruffy 867adj. *disreputable;* foul, rotten, lousy, putrid, stinking, stinky, sickening, revolting, nauseous, nauseating 861adj. *disliked;* loathsome, detestable, abomi-

nable 888adj. *hateful;* vulgar, low, indecent, improper, gross, filthy, obscene 951adj. *impure;* shocking, disgusting, reprehensible, monstrous, horrendous 924adj. *disapproved;* plaguey, wretched, miserable 827adj. *annoying.*

damnable, damned, blasted, confounded, blinking, blankety-blank; execrable, accursed, cursed, hellish, infernal, devilish, diabolic, diabolical.

Vb. *harm,* do h., do a hurt, do a mischief, scathe 827vb. *hurt;* cost one dear 811vb. *be dear;* injure, damage, damnify 655vb. *impair;* corrupt 655vb. *pervert;* do no good 641vb. *be useless;* do evil, work e. 914vb. *do wrong;* molest, pain 827 vb. *torment;* plague, vex, trouble 827vb. *incommode;* land one in trouble, spite, mischief, be unkind 898 vb. *be malevolent.*

ill-treat, maltreat, mishandle, abuse 675vb. *misuse;* ill-use, burden, overburden, put upon, tyrannize, bear hard on, tread on, trample on, victimize, prey upon; persecute 735vb. *oppress;* wrong, aggrieve 914vb. *do wrong;* distress 827vb. *torment;* outrage, violate, force 176vb. *be violent;* savage, maul, bite, scratch, tear 655vb. *wound;* stab 263vb. *pierce;* bruise, buffet 279vb. *strike;* agonize, rack, crucify 963vb. *torture;* spite, use dispiteously, wreak one's malice on 898vb. *be malevolent;* crush 165n. *destroy.*

Adv. *badly,* amiss, wrong, ill; to one's cost; where the shoe pinches.

See: 35, 51, 61, 165, 176, 263, 279, 362, 377, 393, 397, 616, 641, 643, 647, 649, 651, 653, 655, 659, 661, 663, 675, 684, 695, 731, 735, 811, 825, 827, 861, 867, 888, 898, 899, 904, 914, 924, 934, 936, 951, 963, 970, 983.

646 Perfection

N. *perfection,* sheer p.; finish, classic quality; perfectness, the ideal; nothing wrong with, immaculacy, faultlessness, flawlessness; correctness, correctitude, irreproachability; impeccancy, impeccability, infallibility, indefectibility; transcendence 34n. *superiority;* quintessence, essence; peak, top 213n. *summit;* height *or* pitch of perfection, acme of p., pink of p., ne plus ultra, extreme, last word; chef d'oeuvre, flawless performance, chanceless innings 694 n. *masterpiece.*

paragon, nonesuch, nonpareil, flower, a beauty 644n. *exceller;* ideal, beau ideal, prince of; classic, pattern, pattern of perfection, standard, norm, model, mirror 23n. *prototype;* phoenix, rarity 84n. *rara avis;* superman, wonderman 864n. *prodigy.*

Adj. *perfect,* perfected, finished, brought to perfection, ripened; ripe, fully r. 669adj. *matured;* just right, ideal, flawless, faultless, impeccable, infallible, indefectible; correct, irreproachable; immaculate, unblemished, unflawed, unstained; spotless, unspotted, without blemish, without a stain; uncontaminated, pure 44adj. *unmixed;* guiltless 935adj. *innocent;* sound, uncracked, sound as a bell, right as a trivet, in perfect condition; tight, seaworthy; whole, entire, hundred per cent; complete 52adj. *intact;* dazzling, beyond praise 644 adj. *excellent;* consummate, unsurpassable 34adj. *supreme;* brilliant, masterly 694adj. *skillful;* pattern, standard, model, classic, classical, Augustan.

undamaged, safe and sound, with a whole skin, unhurt, unscathed, scatheless; unscarred, unscratched, unmarked; unmarred, unspoiled; unreduced, undiminished, without loss, whole, entire 52adj. *intact;* in the pink 650adj. *healthy.*

Vb. *perfect,* consummate, bring to perfection; ripen 669vb. *mature;* correct 654vb. *rectify;* put the finishing touch 213vb. *crown;* complete, leave nothing to be desired 725vb. *carry through.*

Adv. *perfectly,* flawlessly, impeccably, irreproachably, to perfection, as one would wish.

See: 23, 34, 44, 52, 84, 213, 644, 650, 654, 669, 694, 725, 935.

647 Imperfection

N. *imperfection,* imperfectness, not hundred per cent; room for improvement, not one's best; possibility of perfection, perfectibility 654n. *improvement;* faultiness, erroneousness, defectibility, fallibility 495n. *error;* patchiness, unevenness, curate's egg 17n. *non-uniformity;* immaturity, unripeness, underdevelopment 670n. *undevelopment;* defectiveness, incompletion, missing link, broken set 55n. *incompleteness;* lack, want 627 n. *requirement;* deficiency, inadequacy 636n. *insufficiency;* unsoundness 661n. *vulnerability;* failure, failing, weakness 307n. *shortcoming;* low standard, pass degree; inferior ver-

sion, poor relation 35n. *inferiority;* second best, pis aller, consolation prize, makeshift 150n. *substitute;* mediocrity, averageness 30n. *average;* loss of fitness, staleness 684n. *fatigue;* adulteration 43n. *mixture.*
defect, fault 495n. *error;* flaw, rift, leak, loophole, crack 201n. *gap;* deficiency, limitation 307n. *shortcoming;* kink, twist, screw loose 503n. *eccentricity;* weak point, soft spot, vulnerable point, chink in one's armor, Achilles' heel 661n. *vulnerability;* feet of clay, weak link in the chain 163n. *weakness;* scratch, taint, stain, spot, streak, touch of the tarbrush 845n. *blemish;* drawback, snag, fly in the ointment 702n. *obstacle;* half-blood 43n. *hybrid.*
Adj. *imperfect,* not quite right, not ideal, less than perfect, not classic; fallible, peccable; uneven, patchy, good in parts, like the curate's egg 17adj. *non-uniform;* faulty, botched 695adj. *bungled;* flawed, cracked; unstaunch, leaky, not proof; unsound 661adj. *vulnerable;* soiled, shop-s., tainted, stained, marked, scratched 845adj. *blemished;* not at one's best, below par, off form; stale 684adj. *fatigued;* off-color, not in the pink 651adj. *unhealthy;* not good enough, inadequate, deficient, wanting, lacking 636adj. *insufficient;* defective, not entire 55adj. *incomplete;* partial, broken 53adj. *fragmentary;* maimed, legless, armless 163adj. *crippled;* unfilled, half-filled, under-manned, short-handed, below strength, under complement 670adj. *unequipped;* half-finished 55adj. *unfinished;* unthorough, perfunctory 456adj. *inattentive;* over-wrought, over-elaborated, overdone 546adj. *exaggerated;* warped, twisted, distorted 246adj. *deformed;* mutilated, maimed, lame, halt 163adj. *weakened;* undeveloped, raw, crude, untrained, scratch 670adj. *immature;* makeshift, provisional, substitutionary, substitutional 150adj. *substituted;* secondary 639adj. *unimportant;* second-best, second-rate 35adj. *inferior;* poor, unimpressive, negative 645adj. *bad;* ordinary, much of a muchness, so-so, middling, middle-grade, average 30adj. *median;* moderate, unheroic; only passable, tolerable, bearable, better than nothing 923 adj. *approvable.*
Vb. *be imperfect,* fail of perfection, have a fault; be defective 307vb. *fall short;* lie open to criticism, not bear inspection, not pass muster, fail the test, dissatisfy 636vb. *not suffice;* barely pass, scrape through; fail of approval, not impress, not make the grade 924vb. *incur blame;* have feet of clay 163vb. *be weak;* show a crack, not hold water, leak 298vb. *flow out.*
Adv. *imperfectly,* to a limited extent, barely, almost, not quite, all but; with all its faults.
See: 17, 30, 35, 43, 53, 55, 150, 163, 201, 246, 298, 307, 456, 495, 503, 546, 627, 636, 639, 645, 651, 654, 661, 670, 684, 695, 702, 845, 923, 924. 924.

648 Cleanness

N. *cleanliness,* freedom from dirt, absence of dust, immaculateness 950n. *purity;* freshness, dewiness, whiteness; shine, polish, spit and polish; cleanliness, kid gloves, daintiness, dainty habits 862n. *fastidiousness.*
cleansing, clean, spring-c., dry-c.; washing, cleaning up, mopping up, washing up, wiping up; refining, clarification, purification, epuration; sprinkling, asperges, lustration, mundation, purgation; washing out, flushing; purging, defecation 302n. *excretion;* airing, ventilation, fumigation 338n. *vaporization;* deodorization 395n. *inodorousness;* antisepsis, sterilization, disinfection, disinfestation, delousing; sanitation, conservancy, drainage, sewerage, plumbing, water system 652n. *hygiene;* water closet, flush 649n. *latrine.*
ablution, washing, detersion; lavage, lavation, douche, flush, wash; balneation, bathing, dipping; soaping, scrubbing, sponging, rinsing, shampoo; dip 313n. *plunge;* bath, tub; bath-tub., wash-t., hip-bath, bidet; wash-basin, wash pot, ewer, lota; hot bath, cold b., steam b., vapor b., blanket b.; shower bath, shower, cold s.; Turkish bath, Russian b., Swedish b.; Finnish bath, sauna; wash-house, lavatory, bath-house, bathroom, washroom, public baths, thermae, hummum, sudatorium; plunge bath, swimming bath, swimming pool, natatorium; bathing machine; wash, laundry, home-l., washing machine, launderette.
cleanser, purifier; disinfectant, carbolic, quicklime, deodorant; soda, washing s., lye, spirit; fuller's earth, detergent, soap, scented s., soap flakes; water, hot water, soap and w.; wash, hair-w., mouth w., gargle,

lotion, hand-l.; cream, hand-c., face-c., glycerin; dentifrice, toothpaste, tooth-powder; pumice stone, hearth-s., holy-s.; polish, furniture p., boot p., blacking; wax, varnish; whitewash, paint 427n. *whiting;* blacklead 428n. *black pigment;* diuretic, pull-through 658n. *cathartic;* sewer, drain-pipe, waste-pipe 351n. *drain.*

cleaning utensil, broom, besom, mop, sponge, swab, swabber; washing board; duster, feather-d., whisk, brush, scrubbing-b., nail-b., toothbrush, toothpick, toothstick; dustpan, dustpan and brush, crumb-tray; dustbin, ashcan; carpet-sweeper, carpet-beater, vacuum cleaner; fulling mill; doormat, foot-scraper; scraper, tongue-s., strigil; squeegee, squilgee; pipe-cleaner, pull-through, reamer; windshield wiper; screen, sieve, riddle, strainer 263n. *porosity;* filter, air-f., oil-f., water-f.; blotter, eraser 550n. *obliteration;* comb, hair-c., pocket-c.; rake, hoe; snowplow, water-cart, dust-c.; sprinkler, hose 341n. *irrigator;* washing machine.

cleaning cloth, duster, jharan, dishcloth, dish-clout, dish-rag; glass-cloth, leather, wash-l.; buff, flannel, face-f., towel, hand-t., face-t., bath-t., peignoir; bib, handkerchief, paper h., tissue; face-cloth, sudary, sweat-rag; napery, napkin, table-n., table-mat, doily, tablecloth; mat, drugget 226n. *floor-cover;* cover, chair-c., dust-c. 226n. *coverlet.*

cleaner, refiner, distiller; dry cleaner, launderer, laundryman, laundress, washer-woman, dhobi; fuller; scrub, scrubber, swabber; washer-up, dishwasher, scullion, masalchi; charwoman, char, help; scavenger, dustman, sweeper, road-s., crossing-s.; lavatory attendant, sanitary engineer; chimney-sweep, window-cleaner; shoeblack, shoe-shiner; barber, hairdresser 843n. *beautician;* gleaner, picker; scavenger bird, crow, vulture, kite.

Adj. clean, dirt-free; whitened 427 adj. *white;* polished, clean, bright, shiny, shining 417adj. *undimmed;* cleanly, dainty, nice 862adj. *fastidious;* dewy, fresh; cleaned, well-c., washed etc.vb.; shaven, shorn, barbered, trimmed; cleaned up, laundered, starched; spruce, natty, spick and span, neat, tidy 60adj. *orderly;* deodorized, disinfected, aseptic, antiseptic, hygienic, sterilized, sterile 652adj. *salubrious;* pure, purified, refined, immaculate, spotless, stainless, unsoiled, unmuddied, untarnished, unsullied 646adj. *perfect;* untouched, blank; ritually clean, kosher 301adj. *edible.*

cleansing, lustral, purificatory; disinfectant; hygienic; purgative, purgatory; detergent, abstersive; ablutionary, balneal.

Vb. *clean,* spring-clean, clean up; take the dirt off, lay the dust; valet, spruce, neaten, trim 62vb. *arrange;* wash, wipe, wash clean, wipe c., wash up, wipe up, dry, wring, wring out; sponge, mop, mop up, swab, wash down; scrub, scour; flush, flush out; holystone, scrape 333vb. *rub;* do the washing, launder, starch, iron; buck, bleach, dry-clean; soap, lather, shampoo; bathe, dip, rinse, sluice, douche 341vb. *drench;* dust, whisk, sweep, sweep up, broom, beat, vacuum-clean; brush, brush up; comb, rake; buff, polish; shine, black, blacklead 417vb. *make bright;* whitewash 427vb. *whiten;* blot, erase 550vb. *obliterate;* strip, pick, pick clean, clean out, clear, clear out, rake o., make a clean sweep 300vb. *eject.*

purify, purge, clean up; bowdlerize, expurgate; sublimate, elevate 654vb. *make better;* cleanse, lave, lustrate, asperge; purify oneself, wash one's hands of; freshen, ventilate, fan, deodorize, fumigate; edulcorate, desalt 392vb. *sweeten;* disinfect, sterilize, antisepticize, chlorinate, pasteurize 652vb. *sanitate;* free from impurities, depurate, refine, distill, clarify, rack, skim, scum, despumate; decarbonize; elutriate, strain, filter, percolate, lixiviate, leach 341 vb. *drench;* sift, winnow, van, bolt, riddle, screen, sieve 44vb. *eliminate;* sort out, weed; flush, clean out, wash o., drain 652vb. *sanitate.*

See: 44, 60, 62, 226, 263, 300, 301, 302, 313, 333, 338, 341, 351, 392, 395, 417, 427, 428, 550, 646, 649, 652, 654, 658, 843, 862, 950.

649 Uncleanness

N. *uncleanness,* immundity, immundicity, uncleanliness, dirty habits, wallowing, beastliness; dirtiness (**see** *dirt*); muckiness, miriness 347n. *marsh;* soilure, soiliness; scruffiness, scurfiness, filthiness; lousiness, pediculosis, phthiriasis; squalidity, squalidness, squalor, slumminess 801n. *poverty;* untidiness, sluttishness, slovenliness 61n. *disorder;* stink 397n. *fetor;* pollution, defilement, defedation; corruption, taint, tainting, putrescence, putrefaction 51n. *decomposition;* contamination 651n. *infection;* abomination, scatology, obscenity 951n. *impurity;* unwashed body, dirty linen.

dirt, filth, stain, patch, blot; muck, mud, clay 344n. *soil;* quagmire, bog 347n. *marsh;* night-soil, dung, ordure, feces, stool 302n. *excrement;* snot, mucus; dust, mote 332n. *pulverulence;* cobweb, grime, smut, smudge, soot, smoke; grounds, grouts, dregs, lees, heeltap; sordes, sweepings, rinsings, scourings, offscourings 41n. *leavings;* sediment, sedimentation, deposit, precipitate, residuum, fur; scum, off-scum, dross, froth; scoriae, ashes, cinders, clinker, slag 381n. *ash;* recrement, waste product; drainage, sewerage; cast-offs, cast skin, exuviae, slough; scurf, dandruff; furfur, tartar, argol; pus, matter, feculence; raff, refuse, garbage 641n. *rubbish;* rot, dry-r., wet-r., rust, mildew, mold, fungus 51n. *decay;* carrion, offal; flea, nit 365n. *vermin.*

swill, pig-s., hogwash, draff; bilge, bilge-water; ditch-w., dish-w., slops; sewage, drainage; wallow, hog-w., sough.

latrine, privy, jakes, bogs, necessary house, comfort-station; closet, earth-c., water c., WC; indoor sanitation, out-door sanitation, septic tank; cloakroom, lavatory, loo, toilet; urinal, public convenience; close-stool, commode, thunderbox, bedpan, jerry 302n. *cacation.*

sink, sink of corruption; kitchen sink, draining board; cesspool, sump, slough; gutter, sewer, main, cloaca 351n. *drain;* laystall, dunghill, midden, rubbish-heap, dust-h., compost-h.; dustbin, trash-can, garbage-c., gubbins 194n. *vessel;* dust-hole 194n. *cellar;* colluvies, Augean stables, sty, pig-s., pigpen 192n. *stable;* slum, tenement 192n. *housing;* shambles 362n. *slaughter-house;* plague-spot 651n. *infection;* spittoon, cuspidor.

dirty person, sloven, slattern, slammerkin, drab, draggletail, traipse 61 n. *slut;* litterer, litter lout; mudlark, street-arab; dustman, sweep, chimney-s., scavenger 648n. *cleaner;* beast, pig, wallower, leper.

Adj. *unclean*, unhallowed, unholy 980 adj. *profane;* obscene, corrupt 951 adj. *impure;* coarse, unrefined, unpurified; septic, festering, poisonous 653adj. *toxic;* unsterilized, non-sterile 653adj. *infectious;* squalid, slummy 653adj. *insalubrious;* foul, offensive, nasty, noisome, abominable, disgusting, repulsive, nauseous, nauseating, stinking, malodorous 397adj. *fetid;* uncleanly, unfastidious, beastly, hoggish; scrofulous, scruffy, scurfy, scorbutic, impetiginous; leprous, scabby; lousy, pediculous, crawling; fecal, dungy, stercoraceous, excrementitious 302adj. *excretory;* carious, rotting, rotted, tainted, high; fly-blown, maggoty, carrion 51adj. *decomposed.*

dirty, filthy; dusty, grimy, sooty, smoky, snuffy; thick with dust, unswept, ungarnished, Augean; untidy, unkempt, slovenly, sluttish, bedraggled 61adj. *disordered;* unsoaped, unwashed, unwashen, unscoured, unrinsed, unwiped; black, dingy, uncleaned, unpolished, unburnished; tarnished, stained, soiled; greasy, oily; clotted, caked, matted, begrimed, collied; messy, mucky, muddy, slimy 347adj. *marshy;* thick, turbid; dreggy, scummy; musty, fusty, cobwebby; moth-eaten, threadbare, patched 801adj. *beggarly.*

Vb. *be unclean,*—dirty etc. adj.; get dirty, collect dust, foul up, clog; rust, mildew, molder, fester, gangrene, mortify, putrify, rot, go bad, addle 51vb. *decompose;* grow rank, smell 397vb. *stink;* wallow, roll in the mud.

make unclean, foul, befoul; dirty, dirt, soil; grime, begrime, cover with dust; stain, blot, sully, tarnish; muck, mess, untidy 61vb. *disorder;* daub, smirch, smut, smutch, smudge, blur, smoke 419vb. *bedim;* spot, patch, maculate 437vb. *variegate;* streak, smear, besmear, grease; cake, clog, bemire, beslime, muddy, roil, rile; draggle, drabble, daggle; spatter, bespatter, splash, slobber, slubber, slaver 341vb. *moisten;* poison, taint, infect, contaminate 655vb. *impair;* corrupt 655vb. *pervert;* pollute, defile, profane, desecrate, unhallow 980vb. *be impious.*

See: 41, 51, 61, 192, 194, 302, 332, 341, 344, 347, 351, 362, 365, 381, 397, 419, 437, 641, 648, 651, 653, 655, 801, 951, 980.

650 Health

N. *health*, rude h., robust h., good h.; healthiness, good constitution, health and strength 162n. *vitality;* fitness, condition, good c., pink of condition; bloom, rosiness, rosy cheeks; well-being, physical w.; eupepsia 376n. *euphoria;* whole skin, soundness; incorruption, incorruptibility 644n. *goodness;* long life, longevity, ripe old age 131n. *age;* hygiene, healthy state, clean bill of health; goddess of health, Hygeia.

Adj. *healthy*, healthful, wholesome, hygienic, sanitary 652adj. *salubrious;* in health, in good h., bursting with h., eupeptic, euphoric; fresh, blooming, ruddy, rosy, rosy-cheeked, florid; hale, hearty, hale and hearty, sound, fit, well, fine, bobbish, full of beans; of good constitution, never ill, robust, hardy, strong, vigorous, robustious, staunch 162adj. *stalwart;* fighting fit, in condition, in good condition, in the pink, in good case, in good heart, in fine fettle, in fine feather; sound in wind and limb, sound as a bell, sound as a roach, fit as a fiddle; fresh as a daisy, fresh as April; a picture of health, feeling good; getting well, convalescent, on the up-grade, well again, on one's legs 656adj. *restored;* pretty well, no worse, as well as can be expected; safe and sound, unharmed 646adj. *undamaged;* fat and well-liking.

Vb. *be healthy*,—well etc. adj.; mind one's health, look after oneself; feel fine, bloom, flourish, enjoy good health; be in the pink, have never felt better; wear well, look young; keep one's health, keep fit, keep well, keep body and soul together, keep on one's legs; have a clean bill of health, have no mortality.

get healthy,—fit etc.adj.; recuperate, be well again, return to health, recover one's health, get the color back in one's cheeks; mend, convalesce, become convalescent, take a fresh lease on life, become a new man 656vb. *revive.*

See: 131, 162, 376, 644, 646, 652, 656.

651 Ill-health. Disease

N. *ill-health*, bad h., delicate h., failing h.; delicacy, weak constitution, unhealthiness, weakliness, infirmity, debility 163n. *weakness;* seediness, loss of condition, manginess; morbidity, indisposition, cachexia; chronic complaint, allergy, hay-fever, catarrh; chronic ill-health, invalidism, valetudinarianism, hypochondria, medicine habit.

illness, loss of health 655n. *deterioration;* affliction, disability, handicap, infirmity, inanition 163n. *weakness;* sickness, ailment, complaint, complication; condition, history of; bout of sickness, visitation, attack, acute a.; spasm, stroke, seizure, apoplexy, fit; shock, shellshock; sign of illness, headache, migraine 377n. *pain;* temperature, feverishness, fever, shivers, shakes, rigor 318n. *spasm;* pyrexia, calenture; delirium 503n. *frenzy;* break-down, collapse, prostration; last illness 36n. *decease;* sick-bed, deathbed.

disease, malady, distemper, disorder; epidemic disease, endemic d.; congenital disease; occupational disease; deficiency disease, malnutrition, avitaminosis, beri-beri, pellagra, rickets, scurvy; degenerative disease, wasting d., marasmus, atrophy; traumatic disease, trauma; organic disease, functional d., circulatory d., neurological d., nervous d., epilepsy, falling sickness; musculoskeletal disease; cardiovascular d.; endocrine disease, diabetes; urogenital disease; hemopoietic disease; dermatological disease; neoplasmic disease; respiratory disease; gastrointestinal disease; infectious disease, communicable d.; virus disease, bacillary d., waterborne d., filth d.; brain disease 503n. *insanity;* febrile disease, sweating sickness; hydrocele, dropsy.

plague, pest, scourge 659n. *bane;* pestilence, murrain, infection, contagion; epidemic, pandemic; pneumonic plague, bubonic p., black death.

infection, contagion, miasma, pollution, taint; infectiousness, contagiousness 653n. *insalubrity;* toxicity, sepsis, poisoning 659n. *poison;* plague-spot, hotbed; vector, carrier, germ-c.; virus, bacillus, bacteria, germ, pathogen; blood-poisoning, toxemia, septicemia; food-poisoning, ptomaine p., botulism; gastroenteritis, diarrhea and vomiting, D and V; pyrogenic infection, pyrogenesis, pyemia, suppuration, festering, purulence; infectious disease, cold, common c., influenza, diphtheria, pneumonia; measles, morbilli; German measles, rubella; whooping-cough, pertussis; mumps, parotitis; scarlet fever, scarlatina; chicken-pox, varicella; smallpox, variola; cholera morbus, cholera, Asiatic c.; blackwater fever, yellow f., kala azar, dengue; typhus, prison fever, trench f.; typhoid, paratyphoid; glandular fever; encephalitis, meningitis; poliomyelitis, polio-

encephalitis; tetanus, lockjaw; gangrene.
malaria, ague, malarial fever, remittent f., quotidian f., quartern f., tertian f., benign, tertian, subtertian, malignant s.; enlarged spleen.
dysentery, protozoal d., amoebic d., bacillary d., blood d.; diarrhea, loose stool 302n. *cacation;* diarrhea and vomiting, gastroenteritis; enteritis; colitis.
indigestion, fat i., steatorrhea; dyspepsia, liverishness, liver spots, dizziness, vertigo; biliousness, nausea, vomiting, retching; flatulence, wind; acidosis, heartburn; colic, gripes; gastralgia, stomach-ache, tummy a., belly a.; stomach ulcer, peptic u.; stomach disorder, gastritis, esophagitis, duodenitis; jaundice, hepatogenous j., hematogenous j., toxic j.; cholecystitis, cholelithiasis, gallstones, biliary calculus; constipation, autointoxication.
respiratory disease, cough, cold, sore throat, common cold, infectious catarrh, coryza; rhinitis, rhinorrhea; sinusitis, frontal s., maxillary s., sphenoidal s., ethmoidal s.; tonsilitis, pharyngitis; laryngitis, laryngotracheitis, tracheitis, perichondritis; bronchitis; asthma; pneumonia, bronchopneumonia; diphtheria; whooping-cough, pertussis.
heart disease, cardiac d., cardiovascular d.; carditis, pancarditis, endocarditis, myocarditis, pericarditis, angina pectoris; breast-pang, heartstroke, chest-spasm; brachycardia; tachycardia; gallop rhythm, palpitation, dyspnea; valvular lesion; enlarged heart, cardiac hypertrophy, athlete's heart; fatty degeneration of the heart; heart condition, bad heart, weak h.
blood pressure, high blood p., hypertension; hypotension, low blood pressure; vascular disease, atheroma, aneurysm; angiospasm; hardened arteries, arteriosclerosis; arteritis, endarteritis, aortitis; phlebitis, thrombophlebitis, varicose veins; thrombosis, coronary t., clot, blood-c.
blood disease, anemia, aplastic a., hemolytic a., pernicious a., leukemia; hemophilia; hemorrhage.
phthisis, wasting disease, consumptiveness, decline, graveyard cough, tuberculosis, consumption, galloping c.
carcinosis, epithelioma, cancer; neoplasm, growth; tumor, indolent t., benign t.; malignant tumor, cancerous growth; melanoma, black cancer.
skin disease, cutaneous d.; mange; leucoderma; leprosy; albinism; dermatitis, erythema, flush; erysipelas, St. Anthony's fire, the rose; tetters, impetigo, herpes, herpes zoster, shingles; eczema, serpigo, ringworm, itch, dhobies i. 378n. *formication;* hives, urticaria; rash, eruption, breaking out, ecchymosis, acne, spots, macule, pustule, favus, papule, vesicle, pimple, blister, wart, verruca 253n. *swelling;* miliaria, yaws, framboesia; athlete's foot, Bengal rot, Singapore ear; mole, freckle, birthmark, pockmark 845n. *blemish;* dry skin, xeroma, xeroderma; cowpox, vaccinia; pox, smallpox, chicken-pox.
venereal disease, French disease, pox; syphilis, gonorrhea, clap; venereal ulcer, chancre, syphilitic sore.
ulcer, ulceration, gathering, festering, purulence; inflammation, -itis; sore, impostume, abscess, fistula; blain, chilblain, kibe; corn, hard c., soft c. 253n. *swelling;* gangrene, rot 51n. *decay;* discharge, pus, matter.
rheumatism, rheumatics; articular rheumatism, rheumatic fever; muscular rheumatism, myalgia; fibrositis; frozen shoulder; arthritis, rheumatoid a.; gout.
paralysis, involuntary movements, palsy, tic, tremor 318n. *spasm;* general paralysis, atrophy 375n. *insensibility;* cerebral paralysis, stroke, spasm, seizure, hemiplagia, diplegia, paraplegia; petit mal, epilepsy, falling sickness; infantile paralysis, poliomyelitis, polio; arthropathy, spasticity; Parkinson's disease; sleeping sickness.
animal disease, veterinary d.; distemper, foot-and-mouth disease; rinderpest, murrain; splenic disease, anthrax, sheep rot, bloat; pine; megrims, staggers; glanders, farcy, sweeny, spavin, thrush; psittacosis; hard pad; mange.
sick person, sick man, sufferer; patient, in-p., out-p.; case, stretcher-c., hospital-c.; mental case 504n. *madman;* invalid, chronic i., chronic; valetudinarian, hypochondriac, martyr to ill-health; consumptive, asthmatic, bronchitic, dyspeptic, diabetic; hemophiliac, bleeder; insomniac; neuropath, addict, alcoholic; spastic, arthritic, paralytic; crock, old c., cripple 163n. *weakling;* sick-list.

pathology, case-making, diagnosis, prognosis; etiology, nosology, epidemiology, bacteriology, parasitology 658n. *therapy*.

Adj. *unhealthy*, healthless, unsound, sickly; infirm, decrepit, weakly 163 adj. *weak;* delicate, of weak constitution, liable to illness, always ill; in bad health, in poor h.; in poor condition, mangy; undernourished, under-vitaminized 636adj. *underfed;* sallow, pale 426adj. *colorless;* bilious 433adj. *yellow;* invalid, valetudinarian, hypochondriac.

sick, ill, unwell, not well, indisposed, out of sorts, under the weather, off-color; poorly, seedy, squeamish, groggy, queer, ailing; sickening for, showing symptoms of; feverish, headachy; confined, laid up, bedridden, on one's back, in bed, in hospital, on the sick-list, invalided; seized, taken ill, taken bad; prostrate, collapsed; on the danger list, not allowed visitors; chronic, incurable, inoperable; mortally ill, moribund 361adj. *dying;* peaky, drooping, flagging, pining, languishing, wasting away, in a decline.

diseased, pathological, disordered, distempered; affected, infected, plague-stricken; contaminated, tainted, vitiated, tabid, rotten, rotting, gangrenous 51adj. *decomposed;* peccant, morbid, morbose, morbific, pathogenic; infectious, poisonous, festering, purulent 653adj. *toxic;* measly, morbillous; degenerative, consumptive, phthisical, tuberculous, tubercular; diabetic, dropsical, hydrocephalic; anemic; bloodless, leukemic, hemophilic; arthritic, rheumatic, rheumatoid, rheumaticky; rickety, palsied, paralyzed, paralytic, spastic; leprous, leucodermatous; carcinomatous, cancerous, cankered; syphilitic, venereal; swollen, edematous; gouty; bronchial, throaty, bronchitic, croupy, coughy, coldy; asthmatic; allergic; pyretic, febrile, fevered, shivering, aguish, feverish, delirious; sore, tender; ulcerous, fistular; ulcerated, inflamed; rashy, spotty, erythematous, erysipelatous; spavined, broken-winded; mangy.

Vb. *be ill*, —sick etc.adj.; enjoy ill-health; ail, suffer, labor under, have treatment; have a complaint, have an affliction, be a chronic invalid; not feel well, complain of; feel queer etc. adj.; lose one's health, sicken, fall sick, fall ill; catch, take an infection, contract a disease; break out with, break out in; be seized, be stricken, be taken, be taken bad, not feel so good; have a stroke, collapse; be laid up, take to one's bed, go to hospital, become a patient; languish, pine, peak, droop, waste away, go into a decline, fall into a consumption; fail, flag, lose strength, get worse 655vb. *deteriorate;* grow weak 163vb. *be weak;* gather, fester, suppurate.

Adv. *morbidly*, unhealthily 653adv. *unwholesomely;* in sickness; in hospital, in the doctor's hands, under treatment.

See: 51, 163, 253, 302, 318, 361, 375, 377, 378, 426, 433, 503, 504, 636, 653, 655, 658, 659, 845.

652 Salubrity

N. *salubrity*, healthiness, state of health; well-being 650n. *health;* salubriousness, healthfulness, wholesomeness; ventilation, fresh air, open a., sea a., ozone 340n. *air;* sunshine, out-doors; fine climate, genial c. 340n. *weather*.

hygiene, sanitation, cleanliness 648n. *cleanness*; preventive medicine, prophylaxis 658n. *prophylactic;* quarantine, cordon sanitaire 660n. *protection;* immunity, immunization, inoculation, autoinoculation, vaccination, pasteurization; antisepsis, sterilization, disinfection, chlorination; sanitarium, sanatorium, spa 658n. *hospital;* hot-springs, thermae 658n. *therapy;* keeping fit, exercise, outdoor e., tonic e.; science of health, hygiology, hygienics.

sanitarian, hygienist, sanitationist, sanitary inspector, public health officer; sanitary engineer; Public Health Department; fresh-air fiend, sun-worshiper, nudist.

Adj. *salubrious*, healthful, healthy, wholesome; pure, fresh 648adj. *clean;* ventilated 340adv. *airy;* tonic, bracing, invigorating, refreshing, sanative 656adj. *restorative;* hygienic, sanitary, disinfected, chlorinated, pasteurized, sterilized, sterile, aseptic, antiseptic; prophylactic, immunizing, protective 658adj. *remedial;* good for, salutary, what the doctor ordered 644adj. *beneficial;* nutritious, nourishing, health-preserving; uninjurious, harmless, benign, non-malignant; uninfectious, non-infectious, innoxious, innocuous; immune, immunized, vaccinated, inoculated, protected 660adj. *invulnerable*.

Vb. *be salubrious*, —bracing etc.adj.; be good for one's health, agree with one, make one fit; have a good climate; prevent disease; keep fit 650vb. *be healthy.*

sanitate, disinfect, sterilize, antisepticize, chlorinate, pasteurize; immunize, inoculate, vaccinate; quarantine, put in q., isolate, segregate 833vb. *seclude;* ventilate, freshen 648vb. *purify;* cleanse 648vb. *clean;* drain 342vb. *dry;* conserve 666vb. *preserve.*

Adv. *healthily*, wholesomely, salubriously, hygienically.

See: 340, 342, 644, 648, 650, 656, 658, 660, 666, 883.

653 Insalubrity

N. *insalubrity*, unhealthiness, unwholesomeness; uncleanliness, lack of hygiene, lack of sanitation; dirty habits, verminousness 649n. *uncleanness;* unhealthy conditions, unwholesome surroundings; mephitism, bad air, bad climate; infectiousness, contagiousness; bad drains, slum, sewer 649n. *sink;* infectious person, carrier, germ-c., vector; plague-spot, pesthouse, contagion 651n. *infection;* pollution, radioactivity, fall-out; deadliness, poisonousness 659n. *bane;* non-naturals.

Adj. *insalubrious*, unwholesome, unhealthful, unhealthy; bad for one's health, insanitary, unhygienic; ungenial, bad, nasty, noxious, noisome, injurious 645adj. *harmful;* verminous, infested; undrained 347adj. *marshy;* foul, polluted, undrinkable, inedible; indigestible, unnutritious, non-vitaminous; unsound, unfresh, stale, gone bad 655adj. *deteriorated;* unventilated, windowless, airless; stuffy; overheated, underheated.

infectious, morbific, morbiferous, pathogenic; infective, germ-laden; zymotic; contagious, catching, taking, communicable; pestiferous, pestilent, pestful, plaguey, plague-stricken; malarious, malarial, aguish; epidemic, pandemic, endemic; epizootic, enzootic, sporadic; unsterilized, non-sterile, infected 649adj. *dirty.*

toxic, narcotic, azotic; poisonous, mephitic, pestilential, germ-laden; venomous, envenomed, poisoned, steeped in poison; septic, pussy, mattery, gathering, festering, purulent, suppurating; mortiferous 362 adj. *deadly.*

Adv. *unwholesomely*, insalubriously, poisonously; unhealthily, unhygienically 651adv. *morbidly.*

See: 347, 362, 645, 649, 651, 655, 659.

654 Improvement

N. *improvement*, betterment, uplift, amelioration, melioration; good influence, the making of 178n. *influence;* change for the better, transfiguration 143n. *transformation;* conversion, new leaf 939n. *penitence;* revival, recovery 656n. *restoration;* evolution, development, perfectibility; elaboration, enrichment; decoration 844n. *ornamentation;* advance, onward march, march of time, progress 285n. *progression;* furtherance, advancement, preferment, promotion, kick upstairs, rise, raise, lift, jump 308n. *ascent;* uptrend, upswing 310n. *elevation;* revaluation, enhancement 36n. *increase.*

amendment, mending etc.vb.; mend 656n. *repair;* organization, better o. 62n. *arrangement;* reformation, reform, radical r. (**see** *reformism*); Borstal, reformatory, house of correction 539n. *school*; purification, sublimation 648n. *cleansing;* refining, rectification, putting right, removal of errors; redaction, castigation, correction, revision, red ink, blue pencil; emendation, happy conjecture; recension, revised edition, new e., improved version 589n. *edition;* revise, proof, corrected copy; second thoughts, better t., review, reconsideration, reexamination; further reflection 67n. *sequel;* polish, finishing touch 725n. *completion;* perfectionism 862n. *fastidiousness.*

civilization, culture, kultur; civility, refinement 846n. *good taste;* training 534n. *education;* cultivation, polish, improvement of the mind, menticulture; improvement of the race, eugenics; physical culture, calisthenics 682n. *exercise;* telesis, euthenics.

reformism, meliorism, perfectionism, idealism; radicalism; extremism, revolution 738n. *sedition;* minimalism, maximalism; progressivism, progressism, onward-and-upward department; gradualism, Fabianism; social adjustment 901n. *sociology.*

reformer, improver, repairer, restorer 656n. *mender;* emender, corrector, castigator, editor, reviser, second hand; progressive, progressist, progressionist; minimalist, gradualist, Fabian 625n. *moderate;* radical, extremist, maximalist, revolutionary 738n. *agitator;* communist, Marxist, red; reformist, new dealer; idealist, utopian 862n. *perfectionist;* sociologist, social worker, muckraker, slummer 901n. *philanthropist.*

Adj. *improved,* bettered, enhanced; touched up 843adj. *beautified;* reformed, revised 34adj. *superior;* better, better off, all the better for; better advised, wiser 498adj. *wise;* improvable, corrigible, curable, reformable, perfectible.

improving, reformative, reformatory, remedial, medicinal 656adj. *restorative;* reforming, reformist, progressive, radical; civilizing, cultural, acultural; idealistic, perfectionist, utopian, millenarian, chiliastic; perfectionist 862n. *fastidious.*

Vb. *get better,* grow b., improve, mend, take a turn for the better, turn the corner; pick up, rally, revive, recover 656vb. *be restored;* make progress, advance, develop, evolve 285vb. *progress;* mellow, ripen 669vb. *mature;* fructify 171vb. *be fruitful;* rise 308vb. *ascend;* graduate 727vb. *succeed;* rise in the world, better oneself, make one's way 730vb. *prosper;* mend one's ways, reform, turn a new leaf, go straight 939n. *be penitent;* improve oneself, learn by experience 536vb. *learn;* take advantage of, make capital out of, cash in on 137vb. *profit by.*

make better, better, improve, ameliorate, meliorate, reform; make improvements, improve upon, refine u.; polish, elaborate, enrich, enhance; improve out of recognition, transfigure 147n. *transform;* make, be the making of, have a good influence, leaven 178vb. *influence;* refine, uplift, elevate, sublimate 648 vb. *purify;* moralize; civilize, socialize, teach manners; mend 656vb. *repair;* restore 656vb. *cure;* recruit, revive, infuse fresh blood into 685 vb. *refresh;* soften, lenify, mitigate, palliate, lessen an evil 177vb. *moderate;* forward, advance, upgrade 285 vb. *promote;* foster, fatten, mellow 669vb. *mature;* make the most of, get the best out of 673vb. *use;* develop, open up, reclaim; plant, till, dress, water 370vb. *cultivate;* weed 44vb. *eliminate;* tidy, tidy up, neaten 62vb. *arrange;* spruce, freshen, valet, freshen up 648vb. *clean;* do up, vamp up, tone up, tighten up; renovate, refurbish, reface, renew; bring up to date 126vb. *modernize;* touch up 841vb. *beautify;* improve on nature, make up, titivate 843vb. *primp;* embellish, adorn, ornament 844vb. *decorate;* straighten, straighten out (**see** *rectify*).

rectify, refine 648vb. *purify;* put right, set right, straighten, straighten out 24vb. *adjust;* mend, patch 656vb. *repair;* correct, make corrections, blue-pencil, proofread, remove errors; revise, redact, edit, amend, emend; rewrite, redraft, retell, recast, remold, refashion, remodel, new-model, recreate, refound, reform; reorganize 62vb. *regularize;* make improvements, streamline; review, reexamine, reconsider; correct one's mistakes, stop in time, think again, think better of, have second thoughts; appeal from Philip drunk to Philip sober.

See: 24, 32, 34, 36, 44, 62, 67, 126, 137, 147, 171, 177, 178, 285, 308, 310, 370, 498, 534, 536, 539, 589, 625, 648, 656, 669, 673, 682, 685, 725, 727, 730, 738, 841, 843, 844, 846, 862, 901, 939.

655 Deterioration

N. *deterioration,* debasement, coarsening; cheapening, devaluation; retrogradation, retrogression, slipping back, losing ground 286n. *regression;* reversion to type, throw-back 5n. heredity; decline, declension, declination, ebb 37n. *decrease;* twilight, obscuration, fading 419n. *dimness;* falling off, down-trend, slump, depression 290n. *recession;* impoverishment 801n. *poverty;* law of diminishing returns; Gresham's law; Malthusianism; exhaustion, consumption 634n. *waste;* vitiation, corruption, perversion, prostitution, depravation, demoralization, degeneration, loss of morale, degeneracy, degenerateness, decadence, depravity 934n. *wickedness;* downward course, primrose path 309n. *descent;* recidivism 603n. *tergiversation;* setback 657n. *relapse;* bad ending, tragedy 731n. *ill fortune.*

dilapidation, caducity, collapse, ruination 165n. *destruction;* lack of maintenance, disrepair, neglect 458 n. *negligence;* slum, backstreet 801 n. *poverty;* ravages of time, wear and tear, erosion, corrosion, oxidization, rustiness, rust, moth and rust, canker, corruption, gangrene, rot, dry-r., rottenness 51n. *decay;* moldiness, mildew 659n. *blight;* decrepitude, senility 131n. *age;* marasmus, atrophy 651n. *disease;* shadow, shadow of one's former self, ruin, wreck, mere w., perfect w., physical w., shotten herring.

impairment, spoiling 675n. *misuse;* detriment, damage, inroad, waste 772n. *loss;* discoloration, weathering, patina; pollution, inquination, defilement, corruption, defedation 649n. *uncleanness;* ulceration, venenation, poisoning, intoxication, autointoxication, suppuration, contamination, contagion 651n. *infection;* adulteration, sophistication, watering down, alloy 43n. *mixture;* assault, insult, outrage 712n. *attack;* ruination, dilaceration, demolishment 165n. *destruction;* injuriousness, injury, mischief, ravage, scathe, harm 165n. *havoc;* disablement, crippling, laming, hobbling, nobbling, disabling, mutilation, weakening 163n. *weakness;* disorganization, bedevilment, sabotage 63n. *derangement;* exacerbation 832n. *aggravation.*

wound, injury, trauma; open wound, fresh w., bloody nose; sore, running s. 651n. *ulcer;* laceration, lesion; cut, gash, incision, abrasion, scratch 46 n. *scission;* stab, prick, jab, puncture 263n. *perforation;* contusion, bruise, bump, discoloration, black eye, thick ear 253n. *swelling;* burn, scald; rupture, broken head, broken bones 46n. *disjunction;* scar, mark, cicatrice 845n. *blemish.*

Adj. *deteriorated*, not improved, the worse for; exacerbated 832adj. *aggravated;* spoiled, impaired, damaged, hurt, ruined etc.vb.; worn out, effete, exhausted, shotten, worthless 641adj. *useless;* stale, gone bad, rotten 645adj. *bad;* corked, flat 387 adj. *tasteless;* undermined, sapped, honeycombed, shaken 163adj. *weakened;* tired, over-t., done up 684adj. *fatigued;* no better, deteriorating, worse, getting w., worse and worse, in a bad way; failing, past one's best, declining, in decline, on the d.; aging, senile, senescent 131adj. *aged;* on the way out, on the downgrade, on the downward path; falling, slipping, nodding, tottering, deciduous 309adj. *descending;* faded, withered, sere, decaying 51adj. *decomposed;* consuming, wasting, wasting away, ebbing, at low ebb; slumping, falling off 37adj. *decreasing;* degenerative, retrogressive, retrograde, unprogressive, unimproved, backward 286adj. *regressive;* lapsed, recidivist 603adj. *tergiversating;* degenerate, depraved, vitiated, corrupt 934adj. *vicious;* come down in the world, impoverished 801adj. *poor.*

dilapidated, the worse for wear, in ruins, in shreds; broken, in bits, in pieces; cracked, battered, weatherbeaten; decrepit, ruinous, ramshackle, tottery, tumbledown, on its last legs; slummy, condemned; worn, well-w., frayed, shabby, tatty, holey, in holes, in tatters, in rags; worn out, worn to a frazzle, worn to a shadow, done for 641adj. *useless;* seedy, down at heel, down and out 801adj. *poor;* rusty, rotten, mildewed, moldering, moss-grown, moth-eaten, worm-e., dog-eared 51 adj. *decomposed;* dingy, drab.

Vb. *deteriorate*, not improve, get no better; worsen, get worse, go from bad to worse; slip, slide, go downhill, take the downgrade; not maintain 657vb. *relapse;* fall off, slump, decline, wane, ebb, sink, fail 37vb. *decrease;* slip back, retrograde 286 vb. *regress;* lapse 603vb. *tergiversate;* degenerate, lose morale; tread the primrose path, go to the bad, spoil oneself, ruin o. 934vb. *be wicked;* collapse, break down, fall, totter, droop, stoop 309vb. *tumble;* contract, shrink 198vb. *become small;* wear out, age 131vb. *grow old;* fade, wither, wilt, shrivel, perish, crumble, molder, mildew, grow moss, grow weeds; bolt, run to seed; weather, rust, rot, decay 51vb. *decompose;* spoil, stale, fust, lose its sap, lose its taste, lose its flavor, grow stale, go flat, cork 391vb. *be unpalatable;* go bad, smell 397vb. *stink;* corrupt, putrefy, rankle, fester, suppurate, gangrene, sicken 651vb. *be ill;* do worse, make things worse, jump from the frying pan into the fire, go farther and fare worse 832 vb. *aggravate.*

pervert, deform, warp, twist 246vb. *distort;* abuse, prostitute 675vb. *misuse;* demoralize, deprave, deflower 951vb. *debauch;* vitiate, corrupt 934vb. *make wicked;* lower, degrade, debase, embase 311vb. *abase;* brutalize, dehumanize, barbarize, decivilize; denature, denaturalize 147vb. *transform;* denationalize, detribalize; propagandize, brainwash 535vb. *misteach.*

impair, damage, damnify, hurt, injure, mischieve, scathe, shend 645vb. *harm;* jumble, mess up, muck up, untidy, crease 63vb. *derange;* disorganize, dismantle, dismast; spoil, maul, mar, botch 695vb. *be clumsy;* touch, tinker, tamper, meddle with, fool w., monkey w. 678vb. *meddle;* not improve, worsen, deteriorate, exacerbate, embitter 832vb. *aggravate;* do no good, kill with kindness 499vb. *be foolish;* stale, degrade, lower, coarsen 847vb. *vulgarize;* devalue, debase 812vb. *cheapen*; blacken, blot, spot, stain, uglify 842vb. *make ugly;* scar, mark, wrinkle 845vb. *blemish;* deface, disfigure, deform, warp 246vb. *distort;* corrupt, vitiate (**see** *pervert*); mutilate, maim, lame, cripple, hobble, nobble, hock, hough, hamstring 161 vb. *disable;* scotch, clip the wings, cramp, hamper 702vb. *hinder;* castrate, caponize 161vb. *unman;* expurgate, eviscerate, bowdlerize; curtail, dock 204vb. *shorten;* cream, skim, take the heart out of; adulterate, sophisticate, alloy 43vb. *mix;* denature, deactivate 679vb. *make inactive;* subvert, shake, sap, mine, undermine, labefy 163vb. *weaken;* honeycomb, bore, gnaw, gnaw at the roots, eat away, erode, corrode, rust, rot, mildew 51vb. *decompose;* blight, blast; ravage, waste, scorch, overrun 165vb. *lay waste;* wreck, ruin, overthrow 165vb. *destroy;* crumble 332vb. *pulverize;* dilapidate, fray, wear out, reduce to rags; exhaust, consume, use up 634vb. *waste;* infect, contaminate, poison, envenom, ulcerate; taint, canker, foul, pollute 649vb. *make unclean;* defile, desecrate, profane, unhallow 980vb. *be impious.*

wound, scotch, draw blood, let b.; tear, rend, lacerate, laniate, mangle, rip, rip up 46vb. *disjoin;* maul, savage 176vb. *be violent;* bite, scratch, claw; hack, incise 46vb. *cut;* scarify, score 262vb. *groove;* nick 260vb. *notch;* sting, prick, pink, stab, run through 263vb. *pierce;* bruise, contuse, buffet 279vb. *strike;* crush, grind 332vb. *pulverize;* chafe 333vb. *rub;* smash 46vb. *break;* graze, pepper, wing.

See: 5, 37, 43, 46, 51, 63, 131, 147, 161, 163, 165, 176, 198, 204, 246, 253, 260, 262, 263, 279, 286, 290, 309, 311, 332, 333, 387, 391, 397, 419, 458, 499, 535, 603, 634, 641, 645, 649, 651, 657, 659, 675, 678, 679, 684, 695, 702, 712, 731, 772, 801, 812, 832, 842, 845, 847, 934, 951, 980.

656 Restoration

N. *restoration*, returning, giving back, retrocession 787n. *restitution;* redress, amends, reparation, reparations 941n. *atonement;* finding again, getting back, retrieval, recovery 786 n. *taking;* refoundation, reestablishment, reinstallation, reinvestment, restauration, recall, replacement, reinstatement, reinstallment; rehabilitation; replanting, reforestation, reclamation; rescue, salvage, redemption, ransom, salvation 668n. *deliverance;* reconstitution, reerection, rebuilding, reformation, reconstruction, reorganization; readjustment; remodeling 654n. *reformism;* reconversion, revalorization; rehash, réchauffé; reaction, counterreformation 182n. *counteraction;* resumption, return to normal, derestriction; recruitment, reinforcement 162n. *strengthening;* replenishment 633n. *provision.*

repair, reparation, repairs, renovation, renewal, reconditioning, redintegration, reassembling; rectification, emendation; restoration, making like new 126n. *newness;* mending, invisible m., darning, patching, patching up; cobbling, soling, heeling, tinkering etc.vb.; clout, patch, darn, insertion, reinforcement; new look, face-lift 843n. *beautification.*

revival, recruitment, recovery 685n. *refreshment;* renewal, reawakening, revivescence, resurgence, recurrence, recovery, come-back, break-b.; fresh spurt, new energy; economic recovery, economic miracle, boom 730n. *prosperity;* reactivation, revivification, reanimation, resuscitation, artificial respiration; rejuvenation, rejuvenescence, second youth, Indian summer; face-lift, new look; rebirth, renaissance, new birth, second b.; regeneration, regeneracy, regenerateness 654n. *amendment;* new life, resurrection, awaking from the dead, recall from the grave; resurrection-day 124n. *future state.*

sanation, cure, certain c., perfect c.; recure, healing, mending; cicatrization, closing, scabbing over, healing o.; convalescence, recuperation, recovery, pulling through, restoration to health 658n. *remedy;* moderation, easing 831n. *relief;* psychological cure, catharsis, abreaction; curability.

mender, restorer, repairer, renovator, decorator; emendator, rectifier; rebuilder, second founder; refurbisher, face-lifter; patcher, darner, cobbler, boot-repairer, botcher; thatcher; knife-grinder, tinker, plumber, fixer; salvor, salvager; curer, healer, bonesetter, witch-doctor 658n. *doctor;* faith-healer; psychiatrist; reformist 654n. *reformer.*

Adj. *restored*, revived, refreshed etc. vb.; remade, reconditioned, redone, rectified; like new, renewed; reborn, redivivus, renascent, phoenix-like; cured, none the worse, better, convalescent, on the mend, pulling through; in one's right mind, back to normal; retrievable, restorable, recoverable; mendable, amendable; medicable, curable, sanable, operable; found, recovered, salvaged, reclaimed.

restorative, reparative, analeptic, recuperative, curative, sanative, healing, medicated, medicinal 658adj. *remedial.*

Vb. *be restored*, recover, come round, come to, revive, pick up, rally 685 vb. *be refreshed;* pull through, get over, get up, get well, convalesce, recuperate; weather the storm, survive, live through; reawake, live again, relive, resurrect, come to life again, arise from the dead, return from the grave; reappear, make a come-back; find one's strength, be oneself again, sleep off; return to normal, get back to n., go on as before; resume, start again 68vb. *begin;* look like new, undergo repairs.

restore, give back, hand b., retrocede, yield up 787vb. *restitute;* make amends 941vb. *atone;* put back, bring b., replace; recall, reappoint, reinstall, refound, reestablish, rehabilitate; reconstitute, reconstruct, reform, reorganize 654vb. *make better;* renovate, renew, rehash, warm up; rebuild, reerect, remake, redo; refurbish, make like new 126vb. *modernize;* make whole, redintegrate; reforest, reafforest, replant, reclaim; revalidate, reinforce, recruit 162vb. *strengthen;* fill up, fill up the ranks 633vb. *replenish;* rally, reassemble 74vb. *bring together;* redeem, ransom, rescue, salvage 668 vb. *deliver;* release, derestrict 746vb. *liberate.*

revive, revivify, revitalize, resuscitate, regenerate, recall to life, resurrect, reanimate, reinspire, rekindle; breathe fresh life into, rejuvenate; freshen, recruit 685vb. *refresh;* service; valet.

cure, recure, heal, make well, cure of, break of; nurse, physic, medicine, medicate 658vb. *doctor;* bandage, bind up one's wounds; nurse through, work a cure, snatch from the grave, restore to health, set up; set (a bone); cicatrize, heal over, scab o., skin o., close; right itself, put itself right, work its own cure.

repair, do repairs; amend, emend, right, set to rights, put right, make all square, straighten 654vb. *rectify;* overhaul, mend, fix; tinker, cobble, botch, sole, resole, heel, heel-piece; reface, retread, re-cover, thatch 226 vb. *cover;* reline 227vb. *line;* darn, patch, repatch, patch up, clout; stop, fill (teeth); make over, do up, touch up, freshen up, retouch, vamp, vamp up, plaster up, fill in the cracks, paper over; stanch, stop a gap, plug a hole 350vb. *stanch;* caulk, careen 264vb. *close;* splice, bind, bind up 45vb. *tie*; pick up the pieces, piece together, refit, reassemble, cannibalize 45vb. *join;* face-lift, refurbish, recondition, renovate, renew, remodel, reform.

retrieve, get back, recover, regain, retake, recapture; find again, reclaim, claim back, compensate oneself 31vb. *recoup;* make up for, make up time, make up leeway, take up the slack.

See: 31, 45, 68, 74, 124, 126, 162, 182, 226, 227, 264, 350, 633, 654, 658, 668, 685, 730, 746, 786, 787, 831, 843, 941.

657 Relapse

N. *relapse*, lapse, falling back; throwback, return; retrogression, retrogradation 286n. *regression;* sinking, falling off, fall 655n. *deterioration;* backsliding, recidivation, recidivism, apostasy 603n. *tergiversation;* recrudescence, reinfection, recurrence, fresh outbreak.

Vb. *relapse*, slip back, slide b., sink b., fall b.; throw back, return, retrograde 286vb. *regress;* degenerate 655 vb. *deteriorate;* backslide, recidivate, lapse, fall from grace 603vb. *apostatize;* fall off again, return to one's vomit; have a relapse, suffer a recurrence, not maintain an improvement.

See: 286, 603, 655.

658 Remedy

N. *remedy*, succor, help, present help in time of trouble 703n. *aid;* oil on troubled waters 177n. *moderator;* remedial measure, corrective, correction 654n. *amendment;* redress, amends 787n. *restitution;* expiation 941n. *atonement;* cure, radical c., certain c., perfect c. 656n. *sanation;* medicinal value, healing gift, healing quality *or* property; sovereign remedy, specific r., specific, answer, right a., solution; prescribed remedy, prescription, recipe, receipt, nostrum; universal remedy, panacea, cure-all, catholicon; elixir, elixir vitae, philosopher's stone.

medicine, materia medica, pharmacopoeia; vegetable remedy, galenical, herb, simple; medicinal herb, balm, agaric, linseed, camomile, orris root, mandrake; medication, medicament, patent medicine, drug, proprietary d.; tablet, tabloid, capsule, lozenge; physic, draft, potion, dose, drench, drenching; pill, purge, bolus; preparation, mixture, powder, electuary, linctus; plaster (**see** *surgical dressing*); medicine chest, medicine bottle.

prophylactic, preventive; sanitation, sanitary precaution, cordon sanitaire, quarantine 652n. *hygiene;* prophylaxis, immunization, inoculation, vaccination; antisepsis, disinfection, sterilization; antiseptic, disinfectant, iodine, creosote, carbolic, boric acid, boracic a., chloride of lime; mothball, camphor, lavender; bactericide, germicide, insecticide 659n. *poison;* incense, fumigant; dentifrice, toothpaste, tooth-powder 648n. *cleanser;* mouthwash, gargle; essential oils; quinine.

antidote, abirritant; analgesic, painkiller; counter-irritant, urtication, bee-sting; counter-poison, antitoxin, mithridate, theriac; antidysenteric; antemetic; antaphrodisiac; antifebrile, antifebrific, anticaustic, febrifuge, quinine; cold water; vermifuge, helminthagogue, anthelmintic; antigen, antibody; antibiosis, antibiotic; antispasmodic, mescal; anticoagulant.

cathartic, purge, purgative, laxative, aperient, pull-through; agaric, castor oil, Epsom salts, calomel, senna pods; isaf gul, flea-seed; expectorant, emetic, nauseant, emetine, ipecac, nux vomica; carminative, digestive, pepastic, milk of magnesia.

tonic, corroborant, restorative, analeptic; cordial, tonic water; bracer, reviver, refresher, pick-me-up 174n. *stimulant;* spirits, smelling salts, sal volatile, hartshorn; camomile, effusion, tisane, ptisan; vitamin; benzedrine.

drug, dope, opium, cocaine, snow, morphia, morphine, codeine, caffeine, mescaline; synthetic drug, wonder d., miracle d.; antibiotic, sulpha drug; penicillin; aureomycin, streptomycin, insulin, cortisone; tranquilizer, aspirin, narcotic, analgesic 375n. *anesthetic;* nepenthe, kef, kief.

balm, balsam, oil, soothing syrup, emollient, lenitive 177n. *moderator;* salve, cerate, ointment, collyrium, eye-salve, cream, face-c. 843n. *cosmetic;* vaseline, lanolin, liniment, embrocation; lotion, wash.

surgical dressing, dressing, lint, gauze; swab; bandage, suspensory, sling, splint, cast, tourniquet; fingerstall; patch; cataplasm, vesicant, vesicatory; application, external a., cataplasm, epithem, epithemation; plaster, sticking p., corn p., court p., mustard p., sinapism, fomentation, poultice, compress; tampion, tent, roll, pledget; pessary, suppository; vulnerary, traumatic.

medical art, leechcraft; therapeutics, acology, art of healing, healing touch 656n. *sanation;* medical advice, practice, medical p.; allopathy, homeopathy, ayurvedic system, unani s.; medicine, clinical m., preventive m., virology; diagnosis, prognosis 651n. *pathology;* healing, faith-h., Christian Science; sexology, gynecology, midwifery 164n. *obstetrics;* gerontology, geriatrics, pediatrics; psychopedics; iatrochemistry, psychopharmacology; pharmaceutics, pharmacology, posology, dosology; veterinary medicine.

surgery, chirurgery, general surgery, brain s., heart s.; plastic surgery, anaplasty, rhinoplasty; manipulative surgery, chiropraxis, chiropractic; operation, surgical o., op.; phlebotomy, venesection; bleeding, bloodletting, cupping, transfusion, perfusion; amputation, trephination, tonsillectomy, appendectomy, colostomy, laparotomy; dentistry, drawing, extracting, stopping, filling, crowning; massage, shampoo; chiropody, pedicure, manicure.

therapy, therapeutics, medical care; treatment, medical t., clinical t.; nursing, bedside manner; first aid, after-care; course, cure, faith c., nature c., cold-water c., hydrotherapy; regimen, diet, dietary; chiropody, bone-setting, orthopedics, osteopathy, osteotherapy, orthopraxy; hypnotherapy, hypnopedagogics; physiotherapy, radiotherapy, phototherapy; occupational therapy; electrotherapy, shock treatment; mental treatment, clinical psychology; child psychology, psychopedics; psychotherapy, psychiatry, psychoanalysis; acupuncture, needling; injection, shot, stab, jab; enema, clyster, purge, bowel-wash, douche; cathetic, cathe-

terism, catheterization; fomentation, poulticing.
hospital, infirmary, general hospital, fever h., maternity h., children's h.; mental hospital 503n. *madhouse;* dispensary, clinic, prenatal c.; nursing home, convalescent h., rest h.; home for the dying, terminal home; lazaret, lazaretto, hospice, pest-house; lazar-house, leper asylum, leper colony; hospital ship, hospital train; stretcher, ambulance; ward, hospital w., casualty w., isolation w., sickbay, sickroom, sickbed; hospital bed, ripple-b.; tent, oxygen t., iron lung; dressing station, first-aid s., casualty s.; operation room, operating theater, operating table; consulting room, surgery, clinic; sanatorium, spa, hydro, watering place; pump-room, baths, hot springs, thermae; solarium, sun-deck, sun lamp.
doctor, medical man; leech, quack; veterinary surgeon, vet, horse-doctor; herbalist, herb-doctor; faith-healer, Christian Scientist; allopath, homeopath, ayurvedist, hakim; witch-doctor, medicine-man 983n. *sorcerer;* medico, medical student; houseman, intern, house physician, resident p., house surgeon, resident s., registrar; medical practitioner, general p., GP; locum tenens, locum; physician, clinician, therapeutist, healer; operator, surgeon, general s.; plastic s., neurosurgeon; chirurgeon, barber, barber-surgeon, sawbones; medical officer, health o., sanitary inspector; medical adviser, consultant, specialist; diagnostician, pathologist; alienist, psychiatrist, psychoanalyst, psychopathologist, brain-specialist, neurologist, neuropath; anesthetist, radiotherapist; pediatrician, geriatrician; obstetrician, accoucheur, midwife; gynecologist; sexologist; dermatologist; orthopedist, osteopath, bonesetter, chiropractor, masseur, masseuse; pedicurist, chiropodist, manicurist; ophthalmologist, optician, oculist; aurist; dentist, dental surgeon, tooth-drawer; nutritionist, dietician; medical profession, Harley Street; Red Cross, St. John's Ambulance; Aesculapius, Hippocrates, Galen.
druggist, apothecary, chemist, pharmaceutical c., pharmacopolist, pharmacist; dispenser, posologist, pharmacologist; drugstore, pharmacy.
nurse, male n., probationer n., pro; sister, night s., ward s., theater s., sister tutor, matron, hospital m.; Nightingale, registered nurse, RN, registered sick children's nurse, R.S.C.N.; special nurse, day n., night n.; district nurse, home-n., Sairy Gamp; nursing auxiliary, ward orderly, dresser, medical attendant, stretcher-bearer, ambulance-driver; probationer officer, court missionary, lady almoner 901n. *sociology.*

Adj. *remedial*, corrective, analeptic, curative, first-aid 656adj. *restorative;* helpful 644adj. *beneficial;* therapeutic, medicinal, sanative, hygienic, salutiferous 652adj. *salubrious;* specific, sovereign; panacean, all-healing; soothing, paregoric, balsamic, demulcent, emollient, palliative 177adj. *lenitive;* anodyne, analgesic, narcotic, hypnotic, anesthetic 375adj. *insensible;* peptic, digestive; depurative, detersive 648adj. *cleansing;* cathartic, emetic, vomitory, laxative; antidotal 182adj. *counteracting;* alexipharmic, theriacal, therial; prophylactic, disinfectant, antiseptic; febrifugal, alexipyretic; tonic, stimulative, corroborant; enlivening; dietetic, alimentary, nutritive, nutritional.
medical, pathological, physicianly, Aesculapian, Hippocratic, Galenic; allopathic, homeopathic, ayurvedic; surgical, chirurgical, anaplastic, rhinoplastic, orthopedic, chiropractic; chiropodical, pedicuristic, manicuristic; vulnerary, traumatic; obstetric, obstetrical; medicable, medicinable, operable, curable.

Vb. *remedy*, fix, put right, correct 656vb. *restore;* succor, help 703vb. *aid;* apply a remedy, treat, heal, work a cure 656vb. *cure;* palliate, soothe, neutralize 831vb. *relieve.*
doctor, be a d., practice, have a practice; treat, prescribe, advise; attend 703vb. *minister to;* tend, nurse; give first aid, call an ambulance, hospitalize, put on the sick-list; physic, medicine, medicate, drench, dose, purge; inject, poke, stab, jab; dress, bind, swathe, bandage; stop the bleeding, apply a tourniquet 350vb. *stanch;* poultice, plaster, foment; set, put in splints; drug, dope, anesthetize; operate, use the knife, cut open, amputate; trepan, trephine; curette; cauterize; bleed, leech, cup, let blood, venesect, phlebotomize; transfuse, perfuse; massage, rub, shampoo; draw, extract, pull, stop, fill, crown; pedicure, manicure; immunize, vaccinate, inoculate; sterilize, pasteurize, antisepticize, disinfect 652vb. *sanitate.*

See: 164, 174, 177, 182, 350, 375, 503, 644, 648, 651, 652, 654, 656, 659, 703, 787, 831, 843, 901, 941, 983.

659 Bane

N. *bane,* cause of injury, malevolent influence; curse, plague, pest, scourge, run 616n. *evil;* malady 651 n. *disease;* weakness, bad habit, besetting sin 934n. *vice*; hell, cup, visitation, affliction 731n. *adversity;* woe, funeral 825n. *sorrow;* cross, trial; bore 838n. *tedium;* bugbear, bête noire 827n. *annoyance;* burden, imposition, tax, white elephant; thorn in the flesh, stone round one's neck; perpetual worry, constant anxiety, torment, nagging pain 825n. *worry;* running sore 651n. *ulcer;* bitterness, acid, gall, wormwood 393n. *sourness;* sickener, emetic 391n. *unsavoriness;* sword, sting, serpent's tooth, fang, bramble, brier, nettle 256n. *sharp point;* source of trouble, hornet's nest 663n. *pitfall;* viper, adder, serpent 365n. *reptile;* snake, snake in the grass 663n. *troublemaker;* parasite, leech, locust 168n. *destroyer;* oppressor, terror 735n. *tyrant.*

blight, blast, rust, rubigo, rot, dry r.; mildew, mold, fungus; moth, moth and rust; worm, canker-w., canker, cancer; visitation 651n. *plague;* frost, nip, cold 380n. *coldness;* drought 342n. *desiccation.*

poison, poisonousness, virulence, venomousness, toxicity; bad food, bad water; bacteria, bacillus, germ, virus 651n. *infection;* venom, toxicant, toxin; deadly poison, snake p., rat p., ratsbane, germicide, insecticide, pesticide, acaricide, vulpicide, fungicide, weed-killer, DDT; acid, corrosive; hemlock, arsenic, strychnine, cyanide, hyocyamine, prussic acid, vitriol; nicotine, verdigris; asphyxiant, poison gas, Lewisite, mustard g., tear g., lacrimatory g.; carbon monoxide, carbon dioxide, carbonic acid gas, choke damp, after-d.; foul air, mephitis, miasma, effluvium, sewer gas 653n. *insalubrity;* smog 355n. *cloud;* radioactivity, radioactive cloud, mushroom, fall-out, strontium 90 417n. *radiation;* dope, opium, hashish, bhang, marihuana, morphine, cocaine, snow 658n. *drug;* intoxicant, depressant 949n. *alcoholism;* toxicology.

poisonous plant, hemlock, deadly nightshade, belladonna, datura, henbane, wolfsbane, monkshood, aconite, hellebore, digitalis, foxglove; opium poppy, Indian hemp, bhang, hashish, upas tree.

poisoning, venenation, venefice 362n. *homicide;* blood poisoning, toxemia 651n. *infection*; food poisoning, ptomaine p., botulism; poisoner 362n. *murderer.*

Adj. *baneful,* plaguey, pestilent, noisome 645adj. *harmful;* blighting, withering, poisonous, venomous 653 adj. *toxic;* cursed, accursed 616adj. *evil.*

See: 168, 256, 342, 355, 362, 365, 380, 391, 393, 417, 616, 645, 651, 653, 658, 663, 731, 735, 825, 827, 838, 934, 949.

660 Safety

N. *safety,* safeness, security, surety; social security, welfare state 901n. *sociology;* invulnerability, impregnability, immunity, charmed life; numbers, safety in n. 104n. *multitude;* secure position, permanent post, safe job; safe distance, wide berth 620n. *avoidance;* all clear, coast c., danger past, danger over, storm blown over; guarantee, warrant 473n. *certainty;* sense of security, assurance, confidence 855n. *courage;* safety-valve 667n. *means of escape;* close shave, narrow escape 667n. *escape;* rescue 668n. *deliverance.*

protection, self-p., self-preservation 666n. *preservation;* insurance, reinsurance, self-insurance 858n. *caution;* patronage, auspices, fatherly eye; protectorate, guardianship, wardenship, wardship, tutelage, custody, protective c. 747n. *restraint;* custodianship, safe-keeping, keeping, charge, safe hands, grasp, grip, embrace 778n. *retention;* ward, watch and w. 457n. *surveillance;* safeguard, precaution, preventive measure 713n. *defense;* sanitary precaution, sanitation, immunization, prophylaxis, quarantine, cordon sanitaire 652n. *hygiene;* segregation 883 n. *seclusion;* cushion, screen; means of protection, deterrent 723n. *weapon;* safe-conduct, passport, pass 756 n. *permit;* escort, convoy, guard 722n. *armed force;* defense, sure d., bastion, bulwark, tower of strength 713n. *defenses;* ark, palladium, haven, sanctuary, asylum, earth, hole 662n. *refuge;* anchor, sheet-a. 662n. *safeguard;* moat, ditch, palisade, stockade 235n. *fence;* shield, breastplate, panoply, armor plate 713n. *armor;* umbrella, aegis.

protector, protectress, guardian, tutor;

guardian angel, tutelary god, liege lord, feudal l., patroness 707n. *patron;* defender, preserver, shepherd; bodyguard, lifeguard, strong-arm man 742n. *retainer;* conservator, custodian, curator, warden; warder, castellan, guard; chaperon, duenna, governess, nurse, nursemaid, nanny, mammy, ayah, amah 749n. *keeper;* watcher, look-out, watch, watchman, night-w., chokidar 441n. *spectator;* fire-watcher, fire-fighter, fireman; policeman, police constable, police sergeant, sheriff; bobby, peeler, bluebottle, copper, cop, traffic c., bull, flat-foot, Charley, Dogberry 955n. *police;* tec., dick, private eye 459n. *detective;* sentry, sentinel, garrison 722n. *soldiery;* watch-dog, ban-d., police d. 365n. *dog;* Cerberus, Argus 457n. *surveillance.*

Adj. *safe,* without risk, unhazardous; assured, secure, sure; safe and sound, spared 666adj. *preserved;* with a whole skin, intact, unharmed 646 adj. *undamaged;* garrisoned, well-kept, well-preserved, well-defended; insured, covered; immunized, vaccinated, inoculated; disinfected, hygienic 652adj. *salubrious;* in safety, in security, on the safe side, on sure ground, on terra firma; in harbor, in port, at anchor; above water, high and dry; out of danger, out of harm's way; clear, in the clear, unaccused, unthreatened, unmolested; unexposed, unhazarded; under shelter, sheltered, shielded, screened, protected etc.vb.; patronized, under the wing of; in safe hands, held, in custody, behind bars, under lock and key 747adj. *imprisoned;* reliable, guaranteed, warranted 929adj. *trustworthy;* benign, harmless, unthreatening 615adj. *good.*

invulnerable, immune, impregnable, inexpugnable, unassailable, unattackable, unbreakable, unchallengeable; founded on a rock, defensible, tenable 162adj. *strong;* proof, foolproof; weatherproof, waterproof, leak-p., gas-p., fire-p, bullet-p., bomb-p., shatter-p.; snug, tight, seaworthy, airworthy; armored, steel-clad, panoplied.

tutelary, custodial, guardian, protective, shepherdlike; ready to die for 931adj. *disinterested;* watchful 457 adj. *vigilant;* keeping, protecting 666 adj. *preserving;* antiseptic, disinfectant 652adj. *salubrious.*

Vb. *be safe,*—invulnerable etc.adj.; find safety, reach s., save one's bacon 667vb. *escape;* land on one's feet, tide over, keep one's head above water, weather the storm, ride it out; keep a whole skin, bear a charmed life, have nine lives; be snug, nestle, stay at home, be under shelter, have a roof over one's head; be under cover 523vb. *lurk;* keep a safe distance, give a wide berth 620vb. *avoid.*

safeguard, keep safe, guard, protect; spare 905vb. *show mercy;* stand up for, go bail for 713vb. *defend;* shield, grant asylum, afford sanctuary; cover up for 703vb. *patronize;* keep, bottle, conserve 666vb. *preserve;* treassure, hoard 632vb. *store;* keep in custody 747vb. *imprison;* ward, watch over, nurse, foster, cherish; have charge of, take charge of, keep an eye on, chaperon, play gooseberry 457vb. *look after;* hide, put in a safe place, earth 525vb. *conceal;* cushion 218vb. *support;* cover, shroud, cloak, shade, shadow 421vb. *screen;* keep under cover, garage, lock up; house, shelter, fold; ensconce, embay, enfold, embrace 235 vb. *enclose;* make safe, secure, fortify 162vb. *strengthen;* entrench, fence, fence round 232vb. *circumscribe;* arm, armor, clothe in steel; shepherd, convoy, escort; flank, support; garrison, mount guard; immunize, inoculate, vaccinate; pasteurize, chlorinate, disinfect 652vb. *sanitate;* give assurances, warrant, guarantee 473vb. *make certain;* keep order, police, patrol.

seek safety, demand assurances, take precautions, play for safety, hedge, insure, reinsure 858vb. *be cautious;* make assurance doubly sure 473vb. *be certain;* dig in 599vb. *stand firm;* run away 667vb. *escape;* cut and run 277vb. *move fast;* live to fight another day, think better of it; shorten sail, take in a reef, run for port, take refuge 662vb. *seek refuge.*

Adv. *under shelter,* under cover, in the lee of; out of harm's way, safely, with impunity.

See: 104, 162, 218, 232, 235, 277, 365, 421, 441, 457, 459, 473, 523, 525, 599, 615, 620, 632, 646, 652, 662, 666, 667, 668, 703, 707, 713, 722, 723, 742, 747, 749, 756, 778, 855, 858, 883, 901, 929, 931, 955.

661 Danger

N. *danger,* peril; dangerousness, perilousness, shadow of death, jaws of d., dragon's mouth; dangerous situation, unhealthy s., desperate s., parlous state, forlorn hope **700n.** *predicament;* emergency 137n. *crisis;* insecurity, jeopardy, risk, hazard, ticklishness, precariousness, slipperiness, ticklish business, razor's edge 474n. *uncertainty;* black spot, snag 663n. *pitfall;* trap, death-t. 527n. *ambush;* endangerment, imperilment, hazarding, dangerous course; venturesomeness, daring, overdaring 857n. *rashness;* venture, risky v. 672n. *undertaking;* leap in the dark 618n. *gambling;* slippery slope, road to ruin 655n. *deterioration;* approach of danger, sword of Damocles, menace 900 n. *threat;* sense of danger, apprehension, fears 854n. *nervousness;* cause for alarm, rocks ahead, breakers a., storm brewing, gathering clouds, cloud on the horizon 665n. *danger signal;* narrow escape, hairbreadth e., close shave, near thing, Dunkirk 667n. *escape.*

vulnerability, non-immunity, susceptibility, danger of 180n. *liability;* exposure, nakedness, defenselessness 161n. *helplessness;* instability, insecurity, slipperiness 152n. *changeableness;* exposed part, vulnerable point, chink in the armor, Achilles' heel 163n. *weakness;* tender spot, soft s., soft underbelly 327n. *softness;* unsoundness, feet of clay 647n. *imperfection.*

Adj. *dangerous,* perilous, fraught with danger, treacherous, snaggy; exposed to risk, beset with perils; risky, hazardous, venturous, venturesome, aleatory, dicey, chancy 618n. *speculative;* serious, ugly, emergent, critical; at stake, in question; menacing, ominous, foreboding, alarming 900adj. *threatening;* septic, poisonous 653n. *toxic;* unhealthy, infectious 653 adj. *insalubrious;* inflammable, explosive.

unsafe, not safe, slippery, treacherous, untrustworthy 474adj. *unreliable;* insecure, unsecure, precarious; top-heavy, unsteady 152adj. *unstable;* shaky, tottering, crumbling, nodding to its fall, tumbledown, ramshackle, frail 655adj. *dilapidated;* jerry-built, gimcrack, crazy 163adj. *weak;* built on sand, on shaky foundations; leaky, waterlogged; critical, ticklish, touch and go, hanging by a thread, trembling in the balance, on the edge, on the brink, on the verge.

vulnerable, expugnable, in danger of, not immune 180adj. *liable;* open to, exposed, naked, bare 229adj. *uncovered;* unarmored, unfortified, unprotected 161adj. *defenseless;* unshielded, shelterless, helpless, guideless; unguarded, guardless, unescorted, unshepherded, unconvoyed, unsupported, unflanked; unwarned, unadvised 508adj. *inexpectant.*

endangered, in danger, in peril etc.n.; facing death, in a bad way; slipping, drifting; on the rocks, in shoal water; on slippery ground, on thin ice; surrounded, trapped, under fire; in the lion's den, on the razor's edge; between two fires, between the hammer and the anvil, between the devil and the deep blue sea, between Scylla and Charybdis; on the run, not out of the wood; at bay, with one's back to the wall, at the last stand, reduced to the last extremity; under sentence, with a halter round one's neck, awaiting execution 961 adj. *condemned.*

Vb. *be in danger,* run the risk of 180vb. *be liable;* run into danger, enter the lion's den, walk into a trap 527vb. *ambush;* skate on thin ice, sail too near the wind, sit on a powder-barrel, sleep on a volcano; lean on a broken reed, feel the ground slipping; hang by a thread, tremble in the balance, hover on the brink 474vb. *be uncertain;* totter, slip, slide, sideslip 309vb. *tumble;* get lost 282vb. *stray.*

face danger, face death 855vb. *be courageous;* expose oneself, lay oneself open, live in a glass house; bare one's breast, stand in the breach 711 vb. *defy;* look danger in the face, look down a gun-barrel; brave all hazards, face heavy odds, have the odds against one; engage in a forlorn hope, spurn the odds; challenge fate, tempt providence, court disaster; put one's head in the lion's mouth 857vb. *be rash;* run the gauntlet, come under fire; venture, dare, risk it, take a chance, accept the hazard 618vb. *gamble;* stand condemned, lodge in the condemned cell.

endanger, be dangerous, spell danger, expose to d., put in d., face with, confront w.; imperil, hazard, jeopardize, compromise; risk, stake, venture 618vb. *gamble;* drive headlong, run on the rocks; drive to the danger of the public, put one in fear of his life; be dangerous, threaten danger, loom, forebode, bode ill, menace 960vb. *threaten;* run one hard, overtake 306vb. *outdo.*

See: 137, 152, 161, 163, 180, 229,

282, 306, 309, 327, 474, 508, 527, 618, 647, 653, 655, 665, 672, 700, 711, 854, 855, 857, 900, 961.

662 Refuge. Safeguard

N. *refuge*, sanctuary, asylum, retreat, safe r., safe place; traffic island, zebra crossing; last resort, funk-hole, bolt-hole, fox-hole, burrow; trench, dug-out, air-raid shelter; earth, hole, den, lair, covert, nest, lap, hearth 192n. *home;* sanctum 194n. *room;* cloister, cell, hermitage 192n. *retreat;* sanctum sanctorum, temple, ark, palladium; acropolis, citadel; wall, rampart, bulwark, bastion; stronghold, fastness, fort 713n. *fort;* keep, ward; cache 527n. *hiding place;* dungeon 748n. *prison;* rock, pillar, tower, tower of strength, mainstay 218n. *support.*

shelter, roof, cover; covert, earth, hole; fold, sheepfold, pinfold; lee; lee-wall, windbreak, hedge 235n. *fence;* camp, stockade, zareba; umbrella, wing, shield; fireguard, fender, bumper, life-guard, mudguard, splashboard, windshield 421n. *screen;* sola topi, sun-helmet, spine pad, sun-glasses, eye-shade; haven, harbor, port 295n. *goal;* harborage, anchorage, roadstead, roads; quay, jetty, ghat, marina, dock, dry d., bandar 194n. *stable;* asylum, padded cell 503n. *madhouse;* almshouse, poorhouse, orphanage, cat's home, dog's h., charitable institution, home for the dying, Welfare State.

safeguard, means of safety, protection 660n. *safety;* mail 713n. *armor;* arms, deterrent 723n. *weapon;* respirator, gas-mask; safety device, dead man's handle, safety catch, safety match, safety-valve, vent peg, lightning rod, lightning conductor, fuse; crash helmet; ejector-seat, parachute; lifeboat, rubber dinghy, life-raft 275 n. *raft;* life-preserver, life-belt, life-jacket, cork j., Mae West, life-line, breeches buoy; rope, plank 667n. *means of escape;* anchor, sheet-a., mushroom a., kedge, grapnel, grappling iron, killick, drogue; drag, brake, curb 748n. *fetter;* bolt, bar, lock, key 264n. *stopper;* ballast 31n. *offset;* mole, breakwater, groin, seawall, embankment; lighthouse, lightship 269n. *sailing aid;* jury mast, spare parts 40n. *extra;* safety belt, safety harness.

Vb. *seek refuge,* take refuge 660vb. *seek safety;* take to the woods, take to the hills; turn to, throw oneself in the arms of, shelter under the wing of, put up one's umbrella; claim sanctuary, clasp the knees of, nestle under one's wing, hide behind the skirts of; make port, reach safety, reach home, find shelter; lock oneself in, bolt the door, bar the entrance, let down the portcullis, raise the drawbridge.

See: 31, 40, 192, 194, 218, 235, 264, 269, 275, 295, 421, 503, 527, 660, 667, 713, 723, 748.

663 Pitfall: source of danger

N. *pitfall*, pit, trapdoor, trap for the unwary, catch; snag, pons asinorum 702n. *obstacle;* booby-trap, death-t. 542n. *trap;* surprise 508n. *inexpectation;* lying in wait 527n. *ambush;* sleeping dog; thin ice; quagmire, quicksands, Goodwin Sands, sandbar, flat 347n. *marsh;* shoal, shoal water, breakers, shallows 212n. *shallowness;* reef, sunken r., coral r., rock 344n. *rock;* iron-bound coast, lee shore 344n. *shore;* steep, chasm, abyss, crevasse, precipice 209n. *high land;* rapids, cross-current, undertow 350n. *current;* vortex, maelstrom, whirlpool 350n. *eddy;* tidal wave, tsunami, bore 350n. *wave;* storm, squall, hurricane 352n. *gale;* volcano 383n. *furnace;* dynamite, powder magazine, powder-keg 723n. *explosive;* trouble-spot, danger-spot 661n. *danger;* plague-spot, hotbed 651n. *infection;* source of trouble, hornet's nest, hazard 659n. *bane.*

trouble-maker, mischief-m., wrecker; ill-wisher 881n. *enemy;* firebrand 738 n. *agitator;* dangerous person, ugly customer, undesirable, delinquent 904n. *ruffian;* nigger in the woodpile, snake in the grass, viper in the bosom; hidden hand 178n. *influence;* yellow peril, red p.; Nemesis 910n. *avenger.*

See: 178, 209, 212, 344, 347, 350, 352, 383, 508, 527, 542, 651, 659, 661, 702, 723, 738, 881, 904, 910.

664 Warning

N. *warning*, caution, caveat; example, warning e., lesson, object l.; notice, advance n. 524n. *information;* word, word in the ear, word to the wise 524n. *hint;* final warning, final notice, ultimatum 737n. *demand;* dun 761n. *request;* monition, admonition, admonishment 924n. *reprimand;* dehortation 613n. *dissuasion;* protest, expostulation 762n. *deprecation;*

foreboding, premonition 511n. *prediction;* voice, voice of conscience, warning voice 917n. *conscience;* alarm, siren, foghorn, fog signal, storm s. 665n. *danger signal;* Mother Carey's chickens, stormy petrel, bird of ill omen 511n. *omen;* gathering cloud, cloud on the horizon 661n. *danger;* signs of the times, writing on the wall, symptom, sign 547n. *indication;* knell, death-k. 364n. *obsequies;* beacon, light 547n. *signal, indicator;* menace 900n. *threat.*

warner, monitor, admonitor, admonitrix, admonisher 691n. *adviser;* prophet, Cassandra 511n. *diviner;* flagman, signaler; lighthouse-keeper; watchman, look-out, watch; scout, spy; picket, sentinel, sentry 660n. *protector;* advance guard, rearguard; watch-dog, house-d.; run 763 n. *petitioner.*

Adj. *cautionary*, hinting, warning, monitorial, monitory, admonitory; dehortative, dehortatory 762adj. *deprecatory;* exemplary, instructive 524 adj. *informative;* symptomatic, prognostic 547n. *indicating;* premonitory, boding, ill-omened, ominous 511adj. *presageful;* menacing, minatory 900 adj. *threatening;* deterrent 854adj. *frightening.*

warned, cautioned etc.vb.; once bitten 858adj. *cautious;* forewarned 507adj. *expectant;* forearmed 669adj. *prepared.*

Vb. *warn*, caution; give fair warning, give notice, notify 524vb. *inform;* drop a hint 524vb. *hint;* counsel 691vb. *advise;* put one in mind 505 vb. *remind;* admonish 924vb. *reprove;* spell danger, premonish, forewarn 511vb. *predict;* forearm, put one on his guard 669vb. *prepare;* lower, menace 900vb. *threaten;* contra-indicate 14vb. *be contrary;* advise against 613vb. *dissuade;* dehort, protest 762vb. *deprecate;* sound the alarm 665vb. *raise the alarm.*

be warned, receive notice; beware, take heed, mind what one is about 457vb. *be careful;* be taught a good lesson, learn one's l., profit by the example.

Int. look out! watch out! mind your step! look where you are going!

See: 14, 364, 457, 505, 507, 511, 524, 547, 613, 660, 661, 665, 669, 691, 737, 761, 762, 763, 854, 858, 900, 917, 924.

665 Danger signal

N. *danger signal*, note of warning 664n. *warning;* murmur, muttering 829n. *discontent;* writing on the wall, black cap, evil omen 511n. *omen;* warning sound, alarum, alarm clock, alarm-bell, burglar alarm, police whistle, watchman's rattle; fire-alarm, fire-bell, foghorn, fog signal, motor-horn, klaxon; blast, honk, toot 400n. *loudness;* curfew, tocsin, siren; alert, alarm, beat of drum, trumpet-call 528n. *publication;* war-cry, war-whoop, rallying cry, Fiery Cross; warning light, red l., Very l., beacon; red flag, yellow f.; distress signal, SOS 547n. *signal;* sign of alarm, start, tremor, sweat, hair on end 854n. *fear.*

false alarm, cry of "wolf," scare, scarecrow, bugbear, bugaboo, bogey, nightmare, bad dream 854n. *intimidation;* blank cartridge, flash in the pan 4n. *insubstantiality;* canard 543 n. *untruth;* scaremonger 854n. *alarmist.*

Vb. *raise the alarm*, beat the a., sound the a., give the a., alarm, alert, arouse, scare, startle 854vb. *frighten;* sound one's horn, honk, toot; turn out the guard, raise a hue and cry 528vb. *proclaim;* give a false alarm, cry wolf, cry too soon; sound a warning, toll, knell.

See: 400, 511, 528, 543, 547, 664, 829, 854.

666 Preservation

N. *preservation*, safe-keeping, keeping alive; safe-conduct 660n. *protection;* saving, salvation 668n. *deliverance;* conservation, conservatism, vis conservatrix 144n. *permanence;* upkeep, maintenance, sustentation, support 633n. *provision;* service, servicing, valeting 648n. *cleansing;* saving up 632n. *storage;* frugality 814n. *economy;* self-preservation 932n. *selfishness;* keeping fresh, mummification, embalmment, embalming 364n. *interment;* deep-freeze, cold pack 382n. *refrigeration;* boiling, drying, sun-d., *dehydration* 342n. *desiccation;* ensilage; canning, tinning, packing; prophylaxis, preventive medicine, quarantine, cordon sanitaire 652n. *hygiene.*

preserver, savior, rescuer, deliverer 668n. *deliverance;* amulet, charm, mascot 983n. *talisman;* preservative, ice, cold; camphor, moth-ball, flit; lavender, amber; spice, pickle, brine 389n. *condiment;* refrigerator, fridge 382n. *refrigeration;* thermos flask; silo; cannery, canning factory, canned goods, tinned g.; safety device, life-belt, respirator, gas-mask 662n. *safeguard;* drugget, chair-cover, dust-c. 226n. *covering;* embalmer, mummifier; canner, bottler.

Adj. *preserving,* conserving etc. vb. preservatory, preservative, conservative; prophylactic, protective, preventive, hygienic 652adj. *salubrious.*

preserved, well-p., kept, well-k., fresh, undecayed, intact, whole 646adj. *perfect;* iced, frozen, on ice, in the refrigerator; pickled, salted, corned, tinned, canned, potted, bottled; mummified, embalmed, laid up in lavender, treasured 632adj. *stored.*

Vb. *preserve,* conserve, keep alive, keep fresh, ice, freeze, keep on ice; embalm, mummify; pickle, salt, corn, spice 388vb. *season;* souse, marinate; cure, smoke, kipper, dehydrate, sun-dry 342vb. *dry;* pot, bottle, tin, can; protect, paint, coat, whitewash, kyanize, waterproof; maintain, keep up, keep in repair, service, valet 656vb. *repair;* shore, shore up, embank 218vb. *support;* keep alive, feed, provision, supply 633vb. *provide*; keep safe, keep under cover, garage 660vb. *safeguard;* save up, bottle up 632vb. *store;* spare 814vb. *economize;* nurse, tend 58vb. *doctor;* tender, cherish, treasure 457vb. *look after;* not let go, hug, hold 778vb. *retain;* save, save alive, rescue 668vb. *deliver.*

See: 144, 218, 226, 342, 364, 382, 388, 389, 457, 632, 633, 646, 648, 652, 656, 658, 660, 662, 668, 778, 814, 932, 983.

667 Escape

N. *escape,* leak, leakage, short circuit 298n. *egress;* extrication, delivery, rescue 668n. *deliverance;* riddance, good r. 831n. *relief;* getaway, breakout, prison-breaking; decampment, avolation, flight, flit, French leave 296n. *departure;* withdrawal, retreat, timely r. 286n. *regression;* disappearing trick 446n. *disappearance;* elopement, runaway match; evasion, truancy, tax-dodging 620n. *avoidance;* narrow escape, hairbreadth e., close shave, narrow squeak, near thing 661n. *danger;* come-off, discharge, reprieve 960n. *acquittal;* setting free 746n. *liberation;* immunity, impunity, exemption 919n. *non-liability;* escapology, escapism; literature of escape.

means of escape, exit, way out, back door, secret passage 298n. *egress;* ladder, fire-escape, escape hatch; drawbridge 624n. *bridge;* vent, safety-valve 662n. *safeguard;* dodge, device, trick 623n. *contrivance;* loophole, saving clause, escape c. 468n. *qualification.*

escaper, escapee, runaway; truant, escaped prisoner, prison-breaker; fugitive, refugee prisoner, prison-breaker; fugitive, refugee; survivor; escapologist.

Adj. *escaped,* fled, flown, stolen away; eloping, truant; fugitive, runaway; slippery, elusive, tip-and-run 620adj. *avoiding;* free, at large, scot free, acquitted; relieved, rid of, well out of, well rid of; exempt 919adj. *non-liable.*

Vb. *escape,* find *or* win freedom 746 vb. *achieve liberty;* effect one's escape, make good one's e., make a getaway, break prison; flit, elope, skip 620vb. *run away;* steal away, sneak off; take it on the lam 296vb. *decamp;* slip through, break t., break out, break loose, break away, get free, break one's chains, slip the collar; get out, bluff one's way o., sneak o. 298vb. *emerge;* get away, slip through one's fingers; get off, come off, secure an acquittal, go scot free, go unpunished; scrape through, save one's bacon, weather the storm, survive; get away with it, secure exemption 919vb. *be exempt;* relieve oneself, rid o., be well rid of find relief 831vb. *relieve;* leak, leak away 298vb. *flow out.*

elude, evade, welsh, abscond, dodge 620vb. *avoid;* lie low 523vb. *lurk;* make oneself scarce, give one the slip, baffle one's pursuers, give one a run for one's money; escape notice, be found missing 190vb. *be absent.*

See: 190, 286, 296, 298, 446, 468, 523, 620, 623, 624, 661, 662, 668, 746, 831, 919, 960.

668 Deliverance

N. *deliverance,* delivery, extrication 304n. *extraction*; disburdenment, disencumberment, riddance 831n. *relief;* emancipation 746n. *liberation;* rescue, life-saving; salvage, retrieval 656n. *restoration;* salvation, redemption 965n. *divine function;* ransom, buying off 792n. *purchase;* release, let-off; discharge, reprieve, reprieval 960n. *acquittal;* day of grace, respite 136n. *delay;* truce, standstill 145n. *cessation;* way out 667n. *escape*; dispensation, exemption 919n. *non-liability*.

Adj. *extricable*, rescuable, deliverable, redeemable, fit for release; riddable.

Vb. *deliver*, save, rescue, come to the r., throw a life-line; get one out of 304vb. *extract;* extricate 62vb. *unravel;* unloose, untie, unbind 46vb. *disjoin;* bring to birth, act as a midwife, accouche 164vb. *generate;* disburden 701vb. *disencumber;* rid, save from 831vb. *relieve;* release, unlock, unbar; emancipate, free, set free, set at large 746vb. *liberate;* bring one off, get one off 960vb. *acquit;* deliver oneself 667vb. *escape;* save oneself, rid oneself, get rid of, be rid of, make a good riddance; snatch a brand from the burning, be the salvation of; redeem, ransom, buy off 792vb. *purchase;* salvage, retrieve, recover, bring back 656vb. *restore;* spare, excuse, dispense from 919vb. *exempt*.

Int. to the rescue! all hands to the pump! help!

See: 46, 62, 136, 145, 164, 304, 656, 667, 701, 746, 792, 831, 919, 960, 965.

669 Preparation

N. *preparation*, preparing, making ready, bundobust; clearance, clearing the decks; preliminaries, preliminary step, tuning, priming, loading; mobilization 718n. *war measures;* preliminary course, trial run, trial, trials 461n. *experiment;* practice, rehearsal, dress r.; brief, briefing; training, hard t., inurement, novitiate, baptism 534n. *teaching;* study, prep., homework 536n. *learning;* spadework 68n. *beginning;* groundwork, foundation 218n. *basis;* scaffold, scaffolding 218n. *frame;* planning, rough sketch, first draft, outline, blueprint, scheme, pilot s. 623n. *plan;* shadow cabinet, shadow factory; arrangement, prearrangement, preconcertation, premeditation 608n. *predetermination;* consultation, preconsultation 695n. *advice;* foretaste, forecast, anticipation, encasement 510n. *foresight;* bottom drawer, hope chest 632n. *store*.

fitting out, provisioning, furnishing, furnishment, logistics 663n. *provision;* appointment, commission, equipment, accouterment, array, marshaling, armament; promotion, company-promoting; inauguration, flotation, launching 68n. *debut*.

maturation, ripening, seasoning, bringing to a head; concoction, brewing, digestion; gestation, hatching, incubation, sitting 164n. *propagation;* culinary art 301n. *cookery;* nursing, nurture; cultivation, tilling, tillage, plowing, sowing, planting, plantation 370n. *agriculture*.

preparedness, readiness, ripeness, mellowness, maturity; puberty, nubility 134n. *adultness;* fitness, shipshape condition, height of training, pitch of perfection 646n. *perfection*.

preparer, trainer, coach, gymnasiarch, drill-sergeant 537n. *trainer;* torch-bearer, pioneer, bridge-builder 66n. *precursor;* sappers and miners 722n. *soldiery;* paver, pavior; loader, packer, stevedore; fitter, equipper, provisioner 633n. *provider;* cultivator, agriculturist, plowman, sower, planter 370n. *husbandman;* brewer, cook 301n. *cookery*.

Adj. *preparatory*, preparative; preparing etc. adj.; precautionary, preliminary 64adj. *preceding;* provisional, stop-gap 150adj. *substituted;* brewing, cooking, stewing; brooding, hatching, incubating, maturing; brooding, gestatory, in embryo; in preparation, on foot, on the stocks, on the anvil; in store, in the offing, forthcoming 155adj. *impending;* under consideration, agitated, mooted 623adj. *planned;* under training, learning 536adj. *studious*.

prepared, ready, always r., semper paratus, alert 457adj. *vigilant;* made ready, readied, in readiness, at the ready; mobilized, standing by, on call; teed up, keyed up, spoiling for; trained, fully t., qualified, well-prepared, practiced, in practice, at concert pitch; primed, briefed, instructed 524adj. *informed;* forewarned, forearmed 664adj. *warned;* saddled, ready s., booted and spurred, in the saddle; tight, snug, battened down; groomed, fully dressed, in one's best bib and tucker, in full feather, dressed to kill, got up to k., in full war-paint 228 adj. *dressed;* armed, in armor, in harness, fully armed, armed to the teeth, armed at all points, armed cap-a-pie; rigged, fully r.; equipped, furnished, fully f., well-appointed, provided 633adj. *provisionary;* in store, in hand 632adj. *stored;* in reserve, ready to hand, ready for use; fit for use, in working order; running, in gear.

matured, ripened, cooked, digested, hatched etc.vb.; ripe, seasoned, weathered, hardened; tried, experienced, veteran 694adj. *expert;* adult, grown, full-g., fledged 134adj. *grown up;* overripe, overmature; well-cooked, well-done; elaborate, over-e., wrought, highly w., over-w., worked up, labored, smelling of the lamp; deep-laid.

ready-made, cut and dried, ready for wear, reach-me-down, off the peg; ready-formed, ready-furnished; oven-ready; predigested, ready-cooked, instant.

Vb. *prepare*, take steps, take measures; make preparations, make a bundobust, mount; make ready, pave, pave the way, show the w., bridge, build a b., lead up to, pioneer 64vb. *come before;* choose one's ground, erect the scaffolding, lay *or* dig the foundations, lay the groundwork, provide the basis; predispose, incline; prepare the ground, sow the seed 370vb. *cultivate;* lay a train, dig a mine; set to work, address oneself to, take one's coat off, limber up 68vb. *begin;* rough-hew, cut out, block o.; sketch, outline, blueprint 623vb. *plan;* plot, concert, prearrange 608vb. *predetermine;* prepare for, forearm, guard against, insure, prepare for a rainy day, feather one's nest 660vb. *seek safety;* anticipate 507vb. *expect.*

make ready, ready, have r., finish one's preparations; set in order, put in readiness; stow, stow away, pack 632vb. *store;* trim, make tight, make all snug; commission, put in c.; put one's house in order, put in working order, bring up to scratch, wind up, screw up, tune, tune up, adjust 62vb. *arrange;* lay the table, spread the table, dish up, serve up; settle preliminaries, clear the decks, close the ranks, array; mobilize 74vb. *bring together;* whet the knife, trim the foils, shuffle the cards, tee up; set, cock, prime, load; fledge, feather; raise steam, warm up, crank, crank up, put in gear; equip, fit, fit out, furnish, accouter, harness, rig, dress; arm, provide with arms, provide with teeth 633 vb. *provide;* improvise, rustle up; rehearse, drill, groom, exercise 534 vb. *train;* inure 610vb. *habituate;* coach, brief 524vb. *inform.*

mature, mellow, ripen, bring to fruition 646vb. *perfect;* force, bring on 174vb. *invigorate;* bring to a head 725vb. *climax;* digest, stew, brew 301vb. *cook;* gestate, hatch, incubate, breed 369vb. *breed stock;* grow, farm 370vb. *cultivate;* fledge, nurse, nurture; elaborate, work out 725vb. *carry through;* season, weather, smoke, dry, cure; temper, anneal 326vb. *harden.*

prepare oneself, brace o.; qualify oneself, serve an apprenticeship; study, train, exercise, rehearse, practice 536vb. *learn;* take one's coat off, gird up one's loins, limber up, warm up, flex one's muscles; put on one's armor, buckle on one's breastplate, take sword in hand; be prepared, stand ready, stand by, hold oneself in readiness, keep one's powder dry; anticipate, forearm, set the alarm.

Adv. *in preparation*, in anticipation, in readiness, acock; on the stocks, on the anvil, under construction.

See: 62, 64, 66, 68, 74, 134, 150, 155, 164, 174, 218, 228, 301, 326, 369, 370, 457, 461, 507, 510, 524, 534, 536, 537, 608, 610, 623, 632, 633, 646, 660, 664, 694, 718, 722, 725.

670 Non-preparation

N. *non-preparation*, lack of preparation; pot-luck; unpreparedness, unreadiness; lack of training, want of practice; disqualification, unfitness; rawness, immaturity, crudity, greenness, unripeness 126n. *newness;* belatedness 136n. *lateness;* improvidence, non-provision, neglect 458n. *negligence;* no deliberation 857n. *rashness;* hastiness, precipitance, rush 680n. *haste;* improvisation, impromptu, snap answer 609n. *spontaneity;* surprise 508n. *inexpectation;* forwardness, precocity 135n. *earliness;* imperfection 55n. *incompleteness.*

undevelopment, delayed maturity, slow ripening; native state, undeveloped s., virgin soil; unweeded garden 458n. *negligence;* raw material, unlicked cub, rough diamond; rough copy, unfinished attempt; embryo, abortion.

Adj. *unprepared*, unready, not ready, backward, behindhand 136adj. *late;* unorganized, unarranged, makeshift; without preparation, ad hoc, extemporized, improvised, impromptu, snap, catch-as-catch-can 609adj. *spontaneous;* unstudied 699adj. *artless;* rash, careless 458adj. *negligent;* rush, precipitant, overhasty 680adj. *hasty;* unguarded, exposed 661adj. *vulnerable;* unwarned, caught unawares, caught napping, in the wrong foot, unexpecting 508adj. *inexpectant;* shiftless, improvident, unthrifty, thoughtless, happy-go-lucky 456adj. *light-minded;* scratch, untrained, untaught, untutored 491 adj. *uninstructed;* undrilled, unpracticed, unexercised, unrehearsed 611 adj. *unhabituated;* unworked, untilled, fallow, unhandselled, virgin 674adj. *unused.*

immature, ungrown, half-grown, unripe, green, underripe, half-ripe, unripened, unmellowed; unblown, half-blown; unfledged, unlicked, callow; non-adult, adolescent, juvenile, boyish, girlish 130adj. *young;* undeveloped, half-developed, half-baked, raw 647adj. *imperfect;* underdeveloped, backward 136adj. *late;* unhatched, unborn, embryonic, rudimentary 68adj. *beginning;* unformed, unfashioned, unhewn, unwrought, unlabored, rough-hewn, uncut, unpolished, half-finished, unfinished; undigested, ill-digested; before time, premature, abortive, at half-cock 728 adj. *unsuccessful;* untrained, prentice, undergraduate 695adj. *unskilled;* crude, coarse, rude, savage, uncivilized 699adj. *artless;* early matured, forced, precocious.

uncooked, unbaked, unroasted, unboiled; raw, red, rare, underdone; browned, half-baked, cold, unwarmed; unprepared, undressed, ungarnished; indigestible, inedible 329adj. *tough;* undigested, unconcocted; unseasoned, uncured.

unequipped, untrimmed, unrigged, dismasted, dismantled, undressed 229 adj. *uncovered;* unfound, unfurnished, half-furnished, ill-provided 307adj. *deficient;* unfitted, unqualified, disqualified.

Vb. *be unprepared,*—unready etc.adj.; lack preparation 55vb. *be incomplete;* lie fallow, rust 655vb. *deteriorate;* need exercise, want practice, need training; not plan, make no preparation, offer pot-luck, extemporize, speak off-hand 609vb. *improvize;* be premature, go off at half-cock 135vb. *be early;* take no precautions, drop one's guard 456vb. *be inattentive;* catch unawares 508 vb. *surprise.*

Adv. *unreadily,* extempore, off the cuff, ad hoc, off-hand.

See: 55, 68, 126, 130, 135, 136, 229, 307, 329, 456, 458, 491, 508, 609, 611, 647, 655, 661, 674, 680, 695, 699, 728, 857.

671 Essay

N. *essay,* attempt, bid; step, move, gambit 676n. *deed;* endeavor, struggle, effort 682n. *exertion;* coup d'essai, tackle, try, some attempt; good try, stout *or* brave *or* valiant effort; best effort, best one can do; random effort, catch-as-catch-can; determined effort, set, dead s. 712n. *attack;* trial, probation 461n. *experiment;* go of it, go at, shot at, stab at, jab at, dab at, crack at, whack at; first attempt, first go, first shot, first offense 68n. *debut;* final attempt, last bid, last throw; thing attempted, operation, exercise, venture, adventure, quest, speculation 672n. *undertaking;* aim, goal 617n. *objective;* strain, high endeavor, perfectionism 862n. *fastidiousness.*

essayer, bidder, tackler, trier 852n. *hoper;* assayer, tester 461n. *experimenter;* searcher, quester 459n. *inquirer;* struggler, striver, fighter 716 n. *contender;* idealist 862n. *perfectionist;* activist 654n. *reformer;* undertaker, contractor, entrepreneur, jobber.

Adj. *essaying,* tackling, trying, striving, doing one's best; game, nothing daunted 599adj. *resolute;* questing, searching 459adj. *inquiring;* tentative, catch-as-catch-can; testing, probationary 461adj. *experimental;* ambitious, venturesome, daring 672adj. *enterprising.*

Vb. *essay,* quest, seek 459vb. *search;* seek to, aim, make it one's a. 617 vb. *intend;* offer, bid, make a b.; try, attempt, make an a., make a shift to, make the effort, do something about; endeavor, struggle, strive, try hard, try and try again 599vb. *be resolute;* try one's best, do one's b., use one's best endeavors 682vb. *exert oneself;* pull hard, push h., strain, sweat blood 682vb. *work;* tackle, take on, have a go, give it a try, have a shot at, have a crack at, have a stab at 672vb. *undertake;* get down to, get to grips with, take the bull by the horns, make a go of; take a chance, chance one's arm, try one's luck, venture, speculate 618vb. *gamble;* tempt, tempt providence 461vb. *experiment;* test, make trial of, assay; grope, feel one's way 461vb. *be tentative;* be ambitious, attempt too much, bite off more than one can chew, die in the attempt 728vb. *fail.*

See: 68, 459, 461, 599, 617, 618, 654, 672, 676, 682, 712, 716, 728, 852, 862.

672 Undertaking

N. *undertaking,* contract, engagement, pledged word, obligation 764 n. *promise;* job, task; self-imposed task, labor of love, pilgrimage 597n. *voluntary work;* operation, exercise; program, project, design 623n. *plan;* tall order, large assumption, large undertaking 700n. *hard task;* enterprise, emprise; quest, search, adventure 459n. *inquiry;* venture, speculation, stake 618n. *gambling;* occupation, matter in hand 622n. *business;* struggle, effort, campaign 671n. *essay.*

Adj. *enterprising,* pioneering, adventurous, venturesome, daring; go-ahead, progressive; opportunist, alive to opportunity; ambitious 859adj. *desiring;* overambitious 857adj. *rash;* responsible, owning responsibility.

Vb. *undertake,* engage in, betake oneself, take up, go in for, devote oneself to; venture on, take on, tackle 671vb. *essay;* go about, take in hand, turn one's hand to, put one's hand to; set forward, set going 285 vb. *promote;* proceed to, broach, embark on, launch into, plunge into, fall to, set to, buckle to, set one's shoulder to the wheel 68vb. *begin;* assume, take charge of 689vb. *manage;* execute 725vb. *carry out;* set up shop, have irons in the fire 622vb. *busy oneself;* take on one's shoulders, take upon oneself, assume responsibility, assume an obligation 917vb. *incur a duty;* engage to, commit oneself, contract 764vb. *promise;* volunteer 597vb. *be willing;* show enterprise, pioneer; venture, dare 661vb. *face danger;* apprentice oneself 669vb. *prepare oneself.*

See: 65, 285, 459, 597, 618, 622, 623, 661, 669, 671, 689, 700, 725, 764, 857, 859, 917.

673 Use

N. use, usufruct, enjoyment, disposal 773n. *possession;* conversion to use, conversion, utilization, exploitation; employment, employ, application, appliance; adhibition, administration; exercise, exercitation 610n. *practice;* resort, recourse; mode of use, treatment, good usage, proper treatment 457n. *carefulness;* ill-treatment, hard usage, wrong use 675n. *misuse;* effect of use, wear, wear and tear 655n. *dilapidation;* exhaustion, consumption 634n. *waste;* usefulness, benefit, service, avail 640n. *utility;* serviceability, practicality, convertibility, applicability 642n. *expedience;* office, purpose, point 622 n. *function;* long use, wont, beaten track 610n. *custom.*

Adj. *used,* applied, employed, availed of etc.vb.; in service, in use, in constant u., in practice; worn, second-hand, well-used, well-thumbed, dog-eared, well-worn 655adj. *dilapidated;* beaten, well-trodden 490adj. *known;* staled, vulgarized; pragmatical, practical, utilitarian 640adj. *useful;* makeshift, provisional 150adj. *substituted;* subservient, like wax *or* putty in one's hands 628adj. *instrumental;* available, usable, employable, utilizable, convertible 642adj. *expedient;* at one's service, consumable, disposable.

Vb. *use,* employ, exercise, practice; apply, exert, bring to bear, adhibit, administer; consume, spend on, give to, devote to, consecrate to, dedicate to; assign to, allot (**see** *dispose of*); utilize, make use of, convert, convert to use 640vb. *find useful;* exploit, use to the full, get the best out of, make the most of, exhaust the possibilities; turn to use, turn to account, capitalize, make hay with 137vb. *profit by;* make play with, play off, play off against; make a tool *or* handle of; make a pawn *or* cat's-paw of; put to use, wear, submit to w., wear out, use up 634 vb. *waste;* handle, thumb 378vb. *touch;* tread, follow, beat (a path); work, drive, manipulate 173vb. *operate;* wield, ply, brandish; overwork, tax, task 684vb. *fatigue;* over-use, stale 847vb. *vulgarize;* prepare for use, work on, work up, mold 243vb. *efform.*

avail of, take up, adopt; avail oneself of, try; resort to, run to, betake oneself to, have recourse to, recur to, fall back on; avail of unduly, presume on; press into service, enlist in one's s.; make do with, make shift w., do what one can w., make the most of, make the best of.

dispose of, command; have at one's disposal, control, have at one's command, do what one likes with; allot, assign 783vb. *apportion;* give to, devote to, spare, have to s.; draw forth, call f., put in requisition, call into play, set in play, set in motion, set in action, set going, deploy 612 vb. *motivate;* enjoy, have the usufruct 773vb. *possess;* consume, expend, absorb, use up 634vb. *waste.*

See: 137, 173, 243, 317, 378, 457, 490, 610, 612, 622, 628, 634, 640,

642, 648, 655, 675, 684, 773, 783, 847.

674 Non-use

N. *non-use*, abeyance, suspension 677 n. *inaction;* non-availability 190n. *absence*; stagnation, unemployment 679n. *inactivity;* forbearance, abstinence 620n. *avoidance;* savings, unspent balance 666n. *preservation;* disuse, obsolescence 611n. *desuetude;* dismissal 300n. *ejection;* waiver, giving up, surrender 621n. *relinquishment;* withdrawal, cancellation 752n. *abrogation;* uselessness, write-off 641 n. *inutility;* superannuation.

Adj. *unused*, not used; not available 190adj. *absent;* out of order, not in service, unusable, unemployable 641 adj. *useless;* unutilized, unapplied, unconverted; undisposed of, in hand, saved 632adj. *stored;* spare, extra; unspent, unconsumed 666adj. *preserved;* unessayed, untried; unexercised, in abeyance, suspended; untrodden, unbeaten; untouched, unhandled; ungathered, unculled, unplucked; unnecessary, not wanted, not required, unrequired, unengaged 860adj. *unwanted;* dispensed with, waived; not made use of, resting, unemployed, idle 679adj. *inactive;* jobless, out of work, out of employment, briefless.

disused, derelict, discarded, cast-off, jettisoned, scrapped, written off; sacked, discharged, laid off etc.vb.; laid up, moth-balled, out of commission, rusting; done with, used up, run down; on the shelf, retired; superseded, obsolete, discredited 127 adj. *antiquated.*

Vb. *not use*, not utilize, hold in abeyance; not touch, have no use for; abstain, forbear, hold off 620vb. *avoid;* dispense with, waive, not proceed with 621vb. *relinquish;* overlook, disregard 458vb. *neglect;* spare, save, reserve, keep in hand 632vb. *store;* not accept, decline 607vb. *reject.*

disuse, leave off 611vb. *disaccustom;* stop using, leave to rust, lay up, put in moth-balls, put out of commission, dismantle 641vb. *make useless;* have done with, lay aside, put on the shelf, hang up; pension off, put out to grass; discard, dump, ditch, scrap, write off; jettison, throw away, throw overboard 300vb. *eject;* slough, cast off 229vb. *doff;* give up, relinquish, resign 779vb. *not retain;* suspend, withdraw, cancel 752vb. *abrogate;* discharge, lay off, pay off 300vb. *dismiss;* drop, supersede, replace 150vb. *substitute;* be unused, rust 655vb. *deteriorate.*

See: 127, 150, 190, 229, 300, 458, 607, 611, 620, 621, 632, 641, 655, 666, 677, 679, 752, 779, 860.

675 Misuse

N. *misuse*, abuse, wrong use; misemployment, misapplication; misdirection, diversion; mismanagement, maladministration 695n. *unskillfulness;* misappropriation, malversation 788n. *peculation;* perversion 246n. *distortion;* prostitution, violation; profanation, desecration 980n. *impiety;* pollution 649n. *uncleanness;* extravagance 634n. *waste*; misusage, mishandling, ill-usage, ill-treatment, force 176n. *violence;* outrage, injury 616n. *evil.*

Vb. *misuse*, abuse; use wrongly, misemploy, misdirect; divert, manipulate, misappropriate 788vb. *defraud;* violate, desecrate, take in vain 980 vb. *profane;* prostitute 655vb. *pervert;* pollute 649vb. *make unclean;* do violence to, strain 176vb. *force;* maltreat 246vb. *distort;* outrage, ill-treat 735vb. *oppress;* misgovern, misrule, mishandle, mismanage 695vb. *be unskillful;* overwork, overtask, overtax 684vb. *fatigue;* use hard, wear out 655vb. *impair;* consume, squander, throw away 634vb. *waste;* misapply, cut a whetstone with a razor, use a sledgehammer to crack a nut 695vb. *stultify oneself.*

See: 176, 246, 616, 634, 649, 655, 684, 695, 735, 788, 980.

676 Action

N. *action*, doing, militancy; positive action, commission; negative action, omission; steps, measures, move 623 n. *policy;* transaction, enactment, performance, perpetration; dispatch, execution, effectuation, accomplishment 725n. *completion;* procedure, routine 610n. *practice;* exercitation, praxis; behavior 688n. *conduct;* movement, play, swing 265n. *motion;* operation, working, interaction, evolution 173n. *agency;* force, pressure 178n. *influence;* work, labor 682n. *exertion;* activism, activeness, drama 678n. *activity;* occupation 622 n. *business;* manufacture 164n. *production;* employment 673n. *use;* effort, endeavor, campaign 671n. *essay;* implementation, administration, handling 689n. *management;* plot 594n. *dramaturgy.*

deed, act, overt a.; action, gest, exploit, feat, achievement 855n. *prowess;* bad deed, crime 930n. *foul play;* stunt, tour de force 875n. *ostentation;* measure, step, move 623n. *policy;* maneuver, evolution 688n. *tactics;* stroke, blow, coup, coup de main, coup d'état 623n. *contrivance;* job, task, operation, exercise 672n. *undertaking;* proceeding, transaction, deal, doings, dealings 154n. *affairs;* work, handiwork, workmanship, craftsmanship 694n. *skill;* pièce de résistance, chef d'oeuvre 694n. *masterpiece;* drama, scene; acts, aretalogy 590n. *narrative.*

doer, man of deeds, man of action, activist 678n. *busy person;* practical man, realist; achiever, finisher; hero 855n. *brave person;* practitioner 696 n. *expert;* stunter, stunt-merchant, executant, performer, player 594n. *actor;* perpetrator, committer; offender, criminal 904n. *evildoer;* mover, controller, manipulator 612n. *motivator;* operator 686n. *agent;* contractor, undertaker, entrepreneur, campaigner; executor, executive, administrator, manager 690n. *director;* hand, workman, operative 686n. *worker;* craftsman 696n. *artisan;* creative worker 556n. *artist.*

Adj. *doing,* acting, operating, performing, in the act, red-handed; of commission, of omission; working, in action, in operation, in harness 173adj. *operative;* up and doing, industrious, busy 678adj. *active;* occupational 610adj. *habitual.*

Vb. *do,* be in action, come into operation; act, perform, do one's stuff 173vb. *operate;* militate, act upon 178vb. *influence;* manipulate 612vb. *motivate;* use tactics, twist, turn, maneuver 698vb. *be cunning;* do something, lift a finger, stretch forth one's hand; proceed, proceed with, get going, move, take action, take steps; attempt, try 671vb. *essay;* tackle, take on 672vb. *undertake;* adopt a measure, enact, legislate 953vb. *make legal;* do the deed, perpetrate, commit, inflict, achieve, accomplish, complete 725vb. *carry through;* do the needful, take care of, dispatch, execute, implement, fulfill, put through 725vb. *carry out;* solemnize, observe; act greatly, make history, win renown 866vb. *have repute;* practice, exercise, carry on, prosecute, wage, ply, ply one's task, employ oneself, be at work 622vb. *busy oneself;* officiate 622vb. *function;* transact, proceed 622vb. *do business;* administer, administrate, manage, control 689vb. *direct;* have to do with 688vb. *deal with;* sweat, labor, campaign 682vb. *work;* exploit, make the most of 673vb. *use;* intervene, strike a blow 703vb. *aid;* have a hand in, play a part in, pull an oar 775vb. *participate;* deal in, have a finger in, get mixed up in 678vb. *meddle;* conduct oneself, indulge in 688vb. *behave;* play about, act a., fool a. 497vb. *be absurd;* stunt, show off 875vb. *be ostentatious.*

Adv. *in the act,* in flagrante delicto, red-handed; in the midst of, in the thick of; while one's hand is in, while one is about it.

See: 154, 164, 173, 178, 265, 497, 556, 590, 594, 610, 612, 622, 623, 671, 672, 673, 678, 682, 686, 688, 689, 690, 694, 696, 698, 703, 725, 755, 775, 855, 866, 875, 904, 930, 953.

677 Inaction

N. *inaction,* non-action, nothing doing, inertia 175n. *inertness;* inability to act 161n. *impotence;* failure to act, neglect 458n. *negligence;* abstinence from action, abstention, refraining 620n. *avoidance;* suspension, abeyance, dormancy 674n. *non-use;* immobility, paralysis, impassivity, insensitivity 375n. *insensibility;* passivity, stagnation, vegetation, doldrums, stillness, quiet, calm 266n. *quiescence;* time on one's hands, idle hours, hours of idleness, dolce far niente 681n. *leisure;* rest 683n. *repose;* no work, sinecure; non-employment, under-e., unemployment, loafing, idleness, indolence 679n. *inactivity;* do-nothingness, masterly inactivity, Fabian policy, cunctation 136n. *delay;* unprogressiveness, rust 654n. *deterioration;* non-interference, neutrality 860n. *indifference;* defeatism 856n. *cowardice.*

Adj. *non-active,* inoperative, suspended, in abeyance; dull, sluggish 175adj. *inert;* unoccupied, leisured 681adj. *leisurely;* do-nothing, unprogressive; Fabian, cunctative, delaying, procrastinating; defeatist 853 adj. *hopeless;* stationary, motionless, immobile 266adj. *quiescent;* cold, extinct; not stirring, without a sign of life, dead or dying 361adj. *dead;* idle, unemployed, jobless, briefless, out of work, on the dole, without employment 679adj. *inactive;* incapable of action 161adj. *impotent;* benumbed, paralyzed 375adj. *insensible;* apathetic, phlegmatic 820adj. *impassive;* neutral 860adj. *indifferent;* unhearing 416adj. *deaf.*

Vb. *not act,* fail to a., refuse to a., hang fire 599vb. *be loath;* refrain, abstain 620vb. *avoid;* look on, stand by 441vb. *watch;* watch and wait, wait and see, tide it over, bide one's time 136vb. *wait;* procrastinate 136vb. *put off;* live and let live, let it rip, laisser aller, laisser faire, let sleeping dogs lie, let well alone; hold no brief for, stay neutral, observe neutrality 860vb. *be indifferent;* do nothing, tolerate, squat, fold one's hands, fold one's arms, not move, not budge, not stir, show no sign, not lift a finger, not even attempt 175vb. *be inert;* drift, slide, coast; have no hope 853vb. *despair;* let pass, let go by, leave alone, let a., give it a miss 458adj. *neglect;* stay still, keep quiet 266vb. *be quiescent;* relax, rest and be thankful 683vb. *repose;* have no function 641vb. *be useless;* have nothing to do, kick one's heels 681vb. *have leisure;* pause, desist 145vb. *cease;* rust, lie idle, stay on the shelf, lie fallow 674vb. *not use;* have no life, lie stiff, lie dead 361vb. *die.*

Adv. *without action,* nothing doing, without movement; hands in one's pockets, with folded arms; with the job half done.

See: 136, 145, 161, 175, 266, 361, 375, 416, 441, 458, 599, 620, 641, 654, 674, 679, 681, 683, 820, 853, 856, 860.

678 Activity

N. *activity,* activeness, activism, militancy 676n. *action;* interest, active i. 775n. *participation;* social activity, group a. 882n. *sociability;* activation 612n. *motivation;* excitation 174n. *stimulation;* agitation, movement, mass m. 738n. *sedition;* life, stir 265n. *motion;* nimbleness, briskness, smartness, alacrity, promptitude 597n. *willingness;* readiness 135n. *punctuality;* quickness, dispatch, expedition 277n. *velocity;* spurt, burst, fit 318n. *spasm;* hurry, flurry, hurry-skurry, hustle, bustle, over-haste, frantic haste 680n. *haste;* fuss, bother, botheration, ado, to-do, racketing, tumult, frenzy 61n. *turmoil;* whirl, scramble, mad s., rat-race, maelstrom 315n. *vortex;* drama, great doings, much ado, thick of things, thick of action; working life, battle of l.; plenty to do, irons in the fire 622n. *business;* call on one's time, press of business; pressure of work, no sinecure; busy place, busy street, market-place, heavy traffic; press, madding crowd, seething mob; hum, hive, hive of industry 687n. *workshop.*

restlessness, pottering, aimless activity, desultoriness, no concentration 456n. *inattention;* unquiet, fidgets, fidgetiness 318n. *agitation;* jumpiness, jerkiness 822n. *excitability;* fever, fret 503n. *frenzy;* eagerness, enthusiasm, ardor, fervor, abandon, vehemence 818n. *warm feeling;* vigor, energy, ceaseless e., dynamic e., dynamism, aggressiveness, militancy, enterprise, initiative, push, drive, go, pep 174n. *vigorousness;* vivacity, spirit, animation, liveliness, vitality 360n. *life;* watchfulness, wakefulness, vigilance 457n. *carefulness;* sleeplessness, insomnia; tirelessness, indefatigability.

assiduity, application, concentration, intentness 455n. *attention;* sedulity, industriousness, industry, laboriousness, drudgery 682n. *labor;* determination, earnestness, empressement 599n. *resolution;* tirelessness, indefatigability 600n. *perseverance;* studiousness, painstaking, diligence, habits of business; whole-heartedness, devotedness; Stakhanovism.

overactivity, overextension, overexpansion, excess 637n. *redundance;* futile activity, chasing one's own tail 641n. *lost labor;* thyrotoxic condition, overexertion, Stakhanovism; officiousness, ultracrepidarianism, meddlesomeness, interference, intrusiveness, interruption, meddling, intermeddling, interfering, finger in every pie; tampering, intrigue 623n. *plot.*

busy person, new broom, enthusiast, bustler, hustler, man in a hurry; zealot, fanatic 602n. *opinionist;* slogger, hard worker, tireless w., high-pressure w., Stakhanovite, demon for work, glutton for w. 686n. *worker;* factotum, maid-of-all-work, housewife, drudge, fag, nigger, slave, galley-s., Trojan; horse, beaver, ant, busy bee; man of active habits, man of action, activist; participator; sharp fellow, blade, live wire, go-getter, pusher, thruster; careerist.

meddler, dabbler, intermeddler, officious person, spoilsport, Nosy Parker, ultracrepidarian, busybody, pickthank; tamperer, intriguer 623n. *planner;* interferer, butter-in; kibitzer, back-seat driver 691n. *adviser;* fusspot, nuisance.

Adj. *active,* stirring 265adj. *moving;* going, working, incessant 146adj. *unceasing;* full of dispatch 622vb. *businesslike;* able, able-bodied 162 adj. *strong;* quick, brisk, nippy, spry, smart, gleg 277adj. *speedy;* nimble, light-footed, featly, tripping; energetic, forceful, thrustful 174adj. *vigorous;* pushing, go-getting, up-and-coming 672adj. *enterprising;* frisky, coltish, dashing, sprightly, spirited, mettlesome, live, alive and kicking, full of beans, animated, vivacious 819adj. *lively;* eager, ardent, perfervid 818adj. *fervent;* fierce, desperate 599adj. *resolute;* enthusiastic, zealous, prompt, instant, ready, on one's toes 597adj. *willing;* expeditious, full of dispatch 622vb. *businesslike;* awake, alert, watchful, wakeful 457adj. *vigilant;* sleepless, tireless, restless, feverish, fretful, tossing, dancing, fidgety, jumpy, fussy, nervy, like a cat on hot bricks 318adj. *agitated;* frantic, demonic 503adj. *frenzied;* overactive, overextended; overexerted, thyrotoxic; aggressive, militant, up in arms 718adj. *warlike.*

busy, bustling, hustling, humming, coming and going, rushing to and fro; pottering, doing chores; up and doing, stirring, eventful; astir, afoot, a-doing, on the move, on the go, in full swing; slogging, hard at work, hard at it, up to one's eyes, full of business, fully engaged; in harness, at work, at one's desk; occupied, fully o., employed, over-e.; busy as a bee, busy as a hen with chickens.

industrious, studious, sedulous, assiduous 600adj. *persevering;* laboring, hardworking, plodding, slogging, strenuous 682adj. *laborious;* unflagging, unwearied, unsleeping, tireless, indefatigable, keeping long hours, never-tiring, never-resting, never-sleeping; efficient, workmanlike 622 adj. *businesslike.*

meddling, over-busy, officious, ultracrepidarian, interfering, meddlesome, intriguing; dabbling; participating, in the business.

Vb. *be active,* show interest, interest oneself in, trouble oneself, join in 775vb. *participate;* be stirring, stir, come and go, rush to and fro 265 vb. *move;* run riot, have one's fling 61vb. *rampage;* not sleep, wake up, rouse oneself, bestir o., be up and doing; hum, thrive 730vb. *prosper;* make progress 285vb. *progress;* keep moving, keep on the go, keep the ball rolling 146vb. *go on;* push, shove, thrust, drive 279vb. *impel;* elbow one's way 174vb. *be vigorous;* rush, surge 350vb. *flow;* roar, rage, bluster 352vb. *blow;* explode, burst 176vb. *be violent;* dash, fly, run 277 vb. *move fast;* make the effort, do one's best 671vb. *essay;* take pains 455vb. *be attentive;* be about it, be hard at it 682vb. *exert oneself;* persist 600vb. *persevere;* polish off, dispatch, make short work of, not let the grass grow under one's feet; rise to the occasion, work wonders 727vb. *be successful;* jump to it, show zeal, burn with z., be on fire, anticipate 597vb. *be willing;* be on one's toes, keep awake, wake, watch 457vb. *be careful;* seize the opportunity, take one's chance 137vb. *profit by;* assert oneself, not take it lying down, be up in arms, react, react sharply, show fight 711vb. *defy;* protest, agitate, kick up a shindy, raise the dust 762vb. *deprecate.*

be busy, keep b., have irons in the fire 622vb. *busy oneself;* bustle, hurry, scurry 680vb. *hasten;* live in a whirl, join the rat-race, go all ways at once, run round in circles; chase one's own tail 641vb. *waste effort;* not know which way to turn 700vb. *be in difficulty;* have one's hands full, have not a moment to spare, have no time to lose, rise early, go to bed late; fuss, fret, fume, stamp with impatience 822vb. *be excitable;* have other things to do, have other fish to fry 138vb. *be engaged;* slave, slag 682vb. *work;* overwork, overdo it, make work, make a toil of a pleasure; never stop, improve the shining hour; affect zeal, show work 850vb. *be affected.*

meddle, intermeddle, interpose, intervene, interfere, be officious, not mind one's own business, have a finger in every pie; poke one's nose in, shove one's oar in, butt in 297 vb. *intrude;* pester, bother, dun, annoy 827vb. *incommode;* be bossy, boss, boss one around, tyrannize 735vb. *oppress;* tinker, tamper, touch 655vb. *impair.*

Adv. *actively,* on the go, on one's toes; full tilt, whole hog; with might and main, with life and spirit, for all one is worth.

See: 61, 135, 137, 138, 146, 162, 174, 176, 265, 277, 279, 285, 297, 315, 318, 350, 352, 360, 455, 456, 457, 503, 597, 599, 600, 602, 612, 622, 623, 637, 641, 655, 671, 672, 676, 680, 682, 686, 687, 691, 700, 711, 718, 727, 730, 735, 738, 762, 775, 818, 819, 822, 827, 805, 882.

679 Inactivity

N. *inactivity*, inactiveness 677n. *inaction;* inertia, heaviness, torpor 175n. *inertness;* lull, suspension, suspended animation 145n. *cessation;* immobility, stillness, quietude, doldrums, grave, morgue 266n. *quiescence;* no progress, stagnation 654n. *deterioration;* rust, rustiness 674n. *non-use;* sag, slump, recession 37n. *decrease;* unemployed, smokeless chimneys; absenteeism 598n. *unwillingness;* procrastination 136n. *delay;* idleness, loafing, killing time, dolce far niente; idle hands, idle hours 681n. *leisure.*

sluggishness, stiffness, segnity, segnitude; laziness, indolence, sloth; lethargy, acedia, accidie; remissness 458 n. *negligence;* dawdling, slow progress 278n. *slowness;* inanimation, lifelessness; languor, lentor, dullness, listlessness 819n. *moral insensibility;* stupor, torpor, torpescence, torpidity, numbness 375n. *insensibility;* apathy 860n. *indifference;* phlegm, impassivity 823n. *inexcitability;* supineness, no resistance, line of least r. 721n. *submission.*

sleepiness, tiredness, weariness, lassitude 684n. *fatigue;* somnolence, doziness, drowsiness, heaviness, nodding; oscitation, oscitancy, yawning; stretching, pandiculation; tired head, tired eyes, heavy lids, sand in the eyes; dreaminess 513n. *fantasy.*

sleep, slumber, bye-byes; deep sleep, sound s., heavy s.; untroubled sleep, sleep of the just; arms of Morpheus, Hypnos, sandman; half-sleep, drowse; first sleep, beauty s.; light sleep, nap, catnap, forty winks, shut-eye, snooze, doze, siesta, afternoon rest 683n. *repose;* winter sleep, hibernation; unconsciousness, coma, trance, catalepsy, hypnosis, somnipathy 375n. *insensibility;* sleep-walking, somnambulism; sleeping sickness, encephalitis lethargica 651 n. *disease;* dreams, dreamland, Land of Nod; cradle, pillow, bed, shake-down.

soporific, somnifacient, sleeping draft, nightcap; sleeping pill, sleeping tablet; sedative, barbiturate; opiate, poppy, mandragora, opium, morphia 375n. *anesthetic;* lullaby, berceuse, cradle-song.

idler, drone, lazybones, lie-abed, loafer, lounger, flâneur, sloucher, slug, sluggard; moper, mopus, sleepy-head; lubber, lubbard; dawdle, dawdler 278n. *slowcoach;* hobo, bum, tramp 268n. *wanderer;* mendicant 763n. *beggar;* spiv, parasite, cadger, sponger; floater, drifter; opium-eater, lotus-e., waiter on Providence 596n. *fatalist;* non-worker, sinecurist, rentier; fainéant, dummy, passenger, sleeping partner, absentee landlord, afternoon farmer; dreamer, sleeper, slumberer, dozer, drowser; hibernator, dormouse, marmot; Seven Sleepers, Rip van Winkle, Barbarossa, Sleeping Beauty.

Adj. *inactive*, motionless, stationary, at a standstill, still, hushed, extinct 266adj. *quiescent;* suspended, discontinued, taken off, not working, not operating, not in use, laid up, out of commission 674adj. *disused;* inanimate, lifeless, exanimate 175 adj. *inert;* torpid, benumbed, unconscious, dopey, drugged 375adj. *insensible;* sluggish, stiff, rusty 677 adj. *non-active;* listless, lackadaisical 834adj. *dejected;* tired, faint, languid, languorous 684adj. *fatigued;* dull, heavy, leaden 838adj. *tedious;* soulless, lumpish, stolid 820adj. *impassive;* unresisting, supine, submissive 721adj. submitting, uninterested 454 adj. *incurious;* apathetic 860adj. *indifferent;* lethargic, unaroused, unawakened 823adj. *inexcitable;* non-participating, sleeping 190adj. *absent;* leisured, idle, empty, otiose, unoccupied, disengaged 681adj. *leisurely;* on strike, out.

lazy, bone-l., do-nothing, fainéant; slothful, sluggish, work-shy, indolent, idle; dronish, spivvish, parasitical; idling, lolling, loafing 681adj. *leisurely;* dawdling 278adj. *slow;* tardy, laggard, dilatory, procrastinating 136adj. *late;* slack, remiss, careless 458adj. *negligent.*

sleepy, ready for bed, tired 684adj. *fatigued;* half-awake, half-asleep; slumbrous, somnolent, heavy-eyed, heavy with sleep, stupid with s.; drowsy, dozy, nodding, yawning; napping, dozing; asleep, dreaming, fast asleep, sound a., dead a., dead, dead to the world; unconscious, out; dormant, hibernating, comatose; in dreamland, in the arms of Morpheus, in bed.

somnific, soporific, somniferous, somnifacient, sleep-inducing, sedative, hypnotic.

Vb. *be inactive*, do nothing, rust, stagnate, vegetate, smolder, hang fire 677vb. *not act;* let the grass grow under one's feet, delay 136vb. *put off;* not bother, take it easy, let it rip, laisser faire 458vb. *be neglectful;* hang about, kick one's heels 136vb. *wait;* take one's time, slouch, lag, loiter, dawdle 278vb. *move slowly;* daily, tarry, stay 136vb. *be late;* stand, sit, lie, lollop, loll, lounge, laze, rest, take one's ease 683vb. *repose;* not work, fold one's arms, sit on one's hands; have nothing to do, loaf, idle, mooch, moon, while away the time, twiddle one's thumbs; waste time, consume the golden hours, trifle, dabble, fribble, fiddle-faddle, fritter away the time, piddle, potter, putter 641vb. *waste effort;* slow down, come to a standstill 278vb. *decelerate;* dilly-dally, hesitate 474vb. *be uncertain;* droop, faint, fail, languish, slacken 266vb. *come to rest;* sag, slump 37vb. *decrease;* be still, be hushed 266vb. *be quiescent;* discontinue, stop, come to an end 145vb. *cease;* strike, come out.

sleep, slumber, snooze, nap; estivate, hibernate; sleep sound, sleep well, sleep like a log, sleep like a top, lie in the arms of Morpheus; dream; snore; go to sleep, drop off, fall asleep, take a nap, have forty winks; close one's eyes, feel sleepy, yawn, nod, doze, drowse; go to bed, turn in, doss down, kip d., shake d.; settle down, bed, roost, perch.

make inactive, put to sleep, put to bed, seal up the eyelids; send to sleep, lull, rock, cradle; soothe 177 vb. *assuage;* make lazy, sluggardize; deaden, paralyze, benumb, chill dope, drug, narcotize, put out 375 vb. *render insensible;* stiffen, cramp, immobilize 747vb. *fetter;* lay up, put out of commission 674vb. *disuse;* dismantle 641vb. *make useless;* pay off, stand o., lay o., 300vb. *dismiss.*

See: 37, 136, 145, 175, 177, 190, 266, 268, 278, 300, 375, 454, 458, 474, 513, 596, 598, 641, 651, 654, 674, 677, 681, 683, 684, 721, 747, 763, 819, 820, 823, 834, 838, 860.

680 Haste

N. *haste*, hurry, scurry, hurry-scurry, hustle, bustle, scuttle, scramble 678n. *activity;* splutter, flutter, fidget, fuss 318n. *agitation;* rush, rush job 670 n. *non-preparation;* race, feverish haste, tearing hurry, no time to lose 136n. *lateness;* push, drive, expedition, dispatch 277n. *velocity;* hastening, acceleration, forced march, dash 277n. *spurt;* overhaste, precipitance, impetuosity 857n. *rashness;* inability to wait, hastiness, impatience 822n. *excitability;* cause for haste, immediacy, urgency 638n. *importance.*

Adj. *hasty*, over-h., impetuous, hot-headed, precipitant 857adj. *rash;* feverish, impatient, all impatience, ardent 818adj. *fervent;* pushing, shoving; uncontrolled, boisterous, furious 176adj. *violent;* precipitate, headlong, breathless, scrambling 277 adj. *speedy;* expeditious, prompt, without delay; hasting, hastening, making speed; in haste, in all h., in hot h., hot-foot, running, racing; in a hurry, unable to wait, pressed for time, hard-pressed, driven; done in haste, hurried, scamped, rough and ready, forced, rushed, rush, last-minute 670adj. *unprepared;* allowing no time, brooking no delay, urgent, immediate 638adj. *important.*

Vb. *hasten*, expedite, dispatch; urge, drive, spur, goad, whip, lash, flog 612vb. *incite;* rush, allow no time, brook no delay; be hasty, be precipitate, rush headlong 857vb. *be rash;* haste, make haste; post, race, run, dash off, tear off 277vb. *move fast;* catch up, make up for lost time, overtake 277vb. *outstrip;* spurt, dash, make a forced march 277vb. *accelerate;* hurry, scurry, hustle, bustle, fret, fume, fidget, rush to and fro, dart to and fro 678vb. *be active;* be in a hurry, have no time to spare, have no time to lose, cut short the preliminaries, brush aside; cut corners, rush one's fences; rush through, dash through, make short work of; be pressed for time, work against time, work under pressure; do at the last moment 136vb. *be late;* lose no time, lose not a moment, make every minute count; hasten away, cut one's cable, cut and run, make oneself scarce, stand not upon the order of one's going 296vb. *decamp.*

Adv. *hastily*, hurriedly, precipitately, feverishly, post-haste, hot-foot, apace 277vb. *swiftly;* with all haste, at short notice, on the spur of the moment; immediately, urgently, with urgency, under pressure, by forced marches, with not a moment to lose.

See: 136, 176, 277, 296, 318, 612, 638, 670, 678, 818, 822, 857.

681 Leisure

N. *leisure*, spare time, convenience; spare hours, vacant moments; time on one's hands, time to kill; not enough work, sinecure; no work, idleness, dolce far niente; off duty, time off, day off, holiday, half-h., vacation, leave, furlough 679n. *inactivity;* time to spare, no hurry, ample time, all the time in the world; rest, ease, slippered e. 683n. *repose;* no more work, retirement 753n. *resignation.*

Adj. *leisurely*, deliberate, unhurried 278adj. *slow;* at one's convenience, at one's own time, at any odd moment; leisured, at leisure, disengaged, unoccupied; at loose ends, at ease; off duty, on holiday, on vacation, on leave, on furlough; retired, in retirement; affording leisure, labor-saving.

Vb. *have leisure,* have time enough, have plenty of time, have all the time in the world, have time to spare; be master of one's time, take one's ease, spend, pass, while away; see no cause for haste, take one's time 278vb. *more slowly;* want something to do, find time lie heavy on one's hands 679vb. *be inactive;* take a holiday 683vb. *repose;* give up work, go into retirement, retire 753vb. *resign;* find time for, make leisure, save labor.

See: 278, 679, 683, 753.

682 Exertion

N. *exertion*, effort, struggle, strife 671 n. *essay;* straining, strain, stress, might and main; tug, pull, stretch, heave, lift, throw, a strong pull, a long pull and a pull all together; drive, force, pressure, full p., maximum p., applied energy 160n. *energy;* ado, trouble, toil and t., mighty efforts, the hard way; muscle, elbow grease, sweat of one's brow; pains, painstaking, operoseness 678n. *assiduity;* elaboration, artificiality; overwork, overexertion, overexpansion 678n. *overactivity;* extra work, overtime, busman's holiday; battle, campaign.

exercise, exercitation; employment 673n. *use;* practice, regular p., training workout 669n. *preparation;* bodily exercise, physical e., gymnastics 162n. *athletics;* eurythmics, calisthenics; games, sports, outdoor s., races 837n. *sport.*

labor, work, hard w., heavy w., uphill w., warm w., punishing w., long haul; spade-work, donkey-work; manual labor, sweat of one's brow; housework, chores, toil, travail, swink, drudgery, slavery, sweat, fag, grind, strain, treadmill, grindstone; penal work, hard labor, picking oakum, breaking stones 963n. *penalty;* forced labor, corvée 740n. *compulsion;* fatigue, fatigue duty, spell of d. 917n. *duty;* piecework, taskwork; task, chore, job, operation, exercise 676n. *deed;* shift, trick, stint, stretch, spell of work 110n. *period;* job of work, stroke of w., stitch of w., hand's turn; working life, working day, man-hours.

Adj. *laboring*, born to toil, horny-handed; working, drudging, sweating, grinding, etc.vb.; on the go, on the stretch, hard at it 678adj. *busy;* hard-working, laborious, operose 678adj. *industrious;* slogging, plodding 600adj. *persevering;* strenuous, energetic 678adj. *active;* painstaking, thorough 455adj. *attentive;* exercising, taking exercise, practicing; palaestric, gymnastic, athletic.

laborious, full of labor, involving effort; operose, crushing, killing, backbreaking; grueling, punishing; toilsome, troublesome, weary, wearisome, painful, burdensome; heroic, Herculean; arduous, hard, warm, heavy, uphill 700adj. *difficult;* hard-fought, hard-won; thorough, painstaking, labored; elaborate, artificial; detailed, fiddling; effort-wasting 641 adj. *useless.*

Vb. *exert oneself*, apply oneself, use one's exertions, make an effort, try 671vb. *essay;* struggle, strain, strive, sweat blood; trouble oneself, bestir oneself, put oneself out; spare no effort, turn every stone, do one's utmost, try one's best, use one's best endeavors, do all one can, go to all lengths; put one's heart and soul into it, put out one's whole strength, put one's back into it, strain every nerve, use every muscle; love one's job, have one's heart in one's work 597vb. *be willing;* force one's way, drive through, wade t.; hammer at, slog at 600 vb. *persevere;* battle, campaign.

work, labor, toil, moil, drudge, fag, grind, slog, sweat; sweat blood; pull, haul, tug, heave, ply the oar; dig, spade, lumber; do the work, soil one's hands; spit on one's palms, get down to it, set to, take one's coat off 68vb. *begin;* keep at it, plod 600vb. *persevere;* work hard, work overtime, work double shift, work double tides, work all hours, work night and day, overwork 678vb. *be busy;* slave, work one's fingers to the bone, work like a nigger, work like a slave *or* like a galley-s., work like a horse, work like a Trojan, work like a steam engine; overdo it, make work; work for, serve 703vb. *minister to;* put to work, give work to, task, tax 684vb. *fatigue;* handle, ply 173vb. *operate.*

Adv. *laboriously,* the hard way; arduously, strenuously, energetically; lustily, heartily, heart and soul, with might and main, with all one's might, tooth and nail, hammer and tongs, for all one is worth.

See: 68, 110, 160, 162, 173, 455, 597, 600, 641, 669, 671, 673, 676, 678, 684, 700, 703, 740, 837, 917, 963.

683 Repose

N. *repose,* rest, rest from one's labors 679n. *inactivity;* restfulness, ease, comfort, snugness 376n. *euphoria;* sweet sleep, happy dreams 679n. *sleep;* relaxation, breathing time, breather 685n. *refreshment;* pause, respite, recess, break 145n. *lull;* interval 108n. *interim;* holiday, vacation, leave, furlough, day off, sabbatical year 681n. *leisure;* day of rest, sabbath, Lord's day.

Adj. *reposeful,* restful, easeful, slippered, unbelted, unbuttoned; cushioned, pillowed, snug 376adj. *comfortable;* peaceful, quiet 266adj. *tranquil;* leisured, sabbatical, vacational, holiday 687adj. *leisurely;* postprandial, after-dinner.

Vb. *repose,* rest, take r., enjoy peace, take it easy, take one's ease; mop one's brow, stretch one's legs; recline, lie down, loll, sprawl 216vb. *be horizontal;* perch, roost 311vb. *sit down;* couch, go to bed, kip down, go to sleep 679vb. *sleep;* relax, unbend, forget work, put on one's slippers, rest and be thankful; breathe, take a breather 685vb. *be refreshed;* rest on one's oars 266 vb. *come to rest;* take a holiday, go on leave 681vb. *have leisure.*

Adv. *at rest,* reposefully, restfully, peacefully, on holiday, on vacation.

See: 108, 145, 216, 266, 311, 376, 679, 681, 685.

684 Fatigue

N. *fatigue,* tiredness, weariness, lassitude, languor; physical fatigue, aching muscles; mental fatigue, brain-fag, staleness; jadedness, distress; limit of endurance, exhaustion, collapse, prostration, done-up feeling; strain, overtiredness, overexertion 682n. *exertion;* sign of fatigue, shortness of breath, hard breathing, dyspnea, panting, palpitations 352n. *respiration;* languishment, faintness, fainting, faint, swoon, black-out, deliquium, lipothymy, coma, syncope 375n. *insensibility.*

Adj. *fatigued,* tired, ready for bed 679adj. *sleepy;* tired out, exhausted, spent, fordone; done, done up, done for, pooped, fagged, fagged out, knocked out, washed up, washed out; stupid with fatigue, dull, stale; strained, overworked, overtired, overdriven, overwearied, overfatigued, overstrained; dog-tired, dog-weary, tired to death, dropping, ready to drop, all in, dead beat, beat, whacked; more dead than alive, swooning, fainting, out; aching, sore, toilworn; way-worn, footsore, footweary, walked off one's legs; overwatched, tired-eyed, heavy-e., hollow-e.; tired-looking, haggard, worn; faint, drooping, flagging, languid, languorous; still tired, unrefreshed; tired of, bored with 838 adj. *bored;* jaded, satiated 863adj. *sated.*

panting, anhelous, out of breath, short of b.; breathed, breathless, gasping, puffing and blowing, snorting, winded, blown, broken-winded 352adj. *puffing.*

fatiguing, grueling, punishing, 682 adj. *laborious;* tiresome, wearisome; exacting, demanding; irksome, trying 838adj. *tedious.*

Vb. *be fatigued,*—fagged etc.adj.; get weary, ache in every muscle, gasp, pant, puff, blow, grunt, lose one's wind 352vb. breathe; languish, droop, drop, sink, flag, fail 163vb. *be weak;* stagger, faint, swoon, get giddy, swim; yawn, nod, drowse 679vb. *sleep;* succumb, drop, collapse, crack up, crock up, pack up; cry out for rest, have no strength left, be at the end of one's strength; can go *or* do no more, must have a rest, must sit down; overwork, get stale, need a rest, need a break, need a change, need a holiday.

fatigue, tire, tire out, wear, fag, wear out, exhaust, do up, whack, knock up, crock up, prostrate; double up, wind; demand too much, task, tax, strain, work, drive, overdrive, flog, overwork, overtax, overtask, overburden, overstrain; distress, harass, irk, jade 827vb. *incommode;* tire to death, weary, bore, send to sleep 838vb. *be tedious;* keep from sleep, deprive of rest, stint of r., allow no r.

See: 163, 352, 375, 679, 682, 827, 838, 863.

685 Refreshment

N. *refreshment,* breather, break, recess 145n. *lull;* renewal, recreation, recruitment, recuperation 656n. *restoration;* reanimation, refocillation 656n. *revival;* easing 831n. *relief;* stimulation, refresher, reviver, nineteenth hole 174n. *stimulant;* regalement, refection 301n. *food;* wash, wash and brush up, tidy-up 648n. *cleansing.*

Adj. *refreshing,* cooling, cool 380adj. *cold;* comforting 831adj. *relieving;* bracing, reviving, recruiting 656adj. *restorative;* easy on, labor-saving.

refreshed, freshened up, breathed, recovered, revived, enlivened 656adj. *restored;* like a giant refreshed, twice the man one was; perked up, ready for more.

Vb. *refresh,* freshen, freshen up 648 vb. *clean;* air, fan, ventilate 340vb. *aerify;* shade, cool, cool off, cool one down 382vb. *refrigerate;* brace, stimulate 174vb. *invigorate;* recruit, recreate, revive, reanimate, refocillate, recuperate 656vb. *restore;* ease 831vb. *relieve;* allow rest, give a breather; regale 301vb. *feed.*

be refreshed, breathe, draw breath, get one's breath back, regain *or* recover one's breath, take a deep b., respire, clear one's head; come to, perk up, feel like a giant refreshed; recrudesce, revive 656vb. *be restored;* mop one's brow, renew oneself, recreate o., take a breather, sleep off; go for a change, have a rest 683vb. *repose.*

See: 145, 174, 301, 340, 380, 382, 648, 656, 683, 831.

686 Agent

N. *agent,* operator, actor, performer, player, executant, practitioner; perpetrator 676n. *doer;* minister, tool 628n. *instrument;* factor 754n. *consignee;* representative 754n. *delegate;* deputizer, spokesman 755n. *deputy;* proxy 150n. *substitute;* executor, executrix, executive, administrator, dealer; employer, manufacturer, industrialist 167n. *producer.*

worker, voluntary w. 597n. *volunteer;* social worker 901n. *philanthropist;* independent worker, free-lance, self-employed person; toiler, moiler, drudge, fag, erk, hack; menial, factotum, maid-of-all-work, domestic servant 742n. *servant;* hewer of wood and drawer of water, beast of burden 742n. *slave;* ant, beaver, Stakhanovite 678n. *busy person;* professional man, business m., business woman, career w., breadwinner, earner, salary-e., wage-e., wage-slave, employee; brainworker, boffin; clerical worker, desk-w., white-collar w., black-coat w.; pieceworker, manual w., charwoman, charlady, char, help, daily h., cleaner; laborer, casual l., day-l., agricultural l., farm worker, land-girl, farmer's boy 370 n. *husbandman;* ditcher, thatcher; lumberer, lumberjack, woodcutter; working man, workman, man, hand, operative, factory-worker, factory-hand; navvy, ganger, plate-layer; docker, stevedore, packer; porter, coolie, khalasi, coalheaver; dustman 648n. *cleaner.*

artisan, artificer, tradesman, technician; skilled worker, semiskilled w., past master 696n. *proficient;* journeyman, apprentice 538n. *learner;* craftsman, turner, potter, joiner, cabinet-maker, carpenter, carver, woodworker, sawyer, cooper; wright, wheelwright, wainwright, coachbuilder; shipwright, ship-builder, boat-builder; builder, architect, master mason, mason, housebuilder, bricklayer, hodman, tiler, thatcher, decorator, house-d.; forger, smith, blacksmith, copper-smith, tin-smith, brass-smith, goldsmith, silversmith, gunsmith, locksmith; iron-worker, steel-w., metal-w.; tinker, knife-grinder; collier, worker at the coal-face, miner, tin-m., gold-m.; mechanic, machinist, rigger, fitter, plumber; engineer, civil e., mining e.; electrician, gas-fitter; tailor, cutter, seamstress, needlewoman, shirt-maker, bootmaker, cordwainer, cobbler 228n. *clothier;* watchmaker, clockmaker; jeweler, jewel-cutter; glass-blower.

personnel, staff, force, company, gang, squad, crew, complement, cadre 74n. *band;* dramatis personae 594n. *actor;* coworker, fellow-w., mate, colleague, associate, partner, participator, cooperator 707n. *colleague;* workpeople, hands, men, payroll; labor, casual l.; labor pool, labor force, man-power, working classes.

See: 74, 150, 167, 228, 370, 538, 594, 597, 628, 648, 676, 678, 696, 707, 742, 754, 755, 901.

687 Workshop

N. *workshop*, studio, atelier; workroom, study; laboratory, research l.; workhouse, sweatshop; plant, installation; shop, workshop, yard; mill, cotton-m., loom; sawmill, factory, manufactory; foundry, works, iron-w., brassworks; steelyard, steelworks, smelting-w., tin-w., gas-w., gasification plant; blast-furnace, forge, smithy, stithy, crucible, melting-pot 383n. *furnace;* powerhouse, power station 160n. *energy;* quarry, mine 630n. *store;* coal-mine, colliery, coal-face; tin-mine, stannary; mint; arsenal, armory; dockyard, shipyard, slips; wharf, dock 192n. *stable;* refinery, distillery, brewery; saltworks; shop, shopfloor, bench, production line; nursery 370n. *farm;* dairy, creamery 369n. *stock farm;* kitchen, cookhouse, laundry; office, bureau, business house, firm, company; secretariat, Whitehall, offices, administrative buildings; manufacturing town, hive of industry, hive 678n. *activity.*

See: 160, 192, 369, 370, 383, 630, 678.

688 Conduct

N. *conduct*, behavior, deportment; bearing, personal b., comportment, carriage, port; demeanor, attitude, posture 445n. *mien;* aspect, look, look in one's eyes 445n. *appearance;* tone, tone of voice, delivery 577n. *voice;* motion, action, gesticulation 547n. *gesture;* manner, guise, air; poise, dignity; graciousness 884n. *courtesy;* ungraciousness, rudeness 885n. *discourtesy;* pose 850n. *affectation;* mental attitude, outlook 485 n. *opinion;* psychology, mood 818n. *feeling;* good behavior 933n. *virtue;* misbehavior, misconduct 934n. *wickedness;* democratic behavior, common touch; past behavior, record, history; reward of conduct, deserts 915n. *dueness;* way of life, ethos, morals, ideals, customs, manners 610n. *habit;* course of conduct, line of action, speech from the throne, Queen's speech 623n. *policy;* career, course, race, walk, walk of life 622 n. *vocation;* observance, routine, rules of business 610n. *practice;* procedure, process, method, modus operandi 624n. *way;* treatment, handling, manipulation, direction 689n. *management;* gentle handling, kid gloves, velvet glove 736n. *lenity;* rough handling, jackboot, iron hand 735n. *severity;* dealings, transactions 154n. *affairs;* deeds 676n. *deed.*

tactics, strategy, campaign, plan of c., program 623n. *plan;* line, party l. 623n. *policy;* political science, art of the possible, politics, realpolitik, statesmanship 733n. *governance;* lifemanship, gamesmanship, one-upmanship 698n. *cunning;* brinkmanship, generalship, seamanship 694n. *skill;* maneuvers, maneuvering, marching and countermarching, jockeying, jockeying for position; tactical advantage, vantage ground, weather gauge 34n. *vantage;* maneuver, shift 623n. *contrivance;* move, gambit 676 n. *deed;* game, little g. 698n. *stratagem.*

Adj. *behaving*, behaviorist; psychological; tactical, strategic; political, statesmanlike 622adj. *businesslike.*

Vb. *behave,* act 676vb. *do;* behave well, play the game 933vb. *be virtuous;* behave badly, behave ill, misbehave, carry on 934vb. be *wicked;* deserve well, deserve ill; gesture 547vb. *gesticulate;* posture, pose, affect 850vb. *be affected;* conduct oneself, behave o., carry o., bear o., comport o., demean o.; lead one's life, lead a good l., lead a bad l.; indulge in 678vb. *be active;* play one's part 775n. *participate;* run one's race, follow one's career, conduct one's affairs 622vb. *busy oneself;* follow a course, take a c., shape a c., steer a c. 281vb. *steer for;* paddle one's own canoe, shift for oneself 744vb. *be free;* employ tactics, maneuver, jockey, twist, turn; behave towards, treat.

deal with, have on one's plate, have to do with 676vb. *do;* handle, manipulate 173vb. *operate;* conduct, carry on, run 689n. *manage;* take order, see to, cope with, do the needful; transact, enact, execute, dispatch, carry through, put t., put into practice 725vb. *carry out;* work out 623vb. *plan;* work at, work through, wade t. 682vb. *work;* go through, read 536vb. *study.*

See: 34, 154, 173, 281, 445, 485, 536, 547, 577, 610, 622, 623, 624, 676,

678, 682, 689, 694, 698, 725, 733, 735, 736, 744, 775, 818, 850, 884, 885, 915, 933, 934.

689 Management

N. *management*, conduct, conduct of affairs, manipulation, running, handling; managership, stewardship, proctorship, agency 751n. *commission;* care, charge, control 733n. *authority;* superintendence, oversight 457n. *surveillance;* patronage 660n. *protection;* art of management, tact, way with 694n. *skill;* business management, work study, time and motion s.; ménage, regimen, regime, dispensation; housekeeping, housewifery, housework; husbandry, economics, political economy; kingcraft, statecraft, statesmanship; government 733n. *governance;* regulation, law-making 953n. *legislation;* reins, reins of government, ministry, cabinet, inner c.; staff work, administration; bureaucracy, civil service; secretariat, government office, cutcherry 687n. *workshop.*

directorship, direction, responsibility, control, supreme c. 737n. *command;* dictatorship, leadership, premiership, chairmanship, captaincy 34n. *superiority;* guidance, steering, steerage, pilotage, steersmanship, pilotship, pilotism; sailing instructions 737n. *command;* pole-star, lodestar 520n. *guide;* steering instrument, steering oar, joy-stick, controls, helm, rudder, wheel, tiller; needle, magnetic n., compass, binnacle; gyrocompass, gyropilot, autopilot 269n. *sailing aid;* direction-finding, beam, radar 281n. *direction;* remote control, telearchics.

Adj. *directing*, directorial, leading, hegemonic; directional, guiding, steering, holding the rudder; governing, controlling, gubernatorial, holding the reins, in the chair 733adj. *authoritative;* dictatorial 735adj. *authoritarian;* supervisory, managing, managerial; executive, administrative; legislative, nomothetic; high-level, top-l. 638adj. *important;* economic, political: official, bureaucratic 733adj. *governmental.*

Vb. *manage*, manipulate, maneuver, pull the strings 178vb. *influence;* have taped, have the measure of 490vb. *know;* handle, conduct, run, carry on; minister, administer, prescribe; supervise, superintend, oversee, caretake 457vb. *invigilate;* nurse 457vb. *look after;* have charge of, have in charge, hold the portfolio, hold the reins, handle the ribbons 612vb. *motivate* (**see** *direct*); keep order, police, regulate; legislate, pass laws 953vb. *make legal;* control, govern, sway 733vb. *rule;* know how to manage, have a way with.

direct, lead, pioneer, precede 64vb. *come before;* boss, dictate 737vb. *command;* hold office, hold a responsible position, have responsibility; assume responsibility 917vb. *incur a duty;* preside, take the chair, be chairman, be in the chair; head, captain; stroke, pull the stroke oar; pilot, cox, steer, take the helm, hold the tiller, wield the rudder 269vb. *navigate;* point 281vb. *point to;* show the way 547vb. *indicate;* shepherd, guide, conduct, lead on; introduce, compère; escort 89vb. *accompany;* channel, canalize; route, train, lead, lead over, lead through; furnish the address 524vb. *inform.*

Adv. *in control*, in charge, at the wheel, at the head, in the chair; ex officio.

See: 34, 64, 89, 178, 269, 281, 457, 490, 520, 524, 547, 612, 638, 660, 687, 694, 733, 735, 737, 751, 917, 953.

690 Director

N. *director*, governing body 741n. *governor;* steering committee; cabinet, inner c. 692n. *council;* board of directors, board, chair; staff, brass, top b., management; manager, controller; legislator, law-giver, lawmaker; employer, capitalist, boss 741 n. *master;* headman, chief 34n. *superior;* principal, headmaster, head, rector, moderator, vice-chancellor, chancellor; president, vice-p.; chairman, speaker; premier, prime minister; captain, team-c; stroke, cox, master, ship-m., sailing-m., trierarch 270n. *mariner;* man on the bridge, steersman, helmsman 270 n. *navigator;* pilot 520n. *guide;* forerunner, torch-bearer, link-boy 66n. *precursor;* drill-sergeant 537n. *trainer;* director of studies 537n. *teacher;* backseat driver 691n. *adviser;* kingmaker, wire-puller, animator 612n. *motivator;* traffic cop, traffic warden 305n. *traffic control.*

leader, charismatic l., judge (Old Testament) 741n. *governor;* messiah, Mahdi; leader of the House, leader of the opposition; spearhead, center-forward; shepherd, teamster, drover 369n. *herdsman;* bell-wether; fugleman, file-leader; pacemaker; symposiarch, master of ceremonies, director of the feast; high priest, mystagogue; coryphaeus, chorus-leader, choragus, conductor, band-c., orchestra leader, first violin; precentor; Fuehrer, Duce 741n. *autocrat;* ringleader, demagogue, rabble-rouser, firebrand 738n. *agitator;* chauffeur, jehu 268n. *driver;* captain; condottiere.

manager, person in responsibility, responsible person; man in charge, key man, kingpin 638n. *bigwig;* procurator, administrator, executive, executor 676n. *doer;* statesman, statist, politician; economist, political e.; housekeeper, husband, housewife; steward, bailiff, landreeve; farm-bailiff, reeve, grieve; agent, factor 754n. *consignee;* superintendent, supervisor, inspector, overseer, foreman; warden, housemaster, matron, nurse, tutor 660n. *protector;* proctor, disciplinarian; party-manager, whip; custodian, caretaker, curator, librarian 749n. *keeper;* master of hounds, whipper-in, huntsman; circus manager, ringmaster; compère.

official, office-holder, office-bearer, jack-in-office, tin god; shop steward; government servant, state-s., public s., civil s. 742n. *servant;* officer of state, high official, vizier, grand v., minister, cabinet m., secretary of state, secretary-general, secretary, under-s.; secretariat-wallah, bureaucrat, mandarin, red-tapeist 741n. *officer;* judicial officer, district o., collector, magistrate 733n. *magistrature;* commissioner, prefect, intendant; consul, pro-consul, praetor, quaestor, aedile; first secretary, counselor 754n. *envoy;* alderman, mayor 692n. *councillor;* functionary, party-official, petty o., clerk; school prefect, monitor.

See: 34, 66, 268, 270, 305, 369, 520, 537, 612, 638, 660, 676, 691, 692, 733, 738, 741, 742, 749, 754.

691 Advice

N. *advice,* word of a., piece of a.; words of wisdom, rede 498n. *wisdom;* counsel, adhortation; criticism, constructive c. 480n. *estimate;* didacticism, moralizing, moral injunction, prescription 693n. *precept;* recommendation, proposition, proposal, motion 512n. *supposition;* suggestion, submonition, submission; tip 524n. *hint;* guidance, briefing, instruction 524n. *information;* charge, charge to the jury 955n. *legal trial;* taking counsel, consultation, mutual c., huddle, powwow, parley, pourparler, talks, conversations, talks across the table, summitry 584n. *conference;* seeking advice, reference, referment 584n. *conference;* advice against 762n. *deprecation.*

adviser, counselor, consultant; professional consultant 696n. *expert;* referee, arbiter 480n. *estimator;* prescriber, commender, advocate, recommender, mover, prompter 612 n. *motivator;* medical adviser 658n. *doctor;* legal adviser, counsel 958n. *lawyer;* guide, philosopher and friend, mentor, confidant 537n. *teacher;* monitor, admonisher, remembrancer 505n. *reminder;* Nestor, Egeria, Gray Eminence, Dutch uncle; oracle, wise man 500n. *sage;* backseat driver, kibitzer, busybody 678n. *meddler;* committee of inquiry, consultative body 692n. **council.**

Adj. *advising,* advisory, consultative, deliberative; hortative, recommendatory 612adj. *inducive;* dehortatory 613adj. *dissuasive;* admonitory, warning 664n. *cautionary;* didactic; moral, moralizing.

Vb. *advise,* give advice, counsel, offer c., press advice on; think best, recommend, prescribe, advocate, commend; propose, move, put to, submit, suggest 512vb. *propound;* prompt 524vb. *hint;* press, urge, exhort 612vb. *incite;* dehort, advise against 613vb. *dissuade;* admonish 664vb. *warn;* enjoin, charge, dictate 737vb. *command;* advise well, speak to one's condition 642vb.

consult, seek advice, refer, make a reference, call in, call on; confide in, be closeted with, have at one's elbow; take advice, listen to, be advised, accept advice, take one's cue from, submit one's judgment to another's, follow advice; sit in council, sit in conclave, lay heads together, advise with, hold a consultation, hold a council of war, deliberate, parley, sit round a table, compare notes 584vb. *confer.*

See: 480, 498, 500, 505, 512, 524, 537, 584, 612, 613, 642, 658, 664, 678, 692, 693, 696, 737, 762, 955, 958.

692 Council

N. *council,* council board, round table; council chamber, board room; Star Chamber, court 956n.

tribunal; Privy Council, Aulic C., presidium; ecclesiastical council, curia, consistory, Bench of Bishops; vestry; cabinet, board, advisory b., consultative body, Royal Commission; staff college; assembly, conventicle, congregation 74n. *assemblage;* conclave, convocation 985n. *synod;* convention, congress, meeting, top-level m., summit; durbar, diet; folkmoot, moot, comitia, ecclesia; federal council, amphictyonic c., amphictyony, League of Nations, U.N., parliament of nations; municipal council, county c., borough c., town c., parish c.; local board, union b.; zemstvo, soviet; council of elders, genro, Sanhedrin; sitting, session, séance, audience, hearing 584n. *conference.*

parliament, Mother of Parliaments, Westminster, Upper House, House of Lords, House of Peers, "another place"; Lower House, House of Commons; senate, senatus; legislative assembly, deliberative a., consultative a.; States-General, Cortes, witenagemot; Chambre des Députés, Reichstag, Reichsrath, Rigsdag, Storthing, Duma, Dail Eireann; Senate, Congress; Legislative Council, Lok Sabha, Majlis, Sejm, Knesset; quorum, division.

councillor, privy councillor; senator, conscript fathers, Areopagite, Sanhedrist; peer, life-peer; representative, deputy, congressman, member of Parliament, M.P. 754n. *delegate;* back-bencher, lobby-fodder; parliamentarian, legislator; municipal councillor, mayor, alderman 690n. *official.*

Adj. *parliamentary*, senatorial, congressional; unicameral, bicameral; curule, conciliar; convocational, synodal.

See: 74, 584, 690, 754, 956, 985.

693 Precept

N. *precept,* firm advice 691n. *advice;* direction, instruction, general i.; injunction, charge 737n. *command;* commission 751n. *mandate;* order, written o., writ 737n. *warrant;* rescript, decretal epistle, authoritative reply 480n. *judgment;* prescript, prescription, ordinance, regulation 737 n. *decree;* canon, form, norm, formula, formulary, rubric; rule, golden r., moral 496n. *maxim;* recipe, receipt 658n. *remedy;* commandment, statute, enactment, act, code, penal c., corpus juris 953n. *legislation;* tenet, article, set of rules, constitution; ticket, party line; Ten Commandments, Twelve Tables, laws of the Medes and the Persians; canon law, common l., unwritten l. 953n. *law;* rule of custom, convention 610 n. *practice;* technicality, nice point 530n. *enigma;* precedent, leading case, text 83n. *example.*

Adj. *preceptive*, prescriptive, decretal, mandatory, binding; canonical, rubrical, statutory 953adj. *legal;* moralizing 496adj. *aphoristic;* customary, conventional 610adj. *usual.*

See: 83, 480, 496, 530, 658, 737, 751, 610, 691, 953.

694 Skill

N. *skill,* skillfulness, dexterity, dexterousness, handiness, ambidexterity; grace, style 575n. *elegance;* neatness, deftness, adroitness, address; ease 701n. *facility;* proficiency, competence, efficiency, faculty, capability, capacity 160n. *ability;* many-sidedness, all-round capacity, universal c., versatility, amphibiousness; adaptability, flexibility, suppleness; touch, grip, control; mastery, mastership, wizardry, virtuosity, excellence, prowess 644n. *goodness;* strong point, métier, forte, major suit; acquirement, attainment, accomplishment; skills, seamanship, airmanship, horsemanship, marksmanship; experience, expertise, professionalism; specialism; technology, science, know-how, technique, technical knowledge, practical k. 490n. *knowledge;* practical ability, do-it-yourself habit; craftsmanship, art, artistry, ars celare artem, art that conceals art; finish, execution 646n. *perfection;* ingenuity, resourcefulness, craft, craftiness, callidity 698n. *cunning;* cleverness, sharpness, worldly wisdom, sophistication, lifemanship 498n. *sagacity;* savoir faire, tact, discretion 463n. *discrimination;* feat of skill, trick, hat-t., gimmick, dodge 623n. *contrivance;* sleight of hand, conjuring 542n. *sleight;* funambulism, rope dancing, tightrope walking, brinkmanship; generalship 688n. *tactics;* skillful use, exploitation 673 n. *use.*

aptitude, inborn a., innate ability; bent, natural b. 179n. tendency; faculty, endowment, gift, flair, parts, natural p.; turn, knack, green fingers; talent, genius, genius for; aptness, fitness, qualification.

masterpiece, chef d'oeuvre, a beauty;

pièce de résistance; finished work, workmanlike job, craftsman's j.; masterstroke, coup-de-maître, feat, exploit, hat-trick 676n. *deed;* tour de force, bravura, fireworks; ace, trump, clincher 644n. *exceller;* work of art, objet d'art, curio, collector's piece.

Adj. *skillful,* good, good at 644adj. *excellent;* skilled, crack; apt, handy, dexterous, ambidexterous, deft, adroit, slick, neat; neat-fingered, green-f., fine-f., sure-footed; cunning, clever, quick, shrewd, callid, ingenious 498adj. *intelligent;* politic, statesmanlike 498adj. *wise;* adaptable, flexible, resourceful, ready; many-sided, versatile; ready for anything, panurgic; sound, able, competent, efficient, competitive; wizard, masterly, like a master, magisterial, accomplished, finished 646adj. *perfect.*

gifted, taught by nature; of parts, talented, endowed, well-e., born for, just made for.

expert, experienced, veteran, seasoned, tried, versed in, up in, well up in, knowing 490adj. *instructed;* skilled, trained, practiced, well-p. 669adj. *prepared;* finished, passed, specialized 669adj. *matured;* proficient, efficient, qualified, competent, up to the mark; professional 622adj. *businesslike;* sailorly 270adj. *seamanlike.*

well-made, well-done, craftily contrived, deep-laid; finished, felicitous, happy; artistic, artificial, sophisticated, stylish 575adj. *elegant;* daedalian, cunning; technical, scientific; shipshape, workmanlike.

Vb. *be skillful,* — deft etc.adj.; be good at, do well 644n. *be good;* shine, excel 34vb. *be superior;* have a turn for, have a gift for, be born for, show aptitude, show a talent for; have the knack, have the trick of, have the right touch; be in practice, be on form, be in good f., have one's eye in, have one's hand in; hit the right nail on the head, put the saddle on the right horse; play one's cards well, not put a foot wrong, know just when to stop; use skillfully, exploit, squeeze the last ounce out of 673 vb. *use;* take advantage of, make hay while the sun shines 137vb. *profit by;* live by one's wits, know how to live, get around, know all the answers, have one's wits about one 498vb. *be wise;* exercise discretion 463vb. *discriminate.*

be expert, turn professional; be master of one's profession, know one's job, have the know-how; acquire the technique, qualify oneself 536 vb. *learn;* have experience, know the ropes, know all the ins and outs, know backwards, be up to every trick, take in one's stride 490vb. *know;* know what's what, know a hawk from a handsaw, have cut one's wisdom teeth; show one's skill, play with, demonstrate, stunt 875vb. *be ostentatious.*

Adv. *skillfully,* craftily, artfully; well, with skill, like a master; handily, neatly, featly; stylishly, artistically; knowledgeably, expertly, scientifically; faultlessly, like a machine; naturally, as to the manner born, in one's stride.

See: 34, 137, 160, 179, 270, 463, 490, 498, 536, 542, 575, 622, 623, 644, 646, 669, 673, 676, 688, 698, 701, 875.

695 Unskillfulness

N. *unskillfulness,* want of skill, no gift; lack of practice, rustiness 674 n. *non-use;* rawness, unripeness, immaturity, crudity 670n. *undevelopment;* inexperience, inexpertness 491n. *ignorance;* incapacity, inability, incompetence, inefficiency 161 n. *ineffectuality;* disqualification, unproficiency; quackery, charlatanism 850n. *pretension;* clumsiness, indexterity, unhandiness, lubberliness, left-handedness, awkwardness, gaucherie, étourderie (**see** *bungling*); folly, stupidity 499n. *unintelligence.*

bungling, botching, tinkering, half-measures, pale imitation 726n. *noncompletion;* bungle, botch, botchery; off day, botched performance, bad job, sad work, flop 728n. *failure;* missed chance 138n. *intempestivity;* hamhandedness, dropped catch, fumble, foozle, muff, fluff, miss, mishit, slice, pull, bosh shot, overthrow, misthrow, misfire 495n. *mistake;* thoughtlessness 456n. *inattention;* tactlessness, infelicity, indiscretion 464n. *indiscrimination;* mishandling, misapplication 675n. *misuse;* impolicy, mismanagement, misrule, misgovernment, maladministration 481n. *misjudgment;* misdoing, misconduct, antics; much ado about nothing, wild-goose chase 641n. *lost labor.*

Adj. *unskillful,* ungifted, untalented, unendowed, unaccomplished; stick-in-the-mud, unversatile 679adj. *inactive;* undexterous, unadroit; disqualified, unadapted, unadaptable, unfit, inept 25adj. *unapt;* unable, lame 161adj. *impotent;* incompetent, inefficient, ineffectual; unpractical, unbusinesslike, unstatesmanlike; impolitic, ill-considered, stupid, foolish 499adj. *unwise;* thoughtless 456 adj. *inattentive;* wild, giddy, happy-go-lucky 456adj. *light-minded;* reckless 857adj. *rash;* backward, unforward, failed 728adj. *unsuccessful;* inadequate 636adj. *insufficient;* futile, feckless.

unskilled, skill-less, raw, green, unripe, undeveloped 670adj. *immature;* uninitiated, under training, untrained, half-baked, half-skilled, semiskilled 670adj. *unprepared;* unqualified, inexpert, scratch, inexperienced, ignorant, unversed, unconversant, untaught 491adj. *uninstructed;* non-professional, ham, lay, amateurish, amateur, bumble-puppy; unscientific, unsound, charlatan, quack, quackish; specious, pretentious 850adj. *affected.*

clumsy, awkward, gauche, gawkish; stuttering 580adj. *stammering;* tactless 464adj. *indiscriminating;* lubberly, unhandy, all thumbs, butter-fingered, thick-f.; left-handed, one-h., heavy-h., ham-h., heavy-footed; ungainly, lumbering, hulking, gangling, stumbling; stiff, rusty 674adj. *unused;* unaccustomed, unpracticed, out of practice, out of training, out of form 611adj. *unhabituated;* losing one's touch, slipping, skidding; slovenly, slatternly, slapdash 458 adj. *negligent;* fumbling, groping, tentative 461adj. *experimental;* ungraceful, graceless, clownish 576adj. *inelegant;* top-heavy, ill-balanced, lopsided 29adj. *unequal;* cumbersome, ponderous, clumsily built, unmanageable, unsteerable 195adj. *unwieldy;* maladjusted, creaking, out of joint 495adj. *inexact.*

bungled, ill-done, botched, foozled, mismanaged, mishandled etc.vb.; misguided, misadvised, ill-advised, ill-considered, ill-judged; unplanned 670adj. *unprepared;* ill-contrived, ill-devised, ill-prepared, ill-conducted; unhappy, infelicitous, ill-chosen; crude, rough and ready, inartistic, home-made, do-it-yourself 699adj. *artless;* slapdash, superficial, perfunctory 458adj. *neglected;* foolish, wild, giddy, thoughtless 456adj. *light-minded.*

Vb. *be unskillful*,—inept,—unqualified etc. adj.; not know how 491vb. *not know;* show one's ignorance, set the wrong way about it, start at the wrong end, get hold of the wrong end of the stick; do things by halves, tinker, paper over the cracks 726vb. *not complete;* burn one's fingers, catch a Tartar, reckon without one's host 508vb. *not expect;* maladminister, mishandle, mismanage, misconduct, misrule, misgovern; misapply 674vb. *misuse;* misdirect, missend 495vb. *blunder;* oversleep 138vb. *lose a chance;* forget one's piece, miss one's cue 506 vb. *forget;* ham, overact, underact; lose one's cunning, lose one's skill, go rusty, get out of practice 611vb. *be unused;* lose one's nerve, lose one's head 854vb. *be nervous.*

stultify oneself, not know what one is about, not know one's own interest *or* business, stand in one's own light, cut one's own throat, make a fool of oneself 497vb. *be absurd;* become an object lesson, quarrel with one's bread and butter, kill the goose that lays the golden eggs, throw a stone into one's own garden, bring one's house about one's ears, knock one's head against a stone wall, put the cart before the horse, have too many eggs in one basket, have too many irons in the fire; put a square peg in a round hole, put new wine into old bottles 495vb. *blunder;* labor in vain 470vb. *try impossibilities;* go on a fool's errand 641vb. *waste effort;* lean on a broken reed, strain at a gnat and swallow a camel; catch a Tartar, burn one's fingers.

be clumsy, lumber, hulk, get in the way, stand in the light; trip, trip over, stumble, hobble, limp, go lame 161vb. *be impotent;* not look where one is going 456vb. *be inattentive;* stutter 580vb. *stammer;* fumble, grope, flounder 461vb. *be tentative;* muff, fluff, foozle; pull, slice, mishit, misthrow; overthrow, overshoot 306vb. *overstep;* play into the hands of, give a catch, give a chance; drop, drop a catch, drop a sitter 311vb. *let fall;* catch a crab; bungle, drop a brick, put one's foot in it, make a faux pas 495vb. *blunder;* botch, spoil, mar, slubber, blot, vitiate 655vb. *impair;* fool with 678vb. *meddle;* make a mess of it, make a hash of it, mash, hash, bosh 728vb. *miscarry;* perpetrate, do a bad job, make sad work of, make a poor fist of 728vb. *fail.*

See: 25, 29, 138, 161, 195, 306, 311, 456, 458, 461, 464, 470, 481, 491, 495, 497, 499, 506, 508, 576, 580,

611, 636, 641, 655, 674, 675, 678, 679, 726, 728, 854, 857.

696 Proficient

N. *proficient,* sound player, expert, adept, dab, dabster; do-it-yourself type, all-rounder, jack-of-all-trades, handyman, Admirable Crichton 646 n. *paragon;* master, past master, graduate, cordon bleu; intellectual, master mind, master spirit 500n. *sage;* genius, wizard 864n. *prodigy;* magician 545n. *conjuror;* man of parts, virtuoso; bravura player 413 n. *musician;* prima donna, first fiddle, top-sawyer, protagonist, prize-man, prize-winner, medalist, champion, holder, cup-h. 644n. *exceller;* picked man, seeded player, hope, white h.; crack, crack shot, dead s., good s., marksman 287n. *shooter;* acrobat, rope-dancer, funambulist 159n. *athlete.*

expert, no novice, practitioner; professional, specialist, professor 537n. teacher; connoisseur, savant, pantologist, walking encyclopedia 492 n. *scholar;* veteran, old hand, old stager, old file, old soldier, sea dog, shellback; practiced hand, practiced eye; sophisticate, knowing person, sharp blade, cunning fellow 698n. *slyboots;* sharp, sharper 545n. *trickster;* man of the world, man of business, tactician, strategist, politician; diplomat, diplomatist; technician, skilled worker 686n. *artisan;* experienced hand, right man for the job, key man; consultant 691n. *adviser;* boffin, backroom boy 623n. *planner;* connoisseur, fancier.

See: 159, 287, 413, 492, 500, 537, 545, 619, 623, 644, 646, 686, 691, 698, 864.

697 Bungler

N. *bungler,* failure 728n. *loser;* bad learner, one's despair; botcher, tinker; blunderer, blunderhead, marplot; mismanager, fumbler, muffer, muff, butterfingers; hulker, lump, lout, clumsy l., clumsy, lubber, looby, swab, awkward squad, jaywalker; duffer, stooge, clown, galoot, clot, clod, stick, hick, oaf, ass, calf; Lord of Misrule 501n. *fool;* slob, sloven, slattern, traipse 61n. *slut;* cacographer, dauber, bad hand, poor h., bad shot, poor s., no marksman, no conjuror; novice, greenhorn, colt, raw recruit, apprentice, sorcerer's a. 538n. *beginner;* tail 35n. *inferior;* quack 545n. *impostor;* fair-weather sailor, fresh-water s., horse marine; ass in a lion's skin, jackdaw in peacock's feathers; fish out of water, square peg in a round hole 25n. *misfit;* spoilsport 678n. *meddler.*

See: 25, 35, 61, 501, 538, 545, 678, 728.

698 Cunning

N. *cunning,* craft 694n. *skill;* lore 490n. *knowledge;* resourcefulness, inventiveness, ingenuity 513n. *imagination;* guile, gamesmanship, cunningness, craftiness, artfulness, subtlety, wiliness, slyness, foxiness; stealthiness, stealth 523n. *latency;* cageyness 525n. *reticence;* suppleness, slipperiness, shiftiness; sharp practice, knavery, chicanery, chicane 930n. *foul play;* finesse, jugglery 542n. *sleight;* cheating, circumvention 542n. *deception;* double-dealing, imposture 541n. *duplicity;* smoothness 925n. *flattery;* disguise 525n. *concealment;* maneuvering, temporizing 688n. *tactics;* policy, diplomacy, Machiavellianism; jobbery, gerrymandering 930n. *improbity;* underhand dealing, practice; backstairs influence 178n. *influence;* intrigue 623n. *plot.*

stratagem, ruse, wile, art, artifice, resource, resort, device, wrinkle, ploy, shift, dodge, artful d. 623n. *contrivance;* machination, game, little g. 623n. *plot;* subterfuge, evasion; excuse 614n. *pretext;* white lie 543n. *mental dishonesty;* juggle, cheat 541 n. *deception;* trick, old t., box of tricks, tricks of the trade, rules of the game 542n. *trickery;* feint, catch, net, web, ambush, Trojan horse 542 n. *trap;* ditch, pit 663n. *pitfall;* side-blow, Parthian shot; web of cunning, web of deceit; blind, dust thrown in the eyes, flag of convenience 542n. *sham;* thin end of the wedge, maneuver, move, piece of tactics 688n. *tactics.*

slyboots, crafty fellow, artful dodger, wily person, serpent, snake, fox, Reynard; lurker 527n. *hider;* nigger in the woodpile 663n. *trouble-maker;* fraud, shammer, dissembler, hypocrite 545n. *deceiver;* cheat, sharper 545n. *trickster;* juggler 545n. *conjuror;* smooth citizen, glib tongue 925n. *flatterer;* diplomatist, Machiavellian, intriguer, plotter, schemer 623n. *planner;* strategist, tactician, maneuverer; wire-puller 612n. *motivator.*

Adj. *cunning*, learned, knowledgeable 498adj. *wise;* crafty, artful, sly, wily, subtle, snaky, serpentine, foxy, vulpine, feline; rusy, full of ruses, tricky, tricksy; secret 525adj. *stealthy;* scheming, contriving, practicing, plotting, intriguing, Machiavellian 623adj. *planning;* knowing, fly, canny, sharp, astute, shrewd, acute; too clever for, too clever by half, up to everything, not to be caught with chaff, not born yesterday 498adj. *intelligent;* not to be drawn, cagey 525adj. *reticent;* experienced 694adj. *skillful;* resourceful, ingenious; deep as water 211 adj. *deep;* tactical, strategic, deep-laid, well-l., well-planned; full of snares, insidious 930adj. *perfidious;* shifty, slippery, time-serving, temporizing 518adj. *equivocal;* deceitful, flattering 542adj. *deceiving;* knavish 930adj. *rascally;* crooked, devious 930adj. *dishonest.*

Vb. *be cunning,*—sly etc.adj.; proceed by stratagem, play the fox, have a dodge, try a ruse, finesse, shift, dodge; maneuver, double cross, twist, turn 251vb. *wriggle;* lie low 523vb. *lurk;* intrigue, scheme, practice, play a deep game, spin a web, weave a plot, have an ax to grind 623vb. *plot;* contrive, devise 623vb. *plan;* play tricks with, tinker, gerrymander; circumvent, overreach, pull a fast one, steal a march on, trick, cheat 542vb. *deceive;* blarney 925vb. *flatter;* be too clever for, outsmart, go one better, know a trick worth two of that 306vb. *outdo;* be too quick for, snatch from under one's nose; waylay, dig a pit, undermine, bait the trap 527vb. *ambush;* introduce the thin end of the wedge; match in cunning, see the catch, avoid the trap; have a card up one's sleeve, have a shot in one's locker; know all the answers, live by one's wits.

Adv. *cunningly*, artfully, slyly, on the sly, by a side wind.

See: 178, 211, 251, 306, 490, 498, 513, 518, 523, 525, 527, 541, 542, 543, 545, 612, 614, 623, 663, 688, 694, 925, 930.

699 Artlessness

N. *artlessness*, simplicity, simple-mindedness; naïveté, ingenuousness, guilelessness 935n. *innocence;* unaffectedness, unsophistication, naturalness, freedom from artifice 573n. *plainness;* single-mindedness, sincerity, candor, frankness; bluntness, matter-of-factness, outspokenness 540n. *veracity;* truth, honesty 929 n. *probity;* purity 874n. *modesty;* uncivilized state, savagery; darkness, no science, no art 491n. *ignorance;* indifference to art, philistinism; no artistry 647n. *imperfection;* uncouthness, vulgarity, crudity 847n. *bad taste.*

ingenue, unsophisticated person, child of nature, savage, noble s.; enfant terrible; lamb, innocent l. 935n. *innocent;* greenhorn, novice 538n. *beginner;* rough diamond, plain man, philistine; simple mind, frank heart; hick, hayseed, rube, hillbilly 869n. *countryman.*

Adj. *artless*, without art, without artifice, without tricks; uncomplicated 44adj. *simple;* unadorned, unvarnished 573adj. *plain;* native, natural, unartificial, homespun, home-made; do-it-yourself 695adj. *unskilled;* in a state of nature, uncivilized, wild, savage, unguided, untutored, unlearned, unscientific, backward 491 adj. *ignorant;* arcadian, unsophisticated, ingenuous, naïve, childlike, born yesterday 935adj. *innocent;* guileless, free from guile, unsuspicious, confiding; unaffected, unreserved 609adj. *spontaneous;* candid, frank, open, undissembling, straightforward 540n. *veracious;* undesigning, single, single-minded, single-hearted, true, honest, sincere 929adj. *honorable;* blunt, outspoken, free-spoken; transparent 522adj. *undisguised;* unpoetical, prosaic, matter-of-fact, literal, literal-minded 494adj. *accurate;* shy, inarticulate, unassuming, unpretending 874adj. *modest;* inartistic, philistine; unmusical, tone-deaf 416adj. *deaf;* unrefined, unpolished, uncultured, uncouth, jungly, bush 847adj. *vulgar;* hoydenish 847adj. *ill-bred.*

Vb. *be artless,*—natural etc.adj.; live in a state of nature, know no better; have no guile, have no tricks 935vb. *be innocent;* have no affectations, eschew artifice; confide, wear one's heart upon one's sleeve, look one in the face, look one straight in the eyes, call a spade a spade, say what is in one's mind 573vb. *speak plainly;* not gloze, not flatter 540vb. *be truthful.*

Adv. *artlessly*, without art, without pretensions, without affectations; frankly, sincerely, openly, with an open heart; inartistically, like a philistine.

See: 44, 416, 491, 494, 522, 538, 540, 573, 609, 647, 695, 847, 874, 929, 935.

700 Difficulty

N. *difficulty*, hardness, arduousness, laboriousness, the hard way 682n. *exertion;* impracticability, one's despair 470n. *impossibility;* intricacy, perplexity, inextricability, involvement 61n. *complexity;* complication 832n. *aggravation;* obscurity, impenetrability 517n. *unintelligibility;* inconvenience, awkwardness, embarrassment 643n. *inexpedience;* drag 333n. *friction;* rough ground, hard going, bad patch 259n. *roughness;* quagmire, slough 347n. *marsh;* knot, Gordian k. 251n. *coil;* problem, thorny p., crux, hard nut to crack, poser, teaser, puzzle, headache 530n. *enigma;* impediment, handicap, obstacle, snag, rub, where the shoe pinches 702n. *hindrance;* teething troubles 702n. *hitch;* maze, crooked path 251n. *convolution;* cul-de-sac, dead end, impasse 264n. *closure;* deadlock, stand, stoppage 145n. *stop;* stress, brunt, burden 684n. *fatigue;* trial, temptation, tribulation, vexation 825n. *suffering;* trouble, sea of troubles 731n. *adversity;* difficult person, handful, one's despair, kittle cattle.

hard task, test, real t., test of strength; labors of Hercules, Herculean task, Augean stables, Sisyphean labor; task, job, work cut out, hard row to hoe; handful, tall order, tough assignment, stiff job, hard work, uphill work 682n. *labor;* dead weight, dead lift 322n. *gravity.*

predicament, embarrassment, false position; nonplus, quandary, dilemma, cleft stick, option of difficulties, delicate point, nice p., borderline case 474n. *dubiety;* fix, jam, hole, scrape, hot water, trouble, peck of troubles, kettle of fish, pickle, stew, imbroglio, mess, muddle; pinch, strait, straits, pass, pretty p.; slippery slope, sticky wicket, tight corner, situation, ticklish s. 661n. *danger;* critical situation, exigency, emergency 137n. *crisis.*

Adj. *difficult*, hard, tough, formidable; steep, arduous, uphill; inconvenient, onerous, burdensome, irksome, toilsome, bothersome, plaguey, operose 682adj. *laborious;* exacting, demanding 684adj. *fatiguing;* big, of Herculean *or* Sisyphean proportions; insuperable, impracticable 470adj. *impossible;* offering a problem, problematic; delicate, ticklish, kittle; sooner said than done, more easily said than done; not to be handled with kid gloves, not made with rose water; embarrassing, awkward, unwieldy, unmanageable, hard to cope with, not easily tackled; out of hand, intractable, refractory 738adj. *disobedient;* stubborn, unyielding, perverse 602adj. *obstinate;* ill-behaved, naughty 934adj. *wicked;* perplexing, clueless, obscure 517adj. *unintelligible;* knotty, complex, complicated, inextricable, labyrinthine 251adj. intricate; impenetrable, impassable, trackless, pathless, invious, unnavigable; thorny, rugged, craggy 259adj. *rough;* sticky, critical, emergent 661adj. *dangerous.*

in difficulties, bested, ill-b.; hampered 702adj. *hindered;* laboring, laboring under difficulties; in a quandary, in a dilemma, in a cleft stick, between two stools, between Scylla and Charybdis 474adj. *doubting;* baffled, clueless, nonplussed, at a stand 517 adj. *puzzled;* in a jam, in a fix, up a gum tree, in a spot, in a hole, in a scrape, in hot water, in the soup, in a pickle; in deep water, out of one's depth, under cross-fire, not out of the woods, in danger 661adj. *endangered;* worried, beset with difficulties, harassed with problems, tormented with anxiety 825adj. *suffering;* up against it, hard pressed, sore p., hard run, hard set, hard put to it, put to it, put to one's shifts, driven to extremities; in straits, reduced to s., straitened, pinched; at one's wits end, at the end of one's tether, cornered, at bay, up a tree; stuck, graveled, aground 728adj. *grounded.*

Vb. *be difficult*,—hard etc.adj.; make things difficult, make difficulties for; complicate, complicate matters 63vb. *bedevil;* trouble, inconvenience, put to i., bother, irk, plague, try one's patience, lead one a dance, be a thorn in one's flesh, go against the grain 827vb. *incommode;* present difficulties, set one a problem, pose, perplex, baffle, nonplus, ground, stump, gravel, bring one to a stand 474vb. *puzzle;* encumber, clog, hamper, obstruct 702vb. *hinder;* make things worse 832vb. *aggravate;* lead to an impasse, create a deadlock 470vb. *make impossible;* go hard with, run one hard, put one to his shifts, drive to the wall 661vb. *endanger.*

be in difficulty, have a problem; walk among eggs, pick one's way 461vb. *be tentative;* have one's hands full, have all one can do 678vb. *be busy;* not know which way to turn, be at a loss 474vb. *be uncertain;* have difficulties, have one's work cut out, be put to it, be put to trouble, have trouble with; run into trouble, fall into difficulties, strike a bad patch, let oneself in for, embarrass oneself, catch a packet, catch a Tartar, rouse a hornet's nest; have a hard time of it, have the wolf by the ears 731vb. *have trouble;* bear the brunt, feel the wind, feel the pinch 825vb. *suffer;* have more than enough, sink under the burden 684vb. *be fatigued;* invite difficulty, make it hard for oneself, make a problem of, make heavy weather, flounder; stick, come unstuck 728vb. *miscarry;* try it the hard way, swim upstream, breast the current, struggle, fight 716vb. *contend;* have to face it, live dangerously 661vb. *face danger;* labor under difficulties, labor under a disadvantage, be handicapped 35vb. *be inferior.*

Adv. *with difficulty,* with much ado, hardly; the hard way, uphill, against the stream, against the wind, against the grain; despite, in spite of, in the teeth of; in a pinch; in difficulty.

See: 35, 61, 63, 137, 145, 251, 259, 264, 322, 333, 347, 461, 470, 474, 517, 530, 602, 643, 661, 678, 682, 684, 702, 716, 728, 731, 738, 825, 827, 832, 934.

701 Facility

N. *facility,* easiness, ease, convenience, comfort; wieldiness, ease of handling; flexibility, pliancy 327n. *softness;* capability, capacity, feasibility 469n. *possibility;* comprehensibility 516n. *intelligibility;* facilitation 703n. *aid;* easing, making easy, simplification, making smooth, disencumbrance, disentanglement, disengagement, deoppilation, removal of difficulties 746n. *liberation;* full play, full scope, clean slate, tabula rasa 744n. *scope;* facilities, provision of f. 703n. *aid;* leave 760n. *permission;* simplicity, no complication 44n. *simpleness;* straightforwardness, no difficulty, no competition; no friction, easy going, smooth water 258n. *smoothness;* fair wind, clear coast, clear road 137n. *opportunity;* straight road, royal r., highway, primrose path 624n. *road;* downhill 309n. *descent.*

easy thing, no effort, child's play; short work, holiday task, light work, sinecure 679n. *inactivity;* picnic, play 837n. *amusement;* pie, piece of cake, money for jam; smooth sailing, plain s., joy-ride; nothing to it, sitter, easy target, sitting shot; walkover 727n. *victory;* cinch, sure thing 473n. *certainty;* no trouble, pleasure.

Adj. *easy*, facile, undemanding; effortless, painless; light, short; frictionless 258adj. *smooth;* uncomplicated 44adj. *simple;* not hard, not difficult, foolproof; easy as pie, easily done, easily managed, no sooner said than done; feasible 469 adj. *possible;* easing, facilitating, deoppilant, helpful 703adj. *aiding;* downhill, downstream 309adj. *descending;* with the stream, with the current, with the tide; convenient 376adj. *comfortable;* approachable, within reach 289adj. *accessible;* open to all 263adj. *open;* within comprehension, for the million 516adj. *intelligible.*

wieldy, manageable, tractable, towardly, easy-going, facile 597adj. *willing;* submissive 721adj. *submitting;* yielding, soft, ductile, pliant 327adj. *flexible;* smooth-running, well-oiled, frictionless, on friction wheels; handy, maneuverable, labor-saving.

facilitated, simplified, made easy; disembarrassed, disencumbered, disburdened, untrammeled, unloaded, light; disengaged, unimpeded, unobstructed, untrammeled, unfettered, unrestrained 744vb. *unconfined;* aided, given a chance, helped on one's way; in one's element, at home, quite at home, at ease, on velvet 376adj. *comfortable.*

Vb. *be easy,*—simple etc.adj.; require no effort, present no difficulties, give no trouble, make no demands; lie open to all, be had for the asking; come out, come out easily, be easily solved, have a simple answer 516vb. *be intelligible;* run well, go w., work w., work like a machine, go like clockwork, run on smoothly 258vb. *go smoothly.*

do easily, have no trouble, see one's way; make nothing of, make light of, make no bones about, make short work of, do it in one's head, do it with one hand behind one's back, do it with both eyes shut; have it all one's own way, carry all before one, have the game in one's hands, hold all the trumps, win hands down, win at a canter, walk over the course, have a walkover 727vb. *win;* be at ease, be at home, be in one's element, take in one's stride; take it easy 658vb. *be refreshed;* not strain oneself, drift with the tide, swim with the stream 721vb. *submit;* spare effort, save oneself, take the easy way out, take the easiest way, look for a short cut.

facilitate, ease, make easy; iron out 258vb. *smooth;* grease, oil 334vb. *lubricate;* explain, simplify, vulgarize, popularize 520vb. *interpret;* provide the means, enable 160vb. *empower;* make way for, not stand in the way, leave it open, allow 756vb. *permit;* give a chance to, put one in the way of 469vb. *make possible;* help, help on, speed 703vb. *aid;* pioneer, open up, clear the way, make a path for 64vb. *precede;* pave the way, bridge over; give full play to, make an opening for, leave open, leave a loophole, leave a hole to creep out of 744vb. *give scope.*

disencumber, free, liberate, unshackle, unfetter 668vb. *deliver;* clear, clear the ground, weed, clear away 648 vb. *clean;* derestrict, deobstruct; deoppilate, disengage, disembarrass; disentangle, extricate 62vb. *unravel;* unknot, untie 46vb. *disjoin;* cut the knot, cut the Gordian k. 46vb. *cut;* unclog, take the brake off; ease, lighten, take off one's shoulders, unload, unburden, disburden, ease the burden, alleviate 831vb. *relieve.*

Adv. *easily*, readily, smoothly, without friction; on wheels, swimmingly; effortlessly, with no effort, without difficulty, by the flick of a switch; without a hitch, without let or hindrance, freely, without obstruction; on easy terms.

See: 44, 46, 62, 64, 137, 160, 258, 263, 285, 309, 327, 334, 376, 469, 473, 516, 520, 597, 624, 648, 668, 679, 703, 721, 727, 744, 746, 831, 837.

702 Hindrance

N. *hindrance*, let or h., impedition, impediment, rub; psychological impediment, inhibition, fixation; stalling, thwarting, obstruction, frustration; hampering, shackling, clogging etc.vb.; occlusion, obturation, oppilation, stopping, stopping up, blockage, blocking, shutting 264n. *closure;* blockade, siege 712n. *attack;* limitation, restriction, control 747n. *restraint;* squeezing, coarctation, stricture 198n. *compression;* arrest 747n. *detention;* check, retardation, retardment, deceleration 278n. *slowness;* drag 333n. *friction;* cramp 651n. *paralysis;* interference, meddling 678 n. *overactivity;* interruption, interception, interclusion, interposition, intervention 231n. *interjacence;* obtrusion 303n. *insertion;* objection 762n. *deprecation;* obstructiveness, picketing, sabotage 704n. *opposition;* counter-measure, strike-breaking 182 n. *counteraction;* defense 715n. *resistance;* discouragement, active d., disincentive 613n. *dissuasion;* disapproval, frown 924n. *disapprobation;* boycott, "angry silence" 57n. *exclusion;* forestalling, prevention, prophylaxis, sanitation 652n. *hygiene;* sterilization, birth-control, contraception, contraceptive 172n. *unproductivity;* inability, disability 161n. *impotence;* ban, embargo, estoppal 757n. *prohibition;* capacity for hindrance, nuisance value.

obstacle, impediment, drawback, inconvenience, handicap 700n. *difficulty;* bunker, hazard; bottleneck, blockage, road-block, jam, traffic j., log-j.; hindrance, hamper, let, stay; tie, tether 47n. *bond;* preoccupation, previous engagement 138n. *intempestivity;* snag, block, stop, stymie; stumbling-block, trip-wire, hurdle, hedge, ditch, moat; jump, water-j.; something in the way, lion in the path (**see** *hinderer*); barrier, bulkhead, wall, brick w., seaw., groin, boom, dam, weir, bourock, dike, embankment 662n. *safeguard;* bulwark, breastplate, buffer, parapet, portcullis, barbed wire 713n. *defenses;* fence, ring, blockade 235n. *enclosure;* curtain, iron curtain, bamboo c. 231n. *partition;* stile, five-barred gate, turnstile, turnpike; check, brake, clog, shoe, skid, trammel, shackle, gag, curb 748n. *fetter;* ill wind, cross-w., headwind, crosscurrent; impasse, deadlock, stalemate, vicious circle; cul-de-sac, blind alley, dead end.

hitch, unexpected obstacle, snag, catch, lightning strike 145n. *strike;* repulse, rebuff 760n. *refusal;* contretemps, spot of trouble; teething troubles; technical hitch, breakdown, failure, engine f., engine trouble; puncture, flat; leak, burst pipe; fuse, short circuit; stoppage, stop, dead s., hold-up, traffic block, traffic jam

145n. *stop;* something wrong, screw loose, spanner in the works, grit in the oil, fly in the ointment.

encumbrance, handicap, remora; drag, clog, shackle, chain 748b. *fetter;* trammels, meshes; impedimenta, baggage, lumber, weight, dead-weight, millstone, millstone round one's neck, weight on one's shoulders, load on one's back 322n. *gravity;* pack, fardel, burden, load, overload, last straw; onus, incubus, Old Man of the Sea, white elephant; women and children, passenger; mortgage, debts 803n. *debt.*

hinderer, hindrance; tripper, tripper-up; red herring 10n. *irrelevance;* wet blanket, damper, spoilsport, kill-joy, pussyfoot; marplot 697n. *bungler;* dog in the manger, thwarter, frustrator; obstructor, staller; obstructionist, filibuster, saboteur; botherer, heckler, interrupter, interjector, barracker; intervener, interferer 678n. *meddler;* interloper, intruder, gate-crasher, uninvited guest 59n. *intruder;* mischief-maker, spoiler, poltergeist, gremlin 663n. *trouble-maker;* lion in the path, challenger 705n. *opponent;* rival, competitor 716n. *contender.*

interceptor, tertius gaudens; fieldsman, fielder, wicket-keeper, keeper, stumper, catcher; stop, longstop, back-stop; goalkeeper, goalie, custodian, back.

Adj. *hindering*, impeditive, impedient, obstructive, strike-happy; stalling, delaying, dragging; frustrating, thwarting etc.vb.; cross, contrary, unfavorable 731adj. *adverse;* restrictive, cramping, clogging 747adj. *restraining;* prohibitive, preventive 757 adj. *prohibiting;* prophylactic, counteractive 182adj. *counteracting;* upsetting, disconcerting, confusing; foreign, intrusive, obtrusive, not wanted 59adj. *extraneous;* interloping, intercipient, interfering 678adj. *meddling;* blocking, in the way, in the light; inconvenient, incommodious 643adj. *inexpedient;* hard, rough, snaggy 700adj. *difficult;* onerous, crushing, burdensome, cumbrous 322adj. *weighty;* tripping, entangling; choking, strangling, stifling; disincentive, discouraging; disheartening, damping 613adj. *dissuasive;* unhelpful, uncooperative, unaccommodating 598adj. *unwilling;* defensive, oppositional 704adj. *opposing.*

hindered, clogged, cramped, waterlogged; handicapped, encumbered, burdened with, saddled w., stuck w.; frustrated, thwarted, stymied etc.vb.; held up, delayed, held back, stuck, wind-bound, fog-b. 747adj. *restrained;* stopped, prevented 757adj. *prohibited;* in check, hard-pressed, cornered, treed, checkmated, stalemated 700adj. *in difficulties;* heavy-laden, overburdened 684adj. *fatigued;* left in the lurch, unaided, single-handed.

Vb. *hinder*, let, obstruct, impede; bother, annoy, inconvenience 827vb. *incommode;* embarrass, disconcert, upset, disorder 63vb. *derange;* trip, trip up, give one a fall; tangle, entangle, enmesh 542vb. *ensnare;* get in the way, stand in the w., cross one's path; come between, intervene, interpose 678vb. *meddle;* intercept, cut off, head off, undermine, cut the ground from under one's feet, nip, nip in the bud, stifle, choke, overgrow; gag, muzzle 578vb. *make mute;* suffocate, repress 165vb. *suppress;* quell, kill dead 362 vb. *kill;* hamper, burden, cumber, encumber; press, press down, hang like a millstone round one's neck 322vb. *weigh;* lade, load with, saddle w. 193vb. *load;* cramp, handicap; shackle, trammel, clog, tie one's hands 747vb. *fetter;* restrict, circumscribe 236vb. *limit;* check, brake, drag, be a drag on, hold back 747vb. *restrain;* hold up, slow down, set one back 278vb. *retard;* lame, cripple, hobble, hamstring, paralyze 161vb. *disable;* scotch, wing 655vb. *wound;* clip the wings, cramp the style of, take the wind out of one's sails; discountenance, put out of countenance 867vb. *shame;* intimidate, deter 854vb. *frighten;* discourage, dishearten 613 vb. *dissuade;* be the specter at the feast, mar, spoil, spoil the sport 655vb. *impair;* damp, damp down, throw cold water on 341vb. *moisten;* snub, rebuff 760vb. *refuse.*

obstruct, intervene, interpose, interfere 678vb. *meddle;* obtrude, interlope 297vb. *intrude;* stymie, stand in the way 231vb. *lie between;* buzz, jostle, crowd, squeeze; sit on one's tail 284vb. *follow;* stop, intercept, occlude, interclude, obturate, stop up, block, block up, wall up 264vb. *close;* jam, jam tight, make a bottleneck, create a stoppage; bandage, bind, stop the flow 350vb. *stanch;* dam, dam up, earth up, embank; divert, avert, draw off 495vb. *mislead;* fend off, stave off, stall off 713vb. *parry;* barricade 235vb. *en-*

close; encompass, fence, hedge in, blockade 232vb. *circumscribe;* deny access, keep out 57vb. *exclude;* prevent, not allow, cohibit, inhibit, ban, bar, debar, estop 757vb. *prohibit.*
be obstructive, make it hard for, give trouble 700vb. *be difficult;* stall, keep one in play, occupy; not play, non-cooperate 598vb. *be loath;* thwart, frustrate, stultify, baffle, foil, stymie, balk, be a dog in the manger; counter 182vb. *counteract;* check, countercheck, put in check, checkmate; traverse, contravene 533 vb. *negate;* object, raise objections 704vb. *oppose;* interrupt, interject, heckle, barrack; refuse a hearing, shout down 400vb. *be loud;* take evasive action 620vb. *avoid;* talk out time, filibuster 581vb. *be loquacious;* protract, drag out 113vb. *spin out;* strike, strike work 145vb. *halt;* picket, molest; sabotage, throw a spanner in the works, put grit in the machine, draw the teeth, spike the guns; cross one's bows, take the wind out of one's sails 269vb. *navigate.*

See: 10, 47, 57, 59, 63, 113, 138, 145, 161, 165, 172, 182, 193, 198, 231, 232, 235, 236, 264, 269, 278, 284, 297, 303, 322, 333, 341, 350, 362, 400, 495, 533, 542, 578, 581, 598, 613, 620, 643, 651, 652, 655, 662, 663, 678, 684, 697, 700, 704, 705, 712, 713, 715, 716, 731, 747, 748, 757, 760, 762, 803, 827, 854, 867, 924.

703 Aid

N. *aid*, assistance, help, helping hand, leg-up, lift; succor, rescue 668n. *deliverance;* comfort, support, stead, backing, seconding, abetment, encouragement; reinforcement 162n. *strengthening;* helpfulness, willing help, cordial assistance 706n. *cooperation;* service, ministry, ministration, subministration 897n. *kind act;* interest, friendly i., kindly i., good offices; custom 792n. *purchase;* patronage, auspices, sponsorship, countenance, suffrage, favor 660n. *protection;* good will, charity, sympathy 897n. *benevolence;* intercession 981n. *prayers;* advocacy, championship; good advice, constructive criticism 691n. *advice;* promotion, furtherance, advancement 654n. *improvement;* nursing, spoonfeeding; first aid, medical assistance 658n. *medical art;* relief, recruitment 685n. *refreshment;* preferential treatment, most-favored-nation t.; favorable conditions, favorable circumstances 730n. *prosperity;* fair wind, following w., tail w. 287n. *propulsion;* facilitation, facilities, magic carpet, Aladdin's lamp 701n. *facility;* self-help, do-it-yourself habit 744n. *independence.*
subvention, economic aid, monetary help, pecuniary assistance; state assistance, poor relief 901n. *philanthropy;* benefit, sick b.; loan, accommodation, temporary a., benevolence 802n. *credit;* subsidy, bounty, grant, allowance, expense account; stipend, scholarship, sizarship 962n. *reward;* supplies, maintenance, support, keep, upkeep, free board and lodging, alimentation, nutrition 633n. *provision;* manna, manna in the wilderness 301n. *food.*
aider, help, helper, assister, assistant, lieutenant, right-hand man; standby, support; tower of strength, someone to hold one's hand; nurse, spoonfeeder; abettor, instigator 612 n. *motivator;* factor, useful ingredient 58n. *component;* coadjutor, adjunct, ally, brother-in-arms 707n. *collaborator;* succors, contingents, supports, relieving force, reinforcements, recruits 707n. *auxiliary;* deus ex machina, genie of the lamp; promoter 707n. *patron;* booster, friendly critic 923n. *commender;* fairy godmother 903n. *benefactor;* springboard, jump-off 628n. *instrument.*

Adj. *aiding*, cooperative, helpful, obliging 706adj. *cooperative;* kind, well-disposed, well-intentioned 897 adj. *benevolent;* amicable, neighborly 880adj. *friendly;* favorable, propitious; supporting, seconding, abetting; encouraging 612adj. *inducive;* of service, of help, of great assistance 640adj. *useful;* constructive, well-meant; adjuvant, assistant, auxiliary, subsidiary, ancillary, accessory; in aid of, contributory, promoting; at one's beck and call, subservient 768adj. *observant;* ministrant 628adj. *instrumental.*

Vb. *aid*, help, assist, lend a hand, bear a h., lend one's aid, render assistance; hold out a hand to, take by the hand, take in tow, give a lift to; hold one's hand, spoonfeed; be kind to, give a leg-up to, help a lame dog over a stile 897vb. *be benevolent;* oblige, accommodate, lend money to 784vb. *lend;* find the money, help with m., subsidize, subvention, subventionize; facilitate, speed, lend wings to, feather the shaft, further, advance, boost 285vb. *promote;* abet, instigate, foment, nourish, feed the flame, fan the f. 612vb. *induce;* make for, contribute to, conduce to, be accessory to, be a factor in 156vb. *conduce;* lend support to, second, back, back up, stand by, bolster, prop up, stead 218vb. *support;* comfort, sustain, hearten, give heart to, encourage, rally, embolden 855vb. *give courage;* succor, come to the help of, send help to, furnish assistance to, relieve 668vb. *deliver;* reinforce, fortify 162 vb. *strengthen;* recruit 685vb. *refresh;* set one on his legs 656vb. *restore.*

patronize, favor, smile on, shine on 730vb. *be auspicious;* sponsor, back, guarantee; recommend, put up for; propose, second; countenance, give countenance to, connive at, protect 660vb. *safeguard;* join, enlist under 78vb. *be included;* contribute to, subscribe to, lend one's name 488 vb. *endorse;* take an interest in, have a kindness for 880vb. *befriend;* espouse the cause of, take the side of, side with, champion, take up the cudgels for, stick up for, stand up f., stand by 713vb. *defend;* make interest for, canvass f., vote f. 605 vb. *vote;* give moral support to, pray for, intercede; pay for, pay the piper 804vb. *defray;* entertain, keep, cherish, foster, nurse, wet-nurse, mother 889vb. *pet;* force, manure 370vb. *cultivate;* bestow one's custom, buy from 792vb. *purchase.*

minister to, wait on, do for, help, oblige 742vb. *serve;* give first aid to, nurse 658vb. *doctor;* squire, valet, mother; subserve, be of service to, make oneself useful to 640vb. *be useful;* anticipate the wishes of, consult the wishes of 597vb. *be willing;* pander to, toady, humor, suck up to 925vb. *flatter;* slave, make oneself the slave of, do all one can for, do everything for 682vb. *work;* be assistant to, be one's lieutenant, make oneself the tool of 628vb. *be instrumental.*

Adv. *in aid of*, in the cause of, for the sake of, on behalf of; by the aid of, thanks to; in the service of, in the name of.

See: 78, 156, 162, 218, 285, 287, 301, 370, 488, 597, 605, 612, 628, 633, 640, 654, 656, 658, 660, 668, 682, 685, 691, 701, 706, 707, 713, 730, 742, 744, 768, 784, 792, 804, 855, 880, 889, 897, 903, 923, 925, 981.

704 Opposition

N. *opposition*, oppositeness, polarity 240n. *contraposition;* contrast 14n. *contrariety;* repugnance 861n. *dislike;* antagonism, hostility 881n. *enmity;* clashing, conflict, friction, lack of harmony 709n. *dissension;* dissociation, non-association, non-cooperation, unhelpful attitude 598n. *unwillingness;* contrariness, cussedness, recalcitrance 602n. *obstinacy;* impugnation, counter-argument 479 n. *confutation;* contradiction, denial 533n. *negation;* challenge 711n. *defiance;* oppugnancy, oppugnation, firm opposition, stout o., stand 715n. *resistance;* contravention, infringement 738n. *revolt;* going against, siding a., voting a. 924n. *disapprobation;* withdrawal, walk-out 489n. *dissent;* physical opposition, headwind, cross-current 702n. *obstacle;* mutual opposition, cross purposes, tug of war; faction, rivalry, corrivalry, emulation, competition, race 716n. *contention;* political opposition, the Opposition, Her Majesty's O., the other party, the party in opposition; the other side, wrong s., ranks of Tuscany.

opposites, contraries, extremes, opposite poles 14n. *contrariety;* rivals, duelists, competitors 716n. *contender;* opposite parties, factions 709n. *quarreler;* town and gown, the right and the left, light and darkness, capital and labor, Democrat and Republican.

Adj. *opposing*, oppositional, opposed; in opposition, on the other side, on the wrong s.; anti, against, agin; antagonistic, hostile, unfriendly, antipathetic, unsympathetic 881adj. *inimical;* unfavorable, unpropitious 731 adj. *adverse;* cross, thwarting 702 adj. *hindering;* contrarious 14adj. *contrary;* cussed 602adj. *obstinate;* refractory, recalcitrant 738adj. *disobedient;* resistant, frictional 182adj. *counteracting;* clashing, conflicting, at variance 709adj. *quarreling;* militant, at daggers drawn, with crossed bayonets 716adj. *contending;* facing, face to face, fronting 237adj. *fore;* polarized, at opposite extremes 240 adj. *opposite;* mutually opposed, rival, emulous, competitive 911adj. *jealous.*

Vb. *oppose*, go against, militate a. 14vb. *be contrary;* side against, stand a., hold out a., fight a. 715vb. *resist;* set one's face against, make a dead set a. 607vb. *reject;* object, kick, protest, protest against 762vb.

deprecate; run one's head against, beat a. 279vb. *collide;* vote against, vote down 924vb. *disapprove;* not support, dissociate oneself; contradict, belie 533vb. *negate;* traverse, counter 479vb. *confute;* work against 182vb. *counteract;* countermine, thwart, baffle, foil 702vb. *be obstructive;* be at cross purposes, play at c.; stand up to, challenge, dare 711vb. *defy;* set at naught 922vb. *hold cheap;* fly in the face of 738vb. *disobey;* rebuff, spurn, slap in the face, slam the door in one's f. 760 vb. *refuse;* emulate, rival, match oneself with, compete with, play against, bid a. 716vb. *contend;* set against, pit a., match a.

withstand, confront, face, look in the f., stand up to 661vb. *face danger;* rise against 738vb. *revolt;* meet, encounter, cross swords with 716vb. *fight;* struggle against, make head a., breast, stem, breast the tide, stem the t., swim against the stream; cope with, grapple w., wrestle w. 671vb. *essay;* not be beaten 599vb. *stand firm;* hold one's own, bear the brunt 715vb. *resist.*

Adv. *in opposition*, against, versus, agin; in conflict with, against the tide, against the stream, against the wind, with the wind in one's teeth, against the grain, in the teeth of, in the face of, in spite of, despite.

See: 14, 182, 237, 240, 279, 479, 489, 533, 598, 599, 602, 607, 661, 671, 702, 709, 711, 715, 716, 731, 738, 760, 762, 861, 881, 911, 922, 924.

705 Opponent

N. *opponent*, opposer, lion in the path; adversary, antagonist, foe, foeman 881n. *enemy;* assailant 712n. *attacker;* opposing party, opposition p., the opposition, ranks of Tuscany, opposite camp; oppositionist, radical; obstructionist, filibuster 702n. *hinderer;* independent party, crossbenches; die-hard, bitter-ender, last-ditcher, irreconcilable; radical of the right, reactionist, reactionary, counterrevolutionary, obscurantist; objector, conscientious o. 489n. *dissentient;* resister, passive r.; noncooperator 829n. *malcontent;* agitator, incendiary, terrorist, extremist, ultraist, Jacobin, Fenian 738n. *revolter;* challenger, other candidate, rival, emulator, corrival, competitor, runner-up; battler, fighter, contestant, duelist; entrant, the field, all comers 716n. *contender;* factionary, factioneer, brawler, wrangler 709n. *quarreler;* common enemy, public e., universal foe, outlaw 904n. *offender.*

See: 489, 702, 709, 712, 716, 738, 829, 881, 904.

706 Cooperation

N. *cooperation*, helpfulness 597n. *willingness;* contribution, coadjuvancy, coagency, coefficiency, synergy, symbiosis; duet, double harness, collaboration, joint effort, combined operation; team work, working together, "a long pull, a strong pull and a pull all together"; relay, relay-race, team-r.; team spirit, esprit de corps; lack of friction, unanimity, agreement, concurrence, bipartisanship 710n. *concord;* clanship, clannishness, party spirit, cliquishness, partisanship; connivance, collusion, abetment 612n. *motivation;* conspiracy, complot 623n. *plot;* complicity, participation; sympathy, fraternity, solidarity, fellowship, freemasonry, fellow-feeling, comradeship, fellow-traveling; common cause, mutual assistance, helping one another, back-scratching, log-rolling; reciprocity, give and take, mutual concession 770n. *compromise;* mutual advice, consultation 584n. *conference.*

association, coming together; colleagueship, copartnership, partnership 775n. *participation;* nationalization, internationalization 775n. *joint possession;* pooling, pool; membership, affiliation 78n. *inclusion;* connection, hook-up, tie-up 9n. *relation;* combination, consolidation, centralization 45n. *junction;* integration, solidarity 52n. *whole;* unification, union, synoecism 88n. *unity;* amalgamation, fusion, merger, Anschluss; voluntary association, coalition, alliance, league, federation, confederation, confederacy; axis, united front, common f., popular f. 708n. *political party;* an association, fellowship, college, club, sodality, fraternity 708n. *society;* set, clique, cell 708n. *party;* workers' association, trade union, chapel; business association, company, joint-stock c., interlocking directorship, combine, consortium, trust, cartel, ring 708n. *corporation;* Zollverein, common market, Benelux 708n. *community.*

Adj. *cooperative*, helpful 703adj. *aiding;* frictionless 710adj. *concordant;* coadjutant, coadjuvant; symbiotic, synergic; collaborating, in double harness; married, associating, associated, leagued, in league, hand in glove with; bipartisan; federal 708 adj. *corporate.*

Vb. *cooperate*, collaborate, work together, pull t., work in t., work as a team; go hand in hand, hunt in pairs, run in double harness; team up, partner, go into partnership 775 vb. *participate;* play ball, reciprocate, respond; lend oneself to, espouse 703vb. *patronize;* join in, take part, enter into, take a hand in, strike in with; hang together, hold t., sail *or* row in the same boat, stand shoulder to shoulder, stand by each other, sink or swim together; be in league with, make common cause with, take in each other's washing; band, gang up, associate, league, confederate, federate, ally; coalesce, merge, unite 43vb. *be mixed;* combine, make common cause, club together; understand one another, think alike; conspire 623vb. *plot;* lay heads together, get into a huddle 691vb. *consult;* collude, connive, play another's game; work for an understanding, treat with, negotiate 766vb. *make terms.*

Adv. *cooperatively*, hand in hand, jointly, unanimously, as one man, as one.

See: 9, 43, 45, 52, 78, 88, 584, 597, 612, 623, 691, 703, 708, 710, 766, 770, 775.

707 Auxiliary

N. *auxiliary*, relay, recruit, fresh troops, reinforcement; second line, paramilitary formation 722n. *soldiery;* ally, brother-in-arms, confederate (**see** *colleague*); coadjutor, adjuvant, assistant, helper, helpmate, helping hand 703n. *aider;* right hand, right-hand man, stand-by, support, tower of strength; candle-holder, bottle-h.; gagman, prompter; adjutant, lieutenant, aide-de-camp; secretary, clerk; midwife, handmaid 742n. *servant;* acolyte, server; paranymph, best man; friend in need 880n. *friend;* hanger-on, satellite, henchman, follower 742n. *dependent;* disciple, adherent, votary, sectary 978n. *sectarist;* loyalist, legitimist; stooge, cat's-paw, puppet 628n. *instrument;* jackal, running dog, creature, âme damnée.

collaborator, cooperator, coworker, fellow-w.; team-mate, yoke-fellow, work-f.; sympathizer, fellow-traveler, fifth column, fifth columnist.

colleague, associate, confrère, brother; codirector, partner, comate, fellow; sharer 775n. *participator;* comrade, companion, playmate; confidant, alter ego, second self, faithful companion, fidus Achates, Man Friday; mate, chum, pal, buddy, amigo 880n. *friend;* stand-by, stalwart; ally, confederate; accomplice, accessory, abettor, aider and abettor, fellow-conspirator, particeps criminis; coreligionist; one's fellows, one's own side.

patron, defender, guardian angel, tutelary genius, special providence 660 n. *protector;* well-wisher, sympathizer; champion advocate, friend at court; supporter, backer, guarantor; proposer, seconder, voter; favorer, sider, partisan, votary, aficionado, fan 887n. *lover;* good friend, jack-at-a-pinch, friend in need, deus ex machina; fairy godmother, rich uncle 903n. *benefactor;* promoter, founder, refounder; patron of art, Maecenas 492n. *collector;* customer, client 792n. *purchaser.*

See: 492, 628, 660, 703, 722, 742, 775, 792, 880, 887, 903, 978.

708 Party

N. *party*, movement; group, class 77 n. *classification;* subsect, confession, communion, denomination, church 978n. *sect;* faction, cave, splinter group 489n. *dissentient;* circle, inner c., closed c., charmed c.; set, clique, coterie; caucus, junto, junta, camarilla, committee, club, cell, ring, closed shop; team, eight, eleven, fifteen; crew, complement, dramatis personae 686n. *personnel;* troupe, concert-party 594n. *actor;* gang, knot, bunch, outfit, push 74n. *band;* phalanx, horde 74n. *crowd;* side, camp.

political party, right, left, center; Conservative, Tories, Unionists; Liberals, Radicals, Whigs; Socialists, Labour, National Liberal, Liblab; Democrats, Republicans; Marxists, Communists, Reds, Bolsheviks, Mensheviks, Maximalists, Minimalists; Fascists, Nazis, Falangists; Blue-shirts, Black-shirts, Red-shirts, Brown-shirts; Jacobins, Girondists; coalition, popular front, bloc, political b.; citoyen, comrade, tovarich, red, commie; socialist, laborite, Fabian, syndicalist, anarchist; right-winger, rightist; left-winger, leftist; moderate, centrist; party man, party member, politician.

society, partnership, coalition, combination, combine 706n. *association;* league, alliance, axis; federation, confederation, confederacy; economic association, cooperative, Bund, union, customs u., sodality, Zollverein, Benelux, common market, free trade area; private society, club 76n. *focus;* secret society, Ku Klux Klan, Freemasonry, lodge, cell, club; trade union; chapel; group, division, branch, local b. 53n. *subdivision;* movement, Boy Scouts, Brownies, Cubs, Rovers, Rangers, Sea-scouts; Girl Guides, Blue Birds; Mothers' Union, Church Army, Church Lads' Brigade; Band of Hope; Colonial Dames, Daughters of the American Revolution, D.A.R.; fellow, honorary f., associate, member; party member, comrade; corresponding member, branch m., affiliate 58n. *component.*

community, fellowship, brotherhood, body, band of brother, fraternity, confraternity, sorority, sisterhood; guild, sodality; race, tribe, clan, sect 11n. *family;* order 77n. *classification;* social class 371n. *social group;* state, nation-s., multiracial s. 371n. *nation.*

corporation, body; incorporated society, body corporate, mayor and corporation 692n. *council;* company, livery c., joint-stock c., limited liability c., holding c.; firm, concern, joint c., partnership; house, business h.; establishment, organization, institute; trust, combine, monopoly, cartel, syndicate 706n. *association;* trade association, chamber of commerce, guild, consumers g., housewives union, cooperative society.

Adj. *corporate*, incorporate, corporative, joint-stock; joint, partnered, bonded, banded, leagued, federal, federative; allied, federate, confederate; social, clubby, clubbish, clubbable 882adj. *sociable;* fraternal, comradely 880adj. *friendly;* cooperative, syndicalist.

sectional, denominational, Masonic 978adj. *sectarian;* partisan, communal, clannish, cliquish, cliquey, exclusive; class-conscious; rightist, leftist, left-wing, pink, red; Whiggish, Tory; radical, conservative.

Vb. join a party, put one's name down, subscribe; join, swell the ranks, become a member, take out membership; sign on, enlist, enroll oneself, get elected; cut in, creep in 279vb. *enter;* belong to, fit in, make one of 78vb. *be included;* align oneself, side, take sides, range oneself with, team up w. 706vb. *cooperate;* club together, associate, ally, league, federate; cement a union, merge; make a party, found a p., lead a p.

Adv. in league, in partnership, in the same boat, in cahoots with; hand in hand, side by side, shoulder to shoulder, back to back; all together, en masse, jointly, collectively; unitedly, as one; with all the rest, in the swim.

See: 11, 53, 58, 74, 76, 77, 78, 297, 371, 489, 594, 686, 692, 706, 880, 882, 978.

709 Dissension

N. *dissension*, dissentience 489n. *dissent;* non-cooperation 704n. *opposition;* disharmony, dissonance, disaccord, jar, jangle, jarring note, discordant n., rift, rift within the lute 411n. *discord;* recrimination 714n. *retaliation;* bickering, cat-and-dog life; differences, odds, variance, friction, unpleasantness; soreness 891n. *resentment;* no love lost, hostility, mutual h., class war 888n. *hatred;* disunity, disunion, internal dissension, division in the camp, house divided against itself 25n. *disagreement;* cleavage, cleavage of opinion, parting of the ways, separation 294n. *divergence;* split, faction 978n. schism; misunderstanding, cross purposes 481n. *misjudgment;* imbroglio, embroilment, embranglement 61n. *confusion;* breach, rupture, open r., severance of relations, recall of ambassadors; challenge 711n. *defiance;* ultimatum, declaration of war 718n. *war.*

quarrelsomeness, factiousness, litigiousness; aggressiveness, combativeness, pugnacity, warlike behavior 718 n. *bellicosity;* provocativeness, trailing one's coat 711n. *defiance;* cantankerousness, awkwardness, prickliness, fieriness 892n. *irascibility;* shrewishness, sharp tongue 899n. *scurrility;* contentiousness 716n. *contention;* rivalry, emulation 911n. *jealousy;* thirst for revenge 910n. *revengefulness;* mischievousness, mischief, spite 898n. *malevolence;* apple of discord, spirit of mischief; Ate, Mars.

quarrel, open q.; feud, blood-f., vendetta 910n. *revenge;* war 718n. *warfare;* strife 716n. *contention;* conflict, clash 279n. *collision;* legal battle 959n. *litigation;* controversy, dispute, wrangle, polemic, battle of arguments, paper war 475n. *argument;* wordy warfare, words, war of w., high w., stormy exchange, altercation, rixation, abuse, slanging 899n. *scurrility;* spat, tiff, squabble, jangle, brabble, breeze, squall, storm in a tea-cup; rumpus, hubbub, racket, row, shindy, commotion, scrimmage, fracas, brawl, fisticuffs, breach of the peace, Donnybrook Fair 61n. *turmoil;* gang warfare, street fighting, riot 716n. *fight;* domestic difficulties, family jars, cat-and-dog life 411n. *discord.*

casus belli, ground of quarrel, root of dissension, breaking point; tender spot, sore point; apple of discord, bone of contention, bone to pick; disputed point, point at issue, area of disagreement 724n. *battleground.*

quarreler, disputer, eristic, wrangler 475n. *reasoner;* duelist, rival, emulator 716n. *contender;* strange bedfellows, Kilkenny cats, Montagues and Capulets; quarrel-monger, mischief-maker 663n. *trouble-maker;* scold, bitter tongue 892n. *shrew;* aggressor 712n. *attacker.*

Adj. *quarreling*, discordant, discrepant, clashing, conflicting, ill-mated, ill-matched 14adj. *contrary;* on bad terms, at feud, at odds, at sixes and sevens, at loggerheads, at variance, at daggers drawn, up in arms 881 adj. *inimical;* divided, factious, schismatic 489adj. *dissentient;* mutinous, rebellious 738adj. *disobedient;* uncooperative, non-cooperating 704 adj. *opposing;* sore 891adj. *resentful;* awkward, cantankerous 892adj. *irascible;* sulky 893adj. *sullen;* implacable 910vb. *revengeful;* litigant, litigious 959adj. *litigating;* quarrelsome, non-pacific, unpacific, bellicose 718adj. *warlike;* pugnacious, combative, spoiling for a fight, trailing one's coat, aggressive, militant 712adj. *attacking;* abusive, shrewish, scolding, scurrilous 899adj. *maledicent;* contentious, disputatious, eristic, wrangling, polemical, controversial 475adj. *arguing.*

Vb. *quarrel,* disagree 489vb. *dissent;* clash, conflict 279vb. *collide;* misunderstand, be at cross purposes, pull different ways, be at variance, have differences, have a bone to pick 15vb. *differ;* recriminate 714vb. *retaliate;* fall out, part company, split, break, break with, break squares with; break away 978vb. *schismatize;* break off relations, declare war 718vb. *go to war;* go to law, take it to court 959vb. *litigate;* dispute, try conclusions with, controvert 479vb. *confute;* have a feud with, cherish a vendetta 910vb. *be revengeful;* turn sulky, sulk 893vb. *be sullen;* non-cooperate 704vb. *oppose.*

make quarrels, pick q., fasten a quarrel on; look for trouble, be spoiling for a fight, trail one's coat, challenge 711vb. *defy;* irritate, rub the wrong way, tread on one's toes, provoke 891vb. *enrage;* have a bone to pick, have a crow to pluck; cherish a feud, enjoy a quarrel 881 vb. *make enemies;* embroil, entangle, bedevil relations, estrange, set at odds, set at variance, set by the ears 888vb. *excite hate;* create discord, sound a discordant note 411vb. *discord;* sow dissension, stir up strife, be a quarrel-monger, make mischief, make trouble; divide, draw apart, disunite, drive a wedge between 46vb. *sunder;* widen the breach, fan the flame 832vb. *aggravate;* set against, pit a., match with; egg on, incite 612vb. *motivate.*

bicker, spat, tiff, squabble, nag; peck, henpeck, jar, spar, spar with, live a cat-and-dog life; jangle, brangle, wrangle, dispute with 475vb. *argue;* scold 899vb. *cuss;* have words with, altercate, pick a bone w., pluck a crow w., row, row with, have a row, brawl, kick up a shindy, break the peace, make the fur fly, raise the dust, raise a breeze 61vb. *rampage.*

See: 14, 15, 25, 46, 61, 272, 279, 294, 411, 475, 479, 481, 489, 612, 663, 704, 711, 712, 714, 716, 718, 724, 738, 832, 881, 888, 891, 892, 893, 898, 899, 910, 911, 959, 978.

710 Concord

N. *concord,* harmony 410n. *melody;* unison, unity, duet 24n. *agreement;* unanimity, bipartisanship 488n. *consensus;* lack of friction, understanding, good u., mutual u., rapport; solidarity, team-spirit 706n. *cooperation;* reciprocity 12n. *correlation;* sympathy, fellow-feeling 887n. *love;* compatibility, coexistence, league, amity 880n. *friendship;* rapprochement, reunion, reconciliation, conciliation, peace-making 719n. *pacification;* good offices, arbitration 720n. *mediation;* entente cordiale, happy family, peace and quiet, "married calm" 717n. *peace;* good will, goodwill among men, honeymoon.

Adj. *concordant,* blended 410adj. *harmonious;* en rapport, eye to eye, unanimous, of one mind, bipartisan 24adj. *agreeing;* coexistent, compatible, united, cemented, bonded, allied, leagued; fraternal, loving, amicable, on good terms 880adj. *friendly;* frictionless, happy, peaceable, pacific, at peace 717adj. *peaceful;* conciliatory 719adj. *pacificatory;* agreeable, congenial 826vb. *pleasurable.*

Vb. *concord* 410vb. *harmonize;* bring into concord 719vb. *pacify;* agree 24vb. *accord;* see eye to eye, play a duet, chime in with, pull together 706vb. *cooperate;* reciprocate, respond, run parallel 181vb. *concur;* fraternize 880vb. *be friendly;* keep the peace, remain at peace 717vb. *be at peace.*

See: 12, 24, 181, 410, 488, 706, 717, 719, 720, 826, 880, 887.

711 Defiance

N. *defiance,* dare, daring, challenge, cartel, gage, gauntlet, hat in the ring; bold front, brave face 855n. *courage;* war-cry, war-whoop, war-song, battle-cry 900n. *threat;* high tone 878n. *insolence;* demonstration, display, bravura 875n. *ostentation.*

Adj. *defiant,* defying, challenging, proud, provocative, bellicose, militant 718adj. *warlike;* saucy, insulting 878adj. *insolent;* greatly daring 855 adj. *courageous;* high-toned 871adj. *proud;* reckless, trigger-happy 857 adj. *rash.*

Vb. *defy,* challenge, take one up on, demur 489vb. *dissent;* stand up to 704vb. *oppose;* caution 664vb. *warn;* throw in one's teeth, throw down the gauntlet, throw one's hat in the ring; demand satisfaction, call out, send one's seconds, offer choice of weapons; dare, outdare, beard, singe Philip's b.; brave, run the gauntlet 661vb. *face danger;* laugh to scorn, laugh in one's face, laugh in one's beard, set at naught, snap one's fingers at 922vb. *hold cheap;* bid defiance, set at d., hurl d.; call one's bluff, double the bid; show fight, bare one's teeth, show one's fangs, double one's fist, clench one's f., shake one's f. 900vb. *threaten;* take a high tone 871vb. *be proud;* look big, throw out one's chest, slap one's c., show a bold front; wave 317vb. *brandish;* demonstrate, make a demonstration; crow, bluster, brag 877vb. *boast;* cock a snook 878vb. *be insolent;* trail one's coat 709vb. *make quarrels;* crow over, shout 727vb. *triumph.*

Adv. *defiantly,* challengingly, in defiance of, in spite of one's teeth; under the very nose of.

Int. do your worst! come if you dare!

See: 317, 489, 661, 664, 704, 709, 718, 727, 855, 857, 871, 875, 877, 878, 900, 922.

712 Attack

N. *attack,* hostile a., best method of defense; pugnacity, combativeness, aggressiveness 718n. *bellicosity;* aggression, unprovoked a. 914n. *injustice;* stab in the back 930n. *foul play;* assault, assault and battery 176n. *violence;* armed attack, offensive, drive, push, thrust, pincer movement 688n. *tactics;* run at, dead set at; onslaught, onset, rush, shock, charge, sally, sortie, break-out, break-through; counter-attack 714n. *retaliation;* shock tactics, blitzkrieg, coup de main, surprise; encroachment, infringement 306n. *overstepping;* invasion, inroad, incursion, irruption, over-running 297n. *ingress;* raid, razzia, chappow, foray 788n. *brigandage;* blitz, air-raid, air attack, sea a., land a.; night attack, camisado; storm, taking by s., escalade; boarding, cutting-out expedition; investment, obsession, siege, leaguer, blockade, encirclement 230n. *circumjacence;* challenge, tilt.

terror tactics, intimidation, schrecklichkeit, frightfulness 854n. *intimidation;* war to the knife 735n. *severity;* whiff of grapeshot, battue, dragonnade, noyade, jacquerie, bloodbath 362n. *slaughter;* devastation, laying waste 165n. *havoc.*

bombardment, cannonade, barrage, strafe, blitz; broadside, volley, salvo; bomb-dropping, laying eggs, bombing, saturation b.; firing, shooting, fire, gun-f., machine-gun f., rifle f., fusillade, burst of fire, rapid f., cross-f., plunging f.; raking f., enfilade; platoon fire, file f.; antiaircraft fire, flak; sharp-shooting, sniping, Parthian shot; gunnery, musketry, practice.

foin, thrust, home-t., lunge, pass, passado, carte and tierce; cut, cut and thrust, stoccado, stab, jab; bayonet, cold steel; estrapade; punch, swipe, kick 279n. *knock.*

attacker, assailant, aggressor; militant, war party; spearhead, storm troops, shock t.; fighter pilot, air ace, bomber 722n. *armed force;* sharp-shooter, sniper, guerrilla; in-

vader, raider, tip-and-run r.; besieger, blockader, stormer, escalader.
Adj. *attacking*, assailing, assaulting etc.vb.; pugnacious, combative, aggressive, offensive 718adj. *warlike;* militant, spoiling for a fight, hostile 881adj. *inimical;* up in arms, on the warpath 718adj. *warring;* storming, changing, cutting-out, boarding, over the top; besieging, obsidional, besetting, obsidious.
Vb. *attack*, aggress, be spoiling for a fight; start a war, start a fight, declare war 718vb. *go to war;* strike the first blow, fire the first shot; assault, assail, make a dead set at, go for, set on, pounce upon, fall u., pitch into, sail i., have at; attack tooth and nail, savage, maul, draw blood 655vb. *wound;* launch out at, let fly at, round on; surprise, blitz, overwhelm; move in, invade 306vb. *encroach;* raid, foray, overrun, infest 297vb. *irrupt;* show fight, take the offensive, assume the o., go over to the o., go over to the attack; counter-attack 714vb. *retaliate;* thrust, push, make a drive 279 vb. *impel;* erupt, sally, make a sortie, break out, break through 298 vb. *emerge;* board, lay aboard, grapple; escalade, storm, take by storm, carry, capture 727vb. *overmaster;* ravage, make havoc, scorch, burn 165vb. *lay waste;* harry, drive, beat, beat up, corner, bring to bay 619vb. *hunt;* challenge, enter the lists 711 vb. *defy;* take on 704vb. *oppose;* take up the cudgels, draw the sword, couch one's lance, break a lance 716vb. *fight.*
besiege, lay siege, beleaguer, sit down before, invest, surround, beset, blockade 235vb. *enclose;* engage in siege operations, open the trenches, plant a battery; sap, mine, undermine, spring a mine.
strike at, raise one's hand against; lay about one, swipe, flail, hammer 279vb. *strike, kick;* go berserk, run amok 176vb. *be violent;* have at, have a fling at, fetch a blow, have a cut at, have a shot at; clash, ram 279vb. *collide;* make a pass at, lunge; close with, grapple w., come to close quarters, fight hand to hand, cut and thrust; push, butt, thrust, poke at, thrust at; stab, spear, lance, bayonet, run through, cut down 263 vb. *pierce;* strike home, lay low, bring down 311vb. *abase;* torpedo, sink 313vb. *plunge;* stab in the back 930vb. *be dishonest.*
charge, sound the c., advance against, march a., run a., drive a., sail a., fly a.; bear down on, come on, sail in; rush, mob 61vb. *rampage;* make a rush, rush at, run at, dash at, tilt at, ride full tilt at; ride down, run down, ram, shock 279vb. *collide;* go over the top.
fire at, shoot at, fire upon; fire a shot at, take a pot-shot, pop at, snipe, pick off 287vb. *shoot;* shoot down, bring d.; torpedo, sink; soften up, strafe, bombard, blitz, cannonade, shell, fusillade, pepper; bomb, throw bombs, drop b., lay eggs, plaster, prang; open fire, let fly, volley; spend powder and shot, volley and thunder, rattle, blast, pour a broadside into, rake, straddle, enfilade; take aim, level, draw a bead on 281vb. *aim.*
lapidate, stone, throw a stone, heave a brick; shy, sling, pelt; hurl at, hurl at the head of 287vb. *propel.*
Adv. *aggressively*, offensively, on the offensive, on the attack.
See: 61, 165, 176, 230, 235, 263, 279, 281, 287, 297, 298, 306, 311, 313, 362, 619, 655, 688, 704, 711, 714, 716, 718, 722, 727, 735, 788, 854, 881, 914, 930.

713 Defense

N. *defense*, the defensive, self-defense 715n. *resistance;* art of self-defense, boxing 716n. *pugilism;* judo, jujitsu 716n. *wrestling;* counter, counterstroke, parry, warding off 182n. *counteraction;* repression, suppression, insulation; defensiveness 854n. *nervousness;* posture of defense, guard, ward; defensive arrangement, balance of power; safekeeping 666n. *preservation;* self-protection 660n. *protection;* a defense, rampart, bulwark, ward, screen, buffer, fender, bumper 662n. *safeguard;* deterrent 723n. *weapon;* sinews of war, munitions 723n. *ammunition.*
defenses, muniment; lines, entrenchment, fieldwork, redan, lunette; breastwork, parados, contravallation; outwork, circumvallation; earthwork, embankment, mound; mole, boom; wall, barricade, fence 235n. *barrier;* abatis, palisade, paling, stockade, zareba, laager, sangar; moat, ditch, dike, fosse; trench, dugout; traverse, parallel; trip-wire, booby-trap 542n. *trap;* barbed wire, barbed wire entanglements; spike, caltrop, chevaux de frise; Maginot Line, Siegfried L., Hadrian's Wall,

Wall of Antonine, Great Wall of China; air-raid shelter, underground s. 662n. *shelter;* barrage, antiaircraft fire, flak; barrage-balloon; wooden walls; minefield, mine, countermine; smoke-screen 421n. *screen.*

fortification (**see** *fort*); circumvallation, bulwark, rampart, wall; parapet, battlement, machicolation, embrasure, casemate, merlon, loophole; banquette, barbette, emplacement, gun-e.; vallum, scarp, counterscarp, glacis; curtain, bastion; ravelin, demilune, outwork, hornwork, demibastion; buttress, abutment; gabionage, gabion, gabionade.

fort, fortress, fortalice, stronghold, fastness; citadel, capitol, acropolis 662n. *refuge;* air-raid shelter, underground s. 662n. *shelter;* castle, keep, ward, barbican, tower, turret, bartizan, donjon; portcullis, drawbridge; gate, postern, sally-port; turret, peelhouse, pill-h., martello tower, pillbox, cassine; blockhouse, strong point, redan, lunette; laager, zareba, sangar, enclosure, encampment, camp 235n. *enclosure;* Roman camp, castrum; British camp, Maiden Castle; seafort, military type s., naval type s.

armor, body a., harness; full armor, panoply; mail, chain m.; plate armor, armor-plate; breastplate, poitrel; cuirass lorica, plastron; hauberk, habergeon, brigandine, coat of mail, corselet; cheek-piece, head-p.; helmet, helm, casque, basinet, sallet, morion; visor, beaver; siege cap, steel helmet, tin hat; shako, bearskin, busby, pickelhaube 228n. *headgear;* greaves, gauntlet, vambrace, rerebrace; aegis, shield, buckler; scutum, targe, target; mantelet, testudo, tortoise; carapace, shell; thimble, finger-stall; protective clothing, gasmask.

defender, champion 927n. *vindicator;* patron 703n. *aider;* knight-errant, paladin; loyalist, legitimist, patriot; house-carl, body-guard, life-guard, Praetorian, National Guard; watch, sentry, sentinel; patrol, patrolman; garrison, picket, guard, escort, rearguard; Home Guard, militia, fencible 722n. *soldiery;* fireman, firefighter, fire-watcher; guardian, General Winter 660n. *protector;* warder 749n. *keeper;* wicket-keeper, goal-k., custodian 702n. *interceptor;* deliverer, rescuer, ready help in time of trouble 668n. *deliverance;* challengee, title-defender, title-holder.

Adj. *defending,* challenged, on the defensive 715adj. *resisting;* propugnant, defensive, protective, patriotic 660adj. *tutelary;* exculpatory, self-excusing 927adj. *vindicating.*

defended, armored, plated, panoplied; heavy-armed, mailed, mailclad, armor-c., iron-c.; accoutered, harnessed, armed to the teeth, armed cap-a-pie, armed at all points 669 adj. *prepared;* moated, palisaded, barricaded, walled, fortified, machicolated, castellated, battlemented, loopholed; entrenched, dug in; defensible, proof, bomb-p., bullet-p. 660adj. *invulnerable.*

Vb. *defend,* guard, protect, keep, watch, ward 660vb. *safeguard;* fence, hedge, moat 232vb. *circumscribe;* palisade, barricade 235vb. *enclose;* block 702vb. *obstruct;* cushion, pad, shield, curtain, shroud, shade, cover 421vb. *screen;* cloak 525vb. *conceal;* provide with arms, munition, arm, accouter 669vb. *make ready;* harness, armor, clothe in a., plate, panoply; reinforce, fortify, wall, crenellate, machicolate, loophole 162vb. *strengthen;* entrench, dig in 599vb. *stand firm;* stand in front, stand by; garrison, man, man the defenses, man the breach, stop the gap; champion 927vb. *vindicate;* fight for, unsheathe one's sword for, take up arms for, break a lance for, take up the cudgels for, cover up f. 703vb. *patronize;* rescue, come to the r. 668vb. *deliver.*

parry, counter, riposte, fend, forfend, fend off, ward off, hold off, keep off, fight off, hold *or* keep at bay, keep at arm's length 620vb. *avoid;* turn, avert 282vb. *deflect;* fence, foin; play, play with, keep in play; stall, stonewall, block 702vb. *obstruct;* act on the defensive, fight a defensive battle, play for a draw, stalemate; fight back, show fight, give a warm reception to 715vb. *resist;* butt away, repulse 292vb. *repel;* bear the brunt, hold one's own 704vb. *withstand;* fall back on 673vb. *avail of;* beat a strategic retreat 286vb. *turn back;* survive, scrape through, live to fight another day 667vb. *escape.*

Adv. *defensively,* on the defensive, at bay; in defense, pro patria, in self-defense.

See: 162, 182, 228, 232, 235, 286, 292, 421, 525, 542, 599, 620, 660, 662, 666, 667, 668, 669, 673, 702, 703, 704, 715, 716, 722, 723, 749, 854, 927.

714 Retaliation

N. *retaliation,* reprisal, lex talionis 910n. *revenge;* requital, recompense 962n. *reward;* desert, deserts 915n. *dueness;* punitive action, poetic justice, retribution, Nemesis 963n. *punishment;* repayment 787n. *restitution;* indemnification 31n. *compensation;* reaction, boomerang 280 n. *recoil;* counter, counterstroke, counterblast, counterplot, countermine 182n. *counteraction;* counterattack, sally, sortie 712n. *attack;* recrimination, answering back, riposte, retort, retort courteous 460n. *rejoinder;* returning good for evil, heaping coals of fire; reciprocation, give and take, like for like, tit for tat, quid pro quo, measure for measure, blow for blow, an eye for an eye and a tooth for a tooth, a Roland for an Oliver, diamond cut diamond, biter bit, a game at which two can play; potential retaliation, deterrent 854n. *intimidation.*

Adj. *retaliatory,* in retaliation, in reprisal, in self-defense; retaliative, retributive, punitive, recriminatory; like for like, reciprocal; rightly served.

Vb. *retaliate,* return, retort upon; serve rightly, teach one a lesson, exact compensation, take reprisals; make a requital, pay one out, pay off old scores, wipe out a score, square the account, be quits, get even with, get one's own back 910vb. *avenge;* requite, recompense, compensate 962 vb. *reward;* counter, riposte 713vb. *parry;* do unto others as you would be done by, return good for evil; heap coals of fire on one's head; reciprocate, give and take, return like for like; return the compliment, give as good as one got, pay in the same coin, give a quid pro quo; retort, cap, answer back 460vb. *answer;* recriminate 928vb. *accuse;* react, boomerang 280vb. *recoil;* round on, kick back, hit b., not take it lying down 715vb. *resist;* turn the tables on, hoist one with his own petard.

be rightly served, have had one's lesson; pay compensation, have to pay c. 787n. *restitute;* find one's match, catch a Tartar; get one's deserts, get a dose of one's own medicine 963vb. *be punished;* it serves one right.

Adv. *en revanche,* by way of return, in requital.

See: 31, 182, 280, 460, 712, 713, 715, 787, 854, 910, 915, 928, 962, 963.

715 Resistance

N. *resistance,* oppugnation, front, stand, firm s. 704n. *opposition;* contumacy 602n. *obstinacy;* reluctance, renitence 598n. *unwillingness;* repugnance 861n. *dislike;* objection, demur 468n. *qualification;* recalcitrance, kicking, protest 762n. *deprecation;* non-cooperation, passive resistance, satyagraha; rising, insurrection, resistance movement 738 n. *revolt;* repulsion, repulse, rebuff, bloody nose 760n. *refusal;* refusal to work 145n. *strike.*

Adj. *resisting* etc.vb.; firm against 704adj. *opposing;* protesting, unconsenting, reluctant 598adj. *unwilling;* recalcitrant, renitent, unsubmissive, mutinous, insurrectional 738adj. *disobedient;* contumacious 602adj. *obstinate;* holding out, unyielding, unconquerable, indomitable, unsubdued, undefeated 727adj. *unbeaten;* resistant, proof, proofed, grease-p., bullet-p., bomb-p., waterproof; repugnant, repelling 292adj. *repellent.*

Vb. *resist,* offer resistance, give a warm reception, stand against 704vb. *withstand;* obstruct 702vb. *hinder;* challenge, try a fall 711vb. *defy;* stand out, front, confront, outface 661vb. *face danger;* struggle against, contend with, stem the tide, breast the current 704vb. *oppose;* reluctate, recalcitrate, kick, kick against the pricks, protest 762vb. *deprecate;* demur, object 468vb. *qualify;* strike work, strike, come out 145vb. *cease;* engineer a strike, call out 145vb. *halt;* mutiny, rise, not take it lying down 738vb. *revolt;* make a stand, fight off, keep at arm's length, keep at bay, hold off 713vb. *parry;* hold out, not submit, die hard, sell one's life dearly 599vb. *stand firm;* bear up, bear the brunt, endure 825vb. *suffer;* be proof against, not admit, repel, rebuff 760vb. *refuse;* resist temptation, not be tempted; last 113vb. *outlast.*

See: 113, 145, 292, 468, 598, 599, 602, 661, 702, 704, 711, 713, 727, 738, 760, 762, 825, 861.

716 Contention

N. *contention,* strife, tussle, conflict, clash 709n. *dissension;* combat, fighting, war 718n. *warfare;* debate, dispute, controversy, polemics, paper war, ink-slinging 475n. *argument;* altercation, words, war of w. 709n. *quarrel;* a word and a blow 892n. *irascibility;* stakes, bone of contention 709n. *casus belli;* competition, rivalry, corrivalry, emulation, prestige-chasing 911n. *jealousy;* competitiveness, gamesmanship, survival of the fittest; cut-throat competition, war to the knife, no holds barred; sporting, athletics 837n. *sport.*

contest, trial, trial of strength 461n. *experiment;* test of endurance, marathon, pentathlon, decathlon, tug-of-war 682n. *exertion;* tussle, struggle 671n. *essay;* equal contest, ding-dong fight; close finish, photo f. 200n. *short distance;* competition, open c., free-for-all; knock-out competition, tournament; tourney, jousting, joust, tilting, tilt; prize-competition, stakes, Ashes; match, test m.; concourse, rally; event, handicap, run-off; heat, final, semifinal, quarterfinal, Cup final, Cup tie; set, game, rubber; sporting event, wager, bet 837n. *sport;* field day 837n. *amusement;* Derby day (**see** *racing*); agonism, athletics, gymnastics; gymkhana, horseshow, rodeo; games, Highland Games, Olympics, Olympic g., Pythian g., Isthmian g.; Olympia, Delphi, Isthmus; Wimbledon, Forest Hills; Oval, Lords; Henley 724n. *arena.*

racing, speed contest 277n. *speeding;* races, race, foot r., flat r., sprint, dash, quarter-mile, half-m., mile, marathon; long-distance race, cross-country r.; relay race, team-r., torch r., lampadedromy, lampadophoria; the Turf, horse-racing, sport of kings; horse-race, point-to-point, steeplechase, paperchase, hurdles, sticks 312n. *leap;* chariot-race, trotting-r.; motor race, motor-rally, dirt-track racing, bicycle r.; dog-racing; boat-race, yacht-r., America's Cup competition; regatta, eights, torpids, Lent races, May r., Henley; Epsom, racecourse, track, stadium 724n. *arena.*

pugilism, noble art of self-defense, boxing, shadow-b., sparring, milling, fisticuffs; prize-fighting, boxing match, prize-fight; mill, spar, clinch, in-fighting; round, bout; the ring, the fancy 837n. *sport.*

wrestling, jujitsu, judo, all-in-wrestling, catch-as-catch-can, no holds barred; catch, hold; wrestle, grapple, wrestling match.

duel, triangular d.; affair of honor, pistols for two and coffee for one; match, monomachy, single combat, gladiatorial c.; jousting, joust, tilting, tilt, tourney, tournament; fencing, fence, digladiation, sword-play, lathi-p., single-stick, quarter-s.; hand-to-hand fighting, close grips; bull-fight, tauromachy, dog-fight, cock-fight; bull-ring, cockpit, lists 724n. *arena.*

fight, hostilities, appeal to arms 718n. *warfare;* battle royal, free fight, free-for-all, rough and tumble, rough-house, horse-play, shindy, scuffle, scrum, scrimmage, scramble, dog-fight, melee, fracas, uproar, rumpus, ruction 61n. *turmoil;* gang-warfare, street-fight, riot, rumble; brawl, broil, brabble 709n. *quarrel;* fisticuffs, blows, hard knocks; give and take, cut and thrust; affray, set-to, tussle; running fight, ding-dong f., in-fighting, close f., hand-to-hand f.; close grips, close quarters; combat, fray, clash, conflict 279n. *collision;* encounter, rencounter, scrap, brush; skirmish, skirmishing, velitation; engagement, action, affair, pitched battle, stand-up fight, set-to, grapple 718n. *battle;* deed of arms, feat of a., passage of a. 676n. *deed;* campaign, struggle; death struggle, death grapple, death grips, war to the knife, war to the death; Armageddon, theomachy, gigantomachy; field of battle, battlefield 724n. *battle-ground.*

contender, struggler, trier, striver; tussler, fighter, battler, gamecock; gladiator, bull-fighter 722n. *combatant;* prize-fighter 722n. *pugilist;* duelist 709n. *quarreler;* fencer, swordsman; candidate, entrant, examinee; competitor, rival, corrival, emulator; challenger, runner-up, finalist, semifinalist; starter, also-ran, the field, all comers; contester, pot-hunter; racer, runner, sprinter, miler, team-racer, relay-r., lampadist 277n. *speeder;* agonist 162n. *athlete.*

Adj. *contending*, struggling, grappling etc.vb.; rival, rivaling, racing, outdoing 306adj. *surpassing;* competing, in the business, in the same b.; agonistic, sporting, pot-hunting; starting, running, in the running; agonistic, athletic, palaestric, pugilistic, gladiatorial; contentious, quarrelsome 709adj. *quarreling;* aggressive, combative, fight-hungry, spoiling for a fight, pugnacious, bellicose, warmongering, non-pacific, militant, unpeaceful 718adj. *warlike;* at loggerheads, at odds, at issue, at war, belligerent 718adj. *warring;* competitive, keen, cut-throat; hand to hand, close, at close grips; keenly contested, ding-dong; close run; well-fought, fought to a finish.

Vb. *contend*, combat, strive, struggle, battle, fight, tussle, wrestle, grapple 671vb. *essay;* oppose 715vb. *resist;* argue for, stick out for, make a point of, insist 532vb. *emphasize;* contest, compete, challenge, stake, wager, bet; play, play against, match oneself, vie with, race, run a race; emulate, rival 911vb. *be jealous;* outrival 306vb. *outdo;* enter, enter for, take on, enter the lists, descend into the arena, take up the challenge, pick up the glove; couch one's lance, tilt with, joust w., break a lance w.; take on, try a fall, try conclusions with, close w., grapple w., engage w. 712vb. *strike at;* have a hard fight, fight to a finish.

fight, break the peace, have a fight, scuffle, row, scrimmage, scrap, set to 176vb. *be violent;* pitch into, sail i. 712vb. *attack;* lay on, lay about one 712vb. *strike at;* mix it, join in the melee; square up to, come to blows, exchange b., exchange fisticuffs, give hard knocks, give and take; box, spar, fib, pummel, jostle, kick, scratch, bite 279vb. *strike;* fall foul of, join issue with 709vb. *quarrel;* duel, call out, meet, give satisfaction; encounter, have a brush with, scrap w., exchange shots, skirmish; take on, engage, fight a pitched battle 718 vb. *give battle;* come to grips, come to close quarters, close with, grapple, lock horns; fence, cross swords, measure s.; fight hand to hand, use cold steel; appeal to arms, appeal to the arbitrament of war 718vb. *go to war;* combat, campaign, fight the good fight 718vb. *wage war;* fight hard, fight like devils, fight it out 599vb. *be resolute*.

See: 61, 162, 176, 200, 277, 279, 306, 312, 461, 475, 532, 599, 671, 676, 682, 709, 712, 715, 718, 722, 724, 837, 892, 911.

717 Peace

N. *peace*, state of p., peacefulness, peace and quiet 266n. *quiescence;* piping times of peace 730n. *palmy days;* universal peace, Pax Romana, Pax Britannica; end of hostilities, demobilization 145n. *cessation;* truce, uneasy t., armistice 145n. *lull;* freedom from war, cold w., coexistence, armed neutrality; neutrality; non-involvement 860n. *indifference;* non-intervention 620n. *avoidance;* peaceability, non-aggression 177n. *moderation;* cordial relations 880n. *friendship;* pacifism, peace at any price, non-violence, ahimsa; disarmament, peace-making, irenics 719n. *pacification;* pipe of peace, calumet; league of peace, peace treaty, non-aggression pact 765n. *treaty;* burial of the hatchet 506n. *amnesty*.

pacifist, man of peace, peace-lover, peace-monger; peace-party 177n. *moderator;* neutral, non-combatant, non-belligerent; civilian, women and children; passive resister, conscientious objector, conchy; peacemaker 720n. *mediator*.

Adj. *peaceful*, quiet, halcyon 266adj. *tranquil;* piping 730adj. *palmy;* without war, without bloodshed, bloodless; harmless, dovelike 935adj. *innocent;* peaceable, law-abiding, peace-loving, pacific, unmilitary, unwarlike, unmilitant, unaggressive, war-weary; pacifist, non-violent; unarmed, non-combatant, civilian; unresisting, passive, submissive 721adj. *submitting;* peace-making, conciliatory, irenic 720adj. *mediatory;* without enemies, at peace; not at war, neutral; postwar, prewar.

Vb. *be at peace*, enjoy p., stay at p., observe neutrality, keep out of war, keep out of trouble; mean no harm, be pacific 935vb. *be innocent;* keep the peace, avoid bloodshed; work for peace, make p. 720vb. *mediate;* beat one's sword into a plowshare, make the lion lie down with the lamb, smoke the pipe of peace.

Adv. *peacefully*, peaceably, pacifically; without violence, bloodlessly; quietly, tranquilly, happily.

See: 145, 177, 266, 506, 620, 719, 720, 721, 730, 765, 860, 880, 935.

718 War

N. *war*, arms, the sword; grim-visaged war, horrida bella, ultima ratio regum; appeal to arms, arbitrament of war, fortune of w., wager of battle, ordeal of b.; undeclared war, cold w.; paper war, polemic 709n. *quarrel;* war of nerves 854n. *intimidation;* half-war, doubtful w., armed neutrality; disguised war, intervention, armed i., police action; real war, hot w.; internecine war, civil w., war of revolution, war of independence; wars of religion, religious war, holy w., crusade, jihad; aggressive war, war of expansion; colonial war, gunboat w., limited w., localized w.; major war, general w., world w., global w.; total war, blitzkrieg, atomic war; war of attrition, truceless war, war to the knife, war to the death, no holds barred; pomp and circumstance of war, chivalry, nodding plumes, gorgeous uniforms; martial music, bugle, trumpet, tucket, pibroch; call to arms, bugle-call 547n. *call;* battle-cry, war-whoop, war-song 711n. *defiance;* god of war, god of battles, war-god, Ares, Mars, Bellona. **See** *warfare.*

belligerency, state of war, state of siege; resort to arms, declaration of war, outbreak of w., militancy, hostilities; war-time, war-time conditions, time of war, duration of w.

bellicosity, war fever; love of war, warlike habits, military spirit, pugnacity, combativeness, aggressiveness, militancy 709n. *quarrelsomeness;* militarism, Prussianism, expansionism, war policy; jingoism, chauvinism 481n. *prejudice.*

art of war, warcraft, siegecraft, strategy, grand s. 688n. *tactics;* castrametation 713n. *fortification;* generalship, soldiership, seamanship, airmanship 649n. *skill;* ballistics, gunnery, musketry practice; drill, training 534n. *teaching;* staff-work, logistics, planning 623n. *plan;* military evolutions, maneuvers; military experience, skill in arms 490n. *knowledge.*

war measures, war footing, war preparations, martial p., arming 669 n. *preparation;* call to arms, clarion call, Fiery Cross 547n. *call;* war effort, call-up, mobilization, recruitment, conscription, national service, military duty; volunteering, join-up; rationing; black-out; censorship; internment.

warfare, war, warring, warpath, making war, waging w.; warlike operations, ops.; deeds of blood, bloodshed, battles, sieges 176n. *violence;* fighting, campaigning, soldiering, active service; military service, naval s., air s.; bombing, saturation b. 712 n. *bombardment;* raiding, sea-r.; besieging, blockading, investment 235 n. *enclosure;* aerial warfare, air w., naval w., submarine w., undersea w., chemical w., gas w., germ w., bacteriological w., atomic w., nuclear w.; economic warfare, blockade, attrition, scorched earth, denial policy; psychological warfare, propaganda; offensive warfare 712n. *attack;* defensive warfare 713n. *defense;* mobile warfare, static w., trench w., desert w., jungle w.; bush-fighting, guerrilla warfare; campaign, expedition; operations, land o., sea o., naval o., air o., combined o., joint o., amphibious o.; incursion, invasion, raid; order, word of command, orders 737n. *command;* password, watchword; battle-cry, slogan 547n. *call;* plan of campaign, battle-orders 623n. *plan.*

battle, ordeal of b., pitched b., battle royal 716n. *fight;* line of battle, order of b., array; line, firing l., first l., front l., front, battle f.; armed conflict, action, scrap, skirmish, brush, collision, clash; offensive, blitz 712n. *attack;* defensive battle, stand 713n. *defense;* engagement, naval e., sea e., air e.; sea fight, air f.; arena, battlefield, field of battle, area of hostilities 724n. *battleground.*

Adj. *warring*, on the warpath; campaigning, battling etc. vb.; at war, in a state of w.; belligerent, militant, engaged in war, mobilized, uniformed, under arms, in the army, at the front, on active service; militant, up in arms; armed, sword in hand 669adj. *prepared;* arrayed, embattled; engaged, at grips, at loggerheads 709adj. *quarreling;* on the offensive 712adj. *attacking.*

warlike, militaristic, bellicose, unpacific; militant, aggressive, pugnacious, combative; war-loving, peace-hating, fierce, untamed 898adj. *cruel;* bloodthirsty, battle-hungry, war-fevered; military, martial, exercised in arms, bearing a.; veteran, battle-scarred; armigerent, knightly, chivalrous; soldierly, soldierlike; Napoleonic; military, naval; operational, strategical, tactical.

Vb. *go to war*, resort to arms; declare war, dig up the hatchet; acknowledge belligerency, commit hostilities; appeal to arms, unsheathe the sword, throw away the scabbard, whet the sword, take up the cudgels 716vb. *fight;* take to arms, fly to a., rise, rebel 738vb. *revolt;* raise one's banner, set up one's standard, call to arms, send round the Fiery Cross; arm, militarize, mobilize, put on a war footing; call up, call to the colors, recruit, conscript; join the army, join up, enlist, enroll, take the shilling, don a uniform, take a commission.

wage war, make w., warray; go on the warpath, march to war, engage in hostilities, war, war against, war upon; campaign, open a c., open a front, take the field; go on active service, shoulder a musket, smell powder, flesh one's sword; soldier, be at the front; take the offensive, invade 712vb. *attack;* keep the field, hold one's ground 599vb. *stand firm;* act on the defensive 713vb. *defend;* maneuver, march, counter-march; blockade, beleaguer, besiege, invest 230vb. *surround;* shed blood, put to the sword 362vb. *slaughter;* ravage, burn, scorch 165vb. *lay waste.*

give battle, battle, offer b., accept b.; join battle, meet on the battlefield; engage, provoke an engagement; combat, fight the good fight, fight it out 716vb. *fight;* take a position, choose one's ground, dig in; rally, close the ranks, stand, make a s. 715vb. *resist;* sound the charge, go over the top 712vb. *charge;* open fire, cannonade, spend powder and shot 712vb. *fire at;* skirmish, brush.

Adv. *at war*, at the sword's point, at the point of the bayonet, in the thick of the fray, at the cannon's mouth.

See: 165, 176, 230, 235, 362, 481, 490, 534, 547, 599, 623, 669, 688, 694, 709, 711, 712, 713, 715, 716, 724, 737, 738, 854, 898.

719 Pacification

N. *pacification*, pacifying, peace-making; conciliation, appeasement, mollification 177n. *moderation;* reconciliation, reconcilement, détente, improved relations, rapprochement; accommodation, adjustment 24n. *agreement;* composition 770n. *compromise;* good offices 720n. *mediation;* convention, entente, understanding, peace-treaty, peace pact, non-aggression p., league of peace 765vb. *treaty;* suspension of hostilities, truce, armistice, cease-fire, standstill 145n. *lull;* disarmament, demobilization, disbanding; imposed peace, forced reconciliation, shot-gun wedding 740n. *compulsion.*

irenics, irenicon, peace-offering 177n. *moderator;* propitiation, appeasement 736n. *lenity;* olive branch, overture, peaceful approach, friendly a., hand of friendship, outstretched hand 880n. *friendliness;* flag of truce, white flag, parlementaire, cartel, pipe of peace, calumet 717n. *peace;* wergild, blood-money, compensation 787n. *restitution;* fair offer, easy terms 177n. *moderation;* plea for peace, peace speech 506n. *amnesty;* mercy 909n. *forgiveness.*

Adj. *pacificatory*, conciliatory, placatory, propitiatory; irenic 880adj. *friendly;* disarming, emollient 177 adj. *lenitive;* peace-making, mediatory, trucial; pacified, happy 828adj. *content.*

Vb. *pacify*, make peace, impose p., give to; allay, tranquilize, mollify, take the sting out of 177vb. *assuage;* heal 656vb. *cure;* hold out the olive branch, hold out one's hand, return a soft answer, coo like a dove 880vb. *be friendly;* conciliate, propitiate, disarm, reconcile, placate, appease, satisfy 828vb. *content;* restore harmony 410vb. *harmonize;* win over, bring to terms, meet halfway 770vb. *compromise;* compose differences, settle d., accommodate 24vb. *adjust;* bridge over, bring together 720vb. *mediate;* show mercy 736vb. *be lenient;* grant a truce, grant an armistice, grant peace 766vb. *give terms;* keep the peace 717vb. *be at peace.*

make peace, stop fighting; bury the hatchet, let bygones be bygones, forgive and forget 506vb. *forget;* shake hands, make it up, make friends, patch up a quarrel; lay down one's arms, sheathe the sword, beat swords into plowshares; make a truce, suspend hostilities, demilitarize, disarm, demobilize; close the gates of Janus, smoke the pipe of peace.

See: 24, 145, 177, 410, 506, 656, 717, 720, 736, 740, 765, 766, 770, 787, 828, 880, 909.

720 Mediation

N. *mediation*, good offices, mediatorship, intercession; umpirage, arbitrage, arbitration; intervention, interposition 231n. *interjacence;* intermeddling 678n. *overactivity;* diplomatics, *diplomacy;* parley, negotiation 584n. *conference.*

mediator, common friend, middleman, intermedium, match-maker, go-between, negotiator 231n. *intermediary;* arbitrator, umpire, referee 480n. *estimator;* diplomat, diplomatist, representative, attorney, agent 754n. *delegate;* intercessor, pleader, propitiator; moderating influence, peace party 177n. *moderator;* pacifier, pacificator, trouble-shooter; marriage adviser; peacemaker, make-peace, dove.

Adj. *mediatory*, mediatorial, intercessory, intercessorial, propitiatory 719 adj. *pacificatory.*

Vb. mediate, intervene, intermeddle 678vb. *meddle;* step in, put oneself between, interpose 231vb. *put between;* proffer one's good offices, of-

fer one's intercession, intercede for, beg off, propitiate; run messages for, be a go-between; bring together, negotiate, act as agent; arbitrate, umpire 480vb. *judge;* compose differences 719vb. *pacify.*
See: 177, 231, 480, 584, 678, 719, 754.

721 Submission
N. *submission,* submissiveness 739n. *obedience;* subservience, slavishness 745n. *servitude;* acquiescence, compliance, consent 488n. *assent;* supineness, peace at any price, line of least resistance, non-resistance, passiveness, resignation, fatalism 679n. *inactivity;* yielding, giving way, white flag, capitulation, surrender, unconditional s., rendition, cession, abandonment 621n. *relinquishment;* deference, humble submission 872n. *humility;* act of submission, homage 739n. *loyalty;* kneeling, genuflection, kowtow, prostration 311n. *obeisance.*
Adj. *submitting,* surrendering etc. vb.; quiet, meek, unresisting, non-resisting, law-abiding 717adj. *peaceful;* submissive 739adj. *obedient;* fatalistic, resigned, acquiescent 488adj. *assenting;* pliant 327adj. *soft;* weak-kneed, bending; crouching, crawling, lying down, supine, prostrate; kneeling, on bended knees, down on one's marrow-bones 872adj. *humble.*
Vb. *submit,* yield, give in; not resist, not insist, defer to; bow to, make a virtue of necessity, yield with a good grace, admit defeat, yield the palm 728vb. *be defeated;* resign oneself, be resigned 488vb. *acquiesce;* accept 488vb. *assent;* shrug one's shoulders 860vb. *be indifferent;* withdraw, make way for, draw in one's horns 286vb. *turn back;* not contest, let judgment go by default 679vb. *be inactive;* cease resistance, stop fighting, have no fight left, give up, cry quits, have had enough, throw up the sponge, surrender, hold up one's hands, show the white flag, ask for terms; surrender on terms, capitulate; surrender at discretion, throw oneself on another's mercy; give oneself up, yield oneself, throw down one's arms, hand over one's sword, give one's parole; haul down the flag, strike one's colors; renounce authority, deliver the keys.
knuckle under, succumb, take the count, cave in, collapse; sag, wilt, faint, drop 684vb. *be fatigued;* show no fight, take the line of least resistance, bow before the storm; be submissive, learn obedience, bow one's neck to the yoke, homage, do h. 745vb. *be subject;* take one's medicine, swallow the pill 963vb. *be punished;* apologize, eat humble pie, eat dirt 872vb. *be humbled;* take it, take it from one, take it lying down, pocket the insult, grin and bear it, suffer in patience, digest, stomach, put up with 825vb. *suffer;* bend, bow, kneel, kowtow, crouch, cringe, crawl 311vb. *stoop;* grovel, lick the dust, lick the boots of, kiss the rod; fall on one's knees, throw oneself at the feet of, beg for mercy, cry *or* howl for m. 905vb. *ask mercy;* yield to temptation, indulge.
Int. Kamerad! aman! hands up!
See: 286, 311, 327, 488, 621, 679, 684, 717, 728, 739, 745, 825, 860, 872, 905, 963.

722 Combatant. Army. Navy
N. *combatant,* fighter, battler, tussler, struggler 716n. *contender;* aggressor, assailant, assaulter 712n. *attacker;* besieger, stormer, escalader; storm troops, shock t., forlorn hope; belligerent, fighting man, warrior, brave; bodyguard 713n. *defender;* gunman, bludgeon man, strong-arm m. 362n. *killer;* bully, bravo, rough, rowdy 904n. *ruffian;* fire-eater, swashbuckler, swaggerer, miles gloriosus, Pistol 877n. *boaster;* duelist 709n. *quarreler;* swordsman, sabreur, foilsman, fencer, sword, good s., blade; agonist 162n. *athlete;* gladiator, retiarius; fighting cock, gamecock; bull-fighter, toreador, matador, picador; grappler, wrestler, jujitsuist, judoist 716n. *wrestling;* competitor 716n. *contender;* champion, champ 644n. *exceller;* jouster, tilter; knight, knight-errant, paladin 707n. *patron;* wrangler, disputer, controversialist 475n. *reasoner;* barrister, advocate 959n. *litigant.*
pugilist, pug, boxer, bruiser, sparring partner; prize-fighter, flyweight, bantam-w., feather-w., welter-w., middle-w., cruiser-w., heavy-w.; knuckle-fighter, glove-f. 716n. *pugilism.*
militarist, jingoist, chauvinist, expansionist, militant, crusader, ghazi; Rajput, Kshatriya, Samurai, Mamluke; professional soldier, free-lance, mercenary, free companion, soldier of fortune, adventurer, condottiere, war-lord; freebooter, night-rider, marauder, pirate, land p. 789n. *robber;* war-monger.

soldier, army man, pongo; military man, soldier man, long-term soldier, regular; armed man, soldiery, troops (see *armed force*); campaigner, old c., conquistador; old soldier, veteran, Chelsea pensioner; fighting man, warrior, brave, myrmidon; man-at-arms, gendarme, redcoat, legionary, legionnaire, centurion; vexillary, standard-bearer, color escort, color sergeant, ensign, cornet; heavy-armed soldier, hoplite, phalangist; light-armed soldier, peltast; velites, skirmisher; sharp-shooter, sniper, franc-tireur 287n. *shooter;* auxiliary, territorial, Home Guard, militiaman, fencible; yeomanry, yeoman; irregular, irregular troops, guerrilla, moss-trooper, cateran, kern, gallow-glass, comitadji, bashi-bazouk; raider, tip-and-run r., fedayeen; underground fighter, maquis; picked troops 644n. *elite;* guards, Swiss Guard, Switzer, Praetorian, Immortal, janissary, house-carl; Varangian Guard (see *armed force*); effective, enlisted man; reservist; volunteer; pressed man; conscript, recruit, rookie; serviceman, Tommy, Tommy Atkins, GI, doughboy, bingboy, Aussie, Anzac, poilu, sepoy, sowar, Gurkha, Sikh, askari; woman soldier, female warrior, amazon; battle-maid, valkyrie; Wren, WASP, WAAC (see *women's army*).

soldiery, cannon fodder, food for powder; gallant company, merry men, heroes; private, private soldier, common s., man-at-arms; targeteer, slinger, archer, bowyer, bowman, cross-b., arbalester; spearman, pikeman, pike, halberdier, hoplite, phalangist, lancer; harquebusier, matchlockman, musketeer, fusilier, rifleman, rifles, pistoleer, carabineer, bazookaman, grenadier, bombardier, gunner, matross, cannoneer, artilleryman; pioneer, sapper, miner, engineer; signalman; aircraftman; corporal, sergeant, top-s., ensign, cornet, lieutenant, shavetail 741n. *army officer.*

army, host, camp; phalanx, legion; cohorts, big battalions; horde, mass 104n. *multitude;* warlike people, martial race; nation in arms, levy en masse, general levy, arrière-ban; National Guard, Home G.; militia, yeomanry; landsturm, landwehr; regular army, standing a., professional a., mercenary a., volunteer a., territorial a., conscript a., draft, class; the services, armed forces, all arms, air arm, naval a.

armed force, forces, troops, contingents, effectives, men, personnel; armament, armada; corps d'élite, ceremonial troops, guards, household troops; Household Cavalry, Royal Horse Guards, The Blues; Life Guards, The Tins; Old Guard, Young G., Swiss G., Praetorian G., Varangian G., Immortals, janissaries; picked troops, crack t., shock t., storm t., forlorn hope; spearhead, expeditionary force, striking f., flying column, parachute troops, paratroops, commando, commandos, task force, raiding party, guerrilla force; combat troops, field army, line, thin red l., front l., front-line troops, first echelon; wing, van, vanguard, rear, rearguard, center, main body; second echelon, base troops, reserves, recruits, reinforcements, draft, levy; base, staff; detachment, picket, party, detail; patrol, night patrol, night-watch, sentry, sentinel, vedette 660n. *protector;* garrison, occupying force, occupation troops, army of occupation.

formation, array, line; square, British s., skeltron, phalanx; legion, cohort, century, decury, maniple; column, file, rank; unit, group, army g., corps, army c., division, armored d., panzer d.; brigade, rifle b., light b., heavy b.; artillery brigade, battery; regiment, cavalry r., squadron, troop; battalion, company, platoon, section, squad, detail, party 74n. *band.*

infantry, bayonets, foot-regiment, infantryman, foot-soldier, foot, peon; foot-slogger, PBI; mountain infantry, light i.; chasseur, Jäger, Zouave.

cavalry, yeomanry; heavy cavalry, light c., sabers, horse, light h., cavalry regiment; horseman, cameleer, rider; mounted troops, mounted rifles, mounted police, mounted infantry, horse artillery; horse soldier, cavalryman, yeoman; trooper, sowar; chivalry, knight; man-at-arms, lancer, Uhlan, Hussar, cuirassier, dragoon, light d., heavy d., "big men on big horses"; Ironsides, cossack, spahi, Croat, Pandour, rough-rider; armor, armored car, tank, Panzer; charger, destrier 273n. *war-horse.*

navy, sea power, admiralty; sail, wooden walls; fleet arm, naval armament, armada; fleet, moth-ball f., flotilla, squadron; "little ships."

navy man, naval service, navy, senior service, silent s.; admiral, sea lord 741n. *naval officer;* naval architect, Seabee; sailor boy, sailor, sailor man 270n. *mariner;* blue-jacket, man-of-war man, able seaman, rating, pressed man; foretopman; powder-monkey; coastguardsman; gobbie, gob, swab, swabbie; marine, jolly, leatherneck, Marine Corps; submariner, naval airman 270n. *naval man;* privateer; naval reserve, RNR, Royal Naval Reserve; RNVR, Royal Naval Volunteer Reserve, Wavy Navy.

warship, war vessel, war junk, war galley, trireme, quinquereme, galleon, galleass 275n. *ship;* man-of-war, ship of the line, first-rater, seventy-four; armored vessel, capital ship, battleship, dreadnought; turret ship, monitor, ironclad; cruiser, light c., armored c.; raider, surface r., privateer, pirate ship; frigate, sloop, corvette, scout; patrol-boat, dispatch-b., gunboat, torpedo-boat, mosquito b.; destroyer, torpedo-boat d., catamaran; fire-ship, hell-burner, bomb-vessel; block ship, mine-layer, mine-sweeper; submarine, atomic-powered s., U-boat; submarine chaser, eagle-boat, E-b.; Q-boat, mystery b.; aircraft carrier, flat-top; floating battery; landing-craft, duck, amphibian; transport, troopship, trooper; tender, store ship, supply s., ammunition s., fuel s., depot s., parent s., guard-s., hospital s.; flagship, flotilla-leader.

air force, RAF, U.S. Air Force; Royal Air Force Volunteer Reserve; air arm, flying corps, air service, fleet air arm; squadron, flight, group, wing; warplane 276n. *aircraft;* battle-plane, bomber, heavy b., light b., pilotless b., fighter, night f.; flying boat, Catalina, patrol plane, scout; transport plane, troop-carrier; zeppelin, captive balloon, observation b., barrage-b. 276n. *airship;* air troops, airborne division; parachute troops, paratroopers; aircraftman, ground staff; fighter pilot, bomber p., air crew, bomb-aimer, weaponeer; air-force reserve.

women's army, QARNS (Queen Alexandra's Royal Nursing Service); FANY (First Aid Nursing Yeomanry); AFS (Auxiliary Fire Service); VAD (Voluntary Aid Detachment); WVS (Women's Voluntary Service); WAVES, Waves (Women Accepted for Voluntary Emergency Service); WAC (Women's Army Corps); WAAC (Women's Auxiliary Army Corps); WRAC (Women's Royal Army Corps); WRAF (Women's Royal Air Force); WAF (Women in the Air Force); WASP (Women's Air Force Service Pilots); WAFS (Women's Auxiliary Ferrying Squadron); WRNS, Wrens (Women's Royal Navy Service).

See: 74, 104, 162, 270, 273, 275, 276, 287, 362, 475, 644, 660, 707, 709, 712, 713, 716, 741, 789, 877, 904, 959.

723 Arms

N. *arm* (**see** *weapon*); fleet arm, air a. 722n. *combatant;* arming, armament, munitioning, munitions, manufacture of m.; armaments, armaments race; arms traffic, gun-running; ballistics, rocketry, gunnery, musketry, archery, bowmanship.

arsenal, armory, gun-room, gun-rack, arms chest, stand of arms; arms depot 632n. *storage;* magazine, powder-m., powder-barrel, powder-keg, powder-flask, powder-horn; caisson, limber-box, magazine-chamber; bullet-pouch, cartridge-belt, bandolier, cartridge-clip; arrow-case, quiver; scabbard, sheath; holster, pistol-case 194n. *receptacle.*

weapon, arm, deterrent; deadly weapon, defensive w.; armor, plate, mail 713vb. *defense;* offensive weapon 712n. *attack;* conventional weapon, ABC weapons (atomic w., bacteriological w., chemical w.), TNW (Tactical Nuclear Weapon); antimissile weapon; weapon of reprisal, Vergeltungswaffe, V-1, V-2; secret weapon, death ray; gas, poison g., mustard g., lacrimatory g., tear g. 659n. *poison;* natural weapon, teeth, claws, nails, horn, antler.

missile weapon, javelin, knobkerrie, harpoon, dart, discus; bola, lasso; boomerang, woomerang, woomera, throwstick; arrow, reed-a., cloth-yard a., barbed a., shaft, bolt, quarrel; arrowhead, barb; stone, brick, brickbat; slingstone, shot, ball, bullet, pellet, shell, star s., gas s., shrapnel, whizbang, rocket (**see** *ammunition*); bow, long-b., cross-b., arbalest, balister, catapult, mangonel, sling; blow-pipe; bazooka, rocket-thrower (**see** *gun*); ballistic missile, ICBM, Inter-Continental Ballistic Missile; thunderbolt.

club, mace, knobkerrie, knobstick, war-hammer 279n. *hammer;* battering-ram 279n. *ram*; bat, staff, stave, stick, cane, ferule, ruler, switch, rattan, lathi, quarter-staff, hand-s.; life-preserver, bludgeon, cudgel, shillelagh, blackjack, sandbag, knuckle-duster, brass knuckle, cosh, bicycle-chain, truncheon.

spear, hunting s., fishing s., eel-s., harpoon, gaff; lance, javelin, jerid,

pike, sarissa; partisan, bill, halberd 256n. *sharp point.*
ax, battle-ax, tomahawk, hatchet, war-h., halberd, bill, gisarme; pole-ax, chopper 256n. *sharp edge.*
side-arms, sword; heraldic sword, sax; dagger, bayonet, sword-b.; cold steel, naked s.; broadsword, glaive, claymore, two-edged sword, two-handed s.; cutlass, hanger, whinyard, short sword, sword-stick; saber, scimitar, yataghan, falchion, snickersnee; blade, fine b., bilbo, Toledo, Ferrara; rapier, tuck; fencing sword, épée, foil; dirk, skean, poniard, dudgeon, misericord, stylet, stiletto 256n. *sharp point;* matchet, machete, kukri, creese, kris, parang, knife, bowie-k., flick-k., gravity-blade k., pigsticker 256n. *sharp edge.*
fire arm, small arms, portable gun, hand g., caliver, harquebus, hackbut, hackbush; matchlock; wheel-lock, flint-l., fusil, musket, Brown Bess; blunderbuss, muzzle-loader, smoothbore, escopette, carbine; breechloader, chassepot, needle-gun; rifle, magazine r., repeating-r., Winchester; fowling-piece, sporting gun, shot-g., single-barreled g., double-barreled g., elephant g.; Enfield rifle, Lee-Enfield, Lee-Metford, Martini-Henry, Mauser, Snider, Hotchkiss; bore, caliber; muzzle; trigger, lock; magazine; breech, butt, gunstock; sight, backsight; ramrod.
pistol, dueling p., horse-p.; petronel, pistolet; six-shooter, colt, revolver, repeater, zipgun, rod, gat, shooting-iron; automatic pistol; Beretta, Luger, Webley-Scott.
toy gun, pop-g., air-g., wind-g., water pistol, pea-shooter, blow-pipe 287n. *propellant.*
gun, guns, ordnance, cannonry, artillery, light a., heavy a., mountain a.; horse artillery, galloping guns; battery, broadside; park, artillery p., gun-p.; cannon, brass c., bombard, falconet, swivel, gingal, basilisk, petard, pedrero, paterero, carronade, culverin, demi-c.; serpentine, sling; demi-cannon, saker, drake, rabinet, base, murderer, perier, mortar; stern-chaser, bow-c.; piece, field-piece, field-gun, siege-g.; great gun, heavy g., cannon-royal, seventy-four, heavy metal, Big Bertha; howitzer, trench-mortar, mine-thrower, minenwerfer, Minnie, trench gun; antiaircraft gun, antitank g., bazooka; gun, quick-firing g., Gatling g., mitrailleuse, pom-pom, Maxim, Maxim-Nordenfelt g., Lewis g., machine-g., light machine-g., Bren g., Sten g., submachine g., Thompson submachine-g., Tommy g.; flammenwerfer, flame-thrower; gun-lock, gun-carriage, limber, caisson; gun-emplacement, rocket site.
ammunition, live a., live shot, sharp s.; round of ammunition, round; powder and shot, powder and ball; shot, round s., case s., langrage, langrel, canister shot, grape s., chain s., small s., mitraille, buckshot; ball, cannon b., bullet, expanding b., soft-nosed b., dum-dum b.; projectile 287n. *missile;* slug, stone, sling-shot, pellet; shell, shrapnel-s.; charge, priming, warhead; wad, cartouche, cartridge, ball-c., live c.; spent cartridge, dud; cartridge-belt, cartridge-clip; cartridge-case, shell-c.; cap, detonator, fuse.
explosive, propellant; powder, blasting p., gunpowder; saltpeter, "villainous s."; high explosive, lyddite, cordite, melinite, gun-cotton, dynamite, gelignite, TNT, trinitrotoluene, nitroglycerine, fulgurite; Greek fire; cap, detonator; priming, charge, warhead, atomic w.; fissionable material.
bomb, explosive device; bombshell, egg; grenade, hand-g., Mills bomb; megaton bomb, atomic b., nuclear b., hydrogen b.; mushroom, fall-out; blockbuster, Molotov cocktail; stink-bomb, gas-b., incendiary b., napalm b.; carcass, Greek fire; mine, land-m., magnetic m., acoustic m.; booby-trap; depth-charge, ash-can, torpedo, submarine t., aerial t.; flying bomb, P-plane, V-1, doodlebug, V-2; rocket bomb; time-bomb, infernal machine.
See: 194, 256, 279, 287, 632, 659, 712, 713, 722.

724 Arena

N. *arena,* field, field of action; ground, terrain; center, scene, stage, theater; hustings, platform, floor; airfield, flying ground, landing g.; flight deck 276n. *aircraft;* amphitheater, Flavian a., Colosseum; stadium, stand, grandstand; campus, Campus Martius, Champs de Mars, parade ground, training g. 539n. *training school;* forum, market-place 76n. *focus;* hippodrome, circus, course, racecourse, turf; track, running-t., cinder-t., dog-t.; ring, bull-r., boxing r., ropes; rink, skating r., ice-r.; palaestra, calisthenium, gymnasium, gym; range, shooting r., rifle-r., butt, Bisley; riding-school; hunting field; playground, gutter, beach, lido, pier, fair-ground

837n. *pleasure ground;* playing ground, playing field, football f., gridiron, diamond, pitch, cricket p.; court, tennis c., fives c., squash c.; bowling-green, bowling-alley, skittle a.; lists, tilt-yard, tilting-ground; cockpit, beargarden; chess-board, checker-board; bridge-table; auction room; examination hall; court-room 956n. *law-court.*

battle-ground, battlefield, field of battle, tented field; field of blood, Aceldama; theater of war, war theater, front, front line, firing l., trenches, no-man's-land; sector, salient, bulge, pocket; beach-head, bridge-h.; camp, enemy's c.

See: 76, 276, 539, 837, 956.

725 Completion

N. *completion,* finish, termination, conclusion, end of the matter 69n. *end;* terminus 295n. *goal;* issue, upshot 154n. *eventuality;* result, end r., final r., end product 157n. *effect;* fullness 54n. *completeness;* fulfillment 635n. *sufficiency;* maturity, readiness, perfect r. 669n. *maturation;* consummation, culmination, climax, ne plus ultra 646n. *perfection;* exhaustiveness, thoroughness 455n. *attention;* elaboration, rounding off, finishing off, mopping up, winding up; roofing, topping out; top, crown, superstructure, keystone, coping-stone 213 n. *summit;* missing link 627n. *requirement;* last touch, last stroke, crowning s., final s., finishing s., coup de grâce; achievement, fait accompli, work done, finished product (**see** *effectuation*); boiling point, danger p., breaking p., last straw 236n. *limit;* denouement, catastrophe, last act, final scene 69n. *finality.*

effectuation, carrying through, follow-t.; execution, discharge, implementation; dispatch, performance 676n. *action;* accomplishment, achievement 727n. *success;* elaboration, working out; holing out.

Adj. *completive,* completory, completing, perfective; crowning, culminating 213adj. *topmost;* finishing, conclusive, final, last 69adj. *ending;* unanswerable, crushing; thorough, thoroughgoing, whole-hogging 599 adj. *resolute.*

completed, well-c., full 54adj. *complete;* done, well-d., achieved, accomplished etc.vb.; wrought out, highly wrought, elaborate 646adj. *perfect;* sped, well-s. 727adj. *successful.*

Vb. *carry through,* follow t., follow up, hole out; drive home, clinch, seal, set the seal on, put the seal to, seal up; clear up, mop up, wipe up, finish off, polish off; dispose of, dispatch, give the coup de grâce; complete, consummate, put the finishing touch, cast off (knitting), nail the roof on, top out 54vb. *make complete;* elaborate, hammer out, work o. 646vb. *perfect;* ripen, bring to a head, bring to the boil, bring to boiling point 669vb. *mature;* sit out, see out, see it through (**see** *carry out*); get through, get shut of, dispose of, bring to its close 69vb. *terminate;* set at rest 266vb. *bring to rest.*

carry out, see through, effect, enact 676vb. *do;* dispatch, execute, discharge, implement, effectuate, realize, compass, bring about, accomplish, consummate, achieve 727vb. *succeed;* make short work of, make no bones of; do thoroughly, leave no ends hanging, not do by halves, go the whole hog, be in at the death; deliver the goods, bring home the bacon, be as good as one's word, fill the bill.

climax, cap, crown all 213vb. *crown;* culminate, stand at its peak; scale the heights, conquer Everest; reach boiling point, come to a crisis; reach the limit, touch bottom; put the lid on, add the last straw; come to its end, attain one's e., touch the goal 295vb. *arrive;* die a natural death, die in one's bed; have enough of, be through with 635vb. *have enough.*

See: 54, 69, 154, 157, 213, 236, 266, 295, 455, 599, 627, 635, 646, 669, 676, 727.

726 Non-completion

N. *non-completion,* non-success 728n. *failure;* non-performance, inexecution, neglect 458n. *negligence;* non-fulfillment 636n. *insufficiency;* deficiency, deficit 307n. *shortcoming;* lack 55n. *incompleteness;* unripeness, immaturity 670n. *undevelopment;* never-ending task, Penelope's web, Sisyphean labor, argument in a circle, recurring decimal 71n. *continuity;* perfunctoriness, superficiality, a lick and a promise 456n. *inattention;* tinkering, work undone, job half-done, ends left hanging, points uncleared; no finality, no result, drawn battle, drawn game; stalemate, deadlock; semicompletion, launching stage.

Adj. *uncompleted,* partial, fragmentary 55adj. *incomplete;* unfinalized, unbegun 55adj. *unfinished;* undone, unperformed, unexecuted, unachieved, unaccomplished; unrealized, half-done, half-finished, half-begun, hardly b. 458adj. *neglected;* half-baked, underdone, unripe 670 adj. *immature;* unthorough, perfunctory, superficial; not cleared up, left hanging, left in the air; lacking finish, unelaborated, not worked out, inchoate, sketchy, in outline 647adj. *imperfect;* unbleached, unprocessed, semiprocessed; never-ending 71adj. *continuous.*

Vb. *not complete,* hardly begin, leave undone, leave in the air, leave hanging 458vb. *neglect;* skip, scamp, do by halves, tinker, paper over the cracks 636vb. *not suffice;* scotch the snake not kill it 655vb. *wound;* give up, not follow up, not follow through; fall out, drop o., not stay the course; fail of one's goal, fail of one's end, fall down on 728vb. *fail;* defer, postpone, put off to tomorrow 136vb. *put off.*

Adv. *on the stocks,* under construction, on the anvil, in preparation, in process of; before the finish.

See: 55, 71, 136, 307, 456, 458, 636, 647, 655, 670, 728.

727 Success

N. *success,* glory 866n. *famousness;* success all round, happy outcome, happy ending, favorable issue; prowess, success story, progress, steady advance, God-speed, good s., time well spent 285n. *progression;* fresh advance, breakthrough; one's day, continued success, run of luck, good fortune 730n. *prosperity;* advantage, lead, temporary l., first blood 34n. *vantage;* momentary success, flash in the pan; exploit, feat, achievement 676n. *deed;* accomplishment, goal 725n. *completion;* a success, feather in one's cap, triumph, hit, smash h., triumphant success, howling s., knock-out, kill; good hit, winning h., good shot 694n. *skill;* lucky stroke, fluke 618n. *non-design;* hat-trick, stroke of genius, master-stroke, happy s., scoring s. 694n. *masterpiece;* trump, trump card, winning c., card up one's sleeve 623n. *contrivance;* success in examination, pass, qualification; match-winning 34n. *superiority.*

victory, infliction of defeat, beating, whipping, licking, trouncing 728n. *defeat;* conquest, subdual 745n. *subjection;* successful attack, expugnation, storm, escalade 712n. *attack;* honors of battle, the best of it, triumph; win, game and match; outright win, complete victory, checkmate; narrow win, pyrrhic victory, well-fought field; easy win, runaway victory, love game, walk-over, push-o., picnic; crushing victory, quelling v., slam, grand s.; kill, knock-out, KO; mastery, ascendancy, upper hand, whip-h., advantage, edge, winning position, certain victory 34n. *vantage;* no defeat, stalemate 28n. *draw;* celebration of victory, triumph, ovation, epinician ode 876n. *celebration.*

victor, winner, match-winner, champion, world-beater, medalist, prizeman, first, double f. 644n. *exceller;* winning side, the winners; conqueror, conquistador, thunderbolt of war; defeater, beater, vanquisher, overcomer, subjugator, subduer, queller; master, master of the field, master of the situation; a success, successful rival, successful man, self-made m., rising m. 730n. *made man;* triumpher, triumphator, conquering hero.

Adj. *successful,* effective, efficacious; crushing, quelling; efficient; sovereign 658n. *remedial;* well-spent, fruitful 640adj. *profitable;* happy, lucky; felicitous, masterly 694adj. *skillful;* ever-victorious, unbeatable (**see** *unbeaten*); match-winning, never-failing, surefire, foolproof; unerring, infallible, sure-footed 473adj. *certain;* prize-winning, victorious, world-beating 644adj. *excellent;* winning, leading, up, one up 34adj. *superior;* on top, in the ascendant, rising, on the up and up, sitting pretty 730adj. *prosperous;* triumphant, crowning; triumphal, epinician; crowned with success, flushed with victory; glorious 866adj. *renowned.*

unbeaten, undefeated, unsubdued, unquelled, unvanquished, unovercome 599adj. *resolute;* unbeatable, unconquerable, ever-victorious, invincible.

Vb. *succeed,* succeed in, effect, accomplish, achieve, compass 725vb. *carry through;* be successful, make out, win one's spurs; make a success of, make a go of, make short work of, rise to the occasion; make good, rise, do well, get promotion, work one's way up the ladder, work one's way up, come to the top 730vb. *prosper;* pass, make the grade, qualify, graduate, come off well, come well out of it, come off with flying colors, come out on top, have the best of it 34vb. *be superior;* advance, break through, make a breakthrough 285vb. *pro-*

gress; speed well, strive to some purpose, gain one's end, reach one's goal, secure one's object, obtain one's objective, attain one's purpose; pull it off, be as good as one's word, bring home the bacon; have a success, score a s., make a hit, make a kill; hit the jackpot, break the bank; score a point, win a p., carry a p.; arrive, be a success, get around, make one's mark, click.

be successful, be efficacious, be effective, come off, come right in the end; answer, answer the purpose, do the trick, ring the bell, show results, turn out well; turn up trumps, rise to the occasion; do the job, do wonders, do marvels; compass, manage 676vb. *do;* work, act, work like magic, act like a charm 173vb. *operate;* take effect, tell, pull its weight 178vb. *influence;* bear fruit 171vb. *be fruitful;* get it, hit it, hit the nail on the head; play one's hand well, not put a foot wrong, never go w.; be sure-footed, keep on the right side of; have the ball at one's feet, hold all the trumps; be irresistible, not know the meaning of failure, brush obstacles aside 701vb. *do easily;* not know when one is beaten, come up smiling 599vb. *be resolute;* avoid defeat, hold one's own, maintain one's position 599vb. *stand firm.*

triumph, have one's day, be crowned with success, wear the laurels of victory, erect a trophy 876vb. *celebrate;* crow, crow over 877vb. *boast;* score, score off, be one up on; triumph over difficulties, contrive a success, manage, surmount, overcome obstacles, get over a snag, sweep difficulties out of the way; find a loophole, find a way out, tide over 667vb. *escape;* make head against, stem the current, weather the storm 715vb. *resist;* reap the fruits, reap the harvest 771vb. *gain.*

overmaster, be too much for, be more than a match for 34vb. *be superior;* master, overcome, overpower, overmatch, overthrow, overturn, override, overtrump 306vb. *outdo;* have the advantage, take the a., seize the a., hold the a., keep the a., prevail 34vb. *predominate;* have one on the hip, checkmate, mate, euchre, trump, ruff; conquer, vanquish, quell, subdue, subject, suppress, put down, crush, reduce 745vb. *subjugate;* capture, carry, take, storm, take by s., escalade 712vb. *attack.*

defeat (**see** *overmaster*); discomfit, dash, put another's nose out of joint, cook one's goose; repulse, rebuff 292vb. *repel;* confound, dismay 854vb. *frighten;* best, be too good for, get the better of, get the upper hand, get the whip-h. 34vb. *be superior;* worst, outplay, outpoint, outflank, outmaneuver, outgeneral, outclass, outshine 306vb. *outdo;* disconcert, cut the ground from under one's feet, trip, lay by the heels, baffle, bring to a stand 702vb. *obstruct;* gravel, nonplus 474vb. *puzzle;* beat, lick, thrash, whip, trounce, swamp, overwhelm, crush, drub, give a drubbing, roll in the dust, trample underfoot, trample upon; beat hollow, rout, put to flight, scatter 75vb. *disperse;* silence, put the lid on, put hors de combat, put out of court 165vb. *suppress;* down one's opponent, flatten, crush, put out for the count, knock out; knock for six, hit for s.; bowl out, skittle o.; run hard, corner, bay, drive to the wall, check, put in check 661vb. *endanger;* put an end to, wipe out, do for, dish 165vb. *destroy;* sink, send to the bottom 313 vb. *founder;* break, bankrupt 801vb. *impoverish.*

win, win the battle, gain the day, achieve victory, defeat the enemy, down one's opponent (**see** defeat); be victorious, remain in possession of the field, erect a trophy, claim the victory; come off best, come off with flying colors; win hands down, carry all before one, have it all one's own way, romp home, have a walk-over 701vb. *do easily;* win on points, scrape home, survive; win the last battle, win the last round, succeed in the final; win the match, take the prize, take the cup, walk off with the pot, gain the palm, wear the crown, wear the laurel-wreath; become champion, beat all comers 34vb. *be superior.*

Adv. *successfully,* swimmingly, marvelously well; to some purpose, to good p., with good result, with good effect, with magical e.; to one's heart's content, beyond one's fondest dreams, beyond all expectation; with flying colors, in triumph.

See: 28, 34, 75, 165, 171, 173, 178, 285, 292, 306, 313, 473, 474, 599, 618, 623, 640, 644, 658, 661, 667, 676, 694, 701, 702, 712, 715, 725, 728, 730, 745, 771, 801, 854, 866, 876, 877.

728 Failure

N. *failure,* non-success, successlessness, negative result; no luck, off day 731n. *ill fortune;* non-fulfillment 726n.

non-completion; frustration, slip 'twixt the cup and the lip 702n. *hindrance;* inefficacy, ineffectiveness 161n. *ineffectuality;* vain attempt, abortive a., wild-goose chase, futile effort, no result 641n. *lost labor;* mess, muddle, bungle, foozle 695n. *bungling;* abortion, miscarriage 172n. *unproductivity;* hopeless failure, dead f., dud show, wash-out, fiasco, flop, frost; flunk, no ball, bosh shot, misaim, misfire, slip, omission, faux pas 495n. *mistake;* no go, dead stop, halt 145n. *stop;* engine failure, seizing up, breakdown 702n. *hitch;* collapse, fall, stumble, trip 309n. *descent;* claudication, titubation 161n. *impotence;* anticlimax, lame and impotent conclusion 509n. *disappointment;* losses 772n. *loss;* bankruptcy 805n. *insolvency.*

defeat, bafflement, bewilderment, puzzlement 474n. *uncertainty;* nonplus, deadlock, stalemate, stand 145n. *stop;* lost battle, repulse, rebuff, bloody nose, check, reverse; no move left, checkmate, mate, fool's m.; the worst of it, discomfiture, beating, drubbing, hiding, licking, thrashing, trouncing; retreat; flight 290n. *recession;* dispersal 75n. *dispersion;* stampede, panic 854n. *fear;* rout, landslide; fall, downfall, collapse, debacle; wreck, perdition, graveyard 165n. *ruin;* lost cause, losing game, lost g., non-suit; deathblow, quietus; utter defeat, total d., final d., Waterloo; conquest, subjugation 745n. *subjection.*

loser, unsuccessful competitor, baffled enemy, defeated rival; also-ran, non-starter; has-been, extinct volcano; defeatist, pessimist, misery 834n. *moper;* foozler, sorcerer's apprentice 697n. *bungler;* dud, failure, plucked examinee; sacrifice, victim, prey 544n. *dupe;* underdog 35n. *inferior;* beat generation, beatnik 25n. *misfit;* bankrupt, insolvent 805n. *non-payer;* the losers, losing side, the defeated, the conquered, the vanquished, the fallen.

Adj. *unsuccessful,* ineffective, pale; inglorious, successless, empty-handed; unlucky 731adj. *unfortunate;* vain, bootless, negative, profitless; dud, misfired, hanging fire; miscarried, stillborn, aborted, abortive, premature; stultified; jilted, ditched, left holding the baby; feckless, manqué, failed, plucked, plowed, flunked; unplaced, losing, failing; stumbling, tripping, groping, wandering, out of one's depth 474adj. *uncertain.*

defeated, beaten, bested, worsted, pipped; non-suited, cast; baffled, thwarted, foiled 702adj. *hindered;* disconcerted, dashed, discomfited, hoist with one's own petard; outmaneuvered, outmatched, outplayed, outvoted; outclassed, outshone 35adj. *inferior;* thrashed, licked, whacked; on the losing side, among the also-rans, unplaced; in retreat, in flight 290adj. *receding;* routed, scattered, put to flight; swamped, overwhelmed, sunk; overborne, overthrown, struck down, borne down, knocked out, kaput, brought low, fallen; captured, made a prey, victimized, sacrificed.

grounded, stranded, wrecked, on the rocks, on one's beam-ends 165adj. *destroyed;* unhorsed, dismounted, thrown, thrown on one's back, brought low; ruined, bankrupt, insolvent 805adj. *non-paying.*

Vb. *fail,* not succeed, have no success, have no result; be unsuccessful,—plowed,—plucked etc.adj.; fall down on, flunk, foozle, muddle, botch, bungle 495vb. *blunder;* not make the grade, be found wanting 636vb. *not suffice;* fail one, let one down 509vb. *disappoint;* misaim, misdirect, miss one's aim, go wide, make a bosh shot, miss, hit the wrong target 282vb. *deviate;* get nothing out of it, get no change out of it, draw a blank, return empty-handed, lose one's pains, labor in vain, have shot one's bolt 641vb. *waste effort;* fall, collapse, slide, tumble off one's perch 309vb. *tumble;* break down, come to pieces, come unstuck; seize, seize up, conk out; stop, come to a dead stop, come up against a blank wall, come to a dead end; stick, stick in the mud, bog down, get bogged d. 145vb. *cease;* come to a sticky end, come to a bad e. 655vb. *deteriorate;* go on the rocks, run aground, ground, sink 313vb. *founder;* make a loss, make losses, crash, bust, break, go bankrupt 805 vb. *not pay.*

miscarry, fall still-born, abort; misfire, hang fire, flash in the pan, fizzle out; fall, fall to the ground, crash 309vb. *tumble;* come to naught, come to nothing, end in futility 641 vb. *be useless;* fail of success, come to grief, burst, bust, explode, blow up; flop, prove a fiasco, turn out a frost; not go well, go wrong, go amiss, go awry, gang agley, take a wrong turn, take an ugly turn; do no good, make things worse 832vb. *aggravate;* dash one's hopes, frustrate one's expectations 509vb. *dis-*

appoint; falter, limp, hobble 278 vb. *move slowly.*

be defeated, lose, lose out, suffer defeat, take a beating, lose the day, lose the battle, lose the match; lose the election, lose one's seat, lose the vote, be outvoted; just lose, just miss, get pipped on the post; get the worst of it, come off second best, go off with one's tail between one's legs, lick one's wounds; lose hands down, come in last, not win a point; take the count, bite the dust; fall, succumb 745vb. *be subject;* be captured, fall a prey to, be victimized; retreat, lose ground 290vb. *recede;* take to flight 620vb. *run away;* admit defeat, give one best, have enough, cry quits 721vb. *submit;* have not a leg to stand on, have the ground cut from under one's feet; go downhill 655vb. *deteriorate;* go to the wall, go to the dogs 165vb. *be destroyed.*

Adv. *unsuccessfully,* like a loser, to no purpose, to little or no p., in vain.

See: 25, 35, 75, 145, 161, 165, 172, 278, 282, 290, 309, 313, 474, 495, 509, 544, 620, 636, 641, 655, 695, 697, 702, 721, 726, 731, 745, 772, 805, 832, 834, 854.

729 Trophy

N. *trophy,* sign of success; war-trophy, spoils, capture, captives 790n. *booty;* spolia opima, scalp, head; scars, wounds 655n. *wound;* memorial, war-m., memento 505n. *reminder;* triumphal arch 548n. *monument;* triumph, ovation 876n. *celebration;* plum, benefit, benefit match; prize, first p., booby p., consolation p. 962n. *reward;* sports trophy, Ashes, cup, pot, plate; award, Oscar a.; bays, laurels, crown, laurel c., bay c., coronal, chaplet, garland, wreath, palm, palm of victory; epinician ode, pat on the back; favor, feather in one's cap, sleeve, love-knot 547n. *badge;* flying colors 875n. *ostentation;* glory 866n. *repute.*

decoration, honor 870n. *title;* blushing honors, battle h., spurs 866n. *honors;* citation, mention in dispatches; ribbon, blue r., cordon bleu; athletic honor, blue, oar; medal, gong, star, cross, garter, order, khilat; service stripe, long-service medal, war-m., campaign m.; Victoria Cross, Military C., Croix de Guerre, Iron Cross, Pour le Mérite; Distinguished Service Order; Distinguished Service Cross, Distinguished Flying C., Air Force C., Congressional Medal, Medal of Honor; George Cross, Medal for Merit, civic crown.

See: 505, 547, 548, 655, 790, 866, 870, 875, 876, 962.

730 Prosperity

N. *prosperity,* well-being; economic prosperity, welfare, weal 824n. *happiness;* thriving, health and wealth, having it good 727n. *success;* booming economy, boom; roaring trade, seller's market, favorable trade balance, no unemployment; crest of the wave, high tide, flood, affluence 635 n. *plenty;* luxury 800n. *wealth;* golden touch, Midas t.; flesh-pots, fat of the land, milk and honey, loaves and fishes, flesh-pots of Egypt, chicken in every pot, full dinner-pail; auspiciousness, favor, smiles of fortune, good f., blessings godsend, crowning mercy, goodness and mercy 615n. *good;* luck, run of l., good l., break, lucky b., luck of the draw 159n. *chance;* glory, honor and g., renown 866n. *prestige.*

palmy days, heyday, floruit; halcyon days, bright d., summer, sunshine, fair weather, fair wind, break in the clouds, blue streak; piping times, easy t.; clover, velvet, bed of roses 376n. *euphoria;* bonanza, golden times, Golden Age, Saturnia Regna, Saturnian Age, Ram Raj 824n. *happiness;* spacious times, Periclean Age, Augustan A., Pax Romana, Elizabethan Age.

made man, man of substance, man of property 800n. *rich man;* rising man, prosperous m., successful m.; favorite of the gods, child of fortune, lucky fellow, lucky dog; arriviste, upstart, parvenu, nouveau riche, profiteer; celebrity, hero 866n. *person of repute;* lion 890n. *favorite.*

Adj. *prosperous,* thriving, flourishing, booming 727adj. *successful;* rising, doing well, up and coming, on the up and up; on the make, profiteering; set-up, established, well-to-do, well-off, warm, comfortable, comfortably off 800adj. *moneyed;* riding high on the hog's back, riding on the crest of a wave, buoyant; fortunate, lucky, born with a silver spoon in one's mouth, born under a lucky star; in clover, on velvet; at ease, in bliss; looking prosperous, fat, sleek, euphoric.

palmy, balmy, halcyon, golden, couleur de rose, rosy; piping, blissful, blessed; providential, favorable, promising, auspicious, propitious, cloudless, clear, fine, fair, set f.; glorious, spacious, ample; euphoric, agreeable, cozy 376adj. *comfortable.*

Vb. *prosper,* thrive, flourish, have one's day; do well, fare w., have a good time of it 376vb. *enjoy;* bask in sunshine, make hay, live in clover, lie on velvet, have it easy, live on milk and honey, live on the fat of the land, "never have had it so good"; batten on, grow fat, feed well 301vb. *eat;* blossom, bloom, flower 171vb. *be fruitful;* win glory 866vb. *have repute;* boom, drive a roaring trade, enjoy a seller's market; profiteer 771vb. *gain;* get on, rise in the world, make one's way, work one's way up, arrive 727vb. *succeed;* make money, make a fortune, make one's pile, feather one's nest 800vb. *get rich;* go on well, run smoothly, run on oiled wheels 258vb. *go smoothly;* go on swimmingly, swim with the tide, sail before the wind; keep afloat, keep one's head above water, do well enough.

have luck, have all the l., have a stroke of l., have a good break, have a run of luck; strike lucky, strike oil, strike a rich vein, be on to a good thing; fall on one's feet, enjoy the smiles of fortune, bear a charmed life, be born under a lucky star, be born with a silver spoon in one's mouth, have the ball at one's feet.

be auspicious,—propitious etc.adj.; promise, promise well, set fair; favor, prosper, profit; look kindly on, look benignly on, smile on, shine on, bless, shed blessings on; water, fertilize, make blossom like the rose; turn out well, take a good turn, take a favorable t., turn up trumps 644vb. *do good;* glorify 866 vb. *honor.*

Adv. *prosperously,* swimmingly 727 adv. *successfully;* beyond one's wildest dreams, beyond the dreams of avarice; in the swim, in clover, on velvet.

See: 159, 171, 258, 301, 376, 615, 635, 644, 727, 771, 800, 824, 866, 890.

731 Adversity

N. *adversity,* adverse circumstances, misfortune, frowns of fortune, mixed blessing (**see** *ill fortune*); continual struggle, weary way 700n. *difficulty;* hardship, hard life, no bed of roses 825n. *suffering;* groaning, travail 377 n. *pain;* bad times, hard t., ill t., iron age, ice a., dark a., hell upon earth, vale of sorrows 616n. *evil;* burden, load, pressure, pressure of the times; ups and downs of life, vicissitude 154n. *eventuality;* troubles, sea of t., peck of t., trials, cares, worries 825n. *worry;* wretchedness, misery, despondency, Slough of Despond 834n. *dejection;* bitter cup, bitter pill 872n. *humiliation;* cup, cup of sorrows 825n. *sorrow;* curse, blight, blast, plague, scourge, infliction, visitation 659n. *bane;* bleakness, cold wind, draft, chill, cold, winter 380n. *coldness;* gloom 418n. *darkness;* ill wind, cross w.; blow, hard b., blow between the eyes 704 n. *opposition;* setback, check, rebuff, reverse 728n. *defeat;* rub, pinch, plight, funeral 700n. *predicament;* bad patch, rainy day 655 n. *deterioration;* slump, recession, depression 679n. *inactivity;* dark clouds, gathering c. 900n. *threat;* decline, fall, downfall 165n. *ruin;* broken fortune, want, need, distress, extremity 801n. *poverty.*

ill fortune, misfortune, bad fortune, outrageous f.; bad luck, bad cess, ill luck; no luck, no luck this time, ill success 728n. *failure;* evil dispensation, evil star, malign influence 645n. *badness;* hard case, raw deal, rotten hand, chicane, Yarborough; ill lot, hard l., hard fate, hard lines; ill hap, mishap, mischance, misadventure, contretemps, accident, casualty 159n. *chance;* disaster, calamity, catastrophe, the worst.

unlucky person, constant loser, poor risk; sport of fortune, plaything of fate, Jonah; star-crossed lover 728 n. *loser;* underdog 35n. *inferior;* new poor 801n. *poor man;* lame dog, lame duck 163n. *weakling;* scapegoat, victim, anvil, chopping-block, wretch, poor w. 825n. *sufferer;* prey 544n. *dupe.*

Adj. *adverse,* hostile, frowning, ominous, sinister, inauspicious, unfavorable; bleak, cold; opposed, cross, thwart, contrary, untoward 704adj. *opposing;* malign 645adj. *harmful;* dire, dreadful, ruinous 165adj. *destructive;* disastrous, calamitous,

catastrophic; too bad 645adj. *bad.*
unprosperous, unblessed, inglorious 728adj. *unsuccessful;* not doing well, badly off, not well off 801adj. *poor;* in trouble, up against it, under adverse circumstances, clouded, under a cloud 700adj. *in difficulty;* declining, on the wane, on the downgrade, on one's last legs, on the road to ruin 655adj. *deteriorated;* in the wars, in hard case, in an ill plight, in extremities, in utmost need.
unfortunate, ill-fated, unlucky, ill-starred, star-crossed, planet-struck, blasted; unblessed, luckless, hapless, poor, wretched, miserable, undone, unhappy; stricken, doomed, devoted, accursed; not lucky, out of luck, down on one's luck; out of favor, under a cloud, out of the sun 924 adj. *disapproved;* born to evil, born under an evil star; liable to accident, accident-prone.
Vb. *have trouble,* be in t., be born to t., be one's own worst enemy; stew in one's own juice; be fortune's sport, be the victim of fate, have no luck; be in for it, go through it, be hard pressed, be up against it, fall foul of 700vb. *be in difficulty;* strike a bad patch, meet adversity 825vb. *suffer;* suffer humiliation 872 vb. *be humbled;* come to grief 728 vb. *miscarry;* be in low water, feel the pinch, feel the draft, fall on evil days, have seen better d. 801 vb. *be poor;* go downhill, go down in the world, fall from one's high estate, decline 655vb. *deteriorate;* sink 313vb. *founder;* come to a bad end 728vb. *fail;* go to rack and ruin, go to the dogs 165vb. *be destroyed;* go hard with, be difficult for 700vb. *be difficult.*
Adv. *in adversity,* from bad to worse, from the frying pan into the fire; as ill luck would have it, by mischance, by misadventure.
See: 35, 154, 159, 163, 165, 313, 377, 380, 418, 544, 616, 645, 655, 659, 679, 700, 704, 728, 801, 825, 834, 872, 900, 924.

732 Mediocrity

N. *mediocrity,* mediety, averageness 30n. *average;* golden mean, neither too much nor too little; common lot, ups and downs, mixed blessing; average circumstances, moderate c., a modest competence, enough to get by; modesty, plain living, no excess 177n. *moderation;* respectability, middle classes, bourgeoisie 30n. *middle class;* suburbia, subtopia, villadom; new poor, common man, everyman, man in the street 869n. *commoner.*
Adj. *mediocre,* average, middling; neither good nor bad, betwixt and between, ordinary, commonplace 30 adj. *median;* common, representative 83adj. *typical;* non-extreme 177 adj. *moderate;* decent, quiet 874 adj. *modest;* not striking, undistinguished, inglorious, nothing to boast of; minor, second-rate, second best 35adj. *inferior;* fair, fair to middling; unobjectionable, tolerable, passable, fifty-fifty, much of a muchness; medium, middle, colorless, gray 625adj. *neutral.*
Vb. *be middling,*—mediocre etc.adj.; follow the mean 30vb. *average out;* pass muster 635vb. *suffice;* jog on, manage well enough, go on quietly, avoid excess, keep to the middle 625vb. *be halfway;* live in a suburb; leave something to be desired 647 vb. *be imperfect.*
See: 30, 35, 83, 177, 625, 635, 647, 869, 874.

733 Authority

N. *authority,* power; powers that be, "them," the establishment, ruling classes 741n. *master;* right, divine r., prerogative, royal p.; dynasticism, legitimacy; law, rightful power, legal p., lawful authority 953n. *legality;* delegated authority, regency, committee 751n. *commission;* office of authority, office, place (**see** *magistrature*); portfolio 955n. *jurisdiction;* vicarious authority, power behind the throne 178n. *influence;* indirect authority, patronage, prestige, credit; leadership, hegemony 689n. *directorship;* ascendance, preponderance, prepollence, predominance, supremacy 34n. *superiority;* pride of place, seniority, priority 64n. *precedence;* majesty, royalty, kingliness, crown, kingly c. 868n. *nobility;* lordliness, authoritativeness, dignity; power of the purse, financial control; sea power, admiralty, trident, Britannia; acquisition of power, succession, legitimate s., accession; seizure of power, usurpation.
governance, rule, sway, iron s., reins of government, direction, command 689n. *directorship;* control, supreme c.; hold, grip, gripe, clutches, talon, fangs 778n. *retention;* domina-

tion, mastery, whip-hand, effective control, reach, long arm; dominion, joint d., condominium, sovereignty, suzerainty, overlordship, supremacy 34n. *superiority;* reign, regnancy, regency, dynasty; foreign rule, heterarchy, heteronomy, empery, empire, rod of e. 745n. *subjection;* imperialism, colonialism, expansionism; regime, regiment, regimen; state control, statism, dirigisme, paternalism; bureaucracy, civil service, officialism, red-tapeism, beadledom, bumbledom; droit administratif; Parkinson's law 197n. *expansion.*

gynocracy, gynarchy, regiment of women, petticoat government, women's rule; matriarchy, matriarchate; feminism, suffragettism, suffragism, votes for women.

despotism, benevolent d., paternalism; one-man rule, monocracy, tyranny; dictatorship, Caesarism, kaiserism, czarism, Stalinism; absolutism, autocracy, absolute monarchy; statism, étatism, omnicompetent state, dictatorship of the proletariat; guided democracy, totalitarianism; police state, dinarchy, rule of terror 735n. *brute force.*

government, direction 689n. *management;* form of government, state system, polity; constitutional government, constitutionalism, rule of law 953n. *legality;* misgovernment 734n. *anarchy;* theocracy, thearchy, priestly government, hierocracy, clericalism 985n. *ecclesiasticism;* monarchy, constitutional m., monarchical government, kingship; republicanism, federalism; tribal system, tribalism; feudalism, feudality; aristocracy, meritocracy, oligarchy, minority rule; gerontocracy, senatorial government; duumvirate, triumvirate; rule of wealth, plutocracy; representative government, parliamentary g., government by the ballot box, party system; democracy, people's rule, government of the people, by the people, for the people; democracy unlimited, demagogy, popular will, vox populi; isocracy, pantisocracy, collectivism, proletarianism, ergatocracy; communism, Leninism; party rule, bolshevism, fascism; committee rule, sovietism; imperium in imperio, stratocracy, army rule, military government, martial law; ochlocracy, mobocracy, mob rule, mob law; syndicalism, socialism, guild s., Fabianism, statism; bureaucracy, technocracy; self-government, autonomy, home rule, Dominion status, autarchy 744 n. *independence;* caretaker government, regency, interregnum; sphere of influence, mandate, mandated territory.

magistrature, magistracy, office, place, office of power, office of dignity; kingship, kinghood, czardom, royalty, regality; regency, regentship, protectorship; rulership, burgraviate, chieftainship, sheikhdom, emirate, principate, lordship, seigniory; sultanate, caliphate, wazirate, pashalic, governorship, vice-royalty; satrapy, exarchate, nomarchy, ethnarchy; consulate, consulship, proconsulate, prefecture, tribunate, aedileship; mayoralty, aldermanship; headship, presidentship, presidency, premiership, chairmanship 689n. *directorship;* overlordship, superintendency, inspectorship; mastery, mastership; seat of government, capital, metropolis, palace, White House, Kremlin, Chequers, Whitehall; secretariat 687n. *workshop.*

polity, state, commonwealth, commonweal; country, realm, kingdom, sultanate; republic, city state, city, free c., polis; temple state; federation, confederation; principality, duchy, arch-d., dukedom, palatinate; empire, dominion, colony, dependency, protectorate, mandate, mandated territory 184n. *territory;* province, county 184n. *district;* body politic, corporative state, social s., welfare s.; laws, constitution.

Adj. authoritative, empowered, competent; in office, in authority, clothed with a., magisterial, official, ex officio; mandatory, binding, compulsory 740adj. *compelling;* masterful, domineering; commanding, lordly, dignified, majestic; overruling, imperious, bossy; peremptory, arbitrary, absolute, autocratic, tyrannical, dictatorial, totalitarian 735 adj. *authoritarian;* powerful, puissant 162adj. *strong;* hegemonic, leading 178adj. *influential;* preeminent, preponderant, predominant, prepollent, dominant, paramount 34adj. *supreme.*

ruling, reigning, regnant, regnal; sovereign, holding the scepter, on the throne; royal, regal, majestic, kinglike, kingly, queenly, princely, lordly; dynastic; imperial; magisterial; governing, controlling, dictating etc.vb.

governmental, gubernatorial, political, constitutional; administrative, ministerial, official, bureaucratic, centralized; technocratic; matriarchal, patriarchal; mononarchic, feudal, aristocratic, oligarchic, plutocratic, democratic, popular, classless, republican; self-governing, autonomous, autarchic 744adj. *independent.*

Vb. *rule*, bear r., sway, reign, reign supreme, sit on the throne, wear the crown, wield the scepter; govern, control 737vb. *command;* manage, hold the reins, hold office 689vb. *direct;* hold place, occupy a post, fill a p.; be in power, have authority, wield a., exercise a., exert a., use one's a.; rule absolutely, tyrannize 735vb. *oppress;* dictate, lay down the law; plan, give laws to, legislate for; divide and rule; keep order, police.

take authority, mount the throne, ascend the t., accede to the t., succeed to the t., take command, assume c., take over; assume authority, form a government; get hold of, get a hold on, get the whip hand, get control; seize power, get the power into one's hands, usurp, usurp the throne.

dominate, have the power, have the prestige; preponderate, turn the scale 34vb. *predominate;* lord it over, boss, rule the roost, wear the breeches 737vb. *command;* have the mastery, have the upper hand, hold the whip h. 727vb. *overmaster;* lead by the nose, turn round one's little finger, hold in the hollow of one's hand 178vb. *influence;* regiment, discipline, drill, drive 735vb. *be severe;* dictate, coerce 740vb. *compel;* subject to one's influence, hold by the short hairs, hold down, hold under 745vb. *subjugate;* override, overrule, overawe; overshadow, bestride 226vb. *overlie;* have it all one's own way, do as one will 744 vb. *be free.*

be governed, have laws, have a constitution; be ruled, be swayed by, be dictated to; be under authority, owe obedience, owe fealty, owe loyalty 745vb. *be subject.*

Adv. *by authority,* in the name of, de par le Roi; by warrant of, in virtue of one's authority.

See: 34, 64, 162, 178, 184, 197, 226, 687, 689, 727, 734, 735, 737, 740, 741, 744, 745, 751, 778, 868, 953, 955, 985.

734 Laxity

N. *laxity,* slackness, remissness, indifference 458n. *negligence;* informality 769n. *non-observance;* looseness, loosening, relaxation, unbinding 46n. *disjunction;* loose organization, decentralization; connivance 756n. *permission;* indulgence, toleration, gentleness, license, over-indulgence, over-kindness, softness 736n. *lenity;* line of least resistance 721n. *submission;* weak will, feeble grasp, weak administration, disordered routine, crumbling power 163n. *weakness;* no grip, no drive, no push, inertia 175n. *inertness;* no control, abdication of authority, surrender of control 753n. *resignation;* renunciation 621n. *relinquishment;* concession 770n. *compromise.*

anarchy, breakdown of administration, no authority, writ not running; disorder, disorganization, chaos 61n. *turmoil;* license, licentiousness, insubordination, indiscipline 738n. *disobedience;* anarchism, nihilism, antinomianism 769n. *non-observance;* interregnum, power vacuum, powerlessness 161n. *impotence;* misrule, misgovernment; mob law, lynch l., club l., reign of terror 954n. *lawlessness;* defiance of authority, unauthorized power, usurpation 916n. *arrogation;* dethronement, deposition, uncrowning 752n. *deposal.*

Adj. *lax,* loose, slack, decentralized, disorganized, unorganized 61adj. *orderless;* feeble, infirm 163adj. *weak;* crippled 163adj. *weakened;* remiss 458adj. *negligent;* uncaring 860adj. *indifferent;* relaxed, unstrict, informal, slipshod; tolerant, undemanding, easy, gentle, indulgent, over-i. 736adj. *lenient;* weak-willed, weak-kneed, infirm of purpose 601adj. *irresolute;* unmasterful, lacking authority, uninfluential.

anarchic, anarchical; ungoverned, uncontrolled, unbridled, unsubmissive; licentious 878adj. *insolent;* rebellious 738adj. *disobedient;* disorderly, unruly 738adj. *riotous;* unauthorized, without a writ 954adj. *illegal;* lawless, nihilistic, anarchistic, antinomian 769adj. *non-observant.*

Vb. *be lax,* not enforce; hold a loose rein, give the reins to, give one his head, give rope enough 744vb. *give scope;* stretch a point, connive at; tolerate, put up with, suffer; laisser faire, laisser aller 756vb. *permit;* let one get away with, not say boo to a goose; spoonfeed, indulge 736 vb. *be lenient;* make concessions 770vb. *compromise;* relax, unbind 46vb. *disjoin;* lose control 161vb. *be* *impotent;* renounce authority 621 vb. *relinquish;* stand down, abdicate 753vb. *resign;* misrule, misgovern, mismanage, reduce to chaos 63vb. *derange.*

please oneself, let oneself go, indulge oneself 943vb. *be intemperate;* be a law to oneself, stand in no awe of, defy authority, defy control 738vb. *disobey;* take on oneself, act without authority, act without instructions, act on one's own responsibility; arrogate, usurp authority 916vb. *be undue.*

unthrone, disthrone, uncrown, unseat, force to resign 752vb. *depose;* usurp, snatch the scepter, seize the crown.

See: 46, 61, 63, 161, 163, 175, 458, 601, 621, 721, 736, 738, 744, 752, 753, 756, 769, 770, 860, 878, 916, 943, 954.

735 Severity

N. *severity*, no weakness, rigorousness, strictness, stringency; formalism, pedantry; high standards 862 n. *fastidiousness;* rigidity, inflexibility 326n. *hardness;* discipline, firm control, strong hand, tight h., tight grasp 733n. *authority;* rod of iron, heavy hand, draconian laws; harshness, rigor, extremity, extremes; no concession, no compromise, letter of the law, pound of flesh; intolerance, fanaticism, bigotry 602n. *opiniatrety;* press laws, censorship, suppression 747n. *restraint;* blue laws, puritanism 950n. *prudery;* infliction, visitation, inquisition, persecution, harassment, oppression; spite, victimization 910n. *revenge;* lack of feeling, lack of mercy, inclemency, inexorability, no appeal 906n. *pitilessness;* hard measure, harsh treatment, the hard way, tender mercies, cruelty 898n. *inhumanity;* self-mortification, self-denial, austerity 945n. *asceticism.*

brute force, naked f.; rule of might, big battalions 160n. *power;* coercion, bludgeoning 740n. *compulsion;* bloodiness 176n. *violence;* subjugation 745n. *subjection;* arbitrary power, absolutism, Hobbism, czarism; autocracy, dictatorship 733n. *despotism;* tyranny, liberticide; fascism, Nazism, Hitlerism, Stalinism, totalitarianism; Prussianism, militarism; martial law, iron rule, iron sway, iron hand, iron heel, jackboot, bludgeon.

tyrant, rigorist, pedant, precisian, formalist, stickler, red-tapeist; petty tyrant, jack-in-office; disciplinarian, martinet, drill-sergeant; militarist, Prussian, jackboot; hanging judge, Draco; heavy father, Dutch uncle; Big Brother, authoritarian, despot, dictator, pasha, shogun 741n. *autocrat;* boss, commissar, gauleiter; inquisitor, persecutor; oppressor, bully, hard master, taskmaster, slave-driver, slaver; extortioner, bloodsucker, tax-gatherer, publican, predator, harpy, vulture, octopus; brute 938n. *monster.*

Adj. *severe*, austere, Spartan 945adj. *ascetic;* strict, rigorous, extreme; strait-laced, puritanical, prudish; donnish, pedagogic, formalistic, pedantic; bigoted, fanatical; hypercritical 862adj. *fastidious;* intolerant, censorious 924adj. *disapproving;* rigid 326adj. *hard;* hard-headed, hard-boiled, dour; inflexible, obdurate, uncompromising 602adj. *obstinate;* inexorable, relentless, merciless, unsparing, inclement, unforgiving 906adj. *pitiless;* heavy, stern, stiff; exemplary, stringent, draconian, drastic, savage.

authoritarian, masterful, domineering, lordly, arrogant, haughty 878adj. *insolent;* despotic, absolute, unfettered, arbitrary; totalitarian, fascist, communistic; anti-democratic, undemocratic; coercive, imperative, compulsive 740adj. *compelling;* fussy, bossy, governessy.

oppressive, hard on 914adj. *unjust;* tyrannical, despotic, arbitrary; tyrannous, harsh, over-h.; grinding, withering; exigent, exacting, grasping, griping, extortionate, vulturine, predatory; persecuting, inquisitorial, searching, unsparing; high-handed, overbearing, overmighty, domineering; heavy-handed, iron-h., iron-heeled; ungentle, rough, bloody 176 adj. *violent;* brutal 898adj. *cruel;* totalitarian, Hitlerite, Stalinist.

Vb. *be severe,*—harsh,—strict etc. adj.; exert authority, put one's foot down, discipline; bear hard on, deal hard measure, deal hardly with, lay a heavy hand on; permit no liberties, keep a tight rein on 747vb. *restrain;* be down on, have a down on (**see** *oppress*); come down on, crack down on, stamp on 165vb. *suppress;* not tolerate, persecute, hunt down 619vb. *pursue;* ill-treat, mishandle, use hard, strain 675vb. *misuse;* treat rough, get tough with, pull no punches; inflict, visit, visit on, visit with, chastise, chastise with scorpions 963vb. *punish;* mete stern punishment, wreak vengeance 910 vb. *avenge;* exact reprisals 714vb. *retaliate;* strain one's authority 954 vb. *be illegal;* be extreme, proceed to extremities, have one's pound of flesh; harden one's heart, show no mercy 906vb. *be pitiless;* give no quarter, put to the sword 362vb. *slaughter.*

oppress, tyrannize, play the tyrant, play the despot; take liberties, strain one's authority 734vb. *please oneself;* assume, arrogate 916vb. *be undue;* domineer, lord it; overawe, intimidate, terrorize 854vb. *frighten;* bludgeon 740vb. *compel;* shove around, put upon; bully, haze, harass, plague, annoy 827vb. *torment;* persecute, spite, victimize 898vb. *be malevolent;* break, break the spirit, tame 369vb. *break in;* task, tax, drive 684vb. *fatigue;* overtax, extort, suck, squeeze, grind 809vb. *tax;* trample, tread down, tread underfoot, stamp on, hold down 165 vb. *suppress;* kill liberty, enthrall, enslave, rivet the yoke 745vb. *subjugate;* ride roughshod, injure, inflict injustice 914vb. *do wrong;* misgovern, misrule; rule with a rod of iron, whip, scourge, rack, put the screw on 963vb. *torture;* shed blood, dye with b. 362vb. *murder;* be heavy, weigh on, burden, crush 322 vb. *weigh.*

Adv. *severely,* sternly, strictly etc. adj.; tyrannically, despotically, arbitrarily; the hard way, with a high hand, heavy handedly; cruelly, mercilessly.

See: 160, 165, 176, 322, 326, 362, 369, 602, 619, 675, 684, 714, 733, 734, 740, 745, 747, 809, 827, 854, 862, 878, 898, 906, 910, 914, 916, 924, 938, 945, 950, 954, 963.

736 Lenity

N. *lenity,* softness 734n. *laxity;* lenience, leniency, mildness, gentleness, tenderness; forbearance 823n. *patience;* pardon 909n. *forgiveness;* quarter, mercy, clemency, mercifulness, compassion 905n. *pity;* humanity, kindness 897n. *benevolence;* favor, sop, concession; indulgence, toleration; sufferance, allowance, leave 756n. permission; connivance, complaisance; justice with mercy 177n. *moderation;* light rein, light hand, velvet glove, kid gloves.

Adj. *lenient,* soft, gentle, mild, mild as milk; indulgent, tolerant; conniving, complaisant; unstrict, easy, easy-going, undemanding 734adj. *lax;* forbearing, long-suffering 823adj. *patient;* clement, merciful 909adj. *forgiving;* tender 905adj. *pitying;* too soft, over-merciful; tender towards, afraid to touch, velvet-gloved.

Vb. *be lenient,* show consideration, make no demands, make few d.; deal gently, handle tenderly, go easy, pull one's punches, temper the wind to the shorn lamb 177vb. *moderate;* stroke, pat, featherbed, spoonfeed, spoil, indulge, humor 889vb. *pet;* gratify, favor 925vb. *flatter;* tolerate, allow, connive 756 vb. *permit;* stretch a point 734vb. *be lax;* concede 758vb. *consent;* not press, refrain, forbear 823vb. *be patient;* pity, spare, give quarter 905vb. *show mercy;* pardon 909vb. *forgive;* amnesty 506vb. *forget;* relax, relax the rigor, humanize 897vb. *be benevolent.*

See: 177, 506, 734, 756, 758, 823, 889, 897, 905, 909, 925.

737 Command

N. *command,* royal c., invitation, summons; commandment, ordinance; injunction, imposition; dictation, bidding, behest, hest, hookum, will and pleasure; dictum, say-so 532n. *affirmation;* charge, commission, appointment 751n. *mandate;* instructions, rules, regulations; brief 524n. *information;* directive, order, order of the day; word of command, word; beck, nod, sign 547n. *gesture;* signal, bugle-call, trumpet-c. 547n. *call;* summons, imperative summons; whip, three-line w.; categorical imperative, dictate 740n. *compulsion;* negative command, taboo, ban, embargo, inhibition, proscription 757vb. *prohibition;* countermand, counter-order 752n. *abrogation.*

decree, edict, fiat, ukase, firman, ipse dixit; law, canon, rescript, prescript, prescription 693n. *precept;* bull, papal decree, decretal; circular, encyclical; decree having the force of law, ordinance, order in council; decree nisi, decree absolute; decision, placet, senatus consultum, placitum 480n. *judgment;* enactment, act 953n. *legislation;* plebiscite, electoral mandate 605n. *vote;* dictate, diktat, dictation.

demand, demand as of right, claim, revendication 915n. *dueness;* requisition 761n. *request;* notice, warning

n., final n., final demand, peremptory d., ultimatum; foreclosure; blackmail 900n. *threat;* imposition, exaction, levy, tax demand 809n. *tax.*
warrant, commission, brevet, authorization, written authority, letters patent, passport 756n. *permit;* writ, summons, subpoena, citation, mandamus, habeas corpus 959n. *legal process.*

Adj. *commanding*, imperative, imperatival, categorical, dictatorial; jussive, mandative, mandatory, obligatory, peremptory, compulsive 740 adj. *compelling;* decretory, decretal; exacting obedience 733adj. *authoritative;* decisive, conclusive, final, non-appealable; demanding, clamant, vocal.

Vb. *command*, bid, invite; order, tell, issue a command, pass orders, give an order, send an o.; signal, call, nod, beck, motion, sign, make a s. 547vb. *gesticulate;* wink, tip the wink 524vb. *hint;* direct, give a directive, instruct, brief, circularize, send round instructions; rule, lay down, enjoin; give a mandate, charge, call upon 751vb. *commission;* impose, lay upon, set, set a task, make obligatory 917vb. *impose a duty;* detail, tell off; call together, convene 74vb. *bring together;* send for, summon; cite, subpoena, issue a writ 959vb. *litigate;* send back, remand; dictate, enforce obedience, put one's foot down 740vb. *compel;* countermand 752vb. *abrogate;* lay an embargo, ban, taboo, proscribe 757vb. *prohibit.*
decree, pass a d., sign a d., pass an order in council, issue a ukase, issue a firman, issue one's fiat; promulgate 528vb. *proclaim;* declare, say, say so, lay down the law 532vb. *affirm;* signify one's will and pleasure, prescribe, ordain, appoint 608 vb. *predetermine;* enact, make law, pass a l., legislate 953vb. *make legal;* pass judgment, give j., decide, rule, give a ruling 480vb. *judge.*
demand, require, requisition 627vb. *require;* order, order up, indent 761 vb. *request;* make demands on, send a final demand, give final notice, present an ultimatum, demand with threats, blackmail 900vb. *threaten;* present one's claim, make claims upon, revendicate, reclaim 915vb. *claim;* demand payment, dun, bill, invoice, foreclose; charge 809vb. *price;* exact, levy 809vb. *tax.*

Adv. *commandingly*, imperatively, categorically, authoritatively; at the word of command.

See: 74, 480, 524, 528, 532, 547, 605, 608, 627, 693, 733, 740, 751, 752, 756, 757, 761, 809, 900, 915, 917, 953, 959.

738 Disobedience

N. *disobedience*, indiscipline, unbiddableness, naughtiness, refractoriness 598n. *unwillingness;* insubordination, mutinousness, mutineering; refusal to obey orders, defiance of o. 711n. *defiance;* disregard of orders, non-compliance 769n. *non-observance;* disloyalty, defection, desertion 918n. *dutilessness;* violation of orders, violation of the law, infraction, infringement, criminality, crime, sin 936n. *guilty act;* non-cooperation, non-violent non-c., satyagraha, passive resistance 715n. *resistance;* conscientious objection 704n. *opposition;* obstructionism 702n. hindrance; murmuring, restlessness 829 n. *discontent;* seditiousness, kulakism, Chartism, sansculottism, sansculotterie (**see** *sedition*); wildness 954n. *lawlessness;* banditry, Mafia 788n. *brigandage.*
revolt, mutiny; direct action 145n. *strike;* faction 709n. *dissension;* breakaway, secession 978n. *schism;* defection, Titoism 603n. *tergiversation;* explosive situation, restlessness, restiveness 318n. *agitation;* sabotage, wrecking activities 165n. *destruction;* breach of the peace, disturbance, disorder, riot, street-r., bread-r., rioting, gang warfare, street fighting, émeute, tumult, barricades 61n. *turmoil;* rebellion, insurrection, rising, uprising 176n. *outbreak;* putsch, coup d'état; resistance movement, insurgency, insurgence 715n. *resistance;* subversion 149n. *revolution;* terrorism 954n. *lawlessness;* civil war 718n. *war;* regicide, tyrannicide 362n. *homicide.*
sedition, seditiousness, Chartism, kulakism; agitation, cabal, intrigue 623n. *plot;* subversion, infiltration, fifth-columnism; underground activities 523n. *latency;* terrorism, anarchism, nihilism; treasonable activities, disloyalty, treason, petty t., high t., misprision of t., lese majesty 930n. *perfidy.*
revolter, awkward person, difficult character, handful, naughty boy, kittle cattle; mutineer, rebel; striker 705n. *opponent;* secessionist, seceder, splinter group, cave 978n.

schismatic; Titoist, deviationist; blackleg, scab, non-striker 84n. *nonconformist;* independent, maverick, lone wolf; seditionary, seditionist; traitor, Quisling, fifth-columnist 603 n. *tergiversator;* insurrectionist, insurgent; guerrilla, partisan; resistance, underground, Maquis; Frondeur, Roundhead; tyrannicide, regicide; extremist, Fenian, Jacobin, sansculotte, carbonaro, Decembrist, Bolshevist, Bolshevik, red, red republican, maximalist 149n. *revolutionary;* counter-revolutionary, reactionary, monarchist, White Russian, Chouan, Cagoulard; terrorist, anarchist, nihilist; Mafia, bandit 789 n. *robber;* rebel against all laws, antinomian.

agitator, factionary, factioneer, protester, demonstrator, marcher; tubthumper, ranter, rabble-rouser, demagogue; firebrand, stormy petrel, mischief-maker 663n. *trouble-maker;* seditionist, sedition-monger; red, communist, commie; ringleader, "leader of revolt," Spartacus, Wat Tyler, Jack Cade, John Brown, Jameson, Young Turk.

rioter, street-r., brawler, corner-boy 904n. *ruffian;* demonstrator, suffragette, Chartist, sansculotte; saboteur, wrecker, Luddite; secret society, Ku Klux Klan.

Adj. *disobedient,* undisciplined, ill-disciplined; disobeying, naughty; unfilial, undaughterly; unbiddable, awkward, difficult, self-willed, wayward, restive, impatient of control, vicious, unruly, intractable, ungovernable 598adj. *unwilling;* insubordinate, mutinous, rebellious, bolshie; nonconformist 84adj. *unconformable;* unsubmissive, recusant, uncomplying; uncompliant 769adj. *non-observant;* recalcitrant 715adj. *resisting;* challenging 711adj. *defiant;* contumacious 602adj. *obstinate;* subversive, revolutionary, reactionary; seditious, trouble-making; traitorous, disloyal 918adj. *dutiless;* antinomian 734adj. *anarchic;* gate-crashing, intrusive, uninvited, unbidden; wild, untamed, ferine, savage.

riotous, rioting; anarchic, tumultuary, rumbustious, sansculottic, unruly, wild, rackety 61adj. *disorderly;* law-breaking 954adj. *lawless;* mutinous, mutine; insurrectionary, uprisen, rebellious, in rebellion, up in arms 715adj. *resisting.*

Vb. *disobey,* not obey, not listen, not hearken; not conform 769vb. *not observe;* not do as one is told, disobey orders, show insubordination 711vb. *defy;* defy the whip, cross-vote; snap one's fingers, fly in the face of 704vb. *oppose;* set the law at defiance, break the law, commit a crime 954vb. *be illegal;* violate, infringe, transgress, trespass 306vb. *encroach;* not obey the helm, turn restive, kick, chafe, fret, champ at the bit, play up; kick over the traces, take the bit between one's teeth, bolt, take French leave, take the law into one's own hands, be a law to oneself 734vb. *please oneself;* come uninvited, gate-crash.

revolt, rebel, mutiny; down tools, strike work, come out 145vb. *cease;* sabotage 702vb. *obstruct;* undermine, work underground; secede, break away 978vb. *schismatize;* betray 603vb. *tergiversate;* agitate, demonstrate, protest 762vb. *deprecate;* start a riot, raise Cain, raise a revolt, lead a rebellion; rise, rise up, rise in arms, throw off the yoke, renounce allegiance, fight for independence 746vb. *achieve liberty;* overthrow, upset 149vb. *revolutionize.*

See: 61, 74, 84, 145, 149, 165, 176, 306, 318, 362, 523, 598, 602, 603, 623, 663, 702, 704, 705, 709, 711, 715, 718, 734, 746, 762, 769, 788, 789, 829, 904, 918, 930, 936, 954, 978.

739 Obedience

N. *obedience,* compliance 768n. *observance;* goodness, meekness, biddability, discipline; ductibility, pliancy, malleability 327n. *softness;* readiness 597n. *willingness;* nonresistance, submissiveness, acquiescence 721n. *submission;* passiveness, passivity 679n. *inactivity;* dutifulness, morale, discipline, good d., service d. 917n. *duty;* deference, obsequiousness, slavishness 879n. *servility;* command performance; dumb driven cattle 742n. *slave.*

loyalty, constancy, devotion, fidelity, faithfulness, faith 929n. *probity;* allegiance, fealty, homage, service, deference, submission; vote of confidence.

Adj. *obedient,* complying, compliant, conforming 768adj. *observant;* loyal, leal, faithful, true-blue, steadfast, constant; devoted, dedicated, sworn; offering homage, homageable, submissive 721adj. *submitting;* law-abiding 717adj. *peaceful;* complaisant, docile; good, well-behaved; filial, daughterly; ready 597adj.

willing; acquiescent, resigned, unresisting, non-resisting, passive 679 adj. *inactive;* meek, biddable, dutiful, disciplined, under discipline; at one's beck and call, at one's orders, on a string, on leading strings, under control; disciplined, regimented 917 adj. *dutied;* deferential, obsequious, slavish 879adj. *servile.*

Vb. *obey*, comply, do to order, act upon 768vb. *observe;* sign on the dotted line, toe the l., come to heel 83vb. *conform;* assent 758vb. *consent;* listen, hearken, obey orders, attend to instructions, do as one is told; observe discipline, wait for the word of command; hold oneself ready, put oneself at one's service 598vb. *be willing;* answer the helm, obey the rein, obey the spur; obey the whip, vote to order; do one's bidding, come at one's call, wait upon, follow, follow to the world's end 742vb. *serve;* be loyal, owe loyalty, bear allegiance, do suit and service, homage, pay h., offer h. 768vb. *observe faith;* be under, pay tribute 745vb. *be subject;* know one's duty 917vb. *do one's duty;* make oneself useful, do Trojan service 703vb. *minister to;* yield, bow, bend, stoop, be submissive 721vb. *submit;* grovel, cringe 879vb. *be servile;* play second fiddle 35vb. *be inferior.*

Adv. *obediently*, complaisantly, submissively etc.adj.; under orders, to order, as ordered, in obedience to.

See: 35, 83, 327, 597, 598, 679, 703, 717, 721, 742, 745, 758, 768, 879, 917, 929.

740 Compulsion

N. *compulsion*, spur of necessity 596 n. *necessity;* law of nature 953n. *law;* moral compulsion 917n. *conscience;* Hobson's choice 606n. *no choice;* dictation, coercion, regimentation; blackmail 900n. *threat;* negative compulsion 747n. *restraint;* sanction, sanctions 963n. *penalty;* enforcement, constraint, duress, force, main force, physical f.; right of the stronger, force majeure, mailed fist, big stick, bludgeon, strong arm, strong arm tactics 735n. *brute force;* droit administratif; forcible feeding; impressment, press, press-gang, conscription, call-up, draft 718n. *war measures;* exaction, extortion 786n. *taking;* slavery, corvée, forced labor, labor camp 745n. *servitude;* command performance 733n. *command.*

Adj. *compelling*, compulsive, involuntary, of necessity, unavoidable, inevitable 596adj. *necessary;* imperative, dictatorial, peremptory 737adj. *commanding;* compulsory, mandatory, binding 917adj. *obligatory;* urgent, pressing; overriding, constraining, coercive; omnipotent, irresistible, not to be trifled with 160adj. *powerful;* forcible, forceful, cogent; high-pressure, strong-arm, bludgeoning 735adj. *oppressive.*

Vb. *compel*, constrain, coerce 176vb. *force;* enforce, put into force; dictate, necessitate, oblige, bind; order 737vb. *command;* impose 917vb. *impose a duty;* make, leave no option; leave no escape, pin down, tie d.; press, impress, draft, conscript; drive, dragoon, regiment, discipline; force one's hand; bludgeon 735vb. *oppress;* take by force, requisition, commandeer, extort, exact, wring from, drag f. 786vb. *take;* apply pressure, squeeze, turn the screw, put the screw on, twist one's arm 963vb. *torture;* blackmail 900vb. *threaten;* be peremptory, insist, make a point of, press, urge 532vb. *emphasize;* say it must be done, take no denial, not take no for an answer 532vb. *affirm;* compel to accept, force upon, cram down one's throat, ram down one's t., inflict, foist, fob off on; hold back 747vb. *restrain.*

Adv. *by force*, perforce, compulsorily, of necessity, on compulsion, under pressure, under protest, in spite of one's teeth, nolens volens; forcibly, by force majeure, by the strong arm, at the sword's point, at the point of the bayonet.

See: 60, 176, 532, 596, 606, 718, 735, 737, 745, 747, 786, 900, 917, 953, 963.

741 Master

N. *master*, mistress; master of, captor, possessor 776n. *owner;* sire, lord, lady, dame; liege lord, lord paramount, overlord, lord's lord, suzerain; protector 707n. *patron;* seigneur, lord of the manor, squire, laird 868n. *aristocrat;* senator, signor, oligarch, plutocrat; mister, sir, don, mirza, sahib, thakur 372n. *male;* madam 373n. *lady;* master of the house, husband, goodman; patriarch, matriarch 169n. *parent;* senior, head, principal, provost 34n. *superior;* schoolmaster, dominie 537 n. *teacher;* president, chairman, speaker 690n. *director;* employer, capitalist, boss; leader, duce, fuehrer (**see** *autocrat*); commissar, gauleiter (**see** *officer*); lord of the ascendant, cock of the walk, lord of creation 638n. *bigwig;* ruling class, ruling party, dominant interest, the Establishment; the authorities, principalities and powers, the powers that be, "them," Government, Sarkar, Delhi, Whitehall, Pentagon 733n. *government;* staff, état-major, High Command 689n. *directorship.*

autocrat, autarch, absolute ruler, absolute master, despot, tyrant, dictator, duce, fuehrer; tycoon, boss, shogun; petty tyrant, gauleiter, commissar, jack-in-office, tin god 690n. *official.*

sovereign, suzerain, crowned head, anointed king; Majesty, Highness, Royal H., Excellence; dynasty, house, royal h., royal line, royal blood; royalty, monarch, king, queen; divine king, pharaoh, Inca; imperator, emperor, empress, King Emperor, Holy Roman E.; Caesar, kaiser, kaiserin, czar, czarina, czarevitch; prince, raj kumar, princess, infante, infanta, dauphin, Prince of Wales; Great King, King of Kings, Shahanshah, padishah, shah, sophy; khan, khan khanan, Great Khan, Grand Cham; Celestial Emperor; mikado; Mogul, Great Mogul; sultan, sultana, Grand Turk, Sublime Porte, Sick Man of Europe; mpret, Negus, Prester John; pope, Dalai Lama, Teshu L.; caliph, Commander of the Faithful.

potentate, dynast, ruler; zamorin, chief, chieftain, Highland chief, sheik, cacique, sachem, sagamore; prince, ruling p., princeling, tetrarch; raja, rani, rao, rawal, thakur, thakurani, maharaja, maharani; emir, sirdar, mehtar, sharif; nawab, begum; nizam, Peshwa, Gaekwar, Holkar, Scindia, Jam Sahib; archduke, duke, duchess, burgrave, margrave, margravine, palatine, elector, Prince Bishop; regent, interrex.

governor, military g., lieutenant g., High Commissioner, Governor-General, Crown Representative, viceroy, vicereine, khedive; corregidor, adelantado; proconsul, satrap, kshatrapa, vali, wali, hospodar, hetman, vaivode, stadholder, ethnarch, exarch, eparch, nomarch; grand vizier, beglerbeg, beg, bey, pasha, three-tailed p.; ecclesiastical governor, Prince Bishop; ethnarch, eparch, patriarch, metropolitan, archbishop, cardinal 986n. *ecclesiarch;* judge, charismatic leader (Old Testament).

officer, man in office, functionary, mandarin, bureaucrat 690n. *official;* civil servant, public s. 742n. *servant;* gauleiter, commissar; chief officer, aga, prime minister, grand vizier, vizier, wazir, dewan; chancellor, vice-c., Great Seal; constable, marshall, seneschal, warden; burgomaster, mayor, lord m., lady m., mayoress, alderman, bailie, city father, councillor, syndic, sheriff, bailiff, portreeve, reeve; justice, justice of the peace, alcalde, caid, cadi, moonsif, hakim 957n. *judge;* archon, archon eponymous, probulus, ephor; magistrate, chief m., city m., podestà; president, doge; consul, proconsul, praetor, quaestor, aedile; prefect, intendant, district officer, landamman; district magistrate, deputy m., subdivisional officer; commissioner, deputy c.; revenue officer, collector, subcollector, talukdar, patel, headman; lictor, apparitor, macebearer, beadle, bedel; process-server, pursuivant, bumbaliff, catchpole, tipstaff 995n. *law officer;* sexton, verger, bell-ringer 986n. *church officer;* office-boy 531n. *messenger;* party official, whip.

naval officer, sea lord, first s.; senior naval officer, SNO, naval attaché; admiral of the fleet, admiral, vice a., rear a., port a.; commodore, captain, post c., flag c., commander, lieutenant c., lieutenant, flag l., sublieutenant, midshipman, middy, petty officer, warrant o., leading seaman 270n. *naval man;* trierarch, nauarch.

army officer, staff, High Command, staff officer, brass hat, red-tab; commissioned officer, brevet o.; marshal, field m., commander-in-chief, seraskier, generalissimo, general, captain g., lieutenant g., major g., colonel g., commandant general; brigadier, colonel, lieutenant c., major, captain, lieutenant, second l., subaltern, shavetail, company commander, platoon c.; ensign, cornet, cadet; warrant officer, non-commissioned o., NCO, brigade major, drum m., sergeant m., sergeant, troop s., top s., color s., corporal, corporal major, lance corporal; adjutant, aide-de-camp, quartermaster, orderly officer; imperator, military tribune, legate, centurion, decurion, vexillary; chiliarch, hipparch; subahdar, jemadar, havildar, naik, lance n. 722n. *soldiery;* war-lord, war min-

ister, commanding officer, commander, commandant.
air officer, marshal of the air force, air marshal, air commodore, group-captain, wing-commander, squadron-leader, flight-lieutenant, pilot-officer, flight-sergeant 722n. *air force*.
See: 34, 169, 270, 372, 373, 531, 537, 638, 689, 690, 707, 722, 733, 742, 776, 868, 955, 957, 986.

742 Servant

N. *servant*, public s., civil s. 690n. *official;* unpaid servant, fag, slave; general servant, factotum 678n. *busy person;* humble servant, menial; orderly, peon; temple servant, hierodule; verger, sexton, bell-ringer 986n. *church officer;* subordinate, underling, understrapper 35n. *inferior;* subaltern, helper, assistant, confidential a., secretary, right-hand man 703n. *aider;* paid servant, mercenary, hireling, creature, employee, hand, hired man; odd-job man, chore boy, laborer 686n. *worker;* hewer of wood and drawer of water, hack, drudge, erk; farm-hand 370n. *husbandman;* shepherd, cowherd, milkmaid 369n. *herdsman;* shop-assistant, counter-jumper, shop-walker, floor-w. 793n. *seller;* steward, stewardess, cabin-boy; table servant, waiter, waitress, nippy, table-boy, khidmatgar; head-waiter, wine-w.; bar-tender, barman, barmaid, pot-boy, tapster, drawer, skinker 192n. *tavern;* stableman, hostler, groom, syce, stable-boy, postilion, post-boy; messenger, runner 531n. *courier;* doorman, door-keeper, commissionaire, durwan, concierge, caretaker, housekeeper 264n. *janitor;* porter, night-p.; caddie 273n. *bearer;* buttons, call-boy, page-boy, bell-hop, bell-captain; boots, sweeper, mehtar, jemadar, chambermaid 648n. *cleaner;* occasional servant, help, daily, char, charwoman; universal aunt; baby-sitter; nurse, nursemaid, governess, tutor 749n. *keeper;* companion, confidante; mistress of the robes, dresser.
domestic, servantry, staff; servant's hall 686n. *personnel;* servitor, domestic servant, general s., man-servant, man, serving m.; livery servant, footman, flunky, lackey, houseman; servant girl, abigail, maid, parlor-m., house-m., chamber-maid, femme de chambre, camarista; domestic drudge, maid-of-all-work, tweeny, skivvy, slavey; kitchen-maid, scullery m., dairy m., laundry m.; kitchen boy, turnspit, scullion, cook's mate, masalchi, dish-washer; bheesty; sweeper, jamadar, mehtar, mehtarani; upper servant, housekeeper, steward, chaplain, governess, tutor, nurse, nanny; butler, cook, khansamah, cook-general, cook-bearer; personal servant, page, squire, valet, gentlemen's gentleman, batman; bearer, sirdar; lady's maid, waiting woman; nursemaid, ayah, amah, bonne; gyp, scout, bed-maker, bedder; outdoor staff, gardener, under-g., groom, syce, grasscutter; coachman, tiger, chauffeur 268n. *driver.*
retainer, follower, following, suite, train, cortege 67n. *retinue;* court, courtier; bodyguard, housecarl, henchman, squire, page, page of honor, donzel, armor-bearer, shield-b., train-b.; household staff, major-domo, chamberlain, equerry, steward, bailiff, castellan, chatelain, seneschal; chatelaine, housekeeper; cellarer, butler, cup-bearer; taster, sewer; groom of the chamber, eunuch; chaplain, beadsman, bedesman; lady-in-waiting, companion, confidante; governess, nurse, nanny 749n. *keeper.*
dependent, clientele, client; hanger-on, led-captain, parasite, satellite, camp-follower, creature, jackal 284 n. *follower;* stooge, puppet 628n. *instrument;* subordinate 35n. *inferior;* minion, lackey, flunky (**see** *domestic*); man, henchman, liege-man, homager, vassal; feudary, feudatory; pensioner, pensionary, beadsman; protégé, ward, charge, nursling, foster-child.
subject, state s., national, citizen 191 n. *native;* liege, lieger, vassal, feudatory, homager, man; people, citizenry 869n. *commonalty;* subject population, dependency, colony, provincial, colonial, helot; satellite; helotry (**see** *slave*).
slave, thrall, bondman, bondwoman, broadwife, bondmaid, slave-girl; helot, helotry, hewer of wood and drawer of water, doormat; serf, ascriptus glebae, villein; galley-slave, wage-s., sweated labor 686n. *worker;* hierodule, temple prostitute; odalisque, eunuch; chattel, puppet, chessman, pawn; machine, robot 628n. *instrument;* captive, chain-gang 750n. *prisoner.*

Adj. *serving*, ministering, fagging 703 adj. *aiding;* in service, in domestic s., menial; working, in employment, on the payroll; on the staff, in the train of; at one's beck and call 739adj. *obedient;* unfree, unfranchised, unprivileged; in servitude, in slavery, in captivity, in bonds 745adj. *subject.*

Vb. *serve,* be in service, wait upon, wait on hand and foot 703vb. *minister to;* attend upon, follow, do suit and service 739vb. *obey;* tend, squire, valet, dress; char, chore, do chores, do for, oblige; fag for, do service, make oneself useful 640vb. *be useful;* work for 622vb. *function.*

See: 35, 67, 191, 192, 264, 268, 273, 284, 369, 370, 531, 622, 628, 640, 648, 678, 686, 690, 703, 739, 745, 749, 793, 869, 986.

743 Badge of rule

N. *regalia,* royal trappings, emblem of royalty, insignia of r.; crown, kingly c., orb, scepter; coronet, tiara, diadem; rod of empire; sword of state 733n. *authority;* robe of state, coronation robes, royal robe, pall; ermine, royal purple; throne, Peacock t., royal seat, seat of kings, guddee, musnud; ensign 547n. *flag;* royal standard, royal arms 547n. *heraldry;* lion eagle; Prince of Wales's feathers; uraeus.

badge of rule, emblem of authority, staff, wand, wand of office, rod, Black Rod, baton, truncheon, gavel; herald's wand, caduceus; wand of Dionysus, thyrsus; signet, seal, privy s., keys, ring; sword of state, sword of justice, mace, fasces, axes; pastoral staff, crosier; ankh, ansate cross; woolsack, chair, bench; sartorial insignia, triple crown, miter, bishop's hat, cardinal's hat, shovel h., biretta; bishop's apron, gaiters, lawn sleeves 989n. *canonicals;* judge's cap, black c. 961n. *condemnation;* peer's cap, cap of maintenance, cap of dignity; robe, mantle, toga; royal robe, pall; robe of honor, khilat 547n. *livery.*

badge of rank, sword, belt, sash, spurs, cocked hat, epaulet, tab 547n. *badge;* uniform 547n. *livery;* brass, star, pips, crown, crossed batons; chevron, stripe, anchor, curl, brassard, armlet; garter, order 729n. *decoration.*

See: 547, 729, 733, 989.

744 Freedom

N. *freedom,* liberty, being at large; freedom of action, initiative; free will, free thought, free speech, freedom of the press, the four freedoms; rights, privilege, prerogative, exemption, immunity, diplomatic i. 919n. *non-liability;* liberalism, libertarianism, latitudinarianism 913n. *right;* license, excess of freedom, indiscipline 738n. *disobedience;* free love 951n. *illicit love;* laisser faire, non-interference; non-involvement, non-attachment, detachment, neutralism 860n. *indifference;* non-alignment, cross benches; isolationism, isolation, splendid i. 883n. *seclusion;* emancipation, setting free 746 n. *liberation;* enfranchisement, denization, naturalization, citizenship; franchise, secret ballot 605n. *vote.*

independence, freedom of action, unilaterality; freedom of choice 605n. *choice;* floating vote 606n. *no choice;* freedom of thought, emancipation, bohemianism 84n. *unconformity;* singleness, bachelorhood 895n. *celibacy;* individualism, self-expression, individuality 80n. *particularism;* self-determination, statehood, nationhood, national status 371n. *nation;* autonomy, autarchy, self-rule, home-r., dominion status; autarky, self-support, self-sufficiency 635n. *sufficiency;* freehold 777n. *property;* independent means, competence 800n. *wealth.*

scope, free s., full s., play, free p., full p. 183n. *range;* swing, rope, long r.; maneuverability, leverage; field, room, living r., lebensraum, living space, elbow-room, sea r., wide berth, leeway, margin, clearance 183n. *room;* unstrictness, latitude, liberty, Liberty Hall; the run of; fling, license, excess 734n. *laxity;* one's head, one's own way, one's own devices; ball at one's feet 137n. *opportunity;* facilities, free hand, blank check, carte blanche; free field, free trade, free port, open market, free-trade area, non-tariff zone; "open skies," high seas.

free man, freeman, liveryman, citizen, free c., voter; no slave, freedman, ex-slave; ex-convict, released prisoner; escapee 667n. *escaper;* free agent, free-lance; independent, cross-bencher; isolationist, neutral 625n. *moderate;* interloper, free-trader 59n. *intruder;* antimonopolist, smuggler; free-thinker, latitudinarian, liberal; libertarian, bohemian 84n. *nonconformist;* lone wolf 883n. *solitary.*

Adj. *free,* free-born, free-bred, enfranchised, admitted to citizenship; heart-whole, fancy-free; scot-free 960 adj. *acquitted;* uncaught 667adj. *es-*

caped; released, freed 746adj. *liberated;* at large, free as air, free as the wind; footloose, go-as-you-please, ranging 267adj. *traveling;* ranging freely, having full play (**see** *unconfined*); licensed, chartered, privileged 756adj. *permitted;* exempt, immune 919adj. *non-liable;* free-speaking, plain-spoken 573adj. *plain;* free-thinking, emancipated, broad, broadminded, latitudinarian (**see** *independent*); unbiased, unprejudiced, independent, uninfluenced 913adj. *just;* free and easy, all things to all men 882adj. *sociable;* loose, licentious, unbridled, incontinent, wanton 951adj. *impure;* leisured, out of harness; relaxed, unbottoned, at home, at rest 681adj. *leisurely;* free of cost, gratis, unpaid for 812adj. *uncharged;* unclaimed, going begging 860adj. *unwanted;* free for all, unreserved 289adj. *accessible.*

unconfined, uncribbed, uncabined, untrammeled, unshackled, unfettered, unreined, unbridled, uncurbed, unchained, unbound, unmuzzled, unkenneled; unchecked, unrestrained; unprevented, unhindered, unimpeded, unobstructed; wandering, random; left to one's choice, at one's own devices.

independent, unnecessitated, uncontrolled; uninduced, unilateral 609 adj. *spontaneous;* unforced, uncompelled, uninfluenced; unattached, detached 860adj. *indifferent;* free to choose, uncommitted, uninvolved; non-partisan 625adj. *neutral;* isolationist 883adj. *unsociable;* unvanquished, unconquered, unconquerable, irrepressible 727adj. *unbeaten;* enjoying liberty, unsubjected, unenthralled, unenslaved; autonomous, autarchic, self-governing, self-ruling; autarkic, self-sufficient, self-supporting, self-contained; ungoverned, masterless, owning no master, ungovernable 734adj. *anarchic;* free-lance, unofficial, wildcat; free-minded, free-spirited, free-souled; single, bachelor 895adj. *unwedded;* breakaway 978adj. *schismatical.*

unconditional, unconditioned, without strings; unrestricted, unlimited, absolute; discretionary, arbitrary; freehold, allodial.

Vb. *be free*, enjoy liberty, breathe l.; go free, get f., save oneself 667vb. *escape;* take French leave 738vb. *disobey;* have the run of, be free of, have the freedom of, feel at home, make oneself at h.; range, have scope, have play, have elbow-room; have rope enough, have one's head, have one's fling, have one's way, have it one's own w., do as one likes *or* chooses 734vb. *please oneself;* follow one's bent 179vb. *tend;* go as you please, drift, wander, roam 282vb. *stray;* go one's own way, go it alone, shift for oneself, paddle one's own canoe, stand alone 88vb. *be one;* have a will of one's own 595vb. *will;* have a free mind, worship freedom; be independent, call no man master; stand up for one's rights, defy the whip, cross-vote 711vb. *defy;* stand on one's own feet, suffice for oneself, ask no favors 635vb. *suffice;* take liberties, make free with, presume, presume on 878vb. *be insolent;* dare, venture, make bold to, permit oneself.

give scope, allow initiative, give one his head, allow enough rope 734vb. *be lax;* allow full play 469vb. *make possible;* release, set free, enfranchise 746vb. *liberate;* let, license, charter 756vb. *permit;* let alone, allow to drift, not interfere, live and let live, laisser aller, laisser faire; leave one to his own devices; leave it open, leave to one's own choice; keep the door open.

Adv. *freely*, liberally, ad libitum.

See: 59, 80, 84, 88, 137, 179, 183, 267, 282, 289, 371, 469, 573, 595, 605, 606, 609, 625, 635, 667, 681, 711, 727, 734, 738, 746, 756, 777, 800, 812, 860, 878, 882, 883, 895, 913, 919, 951, 960.

745 Subjection

N. *subjection*, subordination, subordinate position, inferior rank, cadetship, juniority, inferior status, satellite s. 35n. *inferiority;* creaturehood, creatureliness; dependence, clientship, tutelage, guardianship, wardship, chancery, apron strings, leading s.; mutual dependence, symbiosis 12n. *correlation;* subjecthood, allegiance, vassalage, nationality, citizenship; subjugation, conquest, colonialism; loss of freedom, disfranchisement, enslavement 721n. *submission;* constraint, discipline 747n. *restrain;* oppression 735n. *severity;* yoke 748n. *fetter;* slavishness 879n. *servility.*

service, domestic s., government s., employ, employment; servantship, servitorship, flunkydom, flunkyism 739n. *obedience;* tribute, suit and service; vassalage, vassalship, feudality, feudalism 739n. *loyalty;* com-

pulsory service, corvée, forced labor 740n. *compulsion;* conscription 718 n. *war measures.*
servitude, involuntary s., slavery, abject s.; enslavement, captivity, thralldom, bondage, yoke; helotry, helotage, helotism, serfdom, villenage.
Adj. *subjected* etc.vb.; subjugated, overborne, overwhelmed 728vb. *defeated;* reduced, pacified; captived, taken prisoner, deprived of freedom, robbed of f., disfranchised; colonized, enthralled, enslaved, reduced to slavery, sold into s.; under the lash, under the heel, tyrannized over, oppressed, down-trodden, underfoot; treated like dirt, henpecked; regimented, planned; quelled, tame, domesticated 369adj. *tamed;* eating out of one's hand, submissive 721 adj. *submitting;* subservient, slavish 879adj. *servile.*
subject, unfree, not independent, unfranchised, unprivileged; satellite, satellitic 879adj. *servile;* bond, bound, bounden, tributary, colonial; owing service, owing fealty, vassal, feudal, feudatory 739adj. *obedient;* under, subordinate, of lower rank, junior, cadet 35adj. *inferior;* dependent, in chancery, in statu pupillari, in leading strings, tied to the apron s.; subject to, liable to, exposed to 180adj. *liable;* a slave to 610adj. *habituated;* in the hands of, in the clutches of, under the control of, in the power of, at the mercy of; parasitical, hanging on; paid, in the pay of, stipendiary; encumbranced, mortgaged, pawned, in pawn 780adj. *transferred.*
Vb. *be subject,* live under, own the sway of, homage, pay tribute, be under 739vb. *obey;* obey the whip, vote to order; depend on, lean on, hang on 35vb. *be inferior;* be a doormat, let oneself be trampled on; serve, live in subjection, be a slave, drag a chain, grace the triumph of; lose one's independence 721vb. *submit;* pawn, mortgage 780 vb. *convey;* sacrifice one's freedom, have no will of one's own, be a passive instrument 628vb. *be instrumental;* cringe, fawn 879vb. *be servile.*
subjugate, subdue, reduce, subject 727 vb. *overmaster;* colonize, make tributary, vassalize, mediatize; take captive, lead in triumph, drag at one's chariot wheels 727vb. *triumph;* take, capture, lead captive, lay one's yoke upon, reduce to servitude, enslave, helotize, sell into slavery; fetter, bind, hold in bondage 747vb. *imprison;* rob of freedom, disfranchise; trample on, tread on, wipe one's feet on, treat like dirt 735vb. *oppress;* keep under, keep down, hold d., repress, sit on, stamp out 165vb. *suppress;* enthrall, captivate 821vb. *impress;* enchant 983vb. *bewitch;* dominate, lead by the nose, keep in leading strings, tie to one's apron 178vb. *influence;* discipline, regiment, plan; tame, quell 369vb. *break in;* have eating out of one's hand, bring to heel, have at one's beck and call; make one's plaything, do what one likes with 673vb. *dispose of.*
See: 12, 35, 165, 178, 180, 369, 610, 628, 673, 718, 721, 727, 728, 735, 739, 740, 747, 748, 780, 821, 879, 983.

746 Liberation

N. *liberation,* setting free, unshackling, unbinding, release, discharge, enlargement 960n. *acquittal;* unraveling, extrication, disinvolvement 46n. *separation;* riddance, good r. 831n. *relief;* rescue, redemption, salvation, mukti 668n. *deliverance;* manumission, emancipation, enfranchisement; parole; liberalization, relaxation (of control) 734n. *laxity;* decontrol, derationing 752n. *abrogation;* demobilization, disbandment 75n. *dispersion;* forgiveness of sins, absolution 909n. *forgiveness;* justification 927n. *vindication;* acquittance, deed of release, quittance, receipt, quitclaim.
Adj. *liberated,* rescued, delivered, saved 668adj. *extricable;* rid of, relieved; paroled, set free, freed, manumitted, unbound 744vb. *unconfined;* released, enlarged, discharged, acquitted; emancipated, enfranchised etc.vb.
Vb. *liberate,* rescue, save 668vb. *deliver;* excuse, justify 927vb. *vindicate;* dispense 919vb. *exempt;* pardon 909vb. *forgive;* discharge, absolve 960vb. *acquit;* make free, emancipate, manumit; enfranchise, give the vote; release, set free, set at liberty, enlarge, let out; release conditionally, parole 766vb. *give terms;* strike off the fetters, unfetter, unshackle, unchain; unbar, unbolt, unlock 263vb. *open;* loosen, unloose, loose, unbind, extricate, disengage, clear 62vb. *unravel;* unstop, uncork, unclog; ungag, unmuzzle; uncoop, uncage, unkennel; unleash, let slip; let loose, leave to wander, turn

adrift; license, charter; give play to 744vb. *give scope;* let out, vent, give vent to 300vb. *void;* leave hold, unhand, unclinch 779vb. *not retain;* relax, liberalize 734vb. *be lax;* lift, lift off 831vb. *relieve;* rid, dispel 300vb. *eject;* lift controls, decontrol, deration 752vb. *abrogate;* demobilize, disband, send home 75vb. *disperse;* unyoke, unharness, unload 701vb. *disencumber;* disentail, pay off the mortgage, clear the debt.
achieve liberty, gain one's freedom, breathe freely; assert oneself, claim freedom of action; free oneself, shake oneself free; break loose, throw off the yoke, cast off one's shackles, slip the collar, kick over the traces, get away 667vb. *escape*.
See: 46, 62, 75, 263, 300, 667, 668, 701, 734, 744, 752, 766, 779, 831, 909, 919, 927, 960.

747 Restraint

N. *restraint*, self-r., self-control 942n. *temperance;* suppression, repression, coercion, constraint 740n. *compulsion;* cramp, check 702n. *hindrance;* curb, drag, brake, snaffle, bridle 748 n. *fetter;* arrest, retardation, deceleration 278n. *slowness;* prevention, birth-control; cohibition, inhibition, veto, ban, bar, embargo 757n. *prohibition;* legal restraint 953n. *law;* control, strict c., discipline 733n. *authority;* censorship 550n. *obliteration;* press laws 735n. *severity;* binding over 963n. *penalty*.
restriction, limitation, limiting factor 236n. *limit;* localization, keeping within limits 232n. *circumscription;* restriction on movement, curfew; coarctation, constriction, squeeze 198 n. *compression;* duress, pressure 740 n. *compulsion;* control, food-c., rationing; restrictive practice, restraint of trade, exclusive rights, exclusivity 57n. *exclusion;* monopoly, price ring, closed shop; ring, circle, charmed c.; protection, protectionism, mercantilism, mercantile system, protective s., tariff, protective t., tariff wall; most-favored-nation treatment, preference, imperial p.; retrenchment 814n. *economy;* economic pressure, credit squeeze; blockade, starving out; monopolist, protectionist, restrictionist, mercantilist.
detention, preventive d., custody, protective c. 660n. *protection;* arrest, house a., open a., restriction on movement; custodianship, keeping, guarding, keep, care, charge, ward; quarantine, internment; lettre de cachet; captivity, durance, durance vile; thralldom, slavery 745n. *servitude;* entombment, burial 364n. *interment;* immurement, walling up; herding, impoundment, confinement, incarceration, imprisonment; remand, refusal of bail.
Adj. *restraining* etc.vb.; restrictive, conditioned, with strings; restringent, limiting, limitary; custodial, keeping; cramping, hidebound; strait-laced, unbending, unyielding, strict 735adj. *severe;* stiff 326adj. *rigid;* strait 206adj. *narrow;* straitening, confining, close 198adj. *compressive;* confined, poky; coercive, coactive 740 adj. *compelling;* repressive, inhibiting 757adj. *prohibiting;* monopolistic, protectionist, protective, mercantilist.
restrained, self-r., self-controlled 942 adj. *temperate;* disciplined, controlled, under discipline, under control 739adj. *obedient;* on a lead, kept on a leash, kept under restraint 232adj. *circumscribed;* pinned, pinned down; on parole 917adj. *dutied;* protected, rationed; restricted, scant, tight; cramped, hampered, trammeled, shackled 702adj. *hindered;* tied, bound; held up, weatherbound, wind-b., snow-b., ice-b.
imprisoned, detained, kept in; confined, earth-bound, land-locked 232 adj. *circumscribed;* entombed, confined 364adj. *buried;* quarantined, in quarantine; interned, in internment; under detention, kept close, incommunicado; under arrest, laid by the heels, in custody; refused bail, in the lock-up, in hazat; behind bars, incarcerated, locked up; inside, in jug, in quod, in a cell; under hatches, confined to barracks; herded, corralled, impounded, in the pound; in irons, fettered, shackled; pilloried, in the stocks; serving sentence, doing time; mewed, caged, in captivity 750adj. *captive;* trapped.
Vb. *restrain*, hold back, pull b., call b.; arrest, check, curb, rein in, brake, put a brake on, put a drag on, act as a brake 278vb. *retard;* cramp, clog, hamper 702vb. *hinder;* swathe, swaddle 45vb. *tie;* call off, call a halt, stop, put a stop to 145 vb. *halt;* cohibit, inhibit, veto, ban, bar 757vb. *prohibit;* bit, bridle, discipline, control 735vb. *be severe;* subdue 745vb. *subjugate;* grip, hold, pin, keep a tight hold *or* rein on, hold in leading strings, hold in leash, trash 778vb. *retain;* hold in,

keep in, bottle up; restrict, tighten, limit, keep within bounds, stop from spreading, localize, put a ring round, draw the line 232vb. *circumscribe;* stanch, damp down, pour water on, assuage 177vb. *moderate;* hold down, clamp down on, crack down on, keep under, sit on, jump on, repress 165vb. *suppress;* muzzle, gag, silence 578vb. *make mute;* censor, black out 550vb. *obliterate;* restrict access, debar from, rope off, keep out 57vb. *exclude;* restrict imports, put on a tariff, introduce protection; restrict supplies, withhold, keep back; restrict consumption, ration, dole out, be sparing, retrench 814vb. *economize;* try to stop, resist 704vb. *oppose;* police, patrol, keep order.

arrest, make an a., apprehend, lay by the heels, catch, cop, nab, collar, pinch, pick up; handcuff, put the handcuffs on (**see** *fetter*); take, make a prisoner, take prisoner, capture, lead captive; accept the surrender of, put on parole; put under arrest, take into custody, take charge of, clap in the lock-up, hold.

fetter, manacle, bind, pinion, tie up, handcuff, put in irons, put into bilboes; pillory, put in the stocks; tether, picket 45vb. *tie;* shackle, trammel, hobble; enchain, chain, load with chains; condition, attach strings.

imprison, confine, quarantine, intern; hold, detain, keep in, gate; keep in detention, keep under arrest, keep close, hold, incommunicado; cloister 883vb. *seclude;* entomb, bury 364vb. *inter;* wall up, seal up, immure; cage, kennel, impound, corral, herd, pen, mew, crib, cabin, box up, shut up, shut in, trap 235vb. *enclose;* put under restraint, straiten, put in a straitjacket; incarcerate, throw into prison, send to p., commit to p., remand, give in charge; jug, lock up; turn the key on, keep under lock and key, put in a cell, keep behind bars, lay under hatches, clap in irons; keep prisoner, keep in captivity, keep in custody, refuse bail.

See: 45, 57, 145, 165, 177, 198, 206, 232, 235, 236, 278, 326, 364, 550, 578, 660, 702, 704, 733, 735, 739, 740, 745, 748, 750, 757, 778, 814, 883, 917, 942, 953, 963.

748 Prison

N. *prison,* state p., common p., calaboose; prison-house, panopticon, prison without bars; house of detention, house of correction, penitentiary, federal p., reformatory, approved home, Borstal; prison ship, hulks; dungeon, oubliette, limbo; Bastille, Tower; debtor's prison, sponging house; Fleet, Marshalsea, Newgate, Wormwood Scrubs, Holloway, Sing Sing, Dannemora, Alcatraz; criminal lunatic asylum, Broadmoor.

jail, gaol, quod, clink, tronk, jug, can, stir, cooler, big house, glasshouse, booby hatch.

lock-up, hazat, chauki, choky, thana, police station; guard-room, roundhouse; cell, prison c., condemned c., dungeon c., dungeon, oubliette, torture-chamber; prison van, Black Maria; dock, bar; hold, hatches, hulks; pound, cattle-p., pen, cage, coop, kennel, den, barracoon, barrack, keddah 235n. *enclosure;* ghetto, reserve; stocks, pillory; lock, padlock, bolt, bar, barred window.

prison camp, detention c., internment c., prisoner of war c., stalag, oflag; concentration camp, slave c.; Belsen, Auschwitz, Buchenwald; deathhouse, gas chamber, execution c.; penal settlement, convict s., Botany Bay, Andaman Islands, Devil's Island.

fetter, shackle, trammel, bond, chain, ball and c., ring-bolt, irons, gyve, bilboes, hobble; manacle, pinion, handcuff, bracelet, darbies; strait waistcoat, strait jacket, whalebone, corset; muzzle, gag, bit, bridle, snaffle, headstall, halter; rein, bearing r., martingale; reins, ribbons, traces; yoke, collar, harness; curb, brake, skid, shoe, clog, drag, hobble 702n. *hindrance;* tether, rope, leading string 47n. *halter.*

See: 47, 235, 702.

749 Keeper

N. *keeper,* custodian, curator, custos; archivist, record keeper 549n. *recorder;* charge officer, officer in charge; caretaker, concierge, housekeeper; castellan, seneschal, chatelaine, warden; ranger, gamekeeper; guard, escort, convoy; watch-dog, sentry, sentinel, look-out, watchman, night-w., watch, coastguard, garrison 660n. *protector;* invigilator, tutor, chaperon, duenna, governess, nurse, foster-n., wet-n., mammy, nanny, nursemaid, bonne, ayah, amah, baby-sitter 742n. *domestic;*

foster-parent, adoptive p.; guardian, legal g.
jailer, gaoler, turnkey, warder, head w., wardress, prison guard, prison governor; Argus.
See: 549, 660.

750 Prisoner

N. *prisoner*, captive, capture, prisoner of war; parolee, ticket-of-leave man; close prisoner, person under arrest, charge; detenue, detainee, state prisoner, prisoner of state; prisoner at the bar, defendant, accused 928n. *accused person;* first offender, Borstal boy, jail-bird 904n. *offender;* jail inmate, prisoner behind bars, condemned prisoner, convict; chain-gang, galley-slave 742n. *slave;* hostage 767n. *security*.
Adj. *captive*, imprisoned, chained, fettered, shackled in irons, behind bars, under lock and key, under hatches, cooling one's heels; jailed, in prison, in Dartmoor, in Borstal; in the pillory, in the stocks, in the galleys; in custody, under arrest, without bail, remanded; detained, under detention, detained at her Majesty's pleasure.
See: 742, 904, 928.

751 Commission: vicarious authority

N. *commission*, vicarious authority; committal, delegation; devolution, decentralization; deputation, ablegation; legation, mission, embassy, embassage, High Commission 754n. *envoy;* regency, regentship, vice-regentship, vice-royalty 733n. *authority;* representation, procuracy, procuration, proxy; card vote; agency, agentship, factorship; trusteeship, executorship 689n. *management;* clerkship, public service, civil s., bureaucracy 733n. *government*.
mandate, doctor's m., trust, charge 737n. *command;* commission, assignment, appointment, office, task, errand, mission; enterprise 672n. *undertaking;* nomination, return, election 605n. *vote;* posting, translation, transfer, mutual transfer, cross-posting 272n. *transference;* investment, investiture, installation, inauguration, ordination, enthronement, coronation; power, attorney, power of a., letter of a., written authority, charter, writ 737n. *warrant;* brevet, diploma 756n. *permit;* terms of reference 766n. *conditions;* responsibility, care, cure (of souls); baby, ward, charge.
Adj. *commissioned*, empowered, entrusted etc.vb.; deputed, delegated, accredited; vicarious, representational, agential, procuratory.
Vb. *commission*, put in c.; empower, authorize, charge, sanction, charter, license 756vb. *permit;* post, accredit, appoint, assign, name, nominate; engage, hire, staff 622vb. *employ;* invest, induct, install, collate, ordain; raise to the throne, enthrone, crown, anoint; commit, put in one's hands, turn over to, leave it to; consign, entrust, trust with, grant powers of attorney; delegate, depute, send on a mission, send on an errand, send out, ablegate; return, elect, give a mandate 605vb. *vote*.
Adv. *by proxy*, by procuration, per procurationem, by delegated authority.
See: 272, 605, 622, 672, 689, 733, 737, 754, 756, 766.

752 Abrogation

N. *abrogation*, annulment, invalidation; voidance, nullification, vacation, defeasance; canceling, cancellation, cassation, suppression; recall, repeal, revocation, revokement, rescission; abolition, abolishment, dissolution; neonomianism 126n. *newness;* repudiation 533n. *negation;* retractation 603n. *recantation;* suspension, discontinuance, disuse, dead letter 674n. *non-use;* reversal, undoing 148n. *reversion;* counter-order, countermand, nolle prosequi; cancel, cancel-page.
deposal, deposition, dethronement; demotion, degradation; disestablishment, disendowment; deconsecration, secularization; discharge, congé, dismissal, sack, removal 300n. *ejection;* unfrocking 963n. *punishment;* ousting, deprivation 786n. *expropriation;* replacement, supersession 150n. *substitution;* recall, transfer, relief 272n. *transference*.
Adj. *abrogated*, voided, vacated, set aside, quashed, canceled etc.vb.; void, null and void; functus officio, dead; dormant, sleeping 674adj. *unused;* recalled, revoked.
Vb. *abrogate*, annul, disannul, cancel; scrub, scrub out, rub o., wipe o. 550 vb. *obliterate;* invalidate, abolish, dissolve, nullify, void, vacate, render null and void; quash, set aside, reverse, overrule; repeal, revoke, recall; rescind, tear up; unmake, undo

148vb. *revert;* countermand, counter-order; disclaim, disown, deny 533vb. *negate;* repudiate, retract 603vb. *recant;* ignore 458vb. *disregard;* call off, call a halt 747vb. *restrain;* suspend, discontinue, make a dead letter of 674vb. *disuse;* unwish, wish undone 830vb. *regret;* not proceed with 621vb. *relinquish.*

depose, discrown, uncrown, dethrone; unseat, unsaddle; divest 786vb. *deprive;* unfrock, disordain; disbench, disbar, strike off the roll 57vb. *exclude;* disaffiliate, disestablish, disendow; deconsecrate, secularize; suspend, cashier, break 300vb. *dismiss;* ease out, oust 300vb. *eject;* demote, degrade, reduce to the ranks; recall, relieve, supersede, replace, remove 272vb. *transfer.*

See: 57, 126, 148, 150, 272, 300, 458, 533, 550, 603, 621, 674, 747, 786, 830, 963.

753 Resignation

N. *resignation*, demission, good-bye to office; retirement, retiral; leaving, withdrawal, handshake 296n. *departure;* pension, compensation, golden handshake 962n. *reward;* waiver, surrender, abandonment, abdication, renunciation 621n. *relinquishment;* declaration (of innings at cricket); abjuration, disclaimer 533n. *negation;* state of retirement 681vb. *leisure;* feeling of resignation, acquiescence 721n. *submission;* resigner, quitter; man in retirement, pensioner, Cincinnatus.

Adj. *resigning*, abdicatory, abdicant, renunciatory; outgoing, former, retired, quondam, one-time, ci-devant, passé; stickit, discouraged from.

Vb. *resign*, tender one's resignation, send in one's papers, demit, lay down one's office, break one's staff; be relieved, hand over, vacate, vacate office; vacate one's seat, apply for the Chiltern Hundreds; stand down, stand aside, make way for, leave it to; sign off, declare, declare one's innings closed; scratch, withdraw, back out, retire from the contest, throw in one's hand, surrender, give up 721vb. *submit;* quit, throw up, chuck it; sign away, give a. 780vb. *convey;* abdicate, abandon, renounce 621vb. *relinquish;* retire, go into retirement, take one's pension, find one's occupation gone, lie on the shelf; retire in rotation, finish one's term, conclude one's term of office; decline to stand again, not renew the fight, refuse battle; waive, disclaim, abjure 533vb. *negate;* retract 603vb. *recant.*

See: 296, 533, 603, 621, 681, 721, 780, 962.

754 Consignee

N. *consignee*, committee, panel 692n. *council;* counselor, wise man, team of experts, working party 691n. *adviser;* bailee, resignee, stakeholder; nominee, appointee, licensee; trustee, executor 686n. *agent;* factor, one's man of business, bailiff, steward 690 n. *manager;* caretaker, curator 749n. *keeper;* representative (**see** *delegate*); legal representative, attorney, vakeel, mukhtar, counsel, advocate 958n. *law agent;* procurator, proctor, proxy 955n. *deputy;* negotiator, middleman, broker, stockbroker 231n. *intermediary;* underwriter, insurer; purser, bursar 798n. *treasurer;* bill-collector, tax-c., revenue-c., tahsildar, income-tax officer; holder of an office of trust, office-bearer, secretary of state 741n. *officer;* functionary, placeman 690n. *official.*

delegate, walking d., shop steward; nominee, representative, elected r., member; official representative, commissary, commissioner; man on the spot, correspondent, war c., one's own c., special c. 588n. *correspondent;* emissary, special messenger 531n. *messenger;* plenipotentiary (**see** *envoy*); delegation, trade d., mission.

envoy, emissary, legate, ablegate, nuncio, papal n., internuncio, permanent representative, resident, resident minister, ambassador, ambassadress, High Commissioner, chargé d'affaires; corps diplomatique, diplomatic corps; minister, diplomat, doyen of the diplomatic corps; consul, vice-c.; first secretary, attaché; embassy, legation, mission, consulate, High Commission; diplomatist, negotiator, plenipotentiary.

See: 231, 531, 588, 686, 690, 691, 692, 741, 749, 798, 955, 958.

755 Deputy

N. *deputy*, surrogate, alternate, proxy; scapegoat, chopping block, substitute, locum tenens, understudy, stand-in 150n. *substitution;* pro, vice, vice-gerent, vice-regent, viceroy, vice-president, vice-chairman, vice-chancellor, vice-admiral, vice-captain, vice-consul; proconsul, propraetor;

vicar, vicar-general; second-in-command, deputy prime-minister; right-hand man, lieutenant, secretary 703 n. *aider;* alter ego. Gray Eminence, power behind the throne 612n. *motivator;* heir, heir apparent, successor designate 776n. *beneficiary;* spokesman, mouthpiece, herald 531n. *messenger;* next friend; advocate, champion 707n. *patron;* agent, factor, attorney 754n. *consignee.*

Adj. *deputizing*, representing, acting for, agential; vice, pro; diplomatic, ambassadorial, plenipotentiary; standing in for 150adj. *substituted;* negotiatory, intermediary 231adj. *interjacent.*

Vb. *deputize,* act for 622vb. *function;* attorney, act on behalf of, represent, hold a mandate for, hold a proxy f., appear for, speak f., answer f., hold a brief f., state the case f.; hold in trust, manage the business of, be executor 689vb. *manage;* negotiate, broke for; replace, stand for, stand in the stead of, do duty for, stand in another's shoes 150vb. *substitute;* be the chopping block for, act as scapegoat, hold the baby.

Adv. *on behalf*, for, pro; by proxy.

See: 150, 231, 531, 612, 622, 689, 703, 707, 754, 776.

756 Permission

N. *permission*, general p., liberty 744 n. *freedom;* leave, sanction, clearance; vouchsafement, accordance, grant; license, authorization, warrant, warranty; allowance, sufferance, tolerance, toleration, indulgence 736n. *lenity;* acquiescence, passive consent, implied c. 758n. *consent;* connivance 703n. *aid;* blessing, approval 923n. *approbation;* grace, grace and favor 897n. *benevolence;* concession, dispensation, exemption 919n. *nonliability;* release 746n. *liberation.*

permit, express permission, written p.; authority, law 737n. *warrant;* commission 751n. *mandate;* brevet, grant, charter, patent, letters p.; pass, password, passport, visa, safe-conduct; ticket, rain check; license, driving l.; universal license, free hand, carte blanche, blank check 744n. *scope;* leave, compassionate l., leave of absence, furlough, holiday; parole, ticket of leave; all clear, green light, clearance; nihil obstat, imprimatur.

Adj. *permitting*, permissive, indulgent, complaisant, tolerant 736adj. *lenient;* conniving 704adj. *aiding.*

permitted, allowed etc.vb.; licit, legalized 953adj. *legal;* licensed, chartered, patent; unforbidden, unprohibited, open, optional, discretional, without strings 744adj. *unconditional;* permissible, allowable; printable, sayable; not strictly necessary, dispensable.

Vb. *permit,* let 469vb. *make possible;* give permission, grant leave, grant, accord, vouchsafe 781vb. *give;* nod, say yes 758vb. *consent;* bless, give one's blessing; go out of one's way to 759vb. *offer;* sanction, pass 923vb. *approve;* entitle, authorize, warrant, charter, patent, license, enable 160 vb. *empower;* ratify, legalize 953vb. *make legal;* restore permission, decontrol; lift, lift a ban, dispense, release 919vb. *exempt;* clear, give clearance 746vb. *liberate;* give the all clear, give the green light, tip the wink; recognize, concede, allow 488vb. *assent;* provide for, make provision for 633vb. *provide;* make it easy for, favor, privilege, indulge 701vb. *facilitate;* leave the way open, open the door to, open the floodgates 263vb. *open;* foster, encourage 156vb. *conduce;* suffer, tolerate, put up with 736vb. *be lenient;* connive, shut one's eyes to, wink at 734vb. *be lax;* laisser faire, laisser aller, allow a free hand, give carte blanche, issue a blank check 744vb. *give scope;* permit oneself, allow o., take the liberty 734vb. *please oneself.*

ask leave, beg l., beg permission, ask if one may, ask one's blessing; apply for leave, request sanction; seek a favor, petition 761vb. *request;* get leave, have permission; receive a charter, take out a patent.

Adv. *by leave*, with permission, by favor of, under favor, under license; permissibly, allowably, legally, legitimately, licitly.

See: 156, 160, 263, 469, 488, 633, 701, 703, 704, 734, 736, 737, 744, 746, 751, 758, 759, 761, 781, 897, 919, 923, 953.

757 Prohibition

N. *prohibition*, inhibition, interdiction, disallowance, injunction; countermand, counter-order; intervention, interference; interdict, veto, ban, embargo, out-lawry; cohibition, restriction, curfew 747n. *restraint;* proscription, taboo, index expurgatorius; disfavor, rejection 760n. *refusal;* non-recognition, intolerance 924n. *disapprobation;* prohibition of drink, pussyfootism, licensing laws 942n. *temperance;* sumptuary law 814n. *economy;* repressive legislation, censorship, press laws, repression, suppression 735n. *severity;* abolition, cancellation, suspension 752n. *abrogation;* black-out 550n. *obliteration;* forbidden fruit, contraband article 859n. *desired object.*

Adj. *prohibiting*, prohibitory, forbidding, prohibitive, excessive 470adj. *impossible;* penal 963adj. *punitive;* hostile 881adj. *inimical;* exclusive 57 adj. *excluding.*

prohibited, forbidden, barred, banned, under ban; censored, blue-penciled, blacked-out; contraband, illicit, unlawful, outlawed, against the law 954adj. *illegal;* verboten, taboo, untouchable, black; frowned on, not to be thought of, not done; not to be spoken, unmentionable, unsayable, unprintable; out of bounds 57 adj. *excluded.*

Vb. *prohibit*, forbid, forfend; disallow, veto, refuse permission, withhold p., refuse leave, forbid the banns 760vb. *refuse;* withdraw permission, cancel leave; countermand, counter-order, revoke, suspend 752 vb. *abrogate;* inhibit, prevent, paralyze 702vb. *hinder;* cohibit, restrict, stop 747vb. *restrain;* ban, interdict, taboo, proscribe, outlaw; black, declare b.; impose a ban, lay under interdict, place out of bounds; bar, debar, warn off 57vb. *exclude;* excommunicate 300vb. *eject;* repress, stifle, kill 165vb. *suppress;* censor, blue-pencil, black-out 550vb. *obliterate;* frown on, discountenance, disfavor 924vb. *disapprove;* discourage 613vb. *dissuade;* clip, narrow, pinch, cramp 232vb. *circumscribe;* draw the line, block; intervene, interpose, interfere, dash the cup from one's lips.

See: 57, 165, 232, 300, 470, 550, 613, 702, 735, 747, 752, 760, 814, 859, 881, 924, 942, 954, 963.

758 Consent

N. *consent*, free c., full c., willing c. 597n. *willingness;* implied consent, implicit c.; agreement 488n. *assent;* compliance 768n. *observance;* concession, grant, accord; acquiescence, acceptance, entertainment, allowance 756n. *permission;* sanction, endorsement, ratification, confirmation; partial consent 770n. *compromise.*

Adj. *consenting*, agreeable, compliant, ready, ready enough 597adj. *willing;* winking at, conniving 703adj. *aiding;* yielding 721adj. *submitting.*

Vb. *consent*, entertain; entertain the idea, say yes, nod; give consent, ratify, confirm 488vb. *endorse;* sanction, pass 756vb. *permit;* accord one's approval 923vb. *approve;* agree, fall in with, accede 488vb. *assent;* have no objection 488vb. *acquiesce;* be persuaded, come over, come round 612vb. *be induced;* yield, give way 721vb. *submit;* comply, grant a request, do as asked; grant, accord, concede, vouchsafe 781vb. *give;* deign, condescend 884 vb. *be courteous;* listen, hearken 415 vb. *hear;* turn a willing ear, go halfway to meet 597vb. *be willing;* meet one's wishes, do all one is asked 828vb. *content;* satisfy, come up to scratch 635vb. *suffice;* accept, take one at one's word, embrace an offer, jump at; clinch a deal, close with, settle 766vb. *make terms;* tolerate, recognize, allow, connive 736vb. *be lenient;* consent unwillingly, drag oneself, make o.

See: 415, 488, 597, 612, 635, 703, 721, 736, 756, 766, 770, 781, 828, 884, 923.

759 Offer

N. *offer*, fair o., proffer; improper offer, bribery, bribe 612n. *inducement;* tender, bid, take-over b.; declaration, motion, proposition, proposal; approach, overture, advance, invitation; tentative approach, feeler; present, presentation, offering, gratuity, sacrifice 781n. *gift;* dedication, consecration; candidature, application, solicitation 761n. *request.*

Adj. *offering*, inviting; offered, advertised; open, available; on offer, on the market, in the m.; on hire, to let, for sale; on bid, on auction.

Vb. *offer*, proffer, hold out, make an offer, bid, tender; come with, bring, fetch; present, lay at one's feet, place in one's hands 781vb. *give;* dedicate, consecrate; sacrifice to; introduce, broach, move, propose, make a proposition, put forward, suggest 512vb. *propound;* not wait to be asked, approach, approach with, make overtures, make advances, hold out one's hand; keep the door ajar, keep one's offer open; induce 612vb. *bribe;* press, invite, send an invitation, ask one in 882 vb. *be hospitable;* hawk, hawk about, invite tenders, offer for sale 793vb. *sell;* auction, declare the bidding open; cater, cater for 633vb.

provide; make available, place at one's disposal, place in one's way, make a present of 469vb. *make possible;* pose, confront with.
offer oneself, sacrifice o.; stand, make one's candidature, compete, run for, enter 716vb. *contend;* volunteer, come forward 597vb. *be willing;* apply, put in for 761vb. *request;* be on offer, look for takers, go begging.
See: 469, 512, 597, 612, 633, 716, 761, 781, 793, 882.

760 Refusal

N. *refusal,* non-acceptance, declining, declension, turning down 607n. *rejection;* denial, negative answer, no, nay 533n. *negation;* uncompromising answer, flat refusal, point-blank r., peremptory r. 711n. *defiance;* repulse, rebuff, slap in the face 292n. *repulsion;* no facilities, denial policy 715n. *resistance;* withholding 778n. *retention;* recalcitrance 738n. *disobedience;* non-compliance 769n. *non-observance;* recusancy 598n. *unwillingness;* objection, protest 762n. *deprecation;* self-denial 945n. *asceticism;* restraint 942n. *temperance;* renunciation, abnegation 621n. *relinquishment.*
Adj. *refusing,* denying, withholding, rejecting etc.vb.; uncomplaisant, recusant, non-compliant, uncompliant 769adj. *non-observant;* jibbing, objecting 762adj. *deprecatory;* deaf to, unhearing 598adj. *unwilling.*
refused, not granted, turned down, ungratified, rebuffed etc.vb.; inadmissible, out of the question 470 adj. *impossible;* unoffered, withheld 778adj. *retained.*
Vb. *refuse,* say no, shake one's head; disagree 489vb. *dissent;* deny, negative, repudiate, disclaim 533vb. *negate;* decline, turn down 607vb. *reject;* deny firmly, repulse, rebuff 292vb. *repel;* turn away 300vb. *dismiss;* resist persuasion, be unmoved, harden one's heart 602vb. *be obstinate;* not hear, not listen, turn a deaf ear 416vb. *be deaf;* not give, close one's hand, close one's purse; not consent, will otherwise, have other fish to fry; be slow to, hang fire, can't drag *or* make oneself 598 vb. *be loath;* turn from, have nothing to do with, shy at, jib at 620vb. *avoid;* debar, keep out, shut the door 57vb. *exclude;* not want, not cater for; look askance at, dislike, disfavor, discountenance, not hear of 924vb. *disapprove;* frown on, disallow 757vb. *prohibit;* set one's face against 715vb. *resist;* oppose 704vb. *withstand;* kick, protest 762vb. *deprecate;* not comply 769vb. *not observe;* grudge, begrudge, withhold, keep from 778vb. *retain;* deny oneself, waive, renounce, give up 621vb. *relinquish*; deprive oneself, go without, do w. 945vb. *be ascetic.*
Adv. *denyingly,* with a refusal, without acceptance; no, never, over one's dead body, not for all the tea in China.
See: 57, 292, 300, 416, 470, 489, 533, 598, 607, 620, 621, 704, 711, 715, 738, 757, 762, 769, 778, 924, 942, 945.

761 Request

N. *request,* simple r., modest r., humble petition; negative request 762n. *deprecation;* asking, first time of a.; canvass, canvassing, hawking 793n. *sale;* strong request, forcible demand, requisition; last demand, final d., last time of asking, ultimatum 737n. *demand;* demand with threats, blackmail 900n. *threat;* postulation, assertion 532n. *affirmation;* assertion of one's rights, claim, counter-c. 915 n. *dueness;* consumer demand, firm d., steady d., strong d., seller's market 627n. *requirement;* postulate 475n. *premise;* proposition, proposal, motion, rogation, prompting, suggestion; overture, approach 759vb. *offer;* bid, application, suit; petition, memorial, round robin; prayer, appeal, plea (**see** *entreaty*); pressure, instance, insistence, urgency 740n. *compulsion;* clamor, cry, cri de coeur 836n. *lamentation;* dunning, importunity; soliciting, accosting, solicitation, invitation, temptation; mendicancy, begging, street-b., panhandling; appeal for funds, begging letter, subscription list, flag day, bazaar, charity performance; advertising 528n. *advertisement;* want ad, want column; want 859n. *desire.*
entreaty, imploration, imploring, beseeching; submission, humble s., folded hands, bended knees, one's k.; supplication, prayer, hard p., orison 981n. *prayers;* appeal, invocation, apostrophe 583n. *allocution;* solemn entreaty, adjuration, adjurement, conjuration, conjurement, obtestation, obsecration, imprecation; successful entreaty, impetration.
Adj. *requesting,* asking, inviting, begging etc.vb.; mendicant, alms-

hunting; invitatory 759adj. *offering;* claiming 627adj. *demanding;* insisting, insistent; importunate, pressing, urgent, instant; clamorous, dunning.

supplicatory, entreating, suppliant, praying, prayerful; on bended knees, with folded hands, cap in hand; precatory, imploratory, beseeching, with tears in one's eyes; invocatory, adjuratory, imprecatory; precative.

Vb. *request*, ask, invite, solicit; make overtures, approach, accost 759vb. *offer;* sue, sigh, woo, pop the question, put up the banns 889vb. *court;* seek, look for 459vb. *search;* need, have in request, call for, clamor f. 627vb. *require;* crave, make a request, prefer an appeal, beg a favor, ask a boon, have a request to make, make bold to ask, trouble one for 859vb. *desire;* apply, make application, put in for, bid, bid for, make a bid f.; apply to, call on, appeal to, run to, address oneself to, go cap in hand to; tout, hawk, canvass, solicit orders 793vb. *sell;* petition, memorialize; make interest for, press a claim, expect 915vb. *claim;* make demands 737vb. *demand;* blackmail 900vb. *threaten;* be instant, insist 532vb. *emphasize;* urge, persuade 612vb. *induce;* importune, ply, press, dun, besiege, beset; knock at the door, demand entrance; impetrate; touch, touch for 785vb. *borrow;* requisition 786vb. *take;* raise money, tax 786vb. *levy;* formulate one's demands, state one's terms, send an ultimatum 766vb. *give terms.*

beg, cadge, crave, sponge, play the parasite; mump, scrounge, sorn; thumb, hitchhike; panhandle, mendicate; beg one's bread, beg from door to door, knock at every d.; appeal for funds, pass the hat, make a collection, raise subscriptions, open a subscription-list 786vb. *levy;* beg in vain, whistle for 627vb. *require.*

entreat, make entreaty, beg hard; supplicate, be a suppliant; pray, implore, beseech, appeal, conjure, adjure, obtest, obsecrate, imprecate; invoke, apostrophize, appeal to, address 583vb. *speak to;* address one's prayers to, pray to 981vb. *offer worship;* kneel to, go down on one's knees, go down on one's marrow bones; sue, sigh, sigh at one's feet, fall at one's f.; gain by entreaty, impetrate 771vb. *acquire.*

See: 459, 475, 528, 532, 583, 612, 627, 737, 740, 759, 762, 766, 771, 785, 786, 793, 836, 859, 889, 900, 915, 981.

762 Deprecation: negative request

N. *deprecation,* negative request, contrary advice, dehortation 613n. *dissuasion;* begging off, plea for mercy, crossed fingers; intercession, mediation 981n. *prayers;* counter-petition, counter-claim 761n. *request;* murmur, cheep, squeak, complaint 829n. *discontent;* exception, demur, expostulation, remonstrance, protest 704n. *opposition;* reaction, kick 182n. *counteraction;* gesture of protest, tut-tut, raised eyebrows, groans, jeers 924n. *disapprobation;* open letter, round robin; demonstration, indignation meeting, march, hunger-m.; non-compliance 760n. *refusal;* refusal to work 145n. *strike.*

Adj. *deprecatory,* dehortative 613adj. *dissuasive;* protesting, protestant, expostulatory; clamant, vocal; intercessory, mediatorial; averting, apotropaic.

Vb. *deprecate,* ask one not to, dehort, advise against, have a better idea, make a counter-proposal 613 vb. *dissuade;* avert the omen, touch wood, knock on w., cross one's fingers, keep one's fingers crossed 983vb. *practice sorcery;* beg off, plead for, intercede 720vb. *mediate;* pray, appeal 761vb. *entreat;* cry for mercy 905vb. *ask mercy;* show embarrassment, tut-tut, shake one's head, raise one's eyebrows 924vb. *disapprove;* remonstrate, expostulate 924vb. *reprove;* jeer, groan, stamp 926vb. *detract;* murmur, beef, complain 829vb. *be discontented;* demur, jib, kick, squeak, protest against, appeal a., petition a., raise one's voice a., cry out a., cry blue murder 704vb. *oppose;* demonstrate, hold an indignation meeting; strike, strike work, call out, come out, walk o. 145vb. *cease.*

See: 145, 182, 613, 704, 720, 760, 761, 829, 905, 924, 926, 981, 983.

763 Petitioner

N. *petitioner*, humble p., suppliant, supplicant; appealer, appellant; claimant, pretender; postulant, aspirant, expectant; solicitor, asker, seeker, inquirer, advertiser; customer, bidder, tenderer; suitor, courter, wooer; canvasser, hawker, touter, tout, ambulance-chaser, barker, spieler; dun, dunner; pressure group, lobby, lobbyist; applicant, candidate, entrant; competitor, runner 716n. *contender;* complainer, grouser, man with a grievance, ir-

redentist 829n. *malcontent.*
beggar, street-b., sturdy b., professional b., schnorrer, panhandler; mendicant, almshunter; mendicant friar, beghard, bhikshu, bhikkhu; tramp, bum 268n. *wanderer;* cadger, borrower, scrounger, sorner, mumper, hitch-hiker; sponger, parasite 879n. *toady.*
See: 268, 716, 829, 879.

764 Promise

N. *promise,* promise-making, pollicitation 759n. *offer;* undertaking, engagement, commitment; espousal, betrothal, affiance, unofficial engagement 894n. *marriage;* troth, plight, plighted word, word, one's bare w., parole, word of honor, sacred pledge, vow, marriage v. 532n. *oath;* declaration, solemn d. 532n. *affirmation;* declared intention 617n. *intention;* profession, professions, fair words; assurance, pledge, credit, honor, warrant, warranty, guarantee, insurance 767n. *security;* voluntary commitment, gentlemen's agreement, mutual a. 765n. *compact;* covenant, bond, promise to pay 803 n. *debt;* obligation, debt of honor 917n. *duty;* preengagement, firm date, delivery d. 672n. *undertaking;* promiser, promise-maker, votary; engager, party 765n. *signatory.*
Adj. *promissory,* promising, votive; on oath, under o., under hand and seal; on credit, on parole.
promised, covenanted, guaranteed, secured 767adj. *pledged;* engaged, bespoke, reserved; betrothed, affianced; committed, in for it; bound, obliged, obligated 917adj. *dutied.*
Vb. *promise,* say one will 532vb. *affirm;* hold out, proffer 759vb. *offer;* make a promise, give one's word, pledge one's w.; vow, vow and protest, take oath upon it 532vb. *swear;* vouch for, go bail for, warrant, guarantee, assure, confirm, secure, insure, underwrite 767vb. *give security;* pledge, stake; parole oneself, pledge one's honor, plight one's word, stake one's credit; engage, engage for, enter into an engagement, give a firm date 672vb. *undertake;* make a gentleman's agreement, commit oneself, bind oneself, be bound, covenant 765vb. *contract;* accept an obligation, take on oneself, answer for, accept responsibility 917vb. *incur a duty;* accept a liability, promise to pay, incur a debt of honor 785vb. *borrow;* bespeak, preengage, reserve 617vb. *intend;* plight one's faith, exchange vows 894vb. *wed.*
take a pledge, demand security 473vb. *make certain;* put on oath, administer an o., adjure, swear, make one s. 466vb. *testify;* make one promise, exact a p.; take on credit, take one's word, accept one's parole, parole 485vb. *believe;* rely on, expect 473 vb. *be certain.*
Adv. *as promised,* according to contract, duly; professedly, upon one's word, upon one's honor, upon one's guarantee, truly 540adv. *truthfully.*
See: 466, 473, 485, 532, 540, 617, 672, 759, 765, 767, 785, 803, 894, 917.

765 Compact

N. *compact,* contract, bargain, agreement, mutual a., mutual undertaking 672n. *undertaking;* gentleman's agreement, debt of honor 764n. *promise;* mutual pledge, exchange of vows; espousal, betrothal 894n. *marriage;* covenant, indenture, bond 767n. *security;* league, alliance, cartel 706n. *cooperation;* pact, paction, convention, understanding 24n. *agreement;* private understanding, something between them; secret pact, conspiracy 623n. *plot;* negotiation 766n. *conditions;* deal, give and take 770n. *compromise;* adjustment, composition, arrangement, settlement; completion, signature, ratification, confirmation 488n. *assent;* seal, sigil, signet, signature, counter-s.; deed of agreement, indenture 767n. *title-deed.*
treaty, international agreement; peace treaty, non-aggression pact; convention, concordat, protocol; Zollverein, Sonderbund; Pragmatic Sanction, Berne Convention.
signatory, signer, counter-signer, subscriber, the undersigned; swearer, attester, attestant 466n. *witness;* endorser, ratifier; adherent, party, consenting p. 488n. *assenter;* contractor, contracting party, high contracting p.; treaty-maker, negotiator.
Adj. *contractual,* conventional, consensual 488adj. *assenting;* bilateral, multilateral; agreed to, negotiated, signed, undersigned, sworn, ratified; signed, sealed and delivered; under one's hand and seal.
Vb. *contract,* enter into a contract, engage 672vb. *undertake;* precontract 764vb. *promise;* covenant, make a compact, strike a bargain, sign a pact, strike hands, do a deal, clinch a d.; join in a compact, adhere;

league, ally 706vb. *cooperate;* treat, negotiate 791vb. *bargain;* give and take 770vb. *compromise;* stipulate 766vb. *give terms;* agree, arrive at a formula, come to terms 766vb. *make terms;* conclude, set at rest, settle; indent, execute, sign, subscribe, ratify, attest, confirm 488vb. *endorse*; insure, underwrite 767vb. *give security.*

See: 24, 466, 488, 623, 672, 706, 764, 766, 767, 770, 791, 894.

766 Conditions

N. conditions, making terms, treaty-making, negotiation, bargaining, collective b.; hard bargaining, horse-dealing 791n. *barter;* formula, terms, set t., written t., stated t., terms for agreement; final terms, ultimatum, time limit 900n. *threat;* dictated terms 740n. *compulsion;* part of the bargain, condition, set of terms, frame of reference; articles, articles of agreement; provision, clause, entrenched c., escape c., saving c., proviso, limitation, strings, reservation, exception 468n. *qualification;* stipulation, sine qua non, essential clause 627n. *requirement;* rule 693n. *precept;* contractual terms, casus foederis, the letter of the treaty; embodied terms 765n. *treaty;* terms of reference 751n. *mandate.*

Adj. *conditional*, with strings attached, binding 917adj. *obligatory;* provisional, stipulatory, qualificatory, provisory 468adj. *qualifying;* limiting, subject to terms, conditioned, contingent; guarded, safeguarded, fenced, entrenched.

Vb. *give terms*, read out the t., propose conditions; condition, bind, tie down, attach strings; hold out for, insist on one's terms, make demands 737vb. *demand;* stipulate, make it a sine qua non 627vb. *require;* allow no exception 735vb. *be severe;* insert a proviso, allow an exception 468vb. *qualify;* fix the terms, impose the conditions, write the articles, draft the clauses; add a clause, write in.

make terms, negotiate, treat, be in treaty, parley, hold conversations 584vb. *confer;* deal with, treat w., negotiate w.; make overtures, throw out a feeler 461vb. *be tentative;* haggle, higgle 791vb. *bargain;* proffer, make proposals, make a counter-proposal 759vb. *offer;* give and take, yield a point, stretch a p. 770vb. *compromise;* negotiate a treaty, do a deal 765vb. *contract.*

Adv. *on terms*, on one's own t.; conditionally, provisionally, subject to, with a reservation; strictly, to the letter; necessarily, sine qua non; peremptorily, for the last time.

See: 461, 468, 584, 627, 693, 735, 737, 740, 751, 759, 765, 770, 791, 900, 917.

767 Security

N. *security*, precaution 858n. *caution;* guarantee, warranty, authorization, writ 737n. *warrant;* sponsorship, sponsion, patronage 660n. *protection;* suretyship, cautionary, mainprize; surety, bail, caution, replevin, recognizance, personal r., parole; bailor, cautioner, mainpernor; gage, pledge, pawn, pignus, pignoration, hostage; stake, stake money, deposit, earnest, handsel, token, installment; color of one's money, earnest m., caution m.; token payment 804n. *payment;* insurance, underwriting 660n. *safety;* transfer of security, hypothecation, mortgage, bottomry 780n. *transfer;* collateral, collateral security, real s.

title-deed, deed, instrument; unilateral deed, deed-poll; bilateral deed, indenture; charter, covenant, bond 765n. *compact;* receipt, IOU, voucher, acquittance, quittance; certificate, authentication, marriage lines; verification, seal, stamp, signature, endorsement, acceptance 466n. *credential;* valuable security, banknote, treasury n., promissory n., note of hand, hundi, bill, bill of exchange; paper, government p., gilt-edged security; portfolio scrip, share, debenture; mortgage deed, policy, insurance p.; will, testament, codicil, certificate of probate; matter of record, muniment, archive 548n. *record.*

Adj. *pledged*, pawned, popped, deposited; in pawn, on deposit; on lease, on mortgage; on bail, on recognizance.

secured, covered, hedged, insured, mortgaged; gilt-edged; guaranteed, convenanted 764adj. *promised.*

Vb. *give bail*, go b., bail one out, go surety, give s.; take bail, take recognizance, release on bail; hold in pledge, keep in pawn 764vb. *take a pledge.*

give security, offer collateral, hypothecate, bottomry, mortgage; pledge, impignorate, pawn, pop, hock, spout 785vb. *borrow;* guaran-

tee, warrant 473vb. *make certain;* authenticate, verify 466vb. *corroborate;* execute, endorse, seal, stamp, sign, counter-s., subscribe, give one's signature 488vb. *endorse;* accept, grant a receipt, write an IOU 782vb. *receive;* secure, insure, assure, underwrite 660vb. *safeguard.*
See: 466, 473, 488, 548, 660, 737, 764, 765, 780, 782, 785, 804, 858.

768 Observance

N. *observance,* close o. 610n. *practice;* full observance, fulfillment, satisfaction 635n. *sufficiency;* adherence to, attention to, paying respect to, acknowledgment; performance, discharge, acquittance, acquittal 676n. *action;* compliance 739n. *obedience;* conformance 83n. *conformity;* attachment, fidelity, faith, good f. 739n. *loyalty;* sense of responsibility, dependability, reliability 929 n. *probity.*

Adj. *observant,* practicing 676adj. *doing;* heedful, watchful, careful of, attentive to 455adj. *attentive;* conscientious, punctual, diligent, earnest, religious, punctilious; overconscientious, perfectionist 862adj. *fastidious;* literal, pedantic, exact 494adj. *accurate;* responsible, reliable, dependable 929adj. *trustworthy;* loyal, true, compliant 739 adj. *obedient;* adherent to, adhering to 83adj. *conformable;* faithful 929 adj. *honorable.*

Vb. *observe,* heed, respect, regard, have regard to, pay respect to, acknowledge, pay attention to, attend to 455vb. *be attentive;* keep, practice, adhere to, cling to, follow, hold by, abide by, be loyal to 83vb. *conform;* comply 739vb. *obey;* fulfill, discharge, perform, execute, carry out, carry out to the letter 676vb. *do;* satisfy 635vb. *suffice.*

observe faith, keep f., be faithful to, have loyalty; discharge one's functions 917vb. *do one's duty;* act up to one's obligations, meet one's o., be as good as one's word, make good one's promise, fulfill one's engagement, be true to the spirit of, stand by 929vb. *be honorable;* come up to scratch, redeem one's pledge, pay one's debt, pay up 805vb. *pay;* give one his due, deny no just claim 915vb. *grant claims.*

Adv. *with observance,* faithfully, religiously, loyally; literally, meticulously, according to the spirit of.

See: 83, 455, 494, 610, 635, 676, 739, 805, 862, 915, 917, 929.

769 Non-observance

N. *non-observance,* no such practice; inobservance, informality, indifference 734n. *laxity;* inattention, omission, laches 458n. *negligence;* non-conformity, non-adherence 84n. *unconformity;* abhorrence 607n. *rejection;* antinomianism, anarchism 734n. *anarchy;* non-performance, non-feasance 679n. *inactivity;* non-fulfillment, shortcoming 726n. *non-completion;* infringement, violation, transgression 306n. *overstepping;* non-compliance, disloyalty 738n. *disobedience;* protest 762n. *deprecation;* disregard, discourtesy 921n. *disrespect;* bad faith, breach of f., breach of promise 930n. *perfidy;* retractation 603n. *tergiversation;* repudiation, denial 533n. *negation;* failure, bankruptcy 805n. *insolvency;* forfeiture 963n. *penalty.*

Adj. *non-observant,* non-practicing; non-conforming, standing out, blacklegging, non-adhering, nonconformist 84adj. *unconformable;* inattentive to, disregarding, neglectful 458adj. *negligent;* unprofessional, uncanonical, misbehaving; indifferent, informal 734adj. *lax;* non-compliant 738adj. *disobedient;* transgressive, infringing, unlawful 954adj. *lawbreaking;* disloyal 918adj. *dutiless;* unfaithful 930adj. *perfidious;* antinomian, anarchical 734adj. *anarchic.*

Vb. *not observe,* not practice, abhor 607vb. *reject;* not conform, not adhere, not follow, stand out 84vb. *be unconformable;* discard 674vb. *disuse;* set aside 752vb. *abrogate;* omit, ignore 458vb. *neglect;* disregard, slight, show no respect for, snap one's fingers at 921vb. *not respect;* stretch a point 734vb. *be lax;* violate, do violence to 176vb. *force;* transgress 306vb. *overstep;* not comply with 738vb. *disobey;* desert 918vb. *fail in duty;* fail, not come up to scratch 636vb. *not suffice;* perform less than one promised 726vb. *not complete;* break faith, break one's promise, break one's word, neglect one's vow, repudiate one's obligations, dishonor 533vb. *negate;* not stand by one's engagement, go back on, back out 603vb. *tergiversate;* prove unreliable 930vb. *be dishonest;* give the go-by, cut, shirk, dodge, evade, elude 620 vb. *avoid;* shuffle, palter, quibble,

resort to shifts, equivocate 518vb. *be equivocal;* forfeit, incur a penalty 963vb. *be punished.*
See: 84, 176, 306, 458, 518, 533, 603, 607, 620, 636, 674, 679, 726, 734, 738, 752, 762, 805, 918, 921, 930, 954, 963.

770 Compromise

N. *compromise,* non-insistence, concession; mutual concession, give and take, adjustment, formula 765n. *compact;* composition, commutation; second best, pis aller 35n. *inferiority;* modus vivendi, working arrangement 624n. *way;* middle term, splitting the difference 30n. *average;* halfway 625n. *mid-course;* balancing act.

Vb. *compromise,* make a c., find a formula, find a basis; make mutual concessions, give and take, meet one halfway 625vb. *be halfway;* live and let live, not insist, stretch a point 734vb. *be lax;* strike an average, take the mean, go half and half, split the difference 30vb. *average out;* compound, commute; compose differences, adjust d., arbitrate, go to arbitration; patch up, bridge over 719vb. *pacify;* take the good with the bad, take what is offered, make a virtue of necessity, take the will for the deed; make the best of a bad job.
See: 30, 35, 624, 625, 719, 734, 765.

771 Acquisition

N. *acquisition,* getting, winning; breadwinning, earning; acquirement, obtainment, procurement, milking; collection 74n. *assemblage;* realization, profit-taking 793n. *sale;* conversion, encashment 780n. *transfer;* money-getting, money-grubbing 816 n. *avarice;* heap, stack, pile, pool, scoop, jackpot 74n. *accumulation;* trove, finding, picking up 484n. *discovery;* finding again, recovery, retrieval, revendication, recoupment, reentrance, replevin 656n. *restoration;* redemption 792n. *purchase;* getting hold of 786n. *taking;* subreption, theft 788n. *stealing;* coming into, inheritance, heirship, patrimony; thing acquired, acquest, find, trouvaille, windfall, treasure, treasure-trove; something for nothing, free gift 781n. *gift;* gratuity, baksheesh 962n. *reward;* benefit, benefit match, prize, plum 729n. *trophy;* pelf, lucre 797n. *money;* plunder 790n. *booty.*
earnings, income, earned i., wage, salary, screw, pay-packet 804n. *pay;* rate for the job, pay-scale, differential; pension, compensation, "golden handshake"; reward of office, remuneration, emolument 962 n. *reward;* allowance, expense account; pickings, perquisite, perks; cabbage, totting; commission, rake-off 810n. *discount;* return, net r., gross r., receipts, proceeds, sale p., turnover, takings, innings, revenue, taxes 807n. *receipt;* reaping, harvest, vintage, crop, second c., aftermath, gleanings; output, produce 164n. *product.*
gain, thrift, savings 814n. *economy;* no loss, credit side, profit, net p., winnings; dividend, share-out 775n. *participation;* interest, high i., compound i., simple i. 36n. *increment;* paying transaction, profitable t., lucrative deal, successful speculation, main chance; increase of pay, enhanced salary, rise, raise 36n. *increase;* advantage, benefit; selfish advantage, personal benefit 932n. *selfishness.*

Adj. *acquiring,* acquisitive, accumulative; on the make, getting, winning; hoarding, saving.
gainful, paying, profitable, lucrative, remunerative 962adj. *rewarding;* advantageous 644adj. *beneficial;* fruitful, fertile 164adj. *productive;* not honorary, attended with pay, paid, remunerated, breadwinning.
acquired, had, got, gotten, ill-gotten; inherited, patrimonial; on the credit side.

Vb. *acquire,* get, come by; get by effort, earn, gain, obtain, procure, get at; find, strike, come across, pick up, pitch upon, light u. 484 vb. *discover;* get hold of, get possession of, get in one's hand, get between finger and thumb; make one's own, annex 786vb. *appropriate;* win, capture, catch, land, net, bag 786vb. *take;* pick, tot, glean; gather, reap, crop, harvest; derive, draw, tap, milk, mine 304vb. *extract;* collect, accumulate, heap, pile up 74vb. *bring together;* collect funds, raise, levy, raise the wind; save, save up, hoard 632vb. *store;* get by purchase, buy, preempt 792vb. *purchase;* get in advance, reserve, book, engage, preengage 135vb. *be early;* get somehow, beg, borrow or steal; get a living, earn a l., win one's bread; get money, draw a salary, draw a pension, receive one's wages, be paid one's hire; have an income, be in receipt of, have a turnover, gross, take 782vb. *receive;* turn into money, convert, cash, encash, realize; get back, come by one's own, recover, regain, redeem, recapture, reconquer 656vb. *retrieve;* take back, resume, reassume, reclaim, reenter; compensate oneself, recover one's losses 31vb. *recoup;* recover one's costs, break even, balance accounts 28vb. *equalize;* attain, reach; come in for, catch, incur, contract.

inherit, come into, be left, receive a legacy, enjoy an inheritance, take one's patrimony; succeed, succeed to, step into the shoes of, be the heir of.

gain, profit, make a p., draw a p., reap a p., earn a dividend; make, win; make money, coin m., make a fortune, make one's pile, rake in the shekels, turn a pretty penny 800vb. *get rich;* scoop, make a s., win, win the jackpot, break the bank; see one's advantage, sell at a profit; draw one's interest, collect one's profit, credit to one's account.

be profitable, profit, repay, be worthwhile 640vb. *be useful;* pay, pay well; bring in, gross, yield 164vb. *produce;* bring in a return, pay a dividend, show a profit 730vb. *prosper;* accrue, roll in, come into the till, bring grist to the mill, stick to one's fingers.

See: 28, 31, 36, 74, 135, 164, 304, 484, 632, 644, 656, 729, 730, 775, 780, 781, 782, 786, 792, 793, 797, 800, 804, 807, 810, 814, 816, 932, 962.

772 Loss

N. *loss*, deprivation, privation, bereavement, funeral; dispossession, eviction 786n. *expropriation;* sacrifice, forfeiture, forfeit, lapse; hopeless loss, dead l., total l., utter l., irretrievable l., perdition, deperdition 165n. *ruin;* depreciation 655n. *deterioration;* diminishing returns 42 n. *decrement;* set-back, check, reverse; loss of profit, lack of p.; overdraft, failure, bankruptcy 805n. *insolvency;* consumption 806n. *expenditure;* nonrecovery, spilled milk, wastage, leakage 634n. *waste;* dissipation, evaporation, drain, running sore 37n. *decrease;* riddance, good r. 746n. *liberation;* losing battle 728n. *defeat.*

Adj. losing, unprofitable 641adj. *profitless;* squandering 815adj. *prodigal;* the worse for 655adj. *deteriorated;* forfeiting, sacrificing, sacrificial; deprived, dispossessed, robbed 774adj. *unpossessed;* denuded, stripped of, shorn of, reft of, bereft, bereaved; minus, without, lacking; rid of, quit of; set back, out of pocket, down, in the red, overdrawn, bankrupt, insolvent 805adj. *non-paying;* nonprofitmaking 931adj. *disinterested.*

lost, long l., gone, gone for ever; missing, mislaid 188adj. *misplaced;* untraced, untraceable, lost, stolen or strayed 190adj. *absent;* rid, off one's hands; wanting, lacking, short 307adj. *deficient;* irrecoverable, irretrievable, irredeemable, spent, wasted, gone down the drain, squandered 806adj. *expended;* forfeit, forfeited, sacrificed.

Vb. lose, not find, be unable to f., look in vain for; mislay 188vb. *misplace;* miss, let slip, let slip through one's fingers, say good-bye to 138 vb. *lose a chance;* have nothing to show for, squander, throw away 634vb. *waste;* deserve to lose, forfeit, sacrifice; spill the milk, allow to leak, let go down the drain; not improve matters, be the worse for 832vb. *aggravate;* be a loser 728vb. *be defeated;* lose one's stake, lose one's bet, pay out, pay the table; make no profit, be down, be out of pocket; be set back, incur losses, meet with l., sell at a loss; be unable to pay, break, go bankrupt 805vb. *not pay;* overdraw, be overdrawn, be in the red, be minus.

be lost, be missing, be declared m., lose one's way 282vb. *stray;* lapse, go down the drain, go down the spout, go to pot 165vb. *be destroyed;* melt away, never return 446vb. *disappear;* be a good riddance 831vb. *relieve.*

See: 37, 42, 138, 165, 188, 190, 282, 307, 446, 634, 641, 655, 728, 746, 774, 786, 801, 805, 806, 815, 831, 832, 931.

773 Possession

N. *possession*, right of p., de jure p., ownership, proprietorship, rightful possession, lawful p., peaceful p., enjoyment, uti possidetis; seisin, occupancy, nine points of the law, bird in the hand; mastery, hold, grasp, grip, de facto possession 778n. *retention;* a possession 777n. *property;* tenancy, holding 777n. *estate;* tenure, fee, fief, feud, feodality, seigniory, knight service, chivalry, socage, villenage; long possession, prescription 610n. *habit;* exclusive possession, sole p., monopoly, corner, ring; prepossession, preoccupancy, preemption, forestallment, squatting; future possession, expectations, heirship, heirdom, inheritance, heritage, patrimony, reversion, remaindership; taking possession, impropriation, engrossment, making one's own, claiming, hoisting one's flag over 786n. *taking.*

Adj. *possessing,* seized of, having, holding, owning, enjoying etc.vb.; having possessions, propertied; possessed of, in possession, occupying, squatting; endowed with, blessed w., fraught w., instinct w.; exclusive, monopolistic, possessive.

possessed, enjoyed, had, held; in the possession of, in the ownership of, in one's hand, in one's grasp, in one's hold; in the bank, in one's account, to one's credit; at one's disposal, on hand, in store; proper, personal 80adj. *special;* belonging, one's own, one's very o., unshared, private, personal; monopolized by, engrossed by, devoured by; booked, reserved, engaged, occupied; included in, inherent, appertaining, attaching; unsold, undisposed of, on one's hands.

Vb. *possess,* be possessed of, own, have; die possessed of, cut up well 780vb. *bequeath;* hold, have and hold, have a firm grip on, hold in one's grasp, grip 778vb. *retain;* have at one's command, have absolute disposal of, command 673vb. *dispose of;* call oneself owner, boast of 915vb. *claim;* contain, include 78 vb. *comprise;* fill, occupy; squat, sit on, settle upon, inhabit; enjoy, have for one's own 673vb. *use;* have all to oneself, be a dog in the manger, monopolize, engross, corner; get, take possession, make one's own, impropriate 786vb. *take;* recover, reoccupy, reenter 656vb. *retrieve;* preoccupy, forestall, preempt, reserve, book, engage 135vb. *be early;* inherit, come into, come in for, step into, succeed 771vb. *acquire.*

belong, vest, vest in, belong to; be included in, inhere, attach, pertain, appertain, apply; be subject to, owe service to 745vb. *be subject.*

Adv. *possessively,* monopolistically; in one's own right, in full ownership, by right of possession, by prescription.

See: 78, 80, 135, 191, 610, 656, 673, 745, 771, 777, 778, 780, 786, 915.

774 Non-ownership

N. *non-ownership,* non-possession, non-occupancy; tenancy at will, temporary lease; dependence 745n. *subjection;* pauperism 801n. *poverty;* loss of possession 57n. *exclusion;* deprivation, disentitlement 772n. *loss;* exemption, dispensation 919n. *non-liability;* no man's land, debatable territory, Tom Tiddler's ground 184n. *territory.*

Adj. *not owning,* not possessing, dependent 745adj. *subject;* owning nothing, destitute, penniless, propertyless 801adj. *poor;* unblessed with, barren; lacking, minus, without 627 adj. *required;* dispossessed, disentitled 57adj. *excluded.*

unpossessed, unattached, not belonging; masterless, ownerless, nobody's, no man's; international; not owned, unowned, unappropriated; unclaimed, disowned; unheld, unoccupied, untenanted, unleased; vacant 190adj. *empty;* derelict, abandoned 779adj. *not retained;* ungot, unhad, unobtained, unacquired, untaken, going begging 860adj. *unwanted.*

See: 52, 57, 184, 190, 627, 745, 772, 779, 801, 860, 919.

775 Joint Possession

N. *joint possession,* jointness, possession in common; joint tenancy, tenancy in common; gavel-kind; joint ownership, common o.; public property, public domain 777n. *property;* joint government, condominium 733 n. *polity;* joint stock, common stock, pool, kitty 632n. *store;* cooperative system, mutualization, mutualism 706n. *cooperation;* public ownership, state o., socialism, communism, collectivism; community of possessions, community of women; collective farm, collective, kolkhoz, kibbutz 370n. *farm;* share-cropping, métayage.

participation, membership, affiliation 78n. *inclusion;* sharing, cosharing, partnership, copartnership, profit-sharing 706n. *association;* joint mess, syssitia; Dutch party, picnic; dividend, share-out; share, fair s., coportion, lot, whack 783n. *portion;* complicity, involvement, sympathy; fellow-feeling, sympathetic strike, joint action.

participator, member, cosharer, partner, copartner, sharer, coparcener, coheir, joint h,; shareholder, stockholder 776n. *possessor;* cotenant, joint t., tenants in common; sharecropper, métayer 370n. *husbandman;* cooperator, mutualist; collectivist, socialist, communist; sympathizer 707n. *patron.*

Adj. *sharing*, cosharing, joint, profit-sharing, cooperative; common, communal, international; collective, socialistic, communistic; partaking, participating, participatory, in on, involved, in the same boat; in the swim, in the thick of things; sympathetic, condoling.

Vb. *participate*, have a hand in, join in, be in on 706vb. *cooperate;* partake of, share in, take a share, come in for a s.; snack, share, go shares, go snacks, go halves, go fifty-fifty, share and share alike 783 vb. *apportion;* share expenses, go Dutch 804vb. *defray.*

socialize, mutualize, nationalize, internationalize, communize; have in common, put in the kitty, pool, throw in to the common p., hold in common, have all in c., live in joint mess.

Adv. *in common*, by shares, share and share alike; jointly, collectively, unitedly.

See: 78, 370, 632, 706, 707, 733, 776, 777, 783, 804.

776 Possessor

N. *possessor*, holder, person in possession, impropriator; taker, captor, conqueror; trespasser, squatter; monopolizer, dog in the manger; occupant, lodger, occupier, incumbent; mortgagee, bailee, trustee; renter, hirer, lessee, lease-holder, copyholder, rent-payer; tenantry, tenant, tenant-at-will, tenant for life; householder, freeholder, franklin, yeoman; feudatory, feoffee, tenant in fee, vassal 742n. *dependent;* peasant, actual cultivator of the soil, serf, villein, kulak, mujhik, ryot, zamindar 370n. *husbandman;* sublessee, under-tenant, korfa ryot.

owner, monarch, monarch of all one surveys; master, mistress, proprietor, proprietress; purchaser, vendee, buyer 792n. *purchaser;* lord, lord paramount, lord of the manor, mesne lord, feoffer; landed gentry, landed interest 868n. *aristocracy;* man of property, property-owner, property-holder, shareholder, stockholder, landholder, zamindar, landowner, landlord, landlady; mortgagor; testator, testatrix, bequeather, devisor 781n. *giver.*

beneficiary, cestui que trust, cestui que vie; feoffee, releasee, grantee, patentee; impropriator, lay i. 782n. *recipient;* incumbent 986n. *cleric;* devisee, legatee, legatary; inheritor, heritor, successor, successor apparent, tanist; next of kin 11n. *kinsman;* heir, expectant, expectant heir, heiress, "lady richly left"; heir of the body, heir-at-law, heir general, heir male, heir apparent, heir presumptive; crown prince 741n. *sovereign;* reversioner, remainderman; tertius gaudens; coheir, joint heir, cosharer 775n. *participator.*

See: 11, 370, 741, 742, 775, 781, 782, 792, 868, 986.

777 Property

N. *property*, meum et tuum, suum cuique; possession, possessions, one's all; stake, venture; personalty, personal property, public p., common p.; church property, temporalities; chose in possession, chattel, real property, movables, immovables; goods and chattels, parcels, appurtenances, belongings, paraphernalia, effects, personal e., impedimenta, baggage, luggage, traps, things; cargo, lading 193n. *contents;* goods, wares, stock, stock-in-trade 795n. *merchandise;* plant, fixtures, furniture.

estate, estate and effects, assets, frozen a., liquid a., assets and liabilities; circumstances, what one is worth, what one will cut up for; resources 629n. *means;* substance, one's money, one's gold 800n. *wealth;* revenue, income, rent-roll 807n. *receipt;* valuables, securities, stocks and shares, portfolio; stake, holding, investment; copyright, patent; chose in action, claim, demand, good debts, bad d.; right, title, easement, interest, vested i., contingent i., beneficial i., equitable i., life i.; absolute i., paramount estate; lease, tenure, freehold, copyhold, fee, fee simple, fee tail, estate in tail male, estate in tail female; tenement, hereditament, corporeal h., incorporeal h.

lands, land, acres, broad a.; estate, landed e., property, landed p., zamindar, khas mahall; real estate, real property, realty; hereditament, tenement, holding, tenure, allodium,

freehold, copyhold, fief, feud, manor, honor, seigniory, lordship, domain, demesne; messuage, capital m.; farm, home f., ranch, hacienda; crown lands, folk l., common land, common; dependency, dominion, state 184n. *territory.*
dower, dowry, dot, portion, marriage p., jointure, settlement, peculium; allotment, allowance, pin-money; alimony, patrimony, birthright 915n. *dueness;* appanage, heritage; inheritance, legacy, bequest; expectations, remainder, reversion; limitation, strict settlement, estate for life, estate for years; heirloom.
Adj. *proprietary*, branded, patented; movable, immovable, real, personal; propertied, landed, praedial, manorial, seignorial, feudal, feodal, allodial, freehold, leasehold, copyhold; patrimonial, hereditary, heritable, testamentary; entailed, limited; dowered, endowed, established.
Vb. dower, endow, possess with, bless w. 781vb. *give;* devise 780vb. *bequeath;* grant, assign, allot 780vb. *convey;* possess, put in possession, install 751vb. *commission;* establish, found.
Adv. *at credit*, in one's account; to one's heirs and successors.
See: 184, 193, 629, 751, 780, 781, 795, 800, 807, 915.

778 Retention

N. *retention*, prehensility, tenacity; stickiness 354n. *viscidity;* holding on, hanging on, clinging to, prehension; handhold, foothold, toe-hold 218n. *support;* bridge-head, beach-head 34 n. *vantage;* clutches, grip, iron g., gripe, grasp, hold, firm h., stranglehold, half-nelson; squeeze 198n. *compression;* clinch, lock; clip, hug, embrace 889n. *endearment;* keep, ward, keeping in 747n. *detention;* containment, holding action, pincer movement 235n. *enclosure;* plug, stop 264n. *stopper;* ligament 47n. *bond.*
nippers, pincers, tweezers, pliers, wrench, tongs, forceps, vise, clamp 47n. *fastening;* talon, claw, nails 256n. *sharp point;* tentacle, tenaculum 378n. *feeler;* teeth, fangs 256 n. *tooth;* paw, hand, fingers 378n. *finger;* fist, clenched f., nieve.
Adj. *retentive*, retaining 747adj. *restraining;* clinging, adhesive, sticky, gummy, gooey 48adj. *cohesive;* firm, unshakable, indissoluble 45adj. *tied;* tight, strangling, throttling; costive, bound; fast shut 264adj. *closed.*
retained, in the grip of, gripped, pinned, clutched, strangled; fast, held; kept in, detained 747adj. *imprisoned;* penned, held in, contained 232adj. *circumscribed;* saved, kept 666adj. *preserved;* booked, reserved, engaged; undisposed of, unsold, not for sale; unforfeited, undeprived; kept back, withheld 760adj. *refused;* uncommunicated, esoteric, incommunicable 523adj. *occult;* non-transferable, inalienable; entailed, in mortmain, in strict settlement.
Vb. *retain*, hold; hold up, catch, steady 218vb. *support;* hold on, hold fast, hold tight, keep a firm hold of, maintain one's hold; cling to, hang on to, freeze on to, stick to, adhere 48vb. *agglutinate;* fasten on, grip, gripe, grasp, clench, clinch, lock; hug, clip, embrace; pin, pin down, hold d.; have by the throat, throttle, strangle, keep a stranglehold on, put the half-nelson on, tighten one's grip 747vb. *restrain;* fix one's teeth in, dig one's nails in, dig one's toes in; keep in, detain 747vb. *imprison;* contain, keep within limits, draw the line 235vb. *enclose;* keep to oneself, keep in one's own hands, keep back, withhold 525vb. *keep secret;* keep in one's hand, have in hand, not dispose of 632vb. *store;* save, keep 666vb. *preserve;* not part with, keep back, withhold 760vb. *refuse.*
See: 34, 45, 47, 48, 198, 218, 232, 235, 256, 264, 354, 378, 523, 525, 632, 666, 747, 760, 889.

779 Non-retention

N. *non-retention*, parting with, disposal, alienation 780n. *transfer;* selling off 793n. *sale;* letting go, leaving hold of, release 746n. *liberation;* unfreezing, decontrol; dispensation, exemption 919n. *non-liability;* dissolution (of a marriage) 896n. *divorce;* cession, abandonment, renunciation 621n. *relinquishment;* cancellation 752n. *abrogation;* disuse 611n. *desuetude;* availability, salability, disposability; unsoundness, leaking, leak 298n. *outflow.*
derelict, deserted village, abandoned position; jetsam, flotsam 641n. *rubbish;* cast-off, slough; waif, stray, foundling, orphan, maroon; outcaste, untouchable.
Adj. *not retained*, not kept, under notice to quit; alienated, disposed of, sold off; dispensed with, aban-

doned 621adj. *relinquished;* released 746adj. *liberated;* derelict, unclaimed, unappropriated; unowned 774adj. *unpossessed;* disowned, divorced, disinherited; heritable, inheritable, transferable; available, for sale 793 n. *salable;* givable, bestowable.

Vb. *not retain,* part with, alienate, transfer 780vb. *convey;* sell off, dispose of 793vb. *sell;* let go, let slip, unhand, leave hold of, relax one's grip, release one's hold; unlock, unclinch, unclench 263vb. *open;* unbind, untie, disentangle 46vb. *disjoin;* forego, dispense with, do without, spare, give up, waive, abandon, cede, yield 621vb. *relinquish;* renounce, abjure 603vb. *recant;* cancel, revoke 752vb. *abrogate;* lift, lift restrictions, derestrict, decontrol, deration 746vb. *liberate;* supersede, replace 150vb. *substitute;* wash one's hands of, disown, disclaim 533vb. *negate;* dissolve (a marriage) 896 vb. *divorce;* disinherit, cut off with a shilling 801vb. *impoverish;* marry off 894vb. *marry;* get rid of, cast off, ditch, jettison 300vb. *eject;* cast away, maroon; pension off, invalid out, retire; discharge, give notice to quit, ease out, kick o. 300vb. *dismiss;* lay off, stand o.; drop, discard 674vb. *disuse;* withdraw, abandon one's position 753vb. *resign;* lose friends, estrange 881vb. *make enemies;* sit loose to 860vb. *be indifferent;* let out, leak 300vb. *emit.*

See: 46, 150, 263, 298, 300, 533, 603, 611, 621, 641, 674, 746, 752, 753, 774, 780, 793, 801, 860, 881, 894, 896, 919.

780 Transfer (of property)

N. *transfer,* transmission, consignment, delivery, livery, hand-over 272 n. *transference;* enfeoffment, feoffment, livery of seisin; impropriation; settlement, limitation; conveyancing, conveyance; bequeathal, testamentary disposition; assignment; alienation, abalienation 779n. *non-retention;* demise, devise, bequest 781n. *gift;* lease, let, lease and release; bargain and sale 793n. *sale;* trade 791n. *barter;* conversion, exchange 151n. *interchange;* change of hands, change-over 150n. *substitution;* shifting use, shifting trust; devolution, delegation 751n. *commission;* heritability, succession, reversion, inheritance; pledge, pawn, hostage.

Adj. *transferred,* made over, impropriated, feoffed; borrowed, lent, pawned, leased; transferable, conveyable, alienable, exchangeable, negotiable; heritable, reversional, reversionary; givable, bestowable.

Vb. *convey,* transfer by deed; transfer by will (**see** *bequeath*); grant, assign, sign away, give a. 781vb. *give;* demise, let, rent, hire 784vb. *lease;* alienate, abalienate 793vb. *sell;* negotiate, barter 791vb. *trade;* change over 150vb. *substitute;* exchange, convert 151vb. *interchange;* confer, confer ownership, put in possession, impropriate, invest with, enfeoff; confer citizenship, naturalize; commit, devolve, delegate, entrust 751vb. *commission;* give away, marry off 894vb. *marry;* deliver, give delivery, transmit, hand over, make o., pass to, pass the buck 272vb. *transfer;* pledge, pawn 784 vb. *lend;* leave to 756vb. *permit;* transfer ownership, withdraw a gift, give to another; disinherit, cut off, cut off with a shilling 801vb. *impoverish;* dispossess, expropriate, relieve of 786vb. *deprive;* transfer to the state, nationalize, municipalize 775vb. *socialize.*

bequeath, will, will and bequeath, devise, demise; grant, assign; leave, leave by will, make a bequest, leave a legacy; make a will, make one's last will and testament, put in one's will, make testamentary dispositions, add a codicil; leave a fortune, cut up well 800vb. *be rich;* have something to leave.

change hands, pass to another, come into the hands of; change places 151vb. *interchange;* be transferred, pass, shift; revert to, devolve upon; pass from one to another, pass from hand to hand, circulate, go the rounds 314vb. *circle;* succeed, inherit 771n. *acquire.*

See: 150, 151, 272, 314, 751, 756, 771, 775, 779, 781, 784, 786, 791, 793, 800, 801, 894.

781 Giving

N. *giving,* bestowal, donation; almsgiving, charity 901n. *philanthropy;* generosity, generous giving, habit of g. 813n. *liberality;* contribution, subscription to 703n. *subvention;* prize-giving, presentation, award 962n. *reward;* delivery, commitment, consignment, conveyance 780n. *transfer;* endowment, dotation, settlement 777 n. *dower;* grant, accordance, presentment, conferment; investment, investiture, enfeoffment, infeudation; bequeathal, leaving, will-making.

gift, fairing, cadeau, present, birthday p., Christmas p.; good-luck present, handsel; Christmas box, tip, vail, bribe, fee, honorarium, baksheesh, gratuity, sweetener, douceur, pourboire, trinkgeld, drink money 962n. *reward;* token, consideration; prize, award, presentation 729n. *trophy;* benefit, benefit match, benefit performance; alms, maundy money, dole, benefaction, charity 901n. *philanthropy;* sportula, food parcel, free meal; bounty, manna; largess, donation, donative, hand-out; bonus, bonus shares, bonanza; something extra, extras, gracemarks; perks, perquisites, expense account; grant, allowance, compassionate a.; subsidy 703n. *subvention;* boon, grace, favor, grace and f.; unremunerated service, labor of love 597n. *voluntary work;* free gift, outright g., ex gratia payment; piece of luck, windfall; repayment, unsolicited r., conscience-money 804n. *payment;* forced loan, benevolence, tribute 809n. *tax;* bequest, legacy 780n. *transfer.*

offering, dedication, consecration; votive-offering, vow 979n. *piety;* peace-offering, thank-o., offertory, collection, sacrifice, self-s. 981n. *oblation;* Easter-offering, widow's mite; contribution, subscription, flag-day; tribute, free t., Peter's pence; offering of land, bhoodan; ante, stake.

giver, donor, bestower; rewarder, tipper; grantor, feoffer, investor; presenter, awarder, prize-giver; settlor, testator, devisor, bequeather; donator, subscriber, contributor; sacrificer, oblationer 981n. *worshiper;* tributary, tribute-payer 742n. *subject;* almoner, lady a., almsgiver, blood-donor 903n. *benefactor;* generous giver, distributor of largess, Lady Bountiful, rich uncle, Santa Claus, Father Christmas 813n. *good giver.*

Adj. *giving*, granting etc.vb.; tributary 745adj. *subject;* subscribing, contributory 703adj. *aiding;* almsgiving, charitable, eleemosynary, compassionate 897adj. *benevolent;* sacrificial, votive, sacrificing, oblatory 981adj. *worshiping;* generous, bountiful 813adj. *liberal.*

given, bestowed, gifted; given away, gratuitous, gratis, for nothing, free 812adj. *uncharged;* givable, bestowable, allowed, allowable, concessional 756adj. *permitted.*

Vb. give, bestow, lend, render; afford, provide; vouchsafe, favor with, honor w., indulge w., show favor, grant a boon 736vb. *be lenient;* grant, accord 756vb. *permit;* gift, donate, make a present of; give by will, leave, devise, make legacies 780vb. *bequeath;* dower, endow, enrich; give a prize, present, award 962vb. *reward;* confer, bestow upon, vest, invest with; dedicate, consecrate, vow to 759vb. *offer;* devote, offer up, immolate, sacrifice 981vb. *offer worship;* spare for, have time for; give a present, gratify, tip, consider, remember; grease the palm 612vb. *bribe;* bestow alms, make a benefaction, put in the collection 897vb. *philanthropize;* give freely, open one's hand, open one's purse, put one's hand in one's pocket, lavish, pour out, shower upon 813 vb. *be liberal;* spare, give free, give away, not charge; stand, treat, entertain 882vb. *be hospitable;* give out, dispense, dole out, mete o., share o., allot, deal, deal to 783vb. *apportion;* contribute, subscribe, pay towards, subsidize, help, help with money 703vb. *aid;* pay one's share *or* whack, ante up, divvy up 775vb. *participate;* part with, fork out 804 vb. *pay;* share, share with, impart 524vb. *communicate;* render one's due, furnish one's quota 917vb. *do one's duty;* give one his due 915vb. *grant claims;* pay tribute 923vb. *praise;* give up, cede, yield 621vb. *relinquish;* hand over, give o., make o., deliver 780vb. *convey;* commit, consign, entrust 751vb. *commission;* dispatch 272vb. *send.*

See: 272, 524, 597, 612, 621, 703, 729, 736, 742, 745, 751, 756, 759, 775, 777, 780, 783, 804, 809, 812, 813, 882, 897, 901, 903, 915, 917, 923, 962, 979, 981.

782 Receiving

N. *receiving*, admittance 299n. *reception;* getting 771n. *acquisition;* acceptance, recipience, suscipience, assumption; inheritance, succession, heirship; collection, collectorship, receivership, receipt of custom; a receipt, windfall 781n. *gift;* toll, tribute, dues, receipts, proceeds, winnings, gettings, takings 771n. *earnings;* receiving end.

recipient, acceptor, taker, biter; trustee 754n. *consignee;* addressee 588n. *correspondent;* buyer, vendee 792n. *purchaser;* transferee, donee, grantee, feoffee, assignee, allottee, licensee, patentee, concessionaire, lessee, releasee; devisee, legatee, legatary, inheritor, heir, successor 776n. *beneficiary;* payee, earner, stipendiary, wage-earner; pensioner, old-age p., pensionary, annuitant; remittanceman 742n. *dependent;* winner, prize-w., scholarship-holder, exhibitioner, sizar 644n. *exceller;* free-ticket-holder, deadhead; object of charity, sportulary 763n. *beggar;* almsman, beadsman; one at the receiving end, receiver, striker (tennis), batter, batsman (cricket).

receiver, official r., liquidator 798n. *treasurer;* payee, collector, bill-c., rent-c., tax-c., tax-farmer, publican, income-tax officer, excise o., excisemen, customs officer, douanier; booking-clerk; shareholder, bondholder, rentier; oblationary.

Adj. *receiving,* recipient, suscipient; receptive, welcoming; impressionable 819adj. *sensitive;* receiving pay, paid, stipendiary, wage-earning; pensionary, pensioned; awarded, given, favored.

Vb. *receive,* be given, have from; get 771vb. *acquire;* collect, take up, levy, toll, take its t. 786vb. *take;* gross, net, pocket, pouch; be in receipt of, have received; get one's share; be dealt a hand; accept, take in 299vb. *admit;* accept from, take f., draw, encash, be paid; have an income, draw a pension; inherit, succeed, come into, come in for; receipt, give a r., acknowledge.

be received, be drawn, be receipted; be credited, be added unto 38vb. *accrue;* come to hand, come in, roll in, fill the till; pass into one's hands, stick to one's fingers, fall to one's share, fall to one's lot.

See: 38, 299, 588, 644, 742, 754, 763, 771, 776, 781, 786, 792, 798, 819.

783 Apportionment

N. *apportionment,* appointment, assignment, allotment, allocation, appropriation; division, partition, repartition, sharing out; shares, fair s., distribution, deal, new d.; dispensing, dispensation, administration; demarcation, delimitation 236n. *limit;* place, assigned p., allotted sphere, seat, station 27n. *degree;* public sector, private s.

portion, share, share-out, cut, split; dividend, interim d., final d.; allocation, allotment, budget a., block a., blanket a.; lot, contingent; proportion, ratio; quantum, quota; halves, bigger half, moiety 53n. *part;* deal, hand (at cards); dole, mess, meed, modicum, pittance, allowance; ration, iron rations, ration book, coupon; dose, dosage, measure, dollop, whack, helping, melon-cutting, slice 53n. *piece;* rake-off, commission 810 n. *discount;* stake, ante; allotted task, taskwork, task, stint 682n. *labor.*

Vb. *apportion,* allot, allocate, appropriate; appoint, assign; assign a part, cast, cast for a role; assign a place, detail, billet; partition, zone; demarcate, delimit 236vb. *limit;* divide, divvy, carve, carve up, split, cut; halve 92vb. *bisect;* share, share out, distribute; dispense, administer, serve, deal, deal out, portion out, dole out, parcel out; mete, measure, ration, dose; divide proportionately, prorate; get a share, take one's whack.

Adv. *pro rata,* to each according to his share; proportionately, respectively, each to each, per head, per capita; as dealt.

See: 27, 53, 92, 236, 682, 810.

784 Lending

N. *lending,* hiring, leasing, farming out; letting, subletting, subinfeudation; lending at interest, loan transaction, feneration, usury, giving credit 802n. *credit;* investment; mortgage; advance, imprest, loan, accommodation, temporary a.; lending on security, pawnbroking; lease, long l.; let, sublet.

pawnshop, mont-de-piété, pop-shop, hock s.; house of credit, finance corporation, International Monetary Fund.

lender, creditor; harsh creditor, extortioner; investor, financier, banker, banian; money-lender, usurer, shark, Shylock; pawnbroker, uncle; mortgagee, lessor, hirer, renter; backer, angel; seller on credit, tallyman; hire-purchase dealer.

Adj. *lending,* investing, laying out; usurious, extortionate; lent, loaned, on credit.

Vb. *lend,* loan, put out at interest; advance, accommodate, allow credit, give one an imprest account 802vb. *credit;* lend on security, do pawnbroking; put up the money, back, finance; invest, sink; risk one's money 791vb. *speculate.*

lease, let, demise, let out, hire out,

let out on hire, farm out; sublet, subinfeudate.

Adv. *on loan,* on credit, on advance; on security.

See: 791, 802.

785 Borrowing

N. *borrowing,* touching; request for credit, loan application; loan transaction, mortgage 803n. *debt;* hire purchase, H.P., never-never system; pledging, pawning; temporary misappropriation, joy-ride 788n. *stealing;* something borrowed, loan, repayable amount 784n. *lending;* forced loan, benevolence 809n. *tax;* unauthorized borrowing, infringement, plagiarism, copying 20n. *imitation;* borrowed plumes 542n. *deception;* loan-word.

Vb. *borrow,* borrow short, borrow long; touch, touch for; mortgage, pawn, pledge, pop, hock; take a loan, exact a benevolence; get credit, get accommodation, take on loan, take on credit, take on tick; buy in installments, hire-purchase 792vb. *purchase;* incur liabilities, run into debt 803vb. *be in debt;* promise to pay, ask for credit, apply for a loan, raise a loan, raise the wind, float a loan; invite investment, issue debentures, accept deposits; beg, borrow, or steal; cheat, crib, plagiarize, infringe 20vb. *copy.*

hire, rent, farm, lease, take on lease, take on let, charter.

See: 20, 542, 784, 788, 792, 803, 809.

786 Taking

N. *taking,* snatching; seizure, capture, rape; taking hold, grasp, prehension, apprehension 778n. *retention;* taking possession, assuming ownership, impropriation, appropriation, assumption 916n. *arrogation;* requisition, commandeering, nationalization, municipalization, compulsory acquisition 771n. *acquisition;* compulsory saving, postwar credit, compulsory loan, benevolence 785n. *borrowing;* exaction, taxation, raising taxes, impost, levy, capital l. 809n. *tax;* taking back, recovery, retrieval, recoupment; resumption, reprise, reentry; ablation, taking away; taking in advance, prolepsis 135n. *anticipation;* removal 188n. *displacement;* furtive removal, conveyance 788n. *stealing;* snatching away, abreption; scrounging, totting; bodily removal, abduction, kidnapping, slave-raiding, androlepsy, body-snatching; raid, slave-r. 788n. *spoliation;* thing taken, take, haul, catch, capture, prize, plum 790n. *booty;* receipts, takings, winnings, pickings, gleanings 771n. *earnings.*

expropriation, dispossession, extortion, angary; forcible seizure, attachment, distraint, distress, foreclosure; eviction, expulsion 300n. *ejection;* take-over, deprivation, divestment 752n. *abrogation;* disinheritance, disherison 780n. *transfer;* taking without compensation, confiscation, capital levy; diversion, sequestration.

rapacity, rapaciousness, predacity, thirst for loot; avidity, thirst 859n. *hunger;* greed, insatiable g., insatiability 816n. *avarice;* vampirism, blood-sucking; extortion, blackmail.

taker, appropriator, impropriator, impropriatrix; remover, conveyor; seizer, snatcher, grabber; lifter, spoiler, raider, ransacker, sacker, looter, despoiler, depredator 789n. *robber;* slave-raider, kidnapper, abductor, crimp, press-gang; slave-raider, slaver; captor, capturer 741n. *master;* usurper, arrogator; extortioner, blackmailer; locust, devourer 168n. *destroyer;* bloodsucker, leech, parasite, vampire, harpy, vulture, wolf, shark; beast of prey, predator; confiscator, sequestrator 782n. *receiver;* expropriator, disseisor.

Adj. *taking,* prehensile, clinging 778 adj. *retentive;* abstractive, ablatitious; grasping, extortionate, rapacious, wolfish, lupine, vulturine; harpyian, harpy-ish; devouring, all-d., all-engulfing, voracious, ravening, ravenous 859adj. *hungry;* raptorial, predatory 788adj. *thieving;* privative, expropriatory, confiscatory; commandeering, requisitory; acquisitive, possessive 771adj. *acquiring;* anticipative, proleptic.

Vb. *take,* accept, be given 782vb. *receive;* take over, take back (**see** *appropriate*); take in, let in 299vb. *admit;* take to, bring, fetch 273vb. *carry;* take up, snatch up, lift, raise 310vb. *elevate;* take in advance, anticipate 135vb. *be early;* take hold, fasten on, clutch, grip, cling 778vb. *retain;* lay hands upon, seize, snatch, grab, pounce, pounce on, spring; snatch at, reach, reach out for, make a long arm; grasp at, clutch at, grab at, make a grab, scramble for, rush f.; capture, rape, storm, take by s. 727vb. *overmaster;* conquer, captive, lead c. 745vb. *subjugate;* catch, overtake, intercept

277vb. *outstrip;* apprehend, take into custody, make an arrest, nab, nobble, collar, lay by the heels 747vb. *arrest;* make sure of, fasten, pinion 747vb. *fetter;* hook, fish, angle, trap, snare, lime 542vb. *ensnare;* net, land, bag, pocket, pouch; gross, have a turnover 771vb. *acquire;* gather, accumulate, collect 74vb. *bring together;* cull, pick, pluck; reap, crop, harvest, glean 370vb. *cultivate;* scrounge, tot, scrabble, pick over, rummage, ransack 459vb. *search;* pick up, snap up, snaffle; knock off 788vb. *steal;* pick clean, strip 229vb. *uncover;* remove (**see** *take away*); take out, unload, unlade 188vb. *displace;* draw, draw out, draw off, milk, tap, mine 304vb. *extract;* withdraw (**see** *take away*).

appropriate, take to *or* for oneself, make one's own, spheterize, annex; take possession, stake one's claim; take over, assume, assume ownership, impropriate 773vb. *possess;* enter, enter into, come i., succeed 771vb. *inherit;* install oneself, seat o. 187vb. *place oneself;* overrun, swarm over, people, populate, occupy, settle, colonize; win, conquer; take back, get back one's own, recover, resume, repossess, reenter, recapture, reconquer 656vb. *retrieve;* reclaim 915vb. *claim;* commandeer, requisition 737 vb. *demand;* nationalize, secularize 775vb. *socialize;* usurp, arrogate, jump a claim, trespass, squat 916vb. *be undue;* dispossess (**see** *deprive*); treat as one's own, make free with; monopolize, engross, hog, be a dog in the manger; engulf, suck in, suck up, swallow 299vb. *absorb;* devour, eat up (**see** *fleece*).

levy, raise, extort, exact, wrest from, force f. 304vb. *extract;* exact a benevolence, compel to lend 785vb. *borrow;* exact tribute, make pay, lay under contribution, toll, take one's t.; raise taxes 809vb. *tax;* overtax, rack-rent, suck, suck like a leech (**see** *fleece*); draw off, exhaust, drain, empty 300vb. *void;* wring, squeeze, squeeze to the last drop, squeeze till the pips squeak 735vb. *oppress;* divert resources, sequestrate, make a raid on, raid a fund.

take away, remove, shift, unload 188vb. *displace;* send away 272vb. *send;* lighten 701vb. *disencumber;* convey, abstract, relieve, relieve of 788vb. *steal;* remove bodily, escort 89vb. *accompany;* kidnap, crimp, shanghai, press, impress, abduct, ravish, carry off, bear off, bear away; hurry off with, run away w., run off w., elope w., clear off w. 296vb. *decamp;* raid, loot, plunder 788vb. *rob.*

deprive, bereave, orphan, widow; divest, denude, strip 229vb. *uncover;* unfrock, unthrone 752vb. *depose;* dispossess, usurp 916vb. *disentitle;* disseise, oust, evict, expel 300vb. *eject;* expropriate, compulsorily acquire, impose a capital levy; confiscate, forfeit, sequester, sequestrate, distrain, attach, foreclose; disinherit, cut out of one's will, cut off, cut off with a shilling.

fleece, pluck, skin, shear, gut; strip, strip bare 229vb. *uncover;* blackmail, bleed, bleed white, sponge, suck, suck like a leech, suck dry; devour, eat up, eat out of house and home 301vb. *eat;* take one's all, bankrupt, leave one without a penny *or* cent 801vb. *impoverish.*

See: 74, 89, 135, 168, 187, 188, 191, 229, 272, 273, 277, 296, 299, 300, 301, 304, 310, 370, 459, 542, 656, 701, 727, 735, 737, 741, 745, 747, 752, 771, 773, 775, 778, 780, 782, 785, 788, 789, 790, 801, 809, 816, 859, 915, 916.

787 Restitution

N. *restitution*, giving back, return, reversion, rendition; bringing back, repatriation; reinstatement, reenthronement, reinvestment; rehabilitation 656n. *restoration;* redemption, ransom, rescue 668n. *deliverance;* recuperation, replevin, recovery; compensation, indemnification; repayment, recoupment; refund, reimbursement, disgorgement; indemnity, damages 963n. *penalty;* conscience money 941n. *atonement.*

Adj. *restoring*, restitutory, rendering, refunding; indemnificatory, compensatory 941adj. *atoning.*

Vb. *restitute*, make restitution, return, render, give back 656vb. *restore;* pay up, cough up, disgorge 804vb. *pay;* refund, repay, recoup, reimburse; indemnify, pay an indemnity, pay damages, compensate, make it up to; pay compensation, pay reparations, make reparation, pay conscience-money 941vb. *atone;* bring back, repatriate; ransom, redeem 668vb. *deliver;* reinstate, reinvest, rehabilitate, set up again, raise one to his feet, restore one to favor; recover 656vb. *retrieve.*

See: 656, 668, 804, 941, 963.

788 Stealing

N. *stealing*, thieving, lifting, robbing; theft, larceny, petty l., grand l., compound l.; pilfering, filching, robbing the till, pickpocketing, shoplifting; scrounging, totting; burglary, house-breaking; robbery, highway r., gang r., dacoity, thuggee, latrociny; robbery with violence, stick-up, hold-up, smash-and-grab raid; cattle-lifting, rustling; rape, abduction, kidnapping, androlepsy, man-stealing, plagium, slave-raiding; body-snatching; conveyance, abstraction, removal 786n. *taking;* literary theft, cribbing, plagiary, plagiarism, copyright infringement 20n. *imitation;* temporary misappropriation, joy-ride 785n. *borrowing;* thievery, act of theft; job, fiddle.

brigandage, banditry, outlawry, predacity, piracy, buccaneering, filibustering, filibusterism; privateering, letters of marque 718n. *warfare;* raiding, raid, razzia, foray 712n. *attack.*

spoliation, plundering, looting; plundering expedition, chappow (**see** *brigandage*); direption, sack, sacking; depredation, rapine, ravaging 165n. *havoc.*

peculation, embezzlement, misappropriation, malversation, breach of trust, fraudulent conversion; illegal evasion, fraud, fiddle, swindle, cheating 542n. *deception.*

thievishness, thievery, pickery, light-fingeredness, light fingers, kleptomania; predacity 786n. *rapacity;* dishonesty, unreliability in money matters 930n. *improbity;* burglarious intent, intention to steal; den of thieves, thieves' kitchen, Alsatia.

Adj. *thieving*, in the act of theft; with intent to steal; thievish, light-fingered; kleptomaniac; furacious, furative, larcenous, burglarious; predatory, predacious, raptorial; piratical, buccaneering, filibustering, privateering, raiding, marauding; scounging, foraging; dishonest, fraudulent, unreliable in money matters 930adj. *dishonest.*

Vb. *steal*, lift, thieve, pilfer, shoplift; cabbage, mooch, tot; be light-fingered, sneak, pick pockets, rob the till; pick locks, blow a safe; burgle, burglarize, house-break; rob, relieve of; rifle, sack, clean out; swipe, nobble, nick, pinch, bone, nim, prig, snaffle, snitch, knock off, annex 786vb. *take;* forage, scrounge; lift cattle, rustle, drive off, make off with; abduct, kidnap, crimp, shanghai, press, impress; abstract, convey, purloin, filch; make away with, spirit away; crib, copy, plagiarize, infringe copyright, pirate 20vb. *copy;* smuggle, run, poach, hijack.

defraud, embezzle, peculate, purloin, let stick to one's fingers; fiddle, cook the accounts, commit breach of trust, obtain money on false pretenses; swindle, cheat, diddle, chisel, do out of, bilk 542vb. *deceive;* rook, pigeon, gull, dupe; pluck, skin 786vb. *fleece;* welsh, levant.

rob, rob with violence, commit highway robbery, hold up, stick up, make stand and deliver; raid, smash and grab; rob in gangs, dacoit; pirate, sail under the skull and crossbones, buccaneer, filibuster, pickeer, maraud, reave, reive, go free-booting; foray, forage, scrounge; raid; sweep, ransack; plunder, pillage, loot, sack, put to the s., despoil, ravage, depredate, spoil 165vb. *lay waste;* make a prey of, victimize, blackmail, levy b., extort, screw, squeeze 735vb. *oppress.*

See: 20, 165, 542, 712, 718, 735, 785, 786, 930.

789 Thief

N. *thief*, thieving fraternity, swell mob, light-fingered gentry, den of thieves, Alsatia; crook; branded thief, homo trium litterarum; pickers and stealers, light fingers; stealer, lifter, filcher, purloiner, pilferer, snapper-up of unconsidered trifles; sneaker, sneak thief, shoplifter; pickpocket, swell mobsman, cutpurse, purse-snatcher, bag-s.; cattle-lifter, cattle-thief, rustler; burglar, cat-b., house-breaker, safe-b., safe-blower, cracksman, picklock, yegg, yeggman, peteman; free-trader, fair-t., poacher, smuggler, runner, night-r., gun-r., blockade-r.; abductor, kidnapper, crimp 786n. *taker;* slaver, slave-raider; body-snatcher, resurrectionist; fence, receiver of stolen property; plagiarist, infringer.

robber, robber band, forty thieves; brigand, klepht; ranger, rover, bush-ranger, bandit, outlaw, Robin Hood; footpad, highwayman, knight of the road, land-pirate, road agent, hold-up man, stick-up m.; Dick Turpin, Jack Sheppard, Jonathan Wild; thug, dacoit, gang-robber; gangster, gunman, hijacker; sea robber, sea rover, Viking, pirate, buccaneer, picaroon, corsair, filibuster, privateer; reaver, marauder, pindarri, fedayeen, raider, night-rider, freebooter, moss-trooper, cateran, rapparee; plunderer, pillager, sacker, ravager, spoiler, despoiler, depredator; wrecker; beast of prey, predator.

defrauder, embezzler, peculator, fiddler; defaulter, levanter, welsher, bilker; swindler, sharper, cheat, shark, magsman, chevalier d'industrie 545n. *deceiver;* forger, counterfeiter, coin-clipper.

See: 545, 786.

790 Booty

N. *booty*, spoil, spoils; spoils of war, spolia opima 729n. *trophy;* plunder, loot, pillage; prey, victim, quarry; find, strike, prize, purchase, haul, catch, winnings, takings 771n. *gain;* cabbage, pickings, tottings; stolen article, stolen goods, swag, boodle; moonshine, hooch, contraband; illicit gains, graft, blackmail; dole, grant, pork barrel 703n. *subvention.*

See: 703, 729, 771.

791 Barter

N. *barter*, exchange, chop, swap 151n. *interchange;* exchange of goods, silent trade, truck, truck system, scorse; traffic, trading, dealing, buying and selling, bargain and sale, nundination, mercature; factorage, factorship, brokerage, agiotage, arbitrage, jobbing, stock-jobbing, share-pushing; negotiation, bargaining, hard b., higgling, haggling, horse dealing.

trade, commercial intercourse; free trade, black market; open market, free m. 796n. *mart;* trading, traffic, drug t., white slave t., slaving, slave-trade, slave dealing; mercantilism, merchantry; capitalism, free economy, laisser faire 744n. *freedom;* market economy, boom and bust 317n. *fluctuation;* profit-making, mutual profit; commerce, business affairs 622n. *business;* private enterprise, state e., state trading; private sector, public s.; venture, business v. 672n. *undertaking;* speculation 618n. *gambling;* transaction, commercial t., deal, business d., bargain, negotiation 765n. *compact;* clientele, custom 792n. *purchase.*

Adj. *trading*, trafficking, exchanging; commercial, commercialistic, mercantile; mercantilist; wholesale, retail; exchangeable, marketable, merchantable 793adj. *salable;* for profit 618adj. *speculative.*

Vb. *trade*, exchange 151vb. *interchange;* barter, chop, swap, truck, scorse; nundinate, traffic, merchandise; buy and sell, buy cheap and sell dear, export and import; open a trade, drive a t., merchant 622vb. *do business;* traffic in, deal in, handle; turn over, turn over one's stock 793vb. *sell;* commercialize, put on a business footing; trade with, do business w., deal w., have dealings w., open an account w.; finance, back, promote; look to one's profit, have an eye to business, go out for trade; be a thorough businessman, know the price of everything and the value of nothing.

speculate, venture, risk 618vb. *gamble;* invest, sink one's capital in, employ one's capital; give a sprat to catch a whale, rig the market, racketeer, profiteer; black-market, deal in the b., sell under the counter; deal in futures, dabble in shares, play the market, go a bust; go on the stock exchange, operate, bull, bear, stag.

bargain, negotiate, chaffer, cheap, cheapen; beat up, beat down; merchant, huckster, haggle, higgle, dicker 766vb. *make terms;* bid for, make a bid, make a take-over bid, preempt; raise the bid, outbid 759vb. *offer;* overbid 482vb. *overrate;* underbid 483vb. *underestimate;* stickle, stickle for, hold out for, state one's terms, ask for, charge 766vb. *give terms;* drive a bargain, do a deal, shake hands on 765vb. *contract;* settle for, take.

Adv. *in trade*, commerce, in business, on 'change; across the counter, under the counter.

See: 151, 317, 482, 483, 618, 622, 672, 744, 759, 765, 766, 792, 793, 796.

792 Purchase

N. *purchase*, emption; buying up, coemption, cornering, forestalling, preemption; redemption, ransom 668n. *deliverance;* purchase on account, purchase on credit 785n. *borrowing;* hire purchase, never-never system; buying, shopping, window-s., spending on, shopping spree 806n. *expenditure;* regular buying, custom, patronage, demand 627n. *requirement;* buying over, bribery 612n. *inducement;* bid, take-over b. 759n. *offer;* first refusal, right of purchase; a purchase, buy, good b., bargain, real b., something worth buying; purchases, shopping list, requirements.

purchaser, buyer, emptor, coemptor, preemptor; vendee, transferee, consignee; hire purchaser, hirer, renter, leaser, lessee; buyer of labor, employer; marketer, shopper, window-s.; customer, patron, client, clientele, consumer; offerer, bidder, by-b., highest b.; taker, acceptor; bargainer, higgler, haggler; ransomer, redeemer; share-buyer, bull, stag.

Adj. *bought*, paid for, ransomed, redeemed; purchased, bribed; emptional, purchasable, bribable; worth buying 644adj. *valuable.*

buying, purchasing, shopping, marketing; coemptive, preemptive, redemptive; bidding, bargaining, haggling; bullish.

Vb. *purchase*, make a p., complete a p.; buy, acquire by purchase 771 vb. *acquire;* shop, window-s., market, go shopping; have a shopping list 627vb. *require;* make a good buy, get one's money's worth; buy outright, buy over the counter, pay cash for, offer cash for; buy on credit, hire-purchase; buy on account, buy on credit, pay by check; buy in 632vb. *store;* buy up, preempt, regrate, corner, make a corner in; monopolize, engross; buy out, make a take-over bid; buy over, suborn 612vb. *bribe;* buy back, redeem, repurchase, ransom 668vb. *deliver;* pay for, bear the cost of 804vb. *defray;* buy oneself in, invest in, sink one's money in 791vb. *speculate;* buy service, rent 785vb. *hire;* bid, bid for, bid up 759vb. *offer;* buy shares, bull, stag.

See: 612, 627, 632, 644, 688, 759, 771, 785, 791, 804, 806.

793 Sale

N. *sale*, selling, putting on sale, marketing; vent; disposal, alienation 779n. *nonretention;* clearance, sell-out; clearance sale, summer s., winter s., spring s., white s., jumble s., charity s., bazaar; sale of office, simony 930n. *improbity;* exclusive sale, monopoly 747n. *restraint;* public sale, auctioneering, auction, sale by a., roup, Dutch auction, American a.; good market, market for; sales, good s., boom 730n. *prosperity;* bad sales 731n. *adversity;* salesmanship, service, sales talk; competition, customer-snatching; salability, vendibility, marketability; vendible, thing sold, seller, good s., best s., selling line 795n. *merchandise.*

seller, vendor, consignor, transferer; shareseller, bear; auctioneer, crier, rouper; huckster, hawker, monger, chapman, colporteur, smouse, smouch, barrow-boy, coster, costermonger 794n. *peddler;* shopman, dealer 633n. *caterer;* wholesaler, retailer 794n. *tradesman;* salesman, traveling s., traveler, commercial t., commission agent, canvasser, tout; shop-walker, floor-w., counter-jumper; shop-assistant, shop girl, shopman, shopwoman, saleswoman; clerk, booking c., ticket-agent; roundsman, milkman.

Adj. *salable*, vendible, marketable, on sale; sold, sold out; in demand, commanding a sale; available, in the market, up for sale; bearish; on auction, under the hammer.

Vb. *sell*, vend, make a sale; flog, alienate, dispose of; market, put on sale, offer for s., have for s.; bring to market, unload, unload on the market, dump; hawk, smouse, peddle, monger; canvass, tout; cater, cater for the market 633vb. *provide;* put up for sale, auction, put to a., sell by a., bring under the hammer, sell to the highest bidder, knock down to; regrate, wholesale; retail, sell over the counter; turn over, turn over one's stock 791vb. *trade;* realize one's capital, encash; sell at a profit 771vb. *gain;* sell at a loss, sacrifice 772vb. *lose;* undercut 812vb. *cheapen;* sell off, remainder; sell up, sell out, wind up 145vb. *cease;* clear stock, hold a sale; sell again, resell; sell forward.

be sold, be on sale, pass by sale, come under the hammer 780vb. *change hands;* sell, have a sale, have a market, meet a demand, be in d., sell well, sell out, boom; be a selling line, be a best-seller; sell badly, stay on the shelf.

See: 145, 633, 730, 731, 747, 771, 772, 779, 780, 791, 794, 795, 812, 930.

794 Merchant

N. *merchant*, merchant prince, merchant adventurer; liveryman, livery company, guild, chamber of commerce, concern, firm 708n. *corporation;* businessman, man of business; trader, trafficker; slaver, slave-trader; importer, exporter; wholesale merchant, wholesaler, regrater; merchandiser, dealer, chandler, corn-c., ship-c.; middleman, broker, stock-b.; stock-jobber, share-pusher; estate agent, realtor; financier, company promoter; banker, sowkar, banian 784n. *lender;* moneyer, money-changer, cambist, shroff; gold merchant, bullioner.

tradesman, tradespeople, tradesfolk; retailer, middleman, regrater, tallyman; shopkeeper, storekeeper, shopman, storesman 793n. *seller;* monger, ironmonger, mercer, haberdasher, grocer, provision merchant 633n. *caterer.*

peddler, pedlar 793n. *seller;* stall-keeper, booth-k.; huckster, traveling hawker, itinerant tradesman, street-seller, cadger, higgler, smouse, hawker, colporteur, bagman, chapman, cheapjack; rag-and-bone man, coster, costerman, costermonger, barrow-boy; market woman; sutler, vivandière 633n. *caterer.*

See: 633, 708, 784, 793.

795 Merchandise

N. *merchandise,* article of commerce, line; article, commodity, salable c., vendible, stock, stock-in-trade, range, repertoire 632n. *store;* freight, cargo 193n. *contents;* stuff, things for sale, supplies, ware, wares, goods, capital g., durables; shop goods, consumer g., consumer durables; perishable goods, canned g., dry g., white g.

See: 193, 632.

796 Mart

N. *mart,* market, daily m., weekly m.; open market, European open m.; market overt, free market; black market, gray m.; seller's market, buyer's m.; market-place, staple, forum, agora; auction room, Tattersall's, Christie's, Sotheby's; fair, world f., international f., trade f., industries f., horse f., goose f., motor show; exhibition, exposition, shop-window 522n. *manifestation;* corn-market, wheat pit, corn-exchange; exchange, stock e., 'change, bourse, curb-market, Wall Street; Rialto, guildhall; tollbooth, custom-house.

emporium, free port, entrepôt, depot, bandar, warehouse 632n. *storage;* wharf; trading center, trading post; general market, bazaar, arcade, covered market, supermarket, shopping center.

shop, retailer's; store, multiple s., department s., chain s.; emporium, bazaar, supermarket; concern, establishment, house, trading h.; corner shop, stall, booth, stand, newsstand, kiosk, barrow; shopboard, counter, bargain c.; shop-floor, shop-window; office, bureau, chambers, counting-house, counting-room; premises, place of business 687n. *workshop.*

See: 522, 632, 687.

797 Money

N. *money,* numismatics, chrysology; pelf, mammon 800n. *wealth;* lucre, filthy l., root of all evil; medium of exchange, circulating medium; currency, decimal c., managed c., fluctuating c., hard c., soft c., falling c.; sound currency, honest money; money of account, sterling, pound s., £. s. d., pounds, shillings and pence; rupees, annas and pies; precious metal, gold, ocher, ringing gold, clinking g.; silver, siller (**see** *bullion*); ready money, the ready, the best, blunt, cash, spot c., hard c.; change, small c., coppers 33n. *small coin;* pocket money, pin m. *dibs,* shekels, spondulicks, blunt, brass, tin, rhino, jack, dough, lolly, sugar, salt; dosh, 'ackers, oof, mopus, boodle; soap, palm oil, palm grease.

funds, temporary f., hot money; liquidity, account, bank a., money in the bank, bank annuities; wherewithal, the needful 629n. *means;* sinews of war, ready money, the ready, the actual, financial provision, cash supplies, treasure 633n. *provision;* remittance 804n. *payment;* funds for investment, capital; funds in hand, reserves, balances, sterling b.; sum of money, amount, figure, sum, round s., lump s.; fiver, tenner, pony, monkey, grand; mint of money, wads, scads, pile, packet, millions, billions, crores, lakhs 32n. *great quantity;* moneybags, purse, bottomless p. 632n. *store.*

finance, high f., financial world; financial control, money power, purse-strings, power of the purse, almighty dollar; money dealings, cash transaction; money market, exchange 796n. *mart;* exchange rate, valuta, parity, par 28n. *equality;* devaluation, depreciation, falling exchange 655n. *deterioration;* rising exchange 654n. *improvement;* bimetallism; gold standard, managed currency, equalization fund, sinking fund, revolving f.; deficit, finance, inflation, inflationary spiral; disinflation, deflation.

coinage, minting, issue; metallic currency, stamped coinage, gold c., silver c., electrum c., copper c., nickel c., billon c., iron c.; specie, minted coinage, coin, coin of the realm; monetary unit, monetary denomination, guinea, sovereign, pound, quid, shiner, chip; half-sovereign, ten bob; crown, cartwheel; half-crown, two-and-six; florin, shilling, bob; six-pence, tanner; threepenny bit, penny, copper, halfpenny, farthing; mohur, gold m., rupee, sicca r., Burmese r., kyen; anna, pice, pie; decimal coinage, dollar, simoleon, buck, half dollar, quarter, dime, nickel, cent; silver dollar; ten-dollar piece, eagle; twenty-dollar piece, double-eagle; napoleon, louis d'or; franc, heavy f., new f.; mark, Reichsmark; gulden, guilder, kroner, lira, scudo, peseta, peso, bolivar, balboa, colon, milreis, reis; drachma, piaster, ruble, kopeck, zloty, yen, sen; talent, mina, obol; daric, dinar, dirham, shekel; solidus, gold s., bezant, ducat, angel, noble, moidore, piece of eight, pistole; change, small c., centime, sou, naya paisa, cash 33n. *small coin;* shell money, cowrie, wampum.

paper money, fiat m., fiduciary currency, assignat, shinplaster; note, banknote, bank paper, treasury note, ten-shilling note, pound note, five-pound note, smacker; bill, dollar b., greenback, buck, ten-dollar bill, sawbuck; bill of exchange, exchequer bill, negotiable instrument; draft, sight d., order, money o., postal o., check, cheque, travelers c., letter of credit; certificate, gold c., silver c.; promissory note, note of hand, hundi; coupon, warrant, scrip, debenture, bond, premium b. 767n. *security*.

false money, bad m., counterfeit m., base coin, snide, rap; forged note, flash n., forgery, slip, kite; dud check; clipped coinage, depreciated currency, devalued c.; demonetized coinage, withdrawn c., obsolete c.

bullion, bar, gold b., ingot, nugget; solid gold, solid silver; precious metal, yellow m., platinum, gold, white g., electrum, silver, billon.

moneyer, minter, mint master; coiner, forger, penman; bullionist; bullioner, money-dealer, money-changer, cambist 794n. *merchant;* cashier 798n. *treasurer;* drawer, drawee, obligor, obligee; financier, capitalist; moneyed man, money-bags, money-spinner 800n. *rich man*.

Adj. monetary, numismatical, chrysological; pecuniary, financial, fiscal, budgetary, sumptuary; coined, stamped, minted, issued; nummary, fiduciary; gold-based, sterling, sound, solvent 800adj. *rich;* inflationary, deflationary; clipped, devalued, depreciated; withdrawn, demonetized; touching the pocket, crumenal.

Vb. *mint,* coin, stamp; monetize, issue, circulate; pass, utter; forge, counterfeit.

demonetize, withdraw, withdraw from circulation, call in an issue; clip, debase, debase the coinage; devalue, depreciate, inflate 812vb. *cheapen*.

draw money, cash, encash, realize, turn into cash, draw upon, cash a check, endorse a c., write a c., 804 vb. *pay*.

See: 28, 32, 33, 629, 632, 633, 654, 655, 767, 794, 796, 798, 800, 804, 812. 812.

798 Treasurer

N. *treasurer,* honorary t.; purse-bearer, bursar, purser, quaestor; cash-keeper, cashier, teller, croupier; depositary, stake-holder, pawnee, pledgee, trustee, steward 754n. *consignee;* liquidator 782n. *receiver;* bookkeeper 808n. *accountant;* banker, financier; keeper of the purse, paymaster, almoner, budgeteer, Chancellor of the Exchequer, Secretary of the Treasury, Controller of Currency; mint master 797n. *moneyer;* bank 799n. *treasury*.

See: 754, 782, 797, 799, 808.

799 Treasury

N. *treasury,* treasure-house, thesaurus; exchequer, fisc, public purse, pork barrel; hanaper, counting-house, custom-house; bursary, almonry; bank, Bank of England, savings bank, post office savings b., penny b.; coffer, chest 194n. *box;* treasure chest, depository 632n. *store;* strong room, strong box, safe, safe deposit, cash box, money-box, stocking; till, cash register, cash desk, slot-machine; receipt of custom, box-office, gate, turnstile; money-bag, purse, purse-strings 194n. *pocket;* wallet, bill-fold, porte-monnaie, wad, rouleau 194n. *case*.

See: 194, 632.

800 Wealth

N. *wealth*, mammon, lucre, pelf, tin, money-bags 797n. *money;* money-making, golden touch, Midas t.; riches, flesh-pots, fat 635n. *plenty;* luxury 637n. *superfluity;* opulence, affluence, well-being 730n. *prosperity;* ease, comfort, easy circumstances, good c., comfortable c. 376n. *euphoria;* solvency, soundness, creditworthiness 802n. *credit;* solidity, substance 3n. *substantiality;* independence, competence, self-sufficiency 635n. *sufficiency;* high income, supertax bracket 782n. *receiving;* gains 771n. *gain*; resources, large r., long purse, capital, substantial c. 629n. *means;* liquid assets, bank account; limitless resources, bottomless purse, purse of Fortunatus, kamadhuk, golden eggs; nest-egg 633n. *provision;* tidy sum, pile, scads, wad, packet 32n. *great quantity;* fortune, great f., handsome f., large inheritance, ample endowment; broad acres, great possessions 777n. *property;* bonanza, mine, gold m. 632n. *store;* Pactolus, Potosi, Golconda, El Dorado, riches of Solomon; plutocracy, capitalism.

rich man, wealthy man, well-to-do man, warm m., man of means; money-baron, nabob, moneybags, millionaire, multi-m., milliardaire, billiardaire; Croesus, Midas, Dives, Plutus; money-maker, money-spinner, capitalist, plutocrat; heiress, "lady richly left" 776n. *beneficiary;* the haves, moneyed class, propertied c., leisured c., jeunesse dorée; new rich, nouveau riche, parvenu 730n. *made man;* plutocracy, timocracy.

Adj. *rich*, richly endowed, flowing with milk and honey, fat, fertile 164adj. *productive;* abundant 635 adj. *plenteous;* richly furnished, luxurious, upholstered, plush, plushy, ritzy, slap-up; diamond-studded 875 adj. *ostentatious;* wealthy, blessed with this world's goods, well-endowed, well-provided for, born in the purple, born with a silver spoon in one's mouth; opulent, affluent 730 adj. *prosperous;* well-off, well-to-do, warm, well-feathered, in easy circumstances, overpaid 376adj. *comfortable.*

moneyed, monied, propertied, worth a lot, worth a packet, worth millions, made of money, lousy with m., rolling in m., rolling dripping; rich as Croesus, rich as Solomon; high-income, millionaire; in funds, in cash, in credit, on the right side; pecunious, tinny, well-heeled, flush, flush of cash, in the dough; creditworthy, solvent, sound, able to pay 929adj. *trustworthy;* out of debt, all straight 804adj. *paying;* keeping up with the Joneses.

Vb. *be rich*, flow with milk and honey, turn to gold 635vb. *abound;* have money, have a power of m., have means, draw a large income; roll in money, stink of m., wallow in riches; be born in the purple, be born with a silver spoon in one's mouth; be flush, be in funds etc. adj.; have credit, command capital, have money to burn; die rich, cut up well 780vb. *bequeath.*

afford, have the means, have the wherewithal, be able to pay, be solvent, make both ends meet, keep one's head above water, keep the wolf from the door, keep up with the Joneses 635vb. *have enough.*

get rich, come into money 771vb. *inherit;* enrich oneself, make money, mint m., coin m., spin m., make a packet, make a pile, make a fortune, feather one's nest, line one's pocket, strike oil 771vb. *gain;* seek riches, worship the golden calf, pay tribute to mammon.

make rich, enrich, make one's fortune, put money in one's pocket, line one's p.; leave one a fortune 780vb. *bequeath;* enhance 36vb. *augment;* improve 654vb. *make better.*

See: 3, 32, 36, 164, 376, 629, 632, 633, 635, 637, 654, 730, 771, 776, 777, 780, 782, 797, 802, 804, 875, 929.

801 Poverty

N. *poverty*, Lady Poverty 945n. *asceticism;* renunciation of wealth, voluntary poverty 931n. *disinterestedness;* poorness, meagerness 645n. *badness;* impecuniosity, hardupness, embarrassment, difficulties, Queer Street 805n. *insolvency;* impoverishment, loss of fortune, broken f., beggary, mendicancy; utter poverty, penury, pennilessness, pauperism, destitution; privation, indigence, neediness, necessitousness, necessity, need, want, pinch, lack 627n. *requirement;* bare cupboard, empty larder 636n. *scarcity;* wolf at the door, famine 946n. *fasting;* light pocket, empty purse, insufficient income, slender means, narrow m., reduced circumstances, straitened c., low water 636n. *insufficiency;* straits, distress 825n. *suffering;* grinding poverty, subsistence level, hand-to-mouth existence, mere e., bare e.; seediness, beggarliness, raggedness, shreds and tatters, "looped and windowed raggedness"; general poverty, slump, depression 655n. *deterioration;* squalor, slum, back street 655n. *dilapidation.*

poor man, broken man, bankrupt, insolvent 805adj. *non-payer;* pauper, indigent, mendicant, beggar, poor b., rag-picker, starveling, down-and-out 763n. *beggar;* slum-dweller, sansculotte 869n. *rabble;* the poor, new poor, the have-nots, the underprivileged; Cinderella 867n. *object of scorn;* poor relation 35n. *inferior.*

Adj. poor, not well-off, badly o., poorly o., ill-o., not blessed with this world's goods, hard up, impecunious, short, short of funds, short of cash, in the red; broke, stony b., bankrupt, insolvent 805adj. *nonpaying;* reduced to poverty *or* beggary, impoverished, pauperized, broken, beggared; dispossessed, deprived, stripped, fleeced, robbed; penurious, poverty-stricken; needy, indigent, in want, in need 627adj. *necessitous;* in distress, straitened, pinched, hard put to it, put to one's shifts, on one's beam ends 700adj. *in difficulties;* unable to make both ends meet, unable to raise the wind, unable to keep the wolf from the door, unprovided, dowerless, portionless; penniless, moneyless, destitute; down to one's last penny, without a bean, without a cent, without a sou, without prospects; poor in, lacking, wanting; poor in quality 645adj. *bad;* meager, sterile 172adj. *unproductive.*

beggarly, starveling, shabby, seedy, down at heel, down and out, in rags, tattered, patched, barefoot, threadbare, tatty 655adj. *dilapidated;* scruffy, squalid, slummy, back-street 649adj. *dirty;* poverty-stricken, pinched with poverty, poor as a rat, poor as a church mouse, poor as Job's turkey.

Vb. *be poor*, earn nothing, live on a pittance, eke out a livelihood, scrape an existence, live from hand to mouth; not keep the wolf from the door, starve 859vb. *be hungry;* want, lack 627vb. *require;* have not a penny, not have a shot in one's locker; become poor, break, go broke 805vb. *not pay;* decline in fortune, lose one's money, come down in the world 655vb. *deteriorate;* take National Assistance, come on the parish, go on relief, go on the dole, go on the rates, go to the workhouse.

impoverish, reduce to poverty, leave destitute, beggar, pauperize; ruin 165vb. *destroy;* rob, strip 786vb. *fleece;* dispossess, disinherit, disendow, cut off, cut off with a shilling 786vb. *deprive.*

See: 35, 165, 172, 627, 636, 645, 649, 655, 700, 763, 786, 805, 825, 859, 867, 869, 931, 945, 946.

802 Credit

N. *credit*, repute, reputation 866n. *prestige;* credit-worthiness, sound credit, trust, confidence, reliability 929n. *probity;* borrowing capacity, limit of credit; line of credit, tick; banker's credit, letter of c., paper c., credit note, sum to one's account, credit a., right side; credits, balances, credit balance 807n. *receipt;* postponed payment, unpaid bill, account, score, tally, bill 808n. *accounts;* national credit, floating debt 803n. *debt;* loan, mortgage 784 n. *lending;* sum entrusted, sum voted, vote.

creditor, mortgagee, pledgee, pawnee 784n. *lender;* depositor, bank d., investor.

Vb. *credit*, give *or* furnish c., extend c., forgo repayment, grant a loan 784 vb. *lend;* place to one's credit, credit one's account, place to one's a.; grant, vote; await payment, charge to one's account, sell on credit; take credit, open an account, keep an account with, run up an account, run up a bill 785vb. *borrow.*

See: 784, 785, 803, 807, 808, 866, 929.

803 Debt

N. *debt*, indebtedness, state of i. 785n. *borrowing;* liability, obligation, commitment; encumbrance, mortgage 767n. *security;* something owing, indebtment, debit, charge; what one owes, debts, bills, hire-purchase debt; national debt, floating d., funded d.; promise to pay, debt of honor, unsecured debt 764n. *promise;* bad debt, write-off 772n. *loss;* good debt 771n. *gain;* tally, account, account owing; deficit, overdraft, unfavorable balance, balance to pay 307n. *shortcoming;* inability to pay 805n. *insolvency;* payment refused, frozen balance, blocked b., blocked account, frozen assets 805n. *nonpayment;* deferred payment 802n. *credit;* overdue payment, arrears, accumulated a., back pay, back rent; no more credit, foreclosure.

interest, simple i., compound i., high i., excessive i., usury, pound of flesh 784n. *lending;* premium, rate of interest, bank rate.

debtor, debitor; loanee, borrower, loan applicant; obligor, drawee; mortgagor, pledgor; bad debtor, defaulter, insolvent 805n. *non-payer*.

Adj. *indebted*, in debt, borrowing, indebted; pledged, liable, obliged, committed, responsible, answerable, bound 917adj. *dutied;* owing, overdrawn, in the red, minus; encumbered, mortgaged; deep in debt, plunged in d., burdened with d., over head and ears in d. 700adj. *in difficulties;* defaulting, unable to pay, insolvent 805adj. *non-paying;* at the mercy of one's creditors, in the hands of the receiver.

owed, unpaid, still u.; owing, due, overdue, in arrears; outstanding, unbalanced; on the debit side, chargeable, payable, debited, on credit, on deposit, repayable, returnable, bearing, payable on delivery, COD.

Vb. *be in debt*, owe, have to repay; owe money, pay interest; accept a charge, be debited with, be liable; get credit, overdraw (one's account); go on tick 785vb. *borrow;* live on credit, buy on c., keep an account with, have charged to one's a.; run up an account, run into debt, have bills to pay; be in the red, be overdrawn; leave one's bills unpaid, cheat one's creditors, bilk, do a moonlight flit, outrun the constable, welsh, levant 805vb. *not pay;* back another's credit, make oneself responsible, go bail for, be obliged, be bound 917vb. *incur a duty*.

See: 307, 700, 764, 767, 771, 772, 784, 785, 917, 967, 802, 805.

804 Payment

N. *payment*, paying for, bearing the cost, defrayment; paying off, discharge, quittance, acquittance, release, satisfaction, full s., liquidation, clearance, settlement, settlement on account; receipted payment, receipt for payment, receipt in full 807n. *receipt;* cash payment, down p.; first payment, earnest, earnest money, deposit; installment, kist; deferred payment, hire purchase 785n. *borrowing;* due payment, subscription, tribute 809n. *tax;* voluntary payment, contribution, collection 781n. *offering;* payment in lieu, composition, scutage 150n. *substitution;* repayment, compensation, indemnity 787n. *restitution;* disbursement, remittance 806n. *expenditure*.

pay, pay-out, pay-off, pay envelope; pay day 108n. *date;* wages bill, wages, salary 771n. *earnings;* grant, grant-in-aid, subsidy 703n. *subvention;* salary, pension, annuity, remuneration, emolument, fee, garnish, bribe 962n. *reward;* brokerage, factorage 810n. *discount;* something paid, contribution, subscription, collection, mass-money, tribute 809n. *tax;* damages, indemnity 963n. *penalty;* compensation, golden handshake; payer, liquidator, paymaster, purser, cashier 789n. *treasurer*.

Adj. *paying*, disbursing 806adj. *expending;* paying in full, paying cash, never indebted, unindebted; out of debt, owing nothing.

Vb. *pay,* disburse 806vb. *expend;* contribute 781vb. *give;* pay in kind, barter 791vb. *trade;* make payment, pay out, shell o., fork o., stump up, cough up; come across, do the needful, unloose the purse-strings, open one's purse; pay back, disgorge, repay, reimburse, compensate 787vb. *restitute;* tickle the palm, grease the palm, gratify, tip 612vb. *bribe;* pay wages, remunerate, wage 962vb. *reward;* pay in advance, pay on sight, pay on call, pay on demand; pay on the nail, pay on the dot, pay cash, pay cash down, pay down, put d.; honor (a bill), pay up, pay in full, satisfy, redeem, discharge, get a receipt; discount, take up, meet; clear, liquidate, settle, settle an account, clear accounts with, balance accounts w., account w., reckon w., square accounts w., strike a balance 808vb. *account;* settle accounts with, settle a score, quit scores; pay off old scores, wipe off old s., pay one out 714vb. *retaliate*.

defray, pay for, defray the cost, bear the c., stand the c.; pay one's way, pay one's footing, pay one's shot; foot the bill, meet the b., pay the piper; pay sauce for all; stand treat 781vb. *give;* share expenses, go Dutch 775vb. *participate*.

Adv. *cash down*, money d.; cash on delivery, COD; with ready money, on the nail, on the dot, on demand, on sight; without credit, slap-bang; costing, to the tune of.

See: 108, 150, 612, 703, 714, 771, 775, 781, 785, 787, 789, 791, 806, 807, 808, 809, 810, 962, 963.

805 Non-payment

N. *non-payment*, default; defalcation 930n. *improbity;* reduced payment, stoppage, deduction 963n. *penalty;* moratorium, embargo, freeze; dishonoring, refusal to pay, protest, repudiation 760n. *refusal;* deferred payment, hire purchase 785n. *borrowing;* application of the sponge, forgiveness of debts, cancellation of d., seisachtheia 752n. *abrogation;* waste paper bonds, protested bill, dishonored check, bogus c., dud c.; depreciation, devaluation, devalued currency 797n. *false money.*

insolvency, inability to pay, failure to meet one's obligations; crash, failure; failure of credit, run upon a bank; bankruptcy, bankruptcy court, proceedings in bankruptcy, whitewash; nothing to pay with, nothing in the kitty, overdrawn account, overdraft 636n. *insufficiency;* hopeless indebtedness, unpayable debt 803n. *debt.*

non-payer, defaulter, defalcator, embezzler 789n. *defrauder;* bilker, welsher, absconder, levanter; failure, lame duck, man of straw; bankrupt, discharged b., undischarged b., insolvent debtor.

Adj. *non-paying*, defaulting, behindhand, in arrears; unable to pay, insolvent, bankrupt, gazetted; overwhelmed with debt, always owing 803adj. *indebted;* beggared, ruined 801adj. *poor.*

Vb. *not pay*, default, embezzle, swindle 788vb. *defraud;* fall into arrears, get behindhand, forget an installment; stop payment, withhold p., freeze, block; refuse payment, protest a bill; disallow payment, hold an item under objection; divert, sequester 786vb. *deprive;* bounce one's check, dishonor, repudiate; become insolvent, go bankrupt, go through the bankruptcy court, be gazetted, get whitewashed; sink, fail, break, go bust, crash, wind up, go into liquidation; evade one's creditors, outrun the constable, welsh, bilk 542vb. *deceive;* levant, abscond 296vb. *decamp;* have no money to pay with 801vb. *be poor;* go off the gold standard, devalue *or* depreciate the currency 797vb. *demonetize;* draw the purse-strings, button up one's pocket, sit on the money-bags 816vb. *be parsimonious;* relieve of payment, cancel a debt, wipe the slate clean, discharge a bankrupt 752vb. *abrogate.*

See: 296, 542, 636, 752, 760, 785, 786, 788, 789, 797, 801, 803, 816, 930, 963.

806 Expenditure

N. *expenditure*, spending, disbursement 804n. *payment;* spendings, outgoings, costs, cost incurred, expenses, out-of-pocket e., expense account; expense, outlay, investment; dissaving, disinvestment, run on savings; fee, garnish, tribute 804n. *pay;* extravagance, spending spree 815n. *prodigality.*

Adj. *expending*, spending, sumptuary; generous 813adj. *liberal;* extravagant, splashing one's money 813adj. *prodigal;* out of pocket, lighter in one's purse.

expended, spent, disbursed, paid, paid out; laid out, invested; costing, at one's expense.

Vb. *expend*, make expenditure, spend; buy 792vb. *purchase;* lay out, outlay, invest, sink money; be out of pocket, incur costs, incur expenses; meet charges, disburse, pay out 804 vb. *pay;* run down one's account, draw on one's savings, unsave, dissave, disinvest; unhoard, unbelt, untie the purse-strings, open one's purse, empty one's pocket; give money, donate 781vb. *give;* spare no expense, go a bust, do it proud, lavish 813vb. *be liberal;* fling money around, splash one's money, bust, blow, blow one's cash 815vb. *be prodigal;* use up, spend up, consume, run through, get t. 634vb. *waste.*

See: 634, 781, 792, 804, 813, 815.

807 Receipt

N. *receipt*, accountable r., voucher, acknowledgment of payment, value received; money received, credits, innings, revenue, royalty, rents, rent-roll, dues; customs, taxes 809n. *tax;* money coming in, turnover, takings, proceeds, returns, receipts, gross r., net r., box-office r., gate-money, gate; income, national i., private i., privy purse; emolument, regular income, pay, half p., salary, wages 771n. *earnings;* remuneration 962n. *reward;* pension, annuity, tontine; allowance, personal a.; pocket-money, pin-m.; inadequate allowance, pittance; alimony, maintenance; exhibition, sizarship, perquisite 771n. *acquisition;* rake-off 810n. *discount;* interest, return; winnings, profits, gross p., net p., mesne p. 771n. *gain;* bonus, premium 40n. *extra;* prize 729n. *trophy;* draw, lucky d.; legacy, inheritance 777n. *dower.*

Adj. *received,* paid, receipted, acknowledged, acknowledged with thanks.

Vb. see 781vb. *acquire,* 782vb. *receive, be received,* 786vb. *take.*

See: 40, 729, 771, 781, 782, 786, 809, 810, 962.

808 Accounts

N. *accounts,* accompts; accountancy, accounting, commercial arithmetic; bookkeeping, entry, double e., single e.; audit, inspection of accounts; account, profit-and-loss a., balance sheet, debit and credit, debtor-and-creditor account, receipts and expenditures; budgeting, budget, budget estimates 633n. *provision;* running account, current a., cash a., suspense a., expense a.; statement of account, account rendered, compte rendu, statement, bill, waybill, invoice, manifest 87n. *list;* college accounts, battels; account paid, account settled 804n. *payment;* reckoning, computation, score, tally, facts and figures 86n. *numeration.*

account book, passbook, checkbook, cash book, day-b., cost-b., journal, ledger, register, books 548n. *record.*

accountant, chartered a., certified public a.; bookkeeper, storekeeper; accounting party, cashier 798n. *treasurer;* inspector of accounts, examiner of a., auditor; actuary, statistician.

Adj. *accounting,* book-keeping, in charge of accounts; actuarial, reckoning, computing, inventorial, budgetary; accountable.

Vb. *account,* keep the books, keep accounts, keep the cash; make up an account, cast an a.; budget, prepare a b.; cost, value, write up, write down 480vb. *estimate;* book, bring to book, enter, journalize, post, carry over, debit, credit 548vb. *register;* prepare a balance sheet, balance accounts; settle accounts, square a., finalize a., wind up a.; prepare a statement, present an account, charge, bill, invoice; overcharge, surcharge, undercharge 809 vb. *price;* cook the accounts, falsify the a., fiddle, garble, doctor 788vb. *defraud;* audit, inspect accounts, examine the a., go through the books; take stock, check s., inventory, catalog 87vb. *list.*

See: 86, 87, 480, 548, 633, 788, 798, 804, 809.

809 Price

price, selling p., world p., market p., standard p., list p., price current; rate, rate for the job; rate, piece r., flat r.; high rate 811n. *dearness;* low rate 812n. *cheapness;* price control, fixed price, prix fixe 747n. *restraint;* value, face v., par v., fair v., worth, money's w., what it will fetch; scarcity value, famine price; price list, tariff; quoted price, quotation, price charged; amount, figure, sum asked for; ransom, fine 963n. *penalty;* demand, dues, charge; surcharge, supplement 40n. *extra;* overcharge, excessive charge, extortion, ransom; fare, hire, rental, rent, ground r., house r., quit r., rate of r.; fee, refresher, salami, commission, rake-off; charges, freightage, wharfage, lighterage; salvage; postage; cover charge, corkage; bill, invoice, reckoning, shot.

cost, buying price, purchase p.; damage, costs, expenses 806n. *expenditure;* business costs, running c., overheads; wages, wage bill, wage-packet; legal costs, damages 963n. *penalty;* cost of living, cost-of-living index.

tax, taxes, dues; taxation, tax demand 737n. *demand;* rating, assessment, appraisement, valorization 480 n. *estimate;* cess, rate, general r., water r.; levy, toll, duty; imposition, impost; tallage; ship-money; charge, scot, scot and lot (**see** *price*); exaction, forced loan, aid, benevolence 740n. *compulsion;* forced savings 785n. *borrowing;* punitive tax, collective t. 963n. *penalty;* tribute, danegeld, blackmail, ransom 804n. *payment;* ecclesiastical tax, Peter's pence, tithe, tenths; poll tax, capitation t.; property tax, schedule A, death duty; direct taxation, income tax, surtax, supertax, company tax, profits t., excess-profits t.; capital levy, capital-gains tax 786n. *expropriation;* indirect taxation, excise, customs, tariff, tonnage and poundage; local tax, octroi; purchase tax, sales t., multipoint sales t.; salt tax, gabelle; feudal tax, scutage.

Adj. *priced,* charged, fixed; chargeable, leviable, taxable, assessable, ratable, customable, dutiable, excisable; ad valorem; to the tune of, for the price of; taxed, rated, assessed; paid, stipendiary.

Vb. *price*, cost, assess, value, rate 480vb. *estimate;* put a price on, set a price on; place a value on, fix a price for; raise a price, lower a p.; control the p., fix the p.; ask a price, charge, require 737vb. *demand;* bill, invoice.

cost, be worth, fetch, bring in; amount to, come to, mount up to; be priced at, be valued at; bear a price, have a p., have its p.; sell for, go f., be going f.

tax, lay a tax on, impose a tax; fix a tariff, levy a rate, assess for tax, value, valorize; toll, excise, subject to duty, make dutiable; raise taxes, collect t., take one's toll 786vb. *levy;* take a collection, pass round the hat 761vb. *beg;* exact a penalty, fine, punish by f., mulct 963vb. *punish.*

See: 40, 480, 737, 740, 747, 761, 785, 786, 804, 806, 811, 812, 963.

810 Discount

N. *discount*, something off, reduction, rebate, cut 42n. *decrement;* stoppage, deduction; concession, allowance, margin, special price; tare, rate and tret; drawback, rebatement, backwardation, contango, deferment; cut price, bargain p., cut rate, bargain sale 812n. *cheapness;* poundage, percentage; agio, brokerage; something for oneself, rake-off, dastur.

Vb. *discount,* deduct 39vb. *subtract;* allow a margin, tare; reduce, depreciate, abate, rebate 37vb. *bate;* offer a discount, allow a d.; mark down, take off, cut, slash 812vb. *cheapen;* let stick to one's fingers, rake off, get one's rake-off; take a discount, take one's percentage.

Adv. *at a discount*, below par, less than the market rate.

See: 37, 39, 42, 812.

811 Dearness

N. *dearness*, costliness, expensiveness; value, high v., high worth, pricelessness; famine price, scarcity value, rarity, dearth 636n. *scarcity;* exorbitance, extortion, overcharge, excessive charge, unfair price, bad value, poor v.; high price, fancy p., luxury p.; cost, high c., heavy c., pretty penny; extravagant price. Pyrrhic victory, white elephant; tax on one's pocket, ruinous charge; rising costs, rising prices, sellers' market, bull m., climbing prices, soaring p.; cheap money, inflation, inflationary pressure, bullish tendency.

Adj. *dear*, high-priced, expensive, ritzy; costly, multimillion; extravagant, dear-bought, Pyrrhic; dear at the price, overrated, overcharged, overpriced, overpaid; exorbitant, excessive, extortionate; beyond one's means, not affordable, prohibitive, unpayable, more than one can afford, more than one's pocket can stand; rising in price, hardening, rising, soaring, climbing, mounting, inflationary; bullish, at a premium, odds on.

of price, of value, of worth 644adj. *valuable;* priceless, beyond price, above p.; unpayable; invaluable 640adj. *useful;* inestimable, worth a king's ransom, worth a Jew's eye; precious, rare, scarce 140adj. *infrequent;* at a premium, not to be had for love or money.

Vb. *be dear,* cost much, cost a lot, cost a packet, cost a pretty penny, be high priced; gain in value, rise in price, harden; go up, appreciate, soar, mount, climb; get too dear, price itself out of the market; prove expensive, cost one dear, be a white elephant.

overcharge, overprice, sell dear, oversell, ask too much; profiteer, soak, sting, bleed, skin, extort, rack-rent, hold to ransom 786vb. *fleece;* bull, raise the price, raise the bid, bid up, auction 793vb. *sell.*

pay too much, pay through the nose, pay the devil, be stung, be had; pay high, pay dear, buy a white elephant, achieve a Pyrrhic victory; pay beyond one's means, ruin oneself.

Adv. *dearly*, dear, at a price, at great cost, at heavy c., at huge expense; exorbitantly, extravagantly.

See: 140, 636, 640, 644, 786, 793.

812 Cheapness

N. *cheapness*, inexpensiveness, affordability; good value, value for money, bargain, good b., good penny, bon marché; low price, reasonable charge, reasonableness; cheap rate, off-season r., concessional r., excursion fare 810n. *discount;* nominal price, reduced p., knock-down p., cut p., sale p., sacrificial p.; peppercorn rent, easy terms; buyers' market, sluggish m.; cheapening, Dutch auction; falling prices, declining p., bearishness, bearish tendency, easiness; depreciation, fall, slump, deflation; glut, drug on the market 635n. *plenty;* superfluity 637 n. *redundance.*

no charge, absence of c., nominal c. 781n. *gift;* gratuitousness, labor of love 597n. *voluntary work;* free trade, free port; free entry, free admission, free seats, free pass, free ticket; free quarters, grace and favor; free board, run of one's teeth; free service, free delivery; everything for nothing.

Adj. *cheap,* inexpensive, uncostly, moderate, reasonable, fair; affordable, within one's means; economical, economy, economy size; not dear, worth its price, worth the money; low, low-priced, cheap-p., dirt-cheap, for a song, for peanuts; bargain-rate, cut-price, concessional, marked down, half-price; tourist-class, off-season; easy to buy, two-a-penny; worth nothing, cheap and nasty, brummagem 641adj. *useless;* cheapening, bearish, falling, declining, slumping; unsalable, unmarketable; unchargeable, valueless 860adj. *unwanted;* underpaid, underpriced.

uncharged, not charged for, gratuitous, complimentary; gratis, for nothing, for love, for kicks, for nix, for the asking; costing nothing, free, scot-f., free of cost; untaxed, tax-free, rent-f., post-f., postpaid, carriage paid, FOB, including extras; unpaid, unsalaried, honorary 597adj. *voluntary;* given away, unbought, as a gift 781adj. *given;* costless, free, gratis and for nothing; had for the asking.

Vb. *be cheap,*—inexpensive etc. adj.; cost little, be economical, be easily afforded; be worth the money, be cheap at the price; be bought for an old song, be picked up for nothing, go dirt-cheap; cost nothing, be without charge, be free, be had for the asking; cheapen, get cheaper, fall in price, depreciate, come down, decline, sag, fall, slump, plunge.

cheapen, lower, lower the price, reduce the p.; put a low price on, price low, keep cheap, bate one's charges, trim one's prices, shave one's p., mark down, cut, slash; undercharge, underrate, let go for a song, sacrifice, give away, make a present of 781vb. *give;* beat down, undercut, undersell, engage in cut-throat competition; dump, unload; spoil the market, glut 637vb. *superabound;* depress the market, bear; stale, lower, vulgarize 655vb. *impair.*

Adv. *cheaply,* on the cheap; at cost price, at prime cost, at half-price, for a song, for nothing.

See: 597, 635, 637, 641, 655, 781, 810, 860.

813 Liberality

N. *liberality,* liberalness, bounteousness, bountifulness, munificence, generosity 931n. *disinterestedness;* open-handedness, open heart, open hand, open purse, hospitality, open house 882n. *sociability;* free hand, blank check, carte blanche 744n. *scope;* cornucopia 635n. *plenty;* lavishness 815n. *prodigality;* bounty, largess 781n. *gift;* handsome offer, sporting o. 759n. *offer;* benefaction, charity 897n. *kind act.*

good giver, free g., princely g., generous g., cheerful g., liberal donor, unselfish d., blood d.; good spender, good tipper; Lady Bountiful, Father Christmas, Santa Claus, rich uncle 903n. *benefactor.*

Adj. *liberal,* free, freely spending, free-handed, open-h., lavish 815adj. *prodigal;* large-hearted, free-h. 931 adj. *disinterested;* bountiful, charitable 897adj. *benevolent;* hospitable 882adj. *sociable;* handsome, generous, munificent, splendid, slap-up; lordly, princely, royal 868adj. *noble;* ungrudging, unstinting, unsparing, unfailing; in liberal quantities, ample, bounteous, profuse, full, pressed down and running over 635adj. *plenteous;* overflowing 637adj. *redundant.*

Vb. *be liberal,*—generous etc.adj.; lavish, shower largess, shower upon 781vb. *give;* unbelt, open the purse-strings, head the subscription list; give largely, give with both hands, give till it hurts 897vb. *philanthropize;* give more than asked, overpay, pay well, tip w.; keep open house 882vb. *be hospitable;* do it proud, not count the cost, spare no expense; give carte blanche, give a blank check 744vb. *give scope;* spend freely, not ask for the change, throw one's money around 815vb. *be prodigal.*

Adv. *liberally,* ungrudgingly, with open hand, with both hands.

See: 635, 637, 744, 759, 781, 815, 868, 882, 897, 903, 931.

814 Economy

N. *economy,* thrift, thriftiness, frugality; prudence, care, carefulness; husbandry, good h., good housekeeping, good housewifery; sound stewardship, good management, careful m.; watchful eye on expense, avoidance of waste, sumptuary law, credit squeeze 747n. *restriction;* economy drive, economy slip; time-saving, labor-s., time-and-motion study; husbanding of resources, economizing, saving, sparing, pinching, paring, cheese-p.; retrenchment, economies; savings, hoarded s. 632n. *store;* economizer, save-all 816n. *niggard;* economist, physiocrat; good housewife, careful steward.

Adj. *economical*, time-saving, labor-s., money-s., cost-reducing; money-conscious, chary of expense, counting the pence 816adj. *parsimonious;* thrifty, frugal, saving, sparing; unlavish, meager; marginal, with nothing to spare.

Vb. *economize*, be economical,—sparing etc.adj.; avoid extravagance, keep costs down, waste nothing, find a use for everything; keep within one's budget, keep within compass, cut one's coat according to one's cloth, make both ends meet; watch expenses, pare e., cut down expenditure, trim e., make economies, retrench; pinch, scrape 816vb. *be parsimonious;* save, spare, hoard 632vb. *store;* plow back, reinvest, get interest on one's money, not leave money idle, make every penny work 800vb. *get rich.*

Adv. *sparingly*, economically, frugally, nothing in excess.

See: 632, 747, 800, 816.

815 Prodigality

N. *prodigality*, lavishness, profusion, profuseness 637n. *redundance;* idle display, idle expenditure 875n. *ostentation;* extravagance, wasteful expenditure, spendthrift e., reckless e.; wastefulness, dissipation, squandering, squandermania, orgy of spending, spending spree 634n. *waste;* unthriftiness, indifference to economy, uneconomy, uncontrolled expenditure, unregulated e., deficit finance; misapplication, misuse of funds 675n. *misuse;* malversation 788 n. *peculation.*

prodigal, prodigal son, spender, reckless s., waster, spend-all, spendthrift, wastethrift, scattergood, squanderer, squandermaniac.

Adj. *prodigal,* lavish 813n. *liberal;* profuse, overlavish, over-liberal; extravagant, regardless of cost, wasteful, squandering; uneconomic, uneconomical, unthrifty, thriftless, spendthrift, improvident, reckless, dissipated; ill-balanced, penny wise and pound foolish.

Vb. *be prodigal*, prodigalize, go the pace, go a bust, blow; overspend, pour money out, splash money around, flash dollar bills; spill, spend money like water, pour one's money through a sieve; spill one's money, burn one's m., run through one's savings, exhaust one's resources, spend to the last farthing, spend up to the hilt, blow everything, waste one's inheritance, consume one's substance, squander 634 vb. *waste;* play ducks and drakes, burn the candle at both ends, fritter away, throw a., fling a., gamble a., dissipate, pour down the drain; not count the cost, keep no check on expenditure; misspend, fool one's money away, throw good money after bad, throw the helve after the hatchet; have no thought for the morrow, anticipate one's income, spend more than one has, overdraw, outrun the constable; eat up one's capital, kill the goose that lays the golden eggs; save nothing, put nothing by, keep nothing for a rainy day.

Adv. *prodigally*, profusely; like a prodigal, like a spendthrift.

Int. hang the expense! a short life and a merry one! easy come, easy go!

See: 634, 637, 675, 788, 813, 875.

816 Parsimony

N. *parsimony*, parsimoniousness; credit squeeze 814n. *economy;* false economy, misplaced e., cheese-paring e., policy of penny wise and pound foolish; cheese-paring, scrimping, pinching, scraping; niggardliness, meanness, minginess, stinginess, miserliness; illiberality, ungenerosity, uncharity, grudging hand, closed purse 932n. *selfishness.*

avarice, cupidity, acquisitiveness, possessiveness, monopoly; money-grubbing, itch for pelf, itching palm; rapacity, avidity, greed 859n. *desire;* mercenariness, venality, hireling character.

niggard, skinflint, screw, scrimp, scraper, pinchfist, tightwad, no tipper; miser, money-grubber, lickpenny, muckworm; cadger; save-all, hoarder, magpie; hunks, churl, codger, curmudgeon; usurer 784n.

lender; Harpagon, Scrooge.

Adj. *parsimonious*, penurious 814adj. *economical;* over-economical, over-frugal, frugal to excess; money-conscious, penny-wise, miserly, mean, mingy, stingy, near, close, tight; tight-fisted, close-f., hard f., close-handed 778adj. *retentive;* grudging, curmudgeonly, churlish, illiberal, ungenerous, uncharitable, empty-handed, giftless; chary, sparing, pinching, scraping, scrimping; shabby, peddling.

avaricious, grasping, griping, monopolistic 932adj. *selfish;* possessive, acquisitive 771adj. *acquiring;* hoarding, saving; pinching; miserly; cadging; money-grubbing, money-conscious, money-mad, covetous 859 adj. *greedy;* usurious, rapacious, extortionate; mercenary, venal, sordid.

Vb. *be parsimonious*,—niggardly etc. adj.; keep one's fist closed, keep one's purse shut 778vb. *retain;* grudge, begrudge, withhold, keep back 760vb. *refuse;* dole out, stint, skimp, starve, famish 636vb. *make insufficient;* scrape, pinch, gripe, screw, rack-rent, skin a flint 786vb. *fleece;* be penny-wise, spoil the ship for a ha'porth of tar, stop one hole in a sieve; starve oneself, live like a pauper; hoard wealth, never spend a penny; grudge every farthing, beat down, haggle 791vb. *bargain;* cadge, beg, borrow; hoard, sit on.

Adv. *parsimoniously*, niggardly, sparingly, on a shoestring.

See: 636, 760, 771, 778, 784, 786, 791, 814, 859, 932.

817 Affections

N. *affections*, qualities, instincts; passions, emotional life; nature, disposition 5n. *character;* spirit, temper, tone, grain, mettle 5n. *temperament;* cast of soul, cast of mind, habit of m., trait, touch 7n. *state;* personality, psychology, psychological endowment, psychological complex, mental and spiritual makeup, inherited characteristics 5n. *heredity;* being, innermost b., breast, bosom, heart, soul, core, inmost soul, inner man, cockles of the heart, heart of hearts 5n. *essential part;* animus, attitude, frame of mind, state of m., vein, strain, humor, mood; predilection, predisposition, turn, bent, bias 179n. *tendency;* passion, ruling p., master p. 481n. *prejudice;* fullness of heart, flow of soul, heyday of the blood; force of character; fettle, form, shape 7n. *state.*

Adj. *with affections*, affected, characterized, formed, molded, cast, tempered, framed; instinct with, imbued w., tinctured w., penetrated w., eaten up w., possessed w., obsessed w., devoured w.; inborn, inbred, congenital 5adj. *genetic;* deep-rooted, ineffaceable 5adj. *intrinsic;* emotional, demonstrative 818adj. *feeling.*

See: 5, 7, 179, 481, 818.

818 Feeling

N. *feeling*, experience, emotional life; sentience, sensation, sense of 374n. *sense;* sensory perception, sense p. 378n. *touch;* relish, gusto 386n. *taste;* emotion, crystallized e., sentiment; true feeling, sincerity 540 n. *veracity;* impulse 609n. *spontaneity;* responsiveness, response, reaction, fellow-feeling, sympathy, involvement, personal i. 880n. *friendliness;* appreciation, realization, understanding 490n. *knowledge;* impression, deep feeling, deep sense of 819n. *moral sensibility;* religious feeling, unction 979n. *piety;* finer feelings 897n. *benevolence;* hard feelings 891n. *resentment;* stirred feeling, thrill, kick 318n. *spasm;* shock, turn 508n. *inexpectation;* pathos 825n. *suffering;* actuating feeling, animus, emotionality, emotionalism, affectivity 822n. *excitability;* manifestation of feeling, demonstration, demonstrativeness; expression, facial e., play of feature 547n. *gesture;* blush, flush, hectic f., suffusion; tingling, goose-flesh, tremor, trembling, quiver, flutter, flurry, palpitation, pulsation, heaving, panting, throbbing 318n. *agitation;* stew, ferment 318n. *commotion;* control of feeling, stoicism, endurance, sufferance, supportance, toleration 823n. *patience.*

warm feeling, cordiality, empressement, effusiveness, heartiness, full heart, overflowing h.; hot head, impatience; unction, earnestness 834 n. *seriousness;* eagerness, keenness, fervor, ardor, vehemence, enthusiasm, dash, fire 174n. *vigorousness;* vigor, zeal 678n. *activity;* fanaticism, mania 481n. *prejudice;* emotion, passion, ecstasy, inspiration, elevation, transports 822n. *excitable state.*

Adj. *feeling*, affective, sensible, sensorial, sensory 374adj. *sentient;*

spirited, vivacious, lively 819adj. *sensitive;* sensuous 944adj. *sensual;* experiencing, living; enduring, bearing 825adj. *suffering;* responsive, reacting; involved, sympathetic, condoling 775adj. *sharing;* emotional, passionate, full of feeling; unctuous, soulful; intense, tense 821adj. *excited;* cordial, hearty; gushing, effusive; sentimental, romantic; mawkish, treacly, sloppy; thrilling, tingling, throbbing; blushing, flushing.

impressed, affected, influenced; stirred, aroused, moved, touched 821adj. *excited;* struck, awed, awe-struck, overwhelmed; penetrated, imbued with, aflame w., consumed w., devoured by, inspired by; rapt, enraptured, enthralled, ecstatic; lyrical, raving 822adj. *excitable.*

fervent, fervid, perfervid, passionate, tense, intense; eager, breathless, panting, throbbing; impassioned, earnest, zealous, enthusiastic; hotheaded, impetuous, impatient 822 adj. *excitable;* warm, fiery, glowing, burning, red-hot, flaming, boiling 379n. *hot;* hysterical, delirious, overwrought, feverish, hectic 503adj. *frenzied;* strong, uncontrollable, furious 176adj. *violent.*

felt, experienced, lived; heartfelt, cordial, hearty, warm, sincerely felt, sincere 540adj. *veracious;* deeply-felt, profound 211adj. *deep;* stirring, soul-s., heart-warming, heart-expanding; emotive, impressive, strong, overwhelming 821adj. *impressive;* smart, acute, keen, poignant, piercing, trenchant 256adj. *sharp;* caustic, burning, smarting 388adj. *pungent;* penetrating, absorbing; thrilling, tingling, rapturous, ecstatic 826adj. *pleasurable;* pathetic, affecting 827 adj. *distressing.*

Vb. *feel,* sense, receive an impression; entertain, entertain feelings, have f., cherish f., harbor f., feel deeply, take to heart 374adj. *have feelings;* know the feeling, experience, live, live through, go t., pass t., taste, prove; bear, endure, undergo, smart, smart under 825vb. *suffer;* suffer with, feel w., sympathize, condole, share 775vb. *participate;* respond, react, tingle, warm to, fire, kindle, catch, catch the flame, catch the infection, be inspired 821vb. *be excited;* cause feeling 821vb. *impress.*

show feeling, exhibit f., show signs of emotion; demonstrate, not hide one's feelings 522vb. *manifest;* go into ecstasies 824vb. *be pleased;* fly into a passion 891vb. *get angry;* turn color, change c., look blue, look black; go livid, go black in the face, go purple 428vb. *blacken;* look pale, blench, turn pale, go white 427vb. *whiten;* color, blush, flush, glow, mantle, turn red, turn crimson, warm up, go red in the face 431vb. *redden;* quiver, tremble, wince; flutter, shake, quake 318vb. *be agitated;* tingle, thrill, throb, beat 317vb. *oscillate;* palpitate, pant, heave, draw a deep breath 352vb. *breathe;* reel, lurch, stagger 317vb. *fluctuate;* stutter 580vb. stammer.

Adv. *feelingly,* unctuously, earnestly, con amore, heart and soul; with a full heart, with a swelling h., with a bursting h., with a melting h., sympathetically; cordially, heartily, devoutly, sincerely, from the bottom of one's heart.

See: 174, 176, 211, 256, 317, 318, 352, 374, 378, 379, 386, 388, 427, 428, 431, 481, 490, 503, 508, 522, 540, 547, 580, 609, 678, 775, 819, 821, 822, 823, 824, 825, 826, 827, 834, 880, 891, 897, 944, 979.

819 Sensibility

N. *moral sensibility,* sensitivity, sensitiveness; touchiness, prickliness, irritability 892n. *irascibility;* raw feelings, tender f., soft spot, tender spot, quick; sore point, where the shoe pinches 891n. *resentment;* impressibility, affectibility, susceptibility; plasticity, malleability 327n. *softness;* finer feelings, sentimentality, sentimentalism; tenderness, affection 887n. *love;* spirit, spiritedness, vivacity, vivaciousness, liveliness, verve 571n. *vigor;* emotionalism, ebullience, effervescence 822n. *excitability;* fastidiousness, finickiness, aestheticism 463n. *discrimination;* temperament, mobility, changeability 152n. *changeableness;* physical sensitivity, allergy 374n. *sensibility;* touchy person, sensitive plant, mass of nerves.

Adj. *impressible,* malleable, plastic 327adj. *soft;* sensible, aware, conscious of, awake to, alive to, responsive 374adj. *sentient;* impressed with, touched, moved, touched to the quick 818adj. *impressed;* persuasible 612adj. *induced;* impressionable, impassionable 822adj. *excitable;* susceptible, susceptive; romantic, sentimental; sentimentalizing, gushing; emotional, warmhearted; soft, tender, tender as a chicken, tender-hearted, soft-h.,

compassionate 905adj. *pitying.*
sensitive, sensitized; tingling, physically sensitive, sore, raw, tender, allergic; aesthetic, fastidious, particular 463adj. *discriminating;* oversensitive, all feeling 822adj. *excitable;* touchy, irritable, impatient, thin-skinned, easily stung, easily aroused 892adj. *irascible.*
lively, alive, tremblingly a.; vital, vivacious, animated; gamesome, skittish; irrepressible, ebullient, effervescent; mettlesome, spirited, high-s., high-flying; alert, aware, on one's toes 455adj. *attentive;* overquick, impatient; nervous, high-strung, overstrung, temperamental; mobile, changeable; enthusiastic, impassioned; over-enthusiastic, overzealous, fanatic; lively in style, expressive, racy 571adj. *forceful.*
Vb. *be sensitive,*—sentimental etc. adj.; have a soft heart; be all feeling, "die of a rose in aromatic pain"; soften one's heart, let one's heart be touched, weep for 905vb. *pity;* scratch, tingle 378vb. *itch.*
Adv. *on the raw,* to the quick, where the shoe pinches, where it hurts most.
See: 152, 327, 374, 378, 455, 463, 571, 612, 818, 822, 887, 891, 892, 905.

820 Insensibility

N. *moral insensibility,* insentience, no sensation, numbness, stupor 375 n. *insensibility;* inertia 175n. *inertness;* lethargy 679n. *inactivity;* quietism, stagnation, vegetation 266 n. *quiescence;* woodenness, blockishness, obtuseness, stupidity, dullness, no imagination 499n. *unintelligence;* slowness, delayed reaction 456n. *inattention;* uninterest 454n. *incuriosity;* nonchalance, insouciance, unconcern, detachment, apathy 860n. *indifference;* no nerves, imperturbation, phlegm, calmness, steadiness, coolness, sangfroid 823 n. *inexcitability;* no feelings, aloofness, impassibility, impassivity, impassiveness; repression, repression of feeling, stoicism 823n. *patience;* inscrutability, poker-face, dead pan 834n. *seriousness;* insensitivity, coarseness, philistinism 699n. *artlessness;* imperception, thick skin, rhinoceros hide; no pride, no honor; cold heart, frigidity; unsusceptibility, unimpressibility, dourness; unsentimentality, cynicism; callousness 326n. *hardness;* lack of feeling, dry eyes, no heart, heart of stone, heart of marble, brutishness, brutality, brutalization 898n. *inhumanity;* no joy, no humor, no life, no animation 838n. *tedium;* no admiration for 865 n. *non-wonder.*
unfeeling person, iceberg, icicle, cold fish, cold heart, cold-blooded animal; stoic, ascetic; stock, stone, block, marble.
Adj. *impassive,* unconscious 375adj. *insensible;* unsusceptible, insensitive, unimaginative; unresponsive, unimpressionable, unimpressible 823 adj. *inexcitable;* phlegmatic, stolid; wooden, blockish; dull, slow 499 adj. *unintelligent;* unemotional, passionless, impassible; proof, proof against, steeled a.; stoical, ascetic, controlled, undemonstrative; unconcerned, aloof, distant, detached, disengaged, dégagé 860adj. *indifferent;* unaffected, calm 266adj. *tranquil;* steady, unruffled, unshaken, unshocked; imperturbable, without nerves, cool, sangfroid; inscrutable, blank, expressionless, dead-pan, poker-faced; unseeing 439adj. *blind;* unhearing 416adj. *deaf;* unsentimental, cynical; impersonal, dispassionate, without warmth, unforthcoming, frigid, icy, cold, cold-blooded, cold-hearted, cold as charity; unfeeling, heartless, soulless, inhuman; unsmitten, heart-free, fancy-f., heart-whole; unloving, unaffectionate, undemonstrative.
apathetic, unenthusiastic, unambitious; unimpassioned, uninspired, unexcited, unwarmed, unmoved, unstirred, untouched, unsmitten, unstruck, unaroused, unstung; half-hearted, lukewarm, Laodicean 860 adj. *indifferent;* uninterested 454 adj. *incurious;* nonchalant, insouciant, pococurante, careless, regardless, neglectful 458adj. *negligent;* unspirited, spiritless, lackadaisical; lotus-eating, vegetative, stagnant 266 adj. *quiescent;* sluggish, supine 679 adj. *inactive;* blunted 257adj. *unsharpened;* cloyed 863adj. *sated;* torpid, numb, benumbed, palsied, comatose 375adj. *insensible.*
thick-skinned, pachydermatous; impenetrable, impervious; blind to, deaf to, dead to, close to; obtuse, unimaginative, insensitive; callous, insensate, tough, toughened, hardened, case-h. 326adj. *hard;* hard-bitten, hard-boiled, inured 669adj. *matured;* shameless, unblushing, unmoral, amoral.
Vb. *be insensitive,*—impassive etc.

adj.; have no sensation, have no feelings 375vb. *be insensible;* not see, miss the point of, be blind to 439vb. *be blind;* lack animation, lack spirit, lack verve; harden oneself, steel o., harden one's heart against, own no pity 906vb. *be pitiless;* feel indifference 860vb. *be indifferent;* feel no emotion, despise e., have no finer feelings, be a philistine, nil admirari 865vb. *not wonder;* show no regard for 922vb. *despise;* take no interest 454vb. *be incurious;* ignore 458vb. *disregard;* control one's feelings, quell one's desires 942vb. *be temperate;* stagnate, vegetate 679vb. *be inactive;* not stir, not turn a hair, not bat an eyelid 599vb. *be resolute.*

make insensitive, benumb 375vb. *render insensible;* render callous, steel, toughen 326vb. *harden;* sear, dry up 342vb. *dry;* deafen, stop the ears 399vb. *silence;* shut the eyes of 439vb. *blind;* brutalize 655vb. *pervert;* stale, coarsen 847vb. *vulgarize;* satiate, cloy 863vb. *sate;* deaden, obtund, take the edge off 257vb. *blunt.*

Adv. *in cold blood,* with dry eyes, without emotion, with steady pulse; without enthusiasm.

See: 175, 257, 266, 326, 342, 375, 399, 416, 439, 454, 456, 458, 499, 599, 655, 669, 679, 699, 823, 834, 838, 847, 860, 863, 865, 898, 906, 922, 942.

821 Excitation

N. *excitation,* rousing, arousing, stirring up, working up, whipping up; galvanization, galvanism, electrification 174n. *stimulation;* possession, inspiration, afflatus, exhilaration, intoxication, headiness; evocation, calling forth; encouragement, animation, incitement, invitation, appeal 612n. *inducement;* provocation, irritation, casus belli; impression, image, impact 178n. *influence;* fascination, bewitchment, enchantment 983n. *sorcery;* rapture, ravishment 824n. *joy;* emotional appeal, human interest, sentiment, sentimentalism, sob-stuff, pathos; sensationalism, thrill-seeking, melodrama; scandalmongering, muck-raking 926 n. *detraction;* excitement, high pressure, tension 160n. *energy;* state of excitement, perturbation, effervescence, ebullience 318n. *agitation;* shock, thrill 318n. *spasm;* stew, ferment, flurry, furor, breeze 318n. *commotion;* pitch of excitement 503n. *frenzy;* climax 137n. *crisis;* excited feeling, passion, emotion, enthusiasm, lyricism 818n. *feeling;* fuss, drama; temper, fury, rage 891 n. *anger;* interest 453n. *curiosity;* amazement 864n. *wonder;* awe 845n. *fear.*

excitant, stimulator, agent-provocateur, rabble-rouser, tub-thumper 738 n. *agitator;* sensationalist, sob-sister, scandalmonger; headline, banner-h. 528n. *publicity;* fillip, ginger, tonic, pick-me-up 174n. *stimulant;* sting, prick, goad, spur, whip, lash 612n. *incentive;* fan; irritant, gadfly, breeze.

Adj. *excited,* activated, stimulated, stung etc. vb.; busy, astir, bustling, rushing 678adj. *active;* ebullient, effervescent, boiling, seething 355 adj. *bubbly;* tense, wrought up, strung up; overheated, feverish, hectic; delirious, frantic 503adj. *frenzied;* glowing 818adj. *fervent;* heated, flushed 379adj. *hot;* red-hot with excitement, violent 176adj. *furious;* seeing red, wild, mad, foaming at the mouth, frothing, ramping, stamping, roaring, raging 891n. *angry;* avid, eager, itching, agog, thrill-seeking, watering at the mouth 859 adj. *desiring;* tingling, a-tremble, a-quiver 818adj. *feeling;* flurried, a-twitter, all of a flutter 318adj. *agitated;* restless, restive, over-excited, over-wrought, distraught, distracted; beside oneself, hysterical, out of control, uncontrollable, running amok, carried away, a prey to passion; inspired, possessed, impassioned, enthusiastic, lyrical, raving 822adj. *excitable.*

exciting, stimulating, sparkling, intoxicating, heady, exhilarating; provocative, piquant, tantalizing; salty, spicy, appetizing; evocative, suggestive; thrilling, agitating; inspiring, possessing; heating, kindling, rousing, stirring, soul-s., heart-swelling, heart-thrilling; cheering, rousing, rabble-r.; sensational, dramatic, melodramatic, stunning; interesting, gripping, absorbing.

impressive, imposing, grand, stately; dignified, majestic, regal, royal, kingly, queenly 868adj. *noble;* high-wrought, awe-inspiring, soul-subduing, sublime, humbling; overwhelming, overpowering; picturesque, scenic; striking, arresting, dramatic; telling, forceful 178adj. *influential.*

Vb. *excite,* affect, infect 178vb. *influence;* touch, move, draw tears

834vb. *sadden;* impassion, touch the heart-strings, arouse the emotions, stir the feelings, play on one's f.; quicken the pulse, startle, electrify, galvanize; warm, warm the blood, raise the temperature, raise to fever-pitch, bring to the boil, make one's blood boil 381vb. *heat;* inflame, enkindle, kindle, draw a spark, set on fire 381vb. *burn;* sting, pique, irritate 891vb. *enrage;* tantalize, tease 827vb. *torment;* touch on the raw, cut to the quick; rip up, open the wound 827vb. *hurt;* work on, work up, breathe on 612vb. *incite;* breathe into, enthuse, inspire, possess; stir, rouse, arouse, wake, awaken (**see** *animate*); evoke, summon up, call forth; thrill, exhilarate, intoxicate; transport, send, send into ecstasies 826vb. *delight.*

animate, vivify, enliven, quicken 360 vb. *vitalize;* revive, rekindle, resuscitate, breathe fresh life into, bring in new blood 656vb. *restore;* inspire, inspirit, put one on his mettle; infuse courage into, encourage, hearten 855vb. *give courage;* give an edge, put teeth into, whet 256vb. *sharpen;* urge, nag, spur, goad, lash 277vb. *accelerate;* fillip, give a fillip to, stimulate, ginger 174vb. *invigorate;* cherish, foster, foment 162vb. *strengthen;* intensify, fan, fan the flame, blow the coals, stir the embers, poke the fire.

impress, sink in, leave an impression; project *or* present an image; interest, hold, grip, absorb; intrigue, rouse curiosity; strike, claim attention 455vb. *attract notice;* affect 178 vb. *influence;* let sink in, bring home to, drive home 532vb. *emphasize;* come home to, make one realize, penetrate, pierce 516vb. *be intelligible;* arrest, shake, smite, stun, amaze, astound, stagger 508vb. *surprise;* sensationalize, stupefy, gorgonize, petrify 864vb. *be wonderful;* dazzle, fill with admiration; inspire with awe, humble; take one's breath away, overwhelm 727vb. *overmaster;* oppress, perturb, disquiet, upset, worry 827vb. *incommode.*

be excited, flare, flare up, flame, burn 379vb. *be hot;* seethe, boil, explode 318vb. *effervesce;* catch the infection, catch the flame, thrill to 818vb. *feel;* tingle, tremble, quiver, flutter, palpitate 318vb. *be agitated;* mantle, flush 818vb. *show feeling;* squirm, writhe 251vb. *wriggle;* dance, stamp, ramp; jump 312vb. *leap;* seek a thrill, capture a t.

Adv. *excitedly*, uncontrollably, frenziedly; all agog, with one's heart in one's mouth, with one's heart beating, with hair on end; a-quiver, a-tremble.

See: 137, 160, 162, 174, 176, 178, 251, 256, 277, 312, 318, 355, 360, 379, 381, 453, 455, 503, 508, 516, 528, 532, 612, 656, 678, 727, 738, 818, 822, 824, 826, 827, 834, 855, 859, 864, 868, 891, 926, 983.

822 Excitability

N. *excitability*, excitableness, explosiveness, inflammability; instability, temperament, emotionalism; hot blood, hot temper, irritability, scratchiness, touchiness 892n. *irascibility;* impatience, nonendurance; incontinence; intolerance, fanaticism 481n. *bias;* passionateness, vehemence, impetuosity, recklessness, headstrong behavior 857n. *rashness;* hastiness 680n. *haste;* effervescence, ebullition; turbulence, boisterousness; restlessness, fidgetiness, fidgets, nerves, flap 318n. *agitation.*

excitable state, exhilaration, elevation, intoxication, abandon, abandonment; thrill, transport, ecstasy, inspiration, lyricism; fever, fever of excitement, fret, fume, perturbation, trepidation, bother, fuss, flurry, whirl 318n. *agitation;* warmth 379n. *heat;* ferment, pother, stew; gust, whiff, storm, tempest 352n. *gale;* effervescence, ebullition, outburst, outbreak, explosion, scene, song and dance 318n. *commotion;* brainstorm, hysterics, delirium, fit, agony 503n. *frenzy;* distraction, madness 503n. *insanity;* mania, passion, master p., ruling p. 817n. *affections;* rage, fury 176n. *violence;* temper, tantrums, rampage 891n. *anger.*

Adj. *excitable*, sensitized, over-sensitive, raw 819adj. *sensitive;* passionate, emotional; susceptible, romantic; out for thrills, thrill-loving, thrill-seeking; suggestible, inflammable, like tinder; unstable, easily exhilarated, easily depressed; easily impressed, impressionable; variable, unstaid; temperamental, mercurial, volatile 152adj. *changeful;* fitful 604 adj. *capricious;* restless, unquiet, nervy, fidgety, edgy, on edge, ruffled 318adj. *agitated;* high-strung, nervous, startlish, skittish, mettlesome 819adj. *lively;* easily provoked, irritable, fiery, hot-tempered, hot-headed 892adj. *irascible;* impatient 680adj. *hasty;* impetuous, impulsive, madcap 857adj. *rash;* savage, fierce; vehement, boisterous, rumbustious, tempestuous, turbulent, stormy, uproarious, clamorous 176adj. *violent;* restive, uncontrollable 738adj. *riotous;* effervescent, simmering, seething, boiling; volcanic, explosive, ready to burst; fanatical, intolerant; rabid 176adj. *furious;* feverish, febrile, frantic, hysterical, delirious 503adj. *frenzied;* dancing, stamping; like a cat on hot bricks, like a cat on a hot tin roof; tense, electric, atmospheric; inspired, raving, lyrical 821adj. *excited.*

Vb. *be excitable,*—impatient etc.adj.; show impatience, fret, fume, stamp; dance, shuffle; show excitement, show temperament 818vb. *show feeling;* be on edge, have nerves, be in a stew, be in a fuss, flap 318vb. *be agitated;* startle, start, jump 854 vb. *be nervous;* be under strain, break down, be on the verge of a breakdown; have a temper 892vb. *be irascible;* foam, froth, throw fits, have hysterics 503vb. *go mad;* abandon oneself, let oneself go, go wild, run riot, run amok, get out of control, see red; storm, rush about 61 vb. *rampage;* ramp, rage, roar 176 vb. *be violent;* fly into a temper, fly off the handle, burst out, break o., explode, create 891vb. *get angry;* kindle, burn, catch fire, flare up 821vb. *be excited;* scratch, tingle 378vb. *itch.*

See: 61, 152, 176, 318, 352, 378, 379, 481, 503, 604, 680, 738, 817, 818, 819, 821, 854, 857, 891, 892.

823 Inexcitability

N. *inexcitability,* inirritability, imperturbability, good temper; calmness, steadiness, composure; coolness, sangfroid, nonchalance; frigidity, coldness, impassibility 820n. *moral insensibility;* unruffled state, tranquillity 266n. *quietude;* serenity, placidity, peace of mind, calm of m. 828n. *content;* equanimity, balance, poise, even temper, level t., philosophic t., philosophy, balanced mind 28n. *equilibrium;* self-possession, self-command, self-control, self-restraint 942n. *temperance;* repression, self-r., stoicism 945n. *asceticism;* detachment, non-attachment, dispassion, dispassionateness 860n. *indifference;* gravity, staidness, demureness, sobriety 834n. *seriousness;* quietism, Quakerism 679n. *inactivity;* sweetness, gentleness 884n. *courtesy;* tameness, meekness, lack of spirit, lack of mettle 734n. *laxity;* tranquilization, soothing 177n. *moderation.*

patience, patience of Job, patience on a monument; forbearance, endurance, long-suffering, longanimity; tolerance, toleration, refusal to be provoked; sufferance, supportance, stoicism; resignation, acquiescence 721n. *submission.*

Adj. *inexcitable,* impassible, cold, frigid, heavy, dull, immune to stimulation; stable 153adj. *unchangeable;* not given to worry, unworrying, unworried, cool, imperturbable, unflappable; steady, composed, controlled; self-controlled, moderate 942 adj. *temperate;* inscrutable, deadpan 820adj. *impassive;* deliberate, unhurried, unhasty 278adj. *slow;* even, level, equable 16adj. *uniform;* unirritable, good-tempered, sunny; staid, sedate, sober, sober-minded, demure, reserved, grave 834adj. *serious;* quiet, unemphatic 266adj. *quiescent;* placid, unruffled, calm, serene 266adj. *tranquil;* sweet, gentle, mild, lamblike, meek 935adj. *innocent;* unwarlike 717adj. *peaceful;* easy, easy-going, undemanding 736adj. *lenient;* comfortable, gemütlich 828adj. *content;* philosophic, unambitious 860adj. *indifferent;* acquiescent, resigned, submissive 739 adj. *obedient;* unlively, unspirited, spiritless, lackadaisical, torpid, passive 175adj. *inert;* calmed down, in a reasonable frame of mind, tame 369adj. *tamed;* unenthusiastic, unsentimental, unromantic, unpoetic 593adj. *prosaic.*

patient, meek, patient as Job, like patience on a monument, armed with patience; tolerant, long-suffering, longanimous, forbearing, enduring; stoic, stoical, philosophic, philosophical, uncomplaining.

Vb. *keep calm,* be composed, be collected; compose oneself, collect o., keep cool; master one's feelings, swallow one's resentment, control one's temper, keep one's hair on; not turn a hair, not bat an eyelid 820vb. *be insensitive;* relax, not excite oneself, not worry, stop worrying, take things easy 683vb. *repose;* resign oneself, take in good part, take philosophically, have patience, be resigned 721vb. *submit.*

be patient, show patience, show restraint, forbear; put up with, stand, tolerate, bear, endure, support, sustain, suffer, thole, aby, abide; resign oneself, grin and bear it; brook, take, take it from, swallow, digest, stomach, pocket 721vb. *knuckle under;* turn the other cheek 909vb. *forgive;* be tolerant, condone 736vb. *be lenient;* turn a blind eye, overlook 734vb. *be lax;* allow 756vb. *permit;* ignore provocation, keep the peace 717vb. *be at peace;* find a modus vivendi, coexist 770vb. *compromise.*

tranquilize, steady, moderate, moderate one's transports 177vb. *assuage;* calm, rock, lull 266vb. *bring to rest;* cool down, compose 719vb. *pacify;* make one's mind easy, set one's mind at rest 831vb. *relieve;* control, repress 747vb. *restrain.*

See: 16, 28, 153, 175, 177, 266, 278, 369, 593, 679, 683, 717, 719, 721, 734, 736, 739, 747, 756, 770, 820, 828, 831, 834, 860, 884, 909, 935, 942, 945.

824 Joy

N. *joy* 376n. *pleasure;* great pleasure, keen p.; sensation of pleasure, enjoyment, thrill, kick, tickle, piquancy 826n. *pleasurableness;* joyfulness, joyousness 835n. *rejoicing;* delight, gladness, rapture, exaltation, exhilaration, transport, abandonment, ecstasy, enchantment, bewitchment, ravishment; unholy joy, gloating, schadenfreude, malice 898n. *malevolence;* life of pleasure, joys of life, pleasant time, halcyon days, holidays, honeymoon 730n. *palmy days.*

happiness, felicity, good fortune, wellbeing, snugness, comfort, ease 376n. *euphoria;* flourishing time, palmy days, Saturnia Regna, Ram Raj, golden age 730n. *prosperity;* blessedness, bliss, beatitude, summum bonum; seventh heaven, paradise, happy home, Fortunate Isles, Isles of the Blessed, Hesperides, Eden, Arcadia, Cockaigne; happy valley, Bower of Bliss.

enjoyment, fruition, gratification, satisfaction, fulfillment 725n. *completion;* usufruct 773n. *possession;* delectation, oblectation, relish, zest, gusto 386n. *taste;* indulgence, luxuriation, wallowing, hedonism 943n. *intemperance;* full life, eudaemonism, epicureanism 944n. *sensualism;* glee, merry-making, lark, frolic, gambol 833n. *merriment;* fun, treat, excursion, outing 837n. *amusement;* refreshment, good cheer, cakes and ale, beer and skittles, panem et circenses 301n. *eating.*

Adj. *pleased,* glad, not sorry; welcoming, receiving with open arms; satisfied, happy 828adj. *content;* gratified, flattered, pleased as Punch; enjoying, loving it, tickled, tickled to death, tickled pink 837adj. *amused;* exhilarated 833adj. *gay;* exalted, elated, elate, overjoyed 833 adj. *jubilant;* cheering, shouting 835 adj. *rejoicing;* delighted, transported, enraptured, ravished, rapturous, ecstatic, raving 923adj. *approving;* in raptures, in ecstasies, in transports, in the seventh heaven; captivated, charmed, enchanted, fascinated 818 adj. *impressed;* maliciously pleased, gloating.

happy, happy as a king, happy as a sandboy; blithe, joyful, joyous, gladsome, merry 833adj. *gay;* beaming, smiling 835adj. *laughing;* radiant, radiating joy, sparkling, starry-eyed; felicitous, lucky, fortunate, to be congratulated 730adj. *prosperous;* blissful, blest, blessed, beatified; in felicity, in bliss, in paradise; at ease, made comfortable 376adj. *comfortable.*

Vb. *be pleased* etc. adj.; have the pleasure; feel *or* experience pleasure, hug oneself, congratulate o., purr, purr with pleasure, dance with p., jubilate 833vb. *be cheerful;* laugh, smile 835vb. *rejoice;* get pleasure from, get a kick out of, take pleasure in, delight in, rejoice in; go into ecstasies, rave, rave about 821vb. *show feeling;* indulge in, have time for, luxuriate in, solace oneself with, refresh oneself w., bask in, wallow 376vb. *enjoy;* have fun 837vb. *amuse oneself;* gloat, gloat over; appreciate, relish, smack one's lips 386vb. *taste;* take a fancy to, like 887vb. *love;* think well of 923vb. *approve;* take in good part, take no offense.

See: 301, 376, 386, 725, 730, 773, 818, 821, 826, 828, 833, 835, 837, 887, 898, 923, 943, 944.

825 Suffering

N. *suffering,* suffering felt, inconvenience, discomfort, disagreeableness, malaise; sufferance, endurance; heart-ache, weltschmerz, lacrimae rerum 834n. *dejection;* longing, homesickness, nostalgia 859n. *desire;* unsatisfied desire 829n. *discontent;* weariness 684n. *fatigue;* weight on the spirit, nightmare, ephialtes, incubus; affliction, teen, tine, dolor, anguish, angst, agony, passion, torture, torment, mental t. 377n. *pain;* twinge, stab, smart, sting, thorn 377

n. *pang;* suffering imposed, crucifixion, cup, calvary, martyrdom; rack, the stake 963n. *punishment;* purgatory, hell, pains of h., damnation, eternal d. 961n. *condemnation;* unpleasantness, mauvais quart d'heure; the hard way, trial, ordeal, fiery o.; shock, blow, infliction, visitation, tribulation 659n. *bane;* extremity, death's door 651n. *illness;* living death, death in life, fate worse than death 616n. *evil;* evil days, unhappy times, iron age 731n. *adversity.*

sorrow, grief, sadness, mournfulness, gloom 834n. *melancholy;* dole, woe, wretchedness, misery, depths of m.; prostration, despair, desolation 853n. *hopelessness;* unhappiness, infelicity, tale of woe 731n. *adversity;* vexation of spirit, weariness of s., aching heart, bleeding h., broken h.; displeasure, dissatisfaction 829n. *discontent;* vexation, bitterness, mortification, chagrin, heart-burning, fretting, repining, remorse 830n. *regret.*

worry, worrying, worriedness, uneasiness, discomfort, disquiet, unquiet, inquietude, fret, fretting 318n. *agitation;* discomposure, dismay 63n. *derangement;* something on one's mind, weight on one's m., anxiety, concern, solicitude, thought, care, carking c.; responsibility, weight of r., load, burden, strain, tension; a worry, worries, cares, cares of the world; trouble, troubles 616n. *evil;* bother, botheration, annoyance, irritation, pest, thorn in the flesh, death of 659n. *bane;* bothersome task 838 n. *bore;* something to worry about, look-out, funeral; headache, teaser, puzzle, problem 530n. *enigma.*

sufferer, victim, scapegoat, sacrifice; prey, shorn lamb, plucked pigeon 544n. *dupe;* willing sacrifice, martyr; object of compassion, wretch, poor w., misery 731n. *unlucky person;* patient, chronic 651n. *sick person.*

Adj. *suffering,* ill 651adj. *sick;* agonizing, writhing, aching, griped, in pain, on a bed of p., ravaged with p., bleeding, harrowed, on the rack, in torment, in hell 377adj. *pained;* inconvenienced, uncomfortable, ill at ease; anguished, anguishous; anxious, unhappy about, worried, troubled, disquieted, apprehensive, dismayed 854adj. *nervous;* discomposed, disconcerted 63adj. *deranged;* ill-used, maltreated, severely handled; downtrodden 745adj. *subjected;* victimized, made a prey, sacrificed; stricken, wounded; heavy-laden, crushed 684adj. *fatigued;* care-worn, sad-looking, worried-l., harassed-l.; woeful, woebegone, haggard, wild-eyed.

unhappy, infelicitous, unlucky, accursed 731adj. *unfortunate;* despairing 853adj. *hopeless;* doomed 961adj. *condemned;* to be pitied, pitiable; poor, wretched, miserable; sad, melancholy, despondent; cut up, heart-broken, heart-scalded, broken-hearted, heavy-h., sick at heart; sorrowful, sorrowing, grieved, grieving, grief-stricken, woebegone 834 adj. *dejected;* plunged in grief, weeping, weepy, wet-eyed, tearful, in tears, in a taking 836adj. *lamenting;* nostalgic, longing 859adj. *desiring;* discontent, displeased, dissatisfied, disappointed 829adj. *discontented;* offended, vexed, annoyed, pained 924adj. *disapproving;* piqued, chagrined, mortified, humiliated 891adj. *resentful;* sickened, disgusted, nauseated 861adj. *disliking;* sorry, remorseful, compunctious, regretful 830adj. *regretting.*

Vb. *suffer,* undergo, endure, go through, experience 818vb. *feel;* bear, put up with; bear pain, suffer p., suffer torment, bleed; hurt oneself, be hurt, smart, chafe, ache 377vb. *feel pain;* wince, flinch, agonize, writhe, squirm 251vb. *wriggle;* take up one's cross, become a martyr, sacrifice oneself; quaff the bitter cup, have a thin time, have a bad t., go through it, have trouble enough, sup full of horrors 731vb. *have trouble;* trouble oneself, distress o., worry, worry to death, fret, sit on thorns, be on pins and needles 318 vb. *be agitated;* mind, let weigh upon one, take it badly; sorrow, passion, teen, grieve, weep, sigh 836vb. *lament;* pity oneself, despond 834vb. *be dejected;* have regrets, kick oneself 830vb. *regret.*

See: 63, 251, 318, 377, 530, 544, 616, 651, 659, 684, 731, 745, 818, 829, 830, 834, 836, 838, 853, 854, 859, 861, 891, 924, 961, 963.

826 Pleasurableness

N. *pleasurableness,* pleasures of, pleasantness, niceness, delectableness, delectability, delightfulness, amenity, sunny side, bright s.; invitingness, attractiveness, appeal, sex a., come-hither look 291n. *attraction;* winning ways 925n. *flattery;* amiability, winsomeness, charm, fascination, enchantment, witchery, loveliness, sight for sore eyes 841n. *beauty;* joyfulness, honeymoon 824 n. *joy;* something nice, a delight, a treat, a joy; pastime, fun 837n. *amusement;* interest, human i.; melody, harmony 412n. *music;* tastiness, deliciousness 390n. *savoriness;* spice, sauce piquante, relish 389n. *condiment;* dainty, tidbit, sweet 392n. *sweetness;* manna in the wilderness, grateful refreshment, balm 685n. *refreshment;* land flowing with milk and honey 635n. *plenty;* peace, perfect p., peace and quiet, tranquillity 266n. *quietude;* pipe-dream 513n. *fantasy.*

Adj. *pleasurable,* pleasant, nice, good; pleasure-giving 837adj. *amusing;* pleasing, agreeable, grateful, gratifying, flattering; acceptable, welcome, welcome as flowers in May; well-liked, to one's taste, to one's liking; wonderful, marvelous, splendid 644 adj. *excellent;* frictionless, painless 376adj. *comfortable;* cushy, easeful, refreshing 685adj.; *reposeful;* peaceful, quiet 266adj. *tranquil;* bowery, luxurious, voluptuous 376adj. *sensuous;* genial, warm, sunny 833adj. *cheering;* delightful, delectable, delicious, exquisite, choice; luscious, juicy 356adj. *pulpy;* delicate, tasty 390adj. *savory;* sugary 392adj. *sweet;* dulcet, musical, harmonious 410adj. *melodious;* picturesque, scenic, lovely 841adj. *beautiful;* amiable, dear, winning, endearing 887 adj. *lovable;* attractive, fetching, appealing, interesting 291adj. *attracting;* seductive, enticing, inviting, captivating; charming, enchanting, bewitching, ravishing; haunting, thrilling, heart-melting, heart-warming 821adj. *exciting;* homely, cozy; pastoral, idyllic; elysian, paradisical, heavenly, out of this world; beatific, blessed, blissful 824adj. *happy.*

Vb. *please,* give pleasure, afford p., yield p., agree with; make things pleasant 925vb. *flatter;* lull, soothe 177vb. *assuage;* comfort 833vb. *cheer;* put on ease, make comfortable 831vb. *relieve;* sugar, gild the pill 392vb. *sweeten;* stroke, pat, pet, baby, coddle, nurse 889vb. *caress;* indulge, pander 734vb. *be lax;* charm, interest 837vb. *amuse;* rejoice, gladden, make happy; gratify, satisfy, crown one's wishes, leave nothing more to desire 828vb. *content;* bless, crown one's bliss, raise to the seventh heaven, beatify.

delight, surprise with joy; rejoice, exhilarate, elate, elevate, uplift; rejoice one's heart, warm the cockles of one's h., do one's heart good; thrill, intoxicate, ravish; transport, fetch, send, send one into raptures *or* ecstasies 821vb. *excite;* make music in one's ears 925vb. *flatter;* take one's fancy, tickle one's f., hit one's f. 887vb. *excite love;* tickle one's palate 390vb. *appetize;* regale, refresh; tickle, titillate, tease, tantalize; invite, prove inviting, entrance, enrapture; enchant, take, charm, becharm 983vb. *bewitch;* take one's breath away 821vb. *impress;* allure, seduce 291vb. *attract.*

See: 177, 266, 291, 356, 376, 389, 390, 392, 410, 412, 635, 644, 685, 734, 821, 824, 828, 831, 833, 837, 841, 887, 889, 925, 983.

827 Painfulness

N. *painfulness,* painful treatment, harshness, roughness, harassment, persecution 735n. *severity;* hurtfulness, harmfulness 645n. *badness;* disagreeableness, unpleasantness; loathsomeness, hatefulness, beastliness 616n. *evil;* grimness 842n. *ugliness;* hideosity 842n. *eyesore;* friction, irritation, ulceration, inflammation, exacerbation 832n. *aggravation;* soreness, tenderness 377n. *pain;* irritability, inflammability 822n. *excitability;* sore subject, sore point, rub, soft spot, tender s. 819n. *sensibility;* sore, running s., ulcer, thorn in the flesh, pin-prick, where the shoe pinches 659n. *bane;* shock 508n. *inexpectation;* unpalatability, disgust, nausea, sickener 391n. *unsavoriness;* sharpness, bitterness, waters of bitterness, bitter cup, bitter draft, bitter pill, gall and wormwood, vinegar 393n. *sourness;* bread of affliction 731n. *adversity;* tribulation, ordeal, cross, cup, calvary 825n. *suffering;* trouble, care 825n. *worry;* dreariness, cheerlessness; pitifulness, pathos; sorry sight, pathetic s., painful s., sad spectacle, object of pity 731n. *unlucky person;* heavy news 825n. *sorrow;* disenchantment, disillusionment 509n. *disappointment;* hornet's nest, hot water 700n. *predicament.*

annoyance, vexation, pain and grief, death of, pest, curse, plague, botheration, embarrassment 825n. *worry;* cause for annoyance, nuisance, pinprick; grievance, complaint; hardship, troubles 616n. *evil;* last straw, limit, outside edge; offense, affront, insult, provocation 921n. *indignity;*

molestation, infestation, persecution, malignity 898n. *malevolence;* feeling of annoyance, displeasure, mortification 891n. *resentment.*

Adj. *paining,* hurting, aching, sore, tender; dolorific, dolorous, agonizing, racking, purgatorial 377adj. *painful;* scathing, searing, scalding, burning, sharp, biting, nipping, gnawing; burning, caustic, corrosive, vitriolic; harsh, hard, rough, cruel 735adj. *severe;* grinding, grueling, punishing, searching, exquisite, extreme; hurtful, harmful, poisonous 659adj. *baneful.*

unpleasant, unpleasing, disagreeable; uncomfortable, comfortless, joyless, dreary, dismal, depressing 834adj. *cheerless;* unattractive, uninviting; hideous 842adj. *ugly;* unwelcome, undesired, unacceptable 860adj. *unwanted;* thankless, unpopular, displeasing 924adj. *disapproved;* disappointing, unsatisfactory 829adj. *discontenting;* distasteful, unpalatable, off 391adj. *unsavory;* foul, nasty, beastly, horrible 645adj. *not nice;* fulsome, malodorous, stinking 397 adj. *fetid;* bitter, sharp 393adj. *sour;* invidious, obnoxious, offensive, objectionable, undesirable, odious, hateful, loathsome, nauseous, disgusting, revolting, repellent 861adj. *disliked;* execrable, accursed 645adj. *damnable.*

annoying, too bad; troublesome, embarrassing, worrying; bothersome, bothering, wearisome, irksome, tiresome, boring 838adj. *tedious;* burdensome, onerous, oppressive 322 adj. *weighty;* disappointing, unlucky, unfortunate, untoward 731adj. *adverse;* awkward, unaccommodating, impossible, pesky, plaguey, harassing 702adj. *hindering;* importunate, pestering; teasing, trying, irritating, vexatious, aggravating, provoking, maddening; galling, stinging, biting, mortifying.

distressing, afflicting, crushing, grievous; moving, affecting, touching, grieving; harrowing, heartbreaking, heart-rending, tear-jerking; pathetic, tragic, tragical, sad, woeful, rueful, mournful, pitiful, lamentable, deplorable 905adj. *pitiable;* ghastly, grim, dreadful, shocking, appalling, horrifying, horrific, nerve-racking 854adj. *frightening.*

intolerable, insufferable, impossible, insupportable, unendurable, unbearable, past bearing, past enduring, not to be borne, not to be endured, not to be put up with; extreme, beyond the limits of tolerance, more than flesh and blood can stand, enough to make one mad, enough to make a parson swear, enough to try the patience of Job, enough to provoke a saint.

Vb. *hurt,* do h., disagree with, injure 645vb. *harm;* pain, cause p. 377vb. *give pain;* knock out, wind, double up 279vb. *strike;* bite, cut, tear, rend 655vb. *wound;* wound the feelings, hurt the f., gall, pique, nettle, mortify 891vb. *huff;* rub the wrong way, tread on one's corns; touch a soft spot, cut to the quick, pierce the heart, rend the heart-strings, draw tears, grieve, afflict, distress, cut up 834vb. *sadden;* plunge into sorrow, bring grief to one's heart, plant an arrow in one's breast, plant a thorn in one's side; corrode, embitter, exacerbate, keep the wound green, gnaw, chafe, rankle, fester 832vb. *aggravate;* offend, aggrieve (**see** *displease*); insult, affront 921vb. *not respect.*

torment, excruciate, martyr; harrow, rack, put to the r., break on the wheel 963vb. *torture;* put to the question, give the third degree, give one the works; put through the hoop, give one a bad time, maltreat, bait, bully, rag, bullyrag, haze, persecute, assail 735vb. *oppress;* be offensive, snap at, bark at 885vb. *be rude;* importune, dun, beset, besiege 737vb. *demand;* haunt, obsess; annoy, do it to a., pin-prick; tease, pester, plague, nag, badger, wherret, worry, try, chivvy, harass, harry, heckle; molest, bother, vex, provoke, ruffle, irritate, needle, sting, chafe, fret, gall, irk, roil, rile 891vb. *enrage.*

incommode, discomfort, disquiet, disturb, distemper, discompose, disconcert, throw one out, upset 63vb. *derange;* worry, embarrass, trouble, perplex 474vb. *puzzle;* exercise, tire 684vb. *fatigue;* weary, bore 838vb. *be tedious;* obsess, haunt, bedevil; weigh upon one, prey on the mind, weigh on the spirits, press on the heart, depress 834vb. *deject;* infest, get in one's hair, get in one's way, thwart 702vb. *obstruct.*

displease, not please, not appeal, find no favor 924vb. *incur blame;* grate, jar, grate on, jar on, set the teeth on edge, go against the grain; disenchant, disillusion, undeceive 509vb. *disappoint;* dissatisfy, give cause for complaint, aggrieve 829 vb. *discontent;* offend, shock, horrify, scandalize, disgust, revolt, repel, sicken, nauseate, fill one with loathing, stink in the nostrils, stick in the throat, stick in the gizzard, make one's gorge rise, turn one's stomach, make one sick, make one vomit, make one throw up 861vb. *cause dislike;* make one's flesh creep, make one's blood run cold, curdle the blood, appal 854vb. *frighten.*

See: 63, 279, 322, 377, 391, 393, 397, 474, 508, 509, 616, 645, 655, 659, 684, 700, 702, 731, 735, 737, 819, 822, 825, 829, 832, 834, 838, 842, 854, 860, 861, 891, 898, 905, 921, 924, 963.

828 Content

N. *content,* contentment, contentedness, satisfaction, entire s., complacence, complacency; self-complacence, self-satisfaction, smugness 873n. *vanity;* partial content, half-smile, ray of comfort; serenity, quietism, tranquillity, resignation 266 n. *quietude;* ease of mind, trouble-free m., easy m., peace of m., heart's ease, nothing left to worry about 376n. *euphoria;* conciliation, reconciliation 719n. *pacification;* snugness, comfort, sitting pretty; wish-fulfillment, desires fulfilled, ambition achieved, port after stormy seas 730n. *prosperity;* acquiescence 758n. *consent;* resignation 721n. *submission.*

Adj. *content,* contented, satisfied, well-s., sweet 824adj. *happy;* appeased, pacified 717adj. *peaceful;* cushy, feeling just right 376adj. *comfortable;* at ease 683adj. *reposeful;* easy in mind, smiling 833adj. *cheerful;* flattered 824adj. *pleased;* with nothing left to wish for, having no desire unfulfilled, having nothing to grumble at 863adj. *sated;* unrepining, uncomplaining, with no regrets, without complaints; unenvious, unjealous 931adj. *disinterested;* philosophic, without desire, without passion 823adj. *inexcitable;* resigned, acquiescent 721adj. *submitting;* fairly content, better satisfied; easily pleased, easy-going 736 adj. *lenient;* secure 660adj. *safe;* unmolested, untroubled, unworried, unafflicted, unvexed, unplagued; blessed with contentment, thankful, gratified 907adj. *grateful.*

contenting, satisfying, satisfactory 635 adj. *sufficient;* lulling, pacifying, appeasing 719adj. *pacificatory;* tolerable, bearable, endurable, livable; unobjectionable, passable 923adj. *approvable;* desirable, wished for, all that is wished for 859adj. *desired.*

Vb. *be content,*—satisfied etc.adj.; purr, purr with content 824vb. *be pleased;* rest and be thankful, rest satisfied, take the good that the gods provide; thank, be thankful, be grateful, have much to be thankful for 907vb. *be grateful;* have all one asks for, have one's wish, attain one's desire, reach the goal of one's ambition 730vb. *prosper;* congratulate oneself, hug o., lay the flattering unction to one's soul 835vb. *rejoice;* be at ease, be at home, sit pat, sit pretty 376vb. *enjoy;* be reconciled 719vb. *make peace;* get over it, take comfort, take heart of grace 831vb. *be relieved;* rest content, take in good part; complain of nothing, have no complaints, have nothing to grouse about, have no regrets, not repine; put up with, acquiesce 721 vb. *submit.*

content, make contented, satisfy, gratify, make one's day 826vb. *please;* meet with approval, go down well 923vb. *be praised;* make happy, bless with contentment; grant a boon, 781vb. *give;* crown one's wishes, leave no desire unfulfilled, appease one's desires, quench one's thirst 863vb. *sate;* comfort 833vb. *cheer;* bring comfort to, speak peace to 831vb. *relieve;* be kind to 897vb. *philanthropize;* lull, set at ease, set at rest; propitiate, disarm, reconcile, conciliate, appease 719vb. *pacify.*

Adv. *contentedly,* complacently, with satisfaction, to one's heart's content, as one would wish.

See: 266, 376, 635, 660, 683, 717, 719, 721, 730, 736, 758, 781, 823, 824, 826, 831, 833, 835, 859, 863, 873, 897, 907, 923, 931.

829 Discontent

N. *discontent,* discontentment, disgruntlement, slow burn; displeasure, pain, dissatisfaction, acute d. 924n. *disapprobation;* cold comfort, not what one expected 509n. *disappointment;* soreness, chagrin, pique, mortification, heart-burning, bitterness, bile, spleen 891n. *resentment;* uneasiness, disquiet 825n. *worry;* grief, vexation of spirit 825n. *sorrow;* maladjustment, strain, tension; restlessness, "winter of our discontent"; unrest, state of u., restiveness 738n. *disobedience;* agitation 318n. *commotion;* finickiness, faddiness, hypercriticism, perfectionism 862n. *fastid-*

iousness; querulousness 709n. *quarrelsomeness;* ill-will 912n. *envy;* competition 911n. *jealousy; objection,* kick; chip on one's shoulder, grievance, grudge, complaint, plaint 709n. *quarrel;* melancholy 834n. *dejection;* sulkiness, sulks, dirty look, grimace, scowl, frown 893n. *sullenness;* groan, curse 899n. *malediction;* cheep, squeak, murmur, murmuring, whispering campaign, "curses not loud but deep."

malcontent, grumbler, grouch, grouser, growler, mutterer, croaker, complainer, whiner, bleater, bellyacher, Jonah; plaintiff 763n. *petitioner;* faultfinder, critic, censurer, crabber, envier 709n. *quarreler;* sorehead, man with a grievance, man with a chip on his shoulder, angry young man; laudator temporis acti; irredentist; murmurer, seditionist 738n. *agitator;* indignation meeting, protest m. 762n. *deprecation;* the Opposition, Her Majesty's O., leader of the opposition; irreconcilable, bitter-ender, last-ditcher, die-hard 705n. *opponent;* hard taskmaster, exacting critic 735n. *tyrant.*

Adj. *discontented,* displeased, not best pleased; dissatisfied 924adj. *disapproving;* unsatisfied, ungratified 509adj. *disappointed;* defeated 728 adj. *unsuccessful;* malcontent, dissident 489adj. *dissenting;* non-cooperative, obstructive 702adj. *hindering;* restless, restive 738adj. *disobedient;* disgruntled, ill content, browned off, cheesed o., upset 825 adj. *unhappy;* repining 830adj. *regretting;* sad, uncomforted, unconsoled, unrelieved 834adj. *dejected;* ill-disposed, grudging, jealous, envious; bileful, spleenful, bitter, embittered, soured 393adj. *sour;* cross, sulky, sulking 893adj. *sullen;* grouchy, grumbling, grousing, whining, murmuring, cursing, swearing 899adj. *maledicent;* protesting 762 adj. *deprecatory;* unflattered, smarting, sore, mortified, insulted, affronted 891adj. *resentful;* hard to please, hard to satisfy, never satisfied, exigent, exacting 862adj. *fastidious;* fault-finding, critical, hypercritical, censorious 926adj. *detracting;* irreconcilable, hostile 881adj. *inimical;* resisting 704adj. *opposing.*

discontenting, unsatisfactory 636adj. *insufficient;* leaving unsatisfied, unfilling; sickening, nauseating 861 adj. *disliked;* upsetting, mortifying 827adj. *annoying;* frustrating 509adj. *disappointing;* baffling, obstructive 702adj. *hindering;* discouraging, disheartening 613adj. *dissuasive.*

Vb. *be discontented,*—dissatisfied etc. adj.; be critical, crab, criticize, find fault 862vb. *be fastidious;* lack, miss, feel something is missing 627 vb. *require;* sneer, groan, jeer 924 vb. *disapprove;* mind, take offense, take amiss, take ill, take to heart, take on, be offended, smart under 891vb. *resent;* get the hump, sulk 893vb. *be sullen;* look blue, look glum, make a wry face, pull a long f. 834vb. *be dejected;* moan, mutter, murmur, whine, bleat, beef, protest, complain, object, cry blue murder 762vb. *deprecate;* bellyache, grumble, grouse, croak, snap, grin; wail 836vb. *lament;* be aggrieved, have a grievance, cherish a g., have a chip on one's shoulder; join the opposition 704vb. *oppose;* rise up 738vb. *revolt;* grudge 912vb. *envy;* quarrel with one's bread and butter 709vb. *quarrel;* not know when one is well off, refuse God's gifts, look a gift horse in the mouth; be unwilling, make a piece of work of it 598vb. *be loath;* refuse to be satisfied, ask for one's money back, return 607vb. *reject;* remain irreconcilable, be an irredentist; repine 830vb. *regret.*

cause discontent, dissatisfy 636vb. *not suffice;* leave dissatisfied, leave room for complaint 509vb. *disappoint;* spoil for one, spoil one's pleasure, get one down 834vb. *deject;* dishearten, discourage 613vb. *dissuade;* sour, embitter, disgruntle; upset, chafe, fret, bite, put on edge, put out of humor, irritate 891vb. *huff;* put out of countenance, mortify 872vb. *humiliate;* offend, cause resentment 827vb. *displease;* shock, scandalize 924vb. *incur blame;* nauseate, sicken, disgust 861vb. *cause dislike;* arouse discontent, sow the seeds of d., make trouble, stir up t., agitate 738vb. *revolt.*

See: 318, 393, 489, 509, 598, 607, 613, 627, 636, 702, 704, 705, 709, 728, 735, 738, 762, 763, 825, 827, 830, 834, 836, 861, 862, 872, 881, 891, 893, 899, 911, 912, 924, 926.

830 Regret

N. *regret,* regretfulness, regretting, repining; mortification, heart-burning 891n. *resentment;* futile regret, vain r., crying over spilled milk; soul-searching, self-reproach, remorse, contrition, repentance, compunction, regrets, apologies 939 n. *penitence;* disillusion, second thoughts, better t. 67n. *sequel;* longing, desiderium, homesickness, maladie du pays, nostalgia, nostalgie de la boue 859n. *desire;* sense of loss, irredentism 737n. *demand;* laudator temporis acti, irredentist 859n. *desirer;* matter of regret, pity of it.

Adj. *regretting*, missing, homesick, nostalgic; irredentist; harking back, looking over one's shoulder 125adj. *retrospective;* mortified, repining, bitter 891adj. *resentful;* irreconcilable, inconsolable, crying over spilt milk 836adj. *lamenting;* compunctious, regretful, remorseful, rueful, sorry, full of regrets, apologetic, soul-searching, penitent 939adj. *repentant;* undeceived, disillusioned, sadder and wiser.

regretted, much r., sadly missed, badly wanted; regrettable, deplorable, much to be deplored, too bad.

Vb. *regret,* rue, deplore, rue the day; curse one's folly, blame oneself, accuse o., reproach o., kick o.; unwish, wish undone, repine, wring one's hands, cry over spilt milk, spend time in vain regrets 836vb. *lament;* want one's time over again, sigh for the good old days, fight one's battles over again, reopen old wounds, hark back, evoke the past 505vb. *retrospect;* look back, look over one's shoulder, cast a longing, lingering look behind; miss, sadly m., miss badly, regret the loss, want back; long for, be homesick 859vb. *desire;* express regrets, apologize, feel compunction, feel remorse, be sorry 939vb. *be penitent;* ask for another chance 905vb. *ask mercy;* deplore, deprecate, lament 924vb. *disapprove;* feel mortified, gnash one's teeth 891vb. *resent;* have cause for regret, have had one's lesson, regret it, smart for it 963vb. *be punished.*

See: 67, 125, 505, 737, 836, 859, 891, 905, 924, 939, 963.

831 Relief

N. *relief,* recruitment 685n. *refreshment;* easing, alleviation, mitigation, palliation, abatement 177n. *moderation;* good riddance; exemption 668 n. *deliverance;* solace, consolation, comfort, ray of c., crumb of c.; blue streak, rift in the clouds; feeling better, load off one's mind, sigh of relief 656n. *revival;* lulling, lullaby, cradle-song, berceuse; soothing, soothing syrup, lenitive 177n. *moderator;* pain-killer, analgesic 375 n. *anesthetic;* sleeping draft, sleeping pill 679n. *soporific;* pillow 218n. *cushion;* comforter, consoler, ray of sunshine.

Adj. *relieving*, soothing, smoothing, balsamic 685adj. *refreshing;* lulling, assuaging, pain-killing, analgesic, anodyne 177adj. *lenitive;* curative, restorative 658adj. *remedial;* consoling, consolatory, comforting.

Vb. *relieve*, ease, soften, cushion; relax, lessen the strain; temper, temper the wind to the shorn lamb 177vb. *moderate;* lift, raise, take off, lighten, unburden, disburden, take the load off one's mind 701vb. *disencumber;* spare, exempt from 919 vb. *exempt;* save 668vb. *deliver;* console, dry the eyes, wipe the e., wipe away the tears, solace, comfort, bring c., offer a crumb of c.; cheer up, buck up, encourage, hearten, pat on the back 833vb. *cheer;* recruit, shade, cool, fan, ventilate 685vb. *refresh;* restore, repair 656vb. *cure;* bandage, bind up, poultice, plaster 658vb. *doctor;* calm, soothe, pour balm, pour oil, palliate, mitigate, moderate, alleviate, deaden 177vb. *assuage;* smooth the brow, take out the wrinkles 258vb. *smooth;* stroke, pat 889vb. *caress;* cradle, lull, put to sleep 679vb. *sleep;* anesthetize, kill the pain 375vb. *render insensible;* take pity on, put one out of one's misery, give the coup de grâce 905vb. *pity.*

be relieved, relieve oneself, ease o., obtain relief; feel relief, heave a sigh of r., draw breath again; console oneself, solace o.; take comfort, feel better, dry one's eyes, smile again 833vb. *be cheerful;* recover from the blow, get over it, come to, be oneself again, pull oneself together, snap out of it, buck up, perk up, sleep off 656vb. *be restored;* rest content 828vb. *be content.*

See: 177, 218, 258, 375, 656, 658, 668, 679, 685, 701, 828, 833, 889, 905, 919.

832 Aggravation

N. *aggravation,* exacerbation, exasperation, irritation, embittering, embitterment; enhancement, augmentation 36n. *increase;* intensification 162 n. *strengthening;* heightening, deepening, adding to 482n. *overestima-*

tion; making worse 655n. *deterioration;* complication 700n. *difficulty;* irritant 821n. *excitant;* previous offense 936n. *guilt.*

Adj. aggravated, intensified; exacerbated, complicated; unrelieved, made worse, not improved 655adj. *deteriorated;* aggravable.

Vb. *aggravate,* intensify 162vb. *strengthen;* enhance, heighten, deepen; increase 36vb. *augment;* worsen, make worse, render w., make things w., not improve matters 655vb. *deteriorate;* exacerbate, embitter, further embitter, sour, envenom, inflame 821vb. *excite;* exasperate, irritate 891vb. *enrage;* add fuel to the flame, blow the coals; complicate, make bad worse, go from bad to worse, jump from the frying pan into the fire.

Adv. *aggravatedly,* worse and worse, from bad to worse, out of the frying pan into the fire.

Int. so much the worse! tant pis!

See: 36, 162, 482, 655, 700, 821, 891, 936.

833 Cheerfulness

N. *cheerfulness,* alacrity 597n. *willingness;* optimism, hopefulness 852n. *hope;* cheeriness, happiness, blitheness 824n. *joy;* geniality, sunniness, breeziness, smiles, good humor, bon naturel; vitality, spirits, animal s., flow of s., joie de vivre 360n. *life;* light-heartedness, sunshine in the breast, light heart, optimistic soul, carefree mind; liveliness, sparkle, vivacity, animation, exhilaration, elevation, abandon; life and soul of the party, party spirit 882n. *sociality;* optimist, perennial o., Pollyanna.

merriment, laughter and joy; cheer, good c.; exhilaration, high spirits, abandon; jollity, joviality, jocularity, gaiety, glee, mirth, hilarity 835 n. *laughter;* levity, frivolity 499n. *folly;* merry-making, fun, fun and games, sport, good s. 837n. *amusement;* marriage bells, jubilee 876n. *celebration.*

Adj. *cheerful,* cheery, cheerly, blithe, blithesome 824adj. *happy;* hearty, genial 882adj. *sociable;* smiling, sunny, bright, beaming, radiant 835 adj. *laughing;* breezy, of good cheer, in spirits, in good s., in a good humor; in good heart, unrepining, optimistic, hopeful, buoyant, resilient, irrepressible; carefree, light-hearted; debonair, bonny, buxom, bouncing; pert, jaunty, perky, chirpy, canty, spry, spirited, sprightly, vivacious, animated, vital, sparkling, on the top of one's form 819adj. *lively;* alacritous 597adj. *willing.*

gay, light, frivolous 456adj. *light-minded;* joyous, joyful, merry as a cricket, merry as a thrush, happy as a sandboy, happy as a king, gay as a lark, happy as the day is long; sparkling, mirth-loving, laughter-l., waggish, jocular 839adj. *witty;* playful, sportive, frisky, frolic, gamesome, frolicsome, kittenish 837adj. *amusing;* roguish, arch, sly, tricksy; merry, merry-making, mirthful, jocund, jovial, jolly, joking, dancing, laughing, singing, drinking, Anacreontic; wild, rackety, shouting, roaring with laughter, hilarious, uproarious, rip-roaring, rollicking, rattling, splitting one's sides, tickled pink 837adj. *amused.*

jubilant, jubilous, jubilating, gleeful, gleesome, delighted 824adj. *pleased;* elate, erect, flushed, exulting, exultant, triumphant, cock-a-hoop 727adj. *successful;* triumphing, celebrating, riotous, rioting 876adj. *celebrative.*

cheering, exhilarating, enlivening, encouraging etc. vb.; warming, heart-w., raising the spirits, exhilarating, animating, intoxicating 821adj. *exciting;* optimistic, tonic, comforting, like a ray of sunshine, just what the doctor ordered; balmy, palmy, bracing, invigorating 652adj. *salubrious.*

Vb. *be cheerful,* be in good spirits, be in good humor, be in good heart; keep cheerful, look on the bright side, keep one's spirits up 852vb. *hope;* keep one's pecker up, grin and bear it, put a good face upon it 599vb. *be resolute;* take heart, take heart of grace, cheer up, perk up, buck up 831vb. *be relieved;* brighten, liven up, grow animated, let oneself go, abandon oneself, drive dull care away; radiate good humor, smile, beam, sparkle; dance, sing, carol, lilt, chirrup, chirp, whistle, laugh 835vb. *rejoice;* whoop, cheer 876vb. *celebrate;* have fun, frisk, frolic, rollick, romp, sport, disport oneself, enjoy o., have a good time 837vb. *amuse oneself;* go gay, have a party, 882vb. *be sociable.*

cheer, gladden, warm, warm the heart 828vb. *content;* comfort, console 831vb. *relieve;* rejoice the heart, put in a good humor 826vb. *please;* inspire, enliven 821vb. *animate;* exhilarate, elate 826vb. *delight;* encourage, inspirit, raise the spirits, buck up, jolly along, bolster, bolster up 855vb. *give courage;* act like a tonic, energize 174vb. *invigorate.*

Adv. *cheerfully*, willingly, joyfully, gaily, joyously, light-heartedly, optimistically, carelessly; airily, breezily.

See: 174, 360, 456, 499, 597, 599, 652, 727, 819, 821, 824, 826, 828, 831, 835, 837, 839, 852, 855, 876, 882.

834 Dejection. Seriousness

N. *dejection*, joylessness, unhappiness, cheerlessness, dreariness, dejectedness, low spirits, dumps, doldrums; droopiness, dispiritedness, heart-sinking; disillusion 509n. *disappointment;* defeatism, pessimism, cynicism, despair, death-wish, suicidal tendency 853n. *hopelessness;* weariness, oppression, exhaustion 684n. *fatigue;* oppression of spirit, heart-ache, heaviness, sadness, misery, wretchedness, disconsolateness, dolefulness 825n. *sorrow;* despondency, prosternation, prostration, languishment; Slough of Despond, gray dawn; gloominess, gloom, settled g.; glumness, dejected look, haggardness, funereal aspect, long face, downcast countenance, lack-luster eye; cause of dejection, sorry sight, memento mori, depressant 838n. *bore;* care, thought, trouble 825n. *worry.*

melancholy, melancholia, hypochondria, hypochondriasis; black mood, blue devils, blues, horrors, mumps, mopes, moping, mopiness, sighing, sigh; dismals, lachrymals, vapors, megrims, spleen, bile 829n. *discontent;* disgust of life, taedium vitae, weltschmerz, angst, nostalgia, mal du pays, homesickness 825n. *suffering.*

seriousness, earnestness; gravity, solemnity, sobriety, demureness, staidness, grimness 893n. *sullenness;* primness, humorlessness, heaviness, dullness; straight face, dead pan; sternness, heavy stuff; earnest, dead e.; no laughing matter, chastening thought.

moper, croaker, complainer, Jonah 829n. *malcontent;* pessimist, damper, wet blanket, Job's comforter, misery, agelast, sobersides; death's-head, skeleton at the feast; hypochondriac, malade imaginaire, seek-sorrow, self-tormentor.

Adj. *dejected*, joyless, dreary, cheerless, unhappy, sad (**see** *melancholic*); gloomy, despondent, desponding, unhopeful, pessimistic, defeatist, despairing 853adj. *hopeless;* beaten, overcome 728adj. *defeated;* dispirited, unnerved, unmanned 854 adj. *nervous;* troubled, worried 825 adj. *suffering;* downcast, droopy, low, down, down in the mouth, low-spirited, depressed; unlively, out of sorts, not oneself, out of spirits; sluggish, listless, lackadaisical 679 adj. *inactive;* lack-luster 419adj. *dim;* out of countenance, discountenanced, humbled, crushed, chapfallen, chop-f., crestfallen, ready to cry 509adj. *disappointed;* in the doldrums, in low water, out of luck 731adj. *unprosperous;* chastened, sobered, sadder and wiser 830adj. *regretting;* subdued, piano; cynical, disillusioned 509adj. *disappointed.*

melancholic, in the blues, bilious, atrabilious, vaporish, hypochondriacal; jaundiced, sour, hipped, hippish; thoughtful, pensive, penseroso, full of thought; melancholy, sad, triste, tristful; saddened, cut up, heavy, heavy-hearted, full of heaviness, sick at heart, heart-sick, souls. 825adj. *unhappy;* sorry, rueful 830adj. *regretting;* mournful, doleful, woeful, tearful, lachrymose 836adj. *lamenting;* uncheerful, cheerless, joyless, dreary, spiritless, comfortless; miserable, wretched, unrelieved, refusing comfort, disconsolate; moody, sulky, sulking 893adj. *sullen;* mumpish, mopish, dumpish, dull, dismal, gloomy, glum; long-faced, long in the face, woebegone; wan, haggard, care-worn.

serious, sober, sober as a judge, solemn, sedate, staid, demure, muted, grave, grave as an undertaker, stern 735adj. *severe;* sour, puritan, grim, grim-visaged, dark, frowning, scowling, forbidding, saturnine 893adj. *sullen;* unlaughing, unsmiling; inscrutable, straight-faced, poker-f., dead-pan; prim, unlively, humorless; unfunny, unwitty, without a laugh in it, heavy, dull 838adj. *tedious;* chastening, sobering.

cheerless, comfortless, uncomforting, unconsoling, out of comfort; uncongenial, uninviting; depressing, unrelieved, dreary, dull, flat 838adj. *tedious;* dismal, lugubrious, funereal, gloomy, dark, forbidding; drab, gray, somber, overcast, clouded, murky, lowering; ungenial, cold.

Vb. *be dejected*, despond, admit defeat 853vb. *despair;* succumb, lie down 728vb. *be defeated;* languish, sink, droop, sag, wilt, flag, give up 684vb. *be fatigued;* look downcast, look blue, hang the head, pull a long face, laugh on the wrong side of one's mouth; mope, brood 449vb. *think;* lay to heart, take to h., sulk 893vb. *be sullen;* eat one's heart out, yearn, long 859vb. *desire;* sigh, grieve 829vb. *be discontent;* groan 825adj. *suffer;* weep 836vb. *lament;* repine 830vb. *regret.*

be serious, not smile, repress a s.; not laugh, keep a straight face, keep countenance, maintain one's gravity, recover one's g., sober up; look grave, look glum; lack sparkle, lack humor, not see the joke, take oneself seriously, be a bore 838vb. *be tedious;* sober, chasten.

sadden, grieve, grieve to the heart, bring grief, bring sorrow, cut up; turn one's hair gray, break one's heart, crack one's heart-strings; draw tears, touch the heart, melt the h., leave not a dry eye 821vb. *impress;* annoy, pain, spoil one's pleasure 829vb. *discontent;* deny comfort, render disconsolate, drive to despair 853vb. *leave no hope;* crush, overcome, overwhelm, prostrate; orphan, bereave 786vb. *deprive.*

deject, depress, down, get one down; cause alarm and despondency, dishearten, discourage, dispirit, take the heart out of, unman, unnerve 854vb. *frighten;* spoil the fun, take the joy out of, cast a shade, cast a shadow, cast a gloom over 418vb. *darken;* damp, dampen, damp the spirits, throw cold water, frown upon 613vb. *dissuade;* dull the spirits, lie on the mind, weigh heavy on one's heart, oppress the breast; make the heart sick, disgust 827vb. *displease;* strain, weary 684vb. *fatigue;* bore 838vb. *be tedious;* chasten, sober 534vb. *teach.*

See: 418, 419, 449, 509, 534, 613, 679, 684, 728, 731, 735, 786, 821, 825, 827, 829, 830, 836, 838, 853, 854, 893.

835 Rejoicing

N. *rejoicing,* manifestation of joy 837 n. *festivity;* jubilation, jubilee, triumph, exultation 876n. *celebration;* congratulations, felicitation, self-congratulation, mutual c., self-applause 886n. *congratulation;* plaudits, clapping, shout, yell 923n. *applause;* cheers, rousing c., three c., huzzah, hurrah, hosanna, hallelujah 923n. *praise;* thanksgiving 907n. *thanks;* paean, psalm, Te Deum 981 n. *hymn;* reveling, revels 837n. *revel;* merrymaking, abandon, abandonment 833n. *merriment.*

laughter, faculty of l., risibility; loud laughter, hearty l., rollicking l. Homeric l.; roar of laughter, shout of l., burst of l., peal of l., immoderate l., cachinnation; mocking laughter, derision 851n. *ridicule;* laugh, horse l., guffaw; chuckle, throaty c., chortle, gurgle, cackle, crow, coo; giggle, snigger, snicker, titter, tee-hee; fit of laughing, the giggles; smile, sweet s., simper, smirk, grin, broad g., sardonic g.; laughingness, inclination to laughter, twinkle, half-smile; humor, sense of h. 839n. *wit;* laughableness, laughing matter, comedy, farce 497n. *absurdity.*

laugher, chuckler, giggler, cackler, sniggerer, titterer; smiler, grinner, smirker, simperer, Cheshire cat; mocker, derider 926n. *detractor;* rejoicer, rollicker 837n. *reveler;* god of laughter, Momus; comic muse, Thalia.

Adj. *rejoicing,* reveling, rollicking, cheering, shouting, yelling etc. vb.; exultant, flushed, elated 833adj. *jubilant;* lyrical, ecstatic 923adj. *approving.*

laughing, guffawing etc. vb.; splitting one's sides, convulsed with laughter, dying with l.; inclined to laughter, risible; humorous; mocking 851adj. *derisive;* laughable, derisory 849adj. *ridiculous;* comic, farcical 497adj. *absurd.*

Vb. rejoice, be joyful, sing for joy, shout for j., leap for j., dance for j., dance, skip 312vb. *leap;* clap, clap one's hands, throw one's cap in the air whoop, cheer, huzza, hurrah 923 vb. *applaud;* shout 408vb. *vociferate;* carol 413vb. *sing;* sing paeans, shout hosannas, sing the Te Deum 923vb. *praise;* exult, triumph, jubilate 876 vb. *celebrate;* felicitate, congratulate 886vb. *gratulate;* bless, give thanks 907vb. *thank;* abandon oneself, let oneself go, riot, go mad for joy, run in the streets, maffick 61vb. *rampage;* make merry 833vb. *be cheerful;* have a good time, frolic, frisk, rollick 837vb. *revel;* have a party, celebrate 882vb. *be sociable;* feel pleased, congratulate oneself, hug o., rub one's hands, smack one's lips, gloat 824vb. *be pleased;* sigh for pleasure, cry for joy 408vb.

cry; purr, coo, gurgle, crow, chirrup, chirp 409vb. *ululate.*
laugh, laugh outright, start laughing, burst out l., get the giggles; hoot, chuckle, chortle, crow, cackle; giggle, snigger, snicker, titter, tee-hee; make merry over, laugh at, laugh in one's sleeve, mock, deride 851vb. *ridicule;* shake, hold one's sides, shake one's s., split one's s., burst with laughter, split with l., rock with l., roll with l., hoot with l., roar with l., stifle with l., die with l.
smile, grin, show one's teeth; grimace, curl one's lips, grin like a Cheshire cat; smirk, simper; twinkle, beam, flash a smile.
Int. cheers! three c.! huzzah! hurrah! hooray! hosanna! hallelujah! hail the conquering hero! io triumphe!
See: 61, 312, 408, 409, 413, 497, 824, 833, 837, 839, 849, 851, 876, 882, 886, 907, 923, 926, 981.

836 Lamentation

N. *lamentation*, lamenting, ululation, wail, wail of woe, groaning, weeping, wailing; plangency, weeping and wailing, weeping and gnashing of teeth, beating the breast, tearing one's hair; mourning, deep m. 364n. *obsequies;* rending one's garments, sackcloth and ashes; widow's weeds, weepers, crape, black, mourning ring; cypress, willow; Wailing Wall; crying, sobbing, sighing, blubbering, whimpering, whining, greeting, grizzling, sniveling; tears, tearfulness, dolefulness; tenderness, melting mood, starting tears, tears of pity 905n. *pity;* wet eyes, red e.; falling tears, fit of t., flood of t., burst of t.; breakdown, hysterics; cry, good c.; tear, tear-drop; sob, sigh, whimper, whine, grizzle, boo-hoo.
lament, plaint, complaint, jeremiad, dirge, knell, requiem, threnody, elegy, nenia, epicedium, Hari bol, death song, swansong, funeral oration 364n. *obsequies;* keen, coronach, wake 905n. *condolence;* howl, shriek, scream, outcry 409n. *ululation;* tears of grief, tears of rage; sobstuff, sob-story, hard-luck s., tale of woe, jeremiad; cri de coeur; show of grief, crocodile tears 542n. *sham.*
weeper, wailer, keener, lamenter, threnodist, elegist; mourner, professional m., mute 364n. *funeral;* sobber, sigher, grizzler, sniveler, whimperer, whiner, blubberer, cry-baby; complainer, grouser 829n. *malcontent;* Jeremiah, Heraclitus, Niobe; dying duck, dying swan.
Adj. *lamenting,* crying etc. vb.; lachrymatory, tear-shedding, tear-dropping; in tears, bathed in t., dissolved in t.; tearful, lachrymose, in melting mood; wet-eyed, red-e., with moistened eyes; mourning, mournful, doleful 825adj. *unhappy;* woeful, woebegone, haggard, wild-eyed, wringing one's hands 834adj. *dejected;* complaining, planning, plangent, plaintive, plaintiful; elegiac, epicedial, threnodic, threnodial, dirgelike 364adj. *funereal;* condoling, in mourning, in black, in funeral garments, in sackcloth and ashes; half-masted, at half-mast; whining, canting, querulous, querimonious, with a hard-luck story, with a tale of woe; pathetic, pitiful, lamentable, fit for tears, tear-jerking 905adj. *pitiable;* lamented, deplorable 830 adj. *regretted.*
Vb. *lament*, grieve, sorrow, sigh 825 vb. *suffer;* deplore 830vb. *regret;* condole, grieve for, sigh for, plain, weep over, cry o., bewail, bemoan, elegize, threnodize; bury with lamentation, sing the dirge, sing a requiem, toll the knell 364vb. *inter;* mourn, wail, keen, sit at the wake; express grief, put on black, go into mourning, wear m., wear the willow, put on sackcloth and ashes, wring one's hands, beat the breast, tear one's hair, roll in the dust; take on, carry on, take it badly; complain, bellyache, grouse, tell one's tale of woe 829vb. *be discontented.*
weep, wail, greet, pipe one's eye; shed tears, drop t., burst into t., melt in t., dissolve in t., melt, fall into the melting mood; hold back one's tears, be ready to cry; cry, break down, cry like a child, cry like a baby, boo-hoo, cry one's eyes out; howl, cry out, squall, yell, yammer, clamor, scream, shriek 409vb. *ululate;* sob, sigh, moan, groan 825vb. *suffer;* snivel, grizzle, blubber, pule, whine, whimper; get ready to cry, weep without cause, cry for nothing, cry out before one is hurt.
Adv. *tearfully*, painfully, de profundis,
See: 364, 409, 542, 825, 829, 830, 834, 905.

837 Amusement

N. *amusement*, pleasure, interest, delight 826n. *pleasurableness;* diversion, divertissement, entertainment, light e., popular e.; dramatic entertainment 594n. *drama;* pastime, hobby, labor of love 597n. *voluntary work;* solace, recreation, recruitment 685n. *refreshment;* relaxation 683n. *repose;* holiday, Bank h. 681 n. *leisure;* April Fool's Day, gala day, red-letter d., banner d. 876n. *special day;* play, sport, fun, good clean f., good cheer, joviality, jocundity 833n. *merriment;* occasion, do, show, tamasha, rout, commemoration, Gaudy night 876n. *celebration;* outing, excursion, cheap e., jaunt, pleasure trip; treat, Dutch t., wayzgoose, fête champêtre, picnic (**see** *festivity*); garden party, bunfight, fete, jamboree, conversazione 74n. *assembly;* game, game of chance, game of skill, whist drive, bridge d. (**see** *card game*); round games, party g., knitting bee, spelling b. (**see** *indoor game*).

festivity, playtime, holiday-making, holidaying; visiting 882n. *social round;* fun 835n. *laughter;* whirl, round of pleasure, round of gaiety; seeing life, high life, night l.; good time, hot t.; beating it up, burning the candle at both ends, a short life and a merry one 943n. *intemperance;* festival, high f., fair, fun-f., fun of the fair, kermis, carnival, fiesta, mi-carême, gala; masque, masqueing, mummery; festivities, fun and games, merry-making, revels, Saturnalia, Yule-tide, puja, Durga Puja 833n. *merriment;* high day, feast d. 876n. *special day;* carouse, carousal, wassail, wake 301n. *feasting;* conviviality, symposium, party, Dutch p., bottle p. 882n. *social gathering;* drinking party, drinking bout 301n. *drinking;* orgy, debauch, carouse 494 n. *drunkenness;* bust, binge, beano; barbecue, cookout, clambake, wiener roast, bump-supper, harvest s., kirn, dinner, grand d., banquet 301n. *meal.*

revel, rout, jollification, whoopee, fun; fun fast and furious, high jinks, spree, junket, junketing; night out, night on the tiles; bonfire, pyrotechnics, Fourth of July 420n. *fireworks;* play, game, romp, rollick, frolic, lark, skylarking, escapade, prank, rag, trick, monkey-t. 497n. *foolery.*

pleasure-ground, park, deer-p.; green, village g.; arbor, gardens, pleasure-g., Vauxhall 192n. *pleasance;* seaside, Riviera, lido, bathing-beach, holiday camp; playground, recreation ground, cricket g.; field, flying f., playing-f., football f., hunting-f., links, golf l., golf course; rink, skating r., ice r.; squash-court, fives-c., tennis c., croquet lawn 724n. *arena;* circus, fair, funfair, carousel, wonderland; peep-show, raree show 522n. *exhibit;* swing, roundabout, merry-go-round, scenic railway, tunnel of love, switchback, Ferris wheel, big dipper; see-saw, slide, chute.

place of amusement, amusement park, fun-fair, shooting-gallery, skittle-alley, bowling a., covered court, billiard room, card-r., assembly r., pump-r., concert r.; concert hall, music h., vaudeville, hippodrome; picture-house 445n. *cinema;* playhouse 594n. *theater;* dance-room, ballroom, dance-floor; dance-hall, palais de danse; carbaret, night club, boite de nuit; casino, kursaal, gambling hell 618n. *gaming house.*

sport, outdoor life; sportsmanship, gamesmanship 694n. *skill;* sports, field s.; agonism, games, gymnastics 162n. *athletics*, 716n. *contest, racing, pugilism, wrestling;* outdoor sports, camping, picnicking; riding, hacking; archery, shooting, clay-pigeon s.; hunting, shooting, fishing; water sports, swimming, bathing, surf-b., surf-riding, skindiving, aquaplaning, water-polo, boating, rowing, yachting, sailing 269n. *aquatics;* climbing, mountaineering, alpinism 308n. *ascent;* exploring, cave-e., speleology; winter sports, skiing, ski-jumping, bobsleighing, Cresta-running, tobogganing, luging, skating, ice-s., sliding; ice-hockey; curling; flying, gliding 271n. *aeronautics;* tourism, touring, traveling, exploration 267n. *land travel.*

ball game, pat-ball, bat-and-ball game; King Willow, cricket, Test c., league c., single-wicket; baseball, softball, rounders; trapball, knurr and spell; tennis, real t., Royal t.; deck tennis; table tennis, ping-pong; badminton, battledore and shuttlecock; squash, rackets; hand-ball, hurling; fives, pelota; lacrosse, pallone; wall-game, net-ball, volley-b., basket-b.; football, Association f., soccer; Rugby football, rugger; hockey, ice-h., polo, Kop-Karri, water-polo; croquet, table-c., pall mall, golf, clock-g.; skittles, ninepins, bowls, curling; marbles, dibs; quoits, deck q., hoop-la, discus-throwing; billiards, French b., Carolina, snooker, pyramids, pool, bagatelle; carom, shove ha'penny, shovelboard.

indoor game, nursery g., parlor g., round g., party g.; musical bumps, musical chairs, hunt the thimble, hunt the slipper, postman's knock, kiss in the ring, nuts in May; sardines, rabbits, murders; forfeits, guessing game, Kim's g.; crosswords and crooked answers, twenty questions, what's my line; charades, dumb c., crambo, dumb c., parson's cat; word game, spelling-bee, scrabble, lexicon, word making and word taking; riddles, crosswords, acrostics; paper game, consequences, tic-tac-toe; dominoes, Mah-jongg, tiddlywinks, jig-saw puzzle.

board game, chess, three-dimensional c.; draughts, checkers, Chinese c., fox and geese; pachisi; backgammon; race-game, ludo, snakes and ladders, crown and anchor, monopoly, totopoly.

children's games, skipping, swinging, jumping, leap-frog, hop-scotch 312 n. *leap;* he, chain he, hide-and-seek, cache-cache, blindman's buff, hares and hounds, French and English, prisoner's base, Tom Tiddler's ground.

card game, cards, game of cards, rubber of whist, rubber of bridge; Boston, whist, solo w., auction w., auction bridge, contract b.; nap, Napoleon; euchre, écarté, loo, picquet, cribbage, quadrille, ombre, bezique, pinochle, quinze; rummy, gin r., canasta, option, hearts, Black Maria, casino, Parliament, Newmarket, commerce, speculation, Red Dog; solo, solitaire, patience; snap, snip snap snorum, beggar-my-neighbor, old maid, ragged robin, racing demon, slap jack, Happy Families, animal grab, cheating; lotto, keno, housey-housey, bingo, skat; vingt-et-un, pontoon, black jack; drag, poker, strip p., stud p., seven-card stud p., five-card stud p.; Russian bank, Polish b., banker, baccarat, faro, fantan, chemin de fer, chemmy; monte, three-card m., rivers, high low, race the ace, cutting for aces (**see** *gambling game*).

gambling game, dice g., craps, dice, lie d., dicing; roulette, rouge et noir; coin-spinning, king-bee game; numbers, sweepstake, football pool 618 n. *gambling.*

dancing, dance, ball, nautch; bal masqué, masquerade; bal costumé, fancy-dress dance, pagal nautch; thé dansant, tea dance; hop, jam session; ballet, Imperial b., Indian b.; ballet dancing, classical d., Brahmanatya; ballroom dancing, dance competition; choreography; eurythmics; muse of dancing, Terpsichore.

dance, war-dance, sword-d., corroboree; shuffle, double-s., cakewalk, shag, breakdown; solo dance, pas seul; clog-dance, step-d., tap-d.; fan dance, skirt-d., hula-hula; high kicks, cancan; belly-roll, danse due ventre; gipsy dance, flamenco; country dance, morris d., morisco; barn dance, lindy hop, Sir Roger de Coverley; sailor's dance, hornpipe, keel row; folk-dance, Russian d., Cossack d., polonaise, mazurka; jig, Irish j., Walls of Limerick, Waves of Torres; fling, Highland f.; square dance, reel, Virginia r., Scotch r., eightsome, foursome, Strathspey, Gay Gordons, Petronella, Hamilton House, Duke of Perth, strip the willow, Dashing White Sergeant; rigadoon, tarantella, saraband, bolero, fandango, pavane, gavotte, quadrille, cotillion, minuet, allemande, galop, polka; valse, waltz, Viennese w., hesitation w., St. Bernard; fox-trot, turkey-t., bunny-hug, valeta, Lancers; Charleston, black bottom, blues, one-step, quick-s., two-s., paso-doble, tango, rumba, samba, mambo, conga, conga line, bongo, la raspa, cha-cha; Big Apple, Boomps-a-Daisy, hokey-cokey, Lambeth Walk, Palais Glide; jazz, shimmy, jive, jitterbug, rock 'n' roll, creep; excuse-me dance, Paul Jones; dancer, tap-d., clog-d., ballet d., ballerina, corps de ballet; nautch-girl; high-kicker, cancanière; waltzer, foxtrotter, shuffler, hoofer, jiver 312n. *jumper.*

plaything, bauble, knick-knack, souvenir, trinket, toy 639n. *bauble;* children's toy, bricks, building b., jack-in-the-box, teddy bear, doll, rag d., doll's house, doll's furniture, doll's carriage; top, whipping t., teetotum, yo-yo, diabolo; jacks, jackstones, fivestones, marbles; ball, bowl, wood 252n. *sphere;* hoop, jump-rope, stilts, pogo-stick, rocking horse; popgun, air-gun, water pistol, toy p., toy cannon 723vb. *toy gun;* toy soldier, tin s., lead s.; model, model yacht, model airplane; magic lantern, raree show, peep-show 522n. *exhibit;* puppet-show, marionettes, Punch and Judy 551n. *image;* space suit; pin-table, billiard table; card, cards, pack, stack, deck; domino, tile; checker; counter, chip; tiddly-wink.

chessman, man, piece, red p., white p., black p.; pawn, knight, bishop; castle, rook; queen, king.

player, sportsman, sporting man; pothunter 716n. *contender;* gamesman, games-player, all-rounder; ballplayer, cricketer, footballer, baseballer, bowler, hockey-player, tennis-p.; toxophilite 287n. *shooter;* dicer, gamester 618n. *gambler;* card-player, chess-p.; fellow-sportsman, playmate 707n. *colleague*.

reveler, merry-maker, rioter, roisterer, gamboler, rollicker, frolicker; skylarker, ragger; drinker, drunk 949n. *drunkard;* feaster, diner-out 301n. *eater;* pleasure-seeker, thrill-s.; playboy, good-time girl; debauchee 952n. *libertine;* holiday-maker, excursionist, tripper, tourist 268n. *traveler;* King of Misrule, master of the revels, master of ceremonies, toastmaster, symposiarch, arbiter elegantiarum; quizmaster.

Adj. *amusing*, entertaining, diverting etc. vb.; lusory, fun-making, sportive, full of fun 833adj. *gay;* laying oneself out to please, pleasant 826adj. *pleasurable;* laughable, ridiculous, clownish 849adj. *funny;* recreative, recreational 685adj. *refreshing;* festal, festive, holiday.

amused, entertained, tickled 824adj. *pleased;* having fun, festive, sportive, rompish, rollicking, roisterous, prankish, playful, kittenish, roguish, waggish, jolly, jovial; out to enjoy oneself, in festal mood, in holiday spirit 835adj. *rejoicing;* horsey, sporty, sporting, gamesome, games-playing 162adj. *athletic;* disporting, playing, at play; working for pleasure, following one's hobby; entertainable, easy to please, ready to be amused.

Vb. *amuse*, interest, entertain, divert, tickle, make one laugh, take one out of oneself; tickle the fancy, titillate, please 826vb. *delight;* recreate 685vb. *refresh;* solace, enliven 833vb. *cheer;* treat, regale, take out, take for an outing; raise a smile, wake laughter, stir l., convulse with l., set the table in a roar, lay them in the aisles, be the death of one 849vb. *be ridiculous;* humor, keep amused, put in good humor; provide fun, give a party, play the host 882vb. *be hospitable;* be a sport, be a good s., be great fun.

amuse oneself, kill time, while away the t., pass the t. 681vb. *have leisure;* ride one's hobby, dabble, trifle, fribble; play, have fun, enjoy oneself, drown care 833vb. *be cheerful;* make holiday, go a-Maying, have an outing, have a field-day; sport, disport oneself; take one's pleasure, dally, toy, wanton; frisk, frolic, rollick, romp, gambol, caper; cut capers, play tricks, play pranks, fool about, play the fool 497vb. *be absurd;* jest, jape 839vb. *be witty;* play cards, take a hand; game, dice 618vb. *gamble;* play games, be devoted to sport; live the outdoor life, camp, picnic; sail, yacht, fly; hunt, shoot, fish; golf; ride, hack; run, race, jump; bathe, swim; skate, ski, toboggan.

dance, nautch; join the dance, go dancing, attend a jam session; tap-dance, waltz, foxtrot, Charleston, tango, rumba, jive, jitterbug, rock 'n' roll; cavort, caper, schuffle, hoof, trip, tread a measure, trip the light fantastic toe 312vb. *leap*.

revel, make merry, make whoopee, celebrate 835vb. *rejoice;* drive dull care away, make it a party, have a good time; go on the razzle, have a night out, have a night on the tiles, beat it up, paint the town red; junket, roister, drown care; feast, banquet, quaff, carouse, wassail, make the rafters ring; commit a debauch, go on a binge, go on a bust 301vb. *drink;* drown one's sorrows 949vb. *get drunk;* wanton, run a rig, sow one's wild oats, never go to sleep, burn the candle at both ends.

Int. carpe diem! eat, drink and be merry! vogue la galère! vive la bagatelle!

See: 74, 162, 192, 252, 267, 268, 269, 271, 287, 301, 308, 312, 420, 445, 497, 522, 551, 594, 597, 618, 639, 681, 683, 685, 694, 707, 716, 723, 724, 824, 826, 833, 835, 839, 849, 876, 882, 943, 949, 952.

838 Tedium

N. *tedium*, taedium vitae, world-weariness 834n. *melancholy;* lack of interest, uninterest 860n. *indifference;* weariness 684n. *fatigue;* wearisomeness, tediousness, irksomeness; dryness, stodginess, heaviness; too much of a good thing, satiation 863n. *satiety;* disgust, loathing, nausea 861n. *dislike;* flatness, staleness 387n. *insipidity;* stuffiness 840n. *dullness;* prolixity 570n. *diffuseness;* sameness 16n. *uniformity;* monotony, dull m. 106n. *repetition;* leaden hours, time to kill, time the enemy 679n. *inactivity*.

bore, utter b., no fun; boring thing, twice-told tale, crambe repetita; irk, bind; dull work, boring w.; beaten track, daily round 610n. *habit;* grindstone, treadmill 682n. *labor;* boring man, pain in the neck, dry-as-dust, proser, buttonholer, club bore; drip, wet blanket, misery; too much of a good thing.

Adj. *tedious*, uninteresting, devoid of interest; unenjoyable, unexciting, unentertaining, unamusing, unfunny; slow, dragging, leaden, heavy; dry, dry-as-dust, arid; flat, stale, insipid 387adj. *tasteless;* bald 573adj. *plain;* humdrum, suburban, depressing, dreary, stuffy 840adj. *dull;* stodgy, prosaic, uninspired, unreadable, unread; prosy, long, overlong 570adj. *prolix;* drowsy, soporific 679adj. *somnific;* boring, binding, wearisome, tiresome, irksome; wearing, chronic, mortal 684adj. *fatiguing;* repetitive, repetitious 106adj. *repeated;* same, unvarying, invariable, monotonous 16adj. *uniform;* too much, cloying, satiating; disgusting, nauseating, nauseous.

bored, unentertained, unamused, unexcited; afflicted with boredom, counting sheep 679adj. *inactive;* stale, weary, jaded 684adj. *fatigued;* blue, world-weary, life-w., weary of life 834adj. *melancholic;* blasé, uninterested 860adj. *indifferent;* satiated, cloyed 863adj. *sated;* nauseated, sick of, fed up, loathing 861 adj. *disliking.*

Vb. *be tedious*, pall, cloy, glut, jade, satiate 863vb. *sate;* nauseate, sicken, disgust 861vb. *cause dislike;* bore, irk, try, weary 684vb. *fatigue;* bore to death, weary to d., tire out, wear o.; get one down, try one's patience, outstay one's welcome, stay too long; fail to interest, make one yawn, send one to sleep; drag 278 vb. *move slowly;* drag its slow length along, go on and on, never end; harp on, prove monotonous 106vb. *repeat oneself;* buttonhole, be prolix 570vb. *be diffuse.*

Adv. *boringly*, ad nauseam.

See: 16, 106, 387, 570, 573, 610, 679, 682, 684, 834, 840, 860, 861, 863.

839 Wit

N. *wit*, wittiness, pointedness, point, smartness, epigrammatism; esprit, ready, wit, verbal readiness; esprit d'escalier 67n. *sequel;* saltiness, salt, Attic s. 575n. *elegance;* sparkle, scintillation, brightness 498n. *intelligence;* humor, sense of h., pleasant h.; wry humor, pawkiness, dryness, slyness; drollery, pleasantry, waggishness, waggery, facetiousness; jocularity, jocosity, jocoseness 833n. *merriment;* comicality, vis comica 849n. *ridiculousness;* lack of seriousness, trifling, flippancy 456adj. *inattention;* joking, practical j., jesting, tomfoolery, buffoonery 497n. *foolery;* broad humor, low h., vulgarity 847n. *bad taste;* farce, broad f., slapstick, ham, harlequinade 594 n. *dramaturgy;* whimsicality, fancy 604n. *whim;* biting wit, cruel humor, satire, sarcasm 851n. *ridicule;* irony 850n. *affectation;* word-fence 477n. *sophistry;* word-play, play upon words, punning, equivocation 518n. *equivocalness.*

witticism, piece of humor, stroke of wit, jeu d'esprit, saily, mot, bon mot; Wellerism, spoonerism; epigram, smart saying, conceit; pun, play upon words, equivoque, calembour 518n. *equivocalness;* point of the joke, cream of the jest; banter, badinage, persiflage; quiz, retort, repartee, quid pro quo, backchat, back-talk 460n. *rejoinder;* sarcasm 851n. *satire;* joke, practical j., standing j., private j., jest, family j., dry j.; quip, jape, quirk, crank, quips and cranks, gag, crack, wisecrack; old joke, stale jest, salt that has lost its savor, chestnut, Joe Miller, bromide; broad jest, low joke, smoking-room story, limerick; story, funny s.; jest-book, joke-book.

humorist, wit, bel esprit, epigrammatist, reparteeist; conversationalist; joker, japer; life of the party, wag, witcracker, witsnapper; witworm, witling; joker, Joe Miller, Sam' Weller; jokesmith, funnyman, gagman, gagster, punster; banterer, persifleur, quizzer, leg-puller, ragger, teaser; ironist 850n. *affector;* mocker, scoffer, satirist, lampooner 926n. *detractor;* comedian, comic 594n. *entertainer;* comic writer, comic author, cartoonist, caricaturist; burlesquer, parodist 20n. *imitator;* jester, court j., wearer of the cap and bells, motley fool, clown, farceur, buffoon 501n. *fool.*

Adj. *witty*, spirituel, nimble-witted, quick; Attic, salty 575adj. *elegant;* pointed, full of point, ben trovato, epigrammatic; brilliant, sparkling, smart, clever, too clever by half 498adj. *intelligent;* snappy, biting, pungent, keen, sharp, sarcastic; dry, sly, pawky; unserious, facetious, flippant 456adj. *light-minded;* jocular, jocose, joking, joshing, waggish, roguish; lively, pleasant, merry, merry and wise 833adj. *gay*; comic, funny, rib-tickling 849adj. *funny;* humorous, droll; whimsical 604adj. *capricious;* playful, sportive, fooling 497adj. *absurd.*

Vb. *be witty*, scintillate, sparkle, flash; jest, joke, crack a j., cut a j., gag, wisecrack; tell a good story, set the table in a roar, lay them in the aisles 837vb. *amuse;* pun, make a p., play upon words, equivocate 518vb. *be equivocal;* fool, jape 497 vb. *be absurd;* play with, tease, chaff, rag, banter, quip, quiz, twit, pull one's leg, make merry with, make fun of, poke fun at, exercise one's wit upon 851vb. *ridicule;* mock, caricature, burlesque 851vb. *satirize;* retort, flash back, come back at 460vb. *answer;* have a sense of humor, enjoy a joke, see the point.

Adv. *in jest*, in joke, in fun, in sport, in play.

See: 20, 67, 456, 460, 477, 497, 498, 501, 518, 575, 594, 604, 833, 837, 847, 849, 850, 851, 926.

840 Dullness

N. *dullness*, heaviness, infestivity, mopiness 834n. *defection;* stuffiness, dreariness, deadliness; monotony, boringness 838n. *tedium;* colorlessness, drabness; lack of sparkle, lack of inspiration, want of originality; stodginess, unreadability, prosiness; staleness, flatness 387n. *insipidity;* banality, triteness, superficiality; lack of humor, no sense of h., inability to see a joke, primness, impenetrability, gravity, grimness 834n. *seriousness;* prose, matter of fact 573n. *plainness.*

Adj. *dull*, unamusing, uninteresting, unentertaining; unfunny, uncomical, straight; uncharming, uncaptivating; deadly dull, dull as ditchwater; stuffy, dreary, deadly; pointless, meaningless 838adj. *tedious;* unvivid, unlively, colorless, drab; flat, insipid 387adj. *tasteless;* unimaginative, uninventive, unoriginal, derivative, superficial; stupid 499adj. *unintelligent;* without laughter, humorless, grave, prim 834adj. *serious;* unwitty, unsparkling, unscintillating; graceless, insulse, lacking salt 576 adj. *inelegant;* heavy, heavy-gaited, clod-hopping, ponderous, sluggish 278adj. *slow;* stodgy, prosaic, pedestrian, unreadable; stale, banal, commonplace, trite, platitudinous 610 adj. *usual.*

Vb. *be dull,* bore 838adj. *be tedious;* platitudinize, prose, outwrite oneself; hate fun, have no humor in one's composition, never see a joke, not see the point, miss the cream of the jest.

See: 278, 387, 499, 573, 576, 610, 834, 838.

841 Beauty

N. *beauty*, pulchritude, the beautiful; ripe perfection, highest p. 646n. *perfection;* the sublime, sublimity, grandeur, magnificence 868n. *nobility;* splendor, gorgeousness, brilliance, brightness, radiance 417n. *light;* transfiguration 843n. *beautification;* polish, gloss, ornament 844 n. *ornamentation;* scenic beauty, scenery, view, landscape, seascape, cloudscape 445n. *spectacle;* form, fair proportions, regular features, classic f. 245n. *symmetry;* physical beauty, loveliness, comeliness, fairness, handsomeness, bonniness, prettiness; attraction, attractiveness, agreeableness, charm, appeal, glamour, sex appeal, cuteness, kissability; attractions, charms, graces, perfections, ripe p.; good looks, handsome features, pretty face, beaux yeux; shapeliness, belle tournure, trim figure, curves, curvaceousness, vital statistics; gracefulness, grace, concinnity 575n. *elegance;* chic, style 838n. *fashion;* delicacy, refinement 846n. *good taste;* appreciation of beauty, aesthetics, callaesthetics, aestheticism; landscape architecture.

a beauty, thing of beauty, work of art, masterpiece 644n. *exceller;* bijou, jewel, pearl, treasure 646n. *paragon*; fair, fair one, lady bright; belle, raving beauty, reigning b., toast, idol 890n. *favorite;* beau idéal, dream girl; beauty queen, Miss Universe; bathing belle, pin-up girl, cover g., chocolate-box type; pretty, brighteyes; dream, vision, picture, perfect p., sight for sore eyes; angel, charmer, dazzler; enchantress, femme fatale, witch 983n. *sorceress;* smasher, scorcher, lovely, cutie, bird, beaut, peach, dish, lulu; flower, rose, lily; fairy, peri, houri; Grace, the Graces, Hebe, Venus, Aphrodite, Helen of Troy; Apollo, Hyperion, Cupid, Endymion, Adonis, Narcissus, Ganymede, Hylas, Antinous; peacock, swan.

Adj. *beautiful*, pulchritudinous, beauteous, of beauty; lovely, fair, bright, radiant; comely, goodly, bonny, pretty; sweet, sweetly pretty, pretty-pretty, nice, good enough to eat; pretty as a picture, paintable, photogenic; handsome, good-looking, well-favored; graced, well-g.; gracious, stately, statuesque, majestic; leonine, manly; adorable, godlike, goddess-like, divine, "divinely tall and most divinely fair"; picturesque, scenic, ornamental; artistic, well-grouped, well-composed, cunning, curious, quaint 694adj. *well-made;* aesthetic 846adj. *tasteful;* exquisite, choice 605adj. *chosen;* unspotted, unblemished 646adj. *perfect.*

splendid, sublime, superb, fine 644 adj. *excellent;* grand 868adj. *noble;* colored, in color, rich, gorgeous, highly colored 425adj. *florid;* bright, resplendent, dazzling, beaming, radiant, sparkling, glowing 417adj. *radiating;* glossy, polished, magnificent, specious 875adj. *showy;* ornate, loaded 844adj. *ornamented.*

shapely, well-proportioned, regular, classic 245adj. *symmetrical;* formed, well-f., well-turned; rounded, buxom, curved, curvaceous, callipygian, callipygic; clean-limbed, straight-l., straight, slender, slim, svelte, willowy 206adj. *lean;* petite, dainty, delicate; undeformed, undefaced, unwarped, untwisted.

personable, prepossessing, agreeable, comfortable, buxom, sonsy; attractive, fetching, appealing; snappy, cute, kissable; charming, enchanting, glamorous; lovesome, winsome 887adj. *lovable;* of good appearance, with a fair outside; blooming, in bloom, ruddy 431adj. *red;* rosy, rosy-cheeked, apple-c., cherry-lipped, peachy; bright, bright-eyed; sightly, becoming, fit to be seen, passable, not amiss; presentable, proper, decent, neat, natty, tidy, trim; tight, spruce, jimp, dapper, glossy, sleek; well-dressed, well turned out, smart, stylish 848adj. *fashionable;* elegant, dainty, delicate, refined 846adj. *tasteful.*

Vb. *be beautiful*, grow b., be photogenic, photograph well; have good looks, have bright eyes; bloom, glow, beam, dazzle 417vb. *shine;* be dressed to kill; do one credit, win a beauty contest.

beautify, trim, neaten, improve; brighten 417vb. *make bright;* prettify, bejewel, tattoo 844vb. *decorate;* set (a jewel); set off, grace, suit, fit, become, go well, show one off, flatter; bring out the highlights, enhance one's looks, glamorize, transfigure, face-lift; prink, prank, titivate, powder, rouge 843vb. *primp.*

See: 206, 245, 417, 425, 431, 445, 575, 605, 644, 646, 843, 844, 846, 848, 868, 875, 887, 890.

842 Ugliness

N. *ugliness*, unsightliness, hideousness, repulsiveness; lack of beauty, inconcinnity, gracelessness, clumsiness 576n. *inelegance;* want of symmetry, asymmetry 246n. *distortion;* unshapeliness, lack of form 246n. *deformity;* mutilation, disfigurement 845n. *blemish;* uglification, disfiguration, defacement, blackening; squalor, filth, beastliness 649n. *uncleanness;* homeliness, plainness, plain features, ugly face; no beauty, no oil painting, a face to stop a clock; wry face, snarl, forbidding countenance, vinegar aspect, grim look, sour l., hanging l. 893n. *sullenness;* haggardness, haggard look; fading beauty, dim eyes, wrinkles, hand of time 131n. *age.*

eyesore, hideosity, botch, blot, patch 845n. *blemish;* aesthetic crime; blot on the landscape, slum; ugly person, fright, sight, figure, object, not one's type; scarecrow, horror, death's-head, gargoyle, grotesque; monster, abortion; harridan, witch; toad, gorilla, baboon, crow; plain Jane, ugly duckling; satyr, Caliban; Aesop; Beast.

Adj. *ugly*, lacking beauty, beautiless, unbeautiful, unlovely, uncomely, unhandsome; not fair, black; ugly as sin, hideous, foul 649adj. *unclean;* frightful, shocking, monstrous; repulsive, repellent, odious, loathsome 861adj. *disliked;* beastly, nasty 645 adj. *not nice;* unpretty, homely, plain, plain-featured, with no looks, without any looks; forbidding, unprepossessing, ill-favored, ill-featured, hard-f., villainous, grim-visaged, grim, saturnine 893adj. *sullen.*

unsightly, faded, withered, worn, ravaged, wrinkled 131adj. *aged;* not worth looking at, not fit to be seen, unseemly; unshapely, shapeless, formless, irregular, asymmetrical 244adj. *amorphous;* twisted, deformed, disfigured, defaced 246adj. *distorted;* ill-made, ill-shaped, ill-formed, ill-proportioned, disproportioned, mis-proportioned, misshapen, misbegotten, curtailed of its fair proportions; dumpy, squat 196adj. *dwarfish;* stained, discolored 426adj.

colorless; ghastly, wan, grisly, gruesome; tousled, in disarray 61adj. *orderless.*
graceless, ungraced, ungraceful 576 adj. *inelegant;* inartistic, unaesthetic; unbecoming, unornamental, unpicturesque; squalid, dingy, poky, dreary, drab; garish, gaudy, gross, indelicate, coarse 847adj. *vulgar;* dowdy, ill-dressed; rude, crude, rough, rugged, uncouth 699adj. *artless;* clumsy, awkward, ungainly, cumbersome, hulky, hulking, slouching, clod-hopping 195adj. *unwieldy.*
Vb. *be ugly*, lack beauty, have no looks, lose one's l.; fade, wither, age, show one's a. 131vb. *grow old;* look ill, look a wreck, look a mess, look a fright.
make ugly, uglify; fade, wither, discolor 426vb. *decolorize;* darken, shadow 428vb. *blacken;* spoil 655vb. *deteriorate;* soil 649vb. *make unclean;* deface, disfigure, blemish, blot; misshape 244vb. *deform;* torture, twist 246vb. *distort;* mutilate 655vb. *impair.*
See: 61, 131, 195, 196, 244, 246, 426, 428, 576, 645, 649, 655, 699, 845, 847, 861, 893.

843 Beautification

N. *beautification*, beautifying 844n. *ornamentation;* transfiguration 143n. *transformation;* scenic improvement, landscape gardening, landscape architecture; plastic surgery, rhinoplasty, nose-straightening, skin-grafting, face-lift 658n. *surgery;* beauty treatment, skin t., scalp t., face-lifting, mole-removing, depilation, eyebrow plucking, eyebrow penciling; pack, face p., mud p., oatmeal p., facial; massage, face m., skin m., manicure, nail-filing, nail-varnishing, nail-polishing, buffing; pedicure, chiropody; tattooing 844n. *ornamental art;* ear-piercing, nose-p.; sun-tanning, browning, sun lamp, ultraviolet rays; toilet, makeup, art of m., cosmetology; creaming, farding, larding, rouging, painting, shadowing, dyeing, powdering, patching, scenting, soaping, shampooing; wash and brush-up 648n. *ablution.*
hair-dressing, trichology, hair-treatment, scalp massage; barbering, shaving, shampooing, clipping, trimming, thinning, singeing; depilation, plucking; cutting, hair-c., bobbing, shingling; shave, haircut, cut, clip, trim, singe, tidy-up; hair-style, coiffure, crop, Eton c., bob, shingle; crew-cut, cut en brosse, urchin cut, baby-doll c., Italian c., chrysanthemum c., bouffant c.; styling, hair-s., curling, frizzing, tonging, waving, setting, hair-straightening, defrizzing; hair-do, shape, set, wave, permanent w., home permanent w., marcel w., finger w., pin w., hot w., cold w.; curl 251n. *coil;* bang, fringe, ponytail, chignon, bun, pompadour, cowlick, quiff 259n. *hair;* false hair, switch 228n. *wig;* curling-iron, tongs, curlers, pin-c., rollers, crackers, rags; slide, hair-s., barrette, grip, kirby g.; bandeau, Alice band; comb, hair-pin, bobby p., hat-p., hair-net, snood 228n. *headgear.*
hairwash, shampoo, dry s., wet s., liquid s., cream s., powder s., egg s., beer s., vinegar s., medicinal s., antiseptic s.; rinse, tinting, color tone, highlights, lightening, bleach, dye, hair-d., peroxide; hair-spray, lacquer, hair-oil, hair-cream, grease, vaseline, brilliantine, macassar oil, hair-restorer.
cosmetic, beautifier, glamorizer, aid to beauty, patch, beauty spot; makeup, liquid m., stick m.; paint, greasepaint, warpaint, rouge, liquid r., fard, pomade, cream, face-c., cold c., cleansing c., vanishing c., foundation c., night c., hormone c., healing c., skin-ointment, lanolin 357n. *unguent;* lipstick, lipsalve; burnt cork; nail polish, nail varnish, varnish remover; powder, face-p., compressed p., silk p., talcum p.; kohl, collyrium, mascara, eye-shadow; eye-salve, eye lotion; hand lotion, astringent l., sun-tan l.; scented soap, bath salts, bath oil, bath essence 648n. *cleanser;* scent, perfume, essence, eau-de-cologne, toilet water, cologne stick; eyebrow pencil, eyelash curler; hare's foot, rabbit's f.; powder puff, compact, flapjack; makeup set, manicure s., nail-file, nail scissors, clippers; nail polisher, buffer; styptic pencil; dental floss; toiletry, toiletries.
beauty parlor, beauty shop, beauty salon, reducing s.; parfumerie; boudoir, makeup room, dressing r., powder r., powder closet.
beautician, beauty specialist, beauty doctor; fact-lifter, plastic surgeon; makeup artist, glamorizer, tattooer; cosmetician, cosmetologist; barber, hairdresser, hair-stylist; trichologist; manicurist, pedicurist, chiropodist.
Adj. *beautified*, transfigured, transformed; prettified, glamorized, bedizened, madeup, rouged, painted,

powdered, raddled, patched, scented, curled; primped, dressed up, dolled up 841adj. *beautiful.*

Vb. *primp*, prettify, doll up, dress up, bedizen, bejewel; prink, prank, trick out; preen; titivate, make up, put on makeup, apply cosmetics, rouge, paint, shadow, powder; scent oneself; oil, shave, pluck one's eyebrows, varnish one's nails, dye one's hair; curl, wave; have a hair-do, have a facial, have a manicure 841 vb. *beautify.*

See: 143, 228, 251, 259, 357, 648, 658, 841, 844.

844 Ornamentation

N. *ornamentation*, ornature, decoration, adornment, garnish; ornate style, ornateness 574n. *ornament;* prettyism, pretty-pretty; gaudiness, richness, gilt 875n. *ostentation;* enhancement, enrichment, embellishment; setting, background; table decoration, centerpiece, epergne, silver, china, glass; floral decoration, flower arrangement, wreath, coronal, crown, bouquet, nosegay, posy, button-hole; objet d'art, article of virtue, bric-a-brac, curio, medal, medallion.

ornamental art, gardening, landscape g., topiarism; architecture, landscape a., building; interior decoration, furnishing, draping, house-painting 553n. *painting;* statuary 554 n. *sculpture;* cartouche, metope, triglyph; capital, acanthus; pilaster, caryatid; boss, cornice, gargoyle; molding, astragal, beading, fluting, fretting, tracery; varnishing 226n. *facing;* pargeting, veneering, paneling, graining; ormolu, gilding, gilt, gold leaf; lettering, illumination, illustration, illustrating 551n. *art;* heraldic art 547n. *heraldry;* tattooing; reeding, strap-work, coquillage; etching 555n. *engraving;* work, fancy-w., woodwork, fretwork; pokerwork, pyrography; open-work, filigree; relief, embossing, chasing, intaglio 254 n. *relievo;* inlay, inset, enameling, smalto, mosaic 437n. *variegation;* wrought-work, toreutics; gem-cutting, setting; cut glass, wrought iron, figurehead.

pattern, key-p., motif, print, design, composition 331n. *structure;* detail, elaborate d.; geometrical style, decorated s., rose window, cyma, ogee, spandrel, fleur-de-lis; alpana, tracery, scrollwork, fiddlehead, arabesque, flourish, curlicue 251n. *coil;* weave, diaper, Fair Isle 331n. *texture;* check 437n. *checker;* stripe, pin-s. 437n. *striation;* spot, coin s., dot, polka d. 437n. *maculation;* herring-bone, zigzag, dog's tooth, hound's t. 220n. *obliquity;* water-pattern, watermark 547n. *identification.*

needlework, stitchery, tapestry, arras; embossed needlework, sampler; laid-work, patchwork, appliqué work, open w., drawn-thread w.; embroidery, broidery, brocade, brocatelle; crochet, lace, broderie anglaise; smocking, tatting, knitting; stitch, purl, plain, gros point, petit p., needle p.; cross stitch, chain s., cable s., moss s., garter s., hem s., stem s., blanket s., feather s., back s., satin s., herring-bone s., lace s., French knotting, lazy-daisy.

trimming, passementerie, piping, valance, border, fringe, frieze, frill, galloon, gimp 234n. *edging;* binding 589n. *bookbinding;* trapping, frog, lapel, epaulet, shoulder knot, rosette, cockade 547n. *badge;* bow knot 47n. *ligature;* bobble, pom-pom; tassel, danglums, bead, bugle 217n. *pendant;* ermine, fur 259n. *hair;* feather, ostrich f., osprey, plume, panache 259n. *plumage;* streamer, ribbon.

finery, togs, braws, Sunday best 228n. *clothing;* folderol, frippery, frills and furbelows, ribbons, chiffon; gaudery, gaud, trinket, knick-knack, gewgaw, bric-a-brac, tinsel, spangle, sequin, clinquant; costume jewelry, glass, paste, paste diamond, rhinestone 638n. *bauble.*

jewellery, bijouterie, jewel-work; crown jewels, diadem, tiara 743n. *regalia;* drop, locket 217n. *pendant;* crucifix 222n. *cross;* amulet, charm 983n. *talisman;* rope, string, necklet, necklace, chain, watch-c., albert, chatelaine, carcanet 250n. *loop;* torque, armlet, anklet, bracelet; wristlet, bangle, ring, earring, nose-ring, signet r., wedding r., eternity r., engagement r., Russian wedding r., mourning r., dress r. 250n. *circle;* ouch, brooch, fibula, badge, crest; stud, pin, gold p., tie p., sorority p., fraternity p. 47n. *fastening;* medal, medallion.

gem, jewel, bijou; stone, precious s., semi-precious s.; uncut gem, cut g.; brilliant, sparkler, diamond, rock, ice; solitaire; carbuncle, ruby, oriental r., spinel r., balas r., balas; pearl, orient p., cultivated p., seed p., pink p., opal, black o., fire o., girasol; sapphire, white s., yellow s., water s.; turquoise, emerald, beryl, aquamarine, chrysoberyl, chrysoprase, alexandrite; garnet, amethyst, oriental a., topaz, oriental t., occidental t., chalcedony, cornelian, carnelian, sard, jasper, agate, onyx, sardonyx, heliotrope; bloodstone, moonstone, sarkstone, cat's-eye, zircon, jacinth, hyacinth, tourmaline, apatite, chrysolite, olivine, peridot; coral, jade, lapis lazuli.

Adj. *ornamental*, decorative, nonfunctional, fancy; glamorous, picturesque, pretty-pretty; scenic, landscape, topiary; geometric; Doric, Ionic, Corinthian, Roman-esque, Decorated; baroque, rococo; Sheraton, Chippendale; daedal, quaint.

ornamented, decorated, embellished, polished 574adj. *ornate;* picked out 437adj. *variegated;* mosaic, inlaid, enameled; worked, embroidered, trimmed; wreathed, festooned, crowned; overdecorated, overloaded 847adj. *vulgar;* overcolored 425adj. *florid;* luscious, plush, gilt, begilt, gilded 800adj. *rich;* gorgeous, garish, glittering, flashy, gaudy, meretricious 875adj. *showy.*

bedecked, groomed, got up, togged up, wearing, sporting; decked, bedight; looking one's best, in one's b., in one's Sunday b., en grande toilette 228adj. *dressed;* beribboned, festooned, studded, bemedaled; bedizened, bejeweled 843adj. *beautified.*

Vb. *decorate*, embellish, enhance, enrich; adorn, load; grace, set, set off 574vb. *ornament;* paint, bedizen, bejewel; adonize, glamorize, prettify 841vb. *beautify;* garnish, trim; shape, topiarize; array, deck, bedeck, dight, bedight 228vb. *dress;* deck out, trick o., prank, preen, titivate 843vb. *primp;* freshen, smarten, spruce up, furbish, burnish 648vb. *clean;* bemedal, beribbon, garland, crown 866vb. *dignify;* stud, spangle, bespangle 437vb. *variegate;* color-wash, whitewash, varnish, grain, japan, lacquer 226vb. *coat;* enamel, gold, silver; blazon 590vb. *describe;* emblazon, illuminate, illustrate 553vb. *paint;* colorize 425vb. *color;* border, trim 234vb. *hem;* work, pick out, broider, embroider, tapestry; lace 222vb. *enlace;* chase, tool 555vb. *engrave;* emboss 254vb. *jut;* bead, mold; fret, carve; wreathe, festoon, trace, scroll 251vb. *twine.*

See: 47, 217, 220, 222, 226, 228, 234, 250, 251, 254, 259, 331, 425, 437, 547, 551, 553, 554, 555, 574, 589, 590, 639, 648, 743, 800, 841, 843, 847, 866, 875, 983.

845 Blemish

N. *blemish*, no ornament; scar, cicatrice, weal, welt, mark, pock-m.; injury, flaw, crack, defect 647n. *imperfection;* disfigurement, deformity 246n. *distortion;* stigma, blot, blot on the landscape, blot on the scutcheon 843n. *eyesore;* blur, blotch, splotch, smudge 550n. *obliteration;* smut, patch, smear, stain, tarnish, rust, patina 649n. *dirt;* spot, speck, speckle, sun-spot, macula, spottiness 437n. *maculation;* mole, birthmark, strawberry m.; excrescence, pimpliness, pimple, blackhead, wen, wart 253n. *swelling;* blotchiness, lentigo, freckle, leucoderma, albinism 651n. *skin disease;* hare-lip, cleft palate; cut, scratch, sear, bruise, black eye, shiner, cauliflower ear, broken nose 655n. *wound.*

Adj. *blemished*, defective, flawed, cracked, damaged 647adj. *imperfect;* stained, soiled 649adj. *dirty;* shop-soiled, spoiled 655adj. *deteriorated;* marked, scarred; spotted, pitted, pock-marked, maculate; spotty, lentiginous, freckled; club-footed, web-f., web-toed, pigeon-t., hammer-t.; knock-kneed, bandy, bandy-legged; hunch-backed, crooked 246 adj. *distorted.*

Vb. *blemish*, flaw, crack, injure, damage 655vb. *impair;* blot, smudge, stain, smear, soil, cast a slur on 649vb. *make unclean;* stigmatize, brand 547vb. *mark;* scar, pit, pock; spoil, spoil the look of 842vb. *make ugly;* disfigure, deface 244vb. *deform.*

See: 244, 246, 253, 437, 547, 550, 647, 649, 651, 655, 842, 843.

846 Good Taste

N. *good taste*, tastefulness, taste, refined t., cultivated t.; simple taste, simplicity 573n. *plainness;* best of taste, choiceness, excellence 644n. *goodness;* refinement, delicacy, euphemism 950n. *purity;* fine feeling, nicety, nice appreciation, palate 463n. *discrimination;* daintiness, finickiness, kid gloves 862n. *fastidiousness;* decency, seemliness; tact, consideration, natural courtesy, dignity, manners, polished m., breeding, civility, urbanity 884n. *courtesy;* correctness, propriety, decorum; grace, polish, sophistication, gracious living 575n. *elegance;* cultivation, culture, connoisseurship, amateurship, dilettantism; epicureanism, gourmandise; aestheticism, aesthetics, criticism, art c. 480n. *judgment;* artistry, virtuosity, virtue 694n. *skill.*

man of taste, sophisticate, connoisseur, cognescente, amateur, dilettante; gourmet, epicure; aesthete, critic, art c. 480n. *estimator;* arbiter of taste, arbiter elegantiarum, Beau Nash 848n. *fop;* purist, precisian 602n. *opinionist;* euphemist 950n. *prude.*

Adj. *tasteful,* gracious, dignified; in good taste, in the best of t.; choice, exquisite 644adj. *excellent;* simple, unmeretricious 573adj. *plain;* graceful, Attic, classical 575adj. *elegant;* chaste, refined, delicate, euphemistic 950n. *pure;* aesthetic, artistic 819n. *sensitive;* discriminatory, epicurean 463adj. *discriminating;* nice, dainty, choosy, finicky 862adj. *fastidious;* critical, appreciative 480adj. *judicial;* decent, seemly; proper, correct, comme il faut 848adj. *fashionable;* house-trained, sophisticated 848adj. *well-bred.*

Vb. *have taste,* show good t., reveal fine feelings 463vb. *discriminate;* appreciate, value, criticize 480vb. *judge;* go in for the best, take only the best 862vb. *be fastidious.*

Adv. *tastefully,* elegantly, in taste, in the right *or* best t.; becomingly, fittingly, properly, agreeably 24adj. *pertinently.*

See: 24, 463, 480, 573, 575, 602, 644, 694, 819, 848, 862, 884, 950.

847 Bad Taste

N. *bad taste,* tastelessness, ill taste, poor t., excruciating t. 645n. *badness;* no taste, lack of t.; bad art, commercial a.; commercialism, commercialization, yellow press, gutter p.; unrefinement, coarseness, barbarism, vulgarism, vandalism, philistinism. Babbittry 699n. *artlessness;* vulgarity, gaudiness, loudness, blatancy, flagrancy; tawdriness, shoddiness; shoddy, frippery, tinsel, false ornament, glass, paste, ersatz, imitation 639n. *bauble;* lack of feeling, insensitivity, crassness, grossness; tactlessness, indelicacy, impropriety, unseemliness; bad joke, untimely jest, misplaced wit; nastiness, obscenity 951n. *impurity;* unfashionableness, dowdiness, frumpishness; frump, dowdy.

ill-breeding, vulgarity, commonness; loudness, heartiness; rusticity, jungliness; inurbanity, incivility, unfashionableness; bad form, incorrectness; no manners, gaucherie, boorishness, rudeness, impoliteness 885n. *discourtesy;* ungentlemanliness, caddishness; brutishness, savagery; misbehavior, indecorum, ribaldry; rowdyism, ruffianism 61n. *disorder.*

vulgarian, snob, social climber, cad, bounder, low person; rough diamond, unlicked cub; arriviste, parvenu, nouveau riche; man of the people, proletarian, prole 869n. *commoner;* Goth, Vandal, philistine, Babbitt; barbarian, savage.

Adj. *vulgar,* undignified; unrefined, unpolished 576adj. *inelegant;* tasteless, in bad taste, out of t., in the worst t.; gross, crass, coarse, coarsegrained; unfastidious, not particular; knowing no better, philistine, barbarian 699adj. *artless;* commercial, commercialized; tawdry, cheap, catchpenny, gingerbread, tinhorn, ersatz; flashy, meretricious, bedizened 875adj. *showy;* obtrusive, blatant, loud, screaming, gaudy, garish; flaunting, shameless; overdressed, underdressed; suburban, shabby, genteel 850adj. *affected;* not respectable, ungenteel; common, low, gutter, sordid 867adj. *disreputable;* improper, indelicate, indecorous; indecent, lowminded, ribald, obscene, risqué.

ill-bred, underbred, unhousetrained; unpresentable; ungentlemanly, unladylike; unfeminine, hoydenish; ungenteel, non-U, not U 869adj. *plebeian;* loud, hearty; tactless, insensitive, blunt; uncourtly, uncivil, impolite, mannerless, unmannered, ill-mannered 885adj. *discourteous;* unfashionable, unsmart, dowdy, rustic, provincial, countrified; rude, boorish, clownish, loutish, clodhopping, uncouth, uncultured, uncultivated, unpolished, unrefined 491 adj. *ignorant;* unsophisticated, knowing no better 699adj. *artless;* uncivilized, barbaric; awkward, gauche, lubberly 695adj. *clumsy;* misbehaving, rowdy, ruffianly, riotous 61adj. *disorderly;* snobbish, uppish, superior 850adj. *affected.*

Vb. *vulgarize,* cheapen, coarsen, lower; commercialize, popularize; show bad taste, know no better 491 adj. *not know;* be unfashionable, dress in last year's fashions.

See: 61, 491, 576, 639, 645, 695, 699, 848, 850, 867, 869, 875, 885, 951.

848 Fashion

N. *fashion,* style, mode, cut 243n. *form;* method 624n. *way;* vogue, cult 610n. *habit;* prevailing taste, current fashion 126n. *modernism;* rage, fad, craze, cry, furore; new look, the latest, latest fashion, newest out 126 n. *newness;* dernier cri, last word, ne plus ultra; extreme of fashion, height of f., pink of f.; dash 875n. *ostentation;* fashionableness, ton, bon t.; fashion show, mannequin parade 522 n. *exhibit;* haute couture, elegance, foppishness, dressiness; foppery 850 n. *affectation;* world of fashion, vanity fair, passing show, way of the world.

etiquette, point of e., punctilio, pundonor 875n. *formality;* protocol, convention, custom, conventionality 610n. *practice;* snobbery, conventions of society, sanctions of s., done thing, good form; proprieties, appearances, Mrs. Grundy; bienséance, decency, decorum, propriety, right note, correctness 846n. *good taste;* civilized behavior, comity 884 n. *courtesy;* breeding, good b., polish; gentility, gentlemanliness; manners, good m., refined m., polished m., drawing-room m., court m., best behavior; grand air, poise, dignity, savoir faire, savvy 688n. *conduct.*

beau monde, society, good s., high s., civilized s., civilization; town, West End; court, drawing-room, salon; high circles, right people, best p., right set, upper ten 868n. *nobility;* cream, upper crust, cream of society 644n. *elite;* café society, jeunesse dorée; fashionable person, glass of fashion, mold of form; man about town, man of fashion, woman of f., high stepper, classy dame; slave to fashion, leader of f., star of f., Beau Nash, arbiter elegantiarum; man of the world, woman of the w., mondain, mondaine, socialite, clubman, clubwoman, cosmopolitan 882n. *social person.*

fop, fine gentleman, macaroni, buck, pearly king; fine lady, belle, pearly queen; debutante, deb; dandy, beau, Beau Brummel, exquisite, curled darling, scented d., fribble; popinjay, peacock, clotheshorse, fashion plate, tailor's dummy, man milliner; coxcomb, puppy, dandiprat, jackanapes, petit-maître; jemmy, johnnie, swell, toff, dude, masher, filbert, knut, nob; Teddy-boy, Teddy-girl; Corinthian, spark, blood, blade, buckeen, bahadur, lad, bhoy, gay dog; carpet knight; squire of dames.

Adj. *fashionable,* modish, stylish, bon ton; correct, comme il faut; in fashion, in the latest f., a la mode, chi-chi; recherché, exquisite, chic, well-dressed, well-groomed 846adj. *tasteful;* clothes-conscious, foppish, dressy; high-stepping, dashing, doggish, rakish; dandy, smart, classy, tony, swanky, swank, swish, posh; up-to-the-minute, ultrafashionable, newfangled 126adj. *modern;* groomed, dandified, braw, dressed to the nines, in full dress, en grande tenue 228adj. *dressed;* in society, in the best s., in the right set, moving in the best circles, knowing the right people, belonging to the best clubs; in the swim 83adj. *conformable;* snobbish 850adj. *affected;* conventional, done 610adj. *usual.*

well-bred, thoroughbred, blue-blooded 875adj. *noble;* cosmopolitan, sophisticated, civilized, citified, urbane; polished, polite, house-trained; U, gentlemanlike, ladylike 868adj. *genteel;* civil, well-mannered, easy-m., good m., well-spoken 884adj. *courteous;* courtly, stately, distingué, dignified 875adj. *formal;* poised, dégagé, easy, unembarrassed, smooth; correct, decorous, proper, convenable, decent; considerate 884adj. *amiable;* punctilious 929adj. *honorable.*

Vb. *be in fashion,* have a run, be done, pass current 610vb. *be wont;* be the rage, be the latest 126vb. *modernize;* follow the fashion, jump on the bandwagon, change with the times 83vb. *conform;* have the entrée, move in the best circles, be seen in the right places; savoir faire, savoir vivre 882vb. *be sociable;* entertain 882vb. *be hospitable;* keep up with the Joneses, keep up appearances; observe decorum, do the right thing; cut a figure, lead the fashion, set the f., set the tone, give a tone; look right, pass; have an air, have style; dress well, have the right clothes, dandify 843vb. *primp.*

Adv. *fashionably,* in style, a la mode; for appearances, for fashion's sake.

See: 83, 126, 228, 243, 522, 610, 624, 644, 688, 843, 846, 850, 868, 875, 882, 884, 929.

849 Ridiculousness

N. *ridiculousness,* ludicrousness, risibility, laughability, height of absurdity 497n. *absurdity;* funniness, pricelessness, comicality, drollery, waggishness 839n. *wit;* quaintness, oddness, queerness, eccentricity 84n. *abnormality;* bathos, anticlimax 509n. *disappointment;* boasting 877n. *boast;* bombast 546n. *extravagance;* comic interlude, light relief; light verse, comic v., doggerel, limerick, spoonerism, malapropism, Hibernicism, Irish bull 839n. *witticism;* comedy, farce, burlesque, slapstick, knock-about, clowning, buffoonery 954n. *stage play;* unexpectedness, paradox, paradoxicality, Gilbertian situation 508n. *inexpectation.*

Adj. *ridiculous,* ludicrous, preposterous, monstrous, grotesque, fantastic 497adj. *absurd;* awkward, clownish 695n. *clumsy;* derisory, contemptible 639adj. *unimportant;* laughable, risible; bizarre, rum, quaint, odd, queer 84adj. *unusual;* strange, outlandish 59adj. *extraneous;* mannered, stilted 850adj. *affected;* inflated, bombastic, extravagant, outré 546adj. *exaggerated;* fanciful 513adj. *imaginary;* whimsical 604adj. *capricious;* paradoxical.

funny, funny-peculiar 841adj. *abnormal;* funny-ha-ha, laughter-making 837adj. *amusing;* comical, droll, drollish, humorous, waggish 839adj. *witty;* rich, priceless, side-splitting; light, comic, seriocomic, tragi-c.; mocking, ironical, satirical 851adj. *derisive;* burlesque, mock-heroic; doggerel; farcical, slapstick, clownish, knock-about; Aristophanic, Shavian, Gilbertian, Pickwickian.

Vb. *be ridiculous,* make one laugh, excite laughter, raise a laugh; tickle, shake *or* disturb one's gravity, give one the giggles; entertain 837vb. *amuse;* look silly, be a figure of fun, cut a ridiculous figure, be a laughing-stock, fool, play the fool 497vb. *be absurd;* come down with a bump, descend to bathos, pass from the sublime to the ridiculous; put oneself out of court 695vb. *stultify oneself;* poke fun at, make one a laughing-stock 851vb. *ridicule.*

See: 59, 84, 497, 508, 509, 513, 546, 604, 639, 695, 837, 839, 841, 850, 851, 877, 954.

850 Affectation

N. *affectation,* cult, fad 848n. *fashion;* affectedness, pretentiousness 875n. *ostentation;* assumption of airs, affected a., grand a. 873n. *airs;* striking attitude, high moral tone; artificiality, mannerism, trick; literary affectation, esoteric vocabulary, prestige terms, grandiloquence 574 n. *magniloquence;* preciosity, euphuism, cultism, Gongorism 574n. *ornament;* mim, moue, grimace 547n. *gesture;* coquetry, minauderie 604n. *caprice;* conceit, conceitedness, foppery, foppishness, dandyism, puppyism, coxcombry 873n. *vanity;* euphemism, mock modesty, false shame, mauvaise honte 874n. *modesty;* irony, Socratic i., backhanded compliment 851n. *ridicule;* insincerity, play-acting, tongue in cheek 541n. *duplicity;* theatricality, histrionics.

pretension, assumption, pretensions, false p., false claim 916n. *arrogation;* artifice, pretense 614n. *pretext;* humbug, quackery, charlatanism, charlatanry 542n. *deception;* superficiality, shallowness, shallow profundity 4n. *insubstantiality;* stiffness, starchiness, buckram 875n. *formality;* pedantry, purism, precisianism 735n. *severity;* demureness, prunes and prisms 950n. *prudery;* sanctimony, sanctimoniousness 979n. *pietism.*

affector, affecter; pretender, false claimant; humbug, quack, charlatan 545n. *imposter;* play-actor 594n. *actor;* hypocrite, flatterer 545n. *deceiver;* bluffer 877n. *boaster;* coquette, flirt; affectationist, mass of affectation, attitudinizer, poser, poseur; ironist 839n. *humorist;* coxcomb, dandy 848n. *fop;* grimacer, simperer; formalist, precisian, purist, pedant; prig, puritan, pietist 950 n. *prude;* mannerist, euphuist, cultist, gongorist 575n. *stylist.*

Adj. *affected,* full of affectations, self-conscious, over-wrought, overdone 546adj. *exaggerated;* mannered, euphuistic, precious, chi-chi 574adj. *ornate;* artificial, unnatural, stilted, stiff, starchy 875adj. *formal;* prim, priggish, prudish, euphemistic, sanctimonious, smug, demure 979 adj. *pietistic;* arch, sly 833adj. *gay;* coquettish, coy, mock-modest, mincing, simpering, grimacing, languishing; humbugging, canting, hypocritical, tongue-in-cheek, ironical 542adj. *deceiving;* bluffing 877adj. *boasting;* shallow, specious, pretentious, big, big-sounding, high-s., big-mouthed, stagy, theatrical, over-dramatized 875adj. *ostentatious;* coxcombical, foppish, conceited, giving oneself airs, showing off, swanking, posturing, posing, striking poses, striking an attitude, attitudinizing 873adj. *vain;* snobbish, climbing, saving appearances 847adj. *ill-bred;* bogus 541adj. *false;* for effect, sought, put on.

Vb. *be affected,* affect, put on, wear, assume; pretend, feign, go through the motions, make a show of, bluff 541vb. *dissemble;* make as if 20vb. *imitate;* affect zeal, show work 678 vb. *be busy;* perform, act a part, play-act 594vb. *act;* overact, ham, barnstorm 546vb. *exaggerate;* try for effect, seek an e., play to the gallery; dramatize oneself, attitudinize, strike attitudes, posture, pose, strike a p. 875vb. *be ostentatious;* have pretensions, put on airs, give oneself a., swank, show off, make a show 873vb. *be vain;* air one's knowledge 490vb. *know;* air one's style, euphuize 566vb. *show style;* brag, vaunt, talk big 877vb. *boast;* grimace, moue, simper, smirk 835 vb. *smile;* coquette, flirt, languish 887vb. *excite love;* play the hypocrite 541vb. *cant;* save appearances, euphemize; make pretexts, pretext 614vb. *plead.*

See: 4, 20, 490, 541, 542, 545, 546, 547, 566, 568, 574, 575, 594, 604, 614, 678, 735, 833, 835, 839, 847, 848, 851, 873, 874, 875, 877, 887, 916, 950, 979.

851 Ridicule

N. *ridicule,* derision, derisiveness, poking fun; mockery, scoffing, flippancy 921n. *disrespect;* sniggering, grinning 835n. *laughter;* raillery, quizzing, banter, persiflage, badinage, leg-pulling, chaff, quiz, leg-pull; buffoonery, horseplay, clowning, practical joke 497n. *foolery;* grin, snigger, laugh; scoff, mock, fleer 926n. *detraction;* irony, tongue in cheek, sarcasm, barbed shaft, backhanded compliment; catcall, hoot, hiss 924n. *censure;* personality, insult 921n. *indignity;* ribaldry, fescennine verses 839n. *witticism.*

satire, denunciation 928n. *accusation;* parody, burlesque, travesty, caricature, cartoon 552n. *misrepresentation;* skit, take-off 20n. *mimicry;* squib, lampoon 926n. *detraction.*

laughing-stock, gazing-s., object of ridicule, figure of fun, butt, universal b., common jest, by-word; mock, sport, game, fair g.; cock-shy, Aunt Sally; April fool, silly f., buffoon, clown, stooge, zany 501n. *fool;* guy, caricature, travesty, mockery of, apology for; eccentric 504n. *crank;* original, card, queer fish, odd f.; fogy, old f., geezer, mumpsimus, museum piece, mossback, back number; gink, screwball; victim 728n. *loser.*

Adj. *derisive,* ridiculing, mocking, chaffing, joshing etc. vb.; flippant 456adj. *lightminded;* sardonic, sarcastic; ironical, quizzical; satirical, Hudibrastic 833adj. *witty;* ribald, fescennine 847adj. *vulgar;* burlesque, mock-heroic.

Vb. *ridicule,* deride, laugh at, grin at, smile at, smirk at; snicker, sniff, laugh in one's sleeve; banter, chaff, rally, twit, josh, roast, rag, pull one's leg, poke fun, make merry with, play w., exercise one's wit on, make fun of, make game of, take the mickey out of, have one on, fool, make a fool of, make an April fool of, fool to the top of one's bent 542vb. *befool;* mock, scoff, fleer, jeer 926vb. *detract;* turn to a jest, make a joke of, turn to ridicule 922vb. *hold cheap;* take down, deflate, debunk, make one look silly, make one laugh on the other side of his face 872vb. *humiliate.*

satirize, lampoon 921vb. *not respect;* mock, fleer, jibe, scold 899vb. *curse;* mimic, take off 20vb. *imitate;* parody, travesty, burlesque, caricature, guy 552vb. *misrepresent;* expose, show up, denounce, pillory 928vb. *accuse.*

See: 20, 456, 497, 501, 504, 542, 552, 728, 833, 835, 839, 847, 872, 899, 921, 922, 924, 926, 928.

852 Hope

N. *hope,* hopes, expectations, something to bank on, assumption, presumption 507n. *expectation;* good hope, certain h., high h., sanguine expectation, hope and belief, conviction 485n. *belief;* reliance, trust, confidence, faith, assurance 473n. *certainty;* eager hope 135n. *anticipation;* hope recovered, heart of grace, reassurance 831n. *relief;* safe hope, security, anchor, sheet a., mainstay, staff 218n. *support;* final hope, last h., last throw 618n. *gambling;* ray of hope, beam of h., gleam of h., glimmer of h. 469n. *possibility;* good omen, happy o., favorable auspices, promise, fair prospect, bright p. 511n. *omen;* blue sky, blue streak, silver lining 831n. *relief;* hopefulness, no cause for despair;

buoyancy, airiness, breeziness, optimism, enthusiasm 833n. *cheerfulness;* wishful thinking, self-hypnotism, couéism 477n. *sophistry;* rosy picture; star of hope; Pandora's box.
aspiration, ambition, purpose 617n. *intention;* pious hope, fervent h., fond h., airy h.; vision, pipe-dream, golden d., utopianism, millenarianism, messianism; castles in Spain, El Dorado, fool's paradise 513n. *fantasy;* promised land, land of promise, utopia, millennium, the day, Der Tag 617n. *objective.*
hoper, aspirant, candidate, waiting list; hopeful, young h.; expectant, heir apparent 776n. *beneficiary;* optimist, prisoner of hope; utopian, millenarian, chiliast 513n. *visionary;* waiter on providence, Micawber.
Adj. *hoping,* aspiring, soaring, starry-eyed; ambitious, would-be 617adj. *intending;* dreaming, dreaming of 513adj. *imaginative;* hopeful, in hopes 507adj. *expectant;* happy in the hope, next in succession, in sight of, on the verge of; in high hopes, sanguine, confident 473adj. *certain;* buoyant, optimistic, airy, uncritical; elated, enthusiastic, flushed 833adj. *jubilant;* hoping for the best, ever-hoping, undespairing, discouraged 855adj. *unfearing;* waiting on providence, Micawberish; not unhopeful, reasonably confident.
promising, full of promise, favorable, auspicious, propitious 730adj. *prosperous;* bright, fair, golden, roseate, rosy, rose-colored, couleur de rose; affording hope, hopeful, encouraging, inspiriting; plausible, likely 471 adj. *probable;* utopian, millennial, chiliastic; wishful, self-deluding 477 adj. *illogical;* visionary 513adj. *imaginary.*
Vb. *hope,* trust, confide; hope in, put one's trust in, rely, lean on, bank on, count on, pin one's hopes on, hope and believe 485vb. *believe;* presume 471vb. *assume;* speculate, look forward 507vb. *expect;* dream of, aspire, promise oneself, soar, aim high 617vb. *intend;* have a hope, be in hopes, have hopes, have expectations, live in hopes; feel hope, cherish h., nourish h., nurse h.; buck up, take heart of grace, take hope, pluck up h., recover h., renew h. 831vb. *be relieved;* remain hopeful, not despair, see no cause for d., not despond 599vb. *stand firm;* hope on, hope against hope, cling to h., keep hope alive, never say die; catch at a straw, keep one's spirits up, look on the bright side, hope for the best 833vb. *be cheerful;* flatter oneself, delude o. 477vb. *reason ill;* anticipate, make drafts on the future, count one's chickens before they are hatched; indulge in wishful thinking, dream 513vb. *imagine.*
give hope, afford h., foster h., inspire h., inspirit, encourage, comfort 833vb. *cheer;* show signs of, have the makings of, promise, show p., promise well, shape w., augur w., bid fair 471vb. *be likely;* raise expectations, paint a rosy picture 511vb. *predict.*
Adv. *hopefully,* expectantly, in all hopefulness, in all confidence; without discouragement, without despair; optimistically, airily, lightly, gaily, uncritically.
See: 135, 218, 469, 471, 473, 477, 485, 507, 511, 513, 599, 617, 618, 730, 776, 831, 833, 855.

853 Hopelessness

N. *hopelessness,* no hope, loss of hope, discouragement, defeatism, despondency 834n. *dejection;* pessimism, cynicism, despair, desperation, no way out, last hope gone; overthrow of hope, dashed hopes, hope deferred, hope extinguished, cheated hope, deluded h. 509n. *disappointment;* chimera, vain hope, forlorn h., futile h., impossible h. 513n. *fantasy;* message of despair, wan smile; hopeless situation, bad job, bad business 700n. *predicament;* counsel of despair, Job's comforter, misery, pessimist, defeatist 834n. *moper.*
Adj. *hopeless,* without hope, desponding, despairing, in despair, desperate; unhopeful, pessimistic, cynical; defeatist, expecting the worst, fearing the w.; sunk in despair, inconsolable, disconsolate, comfortless 834adj. *dejected;* wringing one's hands 836adj. *lamenting;* cheated of one's last hope 509adj. *disappointed;* desolate, forlorn; ruined, undone, without resource 731adj. *unfortunate.*
unpromising, holding no hope, offering no h., hopeless, comfortless, without comfort 834adj. *cheerless;* desperate 661adj. *dangerous;* unpropitious, inauspicious 731adj. *adverse;* ill-omened, boding, threatening, ominous 511adj. *presageful;* inassuageable, immitigable, irremediable, remediless, incurable, cure-

less, immedicable, inoperable; past cure, past hope, past recall; incorrigible, irreparable, irrecoverable, irrevocable, irredeemable, irreclaimable; irreversible, inevitable; impracticable, out of the question 470 adj. *impossible*.

Vb. *despair,* lose hope, have no h., hope no more; despond, give way to despair, wring one's hands 834 vb. *be dejected;* have shot one's last bolt, give up hope, reject h., abandon h., relinquish h.; hope for nothing more from, write off 674 vb. *disuse*.

leave no hope, offer no h., deny h.; drive to despair, bring to d.; shatter one's last hope 509vb. *disappoint;* be incurable,—inoperable etc. adj.

See: 470, 509, 511, 513, 661, 674, 700, 731, 834, 836.

854 Fear

N. *fear,* healthy f., dread, awe 920n. *respect;* abject fear 856n. *cowardice;* fright, stage-f.; affright, funk, wind up; terror, mortal t., panic t.; state of terror, intimidation, trepidation, alarm, false a.; shock, flutter, flap, flat spin 318n. *agitation;* fit, fit of terror, scare, stampede, panic 318n. *spasm;* flight, sauve qui peut; horror, horripilation, hair on end, cold sweat, blood turning to water; consternation, dismay 853n. *despair;* defense reaction, repression, escapism 620n. *avoidance*.

nervousness, want of courage, lack of confidence, cowardliness 856n. *cowardice;* self-distrust, shyness 874 n. *modesty;* defensiveness, blustering, bluster 877n. *boasting;* timidity, fearfulness, hesitation, fighting shy, backing out 620n. *avoidance;* loss of nerve, cold feet, fears, suspicions, misgiving, mistrust, apprehension, apprehensiveness, uneasiness, disquiet, disquietude, solicitude, anxiety, care 825n. *worry;* depression, despondency 834n. *dejection;* defeatism, pessimism 853n. *despair;* perturbation, trepidation, flutter, tremor, palpitation, blushing, trembling, quaking, shaking, shuddering, shivering, stuttering; nerves, willies, butterflies, qualms, needles, creeps, shivers, jumps, jitters, heebie-jeebies 318n. *agitation;* gooseflesh, hair on end, knees knocking.

phobia, claustrophobia, agoraphobia, acrophobia, pyrophobia; fear of death; anti-Semitism, negrophobia, xenophobia 888n. *hatred;* spy-mania, witch-hunting.

intimidation, deterrence, war of nerves, saber-rattling, rocket-r., fee, faw, fum; threatening 900n. *threat;* caution 664n. *warning;* terror, terrorization, terrorism, reign of terror 735n. *severity;* alarmism, scaremongering; sword of Damocles, suspended sentence 963n. *punishment;* deterrent, weapon of retaliation 723 n. *weapon;* object of terror, goblin, hobgoblin 970n. *demon;* spook, specter 970n. *ghost;* gorgon, Medusa, scarecrow, nightmare, daymare; bugbear, bugaboo, mormo, ogre 938n. *monster;* death's head, skull and crossbones, raw-head, bloodybones.

alarmist, scaremonger, causer of alarm and despondency; defeatist, pessimist; terrorist, terrorizer, intimidator, horrifier, frightener, nerve-shaker, saber-rattler.

Adj. *fearing,* afeard, afraid, frightened, funky, panicky; overawed 920 adj. *respectful;* intimidated, terrorized; in fear, in trepidation, in a fright, in a cold sweat, in a flap, in a panic; terror-crazed, panic-stricken, panic-struck; stampeding, in a scare, scared, alarmed, startled; flapping, hysterical, having fits, in hysterics; dismayed, in consternation, consternated, flabbergasted; frozen, petrified, stunned; appalled, shocked, horrified, aghast, horror-struck, awe-s.; unmanned, scared out of one's wits, numbed with fear, palsied with f., frightened to death, fainting with fright, white as a sheet, pale as death, pale as a ghost, pale as ashes; frightened for nothing, more frightened than hurt, suffering from shock.

nervous, defensive, on the d.; defeatist, pessimistic, despairing 853adj. *hopeless;* timid, timorous, shy, diffident, self-conscious, self-distrustful 874adj. *modest;* coy, wary, hesitating, shrinking, treading warily 858 adj. *cautious;* doubtful, distrustful, misdoubting, suspicious 474adj. *doubting;* windy, faint-hearted, cold-footed 601adj. *irresolute;* disturbed, disquieted, dismayed; apprehensive, uneasy, fearful, dreading, anxious, worried 825adj. *unhappy;* haunted, haunted by fears, a prey to f., terror-ridden, high-strung, starting at a sound, afraid of one's own shadow, jittery, jumpy, nervy; tremulous, shaky, shaking, trembling, quaking, cowering, cringing 856adj.

cowardly; on pins and needles, palpitating, breathless 318adj. *agitated.*
frightening, shocking, startling, alarming etc. vb.; formidable, redoubtable 661adj. *dangerous;* tremendous, dreadful, fear-inspiring, awe-i., numinous, fearsome, awesome 821adj. *impressive;* grim, grisly, hideous, ghastly, revolting, horrifying, horrific, horrible, terrible, awful, appalling; horripilant, hair-raising; weird, eerie, creepy, ghoulish, nightmarish, gruesome, macabre, sinister; portentous, ominous, direful 511adj. *presageful;* intimidating, terroristic, saber-rattling, bullying, hectoring 735adj. *oppressive;* minatory, menacing 900adj. *threatening;* horrisonous, roaring 400adj. *loud;* nerve-racking 827adj. *distressing.*
Vb. *fear,* funk, be afraid,—frightened etc.adj.; stand in fear *or* awe, dread 920vb. *respect;* flap, be in a f., have the wind up, have the willies; get the wind up, take fright, take alarm; panic, fall into p., a stampede, take to flight, fly 620vb. *run away;* start, jump, flutter 318vb. *be agitated;* faint, collapse, break down.
quake, shake, tremble, quiver, shiver, shudder, stutter, quaver; quake in one's shoes, shake like a jelly; fear for one's life, be frightened to death, be scared out of one's wits, faint for fear; change color, blench, pale, go white as a sheet; wince, flinch, shrink, shy, quail, jib, blink 620vb. *avoid;* quail, cower, crouch, skulk, come to heel 721vb. *knuckle under;* stand aghast, be horrified, be chilled with fear, freeze, freeze with horror, feel one's blood run cold, feel one's blood turn to water, feel one's hair stand on end.
be nervous,—apprehensive etc.adj.; feel shy 874vb. *be modest;* have misgivings, suspect, distrust, mistrust 486vb. *doubt;* shrink, shy, quail, funk it, not face it, put off the evil day; be anxious, dread, feel solicitude, consult one's fears, have f., have qualms; hesitate, think twice, have second thoughts, think better of it, not dare 858vb. *be cautious;* get the wind up, start at one's own shadow, be on edge, sit on thorns 318vb. *be agitated.*
frighten, fright, affright, play the bogeyman, make faces, grimace; scare, panic, stampede; intimidate, put in fear, menace 900vb. *threaten;* stand over, hang o. 155vb. *impend;* alarm, cause a., raise the a., cry wolf; make one jump, give one a fright, give one a turn, startle, flutter, flurry 318vb. *agitate;* start, flush 619vb. *hunt;* disquiet, disturb, perturb, prey on the mind, haunt, obsess, beset 827vb. *incommode;* raise apprehensions, make nervous, rattle, shake, unnerve; play on one's nerves, wring one's n., unstring one's n.; unman, make a coward of, cowardize; strike with fear, put the fear of God into, awe, overawe 821vb. *impress;* quell, subdue, cow 727vb. *overmaster;* amate, amaze, flabbergast, stun 508vb. *surprise;* dismay, confound, abash, disconcert 63vb. *derange;* frighten off, daunt, deter, discourage 613vb. *dissuade;* terrorize, institute a reign of terror 735vb. *oppress;* browbeat, bully 827 vb. *torment;* terrify, horrify, harrow, make aghast; chill, freeze, benumb, palsy, petrify, gorgonize, mesmerize 375vb. *render insensible;* appall, chill the spine, freeze the blood, make one's blood run cold, turn one's blood to water; make one's flesh creep, make one's hair stand on end, make one's knees knock, make one's teeth chatter, frighten one out of his wits.
See: 63, 155, 318, 375, 400, 474, 486, 508, 511, 601, 613, 619, 620, 661, 664, 721, 727, 733, 735, 821, 825, 827, 834, 853, 856, 858, 874, 877, 900, 920, 938, 963, 970.

855 Courage

N. *courage,* bravery, valiance, valor; moral courage, courage of one's convictions 929n. *probity;* V.C. courage, heroism, gallantry, chivalry; self-confidence, self-reliance, fearlessness, ignorance of fear, intrepidity, daring, nerve; defiance of danger, boldness, hardihood, audacity 857n. *rashness;* spirit, mettle, dash, go, élan 174n. *vigorousness;* enterprise 672n. *undertaking;* tenacity, bulldog courage 600n. *perseverance;* undauntedness, high morale, stoutness of heart, firmness, fortitude, determination, resoluteness 599n. *resolution;* gameness, pluck, spunk, guts, heart, great h., stout h., heart of oak, backbone, bottom, grit 600 n. *stamina;* sham courage, Dutch c., pot-valiance; desperate courage, courage of despair; brave face, bold front 711n. *defiance;* fresh courage, encouragement, animation 612n. *inducement.*
manliness, manhood, feelings of a man; virtue, chivalry; manly spirit,

martial s., heroic qualities, soldierly q., morale, devotion to duty; militancy, aggressiveness, fierceness 718 n. *bellicosity;* endurance, stiff upper lip 599n. *resolution.*

prowess, derring-do, deeds of d., chivalry, knightliness, knighthood, heroism, heroic achievement, knightly deed, gallant act, act of courage, soldierly conduct; feat, feat of arms, emprise, exploit, stroke, bold s. 676n. *deed;* desperate venture 857n. *rashness;* aristeia, heroics.

brave person, hero, heroine, V.C., G.C.; knight, paladin, bahadur; good soldier, stout s., stout fellow, beau sabreur, brave, fighting man 722n. *soldier;* man, true m., he-man, man of mettle, man of spirit, plucky chap, well-plucked 'un, game dog, bulldog; stranger to fear, dare-devil, risk-taker; fire-eater, bully, bravo 857n. *desperado;* Hector, Achilles, Hotspur, Galahad, Greatheart; Joan of Arc, amazon; Hercules, Don Quixote, Bayard, knight-errant; the brave, the bravest of the brave; band of heroes, gallant company; forlorn hope, picked troops 644n. *elite;* lion, tiger, game-cock, fighting c., bulldog.

Adj. *courageous,* brave, valorous, valiant, gallant, heroic; chivalrous, knightly, knight-like; yeomanly, soldierly, soldier-like, martial, amazonian 718adj. *warlike;* stout, doughty, tall, bonny, manful, manly, tough, two-fisted, red-blooded; militant, bellicose, aggressive, fire-eating; fierce, bloody, savage 898adj. *cruel;* bold 711adj. *defiant;* dashing, hardy, audacious, daring, venturesome 857adj. *rash;* adventurous 672 adj. *enterprising;* mettlesome, spirited, high-s., high-hearted, stout-h., lion-hearted, bold as a lion, bold as brass; firm-minded, strong-m., full of courage, full of fight, full of spirit, full of spunk, spunky; full of Dutch courage, pot-valiant; firm, steady, dogged, indomitable 600adj. *persevering;* desperate, determined 599adj. *resolute;* of high morale, game, plucky, sporting; ready for danger, ready for the fray, ready for anything, unflinching, unshrinking, first in the breach 597adj. *willing.*

unfearing, unafraid, intrepid, despising danger, danger-loving; sure of oneself, confident, self-c., self-reliant; fearless, dauntless, dreadless, aweless; unshrinking, untrembling, unblenching, undismayed, undaunted, undashed, unabashed, unawed, unalarmed, unconcerned, unapprehensive, unappalled, unshaken, unshakable.

Vb. *be courageous,*—bold etc. adj.; fight with the best 716vb. *fight;* venture, adventure, bell the cat, take the plunge, take the bull by the horns 672vb. *undertake;* dare 661 vb. *face danger;* show fight, brave, face, outface, outdare, beard, affront 711vb. *defy;* confront, look in the face, look in the eyes; speak out, speak up 532vb. *affirm;* face the music, show a dauntless front, stick to one's guns 599vb. *stand firm;* go over the top 712vb. *charge;* laugh at danger, mock at d. 857vb. *be rash;* show prowess, show valor, win one's spurs; keep one's head 823vb. *keep calm;* bear up, endure, grin and bear it 825vb. *suffer.*

take courage, pluck up c., muster c., take heart of grace, nerve oneself, drink courage from, put a bold face on it, show fight, cast away fear, screw one's courage to the sticking place 599vb. *be resolute;* rally, stand 599vb. *stand firm.*

give courage, infuse c.; animate, put heart into, hearten, nerve, make a man of; embolden, encourage, inspirit, inspire 612vb. *incite;* rally 833vb. *cheer;* pat on the back, keep in countenance, keep in spirits, preserve morale, raise m., keep one's blood up; bolster up, reassure, take away fear, give confidence, increase one's self-reliance.

Adv. *bravely,* courageously, stoutly, doughtily; with one's blood up, as bold as brass.

See: 174, 532, 597, 599, 600, 612, 644, 661, 672, 676, 711, 712, 716, 718, 722, 823, 825, 833, 898, 857, 929.

856 Cowardice

N. *cowardice,* abject fear, funk, sheer f. 854n. *fear;* cowardliness, craven spirit, no grit, no guts 601n. *irresolution;* pusillanimity, timidity, want of courage, lack of daring; absence of morale, faint-heartedness, chicken-heartedness; unmanliness, poltroonery, dastardy, dastardliness; defeatism 853n. *hopelessness;* desertion, quitting, shirking 918n. *dutilessness;* white feather, yellow streak, low morale, faint heart, chicken liver; pot-valiance, Dutch courage, braggadocio 877n. *boasting;* cowering, skulking, leading from behind;

discretion, better part of valor; safety first, overcaution 858n. *caution;* moral cowardice, recantation 603n. *tergiversation.*

coward, utter c., no hero; funk, poltroon, craven; niddering, nidget, white-liver, dastard; sneak, rat, telltale 524n. *informer;* runaway, runagate 603n. *tergiversator;* coward at heart, dunghill cock, braggart 877n. *boaster;* sissy, milksop, baby, cry-b. 163n. *weakling;* skulker, quitter, shirker, flincher, deserter, scuttler; cur, skunk, chicken, rabbit, hare, mouse, deer, jellyfish, doormat; scaremonger, defeatist 854n. *alarmist.*

Adj. *cowardly,* coward, craven, poltroonish; not so brave, pusillanimous, timid, timorous, fearful, niddering, unable to say boo to a goose 854adj. *nervous;* soft, effeminate, womanish, babyish, unmanly, sissy 163adj. *weak;* spiritless, spunkless, without grit, without guts, poor-spirited, weak-minded, faint-hearted, chicken-h., pigeon-h., white-livered, yellow-l., milk-l., lily-l.; sneaking, skulking, cowering, quailing; dastardly, yellow, abject, base, vile, mean-spirited, currish, recreant, caitiff; unsoldierly, unmilitary, unmartial, unwarlike, unaggressive 717 adj. *peaceful;* cowed, without morale, without fight 721adj. *submitting;* defeatist 853adj. *hopeless;* unheroic, unvaliant, uncourageous, prudent, discreet, more discreet than valiant 858adj. *cautious;* bashful, shy, coy 874adj. *modest;* easily frightened, funky, shakable, unstable, unsteady, infirm of purpose 601adj. *irresolute.*

Vb. *be cowardly,* lack courage, have no fight, have no pluck, have no grit, have no guts, have no heart *or* stomach for 601vb. *be irresolute;* have cold feet 854vb. *be nervous;* shrink, funk, shy 620vb. *avoid;* hide, slink, skulk, sneak; quail, cower, cringe 721vb. *knuckle under;* show a yellow streak, show the white feather, show fear, turn tail, panic, stampede, scuttle, desert 620 vb. *run away;* show discretion, live to fight another day, lead from behind, keep well to the rear, march bravely in the r. 858vb. *be cautious.*

Adv. *unbravely,* uncourageously, unheroically, pusillanimously, faintheartedly, funkily, in a blue funk.

See: 163, 524, 601, 603, 620, 717, 721, 853, 854, 858, 874, 877, 918.

857 Rashness

N. *rashness,* lack of caution, incaution, incautiousness, incircumspection, unwariness, heedlessness 456n. *inattention;* carelessness, neglect 458 n. *negligence;* imprudence, improvidence, indiscretion 499n. *folly;* lack of consideration, inconsideration, irresponsibility, frivolity, flippancy, levity, light-mindedness; wildness, indiscipline, haughtiness 738n. *disobedience;* scorn of the consequences, recklessness, foolhardiness, temerity, audacity, presumption, over-confidence, over-daring; hotheadedness, fieriness, impatience 822 n. *excitability;* rushing into things, impetuosity, precipitance, hastiness, over-haste 680n. *haste;* overenthusiasm, quixotry, quixotism, knight-errantry; dangerous game, playing with fire, brinkmanship; desperation, courage of despair 855n. *courage;* needless risk, blind bargain, leap in the dark 661n. *danger;* too many eggs in one basket, underinsurance 661n. *vulnerability;* reckless gamble, last throw 618n. *gambling;* reckless expenditure 815 n. *prodigality.*

desperado, dare-devil, madcap, hothead, Hotspur, fire-eater; brinkman, adventurer, plunger, inveterate gambler 618n. *gambler;* enfant perdu, harum-scarum, scapegrace, ne'er-do-well; one who sticks at nothing, dynamitard; bully, bravo 904n. *ruffian.*

Adj. *rash,* ill-considered, ill-advised, wildcat, injudicious, indiscreet, imprudent 499adj. *unwise;* careless, hit-and-miss, slapdash, free-and-easy, accident-prone 458adj. *negligent;* unforeseeing, not looking, uncircumspect, incautious, unwary, needless, thoughtless, inconsiderate, uncalculating 456adj. *inattentive;* light, frivolous, airy, breezy, flippant, giddy, devil-may-care, harum-scarum, trigger-happy, slap-h. 456adj. *light-minded;* irresponsible, reckless, regardless, couldn't-care-less, don't-care, damning the consequences, wanton, wild, cavalier; bold, daring, temerarious, audacious; over-daring, over-bold, madcap, daredevil, breakneck, suicidal; overambitious, oversanguine, over-sure, over-confident 852adj. *hoping;* overweening, presumptuous, arrogant 878adj. *insolent;* precipitate, headlong, hell-bent, desperate 680adj. *hasty;* headstrong 602adj. *willful;* untaught by experience 491adj. *ignorant;* impatient, hot-blooded, hot-headed, hot-brained, fire-eating, furious 822adj. *excitable;* danger-loving 855adj. *unfearing;* venturesome 618adj. *speculative;* adventurous, risk-taking 672adj. *enterprising;* thriftless 815adj. *prodigal.*

Vb. *be rash,*—reckless etc.adj.; lack caution, want judgment, lean on a broken reed; expose oneself, drop one's guard, stick one's neck out; not look round, go bull-headed, charge at, rush at, rush into 680vb. *hasten;* take a leap in the dark, make a blind bargain, buy a pig in a poke; ignore the consequences, damn the c.; plunge 618vb. *gamble;* put all one's eggs into one basket, not insure, under-insure; not care 456vb. *be inattentive;* play fast and loose 634vb. *waste;* spend to the hilt 815vb. *be prodigal;* play the fool, play with edged tools, play with fire, burn one's fingers; venture to the brink, stand on the edge of a volcano 661vb. *face danger;* court disaster, ask for trouble, tempt providence; anticipate, reckon without one's host, count one's chickens before they are hatched, aim too high 695vb. *stultify oneself.*

Adv. *rashly,* inconsiderately, carelessly, incautiously, lightly, gaily, cheerfully; recklessly, like Gadarene swine.

See: 456, 458, 491, 499, 602, 618, 634, 661, 672, 680, 695, 738, 815, 822, 852, 855, 878, 904.

858 Caution

N. *caution,* cautiousness, wariness, heedfulness, care, heed 457n. *carefulness;* hesitation, doubt, second thoughts 854n. *nervousness;* instinct of self-preservation 932n. *selfishness;* looking before one leaps, looking twice, looking round, circumspection; guardedness, "Deutsche Blick"; secretiveness, reticence 525n. *secrecy;* calculation, careful reckoning, counting the risk, safety first; nothing left to chance 699n. *preparation;* deliberation, mature consideration 480n. *judgment;* sobriety, balance, level-headedness 834n. *seriousness;* prudence, discretion, worldly wisdom 498n. *wisdom;* insurance, reinsurance, self-insurance 662n. *safeguard;* foresight 511n. *prediction;* Fabianism, Fabian policy 823n. *patience;* going slow, watching one's step, festina lente 278n. *slowness;* wait-and-see policy 136n. *delay.*

Adj. *cautious,* cautelous, wary, watchful 455adj. *attentive;* heedful 457adj. *careful;* hesitating, doubtful, suspicious 854n. *nervous;* taking no risks, insured, hedging; guarded, secret, secretive, incommunicative, 525adj. *reticent;* experienced, taught by experience, once bitten, twice shy 669adj. *prepared;* on one's guard, circumspect, looking round, looking all ways, gingerly, stealthy, feeling one's way, watching one's step, tentative 461adj. *experimental;* conservative 660adj. *safe;* responsible 929adj. *trustworthy;* prudent, prudential, discreet 498adj. *wise;* noncommittal 625adj. *neutral;* frugal, counting the cost 814adj. *economical;* canny, counting the risk; timid, overcautious, unenterprising, unadventurous, over-insured; slow, unhasty, deliberate, Fabian 823adj. *patient;* sober, cool-headed, level-h., cool; cold-blooded, calm, self-possessed 823adj. *inexcitable.*

Vb. *be cautious,* take good care 457vb. *be careful;* take no risks, play safe, play for safety, play for a draw; ca' canny, go slow 278vb. *move slowly;* bury, cover up 525vb. *conceal;* not talk 525vb. *keep secret;* keep under cover, keep on the safe side, keep in the rear, keep in the background, hide 523vb. *lurk;* look, look out, see how the land lies 438vb. *scan;* feel one's way 461vb. *be tentative;* tread warily, watch one's step, walk Spanish, pussyfoot 525vb. *be stealthy;* look twice, think t. 455vb. *be mindful;* calculate, reckon 480vb. *judge;* count the cost, cut one's coat according to one's cloth 814vb. *economize;* know when to stop, take one's time, reculer pour mieux sauter; let well alone, let sleeping dogs lie, keep aloof, keep well out of 620vb. *avoid;* consider the consequences, take heed of the results 511vb. *predict;* take precautions 124vb. *look ahead;* look a gift horse in the mouth 480vb. *estimate;* assure oneself, make sure, make assurance doubly sure 473vb. *make certain;* cover oneself, insure, take out a policy, reinsure, hedge, over-insure 660vb. *seek safety;* leave nothing to chance 669vb. *prepare.*

Adv. *cautiously,* with caution, gingerly, conservatively; on prudential considerations.

See: 124, 136, 278, 438, 455, 457, 461, 473, 480, 498, 511, 523, 525,

620, 625, 660, 662, 669, 814, 823, 834, 854, 929, 932.

859 Desire

N. *desire,* wish, will and pleasure 595n. *will;* summons, call, cry 737n. *command;* dun 737n. *demand;* desideration, wanting, want, need, exigency 627n. *requirement;* claim 915 n. *dueness;* desiderium, nostalgia, homesickness 830n. *regret;* wistfulness, longing, hankering, yearning, sheep's eyes; wishing, thinking, daydreaming, daydream 513n. *fantasy;* ambition, aspiration 852n. *hope;* horme, appetency, appetition; yen, urge 279n. *impulse;* itch, itching, prurience, cacoëthes 378n. *formication;* curiousness, thirst for knowledge, intellectual curiosity 453n. *curiosity;* avidity, eagerness, zeal 597n. *willingness;* passion, ardor, warmth, impetuosity, impatience 822 n. *excitability;* rage, fury 503n. *frenzy;* craving, appetite, hunger, thirst, hungry look (**see** *hunger*); land-hunger, expansionism, irredentism; covetise, covetousness, cupidity, itching palm 816n. *avarice;* graspingness, greediness, greed 786n. *rapacity;* voracity, wolfishness, insatiability 947n. *gluttony;* concupiscence, lust (**see** *libido*); inordinate desire, incontinence 943n. *intemperance.*

hunger, famine, famished condition, empty stomach 946n. *fasting;* appetite, good a., sharp a., keen a., edge of a.; thirst, thirstiness, drought, drouth 342n. *dryness;* burning thirst, unquenchable t.; dipsomania 949n. *alcoholism.*

liking, fancy, fondness, infatuation 887n. *love;* stomach, appetite, zest; relish, tooth, sweet t. 386n. *taste;* leaning, propensity, trend 179n. *tendency;* weakness, partiality; affinity, mutual a.; sympathy, involvement 775n. *participation;* inclination, mind 617n. *intention;* predilection, favor 605n. *choice;* whim, whimsy 604n. *caprice;* hobby, craze, fad, mania 481n. *bias;* fascination, allurement, attraction, temptation, titillation, seduction 612n. *inducement.*

libido, Eros, life instinct; concupiscence, sexual desire, carnal d., passion, rage, rut, heat, estrus; ruttishness, mating season; libidinousness, lickerishness, prurience, lust 951n. *impurity;* nymphomania, priapism, satyriasis 84n. *abnormality;* monomania 503n. *mania.*

desired object, one's desire, wish, desire, desirable thing, desideratum 627n. *requirement;* catch, prize, plum 729n. *trophy;* lion, idol, cynosure 890n. *favorite;* forbidden fruit, contraband article, envy, temptation; magnet, lure, draw 291n. *attraction;* aim, goal, star, ambition, aspiration, dream 617n. *objective;* ideal 646n. *perfection;* height of one's ambition, consummation devoutly to be wished.

desirer, coveter, envier; wooer, suer, courter 887n. *lover;* glutton, sucker for; fancier, amateur, dilettante 492 n. *collector;* devotee, votary, votarist, votaress, idolater 981n. *worshiper;* well-wisher, favorer, sympathizer 707n. *patron;* wisher, aspirant 852n. *hoper;* claimant, irredentist; candidate, solicitant, parasite 763n. *petitioner;* ambitious person, careerist; wanton 952n. *libertine.*

Adj. *desiring,* desirous, wishing, wishful, tempted, unable to resist; lustful, libidinous, concupiscent, rutting, in heat, ruttish, musth, estrous 951 adj. *lecherous;* covetous (**see** *greedy*); craving, needing, wanting 627adj. *demanding;* missing, nostalgic 830 adj. *regretting;* fain, inclined, minded, set upon, bent upon 617 adj. *intending;* ambitious, vaulting 852adj. *hoping;* aspiring, would-be, wistful, longing, yearning, hankering; unsatisfied, irredentist; curious, solicitous, sedulous, anxious; eager, keen, mad k., burning, ardent, agog, breathless, impatient, dying for; itching, spoiling for; clamant, vocal; avid, over-eager, over-inclined, mad for, mad after; liking, fond, partial to, with a weakness for.

greedy, acquisitive, possessive 932 adj. *selfish;* ambitious, place-hunting; voracious, omnivorous, open-mouthed 947adj. *gluttonous;* unsated, unsatisfied, unslaked, quenchless, unquenchable, inappeasable, insatiable, insatiate; rapacious, grasping, gripping, retentive 816adj. *avaricious;* exacting, extortionate 735adj. *oppressive.*

hungry, esurient, hungering, a-hungered; unfilled, empty, foodless, supperless, dinnerless 946adj. *fasting;* starving, famished 636adj. *underfed;* with appetite, ravenous, peckish, sharp-set, hungry as a hunter, pinched with hunger; thirsty, thirsting, athirst, dry, droughty, parched, parched with thirst.

desired, wanted, liked; likable, desirable, worth having, appetible, enviable; acceptable, welcome; appetizing 826adj. *pleasurable;* fetching, catchy, attractive, appealing 291 adj. *attracting;* wished, self-sought, invited 597adj. *voluntary.*

Vb. *desire,* want, desiderate, miss, feel the lack of 627vb. *require;* ask for, cry out f., clamor f. 737vb. *demand;* desire the presence of, call, summon, ring for 737vb. *command;* invite 882vb. *be hospitable;* wish, make a w., pray; wish otherwise, unwish 830vb. *regret;* wish for oneself, covet 912vb. *envy;* promise oneself, have a mind to, ambition, set one's heart on, set one's mind on, have designs on, aim at, have at heart 617vb. *intend;* plan for, angle f., fish f., 623vb. *plan;* aspire, raise one's eyes to, dream of, dream, daydream 852vb. *hope;* want a lot, aim high; look for, expect, think one deserves 915vb. *claim;* wish in vain, whistle for, cry for the moon 695 vb. *stultify oneself;* wish for another, pray for, intercede, invoke, wish on, call down on; wish ill 889 vb. *curse;* wish one well 897vb. *be benevolent;* welcome, be glad of jump at, catch at, grasp at, clutch at 786vb. *take;* lean 179vb. *tend;* favor, prefer, select 603vb. *choose;* crave, itch for, hanker after, long for; long, yearn, pine, languish; pant for, gasp f., burn f., die f., be dying f. 636vb. *be unsatisfied;* thirst for, hunger f., raven f. (**see** *be hungry*); can't wait, must have; like, have a liking, affect, have a taste for, care for, care 887vb. *love;* take to, warm to, fall in love with, dote, dote on, sigh, burn 887vb. *be in love;* ogle, make eyes at, make passes, solicit, woo 889vb. *court;* set one's cap at, make a dead set at, run after, chase 619vb. *pursue;* lust, lust for, lust after, run mad a. 951vb. *be impure;* rut, be in rut, be in heat.

be hungry, hunger, famish, starve, have an empty stomach 636vb. *be unsatisfied;* have a good appetite, gape for, open one's mouth for, water at the mouth, raven 301 vb. *eat;* thirst, be athirst, be dry, be dying for a drink.

cause desire, incline 612vb. *motivate;* arouse desire, provoke d., fill with longing 887vb. *excite love;* stimulate 821vb. *excite;* smell good, whet the appetite, parch, raise a thirst 390 vb. *appetize;* dangle, tease, titillate, tantalize 612vb. *tempt;* allure, draw, catch, fetch 291vb. *attract;* hold out hope 852vb. *give hope.*

Adv. *desirously,* wishfully, wistfully, eagerly, with appetite, hungrily, thirstily, greedily; by request, as desired.

See: 84, 179, 279, 291, 301, 342, 378, 386, 390, 453, 481, 492, 503, 513, 595, 597, 603, 604, 605, 612, 617, 619, 623, 627, 636, 646, 695, 707, 729, 735, 737, 763, 775, 786, 816, 821, 822, 826, 830, 852, 882, 887, 889, 890, 912, 915, 932, 943, 946, 947, 949, 951, 952, 981.

860 Indifference

N. *indifference,* unconcern, uninterest 454n. *incuriosity;* lack of interest, half-heartedness, want of zeal, lukewarmness, Laodiceanism 598n. *unwillingness;* coolness, coldness, faint praise, two cheers 823n. *inexcitability;* unsurprise 865n. *nonwonder;* desirelessness, lovelessness; mutual indifference, nothing between them; anorexy, inappetency, no appetite, loss of a. 375n. *insensibility;* inertia, apathy 679n. *inactivity;* nonchalance, insouciance 458n. *negligence;* perfunctoriness, carelessness 456n. *inattention;* don't-care attitude 734n. *laxity;* recklessness, heedlessness 857n. *rashness;* promiscuity 464 n. *indiscrimination;* amorality, indifferentism; open mind, impartiality, equity 913n. *justice;* neutrality 625n. *mid-course;* nil admirari; six of one and half a dozen of the other; indifferentist, neutralist, neutral 625 n. *moderate;* Laodicean 598n. *slacker;* object of indifference, wallflower.

Adj. *indifferent,* uncaring, unconcerned, insolicitous; uninterested 454 adj. *incurious;* lukewarm, Laodicean, halfhearted 598adj. *unwilling;* impersonal, passionless, insensible, phlegmatic 820adj. *impassive;* unimpressed, unwondering, unsurprised 865adj. *unastonished;* calm, cool, cold 823adj. *inexcitable;* nonchalant, insouciant, careless, pococurante, perfunctory 458adj. *negligent;* supine, lackadaisical, listless 679adj. *inactive;* undesirous, unambitious, unaspiring; don't-care, easy-going 734adj. *lax;* unresponsive, unmoved, unallured, unattracted, untempted; loveless, heart-whole, fancy-free, uninvolved; disenchanted, disillusioned, out of love, cooling off, sitting loose; unswerving 625adj. *undeviating;* impartial, inflexible 913adj. *just;* noncommittal, moderate 625adj. *neutral;* promiscuous 464adj. *indiscriminating;* amoral, cynical.

unwanted, undesired, unwished, uninvited, unbidden, unprovoked; loveless, unvalued, uncared for, unmissed 458adj. *neglected;* all one to 606adj. *choiceless;* insipid, tasteless 391adj. *unsavory;* unattractive, unalluring, untempting, undesirable; unwelcome 861adj. *disliked.*

Vb. *be indifferent,*—unconcerned etc. adj.; see nothing wonderful 865n. *not wonder;* take no interest 456 vb. *be inattentive;* not mind, care little for, damn with faint praise; care nothing for, not care a straw about, have no taste for, have no relish f. 861vb. *dislike;* couldn't care less, take it or leave it; not think twice about, not care, shrug, shrug off, dismiss, let go, make light of 922vb. *hold cheap;* not defend, hold no brief for, stand neuter, take neither side 606vb. *be neutral;* grow indifferent, fall out of love, cool off, sit loose to; not repine, have no regrets; fail to move, leave one cold 820vb. *make insensitive.*

See: 375, 391, 454, 456, 458, 464, 598, 606, 625, 679, 734, 820, 823, 857, 861, 865, 913, 922.

861 Dislike

N. *dislike,* disinclination, no fancy for, no stomach for; reluctance, backwardness 598n. *unwillingness;* displeasure 891n. *resentment;* dissatisfaction 829n. *discontent;* disagreement 489n. *dissent;* shyness, aversion 620n. *avoidance;* instinctive dislike, sudden *or* instant d., antipathy, dyspathy, allergy; distaste, disrelish; repugnance, repulsion, disgust, abomination, abhorrence, detestation, loathing; shuddering, horror, mortal h., rooted h. 854n. *fear;* xenophobia 854n. *phobia;* prejudice, sectarian p., odium theologicum 481 n. *bias;* animosity, bad blood, ill-feeling, mutual hatred, common h. 888n. *hatred;* nausea, queasiness, turn, heaving stomach, vomit 300n. *voidance;* sickener, one's fill 863n. *satiety;* gall and wormwood, bitterness 393adj. *sourness;* object of dislike, not one's type, bête noire, pet aversion, Dr. Fell.

Adj. *disliking,* not liking, displeased 829adj. *discontented;* undesirous, disinclined, loath 598adj. *unwilling;* squeamish, qualmish, queasy; allergic, antipathetic, feeling Dr. Fellish; disagreeing 489adj. *dissenting;* averse, hostile 881adj. *inimical;* averse, shy 620adj. *avoiding;* repelled, abhorring, loathing 888adj. *hating;* unfriendly, unloverlike, loveless; unsympathetic, out of sympathy; disenchanted, disillusioned, out of love, out of conceit with 860 adj. *indifferent;* sick of 863adj. *sated;* nauseated, dog-sick 300adj. *vomiting.*

disliked, unwished, undesired, undesirable 860adj. *unwanted;* unchosen 607adj. *rejected;* unpopular, out of favor, avoided; disagreeing, not to one's taste, grating, jarring, unrelished, bitter, uncomforting, unconsoling; repugnant, antipathetic, rebarbative, repulsive 292adj. *repellent;* revolting, abhorrent, loathsome 888adj. *hateful;* abominable, disgusting 924adj. *disapproved;* nauseous, nauseating, sickening, fulsome, foul, stinking 391adj. *unsavory;* disagreeable, insufferable 827 adj. *intolerable;* loveless, unlovable, unsympathetic; unlovely 842adj. *ugly.*

Vb. *dislike,* mislike, disrelish, distaste, find not to one's taste; not care for, have no liking f.; have no stomach for, have no heart for 598vb. *be loath;* not choose, prefer not to 607vb. *reject;* object 762vb. *deprecate;* mind 891vb. *resent;* take a dislike to, feel an aversion for, have a down on 481vb. *be biased;* react against 280vb. *recoil;* feel sick at, want to heave 300vb. *vomit;* shun, turn away, shrink from, have no time for 620vb. *avoid;* look askance at 924vb. *disapprove;* turn up the nose at, sniff at, sneer at 922vb. *despise;* make a face, grimace 893vb. *be sullen;* be unable to abide, not endure, can't stand, detest, loathe, abominate, abhor 888 vb. *hate;* not like the look of, shudder at 854vb. *fear;* unwish, wish undone 830vb. *regret.*

cause dislike, disincline, deter 854vb. *frighten;* go against the grain, rub the wrong way, antagonize, put one's back up 891vb. *enrage;* set against, set at odds, make bad blood 888vb. *excite hate;* satiate, pall, pall on, jade 863vb. *sate;* disagree with, upset 25vb. *disagree;* put off, revolt 292vb. *repel;* offend, grate, jar 827vb. *displease;* disgust, stick in one's gizzard, nauseate, sicken, make one's gorge rise, turn one's stomach, make one sick; shock, scandalize, make a scandal 924vb. *incur blame.*

Adv. *ad nauseam,* disgustingly.

Int. ugh! horrible!
See: 25, 280, 292, 300, 391, 393, 481, 489, 598, 607, 620, 762, 827, 829, 830, 842, 854, 860, 863, 881, 888, 891, 893, 922, 924.

862 Fastidiousness
N. *fastidiousness,* niceness, nicety, daintiness, finicalness, finicality, delicacy; discernment, perspicacity, subtlety 463n. *discrimination;* refinement 846n. *good taste;* dilettantism, connoisseurship, epicurism; meticulosity, particularity 457n. *carefulness;* idealism, artistic conscience, over-developed c. 917n. *conscience;* perfectionism, fussiness, over-nicety, over-refinement, hypercriticism, pedantry; primness, prudishness, puritanism 950n. *prudery.*
perfectionist, idealist, purist, precisian, fusspot, pedant, hard taskmaster; picker and chooser, gourmet, epicure.
Adj. *fastidious,* concerned with quality, quality-minded; nice, mincing, dainty, delicate, epicurean; perspicacious, discerning 463n. *discriminating;* particular, choosy, picksome, finicky, finical; over-nice, overparticular, scrupulous, meticulous, squeamish, qualmish 455adj. *attentive;* punctilious, conscientious, over-c.; critical, hypercritical, overcritical, fussy, pernickety, hard to please, fault-finding, censorious 924 adj. *disapproving;* pedantic, donnish, precise, rigorous, exacting, difficult 735adj. *severe;* prim, prudish, puritanical 950adj. *pure.*
Vb. *be fastidious,*—choosy etc.adj.; have only the best; pick and choose 605vb. *choose;* refine, over-refine, split hairs, mince matters 475vb. *argue;* draw distinctions 463vb. *discriminate;* find fault 924vb. *dispraise;* fuss, turn up one's nose, wrinkle one's n., say ugh!; look a gift horse in the mouth, see spots in the sun; feel superior, disdain 922vb. *despise;* keep oneself to oneself 883vb. *be unsocial.*
See: 455, 457, 463, 475, 605, 735, 846, 883, 917, 922, 924, 950.

863 Satiety
N. *satiety,* jadedness, fullness, repletion 54n. *plenitude;* over-fullness, plethora, stuffing, engorgement, saturation, saturation point 637n. *redundance;* glut, surfeit, too much of a good thing 838n. *tedium;* overdose, excess 637n. *superfluity;* spoiled child, enfant gaté.
Adj. *sated,* satiated, satisfied, replete, saturated, brimming 635adj. *filled;* surfeited, gorged, over-gorged, glutted, cloyed, sick of; jaded, blasé.
Vb. *sate,* satiate; satisfy, quench, slake 635vb. *suffice;* fill up, overfill, saturate 54vb. *fill;* soak 341vb. *drench;* stuff, gorge, glut, surfeit, cloy, jade, pall; overdose, overfeed; spoil, kill with kindness; bore, weary 838vb. *be tedious.*
See: 54, 341, 635, 637, 838.

864 Wonder
N. *wonder,* state of wonder, wonderment, marvel, stound; admiration, hero-worship 887n. *love;* awe, fascination; cry of wonder, gasp of admiration, whistle, wolf-w., exclamation, note of e.; shocked silence 399n. *silence;* open mouth, popping eyes; shock, surprise, surprisal 508n. *inexpectation;* astonishment, astoundment, amazement; stupor, stupefaction; bewilderment, bafflement 474n. *uncertainty;* consternation 854n. *fear.*
thaumaturgy, wonder-working, miracle-making, spellbinding, magic 983 n. *sorcery;* wonderful works, thaumatology, teratology, aretalogy; stroke of genius, feat, exploit 676n. *deed;* transformation scene, coup de théatre 594n. *dramaturgy.*
prodigy, portent, sign, eye-opener 511 n. *omen;* something incredible, prodigiosity, phenomenon, miracle, marvel, wonder; drama, sensation, cause célèbre, nine days' wonder, annus mirabilis; object of wonder *or* admiration, wonderland, fairyland 513n. *fantasy;* seven wonders of the world; sight, breathtaker 445n. *spectacle;* gazing-stock 851n. *laughing-stock;* infant prodigy, calculating boy, genius, man of genius; miracle-worker, thaumaturge, aretalogist 983n. *sorcerer;* cynosure, lion, hero, wonder man, dream man, Admirable Crichton 646n. *paragon;* freak, sport, curiosity, oddity, monster, monstrosity 84n. *rara avis;* puzzle 530n. *enigma.*
Adj. *wondering,* marveling, admiring etc.vb.; awed, awe-struck, fascinated, spellbound 818adj. *impressed;* surprised 508adj. *inexpectant;* astonished, amazed, astounded; in wonderment, lost in wonder, lost in amazement, unable to believe one's eyes *or* senses; wide-eyed, round-

e., pop-e.; open-mouthed, agape, gaping; spellbound, dumb, dumbstruck, inarticulate, speechless, breathless, wordless, left without words, silenced 399adj. *silent;* bowled over, struck all of a heap, thunderstruck; stupent, stupefied, bewildered 517adj. *puzzled;* aghast, flabbergasted; shocked, scandalized 924 adj. *disapproving.*

wonderful, to wonder at, wondrous, marvellous, miraculous, monstrous, prodigious, phenomenal; stupendous, fearful 854adj. frightening; admirable 644adj. *excellent;* record-breaking 644adj. *best;* striking, overwhelming, awesome, awe-inspiring, breath-taking 821adj. *impressive;* dramatic, sensational; shocking, scandalizing; rare, exceptional, extraordinary, unprecedented 84adj. *unusual;* remarkable, noteworthy; strange, passing s., odd, very odd, weird, weird and wonderful, unaccountable, mysterious, enigmatic 517adj. *puzzling;* outlandish, unheard of 59adj. *extraneous;* fantastic 513adj. *imaginary;* impossible, hardly possible, too good *or* bad to be true 472adj. *improbable;* unbelievable, incredible, inconceivable, unimaginable, indescribable; unutterable, unspeakable, ineffable 517adj. *inexpressible;* surprising 508adj. *unexpected;* astounding, amazing, shattering, bewildering etc.vb.; wonder-working, thaumaturgic, aretalogical; magic, like m. 983adj. *magical.*

Vb. *wonder,* marvel, admire, whistle; hold one's breath, gasp, gasp with admiration; hero-worship 887vb. *love;* stare, gaze and gaze, goggle at, gawk, open one's eyes, rub one's e., not believe one's e.; gape, open one's mouth, stand in amaze 508vb. *not expect;* be struck, be overwhelmed, stand in awe 854vb. *fear;* have no words to express, not know what to say 399vb. *be silent.*

be wonderful,—marvelous etc.adj.; do wonders, work miracles, achieve marvels; surpass belief, stagger b. 486vb. *cause doubt;* beggar all description, baffle d., beat everything; spellbind, enchant 983vb. *bewitch;* dazzle, strike with admiration, turn one's head 887vb. *excite love;* strike dumb, awe, electrify 821vb. *impress;* make one's eyes open, take away one's breath, bowl over, stagger; stun, daze, stupefy, petrify, dumbfound, confound, astound, astonish, amaze, flabbergast 508vb. *surprise;* baffle, bewilder 474vb. *puzzle;* startle 854vb. *frighten;* shock, scandalize 924vb. *incur blame.*

Adv. *wonderfully,* marvelously, remarkably, splendidly, fearfully; strange to say, wonderful to relate, to all men's wonder.

See: 59, 84, 399, 445, 472, 474, 486, 508, 511, 513, 517, 518, 530, 594, 644, 646, 676, 818, 821, 851, 854, 887, 924, 983.

865 Non-wonder

N. *non-wonder,* non-astonishment, unastonishment, unamazement, unsurprise; awelessness, irreverence, refusal to be impressed, nil admirari; blankness, stony indifference 860n. *indifference;* quietism, composure, calmness, serenity, tranquillity 266n. *quietude;* imperturbability, equability, impassiveness, cold blood 820 n. *moral insensibility;* taking for granted 610n. *habituation;* lack of imagination, unimaginativeness; disbelief 486n. *unbelief;* matter of course, just what one thought, nothing to wonder at, nothing in it.

Adj. *unastonished,* unamazed, unsurprised; unawed 855adj. *unfearing;* accustomed 610adj. *habituated;* calm, collected, composed; unimpressionable, phlegmatic, impassive 820adj. *apathetic;* undazzled, undazed, unimpressed, unadmiring, unmoved, unstirred, unaroused 860adj. *indifferent;* cold-blooded, unimaginative; blind to 439adj. *blind;* disbelieving 486adj. *unbelieving;* taking for granted, expecting 507adj. *expectant.*

unastonishing; unsurprising, foreseen 507adj. *expected;* customary, common, ordinary, all in the day's work, nothing wonderful 610adj. *usual.*

Vb. *not wonder,* see nothing remarkable 820vb. *be insensitive;* be blind and deaf to; not believe 486vb. *disbelieve;* see through 516vb. *understand;* treat as a matter of course, take for granted, take as one's due; see it coming 507vb. *expect;* keep one's head 823vb. *keep calm.*

Int. no wonder; nothing to it; of course; why notb; as expected; quite so.

See: 266, 439, 486, 507, 516, 610, 820, 823, 855, 860.

866 Repute

N. *repute,* good r., high r., reputation, good r., special r.; report, good r., title to fame, name, honored n., great n., good n., fair n., character, known c., good c., high c., reputability, respectability 802n. *credit;* regard, esteem 920n. *respect;* opinion, good o., good odor, favor, high f., popular f.; popularity, vogue 848n. *fashion;* acclaim, applause, approval, stamp of a., cachet 923n. *approbation.*

prestige, aura, mystique, magic; glamor, dazzle, éclat, luster, splendor; brilliance, prowess; illustriousness, glory, honor, honor and glory, succès d'estime (**see** *famousness*); esteem, estimation, account, high a., worship 638n. *importance;* face, izzat, caste; degree, rank, ranking, standing, footing, status, honorary s., brevet rank 73 n. *serial place;* condition, position, position in society; stardom, precedence 34n. *superiority;* conspicuousness, prominence, eminence, super-e. 443n. *visibility;* distinction, greatness, high rank, exaltedness, high mightiness, majesty 868n. *nobility;* impressiveness, dignity, stateliness, solemnity, grandeur, sublimity, awesomeness; name to conjure with 178 n. *influence;* paramountcy, ascendancy, hegemony, primacy 733n. *authority;* leadership, acknowledged l. 689n. *directorship;* prestige consideration, snob value.

famousness, title to fame, celebrity, notability, remarkability; illustriousness, renown, fame, name, note; glory 727n. *success;* notoriety 687n. *disrepute;* talk of the town 528n. *publicity;* place in history, posthumous fame 505n. *memory;* undying name, immortal n., immortality, deathlessness; remembrance, commemoration, temple of fame, niche in fame's temple.

honors, honor, blaze of glory, cloud of g., crown of g.; crown, martyr's c.; halo, aureole, nimbus, glory; blushing honors, battle h.; laurels, bays, wreath, garland, favor; feather, feather in one's cap 729n. *trophy;* order, star, garter, ribbon, medal 729 n. *decoration;* spurs, sword, shield, arms 547n. *heraldry;* an honor, distinction, accolade, award 962n. *reward;* compliment, praise, flattery, incense; memorial, statue, bust, picture, portrait, niche, plaque, temple, monument 505n. *reminder;* title of honor, dignity, handle 870n. *title;* patent of nobility, knighthood, baronetcy, peerage 868n. *nobility;* academic honor, baccalaureate, doctorate, degree, academic d., honors d., pass d., honorary d., diploma, certificate 870n. *academic title;* source of honor, fount of h., College of Arms; honors list, birthday honors, roll of honor 87n. *list.*

dignification, glorification, honorification, lionization; honoring, complimenting; crowning, commemoration, coronation 876n. *celebration;* sanctification, dedication, consecration, canonization, beatification; deification, apotheosis; enshrinement, enthronement; promotion, advancement, enhancement, aggrandizement 285n. *progression;* exaltation 310n. *elevation;* ennoblement, knighting; rehabilitation 656n. *restoration.*

person of repute, honored sir, gentle reader, candid r.; worthy, sound man, good citizen, loyal subject, pillar, pillar of society, pillar of the church, pillar of the state; man of honor 929n. *gentleman;* knight, peer 868n. *nobleman;* somebody 371n. *person;* great man, big pot, big noise, big wheel, VIP 638n. *bigwig;* man of mark, notable, celebrity, notability, figure, public f.; champion 644n. *exceller;* lion, star, rising star, rising sun; man of the hour, hero of the day, hero, popular h., pop singer, idol, boast 890n. *favorite;* cynosure, model, mirror 646n. *paragon;* cream, cream of society 644 n. *elite;* choice spirit, master s., leading light 690n. *leader;* grand old man, G.O.M. 500n. *sage;* noble army, great company, bevy, galaxy, constellation 74n. *band.*

Adj. *reputable,* of repute, of reputation, of credit; creditworthy 929adj. *trustworthy;* gentlemanly 929adj. *honorable;* worthy, creditable, meritorious 644adj. *excellent;* respectable, regarded, well-r., well thought of 920adj. *respected;* edifying, moral 933adj. *virtuous;* in good odor, in favor, in high f. 923adj. *approved;* popular, modish 848adj. *fashionable;* sanctioned, allowed, admitted 756adj. *permitted.*

worshipful, reverend, honorable; admirable 864adj. *wonderful;* heroic 855adj. *courageous;* imposing, dignified, august, stately, grand, sublime 821adj. *impressive;* lofty, high 310adj. *elevated;* high and mighty, mighty 32adj. *great;* lordly, princely, kingly, queenly, majestic, royal, regal 868adj. *noble;* aristocratic, well-born, high-caste, heaven-born; glorious, in glory, full of g., full of honors, honored, titled, ennobled; time-honored, ancient, age-old 127 adj. *immemorial;* sacrosanct, sacred, holy 979adj. *sanctified;* proud, honorific, dignifying.

noteworthy, notable, remarkable, extraordinary 84adj. *unusual;* fabulous 864adj. *wonderful;* of mark, of distinction, distinguished, distingué 638adj. *important;* conspicuous, prominent, public, in the eye of 443adj. *well-seen;* eminent, preeminent, super-eminent, peerless, foremost, in the forefront 34adj. *superior;* ranking, starring, leading, commanding; brilliant, bright, lustrous 417adj. *luminous;* illustrious, splendid, glorious 875adj. *ostentatious.*

renowned, celebrated, sung; of renown, of name, of fame; famous, fabled, famed, far-f.; historic, illustrious, great, noble, glorious 644 adj. *excellent;* notorious 867adj. *disreputable;* known as, well-known 490adj. *known;* of note, noted (**see** *noteworthy*); talked of, resounding, in all mouths, on every tongue, in the news 528adj. *published;* unfading, never-f., evergreen, imperishable, deathless, immortal, eternal 115adj. *perpetual.*

Vb. *have repute,* be reputed, have a reputation, enjoy a r., wear a halo; have a name, have a name to lose; rank, stand high, have status *or* standing, have a position, enjoy consideration, be looked up to, have a name for, be praised f. 920vb. *command respect;* stand well with, earn golden opinions, do oneself credit, win honor, win renown, gain prestige, gain a reputation, build a r., earn a name, acquire a character, improve one's credit 924vb. *be praised;* win one's spurs, gain the laurels, take one's degree, graduate 727vb. *succeed;* cut a figure, cut a dash, cover oneself with glory 875vb. *be ostentatious;* shine, excel 644vb. *be good;* steal the show, throw into the shade, overshadow 34vb. *be superior;* have precedence, play first fiddle, take the lead, play the l., star 64vb. *come before;* live in glory, have fame, have a great name, bequeath a n.; make history, live in h., be sure of immortality 505vb. *be remembered.*

seek repute, seek the bubble reputation, thirst for honor, strive for glory, nurse one's ambition; be conscious of one's reputation, consider one's position, mind one's prestige 871vb. *be proud;* wear one's honors, show off, flaunt 871vb. *feel pride;* lord it, queen it, prance, strut 875 vb. *be ostentatious;* brag 877vb. *boast.*

honor, revere, regard, look up to, hold in respect, hold in honor 920 vb. *respect;* stand in awe of 854vb. *fear;* bow down to 981vb. *worship;* know how to value, appreciate, prize, value, tender, treasure 887vb. *love;* show honor, pay respect, pay regard, pay one's respects to 920vb. *show respect;* be polite to 884vb. *be courteous;* compliment 925vb. *flatter;* grace with, honor w., dedicate to, inscribe to; praise, sing the praises, glorify, shout for glory, acclaim 923vb. *applaud;* make much of, lionize, chair; credit, give c., honor for 907vb. *thank;* glorify, immortalize, eternize, commemorate 505vb. *remember;* celebrate, renown, blazon 528vb. *proclaim;* reflect honor, shed luster, do credit to, be a credit to.

dignify, glorify, exalt; canonize, beatify, deify, consecrate, dedicate 979vb. *sanctify;* install, enthrone, crown 751vb. *commission;* signalize, mark out, distinguish 547vb. *indicate;* aggrandize, advance, upgrade 285vb. *promote;* honor, delight to h., confer an h.; bemedal, beribbon 844vb. *decorate;* bestow a title, create, elevate, raise to the peerage, ennoble, nobilitate; dub, knight, give the accolade; give one his title, sir, bemadam 561vb. *name;* take a title, take a handle to one's name, accept a knighthood.

See: 32, 34, 64, 73, 74, 84, 87, 115, 127, 178, 285, 310, 371, 417, 443, 490, 500, 505, 528, 547, 561, 638, 644, 646, 656, 687, 689, 690, 727, 729, 733, 751, 756, 802, 821, 844, 848, 854, 855, 864, 867, 868, 870, 871, 875, 876, 877, 884, 887, 890, 907, 920, 923, 924, 925, 929, 933, 962, 979, 981.

867 Disrepute

N. *disrepute,* disreputability, no repute, no reputation, bad r., bad name, bad character, shady reputation, past; disesteem 921n. *disrespect;* notoriety, infamy, ill repute, ill fame; no standing, ingloriousness, obscurity; bad odor, ill favor, bad f., disfavor, discredit, black books, bad light 888n. *odium;* derogation, dishonor, disgrace, shame (**see** *slur*); ignominy, loss of honor, loss of reputation, faded r., withered laurels, tarnished honor; departed glory, Ichabod; dedecoration, demotion, degradation; debasement, abasement, a long farewell to all one's greatness 872n. *humiliation;* abjectness, baseness, vileness, turpitude 934n. *wickedness;* sense of shame, argumentum ad verecundiam.

slur, reproach 924n. *censure;* imputation, aspersion, reflection, slander, obloquy, opprobrium, abuse 926n. *calumny;* insult 921n. *indignity;* scandal, shocking s., disgrace, shame, burning s., crying s.; defilement, pollution 649n. *uncleanness;* stain, smear 649n. *dirt;* stigma, brand, mark, spot, blot, tarnish, taint 845 n. *blemish;* dirty linen; blot on one's scutcheon, badge of infamy, mark of Cain.

object of scorn, scandalous person, reproach, a hissing and a reproach, by-word, by-word of reproach, contempt, discredit 938n. *bad man;* reject, the bottom 645n. *badness;* Cinderella, poor relation 639n. *nonentity;* failure 728n. *loser.*

Adj. *disreputable,* of no repute, of no reputation; characterless, without references; not respectable, disrespectable, shady 930adj. *rascally;* notorious, infamous, of ill fame, nefarious; arrant 645adj. *bad;* doubtful, questionable, objectionable 645 adj. *not nice;* risqué, ribald, improper, indecent, obscene 951adj. *impure;* not thought much of, held in contempt, despised 922adj. *contemptible;* beggarly, pitiful 639adj. *unimportant;* outcast 607adj. *rejected;* degraded, base, abject, despicable, odious 888adj. *hateful;* mean, cheap, low 847adj. *vulgar;* shabby, squalid, dirty, scruffy 649 adj. *unclean;* poor, down at heel, out at elbows 655adj. *dilapidated;* in a bad light, under a cloud, discredited, disgraced, in disgrace (**see** *inglorious*); reproached, blown upon 924adj. *disapproved;* unpopular 861 adj. *disliked.*

discreditable, no credit to, bringing discredit, reflecting upon one, damaging, compromising; ignoble, unworthy; improper, unbecoming 643 adj. *inexpedient;* dishonorable 930 adj. *dishonest;* despicable 922adj. *contemptible;* censurable 924adj. *blameworthy;* shameful, shame-making, disgraceful, infamous, unedifying, scandalous, shocking, outrageous, unmentionable, disgusting; too bad 645adj. *not nice.*

degrading, lowering, demeaning, ignominious, opprobrious, humiliating; dedecorous, derogatory, wounding one's honor; beneath one, beneath one's dignity, infra dignitatem, infra dig.

inglorious, without repute, without prestige, without note; without a name, nameless 562adj. *anonymous;* groveling, unheroic 879adj. *servile;* unaspiring, unambitious 874adj. *modest;* unnoted, unremarked, unnoticed, unmentioned 458adj. *neglected;* renownless, unrenowned, unknown to fame, obscure 491adj. *unknown;* unseen, unheard 444adj. *invisible;* unhymned, unsung, unglorified, unhonored, undecorated; titleless 869adj. *plebeian;* deflated, cut down to size, debunked, humiliated 872adj. *humbled;* sunk low, shorn of glory, faded, withered, tarnished; stripped of reputation, discredited, creditless, disgraced, dishonored, in eclipse; degraded, demoted, reduced to the ranks.

Vb. *have no repute,* have no reputation, have no character, have no name to lose, have a past; have no credit, rank low, stand low in estimation, have no standing, cut no ice 639vb. *be unimportant;* be out of favor, be in bad odor, be unpopular, be discredited, be in disgrace, lie under reproach, stink in the nostrils; play second fiddle, take a back seat, stay in the background 35vb. *be inferior;* blush unseen 444 vb. *be unseen.*

lose repute, fall *or* go out of fashion; fall, sink 309vb. *descend;* fade, wither; fall into disrepute, incur discredit, incur dishonor, incur disgrace, achieve notoriety 924vb. *incur blame;* spoil one's record, disgrace oneself, compromise one's name, risk one's reputation, lose one's r., outlive one's r.; tarnish one's glory, forfeit one's honor, lose one's halo; earn no credit, earn no honor, win no glory 728vb. *fail;* come down in the eyes of, sink in estimation, suffer in reputation, lose prestige, lose face, lose caste; admit defeat, slink away, crawl, crouch 721vb. *knuckle under;* look silly, look foolish, cut a sorry figure, blush for shame, laugh on the wrong side of one's mouth 497vb. *be absurd;* be exposed, be brought to book 963vb. *be punished.*

demean oneself, lower o., degrade o.; derogate, condescend, stoop, marry beneath one; compromise one's dignity, make oneself cheap, cheapen oneself, disgrace o., behave unworthily; sacrifice one's pride, disregard prestige, forfeit self-respect; apologize, excuse oneself 614vb. *plead;* have no class-feeling, affront one's class; have no pride, feel no shame, think no s.

shame, put to s., hold up to s.; pillory, expose, show up, post; scorn, mock 851vb. *ridicule;* snub, take down a peg or two 872vb. *humiliate;* discompose, disconcert, put out of countenance, put one's nose out of joint, deflate, cut down to size, debunk; degrade, downgrade, demote, disrate, reduce to the ranks, disbar, defrock, deprive, strip 963vb. *punish;* blackball 57vb. *exclude;* vilify, malign, disparage 926vb. *defame;* blast one's reputation, take away one's name, ruin one's credit; put in a bad light, reflect upon, breathe u., blow u., taint; sully, blacken, tarnish, stain, blot, besmear, smear, bespatter 649vb. *make unclean;* debase, defile, desecrate, profane 980vb. *be impious;* stigmatize, brand, cast a slur upon, fix a stain, tar 547vb. *mark;* dishonor, disgrace, discredit, involve in shame, bring to s., bring shame upon, scandalize, be a public scandal 924 vb. *incur blame;* heap shame upon, heap dirt u., drag through the mire; trample, tread underfoot, outrage 735vb. *oppress;* contemn, disdain 922vb. *despise;* make one blush, outrage one's modesty 951vb. *debauch;* not spare one's blushes, overpraise.

See: 35, 57, 309, 444, 458, 491, 497, 547, 562, 607, 614, 639, 643, 645, 649, 655, 721, 728, 735, 845, 847, 851, 861, 869, 872, 874, 879, 888, 921, 922, 924, 926, 930, 934, 938, 951, 963, 980.

868 Nobility

N. *nobility,* nobleness, high character 933n. *virtue;* distinction, quality 644n. *goodness;* rank, high r., titled r., station, order 27n. *degree;* royalty, kingliness, queenliness, princeliness, majesty, prerogative 733n. *authority;* birth, high b., gentle b., gentility, noblesse; descent, high d., noble d., ancestry, long a., line, unbroken l., lineage, pedigree, ancient p. 169n. *genealogy;* noble family, noble house, ancient h., royal h., dynasty, royal d. 11n. *family;* blood, blue b., best b.; bloodstock, caste, high c.; badge of rank, patent of nobility, coat of arms, crest, "boast of heraldry" 547n. *heraldry.*

aristocracy, patriciate, grandeeship, optimacy; nobility, hereditary n., lesser n., noblesse, ancien régime; lordship, lords, peerage, House of Lords, House of Peers, lords spiritual and temporal; dukedom, earldom, viscounty, baronage, baronetcy; knightage, chivalry; landed interest, squirearchy, squiredom; county family, gentry, landed g., gentlefolk; the great, great folk, the high and the mighty, notables; noblesse de robe; life peerage.

upper class, the classes, upper classes, upper ten, upper crust, top layer; first families, best people, better sort, chosen few 644n. *elite;* high society, social register, high life, fashionable world 848n. *beau monde;* ruling class, the twice-born, the Establishment 733n. *authority;* high-ups, Olympians; the haves 800n. *rich man;* salaried class, salariat.

aristocrat, patrician, Olympian; man of caste, Brahman, Rajput; descendant of the Prophet, sayyid; bloodstock, thoroughbred; optimate, senator, magnifico, magnate, dignitary; don, grandee, caballero, hidalgo; gentleman, gentlewoman, armiger; squire, squireen, buckeen, laird, boglord; Junker; cadet; emperor, king, prince 741n *sovereign;* nob, swell, gent, panjandrum, superior person 638n. *bigwig.*

nobleman, man of rank, titled person, noble, noblewoman, noble lord, lady, atheling, seigneur, signor; lording, lordship, milord; peer, life p.; peer of the realm, peeress; Prince of Wales, duke, grand d., archduke, duchess; marquis, marquess, marquise, marchioness, margrave, margravine, count, countess, contessa; earl, belted e.; viscount, baron, thane, baronet, knight, carpet k., banneret, knight-bachelor, knight-banneret; pasha, three-tailed p., beg, bey, nawab, begum, emir, khan, sheikh 741n. *potentate, governor.*

Adj. *noble,* of high character 933adj. *virtuous;* chivalrous, knightly; gentlemanly, gentlemanlike, ladylike (**see** *genteel*); majestic, royal, regal, every inch a king; kingly, queenly, princely; ducal, baronial, seigneurial; generous, gentle, of birth, of gentle blood, of family, pedigreed, well-born, high-b., born to the purple; thoroughbred, pur sang, blue-blooded; of rank, ennobled, titled; haughty, high, exalted, high-up, grand 32adj. *great.*

genteel, patrician, senatorial; aristocratic, Olympian; superior, top-drawer, high-class, upper-c., cabin-c., classy, U, highly respectable, comme il faut; of good breeding 848adj. *well-bred.*

See: 11, 27, 32, 169, 547, 638, 644, 733, 741, 800, 848, 933.

869 Commonalty

N. *commonalty,* commons, third estate, bourgeoisie; plebs, plebeians; citizenry, demos, democracy, King Mob; people at large, populace, the people, the common p., plain p., common sort; vulgar herd, great unwashed; the many, the many-headed, the multitude, the million, hoi polloi; the masses, mass of society, mass of the people, admass, proletariat, proles; the general, rank and file, rag, tag and bobtail, hoc genus omne, Tom, Dick and Harry, Brown, Jones and Robinson.

rabble, rabblement, mob, mobile vulgus, mobility, horde 74n. *crowd;* clamjamfry, rout, rabble r., rascal multitude, varletry; riffraff, scum, off-scourings, faex populi, dregs of society, canaille, doggery, cattle, vermin.

lower classes, lower orders, one's inferiors 35n. *inferior;* common sort, small fry, humble folk; lesser breed, great unwashed; working class, servant c.; steerage, steerage class, lower deck; second-class citizens, the have-nots, the underprivileged; proletariat, proles; sansculottes, submerged tenth, slum population; down-and-outs, depressed class, outcasts, outcasts of society, poor whites, white trash; beatniks, beat generation; demimonde, underworld, low company, low life; dunghill, slum 649n. *sink.*

commoner, bourgeois, plebeian; untitled person, plain Mr.; plain man, mere citizen; one of the people, man of the p., democrat, republican; proletarian, prole; workman; little man, small m., man in the street, everyman, everywoman, common type, average t. 30n. *common man;* common person, cockney, groundling, galleryite 35n. *inferior;* backbencher, private; underling 742n. *servant;* ranker, upstart, parvenu, mushroom, social climber, arriviste, nouveau riche, philistine 847n. *vulgarian;* nobody, nobody one knows, nobody knows who 639n. *nonentity;* low-caste person, Sudra, outcaste; villein, serf 742n. *slave.*

countryman, yeoman, rustic, Hodge, swain, gaffer, peasant, tiller of the soil, cultivator 370n. *husbandman;* serf, villein 742n. *slave;* boor, chuff, churl, carl, kern, bog-trotter; yokel, hind, chawbacon, cider-squeezer, pot-walloper, clod, clodhopper, plowman, hobnail, hob, clay-eater, rube, hay-seed, hick; bumpkin, country b., put, country p., joskin, Tony Lumpkin, country cousin, provincial, hillbilly; clown, lout, loon, looby 510n. *fool.*

low fellow, fellow, varlet 938n. *cad;* guttersnipe, slum-dweller 801n. *poor man;* mudlark, street-arab, gamin, ragamuffin, tatterdemalion, sansculotte; down-and-out, poor white; tramp, bum, weary willie, vagabond 268n. *wanderer;* gaberlunzie, panhandler 763n. *beggar;* low type, rough t., bully, ugly customer, plug-ugly, ruffian, rough, roughneck 904n. *ruffian;* rascal 938n. *knave;* Teddy-boy, Teddy-girl, zoot-suiter, hood; criminal, delinquent, juvenile d., felon 904n. *offender;* barbarian, savage, bushman, Goth, Vandal, yahoo, primitive 371n. *mankind.*

Adj. *plebeian,* common, simple, untitled, unennobled, without rank, titleless; ignoble, below the salt; below-stairs, servant-class; lower-deck, rank and file; mean, low, low-down, street-corner 867adj. *disreputable;* base-born, low-born, low-caste, of low origin, of mean parentage, of mean extraction; slave-born, servile; humble, of low estate, of humble condition 35adj. *inferior;* second-class, low-class, working-c., non-U, proletarian; homely, homespun 573adj. *plain;* obscure 867adj. *inglorious;* coarse, brutish, uncouth, unpolished 847adj. *ill-bred;* unfashionable, cockney, suburban, provincial; parvenu, risen from the ranks 847adj. *vulgar;* boorish, churlish, loutish 885adj. *ungracious.*

barbaric, barbarous, barbarian, wild, savage, brutish; uncivilized, uncultured, without arts, primitive, neolithic 699adj. *artless.*

See: 30, 35, 74, 268, 370, 371, 501, 573, 639, 649, 699, 742, 763, 801, 847, 867, 885, 904, 938.

870 Title

N. *title,* title to fame, entitlement, claim 915n. *dueness;* title of honor, courtesy title, honorific, handle, handle to one's name; honor, distinction, order, knighthood 866n. *honors;* dignified style, plural of dignity, royal we, editorial we 875n. *formality;* mode of address, Royal Highness, Serene H., Excellency, Grace, Lordship, Ladyship, noble, most n., my lord, my lady, dame; the Honorable, Right Honorable; Reverend, Very R., Right R., Most R., Monsignor; dom, padre, father, mother, brother; your reverence, your honor, your worship; sire, esquire, sir, dear s., madam, ma'am, master, mister, mistress, miss; monsieur, madame, mademoiselle; don, señor, señora, señorita; signore, signora, signorina; Herr, mynheer; huzur, sahib, babu; memsahib, mem; shri, sri, srijukta, srimati, musammat; effendi, mirza; citoyen, comrade, tovarich.

academic title, doctor, doctor honoris causa; doctor of philosophy, Ph.D.; doctor of literature, D. Litt.; doctor of divinity, D.D.; doctor of laws, LL.D.; doctor of medicine, M.D.; bachelor of arts, B.A.; bachelor of science, B.Sc., B.S.; master of arts, M.A.; master of science, M.Sc.; bachelor of law, B L.; bachelor of music, Mus.B., doctor of music, Mus.D.; Professor, Professor Emeritus; reader, lecturer; doctorate, baccalaureate.

See: 866, 875, 915.

871 Pride

N. *pride,* proudness, proud heart; just pride, modest p., natural p., innocent p., respect, self-r., self-confidence; self-admiration, conceit, self-c., swelled head, swank, side, chest 873n. *vanity;* snobbery 850n. *affectation;* false pride, touchiness, prickliness 819n. *moral sensibility;* dignity, reputation 866n. *prestige;* stateliness, loftiness, high mightiness; condescension, hauteur, haughtiness, unapproachability, disdain 922n. *contempt;* overweening pride, arrogance, hubris 878n. *insolence;* swelling pride, pomp, pomposity, grandiosity, show, display 875n. *ostentation;* self-praise, vainglory 877n *boasting;* class-consciousness, race-prejudice 481n. *prejudice;* object of pride, source of p., boast, joy, pride and j. 890n. *favorite;* cynosure, pick, flower 646n. *paragon.*

proud man, vain person, snob, parvenu; mass of pride, pride incarnate; swelled head, swank, swanker; highflier, high muckamuck, lord of creation 638n. *bigwig;* fine gentleman, grande dame 848n. *fop;* turkey cock, cock of the walk, swaggerer, bragger 877n. *boaster;* purse-proud plutocrat 800n. *rich man;* class-conscious person 868n. *aristocrat.*

Adj. *proud,* elevated, haughty, lofty, sublime 209adj. *high;* plumed, crested 875adj. *showy;* fine, grand 848adj. *fashionable;* grandiose, dignified, stately, statuesque 821adj. *impressive;* majestic, royal, kingly, queenly, lordly 868adj. *noble;* self-respecting, self-confident, proud-hearted, high-souled 855adj. *courageous;* high-stepping, high-spirited, high-mettled 819adj. *lively;* stiff-necked 602adj. *obstinate;* mighty, overmighty 32adj. *great;* imperious, commanding 733adj. *authoritative;* high-handed 735adj. *oppressive;* overweening, overbearing, hubristical, arrogant 878adj. *insolent;* brazen, unblushing, unabashed, flaunting, hardened 522adj. *undisguised.*

prideful, full of pride, blown with p., flushed with p., puffed-up, inflated, swelling, swollen; overproud, high and mighty, stuck-up, high-hatted, snobbish; upstage, uppish; on one's dignity, one's high horse, on stilts; haughty, disdainful, superior, holier than thou, supercilious, patronizing, condescending 922 adj. *despising;* stand-offish, distant, unapproachable, stiff, starchy, unbending, undemocratic 885adj. *ungracious;* taking pride, purse-proud, house-p.; feeling pride, proud of, bursting with pride, inches taller; strutting, swaggering, vainglorious 877adj. *boastful;* cocky, bumptious, conceited 873adj. *vain;* pretentious 850adj. *affected;* swanky, swanking, pompous 875adj. *showy;* proud as Lucifer, proud as a peacock.

Vb. *be proud,* have one's pride, have one's self-respect, be jealous of one's honor, guard one's reputation, hold one's head high, stand erect, refuse to stoop, not bow, stand on one's dignity, mount one's high horse; rear one's head, toss one's h., hold one's nose in the air, hold it beneath one, be too proud to, be too grand to; be stuck-up, swank, show off, swagger, strut 875vb. *be ostentatious;* condescend, patronize; look down on, disdain 922vb. *despise;* display hauteur 878vb. *be insolent;* lord it, queen it, come it over, throw one's weight about, overween 735vb. *oppress.*

feel pride, swell with p., take pride in, glory in, boast of, not blush for 877vb. *boast;* hug oneself, congratulate o. 824vb. *be pleased;* be flattered, flatter oneself, pride o., plume o., preen o., think a lot of oneself, think too much of o. 873vb. *be vain.*

See: 32, 209, 481, 522, 602, 638, 646, 733, 735, 800, 819, 821, 824, 848, 850, 855, 866, 868, 873, 875, 877, 878, 885, 890, 922.

872 Humility. Humiliation

N. *humility,* humbleness, humble spirit 874n. *modesty;* abasement, lowness, lowliness, lowlihood; unpretentiousness, quietness; harmlessness, inoffensiveness 935n. *innocence;* meekness, resignation, submissiveness 721n. *submission;* self-knowledge, self-depreciation, self-abnegation, self-effacement, self-abasement, tapinosis, kenosis 931n. *disinterestedness;* condescension, stooping 884n. *courtesy;* humble person, no boaster, mouse, violet.

humiliation, abasement, humbling, let-down, set-d., climb-d., come-d.; crushing retort; shame, disgrace 867 n. *disrepute;* sense of shame, sense of disgrace, blush, suffusion, confusion; chastening thought, mortification, hurt pride, injured p., offended dignity 891n. *resentment.*

Adj. *humble,* unproud, humble-minded, self-depreciatory, poor in spirit, lowly; meek, submissive, resigned, unprotesting 721adj. *submitting;* self-effacing, self-abnegating 931adj. *disinterested;* self-abasing, stooping, condescending 884adj. *courteous;* mouselike, harmless, inoffensive, unoffending, deprecatory 935adj. *innocent;* unassuming, unpretentious, without airs 874adj. *modest;* mean, low 639adj. *unimportant;* ignoble 869adj. *plebeian.*

humbled, broken-spirited, bowed down; chastened, crushed, dashed, abashed, crestfallen, chap-fallen, disconcerted, out of countenance 834 adj. *dejected;* humiliated, let down, set d., taken d., cut down to size, squashed, deflated, debunked; not proud of, shamed, blushing 867adj. *inglorious;* scorned, rebuked 924adj. *disapproved;* brought low 728adj. *defeated.*

Vb. *be humble,*—lowly etc. adj.; have no pride, humble oneself 867 vb. *demean oneself;* empty oneself 931vb. *be disinterested;* condescend, unbend 884vb. *be courteous;* stoop, bow down, crawl, sing small, eat humble pie 721vb. *knuckle under;* put up with insolence, turn the other cheek, stomach, pocket 909vb. *forgive.*

be humbled,—humiliated etc. adj.; receive a snub, be taken down a peg; be ashamed, be ashamed of oneself, feel shame, blush, redden, color up; feel small, hide one's face, hang one's head, avert one's eyes; stop swanking, come off it.

humiliate, humble, chasten, abash, disconcert; lower, take down a peg, debunk, deflate; make one feel small, make one sing small, teach one his place, make one crawl, rub one's nose in the dirt; snub, crush, squash, sit on 885vb. *be rude;* mortify, hurt one's pride, offend one's dignity, lower in all men's eyes, put to shame 867vb. *shame;* score off, make a fool of, make one look silly 542vb. *befool;* throw in the shade 306vb. *outdo;* get the better of, triumph over, crow o. 727vb. *overmaster;* outstare, outfrown, frown down, daunt 854vb. *frighten.*

See: 306, 542, 639, 721, 727, 728, 834, 854, 867, 869, 874, 884, 885, 891, 909, 924, 931, 935.

873 Vanity

N. *vanity,* emptiness 4n. *insubstantiality;* vain pride, empty p., idle p. 871n. *pride;* immodesty, conceit, conceitedness, self-importance; swank, side, chest, swelled head; cockiness, bumptiousness, assurance, self-a.; good opinion of oneself, self-conceit, self-esteem, amour-propre, self-love, self-admiration, narcissism; self-complacency, self-approbation, self-praise, self-applause, self-flattery, self-congratulation, self-glorification, vainglory 877 n. *boasting;* self-sufficiency, self-centeredness, egotism 932n. *selfishness;* blatancy, exhibitionism, showing off, self-display 875n. *ostentation;* vanity fair 848n. *beau monde.*

airs, fine a., airs and graces, mannerisms, pretensions, absurb p. 850n. *affectation;* swank, gaudery 875n. *ostentation;* coxcombry, priggishness, foppery.

vain person, self-admirer, Narcissus; egotist, only pebble on the beach; self-made man in love with his maker; coxcomb 848n. *fop;* exhibitionist, peacock, show-off; know-all, pantologist; smarty-boots, clever-stick, Sir Oracle; stuffed shirt, vox et praeterea nihil 4n. *insubstantial thing.*

Adj. *vain,* conceited, stuck-up, proud 871n. *prideful;* egotistic, egoistic, self-centered, self-satisfied, self-complacent, full of oneself, self-important 932adj. *selfish;* self-loving, narcissistic; wise in one's own conceit, dogmatic, opinionated, over-subtle, over-clever, too clever by half 498 adj. *intelligent;* swelled-headed, puffed-up, too big for one's boots, overweening, bumptious, cocky, perky; immodest, blatant; showing off, swaggering, vainglorious, self-glorious 877adj. *boastful;* pompous 875adj. *ostentatious;* pretentious, soi-disant, so-called; coxcombical, fantastical 850adj. *affected.*

Vb. *be vain,*—conceited etc. adj., have a swelled head, have one's head turned; have a high opinion of oneself, set a high value on o., think well of o., think too much of o., exaggerate one's own merits, blow one's own trumpet 877vb. *boast;* admire oneself, hug o., flatter o., lay the flattering unction to one's soul; plume oneself, preen o., pride o. 871vb. *feel pride;* swank, stunt, show off, put on airs, show one's paces, display one's talents, talk for effect, talk big, not hide one's light under a bushel, push oneself forward 875vb. *be ostentatious;* lap up flattery, fish for compliments; get above oneself, have pretentions, give oneself airs 850vb. *be affected;* play the fop, dress, dress up, dandify 843vb. *primp.*

make conceited, fill with conceit, puff up, inflate, give a swelled head to, go to one's head, turn one's h. 925vb. *flatter;* tempt with vanity, accept one's pretentions, take one at his own valuation.

Adv. *conceitedly,* vainly, vaingloriously, swankily.

See: 4, 498, 843, 848, 850, 871, 875, 877, 925, 932.

874 Modesty

N. *modesty,* lack of ostentation, unboastfulness, shyness, retiring disposition; diffidence, constraint, self-distrust, timidness, timidity 854n. *nervousness;* mauvaise honte, overmodesty, prudishness 950n. *prudery;* bashfulness, blushfulness, blushing, blush; pudency, shamefastness, verecundity, shockability; chastity, virtue 950n. *purity;* deprecation, self-depreciation, self-effacement 872n. *humility;* unobtrusiveness, unpretentiousness, unassuming nature; demureness, reserve; hidden merit, modest person, shy thing, violet.

Adj. *modest,* unvain, without vanity; self-effacing, unobtrusive, unseen, unheard 872adj. *humble;* deprecating, deprecatory, unboastful; unpushing, unthrustful, unambitious; quiet, unassuming, unpretentious, unpretending; unimposing, unimpressive, moderate, mediocre 639 adj. *unimportant;* shy, retiring, shrinking, timid, diffident, unself-confident, unsure of oneself 854adj. *nervous;* overshy, awkward, constrained, embarrassed, shameful, inarticulate; bashful, blushful, blushing, rosy, shamefaced, sheepish; reserved, demure, coy; shockable, over-modest, prudish 850adj. *affected;* chaste 950adj. *pure.*

Vb. *be modest,* show moderation, ration oneself 942vb. *be temperate;* not blow one's trumpet, have no ambition, shrink from notoriety; efface oneself, yield precedence 872 vb. *be humble;* play second fiddle, keep in the background, take a back seat, know one's place; blush unseen, shun the limelight, hide one's light under a bushel 456vb. *escape notice;* not look for praise, do good by stealth and blush to find it fame; retire, shrink, hang back, be coy 620vb. *avoid;* show bashfulness, feel shame, stand blushing, blush, color, crimson, mantle 431vb. *redden;* preserve one's modesty, keep oneself pure, guard one's virtue 933 vb. *be virtuous.*

Adv. *modestly,* quietly, soberly, demurely; unpretentiously, without ceremony, privately, without beat of drum.

See: 431, 456, 620, 639, 850, 854, 872, 933, 942, 950.

875 Ostentation

N. *ostentation,* demonstration, display, parade, show 522n. *manifestation;* unconcealment, blatancy, flagrancy, shamelessness, brazenness 528n. *publicity;* ostentatiousness, showiness, magnificence, ideas of m., grandiosity; splendor, brilliance; self-consequence, self-importance 873n. *vanity;* pomposity, fuss, swagger, showing off, pretension, pretensions, airs and graces 873n. *airs;* swank, side, chest, strut; bravado, heroics 877n. *boast;* theatricality, histrionics, dramatization, dramatics, sensationalism 546n. *exaggeration;* demonstrativeness, back-slapping, bonhomie 882n. *sociability;* showmanship, effect, window-dressing; solemnity (**see** *formality*); grandeur, dignity, stateliness, impressiveness; declamation, rhetoric 574n. *magniloquence;* flourish, flourish of trumpets, fanfaronade, big drum 528n. *publication;* pageantry, pomp, circumstance, pomp and c., bravery, pride, panache, flying colors, dash, splash, splurge; equipage 844n. *finery;* frippery, gaudiness, glitter, tinsel 844n. *ornamentation;* idle pomp, idle show, false glitter, unsubstantial pageant, mummery, mockery, idle m., hollow m., solemn m. 4n. *insubstantiality;* tomfoolery 497n. *foolery;* travesty 20n. *mimicry;* exterior, gloss, veneer, polish, varnish 223n. *exteriority;* pretense, profession 614n. *pretext;* insincerity 542n. *deception;* lip honor, mouth h. 925n. *flattery.*

formality, state, stateliness, dignity; ceremoniousness, stiffness, starchiness; plural of dignity, royal we, editorial we 870n. *title;* ceremony, ceremonial 988n. *ritual;* drill, smartness, spit and polish, bull; correctness, correctitude, protocol, form, good f., right f. 848n. *etiquette;* punctilio, punctiliousness, preciseness 455n. *attention;* routine, fixed r. 610n. *practice;* solemnity, formal occasion, ceremonial o., state o., function, grand f., official f. 876n. *celebration;* full dress, court d., robes, regalia, finery 228n. *formal dress;* correct dress 228n. *uniform.*

pageant, show 522n. *exhibit;* fete, gala, gala performance, tournament, tattoo; field day, great doings 876n. *celebration;* son et lumière, mis-en-scène, decor, scenery 445n. *spectacle;* set piece, tableau, scene, transformation s., stage effect, stage trick 594n. *stage set;* display, bravura, stunt; pyrotechnics 420n. *fireworks;* carnival, Lord Mayor's Show 837n. *festivity, revel;* procession, promenade, march past, fly-past; changing the guard, trooping the color; turnout, review, grand r., parade, array, muster, wappenschaw 74n. *assembly.*

Adj. *ostentatious,* showy, pompous; aiming at effect, striving for e., done for e.; window-dressing, for show; prestige, for p., for the look of the thing; specious, seeming, hollow 542 adj. *spurious;* consequential, self-important; pretentious, would-be 850 adj. *affected;* showing off, swanking, swanky 873adj. *vain;* inflated, turgid, orotund, windy, magniloquent, declamatory, high-sounding 574adj. *rhetorical;* grand, highfalutin, splendiferous, splendid, brilliant, magnificent, grandiose; superb, royal 813 adj. *liberal;* sumptuous, diamond-studded, luxurious, deluxe, plushy, ritzy, costly, expensive 811adj. *dear;* painted, glorified.

showy, dressy, dressed to kill, foppish 848adj. *fashionable;* colorful, gaudy, gorgeous 425adj. *florid;* tinsel, garish 847adj. *vulgar;* flaming, flaring, flaunting, flagrant, blatant, public; brave, dashing, gallant, gay, jaunty; spectacular, scenic, dramatic, histrionic, theatrical, stagy; sensational, daring; exhibitionist, stunting.

formal, dignified, solemn, stately, majestic, grand, fine; ceremonious, standing on ceremony, punctilious, stickling, correct, precise, stiff, starchy; of state, public, official; ceremonial, ritual 988n. *ritualistic;* for a special occasion 876adj. *celebrative.*

Vb. *be ostentatious,*—showy etc.adj.; keep state, stand on ceremony; cut a dash, make a splash, make a figure; glitter, dazzle 417vb. *shine;* flaunt, sport 228vb. *wear;* dress up 843vb. *primp;* wave, flourish 317vb. *brandish;* blazon, trumpet, beat the big drum 528vb. *proclaim;* make a demonstration, trail one's coat 711 vb. *defy;* demonstrate, exhibit 522 vb. *show;* act the showman, make a display, put up (*or* on) a show; make the most of, put on a front, window-dress; see to the outside, paper the cracks, polish, veneer 226 vb. *coat;* intend for effect, strive for e., sensationalize; talk for effect, shoot a line 877vb. *boast;* take the center of the stage, stand in the limelight 455vb. *attract notice;* put oneself forward, advertise oneself, dramatize o.; play to the gallery, fish for compliments; show off, stunt, show one's paces, prance, promenade; parade, march, march past, fly past; strut, swank, put on side 873vb. *be vain;* become a spectacle, make people stare.

See: 4, 20, 74, 223, 226, 228, 317, 417, 420, 425, 445, 455, 497, 522, 528, 542, 574, 594, 610, 614, 711, 811, 813, 837, 843, 844, 847, 848, 850, 870, 873, 876, 877, 882, 925, 988.

876 Celebration

N. *celebration,* performance, solemnization 676n. *action;* commemoration 505n. *remembrance;* observance, solemn o. 988n. *ritual;* ceremony, function, occasion, do; formal occasion, coronation, enthronement, inauguration, installation, presentation 751n. *commission;* debut, coming out 68n. *beginning;* reception, welcome, hero's w., official reception 923n. *applause;* festive occasion, fete, jubilee, diamond j. 837n. *festivity;* jubilation, cheering, ovation, triumph, salute, salvo, tattoo, roll, roll of drums, fanfare, fanfaronade, flourish of trumpets, flying colors, flag waving, mafficking 835n. *rejoicing;* illuminations 420n. *fireworks;* bonfire 379n. *fire;* triumphal arch 729n. *trophy;* harvest home, thanksgiving, Te Deum 907n. *thanks;* paean, hosanna, hallelujah 886n. *congratulation;* health, toast.

special day, day to remember, great day, red-letter d., banner d., gala d., flag d., field d.; saint's day, feast d., fast d. 988n. *holy-day;* Armistice Day, VJ d., VE d., D day; Fourth of July, Independence Day, Republic D.; birthday, name-day 141n. *anniversary;* wedding anniversary, silver wedding, golden w., diamond w., ruby w.; centenary, bicentenary, tercentenary, quatercentenary, sesquicentenary.

Adj. *celebrative,* celebrating, signalizing, observing, commemorative 505 adj. *remembering;* occasional, anniversary, centennial, bicentennial, millennial 141adj. *seasonal;* festive, jubilant, mafficking 835adj. *rejoicing;* triumphant, triumphal; welcoming, honorific 886adj. *gratulatory.*

Vb. *celebrate,* solemnize, perform 676vb. *do;* hallow, keep holy, keep sacred 979vb. *sanctify;* commemorate 505vb. *remember;* honor, observe, keep, keep up, maintain; signalize, make an occasion, mark the o., mark with a red letter 547vb. *mark;* make much of, welcome, kill the fatted calf, roast an ox whole 882vb. *be hospitable;* do honor to, fete; chair, carry shoulder-high 310 vb. *elevate;* mob, rush 61vb. *rampage;* garland, wreathe, crown 962 vb. *reward;* lionize, give a hero's welcome, fling wide the gates, roll out the red carpet, hang out the flags, beat a tattoo, blow the trumpets, clash the cymbals, fire a salute, fire a salvo, fire a feu de joie 884vb. *pay respects;* cheer, jubilate, triumph, maffick 835n. *rejoice;* make holiday 837vb. *revel;* instate, present, inaugurate, install, induct 751 vb. *commission;* make one's debut, come out 68vb. *begin.*

toast, pledge, clink glasses; drink to, raise one's glass to, fill one's glass to, drain a bumper, drink a health 301vb. *drink.*

Adv. *in honor of,* in memory of, in celebration of, on the occasion of; for the honor of, as an occasion, to make the o.

See: 61, 68, 141, 301, 310, 379, 420, 505, 547, 676, 729, 751, 835, 837, 882, 884, 886, 907, 923, 962, 979, 988.

877 Boasting

N. *boasting,* bragging, braggery, boastfulness, vainglory, gasconism, braggadocio, braggartism; jactitation, jactation, venditation 875n. *ostentation;* self-glorification, self-glory, self-advertisement, swagger, swank, bounce 873n. *vanity;* advertisement 528n. *publicity;* puffery 482n. *overestimation;* grandiloquence, teratology, rodomontade, vaporing, gassing 515n. *empty talk;* heroics, bravado; chauvinism, jingoism, spreadeagleism 481n. *bias;* defensiveness, blustering, bluster 854n. *nervousness;* saber-rattling, intimidation 900n. *threat.*

boast, brag, vaunt, crack; puff 528n. *advertisement;* shout, gasconade, flourish, fanfaronade, bravado, bombast, rant, rodomontade, highfalutin, tall talk 546n. *exaggeration;* gab, hot air, gas, bunkum, much cry and little wool 515n. *empty talk;* bluff, bounce, 542n. *deception;* vain defiance; presumptuous challenge 711 n. *defiance;* big talk, big drum, bluster, idle threat 900n. *threat.*

boaster, vaunter, braggart, braggadocio; brag, big mouth, shouter, prater; blusterer, charlatan, pretender 545n. *imposter;* bouncer, bluffer 545n. *liar;* swank 873n. *vain person;* gasconader, gascon, Thraso, miles gloriosus, Pistol, Hector; advertiser, puffer 528n. *publicizer;* flourisher, fanfaron, trumpeter; ranter, hot-air merchant; jingoist, chauvinist; saber-rattler, intimidator.

Adj. *boastful,* boasting, bragging, vaunting, big-mouthed; braggart, swaggering, vainglorious, self-glorious 873adj. *vain;* bellicose, saber-rattling, jingo, jingoistic, chauvinistic 718adj. *warlike;* bluffing, hollow, pretentious, empty 542adj. *spurious;*

bombastic, magniloquent, grandiloquent 546adj. *exaggerated;* flushed, exultant, triumphant, cock-a-hoop 727adj. *successful.*

Vb. *boast,* brag, vaunt, gab, talk big, shoot one's mouth, shoot a line, bluff, bluster, shout; bid defiance 711vb. *defy;* vapor, prate, gas 515 vb. *mean nothing;* enlarge, magnify 546vb. *exaggerate;* trumpet, jactitate, venditate, show off 528vb. *publish;* puff, crack up, cry one's wares 528vb. *advertise;* sell oneself, advertise o., blow one's trumpet, bang the big drum 875vb. *be ostentatious;* flourish, wave 317vb. *brandish;* play the jingo, make the eagle scream, rattle the saber 900vb. *threaten;* show off, strut, swagger, prance, swank, throw out one's chest 873vb. *be vain;* gloat, pat oneself on the back, hug oneself 824vb. *be pleased;* boast of, plume oneself 871 vb. *be proud;* glory, crow over 727 vb. *triumph;* jubilate, exult 835vb. *rejoice.*

See: 317, 481, 482, 515, 528, 542, 545, 546, 711, 718, 727, 824, 835, 854, 871, 873, 875, 900.

878 Insolence

N. *insolence,* hubris, arrogance, haughtiness, loftiness, overbearing 871n. *pride;* domineering, tyranny 735n. *severity;* high tone 711n. *defiance;* bluster 900n. *threat;* disdain 922n. *contempt;* sneer, sneering 926 n. *detraction;* contumely, contumelious behavior 899n. *scurrility;* assurance, self-a., self-assertion, bumptiousness, cockiness, brashness; presumption 916n. *arrogation;* audacity, hardihood, boldness, effrontery; shamelessness, brazenness, blatancy, flagrancy; face, front, hardened f., face of brass.

sauciness, disrespect, impertinence, impudence; pertness, malapertness; flippancy, nerve, brass, cheek, cool c., calm c.; lip, sauce, snook, snooks; taunt, personality, insult, affront 921 n. *indignity;* rudeness, incivility 885n. *discourtesy;* petulance, defiance, answer, provocation, answering back, backtalk, backchat 460n. *rejoinder;* raillery, banter 851n. *ridicule.*

insolent person, sauce-box, malapert, impertinent, jackanapes; minx, hussy; pup, puppy; upstart, beggar on horseback, jack-in-office, tin god; blusterer, swaggerer, braggart 877n. *boaster;* bantam-cock, cockalorum; bully, Mohawk, Mohock, sons of Belial, hoodlum, roisterer, swashbuckler, fire-eater, desperado 904n. *ruffian;* brazen-face, monument of brass.

Adj. *insolent,* bellicose 718adj. *warlike;* high-toned 711adj. *defiant;* sneering 926adj. *detracting;* insulting, contumelious 921adj. *disrespectful;* injurious, scurrilous 899adj. *maledicent;* lofty, supercilious, disdainful, contemptuous 922adj. *despising;* undemocratic, snobbish, haughty, snorty, snotty, up-stage, high-hat, high and mighty 871n. *proud;* hubristic, arrogant, presumptuous, assuming; brash, bumptious, bouncing 873adj. *vain;* flagrant, blatant; shameless, dead to shame, unblushing, unabashed, brazen, brazen-faced; bold, hardy, audacious 857 adj. *rash;* overweening, domineering, imperious, magisterial, lordly, dictatorial, arbitrary, high-handed, harsh, outrageous, tyrannical 735 adj. *oppressive;* blustering, bullying, fire-eating, ruffianly 877adj. *boastful.*

impertinent, pert, malapert, forward; impudent, saucy, cheeky, brassy, cool, jaunty, cocky, flippant; cavalier, off-hand, familiar, over-f., free-and-easy, breezy, airy 921adj. *disrespectful;* impolite, rude, uncivil, ill-mannered 885adj. *discourteous;* defiant, answering back, provocative, deliberately p., offensive; personal, ridiculing 851adj. *derisive.*

Vb. *be insolent,*—arrogant etc.adj.; forget one's manners 885vb. *be rude;* have a nerve, cheek, sauce, give lip, taunt, provoke 891vb. *enrage;* retort, answer back 460vb. *answer;* shout down 479vb. *confute;* not know one's place, presume, arrogate, assume, take on oneself, make bold, make free with; put on airs, hold one's nose in the air, look one up and down 871vb. *be proud;* look down on, sneer at 922vb. *despise;* banter, rally 851vb. *ridicule;* express contempt, snort; cock a snook, put one's tongue out, send to blazes 711vb. *defy;* outstare, outlook, outface, brazen it out, brave it o.; take a high tone, lord it, queen it, lord it over; hector, bully, browbeat, trample on, ride rough-shod over, treat with a high hand, outrage 735 vb. *oppress;* swank, swagger, swell, look big 873vb. *be vain;* brag, talk big 877vb. *boast;* brook no control, own no law, be a law to oneself 738 vb. *disobey;* defy the lightning, exhibit hubris, tempt providence.

Adv. *insolently,* impertinently, pertly; arrogantly, hubristically, outrageously.

See: 460, 479, 711, 718, 735, 851, 857, 871, 873, 877, 885, 891, 899, 900, 904, 916, 921, 922, 926.

879 Servility

N. *servility,* slavishness, abject spirit, no pride, lack of self-respect 856n. *cowardice;* subservience 721n *submission;* submissiveness, obsequiousness, compliance, pliancy 739n. *obedience;* time-serving 603n. *tergiversation;* abasement 872n. *humility;* prostration, prosternation, genuflection, stooping, stoop, bent back, bow, scrape, duck, bob 311n. *obeisance;* truckling, cringing, crawling, fawning, toadyism, sycophancy, ingratiation 925n. *flattery;* flunkyism 745n. *service;* servile condition, slavery 745n. *servitude.*

toady, toad, toad-eater, pickthank, yes-man 488n. *assenter;* lickspittle, bootlicker, backscratcher, groveler, spaniel, fawner, courtier, fortune-hunter, tuft-h., lion-h. 925n. *flatterer;* sycophant, parasite, leech, sponger, sponge, smell-feast, beggar; jackal, hanger-on, led-captain, cavaliere servente, gigolo 742n. *dependent;* flunky 742n. *retainer;* born slave, slave; tool, cat's-paw 628n. *instrument.*

Adj. *servile,* not free, dependent 745 adj. *subject;* slavish 856adj. *cowardly;* mean-spirited, mean, abject, base, tame 745adj. *subjected;* subservient, submissive 721adj. *submitting;* pliant, compliant, supple 739adj. *obedient;* time-serving 603adj. *tergiversating;* bowed, stooping, prostrate, groveling, truckling, bowing, scraping, cringing, crawling, sneaking, fawning; begging, whining; toadying, sycophantic, parasitic; obsequious, soapy, oily, slimy, over-civil, over-attentive, ingratiating 925adj. *flattering.*

Vb. *be servile,* forfeit one's self-respect, stoop to anything 867vb. *demean oneself;* squirm, roll, sneak, cringe, crouch, creep, crawl, grovel, truckle, kiss the hands of, kiss the hem of one's garment, lick the boots of 721vb. *knuckle under;* bow, scrape, bend, bob, duck, kowtow, make obeisance, kneel 311vb. *stoop;* make up to, toady, spaniel, fawn, ingratiate oneself, pay court to, curry favor, worm oneself into f. 925vb. *flatter;* squire, attend, dance attendance on, fetch and carry for, jackal for 742vb. *serve;* comply 739 vb. *obey;* be the tool of, do one's dirty work, pander to, stooge for 628vb. *be instrumental;* whine, beg for favors, beg for crumbs 761vb. *beg;* play the parasite, batten on, sponge, sponge on, hang on; jump on the bandwagon, run with the hare and hunt with the hounds 83vb. *conform;* serve the times 603vb. *tergiversate.*

Adv. *servilely,* slavishly, with servility, with a bow and a scrape, cap in hand, touching one's forelock.

See: 83, 311, 488, 603, 628, 721, 739, 742, 745, 761, 856, 867, 872, 925.

880 Friendship

N. *friendship,* bonds of f., amity 710 n. *concord;* compatibility, mateyness, chuminess; friendly relations, relations of friendship, intercourse, friendly i., social i., hobnobbing 882 n. *sociality;* alignment, fellowship, comradeship, sodality, freemasonry, brotherhood, sisterhood 706n. *association;* solidarity, support, mutual s. 706n. *cooperation;* acquaintanceship, acquaintance, mutual a., familiarity, intimacy 490n. *knowledge;* fast friendship, close f., warm f., cordial f., passionate f., honeymoon 887n. *love;* making friends, getting acquainted, introduction, recommendation, commendation; overture, rapprochement 289n. *approach;* renewal of friendship, reconciliation 719n. *pacification.*

friendliness, amicability, kindliness, kindness 884n. *courtesy;* heartiness, cordiality, warmth 897n. *benevolence;* fraternization, camaraderie, mateyness; hospitality 882n. *sociability;* greeting, welcome, open arms, handclasp, handshake, hug, rubbing noses 884 n. *courteous act;* regard, mutual r. 920n. *respect;* goodwill, mutual g.; fellow-feeling, sympathy, response 775n. *participation;* understanding, friendly u., good u., entente, entente cordiale, honeymoon 710n. *concord;* partiality 481n. *prejudice;* favoritism, partisanship 914n. *injustice;* support, loyal s. 703n. *aid.*

friend, girl-f., boy-f. 887n. *loved one;* one's friend and acquaintance, acquaintance, intimate a.; lifelong friend, common f., friend's f.; gossip, crony, old c. (**see** *chum*); neighbor, good n., fellow-townsman, fellow-countryman; cater-cousin, clansman 11n. *kinsman;* well-wisher, favorer, partisan, backer 707n. *patron;* proxenus 660n. *protector;* fellow, brother, confrere, partner, associate 707n. *colleague;* ally, brother-in-arms 707 n. *auxiliary;* collaborator, helper, friend in need 703n. *aider;* invitee, guest, welcome g., frequent visitor, persona grata; guest-friend, protegé; host, kind h. 882n. *social person;* former friend, fair-weather f. 603n. *tergiversator.*

close friend, best f., next f., near f.; best man, groomsman 894n. *bridesman;* dear friend, good f., warm f., close f., fast f., firm f., loyal f.; intimate, bosom friend, friend of one's bosom, confidant, fidus Achates; alter ego, other self, shadow; comrade, companion, boon c., pot c.; good friends all, happy family; mutual friends, inseparables, band of brothers, Three Musketeers, David and Jonathan, Pylades and Orestes, Damon and Pythias, Nisus and Euryalus, Castor and Pollux, Heavenly Twins, par nobile fratrum; two minds with but a single thought, Arcades ambo, birds of a feather.

chum, gossip, crony; pal, mate, amigo, bully, bully-boy, buddy, bunkie, butty, side-kick; fellow, comrade, shipmate, messmate, roommate, stable-companion 707n. *colleague;* playmate, classmate, schoolmate, schoolfellow; pen-friend, penpal; hearties, my h.

xenophile, anglophile, Francophile, Russophile, sinophile, friend of all the world 901n. *philanthropist.*

Adj. *friendly,* non-hostile, amicable, well-affected, devoted 887adj. *loving;* loyal, faithful, staunch, fast, firm, tested, tried 929adj. *trustworthy;* fraternal, brotherly, sisterly, cousinly; natural, unstrained, easy, harmonious 710adj. *concordant;* compatible, sympathetic, understanding; well-wishing, well-meaning, well-intentioned, philanthropic 897adj. *benevolent;* hearty, cordial, warm, welcoming, hospitable 882adj. *sociable;* effusive, demonstrative, back-slapping, hail-fellow-well-met; comradely, chummy, pally, matey; friendly with, well w., good friends w., at home w.; acquainted 490adj. *knowing;* free and easy, on familiar terms, on visiting t., on intimate t., on the best of t.; intimate, inseparable, thick, thick as thieves, hand in glove.

Vb. *be friendly,* be friends with, pull on with, get on well w., enjoy friendship w., live on terms of amity w.; have neighborly relations, hold communication with, have dealings w.; fraternize, hobnob, keep company with, keep up w., keep in w., go about together, be inseparable 882vb. *be sociable;* have friends, have a wide circle of friends, have many friendships, have a large acquaintance; shake hands, clasp h., strike h., throw oneself into the arms of, embrace 884vb. *greet;* welcome, entertain 882vb. *be hospitable;* sympathize 516vb. *understand;* like, warm to, cotton on to 887vb. *love;* mean well, have the best intentions, have the friendliest feelings 897vb. *be benevolent.*

befriend, acknowledge, know, accept one's friendship; take up, favor, protect 703vb. *patronize;* overcome hostility, gain one's friendship; strike an acquaintance, scrape an a., knit friendship; break the ice, make overtures 289vb. *approach;* seek one's friendship, pay one's addresses to 889n. *court;* take to, warm to, cotton on to, fraternize with, frat, hobnob, get pally with, get chummy w., chum up w.; make acquainted, make known to each other, introduce, commend, recommend; renew friendship, become reconciled, shake hands 719vb. *make peace.*

Adv. *amicably,* friendly-like; as friends, arm in arm; heartily, cordially.

See: 11, 289, 481, 490, 516, 603, 660, 703, 706, 707, 710, 719, 775, 882, 884, 887, 889, 894, 897, 901, 914, 920, 929.

881 Enmity

N. *enmity,* inimicality, hostility, antagonism 704n. *opposition;* no love lost, unfriendliness, incompatibility, antipathy 861n. *dislike;* loathing 888 n. *hatred;* animosity, animus, spite, grudge, ill-feeling, ill-will, intolerance, persecution 898n. *malevolence;* jealousy 912n. *envy;* coolness, coldness 380n. *ice;* estrangement, alienation, strain, tension, no honeymoon 709n. *dissension;* bitterness, bitter feelings, hard f., rancor, soreness 891 n. *resentment;* unfaithfulness, disloyalty 738n. *disobedience;* breach, open b., breach of friendship 709n. *quarrel;* hostile act 709n. *casus belli;* conflict, hostilities, state of war 718n. *belligerency;* vendetta, feud.

enemy, no friend, bad f., unfriend; ex-friend 603n. *tergiversator;* back friend, traitor, viper in one's bosom

663n. *troublemaker;* unquiet neighbor, ill-wisher; antagonist, opposite side, other s. 705n. *opponent;* competitor, rival 716n. *contender;* open enemy, foe, foeman, hostile, armed enemy 722n. *combatant;* national enemy, Amalekite; general enemy, public e., outlaw, pirate 789n. *robber;* particular enemy, declared e., sworn e., bitter e., confirmed e., irreconcilable e., arch-enemy; misanthropist, misogynist, misogamist 902n. *misanthrope;* xenophobe, anglophobe, Francophobe, negrophobe, anti-Semite 481n. *narrow mind;* persona nongrata, pet aversion, bête noire, Dr. Fell 888n. *hateful object;* aggressor 712n. *attacker;* secret enemy, Trojan horse.

Adj. *inimical,* unfriendly, not well-inclined, disaffected; disloyal, unfaithful 738adj. *disobedient;* distant 883adj. *unsociable;* cool, chilly, frigid, icy 380adj. *cold;* antipathetic, incompatible, unsympathetic 861n. *disliking;* loathing 888adj. *hating;* hostile, conflicting, actively opposed 704adj. *opposing;* antagonized, estranged, alienated, unreconciled, irreconcilable; bitter, embittered, rancorous 891adj. *resentful;* jealous, grudging 912adj. *envious;* spiteful 898adj. *malevolent;* bad friends with, on bad terms, not on speaking t.; at feud, at enmity, at variance, at daggers drawn 709adj. *quarreling;* aggressive, militant, at war with, belligerent 718adj. *warring;* intolerant, persecuting 735adj. *oppressive;* dangerous, venomous, deadly, fell 659adj. *baneful.*

Vb. *be inimical,*—unfriendly etc.adj.; show hostility, harden one's heart, bear ill-will, bear malice 898vb. *be malevolent;* grudge 912vb. *envy;* hound, persecute 735vb. *oppress;* chase, hunt down 619vb. *hunt;* battle 916vb. *fight;* war, make w. 718vb. *wage war;* take offense, take umbrage 891vb. *resent;* fall out, come to blows 709vb. *quarrel;* be incompatible, conflict, collide, clash 14vb. *be contrary;* withstand 704vb. *oppose.*

make enemies, be unpopular, have no friends 883vb. *be unsocial;* get across, cause offense, antagonize, irritate 891vb. *enrage;* estrange, alienate, make bad blood, set at odds 709vb. *make quarrels;* exacerbate 832vb. *aggravate.*

See: 14, 380, 481, 603, 619, 659, 663, 704, 705, 709, 716, 718, 722, 735, 738, 789, 832, 861, 883, 888, 891, 898, 902, 912, 916.

882 Sociality

N. *sociality,* membership, membership of society, intercommunity, consociation 706n. *association;* making one of, being one of; clubbism, esprit de corps; fellowship, consortship, comradeship, companionship, society; comraderie, fraternization, fratting, hobnobbing; intercourse, social i., familiarity, intimacy 880n. *friendship;* social circle, home c., family c., one's friends and acquaintance 880n. *friend;* social ambition, social climbing; society, claims of society, social demands, the world.

sociability, social activity, group a.; social adjustment, compatibility 83 n. *conformity;* sociableness, gregariousness, sociable disposition, sociable inclination, fondness for company 880n. *friendliness;* social success, popularity; social tact, common touch; social graces, savoir vivre, good manners, easy m. 884n. *courtesy;* urbanity 846n. *good taste;* ability to mix, clubbability; affability, conversability 584n. *interlocution;* acceptability, welcome, kind w., hearty w., warm w., reception, fair r., smiling r.; greeting, glad hand, handshake, handclasp, embrace 884n. *courteous act;* hospitality, home from home, open house, Liberty Hall, pot-luck 813n. *liberality;* good company, good fellowship, geniality, cordiality, heartiness, back-slapping, bonhomie; convivialty, joviality, jollity, merry-making 824n. *enjoyment;* gaiety 837n. *revel;* cheer, good c. 301n. *food;* eating and drinking, social board, festive b., groaning b., loving cup 310n. *feasting.*

social gathering, forgathering, meeting 74n. *assembly;* reunion, social r., get-together, conversazione, social, squash, reception, salon, drawing-room; at home, soiree, levee; entertainment 837n. *amusement;* sing-song, smoking concert; symposium, party, hen-p., stag-p., mixed p., partie carrée, tête-a-tête; house-warming, house party, week-end p., birthday p., coming-out p., social meal, feast, banquet 301n. *feasting;* communion, love-feast, agape 988n. *ritual act;* elevenses, teaparty, dish of tea, five-o'clock, drinks, cocktail party, dinner p., supper p., bump supper, barbecue, bottle party,

Dutch p. 837n. *festivity;* dance, ball, hop, thé dansant 837n. *dancing.*

social round, social activities, social whirl, season, social s., social entertainment; calling list, round of visits; leaving one's card, seeing one's friends, visiting, calling, dropping in; week-ending, stay, visit, formal v., call, courtesy c.; visiting terms, frequentation, haunting 880n. *friendship;* social demand, engagement, dating, dating up, trysting, rendezvous, assignation, date, blind d.; meeting place, trysting place, club 76n. *focus.*

social person, active member, keen m.; caller, visitor, dropper-in, frequenter, habitué; convivial person, bon vivant, good fellow, charming f.; good mixer, good company, life and soul of the party; social success, catch, lion 890n. *favorite;* jolly fellow, boon companion, hobnobber, clubman, club woman; Rotarian, good neighbor 880n. *friend;* hostess, host, good h.; guest, welcome g., one of the family; diner-out, parasite, gate-crasher; socialite, ornament of society, social climber 848n. *beau monde.*

Adj. *sociable,* gregarious, social, sociably disposed, fond of company, party-minded, good at a party; companionable, fraternizable, affable, conversable, chatty, gossipy, fond of talk, ready for a chat; clubbable, clubby; cozy, folksy; neighborly, matey, pally 880adj. *friendly;* hospitable, welcoming, smiling, cordial, warm, hearty, black-slapping, hail-fellow-well-met; convivial, festive, Christmassy, jolly, jovial 833adj. *gay;* lively, witty 837 adj. *amusing;* urbane 884adj. *courteous;* easy, free-and-easy, easy-mannered; unbuttoned, postprandial, after-dinner 683adj. *reposeful.*

welcomed, feted, entertained; welcome, ever-w., quite one of the family; popular, liked, sought-after, socially successful, invited, getting around, first on the invitation list.

Vb. *be sociable,*—gregarious etc.adj.; enjoy society, like company, love a party; have friends, like one's f., make friends easily, hobnob, fraternize, mix with, glad-hand, back-slap 880vb. *be friendly;* mix well, be a good mixer, get around, know how to live, mix in society, go out, dine o., go to parties, accept invitations, cadge i., gate-crash; have fun, beat it up 837vb. *amuse oneself;* join in, get together, make it a party, club together, go Dutch, share, go shares 775vb. *participate;* take pot-luck, eat off the same platter 301vb. *eat;* join in a bottle, crack a b. 301vb. *drink;* pledge 876 vb. *toast;* carouse 837vb. *revel;* make oneself welcome, make oneself at home, make one of the family; relax, unbend 683vb. *repose;* make engagements, date, date up; make friends, seek acquaintance, scrape a. 880vb. *befriend;* introduce oneself, exchange cards; extend one's friendships, enlarge one's acquaintance; keep up with, keep in w., write to 588n. *correspond.*

visit, see people, go visiting, go for a visit, pay a v., guest with, sojourn, stay, weekend; keep up with, keep in w., see one's friends; go and see, look one up, call, wait on, drop a card, leave a c.; call at, look in, drop in; exchange visits, be on visiting terms; winter, summer.

be hospitable, keep open house 813 vb. *be liberal;* invite, have, be at home, receive; welcome, make w., bid one w., welcome with open arms, hug, embrace 884vb. *greet;* act the host, do the honors, preside; do proud, kill the fatted calf 876vb. *celebrate;* send invitations, have company, entertain, regale 301vb. *feed;* give a party, throw a p. 837vb. *revel;* accept, cater for, provide entertainment 633vb. *provide.*

Adv. *sociably,* hospitably, in friendly fashion, like friends, en famille; arm in arm, hand in hand.

See: 74, 76, 83, 301, 584, 588, 633, 683, 706, 775, 813, 824, 833, 837, 846, 848, 876, 880, 884, 890, 988.

883 Unsociability. Seclusion

N. *unsociability,* unsociableness, unsocial habits, shyness 620n. *avoidance;* refusal to mix, keeping one's own company, keeping oneself to onself; home-life, domesticity; singleness 895n. *celibacy;* inhospitality 816n. *parsimony;* standoffishness, unapproachability, distance, aloofness, lonely pride 871n. *pride;* unfriendliness, coolness, coldness, moroseness, savageness 893n. *sullenness;* cut, dead c., cut direct 885n. *discourtesy;* silence, inconversability 582n. *taciturnity;* ostracism, boycott 57n. *exclusion;* blacklist, blackball 607n. *rejection.*

seclusion, privacy, private world, world on its own; island universe 321n. *star;* peace and quiet 266n.

quietude; home-life, domesticity; loneliness, solitariness, solitude; retirement, withdrawal; hiddenness, delitescence 523n. *latency;* confinement, purdah 525n. *concealment;* isolation, splendid i. 744n. *independence;* division, estrangement 46n. *separation;* renunciation 621n. *relinquishment;* renunciation of the world 985n. *monasticism;* anchoritism, stylitism; self-exile, expatriation; sequestration, segregation, rustication, excommunication, quarantine, deportation, banishment, exile 57n. *exclusion;* reserve, reservation, ghetto, native quarter; jail 748n. *prison;* sequestered nook, god-forsaken hole, back of beyond; island, desert; hide-out 527n. *hiding-place;* den, study, sanctum, cloister, cell, hermitage, pillar 192n. *retreat;* ivory tower, private quarters, shell; backwater.

solitary, unsocial person, iceberg; lone wolf, rogue elephant; isolationist, island; recluse, stay-at-home; ruralist, troglodyte, cave-dweller; cenobite, anchorite, hermit, eremite, desert-dweller; stylite, pillar-monk, Simeon Stylites, Diogenes and his tub; maroon, castaway 779n. *derelict;* Robinson Crusoe, Alexander Selkirk.

outcaste, outcast, pariah, leper, outsider; expatriate, alien 59n. *foreigner;* exile, expellee, deportee, evacuee, refugee, displaced person, homeless p., stateless p.; proscribed person, outlaw, bandit; Ishmael, vagabond 268n. *wanderer;* waif, stray, orphan 779n. *derelict;* reject, flotsam and jetsam 641n. *rubbish.*

Adj. *unsociable,* unsocial, antisocial, morose, not fit to live with; unassimilated, foreign 59adj. *extraneous;* unclubbable, stay-at-home, home-keeping, quiet, domestic; inhospitable, unwelcoming, forbidding, hostile, savage; distant, aloof, unbending, stiff; stand-offish, offish, haughty 871adj. *prideful;* unwelcoming, frosty, icy, cold 893adj. *sullen;* unforthcoming, in one's shell; unaffable, inconversable, silent 582adj. *taciturn;* cool, impersonal 860adj. *indifferent;* solitary, lonely, lone 88 adj. *alone;* shy, afraid of company, avoiding society 620adj. *avoiding;* wild, ferine; celibate, unmarried 895adj. *unwedded;* anchoritic, eremetic, retiring, the world forgetting, by the world forgot.

friendless, unfriended, lorn, forlorn, desolate, god-forsaken; lonely, lonesome, solitary; on one's own, without company 88adj. *alone;* cold-shouldered, uninvited, without introductions; unpopular, avoided 860 adj. *unwanted;* blacklisted, blackballed, ostracized, boycotted, sent to Coventry 57adj. *excluded;* expelled, disbarred, deported, exiled; under embargo, banned 757adj. *prohibited.*

secluded, private, sequestered, retired, hidden, buried, tucked away 523adj. *latent;* veiled, behind the veil, behind the purdah 421adj. *screened;* quiet, lonely, isolated, enisled; avoided, god-forsaken, unvisited, unexplored, unseen, unfamiliar, off the beaten track 491 adj. *unknown;* uninhabited, deserted, desert, desolate, vacant 190adj. *empty.*

Vb. *be unsocial,* keep one's own company, keep oneself to oneself, shun company, see no one, talk to nobody; go it alone, play a lone hand; keep out, stay o., stew in one's own juice; stay in one's shell, shut oneself up, remain private, maintain one's privacy, stand aloof 620vb. *avoid;* stay at home, cultivate one's garden, bury oneself, vegetate 266vb. *be quiescent;* retire, go into retirement, give up one's friends, leave the world, take the veil; live secluded, live in purdah.

make unwelcome, frown on 924vb. *disapprove;* repel, keep at arm's length, make one keep his distance, look cool; not acknowledge, ignore, cut, cut dead 885vb. *be rude;* cold-shoulder, turn one's back on, shut the door on; turn out, turf o., cast o., expel 300vb. *eject;* ostracize, boycott, send to Coventry, blacklist, blackball 57vb. *exclude;* have no time for, refuse to meet, refuse to mix with, refuse to associate w., have nothing to do with, treat as a leper, treat as an outsider 620vb. *avoid;* excommunicate, banish, outlaw, ban 963vb. *punish.*

seclude, sequester, island, isolate, quarantine; keep in private, keep in purdah; confine, shut up 747vb. *imprison.*

See: 46, 57, 59, 88, 190, 192, 266, 268, 300, 321, 421, 491, 523, 525, 527, 582, 607, 620, 621, 641, 744, 747, 748, 757, 779, 816, 860, 871, 885, 893, 895, 924, 963, 985.

884 Courtesy

N. *courtesy,* chivalry, knightliness, gallantry; deference 920n. *respect;* consideration, condescension 872n. *humility;* graciousness, politeness, civility, manners, good m., noble m., good behavior, best b.; good breeding, gentle b., gentlemanliness, gentility 846n. *good taste;* courtliness, correctness, correctitude 875n. *formality;* comity, amenity, amiability, sweetness, niceness, obligingness, kindness, kindliness 897n. *benevolence;* gentleness, mansuetude, mildness 736n. *lenity;* easy temper, good humor, complacency 734n. *laxity;* agreeableness, affability, suavity, blandness, common touch, social tact 882n. *sociability;* soft tongue, smooth address 925n. *flattery.*

courteous act, act of courtesy, polite act, graceful gesture, courtesy, civility, favor, charity, kindness, complaisance 897n. *kind act;* compliment 886n. *congratulation;* kind words, fair w., sweet w. 889n. *endearment;* introduction, presentation 880n. *friendliness;* welcome, polite w., reception, invitation; acknowledgment, recognition, mark of r., salutation, salute, greeting, affectionate g., welcoming gesture, smile, kiss, hug, squeeze, handclasp, handshake 920n. *respects;* capping, salaam, namaskar, kowtow, bow, nod 311n. *obeisance;* terms of courtesy, respects, regards, kind r., best r., duty, devoir, remembrances, love, best l.; love and kisses, farewell 296n. *valediction.*

Adj. *courteous,* chivalrous, knightly, generous 868adj. *noble;* courtly, gallant, old-world, correct 875adj. *formal;* polite, civil, urbane, gentlemanlike, dignified, well-mannered, fine-m. 848adj. *well-bred;* gracious, condescending 872adj. *humble;* deferential, mannerly 920adj. *respectful;* on one's best behavior, anxious to please 455adj. *attentive;* obliging, complaisant, kind 897adj. *benevolent;* conciliatory, sweet 719adj. *pacificatory;* agreeable, suave, bland, smooth, ingratiating, well-spoken, fair-s., honey-tongued 925adj. *flattering;* obsequious 879adj. *servile.*

amiable, nice, sweet, winning 887adj. *lovable;* affable, conversable, friendly 882adj. *sociable;* considerate, kind 897adj. *benevolent;* inoffensive, harmless 935adj. *innocent;* gentle, easy, mild 736adj. *lenient;* good-tempered, sweet-t., unruffled 823adj. *inexcitable;* well-behaved, good 739 adj. *obedient;* pacific, peaceable 717 adj. *peaceful.*

Vb. *be courteous,* be on one's best behavior, mind one's manners, display good m.; show courtesy, treat with politeness, treat with deference 920vb. *respect;* give one his title, sir, bemadam; oblige, put oneself out 703vb. *aid;* condescend 872vb. *be humble;* notice, have time for 455vb. *be attentive;* conciliate, speak fair 719vb. *pacify;* preserve one's manners, be all things to all men; take no offense, take in good part 823vb. *be patient;* become courteous, mend one's manners, express regrets 941vb. *atone.*

pay respects, give one's regards, send one's r., pay one's devoirs, offer one's duty; send one's compliments, do one the honor; pay compliments 925vb. *flatter;* drink to, pledge 876 vb. *toast;* homage, pay h., show one's respect, kneel, kiss hands 920 vb. *show respect;* honor, crown, wreathe, garland, chair, give a hero's welcome 876n. *celebrate.*

greet, send greetings (**see** *pay respects*); flag, speak 547vb. *signal;* accost, sidle up 289vb. *approach;* acknowledge, recognize, hold out one's hand 455vb. *notice;* shout one's greeting, hail 408vb. *vociferate;* wave, smile, kiss one's fingers, blow a kiss; say hello, bid good morning 583vb. *speak to;* salute, make salutation, raise one's hat, uncap, uncover; cap, touch one's hat, tip *or* tilt one's h., pull one's forelock; bend, bow, bob, duck, curtsy, salaam, make obeisance, kiss hands, prostrate oneself, kowtow 311vb. *stoop;* shake hands, clasp h., shake the hand, press *or* squeeze *or* wring *or* pump the hand; advance to meet 920vb. *show respect;* escort 89vb. *accompany;* make a salute, fire a s., present arms, parade, turn out; welcome, welcome in, welcome home 882vb. *be sociable;* welcome with open arms 824vb. *be pleased;* open one's arms, embrace, hug, kiss 889 vb. *caress;* usher, usher in, present, introduce 299vb. *admit.*

Adv. *courteously,* politely, with respect, with all due deference; condescendingly, graciously.

See: 89, 289, 296, 299, 311, 408, 455, 547, 583, 703, 717, 719, 734, 736, 739, 823, 824, 848, 868, 872, 875, 876, 879, 880, 882, 886, 887, 889, 897, 920, 925, 935, 941.

885 Discourtesy

N. *discourtesy,* impoliteness, bad manners, ill m., beastly m., sheer bad m., shocking bad m.; no manners, mannerlessness, failure of courtesy, want of chivalry, lack of politeness, lack of manners, scant courtesy, incivility, inurbanity; uncouthness, boorishness 847n. *ill-breeding;* unpleasantness, nastiness, beastliness; misbehavior, misconduct, unbecoming conduct; tactlessness, inconsiderateness, want of consideration.

rudeness, ungraciousness, gruffness, bluntness, bluffness; sharpness, tartness, acerbity, acrimony, asperity; ungentleness, roughness, harshness 735n. *severity;* offhandedness 456n. *inattention;* brusquerie, shortness, short answer, plain a. 569n. *conciseness;* sarcasm 851n. *ridicule;* excessive frankness, disregard of circumlocution, unparliamentary language, bad l., bad words, rude w., virulence 899n. *scurrility;* rebuff, insult 921n. *indignity;* personality, impertinence, procacity, pertness, sauce, lip, cheek, truculence 878n. *insolence;* impatience, interruption, shouting 822n. *excitability;* black look, sour l., scowl, frown 893n. *sullenness;* a discourtesy, act of d., piece of bad manners.

rude person, no true knight, no gentleman; savage, barbarian, brute, lout, boor; mannerless imp, unlicked cub 878n. *insolent person;* curmudgeon, crabstick, bear; crosspatch, groucher, grouser, sulker 829 n. *malcontent.*

Adj. *discourteous,* unknightly, ungallant, unchivalrous; uncourtly, unceremonious, ungentlemanly, inurbane, impolite, uncivil, rude; mannerless, unmannerly, ill-mannered, bad-m., boorish, loutish, uncouth, brutish, beastly, savage, barbarian 847adj. *ill-bred;* insolent, impudent; cheeky, saucy, pert, forward 878adj. *impertinent;* unpleasant, disagreeable; cool, not anxious to please, unaccommodating, uncomplaisant 860adj. *indifferent;* off-handed, cavalier, airy, breezy, tactless, inconsiderate 456adj. *inattentive.*

ungracious, unsmiling, grim 834adj. *serious;* gruff, grunting, growling, bearish 893adj. *sullen;* peevish, testy 892adj. *irascible;* difficult, surly, churlish, unfriendly, unneighborly 883adj. *unsociable;* grousing, grumbling, swearing 829adj. *discontented;* ungentle, rough, rugged, harsh, brutal 735adj. *severe;* bluff, free, frank, over-f., blunt, over-b., scant of courtesy; brusque, short 569adj. *concise;* tart, sharp, biting, acrimonious 388adj. *pungent;* sarcastic, uncomplimentary, unflattering 926adj. *detracting;* foul-mouthed, foul-spoken, abusive, vituperative, cursing 899adj. *maledicent;* contumelious, offensive, injurious, insulting, truculent 921adj. *disrespectful.*

Vb. *be rude,*—mannerless etc. adj.; want manners, have no m., flout etiquette; know no better 699vb. *be artless;* scant one's courtesy, display bad manners, show discourtesy 878vb. *be insolent;* have no time for 456vb. *be inattentive;* treat rudely, be beastly to, snub, turn one's back on, cold-shoulder, cut, ignore, cut dead 883vb. *make unwelcome;* show one the door 300vb. *eject;* cause offense, ruffle one's feelings 891vb. *huff;* treat with contumely, insult 921vb. *not respect;* take liberties, make free with, make bold; stare, ogle 438vb. *gaze;* make one blush 867vb. *shame;* lose one's temper, shout, interrupt 891vb. *get angry;* curse, swear, damn 899vb. *cuss;* snarl, growl, frown, scowl, lower, pout, sulk, refuse to say "thank you" 893vb. *be sullen.*

Adv. *impolitely,* discourteously, like a boor, like an ill-mannered fellow.

See: 300, 388, 438, 456, 569, 699, 735, 822, 829, 834, 847, 851, 860, 867, 878, 883, 891, 892, 893, 899, 921, 926.

886 Congratulation

N. *congratulation,* felicitation, gratulation, congratulations, felicitations, compliments, best c., compliments of the season; good wishes, best w., happy returns; salute, toast; welcome, hero's w., official reception 876n. *celebration;* thanks 907n. *gratitude.*

Adj. *gratulatory,* congratulatory, complimentary; honorific, triumphal, welcoming 876adj. *celebrative.*

Vb. *gratulate,* give Heaven thanks for 907vb. *thank;* congratulate, felicitate, compliment; offer one's congratulations, wish one joy, give one joy, wish many happy returns, wish a merry Christmas; send one's congratulations, send one's compliments 884vb. *pay respects;* sanction a triumph, vote an ovation, accord an o., give one a hero's welcome, give three cheers, clap 923vb. *applaud;* fete, mob, rush, lionize 876vb. *cele-*

brate; congratulate oneself, hug o., thank one's stars 824vb. *be pleased.*
See: 824, 876, 884, 907, 923.

887 Love

N. *love,* affection, friendship, charity, Eros; agapism; true love, real thing; natural affection, parental a., maternal a., mother-love, protective l., protectiveness 931n. *disinterestedness;* possessive love, possessiveness 911n. *jealousy;* conjugal love, uxoriousness; sentiment 818n. *feeling;* kindness, tenderness 897n. *benevolence;* mutual love, mutual affection, mutual attraction, compatibility, sympathy, fellow-feeling, understanding; fondness, liking, predilection, inclination 179n. *tendency;* dilection 605n. *choice;* fancy 604n. *caprice;* attachment, sentimental a., firm a.; devotion, loyal d., patriotism 739n. *loyalty;* sentimentality, susceptibility, amorousness 819n. *moral sensibility;* power of love, fascination, enchantment, bewitchment 983n. *sorcery;* lovesickness, Cupid's sting, yearning, longing 859n. *desire;* amativeness, amorism, eroticism, prurience, lust 859n. *libido;* regard 920n. *respect;* admiration, hero-worship 864n. *wonder;* dawn of love, first l., calf l., puppy l., young l.; crush, pash, infatuation; madness 503n. *insanity;* worship 982n. *idolatry;* passion, tender p., fire of love, flames of l., enthusiasm, rapture, ecstasy, transport, transports of love 822n. *excitable state;* erotomania, abnormal affection 84n. *abnormality;* love psychology, narcissism, Oedipus complex, Electra c.; love-hate, odi et amo.

lovableness, amiability, attractiveness, popularity, gift of pleasing; winsomeness, charm, fascination, appeal, sex a., attractions, charms, beauties; winning ways, pleasing qualities, endearing q.; coquetry, flirtatiousness; sentimental value.

love affair, romantic a., affair of the heart, affaire de coeur; romance, love and the world well lost; flirtation, amour, amourette, entanglement; loves, amours; liaison, intrigue, seduction, adultery 951n. *illicit love;* falling in love, soft impeachment, something between them; course of love, the old old story; betrothal, engagement, espousal, wedding bells 894n. *marriage;* broken engagement, broken romance, broken heart.

love-making, flirting, coquetting, honeying, spooning, poodlefaking, billing and cooing 889n. *endearment;* courtship, courting, walking out, sighing, suing, pressing one's suit, laying siege 889n. *wooing;* pursuit of love, hoping for conquests, flirting, coquetry, philandering; gallantry, dalliance, dallying, toying, chambering, chambering and wantonness, libertinage 951n. *unchastity;* bestowal of love, favors.

love-nest, abode of love, bower, Bower of Bliss; honeymoon cottage, bridal suite, nuptial chamber, bridal bed; women's quarters, gyneceum, zenana, harem, seraglio.

lover, love, true l., sweetheart; young man, boy, boy-friend, Romeo; swain, beau, gallant, spark, squire, escort, date; steady, fiancé; wooer, courter, suitor, follower, captive, admirer, hero-worshiper, adorer, votary, worshiper; aficionado, fan, devoted following, fan-mail; sugar-daddy, dotard; cicisbeo, cavaliere servente, squire of dames, ladies' man, lady-killer, gay seducer, lothario, Don Juan; paramour, amorist 952n. *libertine;* flirt, coquette, philanderer, gold-digger, vampire, vamp.

loved one, beloved object, beloved, love 890n. *darling;* friend, dear head; favored suitor, lucky man, intended, betrothed, affianced, fiancé, fiancée, bride-to-be 894n. *spouse;* conquest, inamorata, lady-love, flame, girl-friend, girl, best g., sweetheart, darling, goddess; bird, babe, dear; idol, hero; heart-throb, dream man, dream girl; Amorette, Dulcinea, Amaryllis, Dowsabel; favorite, mistress, leman, concubine 952n. *kept woman;* dangerous woman, femme fatale.

lovers, pair of lovers, loving couple, engaged c., turtle-doves, love-birds; Daphnis and Chloë, Strephon and Chloë; Benedick and Beatrice, Aucassin and Nicolette, Pierrot and Pierrette, Harlequin and Columbine; star-crossed lovers, tragic l., Pyramus and Thisbe, Romeo and Juliet, Hero and Leander, Leila and Majnun, Tristan and Isolde, Lancelot and Guinevere, Paris and Helen, Troilus and Cressida; historic lovers, Héloïse and Abélard, Dante and Beatrice, Petrarch and Laura, Antony and Cleopatra.

love god, goddess of love, Venus, Aphrodite, Astarte, Freya; Amor, Eros, Kama, Cupid, blind boy; cupidon, amoretto.

love emblem, myrtle, turtle-dove; Cupid's bow, Cupid's arrow, Cupid's dart; pierced heart, bleeding h., broken h. 889n. *love-token.*

Adj. *loving,* agapistic; attached, loyal, patriotic 931adj. *disinterested;* wooing, courting, making love, honeying 889adj. *caressing;* affectionate, cuddlesome, demonstrative; tender, motherly, wifely, conjugal; loverlike, gallant, sentimental, lovesick; mooning, moping, lovelorn, languishing 834adj. *dejected;* fond, uxorious, doting; possessive 911adj. *jealous;* admiring, adoring, devoted, enslaved (**see** *enamored*); flirtatious, coquettish 604adj. *capricious;* amatory, amorous, amative, ardent, passionate 818adj. *fervent;* liking, desirous 859adj. *desiring;* lustful, concupiscent, priapic, libidinous 951adj. *lecherous.*

enamored, in love, fallen in l., falling in l., inclined to, sweet on, keen on, set on, stuck on, gone on, sold on; struck with, taken w., smitten, bitten, caught, hooked; charmed, enchanted, fascinated 983adj. *bewitched;* mad on, infatuated, besotted, dippy, crazy, crazy about, wild a. 503adj. *crazed;* happily in love, blissfully in l. 824adj. *happy;* rapturous, ecstatic 821adj. *excited.*

lovable, desirable, likable, congenial, sympathetic, to one's mind, to one's taste, to one's fancy, after one's heart 859adj. *desired;* lovesome, winsome, loveworthy 884adj. *amiable;* sweet, angelic, divine, adorable; lovely, graceful 841adj. *beautiful;* interesting, intriguing, attractive, seductive, alluring 291adj. *attracting;* prepossessing, appealing, engaging, winning, endearing, captivating, irresistible; charming, enchanting, bewitching 983adj. *sorcerous;* liked, beloved, endeared to, dear, darling, pet, fancy, favorite.

erotic, aphrodisiac, erotogenic; amatory, amatorious, amatorial.

Vb. *love,* like, care, rather care for, quite love, take pleasure in, affect, be partial to, take an interest in; sympathize with, feel w., have a kindness for, be fond of; be susceptible, have a heart, have a warm h.; bear love, hold in affection, hold dear, care for, tender, cherish, cling to, embrace; appreciate, value, prize, treasure, think the world of, regard, admire, revere 920vb. *respect;* adore, worship, idolize, make the god of one's idolatry 982vb. *idolatrize;* live for, live only f.; burn with love, be on fire with passion (**see** *be in love*); make love, poodlefake, honey, bestow one's favors; make much of, spoil, pet, fondle, drool over, slobber o. 889vb. *caress.*

be in love, burn, sweat, faint, die of *or* for love 361vb. *die;* burn with love, glow with ardor, flame with passion, love to distraction, dote 503vb. *be insane;* take a fancy to, cotton on to, take to, warm to, look sweet on, look with passion on 859vb. *desire;* form an attachment, fall for, fall in love, get infatuated, get stuck on; go mad about 503vb. *go mad;* set one's heart on, lose one's heart, bestow one's affections; declare one's love, admit the soft impeachment; offer one's heart to, woo, sue, sigh, press one's suit, make one's addresses 889vb. *court;* set one's cap at, chase 619vb. *pursue;* enjoy one's favors; honeymoon 894vb. *wed.*

excite love, arouse desire 859vb. *cause desire;* warm, inflame 381vb. *heat;* rouse, stir, flutter, enrapture, enthrall 821vb. *excite;* dazzle, bedazzle, charm, enchant, fascinate 983vb. *bewitch;* allure, draw 291vb. *attract;* make oneself attractive 843 vb. *primp;* lure, bait, tantalize, seduce 612vb. *tempt;* lead on, flirt, coquet, philander, break hearts; toy, vamp 889vb. *caress;* smile, leer, make eyes, ogle, wink 889vb. *court;* catch one's eye 455vb. *attract notice;* enamor, take one's fancy, steal one's heart, gain one's affections, engage the a.; make a hit, bowl over, sweep off one's feet, turn one's head, infatuate, craze, madden 503 vb. *make mad;* make a conquest, captivate 745vb. *subjugate;* catch, lead to the altar 894vb. *wed;* endear, endear oneself, ingratiate o., insinuate o., wind oneself into the affections; be loved, be amiable, be lovable, make oneself a favorite, become a f., be the rage; steal every heart, set all hearts on fire, have a place in every heart; curry favor 925vb. *flatter.*

Adv. *affectionately,* kindly, lovingly, tenderly 457vb. *carefully;* fondly, dotingly, madly.

See: 84, 179, 291, 361, 381, 455, 457, 503, 604, 605, 612, 619, 739, 745, 818, 819, 821, 822, 824, 834, 841, 843, 859, 864, 884, 889, 890, 894, 897, 911, 920, 925, 931, 951, 952, 982, 983.

888 Hatred

N. *hatred,* hate, no love lost; love-hate, odi et amo; revulsion of feeling, disillusion; aversion, dyspathy, antipathy, allergy, nausea 861n. *dislike;* intense dislike, repugnance, detestation, loathing, abhorrence, abomination; disfavor, displeasure (**see** *odium*); disaffection, estrangement, alienation 709n. *dissension;* hostility, antagonism 881n. *enmity;* animosity, ill-feeling, bad blood, bitterness, acrimony, rancor 891n. *resentment;* malice, ill-will, evil eye, spite, grudge, ancient g. 898n. *malevolence;* jealousy 912n. *envy;* wrath, vials of w. 891n. *anger;* execration, hymn of hate 899n. *malediction;* scowl, snap, snarl, baring one's fangs 893n. *sullenness;* phobia, xenophobia, anglophobia, anti-Semitism, racialism, racism, Aryanism, color prejudice 481n. *prejudice.*

odium, disfavor, unpopularity 924n. *disapprobation;* discredit, black books 867n. *disrepute;* bad odor, malodor; odiousness, hatefulness, loathsomeness, beastliness, obnoxiousness; despicability, contemptibility 922n. *despisedness.*

hateful object, unwelcome necessity, bitter pill; abomination, filth; one's hate 881n. *enemy;* not one's type, one's aversion, pet a., bête noire, Dr. Fell, nobody's darling; pest, menace, good riddance 659n. *bane;* outsider 938n. *cad;* heretic, blackleg, scab 603n. *tergiversator.*

Adj. *hating,* loathing, envying etc. vb.; loveless; antipathetic, revolted, disgusted 861adj. *disliking;* set against 704adj. *opposing;* averse, abhorrent, antagonistic, hostile, antagonized, snarling 881adj. *inimical;* envious, spiteful, spleenful, malicious, full of malice, malignant, fell 898adj. *malevolent;* bitter, rancorous 891adj. *resentful;* full of hate, implacable; vindictive 910adj. *revengeful;* virulent, execrative 899adj. *maledicent;* out of love, disillusioned 509adj. *disappointed.*

hateful, odious, unlovable, unloved; invidious, antagonizing, obnoxious, pestilential 659adj. *baneful;* beastly, nasty, horrid 645adj. *not nice;* abhorrent, loathsome, abominable; accursed, execrable, execrated 899adj. *cursed;* offensive, repulsive, repellent, nauseous, nauseating, revolting, disgusting 861adj. *disliked;* bitter, sharp 393adj. *sour;* unwelcome 860 adj. *unwanted.*

hated, loathed etc. vb.; uncared for 458adj. *neglected;* out of favor, unpopular 861adj. *disliked;* in one's bad books, discredited 924adj. *disapproved;* loveless, unloved, Dr. Fellish; unvalued, unmissed, unregretted, unlamented, unmourned, undeplored, unwept; unchosen, refused, spurned, condemned, jilted, lovelorn, crossed in love 607adj. *rejected.*

Vb. *hate,* bear hatred, have no love for, loathe, abominate, detest, abhor, hold in horror; turn away from, shrink f. 620vb. *avoid;* revolt from, recoil at 280vb. *recoil;* disrelish 861vb. *dislike;* find loathsome, find obnoxious; not choose, refuse 607vb. *reject;* spurn, contemn 922vb. *despise;* execrate, hold accursed, denounce 899vb. *curse;* bear malice 898vb. *be malevolent;* feel envy 912 vb. *envy;* bear a grudge, owe a g. 910vb. *be revengeful;* show spleen 891vb. *resent;* scowl, growl, snap, snarl, bare one's fangs 893vb. *be sullen;* insult 878vb. *be insolent;* conceive a hatred for, fall out of love, turn to hate.

excite hate, grate, jar 292vb. *repel;* cause loathing, disgust, nauseate, stink in the nostrils 861vb. *cause dislike;* shock, horrify 924vb. *incur blame;* antagonize, destroy goodwill, estrange, alienate, sow dissension, create bad blood, snap friendship, turn all to hate 881vb. *make enemies;* poison, envenom, embitter, exacerbate 832vb. *aggravate;* exasperate, incense 891vb. *enrage.*

See: 280, 292, 393, 458, 481, 509, 603, 607, 620, 645, 659, 704, 709, 832, 860, 861, 867, 878, 881, 891, 893, 898, 899, 910, 912, 922, 924, 938.

889 Endearment

N. *endearment,* blandishment, compliment 925n. *flattery;* loving words, affectionate speeches, pretty s., pretty names, pet name; soft nothings, lovers' vows; affectionate behavior, dalliance, billing and cooing, holding hands, slap and tickle; fondling, cuddling, petting, necking, kissing, osculation; caress, embracement, embrace, clip, cuddle, squeeze, pressure, fond p.; salute, kiss, butterfly k., buss, smacker; nibble, bite; stroke, tickle, slap, tap, pat, pinch, nip 378n. *touch;* familiarity, over-f., advances, pass.

wooing, courting, spooning, flirting; play, love-p., love-making; side-glance, glad eye, come-hither look, ogle, amorous glance, sheep's eyes, fond look, languishing l., sigh; flirtation, philandering, coquetry, gallantry, amorous intentions, honorable i.; courtship, suit, love s., addresses, advances; tale of love, serenade, aubade, love-song, love lyric, amorous ditty, caterwauling; love-letter, billet-doux; love-poem, sonnet, love-plight, engagement, betrothal 894n. *marriage.*

love-token, true lover's knot, favor, glove; ring, engagement r., wedding r., eternity r.; valentine, love-letter, billet-doux; language of flowers, posy; arrow, heart, bleeding h.; tattoo-mark.

Adj. *caressing,* clinging, toying, fondling etc. vb.; demonstrative, affectionate 887adj. *loving;* spoony, cuddlesome, flirtatious, coquettish; wooing, sighing, suing.

Vb. *pet,* pamper, spoil, spoonfeed, mother, smother, kill with kindness; cosset, cocker, coddle; make much of, be all over one; treasure, tender 887vb. *love;* cherish, foster, tender 660vb. *safeguard;* nurse, lap, rock, cradle, baby; sing to, croon over; coax, wheedle 925vb. *flatter.*

caress, love, fondle, dandle, take in one's lap; play with, stroke, smooth, pat, tap, pinch one's cheek, pat one on the head, chuck under the chin; osculate, kiss, buss, brush one's cheek; embrace, enlace, enfold, inarm, lap, fold in one's arms, press to one's bosom, hang on one's neck, fly into the arms of; open one's arms, clip, hug, hold one tight, cling, not let go 778vb. *retain;* clasp, squeeze, press, cuddle; snuggle, nestle, nuzzle; play, romp, wanton, toy, trifle, dally, spark; make dalliance, make love, poodlefake, carry on, spoon, bill and coo, hold hands, slap and tickle, pet, neck; vamp 887vb. *excite love;* (of animals) lick, fawn, rub oneself against; (of a crowd) mob, rush, snatch at, swarm over.

court, make advances, give the glad eye, accept a pass; make eyes, make sheep's e., ogle, leer, eye 438vb. *gaze;* get off, try to get off, become familiar, make a pass, make passes; gallivant, philander, flirt, coquet 887vb. *excite love;* look sweet on 887vb. *be in love;* set one's cap at, run after, chase 619vb. *pursue;* squire, escort 89vb. *accompany;* hang about, wait on 284vb. *follow;* walk out with, have a steady; sue, woo, go a-wooing, go courting, pay court to, pay one's addresses to, pay attentions to, pay suit to, press one's suit; serenade, caterwaul; sigh, sigh at the feet of, pine, languish 887vb. *love;* offer one's heart, offer one's hand, offer one's fortune; ask for the hand of, propose, propose marriage, pop the question, plight one's troth, become engaged, announce one's engagement, publish the banns, make a match 894vb. *wed.*

Adv. *caressingly,* endearingly, wooingly, suingly.

See: 89, 284, 378, 438, 619, 660, 778, 887, 894, 925.

890 Darling. Favorite

N. *darling,* dear, my dear; dear friend; dearest, dear one, only one; love, beloved 887n. *loved one;* heart, dear h.; sweetheart, fancy, dowsabel; sweeting, sweetling, sweetie, sugar, honey, honeybunch; precious, jewel, treasure, tesoro; chéri, chou, mavourneen, babe; angel, angel child, cherub; pippin, poppet, popsy, moppet, mopsy, chuck; pet, petkins, lamb, precious l., chick, chicken, duck, ducks, ducky, dearie, lovey; laddie, sonny.

favorite, darling, mignon; spoiled darling, spoiled child, enfant gâté, fondling, cosset, mother's darling, teacher's pet; nursling, foster-child; jewel, heart's-blood, apple of one's eye, blue-eyed boy; persona grata, man after one's own heart, one of the best, good chap, fine fellow, the tops; sport, good s., real s.; first choice, top seed, only possible choice 644n. *exceller;* someone to be proud of, boast; national figure, Grand Old Man 500n. *sage;* hero, popular h., idol, popular i., matinee i.; star, movie s., film s., top-liner, hit, smash h., knock-out; general favorite, universal f., cynosure, toast; world's sweetheart, Queen of Hearts, pinup girl 841n. *a beauty;* center of attraction, cynosure, honey-pot 291n. *attraction;* catch, lion 895n. *desired object.*

See: 291, 500, 644, 841, 859, 887.

891 Resentment. Anger

N. *resentment,* displeasure, dissatisfaction 829n. *discontent;* huffiness, ill-humor, sulks 893n. *sullenness;* sternness 735n. *severity;* heart-burning, heart-swelling, rankling, rancor, soreness, painful feelings; slow burn, growing impatience; indignation (**see** *anger*); umbrage, offense, taking o., huff, tiff, pique; bile, spleen, gall; acerbity, acrimony, bitterness, bitter resentment, hard feelings; virulence, hate 888n. *hatred;* animosity, grudge, ancient g., bone to pick, crow to pluck 881n. *enmity;* vindictiveness, revengefulness, spite 910n. *revenge;* malice 898n. *malevolence;* impatience, fierceness, hot blood 892n. *irascibility;* cause of offense, red rag to a bull, sore point, dangerous subject; pin-prick, irritation 827n. *annoyance;* provocation, aggravation, insult, affront, last straw 921n. *indignity;* wrong, injury 914n. *injustice.*

anger, wrathfulness, irritation, exasperation, vexation, indignation; dudgeon, high d., wrath, ire, choler, dander, wax; rage, tearing r., berserker r., fury, raging f., passion, towering p. 822n. *excitable state;* crossness, temper, tantrum, paddy, paddywhack, fume, fret, pet, fit of temper, ebullition of t., burst of anger, burst, explosion, storm, stew, ferment, taking, paroxysm, tears of rage 318n. *agitation;* rampage, fire and fury, gnashing the teeth, stamping the foot; shout, roar 400n. *loudness;* fierceness, angry look, glare, frown, scowl; growl, snarl, bark, bite, snap, snappishness, asperity 893 n. *sullenness;* warmth, heat, high words, angry w., rixation 709n. *quarrel;* box on the ear, rap on the knuckles, slap in the face 921n. *indignity;* blows, fisticuffs 716n. *fight.*

Fury, Erinys, Alecto, Megaera, Tisiphone, Furies, Eumenides.

Adj. *resentful,* piqued, stung, galled, huffed; stung, hurt, sore, smarting 829adj. *discontented;* surprised, pained, hurt, offended; warm, indignant; unresigned, reproachful 924 adj. *disapproving;* bitter, embittered, acrimonious, full of hate, rancorous, virulent 888adj. *hating;* full of spleen, spleenful, bileful, bilious, spiteful 898adj. *malevolent;* full of revenge, vindictive 910 adj. *revengeful;* jealous, green with envy 912adj. *envious;* grudging 598adj. *unwilling.*

angry, displeased, not amused, stern, frowning 834adj. *serious;* impatient, cross, waxy, ratty, wild, mad; wroth, wrathy, ireful, irate; peeved, annoyed, irritated, vexed, provoked, stung; worked up, wrought up, het up, hot, hot under the collar; indignant, angered, incensed, infuriated; shirty, in a temper, in a paddy, in a wax, in a huff, in a rage, in a boiling r., in a fury, in a taking, in a passion; warm, fuming, boiling, burning; speechless, stuttering, gnashing, spitting with fury, crying with rage; raging, foaming, savage, violent 176adj. *furious;* apoplectic, rabid, foaming at the mouth, mad, hopping m., dancing, rampaging, rampageous 503adj. *frenzied;* seeing red, berserk; roaring, ramping, rearing; snarling, snapping, glaring, glowering 893adj. *sullen;* red with anger, flushed with rage, red-eyed, bloodshot 431adj. *red;* livid, pale with anger; sulfurous, dangerous, fierce 892adj. *irascible.*

Vb. *resent,* be piqued,—offended etc. adj.; find intolerable, not bear, be unable to stomach 825vb. *suffer;* feel, mind, feel resentment, smart under 829vb. *be discontented;* take amiss, take ill, feel insulted, take offense, take umbrage, take exception 709vb. *quarrel;* jib, take in ill part, take in bad p., get sore, cut up rough; burn, smolder, sizzle, simmer, boil with indignation; express resentment, vent one's spleen, indulge one's spite 898vb. *be malevolent;* take to heart, let it rankle, remember an injury, cherish a grudge, bear malice 910vb. *be revengeful;* go green with envy 912 vb. *envy.*

get angry, get cross, get wild, get mad; get peeved, get sore, get in a pet; kindle, grow warm, grow heated, color, redden, flush with anger; take fire, flare up, start up, rear up, ramp; bridle up, bristle up, raise one's hackles, arch one's back; lose patience, lose one's temper, lose control of one's t., forget oneself; get one's dander up, fall into a passion, fly into a temper, fly off the handle; let fly, burst out, let off steam, boil over, blow up, blow one's top, explode; see red, go berserk, go mad, foam at the mouth.

be angry,—impatient etc. adj.; show impatience, interrupt, chafe, fret, fume, fuss, flounce, dance, ramp, stamp, champ, champ the bit, paw the ground; carry on, create, perform, make a scene, make a row 61vb. *rampage;* turn nasty, cut up rough, raise Cain; rage, rant, roar, bellow, bluster, storm, thunder, fulminate 400vb. *be loud;* look like thunder, look black, look daggers, glare, glower, frown, scowl, growl, snarl 893vb. *be sullen;* spit, snap; gnash one's teeth, grind one's t., weep with rage, boil with r., quiver with r., shake with passion, swell with fury, burst with indignation, stamp with rage, dance with fury, lash one's tail; breathe fire and fury, out-Lear Lear; let fly, express one's feelings, vent one's spleen, open the vials of one's wrath; tiff 709vb. *quarrel;* fight it out 716vb. *fight.*

huff, pique, sting, nettle, rankle; ruffle the dignity, wound, wound the feelings 827vb. *hurt;* antagonize, put one's back up, get across, give umbrage, offend, cause offense, cause lasting o., embitter 888vb. *excite hate;* stick in the gizzard, raise one's gorge 861vb. *cause dislike;* affront, insult, outrage 921vb. *not respect.*

enrage, upset, discompose, ruffle, disturb one's equanimity, ruffle one's temper, irritate, rile, peeve; annoy, vex, pester, bother 827vb. *incommode;* do it to annoy, tease, bait, pin-prick, needle 827vb. *torment;* bite, fret, nag; put out of patience, put in an ill-humor, try one's patience; push too far, make one lose one's temper, put into a temper, work into a passion; anger, incense, infuriate, madden, drive mad; goad, sting, taunt, trail one's coat, invite a quarrel; drive into a fury, lash into f., fan one's f., rouse one's ire, rouse one's choler, kindle one's wrath, excite indignation, stir the blood, stir one's bile, make one's gorge rise, get one's dander up, get one's monkey up; make one's blood boil, make one see red; cause resentment, embitter, ulcerate, envenom, poison; exasperate, add fuel to the flame 832vb. *aggravate;* embroil, set at loggerheads, set by the ears 709 vb. *make quarrels.*

Adv. *angrily,* resentfully, bitterly; warmly, heatedly, sulfurously; in anger, in fury, in the heat of the moment, in the height of passion, with one's monkey up, with one's dander up.

See: 61, 176, 318, 400, 431, 503, 598, 709, 716, 735, 822, 825, 827, 829, 832, 834, 861, 881, 888, 892, 893, 898, 910, 912, 914, 921, 924.

892 Irascibility

N. *irascibility,* quick passions, irritability, impatience 822n. *excitability;* grumpiness, gruffness 883n. *unsociability;* sharpness, tartness, asperity, gall, bile, vinegar 393n. *sourness;* sensitivity 819n. *moral sensibility;* huffiness, touchiness, prickliness, readiness to take offense, pugnacity, bellicosity 709n. *quarrelsomeness;* temperament, testiness, pepperiness, peevishness, petulance; bad liver, uncertain temper, doubtful t., sharp t., short t.; hot temper, fierce t., fiery t.; limited patience, snappishness, a word and a blow; fierceness, dangerousness, hot blood, fieriness, inflammable nature; bad temper, dangerous t., foul t., nasty t., evil t.

shrew, scold, fishwife, callet; spitfire, termagant, virago, vixen, battle-ax, fury, Xanthippe; tartar, hornet; bear 902n. *misanthrope;* crosspatch, mad dog; fiery person, redhead.

Adj. *irascible,* impatient, choleric, irritable, peppery, testy, crusty, peevish, cross-grained; short-tempered, hot-t., sharp-t., uncertain-t.; prickly, touchy, tetchy, huffy, thin-skinned 819adj. *sensitive;* inflammable, like tinder; hot-blooded, fierce, fiery, passionate 822adj. *excitable;* quick, warm, hasty, over-h., over-lively, trigger-happy 857adj. *rash;* dangerous, "sudden and quick in quarrel" 709adj. *quarreling;* scolding, shrewish, vixenish, cured; sharp-tongued 899adj. *maledicent;* petulant, cantankerous, snarling, querulous; exceptious, captious, bitter, vinegary 393adj. *sour;* splenetic, spleenful, bilious, liverish, gouty; scratchy, snappish, waspish; tart, sharp, short; fractious, fretful, moody, moodish, temperamental, changeable; gruff, grumpy, pettish, ratty, like a bear with a sore head 829 adj. *discontented;* ill-humored, currish 893adj. *sullen.*

Vb. *be irascible,* have a temper, have an uncontrollable t.; have a devil in one; have a bad liver; snort, bark, snap, bite 893vb. *be sullen.*

See: 393, 709, 819, 822, 829, 857, 883, 893, 899, 902.

893 Sullenness

N. *sullenness,* sternness, grimness 834adj. *seriousness;* sulkiness, ill-humor, ill condition, pettishness; morosity, churlishness, crabbedness, crustiness, unsociableness 883 n. *unsociability;* vinegar 393n. *sourness;* grumpiness, grouchiness, pout, grimace 829n. *discontent;* gruffness 885n. *discourtesy;* crossness, peevishness, ill-temper, bad t., savage t., shocking t. 892n. *irascibility;* spleen, bile, liver; sulks, fit of the s., the pouts, mulligrubs, bouderie, moodiness, temperament; the blues, blue devils 834n. *melancholy;* black look, hangdog l., torvity; glare, glower, frown, scowl; snort, growl, snarl, snap, bite; "curses not loud but deep."

Adj. *sullen,* forbidding, ugly; black, gloomy, overcast, cloudy, sunless 418adj. *dark;* glowering, scowling; stern, frowning, unsmiling, grim 834adj. *serious;* sulky, sulking, cross, out of temper, out of humor, misanthropic 833adj. *unsociable;* morose, crabbed, crusty, cross-grained, ill-conditioned, difficult; snarling, snapping, snappish, shrewish, vixenish, cantankerous, quarrelsome 709adj. *quarreling;* refractory, jibbing 738 adj. *disobedient;* grouchy, grumbling, grumpy 829adj. *discontented;* acid, tart, vinegary 393adj. *sour;* gruff, rough 885adj. *discourteous;* temperamental, moody, humorsome, up and down 152adj. *changeful;* bilious, jaundiced, blue, down, depressed, melancholy 834adj. *melancholic;* petulant, peevish, currish, cursed, shirty, ill-tempered, bad-t. 892adj. *irascible;* smoldering, sultry.

Vb. *be sullen,* gloom, glower, glare; look black, scowl, frown, knit one's brows; bare one's teeth, show one's fangs, spit; snap, snarl, growl, snort; make a face, grimace, pout, sulk 883vb. *be unsocial;* mope, have the pip, have the blues 834vb. *be dejected;* get out of bed on the wrong side; grout, grouch, grouse, crab, complain, grumble, mutter 829vb. *be discontented.*

Adv. *sullenly,* sulkily, gloomily, ill-humoredly.

See: 152, 393, 418, 709, 738, 829, 834, 883, 885, 892.

894 Marriage

N. *marriage,* matrimony, holy m., sacrament of m., one flesh; wedlock, wedded state, married s., state of matrimony, conjugal bliss; match, union, alliance; conjugality, nuptial bond, marriage tie, marriage bed, bed and board, cohabitation, living as man and wife, life together; wifedom, wifehood, wifeliness; coverture, matronage, matronhood; banns, marriage certificate, marriage lines; marriage god, Hymen, Juno, Pronuba.

type of marriage, matrimonial arrangement, monogamy, monandry, polygamy, Mormonism, polygyny, polyandry; bigamy, gamomania; digamy, deuterogamy, second marriage, remarriage, widow r.; leviration, levirate; arranged match, mariage de convenance, marriage of convenience; love-match, swayamvara, Gandharva marriage; mixed marriage, intermarriage, intercaste m., miscegenation 43n. *mixture;* mismarriage, mésalliance, misalliance, morganatic marriage, left-handed m.; spiritual marriage, syneisaktism; companionate marriage, temporary m., probationary m.; free union, free love, concubinage; compulsory marriage, forcible wedlock, shotgun wedding; abduction, Sabine rape.

wedding, getting married, match, match-making; nuptial vows, marriage v., ring, wedding r., betrothal, spousal, espousal, bridal, nuptials, spousals; leading to the altar, tying the knot; marriage rites, marriage ceremony; wedding service, nuptial mass, nuptial benediction 988n. *Christian rite;* church wedding, white w., civil marriage, registry office m.; Gretna Green marriage, run-away match, elopement; solemn wedding, quiet w.; nuptial torch, torch of Hymen, nuptial song, hymeneal, prothalamion, epithalamium; wedding day, wedding morning; wedding bells, wedding hymn, wedding march, marriage procession, bridelope; marriage feast, wedding breakfast, reception; honeymoon; silver wedding, golden w., wedding anniversary 876n. *special day.*

bridesman, brideman, groomsman, best man, paranymph, bridal party; matron of honor, bridesmaid, page, train-bearer; attendant, usher.

spouse, espouser, espoused; one's promised, one's betrothed 887n. *loved one;* marriage partner, man, wife; spouses, man and wife, Mr. and Mrs., Darby and Joan, Philemon and Baucis; married couple, bridal pair, newlyweds, honeymooners; newlywed, bride, blushing b., young matron, bridegroom, benedict; consort, partner, mate, yokemate, soulmate, affinity; married man, husband, goodman, old man, lord and master; much-married man, henpecked husband; injured husband 952n. *cuckold;* married woman, wedded wife, lady, matron, femme couverte, partner of one's bed and board; wife of one's bosom, helpmate, better half, woman, old w., missus, rib, gray mare; squaw, broad-wife; faithful spouse, monogamist; digamist, second husband, second wife, bigamous w.; wife in all but name.

polygamist, polygynist, much-married man, owner of a harem, Turk, Mormon, Solomon; Bluebeard; bigamist.

matchmaker, matrimonial agent, marriage-broker, go-between, ghatak; marriage adviser 720n. *mediator.*

nubility, marriageable age, fitness for marriage, marriageability; eligibility, suitability, good match, proper m., suitable m.; suitable party, eligible p., welcome suitor 887n. *lover.*

Adj. *married,* partnered, paired, mated, matched; wived, husbanded; handfast, tied, spliced, hitched, in double harness; espoused, wedded, united, made man and wife, made one, bone of one's bone and flesh of one's flesh; monogamous; polygynous, polygamous, polyandrous; much-married, polygamistic, Mormonistic; remarried, digamous, bigamous; just married, newly m., newlywed, honeymooning; mismarried, ill-matched.

marriageable, nubile, concubitant, concubitous; fit for marriage, ripe for m., of age, of marriageable a.; eligible, suitable; handfast, betrothed, promised, engaged, affianced, plighted, bespoke.

matrimonial, marital, connubial, concubinal, concubinary; nuptial, bridal, spousal, hymeneal, epithalamic, epithalamial; conjugal, wifely, matronly, husbandly; digamous, bigamous; polyandrous; morganatic; gamomaniac; syneisaktical.

Vb. *marry,* marry off, find a husband *or* wife for, match, mate; matchmake, make a match, arrange a m.; betroth, affiance, espouse, publish the banns, bid the b.; bestow in marriage, give in marriage, give away; ring the wedding bells, celebrate a marriage, conduct a wedding, read the wedding service, join in marriage, make fast in wedlock, declare man and wife; join, couple, handfast, splice, hitch, tie the knot.

wed, marry, espouse; wive, take to oneself a wife, find a husband; quit the single state, get married, get hitched, get spliced, mate with, marry oneself to, unite oneself, espouse o., give oneself in marriage, bestow one's hand, accept a proposal, become engaged, put up the banns; lead to the altar, take for better or worse, be made one; pair off, mate, couple; honeymoon, cohabit, set up house together, share bed and board, live as man and wife; marry well, make a good match; mismarry, make a bad match, repent at leisure; make a love match 887vb. *be in love;* marry in haste, run away, elope; contract matrimony, make one an honest woman, go through a form of marriage, receive one's marriage lines; marry again, remarry, commit bigamy; intermarry, miscegenate.

Adv. *matrimonially,* in the way of marriage; bigamously, polygamously, morganatically.

See: 43, 720, 876, 887, 952, 988.

895 Celibacy

N. *celibacy,* singleness, single state, single blessedness 744n. *independence;* bachelorhood, bachelorship, bachelorism, bachelordom; misogamy, misogyny 883n. *unsociability;* spinsterhood, spinsterdom; monkhood, the veil 985n. *monasticism;* Encratism, spiritual marriage, syneisakism 894n. *type of marriage;* maidenhood, virginity, pucelage, pudicity 950n. *purity.*

celibate, unmarried man, single m., bachelor, benedict, Coelebs; confirmed bachelor, old b., gay b., not the marrying kind; enemy of marriage, agamist, misogamist, misogynist 902n. *misanthrope;* celibatarian, Encratite, monastic 986n. *monk;* hermit 883n. *solitary;* monastic order, celibate o. 985n. *holy orders;* bachelry, bachelordom.

spinster, unmarried woman, femme sole, bachelor girl; maid unwed, debutante; maid, maiden, virgo intacta; maiden aunt, old maid; vestal, vestal virgin 986n. *nun;* amazon, Diana, Artemis.

Adj. *unwedded,* unwed, unmarried; unpartnered, single, mateless, unmated; spouseless, unwived, wifeless; unhusbanded, husbandless; unwooed, unasked; free, uncaught, heart-whole, fancy-free 744n. *independent;* maidenly, virgin, virginal, vestal 950adj. *pure;* spinster, spinsterlike, spinsterish, old-maidish; bachelor, bachelor-like, bachelorly; celibate, celibatarian, monkish, nunnish 986adj. *monastic.*

Vb. *live single,* stay unmarried, live in single blessedness, keep bachelor hall; refuse marriage, keep heart-whole 744vb. *be free;* have no offers, receive no proposals; live like a hermit 883vb. *be unsocial;* take the veil, get oneself to a nunnery 986 vb. *take orders;* enforce celibacy, celibate.

See: 744, 883, 894, 902, 950, 985, 986.

896 Divorce. Widowhood

N. *divorce,* dissolution of marriage, divorcement, putting away, repudiation; bill of divorcement, divorce decree, decree nisi, decree absolute; separation, legal s., judicial s., separatio a mensa et thoro, separatio a vinculo matrimonii; annulment, decree of nullity; no marriage, nonconsummation; nullity, impediment, diriment i., prohibited degree, consanguinity, affinity; desertion, living apart, separate maintenance, alimony; marriage on the rocks, broken marriage, broken engagement, forbidding the banns; divorce court, divorce case, matrimonial cause; divorced person, divorcé, divorcée, nor wife nor maid; corespondent.

widowhood, widowerhood, viduage, viduity, dowagerism; grass widowhood; widows' weeds 228n. *formal dress.*

widowed spouse, widower, widow, widow woman, relict; dowager, doweress, queen dowager, princess d., dowager duchess; grass widow, grass widower, Merry Widow.

Adj. *divorced,* separated, living apart; dissolved.

widowed, husbandless, wifeless; vidual.

Vb. *divorce,* separate, live separately, live apart, desert 621vb. *relinquish;* disespouse, unmarry, untie the knot; put away, banish from bed and board; sue for divorce, file a divorce suit; wear the horns, be cuckolded; get a divorce, revert to bachelorhood, regain one's freedom; put asunder, dissolve marriage, annul a m., grant a decree of nullity, grant a divorce, pronounce a decree absolute.

be widowed, outlive one's spouse, lose one's wife, mourn one's husband, put on widow's weeds, become a relict.

widow, make a widow, leave one's wife a widow.

See: 228, 621.

897 Benevolence

N. *benevolence,* good will, helpfulness 880n. *friendliness;* ahimsa, harmlessness 935n. *innocence;* benignity, kindly disposition, heart of gold; amiability, bonhomie 822n. *sociability;* milk of human kindness, goodness of nature, warmth of heart, warm-heartedness, kind-heartedness, kindliness, kindness, loving-k., goodness and mercy, charity, Christian c. 887n. *love;* godly love, brotherly l., brotherliness, fraternal feeling 880n. *friendship;* squeamishness, tenderness, consideration 736n. *lenity;* understanding, responsiveness, fellow-feeling, sympathy, overflowing s. 818n. *feeling;* condolence 905n. *pity;* decent feeling, humanity, humaneness, humanitarianism 901n. *philanthropy;* utilitarianism 901n. *sociology;* charitableness, hospitality, beneficence, unselfishness, generosity 813n. *liberality;* gentleness, softness, tolerance, toleration 734n. *laxity;* placability, mercy 909n. *forgiveness;* God's love, grace of God.

kind act, kindness, favor, service; good deed, charitable d.; charity, deed of c., relief, alms, almsgiving 781n. *giving;* prayers, good offices, kind o., good turn, helpful act 703n. *aid;* labor of love 597n. *voluntary work.*

kind person, bon enfant, Christian; good neighbor, good Samaritan, well-wisher 880n. *friend;* sympathizer 707n. *patron;* altruist, idealist, do-gooder 901n. *philanthropist.*

Adj. *benevolent,* well-meant, well-intentioned, with the best intentions, for the best 880adj. *friendly;* out of kindness, to oblige; out of charity, eleemosynary; good of one, so good of; sympathetic, wishing well, well-wishing, favoring, praying for; kindly disposed, benign, benignant, kindly, kind-hearted, overflowing with kindness, full of the milk of human k., warm-hearted, large-h., golden-h.; kind, good, human, decent, Christian; affectionate 887adj. *loving;* fatherly, paternal; motherly, maternal; brotherly, fraternal; sisterly, cousinly; good-humored, good-natured, easy, sweet, gentle 884adj. *amiable;* spleenless, *bileless,* placable, merciful 909adj. *forgiving;* tolerant, indulgent 734adj. *lax;* humane, considerate 736adj. *lenient;* soft-hearted, tender, squeamish; pitiful, sympathizing, condolent 905adj. *pitying;* genial, hospitable 882adj. *sociable;* bounteous, bountiful 813 adj. *liberal;* generous, unselfish, unenvious, unjealous, altruistic 931 adj. *disinterested;* beneficent, charitable, humanitarian, doing good 901 adj. *philanthropic;* obliging, accommodating, helpful 703adj. *aiding;* complacent, compaisant, gracious, gallant, chivalrous, chivalric 884adj. *courteous.*

Vb. *be benevolent,*—kind etc. adj.; feel the springs of charity, have one's heart in the right place; sympathize, understand, feel as for oneself, enter into another's feelings, put oneself in another's place, do as one would be done by, practice the golden rule; return good for evil, heap coals of fire 909vb. *forgive;* wish well, pray for, bless, give one's blessing, bestow a benediction; bear good will, wish the best for, have the right intentions, have the best i., mean well; look with a favorable eye, favor 703vb. *patronize;* benefit 644vb. *do good;* be a good Samaritan, do a good turn, render a service, oblige, put one under an obligation 703vb. *aid;* lenify, humanize, reform 654vb. *make better.*

philanthropize, do good, go about doing good, do good works, have a social conscience, show public spirit; reform, improve; relieve the poor, go slumming; visit, nurse 703 vb. *minister to;* mother 889vb. *pet.*

Adv. *benevolently,* kindly, tenderly, lovingly, charitably, generously; in kindness, in charity; out of kindness, to oblige; mercifully, by the grace of God.

See: 597, 644, 654, 703, 707, 734, 736, 781, 813, 818, 880, 882, 884, 887, 889, 901, 905, 909, 931, 935.

898 Malevolence

N. *malevolence,* ill nature, ill will, ill disposition 881n. *enmity;* truculency, cussedness, bitchiness, beastliness, ill intent, bad intention, worst intentions, cloven hoof; spite, gall, spitefulness, viciousness, malignity, malignancy, malice, deliberate m., malice prepense, malice aforethought; bad blood, hate 888n. *hatred;* venom, virulence, deadliness, balefulness 659n. *bane;* bitterness, acrimony, acerbity 393n. *sourness;* mordacity 388n. *pungency;* rancor 891n. *resentment;* gloating, schadenfreude, unholy joy 912n. *envy;* evil eye 983n. *spell.*

inhumanity, lack of humanity, lack of charity, uncharitableness; intolerance, persecution 735n. *severity;* harshness, mercilessness, implacability, hardness of heart, obduracy, heart of stone 906n. *pitilessness;* cold feelings, unkindness, stepmotherly treatment; callousness 326n. *hardness;* cruelty, barbarity, bloodthirstiness, bloodiness, bloodlust; barbarism, savagery, ferocity, barbarousness, savageness, ferociousness; atrociousness, outrageousness, immanity; ghoulishness, sadism, devilishness 934n. *wickedness;* truculency, brutality, rufianism; destructiveness, vandalism 165n. *destruction.*

cruel act, cruel conduct, truculence, brutality; ill-treatment, bad t., ill usage 675n. *misuse;* victimization, "tender mercies" 735n. *severity;* blood, bloodshed 176n. *violence;* excess, extremes, extremity; act of inhumanity, inhuman deed, atrocity, outrage, devilry; cruelty, cruelties, torture, tortures, barbarity, barbarities; cannibalism, murder 362n. *homicide;* mass murder, genocide, unlimited war 362n. *slaughter.*

Adj. *malevolent,* ill-wishing, ill-willed, ill-intentioned, ill-disposed, meaning harm 661adj. *dangerous;* ill-natured, ill-conditioned 893adj. *sullen;* nasty, vicious, bitchy, cussed 602adj. *willful;* malicious, catty, spiteful 962 adj. *detracting;* mischievous, mischief-making (**see** *maleficent*); baleful, malign, malignant 645adj. *harmful;* venomous 362adj. *deadly;* full of spite, spleenful 888adj. *hating;* jealous 912adj. *envious;* disloyal, treacherous 930adj. *perfidious;* bitter, rancorous 891adj. *resentful;* implacable, unforgiving, merciless 906adj. *pitiless;* vindictive, gloating 910adj. *revengeful;* hostile, fell 881 adj. *inimical;* intolerant, persecuting 735adj. *oppressive.*

maleficent, hurtful, damaging 645adj. *harmful;* poisonous, venomous, virulent, caustic, mordacious 659adj. *baneful;* working ill, spreading evil, mischief-making, spreading mischief 645adj. *bad.*

unkind, unamiable, ill-natured 893 adj. *sullen;* unkindly, unbenevolent, unbenign, unloving, unaffectionate, untender, stepmotherly, unmaternal, unbrotherly, unfraternal, undaughterly, unfilial; cold, unfriendly, hostile 881adj. *inimical;* unforthcoming, uncordial, inhospitable 883adj. *unsociable;* uncooperative, unhelpful, disobliging, inofficious; ungenerous, uncharitable, unforgiving; harsh, gruff, beastly 885adj. *ungracious;* unsympathetic, ununderstanding, unresponsive, unfeeling, insensible, unmoved 820adj. *impassive;* stern 735 adj. *severe;* unsqueamish, tough, hardboiled, hardbitten 326adj. *hard;* inhumane, unnatural.

cruel, grim, fell; steely, grim-faced, cold-eyed, steely-e., hard-hearted, flint-h., stony-h.; ruthless, merciless 906adj. *pitiless;* tyrannical 735adj. *oppressive;* gloating, sadistic; bloodthirsty, cannibalistic 362adj. *murderous;* bloody 176adj. *violent;* excessive, extreme; atrocious, outrageous; feline, tigerish, wolfish; unnatural, subhuman, dehumanized, brutalized, brutish; brutal, rough, truculent, fierce, ferocious; savage, barbarous, wild, untamed, untamable, tameless; inhuman, ghoulish, fiendish, devilish, diabolical, demoniac, satanic, hellish, infernal, tartarean.

Vb. *be malevolent,* bear malice, cherish a grudge, harbor spleen 888vb. *hate;* show ill-will, betray the cloven hoof; show envy 912vb. *envy;* disoblige, spite, do one a bad turn; go to extremes, do one's worst, wreak one's spite, break a butterfly on a wheel, have no mercy 906 vb. *be pitiless;* take one's revenge, victimize, gloat 910vb. *be revengeful;* take it out of one, bully, maltreat 645vb. *ill-treat;* molest, hurt, injure, annoy 645vb. *harm;* malign, run down, throw stones at 926vb. *detract;* tease, harry, hound, persecute, tyrannize, torture 735vb. *oppress;* raven, thirst for blood 362vb. *slaughter;* rankle, fester, poison, be a thorn in the flesh; create havoc, blight, blast 165vb. *lay waste;* cast the evil eye 983vb. *bewitch.*

Adv. *malevolently,* with bad intent, with the worst intentions; spitefully, out of spite.

See: 165, 176, 326, 362, 388, 393, 602, 645, 659, 661, 675, 735, 820, 881, 883, 885, 888, 891, 893, 906, 910, 912, 926, 930, 934, 983.

899 Malediction

N. *malediction,* malison, curse, imprecation, anathema; evil eye 983n. *spell;* no blessing, ill wishes, bad wishes, "curses not loud but deep" 898n. *malevolence;* execration, denunciation, commination 900n. *threat;* onslaught 712n. *attack;* fulmination, thunder, thunders of the Vatican; ban, proscription, excommunication; exorcism, bell, book and candle.

scurrility, ribaldry, vulgarity; profanity, swearing, profane s., cursing and swearing, blasting; evil speaking, maledicence, bad language, foul l., filthy l., blue l., shocking l., strong l., unparliamentary l., Limehouse, billingsgate; naughty word, expletive, swear-word, oath, swear, damn, curse, cuss, tinker's c.; invective, vituperation, abuse, volley of a.; mutual abuse, slanging match, stormy exchange; vain abuse, empty curse, more bark than bite 900n. *threat;* no compliment, aspersion, reflection, vilification, slander 926n. *calumny;* cheek, sauce 878n. *sauciness;* personality, affront; insult 921 n. *indignity;* contumely, scorn 922n. *contempt;* scolding, rough edge of one's tongue, basting, tongue-lashing 924n. *reproach.*

Adj. *maledictory,* cursing, imprecative, imprecatory, anathematizing, comminatory, fulminatory, denunciatory, damnatory.

maledicent, evil-speaking, cursing, swearing, damning, blasting; profane, foul-mouthed, foul-tongued, foul-spoken, unparliamentary, scurrilous, scurrile, ribald 847n. *vulgar;* sulfurous, blue; vituperative, abusive, vitriolic, injurious, vilipendious, reproachful 924adj. *disapproving;* unflattering, candid 573adj. *plain;* contumelious, scornful 922adj. *despising.*

cursed, wished, wished on one; maledict, accursed, unblessed, execrable; anathematized, under a ban, excommunicated, damned 961adj. *condemned;* under a spell 983adj. *bewitched.*

Vb. *curse,* cast the evil eye 983vb. *bewitch;* accurse, wish, wish on, call down on; wish one joy of; curse with bell, book and candle, curse up hill and down dale; anathematize, imprecate, invoke curses on, execrate, hold up to execration; fulminate, thunder against, inveigh 924 vb. *reprove;* denounce 928vb. *accuse;* excommunicate, damn, devote to destruction 961vb. *condemn;* round upon, confound, send to the devil, send to blazes; abuse, vituperate, revile, shend, outscorn, rail, chide, flyte; heap abuse, pour vitriol 924vb. *exprobate;* bespatter, throw mud 926 vb. *detract.*

cuss, curse, swear, damn, blast; swear like a trooper, use expletives, use billingsgate, curse and swear; slang, slangwhang, abuse, blackguard 924vb. *exprobate;* rail, scold, beshrew, give the rough edge of one's tongue.

Int. curse! a curse on! woe to! woe betide! ill betide! confusion seize! devil take it! blast! damn! dang! hang!

See: 573, 712, 847, 878, 898, 900, 921, 922, 924, 926, 928, 961, 983.

900 Threat

N. *threat,* menace; commination, fulmination 899n. *malediction;* minacity, threatfulness, ominousness; challenge, dare, 711n. *defiance;* blackmail 737n. *demand;* battle-cry, war-whoop, saber-rattling, war of nerves 854n. *intimidation;* deterrent 723n. *weapon;* black cloud, threatening c. 511n. *omen;* hidden fires, secret weapon 663n. *pitfall;* impending danger, sword of Damocles 661n. *danger;* danger signal, fair warning, writing on the wall 664n. *warning;* bluster, idle threat, hollow t. 877n. *boast;* bark, growl, snarl 893n. *sullenness.*

Adj. *threatening,* menacing, minatory, minatorial, minacious, threatful; saber-rattling 711adj. *defiant;* blustering, bullying, hectoring 877adj. *boastful;* muttering, grumbling 893 adj. *sullen;* bodeful, portentous, ominous, foreboding 511adj. *presageful;* hovering, lowering, hanging over 155adj. *impending;* ready to spring, growling, snarling 891adj. *angry;* abusive 899adj. *maledicent;* comminatory 899adj. *maledictory;* in terrorem, deterrent 854adj. *frightening;* nasty, unpleasant 661adj. *dangerous.*

Vb. *threaten,* threat, menace, use threats, hold out t., utter t.; demand with menaces, blackmail 737vb. *demand;* frighten, deter, intimidate, bully 854vb. *frighten;* roar, bellow 408vb. *vociferate;* fulminate, thunder 899vb. *curse;* bark, talk big, bluster, hector 877vb. *boast;* shake, wave, flaunt 317vb. *brandish;* rattle the saber, clench the fist, draw one's sword, make a pass 711vb *defy;* bare the fangs, snarl, growl, mutter 893vb. *be sullen;* bristle, spit, look daggers, grow nasty 891vb. *get angry;* draw a bead on, cover, have one covered, keep one c. 281vb. *aim;* gather, mass, lower, hang over, hover, stand in terrorem 155vb. *impend;* bode, presage, promise ill, spell danger 511vb. *predict;* serve notice, forewarn 644vb. *warn;* breathe revenge, promise r., threaten reprisals 910vb. *be revengeful.*

Adv. *threateningly,* menacingly, in terrorem, on pain of death.

See: 155, 281, 317, 408, 511, 661, 663, 664, 711, 723, 737, 854, 877, 891, 893, 899, 910.

901 Philanthropy

N. *philanthropy,* humanitarianism, humanity, humaneness, the golden rule 897n. *benevolence;* humanism, cosmopolitanism, internationalism; altruism 931n. *disinterestedness;* idealism, ideals 933n. *virtue;* universal benevolence, the greatest happiness of the greatest number, utilitarianism, Benthamism; passion for improvement, "onward and upward department" 654n. *reformism;* dedication, crusading spirit, missionary s., nonconformist conscience, social c.; good works, mission, civilizing m., "white man's burden"; holy war, crusade, campaign; cause, messianism, messiahship 689n. *directorship.*

sociology, social science, social engineering, social planning, socialism; Poplarism, poor relief, poor rate; social services, welfare state; social service, welfare work, slumming, good works.

patriotism, civism, civic ideals, good citizenship, public spirit, concern for the public, zeal for the common good, devotion to the common weal, love of country; local patriotism, parochialism; nationalism, chauvinism, my country right or wrong; irredentism, Zionism.

philanthropist, friend of all the world 903n. *benefactor;* humanitarian, do-gooder, social worker, slummer 897 n. *kind person;* paladin, champion, crusader, knight, knight errant; messiah 690n. *leader;* missionary, man with a mission, dedicated soul; visionary, ideologist; idealist, altruist; reformist 654n. *reformer;* utilitarian, Benthamite; utopian, millenarian, chiliast; humanist, cosmopolite, cosmopolitan, citizen of the world, internationalist.

patriot, lover of his country, fighter for his c.; pater patriae, father of his people; nationalist, irredentist, chauvinist, Zionist.

Adj. *philanthropic,* humanitarian, humane, human 897adj. *benevolent;* enlightened, humanistic, liberal; cosmopolitan, international, internationally minded; idealistic, altruistic

931adj. *disinterested;* visionary, dedicated; sociological, socialistic; utilitarian.
patriotic, civically minded, public spirited; irredentist, nationalistic, chauvinistic; loyal, true, true-blue.
Vb. See 897vb. *philanthropize.*
See: 654, 689, 690, 897, 903, 931, 933.

902 Misanthropy
N. *misanthropy,* hatred of mankind, distrust of one's fellow man, disillusionment with society, cynicism, unsociality 883n. *unsociability;* moroseness 893n. *sullenness;* inhumanity, non-humanism, incivism; egotism.
misanthrope, hater of the human race, man-hater, woman-h., misogynist, misogamist; cynic, Diogenes, Timon; egotist; no patriot, defeatist; world-hater, unsocial animal 883n. *solitary;* bear, cross-patch, sulker 829n. *malcontent.*
Adj. *misanthropic,* inhuman, antisocial 883adj. *unsociable;* cynical, Diogenic, Diogenean; uncivic, unpatriotic, defeatist.
Vb. *misanthropize,* become a misanthrope, lose faith in human kind.
Adv. *misanthropically,* cynically.
See: 829, 883, 893.

903 Benefactor
N. *benefactor,* benefactress 901n. *philanthropist;* Lady Bountiful, donor, fairy godmother 781n. *giver;* guardian angel, tutelary saint, good genius 660n. *protector;* founder, foundress, supporter 707n. *patron;* tyrannicide, pater patriae, father of his people 901n. *patriot;* savior, ransomer, redeemer, deliverer, rescuer 668n. *deliverance;* champion 713n. *defender;* Lady Godiva, Good Samaritan 897n. *kind person;* good neighbor 880n. *friend;* helper, present help in time of trouble 703n. *aider;* salt of the earth, saint 937n. *good man.*
See: 660, 668, 703, 707, 713, 781, 880, 897, 901, 937.

904 Evildoer
N. *evildoer,* worker of evil, worker of iniquity, wrongdoer, sinner 934n. *wickedness;* villain, blackguard, bad lot; one up to no good, monkey, little devil, mischief-maker 663n. *trouble-maker;* gossip, slanderer, calumniator 926n. *detractor;* snake in the grass, viper in the bosom, traitor 545n. *deceiver;* marplot 702n. *hinderer;* spoiler, despoiler, wrecker, defacer, vandal, Hun, iconoclast 168 n. *destroyer;* nihilist, anarchist 738n. *revolter;* incendiary, pyromaniac 381 n. *incendiarism;* disturber of the peace, bull in a china shop 738n. *rioter.*
ruffian, blackguard, rogue 938n. *knave;* lout, hooligan, hoodlum, larrikin, sansculotte, badmash 869n. *low fellow;* Teddy-boy, gunboy, terror, holy t., terror of the neighborhood; rough, tough, rowdy, ugly customer, plug-ugly, desperado, Apache, Mohawk; bully, bravo, assassin, hired a.; cut-throat, hangman, gunman, bludgeon man, cosh-m., sandbagger; thug, killer, butcher 362n. *murderer;* genocide, mass murderer, plague, scourge, scourge of the human race, Attila 659n. *bane;* petty tyrant, gauleiter 735n. *tyrant;* brute, savage b., beast, savage barbarian, ape-man, cave-m.; cannibal, anthropophagist; homicidal maniac 504n. *madman.*
offender, sinner, black sheep 938n. *bad man;* suspect; culprit, guilty man, law-breaker; wrongdoer, tortfeasor; criminal, misdemeanant, felon; delinquent, juvenile d., first offender; recidivist, backslider, old offender, hardened o., lag, old l., convict, ex-c., jail-bird; lifer, gallowsbird, "quare fellow"; parolee, probationer, ticket-of-leave man; malefactor, gangster, racketeer, barrator, housebreaker 789n. *thief, robber;* forger 789n. *defrauder;* blackmailer, blood-sucker, vampire; poisoner 362n. *murderer;* outlaw, public enemy 881n. *enemy;* intruder, trespasser; criminal world, underworld, sink of iniquity 934n. *wickedness.*
hell-hag, hell-hound, hell-kite; cat, hell-c., wild c., bitch, virago 892n. *shrew;* she-devil, fury, harpy, siren; ogress, witch, beldam, horror 938n. *monster.*
noxious animal, brute, beast, wild b.; beast of prey, predator; tiger, man-eater, wolf, werewolf, hyena, jackal, fox; kite, vulture, vampire, blood-sucker 365n. *bird of prey;* snake, serpent, viper, adder, asp, rattlesnake, cobra 365n. *reptile;* cockatrice, basilisk, salamander 84n. *rara avis;* scorpion, wasp, hornet; pest, locust, Colorado beetle, worm, wire-w., canker-w. 365n. *vermin;* rat 365n. *rodent;* wild cat, mad dog, rogue elephant.
See: 84, 168, 362, 365, 381, 504, 545,

659, 663, 702, 735, 738, 789, 869, 881, 892, 926, 934, 938.

905 Pity

N. *pity,* springs of p., ruth; remorse, compunction 830n. *regret;* compassion, bowels of c., compassionateness, humanity 897n. *benevolence;* soft heart, tender h.; gentleness, softness, squeamishness 736n. *lenity;* commiseration, touched feelings, melting mood, tears of sympathy 825n. *sorrow;* weltschmerz, lacrimae rerum 834n. *dejection;* sympathy, understanding, deep u., fellow-feeling (**see** *condolence*); self-pity, self-compassion, self-commiseration, tears for oneself; plea for pity, argumentum ad misericordiam.

condolence, sympathy and c.; consolation, comfort 831n. *relief;* commiseration, sympathetic grief, sympathy, fellow-feeling, fellowship in sorrow 775n. *participation;* professional condolence, keen, coronach, wake 836n. *lament.*

mercy, tender mercies, clemency, quarter, grace; locus paenitentiae. second chance; mercifulness, exorability, placability, forbearance, long-suffering 909n. *forgiveness;* light sentence 963n. *penalty;* let-off 960n. *acquittal.*

Adj. *pitying,* compassionate, sympathetic, understanding, condolent, commiserating; pitiful, ruthful, merciful, clement, full of mercy 736adj. *lenient;* melting, tender, tender-hearted, soft, soft-hearted; weak 734 adj. *lax;* unhardened, squeamish, easily touched, easily moved; exorable, placable, disposed to mercy 909adj. *forgiving;* remorseful, compunctious; humane, charitable 897 adj. *benevolent;* forbearing 823adj. *patient.*

pitiable, compassionable, commiserable, pitiful, piteous, deserving pity, demanding p., claiming p., challenging sympathy.

Vb. *pity,* feel p., weep for p., bleed; compassionate, show compassion, show pity, take p., take compassion; sympathize, sympathize with, enter into one's feelings, feel for, feel with, share the grief of 775vb. *participate*; sorrow, grieve, feel sorry for, weep f., lament f., commiserate, condole, condole with, express one's condolences, send one's c., testify one's pity, yearn over 836vb. *lament;* console, comfort, offer consolation, afford c. 833vb. *cheer;* have pity, have compassion, melt, thaw, relent 909vb. *forgive.*

show mercy, have m., offer m., spare, spare the life of, give quarter; forget one's anger 909vb. *forgive;* be slow to anger, forbear; allow time for repentance, indulge 736vb. *be lenient;* relax, relent, unbend, not proceed to extremes, relax one's rigor, show consideration, not be too hard upon, let one down gently; put one out of his misery, give the coup de grâce, be cruel to be kind.

ask mercy, plead for m., appeal for m., pray for m., beg for m., throw oneself upon another's mercy, ask for quarter, beg one's life; find mercy, find compassion, propitiate, disarm, melt, thaw, soften 719vb. *pacify.*

Int. alas! how sad! too bad! for pity's sake! for mercy's s.! for the love of God!

See: 719, 734, 736, 775, 823, 825, 830, 831, 833, 834, 836, 897, 909, 960, 963.

906 Pitilessness

N. *pitilessness,* lack of pity, ruthlessness, mercilessness, unmercifulness; inclemency, intolerance, rigor 735n. *severity;* callousness, hardness of heart 898n. *malevolence;* inflexibility 326n. *hardness;* inexorability, relentlessness, remorselessness, unforgivingness 910adj. *revengefulness;* letter of the law, pound of flesh; no pity, no bowels, short shrift, no quarter.

Adj. *pitiless,* unpitying, uncompassionate, uncondoling, uncomforting, unconsoling, unfeeling, unresponsive 820adj. *impassive;* unsympathizing, unsympathetic; unmelting, unmoved, tearless, dry-eyed; unsqueamish, callous, tough, hardened 326adj. *hard;* harsh, rigorous, intolerant, persecuting 735adj. *severe;* brutal, sadistic 898adj. *cruel;* merciless, ruthless, bowelless; indisposed to mercy, inclement, unmerciful, unrelenting, relentless, remorseless, inflexible, inexorable, implacable; unforgiving, unpardoning, vindictive 910adj. *revengeful.*

Vb. *be pitiless,*—ruthless etc. adj.; have no bowels, have no compassion, have no pity, know no p.; show no p., show no mercy, give no quarter, spare none; shut the gates of mercy, harden one's heart, be deaf to appeal, admit no excuse; not tolerate, persecute 735vb. *be severe;*

stand on the letter of the law, insist on one's pound of flesh 735vb. *be severe;* take one's revenge 910vb. *avenge.*
See: 326, 735, 820, 898, 910.

907 Gratitude
N. *gratitude,* gratefulness, thankfulness, grateful heart, feeling of obligation, sense of o.; grateful acceptance, appreciativeness, appreciation, lively sense of favors to come.
thanks, hearty t.; giving thanks, thanksgiving, eucharist, benediction, blessing; praises, paean, Te Deum 876n. *celebration;* grace, bismillah; grace before meat, grace after m., bread-and-butter letter, collins; credit, credit title, acknowledgment, grateful a., recognition, grateful r., ungrudging r., full praise; tribute 923n. *praise;* thank-offering, parting present, tip 962n. *reward;* requital, return, favor returned 714n. *retaliation.*
Adj. *grateful,* thankful, appreciative; showing appreciation, thanking, blessing, praising; acknowledging favors, crediting, giving credit; obliged, much o., under obligation, beholden, indebted.
Vb. *be grateful,* have a grateful heart, overflow with gratitude; thank one's stars, praise heaven; feel an obligation, cherish a favor, never forget; accept gratefully, pocket thankfully, not look a gift-horse in the mouth; be privileged, have the honor to.
thank, give thanks, render t., return t., express t., pour out one's t., praise, bless; acknowledge, express acknowledgments, credit, give c., give full c. 158vb. *attribute;* appreciate, show appreciation, tip 962vb. *reward;* return a favor, requite, repay, repay with interest 714vb. *retaliate;* return with thanks 787vb. *restitute.*
Adv. *gratefully,* thankfully, with gratitude, with thanks, with interest.
Int. thanks! many t.! much obliged! thank Heaven! Heaven be praised!
See: 158, 714, 787, 876, 923, 962.

908 Ingratitude
N. *ingratitude,* ungratefulness, unthankfulness, thanklessness; grudging thanks, cold t., more kicks than ha'pence; no sense of obligation, indifference to favors, oblivion of benefits, "benefits forgot" 506n. *oblivion;* no reward, unrewardingness, thankless task, thankless office; thankless person, ingrate, ungrateful wretch.
Adj. *ungrateful,* unthankful, ingrate; unobliged, not obliged, unbeholden; unmindful 506adj. *forgetful;* unmindful of favors, insensible of benefits, incapable of gratitude 820 adj. *apathetic.*
unthanked, thankless, without credit, unacknowledged, forgotten; rewardless, bootless, unrewarding, unrewarded, unrequited, ill-r., untipped.
Vb. *be ungrateful,* show ingratitude, admit no obligation, acknowledge no favor; take for granted, take as one's due; not thank, omit to t., forget to t.; see no reason to thank, grudge thanks, look a gift-horse in the mouth; forget benefits, return evil for good.
Int. thank you for nothing! no thanks to.
See: 506, 820.

909 Forgiveness
N. *forgiveness,* pardon, free p., full p., reprievement, reprieval, reprieve 506n. *amnesty;* indemnity, act of i., covenant of i., deed of i.; grace, indulgence, plenary i.; cancellation, remission, absolution, shrift 960n. *acquittal;* one-sided forgiveness, condonation; justification, exculpation, exoneration, excuse 927n. *vindication;* mutual forgiveness, reconciliation renewal of love 719n. *pacification;* forgiving nature, placability, exorability 905n. *pity;* long-suffering, longanimity, forbearance 823n. *patience;* forgiver, pardoner, author of forgiveness.
Adj. *forgiving,* placable, exorable, condoning, admitting excuses, conciliatory; unresentful, forbearing, longanimous, long-suffering 823adj. *patient;* reluctant to punish, more in sorrow than in anger.
forgiven, pardoned, forgiven and forgotten, amnestied, reprieved; remitted, canceled, blotted out, extinguished; condoned, excused, exonerated, let off 960adj. *acquitted;* absolved, shriven; unresented, unavenged, unrevenged, unpunished, unchastened; pardonable, forgivable, venial, excusable.
Vb. *forgive,* pardon, reprieve, forgive and forget, amnesty 506n. *forget;* remit, absolve, assoil, shrive; cancel, blot out, blot out one's transgressions 550vb. *obliterate;* re-

lent, unbend, accept an apology 736 vb. *be lenient;* be merciful, not be too hard upon, let one down gently 905vb. *show mercy;* bear with, put up w., forbear, tolerate 823vb. *be patient;* take no offense, take in good part, pocket, stomach; forget an injury, ignore a wrong, overlook, pass over, not punish, leave unavenged, turn the other cheek; return good for evil, heap coals of fire 897 vb. *be benevolent;* connive, wink at, condone 458vb. *disregard;* excuse, find excuses for 927vb. *justify;* recommend to pardon, intercede 720vb. *mediate;* exculpate, exonerate 960vb. *acquit;* bury the hatchet, let bygones be bygones, make it up, shake hands, kiss and be friends, be reconciled 880vb. *be friendly;* restore to favor, kill the fatted calf 876vb. *celebrate.*

beg pardon, plead for forgiveness, offer apologies, ask for absolution 905vb. *ask mercy;* propitiate, placate 941vb. *atone.*

Adv. *forgivingly,* without resentment, more in sorrow than in anger.

See: 458, 506, 550, 719, 720, 736, 823, 876, 880, 897, 905, 927, 941, 960.

910 Revenge

N. *revengefulness,* thirst for revenge, revanchism; vindictiveness, spitefulness, spite 898n. *malevolence;* ruthlessness 906n. *pitilessness;* remorselessness, relentlessness, implacability, irreconcilability, unappeasability; unappeasable resentment, deadly rancor 891n. *resentment.*

revenge, sweet r., "wild justice"; crime passionel 911n. *jealousy;* vengeance, avengement, day of reckoning 963n. *punishment;* victimization, reprisal, reprisals, punitive expedition 714n. *retaliation;* lex talionis, eye for an eye, tooth for a tooth, blood for blood; vendetta, feud, blood-f., death-f. 881n. *enmity.*

avenger, vindicator, punisher, revanchist; Nemesis, Eumenides, avenging furies.

Adj. *revengeful,* vengeful, breathing vengeance, thirsting for revenge; avenging, taking vengeance, retaliative 714adj. *retaliatory;* at feud 881 adj. *inimical;* unforgiving, unforgetting, implacable, unappeasable, unrelenting, relentless, remorseless 960adj. *pitiless;* grudgeful, vindictive, spiteful 898adj. *malevolent;* rancorous 891adj. *resentful;* enjoying revenge, gloating.

Vb. *avenge,* avenge oneself, revenge o., take one's revenge, take vengeance, wreak v., victimize; exact retribution, get one's own back, repay, pay out, pay off *or* settle old scores, put paid to the account; get back on, give tit for tat 714vb. *retaliate;* sate one's vengeance, glut one's revenge, enjoy one's r., gloat.

be revengeful, — vindictive etc.adj.; cry revenge, breathe r., promise vengeance 888vb. *hate;* nurse one's revenge, cherish a grudge, have a feud, have a rod in pickle, have a crow to pluck, have accounts to settle 881vb. *be inimical;* let it rankle, keep a wound green, remember an injury, brood on one's wrongs 891vb. *resent.*

See: 714, 881, 888, 891, 898, 906, 911, 963.

911 Jealousy

N. *jealousy,* pangs of j., jealousness; jaundiced eye, green-eyed monster; distrust, mistrust 486n. *doubt;* heartburning 891n. *resentment;* enviousness 912n. *envy;* hate 888n. *hatred;* inferiority complex, prestige-chasing, emulation, competitiveness, competition, rivalry, jealous r. 716n. *contention;* possessiveness 887n. *love,* sexual jealousy, crime passionel 910 n. *revenge;* object of jealousy, competitor, rival, hated r., the other man, the other woman; sour grapes.

Adj. *jealous,* green-eyed, yellow-e., jaundiced, envying 912adj. *envious;* devoured with jealousy, horn-mad; possessive 887adj. *loving;* suspicious, mistrusting, distrustful 474adj. *doubting;* emulative, competitive, rival, competing, in the business, in the same b.

Vb. *be jealous,* scent a rival, suspect, mistrust, distrust 486vb. *doubt;* view with jealousy, view with a jaundiced eye 912vb. *envy;* resent another's superiority, nurse an inferiority complex; brook no rival, resent competition; strive to keep for oneself.

See: 474, 486, 716, 887, 888, 891, 910, 912.

912 Envy

N. *envy,* envious eye, enviousness, covetousness 859n. *desire;* rivalry 716n. *contention;* envious rivalry, jalousie de métier 911n. *jealousy;* ill-will, spite, spleen, bile 898n. *malevolence;* mortification, unwilling admiration, grudging praise.

Adj. *envious,* envying, envious-eyed, squint-e., green with envy, fain to change places with 911adj. *jealous;* greedy, unsated, unsatisfied 829adj. *discontented;* covetous, longing 859 adj. *desiring;* grudging; mortified 891adj. *resentful.*

Vb. *envy,* view with e., cast envious looks, turn green with e.; covet, crave, lust after, must have for oneself, long to change places with 859 vb. *desire.*

See: 716, 829, 859, 891, 898, 911.

913 Right

N. *right,* rightfulness, rightness, good case for; right lines 642n. *expedience;* freedom from error, correctness, correctitude, exactness 494n. *accuracy;* fittingness, seemliness, propriety, decency 24n. *fitness;* normality 83n. *conformity;* rules, rules and regulations 693n. *precept;* what ought to be, what should be 917n. *duty;* morality, good morals 917n. *morals;* righteousness 933n. *virtue;* uprightness, honor 929n. *probity;* suum cuique, one's right, one's due, deserts, merits, claim; from each according to his ability, to each according to his need 915n. *dueness;* prerogative, privilege, rights and privileges 919n. *non-liability;* rights, interest, vested i., birthright 777n. *property.*

justice, freedom from wrong, justifiability; righting wrong, redress; reform 654n. *reformism,* tardy justice, overdue reform; even-handed justice, impartial j., indifferent j.; scales of justice, justice under the law, process under the l. 953n. *legality;* retribution, retributive justice 962n. *reward;* lex talionis 714n. *retaliation;* fair-mindedness, objectivity, indifference, detachment, impartiality, equalness 28n. *equality;* equity, equitableness, reasonableness, fairness; fair deal, square d., fair break, fair treatment, fair play, fair field and no favor, equal opportunity; good law, Queensberry rules; Astraea, Themis, Nemesis.

Adj. *right,* rightful, proper, right and p., meet and right; on the right lines, fitting, suitable 24adj. *fit;* better, even b. 642adj. *expedient;* good, just right 646adj. *perfect;* quite right, exact, just so, true, correct 494adj. *accurate;* adjusted, put right, redressed, reformed 654adj. *improved;* normal, standard, classical 83adj. *conformable.*

just, upright, righteous, right-minded, on the side of the angels 933adj. *virtuous;* fair-minded, disinterested, unprejudiced, unbiased, unswerving, undeflected 625adj. *neutral;* detached, impersonal, dispassionate, objective; equal, indifferent, impartial, even-handed; fair, square, fair and s., equitable, reasonable, fair enough; in the right, justifiable, justified, unchallengeable, unchallenged, unimpeachable; legitimate, according to law 953adj. *legal;* sporting, sportsmanlike 929adj. *honorable;* deserved, well-d., earned, merited, well-m. 915adj. *due;* overdue, demanded, claimed, rightly c., claimable 627adj. *required.*

Vb. *be right,* stand to reason 494vb. *be true;* have justice, have cause, be in the right, have right on one's side.

be just.—impartial etc. adj.; play the game 929vb. *be honorable;* do justice, give the devil his due, give full marks to, hand it to 915vb. *grant claims;* see justice done, see fair play, hold the scales even, hear both sides, go by merit, consider on the merits 480vb. *judge;* temper justice with mercy 905vb. *show mercy;* see one righted, right a wrong, right wrongs, redress, remedy, cure, mend, reform, put right 654vb. *rectify;* serve one right 714 vb. *retaliate;* try to be fair, lean over backwards, over-compensate; hide nothing, declare one's interest.

Adv. *rightly,* justly, justifiably, with justice; in the right, within one's rights; like a judge, impartially, indifferently, equally, without distinction, without respect of persons; fairly, without favoritism; naturally, by nature's laws.

See: 24, 28, 83, 480, 494, 625, 627, 642, 646, 654, 693, 714, 777, 905, 915, 917, 919, 929, 933, 953, 962.

914 Wrong

N. *wrong,* wrongness, something wrong, oddness, queerness 84n. *abnormality;* something rotten, curse, bane, scandal 645n. *badness;* disgrace, shame, crying s., dishonor 867n. *slur;* impropriety, unfittingness, unsuitability 643n. *inexpedience;* incorrectness, wrong lines, mistake 495n. *error;* wrongheadedness, unreasonableness 481n. *misjudgment;* unreason 477n. *sophistry;* unjustifiability, what ought not to be, what must not be 916n. *undueness;*

inexcusability, culpability, guiltiness 936n. *guilt;* immorality, vice, sin 934 n. *wickedness;* dishonesty, unrighteousness 930n. *improbity;* irregularity, illegitimacy, criminality, crime, lawlessness 954n. *illegality;* wrongfulness, misdoing, tortiousness, misfeasance, transgression, trespass, encroachment; a wrong, injustice, tort, mischief, outrage, foul 930n. *foul play;* sense of wrong, complaint, charge 928n. *accusation;* grievance, just g. 891n. *resentment;* wrong 'un, immoralist, unjust judge 938n. *bad man.*

injustice, no justice; miscarriage of justice, wrong verdict 481n. *misjudgment;* corrupt justice, uneven scales, warped judgment, packed jury 481n. *bias;* one-sidedness, inequity, unfairness; partiality, leaning, favoritism, favor, nepotism; preferential treatment, discrimination, partisanship, party spirit 481n. *prejudice;* unlawfulness, no law 954 n. *illegality;* justice denied, right withheld, privilege curtailed 916n. *undueness;* party capital, mean advantage, "heads I win, tails you lose"; no equality, wolf and the lamb 29n. *inequality;* not cricket 930 n. *foul play;* imposition, robbing Peter to pay Paul.

Adj. *wrong,* not right 645adj. *bad;* odd, queer, suspect 84adj. *abnormal;* unfitting, ill-fitting, ill-seeming, unseemly, unfit, improper, inappropriate 643adj. *inexpedient*; false, incorrect, untrue 495adj. *erroneous;* off the mark, inaccurate 495adj. *inexact;* on the wrong lines, misjudged, ill-advised, wrongheaded, unreasonable 481adj. *misjudging;* wrong from the start, out of court, inadmissible; irregular, against the rules, foul, unauthorized, unwarranted 757adj. *prohibited;* bad in law, illegitimate, illicit, tortious, criminous, criminal, felonious, nefarious 954adj. *illegal;* condemnable, culpable, in the wrong, offside 936 adj. *guilty;* unwarrantable, inexcusable, unpardonable, unforgivable, unjustifiable (**see** *unjust*); open to objection, objectionable, scandalous 861n. *disliked;* wrongous, wrongful, unrightful, injurious, mischievous 645adj. *harmful;* unrighteous 930adj. *dishonest;* iniquitous, sinful, vicious, immoral 934adj. *wicked.*

unjust, unjustifiable; uneven, weighted 29adj. *unequal;* inequitable, iniquitous, unfair; hard, hard on 735 adj. *severe;* foul, not playing the game, below the belt, unsportsmanlike; discriminatory, favoring, one-sided, leaning to one side, partial, partisan, prejudiced 481adj. *biased;* selling justice 930adj. *venal;* wresting the law 954adj. *illegal.*

Vb. *be wrong,*—unjust etc.adj.; be in the wrong, go wrong 495vb. *err.*

do wrong, wrong, hurt, injure, do an injury 645vb. *harm;* be hard on, have a down on 735vb. *be severe;* not play the game, not play cricket, hit below the belt; break the rules, commit a foul; commit a tort, commit a crime, break the law, wrest the l., pervert the l. 954vb. *be illegal;* transgress, infringe, trespass 306vb. *encroach;* reap where one has not sown, give an inch and take an ell; leave unrighted, leave unremedied; do less than justice, withhold justice, deny j., load, weight, load the scales, pack *or* rig the jury; lean, lean to one side, discriminate against, show partiality, show favoritism, discriminate 481vb. *be biased;* favor 703vb. *patronize;* go too far, overcompensate, lean over backwards; commit, perpetrate.

Adv. *wrongly,* unrightfully, untruly; unjustly, wrongously, tortiously, illegally, criminally, feloniously.

See: 29, 84, 306, 477, 481, 495, 643, 645, 703, 735, 757, 861, 867, 891, 916, 928, 930, 934, 936, 938, 954.

915 Dueness

N. *dueness,* what is due, what is owing; accountability, responsibility, obligation 917n. *duty;* the least one can do, bare minimum; what one looks for, expectations; payability, dues 804n. *payment;* something owed, indebtedness 803n. *debt;* tribute, credit 158n. *attribution;* recognition, acknowledgment 907n. *thanks;* something to be said for, case for; qualification, deserts, merits; justification 927n. *vindication;* entitlement, claim, title 913n. *right;* birthright, patrimony 777n. *dower;* interest, vested i., vested right, prescriptive r., absolute r., indefeasible r., inalienable r.; legal right, easement, prescription, ancient rights; constitutional right, civil rights, bill of r.; privilege, exemption, immunity 919n. *non-liability;* prerogative, privilege; charter, warrant, license 756n. *permit;* liberty, franchise 744n. *freedom;* bond, security 767n. *title-deed;* patent, copyright; recovery of rights, restoration, compensation 787n. *restitution;* owner, title-holder 776n. *possessor;* heir 776n. *beneficiary;* claimant, plaintiff, appellant; man with a grievance, agitator 763n. *petitioner.*

Adj. *due,* owing, payable 803adj. *owed;* ascribable, attributable, assignable; merited, well-m., deserved, well-d., richly d., condign, earned, well-e., coming to one; admitted, allowed, sanctioned, warranted, licit, lawful 756adj. *permitted;* constitutional, entrenched, untouchable, uninfringeable, unchallengeable, unimpeachable, inviolable; privileged, sacrosanct; confirmed, vested, prescriptive, inalienable, imprescriptible; secured by law, legalized, legitimate, rightful, of right, de jure 953adj. *legal;* claimable, heritable, inheritable, earmarked, reserved; expected, fit, fitting, befitting; proper, en règle 642adj. *expedient.*

deserving, meriting, worthy of, worthy, meritorious, emeritus; grantworthy, credit-w.; justifiable, justified; entitled, having the right, having the title, claiming the right, asserting one's privilege, standing up for one's rights.

Vb. *be due,*—owing etc.adj.; ought, ought to be, should be, should have been; be one's due, be due to, have it coming; be the least one can offer, be the least one can do, be the bare minimum; behoove, befit, beseem 917vb. *be one's duty.*

claim, claim as a right, lay a claim, stake a c., take possession 786vb. *appropriate;* arrogate, demand one's rights, assert one's r., stand up for one's r., vindicate one's r. 927vb. *vindicate;* draw on, come down on for, lay under contribution, take one's toll 786vb. *levy;* call in (debts), reclaim, revendicate 656vb. *retrieve;* publish one's claims, declare one's right, clarigate; sue, demand redress 761vb. *request;* enforce a claim, exercise a right; establish a right, patent, copyright.

have a right, expect, have a right to e., claim; be entitled, be privileged, have the right to, have a claim to, make out one's case 478vb. *demonstrate;* have the law on one's side, have the court in one's favor, get a verdict.

deserve, merit, be worthy, be found w., have a claim on; earn, receive one's dues, meet with one's deserts, get one's d.; have it coming to one, have only oneself to thank.

grant claims, give every man his due 913vb. *be just;* ascribe, assign, credit 158vb. *attribute;* hand it to, acknowledge, recognize 907vb. *thank;* allow a claim, sanction a c., warrant, authorize 756vb. *permit;* admit a right, acknowledge a claim, satisfy a c., pay one's dues, honor, meet an obligation, honor a bill 804vb. *pay;* privilege, give a right, confer a r., entitle, vest with a title; allot, prescribe 783vb. *apportion;* legalize, legitimize 953vb. *make legal;* confirm, validate 488vb. *endorse.*

Adv. *duly,* by right, in one's own right, by law, de jure, ex officio, by divine right, jure divino; as expected of one, as required of one.

See: 158, 478, 488, 642, 656, 744, 756, 761, 763, 767, 776, 777, 783, 786, 787, 803, 804, 907, 913, 917, 919, 927, 953.

916 Undueness

N. *undueness,* not what one expects or would expect 508n. *inexpectation;* impropriety, unseemliness 847n. *bad taste;* unfittingness 643n. *inexpedience;* unworthiness, demerit 934n. *vice;* illicitness, illegitimacy, bastardy 954n. *illegality;* no thanks to 908n. *ingratitude;* absence of right, want of title, failure of t., nonentitlement; no claim, no right, no title, false t., weak t., empty t., courtesy t.; gratuitousness, gratuity, bonus, grace marks, baker's dozen, unearned increment; inordinacy, excessiveness, too much, overpayment 637n. *redundance;* imposition, exaction 735n. *severity;* unfair share, lion's s. 32n. *main part;* violation, breach, infraction, infringement, encroachment 306n. *overstepping;* profanation, desecration 980n. *impiety.*

arrogation, assumption, unjustified a., presumption, unwarranted p., swollen claims; pretendership, usurpation, tyranny; misappropriation 786n. *expropriation;* encroachment, inroad, trespass 306n. *overstepping.*

loss of right, disentitlement, disfranchisement, disqualification; alienization, denaturalization, detribalization 147n. *conversion;* forfeiture 772n. *loss;* dismissal, deprivation, dethronement 752n. *deposal;* ouster, dispossession 786n. *expropriation;* seizure, forcible s., robbery 788n. *stealing;* cancellation 752n. *abroga-*

tion; waiver, abdication 621n. *relinquishment.*
usurper, arrogator 735n. *tyrant;* pretender 545n. *imposter;* desecrator; violator, infringer, encroacher, trespasser, squatter.
Adj. *undue,* not owing, unattributable; unowed, gratuitous, by favor; not expected, unlooked for, uncalled for 508adj. *unexpected;* improper, unmeet, unseemly, unfitting, unbefitting, inappropriate 643adj. *inexpedient;* preposterous, not to be thought of, out of the question 497 adj. *absurd.*
unwarranted, unwarrantable; unauthorized, unsanctioned, unallowed, unlicensed, unchartered, unconstitutional; unlegalized, illicit, illegitimate, ultra vires 954adj. *illegal;* arrogated, usurped, stolen, borrowed; excessive, presumptuous, assuming 878adj. *insolent;* unjustified, unjustifiable 914adj. *wrong;* unclaimable, undeserved, unmerited, unearned; overpaid, underpaid; invalid, weak; false, spurious 954adj. *bastard;* fictitious, would-be 850adj. *affected.*
unentitled, without title, uncrowned; unqualified, without qualifications, unempowered, incompetent; unworthy, undeserving, meritless, unmeritorious; underprivileged, unprivileged, without rights, unchartered, unfranchised, voteless; disentitled, discrowned; dethroned, deposed; disqualified, invalidated, disfranchised, defrocked; deprived, bereft, dispossessed, expropriated; forfeited, forfeit.
Vb. *be undue,*—undeserved etc.adj.; not be due, be unclaimed, be unclaimable; show ill-taste, misbecome, misbeseem 847vb. *vulgarize;* presume, arrogate 878vb. *be insolent;* usurp, borrow 788vb. *steal;* trespass, squat 306vb. *encroach;* infringe, break, violate 954vb. *be illegal;* desecrate, profane 980vb. *be impious;* underpay, overpay.
disentitle, uncrown, unthrone 752vb. *depose;* disqualify, unfrock, disfranchise, alienize, denaturalize, detribalize, denationalize; invalidate 752vb. *abrogate;* disallow 757vb. *prohibit;* dispossess, expropriate 786 vb. *deprive;* forfeit, declare f.; defeat a claim, mock the claims of; make illegitimate, illegalize 954vb. *make illegal;* bastardize, debase 655vb. *impair.*
Adv. *unduly,* improperly; undeservedly, without desert, no thanks to.
See: 32, 147, 306, 497, 508, 545, 621, 637, 643, 655, 735, 752, 757, 772, 786, 788, 847, 850, 878, 908, 914, 934, 954, 980.

917 Duty

N. *duty,* what ought to be done, what is up to one, the right thing, the proper t., the decent t.; one's duty, bounden d., imperative d., inescapable d.; obligation, liability, onus, responsibility, accountability 915n. *dueness;* fealty, allegiance, loyalty 739n. *obedience;* sense of duty, dutifulness, duteousness 597n. *willingness;* discharge of duty, performance, acquittal, discharge 768n. *observance;* call of duty, claims of conscience, case of c., matter of duty; bond, tie, engagement, commitment, word, pledge 764n. *promise;* task, office, charge 751n. *commission;* walk of life, profession 622n. *vocation.*
conscience, professional c., tender c., nonconformist c., exacting c., peremptory c.; categorical imperative, inward monitor, inner voice, "still, small voice," "stern daughter of the voice of God."
code of duty, code of honor, unwritten code, professional c., Bushido; decalogue, Ten Commandments, Twelve Tables, Hippocratic oath 693n. *precept.*
morals, morality 933n. *virtue;* honor 929n. *probity;* moral principles, ideals, high i., standards, high s., professional s.; ethics, Christian e., professional e.; ethology, deontology, casuistry, ethical philosophy, moral p., moral science, idealism, utilitarianism, behaviorism 449n. *philosophy.*
Adj. *dutied,* on duty, duty-bound, bounden, bound by duty, pressed by d., called by d.; under duty, in duty bound; obliged, obligated, beholden, under obligation; tied, bound, sworn, pledged, committed, engaged; unexempted, liable, amenable, chargeable, answerable, responsible, accountable; in honor bound, bound in conscience, answerable to God; warned by conscience, plagued by c., conscience-struck 939adj. *repentant;* conscientious, observant, duteous, dutiful 739adj. *obedient;* vowed, under a vow.
obligatory, incumbent, imposed, behooving, up to one; binding, de rigueur, compulsive, peremptory, operative 740adj. *compelling;* inescap-

able, unavoidable; strict, unconditional, categorical.
ethical, moral 933adj. virtuous; honest, decent 929adj. *honorable;* moralistic, ethological, casuistical; moralizing; idealistic; utilitarian.
Vb. *be one's duty,* be incumbent, behoove, become, befit, beseem 915 vb. *be due;* devolve on, belong to; pertain to, fall to, be involved in one's office, arise from one's functions; lie, rest, rest on one's shoulders.
incur a duty, make it one's d., take on oneself, accept responsibility, shoulder one's r.; make oneself liable, commit oneself, pledge o., engage for 764vb. *promise;* assume one's functions, enter upon one's office, receive a posting; have the office, have the function, have the charge, have the duty; owe it to oneself, feel it up to one; feel duty's call, accept the c., answer the c., submit to one's vocation.
do one's duty, fulfill one's d. 739vb. *obey;* discharge, acquit, perform 676vb. *do;* do one's office, discharge one's functions 768vb. *observe;* be on duty, stay at one's post, go down with one's ship; come up to what is expected of one, not be found wanting; keep faith with one's conscience, face one's obligations, discharge an obligation, acquit oneself of an o., redeem a pledge; honor, meet, pay up 804vb. *pay.*
impose a duty, require, oblige, look to, call upon; devolve, call to office, swear one in, offer a post, post 751 vb. *commission;* assign a duty, saddle with, detail, order, enjoin, decree 737vb. *command;* tax, task, overtask, o'er-labor 684vb. *fatigue;* exact 735vb. *be severe;* demand obedience, expect it of one 507vb. *expect;* bind, condition 766vb. *give terms;* bind over, take security 764 vb. *take a pledge.*
Adv. *on duty,* under d., in the line of d., as in duty bound; at one's post; in foro conscientiae; with a safe conscience.
See: 449, 507, 597, 622, 676, 684, 693, 735, 737, 739, 740, 751, 764, 766, 768, 804, 915, 929, 933, 939.

918 Dutilessness

N. *dutilessness,* default, want of duty, failure of d., dereliction of d.; neglect, laches, culpable negligence 458 n. *negligence;* undutifulness, unduteousness 921n. *disrespect;* malingering, evasion of duty 620n. *avoidance;* non-practice, non-performance 769n. *non-observance;* idleness, laziness 679n. *sluggishness;* forgetfulness 506n. *oblivion;* noncooperation, want of alacrity 598n. *unwillingness;* truancy, absenteeism 190n. *absence;* abscondence 667n. *escape;* infraction, violation, breach of orders, indiscipline, mutiny, rebellion 738n. *disobedience;* incompetence, mismanagement 695n. *bungling;* obstruction, sabotage 702 n. *hindrance;* desertion, defection 603n. *tergiversation;* disloyalty, prodition, treachery 930n. *perfidy;* secession, breakaway 978n. *schism;* irresponsibility, escapism; truant, absentee, malingerer, defaulter 620n. *avoider;* deserter, absconder 667n. *escaper;* betrayer, traitor 603n. *tergiversator;* saboteur 702n. *hinderer;* mutineer, rebel 738n. *revolter;* seceder 978n. *schismatic;* escapist 620n. *avoider.*
Adj. *dutiless,* wanting in duty, uncooperative 598adj. *unwilling;* undutiful, unduteous, unfilial, undaughterly 921adj. *disrespectful;* mutinous, rebellious 738adj. *disobedient;* disloyal, treacherous 930 adj. *perfidious;* irresponsible, unreliable; truant, absentee 190adj. *absent;* absconding 667adj. *escaped.*
Vb. *fail in duty,* neglect one's d., commit laches 458vb. *neglect;* ignore one's obligations 458vb. *disregard;* oversleep 679vb. *sleep;* default, let one down, leave one in the lurch 728vb. *fail;* mismanage, bungle 495 vb. *blunder;* not remember 506vb. *forget;* shirk, evade, wriggle out of, malinger, dodge the column 620vb. *avoid;* play truant, overstay leave 190vb. *be absent;* abscond 667vb. *escape;* quit, scuttle, abandon, abandon one's post, desert, desert the colors 621vb. *relinquish;* break orders, disobey o., violate o., exceed one's instructions 738vb. *disobey;* mutiny, rebel 738vb. *revolt;* be disloyal, prove treacherous, betray 603vb. *tergiversate;* strike, strike work, come out 145vb. *cease;* sabotage 702vb. *obstruct;* noncooperate, withdraw, walk out, break away, secede 978vb. *schismatize.*
See: 145, 190, 458, 495, 506, 598, 603, 620, 621, 667, 679, 695, 702, 728, 738, 769, 921, 930, 978.

919 Non-liability

N. *non-liability,* non-responsibility,

exemption, dispensation; conscience-clause, escape-c. 468n. *qualification;* immunity, impunity, privilege, special p., clergiability, benefit of clergy; extraterritoriality, capitulations; franchise, charter 915n. *dueness;* independence, liberty, the four freedoms 744n. *freedom;* license, leave 756n. *permission;* congé, aegrotat, certificate of exemption 756n. *permit;* excuse, exoneration, exculpation 960n. *acquittal;* absolution, pardon, amnesty 909n. *forgiveness;* discharge, release 746n. *liberation;* renunciation 621n. *relinquishment;* evasion of responsibility, escapism, self-exemption, washing one's hands, passing the buck. 753n. *resignation.*

Adj. *non-liable,* not responsible, not answerable, unaccountable, unpunishable; unbound, unencumbered, unentailed; excused, exonerated 960 adj. *acquitted;* dispensed, exempted, privileged, prerogatived; clergiable; shielded, protected; untouched, exempt, immune; unaffected, well out of; independent, unconfined, scot-free 744adj. *free;* tax-free, post-f., duty-f. 812adj. *uncharged.*

Vb. *exempt,* set apart, segregate 883 vb. *seclude;* eliminate, count out, rule o. 57vb. *exclude;* excuse, exonerate, exculpate 960vb. *acquit;* grant absolution, absolve, shrive; pardon 909vb. *forgive;* spare 905 vb. *show mercy;* grant immunity, privilege, charter 756vb. *permit;* license, dispense, give dispensation, grant impunity; amnesty 506vb. *forget;* enfranchise, manumit, set at liberty, release 746vb. *liberate;* pass over, stretch a point 736vb. *be lenient.*

be exempt,—exempted etc.adj.; have one's withers unwrung, owe no responsibility, have no liability, not come within the scope of, not come within the mischief of; enjoy immunity, enjoy impunity, enjoy a privileged position, enjoy independence 744vb. *be free;* spare oneself the necessity, exempt oneself, excuse oneself, absent oneself, take leave, go on leave 190vb. *go away;* transfer the responsibility, pass the buck, shift the blame 272vb. *transfer;* evade *or* escape liability, get away with 667vb. *escape;* own *or* admit no responsibility, wash one's hands.

See: 57, 190, 272, 468, 506, 621, 667, 736, 744, 746, 753, 756, 812, 883, 905, 909, 915, 960.

920 Respect

N. *respect,* regard, consideration, esteem, estimation, honor, favor, 866n. *repute;* polite regard, attention, attentions, flattering a. 884n. *courtesy;* due respect, respectfulness, deference, humbleness 872n. *humility;* obsequiousness 879n. *servility;* humble service, fealty, devotion 739n. *loyalty;* admiration, awe 864n. *wonder;* terror 854n. *fear;* reverence, veneration, adoration 981n. *worship.*

respects, regards, duty, devoirs, kind remembrances, greetings 884n. *courteous act;* due respect, address of welcome, illuminated address, salutation, salaam, namaskar; nod, bob, duck, bow, scrape, curtsy, genuflection, one's knees, prostration, kowtow 311n. *obeisance;* reverence, homage; salute, presenting arms; honors of war, flags flying.

Adj. *respectful,* deferential, knowing one's place 872adj. *humble;* obsequious, bootlicking 879adj. *servile;* submissive 721adj. *submitting;* reverent, reverential 981adj. *worshiping;* admiring, awe-struck 864adj. *wondering;* polite 884adj. *courteous;* ceremonious, with hand at the salute, cap in hand, bare-headed; kneeling on one's knees, prostrate; bobbing, ducking, bowing, scraping, bending, stooping; obeisant, showing respect, rising, standing, on one's feet, all standing.

respected, admired, honored, esteemed, revered 866adj. *reputable;* reverend, venerable; time-honored 866adj. *worshipful;* imposing 821 adj. *impressive;* received with respect, received all standing, saluted.

Vb. *respect,* entertain r., hold in r., hold in estimation, hold in honor, think well of, rank high, place h., look up to, esteem, regard, tender, value; admire 864vb. *wonder;* reverence, venerate, exalt, magnify 866vb. *honor;* adore 981vb. *worship;* idolize 982vb. *idolatrize;* revere, stand in awe, have a wholesome respect for 854vb. *fear;* know one's place, defer to 721vb. *submit;* pay tribute to 923vb. *praise;* do homage to, chair, lionize 876vb. *celebrate.*

show respect, render honor, homage, pay h., do the honors 884vb. *pay respects;* make way for, leave room for, keep one's distance, know one's place; go to meet, welcome, hail, meet with flags flying, salute, present arms, turn out the guard 884vb.

greet; cheer, drink to 876vb. *toast;* bob, duck, bow, scrape, make a leg, curtsy, kneel, kowtow, prostrate oneself 311vb. *stoop;* observe decorum, stand on ceremony, stand, rise, rise to one's feet, rise from one's seat, stand bareheaded; humble oneself, condescend 872vb. *be humble.*

command respect, inspire r., awe, strike with a., overawe, impose 821 vb. *impress;* enjoy a reputation, rank high, stand h., stand well in all men's eyes 866vb. *have repute;* compel respect, demand r., extort admiration 864vb. *be wonderful;* dazzle, bedazzle 875vb. *be ostentatious;* receive respect, gain honor, gain a reputation, win golden opinions 923vb. *be praised.*

Adv. *respectfully,* humbly, with all respect, with due deference; obsequiously, reverentially, reverently; saving your grace, saving your presence.

See: 311, 721, 739, 821, 854, 864, 866, 872, 875, 876, 879, 884, 923, 981, 982.

921 Disrespect

N. *disrespect,* want of respect, scant r., disrespectfulness, irreverence, impoliteness, discourtesy 885n. *rudeness;* disesteem, dishonor, disfavor 924n. *disapprobation;* neglect, undervaluation 483n. *underestimation;* low estimation 867n. *disrepute;* depreciation, disparagement 926n. *detraction;* vilipendency, contumely 899n. *scurrility;* scorn 922n. *contempt;* mockery 851n. *ridicule;* desecration 980n. *impiety.*

indignity, humiliation, affront, insult, slight, snub, slap in the face, outrage 878n. *insolence;* snook, snooks 878n. *sauciness;* gibe, taunt, jeer, fling 922n. *contempt;* quip, sarcasm, mock, flout 851n. *ridicule;* hiss, hoot, boo, catcall, brickbat, brick 924n. *disapprobation.*

Adj. *disrespectful,* wanting in respect, slighting, neglectful 458adj. *negligent;* irreverent, irreverential, aweless 865adj. *unastonished;* sacrilegious 980adj. *profane;* outspoken, overcandid 573adj. *plain;* rude, impolite 885adj. *discourteous;* airy, breezy, off-handed, cavalier, familiar, cheeky, saucy 878adj. *impertinent;* insulting, outrageous 878adj. *insolent;* flouting, jeering, gibing, scoffing, mocking, satirical, cynical, sarcastic 851adj. *derisive;* injurious, contumelious, scurrilous, scurrile 899adj. *maledicent;* depreciative, pejorative 483adj. *depreciating;* snobbish, supercilious, disdainful, scornful 922adj. *despising;* unflattering, uncomplimentary 924adj. *disapproving.*

unrespected, disrespected, held in low esteem, of no account 867adj. *disreputable;* ignored, unregarded, disregarded, unsaluted, ungreeted 458 adj. *neglected;* unenvied, unadmired, unflattered, unreverenced, unrevered, unworshiped; underrated, disparaged 483adj. *undervalued;* looked down on, spat on 922adj. *contemptible.*

Vb. *not respect,* deny r., disrespect; be unable to respect, have no respect for, have no regard f., have no use f. 924vb. *disapprove;* misprize, undervalue, underrate 483vb. *underestimate;* look down on, disdain, scorn 922vb. *despise;* run down, disparage 926vb. *defame;* spit on, toss aside 607vb. *reject;* show disrespect, want respect, fail in courtesy, remain seated, remain covered, keep one's hat on, push aside, shove a., crowd, jostle 885vb. *be rude;* ignore, turn one's back 458vb. *disregard;* snub, slight, put a slight upon, insult, affront, outrage 872vb. *humiliate;* dishonor, disgrace, put to shame, drag in the mud 867 vb. *shame;* trifle with, treat lightly 922vb. *hold cheap;* cheapen, lower, degrade 847vb. *vulgarize;* have no awe, not reverence, desecrate, profane 980vb. *be impious;* call names, vilipend, abuse, indulge in scurrilities 899vb. *curse;* taunt, twit, cock a snook 878vb. *be insolent;* laugh at, scoff, mock, flout, deride 851vb. *ridicule;* make mouths at, jeer, hiss, hoot, boo, point at, spit at 924vb. *exprobate;* mob, hound, chase 619 vb. *pursue;* pelt, stone, throw stones, heave a brick 712vb. *lapidate.*

Adv. *disrespectfully,* irreverently, profanely, sacrilegiously, contumeliously, injuriously; mockingly, derisively.

See: 458, 483, 573, 607, 619, 712, 847, 851, 865, 867, 872, 878, 885, 899, 922, 924, 926, 980.

922 Contempt

N. *contempt,* sovereign c., supreme c., utter c., unutterable c.; misprision, scorn, disdain, disdainfulness, superiority, loftiness 871n.

pride; contemptuousness, sniffiness; superciliousness, snobbishness 850n. *affectation;* superior airs, scornful eye, smile of contempt, curl of the lip, snort; slight, humiliation 921n. *disrespect;* sneer 926n. *detraction;* scoff, flout, mock 851n. *ridicule;* snub, rebuff, cut, cut direct 885n. *discourtesy.*

despisedness, unworthiness, contemptibility, insignificance, puerility, pitiability, futility 639n. *unimportance;* pettiness, meanness, littleness, paltriness 33n. *smallness;* reproach, a hissing and a reproach, byword of reproach 867n. *object of scorn.*

Adj. *despising,* full of contempt, contemptuous, disdainful, holier than thou, snooty, sniffy, snobbish; haughty, lofty, airy, supercilious 871adj. *proud;* scornful, contumelious, withering, jeering, sneering, booing 924adj. *disapproving;* disrespectful, impertinent 878adj. *insolent;* slighting, pooh-poohing 483 adj. *depreciating.*

contemptible, despicable, beneath contempt; abject, worthless 645adj. *bad;* petty, paltry, little, mean 33adj. *small;* spurned, spat on 607adj. *rejected;* scorned, despised, contemned, of no account 921adj. *unrespected;* trifling, pitiable, futile 639adj. *unimportant.*

Vb. *despise,* contemn, hold in despite, hold in contempt, feel utter contempt for, have no use for 921 vb. *not respect;* look down on, hold beneath one, be too high for, be too grand for 871vb. *be proud;* disdain, spurn, sniff at, snort at 607vb. *reject;* come it over, turn up one's nose, wrinkle the n., curl one's lips, toss one's head, snort; snub, turn one's back on 885vb. *be rude;* scorn, whistle, hiss, boo, point, point the finger of scorn 924 vb. *exprobate;* laugh at, turn to scorn, laugh to s., scoff, scout, flout, gibe, jeer, mock, deride 851vb. *ridicule;* trample on, ride roughshod over 735vb. *oppress;* disgrace, roll in the mire 867vb. *shame.*

hold cheap, disesteem, misprize 921 vb. *not respect;* ignore, dismiss, not mind 458vb. *disregard;* belittle, disparage, fail to appreciate, underrate, undervalue 483vb. *underestimate;* disprize, decry 926vb. *detract;* set no value on, set no store by, think nothing of, think small beer of, not care a rap for, not care a straw; laugh at, treat as a laughing matter, snap one's fingers at, set at naught, shrug away, pooh-pooh, say bah! slight, trifle with, treat lightly, treat like dirt, lower, degrade 872vb. *humiliate.*

Adv. *contemptuously,* disdainfully, scornfully, with contempt, with disdain.

contemptibly, pitiably, miserably; to one's utter contempt, to all men's contempt.

See: 33, 458, 483, 607, 639, 645, 735, 850, 851, 867, 871, 872, 878, 885, 921, 924, 926.

923 Approbation

N. *approbation,* approval sober a., modified rapture; satisfaction 828n. *content;* appreciation, recognition 907n. *gratitude;* good opinion, golden opinions, kudos, credit 866 n. *prestige;* regard, admiration, esteem 920n. *respect;* good books, good graces, grace, favor, popularity, affection 887n. *love;* adoption, acceptance, welcome, favorable reception 299n. *reception;* sanction 756n. *permission;* nod of approval, seal of a., blessing; nod, wink, thumbs up, consent 488n. *assent;* countenance, patronage, championship, advocacy 703n. *aid;* good word, kind w., testimonial, reference, commendation, recommendation 466n. *credential.*

praise, loud p., lyrical p., praise and glory, laud, laudation, invocation, benediction, blessing, benison; compliment, high c., encomium, eulogy, panegyric, glorification, adulation, idolatry 925n. *flattery;* hero-worship 864n. *wonder;* overpraise 482n. *overestimation;* faint praise, two cheers; shout of praise, hosanna; praises, song of praise, hymn of p., paean of p., dithyramb, doxology; tribute, credit, meed of praise, tribute of p. 907n. *thanks;* complimentary reference, bouquet, citation, commendation, official biography, hagiography; self-praise, self-glorification 877n. *boasting;* letters of gold; puffing, blurb 528n. *advertisement.*

applause, clamorous a., acclaim, universal a.; enthusiasm, excitement 821adj. *excitation;* warm reception, hero's welcome 876n. *celebration;* acclamation, plaudits, clapping, claque, whistling, cheering; clap, three cheers, paean, hosanna; thunderous applause, peal of a., shout of a., chorus of a., round of a., storm of a., ovation; encore, curtain call; bouquet, pat on the back.

commender, praiser, laudator, encomiast, eulogist, panegyrist; clapper, shouter, claqueur, claque; approver, friendly critic, admirer, devoted a., hero-worshiper; advocate, recommender, supporter, speaker for the motion 707n. *patron;* inscriber, dedicator; advertiser, blurb-writer, puffer, booster; agent, tout, touter, barker 528n. *publicizer;* canvasser, electioneer, election agent.

Adj. *approving,* uncensorious, uncomplaining, satisfied 828adj. *content;* favoring, supporting, advocating 703adj. *aiding;* benedictory 907 adj. *grateful;* approbatory, favorable, well-inclined; appreciative, complimentary, commendatory, laudatory, eulogistic, encomiastic, panegyrical, lyrical; admiring, hero-worshiping, idolatrous; lavish, generous; fulsome, over-praising, uncritical, undiscriminating; acclamatory, plausive, clapping, thundering, thunderous, clamorous 400adj. *loud;* dithyrambic, ecstatic 821adj. *excited.*

approvable, admissible, permissible, acceptable; worth-while 640adj. *useful;* deserving, meritorious, commendable, laudable, estimable, worthy, praiseworthy, creditable, admirable, uncensurable, unimpeachable, beyond all praise 646adj. *perfect;* enviable, desirable 859adj. *desired.*

approved, passed, tested, tried; uncensured, free from blame, stamped with approval, blessed; popular, in favor, in high f., in the good graces of, in good odor, in high esteem, thought well of 866adj. *reputable;* favored, backed, odds on 605adj. *chosen.*

Vb. *approve,* see nothing wrong with, sound pleased, have no fault to find, have nothing but praise for; like well 887vb. *love;* think well of, admire, esteem, tender, value, prize, treasure, cherish, set store by 866 vb. *honor;* appreciate, give credit, salute, take one's hat off to, hand it to, give full marks; think no worse of, think the better of; count it for merit, see the good points, see the good in one, think good, think perfect; think desirable 912vb. *envy;* think the best, award the palm; see to be good, find g., pronounce g., mark with approbation, seal *or* stamp with approval; accept, pass, tick off, give marks; nod, wink, nod one's approval, give one's assent 488vb. *assent;* sanction, bless, give one's blessing 756vb. *permit;* ratify 488vb. *endorse;* commend, recommend, advocate, support, back, favor, countenance, stand up for, speak up f., put in a word for, give one a reference, give one a testimonial 703vb. *patronize.*

praise, compliment, pay compliments 925vb. *flatter;* speak well of, speak highly, swear by; bless 907vb. *thank;* salute, pay tribute to, hand it to, take one's hat off to; commend, give praise, bepraise, laud, belaud, eulogize, panegyrize, laud to the skies, hymn, sound the praises, sing the p., hymn the p., swell the p., doxologize, exalt, extol, glorify, magnify; not spare one's blushes 546vb. *exaggerate;* puff, inflate, overpraise, overestimate 482vb. *overrate;* lionize, hero-worship, idolize 982vb. *idolatrize;* trumpet, write up, cry up, crack up, boost 528vb. *advertise;* praise oneself, glorify o. 877vb. *boast.*

applaud, receive with applause, welcome, hail, hail with satisfaction; acclaim, receive with acclamation, clap, clap one's hands, give a hand, stamp, whistle, thunder one's plaudits; cheer, raise a c., give three cheers, give three times three; cheer to the echo, shout for, root; clap on the back, pat on the back; welcome, garland, chair 876vb. *celebrate;* drink to 876vb. *toast.*

be praised,—praiseworthy etc.adj.; get a citation, be mentioned in dispatches; recommend oneself 866vb. *seek repute;* find favor, win praise, gain credit, earn golden opinions 866vb. *have repute;* get a compliment, receive a tribute, get a hand, get a clap, get a cheer; receive an ovation, take the house by storm 727vb. *triumph;* deserve praise, be to one's credit, redound to the honor; pass, do, pass muster, pass the test.

Adv. *approvingly,* admiringly, with admiration, with praises, with compliments; ungrudgingly, without demur; enviously.

commendably, admirably, wonderfully, unimpeachably; acceptably, satisfactorily, to satisfaction, to approval.

Int. bravo! well done! hear hear! encore! bis! three cheers! hurrah! hosanna!

See: 299, 400, 466, 482, 488, 528, 546, 605, 640, 646, 703, 707, 727, 756, 821, 828, 859, 864, 866, 876,

877, 887, 907, 912, 920, 925, 982.

924 Disapprobation

N. *disapprobation,* disapproval, dissatisfaction 829n. *discontent;* non-approval, return 607n. *rejection;* no permission 760n. *refusal;* disfavor, displeasure, unpopularity 861 n. *dislike;* disesteem 921n. *disrespect;* poor opinion, low o. 867n. *disrepute;* disparagement, decrial, crabbing, carping, niggling 926n. *detraction;* censoriousness, fault-finding 862n. *fastidiousness;* hostility 881n. *enmity;* objection, exception, cavil 468n. *qualification;* impugnation, improbation 479n. *confutation;* complaint, clamor, outcry, protest, tut-tut 762n. *deprecation;* indignation, explosion 891n. *anger;* sibilation, hissing, hiss, boo, countercheer, whistle, catcall, brick, brickbat 851 n. *ridicule;* ostracism, boycott, bar, color-b., ban, non-admission 57n. *exclusion;* blackball, blacklist, bad books; index, index expurgatorious.

censure, dispraise, discommendation, blame, reprehension, impeachment, inculpation 928n. *accusation;* home-truth, no compliment, poor c., left-handed c., back-handed c.; criticism, hostile c., stricture; hyper-criticism, fault-finding; hostile attack, slashing a., onslaught 712n. *attack;* bad press, critical review, hostile r., slashing r., slating; open letter, tirade, jeremiad, philippic, diatribe, speech for the opposition 704n. *opposition;* conviction 961n. *condemnation;* false accusation 928 n. *false charge;* slur, slander, insinuation, innuendo 926n. *calumny;* brand, stigma.

reproach, reproaches, exprobation; objurgation, rixation, wordy quarrel 709n. *quarrel;* home-truths, invective, vituperation, calling names, bawling out, shouting down 899n. *scurrility;* execration 899n. *malediction;* personalities, personal remarks, aspersion, reflection 921n. *indignity;* taunt, sneer 878n. *insolence;* sarcasm, irony, satire, biting wit, biting tongue, cut, hit, home-thrust 851n. *ridicule;* rough side of one's tongue, tongue-lashing, hard words, cutting w., bitter w. (**see** *reprimand*); silent reproach, disapproving look, dirty l., black l. 893n. *sullenness.*

reprimand, remonstrance 762n. *deprecation;* stricture, animadversion, reprehension, reprobation; censure, rebuke, reproof, snub; rocket, raspberry; piece of one's mind, expression of displeasure, mark of d., black mark; castigation, correction, rap over the knuckles, box on the ears 963n. *punishment;* inculpation, admonition, admonishment, increpation, tongue-lashing, chiding, upbraiding, scolding, rating, slating, strafing, trouncing, dressing down, blowing up, wigging, trimming, carpeting, mauvais quart d'heure; talking to, lecture, curtain l., jobation.

disapprover, no friend, no admirer; non-favorer, non-supporter, non-voter; damper, death's head, spoil-sport, misery 834n. *moper;* pussy-foot, puritan, rigorist 950n. *prude;* attacker, opposer 705n. *opponent;* critic, hard c., hostile c., captious c., knocker, fault-finder; reprover, castigator, censurer, censor; satirist, lampooner, mocker 926n. *detractor;* brander, stigmatizer; misogynist 902 n. *misanthrope;* grouser, groucher, man with a grievance 829n. *malcontent.*

Adj. *disapproving,* unapproving, unable to approve, not amused, unamused; shocked, scandalized; unadmiring, unimpressed; disillusioned 509adj. *disappointed;* sparing of praise, grudging; silent 582adj. *taciturn;* disapprobatory, unfavorable, spitting, expectoratory; hostile 881adj. *inimical;* objecting, protesting, clamorous 762adj. *deprecatory;* reproachful, chiding, scolding, upbraiding, vituperative, objurgatory, personal, scurrilous 899adj. *maledictory;* critical, unflattering, uncomplimentary; withering, hard-hitting, strongly worded; over-critical, hypercritical, captious, fault-finding, niggling, carping; disparaging, defamatory, damaging 926adj. *detracting;* caustic, sharp, bitter, venomous, trenchant, mordant; sarcastic, sardonic, cynical 851adj. *derisive;* censorious, holier than thou; blaming, faulting, censuring, reprimanding, recriminative, denunciatory, accusatory, condemning, damning, damnatory 928adj. *accusing.*

disapproved, unapproved, blacklisted, blackballed 607adj. *rejected;* unsatisfactory, found wanting 636adj. *insufficient;* plowed, plucked, failed 728adj. *unsuccessful;* canceled 752 adj. *abrogated;* deleted, censored 550adj. *obliterated;* out of favor, under a cloud; unpraised, dispraised, criticized, shot at, decried, run down, slandered, calumniated; lectured, henpecked, nagged, reprimanded, scolded, chid; on the mat, on the carpet; unregretted, unlamented, unbewailed, unpitied 861adj. *disliked;* hooted, hissed, hissed off the stage, exploded, discredited, disowned, out; in bad odor, in one's bad books 867adj. *disreputable.*

blameworthy, not good enough, too bad; blamable, exceptionable, open to criticism, censurable, condemnable 645adj. *damnable;* reprehensible, dishonorable, unjustifiable 867 adj. *discreditable;* unpraiseworthy, uncommendable, not to be recommended, not to be thought of; reprobate, culpable, to blame 928 adj. *accusable.*

Vb. disapprove, not admire, hold no brief for, fail to appreciate, have no praise for, not think much of, think little of; think the worse of, think ill of, disprize 922vb. *despise;* not pass, fail, plow, pluck; return 607 vb. *reject;* disallow 757vb. *prohibit;* cancel 752vb *abrogate;* censor 550vb. *obliterate;* withhold approval, look grave, shake one's head, not hold with 489vb. *dissent;* disfavor, reprehend, lament, deplore 830vb. *regret;* abhor, reprobate 861vb. *dislike;* wash one's hands, disown, look askance, avoid, ignore; keep at a distance, draw the line, ostracize, ban, bar, blacklist 57vb. *exclude;* protest, tut-tut, remonstrate, object, except, demur 762vb. *deprecate;* discountenance, show disapproval, exclaim, shout down, bawl d., hoot, boo, countercheer, hiss, whistle, explode, drive off the stage; throw mud, throw bad eggs, throw bricks, stone, throw stones 712vb. *lapidate;* hound, chase, mob, lynch; make a face, make a moue, make mouths at, spit; look black 893vb. *be sullen;* look daggers 891vb. *be angry.*

dispraise, discommend, not recommend, give no marks to, damn with faint praise, damn 961vb. *condemn;* criticize, fault, pick holes, cut up, crab, cavil, depreciate, run down, belittle 926vb. *detract;* oppose, tilt at, shoot at 712vb. *attack;* weigh in, hit hard, savage, maul, slash, slate, scourge, flay; inveigh, thunder, fulminate, storm against, rage a. 61 vb. *rampage;* shout down, cry shame, slang, call names, gird, rail, revile, abuse, heap a., pour vitriol, vilipend, objurgate, anathematize, execrate 899vb. *curse;* vilify, blacken, bespatter 926vb. *defame;* exprobate, stigmatize, brand, pillory, gibbet, expose; reproach, denounce, recriminate 928vb. *accuse;* sneer, twit, taunt, jibe 921vb. *not respect.*

reprove, reprehend, rebuke, administer a r., snub; call to order, caution, wag one's finger 664vb. *warn;* animadvert, reflect on, notice, take severe n., book, give one a black mark; censure, reprimand, take to task, rap over the knuckles, box the ears; tick off, tell off, have one's head for, carpet, have on the carpet, have on the mat, haul over the coals; remonstrate, expostulate, admonish, castigate, correct; lecture, read one a lecture, read one a lesson, give one a talking to, chide, dress down, trounce, trim, wig, give one a wigging, browbeat, blow up, tear strips off (**see** *exprobate*); chastise 963vb. *punish.*

blame, find fault, carp, pick holes in; hit at, peck at, henpeck 709vb. *bicker;* reprehend, hold to blame, pick on, put the blame on, hold responsible; throw the first stone, inculpate, incriminate, complain against, impute, impeach, charge, criminate 928vb. *accuse;* round on, return the charge, retort the c., recriminate 714b. *retaliate;* think the worst of 961vb. *condemn.*

exprobate, exprobrate, fall foul of, reproach, heap reproaches, load with r.; reprobate, increpate, upbraid, slate, rate, berate, rail, strafe, shend, revile, abuse, blackguard 899vb. *curse;* go for, inveigh, scold, tongue, tongue-lash, lash, lick with the rough edge of one's tongue, give one a piece of one's mind, give one what for, not pull one's punches.

incur blame, take the blame, take the rap, stand the racket, be held responsible, have to answer for; be open to criticism, blot one's copybook, get a bad name 867vb. *lose repute;* be up on a charge, stand accused; stand corrected; be a caution, be an example, be a scandal, scandalize, shock, revolt 861vb. *cause dislike.*

Adv. *disapprovingly,* reluctantly, against one's better judgment, under protest; reproachfully, complainingly.

See: 57, 61, 468, 479, 489, 509, 550, 582, 607, 636, 645, 664, 704, 705, 709, 712, 714, 728, 752, 757, 760, 762, 829, 830, 834, 851, 861, 862, 867, 878, 881, 891, 893, 899, 902,

921, 922, 926, 928, 950, 961, 963.

925 Flattery

N. *flattery,* cajolery, wheedling, taffy, blarney, blandiloquence, blandishment; butter, soft soap, soft-sawder, salve, lip-salve, rose water, incense, adulation; voice of the charmer, honeyed words, soft nothings 889n. *endearment;* compliment, pretty speeches; unctuousness, euphemism, glozing, gloze; captation, coquetry, fawning, backscratching; assentation, obsequiousness, flunkyism, sycophancy, toadying, tuft-hunting 879n. *servility;* insincerity, hypocrisy, tongue in cheek, lip-homage, mouth-honor, claque 542n. *sham.*

flatterer, adulator, blarneyman, cajoler, wheedler; tout, puffer, booster, claqueur 923n. *commender;* courtier, assentator, yes-man 488n. *assenter;* pickthank, placebo, fawner, sycophant, parasite, minion, hanger-on 879n. *toady;* fair-weather friend, hypocrite 545n. *deceiver.*

Adj. *flattering,* overpraising, overdone 546adj. *exaggerated;* boosting, puffing; complimentary, over-complimentary, full of compliments; fulsome, adulatory, incense-breathing; cajoling, wheedling, coaxing, blarneying, blandiloquent, smooth-tongued; mealy-mouthed, glozing, canting; smooth, oily, unctuous, soapy, slimy, smarmy; obsequious, all over one, courtierly, courtier-like, fawning, crawling, back-scratching, sycophantic 879adj. *servile;* specious, plausible, beguiling, ingratiating, insinuating; lulling, soothing; vote-catching, vote-snatching; false, insincere, tongue-in-cheek, unreliable 541adj. *hypocritical.*

Vb. *flatter,* deal in flattery, have kissed the Blarney stone; compliment, overpraise, overdo it, lay it on thick, lay it on with a trowel, not spare one's blushes; puff, boost, cry up 482vb. *overrate;* adulate, burn incense to, assail with flattery, turn one's head 873vb. *make conceited;* butter up, sawder, soap; coo, blarney, flannel; wheedle, coax, cajole, glaver, cog; lull, soothe, beguile 542vb. *deceive;* humor, gild the pill, make things pleasant, tell a flattering tale, gloze, collogue; blandish, smooth, smarm; make much of, be all over one 889vb. *caress;* fawn, fawn on, cultivate, court, pay court to, play the courtier; smirk 835vb. *smile;* scratch one's back, curry favor, make up to, suck up to; truckle to, toady to, pander to 879vb. *be servile;* insinuate oneself, earwig, creep into one's good graces; flatter oneself, lay the flattering unction to one's soul, have a swelled head 873 vb. *be vain.*

Adv. *flatteringly,* speciously; ad captandum.

See: 482, 488, 541, 542, 545, 546, 835, 873, 879, 889, 923.

926 Detraction

N. *detraction,* faint praise, two cheers, understatement 483n. *underestimation;* criticism, hostile c., destructive c., Zoilism, unfavorable appreciation, bad review, bad press 924n. *disapprobation;* onslaught 712n. *attack;* impeachment 928n. *accusation;* exposure, bad light 867n. *disrepute;* decrial, disparagement, depreciation, running down; lowering, derogation; slighting language, scorn 922n. *contempt;* obtrectation, evil speaking, obloquy 899n. *malediction;* contumely, vilification, abuse, invective 899n. *scurrility;* calumniation, defamation, traducement 543n. *untruth;* backbiting, cattiness, spite 898n. *malevolence;* aspersion, reflection (**see** *calumny*); whisper, innuendo, insinuation, whispering campaign; smear campaign, mud-slinging, smirching, denigration; brand, stigma; muckraking, scandal-mongering, chronique scandaleuse; gutter 649n. *sink;* nil admirari, disillusionment, cynicism 865n. *non-wonder.*

calumny, slander, libel, false report, roorback 543n. *untruth;* a defamation, defamatory remark, damaging report; smear, smear-word, dirty word 867n. *slur;* offensive remark, personal r., personality, insult, taunt 921n. *indignity;* scoff, sarcasm 851n. *ridicule;* sneer, sniff; caricature 522 n. *misrepresentation;* skit, lampoon, pasquinade, squib 851n. *satire;* scandal, scandalous talk, gossip.

detractor, decrier, disparager, depreciator, slighter, despiser; non-admirer, laudator temporis acti; debunker, deflater, cynic; mocker, scoffer, satirizer, satirist, lampooner; castigator, denouncer, reprover, censurer, censor 924n. *disapprover;* no respecter of persons, no flatterer, candid friend, candid critic; critic, hostile c., destructive c., attacker; arch-critic, chief accuser, impeacher 928n. *accuser;* captious critic, knocker, Zoilus; fault-finder, carper, caviler, niggler, word-catcher; barracker 702n. *hinderer;* vandal, philistine 847n. *vulgarian.*

defamer, calumniator, traducer, destroyer of reputations; smircher, smearer, slanderer, libeler; backbiter, gossiper, scandal-monger, muckraker; denigrator, mud-slinger; brander, stigmatizer; vituperator, reviler, abusive person, railer, scold, Thersites 892n. *shrew;* poison pen.

Adj. *detracting,* derogative, derogatory, pejorative; disparaging, depreciatory, decrying, crying down, slighting, contemptuous 922adj. *despising;* whispering, insinuating, blackening, denigratory, mud-slinging, smearing; compromising, damaging; scandalous, obloquious, calumnious, calumniatory, defamatory, slanderous, libelous; insulting 921 adj. *disrespectful;* contumelious, injurious, abusive, scurrilous, foul-spoken, evil-speaking 899adj. *maledicent;* shrewish, scolding, caustic, bitter, venomous, denunciatory, castigatory, accusatory, blaming 924adj. *disapproving;* sarcastic, mocking, scoffing, sneering, cynical 851adj. *derisive;* catty, spiteful 898adj. *malevolent;* unflattering, candid 573n. *plain.*

Vb. *detract,* derogate, depreciate, disparage, run down; debunk, deflate, cut down to life-size 921vb. *not respect;* minimize 483vb. *underestimate;* belittle, slight 922vb. *hold cheap;* sneer at, sniff at 922vb. *despise;* decry, cry down, damn with faint praise, fail to appreciate 924 vb. *disapprove;* find nothing to praise, criticize, crab, gird, fault, find f., pick holes in, slash, slate, pull to pieces, tear to p., rend 924 vb. *dispraise;* caricature, guy 552vb. *misrepresent;* lampoon, berhyme, dip one's pen in gall, pour vitriol 851vb. *satirize;* scoff, mock 851vb. *ridicule;* make catty remarks; whisper, insinuate.

defame, dishonor, damage, compromise, scandalize, degrade, lower, put to shame 867vb. *shame;* give a dog a bad name, lower *or* lessen *or* destroy one's reputation; denounce, expose, gibbet, pillory, stigmatize, brand 928vb. *accuse;* calumniate, libel, slander, traduce, malign; vilify, denigrate, blacken, tarnish, sully, breathe upon, blow u.; asperse, cast aspersions, reflect upon, put in a bad light; speak ill of, speak evil, gossip, make scandal, talk about, backbite, talk behind one's back; smear, besmear, smirch, besmirch, spatter, bespatter, throw mud, fling dirt, drag in the gutter; hound, witch-hunt 619vb. *hunt;* look for scandal, smell evil, muckrake, rake in the gutter.

See: 483, 543, 552, 573, 619, 649, 702, 712, 847, 851, 865, 867, 892, 898, 899, 921, 922, 924, 928.

927 Vindication

N. *vindication,* restoration, rehabilitation 787n. *restitution;* triumph of justice, right triumphant, wrong righted, right asserted, truth established; exoneration, exculpation, clearance 960n. *acquitted;* justification, good grounds, just cause, every excuse; compurgation, apologetics, self-defense, apologia, defense, legal d., good d., successful d.; alibi, plea, excuse, whitewash, gloss 614n. *pretext;* fair excuse, good e., just e. 494n. *truth;* partial excuse, extenuation, palliation, mitigation, mitigating circumstance, extenuating c., palliative 468n. *qualification;* counter-argument 479n. *confutation;* reply, reply for the defense, rebuttal 460n. *rejoinder;* recrimination, tu quoque, counter-charge, charge retorted; justifiable charge, true bill 928n. *accusation;* bringing to book, meed of one's deserts, just punishment 963n. *punishment.*

vindicator, vindicatrix, punisher 910n. *avenger;* apologist, advocate, defender, champion; justifier, excuser, whitewasher, varnisher; compurgator, oath-helper 466n. *witness;* self-defender, defendant 928n. *accused person.*

Adj. *vindicating,* vindicatory, vindicative, avenging; apologetic, exculpatory, justifying, defending; extenuatory, mitigating, palliative.

vindicable, justifiable, maintainable, defensible, arguable; specious, plausible; allowable, warrantable, unobjectionable 756adj. *permitted;* excusable, having some excuse, pardonable, forgivable, venial, expiable; vindicated, justified, within one's rights, not guilty 935adj. *innocent;* justified by the event 494adj. *true.*

Vb. *vindicate,* revenge 910vb. *avenge;* rescue, deliver 746vb. *liberate;* do justice to, give the devil his due 915vb. *grant claims;* set right, restore, rehabilitate 787vb. *restitute;* maintain, speak up for, argue f., contend f., advocate 475vb. *argue;*

undertake to prove, bear out, confirm, make good, prove the truth of, prove 478vb. *demonstrate;* champion, stand up for, stick up for 713 vb. *defend;* support, keep one in countenance 703vb. *patronize.*

justify, warrant, justify by the event, give grounds for, provide justification, furnish an excuse, give a handle, give one cause; put one in the right, put one in the clear, clear, exonerate, exculpate 960vb. *acquit;* give color to, color, whitewash, varnish, gloss; salve one's conscience, justify oneself, defend o. 614vb. *plead;* plead one's own cause, take a plea, say in defense, rebut the charge, plead ignorance, confess and avoid.

extenuate, excuse, make excuses for, make allowance for; palliate, mitigate, soften, mince, soft-pedal, slur, slur over, gloss, gloss over, varnish, whitewash; take the will for the deed 736vb. *be lenient.*

See: 460, 466, 468, 475, 478, 479, 494, 614, 703, 713, 736, 746, 756, 787, 910, 915, 928, 935, 960, 963.

928 Accusation

N. *accusation,* complaint, charge, true c., home-truth; censure, blame, stricture 924n. *reproach;* challenge 711n. *defiance;* inculpation, crimination; countercharge, recrimination, tu quoque argument 460n. *rejoinder;* twit, taunt 921n. *indignity;* imputation, allegation, information, delation, denunciation; plaint, suit, action 959n. *litigation;* prosecution, impeachment, attainder, arraignment, indictment, citation, summons; bill of indictment, bill of attainder, true bill; gravamen, substance of a charge, main c., head and front of one's offending; case, case to answer, case for the prosecution 475n. *reasons;* items in the indictment, particular charge, count 466n. *evidence;* no excuses 961n. *condemnation.*

false charge, faked c., cooked-up c., trumped-up c., put-up job, frame-up; false information, designing i., perjured testimony, hostile evidence, suspect e., false e.; counterfeit evidence, plant, illegal prosecution, vexatious p., sycophancy; lie, libel, slander, scandal, stigma 926n. *calumny.*

accuser, complainant, plaintiff, petitioner, appellant, libelant, litigant; challenger, denouncer, charger; approver, peacher, nark, copper's n. 524n. *informer;* common informer, delator, relator; impeacher, indicter, prosecutrix, prosecutor, public p., habitual p., sycophant; libeler, slanderer, calumniator, stigmatizer 926n. *detractor;* hostile witness 881n. *enemy;* critic, arch-c.

accused person, the accused, prisoner, prisoner at the bar; defendant, respondent, corespondent; culprit; suspect, victim of suspicion; slandered person, libelee, victim.

Adj. *accusing,* alleging, accusatory, denunciatory, criminatory, recriminatory; incriminating, pointing to, imputative, stigmatizing, damnatory, condemnatory; delatory, sycophantic, calumnious, defamatory 926adj. *detracting;* suspicious 924adj. *disapproving.*

accused, informed against, reported a., complained a., suspect; delated, denounced, impeached etc.vb.; charged, up on a charge, prosecuted, hauled up, booked, summoned; awaiting trial, on bail, remanded; slandered, libeled, calumniated 924 adj. *disapproved.*

accusable, imputable; actionable, suable, chargeable, justiciable, liable to prosecution; inexcusable, unpardonable, unforgivable, indefensible, unjustifiable 924adj. *blameworthy;* without excuse, without defense, condemnable 834adj. *heinous;* undefended 661adj. *vulnerable.*

Vb. *accuse,* challenge 711vb. *defy;* taunt, twit 878vb. *be insolent;* point, point a finger at, throw in one's teeth, cast the first stone, reproach 924vb. *reprove;* stigmatize, brand, pillory, gibbet, cast a slur on, calumniate 926vb. *defame;* impute, charge with, saddle w., tax w., hold against, lay to one's charge, lay at one's door, hold responsible, make r.; pick on, fix on, hold to blame, put the blame on, pin on, bring home to 924vb. *blame;* point at, expose, show up, name 526vb. *divulge;* denounce, delate, inform against, tell, tell on, peach, blab, split, turn State's evidence 524vb. *inform;* involve, implicate, inculpate, incriminate; recriminate, counter-charge, rebut the charge, turn the tables upon 479vb. *confute;* shift the blame, pass the buck; return to the charge 712vb. *attack;* accuse oneself, admit the charge, plead guilty 526vb. *confess;* involve oneself, implicate o., lay oneself open, put oneself out of court.

indict, impeach, attaint, arraign, inform against, complain a., lodge a complaint, lay an information; complain, charge, bring a charge, swear an indictment 959vb. *litigate;* book, cite, summon, prosecute, sue; bring an action, bring a suit, bring a case; haul up, pull up, put on trial, put in the dock, ask for a verdict against; charge falsely, lie against 541vb. *be false;* frame, trump up, cook the evidence, use false e., fake the e., plant the e. 541vb. *fake.*

Adv. *accusingly,* censoriously.

See: 460, 466, 475, 479, 524, 526, 541, 661, 711, 712, 878, 881, 921, 924, 926, 934, 959, 961.

929 Probity

N. *probity,* rectitude, uprightness, goodness, sanctity 933n. *virtue;* stainlessness 950n. *purity;* character, honesty, soundness, incorruptibility, integrity; high character, nobleness 868n. *nobility;* honorableness, decent feelings, tender conscience, squeamishness; honor, personal h., sense of h., principles; conscientiousness, punctuality 768n. *observance;* scrupulousness, scrupulosity, punctiliousness, meticulosity 457n. *carefulness;* ingenuousness, singleheartedness; trustworthiness, reliability, sense of responsibility; truthfulness 540n. *veracity;* candor, plain-speaking, home-truth 573n. *plainness;* sincerity, good faith, bona fides 494n. *truth;* fidelity, faith, troth, faithfulness, trustiness, constancy 739n. *loyalty;* clean hands 935n. *innocence;* impartiality, fairness, sportsmanship 913n. *justice;* respectability 866n. *repute;* gentlemanliness 846n. *good taste;* principle, point of honor, punctilio, code, code of honor, Bushido 913n. *right;* court of justice, court of honor, field of h.; argumentum ad verecundiam.

gentleman, man of probity, man of honor, man of his word, sound character, true man; squarepusher, square-shooter, knight, true k., chevalier, galantuomo, caballero; Galahad, Bayard; fair fighter, clean f., fair player, good loser, sportsman, white man, Briton; trump, brick, sport, good s., true-penny.

Adj. *honorable,* upright, erect, of integrity, of honor 933adj. *virtuous;* correct, strict; law-abiding, honest, strictly h.; principled, scrupulous, squeamish, soul-searching; incorruptible, unbribable; incorrupt, inviolate, immaculate 935adj. *innocent;* stainless, unstained, untarnished, unsullied 648adj. *clean;* undepraved, undebauched 950adj. *pure;* ingenuous, unsuspicious, guileless, unworldly 699adj. *artless;* good, white, straight, square, on the square, one hundred per cent; fair, fair-dealing, equitable, impartial 913 adj. *just;* manly, sporting, sportsmanlike, playing the game; high-minded, gentlemanly, chivalrous, knightly 868adj. *noble;* jealous of honor, careful of one's h., respectable 866adj. *reputable;* religious 979 adj. *pious.*

trustworthy, creditworthy, reliable, dependable, tried, tested, proven; trusty, true-hearted, true-blue, true to the core, sure, staunch, single-hearted, constant, unchanging, faithful, loyal 739adj. *obedient;* responsible, duteous, dutiful 768adj. *observant;* conscientious, religious, scrupulous, meticulous, punctilious 457adj. *careful;* candid, frank, open, open and above-board, open-hearted, transparent, without guile 494adj. *true;* ingenuous, straightforward, truthful, truth-speaking, as good as one's word 540adj. *veracious;* unperjured, unperfidious, untreacherous.

Vb. *be honorable,*—chivalrous etc. adj.; behave like a gentleman 933 vb. *be virtuous;* be on the square, deal honorably, play fair, play the game, shoot straight 913vb. *be just;* be a sport, be a brick, turn up trumps; preserve one's honor, fear God 979vb. *be pious;* keep faith, keep one's promise, be as good as one's word, be loyal to one's engagements; hate a lie, stick to the truth, speak the truth and shame the devil 540vb. *be truthful;* go straight, reform, turn over a new leaf 654vb. *get better.*

See: 457, 494, 540, 573, 648, 654, 699, 739, 768, 846, 866, 868, 913, 933, 935, 950, 979.

930 Improbity

N. *improbity,* dishonesty; lack of probity, lack of conscience, lack of principle; suppleness, flexibility, laxity; unconscientiousness 456n. *inattention;* unscrupulousness, opportunism; insincerity, disingenuousness, unstraightforwardness, untrustworthiness, unreliability, undependability, untruthfulness 541n. *falsehood;* unfairness, partiality 914n. *injustice;*

shuffling, slipperiness, snakiness, artfulness; fishiness, suspiciousness, shadiness, obliquity, twistiness, deviousness, crookedness, crooked ways, bypaths of dishonor; corruption, corruptibility, venality, bribability, graft, jobbery, nepotism, simony, barratry; Tammany; baseness, shabbiness, abjectness, abjection, debasement, shamefulness, disgrace, dishonor, shame 867n. *disrepute;* worthlessness, good-for-nothingness, scoundrelism, villainousness, villainy, knavery, roguery, rascality, spivery, skulduggery, racketeering; criminality, crime, complicity **954n.** *lawbreaking;* turpitude, moral t. 934 n. *wickedness.*

perfidy, perfidiousness, faithlessness, unfaithfulness, infidelity, unfaith 543 n. *untruth;* bad faith, Punic f., questionable f.; divided allegiance, wavering loyalty, disloyalty 738n. *disobedience;* practice, double-dealing, double-crossing, Judas kiss 541n. *duplicity;* volte face 603n. *tergiversation;* defection, desertion 918n. *dutilessness;* betrayal, prodition, treachery, stab in the back; treason, high t. 738n. *sedition;* fifth column, Trojan horse; mala fides, breach of faith, broken word, broken faith, broken promise, breach of p., oath forsworn, scrap of paper; cry of treason, Perfide Albion!

foul play, dirty trick, stab in the back; not playing the game, foul 914n. *wrong;* trick, shuffle, chicane, chicanery 542n. *trickery;* practice, sharp p., heads I win, tails you lose; misdealing, fishy transaction, dirty work, job, deal, ramp, racket; fiddle, wangle, manipulation, gerrymandering, hanky-panky; false balance-sheet, malversation 788n. *peculation;* crime, felony 954n. *lawbreaking.*

Adj. *dishonest,* misdealing 914adj. *wrong;* not particular, unfastidious, unsqueamish; unprincipled; unscrupulous, conscienceless; shameless, dead to honor, lost to shame; unethical, immoral 934adj. *wicked;* shaky, untrustworthy, unreliable, undependable; supple, versatile 603adj. *tergiversating;* disingenuous, unstraightforward, untruthful, uncandid 543adj. *untrue;* double-tongued, double-faced, insincere 541adj. *hypocritical;* unerect, creeping, crawling; tricky, artful, dodging, opportunist, slippery, snaky, foxy 698adj. *cunning;* shifty, shuffling, prevaricating 518adj. *equivocal;* designing, scheming; sneaking, underhand, subterranean 523adj. *latent;* not straight, unstraight, indirect, crooked, devious, oblique, tortuous, winding 251adj. *labyrinthine;* insidious, dark, sinister; shady, suspicious, doubtful, questionable; fishy, malodorous 397 adj. *fetid;* fraudulent 542adj. *spurious;* illicit 954adj. *illegal;* foul 645 adj. *bad;* unclean 649adj. *dirty;* dishonorable, infamous 867adj. *disreputable;* derogatory, unworthy, undignified; inglorious, ignominious 867adj. *degrading;* ignoble, unchivalrous, unknightly, ungentlemanly, unmanly, unhandsome.

rascally, criminal, criminous, felonious 954adj. *lawless;* knavish, picaresque, spivish, scampish; infamous, blackguard, villainous; scurvy, scabby, arrant, low, low-down, yellow, base, vile, mongrel, currish; mean, scrubby, shabby, paltry, little, pettifogging, abject, wretched, contemptible 639adj. *unimportant;* time-serving, crawling 925adj. *flattering.*

venal, corruptible, purchasable, bribable, for hire, hireling, mercenary 792adj. *bought;* corrupt, jobbing, grafting, simoniacal, nepotistic; barratrous, selling justice.

perfidious, treacherous, unfaithful, inconstant, trothless, faithless 541 adj. *false;* double-dealing, double-crossing, time-serving 541adj. *hypocritical;* apostatizing 603adj. *tergiversating;* false-hearted, guileful, traitorous, treasonous, treasonable, disloyal, untrue 738adj. *disobedient;* plotting, scheming, intriguing 623 adj. *planning;* insidious, dark, Machiavellian; cheating, cozening 542adj. *deceiving;* fraudulent 542 adj. *spurious.*

Vb. *be dishonest,*—dishonorable etc. adj.; ignore ethics, forget one's principles, yield to temptation, be lost to shame; lack honesty, live dishonestly, live by one's wits, lead a life of crime 954vb. *be illegal;* fiddle, wangle, gerrymander, start a racket, racketeer; defalcate, peculate 788vb. *defraud;* cheat, swindle, chisel 542vb. *deceive;* betray, play false, stab in the back; play double, double-cross, gloze 541vb. *dissemble;* fawn 925vb. *flatter;* break faith, break one's word, forswear, jilt, disregard one's promises, lie 541vb. *be false;* shuffle, dodge, prevaricate 518vb. *be equivocal;* sell out, sell down the river, go over 603vb. *apostatize;* sink into crime, sell one's honor, seal one's infamy 867vb. *lose repute.*

Adv. *dishonestly;* shamelessly, by fair means or foul; treacherously, mala fide; knavishly, villainously, without regard for honesty.

See: 251, 397, 456, 518, 523, 541, 542, 543, 603, 623, 639, 645, 649, 698, 738, 788, 792, 867, 914, 918, 925, 934, 954.

931 Disinterestedness

N. *disinterestedness,* impartiality, indifference 913n. *justice;* detachment, noninvolvement, neutrality 625n. *mid-course;* unselfishness, unpossessiveness, selflessness, no thought for self, self-effacement 872n. *humility;* self-control, self-abnegation, self-denial, self-surrender, self-sacrifice, self-immolation, self-devotion, martyrdom, suttee; rising above oneself, heroism, stoicism 855n. *courage;* loftiness of purpose, elevation of soul, idealism, ideals, high i.; sublimity, elevation, loftiness, nobility, magnanimity; knightliness, chivalry, knight-errantry; generosity, liberality, liberalism 897n. *benevolence;* purity of motive, dedication, consecration; loyalty, faith, faithfulness 929n. *probity;* patriotism 901n. *philanthropy;* altruism, thought for others, consideration, considerateness, kindness 884n. *courtesy;* compassion 905n. *pity;* charity 887n. *love.*

Adj. *disinterested,* dispassionate, impersonal, uninvolved, detached, disengaged, neutral, impartial, indifferent 913adj. *just;* self-controlled, stoical 942adj. *temperate;* uncorrupted, unbought, unbribed, honest 929adj. *honorable;* self-effacing, modest 872adj. *humble;* unjealous, unpossessive, unenvious, ungrudging; unselfish, selfless, self-forgetful; self-denying, self-sacrificing, ready to die for, martyr-like; devoted, self-d., dedicated, consecrated; loyal, faithful; heroic 855adj. *courageous;* thoughtful, considerate, kind 884adj. *courteous;* altruistic, philanthropic, patriotic 897adj. *benevolent;* pure, unmixed; undesigning; sacrificial, unmercenary, for love, non-profit-making; idealistic, high-minded, lofty, elevated, sublime, magnanimous, chivalrous, knightly 868adj. *noble;* generous, liberal, unsparing 781adj. *giving.*

Vb. *be disinterested,*—unselfish etc. adj.; sacrifice, make a s., sacrifice oneself, devote o., live for, die f.; think of others, put oneself last, take a back seat 872vb. *be humble;* rise above petty considerations, rise above oneself, surrender personal considerations.

See: 625, 781, 855, 868, 872, 884, 887, 897, 901, 905, 913, 929, 942.

932 Selfishness

N. *selfishness,* self-consideration, self-love, self-admiration, narcissism, self-worship, self-approbation, self-praise 873n. *vanity;* self-pity, self-indulgence 943n. *intemperance;* self-absorption, egocentrism, autism; egoism, egotism, individualism, particularism; self-preservation, each man for himself; ax to grind, personal considerations, personal motives, private ends, personal advantage, selfish benefit, self-interest, concern for number one; charity that begins at home, cupboard love; illiberality, no magnanimity, mean-mindedness, pettiness, paltriness; illiberality, meanness, niggardliness 816n. *parsimony;* greed, acquisitiveness 911n. *jealousy;* worldliness, worldly wisdom; "heads I win tails you lose" 914n. *injustice;* careerism, selfish ambition, naked a., ruthless a.; power politics.

egotist, egoist, self-centered person, narciscist 873n. *vain person;* particularist, individualist, mass of selfishness; self-seeker; careerist, arriviste, go-getter, adventurer, gold-digger, fortune-hunter; money-grubber 816n. *niggard;* monopolist, dog in the manger, hog, road h.; opportunist, time-server. worldling.

Adj. *selfish,* egocentric, autistic, self-absorbed, wrapped up in oneself; egoistic, egotistic, egotistical; personal, individualistic, concerned with number one; self-interested, self-regarding, self-considering; self-indulgent 944adj. *sensual;* self-loving, self-admiring, narcissistic 873adj. *vain;* non-altruistic, interested; unphilanthropic; unpatriotic; uncharitable, unsympathetic, cold-hearted 898adj. *unkind;* mean, mean-minded, petty, paltry; illiberal, ungenerous, niggardly 816adj. *parsimonious;* acquisitive, money-grubbing, mercenary 816adj. *avaricious;* venal 930adj. *dishonest;* covetous 912adj. *envious;* hoggish, hogging, monopolistic 859 adj. *greedy;* possessive, dog-in-the-manger; competitive 911adj. *jealous;* self-seeking, designing, ax-grinding;

go-getting, on the make, gold-digging, opportunist, time-serving, careerist; unidealistic, materialistic, mundane, worldly, earthly, earthy, worldly-minded, worldly-wise.

Vb. *be selfish,*—egoistic etc.adj.; put oneself first, think only of oneself, take care of number one; love oneself, indulge o., look after o., coddle o., have only oneself to please; feather one's nest, look out for oneself, have an eye to the main chance, know on which side one's bread is buttered, give an inch and take an ell; keep for oneself, hang onto, hog, monopolize, be a dog in the manger 778vb. *retain;* have personal motives, have private ends, have an ax to grind, have one's own game to play; grind one's ax, pursue one's interests, advance one's own i., sacrifice the interests of others, be a bad neighbor.

Adv. *selfishly,* self-regardingly, only for oneself; on the make, for profit; ungenerously, illiberally; for one's own sake, from personal motives, for private ends; jealously, possessively.

See: 778, 816, 859, 873, 898, 911, 912, 914, 930, 943, 944.

933 Virtue

N. *virtue,* virtuousness, moral strength, moral tone, morale; goodness, sheer g.; saintliness, holiness, spirituality, odor of sanctity 979n. *sanctity;* righteousness 913n. *justice;* uprightness, rectitude, moral r., character, integrity, honor, personal h. 929n. *probity;* perfect honor, stainlessness, irreproachability; avoidance of guilt, guiltlessness 935n. *innocence;* morality, ethics 917n. *morals;* sexual morality, chastity 950n. *purity;* straight and narrow path, virtuous conduct, Christian c., good behavior, well-spent life, duty done; good conscience, conscious rectitude; self-improvement, moral rearmament; quality, efficacy, power 160n. *ability.*

virtues, moral v., moral laws; theological virtues, faith, hope, charity; cardinal virtues, prudence, justice, temperance, fortitude; qualities, fine q., saving quality, saving grace; a virtue, good fault, fault on the right side; worth, merit, desert; excellence, perfections 646n. *perfection;* nobleness 868n. *nobility;* altruism, unselfishness 931n. *disinterestedness;* idealism, ideals; self-control 942n. *temperance.*

Adj. *virtuous,* moral 917adj. *ethical;* good 644adj. *excellent;* stainless, white 950adj. *pure;* guiltless 935adj. *innocent;* irreproachable, impeccable, above temptation 646adj. *perfect;* saint-like, seraphic, angelic, saintly, holy 979adj. *sanctified;* principled, well-p., right-minded, on the side of the angels 913adj. *right;* righteous 913adj. *just;* upright, sterling, honest 929adj. *honorable;* duteous, dutiful 739adj. *obedient;* unselfish 931adj. *disinterested;* generous, magnanimous 868adj. *noble;* idealistic, well-intentioned, philanthropic 897 adj. *benevolent;* chaste, virginal; proper, edifying, improving; elevated, sublimated; meritorious, worthy, praiseworthy, commendable 923 adj. *approved.*

Vb. *be virtuous,*—good etc. adj.; have all the virtues, qualify for sainthood 644vb. *be good;* behave, be on one's good *or* best behavior; practice virtue, resist temptation, command one's passions 942vb. *be temperate;* rise superior to, have a soul above; keep to the straight and narrow path, follow one's conscience, walk humbly with one's god, fight the good fight; discharge one's obligations 917vb. *do one's duty;* go straight, keep s. 929vb. *be honorable;* love good, hate wrong 913vb. *be just;* edify, set a good example, shame the devil 644 vb. *do good.*

Adv. *virtuously,* well, meritoriously; righteously, purely, innocently; holily.

See: 160, 644, 646, 739, 868, 897, 913, 917, 923, 929, 931, 935, 942, 950, 979.

934 Wickedness

N. *wickedness,* principle of evil 616n. *evil;* devil, cloven hoof 969n. *Satan;* fallen nature, Old Adam; unrighteousness, iniquity, sinfulness, sin 914n. *wrong;* peccability, loss of innocence 936n. *guilt;* ignorance of good, moral illiteracy; amorality, amoralism 860n. *indifference;* hardness of heart 898n. *malevolence;* willfulness, stubbornness 602adj. *obstinacy;* naughtiness 738n. *disobedience;* immorality, turpitude, moral t.; loose morals, carnality, profligacy 951n. *impurity;* demoralization, degeneration, degeneracy, vitiation, degradation 655n. *deterioration;*

recidivism, backsliding 603n. *tergiversation;* corruption, depravity 645n. *badness;* flagitiousness, heinousness, shamelessness, flagrancy; bad character, viciousness, unworthiness; vice, villainy, knavery, roguery 930n. *foul play;* obliquity, laxity, want of principle, dishonesty 930n. *improbity;* crime, criminality 954n. *lawbreaking;* devilry, hellishness 898 n. *inhumanity;* devil worship, diabolism 982n. *idolatry;* shame, scandal, abomination, enormity, infamy 867n. *disrepute;* infamous conduct, misbehavior, delinquency, wrongdoing, evil-doing, transgression, evil courses, wicked ways, career of crime; primrose path, slippery slope; low life 847n. *ill-breeding;* den of vice, sink of iniquity, hell-broth, Alsatian den, criminal world, underworld, demimonde 649n. *sink.*

vice, fault, demerit, unworthiness; human weakness, infirmity, frailty, foible 163n. *weakness;* imperfection, shortcoming, defect, deficiency, failing, weak side, weakness of the flesh; trespass, injury, outrage, enormity 914n. *wrong;* sin, capital s., deadly s.; seven deadly sins, pride, covetousness, lust, anger, gluttony, envy, sloth; venial sin, small fault, slight transgression, peccadillo, scrape; impropriety, indecorum 847 n. *bad taste;* crime, felony, deadly crime, capital c. 954n. *illegality.*

Adj. *wicked,* virtueless, unvirtuous, immoral; amoral, amoralistic 860 adj. *indifferent;* lax, unprincipled, unscrupulous, conscienceless 930adj. *dishonest;* unblushing, hardened, callous, shameless, brazen, flaunting; irreligious, profane 980adj. *impious;* iniquitous, unrighteous 914adj. *unjust;* evil 645adj. *bad;* evil-minded, bad-hearted 898adj. *malevolent;* evil-doing 898adj. *maleficent;* misbehaving, bad, naughty 738adj. *disobedient;* weak (**see** *frail*); peccant, erring, sinning, transgressing; sinful, sin-laden, full of sin 936adj. *guilty;* unworthy, undeserving, unmeritorious; graceless, not in a state of grace, reprobate; hopeless, incorrigible, irreclaimable, unredeemed, irredeemable; accursed, god-forsaken; hellish, infernal, devilish, fiendish, Mephistophelian, Satanic 969adj. *diabolic.*

vicious, steeped in vice, sunk in iniquity; good-for-nothing, ne'er-do-well; hopeless, past praying for; worthless, unworthy, meritless, graceless 924adj. *disapproved;* villainous, knavish, double-dyed 930adj. *rascally;* improper, unseemly, indecent, unedifying 847adj. *vulgar;* moralless, immoral; unvirtuous 951adj. *unchaste;* profligate, abandoned, characterless, lost to virtue, lost to shame 867adj. *disreputable;* vitiated, corrupt, degraded, demoralized, debauched, ruined, depraved, perverted, degenerate, rotten, rotten to the core 655adj. *deteriorated;* brutalized, brutal 898adj. *cruel.*

frail, infirm, feeble 163adj. *weak;* having a weaker side, having one's foibles, human, only h., too h. 734 adj. *lax;* suggestible, easily tempted 661adj. *vulnerable;* not above temptation, not impeccable, not perfect 647adj. *imperfect;* slipping, sliding, recidivous 603adj. *tergiversating.*

heinous, heavy, grave, serious, deadly; black, scarlet, of deepest dye; abysmal, hellish, infernal 211adj. *deep;* sinful, immoral 914adj. *wrong;* demoralizing, unedifying, contra bonos mores; criminal, nefarious, felonious 954adj. *lawbreaking;* flagitious, monstrous, flagrant, scandalous, scandalizing, infamous, shameful, disgraceful, shocking, outrageous; gross, foul, rank; base, vile, abominable, accursed; blameworthy, culpable 928adj. *accusable;* reprehensible, indefensible, unjustifiable 916adj. *unwarranted;* atrocious, brutal 898adj. *cruel;* unforgivable, unpardonable, inexcusable, irremissible, inexpiable, unatonable.

Vb. *be wicked,*—vicious,—sinful etc. adj.; not be in a state of grace, scoff at virtue; fall from grace, spoil one's record, lapse, relapse, backslide 603 vb. *tergiversate;* fall into sin, go to the bad 655vb. *deteriorate;* do amiss, transgress, misbehave, misdemean oneself, carry on, be naughty, sow one's wild oats; trespass, offend, sin, commit s., err, stray, slip, trip, stumble, fall; have one's foibles, have one's weak side 163vb. *be weak.*

make wicked, render evil, corrupt, demoralize, deform one's character, brutalize 655vb. *pervert;* mislead, lead astray, seduce 612vb. *tempt;* set a bad example, teach wickedness, dehumanize, brutalize, diabolize.

Adv. *wickedly,* wrongly, sinfully; viciously, vilely, depravedly, devilishly; unforgivably, unpardonably, irredeemably, inexpiably.

See: 163, 211, 602, 603, 612, 616, 645, 647, 649, 655, 661, 734, 738,

847, 860, 867, 898, 914, 916, 924, 928, 930, 936, 951, 954, 969, 980, 982.

935 Innocence

N. *innocence,* blessed i., freedom from guilt, guiltlessness, clean hands; conscious innocence, clear conscience, irreproachability; nothing to declare, nothing to confess, inculpability, blamelessness, freedom from blame, every excuse; declared innocence 960n. *acquittal;* ignorance of evil 491n. *ignorance;* inexperience, unworldliness 699n. *artlessness;* playfulness, harmlessness, inoffensiveness, innocent intentions, pure motives; freedom from sin, unfallen state, state of grace 933n. *virtue;* undefilement, stainlessness 950n. *purity;* incorruption, incorruptibility 929n. *probity;* impeccability 646n. *perfection;* days of innocence, golden age, Saturnia regna 730n. *palmy days.*

innocent, Holy Innocents, babe, newborn babe, babe unborn, babes and sucklings; child, ingénue; lamb, dove; angel, white soul; milksop, goody-goody; one in the right, innocent party, injured p., not the culprit.

Adj. *innocent,* pure, unspotted, stainless, unblemished, spotless, immaculate, white 648adj. *clean;* incorrupt, uncorrupted, undefiled; unfallen, sinless, free from sin, unerring, impeccable 646adj. *perfect;* green, inexperienced, knowing no better, unhardened, unversed in crime 491adj. *ignorant;* unworldly, guileless 699adj. *artless;* well-meaning, well-intentioned, well-intended, well-motived 897n. *benevolent;* innocuous, harmless, inoffensive, playful, gentle, lamb-like, dove-like, angelic; innocent as a lamb, innocent as a dove, innocent as a babe unborn, innocent as a child; shockable, goody-goody; Saturnian, Arcadian.

guiltless, free from guilt, not responsible, not guilty 960adj. *acquitted;* falsely accused, misunderstood; clean-handed. bloodless; blameless, faultless, unblameworthy, unculpable, unblamable; irreproachable, above suspicion; irreprovable, irreprehensible, unobjectionable, unexceptionable, unimpeachable, entirely defensible, with every excuse 923adj. *approvable;* pardonable, forgivable, excusable, venial, exculpable, expiable.

Vb. *be innocent,* know no wrong, do no man w., have no guile 929vb. *be honorable;* live in a state of grace, not fall from g. 933vb. *be virtuous;* have every excuse, have no need to blush, have clean hands, have a clear conscience, have nothing to confess, have nothing to declare; have the best intentions, mean no harm, mean no guile; know no better 699vb. *be artless;* stand free of blame, stand above suspicion; acquit oneself, salve one's conscience, wash one's hands.

Adv. *innocently,* blamelessly, harmlessly, well-meaningly; with clean hands, with a clear conscience, with a safe c., with an easy c.

See: 491, 646, 648, 699, 730, 897, 923, 929, 933, 950, 960.

936 Guilt

N. *guilt,* guiltiness, blood g., red-handedness; culpability, chargeability; criminality, criminousness, delinquency 954n. *illegality;* sinfulness, original sin 934n. *wickedness;* involvement, complicity; charge, onus, burden, responsibility 180n. *liability;* blame, censure 924n. *reproach;* guilty feeling, guilt-f., conscious guilt, guilty conscience, bad c.; guilty behavior, suspicious conduct, blush, stammer; admitted guilt, confessed g., confession 526n. *disclosure;* twinge of conscience, biting c. 939n. *penitence.*

guilty act, sin, deadly s., venial s. 934 n. *vice;* misdeed, wicked deed, misdoing, sinning, transgression, trespass, offense, crime, corpus delicti 954n. *illegality;* misdemeanor, felony; misconduct, misbehavior, malpractice, malversation; infamous conduct, unprofessional c.; indiscretion, impropriety, peccadillo; naughtiness, scrape; lapse, slip, faux pas, blunder 495n. *mistake;* omission 458n. *negligence;* culpable omission, laches; sin of commission, fault, failure, dereliction 918n. *dutilessness;* injustice, tort, injury 914n. *wrong;* enormity, atrocity, outrage 898n. *cruel act.*

Adj. *guilty,* found g., convicted 961 adj. *condemned;* thought guilty, suspected, blamed, censured, made responsible 924 adj. *disapproved;* responsible 180adj. *liable;* in the wrong, at fault, to blame, culpable, chargeable 928adj. *accusable;* blameful, reprehensible, censurable 924 adj. *blameworthy;* unjustifiable, without excuse, inexcusable, unpardonable, unforgivable; inexpiable, mortal, deadly 934adj. *heinous;* trespassing, transgressing, peccant, sinful 934adj. *wicked;* criminal, criminous 954adj. *illegal;* blood-guilty 362 adj. *murderous;* red-handed, caught in the act, surprised in the attempt; shamefast, shame-faced, blushing.

Vb. *be guilty,* have sins upon one's conscience, have crimes to answer for, have blood upon one's hands; be caught in the act, be caught red-handed; acknowledge one's guilt, plead guilty 526vb. *confess;* have no excuse, stand condemned; trespass, transgress, sin 934vb. *be wicked.*

Adv. *guiltily,* criminally, criminously; inexcusably, without excuse; red-handed, in the very act, flagrante delicto.

See: 180, 362, 458, 495, 526, 898, 914, 918, 924, 928, 934, 939, 954, 961.

937 Good man

N. *good man,* perfect gentleman, fine character 929n. *gentleman;* good example, model of virtue, salt of the earth, perfection 646n. *paragon;* Christian, true C.; saint 979n. *pietist;* mahatma, great saint; seraph, angel 935n. *innocent;* benefactor 897n. *kind person;* idealist 901n. *philanthropist;* the best, one of the b., the tops 890n. *favorite;* hero 855n. *brave person;* good sort, stout fellow, white man, brick, trump, sport; rough diamond, ugly duckling; demigod, god of one's idolatry 982n. *idol.*

See: 646, 855, 890, 897, 901, 929, 935, 979, 982.

938 Bad Man

N. *bad man,* evil m., no saint, sinner, hardened s., limb of Satan, antichrist 904n. *evildoer;* fallen angel, backslider, recidivist, lost sheep, lost soul, âme damnée, man of no morals, immoralist; reprobate, scapegrace, good-for-nothing, ne'er-do-well, black sheep, the despair of; scalawag, scamp, spalpeen; rake, roué, profligate 952n. *libertine;* wastrel, waster, prodigal son 815n. *prodigal;* scandalous person, reproach, outcast, dregs 867n. *object of scorn;* tramp, vagabond; nasty type, ugly customer, undesirable, bad 'un, wrong 'un, badmash, thug, bully, roughneck 904n. *ruffian;* bad lot, bad egg, bad hat, bad character, scaramouch 869n. *low fellow;* bad influence, bad example; bad boy, naughty b., terror, whelp, monkey, little m., little devil; bad girl, naughty g., jade, wench, slut, Jezebel 952n. *loose woman.*

knave, scurvy k., varlet, vagabond, cullion, catiff, wretch, dog, rascal, rapscallion, rogue, first-class r., prince of rogues; criminal 904n. *offender;* thief, pirate, freebooter 789n. *robber;* villain, blackguard, scoundrel; cheat, liar, crook; chiseler, impostor, twister, shyster 545n. *trickster;* sneak, squealer, rat 524n. *informer;* renegade, recreant 603n. *tergiversator;* betrayer, traitor, arch-traitor, treachetour, quisling, Judas; animal, dog, hound, swine, snake, serpent, viper, reptile, vermin 904n. *noxious animal.*

cad, nasty bit of work, scoundrel, blackguard; rotter, blighter, heel, scab; stinker, bad smell, skunk, dirty dog, filthy hound; bastard, twerp, pimp, pander, pervert, degenerate; cur, hound, swine, worm, the bottom; louse, insect 365n. *vermin;* pig, beast, horrid b., cat, bitch.

monster, shocker, horror, unspeakable villain; monster of cruelty, brute, savage, sadist; ogre 735n. *tyrant;* monster of wickedness, monster of iniquity, fiend, demon, ghoul 969n. *devil;* hell-hound 904n. *hell-hag;* devil in human shape, devil incarnate, fiend i.; ape-man, gorilla 842n. *eyesore;* King Kong, Frankenstein's monster, bogey, terror, raw-head, bloody-bones.

See: 365, 524, 545, 603, 735, 789, 815, 842, 867, 869, 904, 952, 969.

939 Penitence

N. *penitence,* repentance, contrition, compunction, remorse, self-reproach 830n. *regret;* self-accusation, self-condemnation, humble confession 526n. *disclosure;* public confession, exomologesis 988n. *Christian rite;* self-humiliation 872n. *humility;* guilt-feeling, voice of conscience, uneasy c., unquiet c., bad c., twinge of c., qualms of c., strings of c., pricks of c., "compunctious visitings of nature" 936n. *guilt;* awakened conscience, resipiscence 603n. *recantation;* last-minute repentance, death-bed r.; room for repentance, locus paenitentiae; penance, white sheet, sack-cloth and ashes, stool of repentance, cutty stool 964n. *pillory;* apology 941n. *atonement;* half-repentance, grudging apology.

penitent, penitential, flagellant 945n. *ascetic;* magdalen, prodigal son, returned prodigal, a sadder and a wiser man; reformed character, brand plucked from the burning.

Adj. *repentant,* contrite, remorseful, regretful, sorry, apologetic, full of regrets 830adj. *regretting;* unhardened, softened, melted, weeping 836adj. *lamenting;* compunctious, relenting, conscience-stricken, conscience-smitten, pricked by conscience, plagued by c.; self-reproachful, self-accusing, self-convicted, self-condemned; confessing, in the confessional; penitent, penitential, penitentiary, doing penance 941adj. *atoning;* chastened, sobered, awakened, resipiscent; reclaimed, reformed, converted, regenerate.

Vb. *be penitent,* repent, have compunction, feel shame, blush for s., feel sorry, say one is s., express regrets, apologize; reproach oneself, blame o., reprove o., accuse o., convict o., condemn o.; go to confession, shrive oneself 526vb. *confess;* do penance, wear a white sheet, repent in sackcloth and ashes 941vb. *atone;* bewail one's sins, cry peccavi; sing Miserere, sing De Profundis 836vb. *lament;* beat one's breast, scourge oneself; rue, have regrets, wish undone 830vb. *regret;* think again, think better of, stop in time; learn one's lesson, learn from experience 536vb. *learn;* reform, amend, be reformed, be reclaimed, turn over a new leaf 654vb. *get better;* see the light, convert, put on the new man, turn from sin 147vb. *be turned to;* recant one's error 603 vb. *recant.*

Adv. *penitently,* like a penitent, on the stool of repentance, in sackcloth and ashes; repentantly, regretfully.

Int. sorry! mea culpa! repent! for pity!

See: 147, 526, 536, 603, 654, 830, 836, 872, 936, 941, 945, 964, 988.

940 Impenitence

N. *impenitence,* irrepentance, noncontrition; contumacy, recusance, refusal to recant, obduracy, stubbornness 602n. *obstinacy;* hardness of heart, induration 326n. *hardness;* no apologies, no regrets, no compunction 906n. *pitilessness;* incorrigibility, seared conscience, unawakened c.; hardened sinner, despair of 938n. *bad man.*

Adj. *impenitent,* unregretting, unapologizing, unrecanting, recusant; contumacious, obdurate, stubborn 602adj. *obstinate;* unconfessing, unrepentant, uncontrite; unregretful, without regrets; unrelenting, relentless 600adj. *persevering;* uncompunctious, without compunction, without a pang, heartless 898adj. *cruel;* hard, hardened, case-h.; unawakened, sleeping 679adj. *sleepy;* conscienceless, unashamed, unblushing, brazen; incorrigible, irreclaimable, irredeemable, hopeless, despaired of, lost 934adj. *wicked;* graceless, shiftless, unconfessed, unshriven; unchastened, unreformed, unreconciled; unreclaimed, unconverted.

unrepented, unregretted, unapologized for, unatoned.

Vb. *be impenitent,* make no excuses, offer no apologies, have no regrets, would do it again; abide in one's error, not see the light, refuse to recant 602vb. *be obstinate;* make no confession, die and make no sign, die in one's sins, die in contumacy; stay unreconciled, want no forgiveness; feel no compunction, harden one's heart, steel one's h. 906vb. *be pitiless.*

Adv. *impenitently,* unregretfully, unashamedly, unblushingly.

See: 326, 600, 602, 679, 898, 906, 934, 938.

941 Atonement

N. *atonement,* making amends, amends, amende honorable, apology, full a., satisfaction; reparation, compensation, indemnity, indemnification, blood-money, wergild, conscience money 787n. *restitution;* repayment, quittance, quits 714n. *retaliation;* composition 770n. *compromise.*

propitiation, expiration, satisfaction, reconciliation, conciliation 719n. *pacification;* reclamation, redemption 965n. *divine function;* sacrifice, offering, burnt o., peace o., sin o. 981n. *oblation;* scapegoat, whipping-boy, chopping-block 150n. *substitute.*

penance, shrift, confession, acknowledgment 939n. *penitence;* sacrament of penance, penitential exercise, austerities, fasting, maceration, flagellation 945adj. *asceticism;* lustration, purgation 648n. *cleansing;* purgatorial torments, purgatory; penitent form, anxious seat, stool of repentance, cutty stool, corner, white sheet 964n. *pillory;* sackcloth and ashes 836n. *lamentation.*

Adj. *atoning,* making amends 939adj. *repentant;* reparatory, compensatory, indemnificatory 787adj. *restoring;* conciliatory, apologetic; propiatory, expiatory, piacular, purgatorial, lustrative, lustral, lustratory 648adj. *cleansing;* sacrificial, sacrificatory, sacrifice 759adj. *offering;* penitential, penitentiary, doing penance, undergoing p. 963adj. *punitive.*

Vb. *atone,* salve one's conscience, make amends, make reparation, offer r., indemnify, compensate, pay compensation, make it up to; apologize, make apologies, offer one's a. 909vb. *beg pardon;* propitiate, conciliate 719vb. *pacify;* give satisfaction, offer s., make the amende honorable 787vb. *restitute;* redeem one's error, repair one's fault, wipe out one's offenses, be restored to favor; sacrifice to, offer sacrifice; expiate, pay the penalty, pay the forfeit, pay the cost, smart for it 963vb. *be punished;* be the chopping-block, become the whipping-boy, make oneself the scapegoat 931vb. *be disinterested.*

do penance, undergo p., perform penitential exercises, perform austerities; pray, fast, flagellate oneself, scourge o.; purge one's contempt, purge one's offenses, suffer purgatory; put on sackcloth and ashes, stand in a white sheet, stand in the corner, sit on the stool of repentance, sit on the anxious seat; take one's punishment, swallow one's medicine 963vb. *be punished;* salve one's conscience, shrive oneself, go to confession 526vb. *confess.*

See: 150, 526, 648, 714, 719, 759, 770, 787, 836, 909, 931, 939, 945, 963, 964, 965, 981.

942 Temperance

N. *temperance,* nothing in excess 177 n. *moderation;* self-denial 931n. *disinterestedness;* self-restraint, self-control, self-discipline, stoicism 747 n. *restraint;* chastity 950n. *purity;* continence, Encratism; soberness 948n. *sobriety;* forbearance 620n. *avoidance;* renunciation 621n. *relinquishment;* abstemiousness, abstinence, abstention, total abstinence, teetotalism; enforced abstention, prohibition, prohibitionism, pussyfootism 747n. *restriction;* vegetarianism, Pythagoreanism; dieting, banting 946n. *fasting;* frugality 814n. *economy;* plain living, frugal diet, Spartan fare 945n. *asceticism.*

abstainer, total a., teetotaler 948n. *sober person;* prohibitionist, pussyfoot; vegetarian, fruitarian, Pythagorean; Encratite; dieter, banter, faster; enemy of excess, Spartan 945n. *ascetic.*

Adj. *temperate,* unexcessive, within bounds, within compass; measured, tempered 177adj. *moderate;* plain, Spartan, sparing 814adj. *economical;* frugal 816adj. *parsimonious;* forbearing, abstemious, abstinent 620 adj. *avoiding;* dry, teetotal 948adj. *sober;* fruitarian, vegetarian, Pythagorean; ungreedy, self-controlled, self-disciplined, continent 747adj. *restrained;* chaste 950adj. *pure;* self-denying 945adj. *ascetic;* hardy, unpampered.

Vb. *be temperate,*—moderate etc. adj.; moderate, temper, keep within bounds, observe a limit, avoid excess, know when one has had enough 177vb. *be moderate;* keep sober 948vb. *be sober;* forbear, spare, refrain, abstain 620vb. *avoid;* control oneself, contain o. 747vb. *restrain;* deny oneself 945vb. *be ascetic;* go dry; take the pledge, sign the p., join the Band of Hope; ration oneself, tighten one's belt 946vb. *fast;* diet, bant, reduce 206vb. *make thin.*

See: 177, 206, 620, 621, 747, 814, 816, 931, 945, 946, 948, 950.

943 Intemperance

N. *intemperance,* want of moderation, immoderation, unrestraint; excess, excessiveness, luxury 637n. *redundance;* too much 637n. *superfluity;* wastefulness, waste 815n. *prodigality;* want of self-control, indiscipline, incontinence 734n. *laxity;* inabstinence, indulgence, self-i., over i.; addiction, bad habit, drug h. 610 n. *habit;* full life, high living, dissipation, orgy, debauch 944n. *sensualism;* intoxication, crapulence, hangover 949n. *drunkenness.*

Adj. *intemperate,* immoderate, exceeding, excessive 637adj. *redundant;* untempered, unmeasured, unlimited 635adj. *plenteous;* unforbearing, unsparing, unfrugal, uneconomical, wasteful, spendthrift 815adj. *prodigal;* luxurious 637adj. *superfluous;* unascetic, un-Spartan, indulgent, over-i.,, self-i., inabstinent, denying oneself nothing; unrestrained, uncontrolled, unself-controlled, undisciplined 738adj. *riotous;* incontinent 951adj. *unchaste;* unsober, non-teetotal, wet 949adj. *drunk;* animal 944adj. *sensual.*

Vb. *be intemperate,* — immoderate etc.adj.; roll in, luxuriate, plunge, wallow; lack self-control, want discipline, lose control 734vb. *be lax;* deny oneself nothing, indulge oneself 734vb. *please oneself;* have one's fling, sow one's wild oats 815vb. *be prodigal;* run to excess, run riot, exceed, have no measure 637vb. *superabound;* observe no limits, go to all lengths, go the limit, stick at nothing, not know when to stop, over-indulge, burn the candle at both ends 634vb. *waste;* beat it up, carouse 837vb. *revel;* overdrink, drink to excess 949vb. *get drunk;* eat to excess, gorge, overeat, make oneself sick 947vb. *gluttonize;* be incontinent, grow dissipated 951vb. *be impure;* addict oneself, become a slave to habit 610vb. *be wont.*

Adv. *intemperately,* immoderately, excessively; without moderation, without control; incontinently, licentiously; not wisely but too well.

See: 610, 634, 635, 637, 734, 738, 815, 837, 944, 947, 949, 951.

944 Sensualism

N. *sensualism,* life of the senses, unspirituality, leanness of soul, earthiness, materialism 319n. *materiality;* cultivation of the senses, sensuality, carnality, the flesh; grossness, beastliness, bestiality, animalism, hoggishness, wallowing, Circean cup; craze for excitement 822n. *excitability;* love of pleasure, search for p., hedonism, epicurism, epicureanism, eudaemonism 376n. *pleassure;* Sybaritism, voluptuousness, voluptuosity, effeminacy, softness, luxuriousness; luxury, lap of l. 637n. *superfluity;* full life, wine of l., life of pleasure, high living, fast l. 824n. *enjoyment;* swollen desires, incontinence, dissipation 943n. *intemperance;* licentiousness, dissoluteness, debauchery 951n. *impurity;* indulgence, self-i., overindulgence, greediness 947n. *gluttony;* eating and drinking, Lucullan banquet 301n. *feasting;* orgy, debauch, Saturnalia, bacchanalia 837 n. *revel.*

sensualist, animal, pig, swine, hog, wallower; no ascetic, hedonist, man of pleasure, pleasure-lover, thrill-seeker; luxury-lover, Sybarite, voluptuary; eudaemonist, epicurean, votary of Epicurus, swine of E.; epicure, gourmand, Sardanapalus, Lucullus 947n. *glutton;* hard drinker 949n. *drunkard;* loose liver, fast man, rake, debauchee 952 *libertine;* degenerate, Heliogabalus, Nero.

Adj. *sensual,* earthy, gross, unspiritual 319adj. *material;* fleshly, carnal, bodily; animal, bestial, beastly, brutish, swinish, hoggish, wallowing; Circean, pleasure-giving 826adj. *pleasurable;* Sybaritic, voluptuous, pleasure-loving, thrill-seeking; hedonistic, eudaemonistic, epicurean, Lucullan, luxury-loving, luxurious; pampered, indulged, over-i., self-i.; overfed, full-f. 947adj. *gluttonous;* high-living, fast-l., incontinent 943 adj. *intemperate;* licentious, dissipated, debauched 951adj. *impure;* riotous, orgiastic, bacchanalian 949 adj. *drunken.*

Vb. *be sensual,*—voluptuous etc.adj.; cultivate one's senses, be the slave of one's desires, live for pleasure, wallow in luxury, live well, indulge oneself, pamper o.; run riot, go the pace, burn the candle at both ends 943vb. *be intemperate.*

Adv. *sensually,* bestially, hoggishly, swinishly.

See: 301, 319, 376, 637, 822, 824, 826, 837, 943, 947, 949, 951, 952.

945 Asceticism

N. *ascetism,* austerity, mortification, self-m., self-torture, self-mutilation; maceration, flagellation 941n. *penance;* ascetic practice, Encratism, yoga, tapas; anchoritism, eremitism 883n. *seclusion;* cynicism, Diogenes and his tub 883n. *unsociability;* Lady Poverty 801n. *poverty;* plain living, Spartan fare, Lenten f. 946n. *fasting;* fast-day 946n. *fast;* self-denial 942n. *temperance;* frugality 814n. *economy;* puritanism, Sabbatarianism, Christian Science; sackcloth, hair-shirt, cilice.

ascetic, spiritual athlete, yogi, sanyasi, fakir, dervish, fire-walker; hermit, eremite, anchoret, anchorite, recluse 883n. *solitary;* cynic, Diogenes; flagellant 939n. *penitent;* water-drinker 948n. *sober person;* faster, vegetarian, fruitarian, Encratite 942n. *abstainer;* puritan, Plymouth Brother, Sabbatarian; spoil-sport, kill-joy, pussyfoot 702n. *hinderer.*

Adj. *ascetic,* yogic, self-mortifying,

fasting, flagellating; hermit-like, eremitical, anchoritic; puritanical; Sabbatarian; austere, rigorous 735 adj. *severe;* Spartan, unpampered 942adj. *temperate;* water-drinking 948adj. *sober;* plain, wholesome 652adj. *salubrious.*

Vb. *be ascetic,* live like a Spartan; fast, live on nothing, live on air 946vb. *starve;* live like a hermit, wear a hair-shirt, put on sackcloth; control one's senses, do tapas, lie on nails, walk through fire.

Adv. *ascetically,* austerely, abstinently, plainly, frugally, painfully.

See: 652, 702, 735, 801, 814, 883, 939, 941, 942, 946, 948.

946 Fasting

N. *fasting,* abstinence from food; no appetite 860n. *indifference;* keeping fast, xerophagy; dieting, banting; Lenten entertainment, Barmecidal feast; Lenten fare, bread and water, spare diet, meager d., starvation d., soupe maigre; iron rations, short commons 636n. *scarcity;* no food, starvation, utter s., famishment 859n. *hunger.*

fast, fast-day, Friday, Good Friday, Lent, Ramadan; day of abstinence, meatless day, fish d., jour maigre, banyan day 945n. *ascetism;* hunger-strike 145n. *strike.*

Adj. *fasting,* not eating, off one's food; abstinent 942adj. *temperate;* keeping fast, keeping Lent, xerophagous; without food, unfed, empty, foodless, dinnerless, supperless; poorly fed, half-starved 636adj. *underfed;* starved, starving, famished, famishing, dying for food 206adj. *lean;* wanting food, a-hungered 859adj. *hungry;* sparing, frugal 814adj. *economical;* scanty 636adj. *scarce;* meager, thin, poor, Spartan; Lenten, quadragesimal.

Vb. *starve,* famish, clem 859vb. *be hungry;* waste with hunger, show one's bones 206vb. *be narrow;* have no food, have nothing to eat, live on water, live on air, dine with Duke Humphrey, have a Barmecidal feast 801vb. *be poor;* fast, go without food, abstain from f., eat no meat; keep fast, keep Lent, keep Ramadan; lay off food, give up eating, eat nothing, refuse one's food, go on hunger-strike; reduce one's food, diet, go on a d., bant, reduce, take off weight 37vb. *bate;* tighten one's belt, go on short commons, live on iron rations; eat sparingly, make two bites of a cherry, control one's appetite 942vb. *be temperate;* keep a poor table 816vb. *be parsimonious.*

See: 37, 145, 206, 636, 801, 814, 816, 859, 860, 942, 945.

947 Gluttony

N. *gluttony,* gluttonishness, greediness, greed, rapacity, insatiability, gulosity, voracity, voraciousness, wolfishness; edacity, polyphagia, insatiable appetite 859n. *hunger;* good living, high l., full-feeding, indulgence, over-i., overeating, overfeeding 943n. *intemperance;* guzzling, gorging, gormandizing, gluttonizing, pampered appetite, belly-worship, gourmandize, epicureanism, epicurism, pleasures of the table 301n. *gastronomy;* bust, blow-out, masses of food 301n. *feasting.*

glutton, glutton for food, guzzler, gormandizer, bolter, gorger, crammer, stuffer; locust, wolf, vulture, cormorant, pig, hog; vampire, bloodsucker; trencherman, good eater, hearty e. 301n. *eater;* coarse feeder, pantophagist; greedy-guts, greedy pig; belly-god, gourmand, gastronome, gourmet, epicure, Lucullus.

Adj. *gluttonous,* gluttonish, rapacious 859adj. *greedy;* devouring, voracious, edacious, wolfish; omnivorous, pantophagous, all-swallowing, all-engulfing 464adj. *indiscriminating;* starving, insatiable, never full 859 adj. *hungry;* pampered, full-fed, overfed, feeding full 301adj. *feeding;* guzzling, gormandizing, gorging, stuffing, cramming, belly-worshiping, licking one's lips, licking one's chops, watering at the mouth; gastronomic, epicurean.

Vb. *gluttonize,* glutton, gormandize; guzzle, bolt, wolf, gobble, gobble up, engulf; fill oneself, gorge, over-g., cram, stuff; glut oneself, overeat 301vb. *eat;* have the run of one's teeth, eat one's head off, eat like a trooper, eat like a horse, eat like a pig, make a beast of oneself, make oneself sick; indulge one's appetite, pamper one's a., tickle one's palate; savor one's food, lick one's lips, lick one's chops, water at the mouth; keep a good table, have the best cook; like one's food, worship one's belly, live only for eating.

Adv. *gluttonously,* ravenously, wolfishly, hungrily; at a gulp, with one bite; gastronomically.

See: 301, 464, 859, 943.

948 Sobriety

N. *sobriety,* soberness 942n. *temperance;* water-drinking, tea-d., teetotalism, nephalism, pussyfootism; state of sobriety, unintoxicated state, clear head, unfuddled brain, no hangover; prohibition zone.

sober person, moderate drinker, poor d., no toper; non-addict, non-alcoholic; water drinker, tea-d., teetotaler, nephalist, total abstainer 942 n. *abstainer;* Good Templar, Rechabite, blue-ribboner, Band of Hope, Blue Ribbon Army, Temperance League; prohibitionist, pussyfoot; sobersides 834n. *moper.*

Adj. *sober,* abstinent, abstemious 620 adj. *avoiding;* water-drinking, tea-d. 942adj. *temperate;* not drinking, off drink, on the water wagon; teetotal, pussyfoot, prohibitionist, dry; unintoxicated, unfuddled, clear-headed, with a clear head, sober as a judge, stone-cold sober; sobered, come to one's senses, sobered up, without a hangover; unfermented, non-alcoholic, soft.

Vb. *be sober,*—abstemious, etc.adj.; drink water, prefer soft drinks; not drink, not imbibe, keep off liquor, never touch drink, drink moderately 942vb. *be temperate;* go on the water wagon, give up alcohol, become teetotal, sign the pledge, join the Band of Hope; go dry, turn prohibitionist; carry one's liquor, hold one's l., keep a clear head, be sober as a judge; sober up, clear one's head, get the fumes out of one's brain, get rid of a hangover, sleep off.

Adv. *soberly,* with sobriety, abstemiously.

See: 620, 942.

949 Drunkenness

N. *drunkenness,* excessive drinking 943n. *intemperance;* ebriosity, insobriety, inebriety, temulence; bibacity, wine-bibbing, weakness for liquor, fondness for the bottle, worship of Bacchus; sottishness, beeriness, vinousness; influence of liquor, inspiration, exhilaration 821n. *excitation;* Dutch courage 855n. *courage;* intoxication, inebriation, befuddlement, fuddledness, blackout; hiccoughing, hiccuping, stammering, stammer, thick speech 580n. *speech defect;* tipsiness, staggering, titubancy 317n. *oscillation;* getting drunk, one over the eight, drop too much, hard drinking, swilling, soaking 301n. *drinking;* compotation, potation, deep potation, libations, libation to Bacchus; one's cups, flowing bowl, booze 301n. *liquor, wine;* drinking bout, spree, jag, lush, blind, debauch, pub-crawl, orgy of drinking, bacchanalia 837n. *revel.*

crapulence, crapula, crapulousness; next-morning feeling, hangover, head, sick headache.

alcoholism, alcoholic addiction, dipsomania, oenomania 503n. *mania;* delirium tremens, dt's, the horrors, heebie-jeebies, jim-jams, pink elephants; grog-blossom, red nose, blue n., bottle n., cirrhosis of the liver.

drunkard, habitual d., inebriate, drunk, regular d., tight; slave to drink, addict, drink a., alcoholic, dipsomaniac, pathological drunk; drinker, hard d., gin-d., dram-d.; bibber, wine-b.; toper, boozer, soaker, soak, souse, sponge, wineskin, tun; sot, love-pot, toss-pot; frothblower, thirsty soul, Pantagruel; intoxicated person, one under the influence of liquor, drunk; devotee of Bacchus, bacchanal, bacchante, maenad; carouser, pubcrawler 837n. *reveler.*

Adj. *drunk,* inebriated, intoxicated, under the influence of liquor; under the influence, having drink taken, having had a drop too much, in one's cups, in liquor, the worse for l.; half-seas over, three sheets in the wind, one over the eight; gilded, boozed up, ginned up, lit up, flushed, merry, gay, happy, nappy, high, elevated, exhilarated 821adj. *excited;* comfortably drunk, nicely thank you, mellow, ripe, full, fou, primed; gloriously drunk, fighting d., drunk and disorderly 61adj. *disorderly;* pot-valiant, "flown with insolence and wine."

tipsy, squiffy, matty, tight, fresh, flush, lushy, faced, foxed, lushed; sozzled, soused, soaked; pickled, oiled, boiled, fried, frazzled, raddled, corned, potted, canned, housed, whittled, screwed, honked, plowed, smashed; overtaken, overcome, disguised, blasted, plastered; maudlin, fuddled, muddled, flustered, muzzy, woozy, obfuscated, clouded, stupefied; bottled, glazed, glassy-eyed, pie-e., gravy-e., seeing double; dizzy, giddy, reeling, staggering 317adj. *oscillating;* hiccoughing 580adj. *stammering.*

dead drunk, stinking d., stinko, blind drunk, blind, blotto; gone, shot, stiff, out; under the table, dead to

the world; drunk as a lord, drunk as a piper, drunk as a fiddler; drunk as an owl, drunk as David's sow.
crapulous, crapulent, with a hangover, with a head; bilious, dizzy, giddy, sick.
drunken, inebriate 943adj. *intemperate;* habitually drunk, always tight, never sober; sottish, sodden, boozy, beery, vinous, smelling of drink, stinking of liquor; thirsty, bibacious, bibulous, bibbing, wine-b., toping, tippling, swilling, swigging, hard-drinking, bottle-cracking, cork-drawing; pub-crawling, carousing, wassailing; red-nosed, blue-n., bottle-n.; bloodshot, gouty, liverish; given to drink, enslaved to d., addicted to d., alcoholic, dipsomaniac.
intoxicating, poisonous, inebriating, inebriative, temulent; exhilarating, going to the head, heady, winy, like wine 821adj. *exciting;* alcoholic, spirituous, vinous, beery; not soft, hard, potent, double-strength, overproof 162adj. *strong;* neat 44adj. *unmixed.*
Vb. *be drunk,*—tipsy etc.adj.; be under the influence of liquor, have had too much; have a weak head, not hold one's liquor, succumb, be overcome, pass out, see double; hiccough, stutter 580vb. *stammer;* not walk straight, lurch, stagger, reel, swim, trip up 317vb. *oscillate.*
get drunk, have too much, drink deep, drink hard, drink like a fish, drink to get tight; liquor up, gin oneself up, lush, bib, tipple, booze, tope, sot, guzzle, swig, swill, soak, souse, hit the bottle 301vb. *drink;* go on the spree, go on a blind, have a buzz on, go pub-crawling, pub-crawl; drown one's sorrows, commit a debauch, quaff, carouse, wassail, sacrifice to Bacchus 837n. *revel.*
inebriate, be intoxicating,—heady etc. adj.; exhilarate, elevate 821vb. *excite;* go to one's head, make one's head swim, be too much, overcome, disguise, fuddle, befuddle, fuzzle, stupefy; make drunk, tipsify, pickle, stew; drink one under the table, put one under.
Adv. *drunkenly,* sottishly, crapulously, boozily, beerily, vinously; intoxicatingly, headily, winily.
See: 44, 61, 162, 301, 317, 503, 580, 821, 837, 855, 943.

950 Purity

N. *purity,* non-mixture, simplicity, nakedness 44n. *simpleness;* faultlessness 646n. *perfection;* sinlessness, immaculacy 935n. *innocence;* moral purity, morals, good m., morality 933n. *virtue;* decency, propriety, delicacy 846n. *good taste;* pudicity, pudency, shame, blushfulness 874n. *modesty;* chastity, continence, Encratism 942n. *temperance;* coldness, frigidity 820n. *moral insensibility;* honor, one's h., woman's h., honesty; virginity, maidenhood, maidenhead 895n. *celibacy.*
prudery, prudishness, squeamishness, shockability, Victorianism; overmodesty, false modesty, false shame, mauvaise honte 874n. *modesty;* demureness, gravity 834n. *seriousness;* priggishness, primness, coyness 850 n. *affectation;* sanctimony, sanctimoniousness 979n. *pietism;* puritanism, blue laws 735n. *severity;* euphemism, genteelism, mealy-mouthedness; censorship, expurgation, bowdlerization 550n. *obliteration.*
virgin, maiden, vestal, vestal virgin, virgo intacta 895n. *celibate;* Encratite, religious celibate 986n. *monk, nun;* Joseph, Hippolytus, Galahad; pure woman, Diana, Lucretia; maid, old m.
prude, prig, Victorian, euphemist 850n. *affector;* puritan, guardian of morality, Watch Committee, Mrs. Grundy; censor, Bowdler.
Adj. *pure,* unadulterated 44adj. *unmixed;* faultless 646adj. *perfect;* undefiled, unfallen, sinless 935adj. *innocent;* maidenly, virginal, vestal, untouched, unhandseled 895adj. *unwedded;* blushful, blushing, rosy 874 adj. *modest;* coy, shy 620adj. *avoiding;* chaste, continent 942adj. *temperate;* unmovable, unassailable, impregnable, incorruptible 660adj. *invulnerable;* unfeeling 820adj. *impassive;* frigid 380adj. *cold;* immaculate, spotless, snowy 427adj. *white;* good 929adj. *honorable;* moral 933adj. *virtuous;* Platonic, sublimated, elevated, purified; decent, decorous, delicate, refined 846 adj. *tasteful;* edifying, printable, quotable, repeatable, mentionable, virginibus puerisque 648adj. *clean;* censored, bowdlerized, expurgated, edited.
prudish, squeamish, shockable, Victorian; overdelicate, overmodest; old-maidish, straitlaced, puritan, priggish; holy, sanctimonious 979 adj. *pietistic.*
See: 44, 380, 427, 550, 620, 646, 648,

660, 735, 820, 834, 846, 850, 874, 895, 929, 933, 935, 942, 979, 986.

951 Impurity

N. *impurity,* impure thoughts, filthiness, defilement 649n. *uncleanness;* indelicacy 847n. *bad taste;* indecency, immodesty, impudicity, shamelessness, exhibitionism; coarseness, grossness, nastiness; ribaldry, bawdry, bawdiness, salaciousness; loose talk, filthy t., blue story, smoking-room s., Milesian s., limerick, double entendre, equivoque; sex, smut, dirt, filth, obscenity, obscene literature, curious l., pornographic l., pornography; pornogram; banned book; blue cinema; prurience, voyeurism, scopophilia, skeptophilia.

unchastity, lightness, folly, wantonness; incontinence, easy virtue, no morals; immorality, sexual delinquency; sex consciousness, roving eye; lickerishness, prurience, concupiscence, lust 859n. *libido;* carnality, sexuality, fleshliness, the flesh 944n. *sensualism;* sex-indulgence, lasciviousness, lewdness, salacity, lubricity; dissoluteness, dissipation, debauchery, licentiousness, license, libertinism, libertinage, gallantry; seduction, stupration, defloration; venery, lechery, priapism, fornication, wenching, womanizing, whoring; promiscuity, harlotry, whorishness, whoredom.

illicit love, guilty l., unlawful desires; extramarital relations, criminal conversation, unlawful carnal knowledge; incestuous affection, Caunian love; incest, sodomy, homosexualism, lesbianism, bestiality 84 n. *abnormality;* satyriasis, priapism, nymphomania; adultery, unfaithfulness, infidelity, marital i., cuckolding, cuckoldry; eternal triangle, liaison intrigue, amour, amourette, seduction 887n. *love affair;* free love, unwedded cohabitation, irregular union, concubinage, companionate marriage 894n. *type of marriage.*

rape, ravishment, violation, forcing, stupration; indecent assault; sex crime, sex murder.

social evil, harlot's trade, harlotry, whoredom; streetwalking, prostitution, open p.; public indecency, indecent exposure; pimping, pandering, panderism, bawd's trade, brothel-keeping, living on immoral earnings, white-slave traffic.

brothel, bordel, bagnio, seraglio, stew, lupanar; bawdy-house, house, tolerated h., disorderly h., house of ill-fame, house of ill-repute; kip, dive, knocking shop; red-light district.

Adj. *impure,* defiling, defiled, unclean, nasty 649adj. *dirty;* unwholesome 653adj. *insalubrious;* indelicate, unsqueamish, not for the squeamish; vulgar, coarse, gross; ribald, bald, broad, free, loose; strong, racy, bawdy, fescennine, Rabelaisian; uncensored, unexpurgated, unbowdlerized; suggestive, provocative, piquant, titillating; spicy, juicy; immoral, risqué, risky, equivocal, naughty, wicked, blue, lurid; unmentionable, unquotable, unprintable; smutty, filthy, scrofulous, scabrous, scatological, stinking, rank, fulsome, offensive; indecent, obscene, lewd, salacious, lubricious; licentious, Milesian, pornographic, porny; prurient, erotic, phallic, priapic; sexual, sexy, hot.

unchaste, unvirtuous 934adj. *vicious;* frail, not impregnable, fallen, seduced, prostituted; of easy virtue, of loose morals, moralless, immoral; incontinent, light, wanton, loose, fast, free, gay, skittish, riggish, naughty; wild, rackety; immodest, daring, revealing; unblushing, shameless, flaunting, scarlet, meretricious, whorish, tarty; promiscuous, pandemic, streetwalking; Paphian, aphrodisian; brothel-keeping, pimping, procuring.

lecherous, carnal, fleshly, carnal-minded, voluptuous 944n. *sensual;* libidinous, lustful, lickerish, goatish; prurient, concupiscent 859n. *desiring;* rampant, in heat, rutting, ruttish, musth, must; hot, sexed-up, skittish, randy, riggish; sex-conscious, man-c., woman-c.; priapic, mad for women, woman-mad, woman-crazy; sex-mad, sex-crazy, nymphomaniac; lewd, licentious, libertine, free, loose, rakish, gallant; debauched, dissolute, dissipated, profligate, whoremongering, brothel-haunting.

extramarital, irregular, concubinary; unlawful, incestuous, homosexual, lesbian, bestial 84n. *abnormal;* adulterous, unfaithful; committing adultery, anticipating marriage; bed-hopping.

Vb. *be impure,*—unchaste etc.adj.; have no morals, go in for sex; talk sex, swap limericks; be unfaithful, deceive one's spouse, break the marriage vow, commit adultery, cuckold; dissipate 943vb. *be intemperate;* fornicate, womanize, whore, wench, haunt brothels; keep women, keep a mistress, concubinize; lech, lust, rut, be in heat, be hot 859vb. *desire;* wanton, rig, be promiscuous, sleep with anyone; become a prostitute, streetwalk, be on the streets; pimp, pander, procure, keep a brothel.

debauch, defile, smirch 649vb. *make unclean;* abuse, dishonor, seduce, lead astray, deflower, wreck, ruin; concubinize, strumpet, prostitute, whore, make a whore of; lay, tumble, copulate, lie with, sleep w. 45vb. *unite with;* rape, commit r., ravish, violate, force; outrage, assault, indecently a.

Adv. *impurely,* immodestly, shamelessly; loosely, bawdily, sexily, erotically; lewdly, salaciously, suggestively; carnally, sexually 944adv. *sensually;* lustfully, pruriently, concupiscently.

See: 45, 84, 649, 653, 847, 859, 887, 894, 934, 943, 944.

952 Libertine

N. *libertine,* no Joseph; gay bachelor, not the marrying kind; philanderer, flirt; free-lover, loose liver, loose fellow, fast man, rip, rake, rakehell, roué, debauchee, profligate; lady-killer, gallant, squire of dames; fancy-man, gigolo, mignon; intrigant, intriguer, seducer, deceiver, gay d., false lover, lothario 887n. *lover;* corespondent, adulterer, cuckolder, bed-hopper; immoralist, amorist, Don Juan, Casanova; woman-hunter, woman-chaser, skirt-c., chaser, curb-crawler; womanizer, fornicator, whoremonger, whoremaster; voyeur, lecher, satyr, goat, one mad for women; raper, rapist, ravisher, Tarquin; homosexual, homo, pederast, sodomite, pansy, fairy, pervert; protector, ponce, bully.

cuckold, deceived husband, injured h., complaisant h.; wittol, wearer of horns.

loose woman, light w., light o' love, wanton, rig, hot stuff; woman of easy virtue, demirep, one no better than she should be; flirt, piece, bit, bint, wench, quean, jade, hussy, minx, miss, nymphet; baggage, trash, trollop, trull, drab, slut, "daughter of the game"; adventuress, temptress, seductress, scarlet woman, painted w., Jezebel; adultress, false wife, fornicatress, fornicatrix; nymphomaniac, Messalina.

kept woman, mistress, paramour, leman, hetaera, concubine, unofficial wife; favorite, sweetheart, girl-friend 887n. *loved one;* petite dame, petite amie, bit of fluff, floozy, moll, mopsy, doxy.

prostitute, common p., white slave, fallen woman, erring sister; frail sisterhood, demimonde; harlot, trollop, whore, strumpet, laced mutton; street-walker, woman of the streets, woman of the town; woman of the stews, brothel-inmate; tart, punk, chippy, broad, hustler; pick-up, casual conquest, call-girl; fille de joie, poule, lorette, cocotte, courtesan; demimondaine, demirep, hetaera, Aspasia, Lais, Thais, Phryne; cyprian, Paphian; temple-prostitute, hierodule 742n. *slave.*

bawd, go-between, conciliatrix, pimp, pander, procurer, procuress, mackerel, brothel-keeper, madam; white slaver, ponce.

See: 742, 887.

953 Legality

N. *legality,* formality, form, formula, rite, due process 959n. *litigation;* form of law, letter of the l., pale of the l., four corners of the l. (**see** *law*); respect for law, constitutionality, constitutionalism; good law, judgment according to the l. 480n. *judgment;* justice under the law 913n. *justice;* keeping within the law, lawfulness, legitimateness, legitimacy, validity.

legislation, legislature, legislatorship, law-giving, law-making, constitution-m.; codification; legalization, legitimization, validation, ratification, confirmation 532n. *affirmation;* passing into law, enacting, enactment, regulation, regulation by law, regulation by statute; plebiscite 605n. *vote;* plebiscitum, psephism, popular decree; law, statute, ordinance, order, standing o., by-law 737n. *decree;* canon, rule, edict, rescript 693n. *precept;* legislator, law-giver, law-maker.

law, law and equity, the law; body of law, corpus juris, constitution, written c., unwritten c.; charter, institution; codification, codified law, statute book, legal code, pandect, Twelve Tables, Ten Commandments, Pentateuch, Laws of Manu; penal code, civil c., Napoleonic c.; written law, statute l., common l., unwritten l., natural l.; personal law, private l., canon l., ecclesiastical l.; international law, jus gentium, law of nations, law of the sea, law of the air; law of commerce, commercial law, lex mercatoria, law of contract, law of crime, criminal law, civil l., constitutional l.; arm of the law, legal process 955n. *jurisdiction;* writ, summons, lawsuit 959n. *legal trial.*

jurisprudence, nomology, science of law, knowledge of l., legal learning; law-book, legal textbook, legal journal; law consultancy, legal advice.

Adj. *legal,* lawful 913adj. *just;* law-abiding 739adj. *obedient;* legitimate, competent; licit, permissible, allowable 756adj. *permitted;* within the law, sanctioned by law, according to l., de jure, legally sound, good in law; statutable, statutory, constitutional; nomothetic, law-giving, legislatorial, legislational, legislative, decretal; legislated, enacted, passed, voted, made law, ordained, decreed, ordered, by order; legalized, legitimized, brought within the law; liable or amenable to law, actionable, justiciable, triable, cognizable 928adj. *accusable;* fit for legislation, suitable for enactment; pertaining to law, jurisprudential, nomological, learned in the law.

Vb. *be legal,*—legitimate etc. adj.; come within the law, respect the l., abide by the l., keep within the l.

make legal, legalize, legitimize, validate, confirm, ratify 488vb. *endorse;* vest, establish 153vb. *stabilize;* legislate, make laws, give l.; pass, enact, ordain, enforce 737vb. *decree.*

Adv. *legally,* by law, by order; legitimately, de jure, in the eye of the law.

See: 153, 480, 488, 532, 605, 693, 737, 739, 756, 913, 928, 955, 959.

954 Illegality

N. *illegality,* bad law, legal flaw, irregularity, informality, error of law, mistake of l.; wrong verdict, bad judgment 481vb. *misjudgment;* contradictory law, antinomy; miscarriage of justice 914n. *injustice;* wrong side of the law, unlawfulness; unauthorization, incompetence, illicitness, illegitimacy, impermissibility 757n. *prohibiton.*

lawbreaking, breach of law, violation of l., transgression, contravention, infringement, encroachment 306n. *overstepping;* trespass, offense, offense against the law, tort, civil wrong; champerty, malpractice 930 n. *foul play;* shadiness, dishonesty 930n. *improbity;* criminality, criminousness 936n. *guilt;* criminal activity, criminal offense, indictable o., crime, capital c., misdemeanor, felony; misprision, misfeasance, malfeasance, wrongdoing 914n. *wrong;* criminology, criminal statistics.

lawlessness, antinomianism; outlawry, disfranchisement; no law, absence of l., paralysis of authority, breakdown of law and order, crime wave 734n. *anarchy;* kangaroo court, gang rule, mob law, lynch l., Lydford l.; riot, race-r., rioting, hooliganism, ruffianism, rebellion 738n. *revolt;* coup d'état, usurpation 916n. *arrogation;* arbitrary rule, arbitrariness, negation of law, abolition of l.; mailed fist, force majeure, droit de plus fort 735n. *brute force.*

bastardy, bastardism, baseness; bastardization, illegitimacy; bastard, illegitimate child, natural c., love c., by-blow, one born out of wedlock; spurious offspring, offspring of adultery, fruit of a.

Adj. *illegal,* illegitimate, illicit, contraband, black-market; impermissible 757adj. *prohibited;* unauthorized, incompetent, without authority, unwarrantable, informal, unofficial; unlawful, wrongous, wrongful 914 adj. *wrong;* unlegislated, not covered by law, exceeding the l., bad in law; unchartered, unconstitutional, unstatutory; no longer law, superseded, suspended, null and void, annulled 752adj. *abrogated;* irregular, contrary to law, not according to l., unknown to l.; injudicial, extrajudicial; on the wrong side of the law, against the l.; outside the law, outlawed, out of bounds, offside; tortious, actionable, cognizable, justiciable, triable, punishable 928adj. *accusable.*

lawbreaking, trespassing, transgressing, infringing, encroaching; sinning 934adj. *wicked;* offending 936adj. *guilty;* criminal, criminous, misdemeanant, felonious; fraudulent, shady 930adj. *dishonest.*

lawless, antinomian, without law, chaotic 734adj. *anarchic;* ungovernable, licentious 738adj. *riotous;* violent, summary; arbitrary, irresponsible, unanswerable, unaccountable; above the law, over-mighty; despotic, tyrannical 735adj. *oppressive.*

bastard, illegitimate, spurious, base; misbegotten, misbegot, adulterine, base-born; without a father, without a name; bastardized.

Vb. *be illegal,* be bad in law, break the law, violate the l., offend against the l., circumvent the l., disregard the statute; wrest the law, twist *or* strain the l., torture the l.; be lawless, defy the law, drive a coach and horses through the l. 914vb. *do wrong;* take the law into one's own hands, strain one's authority, encroach 734vb. *please oneself;* have no law, know no l., stand above the law; stand outside the law, suffer outlawry.

make illegal,—unlawful etc.adj.; put outside the law, outlaw; illegalize 757vb. *prohibit;* forbid by law, penalize 963vb. *punish;* bastardize, illegitimize; suspend, annul, cancel, make the law a dead letter 752vb. *abrogate.*

Adv. *illégally,* illicitly, illegitimately, unlawfully, criminally, criminously, feloniously, tortiously, with malice prepense.

See: 306, 481, 734, 735, 738, 752, 757, 914, 916, 928, 930, 934, 936, 963.

955 Jurisdiction

N. *jurisdiction,* portfolio 622vb. *function;* judicature, magistracy, commission of the peace; mayoralty, shrievalty, bumbledom; competence, legal c., legal authority, arm of the law 733n. *authority;* administration of justice, legal administration, Ministry of Justice; local jurisdiction, local authority, corporation, municipality, borough council, town c., parish c., bailiwick 692n. *council;* vigilance committee 956n. *tribunal;* office, bureau, secretariat 687n. *workshop;* legal authority, competence.

law officer, legal administrator, Minister of Justice, Lord Chancellor, Attorney-General, Advocate-General, Solicitor-General, Legal Remembrancer, Queen's Proctor; Crown Counsel, public prosecutor; Judge Advocate, Procurator Fiscal, district attorney 957n. *judge;* mayor, lord m., sheriff 733n. *magistrature;* court officer, clerk of the court, huissier, tipstaff, bailiff, bum-bailiff; summoner, process-server, catchpoll, Bow-street runner; paritor, apparitor, beadle, mace-bearer 690n. *official.*

police, forces of law and order; police force, the force, Scotland Yard; constabulary, gendarmerie, military police; peace officer, civil o., police officer, limb of the law, policeman, constable, special c., copper, cop, traffic c., motor police; bluebottle, Peeler, bobby, flatfoot, dick; police-sergeant, police inspector, police superintendent, commissioner of police, chief constable, provost marshal; subinspector, daroga; gendarme, sbirro, alguacil, kavass; watch, posse comitatus; press-gang; plain-clothes man 459n. *detective.*

Adj. *jurisdictional,* jurisdictive, competent; executive, administrative, administrational, directive 689adj. *directing;* justiciary, judiciary, juridical, causidical; original, appellate; justiciable, subject to jurisdiction, liable to the law.

Vb. *hold court,* administer justice, sit on the bench, sit in judgment 480vb. *judge;* hear complaints, hear causes 959vb. *try a case;* be seized of, cognize, take cognizance, take judicial notice.

See: 459, 480, 622, 687, 689, 690, 692, 733, 956, 957, 959.

956 Tribunal

N. *tribunal,* seat of justice, woolsack, throne; judgment seat, bar, bar of justice; court of conscience, tribunal of penance, confessional, judgment-day; forum, ecclesia, wardmote, burghmote 692n. *council;* public opinion, vox populi, electorate; judicatory, bench, board, bench of judges, panel of j., judge and jury; judicial assembly, Areopagus; judicial committee, judicial committee of the Privy Council, King's Council; Justices in Eyre, commission of the peace; Congregation of the Holy Office; original side, appellate s.

lawcourt, court, open c.; court of law, court of justice, criminal court, civil c.; Federal Court, High Court, District Court, County Court; Supreme Court, appellate court, Court of Appeal; court of inferior jurisdiction, subordinate court, small cause c., Court of Requests; court of record, Rolls Court; Court-royal, Board of Green Cloth; King's Court, Court of Exchequer, Exchequer of Pleas, Star Chamber; High Court of Parliament 692n. *parliament;* High Court of Judicature, Queen's Bench, Queen's Bench Division, Court of Common Pleas, Court of Claims; Court of Admiralty, Probate and

Divorce; Court of Chancery, court of equity, court of arbitration; Eyre of Justice, court of oyer and terminer, circuit court; assize; sessions, court of session, quarter sessions, petty s.; Central Criminal Court, Old Bailey; magistrate's court, police c.; coroner's court; court of piepowder, court of pie poudre; feudal court, manorial c., Stannary Court, court-baron, court-leet; guild-court, hustings; Vice-Chancellor's court; court-martial, drum-head c., summary court; durbar, divan 692n. *council.*

ecclesiastical court, court of audience, Court of Arches; papal court, curia; Inquisition, Holy Office.

courtroom, court-house, law-courts, cut-cherry; bench, woolsack, jury-box; dock; witness-box, chair.

Adj. *curial,* judicatory, judicial, justiciary, inquisitional, rhadamanthine; original, appellate 955adj. *jurisdictional.*

See: 692, 955.

957 Judge

N. *judge,* justice, his justiceship, his Lordship; bencher, justicer, justiciar, judiciary, podestà; deemster, doomster, doomsman; dicast, Areopagite, praetor urbanus, praetor peregrinus; verderer; Lord Chancellor, Lord Chief Justice, Master of the Rolls, Exchequer judge, baron; military judge, Judge Advocate; chief justice, puisné judge, county court j., recorder, common serjeant; sessions judge, assize j., judge on circuit, circuiteer; district judge, subordinate j.; civil judge, moonsif, mufti, cadi, kazi; criminal judge, magistrate, district m., presidency m., city m., police m.; stipendiary magistrate; coroner; honorary magistrate, justice of the peace, the great unpaid; bench, judiciary.

magistracy, beak, his Worship, his nibs; arbiter, umpire, referee, assessor, arbitrator 480n. *estimator;* revising barrister 549n. *recorder;* Daniel come to judgment, Solomon, Minos, Rhadamanthus, Recording Angel.

jury, twelve good men and true, twelve men in a box; grand jury, special j., petty j., trial j., coroner's j.; juror's panel, jury list, jurors' book; juror, juryman, jurat, recognitor, assessor; foreman of the jury, chancellor; dicast, judex, dicastery.

See: 480, 549.

958 Lawyer

N. *lawyer,* practicing l., legal practitioner, member of the legal profession, man of law; common lawyer, canon l., civil l., criminal l.; one called to the bar, barrister, barrister-at-law, advocate, counsel, learned c., counsel learned in the law; junior barrister, stuff gown, junior counsel; senior barrister, bencher, bencher of the Inns of Court; silk gown, leading counsel, King's C., Queen's C.; serjeant, serjeant at law, King's serjeant, prime s., postman, tubman; circuit barrister, circuiteer; shyster, pettifogger, crooked lawyer.

law agent, attorney, public a., attorney at law, proctor, procurator; writer to the signet, solicitor before the Supreme Court; solicitor, legal adviser; legal representative, legal agent, vakeel, mukhtar, pleader, advocate; equity draftsman; conveyancer.

notary, common n., notary public, commissioner for oaths; scrivener, petition-writer; clerk of the court, cursitor, articler 955n. *law officer;* solicitor's clerk, barrister's c., barrister's devil.

jurist, jurisconsult, legal adviser, legal expert, legal light, master of jurisprudence, pundit, legist, legalist, civilian, canonist; student of law, law student, legal apprentice, devil.

bar, civil b., criminal b., English bar, Scottish b., junior b., senior b.; Inns of Chancery, Inns of Court, Serjeants' Inn, Gray's I., Lincoln's I., Inner Temple, Middle T.; profession of law, legal profession, the Robe, the long robe; barristership, advocacy, pleading; solicitorship, attorneydom, attorneyism, vakeelship; legal consultancy.

Adj. *jurisprudential,* learned in the law, called to the bar, at the b., practicing at the b., barristerial, forensic; solicitorial, notarial.

Vb. *do law,* study l., go in for l., take up l.; eat one's dinners, be called to the bar; take silk, be called within the bar; practice at the bar, accept a brief, take a case, advocate, plead; practice law, write to the signet, solicit; attorney.

See: 955.

959 Litigation

N. *litigation,* going to law, litigiousness 709n. *quarrelsomeness;* legal dispute 709n. *quarrel;* issue, legal i., matter for judgment, case for decision; lawsuit, suit at law, suit, case, cause, action; prosecution, arraignment, impeachment, charge 928n. *accusation;* test case 461n. *experiment;* claim, counter-c. 915n. *dueness;* plea, petition 761n. *request;* affidavit, written statement, averment, pleading, demurrer 532n. *affirmation.*

legal process, proceedings, legal procedure, course of law, arm of the l. 955n. *jurisdiction;* citation, subpoena, summons, search warrant 737n. *warrant;* arrest, apprehension, detention, committal 747n. *restraint;* habeas corpus, bail, surety, security, recognizance, personal r.; injunction, stay order, order to show cause; writ, certiorari, latitat, nisi prius.

legal trial, trial, trial by law, trial by jury, trial at the bar, trial in court, assize, sessions 956n. *lawcourt;* inquest, inquisition, examination 459n. *inquiry;* hearing, prosecution, defense; hearing of evidence, taking of e., recording of e. 466n. *evidence;* examination, cross-e., reexamination, objection sustained, objection overruled 466n. *testimony;* pleadings, arguments 475n. *reasoning;* counter-argument, rebutter, rebuttal 460n. *rejoinder;* proof 478n. *demonstration;* disproof 479n. *confutation;* summing up, charge to the jury; ruling, finding, decision, verdict 480n. *judgment;* favorable verdict 960n. *acquittal;* unfavorable verdict 961n. *condemnation;* execution of judgment 963n. *punishment;* appeal, motion of a., writ of error; successful appeal, reversal of judgment, retrial; precedent, case-law, decided case, reported c.; law reports, Newgate Calendar; cause-list; case-record, dossier 548n. *record.*

litigant, libellant, party, party to a suit, suitor 763n. *petitioner;* claimant, plaintiff, defendant, appellant, respondent, objector, intervener; accused, prisoner at the bar 928n. *accused person;* litigious person, sycophant, common informer 524n. *informer;* prosecutor 928n. *accuser.*

Adj. *litigating,* at law with, litigant, suing 928adj. *accusing;* going to law, appearing in court; contesting, objecting, disputing 475adj. *arguing;* litigious 709adj. *quarreling;* vexatious, sycophantic.

litigated, on trial, coram judice; argued, disputed, contested; up for trial, brought before the court, submitted for judgment, offered for arbitration; sub judice, on the cause-list, down for hearing, ready for h.; litigable, disputable, arguable, suable, actionable, justiciable 928adj. *accusable.*

Vb. *litigate,* go to law, appeal to l., set the law in motion, start an action, bring a suit, file a s., petition 761vb. *request;* prepare a case, prepare a brief, brief counsel; file a claim 915vb. *claim;* have the law on one, make one a party, sue, implead, arraign, impeach, accuse, charge 928vb. *indict;* cite, summon, serve notice on; prosecute, bring to justice, bring to trial, bring to the bar; challenge the jurors; argue one's case, advocate, plead, call evidence 475vb. *argue.*

try a case, take cognizance, put down for hearing, impanel a jury, hear a cause; examine the witnesses, take statements; sit in judgment, rule, find, decide, adjudicate 480vb. *judge;* close the pleadings, sum up, charge the jury; bring in a verdict, pronounce sentence; commit for trial.

stand trial, come before, come up for trial, be put on t., stand in the dock; plead to the charge, ask to be tried, submit to judgment, hear sentence; defend an action, put in one's defense, make one's d.

Adv. *in litigation,* at law, in court, before the judge; coram judice, sub judice, pendente lite; litigiously, sycophantically.

See: 459, 460, 461, 466, 475, 478, 479, 480, 524, 532, 548, 709, 737, 747, 761, 763, 915, 928, 955, 956, 960, 961, 963.

960 Acquittal

N. *acquittal,* favorable verdict, verdict of not guilty, verdict of not proven, benefit of doubt; clearance, exculpation, exoneration 935n. *innocence;* absolution, discharge; let-off, thumbs up 746n. *liberation;* whitewashing, justification, compurgation 927n. *vindication;* successful defense, defeat of the prosecution; no case, withdrawal of the charge, quashing, quietus; reprieve, pardon 909n. *forgiveness;* non-prosecution, exemption, impunity 919n. *non-liability.*

Adj. *acquitted,* not guilty 935adj. *guiltless;* clear, cleared, in the clear, exonerated, exculpated, vindicated; uncondemned, unpunished, unchastised, immune, exempted, exempt 919adj. *non-liable;* let off, discharged, without a stain on one's character 746adj. *liberated;* reprieved 909adj. *forgiven;* recommended to mercy.

Vb. *acquit,* find *or* pronounce not guilty, prove innocent, justify, compurgate, whitewash, get one off 927 vb. *vindicate;* clear, absolve, exonerate, exculpate; find there is no case to answer, not prosecute 919vb. *exempt;* discharge, let go, let off 746 vb. *liberate;* reprieve, respite, pardon, remit the penalty 909vb. *forgive;* quash, quash the conviction, set aside the sentence, allow an appeal 752vb. *abrogate.*

See: 746, 752, 909, 919, 927, 935.

961 Condemnation

N. *condemnation,* unfavorable verdict, hostile v.; finding of guilty, conviction; successful prosecution, unsuccessful defense; final condemnation, damnation; black-list, Index 924n. *disapprobation;* excommunication 899n. *malediction;* doom, judgment, sentence 963n. *punishment;* writing on the wall 511n. *omen;* outlawry, price on one's head, proscription, attainder; death-warrant, condemned cell, execution chamber, Death Row; thumbs down; black cap; knell.

Adj. *condemned,* found guilty, made liable; convicted, sentenced; proscribed, outlawed, with a price on one's head; self-convicted, confessing; without a case, having no case, without a leg to stand on; cast in one's suit, non-suited, damned 924 adj. *disapproved;* lost, in hell, burning, frying.

Vb. *condemn,* prove guilty, bring home the charge; find liable, find against, non-suit, cast one in his suit; find guilty, pronounce g., convict, sentence; sentence to death, put on the black cap, sign one's death warrant; reject one's defense, reject one's appeal 607vb. *reject;* proscribe, attaint, outlaw, bar, put a price on one's head 954vb. *make illegal;* blacklist, put on the index 924vb. *disapprove;* damn, excommunicate 899vb. *curse;* convict oneself, plead guilty 526vb. *confess.*

See: 511, 526, 607, 899, 924, 954, 963.

962 Reward

N. *reward,* guerdon, remuneration, recompense; meed, deserts, just d. 913n. *justice;* recognition, acknowledgement, thanks 907n. *gratitude;* tribute, deserved t., proof of regard 923n. *praise;* prize-giving, award, presentation, prize, crown, cup, pot, certificate, medal 729n. *trophy;* honor 729n. *decoration;* honors 870 n. *title;* prize-money, talent m., money prize, cash p., prize-fellowship, scholarship, bursary, stipend, exhibition, demyship; assistance, alimony, grant, allowance 703n. *subvention;* reward for service, fee, retainer, honorarium, payment, remuneration, emolument, pension, salary, wage, wages, screw, differential, rate of pay, wage scale, Burnham s. 804n. *pay;* overtime pay 612n. *incentive;* perquisite, perks, expense account, dearness allowance; income turnover 771n. *earnings;* return, profitable r., profit, margin of p. 771n. *gain;* compensation, indemnification, satisfaction; consideration, quid pro quo, requital 714n. *retaliation;* avengement 910n. *revenge;* reparation 787n. *restitution;* bounty, honorarium, gratuity, golden handshake, tip, solatium, gratification, douceur, pourboire, trinkgeld, baksheesh, dastur 781n. *gift;* tempting offer 759n. *offer;* bait, lure, bribe 612n. *inducement;* hush money, smart m., protection m., blackmail.

Adj. *rewarding,* prize-giving, munerary; generous, open-handed 813adj. *liberal;* paying, profitable, remunerative 771adj. *gainful;* promising 759 adj. *offering;* compensatory, indemnificatory 714adj. *retaliatory;* reparatory 787adj. *restoring;* retributive 910adj. *revengeful.*

Vb. *reward,* guerdon, recompense; award, present, give a prize, offer a p., offer a reward; bestow a medal, title 866vb. *honor;* recognize, acknowledge, pay tribute, thank, show one's gratitude 907 vb. *be grateful;* remunerate, fee 804vb. *pay;* satisfy, gratify, tip 781vb. *give;* tip well 813vb. *be liberal;* repay, requite 714vb. *retaliate;* compensate, indemnify, make reparation 787vb. *restitute;* make amends 941vb. *atone;* offer a bribe, gain over 612vb. *bribe.*

be rewarded, gain a reward, get a prize, get a medal, receive a title; get paid, draw a salary, earn an income, have a gainful occupation 771vb. *acquire;* accept payment, accept a gratification 782vb. *receive;* take a bribe, have one's palm greased; have one's reward, get one's deserts, receive one's due 915 vb. *deserve;* reap, reap a profit, seize one's advantage 771vb. *gain;* reap the fruits, reap the whirlwind.

Adv. *rewardingly,* profitably; for a consideration, as a reward, in compensation.

See: 612, 703, 714, 729, 759, 771, 781, 782, 787, 804, 813, 866, 870, 907, 910, 913, 915, 923, 941.

963 Punishment

N. *punishment,* sentence 961n. *condemnation;* execution of sentence, exaction of penalty, penalization, victimization; punition, chastisement, heads rolling; chastening, castigation, strafing, strafe 924n. *reprimand;* disciplinary action, discipline; dose, pill, bitter p., hard lines, infliction, trial, visitation, punishing experience 731n. *adversity;* just deserts, meet reward 915n. *dueness;* doom, judgment, day of j., day of reckoning, divine justice 913n. *justice;* poetic justice, retributive j., retribution, Nemesis; reckoning, repayment 787n. *restitution;* requital, reprisal 714n. *retaliation;* avengement 910n. *revenge;* penance, self-punishment 941n. *atonement;* self-mortification, self-discipline 945n. *asceticism;* hara-kiri 362n. *suicide;* penology, penologist.

corporal punishment, bodily chastisement, smacking, slapping, trouncing, hiding, dusting, beating, fustigation, stick law, argumentum ad baculum; caning, whipping, flogging, scourging, flagellation, bastinado, running the gauntlet; defenestration; ducking, keel-hauling; picket, picketing, slap, smack, rap, rap over the knuckles, box on the ear; drubbing, blow, buffet, cuff, clout, stroke, stripe 279n. *knock;* third degree, torture, peine forte et dure, racking, strappado, breaking on the wheel, death by a thousand cuts 377n. *pain.*

capital punishment, extreme penalty 361n. *death;* death sentence, death warrant; execution 362n. *killing;* decapitation, beheading, heading, guillotining, decollation; traitor's death, hanging, drawing and quartering; strangulation, garrote, bow-stringing; hanging, high jump, long drop, "Tyburn ague"; electrocution; stoning, lapidation; crucifixion, impalement, flaying alive; burning, death by burning, auto da fé; drowning, noyade; massacre, mass murder, mass execution, purge, genocide 362 n. *slaughter;* martyrdom, martyrization, persecution to the death; illegal execution, lynching, lynch law; judicial murder.

penalty, penal character, penality; injury, damage 772n. *loss;* infliction, imposition, task, lines; prescribed punishment, sentence, penalization, pains and penalties, penal code, penology; devil to pay, liability, legal l. 915n. *dueness;* damages, costs, compensation, restoration 787 n. *restitution;* amercement, fining, mulct, fine, sconce, deodand, compulsory payment 804n. *payment;* ransom 809n. *price;* forfeit, forfeiture, sequestration, escheat, confiscation, deprivation 786n. *expropriation;* keeping in, gating, imprisonment 747n. *detention;* binding over 747n. *restraint;* penal servitude, hard labor, galley service, galleys; transportation; expulsion, deportation, externment 300n. *ejection;* ostracism, banishment, exile, proscription, ban, outlawing 57n. *exclusion;* reprisal 714n. *retaliation.*

punisher, vindicator, retaliator 910n. *avenger;* inflicter, chastiser, castigator, corrector, chastener, discipliner, persecutor; sentencer, justiciary, magistrate, court, law 957n. *judge;* spanker, whipper, caner, trouncer, flogger, scourger, flagellator; torturer, inquisitor; executioner, headsman, hangman, Jack Ketch; garroter, bow-stringer; fire-party; lyncher 362n. *murderer.*

Adj. *punitive,* penological, penal, punitory; castigatory, disciplinary, corrective; retributive 910adj. *revengeful;* in reprisal 714adj. *retaliatory;* penalizing, inflictive, fining, mulctuary, amercing; confiscatory, expropriatory 786adj. *taking;* scourging, flagellatory, torturing, racking 377adj. *painful.*

punishable, liable, amerceable, mulctable; inflictable.

Vb. *punish,* visit, afflict; persecute, victimize, make an example of 735 vb. *be severe;* inflict, impose, inflict punishment, administer correction; give one a lesson, chasten, discipline, correct, chastise, castigate; reprimand, strafe, rebuke, have one's head for 924vb. *reprove;* penalize, impose a penalty, sentence 961 vb. *condemn;* execute justice, execute judgment, execute a sentence, carry out a s.; exact a penalty, exact retribution, settle with, get even w., pay one out 714vb. *retaliate;* revenge oneself 710vb. *avenge;*

amerce, mulct, fine, forfeit, deprive, sequestrate, confiscate 786vb. *take away;* unfrock, demote, degrade, downgrade, reduce to the ranks, suspend, supersede; tar and feather, toss in a blanket; pillory, set in the stocks, stand one in a corner; masthead; duck, keelhaul; picket, spreadeagle; lock up 747vb. *imprison;* transport; condemn to the galleys.

spank, paddle, slap, smack, slipper; cuff, clout, box on the ears, rap over the knuckles; drub, trounce, beat, belt, strap, leather, larrup, wallop, welt, tan, cane, birch, switch, whack, dust, dust one's jacket 279 vb. *strike.*

flog, whip, horsewhip, thrash, hide, belabor, cudgel, fustigate 279vb. *strike;* scourge, give stripes, give strokes, give one the cat; lash, lay on the l., flay, flay one's back, lay one's back open; flail, flagellate, bastinado.

torture, give the third degree; give one the works 377vb. *give pain;* put one to torture, thumbscrew, rack, put on the r., break on the wheel; mutilate, trim one's ears; persecute, martyrize 827vb. *torment.*

execute, punish with death, put to death 362vb. *kill;* lynch 362vb. *murder;* dismember, tear limb from limb; decimate; crucify, impale; flay, flay alive; stone, stone to death 712vb. *lapidate;* shoot, fusillade, stand against a wall; drown, noyade, burn, burn alive, burn at the stake, send to the s.; bowstring; garrote, strangle; gibbet, hang, hang by the neck, string up, stretch, turn off, bring to the gallows; hang, draw and quarter; send to the scaffold, bring to the block, strike off one's head, behead, head, decapitate, decollate, guillotine; electrocute; gas, put in the gas-chamber; commit genocide, hold mass executions, purge, massacre 362vb. *slaughter.*

be punished, suffer punishment, take the consequences, catch it; take the rap, stand the racket, face the music; take one's medicine, take one's gruel, hold one's hand out; get what is coming, get one's deserts; regret it, smart for it; come to execution, lay one's head on the block, ride in a tumbril; come to the gallows, stretch a rope, swing, take the high jump, dance upon nothing, kick the air; pay for it with one's head, die the death, drink the hemlock.

See: 57, 279, 300, 361, 362, 377, 710, 712, 714, 731, 735, 747, 772, 786, 787, 804, 809, 827, 910, 913, 915, 924, 941, 945, 957, 961.

964 Means of Punishment

N. *scourge,* birch, birch-rod, cat, cat-o'-nine-tails, rope's end, knout, cowhide, sjambok, chabouk, kurbash; whip, horsewhip, switch, quirt; lash, strap, thong, belt; cane, lithe and limber c., rattan; stick, big s., rod, ferule, cudgel, ruler 723n. *club;* rubber hose, bicycle chain, sandbag.

pillory, stocks, whipping post, ducking stool, cucking stool, trebuchet, scold's bridle, branks; stool of repentance, cutty stool, penitent form, white sheet; chain, irons, bilboes 748n. *fetter;* prison house, prison 748n. *jail;* corner.

instrument of torture, rack, thumbscrew, iron boot, pilliwinks; maiden, wooden horse, triangle, wheel, treadmill; torture chamber.

means of execution, scaffold, block, gallows, gibbet, Tyburn tree, tumbril; cross; stake; Tarpeian rock; hemlock 659n. *poison;* bullet, wall; ax, headsman's a., guillotine; halter, rope, noose, drop; garrote, bowstring; electric chair, hot seat; death chamber, lethal c., gas c.; condemned cell, Death Row 961n. *condemnation.*

See: 659, 723, 748, 961.

965 Divineness

N. *divineness,* divinity, deity; godhood, godhead, godship; divine principle, Brahma; numen, numinousness, mana; being of God, divine essence, perfection, the Good, the True and the Beautiful; love, Fatherhood; Brahmahood, nirvana; impersonal God, atman, paramatman, oversoul, supreme soul, world s.; Ens Entium, First Cause, Primum Mobile; divine nature, God's ways, providence.

divine attribute, being 1n. *existence;* perfect being 646n. *perfection;* oneness 88n. *unity;* infinitude 107n. *infinity;* immanence, omnipresence 189 n. *presence;* omniscience, wisdom 490n. *knowledge;* omnipotence, almightiness 160n. *power;* timelessness, eternity 115n. *perpetuity;* immutability, changelessness 153n. *stability;* truth, sanctity, holiness, goodness, justice, mercy; transcendence, sublimity, supremacy, sovereignty,

majesty, glory, light; glory of the Lord, Shekinah.
the Deity, God, personal god, Supreme Being, Divine B.; the Infinite, the Eternal, the All-wise, the Almighty, the All-holy, the All-merciful; Maker of all things, Creator, Preserver; Allah; Elohim, Yahweh, Jehovah, Adonai, ineffable name, I AM; name of God, Tetragrammaton; God of Abraham, God of Moses, Lord of Hosts, God of our fathers; our Father; Demiurge; All-Father, great spirit; Ahura Mazda, Ormuzd; Baal; Krishna.
Trinity, triad, Hindu Triad, Brahma, Shiva, Vishnu; Holy Trinity, Hypostatic Union; Triune God, Three Persons in one God, Three in One and One in Three; God the Father, God the Son, God the Holy Ghost.
Holy Ghost, third person of the Trinity; Holy Spirit, Spirit of Truth; Paraclete, Comforter, Consoler; Dove.
God the Son, second person of the Trinity, Word, Logos, Son of God, the Only Begotten, Word made flesh, Incarnate Son; Messiah, Son of David, the Anointed, Christ; Immanuel; Lamb of God, Son of Man; Son of Mary, Jesus, Jesus of Nazareth, the Nazarene, the Galilean; the Good Shepherd, Savior, Redeemer, Atoner, Mediator, Intercessor, Judge; Bread of Life, the Way, the Truth, the Life; Light of the World, Sun of Righteousness; King of Kings, King of Heaven, King of Glory, Prince of Peace.
divine function, creation, preservation, judgment; mercy, uncovenanted mercies, forgiveness; inspiration, unction, regeneration, comfort, strengthening, consolation, grace, prevenient g.; propitiation, atonement, redemption, justification, salvation, mediation, intercession.
theophany, divine manifestation, divine emanation, descent, descent to earth, divine intervention, irruption into history, incarnation, full incarnation; transfiguration; Shekinah, Glory of the Lord; avatar, avatars of Vishnu, Matsya, Karma, Varah, Narsinha, Vamara, Kalki, Parashurama, Rama, Krishna.
theocracy, divine government, divine dispensation, God's law, Kingdom of God; God's ways, God's dealings, providence, special p., deus ex machina.
Adj. *divine,* holy, hallowed, sanctified, sacred, sacrosanct, heavenly, celestial; transcendental, sublime, ineffable; numinous, mystical, religious, ghostly, spiritual, superhuman, supraphysical, supernatural; unearthly, supramundane, extramundane, not of this world; providential; theophanic; theocratic.
godlike, divine, superhuman; transcendent, immanent; omnipresent 189adj. *ubiquitous;* immeasurable 107adj. *infinite;* absolute, undefined, self-existent, living 1adj. *existing;* timeless, eternal, everlasting, immortal 115adj. *perpetual;* immutable, unchanging, changeless 144adj. *permanent;* almighty, all-powerful, omnipotent 160adj. *powerful;* creative 160adj. *dynamic;* prescient, providential 510adj. *foreseeing;* all-wise, all-seeing, omniscient, all-knowing 490adj. *knowing;* oracular 511adj. *predicting;* all-merciful, merciful 909adj. *forgiving;* compassionate, pitiful 905adj. *pitying;* fatherly 887adj. *loving;* holy, all-h., worshiped 979adj. *sanctified;* sovereign 34adj. *supreme;* majestic 733adj. *authoritative;* transfigured, glorious, all-g. 866adj. *worshipful;* theomorphic, incarnate, in the image of God, deified; messianic, anointed.
deistic, theistic, Jahwistic, Elohistic, Brahmic, Sivaic, Brahmoistic.
redemptive, intercessional, mediatory, propitiatory; incarnational, avataric; soteriological, messianic.
Adv. *divinely,* as God; under God, by God's will, deo volente, DV; by divine right, jure divino; redemptively, soteriologically.
See: 1, 34, 88, 107, 115, 144, 153, 160, 189, 490, 510, 511, 646, 733, 866, 887, 905, 909, 979.

966 Gods in general
N. *god,* goddess, deva, dev; the gods, the immortals; Olympian 967n. *Olympian god;* the unknown god, pagan g., false g., idol; godling, petty god, inferior g., subordinate g. 967n. *lesser god;* demigod, half-god, divine hero, deified person, divine king, object of worship, fetish, totem; numinous presence, mumbo jumbo; theogony; theotechny; pantheon.
mythic god, nature g., Pan, Flora, Faunus; vegetation god, corn g., tree g., fertility g.; Adonis, Thammuz, Atys; earth goddess, mother earth, mother goddess, earth mother, Great Mother, Magna Mater, Cybele; chthonic deity, god of the

underworld, Pluto, Hades, Dis, Persephone, Yama, Yami 967n. *chthonic god;* sky god, Dyaus, Zeus, Jupiter; storm god, Indra, rain g., Jupiter Pluvius; wind god, Aeolus, Maruts; sun god, Apollo, Hyperion, Helios, Surya; river god, sea g., Poseidon, Neptune, Triton, Varuna; war god, Mars, Bellona; god of love, Cupid, Eros, Venus, Aphrodite; household god, Teraphim, Lares, Penates, Hermae, Hestia, Vesta; tutelary god, genius, good g., good angel, ba, ka; the Fates, Parcae, Clotho, Lachesis, Atropos, the Norns 596n. *fate.*

Adj. *theotechnic,* theogonic, mythological, mythical; deiform, theomorphic, deific, deified.

See: 596, 967.

967 Pantheon: classical and non-classical gods

N. *classical gods,* gods of Greece and Rome, Greco-Roman pantheon; Homeric gods, Hesiodic theogony; primeval gods, Chaos, Erebus, Nox; Ge, Gaia, Tellus, Terra; Uranus, Coelus, Kronos, Saturn, Rhea, Ops; Oceanus, Tethys, Nereus; Helios, Sol, Hyperion, Phaethon; Titan, Prometheus, Epimetheus, Typho, Enceladus; the Fates, Parcae, Clotho, Lachesis, Atropos.

Olympian god, Olympian, Zeus, Jupiter, Jove, president of the immortals; Pluto, Hades, Dis; Poseidon, Neptune; Apollo; Hermes, Mercury; Ares, Enyalios, Mars; Hephaestus, Vulcan; Dionysus, Bacchus; Hera, Juno; Demeter, Ceres; Persephone, Proserpina; Athena, Minerva; Aphrodite, Venus; Artemis, Diana; Eros, Cupid; Iris; Hebe.

chthonic god, chthonians, Ge, Gaia, Hades, Pluto, Persephone; Osiris; Cerberus, Charon, Styx; Erectheus, Trophonius, Pytho; Eumenides, Furies; manes, shades, spirits of the dead.

lesser god, Pan, Sylvanus, Flora, Faunus, Silenus, Satyr, Faun; Aurora, Eos; Luna, Selene; Aeolus, Boreas, Orithyia 352n. *wind;* Nereus, Triton, Proteus, Glaucus, Melicerte; Ate, Eris, Bellona, Nike; Astraea; Muses, tuneful Nine, Erato, Euterpe, Terpsichore, Polymnia, Clio, Calliope, Melpomene, Thalia, Urania; Asclepius, Aesculapius; Hypnos, Somnus; Hymen; Hestia, Vesta; Teraphim, Lares, Penates, Hermae; Kabiri; genius.

nymph, wood n., tree n., dryad, oread; water nymph, naiad; sea nymph, Nereid, Oceanid; Thetis, Circe, Calypso; siren, Parthenope, Scylla, Charybdis 970n. *mythical being;* Leto, Maia.

demigod, divine offspring, divine hero; Heracles, Hercules; Dioscuri, Castor and Pollux, Castor and Polydeuces; Amphion, Zethes; Epaphus, Perseus, Achilles, Aeneas, Memnon.

Hindu god, Brahmanic g., Vedic g.; Dyaus, Prithivi, Indra, Mitra, Varuna, Nasatya; Agni, Apam Napat, Brihaspati; Surya, Savitri, Pushan, Asvin, Ushas; Ratri; Vata, Maruts, Rudra; Parjanya, Apas; Soma; Hindu triad, Trimurti, Brahma, Siva, Vishnu; Brahmadeva; Rama, Krishna, Narayan, Bhagava; Jagannath; Kumara, Karttikeya, Mahasena; Kama, Kamadeva, Madana; hanuman; Ganesha, Ganpat; Hindu goddess, Lakshmi, Sarasvati, Indrani, Rati; Sati, Devi, Uma, Parvati, Durga, Gauri, Kali; Manasa, Sitala.

Egyptian gods; theriomorphic deity, theriocephalous d.; Selk (scorpion); Uazit, Nekhebt, Mert-seger, seker (serpent); Hept (frog); Horakhti, Mentu (hawk); Tahuti (ibis); Sebek (crocodile); Taurt (hippopotamus); Hapi, Apis (bull); Khnum (ram); Apuat, Anpu, Anubis (jackal); Sekhet, Bast (lion); anthropomorphic god, Egyptian triad, Isis, Osiris, Horus, elder Horus, younger H.; Set, Nebhat; Amen, Ammon, Jupiter A., Mut, Khonsu, Anher; Net, Neith; cosmic god, Ra, Amen-Ra, Atmu, Nefer-atmu; Khepra, Harakhti (rising sun); Aten; Nut (heaven), Seb (earth), Shu, Tefnut (space); abstract god, Min (all-father), Hathor (all-mother); Ptah (creator), Maat (truth), Imhotep (peace), Khrumu (Modeller), Thoth (writing), Bes (dancing); Serapis.

Semitic gods, El, Baal, Bel, Belus; Ashur; Melkarth, Marduk, Merodach; Adad, Dagon, Rimmon, Moloch, Patekh; Shamash, Astarte; Al-lat, Al-Uzza, Manat.

Nordic gods, Âss, Aesir, Vanir; Odin, Wotan, Woden; brothers of Odin, Frigg, Frija, Frea; sons of Odin, Heimdall, "white God," Vidaar, "silent god"; Balder, son of B., Forseti, Foseti; wife of Balder, Nanna; Thunor, Donar, Thor, wife of T., Sif, son of S., Ullr; Tyr, Tyw, Tin, Zio; Loki, Lothur, Hödr, Hotherus, "blind god"; Hoenir, Bragi, wife of B., Idunn; Nerthus,

Njörd, wife of N., Skadi; son of Njörd, Frey; daughter of Njörd, Freys; Mimri, Aegir; Asynjur, Nordic goddesses; Frigg, Freya, Gefrun, Idunn, Gerd, Eri, Sigyn, Fulla, Saga, Sjofn, Lofn, Var, Vor, Syn, Snotra, Gna, Sol, Bil, Hlin, Jörd, Rind.

Celtic gods, Dadga, Oengus, Ogma, Lug, Belenos, Grannos, Esos, Tentates, Totatis, Taranis, Maponus, Borvo, Bormo, Mogounos; Nodons, Nuada, Nudd; Ler, Lhyr, Manannan, Manawyddan; Taliesin; Celtic goddess, Morrigan, Andrasta, Sul, Brigit, Belisuma, Epona, Cerridwen, Danu.

Mexican gods, Nahuan g., Aztec g.; Cipactli, earth-dragon; Tezcatlipoca, Red T., Black T.; Uitzilopochtli; creative god, Tonacatecutli; creative goddess, Tonicaciuatl; Xipi Totec, Itzpapalotl, Ilamatecutli; gods of growth, maize god, Tlazolteotl, Cinteotl, Chicomecoatl, Ciuacoatl, Xochiquetzal, Xochipilli; drink god, octli g., Mayauel, Totochtin; rain god, water g., Tlaloc, Chalchihuitlicue, Quetzalcoatl; gods of fire, Xiuhtecutli, Chantico, Quaxolotl; sun god, Tonatiuh, Piltzintecutli; moon god, Metztli, Tecciztecutli; sky god, Mixcoatl, Camaxtli; planet god, Tlauizcalpantecutli; demons of the air, Tzitzimime; god of medicine, Patecatl; god of death, Mictlantecutli, Mictecaciuatl, Tepeyollotl.

See: 352, 970.

968 Angel

N. *angel,* archangel, little angel, angelet; heavenly host, angelic h., choir invisible; heavenly hierarchy, thrones, principalities and powers; seraph, seraphim, cherub, cherubim; ministering spirit, Michael, Gabriel, Raphael, Uriel, Abdiel, Zadkiel; angel of death, Azrael; saint, patron s., glorified soul; angelhood, archangelship; angelophany; angelolatry; angelology.

Madonna, Our Lady, Blessed Virgin Mary, Mother of God, Theotokos; Queen of Heaven, Queen of Angels, Stella Maris; Mariolatry.

Adj. *angelic,* angelical, archangelical, seraphic, cherubic, cherubical, cherubinic; saintly, glorified, celestial.

Vb. *angelize,* angelify, angelogize.

969 Devil

N. *Satan,* Lucifer, Son of the Morning, archangel ruined; arch-fiend, Prince of Darkness, Prince of This World; serpent, Old S., Tempter, Adversary, Antichrist, Common Enemy, Enemy of Mankind; Diabolus, Father of Lies, the devil, shaitan, Eblis; Apollyon, Abaddon, angel of the bottomless pit; the Evil One, Wicked O.; spirit of evil, principle of e., Ahriman.

Mephisto, Mephistopheles, His Satanic Majesty, the Old Gentleman, Old Nick, Old Harry, Old Scratch, Old Gooseberry, Old Horney, Old Clootie, cloven hoof.

devil, fiend; deviling, devilet, familiar, imp, imp of Satan, devil's spawn 938n. *bad man;* demon, Asmodeus, Azazel 970n. *demon;* unclean spirit, dybbuk; powers of darkness, diabolic hierarchy; damned spirit, fallen angel, dweller in Pandemonium, denizen of Hell; Mammon, Belial, Beelzebub; devildom, devilship, devilhood, demonship, demonry; cloven hoof.

diabolism, devilry, diablerie 898n. *inhumanity;* satanism, devilism, devility; devil-worship, demonism, demonolatry, demonomy; demonomanic, demonomania, demonopathy, demoniac possession; demonomagy, demonomancy, black magic, Black Mass 983n. *sorcery;* demonology; demonization.

diabolist, satanist, devil-worshiper, demonolater, demonomist; demonologist, demonologer.

Adj. *diabolic,* diabolical, devil-like, Satanic, fiendish, demoniac, devilish 898adj. *malevolent;* abysmal, infernal, hellish, hell-born; devil-worshiping, demonolatrous; demonomanic, possessed; demonic, demonological.

Vb. *diabolize,* demonize; possess, bedevil 983vb. *bewitch;* demonologize.

See: 898, 938, 970, 983.

970 Fairy

N. *fairy,* fairy world, magic w., fairyland, faerie; fairy folk, good f., little people; fairy being, fay, peri; good fairy, fairy godmother, Santa Claus, Father Christmas 903n. *benefactor;* bad fairy, witch, weird sister 983n. *sorceress;* fairy queen, Mab, Queen M., Titania; fairy king, Oberon, Erl King; Puck, Robin Goodfellow; spirit of air, Ariel; elemental spirit; sylph, sylphide; genius; fairy-ring, pixie r.; fairyism, fairylore, fairy tales, folk-lore.

elf, elves, elfin folk, alfar, hidden

folk, Huldu, Light Elves, Dark E.; pixie, brownie; dwarf, dvergar; troll, trow; gnome, goblin, hobgoblin, kobold, flibbertigibbet; imp, sprite, urchin, hob, oaf, changeling; leprechaun, clurichaun; pigwidgeon; poltergeist, gremlin; Puck, Robin Goodfellow; elvishness, goblinry.

ghost, spirit, departed s.; shades, souls of the dead, manes, lemures; revived corpse, zombi, duffy; revenant, haunter, walker, poltergeist; spook, specter, apparition, phantom, phantasm, shape, shade, wraith, presence, doppelgänger, fetch 440n. *visual fallacy;* control 984n. *spiritualism.*

demon, cacodemon, flibbertigibbet, Friar Rush; imp, familiar, familiar spirit 969n. *devil;* afreet, jinn, genie; dev, asura; bhut, rakshasa; she-demon, lamia, rakshasi; kelpie, banshee; troll, troll-woman, ividjur, wood-women; ogre, ogress, giant, giantess, Rime-giant, Hill-g., Sea-g.; bugbear, bugaboo, bogey, bogeyman, raw-head, bloody-bones, Frankenstein's monster 938n. *monster;* ghoul, vampire, lycanthrope, werewolf, werefolk; incubus, succubus, succuba, nightmare; fury, harpy; Gorgon; ogreism, ogreishness, demonry.

mythical being 968n. *angel,* 969n. *devil;* asura, dev; Pitri, Siddha, Yaksha, Gandharva, Vidyadhara, Kinnara, Asvamukha; Yakshini 967n. *nymph;* Apsaras, houri, Valkyrie, battle-maid, wish-m.; sea nymph, river n., water n., Oceanid, naiad, nix, nixie; merfolk, merman, mermaid, merwoman, Lady of the Lake, Lorelei, siren; water-spirit, undine; water-kelpie, water-elf; Old Man of the Sea; yeti, abominable snowman, phoenix 84n. *rara avis.*

Adj. *fairy-like,* fairy, nymphal; sylph-like 206adj. *lean;* dwarf-like 196adj. *dwarfish;* gigantic 195adj. *huge;* ogreish, devilish, demonic 969adj. *diabolic;* vampirish, lycanthropic; Gorgonian, Scyllan; elf-like, elfin, elvish, impish, puckish 898adj. *maleficent;* magic 983adj. *magical;* mythical, mythic, folklorish 513adj. *imaginary.*

spooky, spookish, ghostly, ghostish; haunted, ghosted, gnomed, hagridden; nightmarish, macabre 854adj. *frightening;* weird, uncanny, unearthly, eldritch 84adj. *abnormal;* eerie, numinous, supernatural, supernormal; spectral, apparitional, wraith-like, mopping and mowing; disembodied, discarnate 320adj. *immaterial;* ectoplasmic, astral, spiritualistic, mediumistic 984adj. *psychic.*

Vb. *goblinize,* haunt, visit, walk; gibber, mop and mow.

Adv. *spookishly,* spectrally, uncannily, nightmarishly; elfishly, puckishly.

See: 84, 195, 196, 206, 320, 440, 513, 854, 898, 903, 938, 967, 969, 983, 984.

971 Heaven

N. *heaven,* presence of God, abode of G., throne of G., kingdom of G., kingdom of heaven, heavenly kingdom, kingdom come; paradise, abode of the blessed, abode of the saints, inheritance of the saints in light; Abraham's bosom, eternal home, happy h.; eternal rest, celestial bliss, blessed state; nirvana, seventh heaven; the millennium, Earthly Paradise, Zion, Land of Beulah, New Jerusalem, Holy City, Celestial C.; afterlife, eternal life, eternity 124n. *future state;* resurrection; assumption, translation, glorification; deification, apotheosis.

mythic heaven, Olympus; Odin's hall, Idavoll, Valaskjolf, Gladsheim, Valhalla, abode of warriors; Asgard, Troy, Gimle, abode of the righteous; Thor's place, Thrutheim, Bilskirnir; Heimdall's hall, Himinbjorg; Balder's abode, Breithablik; Forseti's abode, Glitnir; Frey's place, Alfheim; house for goddesses, Vingolf; Indraloka, devaloka, pitriloka; Elysium, Elysian fields, happy hunting grounds; Yima's vara, Earthly Paradise, Eden, Garden of E., garden of the Hesperides, Islands of the Blest, Isle of Avalon 513n. *fantasy.*

Adj. *paradisiac,* paradisiacal, paradisal; heavenly, celestial, supernal, eternal; beatific, blessed, blissful 824 adj. *happy;* resurrectional, glorified; elysian, Olympian; millennial.

See: 124, 513, 824.

972 Hell

N. *hell,* place of the dead, lower world, nether world, nether regions, underworld; grave, limbo, Sheol, Hades; place of the damned, inferno, Satan's palace, Pandemonium; abyss, bottomless pit, Abaddon; place of torment, Tophet, Gehenna, Jahannum, lake of fire and brimstone; hellfire, everlasting fire, unquenchable f., worm that never dies.

mythic hell, Hel, Niflheim; Narak; Aralu, land of no return; realm of Pluto, Hades, Tartarus, Avernus, Erebus; river of hell, Acheron, Styx, Cocytus, Phlegethon, Lethe; stygian ferryman, Charon; infernal watchdog, Cerberus; infernal judge, Minos, Rhadamanthus; nether gods, chthonians, Pluto, Yama, Yima, Osiris 967n. *chthonic god.*

Adj. *infernal,* bottomless 211adj. *deep;* chthonic, subterranean 210 adj. *low;* hellish, plutonian, avernal, avernian, Tartarean, Tartareous; Acherontic, stygian, Lethean; Cerberean, Cerberic; Rhadamanthine; damned, devilish 969adj. *diabolic.*

See: 210, 211, 967, 969.

973 Religion

N. *religion,* religious instinct, religious bias, religious feeling 979n. *piety;* search for truth, religious quest; natural religion, deism; primitive religion, early faith; paganism 982n. *idolatry;* nature religion, orgiastic r., mystery r., mysteries, Eleusinian m., Orphism, Eleusinianism; dharma, revealed religion, historical r., incarnational r., sacramental r.; religion of the spirit, mysticism, Sufism; yoga, dharmayoga, jnanayoga, karmayoga, bhaktiyoga; Eightfold Path; theosophy; theolatry 981n. *worship;* religious cult, state religion, official r. 981n. *cult;* untheological religion, creedless r., personal r.; no religion, atheism 974n. *irreligion.*

deism, belief in a god, theism; animism, pantheism, polytheism, henotheism, monotheism, dualism; gnosticism.

religious faith, faith 485n. *belief;* Christianism, Christianity, Cross; Judaism; Islam, Crescent; Zoroastrianism, Mazdaism, Zarathustrianism; Vedic religion, dharma, Arya D.; Brahmanism, Hinduism, Vedantism; Vaishnavism 978n. *sectarianism;* Jainism; Buddhism, Dhamma, Hinayana, Lesser Vehicle, Mahayana, Greater Vehicle; Brahmoism; Sikhism; Shintoism; Taoism, Confucianism; theosophy.

theology, science of religion, Queen of the sciences; natural theology, revealed t.; religious knowledge, religious learning, divinity; scholastic theology, scholasticism, Thomism; rabbinism; isagogics, theological exegesis; typology; demythologization; soteriology, theodicy; hagiology, hagiography, iconology; dogmatics, dogmatic theology; symbolics, credal theology; tradition, deposit of faith; teaching, doctrine, religious d., received d., defined d.; definition, canon; doxy, dogma, tenet; articles of faith, credenda, credo 485n. *creed;* confession, Thirty-nine Articles; Islamic exposition, fatwa; fundamentalism 976n. *orthodoxism;* bibliology, higher criticism.

theologian, theologer, theologaster, theologue; divinity student, divine; doctor, doctor of the Church; doctor of the Law, rabbi, scribe, mufti; schoolman, scholastic, scholastic theologian, Thomist, talmudist, canonist; theogonist, hagiologist, hagiographer, iconologist; psalmist, hymnwriter; textualist, Masorete; Bible critic, higher c.; scripturalist, fundamentalist.

religious teacher, prophet, rishi, inspired writer; evangelist, apostle, missionary; reformer, religious r.; founder of religion, Messiah, founder of Christianity, Christ; Muhammad, Prophet of God; Zoroaster; Buddha, Gautama B.; Confucius; founder of Mormonism, Joseph Smith; founder of Christian Science, Mary Baker Eddy; expounder, hierophant, gospeler, catechist 520n. *interpreter.*

religionist, deist, theist; monotheist, henotheist, polytheist, pantheist; animist, fetishist 982n. *idolator;* star-worshiper, Sabaist; pagan, gentile 974n. *heathen;* people of the book; believer, true b., orthodoxist 976n. *the orthodox;* Christian, Nazarene; Jew; Muslim, Islamite, Mussulman, Mohammedan; Parsi, Zoroastrian, guebre; Hindu, gymnosophist, Brahmanist; Jain; Buddhist, Zen B.; Taoist; Confucianist; Shintoist; Mormon 978n. *sect;* theosophist 984n. *occultist;* gnostic 977n. *heretic.*

Adj. *religious,* divine, holy, sacred, spiritual, sacramental; deistic, theistic, animistic, pantheistic, henotheistic, monotheistic, dualistic; Christian, Islamic, Judaistic, Mosaic; Zoroastrian, Avestan; Confucian, Taoistic; Buddhistic, Hinduistic, Vedic, Brahmanical, Upanishadic, Vedantic; yogic, mystic; devotional, devout, practicing 981adj. *worshiping.*

theological, theosophical, scholastic, rabbinic, rabbinical; doctrinal, dogmatic, credal, canonical; christological, soteriological; doxological 988 adj. *ritualistic;* hagiological, iconological.

See: 485, 520, 974, 976, 977, 978, 979, 981, 982, 984, 988.

974 Irreligion

N. *irreligion,* indevotion, unspirituality, leanness of soul; nothing sacred, profaneness, ungodliness, godlessness 980n. *impiety;* false religion, heathenism 982n. *idolatry;* no religion, atheism, nullifidianism, dissent from all creeds, disbelief 486n. *unbelief;* agnosticism, skepticism, Pyrrhonism 486n. *doubt;* probabilism, euhemerism 449n. *philosophy;* lack of faith, want of f., infidelity; lapse, lapse from faith, recidivism, backsliding 603n. *tergiversation;* paganization, de-Christianization, post-Christian state; amoralism, apathy, indifferentism 860n. *indifference.*

antichristianity, antichristianism 704n. *opposition;* paganism, heathenism, heathendom, gentilism; satanism 969 n. *diabolism;* free thinking, free thought, rationalism, positivism 449 n. *philosophy;* hylotheism, materialism, dialectical m., Marxism, nihilism; secularism, worldliness, fleshliness 944n. *sensualism;* mammonism 816n. *avarice.*

irreligionist, antichrist; nullifidian, dissenter, dissenter from all creeds, no believer, atheist 486n. *unbeliever;* rationalist, euhemerist, free thinker; agnostic, skeptic, Pyrrhonist; Marxist, nihilist, materialist, positivist; secularist, worldling, amoralist, indifferentist.

heathen, non-Christian, pagan, paynim; misbeliever, infidel, Kafir, giaour, outcast; gentile, the uncircumcised, the unbaptized, the unconverted; backslider, lapsed Christian 603n. *tergiversator.*

Adj. *irreligious,* having no religion, without r., without a god, godless, altarless, profane 980adj. *impious;* nihilistic, atheistic, atheistical; creedless, nullifidian, agnostic, skeptical, Pyrrhonian, Pyrrhonic 486adj. *unbelieving;* free-thinking, rationalizing, rationalistic, euhemeristic; nonreligious, non-worshiping, non-practicing, non-theological, non-credal 769adj. *non-observant;* undevout, devoutless, unspiritual, ungodly 934 adj. *wicked;* amoral, morally neutral 860adj. *indifferent;* secular, mundane, of this world, worldly, mammonistic 944adj. *sensual;* materialistic, Marxist; lacking faith, faithless; backsliding, recidivous, lapsed, paganized, post-Christian 603adj. *tergiversating;* antireligious, anti-Christian, anti-Church, anticlerical.

heathenish, unholy, unhallowed, unsanctified, unblessed, unconsecrated 980adj. *profane;* unchristian, unbaptized, unconfirmed; gentile, gentilic, uncircumcised; heathen, pagan, infidel; pre-Christian, unconverted, in darkness 491adj. *uninstructed.*

Vb. *be irreligious,*—atheistic etc.adj.; have no religion, lack faith; remain unconverted 486vb. *disbelieve;* shut one's eyes to the light, love darkness, serve Mammon; lose one's faith, give up the Church 603vb. *apostatize;* have no use for religion, scoff at r.; euhemerize, rationalize; persecute the faith, deny God, blaspheme 980vb. *be impious.*

paganize, heathenize, de-Christianize, corrupt one's religion; desanctify, deconsecrate, undedicate, secularize.

See: 449, 486, 491, 603, 704, 769, 816, 860, 934, 944, 969, 980, 982.

975 Revelation

N. *revelation,* divine r., apocalypse 526n. *disclosure;* illumination 417n. *light;* afflatus, divine a., sruti, inspiration, divine i., theopneust; prophecy, prophetic inspiration; intuition, mystical i., mysticism; direct communication, the Law, Mosaic L., Ten Commandments; divine message, God's word, gospel, gospel message; God revealed, theophany, burning bush, epiphany, incarnation, word made flesh; avatar, emanation, divine e.

scripture, word of God, inspired text, sacred t., sacred writings; Holy Scripture, Bible, Holy B., the Book; King James Version, Authorized Version, Revised V.; Vulgate, Douai Version, Greek Version, Septuagint; canonical writings, canonical books, canon; Old Testament, Pentateuch, Hexateuch, Octateuch, Major Prophets, Minor P.; Torah, the Law and the Prophets, Hagiographa; New Testament, Gospels, Synoptic G., Epistles, Pastoral E., Pauline E., Johannine E., Petrine E.; Acts of the Apostles, Revelation, Apocalypse; non-canonical writings, Apocrypha, Agrapha, Logia, sayings, non-canonical gospel; patristic writings; psalter, psalm-book, breviary, missal; prayer-book, Book of Common Prayer 981n. *prayers;* hymn-book, hymnal 981n. *hymn;* post-Biblical writings (Hebrew), Targum, Talmud, Mishnah, Gemara; textual commentary, Masora; Higher Criticism; fundamentalism, scripturalism.

non-Biblical scripture, Koran, Alcoran, the Glorious Koran; hadith, sunna; Hindu scripture, Veda, the Four Vedas, Rigveda, Yajurveda, Samaveda, Atharvaveda; Brahmana, Upanishad, Purana; Bhagavad Gita; sruti, smriti, shastra, sutra; Buddhist scripture, Pitaka, Tripitaka, Digha-Nikaya, Majjhima-N., Dhammapada; Iranian and Zoroastrian scripture, Zend-Avesta, Gatha, Vendidad; Book of the Dead (Egyptian); Book of Mormon.

Adj. *revelational,* inspirational, theopneustic, mystic; inspired, prophetic, revealed; apocalyptic; prophetic, evangelical, evangelic; mystagogic.

scriptural, sacred, holy; hierographic, hieratic; revealed, inspired, prophetic; canonical 733adj. *authoritative;* biblical, Mosaic, preexilic, exilic, post-e.; gospel, evangelistic, apostolic; subapostolic, patristic, homiletic; talmudic, Mishnaic; Koranic, uncreated; Vedic, Upanishadic, Puranic; textuary, textual, Masoretic.

See: 417, 526, 733, 981.

976 Orthodoxy

N. *orthodoxy,* orthodoxness, correct opinion, right belief; sound theology, Trinitarianism; religious truth, gospel t., pure gospel 494n. *truth;* scripturality, canonicity; the Faith, the true faith, the whole f., deposit of f., "the faith once delivered unto the saints"; primitive faith, early Church, Apostolic age; ecumenicalism, catholicity, Catholicism, "quod semper, quod ubique, quod ab omnibus"; formulated faith, credo 485n. *creed;* Apostles' Creed, Nicene C., Athanasian C.; Confession of Augsberg, Thirty-nine Articles, Tridentine decrees; textuary, catechism, Church Catechism.

orthodoxism, strictness, strict interpretation; scripturalism, bibliodulia, fundamentalism, literalism, precisianism; Karaism, Karaitism (Jewish); traditionalism, institutionalism, ecclesiasticism, churchianity 985n. *churchdom;* sound churchmanship 83n. *conformity;* Christian practice 768n. *observance;* intolerance, heresy-hunting, persecution; suppression of heresy, extermination of error, Counter-Reformation; religious censorship, Holy Office 956n. *tribunal;* Inquisition 459n. *interrogation;* Index, Expurgatory I., Index Expurgatorius, Index Librorum Prohibitorum 924n. *disapprobation;* guaranteed orthodoxy, imprimatur 923n. *approbation.*

the Church, Christian world, Christendom, undivided Church; Christian fellowship, communion of saints; Holy Church, Mother C.; Body of Christ, universal Church; Church Militant, Church on earth, visible Church; invisible Church, Church Triumphant; established Church, recognized C., denominational C.; Orthodox C., Eastern Orthodox Church, autocephalous c.; Armenian Church; Roman Church, Roman Catholic and Apostolic C.; Church of England, Episcopalian C.; Church of Scotland; Reformed Church, Protestant C., Lutheran C., Calvinist C.

Catholicism, Orthodoxy, Eastern O.; Roman Catholicism, Romanism, popery, papalism, papistry, ultramontanism, Scarlet Woman; Counter-Reformation; Old Catholicism; Anglicanism, Episcopalianism, prelacy; Anglo-Catholicism, High Church, High-Churchmanship, spikiness; Laudianism, Tractarianism, Oxford movement.

Protestantism, the Reformation, Anglicanism, Lutheranism, Zwinglianism, Calvinism; Presbyterianism, Congregationalism, Baptism; Quakerism, Quakery, Society of Friends; Wesleyanism, Methodism, Wesleyan M., Primitive M.

Catholic, Orthodox, Eastern O.; Roman Catholic, Romanist, papist, papalist, ultramontanist; Old Catholic, Anglo-C., Anglican, Episcopalian, Laudian, High-Churchman, Tractarian.

protestant, reformer, Anglican, Lutheran, Zwinglian, Calvinist, Huguenot; Presbyterian, Congregationalist, Baptist, Wesleyan, Methodist, Wesleyan M., Primitive M.; Quaker, Friend; Plymouth Brother.

church member, pillar of the church; Christian, the baptized, the confirmed; practicing Christian, communicant 981n. *worshipper;* the saints, the faithful, the body of the f., church people, chapel p.; congregation, coreligionist, fellow-worshiper, pew-fellow.

the orthodox, the believing, the faithful, the converted; believer, true b.; pillar of orthodoxy, conformer 83n. *conformist;* traditionalist, scripturalist, literalist, fundamentalist; Karaite; rabbinist 973n. *theologian.*

Adj. *orthodox,* orthodoxical, rightly believing, holding the faith, reciting the creed 485adj. *believing;* right-minded, sound, balanced 480adj. *judicial;* non-heretical, unschistimatical 488adj. *assenting;* undivided, seamless 52adj. *whole;* unswerving, undeviating, loyal, devout 739adj. *obedient;* practicing, conforming, conventional 83adj. *conformable;* precise, strict, pedantic; hyper-orthodox, overreligious, holier than thou; intolerant, witch-hunting, heresy-h., inquisitional 459adj. *inquiring;* correct 494adj. *accurate;* of faith, to be believed, doctrinal 485 adj. *credal;* authoritative, defined, canonical, biblical, scriptural, evangelical, gospel 494adj. *genuine;* textual, literal, fundamentalist, fundamentalistic; Trinitarian; Athanasian; catholic, ecumenical, universal; accepted, held, widely h., believed, generally b. 485adj. *credible;* traditional, customary 610adj. *usual.*

popish, papistical, Roman, Romish, Romanizing, ultramontanist; Catholic, Roman Catholic.

Anglican, Episcopalian, prelatical, Laudian; tractarian, Anglo-Catholic, High-Church, high, spiky.

protestant, reformed; denominational 978adj. *sectarian;* Lutheran, Zwinglian, Calvinist, Calvinistic; Presbyterian, Congregational, Methodist, Wesleyan, Quakerish; bishopless, non-episcopal.

Vb. *be orthodox,*—Catholic etc.adj.; hold the faith, recite the creeds 485 vb. *believe;* support the church, go to c. 83vb. *conform;* Catholicize, Romanize; Protestantize; Anglicanize; Lutheranize; Calvinize; Presbyterianize.

Adv. *orthodoxly,* orthodoxically, catholicly.

See: 52, 83, 459, 480, 485, 488, 494, 610, 739, 768, 923, 924, 956, 973, 978, 981, 983, 985.

977 Heterodoxy

N. *heterodoxy,* other men's doxy; unorthodoxy, unauthorized belief, unauthorized doubts, personal judgment; erroneous opinion, wrong belief, misbelief, false creed, superstition 495n. *error;* strange doctrine, queer tenets, new teaching, bad t.; perversion of the truth 535n. *misteaching;* doubtful orthodoxy, heretical tendency, latitudinarianism, modernism, Higher Criticism; unscripturality, non-catholicity, partial truth; heresy, rank h.

heresy, fabrication of h., heresiarchy; heathen theology, gnosticism; monarchianism, modal m., patripassianism, Sabellianism, dynamic, monarchianism, adoptionist m.; Arianism, Arian syllogism, Arian creed, "blasphemy of Sirmium," Socinianism; Unitarianism; Apollinarianism, Nestorianism, Eutychianism; Monophysitism, Monothelitism; Pelagianism, semi-P.; Montanism, Donatism, Manichaeism, Albigensianism, Antinomianism; Wycliffism, Lollardism, Lollardy; Erastianism, anti-papalism.

heretic, arch-h., heresiarch; Gnostic, Manichaean; Monarchian, Unitarian; Arius, Arian; Nestorius, Nestorian; Eutyches, Eutychian; Apollinaris, Apollinarian; Monophysite, Monothelite; Montanus, millenarian, Montanist; Novatian; Donatist; Catharist, Catharan, Paulician, Albigensian, Antinomian; Wycliffist, Lollard, Hussite.

Adj. *heterodox,* differing, unconventional 15n. *different;* dissentient 489 adj. *dissenting;* non-doctrinaire, nonconformist 84adj. *unconformable;* uncatholic, antipapal; less than orthodox, erroneous 495adj. *mistaken;* unorthodox, unbiblical, unscriptural, unauthorized, unsanctioned, proscribed 757adj. *prohibited;* heretical, anathematized, damnable 961adj. *condemned.*

heretical, heretic; heathen, Gnostic, Manichaean, monarchian, patripassian, unitarian, Socinian; Arian, Eutychian, Apollinarian, Nestorian, Monophysite, Monothelite; Pelagian; Antinomian, Albigensian; Wycliffite, Lollard, Hussite.

Vb. *hereticate,* declare heretical, anathematize 961vb. *condemn.*

be heretical,—unorthodox etc.adj.; Arianize, Pelagianize, Socianize, Erastianize.

Adv. *heretically,* unorthodoxly.

See: 15, 84, 489, 495, 535, 757, 961.

978 Sectarianism

N. *sectarianism,* sectarism, sectism; particularism, exclusiveness, clannishness, sectionalism 481n. *prejudice;* bigotry 481n. *bias;* party-mindedness, party-spirit, factiousness 709 n. *quarrelsomeness;* independence,

separatism, schismaticalness, schismatical tendency 738n. *disobedience;* denominationalism, noncomformism, nonconformity, dissent, "the dissidence of dissent" 489n. *dissent;* Lutheranism, Calvinism, Presbyterianism, Puritanism 976n. *Protestantism;* Puseyism, Tractarianism 976n. *Catholicism.*
schism, division, divisions, differences 709n. *quarrel;* dissociation, breakaway, secession, withdrawal 46n. *separation;* non-recognition, mutual excommunication 883n. *seclusion;* non-jury, recusancy 769n. *non-observance;* religious schism, Donatism, Great Schism, Great Western S.
church party, Judaizers, Ebionites; ultramontanists, papalists; Gallicans; Erastians; High-Church party, Laudians, Episcopalians, Puseyites, Tractarians 976n. *Catholic;* Low-Church party, Evangelicals, Puritans 976n. *protestant;* Broad Church party, latitudinarians, modernists.
sect, division, off-shoot, branch, group, 708n. *party;* order, religious o., brotherhood, sisterhood 708n. *community;* nonconformist sect, chapel, conventicle 976n. *Protestantism;* Society of Friends, Friends, Quakers; Unitarians; Plymouth Brethren; Sabbatarians, Seventh-day Adventists; Fifth Monarchy Men; Church of Christ Scientist; Church of Jesus Christ of the Latter-day Saints, Mormons; Peculiar People, British Israelites; Jehovah's Witnesses; Salvation Army, Salvationists; Oxford movement, Buchmanism.
non-Christian sect, Jewish s., Nazirites; Pharisees, Sadducees, Herodians; rabbinists; Karaites; Essenes; Sephardim, Ashkenazim; pagano-Christian sect, Gnostics, Mandaeans, Euchites; Islamic sect, Sunnis, Shiites, Sufis, Wahhabis; Hindu sect, Vedantists, Vaishnavas, Saivites, Tantrikas; Brahmo Samaj, Brahmoists, Adi Samaj, Nava Vidhan; Arya Samaj 973n. *religious faith.*
sectarist, sectist, sectarian, particularist; follower, party-man; sectary, Independant; Puritan, wowser; Presbyterian, Covenanter 976n. *protestant;* Quaker, Friend 977n. *heretic;* Salvationist; Buchmanite, grouper; Sunnite, Shiite, Sufi, Wahhabi; Saivite, Vaishnavite, Vedantist; Arya Samajist; Brahmo, Brahmoist.
schismatic, separated brother; schismatics, separated brethren; separatist, separationist; seceder, secessionist; factioneer, factionist 709n. *quarreler;* rebel, mutineer 738n. *revolter;* recusant, non-juror; dissident, dissenter, nonconformist 489 n. *dissentient;* wrong believer 977n. *heretic;* apostate 603n. *tergiversator.*
Adj. *sectarian,* particularist; party-minded, partisan 481adj. *biased;* clannish, exclusive 708adj. *sectional;* Judaizing, Ebionite; Gallican; Erastian; sectarial, High-Church, Laudian, Episcopalian 976adj. *Anglican;* Low-Church, Evangelical 976adj. *protestant;* Puritan, Independent, Presbyterian, Covenanting; Vaishnavite, Saivite, Tantriki, Brahmo, Brahmoistic; Sunni, Shiite, Sufee; Essene, Pharisaic, Pharisaean, Sadducean, Herodian; Sephardi, Ashkenazi.
schismatical, schismatic, secessionist, seceding, breakaway; divided, separated 46adj. *separate;* excommunicated, excommunicable 977n. *heretical;* dissentient, nonconformist 489adj. *dissenting;* non-juring, recusant 769adj. *non-observant;* rebellious, rebel, contumacious 738adj. *disobedient;* apostate 603adj. *tergiversating.*
Vb. *sectarianize,* follow a sect 708vb. *join a party;* Lutheranize, Calvinize.
schismatize, commit schism, separate, divide, withdraw, secede, break away, hive off 603vb. *apostatize;* be in a state of schism, be contumacious 738vb. *disobey.*
See: 46, 481, 489, 603, 708, 709, 738, 769, 883, 973, 976, 977.

979 Piety
N. *piety,* piousness, goodness 933n. *virtue;* reverence, veneration, honor, decent respect 920n. *respect;* affection, kind feeling, friendly f. 897n. *benevolence;* dutifulness, loyalty, conformity, attendance at worship 968n. *observance;* churchmanship, sound c. 976n. *orthodoxy;* religiousness, religion, theism 973n. *deism;* religious feeling, pious sentiment, theopathy; fear of God, godly fear 854n. *fear;* submissiveness, humbleness 872n. *humility;* pious belief, faith, trust, trust in God 485n. *belief;* devotion, dedication, self-surrender 931n. *disinterestedness;* devoutness, sincerity, earnestness, unction; inspiration, enthusiasm, fervor, exaltation 821n. *excitation;* adoration, prostration 981n. *worship;* prayerfulness, meditation, retreat

981n. *worship;* contemplation, mysticism, communion with God, mystic communion 973n. *religion;* act of piety, pious duty, charity 901n. *philanthropy;* pious fiction, edifying story, moral 496n. *maxim;* Christian behavior, Christian life; pilgrimage, hajj.

sanctity, holiness, hallowedness, sacredness, sacrosanctity; goodness, cardinal virtues, theological v. 933n. *virtue;* cooperation with grace, synergism; state of grace, odor of sanctity 950n. *purity;* godliness, sanctimony, saintliness, holy character; spirituality, otherworldliness; spiritual life, life in God; sainthood, blessedness, blessed state; conversion, regeneration, rebirth, new birth 656n. *revival;* edification, sanctification, justification, adoption 965 n. *divine function;* canonization, beatification, consecration, dedication 866n. *dignification.*

pietism, show of piety, sanctimony; sanctimoniousness, unction, cant 542n. *sham;* religionism, religiosity, religious mania; over-piety, over-orthodoxy 976n. *orthodoxism;* scrupulosity, tender conscience; austerity 945n. *asceticism;* formalism, precisianism, puritanism 481n. *narrow mind;* literalness, fundamentalism, Bible-worship, bibliolatry, bibliodulia 494n. *accuracy;* Sabbatarianism 978n. *sectarianism;* churchianity, churchiness, sacerdotalism, ritualism, spikiness; calendar-worship 985 n. *ecclesiasticism;* preachiness, unctuousness; odium theologicum 888n. *hatred;* bigotry, fanaticism 481n. *prejudice;* persecution, witch-hunting, heresy-h. 735n. *severity;* crusading spirit, missionary s., salvationism 901n. *philanthropy.*

pietist, pious person, real saint 937 *good man;* the good, the righteous, the just; conformist 488n. *assenter;* professing Christian, practicing C., communicant 981n. *worshiper;* confessor, martyr; beatified person, saint; man of prayer, contemplative, mystic, sufi; holy man, sadhu, sannyasi, bhikshu, fakir, dervish 945n. *ascetic;* hermit, anchorite 883 n. *solitary;* monk, nun, religious 986 n. *clergy;* devotee, dedicated soul; convert, neophyte, catechumen, ordinand 538n. *learner;* believer, true b., the faithful, the elect 976n. *church member;* the chosen people, children of delight; pilgrim, palmer, hajji; votary.

religionist, euchite; enthusiast, wowser, fanatic, bigot, zealot, image-breaker, iconoclast 678n. *busy person;* formalist, precisian, puritan; Pharisee, scribe, scribes and Pharisees; fundamentalist, Bible-worshiper, bibliolater, bibliodule, Sabbatarian 978n. *sectarist;* sermonizer, pulpiteer 537n. *preacher;* salvationist, hot-gospeler; missionary 901n. *philanthropist;* champion of the faith, crusader, militant Christian; militant Islamite, ghazi; persecutor 735n. *tyrant.*

Adj. *pious,* good, kind 897adj. *benevolent;* decent, reverent 920adj. *respectful;* faithful, true, loyal, devoted 739adj. *obedient;* conforming, traditional 768adj. *observant;* believing, holding the faith 976adj. *orthodox;* sincere, practicing, professing, confessing 540adj. *veracious;* pure, pure in heart, holy-minded, heavenly-m.; unworldly, otherworldly, spiritual; godly, religious, devout; praying, prayerful, psalm-singing 981adj. *worshiping;* in retreat, meditative, contemplative, mystic; saintly, saintlike, sainted; Christian, Christ-like, full of grace.

pietistic, ardent, fervent, seraphic; enthusiastic, inspired; austere 945 adj. *ascetic;* hermit-like, anchoritic 883adj. *unsociable;* pi, religiose, over-religious, over-pious, over-devout, over-righteous, holier than thou; over-strict, precise, puritan 678adj. *meddling;* formalistic, Pharisaic, ritualistic 978adj. *sectarian;* priest-ridden, churchy, spiky; psalm-singing, hymn-s.; preachy, sanctimonious, canting 850adj. *affected;* goody-goody 933adj. *virtuous;* crusading, missionary-minded.

sanctified, made holy, consecrated, dedicated, enshrined; reverend, holy, sacred, solemn, sacrosanct 866adj. *worshipful;* haloed, sainted, canonized, beatified; saved, redeemed, ransomed 746adj. *liberated;* regenerate, renewed, reborn 656adj. *restored;* adopted, justified.

Vb. *be pious,*—religious etc.adj.; be holy, wear a halo; mind heavenly things, think of God; fear God 854 n. *fear;* have one's religion 485vb. *believe;* keep the faith, fight the good fight 162vb. *be strong;* walk humbly with one's God, humble oneself 872vb. *be humble;* go to church, attend divine worship; pray, say one's prayers 981vb. *worship;* kneel, genuflect, bow 311vb. *stoop;* cross oneself, make the sign of the cross 547vb. *gesticulate;* make offering, sacrifice, devote 759vb. *offer;* give alms and oblations, lend to God 781vb. *give;* give to the poor 897vb. *be benevolent;* glorify God 923vb. *praise;* give God the glory 907vb. *thank;* revere, show reverence 920 vb. *show respect;* hearken, listen 739vb. *obey;* sermonize, preachify, preach at 534vb. *teach;* let one's light shine, set a good example.

become pious, be converted, get religion; change one's religion, go over 603vb. *tergiversate;* see the light, see the error of one's ways 603vb. *recant;* mend one's ways, reform, repent 939vb. *be penitent;* enter the church, become ordained, take holy orders, take vows, take the veil 986 vb. *take orders;* pilgrimize, go on a pilgrimage, do the hajj 267vb. *travel.*

make pious, bring religion to, bring to God, convert 485vb. *convince;* Christianize, win for Christ, baptize, receive into the church 299vb. *admit;* depaganize, spiritualize 648vb. *purify;* edify, confirm, strengthen one's faith, confirm in the f. 162vb. *strengthen;* inspire, fill with grace, uplift 654vb. *make better;* redeem, regenerate 656vb. *restore.*

sanctify, hallow, make holy, keep h. 866vb. *honor;* spiritualize, consecrate, dedicate, enshrine 866vb. *dignify;* make a saint of, saint, canonize, beatify, pronounce blessed, invest with a halo; sain, make the sign of the cross.

See: 162, 267, 299, 311, 481, 485, 488, 494, 534, 537, 538, 540, 542, 547, 603, 648, 654, 656, 678, 735, 739, 746, 759, 768, 781, 821, 850, 854, 866, 872, 883, 888, 897, 901, 920, 931, 933, 937, 939, 945, 950, 965, 968, 973, 976, 978, 981, 985, 986.

980 Impiety

N. *impiety,* impiousness; irreverence, disregard 921n. *disrespect;* non-worship, lack of piety, lack of reverence; undutifulness 918n. *dutilessness;* godlessness 974n. *irreligion;* scoffing, mockery, derision 851n. *ridicule;* scorn, pride 922n. *contempt;* sacrilegiousness, profanity; blasphemy, evil-speaking, cursing, swearing 899n. *malediction;* sacrilege, desecration, violation, profanation, perversion, abuse 675n. *misuse;* sin, pervertedness, immoralism 934 n. *wickedness;* hardening, stubbornness 940n. *impenitence;* declension, regression 655n. *deterioration;* backsliding, recidivism, apostasy, recreancy 603n. *tergiversation;* profaneness, unholiness, worldliness, materialism 319n. *materiality;* amoralism, indifferentism 464n. *indiscrimination;* misdevotion 982n. *idolatry;* paganism, heathenism; rejection, reprobation 924n. *disapprobation.*

false piety, pious fraud 541n. *falsehood;* solemn mockery, mummery, imposture 542n. *sham;* sham piety, sanctimony, sanctimoniousness, Pharisaism 979n. *pietism;* hypocrisy, religious h., lip-service, lip-reverence 541n. *duplicity;* cant, snuffling, holy horror 850n. *affectation.*

impious person, blasphemer, curser, swearer 899n. *malediction;* mocker, scorner, contemner, despiser, defamer, calumniator 926n. *detractor;* sacrilegist, desecrator, violator, profaner, law-breaker 904n. *offender;* profane person, non-worshiper, gentile, pagan, infidel, unbeliever 974n. *heathen;* misbeliever 982n. *idolater;* disbeliever, atheist 974n. *irreligionist;* indifferentist, amoralist; worldling, materialist, immoralist 944n. *sensualist;* sinner, reprobate, the wicked, the unrighteous, sons of Belial, children of darkness 938n. *bad man;* recidivist, backslider, apostate, adulterous generation 603 n. *tergiversator;* fallen angel, Tempter, Wicked One 969n. *Satan;* hypocrite, religious h., Tartuffe 545n. *imposter;* canter, snuffler, lip-worshiper 850n. *affector.*

Adj. *impious,* antireligious, anti-Christian, antichurch 704adj. *opposing;* recusant, dissenting 977adj. *heretical;* unbelieving, non-believing, atheistical, godless 974adj. *irreligious;* non-worshiping, undevout, non-practicing 769adj. *non-observant;* misbelieving 982adj. *idolatrous;* scoffing, mocking, deriding 851adj. *derisive;* blaspheming, blasphemous, cursing, swearing, evil-speaking 899 adj. *maledicent;* irreverent, without reverence 921adj. *disrespectful;* sacrilegious, profaning, desecrating, violating, criminal 954adj. *lawless;* unawed, brazen, bold 855adj. *unfearing;* hard, unmoved, unfeeling 898adj. *cruel;* sinning, sinful, hardened, perverted, reprobate, unregenerate 934adj. *wicked;* backsliding, recidivous, apostate 603adj. *tergiversating;* canting, snuffling, sancti-

monious 850adj. *affected;* Pharisaical 541adj. *hypocritical.*
profane, unholy, unhallowed, unsanctified, unblest, sacrilegious; godforsaken, accursed; undedicated, unconsecrated, deconsecrated; infidel, pagan, gentile; paganized, de-Christianized 974adj. *heathenish.*
Vb. *be impious,*—sacrilegious etc. adj.; rebel against God 871vb. *be proud;* sin 934vb. *be wicked;* swear, blaspheme, revile 899vb. *curse;* have no reverence, show no respect 921 vb. *not respect;* profane, desecrate, violate 675vb. *misuse;* commit sacrilege, lay profane hands on, sully 649vb. *make unclean;* misbelieve, worship false gods; cant, snuffle 850 vb. *be affected;* play the hypocrite, play false 541vb. *dissemble;* backslide 603vb. *apostatize;* sin against the light, grow hardened, harden one's heart 655vb. *deteriorate.*
See: 541, 542, 545, 603, 649, 655, 675, 704, 769, 850, 851, 855, 871, 898, 899, 904, 918, 921, 922, 924, 926, 934, 938, 940, 944, 954, 969, 974, 977, 982.

981 Worship

N. *worship,* honor, reverence, homage 920n. *respect;* holy fear 854n. *fear;* veneration, adoration, prostration of the soul; humbling oneself, humbleness 872n. *humility;* devotion, devotedness 979n. *piety;* prayer, one's devotions, one's prayers; retreat, quiet time, meditation, contemplation, communion.
cult, mystique; type of worship, service 917n. *duty;* service of God, supreme worship, latria; inferior worship, dulia, hyperdulia; iconolatry, image-worship; false worship 982n. *idolatry.*
act of worship, rites, mysteries 988n. *rite;* laud, laudation, praises, doxology 923n. *praise;* glorification, giving glory, extolment 866n. *dignification;* hymning, hymn-singing, psalm-s., psalmody, chanting 412n. *vocal music;* thanksgiving, blessing, benediction 907n. *thanks;* offering, oblation, almsgiving, sacrifice, making s., sacrificing, offering (**see** *oblation*); praying, saying one's prayers, reciting the rosary; self-examination 939n. *penitence;* self-denial, self-discipline 945 *asceticism;* keeping fast 946n. *fasting;* hajj, pilgrimage 267n. *wandering.*
prayers, orisons, devotions; private devotion, retreat, contemplation 449 n. *meditation;* prayer, orison, bidding prayer; petition, petitionary prayer 761n. *request;* invocation, invocatory prayer 583n. *allocution;* intercession, intercessory prayer 762 n. *deprecation;* suffrage, prayers for the dead, vigils; special prayer, intention; rogation, supplication, solemn s., litany, solemn l.; comminatory prayer, commination, denunciation 900n. *threat;* imprecation, imprecatory prayer 899n. *malediction;* excommunication, ban 883n. *seclusion;* exorcism 300n. *ejection;* benediction, benedicite, benison, grace, grace before meat 907n. *thanks;* prayer for the day, collect; liturgical prayer, the Lord's Prayer, Paternoster, Our Father; Ave, Ave Maria, Hail Mary; Kyrie Eleison, Sursum Corda, Sanctus; Nunc Dimittis; dismissal, blessing; rosary, beads, beadroll; prayer-wheel; prayer-book, missal, breviary, book of hours; call to prayer, muezzin's cry 547n. *call.*
hymn, song, religious lyric, psalm, metrical p.; processional hymn, recessional; chant, chaunt, descant 412n. *vocal music;* anthem, cantata, motet; antiphon, response; canticle, Te Deum, Benedicite; song of praise, Magnificat; doxology, Gloria; greater doxology, Gloria in Excelsis; lesser doxology, Gloria Patri; paean, Hallelujah, Hosanna; Homeric hymn; Vedic hymn; hymn-singing, hymnody; psalm-singing, psalmody; hymn-book, hymnal, psalter; Vedic hymns, Rigveda, Samaveda; hymnology, hymnography.
oblation, tribute, Peter's pence, mass money, offertory, collection, alms and oblations 781n. *offering;* pewrent, pewage; libation, incense, censing 988n. *rite;* dedication, consecration 866n. *dignification;* votive offering, de voto o.; thank-offering 907n. *gratitude;* sin-offering, victim, scapegoat 150n. *substitute;* burnt offering, holocaust; sacrifice, devotion; immolation, hecatomb 362n. *slaughter;* human sacrifice 362n. *homicide;* self-sacrifice, self-devotion 931n. *disinterestedness;* self-immolation, suttee, sutteeism 362n. *suicide;* expiation, propitiation 941n. *atonement;* a humble and a contrite heart 939n. *penitence.*
public worship, common prayer, intercommunion; agape, love-feast; service, divine service, mass, matins, evensong, benediction 988n. *rite;*

psalm-singing, psalmody, hymn-singing 412n. *vocal music;* church, church-going, chapel-g., attendance at church 979n. *piety;* meeting for prayer, gathering for worship 74n. *assembly;* prayer-meeting, revivalist m.; open-air service, street evangelism, revivalism; temple worship, state religion 973n. *religion.*

worshiper, fellow-w., coreligionist, pew-fellow 976n. *church member;* adorer, venerator; euchite; votary, devotee, oblate 979n. *pietist;* glorifier, hymner, praiser, idolizer, admirer, ardent a., humble a. 923n. *commender;* homager, follower, server 742n. *servant;* image-worshiper, iconolater 982n. *idolater;* sacrificer, sacrificator, offerer 781n. *giver;* invocator, invoker, caller 583n. *allocution;* supplicator, supplicant, suppliant 763n. *petitioner;* pray-er, man of prayer, beadsman, intercessor; contemplative, mystic, sufi, visionary; dervish, marabout, enthusiast, revivalist, prophet 973n. *religious teacher;* celebrant, officiant 986n. *clergy;* communicant, churchgoer, chapel-g., temple-worshiper; worshiping church, congregation, the faithful 976n. *church member;* psalm-singer, hymn-s., psalmodist 413n. *vocalist;* psalmist, hymn-writer, hymnologist 988n. *ritualist;* pilgrim, palmer, hajji 268n. *traveler.*

Adj. *worshiping,*—adoring etc.vb.; worshiping falsely 982adj. *idolatrous;* devout, devoted 979adj. *pious;* reverent, reverential 920adj. *respectful;* prayerful, fervent, instant in prayer 761adj. *supplicatory;* meditating, praying, interceding; in act of worship, communicating; kneeling, on one's knees; at one's prayers, at one's devotions, in retreat; regular in worship, church-going, chapel-g., communicant 976adj. *orthodox;* participating in worship, hymn-singing, psalm-s.; celebrating, officiating, ministering 988adj. *ritualistic;* mystic, mystical.

devotional, appertaining to worship, latreutic 988adj. *ritualistic;* worshipful, solemn, sacred, holy 979adj. *sanctified;* revered, worshiped 920 adj. *respected;* sacramental, mystic, mystical; invocatory 583adj. *vocative;* precatory, intercessory, petitionary 761adj. *supplicatory;* imprecatory 899adj. *maledictory;* sacrificatory, sacrificial; oblationary, votive, ex voto 759adj. *offering;* doxological, giving glory, praising 923 adj. *approving.*

Vb. *worship,* honor, revere, venerate, adore 920vb. *respect;* honor and obey 854vb. *fear;* do worship to, pay homage to, homage, acknowledge 917vb. *do one's duty;* pay divine honors to, make a god of one, deify, apotheosize 982vb. *idolatrize;* bow, kneel, genuflect, humble oneself, prostrate o. 872vb. *be humbled;* lift up the heart, bless, give thanks 907vb. *thank;* extol, laud, magnify, glorify, give glory to, doxologize 923vb. *praise;* hymn, anthem, celebrate 413vb. *sing;* call on, invoke, name, address 583vb. *speak to;* petition, beseech, supplicate, intercede, make intercession 761vb. *entreat;* pray, say a prayer, say one's prayers, recite the rosary, tell one's beads; meditate, contemplate, commune with God 979vb. *be pious.*

offer worship, celebrate, officiate, minister, administer the sacraments 988vb. *perform ritual;* lead the congregation, lead in prayer; sacrifice, make s., offer up 781vb. *give;* sacrifice to, propitiate, appease 719 vb. *pacify;* vow, make vows 764vb. *promise;* dedicate, consecrate 979vb. *sanctify;* take vows, enter holy orders 986vb. *take orders;* pilgrimize, go on a pilgrimage 267vb. *travel;* go to church, go to chapel, go to meeting, meet for prayer, engage in common prayer 979vb. *be pious;* go to service, hear Mass, take the sacraments, communicate, take Holy Communion, eat the Lord's Supper; fast, undertake a f. 946vb. *starve;* deny oneself, practice asceticism 945vb. *be ascetic;* go into retreat 449vb. *meditate;* sing hymns, sing psalms, hymnodize, psalmodize, anthem, chant 413vb. *sing;* doxologize 923vb. *praise.*

Int. Alleluia! Hallelujah! Hosanna! Glory be to God! Holy, Holy, Holy! Lift up your hearts, Sursum Corda! Lord, have mercy, Kyrie Eleison! Our Father; Lord, bless us! God save!

See: 74, 150, 267, 268, 300, 362, 412, 413, 449, 547, 583, 742, 759, 761, 762, 763, 781, 854, 866, 872, 899, 900, 907, 917, 920, 923, 931, 939, 941, 945, 946, 973, 976, 979, 982, 986, 988.

982 Idolatry

N. *idolatry,* idolatrousness, false worship, superstition 981n. *worship;* heathenishness, heathenism, paganism 973n. *religion;* fetishism, anthropomorphism, zoomorphism; iconolatry, image-worship; idolism, idol-worship, idolodulia, idolomania; idolomancy, mumbo jumbo, hocus-pocus 983n. *sorcery;* heliolatry, sun-worship; star-worship, Sabaism; pyrolatry, fire-worship; zoolatry, animal-worship; ophiolatry, snake-worship; demonolatry, devil-worship 969n. *diabolism;* mammonism, money-worship; bibliolatry, ecclesiolatry; idol-offering, idolothyte.

deification, god-making, apotheosis, apocolocyntosis; idolization 920n. *respect;* king-worship, emperor-w. 981n. *worship.*

idol, statue 554n. *sculpture;* image, graven i., molten i.; cult image, fetish, totem-pole; lingam, yoni; golden calf 966n. *god;* godling, thakur, joss; teraphim, lares et penates, totem, kobong, Mumbo Jumbo.

idolater, idolatress; idol-worshiper, idolatrizer, idolist; anthropomorphite; fetishist, fetisheer, fetish-man, fetish-woman; totemist; iconolater, image-worshiper 981n. *worshiper;* heliolater, sun-worshiper; star-worshiper, Sabaist; pyrolater, fire-worshiper, guebre; bibliolater, ecclesiolater 979n. *pietist;* mammonist, mammon-worshiper; demonolater, demonist, devil-worshiper 969n. *diabolist;* pagan, heathendom 974n. *heathen;* idolizer, deifier 923n. *commender;* idol-maker, image-m., maker of graven images.

Adj. *idolatrous,* pagan, heathen 974n. *heathenish;* idolatric, serving images; fetishistic; anthropomorphic, theriomorphic; anthropomorphitic; fire-worshiping, sun-w., star-w., Sabaist; devil-worshiping 969adj. *diabolic;* offered to an idol, idolothyte.

Vb. *idolatrize,* worship idols, worship the golden calf, bow down to a graven image; anthropomorphize, make God in one's own image; deify, apotheosize 979vb. *sanctify;* idolize, put on a pedestal 923vb. *praise;* heathenize 974vb. *paganize.*

Adv. *idolatrously,* heathenishly.

See: 554, 920, 923, 966, 969, 973, 974, 979, 981.

983 Sorcery

N. *sorcery,* spellbinding, witchery, magic arts, enchantments; witchcraft, sortilege; magianism, gramarye, magic lore 490n. *knowledge;* wizardry, magic skill 694n. *skill;* thaumaturgics, wonder-working, miracle-mongering 864n. *thaumaturgy;* magic, jadu, jugglery, illusionism 542n. *sleight;* sympathetic magic, influence 612n. *inducement;* white magic, theurgy; black magic, goety, black art, necromancy, diablerie, demonry 969n. *diabolism;* priestcraft, superstition, witch-doctoring, shamanism, obeahism, obeah, voodooism, voodoo, hoodoo; psychomancy, spirit-raising 511n. *divination;* spirit-laying, ghost-l., exorcism, exsufflation 988n. *rite;* magic rite, conjuration, invocation, incantation; ghost dance; coven, witches' sabbath, witches' coven; Walpurgisnacht; witching hour.

spell, charm, glamor, enchantment, cantrip, hoodoo, curse; evil eye, jinx, influence; bewitchment, fascination 291n. *attraction;* obsession, possession, demoniac p., bedevilment, nympholepsy; Dionysiac frenzy 503n. *frenzy;* incantation, rune; magic sign, pass; magic word, magic formula, open sesame, abracadabra; hocus-pocus, mumbo jumbo, fee faw fum 515n. *unmeaningness;* philter, love-potion (**see** *magic instrument*).

talisman, telesm, charm, counter-c.; cross, phylactery, demonifuge 662n. *safeguard;* obeah, fetish 982n. *idol;* periapt, amulet, mascot, luck-bringer, lucky charm; swastika, fylfot, gammadion, pentacle; scarab; birth-stone; emblem, flag, national f. 547n. *flag;* relic, holy r.; palladium 662n. *refuge.*

magic instrument, bell, book and candle; wizard's cup, witches' broomstick; magic recipe, witch-broth, hell-b., witches' caldron; philter, potion, moly; magic wheel, rhomb; wand, fairy w.; magic ring, Solomon's seal, Aladdin's lamp, Alf's button, purse of Fortunatus; magic mirror, magic sword, flying carpet; seven-league boots; Excalibur; cap of darkness, cloak of invisibility; wish-fulfiller, wishing-well, kamadhuk, wish-bone, merry-thought; divining rod 484n. *detector.*

sorcerer, wise man, seer, soothsayer, Chaldean, sortileger 511n. *diviner;* astrologer, alchemist 984n. *occultist;* mage, magian, the Magi; thaumaturgist, wonder-worker, miracle-w. 864n. *thaumaturgy;* shaman, witch-doctor, medicine-man, figure-flinger, fetisheer, fetish-man 982n. *idolater;* obi-man, voodooist, hoodooist, spirit-raiser 984n. *occultist;* conjuror, exorcist; charmer, snake-c.; juggler, illusionist 545n. *conjuror;* spellbinder, enchanter, wizard, warlock; magician, theurgist; goetic, necromancer 969n. *diabolist;* familiar, imp, devil, evil spirit 969n. *devil;* sorcerer's apprentice; Merlin, Faust, Pied Piper, Comus.

sorceress, wise woman, sibyl 511n. *diviner;* enchantress, witch, weird sister; hag, hellcat; night-hag; succubus, succuba; lamia; vampire; fairy godmother, wicked fairy, 970n. *fairy;* Witch of Endor, Hecate, Circe, Medea.

Adj. sorcerous, sortilegious; wizardly, witch-like; succubine; Circean; magicianly, magician, Chaldean; thaumaturgic 864adj. *wonderful;* theurgic, theurgical; goetic, necromantic 969adj. *diabolic;* shamanist, shamanistic, voodooistic; spell-like, incantatory, runic; conjuring, spirit-raising; witching, spell-binding, enchanting, fascinating 291adj. *attracting;* malignant, blighting, blasting, withering, casting the evil eye, overlooking 898adj. *maleficent;* occult, esoteric 984adj. *cabalistic.*

magical, witching; otherworldly, supernatural, uncanny, eldritch, weird 970adj. fairy-like; amuletic, talismanic, telesmatic, phylacteric 660 adj. *tutelary;* having magic power, charmed, enchanted 178adj. *influential.*

bewitched, witched, ensorcelled, tranced, enchanted, charmed, becharmed, fay; hypnotized, fascinated, spellbound, under a spell, under a charm; overlooked, under the evil eye; under a curse, cursed; blighted, blasted, withered; hag-ridden, haunted, beghosted.

Vb. *practice sorcery,*—witchcraft etc. n.; cast horoscopes 511vb. *divine;* do magic, weave spells; speak mystically, cabalize; recite a spell, recite an incantation, say the magic word, make passes; conjure, invoke, call up; raise spirits, command s., shamanize; exorcize, lay ghosts; wave a wand, rub the magic ring, spin the magic wheel; put on one's seven-league boots; ride a broomstick.

bewitch, witch, charm, becharm, enchant, fascinate, take 291vb. *attract;* hypnotize; ensorcell, spellbind, cast a spell on, lay under a spell; hoodoo, voodoo, obi, obeah; overlook, cast the evil eye, blight, blast 898 vb. *be malevolent;* put a curse on, lay under a curse 899vb. *curse;* lay under a ban, taboo, make t. 757vb. *prohibit;* hag-ride, haunt, walk, ghost, beghost 970vb. *goblinize.*

Adv. *sorcerously,* by means of enchantment; as under a spell.

See: 178, 291, 484, 490, 503, 511, 515, 542, 545, 547, 612, 660, 662, 694, 757, 864, 898, 899, 969, 970, 982, 984, 988.

984 Occultism

N. *occultism,* esoterism, esotericism, mysticism, transcendentalism 973n. *religion;* mystical interpretation, cabalism, cabala, gematria; theosophy, reincarnationism; yogism, yogeeism; sciosophy, hyperphysics, metapsychics; supernaturalism, psychism, pseudopsychology; secret art, esoteric science, odylism, alchemy, astrology, psychomancy, spiritualism, magic 983n. *sorcery;* mantology, sortilege 511n. *divination;* fortune-telling, crystal-gazing, palmistry, chiromancy 511n. *prediction;* clairvoyance, second sight 438n. *vision;* sixth sense 476n. *intuition;* animal magnetism, mesmerism, hypnotism; hypnosis, hypnotic trance 375n. *insensibility;* odyl, od, biod, thermod.

psychics, parapsychology, psychism 447n. *psychology;* psychic science, psychic research; paranormal perception, extrasensory p.; telegnosis, telesthesia, cryptesthesia, clairaudience, clairvoyance, second sight 476 n. *intuition;* telepathy, telergy; thought-reading, mind-r., thought transference; precognition, psi faculty.

theosophy, esoteric Buddhism, theosophic pantheism, reincarnationism 973n. *religion;* Essence, First Cause, the One; polarization of the One; devas, hierarchies; the Inner Government of the World, the Hierarchy, Great White Lodge; head of the Hierarchy, Lord of the World; Master, Elder Brother, guide.

spiritualism, spiritism; spirit communciation, psychomancy 983n. *sorcery;* mediumism, mediumship; séance, sitting; astral body, spirit b., ethereal b. 320n. *immateriality;* spirit manifestation, materialization, ectoplasm, teleplasm 319n. *materiality;* apport, telekinesis; poltergeistery; spirit-rapping, table-tapping, table-turning; automatism, automatic writing, spirit w., psychography 586n. *writing;* spirit message, psychogram; spiritualistic apparatus, psychograph, planchette, ouija

board, dark room; control; guide; psychic research.
occultist, mystic, transcendentalist, supernaturalist; esoteric, cabalist; reincarnationist; theosophist, seer of the real; spiritualist, believer in spiritualism; Rosicrucian; alchemist 983n. *sorcerer;* astrologer, mantologist, sortileger, fortune-teller, crystal-gazer, palmist 511n. *diviner;* Rosenkrantz, Cagliostro, Katafeltro, Mesmer.
psychic, clairvoyant, clairaudient; telepath, telepathist; mind-reader, thought-r.; mesmerist, hypnotist; medium, spirit-rapper, automatist, psychographer, spirit-writer; seer, prophet 511n. *oracle;* dowser, water-diviner 511n. *diviner.*
psychist, parapsychologist, metapsychologist, psychophysicist, psychic researcher.
Adj. *cabalistic,* esoteric, cryptic, hidden 523adj. *occult;* dark, mysterious 491adj. *unknown;* mystic, transcendental, supernatural 973adj. *religious;* theosophic, theosophical, reincarnational; Rosicrucian; odylic; astrological, alchemistic, necromantic 983adj. *sorcerous;* ghosty, poltergeistish 970adj. *spooky.*
psychic, psychical, fey, second-sighted; mantological, prophetic 511 adj. *predicting;* telepathic, clairvoyant, clairaudient; thought-reading, mind-r.; spiritualistic, mediumistic; ectoplasmic, telekinetic, spirit-rapping; mesmeric, hypnotic.
paranormal, parapsychological, metapsychological, hyperpsychological, supernatural, hyperphysical.
Vb. *practice occultism,* mysterize, mysticize, esoterize; theosophize; cabalize; odize, odylize; alchemize 147vb. *transform;* astrologize, mantologize 511vb. *divine;* hypnotize, mesmerize; practice spiritualism, dabble in s.; hold a séance, attend séances; practice mediumship, have a control, go into a trance, rap tables, write spirit messages; materialize, dematerialize; study spiritualism, engage in psychic research.
See: 147, 319, 320, 375, 438, 447, 476, 491, 511, 523, 586, 970, 973, 983.

985 Churchdom

N. *churchdom,* the church, pale of the c., Christendom 976n. *the Church;* priestly government, hierocracy, theocracy; obedience, Roman o.; rule of the saints 733n. *authority;* the elect, priestly nation, kingdom of priests; church government 733n. *government;* ecclesiastical order, hierarchy 60n. *order;* paparchy, papality, papacy, popedom; popishness, ultramontanism; cardinalism; bishopdom, prelatehood, prelatry, prelacy; archiepiscopacy, episcopacy, lordly e., episcopalianism; presbytery, presbyterianism, congregationalism, independence 978 n. *sectarianism;* ecclosiology, ecclesiologist.
ecclesiasticism, clericalism, sacerdotalism; priestliness, priesthood, Brahmahood; priestdom, priestcraft; Brahmanism; ecclesiastical privilege, benefit of clergy, clergiability 919n. *non-liability;* ecclesiastical censorship, inquisition, Holy Office, Index Expurgatorious 757n. *prohibition.*
monasticism, monastic life, monachism, monachy 895n. *celibacy;* cenobitism 883n. *seclusion;* monkhood, monkishness, friarhood 945n. *asceticism.*
church ministry, ecclesiastical vocation, call, call to the ministry 622n. *vocation;* apostleship, apostolate, mission, mission to the heathen, conversion of the h. 147n. *conversion;* pastorate, pastorship, cure, cure of souls; spiritual comfort, spiritual leadership 901n. *philanthropy;* spiritual guidance, confession, absolution, shrift 988n. *ministration;* preaching office, predication, preaching, homiletics 534n. *teaching.*
holy orders, orders, minor o. 986n. *cleric;* apostolic succession, ordering, ordination, consecration; induction, reading in; installation, enthronement; nomination, presentation, appointment 751n. *commission;* preferment, translation, elevation 285n. *progression;* episcopal election, congé d'élire.
church office 689n. *management;* ecclesiastical rank 27n. *degree;* priesthood, priestliness; apostolate, apostleship; pontificate, papacy, popeship, Holy See, Vatican; cardinalate, cardinalship; patriarchate, patriarchship; exarchate, metropolitanate; primacy, primateship; archiepiscopate, archbishopric; see, bishopric, episcopate, episcopacy, prelacy; abbotcy, abbotship, abbacy, abbotric; priorate, priorship; archdeaconry, archdeaconate, archdeaconship; deanery, deanship; canonry, canonicate; prebendaryship; deaconship; diaconate, subdiaconate; presbyterate,

presbytership, eldership, moderatorship, ministership, pastorship, pastorate; rectorship, vicarship, vicariate; curacy, cure, cure of souls; chaplainship, chaplaincy, chaplainry; incumbency, tenure, benefice 773n. *possession;* preferment, appointment, translation.
parish, deanery; presbytery; diocese, bishopric, see, archbishopric; metropolitanate, patriarchate, province 184n. *district.*
benefice, incumbency, tenure; living, ecclesiastical l., spiritual l., rectorship, parsonage; glebe, tithe; prebend, prebendal stall, canonry; temporalities, church lands, church endowments 777n. *property;* patronage, advowson, right of presentation.
synod, provincial s., convocation, general council, ecumenical c. 692n. *council;* conciliar movement; college of cardinals, consistory, conclave; bench of bishops, episcopal bench; chapter, vestry; kirk session, presbytery, synod, Sanhedrin 956n. *tribunal;* consistorial court, Court of Arches 956n. *ecclesiastical court.*
Adj. *ecclesiastical,* ecclestiastic, churchly, ecclesiological, theocratic; obediental, infallible 733adj. *authoritative;* hierocratic, priest-ridden, ultramontane 976adj. *orthodox;* apostolic; hierarchical, pontifical, papal 976adj. *popish;* patriarchal, metropolitan; archiepiscopal, episcopal, prelatic, prelatical 986adj. *clerical;* episcopalian, presbyterian 978adj. *sectarian;* prioral, abbatical, abbatial; conciliar, synodic, presbyteral, capitular; sanhedral, consistorial; provincial, diocesan, parochial.
priestly, sacerdotal, hieratic, Aaronic, Levitical; Brahmanic; sacramental, spiritual; ministering, apostolic, pastoral.
Vb. *ecclesiasticize,* be churchly,—priestly etc.adj.; episcopize, prelatize; frock, ordain, order, consecrate, enthrone; cowl, tonsure, make a monk of; call, confer, nominate, present; benefice, prefer, bestow a living 781vb. *give;* translate 272vb. *transfer;* elevate 285vb. *promote;* beatify, canonize, saint 979vb. *sanctify;* enter the church 986vb. *take orders;* sanctuarize 660vb. *safeguard.*
Adv. *ecclesiastically,* church-wise.
See: 27, 60, 147, 184, 285, 534, 622, 660, 689, 692, 733, 751, 757, 773, 777, 883, 895, 901, 919, 945, 956, 976, 978, 986, 988.

986 Clergy
N. *clergy,* hierarchy; clerical order, parsondom, the cloth, the ministry; sacerdotal order, priesthood, secular clergy, regular clergy, religious.
cleric, clerical; clerk in holy orders, priest, deacon, subdeacon, acolyte, exorcist, lector, ostiary; churchman, ecclesiastic, divine; clergyman, black coat, reverend, reverend gentleman; father, father in God; padre, sky-pilot, Holy Joe; beneficed clergyman, beneficiary, pluralist, parson, rector, incumbent, residentiary, resident, residenter 776n. *possessor;* hedgepriest, priestling 639n. *nonentity;* ordinand, seminarist 538n. *learner.*
pastor, shepherd, father in God, minister, parish priest, rector, vicar, perpetual curate, curate, abbé; chaplain; confessor, father c., penitentiary, penitencer; spiritual director, spiritual adviser; pardoner; friar; preaching order, predicant; preacher, pulpiteer, lecturer, lay-preacher, woman p. 537n. *preacher;* field preacher, missioner, missionary 901n. *philanthropist;* evangelist, revivalist, salvationist, hot-gospeler.
ecclesiarch, ecclesiastical potentate, hierarch 741n. *potentate;* pope, Supreme Pontiff, Holy Father, Vicar of Christ; cardinal, prince of the church; patriarch, exarch, metropolitan, primate, archbishop; prelate, diocesan, bishop, bishop in partibus; suffragan, assistant bishop, "episcopal curate"; bench of bishops, episcopate, Lords Spiritual; archpriest, archpresbyter; archdeacon, dean, subdean, rural dean; canon, canon regular, canon secular, residentiary; prebendary, capitular; archimandrite; superior, mother s.; abbot, abbess; prior, prioress, Grand Prior; elder, presbyter, moderator; bishopess, she-bishop, Pope Joan 545n. *impostor.*
monk, monastic, cloisterer 895n. *celibate;* hermit, cenobite, Desert Father 883n. *solitary;* vagabond monk, circumcellion; Greek monk, caloyer; Islamic monk, santon, marabout; sufi 979n. *pietist;* dervish, fakir 945n. *ascetic;* Buddhist monk, pongyi, bronze; brother, regular, conventual; superior, archimandrite, abbot, prior; novice, lay brother; cowl, shaveling; friar, begging f., mendicant; discalced friar, discalceate; monks, religious; fraternity, brotherhood, lay b., friarhood, friary; order, religious o. 708n.

community; Black Monk, Benedictine, Cistercian, Bernardine, Trappist; Carthusian; Cluniac; Gilbertine; Premonstratensian, Maturine; Dominicans, Friars Preachers, Black Friars; Franciscans, Poverelli, Grey Friars, Friars Minors, Minorites, Friars Observant, Recollects, Friars Conventual, Capuchins, Augustines, Austin Friars; Carmelites, White Friars; Crutched Friars, Crossed F.; Bonhommes; teaching order, missionary o., Society of Jesus, Jesuits; crusading order, Templars, Knights Templars, Poor Soldiers of the Temple; Hospitalers, Knights Hospitalers, Knights of the Hospital of St. John of Jerusalem, Knights of Malta; Grand Prior; mendicant order, beghard.

nun, cloistress, clergywoman; sister, mother; novice, postulant; lay sister; superioress, mother superior, abbess, prioress, canoness, deaconess; sisterhood, lay s., beguinage, beguine.

church officer, elder, presbyter, moderator 741n. *officer;* priest, chantry p., chaplain, altarist; curate in charge, minister; lay preacher, lay reader, Bible-reader, Bible-woman; acolyte, server, altar-boy; crucifer, thurifer, boat-boy 988n. *ritualist;* chorister, choirboy, choirman, precentor, succentor, cantor 413n. *choir;* sidesman; churchwarden, vestryman, capitular; clerk, vestry c., parish c.; beadle, verger, pew-opener; sacristan, sexton; grave-digger, bell-ringer; sumner 955n. *law officer.*

priest, chief p., high p., archpriest; priestess, vestal, Pythia, pythoness, pythonissa, prophetess, prophet 511 n. *oracle;* Levite; rabbi; imam, mufti, mahdi; Brahman, purohit, pujari; talapoin, pongyi, bonze, lama, Dalai L., Grand L., Teshu L.; pontiff, flamen, archflamen; druid, druidess; shaman, witch-doctor.

church title, Holy Father; Eminence; Monsignor, Monseigneur; Lordship, Lord Spiritual; Most Reverend, Right R., Very R.; the Reverend; parson, rector, vicar; father, brother, Dom; mother, sister.

monastery, monkery, bonzery, lamasery; friary; priory, abbey; convent, nunnery, beguinage; ashram, hermitage 192n. *retreat;* community house 192n. *abode;* theological college, seminary 539n. *training school;* cell 194n. *chamber.*

parsonage, parson's house, presbytery, rectory, vicarage; glebe-house, pastorage, manse; deanery, archdeaconry 192n. *abode;* palace, bishop's p., patriarchate; Lambeth, Vatican; church-house, church-hall; close, cathedral c., papal precincts 235n. *enclosure.*

Adj. *clerical,* in orders, in holy o.; with benefit of clergy, clergiable; regular; secular; ordained, consecrated; gaitered, aproned, mitered 989adj. *vestured;* prebendal, beneficed, pluralistic; unbeneficed, glebeless, lay; parsonical, rectorial, vicarial; pastoral, ministerial, presbyteral, sacerdotal 985adj. *priestly;* diaconal, subdiaconal, archidiaconal, prelatical, episcopal 985adj. *ecclesiastical.*

monastic, monasterial, cloistral, cloisterly; cloistered, conventual, enclosed 232adj. *circumscribed;* monkish, monachic, celibate 895adj. *unwedded;* cowled, capuched 989adj. *vestured;* tonsured, shaven and shorn; bonze-like.

Vb. *take orders,* be ordained, enter the church, enter the ministry, wear the cloth; take vows, take the tonsure, take the cowl; take the veil, become a nun.

Adv. *clerically,* parsonically.

See: 192, 194, 232, 235, 413, 511, 537, 538, 539, 545, 639, 708, 741, 776, 883, 895, 901, 945, 955, 979, 985, 988, 989.

987 Laity

N. *laity,* temporalty, lay people, people, civilians 869n. *commonalty;* cure, charge, parish; flock, sheep, fold; diocesans, parishioners; brethren, congregation, society 976n. *church member;* lay brethren, lay sisterhood, lay community 708n. *community;* the profane, the worldly.

laicality, temporality, secularity; laicization, secularization, deconsecration.

layman, lay woman, laic; lay rector, lay deacon; lay brother, lay sister; catechumen, ordinand, seminarist, novice, postulant 538n. *learner;* lay preacher, lay reader; parishioner, diocesan, member of the flock 976n. *church member;* non-professional, amateur 695n. *unskillfulness;* civilian 869n. *commoner;* profane person; laicizer, secularizer.

Adj. *laical,* parishional, congregational; laic, lay, non-clerical, non-priestly, unordained, not in orders, non-clerigable; non-ecclesiastical, unclerical, unpriestly, secular; temporal, in the world, of the w., nonreligious 974adj. *irreligious;* profane, unholy, unconsecrated; laicized, secularized, deconsecrated; non-professional, amateur, do-it-yourself; amateurish 695adj. *unskilled;* civilian, popular 869adj. *plebeian.*

Vb. *laicize,* secularize, undedicate, deconsecrate, dishallow.

Adv. *laically,* as a layman.

See: 538, 695, 708, 869, 974, 976.

988 Ritual

N. *ritual,* procedure, way of doing things, method 624n. *way;* prescribed procedure, due order, routine, drill, system 60n. *order;* form, order, liturgy 610n. *practice;* symbolization, symbolism 519n. *metaphor;* rituality, ceremonial, ceremony 875n. *formality.*

ritualism, ceremonialism, ceremony, formalism, spikiness; liturgics.

rite, mode of worship 981n. *cult;* institution, observance, ritual *practice;* form, order, ordinance, rubric, formula, formulary 693n. *precept;* ceremony, solemnity, sacrament, mystery 876n. *celebration;* rites, mysteries 551n. *representation;* initiatory rite, circumcision, initiation, baptism 299n. *reception;* christening (**see** *Christian rite*).

ministration, functioning, officiation, performance 676n. *action;* administration, celebration, solemnization; pulpitry, predication, preaching 534 n. *teaching;* preachment, homily 534 n. *lecture;* sacred rhetoric, homiletics 579n. *oratory;* pastorship, pastoral epistle, pastoral letter; confession, auricular c.; shrift, absolution, penance.

Christian rite, rites of the Church; sacrament, the seven sacraments; baptism, infant b., christening 299n. *reception;* immersion, total i. 303n. *immersion;* affusion 341n. *moistening;* confirmation, bishoping; Holy Communion, Eucharist, reservation of the sacraments; paenitentia prima, paenitentia secunda, exomologesis 941n. *penance;* absolution 960 n. *acquittal;* Holy Matrimony 894n. *marriage;* Holy Orders 985n. *churchdom;* Holy Unction, chrismation, chrism; visitation of the sick, extreme unction, last rites, viaticum; burial of the dead; requiem mass; liturgy, order of service, order of baptism, marriage service, solemnization of matrimony, nuptial mass; churching of women; ordination, ordering of deacons, ordering of priests; consecration, consecration of bishops; exorcism 300n. *ejection;* excommunication, ban, bell, book and candle 883n. *seclusion;* canonization, beatification 866n. *dignification;* dedication, undedication.

Holy Communion, Eucharist, eucharistic sacrifice; mass, high m., solemn m., great m., sung m., missa cantata; low mass, little m., dry m., missa sicca; public mass, private m.; communion, the Lord's Supper; celebration, service, order of s., liturgy; preparation, confession, asperges; service of the book, introit, the Kyries, the Gloria, the Lesson, the Gradual, the Collects, the Gospel, the creed; service of the Altar, the offertory, offertory sentence, offertory prayers, the biddings; the blessing, the thanksgiving, Sursum Corda, Preface, Sanctus, Great Amen; the breaking of the bread, the commixture; the Pax; consecration; elevation of the Host; Agnus Dei; the Communion; kiss of peace; prayers of thanksgiving, the dismissal; the blessing.

the sacrament, the Holy Sacrament; Corpus Christi, body and blood of Christ; real presence, transubstantiation, consubstantiation, impanation; the elements, bread and wine, wafer, altar bread; consecrated bread, host; reserved sacrament; viaticum.

church service, office, duty, service; liturgy, celebration, concelebration; canonical hours, matins, lauds, prime, terce, sext, none, vespers, compline; the little hours; morning prayer, matins; evening prayer, evensong, benediction; Tenebrae; vigil, midnight mass, watchnight service; devotional service, three-hour s.; novena.

ritual act, symbolical act, sacramental, symbolism 551n. *representation;* lustration, purification 648n. *cleansing;* thurification 338n. *vaporization;* sprinkling, aspersion, asperges 341n. *moistening;* circumambulation 314n. *circuition;* procession 285n. *progression;* stations of the cross 981n. *act of worship;* obeisance, bowing, kneeling, genuflection, prostration, homage 920n. *respects;* crossing oneself, signation, sign of the cross 547n. *gesture;* eucharistic rite, breaking the bread, commixture; intinction 341n. *moistening;* elevating of the Host; kiss of peace.

ritual object, cross, rood, Holy Rood,

crucifix; altar, Lord's table, communion t.; altar furniture, altar cloth, rowel c.; candle, candlestick; communion wine, communion bread; cup, chalice, grail, Holy Grail, Sangreal; cruet, paten, ciborium, pyx, pyx-chest, tabernacle; monstrance; chrism, chrismatory; collection-plate, salver; incense, incensory, censer, thurible; holy water; aspergillum; asperger; piscina; sacring-bell, Sanctus bell; font, baptismal f., baptistery; baptismal garment, chrisom; wedding garment, bridal veil, wedding-ring; devotional object, relics, sacred relics; reliquary, shrine, casket 194n. *box;* icon, Pietà, Holy Sepulcher, stations of the cross 551n. *image;* osculatory, pax; Agnus Dei, rosary, beads, beadroll 981n. *prayers;* non-Christian objects, Ark of the Covenant, mercy seat; seven-branched candlestick; shewbread; laver; hyssop; sackcloth and ashes; libation dish, patina; joss-stick; sacred thread; prayer-wheel; altar of incense; Urim, Thummim; temple veil.

ritualist, ceremonialist, Sabbatarian, formalist; liturgist, liturgiologist, litanist, euchologist; Sacramentarian, sacramentalist; celebrant, masser, minister 986n. *priest;* server, acolyte; thurifer, boat-boy; crucifer, processionist, processioner.

office-book, service-b., ordinal, lectionary; liturgy, litany, euchologion; formulary, farse, rubric, canon 693n. *precept;* book of hours, breviary; missal, mass-book; euchology, prayer-book, book of common prayer 981n. *prayers;* beads, beadroll, rosary.

hymnal, hymnology, hymn-book, choir-b.; psalter, psalm-book, book of psalms 981n. *hymn.*

holy-day, feast, feast-day, festival 837n. *festivity;* fast-day, meatless d. 946n. *fast;* high day, day of observance, day of obligation 876n. *celebration;* sabbath, sabbath-day, day of rest 681n. *leisure;* Lord's Day, Sunday; proper day 876n. *special day;* saint's day 141n. *anniversary;* All Hallows, All Saints, All Souls, Lady Day, Feast of the Annunciation; Candlemas, Feast of the Purification; Feast of the Assumption; Lammas, Martinmas, Michaelmas; Holy-tide, sacred season; Advent; Christmas, Christmas-tide, Yuletide, Noel, Nativity, Epiphany, Twelfth Night; Lent, Shrove Tuesday, Ash Wednesday, Maundy Thursday, Good Friday; Holy Week, Passion Week; Easter, Eastertide, Easter Sunday; Ascension Day; Whitsuntide, Whitsun, Whitsunday, Pentecost; Corpus Christi; Trinity Sunday; Passover; Feast of Weeks, Pentecost; Feast of Tabernacles, Feast of Ingathering; Day of Atonement, Sabbath of Sabbaths; Ramadan, lesser Bairam, Greater B.; Mohurrum; puja.

Adj. *ritual,* procedural; formal, solemn, ceremonial, liturgical; processional, recessional; symbolic, symbolical, representational 551adj. *representing;* sacramental, eucharistic; chrismal; baptismal; sacrificial, paschal; festal, pentecostal; fasting, Lenten; prescribed, ordained; unleavened; kosher; consecrated, blessed.

ritualistic, ceremonious, ceremonial, formular, formulistic; Sabbatarian; Sacramentarian; observant of ritual, addicted to r., lavish of r.; liturgiological, euchological.

Vb. *perform ritual,* do the rites, say office, celebrate, concelebrate, officiate, function; baptize, christen, confirm, ordain, lay on hands; minister, administer the sacraments, give communion, housel; sacrifice, offer s., make s.; offer prayers, bless, give benediction; anathematize, ban, ban with bell, book and candle; excommunicate, unchurch, unfrock; dedicate, consecrate, deconsecrate; purify, lustrate, asperge; thurify, cense; anoint, anele, give extreme unction; confess, absolve, pronounce absolution, shrive; take communion, receive the sacraments, housel oneself; bow, kneel, genuflect, prostrate oneself; sign oneself, make the sign of the cross, sain; take holy water; tell one's beads, say one's rosary; go one's stations, make one's s.; process, go in procession; circumambulate; fast, flagellate, do penance, stand in a white sheet.

ritualize, ceremonialize, institute a rite, organize a cult; sabbatize, sacramentalize, observe, keep, keep holy.

Adv. *ritually,* ceremonially; symbolically, sacramentally; liturgically.

See: 60, 141, 194, 285, 299, 300, 303, 314, 338, 341, 519, 534, 547, 551, 579, 610, 624, 648, 676, 681, 693, 837, 866, 876, 883, 920, 941, 946, 960, 981, 985.

989 Canonicals

N. *canonicals,* clerical dress, cloth, clerical black 228n. *dress;* frock, soutane, cassock, scapular; cloak, gown, Geneva g. 228n. *cloak;* robe, cowl, hood, capouch, capuche; lappet, bands; chimere, simar, lawn sleeves; apron, gaiters, shovel hat; cardinal's hat; priests' cap, biretta, black b., purple b., red b.; skullcap, calotte, zucchetto; Salvation Army bonnet 228n. *headgear;* tonsure, shaven crown 229n. *bareness;* prayer-cap; tallith; white sheet, white sheet of repentance; sanbenito, simarra.

vestments, ephod, priestly vesture, canonical robes 228n. *dress;* pontificalia, pontificals; cassock, surplice, rochet; cappa magna; cope, tunicle, dalmatic, alb 228n. *robe;* amice, chasuble; stole, deacon's s., orarion; scarf, tippet, pallium; cingulum 47n. *girdle;* maniple, fanon, fannel; biretta 228n. *headgear;* miter, tiara, triple crown 743n. *regalia;* papal vestment, orale, fanon; crosier, crose, staff, pastoral s. 743n. *badge of rank;* pectoral 222n. *cross;* episcopal ring; altar-cloth, frontlet, pall; pyx-cloth; orphrey, orfray, ecclesiastical embroidery 844n. *ornamentation.*

Adj. *vestmental,* vestmentary, vestiary; canonical, pontifical.

vestured, robed 228adj. dressed; surpliced, stoled etc.n.; cowled, hooded, capuched 986adj. *monastic;* gaitered, aproned 986adj. *clerical;* mitered, crosiered; wearing the triple crown, tiara'd.

See: 47, 222, 228, 229, 743, 844, 986.

990 Temple

N. *temple,* fane, pantheon; shrine, sacellum; idol house, joss-h., teocalli 982n. *idolatry;* house of God, tabernacle, the Temple, House of the Lord; place of worship 981n. *worship;* masjid, mosque, Friday m.; mandir, mandap; house of prayer, oratory, oratorium; sacred edifice, pagoda, stupa, tope, dagoba, ziggurat, Tower of Babel 164n. *edifice;* propylaeum; pronaos, portico, cella, naos.

holy place, holy ground, sacred precinct, temenos; sacrarium, sanctuary, adytum, cella, naos; Ark of the Covenant, mercy seat, sanctum, holy of holies, oracle; martyry, sacred tomb, murabit, marabout, sepulcher, Holy Sepulcher; graveyard, Golgotha, God's acre 364n. *cemetery;* place of pilgrimage; Holy City, ion, New Jerusalem; Mecca, Benares, Banaras.

church, God's house; parish church, daughter c., chapel of ease; chapelry, chapelstead; cathedral, minster, pro-cathedral; basilica; abbey; kirk, chapel, tabernacle, temple, bethel, ebenezer; steeple-house, conventicle, meeting-house, prayer-h.; house of prayer, oratory, chantry, chantry-chapel; synagogue, mosque.

altar, sacrarium, sanctuary; altar-stone, altar-slab, mensa; altar-table, Lord's t., communion t.; altar-bread 988n. *the sacrament;* altar pyx; prothesis, credence, credence-table 988n. *ritual object;* canopy, baldachin, altar-piece, altar-screen, reredos; altar-cloth, altar-frontal, altar-facing, antependium; altar-stair, predella, altar-rails; altar of incense; shewbread.

church utensil, font, baptistry; aumbry, stoup, piscina; chalice, paten 988n. *ritual object;* pulpit, lectern; reading-bible, hymnal, prayer-book 981n. *prayers;* hassock, kneeler; salver, collection-plate, collection-bag; organ, harmonium; bell, church-b., carillon 412n. *campanology.*

church interior, nave, cella, body of the kirk; aisle, apse, ambulatory, transept; rood-steeple, rood-tower; chancel, choir, sanctuary; hagioscope, priest's window, squint; chancel screen, rood-s., jube, rood loft, gallery, organ-loft; stall, choir-s., sedile, sedilia, misericord; pew; minister's pew, reading-p.; pulpit, ambo; reader's pew, lectern; chapel, Lady c.; confessional; clerestory, triforium, spandrel; stained glass, stained-glass window, rose w., jesse w., jesse; calvary, stations of the cross, Easter sepulcher; baptistry font; sacristy, vestry; crypt, vault; rood, cross, crucifix.

church exterior, church-door, porch, Galilee, tympanum 263n. *doorway;* tower, steeple, spire 209n. *high structure;* bell-tower, belfry, campanile; buttress, flying b. 218n. *supporter;* cloister, ambulatory; chapter-house, presbytery 692n. *council;* churchyard, kirkyard, lychgate; close 235n. *enclosure;* gopura; torii.

Adj. *churchlike,* basilican, cathedralic; cruciform 222adj. *crossed;* apsidal 248adj. *curved;* Gothic, Romanesque, Norman, Early English, decorated, perpendicular.

See: 164, 209, 218, 222, 235 248, 263, 364, 412, 692, 981, 982, 988.

INDEX

For instructions on how to use this Index
see pages lxxvii-xxc

A

Aaronic
  priestly 985adj.
A1
  supreme 34adj.
  best 644adj.
abacist
  computer 86n.
aback
  rearward 238adv.
abacus
  counting instrument 86n.
abaft
  rearward 238adv.
abalienate
  convey 780vb.
abandon
  exclude 57vb.
  depart 296vb.
  disregard 458vb.
  tergiversate 603vb.
  relinquish 621vb.
  assiduity 678n.
  restlessness 678n.
  resign 753vb.
  not retain 779vb.
  excitable state 822n.
  cheerfulness 833n.
  rejoicing 835n.
abandoned
  separate 46adj.
  unpossessed 774adj.
  vicious 934adj.
abandonment
  tergiversation 603n.
  relinquishment 621n.
  submission 721n.
  resignation 753n.
  non-retention 779n.
  excitable state 822n.
  rejoicing 835n.
abandon one's post
  fail in duty 918vb.
abase
  be low 210vb.
  abase 311vb.
  pervert 655vb.
abasement
  disrepute 867n.
  humility 872n.
  humiliation 872n.
  servility 879n.
abash
  abase 311vb.
  frighten 854vb.
  humiliate 872vb.
abate
  decrease 37vb.
  moderate 177vb.
  qualify 468vb.
  discount 810vb.
abatement
  contraction 198n.
  relief 831n.
abatis
  defenses 713n.
abattoir
  slaughter-house 362n.
abaxial
  oblique 220adj.
abbacy
  church office 985n.
abbatical
  ecclesiastical 985adj.
abbé
  pastor 986n.
abbess
  ecclesiarch 986n.
  nun 986n.
abbey
  house 192n.
  monastery 986n.
  church 990n.
abbot
  ecclesiarch 986n.
  monk 986n.
abbotship
  church office 985n.
abbreviate
  bate 37vb.
  subtract 39vb.
  shorten 204vb.
  be concise 569vb.
  abstract 592vb.
abbreviation
  smallness 33n.
  contraction 198n.
  compendium 592n.
A.B.C.
  beginning 68n.
  guide-book 524n.
  curriculum 534n.
  letter 558n.
abdicate
  relinquish 621vb.
  be lax 734vb.
  resign 753vb.
abdication
  laxity 734n.
  loss of right 916n.
abdomen
  maw 194n.
  insides 224n.
abduct
  take away 786vb.
  steal 788vb.
abduction
  type of marriage 894n.
abeam
  sideways 239adv.
abed
  supine 216adj.
aberrant
  non-uniform 17adj.
  erroneous 495adj.
aberration
  abnormality 84n.
  displacement 188n.
  deviation 282n.
  divergence 294n.
  inattention 456n.
  insanity 503n.
abet
  concur 181vb.
  incite 612vb.
  aid 703vb.
abetment
  causation 156n.
  cooperation 706n.
abettor
  cause 156n.
  assenter 488n.
  motivator 612n.
  colleague 707n.
abeyance
  extinction 2n.
  lull 145n.
  non-use 674n.
  inaction 677n.
abeyance, in
  inert 175adj.
abhor
  not observe 769vb.
  dislike 861vb.
  hate 888vb.
  disapprove 924vb.
abhorrent
  contrary 14adj.
abide
  be 1vb.
  continue 108vb.
  last 113vb.
  stay 144vb.
  go on 146vb.
  dwell 192vb.
  be quiescent 266vb.
  be patient 823vb.
abide by
  acquiesce 488vb.
  observe 768vb.
abiding place
  abode 192n.
abient
  avoiding 620adj.
abient behavior
  recession 290n.
abient response
  recession 290n.
ability
  ability 160n.
  influence 178n.
  intelligence 498n.
  utility 640n.
  skill 694n.
ab initio
  initially 68adv.
abiogenesis
  propagation 164n.
abirritant
  lenitive 177adj.
  antidote 658n.

abject
servile 879adj.
cowardly 856adj.
disreputable 867adj.
contemptible 922adj.
rascally 930adj.
abjure
negate 533vb.
recant 603vb.
resign 753vb.
not retain 779vb.
ablative absolute
grammar 564n.
ablaze
fiery 379adj.
luminous 417adj.
able
powerful 160adj.
possible 469adj.
intelligent 498adj.
useful 640adj.
active 678adj.
skillful 694adj.
able-bodied
stalwart 162adj.
active 678adj.
ablegate
displace 188vb.
commission 751vb.
envoy 754n.
able seaman
mariner 270n.
navy man 722n.
ablution
water 339n.
moistening 341n.
ablution 648n.
abnegate
negate 533vb.
reject 607vb.
relinquish 621vb.
abnegation
refusal 760n.
temperance 942n.
abnormal
non-uniform 17adj.
disagreeing 25adj.
extraneous 59adj.
abnormal 84adj.
deviating 282adj.
insane 503adj.
unexpected 508adj.
ungrammatical 565adj.
funny 849adj.
wrong 914adj.
spooky 970adj.
abnormality
illicit love 951n.
abnormal psychology
psychology 447n.
insanity 503n.
aboard
here 189adv.
afloat 275adv.
abode
territory 184n.
station 187n.
abode 192n.
aboiement
speech defect 580n.
abolish
nullify 2vb.
destroy 165vb.
abrogate 752vb.
abolition
revolution 149n.
desuetude 611n.
abrogation 752n.
prohibition 757n.
abolitionist
revolutionist 149n.
destroyer 168n.
abominable
not nice 645adj.
unclean 649adj.
disliked 861adj.
hateful 888adj.
heinous 934adj.
abominable snowman
animal 365n.
mythical being 970n.
abominably
extremely 32adv.
abomination
badness 645n.
uncleanness 649n.
dislike 861n.
hatred 888n.
hateful object 888n.
wickedness 934n.
aboriginal
beginning 68adj.
primal 127adj.
fundamental 156adj.
native 191n., adj.
aborigine
earliness 135n.
abort
be unproductive 172vb.
miscarry 728vb.
abortion
abnormality 84n.
deformity 246n.
undevelopment 670n.
failure 728n.
eyesore 842n.
abortive
early 135adj.
unproductive 172adj.
disappointing 509adj.
profitless 641adj.
immature 670adj.
unsuccessful 728adj.
abound
abound 635vb.
superabound 637vb.
be rich 800vb.
about
concerning 9adv.
about 33adv.
nearly 200adv.
around 230adv.
about face
turn back 286vb.
about it, be
be active 678vb.
about to
prospectively 124adv.
tending 179adj.
about to be
impending 155adj.
about turn
reversion 148n.
turn round 282vb.
return 286n.
above
before 64adv.
retrospectively 125adv.
aloft 209adv.
prideful 871adj.
above all
eminently 34adv.
importantly 638adv.
above-board
veracious 540adj.
above-mentioned
preceding 64adj.
repeated 106adj.
prior 119adj.
foregoing 125adj.
above par
beyond 34adv.
excellent 644adj.
above price
valuable 644adj.
of price 811adj.
ab ovo
initially 68adv.
abracadabra
spell 983n.
abrade
bate 37vb.
subtract 39vb.
uncover 229vb.
pulverize 332vb.
rub 333vb.
obliterate 550vb.
abrasion
wound 655n.
abrasive
pulverizer 332n.
rubbing 333adj.
obliteration 550n.
abreaction
sanation 656n.
abreast
equal 28adj.
in parallel 219adv.
sideways 239adj.
abridge
bate 37vb.
subtract 39vb.

make smaller 198vb.
shorten 204vb.
translate 520vb.
be concise 569vb.
abstract 592vb.
abridgment
edition 589n.
compendium 592n.
abroad
abroad 59adv.
afar 199adv.
doubting 474adj.
abrogate
nullify 2vb.
disable 161vb.
suppress 165vb.
negate 533vb.
recant 603vb.
reject 607vb.
relinquish 621vb.
disuse 674vb.
liberate 746vb.
abrogate 752vb.
prohibit 757vb.
not observe 769vb.
not retain 779vb.
make illegal 954vb.
abrogation
revolution 149n.
destruction 165n.
desuetude 611n.
abrogation 752n.
abrupt
instantaneous 116adj.
violent 176adj.
vertical 215adj.
sloping 220adj.
inelegant 576adj.
hasty 680adj.
abscess
ulcer 651n.
abscission
subtraction 39n.
scission 46n.
abscond
decamp 296vb.
run away 620vb.
elude 667vb.
not pay 805vb.
fail in duty 918vb.
absence
non-existence 2n.
deficit 55n.
absence 190n.
farness 199n.
invisibility 444n.
oblivion 506n.
non-use 674n.
dutilessness 918n.
absent
abstracted 456adj.
unprovided 636adj.
inactive 679adj.
absentee
absence 190n.
dutilessness 918n.
absenteeism
absence 190n.
inactivity 679n.
dutilessness 918n.
absent-minded
abstracted 456adj.
forgetful 506adj.
absent oneself
be absent 190vb.
disappear 446vb.
run away 620vb.
be exempt 919vb.
absinthe
sourness 393n.
absolute
existing 1adj.
irrelative 10adj.
absolute 32adj.
simple 44adj.
complete 54adj.
self 80n.
one 88adj.
positive 473adj.
credal 485adj.
assertive 532adj.
authoritative 733adj.
authoritarian 735adj.
unconditional 744adj.
godlike 965adj.
absolutely
positively 32adv.
absolution
amnesty 506n.
liberation 746n.
forgiveness 909n.
non-liability 919n.
acquittal 960n.
church ministry 985n.
Christian rite 988n.
ministration 988n.
absolutism
despotism 733n.
absolve
liberate 746vb.
forgive 909vb.
exempt 919vb.
acquit 960vb.
perform ritual 988vb.
absonant
discordant 411adj.
illogical 477adj.
absorb
add 38vb.
combine 50vb.
contain 56vb.
consume 165vb.
absorb 299vb.
eat 301vb.
be attentive 455vb.
dispose of 673vb.
appropriate 786vb.
impress 821vb.
absorbed
thoughtful 449adj.
abstracted 456adj.
absorbent
admitting 299adj.
drier 342n.
absorbing
felt 818adj.
exciting 821adj.
absorption
identity 13n.
combination 50n.
reception 299n.
attention 455n.
abstain
be loath 598vb.
be neutral 606vb.
avoid 620vb.
relinquish 621vb.
not use 674vb.
be temperate 942vb.
abstainer
abstainer 942n.
ascetic 945n.
abstemious
temperate 942adj.
sober 948adj.
abstention
unwillingness 598n.
no choice 606n.
avoidance 620n.
inaction 677n.
temperance 942n.
abstinence
avoidance 620n.
non-use 674n.
temperance 942n.
abstinent
fasting 946adj.
sober 948adj.
abstract
insubstantial 4adj.
shorten 204vb.
mental 447adj.
philosophic 449adj.
be concise 569vb.
description 590n.
compendium 592n.
abstract 592vb.
take away 786vb.
steal 788vb.
abstracted
separate 46adj.
deviating 282adj.
abstracted 456adj.
crazed 503adj.
forgetful 506adj.
compendious 592adj.
abstractedness
abstractedness 456n.
fantasy 513n.
abstraction
insubstantiality 4n.
insubstantial thing 4n.

subtraction 39n.
disjunction 46n.
separation 46n.
incogitance 450n.
abstractedness 456n.
imperspicuity 568n.
stealing 788n.
abstractive
taking 786adj.
abstruse
puzzling 517adj.
imperspicuous 568adj.
absurd
disagreeing 25adj.
abnormal 84adj.
absurd 497adj.
foolish 499adj.
imaginative 513adj.
unmeaning 515adj.
useless 641adj.
absurdity
insubstantiality 4n.
ineffectuality 161n.
argumentation 475n.
error 495n.
absurdity 497n.
ideality 513n.
unmeaningness 515n.
silly talk 515n.
fable 543n.
caprice 604n.
pretext 614n.
trifle 639n.
inutility 641n.
abundance
greatness 32n.
great quantity 32n.
abundance 171n.
store 632n.
plenty 635n.
redundance 637n.
abundant
many 104adj.
diffuse 570adj.
rich 800adj.
abuse
force 176vb.
evil 616n.
waste 634vb.
ill-treat 645vb.
pervert 655vb.
misuse 675n., vb.
quarrel 709n.
slur 867n.
scurrility 899n.
curse 899vb.
not respect 921vb.
dispraise 924vb.
exprobate 924vb.
detraction 926n.
debauch 951vb.
impiety 980n.
abuse of language
neology 560n.
abuse the mind
misteach 535vb.
abusive
quarreling 709adj.
ungracious 885adj.
maledicent 899adj.
threatening 900adj.
detracting 926adj.
abut
be near 200vb.
be contiguous 202vb.
abutment
supporter 218n.
fortification 713n.
abut on
be supported 218vb.
abysmal
deep 211adj.
heinous 934adj.
diabolic 969adj.
abyss
space 183n.
gap 201n.
depth 211n.
cavity 255n.
pitfall 663n.
hell 972n.
acacia
tree 366n.
academic
irrelevant 10adj.
suppositional 512adj.
educational 534adj.
studious 536adj.
academicals
uniform 228n.
academician
intellectual 492n.
artist 556n.
academic title
academic title 870n.
academy
philosopher 449n.
academy 539n.
acarpous
unproductive 172adj.
accede
accrue 39vb.
approach 289vb.
assent 488vb.
consent 758vb.
accede to the throne
take authority 733vb.
accelerando
adagio 412adv.
accelerate
augment 36vb.
be early 135vb.
be vigorous 174vb.
make violent 176vb.
accelerate 277vb.
promote 285vb.
hasten 680vb.
animate 821vb.
accent
sound 398n.
prosody 593n.
affirmation 532n.
emphasize 532vb.
punctuation 547n.
pronunciation 577n.
voice 577vb.
speech defect 580n.
accents
voice 577n.
speech 579n.
accentual
vocal 577adj.
accentuate
emphasize 532vb.
accentuation
grammar 564n.
pronunciation 577n.
prosody 593n.
accept
admit 299vb.
believe 485vb.
acquiesce 488vb.
choose 605vb.
undertake 672vb.
submit 721vb.
consent 758vb.
give security 767vb.
receive 782vb.
take 786vb.
be hospitable 882vb.
approve 923vb.
acceptability
sufficiency 635n.
sociability 882n.
acceptable
admitting 299adj.
rational 475adj.
expedient 642adj.
pleasurable 826adj.
desired 859adj.
approvable 923adj.
acceptance
connotation 514n.
title-deed 767n.
(*see* accept)
accept deposits
borrow 785vb.
accepted
credible 485adj.
usual 610adj.
orthodox 976adj.
acceptor
recipient 782n.
purchaser 792n.
accept responsibility
look after 457vb.
promise 764vb.
incur a duty 917vb.
access
increment 36n.
entrance 68n.
doorway 263n.

approach 289n.
ingress 297n.
way in 297n.
reception 299n.
spasm 318n.
access 624n.
accessible
near 200adj.
open 263adj.
accessible 289adj.
admitting 299adj.
possible 469adj.
easy 701adj.
free 744adj.
accession
increment 36n.
addition 38n.
extra 40n.
approach 289n.
arrival 295n.
authority 733n.
accessory
extrinsicality 6n.
extrinsic 6adj.
adjunct 40n.
concomitant 89n.
accompanying 89adj.
superfluity 637n.
trifle 639n.
aiding 703adj.
colleague 707n.
accidence
grammar 564n.
accident
extrinsicality 6n.
chance 159n.
evil 616n.
non-design 618n.
ill fortune 731n.
accidental
extrinsic 6adj.
happening 154adj.
casual 159adj.
unintentional 618adj.
accident-prone
unfortunate 731adj.
accidie
sluggishness 679n.
acclaim
assent 488vb.
repute 866n.
honor 866vb.
applause 923n.
applaud 923vb.
acclamation
applause 923n.
acclimatize
make conform 83vb.
break in 369vb.
habituate 610vb.
acclivity
acclivity 220n.
ascent 308n.
accolade
honors 866n.
accommodate
adjust 24vb.
equalize 28vb.
comprise 78vb.
make conform 83vb.
place 187vb.
aid 703vb.
pacify 719vb.
lend 784vb.
accommodating
benevolent 897adj.
accommodation
room 183n.
storage 632n.
subvention 703n.
accompaniment
relativeness 9n.
adjunct 40n.
accompaniment 89n.
concomitant 89n.
synchronism 123n.
musical piece 412n.
accompanist
instrumentalist 413n.
accompany
accompany 89vb.
synchronize 123vb.
be contiguous 202vb.
play music 413vb.
direct 689vb.
accomplice
colleague 707n.
accomplish
produce 164vb.
do 676vb.
carry out 725vb.
succeed 727vb.
accomplished
skillful 694adj.
accomplished fact
certainty 473n.
accomplishment
culture 490n.
skill 694n.
(*see* accomplish)
accord
be uniform 16vb.
agreement 24n.
be equal 28vb.
combine 50vb.
conform 83vb.
concur 181vb.
harmonize 410vb.
assent 488vb.
be expedient 642vb.
concord 710vb.
permit 756vb.
consent 758n.
give 781vb.
according as
thus 8adv.
provided 468adv.
according to
conformably 83adv.
accordion
organ 414n.
accordionist
instrumentalist 413n.
accord, with one
unanimously 488adv.
accost
approach 289n.
speak to 583vb.
request 761vb.
greet 884vb.
accouche
deliver 668vb.
accouchement
obstetrics 164n.
accoucheur
obstetrics 164n.
doctor 658n.
account
statistics 86n.
list 87n.
estimate 480vb.
opine 485vb.
report 524n.
description 590n.
narration 590n.
funds 797n.
credit 802n.
debt 803n.
accounts 808n.
account 808vb.
prestige 866n.
accountability
liability 180n.
dueness 915n.
duty 917n.
accountable
accounting 808adj.
accountancy
numeration 86n.
registration 548n.
accounts 808n.
accountant
computer 86n.
recorder 549n.
treasurer 798n.
accountant 808n.
account book
list 87n.
record 548n.
account book 808n.
account for
cause 156vb.
account for 158vb.
interpret 520vb.
account, in one's
at credit 777adv.
account of, take
notice 455vb.
account, on no
in no way 33adv.
account owing
debt 803n.

accounts
accounts 809n.
account with
pay 804vb.
accouplement
joinder 45n.
accouter
dress 228vb.
make ready 669vb.
defend 713vb.
accouterment
dressing 228n.
uniform 228n.
equipment 630n.
fitting out 669n.
accredit
commission 751vb.
accredited
credible 485adj.
credal 485adj.
usual 610adj.
accretion
increment 36n.
addition 38n.
expansion 197n.
accrue
be extrinsic 6vb.
augment 36vb.
accrue 38vb.
result 157vb.
approach 289vb.
be profitable 771vb.
be received 782vb.
accumbent
supine 216adj.
accumulate
grow 36vb.
join 45vb.
bring together 74vb.
store 632vb.
acquire 771vb.
take 786vb.
accumulation
great quantity 32n.
accumulative
acquiring 771adj.
accumulator
accumulator 74n.
accuracy
mimicry 20n.
attention 455n.
carefulness 457n.
discrimination 463n.
accuracy 494n.
veracity 540n.
accurate
careful 457adj.
descriptive 590adj.
orthodox 976adj.
accursed
damnable 645adj.
bad 645adj.
harmful 645adj.
baneful 659adj.
unfortunate 731adj.
unhappy 825adj.
unpleasant 827adj.
hateful 888adj.
cursed 899adj.
heinous 934adj.
wicked 934adj.
profane 980adj.
accusable
accusable 928adj.
illegal 954adj.
accusation
affirmation 532n.
wrong 914n.
detraction 926n.
accusation 928n.
litigation 959n.
accusatory
disapproving 924adj.
detracting 926adj.
accuse
attribute 158vb.
inform 524vb.
oppose 704vb.
satirize 851vb.
defame 926vb.
accuse 928vb.
litigate 959vb.
accuse oneself
be penitent 939vb.
accused, the
prisoner 750n.
accused person 928n.
litigant 959n.
accuser
informer 524n.
detractor 926n.
accuser 928n.
litigant 959n.
accusing
evidential 466adj.
accustom
train 534vb.
habituate 610vb.
accustomed
usual 610adj.
unastonished 865adj.
ace
unit 88n.
means 629n.
masterpiece 694n.
acedia
sluggishness 679n.
acerbity
pungency 388n.
unsavoriness 390n.
sourness 393n.
rudeness 885n.
resentment 891n.
malevolence 898n.
acetify
be sour 393vb.
acetose
sour 393adj.
acetylene
fuel 385n.
ache
pang 377n.
feel pain 377vb.
give pain 377vb.
suffer 825vb.
achievable
possible 469adj.
achieve
terminate 69vb.
produce 164vb.
be instrumental 628vb.
do 676vb.
carry out 725vb.
succeed 727vb.
achievement
progression 282n.
heraldry 547n.
monument 548n.
(*see* achieve)
Achilles' heel
defect 647n.
vulnerability 661n.
achromatic
colorless 426adj.
achromatism
desiccation 342n.
dimness 419n.
achromatism 426n.
acid
destroyer 168n.
keen 174adj.
unsavory 391adj.
sourness 393n.
bane 659n.
poison 659n.
acidify
be sour 393vb.
acidity
pungency 388n.
sourness 393n.
acidosis
sourness 393n.
indigestion 651n.
acid test
experiment 461n.
acidulated
sour 393adj.
acidulous
keen 174adj.
sour 393adj.
aciform
sharp 256adj.
acknowledge
attribute 158vb.
notice 455vb.
answer 460vb.
testify 466vb.
assent 488vb.
confess 526vb.
correspond 588vb.
observe 768vb.
befriend 880vb.

greet 884vb.
thank 907vb.
grant claims 915vb.
reward 962vb.
worship 981vb.
acknowledged
usual 610adj.
received 807adj.
acknowledgment
(*see* acknowledge)
acme
summit 213n.
acne
skin disease 651n.
a-cold
a-cold 380adj.
acology
medical art 658n.
acolyte
auxiliary 707n.
cleric 986n.
church officer 986n.
ritualist 988n.
acomia
bareness 229n.
aconite
poisonous plant 659n.
acoustic
sounding 398adj.
auditory 415adj.
acoustics
acoustics 398n.
hearing 415n.
acquaint
inform 524vb.
acquaintance
knowledge 490n.
information 524n.
friendship 880n.
friend 880n.
acquaint oneself
know 490vb.
acquiesce
concur 181vb.
acquiesce 488vb.
be willing 597vb.
submit 721vb.
consent 758vb.
be content 828vb.
acquiescence
conformity 83n.
obedience 739n.
permission 756n.
patience 823n.
acquiescent
agreeing 24adj.
inexcitable 823adj.
acquire
acquire 771vb.
possess 773vb.
receive 782vb.
take 786vb.
be rewarded 962vb.
acquired
extrinsic 6adj.
acquired characteristic
extrinsicality 6n.
acquirement
skill 694n.
acquisition 771n.
acquirements
culture 490n.
acquisition
increment 36n.
extra 40n.
assemblage 74n.
benefit 615n.
store 632n.
acquisition 771n.
receiving 782n.
taking 786n.
acquisitions
culture 490n.
acquisitive
acquiring 771adj.
taking 786adj.
avaricious 816adj.
greedy 859adj.
selfish 932adj.
acquit
deliver 668n.
liberate 746vb.
forgive 909vb.
do one's duty 917vb.
exempt 919vb.
justify 927vb.
acquit 960vb.
acquittal
escape 667n.
observance 768n.
non-liability 919n.
vindication 927n.
innocence 935n.
legal trial 959n.
acquittal 960n.
acquittance
liberation 746n.
title-deed 767n.
observance 768n.
payment 804n.
acre
measure 183n.
acreage
measure 183n.
acres
land 344n.
lands 777n.
acrid
keen 174adj.
pungent 388adj.
unsavory 391adj.
acrimonious
ungracious 885adj.
resentful 891adj.
acrimony
keenness 174n.
sharpness 256n.
rudeness 885n.
hatred 888n.
resentment 891n.
malevolence 898n.
acrobat
athlete 162n.
proficient 696n.
acrobatic
athletic 162adj.
flexible 327adj.
acrobatics
athletics 162n.
acrophobia
psychopathy 503n.
phobia 854n.
acropolis
vertex 213n.
refuge 662n.
fort 713n.
across
obliquely 220adv.
across 222adv.
acrostic
equivocalness 518n.
enigma 530n.
initials 558n.
act
operate 173vb.
duplicity 541n.
dissemble 541vb.
represent 551vb.
stage show 594n.
act 594vb.
function 622vb.
be instrumental 628vb.
deed 676n.
do 676vb.
behave 688vb.
precept 693n.
be successful 727vb.
decree 737n.
be affected 850vb.
acta
record 548n.
act a part
cant 541vb.
be affected 850vb.
act-drop
stage-set 594n.
acted upon
operative 173adj.
act for
substitute 150vb.
deputize 755vb.
acting
ephemeral 114adj.
operative 173adj.
representation 551n.
acting arrangement
transientness 114n.
actinism
radiation 417n.
actinometer
optical device 442n.

actinometry
optics 417n.
act, in the
in the act 676adv.
action
eventuality 154n.
energy 160n.
production 164n.
agency 173n.
dramaturgy 594n.
policy 623n.
action 676n.
activity 678n.
conduct 688n.
fight 716n.
battle 718n.
effectuation 725n.
litigation 959n.
actionable
accusable 928adj.
legal 953adj.
illegal 954adj.
litigated 959adj.
activate
operate 173vb.
invigorate 174vb.
influence 178vb.
activation
stimulation 174n.
activity 678n.
activator
stimulant 174n.
active
stalwart 162adj.
operative 173adj.
vigorous 174adj.
moving 265adj.
willing 597adj.
businesslike 622adj.
doing 676adj.
active 678adj.
laboring 682adj.
excited 821adj.
active in
influential 178adj.
active list, on the
operative 173adj.
actively
greatly 32adv.
active service
warfare 718n.
activism
action 676n.
activity 678n.
activist
essayer 671n.
doer 676n.
busy person 678n.
activity
vigorousness 174n.
stimulation 174n.
agitation 318n.
business, job 622n.
instrumentality 628n.
action 676n.
activity 678n.
actor
imitator 20n.
deceiver 545n.
actor 594n.
doer 676n.
agent 686n.
personnel 686n.
affector 850n.
actor manager
stage-manager 594n.
act out
terminate 69vb.
actual
real 1adj.
present 121adj.
true 494 adj.
actuarial
accounting 808adj.
actuarial calculation
calculation of chance 159n.
actuary
computer 86n.
accountant 808n.
actuate
influence 178vb.
move 265vb.
motivate 612vb.
act upon
operate 173vb.
motivate 612vb.
acuity
sharpness 256n.
vision 438n.
sagacity 498n.
acumen
discrimination 463n.
sagacity 498n.
acuminate
tapering 256adj.
sharpen 256vb.
acupuncture
perforation 263n.
therapy 658n.
acute
keen 174adj.
violent 176adj.
sharp 256adj.
sentient 374adj.
strident 407adj.
intelligent 498adj.
cunning 698adj.
felt 818adj.
acute accent
punctuation 547n.
acuteness
sharpness 256n.
sagacity 498n.
adage
maxim 496n.
adagio
slowly 278adv.
adagio 412adv.
Adam
precursor 66n.
husbandman 370n.
mankind 371n.
male 372n.
Adam and Eve
parent 169n.
adamant
strength 162n.
hardness 326n.
Adamite
mankind 371adj.
Adamitic
human 371adj.
adapt
adjust 24vb.
translate 520vb.
adaptable
fit 24adj.
conformable 83adj.
flexible 327adj.
useful 640adj.
skillful 694adj.
adaptation
adaptation 24n.
conformity 83n.
transformation 147n.
musical piece 412n.
translation 520n.
edition 589n.
adapted
fit 24adj.
combined 50adj.
conformable 83adj.
adapted to
expedient 642adj.
adapter
alterer 143n.
ad captandum
sophistical 477adj.
flatteringly 925adv.
add
add 38vb.
join, affix 45vb.
agglutinate 48vb.
combine 50vb.
prepose 64vb.
modify 143vb.
enlarge 197vb.
insert 303vb.
misinterpret 521vb.
exaggerate 546vb.
addenda
edition 589n.
addendum
addition 38n.
extra, adjunct 40n.
adder
reptile 365n.
sibilation 406n.
bane 659n.
noxious animal 904n.
add fuel to the flame

augment 36vb.
make violent 176vb.
aggravate 832vb.
enrage 891vb.
addict
habitué 610n.
sick person 651n.
drunkard 949n.
addiction
habit 610n.
intemperance 943n.
adding machine
counting instrument 86n.
addition
quantity 26n.
increment 36n.
increase 36n.
addition 38n.
adjunct 40n.
mixture 43n.
joinder 45n.
whole 52n.
sequence 65n.
numerical result 85n.
numerical operation 86n.
expansion 197n.
insertion 303n.
exaggeration 546n.
additional
extrinsic 6adj.
additional 38adj.
included 78adj.
superfluous 637adj.
additive
additional 38adj.
extra 40n.
component 58n.
addle
sterilize 172vb.
be unclean 649vb.
addled
unproductive 172adj.
light-minded 456adj.
unintelligent 499adj.
addle-head
fool 501n.
address
place 185n.
situation 186n.
locality 187n.
abode 192n.
send 272vb.
oration 579n.
orate 579vb.
allocution 583n.
speak to 583vb.
correspond 587vb.
skill 694n.
entreat 761vb.
address book
reminder 505n.
address card
label 547n.
addressee
resident 191n.
interlocutor 584n.
correspondent 588n.
recipient 782n.
addresses
reading matter 589n.
wooing 889n.
address oneself
begin 68vb.
prepare 669vb.
adduce
corroborate 466vb.
manifest 522vb.
adduction
attraction 291n.
add up
add 38vb.
be intelligible 516vb.
add up to
mean 514vb.
adelantado
governor 741n.
adenography
structure 331n.
adenoidal
stammering 580adj.
adenoids
swelling 253n.
adenology
structure 331n.
adeps
fat 357n.
adept
proficient 696n.
adequacy
sufficiency 635n.
utility 640n.
adhere
accrue 38vb.
unite with 45vb.
cohere 48vb.
be contiguous 202vb.
transfer 272vb.
approach 289vb.
assent 488vb.
be wont 610vb.
contract 765vb.
retain 778vb.
adherence
coherence 48n.
observance 768n.
adherent
cohesive 48adj.
follower 284n.
auxiliary 707n.
signatory 765n.
adhere to
observe 768vb.
adhesion
coherence 48n.
contiguity 202n.
adhesive
conjunctive 45adj.
adhesive 47n.
cohesive 48adj.
tough 329adj.
viscid 354adj.
retentive 778adj.
adhesiveness
viscidity 354n.
adhibit
use 673vb.
ad hoc
spontaneous 609adj.
extempore 609adv.
unprepared 670adj.
unreadily 670vb.
ad hominem
specially 80adv.
adiactinic
opaque 423adj.
adiathermic
cold 380adj.
opaque 423adj.
adieu
valediction 296n.
ad infinitum
infinitely 107adj.
adipocere
decay 51n.
fat 357n.
adipose
fatty 357adj.
adit
doorway 263n.
tunnel 263n.
access 624n.
adjacent
near 200adj.
contiguous 202adj.
adjective
adjunct 40n.
part of speech 564n.
adjoin
be near 200vb.
be contiguous 202vb.
adjourn
put off 136vb.
adjournment
interim 108n.
delay 136n.
adjudge
judge 480vb.
adjudicate
judge 480vb.
try a case 959vb.
adjudication
judgment 480n.
adjudicator
estimator 480n.
adjunct
increment 36n.
adjunct 40n.
part 53n.
component 58n.
extremity 69n.

concomitant 89n.
aider 703n.
adjure
affirm 532vb.
entreat 761vb.
take a pledge 764vb.
adjurement
oath 532n.
adjust
graduate 27vb.
equalize 28vb.
mix 43vb.
regularize 62vb.
make conform 83vb.
synchronize 123vb.
moderate 177vb.
harmonize 410vb.
be true 494vb.
plan 623 vb.
rectify 654vb.
make ready 669vb.
pacify 719vb.
adjustable
conformable 83adj.
adjusted
conformable 83adj.
accurate 494adj.
right 913adj.
adjustment
adaptation 24n.
change 143n.
compact 765n.
compromise 770n.
(*see* adjust)
adjutage
tube 263n.
outlet 298n.
adjutant
auxiliary 707n.
army officer 741n.
adjuvant
aiding 703adj.
auxiliary 707n.
ad-libber
speaker 579n.
ad-libbing
spontaneity 609n.
ad libitum, ad lib
often 139adv.
at will 595adv.
enough 635adv.
freely 744adv.
admass
dupe 544n.
commonalty 869n.
administer
use 673vb.
do 676vb.
manage 689vb.
apportion 783vb.
administration
arrangement 62n.
use 673n.
action 676n.
management 689n.
apportionment 783n.
ministration 988n.
administrative
directing 689adj.
governmental 733adj.
jurisdictional 955adj.
administrator
doer 676n.
agent 686n.
manager 690n.
admirable
excellent 644adj.
wonderful 864adj.
worshipful 866adj.
approvable 923adj.
Admirable Crichton
exceller 644n.
proficient 696n.
prodigy 864n.
admiral
navy man 722n.
naval officer 741n.
admiralty
navy 722n.
authority 733n.
admiration
wonder 864n.
love 887n.
respect 920n.
approbation 923n.
admired
excellent 644adj.
respected 920adj.
admire oneself
be vain 873vb.
admirer
lover 887n.
commender 923n.
worshiper 981n.
admissibility
fitness 24n.
admissible
numerable 86adj.
rational 475adj.
approvable 923adj.
admission
inclusion 78n.
ingress 297n.
reception 299n.
testimony 466n.
assent 488n.
disclosure 526n.
affirmation 532n.
admit
add 38vb.
admit 299vb.
testify 466vb.
be reasonable 475vb.
believe 485vb.
assent 488vb.
confess 526vb.
affirm 532vb.
receive 782vb.
admit of
be possible 469vb.
admitting
provided 468adv.
open 263adj.
admixture
mixture 43n.
tincture 43n.
admonish
warn 664vb.
advise 691vb.
reprove 924vb.
admonition
dissuasion 613n.
warning 664n.
reprimand 924n.
ad nauseam
ad nauseam 861adv.
boringly 838adv.
adnoun
part of speech 564n.
ado
activity 678n.
exertion 682n.
adobe
small house 192n.
materials 631n.
a-doing
happening 154adj.
busy 678adj.
adolescence
youth 130n.
adolescent
young 130adj.
youngster 132n.
immature 670adj.
Adonis
male 372n.
a beauty 841n.
mythic god 966n.
adopt
be akin 11vb.
choose 605vb.
avail of 673vb.
adopted
additional 38adj.
filial 170adj.
sanctified 979adj.
adoption
choice 605n.
approbation 923n.
sanctity 979n.
adoptive
filial 170adj.
adorable
beautiful 841adj.
lovable 887adj.
adoration
respect 920n.
piety 979n.
worship 981n.
adore
love 887vb.

respect 920vb.
worship 981vb.
adorn
ornament 574vb.
make better 654vb.
decorate 844vb.
adornment
ornamentation 844n.
adrift
irrelative 10adj.
irrelevant 10adj.
separate 46adj.
apart 46adv.
unassembled 75adj.
astray 282adv.
doubting 474adj.
adroit
skillful 694adj.
adscititious
extrinsic 6adj.
additional 38adj.
superfluous 637adj.
adulation
exaggeration 546n.
praise 923n.
flattery 925n.
adult
adult 134n.
grown up 134adj.
manly 162adj.
matured 669adj.
adulterate
mix 43vb.
modify 143vb.
weaken 163vb.
abase 311vb.
rarefy 325vb.
add water 339vb.
impair 655vb.
adulterated
spurious 542adj.
adulterer
libertine 952n.
adulterine
spurious 542adj.
bastard 954adj.
adulterous
extramarital 951adj.
adultery
love affair 887n.
illicit love 951n.
adultness
adultness 134n.
preparedness 669n.
adultress
loose woman 952n.
adumbrate
predestine 155vb.
darken 418vb.
propound 512vb.
figure 519vb.
hint 524vb.
represent 551vb.
describe 590vb.
adumbration
similarity 18n.
copy 22n.
latency 523n.
adunation
combination 50n.
aduncity
angularity 247n.
curvature 248n.
adust
heated 381adj.
brown 430adj.
Advaita
philosophy 449n.
ad valorem
priced 809adj.
advance
increase 36n.
augment 36vb.
part 53n.
prepose 64vb.
elapse 111vb.
early 135adj.
go on 146vb.
motion 265n.
marching 267n.
travel 267vb.
progression 285n.
progress 285vb.
promote 285vb.
approach 289n., vb.
be visible 443vb.
affirm 532vb.
be instrumental 628vb.
be useful 640vb.
be expedient 642vb.
improvement 654n.
get better 654vb.
make better 654vb.
aid 703vb.
succeed 727vb.
offer 759n.
lend 784vb.
dignify 866vb.
advance against
charge 712vb.
advanced
modern 126adj.
early 135adj.
progressive 285adj.
advance guard
front 237n.
advance, in
early 135adj.
in front 237adv.
ahead 283adv.
advancement
(*see* advance)
advance notice
prediction 511n.
warning 664n.
advance of, in
beyond 34adv.
advances
approach 289n.
endearment 889n.
wooing 889n.
advantage
vantage 34n.
benefit 615n., vb.
utility 640n.
be useful 640vb.
expedience 642n.
be expedient 642vb.
success, victory 727n.
gain 771n.
advantage, have the
be unequal 29vb.
predominate 34vb.
advantage of, take
befool 542vb.
advantageous
(*see* advantage)
advent
futurity 124n.
eventuality 154n.
approach 289n.
arrival 295n.
holy-day 988n.
adventitious
extrinsic 6adj.
circumstantial 8adj.
casual 159adj.
adventure
eventuality 154n.
pursuit 619n.
essay 671n.
undertaking 672n.
be courageous 855vb.
adventurer
traveler 268n.
experimenter 461n.
impostor 545n.
gambler 618n.
militarist 722n.
desperado 857n.
egotist 932n.
adventures
biography 590n.
adventuress
loose woman 952n.
adventurous
speculative 618adj.
enterprising 672adj.
courageous 855adj.
rash 857adj.
adverb
adjunct 40n.
part of speech 564n.
adversaria
commentary 520n.
record 548n.
adversary
opponent 705n.
Satan 969n.
adversative
contrary 14adj.
negative 533adj.

- adverse
  - *contrary* 14adj.
  - *presageful* 511adj.
  - *unwilling* 598adj.
  - *evil* 616adj.
  - *inexpedient* 643adj.
  - *harmful* 645adj.
  - *hindering* 702adj.
  - *opposing* 704adj.
  - *adverse* 731adj.
  - *annoying* 827adj.
  - *unpromising* 853adj.
  - *disliking* 861adj.
- adversity
  - *ruin* 165n.
  - *evil* 616n.
  - *difficulty* 700n.
  - *adversity* 731n.
  - *suffering* 825n.
  - *painfulness* 827n.
  - *punishment* 963n.
- advert
  - *cognize* 447vb.
  - *be attentive* 455vb.
  - *notice* 455vb.
- advertence
  - *attention* 455n.
- advertise
  - *attract notice* 455vb.
  - *predict* 511vb.
  - *communicate* 524vb.
  - *advertise* 528vb.
  - *make important* 638vb.
  - *boast* 877vb.
  - *praise* 923vb.
- advertisement
  - *exhibit* 522n.
  - *information* 524n.
  - *advertisement* 528n.
  - *inducement* 612n.
  - *request* 761n.
  - *boasting* 877n.
- advertise oneself
  - *be ostentatious* 875vb.
  - *boast* 877vb.
- advertiser
  - *overestimation* 482n.
  - *exhibitor* 522n.
  - *informant* 524n.
  - *publicizer* 528n.
  - *motivator* 612n.
  - *petitioner* 763n.
  - *boaster* 877n.
  - *commender* 923n.
- advice
  - *meditation* 449n.
  - *estimate* 480n.
  - *information* 524n.
  - *hint* 524n.
  - *message* 529n.
  - *news* 529n.
  - *inducement* 612n.
  - *preparation* 669n.
  - *advice* 691n.
  - *precept* 693n.
  - *aid* 703n.
- advisable
  - *expedient* 642adj.
- advise
  - *propound* 512vb.
  - *hint* 524vb.
  - *inform* 524vb.
  - *doctor* 658vb.
  - *warn* 664vb.
  - *advise* 691vb.
- advise against
  - *dissuade* 613vb.
  - *warn* 664vb.
- advised
  - *predetermined* 608adj.
- advisedly
  - *purposely* 617adv.
- adviser
  - *estimator* 480n.
  - *sage* 500n.
  - *teacher* 537n.
  - *director* 690n.
  - *adviser* 691n.
  - *expert* 696n.
  - *consignee* 754n.
- advise with
  - *confer* 584vb.
  - *consult* 691vb.
- advisory
  - *judicial* 480adj.
  - *advising* 691adj.
- advocacy
  - *aid* 703n.
  - *approbation* 923n.
  - *bar* 958n.
- advocate
  - *intermediary* 231n.
  - *speaker* 579n.
  - *motivator* 612n.
  - *adviser* 691n.
  - *advise* 691vb.
  - *patron* 707n.
  - *combatant* 722n.
  - *consignee* 754n.
  - *deputy* 755n.
  - *approve* 923vb.
  - *vindicator* 927n.
  - *vindicate* 927vb.
  - *lawyer* 958n.
  - *litigate* 959vb.
- advowson
  - *benefice* 985n.
- adynamic
  - *weak* 163adj.
- adytum
  - *chamber* 194n.
  - *hiding-place* 527n.
  - *holy place* 990n.
- adz
  - *sharp edge* 256n.
- aedile
  - *official* 690n.
  - *officer* 741n.
- aedileship
  - *magistrature* 733n.
- aegis
  - *protection* 660n.
  - *armor* 713n.
- aegrotat
  - *non-liability* 919n.
- aeolian
  - *windy* 352adj.
- Aeolus
  - *wind* 352n.
  - *mythic god* 966n.
  - *lesser god* 967n.
- aeonian
  - *perpetual* 115adj.
- aeons
  - *diuturnity* 113n.
- aerate
  - *gasify* 336vb.
  - *aerify* 340vb.
  - *bubble* 355vb.
- aerated
  - *light* 323adj.
  - *rare* 325adj.
  - *airy* 340adj.
  - *bubbly* 355adj.
- aerial
  - *high* 209adj.
  - *flying* 271adj.
  - *gaseous* 336adj.
  - *airy* 340adj.
  - *telecommunication* 531n.
- aerie
  - *group* 74n.
  - *nest* 192n.
  - *high structure* 209n.
- aeriform
  - *gaseous* 336adj.
  - *airy* 340adj.
- aerify
  - *lighten* 323vb.
  - *gasify* 336vb.
  - *vaporize* 338vb.
  - *aerify* 340vb.
  - *refrigerate* 382vb.
  - *refresh* 685vb.
- aerobatics
  - *aeronautics* 271n.
- aerodonetics
  - *aeronautics* 271n.
- aerodynamic
  - *flying* 271adj.
  - *aviational* 276adj.
- aerodynamics
  - *aeronautics* 271n.
  - *gaseity* 336n.
  - *pneumatics* 340n.
  - *anemology* 352n.
- aerodyne
  - *aircraft* 276n.
- aerography
  - *pneumatics* 340n.

aerolite
meteor 321n.
aerology
pneumatics 340n.
aeromancy
weather 340n.
theomancy 511n.
aeromechanics
aeronautics 271n.
aerometer
density 324n.
pneumatics 340n.
aeronaut
aeronaut 271n.
aeronautics
aeronautics 271n.
sport 837n.
aeroscopy
pneumatics 340n.
weather 340n.
aerosphere
atmosphere 340n.
aerostat
aeronaut 271n.
airship 276n.
aerostatics
aeronautics 271n.
gaseity 336n.
aesculap
sharp edge 256n.
Aesculapian
medical 658adj.
Aesop
sage 500n.
eyesore 842n.
aesthete
sensibility 374n.
man of taste 846n.
aesthetic
sensitive 819adj.
beautiful 841adj.
tasteful 846adj.
aestheticism
sensibility 374n.
moral sensibility 819n.
beauty 841n.
aesthetics
sensibility 374n.
beauty 841n.
good taste 846n.
aestival
summery 128adj.
warm 379adj.
aestivate
sleep 679vb.
afar
afar 199adv.
affability
sociability 882n.
affable
sociable 882adj.
amiable 884adj.
affair
eventuality 154n.
topic 452n.
badness 645n.
fight 716n.
affairs
affairs 154n.
pursuit 619n.
business 622n.
deed 676n.
affect
be related 9vb.
modify 143vb.
influence 178vb.
tend 179vb.
show 522vb.
dissemble 541vb.
be important 638vb.
behave 688vb.
excite 821vb.
impress 821vb.
be affected 850vb.
desire 859vb.
love 887vb.
affectation
imitation 20n.
mimicry 20n.
underestimation 483n.
sciolism 491n.
foolery 497n.
magniloquence 574n.
inelegance 576n.
speech defect 580n.
fashion 848n.
affectation 850n.
prudery 950n.
false piety 980n.
affected
hypocritical 541adj.
diseased 651adj.
vain 873adj.
(*see* affect, affectation)
affectibility
sensibility 374n.
moral sensibility 819n.
affection
moral sensibility 819n.
love 887n.
approbation 923n.
piety 979n.
affectionate
loving 887adj.
caressing 889adj.
benevolent 897adj.
affections
temperament 5n.
influence 178n.
affections 817n.
affectivity
feeling 818n.
affiance
promise 764n.
marry 894vb.
affianced
promised 764adj.
marriageable 894adj.
loved one 887n.
affiche
exhibit 522n.
advertisement 528n.
affidavit
testimony 466n.
oath 532n.
litigation 959n.
affiliate
be akin 11vb.
society 708n.
affiliation
relation 9n.
consanguinity 11n.
association 706n.
participation 775n.
affinity
relation 9n.
consanguinity 11n.
similarity 18n.
tendency 179n.
attraction 291n.
liking 859n.
spouse 894n.
affinity, have an
combine 50vb.
affirm
believe 485vb.
opine 485vb.
suppose 512vb.
mean 514vb.
affirm 532vb.
speak 579vb.
plead 614vb.
decree 737vb.
promise 764vb.
affirmation
testimony 466n.
assent 488n.
affirmation 532n.
promise 764n.
affirmative
positive 473adj.
meaningful 514adj.
forceful 571adj.
affix
add 38vb.
adjunct 40n.
affix 45vb.
agglutinate 48vb.
sequel 67n.
spoken letter 558n.
word 559n.
part of speech 564n.
afflatus
wind 352n.
imagination 513n.
poetry 593n.
excitation 821n.
revelation 975n.
afflict
hurt 827vb.
punish 963vb.

affliction
evil 616n.
illness 651n.
bane 659n.
affluence
plenty 635n.
superfluity 637n.
prosperity 730n.
wealth 800n.
affluent
approaching 289adj.
stream 350adj.
flowing 350adj.
(*see* affluence)
afflux
approach 289n.
afford
provide 633vb.
have enough 635vb.
give 781vb.
afford 800vb.
affordable
cheap 812adj.
afforest
vegetate 366vb.
afforestation
forestry 366n.
agriculture 370n.
affray
turmoil 61n.
fight 716n.
affright
fear 854n.
frighten 854vb.
affront
annoyance 827n.
hurt 827vb.
be courageous 855vb.
sauciness 878n.
resentment 891n.
huff 891vb.
scurrility 899n.
indignity 921n.
not respect 921vb.
affuse
moisten 341vb.
aficionado
patron 707n.
afire
fiery 379adj.
aflame
luminous 417adj.
aflame with
impressed 818adj.
afloat
existing 1adj.
happening 154adj.
seafaring 269adj.
afloat 275adv.
at sea 343adv.
rumored 529adj.
afore
before 119adv.
aforesaid
preceding 64adj.
repeated 106adj.
prior 119adj.
foregoing 125adj.
aforethought
predetermined 608adj.
intended 617adj.
aforetime
before 119adv.
formerly 125adv.
a fortiori
eminently 34adv.
reasonably 475adv.
afraid
fearing 854adj.
Afreet
demon 970n.
afresh
again 106adv.
newly 126adv.
aft
rearward 238adv.
after
after 65adv.
subsequently 120adv.
back 238adj.
rearward 238adv.
behind 284adv.
pursuant to 619adv.
after, be
pursue 619vb.
afterbirth
sequel 67n.
obstetrics 164n.
after-care
therapy 658n.
afterclap
sequel 67n.
inexpectation 508n.
aftercomer
aftercomer 67n.
substitute 150n.
after-course
sequel 67n.
aftercrop
sequel 67n.
after-damp
gas 336n.
poison 569n.
after-dinner
subsequent 120adj.
reposeful 683adj.
sociable 882adj.
after-effect
sequel 67n.
effect 157n.
afterglow
remainder 41n.
sequel 67n.
glow 417n.
aftergrowth
sequel 67n.
abundance 171n.
afterlife
sequel 67n.
future state 124n.
Heaven 971n.
aftermath
sequel 67n.
posteriority 120n.
effect 157n.
abundance 171n.
earnings 771n.
aftermost
rearward 238adv.
afternoon
evening 129n.
vespertine 129adj.
afterpain
sequel 67n.
afterpart
sequel 67n.
rear 238n.
poop 238n.
afterpiece
sequel 67n.
stage play 594n.
after-taste
sequel 67n.
taste 386n.
afterthought
sequel 67n.
lateness 136n.
thought 449n.
remembrance 505n.
tergiversation 603n.
afterwards
after 65adv.
subsequently 120adv.
afterworld
destiny 155n.
again
again 106adv.
again and again
repeatedly 106adv.
often 139adv.
against
although 182adv.
against 240adv.
opposing 704adj.
in opposition 704adv.
against the grain
with difficulty 700adv.
in opposition 704adv.
agamist
celibate 895n.
agape
open 263adj.
expectant 507adj.
wondering 864adj.
Agape
social gathering 882n.
public worship 981n.
agapism
love 887n.
agaric
medicine 658n.
cathartic 658n.

agate
type size 587n.
gem 844n.
age
date 108n.
pass time 108vb.
era 110n.
diuturnity 113n.
chronology 117n.
oldness 127n.
grow old 131vb.
weakness 163n.
dilapidation 655n.
deteriorate 655vb.
ugliness 842n.
aged
aged 131adj.
age, full
adultness 134n.
age-group
group 74n.
classification 77n.
contemporary 123n.
agelast
moper 834n.
ageless
perpetual 115adj.
young 130adj.
agelong
lasting 113adj.
perpetual 115adj.
agency
agency 173n.
instrumentality 628n.
action 676n.
management 689n.
commission 751n.
agenda
affairs 154n.
topic 452n.
predetermination 608n.
business 622n.
policy 623n.
agent
inferior 35n.
substitute 150n.
cause 156n.
producer 167n.
intermediary 231n.
instrument 628n.
doer 676n.
agent 686n.
manager 690n.
mediator 720n.
consignee 754n.
deputy 755n.
agential
instrumental 628adj.
commissioned 751adj.
deputizing 755adj.
agent provocateur
ambush 527n.
trickster 545n.
motivator 612n.
excitant 821n.
agentship
commission 751n.
age, of
grown up 134adj.
marriageable 894adj.
age-old
immemorial 127adj.
worshipful 866adj.
agglomerate
coherence 48n.
cohere 48vb.
agglomeration
coherence 48n.
accumulation 74n.
agglutinate
join, affix 45vb.
agglutinate 48vb.
retain 778vb.
agglutinative
linguistic 557adj.
aggrandize
augment 36vb.
enlarge 197vb.
dignify 866vb.
aggrandizement
greatness 32n.
aggravate
augment 36vb.
make violent 176vb.
exaggerate 546vb.
impair 655vb.
be difficult 700vb.
miscarry 728vb.
hurt 827vb.
aggravate 832vb.
enrage 891vb.
aggregate
all 52n.
bring together 74vb.
numerical result 85n.
number 86vb.
aggregation
combination 50n.
accumulation 74n.
aggression
attack 712n.
aggressive
vigorous 174adj.
violent 176adj.
active 678adj.
quarreling 709adj.
attacking 712adj.
contending 716adj.
warlike 718adj.
courageous 855adj.
aggressiveness
vitality 162n.
bellicosity 718n.
manliness 855n.
aggressor
quarreler 709n.
attacker 712n.
combatant 722n.
aggrieve
ill-treat 645vb.
displease 827vb.
aghast
fearing 854adj.
agile
speedy 277adj.
agio
discount 810n.
agiotage
barter 791n.
agitate
derange 63vb.
jumble 63vb.
move 265vb.
agitate 318vb.
cause feeling 374vb.
distract 456vb.
inquire 459vb.
be active 678vb.
revolt 738vb.
cause discontent 829vb.
frighten 854vb.
agitated
fitful 142adj.
unstable 152adj.
agitation
derangement 63n.
changeableness 152n.
stimulation 174n.
motion 265n.
agitation 318n.
activity 678n.
restlessness 678n.
haste 680n.
revolt, sedition 738n.
feeling 818n.
excitation 821n.
worry 825n.
discontent 829n.
fear 854n.
agitator
dissentient 489n.
motivator 612n.
reformer 654n.
trouble-maker 663n.
leader 690n.
opponent 705n.
agitator 738n.
excitant 821n.
malcontent 829n.
aglow
fiery 379adj.
luminous 417adj.
agnate
kinsman 11n.
akin 11adj.
agnomen
name 561n.
agnostic
doubting 474adj.
unbeliever 486n.

dissenting 489adj.
irreligionist 974n.
irreligious 974adj.
agnosticism
philosophy 449n.
ago
not now 122adv.
formerly 125adv.
agog
inquisitive 453adj.
expectant 507adj.
desiring 859adj.
excited 821adj.
agonism
athletics 162n.
contention 716n.
sport 837n.
agonize
feel pain 377vb.
ill-treat 645vb.
suffer 825vb.
agony
pain 377n.
excitable state 822n.
suffering 825n.
agony column
advertisement 528n.
agora
focus 76n.
mart 796n.
agoraphobia
psychopathy 503n.
phobia 854n.
agrarian
agrarian 370adj.
agree
resemble 18vb.
accord 24vb.
conform 83vb.
concur 181vb.
believe 485vb.
assent 488vb.
be willing 597vb.
concord 710vb.
consent 758vb.
contract 765vb.
agreeable
agreeing 24adj.
conformable 83adj.
pleasant 376adj.
willing 597adj.
concordant 710adj.
palmy 730adj.
consenting 758adj.
pleasurable 826adj.
personable 841adj.
agreement
relevance 9n.
uniformity 16n.
symmetry 245n.
(*see* agree)
agrestic
agrarian 370adj.
agriculture
agriculture 370n.
maturation 669n.
agronomics
agriculture 370n.
aground
in difficulties 700adj.
ague
spasm 318n.
malaria 651n.
aguish
a-cold 380adj.
diseased 651adj.
infectious 653adj.
ahead
superior 34adj.
future 124adj.
beyond 199adv.
in front 237adv.
ahead 283adv.
forward 285adv.
ahimsa
peace 717n.
benevolence 897n.
aid
support 218n., vb.
instrumentality 628n.
utility 640n.
be useful 640vb.
remedy 658vb.
facility 701n.
facilitate 701vb.
aid 703n., vb.
tax 809n.
be benevolent 897vb.
aid and abet
incite 612vb.
aide-de-camp
auxiliary 707n.
army officer 741n.
aide-mémoire
reminder 505n.
aider
aider 703n.
(*see* auxiliary)
aidless
weak 163adj.
aid of, in
relative 9adj.
in aid of 703adv.
ail
be ill 651vb.
aileron
equilibrium 28n.
wing 271n.
aircraft 276n.
ailment
illness 651n.
aim
direction 281n.
aim 281vb.
objective 617n.
aim at 617vb.
business 622n.
essay 671n., vb.
fire at 712vb.
desired object 859n.
aim at
aim at 617vb.
pursue 619vb.
desire 859vb.
aimless
orderless 61adj.
designless 618adj.
aimlessness
inattention 456n.
air
insubstantial thing 4n.
initiate 68vb.
transport 272n.
element 319n.
levity 323n.
rarity 325n.
gas 336n.
air 340n.
aerify 340vb.
dry 342vb.
tune 412n.
mien 445n.
inquire 459vb.
divulge 526vb.
salubrity 652n.
refresh 685vb.
conduct 688n.
airborne
high 209adj.
flying 271adj.
ascending 308adj.
air-condition
refrigerate 382vb.
air-conditioner
air 340n.
ventilation 352n.
thermometry 379n.
refrigerator 384n.
aircraft
aircraft 276n.
aircraftman
aeronaut 271n.
soldiery 722n.
air force 722n.
aircrew
aeronaut 271n.
air force 722n.
air-current
wind 352n.
airdrome
air travel 271n.
aircraft 276n.
goal 295n.
air-duct
air-pipe 353n.
airfield
air travel 271n.
arena 724n.
air force
air force 722n.
air-gun
toy gun 723n.

plaything 837n.
air-hole
orifice 263n.
air-pipe 353n.
air-hostess
aeronaut 271n.
airiness
rarity 325n.
airing
land travel 267n.
air 340n.
dryness 342n.
ventilation 352n.
inquiry 459n.
cleansing 648n.
air, in the
reportedly 524adv.
airlane
air travel 271n.
route 624n.
airless
tranquil 266adj.
insalubrious 653adj.
air-lift
air travel 271n.
transport 272n.
airline
straightness 249n.
air travel 271n.
direction 281n.
airmail
mails 531n.
correspond 588vb.
airman
aeronaut 271n.
air-pipe
air-pipe 353n.
airplane
aircraft 276n.
air-pocket
emptiness 190n.
air 340n.
wind 352n.
airport
air travel 271n.
goal 295n.
air-proof
sealed off 264adj.
air-raid
attack 712n.
air-raid shelter
refuge 662n.
defenses, fort 713n.
airs
affectation 850n.
airs 873n.
airscrew
rotator 315n.
airship
airship 276n.
air-sick
flying 271adj.
vomiting 300adj.
air space
air travel 271n.
territory 184n.
air-stream
wind 352n.
airstrip
air travel 271n.
air-terminal
goal 295n.
stopping place 145n.
air-tight
sealed off 264adj.
air travel
air travel 271n.
airworthy
flying 271adj.
transferable 272adj.
aviational 276adj.
invulnerable 660adj.
airy
insubstantial 4adj.
light 323adj.
airy 340adj.
windy 352adj.
light-minded 456adj.
trivial 639adj.
salubrious 652adj.
rash 857adj.
impertinent 878adj.
discourteous 884adj.
disrespectful 921adj.
aisle
open space 263n.
path 624n.
church interior 990n.
ajar
open 263adj.
ajutage
(*see* adjutage)
akimbo
angular 247adj.
akin
akin 11adj.
similar 18adj.
alabaster
white thing 427n.
a la carte
optionally 605adv.
alacrity
willingness 597n.
activity 678n.
cheerfulness 833n.
Aladdin's lamp
instrument 628n.
aid 703n.
magic instrument 983n.
a la mode
modern 126adj.
fashionable 848adj.
alar
flying 271adj.
alarm, alarum
timekeeper 117n.
loudness 400n.
megaphone 400n.
signal 547n.
warning 664n.
danger signal 665n.
raise the alarm 665vb.
fear 854n.
frighten 854vb.
alarmism
intimidation 854n.
alarmist
false alarm 665n.
alarmist 854n.
coward 856n.
alb
vestments 989n.
albedo
light 417n.
reflection 417n.
albert
jewelry 844n.
albescence
whiteness 427n.
Albigensian
heretic 977n.
heretical 977adj.
albinism
achromatism 426n.
whiteness 427n.
skin disease 651n.
blemish 845n.
albino
achromatism 426n.
colorless 426adj.
white thing 427n.
album
reminder 505n.
record 548n.
reference book 589n.
anthology 592n.
albumen
semiliquidity 354n.
organism 358n.
alchemist
alterer 143n.
sorcerer 983n.
occultist 984n.
alchemy
conversion 147n.
occultism 984n.
alcohol
stimulant 174n.
liquor 301n.
alcoholic
strong 162adj.
sick person 651n.
drunkard 949n.
drunken 949adj.
intoxicating 949adj.
Alcoran
non-Biblical scripture 975n.
alcove
arbor 194n.
cavity 255n.

alderman
official 690n.
councillor 692n.
officer 741n.
aldermanship
magistrature 733n.
ale
liquor 301n.
aleatory
speculative 618adj.
dangerous 661adj.
alee
sideways 239adv.
alehouse
tavern 192n.
alembic
crucible 147n.
vessel 194n.
heater 383n.
alert
attentive 455adj.
vigilant 457adj.
signal 547vb.
danger signal 665n.
raise the alarm 665vb.
prepared 669adj.
active 678adj.
lively 819adj.
Alexandrine
prosody 593n.
alexipharmic
remedial 658adj.
alfresco
externally 223adv.
alfresco 340adv.
algae
plant 366n.
algebra
mathematics 86n.
algology
botany 368n.
algor
coldness 380n.
algorithm
number 85n.
alias
named 561adj.
misnomer 562n.
alibi
absence 190n.
pretext 614n.
vindication 927n.
alidad
gauge 465n.
alien
irrelative 10adj.
foreigner 59n.
extraneous 59adj.
unconformable 84adj.
settler 191n.
outcaste 883n.
alienable
transferred 780adj.
alienate
set apart 46vb.
not retain 779vb.
convey 780vb.
sell 793n.
make enemies 881vb.
excite hate 888vb.
alienation
insanity 503n.
non-retention 779n.
transfer 780n.
sale 793n.
enmity 881n.
hatred 888n.
alienism
extraneousness 59n.
insanity 503n.
alienist
psychologist 447n.
insanity 503n.
doctor 658n.
alienization
conversion 147n.
loss of right 916n.
aliform
lateral 239adj.
alight
place oneself 187vb.
come to rest 266vb.
land 295vb.
descend 309vb.
sit down 311vb.
fiery 379adj.
align
make uniform 16vb.
adjust 24vb.
arrange 62vb.
flatten 216vb.
print 587vb.
alignment
direction 281n.
friendship 880n.
align oneself
join a party 708vb.
alike
similar 18adj.
aliment
food 301n.
alimentary
nourishing 301adj.
remedial 658adj.
alimony
dower 777n.
receipt 807n.
divorce 896n.
aliquant, aliquot
numerical element 85n.
part 53n.
alive
alive 360adj.
sentient 374adj.
intelligent 498adj.
alive to
attentive 455adj.
knowing 490adj.
impressible 819adj.
alive with
multitudinous 104adj.
alkahest
liquefaction 337n.
all
all 52n.
completeness 54n.
everyman 79n.
universal 79adj.
all along
while 108adv.
all along 113adv.
all and sundry
everyman 79n.
all attention
attentive 455adj.
allay
assuage 177vb.
pacify 719vb.
all but
almost 33adv.
wholly 52adv.
all clear
safety 660n.
permit 756n.
all comers
contender 716n.
all costs, at
resolutely 599adv.
all ears
auditory 415adj.
inquisitive 453adj.
attentive 455adj.
all edges
unconformable 84adj.
allegation
testimony 466n.
affirmation 532n.
pretext 614n.
accusation 928n.
allegiance
loyalty 739n.
subjection 745n.
duty 917n.
allegory
comparison 462n.
metaphor 519n.
latency 523n.
narrative 590n.
allegro
adagio 412adv.
allelomorph
heredity 5n.
all-embracing
extensive 32adj.
comprehensive 52adj.
inclusive 78adj.
general 79adj.
allergy
sensibility 374n.
ill-health 651n.
moral sensibillty 819n.

dislike 861n.
hatred 888n.
alleviate
assuage 177vb.
disencumber 701vb.
relieve 831vb.
alley
street 192n.
sphere 252n.
open space 263n.
road 624n.
all eyes
attentive 455adj.
vigilant 457adj.
all found
provisionary 633adj.
all fours, on
identically 13adv.
agreeing 24adj.
alliance
relation 9n.
consanguinity 11n.
junction 45n.
combination 50n.
concurrence 181n.
association 706n.
society 708n.
compact 765n.
marriage 894n.
allied
corporate 708adj.
concordant 710adj.
alligator
skin 226n.
reptile 365n.
all in
fatigued 684adj.
all in all
on an average 30adv.
wholly 52adv.
alliteration
assimilation 18n.
repetition 106n.
ornament 574n.
prosody 593n.
all manner of
different 15adj.
multiform 82adj.
allocate
arrange 62vb.
apportion 783vb.
allocution
speech 579n.
allocution 583n.
allodial
unconditional 744adj.
proprietary 777adj.
allodium
territory 184n.
lands 777n.
all of
completely 54adv.
all of a piece
uniform 16adj.
all off
ending 69adj.
allogamy
mixture 43n.
all one
equivalent 28adj.
all, one's
property 777n.
allonym
misteaching 535n.
misnomer 562n.
allopath
doctor 658n.
allopathy
medical art 658n.
allophone
speech sound 398n.
allot
quantify 26vb.
arrange 62vb.
dispose of 673vb.
dower 777vb.
apportion 783vb.
grant claims 915vb.
allotment
farm 370n.
allottee
recipient 782n.
(*see* allot)
all out
completely 54adv.
swiftly 277adv.
allow
make possible 469vb.
be reasonable 475vb.
believe 485vb.
assent, acquiesce 488vb.
confess 526vb.
facilitate 701vb.
be lenient 736vb.
permit 756vb.
consent 758vb.
be patient 823vb.
allowable
possible 469adj.
permitted 756adj.
given 781adj.
vindicable 727adj.
legal 953adj.
allowance
offset 31n.
decrement 42n.
qualification 468n.
subvention 703n.
lenity 736n.
permission 756n.
consent 758n.
earnings 771n.
dower 777n.
gift 781n.
portion 783n.
receipt 807n.
discount 810n.
reward 962n.
allow for
set off 31vb.
alloy
a mixture 43n.
mix 43vb.
compound 50n.
impairment 655n.
all-purpose
useful 640adj.
all quarters, in
widely 183adv.
all right
not bad 644adj.
all-round
multiform 82adj.
all-rounder
athlete 162n.
proficient 696n.
player 837n.
all sorts
non-uniform 17adj.
medley 43n.
everyman 79n.
allspice
condiment 389n.
all-star
dramatic 594adj.
excellent 644adj.
all the same
nevertheless 468adv.
all thumbs
clumsy 695adj.
all told
completely 54adv.
allude
relate 9vb.
propound 512vb.
mean 514vb.
figure 519vb.
imply 523vb.
hint 524vb.
allure
influence 178vb.
attraction 291n.
attract 291vb.
tempt 612vb.
delight 826vb.
cause desire 859vb.
excite love 887vb.
allusion
referral 9n.
metaphor 519n.
allusive
relevant 9adj.
suppositional 512adj.
meaningful 514adj.
figurative 519adj.
tacit 523adj.
imperspicuous 568adj.
alluvial
flat 216adj.
territorial 344adj.
alluvium

leavings 41n.
thing transferred 272n.
soil 344n.
all work, of
useful 640adj.
ally
join 45vb.
combine 50vb.
aider 703n.
cooperate 706vb.
colleague 707n.
join a party 708vb.
contract 765vb.
friend 880n.
almagest
dissertation 591n.
almanac
directory 87n.
chronology 117n.
almighty
powerful 160adj.
godlike 965adj.
Almighty, the
the Deity 965n.
almond
fruit 301n.
almoner
giver 781n.
treasurer 798n.
almonry
treasury 799n.
almost
almost 33adv.
nearly 200adv.
imperfectly 647adv.
almost all
main part 52n.
alms
gift 781n.
kind act 897n.
almshouse
retreat 192n.
shelter 662n.
aloft
aloft 209adv.
aloha
arrival 295n.
valediction 296n.
alone
separate 46adj.
alone 88adj.
unsociable 883adj.
friendless 883adj.
along
longwise 203adv.
alongside
nigh 200adv.
in parallel 219adv.
sideways 239adv.
along with
in addition 38adv.
with 89adv.
synchronously 123adv.
aloof
non-adhesive 49adj.
distant 199adj.
incurious 454adj.
impassive 820adj.
unsociable 833adj.
alopecia
bareness 229n.
aloud
loudly 400adv.
vocal 577adj.
Alp
high land 209n.
alpaca
fiber 208n.
textile 222n.
alpana
pattern 844n.
alpenglow
morning 128n.
evening 129n.
alpenstock
supporter 218n.
alpestrine
alpine 209adj.
alpha
beginning 68n.
Alpha and Omega
all 52n.
alphabet
beginning 68n.
letter 558n.
alphabetarian
beginner 538n.
alphabeticize
class 62vb.
alphabetize
spell 558vb.
alpha particle
element 319n.
alpha plus
excellent 644adj.
alpine
alpine 209adj.
Alpinism
ascent 308n.
sport 837n.
alpinist
traveler 268n.
climber 308n.
already
before 119adv.
at present 121adv.
retrospectively 125adv.
Alsatia
thievishness 788n.
thief 789n.
also
in addition 38adv.
also-ran
inferior 35n.
loser 728n.
altar
stand 218n.
ritual object 988n.
altar 990n.
altar-boy
church officer 986n.
altarless
irreligious 974adj.
alter
change 143vb.
qualify 468vb.
alterable
unstable 152adj.
changeful 152adj.
alterant
alterer 143n.
alteration
difference 15n.
change 143n.
altercate
bicker 709vb.
alter course
deviate 282vb.
alter ego
identity 13n.
analogue 18n.
colleague 707n.
deputy 755n.
close friend 880n.
alternate
correlative 12adj.
correlate 12vb.
sequent 65adj.
come after 65vb.
discontinuous 72adj.
periodic 141adj.
be periodic 141vb.
substitute 150n.
vary 152vb.
fluctuate 317vb.
deputy 755n.
alternating current
periodicity 141n.
electricity 160n.
alternative
substitute 150n.
choice 605n.
means 629n.
contrivance 623n.
alternatively
instead 150adv.
alter the case
tell against 467vb.
qualify 468vb.
although
although 182adv.
altimeter
altimetry 209n.
angular measure 247n.
meter 465n.
altimetry
altimetry 209n.
angular measure 247n.
geometry 465n.
altitude
degree 27n.
superiority 34n.

height 209n.
alto
vocalist 413n.
altogether
wholly 52adv.
completely 54adv.
altogether, the
bareness 229n.
altruism
philanthropy 901n.
disinterestedness 931n.
virtues 933n.
altruist
kind person 897n.
altruistic
disinterested 931adj.
alum
sourness 393n.
alumnus
learner 538n.
alveolar, alveolate
concave 255adj.
alveus
cavity 255n.
conduit 351n.
always
generally 79adv.
while 108adv.
amadou
lighter 385n.
amain
violently 176adv.
Amalekite
enemy 881n.
amalgam
a mixture 43n.
compound 50n.
amalgamate
combine 50vb.
amalgamation
association 706n.
amanuensis
recorder 549n.
amaranthine
perpetual 115adj.
amass
bring together 74vb.
store 632vb.
amateur
beginner 338n.
unskilled 695adj.
bungler 697n.
man of taste 846n.
desirer 859n.
layman 987n.
amateurish
ignorant 491adj.
unskilled 695adj.
laical 987adj.
amateurship
good taste 846n.
amativeness
love 887n.
amatory
erotic 887adj.
amaurosis
blindness 439n.
amaurotic
dim-sighted 440adj.
amaze
surprise 508vb.
disappoint 509vb.
impress 821vb.
frighten 854vb.
be wonderful 864vb.
amazement
inexpectation 508n.
excitation 821n.
wonder 864n.
amazing
prodigious 32adj.
amazon
athlete 162n.
woman 373n.
soldier 722n.
brave person 855n.
spinster 895n.
amazonian
manly 162adj.
ambages
meanderings 251n.
pleonasm 570n.
circuit 626n.
ambassador
messenger 531n.
envoy 754n.
ambassadorial
deputizing 755adj.
amber
resin 357n.
brownness 430n.
preserver 666n.
ambergris
resin 357n.
scent 396n.
ambidexterity
dextrality 241n.
skill 694n.
ambience
circumjacence 230n.
painting 553n.
ambiguity
disagreement 25n.
uncertainty 474n.
connotation 514n.
unintelligibility 517n.
equivocalness 518n.
mental dishonesty 543n.
imperspicuity 568n.
ambit
outline 233n.
circuition 314n.
circuit 626n.
ambition
motive 612n.
intention 617n.
business 622n.
aspiration 852n.
desire 859n.
desired object 859n.
ambitious
essaying 671adj.
enterprising 672adj.
greedy 859adj.
ambivalence
contrariety 14n.
disagreement 25n.
equivocalness 518n.
amble
gait 265n.
pedestrianism 267n.
ride 267vb.
slowness 278n.
move slowly 278vb.
ambo
rostrum 539n.
church interior 990n.
ambrosia
food 301n.
savoriness 390n.
ambulance
vehicle 274n.
hospital 658n.
ambulance-chaser
petitioner 763n.
ambulation
pedestrianism 267n.
ambulatory
traveling 267adj.
path 624n.
church interior 990n.
church exterior 990n.
ambush
surprise 508vb.
latency 523n.
ambush 527n., vb.
trap 542n.
danger 661n.
pitfall 663n.
stratagem 698n.
be cunning 698vb.
ambush, in
disguised 525adj.
amebean
sequent 65adj.
amelioration
improvement 654n.
amen
assent 488n.
amenable
liable 180adj.
credulous 487adj.
willing 597adj.
dutied 917adj.
amend
rectify 654vb.
repair 656vb.
be penitent 939vb.
amendable
restored 656adj.
amende honorable

atonement 941n.
amendment
interpretation 520n.
amends
compensation 31n.
restoration 656n.
remedy 658n.
atonement 941n.
amenity
pleasurableness 826n.
courtesy 884n.
amentia
insanity 503n.
amerce
punish 963vb.
amercement
penalty 963n.
amerciable
punishable 963adj.
americanize
transform 147vb.
amethyst
purple 434n.
gem 844n.
amiable
well-bred 848adj.
amiability
pleasurableness 826n.
courtesy 884n.
lovableness 887n.
benevolence 897n.
amicable
aiding 703adj.
concordant 710adj.
friendly 880adj.
amice
vestments 989n.
amid, amidst
between 231adv.
amiss
inopportunely 138adv.
amiss 616adv.
badly 645adv.
amity
concord 710n.
friendship 880n.
ammonia
pungency 388n.
ammonite
coil 251n.
ammunition
means 629n.
defense 713n.
ammunition 723n.
amnesia
oblivion 506n.
amnesty
extinction 2n.
amnesty 506n.
forget 506vb.
obliteration 550n.
peace 717n.
irenics 719n.
be lenient 736vb.
forgive 909vb.
non-liability 919n.
exempt 919vb.
amoeba
animalcule 196n.
among
centrally 225adv.
between 231adv.
amoral
thick-skinned 820adj.
indifferent 860adj.
wicked 934adj.
irreligious 974adj.
amoralism
no choice 606n.
wickedness 934n.
irreligion 974n.
impiety 980n.
amoralist
indifference 860n.
amorist
lover 887n.
libertine 952n.
amorous
foolish 499adj.
loving 887adj.
amorphism
non-uniformity 17n.
amorphism 244n.
amorphous
incomplete 55adj.
amorphous 244adj.
fluidal 335adj.
unsightly 842adj.
amount
quantity 26n.
degree 27n.
funds 797n.
price 809n.
amount to
number 86vb.
cost 809vb.
amour
love affair 887n.
illicit love 951n.
amour-propre
vanity 873n.
amperage
electricity 160n.
ampere, amp
electricity 160n.
ampersand
letter 558n.
amphibian
animal 365n.
reptile 365n.
amphibious
unconformable 84adj.
double 91adj.
amphibology
equivocalness 518n.
amphibrach
prosody 593n.
amphictyony
council 692n.
amphigory
absurdity 497n.
unmeaningness 515n.
amphimacer
prosody 593n.
amphimixis
mixture 43n.
amphisbaena
reptile 365n.
amphitheater
view 438n.
classroom 539n.
theater 594n.
arena 724n.
amphora
vessel 194n.
ample
great 32adj.
many 104adj.
spacious 183adj.
large 195adj.
broad 205adj.
diffuse 570adj.
plenteous 635adj.
palmy 730adj.
liberal 813adj.
amplifier
megaphone 400n.
hearing aid 415n.
amplify
augment 36vb.
enlarge 197vb.
translate 520vb.
be diffuse 570vb.
amplitude
quantity 26n.
degree 27n.
greatness 32n.
plenitude 54n.
range 183n.
size 195n.
breadth 205n.
diffuseness 570n.
plenty 635n.
ampul
receptacle 194n.
ampulla
vessel 194n.
ampullar, ampullaceous
expanded 197adj.
amputate
subtract 39vb.
cut, sunder 46vb.
doctor 658vb.
amulet
non-design 618n.
preserver 666n.
jewelry 844n.
talisman 983n.
amuse
distract 456vb.
amuse 837vb.
be witty 839vb.

amusement
enjoyment 824n.
pleasurableness 826n.
amusement 837n.
amusing
pleasant 376adj.
gay 833adj.
amusing 837adj.
sociable 882adj.
anabatic
increasing 36adj.
ascending 308adj.
anabolism
transformation 143n.
anachronism
anachronism 118n.
different time 122n.
intempestivity 138n.
inexactness 495n.
anachronistic
anachronistic 118adj.
non-contemporary 122adj.
antiquated 127adj.
ill-timed 138adj.
anaclastic
luminous 417adj.
anaclinal
sloping 220adj.
anacoluthon
discontinuity 72n.
anaconda
reptile 365n.
Anacreontic
poem 593n.
gay 833adj.
anacrusis
prelude 66n.
musical piece 412n.
anadiplosis
repetition 106n.
ornament 574n.
anaerobe
animalcule 196n.
anaglyph
sculpture 554n.
anaglyptic
glyptic 554adj.
anagoge
metaphor 519n.
latency 523n.
anagram
equivocalness 518n.
enigma 530n.
initials 558n.
anal
back 238adj.
analects
anthology 592n.
analeptic
restorative 656adj.
tonic 658n.
remedial 658adj.
analgesia
insensibility 375n.
analgesic
antidote 658n.
drug 658n.
remedial 658adj.
relieving 831adj.
analogical
similar 18adj.
compared 462adj.
analogous
correlative 12adj.
symmetrical 245adj.
analogue
identity 13n.
analogue 18n.
copy 22n.
analogy
relativeness 9n.
similarity 18n.
comparison 462n.
analysis
numerical operation 86n.
experiment 461n.
argumentation 475n.
grammar 564n.
compendium 592n.
analyst
inquirer 459n.
experimenter 461n.
analytic
inquiring 459adj.
experimental 461adj.
analyze
sunder 46vb.
decompose 51vb.
class 62vb.
inquire 459vb.
experiment 461vb.
parse 564vb.
rational 475adj.
linguistic 557adj.
anamorphosis
distortion 246n.
visual fallacy 440n.
misrepresentation 552n.
anapest
prosody 593n.
anaphora
repetition 106n.
trope 519n.
ornament 574n.
anaplasty
surgery 658n.
anarch
anarch 61n.
anarchic
disorderly 61adj.
anarchic 734 adj.
riotous 738adj.
disobedient 738adj.
independent 744adj.
non-observant 769adj.
lawless 954adj.
anarchism
sedition 738n.
anarchist
revolutionist 149n.
destroyer 168n.
violent creature 176n.
revolter 738n.
evildoer 904n.
anarchy
anarchy 734n.
anastomosis
junction 45n.
crossing 222n.
anastrophe
inversion 221n.
ornament 574n.
anathema
malediction 899n.
anathematize
curse 899vb.
dispraise 924vb.
hereticate 977vb.
perform ritual 988vb.
anatomic
structural 331adj.
anatomist
zoologist 367n.
anatomize
sunder 46vb.
class 62vb.
anatomy
thinness 206n.
structure 331n.
biology 358n.
zoology 367n.
anatriptic
rubbing 333adj.
ancestor
precursor 66n.
old man 133n.
source 156n.
parent 169n.
ancestral
immemorial 127adj.
former 125adj.
parental 169adj.
ancestry
heredity 5n.
consanguinity 11n.
origin 68n.
source 156n.
genealogy 169n.
nobility 868n.
anchor
affix 45vb.
coupling 47n.
place oneself 187vb.
dwell 192vb.
come to rest 266vb.
navigate 269vb.
protection 660n.
safeguard 662n.
badge of rank 743n.

hope 852n.
anchorage
station 187n.
goal 295n.
shelter 662n.
anchorite
solitary 883n.
ascetic 945n.
pietist 979n.
anchoritic
ascetic 945adj.
unsociable 883adj.
ancien régime
preterition 125n.
archaism 127n.
aristocracy 868n.
ancient
past 125adj.
former 125adj.
olden 127adj.
worshipful 866adj.
ancient history
antiquity 125n.
ancients, the
antiquity 125n.
ancillary
aiding 703adj.
and, and also
in addition 38adv.
andante
slowness 278n.
slow 278adj.
tempo 410n.
adagio 412adv.
and co.
no name 562n.
andirons
furnace 383n.
androcentric
male 372adj.
androgenous
abnormal 84adj.
androgyn
nonconformist 84n.
androgynous
female 373adj.
androgyny
abnormality 84n.
female 373n.
androlepsy
taking 786n.
stealing 788n.
andromania
abnormality 84n.
and so
thus 8adv.
consequently 157adv.
and then some
completely 54adv.
anecdotage
loquacity 581n.
anecdotal, anecdotic
remembering 505adj.
anecdote
narrative 590n.
anele
perform ritual 988vb.
anemia
weakness 163n.
achromatism 426n.
blood disease 651n.
anemography
anemology 352n.
anemology
pneumatics 340n.
anemology 352n.
anemometer
anemology 352n.
meter 465n.
recording instrument 549n.
anemometry
pneumatics 340n.
aneroid barometer
pneumatics 340n.
anesthesia
insensibility 375n.
anesthetic
moderator 177n.
anesthetic 375n.
insensible 375adj.
drug 658n.
remedial 658adj.
soporific 679n.
relief 831n.
anesthetist
doctor 658n.
aneurysm
blood pressure 651n.
anew
again 106adv.
newly 126adv.
anfractuosity
convolution 251n.
angary
expropriation 786n.
angel
stage manager 594n.
lender 784n.
coinage 797n.
a beauty 841n.
darling 890n.
angel 968n.
mythical being 970n.
angelic
virtuous 933adj.
lovable 887adj.
angelic 968adj.
angelus
signal 547n.
anger
excitation 821n.
anger 891n.
enrage 891vb.
disapprobation 924n.
vice 934n.
angina
pang 377n.
angiography
structure 331n.
angiology
structure 331n.
angle
joint 45n.
angle 247n.
angulate 247vb.
bias 481n.
opinion 485n.
hunt 619vb.
take 786vb.
Anglican
Anglican 976adj.
Protestant 976n.
Catholic 976n.
sectarian 978adj.
Anglicanism
Catholicism 976n.
Protestantism 976n.
anglicism
dialect 560n.
anglicize
transform 147vb.
Anglo-Catholic
Catholic 976n.
Anglican 976adj.
anglophile
xenophile 880n.
anglophobe
enemy 881n.
anglophobia
hatred 888n.
angora
fiber 208n.
textile 222n.
angry
angry 891adj.
angry young man
nonconformist 84n.
malcontent 829n.
angst
suffering 825n.
melancholy 834n.
anguilliform
fibrous 208adj.
labyrinthine 251adj.
anguish
pain 377n.
badness 645n.
suffering 825n.
angular
angular 247adj.
angularity
unconformity 84n.
obliquity 220n.
angularity 247n.
angular measure
angular measure 247n.
angustation
narrowing 206n.
anhelous
panting 684adj.
anhydrous

dry 342n.
anile
aged 131adj.
foolish 499adj.
aniline dye
pigment 425n.
anility
age 131n.
folly 499n.
animadversion
reprimand 924n.
animadvert
think 449vb.
notice 455vb.
reprove 924vb.
animal
inferior 35n.
animal 365n., adj.
mindless 448adj.
unthinking 450adj.
intemperate 943adj.
sensualist 944n.
animal and vegetable kingdom
organism 358n.
animalcular
animal 365adj.
animalcule
small animal 33n.
animalcule 196n.
animalism
animality 365n.
sensualism 944n.
animality
life 360n.
animality 365n.
non-intellect 448n.
animal management
animal husbandry 369n.
animal spirits
vitality 162n.
life 360n.
animality 365n.
cheerfulness 833n.
animate
strengthen 162vb.
invigorate 174vb.
incite 612vb.
animate 821vb.
cheer 833vb.
give courage 855vb.
animated cartoon
cinema 445n.
animation
life 360n.
animality 365n.
restlessness 678n.
excitation 821n.
cheerfulness 833n.
courage 855n.
animator
director 690n.
animism
immateriality 320n.
deism 973n.
animist
immateriality 320n.
religionist 973adj.
animosity
dislike 861n.
enmity 881n.
hatred 888n.
resentment 891n.
animus
willingness 597n.
intention 617n.
affections 817n.
feeling 818n.
ankle
joint 45n.
angularity 247n.
anklet
jewelry 844n.
ankus
sharp point 256n.
incentive 612n.
anna
small coin 33n.
coinage 797n.
annalist
chronologist 117n.
chronicler 549n.
narrator 590n.
annals
chronology 117n.
record 548n.
narrative 590n.
anneal
be tough 329vb.
mature 669vb.
annelid
reptile 365n.
annex
add 38vb.
adjunct 40n.
connect 45vb.
require 771vb.
appropriate 786vb.
steal 788vb.
annexation
adjunct 40n.
joinder 45n.
annihilate
nullify 2vb.
destroy 165vb.
slaughter 362vb.
anniversary
date 108n.
anniversary 141n.
seasonal 141adj.
special day 876n.
celebrative 876adj.
holy-day 988n.
anno Domini
anno Domini 108adv.
anciently 127adv.
annotate
interpret 520vb.
mark 547vb.
annotation
commentary 520n.
record 548n.
annotator
interpreter 520n.
announce
happen 154vb.
predict 511vb.
communicate 524vb.
proclaim 528vb.
name 561vb.
announcer
precursor 66n.
informant 524n.
publicizer 528n.
messenger 531n.
nomenclator 561n.
annoy
give pain 377vb.
meddle 678vb.
hinder 702vb.
oppress 735vb.
torment 827vb.
sadden 834vb.
enrage 891vb.
be malevolent 898vb.
annoyance
bane 659n.
worry 825n.
annoyance 827n.
resentment 891n.
annual
periodic 110adj.
seasonal 141adj.
flower 366n.
journal 528n.
annuitant
recipient 782n.
annuity
pay 804n.
receipt 807n.
annul
destroy 165vb.
relinquish 621vb.
abrogate 752vb.
divorce 896vb.
make illegal 954vb.
annular
round 250adj.
annularity
circularity 250n.
annulment
obliteration 550n.
relinquishment 621n.
abrogation 752n.
divorce 896n.
annulus
circle 250n.
annunciate
communicate 524vb.
annus mirabilis
period 110n.

prodigy 864n.
anodyne
moderator 177n.
lenitive 177adj.
remedial 658adj.
relieving 831adj.
anoint
overlay 226vb.
lubricate 334vb.
commission 751vb.
perform ritual 988vb.
anointment
lubrication 334n.
unctuousness 357n.
anomalous
orderless 61adj.
abnormal 84adj.
grammatical 564adj.
anon
betimes 135adv.
anonymity
unknown thing 490n.
latency 523n.
concealment 525n.
no name 562n.
anonymous
anonymous 562adj.
inglorious 867adj.
anopheles
fly 365n.
anorexy
indifference 860n.
anosmia
inodorousness 395n.
another
different 15adj.
another edition of
analogue 18n.
another story
variant 15n.
another time
different time 122n.
Anschauing
opinion 485n.
Anschluss
combination 50n.
association 706n.
anserine
foolish 499adj.
answer
accord 24vb.
numerical result 85n.
reason why 156n.
answer 460n., vb.
counter-evidence 467n.
argue 475vb.
confutation 479n.
confute 479vb.
interpretation 520n.
converse 584vb.
correspondence 588n.
contrivance 623n.
suffice 635vb.
expedience 642n.
be expedient 642vb.
remedy 658n.
retaliate 714vb.
be successful 727vb.
sauciness 878n.
answerable
causal 156adj.
liable 180adj.
indebted 803adj.
dutied 917adj.
answer back
interchange 151vb.
answer 460vb.
argue 475vb.
retaliate 714vb.
be insolent 878vb.
answer for
be liable 180vb.
deputize 755vb.
promise 764vb.
answer one's name
be present 189vb.
answer one's turn
be useful 640vb.
answer to
be related 9vb.
correlate 12vb.
resemble 18vb.
be named 561vb.
ant
animalcule 196n.
vermin 365n.
busy person 678n.
worker 686n.
antagonism
contrariety 14n.
counteraction 182n.
opposition 704n.
enmity 881n.
hatred 888n.
antagonist
opponent 705n.
enemy 881n.
antagonize
counteract 182vb.
cause dislike 861vb.
make enemies 881vb.
excite hate 888vb.
huff 891vb.
antaphrodisiac
moderator 177n.
antidote 658n.
antarctic
opposite 240adj.
cold 380adj.
ante
fore 64adv.
gambling 618n.
give 781vb.
portion 783n.
antecedence
precedence 64n.
priority 119n.
antecedent
precursor 66n.
antedate
misdate 118vb.
antediluvian
precursor 66n.
primal 127adj.
old man 133n.
antelope
speeder 277n.
deer 365n.
antemeridian
matinal 128adj.
antemetic
antidote 658n.
antenna
filament 208n.
projection 254n.
feeler 378n.
telecommunication 531n.
antepenultimate
ending 69adj.
anteposition
precedence 64n.
front 237n.
anterior
preceding 64adj.
prior 119adj.
fore 237adj.
anteroom
lobby 194n.
front 237n.
ant-heap
abundance 171n.
nest 192n.
anthem
vocal music 412n.
hymn 981n.
offer worship 981vb.
ant-hill
nest 192n.
anthologize
abstract 592vb.
select 605vb.
anthology
assemblage 74n.
reading matter 589n.
anthology 592n.
choice 605n.
anthracite
coal 385n.
anthrax
animal disease 651n.
anthropocentric
human 371adj.
anthropogenesis
anthropology 371n.
anthropography
anthropology 371n.
anthropoid
animal 365adj.
human 371adj.
anthropology
zoology 367n.

anthropology 371n.
anthropometry
anthropology 371n.
anthropomorphic
idolatrous 982adj.
anthropomorphize
idolatrize 982vb.
anti
contrary 14adj.
opposing 704adj.
antibiosis
antidote 658n.
antibiotic
drug 658n.
antidote 658n.
antibody
antidote 658n.
antichrist
bad man 938n.
Satan 969n.
irreligionist 974n.
anticipate
misdate 118vb.
do before 119vb.
look ahead 124vb.
be early 135vb.
expect 507vb.
foresee 510vb.
be willing 597vb.
prepare oneself 669vb.
be active 678vb.
take 786vb.
hope 852vb.
be rash 857vb.
anticipation
exclusion 57n.
(*see* anticipate)
anti-clerical
irreligious 974adj.
anticlimax
decrease 37n.
absurdity 497n.
inexpectation 508n.
disappointment 509n.
feebleness 572n.
failure 728n.
ridiculousness 849n.
anticlinal
sloping 220adj.
anticlockwise
toward 281adv.
regressive 286adj.
round and round 315adv.
anticoagulant
antidote 658n.
antics
foolery 497n.
bungling 695n.
anticyclone
weather 340n.
antidemocratic
authoritarian 735adj.
antidotal
counteracting 182adj.
remedial 658adj.
antidote
contrariety 14n.
counteraction 182n.
antidote 658n.
anti-freeze
heating 381adj.
antigen
antidote 658n.
antigropelos
legwear 228n.
antilogarithm
numerical element 85n.
antilogy
sophism 477n.
antimacassar
covering 226n.
antimonopolist
free man 744n.
antinomian
anarchic 734adj.
revolter 738n.
resisting 738adj.
non-observant 769adj.
lawless 954adj.
heretic 977n.
antinomy
contrariety 14n.
illegality 954n.
antiparallel
oblique 220adj.
anti-particle
particle 33n.
antipathetic
unconformable 84adj.
antipathy
contrariety 14n.
difference 15n.
dislike 861n.
enmity 881n.
hatred 888n.
antiphon
answer 460n.
hymn 981n.
antiphony
choral music 412n.
answer 460n.
antiphrasis
neology 560n.
solecism 565n.
antipodean
inverted 221adj.
antipodes
contrariety 14n.
farness 199n.
contraposition 240n.
antipole
contrariety 14n.
antiquarianism
palaetiology 125n.
antiquarium
antiquity 125n.
collection 632n.
antiquary
antiquarian 125n.
collector 492n.
chronicler 549n.
antiquated
past 125adj.
antiquated 127adj.
aged 131adj.
powerless 161adj.
disused 674adj.
antique
archaism 127n.
olden 127adj.
exhibit 522n.
antiquities
archaism 127n.
antiquity
time 108n.
diuturnity 113n.
antiquity 125n.
oldness 127n.
old man 133n.
anti-Semitism
prejudice 481n.
phobia 854n.
hatred 888n.
antiseptic
clean 648adj.
salubrious 652adj.
prophylactic 658n.
remedial 658adj.
tutelary 660adj.
antisepticize
purify 648vb.
sanitate 652vb.
doctor 658vb.
antisocial
unsociable 883adj.
misanthropic 902adj.
antispasmodic
antidote 658n.
antistrophe
verse form 593n.
antithesis
contrariety 14n.
difference 15n.
contraposition 240n.
trope 519n.
ornament 574n.
antithetic
inverted 221adj.
antitoxin
antidote 658n.
antitrades
wind 352n.
antitype
prototype 23n.
antler
protuberance 254n.
sharp point 256n.
weapon 723n.
antonomasia
trope 519n.
nomenclature 561n.

antonym
contrariety 14n.
connotation 514n.
word 559n.
name 561n.
antrum
cavity 255n.
anus
buttocks 238n.
anvil
stand 218n.
unlucky person 731n.
anvil, on the
in preparation 669adv.
on the stocks 726adv.
anxiety
(*see* anxious)
anxiety neurosis
psychopathy 503n.
anxious
careful 457adj.
expectant 507adj.
suffering 825adj.
nervous 854adj.
desiring 859adj.
anxious seat
penance 941n.
anxious to please
courteous 884adj.
any
quantitative 26adj.
no name 562n.
anonymous 562adj.
no choice 606n.
anybody's guess
uncertainty 474n.
anyhow
confusedly 61adv.
negligently 458adv.
anyone
everyman 79n.
anything but
contrary 14adj.
different 15adj.
aorist
time 108n.
aoristic
elapsing 111adj.
uncertain 474adj.
aorta
conduit 351n.
aortitis
blood pressure 651n.
apace
swiftly 277adv.
hastily 680adv.
apache
ruffian 904n.
apart
separate 46adj.
afar 199adv.
apart from
exclusive of 57adv.
apartheid
exclusion 57n.
prejudice 481n.
apartment
flat 192n.
chamber 194n.
apathetic
inert 175adj.
slow 278adj.
incurious 454adj.
inattentive 456adj.
inexpectant 508adj.
choiceless 606adj.
non-active 677adj.
inactive 679adj.
apathetic 820adj.
unastonished 865adj.
apathy
(*see* apathetic)
ape
imitator 20n.
imitate 20vb.
monkey 365n.
ape-man
mankind 371n.
ruffian 904n.
monster 938n.
aperçu
dissertation 591n.
compendium 592n.
aperient
opener 263n.
ejector 300n.
cathartic 658n.
apéritif
stimulant 174n.
liquor 301n.
aperture
opening 263n.
orifice 263n.
apex
summit 213n.
aphaeresis
shortening 204n.
aphasia
speech defect 580n.
aphelion
distance 199n.
aphonic
silent 399adj.
voiceless 578adj.
aphony, aphonia
silence 399n.
aphony 578n.
speech defect 580n.
aphorism
maxim 496n.
conciseness 569n.
aphotic
unlit 418adj.
aphrodisiac
stimulant 174n.
erotic 887adj.
Aphrodite
woman 373n.
a beauty 841n.
love god 887n.
mythic god 966n.
Olympian god 967n.
apiarist
breeder 369n.
apiary
dwelling 192n.
nest 192n.
stock farm 369n.
apical
topmost 213adj.
apiculture
animal husbandry 369n.
apiece
severally 80adv.
apish
imitative 20adj.
foolish 499adj.
aplomb
stability 153n.
resolution 399n.
apnea
decease 361n.
apocalypse
ruin 165n.
prediction 511n.
disclosure 526n.
scripture 975n.
revelation 975n.
apocope
shortening 204n.
apocrypha
scripture 975n.
apocryphal
uncertified 474adj.
erroneous 495adj.
apodixis
demonstration 478n.
apodosis
end 69n.
apogee
distance 199n.
summit 213n.
apograph
copy 22n.
Apollinarian
heretic 977n.
Apollo
musician 413n.
a beauty 841n.
Olympian god 967n.
Apollyon
Satan 969n.
apologetic
arguing 475adj.
excusing 614adj.
regretting 830adj.
vindicating 927adj.
repentant 939adj.
atoning 941adj.
apologetics, apologia
argument 475n.

vindication 927n.
apologies
regret 830n.
apologist
reasoner 475n.
vindicator 927n.
apologize
recant 603vb.
tergiversate 603vb.
plead 614vb.
knuckle under 721vb.
regret 830vb.
demean oneself 867vb.
be penitent 939vb.
atone 941vb.
apologue
metaphor 519n.
lecture 534n.
narrative 590n.
apology
penitence 939n.
atonement 941n.
apology for
copy 22n.
pretext 614n.
laughing stock 851n.
apophysis
swelling 253n.
apoplexy
helplessness 161n.
illness 651n.
aport
sinistral 242adj.
aposiopesis
trope 519n.
conciseness 569n.
ornament 574n.
taciturnity 582n.
apostasy
(*see* apostatize)
apostate
changed person 147n.
dissentient 489n.
(*see* apostatize)
apostatize
dissent 489vb.
be irresolute 601vb.
apostatize 603vb.
reject 607vb.
relinquish 621vb.
relapse 675vb.
be dishonest 930vb.
be irreligious 974vb.
schismatize 978vb.
be impious 980vb.
apostle
messenger 531n.
preacher 537n.
religious teacher 973n.
Apostles' Creed
orthodoxy 976n.
apostolate
vocation 622n.
church office 985n.
church ministry 985n.
apostolic
scriptural 975adj.
ecclesiastical 985adj.
priestly 985adj.
apostolic succession
holy orders 985n.
apostrophe
punctuation 547n.
nomenclature 561n.
apostrophize
orate 579vb.
speak to 583vb.
soliloquize 585vb.
entreat 761vb.
apothecary
druggist 658n.
apothegm
maxim 496n.
apotheosis
dignification 866n.
heaven 971n.
deification 982n.
apotropaic
deprecatory 762adj.
apozem
solution 337n.
appall
displease 827vb.
frighten 854vb.
appanage
dower 777n.
apparatus
tool 630n.
apparatus criticus
commentary 520n.
apparel
clothing 228n.
dress 228vb.
apparent
visible 443adj.
appearing 445adj.
plausible 471adj.
certain 473adj.
manifest 522adj.
apparentation
consanguinity 11n.
attribution 158n.
apparently
apparently 445adv.
probably 471adv.
apparition
visual fallacy 440n.
appearance 445n.
manifestation 522n.
ghost 970n.
apparitor
officer 741n.
law officer 955n.
appeal
influence 178vb.
attraction 291n.
attract 291vb.
affirmation 532n.
affirm 532vb.
allocution 583n.
motivate 612vb.
entreaty 761n.
request 761n.
deprecate 762vb.
excitation 821n.
pleasurableness 826n.
beauty 841n.
lovableness 887n.
legal trial 959n.
appeal against
negate 533vb.
deprecate 762vb.
appeal to
speak to 583vb.
request 761vb.
appear
be visible 443vb.
appear 445vb.
be disclosed 526vb.
appearance
circumstance 8n.
similarity 18n.
situation 186n.
form 243n.
visibility 443n.
appearance 445n.
probability 471n.
manifestation 522n.
appearances
etiquette 848n.
appear for
deputize 755vb.
appease
assuage 177vb.
induce 612vb.
pacify 719vb.
content 828vb.
offer worship 981vb.
appeasement
irenics 719n.
appellant
petitioner 763n.
dueness 915n.
accuser 928n.
litigant 959n.
appellate
curial 956adj.
appellation
nomenclature 561n.
appellative
name 561n.
naming 561adj.
append
add 38vb.
place after 65vb.
hang 217vb.
appendage
adjunct 40n.
sequel 67n.
concomitant 89n.
appendectomy
surgery 658n.

appendix
addition 38n.
adjunct 40n.
sequel 67n.
extremity 69n.
pendant 217n.
edition 589n.
apperception
intellect 447n.
appertain
be related 9vb.
be one of 58vb.
be included 78vb.
belong 773vb.
appetency
relation 9n.
will 595n.
desire 859n.
appetible
desired 859adj.
appetite
eating 301n.
desire, hunger 859n.
liking 859n.
appetize
taste 386vb.
appetize 390vb.
delight 826vb.
cause desire 859vb.
appetizer
stimulant 174n.
savoriness 390n.
applaud
assent 488vb.
rejoice 835vb.
honor 866vb.
gratulate 886vb.
applaud 923vb.
apple
fruit 301n.
apple of discord
quarrelsomeness 709n.
casus belli 709n.
apple of one's eye
favorite 890n.
appliance
causal means 156n.
instrument 628n.
means 629n.
tool 630n.
use 673n.
applicable
relevant 9adj.
apt 24adj.
useful 640adj.
expedient 642adj.
applicant
respondent 460n.
petitioner 763n.
application
referral 9n.
relevance 9n.
meditation 449n.
attention 455n.
connotation 514n.
metaphor 519n.
interpretation 520n.
perseverance 600n.
instrumentality 628n.
surgical dressing 658n.
use 673n.
assiduity 678n.
offer 759n.
request 761n.
applied
instrumental 628adj.
useful 640adj.
appliqué work
needlework 844n.
apply
relate 9vb.
figure 519vb.
use 673vb.
request 761vb.
belong 773vb.
apply oneself
study 536vb.
appoggiatura
musical note 410n.
appoint
select 605vb.
predetermine 608vb.
employ 622vb.
decree 737vb.
commission 751vb.
apportion 783vb.
appointed
fated 596adj.
appointee
consignee 754n.
appointment
job 622n.
fitting out 669n.
(*see* appoint)
appointment, by
chosen 605adj.
appointments
equipment 630n.
apport
spiritualism 984n.
apportion
arrange 62vb.
dispose of 673vb.
apportion 783vb.
apposite
relevant 9adj.
appositeness
fitness 24n.
apposition
relativeness 9n.
contiguity 202n.
grammar 564n.
appraise
discriminate 463vb.
appraise 465vb.
estimate 480vb.
appraiser
appraiser 465n.
estimator 480n.
appreciate
grow 36vb.
cognize 447vb.
appraise 465vb.
know 490vb.
be dear 811vb.
be pleased 824vb.
have taste 846vb.
honor 866vb.
love 887vb.
thank 907vb.
approve 923vb.
appreciation
discrimination 463n.
measurement 465n.
estimate 480n.
feeling 818n.
gratitude 907n.
approbation 923n.
appreciative
judicial 480adj.
tasteful 846adj.
grateful 907adj.
approving 923adj.
apprehend
opine 485vb.
know 490vb.
expect 507vb.
understand 516vb.
arrest 747vb.
take 786vb.
apprehensible
intelligible 516adj.
apprehension
idea 451n.
knowledge 490n.
expectation 507n.
danger 661n.
taking 786n
nervousness 854n.
apprehensive
expectant 507adj.
suffering 825adj.
nervous 854adj.
apprentice
beginner 538n.
artisan 686n.
bungler 697n.
apprenticeship
learning 536n.
apprise
inform 524vb.
approach
resemble 18vb.
entrance 68n.
beginning 68n.
futurity 124n.
be to come 124n.
impend 155vb.
tend 179vb.
nearness 200n.
doorway 263n.

motion 265n.
approach 289vb.
arrival 294n.
speak to 583vb.
pursuit 619n.
policy 623n.
way 624n.
offer 759n., vb.
request 761n., vb.
greet 884vb.
approachable
accessible 289adj.
possible 469adj.
easy 701adj.
approaches
near place 200n.
approbation
permission 488n.
approbation 923n.
appropinquate
approach 289vb.
appropriate
circumstantial 8adj.
relevant 9adj.
apt 24adj.
special 80adj.
acquire 771vb.
apportion 783vb.
appropriate 786vb.
claim 915vb.
appropriation
apportionment 783n.
taking 786n.
approvable
approvable 923adj.
approval
assent 488n.
permission 756n.
repute 866n.
approbation 923n.
approval, on
experimentally 461adv.
chosen 605adj.
approve
choose 605vb.
select 605vb.
permit 756vb.
consent 758vb.
be pleased 824vb.
approve 923vb.
approved
usual 610adj.
approver
informer 524n.
tergiversator 603n.
commender 923n.
accuser 928n.
approximate
be related 9vb.
similar 18adj.
liken 18vb.
resemble 18vb.
near 200adj.
approach 289vb.
approximately
almost 33adv.
approximation
numerical operation 86n.
appulse
contiguity 202n.
collide 279vb.
approach 289n.
appurtenance
adjunct 40n.
component 58n.
concomitant 89n.
property 777n.
appurtenant
relative 9adj.
ingredient 58adj.
apricate
dry 342vb.
enjoy 376vb.
aprication
heating 381n.
apricot
fruit 301n.
orange 436n.
April fool
dupe 544n.
laughing stock 851n.
April Fool's Day
amusement 837n.
April shower
brief span 114n.
changeable thing 152n.
a priori
intrinsic 5 adj.
rational 475adj.
reasonably 475adj.
a priori knowledge
intuition 476n.
apriorism
reasoning 475n.
apron
apron 228n.
canonicals 989n.
apron strings
subjection 745n.
a propos
concerning 9adj.
apt 24adj.
incidentally 137adv.
apse
church interior 990n.
apt
relevant 9adj.
apt 24adj.
opportune 137adj.
plausible 471adj.
skillful 494adj.
intelligent 498adj.
willing 597adj.
apteryx
flightless bird 365n.
aptitude
fitness 24n.
ability 160n.
tendency 179n.
intelligence 498n.
learning 536n.
willingness 597n.
aptitude 694n.
aquamarine
greenness 432n.
blueness 435n.
blue 435adj.
gem 844n.
aquaplane
swim 269vb.
aquaplaning
aquatics 269n.
sport 837n.
aquarelle
picture 553n.
aquarellist
artist 556n.
aquarium
accumulation 74n.
lake 346n.
cattle pen 369n.
zoo 369n.
collection 632n.
Aquarius
zodiac 321n.
aquatic
seafaring 269adj.
watery 339adj.
aquatics
aquatics 269n.
sport 837n.
aquatint
picture 553n.
engraving 555n.
aqueduct
conduit 351n.
aqueous
watery 339adj.
aquiline
curved 248adj.
animal 365adj.
Arab
wanderer 268n.
thoroughbred 273n.
arabesque
crossing 222n.
pattern 844n.
Arabist
linguist 557n.
arable
soil 344n.
farm 370n.
agrarian 370n.
arachnid
animal 365n.
arbalest
missile weapon 723n.
arbiter
adviser 691n.
magistracy 957n.
arbiter elegantiarum

reveler 837n.
man of taste 846n.
beau monde 848n.
arbitrage
judgment 480n.
mediation 720n.
barter 791n.
arbitral
judicial 480adj.
arbitrament
judgment 480n.
arbitrariness
irrelation 10n.
caprice 604n.
lawlessness 957n.
arbitrary
unconformable 84adj.
illogical 477adj.
volitional 595adj.
willful 602adj.
capricious 604adj.
authoritative 733adj.
authoritarian 735adj.
oppressive 735adj.
unconditional 744adj.
insolent 878adj.
lawless 954adj.
arbitrary power
brute force 735n.
arbitrate
judge 480vb.
mediate 720vb.
compromise 770vb.
arbor
pavilion 192n.
arbor 194n.
pivot 218n.
pleasure-ground 837n.
arboreal
reboreal 366adj.
arborescent
symmetrical 245adj.
arboreal 366adj.
arboretum
garden 370n.
arboriculture
agriculture 370n.
arc
arc 250n.
fire 379n.
arcade
pavilion 192n.
street 192n.
curve 248n.
path 624n.
emporium 796n.
arcadia
happiness 824n.
arcadian
artless 699adj.
innocent 935adj.
arcane
unintelligible 517adj.
latent 523adj.
concealed 525adj.
arcanum
secret 530n.
arc-boutant
supporter 218n.
arch
consummate 32adj.
supreme 34adj.
bond 47n.
foot 214n.
supporter 218n.
curve 248n.
make curved 248vb.
be convex 253vb.
gay 833adj.
affected 850adj.
archaeography
palaetiology 125n.
archaeologist
antiquarian 125n.
inquirer 459n.
detector 484n.
archaeology
palaetiology 125n.
archaic
olden 127adj.
neological 562adj.
archaism
antiquity 125n.
archaism 127n.
reversion 148n.
neology 560n.
archaize
look back 125vb.
retrospect 505vb.
archangel
angel 968n.
archbishop
governor 741n.
ecclesiarch 986n.
archbishopric
district 184n.
church office 985n.
parish 985n.
archdeacon
ecclesiarch 986n.
archdeaconry
church office 985n.
parsonage 986n.
archduke
potentate 741n.
nobleman 868n.
archer
shooter 287n.
soldiery 722n.
archery
propulsion 287n.
arm 723n.
sport 837n.
archetypal
unimitative 21adj.
archetype
prototype 23n.
idea 451n.
archiepiscopacy
churchdom 985n.
archiform
curved 248adj.
archimandrite
ecclesiarch 986n.
monk 986n.
archipelago
island 349n.
architect
producer 167n.
artisan 686n.
architectonic
productive 164adj.
architectural 192adj.
architectonics
structure 331n.
architectural
architcetural 192adj.
formative 243adj.
structural 331adj.
architecture
composition 56n.
arrangement 62n.
production 164n.
form 243n.
structure 331n.
art 551n.
ornamental art 844n.
architrave
summit 213n.
beam 218n.
archive(s)
title-deed 767n.
archivist
recorder 549n.
keeper 749n.
archpriest
ecclesiarch 986n.
priest 986n.
archway
doorway 263n.
arc light
lamp 420n.
arctic
opposite 240adj.
coldness 380n.
arcuate
make curved 248vb.
arcuate 253adj.
ardent
(*see* ardor)
ardent spirits
liquor 301n.
ardor
heat 379n.
vigor 571n.
restlessness 678n.
warm feeling 818n.
desire 859n.
arduous
laborious 682adj.
difficult 700adj.
area

quantity 26n.
space 183n.
measure 183n.
region 184n.
place 185n.
size 195n.
arefaction
desiccation 342n.
area
meeting place 192n.
view 438n.
theater 594n.
contest 716n.
battle 718n.
arena 724n.
pleasure-ground 837n.
arenaceous
powdery 332adj.
areola
circle 250n.
Areopagite
councillor 692n.
judge 957n.
Areopagus
tribunal 956n.
law court 956n.
Ares
war 718n.
Olympian god 967n.
aretalogical
descriptive 590adj.
wonderful 864adj.
aretalogist
exaggeration 546n.
narrator 590n.
prodigy 864n.
aretalogy
exaggeration 546n.
biography 590n.
deed 676n.
thaumaturgy 864n.
arête
sharp point 256n.
argent
white 427adj.
heraldry 547n.
argil
soil 344n.
materials 631n.
argilaceous
soft 327adj.
Argo
ship 275n.
argon
air 340n.
argonaut
mariner 270n.
argosy
shipping 275n.
merchant ship 275n.
argot
slang 560n.
arguable
possible 469adj.
uncertain 474adj.
arguing 475adj.
vindicable 927adj.
litigated 959adj.
argue
evidence 466vb.
argue 475vb.
dissent 489vb.
propound 512vb.
affirm 532vb.
indicate 547vb.
confer 584vb.
plead 614vb.
argue against
dissuade 613vb.
argue for
contend 716vb.
argue in a circle
reason ill 477vb.
argument
disagreement 25n.
topic 452n.
argument 475n.
demonstration 478n.
supposition 512n.
conference 584n.
narrative 590n.
quarrel 709n.
contention 716n.
argumentation
argumentation 475n.
argumentative
arguing 475adj.
argumentum ad baculum
corporal punishment 963n.
argumentum ad misreicordiam
pity 905n.
argumentum ad verecundiam
disrepute 867n.
probity 929n.
Argus
janitor 264n.
eye 438n.
protector 660n.
jailer 749n.
aria
tune 412n.
Arian
heretic 977n.
heretical 977adj.
arid
unproductive 172adj.
dry 342adj.
tedious 838adj.
Ariel
speeder 277n.
satellite 321n.
courier 531n.
fairy 970n.
Aries
zodiac 321n.
arietation
impulse 279n.
aright
well 615adv.
aright 644adv.
arise
become 1vb.
begin 68vb.
happen 154vb.
ascend 308vb.
lift oneself 310vb.
be visible 443vb.
appear 445vb.
arise from
result 157vb.
aristeia
prowess 855n.
aristocracy
superiority 34n.
nation 371n.
government 733n.
aristocracy 868n.
aristocrat
aristocrat 868n.
proud man 871n.
aristocratic
governmental 753adj.
worshipful 866adj.
genteel 868adj.
Aristophanic
funny 849adj.
Aristotelianism
philosophy 449n.
arithmetic
numerical 85adj.
mathematics 86n.
statistical 86adj.
arithmetic progression
series 71n.
ratio 85n.
progression 285n.
ark
retreat 192n.
box 194n.
ship 275n.
protection 660n.
refuge 662n.
Ark of the Covenant
ritual object 988n.
holy place 990n.
arm
adjunct 40n.
limb 53n.
empower 160vb.
supporter 218n.
sleeve 228n.
indicator 547n.
tool 630n.
provide 633vb.
safeguard 660vb.
make ready 669vb.
defend 713vb.
go to war 718vb.

arm 723n.
weapon 723n.
armada
armed force 722n.
navy 722n.
Armageddon
fight 716n.
armament
fitting out 669n.
armed force 722n.
arm 723n.
armature
coil 251n.
armband
belt 228n.
armchair
seat 218n.
softness 327n.
armchair critic
theorist 512n.
armed force(s)
armed force 722n.
army 722n.
armed intervention
war 718n.
armful
finite quantity 26n.
armhole
sleeve 228n.
orifice 263n.
armiger
aristocrat 868n.
armillary
gauge 465n.
arm in arm
conjunct 45adj.
with 89adv.
nigh 200adv.
contiguously 202adv.
across 222adv.
sociably 882adv.
armipotent
powerful 160adj.
armistice
lull 145n.
peace 717n.
pacification 719n.
armless
fragmentary 53adj.
incomplete 55adj.
defenseless 161adj.
crippled 163adj.
imperfect 647adj.
armlet
belt 228n.
loop 250n.
badge of rank 743n.
armor
covering 226n.
war-chariot 274n.
protection 660n.
safeguard 662n.
armor 713n.
defend 713vb.
cavalry 722n.
weapon 723n.
armor-bearer
retainer 742n.
armored
invulnerable 660adj.
defended 713adj.
armored car
war-chariot 274n.
cavalry 722n.
armorial
heraldic 547adj.
armorial bearings
heraldry 547n.
armory
accumulation 74n.
heraldry 547n.
storage 632n.
workshop 687n.
arsenal 723n.
armpits
fetor 397n.
arms
heraldry 547n.
vocation 622n.
safeguard 662n.
war 718n.
honors 866n.
arms chest
arsenal 723n
arms, in
infantine 132adj.
warring 718adj.
arm's length, at
afar 199adv.
army
multitude 104n.
army 722n.
army officer
army officer 741n.
aroma
fragrance 396n.
around
nearly 200adv.
around 230adv.
arouse
cause feeling 374vb.
incite 612vb.
raise the alarm 665vb.
excite 821vb.
arpeggio
musical note 410n.
harmonize 410vb.
arrack
liquor 301n.
arraign
indict 928vb.
arraignment
accusation 928n.
litigation 959n.
arrange
arrange 62vb.
modify 143vb.
compose music 413vb.
predetermine 608vb.
plan 623vb.
make ready 669vb.
arrangement
adaptation 24n.
regularity 81n.
musical piece 412n.
preparation 669n.
compact 765n.
arrant
consummate 32adj.
manifest 522adj.
bad 645adj.
disreputable 867adj.
rascally 930adj.
arras
covering 226n.
needlework 844n.
array
order 60n.
arrangement 62n.
arrange 62vb.
series 71n.
multitude 104n.
place 187vb.
dress 228vb.
make ready 669vb.
battle 718n.
formation 722n.
decorate 844vb.
pageant 875n.
arrears
debt 803n.
arrears, in
behindhand 307adv.
owed 803adj.
non-paying 805adj.
arrest
cessation 145n.
halt 145vb.
cause feeling 374vb.
hindrance 702n.
restraint 747n.
detention 747n.
arrest 747vb.
take 786vb.
impress 821vb.
legal process 959n.
arresting
unexpected 508adj.
impressive 821adj.
arrière-ban
publication 528n.
army 722n.
arrière-pensée
sophistry 477n.
concealment 525n.
arrival
junction 45n.
intruder 59n.
beginning 68n.
arrival 295n.
arrive
accrue 38vb.

happen 154vb.
be present 189vb.
approach 289vb.
arrive 295vb.
flourish 615vb.
climax 725vb.
succeed 727vb.
prosper 730vb.

arriviste
made man 730n.
commoner 869n.
egotist 932n.

arrogance
pride 871n.
insolence 878n.

arrogant
authoritarian 735adj.
rash 857adj.

arrogate
please oneself 734vb.
appropriate 786vb.
be insolent 788vb.
claim 915vb.
be undue 916vb.

arrogation
taking 786n.
pretension 850n.
insolence 878n.
arrogation 916n.

arrondissement
district 184n.

arrow
sharp point 256n.
speeder 277n.
missile 287n.
indicator 547n.
missile weapon 723n.
love token 889n.

arroyo
stream 350n.
conduit 351n.

arsenal
accumulation 74n.
storage 632n.
workshop 687n.
arsenal 723n.

arsenic
poison 659n.

arsis
pronunciation 577n.
prosody 593n.

arson
fire 379n.
incendiarism 381n.

art
composition 56n.
production 164n.
art 551n.
business 622n.
skill 694n.
stratagem 698n.

art-critic
spectator 441n.
man of taste 846n.

art equipment
art equipment 553n.

arterial
communicating 624adj.

arteritis
blood pressure 651n.

artery
essential part 5n.
tube 263n.
conduit 351n.
life 360n.
road 624n.

artesian well
outflow 298n.
lake 346n.

artful
intelligent 498adj.
false 541adj.
deceiving 542adj.
cunning 698adj.
dishonest 930adj.

art gallery
collection 632n.

arthritic
impotent 161adj.
crippled 163adj.
sick person 651n.
diseased 651adj.

arthritis
pang 377n.
rheumatism 651n.

arthropathy
paralysis 651n.

artichoke
tuber 301n.
vegetables 301n.

article
product 164n.
object 319n.
publicity 528n.
reading matter 589n.
article 591n.
precept 693n.
merchandise 795n.

article oneself
learn 536vb.

articles
creed 485n.
conditions 766n.

articulate
join 45vb.
phrase 563vb.
vocal 577adj.
voice 577vb.
speak 579vb.

artifact
product 164n.

artifice
contrivance 623n.
stratagem 698n.
pretension 850n.

artificer
producer 167n.
artisan 686n.

artificial
simulating 18adj.
produced 164adj.
horticultural 370adj.
spurious 542adj.
untrue 543adj.
elegant 575adj.
inelegant 576adj.
laborious 682adj.
well-made 694adj.
affected 850adj.

artificial respiration
revival 656n.

artificial satellite
space-ship 276n.
satellite 321n.

artillery
loudness 400n.
gun 723n.

artilleryman
soldiery 722n.

artisan
artist 556n.
machinist 630n.
doer 676n.
artisan 686n.

artist
producer 167n.
visionary 513n.
artist 556n.
entertainer 594n.
doer 676n.

artistic
elegant 575adj.
well-made 694adj.
beautiful 841adj.
tasteful 846adj.

artistry
touch 378n.
imagination 513n.
painting 533n.
skill 694n.
good taste 846n.

artless
simple 44adj.
amorphous 244adj.
ignorant 491adj.
foolish 499adj.
veracious 540adj.
plain 573adj.
inelegant 576adj.
spontaneous 609adj.
unprepared 670adj.
bungled 695adj.
artless 699adj.
graceless 842adj.
vulgar 847adj.
barbaric 869adj.
innocent 935adj.

art master
artist 556n.

arts
culture 490n.
literature 557n.

art, work of
masterpiece 694n.
Aryan
ethnic 11adj.
language type 557n.
Aryanism
prejudice 481n.
asafetida
unsavoriness 391n.
fetor 397n.
asbestos
incombustibility 382n.
ascend
be high 209vb.
be oblique 220vb.
fly 271vb.
ascend 308vb.
ascendancy
power 160n.
influence 178n.
victory 727n.
authority 733n.
prestige 866n.
ascendant, in the
successful 727adj.
ascender
print-type 587n.
ascending order
increase 36n.
series 71n.
expansion 197n.
ascent
series 71n.
acclivity 220n.
motion 265n.
progression 285n.
ascent 308n.
improvement 654n.
ascertain
make certain 473vb.
ascertainment
certainty 473n.
demonstration 478n.
discovery 484n.
ascetic
severe 735adj.
impassive 820adj.
unfeeling person 820n.
abstainer 942n.
temperate 942adj.
ascetic 945n., adj.
pietist 979n.
pietistic 979adj.
monk 986n.
asceticism
temperance 942n.
asceticism 945n.
punishment 963n.
pietism 979n.
act of worship 981n.
monasticism 985n.
ascribable
due 915adj.
ascribe
attribute 158vb.
grant claims 915vb.
ascription
attribution 158n.
ascriptus glebae
husbandman 370n.
slave 742n.
asdic
hearing aid 415n.
detector 484n.
aseity
existence 1n.
aseptic
clean 648adj.
salubrious 652adj.
asexual
simple 44adj.
Asgard
mythic heaven 971n.
as good as
equivalent 28adj.
equally 28adv.
on the whole 52adv.
completely 54adv.
ash
pulverulence 332n.
tree 366n.
ash 381n.
dirt 649n.
ash can
cleaning utensil 648n.
bomb 723n.
ashen
colorless 426adj.
gray 429adj.
Ashes
trophy 729n.
ashes
corpse 363n.
ashlar
building material 631n.
ashore
on land 344adv.
ashram
retreat 192n.
monastery 986n.
Ash Wednesday
holy-day 988n.
ashy
colorless 426adj.
gray 429adj.
aside
sideways 239adv.
faintly 401adv.
latency 523n.
hint 524n.
secretly 525adv.
soliloquy 585n.
aside 585adv.
dramaturgy 594n.
as if
similarly 18adv.
asinine
equine 273adj.
animal 365adj.
absurd 497adj.
foolish 499adj.
as it were
similarly 18adv.
ask
inquire 459vb.
not know 491vb.
request 761vb.
askance
obliquely 220adv.
sideways 239adv.
askew
unequal 29adj.
oblique 220adj.
distorted 246adj.
ask for
inquire 459vb.
bargain 791vb.
desire 859vb.
ask for trouble
be rash 857vb.
aslant
oblique 220adj.
asleep
quiescent 266adj.
sleepy 679adj.
as long as
during pleasure 112adv.
aslope
obliquely 220adv.
asomatous
immaterial 320adj.
asp
reptile 365n.
noxious animal 904n.
asparagus
vegetable 301n.
aspect
character 5n.
modality 7n.
situation 186n.
appearance 445n.
conduct 688n.
aspen
agitation 318n.
tree 366n.
asperge
moisten 341vb.
purify 648vb.
perform ritual 988vb.
asperges
moistening 341n.
asperity
roughness 259n.
rudeness 885n.
anger 891n.
irascibility 892n.
asperse
moisten 341vb.
defame 926vb.
aspersion

moistening 341n.
slur 866n.
scurrility 899n.
reproach 924n.
detraction 926n.
ritual act 988n.
asphalt
smoothness 258n.
resin 357n.
road 624n.
building material 631n.
asphyxia
decease 361n.
asphyxiant
deadly 362adj.
poison 659n.
asphyxiate
close 264vb.
aspirant
petitioner 763n.
hoper 852n.
desirer 859n.
aspirate
breathe 352vb.
speech sound 398n.
rasp 407vb.
spoken letter 558n.
voice 577vb.
aspiration
pronunciation 577n.
motive 612n.
objective 617n.
aspiration 852n.
desire 859n.
desired object 859n.
aspire
ascend 308vb.
hope 852vb.
desire 859vb.
aspirin
drug 658n.
asquint
obliquely 220adv.
sideways 239adv.
as regards
concerning 9adv.
ass
beast of burden 273n.
animal 365n.
fool 501n.
bungler 697n.
assail
attack 712vb.
torment 827vb.
assailant
opponent 705n.
attacker 712n.
combatant 722n.
assassin
destroyer 168n.
violent creature 176n.
murderer 362n.
ruffian 904n.
assassinate
murder 362vb.
assault
knock 279n.
impairment 655n.
attack 712n., vb.
debauch 951vb.
assay
experiment 461n., vb.
essay 671vb.
assemblage
(*see* assemble)
assemble
join 45vb.
compose 56vb.
congregate 74vb.
bring together 74vb.
produce 164vb.
meet 295vb.
call 547n.
assembly
convergence 293n.
conference 584n.
council 692n.
sociability 882n.
(*see* assemble)
assembly line
production 164n.
assembly room
place of amusement 837n.
assent
agreement 24n.
assent 488n., vb.
willingness 597n.
obey 739vb.
permit 756vb.
consent 758n., vb.
assentaneous
assenting 488adj.
assentation
flattery 925n.
assentient
assenting 488adj.
assert
suppose 512vb.
mean 514vb.
affirm 532vb.
assertion
testimony 466n.
assertive
assertive 532adj.
assert oneself
influence 178vb.
be active 678vb.
assess
appraise 465vb.
price, tax 809vb.
assessable
measured 465adj.
priced 809adj.
assessment
measurement 465n.
estimate 480n.
tax 809n.
assessor
appraiser 465n.
estimator 480n.
jury 957n.
assets
sufficiency 635n.
means 629n.
store 632n.
estate 777n.
asseverate
affirm 532vb.
assibilate
hiss 406vb.
assiduity
attention 455n.
carefulness 457n.
perseverance 600n.
assiduity 678n.
exertion 682n.
assiduous
frequent 139 adj.
(*see* assiduity)
assign
arrange 63vb.
attribute 158vb.
transfer 672vb.
dispose of 673vb.
commission 751vb.
dower 777vb.
convey 780vb.
bequeath 780vb.
apportion 783vb.
grant claims 915vb.
assignable
attributed 158adj.
transferable 272adj.
due 915adj.
assignat
paper money 797n.
assignation
focus 76n.
social round 882n.
assignee
recipient 782n.
assignment
mandate 751n.
transfer 780n.
apportionment 783n.
assimilate
identify 13vb.
make uniform 16vb.
liken 18vb.
combine 50vb.
make conform 83vb.
transform 147vb.
absorb 299vb.
learn 536vb.
assimilation
inclusion 78n.
speech sound 398n.
(*see* assimilate)
assimilative
admitting 299adj.
ass in a lion's skin

misfit 25n.
impostor 545n.
bungler 697n.
assist
aid 703vb.
assistance
instrumentality 628n.
provision 633n.
aid 703n.
assistant
inferior 35n.
instrument 628n.
auxiliary 707n.
servant 742n.
assist at
be present 189vb.
assister
aider 703n.
assize
measurement 465n.
law-court 956n.
legal trial 959n.
associate
join 45vb.
combine 50vb.
congregate 74vb.
concomitant 89n.
accompany 89vb.
personnel 686n.
cooperate 706vb.
colleague 707n.
society 708n.
join a party 708vb.
friend 880n.
associate with
unite with 45vb.
association
relation 9n.
junction 45n.
group 74n.
accompaniment 89n.
concurrence 181n.
intuition 476n.
habituation 610n.
association 706n.
corporation 708n.
participation 775n.
sociality 882n.
association of ideas
intellect 447n.
thought 449n.
supposition 512n.
associative
attracting 291adj.
assonance
assimilation 18n.
recurrence 106n.
melody 410n.
prosody 593n.
ornament 574n.
assonant
word 559n.
as soon as
synchronously 123adv.
assort
make uniform 16vb.
assortment
uniformity 16n.
arrangement 62n.
series 71n.
bunch 74n.
accumulation 74n.
sort 77n.
assuage
assuage 177vb.
soften 327vb.
pacify 719vb.
restrain 747vb.
please 826vb.
relieve 831vb.
assuefaction
habituation 610n.
assuetude
habit 610n.
assume
account for 158vb.
wear 228vb.
assume 471vb.
premise 475vb.
believe, opine 485vb.
expect 507vb.
suppose 512vb.
dissemble 541vb.
undertake 672vb.
appropriate 786vb.
be affected 850vb.
hope 852vb.
be insolent 878vb.
assuming
if 8adv.
supposedly 512adv.
insolent 878adj.
unwarranted 916adj.
assumption
attribution 158n.
elevation 310n.
premise 475n.
opinion 485n.
supposition 512n.
receiving 782n.
taking 786n.
pretension 850n.
hope 852n.
arrogation 916n.
heaven 971n.
assurance
calculation of chance 159n.
positiveness 473n.
belief 485n.
affirmation 532n.
safety 660n.
promise 764n.
hope 852n.
vanity 873n.
insolence 878n.
assure
make certain 473vb.
convince 485vb.
promise 764vb.
give security 767vb.
assured
positive 473adj.
believing 485adj.
assertive 532adj.
safe 660adj.
astatic
light 323adj.
asterisk
punctuation 547n.
mark 547vb.
asterism
star 321n.
punctuation 547n.
astern
rearward 238adv.
asteroid
planet 321n.
asthenia
weakness 163n.
asthma
respiratory disease 651n.
asthmatic
puffing 352adj.
sibilant 406adj.
sick person 651n.
diseased 651adj.
astigmatism
dim sight 440n.
astir
busy 678adj.
excited 821adj.
as to
concerning 9adv.
astonish
cause feeling 374vb.
surprise 508vb.
be wonderful 864vb.
astonishing
prodigious 32adj.
unusual 84adj.
astonishment
inexpectation 508n.
wonder 864n.
astound
surprise 508vb.
impress 821vb.
be wonderful 864vb.
astraddle
astride 218adv.
astrakhan
headgear 228n.
astral
immaterial 320adj.
celestial 321adj.
spooky 970adj.
astral body
immateriality 320n.
spiritualism 984n.
astray
irrelative 10adj.

unassembled 75adj.
unconformable 84adj.
deviating 282adj.
astriction
joinder 45n.
contraction 198n.
astride
astride 218adv.
astringent
compressor 198n.
compressive 198adj.
pungent 388adj.
astrodome
view 438n.
astrolabe
astronomy 321n.
gauge 465n.
astrologer
astronomy 321n.
diviner 511n.
sorcerer 983n.
occultist 984n.
astromancy
astronomy 321n.
divination 511n.
astronaut
aeronaut 271n.
astronautical
aviational 276adj.
astronomer
astronomy 321n.
astronomical unit
long measure 203n.
astrophysics
astronomy 321n.
astute
intelligent 498adj.
cunning 698adj.
asunder
apart 46adv.
afar 199adv.
asura
mythical being 970n.
demon 970n.
as usual
conformably 83adv.
as well as
in addition 38adv.
asylum
retreat 192n.
reception 299n.
madhouse 503n.
protection 660n.
refuge, shelter 662n.
asymmetry
irrelation 10n.
non-uniformity 17n.
disagreement 25n.
inequality 29n.
distortion 246n.
ugliness 842n.
asymptote
convergence 293n.
part of speech 564n.
grammatical 564adj.
asyndeton
disjunction 46n.
trope 519n.
grammar 564n.
as you were
reversibly 148adv.
at all events
nevertheless 468adv.
at any moment
in the future 155adv.
at a stretch
continuously 71adv.
atavism
heredity 5n.
consanguinity 11n.
recurrence 106n.
reversion 148n.
reproduction 166n.
influence 178n.
memory 505n.
ataxia
helplessness 161n.
at bottom
intrinsically 5adv.
Ate
quarrelsomeness 709n.
lesser god 967n.
atelier
chamber 194n.
art equipment 553n.
workshop 687n.
athanasia
perpetuity 115n.
athanor
heater 383n.
at heart
inside 224adv.
centrally 225adv.
atheism
philosophy 449n.
unbelief 486n.
irreligion 974n.
atheroma
blood pressure 651n.
athirst
hungry 859adj.
athlete
athlete 162n.
proficient 695n.
contender 716n.
athletics
athletics 162n.
exercise 682n.
contention 716n.
contest 716n.
sport 837n.
at home
apt 24adj.
assembly 74n.
on the spot 189adj.
residing 192adj.
social gathering 882n.
at home with
friendly 880adj.
athwart
oblique 220adj.
across 222adv.
at intervals
discontinuously 72adv.
Atlantis
fantasy 513n.
atlas
arrangement 62n.
directory 87n.
world 321n.
map 551n.
Atlas
athlete 162n.
supporter 218n.
at last
finally 69adv.
late 136adv.
at least
slightly 33adv.
at length
late 136adv.
diffusely 570adv.
Atman
self 80n.
divineness 965n.
atmometer
vaporizer 338n.
atmosphere
influence 178n.
covering 226n.
circumjacence 230n.
atmosphere 340n.
painting 553n.
atmospheric
blue 435adj.
excitable 822adj.
atmospherics
commotion 318n.
discord 411n.
atoll
island 349n.
atom
particle 33n.
unit 88n.
minuteness 196n.
element 319n.
atomic
simple 44adj.
dynamic 160adj.
minute 196adj.
atomize
demolish 165vb.
vaporize 338vb.
atomizer
pulverizer 332n.
vaporizer 338n.
atom-smasher
nucleonics 160n.
atomy
small animal 33n.
dwarf 196n.
atonality

discord 411n.
at one
agreeing 24adj.
atone
restitute 787vb.
be penitent 939vb.
atone 941vb.
atonement
substitution 150n.
atonement 941n.
divine function 965n.
atony
weakness 163n.
atop
aloft 209adv.
atop 213adv.
atrabilious
black 428adj.
melancholic 834adj.
at random
by chance 159adv.
atrocious
cruel 898adj.
heinous 934adj.
atrocity
cruel act 898n.
guilty act 936n.
atrophy
helplessness 161n.
contraction 198n.
paralysis 651n.
dilapidation 655n.
attach
add 38vb.
affix, connect 45vb.
belong 773vb.
attaché
envoy 754n.
attaché case
box 194n.
attached
loving 887adj.
attachment
adjunct 40n.
part 53n.
observance 768n.
expropriation 786n.
love 887n.
attack
beginning 68n.
begin 68vb.
vigorousness 174n.
be vigorous 174vb.
outbreak 176n.
irrupt 297vb.
encroach 306vb.
spasm 318n.
argue 475vb.
cause doubt 486vb.
voice 577n.
resolution 599n.
policy 623n.
plan 623vb.
way 624n.
illness 651n.
essay 671n.
attack 712n., vb.
fight 716vb.
battle 718n.
wage war 718vb.
dispraise 924vb.
detraction 926n.
attacker
opponent 705n.
attacker 712n.
combatant 722n.
attain
arrive 295vb.
acquire 771vb.
attainable
accessible 289adj.
possible 469adj.
attainder
(*see* attaint)
attainment(s)
culture 490n.
intelligence 498n.
learning 536n.
skill 694n.
attaint
indict 928vb.
condemn 961vb.
attar
scent 396n.
attemper
mix 43vb.
moderate 177vb.
attempt
essay 671n., vb.
do 676vb.
attend
accompany 89vb.
be present 189vb.
follow 284vb.
watch 441vb.
be attentive 455vb.
doctor 658vb.
be servile 879vb.
attendance
retinue 67n.
(*see* attend)
attendant
accompanying 89adj.
on the spot 189adj.
follower 284n.
spectator 441n.
bridesman 894n.
attention
listening 415n.
attention 455n.
carefulness 457n.
accuracy 494n.
study 536n.
assiduity 678n.
respect 920n.
attenuate
make smaller 198vb.
make thin 206vb.
rarefy 325vb.
attest
testify 466vb.
endorse 488vb.
swear 532vb.
sign 547vb.
contract 765vb.
attestant
witness 466n.
signatory 765n.
attestation
testimony 466n.
certainty 473n.
attested
evidential 466adj.
certain 473adj.
attic
attic 194n.
Attic
elegant 575adj.
witty 839adj.
tasteful 846adj.
attire
dressing 228n.
dress 228vb.
attitude
situation 186n.
form 243n.
idea 451n.
supposition 512n.
affections 817n.
attitudinize
be affected 850vb.
attorney
mediator 720n.
mandate 751n.
consignee 754n.
deputy 755n.
deputize 755vb.
law agent 958n.
attract
bring together 74vb.
influence 178vb.
attract 291vb.
motivate 612vb.
delight 826vb.
excite love 887vb.
attraction
energy 160n.
influence 178n.
tendency 179n.
traction 288n.
attraction 291n.
grammar 564n.
inducement 612n.
incentive 612n.
pleasurableness 826n.
liking 859n.
favorite 890n.
attractions
beauty 841n.
lovableness 887n.
attractive, -ness
(*see* attraction)

attract notice
attract notice 455vb.
attribute
specialty 80n.
concomitant 89n.
attribute 158vb.
ability 160n.
grant claims 915vb.
attrition
decrease 37n.
pulverulence 322n.
friction 333n.
warfare 718n.
attune
adjust 24vb.
harmonize 410vb.
atypical
non-uniform 17adj.
dissimilar 19adj.
abnormal 84adj.
aubade
vocal music 412n.
musical piece 412n.
wooing 889n.
aubergine
vegetable 301n.
auburn
brown 430adj.
red 431adj.
auction
sale 793n.
sell 793vb.
overcharge 811vb.
auction room
mart 796n.
audacity
courage 855n.
rashness 857n.
insolence 878n.
audible
sounding 398adj.
loud 400adj.
auditory 415adj.
intelligible 516adj.
speaking 579n.
audience
listener 45n.
listening 415n.
onlookers 441n.
allocution 583n.
conference 584n.
playgoer 594n.
audiometer
acoustics 398n.
audiphone
hearing aid 415n.
audit
inquiry 459n.
inquire 459vb.
account 808vb.
accounts 808n.
audition
hearing 415n.
listening 415n.
exam 459n.
experiment 461n.
conference 584n.
auditor
listener 415n.
accountant 808n.
auditorium
meeting place 192n.
listener 415n.
onlookers 441n.
classroom 539n.
conference 584n.
theater 594n.
Augean stables
sink 649n.
auger
sharp point 256n.
perforator 263n.
augment
increment 36n.
augment 36vb.
add 38vb.
adjunct 40n.
strengthen 162vb.
part of speech 564n.
aggravate 832vb.
augur
diviner 511n.
predict 511vb.
augury
divination 511n.
omen 511n.
august
great 32adj.
notable 638adj.
worshipful 866adj.
Augustan
elegant 575adj.
perfect 646adj.
Augustan Age
literature 557n.
palmy days 730n.
auk
animal 365n.
aumbry
church utensil 990n.
aunt
kinsman 11n.
woman 373n.
Aunt Sally
laughing-stock 851n.
au pair
in exchange 151adv.
aura
circumjacence 230n.
light 417n.
prestige 866n.
aural
auditory 415adj.
aureate
yellow 433adj.
aureole
loop 250n.
light 417n.
honors 866n.
Aureomycin
drug 658n.
auricle
ear 415n.
auricular confession
secrecy 525n.
ministration 988n.
aurist
doctor 658n.
aurochs
cattle 365n.
aurora
morning 128n.
glow 417n.
luminary 420n.
redness 431n.
lesser god 967n.
Auschwitz
prison camp 748n.
auscultation
listening 415n.
auspicate
auspicate 68vb.
divine 511vb.
auspice(s)
omen 511n.
protection 660n.
aid 703n.
auspicious
circumstantial 8adj.
opportune 137adj.
presageful 511adj
palmy 730adj.
promising 852adj.
austere
plain 573adj.
severe 735adj.
ascetic 945adj.
pietistic 979adj.
austerities
penance 941n.
austerity
unsavoriness 391n.
plainness 573n.
insufficiency 636n.
severity 735n.
asceticism 945n.
pietism 979n.
Australasian
ethnic 11adj.
Australopithecus
mankind 371n.
autarch
autocrat 741n.
autarchic
governmental 733adj.
independent 744adj.
autarchy
government 733n.
independence 744n.
autarkic
independent 744adj.
autarky

independence 744n.
authentic
unimitated 21adj.
evidential 466adj.
genuine 494adj.
authenticate
testify 466vb.
make certain 473vb.
endorse 488vb.
give security 767vb.
authenticity
identity 13n.
authenticity 494n.
author
cause 156n.
producer 167n.
publicizer 528n.
penman 586n.
author 589n.
narrator 590n.
dissertator 591n.
planner 623n.
authoritarian
tyrant 735n.
authoritarian 735adj.
authoritative
powerful 160adj.
influential 178n.
evidential 466adj.
certain 473adj.
credal 485adj.
directing 689adj.
authoritative 733adj.
commanding 737adj.
scriptural 975adj.
orthodox 976adj.
authorities
evidence 466n.
authorities, the
master 741n.
authority
greatness 32n.
superiority 34n.
power 160n.
influence 178n.
evidence 466n.
credential 466n.
informant 524n.
authority 733n.
commission 751n.
permit 756n.
jurisdiction 955n.
authorize
empower 160vb.
commission 751vb.
permit 756vb.
grant claims 915vb.
authorship
composition 56n.
causation 156n.
production 164n.
writing 586n.
autism
selfishness 932n.
auto
automobile 274n.
autobahn
road 624n.
autobiographer
chronicler 549n.
narrator 590n.
autobiography
biography 590n.
autochthonous
native 191adj.
autocracy
despotism 733n.
brute force 735n.
autocrat
tyrant 735n.
autocrat 741n.
autocratic
volitional 595adj.
authoritative 733adj.
auto da fé
killing 362n.
burning 381n.
capital punishment 963n.
autogenesis
propagation 164n.
autogiro
aircraft 276n.
autograph
no imitation 21n.
identification 457n.
label 547n.
sign 547vb.
script 586n.
written 586adj.
autograph album
reminder 505n.
autohypnosis
insensibility 375n.
auto-intoxication
indigestion 651n.
impairment 655n.
automat
café 192n.
automatic
involuntary 596adj.
spontaneous 609adj.
instrumental 628adj.
mechanical 630adj.
pistol 723n.
automatic writing
spiritualism 984n.
automation
production 164n.
instrumentality 628n.
mechanics 630n.
automatism
incogitance 450n.
spiritualism 984n.
automaton
image 551n.
fatalist 596n.
machine 630n.
automobile
automobile 274n.
vehicular 274adj.
automotive
moving 265adj.
traveling 267adj.
autonomy
government 733n.
independence 744n.
autonymous
genuine 494adj.
semantic 514adj.
autopilot
directorship 689n.
autopsy
death 361n.
inquest 364n.
inspection 438n.
inquiry 459n.
autoptical
manifest 522adj.
autostrada
road 624n.
auto-suggestion
sense 374n.
fantasy 513n.
autumn
autumn 129n.
auxiliary
inferior 35n., adj.
additional 38n.
extra 40n.
supporter 218n.
aider 703n.
aiding 703adj.
auxiliary 707n.
soldier 722n.
avail
benefit 615vb.
utility 640n.
be useful 640vb.
use 673n.
availability
possibility 469n.
available
on the spot 189adj.
accessible 289adj.
possible 469adj.
instrumental 628adj.
stored 632adj.
provisionary 633adj.
useful 640adj.
used 673adj.
offering 759adj.
not retained 779adj.
salable 793adj.
avail of
avail of 673vb.
avalanche
revolution 149n.
descent 309n.
snow 380n.
redundance 637n.
avant-garde

precursor 66n.
modernist 126n.
modern 126adj.
front 237n.
avant-propos
prelude 66n.
avarice
avarice 816n.
desire 859n.
selfishness 932n.
avaricious
acquiring 771adj.
(*see* avarice)
avatar
transformation 143n.
theophany 965n.
revelation 975n.
avenge
retaliate 714vb.
avenge 910vb.
punish 963vb.
avenger
vindicator 927n.
avenue
street 192n.
path 624n.
aver
affirm 532vb.
average
average 30n.
median 30adj.
average out 30vb.
inconsiderable 33adj.
middle 70n.
generality 79n.
general 79adj.
typical 83adj.
not discriminate 464vb.
mid-course 625n.
not bad 644adj.
imperfection 647n.
imperfect 647adj.
mediocre 732n.
averages
statistics 86n.
averment
affirmation 532n.
litigation 959n.
Avernus
mythic hell 972n.
aversion
unwillingness 598n.
dislike 861n.
hatred 888n.
hateful object 888n.
avert
deflect 282vb.
obstruct 702vb.
parry 713vb.
avian
animal 365adj.
aviary
dwelling 192n.
nest 192n.
zoo 369n.
aviation
aeronautics 271n.
aviator
aeronaut 271n.
avidity
rapacity 786n.
avarice 816n.
desire 859n.
avifauna
bird 365n.
avitaminosis
disease 651n.
avocation
pursuit 619n.
avoidance 620n.
business 622n.
avoid
exclude 57vb.
be absent 190vb.
be distant 199vb.
be loath 598vb.
avoid 620vb.
circuit 626vb.
not use 674vb.
parry 713vb.
not observe 769vb.
dislike 861vb.
be unsocial 883vb.
make unwelcome 883vb.
hate 888vb.
disapprove 924vb.
avoidable
avoidable 620adj.
avoidance
escape 667n.
dutilessness 918n.
temperance 942n.
(*see* avoid)
avoirdupois
finite quantity 26n.
weighment 322n.
avouch
affirm 532vb.
avow
testify 466vb.
assent 488vb.
confess 526vb.
affirm 532vb.
avulsion
scission 46n.
extraction 304n.
avuncular
akin 11adj.
await
look ahead 124vb.
wait 136vb.
expect, await 507vb.
awake
attentive 455adj.
active 678adj.
impressible 819adj.
awaken
have feeling 374vb.
cause feeling 374vb.
be informed 524vb.
excite 821vb.
(*see* wake)
award
judgment 480n.
judge 480vb.
trophy 729n.
gift 781n.
give 781vb.
reward 962n., vb.
aware
sentient 374adj.
knowing 490adj.
intelligent 498adj.
lively 819adj.
impressible 819adj.
awareness
intellect 447n.
awash
drenched 341adj.
away
absent 190adj.
afar 199adv.
awe
excitation 821n.
fear 854n.
frighten 854vb.
wonder 864n.
be wonderful 864vb.
respect 920n.
command respect 920vb.
aweless
unfearing 855adj.
disrespectful 921adj.
awesome
(*see* awe)
awesomeness
prestige 866n.
awful
silent 399adj.
not nice 645adj.
bad 645adj.
frightening 854adj.
awfully
greatly 32adv.
awkward
unconformable 84adj.
young 130adj.
unwieldy 195adj.
ignorant 491adj.
foolish 499adj.
inelegant 576adj.
inexpedient 643adj.
clumsy 695adj.
difficult 700adj.
quarreling 709adj.
annoying 827adj.
ill-bred 847adj.
graceless 842adj.
ridiculous 849adj.

modest 874adj.
awkward age
youth 130n.
awkward squad
bungler 697n.
awl
sharp point 256n.
perforator 263n.
awn
prickle 256n.
roughness 259n.
awning
canopy 226n.
screen 421n.
awry
orderless 61adj.
oblique 220adj.
distorted 246adj.
evil 616adj.
amiss 616adj.
ax
shorten 204vb.
sharp edge 256n.
dismiss 300vb.
killer 362n.
ax 723n.
means of execution 964n.
ax-grinder
planner 623n.
egotist 932n.
axial
central 225adj.
directed 281adj.
axiom
certainty 473n.
premise 475n.
axiom 496n.
axis
pivot 218n.
centrality 225n.
rotator 315n.
gauge 465n.
association 706n.
society 708n.
axle
rotator 315n.
axle-load
weighment 322n.
metrology 465n.
ayah
protector 660n.
domestic 742n.
keeper 749n.
aye
perpetuity 115n.
ayes, the
assenter 488n.
ayurvedic
medical 658adj.
azalea
tree 366n.
azimuth
horizontality 216n.
compass point 281n.
azoic
inorganic 359adj.
azotic
toxic 653adj.
azure
blueness 435n.
heraldry 547n.
azygous
alone 88adj.

B

ba
analogue 18n.
spirit 447n.
mythic god 966n.
baa
ululation 409n.
ululate 409vb.
babble
flow 350vb.
sound faint 401vb.
reason ill 477vb.
be foolish 499vb.
be insane 503vb.
empty talk 515n.
mean nothing 515vb.
language 557n.
chatter 581n.
babbler
bird 365n.
fool 501n.
babe
ignoramus 493n.
ninny 501n.
darling 890n.
innocent 935n.
(*see* baby)
Babel
confusion 61n.
discord 411n.
unmeaningness 515n.
language 557n.
baboon
monkey 365n.
eyesore 842n.
babu
male 372n.
recorder 549n.
baby
child 132n.
infantine 132adj.
weakling 163n.
weak 163adj.
little 196adj.
mandate 751n.
please 826vb.
coward 856n.
(*see* babe)
baby-clothes
clothing 228n.
robe 228n.
babyhood
beginning 68n.
youth 130n.
helplessness 161n.
babyish
infantine 132adj.
weak 163adj.
foolish 499adj.
cowardly 856adj.
baby-sit
look after 457vb.
baby-sitter
servant 742n.
keeper 749n.
baccalaureate
academic title 870n.
baccarat
card game 837n.
bacchanal
drunkard 949n.
bacchanalia
sensualism 944n.
drunkenness 949n.
bacchante
madman 504n.
drunkard 949n.
bacchic
disorderly 61adj.
frenzied 503adj.
bacchius
prosody 593n.
Bacchus
Olympian god 967n.
bachelor
male 372n.
independent 744adj.
celibate 895adj.
bachelor girl
woman 373n.
spinster 895n.
bacillus
animalcule 196n.
infection 651n.
poison 659n.
back
change 143vb.
supporter 218n.
be inverted 221vb.
line 227vb.
rear 238n.
back 238adj.
contraposition 240n.
camber 253n.
ride 267vb.
navigate 269vb.
deviate 282vb.
regress 286vb.
backward 286adv.
harden 326vb.
blow 352vb.
break in 369vb.
choose 605vb.
gamble 618vb.
interceptor 702n.

aid, patronize 703vb.
approve 923vb.
back and fill
be irresolute 601vb.
back-bencher
inferior 35n.
councillor 692n.
commoner 869n.
backbite
defame 926vb.
backbone
essential part 5n.
vigorousness 174n.
supporter 218n.
pillar 218n.
centrality 225n.
rear 238n.
resolution 599n.
stamina 600n.
courage 855n.
backbreaking
laborious 682adj.
backchat
answer 460n.
slang 560n.
witticism 839n.
sauciness 878n.
backcloth
spectacle 445n.
stage-set 594n.
backdoor
rear 238n.
doorway 263n.
means of escape 667n.
stealthy 525adj.
back down
regress 286vb.
tergiversate 603vb.
relinquish 621vb.
backdrop
spectacle 445n.
stage-set 594n.
backer
stage manager 594n.
gambler 618n.
patron 707n.
lender 784n.
friend 880n.
back-fire
reversion 148n.
counteraction 182n.
bang 402n., vb.
backgammon
board game 837n.
background
concomitant 89n.
accompanying 89adj.
distance 199n.
circumjacence 230n.
rear 238n.
spectacle 445n.
stage-set 594n.
ornamentation 844n.
background, in the
rearwards 238adv.
latent 523adj.
backing
lining 227n.
(*see* back)
back-lash
counteraction 182n.
recoil 280n.
backlog
store 632n.
back number
archaism 127n.
back out
regress 286vb.
tergiversate 603vb.
resign 753vb.
not observe 769vb.
back-pedal
retard 278vb.
backrest
supporter 218n.
backroom
latent 523adj.
hiding-place 527n.
back-scratcher
toady 879n.
back-scratching
cooperation 706n.
flattery 925n.
back seat
inferiority 35n.
backseat driver
spectator 441n.
director 690n.
adviser 691n.
backset
cultivate 370vb.
backside
rear 238n.
buttocks 238n.
back-slapping
ostentation 875n.
friendly 880adj.
sociability 882n.
sociable 882adj.
backslide
revert 148vb.
tergiversate 603vb.
relapse 657vb.
be wicked 934vb.
be impious 980vb.
backslider
tergiversator 605n.
offender 904n.
bad man 938n.
backstaff
gauge 465n.
backstage
rear 238n.
stage-set 594n.
on stage 594adv.
backstairs
hiding-place 527n.
back street
dilapidation 655n.
backswept
back 238adj.
back-talk
answer 460n.
witticism 839n.
sauciness 878n.
back to back
rearward 238adv.
in league 708adv.
back-to-front
inverted 221adj.
back to the wall, with one's
endangered 661adj.
backward
late 136adj.
rearward 238adv.
backwards
backwards 286adv.
regressive 286adj.
ignorant 491adj.
unintelligent 499adj.
unwilling 598adj.
avoiding 620adj.
deteriorated 655adj.
unprepared 670adj.
immature 670adj.
unskillful 695adj.
artless 699adj.
backwardation
discount 810n.
backward-looking
retrospective 125adj.
regressive 286adj.
backward and forwards
in exchange 151adv.
to and fro 317adv.
backwash
effect 157n.
water travel 269n.
eddy, wave 350n.
back-water
retard 278vb.
regress 286vb.
seclusion 883n.
backwoodsman
dweller 191n.
backyard
place 185n.
bacon
meat 301n.
bacteria
animalcule 196n.
infection 651n.
poison 659n.
bactericide
prophylactic 658n.
bacteriology
pathology 651n.
bad
inferior 35adj.
decomposed 51adj.
fetid 397adj.

feeble 572adj.
evil 616adj.
unimportant 639adj.
bad 645adj.
imperfect 647adj.
insalubrious 653adj.
deteriorated 655adj.
adverse 731adj.
disreputable 867adj.
wrong 914adj.
dishonest 930adj.
wicked 934adj.
bad blood
dislike 861n.
hatred 888n.
malevolence 898n.
bad business
hopelessness 853n.
bad cess
ill fortune 731n.
bad character
bad man 938n.
bad conscience
guilt 936n.
penitence 939n.
bad egg
fetor 397n.
bad man 938n.
bad faith
falsehood 541n.
non-observance 769n.
perfidy 930n.
badge
heraldry 547n.
badge 547n.
badge of rank 743n.
jewelry 844n.
badger
torment 827vb.
bad hand
bungler 697n.
bad hat
bad man 938n.
badinage
witticism 839n.
ridicule 851n.
bad job
bungling 695n.
hopelessness 853n.
bad language
rudeness 885n.
scurrility 899n.
bad light
detraction 926n.
bad lot
bad man 938n.
bad luck
chance 159n.
disappointment 509n.
non-design 618n.
ill fortune 731n.
badly off
unprosperous 731adj.
poor 801adj.
bad man
bad man 938n.
badminton
ball game 837n.
bad name
disrepute 867n.
badness
(*see* bad)
bad odor
fetor 397n.
disrepute 867n.
bad patch
difficulty 700n.
adversity 731n.
bad taste
inelegance 576n.
bad taste 847n.
bad-tempered
sullen 893adj.
bad terms, on
quarreling 709adj.
inimical 881adj.
bad to worse, from
in adversity 731adv.
(*see* aggravation)
bad way, in a
deteriorated 655adj.
endangered 661adj.
bad wishes
malediction 899n.
Baedeker
itinerary 267n.
guide-book 524n.
baffle
be difficult 700vb.
be obstructive 702vb.
oppose 704vb.
defeat 727vb.
be wonderful 864vb.
baffled
impotent 161adj.
puzzled 517adj.
bag
bunch 74n.
stow 187vb.
bag 194n.
bladder 194n.
be convex 253vb.
carrier 273n.
take 786vb.
bagatelle
trifle 639n.
ball game 837n.
bagful
finite quantity 26n.
store 632n.
baggage
youngster 132n
box 194n.
thing transferred 272n.
encumbrance 702n.
property 777n.
loose woman 952n.
baggy
non-adhesive 49adj.
spacious 183adj.
recipient 194adj.
large 195adj.
broad 205adj.
pendent 217adj.
bagman
inquirer 459n.
peddler 794n.
bagnio
brothel 951n.
bagpipes
flute 414n.
bags
great quantity 32n.
trousers 228n.
bail
transpose 272vb.
void 300vb.
security 767n.
legal process 959n.
bailee
consignee 754n.
possessor 776n.
bailie
officer 741n.
bailiff
manager 690n.
officer 741n.
retainer 742n.
consignee 754n.
law officer 955n.
bailiwick
district 184n.
jurisdiction 955n.
bail, on
pledged 767adj.
accused 928adj.
bailor
security 767n.
bairn
child 132n.
bait
attraction 291n.
attract 291vb.
trickery 524n.
trap 542n.
ensnare 542vb.
incentive 612n.
tempt 612vb.
chase 619n.
torment 827vb.
excite love 887vb.
enrage 891vb.
reward 962n.
baize
textile 222n.
bake
cook 301vb.
be hot 379vb.
heat 381vb.
bakehouse
cookery 301n.
baker

cookery 301n.
provider 633n.
bakers' dozen
over five 99n.
undueness 916n.
bakery
cookery 301n.
baking-powder
leaven 323n.
baksheesh
incentive 612n.
acquisition 771n.
gift 781n.
reward 962n.
balalaika
harp 414n.
balance
relate 9vb.
correlate 12vb.
adjust 24vb.
equilibrium 28n.
average 30n.
offset 31n.
set off 31vb.
remainder 41n.
part 53n.
completeness 54n.
stability 153n.
stabilize 153vb.
symmetry 245n.
scales 322n.
weigh 322vb.
compare 462vb.
gauge 465n.
measure 465vb.
sagacity 498n.
elegance 575n.
be irresolute 601vb.
mid-course 625n.
be half-way 625vb.
superfluity 637n.
account 808vb.
inexcitability 823n.
caution 858n.
balance of power
defense 713n.
balances
funds 797n.
credit 802n.
balance sheet
accounts 808n.
balancing act
equivocalness 518n.
compromise 770n.
balas
gem 844n.
balbutiate
stammer 580vb.
balcony
lobby 194n.
projection 254n.
theater 594n.
bald
hairless 229adj.
smooth 258adj.
veracious 540adj.
feeble 572adj.
plain 573adj.
tedious 838adj.
impure 951adj.
baldachin
canopy 226n.
altar 990n.
balderdash
silly talk 515n.
baldness
bareness 229n.
veracity 540n.
feebleness 572n.
plainness 573n.
baldric
outline 233n.
loop 250n.
bale
bunch 74n.
stow 187vb.
receptacle 194n.
cultivate 370vb.
evil 616n.
bale-fire
fire 379n.
signal light 420n.
signal 547n.
baleful
harmful 645adj.
malevolent 898adj.
bale out
fly 271vb.
emerge 298vb.
baler
ladle 194n.
irrigator 341n.
farm tool 370n.
balize
signal 547n.
balk
beam 218n.
partition 231n.
disappointment 509n.
disappoint 509vb.
materials 631n.
be obstructive 702vb.
ball
sphere 252n.
round 252vb.
missile 287n.
missile weapon 723n.
ammunition 723n.
dancing 837n.
plaything 837n.
social gathering 882n.
ballad
vocal music 412n.
ballade
verse form 593n.
balladry
poetry 593n.
doggerel 593n.
ballast
offset 31n.
compensate 31vb.
gravity 322n.
wisdom 498n.
safeguard 662n.
ballerina
jumper 312n.
actor 594n.
dancing 837n.
ballet
composition 56n.
stage play 594n.
dancing 837n.
balletomane
crank 504n.
playgoer 594n.
ball game
ball game 837n.
ballistics
propulsion 287n.
art of war 718n.
arm 723n.
ballon d'essai
empiricism 461n.
balloon
bladder 194n.
expand 197vb.
sphere 252n.
round 252vb.
be convex 253vb.
airship 276n.
be light 323vb.
balloonist
aeronaut 271n.
ballot
affirmation 532n.
vote 605n.
ball-player
player 837n.
ballroom
place of amusement 837n.
ball up
bedevil 63vb.
ballyhoo
loudness 400n.
overestimation 482n.
advertisement 528n.
exaggeration 546n.
balm
moderator 177n.
lubricant 334n.
scent 396n.
balm, medicine 658n.
pleasurableness 826n.
balmoral
headgear 228n.
balmy
warm 379adj.
fragrant 396adj.
palmy 730adj.
cheering 833adj.
balneal

watery 339adj.
cleansing 648adj.
balneation
water 339n.
moistening 341n.
ablution 648n.
baloney
empty talk 515n.
falsehood 541n.
balsam
balm 658n.
balsamic
remedial 658adj.
relieving 831adj.
balustrade
handle 218n.
pillar 218n.
fence 235n.
bambino
child 132n.
bamboo
tree 366n.
bamboozle
puzzle 474vb.
keep secret 525vb.
befool 542vb.
deceive 542vb.
bamboozler
trickster 545n.
ban
exclusion 57n.
exclude 57vb.
publication 528n.
proclaim 528vb.
hindrance 702n.
obstruct 702vb.
command 737n., vb.
restraint 747n.
restrain 747vb.
prohibition 757n.
prohibit 757vb.
make unwelcome 823vb.
malediction 899n.
disapprobation 924n.
disapprove 924vb.
condemn 961vb.
penalty 963n.
banal
usual 610adj.
dull 840adj.
banality
maxim 496n.
banana
fruit 301n.
band
ligature 47n.
bond, girdle 47n.
band 74n.
congregate 74vb.
compressor 198n.
strip 208n.
outline 233n.
loop 250n.
orchestra 413n.
striation 437n.
personnel 686n.
cooperate 607vb.
party 708n.
formation 722n.
bandage
tie 45vb.
ligature 47n.
compressor 198n.
make smaller 198vb.
strip 208n.
supporter 218n.
support 218vb.
wrapping 226n.
cover 226vb.
cure 656vb.
surgical dressing 658n.
doctor 658vb.
obstruct 702vb.
relieve 831vb.
bandanna
neckwear 228n.
bandbox
box 194n.
band-conductor
orchestra 413n.
leader 690n.
bandeau
hairdressing 843n.
banderole
girdle 47n.
flag 547n.
bandicoot
rodent 365n.
bandit
revolter 738n.
robber 789n.
outcaste 883n.
banditry
brigandage 788n.
band-leader
timekeeper 117n.
orchestra 413n.
band-master
orchestra 413n.
band of brothers
community 708n.
close friend 880n.
bandolier
girdle 47n.
belt 228n.
loop 250n.
arsenal 723n.
bands
canonicals 989n.
bandsman
orchestra 413n.
bandy
deformed 246adj.
bandy about
publish 528vb.
bandy arguments
argue 475vb.
bandy words
interchange 151vb.
converse 584vb.
bane
evil 616n.
badness 645n.
plague 651n.
bane 659n.
pitfall 663n.
adversity 731n.
painfulness 827n.
hateful object 888n.
wrong 914n.
baneful
(*see* bane)
bang
be vigorous 174vb.
hair 259n.
close 264vb.
impulse, knock 279n.
impel, strike 279vb.
loudness 400n.
be loud 400vb.
bang 402n., vb.
hair-dressing 843n.
banger
meat 301n.
bangle
jewelry 844n.
banian
vest 228n.
bodywear 228n.
lender 784n.
merchant 794n.
banish
exclude 57vb.
displace 188vb.
eject 300vb.
make unwelcome 883vb.
banishment
seclusion 883n.
penalty 963n.
banjo
harp 414n.
banjoist
instrumentalist 413n.
bank
high land 209n.
seat 218n.
acclivity 220n.
be oblique 220vb.
edge 234n.
laterality 239n.
shore 344n.
storage 632n.
store 632vb.
treasurer 798n.
treasury 799n.
bank account
wealth 800n.
bank down
extinguish 382vb.

banker
lender 784n.
merchant 794n.
treasurer 798n.
card game 837n.
banknote
title-deed 767n.
paper money 797n.
bank on
hope 852vb.
bankrupt
losing 772adj.
fleece 786vb.
poor man 801n.
poor 801adj.
non-payer 805n.
non-paying 805adj.
bankruptcy
insufficiency 636n.
failure 728n.
non-observance 769n.
loss 772n.
insolvency 805n.
banlieu
near place 200n.
circumjacence 230n.
banner
advertisement 528n.
flag 547n.
banneret
flag 547n.
nobleman 868n.
bannister(s)
pillar 218n.
fence 235n.
bannock
pastry 301n.
banns
marriage 894n.
banquet
feasting 301n.
eat, feed 301vb.
plenty 635n.
revel 837vb.
festivity 837n.
social gathering 882n.
banquette
stand 218n.
fortification 713n.
banshee
demon 970n.
bant
decrease 37vb.
make smaller 198vb.
make thin 206vb.
be temperate 942vb.
starve 946vb.
bantam
animalcule 196n.
bantam-weight
pugilist 722n.
banter
witticism 839n.
be witty 839vb.
ridicule 851n., vb.
sauciness 878n.
abstainer 942n.
banterer
humorist 839n.
banting
dieting 301n.
fasting 946n.
bantling
child 132n.
descendant 170n.
banyan
tree 366n.
baptism
reception 299n.
immersion 303n.
moistening 341n.
nomenclature 561n.
preparation 669n.
Christian rite 988n.
baptismal
admitting 299adj.
ritual 988adj.
Baptist
Protestant 976n.
baptistery
ritual object 988n.
church interior 990n.
church utensil 990n.
baptize
auspicate 68vb.
admit 299vb.
immerse 303vb.
drench 341vb.
name 561vb.
make pious 979vb.
perform ritual 988vb.
bar
in deduction 39adv.
fastening 47n.
exclusion 57n.
exclude 57vb.
tavern 192n.
chamber 194n.
line 203n.
barrier 235n.
stopper 264n.
close 264vb.
island 349n.
notation 410n.
safeguard 662n.
obstruct 702vb.
restraint 747n.
restrain 747vb.
lock-up 748n.
bullion 797n.
disapprobation 924n.
disapprove 924vb.
tribunal 956n.
bar 958n.
barb
filament 208n.
sharp point 256n.
sharpen 256vb.
thoroughbred 273n.
missile weapon 723n.
barbarian
foreigner 59n.
extraneous 59adj.
destroyer 168n.
violent creature 176n.
vulgarian 847n.
vulgar 847adj.
low fellow 869n.
plebeian 869adj.
rude person 885n.
ruffian 904n.
barbarism
neology 560n.
solecism 565n.
bad taste 847n.
inhumanity 898n.
barbarity
violence 176n.
cruel act 898n.
inhumanity 898n.
barbarize
pervert 655vb.
barbarous
(*see* barbarian, barbarism)
barbecue
meal, feasting 301n.
festivity 837n.
social gathering 882n.
barbed shaft
ridicule 851n.
barbed wire
sharp point 256n.
obstacle 702n.
defenses 713n.
barber
cleaner 648n.
doctor 658n.
beautician 843n.
barbette
fortification 713n.
barbican
fort 713n.
barbiturate
moderator 177n.
soporific 679n.
barcarole
vocal music 712n.
bard
meat 301n.
cook 301vb.
musician 413n.
poet 593n.
bare
inconsiderable 33adj.
simple 44adj.
weakened 163adj.
demolish 165vb.
empty 190adj.
uncovered 229adj.
uncover 229vb.
open 263vb.

dry 342adj.
undisguised 522adj.
disclose 526vb.
plain 573adj.
unprovided 636adj.
vulnerable 661adj.

barefaced
undisguised 522adj.
false 541adj.

barefoot
uncovered 229adj.
beggarly 801adj.

barehanded
defenseless 161adj.

bare-headed
uncovered 229adj.
respectful 920adj.

barely
almost 33adv.
slightly 33adv.
imperfectly 647adv.

bare minimum
needfulness 627n.
dueness 915n.

bareness
emptiness 190n.
bareness 229n.
plainness 573n.

bargain
consensus 488n.
compact 765n.
contract 765vb.
make terms 766vb.
trade 791n.
bargain 791vb.
purchase 792n.
cheapness 812n.
be parsimonious 816vb.

barge
boat 275n.

barge in
intrude 297vb.
encroach 306vb.

bargeman
boatman 270n.

baritone
resonance 404n.
vocalist 413n.

bark
layer 207n.
skin 226n.
uncover 229vb.
sailing-ship 275n.
cry 408vb.
ululation 409n.
anger 891n.
be irascible 892vb.
sullenness 893n.
threat 900n.
threaten 900vb.

barker
overestimation 482n.
publicizer 528n.
petitioner 763n.
commender 923n.

barkless
smooth 258adj.

barley
cereal 301n.
provender 301n.
corn 366n.

barm
cookery 301n.
leaven 323n.
bubble 355n.

barman
servant 742n.

Barmecidal feast
fasting 946n.

barmy
light 323adj.
unintelligent 499adj.

barn
small house 192n.
farm tool 370n.
storage 632n.
store 632vb.

barnacle
coherence 48n.

barnstorm
act 594vb.
be affected 850vb.

barogram
pneumatics 340n.

barograph
altimetry 209n.
pneumatics 340n.
weather 340n.

barometer
pneumatics 340n.
weather 340n.
meter 465n.

baron
nobleman 868n.
judge 957n.

baronet
nobleman 868n.

baronetcy
honors 866n.
aristocracy 868n.

baronial
noble 868adj.

baroque
school of painting 553n.
ornamental 844adj.

baroscope
pneumatics 340n.

barouche
carriage 274n.

barque
sailing-ship 275n.

barrack
quarters 192n.
be obstructive 702vb.
lock-up 748n.

barracker
hinderer 702n.
detractor 926n.

barrage
roll 403n.
bombardment 712n.
defenses 713n.

barrage-balloon
defenses 713n.
air force 722n.

barranca
high land 209n.
valley 255n.
conduit 351n.

barrator
offender 904n.

barratry
improbity 930n.

barrel
vat 194n.
cylinder 252n.

barrel organ
organ 414n.

barren
impotent 161adj.
unproductive 172adj.
profitless 641adj.

barricade
barrier 235n.
obstruct 702vb.
defenses 713n.
defend 713vb.

barricades
revolt 738n.

barrier
exclusion 57n.
barrier 235n.
obstacle 702n.
defenses 713n.

barrister
lawyer 958n.

barrow
monticle 209n.
pushcart 274n.
tomb 364n.
monument 548n.
shop 796n.

barrow-boy
seller 793n.
peddler 794n.

bar-tender
servant 742n.

barter
equivalence 28n.
interchange 151n., vb.
transference 272n.
conditions 766n.
transfer 780n.
convey 780vb.
barter 791n.
trade 791vb.

bartizan
fort 713n.

barytone
punctuation 547n.

basal
undermost 214adj.
supporting 218adj.
base
inferiority 35n.
serial place 73n.
situation 186n.
station 187n.
place 187vb.
abode 192n.
layer 207n.
lowness 210n.
base 214n.
basis 218n.
limit 236n.
heraldry 547n.
bad 645adj.
cowardly 856adj.
disreputable 867adj.
rascally 930adj.
heinous 934adj.
baseball
ball game 837n.
base-born
plebeian 869adj.
baseless
unreal 2adj.
baseline
place 185n.
base 214n.
basement
cellar 194n.
base 214n.
baseness
disrepute 867n.
improbity 930n.
bash
strike 279vb.
bashaw
(*see* pasha)
bashful
unwilling 598adj.
cowardly 856adj.
modest 874adj.
bashi-bazouk
soldier 722n.
basic
intrinsic 5adj.
simple 44adj.
fundamental 156adj.
undermost 214adj.
important 639adj.
basics
reality 1n.
basilica
church 990n.
basilisk
rara avis 84n.
reptile 365n.
eye 438n.
gun 723n.
noxious animal 904n.
basin
stable 192n.
bowl 194n.
cavity 255n.
lake 346n.
plain 348n.
conduit 351n.
basinet
armor 713n.
basis
basis 218n.
base 214n.
bask
enjoy 376vb.
be hot 379vb.
be pleased 824vb.
basket
basket 194n.
basque
bodywear 228n.
edging 234n.
bas relief
relievo 254n.
bass
table fish 365n.
resonance 404n.
vocalist 413n.
basset
layer 207n.
bassinet
basket 194n.
bed 218n.
pushcart 274n.
bassoon
flute 414n.
bassoonist
instrumentalist 413n.
bast
ligature 47n.
fiber 208n.
bastard
spurious 542adj.
unwarranted 916adj.
cad 938n.
bastard 954adj.
bastardize
disentitle 916vb.
make illegal 954vb.
bastardy
sonship 170n.
undueness 916n.
bastardy 954n.
baste
tie 45vb.
strike 279vb.
cook 301vb.
moisten 341vb.
pinguefy 357vb.
bastille
prison 748n.
bastinado
corporal punishment 963n.
flog 963vb.
bastion
protection 660n.
fortification 713n.
bat
velocity 277n.
hammer 279n.
strike 279vb.
propel 287vb.
bird 365n.
language 557n.
club 723n.
batch
finite quantity 26n.
group 74n.
bate
bate 37vb.
moderate 177vb.
bated breath
aphony 578n.
make smaller 198vb.
blunt 257vb.
discount 810vb.
bated breath, with
faintly 401adv.
expectantly 507adv.
voicelessly 578adv.
bath
vessel 194n.
immersion 303n.
water 339n.
moistening 341n.
ablution 648n.
bath-chair
pushcart 274n.
bathe
swim 269vb.
immerse 303vb.
plunge 313vb.
be wet, drench 341vb.
clean 648vb.
amuse oneself 837vb.
bath-house
chamber 194n.
ablution 648n.
bathing beach
pleasure-ground 837n.
bathing beauty
sea nymph 343n.
bathing costume
beachwear 228n.
bathos
absurdity 497n.
ridiculousness 849n.
bathrobe
informal dress 228n.
bathroom
chamber 194n.
ablution 648n.
baths
hospital 658n.
bath salts
cosmetic 843n.
bathymeter
depth 211n.
oceanography 343n.
bathyphilous

deep 211adj.
bathyscaphe
depth 211n.
oceanography 343n.
bathysphere
depth 211n.
diver 313n.
oceanography 343n.
batman
domestic 742n.
baton
supporter 218n.
badge 547n.
badge of rule 743n.
batrachian
frog 365n.
animal 365n., adj.
bats
crazed 503adj.
battalion
formation 722n.
battalions
multitude 104n.
battels
accounts 808adj.
batten
fastening 47n.
batten down
close 264vb.
batten on
eat 301vb.
prosper 730vb.
be servile 879vb.
battens
theater 594n.
batter
demolish 165vb.
obliquity 220n.
deform 244vb.
distort 246vb.
strike, collide 279vb.
pulpiness 356n.
batterie
musical instrument 414n.
battering-ram
ram 279n.
club 723n.
battery
electricity 160n.
storage 632n.
formation 722n.
gun 723n.
battle
slaughter 362n.
exert oneself 682vb.
fight 716n.
contend 716vb.
battle 718n.
give battle 718vb.
exertion 862n.
battle-ax
sharp edge 256n.
ax 723n.
shrew 892n.
battle-cry
call 547n.
defiance 711n.
war, warfare 718n.
threat 900n.
battledore and shuttlecock
interchange 151n.
ball game 837n.
battle dress
uniform 228n.
battlefield
slaughter-house 362n.
battle 718n.
battleground 724n.
battleground
casus belli 709n.
fight 716n.
battle 718n.
battleground 724n.
battlement
summit 213n.
notch 260n.
fortification 713n.
battler
opponent 705n.
contender 716n.
combatant 722n.
battleship
warship 722n.
battology
repetition 106n.
battue
slaughter 362n.
chase 619n.
terror tactics 712n.
batty
crazed 503adj.
bauble
trifle 639n.
bauble 639n.
plaything 837n.
finery 844n.
baulk
(*see* balk)
bawd
provider 633n.
bawd 952n.
bawdry
impurity 951n.
bawdy-house
brothel 951n.
bawl
cry 408n., vb.
vociferate 408vb.
bawling out
reproach 924n.
bay
compartment 194n.
curve 248n.
cavity 255n.
horse 273n.
potherb 301n.
gulf 345n.
tree 366n.
ululate 409vb.
brown 430adj.
defeat 727vb.
Bayard
brave person 855n.
gentleman 929n.
bay, at
endangered 661adj.
in difficulties 700adj.
defensively 713adv.
bayonet
strike 279vb.
kill 362vb.
foin 712n.
strike at 712vb.
side-arms 723n.
bayou
gulf 345n.
lake 346n.
bays
badge 547n.
trophy 729n.
honors 866n.
bazaar
sale 793n.
shop 796n.
emporium 796n.
bazooka
gun 723n.
missile weapon 723n.
be
be 1vb.
be situate 186vb.
be true 494vb.
beach
edge 234n.
land 295vb.
shore 344n.
arena 724n.
beachcomber
wanderer 268n.
wave 350n.
beachhead
battleground 724n.
retention 778n.
beachwear
beachwear 228n.
aquatics 269n.
beacon
signal light 420n.
telecommunication 531n.
heraldry 547n.
signal 547n.
warning 664n.
danger signal 665n.
bead
sphere 252n.
trimming 844n.
decorate 844vb.
beading
ornamental art 844n.

beadle
officer 741n.
law officer 955n.
church officer 986n.
beadledom
habit 610n.
governance 733n.
beadroll
list 87n.
prayers 981n.
ritual object 988n.
office-book 988n.
beadsman
retainer 742n.
dependent 742n.
recipient 782n.
worshiper 981n.
beady
rotund 252adj.
beagle
dog 365n.
hunt 619vb.
beak
prow 237n.
projection 254n.
teacher 537n.
magistracy 957n.
beaked
curved 248adj.
beaker
cup 194n.
be-all and end-all
all 52n.
intention 617n.
important matter 638n.
beam
beam 218n.
laterality 239n.
direction 281n.
scales 322n.
radiation 417n.
flash 417n.
radiate 417vb.
materials 631n.
directorship 689n.
be cheerful 833vb.
smile 835vb.
be beautiful 841vb.
beam-ends, on one's
grounded 728adj.
beam, off the
irrelevant 10adj.
deviating 282adj.
mistaken 495adj.
beam, on the
straight 249adv.
in flight 271adv.
beamy
broad 205adj.
luminous 417adj.
bean
small coin 33n.
head 213n.
plant 366n.
beanery
café 192n.
beanfeast
feasting 301n.
meal 301n.
beany
headgear 228n.
bear
reproduce itself 164vb.
be fruitful 171vb.
compressor 198n.
support 218vb.
carry 273vb.
orientate 281vb.
animal 365n.
gambler 618n.
speculate 791vb.
seller 793n.
cheapen 812vb.
feel 818vb.
be patient 823vb.
suffer 825vb.
rude person 885n.
shrew 892n.
bearable
imperfect 647adj.
contenting 828adj.
bear a hand
aid 703vb.
beard
filament 208n.
prickle 256n.
hair 259n.
print-type 587n.
defy 711vb.
be courageous 855vb.
beardless
young 130adj.
hairless 229adj.
bear down
approach 289vb.
charge 712vb.
bearer
bearer 273n.
domestic 742n.
bear fruit
reproduce itself 164vb.
be useful 640vb.
be successful 727vb.
beargarden
turmoil 61n.
arena 724n.
bear hard
be violent 176vb.
ill-treat 645vb.
be severe 735vb.
bearing
relation 9n.
supporter 218n.
pivot 218n.
bearing 273adj.
direction 281n.
meaning 514n.
conduct 688n.
owed 803adj.
feeling 818adj.
bearings
circumstance 8n.
bearings 186n.
bearish
salable 793adj.
cheap 812adj.
ungracious 885adj.
bear-leader
teacher 537n.
bear off
deviate 282vb.
take away 786vb.
bear oneself
behave 688vb.
bear out
corroborate 466vb.
demonstrate 478vb.
vindicate 927vb.
bear-pit
cattle pen 369n.
bearskin
headgear 228n.
armor 713n.
bear up
support 218vb.
elevate 310vb.
resist 715vb.
bear upon
be related 9vb.
operate 173vb.
influence 178vb.
bear with
be patient 823vb.
forgive 909vb.
beast
violent creature 176n.
animal 365n.
dirty person 649n.
eyesore 842n.
ruffian 904n.
noxious animal 904n.
cad 938n.
beastly
extremely 32adv.
animal 365adj.
not nice 645adj.
unpleasant 827adj.
ugly 842adj.
discourteous 885adj.
hateful 888adj.
sensual 944adj.
beast of burden
beast of burden 273n.
worker 686n.
beast of prey
killer 362n.
animal 365n.
taker 786n.
noxious animal 904n.
beat
be superior 34vb.

inferior 35adj.
periodicity 141n.
be periodic 141vb.
territory 184n.
place 185n.
impulse 279n.
strike 279vb.
pass 305vb.
outdo 306vb.
oscillation 317n.
oscillate 317vb.
agitate 318vb.
pulverize 332vb.
roll 403vb.
tempo 410n.
play music 413vb.
prosody 593n.
route 624n.
clean 648vb.
use 673vb.
attack 712vb.
defeat 727vb.
reprove 924vb.
spank 963vb.
beat about the bush
sophisticate 477vb.
dissemble 541vb.
be diffuse 570vb.
circuit 626vb.
beat down
cheapen 812vb.
beaten track
habit 610n.
route 624n.
use 673n.
beatific
good 615adj.
pleasurable 826adj.
paradisiac 971adj.
beatify
please 826vb.
dignify 866vb.
sanctify 979vb.
ecclesiasticize 985vb.
beating
knock 279n.
chase 619n.
victory 727n.
defeat 728n.
corporal punishment 963n.
beat it
decamp 296vb.
beatitude
happiness 824n.
beat it up
revel 837vb.
beatnik
loser 728n.
lower classes 869n.
beat of drum
publication 528n.
danger signal 665n.
beat off
repel 292vb.
beat one's brains
think 449vb.
beat, on the
synchronous 123adj.
synchronously 123adv.
beat the air
waste effort 641vb.
beat the bounds
limit 236vb.
traverse 267vb.
measure 465vb.
beat the record
be superior 34vb.
beat time
time 117vb.
play music 413vb.
beat up
strike 279vb.
thicken 354vb.
attack 712vb.
beau
male 372n.
fop 848n.
lover 887n.
Beaufort scale
anemology 352n.
beau ideal
paragon 646n.
a beauty 841n.
beau monde
beau monde 848n.
beautician
beautician 843n.
beautification
beautification 843n.
beautiful
elegant 575adj.
pleasurable 826adj.
beautiful 841adj.
beautified 843adj.
lovable 887adj.
beautify
ornament 574vb.
make better 654vb.
beautify 841vb.
primp 843vb.
decorate 844vb.
beautiless
ugly 842adj.
beauty
symmetry 245n.
beauty 641n.
a beauty 641n.
(*see* beautiful)
masterpiece 694n.
beauty parlor
beauty parlor 843n.
beauty specialist
beautician 843n.
beauty treatment
beautification 843n.
beaux yeux
beauty 841n.
beaver
headgear 228n.
hair 259n.
rodent 365n.
busy person 678n.
worker 686n.
armor 713n.
bebop
music 412n.
because
causally 156adv.
hence 158adv.
beck
stream 350n.
gesture 547n.
gesticulate 547vb.
command 737n.
beck and call, at one's
aiding 703adj.
obedient 739adj.
serving 742adj.
beckon
gesticulate 547vb.
become
become 1vb.
be turned to 147vb.
beautify 841vb.
be one's duty 917vb.
becoming
existence 1n.
appearance 445n.
personable 841adj.
bed
unite with 45vb.
place 187vb.
layer 207n.
base 214n.
basis 218n.
bed 218n.
resting place 266n.
garden 370n.
sleep 679n., vb.
bed and board
provision 633n.
marriage 894n.
bedbug
vermin 365n.
bed-clothes
coverlet 226n.
bedel
officer 741n.
(*see* beadle)
bedesman
(*see* beadsman)
bedevil
bedevil 63vb.
incommode 827vb.
diabolize 969vb.
bedevilment
spell 983n.
bedew
moisten 341vb.
bed-hopper
libertine 952n.

bedim
darken 418vb.
bedim 419vb.
make unclean 649vb.
bedizen
dress 228vb.
decorate 844vb.
bedizened
bedecked 844adj.
vulgar 847adj.
bedlam
confusion 61n.
turmoil 61n.
discord 411n.
madhouse 503n.
bedlamite
madman 504n.
bed of roses
euphoria 376n.
fragrance 396n.
bedouin
dweller 191n.
wanderer 268n.
bed out
cultivate 370vb.
bed-pan
vessel 194n.
latrine 649n.
bedraggled
orderless 61adj.
dirty 649adj.
bedridden
sick 651adj.
bedrock
reality 1n.
simpleness 44n.
permanence 144n.
source 156n.
base 214n.
basis 218n.
chief thing 638n.
important 638adj.
bedroom
chamber 194n.
bedside manner
therapy 658n.
bed-time
clock time 117n.
evening 129n.
vespertine 129adj.
bee
fly 365n.
beech
tree 366n.
beechy
arboreal 366adj.
beef
vitality 162n.
meat 301n.
be discontented 829vb.
beef-witted
unthinking 450adj.
unintelligent 499adj.
beefy
stalwart 162adj.
fleshy 195adj.
beehive
crowd 74n.
dome 253n.
stock farm 369n.
bee in the bonnet
whim 604n.
bee-keeper
breeder 369n.
bee-line
short distance 200n.
straightness 249n.
direction 281n.
mid-course 625n.
Beelzebub
devil 969n.
beer
liquor 301n.
beer and skittles
enjoyment 824n.
beery
intoxicating 949adj.
drunken 949adj.
bee-sting
antidote 658n.
beestings
milk 301n.
beeswax
viscidity 354n.
beetle
be high 209vb.
hammer 279n.
fly 365n.
beetlebrow
projection 254n.
beetling
overhanging 209adj.
pendent 217adj.
beetroot
tuber 301n.
befall
happen 154vb.
befit
accord 24vb.
be expedient 642vb.
be due 915vb.
be one's duty 917vb.
befool
puzzle 474vb.
sophisticate 477vb.
mislead 495vb.
disappoint 509vb.
befool 542vb.
humiliate 872vb.
before
fore 64adv.
before 119adv.
retrospectively 125adv.
here 189adv.
in front 237adv.
ahead 283adv.
beforehand
before 119adv.
beforehand 135adv.
befoul
make unclean 649vb.
befriend
patronize 703vb.
befriend 880vb.
be sociable 882vb.
befuddlement
drunkenness 949n.
beg
governor 741n.
beg 761vb.
be parsimonious 816vb.
nobleman 868n.
be servile 879vb.
beg, borrow or steal
find means 629vb.
beget
cause 156vb.
generate 164vb.
vitalize 360vb.
begetter
cause 156n.
producer 167n.
parent 169n.
beggar
wanderer 268n.
idler 679n.
beggar 763n.
recipient 782n.
poor man 801n.
impoverish 801vb.
low fellow 869n.
toady 879n.
beggarly
dirty 649adj.
beggarly 801adj.
disreputable 867adj.
beggary
poverty 801n.
beghard
monk 986n.
begin
become 1vb.
grow 36vb.
begin 68vb.
be born 360vb.
prepare 669vb.
undertake 672n.
begin again
repeat 106vb.
revert 148vb.
begin from
result 157vb.
beginner
beginner 538n.
bungler 697n.
beginning
new 126adj.
earliness 135n.
source 156n.
beg off

mediate 720vb.
deprecate 762vb.
begotten
born 360adj.
beg pardon
beg pardon 909vb.
begrime
bedim 419vb.
make unclean 649vb.
begrudge
be loath 598vb.
refuse 760vb.
beg the question
reason ill 477vb.
beguile
mislead 495vb.
deceive 542vb.
flatter 925vb.
Beguine
nun 986n.
begum
potentate 741n.
nobleman 868n.
behalf
benefit 615n.
behalf, on
on behalf 755adv.
behave
do 676vb.
behave 688vb.
be virtuous 933vb.
behavior
mien 445n.
way 624n.
action 676n.
conduct 688n.
behaviorism
psychology 447n.
morals 917n.
behead
subtract 39vb.
sunder 46vb.
shorten 204vb.
kill 362vb.
execute 963vb.
behest
command 737n.
behind
rear 238n.
rearward 238adv.
behind 284adv.
behind bars
captive 750adj.
behindhand
late 136adj.
behindhand 307adv.
unprepared 670adj.
non-paying 805adj.
behind the scenes
causally 156adv.
invisibly 444adv.
knowing 490adv.
latent 523adj.
behind the times
anachronistic 118adj.
not now 122adv.
antiquated 127adj.
ignorant 491adj.
behind time
anachronistic 118adj.
late 136adj.
behold
see 438vb.
beholden
grateful 907adj.
dutied 917adj.
beholder
spectator 441n.
behoove
be due 915vb.
be one's duty 917vb.
beige
brown 430adj.
being
existence 1n.
self 80n.
life 360n.
affections 817n.
bejewel
beautify 841vb.
primp 843vb.
decorate 844vb.
belabor
strike 279vb.
flog 963vb.
belated
late 136adj.
belay
tie 45vb.
bel canto
vocal music 412n.
belch
repeat 106vb.
vomit 300vb.
respiration 352n.
breathe 352vb.
beldam
old woman 133n.
maternity 169n.
hell-hag 904n.
beleaguer
circumscribe 232adj.
besiege 712vb.
wage war 718vb.
belfry
high structure 209n.
head 213n.
church exterior 990n.
Belial
devil 969n.
belie
negate 533vb.
oppose 704vb.
belief
belief 485n.
religious faith 973n.
piety 979n.
believable
plausible 471adj.
credible 485adj.
believe
assume 471vb.
believe 485vb.
expect 507vb.
believer
religionist 973n.
pietist 979n.
belike
probably 471adv.
Belisha beacon
traffic control 305n.
signal 547n.
belittle
underestimate 483vb.
hold cheap 922vb.
dispraise 924vb.
detract 926vb.
bell
timekeeper 117n.
megaphone 400n.
ululate 409vb.
campanology 412n.
gong 414n.
signal 547n.
church utensil 990n.
belladonna
poisonous plant 659n.
bell, book and candle
malediction 899n.
Christian rite 988n.
belle
a beauty 841n.
fop 848n.
belles lettres
literature 557n.
belletrist
dissertator 591n.
bell-hop
courier 531n.
servant 742n.
bellicose
violent 176adj.
quarreling 709adj.
defiant 711adj.
contending 716adj.
warring 718adj.
courageous 855adj.
boastful 877adj.
insolent 878adj.
bellicosity
irascibility 892n.
(*see* bellicose)
belligerency
belligerency 718n.
enmity 881n.
belligerent
contending 716adj.
warring 718adj.
combatant 722n.
inimical 881adj.
bellman
publicizer 528n.

messenger 531n.
bellow
blow 352vb.
be loud 400vb.
vociferate 408vb.
ululate 409vb.
be angry 891vb.
threaten 900vb.
bellows
sufflation 352n.
respiration 352n.
heater 383n.
voice 577n.
bell-ringer
campanology 412n.
instrumentalist 413n.
officer 741n.
servant 742n.
church officer 986n.
bell the cat
be courageous 855vb.
bell-tower
church exterior 990n.
bell-wether
precursor 66n.
sheep 365n.
leader 690n.
belly
maw 194n.
expand 197vb.
insides 224n.
swelling 253n.
be convex 253vb.
eater 301n.
belly-ache
pang 377n.
indigestion 651n.
be discontented 829vb.
lament 836vb.
belly-band
girdle 47n.
belt 228n.
belly-flop
descent 309n.
plunge 313n.
bellyful
plenitude 54n.
sufficiency 635n.
redundance 637n.
belly-worship
gluttony 947n.
belong
be intrinsic 5vb.
be related 9vb.
accord 24vb.
constitute 56vb.
be one of 58vb.
be included 78vb.
accompany 89vb.
join a party 708vb.
belong 773vb.
belongings
property 777n.
beloved
loved one 887n.
lovable 887adj.
darling 890n.
below
after 65adv.
under 210adv.
below par
under 210adv.
imperfect 647adj.
at a discount 810adv.
below stairs
under 210adv.
plebeian 869adj.
below the belt
unjust 914adj.
below the salt
plebeian 869adj.
below the surface
latent 523adj.
Belsen
slaughter-house 362n.
prison camp 748n.
belt
girdle 47n.
region 184n.
compressor 198n.
belt 228n.
outline 233n.
loop 250n.
badge of rank 743n.
spank 963vb.
scourge 964n.
belvedere
view 438n.
bema
rostrum 539n.
bemedal
decorate 844vb.
dignify 866vb.
bemire
make unclean 649vb.
bemoan
lament 836vb.
bemused
abstracted 456adj.
bench
stand 218n.
seat 218n.
workshop 687n.
badge of rule 743n.
tribunal 956n.
bencher
judge 957n.
lawyer 958n.
bench-mark
limit 236n.
signpost 547n.
bench of bishops
synod 985n.
ecclesiarch 986n.
bend
tie 45vb.
break 46vb.
ligature 47n
derange 63vb.
conform 83vb.
modify 143vb.
force 176vb.
obliquity 220n.
be oblique 220vb.
distortion 246n.
distort 246vb.
angularity 247n.
angulate 247vb.
curve 248n.
make curved 248vb.
twine 251vb.
point to 281vb.
deviation 282n.
deflect 282vb.
stoop 311vb.
soften 327vb.
heraldry 547n.
motivate 612vb.
knuckle under 721vb.
obey 739vb.
be servile 879vb.
greet 884vb.
beneath
less 35adv.
under 210adv.
beneath one
degrading 867adj.
Benedick
spouse 894n.
celibate 895n.
Benedictine
monk 986n.
benediction
good 615n.
thanks 907n.
praise 923n.
prayers 981n.
act of worship 981n.
church service 988n.
benefaction
gift 781n.
liberality 813n.
benefactor
patron 707n.
giver 781n.
good giver 813n.
philanthropist 901n.
benefactor 903n.
good man 937n.
benefice
benefice 985n.
ecclesiasticize 985vb.
beneficence
goodness 644n.
benevolence 897n.
beneficial
good 615adj.
profitable 640adj.
beneficial 644adj.
salubrious 652adj.
remedial 658adj.

gainful 771adj.
beneficiary
beneficiary 776n.
recipient 782n.
benefit
benefit 615n., vb.
utility 640n.
be useful 640vb.
be expedient 642vb.
do good 644vb.
use 673n.
subvention 703n.
trophy 729n.
acquisition 771n.
gain 771n.
gift 781n.
be benevolent 897vb.
benefit of clergy
non-liability 919n.
ecclesiasticism 985n.
benefit of doubt
acquittal 960n.
benefit performance
gift 781n.
benevolence
goodness 644n.
aid 703n.
subvention 703n.
lenity 736n.
gift 781n.
borrowing 785n.
taking 786n.
tax 809n.
friendliness 880n.
love 887n.
benevolence 897n.
disinterestedness 931n.
piety 979n.
benevolent
liberal 813adj.
friendly 880adj.
benevolent 897adj.
(*see* benevolence)
benighted
vespertine 129adj.
late 136adj.
dark 418adj.
blind 439adj.
ignorant 491adj.
benign, benignant
salubrious 652adj.
safe 660adj.
benevolent 897adj.
benison
good 615n.
praise 923n.
prayers 981n.
bent
tendency 179n.
oblique 220adj.
angular 247adj.
curved 248adj.
grass 366n.
bias 481n.
willingness 597n.
aptitude 694n.
affections 817n.
Benthamism
philanthropy 901n.
benthonic
oceanic 343adj.
benthos
lowness 210n.
ocean 343n.
ben trovato
plausible 471adj.
witty 839adj.
bent upon
resolute 599adj.
desiring 859adj.
benumb
disable 161vb.
render insensible 375vb.
refrigerate 382vb.
make inactive 679vb.
make insensitive 820vb.
frighten 854vb.
benzedrine
tonic 658n.
be off
go away 190vb.
start out 296vb.
run away 620vb.
bequeath
transfer 272vb.
dower 777vb.
bequeath 780vb.
give 781vb.
bequest
(*see* bequeath)
berate
exprobate 924vb.
berceuse
musical piece 412n.
vocal music 412n.
soporific 679n.
relief 831n.
bereave
deprive 786vb.
sadden 834vb.
bereavement
loss 772n.
bereft
defenseless 161adj.
unentitled 916adj.
beret
headgear 228n.
berg
ice 380n.
berhyme
poetize 593vb.
detract 926vb.
beribbon
decorate 844vb.
dignify 866vb.
berlin
carriage 274n.
berm
edge 234n.
berry
fruit 301n.
berserk
furious 176adj.
violent creature 176n.
frenzied 503adj.
angry 891adj.
berth
place 187vb.
quarters 192n.
stable 192n.
dwell 192vb.
goal 295n.
arrive 295vb.
job 622n.
beryl
greenness 432n.
blueness 435n.
gem 844n.
beseech
entreat 761vb.
worship 981vb.
beseem
be due 915vb.
be one's duty 917vb.
beset
surround 230vb.
follow 284vb.
besiege 712vb.
request 761vb.
torment 827vb.
frighten 854vb.
besetting
universal 79adj.
habitual 610adj.
attacking 712adj.
beshrew
cuss 899vb.
beside
in addition 38adv.
unconformably 84adv.
nigh 200adv.
sideways 239adv.
beside oneself
frenzied 503adj.
besiege
surround 230vb.
besiege 712vb.
wage war 718vb.
request 761vb.
besilver
coat 226vb.
beslime
make unclean 649vb.
besmear
overlay 226vb.
bedim 419vb.
make unclean 649vb.
shame 867vb.
defame 926vb.
besmirch

bedim 419vb.
defame 926vb.
besnow
whiten 427vb.
besom
cleaning utensil 648n.
besotted
misjudging 481adj.
foolish 499adj.
enamored 887adj.
bespangle
decorate 844vb.
bespatter
make unclean 649vb.
shame 867vb.
dispraise 924vb.
defame 926vb.
bespeak
be early 135vb.
evidence 466vb.
mean 514vb.
indicate 547vb.
promise 764vb.
bespoke
definite 80adj.
promised 764adj.
best
superior 34n.
supreme 34adj.
be superior 34vb.
best 644adj.
defeat 727vb.
money 797n.
best blood
nobility 868n.
bestead
be useful 640vb.
bested
in difficulties 700adj.
best, for the
well 615adv.
bestial
animal 365adj.
sensual 944adj.
bestiality
sensualism 944n.
illicit love 951n.
best, in one's
bedecked 844adj.
bestir oneself
be active 678vb.
exert oneself 682vb.
best man
auxiliary 707n.
close friend 880n.
bridesman 894n.
best of, make the
avail of 673vb.
best of terms, on the
friendly 880adj.
bestow
place 187vb.
give 781vb.
best part
main part 52n.
best people
élite 644n.
beau monde 848n.
upper class 868n.
bestraddle
overlie 266vb.
bestride
connect 45vb.
influence 178vb.
extend 183vb.
be broad 205vb.
be high 209vb.
overlie 266vb.
dominate 733vb.
best-seller
book 589n.
reading matter 589n.
novel 590n.
exceller 644n.
best wishes
congratulation 886n.
bet
gambling 618n.
gamble 618vb.
contest 716n.
contend 716vb.
betake oneself to
travel 267vb.
avail of 673vb.
beta minus
inconsiderable 33adj.
betatron
nucleonics 160n.
bête noire
bane 659n.
hateful object 888n.
bethel
church 990n.
bethink oneself
meditate 449vb.
remember 505vb.
betide
happen 154vb.
betimes
betimes 135adv.
betoken
evidence 466vb.
predict 511vb.
indicate 547vb.
bet on
be certain 473vb.
betray
disappoint 509vb.
disclose 526vb.
be false 541vb.
deceive 542vb.
indicate 547vb.
apostatize 603vb.
revolt 738vb.
fail in duty 918vb.
be dishonest 930vb.
betray itself
be visible 443vb.
betroth
promise 764vb.
marry 894vb.
betrothal
love affair 887n.
wooing 889n.
wedding 894n.
betrothed
promised 764adj.
loved one 887n.
marriageable 894adj.
better
superior 34adj.
be superior 34vb.
gambler 618n.
excellent 644adj.
improved 654adj.
make better 654vb.
restored 656adj.
betterment
benefit 615n.
improvement 654n.
better sort
upper class 868n.
betting
gambling 618n.
between
between 231adv.
between-decks
compartment 194n.
between ourselves
secretly 525adv.
between two stools
in difficulties 700adj.
betwixt and between
between 231adv.
mediocre 732adj.
bevel
cut 46vb.
obliquity 220n.
beverage
potion 301n.
bevy
group 74n.
bewail
lament 836vb.
beware
be warned 664vb.
bewilder
distract 456vb.
puzzle 474vb.
be wonderful 864vb.
bewitch
engross 449vb.
motivate 612vb.
delight 826vb.
be wonderful 864vb.
excite love 887vb.
be malevolent 898vb.
curse 899vb.
diabolize 969vb.
bewitch 983vb.
bewitchment
conversion 147n.

(*see* bewitch)
bewray
disclose 526vb.
bey
governor 741n.
nobleman 868n.
beyond
beyond 199adv.
beyond one's means
dear 811adj.
beyond one's reach
impracticable 470adj.
beyond praise
perfect 646adj.
beyond price
of price 811adj.
beyond the pale
excluded 57adj.
bezel
obliquity 220n.
furrow 262n.
bezique
card game 837n.
Bhagavad Gita
non-Biblical scripture 975n.
bhaktiyoga
religion 973n.
bhang
poison 659n.
poisonous plant 659n.
bias
inequality 29n.
influence 178vb.
tendency 179n.
obliquity 220n.
render oblique 220vb.
deflect 282vb.
prejudice 481n.
bias 481n., vb.
eccentricity 503n.
willingness 597n.
opiniatry 602n.
choice 605n.
motivate 612vb.
affections 817n.
liking 859n.
dislike 861n.
injustice 914n.
bib
apron 228n.
cleaning cloth 648n.
get drunk 949vb.
bibber
drunkard 949n.
bibelot
bauble 639n.
Bible
certainty 473n.
truth 494n.
oracle 511n.
scripture 975n.
Bible critic
theologian 973n.
bibliodule
religionist 979n.
bibliographer
bookman 589n.
bibliography
list 87n.
reference book 589n.
bibliolatry
pietism 979n.
idolatry 982n.
bibliomania
erudition 490n.
mania 503n.
bibliophile
collector 492n.
bookman 589n.
bibliotheca
library 589n.
bibulous
feeding 301adj.
drunken 949adj.
bicameral
parliamentary 692adj.
bice
green pigment 432n.
blue pigment 435n.
biceps
vitality 162n.
bicker
disagree 25vb.
argue 475vb.
bicker 709vb.
bicolor
variegated 437adj.
bicuspid
bisected 92adj.
bicycle
conveyance 267n.
ride 267vb.
bicycle 274n.
bicycle chain
club 723n.
scourge 964n.
bid
intention 617n.
aim at 617vb.
gambling 618n.
essay 671n., vb.
command 737vb.
offer 759n., vb.
request 761n., vb.
purchase 792n.
bid against
oppose 704vb.
biddable
willing 597adj.
obedient 739adj.
bid defiance
defy 711vb.
boast 877vb.
bidder
petitioner 763n.
purchaser 792n.
biddy
poultry 365n.
bide
stay 144vb.
bide one's time
wait 136vb.
await 507vb.
not act 677vb.
bidet
ablution 648n.
bid fair
tend 179vb.
be likely 471vb.
give hope 852vb.
bid up
overcharge 811vb.
biennial
periodic 110adj.
seasonal 141adj.
flower 366n.
bier
bed 218n.
funeral 364n.
bifacial
double 91adj.
bifarious
double 91adj.
biff
knock 279n.
strike 279vb.
biform
dual 90adj.
double 91adj.
bifurcate
bisected 92n.
bifurcate 92vb.
cross 222vb.
angular 247adj.
angulate 247vb.
diverge 294vb.
big
great 32adj.
older 131adj.
large 195adj.
important 638adj.
affected 850adj.
bigamist
polygamist 894n.
bigamy
type of marriage 894n.
big bug
bigwig 638n.
big drum
boast 877n.
bigener
hybrid 43n.
biggin
caldron 194n.
bight
curve 248n.
cavity 255n.
gulf 345n.
bigness
greatness 32n.
strength 162n.

hugeness 195n.
big noise
bigwig 638n.
person of repute 866n.
bigot
doctrinaire 473n.
opinionist 602n.
religionist 979n.
bigotry
positiveness 473n.
narrow mind 481n.
credulity 487n.
opiniatrety 602n.
severity 735n.
sectarianism 978n.
pietism 979n.
big shot
bigwig 638n.
big stick
incentive 612n.
compulsion 740n.
big-time
notable 638adj.
big way, in a
greatly 32adv.
bigwig
superior 34n.
bigwig 638n.
master 741n.
person of repute 866n.
aristocrat 868n.
proud man 871n.
big with
productive 164adj.
bijou
a beauty 841n.
gem 844n.
bike
crowd 74n.
bicycle 274n.
bikini
beachwear 228n.
aquatics 269n.
bilateral
dual 90adj.
lateral 239adj.
contractual 765adj.
bilberry
fruit 301n.
bilbo
side-arms 723n.
bilboes
fetter 748n.
pillory 964n.
bile
discontent 829n.
melancholy 834n.
resentment 891n.
irascibility 892n.
sullenness 893n.
envy 912n.
bileless
benevolent 897adj.
bilge
leavings 41n.
base 214n.
convexity 253n.
silly talk 515n.
swill 649n.
bilingual
linguistic 557adj.
bilious
green 432adj.
yellow 433adj.
unhealthy 651adj.
melancholic 834adj.
resentful 891adj.
irascible 892adj.
crapulous 949adj.
biliousness
indigestion 651n.
bilk
disappoint 509vb.
deceive 542vb.
defraud 788vb.
be in debt 803vb.
not pay 805vb.
bilker
trickster 545n.
avoider 620n.
defrauder 789n.
non-payer 805n.
bill
numerical result 85n.
list 87n.
sharp edge 256n.
exhibit 522n.
advertisement 528n.
advertise 528vb.
label 547n.
dramatize 594vb.
spear, ax 723n.
demand 737vb.
title-deed 767n.
paper money 797n.
credit 802n.
debt 803n.
account 808vb.
accounts 808n.
price 809n., vb.
bill and coo
caress 889vb.
billboard
exhibit 522n.
advertisement 528n.
bill-collector
consignee 754n.
receiver 782n.
billet
place 185n.
place 187vb.
quarters 192n.
goal 295n.
label 547n.
correspondence 588n.
apportion 783vb.
billet doux
correspondence 588n.
love-token 889n.
billfold
case 194n.
treasury 799n.
bill-hook
sharp edge 256n.
billiards
ball game 837n.
billingsgate
slang 560n.
scurrility 899n.
billion
over one hundred 99n.
bill of exchange
title-deed 767n.
paper money 797n.
bill of fare
list 87n.
meal 301n.
billion
a mixture 43n.
billow
swelling 253n.
wave 350n.
billowy
curved 248adj.
convex 253adj.
bill-sticker
publicizer 528n.
billycock
headgear 228n.
bimetallism
finance 797n.
binary
dual 90adj.
star 321n.
bind
tie 45vb.
combine 50vb.
bring together 74vb.
stabilize 153vb.
make smaller 198vb.
cover 226vb.
close 264vb.
be dense 324vb.
cultivate 370vb.
repair 656vb.
doctor 658vb.
obstruct 702vb.
compel 740vb.
subjugate 745vb.
fetter 747vb.
give terms 766vb.
tedium 838n.
impose a duty 917vb.
binder
bond 47n.
compressor 198n.
farm tool 370n.
bindery
bookbinding 589n.
binding
ligature 47n.
compressive 198adj.

wrapping 226n.
solidifying 324adj.
book-binding 589n.
necessary 596adj.
preceptive 693adj.
authoritative 733adj.
compelling 740adj.
conditional 766adj.
tedious 838adj.
trimming 844n.
obligatory 917adj.
bind oneself
promise 764vb.
bind over
impose a duty 917vb.
bind up
repair 656vb.
relieve 831vb.
bine
plant 366n.
binge
festivity 837n.
binnacle
sailing aid 269n.
binocular
seeing 438adj.
binoculars
telescope 442n.
biochemistry
biology 358n.
biod
occultism 984n.
biogenesis
propagation 164n.
biogenetic
biological 358adj.
biograph
cinema 445n.
biographer
chronicler 549n.
author 589n.
narrator 590n.
biography
record 548n.
reading matter 589n.
biography 590n.
biology
structure 331n.
biology 358n.
life 360n.
bionomics
biology 358n.
bioplasm
organism 358n.
life 360n.
bioplast
organism 358n.
life 360n.
bioscope
cinema 445n.
biotic
alive 360adj.
biotic potential
productiveness 171n.
biotype
prototype 23n.
organism 358n.
biparous
dual 90adj.
bipartisan
agreeing 24adj.
dual 90adj.
concurrent 181adj.
assented 488adj.
cooperative 706adj.
concordant 710adj.
bipartite
disjunct 46adj.
bisected 92adj.
biped
animal 365n.
biplanar
semantic 514adj.
biplane
aircraft 276n.
birch
tree 366n.
spank 963vb.
scourge 964n.
bird
aeronaut 271n.
speeder 277n.
bird 365n.
animal 365n.
woman 373n.
vocalist 413n.
bird-cage
cattle pen 369n.
bird-call
ululation 409n.
vocal music 412n.
bird in the hand
object 319n.
possession 773n.
bird-lime
adhesive 47n.
trap 542n.
bird's-eye view
whole 52n.
generality 79n.
view 438n.
spectacle 445n.
art subject 553n.
compendium 592n.
bird-watching
zoology 367n.
bird-witted
light-minded 456adj.
foolish 499adj.
bireme
galley 275n.
biretta
headgear 228n.
badge of rule 743n.
canonicals 989n.
vestments 989n.
birth
origin 68n.
beginning 68n.
propagation 164n.
obstetrics 164n.
genealogy 169n.
life 360n.
nobility 868n.
birth certificate
label 547n.
record 548n.
birth-control
restraint 747n.
birthday
date 108n.
anniversary 141n.
special day 876n.
birthday suit
bareness 229n.
birthmark
identification 547n.
skin disease 651n.
blemish 845n.
birth-pang
obstetrics 164n.
birthplace
source 156n.
home 192n.
birthrate
statistics 86n.
propagation 164n.
birthright
priority 119n.
dower 777n.
right 913n.
dueness 915n.
birth-stone
talisman 983n.
bis
again 106adv.
biscuit
food 301n.
pastry 301n.
bisect
sunder 46vb.
bisect 92vb.
apportion 783vb.
bisection
equalization 28n.
middle 70n.
bisection 92n.
bishop
chessman 837n.
ecclesiarch 986n.
bishopless
Protestant 976adj.
bishopric
district 184n.
parish 985n.
church office 985n.
bison
cattle 365n.
bisque
vantage 34n.
soup 301n.
bistoury

sharp edge 256n.
bister
brown paint 430n.
bistro
café 192n.
bit
small quantity 33n.
piece 53n.
perforator 263n.
woman 373n.
restrain 747vb.
fetter 748n.
loose woman 952n.
bit by bit
by degrees 27adv.
separately 46adv.
piecemeal 53adv.
severally 80adv.
gradatim 278adv.
bitch
dog 365n.
female animal 373n.
hell-hag 904n.
cad 938n.
bitchy
malevolent 898adj.
bite
small quantity 33n.
cut 46vb.
piece 53n.
vigorousness 174n.
be violent 176vb.
be sharp 256vb.
notch 260vb.
mouthful 301n.
chew 301vb.
give pain 377vb.
refrigerate 382vb.
pungency 388n.
trickery 542n.
deceive 542vb.
engrave 555vb.
vigor 571n.
ill-treat 645vb.
wound 655vb.
fight 716vb.
hurt 827vb.
cause discontent 829vb.
endearment 889n.
anger 891n.
enrage 891vb.
be irascible 892vb.
sullenness 893n.
biter bit
retaliation 714n.
bite the dust
be destroyed 165vb.
tumble 309vb.
be defeated 728vb.
biting tongue
reproach 924n.
bits
rubbish 641n.
bitt
fastening 47n.
bitter
liquor 301n.
painful 377adj.
cold 380adj.
pungent 388adj.
unsavory 391adj.
sour 393adj.
unpleasant 827adj.
discontented 829adj.
regretting 830adj.
disliked 861adj.
inimical 881adj.
hating, hateful 888adj.
resentful 891adj.
irascible 892adj.
malevolent 898adj.
disapproving 924adj.
detracting 926adj.
bitter end
finality 69n.
bitter-ender
opinionist 602n.
opponent 705n.
malcontent 829n.
bitterness
(*see* bitter)
bitter pill
unsavoriness 391n.
adversity 731n.
painfulness 827n.
hateful object 888n.
punishment 963n.
bitters
sourness 393n.
bitter-sweet
contrary 14adj.
painful 377adj.
bitty
fragmentary 53adj.
incomplete 55adj.
bitumen
resin 357n.
bivalent
double 91adj.
bivalve
fish food 301n.
fish 365n.
bivouac
station 187n.
place oneself 187vb.
abode 192n.
dwell 192vb.
resting place 266n.
bizarre
unusual 84adj.
ridiculous 849adj.
blab
inform 524vb.
divulge 526vb.
accuse 928vb.
blabber
informer 524n.
stammer 580vb.
black
exclude 57vb.
funereal 364adj.
dark 418adj.
darken 418vb.
blackness 428n.
negro 428n.
black 428adj.
blacken 428vb.
evil 616adj.
bad 645adj.
clean 648vb.
dirty 649adj.
prohibited 757adj.
lamentation 836n.
ugly 842adj.
sullen 893adj.
heinous 934adj.
black and white
polarity 14n.
light contrast 417n.
achromatism 426n.
blackness 428n.
pied 437adj.
painting 553n.
black and white, in
written 586adj.
black art
sorcery 983n.
blackball
exclusion 57n.
exclude 57vb.
eject 300vb.
shame 867vb.
unsociability 883n.
make unwelcome 883vb.
disapprobation 924n.
blackberry
fruit 301n.
black thing 428n.
blackbird
bird 365n.
vocalist 413n.
black thing 428n.
black books
odium 888n.
black cap
danger signal 665n.
condemnation 961n.
black cloud
threat 900n.
black coat
cleric 986n.
blacken
darken 418vb.
color 425vb.
blacken 428vb.
impair 655vb.
make ugly 842vb.
shame 867vb.
dispraise 924vb.
defame 926vb.

blackguard
cuss 889vb.
ruffian 904n.
evildoer 904n.
exprobate 924vb.
rascally 930adj.
knave 938n.
blackhead
blemish 845n.
blacking
black pigment 428n.
cleanser 648n.
blackjack
vessel 194n.
hammer 279n.
strike 279vb.
kill 362vb.
club 723n.
blacklead
lubricant 334n.
cleanser 648n.
clean 648vb.
blackleg
nonconformist 84n.
tergiversator 603n.
hateful object 888n.
black-letter
antiquated 127adj.
letter 558n.
print-type 587n.
black-list
set apart 46vb.
name 561vb.
unsociability 883n.
make unwelcome 883vb.
disapprobation 924n.
disapprove 924vb.
condemnation 961n.
condemn 961vb.
black magic
diabolism 969n.
sorcery 983n.
blackmail
demand 737n., vb.
compulsion 740n.
compel 740vb.
rapacity 786n.
fleece 786vb.
booty 790n.
tax 809n.
threat 900n.
threaten 900vb.
reward 962n.
Black Maria
vehicle 274n.
lock-up 748n.
card game 837n.
black mark
reprimand 924n.
black market
trade 791n.
speculate 791vb.
mart 796n.
illegal 954adj.
Black Mass
diabolism 969n.
blackness
darkness 418n.
blackness 428n.
black out
darken 418vb.
obliterate 550vb.
restrain 747vb.
prohibit 757vb.
black-out
obscuration 418n.
fatigue 684n.
war measures 718n.
prohibition 757n.
drunkenness 949n.
black sheep
offender 904n.
Blackshirts
political party 708n.
blacksmith
animal husbandry 369n.
artisan 686n.
black spot
danger 661n.
bladder
bladder 194n.
blade
sharp edge 256n.
propeller 269n.
male 372n.
combatant 722n.
side-arms 723n.
fop 848n.
blah-blah
empty talk 515n.
blain
swelling 253n.
hardness 326n.
ulcer 651n.
blame
attribute 158vb.
censure 924n.
blame 924vb.
accusation 928n.
guilt 936n.
blameless
guiltless 935adj.
blame oneself
be penitent 939vb.
blameworthy
discreditable 867adj.
blameworthy 924adj.
accusable 928adj.
heinous 934adj.
guilty 936adj.
blanch
lose color 426vb.
decolorize 426vb.
whiten 427vb.
bland
lenitive 177adj.
smooth 258adj.
courteous 884adj.
blandiloquence
flattery 925n.
blandish
induce 612vb.
tempt 612vb.
flatter 925vb.
blandishment
endearment 889n.
blank
non-existence 2n.
insubstantial 4adj.
uniform 16adj.
zero 103n.
empty 190adj.
centrality 225n.
form 243n.
opaque 423adj.
colorless 426adj.
unthinking 450adj.
ignorant 491adj.
unintelligible 517adj.
punctuation 547n.
clean 648adj.
impassive 820adj.
blank cartridge
insubstantial thing 4n.
ineffectuality 161n.
emptiness 190n.
false alarm 665n.
blank check
scope 744n.
liberality 813n.
blanket
general 79adj.
suppress 165vb.
moderate 177vb.
coverlet 226vb.
cover 226vb.
warm clothes 381n.
screen 421vb.
indiscriminate 464adj.
blankety-blank
damnable 645adj.
blank verse
verse form 593n.
prosody 593n.
blare
loudness 400n.
be loud 400vb.
resonance 404n.
resound 404vb.
stridor 407n.
blarney
empty talk 515n.
mean nothing 515vb.
falsehood 541n.
be cunning 698vb.
flattery 925n.
blasé
bored 838adj.

sated 863adj.
blaspheme
be irreligious 974vb.
be impious 980vb.
blast
outbreak 176n.
air 340n.
wind, gale 352n.
blow 352vb.
loudness 400n.
bang 402n.
crackle 402vb.
impair 655vb.
blight 659n.
danger signal 665n.
fire at 712vb.
adversity 731n.
be malevolent 898vb.
bewitch 983vb.
blat
mean nothing 515vb.
blatancy
bad taste 847n.
vanity 873n.
ostentation 875n.
insolence 878n.
blatant
loud 400adj.
ululant 409adj.
well-known 528adj.
(*see* blatancy)
blather
empty talk 515n.
blatter
ululate 409vb.
blaze
fire 379n.
be hot 379vb.
light 417n.
shine 417vb.
mark 547vb.
blazer
tunic 228n.
livery 547n.
blaze the trail
come before 64vb.
blazon
proclaim 528vb.
heraldry 547n.
register 548vb.
decorate 844vb.
honor 866vb.
be ostentatious 875vb.
blazonry
heraldry 547n.
bleach
dry 342vb.
decolorize 426vb.
whiten 427vb.
clean 648vb.
hairwash 843n.
bleachers
onlookers 441n.
bleak
adverse 731adj.
blear
bedim 419vb.
blear-eyed
dim-sighted 440adj.
bleary
dim 419adj.
bleat
ululate 409vb.
be discontented 829vb.
bleb
swelling 253n.
bleed
flow out 298vb.
void, emit 300vb.
be wet 341vb.
doctor 658vb.
fleece 786vb.
overcharge 811vb.
suffer 825vb.
pity 905vb.
blemish
weakness 163n.
deformity 246n.
impair 655vb.
eyesore 842n.
make ugly 842vb.
blemish 845n., vb.
slur 867n.
blench
be loath 598vb.
avoid 620vb.
show feeling 818vb.
quake 854vb.
blend
a mixture 43n.
mix 43vb.
compound 50n.
combine 50vb.
harmonize 410vb.
bless
benefit 615vb.
be auspicious 730vb.
permit 756vb.
rejoice 835vb.
be benevolent 897vb.
thank 907vb.
approve, praise 923vb.
worship 981vb.
perform ritual 988vb.
blessed
good 615adj.
palmy 730adj.
happy 824adj.
pleasurable 826adj.
paradisiac 971adj.
ritual 988adj.
blessed with
possessing 773adj.
blessing
benefit 615n.
good 615n.
permission 756n.
(*see* bless)
blessings
prosperity 730n.
blether
empty talk 515n.
mean nothing 515vb.
blight
decay 51n.
destroyer 168n.
badness 645n.
dilapidation 655n.
impair 655vb.
blight 659n.
adversity 731n.
be malevolent 898vb.
bewitch 983vb.
blighter
cad 938n.
Blighty
home 192n.
blimp
airship 276n.
opinionist 602n.
blind
shade 226n.
shine 417vb.
curtain 421n.
screened 421adj.
blind 439adj., vb.
be unseen 444vb.
inattentive 456adj.
distract 456vb.
indiscriminating 464adj.
misjudging 481adj.
disguise 527n.
trickery 542n.
deceive 542vb.
involuntary 596adj.
pretext 614n.
stratagem 698n.
impassive 820adj.
unastonished 865adj.
drunkenness 949n.
dead drunk 949adj.
blind alley
cavity 255n.
road 624n.
obstacle 702n.
blind bargain
uncertainty 474n.
gambling 618n.
rashness 857n.
blind corner
invisibility 444n.
blindfold
screen 421vb.
blind 439adj., vb.
keep secret 525vb.
deceive 542vb.
blinding
luminous 417adj.
blindness
blindness 439n.

invisibility 444n.
indiscrimination 464n.
ignorance 491n.
opiniatrety 602n.
blind side
blindness 439n.
inattention 456n.
prejudice 481n.
folly 499n.
opiniatrety 602n.
blind spot
blindness 439n.
invisibility 444n.
inattention 456n.
prejudice 481n.
blink
flash 417n.
reflection 417n.
shine 417vb.
look 438n.
gaze 438vb.
be blind 439vb.
dim sight 440n.
be dim-sighted 440vb.
be irresolute 601vb.
avoid 620vb.
blinker
signal light 420n.
screen 421vb.
blind 439vb.
dim sight 440n.
deceive 542vb.
bliss
happiness 824n.
blissful
palmy 730adj.
happy 824adj.
pleasurable 826adj.
paradisiac 971adj.
blister
bladder 194n.
swelling 253n.
skin disease 651n.
blithe
happy 824adj.
cheerful 833adj.
blitz
havoc 165n.
loudness 400n.
attack 712n.
bombardment 712n.
fire at 712vb.
battle 718n.
blizzard
storm 176n.
gale 352n.
wintriness 380n.
bloat
enlarge 197vb.
animal disease 651n.
bloated
fleshy 195adj.
bloater
fish food 301n.
bloc
political party 708n.
block
housing 192n.
bulk 195n.
stand 218n.
close 264vb.
repel 292vb.
solid body 324n.
hardness 326n.
dunce 501n.
engraving 555n.
stationery 586n.
obstacle 702n.
obstruct 702vb.
defend 713vb.
parry 713vb.
prohibit 757vb.
not pay 805vb.
unfeeling person 820n.
means of execution 964n.
blockade
besiege 212vb.
surround 230vb.
circumscription 232n.
circumscribe 232vb.
closure 264n.
close 264vb.
hindrance 702n.
obstruct 702vb.
attack 712n.
warfare 718n.
wage war 718vb.
restriction 747n.
blockage
stop 145n.
hindrance 702n.
obstacle 702n.
blockhead
ignoramus 493n.
dunce 501n.
blockhouse
fort 713n.
blockish
unintelligent 499adj.
block out
outline 233vb.
efform 243vb.
bloke
person 371n.
male 372n.
blond
achromatism 426n.
colorless 426adj.
whitish 427adj.
yellow 433adj.
blood
consanguinity 11n.
auspicate 68vb.
breed 77n.
genealogy 169n.
vigorousness 174n.
fluid, blood 335n.
life 360n.
redness 431n.
fop 848n.
nobility 868n.
cruel act 898n.
blood bath
slaughter 362n.
terror tactics 712n.
blood feud
quarrel 709n.
revenge 910n.
blood-group
race 11n.
classification 77n.
blood 335n.
blood-guilty
murderous 362adj.
guilty 936adj.
blood-horse
thoroughbred 273n.
bloodhound
dog 365n.
detective 459n.
blcodiness
inhumanity 898n.
bloodless
insubstantial 4adj.
weak 163adj.
colorless 426adj.
diseased 651adj.
peaceful 717adj.
guiltless 935adj.
blood-letting
voidance 300n.
killing 362n.
surgery 658n.
blood-line
genealogy 169n.
blood-lust
violence 176n.
inhumanity 898n.
blood-money
irenics 719n.
atonement 941n.
blood pressure
blood pressure 651n.
bloodshed
slaughter 362n.
warfare 718n.
cruel act 898n.
bloodshot
sanguineous 335adj.
bloodshot 431adj.
angry 891adj.
drunken 949adj.
blood-sport
killing 363n.
chase 619n.
bloodstained
murderous 362adj.
bloodshot 431adj.
bloodstock
thoroughbred 273n.
nobility 868n.

bloodsucker
tyrant 733n.
taker 786n.
noxious animal 904n.
blood-sucking
rapacity 786n.
blood-thirsty
furious 176adj.
murderous 362adj.
harmful 645adj.
warlike 718adj.
cruel 898adj.
blood up, with one's
bravely 855adv
blood vessel
conduit 351n.
bloody
violent 176adj.
sanguineous 335adj.
humid 341adj.
murderous 362adj.
bloodshot 431adj.
oppressive 735adj.
cruel 898adj.
bloody-mindedness
obstinacy 602n.
bloody nose
recoil 280n.
defeat 728n.
bloom
salad days 130n.
adultness 134n.
reproduce 164vb.
expand 197vb.
layer 207n.
open 263vb.
flower 366n.
redness 431n.
health 650n.
be healthy 650vb.
prosper 730vb.
be beautiful 841vb.
bloomer
mistake 495n.
bloomers
trousers 228n.
underwear 228n.
bloomy
vegetal 366adj.
blossom
growth 157n.
product 164n.
reproduce itself 164vb.
be fruitful 171vb.
(*see* bloom)
blot
tincture 43n.
absorb 299vb.
dry 342vb.
blacken 428vb.
variegate 437vb.
mistake 495n.
blunder 495vb.
conceal 525vb.
mark 547vb.
obliteration 550n.
obliterate 550vb.
write 586vb.
clean 648vb.
dirt 649n.
make unclean 649vb.
impair 655vb.
be clumsy 695vb.
eyesore 842n.
make ugly 842vb.
blemish 845n., vb.
slur 867n.
shame 867vb.
blotch
blemish 845n.
blot out
subtract 39vb.
destroy 165vb.
obliterate 550vb.
forgive 909vb.
(*see* blot)
blotter
cleaning utensil 648n.
blotto
dead drunk 949adj.
blouse
bodywear 228n.
blow
be violent 176vb.
expand 197vb.
knock 279n.
meal 301n.
aerify 340vb.
wind, gale 352n.
blow 352vb.
inexpectation 508n.
evil 616n.
deed 676n.
be fatigued 684vb.
expend 806vb.
be prodigal 815vb.
suffering 825n.
corporal punishment 963n.
blow away
propel 287vb.
blow down
demolish 165vb.
blower
orifice 263n.
air 340n.
ventilation 352n.
hearing aid 415n.
blow-hole
orifice 263n.
outlet 298n.
air-pipe 353n.
blow hot and cold
vary 152vb.
be irresolute 601vb.
be capricious 604vb.
blow in
enter 297vb.
blowiness
wind 352n.
blow-lamp
furnace 383n.
blown
panting 684adj.
blow one's own trumpet
boast 877vb.
blow one's top
get angry 891vb.
blow open
force 176vb.
blow-out
feasting 301n.
meal 301n.
bang 402n.
gluttony 947n.
blow out
nullify 2vb.
suppress 165vb.
enlarge 197vb.
extinguish 382vb.
snuff out 418vb.
blow over
be past 125vb.
cease 145vb.
blow-pipe
propellant 287n.
sufflation 352n.
air-pipe 353n.
heater 383n.
missile weapon 723n.
toy gun 723n.
blows
fight 716n.
anger 891n.
blow the gaff
inform 524vb.
divulge 526vb.
blow-up
duplicate 22n.
outbreak 176n.
photography 551n.
blow up
augment 36vb.
break 46vb.
demolish 165vb.
be violent 176vb.
force 176vb.
enlarge 197vb.
sufflate 352vb.
be disclosed 526vb.
photograph 551vb.
miscarry 728vb.
get angry 891vb.
blow upon
defame 926vb.
blowsy
fleshy 195adj.
expanded 197adj.
red 431adj.
blowy
windy 352adj.
blubber

fat 357n.
stammer 580vb.
weep 836vb.
bludgeon
club 723n.
brute force 735n.
oppress 735vb.
compulsion 740n.
compel 740vb.
blue
athlete 162n.
air 340n.
a-cold 380adj.
blueness 435adj.
blue 435adj., vb.
badge 547n.
decoration 729n.
bored 838adj.
impure 951adj.
Bluebeard
polygamist 894n.
blue blood
blood 335n.
nobility 868n.
blue devils
psychopathy 503n.
melancholy 834n.
blue-eyed boy
favorite 890n.
blue moon
neverness 109n.
blue-pencil
subtract 39vb.
obliterate 550vb.
rectify 654vb.
prohibit 757vb.
blueprint
prototype 23n.
representation 551n.
compendium 592n.
plan 623n., vb.
preparation 669n.
blue ribbon
decoration 729n.
blues
music 412n.
psychopathy 503n.
melancholy 834n.
dance 837n.
sullenness 893n.
blue stocking
intellectual 492n.
bluff
violent 176adj.
high land 209n.
verticality 215n.
unsharpened 257adj.
blind 439vb.
duplicity 541n.
trickery 542n.
deceive 542vb.
plead 614vb.
be affected 850vb.
boast 877n.
ungracious 885adj.
bluffer
impostor 545n.
affector 850n.
boaster 877n.
blunder
misjudge 481adj.
mistake 495n.
blunder 495vb.
solecize 565vb.
be unskillful 695vb.
fail 728vb.
blunderbuss
propellant 287n.
fire-arm 723n.
blunderer
fool 501n.
bungler 697n.
blunt
weaken 163vb.
inert 175adj.
moderate 177vb.
low 210adj.
unsharpened 257adj.
blunt 257vb.
smooth 258adj.
render insensible 375vb.
undisguised 522adj.
assertive 532adj.
veracious 540adj.
artless 699adj.
dibs 797n.
make insensitive 820vb.
ill-bred 847adj.
ungracious 885adj.
blur
darken 418vb.
dimness 419n.
blur 440vb.
make unclean 649vb.
blemish 845n.
blurb
advertisement 528n.
praise 923n.
blurb-writer
publicizer 528n.
commender 923n.
blurred
amorphous 244adj.
dim 419adj.
ill-seen 444adj.
blurry
shadowy 419adj.
ill-seen 444adj.
blurt
improvise 609vb.
blurt out
inform 524vb.
divulge 526vb.
voice 577vb.
speak 579vb.
blush
heat 379n.
hue 425n.
redness 431n.
redden 431vb.
disclosure 526n.
indication 547n.
feeling 818n.
show feeling 818vb.
guilt 836n.
humiliation 872n.
be humbled 872vb.
modesty 874n.
be modest 874vb.
blushful
modest 874adj.
pure 950adj.
bluster
violence 176n.
be violent 176vb.
be active 678vb.
defy 711vb.
nervousness 854n.
boast 877n., vb.
insolence 878n.
be angry 891vb.
threaten 900vb.
threat 900n.
blusterer
boaster 877n.
insolent person 878n.
blustery
violent 176adj.
windy 352adj.
boa
neckwear 228n.
boa constrictor
compressor 198n.
reptile 365n.
boar
pig 365n.
male animal 372n.
board
lamina 207n.
stand, shelf 218n.
irrupt 297vb.
provisions 301n.
feed 301vb.
hardness 326n.
materials 631n.
provide 633vb.
director 690n.
council 692n.
attack 712vb.
tribunal 956n.
boarder
resident 191n.
eater 301n.
learner 538n.
boarding house
quarters 192n.
board, on
here 189adv.
under way 269adv.
boardroom

conference 584n.
boards
wrapping 226n.
bookbinding 589n.
theater 594n.
boast
comprise 78vb.
exaggerate 546vb.
triumph 727vb.
possess 773vb.
ridiculousness 849n.
be affected 850vb.
person of repute 866n.
pride 871n.
feel pride 871vb.
be vain 873vb.
be ostentatious 875vb.
boast 877n., vb.
be insolent 878vb.
favorite 890n.
boaster
impostor 545n.
combatant 722n.
(*see* boast)
boasting
overestimation 482n.
empty talk 515n.
magniloquence 574n.
(*see* boast)
boat
voyage, row 269vb.
ship, boat 275n.
boatable
seafaring 269adj.
boat-boy
church officer 986n.
ritualist 988n.
boater
headgear 228n.
boathouse
stable 192n.
boating
aquatics 269n.
sport 837n.
boatman
boatman 270n.
boatswain
mariner 270n.
navigator 270n.
bob
timekeeper 117n.
shorten 204vb.
pendant 217n.
obeisance 311n.
stoop 311vb.
leap 312vb.
oscillation 317n.
be agitated 318vb.
gravity 322n.
coinage 797n.
hair-dressing 843n.
greet 884n.
show respect 920vb.
bobbish
healthy 650adj.
bobble
pendant 217n.
trimming 844n.
bobby
protector 660n.
police 955n.
bobbysoxer
youngster 132n.
bode
predict 511vb.
threaten 900vb.
bodice
bodywear 228n.
bodiless
insubstantial 4adj.
immaterial 320adj.
bodily
substantially 3adv.
collectively 52adv.
material 319adj.
sensual 944adj.
boding
cautionary 664adj.
unpromising 853adj.
bodkin
sharp point 256n.
perforator 263n.
body
substance 3n.
main part 32n.
middle 70n.
band 74n.
frame 218n.
matter 319n.
structure 331n.
corpse 363n.
person 371n.
savoriness 390n.
community 708n.
corporation 708n.
body-building
nourishing 301adj.
body forth
make extrinsic 6vb.
externalize 223vb.
materialize 319vb.
bodyguard
protector 660n.
defender 713n.
combatant 722n.
retainer 742n.
body politic
nation 371n.
polity 733n.
body-snatcher
thief 789n.
boffin
worker 686n.
expert 696n.
bog
marsh 347n.
dirt 649n.
bog down
fail 728vb.
bogey
false alarm 665n.
demon 970n.
boggle
be uncertain 474vb.
doubt 486vb.
dissent 489n.
be loth 598vb.
bogie
train 274n.
bogs
latrine 649n.
bog-trotter
countryman 869n.
bogus
false 541adj.
spurious 542adj.
untrue 543adj.
affected 850adj.
bogy
(*see* bogey)
Bohemian
nonconformist 84n.
wanderer 268n.
free man 744n.
bohunk
foreigner 59n.
boil
swelling 253n.
cook 301vb.
effervesce 318vb.
bubble 355vb.
be hot 379vb.
hiss 406vb.
be excited 821vb.
boil down
bate 37vb.
make smaller 198vb.
shorten 204vb.
boil down to
mean 514vb.
boiler
caldron 194n.
poultry 365n.
heater 383n.
boiling
finite quantity 26n.
boiling point
heat 379n.
completion 725n.
boil over
be violent 176vb.
effervesce 318vb.
get angry 891vb.
boisterous
violent 176adj.
windy 352adj.
hasty 680adj.
excitable 822adj.
bolas
missile weapon 723n.
bold

salient 254adj.
undisguised 522adj.
forceful 571adj.
courageous 855adj.
rash 857adj.
insolent 878adj.
bole
origin 156n.
cylinder 252n.
soil 344n.
tree 366n.
bolero
vest 228n.
dance 837n.
bolet
vegetable 301n.
plant 366n.
bolide
meteor 321n.
boll
sphere 252n.
metrology 465n.
bollard
fastening 47n.
Bolshevik(s)
political party 708n.
revolter 738n.
bolshevism
government 733n.
bolshie
disobedient 738adj.
bolster
cushion 218n.
support 218vb.
aid 703vb.
cheer 833vb.
bolt
eliminate 44vb.
affix 45vb.
fastening 47n.
bunch 74n.
barrier 235n.
sharp point 256n.
stopper 264n.
close 264vb.
move fast 277vb.
missile 287n.
decamp 296vb.
discriminate 463vb.
select 605vb.
run away 620vb.
purify 648vb.
deteriorate 655vb.
safeguard 662n.
missile weapon 723n.
disobey 738vb.
lock-up 748n.
gluttonize 947vb.
bolter
tergiversator 603n.
bolt from the blue
inexpectation 508n.
bolt-hole
tunnel 263n.
refuge 662n.
bolus
medicine 658n.
bomb
destroyer 168n.
bang 402n.
fire at 712vb.
bomb 723n.
bombard
radiate 417vb.
fire at 712vb.
gun 723n.
bombardier
aeronaut 271n.
soldiery 722n.
bombardment
havoc 165n.
loudness 400n.
bombardment 712n.
bombardon
horn 414n.
bombast
lining 227n.
overestimation 482n.
absurdity 497n.
empty talk 515n.
magniloquence 574n.
ridiculousness 849n.
boast 877n.
bomber
aircraft 276n.
air force 722n.
bombination
ululation 409n.
bomb-proof
unyielding 162adj.
invulnerable 660adj.
defended 713adj.
resisting 715adj.
bombshell
inexpectation 508n.
bomb 723n.
bona fide
veracious 540adj.
truthfully 540adv.
bona fides
probity 929n.
bonanza
plenty 635n.
palmy days 730n.
bonbon
sweet 392n.
bond
relation 9n.
junction 45n.
bond 47n.
subject 745adj.
fetter 748n.
promise 764n.
compact 765n.
title-deed 767n.
paper money 797n.
dueness 915n.
duty 917n.
bondage
servitude 745n.
bond-holder
receiver 782n.
bondman
slave 742n.
bone
modality 7n.
vitality 162n.
uncover 229vb.
void 300vb.
cook 301vb.
solid body 324n.
hardness 326n.
structure 331n.
steal 788vb.
bonehead
dunce 501n.
bon enfant
kind person 897n.
bone of contention
question 459n.
casus belli 709n.
contention 716n.
boner
mistake 495n.
bones
gong 414n.
corpse 363n.
gambling 618n.
bone-setter
mender 656n.
bone-setting
therapy 658n.
bone to pick
casus belli 709n.
resentment 891n.
boneyard
cemetery 364n.
bonfire
fire 379n.
revel 837n.
celebration 876n.
bonhomie
ostentation 875n.
sociability 882n.
benevolence 897n.
bon mot
witticism 839n.
bonne
domestic 742n.
keeper 749n.
bonnet
covering 226n.
headgear 228n.
bonny
cheerful 833adj.
beautiful 841adj.
courageous 855adj.
bon ton
fashion 848n.
fashionable 848adj.
bonus
extra 40n.

incentive 612n.
superfluity 637n.
gift 781n.
receipt 807n.
undueness 916n.
bon vivant,– viveur
social person 882n.
bony
lean 206adj.
hard 326adj.
bonze
monk 986n.
priest 986n.
bonzery
monastery 986n.
boo
cry 408n., vb.
vociferate 408vb.
gesture 547n.
not respect 921vb.
despise 922vb.
disapprove 924vb.
boob, booby
dunce 501n.
ninny 501n.
booby hatch
jail 748n.
booby-trap
trap 542n.
defenses 713n.
bomb 723n.
boodle
booty 790n.
dibs 797n.
boo-hoo
cry 408n., vb.
weep 836vb.
book
subdivision 53n.
register 548vb.
book 589n.
require 627vb.
acquire 771vb.
possess 773vb.
account 808vb.
reprove 924vb.
indict 928vb.
bookbinder
bookbinding 589n.
book-case
cabinet 194n.
library 589n.
book-club
library 589n.
book-collector
collector 492n.
bookman 589n.
book-dealer
bookman 589n.
bookie
gambler 618n.
booking-clerk
receiver 782n.
seller 793n.
bookish
instructed 490adj.
studious 536adj.
book-keep
number 86vb.
book-keeper
computer 86n.
recorder 549n.
treasurer 798n.
accountant 808n.
book-keeping
registration 548n.
accounts 808n.
accounting 808adj.
book-learning
erudition 490n.
bookless
uninstructed 491adj.
booklet
book 589n.
book-lover
bookman 589n.
bookmaker
gambler 618n.
book-making
calculation of chance 159n.
bookman
bookman 589n.
books
account book 808n.
bookselling
publication 528n.
bookman 589n.
bibliographical 589adj.
book-shop
library 589n.
book-trade
publication 528n.
bookworm
scholar 492n.
learner 538n.
bookman 589n.
boom
supporter 218n.
impel 279vb.
be loud 400vb.
bang 402vb.
ululate 409vb.
revival 656n.
obstacle 702n.
defenses 713n.
prosperity 730n.
sale 793n.
boomerang
recoil 280n.
retaliation 714n.
missile weapon 723n.
boon
benefit 615n.
gift 781n.
boon companion
close friend 880n.
social person 882n.
boor
countryman 869n.
rude person 885n.
boorish
ill-bred 847adj.
plebeian 869adj.
boorishness
discourtesy 885n.
boost
stimulant 174n.
invigorate 174vb.
impulse 279n.
overrate 482vb.
advertise 528vb.
aider 703n.
praise 923vb.
booster
publicizer 528n.
commender 923n.
boot
box 194n.
stand 218n.
footwear 228n.
kick 279vb.
ejection 300n.
booth
small house 192n.
shop 796n.
bootikin
footwear 228n.
glove 228n.
boot-lace
ligature 47n.
bootless
wasted 634adj.
unsuccessful 728adj.
unthanked 908adj.
bootlicker
toady 879n.
bootmaker
clothier 228n.
artisan 686n.
boots
servant 742n.
boot-tree
mold 23n.
booty
trophy 729n.
acquisition 771n.
booty 790n.
booze
liquor 301n.
get drunk 949vb.
boozer
drunkard 949n.
bopster
musician 413n.
borage
potherb 301n.
border
adjunct 40n.
be near 200vb.
contiguity 202n.
circumjacence 230n.

circumscribe 232vb.
edge, edging 234n.
hem 234vb.
limit 236vb.
flank 239vb.
garden 370n.
trimming 844n.
decorate 844vb.
borderer
dweller 191n.
borderland(s)
contiguity 202n.
borderline
limited 236adj.
borderline case
predicament 700n.
bore
breadth 205n.
make concave 255vb.
perforation 263n.
pierce 263vb.
pass 305vb.
descend 309vb.
current 350n.
wave 350n.
impair 655vb.
bane 659n.
fatigue 684vb.
fire-arm 723n.
worry 825n.
tedium, bore 838n.
be dull 840vb.
sate 863vb.
boreal
windy 352adj.
cold 380adj.
boredom
tedium 838n.
borer
sharp point 256n.
perforator 863n.
boring
tunnel 263n.
descent 309n.
born
born 360adj.
born for
gifted 694adj.
born in the purple
rich 800adj.
noble 868adj.
born of
caused 157adj.
born yesterday
artless 699adj.
borough
district 184n.
electorate 605n.
borrow
copy 20vb.
request 761vb.
borrow 785vb.
be undue 916vb.
borrowed plumes
sham 542n.
borrowed time
opportunity 137n.
borrower
beggar 763n.
debtor 803n.
Borstal
school 539n.
amendment 654n.
prison 748n.
bosh
silly talk 515n.
bosh shot
mistake 495n.
bosky
arboreal 366adj.
bosom
receptacle 194n.
interiority 224n.
bosom 253n.
spirit 447n.
affections 817n.
bosomy
fleshy 195adj.
convex 253adj.
boss
superior 34n.
swelling 253n.
roughen 259vb.
meddle 678vb.
direct 689vb.
director 690n.
dominate 733vb.
tyrant 735n.
master, autocrat 741n.
ornamental art 844n.
bossy
authoritative 733adj.
authoritarian 735adj.
bo'sun
mariner 270n.
Boswell
narrator 590n.
botanical
vegetal 366adj.
botanical 368adj.
botanical garden
botany 368n.
garden 370n.
botanist
botanist 368n.
botany
biology 358n.
botany 368n.
Botany Bay
prison camp 748n.
botch
neglect 458vb.
misrepresent 552vb.
impair 655vb.
repair 656vb.
be clumsy 695vb.
fail 728vb.
eyesore 842n.
botcher
mender 656n.
bungler 697n.
both
dual 90adj.
bother
commotion 318n.
be attentive 455vb.
distract 456vb.
activity 678n.
meddle 678vb.
be difficult 700vb.
hinder 702vb.
excitable state 822n.
worry 825n.
torment 827vb.
enrage 891vb.
bottle
vessel 194n.
potion 301n.
preserve 666vb.
bottleneck
contraction 198n.
narrowness 206n.
obstacle 702n.
bottle party
festivity 837n.
social gathering 882n.
bottle up
conceal 525vb.
preserve 666vb.
bottom
inferiority 35n.
extremity 69n.
lowness 210n.
depth 211n.
base 214n.
undermost 214adj.
support 218vb.
rear 238n.
buttocks 238n.
ship 275n.
marsh 347n.
stamina 600n.
courage 855n.
bottom drawer
store 632n.
preparation 669n.
bottomless
deep 211adj.
infernal 972adj.
bottommost
lesser 35adj.
bottomry
security 767n.
bottom, the
object of scorn 867n.
cad 938n.
bottom up
inverted 221adj.
botulism
infection 651n.
poisoning 659n.
boudoir

chamber 194n.
beauty parlor 843n.
bough
branch 53n.
foliage 366n.
boulder
sphere 252n.
hardness 326n.
rock 344n.
boulevard
street 192n.
path 624n.
bounce
recoil 280n.
eject 300vb.
ascend 308vb.
leap 312vb.
oscillate 317vb.
agitation 318n.
elasticity 328n.
boasting 877n.
bouncer
ejector 300n.
bouncing
cheerful 833adj.
bound
bate 37vb.
tied 45adj.
hem 234vb.
limit 236vb.
spurt 277n.
move fast 277vb.
leap 312n., vb.
certain 473adj.
fated 596adj.
subject 745adj.
restrained 747adj.
retentive 778adj.
indebted 803adj.
dutied 917adj.
boundary
separation 46n.
extremity 69n.
edge 234n.
limit 236n.
bounden
subject 745adj.
dutied 917adj.
bounder
vulgarian 847n.
bound for
directed 281adj.
boundless
infinite 107adj.
spacious 183adj.
bounds
region 184n.
outline 233n.
bounteous
liberal 813adj.
benevolent 897adj.
bountiful
giving 781adj.
bounty
subvention 703n.
gift 781n.
liberality 813n.
reward 962n.
bouquet
bunch 74n.
savoriness 390n.
odor 394n.
fragrance 396n.
ornamentation 844n.
applause, praise 923n.
bourgeois
median 30adj.
type size 587n.
commoner 869n.
bourgeoisie
mediocrity 732n.
commonalty 869n.
bourn
limit 236n.
goal 295n.
stream 350n.
bourse
bourse 618n.
mart 796n.
boustrophedon
writing 586n.
bout
period 110n.
periodicity 141n.
pugilism 716n.
bout rimé
prosody 593n.
bovine
animal 365adj.
unintelligent 499adj.
bow
prow 237n.
curve 248n.
camber 253n.
propellant 287n.
obeisance 311n.
stoop 311vb.
play music 413vb.
viol 414n.
knuckle under 721vb.
missile weapon 723n.
obey 739vb.
trimming 844n.
courteous act 884n.
greet 884vb.
show respect 920vb.
worship 981vb.
perform ritual 988vb.
bow-chaser
gun 723n.
Bowdler
prude 950n.
bowdlerize
impair 655vb.
bow down,– to
stoop 311vb.
honor 866vb.
be humble 872vb.
bowelless
pitiless 906adj.
bowels
insides 224n.
bowel wash
therapy 658n.
bower
pavilion 192n.
arbor 194n.
screen 421n.
love-nest 887n.
bowery
screened 421adj.
pleasurable 826adj.
bowl
bowl 194n.
cavity 255n.
missile 287n.
propel 287vb.
potion 301n.
rotate 315vb.
bowl along
go smoothly 258vb.
move fast 277vb.
bow-legged
deformed 246adj.
curved 248adj.
bowler
thrower 287n.
player 837n.
bowline
tackling 47n.
bowling-alley
arena 724n.
bowling-green
pleasance 192n.
horizontality 216n.
smoothness 258n.
arena 724n.
bowl out
dismiss 300vb.
defeat 727vb.
bowl over
disable 161vb.
fell 311vb.
surprise 508vb.
be wonderful 864vb.
bowls
ball game 837n.
bowman
shooter 287n.
soldiery 722n.
bow out
dismiss 300vb.
bowshot
short distance 200n.
bowsprit
prow 237n.
projection 254n.
Bow-street runner
detective 459n.
law officer 955n.
bowstring
kill 362vb.

means of execution 964n.
bow to
be inferior 35vb.
bowyer
soldiery 722n.
box
disjunction 46n.
small house 192n.
compartment 194n.
box 194n.
seat 218n.
circumscribe 232vb.
enclosure 235n.
strike 279vb.
tree 366n.
theater 594n.
fight 716vb.
boxer
dog 365n.
pugilist 722n.
boxing
pugilism 716n.
box-office
onlookers 441n.
theater 594n.
treasury 799n.
box on the ears
reprimand 924n.
box the compass
orientate 281vb.
rotate 315vb.
box up
imprison 747vb.
boy
youngster 132n.
male 372n.
lover 887n.
boycott
set apart 46vb.
exclusion 57n.
avoid 620n.
hindrance 702n.
make unwelcome 883vb.
disapprobation 924n.
boy-friend
friend 880n.
lover 887n.
boyhood
youth 130n.
boyish
young 130adj.
infantine 132adj.
foolish 499adj.
immature 670adj.
brabble
quarrel 709n.
fight 716n.
brace
tighten 45vb.
group 74n.
duality 90n.
strengthen 162vb.
supporter 218n.
support 218vb.
notation 410n.
punctuation 547n.
refresh 685vb.
brace and bit
perforator 263n.
bracelet(s)
fastening 47n.
loop 250n.
fetter 748n.
jewelry 844n.
brace oneself
prepare oneself 669vb.
bracer
stimulant 174n.
pungency 388n.
tonic 658n.
braces
fastening 47n.
hanger 217n.
supporter 218n.
underwear 228n.
brachial
brachial 53adj.
bracing
salubrious 652adj.
refreshing 685adj.
cheering 833adj.
bracken
plant 366n.
bracket
equalize 28vb.
join 45vb.
bond 47n.
classification 77n.
pair 90vb.
supporter 218n.
shelf 218n.
put between 231vb.
angularity 247n.
punctuation 547n.
bracket with
liken 18vb.
brackish
salty 388adj.
brad
fastening 47n.
bradawl
sharp point 256n.
perforator 263n.
Bradshaw
itinerary 267n.
guide-book 524n.
brae
high land 209n.
brag
be affected 850vb.
seek repute 866vb.
boast 877vb.
be insolent 878vb.
braggadocio
cowardice 856n.
(*see* brag)
braggart
(*see* brag)
Brahma
Trinity 965n.
divineness 965n.
Hindu god 967n.
Brahmana
non-Biblical scripture 975n.
Brahmanism
religious faith 973n.
Brahmi
letter 558n.
Brahmin
aristocrat 868n.
priest 986n.
Brahminic
religious 973adj.
priestly 985adj.
Brahminism
ecclesiasticism 985n.
Brahmo
sectarist 978n.
sectarian 978adj.
Brahmo Samaj
non-Christian sect 978n.
braid
tie 45vb.
ligature 47n.
crossing 222n.
weave 222vb.
variegate 437vb.
brail
tie 45vb.
elevate 310vb.
braille
lettering 586n.
writing 586n.
brain
head 213n.
kill 362vb.
render insensible 375vb.
intellect 447n.
intellectual 492n.
intelligence 498n.
brain-child
idea 451n.
brain-fag
thought 449n.
fatigue 684n.
brainless
mindless 448adj.
foolish 499adj.
brainlessness
non-intellect 447vb.
brainpan
head 213n.
brainsick
light-minded 456adj.
crazed 503adj.
frenzied 503adj.
brain specialist

doctor 658n.
brainstorm
violence 176n.
psychopathy 503n.
excitable state 822n.
brain trust
interrogation 459n.
intellectual 492n.
brainwash
teach 534vb.
misteach 535vb.
pervert 655vb.
brainwashing
conversion 147n.
teaching 534n.
brain-wave
idea 451n.
brain-work
thought 449n.
brain-worker
intellectual 492adj.
brainy
intelligent 498adj.
brake
halt 145vb.
moderator 177n.
bring to rest 266vb.
train 274n.
retard 278vb.
wood 366n.
safeguard 662n.
obstacle 702n.
hinder 702vb.
restraint 747n.
fetter 748n.
brakeman
driver 268n.
brake-van
train 274n.
bramble
prickle 256n.
bane 659n.
brambly
sharp 256adj.
bran
leavings 41n.
powder 332n.
rubbish 641n.
branch
adjunct 40n.
branch 53n.
be dispersed 75vb.
classification 77n.
bifurcate 92vb.
descendant 170n.
extend 183vb.
nest 192n.
filament 208n.
angulate 247vb.
diverge 294vb.
tree, foliage 366n.
society 708n.
sect 978n.
branching
spacious 183adj.
symmetrical 245adj.
branch out
be diffuse 570vb.
branchy
brachial 53adj.
brand
sort 77n.
burn 381vb.
lighter 385n.
torch 420n.
identification 547n.
label 547n.
mark 547vb.
blemish 845vb.
slur 867n.
shame 867vb.
censure 924n.
defame 926vb.
accuse 928vb.
branding-iron
burning 381n.
brandish
operate 173vb.
brandish 317vb.
agitate 318vb.
show 522vb.
be ostentatious 875vb.
threaten 900vb.
brangle
bicker 709vb.
brash
piece 53n.
insolent 878adj.
brass
a mixture 43n.
obsequies 364n.
megaphone 400n.
resonance 404n.
stridor 407n.
orchestra 413n.
musical instrument 414n.
monument 548n.
director 690n.
badge of rank 743n.
dibs 797n.
sauciness 878n.
brassard
livery 547n.
badge of rank 743n.
brasserie
café 192n.
brass hat
army officer 741n.
brassière
underwear 228n.
brass tacks
reality 1n.
brassy
loud 400adj.
strident 407adj.
ornate 574adj.
impertinent 878adj.
brat
child 132n.
brattice
lining 227n.
partition 231n.
bravado
boast 877n.
boasting 877n.
brave
defy 711vb.
combatant 722n.
soldier 722n.
brave person 855n.
courageous 855adj.
be courageous 855vb.
showy 875adj.
bravery
courage 855n.
ostentation 875n.
bravo
violent creature 176n.
desperado 857n.
ruffian 904n.
bravura
musical skill 413n.
masterpiece 694n.
braw
fashionable 848adj.
brawl
loudness 400n.
quarrel 709n.
bicker 709vb.
fight 716n.
brawler
opponent 705n.
rioter 738n.
brawn
vitality 162n.
brawny
stalwart 162adj.
fleshy 195adj.
braws
finery 844n.
bray
pulverize 332vb.
be loud 400vb.
resound 404vb.
rasp 407vb.
ululate 409vb.
braze
join 45vb.
agglutinate 48vb.
brazen
strident 407adj.
undisguised 522adj.
false 541adj.
proud 871adj.
insolent 878adj.
impenitent 940adj.
brazier
heater 383n.
breach
disjunction 46n.
gap 201n.

dissension 709n.
enmity 881n.
undueness 916n.
breach of faith
non-observance 769n.
perfidy 930n.
breach of the peace
quarrel 709n.
breach of trust
peculation 788n.
bread
food 301n.
cereal 301n.
bread and butter
food 301n.
vocation 622n.
bread-and-butter letter
thanks 907n.
bread and water
unsavoriness 391n.
insufficiency 636n.
fasting 946n.
bread-riot
revolt 738n.
breadth
greatness 32n.
measure 183n.
size 195n.
breadth 205n.
breadth of mind
wisdom 498n.
breadwinner
worker 686n.
breadwinning
acquisition 771n.
gainful 771adj.
break
disjunction 46n.
break 46vb.
be disjoined 46vb.
incompleteness 55n.
discontinuity 72n.
numeration 86n.
interim 108n.
change 143n.
lull 145n.
continuance 146n.
demolish 165vb.
interval 201n.
be brittle 330vb.
flow 350vb.
rasp 407vb.
wound 655vb.
repose 683n.
quarrel 709vb.
defeat 727vb.
fail 728vb.
prosperity 730n.
oppress 735vb.
depose 752vb.
lose 772vb.
not pay 805vb.
breakable
brittle 330adj.
breakaway
revolt 738n.
independent 744adj.
break away
be dispersed 75vb.
run away 620vb.
escape 667vb.
revolt 738vb.
schismatize 978vb.
break-back
compensation 31n.
break bulk
void 300vb.
break camp
decamp 296vb.
breakdown
decomposition 51n.
stop 145n.
helplessness 161n.
ruin 165n.
illness 651n.
hitch 702n.
failure 728n.
lamentation 836n.
dance 837n.
breaker
vat 194n.
wave 350n.
breaker-in
trainer 537n.
break even
be equal 28vb.
breakfast
meal 301n.
eat 301vb.
break in
irrupt 297vb.
intrude 297vb.
break in 369vb.
train 534vb.
habituate 610vb.
subjugate 745vb.
breaking point
casus belli 709n.
completion 725n.
breaking voice
aphony 578n.
break in on
derange 63vb.
mistime 138vb.
intrude 297vb.
break it up
be disjoined 46vb.
breakneck
sloping 220adj.
speedy 277adj.
rash 857adj.
break of
cure 656vb.
break of day
morning 128n.
half-light 419n.
break off
be incomplete 55adj.
cease 145vb.
break open
force 176vb.
break out
begin 68vb.
be violent 176vb.
emerge 298vb.
escape 667vb.
attack 712vb.
be excitable 822vb.
break ranks
be dispersed 75vb.
break the news
inform 524vb.
breakthrough
attack 712n.
success 727n.
break-up
disjunction 46n.
decomposition 51n.
finality 69n.
dispersion 75n.
revolution 149n.
ruin 165n.
breakwater
projection 254n.
safeguard 662n.
break wind
eruct 300vb.
break with
quarrel 709vb.
bream
table fish 365n.
breast
interiority 224n.
be in front 237vb.
bosom 253n.
climb 308vb.
spirit 447n.
withstand 704vb.
affections 817n.
breast-feed
feed 301vb.
breastplate
bosom 253n.
protection 660n.
obstacle 702n.
armor 713n.
breastwork
defenses 713n.
breath
insubstantial thing 4n.
instant 116n.
breeze 352n.
life 360n.
odor 394n.
faintness 401n.
breathe
exude 298vb.
breathe 352vb.
live 360vb.
sound faint 401vb.
hint 524vb.
divulge 526vb.

voice 577vb.
speak 579vb.
repose 683vb.
be refreshed 685vb.
breathe down one's neck
impend 155vb.
approach 289vb.
breathe in
breathe 352vb.
smell 394vb.
breathe life into
vitalize 360vb.
breathe of
evidence 466vb.
mean 514vb.
breathe out
emit 300vb.
breathe 352vb.
breather
repose 683n.
breathe upon
shame 867vb.
defame 926vb.
breathing
oscillation 317n.
respiration 352n.
life 360n.
alive 360adj.
breathless
agitated 318adj.
puffing 352adj.
dead 361adj.
voiceless 578adj.
stammering 580adj.
hasty 680adj.
panting 684adj.
fervent 818adj.
nervous 854adj.
wondering 864adj.
breath-taker
prodigy 864n.
breath-taking
prodigious 32adj.
notable 638adj.
wonderful 864adj.
bred
(*see* breed)
breech
dress 228vb.
rear, buttocks 238n.
fire-arm 723n.
breech-cloth
loincloth 228n.
breeches
breeches 228n.
breechloader
fire-arm 723n.
breed
character 5n.
race 11n.
grow 36vb.
breed 77n.
generate 164vb.
posterity 170n.
breed stock 369n.
educate 534vb.
mature 669vb.
breeder
producer 167n.
breeder 369n.
breeder-reactor
nucleonics 160n.
breeding
good taste 846n.
etiquette 848n.
breeding-place
seedbed 156n.
breed with
unite with 45vb.
breeze
breeze 352n.
blow 352vb.
quarrel 709n.
excitation 821n.
breezy
airy 340adj.
windy 352adj.
cheerful 833adj.
disrespectful 921adj.
brethren
laity 987n.
breve
notation 410n.
punctuation 547n.
brevet
warrant 737n.
mandate 751n.
permit 756n.
breviary
textbook 589n.
compendium 592n.
office-book 988n.
brevier
type size 587n.
brevity
smallness 33n.
brief space 114n.
shortness 204n.
conciseness 569n.
brew
a mixture 43n.
mix 43vb.
soup 301n.
liquor 301n.
mature 669vb.
brewer
preparer 669n.
brewis
cereal 301n.
briar
(*see* brier)
bribable
bought 792adj.
venal 930adj.
bribe
incentive 612n.
bribe 612vb.
offer 759vb.
reward 962n.
bribery
(*see* bribe)
bric-a-brac
bauble 639n.
ornamentation 844n.
finery 844n.
brick
component 58n.
lamina 207n.
hardness 326n.
pottery 381n.
building material 631n.
missile weapon 723n.
indignity 921n.
disapprobation 924n.
gentleman 929n.
good man 937n.
brickbat
piece 53n.
missile weapon 723n.
bricklayer
artisan 686n.
bricks
plaything 837n.
bricks and mortar
building material 631n.
brick wall
hardness 326n.
obstacle 702n.
brickwork
edifice 164n.
structure 331n.
bridal
wedding 894n.
matrimonial 894adj.
bride
woman 373n.
spouse 894n.
bridegroom
spouse 894n.
bridesmaid
bridesman 894n.
bridge
connect 45vb.
vertex 213n.
tooth 256n.
passage 305n.
viol 414n.
bridge 624n.
facilitate 701vb.
compromise 770vb.
card game 837vb.
bridgehead
battleground 724n.
bridge-table
arena 724n.
bridle
break in 369vb.
restrain 747vb.
fetter 748n.
bridle up
get angry 891vb.

brief
small 33adj.
brief 114adj.
short 204adj.
inform 524vb.
concise 569adj.
be concise 569vb.
description 590n.
compendium 592n.
preparation 669n.
make ready 669vb.
command 737n., vb.
brief-case
case 194n.
briefing
information 524n.
preparation 669n.
advice 691n.
briefless
unused 674adj.
non-active 677adj.
briefs
underwear 228n.
brier, briar
prickle 256n.
air-pipe 353n.
tobacco 388n.
bane 659n.
briery
sharp 256adj.
brig
sailing-ship 275n.
brigade
combine 50vb.
group 74n.
bring together 74vb.
formation 722n.
brigadier
army officer 741n.
brigand
robber 789n.
brigandage
brigandage 788n.
brigantine
sailing-ship 275n.
bright
undimmed 417adj.
luminous 417adj.
luminescent 420adj.
florid 425adj.
white 427adj.
intelligent 498adj.
clean 648adj.
cheerful 833adj.
beautiful 841adj.
promising 852adj.
brighten
make bright 417vb.
be cheerful 833vb.
beautify 841vb.
bright eyes
a beauty 841n.
brightness
light 417n.
wit 839n.
beauty 841n.
bright side
pleasurableness 826n.
bright young thing
modernist 126n.
brilliance
light 417n.
hue 425n.
intelligence 498n.
beauty 841n.
ostentation 875n.
brilliant
witty 839adj.
gem 844n.
noteworthy 866adj.
(*see* brilliance)
brilliantine
adhesive 47n.
unguent 357n.
hairwash 843n.
brim
fill 54vb.
headgear 228n.
edge 234n.
abound 635vb.
brimstone
fumigator 385n.
brindled
mottled 437adj.
brine
water 339n.
drench 341vb.
ocean 343n.
pungency 388n.
season 388vb.
preserver 666n.
bring
carry 273vb.
offer 759vb.
bring about
cause 156vb.
produce 164vb.
induce 612vb.
carry out 725vb.
bring back
replace 187vb.
deliver 668vb.
restitute 787vb.
bring down
fell 311vb.
strike at 712vb.
bring forth
reproduce itself 164vb.
manifest 522vb.
bring forward
attract notice 455vb.
bring home to
attribute 158vb.
convince 485vb.
impress 821vb.
bring in
be profitable 271vb.
admit 299vb.
bring on
cause 156vb.
promote 285vb.
bring out
manifest 522vb.
bring over
convince 485vb.
induce 612vb.
bring round
make sane 302vb.
convince 485vb.
induce 612vb.
bring to
add 38vb.
bring to rest 266vb.
bring to a head
mature 669vb.
bring to bear
relate 9vb.
use 673vb.
bring to book
account 808vb.
bring together
pacify 719vb.
mediate 720vb.
bring to heel
subjugate 745vb.
bring to life
vitalize 360vb.
bring to light
discover 484vb.
manifest 522vb.
bring to pass
cause 156vb.
bring up
produce 164vb.
vomit 300vb.
argue 475vb.
manifest 522vb.
educate 534vb.
brink
extremity 69n.
nearness 200n.
edge 234n.
brinkman
desperado 857n.
brinkmanship
tactics 688n.
skill 694n.
rashness 857n.
brisk
vigorous 174adj.
active 678adj.
brisling
fish food 301n.
bristle with
be many 104vb.
abound 635vb.
superabound 637vb.
bristly
sharp 256adj.
hairy 259adj.
Briticism
dialect 560n.

British Israelites
sect 978n.
British square
formation 722n.
Briton
native 191n.
gentleman 929n.
brittle
ephemeral 114adj.
flimsy 163adj.
brittle 330adj.
broach
initiate 68vb.
cause 156vb.
sharp point 256n.
perforator 263n.
void 300vb.
make flow 350vb.
publish 528vb.
undertake 672vb.
offer 759vb.
broad
great 32adj.
general 79adj.
spacious 183adj.
large 195adj.
broad 205adj.
lake 346n.
woman 373n.
inexact 495adj.
wise 498adj.
dialectical 560adj.
free 744adj.
impure 951adj.
prostitute 952n.
broad arrow
label 547n.
broad-based
inclusive 78adj.
general 79adj.
broadcast
disperse 75vb.
generalize 79vb.
let fall 311vb.
cultivate 370vb.
communicate 524vb.
publish 528vb.
telecommunication 531n.
oration 579n.
waste 634vb.
broadcloth
textile 222n.
broaden
augment 36vb.
generalize 79vb.
enlarge 197vb.
expand 197vb.
be broad 205vb.
broad-minded
wise 498adj.
free 744adj.
broadness
generality 79n.
breadth 205n.
inexactness 495n.
(*see* broad)
broadsheet
the press 528n.
broadside
laterality 239n.
bombardment 712n.
gun 723n.
broadwife
slave 742n.
spouse 894n.
Brobdingnagian
huge 195adj.
giant 195n.
brocade
textile 222n.
needlework 844n.
brocatelle
needlework 844n.
broccoli
vegetable 301n.
brochette
fastening 47n.
sharp point 256n.
brochure
the press 528n.
book 589n.
brocket
male animal 372n.
brogue
specialty 80n.
dialect 560n.
pronunciation 577n.
speech defect 580n.
brogues
footwear 228n.
broidery
needlework 844n.
broil
cook 301vb.
fight 716n.
broiler
poultry 365n.
broke
poor 801adj.
broke for
deputize 755vb.
broken
rough 259adj.
imperfect 647adj.
tamed 369adj.
(*see* break)
broken reed
weak thing 163n.
broken thread
discontinuity 72n.
broken-winded
diseased 651adj.
panting 684adj.
broker
intermediary 231n.
consignee 754n.
merchant 794n.
brokerage
pay 804n.
discount 810n.
bromide
moderator 177n.
maxim 496n.
witticism 839n.
bronchia
air-pipe 353n.
bronchitis
respiratory disease 651n.
bronchus
air-pipe 353n.
bronco
saddle-horse 273n.
bronco buster
rider 268n.
herdsman 369n.
brontosaur
animal 365n.
bronze
a mixture 43n.
brownness 430n.
sculpture 554n.
Bronze Age
era 110n.
brooch
fastening 47n.
jewelry 844n.
brood
group 74n.
youngling 132n.
posterity 170n.
meditate 449vb.
be dejected 834vb.
brooding
preparatory 669adj.
brood-mare
horse 273n.
broody
productive 164adj.
brook
stream 350n.
be patient 823vb.
brook no denial
affirm 532vb.
necessitate 596vb.
be obstinate 602vb.
broom
plant 366n.
cleaning utensil 648n.
brose
cereal 310n.
broth
soup 301n.
brothel
brothel 951n.
brothel-keeper
bawd 952n.
brother
kinsman 11n.
analogue 18n.
compeer 28n.

male 372n.
colleague 708n.
title 870n.
friend 880n.
monk 986n.
church title 986n.
brotherhood
family 11n.
band 74n.
community 708n.
friendship 880n.
sect 978n.
monk 986n.
brotherly
akin 11adj.
friendly 880adj.
benevolent 897adj.
brougham
carriage 274n.
brow
head 213n.
face 237n.
dome 253n.
projection 254n.
browbeat
induce 612vb.
frighten 854vb.
be insolent 878vb.
reprove 924vb.
brown
dry 342adj.
darken 418vb.
brownness 430n.
browned off
discontented 829adj.
brownie
elf 970n.
brown study
thought 449n.
abstractedness 456n.
fantasy 513n.
browse
graze 301vb.
study 536vb.
bruise
pulverize 332adj.
pain 377n.
touch 378vb.
ill-treat 645vb.
wound 655n., vb.
blemish 845n.
bruiser
pugilist 722n.
bruit
publish 528vb.
rumor 529n.
brumal
wintry 129adj.
cold 380adj.
brummagem
sham 542n.
spurious 542adj.
cheap 812adj.
brunette
woman 373n.
black 428adj.
brown 430adj.
brunt
collision 279n.
difficulty 700n.
brunt, bear the
be in difficulty 700vb.
parry 713vb.
resist 715vb.
brush
be near 200vb.
be contiguous 202vb.
pendant 217n.
rear 238n.
rub 333vb.
cleaning utensil 648n.
fight 716n.
give battle 718vb.
brush off
repel 292vb.
eject 300vb.
brush up
study 536vb.
clean 648vb.
brushwood
wood 366n.
fuel 385n.
brushwork
painting 553n.
brusque
violent 176adj.
concise 569adj.
taciturn 582adj.
hasty 680adj.
ungracious 885adj.
brutal
violent 176adj.
oppressive 735adj.
ungracious 885adj.
cruel 898adj.
vicious 934adj.
heinous 934adj.
brutality
moral insensibility 820n.
(*see* brutal)
brutalize
pervert 655vb.
make insensitive 820vb.
make wicked 934vb.
brute
violent creature 176n.
animal 365n.
mindless 448adj.
tyrant 735n.
rude person 885n.
ruffian 904n.
noxious animal 904n.
monster 938n.
brute creation
animality 365n.
non-intellect 448n.
brute fact
reality 1n.
brute force
strength 162n.
violence 176n.
brute force 735n.
brutish
plebeian 869adj.
discourteous 885adj.
cruel 898adj.
sensual 944adj.
bubble
insubstantial thing 4n
brief span 114n.
stimulation 174n.
bladder 194n.
minuteness 196n.
sphere 252n.
effervesce 318vb.
levity 323n.
brittleness 330n.
flow 350vb.
bubble 355n., vb.
hiss 406vb.
deceive 542vb.
bauble 639n.
bubbly
wine 301n.
bubbly 355adj.
bubo
swelling 253n.
buccal
lateral 239adj.
buccaneer
rob 788vb.
robber 789n.
Buchenwald
prison camp 748n.
Buchmanism
sect 978n.
buck
leap 312n., vb.
flow 350vb.
deer 365n.
male animal 372n.
clean 648vb.
paper money 797n.
fop 848n.
buck-basket
basket 194n.
buckboard
carriage 274n.
bucket
vessel 194n.
bucket shop
bourse 618n.
buckle
join 45vb.
break 46vb.
fastening 47n.
distort 246vb.
make concave 255vb.
buckled
convoluted 251adj.

buckler
armor 713n.
buckle to
be resolute 599vb.
buckling
table fish 365n.
buckram
bookbinding 589n.
pretension 850n.
buckshot
ammunition 723n.
buckskins
breeches 228n.
buck up
relieve 831vb.
cheer, be cheerful 833vb.
hope 852vb.
bucolic
agrarian 370adj.
poetic 593adj.
bud
grow 36vb.
origin 68n.
source 156n.
growth 157n.
result 157vb.
reproduce itself 164vb.
be fruitful 171vb.
expand 197vb.
swelling 253n.
implant 303vb.
flower 366n.
Buddha
sage 500n.
religious teacher 973n.
Buddhism
religious faith 973n.
Buddhist
religionist 973n.
budding
young 130adj.
new 126adj.
buddy
colleague 707n.
chum 880n.
budge
hair 259n.
move 265vb.
budgerigar
bird 365n.
budgerow
small house 192n.
boat 275n.
budget
bunch 74n.
bag 174n.
correspondence 588n.
store 632n.
provide 633vb.
accounts 808n.
budgetary
monetary 797adj.
accounting 808adj.
budgeteer
treasurer 798n.
buff
bareness 229n.
smooth 258vb.
rub 333vb.
brown 430adj.
yellow 433adj.
cleaning cloth 648n.
buffalo
cattle 365n.
buffer
intermediary 231n.
male 372n.
obstacle 702n.
defense 713n.
cosmetic 843n.
buffer state
intermediary 231n.
buffet
cabinet 194n.
knock 279n.
strike 279vb.
ill-treat 645vb.
wound 655vb.
buffoon
entertainer 594n.
humorist 839n.
laughing-stock 851n.
buffoonery
foolery 497n.
ridiculousness 849n.
bug
vermin 365n.
bugaboo
false alarm 665n.
intimidation 854n.
demon 970n.
bugbear
fantasy 513n.
bane 659n.
false alarm 665n.
intimidation 854n.
demon 970n.
buggy
carriage 274n.
bug-house
madhouse 503n.
bugle
play music 413vb.
horn 414n.
call 547n.
heraldry 547n.
war 718n.
trimming 844n.
bugler
instrumentalist 413n.
build
compose 56vb.
produce 164vb.
form 243n.
efform 243vb.
elevate 310vb.
structure 331n.
builder
producer 167n.
elevation 310n.
planner 623n.
artisan 686n.
building
edifice 164n.
production 164n.
house, housing 192n.
ornamental art 844n.
build-up
increase 36n.
composition 56n.
overestimation 482n.
advertisement 528n.
build up
strengthen 162vb.
built-in
ingredient 58adj.
accompanying 89adj.
interior 224adj.
built-up
urban 192adj.
bulb
swelling 253n.
plant 366n.
lamp 420n.
bulbous
expanded 197adj.
rotund 252adj.
convex 253adj.
bulbul
bird 365n.
bulge
vantage 34n.
increment 36n.
fill 54vb.
swelling 253n.
be convex 253vb.
bulk
quantity 26n.
main part 32n.
be great 32vb.
greater number 104n.
bulk 195n.
bulkhead
partition 231n.
obstacle 702n.
bulky
substantial 3adj.
great 32adj.
large 195adj.
bull
cattle 365n.
male animal 372n.
mistake 495n.
solecism 565n.
practice 601n.
gambler 618n.
decree 737n.
speculate 791vb.
purchaser 792n.
formality 875n.
bulldog

dog 368n.
brave person 855n.
bulldoze
demolish 165vb.
collide 279vb.
bulldozer
smoother 258n.
ram 279n.
bull in a china shop
turmoil 61n.
bullet
sphere 252n.
speeder 277n.
missile weapon 723n.
ammunition 723n.
bulletin
report 524n.
news 529n.
correspondence 588n.
bullet-proof
unyielding 162adj.
invulnerable 660adj.
bull-fight
duel 716n.
bull-fighter
combatant 722n.
bullion
textile 222n.
bullion 797n.
bullionist
moneyer 797n.
bullish
buying 792adj.
dear 811adj.
bull market
dearness 811n.
bullock
eunuch 161n.
cattle 365n.
male animal 372n.
bull-ring
arena 724n.
bull's-eye
centrality 225n.
lamp 420n.
objective 617n.
bully
athlete 162n.
violent creature 176n.
combatant 722n.
tyrant 735n.
oppress 735vb.
torment 827vb.
frighten 854vb.
brave person 855n.
desperado 857n.
low fellow 869n.
insolent person 878n.
be insolent 878vb.
chum 880n.
be malevolent 898vb.
threaten 900vb.
ruffian 904n.
libertine 952n.
bulrush
plant 366n.
bulwark
protection 660n.
obstacle 702n.
defense 713n.
fortification 713n.
bum
wander 267vb.
wanderer 268n.
beggar 763n.
bum-bailiff
officer 741n.
law officer 955n.
bumbledom
governance 733n.
jurisdiction 955n.
bumble-puppy
unskilled 695adj.
bumboat
boat 275n.
bummaree
bearer 273n.
bump
swelling 253n.
protuberance 254n.
move slowly 278vb.
collision 279n.
faintness 401n.
sound dead 405vb.
wound 655n.
bumper
plenitude 54n.
intermediary 231n.
potion 301n.
shelter 662n.
defense 713n.
bumper crop
plenty 635n.
bumpiness
roughness 259n.
bump into
collide 217vb.
meet 295vb.
bumpkin
dunce 501n.
countryman 869n.
bump off
murder 362vb.
bump-supper
feasting 301n.
festivity 837n.
social gathering 882n.
bumptious
prideful 871adj.
vain 873adj.
insolent 878adj.
bump up
augment 36vb.
bumpy
non-uniform 17adj.
discontinuous 72adj.
rough 259adj.
bun
hair 259n.
pastry 301n.
hair-dressing 843n.
bunch
cohere 48vb.
bunch, crowd 74n.
congregate 74vb.
party 708n.
bundle
bunch 74n.
bag 194n.
collection 632n.
store 632n., vb.
bundle out
eject 300vb.
bun-fight
amusement 837n.
bung
covering 226n.
stopper 264n.
close 264vb.
bungalow
house 192n.
bungle
lose a chance 138vb.
neglect 458vb.
mistake 495n.
be clumsy 695vb.
fail 728vb.
bungler
fool 501n.
nonentity 639n.
bungler 697n.
hinderer 702n.
loser 728n.
bunion
swelling 253n.
bunk
dwell 192vb.
bed 218n.
empty talk 515n.
run away 620vb.
bunker
cellar 194n.
storage 632n.
provide 633vb.
obstacle 702n.
bunkum
falsehood 141n.
empty talk 515n.
boast 877n.
bunt
be convex 253vb.
collide 279vb.
bunting
flag 547n.
buoy
sailing aid 269n.
elevate 310vb.
levity 323n.
signpost 547n.
buoyancy
energy 160n.
levity 323n.

elasticity 328n.
hope 852n.
buoyant
swimming 269adj.
cheerful 833adj.
hoping 852adj.
buoy up
support 218vb.
bur
(*see* burr)
burble
flow 350vb.
reason ill 477vb.
be foolish 499vb.
burbler
fool 501n.
burden
repetition 106n.
load 193vb.
gravity 322n.
make heavy 322vb.
vocal music 412n.
topic 452n.
verse form 593n.
ill-treat 645vb.
bane 659n.
difficulty 700n.
encumbrance 702n.
adversity 731n.
oppress 735vb.
burdened
bearing 273adj.
burdensome
weighty 322adj.
bad 645adj.
laborious 682adj.
difficult 700adj.
hindering 702adj.
annoying 827adj.
bureau
cabinet 194n.
workshop 687n.
jurisdiction 955n.
bureaucracy
management 689n.
governance 733n.
commission 751n.
bureaucrat
official 690n.
officer 741n.
burgee
flag 547n.
burgeon
grow 36vb.
reproduce itself 164vb.
expand 197vb.
flower 366n.
burgess
native 191n.
burgh
housing 192n.
burgher
native 191n.
burglar
thief 789n.
burglar-alarm
danger signal 665n.
burglarious
thieving 788adj.
burglary
stealing 788n.
burgle
steal 788vb.
burgomaster
officer 741n.
burial
immersion 303n.
interment 364n.
concealment 525n.
obliteration 550n.
detention 747n.
buried
deep 211adj.
dead 361adj.
buried 364adj.
neglected 458adj.
forgotten 506adj.
concealed 525adj.
secluded 883adj.
burin
sculpture 554n.
engraving 555n.
burke
suppress 165vb.
murder 362vb.
burl
solid body 324n.
burlap
textile 222n.
burlesque
mimicry 20n.
foolery 497n.
exaggeration 546n.
misrepresent 552n.
stage play 594n.
ridiculousness 849n.
funny 849adj.
satirize 851vb.
burly
stalwart 162adj.
burn
dry 342vb.
stream 350n.
be hot 379vb.
burn 381vb.
shine 417vb.
embrown 430vb.
waste 634vb.
excite 821vb.
desire 859vb.
be in love 887vb.
resent 891vb.
execute 963vb.
burnable
combustible 385adj.
burner
burning 381n.
furnace 383n.
torch 420n.
burn in
mark 547vb.
burning
pungent 388adj.
fervent 818adj.
angry 891adj.
burning-glass
optical device 442n.
burnish
smooth 258vb.
make bright 417n.
decorate 844vb.
burn one's boats
be resolute 599vb.
burn one's fingers
stultify oneself 695vb.
to rash 857vb.
burnoose
cloak 228n.
burn-proof
incombustible 382adj.
burn the candle at both ends
waste 634vb.
be prodigal 815vb.
be intemperate 943vb.
be sensual 944vb.
burn the ground
move fast 277vb.
burn the midnight oil
be late 136vb.
study 536vb.
burnt offering
propitiation 941n.
oblation 981n.
burp
eruct 300vb.
breathe 352vb.
burr, bur
coherence 48n.
roughness 259n.
perforator 263n.
rasp 407vb.
engraving 555n.
neologize 560vb.
pronunciation 577n.
voice 577vb.
speech defect 580n.
burrow
weaken 163vb.
dwelling 192n.
excavation 255n.
make concave 255vb.
pierce 263vb.
descend 309vb.
lurk 523vb.
refuge 662n.
bursar
treasurer 798n.
bursary
treasury 799n.
reward 962n.
burst

break, rend 46vb.
be dispersed 75vb.
instant 116n.
be violent 175vb.
outbreak 176n.
open 263vb.
spurt 277n.
be brittle 330vb.
have feeling 374vb.
be loud 400vb.
bang 402n., vb.
activity 678n.
miscarry 728vb.
burst forth
begin 68vb.
expand 197vb.
burst in
irrupt, intrude 297vb.
burst open
force 176vb.
burst out
be excitable 822vb.
get angry 891vb.
burst with
superabound 637vb.
bury
insert 303vb.
implant 303vb.
inter 364vb.
conceal 525vb.
obliterate 550vb.
store 632vb.
imprison 747vb.
bury the hatchet
forget 506vb.
make peace 719vb.
forgive 909vb.
bus
conveyance 267n.
bus 274n.
busby
headgear 228n.
bush
line 227vb.
plain 348n.
wood 366n.
artless 699adj.
bushel
great quantity 32n.
certain quantity 104n.
metrology 465n.
Bushido
code of duty 917n.
probity 929n.
bushing
lining 227n.
bushman
low fellow 869n.
bush-ranger
robber 789n.
bushy
dense 325adj.
arboreal 366adj.
business
affairs 154n.
production 164n.
topic 452n.
dramaturgy 594n.
intention 617n.
business 622n.
function 622n.
undertaking 672n.
action 676n.
activity 678n.
trade 791n.
business house
workshop 687n.
corporation 708n.
businesslike
orderly 60adj.
businesslike 622adj.
industrious 678adj.
expert 694adj.
busker
entertainer 594n.
buskin
footwear 228n.
drama 594n.
busman
carrier 273n.
busman's holiday
exertion 682n.
buss
fishing-boat 275n.
caress 889vb.
bust
bosom 253n.
meal 301n.
monument 548n.
image 551n.
sculpture 554n.
gluttony 947n.
bustle
skirt 228n.
be agitated 318vb.
activity 678n.
bustling
eventful 154adj.
excited 821adj.
busy
eventful 154adj.
inquisitive 453adj.
employ 622vb.
doing 676adj.
busy bee
busy person 678n.
busybody
inquisitor 453n.
meddler 678n.
adviser 691n.
but
qualification 468n.
nevertheless 468adv.
butcher
violent creature 176n.
killer 362n.
slaughter 362vb.
provider 633n.
ruffian 904n.
butler
domestic 742n.
retainer 742n.
butt
vat 194n.
limit 236n.
collide 279vb.
repel 292vb.
fool, ninny 501n.
objective 617n.
strike at 712vb.
arena 724n.
laughing-stock 851n.
butte
high land 209n.
butt-end
remainder 41n.
extremity 69n.
butter
overlay 226vb.
smooth 258vb.
lubricate 334vb.
fat 357n.
flatter 925vb.
butter-fingered
clumsy 695adj.
butterfingers
bungler 697n.
butterflies
nervousness 854n.
butterfly
fly 365n.
variegation 437n.
waverer 601n.
butter-in
meddler 678n.
butterscotch
sweetmeat 301n.
sweet 392n.
buttery
provisions 301n.
fatty 357adj.
storage 632n.
butt in
interfere 231vb.
meet 295vb.
meddle 678vb.
buttocks
rear 238n.
button
fastening 47n.
close 264vb.
trifle 639n.
buttoned-up
reticent 525adj.
buttonhole
fastening 47n.
orifice 263n.
fragrance 396n.
be loquacious 581vb.
speak to 583vb.
be tedious 838vb.
ornamentation 844n.

buttonhook
fastening 47n.
buttons
youngster 132n.
courier 531n.
servant 742n.
buttress
strengthen 162vb.
supporter 218n.
projection 254n.
corroborate 466vb.
fortification 713n.
church exterior 990n.
butyraceous
fatty 357adj.
buxom
cheerful 833adj.
shapely 841adj.
buy
acquire 771vb.
purchase 792vb.
expend 806vb.
buy and sell
trade 791vb.
buyer
owner 776n.
recipient 782n.
purchaser 792n.
buyer's market
mart 796n.
cheapness 812n.
buy off
bribe 612vb.
deliver 668vb.
buzz
be near 200vb.
fly 271vb.
roll 403n.
resound 404vb.
hiss 406vb.
ululation 409n.
rumor 529n.
obstruct 702vb.
buzz about
publish 528vb.
be published 528vb.
buzzard
bird of prey 365n.
fool 501n.
buzzer
megaphone 400n.
signal 547n.
buzz off
decamp 296vb.
by
akin 11adj.
born 360adj.
by means of 629adv.
by and large
generally 79adv.
by-blow
bastardy 954n.
bye
extra 40n.
by favor
during pleasure 112adv.
bygone
past 125adj.
forgotten 506adj.
by halves
incompletely 55adv.
by inches
by degrees 27adv.
piecemeal 53adv.
by-law
rule 81n.
by-pass
avoid 620vb.
road 624n.
circuit 626n., vb.
bypath
deviation 282n.
path 624n.
by-play
hint 524n.
gesture 547n.
by-product
sequel 67n.
product 164n.
byre
stable 192n.
cattle pen 369n.
farm tool 370n.
bystander
spectator 441n.
by the book
by rule 81adv.
by the way
concerning 9adv.
incidentally 137adv.
at random 618adv.
by turns
correlatively 12adv.
by-way
path 624n.
byword
maxim 496n.
slang 560n.
laughing-stock 851n.
object of scorn 867n.
Byzantine
olden 127adj.
Byzantinism
art 551n.

C

cab
compartment 194n.
cab 274n.
cabal
latency 523n.
planner 623n.
plot 623n., vb.
sedition 738n.
cabalism
occultism 984n.
cabaret
theater 594n.
stage show 594n.
place of amusement 837n.
cabbage
leavings 41n.
vegetable 301n.
earnings 771n.
steal 788vb.
booty 790n.
cabby
driver 268n.
caber
missile 287n.
cabin
small house 192n.
chamber 194n.
railroad 624n.
imprison 747vb.
cabin-boy
youngster 132n.
mariner 270n.
servant 742n.
cabin-class
genteel 868adj.
cabinet
chamber 194n.
cabinet 194n.
storage 632n.
management 689n.
director 690n.
council 692n.
cable
cable 47n.
electricity 160n.
information 524n.
message 529n.
telecommunication 531n.
cabman
driver 268n.
caboose
train 274n.
heater 383n.
cabriolet
carriage 274n.
ca' canny
be cautious 858vb.
cacation
cacation 302n.
cache
retreat 192n.
concealment 525n.
hiding-place 527n.
store 632n.
refuge 662n.
cachet
label 547n.
repute 866n.
cachexia
weakness 163n.
ill-health 651n.

cachinnation
loudness 400n.
cry 408n.
laughter 835n.
cacique
potentate 741n.
cackle
ululate 409vb.
chatter 581n.
laughter 835n.
cacoëthes
habit 610n.
desire 859n.
cacogenics
biology 358n.
cacography
spelling 558n.
cacology
solecism 565n.
caconym
neology 560n.
cacophony
stridor 407n.
discord 411n.
inelegance 576n.
cactus
prickle 256n.
plant 366n.
cad
nonconformist 84n.
vulgarian 847n.
low fellow 869n.
hateful object 888n.
cad 938n.
cadastral
listed 87adj.
metric 465adj.
cadastre
list 87n.
cadaver
corpse 363n.
cadaverous
lean 206adj.
cadaverous 363adj.
colorless 426adj.
caddie
bearer 273n.
carry 273vb.
servant 742n.
(*see* caddy)
caddishness
ill-breeding 847n.
caddy
small box 194n.
cadence
descent 309n.
sound 398n.
cadenza
musical note 410n.
musical piece 412n.
cadet
posteriority 120n.
subsequent 120adj.
young 130adj.
youngster 132n.
army officer 741n.
cadetship
subjection 745n.
cadge
beg 761vb.
be parsimonious 816vb.
cadger
idler 679n.
beggar 763n.
peddler 794n.
niggard 816n.
cadi
officer 741n.
judge 957n.
cadre
band 74n.
classification 77n.
personnel 686n.
caduceus
badge of rule 743n.
caducity
transientness 114n.
age 131n.
impotence 161n.
weakness 163n.
dilapidation 655n.
Caesar
sovereign 741n.
Caesarism
despotism 733n.
caespitose
vegetal 366adj.
caesura
separation 46n.
discontinuity 72n.
interval 201n.
prosody 593n.
café
café 192n.
café society
beau monde 848n.
caffeine
drug 658n.
caftan
tunic 228n.
cage
stable 192n.
receptacle 194n.
compartment 194n.
frame 218n.
circumscribe 232vb.
enclosure 235n.
break in 369vb.
imprison 747vb.
lock-up 748n.
cagebird
bird 365n.
cagey
reticent 525adj.
cunning 698adj.
cahoots with, in
in league 708adv.
caid
officer 741n.
caiman
reptile 365n.
Cain
murderer 362n.
caïque
sailing-ship 275n.
cairn
tomb 364n.
dog 365n.
signpost 547n.
monument 548n.
caisse
drum 414n.
caisson
box 194n.
war-chariot 274n.
arsenal 723n.
gun 723n.
cajole
befool 542vb.
tempt 612vb.
flatter 925vb.
cake
cohere 48vb.
pastry 301n.
be dense 324vb.
sweet 392n.
make unclean 649vb.
cakes and ale
food 301n.
prosperity 770n.
enjoyment 824n.
cake, take the
be superior 34vb.
calabash
vessel 194n.
calaboose
prison 748n.
calamity
evil 616n.
ill fortune 731n.
calamity prophet
overestimation 482n.
oracle 511n.
calash
carriage 274n.
calcify
harden 326vb.
calcimine
color 425vb.
whiting 427n.
calcine
burn 381vb.
calcite
rock 344n.
calcium
food content 301n.
calculate
do sums 86vb.
measure 465vb.
estimate 480vb.
believe 485vb.
expect 507vb.

intend 617vb.
plan 623vb.
be cautious 858vb.
calculated
tending 179adj.
predetermined 608adj.
calculating
intelligent 498adj.
calculating machine
counting instrument 86n.
calculation
numeration 86n.
caution 858n.
(*see* calculate)
calculator
computer 86n.
calculus
mathematics 86n.
solid body 324n.
caldron
crucible 147n.
caldron 194n.
heater 383n.
calefaction
heating 381n.
calendar
directory 87n.
fix the time 108vb.
timekeeper 117n.
chronology 117n.
time 117vb.
record 548vb.
reference book 589n.
calender
smooth 258vb.
calends
date 108n.
calenture
illness 651n.
calf
youngling 132n.
skin 226n.
leg 267n.
cattle 365n.
male animal 372n.
fool 501n.
bungler 697n.
caliber
size 195n.
breadth 205n.
perforation 263n.
intelligence 498n.
fire-arm 723n.
calibrate
graduate 27vb.
gauge 465vb.
calico
textile 222n.
calidarium
heater 383n.
caliper
gauge 465n.
measure 465vb.
caliph
sovereign 741n.
caliphate
magistrate 733n.
calisthenics
athletics 162n.
education 534n.
civilization 654n.
exercise 682n.
caliver
fire-arm 723n.
call
enter 297vb.
be loud 400vb.
cry 408n.
ululation 409n.
musical note 410n.
communicate 524vb.
publication 528n.
call 547n.
name 561vb.
motive 612n.
command 737n., vb.
desire 859n., vb.
social round 882n.
visit 882vb.
prayers 981n.
call a spade a spade
speak plainly 573vb.
be artless 699vb.
call at
visit 882vb.
call away
distract 456vb.
call-boy
courier 531n.
stage-hand 594n.
caller
incomer 297n.
social person 882n.
call for
require 627vb.
request 761vb.
call-girl
prostitute 952n.
calligraphist
penman 586n.
calligraphy
art 551n.
lettering 586n.
call in
bring together 74vb.
admit 299vb.
consult 691vb.
claim 915vb.
calling
vocation 622n.
call in question
negate 533vb.
callipygian
broad 205adj.
shapely 841adj.
call it a day
cease 145vb.
call names
not respect 921vb.
dispraise 924vb.
call, on
on the spot 189adj.
call on
consult 691vb.
visit 882vb.
worship 981vb.
callosity
hardness 326n.
callous
hard 326adj.
unfeeling 375adj.
thick-skinned 820adj.
pitiless 906adj.
wicked 934adj.
call out
halt 145vb.
defy 711vb.
fight 716vb.
call over
number 86vb.
callow
young 130adj.
immature 670adj.
call to order
reprove 924vb.
call-up
war measures 718n.
call up
go to war 718vb.
practice sorcery 983vb.
calm
assuage 177vb.
flat 216adj.
smoothness 258n.
quietude 266n.
tranquil 266adj.
silent 399adj.
inaction 677n.
impassive 820adj.
inexcitable 823adj.
tranquilize 823vb.
relieve 831vb.
cautious 858adj.
indifferent 860adj.
unastonished 865adj.
calmative
moderator 177n.
lenitive 177adj.
calomel
cathartic 658n.
caloric
heat 379n.
calories
food content 301n.
thermometry 379n.
calorimeter
thermometry 379n.
calotte
canonicals 989n.
calotype
photography 551n.
caloyer

monk 986n.
calque
word 559n.
neology 560n.
caltrop
sharp point 256n.
defenses 713n.
calumet
tobacco 388n.
peace 717n.
irenics 719n.
calumniate
defame 926vb.
calumny
slur 867n.
scurrility 899n.
censure 924n.
calumny 926n.
false charge 928n.
calvary
suffering 825n.
painfulness 827n.
church interior 990n.
calve
reproduce itself 164vb.
Calvinism
Protestantism 976n.
sectarianism 978n.
calypso
vocal music 412n.
calyx
receptacle 194n.
flower 366n.
camaraderie
friendliness 880n.
sociality 882n.
camarilla
party 708n.
camber
obliquity 220n.
be curved 248vb.
camber 253n.
be convex 253vb.
cambist
merchant 794n.
moneyer 797n.
cambric
textile 222n.
camel
beast of burden 273n.
cameleer
driver 268n.
cavalry 722n.
camellia
tree 366n.
cameo
relievo 254n.
camera
camera 442n.
recording instrument 549n.
photography 551n.
camera, in
secretly 525adv.
cameraman
recorder 549n.
camiknickers
underwear 228n.
camisado
attack 712n.
camisole
bodywear 228n.
camomile
medicine 658n.
camouflage
assimilation 18n.
make unlike 19vb.
mimicry 20n.
transform 147vb.
conceal 525vb.
disguise 527n.
camp
place oneself 187vb.
station 187n.
abode 192n.
dwell 192vb.
shelter 662n.
party 708n.
fort 713n.
army 722n.
campagna
space 183n.
plain 348n.
campaign
marching 267n.
undertaking 672n.
action 676n.
exert oneself 682vb.
tactics 688n.
fight 716n., vb.
warfare 718n.
campaigner
soldier 722n.
campaniform
rotund 252adj.
concave 255adj.
campanile
high structure 209n.
church exterior 990n.
campanologist
campanology 412n.
instrumentalist 413n.
campestral
champaign 348adj.
camp-follower
dependent 742n.
camphor
resin 357n.
scent 396n.
prophylactic 658n.
preserver 666n.
campus
focus 76n.
meeting place 192n.
arena 724n.
can
be able 160vb.
cup 194n.
small box 194n.
vessel 194n.
preserve 666vb.
jail 748n.
canaille
rabble 869n.
canal
conduit 351n.
access 624n.
canalize
direct 689vb.
canalular
tubular 263adj.
canard
rumor 529n.
fable 543n.
false alarm 665n.
canary
bird 365n.
yellowness 433n.
canasta
card game 837n.
cancan
dance 837n.
cancel
nullify 2vb.
set off 31vb.
destroy 165vb.
counteract 182vb.
obliterate 550vb.
disuse 674vb.
abrogate 752vb.
cancel out
counteract 182vb.
tell against 467vb.
cancel page
abrogation 752n.
Cancer
zodiac 321n.
cancer
carcinosis 651n.
blight 659n.
candid
true 494adj.
undisguised 522adj.
informative 524adj.
veracious 540adj.
artless 699adj.
maledicent 899adj.
detracting 926adj.
trustworthy 929adj.
candidate
testee 461n.
contender 716n.
petitioner 763n.
hoper 852n.
desirer 859n.
candidature
vote 605n.
offer 759n.
candied
sweet 392adj.
candle
lighter 385n.

torch 420n.
ritual object 988n.
candle-holder
auxiliary 707n.
candlelight
evening 129n.
light 417n.
glimmer 419n.
Candlemas
holy-day 988n.
candle-power
light 417n.
metrology 465n.
candor
(*see* candid)
candy
sweetmeat 301n.
be dense 324vb.
sweeten 392vb.
cane
supporter 218n.
strike 279vb.
tree 366n.
club 723n.
spank 963vb.
scourge 964n.
canescence
whiteness 427n.
gray 429n.
canicule
heat 379n.
canine
dog 365n.
animal 365adj.
caning
corporal punishment 963n.
canister
box 194n.
small box 194n.
basket 194n.
canister shot
ammunition 723n.
canker
dilapidation 655n.
impair 655vb.
blight 659n.
cankerworm
destroyer 168n.
blight 659n.
noxious animal 904n.
cannabis
fiber 208n.
cannery
preserver 666n.
cannibal
eater 301n.
ruffian 904n.
cannibalistic
murderous 362adj.
cruel 898adj.
cannibalize
sunder 46vb.
repair 656vb.
cannikin
cup 194n.
cannonade
shoot 287vb.
bombardment 712n.
cannon-ball
sphere 252n.
speeder 277n.
missile 287n.
ammunition 723n.
cannon fodder
soldiery 722n.
cannot
be impotent 161vb.
cannula
tube 263n.
canny
knowing 490adj.
intelligent 498adj.
cunning 698adj.
cautious 858adj.
canoe
row 269vb.
rowboat 275n.
canoeing
aquatics 269n.
canoeist
boatman 270n.
canon
rule 81n.
musical piece 412n.
creed 485n.
precept 693n.
decree 737n.
legislation 953n.
theology 973n.
scripture 975n.
ecclesiarch 986n.
office-book 988n.
canonical
regular 83adj.
evidential 466adj.
credal 485adj.
preceptive 693adj.
theological 973adj.
scriptural 975adj.
orthodox 976adj.
vestmental 989adj.
canonical books
scripture 975n.
canonical hours
church service 988n.
canonicals
uniform 228n.
badge of rule 743n.
canonicals 989n.
canonicity
orthodoxy 976n.
canonist
jurist 958n.
theologian 973n.
canonization
dignification 866n.
sanctity 979n.
Christian rite 988n.
canon law
precept 693n.
law 953n.
canonry
benefice 985n.
church office 985n.
can-opener
opener 263n.
canopy
canopy 226n.
screen 421n.
altar 990n.
canorous
melodious 410adj.
cant
obliquity 220n.
propel 287vb.
sophisticate 477vb.
falsehood 541n.
duplicity 541n.
cant 541vb.
slang 560n.
dialectical 560adj.
be affected 850vb.
false piety 890n.
cantabile
musical 412adj.
cantaloupe
fruit 301n.
cantankerous
quarreling 709adj.
irascible 892adj.
sullen 893adj.
cantata
vocal music 412n.
hymn 981n.
canteen
café 192n.
box 194n.
chamber 194n.
canter
gait 265n.
ride 267vb.
deceiver 545n.
cantharides
stimulant 174n.
canticle
vocal music 412n.
hymn 981n.
cantilever
supporter 218n.
cantillate
sing 413vb.
cantle
piece 53n.
canto
subdivision 53n.
poem 593n.
canton
district 184n.
flag 547n.
cantor
choir 413n.

church officer 986n.
cantrip
spell 983n.
can't stand
dislike 861vb.
cant term
name 561n.
canty
cheerful 833adj.
Canuck
foreigner 59n.
native 191n.
canvas
textile 222n.
canopy 226n.
sail 269n.
picture 553n.
art equipment 553n.
canvass
inquire 459vb.
argue 475vb.
divulge 526vb.
publish 528vb.
advertise 528vb.
confer 584vb.
dissert 591vb.
vote 605n., vb.
request 761vb.
sell 793vb.
canvasser
commender 923n.
(*see* canvass)
canvass for
patronize 703vb.
canyon
gap 201n.
valley 255n.
caoutchouc
elasticity 328n.
cap
be superior 34vb.
vertex 213n.
crown 213vb.
covering 226n.
headgear 228n.
stopper 264n.
punctuation 547n.
badge 547n.
letter 558n.
retaliate 714vb.
explosive 723n.
climax 725vb.
greet 884vb.
capability
fitness 24n.
ability 160n.
influence 178n.
skill 694n.
facility 701n.
capable
possible 469adj.
intelligent 498adj.
capacious
great 32adj.
spacious 183adj.
recipient 194adj.
large 195adj.
capacitance
electricity 160n.
capacity
greatness 32n.
plenitude 54n.
inclusion 78n.
ability 160n.
room 183n.
size 195n.
limit 236n.
intelligence 498n.
function 622n.
means 629n.
utility 640n.
skill 694n.
facility 701n.
cap and bells
entertainer 594n.
cap and gown
formal dress 228n.
uniform 228n.
caparison
coverlet 226n.
dress 228vb.
cape
cloak 228n.
Cape-colored
hybrid 43n.
caper
potherb 301n.
leap 312n., vb.
condiment 389n.
amuse oneself 837vb.
dance 837vb.
capful
finite quantity 26n.
small quantity 33n.
capillament
filament 208n.
capillary
narrow 206adj.
filament 208n.
fibrous 208adj.
tubular 263adj.
conduit 351n.
capilliform
fibrous 208adj.
cap in hand
respectful 920adj.
capital
supreme 34adj.
abode 192n.
summit 213n.
deadly 362adj.
literal 558adj.
means 629n.
store 632n.
important 638adj.
best 644adj.
magistrature 733n.
funds 797n.
wealth 800n.
ornamental art 844n.
capitalism
barter 791n.
wealth 800n.
capitalist
director 690n.
master 741n.
moneyer 797n.
rich man 800n.
capitalize
profit by 137vb.
use 673vb.
capital letter, capitals
punctuation 547n.
letter 558n.
print-type 587n.
capital levy
taking 786n.
expropriation 786n.
tax 809n.
capital punishment
capital punishment 963n.
capitation
numeration 86n.
capitol
fort 713n.
capitular
ecclesiastical 985adj.
ecclesiarch 986n.
church officer 986n.
capitulate
submit 721vb.
capitulation
submission 721n.
capitulations
non-liability 919n.
capon
eunuch 161n.
poultry 365n.
male animal 372n.
caponize
unman 161vb.
capriccio
musical piece 412n.
caprice
non-uniformity 17n.
fitfulness 142n.
changeableness 152n.
musical piece 412n.
bias 481n.
will 595n.
tergiversation 603n.
caprice 604n.
liking 859n.
capricious
multiform 82adj.
transient 114adj.
light-minded 456adj.
uncertain 474adj.
(*see* caprice)
Capricorn
zodiac 321n.

capriole
leap 312n.
capsicum
vegetable 301n.
condiment 389n.
capsize
be unequal 29vb.
derange 63vb.
invert 221vb.
capstan
lifter 310n.
rotator 315n.
capstone
summit 213n.
capsular
capsular 194adj.
concave 255adj.
capsule
receptacle 194n.
covering 226n.
medicine 658n.
captain
navigate 269vb.
naval man 270n.
direct 689vb.
leader 690n.
army officer 741n.
naval officer 741n.
captaincy
degree 27n.
precedence 64n.
captation
flattery 925n.
caption
commentary 520n.
label 547n.
record 548n.
name 561n.
phrase 563n.
script 586n.
letterpress 587n.
description 590n.
captious
sophistical 477adj.
capricious 604adj.
irascible 892adj.
disapproving 927adj.
captivate
motivate 612vb.
subjugate 745vb.
excite love 887vb.
captive
slave 742n.
subjugate 745vb.
imprisoned 747adj.
prisoner 750n.
take 786vb.
captivity
servitude 745n.
detention 747n.
captor
master 741n.
possessor 776n.
taker 786n.
capture
imagine 513vb.
attack 712vb.
overmaster 727vb.
trophy 729n.
subjugate 745vb.
arrest 747vb.
prisoner 750n.
acquire 771vb.
take 786vb.
capuccino
soft drink 301n.
capuche
canonicals 989n.
car
conveyance 267n.
train 274n.
automobile 274n.
airship 276n.
carabineer
soldiery 722n.
caracole
equitation 267n.
ride 267vb.
leap 312n., vb.
carafe
vessel 194n.
caramel
sweetmeat 301n.
sweet 392n.
carapace
covering 226n.
armor 713n.
carat
weighment 322n.
caravan
procession 71n.
small house 192n.
land travel 267n.
marching 267n.
conveyance 267n.
carriage 274n.
caravansary
inn 192n.
caravel
merchant ship 275n.
caraway
condiment 389n.
carbine
fire-arm 723n.
carbohydrate
food content 301n.
carbolic
cleanser 648n.
prophylactic 658n.
carbon
duplicate 22n.
ash 381n.
carbonaceous
combustible 385adj.
carbon copy
duplication 91n.
record 548n.
carbonize
burn 381vb.
carbuncle
swelling 253n.
redness 431n.
gem 844n.
carcanet
jewelry 844n.
carcass
structure 331n.
corpse 363n.
bomb 723n.
carcinoma
carcinosis 651n.
card
unravel 62vb.
nonconformist 84n.
lamina 207n.
sailing aid 269n.
label 547n.
record 548n.
correspondence 588n.
contrivance 623n.
instrument 628n.
means 629n.
laughing-stock 851n.
cardboard
lamina 207n.
spurious 542adj.
bookbinding 589n.
paper 631n.
card game
card game 837n.
cardigan
vest 228n.
cardinal
intrinsic 5adj.
supreme 34adj.
numerical 85adj.
cloak 228n.
bird 365n.
red color 431n.
important 638adj.
best 644adj.
ecclesiarch 986n.
cardinalate
church office 985n.
cardinal points
compass point 281n.
card index
sorting 62n.
directory 87n.
cardioid
curve 248n.
card-sharper
trickster 545n.
cardsharping
trickery 542n.
cards, on the
liable 180adj.
possible 469adj.
probable 471adj.
cards on the table
disclosure 526n.
care

carefulness 457n.
business 622n.
management 689n.
detention 747n.
mandate 751n.
economy 814n.
worry 825n.
painfulness 827n.
dejection 834n.
nervousness 854n.
caution 858n.
desire 859vb.
love 887vb.
careen
be oblique 220vb.
navigate 269vb.
move fast 277vb.
repair 656vb.
career
continuity 71n.
speeding 277n.
move fast 277vb.
progression 285n.
vocation 622n.
conduct 688n.
careerism
selfishness 932n.
careerist
planner 623n.
busy person 678n.
carefree
cheerful 833adj.
careful
(*see* care)
careful of
observant 768adj.
careless
orderless 61adj.
inattentive 456adj.
negligent 458adj.
feeble 572adj.
unprepared 670adj.
lazy 679adj.
apathetic 820adj.
rash 857adj.
indifferent 860adj.
cares
adversity 731n.
worry 825n.
caress
touch 378vb.
please 826vb.
love 887vb.
endearment 889n.
caress 889vb.
flatter 925vb.
caret
deficit 55n.
punctuation 547n.
caretake
manage 689vb.
caretaker
manager 690n.
servant 742n.
keeper 749n.
consignee 754n.
care-worn
suffering 825adj.
melancholic 834adj.
cargo
contents 193n.
thing transferred 272n.
property 777n.
merchandise 795n.
caribou
deer 365n.
caricature
dissimilarity 19n.
imitate 20vb.
foolery 497n.
be absurd 497vb.
misinterpret 521vb.
exaggeration 546n.
misrepresent 552vb.
picture 553n.
be witty 839vb.
laughing-stock 851n.
satire 851n.
calumny 926n.
detract 926vb.
caricaturist
artist 556n.
humorist 839n.
caries
decay 51n.
carillon
loudness 400n.
roll 403n.
resonance 404n.
campanology 412n.
tune 412n.
gong 414n.
signal 547n.
cariole
sled 274n.
carriage 274n.
Carlylese
imperspicuity 568n.
Carmelites
monk 986n.
carminative
cathartic 658n.
carmine
red color 431n.
carnage
havoc 165n.
slaughter 362n.
carnal
sensual 944adj.
lecherous 951adj.
carnal knowledge
coition 45n.
carnation
red color 431n.
carnelian
redness 431n.
gem 844n.
carnival
festivity 837n.
pageant 875n.
carnivore
eater 301n.
animal 365n.
carol
vocal music 412n.
sing 413vb.
voice 577vb.
be cheerful 833vb.
rejoice 835vb.
carol-singers
choir 413n.
carom
recoil 280n.
carouse
eat 301vb.
festivity 837n.
revel 837vb.
be sociable 882vb.
be intemperate 943vb.
get drunk 949vb.
carousel
pleasure-ground 837n.
carp
fish food 301n.
table fish 365n.
blame 924vb.
car park
enclosure 235n.
carpenter
artisan 686n.
carper
detractor 926n.
carpet
floor-cover 226n.
reprove 924vb.
carpet-bagger
trickster 545n.
carrack
ship 275n.
merchant ship 275n.
carriage
supporter 218n.
transport 272n.
gait 265n.
carrier 273n.
train 274n.
carriage 274n.
mien 445n.
conduct 688n.
carriage-paid
uncharged 812adj.
carriageway
road 624n.
carried
assented 488n.
carried away
excited 821adj.
carrier
supporter 218n.
carrier 273n.
courier 531n.
infection 651n.

insalubrity 653n.
carrier pigeon
bearer 273n.
bird 365n.
courier 531n.
carrion
decay 51n.
food 301n.
corpse 363n.
rubbish 641n.
dirt 649n.
carronade
gun 723n.
carrot
tuber 301n.
incentive 612n.
carroty
red 431adj.
carry
reproduce itself 64vb.
tend 179vb.
be distant 199vb.
support 218vb.
wear 228vb.
carry 273vb.
overmaster 727vb.
carry off
take away 786vb.
carry on
go on 146vb.
do 676vb.
behave 688vb.
deal with 688vb.
manage 689vb.
lament 836vb.
be angry 891vb.
carry out
deal with 688vb.
carry out 725vb.
observe 768vb.
carry-over
remainder 44n.
thing transferred 272n.
carry over
add 38vb.
transfer 272vb.
account 808vb.
carry through
make complete 54vb.
terminate 69vb.
carry through 725vb.
carry weight
influence 178vb.
evidence 466vb.
be important 638vb.
cart
carry 273vb.
cart 274n.
cartage
transport 272n.
carte blanche
scope 744n.
permit 756n.
liberality 813n.
cartel
association 706n.
corporation 708n.
defiance 711n.
compact 765n.
carter
driver 268n.
carrier 273n.
Carthusian
monk 986n.
cartilage
solid body 324n.
hardness 326n.
toughness 329n.
cartload
contents 193n.
cartographer
surveyor 465n.
cartography
map 551n.
carton
small box 194n.
paper 631n.
cartoon
copy 22n.
cinema 445n.
representation 551n.
picture 553n.
satire 851n.
cartoonist
artist 556n.
humorist 839n.
cartouche
script 586n.
ammunition 723n.
ornamental art 844n.
cartridge
ammunition 723n.
cartulary
record 548n.
cartwheel
overturning 221n.
carve
cut, sunder 46vb.
produce 164vb.
efform 243vb.
groove 262vb.
record 548vb.
sculpt 554vb.
apportion 783vb.
decorate 844vb.
carvel
ship 275n.
carver
sharp edge 256n.
sculptor 556n.
artisan 686n.
carve up
apportion 783vb.
carving
sculpture 554n.
writing 586n.
caryatid
pillar 218n.
ornamental art 844n.
cascade
descend 309vb.
waterfall 350n.
case
state 7n.
example 83n.
eventuality 154n.
box 194n.
case 194n.
cover 226vb.
enclosure 235n.
topic 452n.
argument 475n.
report 524n.
grammar 564n.
press 587n.
bookbinding 589n.
business 622n.
sick person 651n.
accusation 928n.
litigation 959n.
caseation
condensation 324n.
case-ending
part of speech 564n.
case-harden
strengthen 162vb.
be tough 329vb.
habituate 610vb.
case-hardened
strong 162adj.
unfeeling 375adj.
obstinate 602adj.
thick-skinned 820adj.
impenitent 940adj.
case-history
evidence 466n.
record 548n.
case, in
if 8adv.
case in point
relevance 9n.
fitness 24n.
example 83n.
case-law
legal trial 959n.
casemate
quarters 192n.
fortification 713n.
casement
window 263n.
case of need
needfulness 627n.
case-record
documentary evidence 465n.
legal trial 959n.
casern
quarters 192n.
cash
small coin 33n.
acquire 771vb.
money 797n.

draw money 797vb.
cash book
record 548n.
account book 808n.
cash box
treasury 799n.
cash desk
treasury 799n.
cash down
cash down 804adv.
cashier
depose 752vb.
moneyer 797n.
treasurer 798n.
pay 804n.
accountant 808n.
cash in on
profit by 137vb.
cashmere
fiber 208n.
textile 222n.
cash register
counting instrument 86n.
recording instrument 549n.
treasury 799n.
casino
gaming-house 618n.
place of amusement 837n.
card game 837n.
cask
vat 194n.
casket
small box 194n.
interment 364n.
ritual object 988n.
casque
headgear 228n.
armor 713n.
Cassandra
oracle 511n.
warner 664n.
cassation
obliteration 550n.
abrogation 752n.
casserole
caldron 194n.
dish 301n.
cook 301vb.
cassock
tunic 228n.
vestments 989n.
cassolette
caldron 194n.
cassowary
flightless bird 365n.
cast
copy 22n.
number 86vb.
produce 164vb.
tendency 179n.
wrapping 226n.
doff 229vb.
form 243n.
efform 243vb.
propel 287vb.
excrement 302n.
liquefy 337vb.
heat 381vb.
hue 425n.
dim sight 440n.
mien 445n.
sculpture 554n.
actor 594n.
dramatize 594vb.
incentive 612n.
surgical dressing 658n.
defeated 728adj.
apportion 783vb.
castanets
gong 414n.
castaway
solitary 883n.
(*see* derelict)
cast before swine
consume 165vb.
waste 634vb.
caste
breed 77n.
prestige 866n.
nobility 868n.
caste consciousness
particularism 80n.
casteism
exclusion 57n.
castellan
protector 660n.
retainer 742n.
keeper 749n.
caster
small box 194n.
wheel 250n.
thrower 287n.
castigate
(*see* castigation)
castigation
amendment 654n.
reprimand 924n.
punishment 963n.
castigator
reformer 654n.
disapprover 924n.
detractor 926n.
punisher 963n.
casting
dramaturgy 594n.
casting vote
inequality 29n.
judgment 480n.
vote 605n.
casting weight
offset 31n.
cast-iron
hard 326adj.
resolute 599adj.
castle
interchange 151vb.
house 192n.
fort 713n.
chessman 837n.
castle-builder
visionary 513n.
castles in Spain
fantasy 513n.
aspiration 852n.
cast lots
divine 511vb.
gamble 618vb.
cast-off
excretory 302adj.
relinquished 621adj.
derelict 779n.
cast off
disjoin 46vb.
navigate 269vb.
start out 296vb.
relinquish 621vb.
disuse 674vb.
carry through 725vb.
not retain 779vb.
cast of mind
affections 817n.
cast on
tie 45vb.
castor
headgear 228n.
castor oil
cathartic 658n.
castrametation
art of war 718n.
castrate
subtract 39vb.
unman 161vb.
sterilize 172vb.
make useless 641vb.
impair 655vb.
castrato
eunuch 161n.
vocalist 413n.
cast up
do sums 86vb.
estimate 480vb.
casual
extrinsic 6adj.
orderless 61adj.
casual 159adj.
negligent 458adj.
uncertain 474adj.
unintentional 618adj.
casualties
death roll 361n.
casualty
extrinsicality 6n.
eventuality 154n.
chance 159n.
evil 616n.
non-design 618n.
ill fortune 731n.
casualty station
hospital 658n.

casuist
reasoner 475n.
sophist 477n.
casuistry
sophistry 477n.
falsehood 541n.
morals 917n.
casus belli
casus belli 709n.
excitation 821n.
casus foederis
conditions 766n.
cat
vomit 300vb.
cat 365n.
hell-hag 904n.
cad 938n.
scourge 964n.
catabasis
decrease 37n.
catabolism
transformation 143n.
catacaustic
curve 248n.
catachresis
metaphor 519n.
misinterpretation 521n.
solecism 564n.
cataclinal
sloping 220adj.
cataclysm
revolution 149n.
havoc 165n.
outbreak 176n.
cataclysmic
flowing 350adj.
(*see* cataclysm)
catacomb
cemetery 364n.
catacoustics
acoustics 398n.
catadupe
waterfall 350n.
catafalque
funeral 364n.
catalectic
short 204adj.
poetic 593adj.
catalepsy
quiescence 266n.
insensibility 375n.
sleep 679n.
catalog
arrangement 62n.
class 62vb.
list 87n., vb.
guide-book 524n.
record 548n.
catalysis
decomposition 51n.
catalyst
alterer 143n.
catamaran
raft 275n.
warship 722n.
catamenia
regular return 141n.
hemorrhage 302n.
catamountain
cat 365n.
cat and dog life
dissension 709n.
cataphonics
acoustics 398n.
cataplasm
surgical dressing 658n.
catapult
propellant 287n.
missile weapon 723n.
cataract
high water 209n.
waterfall 350n.
blindness 439n.
dim sight 440n.
catarrh
excretion 302n.
ill-health 651n.
catastrophe
revolution 149n.
eventuality 154n.
ruin 165n.
disclosure 526n.
evil 616n.
completion 725n.
ill fortune 731n.
catatonia
psychopathy 503n.
catcall
be loud 400vb.
shrill 407vb.
ridicule 851n.
disapprobation 924n.
catch
copy 20vb.
fastening 47n.
bring together 74vb.
halt 145vb.
rub 333vb.
vocal music 412n.
hear 415vb.
question 459n.
know 490vb.
absurdity 497n.
surprise 508vb.
understand 516vb.
ambush 527n.
trap 542n.
befool 542vb.
ensnare 542vb.
represent 551vb.
be induced 612vb.
hunt 619vb.
bigwig 638n.
be ill 651vb.
pitfall 663n.
stratagem 698n.
hitch 702n.
wrestling 716n.
arrest 747vb.
acquire 771vb.
take 786vb.
booty 790n.
feel 818vb.
desired object 859n.
social person 882n.
favorite 890n.
catch a likeness
represent 551vb.
catch-all
receptacle 194n.
catch as catch can
spontaneous 609adj.
essaying 671adj.
wrestling 716n.
catch at
be willing 597vb.
desire 859vb.
catch at straws
overrate 482vb.
be credulous 487vb.
catch a Tartar
be duped 544vb.
stultify oneself 695vb.
be in difficulty 700vb.
be rightly served 714vb.
catch bending
be neglectful 458vb.
surprise 508vb.
catcher
interceptor 702n.
catch fire
be hot 379vb.
be excitable 822vb.
catching
infectious 653adj.
catch on
prevail 178vb.
be wont 610adj.
catch out
dismiss 300vb.
detect 484vb.
discover 526vb.
ensnare 542vb.
catchpenny
spurious 542adj.
trivial 639adj.
vulgar 847adj.
catchpoll
law officer 955n.
catch the breath
breathe 352vb.
rasp 407vb.
catch the eye
attract notice 455vb.
be visible 443vb.
catch up
outstrip 277vb.
approach 289vb.
hasten 680vb.
catchword
maxim 496n.

indication 547n.
call 547n.
catchy
melodious 410adj.
desired 859adj.
catechism
interrogation 459n.
creed 485n.
orthodoxy 976n.
catechist
teacher 537n.
religious teacher 973n.
catechize
interrogate 459vb.
catechumen
changed person 147n.
learner 538n.
beginner 538n.
pietist 979n.
layman 987n.
categorical
positive 473adj.
demonstrating 478adj.
assertive 532adj.
commanding 737adj.
categorical imperative
command 737n.
conscience 917n.
categorization
arrangement 62n.
category
state 7n.
classification 77n.
catena
continuity 71n.
catenary
curve 248n.
catenate
continuate 71vb.
cater
feed 301vb.
provide 633vb.
offer 759vb.
sell 793vb.
cateran
soldier 722n.
robber 789n.
cater-cornered
oblique 220adj.
caterer
caterer 633n.
cater for
be hospitable 882vb.
caterpillar
vermin 365n.
caters
campanology 412n.
caterwaul
be loud 400vb.
shrill 407vb.
cry 408n., vb.
ululate 409vb.
court 889vb.
catgut
viol 414n.
Catharan, Catharist
heretic 977n.
catharsis
sanation 656n.
cathartic
ejector 300n.
expulsive 300adj.
cleanser 648n.
cathartic 658n.
remedial 658adj.
cathead
supporter 218n.
cathedral
church 990n.
catheter
drain 351n.
catheterism
therapy 658n.
catholic
universal 79adj.
orthodox 976adj.
Catholic
popish 976adj.
Catholic 976n.
Catholicism
orthodoxy 976n.
Catholicism 976n.
catholicity
generality 79n.
catholicon
remedy 658n.
catlap
insipidity 387n.
cat-like
stealthy 525adj.
catling
sharp edge 256n.
catnap
sleep 679n.
cat-o'-nine-tails
scourge 964n.
catoptrics
optics 417n.
cat's cradle
crossing 222n.
cat's-eye
gem 844n.
cat's nine lives
diuturnity 113n.
life 360n.
cat's-paw
shallowness 212n.
furrow 262n.
wave 350n.
dupe 544n.
instrument 628n.
auxiliary 707n.
toady 879n.
catsup
sauce 389n.
cattiness
detraction 926n.
cattle
beast of burden 273n.
cattle 365n.
rabble 869n.
cattle farm
stock farm 369n.
cattle-lifter
thief 789n.
cattleman
herdsman 369n.
catty
malevolent 898adj.
detracting 926adj.
catur
galley 275n.
catwalk
aircraft 276n.
bridge 624n.
Caucasian
ethnic 11adj.
caucus
assemblage 74n.
party 708n.
caudal
ending 69adj.
back 238adj.
caudate
pendent 217adj.
back 238adj.
caudex
supporter 218n.
caudiform
back 238adj.
caudle
potion 301n.
liquor 301n.
drink 301vb.
caul
obstetrics 164n.
cauldron
(*see* caldron)
caulicle
foliage 366n.
cauliflower
vegetable 301n.
caulk
repair 656vb.
causal
causal 156adj.
instrumental 628adj.
causality
relativeness 9n.
causation 156n.
causation
causation 156n.
agency 173n.
cause
cause 156n., vb.
reason why 156n.
produce 164vb.
influence 178n.
promote 285vb.
reasons 475n.
predetermine 608vb.

motive 612n.
induce 612vb.
philanthropy 901n.
litigation 959n.
cause and effect
relativeness 9n.
cause célèbre
prodigy 864n.
causeless
causeless 159adj.
designless 618adj.
cause-list
legal trial 959n.
causerie
chat 584n.
interlocution 584n.
article 591n.
causeway
road 624n.
causidical
jurisdictional 955adj.
caustic
keen 174adj.
curve 248n.
burning 381n.
heating 381adj.
pungent 388adj.
felt 818adj.
paining 827adj.
maleficent 898adj.
disapproving 924adj.
detracting 926adj.
caustic line
curve 248n.
cauterant
burning 381n.
cauterize
burn 381vb.
doctor 658vb.
cautery
burning 381n.
caution
delay 136n.
slowness 278n.
carefulness 457n.
foresight 510n.
omen 511n.
hint 524n.
unwillingness 598n.
irresolution 601n.
dissuasion 613n.
warn 664vb.
intimidation 854n.
frighten 854vb.
cowardice 856n.
caution 858n.
reprove 924vb.
cautionary
cautionary 664adj.
advising 691adj.
cautious
doubting 474adj.
taciturn 582adj.
(*see* caution)
cavalcade
procession 71n.
marching 267n.
cavalier
rider 268n.
rash 857adj.
impertinent 878adj.
discourteous 885adj.
disrespectful 921adj.
cavaliere servente
toady 879n.
lover 887n.
cavalry
rider 268n.
cavalry 722n.
cavatina
vocal music 412n.
cave
dwelling 192n.
receptacle 194n.
interiority 224n.
cavity 255n.
dissentient 489n.
party 708n.
caveat
warning 664n.
cave-dweller
dweller 191n.
solitary 883n.
cave in
be concave 255vb.
descend 309vb.
cave man
violent creature 176n.
mankind 371n.
male 372n.
ruffian 904n.
cavern
cavity 255n.
darkness 418n.
cavernous
deep 211adj.
caviar
fish food 301n.
condiment 389n.
savoriness 390n.
cavil
argue 475vb.
sophisticate 477vb.
doubt 486vb.
dissent 489vb.
disapprobation 924n.
dispraise 924vb.
disapprove 924vb.
caviler
(*see* cavil)
cavity
receptacle 194n.
gap 201n.
cavity 255n.
cavort
leap 312vb.
dance 837vb.
caw
rasp 407vb.
ululate 409vb.
cay
island 349n.
cayenne
condiment 389n.
cease
end 69vb.
cease 145vb.
be quiescent 266n.
relinquish 621vb.
be inactive 679vb.
fail 728vb.
cease-fire
lull 145n.
pacification 719n.
ceaseless
perpetual 115adj.
ceaselessly
persistently 600adv.
ceaselessness
perseverance 600n.
cecal
closed 264adj.
cedar
tree 366n.
cede
relinquish 621vb.
not retain 779vb.
give 781vb.
cedilla
punctuation 547n.
ceil
overlay 226vb.
ceiling
finite quantity 26n.
height 209n.
vertex 213n.
roof 226n.
limit 236n.
visibility 443n.
celadon
green color 432n.
celebrant
worshiper 981n.
ritualist 988n.
celebrate
remind 505vb.
proclaim 528vb.
make important 638vb.
be cheerful 833vb.
rejoice 835vb.
revel 837vb.
honor 866vb.
celebrate 876vb.
applaud 923vb.
offer worship 981vb.
perform ritual 988vb.
celebrated
known 490adj.
well-known 528adj.
renowned 866adj.
celebration
(*see* celebrate)

celebrative
celebrative 876adj.
celebrity
made man 730n.
famousness 866n.
person of repute 866n.
celerity
velocity 277n.
celery
vegetable 301n.
celeste
mute 414n.
piano 414n.
blueness 435n.
celestial
foreigner 59n.
celestial 321adj.
divine 965adj.
angelic 968adj.
paradisiac 971adj.
celibacy
unproductivity 172n.
unsociability 883n.
celibacy 895n.
monasticism 985n.
celibate
alone 88adj.
celibate 895n.
virgin 950n.
(*see* celibacy)
cell
electricity 160n.
retreat 192n.
compartment 194n.
insides 224n.
enclosure 235n.
cavity 255n.
organism 358n.
life 360n.
refuge 662n.
party, society 708n.
lock-up 748n.
seclusion 883n.
monastery 986n.
cella
temple 990n.
holy place 990n.
church interior 990n.
cellar
cellar 194n.
depth 211n.
sink 649n.
cellarage
cellar 194n.
lowness 210n.
depth 211n.
cellarer
retainer 742n.
cellarette
cabinet 194n.
cellist
instrumentalist 413n.
cello
viol 414n.
cellophane
wrapping 226n.
cellular
cellular 194adj.
concave 255adj.
cellule
compartment 194n.
celluloid
cinema 445n.
materials 631n.
Celtic fringe
foreigner 59n.
cembalist
instrumentalist 413n.
cement
join 45vb.
bond 47n.
adhesive 47n.
agglutinate 48vb.
overlay 226vb.
solid body 324n.
hardness 326n.
building material 631n.
cemented
firm-set 45adj.
concordant 710adj.
cemetery
cemetery 364n.
holy place 990n.
cenobite
solitary 883n.
monk 986n.
cenobitism
monasticism 985n.
cenotaph
obsequies 364n.
tomb 364n.
cenozoic
secular 110adj.
cense
perform ritual 988vb.
censer
caldron 194n.
scent 396n.
ritual object 988n.
censor
exclude 57vb.
inquirer 459n.
estimator 480n.
inquisitor 543n.
obliterate 550vb.
restrain 747vb.
prohibit 757vb.
disapprove 924vb.
detractor 926n.
prude 950n.
censorial
judicial 480adj.
censorious
judicial 480adj.
severe 735adj.
discontented 829adj.
fastidious 862adj.
disapproving 924adj.
censorship
estimate 480n.
war measures 718n.
severity 735n.
prohibition 757n.
prudery 950n.
censurable
discreditable 867adj.
blameworthy 924adj.
guilty 936adj.
censure
estimate 480n., vb.
slur 867n.
censure 924n.
reprimand 924n.
reprove 924vb.
accusation 928n.
guilt 936n.
censurer
malcontent 829n.
(*see* censure)
census
numeration 86n.
statistics 86n.
cent
small coin 33n.
trifle 639n.
coinage 797n.
centaur
rara avis 84n.
rider 268n.
centenarian
old man 133n.
centenary
hundred 99n.
anniversary 141n.
special day 876n.
centennial
fifth and over 99adj.
center
essence 1n.
middle point 30n.
bring together 74vb.
focus 76n., vb.
place 185n., vb.
arena 224n.
interiority 224n.
center 225n.
converge 293vb.
chief thing 638n.
political party 708n.
armed force 722n.
centerboard
stabilizer 153n.
center forward
leader 690n.
centering
location 187n.
convergent 293adj.
center-line
centrality 225n.
centermost
central 225adj.
center of gravity

centrality 225n.
center on
congregate 74vb.
converge 293vb.
centerpiece
ornamentation 844n.
centesimal
fifth and over 99adj.
multifid 100adj.
centillion
over one hundred 99n.
centime
small coin 33n.
centimeter
long measure 203n.
cento
a mixture 43n.
doggerel 593n.
central
median 30adj.
fundamental 156adj.
interior 224adj.
central 225adj.
inland 344adj.
undeviating 625adj.
important 638adj.
centrality
centrality 225n.
symmetry 245n.
centralization
uniformity 16n.
centrality 225n.
centralize
combine 50vb.
regularize 62vb.
focus 76vb.
centralize 225vb.
centrifugal
unassembled 75adj.
exterior 223adj.
receding 290adj.
repellent 292adj.
divergent 294adj.
avoiding 620adj.
centrifugence
divergence 294n.
centripetal
attracting 291adj.
convergent 293adj.
centripetence
centrality 225n.
centrist
political party 708n.
centuplicate
fifth and over 99adj.
centurial
fifth and over 99adj.
centurion
soldier 722n.
army officer 741n.
century
hundred 99n.
period 110n.
diuturnity 113n.
formation 722n.
cephalic
topmost 213adj.
cephalopod
fish 365n.
ceramics
pottery 381n.
sculpture 554n.
cerastes
reptile 365n.
cerate
unguent 357n.
balm 658n.
Cerberus
rara avis 84n.
janitor 264n.
protector 660n.
chthonic god 967n.
mythic hell 972n.
cereal
cereal 301n.
corn 366n.
cerebral
mental 447adj.
spoken letter 558n.
vocal 577adj.
cerebrate
think 449vb.
cerebration
production 164n.
thought 449n.
cerebrum
intellect 447n.
cerecloth
grave clothes 364n.
cerelein
blue pigment 435n.
cerement(s)
wrapping 226n.
grave clothes 364n.
ceremonial
formality 875n.
formal 875adj.
ritual 988n., adj.
ceremonialist
ritualist 988n.
ceremonious
formal 875adj.
respectful 920adj.
ritualistic 988adj.
ceremony
formality 875n.
celebration 876n.
ritual, rite 988n.
cereous
fatty 357adj.
cerin
fat 357n.
cerise
red color 431n.
cerography
engraving 555n.
writing 586n.
ceroplastics
sculpture 554n.
certain
quantitative 26adj.
definite 80adj.
unchangeable 153adj.
certain 473adj.
demonstrated 478adj.
believing 485adj.
know 490adj.
true 494adj.
expectant 507adj.
anonymous 562adj.
successful 727adj.
certain, a
one 88adj.
certainty
certainty 473n.
positiveness 473n.
demonstration 478n.
discovery 484n.
belief 485n.
expectation 507n.
foresight 510n.
intelligibility 516n.
certifiable
insane 503adj.
certificate
credential 466n.
record 548n.
title-deed 767n.
paper money 797n.
honors 866n.
reward 962n.
certification
certainty 473n.
assent 488n.
certified
positive 473adj.
insane 503adj.
certify
testify 466vb.
make certain 473vb.
inform 524vb.
affirm 532vb.
certiorari
legal process 959n.
certitude
certainty 473n.
cerulean
blue 435adj.
cervical
supporting 218adj.
cervidae
deer 365n.
cervine
animal 365adj.
cervix
supporter 218n.
pillar 218n.
cesarean operation
obstetrics 164n.

cess
tax 809n.
cessation
end 69n.
finality 69n.
cessation 145n.
quiescence 266n.
deliverance 668n.
peace 717n.
cession
offset 31n.
reversion 148n.
relinquishment 621n.
submission 721n.
non-retention 779n.
cesspool
receptacle 194n.
lake 346n.
storage 632n.
sink 649n.
cestui que trust
beneficiary 776n.
cestui que vie
beneficiary 776n.
cestus
girdle 47n.
loop 250n.
cetacean
fish 365n.
ceteris paribus
equally 28adv.
chabouk
scourge 964n.
chad
question 459n.
picture 553n.
chafe
rub 333vb.
give pain 377vb.
heat 381vb.
wound 655vb.
disobey 738vb.
suffer 825vb.
hurt 827vb.
cause discontent 829vb.
be angry 891vb.
chaff
leavings 41n.
corn 366n.
trifle 639n.
rubbish 641n.
be witty 839vb.
ridicule 851n., vb.
chaffer
bargain 791vb.
chafing dish
heater 383n.
chagrin
sorrow 825n.
discontent 829n.
chain
cable 47n.
bond 47n.
coherence 48n.
continuity 71n.
series 71n.
long measure 203n.
gauge 465n.
encumbrance 702n.
fetter 748n.
jewelry 844n.
chain-gang
slave 742n.
prisoner 750n.
chain-reaction
continuity 71n.
chain-reactor
nucleonics 160n.
chain stitch
needlework 844n.
chain together
connect 45vb.
chair
seat 218n.
elevate 310vb.
rostrum 539n.
director 690n.
badge of rule 743n.
honor 866vb.
celebrate 876vb.
pay respects 884vb.
respect 920vb.
applaud 923vb.
courtroom 956n.
chairborne
quiescent 266adj.
chairman
superior 34n.
director 690n.
master 741n.
chairmanship
directorship 689n.
magistrature 733n.
chaise
carriage 274n.
chaise longue
seat 218n.
chalcedony
gem 844n.
chalcography
engraving 555n.
Chalcolithic
secular 110adj.
Chaldean
sorcerer 983n.
sorcerous 983adj.
chalet
house 192n.
chalice
cup 194n.
ritual object 988n.
church utensil 990n.
chalk
soil 344n.
white thing 427n.
mark 547vb.
art equipment 553n.
chalk out
plan 623vb.
chalk up
mark 547vb.
register 548vb.
chalky
territorial 344adj.
white 427adj.
challenge
question 459n.
dissent 489n., vb.
negation 533n.
call 547n.
motivate 612vb.
opposition 704n.
dissension 709n.
defiance 711n.
attack 712n., vb.
resist 715vb.
threat 900vb.
challengee
defender 713n.
challenger
dissentient 489n.
hinderer 702n.
opponent 705n.
contender 716n.
accuser 928n.
chamber
chamber 194n.
chambering
love-making 887n.
chamberlain
retainer 742n.
chambermaid
servant 742n.
domestic 742n.
chamber of commerce
corporation 708n.
merchant 794n.
chamber-pot
vessel 194n.
chameleon
changeable thing 152n.
reptile 365n.
variegation 437n.
iridescent 437adj.
waverer 601n.
chamfer
furrow 262n.
groove 262vb.
champ
be angry 891vb.
champagne
wine 301n.
champaign
open space 263n.
plain 348n.
champerty
lawbreaking 954n.
champion
superior 34n.
supreme 34adj.
athlete 162n.

exceller 644n.
proficient 696n.
patronize 703vb.
patron 707n.
defender 713n.
combatant 722n.
victor 727n.
deputy 755n.
philanthropist 901n.
benefactor 903n.
vindicator 927n.
championship
superiority 34n.
(*see* champion)
chance
opportunity 137n.
eventuality 154n.
happen 154vb.
chance 159n.
possibility 469n.
gambling 618n.
chance, have a
be likely 471vb.
chance it
gamble 618vb.
chancel
compartment 194n.
church interior 990n.
chancellor
director 690n.
officer 741n.
chancery
subjection 745n.
chancery, in
subject 745adj.
chancre
venereal disease 651n.
chancy
casual 159adj.
uncertain 474adj.
speculative 618adj.
dangerous 661adj.
chandelier
pendant 217n.
lamp 420n.
chandler
merchant 794n.
change
difference 15n.
make unlike 19vb.
fitfulness 142n.
change 143n., vb.
be turned to 147adj.
substitute 150n.
changeableness 152n.
vary 152vb.
influence 178vb.
dress 228vb.
doff 229vb.
campanology 412n.
money, coinage 797n.
changeability
caprice 604n.
(*see* changeable)
changeable
non-uniform 17adj.
multiform 82adj.
transient 114adj.
changeable 143adj.
converted 147adj.
changeful 152adj.
uncertain 474adj.
irresolute 601adj.
lively 819adj.
irascible 892adj.
change course
deviate 286vb.
change front
tergiversate 603vb.
changeful
(*see* changeable)
change hands
change hands 780vb.
change into
become 1vb.
(*see* convert)
changeless
unchangeable 153adj.
godlike 965adj.
changeling
child 132n.
substitute 150n.
fool 501n.
elf 970n.
change money
interchange 151vb.
change of hands
transfer 780n.
change of life
age 131n.
unproductivity 172n.
change of mind
tergiversation 603n.
change over
transfer 780n.
convey 780vb.
change places
be in motion 265vb.
change hands 780vb.
change-ringing
campanology 412n.
change round
modify 143vb.
change sides
be irresolute 601vb.
apostatize 603vb.
channel
bond 47n.
cavity 255n.
furrow 262n.
groove 262vb.
way in 297n.
passage 305n.
gulf 345n.
conduit 351n.
informant 524n.
access, path 624n.
instrument 628n.
direct 689vb.
chant
repetition 106n.
vociferate 408vb.
vocal music 412n.
sing 413vb.
voice 577vb.
hymn 981n.
chantey
vocal music 412n.
poem 593n.
chantry
church 990n.
chaos
non-uniformity 17n.
non-coherence 49n.
decomposition 51n.
confusion 61n.
havoc 165n.
amorphism 244n.
anarchy 734n.
chaotic
lawless 954adj.
(*see* chaos)
chap
gap 201n.
roughness 259n.
person 371n.
male 372n.
chapel
association 706n.
sect 978n.
church 990n.
church interior 990n.
chapel-goer
worshiper 981n.
chaperon
accompany 89vb.
look after 457vb.
protector 660n.
keeper 749n.
chaperonage
carefulness 457n.
chap-fallen
dejected 834adj.
humbled 872adj.
chaplain
retainer 742n.
pastor 986n.
church officer 986n.
chaplaincy
church office 985n.
chaplet
loop 250n.
badge 547n.
trophy 729n.
chapman
seller 793n.
peddler 794n.
chaps
laterality 239n.
trousers 288n.
chapter
subdivision 53n.

topic 452n.
edition 589n.
synod 985n.
chapter and verse
situation 186n.
evidence 466n.
accuracy 494n.
chapter-house
church exterior 990n.
char
burn 381vb.
blacken 428vb.
embrown 430vb.
(*see* charwoman)
char-à-banc
carriage 274n.
character
character 5n.
composition 56n.
sort 77n.
nonconformist 84n.
person 371n.
credential 466n.
letter 558n.
acting 594n.
habit 610n.
affections 817n.
repute 866n.
probity 929n.
virtue 933n.
characteristic
intrinsic 5adj.
characteristic 5adj.
specialty 80n.
special 80adj.
tendency 179n.
indicating 547adj.
characterization
representation 551n.
description 590n.
dramaturgy 594n.
characterize
represent 551vb.
name 561vb.
describe 590vb.
characterless
insubstantial 4adj.
uniform 16adj.
empty 190adj.
amorphous 244adj.
disreputable 867adj.
vicious 934adj.
character-sketch
description 590n.
charade
enigma 530n.
gesture 547n.
representation 551n.
drama 594n.
charcoal
ash 381n.
fuel 385n.
black thing 428n.
art equipment 553n.
charge
fill 54vb.
energy 160n.
empower 160vb.
load 193vb.
move fast 277vb.
collide 279vb.
make heavy 322vb.
heraldry 547n.
call 547n.
mark 547vb.
ornament 574vb.
pursue 619vb.
job 622n.
requirement 627n.
protection 660n.
management 689n.
advise 691vb.
precept 693n.
attack 712n.
charge 712vb.
give battle 718vb.
ammunition 723n.
explosive 723n.
demand 737vb.
command 737n., vb.
dependent 742n.
detention 747n.
prisoner 750n.
mandate 751n.
commission 751vb.
debt 803n.
account 808vb.
price 809n., vb.
duty 917n.
blame 924vb.
accusation 928n.
guilt 936n.
chargeable
owed 803adj.
priced 809adj.
dutied 917adj.
accusable 928adj.
guilty 936adj.
charge at
be rash 857vb.
chargé d'affaires
envoy 754n.
charge of, take
safeguard 660vb.
undertake 672vb.
charge on,– to,– with
attribute 158vb.
accuse 928vb.
charger
plate 194n.
war-horse 273n.
cavalry 722n.
chariot
carriage 274n.
charioteer
driver 268n.
charitable
liberal 813adj.
(*see* charity)
charity
aid 703n.
giving, gift 781n.
liberality 813n.
courteous act 884n.
love 887n.
kind act 897n.
benevolence 897n.
disinterestedness 931n.
piety 979n.
charivari
discord 411n.
charlady
worker 686n.
(*see* charwoman)
charlatan
sciolist 493n.
affector 850n.
boaster 877n.
charlatanism
sciolism 491n.
duplicity 541n.
unskillfulness 695n.
pretension 850n.
Charley
ninny 501n.
protector 660n.
charm
attraction 291n.
sweetness 392n.
motivate 612vb.
preserver 666n.
pleasurableness 826n.
delight 826vb.
please 826vb.
beauty 841n.
jewelry 844n.
lovableness 887n.
spell 983n.
talisman 983n.
bewitch 983vb.
charmed
willing 597adj.
charmed circle
elite 644n.
charmed life
safety 660n.
charmer
attraction 291n.
a beauty 841n.
sorcerer 983n.
charms
beauty 841n.
lovableness 887n.
charnel house
death 361n.
interment 364n.
chart
situation 186n.
itinerary 267n.
sailing aid 269n.
guide-book 524n.
map 551n.

represent 551vb.
charter
give scope 744vb.
liberate 746vb.
commission 751n.
permit 756n., vb.
title-deed 767n.
hire 785vb.
chartism
disobedience 738n.
sedition 738n.
charwoman, char
cleaner 648n.
worker 686n.
servant 742n.
chary
parsimonious 816adj.
Charybdis
vortex 315n.
eddy 350n.
nymph 967n.
chase
pleasance 192n.
groove 262n.
grassland 348n.
wood 366n.
objective 617n.
chase 619n.
pursue 619vb.
decorate 844vb.
desire 859vb.
be inimical 881vb.
be in love 887vb.
court 889vb.
disapprove 924vb.
chaser
potion 301n.
engraver 556n.
libertine 952n.
chasm
gap 201n.
depth 211n.
cavity 255n.
pitfall 663n.
chasseur
infantry 722n.
chassis
base 214n.
supporter 218n.
frame 218n.
structure 331n.
chaste
plain 573adj.
elegant 575adj.
tasteful 846adj.
modest 874adj.
virtuous 933adj.
temperate 942adj.
pure 950adj.
chasten
moderate 177vb.
educate 534vb.
deject 834vb.
humiliate 872vb.
punish 963vb.
chastened
repentant 939adj.
chastise
reprove 924vb.
punish 963vb.
chastity
(*see* chaste)
chasuble
vestments 989n.
chat
empty talk 515n.
rumor 529n.
converse 584vb.
chateau
house 192n.
chatelaine
resident 191n.
retainer 742n.
keeper 749n.
jewelry 844n.
chatoyant
iridescent 437adj.
chattel
equipment 630n.
slave 742n.
property 777n.
chatter
roll 403vb.
ululate 409vb.
empty talk 515n.
speak 579vb.
chatter 581n.
be loquacious 581vb.
chatterbox
chatterer 581n.
chatterer
newsmonger 529n.
speaker 579n.
chatterer 581n.
chattering
spasm 318n.
a-cold 380adj.
chatty
informative 524adj.
loquacious 581adj.
conversing 584adj.
sociable 882adj.
chauffeur
driver 268n.
domestic 742n.
chauvinism
nation 371n.
prejudice 481n.
exaggeration 546n.
bellicosity 718n.
boasting 877n.
patriotism 901n.
chauvinist
militarist 722n.
(*see* chauvinism)
cheap
inferior 35adj.
spurious 542adj.
trivial 639adj.
bargain 791vb.
cheap 812adj.
vulgar 847adj.
disreputable 867adj.
cheapen
make useless 641vb.
impair 655vb.
bargain 791vb.
discount 812vb.
vulgarize 847vb.
not respect 921vb.
cheapen oneself
demean oneself 867vb.
cheapjack
peddler 794n.
cheapness
cheapness 812n.
(*see* cheap)
cheat
duplicity 541n.
trickery 542n.
deceive 542vb.
stratagem 698n.
defraud 788vb.
defrauder 789n.
be dishonest 930vb.
knave 938n.
check
delay 136n.
stop 145n.
halt 145vb.
moderate 177vb.
counteraction 182n.
retard 278vb.
checker 437n.
variegate 437vb.
be careful 457vb.
inquiry 459n.
experiment 461n., vb.
comparison 462n.
measurement 465n.
make certain 473vb.
obstacle 702n.
hinder 702vb.
defeat 728n.
adversity 731n.
restraint 747n.
paper money 797n.
pattern 844n.
check-book
record 548n.
checker
blackness 428n.
checker 437n.
variegate 437vb.
checkerboard
checker 437n.
arena 724n.
checkered
changeable 143adj.
checkers
board game 837n.
checkmate

stop 145n.
halt 145vb.
be obstructive 702vb.
victory 727n.
overmaster 727vb.
defeat 728n.
check-up
attention 455n.
cheek
buttocks 238n.
laterality 239n.
sauciness 878n.
be insolent 878vb.
rudeness 885n.
scurrility 899n.
cheek by jowl
contiguously 202adv.
sideways 239adv.
cheek-piece
armor 713n.
cheeky
impertinent 878adj.
disrespectful 921adj.
cheep
ululate 409vb.
deprecation 762n.
discontent 829n.
cheer
invigorate 174vb.
food 301n.
vociferate 408vb.
assent 488vb.
refresh 685vb.
please 826vb.
content 828vb.
relieve 831vb.
merriment 833n.
cheer 833vb.
rejoice 835vb.
amuse 837vb.
give hope 852vb.
give courage 855vb.
celebrate 876vb.
show respect 920vb.
applaud 923vb.
cheerful
cheerful 833adj.
cheerfulness
vitality 162n.
willingness 597n.
cheerfulness 833n.
hope 852n.
cheerless
unhappy 825adj.
cheerless 834adj.
dejected 834adj.
cheers
rejoicing 835n.
cheer up
relieve 831vb.
be cheerful 833vb.
cheery
cheerful 833adj.
cheese
milk product 301n.
cheesed off
discontented 829adj.
cheese-paring
economy 814n.
parsimony 816n.
cheetah
cat 365n.
chef
cookery 301n.
caterer 633n.
chef d'oeuvre
product 164n.
exceller 644n.
deed 676n.
masterpiece 694n.
Cheka
police inquiry 459n.
chela
learner 538n.
chelonian
reptile 365n.
chemise
bodywear 228n.
chemist
experimenter 461n.
druggist 658n.
chemistry
conversion 147n.
chenille
textile 222n.
cherish
look after 457vb.
safeguard 660vb.
preserve 666vb.
patronize 703vb.
animate 821vb.
love 887vb.
pet 889vb.
approve 923vb.
cheroot
tobacco 388n.
cherry
fruit 301n.
redness 431n.
chersonese
projection 254n.
cherub
child 132n.
darling 890n.
angel 968n.
cherubim
angel 968n.
Cheshire cat
laughter 835n.
chess
board game 837n.
chess-board
checker 437n.
arena 724n.
chessman
chessman 837n.
chest
box 194n.
insides 224n.
bosom 253n.
store 632n.
treasury 799n.
pride 871n.
vanity 873n.
ostentation 875n.
Chesterfield
seat 218n.
chestnut
repetition 106n.
horse 273n.
fruit 301n.
tree 366n.
brown 430adj.
witticism 839n.
chest of drawers
cabinet 194n.
chesty
puffing 352adj.
cheval-glass
mirror 442n.
chevaux-de-frise
sharp point 256n.
defenses 713n.
chevron
obliquity 220n.
livery 547n.
heraldry 547n.
badge of rank 743n.
chew
rend 46vb.
chew 301vb.
pulverize 332vb.
smoke 388vb.
chew over
meditate 449vb.
chew the cud
graze 301vb.
meditate 449vb.
chiaroscuro
light contrast 417n.
obscuration 418n.
blackness 428n.
gray 429n.
painting 553n.
chiasma, chiasmus
reversion 148n.
inversion 221n.
crossing 222n.
ornament 574n.
chiastic
reverted 148adj.
inverted 221adj.
crossed 222adj.
chic
elegant 575adj.
beauty 841n.
fashionable 848adj.
chicanery, chicane
sophistry 477n.
trickery 542n.
cunning 698n.
foul play 930n.

chi-chi
dialect 560n.
fashionable 848adj.
affected 850adj.
chick
youngling 132n.
youngster 132n.
curtain 421n.
darling 890n.
chicken
youngling 132n.
table bird 365n.
poultry 365n.
coward 856n.
darling 890n.
chicken-feed
small quantity 33n.
provender 301n.
trifle 639n.
chicken-hearted
cowardly 856adj.
chicken liver
cowardice 856n.
chickenpox
infection 651n.
skin disease 651n.
chicken run
stock farm 369n.
chicory
potherb 301n.
chid
disapproved 924adj.
chide
curse 899vb.
reprove 924vb.
chief
superior 34n.
supreme 34adj.
first 68adj.
central 225adj.
heraldry 547n.
bigwig 639n.
important 639adj.
director 690n.
potentate 741n.
chieftain
potentate 741n.
chieftainship
magistrature 733n.
chiffon
textile 222n.
finery 844n.
chiffonier
cabinet 194n.
chignon
hair 259n.
hair-dressing 843n.
chilblain
hardness 326n.
ulcer 651n.
child
child 132n.
descendant 170n.
posterity 170n.
ninny 501n.
innocent 935n.
childbed, childbirth
obstetrics 164n.
childhood
youth 130n.
childish
young 130adj.
infantine 132adj.
credulous 487adj.
foolish 499adj.
feeble 572adj.
trivial 639adj.
childless
unproductive 172adj.
childlike
infantine 132adj.
artless 699adj.
child of fortune
made man 730n.
child of nature
ingenue 699n.
chili
vegetable 301n.
pungency 388n.
condiment 389n.
chiliad
over one hundred 99n.
chill
moderate 177vb.
coldness 380n.
refrigerate 382vb.
dissuade 613vb.
make inactive 679vb.
adversity 731n.
frighten 854vb.
chilly
cold 380adj.
a-cold 380adj.
inimical 881adj.
chime
repetition 106n.
sound faint 401vb.
roll 403vb.
resonance 404n.
melody 410n.
harmonize 410vb.
tune 412n.
campanology 412n.
chime in (with)
accord 24vb.
conform 83vb.
assent 488vb.
chimera
insubstantial thing 4n.
rara avis 84n.
fantasy 513n.
hopelessness 853n.
chimere
canonicals 989n.
chimerical
(*see* chimera)
chimes
gong 414n.
chiming
campanology 412n.
chimney
chimney 263n.
air-pipe 353n.
furnace 383n.
chimney corner
home 192n.
chimney-stack
air-pipe 353n.
chimney-sweep
cleaner 648n.
dirty person 649n.
chimpanzee
monkey 365n.
chin
face 237n.
projection 254n.
china
brittleness 330n.
pottery 381n.
ornamentation 844n.
China, great wall of
exclusion 57n.
chinaware
receptacle 194n.
pottery 381n.
chinchilla
skin 226n.
chine
high land 209n.
centrality 225n.
rear 238n.
Chinese boxes
small box 194n.
stratification 207n.
chink
gap 201n.
furrow 262n.
sound faint 401vb.
defect 647n.
vulnerability 661n.
chinook
wind 352n.
Chinook
dialect 560n.
chintz
textile 222n.
chinwag
speech 579n.
chatterer 581n.
chip
small thing 33n.
cut 46vb.
piece 53n.
make smaller 198vb.
pulverize 332vb.
label 547n.
sculpt 554vb.
coinage 797n.
plaything 837n.
chipmunk
rodent 365n.
chip off the old block

analogue 18n.
descendant 170n.
chip on one's shoulder, have a
be discontented 829vb.
Chippendale
ornamental 844adj.
chippy
prostitute 952n.
chirk
ululate 409vb.
chirography
writing 586n.
chiromancy
divination 511n.
occultism 984n.
chiropodist
doctor 658n.
beautician 843n.
chiropody
therapy 658n.
surgery 658n.
beautification 843n.
chiropractic
surgery 658n.
chiropractor
doctor 658n.
chiropraxis
surgery 658n.
chirp
ululate 409vb.
sing 413vb.
be cheerful 833vb.
rejoice 835vb.
chirpy
cheerful 833adj.
chirrup
(*see* chirp)
chisel
produce 164vb.
efform 243vb.
sharp edge 256n.
sculpt 554vb.
engraving 555n.
tool 630n.
defraud 788vb.
be dishonest 930vb.
chiseler
trickster 545n.
knave 938n.
chit
youngster 132n.
dwarf 196n.
credential 466n.
correspondence 588n.
chit-chat
chat 584n.
chiton
tunic 228n.
chitterlings
insides 224n.
meat 301n.
chivalrous
warlike 718adj.
courageous 855adj.
noble 868adj.
courteous 884adj.
benevolent 897adj.
honorable 929adj.
disinterested 931adj.
chivalry
rider 268n.
war 718n.
cavalry 722n.
courage 855n.
aristocracy 868n.
courtesy 884n.
disinterestedness 931n.
chive
vegetable 301n.
chivy
torment 827vb.
chlamys
cloak 228n.
chloral
anesthetic 375n.
chlorinate
purify 648vb.
sanitate 652vb.
safeguard 660vb.
chlorine
green 432adj.
chloroform
anesthetic 375n.
render insensible 375vb.
chlorophyll
green pigment 432n.
chock
supporter 218n.
chock-a-block
full 54adj.
chocolate
sweetmeat 301n.
soft drink 301n.
sweet 392n.
brownness 430n.
choice
precedence 64n.
unusual 84adj.
discrimination 463n.
choice 605n.
chosen 605adj.
excellent 644adj.
independence 744n.
pleasurable 826adj.
beautiful 841adj.
tasteful 846adj.
liking 859n.
choiceless
choiceless 606adj.
choicelessness
no choice 606n.
choiceness
good taste 846n.
choice spirit
person of repute 866n.
choir
accord 24vb.
choir 413n.
church officer 986n.
church interior 990n.
choke
close 264vb.
stopper 264n.
kill 362vb.
extinguish 382vb.
rasp 407vb.
superabound 637vb.
hinder 702vb.
choke-damp
gas 336n.
poison 659n.
choke off
dissuade 613vb.
choker
shawl 228n.
neckwear 228n.
chokidar
protector 660n.
choky
lock-up 748n.
cholecystitis
indigestion 651n.
cholelithiasis
indigestion 651n.
choler
anger 891n.
cholera
disease 651n.
choleric
irascible 892adj.
choli
bodywear 228n.
chondrite
meteor 321n.
choose
will 595vb.
be willing 597vb.
choose 605vb.
desire 859vb.
choosy
tasteful 846adj.
fastidious 862adj.
chop, chops
cut 46vb.
piece 53n.
interchange 151vb.
shorten 204vb.
laterality 239n.
meat 301n.
trade 791vb.
chop and change
change 143vb.
vary 152vb.
chop-fallen
dejected 834adj.
chop-house
café 192n.
chop logic
discriminate 463vb.
reason 475n.

chopper
sharp edge 256n.
pulverizer 332n.
ax 723n.
choppiness
roughness 259n.
agitation 318n.
wave 350n.
chopping-block
substitute 150n.
unlucky person 731n.
propitiation 941n.
choppy
non-uniform 17adj.
rough 259adj.
chop-sticks
shovel 274n.
choragus, choregus
stage-manager 594n.
leader 690n.
choragy
dramaturgy 594n.
choral
musical 412adj.
musicianly 413adj.
chorale
vocal music 412n.
chord
bond 47n.
straightness 249n.
musical note 410n.
musical piece 412n.
chords, vocal
voice 577n.
chore
job 622n.
labor 682n.
serve 742vb.
chorea
spasm 318n.
chore boy
servant 742n.
choregus
(*see* choragus)
choreography
composition 56n.
arrangement 62n.
dancing 837n.
choreus
prosody 593n.
chorine
actor 594n.
chorister
choir 413n.
church officer 986n.
chorography
situation 186n.
chortle
laugh 835vb.
chorus
do likewise 20vb.
copy 20vb.
agreement 24n.
accord 24vb.
combination 50n.
repeat oneself 106vb.
periodicity 141n.
cry 408n.
vociferate 402vb.
melody 410n.
harmonize 410vb.
vocal music 412n.
choir 413n.
sing 413vb.
consensus 488n.
speaker 579n.
dramaturgy 594n.
actor 594n.
chorus girl
actor 594n.
chosen
voluntary 597adj
approved 923adj
chosen few
elite 644n.
chosen people
pietist 979n.
chosen race
particularism 80n.
chouse
deceive 542vb.
chow
mouthful 301n.
dog 365n.
chowchow
a mixture 43n.
sweetmeat 301n.
chowder
dish 301n.
chowrie
ventilation 352n.
chrestomathy
literature 557n.
textbook 589n.
anthology 592n.
chrism
Christian rite 988n.
chrismal
ritual 988adj.
chrismation
Christian rite 988n.
chrisom
ritual object 988n.
Christ
God the Son 965n.
religious teacher 973n.
christen
auspicate 68vb.
name 561vb.
perform ritual 988vb.
Christendom
the Church 976n.
churchdom 985n.
christening
nomenclature 561n.
Christian rite 988n.
Christian
kind person 897n.
religious 973adj.
church member 976n.
pious 979adj.
Christianity
religious faith 973n.
christianize
make pious 979vb.
Christian Science
medical art 658n.
asceticism 945n.
Christian Scientist
doctor 658n.
Christmas
anniversary 141n.
holy-day 988n.
Christmas box
gift 781n.
Christmassy
sociable 882adj.
christological
theological 973adj.
chromascope
chromatics 425n.
chromatic
harmonic 410adj.
colored 425adj.
chromatics
chromatics 425n.
chromatic scale
musical note 410n.
color 425n.
chromatin
organism 358n.
chromatism
hue 425n.
chromatodysopia
dim sight 440n.
chromatology
chromatics 425n.
chromolithography
printing 555n.
chromosome
organism 358n.
chromosphere
sun 321n.
chronic
lasting 113adj.
obstinate 602adj.
sick person 651n.
sick 651adj.
sufferer 825n.
tedious 838adj.
chronicle
record 548n., vb.
narrative 590n.
chronicler
chronologist 117n.
chronicler 549n.
narrator 590n.
chronique scandaleuse
detraction 926n.
chronogram
chronology 117n.
chronograph

timekeeper 117n.
chronological
chronological 117adj.
chronological error
anachronism 118n.
chronologist
chronologist 117n.
chronology
date 108n.
chronology 117n.
chronometer
timekeeper 117n.
sailing aid 269n.
chronometry
chronometry 117n.
chrysalis
youngling 132n.
source 156n.
nest 192n.
receptacle 194n.
wrapping 226n.
vermin 365n.
chryselephantine
mixed 43adj.
chrysolite
gem 844n.
chrysoprase
greenness 432n.
gem 844n.
chthonic
infernal 972adj.
chubby
fleshy 195adj.
chuck
propel 287vb.
meat 301n.
darling 890n.
chucker-out
athlete 162n.
ejector 300n.
chuck it
resign 753vb.
chuckle
ululate 409vb.
laughter 835n.
chuck out
eject 300vb.
chuck under the chin
caress 889vb.
chudder
wrapping 226n.
shawl 228n.
chug
be in motion 265vb.
move slowly 278vb.
chug on
travel 267vb.
chukker
period 110n.
periodicity 141n.
chum
colleague 707n.
chum 880n.
chummery
quarters 192n.
chummy
friendly 880adj.
chump
dunce 501n.
chum up with
befriend 880vb.
chum with
dwell 192vb.
chunk
sunder 46vb.
piece 53n.
chunkiness
bulk 195n.
chunky
fleshy 195adj.
rough 259adj.
church
the Church 976n.
churchdom 985n.
church 990n.
church bell(s)
signal 547n.
call 547n.
church utensil 990n.
churchdom
orthodoxism 976n.
churchdom 985n.
church-goer
worshiper 981n.
church government
churchdom 985n.
churchianity
orthodoxism 976n.
pietism 979n.
churchiness
pietism 979n.
churching of women
Christian rite 988n.
churchlike
churchlike 990adj.
churchly
ecclesiastical 985adj.
churchman
cleric 986n.
churchmanship
piety 979n.
church service
church service 988n.
churchwarden
tobacco 388n.
church officer 986n.
churchy
pietistic 979adj.
churchyard
cemetery 364n.
church exterior 990n.
churl
niggard 816n.
countryman 869n.
churlish
parsimonious 816adj.
plebeian 869adj.
ungracious 885adj.
churlishness
sullenness 893n.
churn
rotator 315n.
rotate 315vb.
agitate 318vb.
thicken 354vb.
churn out
produce 164vb.
churr
ululate 409vb.
chute
obliquity 220n.
outlet 298n.
waterfall 350n.
pleasure-ground 837n.
chutney
sauce 389n.
chyle
fluid 335n.
chypre
scent 396n.
cibarious
edible 301adj.
nourishing 301adj.
ciborium
canopy 226n.
ritual object 988n.
cicada, cicala
jumper 312n.
vermin 365n.
cicatrice
wound 655n.
blemish 845n.
cicatrize
cure 656vb.
Cicero
speaker 579n.
cicerone
guide 520n.
cicuration
animal husbandry 369n.
cider
liquor 301n.
ci-devant
prior 119adj.
former 125adj.
resigning 753adj.
cigar, cigarette
tobacco 388n.
cilia
hair 259n.
cilice
asceticism 945n.
cilium
filament 208n.
Cimmerian
dark 418adj.
cinch
tie 45vb.
girdle 47n.
certainty 473n.
easy thing 701n.

Cincinnatus
resignation 753n.
cincture
belt 228n.
loop 250n.
cinder(s)
ash 381n.
coal 385n.
dirt 649n.
Cinderella
nonentity 639n.
poor man 801n.
object of scorn 867n.
ciné-camera
cinema 445n.
cinema
cinema 445n.
photography 551n.
theater 594n.
place of amusement 837n.
cinemagoer
spectator 441n.
cinematograph
cinema 445n.
cinematographer
photography 551n.
cinematographic
moving 265adj.
cinematography
photography 551n.
cinerama
cinema 445n.
cinerary
funereal 364adj.
gray 429adj.
cinerary urn
interment 364n.
cinereous
grey 429adj.
cingle
compressor 198n.
cingulum
vestments 989n.
cinnabar
red pigment 431n.
cinnamon
condiment 389n.
brown 430adj.
cinques
campanology 412n.
cipher
non-existence 2n.
number 85n.
do sums 86vb.
zero 103n.
secrecy 525n.
enigma 530n.
symbology 547n.
indication 547n.
label 547n.
initials 558n.
spell 558vb.
writing 586n.
nonentity 639n.
cipherer
interpreter 520n.
circa
nearly 200adv.
Circe
motivator 612n.
nymph 967n.
sorceress 983n.
Circean
sensual 944adj.
sorcerous 983adj.
circle
family 11n.
continuity 71n.
run on 71vb.
group 74n.
be periodic 141vb.
region 184n.
surround 230vb.
outline 233n.
circle 250n.
circle 314vb.
theater 594n.
circuit 626n.
party 708n.
restriction 747n.
change hands 780vb.
circlet
outline 233n.
circuit
whole 52n.
continuity 71n.
periodicity 141n.
revolution 149n.
electricity 160n.
region 184n.
circumjacence 230n.
outline 233n.
orbit 250n.
circle 250n.
land travel 267n.
deviation 282n.
circuition 314n.
route 624n.
circuit 626n., vb.
circuit court
law-court 956n.
circuit house
inn 192n.
circuition
(*see* circuit)
circuitous
deviating 282adj.
labyrinthine 251adj.
circuitous 314adj.
roundabout 626adj.
circular
uniform 16adj.
continuous 71adj.
generality 79n.
regular 81adj.
curved 248adj.
round 250adj.
publication 528n.
correspondence 588n.
decree 737n.
circularity
continuity 71n.
circularity 250n.
circularize
publish 528vb.
correspond 588vb.
command 737vb.
circular reasoning
sophism 477n.
circulate
disperse 75vb.
go round 250vb.
pass 305n.
circle 314vb.
be published 528vb.
change hands 780vb.
mint 797vb.
circulation
blood 335n.
(*see* circulate)
circulatory
circuitous 626adj.
circumambience
circumjacence 230n.
circumambient
circumjacent 230adj.
circuitous 314adj.
roundabout 626adj.
circumambulate
traverse 267vb.
circle 314vb.
perform ritual 988vb.
circumambulation
circuition 314n.
circuit 626n.
ritual act 988n.
circumbendibus
meanderings 251n.
deviation 282n.
route 624n.
circumcellion
monk 986n.
circumcise
cut 46vb.
circumcision
scission 46n.
rite 988n.
circumduction
obliteration 550n.
circumference
region 184n.
size 195n.
distance 199vb.
exteriority 223n.
circumjacence 230n.
outline 233n.
enclosure 235n.
limit 236n.
circuit 626n.
circumflex
curved 248adj.

circumflex accent
punctuation 547n.
circumfluence
rotation 315n.
circumfluent
circumjacent 230adj.
circuitous 314adj.
circumfluous
insular 349adj.
circumforaneous
traveling 267adj.
circuitous 314adj.
circumfusion
dispersion 75n.
circumgyration
rotation 315n.
circumjacence
exteriority 223n.
circumjacence 230n.
circumlocution
phrase 563n.
pleonasm 570n.
circumlocutory
prolix 570adj.
roundabout 626adj.
circumnavigate
navigate 269vb.
circle 314vb.
circumrotation
rotation 315n.
circumscribe
set apart 46vb.
exclude 57vb.
make smaller 198vb.
surround 230vb.
circumscribe 232vb.
outline 233vb.
enclose 235vb.
limit 236vb.
hinder, obstruct 702vb.
restrain 747vb.
prohibit 757vb.
circumspection
attention 455n.
carefulness 457n.
caution 858n.
circumstance
circumstance 8n.
degree 27n.
concomitant 89n.
eventuality 154n.
affairs 154n.
ostentation 875n.
circumstances
circumstance 8n.
particulars 80n.
estate 777n.
circumstantial
circumstantial 8adj.
complete 54adj.
definite 80adj.
careful 457adj.
veracious 540adj.
diffuse 570adj.
descriptive 590adj.
circumstantiate
corroborate 466vb.
circumvallation
circumscription 232n.
enclosure 235n.
fortification 713n.
defenses 713n.
circumvent
deceive 542vb.
be cunning 698vb.
circumvolution
convolution 251n.
rotation 315n.
circus
band 74n.
housing 192n.
zoo 369n.
theater 594n.
arena 724n.
pleasure-ground 837n.
cirrhosis
hardening 326n.
cirrhosis of the liver
alcoholism 949n.
cirrus
cloud 355n.
cist
box 194n.
tomb 364n.
Cistercian
monk 986n.
cistern
vat 194n.
moistening 341n.
storage 632n.
citadel
refuge 662n.
fort 713n.
citation
referral 9n.
repetition 106n.
evidence 466n.
decoration 729n.
warrant 737n.
praise 923n.
cite
copy 20vb.
exemplify 83vb.
repeat 106vb.
manifest 522vb.
command 737vb.
indict 928vb.
litigate 959vb.
cithara
harp 414n.
citified
urban 192adj.
well-bred 848adj.
citizen
native 191n.
subject 742n.
free man 744n.
citizen of the world
philanthropist 901n.
citizenry
habitancy 191n.
social group 371n.
subject 742n.
commonalty 869n.
citizenship
subjection 745n.
citriculture
agriculture 370n.
citrine
yellow 433adj.
citronella oil
scent 396n.
cittern
harp 414n.
city
district 184n.
abode 192n.
housing 192n.
business 622n.
polity 733n.
city father
officer 741n.
city state
nation 371n.
polity 733n.
civet
scent 396n.
civic
national 371adj.
civic center
focus 76n.
civic crown
decoration 729n.
civil
national 371adj.
well-bred 848adj.
courteous 884adj.
civil code
law 953n.
civilian
pacifist 717n.
peaceful 717adj.
jurist 958n.
layman 987n.
laical 987adj.
civility
civilization 654n.
good taste 846n.
courtesy 884n.
courteous act 884n.
civilization
culture 490n.
civilization 654n.
beau monde 848n.
civilize
make better 654vb.
civilized
well-bred 848adj.
civil law
law 953n.
civil lines

station 187n.
civil war
war 718n.
revolt 738n.
civism
patriotism 901n.
civvies
dress 228n.
clack
roll 403vb.
ululate 409vb.
mean nothing 515vb.
chatter 581n.
be loquacious 581vb.
clad
dressed 228adj.
claim
territory 184n.
enclosure 235n.
affirm 532vb.
plead 614vb.
requirement 627n.
require 627vb.
demand 737n., vb.
request 761n., vb.
possess 773vb.
estate 777n.
appropriate 786vb.
desire 859n., vb.
right 913n.
have a right 915vb.
claim 915vb.
litigation 959n.
claimable
just 913adj.
due 915adj.
claimant
petitioner 763n.
desirer 859n.
dueness 915n.
litigant 959n.
claim relationship
be akin 11vb.
clairaudience
psychics 984n.
clair-obscur
light contrast 417n.
clairschach
harp 414n.
clairvoyance
intuition 476n.
foresight 510n.
divination 511n.
psychics 984n.
clairvoyant
oracle 511n.
(*see* clairvoyance)
clam
table fish 365n.
taciturnity 582n.
clamant
loud 400adj.
crying 408adj.
commanding 737adj.
deprecatory 762adj.
desiring 859adj.
clambake
feasting 301n.
meal 301n.
festivity 837n.
clamber
climb 308vb.
clamjamfry
rabble 869n.
clam-like
reticent 525adj.
clammy
viscid 354adj.
clamor
loudness 400n.
cry 408n.
vociferate 408vb.
request 761n.
weep 836vb.
disapprobation 924n.
clamorous
(*see* clamor)
clamp
affix 45vb.
fastening 47n.
nippers 778n.
clamp down
close 264vb.
restrain 747vb.
clan
group 74n.
breed 77n.
genealogy 169n.
community 708n.
clandestine
occult 523adj.
stealthy 525adj.
concealed 525adj.
clang
loudness 400n.
be loud 400vb.
roll 403n., vb.
resonance 404n.
clanger
mistake 495n.
clangor
loudness 400n.
resonance 404n.
clank
resound 404vb.
rasp 407vb.
clannish
ethnic 11adj.
biased 481adj.
sectional 708adj.
sectarian 978adj.
clannishness
cooperation 706n.
(*see* clannish)
clanship
cooperation 706n.
clansman
kinsman 11n.
friend 880n.
clap
orifice 263n.
strike 279vb.
loudness 400n.
bang 402n.
crackle 402vb.
gesticulate 547vb.
venereal disease 651n.
rejoice 835vb.
gratulate 886vb.
applause 923n.
clap on
add 38vb.
clapper
commender 923n.
clappers
gong 414n.
chatter 581n.
clap together
join 45vb.
claptrap
sophistry 477n.
empty talk 515n.
fable 543n.
claque
playgoer 594n.
applause 923n.
commender 923n.
flattery 925n.
claqueur
playgoer 594n.
commender 923n.
flatterer 925n.
claret
blood 335n.
wine 361n.
redness 431n.
clarification
demonstration 478n.
(*see* clarify)
clarified
unmixed 44adj.
clarify
eliminate 44vb.
liquefy 337vb.
make flow 350vb.
be transparent 422vb.
be intelligible 516vb.
interpret 520vb.
purify 648vb.
clarigate
claim 915vb.
clarinet
flute 414n.
clarinetist
instrumentalist 413n.
clarion
horn 414n.
clarion call
loudness 400n.
war measures 718n.
clarity
transparency 422n.

visibility 443n.
intelligibility 516n.
perspicuity 567n.
elegance 575n.
clash
contrariety 14n.
differ 15vb.
disagreement 25n.
violence 176n.
counteract 182vb.
collide 279vb.
bang 402vb.
rasp 407vb.
discord 411vb.
quarrel 709n., vb.
strike at 712vb.
contention 716n.
battle 718n.
be inimical 881vb.
clasp
fastening 47n.
cohere 48vb.
circumscribe 232vb.
loop 250n.
caress 889vb.
class
degree 27n.
graduate 27vb.
class 62vb.
group 74n.
classification 77n.
contemporary 123n.
study 536n.
party 708n.
army 722n.
class-conscious
sectional 708adj.
class consciousness
particularism 80n.
pride 871n.
classes
curriculum 536n.
classes, the
social group 371n.
upper class 868n.
classic
prototypal 23adj.
olden 127adj.
symmetrical 245adj.
stylist 575n.
elegant 575adj.
book 589n.
excellent 644adj.
perfect 646adj.
classical
literary 557adj.
tasteful 846adj.
right 913adj.
classicist
antiquarian 125n.
classifiability
relation 9n.
classifiable
relative 9adj.
classification
relation 9n.
degree 27n.
subdivision 53n.
arrangement 62n.
classification 77n.
identification 547n.
classificatory
classificatory 77adj.
classify
class 62vb.
make certain 473vb.
indicate 547vb.
classify as
number with 78vb.
classless
governmental 753adj.
classmate
learner 538n.
chum 880n.
class prejudice
prejudice 481n.
classroom
classroom 539n.
class war
prejudice 481n.
dissension 709n.
class-work
study 536n.
classy
fashionable 848adj.
genteel 868adj.
clatter
medley 43n.
loudness 400n.
roll 403n., vb.
claudicate
move slowly 278vb.
clause
subdivision 53n.
phrase 563n.
conditions 766n.
claustral
circumjacent 230adj.
sealed off 264adj.
claustrophobia
psychopathy 503n.
phobia 854n.
claver
chatter 581n.
clavichord
piano 414n.
clavicle
supporter 218n.
clavier
piano 414n.
claw
rend 46vb.
coupling 47n.
foot 214n.
sharp point 256n.
wound 655vb.
nippers 778n.
clay
adhesive 47n.
solid body 324n.
softness 327n.
soil 344n.
corpse 363n.
sculpture 554n.
materials 631n.
dirt 649n.
claymore
side-arms 723n.
clean
unmixed 44adj.
completely 54adv.
empty 190adj.
make bright 417vb.
whiten 427vb.
clean 648adj., vb.
sanitate 652adj.
make better 654vb.
disencumber 701vb.
pure 950adj.
clean-cut
definite 80adj.
positive 473adj.
cleaner
cleaner 648n.
clean hands
probity 929n.
innocence 935n.
clean-limbed
shapely 841adj.
cleanliness
cleanness 648n.
hygiene 652n.
clean out
void 300vb.
search 459vb.
clean 648vb.
steal 788vb.
cleanse
purify 648vb.
sanitate 652vb.
cleanser
cleanser 648n.
clean-shaven
hairless 229adj.
clean slate
revolution 149n.
obliteration 550n.
clean sweep
ejection 300n.
clean up
unravel 62vb.
purify 648vb.
clear
unmixed 44adj.
eliminate 44vb.
orderly 60adj.
displace 188vb.
space 201vb.
be high 209vb.
fly 271vb.
leap 312vb.
fluidal 335adj.

make flow 350vb.
melodious 410adj.
undimmed 417adj.
make bright 417vb.
transparent 422adj.
well-seen 443adj.
certain 473adj.
semantic 514adj.
intelligible 516adj.
manifest 522adj.
informative 524adj.
perspicuous 567adj.
elegant 575adj.
vocal 577adj.
clean 648vb.
safe 660adj.
disencumber 701vb.
liberate 746vb.
permit 756vb.
pay 804vb.
justify 927vb.
acquit 960vb.

clearance
elimination 44n.
room 183n.
interval 201n.
voidance 300n.
cacation 302n.
preparation 669n.
scope 744n.
permission 756n.
sale 793n.
payment 804n.
vindication 927n.
acquittal 960n.

clear coast
facility 701n.

clear conscience
innocence 935n.

clear-cut
definite 80adj.
well-seen 443adj.
positive 473adj.
(*see* clear)

clear field
opportunity 137n.

clear-headed
intelligent 498adj.
sane 502adj.
sober 948adj.

clearing
open space 263n.
wood 366n.

clearness
transparency 422n.
(*see* clear)

clear of
beyond 199adv.

clear off
decamp 296vb.
void 300vb.

clear out
decamp 296vb.
emerge 298vb.
void 300vb.
clean 648vb.

clear-sighted
seeing 438adj.
intelligent 498adj.

clear the air
unravel 62vb.

clear the decks
make ready 669vb.

clear the ground
pass 305vb.
disencumber 701vb.

clear the path
make possible 469vb.

clear the throat
eruct 300vb.
rasp 407vb.

clear the way
come before 64vb.

clear up
cease 145vb.
make bright 417vb.
be intelligible 516vb.
carry through 725vb.

clearway
traffic control 305n.
road 624n.

cleat
fastening 47n.

cleavage
disjunction 46n.
scission 46n.
structure 331n.
dissension 709n.

cleave
cut, sunder 46vb.
bisect 92vb.

cleaver
sharp edge 256n.

cleave to
cohere 48vb.

cledge
soil 344n.

clef
key 410n.
notation 410n.

cleft
disjunction 46n.
disjunct 46adj.
bisected 92adj.
gap 201n.
spaced 201adj.

cleft stick
dubiety 474n.

clemency
lenity 736n.
mercy 905n.

clench
retain 778vb.

clench one's fist
defy 711vb.
threaten 900vb.

clepsydra
timekeeper 117n.

clerestory
church interior 990n.

clergiability
non-liability 919n.
ecclesiasticism 985n.

clergy
clergy 986n.

clergyman
cleric 986n.

clergywoman
nun 986n.

cleric
holy orders 985n.
cleric 986n.

clerical
ecclesiastical 985adj.
cleric 986n.
clerical 986adj.
vestured 989adj.

clericalism
government 733n.
ecclesiasticism 985n.

clerisy
scholar 492n.

clerk
scholar 492n.
intellectual 492n.
recorder 549n.
penman 586n.
official 690n.
auxiliary 707n.
cleric 986n.

clerkly
instructed 490adj.
written 586adj.

clever
intelligent 498adj.
skillful 694adj.
witty 839adj.

cleverstick
vain person 873n.

clew
sphere 252n.
round 252vb.
(*see* clue)

clew line
tackling 47n.

cliché
uniformity 16n.
repetition 106n.
maxim 496n.
empty talk 515n.
word 559n.
neology 560n.
phrase 563n.

cliché-ridden
repeated 106adj.
feeble 572adj.

click
fastening 47n.
speech sound 398n.
sound faint 401vb.
crackle 402vb.
sound dead 405vb.

know 490vb.
understand 516vb.
succeed 727vb.
client
concomitant 89n.
follower 284n.
habitué 610n.
patron 707n.
dependent 742n.
purchaser 792n.
clientele
dependent 742n.
purchaser 792n.
clientship
subjection 745n.
cliff
high land 209n.
verticality 215n.
acclivity 220n.
rock 244n.
climacteric
serial place 73n.
age 131n.
climactic
crowning 34adj.
climate
influence 178n.
region 184n.
weather 340n.
climatology
weather 340n.
climax
degree 27n.
superiority 34n.
augment 36vb.
serial place 73n.
summit 213n.
crown 213vb.
mature 669vb.
completion 725n.
climax 725vb.
excitation 821n.
climb
grow 36vb.
high land 209n.
be oblique 220vb.
fly 271vb.
ascent 308n.
climb 308vb.
be dear 811vb.
climb-down
humiliation 872n.
climber
traveler 268n.
climber 308n.
climbing
great 32adj.
sport 837n.
clime
region 184n.
land 344n.
clinal
oblique 220adj.
clinch
tie 45vb.
unite with 45vb.
ligature 47n.
cohere 48vb.
close 264vb.
make certain 473vb.
pugilism 716n.
carry through 725vb.
retention 778n.
clinch an argument
demonstrate 478vb.
clincher
reasons 475n.
confutation 479n.
masterpiece 694n.
cling
cohere 48vb.
persevere 600vb.
be wont 610vb.
take 786vb.
caress 889vb.
clinging
cohesive 48adj.
tough 329adj.
habitual 610adj.
retentive 778adj.
cling to
be near 200vb.
observe 768vb.
retain 778vb.
clinic
hospital 658n.
clinician
doctor 658n.
clink
faintness 401n.
resonance 404n.
rasp 407vb.
jail 748n.
clinker
ash 381n.
dirt 649n.
clinker-built
layered 207adj.
marine 275adj.
clinometer
angular measure 247n.
clinquant
finery 844n.
clip
subtract 39vb.
connect 45vb.
cut 46vb.
fastening 47n.
bunch 74n.
make smaller 198vb.
shorten 204vb.
circumscribe 232vb.
touch 378vb.
prohibit 757vb.
demonetize 797vb.
hair-dressing 843n.
caress 889vb.
clip one's words
be concise 569vb.
stammer 580vb.
clipper
sailing-ship 275n.
aircraft 276n.
speeder 277n.
clippers
sharp edge 256n.
cosmetic 843n.
clippings
leavings 41n.
piece 53n.
clip the wings
disable 161vb.
retard 278vb.
make useless 641vb.
hinder 702vb.
clique
party 708n.
cliquish, cliquey
biased 481adj.
sectional 708adj.
cliquism
prejudice 481n.
cloaca
sink 649n.
cloak
wrapping 226n.
cloak 228n.
screen 421n.
pretext 614n.
safeguard 660vb.
defend 713vb.
canonicals 989n.
cloak-and-dagger
stealthy 525adj.
cloakroom
chamber 194n.
latrine 649n.
cloche
garden 370n.
clock
timekeeper 117n.
time 117vb.
clock-hand
indicator 547n.
clock in
begin 68vb.
arrive 295vb.
clockmaker
timekeeper 117n.
artisan 686n.
clock out
end 69vb.
depart 296vb.
clockwise
toward 281adv.
round and round 315adv.
clockwork
complexity 61n.
accuracy 494n.
machine 630n.
clod

piece 53n.
bulk 195n.
solid body 324n.
soil 344n.
dunce 501n.
bungler 697n.
countryman 869n.

clod-hopping
dull 840adj.
graceless 842adj.
ill-bred 847adj.

clog
footwear 228n.
make unclean 649vb.
be difficult 700vb.
encumbrance 702n.
hinder 702vb.
restrain 747vb.
fetter 748n.

cloison
partition 231n.

cloister
retreat 192n.
pavilion 192n.
surround 230vb.
circumscribe 232vb.
enclose 235vb.
path 624n.
refuge 662n.
imprison 747vb.
seclusion 883n.
church exterior 990n.

cloistered
monastic 986adj.

cloistress
nun 986n.

close
similar 18adj.
firm-set 45adj.
join 45vb.
cohesive 48adj.
end 69n., vb.
cease 145vb.
impending 155adj.
place 185n.
make smaller 198vb.
near 200adj.
narrow 206adj.
close 264vb.
approach 289vb.
dense 324adj.
warm 379adj.
attentive 455adj.
accurate 494adj.
reticent 525adj.
concise 569adj.
taciturn 582adj.
repair 656vb.
cure 656vb.
restraining 747adj.
parsimonious 816adj.
parsonage 986n.
church exterior 990n.

closed door
exclusion 57n.

closed mind
narrow mind 481n.
predetermination 608n.

closed shop
uniformity 16n.
exclusion 57n.
restriction 747n.

close finish
short distance 200n.
contest 716n.

close-fisted
parsimonious 816adj.

close fit
adaptation 24n.

close grips
duel 716n.

close in
circumscribe 232vb.
converge 293vb.

closeness
(*see* close)

close quarters
short distance 200n.

close season
interim 108n.
period 110n.

close-set
conjunct 45adj.

close shave
danger 661n.
escape 667n.

close-stool
latrine 649n.

closet
cabinet 194n.
chamber 194n.
hiding-place 527n.
latrine 649n.

close the ranks
cohere 48vb.
make ready 669vb.
give battle 718vb.

close to
nigh 200adv.
contiguous 202adj.

close up
become small 198n.

close-up
short distance 200n.
photography 551n.

close upon
almost 33adv.
subsequently 120adv.
prospectively 124adv.
nigh 200adv.

close with
converge 293vb.
assent 488vb.
strike at 712vb.
fight 716vb.
consent 758vb.

closure
joinder 45n.
end 69n.
stop 145n.
contraction 198n.
closure 264n.

clot
be dense 324vb.
solid body 324n.
blood 335n.
semiliquidity 354n.
thicken 354vb.
dunce 501n.
blood pressure 651n
bungler 697n.

cloth
textile 222n.
bookbinding 589n.
materials 631n.
clergy 986n.
canonicals 989n.

clothe
dress 228vb.
provide 633vb.

clothes
clothing 228n.

clotheshorse
hanger 217n.
frame 218n.
fop 848n.

clothier
clothier 228n.
artisan 686n.

clothing
dressing 228n.
clothing 228n.

Clotho
fate 596n.

clotted
dense 324adj.
semiliquid 354adj.
dirty 649adj.

cloud
accumulation 74n.
certain quantity 104n.
gas 336n.
air 340n.
moisture 341n.
cloud 355n., vb.
obfuscation 421n.
screen 421vb.
opacity 423n.
variegate 437vb.
uncertainty 474n.
disguise 527n.

cloud-burst
storm 176n.
rain 350n.

cloud-cuckoo land
fantasy 513n.

clouded
cheerless 834adj.
tipsy 949adj.
(*see* cloudy)

cloudiness
cloud 355n.

dimness 419n.
imperspicuity 568n.
cloudless
dry 342adj.
undimmed 417adj.
palmy 730adj.
cloud on the horizon
danger 661n.
warning 664n.
cloudscape
abstracted 456adj.
art subject 553n.
clouds, in the
abstracted 456adj.
cloud the issue
be unrelated 10vb.
cloudy
humid 341adj.
cloudy 355adj.
unlit 418adj.
dim 419adj.
opaque 423adj.
semitransparent 424adj.
mottled 437adj.
uncertain 474adj.
imaginary 513adj.
imperspicuous 568adj.
sullen 893adj.
clout
strike 279vb.
repair 656n., vb.
corporal punishment 963n.
spank 963vb.
clove
potherb 301n.
condiment 389n.
scent 396n.
clove-hitch
ligature 47n.
cloven
(*see* cleft)
cloven hoof
malevolence 898n.
wickedness 934n.
Mephisto 969n.
clover
grass 366n.
euphoria 376n.
palmy days 730n.
clover leaf
traffic control 305n.
access 624n.
clown
be absurd 497vb.
fool 501n.
entertainer 594n.
bungler 697n.
humorist 839n.
laughing-stock 851n.
countryman 869n.
clownish
clumsy 695adj.
amusing 837adj.
ill-bred 847adj.
ridiculous 849adj.
cloy
render insensible 375vb.
superabound 637vb.
make insensitive 820vb.
be tedious 838vb.
sate 863vb.
club
focus 76n.
meeting place 192n.
strike 279vb.
association 706n.
party, society 708n.
club 723n.
social round 882n.
scourge 964n.
clubbable
corporate 708adj.
sociable 882adj.
clubbism
sociality 882n.
clubfoot
deformity 246n.
club-haul
navigate 269vb.
clubland
district 184n.
club law
anarchy 734n.
clubman
beau monde 848n.
social person 882n.
club together
cooperate 706vb.
join a party 708vb.
be sociable 882vb.
cluck
ululate 409vb.
clue
bunch 74n.
answer 460n.
evidence 466n.
knowledge 490n.
interpretation 520n.
hint 524n.
indication 547n.
(*see* clew)
clueless
doubting 474adj.
ignorant 491adj.
in difficulties 700adj.
clump
bunch 74n.
strike 279vb.
wood 366n.
clumsy
unapt 25adj.
unwieldy 195adj.
slow 278adj.
inexact 495adj.
unintelligent 499adj.
inelegant 576adj.
inexpedient 643adj.
bad 645adj.
clumsy 695adj.
bungler 697n.
graceless 842adj.
ill-bred 847adj.
ridiculous 849adj.
clunk
resound 404vb.
cluster
group 74n.
congregate 74vb.
clutch
group 74n.
certain quantity 104n.
youngling 132n.
take 786vb.
clutch at
desire 859vb.
clutches
governance 733n.
retention 778n.
clutches of, in the
subject 745adj.
clutter
multitude 104n.
clyster
insertion 303n.
drain 351n.
therapy 658n.
coach
train, carriage 274n.
train, educate 534vb.
trainer, teacher 537n.
make ready 669vb.
coach-house
stable 192n.
chamber 194n.
coachman
driver 268n.
domestic 742n.
coadjutant
cooperative 706adj.
coadjutor
aider 703n.
auxiliary 707n.
coagency
accompaniment 89n.
agency 173n.
concurrence 181n.
cooperation 706n.
coagulate
cohere 48vb.
be dense 324vb.
thicken 354vb.
coagulum
solid body 324n.
coal
propellant 287n.
burn 381vb.
heater 383n.
coal, lighter 385n.

fire 385vb.
glimmer 419n.
torch 420n.
black thing 428n.
coalesce
be identical 13vb.
combine 50vb.
coalescence
junction 45n.
coal-face
workshop 687n.
coal-field
coal 385n.
coal-heaver
bearer 273n.
worker 686n.
coal-hole
cellar 194n.
coalition
junction 45n.
political party 708n.
society 708n.
coal measure(s)
mineral 359n.
coal 385n.
coal-mine, coal-pit
excavation 255n.
workshop 687n.
coal-scuttle
vessel 194n.
coaly
combustible 385adj.
coaming
edge 234n.
coaptation
adaptation 24n.
coarctation
compression 198n.
narrowing 206n.
hindrance 702n.
restriction 747n.
coarse
rough 259adj.
textural 331adj.
unsavory 391adj.
indiscriminating 464adj.
inelegant 576adj.
unclean 649adj.
immature 670adj.
graceless 842adj.
vulgar 847adj.
plebeian 869adj.
impure 951adj.
coarsen
impair 655vb.
make insensitive 820vb.
vulgarize 847vb.
coarseness
moral insensibility 820n.
plainness 573n.
coast
edge 234n.
laterality 239n.
flank 239vb.
go smoothly 258vb.
travel 267vb.
voyage 269vb.
approach 289vb.
pass 305vb.
shore 344n.
not act 677vb.
coastal
marginal 234adj.
coastal 344adj.
coaster
stand 218n.
sled 274n.
merchant ship 275n.
coastguard
naval man 270n.
keeper 749n.
coast-line
outline 233n.
shore 344n.
coat
add 38vb.
layer 207n.
laminate 207vb.
skin, wrapping 226n.
coat 226vb.
line 227vb.
tunic, overcoat 228n.
make opaque 423vb.
preserve 666vb.
coatee
tunic 228n.
coating
layer 207n.
covering 226n.
facing 226n.
lining 227n.
coat of arms
heraldry 547n.
coat-tail
extremity 69n.
pendant 217n.
coax
induce, tempt 612vb.
pet 889vb.
flatterer 925vb.
cob
pony 273n.
waterfowl 365n.
male animal 372n.
cobalt
blue pigment 435n.
cobble
paving 226n.
building material 631n.
cobbler
clothier 228n.
mender 656n.
artisan 686n.
cobbles
road 624n.
cobblestone
paving 226n.
coble
fishing-boat 275n.
cobra
reptile 365n.
noxious animal 904n.
cobweb
weak thing 163n.
filament 208n.
network 222n.
levity 323n.
trifle 639n.
dirt 649n.
cocaine
anesthetic 375n.
drug 658n.
poison 659n.
coccyx
buttocks 238n.
cochineal
pigment 425n.
red pigment 431n.
cochlea
ear 415n.
coil 251n.
cock
poultry 365n.
male animal 372n.
tool 630n.
make ready 669vb.
cockade
livery 547n.
trimming 844n.
cock-a-doodle-doo
ululation 409n.
cock-a-hoop
jubilant 833adj.
boastful 877adj.
cockalorum
insolent person 878n.
cock-and-bull story
insubstantial thing 4n.
fable 543n.
cock a snook at
be insolent 878vb.
not respect 921vb.
cockatrice
rara avis 84n.
reptile 365n.
eye 438n.
heraldry 547n.
noxious animal 904n.
cockboat
boat 275n.
cock-crow
morning 128n.
cocker
pet 889vb.
cockerel
poultry 365n.
male animal 372n.
cock-eyed

oblique 220adj.
distorted 246adj.
dim-sighted 440adj.
cock fight
duel 716n.
cockle
fold 261vb.
fish food 301n.
table fish 365n.
cockles of the heart
affections 817n.
cockloft
attic 194n.
cockney
native 191n.
dialectical 560adj.
commoner 869n.
plebeian 869adj.
cock of the walk
exceller 644n.
master 741n.
proud man 871n.
cockpit
chamber 914n.
aircraft 276n.
cattle pen 369n.
duel 716n.
arena 724n.
cockroach
fly 365n.
cockshut
evening 129n.
cock-shy
propulsion 287n.
laughing-stock 851n.
cocksparrow
dwarf 196n.
cocksure
believing 485adj.
cocktail
a mixture 43n.
potion 301n.
liquor 301n.
cock up
be vertical 215vb.
jut 254vb.
cocky
prideful 871adj.
vain 873adj.
impertinent 878adj.
cocoa
soft drink 301n.
coconut
fruit 301n.
cocoon
youngling 132n.
source 156n.
nest 192n.
receptacle 194n.
wrapping 226n.
vermin 365n.
cocotte
prostitute 952n.
coction
heating 381n.
cod
skin 226n.
table fish 365n.
coda
adjunct 40n.
sequel 67n.
end 69n.
rear 238n.
melody 410n.
musical piece 412n.
coddle
cook 301vb.
please 826vb.
pet 889vb.
code
arrangement 62n.
rule 81n.
translate 520vb.
secrecy 525n.
conceal 525vb.
enigma 530n.
symbology 547n.
writing 586n.
precept 693n.
probity 929n.
codeine
drug 658n.
code of honor
code of duty 917n.
probity 929n.
coder
interpreter 520n.
codex
script 586n.
book 589n.
codger
niggard 816n.
codicil
adjunct 40n.
sequel 67n.
title-deed 767n.
codification
law 953n.
legislation 953n.
codify
class 62vb.
codirector
colleague 707n.
codling
youngster 132n.
coeducation
education 534n.
coefficience
accompaniment 89n.
cooperation 706n.
coefficient
numerical element 85n.
concomitant 89n.
coelenterate
animal 365n.
coemption
purchase 792n.
coequal
equal 28adj.
compeer 28n.
coerce
dominate 733vb.
compel 740vb.
coercion
brute force 735n.
compulsion 740n.
restraint 747n.
coeternal
perpetual 115adj.
synchronous 123adj.
coeval
contemporary 123n.
synchronous 123adj.
coexist
be 1vb.
accompany 89vb.
be contiguous 202vb.
be patient 823vb.
coexistence
existence 1n.
accompaniment 89n.
synchronism 123n.
contiguity 202n.
concord 710n.
peace 717n.
coextension
equality 28n.
parallelism 219n.
coextensive
symmetrical 245adj.
(*see* coextension)
coffee
soft drink 301n.
brownness 430n.
coffee house
café 192n.
coffee-pot
caldron 194n.
coffee stall
café 192n.
coffer
box 194n.
storage 632n.
treasury 799n.
coffin
box 194n.
interment 364n.
funeral 364n.
cog
tooth 256n.
notch 260n.
merchant ship 275n.
deceive, befool 542vb.
flatter 925vb.
cogent
powerful 160adj.
rational 475adj.
compelling 740adj.
cogged
toothed 256adj.
cogger
trickster 545n.

coggery
trickery 542n.
cogitate
think 449vb.
cogitation, cogitative
(*see* cogitate)
cognac
liquor 301n.
cognate
relative 9adj.
kinsman 11n.
akin 11adj.
similar 18adj.
verbal 559adj.
cognisance
(*see* cognizance)
cognition
knowledge 490n.
cognitive
mental 447adj.
knowing 490adj.
cognizable
known 490adj.
intelligible 516adj.
legal 953adj.
illegal 954adj.
cognizance
intellect 447n.
knowledge 490n.
cognizance of, take
notice 455vb.
cognizant
mental 447adj.
knowing 490adj.
cognize
cognize 447vb.
know 490vb.
hold court 955vb.
cognomen
name 561n.
cognoscente
man of taste 846n.
cog-wheel
notch 260n.
cohabit
unite with 45vb.
accompany 89vb.
wed 894vb.
coheir
participator 775n.
beneficiary 776n.
cohere
cohere 48vb.
be dense 324vb.
thicken 354vb.
coherence
junction 45n.
coherence 48n.
sanity 501n.
intelligibility 516n.
coherent
(*see* coherence)
cohesion
coherence 48n.
density 324n.
viscidity 354n.
cohesive
firm-set 45adj.
cohesive 48adj.
retentive 778adj.
cohibit
obstruct 702vb.
restrain 747vb.
prohibit 757vb.
cohort(s)
formation 722n.
army 722n.
coif
headgear 228n.
coiffure
wig 228n.
hair-dressing 843n.
coign of vantage
vantage 34n.
coil
complexity 61n.
twine 251vb.
round 252vb.
difficulty 700n.
hair-dressing 843n.
coin
produce 164vb.
efform 243vb.
imagine 513vb.
fake 541vb.
mint 797vb.
coinage
production 164n.
coinage 797n.
coincide
be identical 1vb.
accord 24vb.
accompany 89vb.
coincidence
synchronism 123n.
eventuality 154n.
chance 159n.
concurrence 181n.
contiguity 202n.
(*see* coincide)
coincident
conjunctive 45adj.
(*see* coincidence)
coincidental
accompanying 89adj.
casual 159adj.
unintentional 618adj.
coin-clipper
defrauder 789n.
coiner
moneyer 797n.
coin words
neologize 560vb.
coir
fiber 208n.
coital
conjunctive 45adj.
coition, coitus
coition 45n.
propagation 164n.
coke
soft drink 301n.
ash 381n.
coal 385n.
col
bond 47n.
narrowness 206n.
high land 209n.
cola
soft drink 301n.
colander
bowl 194n.
porosity 263n.
cold
wintry 129adj.
dead 361adj.
insensible 375adj.
coldness 380n.
feeble 572adj.
infection 651n.
respiratory disease 651n.
blight 659n.
preserver 666n.
non-active 677adj.
adversity 731n.
uncooked 760adj.
impassive 820adj.
inexcitable 823adj.
cheerless 834adj.
indifferent 860adj.
inimical 881adj.
unsociable 883adj.
unkind 898adj.
pure 950adj.
cold-blooded
animal 365adj.
impassive 820adj.
cautious 858adj.
unastonished 865adj.
cold comfort
discontent 829n.
cold feet
nervousness 854n.
cold fish
unfeeling person 820n.
cold frame
garden 370n.
cold front
wintriness 380n.
coldness
coldness 380n.
(*see* cold)
cold pack
preservation 666n.
cold-shoulder
exclude 57vb.
disregard 458vb.
reject 607vb.
avoid 620vb.
make unwelcome 833vb.

cold storage
delay 136n.
refrigerator 384n.
cold sweat
fear 854n.
cold war
war 718n.
cold water
moderator 177n.
dissuasion 613n.
antidote 658n.
cole, coleslaw, colewort
vegetable 301n.
colic
pang 377n.
indigestion 651n.
collaborate
be willing 597vb.
apostatize 603vb.
cooperate 706vb.
collaboration
concurrence 181n.
cooperation 706n.
collaborator
tergiversator 603n.
personnel 686n.
collaborator 707n.
friend 880n.
collapse
decrease 37vb.
cease 145vb.
helplessness 161n.
weakness 163n.
ruin 165n.
fall short 307vb.
descent 309n.
illness 651n.
dilapidation 655n.
fatigue 684n.
knuckle under 721vb.
defeat 728n.
fail 728vb.
collar
halter 47n.
girdle 47n.
neckwear 228n.
loop 250n.
meat 301n.
arrest 747vb.
fetter 748n.
take 786vb.
collate
compare 462vb.
commission 751vb.
collateral
relative 9adj.
akin 11adj.
offset 31n.
parallel 219adj.
lateral 239adj.
security 767n.
collaterality
relation 9n.
sonship 170n.
collation
meal 301n.
comparison 462n.
colleague
personnel 686n.
colleague 707n.
friend 880n.
colleagueship
association 706n.
collect
join 45vb.
bring together 74vb.
understand 516vb.
abstract 592vb.
acquire 771vb.
receive 782vb.
take 786vb.
prayers 981n.
collectanea
accumulation 74n.
anthology 592n.
collected
compendious 592adj.
unastonished 865adj.
collection
arrangement 62n.
accumulation 74n.
exhibit 522n.
collection 632n.
offering 781n.
payment 804n.
oblation 981n.
collection bag,—plate
church utensil 990n.
collective
assemblage 74n.
general 79adj.
agrarian 370adj.
joint possession 775n.
sharing 775adj.
collective farm
farm 370n.
joint possession 775n.
collectively
collectively 52adv.
together 74adv.
with 89adv.
in common 755adv.
collectivism
government 733n.
joint possession 775n.
collectivity
whole 52n.
collectivization
assemblage 74n.
collect oneself
keep calm 823vb.
collector
accumulator 74n.
collector 492n.
official 690n.
receiver 782n.
collectorship
receiving 782n.
collector's piece
exhibit 522n.
exceller 644n.
masterpiece 694n.
colleen
youngster 132n.
college
group 74n.
academy 539n.
collegian, colleger
college student 538n.
collegiate
student-like 538adj.
collide
disagree 25vb.
collide 279vb.
approach 289vb.
meet 295vb.
touch 378vb.
strike at 712vb.
be inimical 881vb.
collie
dog 365n.
collied
black 428adj.
dirty 649adj.
collier
merchant ship 275n.
artisan 686n.
colliery
excavation 255n.
store 632n.
workshop 687n.
collimation
parallelism 219n.
direction 281n.
collimator
direction 281n.
colliquation
liquefaction 337n.
collision
violence 176n.
counteraction 182n.
collision 279n.
convergence 293n.
quarrel 709n.
fight 716n.
battle 718n.
collision course
convergence 293n.
collocate
arrange 62vb.
bring together 74vb.
place 187vb.
collocation
(*see* collocate)
collocutor
interlocutor 584n.
collodion
viscidity 354n.
collogue
converse 584vb.
flatter 925vb.
colloid

viscidity 354n.
semiliquidity 354n.
collop
piece 53n.
colloquial
figurative 519adj.
linguistic 557adj.
dialectical 560adj.
colloquialism
trope 519n.
slang 560n.
colloquy
speech 579n.
interlocution 584n.
conference 584n.
collotype
copy 22n.
representation 551n.
collusion
concurrence 181n.
deception 542n.
cooperation 706n.
collusive, collusory
false 541adj.
deceiving 542adj.
colluvies
sink 649n.
collyrium
balm 658n.
cosmetic 843n.
collywobbles
voidance 300n.
pang 377n.
colon
insides 224n.
tube 263n.
drain 351n.
punctuation 547n.
colonel
army officer 741n.
colonelcy
degree 27n.
colonial
foreigner 59n.
settler 191n.
subject 742n.
subject 745adj.
colonialism
governance 733n.
subjection 745n.
colonist
settler 191n.
incomer 297n.
egress 298n.
colonization
location 187n.
colonize
place oneself 187vb.
dwell 192vb.
subjugate 745vb.
appropriate 786vb.
colonnade
series 71n.
pavilion 192n.
path 624n.
colony
crowd 74n.
certain quantity 104n.
descendant 170n.
territory 184n.
station 187n.
habitancy 191n.
polity 733n.
subject 742n.
colophon
sequel 67n.
rear 238n.
label 547n.
letterpress 587n.
edition 589n.
colophony
resin 357n.
color
character 5n.
tincture 43n.
mix 43vb.
sort 77n.
modify 143vb.
influence 187vb.
light 417n.
color 425n., vb.
blackness 428n.
redden 431vb.
mien 445n.
qualify 468vb.
probability 471n.
sophisticate 477vb.
cant 541vb.
paint 553vb.
ornament 574n.
pretext 614n.
show feeling 818vb.
decorate 844vb.
be modest 874vb.
get angry 891vb.
justify 927vb.
colorable
plausible 471adj.
deceiving 542adj.
ostensible 614adj.
Colorado beetle
noxious animal 904n.
coloration
light 417n.
color, hue 425n.
coloratura
vocal music 412n.
vocalist 413n.
color-bar
exclusion 57n.
disapprobation 924n.
color-blind
dim-sighted 440adj.
indiscriminating 464adj.
colored
colored 425adj.
blackish 428adj.
colorful
luminous 417adj.
luminescent 420adj.
colored, florid 425adj.
variegated 437adj.
showy 875adj.
coloring
hue 425n.
qualification 468n.
meaning 514n.
exaggeration 546n.
identification 547n.
painting 553n.
coloring matter
pigment 425n.
colorist
artist 556n.
colorless
weak 163adj.
dim 419adj.
colorless 426adj.
feeble 572adj.
unhealthy 651adj.
mediocre 732adj.
dull 840adj.
color, man of
negro 428n.
colors
flag 547n.
color up
redden 431vb.
be humbled 872vb.
color-wash
pigment 425n.
decorate 844vb.
colossal
enormous 32adj.
stalwart 162adj.
huge 195adj.
tall 209adj.
Colosseum
arena 724n.
colossus
giant 195n.
tall creature 209n.
high structure 209n.
sculpture 554n.
colporteur
seller 793n.
peddler 794n.
colt
youngling 132n.
horse 273n.
male animal 372n.
beginner 538n.
bungler 697n.
colter
sharp edge 256n.
farm tool 370n.
coltish
infantine 132adj.
active 678adj.
colubriform
animal 365adj.

columbaceous
animal 365adj.
columbarium
cemetery 364n.
columbine
entertainer 594n.
columellar
supporting 218adj.
column
high structure 209n.
pillar 218n.
cylinder 252n.
marching 267n.
rostrum 539n.
monument 548n.
formation 722n.
columnar
supporting 218adj.
rotund 252adj.
columnist
informant 524n.
chronicler 549n.
author 589n.
coma
helplessness 161n.
insensibility 375n.
sleep 679n.
fatigue 684n.
co-mate
colleague 707n.
comatose
impotent 161adj.
apathetic 820adj.
(*see* coma)
comb
valley 255n.
tooth 256n.
musical instrument 414n.
cleaning utensil 648n.
clean 648vb.
hair-dressing 843n.
combat
contention, fight 716n.
give battle 718vb.
combatant
contender 716n.
combatant 722n.
combative
quarreling 709adj.
contending 716adj.
warlike 718adj.
combativeness
bellicosity 718n.
comber
wave 350n.
combination
mixture 43n.
junction 45n.
coherence 48n.
combination 50n.
composition 56n.
assemblage 74n.
numerical operation 86n.
association 706n.
society 708n.
combinations
underwear 228n.
combine
be one 88vb.
association 706n.
(*see* combination)
combine-harvester
farm tool 370n.
combings
cleavings 41n
rubbish 641n.
comb out
unravel 62vb.
combustibility
burning 381n.
combustible
fuel 385n.
combustible 385adj.
combustion
burning 381n.
come
arrive 295vb.
come about
be 1vb.
happen 154vb.
come a cropper
tumble 309vb.
come across
acquire 771vb.
pay 804vb.
come again
be unsatisfied 636vb.
come alive
be intelligible 516vb.
come amiss
disagree 25vb.
be inexpedient 643vb.
come and go
fluctuate 317vb.
be active 678vb.
come apart
be disjoined 46vb.
come-back
compensation 31n.
revival 656n.
come by
acquire 771vb.
comedian
actor 594n.
humorist 839n.
come-down
descent 309n.
disappointment 509n.
humiliation 872n.
come down
decrease 37vb.
be poor 301vb.
descend 309vb.
be cheap 812vb.
come down on
be severe 735vb.
restrain 747vb.
come down on for
claim 915vb.
comedy
stage play 594n.
laughter 835n.
ridiculousness 849n.
come forth
emerge 298vb.
be visible 443vb.
come forward
be visible 443vb.
offer oneself 759vb.
come from
result 157vb.
come-hither look
look 438n.
pleasurableness 826n.
wooing 889n.
come in
be included 78vb.
enter 297vb.
be received 782vb.
come in for
receive 782vb.
come into
inherit 771vb.
possess 773vb.
receive 782vb.
come into existence
become 1vb.
happen 154vb.
come into use
be wont 610vb.
comely
symmetrical 245adj.
beautiful 841adj.
come natural
accord 24vb.
come near
resemble 18vb.
approach 289vb.
come of
result 157vb.
come of age
come of age 134vb.
come off
cease 145vb.
happen 154vb.
transfer 272vb.
escape 667vb.
be successful 727vb.
come off it
be humbled 872vb.
come off on
cohere 48vb.
come on
impend 155vb.
progress 285vb.
charge 712vb.
come out
begin 68vb.
emerge 298vb.
be visible 443vb.

be disclosed 526vb.
dramatize 594vb.
relinquish 621vb.
be inactive 679vb.
be easy 701vb.
revolt 738vb.
come out of
result 157vb.
come out with
divulge 526vb.
come over
consent 758vb.
come round
be periodic 141vb.
be restored 656vb.
consent 758vb.
comes
star 321n.
come short
be inferior 35vb.
be incomplete 55vb.
fall short 307vb.
not suffice 636vb.
comestible
food 301n.
edible 301adj.
comet
wanderer 268n.
planet 321n.
cometary
celestial 321adj.
come to
number 86vb.
be turned to 147vb.
be restored 656vb.
be refreshed 685vb.
cost 809vb.
come to a head
culminate 34vb.
be complete 54vb.
come to be
become 1vb.
come to bits
be disjoined 46vb.
come to blows
fight 716vb.
be inimical 881vb.
come together
congregate 74n.
converge 293vb.
come to grief
miscarry 728vb.
have trouble 731vb.
come to hand
arrive 295vb.
be received 782vb.
come to heel
accompany 89vb.
follow 284vb.
obey 739vb.
come to know
be informed 524vb.
come to life
live 360vb.
be restored 656vb.
come to light
be visible 443vb.
be plain 522vb.
be disclosed 526vb.
come to nothing
not be 2vb.
be unproductive 172vb.
fall short 307vb.
miscarry 728vb.
come to pass
happen 154vb.
come to stay
stay 144vb.
come to terms
accord 24vb.
contract 765vb.
come to the point
be related 9vb.
specify 80vb.
be concise 569vb.
speak plainly 573vb.
come under
be included 78vb.
come unstuck
be disjoined 46vb.
come unstuck 49vb.
be dispersed 75vb.
be in difficulty 700vb.
fail 728vb.
come upon
meet 295vb.
discover 484vb.
comfit
sweet 392n.
comfort
euphoria 376n.
repose 682n.
refresh 685vb.
aid 703n., vb.
wealth 800n.
happiness 824n.
please 826vb.
content 828n., vb.
relief 831n.
cheer 833vb.
give hope 852vb.
condolence 905n.
pity 905vb.
comfortable
adjusted 24adj.
tranquil 266adj.
comfortable 376adj.
reposeful 683adj.
easy 701adj.
prosperous, palmy 730adj.
rich 800adj.
inexcitable 823adj.
happy 824adj.
pleasurable 826adj.
content 828adj.
comforter
wrapping 226n.
shawl 228n.
relief 831n.
Comforter
Holy Ghost 965n.
comfortless
unpleasant 827adj.
cheerless 834adj.
unpromising 853adj.
comfort station
latrine 649n.
comic
actor 594n.
dramatic 594adj.
laughing 835adj.
humorist 839n.
witty 839adj.
funny 849adj.
coming
future 124adj.
coming events
futurity 124n.
destiny 155n.
coming out
debut 68n.
celebration 876n.
comitia
council 692n.
comity
etiquette 848n.
courtesy 884n.
comity of nations
mankind 371n.
comma
punctuation 347n.
command
vantage 34n.
be superior 34vb.
influence 178vb.
be high 209vb.
will 595n., vb.
requirement 627n.
dispose of 673vb.
direct 689vb.
precept 693n.
dominate 733vb.
command 737n., vb.
compel 740vb.
mandate 751n.
possess 773vb.
commandant
army officer 741n.
commandeer
appropriate 786vb.
commander
superior 34n.
naval man 270n.
army officer 741n.
naval officer 741n.
commanding
authoritative 733adj.
noteworthy 866adj.
proud 871adj.
(*see* command)
commandment

(*see* command)
commando
armed force 722n.
comme il faut
tasteful 846adj.
fashionable 848adj.
genteel 868adj.
commemorate
remind 505vb.
honor 866vb.
celebrate 876vb.
commemoration
remembrance 505n.
amusement 837n.
(*see* commemorate)
commence
begin 68vb.
commend
advise 691vb.
befriend 880vb.
approve 923vb.
praise 923vb.
commendable
good 615adj.
expedient 642adj.
approvable 923adj.
virtuous 933adj.
commender
adviser 691n.
commender 923n.
commensal
mensal 301adj.
commensurability
fitness 24n.
commensurable
numerical 85adj.
numerable 86adj.
commensurate
relative 9adj.
agreeing 24adj.
numerical 85adj.
numerable 86adj.
sufficient 635adj.
comment
notice 455vb.
estimate 480n., vb.
maxim 496n.
interpret 520vb.
commentary 520n.
affirmation 532n.
speech 579n.
article 591n.
dissert 591vb.
commentary
commentary 520n.
article 591n.
commentator
estimator 480n.
intellectual 492n.
interpreter 520n.
informant 524n.
dissertator 591n.
commerce
interlocution 584n.
business 622n.
trade 791n.
card game 837n.
commercial
businesslike 622adj.
trading 791adj.
vulgar 847adj.
commercialism
trade 791n.
bad taste 847n.
commercialize
trade 791vb.
vulgarize 847vb.
commercial traveler
traveler 268n.
seller 793n.
commination
malediction 899n.
threat 900n.
prayers 981n.
comminute
break 46vb.
pulverize 332vb.
commiseration
pity 905n.
condolence 905n.
commissar
tyrant 735n.
master, officer 741n.
autocrat 741n.
commissarial
provisionary 633adj.
commissariat
provisions 301n.
provision 633n.
commissary
provider 633n.
delegate 754n.
commission
increment 36n.
band 74n.
job 622n.
employ 622vb.
fitting out 669n.
make ready 669vb.
action 676n.
warrant 737n., vb.
commission 751n., vb.
permit 756n.
earnings 771n.
impose a duty 917vb.
commissionaire
janitor 264n.
courier 531n.
servant 742n.
commissioner
official 690n.
officer 741n.
delegate 754n.
commissioner for oaths
notary 958n.
commission of the peace
jurisdiction 955n.
tribunal 956n.
commissure
joint 45n.
commit
transfer 272vb.
do 676vb.
commission 751vb.
convey 780vb.
do wrong 914vb.
commitment
promise 764n.
giving 781n.
debt 803n.
duty 917n.
commit oneself
affirm 532vb.
undertake 762vb.
promise 764vb.
incur a duty 917vb.
committal
transference 272n.
commission 751n.
legal process 959n.
committed
affirmative 532adj.
promised 476adj.
indebted 803adj.
dutied 917adj.
committee
band 74n.
party 708n.
authority 733n.
consignee 754n.
commixture
mixture 43n.
ritual act 988n.
commode
vessel 194n.
cabinet 194n.
latrine 649n.
commodious
useful 640adj.
commodity
object 319n.
benefit 615n.
utility 640n.
merchandise 795n.
commodore
naval man 270n.
naval officer 741n.
common
inferior 35adj.
general 79adj.
typical 83adj.
frequent 139adj.
plain 348n.
mediocre 732adj.
sharing 775adj.
lands 777n.
vulgar 847adj.
unastonishing 865adj.
plebeian 869adj.
commonalty
social group 371n.
commonalty 869n.

common cause
cooperation 706n.
common denominator
relation 9n.
numerical element 85n.
commoner
college student 538n.
mediocrity 732n.
vulgarian 847n.
commoner 869n.
common feature
similarity 18n.
common front
association 706n.
common knowledge
knowledge 490n.
publicity 528n.
common lot
mediocrity 732n.
commonly
often 139adv.
common man
common man 30n.
everyman 79n.
mediocrity 732n.
commonness
(*see* common)
common or garden
typical 83adj.
commonplace
median 30adj.
typical 83adj.
topic 452n.
known 490adj.
maxim 496n.
aphoristic 496adj.
phrase 563n.
plain 573adj.
usual 610adj.
trivial 639adj.
mediocre 732adj.
dull 840adj.
commonplace book
reminder 505n.
anthology 592n.
common prayer
public worship 981n.
common run
habit 610n.
commons
provisions 301n.
commonalty 869n.
common sense
intelligence 498n.
sanity 502n.
common speech
language 557n.
plainness 573n.
common stamp
uniformity 16n.
common stock
joint possession 775n.
common touch
sociability 882n.
courtesy 884n.
commonweal
nation 371n.
good 615n.
utility 640n.
polity 733n.
commonwealth
territory 184n.
nation 371n.
polity 733n.
commorant
dweller 191n.
commotion
violence 176n.
commotion 318n.
exaggeration 546n.
excitable state 822vb.
communal
national 371adj.
sectional 708adj.
sharing 775adj.
commune
district 184n.
meditate 449vb.
communicate 524vb.
converse 584vb.
communicable
transferable 272adj.
infectious 653adj.
communicant
church member 976n.
pietist 979n.
worshiper 981n.
communicate
connect 45vb.
transfer 272vb.
mean 514vb.
communicate 524vb.
give 781vb.
offer worship 981vb.
communicating
accessible 289adj.
communication
information 524n.
disclosure 526n.
message 529n.
interlocution 584n.
correspondence 588n.
(*see* communicate)
communications
access 624n.
communicative
loquacious 581adj.
communicator
informant 524n.
communion
interlocution 584n.
party 708n.
social gathering 882n.
worship 981n.
Holy Communion 988n.
communiqué
report 524n.
news 529n.
communist
reformer 654n.
agitator 738n.
participator 775n.
communistic
authoritarian 735adj.
sharing 775adj.
community
habitancy 191n.
social group 371n.
association 706n.
community 708n.
sect 978n.
monk 986n.
laity 987n.
community-chest
store 632n.
community house
monastery 986n.
communize
socialize 775vb.
commutable
substituted 150adj.
interchanged 151adj.
commutation
compensation 31n.
substitution 150n.
interchange 151n.
compromise 770n.
commute
be periodic 141vb.
substitute 150vb.
interchange 151vb.
compromise 770vb.
commuter
traveler 268n.
rider 268n.
thing transferred 272n.
compact
small 33adj.
cohesive 48adj.
ease 194n.
little 196adj.
contracted 198adj.
short 204adj.
dense 324adj.
concise 569adj.
compact 765n.
cosmetic 843n.
compaction
coherence 48n.
contraction 198n.
structure 331n.
companion
analogue 18n.
concomitant 89n.
window 263n.
colleague 707n.
servant, retainer 742n.
close friend 880n.
companionable

sociable 882adj.
companionate marriage
type of marriage 894n.
illicit love 951n.
companionship
accompaniment 89n.
sociality 882n.
companion-way
entrance 263n.
ascent 308n.
company
assembly 74n.
band 74n.
accompaniment 89n.
actor 594n.
personnel 686n.
workshop 687n.
association 706n.
corporation 708n.
formation 722n.
comparability
relevance 9n.
relativeness 9n.
similarity 18n.
comparable
relative 9adj.
equivalent 28adj.
compared 462adj.
comparative
figurative 519adj.
grammatical 564adj.
comparatively
slightly 33adv.
comparatively 462adv.
compare
relate 9vb.
graduate 27vb.
compare 462vb.
discriminate 463vb.
compare notes
consult 691vb.
compare with
resemble 18vb.
comparison
relativeness 9n.
assimilation 18n.
joinder 45n.
comparison 462n.
metaphor 519n.
compartition
decomposition 51n.
compartment
subdivision 53n.
place 185n.
compartment 194n.
train 274n.
heraldry 547n.
compartmentalize
set apart 46vb.
compartmentalized
cellular 194adj.
compass
ability 160n.
range 183n.
region 184n.
distance 199n.
circumjacence 230n.
surround 230vb.
outline 233n.
sailing aid 269n.
direction 281n.
circle 314vb.
gauge 465n.
signpost 547n.
succeed 727vb.
compassion
lenity 736n.
pity 905n.
disinterestedness 931n.
compassionable
pitiable 905adj.
compassionate
giving 781adj.
impressible 819adj.
pitying 905adj.
pity 905vb.
compass point
compass point 281n.
compatibility
adaptation 24n.
possibility 469n.
concord 710n.
friendship 880n.
sociability 882n.
love 887n.
compatriot
kinsman 11n.
native 191n.
compeer
compeer 28n.
contemporary 123n.
compel
be able 160vb.
influence 178vb.
motivate 612vb.
command 737vb.
compel 740vb.
compellation
nomenclature 561n.
compelling
causal 156adj.
powerful 160adj.
strong 162adj.
influential 178adj.
forceful 571adj.
necessary 596adj.
compelling 740adj.
compendious
small 33adj.
short 204adj.
concise 569adj.
compendious 592adj.
compendium
accumulation 74n.
miniature 196n.
contraction 198n.
compendium 592n.
compensate
correlate 12vb.
equalize 28vb.
compensate 31vb.
retaliate 714vb.
restitute 787vb.
pay 804vb.
atone 941vb.
reward 962vb.
compensation
(*see* compensate)
compère
actor 594n.
stage-manager 594n.
direct 690vb.
compete
do likewise 20vb.
contend 716vb.
offer oneself 759vb.
competence
ability 160n.
sufficiency 635n.
skill 694n.
independence 744n.
wealth 800n.
jurisdiction 955n.
competent
legal 953adj.
jurisdictional 955adj.
(*see* competence)
compete with
oppose 704vb.
competition
imitation 20n.
opposition 704n.
contention 716n.
sale 793n.
jealousy 911n.
competitive
equal 28adj.
skillful 694adj.
selfish 932adj.
competitor
compeer 28n.
incomer 297n.
hinderer 702n.
opponent 705n.
contender 716n.
petitioner 763n.
enemy 881n.
competitors
opposites 704n.
compilation
composition 56n.
assemblage 74n.
accumulation 74n.
dictionary 559n.
anthology 592n.
compile
compose 56vb.
(*see* compilation)
compiler
collector 492n.
etymology 559n.

anthology 592n.
complacence
content 828n.
courtesy 884n.
complacent
benevolent 897adj.
complain
deprecate 762vb.
be discontented 829vb.
lament 836vb.
be sullen 893vb.
blame 924vb.
indict 928vb.
complainant
accuser 928n.
complainer
malcontent 829n.
moper 834n.
weeper 836n.
complain of
be ill 651vb.
complaint
cry 408n.
evil 616n.
illness 651n.
deprecation 762n.
annoyance 827n.
discontent 829n.
lament 836n.
wrong 914n.
disapprobation 924n.
accusation 928n.
complaisance
permission 756n.
courteous act 884n.
complaisant
conformable 83adj.
lenient 736adj.
obedient 739adj.
courteous 884adj.
benevolent 897adj.
complement
analogue 18n.
adjunct 40n.
plenitude 54n.
component 58n.
band 74n.
inclusion 78n.
numerical element 85n.
personnel 686n.
complementary
correlative 12adj.
complete
consummate 32adj.
make complete 54vb.
persevere 600vb.
sufficient 635adj.
perfect 646adj.
do 676vb.
carry through 725vb.
completely
wholly 52adv.
completeness
whole 52n.
completeness 54n.
completion 725n.
completion
sequel 67n.
sufficiency 635n.
completion 725n.
(*see* completeness)
complex
character 5n.
mixed 43adj.
whole 52n.
complex 61adj.
intricate 251adj.
structure 331n.
imperspicuous 568adj.
habituation 610n.
difficult 700adj.
complexion
modality 7n.
state 7n.
hue 425n.
mien 445n.
complexity
medley 43n.
complexity 61n.
enigma 530n.
imperspicuity 568n.
(*see* complex)
compliance
concurrence 181n.
softness 327n.
willingness 597n.
submission 721n.
obedience 739n.
consent 758n.
observance 768n.
servility 879n.
compliant
(*see* compliance)
complicate
bedevil 63vb.
be unintelligible 517vb.
aggravate 832vb.
complication
complexity 61n.
illness 651n.
(*see* complexity)
complicity
cooperation 707n.
participation 775n.
improbity 930n.
guilt 936n.
compliment
honors 866n.
courteous act 884n.
gratulate 886vb.
endearment 889n.
praise 923n., vb.
flatter 925vb.
complimentary
uncharged 812adj.
compline
church service 988n.
comply
(*see* compliance)
compo
facing 226n.
building material 631n.
component
adjunct 40n.
part 53n.
component 58n.
included 78adj.
unit 88n.
contents 193n.
element 319n.
comportment
conduct 688n.
comport with
accord 24vb.
compose
mix 43vb.
combine 50vb.
compose, constitute 56vb.
arrange 62vb.
be included 78vb.
produce 164vb.
assuage 177vb.
harmonize 410vb.
compose music 413vb.
write 586vb.
print 587vb.
tranquilize 823vb.
composed
inexcitable 823adj.
unastonished 865adj.
compose differences
pacify 719vb.
mediate 720vb.
compromise 770vb.
compose oneself
keep calm 823vb.
composer
producer 167n.
musician 413n.
composite
mixed 43adj.
conjunct 45adj.
plural 101adj.
composition
a mixture 43n.
combination 50n.
composition 56n.
arrangement 62n.
substitution 150n.
quid pro quo 150n.
production 164n.
structure 331n.
musical piece 412n.
painting 553n.
writing 586n.
print 587n.
building material 631n.
pacification 719n.

compact 765n.
compromise 770n.
payment 804n.
pattern 844n.
compositor
printer 587n.
compos mentis
sane 502adj.
compost
fertilizer 171n.
composure
inexcitability 823n.
non-wonder 865n.
compote
pudding 301n.
sweetmeat 301n.
compound
a mixture 43n.
compound 50n.
compose 56vb.
substitute 150vb.
enclosure 235n.
compromise 770vb.
comprador
provider 633n.
comprehend
contain 56vb.
comprise 78vb.
know 490vb.
understand 516vb.
comprehensible
intelligible 516adj.
comprehension
connotation 514n.
(*see* comprehend)
comprehensive
extensive 32adj.
comprehensive 52adj.
complete 54adj.
inclusive 78adj.
general 79adj.
large 195adj.
comprehensivity
whole 52n.
(*see* comprehensive)
compress
tighten 45vb.
make smaller 198vb.
shorten 204vb.
make thin 206vb.
be dense 324vb.
stanch 350vb.
be concise 569vb.
surgical dressing 658n.
compressible
contracted 198adj.
rare 325adj.
soft 327adj.
compression
smallness 33n.
diminution 37n.
energy 160n.
compression 198n.
narrowing 206n.
closure 264n.
conciseness 569n.
compendium 592n.
restriction 747n.
compressor
compressor 198n.
stopper 264n.
condensation 324n.
comprise
comprise 78vb.
comprobation
demonstration 478n.
compromise
adaptation 24n.
middle point 30n.
moderation 177n.
irresolution 601n.
mid-course 625n.
endanger 661vb.
pacification 719n.
laxity 734n.
compact 765n.
make terms 766vb.
compromise 770n., vb.
defame 926vb.
compromising
discreditable 867adj.
comptometer
counting instrument 86n.
compulsion
necessity 596n.
no choice 606n.
needfulness 627n.
compulsion 740n.
restraint 747n.
compulsive
powerful 160adj.
strong 162adj.
necessary 596adj.
authoritarian 735adj.
commanding 737adj.
compelling 740adj.
obligatory 917adj.
compulsory
compelling 740adj.
compulsory acquisition
taking 786n.
compunction
regret 830n.
pity 905n.
penitence 939n.
compunctious
unhappy 825adj.
compurgation
credential 466n.
vindication 927n.
acquittal 960n.
compurgator
witness 466n.
vindicator 927n.
computable
numerable 86adj.
measured 465adj.
computation
numeration 86n.
measurement 465n.
accounts 808n.
compute
do sums 86vb.
measure 465vb.
computer
computer 86n.
comrade
concomitant 89n.
male 372n.
colleague 707n.
society 708n.
political party 708n.
title 870n.
chum 880n.
comradely
corporate 708adj.
friendly 880adj.
comradeship
cooperation 706n.
friendship 880n.
sociality 882n.
con
meditate 449vb.
know 490vb.
memorize 505vb.
con amore
willingly 597adj.
feelingly 818adv.
conation
will 595n.
concamerate
make curved 248vb.
concatenate
connect 45vb.
concatenation
joinder 45n.
continuity 71n.
concave
concave 255adj.
conceal
contain 56vb.
cover 226vb.
screen 421vb.
conceal 525vb.
safeguard 660vb.
concealed
unknown 491adj.
latent 523adj.
cabalistic 984adj.
concealment
invisibility 444n.
equivocalness 518n.
concealment 525n.
seclusion 883n.
concede
be reasonable 475vb.
assent 488vb.
confess 526vb.
be induced 612vb.

be lenient 736vb.
permit 756vb.
consent 758vb.
conceit
thought 449n.
idea 451n.
folly 499n.
supposition 512n.
ideality 513n.
witticism 839n.
affectation 850n.
pride 871n.
vanity 873n.
conceivable
possible 469adj.
conceive
produce 164vb.
be fruitful 171vb.
vitalize 360vb.
cognize 447vb.
opine 485vb.
know 490vb.
suppose 512vb.
imagine 513vb.
concent
agreement 24adj.
melody 410n.
concentrate
augment 36vb.
congregate 74vb.
focus 76vb.
centralize 225vb.
converge 293vb.
think 449vb.
be attentive 455vb.
concentration
centrality 225n.
convergence 293n.
condensation 324n.
resolution 599n.
perseverance 600n.
assiduity 678n.
(*see* concentrate)
concentration camp
prison camp 748n.
concentric
parallel 219adj.
central 225adj.
concept
idea 451n.
opinion 485n.
ideality 513n.
conception
product 164n.
propagation 164n.
intellect 447n.
thought 449n.
idea 451n.
opinion 485n.
ideality 513n.
conceptual
mental 447adj.
conceptualism
philosophy 449n.
conceptualize
cognize 447vb.
concern
relation 9n.
be related 9vb.
affairs 154n.
topic 452n.
function, business 622n.
importance 638n.
corporation 708n.
merchant 794n.
shop 796n.
worry 825n.
concern, of no
irrelative 10adj.
concert
agreement 24n.
adjust 24vb.
concurrence 181n.
melody 410n.
harmonize 410vb.
music 412n.
musical instrument 414n.
plot 623vb.
prepare 669vb.
concertina
organ 414n.
concerto
duet 412n.
concert-party
actor 594n.
party 708n.
concert pitch
musical note 410n.
concert-room
place of amusement 837n.
concession
offset 31n.
laxity 734n.
lenity 736n.
consent 758n.
compromise 770n.
discount 810n.
concessionaire
recipient 782n.
concessional
given 781adj.
cheap 812adj.
conch
horn 414n.
conchoid
curve 248n.
conchy
pacifist 717n.
concierge
janitor 264n.
servant 742n.
keeper 749n.
conciliar
parliamentary 692adj.
ecclesiastical 985adj.
conciliate
induce 612vb.
pacify 719vb.
content 828vb.
be courteous 884vb.
atone 941vb.
conciliation
concord 710n.
(*see* conciliate)
conciliatory
pacificatory 719adj.
concinnity
elegance 575n.
beauty 841n.
concise
short 204adj.
compendious 592adj.
conciseness
imperspicuity 568n.
conciseness 569n.
conclave
assembly 74n.
conference 584n.
council 692n.
synod 985n.
conclude
terminate 69vb.
judge 480vb.
be resolute 599vb.
contract 765vb.
conclusion
sequel 67n.
finality 69n.
argumentation 475n.
judgment 480n.
opinion 485n.
affirmation 532n.
completion 725n.
conclusions, try
argue 475vb.
conclusive
positive 473adj.
demonstrating 478adj.
judicial 480adj.
completive 725adj.
commanding 737adj.
concoct
imagine 513vb.
fake 541vb.
write 586vb.
plan 623vb.
concoction
production 164n.
potion 301n.
untruth 543n.
maturation 669n.
concomitance
accompaniment 89adv.
synchronism 123n.
contiguity 202n.
concomitant
adjunct 40n.
concomitant 89n.

synchronous 123adj.
concurrent 181adj.
concord
agreement 24n.
mixture 43n.
order 60n.
concurrence 181n.
melody 410n.
consensus 488n.
cooperation 706n.
concord 710vb.
friendliness 880n.
concordance
agreement 24n.
dictionary 559n.
concordat
treaty 765n.
concourse
junction 45n.
assembly 74n.
convergence 293n.
contest 716n.
concrescence
junction 45n.
concrete
real 1adj.
substantial 3adj.
coherence 48n.
cohesive 48adj.
definite 80adj.
formed 243adj.
material 319adj.
solid body 324n.
dense 324adj.
hard 326adj.
building material 631n.
concreteness
substantiality 3n.
materiality 319n.
density 324n.
concretion
substance 3n.
junction 45n.
condensation 324n.
solid body 324n.
concubinage
type of marriage 894n.
illicit love 951n.
concubinary
matrimonial 894adj.
extramarital 951adj.
concubine
loved one 887n.
kept woman 952n.
concubitous
marriageable 894adj.
concupiscence
libido 859n.
unchastity 951n.
concupiscent
desiring 859adj.
loving 887adj.
lecherous 951adj.
concur
accord 24vb.
accompany 89vb.
concur 181vb.
be parallel 219vb.
assent 488vb.
concurrence
junction 45n.
combination 50n.
assembly 74n.
accompaniment 89n.
synchronism 123n.
eventuality 154n.
concurrence 181n.
convergence 293n.
assent 488n.
cooperation 706n.
concurrent
concurrent 181adj.
(*see* concurrence)
concurrently
synchronously 123adv.
concurrently 181adv.
concuss
strike 279vb.
render insensible 375vb.
concussion
impulse 279n.
condemn
curse 899vb.
condemn 961vb.
punish 963vb.
hereticate 977vb.
condemnable
wrong 914adj.
blameworthy 924adj.
accusable 928adj.
condemned
dilapidated 655adj.
hated 888adj.
condemned 961adj.
heterodox 977adj.
condemned cell
lock-up 748n.
condemn oneself
be penitent 939vb.
condensation
coherence 48n.
crowd 74n.
contraction 198n.
condensation 324n.
solid body 324n.
condense
make smaller 198vb.
be dense 324vb.
be concise 569vb.
abstract 592vb.
condescend
consent 758vb.
demean oneself 867vb.
be proud 871vb.
be humble 872vb.
be courteous 884vb.
show respect 920vb.
condescend to
notice 455vb.
condescension
pride 871n.
humility 872n.
courtesy 884n.
condign
due 915adj.
condiment
adjunct 40n.
food 301n.
condiment 389n.
pleasurableness 826n.
condition
state 7n.
composition 56n.
limit 236vb.
qualification 468n.
supposition 512n.
teach 534vb.
health 650n.
fetter 747vb.
give terms 766vb.
conditional
qualifying 468adj.
uncertain 474adj.
conditional 766adj.
conditionally
conditionally 7adv.
relatively 9adv.
provided 468adv.
conditioned
involuntary 596adj.
conditioned reflex
incogitance 450n.
necessity 596n.
habituation 610n.
condition, in
athletic 162adj.
fleshy 195adj.
healthy 650adj.
conditioning
teaching 534n.
habituation 610n.
conditions
conditions 766n.
condole
feel 818vb.
lament 836vb.
pity 905vb.
condolence
(*see* condole)
condominium
governance 733n.
joint possession 775n.
condone
be patient 823vb.
forgive 909vb.
condottiere
leader 690n.
militarist 722n.
conduce
conduce 156vb.
tend 179vb.

concur 181vb.
promote 285vb.
make likely 471vb.
be useful 640vb.
be expedient 642vb.
aid 703vb.
permit 756vb.
conduct
come before 64vb.
accompany 89vb.
transfer 272vb.
carry 273vb.
precede 283vb.
play music 413vb.
mien 445n.
practice 610n.
action 676n.
conduct 688n.
manage 689vb.
conduction
motion 265n.
transference 272n.
conductive
transferable 272adj.
conductivity
motion 265n.
conduct oneself
behave 688vb.
conductor
timekeeper 117n.
driver 268n.
carrier 273n.
musician 413n.
orchestra 413n.
leader 690n.
conduit
outlet 298n.
passage 305n.
irrigator 341n.
conduit 351n.
condyle, condylema
swelling 253n.
cone
cone 252n.
coney
vermin 365n.
coney-catcher
hunter 619n.
confabulate
speak 579vb.
converse 584vb.
confection
a mixture 43n.
product 164n.
sweet 392n.
confectioner
caterer 633n.
confectionery
pastry 301n.
sweet 392n.
confederate
cooperate 706vb.
colleague 707n.
corporate 708adj.
confederation
combination 50n.
association 706n.
society 708n.
polity 733n.
confer
argue 475vb.
confer 584vb.
consult 691vb.
give 781vb.
conference
inquiry 459n.
speech 579n.
conference 584n.
advice 691n.
confess
testify 466vb.
believe 485vb.
assent 488vb.
confess 526vb.
affirm 532vb.
be guilty 936vb.
be penitent 939vb.
perform ritual 988vb.
confession
creed 485n.
party 708n.
penance 941n.
(*see* confess)
confessional
credal 485adj.
disclosure 526n.
tribunal 956n.
church interior 990n.
confessions
biography 590n.
confessor
questioner 459n.
pietist 979n.
pastor 986n.
confidant
teacher 537n.
adviser 691n.
colleague 707n.
retainer 742n.
close friend 880n.
confide
believe 485vb.
inform 524vb.
divulge 526vb.
be artless 699vb.
hope 852vb.
confide in
consult 691vb.
confidence
positiveness 473n.
belief 485n.
expectation 507n.
information 524n.
secret 530n.
safety 660n.
credit 802n.
hope 852n.
confidence trick
trickery 542n.
confident
positive 473adj.
believing 485adj.
expectant 507adj.
assertive 532adj.
hoping 852adj.
unfearing 855adj.
confidential
concealed 525adj.
confiding
believing 485adj.
credulous 487adj.
artless 699adj.
configuration
form 243n.
configurationism
psychology 447n.
confine
region 184n.
place 185n.
circumscribe 232vb.
hem 234vb.
limit 236vb.
conceal 525vb.
make insufficient 636vb.
imprison 747vb.
seclude 883vb.
confined
narrow-minded 481adj.
sick 651adj.
(*see* confine)
confinement
obstetrics 164n.
detention 747n.
seclusion 883n.
confines
near place 200n.
edge 234n.
confirm
stabilize 153vb.
strengthen 162vb.
corroborate 466vb.
make certain 473vb.
judge 480vb.
endorse 488vb.
affirm 532vb.
consent 758vb.
promise 764vb.
contract 765vb.
grant claims 915vb.
vindicate 927vb.
make legal 953vb.
make pious 979vb.
perform ritual 988vb.
confirmation
Christian rite 988n.
(*see* confirm)
confirmatory
evidential 466adj.
confiscate
deprive 786vb.
punish 963vb.

confiscatory
taking 786adj.
punitive 963adj.
conflagration
fire 379n.
conflation
combination 50n.
conflict
contrariety 14n.
differ 15vb.
disagreement 25n.
counteraction 182n.
opposition 704n.
quarrel 709n., vb.
contention 716n.
enmity 881n.
confluence
junction 45n.
convergence 293n.
current 350n.
conflux
assembly 74n.
convergence 293n.
conform
be uniform 16vb.
do likewise 20vb.
adjust 24vb.
conform 83vb.
acquiesce 488vb.
obey 739vb.
observe 768vb.
be servile 879vb.
be orthodox 976vb.
conformable
agreeing 24adj.
regular 81adj.
conformable 83adj.
conformance
(*see* conformity)
conformation
composition 56n.
form 243n.
conforming
orthodox 976adj.
pious 979adj.
conformist
conformist 83n.
assenter 488n.
the orthodox 976n.
pietist 979n.
conformity
uniformity 16n.
regularity 81n.
conformity 83n.
concurrence 181n.
observance 768n.
orthodoxism 976n.
piety 979n.
confound
derange 63vb.
destroy 165vb.
not discriminate 464vb.
confute 479vb.
defeat 727vb.
frighten 854vb.
be wonderful 864vb.
curse 899vb.
confounded
damnable 645adj.
confoundedly
extremely 32adv.
confraternity
community 708n.
confrere
colleague 707n.
friend 880n.
confront
be present 189vb.
be in front 237vb.
be opposite 240vb.
compare 462vb.
show 522vb.
withstand 704vb.
resist 715vb.
confrontation
comparison 462n.
confronting
opposite 240adj.
Confucianism
religious faith 973n.
Confucius
religious teacher 973n.
confuse
bedevil 63vb.
blur 440vb.
distract 456vb.
not discriminate 464vb.
puzzle 474vb.
be unintelligible 517vb.
confused
mixed 43adj.
orderless 61adj.
shadowy 419adj.
ill-seen 444adj.
indiscriminate 464adj.
ill-reasoned 477adj.
ignorant 491adj.
imperspicuous 568adj.
confusion
medley 43n.
confusion 61n.
havoc 165n.
amorphism 244n.
commotion 318n.
psychopathy 503n.
humiliation 872n.
confutation
rejoinder 460n.
counter-evidence 467n.
argumentation 475n.
confutation 479n.
negation 533n.
conga
dance 837n.
congé
valediction 296n.
deposal 752n.
non-liability 919n.
congeal
be dense 324vb.
refrigerate 382vb.
congener
kinsman 11n.
analogue 18n.
congenerous
akin 11adj.
congenial
genetic 5adj.
relative 9adj.
agreeing 24adj.
pleasant 376adj.
concordant 710adj.
lovable 887adj.
congenital
genetic 5adj.
with affections 817adj.
congeries
accumulation 74n.
congest
superabound 637vb.
congestion
crowd 74n.
redundance 637n.
conglaciation
refrigeration 382n.
conglomerate
cohere 48vb.
bring together 74vb.
solid body 324n.
rock 344n.
conglutination
coherence 48n.
congratulate
gratulate 886vb.
congratulate oneself
be content 828vb.
rejoice 835vb.
feel pride 871vb.
congratulation
rejoicing 835n.
celebration 876n.
courteous act 884n.
congratulation 886n.
congregate
congregate 74vb.
meet 295vb.
congregation
assembly 74n.
council 692n.
church member 976n.
worshiper 981n.
laity 987n.
congregational
laical 987adj.
Congregational
Protestant 976adj.
Congregationalism

Protestantism 976n.
congress
junction 45n.
convergence 293n.
council 692n.
parliament 692n.
congressional
parliamentary 692adj.
congressman
councillor 692n.
congruence, congruity
identity 13n.
similarity 18n.
conformance 24n.
congruent
agreeing 24adj.
equal 28adj.
symmetrical 245adj.
congruity
(*see* congruence)
conical
rotund 252adj.
tapering 256adj.
convergent 293adj.
conic section
curve 248n.
conjectional
suppositional 512adj.
conjecture
attribution 158n.
assume 471vb.
uncertainty 474n.
estimate 480vb.
conjecture 512n.
suppose 512vb.
conjoin
add 38vb.
mix 43vb.
join 45vb.
conjugal
loving 887adj.
matrimonial 894adj.
conjugate
combined 50adj.
dual 90adj.
verbal 559adj.
parse 564vb.
conjugation
arrangement 62n.
(*see* conjugate)
conjunct
conjunct 45adj.
combined 50adj.
indivisible 52adj.
accompanying 89adj.
conjunction
junction 45n.
concurrence 181n.
contiguity 202n.
part of speech 564n.
conjunctive
grammatical 564adj.
conjuration
entreaty 761n.
sorcery 983n.
conjure
deceive 542vb.
entreat 761vb.
practice sorcery 983vb.
conjure into
convert 147vb.
conjure up
imagine 513vb.
conjuror
imitator 20n.
conjuror 545n.
entertainer 594n.
slyboots 698n.
sorcerer 983n.
conk
face 237n.
projection 254n.
conk out
fail 728vb.
con-man
trickster 545n.
connatural
genetic 5adj.
akin 11adj.
connect
relate 9vb.
connect 45vb.
continuate 71vb.
be contiguous 202vb.
connectedness
coherence 48n.
connection
relation 9n.
consanguinity 11n.
bond 47n.
(*see* connect)
conning tower
view 438n.
connivance
concurrence 181n.
cooperation 706n.
laxity 734n.
lenity 736n.
permission 756n.
connive
disregard 458vb.
patronize 703vb.
connoisseur
eater 301n.
collector 492n.
expert 696n.
man of taste 846n.
connoisseurship
good taste 846n.
fastidiousness 862n.
connotation
connotation 514n.
meaning 514n.
indication 547n.
connotative
semantic 514adj.
indicating 547adj.
connote
mean 514vb.
imply 523vb.
connubial
matrimonial 894adj.
conoid
cone 252n.
conoidal, conoid
rotund 252adj.
conquer
overmaster 727vb.
take 786vb.
conquered, the
loser 728n.
conqueror
victor 727n.
possessor 776n.
conquest
victory 727n.
defeat 728n.
subjection 745n.
loved one 887n.
consanguinity
relation 9n.
consanguinity 11n.
parentage 169n.
conscience
knowledge 490n.
motive 612n.
warning 664n.
conscience 917n.
conscience-clause
non-liability 919n.
conscienceless
dishonest 930adj.
wicked 934adj.
impenitent 940adj.
conscience-money
gift 781n.
restitution 787n.
atonement 941n.
conscientious
careful 457adj.
observant 768adj.
fastidious 862adj.
dutied 917adj.
trustworthy 929adj.
conscientious objector
dissentient 489n.
opponent 705n.
pacifist 717n.
conscious
sentient 374adj.
mental 447adj.
attentive 455adj.
knowing 490adj.
conscript
go to war 718vb.
soldier 722n.
compel 740vb.
conscription
war measures 718n.
compulsion 740n.
consecrate
offer 759vb.

give 781vb.
dignify 866vb.
sanctify 979vb.
offer worship 981vb.
ecclesiasticize 985vb.
perform ritual 988vb.
consecrated
disinterested 931adj.
consecrate to
use 673vb.
consecration
offering 781n.
Holy Communion 988n.
Christian rite 988n.
consecution
sequence 65n.
continuity 71n.
consecutive
sequent 65adj.
continuous 71adj.
consensus
agreement 24n.
concurrence 181n.
consensus 488n.
consent
agreement 24n.
accord 24vb.
assent 488n., vb.
endorse 488vb.
willingness 597n.
be induced 612vb.
obey 739vb.
permission 756n.
consent 758n., vb.
approbation 923n.
consentaneous
agreeing 24adj.
assenting 488adj.
consentient
agreeing 24adj.
assenting 488adj.
consequence
sequel 67n.
eventuality 154n.
effect 157n.
importance 638n.
consequential
eventual 154adj.
caused 157adj.
demonstrating 478adj.
ostentatious 875adj.
consequently
consequently 157adv.
reasonably 475adv.
conservancy
cleansing 648n.
conservation
permanence 144n.
forestry 366n.
storage 632n.
preservation 666n.
conservatism
permanence 144n.
habit 610n.
preservation 666n.
conservative
permanent 144adj.
depreciating 483adj.
preserving 666adj.
political party 708n.
sectional 708adj.
cautious 858adj.
conservatoire
music 412n.
academy 539n.
conservator
protector 660n.
conservatory
seedbed 156n.
arbor 194n.
garden 370n.
heater 383n.
(*see* conservatoire)
conserve
sweet 392n.
sanitate 652vb.
safeguard 660vb.
preserve 666vb.
consider
meditate 449vb.
notice 455vb.
inquire 459vb.
estimate 480vb.
opine 485vb.
give 781vb.
considerable
substantial 3adj.
great 32adj.
many 104adj.
large 195adj.
important 638adj.
considerate
thoughtful 449adj.
careful 457adj.
well-bred 848adj.
amiable 884adj.
benevolent 897adj.
disinterested 931adj.
consideration
quid pro quo 150n.
meditation 449n.
qualification 468n.
importance 638n.
gift 781n.
courtesy 884n.
benevolence 897n.
respect 920n.
disinterestedness 931n.
consideration, be a
motivate 612vb.
consideration, of
important 688adj.
consideration, under
preparatory 669adj.
consign
send 272vb.
commission 751vb.
consignee
agent 686n.
consignee 754n.
deputy 755n.
recipient 782n.
purchaser 972n.
consignment
thing transferred 272n.
transfer 780n.
giving 781n.
consignor
seller 793n.
transferrer 272n.
consistence
density 324n.
consistency
uniformity 16n.
regularity 81n.
truth 494n.
consistent
rational 475adj.
(*see* consistency)
consist in
be 1vb.
consist of
comprise 78vb.
consistory
council 692n.
synod 985n.
consolation
relief 831n.
condolence 905n.
consolatory
relieving 831adj.
console
stand 218n.
shelf 218n.
relieve 831vb.
cheer 833vb.
pity 905vb.
consolidate
join 45vb.
cohere 48vb.
bring together 74vb.
centralize 225vb.
be dense 324vb.
abstract 592vb.
consolidation
contraction 198n.
association 706n.
(*see* consolidate)
consommé
soup 301n.
consonance
agreement 24n.
melody 410n.
consonant
speech sound 398n.
consonantal
sounding 398adj.
literal 558adj.
consort
concomitant 89n.

spouse 894n.
consortium
agreement 24n.
association 706n.
consortship
accompaniment 89n.
conspection
inspection 438n.
conspectus
whole 52n.
generality 79n.
view 438n.
compendium 592n.
conspicuous
well-seen 443adj.
manifest 522adj.
notable 638adj.
noteworthy 866adj.
conspiracy
combination 50n.
concurrence 181n.
secrecy 525n.
plot 623n.
cooperation 706n.
compact 765n.
conspirator
deceiver 545n.
planner 623n.
conspiratorial
stealthy 525adj.
planning 623adj.
conspire
combine 50vb.
(*see* conspiracy)
constable
police 955n.
constabulary
police 955n.
constancy
uniformity 16n.
stability 153n.
resolution 599n.
perseverance 600n.
obstinacy 602n.
loyalty 739n.
probity 929n.
constant
characteristic 5adj.
identity 13n.
identical 13adj.
uniform 16adj.
continuous 71adj.
regular 81adj.
lasting 113adj.
perpetual 115adj.
frequent 139adj.
periodic 141adj.
unchangeable 153adj.
colored 425adj.
accurate 494adj.
resolute 599adj.
persevering 600adj.
obedient 739n.
trustworthy 929adj.
constellation
group 74n.
star 321n.
person of repute 866n.
consternation
fear 854n.
wonder 864n.
constipate
be dense 324vb.
constipation
closure 264n.
condensation 324n.
indigestion 651n.
constituency
district 184n.
electorate 605n.
constituent
part 53n.
component 58n.
included 78adj.
electorate 605n.
constituents
contents 193n.
constitute
constitute 56vb.
be included 78vb.
produce 164vb.
constitution
character 5n.
composition 56n.
inclusion 78n.
structure 331n.
precept 693n.
polity 733n.
law 953n.
constitutional
pedestrianism 267n.
habit 610n.
governmental 733adj.
due 915adj.
legal 953adj.
constitutionalism
government 733n.
legality 953n.
constraint
compulsion 740n.
subjection 745n.
restraint 747n.
modesty 874n.
constrict
tighten 45vb.
make smaller 198vb.
constriction
narrowing 206n.
constrictor
compressor 198n.
construction
composition 56n.
arrangement 62n.
production 164n.
structure 331n.
conjecture 512n.
interpretation 520n.
constructional
structural 331adj.
constructive
productive 164adj.
evidential 466adj.
interpretive 520adj.
aiding 703adj.
constructor
producer 167n.
doer 676n.
construe
translation 520n.
interpret 520vb.
parse 564vb.
consubstantial
similar 18adj.
consubstantiation
the sacrament 988n.
consuetude
habit 610n.
consul
official 690n.
envoy 754n.
consulate
magistrature 733n.
envoy 754n.
consult
confer 584vb.
consult 691vb.
cooperate 706vb.
consultant
sage 500n.
oracle 511n.
teacher 537n.
doctor 658n.
adviser 691n.
expert 696n.
consultation
preparation 669n.
advice 691n.
consultative
advising 691adj.
consulting room
hospital 658n.
consumable
used 673adj.
consume
bate 37vb.
decompose 51vb.
disable 161vb.
destroy 165vb.
consume 165vb.
eat 301vb.
require 627vb.
waste 634vb.
impair 655vb.
use, dispose of 673vb.
misuse 675vb.
expend 806vb.
consumer
eater 301n.
purchaser 792n.
consumer goods
merchandise 795n.
consummate

consummate 32adj.
unite with 45vb.
complete 54adj.
crown 213vb.
perfect 646adj., vb.
carry through 725vb.
consummation
coition 45n.
completeness 54n.
(*see* consummate)
consumption
decrement 42n.
thinness 206n.
phthisis 651n.
loss 772n.
(*see* consume)
consumptive
sick person 651n.
diseased 651adj.
contact
junction 45n.
connect 45vb.
be contiguous 202vb.
informant 524n.
communicate 524vb.
messenger 531n.
contact lens
eyeglass 442n.
contact man
messenger 531n.
contact print
copy, duplicate 22n.
contagion
influence 178n.
transference 272n.
infection 651n.
plague 651n.
insalubrity 653n.
impairment 655n.
contagious
(*see* contagion)
contain
contain 56vb.
comprise 78vb.
circumscribe 232vb.
possess 773vb.
container
receptacle 194n.
storage 632n.
containment
circumjacence 230n.
circumscription 232n.
retention 778n.
contain oneself
be temperate 942vb.
contaminate
be mixed 43vb.
influence 178vb.
transfer 272vb.
make unclean 649vb.
impair 655vb.
contamination
badness 645n.
(*see* contaminate)
contango
delay 136n.
discount 810n.
contemn
shame 867vb.
hate 888vb.
despise 922vb.
detract 926vb.
contemplate
meditate 449vb.
expect 507vb.
intend 617vb.
worship 981vb.
contemplation
look 438n.
attention 455n.
(*see* contemplate)
contemplative
pietist 979n.
worshiper 981n.
contemporaneity
accompaniment 89n.
time 108n.
present time 121n.
synchronism 123n.
modernism 126n.
contemporary
present 121adj.
contemporary 123n.
synchronous 123adj.
contempt
object of scorn 867n.
pride 871n.
contempt 922n.
detraction 926n.
contemptibility
odium 888n.
despisedness 922n.
contemptible
inferior 35adj.
unimportant 639adj.
trivial 639adj.
ridiculous 849adj.
discreditable 867adj.
disreputable 867adj.
contemptible 922adj.
rascally 930adj.
contempt of, in
in defiance of 25adv.
contemptuous
insolent 878adj.
despising 922adj.
detracting 926adj.
contend
affirm 532vb.
oppose 704vb.
contend 716vb.
contender
athlete 162n.
essayer 671n.
opponent 705n.
contender 716n.
combatant 722n.
contend for
vindicate 927vb.
content
component 58n.
structure 331n.
euphoria 376n.
comfortable 376adj.
willing 597adj.
suffice 635vb.
pacify 719vb.
inexcitability 823n.
content 828n., adj., vb.
cheer 833vb.
approving 923adj.
contented
content 828adj.
contenting
contenting 828adj.
contention
question 459n.
opposition 704n.
quarrel 709n.
contention 716n.
contentious
quarreling 709adj.
contending 716adj.
contentment
euphoria 376n.
sufficiency 635n.
content 828n.
contents
contents 193n.
topic 452n.
meaning 514n.
compendium 592n.
property 777n.
conterminous
ending 69adj.
synchronous 123adj.
contiguous 202adj.
contesseration
assemblage 74n.
contest
athletics 162n.
contend 716vb.
sport 837n.
contestant
opponent 705n.
contester
contender 716n.
context
circumstance 8n.
relation 9n.
concomitant 89n.
meaning 514n.
connotation 514n.
contextual
circumstantial 8adj.
relative 9adj.
contexture
texture 331n.
contiguity
junction 45n.
nearness 200n.
contiguity 202n.

contiguous
(*see* contiguity)
continence
temperance 942n.
purity 950n.
continent
region 184n.
land 344n.
temperate 942adj.
pure 950adj.
continental
foreigner 59n.
extraneous 59adj.
regional 184adj.
dweller 191n.
inland 344adj.
continental shelf
territory 184n.
shore 344n.
contingency
extrinsicality 6n.
eventuality 154n.
chance 159n.
liability 180n.
possibility 469n.
uncertainty 474n.
expectation 507n.
contingent
extrinsic 6adj.
circumstantial 8adj.
part 53n.
eventual 154adj.
caused 157adj.
casual 159adj.
liable 180adj.
qualifying 468adj.
possible 469adj.
uncertain 474adj.
conditional 766adj.
portion 783n.
contingents
aider 703n.
armed force 722n.
continual
continuous 71adj.
perpetual 115adj.
frequent 139adj.
unceasing 146adj.
continuance
uniformity 16n.
sequence 65n.
course of time 111n.
durability 113n.
perpetuity 115n.
permanence 144n.
continuance 146n.
perseverance 600n.
habit 610n.
continuate
continuate 71vb.
sustain 146vb.
continuation
adjunct 40n.
arrangement 62n.
sequence 65n.
sequel 67n.
continuance 146n.
reading matter 589n.
continue
be 1vb.
run on 71vb.
lengthen 203vb.
(*see* continuance)
continuity
coherence 48n.
order 60n.
continuity 71n.
recurrence 106n.
frequency 139n.
periodicity 141n.
continuance 146n.
contiguity 202n.
continuous
(*see* continuity)
continuum
space 183n.
contort
distort 246vb.
contorted
convoluted 251adj.
contortionist
entertainer 594n.
contour
outline 233n.
form 243n.
feature 445n.
contra
contrarily 14adv.
contraband
prohibited 757adj.
booty 790n.
illegal 954adj.
contraception
unproductivity 172n.
hindrance 702n.
contraceptive
hindrance 702n.
contract
bate, decrease 37vb.
become small 198vb.
shorten 204vb.
make thin 206vb.
be dense 324vb.
be concise 569vb.
undertaking 672n.
compact 765n.
make terms 766vb.
acquire 771vb.
bargain 791vb.
contract bridge
card game 837n.
contractile
contracted 198adj.
contraction
diminution 37n.
contraction 198n.
closure 264n.
writing 568n.
conciseness 569n.
compendium 592n.
contractor
essayer 671n.
signatory 765n.
contractual
agreeing 24adj.
contractual 765adj.
contradict
be contrary 14vb.
disagree 25vb.
answer 460vb.
tell against 467vb.
confute 479vb.
dissent 489vb.
negate 533vb.
oppose 704vb.
contradiction
(*see* contradict)
contradictory
illogical 477adj.
negative 533adj.
contradistinction
contrariety 14n.
differentiation 15n.
contra-indicate
be contrary 14vb.
tell against 467vb.
warn 664n.
contra-indication
counter-evidence 467n.
contralto
resonance 404n.
vocalist 413n.
contraposition
contrariety 14n.
difference 15n.
reversion 148n.
inversion 221n.
contraposition 240n.
contraption
contrivance 623n.
contrapuntal
musical 412adj.
musicianly 413adj.
contrapuntist
musician 413n.
contraries
polarity 14n.
opposites 704n.
contrariety
irrelation 10n.
contrariety 14n.
non-uniformity 17n.
disagreement 25n.
counteraction 182n.
inversion 221n.
contraposition 240n.
counter-evidence 467n.
connotation 514n.
opposition 704n.
contrarious
unconformable 84adj.
opposing 704adj.

contrariwise
against 240adv.
contrary
contrary 14adj.
different 15adj.
disagreeing 25adj.
separate 46adj.
counteracting 182adj.
opposite 240adj.
countervailing 467adj.
negative 533adj.
capricious 604adj.
hindering 702adj.
opposing 704adj.
adverse 731adj.
contrary, on the
no 489adv.
contrast
contrariety 14n.
difference 15n.
differ 15vb.
non-uniformity 17n.
dissimilarity 19n.
compare 462vb.
trope 519n.
opposition 704n.
contravallation
defenses 713n.
contravene
be contrary 14vb.
tell against 467vb.
negate 533vb.
be obstructive 702vb.
contravention
lawbreaking 954n.
(*see* contravene)
contrecoup
recoil 280n.
contrectation
touch 378n.
contretemps
intempestivity 138n.
hitch 702n.
ill fortune 731n.
contribute
concur 181vb.
give 781vb.
pay 804vb.
contribute to
augment 36vb.
add 38vb.
conduce 156vb.
tend 179vb.
aid, patronize 703vb.
contributing
influential 178adj.
concurrent 181adj.
contribution
increment 36n.
cooperation 706n.
giving, offering 781n.
payment 804n.
contributor
cause 156n.
correspondent 588n.
author 589n.
dissertator 591n.
giver 781n.
contributory
additional 38n.
contrition
regret 830n.
penitence 939n.
contrivance
arrangement 62n.
idea 451n.
contrivance 623n.
plan 623n.
instrument 628n.
means 629n.
tool 630n.
tactics 688n.
skill 694n.
stratagem 698n.
contrive
produce 164vb.
predetermine 608vb.
find means 629vb.
contrived
predetermined 608adj.
contriver
planner 623n.
control
order 60vb.
be able 160n.
moderate 177vb.
influence 178n.
comparison 462n.
do 676vb.
management 689n.
skill 694n.
hindrance 702n.
governance 733n.
rule 733vb.
take authority 733vb.
restrain 747vb.
tranquilize 823vb.
ghost 970n.
spiritualism 984n.
controlled
involuntary 596adj.
predetermined 608adj.
restrained 747adj.
impassive 820adj.
inexcitable 823adj.
controller
doer 676n.
director 690n.
control oneself
be temperate 942vb.
controls
aircraft 276n.
directorship 689n.
controversial
uncertain 474adj.
arguing 475adj.
quarreling 709adj.
controversialist
reasoner 475n.
combatant 722n.
controversy
disagreement 25n.
question 459n.
argument 475n.
dissent 489n.
conference 584n.
quarrel 709n.
contention 716n.
controvert
argue 475vb.
negate 533vb.
controvertible
uncertain 474adj.
arguing 475adj.
contumacious
disobedient 738adj.
schismatical 978adj.
(*see* contumacy)
contumacy
obstinacy 602n.
resistance 715n.
impenitence 940n.
contumelious
insolent 878adj.
ungracious 885adj.
maledicent 899adj.
disrespectful 921adj.
despising 922adj.
detracting 926adj.
contumely
insolence 878n.
scurrility 899n.
disrespect 921n.
detraction 926n.
contuse
pulverize 332vb.
contusion
pulverulence 332n.
wound 655n.
conundrum
equivocalness 518n.
enigma 530n.
conurbate
urbanize 192vb.
conurbation
district 184n.
housing 192n.
convalesce
grow 36vb.
be strong 162vb.
get healthy 650vb.
be restored 656vb.
convalescent home
hospital 658n.
convection
transference 272n.
convene
bring together 74vb.
command 737vb.
convenience
opportunity 137n.
euphoria 376n.

means 629n.
utility 640n.
expedience 642n.
leisure 681n.
facility 701n.
convenient
(*see* convenience)
convent
house 192n.
monastery 986n.
conventicle
assembly 74n.
meeting place 192n.
council 692n.
sect 978n.
church 990n.
convention
regularity 81n.
conformity 83n.
conference 584n.
practice 610n.
council 692n.
precept 693n.
pacification 719n.
compact 765n.
treaty 765n.
etiquette 848n.
conventional
orthodox 976adj.
(*see* convention)
conventionalist
conformist 83n.
habitué 610n.
conventionality
conformity 83n.
(*see* convention)
conventionalize
make conform 83vb.
conventual
monk 986n.
monastic 986adj.
converge
congregate 74vb.
focus 76vb.
be near 200vb.
be narrow 206vb.
be oblique 220vb.
centralize 225vb.
converge 293vb.
convergence
junction 45n.
(*see* converge)
conversable
loquacious 581adj.
conversing 584adj.
well-bred 848adj.
sociable 882adj.
amiable 884adj.
conversant
knowing 490adj.
conversation
speech 579n.
interlocution 584n.
conversational
loquacious 581adj.
conversing 584adj.
conversationalist
speaker 579n.
chatterer 581n.
interlocutor 584n.
humorist 839n.
conversation level
faintness 401n.
conversations
conference 584n.
advice 691n.
conversazione
assembly 74n.
conference 584n.
amusement 837n.
social gathering 882n.
converse
contrariety 14n.
countervailing 467adj.
communicate 524vb.
speak 579vb.
be loquacious 581vb.
interlocution 584n.
converse 584vb.
conversely
conversely 467adv.
conversion
change 143n.
conversion 147n.
production 164n.
teaching 534n.
improvement 654n.
use 673n.
acquisition 771n.
transfer 780n.
convert
make unlike 19vb.
modify 143vb.
changed person 147n.
convert 147vb.
interchange 151vb.
convince 485vb.
learner 538n.
tergiversator 603n.
induce 612vb.
use 673vb.
acquire 771vb.
be penitent 939vb.
make pious 979vb.
convertibility
conversion 147n.
use 673n.
convertible
equivalent 28adj.
interchanged 151adj.
automobile 274n.
convexity
curvature 248n.
convexity 253n.
convey
move 265vb.
transfer 272vb.
carry 273vb.
pass 305vb.
mean 514vb.
communicate 524vb.
inform 524vb.
dower 777vb.
not retain 779vb.
convey 780vb.
take away 786vb.
steal 788vb.
conveyance
conveyance 267n.
transport 272n.
transference 272n.
vehicle 274n.
transfer 780n.
taking 786n.
conveyancer
transferrer 272n.
law agent 958n.
conveyor belt
carrier 273n.
conveyor 274n.
convict
confute 479vb.
prisoner 750n.
offender 904n.
condemn 961vb.
conviction
positiveness 473n.
confutation 479n.
belief 485n.
teaching 534n.
hope 852n.
condemnation 961n.
convict settlement
prison camp 748n.
convince
influence 178vb.
make certain 473vb.
demonstrate 478vb.
convince 485vb.
convinced
positive 473adj.
believing 485adj.
convincing
plausible 471adj.
demonstrating 478adj.
credible 485adj.
descriptive 590adj.
conviviality
festivity 837n.
sociability 882n.
convocation
council 692n.
synod 985n.
convocational
parliamentary 692adj.
convoke
bring together 74vb.
convolution
crossing 222n.
curvature 248n.
convolution 251n.
convolvulus

coil 251n.
convoy
concomitant 89n.
accompany 89vb.
carry 273vb.
protection 660n.
keeper 749n.
convoy, in
with 89adv.
convulsion
disorder, turmoil 61n.
derangement 63n.
revolution 149n.
outbreak 176n.
spasm 318n.
pang 377n.
convulsive
violent 176adj.
agitated 318adj.
coo
ululate 409vb.
rejoice 835vb.
caress 889vb.
flatter 925vb.
cook
cook 301vb.
heat 381vb.
fake 541vb.
caterer 633n.
preparer 669n.
mature 669vb.
domestic 742n.
cook-book
cookery 301n.
cooker
furnace 383n.
cookery
cookery 301n.
maturation 669n.
cook-house
chamber 194n.
heater 383n.
workshop 687n.
cook one's goose
destroy 165vb.
defeat 727vb.
overmaster 727vb.
cookout
meal 301n.
feasting 301n.
festivity 837n.
cool
moderate 177vb.
coldness 380n.
refrigerate 382vb.
sane 502adj.
dissuade 613vb.
refresh 685vb.
impassive 820adj.
inexcitable 823adj.
relieve 831vb.
cautious 858adj.
indifferent 860adj.
impertinent 878adj.
inimical 881adj.
unsociable 883adj.
discourteous 885adj.
coolant
refrigerator 384n.
cooler
moderator 177n.
refrigerator 384n.
jail 748n.
coolie
bearer 273n.
worker 686n.
coolness
coldness 380n.
(*see* cool)
cool one's heels
wait 136vb.
coon
vocalist 413n.
coop
stable 192n.
lock-up 748n.
cooper
artisan 686n.
cooperate
concur 181vb.
cooperation
combination 50n.
causation 156n.
agency 173n.
concurrence 181n.
assent 488n.
willingness 597n.
instrumentality 628n.
aid 703n.
cooperation 706n.
concord 710n.
cooperative
cooperative 706adj.
society 708n.
corporate 708adj.
cooperative society
corporation 708n.
cooperative system
joint possession 775n.
cooperator
assenter 488n.
personnel 686n.
collaborator 707n.
participator 775n.
coopt
choose 605vb.
coordinate
equal 28adj.
regularize 62vb.
gauge 465n.
metrology 465n.
coot
waterfowl 365n.
cop
protector 660n.
arrest 747vb.
police 955n.
copal
resin 357n.
coparcener
participator 775n.
cope
vestments 989n.
cope with
be equal 28vb.
deal with 688vb.
withstand 704vb.
coping
summit 213n.
coping stone
summit 213n.
completion 725n.
copious
prolific 171adj.
diffuse 570adj.
plenteous 635adj.
copper
caldron 194n.
heater 383n.
brownness 430n.
orange 436n.
protector 660n.
coinage 797n.
police 955n.
copper-colored
orange 436adj.
copperhead
reptile 365n.
copperplate
engraving 555n.
written 586adj.
coppers
money 797n.
coppice
wood 366n.
coprolith
excrement 302n.
copse
bunch 74n.
wood 366n.
copula
bond 47n.
copulation
coition 45n.
propagation 164n.
copulative
conjunctive 45adj.
grammatical 564adj.
copy
analogue 18n.
copy 20vb.
copy 22n.
prototype 23n.
conform 83vb.
duplication 91n.
repeat 106vb.
reproduce 166vb.
transpose 272vb.
news 529n.
sham 542n.
represent 551vb.
write 586vb.

letterpress 587n.
reading matter 589n.
borrow 785vb.
steal 788vb.
copybook
prototype 23n.
regular 83adj.
copycat
imitator 20n.
conformist 83n.
copyhold
lands, estate 777n.
proprietary 777adj.
copy-holder
possessor 776n.
copyist
imitator 20n.
artist 556n.
penman 586n.
copyright
estate 777n.
dueness 915n.
claim 915vb.
copy-typist
imitator 20n.
copy-writer
publicizer 528n.
coquet
be capricious 604vb.
excite love 887vb.
court 889vb.
coquetry
tergiversation 603n.
whim 604n.
affectation 850n.
love-making 887n.
wooing 889n.
flattery 925n.
coquette
affector 850n.
lover 887n.
coquillage
ornamental art 844n.
coracle
rowboat 275n.
coral
redness 431n.
gem 844n.
corallin
red pigment 431n.
coral reef
island 349n.
coram judice
litigated 959adj.
in litigation 959adv.
cor anglais
flute 414n.
corbel
shelf 218n.
cord
cable, ligature 47n.
line 203n.
fiber 208n.
cordage
tackling 47n.
cordated
curved 248adj.
cordial
soft drink 301n.
pleasant 376adj.
pungency 388n.
willing 597adj.
tonic 658n.
feeling 818adj.
felt 818adj.
friendly 880adj.
sociable 882adj.
cordiality
(*see* cordial)
cordite
propellant 287n.
explosive 723n.
cordon
outline 233n.
barrier 235n.
enclose 235vb.
loop 250n.
stopper 264n.
cordon bleu
proficient 696n.
decoration 729n.
cordon sanitaire
hygiene 652n.
prophylactic 658n.
protection 660n.
preservation 666n.
corduroy
textile 222n.
roughness 259n.
furrow 262n.
cordwainer
clothier 228n.
artisan 686n.
core
essence 1n.
essential part 5n.
focus 76n.
centrality 225n.
chief thing 638n.
affections 817n.
corelation
correlation 12n.
coreligionist
colleague 707n.
church member 976n.
worshiper 981n.
corer
perforator 263n.
corespondent
divorce 896n.
libertine 952n.
coriaceous
tough 329adj.
Corinthian
ornamental 844adj.
fop 848n.
cork
covering 226n.
stopper 264n.
levity 323n.
deteriorate 655vb.
corkage
price 809n.
corked
unsavory 391adj.
deteriorated 655adj.
corker
exceller 644n.
corkscrew
coil 251n.
meander 251vb.
opener 263n.
perforator 263n.
extractor 304n.
cormorant
eater 301n.
bird of prey 365n.
glutton 947n.
corn
swelling 253n.
provender 301n.
hardness 326n.
corn 366n.
ulcer 651n.
preserve 666vb.
corn-chandler
merchant 794n.
corncob
tobacco 388n.
cornea
eye 438n.
cornel
tree 366n.
cornelian
gem 844n.
corneous
hard 326adj.
corner
circumstance 84n.
place 185n.
angularity 247n.
cavity 255n.
circle 314vb.
hiding-place 527n.
attack 712vb.
defeat 727vb.
possession 773n.
purchase 792vb.
pillory 964n.
corner-boy
rioter 738n.
cornered
angular 247adj.
in difficulties 700adj.
hindered 702adj.
cornering
circuition 314n.
purchase 792n.
corner-stone
supporter 218n.
chief thing 638n.
cornet

bag 194n.
cone 252n.
horn 414n.
army officer 741n.
cornetist
instrumentalist 413n.
cornflour
semiliquidity 354n.
cornflower
blueness 435n.
cornice
summit 213n.
cornification
hardening 326n.
cornucopia
abundance 171n.
store 632n.
plenty 635n.
liberality 813n.
cornute
tapering 256adj.
corny
known 490adj.
corollary
adjunct 40n.
judgment 480n.
corona
loop 250n.
sun 321n.
light 417n.
coronach
musical piece 412n.
vocal music 412n.
lament 836n.
condolence 905n.
coronal
ornamentation 844n.
coronary thrombosis
blood pressure 651n.
coronation
mandate 751n.
dignification 866n.
celebration 876n.
coroner
judge 957n.
coronet
headgear 228n.
loop 250n.
heraldry 547n.
trophy 729n.
regalia 743n.
corporal
army officer 741n.
corporality
materiality 319n.
corporal punishment
corporal punishment 963n.
corporate
conjunct 45adj.
cooperative 706adj.
corporate 708adj.
corporation
bulk 195n.
swelling 253n.
association 706n.
corporation 708n.
jurisdiction 955n.
corporative state
polity 733n.
corporeality
materiality 319n.
corporeity
substantiality 3n.
materiality 319n.
corposant
glow-worm 420n.
corps
band 74n.
formation 722n.
corps de ballet
jumper 312n.
actor 594n.
corps d'élite
elite 644n.
armed force 722n.
corps diplomatique
envoy 754n.
corpse
corpse 363n.
corpse-candle
glow-worm 420n.
torch 420n.
corpulence
bulk 195n.
thickness 205n.
corpus
substance 3n.
whole 52n.
assemblage 74n.
matter 319n.
reading matter 589n.
Corpus Christi
the Sacrament 988n.
holy-day 988n.
corpuscle
particle 33n.
blood 335n.
corpuscular
minute 196adj.
corpus delicti
guilty act 936n.
corradiation
focus 76n.
convergence 293n.
corral
bring together 74vb.
circumscribe 232vb.
enclosure 235n.
break in 369vb.
imprison 747vb.
correct
orderly 60adj.
moderate 177vb.
true, accurate 494adj.
grammatical 564adj.
elegant 575adj.
print 587vb.
neutral 625adj.
perfect 646adj.
rectify 654vb.
remedy 658vb.
tasteful 846adj.
fashionable 848adj.
well-bred 848adj.
formal 875adj.
right 913adj.
reprove 924vb.
honorable 929adj.
punish 963vb.
orthodox 976adj.
correction
moderation 177n.
amendment 654n.
remedy 658n.
reprimand 924n.
correctitude
formality 875n.
(*see* correctness)
corrective
counteracting 182adj.
remedial 658adj.
punitive 963adj.
correctness
mid-course 625n.
perfection 646n.
good taste 846n.
etiquette 848n.
formality 875n.
courtesy 884n.
right 913n.
corrector
reformer 654n.
punisher 963n.
correlate
compare 462vb.
(*see* correlation)
correlation
relativeness 9n.
correlation 12n.
similarity 18n.
equalization 28n.
symmetry 245n.
correlative
interchanged 151adj.
correspondence
relativeness 9n.
correlation 12n.
uniformity 16n.
similarity 18n.
conformance 24n.
parallelism 219n.
symmetry 245n.
information 524n.
report 524n.
record 548n.
correspondence 588n.
correspondent
respondent 460n.
informant 524n.
publicizer 528n.
correspondent 588n.

author 589n.
delegate 754n.
recipient 782n.
correspond to
resemble 18vb.
corridor
bond 47n.
entrance 68n.
region 184n.
lobby 194n.
doorway 263n.
open space 263n.
access 624n.
corrigendum
mistake 495n.
corrigible
improved 564adj.
corrival
compeer 28n.
opponent 705n.
contender 716n.
corrivalry
opposition 704n.
contention 716n.
corrivation
current 350n.
corroborant
tonic 658n.
remedial 658adj.
corroborate
corroborate 466vb.
demonstrate 478vb.
affirm 532vb.
corroboration
evidence 466n.
assent 488n.
corroborative
evidential 466adj.
corroboree
dance 837n.
corrode
burn 381vb.
impair 655vb.
hurt 827vb.
corrosion
dilapidation 655n.
corrosive
destroyer 168n.
keen 174adj.
harmful 645adj.
poison 659n.
paining 827adj.
corrugate
crinkle 251vb.
roughen 259vb.
fold 261vb.
groove 262vb.
corrugated
undulatory 251adj.
rough 259adj.
corrugation
(*see* corrugate)
corrupt
decompose 51vb.
misteach 535vb.
neological 560adj.
bribe 612vb.
bad 645adj.
harm 645vb.
unclean 649adj.
make unclean 649vb.
deteriorated 655adj.
deteriorate 655vb.
impair, pervert 655vb.
venal 930adj.
vicious 934adj.
make wicked 934vb.
corruptibility
improbity 930n.
corruptible
venal 930adj.
corruption
fetor 397n.
neology 560n.
badness 645n.
uncleanness 649n.
improbity 930n.
(*see* corrupt)
corsage
bodywear 228n.
corsair
galley 275n.
robber 789n.
corselet
bodywear 228n.
armor 713n.
corset
compressor 198n.
supporter 218n.
underwear 228n.
hardness 326n.
fetter 748n.
cortege
adjunct 40n.
retinue 67n.
procession 71n.
concomitant 89n.
marching 267n.
slowcoach 278n.
follower 284n.
obsequies 364n.
retainer 742n.
cortes
parliament 692n.
cortex
exteriority 223n.
skin 226n.
cortical
exterior 223adj.
dermal 226adj.
cortisone
drug 658n.
coruscation
flash 417n.
corvée
labor 682n.
compulsion 740n.
corvette
sailing-ship 275n.
warship 722n.
Corybant
madman 504n.
Corybantiasm
frenzy 503n.
coryphaeus
teacher 537n.
leader 690n.
coryphée
actor 594n.
cosecant
ratio 85n.
cosh
strike 279vb.
hammer 279n.
club 723n.
cosharer
participator 775n.
cosh-man
ruffian 904n.
cosine
ratio 85n.
cosiness
euphoria 376n.
cosmetic
unguent 357n.
scent 396n.
balm 658n.
cosmetic 843n.
cosmetician
beautician 843n.
cosmetology
beautification 843n.
cosmic
extensive 32adj.
comprehensive 52adj.
cosmic 321adj.
cosmogony
uranometry 321n.
cosmography 321n.
cosmography
situation 186n.
uranometry 321n.
cosmography 321n.
geography 321n.
cosmology
uranometry 321n.
cosmography 321n.
cosmopolitan
universal 79adj.
urban 192adj.
national 371adj.
beau monde 848n.
well-bred 848adj.
philanthropic 901adj.
cosmopolite
philanthropist 901n.
cosmorama
spectacle 445n.
cosmos
whole 52n.
universe 321n.
cosmotron

nucleonics 160n.
cossack
cavalry 722n.
cosset
pet 889vb.
favorite 890n.
cost
appraise 465vb.
account 808vb.
cost 809n., vb.
dearness 811n.
costal
lateral 239adj.
coster,– monger
seller 793n.
peddler 794n.
coster-barrow
pushcart 274n.
costive
dense 324adj.
retentive 778adj.
costless
uncharged 812adj.
costly
destructive 165adj.
valuable 644adj.
harmful 645adj.
dear 811adj.
ostentatious 875adj.
cost-reducing
economical 814adj.
costs
expenditure 806n.
cost 809n.
penalty 963n.
cost, to one's
amiss 616adv.
badly 645adv.
costume
dress 228n.
stage-set 594n.
costumier
clothier 228n.
stage-hand 594n.
cosubstantial
identical 13adj.
cot
small house 192n.
bed 218n.
cotangent
ratio 85n.
cote
stable 192n.
coterie
group, band 74n.
party 708n.
cothurnus
drama 594n.
cotillion
dance 837n.
cottage
small house 192n.
cottager, cotter
resident 191n.
cotter pin
fastening 47n.
cotton
textile 222n.
fiber 208n.
cotton on to
be friendly 880vb.
cottons
clothing 228n.
cotton wool
fiber 208n.
cotyledon
foliage 366n.
couch
be horizontal 216vb.
bed, seat 218n.
sit down 311vb.
repose 683vb.
couchant
supine 216adj.
heraldic 547adj.
couéism
sense 374n.
hope 852n.
cougar
cat 365n.
cough
eruct 300vb.
excretion 302n.
breathe 352vb.
rasp 407vb.
respiratory disease 651n.
cough up
restitute 787vb.
pay 804vb.
coughy
puffing 352adj.
couldn't care less
be incurious 454vb.
be indifferent 860adv.
couldn't-care-less
rash 857adj.
couleur de rose
excellent 644adj.
palmy 730adj.
promising 852adj.
coulisses
theater 594n.
council
assembly 74n.
director 690n.
adviser 691n.
council 692n.
consignee 754n.
conference 884n.
jurisdiction 955n.
tribunal 956n.
synod 985n.
councillor
official 690n.
councillor 692n.
officer 741n.
counsel
incite 612vb.
warning 664n.
advise 691vb.
consignee 754n.
lawyer 958n.
counsel of despair
inexpedience 643n.
hopelessness 853n.
counselor
sage 500n.
official 690n.
adviser 691n.
count
quantify 26vb.
comprise 78vb.
numeration 86n.
measure 465vb.
motivate 612vb.
be important 638vb.
nobleman 868n.
accusation 928n.
countable
numerable 86adj.
count as
substitute 150vb.
countenance
face 237n.
mien 445n.
inducement 612n.
aid 703n.
patronize 703vb.
approve 923vb.
counter
contrary 14adj.
computer 86n.
counteract 182vb.
stand, shelf 118n.
poop 238n.
answer 460vb.
label 547n.
be obstructive 702vb.
oppose 704vb.
parry 713vb.
retaliate 714vb.
shop 796n.
plaything 837n.
counteract
be contrary 14vb.
weaken 163vb.
counteract 182vb.
tell against 467vb.
oppose 704vb.
counteraction
(*see* counteract)
counteractive
contrary 14adj.
counter-argument
opposition 704n.
vindication 927n.
legal trial 959n.
counter-attack
attack 712vb.
retaliation 714n.
counter-attraction

offset 31n.
influence 178n.
counterbalance
offset 31n.
counteract 182n.
counterblast
counteraction 182n.
answer 460n.
retaliation 714n.
counter-caster
computer 86n.
counterchange
correlate 12vb.
interchange 151n., vb.
counter-charge
rejoinder 460n.
vindication 927n.
accusation 928n.
counter-charm
counteraction 182n.
talisman 983n.
countercheck
be obstructive 702vb.
countercheer
disapprobation 924n.
counter-claim
offset 31n.
request 761n.
deprecation 762n.
litigation 959n.
counterdraw
copy 20vb.
counter-espionage
secret service 459n.
counter-evidence
counter-evidence 467n.
counterfeit
imitation 20n.
duplicity 541n.
fake 541vb.
sham 542n.
spurious 542adj.
deceive 542vb.
be untrue 543vb.
mint 797vb.
counterfeiter
deceiver 545n.
defrauder 789n.
counterfoil
label 547n.
counterglow
heavens 321n.
counter-irritant
counteraction 182n.
antidote 658n.
counter-jumper
seller 793n.
countermand
command 737vb.
abrogate 752vb.
prohibition 757n.
countermarch
turn back 286vb.
wage war 718vb.
countermark
label 547n.
counter-meaning
contrariety 14n.
connotation 514n.
countermine
plot 623n., vb.
oppose 704vb.
defenses 713n.
retaliation 714n.
countermovement
return 286n.
counter-order
abrogation 752n.
prohibition 757n.
counterpane
coverlet 226n.
counterpart
identity 13n.
analogue 18n.
copy, duplicate 22n.
counterplot
plot 623n.
retaliation 714n.
counterpoint
contrariety 14n.
combination 50n.
symmetry 245n.
melody 410n.
music 412n.
counterpoise
equalize 28vb.
offset 31n.
counteract 182vb.
gravity 322n.
weigh 322vb.
counterpole
contrariety 14n.
Counter Reformation
restoration 656n.
orthodoxism 976n.
Catholicism 976n.
counter-revolution
reversion 148n.
revolution 149n.
counters
counting instrument 86n.
counterscarp
fortification 713n.
countersense
contrariety 14n.
connotation 514n.
countersign
answer 460n.
testify 466vb.
endorse 488vb.
call 547n.
sign 547vb.
give security 767vb.
counter-signature
credential 466n.
compact 765n.
counterspin
evolution 316n.
counter statement
rejoinder 460n.
counter-stream
contrariety 14n.
counter-stroke
defense 713n.
retaliation 714n.
counter-symptom
contrariety 14n.
counter-tenor
stridor 407n.
vocalist 413n.
counter-term
name 561n.
countertype
prototype 23n.
countervail
be equal 28vb.
set off 31vb.
counteract 182vb.
tell against 467vb.
counterweight
offset 31n.
stabilizer 153n.
counteract 182vb.
weigh 322vb.
countess
nobleman 868n.
count for nothing
be unimportant 639vb.
counting
inclusive 78adj.
numeration 86n.
counting heads
vote 605n.
counting-house
shop 796n.
treasury 799n.
countless
multitudinous 104adj.
infinite 107adj.
count on
assume 471vb.
believe 485vb.
expect 507vb.
count out
exclude 57vb.
reject 607vb.
exempt 919vb.
countrified
provincial 192adj.
ill-bred 847adj.
country
region 184n.
home 192n.
land 344n.
polity 733n.
countryman
dweller 191n.
countryman 869n.
counts
particulars 80n.

count the cost
be cautious 858vb.
count upon
(*see* count on)
count with
number with 78vb.
county
district 184n.
polity 733n.
county family
aristocracy 868n.
coup
instant 116n.
contrivance 623n.
deed 676n.
coup de grâce
end 69n.
killing 362n.
completion 725n.
coup de main
violence 176n.
deed 676n.
attack 712n.
coup-de-maître
masterpiece 694n.
coup d'état
revolution 149n.
policy 623n.
deed 676n.
revolt 738n.
lawlessness 954n.
coup de théâtre
thaumaturgy 864n.
coup d'oeil
inspection 438n.
coupé
train 274n.
automobile 274n.
carriage 274n.
couple
analogue 18n.
join 45vb.
unite with 45vb.
combine 50vb.
duality 90n.
marry 894vb.
coupled
accompanying 89adj.
couplet
duality 90n.
prosody 593n.
verse form 593n.
coupling
joinder 45n.
coition 45n.
coupling 47n.
coupon
portion 783n.
paper money 797n.
courage
resolution 599n.
courage 855n.
courgette
vegetable 301n.
courier
guide 520n.
courier 531n.
course
order 60n.
continuity 71n.
time 108n.
tendency 179n.
layer 207n.
motion 265n.
itinerary 267n.
water travel 269n.
sail 275n.
speeding 277n.
direction 281n.
dish 301n.
flow 350vb.
curriculum 534n.
hunt 619vb.
route 624n.
therapy 658n.
conduct 688n.
arena 724n.
course, of
necessarily 596adv.
course of events
affairs 154n.
course of, in the
while 108adv.
course of law
legal process 959n.
course of study
curriculum 534n.
study 536n.
course of time
course of time 111n.
courser
horse 273n.
war-horse 273n.
speeder 277n.
dog 365n.
hunter 619n.
coursing
chase 619n.
court
place 185n.
housing 192n.
horizontality 216n.
open space 263n.
council 692n.
arena 724n.
retainer 742n.
request 761vb.
beau monde 848n.
desire 859vb.
befriend 880vb.
be in love 887vb.
court 889vb.
flatter 925vb.
law-court 956n.
court dress
formal dress 228n.
formality 875n.
courteous
well-bred 848adj.
benevolent 897adj.
(*see* courtesy)
courtesan
prostitute 952n.
courtesy
obeisance 311n.
humility 872n.
sociability 882n.
courtesy 884n.
courteous act 884n.
disinterestedness 931n.
courtesy, by
insubstantially 4adv.
courtesy call
social round 882n.
courtesy title
insubstantial thing 4n.
title 870n.
undueness 916n.
court-house
courtroom 956n.
courtier
retainer 742n.
toady 879n.
flatterer 925n.
court-leet
law-court 956n.
courtly
well-bred 848adj.
courteous 884adj.
court manners
etiquette 848n.
court-martial
law-court 956n.
Court of Appeal
law-court 956n.
Court of Arches
ecclesiastical court 956n.
synod 985n.
court of audience
ecclesiastical court 956n.
court of law
law-court 956n.
court plaster
surgical dressing 658n.
courtroom
courtroom 956n.
courtship
love-making 887n.
wooing 889n.
courtyard
place 185n.
cousin
kinsman 11n.
couturier
clothier 228n.
artist 556n.
cove
cavity 255n.
gulf 345n.
person 371n.

male 372n.
coven
assembly 74n.
sorcery 983n.
covenant
promise 764n., vb.
compact 765n.
contract 765vb.
title-deed 767n.
covenanted
secured 767adj.
covenanter
assenter 488n.
sectarist 978n.
covenanting
sectarian 978adj.
Coventry, send to
exclude 57vb.
cover
offset 31n.
fill 54vb.
generate 164vb.
extend 183vb.
receptacle 194n.
be high 209vb.
wrapping 226n.
cover 226vb.
stopper 264n.
meal, dish 301n.
darken 418vb.
screen 421vb.
communicate 524vb.
conceal 525vb.
hiding-place 527n.
disguise 527n.
publish 528vb.
deception 542n.
mark 547vb.
obliterate 550vb.
correspondence 588n.
bookbinding 589n.
pretext 614n.
gamble 618vb.
cleaning cloth 648n.
safeguard 660vb.
shelter 662n.
defend 713vb.
threaten 900vb.
coverage
inclusion 78n.
range 183n.
publicity 528n.
cover all cases
be general 79vb.
cover girl
a beauty 841n.
cover ground
progress 285vb.
coverlet
coverlet 226n.
warm clothes 381n.
covert
nest 192n.
wood 366n.
screen 421n.
occult 523adj.
concealed 525adj.
refuge, shelter 662n.
coverts
plumage 259n.
coverture
marriage 894n.
cover up
screen 421vb.
keep secret 525vb.
covet
desire 859vb.
envy 912vb.
covetous
avaricious 816adj.
desiring 859adj.
envious 912adj.
selfish 932adj.
covey
group 74n.
certain quantity 104n.
covinous
false 541adj.
deceiving 542adj.
cow
cattle 365n.
female animal 373n.
dissuade 613vb.
frighten 854vb.
coward
weakling 163n.
avoider 620n.
coward 856n.
cowardice
irresolution 601n.
cowardice 856n.
cowardize
unman 161vb.
frighten 854vb.
cowardly
(*see* cowardice)
cowboy
rider 268n.
herdsman 369n.
cower
stoop 311vb.
avoid 620vb.
quake 854vb.
be cowardly 856vb.
cowherd, cowman
herdsman 369n.
servant 742n.
cowhide
skin 226n.
scourge 964n.
cowhouse, cowshed
stable 192n.
cattle pen 369n.
cowl
covering 226n.
headgear 228n.
ecclesiasticize 985vb.
monk 986vb.
canonicals 989n.
cowlick
hair 259n.
hair-dressing 843n.
cowling
covering 226n.
cowlstaff
supporter 218n.
coworker
personnel 686n.
collaborator 707n.
cow-pat
excrement 302n.
cowpox
skin disease 651n.
cowpuncher
rider 268n.
herdsman 369n.
cowrie
small coin 33n.
coinage 797n.
cox
navigator 270n.
direct 689vb.
coxcomb
entertainer 594n.
vain person 783n.
fop 848n.
affector 850n.
coxcombry
affectation 850n.
airs 873n.
coxswain
navigate 269vb.
(*see* cox)
coy
affected 850adj.
nervous 854adj.
cowardly 856adj.
modest 874adj.
pure 950adj.
coyote
dog 365n.
cozen
deceive 542vb.
cozener
trickster 545n.
motivator 612n.
cozening
perfidious 930adj.
cozy
comfortable 376adj.
palmy 730adj.
pleasurable 826adj.
sociable 882adj.
crab
fish food 301n.
reptile 365n.
table fish 365n.
sourness 393n.
be discontented 829vb.
be sullen 893vb.
dispraise 924vb.
detract 926vb.

crabbed
sour 393adj.
puzzling 517adj.
imperspicuous 568adj.
inelegant 576adj.
sullen 893adj.
crabstick
rude person 885n.
crab-walk
deviation 282n.
crack
disjunction 46n.
break 46vb.
discontinuity 72n.
instant 116n.
weakness 163n.
gap 201n.
space 201vb.
roughness 259n.
furrow 262n.
opening 263n.
knock 279n.
be brittle 330vb.
bang 402n.
crackle 402vb.
rasp 407vb.
striation 437n.
decipher 520vb.
best 644adj.
defect 647n.
skillful 694adj.
witticism 839n.
blemish 845n., vb.
crack a bottle
drink 301vb.
be sociable 882vb.
crack a cipher
decipher 520vb.
crack at
essay 671n.
crack-brain
crank 504n.
crack-brained
foolish 499adj.
crazed 503adj.
crack down on
be severe 735vb.
restrain 747vb.
cracked
spaced 201adj.
non-resonant 405adj.
strident 407adj.
discordant 411adj.
misjudging 481adj.
unintelligent 499adj.
interpreted 520adj.
voiceless 578adj.
imperfect 647adj.
dilapidated 655adj.
blemished 845adj.
cracked-up
overrated 482adj.
cracker
pastry 301n.
bang 402n.
crackerjack
topping 644adj.
crackers
crazed 503adj.
hair-dressing 843n.
crackle
bang 402n.
crackle 402vb.
crack of doom
finality 69n.
future state 124n.
ruin 165n.
death 361n.
crackpot
fool 501n.
crank 504n.
cracksman
thief 789n.
crack up
be fatigued 684vb.
boast 877vb.
praise 923vb.
cradle
origin 68n.
nonage 130n.
seedbed 156n.
assuage 177vb.
nest, home 192n.
basket 194n.
support, bed 218n.
bring to rest 266vb.
make inactive 679vb.
relieve 831vb.
pet 889vb.
cradle-song
vocal music 412n.
soporific 679n.
relief 831n.
craft
ship, shipping 275n.
sagacity 498n.
deception 542n.
vocation 622n.
skill 694n.
cunning 698n.
craftiness
(*see* crafty)
craftsman
producer 167n.
artist 556n.
machinist 630n.
doer 676n.
artisan 686n.
craftsmanship
skill 694n.
crafty
intelligent 498adj.
deceiving 542adj.
cunning 698adj.
crag
high land 209n.
sharp point 256n.
hardness 326n.
rock 344n.
craggy
sharp 256adj.
rough 259adj.
difficult 700adj.
cragsman
traveler 268n.
climber 308n.
cram
fill 54vb.
bring together 74vb.
load 193vb.
enlarge 197vb.
be dense 324vb.
educate 534vb.
study 536n., vb.
superabound 637vb.
gluttonize 947vb.
crambo
doggerel 593n.
indoor game 837n.
cram-full
full 54adj.
cram in
stow 187vb.
crammer
teacher 537n.
training school 539n.
untruth 543n.
glutton 947n.
cramoisie
red color 431n.
cramp
fastening 47n.
disable 161vb.
weaken 163vb.
make smaller 198vb.
spasm 318n.
pang 377n.
make insufficient 636vb.
impair 655vb.
hinder 702vb.
restraint 747n.
cramped
narrow-minded 481adj.
inelegant 576adj.
cran
basket 194n.
crane
hanger 217n.
lifter 310n.
bird of prey 365n.
crane one's neck
scan 438adj.
cranial
topmost 213adj.
craniology
head 213n.
anthropology 371n.
craniometry
head 213n.
anthropology 371n.
cranium

head 213n.
dome 253n.
crank
handle 218n.
meandering 251n.
rotate 315vb.
narrow mind 481n.
fool 501n.
eccentricity 503n.
crank 504n.
visionary 513n.
make ready 669vb.
witticism 839n.
laughing-stock 851n.
crank-handle
handle 218n.
crankiness
(*see* crank, cranky)
crankish
misjudging 481adj.
crankle
meander 251vb.
fold 261n.
cranky
convoluted 251adj.
crazed 503adj.
crannog
dwelling 192n.
cranny
compartment 194n.
furrow 261n.
hiding-place 527n.
crape
convolution 251n.
crinkle 251vb.
black thing 428n.
badge 547n.
lamentation 836n.
craps
gambling 618n.
gambling game 837n.
crapulence
sequel 67n.
pain 377n.
intemperance 943n.
crapulence 949n.
crash
revolution 149n.
textile 222n.
aeronautics 271n.
fly 271vb.
collision 279n.
descent 309n.
be brittle 330vb.
be loud 400vb.
bang 402n., vb.
discord 411vb.
miscarry, fail 728vb.
insolvency 805n.
crash-dive
aeronautics 271n.
plunge 313vb.
crash-landing
aeronautics 271n.
crasis
temperament 5n.
combination 50n.
composition 56n.
crass
consummate 32adj.
dense 324adj.
unintelligent 499adj.
manifest 522adj.
vulgar 847adj.
crate
basket 194n.
vehicle 274n.
crater
bowl 194n.
cavity 255n.
orifice 263n.
cravat
neckwear 228n.
crave
require 627vb.
request 761vb.
desire 859vb.
envy 912vb.
craven
coward 856n.
crawfish
regress 286vb.
table fish 365n.
crawl
pedestrianism 267n.
aquatics 269n.
slowness 278n.
move slowly 278vb.
tergiversate 603vb.
knuckle under 721vb.
lose repute 867vb.
be humble 872vb.
be servile 879vb.
crawlers
breeches 228n.
crawling
multitudinous 104adj.
unclean 649adj.
crawl with
be many 104vb.
superabound 637vb.
crayfish
table fish 365n.
crayon
paint 553vb.
art equipment 553n.
craze
be brittle 330vb.
striation 437n.
bias 481n.
make mad 503vb.
whim 604n.
practice 610n.
fashion 848n.
liking 859n.
excite love 887vb.
crazed
foolish 499adj.
craziness
eccentricity 503n.
crazy
non-uniform 17adj.
aged 131adj.
flimsy 163adj.
distorted 246adj.
brittle 330adj.
variegated 437adj.
crazed 503adj.
unsafe 661adj.
enamored 887adj.
crazy paving
discontinuity 72n.
checker 437n.
creak
move slowly 278vb.
sound faint 401vb.
stridor 407n.
creaking, creaky
strident 407adj.
hoarse 407adj.
clumsy 695adj.
cream
milk 301n.
semiliquidity 354n.
bubble 355vb.
fat 357n.
unguent 357n.
select 605vb.
chief thing 638n.
elite 644n.
cleanser 648n.
balm 658n.
cosmetic 845n.
beau monde 848n.
person of repute 866n.
cream-colored
yellow 433adj.
creamery
workshop 687n.
creamy
semiliquid 354adj.
fatty 357adj.
savory 390adj.
soft-hued 425adj.
whitish 427adj.
yellow 433adj.
crease
joint 45n.
jumble 63vb.
limit 236n.
fold 261n., vb.
impair 655vb.
create
cause 156vb.
produce 164vb.
efform 243vb.
imagine 513vb.
be excitable 822vb.
dignify 866vb.
be angry 891vb.
creation
existence 1n.

non-imitation 21n.
antiquity 125n.
production 164n.
dress 228n.
efformation 243n.
universe 321n.
divine function 965n.
creative
unimitative 21adj.
causal 156adj.
productive 164adj.
prolific 171adj.
imaginative 513adj.
godlike 965adj.
creator
cause 156n.
producer 167n.
the Deity 965n.
creature
substance 3n.
product 164n.
animal 365n.
person 371n.
auxiliary 707n.
dependent 742n.
creature comforts
food 301n.
euphoria 376n.
creaturehood
subjection 745n.
creaturely
produced 164adj.
human 371adj.
creature of habit
repetition 106n.
habitué 610n.
crèche
school 539n.
credal
credal 485adj.
theological 973adj.
orthodox 976adj.
credence
belief 485n.
altar 990n.
credenda
creed 485n.
theology 973n.
credential
credential 465n.
title-deed 767n.
credible
possible 469adj.
plausible 471adj.
credible 485adj.
credit
attribute 158vb.
influence 178n.
believe 485vb.
means 629n.
subvention 703n.
authority 733n.
promise 764n.
lend 784vb.
credit 802n., vb.
account 808vb.
repute 866n.
honor 866vb.
thank 907vb.
dueness 915n.
approbation 923n.
praise 923n.
creditable
excellent 644adj.
reputable 866adj.
approvable 923adj.
creditless
inglorious 867adj.
credit, on
promissory 764adj.
lending 784adj.
owed 803adj.
creditor
provider 633n.
lender 784n.
creditor 802n.
credit side
gain 771n.
credit title
thanks 907n.
credit-worthiness
wealth 800n.
credit 802n.
credit-worthy
reputable 866adj.
deserving 915adj.
credo
(*see* creed)
credulity
credulity 487n.
deception 542n.
persuasibility 612n.
credulous
misjudging 481adj.
credulous 487adj.
gullible 544adj.
creed
creed 485n.
theology 973n.
orthodoxy 976n.
creedless
unbelieving 486adj.
irreligious 974adj.
creek
gap 201n.
cavity 255n.
gulf 345n.
stream 350n.
creel
basket 194n.
creep
drag on 113vb.
be rough 259vb.
move slowly 278vb.
feel pain 377vb.
itch 378vb.
lurk 523adj.
be stealthy 525vb.
dance 837n.
be servile 879vb.
creeper
coil 251n.
plant 366n.
creepers
footwear 228n.
creeping thing
animal 365n.
creeps
formication 378n.
nervousness 854n.
creep upon
surprise 508vb.
creepy
frightening 854adj.
creese
sharp edge 256n.
side arms 723n.
cremation
interment 364n.
burning 381n.
crematorium
interment 364n.
furnace 383n.
crenation
edging 234n.
notch 260n.
crenellate
hem 234vb.
notch 260vb.
defend 713vb.
Creole
foreigner 59n.
settler 191n.
creosote
prophylactic 658n.
crepe
(*see* crape)
crepitate
eruct 300vb.
crackle 402vb.
crepuscule
evening 129n.
half-light 419n.
crescendo
increase 36n.
expansion 197n.
loudness 400n.
crescent
housing 192n.
curve 248n.
arc 250n.
flag 547n.
religious faith 973n.
cress
potherb 301n.
cresset
torch 420n.
crest
superiority 34n.
high land 209n.
crown 213vb.
summit 213n.

plumage 259n.
heraldry 547n.
mark 547vb.
jewelry 844n.
nobility 868n.
crestfallen
disappointed 509adj.
dejected 834adj.
humbled 872adj.
cretaceous
white 427adj.
cretic
prosody 593n.
cretin
fool 501n.
madman 504n.
cretinous
unintelligent 499adj.
insane 503adj.
cretonne
textile 222n.
crevasse
gap 201n.
cavity 255n.
pitfall 633n.
crevice
gap 201n.
crew
component 58n.
band 74n.
resident 191n.
navigate 269vb.
mariner 270n.
personnel 686n.
party 708n.
crew-cut
shortness 204n.
hair-dressing 843n.
crewel-work
textile 222n.
crewless
empty 190adj.
crib
copy 22n.
bed 218n.
translation 520n.
classroom 538n.
imprison 747vb.
borrow 785n.
steal 788vb.
cribbage
card game 837n.
cribble
porosity 263n.
cribriform
perforated 263adj.
crick
pang 377n.
ululate 409vb.
cricket
ball game 837n.
cricketer
player 837n.
cricket pitch
arena 724n.
cri de coeur
request 761n.
lament 836n.
cried-up
overrated 482adj.
crier
cry 408n.
publicizer 528n.
seller 793n.
crime
disobedience 738n.
improbity 930n.
foul play 930n.
wickedness 934n.
vice 934n.
guilty act 936n.
lawbreaking 954n.
crime passionel
homicide 362n.
revenge 910n.
jealousy 911n.
crime story
novel 590n.
crime wave
lawlessness 954n.
criminal
unconformable 84adj.
offender 904n.
wrong 914adj.
rascally 930adj.
heinous 934adj.
guilty 936adj.
knave 938n.
lawbreaking 954adj.
criminal conversation
illicit love 951n.
criminal offence
lawbreaking 954n.
crimination
accusation 928n.
criminologist
detective 459n.
criminology
lawbreaking 954n.
criminous
(*see* criminal)
crimp
crinkle 251vb.
notch 260vb.
brittle 330adj.
ensnare 542vb.
trickster 545n.
taker 786n.
steal 788vb.
thief 789n.
crimson
red color 431n.
be modest 874vb.
cringe
stoop 311vb.
obey 739vb.
be subject 745vb.
be cowardly 856vb.
be servile 879vb.
crinite, crinose
hairy 259adj.
crinkle
distort 246vb.
angulate 247vb.
make curved 248vb.
crinkle 251vb.
roughen 259vb.
fold 261n., vb.
crinkum-crankum
ideality 513n.
crinoline
skirt 228n.
crinose
hairy 259adj.
cripple
disable 161vb.
weaken 163vb.
make useless 641vb.
sick person 651n.
impair 655vb.
hinder 702vb.
crippled
incomplete 55adj.
imperfect 647adj.
crisis
juncture 8n.
degree 27n.
crisis 137n.
eventuality 154n.
limit 236n.
important matter 638n.
danger 661n.
predicament 700n.
excitation 821n.
crisp
crinkle 251vb.
rough 259adj.
roughen 259vb.
brittle 330adj.
criss-cross
crossed 222adj.
criterion
prototype 23n.
testing agent 461n.
comparison 462n.
identification 547n.
critic
estimator 480n.
dissentient 489n.
theorist 512n.
interpreter 520n.
dissertator 591n.
malcontent 829n.
man of taste 846n.
disapprover 924n.
accuser 928n.
critical
circumstantial 8adj.
crucial 137adj.
timely 137adj.
eventful 154adj.
discriminating 463adj.

judicial 480adj.
discursive 591adj.
important 638adj.
dangerous 661adj.
difficult 700adj.
discontented 829adj.
tasteful 846adj.
fastidious 862adj.
disapproving 924adj.
criticism
estimate 480n.
interpretation 520n.
affirmation 532n.
article 591n.
advice 691n.
good taste 846n.
censure 924n.
detraction 926n.
criticize
compare 462vb.
discriminate 463vb.
be discontented 829vb.
critique
(*see* criticism)
croak
die 361vb.
rasp 407vb.
ululation 409n.
ululate 409vb.
be discontented 829vb.
croaker
frog 365n.
malcontent 829n.
moper 834n.
croaking
voiceless 587adj.
crochet
tie 45vb.
network 222n.
needlework 844n.
crock
vessel 194n.
sick person 651n.
crockery
receptacle 194n.
brittleness 330n.
pottery 381n.
materials 631n.
crock up
be fatigued 684vb.
crocodile
procession 71n.
skin 226n.
reptile 365n.
crocodile tears
duplicity 541n.
crocus
yellowness 433n.
Croesus
rich man 800n.
croft
house 192n.
enclosure 235n.
farm 370n.
crofter
resident 191n.
husbandman 370n.
croissant
cereal 301n.
Croix de Guerre
decoration 729n.
cromlech
tomb 364n.
monument 548n.
crone
old woman 133n.
Cronian
primal 127adj.
cronk
ululation 409n.
crony
chum 880n.
friend 880n.
crook
supporter 218n.
render oblique 220vb.
angulate 247vb.
make curved 248vb.
deflect 282vb.
punctuation 547n.
thief 789n.
knave 938n.
crook-backed
deformed 246adj.
crooked
oblique 220adj.
distorted 246adj.
angular 247adj.
deviating 282adj.
occult 523adj.
cunning 698adj.
blemished 845adj.
dishonest 930adj.
croon
sound faint 401vb.
sing 413vb.
crooner
vocalist 413n.
entertainer 594n.
croon over
pet 889vb.
crop
great quantity 32n.
multitude 104n.
growth 157n.
producer 164n.
maw 194n.
shorten 204vb.
graze 301vb.
agriculture 370n.
cultivate 370vb.
store 632n.
earnings 771n.
acquire 771vb.
take 786vb.
hair-dressing 843n.
crop-full
full 54adj.
cropper
descent 309n.
crop up
happen 154vb.
reproduce 166vb.
be visible 443vb.
croquet
ball game 837n.
croquet lawn
horizontality 216n.
pleasure-ground 837n.
crose
vestments 989n.
crosier
badge of rule 743n.
vestments 989n.
cross
hybrid 43n.
counteract 182vb.
be oblique 220vb.
cross 222n., vb.
angularity 247n.
traverse 267vb.
pass 305vb.
assent 488n.
label, badge 547n.
mark 547vb.
script 586n.
bane 659n.
hindering 702adj.
opposing 704adj.
decoration 729n.
adverse 731adj.
painfulness 827n.
jewelry 844n.
angry 891adj.
sullen 893adj.
means of execution 964n.
religious faith 973n.
talisman 983n.
ritual object 988n.
vestments 989n.
church interior 990n.
cross-bencher
free man 744n.
crossbow
propellant 287n.
missile weapon 723n.
cross-breed
hybrid 43n.
mix 43vb.
nonconformist 84n.
cross-connection
junction 45n.
cross-country
directed 281adj.
cross-current
counteraction 182n.
contraposition 240n.
current 350n.
wind 352n.
pitfall 633n.
obstacle 702n.

opposition 704n.
cross-examination
interrogation 459n.
legal trial 959n.
cross-examiner
inquisitor 453n.
questioner 459n.
cross-eyed
dim-sighted 440adj.
cross-fire
bombardment 712n.
cross-grained
rough 259adj.
willful 602adj.
irascible 892adj.
sullen 893adj.
cross-hatch
groove 262vb..
crossing
crossing 222n.
passage 305n.
access, road 624n.
crossing-sweeper
cleaner 648n.
cross oneself
be pious 979vb.
cross one's heart
swear 532vb.
cross one's path
hinder 702vb.
cross, on the
obliquely 220adv.
cross out
subtract 39vb.
eject 300vb.
obliterate 550vb.
cross over
apostatize 603vb.
crosspatch
rude person 885n.
shrew 892n.
cross-purposes
error 495n.
misinterpretation 521n.
opposition 704n.
dissension 709n.
cross-question
question 459n.
interrogate 459vb.
cross-reference
sorting 62n.
class 62vb.
crossroad
juncture 8n.
focus 76n.
crossing 222n.
divergence 294n.
road 624n.
cross section
example 83n.
cross stitch
needlework 844n.
cross swords
argue 475vb.
withstand 704vb.
fight 716vb.
cross the floor
apostatize 603vb.
cross the mind
dawn upon 449vb.
cross the Rubicon
initiate 68vb.
overstep 306vb.
be resolute 599vb.
choose 605vb.
cross-tree
supporter 218n.
cross-vote
disobey 738vb.
be free 744vb.
crossways
juncture 8n.
joint 45n.
focus 76n.
angularity 247n.
road 624n.
crosswise
obliquely 220adv.
across 222adv.
cross with
unite with 45vb.
crossword
enigma 530n.
indoor game 837n.
crotch
angularity 247n.
crotchet
angularity 247n.
notation 410n.
bias 481n.
punctuation 547n.
whim 604n.
crotchety
unconformable 84adj.
misjudging 481adj.
crazed 503adj.
willful 602adj.
capricious 604adj.
crouch
be low 210vb.
stoop 311vb.
knuckle under 721vb.
quake 854vb.
be servile 879vb.
croup
buttocks 238n.
rear 238n.
respiration 352n.
croupier
treasurer 798n.
croupy
diseased 651adj.
crow
bird 365n.
ululate 409vb.
black thing 428n.
tool 630n.
cleaner 648n.
defy 711vb.
triumph 727vb.
rejoice, laugh 835vb.
eyesore 842n.
boast 877vb.
crowbar
tool 630n.
crowd
great quantity 32n.
medley 43n.
crowd 74n.
multitude 104n.
be near 200vb.
be contiguous 202vb.
be dense 324vb.
viol 414n.
redundance 637n.
obstruct 702vb.
party 708n.
crown
completeness 54n.
vertex 213n.
summit, head 213n.
crown 213vb.
headgear 228n.
limit 236vb.
loop 250n.
strike 279vb.
badge, heraldry 547n.
objective 617n.
perfect 646vb.
doctor 658vb.
completion 725n.
climax 725vb.
trophy 729n.
authority 733n.
regalia 743n.
badge of rank 743n.
commission 751vb.
coinage 797n.
ornamentation 844n.
decorate 844vb.
honors 866n.
pay respects 884vb.
reward 962n.
crown all
culminate 34vb.
climax 725vb.
crowned head
sovereign 741n.
crowning
topmost 213adj.
crowning point
summit 213n.
crow over
defy 711vb.
triumph 727vb.
boast 877vb.
crow's feet
fold 261n.
crow's nest
vertex 213n.
view 438n.
crow to pluck

resentment 891n.
crozier
(*see* crosier)
crucial
circumstantial 8adj.
crucial 137adj.
fundamental 156adj.
crossed 222adj.
demonstrating 478adj.
crucial moment
juncture 8n.
crisis 137n.
crucial test
experiment 461n.
crucible
mixture 43n.
crucible 147n.
vessel 194n.
heater 383n.
testing agent 461n.
workshop 687n.
crucifer
church officer 986n.
ritualist 988n.
crucifix
hanger 217n.
cross 222n.
ritual object 988n.
church interior 990n.
crucifixion
killing 362n.
pain 377n.
art subject 553n.
suffering 825n.
capital punishment 963n.
cruciform
crossed 222adj.
churchlike 990adj.
crucify
(*see* crucifixion)
crude
incomplete 55adj.
beginning 68adj.
inelegant 576adj.
imperfect 647adj.
immature 670adj.
bungled 695adj.
graceless 842adj.
cruel
violent 176adj.
harmful 645adj.
warlike 718adj.
oppressive 735adj.
paining 827adj.
cruel 898adj.
pitiless 906adj.
cruelly
painfully 32adv.
cruelty
(*see* cruel)
cruet
vessel 194n.
ritual object 988n.
cruise
be in motion 265vb.
travel 267vb.
water travel 269n.
cruiser
warship 722n.
cruiser-weight
pugilist 722n.
crumb
small thing 33n.
piece 53n.
powder 332n.
crumble
break 46vb.
decompose 51vb.
be weak 163vb.
be destroyed 165vb.
pastry 301n.
be brittle 330vb.
pulverize 332vb.
impair 655vb.
deteriorate 655vb.
crumbling
antiquated 127adj.
weakened 163adj.
powdery 332adj.
unsafe 661adj.
crumbly
fragmentary 53adj.
brittle 330adj.
powdery 332adj.
crumbs
rubbish 641n.
crumenal
monetary 797adj.
crumpet
head 213n.
pastry 301n.
crumple
jumble 63vb.
distort 246vb.
crinkle 251vb.
fold 261n., vb.
impair 655vb.
crumster
merchant ship 275n.
crunch
rend 46vb.
chew 301vb.
pulverize 332vb.
rasp 407vb.
crunk
ululate 409vb.
cruor
blood 335n.
crupper
buttocks 238n.
rear 238n.
crusade
war 718n.
philanthropy 901n.
crusader
militarist 722n.
philanthropist 901n.
religionist 979n.
crusading spirit
philanthropy 901n.
pietism 979n.
cruse
vessel 194n.
crush
jumble 63vb.
crowd 74n.
demolish 165vb.
force 176vb.
make smaller 198vb.
abase 311vb.
pulverize 332vb.
touch 378vb.
confute 479vb.
ill-treat 645vb.
wound 655vb.
overmaster 727vb.
oppress 735vb.
sadden 834vb.
humiliate 872vb.
love 887n.
crusher
pulverizer 332n.
crushing
destructive 165adj.
forceful 571adj.
laborious 682adj.
hindering 702adj.
completive 725adj.
successful 727adj.
distressing 827adj.
crust
piece 53n.
exteriority 223n.
covering 226n.
skin 226n.
mouthful 301n.
cereal 301n.
be dense 324vb.
land 344n.
crustacean
animal 365n.
crusty
irascible 892adj.
sullen 893adj.
crutch
supporter 218n.
angularity 247n.
crux
cross 222n.
unintelligibility 517n.
enigma 530n.
difficulty 700n.
cry
feel pain 377vb.
loudness 400n.
cry 408n., vb.
ululation 409n.
proclaim 528vb.
rumor 529n.
lamentation 836n.
weep 836vb.

fashion 848n.
cry-baby
weakling 163n.
weeper 836n.
coward 856n.
cry down
deprecate 762vb.
detract 926vb.
cry of "wolf"
insubstantial thing 4n.
false alarm 665n.
cry out against
dissuade 613vb.
deprecate 762vb.
cry out for
require 627vb.
cry over spilt milk
regret 830vb.
crypt
cellar 194n.
tomb 364n.
concealment 525n.
hiding-place 527n.
church interior 990n.
cryptesthesia
psychics 984n.
cryptic
uncertain 474adj.
occult 523adj.
concealed 525adj.
cabalistic 984adj.
crypto
latent 523adj.
cryptogram
enigma 530n.
cryptography
latency 523n.
secrecy 525n.
cry quits
submit 721vb.
be defeated 728vb.
cry shame
dispraise 924vb.
crystal
minuteness 196n.
covering 226n.
solid body 324n.
transparency 422n.
optical device 442n.
oracle 511n.
crystal-gazer
diviner 511n.
occultist 984n.
crystalline
symmetrical 245adj.
dense 324adj.
hard 326adj.
transparent 422adj.
crystallization
conversion 147n.
condensation 324n.
hardening 326n.
crystallize
efform 243vb.
be dense 324vb.
harden 326vb.
sweeten 392vb.
cry up
overrate 482vb.
praise 923vb.
flatter 925vb.
cry wolf
misteach 535vb.
be false 541vb.
raise the alarm 665vb.
frighten 854vb.
cub
youngster 132n.
youngling 132n.
cubature
size 195n.
measurement 465n.
cubby-hole
compartment 194n.
cube
do sums 86vb.
treble 94vb.
angular figure 247n.
cube root
numerical element 85n.
cubic
spatial 183adj.
angulated 247adj.
metric 465adj.
cubic content
space 183n.
measure 183n.
metrology 465n.
cubicle
compartment 194n.
chamber 194n.
cubism
school of painting 553n.
cubit
limb 53n.
long measure 203n.
cubital
brachial 53adj.
cuckold
spouse 894n.
be impure 951vb.
cuckold 952n.
cuckoldry
illicit love 951n.
cuckoo
intruder 59n.
repetition 106n.
ejector 300n.
bird 365n.
ululation 409n.
fool 501n.
crazed 503adj.
cucumber
vegetable 301n.
cucurbit
vessel 194n.
plant 366n.
heater 383n.
cud
mouthful 301n.
cuddle
be near 200vb.
caress 889vb.
cuddlesome
loving 878adj.
caressing 878adj.
cuddy
chamber 194n.
beast of burden 273n.
cudgel
strike 279vb.
club 723n.
flog 963vb.
scourge 964n.
cudgel one's brains
think 449vb.
cue
ram 279n.
reminder 505n.
hint 524n.
cuff
sleeve 228n.
fold 261n.
knock 279n.
corporal punishment 963n.
spank 963vb.
cuff-link
fastening 47n.
cuirass
armor 713n.
cuirassier
cavalry 722n.
cuisine
cookery 301n.
cul-de-sac
stopping place 145n.
cavity 255n.
closure 264n.
road 624n.
difficulty 700n.
obstacle 702n.
culex
fly 365n.
culinary
culinary 301adj.
cull
dupe 544n.
select 605vb.
take 786vb.
cully
befool 542vb.
dupe 544n.
culminate
culminate 34vb.
grow 36vb.
be complete 54vb.
be high 209vb.
crown 213vb.
ascend 308vb.
climax 725vb.

culpable
wrong 914adj.
blameworthy 924adj.
heinous 934adj.
guilty 936adj.
culprit
offender 904n.
accused person 928n.
cult
practice 610n.
business 622n.
fashion 848n.
affectation 850n.
religion 973n.
cult 981n.
rite 988n.
cult image
idol 982n.
cultism
ornament 574n.
affectation 850n.
cultivable
agrarian 370adj.
cultivate
produce 164vb.
make fruitful 171vb.
cultivate 370vb.
make better 654vb.
prepare 669vb.
patronize 703vb.
flatter 925vb.
cultivated
instructed 490adj.
cultivation
agriculture 370n.
culture 490n.
learning 536n.
civilization 654n.
maturation 669n.
good taste 846n.
cultivator
husbandman 370n.
countryman 869n.
cultural
educational 534adj.
improving 654adj.
culture
breed stock 369vb.
culture 490n.
learning 536n.
civilization 654n.
good taste 846n.
cultured
horticultural 370adj.
instructed 490adj.
spurious 542adj.
cultus
practice 610n.
culver
bird 365n.
culverin
gun 723n.
culvert
drain 351n.
access 624n.
cumber
weigh 322vb.
hinder 702vb.
cumbersome, cumbrous
weighty 322adj.
clumsy 695adj.
graceless 842adj.
cummerbund
girdle 47n.
belt 228n.
loop 250n.
cumulative
increasing 36adj.
cumulativeness
increase 36n.
continuity 71n.
cumulus
cloud 355n.
cunctation
delay 136n.
slowness 278n.
inaction 677n.
cuneate
angulated 247adj.
cuneiform
angulated 247adj.
letter 558n.
written 586adj.
cunning
sagacity 498n.
skill 694n.
cunning 698n., adj.
dishonest 930adj.
cup
cup 194n.
support 218vb.
cavity 255n.
void 300vb.
liquor 301n.
monument 548n.
doctor 658vb.
bane 659n.
trophy 729n.
adversity 731n.
suffering 825n.
painfulness 827n.
reward 962n.
ritual object 988n.
cup-bearer
retainer 742n.
cupboard
cabinet 194n.
shelf 218n.
storage 632n.
cupel
vessel 194n.
cup 194n.
heat 381vb.
testing agent 461n.
cupful
finite quantity 26n.
cup-holder
superior 34n.
proficient 696n.
Cupid
a beauty 841n.
love god 887n.
cupidity
avarice 816n.
desire 859n.
Cupid's bow
curve 248n.
coil 251n.
love emblem 887n.
cupola
high structure 209n.
roof 226n.
dome 253n.
cupping-glass
vessel 194n.
cupreous
brown 430adj.
orange 436adj.
cups
drunkenness 949n.
cur
dog 365n.
coward 856n.
cad 938n.
curable
improved 654adj.
restored 656adj.
medical 658adj.
curacy
church office 985n.
curate
pastor 986n.
curative
restorative 656adj.
remedial 658adj.
relieving 831adj.
curator
collector 492n.
protector 660n.
manager 690n.
keeper 749n.
curb
moderate 177vb.
edge 234n.
limit 236n.
slowness 278n.
retard 278vb.
road 624n.
safeguard 662n.
obstacle 702n.
restrain 747vb.
fetter 748n.
curb-crawler
libertine 952n.
curb-market
mart 796n.
curculio
vermin 365n.
curd
solid body 324n.
curdle
be dense 324vb.

thicken 354vb.
curds
milk 301n.
milk product 301n.
semiliquidity 354n.
cure
counteract 182vb.
make better 654vb.
sanation 656n.
cure 656vb.
remedy, therapy 658n.
preserve 666vb.
mature 669vb.
relieve 831vb.
church ministry 985n.
laity 987n.
cure-all
remedy 658n.
cureless
unpromising 853adj.
cure of
disaccustom 611vb.
cure of souls
vocation 622n.
mandate 751n.
church ministry 985n.
curette
doctor 658vb.
curfew
evening 129n.
danger signal 665n.
restriction 747n.
prohibition 757n.
curia
council 692n.
ecclesiastical court 956n.
curio
exhibit 522n.
masterpiece 694n.
ornamentation 844n.
curiosity
nonconformist 84n.
curiosity 453n.
excitation 821n.
desire 859n.
prodigy 864n.
curious
beautiful 841adj.
(*see* curiosity)
curious literature
impurity 951n.
curl
filament 208n.
curve 248n.
loop 250n.
coil 251n.
hair 259n.
fold 261vb.
badge of rank 743n.
hair-dressing 843n.
primp 843vb.
curler
thrower 287n.
curlers
fastening 47n.
hair-dressing 843n.
curlicue
coil 251n.
lettering 586n.
pattern 844n.
curling
sport 837n.
curling-iron
heater 383n.
hair-dressing 843n.
curly
undulatory 251adj.
hairy 259adj.
curmudgeon
niggard 816n.
rude person 885n.
curragh
rowboat 275n.
currant
fruit 301n.
currency
existence 1n.
generality 79n.
publicity 528n.
money 797n.
current
existing 1adj.
general 79adj.
present 121adj.
happening 154adj.
electricity 160n.
motion 265n.
direction 281n.
progression 285n.
current 350n.
wind 352n.
known 490adj.
published 528adj.
usual 610adj.
curricle
carriage 274n.
curriculum
curriculum 534n.
curried
pungent 388adj.
currish
cowardly 856adj.
irascible 892adj.
sullen 893adj.
rascally 930adj.
curry
cook 301vb.
rub 333vb.
pungency 388n.
season 388vb.
condiment 389n.
curry-comb
rub 333vb.
groom 369vb.
curry favor
be servile 879vb.
flatter 925vb.
curse
influence 178n.
badness 645n.
bane 659n.
adversity 731n.
annoyance 827n.
discontent 829n.
malediction 899n.
condemn 961vb.
be impious 980vb.
spell 983n.
cursed
damnable 645adj.
sullen 893adj.
cursitor
notary 958n.
cursive
written 586adj.
cursory
inconsiderable 33adj.
transient 114adj.
inattentive 456adj.
hasty 680adj.
curst
irascible 892adj.
sullen 893adj.
curt
short 204adj.
concise 569adj.
taciturn 582adj.
curtail
subtract 39vb.
cut, sunder 46vb.
shorten 204vb.
curtain
separation 46n.
exclusion 57n.
end 69n.
recurrence 106n.
hang 217vb.
surround 230vb.
fence 235n.
partition 321n.
darken 418vb.
screen 421vb.
invisibility 444n.
dramaturgy 594n.
stage-set 594n.
obstacle 702n.
fortification 713n.
curtain-call
recurrence 106n.
dramaturgy 594n.
applause 923n.
curtain lecture
reprimand 924n.
curtain-raiser
beginning 68n.
stage play 594n.
curtsy
stoop 311vb.
obeisance 311n.
greet 884vb.

show respect 920vb.
curule
parliamentary 692adj.
curvaceous
curved 248adj.
convex 253adj.
shapely 841adj.
curvation
curvature 248n.
curvature
obliquity 220n.
curvature 248n.
curve
obliquity 220n.
curve 248n.
deviate 282vb.
circle 314vb.
curves
bluntness 257n.
beauty 841n.
curvet
equitation 267n.
leap 312n., vb.
curvilinear
curved 248adj.
curving
unsharpened 257adj.
cushat
bird 365n.
cushion
moderate 177vb.
seat, cushion 218n.
support 218vb.
line 227vb.
intermediary 231n.
put between 231vb.
soften 327vb.
euphoria 376n.
protection 660n.
defend 713vb.
relieve 831vb.
cushy
pleasurable 826adj.
content 828adj.
cusp
extremity 69n.
vertex 213n.
angularity 247n.
sharp point 256n.
cuspidate
sharp 256adj.
cuspidor
bowl 194n.
cuss
scurrility 899n.
cuss 899vb.
cussedness
opposition 704n.
malevolence 898n.
custard
pudding 301n.
custodial
tutelary 660adj.
restraining 747adj.
custodian
protector 660n.
manager 690n.
interceptor 702n.
defender 713n.
keeper 749n.
custody
protection 660n.
detention 747n.
custody, in
safe 660adj.
imprisoned 747adj.
captive 750adj.
custom
order 60n.
continuity 71n.
generality 79n.
regularity 81n.
tradition 127n.
permanence 144n.
habit 610n.
barter 791n.
purchase 792n.
etiquette 848n.
customable
priced 809adj.
customary
preceptive 693adj.
unastonishing 865adj.
orthodox 976adj.
(*see* custom)
customer
person 371n.
habitué 610n.
patron 707n.
purchaser 792n.
customhouse
mart 796n.
treasury 799n.
customs
conduct 688n.
receipt 807n.
tax 809n.
cut
adjust 24vb.
diminution 37n.
subtract 39vb.
decrement 42n.
cut 46vb.
piece 53n.
discontinuity 72n.
gap 201n.
shorten 204vb.
lamina 207n.
form 243n.
excavation 255n.
be sharp 256vb.
smooth 258vb.
notch 260n.
groove 262vb.
move fast 277vb.
knock 279n.
eject 300vb.
meat 301n.
give pain 377vb.
feature 445n.
disregard 458vb.
sculpt 554vb.
engrave 555vb.
wound 655n., vb.
not observe 769vb.
portion 783n.
discount 810n., vb.
cheapen 812vb.
hurt 827vb.
hair-dressing 843n.
fashion 848n.
make unwelcome 883vb.
be rude 885vb.
cut above, a
superior 34adj.
cut a dash
be important 638vb.
have repute 866vb.
be ostentatious 875vb.
cut a figure
appear 445vb.
be in fashion 848vb.
(*see* cut a dash)
cut and come again
repeat 106vb.
cut and dried
definite 80adj.
ready-made 669adj.
cut and thrust
foin 712n.
fight 716n.
cutaneous
dermal 226adj.
cut back
bate 37vb.
subtract 39vb.
shorten 204vb.
cut both ways
tell against 467vb.
be equivocal 518vb.
cutcherry
management 689n.
courtroom 956n.
cut down
demolish 165vb.
fell 311vb.
slaughter 362vb.
strike at 712vb.
(*see* cut back)
cute
personable 841adj.
cut glass
ornamental art 844n.
cut ice
influence 178vb.
cuticle
skin 226n.
cuticular
dermal 226adj.
cutie
a beauty 841n.

cut in
join a party 708vb.
cutis
skin 226n.
cutlass
sharp edge 256n.
side arms 723n.
cutlery
sharp edge 256n.
cutlet
piece 53n.
(*see* meat)
cut off
set apart 46vb.
suppress 165vb.
circumscribe 232vb.
kill 362vb.
be concise 569vb.
hinder 702vb.
impoverish 801vb.
cut of one's jib
form 243n.
feature 445n.
cut out
be superior 34vb.
substitute 150vb.
efform 243vb.
plan 623vb.
cut out for
fit 24adj.
expedient 642adj.
cut price
discount 810n.
cheap 812adj.
cutpurse
thief 798n.
cut short
halt 145vb.
suppress 165vb.
shorten 204vb.
be concise 569vb.
cutter
clothier 228n.
sharp edge 256n.
boat 275n.
farm tool 370n.
epitomizer 592n.
artisan 686n.
cut the Gordian knot
disencumber 701vb.
cut-throat
destructive 165adj.
murderer 362n.
contending 716adj.
ruffian 904n.
cut through
pierce 263vb.
cutting
scission 46n.
excavation 255n.
sharp 256adj.
cinema 445n.
forceful 571adj.
railroad 624n.
cuttings
record 548n.
anthology 592n.
cut to the quick
hurt 827vb.
cutty stool
penitence 939n.
penance 941n.
pillory 964n.
cut up
unhappy 825adj.
hurt 827vb.
sadden 834vb.
cut up rough
be angry 891vb.
resent 891vb.
cwm
valley 255n.
cyanic
blue 435adj.
cyanide
poison 659n.
cyanin, cyanine
blue pigment 435n.
cyanosis
blueness 435n.
cybernetics
mechanics 630n.
cyclamen
redness 431n.
cycle
recurrence 106n.
era 110n.
regular return 141n.
orbit 250n.
ride 267vb.
bicycle 274n.
cycle-rickshaw
cab 274n.
bicycle 274n.
cycling
land travel 267adj.
cyclist
rider 268n.
cycloid
arc 250n.
cyclometer
meter 465n.
cyclone
vortex 315n.
weather 340n.
gale 352n.
cyclopean
huge 195adj.
cyclopedia
reference book 589n.
Cyclops
rara avis 84n.
giant 195n.
cyclorama
spectacle 445n.
cyclotron
nucleonics 160n.
cygnet
youngling 132n.
waterfowl 365n.
cylinder
cylinder 252n.
cylindrical
rotund 252adj.
tubular 263adj.
cymbalo
piano 414n.
cymbals
gong 414n.
cynic
misanthrope 902n.
detractor 926n.
ascetic 945n.
cynical
indifferent 860adj.
disrespectful 921adj.
disapproving 924adj.
detracting 926adj.
(*see* cynicism)
cynicism
philosophy 449n.
moral insensibility 820n.
dejection 834n.
hopelessness 853n.
misanthropy 902n.
asceticism 945n.
cynosural
well-seen 443adj.
cynosure
prototype 23n.
focus 76n.
attraction 291n.
spectacle 445n.
signpost 547n.
desired object 859n.
prodigy 864n.
person of repute 866n.
pride 871n.
favorite 890n.
cypress
tree 366n.
lamentation 836n.
cyst
bladder 194n.
cystic
capsular 194adj.
cytoblast, cytoplasm
organism 358n.
cytogenetics
biology 358n.
cytology
biology 358n.
czar
sovereign 741n.
czardom
magistrature 733n.
czarism
despotism 733n.
brute force 735n.

D

dab
knock 279n.
leap 312vb.
proficient 696n.
dabble
moisten 341vb.
make unclean 649vb.
be inactive 679vb.
amuse oneself 837vb.
dabbler
experimenter 461n.
sciolist 493n.
meddler 678n.
dabbling
smattering 491adj.
dabchick
waterfowl 365n.
dabs
trace 548n.
dabster
proficient 696n.
da capo
again 106adv.
dace
table fish 365n.
dachshund
dog 365n.
dacoit
robber 789n.
dacoity
stealing 788n.
dactyl
prosody 593n.
dactylogy
deafness 416n.
symbology 547n.
gesture 547n.
dactylonomy
numeration 86n.
dad, daddy
parent 169n.
dadaist
artist 556n.
dado
base 214n.
Daedal, Daedalian
variegated 437adj.
well-made 694adj.
ornamental 844adj.
daffodil
yellowness 433n.
daft, daffy
foolish 499adj.
crazed 503adj.
dagger
sharp point 256n.
punctuation 547n.
sidearms 723n.
daggers drawn, at
opposing 704adj.
quarreling 709adj.
inimical 881adj.
daggle
hang 217vb.
make unclean 649vb.
dago
foreigner 59n.
dagoba
temple 990n.
daguerreotype
photograph 551n.
dah
sharp edge 256n.
dai
obstetrics 164n.
Dail Eireann
parliament 692n.
daily
often 139adv.
seasonal 141adj.
periodically 141adv.
the press, journal 528n.
usual 610adj.
servant 742n.
daily bread
food 301n.
vocation 622n.
daily round
uniformity 16n.
continuity 71n.
regular return 141n.
habit 610n.
business 622n.
dainty
small 33adj.
little 196adj.
food 301n.
savory 390adj.
clean 648adj.
pleasurableness 826n.
shapely 841adj.
personable 841adj.
tasteful 846adj.
fastidious 862adj.
dairy
chamber 194n.
workshop 687n.
dairy farm
stock farm 369n.
farm 370n.
dairymaid
domestic 742n.
dais
stand 218n.
rostrum 539n.
dak bungalow
inn 192n.
Dalai Lama
sovereign 741n.
priest 986n.
dale
plain 348n.
dalesman
dweller 191n.
dalliance
love-making 887n.
endearment 889n.
dally
be late 136vb.
be irresolute 601vb.
be inactive 679vb.
amuse oneself 837vb.
caress 889vb.
dalmatic
vestments 989n.
Daltonism
dim sight 440n.
dam
be akin 11vb.
exclusion 57n.
halt 145vb.
maternity 169n.
close 264vb.
irrigator 341n.
lake 346n.
stanch 350vb.
obstruct 702vb.
damage
break 46vb.
derange 63vb.
weaken 163vb.
lay waste 165vb.
tell against 467vb.
evil 616n.
waste 634n.
make insufficient 636vb.
inutility 641n.
harm 645vb.
impairment 655n.
cost 809n.
blemish 845vb.
defame 926vb.
damages
offset 31n.
restitution 787n.
cost 809n.
penalty 963n.
damaging
harmful 645adj.
discreditable 867adj.
maleficent 898adj.
damascene
variegate 437vb.
damask
textile 222n.
red color 431n.
dame
lady 373n.
teacher 537n.
master 741n.
title 870n.
dammed
born 360adj.
damn
scurrility 899n.
curse, cuss 899vb.
dispraise 924vb.

condemn 961vb.
damnable
evil 616adj.
damnable 645adj.
unpleasant 827adj.
heterodox 977adj.
damnably
extremely 32adv.
damnation
future state 124n.
suffering 825n.
condemnation 961n.
damnatory
maledictory 899adj.
disapproving 924adj.
accusing 928adj.
damnify
harm 645vb.
impair 655vb.
damn the consequences
be obstinate 602vb.
be rash 857vb.
damp
moderate 177vb.
gas 336n.
water 339n.
moisture 341n.
extinguish 382vb.
mute 401vb.
sound dead 405vb.
hinder 702vb.
deject 834vb.
damped
incombustible 382adj.
non-resonant 405adj.
dampen
dissuade 613vb.
(*see* damp)
damper
moderator 177n.
stopper 264n.
heater 383n.
silencer 401n.
non-resonance 405n.
piano, mute 414n.
dissuasion 613n.
hinderer 702n.
moper 834n.
disapprover 924n.
damp-proof
unyielding 162adj.
dry 342adj.
damp squib
insubstantial thing 4n.
disappointment 509n.
damsel
youngster 132n.
damson
fruit 301n.
redness 431n.
dance
vary 152vb.
be in motion 265vb.
walk 267vb.
ascend 308vb.
leap 312n., vb.
fluctuation 317n.
oscillate 317vb.
be agitated 318vb.
shine 417vb.
be excited 821vb.
be excitable 822vb.
be cheerful 833vb.
rejoice 835vb.
dance 837n., vb.
dancing 837n.
social gathering 882n.
be angry 891vb.
dance attendance
accompany 89vb.
wait 136vb.
follow 284vb.
be servile 789vb.
dance-floor, dance-hall
place of amusement 837n.
dancer
jumper 312n.
dance 837n.
dance-step
gait 265n.
leap 312n.
dancing
gay 833adj.
dancing 837n.
dancing girl
entertainer 594n.
dancing-master
trainer 537n.
dancing school
academy 539n.
dander
anger 891n.
dandified
fashionable 848adj.
dandiprat
dwarf 196n.
fop 848n.
dandle
caress 889vb.
dandruff
dirt 649n.
dandy
vehicle 274n.
sailing-ship 275n.
topping 644adj.
fop 848n.
fashionable 848adj.
affector 850n.
dandyism
affectation 850n.
danegeld
tax 809n.
danger
probability 471n.
unreliability 474n.
omen 511n.
latency 523n.
danger 661n.
pitfall 663n.
danger, in
liable 180adj.
endangered 661adj.
in difficulties 700adj.
danger list, on the
sick 651adj.
dangerous
harmful 645adj.
dangerous 661adj.
difficult 700adj.
frightening 854adj.
inimical 881adj.
angry 891adj.
irascible 892adj.
malevolent 898adj.
threatening 900adj.
danger signal
signal 547n.
dissuasion 613n.
danger signal 665n.
threat 900n.
danger-spot
pitfall 663n.
dangle
come unstuck 49vb.
wait 136vb.
pendant 217n.
hang 217vb.
oscillate 317vb.
show 522vb.
cause desire 859vb.
dangler
follower 284n.
Daniel
sage 500n.
dank
humid 341adj.
cheerless 834adj.
danseuse
actor 594n.
dao
sharp edge 256n.
dapper
personable 841adj.
dapple
brown 430adj.
variegate 437vb.
dappled
pied 437adj.
darbies
fetter 748n.
dare
be resolute 599vb.
face danger 661vb.
undertake 672vb.
oppose 704vb.
defy 711vb.
be free 744vb.
be courageous 855vb.
threat 900n.
dare-devil
brave person 855n.

desperado 857n.
rash 857adj.
dare say
assume 471vb.
daric
coinage 797n.
daring
undisguised 522adj.
showy 875adj.
unchaste 951adj.
(*see* dare)
dark
vespertine 129adj.
dark 418adj.
black 428adj.
brown 430adj.
blind 439adj.
invisible 444adj.
unknown 491adj.
ignorant 491adj.
unintelligible 517adj.
latent 523adj.
imperspicuous 568adj.
sullen 893adj.
dishonest 930adj.
cabalistic 984adj.
Dark Ages
antiquity 125n.
unknown thing 491n.
darken
darken 418vb.
blind 439vb.
blur 440vb.
be unseen 444vb.
conceal 525vb.
deject 834vb.
make ugly 842vb.
dark glasses
screen 421n.
eyeglass 442n.
dark horse
unknown thing 491n.
latency 523n.
secret 530n.
dark, in the
darkling 418adv.
invisibly 444adv.
ignorant 491adj.
dark-lantern
glimmer 419n.
lamp 420n.
darkness
uncertainty 474n.
ignorance 491n.
(*see* dark)
darkness, in
heathenish 974adj.
dark-room
darkness 418n.
dark-skinned
blackish 428adj.
darky
negro 428n.
darling
loved one 887n.
lovable 887adj.
darling 890n.
favorite 890n.
darn
join 45vb.
repair 656n., vb.
dart
vary 152vb.
move fast 277vb.
missile 287n.
propel 287vb.
missile weapon 723n.
darting pain
pang 377n.
Darwinism
biology 358n.
dash
small quantity 33n.
tincture 43n.
bond 47n.
vigorousness 174n.
spurt 277n.
move fast 277vb.
be agitated 318vb.
flow 350vb.
punctuation 547n.
mark 547vb.
resolution 599n.
be active 678vb.
hasten 680vb.
racing 716n.
defeat 727vb.
warm feeling 818n.
fashion 848n.
courage 855n.
ostentation 875n.
dash against
collide 279vb.
dash at
charge 712vb.
dash down
fell 311vb.
dashed
humbled 872adj.
dashing
(*see* dash)
dash one's hopes
disappoint 509vb.
miscarry 728vb.
dastard
coward 856n.
dastur
reward 962n.
data, datum
evidence 466n.
premise 475n.
supposition 512n.
datal
chronological 117n.
datary
chronologist 117n.
date
date 108n.
chronology 117n.
fruit 301n.
social round 882n.
lover 887n.
dateless
perpetual 115adj.
datelessness
neverness 109n.
date-line
dividing line 92n.
limit 236n.
date-list
chronology 117n.
date-palm
tree 366n.
date up
be sociable 882vb.
datum
(*see* data)
datura
poisonous plant 659n.
daub
coat 226vb.
color 425vb.
unmeaningness 515n.
misrepresentation 552n.
picture 553n.
paint 553vb.
make unclean 649vb.
dauber
artist 556n.
bungler 697n.
daughter
descendant 170n.
woman 373n.
daughterly
filial 170adj.
obedient 739adj.
daunt
dissuade 613vb.
frighten 854vb.
humiliate 872vb.
dauntless
unfearing 855adj.
dauphin
sovereign 741n.
davenport
cabinet 194n.
davit
hanger 217n.
daw
fool 501n.
dawdle
drag on 113vb.
be late 136vb.
wander 267vb.
walk 267vb.
move slowly 278vb.
be inactive 679vb.
dawdler
slowcoach 278n.
idler 679n.
dawn

precursor 66n.
beginning 68n.
morning 128n.
make bright 417vb.
redness 431n.
appear 445vb.
dawn man
mankind 371n.
dawn upon
be visible 443vb.
dawn upon 449vb.
day
date 108n.
period 110n.
day after day
repeatedly 106adv.
perpetually 139adv.
day and night
perpetually 139adv.
day-book
record 548n.
account book 808n.
daybreak
morning 128n.
half-light 419n.
day by day
repeatedly 106adv.
while 108adv.
all along 113adv.
periodically 141adv.
daydream
fantasy 513n.
desire 959n., vb.
daydreaming
abstractedness 456n.
fantasy 513n.
daylight
interval 201n.
light 417n.
manifestation 522n.
disclosure 526n.
daylight saving
clock time 117n.
day of abstinence
fast 946n.
day off
lull 145n.
leisure 681n.
repose 683n.
day of judgment
finality 69n.
punishment 963n.
day of obligation
holy-day 988n.
day of reckoning
revenge 910n.
punishment 963n.
day of rest
repose 683n.
holy-day 988n.
day of the week
date 108n.
days
time 108n.
era 110n.
days of grace
delay 136n.
day-star
morning 128n.
sun 321n.
daze
blur 440vb.
distract 456vb.
puzzle 474vb.
be wonderful 864vb.
dazed
insensible 375adj.
dim-sighted 440adj.
distracted 456adj.
doubting 474adj.
foolish 499adj.
dazzle
light 417n.
shine 417vb.
blind 439vb.
blur 440vb.
be visible 443vb.
distract 456vb.
deceive 542vb.
impress 821vb.
be beautiful 841vb.
be wonderful 864vb.
prestige 866n.
be ostentatious 875vb.
excite love 887vb.
command respect 920vb.
dazzler
a beauty 841n.
dazzling
excellent 644adj.
(*see* dazzle)
D-day
start 68n.
date 108n.
special day 876n.
deacon
cleric 986n.
deaconess
nun 986n.
deaconship
church office 985n.
deactivate
weaken 163vb.
assuage 177vb.
impair 655vb.
deactivated
inert 175adj.
dead
unborn 2adj.
past 125adj.
inert 175adj.
quiescent 266adj.
dead 361adj.
insensible 375adj.
muted 401adj.
non-resonant 405adj.
soft-hued 425adj.
colorless 426adj.
non-active 677adj.
abrogated 752adj.
dead against
in opposition 704adv.
dead and buried
forgotten 506adj.
dead-beat
impotent 161adj.
impulse 279n.
fatigued 684adj.
dead body
corpse 363n.
dead center
centrality 225n.
dead-center
accurate 494adj.
dead earnest
seriousness 834n.
deaden
disable 161vb.
assuage 177vb.
kill 362vb.
render insensible 375vb.
mute 401vb.
sound dead 405vb.
decolorize 426vb.
make mute 578vb.
make insensitive 820vb.
relieve 831vb.
make inactive 879vb.
dead end
stopping place 145n.
closure 264n.
obstacle 702n.
dead-eye
orifice 263n.
deadfall
trap 542n.
deadhead
playgoer 594n.
recipient 782n.
dead heat
draw 28n.
synchronism 123n.
dead-house
death 361n.
deadish
tasteless 387adj.
dead letter
ineffectuality 161n.
unmeaningness 515n.
rubbish 641n.
abrogation 752n.
dead level
uniformity 16n.
horizontality 216n.
deadlight
glow-worm 420n.
curtain 421n.
deadline
limit 236n.

deadliness
(*see* deadly)
deadlock
draw 28n.
equilibrium 28n.
stop 145n.
quiescence 266n.
impossibility 470n.
difficulty 700n.
obstacle 702n.
non-completion 726n.
defeat 728n.
deadly
destructive 165adj.
vigorous 174adj.
deadly 362adj.
evil 616adj.
harmful 645adj.
toxic 653adj.
dull 840adj.
malevolent 898adj.
heinous 934adj.
dead man's handle
safeguard 662n.
dead march
obsequies 364n.
musical piece 412n.
deadness
(*see* dead)
dead of night
midnight 129n.
darkness 418n.
dead-on
accurate 494adj.
dead-pan
still 266adj.
impassive 820adj.
inexcitable 823adj.
serious 834adj.
dead reckoning
navigation 269n.
measurement 465n.
dead set at
attack 712n.
dead shot
proficient 696n.
dead spit
analogue 18n.
dead stop
stop 145n.
quiescence 266n.
hitch 702n.
failure 728n.
dead to
thick-skinned 820adj.
dead-weight
encumbrance 702n.
dead wood
rubbish 641n.
deaf
deaf 416adj.
inattentive 456adj.
indiscriminating
464adj.
obstinate 602adj.
non-active 677adj.
deaf and dumb
deaf 416adj.
voiceless 578adj.
deaf and dumb language
gesture 547n.
deafen
be loud 400vb.
deafen 416vb.
make insensitive
820vb.
deaf-mute
deafness 416n.
aphony 578n.
deafness
deafness 416n.
deal
great quantity 32n.
arrange 62vb.
disperse 75vb.
deed 676n.
compact 765n.
give 781vb.
portion 783n.
apportion 783vb.
trade 791n.
dealer
agent 686n.
seller 793n.
merchant 794n.
deal in
do 676vb.
trade 791vb.
dealings
deed 676n.
deal with
be related 9vb.
dissert 591vb.
deal with 688vb.
make terms 766vb.
trade 791vb.
dean
ecclesiarch 986n.
deanery
church office 985n.
parish 985n.
parsonage 986n.
deanship
seniority 131n.
church office 985n.
dear
known 490adj.
profitless 641adj.
dear 811adj.
pleasurable 826adj.
loved one 887n.
lovable 887adj.
darling 890n.
dearth
unproductivity 172n.
scarcity 636n.
dearness 811n.
death
extinction 2n.
decay 51n.
destroyer 168n.
quietude 266n.
death 361n.
death-bed
decease 361n.
illness 651n.
death, be in at the
arrive 295vb.
carry out 725vb.
deathblow
end 69n.
death 361n.
killing 362n.
defeat 728n.
death column
death roll 361n.
death-dealing
murderous 362adj.
death-duty
tax 809n.
deathhouse
prison camp 748n.
death-knell
decease 361n.
death 361n.
deathless
perpetual 115adj.
renowned 866adj.
deathlessness
famousness 866n.
deathlike
dying 361adj.
cadaverous 363adj.
silent 399adj.
deathliness
quiescence 266n.
deathly
dying 361adj.
deadly 362adj.
cadaverous 363adj.
colorless 426adj.
death mask
copy 22n.
death of
worry 825n.
annoyance 827n.
death rate
statistics 86n.
death roll 361n.
death-rattle
decease 361n.
death scene
decease 361n.
death sentence
capital punishment
963n.
death's head
moper 834n.
eyesore 842n.
disapprover 924n.
death-trap

danger 661adj.
pitfall 663n.
death-warrant
condemnation 961n.
capital punishment 963n.
death-watch
decease 361n.
death-wish
dejection 834n.
debacle
revolution 149n.
ruin 165n.
descent 309n.
defeat 728n.
debag
uncover 229vb.
debar
obstruct 702vb.
restrain 747vb.
prohibit 757vb.
refuse 760vb.
debase
abase 311vb.
pervert 655vb.
impair 655vb.
demonetize 797vb.
shame 867vb.
disentitle 916vb.
debasement
lowness 210n.
improbity 930n.
(*see* debase)
debatable
topical 452adj.
moot 459adj.
uncertain 474adj.
arguing 475adj.
debate
argument 475n.
conference 584n.
be irresolute 601vb.
contention 716vb.
debater
reasoner 475n.
debauch
pervert 655vb.
festivity 837n.
sensualism 944n.
drunkenness 949n.
debauch 951vb.
debauched
vicious 934adj.
debauchee
reveler 837n.
sensualist 944n.
libertine 952n.
debauchery
sensualism 944n.
unchastity 951n.
debenture
title-deed 767n.
paper money 797n.
debility
weakness 163n.
ill-health 651n.
debit
debt 803n.
account 808vb.
debonair
cheerful 833adj.
debouch
start out 296vb.
emerge, flow out 298vb.
debris
remainder 41n.
piece 53n.
accumulation 74n.
powder 332n.
rubbish 641n.
debt
encumbrance 702n.
debt 803n.
dueness 915n.
debt of honor
promise 764n.
compact 765n.
debtor
debtor 803n.
debunk
abase 311vb.
ridicule 851vb.
shame 867vb.
humiliate 872vb.
detract 926vb.
debut
debut 68n.
celebration 876n.
debutant, -e
beginner 538n.
fop 848n.
spinster 895n.
decad
over five 99n.
decade
over five 99n.
period 110n.
decadence
deterioration 655n.
decagon
angular figure 247n.
decalogue
code of duty 917n.
decamp
decamp 296vb.
disappear 446adj.
run away 620vb.
decant
transpose 272vb.
void 300vb.
let fall 311vb.
infuse 303vb.
decanter
vessel 194n.
transferrer 272n.
decapitate
subtract 39vb.
cut, sunder 46vb.
execute 963vb.
decarbonize
purify 648vb.
decathlon
contest 716n.
decay
extinction 2n.
decrease 37vb.
decay 51n.
be old 127vb.
age 131n.
destroyer 168n.
become small 198vb.
death 361n.
desuetude 611n.
waste 634vb.
badness 645n.
dirt 649n.
dilapidation 655n.
decease
decease 361n.
die 361vb.
deceit
deception 542n.
deceitful
false 541adj.
deceiving 542adj.
cunning 698adj.
deceive
mislead 495vb.
dissemble 541vb.
deceive 542vb.
be cunning 698vb.
be affected 850vb.
flatter 925vb.
be dishonest 930vb.
be impure 951vb.
deceived husband
cuckold 952n.
deceiver
deceiver 545n.
tergiversator 603n.
slyboots 698n.
affector 850n.
libertine 952n.
deceiving
simulating 18adj.
disappointing 509adj.
deceleration
diminution 37n.
delay 136n.
slowness 278n.
hindrance 702n.
restraint 747n.
Decembrist
revolter 738n.
decency
good taste 846n.
etiquette 848n.
right 913n.
purity 950n.
decennial
seasonal 141adj.

decennium
period 110n.
decent
not bad 644adj.
mediocre 732adj.
personable 841adj.
tasteful 846adj.
well-bred 848adj.
ethical 917adj.
pure 950adj.
decentralization
non-uniformity 17n.
decomposition 51n.
arrangement 62n.
dispersion 75n.
laxity 734n.
commission 751n.
deception
insubstantiality 4n.
concealment 525n.
(*see* deceptive)
deceptive
simulating 18adj.
appearing 445adj.
sophistical 477adj.
erroneous 495adj.
disappointing 509adj.
false 541adj.
deceiving 542adj.
de-christianize
paganize 974vb.
de-christianized
profane 980adj.
decibar
weather 340n.
decibel
sound 398n.
metrology 465n.
decide
terminate 69vb.
cause 156vb.
answer 460vb.
make certain 473vb.
judge 480vb.
be resolute 599vb.
choose 605vb.
decree 737vb.
try a case 959vb.
decided
assertive 532adj.
volitional 595adj.
decidedly
positively 32adv.
deciduous
ephemeral 114adj.
descending 309adj.
vegetal 366adj.
deteriorated 655adj.
decimal
numerical element 85n.
decimal point
punctuation 547n.
decimal system
numeration 86n.
decimate
bate 37vb.
multisect 100vb.
render few 105vb.
weaken 163vb.
destroy 165vb.
slaughter 362vb.
execute 963vb.
decipher
decipher 520vb.
decipherable
intelligible 516adj.
decipherment
interpretation 520n.
translation 520n.
decision
vigor 571n.
will 595n.
(*see* decide)
decisive
timely 137adj.
crucial 137adj.
causal 156adj.
influential 178adj.
evidential 466adj.
demonstrating 478adj.
assertive 532adj.
commanding 737adj.
decivilize
pervert 655vb.
deck
compartment 194n.
layer 207n.
roof 226n.
overlay 226vb.
dress 228vb.
plaything 837n.
decorate 844vb.
deckhand
mariner 270n.
deckle-edge
roughness 259n.
declaim
proclaim 528vb.
orate 579vb.
declaimer
speaker 579n.
declamation
vigor 571n.
magniloquence 574n.
oratory 579n.
ostentation 875n.
declarant
foreigner 59n.
declaration
(*see* declare)
declaration of faith
creed 485n.
declaratory
meaningful 514adj.
publishing 528adj.
affirming 532adj.
declare
evidence 466vb.
believe 485vb.
mean 514vb.
divulge 526vb.
proclaim 528vb.
affirm 532vb.
indicate 547vb.
speak 579vb.
decree 737vb.
resign 753vb.
declare war
quarrel 709vb.
attack 712vb.
go to war 718vb.
declassify
exclude 57vb.
derange 63vb.
declension
differentiation 15n.
change 143n.
transition 147n.
grammar 564n.
(*see* decline)
declination
bearings 186n.
divergence 294n.
descent 309n.
decline
inferiority 35n.
decrease 37n., vb.
oldness 127n.
weakness 163n.
be weak 163vb.
contraction 198n.
be oblique 220vb.
regression 286n.
recede 290vb.
descent 309n.
parse 564vb.
reject 607vb.
phthisis 651n.
deterioration 655n.
not use 674vb.
adversity 731n.
declivity
acclivity 220n.
descent 309n.
decoction
potion 301n.
solution 337n.
heating 381n.
decode
decipher 520vb.
decollation
capital punishment 963n.
décolleté
uncovering 229n.
decoloration
achromatism 426n.
decolorize
decolorize 426vb.
make ugly 842vb.

decompose
disjoin 46vb.
decompose 51vb.
disperse 75vb.
perish 361vb.
be unclean 649vb.
deteriorate 655vb.
decompound
decompose 51vb.
deconsecrate
depose 752vb.
paganize 974vb.
laicize 987vb.
deconsecrated
profane 980adj.
decontrol
liberation 746n.
permit 756vb.
non-retention 779n.
decor
spectacle 445n.
stage-set 594n.
pageant 875n.
decorate
beautify 841vb.
(*see* decoration)
decoration
concomitant 89n.
spectacle 445n.
badge 547n.
monument 548n.
ornament 574n.
improvement 654n.
decoration 729n.
badge of rank 743n.
ornamentation 844n.
honors 866n.
reward 962n.
decorative
painted 553adj.
ornamental 844adj.
decorator
mender 656n.
artisan 686n.
decorous
well-bred 848adj.
pure 950adj.
decortication
uncovering 229n.
decorum
good taste 846n.
etiquette 848n.
decoy
attraction 291n.
ambush 527n.
trap 542n.
trickster 545n.
incentive 612n.
decrease
decrease 37n., vb.
subtract 39vb.
unproductivity 172n.
become small 198vb.
disappear 446vb.
waste 634vb.
scarcity 636n.
deterioration 655n.
loss 772n.
decreasing
lesser 35adj.
decreasingly
diminuendo 37adv.
decree
judgment 480n.
publication 528n.
predetermination 608n.
precept 693n.
decree 737n., vb.
impose a duty 917vb.
legislation 953n.
decree absolute
divorce 896n.
decree nisi
divorce 896n.
decrement
decrease 37n.
subtraction 39n.
decrement 42n.
deficit 55n.
contraction 198n.
shortcoming 307n.
loss 772n.
discount 810n.
decrepit
aged 131adj.
weak 163adj.
unhealthy 651adj.
dilapidated 655adj.
decretal
judicial 480adj.
preceptive 693adj.
decree 737n.
commanding 737adj.
legal 983adj.
decrial
disapprobation 924n.
detraction 926n.
decry
hold cheap 922vb.
detract 926vb.
decuple
fifth and over 99adj.
decurion
army officer 741n.
decury
over five 99n.
formation 722n.
decussation
joint 45n.
crossing 222n.
dedecoration
disrepute 867n.
dedicate
offer 759vb.
give 781vb.
dignify 866vb.
sanctify 979vb.
offer worship 981vb.
perform ritual 988vb.
dedicated
habituated 610adj.
obedient 739adj.
philanthropic 901adj.
disinterested 931adj.
dedicate to
use 673vb.
honor 866vb.
dedication
nomenclature 561n.
edition 589n.
willingness 597n.
resolution 599n.
(*see* dedicated)
dedicator
commender 923n.
deduce
assume 471vb.
reason 475n.
demonstrate 478vb.
interpret 520vb.
deducible
evidential 466adj.
demonstrating 478adj.
deduct
disjoin 46vb.
(*see* deduction)
deduction
diminution 37n.
subtraction 39n.
decrement 42n.
reasoning 475n.
demonstration 478n.
judgment 480n.
non-payment 805n.
discount 810n.
deed
deed 676n.
conduct 688n.
title-deed 767n.
prowess 855n.
deed of arms
fight 716n.
deed-poll
title-deed 767n.
deem
opine 485vb.
deemster
judge 957n.
deep
great 32adj.
spacious 183adj.
deep 211adj.
interior 224adj.
ocean 343n.
loud 400adj.
hoarse 407adj.
florid 425adj.
black 428adj.
wise 498adj.
inexpressible 517adj.
concealed 525adj.
imperspicuous 568adj.

cunning 698adj.
felt 818adj.
heinous 934adj.
infernal 972adj.
deep down
intrinsic 5adj.
deepen
augment 36vb.
enlarge 197vb.
be deep 211vb.
blacken 428vb.
aggravate 832vb.
deep-freeze
refrigeration 382n.
cooled 382adj.
refrigerator 384n.
storage 632n.
preservation 666n.
deep in
ingredient 58adj.
attentive 455adj.
studious 536adj.
deep-laid
matured 669adj.
well-made 694adj.
cunning 698adj.
deepness
depth 211n.
deep-rooted
intrinsic 5adj.
lasting 113adj.
fixed 153adj.
strong 162adj.
deep 211adj.
habitual 610adj.
with affections 817adj.
deep-sea
seafaring 269n.
deep-seated
intrinsic 5adj.
lasting 113adj.
fixed 153adj.
deep 211adj.
interior 224adj.
habitual 610adj.
deep water, in
in difficulties 700adj.
deer
speeder 277n.
deer 365n.
coward 856n.
deer-stalker
hunter 619n.
deface
destroy 165vb.
deform 244vb.
obliterate 550vb.
make useless 641vb.
impair 655vb.
make ugly 842vb.
blemish 845vb.
defacer
destroyer 168n.
defalcate
be dishonest 930vb.
defalcation
deficit 55n.
shortcoming 307n.
non-payment 805n.
defamation
detraction 926n.
defamatory
disapproving 924adj.
detracting 926adj.
accusing 928adj.
defame
shame 867vb.
not respect 921vb.
defame 926vb.
accuse 928vb.
default
deficit 55n.
shortcoming 307n.
negligence 458n.
not suffice 636vb.
non-payment 805n.
not pay 805vb.
fail in duty 918vb.
defaulter
defrauder 789n.
debtor 803n.
non-payer 805n.
defeasance
abrogation 752n.
defeat
ruin 165n.
puzzle 474vb.
confute 479vb.
defeat 728n., vb.
defeated, the
loser 728n.
defeatism
inaction 677n.
dejection 834n.
hopelessness 853n.
nervousness 854n.
cowardice 856n.
defeatist
alarmist 854n.
misanthrope 902n.
(*see* defeatism)
defecation
cacation 302n.
cleansing 648n.
defect
inequality 29n.
inferiority 35n.
decrement 42n.
deficit 55n.
shortcoming 307n.
requirement 627n.
insufficiency 636n.
defect 647n.
blemish 845n.
vice 934n.
defectibility
imperfection 647n.
defection
tergiversation 603n.
relinquishment 621n.
disobedience 738n.
revolt 738n.
dutilessness 918n.
perfidy 930n.
defective
deformed 246adj.
insane 503adj.
(*see* defect)
defedation
uncleanness 649n.
impairment 655n.
defend
patronize 703vb.
defend 713vb.
resist 715vb.
defendant
prisoner 750n.
accused person 928n.
litigant 959n.
defended
strong 162adj.
defender
protector 660n.
patron 707n.
defender 713n.
combatant 722n.
vindicator 927n.
defense
counteraction 182n.
rejoinder 460n.
counter-evidence 467n.
argument 475n.
avoidance 620n.
protection 660n.
hindrance 702n.
defense 713n.
warfare 718n.
vindication 927n.
legal trial 959n.
defenseless
defenseless 161adj.
weak 163adj.
vulnerable 661adj.
defenses
protection 660n.
defenses 713n.
defenestrate
propel 287vb.
defenestration
propulsion 287n.
corporal punishment 963n.
defensible
invulnerable 660adj.
defended 713adj.
vindicable 927adj.
defensive
avoiding 620adj.
hindering 702adj.
defending 713adj.
nervous 854adj.
defer

put off 136vb.
not complete 726vb.
deference
submission 721n.
obedience 739n.
loyalty 739n.
courtesy 884n.
respect 920n.
deferential
(*see* deference)
deferment
delay 136n.
discount 810n.
defer to
assent 488vb.
defiance
dissent 489n.
affirmation 532n.
negation 533n.
opposition 704n.
dissension 709n.
defiance 711n.
disobedience 738n.
courage 855n.
boast 877n.
sauciness 878n.
defiant
unconformable 84adj.
undisguised 522adj.
deficiency
inferiority 35n.
incompleteness 55n.
insufficiency 636n.
imperfection 647n.
defect 647n.
non-completion 726n.
vice 934n.
deficient
small 33adj.
deficient 307adj.
unintelligent 499adj.
unprovided 636adj.
unequipped 670adj.
deficit
deficit 55n.
shortcoming 307n.
insufficiency 636n.
non-completion 726n.
debt 803n.
deficit finance
finance 797n.
prodigality 815n.
defile
gap 201n.
walk 267vb.
passage 305n.
access 624n.
make unclean 649vb.
impair, pervert 655vb.
shame 867vb.
debauch 951vb.
defilement
uncleanness 649n.
impairment 655n.
slur 867n.
impurity 951n.
define
specify 80vb.
limit 236vb.
interpret 520vb.
name 561vb.
definite
definite 80adj.
limited 236adj.
well-seen 443adj.
positive 473adj.
accurate 494adj.
intelligible 516adj.
manifest 522adj.
informative 524adj.
assertive 532adj.
perspicuous 567adj.
definition
limit 236n.
interpretation 520n.
perspicuity 567n.
theology 973n.
definitive
ending 69adj.
definite 80adj.
interpretive 520adj.
deflate
bate 37vb.
disable 161vb.
make smaller 198vb.
abase, depress 311vb.
underestimate 483vb.
ridicule 851vb.
shame 867vb.
humiliate 872vb.
detract 926vb.
deflation
finance 797n.
cheapness 812n.
deflationary
monetary 797adj.
deflect
render oblique 220vb.
make curved 248vb.
impel 279n.
deflect 282vb.
repel 292vb.
dissuade 613vb.
avoid 620vb.
parry 713vb.
deflection
curvature 248n.
deviation 282n.
defloration
(*see* deflower)
deflower
unite with 45vb.
pervert 655vb.
debauch 951vb.
deforest
extract 304vb.
deform
force 176vb.
deform 244vb.
distort 246vb.
misrepresent 552vb.
impair, pervert 655vb.
make ugly 842vb.
blemish 845vb.
deformed
abnormal 84adj.
disguised 525adj.
deformity
amorphism 244n.
deformity 246n.
ugliness 842n.
blemish 845n.
defraud
deceive 542vb.
defraud 788vb.
not pay 804vb.
be dishonest 930vb.
defrauder
trickster 545n.
defrayment
payment 804n.
defrock
depose 752vb.
shame 867vb.
defrost
heat 381vb.
deft
skillful 694adj.
defumigate
have no smell 395vb.
defunct
extinct 2adj.
dead 361adj.
corpse 363n.
unwonted 611adj.
defy
counteract 182vb.
dissent 489vb.
negate 533vb.
be resolute 599vb.
face danger 661vb.
oppose 704vb.
defy 711vb.
resist 715vb.
disobey 738vb.
be free 744vb.
be insolent 878vb.
degauss
counteract 182vb.
degeneracy
deterioration 655n.
wickedness 934n.
degenerate
changed person 147n.
be turned to 147vb.
deteriorated 655adj.
deteriorate 655vb.
relapse 657vb.
vicious 934adj.
cad 938n.
sensualist 944n.
degenerative

harmful 645adj.
diseased 651adj.
deglutition
eating 301n.
degrade
bate 37vb.
impair, pervert 655vb.
depose 752vb.
shame 867vb.
not respect 921vb.
hold cheap 922vb.
defame 926vb.
punish 963vb.
degree
relativeness 9n.
degree 27n.
series 71n.
angular measure 247n.
measurement 465n.
prestige 866n.
nobility 868n.
degree-holder
scholar 492n.
degree-hungry
studious 536adj.
degree of latitude
long measure 203n.
degree of longitude
long measure 203n.
degrees, by
gradatim 278adv.
degree, to some
partially 33adv.
degustation
taste 386n.
dehortation
dissuasion 613n.
warning 664n.
deprecation 762n.
dehumanize
pervert 655vb.
make wicked 934vb.
dehumanized
cruel 898adj.
dehumidify
dry 342vb.
dehydration
desiccation 342n.
preservation 666n.
de-ice
heat 381vb.
deific
theotechnic 966adj.
deification
dignification 866n.
deification 982n.
deify
dignify 866vb.
worship 891vb.
idolatrize 982vb.
deign
consent 758vb.
deism
philosophy 449n.
religion, deism 973n.
deist
religionist 973n.
deity
divineness 965n.
Deity, the
cause 156n.
the Deity 965n.
dejected
unhappy 825adj.
dejection
discontent 829n.
dejection 834n.
hopelessness 853n.
de jure
due 915adj.
duly 915adv.
legal 953adj.
legally 953adv.
dekink
straighten 249vb.
dekko
inspection 438n.
delaminate
laminate 207vb.
delation
accusation 928n.
delator
informer 524n.
accuser 928n.
delay
protraction 113n.
delay 136n.
lull 145n.
slowness 278n.
be irresolute 601vb.
inaction 677n.
be inactive 679vb.
caution 858n.
delaying
hindering 702adj.
delaying action
avoidance 620n.
dele
obliterate 550vb.
delectable
savory 390adj.
pleasurable 826adj.
delectation
enjoyment 824n.
delectus
textbook 589n.
reading matter 589n.
anthology 592n.
delegate
agent 686n.
councillor 692n.
mediator 720n.
commission 751vb.
delegate 754n.
delegation
commission 751n.
delegate 754n.
transfer 780n.
deleted
disapproved 924adj.
deleterious
harmful 645adj.
deletion
subtraction 39n.
obliteration 550n.
deliberate
slow 278adj.
predetermined 608adj.
intended 617adj.
leisurely 681adj.
consult 691vb.
cautious 858adj.
deliberation
meditation 449n.
slowness 278n.
caution 858n.
deliberative
thoughtful 449adj.
advising 691adj.
deliberative assembly
parliament 692n.
delicacy
weakness 163n.
savoriness 390n.
discrimination 463n.
ill-health 651n.
beauty 841n.
good taste 846n.
fastidiousness 862n.
purity 950n.
delicate
brittle 330adj.
textural 331adj.
soft-hued 425adj.
accurate 494adj.
difficult 700adj.
pleasurable 826adj.
(*see* delicacy)
delicatessen
pastry 301n.
delicious
edible 301adj.
pleasant 376adj.
savory 390adj.
topping 644adj.
pleasurable 826adj.
delight
pleasure 376n.
excite 821vb.
joy 824n.
pleasurableness 826n.
delight 826vb.
amusement 837n.
amuse 837vb.
delighted
willing 597adj.
jubilant 833adj.
delightful
pleasant 376adj.
pleasurable 826adj.
delight in

be pleased 824vb.
delimit
limit 236vb.
mark 547vb.
apportion 783vb.
delineation
outline 233n.
representation 551n.
description 590n.
delinquency
shortcoming 307n.
wickedness 934n.
guilt 936n.
delinquent
trouble-maker 663n.
low fellow 869n.
offender 904n.
deliquescence
decrease 37n.
liquefaction 337n.
deliquium
helplessness 161n.
fatigue 684n.
delirium
frenzy 503n.
fantasy 513n.
unmeaningness 515n.
illness 651n.
excitable state 822n.
delirium tremens
frenzy 503n.
alcoholism 949n.
delitescence
invisibility 444n.
latency 523n.
seclusion 883n.
deliver
transfer 272vb.
provide 633vb.
restore 656vb.
preserve 666vb.
deliver 668vb.
disencumber 701vb.
aid 703vb.
liberate 746vb.
convey 780vb.
give 781vb.
restitute 787vb.
relieve 831vb.
vindicate 927vb.
deliverance
safety 660n.
escape 667n.
(*see* deliver)
deliverer
preserver 666n.
defender 713n.
benefactor 903n.
deliver the goods
be expedient 642vb.
carry out 725vb.
delivery
obstetrics 164n.
transference 272n.
voice 577n.
speech 579n.
provision 633n.
deliverance 668n.
transfer 780n.
dell
valley 255n.
delousing
cleansing 648n.
delta
land 344n.
gulf 345n.
plain 348n.
delude
deceive 542vb.
(*see* delusion)
deluge
crowd 74n.
drench 341vb.
flow 350vb.
superabound 637vb.
delusion
error 495n.
fantasy 513n.
deception 542n.
delusions
psychopathy 503n.
delusive
erroneous 495adj.
deceiving 542adj.
deluxe
comfortable 376adj.
ostentatious 875adj.
delve
make concave 255vb.
cultivate 370vb.
delve into
inquire 459vb.
demagogue
leader 690n.
agitator 738n.
demagogy
government 733n.
demand
inquire 459vb.
require 627vb.
warning 664n.
demand 737n., vb.
request 761n., vb.
give terms 766vb.
purchase 792n.
desire 859n., vb.
claim 915vb.
demanding
fatiguing 684adj.
demarcate
limit 236vb.
mark 547vb.
apportion 783vb.
demarche
debut 68n.
dematerialize
not be 2vb.
disembody 320vb.
disappear 446vb.
practise occultism 984vb.
demeaning
degrading 867adj.
demean oneself
behave 688vb.
demean oneself 867vb.
demeanor
mien 445n.
gesture 547n.
conduct 688n.
dement
make mad 503vb.
démenti
negation 533n.
dementia
insanity 503n.
demerit
undueness 916n.
vice 934n.
demesne
farm 370n.
lands 777n.
demi-
bisected 92adj.
demibastion
fortification 713n.
demigod
god 966n.
demigod 967n.
demigration
wandering 267n.
demijohn
vessel 194n.
demilitarize
disable 161vb.
make peace 719vb.
demilune
fortification 713n.
demi-monde
lower classes 869n.
wickedness 934n.
prostitute 952n.
demi-rep
prostitute 952n.
loose woman 952n.
demise
decease 361n.
die 361vb.
bequeath 780vb.
lease 784vb.
demission
resignation 753n.
demiurge
the Deity 965n.
demivolt
leap 312n.
demobilization
dispersion 75n.
impotence 161n.
peace 717n.
pacification 719n.

liberation 746n.
democracy
nation 371n.
government 733n.
commonalty 869n.
democrat
commoner 869n.
democratic
equal 28adj.
governmental 733adj.
demography
statistics 86n.
anthropology 371n.
demolish
break 46vb.
revolutionize 149vb.
demolish 165vb.
fell 311vb.
confute 479vb.
demolition
destruction 165n.
demon
violent creature 176n.
monster 938n.
devil 969n.
demon 970n.
demonetize
demonetize 797vb.
not pay 805vb.
demoniac
cruel 898adj.
diabolic 969adj.
demoniac possession
spell 983n.
demonic
active 678adj.
diabolic 969adj.
fairylike 970adj.
demonifuge
talisman 983n.
demonism
diabolism 969n.
demonist
idolater 982n.
demonolater
diabolist 969n.
idolater 982n.
demonology
diabolism 969n.
demonstrable
certain 473adj.
demonstrate
demonstrate 478vb.
interpret 520vb.
show 522vb.
be expert 694vb.
defy 711vb.
revolt 738vb.
deprecate 762vb.
show feeling 818vb.
demonstrated
true 494adj.
demonstration
ostentation 875n.
(*see* demonstrate)
demonstrative
evidential 466adj.
indicating 547adj.
with affections 817adj.
friendly 880adj.
loving 887adj.
caressing 889adj.
demonstrator
guide 520n.
exhibitor 522n.
agitator 738n.
rioter 738n.
demoralization
deterioration 655n.
wickedness 934n.
demos
nation 371n.
commonalty 869n.
demote
punish 963vb.
(*see* demotion)
demotic
linguistic 557adj.
written 586adj.
demotion
diminution 37n.
descent 309n.
depression 311n.
deposal 752n.
disrepute 867n.
demur
qualification 468n.
argue 475vb.
doubt 486n., vb.
dissent 489n., vb.
negate 533vb.
be loath 598vb.
defy 711vb.
resistance 715n.
deprecate 762vb.
disapprove 924vb.
demure
inexcitable 823adj.
serious 834adj.
affected 850adj.
modest 874adj.
demurrage
delay 136n.
demurrer
litigation 959n.
(*see* demur)
demyship
reward 962n.
demythologization
interpretation 520n.
theology 973n.
den
dwelling, retreat 192n.
chamber 194n.
cavity 255n.
hiding-place 527n.
refuge 662n.
lock-up 748n.
seclusion 883n.
denary
fifth and over 99adj.
denationalize
derange 63vb.
pervert 655vb.
disentitle 916vb.
denaturalization
conversion 147n.
loss of right 916n.
denaturalize
pervert 655vb.
disentitle 916vb.
denature
modify 143vb.
weaken 163vb.
impair, pervert 655vb.
denazify
void 300vb.
dendrific
arboreal 366adj.
dendriform
symmetrical 245adj.
arboreal 366adj.
dendrological
arboreal 366adj.
dendrology
forestry 366n.
botany 368n.
dene
valley 255n.
plain 348n.
dengue
infection 651n.
denial
confutation 479n.
unbelief 486n.
dissent 489n.
negation 533n.
recantation 603n.
rejection 607n.
opposition 704n.
refusal 760n.
denier
texture 331n.
unbeliever 486n.
denigration
blackness 428n.
detraction 926n.
denims
trousers 228n.
denization
freedom 744n.
denizen
dweller 191n.
denomination
classification 77n.
nomenclature 561n.
party 708n.
denominational
sectional 708adj.
Protestant 976adj.
sectarianism 978n.
denominative

part of speech 564n.
denominator
numerical element 85n.
denotable
marked 547adj.
denotation
connotation 514n.
denotative
semantic 514adj.
denote
specify 80vb.
mean 514vb.
indicate 547vb.
denouement
eventuality 154n.
effect 157n.
evolution 316n.
disclosure 526n.
completion 725n.
denounce
inform 524vb.
proclaim 528vb.
satirize 851vb.
hate 888vb.
curse 899vb.
dispraise 924vb.
defame 926vb.
accuse 928vb.
de novo
again 106adv.
dense
firm-set 45adj.
multitudinous 104adj.
unyielding 162adj.
thick 205adj.
closed 264n.
dense 324adj.
tactual 378adj.
ignorant 491adj.
unintelligent 499adj.
densen
be dense 324vb.
densimeter
density 324n.
density
materiality 319n.
density 324n.
semiliquidity 354n.
opacity 423n.
(*see* dense)
dent
concavity 255n.
notch 260n., vb.
depression 311n.
dental
toothed 256adj.
speech sound 398n.
spoken letter 558n.
dentate
notched 260adj.
denticulation
tooth 256n.
dentifrice
cleanser 648n.
prophylactic 658n.
dentist
doctor 658n.
dentistry
surgery 658n.
dentition, denture
tooth 256n.
denudation
separation 46n.
uncovering 229n.
denude
subtract 39vb.
uncover 229vb.
disclose 526vb.
deprive 786vb.
denunciation
(*see* denounce)
denunciatory
maledictory 899adj.
disapproving 924adj.
detracting 926adj.
accusing 928adj.
deny
exclude 57vb.
put off 136vb.
confute 479vb.
disbelieve 486vb.
disappoint 509vb.
negate 533vb.
recant 603vb.
reject 607vb.
avoid 620vb.
abrogate 752vb.
refuse 760vb.
deny oneself
relinquish 621vb.
be temperate 942vb.
deodand
penalty 963n.
deodorant
inodorousness 395n.
cleanser 648n.
deodorize
aerify 340vb.
have no smell 395vb.
purify 648vb.
deontology
morals 917n.
deoppilation
facility 701n.
Deo volente, D. V.
possibly 469adv.
divinely 965adv.
depaganize
make pious 979vb.
depart
be disjoined 46vb.
recede 290vb.
depart 296vb.
emerge 298vb.
disappear 446vb.
relinquish 621vb.
departed
dead 361adj.
depart from
differ 15vb.
deviate 282vb.
department
subdivision 53n.
classification 77n.
district 184n.
function 622n.
departmentalized
fragmentary 53adj.
departure
start 68n.
deviation 282n.
recession 290n.
departure 296n.
decease 361n.
(*see* depart)
depend
depend 157vb.
hang 217vb.
be possible 469vb.
be uncertain 474vb.
dependability
observance 768n.
dependable
willing 597adj.
observant 768adj.
trustworthy 929adj.
dependence
relativeness 9n.
inferiority 35n.
pendency 217n.
subjection 745n.
non-ownership 774n.
dependency
territory 184n.
polity 733n.
subject 742n.
lands 777n.
dependent
inferior 35n., adj.
pendent 217adj.
uncertain 474adj.
auxiliary 707n.
dependent 742n.
subject 745adj.
not owning 774adj.
recipient 782n.
servile 879adj.
dependent on
caused 157adj.
liable 180adj.
depend on
believe 485vb.
be subject 745vb.
depict
represent 551vb.
describe 590vb.
depilation
uncovering 229n.
beautification 843n.
hair-dressing 843n.
deplete

waste 634vb.
make insufficient 636vb.
deplorable
bad 645adj.
distressing 827adj.
regretted 830adj.
deplore
regret 830vb.
lament 836vb.
disapprove 924vb.
deploy
place 187vb.
expand 197vb.
lengthen 203vb.
be broad 205vb.
flank 239vb.
open 263vb.
diverge 294vb.
dispose of 673vb.
deponent
witness 466n.
depopulate
bate 37vb.
lay waste 165vb.
void 300vb.
deport
exclude 57vb.
deportation
exclusion 57n.
transference 272n.
ejection 300n.
seclusion 883n.
penalty 963n.
deportee
ejection 300n.
outcaste 883n.
deportment
conduct 688n.
deposal
deposal 752n.
depose
displace 188vb.
abase 311vb.
testify 466vb.
unthrone 734vb.
depose 752vb.
deprive 786vb.
deposed
powerless 161adj.
unentitled 916adj.
deposit
leavings 41n.
place 187vb.
thing transferred 272n.
solid body 324n.
soil 344n.
store 632n., vb.
security 767n.
payment 804n.
depositary
treasurer 798n.
deposition
location 187n.
testimony 466n.
oath 532n.
deposal 752n.
deposit of faith
theology 973n.
orthodoxy 976n.
depositor
creditor 802n.
depository
storage 632n.
treasury 799n.
depot
station 187n.
storage 632n.
emporium 796n.
deprave
pervert 655vb.
depraved
bad 645adj.
deteriorated 655adj.
vicious 934adj.
depravity
badness 645n.
deterioration 655n.
wickedness 934n.
deprecate
dissent 489vb.
dissuade 613vb.
warn 664vb.
oppose 704vb.
resist 715vb.
deprecate 762vb.
regret 830vb.
deprecation
disapprobation 924n.
(*see* deprecate)
deprecatory
humble 872adj.
modest 874adj.
depreciation
decrease 37n.
underestimation 483n.
misinterpretation 521n.
loss 772n.
finance 797n.
non-payment 805n.
cheapness 812n.
disrespect 921n.
detraction 926n.
depredation
havoc 165n.
spoliation 788n.
depredator
taker 786n.
robber 789n.
depress
make concave 255vb.
depress 311vb.
incommode 827vb.
deject 834vb.
depressant
poison 659n.
dejection 834n.
depressed
sullen 893adj.
depressed class
lower classes 869n.
depressed state
psychopathy 503n.
depressing
unpleasant 827adj.
cheerless 834adj.
tedious 838adj.
depression
lowness 210n.
depth 211n.
valley 255n.
descent 309n.
depression 311n.
psychopathy 503n.
deterioration 655n.
adversity 731n.
poverty 801n.
nervousness 854n.
deprivation
separation 46n.
absence 190n.
ejection 300n.
deposal 752n.
loss 772n.
non-ownership 774n.
expropriation 786n.
loss of right 916n.
penalty 963n.
deprive
make insufficient 636vb.
impoverish 801vb.
not pay 805vb.
(*see* deprivation)
de profundis
tearfully 836adv.
depth
greatness 32n.
space 183n.
size 195n.
depth 211n.
interiority 224n.
wisdom 498n.
imperspicuity 568n.
depth-charge
bomb 723n.
depths
rear 238n.
depurate
purify 648vb.
depurative
remedial 65adj.
deputation
commission 751n.
depute
commission 751vb.
deputize
substitute 150vb.
represent 551vb.
function 622vb.
deputize 755vb.
deputy

inferior 35n.
substitute 150n.
agent 686n.
councillor 692n.
consignee 754n.
deputy 755n.
deracinate
destroy 165vb.
eject 300vb.
extract 304vb.
déraciné
foreigner 59n.
wanderer 268n.
derail
derange 63vb.
displace 188vb.
derange
derange 63vb.
deform 244vb.
agitate 318vb.
distract 456vb.
make mad 503vb.
impair 655vb.
hinder 702vb.
incommode 827vb.
deranged
insane 503adj.
derangement
non-uniformity 17n.
disorder 61n.
unconformity 84n.
displacement 188n.
(*see* derange)
deration
liberate 746vb.
not retain 779vb.
derby
headgear 228n.
derelict
survivor 41n.
disused 674adj.
unpossessed 774adj.
derelict 779n.
not retained 779adj.
solitary, outcaste 883n.
dereliction
relinquishment 621n.
dutilessness 918n.
guilty act 936n.
derestrict
revert 148vb.
restore 656vb.
not retain 779vb.
deride
reject 607vb.
laugh 835vb.
ridicule 851vb.
not respect 921vb.
despise 922vb.
de rigueur
usual 610adj.
obligatory 917adj.
derision
unbelief 486n.
laughter 835n.
ridicule 851n.
impiety 980n.
derisive
derisive 851adj.
derisory
ridiculous 849adj.
derivable
caused 157adj.
attributed 158adj.
derivation
origin 68n.
reversion 148n.
source 156n.
effect 157n.
attribution 158n.
connotation 514n.
etymology 559n.
derivative
imitative 20adj.
effect 157n.
word 559n.
dull 840adj.
derive
result 158vb.
attribute 158vb.
acquire 771vb.
derm
skin 226n.
dermal
dermal 226adj.
dermatitis
skin disease 651n.
dermatologist
doctor 658n.
dernier cri
modernism 126n.
fashion 848n.
derogation
disrepute 867n.
detraction 926n.
derogatory
degrading 867adj.
detracting 926adj.
dishonest 930adj.
derrick
hanger 217n.
lifter 310n.
dervish
ascetic 945n.
pietist 979n.
worshiper 981n.
monk 986n.
desanctify
paganize 974vb.
descant
vocal music 412n.
sing 413vb.
be diffuse 570vb.
dissertation 591n.
hymn 981n.
descend
decrease 37vb.
be oblique 220vb.
descend 309vb.
descendant
survivor 41n.
aftercomer 67n.
posteriority 120n.
descendant 170n.
descendants
futurity 124n.
descender
print-type 587n.
descend from
result 157vb.
descending order
decrease 37n.
series 71n.
contraction 198n.
descent
consanguinity 11n.
decrease 37n.
sequence 65n.
continuity 71n.
posteriority 120n.
revolution 149n.
source 156n.
genealogy 169n.
sonship 170n.
presence 189n.
acclivity 220n.
motion 265n.
descent 309n.
plunge 313n.
deterioration 655n.
nobility 868n.
theophany 965n.
describe
communicate 524vb.
represent 551vb.
describe 590vb.
description
sort 77n.
indication 547n.
nomenclature 561n.
writing 586n.
description 590n.
descriptive
expressive 516adj.
descriptive 590adj.
descry
see 438vb.
understand 516vb.
desecrate
make unclean 649vb.
impair 655vb.
misuse 675vb.
shame 867vb.
be undue 916vb.
not respect 921vb.
be impious 980vb.
desecrator
usurper 916n.
impious person 980n.
desert
havoc 165n.
desert 172n.

unproductive 172adj.
emptiness 190n.
dryness 342n.
dry 342n.
land 344n.
tergiversate 603vb.
run away 620vb.
relinquish 621vb.
goodness 644n.
retaliation 714n.
not observe 769vb.
be cowardly 856vb.
seclusion 883n.
fail in duty 918vb.
virtues 933n.
(*see* deserts)

deserter
tergiversator 603n.
avoider 620n.
coward 856n.
dutilessness 918n.

desertion
disobedience 738n.
divorce 896n.
perfidy 930n.

desert-dweller
dweller 191n.
solitary 883n.

deserts
conduct 688n.
retaliation 714n.
right 913n.
dueness 915n.
reward 962n.

deserve
be good 644vb.
deserve 915vb.
be rewarded 962vb.

deserved
just 913adj.
due 915adj.

deserving
excellent 644adj.
approvable 923adj.

deshabille
informal dress 228n.
uncovering 229n.

desiccation
desiccation 342n.
blight 659n.
preservation 666n.

desiderate
require 627vb.
be unsatisfied 636vb.
desire 859vb.

desideration, desideratum
requirement 627n.
desire 859n.
desired object 859n.

desiderium
regret 830n.
desire 859n.

design
prototype 23n.
composition 56n.
form 243n.
representation 551n.
painting 553n.
intention 617n.
plan 623n.
undertaking 672n.
pattern 844n.

designate
specify 80vb.
future 124adj.
mark 547vb.
chosen 605adj.
select 605vb.

designation
classification 77n.
nomenclature 561n.
name 561n.

designer
producer 167n.
artist 556n.
planner 623n.

designing
dishonest 930adj.
selfish 932adj.

designless
designless 618adj.

desinence
extremity 69n.
cessation 145n.

desipience
folly 499n.

desirability
needfulness 627n.
expedience 642n.

desirable
expedient 642adj.
contenting 828adj.
desired 859adj.
lovable 887adj.
approvable 923adj.

desire
attraction 291n.
will 595n., vb.
motive 612n.
intention 617n.
require 627vb.
request 761n., vb.
desire 859n., vb.
desired object 859n.
love 887n.

desirous
willing 597adj.

desist
cease 145vb.
not act 677vb.

desk
cabinet 194n.
stand 218n.
classroom 539n.

deskbook
reading matter 589n.

desk-work
study 536n.

desolate
lay waste 165vb.
unproductive 172adj.
void 300vb.
hopeless 853adj.
friendless 883adj.
secluded 883adj.

desolation
havoc 165n.
desert 172n.
emptiness 190n.
sorrow 825n.

despair
not expect 508vb.
be disappointed 509vb.
sorrow 825n.
dejection 834n.
hopelessness 853n.

despair, counsel of
inexpedience 643n.
hopelessness 853n.

despair of
impenitence 940n.

despair, one's
bungler 697n.
difficulty 700n.

despatch
(*see* dispatch)

desperado
murderer 362n.
brave person 855n.
desperado 857n.
insolent person 878n.
ruffian 904n.

desperate
consummate 32adj.
furious 176adj.
resolute 599adj.
active 678adj.
hopeless 853adj.
courageous 855adj.
rash 857adj.

desperately
extremely 32adv.

desperation
(*see* desperate)

despicable
discreditable 867adj.
disreputable 867adj.
contemptible 922adj.

despicability
odium 888n.

despise
underestimate 483vb.
be proud 871vb.
hate 888vb.
not respect 921vb.
despise 922vb.

despised
contemptible 922adj.

despisedness
unimportance 639n.
despisedness 922n.

despite

in defiance of 25adv.
although 182adv.
nevertheless 468adj.
with difficulty 700adv.
in opposition 704adv.
despoil
lay waste 165vb.
impair 655vb.
rob 788vb.
despoiler
taker 786n.
robber 789n.
evildoer 904n.
despondency
adversity 731n.
dejection 834n.
hopelessness 853n.
nervousness 854n.
despot
tyrant 735n.
autocrat 741n.
despotic
oppressive 735adj.
authoritarian 735adj.
lawless 954adj.
despotism
despotism 733n.
brute force 735n.
desquamation
uncovering 229n.
dessert
sequel 67n.
dish 301n.
dessous
underwear 228n.
destination
stopping place 145n.
objective 617n.
destine
predestine 155vb.
necessitate 596vb.
predetermine 608vb.
intend 617vb.
destined
future 124adj.
impending 155adj.
fated 596adj.
destiny
finality 69n.
futurity 124n.
destiny 155n.
cause 156n.
influence 178n.
expectation 507n.
necessity 596n.
predetermination 608n.
destitute
necessitous 627adj.
not owning 774adj.
poor 801adj.
destitution
poverty 801n.
destroy
nullify 2vb.
destroy 165vb.
slaughter 362vb.
confute 479vb.
waste 634vb.
defeat 727vb.
impoverish 801vb.
destroyer
revolutionist 149n.
destroyer 168n.
violent creature 176n.
bane 659n.
warship 722n.
destruction
extinction 2n.
disorder 61n.
revolution 149n.
destruction 165n.
killing 362n.
destructive
destructive 165adj.
wasteful 634adj.
harmful 645adj.
adverse 731adj.
destructiveness
waste 634n.
destructor
furnace 383n.
desuetude
desuetude 611n.
non-retention 779n.
desultoriness
inattention 456n.
desultory
orderless 61adj.
discontinuous 72adj.
fitful 142adj.
unstable 152adj.
deviating 282adj.
light-minded 456adj.
prolix 570adj.
detach
disjoin 46vb.
unstick 49vb.
disperse 75vb.
send 272vb.
detachable
severable 46adj.
detached
irrelative 10adj.
non-adhesive 49adj.
neutral 625adj.
independent 744adj.
impassive 820adj.
just 913adj.
disinterested 931adj.
detachment
separation 46n.
part 53n.
inattention 456n.
armed force 722n.
moral insensibility 820n.
inexcitability 823n.
justice 913n.
disinterestedness 931n.
detail
small quantity 33n.
part 53n.
specify 80vb.
send 272vb.
be diffuse 570vb.
describe 590vb.
trifle 639n.
armed force 722n.
command 737vb.
apportion 783vb.
pattern 844n.
detailed
complete 54adj.
definite 80adj.
diffuse 570adj.
descriptive 590adj.
laborious 682adj.
details
particulars 80n.
detain
imprison 747vb.
retain 778vb.
detainee
prisoner 750n.
detect
see 438vb.
detect 484vb.
understand 516vb.
disclose 526vb.
detectable
visible 443adj.
detection
police inquiry 459n.
discovery 484n.
knowledge 490n.
detective
inquisitor 453n.
detective 459n.
detector
detector 484n.
detent
fastening 47n.
détente
moderation 177n.
pacification 719n.
detention
delay 136n.
hindrance 702n.
detention 747n.
retention 778n.
detention camp
prison camp 748n.
détenue
prisoner 750n.
deter
cause doubt 486vb.
dissuade 613vb.
hinder 702vb.
frighten 854vb.
cause dislike 861vb.
threaten 900vb.

detergent
cleanser 648n.
deteriorate
decompose 51vb.
be old 127vb.
be weak 163vb.
disuse 674vb.
deterioration
inferiority 35n.
decrease 37n.
mixture 43n.
change 143n.
ruin 165n.
regression 286n.
desuetude 611n.
waste 634n.
badness 645n.
illness 651n.
deterioration 655n.
relapse 657n.
loss 772n.
wickedness 934n.
determinant
cause 156n.
determinate
definite 80adj.
determination
will 595n.
resolution 599n.
obstinacy 602n.
intention 617n.
assiduity 678n.
courage 855n.
determinative
judicial 480adj.
determine
arrange 62vb.
terminate 69vb.
specify 80vb.
cause 156vb.
will 595vb.
be resolute 599vb.
determinism
necessity 596n.
determinist
fatalist 596n.
deterrence
dissuasion 613n.
intimidation 854n.
deterrent
counteraction 182n.
dissuasion 613n.
protection 660n.
safeguard 662n.
cautionary 664adj.
defense 713n.
retaliation 714n.
weapon 723n.
threat 900n.
detersion
ablution 648n.
detersive
remedial 658adj.
detest
(*see* detestation)
detestable
not nice 645adj.
detestation
dislike 861n.
hatred 888n.
dethrone
depose 752vb.
dethroned
unentitled 916adj.
dethronement
anarchy 734n.
deposal 752n.
loss of right 916n.
detonation
outbreak 176n.
bang 402n.
detonator
lighter 385n.
ammunition 723n.
explosive 723n.
detour
curvature 248n.
deviation 282n.
route 624n.
circuit 626n.
detract
subtract 39vb.
detraction
diminution 37n.
underestimation 483n.
contempt 922n.
detraction 926n.
detrain
land 295vb.
detribalize
derange 63vb.
pervert 655vb.
disentitle 916vb.
detriment
inutility 641n.
inexpedience 643n.
badness 645n.
impairment 655n.
detrition
subtraction 39n.
pulverulence 332n.
detritus
leavings 41n.
piece 53n.
accumulation 74n.
thing transferred 272n.
powder 332n.
de trop
superfluous 637adj.
detrusion
depression 311n.
deuce
draw 28n.
duality 90n.
deucedly
extremely 32adv.
deus ex machina
aider 703n.
patron 707n.
deuteragonist
actor 594n.
deuterium
gas 336n.
deuterogamy
type of marriage 894n.
dev, deva
god 966n.
mythical being 970n.
demon 970n.
devaloka
mythic heaven 971n.
devalue
make useless 641vb.
impair 655vb.
demonetize 797vb.
Devanagari
letter 558n.
devastate
lay waste 165vb.
devastation
havoc 165n.
terror tactics 712n.
develop
become 1vb.
augment 36vb.
result 157vb.
be visible 443vb.
manifest 522vb.
educate 534vb.
photograph 551vb.
(*see* development)
development
increase 36n.
conversion 147n.
growth 157n.
production 164n.
propagation 164n.
expansion 197n.
progression 285n.
evolution 316n.
musical piece 412n.
improvement 654n.
development area
room 183n.
deverbal
grammatical 564adj.
deverbative
part of speech 564n.
devexity
acclivity 220n.
curvature 248n.
deviate
be oblique 220vb.
(*see* deviation)
deviation
difference 15n.
non-uniformity 17n.
unconformity 84n.
change 143n.
displacement 188n.
distance 199n.

curvature 248n.
deviation 282n.
divergence 294n.
error 495n.
tergiversation 603n.
deviationism
unconformity 84n.
deviationist
nonconformist 84n.
crank 504n.
tergiversator 603n.
revolter 738n.
device
idea 451n.
heraldry 547n.
contrivance 623n.
instrument 628n.
means 629n.
tool 630n.
means of escape 667n.
stratagem 698n.
devil
violent creature 176n.
cook 301vb.
season 388vb.
wickedness 934n.
monster 938n.
jurist 958n.
devil 969n.
mythical being 970n.
demon 970n.
sorcerer 983n.
devilish
cruel 898adj.
wicked 934adj.
diabolic 969adj.
fairylike 970adj.
infernal 972adj.
devil-may-care
rash 857adj.
devilment
evil 616n.
devilry
cruel act 898n.
wickedness 934n.
diabolism 969n.
devil's advocate
sophist 477n.
Devil's Island
prison camp 748n.
devil's tattoo
roll 403n.
Devil, the
Satan 969n.
devil to pay
turmoil 61n.
devil-worship
wickedness 934n.
diabolism 969n.
idolatry 982n.
devious
deviating 282adj.
circuitous 314adj.
cunning 698adj.
dishonest 930adj.
devisable
transferable 272adj.
devise
transfer 272vb.
think 449vb.
imagine 513vb.
plan 623vb.
be cunning 698vb.
dower 777vb.
bequeath 780vb.
give 781vb.
devisee
beneficiary 776n.
recipient 782n.
deviser
producer 167n.
devisor
owner 776n.
giver 781n.
devitalize
unman 161vb.
weaken 163vb.
devitrify
make opaque 423vb.
devoid
empty 190adj.
devoir
courteous act 884n.
respects 920n.
devolution
commission 751n.
transfer 780n.
devolve
convey 780vb.
impose a duty 917vb.
devolve on
be one's duty 917vb.
devote
use 673vb.
give 781vb.
be pious 979vb.
devoted
resolute 599adj.
unfortunate 731adj.
obedient 739adj.
friendly 880adj.
loving 887adj.
disinterested 931adj.
pious 979adj.
worshiping 981adj.
devotedness
assiduity 678n.
devoted to
habituated 610adj.
devotee
habitué 610n.
desirer 859n.
pietist 979n.
worshiper 981n.
devote to destruction
curse 899vb.
devotion
resolution 599n.
loyalty 739n.
love 887n.
respect 920n.
piety 979n.
oblation 981n.
worship 981n.
devotional
religious 973adj.
devotional 981adj.
devotions
prayers 981n.
devour
destroy 165vb.
eat 301vb.
give pain 377vb.
waste 634n.
appropriate, fleece 786vb.
devoured by
possessed 773adj.
devouring
gluttonous 947adj.
devout
religious 973adj.
orthodox 976adj.
pious 979adj.
worshiping 981adj.
devoutly
feelingly 818adv
devoutness
piety 979n.
dew
moisture 341n.
dewan
officer 741n.
dewiness
newness 126n.
moisture 341n.
cleanness 648n.
(*see* dewy)
dewlap
pendant 217n.
dewy
matinal 128adj.
humid 341adj.
clean 648adj.
dexiotropic
dextral 241n.
dexter
dextrality 241n.
dexterity
skill 694n.
dexterous
dextral 241adj.
skillful 694adj.
dextral, dextrad
dextral 241adj.
dextrose
sweet 392n.
Dhamma
religious faith 973n.
dharma
religion 973n.
religious faith 973n.

dhobi
cleaner 648n.
dhobie itch
formication 378n.
skin disease 651n.
dhoti
dress 228n.
dhow
sailing-ship 275n.
diabetes
disease 651n.
diabetic
sick person 651n.
diablerie
diabolism 969n.
sorcery 983n.
diabolic
evil 616adj.
damnable 645adj.
cruel 898adj.
wicked 934adj.
diabolic 969adj.
fairylike 970adj.
infernal 972adj.
idolatrous 982adj.
sorcerous 983adj.
diabolist
diabolist 969n.
idolater 982n.
sorcerer 983n.
diabolo
plaything 837n.
diacaustic
curve 248n.
diaconal
clerical 986adj.
diaconate
church office 985n.
diacritic
indicating 547adj.
diacritic mark
punctuation 547n.
diadem
regalia 743n.
jewelry 844n.
diaeresis
decomposition 51n.
punctuation 547n.
prosody 593n.
diagnose
discriminate 463vb.
diagnosis
character 5n.
classification 77n.
discrimination 463n.
pathology 651n.
medical art 658n.
diagnostic
characteristic 5adj.
distinctive 15adj.
special 80adj.
identification 547n.
diagnostician
doctor 658n.
diagnostics
discrimination 463n.
diagonal
dividing line 92n.
obliquity 220n.
crossed 222adj.
directed 281adj.
diagram
copy 22n.
outline 233n.
representation 551n.
diagrammatize
abstract 592vb.
diagraph
representation 551n.
dial
timekeeper 117n.
face 237n.
communicate 524vb.
dialect
speciality 80n.
unintelligibility 517n.
language 557n.
dialect 560n.
speech defect 580n.
dialectic
inquiring 459adj.
interrogation 459n.
reasoning 475n.
rational 475adj.
dialectical
linguistic 557adj.
dialectical 560adj.
dialectical materialism
materiality 319n.
philosophy 449n.
dialectics
reasoning 475n.
dialectology
linguistics 557n.
dialogism
allocution 583n.
dialogue
interrogation 459n.
answer 460n.
argument 475n.
interlocution 584n.
dramaturgy 594n.
diameter
dividing line 92n.
breadth 205n.
diamond
angular figure 247n.
hardness 326n.
type size 587n.
exceller 644n.
arena 724n.
gem 844n.
diamond cut diamond
retaliation 714n.
diamond jubilee
celebration 876n.
Diana
moon 321n.
hunter 619n.
spinster 895n.
virgin 950n.
Olympian god 967n.
dianoetic
rational 475adj.
diapason
loudness 400n.
musical note 410n.
diaper
loincloth 228n.
pattern 844n.
diaphane
transparency 422n.
diaphanous
transparent 422adj.
diaphonics
acoustics 398n.
diaphoresis
outflow 298n.
excretion 302n.
diaphragm
middle 70n.
partition 231n.
musical instrument 414n.
phonograph 414n.
diarist
chronologist 117n.
chronicler 549n.
author 589n.
narrator 590n.
diarize
time 117vb.
register 548vb.
diarrhea
cacation 302n.
dysentery 651n.
diary
chronology 117n.
reminder 505n.
record 548n.
reference book 589n.
biography 590n.
diaspora
foreigner 59n.
dispersion 75n.
diastole
dilation 197n.
diatessaron
musical note 410n.
diathermancy
heat 379n.
heating 381n.
diathermometer
thermometry 379n.
diathesis
character 5n.
state 7n.
diatonic
harmonic 410adj.
diatribe
oration 579n.

censure 924n.
dibble
perforator 263n.
farm tool 370n.
cultivate 370vb.
dibs
dibs 797n.
ball game 837n.
dicast, dicastery
judge, jury 957n.
dice
oracle 511n.
gambling 618n.
gambling game 837n.
dice, on the
possible 469adj.
dicer
gambler 618n.
player 837n.
dicer's oath
unreliability 474n.
untruth 543n.
dicey
casual 159adj.
speculative 618adj.
dangerous 661adj.
dichotomize
sunder 46vb.
bisect 92vb.
dichotomy
disjunction 46n.
bisection 92n.
dichroism
variegation 437n.
dim sight 440n.
dick
detective 459n.
protector 660n.
police 955n.
dicker
bargain 791vb.
dickey
seat 218n.
apron 228n.
dictaphone
hearing aid 415n.
recording instrument 549n.
dictate
teach 534vb.
speak 579vb.
direct 689vb.
advise 691vb.
rule, dominate 733vb.
decree 737n.
compel 740vb.
dictated
vocal 577adj.
necessary 596adj.
dictation
necessity 596n.
no choice 606n.
(*see* dictate)
dictator
tyrant 735n.
autocrat 741n.
dictatorial
narrow-minded 481adj.
volitional 595adj.
directing 689adj.
authoritative 733adj.
commanding 737adj.
compelling 740adj.
insolent 878adj.
dictatorship
directorship 689n.
despotism 733n.
brute force 735n.
diction
meaning 514n.
phrase 563n.
style 566n.
dictionary
commentary 520n.
dictionary 559n.
collection 632n.
dictum
maxim 496n.
affirmation 532n.
command 737n.
didactic
educational 534adj.
advising 691adj.
diddle
deceive 542vb.
defraud 788vb.
diddler
trickster 545n.
die
mold 23n.
end 69vb.
die 361vb.
printing 555n.
gambling 618n.
die away
shade off 27vb.
decrease 37vb.
cease 145vb.
died out
extinct 2adj.
die down
decrease 37vb.
be quiescent 266vb.
extinguish 382vb.
die for
desire 859vb.
be disinterested 931vb.
die hard
stand firm 599vb.
resist 715vb.
die-hard
unchangeable 153adj.
opinionist 602n.
opponent 705n.
malcontent 829n.
die in harness
persevere 600vb.
die on the ear
sound faint 401vb.
die out
pass away 2vb.
diesel
locomotive 274n.
Dies Irae
obsequies 364n.
dies non
neverness 109n.
diet
make smaller 198vb.
dieting 301n.
therapy 658n.
council 692n.
be temperate 942vb.
starve 946vb.
dietary
dieting 301n.
meal 301n.
therapy 658n.
dietetic
nourishing 301adj.
remedial 658adj.
dietetics
dieting 301n.
die the death
be punished 963vb.
dietician
dieting 301n.
doctor 658n.
difference
irrelation 10n.
contrariety 14n.
difference 15n.
dissimilarity 19n.
disagreement 25n.
inequality 29n.
remainder 41n.
numerical result 85n.
divergence 294n.
discrimination 463n.
dissent 489n.
heraldry 547n.
dissension 709n.
schism 978n.
difference, see the
discriminate 463vb.
different
contrary 14adj.
non-uniform 17adj.
superior 34adj.
changeful 152adj.
differentia
speciality 80n.
differential
variant 15n.
degree 27n.
inequality 29n.
numerical element 85n.
earnings 771n.
reward 962n.
differentiate
set apart 46vb.

specify 80vb.
discriminate 463vb.
differentiation
differentiation 15n.
degree 27n.
numerical operation 86n.
comparison 462n.
difficult
impracticable 470adj.
puzzling 517adj.
imperspicuous 568adj.
laborious 682adj.
difficult 700adj.
fastidious 862adj.
ungracious 885adj.
sullen 893adj.
difficulty
unintelligibility 517n.
enigma 530n.
imperspicuity 568n.
difficulty 700n.
obstacle 702n.
adversity 731n.
diffidence
modesty 874n.
diffident
nervous 854adj.
modest 874adj.
diffluent
flowing 350adj.
diffraction
dispersion 75n.
obliquity 220n.
diffraction grating
optical device 442n.
diffuse
irrelevant 10adj.
diffuse 570adj.
(see diffusion)
diffused through
ubiquitous 189adj.
diffuseness
repetition 106n.
empty talk 515n.
diffuseness 570n.
loquacity 581n.
diffusion
disjunction 46n.
dispersion 75n.
presence 189n.
transference 272n.
ingress 297n.
information 524n.
diffusive
prolix 570adj.
dig
excavation 255n.
make concave 255vb.
knock 279n.
cultivate 370vb.
search 459n., vb.
work 682vb.
digamy
type of marriage 894n.
digest
arrangement 62n.
class 62vb.
absorb 299vb.
eat 301vb.
meditate 449vb.
be attentive 455vb.
literature 557n.
compendium 592n.
mature 669vb.
knuckle under 721vb.
be patient 823vb.
digestible
light 323adj.
digestion
combination 50n.
(see digest)
digestive
cathartic 658n.
remedial 658adj.
digger
excavator 255n.
gardener 370n.
diggings, digs
quarters 192n.
digging-stick
perforator 263n.
farm tool 370n.
dight
dressed 228adj.
dress 228vb.
decorate 844vb.
dig in
place oneself 187vb.
stand firm 599vb.
defend 713vb.
give battle 718vb.
digit
number 85n.
feeler 378n.
digital
handed 378adj.
digitalis
poisonous plant 659n.
digitate
disjunct 46adj.
diglot
linguistic 557adj.
dignification
dignification 866n.
dignified
elegant 575adj.
authoritative 733adj.
impressive 821adj.
well-bred 848adj.
worshipful 866adj.
proud 871adj.
formal 875adj.
courteous 884adj.
dignify
decorate 844vb.
dignify 866vb.
dignitary
aristocrat 868n.
dignity
elegance 575n.
conduct 688n.
authority 733n.
good taste 846n.
beau monde 848n.
prestige 866n.
honors 866n.
title 870n.
pride 871n.
formality 875n.
ostentation 875n.
dig one's toes in
stay 144vb.
stand firm 599vb.
retain 778vb.
dig out
make concave 255vb.
extract 304vb.
digression
deviation 282n.
pleonasm 570n.
circuit 626n.
dig up
extract 304vb.
exhume 364vb.
be curious 453vb.
discover 484vb.
dig up the past
look back 125vb.
retrospect 505vb.
dihedral
dual 90adj.
dike
gap 201n.
fence 235n.
furrow 262n.
lake 346n.
conduit 351n.
obstacle 702n.
defenses 713n.
diktat
(see dictate)
dilaceration
scission 46n.
impairment 655n.
dilapidate
waste 634vb.
(see dilapidation)
dilapidation
decay 51n.
destruction 165n.
dilapidation 655n.
use 673n.
poverty 801n.
dilatation
dilation 197n.
thickness 205n.
rarity 325n.
dilate
grow 36vb.
expand 197vb.

rarefy 325vb.
sufflate 352vb.
be diffuse 570vb.
dilatory
late 136adj.
slow 278adj.
lazy 679adj.
dilection
love 887n.
dilemma
circumstance 8n.
dubiety 474n.
argumentation 475n.
choice 605n.
predicament 700n.
dilettante
smattering 491adj.
sciolist 493n.
man of taste 846n.
dilettantism
erudition 490n.
good taste 846n.
fastidiousness 862n.
diligence
stage-coach 274n.
attention 455n.
carefulness 457n.
assiduity 678n.
diligent
studious 536adj.
observant 768adj.
dill
potherb 301n.
dilly-dally
be late 136vb.
be irresolute 601vb.
be inactive 679vb.
diluent
liquefaction 337n.
water 339n.
dilute
bate 37vb.
weaken 163vb.
rarefy 325vb.
add water 339vb.
moisten 341vb.
diluvian
primal 127adj.
dim
darken 418vb.
bedim 419vb.
dim 419adj.
decolorize 426vb.
blackish 428adj.
blur 440vb.
ill-seen 444adj.
unintelligent 499adj.
puzzling 517adj.
dime
small coin 33n.
coinage 797n.
dimension
quantity 26n.
measure 183n.
appearance 445n.
dimensional
metric 465adj.
dimensions
size 195n.
dimeter
prosody 593n.
dim-eyed
dim-sighted 440adj.
dimidiate
bisect 92vb.
mark 547vb.
diminish
bate 37vb.
subtract 39vb.
render few 105vb.
moderate 177vb.
diminished
lesser 35adj.
diminishing returns
loss 772n.
diminuendo
diminuendo 37adv.
diminution
smallness 33n.
diminution 37n.
subtraction 39n.
decrement 42n.
contraction 198n.
diminutive
small 33adj.
little 196adj.
word 559n.
part of speech 564n.
dimity
textile 222n.
dimmer
obscuration 418n.
dimness
darkness 418n.
dimness 419n.
invisibility 444n.
latency 523n.
dimple
cavity 255n.
notch 260n.
dimpled
fleshy 195adj.
dim sight
dim sight 440n.
dim-witted
unintelligent 499adj.
din
commotion 318n.
loudness 400n.
be loud 400vb.
roll 403n.
advertise 528vb.
dinar
coinage 797n.
dinarchy
despotism 733n.
dine
eat 301vb.
feed 301vb.
dine out
be sociable 882vb.
diner
café 192n.
train 274n.
eater 301n.
diner-out
reveler 837n.
social person 882n.
dinette
café 192n.
ding
resound 404vb.
ding-dong
draw 28n.
equal 28adj.
repeated 106adj.
roll 403n.
contending 716adj.
dinghy
rowboat 275n.
dingle
valley 255n.
dingy
dark 418adj.
dim 419adj.
soft-hued 425adj.
colorless 426adj.
dirty 649adj.
graceless 842adj.
dining car
train 274n.
dining room
chamber 194n.
feasting 301n.
din in the ears
repeat oneself 106vb.
advertise 528vb.
be loquacious 581vb.
dinkum
truth 494n.
dinky
orderly 60adj.
little 196adj.
dinner
meal 301n.
festivity 837n.
dinner jacket
informal dress 228n.
tunic 228n.
dinnerless
hungry 859adj.
fasting 946adj.
dinosaur
giant 195n.
animal 365n.
dint
power 160n.
be vigorous 174vb.
concavity 255n.
make concave 255vb.
knock 279n.
collide 279vb.

diocesan
ecclesiastical 985adj.
ecclesiarch 986n.
layman 987n.
diocese
district 184n.
parish 985n.
Diogenes
solitary 883n.
misanthrope 902n.
ascetic 945n.
Dionysiac
disorderly 61adj.
Dionysiac frenzy
spell 983n.
Dionysus
vegetability 366n.
Olympian god 967n.
dioptrics
optics 417n.
diorama
spectacle 445n.
art subject 553n.
diorism
discrimination 463n.
dip
acclivity 220n.
cavity, valley 255n.
swim 269vb.
transpose 272vb.
retard 278vb.
impel 279vb.
point to 281vb.
immerse 303vb.
descent 309n.
depression 311n.
plunge 313n., vb.
be wet 341vb.
drench 341vb.
snuff out 418vb.
glimmer 419n.
bedim 419vb.
torch 420n.
color 425vb.
signal 547vb.
ablution 648n.
diphtheria
infection 651n.
respiratory disease 651n.
diphthong
speech sound 398n.
spoken letter 558n.
voice 577n.
dip into
be attentive 455vb.
diplegia
paralysis 651n.
diploma
credential 466n.
record 548n.
mandate 751n.
honors 866n.
diplomacy
duplicity 541n.
cunning 698n.
mediation 720n.
diplomat
mediator 720n.
envoy 754n.
diplomatic
hypocritical 541adj.
diplomatics
mediation 720n.
diplomatist
expert 696n.
slyboots 698n.
mediator 720n.
envoy 754n.
dipper
ladle 194n.
star 321n.
irrigator 341n.
obscuration 418n.
dippy
crazed 503adj.
enamored 887adj.
dipsomania
alcoholism 949n.
dipsomaniac
madman 504n.
drunkard 949n.
diptych
picture 553n.
dire
harmful 645adj.
adverse 731adj.
direct
simple 44adj.
orderly 60adj.
continuous 71adj.
straight 249adj.
send 272vb.
orientate 281vb.
toward 281adv.
intuitive 476adj.
accurate 494adj.
educate 534vb.
indicate 547vb.
perspicuous 567adj.
dramatize 594vb.
motivate 612vb.
undeviating 625adj.
direct 689vb.
rule 733vb.
command 737vb.
direct action
revolt 738n.
direction
relation 9n.
laterality 239n.
direction 281n.
teaching 534n.
dramaturgy 594n.
route 624n.
directorship 689n.
precept 693n.
governance 733n.
direction-finder
direction 281n.
indicator 547n.
directive
command 737n.
jurisdictional 955adj.
direct line
straightness 249n.
directly
suddenly 135adv.
straight on 249adv.
towards 281adv.
plainly 573adv.
directness
continuity 71n.
straightness 249n.
perspicuity 567n.
director
stage-manager 594n.
director 690n.
master 741n.
directorial
directing 689adj.
directorship
directorship 689n.
directory
directory 87n.
guide-book 524n.
direful
frightening 854adj.
diremption
separation 46n.
direption
spoliation 788n.
dirge
obsequies 364n.
musical piece 412n.
poem 593n.
lament 836n.
dirigible
airship 276n.
dirigisme
governance 733n.
dirk
side-arms 723n.
dirt
excrement 302n.
opacity 423n.
rubbish 641n.
dirt 649n.
slur 867n.
impurity 951n.
dirty
windy 352adj.
bedim 419vb.
opaque 423adj.
black 428adj.
dirty 649adj.
make unclean 649vb.
infectious 653adj.
disreputable 867adj.
dishonest 930adj.
impure 951adj.
dirty dog

cad 938n.
dirty linen
uncleanness 649n.
slur 867n.
dirty look
look 438n.
reproach 924n.
dirty trick
foul play 930n.
dirty weather
storm 176n.
gale 352n.
dirty work
foul play 930n.
disability
impotence 161n.
inexpedience 643n.
illness 651n.
hindrance 702n.
disable
disable 161vb.
weaken 163vb.
impair 655vb.
hinder 702vb.
disabuse
inform 524vb.
disclose 526vb.
educate 534vb.
disaccharide
food content 301n.
disaccord
disagreement 25n.
disorder 61n.
dissension 709n.
disaccustom
disaccustom 611vb.
relinquish 621vb.
disuse 674vb.
disadvantage
inferiority 35n.
evil 616n.
inexpedience 643n.
disadvantageous
harmful 645adj.
disaffect
dissuade 613vb.
disaffection
dissent 489n.
hatred 888n.
disaffiliate
depose 752vb.
disaffirm
negate 533vb.
disagree
cause dislike 861vb.
(*see* disagreement)
disagreeable
painful 377adj.
fetid 397adj.
unpleasant 827adj.
disliked 861adj.
discourteous 885adj.
disagreement
contrariety 14n.
difference 15n.
dissimilarity 19n.
disagreement 25n.
inequality 29n.
unconformity 84n.
unbelief 486n.
dissent 489n.
negation 533n.
unwillingness 598n.
dissension 709n.
disallow
exclude 57vb.
make impossible 470vb.
dissent 489vb.
negate 533vb.
reject 607vb.
refuse 760vb.
disentitle 916vb.
disapprove 924vb.
disappear
pass away 2vb.
cease 145vb.
decamp 296vb.
be unseen 444vb.
disappear 446vb.
be stealthy 525vb.
be lost 772vb.
disappearance
transientness 114n.
absence 190n.
obscuration 418n.
disappearance 446n.
escape 667n.
disappoint
disappoint 509vb.
deceive 542n.
miscarry 728vb.
displease 827vb.
cause discontent 829vb.
leave no hope 853vb.
disappointment
inexpectation 508n.
(*see* disappoint)
disapprobation
dissent 489n.
rejection 607n.
disrespect 921n.
disapprobation 924n.
detraction 926n.
condemnation 961n.
disapproval
(*see* disapprobation)
disapprove
oppose 704vb.
deprecate 762vb.
prohibit 757vb.
dislike 861vb.
make unwelcome 883vb.
(*see* disapprobation)
disarm
disable 161vb.
weaken 163vb.
be moderate 177vb.
assuage 177vb.
make useless 641vb.
pacify 719vb.
disarmament
impotence 161n.
peace 717n.
pacification 719n.
disarming
pacificatory 719adj.
disarrangement
derangement 63n.
disarray
disorder 61n.
disassemble
make useless 641vb.
disaster
ill fortune 731n.
disastrous
evil 616adj.
harmful 645adj.
disavow
negate 533vb.
recant 603vb.
reject 607vb.
disband
disjoin 46vb.
disperse 75vb.
liberate 746vb.
disbar
exclude 57vb.
eject 300vb.
depose 752vb.
shame 867vb.
disbelief
unbelief 486n.
negation 533n.
non-wonder 865n.
irreligion 974n.
disbeliever
unbeliever 486n.
impious person 980n.
disburden
deliver 668vb.
disencumber 701vb.
relieve 831vb.
disbursement
payment 804n.
expenditure 806n.
disc
face 237n.
circle 250n.
phonograph 414n.
recording instrument 549n.
discalceate
monk 986n.
discard
eject 300vb.
rejection 607n.
reject 607vb.

relinquish 621vb.
rubbish 641n.
disuse 674vb.
not observe 769vb.
not retain 779vb.
discarded
unwonted 611adj.
discargo
void 300vb.
discarnate
immaterial 320adj.
spooky 970adj.
disceptation
argument 475n.
discern
see 438vb.
discriminate 463vb.
know 490vb.
understand 516vb.
discernible
visible 443adj.
discernment
inspection 438n.
discrimination 463n.
sagacity 498n.
fastidiousness 862n.
discerption
scission 46n.
discharge
displace 188vb.
propulsion 287n.
land 295vb.
outflow 298n.
ejection 300n.
dismiss, void 300vb.
excretion 302n.
ulcer 651n.
deliverance 668n.
disuse 674vb.
carry out 725vb.
liberation 746n.
deposal 752n.
observance 768n.
not retain 779vb.
pay 804vb.
do one's duty 917vb.
non-liability 919n.
acquittal 960n.
disciple
changed person 147n.
listener 415n.
learner 538n.
auxiliary 707n.
disciplinarian
teacher, trainer 537n.
tyrant 735n.
disciplinary
punitive 963adj.
discipline
order 60n.
teaching 534n.
dominate 733vb.
severity 735n.
obedience 739n.
subjugate 745vb.
restraint 747n.
punishment 963n.
disciplined
orderly 60adj.
obedient 739adj.
discipular
student-like 538adj.
disclaim
negate 533vb.
recant 603vb.
reject 607vb.
resign 753vb.
refuse 760vb.
not retain 779vb.
disclaimer
negation 533n.
recantation 603n.
resignation 753n.
disclose
inform 524vb.
disclose 526vb.
indicate 547vb.
disclosure
manifestation 522n.
disclosure 526n.
discoid
round 250adj.
(*see* discous)
discolor
variegate 437vb.
make ugly 842vb.
(*see* discoloration)
discoloration
hue 425n.
achromatism 426n.
impairment 655n.
wound 655n.
discomfiture
defeat 728n.
discomfort
pain 377n.
evil 616n.
suffering, worry 825n.
incommode 827vb.
discommendation
censure 924n.
discompose
derange 63vb.
agitate 318vb.
distract 456vb.
incommode 827vb.
enrage 891vb.
discomposure
disorder 61n.
worry 825n.
disconcert
derange 63vb.
distract 456vb.
disappoint 509vb.
hinder 702vb.
defeat 727vb.
incommode 827vb.
frignten 854vb.
shame 867vb.
humiliate 972vb.
disconcerted
inexpectant 508adj.
disappointed 509adj.
(*see* disconcert)
disconformity
unconformity 84n.
disconnect
disjoin 46vb.
discontinue 72vb.
disconnectedness
discontinuity 72n.
disconnection
irrelation 10n.
disjunction 46n.
disconsolate
melancholic 834adj.
hopeless 853adj.
discontent
dissent 489n.
disappointment 509n.
sorrow 825n.
displease 827vb.
discontent 829n.
sadden 834vb.
resentment 891n.
sullenness 893n.
disapprobation 924n.
discontinuance
discontinuity 72n.
cessation 145n.
desuetude 611n.
abrogation 752n.
discontinuation
discontinuity 72n.
discontinuity
irrelation 10n.
non-uniformity 17n.
disjunction 46n.
non-coherence 49n.
incompleteness 55n.
discontinuity 72n.
intempestivity 138n.
stop 145n.
interval 201n.
discord
contrariety 14n.
difference 15n.
disagreement 25n.
medley 43n.
disorder 61n.
rasp 407vb.
discord 411n., vb.
dissension 709n.
discount
subtraction 39n.
decrement 42n.
disregard 458vb.
qualification 468n.
underestimate 483vb.
pay 804n., vb.
discount 810n., vb.
discountenance

hinder 702vb.
prohibit 757vb.
refuse 760vb.
disapprove 924vb.
discourage
dissuade 613vb.
hinder 702vb.
prohibit 757vb.
cause discontent 829vb.
deject 834vb.
frighten 854vb.
discouragement
hopelessness 853n.
discourse
lecture 534n.
teach 534vb.
oration 579n.
dissertation 591n.
discourteous
impertinent 878adj.
discourtesy
ill-breeding 847n.
unsociability 883n.
discourtesy 885n.
disrespect 921n.
discous
broad 205adj.
(*see* discoid)
discover
come before 64vb.
meet with 154vb.
cause 156vb.
produce 164vb.
see 438vb.
think 449vb.
discover 484vb.
manifest 522vb.
be informed 524vb.
discoverable
intelligible 516adj.
discoverer
precursor 66n.
producer 167n.
inquirer 459n.
detector 484n.
discovery
beginning 68n.
appearance 445n.
discovery 484n.
knowledge 490n.
manifestation 522n.
disclosure 526n.
discredit
unbelief 486n.
disbelieve 486vb.
cause doubt 486vb.
disrepute 867n.
odium 888n.
discreditable
bad 645adj.
discreditable 867adj.
discredited
disused 674adj.
disreputable 867adj.
disapproved 924adj.
discreet
discriminating 463adj.
reticent 525adj.
cowardly 856adj.
cautious 858adj.
discrepancy
difference 15n.
disagreement 25n.
discrepant
quarreling 709adj.
discrete
separate 46adj.
discontinuous 72adj.
discretion
discrimination 463n.
judgment 480n.
sagacity 498n.
will 595n.
choice 605n.
skill 694n.
cowardice 856n.
caution 858n.
discretional
volitional 595adj.
voluntary 597adj.
choosing 605adj.
unconditional 744adj.
discriminate
make unlike 19vb.
set apart 46vb.
specify 80vb.
discriminate 463vb
know 490vb.
be wise 498vb.
select 605vb.
be skillful 694vb.
have taste 846vb.
be fastidious 862vb.
discriminate against
do wrong 914vb.
discrimination
contrariety 14n.
discrimination 463n.
judgment 480n.
moral sensibility 819n.
fastidiousness 862n.
injustice 914n.
(*see* discriminate)
discriminatory
tasteful 846adj.
unjust 914adj.
discursive
traveling 267adj.
deviating 282adj.
rational 475adj.
prolix 570adj.
conversing 584adj.
discursive 591adj.
discursory
rational 475adj.
discursive 591adj.
discus
circle 250n.
missile 287n.
missile weapon 723n.
discuss
eat 301vb.
meditate 449vb.
argue 475vb.
publish 528vb.
confer 584vb.
dissert 591vb.
discussion
inquiry 459n.
dissertation 591n.
discussion play
lecture 534n.
disdain
reject 607vb.
be fastidious 862vb.
pride 871n.
insolence 878n.
contempt 922n.
disease
disease 651n.
bane 659n.
disembark
land 295vb.
disembarkation
arrival 295n.
disembarrass
disencumber 701vb.
disembodied
immaterial 320adj.
spooky 970adj.
disembody
disperse 75vb.
disembody 320vb.
disemboguement
outflow 298n.
disembowel
void 300vb.
disenchant
dissuade 613vb.
displease 827vb.
disenchanted
indifferent 860adj.
disenchantment
reversion 148n.
discovery 484n.
painfulness 827n.
disencumber
lighten 323vb.
deliver 668vb.
disencumber 701vb.
liberate 746vb.
take away 786vb.
disencumbrance
displacement 188n.
facility 701n.
disendow
depose 752vb.
impoverish 801vb.
disengage
disencumber 701vb.
liberate 746vb.

disengaged
inactive 679adj.
leisurely 681adj.
impassive 820adj.
disinterested 931adj.
disengagement
disjunction 46n.
regression 286n.
extraction 304n.
facility 701n.
disentail
liberate 746vb.
disentangle
simplify 44vb.
disjoin 46vb.
unravel 62vb.
evolve 316vb.
decipher 520vb.
disencumber 701vb.
not retain 779vb.
disentitle
deprive 786vb.
disentitlement
non-ownership 774n.
loss of right 916n.
disentomb
exhume 364vb.
disequilibrium
inequality 29n.
disestablishment
deposal 752n.
disesteem
disrepute 867n.
disrespect 921n.
hold cheap 922vb.
disapprobation 924n.
diseuse
entertainer 594n.
disfavor
prohibition 757n.
refuse 760vb.
disrepute 867n.
odium 888n.
not respect 921vb.
disapprobation 924n.
disfigure
deform 244vb.
mark 547vb.
impair 655vb.
make ugly 842vb.
blemish 845vb.
disfranchisement
subjection 745n.
loss of right 916n.
lawlessness 954n.
disgorge
void, vomit 300vb.
restitute 787vb.
pay 804vb.
disgrace
disrepute, slur 867n.
shame 867vb.
humiliation 872n.
not respect 921vb.
disgraceful
discreditable 867adj.
heinous 934adj.
disgruntle
disappoint 509vb.
cause discontent 829vb.
disguise
assimilation 18n.
dissimilarity 19n.
mimicry 20n.
modify 143vb.
transform 147vb.
screen 421n.
conceal 525vb.
disguise 527n.
dissemble 541vb.
cunning 698n.
disguised
unknown 491adj.
disgust
be unpalatable 391n.
dissuade 613vb.
displease 827vb.
cause discontent 829vb.
tedium 838n.
dislike 861n.
excite hate 888vb.
disgusting
unsavory 391adj.
not nice 645adj.
unclean 649adj.
dish
destroy 165vb.
plate 194n.
horizontality 216n.
dish 301n.
defeat 727vb.
dishabille
informal dress 228n.
uncovering 229n.
disharmony
disagreement 25n.
disorder 61n.
discord 411n.
dissension 709n.
dish-cloth
cleaning cloth 648n.
dishearten
dissuade 613vb.
hinder 702vb.
cause discontent 829vb.
deject 834vb.
disherison
expropriation 876n.
dishevelment
non-uniformity 17n.
disorder 61n.
derangement 63n.
dishonest
false 541adj.
discreditable 867adj.
dishonest 930adj.
dishonesty
thievishness 788n.
wrong 914n.
improbity 930n.
wickedness 934n.
lawbreaking 954n.
dishonor
not observe 769vb.
not pay 805vb.
disrepute 867n.
wrong 914n.
disrespect 921n.
defame 926vb.
improbity 930n.
debauch 951vb.
dishonorable
discreditable 867adj.
blameworthy 924adj.
dishonest 930adj.
dish-rag
cleaning cloth 648n.
dish up
make ready 669vb.
dish-washer
cleaner 648n.
domestic 742n.
dish-water
weak thing 163n.
swill 649n.
disillusion
disappoint 509vb.
disclose 526vb.
dissuade 613vb.
displease 827vb.
regret 830n.
dejection 834n.
hatred 888n.
disillusioned
impassive 820adj.
indifferent 860adj.
disincarnate
disembody 320vb.
disincentive
dissuasion 613n.
hindrance 702n.
disinclination
unwillingness 598n.
dislike 861n.
disincline
dissuade 613vb.
cause dislike 861vb.
disinfect
sterilize 172vb.
purify 648vb.
sanitate 652vb.
doctor 658vb.
safeguard 660vb.
disinfectant
cleanser 648n.
prophylactic 658n.
remedial 658adj.
tutelary 660adj.
disinfected

clean 648adj.
salubrious 652adj.
safe 660adj.
disinfection
hygiene 652n.
disinfest
void 300vb.
disinfestation
cleansing 648n.
disinflation
finance 797n.
disingenuous
false 541adj.
dishonest 930adj.
disinherit
not retain 779vb.
convey 780vb.
deprive 786vb.
impoverish 801vb.
disintegrate
be disjoined 46vb.
break, disjoin 46vb.
decompose 51vb.
disperse 75vb.
pulverize 332vb.
disinter
exhume 364vb.
discover 484vb.
disinterested
choiceless 606adj.
benevolent 897adj.
philanthropic 901adj.
just 913adj.
disinterested 931adj.
virtuous 933adj.
disinterment
inquest 364n.
disinvestment
expenditure 806n.
disjoin
simplify 44vb.
disjoin 46vb.
unstick 49vb.
decompose 51vb.
disperse 75vb.
displace 188vb.
disjunct
disjunct 46adj.
fragmentary 53adj.
orderless 61adj.
discontinuous 72adj.
disjunction
irrelation 10n.
subtraction 39n.
discontinuity 72n.
laxity 734n.
(*see* disjoin)
disjunctive
separate 46adj.
disk
face 237n.
circle 250n.
(*see* disc)
dislike
unwillingness 598n.
be loath 598vb.
refuse 760vb.
dislike 861n., vb.
enmity 881n.
hatred 888n.
dislimb
rend 46vb.
dislocate
disjoin 46vb.
derange 63vb.
disable 161vb.
force 176vb.
displace 188vb.
distort 246vb.
dislodge
derange 63vb.
displace 188vb.
eject 300vb.
disloyal
changeful 152adj.
disloyalty
disobedience 738n.
sedition 738n.
non-observance 769n.
enmity 881n.
dutilessness 918n.
perfidy 930n.
dismal
dark 418adj.
unpleasant 827adj.
melancholic 834adj.
cheerless 834adj.
dismals
melancholy 834n.
dismantle
break, sunder 46vb.
weaken 163vb.
demolish 165vb.
uncover 229vb.
make useless 641vb.
impair 655vb.
disuse 674vb.
make inactive 679vb.
dismantled
unequipped 670adj.
dismay
defeat 727vb.
worry 825n.
fear 854n.
dismember
sunder, rend 46vb.
execute 963vb.
dismemberment
decomposition 51n.
dismiss
be dispersed 75vb.
displace 188vb.
dismiss 300vb.
disregard 458vb.
dismissal
exclusion 57n.
valediction 296n.
ejection 300n.
non-use 674n.
deposal 752n.
loss of right 916n.
dismount
disjoin 46vb.
unstick 49vb.
land 295vb.
descend 309vb.
disobedience
unwillingness 598n.
disobedience 738n.
refusal 760n.
non-observance 769n.
disobedient
willful 602adj.
difficult 700adj.
sullen 893adj.
schismatical 978adj.
(*see* disobedience)
disobey
fail in duty 918vb.
disoblige
be malevolent 898vb.
disordain
depose 752vb.
disorder
non-uniformity 17n.
decompose 51vb.
disorder 61n.
derangement 63n.
discontinuity 72n.
disperse 75vb.
deform 244vb.
negligence 458n.
badness 645n.
disease 651n.
hinder 702vb.
anarchy 734n.
revolt 738n.
disorderly
violent 176adj.
anarchic 734adj.
riotous 738adj.
ill-bred 847adj.
disorderly house
brothel 951n.
disorganization
derangement 63n.
destruction 165n.
impairment 655n.
anarchy 734n.
disorganized
lax 734adj.
disorientate
derange 63vb.
displace 188vb.
disorientation
deviation 282n.
disown
be unrelated 10vb.
negate 533vb.
avoid 620vb.
abrogate 752vb.
not retain 779vb.

disapprove 924vb.
disparage
underestimate 483vb.
shame 867vb.
not respect 921vb.
hold cheap 922vb.
detract 926vb.
disparagement
disrespect 921n.
disapprobation 924n.
detraction 926n.
disparity
irrelation 10n.
difference 15n.
dissimilarity 19n.
disagreement 25n.
inequality 29n.
dispart
disjoin 46vb.
dispassion
inexcitability 823n.
justice 913n.
dispassionate
impassive 820adj.
just 913adj.
disinterested 931adj.
dispatch
punctuality 135n.
move 265vb.
send 272vb.
kill 362vb.
report 523n.
correspondence 588n.
do 676vb.
activity 678n.
haste 680n.
deal with 688vb.
effectuation 725n.
dispatcher
transferrer 272n.
dispatches
report 524n.
dispatch-rider
courier 531n.
dispel
disjoin 46vb.
disperse 75vb.
destroy 165vb.
displace 188vb.
repel 292vb.
disappear 446vb.
liberate 746vb.
dispensable
superfluous 637adj.
useless 641adj.
permitted 756adj.
dispensary
hospital 658n.
dispensation
exclusion 57n.
deliverance 668n.
management 689n.
permission 756n.
non-retention 779n.
apportionment 783n.
non-liability 919n.
dispense
give 781vb.
exempt 919vb.
(*see* dispensation)
dispenser
druggist 658n.
dispense with
not use 674vb.
not retain 779vb.
dispeople
void 300vb.
dispersal
diminution 37n.
disjunction 46n.
dispersion 75n.
transference 272n.
disperse
disappear 446vb.
defeat 727vb.
dispersion
separation 46n.
non-coherence 49n.
disorder 61n.
dispersion 75n.
expansion 197n.
distance 199n.
transference 272n.
divergence 294n.
reflection 417n.
waste 634n.
dispirit
dissuade 613vb.
deject 834vb.
displace
disjoin 46vb.
exclude 57vb.
derange 63vb.
substitute 150vb.
displace 188vb.
move 265vb.
transpose 272vb.
eject 300vb.
displaced person
foreigner 59n.
displacement 188n.
wanderer 268n.
outcaste 883n.
displacement
displacement 188n.
depth 211n.
gravity 322n.
(*see* displace)
displant
displace 188vb.
display
accumulation 74n.
spectacle 445n.
exhibit 522n.
show 522vb.
publicity 528n.
pride 871n.
ostentation 875n.
pageant 875n.
displease
displease 827vb.
cause discontent 829vb.
cause dislike 861vb.
displeasure
sorrow 825n.
annoyance 827n.
discontent 829n.
dislike 861n.
hatred 888n.
resentment 891n.
disapprobation 924n.
disport oneself
be cheerful 833vb.
amuse oneself 837vb.
disposability
non-retention 779n.
disposable
useful 640adj.
used 673adj.
disposal
arrangement 62n.
use 673n.
non-retention 779n.
sale 793n.
disposal, at one's
possessed 773adj.
dispose
order 60vb.
arrange 62vb.
influence 178vb.
tend 179vb.
motivate 612vb.
disposed
willing 597adj.
intending 617adj.
dispose of
dispose of 673vb.
carry through 725vb.
possess 773vb.
sell 793vb.
disposition
temperament 5n.
order 60n.
arrangement 62n.
location 187n.
will 595n.
willingness 597n.
affections 817n.
dispossess
eject 300vb.
convey 780vb.
deprive 786vb.
appropriate 786vb.
impoverish 801vb.
disentitle 916vb.
dispossessed
losing 772adj.
not owning 774adj.
poor 801adj.
unentitled 916adj.

dispossession
ejection 300n.
loss 772n.
loss of right 916n.
dispraise
censure 924n.
dispraise 924vb.
dispread
unassembled 75adj.
disperse 75vb.
disprize
hold cheap 922vb.
disapprove 924vb.
disproof
counter-evidence 467n.
confutation 479n.
negation 533n.
disproportion
irrelation 10n.
disagreement 25n.
inequality 29n.
distortion 246n.
exaggeration 546n.
disproportioned
unsightly 842adj.
disprovable
confuted 479adj.
disprove
(*see* disproof)
disproved
erroneous 495adj.
disputable
uncertain 474adj.
arguing 475adj.
unbelieved 486adj.
litigated 959adj.
disputant
reasoner 475n.
disputation
argument 475n.
disputatious
arguing 475adj.
quarreling 709adj.
dispute
disagree 25vb.
argue 475vb.
quarrel 709n., vb.
contention 716n.
disputer
combatant 722n.
dispute with
bicker 709vb.
disqualification
impotence 161n.
ejection 300n.
inexpedience 643n.
non-preparation 670n.
unskillfulness 695n.
loss of right 916n.
disqualify
exclude 57vb.
disable 161vb.
make useless 641vb.
disentitle 916vb.
disquiet
changeableness 152n.
agitation 318n.
impress 821vb.
worry 825n.
incommode 827vb.
discontent 829n.
nervousness 854n.
disquisition
lecture 534n.
diffuseness 570n.
dissertation 591n.
disquisitional
discursive 591adj.
disrate
shame 867vb.
disregard
exclude 57vb.
be deaf 416vb.
not think 450vb.
be incurious 454vb.
inattention 456n.
disregard 458vb.
not know 491vb.
reject 607vb.
not use 674vb.
abrogate 752vb.
non-observance 769n.
fail in duty 918vb.
not respect 921vb.
impiety 980n.
disregarded
unimportant 639adj.
(*see* disregard)
disrelish
dislike 861n., vb.
hate 888vb.
disremember
forget 506vb.
disrepair
dilapidation 655n.
disreputable
not nice 645adj.
vulgar 847adj.
disreputable 867adj.
plebeian 869adj.
dishonest 930adj.
disrepute
disrepute 867n.
humiliation 872n.
odium 888n.
disrespect
non-observance 769n.
ridicule 851n.
disrepute 867n.
dutilessness 918n.
disrespect 921n.
not respect 921vb.
disapprobation 924n.
disrespectful
non-observant 769adj.
insolent 878adj.
impertinent 878adj.
dutiless 918adj.
disrespectful 921adj.
despising 922adj.
detracting 926adj.
disrobe
doff 229vb.
disruption
separation 46n.
destruction 165n.
dissatisfaction
dissent 489n.
sorrow 825n.
discontent 829n.
dislike 861n.
resentment 891n.
disapprobation 924n.
dissatisfy
disappoint 509vb.
be imperfect 647vb.
displease 827vb.
cause discontent 829vb.
dissaving
expenditure 806n.
dissect
sunder 46vb.
decompose 51vb.
class 62vb.
inquire 459vb.
disseisin
expropriation 786n.
disseisor
taker 786n.
dissemblance
dissimilarity 19n.
dissemble
make unlike 19vb.
mislead 495vb.
be equivocal 518vb.
conceal 525vb.
dissemble 541vb.
deceive 542vb.
be affected 850vb.
dissembler
deceiver 545n.
slyboots 698n.
dissemination
dispersion 75n.
information 524n.
publication 528n.
dissension
difference 15n.
disagreement 25n.
dissent 489n.
opposition 704n.
dissension 709n.
contention 716n.
enmity 881n.
dissent
disagreement 25n.
unbelief 486n.
dissent 489n., vb.
negation 533n.
reject 607vb.
opposition 704n.

dissension 709n.
refuse 760vb.
sectarianism 978n.
dissenter
nonconformist 84n.
unbeliever 486n.
dissentient 489n.
schismatic 978n.
dissentience
dissent 489n.
dissentient
nonconformist 84n.
unbeliever 486n.
dissentient 489n.
opponent 705n.
heterodox 977adj.
schismatical 978adj.
dissenting
unconformable 84adj.
heterodox 977adj.
schismatical 978adj.
dissert
write 586vb.
dissert 591vb.
dissertation
diffuseness 570n.
oration 579n.
dissertation 591n.
disserve
harm 645vb.
disservice
evil 616n.
inutility 641n.
dissever
disjoin 46vb.
dissidence
disagreement 25n.
unconformity 84n.
dissent 489n.
sectarianism 978n.
dissident
nonconformist 84n.
dissentient 489n.
discontented 829adj.
schismatic 978n.
dissilience
disjunction 46n.
outbreak 176n.
dissimilar
different 15adj.
non-uniform 17adj.
dissimilar 19adj.
unequal 29adj.
dissimilation
dissimilarity 19n.
speech sound 398n.
grammar 654n.
dissimilitude
dissimilarity 19n.
dissimulate
dissemble 541vb.
dissimulation
mimicry 20n.
concealment 525n.
duplicity 541n.
dissipated
prodigal 815adj.
lecherous 951adj.
dissipation
dispersion 75n.
pleasure 376n.
disappearance 446n.
waste 634n.
loss 772n.
prodigality 815n.
intemperance 943n.
sensualism 944n.
unchastity 951n.
dissociation
irrelation 10n.
disjunction 46n.
unwillingness 598n.
opposition 704n.
schism 978n.
dissoluble
severable 46adj.
liquefied 337adj.
dissoluteness
sensualism 944n.
unchastity 951n.
dissolution
diminution 37n.
separation 46n.
decomposition 51n.
disorder 61n.
finality 69n.
destruction 165n.
liquefaction 337n.
disappearance 446n.
abrogation 752n.
non-retention 779n.
dissolvable
severable 46adj.
dissolve
not be 2vb.
shade off 27vb.
decompose 51vb.
be dispersed 75vb.
destroy 165vb.
deform 244vb.
(*see* dissolution)
dissolvent
liquefaction 337n.
dissonance
disagreement 25n.
discord 411n.
dissension 709n.
dissuade
cause doubt 486vb.
dissuade 613vb.
advise 691vb.
hinder 702vb.
deprecate 762vb.
cause discontent 829vb.
frighten 854vb.
dissuasive
dissuasive 613adj.
advising 691adj.
deprecatory 762adj.
distaff
weaving 222n.
distaff side
womankind 373n.
distance
difference 15n.
range 183n.
distance 199n.
length 203n.
outstrip 277vb.
progress 285vb.
outdo 306vb.
invisibility 444n.
unsociability 883n.
distance apart
disjunction 46n.
distance of time
diuturnity 113n.
antiquity 125n.
distant
extraneous 59adj.
distant 199adj.
exterior 223adj.
incurious 454adj.
impassive 820adj.
prideful 871adj.
inimical 881adj.
unsociable 883adj.
distant past
preterition 125n.
distaste
dislike 861n., vb.
distasteful
unpleasant 827adj.
distemper
weaken 163vb.
facing 226n.
color, pigment 425n.
art equipment 553n.
disease 651n.
animal disease 651n.
incommode 827vb.
distend
augment 36vb.
expand 197vb.
distension
dilation 197n.
disthrone
unthrone 734vb.
distich
verse form 593n.
distill
exude 298vb.
extract 304vb.
vaporize 338vb.
purify 648vb.
distillation
outflow 298n.
heating 381n.
distillery
vaporizer 338n.
workshop 687n.

distinct
different 15adj.
separate 46adj.
definite 80adj.
sounding 398adj.
loud 400adj.
well-seen 443adj.
intelligible 516adj.
assertive 532adj.
vocal 577adj.
distinction
differentiation 15n.
specialty 80n.
discrimination 463n.
reasoning 475n.
elegance 575n.
importance 638n.
prestige, honors 866n.
nobility 868n.
title 870n.
distinctive
distinctive 15adj.
special 80adj.
distinctness
sound 398n.
loudness 400n.
voice 577n.
(*see* distinct)
distinguish
differentiate 15vb.
set apart 46vb.
see 438vb.
distinguish 463vb.
be wise 498vb.
understand 516vb.
name 561vb.
dignify 866vb.
distinguishable
separate 46adj.
distinguished
superior 34adj.
elegant 575adj.
notable 638adj.
noteworthy 866adj.
distort
make unlike 19vb.
transform 147vb.
render oblique 220vb.
distort 246vb.
be false 541vb.
misinterpret 521vb.
misteach 535vb.
exaggerate 546vb.
misrepresent 552vb.
pervert 655vb.
misuse 675vb.
make ugly 842vb.
distorted
abnormal 84adj.
imperfect 647adj.
distorting mirror
visual fallacy 440n.
mirror 442n.
misrepresentation 552n.
distortion
irrelation 10n.
mimicry 20n.
violence 176n.
visual fallacy 440n.
falsehood 541n.
untruth 543n.
blemish 845n.
(*see* distort)
distract
distract 456vb.
distraction
abstractedness 456n.
frenzy 503n.
excitable state 822n.
distraint
expropriation 786n.
distrait
abstracted 456adj.
distraught
doubting 474adj.
frenzied 503adj.
excited 821adj.
distress
pain 377n.
give pain 377vb.
evil 616n.
ill-treat 645vb.
fatigue 684n., vb.
adversity 731n.
expropriation 786n.
poverty 801n.
hurt 827vb.
distressing
felt 818adj.
distressing 827adj.
distress signal
danger signal 665n.
distributary
stream 350n.
distribution
arrangement 62n.
dispersion 75n.
apportionment 783n.
district
subdivision 53n.
district 184n.
regional 184adj.
place 185n.
locality 187n.
land 344n.
parish 985n.
distrust
doubt 486n., vb.
be nervous 854vb.
jealousy 911n.
disturb
decompose 51vb.
derange 63vb.
mistime 138vb.
modify 143vb.
displace 188vb.
agitate 318vb.
cause feeling 374vb.
distract 456vb.
incommode 827vb.
frighten 854vb.
disturbance
turmoil 61n.
derangement 63n.
intempestivity 138n.
commotion 318n.
revolt 738n.
disturbed
violent 176adj.
nervous 854adj.
disunion, disunity
disjunction 46n.
disorder 61n.
dissension 709n.
disunite
disjoin 46vb.
disuse
rejection 607n.
desuetude 611n.
relinquishment 621n.
non-use 674n.
make inactive 679vb.
abrogation 752n.
non-retention 779n.
disused
past 125adj.
antiquated 127adj.
disyllable
spoken letter 558n.
ditch
gap 201n.
fence 235n.
cavity 255n.
furrow 262n.
dry 342vb.
lake 346n.
conduit 351n.
drain 351n.
cultivate 370vb.
tergiversate 603vb.
reject 607vb.
relinquish 621vb.
protection 660n.
disuse 674vb.
stratagem 698n.
obstacle 702n.
defenses 713n.
not retain 779vb.
ditch-water
swill 649n.
dither
be agitated 318vb.
be uncertain 474vb.
be irresolute 601vb.
dithyramb
vocal music 412n.
poem 593n.
praise 923n.
dithyrambic
approving 923adj.
dithyrambist

poet 593n.
ditto
identity 13n.
accord 24vb.
repetition 106n.
again 106adv.
assent 488vb.
ditty
vocal music 412n.
ditty-bag
bag 194n.
diuretic
excretory 302adj.
cleanser 648n.
diurnal
seasonal 141adj.
diuturnity
diuturnity 113n.
perpetuity 115n.
diva
vocalist 413n.
actor 594n.
divagate
stray 282vb.
circuit 626vb.
divan
seat 218n.
reading matter 589n.
anthology 592n.
poem 593n.
law court 956n.
divaricate
differ 15vb.
bifurcate 92vb.
angulate 247vb.
deviate 282vb.
diverge 294vb.
dive
tavern 192n.
swim 269vb.
navigate 269vb.
fly 271vb.
spurt 277n.
descent 309n.
plunge 313n., vb.
be wet 341vb.
divellicate
rend 46vb.
diver
depth 211n.
diver 313n.
waterfowl 365n.
diverge
be oblique 220vb.
(*see* divergence)
divergence
difference 15n.
non-uniformity 17n.
dissimilarity 19n.
disagreement 25n.
disjunction 46n.
dispersion 75n.
bifurcation 92n.
deviation 282n.
divergence 294n.
dissension 709n.
divers
different 15adj.
multiform 82adj.
many 104adj.
diverse
(*see* diversity)
diversification
variegation 437n.
diversify
modify 143vb.
variegate 437vb.
diversion
change 143n.
deviation 282n.
pleasure 367n.
trickery, trap 542n.
misuse 675n.
expropriation 786n.
amusement 837n.
diversity
irrelation 10n.
difference 15n.
non-uniformity 17n.
dissimilarity 19n.
multiformity 82n.
variegation 437n.
divert
render oblique 220vb.
deflect 282vb.
distract 456vb.
ensnare 542vb.
misuse 675vb.
obstruct 702vb.
not pay 805vb.
amuse 837vb.
divertissement
pleasure 376n.
musical piece 412n.
stage play 594n.
amusement 837n.
divest
subtract 39vb.
uncover 229vb.
relinquish 621vb.
depose 752vb.
deprive 786vb.
divide
sunder 46vb.
part 53vb.
class 62vb.
do sums 86vb.
bisect 92vb.
summit 213n.
partition 231n.
limit 236n.
mete out 465vb.
vote 605vb.
make quarrels 709vb.
apportion 783vb.
schismatize 978vb.
dividend
part 53n.
numerical element 85n.
gain 771n.
participation 775n.
portion 783n.
dividers
gauge 465n.
dividing line
dividing line 92n.
divination
intuition 476n.
divination 511n.
hermeneutics 520n.
sorcery 983n.
occultism 984n.
divine
foresee 510vb.
divine 511vb.
suppose 512vb.
beautiful 841adj.
lovable 887adj.
divine 965adj.
godlike 965adj.
theologian 973n.
religious 973adj.
cleric 986n.
divineness
divineness 965n.
diviner
diviner 511n.
interpreter 520n.
sorcerer 983n.
sorceress 983n.
occultist, psychic 984n.
divine right
authority 733n.
divine service
public worship 981n.
diving
aquatics 269n.
diving-bell
diver 313n.
divining rod
magic instrument 983n.
divinity
divineness 965n.
theology 973n.
divisible
severable 46adj.
numerical 85adj.
division
scission 46n.
decomposition 51n.
subdivision 53n.
arrangement 62n.
discontinuity 72n.
classification 77n.
numerical operation 86n.
district 184n.
partition 231n.
vote 605n.
parliament 692n.

dissension 709n.
formation 722n.
apportionment 783n.
seclusion 833n.
schism, sect 978n.
divisor
numerical element 85n.
divorce
separation 46n.
non-retention 779n.
divorce 896n., vb.
divot
piece 53n.
soil 344n.
grass 366n.
divulgation
publication 528n.
divulgatory
disclosing 526adj.
divulge
manifest 522vb.
divulge 526vb.
publish 528vb.
divulsion
scission 46n.
divvy
apportion 783vb.
dizzy
unequal 29adj.
changeful 152adj.
high 209adj.
rotary 315adj.
dim-sighted 440adj.
light-minded 456adj.
foolish 499adj.
ninny 501n.
fool 501n.
crazed 503adj.
crapulous 949adj.
tipsy 949adj.
do
be in a state 7vb.
accord 24vb.
cause 156vb.
produce 164vb.
operate 173vb.
deceive 542vb.
represent 551vb.
be instrumental 628vb.
suffice 635vb.
be useful 640vb.
be expedient 642vb.
do 676vb.
deal with 688vb.
amusement 837n.
celebration 876n.
doable
possible 469adj.
do after
do likewise 20vb.
do again
repeat 106vb.
do all one can
exert oneself 682vb.
do as others do
conform 83vb.
do away with
destroy 165vb.
kill 362vb.
dobbin
horse 273n.
doch-an-dorrach
valediction 296n.
docile
tamed 369adj.
studious 536adj.
willing 597adj.
induced 612adj.
obedient 739adj.
docility
learning 536n.
willingness 597n.
persuasibility 612n.
docimasy
experiment 461n.
dock
subtract 39vb.
cut 46vb.
stable 192n.
shorten 204vb.
navigate 269vb.
goal 295n.
arrive 295vb.
storage 632n.
impair 655vb.
shelter 662n.
workshop 687n.
lock-up 748n.
courtroom 956n.
docker
boatman 270n.
worker 686n.
docket
list 87n., vb.
credential 466n.
label 547n.
mark 547vb.
registration 548n.
compendium 592n.
abstract 592vb.
dockland
district 184n.
dockyard
workshop 687n.
doctor
mix 43vb.
modify 143vb.
scholar 492n.
sage 500n.
bribe 612vb.
cure 656vb.
doctor 658n., vb.
relieve 831vb.
academic title 870n.
theologian 973n.
doctorate
academic title 870n.
doctrinaire
doctrinaire 473n.
positive 473adj.
narrow mind 481n.
theorist 512n.
doctrinal
credal 485adj.
educational 534adj.
theological 973adj.
orthodox 976adj.
doctrine
creed 485n.
theology 973n.
document
evidence 466n.
corroborate 466vb.
demonstrate 478vb.
record 548n.
documentary
cinema 445n.
evidential 466adj.
informative 524adj.
descriptive 590adj.
documentation
(*see* document)
dodder
be agitated 318vb.
be irresolute 601vb.
dodderer
waverer 601n.
dodge
vary 152vb.
be in motion 265vb.
deviate 282vb.
campanology 412n.
disregard 458vb.
sophisticate 477vb.
be stealthy 525vb.
dissemble 541vb.
trickery 542n.
pretext 614n.
avoid 620vb.
contrivance 623n.
means of escape 667n.
elude 667vb.
skill 694n.
stratagem 698n.
not observe 769vb.
be dishonest 930vb.
dodger
hider 527n.
avoider 620n.
dodo
flightless bird 365n.
do duty
function 622vb.
deputize 755vb.
doe
speeder 277n.
female animal 373n.
doer
producer 167n.
doer 676n.

doeskin
skin 226n.
doff
doff 229vb.
do for
destroy 165vb.
murder 362vb.
kill 362vb.
minister to 703vb.
defeat 727vb.
serve 742vb.
dog
accompany 89vb.
be behind 238vb.
follow 284vb.
dog 365n.
male animal 372n.
pursue 619vb.
knave 938n.
dog-cart
carriage, cart 274n.
dog-collar
neckwear 228n.
canonicals 989n.
dog-days
heat 379n.
doge
officer 741n.
dog-eared
folded 261adj.
dilapidated 655adj.
used 673adj.
dog-fight
duel 716n.
fight 716n.
dogged
obstinate 602adj.
courageous 855adj.
doggedness
perseverance 600n.
obstinacy 602n.
dogger
fishing-boat 275n.
hunter 619n.
doggerel
inelegant 576adj.
doggerel 593n.
poetic 593adj.
ridiculousness 849n.
funny 849adj.
doggish
fashionable 848adj.
dog in the manger
hinderer 702n.
egotist 932n.
dogma
certainty 473n.
creed 485n.
theology 973n.
dogmatic
certain, positive 473adj.
narrow-minded 481adj.
credal 485adj.
assertive 532adj.
obstinate 602adj.
vain 873adj.
dogmatics
theology 973n.
dogmatism
positiveness 473n.
affirmation 532n.
opiniatrety 602n.
dogmatist
doctrinaire 473n.
opinionist 602n.
dogmatize
dogmatize 473vb.
be biased 481vb.
affirm 532vb.
do good
benefit 615vb.
be useful 640vb.
do good 644vb.
philanthropize 897vb.
do-gooder
kind person 897n.
philanthropist 901n.
dogsbody
food 301n.
dog's tooth
notch 260n.
pattern 844n.
dog-tired
fatigued 684adj.
dog-track
meeting place 192n.
arena 724n.
dog-trot
gait 265n.
slowness 278n.
dog-watch
period 110n.
evening 129n.
doily
cleaning cloth 648n.
do in
destroy 165vb.
kill 362vb.
doing
happening 154adj.
production 164n.
agency 173n.
operative 173adj.
representation 551n.
action 676n.
doing 676adj.
doing, be
busy oneself 622vb.
doings
affairs 154n.
clothing 228n.
deed 676n.
doing time
imprisoned 747adj.
doing well
prosperous 730adj.
do instead
compensate 31vb.
do into
translate 520vb.
doit
small coin 33n.
trifle 639n.
doited
aged 131adj.
do-it-yourself
bungled 695adj.
artless 699adj.
laical 987adj.
do justice to
be just 913vb.
vindicate 927vb.
doldrums
weather 340n.
inaction 677n.
inactivity 769n.
dejection 834n.
dole
small quantity 33n.
insufficiency 636n.
gift 781n.
portion 783n.
booty 790n.
sorrow 825n.
doleful
melancholic 834adj.
lamenting 836adj.
dole out
mete out 465vb.
give 781vb.
apportion 783vb.
be parsimonious 816vb.
doll
dwarf 196n.
woman 373n.
image 551n.
plaything 837n.
dollar
coinage 797n.
dollop
piece 53n.
portion 783n.
doll's house
plaything 837n.
doll up
primp 843vb.
dolly
infantine 132adj.
little 196adj.
dolman
tunic 228n.
dolmen
tomb 364n.
monument 548n.
dolor
pain 377n.
suffering 825n.
dolorific
paining 827adj.

dolphin
fish 365n.
dolt
dunce 501n.
doltish
unintelligent 499adj.
Dom
church title 986n.
domain
territory 184n.
lands 777n.
dome
edifice 164n.
house 192n.
high structure 209n.
head 213n.
roof 226n.
sphere 252n.
dome 253n.
Domesday Book
list 87n.
domestic
native 191adj.
provincial 192adj.
interior 224adj.
tamed 369adj.
domestic 742n.
unsociable 883adj.
domesticate
break in 369vb.
habituate 610vb.
domesticated
native 191adj.
quiescent 266adj.
tamed 369adj.
subjected 745adj.
domestication
location 187n.
animal husbandry 369n.
domesticity
quietude 266n.
unsociability 883n.
domestic science
cookery 301n.
domicile
abode 192n.
domiciled
native 191adj.
domiciliary visit
search 459n.
dominance
influence 178n.
dominant
supreme 34adj.
influential 178adj.
musical note 410n.
authoritative 733adj.
dominate
be able 160vb.
influence 178vb.
prevail 178vb.
dominate 733vb.
subjugate 745vb.
dominating
overhanging 209adj.
domination
superiority 34n.
influence 178n.
governance 733n.
domineer
oppress 735vb.
domineering
authoritative 733adj.
oppressive 735adj.
insolent 878adj.
dominie
teacher 537n.
master 741n.
dominion
territory 184n.
governance 733n.
polity 733n.
lands 777n.
dominion status
government 733n.
independence 744n.
domino
lamina 207n.
robe, cloak 228n.
disguise 527n.
plaything 837n.
don
wear 228vb.
male 372n.
scholar 492n.
teacher 537n.
master 741n.
aristocrat 868n.
title 870n.
donation
incentive 612n.
giving 781n.
Donatism
heresy 977n.
schism 978n.
donative
incentive 612n.
gift 781n.
done
culinary 301adj.
usual 610adj.
fashionable 848adj.
donee
recipient 782n.
done for
fatigued 684adj.
done thing
practice 610n.
etiquette 848n.
done up
fatigued 684adj.
done with
disused 674adj.
donjon
fort 713n.
Don Juan
libertine 952n.
donkey
beast of burden 273n.
animal 365n.
fool 501n.
donna
lady 373n.
donnish
narrow-minded 481adj.
instructed 490adj.
severe 735adj.
fastidious 862adj.
donor
provider 633n.
giver 781n.
benefactor 903n.
do-nothing
non-active 677adj.
idler 679n.
lazy 679adj.
do nothing but
recur 139vb.
Don Quixote
crank 504n.
visionary 513n.
brave person 835n.
don't-care
rash 857adj.
indifferent 860adj.
donzel
retainer 742n.
doodle
play music 413vb.
be inattentive 456vb.
doodlebug
rocket 276n.
bomb 723n.
dooly
vehicle 274n.
doom
finality 69n.
predestine 155vb.
ruin 165n.
death 361n.
judge 480vb.
fate 596n.
necessitate 596vb.
intend 617vb.
condemnation 961n.
punishment 963n.
doomed
ephemeral 114adj.
unfortunate 731adj.
unhappy 825adj.
doomsday
future state 124n.
doomsman
judge 957n.
door
entrance 68n.
threshold 234n.
barrier 235n.
doorway 263n.
access 624n.
door-bell

signal 547n.
door-keeper, doorman
janitor 264n.
servant 742n.
door-knocker
hammer 279n.
signal 547n.
doormat
weakling 163n.
floor-cover 226n.
cleaning utensil 648n.
slave 742n.
coward 856n.
doorstep
stand 218n.
threshold 234n.
doorway 263n.
doorway
doorway 263n.
way in 297n.
access 624n.
do out of
deceive 542vb.
defraud 788vb.
do over
coat 226vb.
dope
anesthetic 375n.
ninny 501n.
information 524n.
befool 542vb.
drug 658n.
doctor 658vb.
make inactive 679vb.
dope-addict, dope-fiend
madman 504n.
habitué 610n.
doppelgänger
ghost 970n.
Doppler effect
displacement 188n.
Doric
harmonic 410adj.
dialect 560n.
ornamental 844adj.
dormancy
inaction 677n.
(*see* dormant)
dormant
inert 175adj.
quiescent 266adj.
latent 523adj.
sleepy 679adj.
abrogated 752adj.
dormer
window 263n.
dormitory
quarters 192n.
chamber 194n.
dormitory area
housing 192n.
dormouse
idler 679n.
dorsal
back 238adj.
dorsum
rear 238n.
camber 253n.
dory
fishing-boat 275n.
table fish 365n.
dose
finite quantity 26n.
piece 53n.
measurement 465n.
medicine 658n.
portion 783n.
punishment 963n.
dosology
medical art 658n.
doss down
be quiescent 266vb.
sleep 679vb.
dosser
basket 194n.
doss-house
inn 192n.
dossier
documentary evidence 465n.
information 524n.
record 548n.
dossil
covering 226n.
stopper 264n.
dot
small thing 33n.
place 185n.
punctuation 547n.
mark 547vb.
lettering 586n.
dower 777n.
pattern 844n.
dotage
age 131n.
credulity 487n.
folly 499n.
insanity 503n.
dotard
old man 133n.
fool 501n.
lover 887n.
dote
be foolish 499vb.
desire 859vb.
be in love 887vb.
do the honors
be hospitable 882vb.
show respect 920vb.
do the needful
suffice 635vb.
do 676vb.
deal with 688vb.
pay 804vb.
dot, on the
instantaneously 116adv.
dottle
leavings 41n.
rubbish 641n.
dotty
foolish 499adj.
crazed 503adj.
double
identity 13n.
analogue 18n.
augment 36vb.
double 91adj., vb.
repeat 106vb.
substitute 150n.
vary 152vb.
invigorate 174vb.
enlarge 197vb.
fold 261vb.
gait 265n.
walk 267vb.
speeding 277n.
turn back 286vb.
spirit 447n.
hypocritical 541adj.
representation 551n.
equivocal 578adj.
double-bass
viol 414n.
double-cross
deceive 542vb.
be cunning 698vb.
be dishonest 930vb.
double-dealing
duplicity 541n.
tergiversating 603adj.
cunning 698n.
perfidy 930n.
double Dutch
unmeaningness 515n.
unintelligibility 517n.
double-dyed
colored 425adj.
vicious 934adj.
double entendre
equivocalness 518n.
impurity 951n.
double entry
registration 548n.
accounts 808n.
double-faced
double 91adj.
dishonest 930adj.
double figures
over five 99n.
double-fronted
architectural 192adj.
double harness
duality 90n.
cooperation 706n.
double-jointed
flexible 327adj.
double meaning
equivocalness 518n.
doubles
campanology 412n.
double-shuffle

dance 837n.
double-sided
dual 90adj.
double-strength
strong 162adj.
intoxicating 949adj.
doublet
substitute 150n.
tunic 228n.
word 559n.
double-take
sequel 67n.
inspection 438n.
doubletalk
unmeaningness 515n.
equivocalness 518n.
slang 560n.
double-tongued
equivocal 518adj.
hypocritical 541adj.
dishonest 930adj.
double up
disable 161vb.
hurt 827vb.
double vision
vision 438n.
dim sight 440n.
doublure
lining 227n.
doubly
greatly 32adv.
doubt
improbability 472n.
dubiety 474n.
doubt 486n., vb.
dissent 489n.
not know 491vb.
be nervous 854vb.
caution 858n.
doubter
unbeliever 486n.
doubtful
moot 459adj.
disreputable 867adj.
dishonest 930adj.
(*see* doubt)
doubtful meaning, of
puzzling 517adj.
doubting
irresolute 601adj.
nervous 854adj.
doubtless
certainly 473adv.
douceur
gift 781n.
reward 962n.
douche
water 339n.
ablution 648n.
therapy 658n.
dough
softness 327n.
pulpiness 356n.
dibs 797n.
doughboy
soldier 722n.
doughnut
pastry 301n.
doughty
courageous 855adj.
do up
join 45vb.
make better 654vb.
repair 656vb.
fatigue 684vb.
dour
obstinate 602adj.
severe 735adj.
douse
retard 278vb.
depress 311vb.
plunge 313vb.
drench 341vb.
extinguish 382vb.
snuff out 418vb.
dove
bird 365n.
mediator 720n.
innocent 935n.
Holy Ghost 965n.
dovecote
stable 192n.
dovelike
peaceful 717adj
dovetail
accord 24vb.
join 45vb.
cross 222vb.
intromit 231vb.
implant 303vb.
dowager
woman 373n.
widowed spouse 896n.
dowdy
graceless 842adj.
bad taste 847n.
ill-bred 847adj.
dower
giving 718n., vb.
dower 777n., vb.
dowerless
poor 801adj.
do with, have to
be related 9vb.
do without
not retain 779vb.
dowlas
textile 222n.
down
filament 208n.
under 210adv.
smoothness 258n.
hair 259n.
down 309adv.
levity 323n.
softness 327n.
recorded 548adj.
dejected 834adj.
sullen 893adj.
down-and-out
powerless 161adj.
dilapidated 655adj.
poor man 801n.
low fellow 869n.
down-at-heel
dilapidated 655adj.
beggarly 801adj.
disreputable 867adj.
downcast
dejected 834adj.
downdraft
descent 309n.
wind 352n.
downfall
ruin 165n.
descent 309n.
defeat 728n.
adversity 731n.
downgrade
shame 867vb.
punish 963vb.
downhill
acclivity 220n.
sloping 220adj.
down 309adv.
facility 701n.
easy 701adj.
downiness
(*see* downy)
down in the mouth
dejected 834adj.
down on one's luck
unfortunate 731adj.
downpour
descent 309n.
rain 350n.
downright
consummate 32adj.
positively 32adv.
simple 44adj.
complete 54adj.
intelligible 516adj.
undisguised 522adj.
veracious 540adj.
downrush
spurt 277n.
descent 309n.
downs
high land 209n.
down stage
stage-set 594n.
on stage 594adv.
downstairs
under 210adv.
down 309adv.
downstream
toward 281adv.
down 309adv.
easy 701adj.
down to earth
true 494adj.
down to the ground

completely 54adv.
down tools
cease 154vb.
revolt 738vb.
downtown
afar 199adv.
directed 281adj.
downtrend
deterioration 655n.
downtrodden
subjected 745adj.
suffering 825adj.
down under
beyond 199adv.
downwards
under 210adv.
down 309adv.
downwind
directed 281adj.
toward 281adv.
downy
fibrous 208adj.
smooth 258adj.
downy 259adj.
soft 327adj.
comfortable 376adj.
dowry
store 632n.
dower 777n.
dowse
search 459vb.
(*see* douse)
dowser
inquirer 459n.
detector 484n.
diviner 511n.
psychic 984n.
dowsing
intuition 476n.
divination 511n.
doxological
theological 973adj.
devotional 981adj.
doxology
praise 923n.
act of worship 981n.
hymn 981n.
doxy
creed 485n.
kept woman 952n.
theology 973n.
doyen
seniority 131n.
doyley, doily
cleaning cloth 648n.
doze
be neglectful 458vb.
sleep 679n., vb.
dozen
over five 99n.
drab
uniform 16adj.
soft-hued 425adj.
dirty person 649n.
dilapidated 655adj.
cheerless 834adj.
dull 840adj.
graceless 842n.
loose woman 952n.
drachma
weighment 322n.
coinage 797n.
draconian
severe 735adj.
draff
swill 649n.
draft
copy 22n.
prototype 23n.
compose 56vb.
depth 211n.
transport 272n.
traction 288n.
potion 301n.
gravity 322n.
wind 352n.
representation 551n.
write 586vb.
compendium 592n.
plan 623n., vb.
medicine 658n.
army 722n.
armed force 722n.
adversity 731n.
compel 740vb.
paper money 797n.
plaything 837n.
drafthorse
drafthorse 273n.
draft off
disperse 75vb.
displace 188vb.
transpose 272vb.
draftsman
recorder 549n.
artist 556n.
draftsmanship
painting 553n.
drag
pend 136vb.
influence 178n.
counteraction 182n.
be long 203vb.
transpose 272vb.
carriage 274n.
slowness 278n.
draw 288vb.
attract 291vb.
friction 333vb.
motivate 612vb.
safeguard 662n.
difficulty 700n.
encumbrance 702n.
restraint 747n.
fetter 748n.
card game 837n.
be tedious 838vb.
drag from
extract 304vb.
compel 740vb.
dragging
slow 278adj.
unwilling 598adj.
dragging out
protraction 113n.
draggle
make unclean 649vb.
draggletail
slut 61n.
dirty person 649n.
dragnet
generality 79n.
network 222n.
traction 288n.
dragoman
guide 520n.
drag on
continue 108vb.
elapse 111vb.
drag on 113vb.
pend 136vb.
be long 203vb.
dragon
rara avis 84n.
violent creature 176n.
drag oneself
consent 758vb.
drag one's feet
move slowly 278vb.
be loath 598vb.
dragonfly
fly 365n.
dragonnade
terror tactics 712n.
penalty 963n.
dragon's blood
red pigment 431n.
dragon's mouth
danger 661n.
dragoon
cavalry 722n.
compel 740vb.
drag out
spin out 113vb.
extract 304vb.
manifest 522vb.
drain
bate 37vb.
receptacle 194n.
outflow 298n.
void 300vb.
drink 301vb.
dry 342vb.
drain 351n.
cultivate 370vb.
storage 632n.
waste 634vb.
purify 648vb.
sink 649n.
sanitate 652vb.
loss 772n.
levy 786vb.

drainage
outflow 298n.
voidance 300n.
desiccation 342n.
waste 634n.
cleansing 648n.
dirt, swill 649n.
drain of color
decolorize 426vb.
drain-pipe
cylinder 252n.
outlet 298n.
drain 351n.
cleanser 648n.
drake
waterfowl 365n.
male animal 372n.
gun 723n.
dram
potion 301n.
pungency 388n.
metrology 465n.
incentive 612n.
(*see* drachma)
drama, dramatics
drama, stage play 594n.
action 676n.
activity 678n.
excitation 821n.
ostentation 875n.
dramatic
dramatic 594adj.
impressive 821adj.
wonderful 864adj.
showy 875adj.
dramatis personae
list 87n.
person 371n.
actor 594n.
personnel 686n.
party 708n.
dramatist
dramatist 594n.
dramatize
exaggerate 546vb.
represent 551vb.
dramatize 594vb.
dramatize oneself
be affected 850vb.
dramaturgy
mimicry 20n.
dramaturgy 594n.
drape
hang 217vb.
dress 228vb.
draper
clothier 228n.
drapery
pendant 217n.
robe 228n.
drapes
covering 226n.
robe 228n.
drastic
vigorous 174adj.
severe 735adj.
draught-board
checker 437n.
draughts
board game 837n.
draw
copy 20vb.
draw 28n.
be equal 28vb.
compose 56vb.
bring together 74vb.
displace 188vb.
make thin 206vb.
uncover 229vb.
outline 233vb.
efform 243vb.
draw 288vb.
attraction 291n.
attract 291vb.
cook 301vb.
extract 304vb.
blow, breathe 352vb.
be hot 379vb.
smoke 388vb.
represent 551vb.
paint 553vb.
describe 590vb.
motivate 612vb.
gambling 618n.
provide 633vb.
acquire 771vb.
receive 782vb.
take 786vb.
receipt 807n.
desired object 859n.
excite love 887vb.
draw a bead on
aim 281vb.
shoot 287vb.
fire at 712vb.
threaten 900vb.
draw a blank
fail 728vb.
draw aside
deflect 282vb.
draw attention
attract notice 455vb.
show 522vb.
draw back
regress 286vb.
recede 290vb.
avoid 620vb.
drawback
decrement 42n.
evil 616n.
obstacle 702n.
discount 810n.
draw-bar
coupling 47n.
draw blood
void 300vb.
attack 712vb.
draw breath
be 1vb.
live 360vb.
be born 360vb.
be refreshed 685vb.
drawbridge
bridge 624n.
means of escape 667n.
fort 713n.
drawee
debtor 803n.
drawer
compartment 194n.
traction 288n.
artist 556n.
servant 742n.
drawers
trousers 228n.
underwear 228n.
draw in
make smaller 198vb.
drawing
representation 551n.
picture 553n.
drawing and quartering
capital punishment 963n.
drawing-room
assembly 74n.
chamber 194n.
beau monde 848n.
social gathering 882n.
draw in one's horns
submit 721vb.
drawl
move slowly 278vb.
speech defect 580n.
draw lots
gamble 618vb.
drawn
equal 28adj.
closed 264adj.
drawn game
draw 28n.
non-completion 726n.
drawn-thread work
needlework 844n.
draw off
extract 304vb.
obstruct 702vb.
levy 786vb.
draw out
spin out 113vb.
enlarge 197vb.
extract 304vb.
be diffuse 570vb.
drawstring
fastening 47n.
ligature 47n.
draw stumps
terminate 69vb.
draw the curtain
screen 421vb.
conceal 525vb.

draw the line
exclude 57vb.
discriminate 463vb.
reject 607vb.
restrain 747vb.
prohibit 757vb.
draw the teeth
disable 161vb.
counteract 182vb.
be obstructive 702vb.
draw together
join 45vb.
bring together 74vb.
draw up
compose 56vb.
be in order 60vb.
come to rest 266vb.
write 586vb.
draw upon
draw money 797vb.
dray
cart 274n.
drayage
transport 272n.
drayman
driver 268n.
dread
expectation 507n.
fear 854n., vb.
dreadful
harmful 645adj.
not nice 645adj.
adverse 731adj.
distressing 827adj.
frightening 854adj.
dreadfully
painfully 32adv.
dreadnought
warship 722n.
dream
insubstantial thing 4n.
vision 438n.
visual fallacy 440n.
not think 450vb.
be inattentive 456vb.
error 495n.
suppose 512vb.
fantasy 513n.
objective 617n.
sleep 679vb.
a beauty 841n.
hope 852vb.
desired object 859n.
dreamer
crank 504n.
visionary 513n.
idler 679n.
dreamland
fantasy 513n.
sleep 679n.
dreamlike
shadowy 419adj.
dream, not a
reality 1n.
dream up
imagine 513vb.
dream world
fantasy 513n.
dreamy
insubstantial 4adj.
thoughtful 449adj.
abstracted 456adj.
imaginary 513adj.
dreary
unpleasant 827adj.
cheerless 834adj.
dejected 834adj.
melancholic 834adj.
tedious 838adj.
dull 840adj.
graceless 842adj.
dredge
extract 304vb.
elevate 310vb.
dredger
excavator 255n.
ship 275n.
extractor 304n.
lifter 310n.
dree one's weird
be forced 596vb.
dreggy
dirty 649adj.
dregs
leavings 41n.
extremity 69n.
rubbish 641n.
dirt 649n.
rabble 869n.
bad man 938n.
drench
potion 301n.
soften 327vb.
add water 339vb.
drench 341vb.
groom 369vb.
clean 648vb.
medicine 658n.
sate 863vb.
drencher
rain 350n.
dress
be uniform 16vb.
adjust 24vb.
equalize 28vb.
cover 226vb.
dress 228n., vb.
cook 301vb.
livery 547n.
doctor 658vb.
make ready 669vb.
dressage
equitation 267n.
dress down
reprove 924vb.
dresser
cabinet 194n.
stand, shelf 218n.
clothier 228n.
nurse 658n.
servant 742n.
dressiness
fashion 848n.
dressing
wrapping 226n.
dressing 228n.
cookery 301n.
condiment 389n.
surgical dressing 658n.
dressing down
reprimand 924n.
dressing gown
informal dress 228n.
dressing room
chamber 194n.
theater 594n.
beauty parlor 843n.
dressing station
hospital 658n.
dressmaker
clothier 228n.
dress rehearsal
dramaturgy 594n.
preparation 669n.
dress show
exhibit 522n.
dress up
dress 228vb.
dissemble 541vb.
primp 843vb.
dressy
fashionable 848adj.
showy 875adj.
dribble
small quantity 33n.
move slowly 278vb.
kick 279vb.
propel 287vb.
exude 298vb.
emit 300vb.
flow 350vb.
driblet
finite quantity 26n.
small thing 33n.
drier
drier 342n.
drift
leavings 41n.
accumulation 74n.
vary 152vb.
tendency 179n.
distance 199n.
fly 271vb.
thing transferred 272n.
move slowly 278vb.
direction 281n.
deviation 282n.
shortcoming 307n.
be neglectful 458vb.
be uncertain 474vb.
meaning 514n.
intention 617n.

not act 677vb.
be free 744vb.
drifter
wanderer 268n.
fishing-boat 275n.
idler 679n.
drifting
impotent 161adj.
driftway
water travel 269n.
drift with the tide
conform 83vb.
driftwood
thing transferred 272n.
drill
make uniform 16vb.
regularity 81n.
make conform 83vb.
textile 222n.
sharp point 256n.
perforator 263n.
train 534vb.
habituation 610n.
make ready 669vb.
art of war 718n.
dominate 733vb.
formality 875n.
ritual 988n.
drill dress
tunic 228n.
drill-sergeant
uniformist 16n.
trainer 537n.
preparer 669n.
director 690n.
tyrant 735n.
drink
stimulant 174n.
absorb 299vb.
potion 301n.
drink 301vb.
waste 634vb.
revel 837vb.
get drunk 949vb.
drinkable
edible 301adj.
drink a health
toast 876vb.
drinker
drinking 301n.
reveler 837n.
drunkard 949n.
drink in
be attentive 455vb.
learn 536vb.
drinking bout
festivity 837n.
drunkenness 949n.
drinking-water
soft drink 301n.
water 339n.
drinks
social gathering 882n.
drink to
toast 876vb.
pay respects 884vb.
drip
move slowly 278vb.
exude 298vb.
emit 300vb.
descend 309vb.
be wet 341vb.
flow, rain 350vb.
ninny 501n.
bore 838n.
dripping
meat 301n.
fat 357n.
dripping with
full 54adj.
drive
operate 173vb.
vigorousness 174n.
influence 178n.
doorway 263n.
move 265vb.
ride 267vb.
spurt 277n.
accelerate 277vb.
impel 279vb.
propulsion 287n.
vigor 571n.
resolution 599n.
incite 612vb.
chase 619n.
access, path 624n.
be active 678vb.
haste 680n.
exertion 682n.
fatigue 684vb.
attack 712n., vb.
oppress 735vb.
compel 740vb.
drive at
mean 514vb.
aim at 617vb.
drive away
repel 292vb.
drive home
carry through 725vb.
drive in
affix 45vb.
insert 303vb.
drive-in
doorway 263n.
approachable 289adj.
drive into a corner
necessitate 596vb.
drivel
emit, exude 298vb.
be foolish 499vb.
be insane 503vb.
silly talk 515n.
diffuseness 570n.
be loquacious 581vb.
driveler
fool 501n.
chatterer 581n.
driven
hasty 680adj.
driven snow
ice 380n.
white thing 427n.
driver
driver 268n.
carrier 273n.
machinist 630adj.
leader 690n.
drive off
rob 788vb.
drive on
progress 285vb.
drive out
eject 300vb.
drive to the wall
be difficult 700vb.
defeat 727vb.
drizzle
moisture 341n.
rain 350n., vb.
drogue
safeguard 662n.
droit administratif
governance 733n.
compulsion 740n.
droll
witty 839adj.
funny 849adj.
drollery
foolery 497n.
wit 839n.
ridiculousness 849n.
dromedary
beast of burden 273n.
dromond
ship 275n.
drone
uniformity 16n.
fly 265n.
slowcoach 278n.
roll 403vb.
stridor 407n.
ululation 409n.
musical note 410n.
discord 411vb.
be loquacious 581vb.
idler 679n.
drool
exude 298vb.
emit 300vb.
mean nothing 515vb.
droop
be weak 163vb.
hang 217vb.
descend 309vb.
be ill 651vb.
deteriorate 655vb.
be inactive 679vb.
be fatigued 684vb.
be dejected 834vb.
droopy
dejected 834adj.

drop
small thing 33n.
decrease 37n., vb.
tincture 43n.
be weak 163vb.
reproduce itself 164vb.
minuteness 196n.
pendant 217n.
exude 298vb.
dismiss 300vb.
insert 303vb.
descent 309n.
let fall 311vb.
moisture 341n.
flow, rain 350vb.
stage-set 594n.
relinquish 621vb.
disuse 674vb.
be clumsy 695vb.
not retain 779vb.
jewelry 844n.
means of execution 964n.
drop a line
correspond 588vb.
drop anchor
place oneself 187vb.
navigate 269vb.
arrive 295vb.
drop a sitter
lose a chance 138vb.
be clumsy 695vb.
drop behind
be behind 238vb.
follow 284vb.
drop by drop
by degrees 27adv.
piecemeal 53adv.
drop from the clouds
surprise 508vb.
drop in
arrive 295vb.
enter 297vb.
visit 882vb.
drop in the ocean
trifle 639n.
drop into place
grade 73vb.
droplet
small thing 33n.
minuteness 196n.
drop off
die 361vb.
sleep 679vb.
drop of the curtain
finality 69n.
drop one's voice
speak low 578vb.
drop out
not complete 726vb.
dropping
fatigued 684adj.
droppings
excrement 302n.
drop-scene
stage-set 594n.
dropsy
dilation 197n.
fluid 335n.
disease 651n.
drop the mask
disclose 526vb.
be truthful 540vb.
drop the pilot
start out 296vb.
drop too much
drunkenness 949n.
droshky
cab 274n.
carriage 274n.
dross
leavings 41n.
layer 207n.
ash 381n.
rubbish 641n.
dirt 649n.
drought
dryness 342n.
scarcity 636n.
blight 659n.
hunger 859n.
drove
group 74n.
drover
driver 268n.
leader 690n.
drown
fill 54vb.
destroy, suppress 165vb.
descend 309vb.
depress 311vb.
founder 313vb.
drench 341vb.
perish 361vb.
kill 362vb.
silence 399vb.
obliterate 550vb.
drowned
deep 211adj.
drowse
be inattentive 456vb.
be neglectful 458vb.
sleep 679n.
be fatigued 684vb.
drowser
idler 679n.
drowsy
sleepy 679adj.
tedious 838adj.
drub
defeat 727vb.
spank 963vb.
drudge
busy person 678n.
work 682vb.
worker 686n.
servant 742n.
drudgery
assiduity 678n.
labor 682n.
drug
anesthetic 375n.
drug 658n.
doctor 658vb.
poison 659n.
make inactive 679vb.
drugget
floor-cover 226n.
cleaning cloth 648n.
preserver 666n.
druggist
druggist 658n.
drug habit
intemperance 943n.
drug on the market
superfluity 637n.
cheapness 812n.
drugstore
druggist 658n.
druid
priest 986n.
drum
repeat oneself 106vb.
cylinder 252n.
oscillate 317vb.
roll 403vb.
play music 413vb.
drum 414n.
call 547n.
drum-beat
periodicity 141n.
call 547n.
drumfire
roll 403n.
drumly
opaque 423adj.
drummer
instrumentalist 413n.
drum out
eject 300vb.
drunk
reveler 837n.
intemperate 943adj.
drunkard 949n.
drunk 949adj.
drunkard
reveler 837n.
drunkard 949n.
drunken
sensual 944adj.
drunken 949adj.
drunkenness
intemperance 943n.
drunkenness 949n.
drupe
fruit 301n.
dry
non-adhesive 49adj.
unproductive 172adj.
dry 342adj., vb.

stanch 350vb.
hot 379adj.
sour 393adj.
strident 407adj.
feeble 572adj.
plain 573adj.
voiceless 578adj.
clean 648vb.
sanitate 652vb.
preserve 666vb.
mature 669vb.
tedious 838adj.
witty 839adj.
hungry 859adj.
temperate 942adj.
sober 948adj.
dryad
vegetability 366n.
nymph 967n.
dry-as-dust
antiquarian 125n.
bore 838n.
tedious 838adj.
dry cleaner
cleaner 648n.
dry-dock
goal 295n.
shelter 662n.
dryer
(*see* drier)
dry-eyed
pitiless 906adj.
dry eyes
moral insensibility 820n.
dry goods
merchandise 795n.
dry measure
metrology 465n.
dryness
desert 172n.
dryness 342n.
tedium 838n.
wit 839n.
hunger 859n.
dry-nurse
teacher 537n.
drypoint
engraving 555n.
dry rot
rot 649n.
dilapidation 655n.
blight 659n.
drysaltery
art equipment 553n.
dry up
decrease 37vb.
cease 145vb.
dry 342vb.
be mute 578vb.
waste 634vb.
not suffice 636vb.
dual
dual 90adj.
double 91adj.
grammatical 564adj.
dualism
duality 90n.
deism 973n.
duality
duality 90n.
dual personality
spirit 447n.
psychopathy 503n.
dub
name 561vb.
misname 562vb.
dignify 866vb.
dubiety
dubiety 474n.
irresolution 601n.
no choice 606n.
predicament 700n.
dubious
improbable 472adj.
uncertain 474adj.
doubting 474adj.
ducal
noble 868adj.
ducat
coinage 797n.
duce
leader 690n.
master 741n.
autocrat 741n.
duchess
potentate 741n.
nobleman 868n.
duchy
territory 184n.
polity 733n.
duck
zero 103n.
textile 222n.
swim 269vb.
immerse 303vb.
descend 309vb.
stoop 311vb.
plunge 313vb.
drench 341vb.
table bird 365n.
waterfowl 365n.
be loath 598vb.
avoid 620vb.
darling 890n.
show respect 920vb.
punish 963vb.
duck-boards
paving 226n.
bridge 624n.
ducking
plunge 313n.
moistening 341n.
corporal punishment 963n.
ducking-stool
pillory 964n.
duckling
youngling 132n.
waterfowl 365n.
duck-pond
stock farm 369n.
duck's egg
zero 103n.
ducky
darling 890n.
duct
conduit 351n.
ductile
drawing 288adj.
flexible 327adj.
elastic 328adj.
wieldy 701adj.
dud
powerless 161adj.
ammunition 723n.
loser 728n.
unsuccessful 728adj.
dud check
false money 797n.
dude
dupe 544n.
fop 848n.
dudeen
tobacco 388n.
dudgeon
anger 891n.
duds
clothing 228n.
due
future 124n.
expedient 642adj.
owed 803adj.
due 915adj.
due course, in
prospectively 124adv.
opportunely 137adv.
duel
duality 90n.
duel 716n.
duelist
opponent 705n.
quarreler 709n.
contender 716n.
combatant 722n.
dueness
attribution 158n.
expedience 642n.
right 913n.
dueness 915n.
(*see* duty)
duenna
teacher 537n.
protector 660n.
keeper 749n.
due order
ritual 988n.
due process
legality 953n.
dues
receipt 807n.
tax 809n.

dueness 915n.
duet
duality 90n.
duet 412n.
cooperation 706n.
concord 710n.
due to
caused 157adj.
duff
pudding 301n.
duffel
textile 222n.
duffer
ignoramus 493n.
dunce 501n.
bungler 697n.
duffy
ghost 970n.
dug
bosom 253n.
dug-in
defended 713adj.
dug-out
old man 133n.
excavation 255n.
furrow 261n.
rowboat 275n.
refuge 662n.
defenses 713n.
duke
potentate 741n.
nobleman 868n.
dukedom
polity 733n.
aristocracy 868n.
dulcet
sweet 392adj.
melodious 410adj.
pleasurable 826adj.
dulcify
assuage 177vb.
sweeten 392vb.
dulcimer
piano 414n.
dulcinea
loved one 887n.
dulia
cult 981n.
dull
assuage 177vb.
inert 175adj.
blunt 257vb.
render insensible 375vb.
mute 401vb.
non-resonant 405adj.
dim 419adj.
soft-hued 425adj.
colorless 426adj.
gray 429adj.
ignorant 491adj.
unintelligent 499adj.
feeble 572adj.
inactive 679adj.
fatigued 684adj.
impassive 820adj.
cheerless 834adj.
melancholic 834adj.
tedious 838adj.
dull 840adj.
dullard
dunce 501n.
dullness
seriousness 834n.
dullness 840n.
(*see* dull)
duly
as promised 764adv.
duly 915adv.
duma
parliament 692n.
dumb
ignorant 491adj.
unintelligent 499adj.
voiceless 578adj.
wondering 864adj.
dumbbell
dunce 501n.
dumb charade
enigma 530n.
gesture 547n.
drama 594n.
indoor game 837n.
dumbfound
surprise 508vb.
disappoint 509vb.
make mute 578vb.
be wonderful 864vb.
dumbness
aphony 578n.
dumb show
gesture 547n.
representation 551n.
stage play 594n.
dumb show, in
symbolically 547adv.
dumbstruck
wondering 864adj.
dumbwaiter
cabinet 194n.
lifter 310n.
dummy
insubstantial thing 4n.
prototype 23n.
substitute 150n.
ineffectuality 161n.
disguise 527n.
sham 542n.
image 551n.
aphony 578n.
letterpress 587n.
plan 623n.
idler 679n.
dump
accumulation 74n.
storage 632n.
rubbish 641n.
disuse 674vb.
sell 793vb.
cheapen 812vb.
dumpling
pudding 301n.
dumps
dejection 834n.
dumpy
fleshy 195adj.
dwarfish 196adj.
short 204adj.
thick 205adj.
unsightly 842adj.
dun
horse 273n.
dim 419adj.
warner 664n.
demand 737vb.
request 761vb.
petitioner 763n.
torment 827vb.
dunce
ignoramus 493n.
dunce 501n.
dunderhead
dunce 501n.
dune
monticle 209n.
dung
fertilizer 171n.
invigorate 174vb.
excrement 302n.
agriculture 370n.
fetor 397n.
dirt 649n.
dungarees
trousers 228n.
dungeon
cellar 194n.
darkness 418n.
refuge 662n.
prison 748n.
dunghill
sink 649n.
lower classes 869n.
dunghill cock
coward 856n.
dunnage
lining 227n.
duo
duet 412n.
duodecimo
miniature 196n.
little 196adj.
edition 589n.
duodenitis
indigestion 651n.
duologue
interlocution 584n.
dupe
weakling 163n.
ignoramus 493n.
befool 542vb.
dupe 544n.
loser 728n.

defraud 788vb.
sufferer 825n.
duplex
dual 90adj.
double 91adj.
flat 192n.
duplicate
identity 13n.
copy 20vb.
duplicate 22n.
augment 36vb.
double 91adj., vb.
repeat 106n.
reproduce 166vb.
label 547n.
record 548n.
representation 551n.
be superfluous 637vb.
duplicity
equivocalness 518n.
duplicity 541n.
deception 542n.
mental dishonesty 543n.
cunning 698n.
affectation 850n.
perfidy 930n.
durability
toughness 329n.
durable
lasting 113adj.
perpetual 115adj.
permanent 144adj.
unchangeable 153adj.
tough 329adj.
durables
merchandise 795n.
duralumin
hardness 326n.
dura mater
head 213n.
intellect 447n.
duramen
hardness 326n.
durance
detention 747n.
duration
time 108n.
course of time 111n.
permanence 144n.
durbar
conference 584n.
council 692n.
law-court 956n.
duress
compulsion 740n.
restriction 747n.
during
while 108adv.
durra
corn 366n.
durwan
janitor 264n.
servant 742n.
dusk
evening 129n.
darkness 418n.
half-light 419n.
dusky
vespertine 129adj.
dim 419adj.
dust
oldness 127n.
minuteness 196n.
overlay 226vb.
strike 279vb.
let fall 311vb.
levity 323n.
powder 332n.
soil 344n.
corpse 363n.
obfuscation 421n.
variegate 437vb.
trickery 542n.
rubbish 641n.
clean 648vb.
dirt 649n.
spank 963vb.
dustbin
cellar 194n.
vessel 194n.
cleaning utensil 648n.
sink 649n.
dust-bowl
desert 172n.
dust-cover
screen 421n.
cleaning cloth 648n.
preserver 666n.
dusted
mottled 437adj.
duster
obliteration 550n.
cleaning cloth 648n.
dust-heap
accumulation 74n.
rubbish 641n.
sink 649n.
dust-hole
cellar 194n.
rubbish 641n.
sink 649n.
dustiness
pulverulence 332n.
dusting
corporal punishment 963n.
dust in the eyes
pretext 614n.
stratagem 698n.
dust-jacket
wrapping 226n.
dustman
cleaner 648n.
dirty person 649n.
worker 686n.
dustpan
cleaning utensil 648n.
dusty
traveling 267adj.
powdery 332adj.
dry 342adj.
soft-hued 425adj.
mottled 437adj.
dirty 649adj.
Dutch auction
sale 793n.
cheapness 812n.
Dutch courage
courage 855n.
cowardice 856n.
Dutch party
participation 775n.
festivity 837n.
social gathering 882n.
Dutch uncle
adviser 691n.
tyrant 735n.
Dutch wife
cushion 218n.
duteous
(*see* dutiful)
dutiable
priced 809adj.
dutiful
obedient 739adj.
dutied 917adj.
trustworthy 929adj.
virtuous 933adj.
dutiless
negligent 458adj.
disobedient 738n.
non-observant 769adj.
dutiless 918adj.
duty
necessity 596n.
motive 612n.
function 622n.
needfulness 627n.
labor 682n.
tax 809n.
courteous act 884n.
right 913n.
dueness 915n.
duty 917n.
duty-bound
dutied 917adj.
duty-free
non-liable 919adj.
duty, on
dutied 917adj.
duumvirate
government 733n.
D.V.
possibly 469adv.
Dvaita
philosophy 449n.
dwarf
small animal 33n.
bate 37vb.
dwarf 196n.
make smaller 198vb.

star 321n.
elf 970n.
dwarfish
small 33adj.
dwarfish 196adj.
short 204adj.
unsightly 842adj.
fairylike 970adj.
dwell
stay 144vb.
be situate 186vb.
place oneself 187vb.
dwell 192vb.
be quiescent 266vb.
dweller
dweller 191n.
dwelling
dwelling 192n.
dwell on
emphasize 532vb.
dwell on the past
retrospect 505vb.
dwindle
decrease 37vb.
be little 196vb.
become small 198vb.
disappear 446vb.
dyad
duality 90n.
dyarchy
duality 90n.
dye
tincture 43n.
modify 143vb.
hue, pigment 425n.
color 425vb.
hairwash 843n.
dyed
habitual 610adj.
dyeing
beautification 843n.
dyer
alterer 143n.
dyestuff
pigment 425n.
dying
ephemeral 114adj.
quiescent 266adj.
sick 651adj.
dying breath
decease 361n.
dying day
decease 361n.
dying duck
weeper 836n.
dying to
willing 597adj.
dynamic
powerful 160adj.
operative 173adj.
vigorous 174adj.
impelling 279adj.
dynamics
science of forces 162n.
motion 265n.
impulse 279n.
dynamism
energy 160n.
vigorousness 174n.
restlessness 678n.
dynamitard
desperado 857n.
dynamite
destroyer 168n.
vigorousness 174n.
propellant 287n.
pitfall 663n.
explosive 723n.
dynamo
causal means 156n.
electricity 160n.
vigorousness 174n.
dynamometer
meter 465n.
dynast
potentate 741n.
dynastic
ruling 733adj.
dynasticism
authority 733n.
dynasty
continuity 71n.
governance 733n.
sovereign 741n.
nobility 868n.
dysentery
cacation 302n.
dysentery 651n.
dyspathy
dislike 861n.
hatred 888n.
dyspepsia
indigestion 651n.
dysphony
aphony 578n.
speech defect 580n.
dyspnea
fatigue 684n.

E

each
universal 79adj.
severally 80adv.
each man for himself
selfishness 932n.
each other
correlation 12n.
correlatively 12adv.
eager
willing 597adj.
active 678adj.
fervent 818adj.
excited 821adj.
desiring 859adj.
eagle
speeder 277n.
bird of prey 365n.
eye 438n.
flag, heraldry 547n.
regalia 743n.
coinage 797n.
eagle-eyed
seeing 438adj.
eaglet
bird of prey 365n.
eagre
current, wave 350n.
ear
growth 157n.
reproduce itself 164vb.
handle 218n.
ear 415n.
eardrop
pendant 217n.
ear-drum, ear-hole
ear 415n.
earful
hearing 415n.
oration 579n.
earl
nobleman 868n.
earless
deaf 416adj.
earlier
before 64adv.
prior 119adj.
before 119adv.
not now 122adv.
earliest
prior 119adj.
earliness
earliness 134n.
early
past 125adj.
matinal 128adj.
early 135adj.
betimes 135adv.
ill-timed 138adj.
immature 670adj.
earmark
label 547n.
mark 547vb.
select 605vb.
intend 617vb.
require 627vb.
earmarked
future 124adj.
due 915adj.
earn
acquire 771vb.
deserve 915vb.
earned
just 913adj.
due 915adj.
earned income
earnings 771n.
earner
worker 686n.
recipient 782n.

earnest
attentive 455adj.
affirmative 532adj.
willing 597adj.
resolute 599adj.
security 767n.
observant 768adj.
fervent 818adj.
seriousness 834n.
earnest money
part 53n.
security 767n.
earnestness
assiduity 678n.
piety 979n.
(*see* earnest)
earning capacity
utility 640n.
earnings
earnings 771n.
receiving 782n.
reward 962n.
earn interest
grow 36vb.
earn one's living
do business 622vb.
earphone
hearing aid 415n.
telecommunication 531n.
earphones
hair 259n.
ear-piercing
strident 407adj.
beautification 843n.
ear-ring
pendant 217n.
jewelry 844n.
earshot
short distance 200n.
hearing 415n.
earth
connect 45vb.
dwelling 192n.
base 214n.
planet 231n.
implant 303vb.
element 319n.
world 321n.
land 344n.
corpse 363n.
refuge 662n.
earthborn
human 371adj.
earth-bound
native 191adj.
imprisoned 747adj.
earth-closet
latrine 649n.
earth-dweller
native 191n.
earthenware
pottery 381n.
earthlight
glimmer 419n.
earthling
mankind 371n.
person 371n.
earthly
telluric 321adj.
selfish 932adj.
Earthly Paradise
mythic heaven 971n.
heaven 971n.
Earth-mother
abundance 171n.
earth, on
under the sun 321adv.
earthquake
revolution 149n.
destroyer 168n.
oscillation 317n.
earth satellite
satellite 321n.
earth-shaking
influential 178adj.
important 638adj.
earth up
obstruct 702vb.
earth-wire
cable 47n.
earthwork
defenses 713n.
earthworm
reptile 365n.
earthy
territorial 344adj.
selfish 932adj.
sensual 944adj.
ear-trumpet
megaphone 400n.
hearing aid 415n.
earwig
vermin 365n.
flatter 925vb.
ear-witness
witness 466n.
ease
bate 37vb.
assuage 177vb.
lighten 323vb.
euphoria 376n.
elegance 575n.
leisure 681n.
repose 683n.
refresh 685vb.
skill 694n.
facility 701n.
disencumber 701vb.
facilitate 701vb.
wealth 800n.
happiness 824n.
relieve 831vb.
ease along
move slowly 278vb.
propel 287vb.
ease, at
in comfort 376adv.
leisurely 681adj.
content 828adj.
easeful
tranquil 266adj.
comfortable 376adj.
reposeful 683adj.
pleasurable 826adj.
easel
frame 218n.
art equipment 553n.
easement
estate 777n.
dueness 915n.
ease off
deviate 282vb.
ease of mind
content 828n.
ease oneself
excrete 302vb.
ease out
depose 752vb.
ease up
decelerate 278vb.
easiness
cheapness 812n.
(*see* easy)
easing
(*see* ease)
east
laterality 239n.
compass point 281n.
wind 352n.
east and west
polarity 14n.
Easter
anniversary 141n.
holy-day 988n.
easterly, eastern
lateral 239adj.
Easterner
foreigner 59n.
Eastertide
holy-day 988n.
East Indiaman
merchant ship 275n.
eastward
lateral 239adj.
easy
comfortable 376adj.
possible 469adj.
intelligible 516adj.
elegant 575adj.
easy 701adj.
lax 734n.
lenient 736adj.
inexcitable 823adj.
well-bred 848adj.
friendly 880adj.
sociable 882adj.
amiable 884adj.
easy circumstances
wealth 800n.
easy going
facility 701n.

easy-going
tranquil 266adj.
irresolute 601adj.
wieldy 701adj.
lenient 736adj.
inexcitable 823adj.
content 828adj.
indifferent 860adj.
easy-mannered
well-bred 848adj.
sociable 882adj.
easy prey
dupe 544n.
easy terms
irenics 719n.
cheapness 812n.
easy virtue
unchastity 951n.
eat
absorb 299vb.
eat 301vb.
give pain 377vb.
waste 634vb.
gluttonize 947vb.
eatable
food 301n.
edible 301adj.
eat away
bate 37vb.
impair 655vb.
eat dirt
knuckle under 721vb.
eater
eater 301n.
glutton 947n.
eat humble pie
recant 603vb.
knuckle under 721vb.
be humble 872vb.
eating and drinking
sociability 882n.
eating house
café 192n.
eat one's dinners
do law 958vb.
eat one's heart out
be dejected 834vb.
eat one's words
recant 603vb.
eats
food 301n.
eat up
destroy 165vb.
consume 165vb.
eat 301vb.
appropriate 786vb.
eau-de-cologne
scent 396n.
cosmetic 843n.
eau-de-vie
liquor 301n.
eave
roof 226n.
edge 234n.
projection 254n.
eavesdrop
hear 415vb.
be curious 453vb.
eavesdropper
inquisitor 453n.
informer 524n.
ebb
decrease 37n.
reversion 148n.
revert 148vb.
become small 198vb.
regress 286vb.
recede 290vb.
flow 350vb.
waste 634n., vb.
scarcity 636n.
deterioration 655n.
ebb and flow
periodicity 141n.
fluctuation 317n.
current 350n.
ebb-tide
lowness 210n.
ebenezer
church 990n.
Ebionite
sectarian 978adj.
Eblis
Satan 969n.
ebony
tree 366n.
black thing 428n.
ebriosity
drunkenness 949n.
ebullience
stimulation 174n.
moral sensibility 819n.
excitation 821n.
ebullient
violent 176adj.
hot 379adj.
lively 819adj.
excited 821adj.
ebullition
stimulation 174n.
outbreak 176n.
commotion 318n.
heat 379n.
excitability 822n.
excitable state 822n.
eburnean
whitish 427adj.
écarté
card game 837n.
eccentric
unimitative 21adj.
misfit 25n.
fitful 142adj.
exterior 223adj.
deviating 282adj.
foolish 499adj.
fool 501n.
crazed 503adj.
crank 504n.
laughing-stock 851n.
eccentricity
unconformity 84n.
(*see* eccentric)
ecchymosis
excretion 302n.
skin disease 651n.
ecclesia
council 692n.
tribunal 956n.
ecclesiarch
governor 741n.
ecclesiarch 986n.
ecclesiastic
ecclesiastical 985adj.
cleric 986n.
ecclesiasticism
orthodoxism 976n.
ecclesiasticism 985n.
ecclesiolatry
idolatry 982n.
ecclesiology
churchdom 985n.
ecdysiast
stripper 229n.
echelon
series 71n.
echo
imitation 20n.
do likewise 20vb.
accord 24vb.
conform 83vb.
duplication 91n.
repetition 106n.
recoil 280n.
resonance 404n.
answer 460n., vb.
assent 488vb.
echo balloon
space-ship 276n.
echoing
loud 400adj.
resonant 404adj.
echolalia
imitation 20n.
éclat
prestige 866n.
eclecticism
mixture 43n.
philosophy 449n.
choice 605n.
eclipse
be superior 34vb.
obscuration 418n.
blind 439vb.
be invisible 444vb.
disappearance 446n.
conceal 525vb.
ecliptic
zodiac 321n.
eclogue
description 590n.
poem 593n.

école normale
training school 539n.
ecology
biology 358n.
economic
directing 689adj.
economical
cheap 812adj.
economical 814adj.
cautious 858adj.
temperate 942adj.
economics
management 689n.
economist
manager 690n.
economy 814n.
economize
bate 37vb.
shorten 204vb.
preserve 666vb.
restrain 747vb.
economize 814vb.
be cautious 858vb.
economy
order 60n.
restriction 747n.
economy 814n.
ecru
brown 430adj.
ecstasy
transition 147n.
frenzy 503n.
imagination 513n.
warm feeling 818n.
excitable state 822n.
joy 824n.
love 887n.
ecstatic
approving 923adj.
(*see* ecstasy)
ectopia
disorder 61n.
unconformity 84n.
displacement 188n.
ectoplasm
spiritualism 984n.
ectoplasmic
spooky 970adj.
psychical 984adj.
ectype
copy 22n.
ecumenical
universal 79adj.
orthodox 976adj.
ecumenicalism
generality 79n.
orthodoxy 976n.
eczema
skin disease 651n.
edacity
gluttony 947n.
eddy
coil 251n.
vortex 315n.
eddy 350n.
edema
swelling 253n.
edematous
expanded 197adj.
soft 327adj.
diseased 651adj.
Eden
happiness 824n.
mythic heaven 971n.
edentate
unsharpened 257adj.
edge
vantage 34n.
extremity 69n.
keenness 174n.
nearness 200n.
contiguity 202n.
circumscribe 232vb.
outline 233n.
edge 234n.
limit 236n., vb.
laterality 239n.
sharpen 256vb.
pungency 383n.
edge, have the
predominate 34vb.
edge in
intromit 231vb.
edge off
deviate 282vb.
edge, on
on edge 259adv.
expectantly 507adv.
excitable 822adj.
edge-tool
sharp edge 256n.
edgewise
obliquely 220adv.
edging
adjunct 40n.
edging 234n.
trimming 844n.
edgy
excitable 822adj.
edible
food 301n.
edible 301adj.
clean 648adj.
edict
publication 528n.
decree 737n.
legislation 953n.
edification
production 164n.
teaching 543n.
sanctity 979n.
edifice
edifice 164n.
edificial
architectural 190adj.
edify
educate 534vb.
benefit 615vb.
do good 644vb.
be virtuous 933vb.
make pious 979vb.
edifying
reputable 866adj.
pure 950adj.
edit
interpret 520vb.
publish 528vb.
rectify 654vb.
edited
pure 950adj.
edition
the press 528n.
edition 589n.
editor
interpreter 520n.
author 589n.
bookman 589n.
dissertator 591n.
reformer 654n.
editorial
interpretive 520adj.
publicity 528n.
article 591n.
educate
inform 524vb.
educated
instructed 490adj.
education
culture 490n.
education 534n.
teaching 534n.
vocation 622n.
civilization 654n.
educational
influential 178adj.
informative 524adj.
educational 534adj.
educe
extract 304vb.
educt
remainder 41n.
edulcorate
sweeten 392vb.
purify 648vb.
eel
serpent 251n.
table fish 365n.
eerie
frightening 854adj.
spooky 970adj.
efface
destroy 165vb.
forget 506vb.
obliterate 550vb.
efface oneself
be modest 874vb.
effect
sequel 67n.
end 69n.
eventuality 154n.
cause 156vb.

effect 157n.
product 164n.
sense 374n.
spectacle 445n.
meaning 514n.
be instrumental 628vb.
completion 725n.
effective
causal 156adj.
powerful 160adj.
influential 178adj.
forceful 571adj.
instrumental 628adj.
useful 640adj.
expedient 642adj.
soldier 722n.
successful 727adj.
effectiveness
agency 173n.
effects
property 777n.
effectual
operative 173adj.
(*see* effective)
effectuation
agency 173n.
action 676n.
effectuation 725n.
effeminacy
weakness 163n.
female 373n.
sensualism 944n.
effeminate
unman 161vb.
weak 163adj.
female 373adj.
cowardly 856adj.
effendi
title 870n.
effervesce
hiss 406vb.
(*see* effervescence)
effervescence
outbreak 176n.
commotion 318n.
bubble 355n.
moral sensibility 819n.
excitation 821n.
excitable state 822n.
effervescent
bubbly 355adj.
effete
aged 131adj.
impotent 161adj.
weakened 163adj.
useless 641adj.
deteriorated 655adj.
efficacious
successful 727adj.
efficacy
ability 160n.
agency 173n.
instrumentality 628n.
utility 640n.
skill 694n.
virtue 933n.
efficient
powerful 160adj.
operative 173adj.
businesslike 622adj.
instrumental 628adj.
useful 640adj.
industrious 678adj.
skillful 694adj.
effigy
copy 22n.
image 551n.
efflorescence
propagation 164n.
pulverulence 332n.
powder 332n.
effluence
outflow 298n.
current 350n.
effluvium
gas 336n.
odor 394n.
poison 659n.
efflux
egress 298n.
outflow 298n.
efflux-tube
drain 351n.
efformation
production 164n.
efformation 243n.
effort
power 160n.
production 164n.
vigorousness 174n.
essay 671n.
undertaking 672n.
action 676n.
exertion 682n.
effortless
easy 701adj.
effort-wasting
useless 641adj.
effrontery
insolence 878n.
effulgence
light 417n.
effuse
be loquacious 581vb.
effusion
outflow 298n.
ejection 300n.
excretion 302n.
diffuseness 570n.
speech 579n.
tonic 658n.
effusive
diffuse 570adj.
loquacious 581adj.
friendly 880adj.
effusiveness
warm feeling 818n.
egalitarian
uniformist 16n.
Egeria
adviser 691n.
egesta
excrement 302n.
egestion
voidance 300n.
egg
origin 68n.
source 156n.
product 164n.
egg-cup
cup 194n.
egg-glass
timekeeper 117n.
egghead
intellectual 492n.
sage 500n.
eggnog
liquor 301n.
egg on
incite 612vb.
make quarrels 709vb.
egg-shaped
round 250adj.
rotund 252adj.
eggshell
weak thing 163n.
brittleness 330n.
ego
intrinsicality 5n.
subjectivity 320n.
spirit 447n.
egocentric
selfish 932adj.
egocentrism
interiority 224n.
selfishness 932n.
egoism
interiority 224n.
selfishness 932n.
egoistic
vain 873adj.
selfish 932adj.
egotism
interiority 224n.
overestimation 482n.
vanity 873n.
misanthropy 902n.
selfishness 932n.
egregious
unconformable 84adj.
exterior 223adj.
absurd 497adj.
exaggerated 546adj.
notable 638adj.
egregiously
eminently 34adv.
egress
departure 296n.
egress 298n.
passage 305n.
means of escape 667n.

Egyptologist
antiquarian 125n.
eiderdown
coverlet 226n.
softness 327n.
eidetic
lifelike 18adj.
well-seen 443adj.
imaginative 513adj.
eidotropic
(*see* eidetic)
Eiffel Tower
high structure 209n.
eight
band 74n.
rowboat 275n.
party 708n.
eight bells
noon 128n.
Eightfold Path
religion 973n.
eights
racing 716n.
eightsome
dance 837n.
eisteddfod
assembly 74n.
music 412n.
choir 413n.
either . . . or
optionally 605adv.
ejaculation
ejection 300n.
cry 408n.
voice 577n.
eject
propel 287vb.
reject 607vb.
make unwelcome 883vb.
(*see* ejection)
ejecta
excrement 302n.
ejection
displacement 188n.
ejection 300n.
extraction 304n.
deposal 752n.
expropriation 786n.
penalty 963n.
ejective
excretory 302adj.
ejector-seat
ejector 300n.
safeguard 662n.
eke out
make complete 54vb.
elaborate
ornament 574vb.
mature 669vb.
elaboration
elegance 575n.
improvement 654n.
exertion 682n.
completion 725n.
effectuation 725n.
élan
vigorousness 174n.
collision 279n.
resolution 599n.
courage 855n.
eland
deer 365n.
elapse
end 69vb.
continue 108vb.
elapse 111vb.
be past 125vb.
elasticity
energy 160n.
strength 162n.
expansion 197n.
recoil 280n.
elasticity 328n.
elate
pleased 824adj.
delight 826vb.
cheer 833vb.
elation
psychopathy 503n.
elative
superior 34adj.
grammatical 564adj.
elbow
joint 45n.
limb 53n.
angularity 247n.
camber 253n.
fold 261n.
impel 279vb.
elbow-grease
friction 333n.
exertion 682n.
elbow-room
opportunity 137n.
room 183n.
scope 744n.
eld
antiquity 125n.
oldness 127n.
age 131n.
elder
superior 34n.
prior 119adj.
olden 127adj.
older 131adj.
old man 133n.
ecclesiarch 986n.
church officer 986n.
elderberry
fruit 301n.
Elder Brother
theosophy 984n.
elderly
aged 131adj.
eldership
oldness 127n.
seniority 131n.
church office 985n.
El Dorado
fantasy 513n.
objective 617n.
wealth 800n.
aspiration 852n.
eldritch
spooky 970adj.
Eleatics
philosopher 449n.
elect
pietist 979n.
churchdom 985n.
election
fate 596n.
vote 605n.
choice 605n.
mandate 751n.
electioneer
vote 605vb.
elective, electoral
choosing 605adj.
elector
electorate 605n.
potentate 741n.
electoral college
electorate 605n.
electoral roll
list 87n.
electorate 605n.
electoral system
vote 605n.
electorate
electorate 605n.
tribunal 956n.
electric
dynamic 160adj.
speedy 277adj.
excitable 822adj.
electric chair
means of execution 964n.
electrician
stage-hand 594n.
artisan 686n.
electricity
electricity 160n.
velocity 277n.
heater 383n.
electrify
empower 160vb.
surprise 508vb.
excite 821vb.
be wonderful 866vb.
electrocution
capital punishment 963n.
electrodynamics
electricity 160n.
science of forces 162n.
electrolier
pendant 217n.
electrolysis
decomposition 51n.

electromagnetism
electricity 160n.
electron
particle 33n.
minuteness 196n.
element 319n.
electronic brain
mnemonics 505n.
electronics
nucleonics 160n.
electroplate
coat 226vb.
electrostatics
electricity 160n.
science of forces 162n.
electrotherapy
therapy 658n.
electrotype
copy 22n.
print 587n.
electrum
a mixture 43n.
bullion 797n.
electuary
medicine 658n.
eleemosynary
giving 781adj.
benevolent 897adj.
elegance
elegance 575n.
skill 694n.
beauty 841n.
good taste 846n.
fashion 848n.
elegiac
funereal 364adj.
poetic 593adj.
lamenting 836adj.
elegist
poet 593n.
weeper 836n.
elegy
obsequies 364n.
poem 593n.
lament 836n.
element
part 53n.
component 58n.
source 156n.
filament 208n.
element 319n.
person 371n.
elemental
intrinsic 5adj.
simple 44adj.
beginning 68adj.
elementary
simple 44adj.
beginning 68adj.
immature 670adj.
element, in one's
apt 24adj.
facilitated 701adj.
elements
beginning 68n.
weather 340n.
the sacrament 988n.
elench
argumentation 475n.
elenchus
confutation 479n.
elenctic
inquiring 459adj.
elephant
giant 195n.
beast of burden 273n.
animal 365n.
elephantine
unwieldy 195adj.
Eleusinianism
religion 973n.
elevate
(*see* elevation)
elevated
train 274n.
worshipful 866adj.
proud 871adj.
drunk 949adj.
elevated railway
railroad 624n.
elevation
height 209n.
verticality 215n.
progression 285n.
elevation 310n.
feature 445n.
map 551n.
vigor 571n.
improvement 654n.
warm feeling 818n.
excitable state 822n.
cheerfulness 833n.
dignification 866n.
disinterestedness 931n.
elevation of the Host
ritual act 988n.
Holy Communion 988n.
elevator
lifter 310n.
eleven
band 74n.
party 708n.
elevenses
meal 301n.
social gathering 882n.
eleventh hour
lateness 136n.
occasion, crisis 137n.
elf
child 132n.
dwarf 196n.
elf 970n.
elfin
little 196adj.
fairylike 970adj.
elf-lock
hair 259n.
elicit
cause 156vb.
extract 304vb.
discover 484vb.
manifest 522vb.
elide
(*see* elision)
eligibility
inclusion 78n.
nubility 894n.
eligible
numerable 86adj.
expedient 642adj.
marriageable 894adj.
Elijah's mantle
sequence 65n.
eliminate
bate 37vb.
eliminate 44vb.
exclude 57vb.
render few 105vb.
eject, void 300vb.
extract 304vb.
reject 607vb.
purify 648vb.
exempt 919vb.
elimination
destruction 165n.
(*see* eliminate)
elision
scission 46n.
contraction 198n.
shortening 204n.
prosody 593n.
elite
chief thing 638n.
elite 644n.
beau monde 848n.
person of repute 866n.
upper class 868n.
elixir
remedy 658n.
elk
skin 226n.
deer 365n.
ell
long measure 203n.
ellipse
arc 250n.
ellipsis
shortening 204n.
grammar 564n.
imperspicuity 568n.
conciseness 569n.
ellipsoid
arc 250n.
sphere 252n.
elliptic
short 204adj.
round 250adj.
concise 569adj.
elm

tree 366n.
elocution
pronunciation 577n.
speech, oratory 579n.
elocutionary
speaking 579n.
Elohim
the Deity 965n.
elongate
lengthen 203vb.
elongation
distance 199n.
elope
decamp 296vb.
run away 620vb.
escape 667vb.
wed 894vb.
elope with
take away 786vb.
eloquence
vigor 571n.
magniloquence 574n.
eloquence 579n.
loquacity 581n.
eloquent
inducive 612adj.
else
in addition 38adv.
elsewhere
not here 190adv.
elucidate
be intelligible 516vb.
interpret 520vb.
manifest 522vb.
teach 534vb.
elude
sophisticate 477vb.
avoid 620vb.
elude 667vb.
not observe 769vb.
elusive
puzzling 517adj.
deceiving 542adj.
avoiding 620adj.
escaped 667adj.
elutriate
purify 648vb.
elver
table fish 365n.
elvish
fairylike 970adj.
elysian
pleasurable 826adj.
paradisiac 971adj.
Elysium
the dead 361n.
mythic heaven 971n.
emaciation
contraction 198n.
thinness 206n.
emanate
happen 154vb.
result 157vb.
emerge 298vb.
be plain 522vb.
emanation
egress 298n.
excretion 302n.
odor 394n.
appearance 445n.
revelation 975n.
emancipation
deliverance 668n.
freedom 744n.
independence 744n.
liberation 746n.
emarginate
toothed 256adj.
notched 260adj.
emasculate
subtract 39vb.
unman 161vb.
emasculation
weakness 163n.
embalm
inter 364vb.
be fragrant 396vb.
preserve 666vb.
embalmer
interment 364n.
preserver 666n.
embalmment
preservation 666n.
embank
preserve 666vb.
obstruct 702vb.
embankment
street 192n.
supporter 218n.
safeguard 662n.
obstacle 702n.
defenses 713n.
embarcation
(*see* embarkation)
embargo
quiescence 266n.
hindrance 702n.
command 737n.
restraint 747n.
prohibition 757n.
non-payment 805n.
embark
voyage 269vb.
embarkation
start 68n.
departure 296n.
embark on
begin 68vb.
undertake 672vb.
embarras de choix
choice 605n.
embarrass
be inexpedient 643vb.
hinder 702vb.
incommode 827vb.
embarrassed
modest 874adj.
embarrassment
dubiety 474n.
predicament 700n.
poverty 801n.
annoyance 827n.
embassy
house 192n.
message 529n.
commission 751n.
envoy 754n.
embattled
warring 718adj.
embay
surround 230vb.
circumscribe 232vb.
safeguard 660vb.
embed
place 187vb.
support 218vb.
be inside 224vb.
implant 303vb.
embellish
make better 654vb.
decorate 844vb.
embellished
false 541adj.
embellishment
ornament 574n.
ornamentation 844n.
ember
ash 381n.
coal, lighter 385n.
glimmer 419n.
torch 420n.
embezzle
defraud 788vb.
not pay 805vb.
embezzlement
peculation 788n.
embezzler
defrauder 789n.
non-payer 805n.
embitter
impair 655vb.
hurt 827vb.
cause discontent 829vb.
aggravate 832vb.
excite hate 888vb.
huff, enrage 891vb.
embittered
biased 481adj.
resentful 891adj.
embitterment
aggravation 832n.
emblazon
color 425vb.
mark 547vb.
represent 551vb.
decorate 844vb.
emblazoned
heraldic 547adj.
emblem
insubstantial thing 4n.

heraldry 547n.
badge 547n.
talisman 983n.
emblematic
representing 551adj.
embodiment
essential part 5n.
combination 50n.
composition 56n.
inclusion 78n.
materiality 319n.
appearance 445n.
representation 551n.
embody
join 45vb.
figure 519vb.
(*see* embodiment)
embolden
aid 703vb.
give courage 855vb.
embolism
closure 264n.
interjection 231n.
insertion 303n.
embolismal
interjacent 231adj.
embolus
stopper 264n.
solid body 324n.
embosomed
located 187adj.
interjacent 231adj.
circumscribed 232adj.
emboss
be convex 253vb.
mark 547vb.
decorate 844vb.
embossment
relievo 254n.
embouchure
orifice 263n.
embower
comprise 78vb.
embox
comprise 78vb.
enclose 235vb.
insert 303vb.
embrace
unite with 45vb.
cohere 48vb.
contain 56vb.
comprise 78vb.
surround 230vb.
circumscribe 232vb.
enclose 235vb.
choose 605vb.
circuit 626vb.
protection 660n.
safeguard 660vb.
retention 778n.
be friendly 880vb.
sociability 882n.
greet 884vb.
love 887vb.
endearment 889n.
embrace an offer
consent 758vb.
embrace an opinion
opine 485vb.
embranglement
dissension 709n.
embrasure
notch 260n.
window 263n.
fortification 713n.
embrocation
unguent 357n.
balm 658n.
embroider
variegate 437vb.
cant 541vb.
exaggerate 546vb.
decorate 844vb.
embroidery
adjunct 40n.
art 551n.
needlework 844n.
(*see* embroider)
embroil
enrage 891vb.
embroilment
confusion 61n.
dissension 709n.
embrown
embrown 430vb.
embryo
source 156n.
undevelopment 670n.
embryo, in
impending 155adj.
preparatory 669adj.
embryology
biology 358n.
embryonic
beginning 68adj.
causal 156adj.
exiguous 196adj.
amorphous 244adj.
immature 670adj.
emendation
interpretation 520n.
amendment 654n.
repair 656n.
emendator
interpreter 520n.
mender 656n.
emender
interpreter 520n.
reformer 654n.
emerald
greenness 432n.
gem 844n.
emerge
result 157vb.
depart 296vb.
emerge 298vb.
be visible 443vb.
be proved 478vb.
be disclosed 526vb.
emergence
egress 298n.
emergency
juncture 8n.
crisis 137n.
eventuality 154n.
needfulness 627n.
danger 661n.
predicament 700n.
emeritus
deserving 915adj.
emery
sharpener 256n.
emery paper
sharpener 256n.
smoother 258n.
pulverizer 332n.
emetic
ejector 300n.
expulsive 300adj.
unsavory 391adj.
cathartic 658n.
bane 659n.
emetine
cathartic 658n.
emeto-cathartic
expulsive 300adj.
émeute
revolt 738n.
emication
flash 417n.
emigrant
foreigner 59n.
wanderer 268n.
egress 298n.
emigration
wandering 267n.
departure 296n.
egress 298n.
émigré
wanderer 268n.
egress 298n.
eminence
greatness 32n.
superiority 34n.
height 209n.
prominence 254n.
elevation 310n.
importance 638n.
goodness 644n.
prestige 866n.
church title 986n.
eminently
remarkably 32adv.
emir
potentate 741n.
nobleman 868n.
emissary
messenger 531n.
delegate, envoy 754n.
emission
ejection 300n.
speech 579n.

emit
emit 300vb.
publish 528vb.
speak 579vb.
emmenagogic
expulsive 300adj.
emmer
corn 366n.
emmet
animalcule 196n.
vermin 365n.
emollient
lenitive 177adj.
soft 327adj.
lubricant 334n.
balm 658n.
remedial 658adj.
pacificatory 719adj.
emolument
earnings 771n.
pay 804n.
receipt 807n.
reward 962n.
emotion
influence 178n.
warm feeling 818n.
emotional
spontaneous 609adj.
with affections 817adj.
feeling 818adj.
impressible 819adj.
excitable 822adj.
emotionalism
persuasibility 612n.
feeling 818n.
moral sensibility 819n.
excitability 822n.
emotive
felt 818adj.
empathy
imagination 513n.
emperor
sovereign 741n.
aristocrat 868n.
emphasis
(*see* emphasize)
emphasize
strengthen 162vb.
attract notice 455vb.
argue 475vb.
be intelligible 516vb.
manifest 522vb.
emphasize 532vb.
indicate 547vb.
make important 638vb.
impress 821vb.
emphatic
strong 162adj.
florid 425adj.
expressive 516adj.
undisguised 522adj.
assertive 532adj.
forceful 571adj.
emphatically
positively 32adv.
emphysema
swelling 253n.
empire
territory 184n.
polity 733n.
governance 733n.
empiric
imposter 545n.
empirical
inquiring 459adj.
experimental 461adj.
empiricism
empiricism 461n.
empiricist
experimenter 461n.
learner 538n.
emplacement
place 185n.
situation 186n.
location, station 187n.
stand 218n.
fortification 713n.
employ
employ 622vb.
use 673n., vb.
service 745n.
commission 751vb.
employable
instrumental 628adj.
useful 640adj.
used 673adj.
employee
worker 686n.
servant 742n.
consignee 754n.
employer
agent 686n.
director 690n.
master 741n.
purchaser 792n.
employment
job 622n.
business 622n.
instrumentality 628n.
utility 640n.
use 673n.
action 676n.
exercise 682n.
service 745n.
employ oneself
do 676vb.
emporium
emporium, shop 796n.
empower
empower 160vb.
make possible 469vb.
facilitate 701vb.
commission 751vb.
permit 756vb.
empowered
authoritative 733adj.
empress
sovereign 741n.
empressement
assiduity 678n.
warm feeling 818n.
emprise
undertaking 672n.
prowess 855n.
empties
emptiness 190n.
rubbish 641n.
emptiness
non-existence 2n.
insubstantiality 4n.
emptiness 190n.
rarity 325n.
unmeaningness 515n.
unimportance 639n.
vanity 873n.
emption
purchase 792n.
empty
subtract 39vb.
displace 188vb.
empty 190adj.
make smaller 198vb.
transpose 272vb.
void 300vb.
rare 325adj.
make flow 350vb.
unthinking 450adj.
sophistical 477adj.
unmeaning 515adj.
hypocritical 541adj.
untrue 543adj.
feeble 572adj.
unprovided 636adj.
inactive 679adj.
unpossessed 774adj.
hungry 859adj.
boastful 877adj.
fasting 946adj.
empty-handed
unprovided 636adj.
unsuccessful 728adj.
parsimonious 816adj.
empty-headed
mindless 448adj.
unthinking 450adj.
empty-headedness
folly 499n.
empty into
flow 350vb.
empty purse
poverty 801n.
empty stomach
hunger 859n.
empty talk
empty talk 315n.
empurple
empurple 434vb.
empyrean
heavens 321n.
empyreuma
fire 379n.
burning 381n.

fetor 397n.
empyrosis
fire 379n.
emu
flightless bird 365n.
emulation
imitation 20n.
opposition 704n.
quarrelsomeness 709n.
contention 716n.
jealousy 911n.
emulator
opponent 705n.
quarreler 709n.
contender 716n.
emulous
opposing 704adj.
emulsification
thickening 354n.
emulsion
viscidity 354n.
emulsive
semiliquid 354adj.
emunctory
drain 351n.
enable
empower 160vb.
make possible 469vb.
facilitate 701vb.
permit 756vb.
enact
show 522vb.
represent 551vb.
do 676vb.
deal with 688vb.
carry out 725vb.
decree 737vb.
make legal 953vb.
enactment
dramaturgy 594n.
action 676n.
precept 693n.
(*see* enact)
enallage
trope 519n.
enamel
coat 226vb.
facing 226n.
smooth 258vb.
color 425vb.
decorate 844vb.
enameler
engraver 556n.
enamor
motivate 612vb.
excite love 887vb.
en bloc
collectively 52adv.
encamp
place oneself 187vb.
dwell 192vb.
encampment
station 187n.
abode 192n.
fort 713n.
encapsulate
comprise 78vb.
cover 226vb.
insert 303vb.
encapsulation
inclusion 78n.
encase
comprise 78vb.
circumscribe 232vb.
cover 226vb.
insert 303vb.
encasement
requirement 627n.
provision 633n.
encash
acquire 771vb.
receive 782vb.
sell 793vb.
draw money 797vb.
enceinte
productive 164adj.
enclosure 235n.
encephalitis
infection 651n.
sleep 679n.
enchain
fetter 747vb.
enchant
subjugate 745vb.
delight 826vb.
be wonderful 864vb.
excite love 887vb.
bewitch 983vb.
enchanter
sorcerer 983n.
enchantment
conversion 147n.
excitation 821n.
joy 824n.
pleasurableness 826n.
love 887n.
spell 983n.
enchantress
a beauty 841n.
sorceress 983n.
enchase
affix 45vb.
enchiridion
reading matter 589n.
enchorial
native 191adj.
linguistic 557adj.
encircle
comprise 78vb.
surround 230vb.
circumscribe 232vb.
go round 250vb.
circuit 626vb.
encirclement
circumscription 232n.
attack 712n.
enclave
region 184n.
enclitic
sequel 67n.
enclose
be exterior 223vb.
surround 230vb.
circumscribe 232vb.
enclose 235vb.
close 264vb.
cultivate 370vb.
obstruct 702vb.
besiege 712vb.
imprison 747vb.
retain 778vb.
enclosed
interior 234adj.
monastic 986adj.
enclosure
region 184n.
place 185n.
contents 193n.
receptacle 194n.
frame 218n.
circumscription 232n.
enclosure 235n.
correspondence 588n.
fort 713n.
encomiast
commender 923n.
encomium
praise 923n.
encompass
surround 230vb.
limit 236vb.
circumscribe 232vb.
circuit 626vb.
obstruct 702vb.
encore
duplication 91n.
double 91vb.
repetition 106n.
again 106adv.
dramaturgy 594n.
applause 923n.
encounter
synchronize 123vb.
eventuality 154n.
meet with 154vb.
contiguity 202n.
collision 279n.
meet 295vb.
discover 484vb.
withstand 704vb.
fight 716n., vb.
encourage
incite 612vb.
aid 703vb.
animate 821vb.
relieve 831vb.
cheer 833vb.
give hope 852vb.
give courage 855vb.
encouragement
causation 156n.
encouraging

influential 178adj.
encratism
celibacy 895n.
temperance 942n.
asceticism 945n.
Encratite
celibate 895n.
abstainer 942n.
sober person 948n.
virgin 950n.
encroach
be near 200vb.
interfere 231vb.
encroach 306vb.
be illegal 954vb.
encroacher
usurper 916n.
encroachment
progression 285n.
overstepping 306n.
attack 712n.
wrong 914n.
undueness 916n.
encrust
coat 226vb.
line 227vb.
encumber
be difficult 700vb.
hinder 702vb.
encumbrance
gravity 322n.
encumbrance 702n.
debt 803n.
encyclical
publication 528n.
decree 737n.
encyclopedia
erudition 490n.
reference book 589n.
encyclopedic
general 79adj.
encyclopedist
scholar 492n.
end
be complete 54vb.
sequel 67n.
extremity 69n.
end 69n., vb.
cease 145vb.
eventuality 154n.
effect 157n.
destroy 165vb.
vertex 213n.
limit 236n.
decease 261n.
intention 617n.
objective 617n.
completion 725n.
endanger
endanger 661vb.
be difficult 700vb.
endarteritis
blood pressure 651n.
endear
excite love 887vb.
endearing
pleasurable 826adj.
lovable 887adj.
endearment
inducement 612n.
courteous act 884n.
love-making 887n.
endearment 889n.
endeavor
essay 671n., vb.
action 676n.
ended
past 125adj.
endemic
interior 224adj.
infectious 653adj.
endenizen
place oneself 187vb.
endive
vegetable 301n.
endless
multitudinous 104adj.
infinite 107adj.
perpetual 115adj.
endlessness
continuity 71n.
endlong
longwise 203adv.
endocardial
interior 224adj.
endocarditis
heart disease 651n.
endocrine
interiority 224n.
endoderm
interiority 224n.
end of one's tether, at the
in difficulties 700adj.
endogamy
interiority 224n.
(*see* marriage)
endogenous
interior 224adj.
vegetal 366adj.
endorse
testify 446vb.
endorse 488vb.
sign 547vb.
patronize 703vb.
consent 758vb.
give security 767vb.
approve 923vb.
endorsement
label 547n.
consent 758n.
endorser
signatory 765n.
endosmose
passage 305n.
endow
empower 160vb.
dower 777vb.
give 781vb.
endowed with
possessing 773adj.
endowment
heredity 5n.
ability 160n.
aptitude 694n.
end-paper
ligature 47n.
end to end
contiguous 202adj.
contiguously 202adv.
longwise 203adv.
endurable
contenting 828adj.
endurance
durability 113n.
permanence 144n.
power 160n.
perseverance 600n.
feeling 818n.
patience 823n.
suffering 825n.
manliness 855n.
endure
be 1vb.
continue 108vb.
last 113vb.
stay 144vb.
go on 146vb.
meet with 154vb.
support 218vb.
carry 273vb.
acquiesce 488vb.
be resolute 599vb.
stand firm 599vb.
persevere 600vb.
resist 715vb.
feel 818vb.
be patient 823vb.
suffer 825vb.
be courageous 855vb.
enema
insertion 303n.
therapy 658n.
enema-can
drain 351n.
enemy
trouble-maker 663n.
opponent 705n.
enemy 881n.
hateful object 888n.
energetic
(*see* energy)
energize
augment 36vb.
strengthen 162vb.
invigorate 174vb.
incite 612vb.
cheer 833vb.
energy
energy 160n.
power 160n.
strength 162n.

vigorousness 174n.
vigor 571n.
resolution 599n.
restlessness 678n.
exertion 682n.

enervate
unman 161vb.
weaken 163vb.

en famille
sociably 882adv.

enfant gâté
satiety 863n.
favorite 890n.

enfant perdu
desperado 857n.

enfant terrible
inquisitor 453n.
questioner 459n.
ingenue 699n.

enfeeble
weaken 163vb.

enfeoffment
transfer 780n.
giving 781n.

enfilade
look along 203vb.
pierce 263vb.
pass 305vb.
bombardment 712n.
fire at 712vb.

enfold
dress 228vb.
circumscribe 232vb.
fold 261vb.
safeguard 660vb.
caress 889vb.

enforce
motivate 612vb.
compel 740vb.
make legal 953vb.

enfranchise
give scope 744vb.
liberate 746vb.
exempt 919vb.

engage
join 45vb.
induce 612vb.
employ 622vb.
undertake 672vb.
contend, fight 716vb.
give battle 718vb.
commission 751vb.
promise 764vb.
contract 765vb.
incur a duty 917vb.
acquire 771vb.
possess 773vb.

engaged
retained 778adj.
marriageable 894adj.

engaged couple
lovers 887n.

engage gear
enlace 222vb.

engage in
busy oneself 622vb.
undertake 672vb.

engagement
intention 617n.
undertaking 672n.
fight 716n.
battle 718n.
promise 764n.
social round 882n.
love affair 887n.
duty 917n.

engagement diary
reminder 505n.

engagement ring
jewelry 844n.
love-token 889n.

engaging
lovable 887adj.

engender
generate 164vb.

engine
causal means 156n.
empower 160vb.
strengthen 162vb.
machine 630n.

engine-driver
driver 208n.

engineer
cause 156vb.
produce 164vb.
producer 167n.
driver 268n.
planner 623n.
plan 623vb.
machinist 630n.
artisan 686n.
soldiery 722n.

engineered
false 541adj.

engineering
mechanics 630n.

English
translate 520vb.
type size 587n.

engorge
absorb 299vb.

engorgement
redundance 637n.

engraft
add 38vb.
affix 45vb.
implant 303vb.
cultivate 370vb.
educate 534vb.
habituate 610vb.

engrafted
extrinsic 6adj.

engrail
roughen 259vb.

en grande tenue
fashionable 848adj.

en grande toilette
bedecked 844adj.

engrave
cut 46vb.
groove 262vb.
mark 547vb.
record 548vb.
represent 551vb.
engrave 555vb.
write 586vb.

engraver
recorder 549n.
engraver 556n.

engraving
copy 22n.
picture 553n.
engraving 555n.

engross
absorb 299vb.
engross 449vb.
bias 481vb.
write 586vb.
possess 773vb.
appropriate 786vb.
purchase 792vb.

engrossed
obsessed 455adj.
distracted 456adj.

engrossment
possession 773n.

engulf
consume 165vb.
destroy 165vb.
absorb 299vb.
appropriate 786vb.
gluttonize 947vb.

enhance
manifest 522vb.
make important 638vb.
beautify 841vb.

enhancement
increase 36n.
improvement 654n.
aggravation 832n.
ornamentation 844n.
dignification 866n.

enharmonic
harmonic 410adj.

enigma
question 459n.
dubiety 474n.
unknown thing 491n.
unmeaningness 515n.
unintelligibility 517n.
enigma 530n.
difficulty 700n.
prodigy 864n.

enigmatic
aphoristic 496adj.
imperspicuous 568adj.

enigmatist
questioner 459n.

enisled
alone 88adj.
distant 199adj.
secluded 883adj.

enjambment
ornament 574n.
prosody 593n.
enjoin
advise 691vb.
command 737vb.
impose a duty 917vb.
enjoy
unite with 45vb.
enjoy 376vb.
find useful 640vb.
dispose of 673vb.
prosper 730vb.
possess 773vb.
be pleased 824adj.
enjoyable
pleasant 376adj.
enjoyment
coition 45n.
sociability 882n.
sensualism 944n.
(*see* enjoy)
enjoy oneself
be cheerful 833vb.
amuse oneself 837vb.
enkindle
kindle 381vb.
excite 821vb.
enkindled
fiery 379adj.
enlace
enlace 222vb.
caress 889vb.
enlarge
make important 638vb.
boast 877vb.
(*see* enlargement)
enlargement
duplicate 22n.
increase 36n.
expansion 197n.
exaggeration 546n.
photography 551n.
liberation 746n.
enlarge upon
be diffuse 570vb.
enlighten
interpret 520vb.
manifest 522vb.
inform 524vb.
educate 534vb.
enlightened
wise 498adj.
philanthropic 901adj.
enlightenment
knowledge 490n.
wisdom 498n.
information 524n.
enlist
be included 78vb.
list 87vb.
enter 297vb.
admit 299vb.
register 548vb.
induce 612vb.
employ 622vb.
avail of 673vb.
go to war 718vb.
enlisted man
soldier 722n.
enlistment
reception 299n.
registration 548n.
enlist under
patronize 703vb.
enliven
strengthen 162vb.
invigorate 174vb.
vitalize 360vb.
animate 821vb.
cheer 833vb.
amuse 837vb.
enlivened
refreshed 685adj.
en masse
collectively 52adv.
together 74adv.
in league 708adv.
enmesh
enlace 222vb.
ensnare 542vb.
hinder 702vb.
enmity
enmity 881n.
malevolence 898n.
ennead
over five 99n.
ennoblement
dignification 866n.
ennui
tedium 838n.
enormity
greatness 32n.
hugeness 195n.
wickedness 934n.
vice 934n.
guilty act 936n.
enormous
enormous 32adj.
huge 195adj.
Enosis
combination 50n.
enough
sufficiency 635n.
sufficient 635adj.
enough 635adv.
enough and to spare
plenteous 635adj.
redundantly 637adv.
en passant
incidentally 137adv.
en passant 305adv.
enplane
start out 296vb.
enrage
make violent 176vb.
make mad 503vb.
excite 821vb.
excite hate 888vb.
enrage 891vb.
en rapport
relative 9adj.
concordant 710adj.
enrapture
excite love 887vb.
enrich
ornament 574vb.
make better 654vb.
give 781vb.
make rich 800vb.
decorate 844vb.
enrobe
dress 228vb.
enroll
list 87vb.
admit 299vb.
register 548vb.
enroll oneself
be included 78vb.
enter 297vb.
join a party 708vb.
en route
on foot 267adv.
in transit 272adv.
ens
existence 1n.
ensconce
place 187vb.
conceal 525vb.
safeguard 660vb.
enscroll
register 548vb.
ensemble
all, whole 52n.
duet 412n.
enshrine
circumscribe 232vb.
sanctify 979vb.
enshrinement
dignification 866n.
enshrouded
invisible 444adj.
ensiform
sharp 256adj.
ensign
flag 547n.
army officer 741n.
regalia 743n.
ensilage
agriculture 370n.
preservation 666n.
enslave
oppress 735vb.
subjugate 745vb.
enslaved
loving 887adj.
enslavement
(*see* enslave)
ensnare
ambush 527vb.
ensnare 542vb.
tempt 612vb.

hunt 619vb.
take 786vb.
ensue
come after 65vb.
ensue 120vb.
ensure
make certain 473vb.
predetermine 608vb.
(*see* insure)
entablature
summit 213n.
entail
conduce 156vb.
make likely 471vb.
entailed
proprietary 777adj.
retained 778adj.
entangle
bedevil 63vb.
enlace 222vb.
be unintelligible 517vb.
ensnare 542vb.
hinder 702vb.
make quarrels 709vb.
entangled
complex 61adj.
entanglement
medley 43n.
crossing 222n.
love affair 887n.
entelechy
reality 1n.
existence 1n.
entente
agreement 24n.
concord 710n.
pacification 719n.
friendliness 880n.
enter
fill 54vb.
begin 68vb.
be included 78vb.
list 87vb.
approach 289vb.
converge 293vb.
arrive 295vb.
enter 297vb.
insert 303vb.
be visible 443vb.
register 548vb.
join a party 708vb.
contend 716vb.
offer oneself 759vb.
appropriate 786vb.
account 808vb.
enter into
be one of 58vb.
imagine 513vb.
describe 590vb.
contract 765vb.
enter into detail
specify 80vb.
enterprise
vigorousness 174n.
progression 285n.
intention 617n.
pursuit 619n.
business 622n.
undertaking 672n.
restlessness 678n.
mandate 751n.
courage 855n.
enterprising
speculative 618adj.
entertain
employ 622vb.
patronize 703vb.
consent 758vb.
give 781vb.
feel 818vb.
amuse 837vb.
be ridiculous 849vb.
be friendly 880vb.
be hospitable 882vb.
entertainable
amused 837adj.
entertainer
entertainer 594n.
humorist 839n.
entertainment
provisions 301n.
pleasure 376n.
provision 633n.
amusement 837n.
social gathering 882n.
entêté
willful 602adj.
enthrall
oppress 735vb.
subjugate 745vb.
excite love 887vb.
enthronement
mandate 751n.
dignification 866n.
celebration 876n.
holy orders 985n.
enthuse
excite 821vb.
enthusiasm
vigor 571n.
willingness 579n.
restlessness 678n.
warm feeling 818n.
excitation 821n.
hope 852n.
love 887n.
applause 923n.
piety 979n.
enthusiast
crank 504n.
visionary 513n.
busy person 678n.
religionist 979n.
worshiper 981n.
enthusiastic
optimistc 482adj.
imaginative 513adj.
(*see* enthusiasm)
enthymeme
reasoning 475n.
entice
distract 456vb.
ensnare 542vb.
induce, tempt 612vb.
enticing
pleasurable 826adj.
entire
consummate 32adj.
whole 52adj.
complete 54adj.
perfect 646adj.
undamaged 646adj.
entirety
whole 52n.
completeness 54n.
entitative
existing 1adj.
entitle
name 561vb.
permit 756vb.
grant claims 915vb.
entitled
deserving 915adj.
entitlement
dueness 915n.
entity
existence 1n.
unit 88n.
entombment
interment 364n.
detention 747n.
entomology
zoology 367n.
entourage
concomitant 89n.
circumjacence 230n.
entozoon
animalcule 196n.
entr'acte
interim 108n.
stage play 594n.
entrails
insides 224n.
entrain
start out 296vb.
entrance
entrance 68n.
front 237n.
entrance 263n.
doorway 263n.
way in 297n.
ingress 297n.
dramaturgy 594n.
delight 826vb.
entrant
incomer 297n.
respondent 460vb.
testee 461n.
opponent 705n.
contender 716n.
petitioner 763n.

entrap
ensnare 542vb.
entreaty
entreaty 761n.
entrée
ingress 297n.
reception 299n.
entrench
stabilize 153vb.
strengthen 162vb.
place oneself 187vb.
encroach 306vb.
safeguard 660vb.
defend 713vb.
entrenched
vested 153adj.
conditional 766adj.
due 915adj.
entrenched clause
fixture 153n.
conditions 766n.
entrenchment
defenses 713n.
entre nous
secretly 525adv.
entrepôt
storage 632n.
emporium 796n.
entrepreneur
gambler 618n.
essayer 671n.
doer 676n.
entresol
compartment 194n.
layer 207n.
entrust
transfer 272vb.
commission 751vb.
give 781vb.
convey 780vb.
entry
doorway 263n.
way in 297n.
ingress 297n.
registration 548n.
entwine
relate 9vb.
connect 45vb.
unite with 45vb.
enlace 222vb.
twine 251vb.
enucleation
interpretation 520n.
enumerate
specify 80vb.
enumeration
numeration 86n.
list 87n.
enunciate
affirm 532vb.
enunciation
voice 577n.
pronunciation 577n.
speech 579n.
envelop
comprise 78vb.
dress 228vb.
circumscribe 232vb.
envelope
receptacle 194n.
covering 226n.
enclosure 235n.
correspondence 588n.
envelopment
circumscription 232n.
envenom
impair 655vb.
aggravate 832vb.
excite hate 888vb.
envenomed
bad 645adj.
toxic 653adj.
enviable
desired 859adj.
approvable 923adj.
envier
malcontent 829n.
envious
inimical 881adj.
hating 888adj.
malevolent 898adj.
jealous 911adj.
envious 912adj.
environment
circumstance 8n.
relation 9n.
locality 187n.
circumjacence 230n.
environmental
circumstantial 8adj.
relative 9adj.
environs
entrance 68n.
locality 187n.
near place 200n.
circumjacence 230n.
envisage
imagine 513vb.
envoi
adjunct 40n.
sequel 67n.
end 69n.
verse form 593n.
envoy
messenger 531n.
official 690n.
envoy 754n.
envy
discontent 829n.
be discontented 829vb.
desire 859vb.
desired object 859n.
enmity 881n.
be inimical 881vb.
hatred 888n.
resent 891vb.
malevolence 898n.
jealousy 911n.
envy 912n., vb.
approve 923vb.
enwrap
fold 261vb.
enzootic
infectious 653adj.
enzyme
alterer 143n.
leaven 323n.
Eoanthropus
mankind 371n.
Eocene
secular 110adj.
eolith
antiquity 125n.
Eolithic
secular 110adj.
Eos
morning 128n.
lesser god 967n.
epagoge
argumentation 475n.
epaulet
badge 547n.
livery 547n.
badge of rank 743n.
trimming 844n.
épée
side-arms 723n.
epenthesis
addition 38n.
epergne
plate 194n.
ornamentation 844n.
epexegesis
interpretation 520n.
ephah
metrology 465n.
ephemeral
ephemeral 114adj.
dying 361adj.
ephemeris
chronology 117n.
guide-book 524n.
ephialtes
pain 377n.
suffering 825n.
ephod
vestments 989n.
ephor
officer 741n.
epic
prolix 570adj.
narrative 590n.
descriptive 590adj.
poem 593n.
epicedium
lament 836n.
epicene
multiform 82adj.
abnormal 84adj.
equivocal 518adj.
epicenter
centrality 225n.

epicranium
head 213n.
epicure
eater 301n.
gastronomy 301n.
man of taste 846n.
perfectionist 862n.
sensualist 944n.
glutton 947n.
epicurean
sensuous 376adj.
savory 390adj.
epicureanism
gastronomy 301n.
philosophy 449n.
enjoyment 824n.
good taste 846n.
sensualism 944n.
gluttony 947n.
epicycle
orbit 250n.
epidemic
extensive 32adj.
comprehensive 52adj.
universal 79adj.
plague 651n.
infectious 653adj.
epidemiology
pathology 651n.
epidermic
exterior 223adj.
dermal 226adj.
epidermis
skin 226n.
epidiascope
optical device 442n.
epigenesis
propagation 164n.
epigram
maxim 496n.
phrase 563n.
conciseness 569n.
witticism 839n.
epigrammatist
phrase 563n.
humorist 839n.
epigraph
indication 547n.
script 586n.
epigrapher
penman 586n.
epigraphic
recording 548adj.
epigraphist
interpreter 520n.
phrase 563n.
epigraphy
hermeneutics 520n.
registration 548n.
epilepsy
spasm 318n.
frenzy 503n.
paralysis 651n.
epilogue
sequel 67n.
extremity 69n.
dramaturgy 594n.
epinician ode
trophy 729n.
epiphany
revelation 975n.
holy-day 988n.
epiphenomenon
concomitant 89n.
appearance 445n.
episcopacy
churchdom 985n.
church office 985n.
episcopal
clerical 986adj.
Episcopalian
Anglican 976adj.
Catholic 976adj.
ecclesiastical 985adj.
episcopate
church office 985n.
ecclesiarch 986n.
episode
irrelevance 10n.
adjunct 40n.
discontinuity 72n.
interim 108n.
interjection 231n.
pleonasm 570n.
epistemology
knowledge 490n.
epistle
correspondence 588n.
epistolary
epistolary 588adj.
epistrophe
ornament 574n.
epistyle
beam 218n.
summit 213n.
epitaph
valediction 296n.
obsequies 364n.
indication 547n.
phrase 563n.
description 590n.
epithalamium
vocal music 412n.
poem 593n.
wedding 894n.
epithelioma
carcinosis 651n.
epitherm
surgical dressing 658n.
epithet
name 561n.
epitome
miniature 196n.
contraction 198n.
shortening 204n.
conciseness 569n.
compendium 592n.
epitomize
shorten 204vb.
abstract 592vb.
epizootic
infectious 653adj.
epoch
era 110n.
chronology 117n.
epochal
secular 110adj.
epoch-making
notable 638adj.
epode
poem 593n.
eponym
name 561n.
eponymous
named 561adj.
epos
narrative 590n.
Epsom salts
cathartic 658n.
epuration
cleansing 648n.
equability
equality 28n.
non-wonder 865n.
equable
inexcitable 823adj.
equal
similar 18adj.
compeer 28n.
equal 28adj.
just 913adj.
equality
relativeness 9n.
identity 13n.
equality 28n.
synchronism 123n.
equal chance 159n.
parallelism 219n.
equalization
equalization 28n.
equalize
equalize 28vb.
average out 30vb.
flatten 216vb.
compare 462vb.
equanimity
inexcitability 823n.
equate
identify 13vb.
equalize 28vb.
equation
equalization 28n.
equivalence 28n.
numerical result 85n.
numerical operation 86n.
equator
equalization 28n.
girdle 47n.
middle 70n.
dividing line 92n.
limit 236n.

circle 250n.
equatorial
middle 70adj.
telluric 321adj.
warm 379adj.
equerry
retainer 742n.
equestrian
rider 268n.
equestrianism
equitation 267n.
equidistance
middle 70n.
parallelism 219n.
equilateral
uniform 16adj.
equal 28adj.
symmetrical 245adj.
angular figure 247n.
equilibrant
equilibrium 28n.
equilibration
equilibrium 28n.
equilibrist
entertainer 594n.
equilibrium
equilibrium 28n.
stability 153n.
quiescence 266n.
equine
equine 273adj.
animal 365adj.
equinoctial
vernal 128adj.
autumnal 129adj.
celestial 321adj.
equinoctial colure
uranometry 321n.
equinox
spring 128n.
autumn 129n.
equip
dress 228vb.
find means 629vb.
provide 633vb.
make ready 669vb.
give 781vb.
equipage
carriage 274n.
ostentation 875n.
equiparation
equalization 28n.
equipendent
equal 28adj.
equipment
adjunct 40n.
contents 193n.
means 629n.
equipment 630n.
provision 633n.
fitting out 669n.
equipoise
equilibrium 28n.
weighment 322n.
equiponderance
equilibrium 28n.
equipper
preparer 669n.
equitable
just 913adj.
honorable 929adj.
equitation
motion 265n.
equitation 267n.
equity
indifference 860n.
justice 913n.
equivalence
identity 13n.
similarity 18n.
equivalence 28n.
connotation 514n.
equivalent
offset 31n.
quid pro quo 150n.
interpretive 520adj.
equivocal
uncertain 474adj.
puzzling 517adj.
equivocal 518adj.
false 541adj.
imperspicuous 568adj.
tergiversating 603adj.
dishonest 930adj.
equivocalness
connotation 514n.
(*see* equivocation)
equivocate
misinterpret 521vb.
equivocation
sophistry 477n.
equivocalness 518n.
falsehood 541n.
pretext 614n.
wit 839n.
equivocator
sophist 477n.
liar 545n.
equivoque
assimilation 18n.
absurdity 497n.
equivocalness 518n.
witticism 839n.
impurity 951n.
era
date 108n.
era 110n.
chronology 117n.
eradicate
subtract 39vb.
exclude 57vb.
destroy 165vb.
displace 188vb.
eject 300vb.
extract 304vb.
erase
destroy 165vb.
eject 300vb.
rub 333vb.
obliterate 550vb.
clean 648vb.
Erastianism
heresy 977n.
erasure
friction 333n.
obliteration 550n.
ere
before 119adv.
Erebus
darkness 418n.
classical gods 967n.
mythic hell 972n.
erect
stabilize 153vb.
cause 156vb.
produce 164vb.
place 187vb.
make vertical 215vb.
elevate 310vb.
jubilant 833adj.
honorable 929adj.
erectile
elevated 310adj.
erection
edifice 164n.
erectness
verticality 215n.
erector
lifter 310n.
ere long
betimes 135adv.
eremitical
unconformable 84adj.
alone 88adj.
unsociable 883adj.
ascetic 945adj.
ere now
before 119adv.
retrospectively 125adv.
erewhile
before 119adv.
formerly 125adv.
erewhon
fantasy 513n.
erg
energy 160n.
ergatocracy
government 733n.
ergo
hence 158adv.
ergotism
argument 475n.
judgment 480n.
Erinys
violent creature 176n.
Fury 891n.
eriometer
optical device 442n.
eristic
reasoner 475n.
arguing 475adj.

quarreler 709n.
erk
servant 742n.
Erl King
fairy 970n.
ermine
skin 226n.
heraldry 547n.
regalia 743n.
trimming 844n.
erne
bird of prey 365n.
Ernie
counting instrument 86n.
erode
bate 37vb.
subtract 39vb.
decompose 51vb.
encroach 306vb.
pulverize 332vb.
rub 333vb.
impair 655vb.
Eros
libido 859n.
love 887n.
erotic
erotic 887adj.
impure 951adj.
eroticism
love 887n.
erotogenic
erotic 887adj.
erotomania
love 887n.
err
stray 282vb.
err 495vb.
be wicked 934vb.
errancy
error 495n.
errand
land travel 267n.
message 529n.
job 622n.
mandate 751n.
errand boy
courier 531n.
errant
traveling 267adj.
deviating 282adj.
errantry
wandering 267n.
errata
edition 589n.
erratic
non-uniform 17adj.
fitful 142adj.
unstable 152adj.
moving 265adj.
deviating 282adj.
inexact 495adj.
crazed 503adj.
capricious 604adj.
erratum
mistake 495n.
erring
wicked 934adj.
erroneous
unreal 2adj.
illogical 477adj.
erroneous 495adj.
wrong 914adj.
heterodox 977adj.
error
deviation 282n.
misjudgment 481n.
error 495n.
deception 542n.
inexpedience 643n.
wrong 914n.
heterodoxy 977n.
ersatz
simulating 18adj.
imitative 20adj.
substitute 150n.
spurious 542adj.
vulgar 847adj.
erst
formerly 125adv.
erstwhile
prior 119adj.
former 125adj.
erubescence
redness 431n.
eructation
voidance 300n.
respiration 352n.
erudition
erudition 490n.
learning 536n.
erupt
attack 712vb.
(*see* eruption)
erupting
fiery 379adj.
eruption
revolution 149n.
outbreak 176n.
egress 298n.
voidance 300n.
skin disease 651n.
erysipelatous
diseased 651adj.
erythematous
diseased 651adj.
escalade
irrupt 297vb.
ascent 308n.
climb 308vb.
attack 712n., vb.
escalator
transport 272n.
carrier 273n.
conveyor 274n.
ascent 308n.
lifter 310n.
escalator clause
qualification 468n.
escapable
avoidable 620adj.
escapade
foolery 497n.
whim 604n.
revel 837n.
escape
decrement 42n.
decamp 296vb.
outflow 298n.
flow out 298vb.
outlet, egress 298n.
run away 620vb.
seek safety 660vb.
escape 667n., vb.
deliverance 668n.
achieve liberty 745vb.
dutilessness 918n.
escape clause
qualification 468n.
conditions 766n.
escapee
wanderer 268n.
escaper 667n.
free man 744n.
escape notice
be unseen 444vb.
escape notice 456vb.
elude 667vb.
escapism
fantasy 513n.
avoidance 620n.
escape 667n.
fear 854n.
non-liability 919n.
escapist
visionary 513n.
avoider 620n.
escapology
escape 667n.
escarpment
high land 209n.
acclivity 220n.
escharotic
keen 174adj.
eschatology
finality 69n.
escheat
revert 148vb.
penalty 963n.
eschew
avoid 620vb.
dislike 861vb.
escort
accompaniment 89n.
concomitant 89n.
carry 273vb.
protection 660n.
direct 689vb.
defender 713n.
keeper 749n.
take away 786vb.
lover 887n.

court 889vb.
escritoire
cabinet 194n.
esculent
edible 301adj.
escutcheon
heraldry 547n.
esophagitis
indigestion 651n.
esophagus
maw 194n.
orifice 263n.
esoteric
private 80adj.
unintelligible 517adj.
occult 523adj.
retained 778adj.
sorcerous 983adj.
occultist 984n.
esoterism
latency 523n.
secret 530n.
occultism 984n.
espadrilles
footwear 228n.
espalier
fence 235n.
especial
(*see* special)
especially
eminently 34adv.
specially 80adv.
Esperanto
language 557n.
espial
inspection 438n.
discovery 484n.
espionage
secret service 459n.
esplanade
horizontality 216n.
path 624n.
espousal
promise 764n.
compact 765n.
love affair 887n.
wedding 894n.
espouse
choose 605vb.
patronize 703vb.
cooperate 706vb.
marry 894vb.
esprit
intelligence 498n.
wit 839n.
esprit de corps
prejudice 481n.
cooperation 706n.
sociality 882n.
esprit d'escalier
sequel 67n.
thought 449n.
wit 839n.
espy
see 438vb.
esquire
male 372n.
title 870n.
essay
experiment 461n.
reading matter 589n.
article 591n.
dissertation 591n.
essay 671n., vb.
undertaking 672n.
be active 678vb.
exert oneself 682vb.
action 766n.
essayist
author 589n.
dissertator 591n.
esse
existence 1n.
essence
essence 1n.
essential part 5n.
main part 32n.
product 164n.
form 243n.
extraction 304n.
odor 394n.
meaning 514n.
goodness 644n.
perfection 646n.
cosmetic 843n.
theosophy 984n.
essence, in
actually 1adv.
Essenes
non-Christian sect 978n.
essential
real 1adj.
existing 1adj.
intrinsic 5adj.
absolute 32adj.
requirement 627n.
chief thing 638n.
essentiality
substantiality 3n.
needfulness 627n.
importance 638n.
essentially
actually 1adv.
substantially 3adv.
intrinsically 5adv.
wholly 52adv.
essential oils
prophylactic 658n.
establish
auspicate 68vb.
perpetuate 115vb.
stabilize 153vb.
produce 164vb.
place 187vb.
corroborate 466vb.
demonstrate 478vb.
dower 777vb.
make legal 953vb.
established
immemorial 127adj.
permanent 144adj.
vested 153adj.
usual 610adj.
prosperous 730adj.
proprietary 777adj.
establishment
beginning 68n.
band 74n.
fixture 153n.
production 164n.
location 187n.
demonstration 478n.
bigwig 638n.
corporation 708n.
shop 796n.
Establishment, the
influence 178n.
master 741n.
upper class 868n.
estafette
courier 531n.
estaminet
tavern 192n.
estate
state 7n.
territory 184n.
land 344n.
farm 370n.
estate, lands 777n.
estate-car
automobile 274n.
estate for life
dower 777n.
estate for years
dower 777n.
esteem
opine 485vb.
repute, prestige 866n.
respect 920n., vb.
approbation 923n.
estimable
excellent 644adj.
approvable 923adj.
estimate
do sums 86vb.
cognize 447vb.
discriminate 463vb.
measurement 465n.
estimate 480n., vb.
expectation 507n.
report 524n.
price 809vb.
estimation
measurement 465n.
estimate 480n.
(*see* esteem)
estop
obstruct 702vb.
estoppel
hindrance 702n.
estrange

set apart 46vb.
make quarrels 709vb.
not retain 779vb.
make enemies 881vb.
excite hate 888vb.
estrangement
seclusion 883n.
(*see* estrange)
estrapade
foin 712n.
estrous
libido 859n.
estuary
open space 263n.
gulf 345n.
esurient
hungry 859adj.
etatism
despotism 733n.
et cetera
in addition 38adv.
including 78adv.
et cetera 101adv.
etch
outline 233vb.
groove 262vb.
mark 547vb.
engrave 555vb.
etcher
engraver 556n.
etching
representation 551n.
engraving 555n.
ornamental art 844n.
eternal
lasting 113adj.
unceasing 146adj.
(*see* eternity)
eternalize, eternize
perpetuate 115vb.
honor 866vb.
eternal triangle
illicit love 951n.
eternity
existence 1n.
infinity 107n.
neverness 109n.
perpetuity 115n.
immateriality 320n.
divine attribute 965n.
heaven 971n.
eternity ring
jewelry 844n.
love-token 889n.
ether
heavens 321n.
levity 323n.
rarity 325n.
gas 336n.
anesthetic 375n.
ethereal
insubstantial 4adj.
light 323adj.
rare 325adj.
ethereal body
spiritualism 984n.
etherial
(*see* ethereal)
ethics
morals 917n.
virtue 933n.
ethnarch
governor 741n.
ethnic
ethnic 11adj.
human 371adj.
ethnic group
race 11n.
ethnic type
mankind 371n.
ethnology
anthropology 371n.
ethos
character 5n.
conduct 688n.
etiolation
achromatism 426n.
whiteness 427n.
etiolin
green pigment 432n.
etiology
causation 156n.
attribution 158n.
science 490n.
pathology 651n.
etiquette
conformity 83n.
practice 610n.
etiquette 848n.
formality 875n.
Eton crop
shortening 204n.
hair-dressing 843n.
Eton-jacket
tunic 228n.
étourderie
inattention 456n.
unskillfulness 695n.
étude
musical piece 412n.
etui
case 194n.
etymology
source 156n.
efformation 243n.
linguistics 557n.
etymology 559n.
etymon
source 156n.
word 559n.
Eucharist
Holy Communion
988n.
Euchites
non-Christian sect
978n.
euchologion
office-book 988n.
euchology
office-book 988n.
euchre
overmaster 727vb.
card game 837n.
eugenics
biology 358n.
civilization 654n.
euhemerism
reasoning 475n.
interpretation 520n.
irreligion 974n.
eulogist
commender 923n.
eulogy
description 590n.
praise 923n.
eunuch
eunuch 161n.
slave 742n.
eupepsia
health 650n.
euphemism
underestimation 483n.
trope 519n.
falsehood 541n.
ornament 574n.
good taste 846n.
affectation 850n.
flattery 924n.
prudery 950n.
euphemist
phrasemonger 574n.
euphemize
moderate 177vb.
underestimate 483vb.
cant 541vb.
ornament 547vb.
be affected 850vb.
euphonious
(*see* euphony)
euphonium
horn 414n.
euphony
melody 410n.
elegance 575n.
euphoria
euphoria 376n.
health 650n.
palmy days 730n.
happiness 824n.
content 828n.
euphuism
trope 519n.
ornament 574n.
affectation 850n.
euphuist
phrasemonger 574n.
affector 850n.
Eurasian
hybrid 43n.
euripus
narrowness 206n.
gulf 345n.

europeanize
transform 147vb.
eurythmics
education 534n.
exercise 862n.
dancing 837n.
eurythmy
symmetry 245n.
euthanasia
decease 361n.
killing 362n.
euphoria 376n.
euthenics
civilization 654n.
Eutychianism
heresy 977n.
evacuate
be absent 190vb.
go away 190vb.
decamp 296vb.
evacuation
recession 290n.
egress 298n.
voidance 300n.
cacation 302n.
relinquishment 621n.
evacuee
outcaste 883n.
evade
sophisticate 477vb.
be stealthy 525vb.
avoid 620vb.
elude 667vb.
not observe 769vb.
fail in duty 918vb.
evagation
deviation 282n.
evaginate
invert 221vb.
evaluate
class 62vb.
appraise 465vb.
estimate 480vb.
evanescence
transientness 114n.
disappearance 446n.
evanescent
inconsiderable 33adj.
evangel
news 529n.
evangelic
revelational 975adj.
evangelical
revelational 975adj.
orthodox 976adj.
sectarian 978adj.
evangelist
preacher 537n.
religious teacher 973n.
pastor 986n.
evangelistic
scriptural 975adj.
evangelize
convert 147vb.
convince 485vb.
evaporate
not be 2vb.
decrease 37vb.
be dispersed 75vb.
be transient 114vb.
destroy 165vb.
become small 198vb.
vaporize 338vb.
dry 343vb.
disappear 446vb.
waste 634vb.
evaporation
loss 772n.
(*see* evaporate)
evaporator
drier 342n.
evasion
sophistry 477n.
concealment 525n.
falsehood 541n.
mental dishonesty 543n.
pretext 614n.
avoidance 620n.
escape 667n.
stratagem 698n.
evasive
equivocal 518adj.
reticent 541adj.
untrue 543adj.
evasive action
avoidance 620n.
eve
precursor 66n.
priority 119n.
evening 129n.
evection
derangement 63n.
even
uniform 16adj.
equal 28adj.
regular 81adj.
numerical 85adj.
evening 129n.
periodic 141adj.
flatten 216vb.
symmetrical 245adj.
straight 249adj.
smooth 258adj., vb.
inexcitable 823adj.
even date
present time 121n.
even-handed
just 913adj.
evening
end 69n.
period 110n.
evening 129n.
obscuration 418n.
half-light 419n.
evening dress
formal dress 228n.
even keel
equilibrium 28n.
even money
equivalence 28n.
even-sided
equal 28adj.
symmetrical 245adj.
even so
nevertheless 468adv.
Evensong
evening 129n.
public worship 981n.
church service 988n.
event
reality 1n.
occasion 137n.
eventuality 154n.
appearance 445n.
contest 716n.
even temper
inexcitability 823n.
even tenor
uniformity 16n.
order 60n.
eventful
circumstantial 8adj.
eventful 154adj.
notable 638adj.
eventual
future 124adj.
eventual 154adj.
eventuality
juncture 8n.
futurity 124n.
occasion 137n.
eventuality 154n.
chance 159n.
appearance 445n.
eventually
prospectively 124adv.
eventually 154adv.
in the future 155adv.
consequently 157adv.
eventuate
happen 154vb.
result 157vb.
appear 445vb.
ever and ever
forever 115adv.
everglade
marsh 347n.
evergreen
continuous 71adj.
lasting 113adj.
perpetual 115adj.
new 126adj.
young 130adj.
unchangeable 153adj.
unyielding 162adj.
vegetal 366adj.
renowned 866adj.
everlasting
perpetual 115adj.
godlike 965adj.
ever less

diminuendo 37adv.
evermore
forever 115adv.
ever since
all along 113adv.
eversion
change 143n.
inversion 221n.
evolution 316n.
ever so
greatly 32adv.
evert
modify 143vb.
every
universal 79adj.
everybody
medley 43n.
all 52n.
everyman 79n.
mankind 371n.
every day
often 139adv.
everyday
typical 83adj.
plain 573adj.
usual 610adj.
everyday language
prose 593n.
every excuse
vindication 927n.
innocence 935n.
every inch
wholly 52adj.
completely 54adv.
everyman
prototype 23n.
common man 30n.
everyman 79n.
person 371n.
mediocrity 732n.
commoner 869n.
everyone
(*see* everybody)
every other
sequent 65adj.
by turns 141adj.
every side, on
around 230adv.
every so often
sometimes 139adv.
at intervals 201adv.
every tongue, on
renowned 866adj.
every way
completely 54adv.
everywhere
space 183n.
widely 183adv.
here 189adv.
eviction
ejection 300n.
loss 772n.
expropriation 786n.
evidence
evidence 466n., vb.
make likely 471vb.
demonstrate 478vb.
mean 514vb.
manifest 522vb.
indication 547n.
trace 548n.
legal trial 959n.
evidence against
counter-evidence 467n.
evident
visible 443adj.
certain 473adj.
demonstrated 478adj.
manifest 522adj.
evidential
evidential 466adj.
evil
evil 616n.
harmful 645adj.
bane 659n.
adversity 731n.
suffering 825n.
wickedness 934n.
evil day
adversity 731n.
evildoer
evildoer 904n.
bad man 938n.
evil eye
look 438n.
hatred 888n.
malediction 899n.
spell 983n.
evil hour
intempestivity 138n.
evil-minded
wicked 934adj.
evil-speaking
scurrility 899n.
detraction 926n.
impiety 980n.
evil spirit
sorcerer 983n.
evil star
badness 645n.
ill fortune 731n.
evince
evidence 466vb.
demonstrate 478vb.
manifest 522vb.
indicate 547vb.
eviscerate
void 300vb.
extract 304vb.
impair 655vb.
evitable
possible 469adj.
evocation
causation 156n.
remembrance 505n.
representation 551n.
description 590n.
excitation 831n.
evoke
incite 612vb.
(*see* evocation)
evolution
existence 1n.
numerical operation 86n.
conversion 147n.
production 164n.
motion 265n.
progression 285n.
circuition 314n.
evolution 316n.
biology 358n.
improvement 654n.
action 676n.
evolutionary
evolving 316adj.
biological 358adj.
evolutionist
biology 358n.
evolve
become 1vb.
result 157vb.
extract 304vb.
evolve 316vb.
(*see* evolution)
evolved from
caused 157adj.
evulsion
extraction 304n.
ewe
sheep 365n.
female animal 373n.
ewe-lamb
youngling 132n.
ewer
vessel 194n.
water 339n.
ablution 648n.
ex
prior 119adj.
exacerbate
augment 36vb.
make violent 176vb.
impair 655vb.
hurt 827vb.
aggravate 832vb.
make enemies 881vb.
excite hate 888vb.
exact
lifelike 18adj.
definite 80adj.
careful 457adj.
accurate 494adj.
veracious 540adj.
perspicuous 567adj.
concise 569adj.
demand 737vb.
observant 768adj.
levy 786vb.
right 913adj.
impose a duty 917vb.

exacting
fatiguing 684adj.
difficult 700adj.
oppressive 735adj.
discontented 829adj.
greedy 859adj.
fastidious 862adj.
exaction
demand 737n.
compulsion 740n.
taking 786n.
tax 809n.
undueness 916n.
exactitude
(*see* exactness)
exactness
carefulness 457n.
accuracy 494n.
perspicuity 567n.
right 913n.
exaggerate
misinterpret 521vb.
make important 638vb.
be affected 850vb.
(*see* exaggeration)
exaggerated
exorbitant 32adj.
exaggeration
greatness 32n.
increase 36n.
expansion 197n.
overstepping 306n.
overestimation 482n.
absurdity 497n.
ideality 513n.
misinterpretation 521n.
untruth 543n.
exaggeration 545n.
misrepresentation 552n.
magniloquence 574n.
redundance 637n.
ostentation 875n.
boast 877n.
exalt
augment 36vb.
elevate 310vb.
make important 638vb.
respect 920vb.
praise 923vb.
exaltation
elevation 310n.
warm feeling 818n.
joy 824n.
piety 979n.
exalted
great 32adj.
high 209adj.
notable 638adj.
noble 868adj.
exaltedness
prestige 866n.
examination
meditation 449n.
attention 455n.
inquiry 459n.
exam 459n.
experiment 461n.
dissertation 591n.
legal trial 959n.
examination-in-chief
interrogation 459n.
examination paper
question 459n.
examine
scan 438vb.
interrogate 459vb.
examinee
exam 459n.
respondent 460n.
testee 461n.
beginner 538n.
contender 716n.
examiner
listener 415n.
spectator 441n.
inquisitor 453n.
inquirer 459n.
estimator 480n.
interlocutor 584n.
example
relevance 9n.
non-imitation 21n.
duplicate 22n.
prototype 23n.
part 53n.
precursor 66n.
rule 81n.
example 83n.
exhibit 522n.
warning 664n.
exanimate
dead 361adj.
inactive 679adj.
exarch
governor 741n.
ecclesiarch 986n.
exarchate
church office 985n.
exasperate
make violent 176vb.
aggravate 832vb.
excite hate 888vb.
enrage 891vb.
ex cathedra
assertive 532adj.
affirmatively 532adv.
ex cathedra utterance
certainty 473n.
excavation
excavation 255n.
extraction 304n.
search 459n.
excecate
blind 439adj., vb.
exceed
be great 32vb.
be superior 34vb.
grow 36vb.
overstep, outdo 306vb.
be intemperate 943vb.
exceeding
exorbitant 32adj.
excel
have repute 866vb.
excellence
superiority 34n.
precedence 64n.
importance 638n.
goodness 644n.
skill 694n.
good taste 846n.
virtues 933n.
Excellence, Excellency
sovereign 741n.
title 870n.
excellent
great 32adj.
supreme 34adj.
perfect 646adj.
splendid 841adj.
exceller
exceller 644n.
excelsior
up 308adv.
type size 587n.
except
if 8adv.
subtract 39vb.
in deduction 39adv.
exclusive of 57adv.
(*see* exception)
exception
non-uniformity 17n.
separation 46n.
exclusion 57n.
specialty 80n.
unconformity 84n.
qualification 468n.
rejection 607n.
deprecation 762n.
conditions 766n.
disapprobation 924n.
exceptionable
blameworthy 924adj.
exceptional
non-uniform 17adj.
disagreeing 25adj.
remarkable 32adj.
extraneous 59adj.
exceptionally
greatly 32adv.
exceptious
irascible 892adj.
excerpt
part 53n.
edition 589n.
abstract 592vb.
select 605vb.
excerpta, excerpts
anthology 592n.
choice 605n.

excess
superiority 34n.
exaggeration 546n.
inelegance 576n.
redundance 637n.
overactivity 678n.
scope 744n.
satiety 863n.
cruel act 898n.
intemperance 943n.
excessive
exorbitant 32adj.
surpassing 306adj.
exaggerated 546adj.
pleonastic 570adj.
inelegant 576adj.
superfluous 637adj.
redundant 637adj.
dear 811adj.
cruel 898adj.
unwarranted 916adj.
intemperate 943adj.
excessively
extremely 32adv.
exchange
correlation 12n.
equivalence 28n.
focus 76n.
substitution 150n.
interchange 151n., vb.
interlocution 584n.
bourse 618n.
transfer 780n.
barter, trade 791vb.
mart 796n.
finance 797n.
exchange, in
in exchange 151adv.
exchange views
compare 462vb.
exchequer
storage 632n.
treasury 799n.
excise
subtract 39vb.
tax 809n.
exciseman
receiver 782n.
excision
subtraction 39n.
excitable
impressible 819adj.
excited 821adj.
excitable 822adj.
irascible 892adj.
excitant
stimulant 174n.
excitant 821n.
aggravation 832n.
excitation
(*see* excite)
excite
cause 156vb.
strengthen 162vb.
operate 173vb.
invigorate 174vb.
make violent 176vb.
cause feeling 374vb.
itch 378vb.
incite 612vb.
excite 821vb.
delight 826vb.
aggravate 832vb.
excite love 887vb.
excitement
stimulation 174n.
excitation 821n.
exciting
pleasurable 826adj.
exclaim
cry 408vb.
voice 577vb.
disapprove 924vb.
exclamation
cry 408n.
voice 577n.
wonder 864n.
exclamation mark
punctuation 547n.
exclave
region 184n.
exclude
bate 37vb.
disregard 458vb.
make impossible 470vb.
obstruct 702vb.
restrain 747vb.
depose 752vb.
prohibit 757vb.
refuse 760vb.
(*see* exclusion)
excluded
extraneous 59adj.
displaced 188adj.
impossible 470adj.
exclusion
separation 46n.
exclusion 57n.
unconformity 84n.
exteriority 223n.
ejection 300n.
rejection 607n.
non-ownership 774n.
seclusion 883n.
unsociability 883n.
(*see* exclude)
exclusive
unmixed 44adj.
private 80adj.
unconformable 84adj.
excellent 644adj.
sectional 708adj.
sectarian 978adj.
exclusiveness
contrariety 14n.
particularism 80n.
sectarianism 978n.
exclusivity
restriction 747n.
excogitation
thought 449n.
meditation 449n.
ideality 513n.
excommunicate
exclude 57vb.
prohibit 757vb.
make unwelcome 883vb.
curse 899vb.
condemn 961vb.
perform ritual 988vb.
excommunicated
cursed 899adj.
schismatical 978adj.
excoriation
uncovering 229n.
excrement, excreta
excrement 302n.
dirt 649n.
excrementitious
unclean 649adj.
excrescence
swelling 253n.
superfluity 637n.
blemish 845n.
excrescent
useless 641adj.
excretion
ejection 300n.
voidance 300n.
excretion 302n.
excruciate
give pain 377vb.
torment 827vb.
excruciating
painful 377adj.
exculpable
guiltless 935adj.
exculpation
forgiveness 909n.
non-liability 919n.
vindication 927n.
acquittal 960n.
excursion
land travel 267n.
overstepping 306n.
pleonasm 570n.
enjoyment 824n.
amusement 837n.
excursionist
traveler 268n.
reveler 837n.
excursive
deviating 282adj.
prolix 570adj.
excursus
pleonasm 570n.
dissertation 591n.
excusable
forgiven 908adj.
vindicable 927adj.

guiltless 935adj.
excuse
exclude 57vb.
reason why 156n.
disregard 458vb.
qualify 468vb.
mental dishonesty 543n.
pretext 614n.
stratagem 698n.
liberate 746vb.
forgiveness 909n.
non-liability 919n.
vindication 927n.
extenuate 927vb.
execrable
bad 645adj.
execrate
curse 899vb.
dispraise 924vb.
execration
hatred 888n.
malediction 899n.
reproach 924n.
executant
musician 413n.
doer 676n.
execution
killing 362n.
action 676n.
effectuation 725n.
capital punishment 963n.
executive
agent 686n.
directing 689adj.
manager 690n.
executor
doer 676n.
agent 686n.
manager 690n.
exegesis
interpretation 520n.
exemplar
prototype 23n.
example 83n.
exemplary
typical 33adj.
excellent 644adj.
exemplify
exemplify 83adj.
exempt
liberate 746vb.
exemption
exclusion 57n.
permission 756n.
non-liability 919n.
exercise
train 534vb.
function 622vb.
prepare oneself 669vb.
use 673n., vb.
deed 676n.
exercise 682n.
incommode 827vb.
exercitation
teaching 534n.
(*see* exercise)
exergue
edging 234n.
exert
use 673vb.
exertion
power 160n.
vigorousness 174n.
perseverance 600n.
essay 671n.
action 676n.
exertion 682n.
fatigue 684n.
difficulty 700n.
contest 716n.
exfoliation
uncovering 229n.
egress 298n.
exhalation
gas 336n.
exhale
exude 298vb.
emit 300vb.
vaporize 338vb.
breathe 352vb.
smell 394vb.
exhaust
bate 37vb.
disable 161vb.
make smaller 198vb.
outlet 298n.
rarefy 325vb.
sufflate 352vb.
waste 634n., vb.
make insufficient 636vb.
impair 655vb.
fatigue 684vb.
levy 786vb.
exhaustion
helplessness 161n.
weakness 163n.
(*see* exhaust)
exhaustive
complete 54adj.
exhaust pipe
outlet 298n.
sufflation 352n.
exhibit
evidence 466n.
exhibit 522n.
show 522vb.
advertisement 528n.
indicate 547vb.
be ostentatious 875vb.
exhibition
spectacle 445n.
appearance 445n.
foolery 497n.
manifestation 522n.
collection 632n.
mart 796n.
receipt 807n.
reward 962n.
exhibitioner
college student 538n.
recipient 782n.
exhibitionism
inelegance 576n.
vanity 873n.
impurity 951n.
exhibitionist
vain person 873n.
showy 875adj.
exhibitor
exhibitor 522n.
exhilarate
excite 821vb.
delight 826vb.
cheer 833vb.
inebriate 949vb.
exhilarated
pleased 824adj.
drunk 949adj.
exhilaration
excitable state 822n.
(*see* exhilarate)
exhort
incite 612vb.
advise 691vb.
exhortation
oration 579n.
inducement 612n.
exhumation
inquest 364n.
exhume
look back 125vb.
exhume 364vb.
ex hypothesi
supposedly 512adv.
exigence
needfulness 627n.
predicament 700n.
desire 859n.
exigent
demanding 627adj.
oppressive 735adj.
discontented 829adj.
exiguity
smallness 33n.
fewness 105n.
littleness 196n.
shortness 204n.
exile
exclusion 57n.
displacement 188n.
egress 298n.
ejection 300n.
seclusion 883n.
outcaste 883n.
penalty 963n.
exilic
scriptural 975adj.
exility

thinness 206n.
eximious
excellent 644adj.
exist
be 1vb.
be present 189vb.
live 360vb.
be true 494vb.
existence
existence 1n.
essence 1n.
presence 189n.
life 360n.
existential
existing 1adj.
existentialism
existence 1n.
philosophy 449n.
exit
doorway 263n.
departure 296n.
egress, outlet 298n.
decease 361n.
disappearance 446n.
dramaturgy 594n.
means of escape 667n.
exode
stage play 594n.
exodos
dramaturgy 594n.
exodus
departure 296n.
egress 298n.
ex officio
in control 689adv.
authoritative 733adj.
duly 915adv.
exogenous
exterior 223adj.
vegetal 366adj.
exomologesis
penitence 939n.
Christian rite 988n.
exoneration
forgiveness 909n.
non-liability 919n.
vindication 927n.
acquittal 960n.
exorability
mercy 905n.
forgiveness 909n.
exorbitance
greatness 32n.
exaggeration 546n.
redundance 637n.
dearness 811n.
exorbitant
huge 195adj.
deviating 282adj.
surpassing 306adj.
exorbitation
deviation 282n.
exorcise
eject 300vb.
dismiss 300vb.
practice sorcery 983vb.
prayers 981n.
sorcery 983n.
Christian rite 988n.
exorcism
malediction 899n.
exorcist
sorcerer 983n.
cleric 986n.
exordium
prelude 66n.
beginning 68n.
exosmose
passage 305n.
exostosis
swelling 253n.
exoteric
undisguised 522adj.
published 528adj.
exotic
irrelation 10n.
dissimilar 19adj.
extraneous 59adj.
unconformable 84adj.
flower 366n.
horticultural 370adj.
expand
add 38vb.
lengthen 203vb.
be broad 205vb.
progress 285vb.
rarefy 325vb.
exaggerate 546vb.
(*see* expansion)
expanse
greatness 32n.
space 183n.
size 195n.
breadth 205n.
expansion
increase 36n.
space 183n.
expansion 197n.
diffuseness 570n.
expansionism
ingress 297n.
overstepping 306n.
nation 371n.
bellicosity 718n.
governance 733n.
expansionist
militarist 722n.
expansive
spacious 183adj.
expanded 197adj.
broad 205adj.
expatiate
be diffuse 570vb.
speak 579vb.
be loquacious 581vb.
expatriate
exclude 57vb.
foreigner 59n.
eject 300vb.
outcaste 883n.
expatriation
egress 298n.
seclusion 883n.
expect
look ahead 124vb.
assume 471vb.
expect 507vb.
intend 617vb.
hope 852vb.
desire 859vb.
not wonder 865vb.
have a right 915vb.
expectance
expectation 507n.
expectant
future 124adj.
attentive 455adj.
expectant 507adj.
petitioner 763n.
beneficiary 776n.
hoper 852n.
expectation
destiny 155n.
probability 471n.
dubiety 474n.
belief 485n.
expectation 507n.
hope 852n.
expectations
dueness 915n.
expected
future 124adj.
expected, as
probably 471adv.
duly 915adv.
expecting
productive 164adj.
expectorant
cathartic 658n.
expectorate
eruct 300vb.
expectoration
excretion 302n.
expectoratory
disapproving 924adj.
expedience
fitness 24n.
utility 640n.
expedience 642n.
right 913n.
expedient
opportune 137adj.
operative 173adj.
possible 469adj.
wise 498adj.
contrivance 623n.
instrument 628n.
means 629n.
expedite
be early 135vb.
accelerate 277vb.
hasten 680vb.

expedition
land travel 267n.
velocity 277n.
activity 678n.
haste 680n.
warfare 718n.
expel
impel 279n.
propel 287vb.
reject 607vb.
make unwelcome 883vb.
(*see* expulsion)
expellee
outcaste 883n.
expend
dispose of 673vb.
pay 804vb.
expend 806vb.
expendable
superfluous 637adj.
unimportant 639adj.
useless 641adj.
expenditure
waste 634n.
loss 772vb.
purchase 792n.
expenditure 806n.
cost 809n.
expense
(*see* expenditure)
expense account
earnings 771n.
gift 781n.
reward 962n.
expensive
dear 811adj.
ostentatious 875adj.
experience
meet with 154vb.
empiricism 461n.
knowledge 490n.
wisdom 498n.
skill 694n.
feel 818vb.
experienced
matured 669adj.
expert 694adj.
cautious 858adj.
experiences
biography 590n.
experiment
be curious 453vb.
inquire 459vb.
experiment 461n., vb.
demonstration 478n.
gambling 618n.
preparation 669n.
essay 671n., vb.
experimental
new 126adj.
experimental 461adj.
speculative 618adj.
cautious 858adj.
experimentalist
experimenter 461n.
experimentation
experiment 461n.
experimenter
experimenter 461n.
learner 538n.
gambler 618n.
essayer 671n.
expert
knowing 490adj.
sage 500n.
matured 669adj.
adviser 691n.
expert 694adj.
proficient, expert 696n.
expertise
skill 694n.
expiable
vindicable 927adj.
expiation
compensation 31n.
remedy 658n.
propitiation 941n.
oblation 981n.
expiration
respiration 352n.
expire
end 69vb.
elapse 111vb.
die 361vb.
expired
past 125adj.
explain
specify 80vb.
facilitate 701vb.
explain away
reason 475vb.
confute 479vb.
disbelieve 486vb.
misteach 535vb.
explained
intelligible 516adj.
explanation
reason why 156n.
attribution 158n.
answer 460n.
discovery 484n.
interpretation 520n.
explanations
disclosure 526n.
expletive
pleonasm 570n.
superfluous 637adj.
scurrility 899n.
explicable
intelligible 516adj.
explicate
evolve 316vb.
explication
evolution 316n.
interpretation 520n.
explicit
meaningful 514adj.
intelligible 516adj.
undisguised 522adj.
informative 524adj.
perspicuous 567adj.
explode
break 46vb.
be dispersed 75vb.
open 263vb.
shoot 287vb.
be brittle 330vb.
confute 479vb.
be active 678vb.
miscarry 728vb.
(*see* explosion)
exploded
past 125adj.
antiquated 127adj.
unbelieved 486adj.
erroneous 495adj.
disapproved 924adj.
exploit
important matter 638n.
use 673vb.
deed 676n.
masterpiece 694n.
be skillful 694vb.
success 727n.
thaumaturgy 864n.
prowess 855n.
exploitation
(*see* exploit)
exploration
land travel 267n.
inquiry, search 459n.
experiment 461n.
discovery 484n.
exploratory
precursory 66adj.
experimental 461adj.
explore
(*see* exploration)
explored
known 490adj.
explorer
precursor 66n.
traveler 268n.
inquisitor 453n.
inquirer 459n.
experimenter 461n.
detector 484n.
explosion
outbreak 176n.
bang 402n.
excitable state 822n.
anger 891n.
disapprobation 924n.
(*see* explode)
explosive
destroyer 168n.
violent 176adj.
propellant 287n.

brittle 330adj.
combustible 385adj.
dangerous 661adj.
pitfall 663n.
explosive 723n.
exponent
numerical element 85n.
interpreter 520n.
teacher 537n.
indication 547n.
exponential
numerical 85adj.
indicating 547adj.
export
transference 272n.
egress 298n.
eject 300vb.
provide 633vb.
export and import
trade 791vb.
exporter
transferrer 272n.
carrier 273n.
merchant 794n.
expose
uncover 229vb.
aerify 340vb.
be visible 443vb.
confute 479vb.
detect 484vb.
show 522vb.
disclose 526vb.
photograph 551vb.
satirize 851vb.
shame 867vb.
dispraise 924vb.
defame 926vb.
accuse 928vb.
exposé
description 590n.
exposed
defenseless 161adj.
weakened 163adj.
liable 180adj.
windy 352adj.
sentient 374adj.
painful 377adj.
vulnerable 661adj.
subject 745adj.
expose oneself
be liable 180vb.
face danger 661vb.
exposition
musical piece 412n.
spectacle 445n.
demonstration 478n.
interpretation 520n.
exhibit 522n.
dissertation 591n.
mart 796n.
expositor
interpreter 520n.
teacher 537n.
dissertator 591n.
expository
interpretive 520adj.
informative 524adj.
disclosing 526adj.
discursive 591adj.
ex post facto
subsequently 120adv.
retrospectively 125adv.
expostulate
reprove 924vb.
expostulation
dissent 489n.
dissuasion 613n.
warning 664n.
deprecation 762n.
exposure
liability 180n.
uncovering 229n.
air 340n.
homicide 362n.
refrigeration 382n.
visibility 443n.
confutation 479n.
discovery 484n.
photography 551n.
vulnerability 661n.
detraction 926n.
expound
interpret 520vb.
teach 534vb.
express
definite 80adj.
specify 80vb.
efform 243vb.
bearer 273n.
vehicular 274adj.
speeder 277n.
extract 304vb.
mean 514vb.
manifest 522vb.
courier 531n.
assertive 532adj.
affirm 532vb.
phrase 563vb.
voice 577vb.
express delivery
mails 531n.
expressible
shown 522adj.
expression
number 85n.
efformation 243n.
musical skill 413n.
mien 445n.
meaning 514n.
manifestation 522n.
affirmation 532n.
word 559n.
phrase 563n.
feeling 818n.
expressionism
art 551n.
school of painting 553n.
expressionless
still 266adj.
unintelligible 517adj.
impassive 820adj.
expressive
meaningful 514adj.
expressive 516adj.
informative 524adj.
elegant 575adj.
lively 819adj.
expressway
road 624n.
exprobate
curse 899vb.
exprobate 924vb.
exprobation
reproach 924n.
expropriate
convey 780vb.
disentitle 916vb.
expropriation
ejection 300n.
loss 772n.
expropriation 786n.
penalty 963n.
expropriator
taker 786n.
expropriatory
taking 786adj.
punitive 963adj.
expugnable
vulnerable 661adj.
expugnation
victory 727n.
expulsion
subtraction 39n.
elimination 44n.
separation 46n.
exclusion 57n.
transference 272n.
ejection 300n.
expropriation 786n.
penalty 963n.
(*see* expel)
expulsive
propulsive 287adj.
expulsive 300adj.
expunge
destroy 165vb.
obliterate 550vb.
expurgate
exclude 57vb.
purify 648vb.
impair 655vb.
expurgation
prudery 950n.
Expurgatory Index
orthodoxism 976n.
exquisite
painful 377adj.
savory 390adj.
excellent 644adj.
pleasurable 826adj.

paining 827adj.
beautiful 841adj.
tasteful 846adj.
fop 848n.
fashionable 848adj.
exquisitely
greatly 32adv.
exsanguine
colorless 426adj.
exsection
extraction 304n.
exsuction
extraction 304n.
exsufflation
sorcery 983n.
extant
existing 1adj.
recorded 548adj.
extemporaneous
spontaneous 609adj.
extempore
instantaneously 116adv.
at present 121adv.
suddenly 135adv.
incidentally 137adv.
extempore 609adv.
unreadily 670adv.
extemporization
spontaneity 609n.
extemporize
compose music 413vb.
improvise 609vb.
be unprepared 670vb.
extend
add 38vb.
continuate 71vb.
extend 183vb.
enlarge 197vb.
lengthen 203vb.
extend to
fill 54vb.
be distant 199vb.
be contiguous 202vb.
extensibility
expansion 197n.
extensible
elastic 328adj.
extensile
flexible 327adj.
elastic 328adj.
extension
increase 36n.
adjunct 40n.
protraction 113n.
continuance 146n.
space 183n.
expansion 197n.
lengthening 203n.
(*see* extent)
extensive
extensive 32adj.
spacious 183adj.
large 195adj.
extenso, in
diffusely 570adv.
extent
quantity 26n.
degree 27n.
greatness 32n.
space 183n.
size 195n.
length 203n.
(*see* extension)
extenuate
bate 37vb.
weaken 163vb.
moderate 177vb.
qualify 468vb.
plead 614vb.
extenuate 927vb.
extenuated
lean 206adj.
extenuating circumstances
qualification 468n.
vindication 927n.
extenuation
vindication 927n.
exterior
extrinsic 6adj.
separate 46adj.
exteriority 223n.
appearing 445adj.
ostentation 875n.
exteriority
extraneousness 59n.
farness 199n.
exteriority 223n.
exterminate
destroy 165vb.
extermination
extraction 304n.
slaughter 362n.
exterminator
killer 362n.
extern
externalize 223vb.
eject 300vb.
external
extrinsic 6adj.
separate 46adj.
exterior 223adj.
appearing 445adj.
externalize
make extrinsic 6vb.
externalize 223vb.
materialize 319vb.
manifest 522vb.
external origin, of
extraneous 59adj.
externment
ejection 300n.
penalty 963n.
extinct
extinct 2adj.
past 125adj.
dead 361adj.
non-active 677adj.
inactive 679adj.
extinction
extinction 2n.
destruction 165n.
death 361n.
disappearance 446n.
extinguish
bate 37vb.
suppress 165vb.
extinguish 382vb.
snuff out 418vb.
extinguisher
extinguisher 382n.
extirpation
destruction 165n.
extraction 304n.
extol
praise 923vb.
worship 981vb.
extort
extract 304vb.
oppress 735vb.
rob 788vb.
extortion
compulsion 740n.
expropriation 786n.
rapacity 786n.
dearness 811n.
extortionate
oppressive 735adj.
lending 784adj.
taking 786adj.
dear 811adj.
avaricious 816adj.
greedy 859adj.
extortioner
tyrant 735n.
lender 784n.
taker 786n.
extra
increment 36n.
additional 38adj.
extra 40n.
ingredient 58adj.
superfluity 637n.
unused 674adj.
extract
part 53n.
product 164n.
uncover 229vb.
draw 288vb.
eject 300vb.
extract 304vb.
manifest 522vb.
acquire 771vb.
take, levy 786vb.
extraction
subtraction 39n.
genealogy 169n.
displacement 188n.
transference 272n.
extraction 304n.
deliverance 668n.

extractive
extracted 304adj.
extradition
transference 272n.
ejection 300n.
extrajudicial
illegal 954adj.
extramarital
extramarital 951adj.
extramundane
immaterial 320adj.
divine 965adj.
extramural
extrinsic 6adj.
exterior 223adj.
extraneous
non-uniform 17adj.
disagreeing 25adj.
separate 46adj.
excluded 57adj.
extraneous 59adj.
unconformable 84adj.
exterior 223adj.
extraneousness
extrinsicality 6n.
irrelation 10n.
extraneousness 59n.
farness 199n.
extraordinary
unusual 84n.
wonderful 864adj.
noteworthy 866adj.
extrapolate
make intrinsic 6vb.
externalize 223vb.
extrasensory perception
sense 374n.
intellect 447n.
extrasensivity
extrinsicality 6n.
extraterritorial
exterior 223adj.
extraterritoriality
exteriority 223n.
non-liability 919n.
extra time
protraction 113n.
extravagance
foolery 497n.
folly 499n.
exaggeration 546n.
waste 634n.
misuse 675n.
expenditure 806n.
prodigality 815n.
ridiculousness 849n.
extravagant
exorbitant 32adj.
violent 176adj.
deviating 282adj.
imaginative 513adj.
plenteous 635adj.
dear 811adj.
extravaganza
musical piece 412n.
spectacle 445n.
ideality 513n.
stage play 594n.
extravagation
overstepping 306n.
extravasation
outflow 298n.
excretion 302n.
extraversion
(*see* extroversion)
extreme
exorbitant 32adj.
complete 54adj.
ending 69adj.
(*see* extremes, extremity)
extremely
extremely 32adv.
extreme penalty
capital punishment 963n.
extremes
exaggeration 546n.
redundance 637n.
opposites 704n.
severity 735n.
cruel act 898n.
extreme unction
decease 361n.
Christian rite 988n.
extremism
exaggeration 546n.
reformism 654n.
extremist
crank 504n.
exaggeration 546n.
reformer 654n.
opponent 705n.
revolter 738n.
extremities
violence 176n.
extremities, in
unprosperous 731adj.
extremity
adjunct 40n.
extremity 69n.
crisis 137n.
vertex 213n.
edge 234n.
limit 236n.
rear 238n.
adversity 731n.
severity 735n.
suffering 825n.
extricate
disencumber 701vb.
extrication
extraction 304n.
escape 667n.
deliverance 668n.
liberation 746n.
extrinsic
separate 46adj.
extrinsicality
extrinsicality 6n.
extraneousness 59n.
exteriority 223n.
extroitive
extrinsic 6adj.
extroversion
extrinsicality 6n.
extrovert
extrinsicality 6n.
exteriority 223n.
extrusion
exclusion 57n.
ejection 300n.
excretion 302n.
extrusive
expulsive 300adj.
exuberance
productiveness 171n.
diffuseness 570n.
redundance 637n.
exuberate
abound 635vb.
exudation
outflow 298n.
excretion 302n.
exude
exude 298vb.
emit 300vb.
be wet 341vb.
exult
vociferate 408vb.
rejoice 835vb.
boast 877vb.
exultant
jubilant 833adj.
exultation
rejoicing 835n.
exuviae
excrement 302n.
dirt 649n.
exuvial
excretory 302adj.
ex voto
devotional 981adj.
eyas
youngling 132n.
eye
centrality 225n.
circle 250n.
orifice 263n.
eye 438n.
gaze 438vb.
watch 441vb.
surveillance 457n.
eyeball
eye 438n.
eyebrows
hair 259n.
eye-catching
well-seen 443adj.
manifest 522adj.
eye-disease
blindness 439n.

eye for an eye
interchange 151n.
retaliation 714n.
revenge 910n.
eyeful
view 438n.
spectacle 445n.
eyeglass
eyeglass 442n.
eyelash
filament 208n.
shade 226n.
hair 259n.
screen 421n.
eyeless
crippled 163adj.
blind 439adj.
eyelet
fastening 47n.
orifice 263n.
perforation 263n.
eyelid
shade 226n.
screen 421n.
eye-opener
discovery 484n.
inexpectation 508n.
prodigy 864n.
eye-piece
astronomy 321n.
transparency 422n.
optical device 442n.
eyer
spectator 441n.
eye-range
visibility 443n.
eye-salve
balm 658n.
cosmetic 843n.
eye-shade
screen 421n.
dim sight 440n.
safeguard 662n.
eye-shadow
cosmetic 843n.
eye-shot
visibility 443n.
eyesight
vision 438n.
eyes of, in the
apparently 445adv.
eyes on
attention 455n.
surveillance 457n.
eyes open, with one's
at sight 438adv.
purposely 617adv.
eyesore
deformity 246n.
eyesore 842n.
monster 938n.
eyestrain
dim sight 440n.
eye-testing
vision 438n.
eye to eye
concordant 710adj.
eyewash
falsehood 541n.
eye-witness
spectator 441n.
visibility 443n.
witness 466n.
eyrie
(*see* aerie)

F

Fabian
reformer 654n.
political party 708n.
Fabianism
continuity 71n.
slowness 278n.
reformism 654n.
government 733n.
caution 858n.
Fabian policy
delay 136n.
caution 858n.
fable
fantasy 513n.
metaphor 519n.
fable 543n.
narrative 590n.
describe 590vb.
fabliau
narrative 590n.
fabric
modality 7n.
edifice 164n.
textile 222n.
structure, texture 331n.
materials 631n.
fabricate
compose 56vb.
produce 164vb.
imagine 513vb.
fake 541vb.
fabricated
unattested 467adj.
imaginary 513adj.
fabrication
production 164n.
falsehood 541n.
untruth 543n.
fabricator
liar 545n.
fabulist
liar 545n.
narrator 590n.
fabulous
unreal 2adj.
prodigious 32adj.
imaginary 513adj.
untrue 543adj.
noteworthy 866adj.
faburden
melody 410n.
facade
exteriority 223n.
face 237n.
duplicity 541n.
face
prepose 64vb.
impend 155vb.
be present 189vb.
exteriority 223n.
coat 226vb.
line 227vb.
face 237n.
be opposite 240vb.
orientate 281vb.
mien 445n.
expect 507vb.
be resolute 599vb.
withstand 704vb.
resist 715vb.
be courageous 855vb.
prestige 866n.
insolence 878n.
face about
revert 148vb.
turn round 282vb.
face both ways
tergiversate 603vb.
face cream
unguent 357n.
cleanser 648n.
balm 658n.
cosmetic 843n.
face death
face danger 661vb.
face down
under 210adv.
supine 216adj.
inversely 221adv.
faceless
uniform 16adj.
face-lift
beautification 843n.
face of it, on the
externally 223adv.
apparently 445adv.
manifestly 522adv.
face powder
powder 332n.
scent 396n.
cosmetic 843n.
facet
exteriority 223n.
face the music
be courageous 855vb.
face the odds
be resolute 599vb.
facetiousness
wit 839n.
face to face
in front 237adv.
against 240adv.

opposing 704adj.
face-towel
cleaning cloth 648n.
face value
appearance 445n.
price 809n.
facia
face 237n.
facial
exterior 223adj.
beautification 843n.
facile
easy 701adj.
facile princeps
supreme 34adj.
facilitate
facilitate 701vb.
aid 703vb.
permit 756vb.
facilities
means 629n.
expedience 642n.
facility 701n.
aid 703n.
scope 744n.
facility
skill 694n.
facility 701n.
aid 703n.
facing
near 200adj.
facing 226n.
opposite 240adj.
against 240adv.
toward 281adv.
opposing 704adj.
façon de parler
trope 519n.
facsimile
identity 13n.
copy 22n.
fact
reality 1n.
eventuality 154n.
evidence 466n.
certainty 473n.
truth 494n.
chief thing 638n.
(*see* facts)
fact-finding
inquiring 459adj.
fact, in
actually 1adv.
positively 32adj.
faction
disagreement 25n.
part 53n.
dissentient 489n.
opposition 704n.
party 708n.
dissension 709n.
revolt 738n.
sect 978n.
factionary
opponent 705n.
agitator 738n.
factionist
schismatic 978n.
factiousness
quarrelsomeness 709n.
sectarianism 978n.
factitious
untrue 543adj.
factitive
causal 156adj.
factor
part 53n.
component 58n.
numerical element 85n.
cause 156n.
influence 178n.
element 319n.
agent 686n.
manager 690n.
consignee 754n.
deputy 755n.
factorize
simplify 44vb.
decompose 51vb.
factors
circumstance 8n.
factorship
commission 751n.
factory
workshop 687n.
factory-hand
worker 686n.
factotum
busy person 678n.
worker 686n.
servant 742n.
facts
evidence 466n.
accuracy 494n.
information 524n.
facts and figures
accounts 808n.
factual
real 1adj.
evidential 466adj.
certain 473adj.
true 494adj.
descriptive 590adj.
facula
sun 321n.
faculty
classification 77n.
ability 160n.
erudition 490n.
teacher 537n.
aptitude 694n.
facundity
eloquence 579n.
fad
bias 481n.
eccentricity 503n.
insanity 503n.
crank 504n.
whim 604n.
fashion 848n.
affectation 850n.
liking 859n.
faddiness
caprice 604n.
discontent 829n.
faddishness
eccentricity 503n.
caprice 604n.
faddist
narrow mind 481n.
crank 504n.
faddy
misjudging 481adj.
crazed 503adj.
capricious 604adj.
fade
shade off 27vb.
decrease 37vb.
be transient 114vb.
be old 127vb.
cease 145vb.
be dim 419vb.
achromatism 426n.
whiten 427vb.
be unseen 444vb.
disappear 446vb.
deteriorate 655vb.
make ugly 842vb.
lose repute 867vb.
fade away
end 69vb.
cease 145vb.
disappear 446vb.
faded
dry 342n.
soft-hued 425adj.
colorless 426adj.
fade-out
decrease 37n.
obscuration 418n.
disappearance 446n.
fadge with
accord 24vb.
faerie
fairy 970n.
fag
tobacco 388n.
beginner 538n.
busy person 678n.
labor 682n.
fatigue 684vb.
worker 686n.
fag-end
remainder 41n.
extremity 69n.
fagot
bunch 74n.
fuel 385n.
materials 631n.
faience
pottery 381n.

fail
be inferior 35vb.
decrease 37vb.
lose a chance 138vb.
cease 145vb.
be weak 163vb.
fall short 307vb.
blunder 495vb.
be disappointed 509vb.
not suffice 636vb.
be useless 641vb.
be ill 651vb.
deteriorate 655vb.
be fatigued 684vb.
not complete 726vb.
fail 728vb.
not observe 769vb.
not pay 805vb.
fail in duty 918vb.
disapprove 924vb.
failing
aged 131adj.
imperfection 647n.
vice 934n.
failure
inferior 35n.
stop 145n.
impotence 161n.
mistake 495n.
insufficiency 636n.
lost labor 641n.
imperfection 647n.
bungling 695n.
bungler 697n.
hitch 702n.
non-completion 726n.
failure, loser 728n.
ill fortune 731n.
non-observance 769n.
loss 772n.
insolvency 805n.
object of scorn 867n.
guilty act 936n.
fain
willing 597adj.
desiring 859adj.
fainéant
idler 679n.
lazy 679adj.
faint
small 33adj.
be impotent 161vb.
weak 163adj.
silent 398n.
muted 401adj.
dim 419adj.
ill-seen 444adj.
irresolute 601adj.
fatigue 684n.
fear 854vb.
faint-heart
waverer 601n.
faint-heartedness
irresolution 601n.
cowardice 856n.
faintness
faintness 401n.
non-resonance 405n.
dimness 419n.
unintelligibility 517n.
fatigue 684n.
faint praise
detraction 926n.
fair
inconsiderable 33adj.
dry 342adj.
warm 379adj.
undimmed 417adj.
whitish 427adj.
rational 475adj.
exhibit 522n.
not bad 644adj.
palmy 730adj.
mediocre 732adj.
mart 796n.
festivity 837n.
pleasure ground 837n.
a beauty 841n.
beautiful 841adj.
promising 852adj.
just 913adj.
honorable 929adj.
fair chance
opportunity 137n.
fair chance 159n.
probability 471n.
fair comparison
similarity 18n.
fair copy
copy 22n.
script 586n.
write 586vb.
fair-dealing
honorable 929adj.
fair exchange
equivalence 28n.
fair excuse
vindication 927n.
fair field
opportunity 137n.
fair game
laughing-stock 851n.
fair-ground
arena 724n.
fair-haired
whitish 427adj.
yellow 433adj.
fairing
gift 781n.
Fair Isle
pattern 844n.
fair-minded
wise 498adj.
just 913adj.
fair name
repute 866n.
fairness
beauty 841n.
justice 913n.
probity 929n.
fair offer
irenics 719n.
offer 759n.
fair play
justice 913n.
fair sex
womankind 373n.
fair shares
apportionment 783n.
fair-sized
great 32adj.
big 195adj.
fair-spoken
courteous 884adj.
fair value
equivalence 28n.
price 809n.
fairway
plain 348n.
path 624n.
fair way, in a
almost 33adv.
tending 179adj.
probable 471adj.
fair weather
weather 340n.
palmy days 730n.
fair-weather
transient 114adj.
fair-weather friend
deceiver 545n.
flatterer 925n.
fair words
promise 764n.
courteous act 884n.
fairy
nonconformist 84n.
a beauty 841n.
libertine 952n.
fairy 970n.
sorceress 983n.
fairy godmother
patron 707n.
benefactor 903n.
fairyland
fantasy 513n.
prodigy 864n.
fairy 970n.
fairylike
fairylike 970adj.
magical 983adj.
fairy-tale
fable 543n.
narrative 590n.
fairy wand
magic instrument 983n.
fait accompli
reality 1n.
certainty 473n.
completion 725n.
faith

belief 485n.
loyalty 739n.
observance 768n.
hope 852n.
probity 929n.
disinterestedness 931n.
religious faith 973n.
orthodoxy 976n.
piety 979n.
faith cure
therapy 658n.
faithful
lifelike 18adj.
conformable 83adj.
true, accurate 494adj.
interpretive 520adj.
obedient 739adj.
observant 768adj.
friendly 880adj.
trustworthy 929adj.
pious 979adj.
faithfulness
conformity 83n.
loyalty 739n.
probity 929n.
faithful, the
church member 976n.
pietist 979n.
worshiper 981n.
faith-healer
doctor 658n.
faith-healing
medical art 658n.
faith, hope, and charity
virtues 933n.
faithless
perfidious 930adj.
irreligious 974adj.
faithlessness
perfidy 930n.
faith, of
credal 485adj.
orthodox 976adj.
fake
imitation 20n.
duplicity 541n.
false 541adj.
fake 541vb.
sham 542n.
spurious 542adj.
imposter 545n.
faker
imitator 20n.
fakir
ascetic 945n.
pietist 979n.
monk 986n.
Falangists
political party 708n.
falcated
angular 247adj.
curved 248adj.
falchion
sharp edge 256n.
side-arms 723n.
falcon
bird of prey 365n.
heraldry 547n.
falconer
hunter 619n.
falconet
gun 723n.
falconry
chase 619n.
faldstool
seat 218n.
fall
decrease 37n.
autumn 129n.
be weak 163vb.
be destroyed 165vb.
acclivity 220n.
deviation 282n.
regression 286n.
descent 309n.
perish 361vb.
deteriorate 655vb.
miscarry 728vb.
adversity 731n.
cheapness 812n.
lose repute 867vb.
be wicked 934vb.
fallacy
sophism 477n.
error 495n.
deception 542n.
fall apart
be disjoined 46vb.
fall asleep
die 361vb.
sleep 679vb.
fall back on
avail of 673vb.
parry 713vb.
fall below
not suffice 636vb.
fall down
descend 309vb.
fallen
death roll 361n.
unchaste 951adj.
fallen angel
bad man 938n.
devil 969n.
impious person 980n.
fallen woman
prostitute 952n.
fall for
be credulous 487vb.
be duped 544vb.
be in love 887vb.
fall foul of
collide 279vb.
fight 716vb.
have trouble 731vb.
fall from grace
relapse 657vb.
be wicked 934vb.
fallibility
unreliability 474n.
misjudgment 481n.
error 495n.
unintelligence 499n.
imperfection 647n.
fallible
illogical 477adj.
fall in
be uniform 16vb.
be in order 60vb.
be brittle 330vb.
falling off
decrease 37n.
deterioration 655n.
relapse 657n.
falling sickness
spasm 318n.
paralysis 651n.
falling star
meteor 321n.
fall in love
be in love 887vb.
fall into
be turned to 147vb.
enter 297vb.
flow 350vb.
fall into line
conform 83vb.
fall into place
be in order 60vb.
have rank 73vb.
fall in with
conform 83vb.
converge 293vb.
consent 758vb.
fall off
be disjoined 46vb.
deteriorate 655vb.
fall on
(*see* fall upon)
fall on one's feet
have luck 730vb.
fallopian tubes
genitalia 164n.
fall out
be dispersed 75vb.
happen 154vb.
quarrel 709vb.
not complete 726vb.
be inimical 881vb.
fall-out
nucleonics 160n.
radiation 417n.
insalubrity 653n.
poison 659n.
bomb 723n.
fallow
unproductive 172adj.
farm 370n.
yellow 433adj.
unprepared 670adj.
fall pat

accord 24vb.
fall short
be unequal 29vb.
be inferior 35vb.
be incomplete 55vb.
fall short 307vb.
fall through
fall short 307vb.
(*see* miscarry)
fall to
eat 301vb.
undertake 672vb.
be one's duty 917vb.
fall to the ground
be confuted 479vb.
miscarry 728vb.
fall under
be included 78vb.
fall upon
surprise 508vb.
attack 712vb.
false
unreal 2adj.
unattested 467adj.
illogical 477adj.
erroneous 495adj.
false 541adj.
spurious 542adj.
affected 850adj.
wrong 914adj.
unwarranted 916adj.
flattering 925adj.
perfidious 930adj.
false alarm
insubstantial thing 4n.
false alarm 665n.
false charge
false charge 928n.
false coloring
misinterpretation 521n.
falsehood 541n.
false colors
sham 542n.
false copy
dissimilarity 19n.
false dawn
precursor 66n.
misjudgment 481n.
error 495n.
disappointment 509n.
falsehood
error 495n.
ideality 513n.
misteaching 535n.
falsehood 541n.
deception 542n.
improbity 930n.
false impression
error 495n.
false light
visual fallacy 440n.
error 495n.
false modesty
underestimation 483n.
(*see* false shame)
false name
misteaching 535n.
misnomer 562n.
false note
misfit 25n.
false position
predicament 700n.
false pretensions
pretension 850n.
false shame
affectation 850n.
false teeth
tooth 256n.
falsetto
stridor 407n.
aphony 578n.
falsification
imitation 20n.
falsify
mislead 495vb.
misinterpret 521vb.
be false 541vb.
be untrue 543vb.
falsity
(*see* false, falsehood)
falter
move slowly 278vb.
be uncertain 474vb.
stammer 580vb.
be irresolute 601vb.
miscarry 728vb.
fame
greatness 32n.
remembrance 505n.
publicity 528n.
famousness 866n.
familiar
interior 224adj.
known 490adj.
habitual, usual 610adj.
impertinent 878adj.
disrespectful 921adj.
devil 969n.
demon 970n.
sorcerer 983n.
familiarity
knowledge 490n.
habit 610n.
friendship 880n.
sociality 882n.
familiarize
know 490vb.
train 534vb.
family
family 11n.
all 52n.
subdivision 53n.
breed 77n.
genealogy 169n.
parental 169adj.
posterity 170n.
community 708n.
nobility 868n.
family circle
family 11n.
sociality 882n.
family connection
consanguinity 11n.
family likeness
similarity 18n.
family man
resident 191n.
family tree
series 71n.
list 87n.
genealogy 169n.
family way, in the
productive 164adj.
famine
unproductivity 172n.
scarcity 636n.
poverty 801n.
hunger 859n.
famish
be parsimonious 816vb.
be hungry 859vb.
starve 946vb.
famous
great 32adj.
known 490adj.
well-known 528adj.
topping 644adj.
renowned 866adj.
famously
well 644adv.
fan
rotator 315n.
aerify 340vb.
ventilation 352n.
refrigerator 384n.
crank 504n.
habitué 610n.
purify 648vb.
refresh 685vb.
patron 707n.
animate 821vb.
relieve 831vb.
lover 887n.
fanatic
doctrinaire 473n.
narrow mind 481n.
biased 481adj.
crank 504n.
opinionist 602n.
obstinate 602adj.
busy person 678n.
lively 819adj.
religionist 979n.
fanatical
positive 473adj.
severe 735adj.
excitable 822adj.
fanatically
extremely 32adv.
fanaticism

narrow mind 481n.
credulity 487n.
insanity 503n.
opiniatrety 602n.
severity 735n.
warm feeling 818n.
excitability 822n.
pietism 979n.
fancier
breeder 369n.
expert 696n.
desirer 859n.
fanciful
absurd 497adj.
imaginary 513adj.
exaggerated 546adj.
capricious 604adj.
ridiculous 849adj.
fancy
think 449vb.
idea 451n.
opine 485vb.
supposition 512n.
imagination 513n.
caprice 604n.
choice 605n.
pugilism 716n.
wit 839n.
ornamental 844adj.
liking 859n.
love 887n.
darling 890n.
fancy dress
clothing 228n.
disguise 527n.
fancy-free
free 744adj.
impassive 820adj.
indifferent 860adj.
unwedded 895adj.
fancy-man
libertine 952n.
fancy-work
ornamental art 844n.
fandango
dance 837n.
fane
temple 990n.
fanfare
loudness 400n.
celebration 876n.
fanfaronade
ostentation 875n.
celebration 876n.
boast 877n.
fang
tooth 256n.
bane 659n.
fangs
governance 733n.
nippers 778n.
fanlight
window 263n.
fanlike
broad 205adj.
fannel
vestments 989n.
fanny
buttocks 238n.
fanon
vestments 989n.
fan out
be dispersed 75vb.
expand 197vb.
be broad 205vb.
diverge 294vb.
fantan
card game 837n.
fantasia
musical piece 412n.
fantastic
unusual 84adj.
absurd 497adj.
capricious 604adj.
ridiculous 849adj.
wonderful 864adj.
fantastical
insubstantial 4adj.
erroneous 495adj.
imaginative 513adj.
fantasy
insubstantiality 4n.
insubstantial thing 4n.
visual fallacy 440n.
appearance 445n.
error 495n.
fantasy 513n.
caprice 604n.
pleasurableness 826n.
aspiration 852n.
desire 859n.
fantoccini
image 551n.
stage play 594n.
far
distant 199adj.
afar 199adv.
far and away
eminently 34adv.
far and near
widely 183adv.
far and wide
widely 183adv.
afar 199adv.
far away
afar 199adv.
abstracted 456adj.
far between
spaced 201adj.
farce
foolery 497n.
fable 543n.
stage play 594n.
trifle 639n.
laughter 835n.
wit 839n.
ridiculousness 849n.
farceur
humorist 839n.
farcical
(*see* farce)
far corner
rear 238n.
far cry
distance 199n.
farcy
animal disease 651n.
fard
cosmetic 843n.
fare
be in a state 7vb.
travel 267vb.
meal 301n.
eat 301vb.
price 809n.
farewell
valediction 296n.
courteous act 884n.
far-fetched
irrelevant 10adj.
far-flung
unassembled 75adj.
farflying
extensive 32adj.
far from
different 15adj.
far-going
exorbitant 32adj.
far-gone
consummate 32adj.
farinaceous
powdery 332adj.
farm
produce 164vb.
breed stock 369vb.
farm 370n.
cultivate 370vb.
mature 669vb.
workshop 687n.
lands 777n.
hire 785vb.
farmer
husbandman 370n.
farm-hand
servant 742n.
farming
territorial 344adj.
agriculture 370n.
farmland
soil 344n.
farm 370n.
farm out
lease 784vb.
farmstead
house 192n.
farmyard
farm 370n.
farness
farness 199n.
faro
card game 837n.
farrago

medley 43n.
confusion 61n.
absurdity 497n.
far-reaching
extensive 32adj.
spacious 183adj.
farrier
animal husbandry 369n.
farrow
youngling 132n.
reproduce itself 164vb.
posterity 170n.
farse
office-book 988n.
far-sighted
seeing 438adj.
vigilant 457adj.
intelligent 498adj.
foreseeing 510adj.
farther
distant 199adj.
beyond 199adv.
farthest point
extremity 69n.
farthing
small coin 33n.
quadrisection 98n.
coinage 797n.
farthingale
frame 218n.
skirt 228n.
fasces
bunch 74n.
badge of rule 743n.
fascia
strip 208n.
loop 250n.
fascicle
subdivision 53n.
bunch 74n.
fascinate
engross 449vb.
attract notice 455vb.
(*see* fascination)
fascination
influence 178n.
inducement 612n.
excitation 821n.
pleasurableness 826n.
liking 859n.
wonder 864n.
love 887n.
lovableness 887n.
spell 983n.
fascine
bunch 74n.
fascism
government 733n.
brute force 735n.
fashion
modality 7n.
similarity 18n.
generality 79n.
conformity 83n.
modernism 126n.
dressing 228n.
form 243n.
efform 243vb.
feature 445n.
style 566n.
practice 610n.
way 624n.
fashion 848n.
affectation 850n.
fashionable
tasteful 846adj.
(*see* fashion)
fashion, in
fashionable 848adj.
fashion model
living model 23n.
fashion plate
fop 848n.
fashion upon
represent 551vb.
fast
tied 45adj.
firm-set 45adj.
anachronistic 118adj.
fixed 153adj.
speedy 277adj.
colored 425adj.
retained 778adj.
do penance 941vb.
be temperate 942vb.
asceticism 944vb.
fast 946n.
starve 946vb.
unchaste 951adj.
offer worship 981vb.
holy-day 988n.
fast by
nigh 200adv.
fast color
fixture 153n.
fast-day
insufficiency 636n.
special day 876n.
asceticism 944adj.
fast 946n.
holy-day 988n.
fast dye
fixture 153n.
pigment 425n.
fasten
affix, tighten 45vb.
close 264vb.
fastener
fastening 47n.
fastening
joinder 45n.
fastening 47n.
nippers 778n.
fasten on
be attentive 455vb.
make important 638vb.
take 786vb.
fasten to
hang 217vb.
faster
abstainer 942n.
ascetic 945n.
fasti
chronology 117n.
fastidious
careful 457adj.
discriminating 463adj.
accurate 494adj.
capricious 604adj.
clean 648n.
severe 735adj.
observant 768adj.
sensitive 819adj.
tasteful 846adj.
fastidious 862adj.
fastigium
vertex 213n.
fasting
underfed 636adj.
hungry 859adj.
fast-living
sensual 944adj.
fastness
refuge 662n.
fort 713n.
fat
prolific 171adj.
fleshy 195adj.
expanded 197adj.
food content 301n.
fat 357n.
plenty 635n.
redundant 637adj.
prosperous 730adj.
rich 800adj.
fatal
deadly 362adj.
evil 616adj.
harmful 645adj.
fatalism
philosophy 449n.
necessity 596n.
submission 721n.
fatalist
fatalist 596n.
fatality
decease 361n.
necessity 596n.
evil 616n.
fata morgana
glow-worm 420n.
visual fallacy 440n.
mirage 513n.
fate
finality 69n.
futurity 124n.
destiny 155n.
cause 156n.
chance 159n.

influence 178n.
certainty 473n.
fate 596n.
non-design 618n.
fated
fated 596adj.
Fates, the
fate 596n.
mythic god 966n.
classical gods 967n.
fathead
dunce 501n.
father
kinsman 11n.
cause 156n.
generate 164vb.
parent 169n.
male 372n.
church title 986n.
cleric 986n.
father and mother of
whopping 32adj.
Father Christmas
good giver 813n.
fairy 970n.
fathered
born 360adj.
fatherhood
family 11n.
propagation 164n.
parentage 169n.
life 360n.
divineness 965n.
fatherland
territory 184n.
home 192n.
fatherless
defenseless 161adj.
fatherly
parental 169adj.
godlike 965adj.
fatherly eye
protection 660n.
father upon
attribute 158vb.
fathom
long measure 203n.
be deep 211vb.
plunge 313vb.
inquire 459vb.
measure 465vb.
understand 516vb.
fathometer
diver 313n.
gauge 465n.
fathomless
deep 211adj.
fatidical
predicting 511adj.
fatigue
weakness 163n.
pain 377n.
use 673vb.
misuse 675vb.
sleepiness 679n.
labor 682n.
fatigue 684n., vb.
oppress 735vb.
suffering 825n.
incommode 827vb.
be tedious 838vb.
fatigues
uniform 228n.
fat in the fire
turmoil 61n.
fatiscence
gap 201n.
opening 263n.
fatling
cattle 365n.
fat lot
great quantity 32n.
fatness
bulk 195n.
fat of the land
plenty 635n.
prosperity 730n.
fatten
grow 36vb.
enlarge 197vb.
be broad 205vb.
feed 301vb.
pinguefy 357vb.
breed stock 369vb.
make better 654vb.
fattening
nourishing 301adj.
fatty
fatty 357adj.
fatuity
insubstantiality 4n.
incogitance 450n.
absurdity 497n.
folly 499n.
fatuous
absurd 497adj.
foolish 499adj.
unmeaning 515adj.
fatwa
theology 973n.
faubourgs
circumjacence 230n.
fauces
threshold 234n.
faucet
tube 263n.
stopper 264n.
fault
discontinuity 72n.
weakness 163n.
gap 201n.
shortcoming 307n.
blunder 495n.
evil 616n.
defect 647n.
dispraise 924vb.
detract 926vb.
vice 934n.
guilty act 966n.
fault, at
doubting 474adj.
fault-finder
malcontent 829n.
disapprover 924n.
detractor 926n.
fault-finding
discontented 829adj.
fastidious 862adj.
disapprobation 924n.
censure 924n.
faultiness
inferiority 35n.
inexactness 495n.
badness 645n.
imperfection 647n.
faultless
perfect 646adj.
guiltless 935adj.
pure 950adj.
fault on the right side
virtues 933n.
fault, to a
extremely 32adv.
faulty
inexact 495adj.
ungrammatical 565adj.
inelegant 576adj.
bad 645adj.
imperfect 647adj.
faun
vegetability 366n.
lesser god 967n.
fauna
organism 358n.
animality 365n.
Faust
sorcerer 983n.
fauteuil
seat 218n.
theater 594n.
faux-bourdon
melody 410n.
faux pas
mistake 495n.
solecism 565n.
failure 728n.
guilty act 936n.
favor
vantage 34n.
influence 178n.
promote 285vb.
mien 445n.
be biased 481vb.
assent 488n.
badge 547n.
correspondence 588n.
choose 605vb.
benefit 615n., vb.
do good 644vb.
aid 703n.
trophy 729n.

be auspicious 730vb.
lenity 736n.
permit 756vb.
liking 859n.
repute, honors 866n.
befriend 880vb.
courteous act 884n.
love-token 889n.
kind act 897n.
approbation 923n.
favorable
opportune 137adj.
presageful 511adj.
willing 597adj.
aiding 703adj.
promising 852adj.
approving 923adj.
favorable auspices
hope 852n.
favorable chance
fair chance 159n.
probability 471n.
favorable issue
success 727n.
favorable verdict
legal trial 959n.
acquittal 960n.
favor, by
by leave 756adv.
undue 916adj.
favorer
patron 707n.
friend 880n.
favor, in
reputable 866adj.
approved 923adj.
favorite
chosen 605adj.
bigwig 638n.
made man 730n.
person of repute 866n.
social person 882n.
loved one 887n.
favorite 890n.
kept woman 952n.
favoritism
prejudice 481n.
choice 605n.
friendliness 880n.
injustice 914n.
favors
love-making 887n.
favus
skin disease 651n.
fawn
youngling 132n.
deer 365n.
male animal 372n.
brown 430adj.
be subject 745vb.
be servile 879vb.
caress 889vb.
flatter 925vb.
fawner
toady 879n.
fawn on
be near 200vb.
befool 542vb.
flatter 925vb.
fay
fairy 970n.
fealty
loyalty 739n.
duty 917n.
respect 920n.
fear
doubt 486n.
avoidance 620n.
fear 854n., vb.
cowardice 856n.
dislike 861vb.
wonder 864n., vb.
honor 866vb.
respect 920n.
piety 979n.
worship 981n., vb.
fearful
nervous 854adj.
cowardly 856adj.
wonderful 864adj.
fearfully
extremely 32adv.
wonderfully 864adv.
fearing the worst
hopeless 853adj.
fearless
unfearing 855adj.
fear of God
piety 979n.
fears
danger 661n.
fearsome
frightening 854adj.
feasibility
possibility 469n.
facility 701n.
feast
regular return 141n.
feasting 301n.
feed 301vb.
pleasure 376n.
plenty 635n.
revel 837vb.
social gathering 882n.
holy-day 988n.
feast-day
festivity 837n.
special day 876n.
holy-day 988n.
feasting
sociability 882n.
sensualism 944n.
gluttony 947n.
feat
contrivance 623n.
deed 676n.
masterpiece 694n.
prowess 855n.
thaumaturgy 864n.
feather
sort 77n.
row 269vb.
levity 323n.
waverer 601n.
trifle 639n.
make ready 669vb.
trimming 844n.
honors 866n.
(*see* feathers)
featherbed
softness 327n.
euphoria 376n.
be lenient 736vb.
feather-brained
foolish 499adj.
irresolute 601adj.
feathering
plumage 259n.
feather in one's cap
trophy 729n.
honors 866n.
feather one's nest
prepare 669vb.
prosper 730vb.
get rich 800vb.
be selfish 932vb.
feathers
skin 226n.
headgear 228n.
plumage 259n.
wing 271n.
softness 327n.
(*see* feather)
feather-weight
levity 323n.
pugilist 722n.
feathery
downy 259adj.
light 323adj.
featly
skillfully 694adj.
feature
character 5n.
component 58n.
specialty 80n.
face 237n.
form 243n.
feature 445n.
show 522vb.
advertise 528vb.
identification 547n.
dramatize 594vb.
featureless
insubstantial 4adj.
uniform 16adj.
empty 190adj.
flat 216adj.
amorphous 244adj.
irresolute 601adj.
febrifuge
antidote 658n.
febrile

hot 379adj.
diseased 651adj.
excitable 822adj.
feces
excrement 302n.
feckless
useless 641adj.
unskillful 695adj.
unsuccessful 728adj.
feculence
excrement 302n.
dirt 649n.
fecundation
propagation 164n.
productiveness 171n.
fecundity
propagation 164n.
productiveness 171n.
fedayeen
soldier 722n.
robber 789n.
federal
cooperative 706adj.
corporate 708adj.
Federal agent
detective 459n.
Federal Courts
law-court 956n.
federalism
government 733n.
federate
cooperate 706vb.
join a party 708vb.
federation
combination 50n.
association 706n.
society 708n.
polity 733n.
federative
corporate 708adj.
fedora
headgear 228n.
fed up
bored 838adj.
fee
possession 773n.
estate 777n.
gift 781n.
pay 804n.
expenditure 806n.
price 809n.
reward 962n., vb.
feeble
small 33adj.
powerless 161adj.
weak 163adj.
muted 401adj.
ill-reasoned 477adj.
feeble 572adj.
lax 734adj.
feeble-minded
weak 163adj.
unintelligent 499adj.
insane 503adj.
feed
support 218vb.
meal 301n.
provender 301n.
eat 301vb.
vitalize 360vb.
groom 369vb.
fire 385vb.
provide 633vb.
be hospitable 882vb.
feeder
eater 301n.
stream 350n.
provider 633n.
fee, faw, fum
intimidation 854n.
spell 983n.
feel
meet with 154vb.
texture 331n.
have feeling 374vb.
touch 378n.
be tentative 461vb.
discrimination 463n.
opine 485vb.
feel 818vb.
suffer 825vb.
resent 891vb.
feeler
projection 254n.
feeler 378n.
question 459n.
empiricism 461n.
offer 759n.
feel for
search 459vb.
pity 905vb.
feeling
influence 178n.
sense 374n.
touch 378n.
intuition 476n.
opinion 485n.
interpretation 520n.
vigor 571n.
with affections 817adj.
feeling 818n., adj.
excitation 821n.
benevolence 897n.
feeling the pinch
necessitous 627adj.
feel in one's bones
intuit 476vb.
feel like
be willing 597vb.
feel one's oats
be vigorous 174vb.
feel one's way
be tentative 461vb.
foresee 510vb.
essay 671vb.
be cautious 858vb.
feel small
be humbled 872vb.
feel the pinch
be in difficulty 700vb.
have trouble 731vb.
feel the pulse
inquire 459vb.
be tentative 461vb.
feel with
love 887vb.
pity 905vb.
fee simple
estate 777n.
fee tail
estate 777n.
feet of clay
weakness 163n.
defect 647n.
vulnerability 661n.
feign
dissemble 541vb.
be affected 850vb.
feigned
hypocritical 541adj.
deceiving 542adj.
feint
trickery 542n.
stratagem 698n.
felicitation
rejoicing 835n.
congratulation 886n.
felicitous
apt 24adj.
elegant 575adj.
well-made 694adj.
successful 727adj.
happy 824adj.
felicity
elegance 575n.
happiness 824n.
feline
cat 365n.
stealthy 525adj.
cunning 698adj.
cruel 898adj.
fell
demolish 165vb.
skin 226n.
high land 209n.
flatten 216vb.
strike 279vb.
fell 311vb.
plain 348n.
deadly 362adj.
evil 616adj.
inimical 881adj.
hating 888adj.
cruel 898adj.
felloe, felly
edge 234n.
wheel 250n.
fellow
analogue 18n.
compeer 28n.
adjunct 40n.
concomitant 89n.

person 371n.
male 372n.
college 538n.
colleague 707n.
society 708n.
low fellow 869n.
friend, chum 880n.
fellow-citizen
native 191n.
fellow-countryman
native 191n.
friend 880n.
fellow-creature
person 371n.
fellow-feeling
cooperation 706n.
concord 710n.
participation 775n.
feeling 818n.
friendliness 880n.
love 887n.
benevolence 897n.
condolence 905n.
pity 905n.
fellowless
alone 88adj.
fellows
duality 90n.
fellowship
group 74n.
association 706n.
community 708n.
friendship 880n.
sociality 882n.
fellow-traveler
concomitant 89n.
assenter 488n.
collaborator 707n.
fellow-worker
personnel 686n.
collaborator 707n.
felly
edge 234n.
wheel 250n.
felo-de-se
suicide 362n.
felon
low fellow 869n.
offender 904n.
felonious
wrong 914adj.
rascally 930adj.
heinous 934adj.
lawbreaking 954adj.
felony
vice 934n.
guilty act 936n.
lawbreaking 954n.
felt
textile 222n.
weave 222vb.
felt 818adj.
felucca
sailing-ship 275n.
female
female 373n., adj.
feminine
generic 77adj.
female 373adj.
grammatical 564adj.
femininity
female 373n.
feminism
female 373n.
gynocracy 733n.
feminist
female 373adj.
femme couverte
spouse 894n.
femme de chambre
domestic 742n.
femme fatale
a beauty 841n.
femme sole
spinster 895n.
femoral
crural 267adj.
fen
moisture 341n.
marsh 347n.
fence
partition 231n.
fence 235n.
stopper 264n.
cultivate 370vb.
screen 421n.
sophisticate 477vb.
protection 660n.
shelter 662n.
obstacle 702n.
defenses 713n.
parry 713vb.
duel 716n.
fight 716vb.
thief 789n.
fencer
thoroughbred 273n.
contender 716n.
combatant 722n.
fencible
defender 713n.
soldier 722n.
fend
obstruct 702vb.
parry 713vb.
fender
intermediary 231n.
furnace 383n.
shelter 662n.
defense 713n.
feneration
lending 784n.
fenestration
window 263n.
Fenian
opponent 705n.
revolter 738n.
fennel
potherb 301n.
fenny
humid 341adj.
marshy 347adj.
feodal
proprietary 777adj.
feodality
possession 773n.
feoffee
possessor 776n.
beneficiary 776n.
recipient 782n.
feoffer
owner 776n.
giver 781n.
feoffment
transfer 780n.
feracious
prolific 171adj.
ferine
disobedient 738adj.
unsociable 883adj.
ferment
turmoil 61n.
alterer 143n.
conversion 147n.
be turned to 147vb.
convert 147vb.
stimulation 174n.
storm 176n.
commotion 318n.
effervesce 318vb.
leaven 323n.
bubble 355vb.
be sour 393vb.
feeling 818n.
excitation 821n.
excitable state 822n.
anger 891n.
fern
plant 366n.
ferocious
furious 176adj.
cruel 898adj.
ferret
vermin 365n.
eye 438n.
ferret out
discover 484vb.
ferriage
transference 272n.
ferro-concrete
hardness 326n.
hard 326adj.
building material 631n.
ferruginous
red 431adj.
ferrule, ferrel
covering 226n.
ferry
voyage 269vb.
transfer 272vb.
carry 273vb.

ship, boat 275n.
ferryman
boatman 270n.
transferrer 272n.
carrier 273n.
fertile
imaginative 513adj.
profitable 640adj.
gainful 771adj.
rich 800adj.
fertility
propagation 164n.
productiveness 171n.
diffuseness 570n.
plenty 635n.
fertilization
propagation 164n.
fertilize
make fruitful 171vb.
invigorate 174vb.
cultivate 370vb.
be auspicious 730vb.
fertilizer
producer 167n.
fertilizer 171n.
agriculture 370n.
ferule
club 723n.
scourge 964n.
fervent
hot 379adj.
active 678adj.
fervent 818adj.
loving 887adj.
pietistic 979adj.
worshiping 981adj.
fervor
heat 379n.
restlessness 678n.
warm feeling 818n.
piety 979n.
fescennine verses
doggerel 593n.
ridicule 851n.
fess
heraldry 547n.
fesswise
horizontally 216adj.
festal
amusing 837adj.
ritual 988adj.
fester
be unclean 649vb.
be ill 651vb.
deteriorate 655vb.
be malevolent 898vb.
festering
infection 651n.
toxic 653adj.
festina lente
caution 858n.
festival
assembly 74n.
festivity 837n.
holy-day 988n.
festive
celebrative 876adj.
sociable 882adj.
festivity
meal 301n.
rejoicing 835n.
festivity 837n.
celebration 876n.
social gathering 882n.
festoon
curve 448n.
decorate 844vb.
fetch
carry 273vb.
trickery 542n.
cost 809vb.
delight 826vb.
cause desire 859vb.
ghost 970n.
fetch and carry
be servile 879vb.
fetching
personable 841adj.
fetch up at
arrive 295vb.
fete
rampage 61vb.
meal 301n.
amusement 837n.
pageant 875n.
celebration 876n.
gratulate 886vb.
fête champêtre
amusement 837n.
feted
welcomed 882adj.
fetid
unsavory 391adj.
odorous 394adj.
fetid 397adj.
bad, not nice 645adj.
unclean 649adj.
unpleasant 827adj.
fetish
god 966n.
idol 982n.
talisman 983n.
fetishism
idolatry 982n.
fetishist
religionist 973n.
idolator 982n.
fetish-man
sorcerer 983n.
fetor
(*see* fetid)
fetter
tie 45vb.
safeguard 662n.
make inactive 679vb.
hinder 702vb.
subjection 745n.
fetter 748n.
fettered
captive 750adj.
fettle
state 7n.
affections 817n.
fetus
source 156n.
feud
quarrel 709n.
possession 773n.
lands 777n.
enmity 881n.
revenge 910n.
feudal
olden 127adj.
governmental 733adj.
subject 745adj.
proprietary 777adj.
feudalism
government 733n.
service 745n.
feudatory
dependent 742n.
subject 745adj.
possessor 776n.
feuillemorte
brown 430adj.
fever
agitation 318n.
heat 379n.
illness 651n.
restlessness 678n.
excitable state 822n.
feverish
hasty 680adj.
fervent 818adj.
excited 821adj.
feverishness
(*see* fever)
few
inconsiderable 33adj.
few 105adj.
infrequent 140adj.
scarce 636adj.
few, a
plurality 101n.
fewness 105n.
few and far between
discontinuous 72adj.
unassembled 75adj.
few 105adj.
seldom 140adv.
fewness
finite quantity 26n.
inferiority 35n.
fey
dying 361adj.
bewitched 983adj.
psychical 984adj.
fez
headgear 228n.
fiacre
cab 274n.
fiancé, fiancée

lover 887n.
loved one 887n.
fiasco
failure 728n.
fiat
decree 737n.
fiat money
paper money 797n.
fib
untruth 543n.
fight 716vb.
fibber, fibster
liar 545n.
fiber
essential part 5n.
fiber 208n.
texture 331n.
materials 631n.
fibril
filament 208n.
fibrositis
pang 377n.
rheumatism 651n.
fibrous
fibrous 208adj.
tough 329adj.
fibula
fastening 47n.
jewelry 844n.
fichu
apron 228n.
fickle
transient 114adj.
changeable 143adj.
changeful 152adj.
unreliable 474adj.
tergiversating 603adj.
capricious 604adj.
fickleness
irresolution 601n.
fictile
formed 243adj.
fiction
product 164n.
idea 451n.
ideality 513n.
falsehood 541n.
untruth 543n.
novel 590n.
fictional
imaginative 513adj.
descriptive 590adj.
fiction-writer
narrator 590n.
fictitious
insubstantial 4adj.
imaginary 513adj.
untrue 543adj.
unwarranted 916adj.
fid
supporter 218n.
tobacco 388n.
fiddle
modify 143vb.
play music 413vb.
viol 414n.
trickery 542n.
contrivance 623n.
foul play 930n.
fiddle-faddle
silly talk 515n.
fiddlehead
coil 251n.
pattern 844n.
fiddler
instrumentalist 413n.
trickster 545n.
defrauder 789n.
fiddlestick
viol 414n.
fiddlesticks
trifle 639n.
fiddle with
touch 378vb.
fiddling
trivial 639adj.
laborious 682adj.
fidelity
accuracy 494n.
veracity 540n.
loyalty 739n.
observance 768n.
probity 929n.
fidget
hasten 680vb.
fidgets
changeableness 152n.
agitation 318n.
restlessness 678n.
excitability 822n.
fidgety
unstable 152adj.
irresolute 601adj.
active 678adj.
excitable 822adj.
fiducial
unchangeable 153adj.
credible 485adj.
fiduciary
credible 485adj.
monetary 797adj.
fief
possession 773n.
lands 777n.
field
opportunity 137n.
range 183n.
region 184n.
place 185n.
enclosure 235n.
grassland 348n.
topic 542n.
hunter 619n.
function 622n.
opponent 705n.
contender 716n.
arena 724n.
scope 744n.
pleasure-ground 837n.
field day
contest 716n.
pageant 875n.
special day 876n.
fielder, fieldsman
interceptor 702n.
field-glass
telescope 442n.
field marshal
army officer 741n.
field of action
arena 724n.
field of battle
slaughter-house 362n.
fight 716n.
battle 718n.
battleground 724n.
field of force
energy 160n.
field of view
view 438n.
visibility 443n.
fieldpiece
gun 723n.
fields
land 344n.
plain 348n.
farm 370n.
field sports
sport 837n.
field-work
defenses 713n.
fiend
monster 938n.
devil 969n.
fiendish
cruel 898adj.
wicked 934adj.
fierce
active 678adj.
warlike 718adj.
excitable 822adj.
courageous 855adj.
angry 891adj.
irascible 892adj.
cruel 898adj.
fiercely
greatly 32adv.
fieriness
quarrelsomeness 709n.
rashness 857n.
fiery
violent 176adj.
fiery 379adj.
luminous 417adj.
red 431adj.
forceful 571adj.
fervent 818adj.
excitable 822adj.
irascible 892adj.
Fiery Cross
danger signal 665n.

war measures 718n.
fiesta
festivity 837n.
fife
stridor 407n.
flute 414n.
fifer
instrumentalist 413n.
fifteen
party 708n.
fifth
interval 201n.
musical note 410n.
fifth column
planner 623n.
collaborator 707n.
perfidy 930n.
fifth-columnism
sedition 738n.
fifth columnist
tergiversator 603n.
Fifth Monarchy Men
sect 978n.
fifth wheel of the coach
extra 40n.
fifty-fifty
equal 28adj.
median 30adj.
mediocre 732adj.
fig
state 7n.
fruit 301n.
fight
turmoil 61n.
be in difficulty 700vb.
withstand 704vb.
fight 716n., vb.
go to war 718vb.
be courageous 855vb.
fight against
oppose 704vb.
fight back, fight off
parry 713vb.
fighter
aircraft 276n.
essayer 671n.
opponent 705n.
contender 716n.
combatant 722n.
air force 722n.
fight for
defend 713vb.
fight-hungry
contending 716adj.
fighting
athletic 162adj.
contention 716n.
warfare 718n.
fighting cock
combatant 722n.
brave person 855n.
fighting man
soldier 722n.
combatant 722n.
brave person 855n.
fight on
stand firm 599vb.
fight shy
be loath 598vb.
avoid 620vb.
fight the good fight
be virtuous 933vb.
be pious 979vb.
figment
insubstantial thing 4n.
product 164n.
idea 451n.
ideality 513n.
figurante
actor 594n.
figurate
numerical 85adj.
figurative
semantic 514adj.
figurative 519adj.
occult 523adj.
representing 551adj.
rhetorical 574adj.
figure
number 85n.
do sums 86vb.
outline 233n.
form 243n.
person 371n.
feature 445n.
trope 519n.
indication 547n.
image 551n.
represent 551vb.
funds 797n.
price 809n.
eyesore 842n.
person of repute 866n.
figure-flinger
sorcerer 983n.
figurehead
insubstantial thing 4n.
ineffectuality 161n.
face, prow 237n.
projection 254n.
badge 547n.
nonentity 639n.
ornamental art 844n.
figure in
appear 445vb.
figure eight
curve 248n.
loop 250n.
figure of fun
laughing-stock 851n.
figure of speech
trope 519n.
exaggeration 546n.
ornament 574n.
figures
statistics 86n.
figure-work
numerical operation 86n.
filacious
fibrous 208adj.
filament
narrowness 206n.
filament 208n.
lamp 420n.
filamentous
fibrous 208adj.
hairy 259adj.
filbert
fruit 301n.
fop 848n.
filch
steal 788vb.
filcher
thief 789n.
file
bate 37vb.
sorting 62n.
class 62vb.
procession 71n.
series 71n.
bunch 74n.
list 87n., vb.
put off 136vb.
receptacle 194n.
make smaller 198vb.
sharpener 256n.
sharpen 256vb.
smoother 258n.
roughness 259n.
walk 267vb.
pulverize 332vb.
rub 333vb.
information 524n.
record 548n., vb.
collection 632n.
store 632vb.
formation 722n.
file off
walk 267vb.
diverge 294vb.
filial
filial 170adj.
obedient 739adj.
filiation
relation 9n.
consanguinity 11n.
attribution 158n.
sonship 170n.
filibeg
skirt 228n.
filibuster
spin out 113vb.
delay 136n.
be loquacious 581vb.
hinderer 702n.
opponent 705n.
robber 789n.
filiform
fibrous 208adj.
filigree

network 222n.
ornamental art 844n.
filing
pulverulence 332n.
friction 333n.
registration 548n.
filings
leavings 41n.
powder 332n.
filing system
sorting 62n.
fill
grow 36vb.
fill 54vb.
be many 104vb.
stow 187vb.
pervade 189vb.
load 193vb.
enlarge 197vb.
line 227vb.
close 264vb.
store 632vb.
replenish 633vb.
suffice 635vb.
superabound 637vb.
doctor 658vb.
possess 773vb.
sate 863vb.
filler
news 529n.
fillet
girdle 47n.
ligature 47n.
strip 208n.
headgear 228n.
uncover 229vb.
loop 250n.
void 300vb.
cook 301vb.
fill in
darken 418vb.
filling
contents 193n.
lining 227n.
surgery 658n.
filling station
storage 632n.
fillip
knock 279n.
incentive 612n.
excitant 821n.
animate 821vb.
fill, one's
sufficiency 635n.
dislike 861n.
fill out
expand 197vb.
fill the air
be loud 400vb.
fill the bill
suffice 635vb.
be expedient 642vb.
carry out 725vb.
fill the gap
accrue 38vb.
fill the mind
engross 449vb.
fill up
replenish 633vb.
suffice 635vb.
sate 863vb.
filly
youngling 132n.
horse 273n.
woman 373n.
female animal 373n.
film
layer 207n.
skin, shade 226n.
cloud 355n.
obfuscation 421n.
opacity 423n.
dim sight 440n.
camera 442n.
cinema 445n.
photography 551n.
film-goer
playgoer 594n.
films
cinema 445n.
filmy
layered 207adj.
textural 331adj.
dim 419adj.
opaque 423adj.
filter
deviate 282vb.
exude 298vb.
screen 421n., vb.
cleaning utensil 648n.
purify 648vb.
filter in
infiltrate 297vb.
filth
badness 645n.
dirt 649n.
ugliness 842n.
hateful object 888n.
impurity 951n.
filthy
unsavory 391adj.
not nice 645adj.
filthy language
scurrility 899n.
filthy lucre
money 797n.
filtrate
exude 298vb.
fimbriated
hairy 259adj.
fin
equilibrium 28n.
limb 53n.
laterality 239n.
propeller 269n.
final
ending 69adj.
answering 460adj.
positive 473adj.
contest 716n.
completive 725adj.
final cause
cause 156n.
intention 617n.
finale
end 69n.
musical piece 412n.
dramaturgy 594n.
finalist
aftercomer 67n.
contender 716n.
finality
completeness 54n.
(*see final*)
finalize
make certain 473vb.
final notice
warning 664n.
demand 737n.
final point
goal 295n.
finals
exam. 459n.
final stroke
killing 362n.
completion 725n.
finance
means 629n.
lend 784vb.
finance 797n.
financial
monetary 797adj.
financier
lender 784n.
merchant 794n.
moneyer 797n.
treasurer 798n.
finch
bird 365n.
find
extra 40n.
meet with 154vb.
judge 480vb.
discovery 484n.
benefit 615n.
find means 629vb.
provide 633vb.
acquisition 771n.
booty 790n.
try a case 959vb.
acquire 771vb.
find again
retrieve 656vb.
find against
condemn 961vb.
find fault
be discontented 829vb.
be fastidious 862vb.
blame 924vb.
detract 926vb.

find favor
be praised 923vb.
find guilty
condemn 961vb.
finding
judgment 480n.
discovery 484n.
acquisition 771n.
legal trial 959n.
find means
find means 629vb.
find out
discover 484vb.
find room for
comprise 78vb.
place 187vb.
find the place
place 187vb.
find time for
have leisure 681vb.
find words for
phrase 563vb.
fine
small 33adj.
large 195adj.
narrow 206adj.
rare 325adj.
textural 331adj.
dry 342adj.
transparent 422adj.
discriminating 463adj.
accurate 494adj.
good 615adj.
excellent 644adj.
healthy 650adj.
palmy 730adj.
price 809n.
tax 809vb.
splendid 841adj.
proud 871adj.
formal 875adj.
penalty 963n.
fine airs
airs 873n.
fine feather, in
healthy 650adj.
fine feeling
good taste 846n.
fine fettle, in
strong 162adj.
healthy 650adj.
fine gentleman
fop 848n.
proud man 871n.
fine-mannered
courteous 884adj.
finer feelings
feeling 818n.
moral sensibility 819n.
finery
clothing 228n.
finery 844n.
ostentation 875n.
fine shade
differentiation 15n.
discrimination 463n.
fine-spun
narrow 206adj.
fibrous 208adj.
sophistical 477adj.
textural 331adj.
finesse
cunning 698n.
fine-woven
textural 331adj.
fine-writing
ornament 574n.
finger
small thing 33n.
piece 53n.
long measure 203n.
finger 378n.
touch 378vb.
indicator 547n.
nippers 778n.
fingering
musical skill 413n.
finger in the pie, have a
interfere 231vb.
meddle 678vb.
finger-mark
trace 548n.
finger-nail
finger 378n.
finger-post
direction 281n.
signpost 547n.
fingerprint
identification 547n.
label 547n.
trace 548n.
finger's breadth
short distance 200n.
narrowness 206n.
finger-stall
case 194n.
covering 226n.
surgical dressing 658n.
armor 713n.
finial
vertex 213n.
summit 213n.
finical
attentive 455adj.
fastidious 862adj.
finickiness
moral sensibility 819n.
discontent 829n.
good taste 846n.
finicky
fastidious 862adj.
finish
completion 54n.
end 69n., vb.
cease 145n.
symmetry 245n.
smoothness 258n.
arrival 295n.
elegance 575n.
perfection 646n.
finished
extinct 2adj.
consummate 32adj.
past 125adj.
expert, well-made 694adj.
finisher
survivor 41n.
aftercomer 67n.
finishing school
academy 539n.
training school 539n.
finish off
carry through 725vb.
finite
circumscribed 232adj.
limited 236adj.
fink
informer 524n.
fir
tree 366n.
fire
destroyer 168n.
vigorousness 174n.
shoot 287vb.
dismiss 300vb.
element 319n.
fire 379n.
kindle 381vb.
furnace 383n.
fire 385vb.
light 417n.
luminary 420n.
signal 547n.
vigor 571n.
bombardment 712n.
warm feeling 818adj.
fire-alarm
danger signal 665n.
fire and water
polarity 14n.
fire-arm
fire-arm 723n.
fire-ball
meteor 321n.
fuel 385n.
luminary 420n.
fire-balloon
airship 276n.
fire-barrel
lighter 385n.
fire-bell
danger signal 665n.
fire-box
furnace 383n.
firebrand
violent creature 176n.
incendiarism 381n.
lighter 385n.

dissentient 489n.
motivator 612n.
trouble-maker 663n.
leader 690n.
agitator 738n.
fire-brigade
extinguisher 382n.
fire-bug
incendiarism 381n.
fire damp
gas 336n.
fire-dog
furnace 383n.
fire-drake
glow-worm 420n.
fire-eater
violent creature 176n.
combatant 722n.
brave person 855n.
desperado 857n.
insolent person 878n.
fire-engine
vehicle 274n.
irrigator 341n.
extinguisher 382n.
fire-escape
means of escape 667n.
fire-fighter
extinguisher 382n.
protector 660n.
defender 713n.
firefly
fly 365n.
flash 417n.
glimmer 419n.
glow-worm 420n.
fireguard
furnace 383n.
shelter 662n.
fire-irons
furnace 383n.
fireman
extinguisher 382n.
protector 660n.
defender 713n.
fire-new
new 126adj.
fire-party
punisher 963n.
fireplace
furnace 383n.
fire-proof
coat 226vb.
incombustible 382adj.
invulnerable 660adj.
fire-raising
incendiarism 381n.
fire-ship
ship 275n.
lighter 385n.
warship 722n.
fireside
focus 76n.
home 192n.
fire-station
extinguisher 382n.
fire-step
stand 218n.
fire-walker
ascetic 945n.
fire-watcher
protector 660n.
defender 713n.
firewater
liquor 301n.
firewood
fuel 385n.
fireworks
fire 379n.
fireworks 420n.
spectacle 445n.
masterpiece 694n.
revel 837n.
celebration 876n.
fire-worship
fire 379n.
idolatry 982n.
firing line
battle 718n.
battleground 724n.
firkin
vat 194n.
firlot
metrology 465n.
firm
firm-set 45adj.
fixed 153adj.
strong 162adj.
dense 324adj.
rigid 326adj.
resolute 599adj.
obstinate 602adj.
workshop 687n.
corporation 708n.
retentive 778adj.
merchant 794n.
courageous 855adj.
firmament
heavens 321n.
firman
decree 737n.
firm date
promise 764n.
firmness
permanence 144n.
stability 153n.
hardness 326n.
resolution 599n.
courage 855n.
first
unimitative 21adj.
supreme 34adj.
first 68adj.
prior 119adj.
fundamental 156adj.
foremost 283adj.
best 644adj.
victor 727n.
first aid
therapy 658n.
aid 703n.
first appearance
debut 68n.
first arrival
earliness 135n.
first blood
success 727n.
first blush
beginning 68n.
appearance 445n.
first-born
superior 34n.
precursor 66n.
priority 119n.
older 131adj.
prior 119adj.
olden 127adj.
First Cause
cause 156n.
divineness 965n.
theosophy 984n.
first choice
superior 34n.
choice 605n.
chief thing 638n.
first-class
supreme 34adj.
first come first served
no choice 606n.
first-comer(s)
earliness 135n.
native 191n.
first draft
experiment 461n.
plan 623n.
preparation 669n.
first go
essay 671n.
first-hand
unimitative 21adj.
evidential 466adj.
first lady
superior 34n.
first move
debut 68n.
first-nighter
playgoer 594n.
first offence
debut 68n.
essay 671n.
first offender
beginner 538n.
prisoner 750n.
offender 904n.
first point of Aries
uranometry 321n.
first principle
source 156n.
premise 475n.
first-rate

supreme 34adj.
notable 638adj.
best 644adj.
first-rater
exceller 644n.
warship 722n.
first refusal
purchase 792n.
first round
beginning 68n.
first sight, at
at sight 438n.
apparently 445adv.
first step
debut 68n.
first steps
learning 536n.
first thing
betimes 135adv.
first violin
orchestra 413n.
leader 690n.
first water, of the
excellent 644adj.
firth
gulf 345n.
fisc
treasury 799n.
fiscal
monetary 797adj.
fish
fish food 301n.
animal, fish 365n.
search 459vb.
be tentative 461vb.
hunt 619vb.
take 786vb.
amuse oneself 837vb.
fish day
fast 946n.
fisher
hunter 619n.
fisherman's yarn
fable 543n.
fishery
stock farm 369n.
fish for
search 459vb.
be tentative 461vb.
pursue 619vb.
desire 859vb.
fishglue
adhesive 47n.
fishiness
improbity 930n.
fishing
chase 619n.
sport 837n.
fish manure
fertilizer 171n.
fishmonger
provider 633n.
fish-net
network 222n.
enclosure 235n.
fish out of water
misfit 25n.
nonconformist 84n.
displacement 188n.
bungler 697n.
fish pond
lake 346n.
stock farm 369n.
fish up
elevate 310vb.
discover 484vb.
fishwife
shrew 892n.
fishy
animal 365adj.
dishonest 930adj.
fishy story
fable 543n.
fissile
brittle 330adj.
fission
separation 46n.
decompose 51vb.
fissionable
severable 46adj.
fissure
disjunction 46n.
gap 201n.
fist
finger 378n.
lettering 586n.
nippers 778n.
fisticuffs
knock 279n.
quarrel 709n.
pugilism 716n.
fistula
tube 263n.
ulcer 651n.
fit
modality 7n.
adjust 24vb.
join 45vb.
cohere 48vb.
subdivision 53n.
make conform 83vb.
athletic 162adj.
violence 176n.
spasm 318n.
frenzy 503n.
poem 593n.
whim 604n.
expedient 642adj.
healthy 650adj.
illness 651n.
make ready 669vb.
excitable state 822n.
right 913adj.
due 915adj.
fit for
useful 640adj.
fit for consideration
topical 452adj.
fit for inquiry
moot 459adj.
fit for nothing
useless 641adj.
fitful
excitable 822adj.
fitfulness
discontinuity 72n.
fitfulness 142n.
changeableness 152n.
caprice 604n.
fit in
accord 24vb.
conform 83vb.
load 193vb.
join a party 708vb.
fitness
relevance 9n.
fitness 24n.
occasion 137n.
ability 160n.
expedience 642n.
health 650n.
aptitude 694n.
preparedness 669n.
right 913n.
fit out
dress 228vb.
find means 629vb.
provide 633vb.
make ready 669vb.
fits and starts
fitfulness 142n.
agitation 318n.
fits and starts, by
fitfully 142adv.
jerkily 318adv.
capriciously 604adv.
fitter
machinist 630n.
preparer 669n.
artisan 686n.
fit tight
cohere 48vb.
fill 54vb.
fitting
relevant 9adj.
adjusted 24adj.
cohesive 48adj.
opportune 137adj.
expedient 642adj.
fittings
equipment 630n.
fit to be seen
personable 841adj.
fit together
join 45vb.
combine 50vb.
five by five
fleshy 195adj.
five-finger
handed 378adj.
five o'clock
meal 301n.

social gathering 882n.
fiver
funds 797n.
fives
ball game 837n.
five-stones
plaything 837n.
fix
affix 45vb.
arrange 62vb.
stabilize 153vb.
place 187vb.
close 264vb.
quiescence 266n.
be resolute 599vb.
repair 656vb.
remedy 658vb.
predicament 700n.
fixation
location 187n.
habituation 610n.
hindrance 702n.
fixative
adhesive 47n.
pigment 425n.
fixed
firm-set 45adj.
immemorial 127adj.
permanent 144adj.
fixed 153adj.
located 187adj.
still 266adj.
positive 473adj.
habitual 610adj.
fixed interval
regular return 141n.
fixer
trickster 545n.
mender 656n.
fix, in a
in difficulties 700adj.
fixity
permanence 144n.
stability 153n.
quiescence 266n.
positiveness 473n.
resolution 599n.
obstinacy 602n.
fix on
be attentive 455vb.
fixture
adjunct 40n.
joinder 45n.
part 53n.
concomitant 89adj.
fixture 153n.
equipment 630n.
fixtures
property 777n.
fizgig
fireworks 420n.
fizz
vigorousness 174n.
wine 301n.
soft drink 301n.
bubble 355n., vb.
hiss 406vb.
fizzer
exceller 644n.
fizzle
bubble 355vb.
crackle 402vb.
hiss 406vb.
fizzle out
fall short 307vb.
miscarry 728vb.
fizzy
vigorous 174adj.
watery 339adj.
windy 352adj.
bubbly 355adj.
fjord
gulf 345n.
flabbergast
frighten 854vb.
be wonderful 864vb.
flabby
weak 163adj.
soft 327adj.
pulpy 356adj.
flabelliform
expanded 197adj.
broad 205adj.
flaccidity
weakness 163n.
softness 327n.
feebleness 572n.
flag
be weak 163vb.
lamina 207n.
base 214n.
decelerate 278vb.
foliage 366n.
signal, flag 547n.
road 624n.
building material 631n.
be ill 651n.
be fatigued 684vb.
regalia 743n.
be dejected 834vb.
greet 884vb.
flag-bearer
messenger 531n.
flag-captain
naval officer 741n.
flag day
request 671n.
special day 876n.
flagellant
penitent 939n.
ascetic 945n.
flagellate
perform ritual 988vb.
flagellation
penance 941n.
asceticism 945n.
corporal punishment 963n.
flagelliform
fibrous 208adj.
flageolet
flute 414n.
flagitiousness
wickedness 934n.
flag-lieutenant
naval officer 741n.
flag-man
warner 664n.
flag of convenience
contrivance 623n.
stratagem 698n.
flag officer
naval man 270n.
flag of truce
irenics 719n.
flagon
vessel 194n.
flag-pole
flag 547n.
flagrancy
manifestation 522n.
publicity 528n.
bad taste 847n.
ostentation 875n.
insolence 878n.
wickedness 934n.
flagrant
whopping 32adj.
(*see* flagrancy)
flagrante delicto
guiltily 936adv.
flagration
burning 381n.
flags
paving 226n.
smoothness 258n.
flagship
warship 722n.
flag-signaling
telecommunication 531n.
flagstaff
high structure 209n.
support 218n.
flagstones
road 624n.
flag-waving
celebration 876n.
flail
hammer 279n.
cultivate 370vb.
strike at 712vb.
flog 963vb.
flair
odor 394n.
intellect 447n.
discrimination 463n.
discovery 484n.
aptitude 694n.
flak
bombardment 712n.

defenses 713n.
flake
small thing 33n.
piece 53n.
lamina 207n.
powder 332n.
pulverize 332vb.
flakiness
stratification 207n.
brittleness 330n.
flaky
brittle 330adj.
flambeau
torch 420n.
flamboyant
ornate 574adj.
undulatory 251adj.
flame
fire 379n.
heat 379n.
heater 383n.
shine 417vb.
light 417n.
luminary 420n.
redness 431n.
orange 436n.
be excited 821vb.
loved one 887n.
flame-colored
orange 436adj.
flamen
priest 986n.
flamenco
dance 837n.
flame-proof
incombustible 382adj.
flame-thrower
propellant 287n.
gun 723n.
flaming
violent 176adj.
fiery 379adj.
fervent 818adj.
showy 875adj.
flamingo
bird of prey 365n.
flan
pastry 301n.
flaneur
idler 679n.
flange
edge 234n.
projection 254n.
flank
laterality 239n.
safeguard 660vb.
flannel
textile 222n.
warm clothes 381n.
cleaning cloth 648n.
flatter 925vb.
flannelette
textile 222n.
flap
adjunct 40n.
come unstuck 49vb.
pendant 217n.
hang 217vb.
covering 226n.
be in motion 265vb.
strike 279vb.
agitation 318n.
blow 352vb.
sound dead 405vb.
excitability 822n.
fear 854n., vb.
flapdoodle
empty talk 515n.
flapjack
cereal 301n.
cosmetic 843n.
flapper
youngster 132n.
reminder 305n.
(*see* woman)
flaps
wing 271n.
aircraft 276n.
flare
be violent 176vb.
move fast 277vb.
be hot 379vb.
shine 417vb.
torch 420n.
signal light 420n.
luminary 420adj.
be excited 821vb.
flare up
be excitable 882vb.
get angry 891vb.
flaring
whopping 32adj.
fiery 379adj.
florid 425adj.
showy 875adj.
flash
small quantity 33n.
instant 116n.
changeableness 152n.
be violent 176vb.
velocity 277n.
pass 305vb.
agitation 318n.
fire 379n.
flash 417n.
luminary 420n.
communicate 524vb.
news 529n.
spurious 542adj.
signal, livery 547n.
spontaneity 609n.
flash-back
remembrance 505n.
flashbulb
lamp 420n.
flash in the pan
insubstantial thing 4n.
brief span 114n.
ineffectuality 161n.
be unproductive 172vb.
false alarm 665n.
miscarry 728vb.
flashlight
lamp 420n.
flash point
heat 379n.
flashy
florid 425adj.
ornate 574adj.
ornamented 844adj.
vulgar 847adj.
flask
vessel 194n.
flat
uniform 16adj.
impotent 161adj.
inert 175adj.
spatial 183adj.
flat 192n.
chamber 194n.
short 204adj.
low 210adj.
flat 216adj.
inverted 221adj.
unsharpened 257adj.
smooth 258adj.
still 266adj.
marsh 347n.
champaign 348adj.
tasteless 387adj.
unsavory 391adj.
non-resonant 405adj.
strident 407adj.
musical note 410n.
harmonic 410adj.
discordant 411adj.
soft-hued 425adj.
mirror 442n.
ninny 501n.
assertive 532adj.
dupe 544n.
feeble 572adj.
stage-set 594n.
deteriorated 655adj.
hitch 702n.
cheerless 834adj.
tedious 838adj.
dull 840adj.
flatbed
horizontality 216n.
press 587n.
flat-car
train 274n.
flat-foot
detective 459n.
protector 660n.
police 955n.
flat-iron
flattener 216n.
smoother 258n.
flatland
lowness 210n.

flatlet
small house 192n.
flatness
lowness 210n.
horizontality 216n.
(*see* flat)
flat out
swiftly 277adj.
flats
plain 348n.
flat spin
fear 854n.
flatten
demolish 165vb.
make smaller 198vb.
flatten 216vb.
smooth 258vb.
fell 311vb.
flattened
unsharpened 257adj.
flatten out
fly 271vb.
flatter
imitate 20vb.
mislead 495vb.
befool 542vb.
exaggerate 546vb.
misrepresent 552vb.
tempt 612vb.
please 826vb.
beautify 841vb.
honor 866vb.
flatter 925vb.
be dishonest 930vb.
(*see* flattery)
flatterer
slyboots 698n.
affector 850n.
toady 879n.
flatterer 925n.
flattering
erroneous 495adj.
hypocritical 541adj.
deceiving 542adj.
flattering portrait
misrepresentation 552n.
flatter oneself
assume 471vb.
hope 852vb.
feel pride 871vb.
be vain 873vb.
flattery
conformity 83n.
assent 488n.
empty talk 515n.
falsehood 541n.
inducement 612n.
cunning 698n.
servility 879n.
courtesy 884n.
endearment 889n.
praise 923n.
flattery 925n.
(*see* flatter)
flat-top
warship 722n.
flatulence
gaseity 336n.
diffuseness 570n.
magniloquence 574n.
indigestion 651n.
flatulent
feeble 572adj.
flatus
gas 336n.
wind 352n.
flaunches
heraldry 547n.
flaunt
show 522vb.
seek repute 866vb.
be ostentatious 875vb.
threaten 900vb.
flautist
instrumentalist 413n.
flavor
cook 301vb.
taste 386n.
season 388vb.
flavoring
food 301n.
taste 386n.
condiment 389n.
flavorless
tasteless 387adj.
flavous
yellow 433adj.
flaw
discontinuity 72n.
weakness 163n.
gap 201n.
gale 352n.
sophism 477n.
mistake 495n.
badness 645n.
defect 647n.
blemish 845n., vb.
flawless
consummate 32adj.
elegant 575adj.
perfect 646adj.
flax
fiber 208n.
flaxen
yellow 433adj.
flay
rend 46vb.
uncover 229vb.
dispraise 924vb.
execute 963vb.
flea
athlete 162n.
jumper 312n.
vermin 365n.
dirt 649n.
flea-bag
bag 194n.
flea-bite
small quantity 33n.
trifle 639n.
flea-bitten
mottled 437adj.
fleam
sharp point 256n.
perforator 263n.
flèche
sharp point 256n.
fleck
small thing 33n.
(*see* blemish)
flection
deviation 282n.
fled
escaped 667adj.
fledge
mature 669vb.
fledgling
new 126adj.
youngling 132n.
bird 365n.
flee
decamp 296vb.
run away 620vb.
fleece
skin 226n.
hair 259n.
softness 327n.
groom 369vb.
fleece 786vb.
defraud 788vb.
impoverish 801vb.
overcharge 811vb.
fleecy
fibrous 208adj.
fleecy 259adj.
fleer
ridicule 851n., vb.
satirize 851vb.
fleet
be transient 114vb.
shipping 275n.
speedy 277adj.
navy 722n.
fleeting
insubstantial 4adj.
transient 114adj.
Fleet Street
the press 528n.
flesh
auspicate 68vb.
matter 319n.
animality 365n.
mankind 371n.
sensualism 944n.
unchastity 951n.
flesh and blood
substance 3n.
bulk 195n.
matter 319n.
animality 365n.

fleshings
legwear 228n.
flesh, in the
alive 360adj.
fleshless
lean 206adj.
fleshliness
sensualism 944n.
unchastity 951n.
fleshly
material 319adj.
human 371adj.
flesh-pots
feasting 301n.
prosperity 730n.
wealth 800n.
flesh show
stage show 594n.
fleshy
fleshy 195adj.
pulpy 356adj.
fatty 357adj.
fleur-de-lys
heraldry 547n.
pattern 844n
flexed
curved 248adj.
flexibility
softness 327n.
skill 694n.
improbity 930n.
flexible
conformable 83adj.
flexible 327adj.
irresolute 601adj.
wieldy 701adj.
flexion
curvature 248n.
fold 261n.
deviation 282n.
flex one's muscles
prepare oneself 669vb.
flexuosity
convolution 251n.
flexure
angularity 247n.
curvature 248n.
fold 261n.
flibbertigibbet
demon, elf 970n.
flick
move 265vb.
impel 279vb.
touch 378n., vb.
flicker
be transient 114vb.
changeableness 152n.
flash 417n.
shine 417vb.
glimmer 419n.
flickers, flicks
cinema 445n.
flier
aeronaut 271n.
speeder 277n.
flies
theater 594n.
flight
group 74n.
transientness 114n.
aeronautics 271n.
fly 271vb.
velocity 277n.
propel 287vb.
recession 290n.
departure 296n.
avoidance 620n.
escape 667n.
air force 722n.
defeat 728n.
fear 854n.
flightiness
changeableness 152n.
(*see* flighty)
flight lieutenant
air officer 741n.
flight of fancy
insubstantial thing 4n.
ideality 513n.
exaggeration 546n.
flight of stairs
ascent 308n.
access 624n.
flight of time
course of time 111n.
flight sergeant
air officer 741n.
flighty
transient 114adj.
light-minded 456adj.
irresolute 601adj.
flim-flam
falsehood 541n.
flimsy
flimsy 163adj.
rare 325adj.
brittle 330adj.
ill-reasoned 477adj.
unimportant 639adj.
flinch
recoil 280vb.
feel pain 377vb.
avoid 620vb.
suffer 825vb.
quake 854vb.
flincher
tergiversator 603n.
coward 856n.
flinders
small thing 33n.
fling
move 265vb.
impel 279vb.
propulsion 287n.
scope 744n.
dance 837n.
indignity 921n.
fling about
jumble 63vb.
fling away
be prodigal 815vb.
fling, have one's
be intemperate 943vb.
fling out
eject 300vb.
reject 607vb.
flint
hardness 326n.
soil 344n.
lighter 385n.
tool 630n.
flint-lock
fire-arm 723n.
flinty
hard 326adj.
territorial 344adj.
flip
move 265vb.
impulse 279n.
touch 378n., vb.
incentive 612n.
flippancy
inattention 456n.
unimportance 639n.
wit 839n.
ridicule 851n.
rashness 857n.
sauciness 878n.
flippant
light-minded 456adj.
flipper
limb 53n.
propeller 269n.
feeler 378n.
flirt
tergiversator 603n.
be capricious 604vb.
affector 850n.
excite love 887vb.
court 889vb.
libertine 952n.
loose woman 952n.
flirtation
whim 604n.
love affair 887n.
wooing 889n.
flirtatiousness
caprice 604n.
love 887n.
flirting
love-making 887n.
wooing 889n.
flit
elapse 111vb.
be transient 114vb.
vary 152vb.
move 265vb.
travel 267vb.
decamp 296vb.
run away 620vb.

preserver 666n.
escape 667n., vb.
flit about
wander 267vb.
flitter
vary 152vb.
be in motion 265vb.
float
stabilize 153vb.
hang 217vb.
go smoothly 258vb.
swim 269vb.
fly 271vb.
cart 274n.
raft 275n.
be light 323vb.
be uncertain 474vb.
theater 594n.
find means 629vb.
floater
missile 287n.
idler 679n.
floating
unstable 152adj.
floating vote
changeableness 152n.
dubiety 474n.
irresolution 601vb.
float on the air
sound faint 401vb.
floats
theater 594n.
float up
ascend 308vb.
flocculent
soft 327adj.
powdery 332adj.
flocculi
sun 321n.
powder 332n.
flock
group 74n.
congregate 74vb.
certain quantity 104n.
be many 104vb.
filament 208n.
hair 259n.
animal 365n.
laity 987n.
floe
island 349n.
ice 380n.
flog
strike 279vb.
give pain 377vb.
incite 612vb.
fatigue 684vb.
sell 793vb.
flog 963vb.
flog a dead horse
be superfluous 637vb.
waste effort 641vb.
flood
great quantity 32n.
increase 36n.
crowd 74n.
congregate 74vb.
be dispersed 75vb.
be many 104vb.
destroyer 168n.
outbreak 176n.
high water 209n.
progression 285n.
irrupt 297vb.
flow out 298vb.
immerse 303vb.
encroach 306vb.
irrigate 341vb.
flow 350vb.
plenty 635n.
redundance 637n.
flooded
covered 226adj.
flood-gate
outlet 298n.
conduit 351n.
flood level
high water 209n.
flood-lighting
lighting 420n.
flood-lit
luminous 417adj.
flood tide
high water 209n.
floor
compartment 194n.
layer 207n.
lowness 210n.
base 214n.
horizontality 216n.
flatten 216vb.
basis 218n.
paving 226n.
overlay 226vb.
strike 279vb.
fell 311vb.
confute 479vb.
arena 724n.
floor-boards
paving 226n.
floor-cover
floor-cover 226n.
floor-show
stage show 594n.
floor-walker
servant 742n.
seller 793n.
flop
descend 309vb.
be agitated 318vb.
bungling 695n.
failure 728n.
miscarry 728n.
(*see* fatigue)
floppy
non-adhesive 49adj.
weak 163adj.
soft 327adj.
Flora
vegetability 366n.
flora
organism 358n.
vegetability 366n.
floral
vegetal 366adj.
floresce
expand 197vb.
florescence
salad days 130n.
adultness 134n.
growth 157n.
propagation 164n.
vegetability 366n.
florescent
vernal 128adj.
young 130adj.
grown up 134adj.
floriculture
flower 366n.
agriculture 370n.
florid
florid 425adj.
red 431adj.
ornate 574adj.
healthy 650adj.
splendid 841adj.
ornamental 844adj.
florin
coinage 797n.
floruit
adultness 134n.
palmy days 730n.
floss
hair 259n.
flotation
fitting out 669n.
flotilla
shipping 275n.
navy 722n.
flotsam
thing transferred 272n.
derelict 779n.
flotsam and jetsam
piece 53n.
dispersion 75n.
outcaste 883n.
flounce
edging 234n.
fold 261n.
leap 312vb.
be angry 891vb.
flounder
leap 312vb.
fluctuate 317vb.
be agitated 318vb.
table fish 365n.
be uncertain 474vb.
be clumsy 695vb.
be in difficulty 700vb.
flour
cereal 301n.

powder 332n.
thickening 345n.
corn 366n.
white thing 427n.
flourish
coil 251n.
brandish 317vb.
agitate 318vb.
loudness 400n.
musical note 410n.
trope 519n.
show 522vb.
publication 528n.
call 547n.
ornament 574n.
orate 579vb.
lettering 586n.
flourish 615vb.
be healthy 650vb.
prosper 730vb.
pattern 844n.
ostentation 875n.
boast 877n.
floury
powdery 332adj.
flout
despise 922vb.
flow
quantity 26n.
continuity 71n.
elapse 111vb.
hang 217vb.
motion 265n.
irrupt 297vb.
be fluid 335vb.
current 350n.
flow 350vb.
diffuseness 570n.
elegance 575n.
abound 635vb.
be active 678vb.
flow between
sunder 46vb.
flower
essential part 5n.
grow 36vb.
reproduce itself 164vb.
expand 197vb.
flower 366n.
elite 644n.
paragon 646n.
prosper 730vb.
a beauty 841n.
flower-bed
flower 366n.
garden 370n.
flower-growing
agriculture 370n.
flowering
vernal 128adj.
young 130adv.
flower of life
salad days 130n.
flowers
regular return 141n.
hemorrhage 302n.
pulverulence 332n.
reading matter 589n.
anthology 592n.
flowery
vegetal 366adj.
figurative 519adj.
ornate 574adj.
flowing
perpetual 115adj.
unstable 152adj.
diffuse 570adj.
elegant 575adj.
flowing bowl
drunkenness 949n.
flowing tongue
loquacity 581n.
flown
absent 190adj.
escaped 667adj.
flow of spirits
cheerfulness 833n.
flow on
progress 285vb.
fluctuate
be unequal 29vb.
be periodic 141vb.
vary 152vb.
fluctuate 317vb.
be capricious 604vb.
fluctuation
changeableness 152n.
motion 265n.
fluctuation 317n.
current 350n.
uncertainty 474n.
irresolution 601n.
flue
chimney 263n.
air-pipe 353n.
furnace 383n.
fluency
diffuseness 570n.
elegance 575n.
speech, eloquence 575n.
loquacity 581n.
fluent
numerical element 85n.
fluidal 335adj.
flowing 350adj.
(*see* fluency)
flue-pipe
orifice 263n.
air-pipe 353n.
fluff
jumble 63vb.
hair 259n.
levity 323n.
be clumsy 695vb.
fluffy
downy 259adj.
fleecy 259adj.
flugelhorn
horn 414n.
fluid
unstable 152adj.
amorphous 244adj.
liquor 301n.
fluid 335n.
moisture 341n.
flowing 350adj.
fluidity
non-coherence 49n.
weakness 163n.
softness 327n.
fluidity 335n.
liquefaction 337n.
unreliability 474n.
fluke
chance 159n.
angularity 247n.
non-design 618n.
success 727n.
fluky
casual 159adj.
flummery
empty talk 515n.
fable 534n.
flummox
distract 456vb.
puzzle 474vb.
flunk
failure 728n.
flunky
domestic 742n.
dependent 742n.
toady 879n.
flunkyism
service 745n.
servility 879n.
flattery 925n.
fluorescence
glow 417n.
fluorescent
luminescent 420adj.
fluorometer
meter 465n.
flurry
derange 63vb.
velocity 277n.
rain 350n.
gale 352n.
distract 456vb.
activity 678n.
feeling 818n.
excitation 821n.
excitable state 822n.
frighten 854vb.
flush
uniform 16adj.
equal 28adj.
full 54adj.
flat 216adj.
smooth 258adj.

waterfall 350n.
be hot 379vb.
glow 417n.
hue 425n.
redness 431n.
hunt 619vb.
filled 635adj.
clean, purify 648vb.
skin disease 651n.
moneyed 800adj.
show feeling 818vb.
be excited 821vb.
frighten 854vb.
tipsy 949adj.
fluster
derange 63vb.
distract 456vb.
flute
groove 262vb.
stridor 407n.
shrill 407vb.
play music 413vb.
flute 414n.
fluting
furrow 262n.
ornamental art 844n.
flutist
instrumentalist 413n.
flutter
vary 152vb.
be in motion 265vb.
fly 271vb.
oscillation 317n.
brandish 317vb.
agitation 318n.
gambling 618n.
haste 680n.
feeling 818n.
be excited 821vb.
nervousness 854n.
frighten 854vb.
excite love 887vb.
fluvial
flowing 350adj.
flux
conversion 147n.
motion 265n.
liquefaction 337n.
current 350n.
flux and reflux
fluctuation 317n.
fluxibility
fluidity 335n.
liquefaction 337n.
fluxion
numerical element 85n.
fluxions
mathematics 86n.
fluxure
fluidity 335n.
fly
elapse 111vb.
be transient 114vb.
be violent 176vb.
animalcule 196n.
edge 234n.
fly 271vb.
carry 273vb.
cab 274n.
move fast 277vb.
decamp 296vb.
agitate 318vb.
be brittle 330vb.
fly 365n.
knowing 490adj.
intelligent 498adj.
flag 547n.
run away 620vb.
be active 678vb.
cunning 698adj.
fear 854vb.
fly about
be published 528vb.
fly against
charge 712vb.
fly a kite
be tentative 461vb.
fly along
travel 267vb.
fly apart
be dispersed 75vb.
flyblown
unclean 649adj.
fly-by-night
avoiding 620adj.
fly-fishing
chase 619n.
flying
transient 114adj.
high 209adj.
aeronautics 271n.
flying buttress
supporter 218n.
church exterior 990n.
flying carpet
magic instrument 983n.
flying colors
trophy 729n.
ostentation 875n.
celebration 876n.
flying colors, with
successfully 727adv.
flying column
armed force 722n.
Flying Dutchman
wanderer 268n.
mariner 270n.
fantasy 513n.
flying ground
arena 724n.
flying instruments
aircraft 276n.
flying saucer
space-ship 276n.
flying start
vantage 34n.
start 68n.
priority 119n.
spurt 277n.
precession 283n.
fly in the face of
oppose 704vb.
disobey 738vb.
fly in the ointment
defect 647n.
hitch 702n.
fly-leaf
interjection 231n.
partition 231n.
edition 589n.
fly off at a tangent
deviate 282vb.
diverge 294vb.
fly off the handle
be excitable 822vb.
get angry 891vb.
fly-over
crossing 222n.
traffic control 305n.
passage 305n.
bridge 624n.
communicating 624adj.
fly-paper
adhesive 47n.
trap 542n.
fly-past
pageant 875n.
flyte
curse 899vb.
flyweight
pugilist 722n.
fly-wheel
rotator 315n.
foal
youngling 132n.
reproduce itself 164vb.
horse 273n.
male animal 372n.
foam
stimulation 174n.
be violent 176vb.
excrement 302n.
effervesce 318vb.
moisture 341n.
bubble 355n., vb.
bauble 639n.
be excitable 822vb.
foam at the mouth
effervesce 318vb.
be insane 503vb.
go mad 503vb.
get angry 891vb.
foamy
light 323adj.
bubbly 355adj.
white 427adj.
fob

pocket 194n.
deceive 542vb.
focal
central 225adj.
focalization
centrality 225n.
convergence 293n.
focal point
focus 76n.
centrality 225n.
focimetry
measurement 464n.
fo'c'sle
prow 237n.
focus
junction 45n.
bring together 74vb.
focus 76n., vb.
meeting place 192n.
centralize 225vb.
convergence 293n.
gaze 438vb.
be attentive 455vb.
arena 724n.
focus, in
well-seen 443adj.
focus the attention
attract notice 455vb.
fodder
provender 301n.
groom 369vb.
agriculture 370n.
materials 631n.
foe
opponent 705n.
enemy 881n.
fog
moisture 341n.
cloud 355n.
dimness 419n.
screen 421vb.
opacity 423n.
blur 440vb.
invisibility 444n.
puzzle 474vb.
fog-bound
hindered 702adj.
fogginess
dimness 419n.
imperspicuity 568n.
foggy
dense 324adj.
humid 341adj.
cloudy 355adj.
dim 419adj.
opaque 423adj.
fog-signal
warning 664n.
danger signal 665n.
fogy
archaism 127n.
crank 504n.
opinionist 602n.
laughing-stock 851n.
foible
vice 934n.
(*see* defect)
foil
lamina 207n.
bluntness 257n.
disappoint 509vb.
be obstructive 702vb.
oppose 704vb.
side-arms 723n.
foiled
defeated 728adj.
foin
collide 279vb.
foin 712n.
parry 713vb.
foison
plenty 635n.
foist
galley 275n.
compel 740vb.
foist in
intromit 231vb.
foist off
deceive 542vb.
fold
joint 45n.
duplication 91n.
stable 192n.
receptacle 194n.
make smaller 198vb.
enclosure 235n.
angularity 247n.
make curved 248vb.
fold 261n., vb.
safeguard 660vb.
shelter 662n.
laity 987n.
folded hands
entreaty 761n.
folder
receptacle 194n.
collection 632n.
folderol
finery 844n.
fold one's arms
not act 677vb.
fold up
cease 145vb.
make smaller 198vb.
foliaceous
layered 207adj.
foliage
foliage 366n.
greenness 432n.
foliate
number 86vb.
layered 207adj.
foliation
foliage 366n.
folio
part 53n.
edition 889n.
folk
tradition 127n.
social group 371n.
folklore
anthropology 371n.
folklorish
fairylike 970adj.
folkmoot
council 692n.
folksy
sociable 882adj.
follicle
compartment 194n.
cavity 255n.
follow
do likewise 20vb.
be inferior 35vb.
come after 65vb.
conform 83vb.
accompany 89vb.
be late 136vb.
happen 154adj.
result 157vb.
be behind 238vb.
follow 284vb.
watch 441vb.
be reasonable 475vb.
be proved 478vb.
detect 484vb.
understand 516vb.
use 673vb.
obey 739vb.
serve 742vb.
observe 768vb.
follow a calling
do business 622vb.
follow a course
behave 688vb.
follow advice
consult 691vb.
follower
imitator 20n.
inferior 35n.
retinue 67n.
conformist 83n.
concomitant 89n.
follower 284n.
learner 538n.
auxiliary 707n.
dependent 742n.
lover 887n.
sectarist 978n.
worshiper 981n.
following
retinue 67n.
(*see* follower)
following wind
aid 703n.
follow suit
do likewise 20vb.
follow the scent
pursue 619vb.
follow-through
sequel 67n.
effectuation 725n.

follow through
sustain 146vb.
carry through 725vb.
follow-up
sequel 67n.
follow-up
carry through 725vb.
folly
insubstantial thing 4n.
pavilion 192n.
ignorance 491n.
folly 499n.
rashness 857n.
foment
make violent 176vb.
heat 381vb.
doctor 658vb.
aid 703vb.
animate 821vb.
fomentation
causation 156n.
surgical dressing 658n.
therapy 658n.
fond
foolish 499adj.
crazed 503adj.
desiring 859adj.
loving 887adj.
fondle
touch 378vb.
love 887vb.
caress 889vb.
fondling
favorite 890n.
fondness
(*see* fond)
fons et origo
origin 68n.
source 156n.
font
print-type 587n.
ritual object 988n.
church utensil 990n.
fontanel
head 213n.
food
food 301n.
life 360n.
materials 631n.
provision 633n.
refreshment 685n.
food content
food content 301n.
food for thought
topic 452n.
foodless
hungry 859adj.
fasting 946adj.
food-poisoning
infection 651n.
poisoning 659n.
foodstuff(s)
food 301n.
provisions 301n.
provender 301n.
fool
pulpiness 356n.
ignoramus 493n.
be absurd 497vb.
fool 501n.
madman 504n.
befool 542vb.
dupe 544n.
entertainer 594n.
bungler 697n.
humorist 839n.
be ridiculous 849vb.
laughing-stock 851n.
foolery
foolery 497n.
folly 499n.
revel 837n.
wit 839n.
witticism 851n.
foolhardiness
rashness 857n.
foolish
aged 131adj.
mindless 448adj.
credulous 487adj.
ignorant 491adj.
absurd 497adj.
foolish 499adj.
crazed 503adj.
trivial 639adj.
foolishness
(*see* folly)
fool-proof
certain 473adj.
invulnerable 660adj.
easy 701adj.
successful 727adj.
foolscap
label 547n.
stationery 586n.
paper 631n.
fool's errand
lost labor 641n.
fool's paradise
insubstantial thing 4n.
misjudgment 481n.
disappointment 509n.
aspiration 852n.
foot
long measure 203n.
lowness 210n.
base, foot 214n.
stand 218adj.
prosody 593n.
infantry 722n.
footage
distance 119n.
length 203n.
foot and mouth disease
animal disease 651n.
football
sphere 252n.
missile 287n.
ball game 837n.
footballer
player 837n.
football pool
chance 159n.
gambling 618n.
gambling game 837n.
foot by foot
piecemeal 53adv.
footfall
gait 265n.
indication 547n.
footgear
footwear 228n.
foothill(s)
entrance 68n.
high land 209n.
foothold
basis 218n.
retention 778n.
footing
state 7n.
circumstance 8n.
degree 27n.
serial place 73n.
influence 178n.
situation 186n.
base 214n.
support, basis 218n.
foot it
walk 267vb.
leap 312vb.
footlet
footwear 228n.
footlight(s)
lighting 420n.
drama, theater 594n.
footling
trivial 639adj.
footloose
traveling 267adj.
designless 618adj.
footman
pedestrian 268n.
domestic 742n.
(*see* infantry)
footmark
trace 548n.
footnote(s)
adjunct 40n.
commentary 520n.
foot, on
continuing 108adj.
happening 154adj.
operative 173adj.
on foot 267adv.
preparatory 669adj.
footpad
pedestrian 268n.
robber 789n.
footpath

path 624n.
foot-plate man
driver 68n.
footprint
concavity 255n.
identification 547n.
trace 548n.
footrest
supporter 218n.
footrule
gauge 465n.
foot-slogger
pedestrian 268n.
infantry 722n.
foot-soldier
infantry 722n.
footsore
fatigued 684adj.
footstep
trace 548n.
footstool
seat 218n.
foot the bill
defray 804vb.
footwear
footwear 228n.
foozle
be clumsy 695vb.
failure 728n.
fop
fop 848n.
affector 850n.
foppery
fashion 848n.
affectation 850n.
airs 873n.
foppish
fashionable 848adj.
affected 850adj.
showy 875adj.
forage
provender 301n.
provide 633vb.
steal 788vb.
foramen
orifice 263n.
forasmuch
concerning 9adv.
forasmuch as
hence 158adv.
foray
attack 712n.
brigandage 788n.
forbear
precursor 66n.
disregard 458vb.
(*see* forebearance, forebear)
forbearance
avoidance 620n.
non-use 674n.
lenity 736n.
patience 823n.
mercy 905n.
forgiveness 909n.
temperance 942n.
forbid
prohibit 757vb.
forbidden fruit
incentive 612n.
prohibition 757n.
forbidding
cheerless 834adj.
serious 834adj.
ugly 842adj.
unsociable 883adj.
sullen 893adj.
force
be unrelated 10vb.
quantity 26n.
derange 63vb.
band 74n.
make conform 83vb.
cause 156n.
energy 160n.
strength 162n.
agency 173n.
vigorousness 174n.
force 176vb.
influence 178vb.
promote 285vb.
waterfall 350n.
cultivate 370vb.
meaning 514n.
vigor 571n.
motivate 612vb.
ill-treat 645vb.
mature 669vb.
misuse 675n., vb.
action 676n.
exertion 682n.
personnel 686n.
armed force 722n.
compulsion 740n.
debauch 951vb.
forced
irrelevant 10adj.
feeble 572adj.
inelegant 576adj.
unwilling 598adj.
forced labor
slacker 598n.
labor 682n.
compulsion 740n.
forced landing
aeronautics 271n.
forced march
haste 680n.
forceful
strong 162adj.
vigorous 174adj.
assertive 532adj.
stylistic 566adj.
forceful 571adj.
resolute 599adj.
active 678adj.
compelling 740adj.
impressive 821adj.
force, in
operative 173adj.
forcene
heraldic 547adj.
force of character
affections 817n.
force of circumstances
necessity 596n.
force one's hand
compel 740vb.
force one's way
exert oneself 682vb.
force open
sunder 46vb.
force 176vb.
forceps
cross 222n.
extractor 304n.
nippers 778n.
force, the
police 955n.
forcible
(*see* forceful)
forcible-feeble
feeble 572adj.
ford
pass 305vb.
be wet 341vb.
bridge 624n.
fordone
fatigued 684adj.
fore
before 64adv.
prior 119adj.
front 237n.
fore and aft
throughout 54adv.
longwise 203adv.
forearm
limb 53n.
warn 664vb.
prepare 669vb.
forebear
precursor 66n.
parent 66n.
(*see* forbear)
forebode
predict 511vb.
indicate 547vb.
endanger 661vb.
foreboding
foresight 510n.
prediction 511n.
dangerous 661adj.
warning 664n.
threatening 900adj.
forecast
destiny 155n.
impending 155adj.
expectation 507n.
foresee 510vb.
predict 511vb.
policy 623n.
preparation 669n.

forecastle
prow 237n.
forechosen
fated 596adj.
foreclose
obstruct 702vb.
demand 737vb.
deprive 786vb.
foreclosure
expropriation 786n.
debt 803n.
forecourse
sail 275n.
forecourt
front 237n.
foredate
misdate 118vb.
foredoom
predestine 155vb.
fate 596n.
necessitate 596vb.
forefather
parent 169n.
forefathers
the dead 361n.
forefinger
finger 378n.
forefoot
foot 214n.
forefront
beginning 68n.
front 237n.
foreglimpse
foresight 510n.
foregoing
preceding 64adj.
prior 119adj.
foregoing 125adj.
foregone conclusion
prejudgment 481n.
foresight 510n.
predetermination 608n.
foreground
front 237n.
stage set 594n.
forehanded
vigilant 457adj.
forehead
head 213n.
face 237n.
foreign
irrelative 10adj.
disagreeing 25adj.
separate 46adj.
extraneous 59adj.
foreign body
misfit 25n.
extraneousness 59n.
foreigner
misfit 25n.
foreigner 59n.
outcaste 883n.
foreignness
exteriority 223n.
foreign parts
extraneousness 59n.
farness 199n.
forejudge
prejudge 481vb.
foresee 510vb.
foreknowledge
foresight 510n.
foreland
projection 254n.
forelay
ensnare 542vb.
foreleg
leg 267n.
forelimb
limb 53n.
forelock
front 237n.
hair 259n.
foreman
superior 34n.
manager 690n.
foremast
prow 237n.
foremost
supreme 34adj.
first 68adj.
foremost 283adj.
ahead 283adv.
important 638adj.
noteworthy 866adj.
forename
name 561n.
forenoon
morning 128n.
forensic
jurisprudential 958adj.
foreordain
predestine 155vb.
predetermine 608vb.
forepart
front 237n.
forepeak
prow 237n.
forepiece
front 237n.
forerake
projection 254n.
forerun
come before 64vb.
be before 119vb.
precede 283vb.
forerunner
precursor 66n.
front 237n.
messenger 531n.
director 690n.
foresail
sail 275n.
foresee
look ahead 124vb.
be wise 498vb.
expect 507vb.
foresee 510vb.
intend 617vb.
foreseeable
future 124adj.
expected 507adj.
foreseen
expected 507adj.
unastonishing 865adj.
foreshadow
predestine 155vb.
predict 511vb.
foreshorten
shorten 204vb.
foreshow
predict 511vb.
foresight
priority 119n.
looking ahead 124n.
carefulness 457n.
sagacity 498n.
foresight 510n.
prediction 511n.
policy 623n.
preparation 669n.
caution 858n.
foreskin
front 237n.
forest
wood 366n.
forestall
exclude 57vb.
do before 119vb.
look ahead 124vb.
be early 135vb.
expect 507vb.
foresee 510vb.
deceive 542vb.
possess 773vb.
forestay
prow 237n.
forester
dweller 191n.
forestry 366n.
gardener 370n.
forestry
forestry 366n.
botany 368n.
agriculture 370n.
foretaste
precursor 66n.
example 83n.
expectation 507n.
foresight 510n.
preparation 669n.
foretell
predict 511vb.
forethought
thought 449n.
carefulness 457n.
sagacity 498n.
foresight 510n.
policy 623n.
foretoken

omen 511n.
foretopman
navigator 270n.
climber 308n.
forever
forever 115adv.
for everybody
general 79adj.
forewarn
foresee 510vb.
predict 511vb.
warn 664vb.
threaten 900vb.
forewarning
precursor 66n.
foreword
prelude 66n.
for example
conformably 83adv.
forfeit
decrease 37n., vb.
decrement 42n.
relinquish 621vb.
loss 772n.
deprive 786vb.
disentitle 916vb.
penalty 963n.
forfeiture
(*see* forfeit)
forfend
parry 713vb.
prohibit 757vb.
forgathering
junction 45n.
assembly 74n.
social gathering 882n.
forge
copy 20vb.
produce 164vb.
efform 243vb.
furnace 383n.
fake 541vb.
be untrue 543vb.
workshop 687n.
mint 797vb.
forge ahead
be in front 237vb.
progress 285vb.
forger
imitator 20n.
deceiver 545n.
artisan 686n.
defrauder 789n.
moneyer 797n.
offender 904n.
forgery
imitation 20n.
copy 22n.
falsehood 541n.
sham 542n.
false money 797n.
forget
be inattentive 456vb.
forget 506vb.
obliterate 550vb.
relinquish 621vb.
be lenient 736vb.
fail in duty 918vb.
forgetful
negligent 458adj.
forgetful 506adj.
forget-me-not
blueness 435n.
forgivable
trivial 639adj.
forgiven 909adj.
vindicable 927adj.
guiltless 935adj.
forgive
disregard 458vb.
forgive 909vb.
forgiveness
amnesty 506n.
irenics 719n.
lenity 736n.
benevolence 897n.
forgiveness 909n.
acquittal 960n.
divine function 965n.
forgo
relinquish 621vb.
not retain 779vb.
forgone
relinquished 621adj.
for good
for long 113adv.
for good and all
throughout 54adv.
forever 115adv.
forgotten
past 125adj.
unknown 491adj.
forgotten 506adj.
unthanked 908adj.
fork
bifurcation 92n.
cross 222vb.
angularity 247n.
sharp point 256n.
diverge 294vb.
fork out
give 781vb.
pay 804vb.
forlorn
hopeless 853adj.
friendless 883adj.
forlorn hope
danger 661n.
combatant 722n.
armed force 722n.
brave person 855n.
form
similarity 18n.
copy 22n.
constitute 56vb.
arrange 62vb.
rule 81n.
conformity 83n.
convert 147vb.
produce 164vb.
seat 218n.
form 243n.
appearance 445n.
educate 534vb.
class 538n.
record 548n.
letterpress 587n.
edition 589n.
practice 610n.
beauty 841n.
fashion 848n.
formality 875n.
legality 953n.
ritual 988n.
formal
conditionate 7adj.
regular 83adj.
formal dress
formal dress 228n.
formalism
severity 735n.
pietism 979n.
ritualism 988n.
formalist
tyrant 735n.
affector 850n.
religionist 979n.
ritualist 988n.
formality
formality 875n.
courtesy 884n.
format
form 243n.
formation
group 74n.
efformation 243n.
production 164n.
formation 722n.
formative
formative 243adj.
form, bad
ill-breeding 847n.
form, be on
be skillful 694vb.
former
preceding 64adj.
prior 119adj.
former 125adj.
resigning 753adj.
formerly
long ago 113adv.
formerly 125adv.
formication
formication 378n.
skin disease 651n.
formidable
difficult 700adj.
frightening 854adj.
formless
amorphous 244adj.
unsightly 842adj.
form of law

legality 953n.
formula
rule 81n.
number 85n.
axiom 496n.
phrase 563n.
precept 693n.
legality 953n.
rite 988n.
formular
ritualistic 988adj.
formulary
maxim 496n.
precept 693n.
office-book 988n.
rite 988n.
formulate
arrange 62vb.
efform 243vb.
affirm 532vb.
write 586vb.
fornication
unchastity 951n.
fornicator
libertine 952n.
forsake
tergiversate 603vb.
relinquish 621vb.
for sale
offering 759adj.
(*see* saleable)
forswear
negate 533vb.
be false 541vb.
recant 603vb.
avoid 620vb.
relinquish 621vb.
be dishonest 930vb.
fort
refuge 662n.
fort 713n.
forte
skill 694n.
forth
forward 285adv.
forthcoming
early 135adj.
impending 155adj.
veracious 540adj.
feeling 818adj.
for the million
easy 701adj.
for the moment
transiently 114adj.
for the nonce
singly 88adv.
for the occasion
present 121adj.
for the sake of
in aid of 703adv.
forthright
intelligible 516adj.
undisguised 522adj.
veracious 540adj.
forthwith
suddenly 135adv.
fortification
fortification 713n.
art of war 718n.
fortified
strong 162adj.
hard 326adj.
defended 713adj.
fortify
strengthen 162vb.
safeguard 660vb.
aid 703vb.
defend 713vb.
fortissimo
loud 400adj.
loudness 400n.
loudly 400adv.
fortitude
courage 855n.
virtues 933n.
fortnight
period 110n.
fortnightly
seasonal 141adj.
fortress
fort 713n.
fortuitous
extrinsic 6adj.
casual 159adj.
unintentional 618adj.
fortunate
opportune 137adj.
prosperous 730adj.
happy 824adj.
fortune
eventuality 154n.
chance 159n.
prediction 511n.
fate 596n.
good 615n.
wealth 800n.
fortune-hunter
toady 879n.
egotist 932n.
fortunes
biography 590n.
fortune-teller
diviner 511n.
occultist 984n.
fortune-telling
divination 511n.
occultism 984n.
forty-niner
traveler 268n.
forty winks
sleep 679n.
forum
focus 76n.
meeting place 192n.
rostrum 539n.
arena 724n.
mart 796n.
tribunal 956n.
forward
early 135adj.
fore 237adj.
send 272vb.
forward 285adv.
intelligent 498adj.
correspond 588vb.
willing 597adj.
willful 602adj.
be expedient 642vb.
make better 654vb.
impertinent 878adj.
discourteous 885adj.
forward-looking
progressive 285adj.
forwardness
intelligence 498n.
willingness 597n.
non-preparation 670n.
(*see* precocity)
forward, set
undertake 672vb.
fosse
fence 235n.
furrow 262n.
defenses 713n.
fossil
remainder 41n.
antiquity 125n.
archaism 127n.
old man 133n.
organism 358n.
corpse 363n.
fossilization
condensation 324n.
hardening 326n.
fossor
excavator 255n.
foster
look after 457vb.
train 534vb.
make better 654vb.
safeguard 660vb.
patronize 703vb.
permit 756vb.
animate 821vb.
pet 889vb.
foster-child
favorite 890n.
foster-father
parent 169n.
fosterling
child 132n.
fother
line 227vb.
close 264vb.
foul
collide 279vb.
windy 352adj.
fetid 397adj.
evil 616adj.
bad 645adj.
unclean 649adj.
insalubrious 653adj.

unpleasant 827adj.
ugly 842adj.
disliked 861adj.
wrong 914adj.
foul play 930n.
heinous 934adj.
foulard
textile 222n.
foul language
scurrility 899n.
foul play
evil 616n.
injustice 914n.
foul play 930n.
found
stabilize 153vb.
cause 156vb.
liquefy 337vb.
heat 381vb.
dower 777vb.
foundation
composition 56n.
beginning 68n.
permanence 144n.
source 156n.
base 214n.
basis 218n.
preparation 669n.
foundational
fundamental 156adj.
founder
cause 156n.
producer 167n.
descend 309vb.
founder 313vb.
perish 361vb.
planner 623n.
patron 707n.
fail 728vb.
benefactor 903n.
foundered
impotent 161adj.
deep 211adj.
foundling
derelict 779n.
foundry
workshop 687n.
found upon
attribute 158vb.
fount
origin 68n.
source 156n.
stream 350n.
store 632n.
(*see* font)
fountain
source 156n.
outflow 298n.
soft drink 301n.
climber 308n.
stream 350n.
store 632n.
four
quaternity 96n.
four corners
whole 52n.
four-dimensional
metric 465adj.
four-flusher
deceiver 545n.
fourfold
fourfold 97adj.
four-in-hand
carriage 274n.
four-letter word
plainness 573n.
fourposter
bed 218n.
four-sided
symmetrical 245adj.
foursome
quaternity 96n.
dance 837n.
four-square
four 96adj.
angulated 247adj.
fourth dimension
time 108n.
fourth estate
the press 528n.
four-wheeler
cab 274n.
fowl
bird 365n.
hunt 619vb.
fowler
hunter 619n.
fowling-piece
chase 619n.
fire-arm 723n.
fox
vermin 365n.
puzzle 474vb.
trickster 545n.
slyboots 698n.
noxious animal 904n.
foxglove
poisonous plant 659n.
foxhole
tunnel 263n.
refuge 662n.
fox-hound
dog 365n.
hunter 619n.
foxiness
cunning 698n.
fox-trot
dance 837n., vb.
foxy
brown 430adj.
red 431adj.
intelligent 498adj.
cunning 698adj.
dishonest 930adj.
foyer
lobby 194n.
theater 594n.
fracas
turmoil 61n.
loudness 400n.
quarrel 709n.
fight 716n.
fraction
quantity 26n.
part 53n.
numerical element 85n.
fraction 102n.
trifle 639n.
fractionize
sunder 46vb.
fractious
unwilling 598adj.
irascible 892adj.
fracture
separation 46n.
break 46vb.
discontinuity 72n.
gap 201n.
be brittle 330vb.
fragile
unsubstantial 4adj.
flimsy 163adj.
brittle 330adj.
fragility
transientness 114n.
fragment
small thing 33n.
break 46vb.
part, piece 53n.
fraction 102n.
be brittle 330vb.
pulverize 332vb.
fragmentary
fragmentary 53adj.
incomplete 55adj.
fractional 102adj.
exiguous 196adj.
imperfect 647adj.
uncompleted 726adj.
fragmentation
separation 46n.
pulverulence 332n.
fragrance
sweetness 392n.
odor 394n.
fragrance 396n.
fragrant
pleasant 376adj.
frail
ephemeral 114adj.
flimsy 163adj.
basket 194n.
brittle 330adj.
unsafe 661adj.
wicked, frail 934adj.
unchaste 951adj.
frailty
vice 934n.
(*see* fragility)
framboesia
skin disease 651n.

frame
modality 7n.
relate 9vb.
mold 23n.
affix 45vb.
produce 164vb.
receptacle 194n.
basket 194n.
hanger 217n.
frame 218n.
be exterior 223vb.
circumscribe 232vb.
outline 233n., vb.
edging 234n.
enclose 235vb.
form 243n.
efform 243vb.
structure 331n.
garden 370n.
fake 541vb.
predetermine 608vb.
plot 623vb.
indict 928vb.
frame of mind
affections 817n.
frame of reference
referral 9n.
prototype 23n.
frame-up
trap 542n.
untruth 543n.
predetermination 608n.
plot 623n.
false charge 928n.
framework
basket 194n.
frame 218n.
outline 233n.
structure 331n.
framing
circumjacent 230adj.
franchise
vote 605n.
freedom 744n.
dueness 915n.
non-liability 919n.
Franciscans
monk 986n.
francophile
xenophile 880n.
franc-tireur
soldier 722n.
frangibility
non-coherence 49n.
brittleness 330n.
frangipane
scent 396n.
frank
undisguised 522adj.
correspond 588vb.
artless 699adj.
ungracious 885adj.
trustworthy 929adj.
Frankenstein's monster
monster 938n.
demon 970n.
frankfurter
meat 301n.
frankincense
resin 357n.
scent 396n.
franklin
possessor 776n.
frankness
truth 494n.
veracity 540n.
artlessness 699n.
plainness 573n.
frantic
disorderly 61adj.
furious 176adj.
absurd 497adj.
frenzied 503adj.
active 678adj.
excitable 822adj.
frantically
extremely 32adv.
frap
tie 45vb.
tighten 45vb.
fraternal
akin 11adj.
corporate 708adj.
concordant 710adj.
friendly 880adj.
benevolent 897adj.
fraternity
family 11n.
association 706n.
community 708n.
monk 986n.
fraternize
accord 24vb.
combine 50vb.
concord 710vb.
be friendly 880vb.
be sociable 882vb.
fratricide
homicide 362n.
Frau
lady 373n.
fraud
duplicity 541n.
deception 542n.
trickery 542n.
imposter 545n.
slyboots 698n.
peculation 788n.
fraudulence
deception 542n.
fraudulent
false 541adj.
thieving 788adj.
perfidious 930adj.
dishonest 930adj.
lawbreaking 954adj.
fraught
full 54adj.
fraught with
productive 164adj.
possessing 773adj.
fray
rend 46vb.
rub 333vb.
impair 655vb.
fight 716n.
freak
nonconformist 84n.
crank 504n.
whim 604n.
prodigy 864n.
freakish
unexpected 508adj.
(*see* freak)
freakishness
caprice 604n.
freckle
maculation 437n.
variegate 437vb.
skin disease 651n.
blemish 845n., vb.
free
disjoin 46vb.
unstick 49vb.
veracious 540adj.
voluntary 597adj.
escaped 667adj.
deliver 668vb.
disencumber 701vb.
free 744adj.
given 781adj.
uncharged 812adj.
liberal 813adj.
ungracious 885adj.
unwedded 895adj.
unchaste 951adj.
free agent
free man 744n.
free allowance
decrement 42n.
free-and-easy
rash 857adj.
impertinent 878adj.
sociable 882adj.
freeboard
interval 201n.
freebooter
militarist 722n.
robber 789n.
knave 938n.
free-born
free 744adj.
free choice
willingness 597n.
free companion
militarist 722n.
freed
liberated 746adj.
freedman
free man 744n.
freedom

opportunity 137n.
freedom 744n.
permission 756n.
dueness 915n.
freedom of action
independence 744n.
free field
scope 744n.
free-for-all
turmoil 61n.
fight 716n.
free from
unmixed 44adj.
free hand
scope 744n.
permit 756n.
liberality 813n.
freehold
independence 744n.
unconditional 744adj.
lands 777n.
proprietary 777adj.
free-holder
possessor 776n.
freelance
worker 686n.
militarist 722n.
free man 744n.
free love
type of marriage 894n.
illicit love 951n.
freely
easily 701adv.
freely 744adv.
freeman
free man 744n.
freemartin
eunuch 161n.
freemasonry
secrecy 525n.
society 708n.
friendship 880n.
free pardon
amnesty 506n.
forgiveness 909n.
free play
scope 744n.
free range
stock farm 369n.
free speech
freedom 744n.
free-spoken
artless 699adj.
free-thinker
irreligionist 971n.
free thought
freedom 744n.
antichristianity 974n.
free trade
ingress 297n.
scope 744n.
trade 791n.
no charge 812n.
freetrader
free man 744n.
free verse
verse form 593n.
freewheel
go smoothly 258vb.
free will
will 595n.
freedom 744n.
freeze
cohere 48vb.
halt 145vb.
be dense 324vb.
harden 326vb.
render insensible 375vb.
be cold 380vb.
refrigerate 382vb.
preserve 666vb.
not pay 805vb.
quake 854vb.
frighten 854vb.
freezer
refrigerator 384n.
freeze on to
retain 778vb.
freight
fill 54vb.
stow 187vb.
contents 193n.
load 193vb.
thing transferred 272n.
gravity 322n.
merchandise 795n.
freightage
transport 272n.
price 809n.
freight-car
train 274n.
freighted
full 54adj.
bearing 273adj.
freighter
carrier 273n.
merchant ship 275n.
frenzied
furious 176adj.
angry 891adj.
frenzy
turmoil 61n.
spasm 318n.
commotion 318n.
frenzy 503n.
fantasy 513n.
unmeaningness 515n.
illness 651n.
activity 678n.
restlessness 678n.
excitable state 822n.
desire 859n.
frequency
degree 27n.
continuity 71n.
recurrence 106n.
frequency 139n.
periodicity 141n.
cacation 302n.
oscillation 317n.
frequent
many 104adj.
go on 146vb.
be present 189vb.
dwell 192vb.
usual 610adj.
be wont 610vb.
frequentation
social round 882n.
frequenter
habitué 610n.
fresco
picture 553n.
fresh
unimitative 21adj.
new 126adj.
matinal 128adj.
early 135adj.
airy 340adj.
humid 341adj.
windy 352adj.
cold 380adj.
remembered 505adj.
unhabituated 611adj.
not bad 644adj.
clean 648adj.
healthy 650adj.
salubrious 652adj.
preserved 666adj.
impertinent 878adj.
tipsy 949adj.
fresh air
salubrity 652n.
fresh-air fiend
sanatarian 652n.
fresh blood
aftercomer 67n.
freshen
be strong 162vb.
invigorate 174vb.
aerify 340vb.
blow 352vb.
refrigerate 382vb.
purify 648vb.
sanitate 652vb.
make better 654vb.
revive 656vb.
refresh 685vb.
decorate 844vb.
freshened up
modernized 126n.
freshet
stream 350n.
freshman
college student 538n.
freshness
non-imitation 21n.
(*see* fresh)
fresh outbreak
relapse 657n.

fresh spurt
revival 656n.
fresh start
start 68n.
fresh-water sailor
bungler 697n.
fret
rend 46vb.
rub 333vb.
give pain 377vb.
cry 408vb.
play music 413vb.
harp 414n.
variegate 437vb.
restlessness 678n.
disobey 738vb.
excitable state 822n
worry 825n.
torment 827vb.
cause discontent 829vb.
decorate 844vb.
enrage 891vb.
fretful
crying 408adj.
capricious 604adj.
active 678adj.
irascible 892adj.
fretting
ornamental art 844n.
fretwork
network 222n.
ornamental art 844n.
Freudianism
psychology 447n.
friable
flimsy 163adj.
brittle 330adj.
powdery 332adj.
friar
monk 986n.
pastor 986n.
friarhood
monasticism 985n.
friary
monastery 986n.
fribble
neglect 458vb.
nonentity 639n.
trifle 639n.
be inactive 679vb.
amuse oneself 837vb.
fop 848n.
fricassee
dish 301n.
frication
friction 333n.
fricative
rubbing 333adj.
speech sound 398n.
spoken letter 558n.
vocal 577adj.
friction
energy 160n.
counteraction 182n.
collision 279n.
pulverulence 332n.
friction 333n.
stridor 407n.
difficulty 700n.
opposition 704n.
dissension 709n.
painfulness 827n.
frictionless
silent 399adj.
easy, wieldly 701adj.
cooperating 706adj.
pleasurable 826adj.
Friday
fast 946n.
fridge
provisions 301n.
refrigerator 384n.
storage 632n.
preserver 666n.
friend
auxiliary 707n.
colleague 707n.
friend 880n.
loved one 887n.
kind person 897n.
benefactor 903n.
Protestant 976n.
sectarist 978n.
friend at court
latency 523n.
patron 707n.
friendless
alone 88adj.
defenseless 161adj.
friendless 883adj.
friendliness
irenics 719n.
friendliness 880n.
sociability 882n.
courteous act 884n.
benevolence 897n.
friendly
aiding 703adj.
concordant 710adj.
friendly 880adj.
sociable 882adj.
amiable 884adj.
friend of all the world
xenophile 880n.
Friends
sect 978n.
friendship
relation 9n.
peace 717n.
friendship 880n.
sociality 882n.
love 887n.
benevolence 897n.
frieze
summit 213n.
textile 222n.
trimming 844n.
frigate
sailing-ship 275n.
warship 722n.
fright
eyesore 842n.
fear 854n.
frighten
dissuade 613vb.
raise the alarm 665vb.
hinder 702vb.
deject 834vb.
frighten 854vb.
frightful
prodigious 32adj.
ugly 842adj.
frightfulness
terror tactics 712n.
frigid
cold 380adj.
feeble 572adj.
impassive 820adj.
inexcitable 823adj.
pure 950adj.
frigidaire
provisions 301n.
refrigerator 384n.
frigidarium
refrigerator 384n.
frigidity
coldness 380n.
feebleness 572n.
moral insensibility 820n.
purity 950n.
frigorific
cooled 382adj.
frill
adjunct 40n.
edging 234n.
trimming 844n.
frillies
underwear 228n.
frills
ornament 574n.
frills and furbelows
finery 844n.
fringe
adjunct 40n.
extremity 69n.
concomitant 89n.
contiguity 202n.
edging 234n.
hair 259n.
hair-dressing 843n.
trimming 844n.
frippery
clothing 228n.
bauble 639n.
finery 844n.
bad taste 847n.
ostentation 875n.
frisk
move fast 277vb.
leap 312vb.

search 459vb.
be cheerful 833vb.
rejoice 835vb.
amuse oneself 837vb.
frisky
leaping 312adj.
active 678adj.
gay 833adj.
frisson
agitation 318n.
frith
gulf 345n.
wood 366n.
fritinancy
ululation 409n.
fritter away
bate 37vb.
waste 634vb.
be prodigal 815vb.
fritters
pudding 301n.
frivolity
folly 499n.
unimportance 639n.
merriment 833n.
rashness 857n.
frivolous
light-minded 456adj.
ill-reasoned 477adj.
capricious 604adj.
(*see* frivolity)
frizz
crinkle 251vb.
fold 261vb.
frizzing
hair-dressing 843n.
frizzle
make curved 248vb.
fold 261vb.
be hot 379vb.
frizzy
undulatory 251adj.
hairy 259adj.
frock
dress 228n.
ecclesiasticize 985vb.
canonicals 989n.
frock coat
tunic 228n.
Froebelism
education 534n.
frog
fastening 47n.
jumper 312n.
frog 365n.
trimming 844n.
frogman
diver 313n.
frogmarch
impel 279vb.
frolic
leap 312n.
enjoyment 824n.
be cheerful 833vb.
rejoice 835vb.
amuse oneself 837vb.
from A to Z
including 78adv.
from beginning to end
throughout 54adv.
from now on
henceforth 124adv.
from scratch
at zero 103adv.
frondescence
vegetability 366n.
foliage 366n.
Frondeur
revolter 738n.
front
precedence 64n.
beginning 68n.
impend 155vb.
nearness 200n.
exteriority 223n.
apron 228n.
edge 234n.
front 237n.
orientate 281vb.
duplicity 541n.
resistance 715n.
battle 718n.
battleground 724n.
insolence 878n.
frontage
face 237n.
frontier
entrance 68n.
extremity 69n.
farness 199n.
contiguity 202n.
edge 234n.
limit 236n.
frontiersman
dweller 191n.
front, in
ahead 283adv.
in front 237adv.
fronting
opposite 240adj.
frontispiece
prelude 66n.
front, face 237n.
frontlet
vestments 989n.
front-page
notable 638adj.
front-rank
supreme 34adj.
front window
exhibit 522n.
frosh
college student 538n.
frost
powder 332n.
wintriness 380n.
refrigerate 382vb.
opacity 423n.
whiten 427vb.
blight 659n.
failure 728n.
frostbite
coldness 380n.
refrigerate 382vb.
frosting
pulverulence 332n.
frosty
cold 380adj.
white 427adj.
unsociable 883adj.
froth
stimulation 174n.
excrement 302n.
effervesce 318vb.
moisture 341n.
bubble 355n., vb.
chatter 581n.
bauble 639n.
dirt 649n.
be excitable 822vb.
frothblower
drunkard 949n.
frothy
light 323adj.
bubbly 355adj.
diffuse 570adj.
ornate 574adj.
trivial 639adj.
frou-frou
faintness 401n.
sibilation 406n.
frounce
fold 261n., vb.
frown
distort 246vb.
fold 261n.
gesture 547n.
hindrance 702n.
dicontent 829n.
rudeness 885n.
anger 891n.
be sullen 893vb.
frown down
humiliate 872vb.
frowning
adverse 731adj.
serious 834adj.
frown on
prohibit 757vb.
deject 834vb.
(*see* disapprove)
frowsty
fetid 397adj.
frowzy
fetid 397adj.
frozen
cohesive 48adj.
still 266adj.
dense 324adj.
hard 326adj.
insensible 375adj.
a-cold 380adj.

cooled 382adj.
preserved 666adj.
fearing 854adj.
frozen assets
estate 777n.
debt 803n.
fructification
propagation 164n.
productiveness 171n.
fructose
food content 301n.
sweet 392n.
frugal
cautious 858adj.
fasting 946adj.
frugality
preservation 666n.
economy 814n.
temperance 942n.
asceticism 945n.
frugivorous
feeding 301adj.
fruit
growth 157n.
product 164n.
fruit 301n.
fruitarian
abstainer 942n.
ascetic 945n.
fruitful
increasing 36adj.
prolific 171adj.
successful 727adj.
acquiring 771adj.
fruit-growing
agriculture 370n.
fruition
propagation 164n.
use 673n.
enjoyment 824n.
fruit juice
soft drink 301n.
fruitless
unproductive 172adj.
wasted 634adj.
profitless 641adj.
fruity
fragrant 396adj.
fetid 397adj.
frump
bad taste 847n.
frustrating
discontenting 829adj.
frustration
psychopathy 503n.
disappointment 509n.
hindrance 702n.
failure 728n.
frustum, frustulum
piece, part 53n.
fry
youngling 132n.
cook 301vb.
be hot 379vb.
heat 381vb.
frying-pan
caldron 194n.
heater 383n.
frying-pan into the fire, out of the
in adversity 731adv.
aggravatedly 832adv.
fubsy
fleshy 195adj.
fuddle
distract 456vb.
inebriate 949vb.
fuddled
foolish 499adj.
tipsy 949adj.
fudge
sweet 392n.
silly talk 515n.
trifle 639n.
Fuehrer
leader 690n.
master 741n.
autocrat 741n.
fuel
propellant 287n.
oil 357n.
kindle 381vb.
heater 383n.
fuel 385n.
fire 385vb.
materials 631n.
store 632vb.
provide 633vb.
fugacity
transientness 114n.
fugitive
disjunct 46adj.
transient 114adj.
wanderer 268n.
avoider 620n.
escaper 667n.
fugitive pieces
reading matter 589n.
anthology 592n.
fugleman
living model 23n.
leader 690n.
fugue
musical piece 412n.
oblivion 506n.
fulcrum
pivot 218n.
centrality 225n.
fulfill
do 676vb.
observe 768vb.
fulfilled
veracious 540adj.
fulfillment
completeness 54adj.
sufficiency 635n.
completion 725n.
observance 768n.
enjoyment 824n.
fulguration
storm 176n.
flash 417n.
luminary 420n.
fulgurite
explosive 723n.
fuliginous
opaque 423adj.
black 428adj.
full
whole 52adj.
plenitude 54n.
assembled 74adj.
multitudinous 104adj.
fleshy 195adj.
broad 205adj.
loud 400adj.
veracious 540adj.
descriptive 590adj.
filled 635adj.
clean 648vb.
completed 725adj.
drunk 949adj.
full bat
speeding 277n.
full blast
loudness 400n.
full-blooded
vigorous 174adj.
full-blown
grown up 134adj.
expanded 197adj.
full-bodied
tasty 386adj.
odorous 394adj.
full career
speeding 277n.
full chorus
agreement 24n.
loudness 400n.
full circle
revolution 149n.
circuition 314n.
rotation 315n.
full-colored
florid 425adj.
full coverage
inclusion 78n.
full cry, in
loudly 400adv.
pursuing 619adj.
full dress
formal dress 228n.
uniform 228n.
formality 875n.
fuller
cleaner 648n.
full-fed
sensual 944adj.
gluttonous 947adj.
full force, in
strong 162adj.
full-grown

grown up 134adj.
expanded 197adj.
full heart
warm feeling 818n.
full house
plenitude 54n.
crowd 74n.
playgoer 594n.
full-length
comprehensive 52adj.
long 203adj.
full life
enjoyment 824n.
intemperance 943n.
sensualism 944n.
full measure
plenitude 54n.
sufficiency 635n.
full-mouthed
ululant 409adj.
fullness
greatness 32n.
whole 52n.
plenitude 54n.
breadth 205n.
plenty 635n.
completion 725n.
fullness of time, in the
in time 111adv.
prospectively 124adv.
opportunely 137adv.
full of beans
healthy 650adj.
active 678adj.
full play
facility 701n.
scope 744n.
full pressure
energy 160n.
exertion 682n.
full-size
great 32adj.
full speed
speeding 277n.
full stop
stop 145n.
quiescence 266n.
punctuation 547n.
full-tilt
actively 678adv.
full, to the
enough 635adv.
fully
completely 54adv.
fulminate
be violent 176vb.
propel 287vb.
be loud 400vb.
emphasize 532adj.
be angry 891vb.
curse 899vb.
threaten 900vb.
dispraise 924vb.
fulsome
fetid 397adj.
bad 645adj.
unpleasant 827adj.
disliked 861adj.
flattering 925adj.
impure 951adj.
fulvous
yellow 433adj.
fumarole
chimney 263n.
furnace 383n.
fumble
touch 378vb.
be tentative 461vb.
be uncertain 474vb.
be clumsy 695vb.
fumbler
bungler 697n.
fume
be violent 176vb.
emit 300vb.
gas 336n.
vaporize 338vb.
be hot 379vb.
odor 394n.
hasten 680vb.
excitable state 822n.
be busy 678vb.
be excitable 822vb.
be angry 891vb.
fumé
semitransparent 424adj.
fumid
opaque 423adj.
fumigant
prophylactic 658n.
fumigation
vaporization 338n.
inodorousness 395n.
fragrance 396n.
cleaning 648n.
fumigator
fumigator 385n.
fun
enjoyment 824n.
pleasurableness 826n.
merriment 833n.
amusement 837n.
funambulism
skill 694n.
funambulist
proficient 696n.
function
relativeness 9n.
number 85n.
agency 173n.
function 622vb.
utility 640n.
do 676vb.
formality 875n.
celebration 876n.
jurisdiction 955n.
functional
correlative 12adj.
instrumental 628adj.
useful 640adj.
Functionalism
school of painting 553n.
functionary
official 690n.
officer 741n.
consignee 754n.
functionless
useless 641adj.
functus officio
extinct 2adj.
abrogated 752adj.
fund
store 632n., vb.
funds 797n.
fundament
base 214n.
rear, buttocks 238n.
fundamental
intrinsic 5adj.
simple 44adj.
beginning 68adj.
fundamental 156adj.
undermost 214adj.
supporting 218adj.
important 638adj.
fundamentalism
theology 973n.
scripture 975n.
orthodoxism 976n.
pietism 979n.
fundamentally
intrinsically 5adv.
positively 32adv.
fundamentals
reality 1n.
base 214n.
chief thing 638n.
funds, in
moneyed 800adj.
fundus
base 214n.
funeral
funeral 364n.
worry 825n.
funeral oration
valediction 296n.
obsequies 364n.
oration 579n.
lament 836n.
funereal
funereal 364adj.
dark 418adj.
black 428adj.
cheerless 834adj.
fun-fair
pleasure-ground 837n.
fungicide
poison 659n.
fungiform
rotund 252adj.

vegetal 366adj.
fungoid
vegetal 366adj.
fungology
botany 368n.
fungus
plant 366n.
fetor 397n.
dirt 649n.
blight 659n.
funicle
filament 208n.
funicular
fibrous 208adj.
train 274n.
railroad 624n.
funk
smoke 388vb.
stink 397vb.
fear 854n.
coward 856n.
funk-hole
hiding-place 527n.
refuge 662n.
funnel
cylinder 252n.
cavity 255n.
tunnel, tube 263n.
chimney 263n.
conduit 351n.
air-pipe 353n.
funny
unusual 84adj.
rowboat 275n.
crazed 503adj.
witty 839adj.
funny 849adj.
funnybone
limb 53n.
fur
skin 226n.
covering 226n.
neckwear 228n.
hair 259n.
warm clothes 381n.
heraldry 547n.
dirt 649n.
trimming 844n.
furacious
thieving 788adj.
furbelow
edging 234n.
furbish
decorate 844vb.
(*see* refurbish)
furcate
crossed 222adj.
angular 247adj.
furfur
dirt 649n.
furfuraceous
powdery 332adj.
Furies
Fury 891n.
chthonic god 967n.
furious
destructive 165adj.
furious 176adj.
frenzied 503adj.
harmful 645adj.
hasty 680adj.
fervent 818adj.
excited 821adj.
excitable 822adj.
rash 857adj.
angry 891adj.
furiously
extremely 32adv.
furl
fold 261vb.
elevate 310vb.
rotate 315vb.
furlough
absence 190n.
leisure 681n.
repose 683n.
permit 756n.
furnace
fire 379n.
furnace 383n.
workshop 687n.
furnish
find means 629vb.
provide 633vb.
make ready 669vb.
give 781vb.
furnishing(s)
adjunct 40n.
contents 193n.
equipment 630n.
ornamental art 844n.
furnishment
fitting out 669n.
furniture
equipment 630n.
property 776n.
furor
frenzy 503n.
excitation 821n.
(*see* furore)
furore
violence 176n.
commotion 318n.
fashion 848n.
furrier
stripper 229n.
furrow
gap 201n.
roughness 259n.
fold 261vb.
furrow 262n.
furrowing
concavity 255n.
furry
hairy 259adj.
further
in addition 38adv.
beyond 199adv.
in front 237adv.
promote 285vb.
aid 703vb.
furtherance
progression 285n.
improvement 654n.
aid 703n.
furthermost
distant 199adj.
further reflection
amendment 654n.
furtive
stealthy 525adj.
furuncle
swelling 253n.
fury
violence 176n.
violent creature 176n.
excitation 821n.
excitable state 822n.
anger, Fury 891n.
shrew 892n.
hell-hag 904n.
demon 970n.
furze
plant 366n.
fuscous
brown 430adj.
fuse
heat 381vb.
lighter 385n.
safeguard 662n.
hitch 702n.
ammunition 723n.
(*see* fusion)
fusee
lighter 385n.
fuselage
frame 218n.
fusiform
angulated 247adj.
tapering 256adj.
fusil
fire-arm 723n.
fusilier
soldiery 722n.
fusillade
slaughter 362n.
bombardment 712n.
execute 963vb.
fusion
mixture 43n.
junction 45n.
combination 50n.
liquefaction 337n.
association 706n.
fuss
commotion 318n.
exaggeration 546n.
activity 678n.
haste 680n.
excitation 821n.
excitable state 822n.
be fastidious 862vb.

ostentation 875n.
be angry 891vb.
fussiness
fastidiousness 862n.
fusspot
meddler 678n.
perfectionist 861n.
fussy
narrow-minded 481adj.
active 678adj.
authoritarian 735adj.
fastidious 862adj.
fust
be old 127vb.
deteriorate 655vb.
fustian
textile 222n.
absurdity 497n.
empty talk 515n.
magniloquence 574n.
fustigate
flog 963vb.
fusty
antiquated 127adj.
fetid 397adj.
dirty 649adj.
futhark
letter 558n.
futile
wasted 634adj.
unskillful 695adj.
futilitarian
underestimation 483n.
futility
ineffectuality 161n.
foolery 497n.
absurdity 497n.
inutility 641n.
despisedness 922n.
future
unborn 2adj.
subsequent 120adj.
futurity 124n.
impending 155adj.
unknown 491adj.
expected 507adj.
future, in
henceforth 124adv.
future life
destiny 155n.
futures
gambling 618n.
future state
future state 124n.
Futurism
school of painting 553n.
futurist
modernist 126n.
artist 556n.
futuristic
modern 126adj.
futurity
time 108n.
posteriority 120n.
different time 122n.
futurity 124n.
fuzzle
inebriate 949vb.
fuzzy
amorphous 244adj.
hairy 259adj.
shadowy 419adj.
ill-seen 444adj.
fylfot
heraldry 547n.
talisman 983n.

G

gab
loquacity 581n.
boast 877n., vb.
gabber
speaker 579n.
chatterer 581n.
gabble
ululate 409vb.
empty talk 515n.
speak 579vb.
stammer 580vb.
chatter 581vb.
gabelle
tax 809n
gaberdine
tunic 228n.
gaberlunzie
low fellow 869n.
gabert
sailing-ship 275n.
gabion
fortification 713n.
gable
vertex 213n.
roof 226n.
laterality 239n.
gable-end
extremity 69n.
gaby
ninny 501n.
gad
wander 267vb.
gadfly
fly 365n.
excitant 821n.
gadget
object 319n.
contrivance 623n.
instrument 628n.
tool 630n.
gaff
sharp point 256n.
spear 723n.
gaffe
mistake 495n.
gaffer
old man 133n.
male 372n.
fool 501n.
countryman 869n.
gaffle
sharp point 256n.
gag
stopper 264n.
silence 399vb.
make mute 578vb.
act 594vb.
obstacle 702n.
restrain 747vb.
fetter 748n.
witticism 839n.
gaga
foolish 499adj.
gage
defiance 711n.
security 767n.
gaggle
group 74n.
ululate 409vb.
gagman
dramatist 594n.
auxiliary 707n.
humorist 839n.
gaiety
merriment 833n.
sociability 882n.
gaily
inadvertently 456adv.
hopefully 852adv.
rashly 857adv.
gain
increment 36n.
be early 135vb.
growth 157n.
product 164n.
progression 284n.
arrive 295vb.
benefit 615n.
utility 640n.
gain 771n., vb.
booty 790n.
be rewarded 962vb.
gain a footing
prevail 178vb.
gainful
profitable 640adj.
gainful 771adj.
rewarding 962adj.
gaingiving
doubt 486n.
gaining
non-uniform 17adj.
anachronistic 118adj.
gaining time
delay 136n.
gain on
outstrip 277vb.
approach 289vb.
outdo 306vb.
gain over
induce 612vb.

gains
wealth 800n.
gainsay
negate 533vb.
gain time
spin out 113vb.
be early 135vb.
put off 136vb.
gain upon one
be wont 610vb.
gait
gait 265n.
way 624n.
gaiters
legwear 228n.
badge of rule 743n.
canonicals 989n.
gala
festivity 837n.
pageant 875n.
galactic
cosmic 321adj.
galactose
food content 301n.
sweet 392n.
Galahad
brave person 855n.
gentleman 929n.
virgin 950n.
galanty show
spectacle 445n.
gala performance
pageant 875n.
galaxy
group 74n.
star 321n.
island 349n.
glow 417n.
luminary 420n.
gale
gale 352n.
excitable state 822n.
gale force
storm 176n.
galenic
medical 658adj.
galenical
medicine 658n.
gali-gali man
conjuror 545n.
galilee
church exterior 990n.
galimatias
unmeaningness 515n.
galingale
condiment 389n.
gall
swelling 253n.
rub 333vb.
give pain 377vb.
sourness 393n.
bane 659n.
torment 827vb.
irascibility 892n.
malevolence 898n.
gall and wormwood
painfulness 827n.
gallant
courageous 855adj.
showy 875adj.
courteous 884adj.
lover 887n.
libertine 952n.
gallantry
(*see* gallant)
galleass
galley 275n.
warship 722n.
galleon
ship 275n.
merchant ship 275n.
warship 722n.
gallery
tunnel 263n.
doorway 263n.
listener 415n.
onlookers 441n.
exhibit 522n.
theater 594n.
playgoer 594n.
collection 632n.
church interior 990n.
galley
chamber 194n.
galley, rowboat 275n.
heater 383n.
galley proof
letterpress 587n.
galleys
penalty 963n.
galley-slave
mariner 270n.
busy person 678n.
prisoner 750n.
galliard
musical piece 412n.
Gallicans
church party 978n.
gallicism
dialect 560n.
galligaskins
breeches 228n.
legwear 228n.
gallimaufry
medley 43n.
gallinipper
fly 365n.
galliot
galley 275n.
merchant ship 275n.
gallipot
vessel 194n.
gallivant
wander 267vb.
court 889vb.
gallivat
sailing-ship 275n.
gallon
metrology 465n.
gallons
great quantity 32n.
galloon
trimming 844n.
gallop
be transient 114vb.
gait 265n.
ride 267vb.
move fast 277vb.
gallowglass
soldier 722n.
gallows
hanger 217n.
means of execution 964n.
gallowsbird
offender 904n.
gall-stone
indigestion 651n.
Gallup poll
statistics 86n.
inquiry 459n.
empiricism 461n.
vote 605n.
galoot
ninny 501n.
bungler 697n.
galop
dance 837n.
galore
great quantity 32n.
many 104adj.
plenty 635n.
galosh
footwear 228n.
galvanism
electricity 160n.
excitation 821n.
gambado
legwear 228n.
footwear 228n.
leap 312n.
gambison
tunic 228n.
gambit
debut 68n.
essay 671n.
tactics 688n.
gamble
chance 159vb.
be tentative 461vb.
uncertainty 474n.
conjecture 512n.
gamble 618vb.
face danger 661vb.
speculate 791vb.
be rash 857vb.
gamble away
be prodigal 815vb.
gambler
experimenter 461n.
diviner 511n.
theorist 512n.

G H

gambler 618n.
desperado 857n.
gambling game
gambling game 837n.
gambling hell
gaming-house 618n.
place of amusement 837n.
gamboge
yellow pigment 433n.
gambol
leap 312n., vb.
enjoyment 824n.
amuse oneself 837vb.
game
crippled 163adj.
meat 301n.
animal 365n.
savoriness 390n.
trickery 542n.
resolute 599adj.
stamina 600n.
persevering 601adj.
objective 617n.
gamble 618vb.
chase 619n.
stratagem 698n.
contest 716n.
amusement 837n.
laughing-stock 851n.
courageous 855adj.
game at which two can play
retaliation 714n.
gamecock
contender 716n.
combatant 722n.
brave person 855n.
gamekeeper
animal husbandry 369n.
keeper 749n.
game of, make
befool 542vb.
game reserve
pleasance 192n.
wood 366n.
games
exercise 682n.
contest 716n.
sport 837n.
gamesman
player 837n.
gamesmanship
tactics 688n.
cunning 698n.
gamesome
gay 833adj.
lively 819adj.
amused 837adj.
gamester
experimenter 461n.
gambler 618n.
player 837n.
gametophyte
plant 366n.
gamin
low fellow 869n.
gammadion
talisman 983n.
gamma ray
radiation 417n.
gammer
old woman 133n.
lady 373n.
gammon
meat 301n.
absurdity 497n.
silly talk 515n.
falsehood 541n.
deceive 542vb.
gamomania
mania 502n.
type of marriage 894n.
gamp
shade 226n.
gamut
series 71n.
musical note 410n.
gamy
pungent 388adj.
fetid 397adj.
gander
waterfowl 365n.
male animal 372n.
gang
band 74n.
move 265vb.
personnel 686n.
party 708n.
ganger
worker 686n.
gangling
unwieldy 195adj.
clumsy 695adj.
gangplank
bridge 624n.
gangrene
decay 51n.
be unclean 649vb.
ulcer 651n.
deteriorate 654vb.
gang rule
lawlessness 954n.
gangster
murderer 362n.
robber 789n.
offender 904n.
gang up
congregate 74vb.
cooperate 706vb.
gang up with
accompany 89vb.
gangway
doorway 263n.
access, bridge 624n.
gannet
bird of prey 365n.
gantry
stand 218n.
Ganymede
satellite 321n.
a beauty 841n.
gap
disjunction 46n.
incompleteness 55n.
discontinuity 72n.
gap 201n.
concavity 255n.
opening 263n.
defect 647n.
gape
space 201vb.
be deep 211vb.
open 263vb.
gaze 438vb.
watch 441vb.
be curious 453vb.
wonder 864vb.
gape for
be hungry 859vb.
gaper
spectator 441n.
ninny 501n.
gaping
expanded 197adj.
gappy
spaced 201adj.
garage
small house 192n.
stable 192n.
chamber 194n.
cover 226vb.
storage 632n.
safeguard 660vb.
garb
dressing 228n.
dress 228vb.
heraldry 547n.
garbage
dirt 649n.
garbage can
vessel 194n.
garble
subtract 39vb.
exclude 57vb.
misteach 495vb.
misinterpret 521vb.
be false 541vb.
garden
enclosure 235n.
garden 370n.
gardener
gardener 370n.
domestic 742n.
gardening
agriculture 370n.
ornamental art 844n.
garden-party
amusement 837n.
gardens

pleasance 192n.
pleasure-ground 837n.
gargantuan
huge 195adj.
gargle
moisten 341vb.
cleanser 648n.
prophylactic 658n.
gargoyle
outlet 298n.
conduit 351n.
drain 351n.
eyesore 842n.
ornamental art 844n.
garish
luminous 417adj.
florid 425adj.
graceless 842adj.
ornamental 844adj.
vulgar 847adj.
showy 875adj.
garland
loop 250n.
badge 547n.
trophy 729n.
decorate 844vb.
honors 866n.
celebrate 876vb.
pay respects 884vb.
garlic
condiment 389n.
fetor 397n.
vegetable 301n.
garment
dress 228n., vb.
garner
store 632vb.
garnet
redness 431n.
gem 844n.
garnish
adjunct 40n.
cook 301vb.
pay 804n.
expenditure 806n.
ornamentation 844n.
garniture
dressing 228n.
garret
attic 194n.
vertex 213n.
garrison
resident 191n.
safeguard 660vb.
defender 713n.
armed force 722n.
keeper 749n.
garron
pony 273n.
garrote
kill 362vb.
execute 963vb.
means of execution 964n.
garroter
murderer 362n.
punisher 963n.
garrulous
disclosing 526adj.
loquacious 581adj.
garter
fastening 47n.
compressor 198n.
hanger 217n.
supporter 218n.
underwear 228n.
badge 547n.
decoration 729n.
badge of rank 743n.
honors 866n.
garth
enclosure 235n.
gas
propellant 287n.
lifter 310n.
levity 323n.
rarity 325n.
fluid 335n.
gas 336n.
oil 357n.
murder 362vb.
anesthetic 375n.
heater 383n.
fuel 385n.
empty talk 515n.
be loquacious 581vb.
weapon 723n.
boast 877n.
execute 963vb.
gasalier
pendant 217n.
gas 336n.
lamp 420n.
gas-bag
bladder 194n.
chatterer 581n.
gas-chamber
slaughter-house 362n.
prison camp 748n.
means of execution 964n.
gas-coke
coal 385n.
gasconism
boasting 877n.
gaseous
light 323adj.
gaseous 336adj.
gas-flare
torch 420n.
gash
cut 46vb.
gap 201n.
notch 260n.
wound 655n.
gas-holder
gas 336n.
storage 632n.
gasify
lighten 323vb.
rarefy 325vb.
gasify 336vb.
vaporize 338vb.
gasket
lining 227n.
gaskins
legwear 228n.
gas mantle
lamp 420n.
gas-mask
covering 226n.
safeguard 662n.
preserver 666n.
armor 713n.
gasoline
propellant 287n.
oil 357n.
fuel 385n.
gasometer
gas 336n.
storage 632n.
gasp
breathe 352vb.
rasp 407vb.
cry 408n., vb.
voice 577n.
be fatigued 684vb.
wonder 864vb.
gasper
tobacco 388n.
gasp for
desire 859vb.
gas-pipe
air-pipe 353n.
gas-proof
sealed off 264adj.
invulnerable 660adj.
gas, put under
render insensible 375vb.
gas-ring
furnace 383n.
gasser
chatterer 581n.
gassy
gaseous 336adj.
vaporific 338adj.
windy 352adj.
loquacious 581adj.
gastral
cellular 194adj.
gastralgia
indigestion 651n.
gastriloquism
voice 577n.
gastritis
indigestion 651n.
gastro-enteritis
dysentery 651n.
gastronomy
gastronomy 301n.

gluttony 947n.
gasworks
gas 336n.
workshop 687n.
gat
gap 201n.
opening 263n.
pistol 723n.
gate
entrance 68n.
barrier 235n.
doorway 263n.
incomer 297n.
onlookers 441n.
fort 713n.
imprison 747vb.
receipt 807n.
gateau
pastry 301n.
gate-crash
intrude 297vb.
be sociable 882vb.
gate-crasher
intruder 59n.
gate-keeper
janitor 264n.
gate-money
receipt 807n.
gate-post
doorway 263n.
gateway
entrance 68n.
gather
join 45vb.
congregate 74vb.
expand 197vb.
fold 261vb.
meet 295vb.
cultivate 370vb.
be informed 524vb.
store 632vb.
acquire 771vb.
take 786vb.
gatherer
accumulator 74n.
gathering
assembly 74n.
conference 584n.
bookbinding 589n.
ulcer 651n.
toxic 653adj.
(*see* gather)
gathering cloud(s)
omen 511n.
danger 661n.
warning 664n.
adversity 731n.
gather together
converge 293vb.
gather way
navigate 269vb.
gauche
sinistral 242adj.
ignorant 491adj.
foolish 499adj.
inelegant 576adj.
clumsy 695adj.
ill-bred 847adj.
gaucherie
ignorance 491n.
gaucho
rider 268n.
herdsman 369n.
gaudery
finery 844n.
airs 873n.
gaudy
florid 425adj.
graceless 842adj.
ornamented 844adj.
vulgar 847adj.
showy 875adj.
gauge
breadth 205n.
testing agent 461n.
gauge 465n., vb.
gauleiter
tyrant 735n.
autocrat 741n.
officer 741n.
ruffian 904n.
gaumless
foolish 499adj.
gaunt
lean 206adj.
deformed 246adj.
gauntlet
glove 228n.
defiance 711n.
armor 713n.
gauze
transparency 422n.
semitransparency 424n.
gauzy
insubstantial 4adj.
gavel
badge of rule 743n.
gavelkind
joint possession 775n.
gavial
reptile 365n.
gavotte
musical piece 412n.
dance 837n.
gawk
gaze 438vb.
watch 441vb.
be curious 453vb.
ninny 501n.
wonder 864vb.
gawky
foolish 499adj.
clumsy 695adj.
gay
luminescent 420adj.
florid 425adj.
pleased, happy 824adj.
gay 833adj.
amusing 837adj.
showy 875adj.
drunk 949adj.
unchaste 951adj.
gaze
look, gaze 438vb.
watch 441vb.
be curious 453vb.
be attentive 455vb.
gazebo
view 438n.
arbor 194n.
gazelle
deer 365n.
gazette
advertisement 528n.
journal 528n.
proclaim 528vb.
record 548n.
gazetteer
directory 87n.
guide-book 524n.
reference book 589n.
gazing-stock
laughing-stock 851n.
prodigy 864n.
gear
clothing 228n.
equipment 630n.
geared
correlative 12adj.
gear, out of
orderless 61adj.
gears
machine 630n.
gear to, gear with
relate 9vb.
accord 24vb.
join 45vb.
gecko
reptile 365n.
geest
soil 344n.
geezer
laughing-stock 851n.
gegenschein
heavens 321n.
glow 417n.
luminary 420n.
Gehenna
hell 972n.
Geiger counter
meter 465n.
geisha girl
entertainer 594n.
gel
thicken 354vb.
gelatin
thickening 354n.
gelatination
condensation 324n.
geld

subtract 39vb.
unman 161vb.
sterilize 172vb.
gelding
eunuch 161n.
horse 273n.
male animal 372n.
gelefaction
thickening 354n.
gelidity
coldness 380n.
gelignite
explosive 723n.
gem
exceller 644n.
gem 844n.
gematria
occultism 984n.
gem-cutting
engraving 555n.
ornamental art 844n.
gemination
duplication 91n.
Gemini
duality 90n.
zodiac 321n.
gemot
assembly 74n.
gemütlich
inexcitable 823adj.
gen
information 524n.
gendarme
soldier 722n.
police 955n.
gender
classification 77n.
grammar 564n.
gene
heredity 5n.
genealogy
series 71n.
genealogy 169n.
general
broad 205adj.
national 371adj.
usual 610adj.
army officer 741n.
commonality 869n.
(*see* generality)
general council
synod 985n.
generalissimo
army officer 741n.
generality
average 30n.
whole 52n.
inclusion 78n.
generality 79n.
conformity 83n.
indiscrimination 464n.
inexactness 495n.
generalization
reasoning 475n.
generalize
generalize 79vb.
(*see* generality)
general practitioner
doctor 658n.
general principle
premise 475n.
generalship
tactics 688n.
skill 694n.
art of war 718n.
generate
make fruitful 171adj.
vitalize 360vb.
generation
race 11n.
coition 45n.
causation 156n.
propagation 164n.
generationism
heredity 5n.
generations
diuturnity 113n.
generations of man
mankind 371n.
generator
causal means 156n.
electricity 160n.
producer 167n.
generic
generic 77adj.
general 79adj.
generification
classification 77n.
generosity
(*see* generous)
generous
great 32adj.
many 104adj.
tasty 386adj.
plenteous 635adj.
giving 781adj.
expending 806adj.
liberal 813adj.
noble 868adj.
courteous 884adj.
benevolent 897adj.
approving 923adj.
disinterested 931adj.
virtuous 933adj.
rewarding 962adj.
genesiology
propagation 164n.
genesis
origin 68n.
source 156n.
propagation 164n.
genet
saddle-horse 273n.
genethliacs
divination 511n.
genetic
genetic 5adj.
productive 164adj.
genetics
biology 358n.
Geneva gown
canonicals 989n.
genial
productive 164adj.
pleasant 376adj.
warm 379adj.
willing 597adj.
pleasurable 826adj.
cheerful 833adj.
benevolent 897adj.
genial climate
salubrity 652n.
geniculated
angular 247adj.
genie
demon 970n.
genital
productive 164adj.
genitalia
genitalia 164n.
genius
identity 13n.
analogue 18n.
intellect, spirit 447n.
intellectual 492n.
intelligence 498n.
sage 500n.
exceller 644n.
aptitude 694n.
proficient 696n.
prodigy 864n.
mythic god 966n.
lesser god 967n.
fairy 970n.
genocide
slaughter 362n.
cruel act 898n.
ruffian 904n.
capital punishment 963n.
genotype
breed 77n.
genre
sort 77n.
art style 553n.
genro
council 692n.
genteel
well-bred 848adj.
genteel 868adj.
genteelism
prudery 950n.
gentian violet
purple 434n.
gentile
ethnic 11adj.
religionist 973n.
heathen 974n.
impious person 980n.
profane 980adj.
gentility
race 11n.

etiquette 848n.
nobility 868n.
courtesy 884n.
gentle
moderate 177adj.
soft 327adj.
tamed 369adj.
muted 401adj.
lax 734adj.
lenient 736adj.
inexcitable 823adj.
noble 868adj.
amiable 884adj.
benevolent 897adj.
innocent 935adj.
gentlefolk
aristocracy 868n.
gentleman
male 372n.
person of repute 866n.
aristocrat 868n.
gentleman 929n.
good man 937n.
gentlemanlike
well-bred 848adj.
noble 868adj.
gentlemanly
reputable 866adj.
noble 868adj.
honorable 929adj.
gentleman of fortune
gambler 618n.
gentleman's agreement
promise 764n.
compact 765n.
gentleman's gentleman
domestic 742n.
gentleness
pity 905n.
(*see* gentle)
gentle sex
womankind 373n.
gentlewoman
lady 373n.
aristocrat 868n.
gentry
aristocracy 868n.
genual
crural 267adj.
genuant
heraldic 547adj.
genuflect
stoop 311vb.
perform ritual 988vb.
genuflection
obeisance 311n.
submission 721n.
servility 879n.
respects 920n.
ritual act 988n.
genuine
orthodox 976adj.
(*see* genuineness)
genuine article
no imitation 21n.
genuineness
identity 13n.
no imitation 21n.
authenticity 494n.
genus
group 74n.
breed 77n.
geocentric
central 225adj.
celestial 321adj.
geodesy
geography 321n.
uranometry 321n.
measurement 465n.
geognosy
mineralogy 359n.
geographer
uranometry 321n.
geography
situation 186n.
geography 321n.
uranometry 321n.
land 344n.
geoid
sphere 252n.
world 321n.
geological period
era 110n.
geological times
antiquity 125n.
geologist
uranometry 321n.
geology
geography 321n.
uranometry 321n.
land 344n.
mineralogy 359n.
geomancy
theomancy 511n.
geometer
computer 86n.
geometry 465n.
surveyor 465n.
geometric
ornamental 844adj.
geometric progression
series 71n.
ratio 85n.
progression 285n.
geometric style
pattern 844n.
geometry
mathematics 86n.
geometry 465n.
curriculum 536n.
geophone
meter 465n.
geoponics
agriculture 370n.
georama
spectacle 445n.
George Cross
badge 547n.
decoration 729n.
georgette
textile 222n.
georgic
agrarian 370adj.
poem 593n.
geoscopy
mineralogy 359n.
geostatics
gravity 322n.
geranium
redness 431n.
geriatrics
gerontology 131n.
medical art 658n.
germ
origin 68n.
source 156n.
animalcule 196n.
infection 651n.
poison 659n.
german
akin 11adj.
germane
apt 24adj.
germ-carrier
carrier 273n.
infection 651n.
insolubrity 653n.
germen
source 156n.
germicide
prophylactic 658n.
poison 659n.
germinal
causal 156adj.
productive 164adj.
generative 171adj.
germinate
result 157vb.
be fruitful 171vb.
expand 197vb.
vegetate 366vb.
germ-laden
infectious 653adj.
toxic 653adj.
germ plasm
organism 358n.
gerontic
aged 131adj.
gerontocracy
government 733n.
gerontology
gerontology 131n.
medical art 658n.
gerontotherapy
gerontology 131n.
gerousia
seniority 131n.
gerrymander
deceive 542vb.
be cunning 698vb.
foul play 930n.

be dishonest 930vb.
gesso
art equipment 553n.
gestapo
police inquiry 459n.
gestation
propagation 164n.
maturation 669n.
gesticulate
be mute 578vb.
speak 579vb.
gesticulation
mimicry 20n.
(*see* gesture)
gesticulatory
indicating 547adj.
gesture
motion 265n.
mien 445n.
hint 524n.
gesture 547n.
gesticulate 547vb.
conduct 688n.
command 737n.
ritual act 988n.
gestureless
still 266adj.
get
be turned to 147vb.
generate 164vb.
understand 516vb.
acquire 771vb.
possess 773vb.
receive 782vb.
get about
be published 528vb.
get above oneself
be vain 873vb.
get across
communicate 524vb.
make enemies 881vb.
get a move on
accelerate 277vb.
get-at-able
accessible 289adj.
get-away
departure 296n.
escape 667n.
get back
recoup 31vb.
retrieve 656vb.
acquire 771vb.
get even with
retaliate 714vb.
punish 963vb.
get going
start out 296vb.
do 676vb.
get in one's hair
incommode 827vb.
get into
be mixed 43vb.
wear 228vb.
get in touch
be contiguous 202vb.
communicate 524vb.
get off
land 295vb.
escape 667vb.
court 889vb.
get on
accord 24vb.
grow 36vb.
progress 285vb.
get over
be restored 656vb.
get religion
become pious 979vb.
get rid of
destroy 165vb.
eject 300vb.
kill 362vb.
deliver 668vb.
not retain 779vb.
get round
befool 542vb.
get there
arrive 295vb.
get through
terminate 69vb.
communicate 524vb.
expend 806vb.
get-together
assembly 74n.
social gathering 882n.
get up
lift oneself 310vb.
study 536vb.
fake 541vb.
be restored 656vb.
get what is coming
be punished 963vb.
get wind of
smell 394vb.
discover 484vb.
get wrong
misinterpret 521vb.
gewgaw
bauble 639n.
finery 844n.
geyser
outflow 298n.
stream 350n.
heat 379n.
ghastly
colorless 426adj.
not nice 645adj.
distressing 827adj.
unsightly 842adj.
frightening 854adj.
ghat
entrance 68n.
gap 201n.
narrowness 206n.
passage 305n.
ghazel
verse form 593n.
ghazi
militarist 722n.
religionist 979n.
ghee
fat 357n.
ghetto
exclusion 57n.
retreat 192n.
lock-up 748n.
seclusion 883n.
ghost
insubstantial thing 4n.
substitute 150n.
immateriality 320n.
corpse 363n.
dimness 419n.
visual fallacy 440n.
appearance 445n.
fantasy 513n.
author 589n.
ghost 970n.
bewitch 983vb.
ghostly
insubstantial 4adj.
immaterial 320adj.
shadowy 419adj.
divine 965adj.
spooky 970adj.
ghosts
the dead 361n.
ghoul
monster 938n.
demon 970n.
ghoulish
inquisitive 453adj.
frightening 854adj.
cruel 898adj.
giant
enormous 32adj.
giant 195n.
tall creature 209n.
demon 970n.
giantism
size 195n.
giaour
heathen 974n.
gibber
be absurd 497vb.
goblinize 970vb.
gibberish
absurdity 497n.
unmeaningness 515n.
unintelligibility 517n.
slang 560n.
gibbet
hanger 217n.
killer 362n.
dispraise 924vb.
defame 926vb.
accuse 928vb.
execute 963vb.
means of execution

964n.
gibble-gabble
chatter 581n.
gibbosity
rotundity 252n.
convexity 253n.
gibe
satirize 851vb.
indignity 921n.
despise 922vb.
dispraise 924vb.
gibing
disrespectful 921adj.
giblets
meat 301n.
gibus
headgear 228n.
giddiness
weakness 163n.
folly 499n.
giddy
changeful 152adj.
light-minded 456adj.
crazed 503adj.
irresolute 601adj.
capricious 604adj.
rash 857adj.
tipsy 949adj.
gift
extra 40n.
ability 160n.
tendency 179n.
aptitude 694n.
offer 759n.
acquisition 771n.
transfer 780n.
gift 781n.
no charge 812n.
(*see* give)
gifted
gifted 694adj.
giftedness
intelligence 498n.
giftless
parsimonious 816adj.
gift of the gab
eloquence 579n.
loquacity 581n.
gig
carriage 274n.
boat 275n.
gigantic
enormous 32adj.
stalwart 162adj.
huge 195adj.
tall 209adj.
fairylike 970adj.
gigantism
greatness 32n.
hugeness 195n.
size 195n.
expansion 197n.
gigantomachy
fight 716n.
giggle
laughter 835n.
giglet
youngster 132n.
gigolo
toady 879n.
libertine 952n.
gigsman
boatman 270n.
Gilbertian
funny 849adj.
gild
coat 226vb.
color 425vb.
gild 433vb.
decorate 844vb.
gild the pill
deceive 542vb.
tempt 612vb.
please 826vb.
flatter 925vb.
gilgal
monument 548n.
gill
laterality 239n.
stream 350n.
metrology 465n.
gillie
animal husbandry 369n.
gilt
ornamentation 844n.
gilt-edged
valuable 644adj.
secured 767adj.
gimcrack
flimsy 163adj.
brittle 330adj.
trivial 639adj.
unsafe 661adj.
gimlet
perforator 263n.
gimmick
contrivance 623n.
skill 694n.
gimp
trimming 844n.
gin
liquor 301n.
trap 542n.
ginger
vigorousness 714n.
sweetmeat 301n.
tuber 301n.
pungency 388n.
condiment 389n.
orange 436n., adj.
excitant 821n.
ginger beer
soft drink 301n.
gingerbread
pastry 301n.
vulgar 847adj.
gingerly
moderately 177adv.
careful 457adj.
cautiously 858adv.
gingham
textile 222n.
ginglymus
joint 45n.
gink
laughing-stock 851n.
gin palace
tavern 192n.
gippo
fluid 335n.
gipsy
stream 350n.
(*see* gypsy)
giraffe
tall creature 209n.
girandole
lamp 420n.
girasol
gem 844n.
gird
tie 45vb.
dispraise 924vb.
detract 926vb.
girder
bond 47n.
beam 218n.
girdle
tie 45vb.
girdle 47n.
compressor 198n.
underwear 228n.
surround 230n.
outline 233n.
enclosure 235n.
loop 250n.
go round 250vb.
gird up one's loins
be strong 162vb.
prepare oneself 669vb.
girl
youngster 132n.
woman 373n.
loved one 887n.
girlhood
youth 130n.
girlish
young 130adj.
infantine 132adj.
immature 670adj.
girn
be discontented 829vb.
girth
greatness 32n.
girdle 47n.
size 195n.
belt 228n.
outline 233n.
gisarme

ax 723n.
gist
essential part 5n.
chief part 52n.
topic 452n.
meaning 514n.
chief thing 638n.
gittern
harp 414n.
givable
not retained 779adj.
give
oscillate 317vb.
soften 327vb.
elasticity 328n.
provide 633vb.
convey 780vb.
give 781vb.
expand 805vb.
be liberal 813vb.
reward 962vb.
(*see* gift)
give a hand
applaud 923vb.
give a handle
justify 927vb.
give and take
correlation 12n.
set off 31vb.
interchange 151n., vb.
answer 460n.
argument 475n.
retaliation 714n.
fight 716n., vb.
compromise 770n., vb.
give away
disclose 526vb.
give 781vb.
cheapen 812vb.
marry 894vb.
give back
restitute 787vb.
give birth
reproduce itself 164vb.
vitalize 360vb.
give ground
regress 286vb.
give grounds
justify 927vb.
give in
relinquish 621vb.
submit 721vb.
given
existing 1adj.
circumstantial 8adj.
prior 119adj.
supposed 512adj.
uncharged 812adj.
givenness
existence 1n.
given to
habituated 610adj.
give occasion
cause 156vb.
give off
emit 300vb.
give one joy
gratulate 886vb.
give one pause
dissuade 613vb.
give oneself airs
be affected 850vb.
be vain 873vb.
give oneself up
submit 721vb.
give one's mind to
be attentive 455vb.
give one the slip
decamp 296vb.
elude 667vb.
give one the works
torment 827vb.
torture 963vb.
give out
communicate 524vb.
publish 528vb.
give over
cease 145vb.
give points to
equalize 28vb.
be unequal 29vb.
giver
giver 781n.
give rise to
conduce 156vb.
give suck
feed 301vb.
give the lie
negate 533vb.
give tongue
be loud 400vb.
speak 579vb.
give up
cease 145vb.
not understand 517vb.
relinquish 621vb.
disuse 674vb.
submit 721vb.
not complete 726vb.
resign 753vb.
not retain 779vb.
give way
be weak 163vb.
regress 286vb.
descend 309vb.
be brittle 330vb.
be irresolute 601vb.
gizzard
maw 194n.
glabella
face 237n.
glabreity
smoothness 258n.
glacé
cooled 382adj.
glacial
cold 380adj.
glaciation
condensation 324n.
hardening 326n.
refrigeration 382n.
glacier
ice 380n.
glaciology
mineralogy 359n.
glacis
acclivity 220n.
fortification 713n.
glad
willing 597adj.
gladden
please 826vb.
cheer 833vb.
glade
valley 255n.
open space 263n.
screen 421n.
path 624n.
glad eye
look 438n.
wooing 889n.
glad-hand
be sociable 882vb.
gladiator
entertainer 594n.
contender 716n.
combatant 722n.
gladness
joy 824n.
glad of, be
desire 859vb.
glair
viscidity 354n.
glamorize
beautify 841vb.
decorate 844vb.
glamorizer
beautician 843n.
cosmetic 843n.
glamorous
personable 841adj.
glamour
beauty 841n.
prestige 866n.
spell 983n.
glance
deflect 282vb.
propel 287vb.
shine 417vb.
look 438n.
gesture 547n.
glancing
lateral 239adj.
glancing light
variegation 437n.
gland
insides 224n.
glanders
animal disease 651n.

glare
light 417n.
gaze 438vb.
blur 440vb.
be visible 443vb.
anger 891n.
glaring
whopping 32adj.
florid 425adj.
manifest 522adj.
well-known 528adj.
glass
weak thing 163n.
cup 194n.
smoothness 258n.
potion 301n.
brittleness 330n.
weather 340n.
transparency 422n.
mirror 442n.
finery 844n.
bad taste 847n.
glasses
eyeglass 442n.
glass house
brittleness 330n.
glasshouse
arbor 194n.
garden 370n.
glassiness
transparency 422n.
glass of fashion
beau monde 848n.
glassware
receptacle 194n.
glassy
smooth 258adj.
tranquil 266adj.
hard 326adj.
brittle 330adj.
undimmed 417adj.
dim 419adj.
transparent 422adj.
colorless 426adj.
glassy-eyed
tipsy 949adj.
glaucoma
blindness 439n.
dim sight 440n.
glaucous
gray 429adj.
green 432adj.
glaze
facing 226n.
coat 226vb.
smoothness 258n.
viscidity 354n.
screen 421vb.
glazed ware
pottery 381n.
gleam
small quantity 33n.
flash 417n.
shine 417vb.
incentive 612n.
glean
cultivate 370vb.
abstract 592vb.
select 605vb.
store 632vb.
acquire 771vb.
take 786vb.
gleaner
aftercomer 67n.
accumulator 74n.
husbandman 370n.
cleaner 648n.
gleanings
anthology 592n.
choice 605n.
earnings 771n.
glebe
soil 344n.
benefice 985n.
glee
vocal music 412n.
enjoyment 824n.
merriment 833n.
glee-club
choir 413n.
gleeful
jubilant 833adj.
gleeman
vocalist 413n.
glen
valley 255n.
glengarry
headgear 228n.
glib
loquacious 581adj.
glide
elapse 111vb.
interjection 231n.
go smoothly 258vb.
move 265vb.
travel 267vb.
fly 271vb.
glider
aeronaut 271n.
aircraft 276n.
glide-sound
interjection 231n.
glim
lamp 420n.
glimmer
flash 417n.
glimmer 419n.
be dim 419vb.
be visible 443vb.
hint 524n.
glimmering
sciolism 491n.
glimpse
look 438n.
see 438vb.
knowledge 490n.
glint
flash 417n.
look 438n.
glinting
luminous 417adj.
glissade
descent 309n.
glisten, glister
shine 417vb.
glitter
shine 417vb.
flash 417n.
be visible 443vb.
ostentation 875n.
glittering
ornamented 844adj.
gloaming
evening 129n.
half-light 419n.
gloat
enjoy 376vb.
gaze 438vb.
be pleased 824vb.
rejoice 835vb.
boast 877vb.
be malevolent 898vb.
gloating
revengeful 910adj.
global
inclusive 78adj.
universal 79adj.
spacious 183adj.
ubiquitous 189adj.
rotund 252adj.
telluric 321adj.
globe
sphere 252n.
world 321n.
globe-trotter
traveler 268n.
spectator 441n.
globularity
rotundity 252n.
globule
sphere 252n.
glockenspiel
gong 414n.
gloom
darkness 418n.
dimness 419n.
adversity 731n.
sorrow 825n.
dejection 834n.
be sullen 893vb.
Gloria
hymn 981n.
glorification
dignification 866n.
praise 923n.
act of worship 981n.
glorified
ostentatious 875adj.
angelic 968adj.

paradisiac 971adj.
glorify
advertise 528vb.
make important 638vb.
honor 866vb.
praise 923vb.
worship 981vb.
gloriole
light 417n.
glorious
great 32adj.
excellent 644adj.
noteworthy 866adj.
godlike 965adj.
(*see* glory)
Glorious Koran
non-Biblical scripture 975n.
glory
light 417n.
manifestation 522n.
success 727n.
trophy 729n.
prosperity 730n.
prestige 866n.
famousness 866n.
feel pride 871vb.
boast 877vb.
divine attribute 965n.
gloss
smoothness 258n.
light 417n.
reflection 417n.
commentary 520n.
sham 542n.
untruth 543n.
word 559n.
pretext 614n.
beauty 841n.
ostentation 875n.
extenuate 927vb.
glossarist
interpreter 520n.
glossary
word list 87n.
commentary 520n.
dictionary 559n.
glossless
colorless 426adj.
glossographer
collector 492n.
interpreter 520n.
glossography
commentary 520n.
glossology
linguistics 557n.
gloss over
neglect 458vb.
sophisticate 477vb.
conceal 525vb.
cant 541vb.
plead 614vb.
extenuate 927vb.
glossy
luminous 417adj.
splendid 841adj.
personable 841adj.
glottal stop
pronunciation 577n.
glottologist
linguist 557n.
glottology
linguistics 557n.
glove
glove 228n.
love-token 889n.
glow
heat 379n.
glow 417n.
hue 425n.
redness 431n.
be visible 443vb.
vigor 571n.
show feeling 818vb.
be beautiful 841vb.
glower
be angry 891vb.
be sullen 893vb.
glow-worm
glimmer 419n.
glow-worm 420n.
gloze
underestimate 483vb.
mislead 495vb.
interpret 520vb.
misinterpret 521vb.
cant 541vb.
flatter 925vb.
be dishonest 930vb.
glucose
food content 301n.
sweet 392n.
glue
adhesive 47n.
agglutinate 48vb.
viscidity 354n.
glued
firm-set 45adj.
glue on
affix 45vb.
glum
melancholic 834adj.
glut
productiveness 171n.
superfluity 637n.
cheapness 812n.
satiety 863vb.
gluteal
back 238adj.
crural 267adj.
glutinosity
viscidity 354n.
glut oneself
gluttonize 947vb.
glutton
desirer 859n.
sensualist 944n.
glutton 947n.
glutton for work
busy person 678n.
gluttonous
greedy 859adj.
gluttony
gastronomy 301n.
desire 859n.
vice 934n.
sensualism 944n.
gluttony 947n.
glycerin
lubricant 334n.
fat 357n.
cleanser 648n.
glyconic
prosody 593n.
glyph
furrow 262n.
glyptic
formative 243adj.
glyptic 554adj.
glyptography
engraving 555n.
G-man
detective 459n.
gnar
ululate 409vb.
gnarled
distorted 246adj.
rough 259adj.
dense 324adj.
gnashing
angry 891adj.
gnash one's teeth
be impotent 161vb.
regret 830vb.
be angry 891vb.
gnat
fly 365n.
animalcule 196n.
gnaw
bate 37vb.
rend 46vb.
chew 301vb.
rub 333vb.
give pain 377vb.
impair 655vb.
hurt 827vb.
gnome
maxim 496n.
elf 970n.
gnomic
aphoristic 496adj.
gnomon
timekeeper 117n.
gnostic
religionist 973n.
gnosticism
philosophy 449n.
deism 973n.

heresy 977n.
Gnostics
non-Christian sect 978n.
gnu
deer 365n.
go
be disjoined 46vb.
operate 173vb.
vigorousness 174n.
move 265vb.
travel, walk 267vb.
recede 290vb.
die 361vb.
function 622vb.
restlessness 678n.
courage 855n.
go a-begging
be superfluous 637vb.
be useless 641vb.
go about
undertake 672vb.
goad
stimulant 174n.
make violent 176vb.
sharp point 256n.
impel 279vb.
incentive 612n.
excitant 821n.
enrage 891vb.
go against
counteract 182vb.
oppose 704vb.
go against the grain
be rough 259vb.
be difficult 700vb.
displease 827vb.
cause dislike 861vb.
go-ahead
vigorous 174adj.
enterprising 672adj.
goal
extremity 69n.
focus 76n.
stopping place 145n.
limit 236n.
resting place 266n.
direction 281n.
goal 295n.
objective 617n.
completion 725n.
success 727n.
desired object 859n.
goal-keeper
interceptor 702n.
defender 713n.
go along with
concur 181vb.
assent 488vb.
go-as-you-please
free 744adj.
go at
essay 671n.
goat
jumper 312n.
cattle 365n.
libertine 952n.
goatee
hair 259n.
goatherd
herdsman 369n.
goatish
lecherous 951adj.
go away
go away 190vb.
recede 290vb.
depart 296vb.
gob
orifice 263n.
naval man 270n.
eruct 300vb.
navy man 722n.
go back
repeat oneself 106vb.
turn round 282vb.
turn back 286vb.
go back on
negate 533vb.
relinquish 621vb.
not observe 769vb.
(*see* tergiversate)
go bad
be unclean 649vb.
deteriorate 655vb.
gobbet
small thing 33n.
mouthful 301n.
gobble
absorb 299vb.
ululate 409vb.
gluttonize 947vb.
go-between
joinder 45n.
intermediary 231n.
informant 524n.
messenger 531n.
mediator 720n.
matchmaker 894n.
bawd 952n.
goblet
cup 194n.
goblin
intimidation 854n.
elf 970n.
gobstopper
stopper 264n.
mouthful 301n.
go by
elapse 111vb.
goby
fish 365n.
go-cart
pushcart 274n.
god
cause 156n.
the Deity 965n.
god 966n.
idol 982n.
goddess
woman 373n.
loved one 887n.
god-forsaken
empty 190adj.
secluded 883adj.
profane 980adj.
godhead
divineness 965n.
godless
irreligious 974adj.
impious 980adj.
godlike
beautiful 841adj.
godlike 965adj.
godly
pious 979adj.
god-making
deification 982n.
godown
storage 632n.
go down
descend 309vb.
founder 313vb.
be believed 485vb.
go downhill
deteriorate 655vb.
have trouble 731vb.
godparents
family 11n.
gods
theater 594n.
playgoer 594n.
godsend
benefit 615n.
prosperity 730n.
godson
family 11n.
God's own
chosen 605adj.
God-speed
success 727n.
God's ways
divineness 965n.
theocracy 965n.
God's will
fate 596n.
God's word
revelation 975n.
go Dutch
be sociable 882vb.
God willing
possibly 469adv.
goer
thoroughbred 273n.
goetic
sorcerous 983adj.
goffer
groove 262vb.
go for
aim at 617vb.

attack 712vb.
cost 809vb.
desire 859vb.
go from bad to worse
deteriorate 655vb.
aggravate 832vb.
go-getter
progression 285n.
planner 623n.
busy person 678n.
egotist 932n.
goggle
gaze 438vb.
wonder 864vb.
goggles
eyeglass 442n.
go half-way
be half-way 625vb.
consent 758vb.
(*see* compromise)
go halves
participate 775vb.
go hard with
have trouble 731vb.
go in for
be resolute 599vb.
choose 605vb.
aim at 617vb.
busy oneself 622vb.
undertake 672vb.
going
relinquishment 621n.
active 678adj.
going, be
depart 296vb.
going begging
free 744adj.
unpossessed 774adj.
going on
unfinished 55adj.
go into
inquire 459vb.
dissert 591vb.
go it alone
be free 744vb.
Golconda
wealth 800n.
gold
yellowness 433n.
orange 436n.
incentive 612n.
exceller 644n.
money, bullion 797n.
gold-digger
lover 887n.
egotist 932n.
golden
yellow 433adj.
valuable 644adj.
palmy 730adj.
promising 852adj.
Golden Age
era 110n.
literature 557n.
palmy days 730n.
happiness 824n.
innocence 935n.
golden calf
idol 982n.
golden mean
average 30n.
moderation 177n.
mid-course 625n.
golden opinions
approbation 923n.
golden rule
precept 693n.
golden touch
prosperity 730n.
wealth 800n.
golden wedding
period 110n.
anniversary 141n.
special day 876n.
wedding 897n.
goldfish
fish 365n.
gold-mine
store 632n.
wealth 800n.
gold-rush
land travel 267n.
goldsmith
artisan 686n.
gold standard
finance 797n.
golf
ball game 837n.
golf-links
pleasure-ground 837n.
Golgotha
cemetery 364n.
holy place 990n.
Goliath
athlete 162n.
giant 195n.
golliwog
image 551n.
gondola
rowboat 275n.
airship 276n.
gondolier
boatman 270n.
carrier 273n.
gone
past 125adj.
absent 190adj.
dead 361adj.
disappearing 446adj.
lost 772adj.
dead drunk 949adj.
gone on
enamored 887adj.
goner
corpse 363n.
gonfalon
flag 547n.
gong
timekeeper 117n.
resound 404vb.
gong 414n.
signal, badge 547n.
decoration 729n.
Gongorism
ornament 574n.
goniometer
angular measure 247n.
meter 465n.
gonorrhea
venereal disease 651n.
good
savory 390adj.
elegant 575adj.
good 615n., adj.
utility 640n.
excellent 644adj.
skillful 694adj.
prosperity 730n.
obedient 739adj.
pleasurable 826n.
amiable 884adj.
benevolent 897adj.
right 913adj.
honorable 929adj.
virtuous 933adj.
pure 950adj.
pious 979adj.
good angel
mythic god 966n.
(*see* benefactor)
good as, as
nearly 200adv.
good as one's word
veracious 540adj.
trustworthy 929adj.
good behavior
courtesy 884n.
virtue 933n.
good bet
fair chance 159n.
good books
approbation 923n.
good breeding
etiquette 848n.
courtesy 884n.
goodbye
valediction 296n.
good chance
fair chance 159n.
possibility 469n.
probability 471n.
good cheer
food 301n.
enjoyment 824n.
merriment 833n.
amusement 837n.
sociability 882n.
good company
social person 882n.

good constitution
health 650n.
good deal
great quantity 32n.
good defense
vindication 927n.
good delivery
eloquence 579n.
good earnest, in
resolutely 599adv.
good example
relevance 9n.
analogue 18n.
fitness 24n.
good man 937n.
good faith
probity 929n.
good fault
virtues 933n.
good fellowship
sociability 882n.
good for
useful 640adj.
salubrious 652adj.
good form
practice 610n.
etiquette 848n.
formality 875n.
good for nothing
powerless 161adj.
profitless 641adj.
vicious 934adj.
bad man 938n.
Good Friday
fast 946n.
holy-day 988n.
good genius
benefactor 903n.
mythic god 966n.
good graces
approbation 923n.
good grace, with a
willingly 597adv.
good grounds
vindication 927n.
good humor
cheerfulness 833n.
courtesy 884n.
good in parts
imperfect 647adj.
good living
gastronomy 301n.
gluttony 947n.
good-looking
beautiful 841adj.
good loser
gentleman 929n.
good luck
chance 159n.
non-design 618n.
prosperity 730n.
goodly
great 32adj.
fleshy 195adj.
good 615adj.
beautiful 841adj.
good man
good man 937n.
pietist 979n.
goodman
resident 191n.
male 372n.
master 741n.
spouse 894n.
good-mannnered
well-bred 848adj.
good name
repute 866n.
good-natured
irresolute 601adj.
benevolent 897adj.
good neighbour
friend 880n.
social person 882n.
kind person 897n.
goodness
(*see* good)
goodnight
valediction 296n.
good odor
repute 866n.
good offices
aid 703n.
concord 710n.
pacification 719n.
mediation 720n.
kind act 897n.
good of one
lifelike 18adj.
benevolent 897adj.
good points
goodness 644n.
good purpose, to
successfully 727adv.
good reason
probability 471n.
good report
repute 866n.
good riddance
rubbish 641n.
relief 831n.
hateful object 888n.
goods
thing transferred 272n.
property 777n.
merchandise 795n.
Good Samaritan
kind person 897n.
benefactor 903n.
goods and chattels
property 777n.
good sense
intelligence 498n.
good sort
good man 937n.
good spirits, in
cheerful 833adj.
good taste
elegance 575n.
good taste 846n.
good-tempered
inexcitable 823adj.
amiable 884adj.
good terms, on
concordant 710adj.
goods, the
information 524n.
goods-train
carrier 273n.
train 274n.
good time, have a
rejoice 835vb.
good turn
benefit 615n.
kind act 897n.
good value
cheapness 812n.
goodwife
lady 373n.
goodwill, good will
willingness 597n.
friendliness 880n.
benevolence 897n.
good wishes
congratulation 886n.
goody
lady 373n.
goody-goody
foolish 499adj.
ninny 501n.
innocent 935n., adj.
pietistic 979adj.
gooey
retentive 778adj.
goof
ignoramus 493n.
ninny 501n.
go off
happen 154vb.
be violent 176vb.
goofy
foolish 499adj.
googly
deviation 282n.
sleight 542n.
go on
last 113vb.
stay 144vb.
go on 146vb.
happen 154vb.
be in motion 265vb.
progress 285vb.
be active 678vb.
go on and on
be tedious 838vb.
go one better
be superior 34vb.
be cunning 698vb.

go one's own way
be dispersed 75vb.
diverge 294vb.
be incurious 454vb.
dissent 489vb.
will 595vb.
be free 744vb.
go, on the
on the move 265adv.
laboring 682adj.
goose
table-bird 365n.
waterfowl 365n.
female animal 373n.
sibilation 406n.
ignoramus 493n.
fool 501n.
gooseberry
fruit 301n.
gooseberry, play
look after 457vb.
gooseflesh
roughness 259n.
formication 378n.
coldness 380n.
nervousness 854n.
goosegirl
herdsman 369n.
goosery
cattle pen 369n.
goose-step
gait 265n.
walk 267vb.
go out of one's way
deviate 282vb.
be willing 597vb.
circuit 626vb.
go over
number 86vb.
repeat 106vb.
be inverted 221vb.
pass 305vb.
search 459vb.
study 536vb.
be irresolute 601vb.
be dishonest 930vb.
go over the top
charge 712vb.
be courageous 855vb.
gopher
rodent 365n.
go places
travel 267vb.
(*see* sociability)
gopura
high structure 209n.
church exterior 990n.
gorbelly
bulk 195n.
Gordian knot
ligature 47n.
complexity 61n.
difficulty 700n.
gore
pierce 263n.
blood 335n.
pulpiness 356n.
redness 431n.
gorge
gap 201n.
valley 255n.
conduit 351n.
superabound 637vb.
sate 863vb.
be intemperate 943vb.
gluttonize 947vb.
gorged
full 45adj.
gorge-de-pigeon
variegation 437n.
gorgeous
florid 425adj.
splendid 841adj.
ornamented 844adj.
showy 875adj.
gorgon
rara avis 84n.
intimidation 854n.
demon 970n.
gorgonzola
milk product 301n.
gorilla
monkey 365n.
eyesore 842n.
monster 938n.
gormandize
eat 301vb.
gluttonize 947vb.
gorse
plant 366n.
gory
sanguineous 335adj.
murderous 362adj.
bloodshot 431adj.
go shares
be equal 28vb.
participate 775vb.
be sociable 882vb.
gosling
youngling 132n.
child 132n.
waterfowl 365n.
go-slow
slowness 278n.
unwilling 598adj.
gospel
certainty 473n.
authenticity 494n.
news 529n.
revelation 975n.
scriptural 975adj.
orthodox 976adj.
gospeler
preacher 537n.
religious teacher 973n.
Gospels
scripture 975n.
gospel, take for
believe 485vb.
gossamer
insubstantial thing 4n.
weak thing 163n.
filament 208n.
levity 323n.
transparency 422n.
trifle 639n.
gossip
insubstantial thing 4n.
family 11n.
topic 452n.
inquisitor 453n.
informer 524n.
newsmonger 529n.
fable 543n.
be loquacious 581vb.
chat 584n.
chum 880n.
calumny 926n.
gossip-writer
informant 524n.
chronicler 549n.
author 589n.
gossipy
loquacious 581adj.
conversing 584adj.
sociable 882adj.
got
acquired 771adj.
Goth
vulgarian 847n.
low fellow 869n.
go the pace
be prodigal 815vb.
be sensual 944vb.
go the rounds
traverse 267vb.
be published 528vb.
change hands 780vb.
Gothic
architectural 192adj.
amorphous 244adj.
literal 558adj.
inelegant 576adj.
written 586adj.
print-type 587n.
go through
meet with 154vb.
pass 305vb.
search 459vb.
deal with 688vb.
suffer 825vb.
go through fire and water
be resolute 599vb.
go through the motions
dissemble 541vb.
go to all lengths

exaggerate 546vb.
be resolute 599vb.
exert oneself 682vb.
be intemperate 943vb.
go to it
begin 68vb.
go to law
quarrel 709vb.
litigate 959vb.
go too far
overstep 306vb.
go to one's head
make conceited 873vb.
inebriate 949vb.
go to pieces
decompose 51vb.
be destroyed 165vb.
go to sea
sail 269vb.
go to the wall
be destroyed 165vb.
perish 361vb.
be defeated 728vb.
gotra
family 11n.
breed 77n.
gotten
acquired 771adj.
Götterdämmerung
finality 69n.
got up
bedecked 844adj.
gouache
art equipment 553n.
gouge (out)
make concave 255vb.
extract 304vb.
goulash
dish 301n.
gourd
vessel 194n.
vegetable 301n.
plant 366n.
gourmandise
gastronomy 301n.
good taste 846n.
gluttony 947n.
gourmet
eater 301n.
gastronomy 301n.
man of taste 846n.
perfectionist 862n.
glutton 947n.
gout
rheumatism 651n.
gouty
crippled 163adj.
diseased 651adj.
irascible 892adj.
govern
order 60vb.
moderate 177vb.
manage 689vb.
rule 733vb.
governance
power 160n.
influence 178n.
(*see* government)
governess
teacher 537n.
protector 660n.
retainer 742n.
keeper 749n.
governessy
authoritarian 735adj.
governing body
director 690n.
government
management 689n.
government 733n.
master 741n.
governmental
businesslike 622adj.
government servant
official 690n.
governor
teacher 537n.
director 690n.
governor 741n.
governorship
magistrature 733n.
go with
accord 24vb.
accompany 89vb.
concur 181vb.
go without saying
be plain 522vb.
gowk
ninny 501n.
fool 501n.
gown
dress 228n.
canonicals 989n.
go wrong
err 495vb.
miscarry 728vb.
be wrong 914vb.
grab
sailing ship 275n.
take 786vb.
grabble
touch 378vb.
grace
musical note 410n.
style 566n.
ornament 574vb.
elegance 575n.
skill 694n.
permission 756n.
gift 781n.
beauty 841n.
decorate 844vb.
good taste 846n.
title 870n.
mercy 905n.
thanks 907n.
forgiveness 909n.
divine function 965n.
prayers 981n.
grace and favor
permission 756n.
gift 781n.
no charge 812n.
graceful
lovable 887adj.
gracefulness
elegance 575n.
beauty 841n.
graceless
inelegant 576adj.
clumsy 695adj.
dull 840adj.
graceless 842adj.
vicious 934adj.
impenitent 940adj.
grace marks
extra 40n.
gift 781n.
undueness 916n.
grace-note
musical note 410n.
graces
beauty 841n.
gracile
narrow 206adj.
gracious
willing 597adj.
beautiful 841adj.
tasteful 846adj.
courteous 884adj.
benevolent 897adj.
gracious living
euphoria 376n.
gradatim
in order 60adv.
gradatim 278adv.
gradation
degree 27n.
order 60n.
arrangement 62n.
series 71n.
grade
degree 27n.
graduate 27vb.
arrange, class 62vb.
serial place 73n.
grade 73vb.
sort 77n.
acclivity 220n.
gauge 465vb.
class 538n.
gradient
acclivity 220n.
ascent 308n.
gradual
gradational 27adj.
continuous 71adj.
slow 278adj.
gradualism

continuity 71n.
slowness 278n.
reformism 654n.

gradualist
reformer 654n.

gradually
gradatim 278adv.

graduate
graduate 27vb.
grade 73vb.
pass 305vb.
gauge 465vb.
learn 536vb.
college student 538n.
get better 654vb.
proficient 696n.

graduation
adaptation 24n.
(*see* grade)

gradus
word list 87n.
dictionary 559n.
textbook 589n.

graffito
record 548n.
script 586n.

graft
descendant 170n.
implant 303vb.
cultivate 370vb.
booty 790n.
improbity 930n.

grafting
venal 930adj.

grail
ritual object 988n.

grain
temperament 5n.
small thing 33n.
tendency 179n.
minuteness 196n.
cereal 301n.
provender 301n.
weighment 322n.
texture 331n.
powder 332n.
corn 366n.
pigment 425n.
color 425vb.
red pigment 431n.
affections 817n.
decorate 844vb.

grain, in
fixed 153adj.

graining
ornamental art 844n.

grains of allowance
qualification 468n.

gram
weighment 322n.

gramarye
sorcery 983n.

gramineous
vegetal 366adj.

graminivorous
feeding 301adj.

grammar
curriculum 536n.
grammar 564n.
textbook 589n.

grammarian
linguist 557n.

gramaphone
phonograph 414n.
hearing aid 415n.

grampus
fish 365n.

granadilla
fruit 301n.

granary
storage 632n.

grand
whole 52adj.
over one hundred 99n.
topping 644adj.
funds 797n.
impressive 821adj.
splendid 841adj.
noble 868adj.
proud 871adj.
formal 875adj.
(*see* grandeur)

grand airs
affectation 850n.

grandam
old woman 133n.
maternity 169n.

grandchildren
posterity 170n.

grand climacteric
age 131n.

grand duchy
territory 184n.

grand duke
nobleman 868n.

grande dame
proud man 871n.

grandee
aristocrat 868n.

grande toilette
formal dress 228n.

grandeur
greatness 32n.
vigor 571n.
beauty 841n.
prestige 866n.
ostentation 875n.

grandfather
old man 133n.
parent 169n.

grandiloquence
exaggeration 546n.
vigor 571n.
magniloquence 574n.
eloquence 579n.
affectation 850n.
boasting 877n.

grandiose
huge 195adj.
rhetorical 574adj.
proud 871adj.
ostentatious 875adj.

Grand Lama
priest 986n.

grandmother
old woman 133n.
maternity 169n.
woman 373n.

grandsire
old man 133n.
parent 169n.

grand slam
victory 727n.

grandstand
view 438n.
onlookers 441n.

grand view
whole 52n.

grange
house 192n.
farm 370n.

granger
husbandman 370n.

granite
hardness 326n.
rock 344n.

granny knot
ligature 47n.

grant
be reasonable 475adj.
believe 485vb.
confess 526vb.
subvention 703n.
be lenient 736vb.
permission 756n.
consent 758n.
dower 777vb.
convey 780vb.
gift 781n.
pay 804n.
reward 962n.

grant asylum
admit 299vb.

granted
assented 488adj.
supposed 512adj.

grantee
beneficiary 776n.
recipient 782n.

grant-in-aid
pay 804n.

granting
if 8adv.

grantor
giver 781n.

grant-worthy
deserving 915adj.

granular
minute 196adj.
textural 331adj.

powdery 332adj.
granulation
texture 331n.
pulverulence 332n.
granule
small quantity 33n.
powder 332n.
grape
fruit 301n.
grape-shot
missile 287n.
ammunition 723n.
grape-vine
informant 524n.
graph
mathematics 86n.
graphic
expressive 516adj.
representing 551adj.
painted 553adj.
forceful 571adj.
descriptive 590adj.
graphic art
art 551n.
painting 553n.
graphite
lubricant 334n.
graphology
writing 586n.
graphometer
angular measure 247n.
graphotype
printing 555n.
grapnel
safeguard 662n.
grapple
join, tie 45vb.
be resolute 599vb.
attack 712vb.
wrestling 716n.
contend 716vb.
grappler
combatant 722n.
grapple with
withstand 704vb.
grappling iron
coupling 47n.
safeguard 662n.
grasp
ability 160n.
range 183n.
distance 199n.
knowledge 490n.
be wise 498vb.
understand 516vb.
protection 660n.
possession 773n.
retention 778n.
taking 786n.
grasp at
desire 859vb.
grasping
oppressive 735adj.
taking 786adj.
avaricious 816adj.
greedy 859adj.
grass
provender 301n.
grass 366n.
garden 370n.
greenness 432n.
grasshopper
jumper 312n.
vermin 365n.
grassland
grassland 348n.
grassless
dry 342adj.
grassy
soft 327adj.
vegetal 366adj.
green 432adj.
grate
rub 333vb.
give pain 377vb.
furnace 383n.
rasp 407vb.
ululate 409vb.
discord 411vb.
pulverize 332vb.
displease 827vb.
cause dislike 861vb.
excite hate 888vb.
grateful
pleasant 376adj.
pleasurable 826adj.
content 828adj.
grateful 907adj.
grater
roughness 259n.
pulverizer 332n.
gratification
pleasure 376n.
(*see* gratify)
gratify
bribe 612vb.
be lenient 736vb.
give 781vb.
pay 804vb.
please 826vb.
content 828vb.
reward 962vb.
grating
disagreeing 25adj.
network 222n.
(*see* grate)
gratis
free 744adj.
given 781adj.
uncharged 812adj.
gratitude
gratitude 907n.
gratuitous
suppositional 512adj.
voluntary 597adj.
given 781adj.
uncharged 812adj.
undue 916adj.
gratuity
extra 40n.
acquisition 771n.
gift 781n.
undueness 916n.
reward 962n.
gratulation
congratulation 886n.
gravamen
accusation 928n.
grave
great 32adj.
excavation 255n.
groove 262vb.
resting place 266n.
death 361n.
tomb 364n.
record 548vb.
engrave 555vb.
forceful 571adj.
important 638adj.
inexcitable 823adj.
serious 834adj.
dull 840adj.
heinous 934adj.
grave accent
punctuation 547n.
grave clothes
grave clothes 364n.
grave-digger
excavator 255n.
interment 364n.
church officer 986n.
gravel
flatten 216vb.
powder 332n.
soil 344n.
puzzle 474vb.
confute 479vb.
be difficult 700n.
defeat 727vb.
gravelly
hard 326adj.
powdery 332adj.
territorial 344adj.
graven image
image 551n.
idol 982n.
graveolence
odor 394n.
fetor 397n.
gravestone
covering 226n.
obsequies 364n.
graveyard
cemetery 364n.
holy place 990n.
gravid
productive 164adj.
graving dock
stable 192n.

gravitate
tend 179vb.
descend 309vb.
weigh 322vb.
gravitation
influence 178n.
gravity 322n.
gravity
influence 178n.
attraction 291n.
materiality 319n.
gravity 322n.
vigor 571n.
importance 638n.
inexcitability 823n.
seriousness 834n.
prudery 950n.
gravy
fluid 335n.
semiliquidity 354n.
gravy-boat
bowl 194n.
gray
uniform 16adj.
median 30adj.
horse 273n.
dim 419adj.
colorless 426adj.
whitish 427adj.
gray 429n., adj.
neutral 625adj.
mediocre 732adj.
cheerless 834adj.
graybeard
old man 133n.
gray dawn
half-light 419n.
dejection 834n.
Gray Eminence
adviser 691n.
gray mare
spouse 894n.
gray matter
head 213n.
intelligence 498n.
graze
be near 200vb.
be contiguous 202vb.
shallowness 212n.
collide 279vb.
feed 301vb.
rub 333vb.
touch 378n., vb.
wound 655vb.
grazing
grassland 348n.
stock farm 369n.
grease
adhesive 47n.
coat 226vb.
smoother 258n.
meat 301n.
soften 327vb.
lubricant 334n.
fat 357n.
silencer 401n.
make unclean 649vb.
facilitate 701vb.
hairwash 843n.
grease-gun
lubricant 334n.
grease-paint
stage-set 594n.
cosmetic 843n.
grease-proof
resisting 715adj.
greaser
foreigner 59n.
grease the palm
bribe 612vb.
greasy
smooth 258adj.
unctuous 357adj.
savory 390adj.
dirty 649adj.
great
great 32adj.
superior 34adj.
powerful 160adj.
strong 162adj.
influential 178adj.
large 195adj.
plenteous 635adj.
important 638adj.
excellent 644adj.
worshipful 866adj.
noble 868adj.
proud 871adj.
great circle
circle 250n.
uranometry 321n.
greatcoat
overcoat 228n.
great deal
greatly 32adv.
great doings
important matter 638n.
activity 678n.
pageant 875n.
greaten
expand 197vb.
enlarge 197vb.
greater than ever
increasing 36adj.
greatest
supreme 34adj.
great folk
aristocracy 868n.
great majority
greater number 104n.
the dead 361n.
great man
bigwig 638n.
great name
repute 866n.
greatness
(*see* great)
Greats
exam. 459n.
curriculum 536n.
Great Seal
officer 741n.
great spirit
the Deity 965n.
great thing
chief thing 638n.
great unpaid
judge 957n.
Great Wall of China
partition 231n.
defenses 713n.
Great Year
era 110n.
greaves
legwear 228n.
armor 713n.
grebe
waterfowl 365n.
greed
rapacity 786n.
avarice 816n.
desire 859n.
selfishness 932n.
gluttony 947n.
greediness
overstepping 306n.
sensualism 944n.
(*see* greed)
greedy
feeding 301adj.
unprovided 636adj.
greedy 859adj.
envious 912adj.
Greek
unknown thing 491n.
unmeaningness 515n.
Greek fire
fireworks 420n.
explosive 723n.
Greek kalends
neverness 109n.
Greek mode
key 410n.
green
new 126adj.
young 130adj.
pleasance 192n.
grassland 348n.
vegetal 366adj.
sour 393adj.
greenness 432n.
credulous 487adj.
ignorant 491adj.
unhabituated 611adj.
immature 670adj.
unskilled 695adj.
pleasure-ground 837n.
innocent 935adj.
greenback

paper money 797n.
green belt
space 183n.
limit 236n.
plain 348n.
vegetability 366n.
greenery
plant 366n.
greenness 432n.
green-eyed
jealous 911adj.
green fingers
feeler 378n.
aptitude 694n.
greenfly
fly 365n.
greengrocer
provider 633n.
greenhorn
ignoramus 493n.
ninny 501n.
beginner 538n.
dupe 544n.
bungler 697n.
ingenue 699n.
greenhouse
arbor 194n.
garden 370n.
green light
signal light 420n.
assent 488n.
signal 547n.
permit 756n.
green-room
theater 594n.
greens
vegetable 301n.
greensward
grassland 348n.
greet
meet 295vb.
speak to 583vb.
weep 836vb.
be friendly 880vb.
be hospitable 882vb.
greet 884vb.
greetings
respects 920n.
gregarious
sociable 882adj.
Gregorian
musicianly 413adj.
gremlin
hinderer 702n.
elf 970n.
grenade
bang 402n.
bomb 723n.
grenadier
tall creature 209n.
soldiery 722n.
Gresham's law
deterioration 655n.
grey
(*see* gray)
greyhound
speeder 277n.
dog 365n.
grid
correlation 12n.
electricity 160n.
network 222n.
griddle
cook 301vb.
gridiron
network 222n.
heater 383n.
arena 724n.
grief
evil 616n.
sorrow 825n.
discontent 829n.
grievance
evil 616n.
annoyance 827n.
discontent 829n.
wrong 914n.
grieve
manager 690n.
suffer 825vb.
hurt 827vb.
sadden 834vb.
lament 836vb.
pity 905vb.
grievous
bad 645adj.
distressing 827adj.
griff
hybrid 43n.
griffin
hybrid 43n.
rara avis 84n.
animal 365n.
ignoramus 493n.
heraldry 547n.
grig
table fish 365n.
grill
network 222n.
window 263n.
cook 301vb.
be hot 379vb.
heat 381vb.
heater 383n.
interrogate 459vb.
grill-room
café 192n.
chamber 194n.
grilse
table fish 365n.
grim
resolute 599adj.
obstinate 602adj.
distressing 827adj.
serious 834adj.
frightening 854adj.
ungracious 885adj.
ugly 892adj.
sullen 893adj.
cruel 898adj.
grimace
distortion 246n.
look 438n.
gesture 547n.
be loath 598vb.
discontent 829n.
smile 835vb.
affectation 850n.
frighten 854vb.
dislike 861vb.
sullenness 893n.
grimalkin
cat 365n.
grime
dirt 649n.
Grimm's law
linguistics 557n.
grimness
dullness 840n.
(*see* grim)
grimy
dim 419adj.
dirty 649adj.
grin
smile 835vb.
ridicule 851n.
grin and bear it
stand firm 599vb.
be patient 823vb.
be cheerful 833vb.
grind
bate 37vb.
rend, break 46vb.
demolish 165vb.
make smaller 198vb.
sharpen 256vb.
chew 301vb.
pulverize 332vb.
rub 333vb.
give pain 377vb.
rasp 407vb.
study 536n., vb.
wound 655vb.
labor 682n.
oppress 735vb.
grinder
tooth 256n.
meal 301n.
pulverizer 332n.
grindstone
sharpener 256n.
pulverizer 332n.
labor 682n.
bore 838n.
gringo
foreigner 59n.
grip
join, tie 45vb.
fastening 47n.
cohere 48vb.
vitality 162n.
vigorousness 174n.

bag 194n.
handle 218n.
gesture 547n.
protection 660n.
skill 694n.
governance 733n.
restrain 747vb.
possession 773n.
retention 778n.
impress 821vb.
hair-dressing 843n.
gripe
pang 377n.
indigestion 651n.
be parsimonious 816vb.
griping
oppressive 735adj.
avaricious 816adj.
greedy 859adj.
gripping
influential 178n.
exiting 821adj.
grip-sack
bag 194n.
grips, at
warring 718adj.
grisaille
gray 429n.
painting 553n.
grisette
woman 373n.
grisly
unsightly 842adj.
frightening 854adj.
grist
powder 332n.
materials 631n.
provision 633n.
gristle
vigorousness 174n.
solid body 324n.
hardness 326n.
toughness 329n.
grit
strength 162n.
hardness 326n.
texture 331n.
powder 332n.
resolution 599n.
stamina 600n.
courage 855n.
grizzle
whiten 427vb.
weep 836vb.
grizzled
whitish 427adj.
gray 429adj.
pied 437adj.
grizzly
gray 429adj.
groan
feel pain 377vb.
cry 408vb.
deprecate 762vb.
discontent 829n.
be dejected 834vb.
weep 836vb.
groat
small coin 33n.
groats
small thing 33n.
grocer
provider 633n.
tradesman 794n.
groceries
provisions 301n.
grog
liquor 301n.
grog-blossom
alcoholism 949n.
groggy
weakly 163adj.
oscillating 317adj.
sick 651adj.
grogshop
tavern 192n.
groin
angularity 247n.
projection 254n.
safeguard 662n.
obstacle 702n.
grommet
orifice 263n.
groom
animal husbandry 369n.
man 372n.
train 534vb.
make ready 669vb.
domestic 742n.
groomed
bedecked 844adj.
fashionable 848adj.
groomsman
close friend 880n.
bridesman 894n.
groove
cut 46vb.
regularity 81n.
place 185n.
receptacle 194n.
gap 201n.
furrow 262n.
habit 610n.
grope
move slowly 278vb.
touch 378vb.
be dim-sighted 440vb.
be tentative 461vb.
be uncertain 474vb.
essay 671vb.
be clumsy 695vb.
grope for
search 459vb.
groping
ignorant 491adj.
clumsy 695adj.
unsuccessful 728adj.
grosgrain
textile 222n.
gross
consummate 32adj.
whole 52adj.
unintelligent 499adj.
manifest 522adj.
bad 645adj.
acquire 771vb.
receive 782vb.
take 786vb.
graceless 842adj.
vulgar 847adj.
heinous 934adj.
sensual 944adj.
impure 951adj.
gross, a
over one hundred 99n.
grot, grotto
pavilion 192n.
arbor 194n.
cavity 255n.
grotesque
unusual 84adj.
distorted 246adj.
absurd 497adj.
inelegant 576adj.
eyesore 842n.
ridiculous 849adj.
grouch
(*see* grouse)
ground
reason why 156n.
territory 184n.
situation 186n.
base 214n.
flatten 216vb.
basis 218n.
come to rest 266vb.
navigate 269vb.
land 295vb.
powdery 332adj.
land 344n.
evidence 466n.
educate 534vb.
motive 612n.
be difficult 700vb.
arena 724n.
fail 728vb.
ground and consequent
causation 156vb.
grounded
real 1adj.
fixed 153adj.
impotent 161adj.
evidential 466adj.
in difficulties 700adj.
grounded 728adj.
ground floor
base 214n.
groundless
unreal 2adj.

insubstantial 4adj.
causeless 159adj.
illogical 477adj.
groundling
playgoer 594n.
commoner 869n.
ground-plan
map 551n.
plan 623n.
grounds
leavings 41n.
pleasance 192n.
grassland 348n.
dirt 649n.
pleasure-ground 837n.
ground upon
attribute 158vb.
groundwork
prelude 66n.
source 156n.
base 214n.
basis 218n.
preparation 669n.
group
combine 50vb.
subdivision 53n.
arrange 62vb.
series 71n.
group 74n.
sculpture 554n.
party 708n.
formation 722n.
sect 978n.
group captain
air officer 741n.
grouper
sectarist 978n.
grouse
table bird 365n.
be discontented 829vb.
lament 836vb.
be sullen 893vb.
grouser
dissentient 489n.
malcontent 829n.
rude person 885n.
disapprover 924n.
grout
adhesive 47n.
coat 226vb.
dirt 649n.
be sullen 893vb.
grove
street 192n.
wood 366n.
grovel
be low 210vb.
be horizontal 216vb.
knuckle under 721vb.
obey 739vb.
be servile 879vb.
grow
become 1vb.
grow 36vb.
be turned to 147vb.
result 157vb.
generate 164vb.
expand 197vb.
progress 285vb.
breed stock 369vb.
cultivate 370vb.
mature 669vb.
grower
producer 167n.
growing
young 130adj.
growing pains
increase 36n.
youth 130n.
growl
ululation 409n.
be rude 885vb.
hate 888vb.
anger 891n.
sullenness 893n.
threat 900n.
growler
cab 274n.
malcontent 829n.
growling
hoarse 407adj.
grow moss
stay 144vb.
deteriorate 655vb.
grown-up
grown-up 134adj.
grow on one
be wont 610vb.
growth
increase 36n.
sequel 67n.
conversion 147n.
growth 157n.
propagation 164n.
expansion 197n.
swelling 253n.
agriculture 370n.
grow together
cohere 48vb.
combine 50vb.
grub
small animal 33n.
animalcule 196n.
food 301n.
extract 304vb.
grubble
touch 378vb.
Grub Street hack
author 589n.
grudge
be loath 598vb.
refuse 760vb.
be parsimonious 816vb.
be discontented 829vb.
enmity 881n.
hatred 888n.
resentment 891n.
grudgeful
revengeful 910adj.
gruel
cereal 301n.
grueling
fatiguing 684adj.
paining 827adj.
gruesome
unsightly 842adj.
frightening 854adj.
gruff
hoarse 407adj.
taciturn 582adj.
ungracious 885adj.
irascible 892adj.
sullen 893adj.
unkind 898adj.
grumble
roll 403vb.
cry 408vb.
be discontented 829vb.
be sullen 893vb.
grumbling
threatening 900adj.
grume
solid body 324n.
blood 335n.
semiliquidity 354n.
pulpiness 356n.
grumpy
irascible 892adj.
sullen 893adj.
grunt
rasp 407vb.
cry 408n., vb.
ululate 409vb.
be fatigued 684vb.
grunting
ungracious 885adj.
guano
fertilizer 171n.
excrement 302n.
guarantee
make certain 473vb.
affirm 532vb.
safeguard 660vb.
patronize 703vb.
promise 764n.
security 767n.
guarantor
patron 707n.
guard
janitor 264n.
driver 268n.
attention 455n.
surveillance 457n.
protection 660n.
safeguard 660vb.
defender 713n.
keeper 749n.
guardant
heraldic 547adj.
guarded
taciturn 582adj.

conditional 766adj.
cautious 858adj.
guardian
(*see* guard)
guardian angel
patron 707n.
benefactor 903n.
guardless
vulnerable 661adj.
guard, on
vigilant 457adj.
cautious 858adj.
guard-room
lock-up 748n.
guards
armed force 722n.
guard's van
train 274n.
guava
fruit 301n.
gubbins
vessel 194n.
sink 649n.
gubernatorial
directing 689adj.
governmental 733adj.
guddee
seat 218n.
regalia 743n.
gudgeon
pivot 218n.
fish 365n.
guebre
religionist 973n.
idolater 982n.
guerdon
reward 962n., vb.
guernsey
vest 228n.
guerrilla
attacker 712n.
soldier 722n.
revolter 738n.
guess
assume 471vb.
intuit 476vb.
estimate 480vb.
opinion 485n.
not know 491vb.
conjecture 512n.
hint 524n.
guess, at a
about 33adv.
guess-warp
cable 47n.
guesswork
empiricism 461n.
uncertainty 474n.
intuition 476n.
conjecture 512n.
guest
resident 191n.
friend 880n.
social person 882n.
guest-friend
friend 880n.
guest-house
quarters 192n.
guest-rope
cable 47n.
guff
insubstantial thing 4n.
empty talk 515n.
fable 543n.
guffaw
laughter 835n.
guggle
flow 350vb.
bubble 355vb.
sound faint 401vb.
resound 404vb.
ululate 409vb.
gugglet
vessel 194n.
guidance
teaching 534n.
directorship 689n.
advice 691n.
guide
prototype 23n.
superior 34n.
come before 64vb.
precursor 66n.
rule 81n.
accompany 89vb.
influence 178vb.
itinerary 267n.
precede 283vb.
sage 500n.
guide 520n.
show 522vb.
informant 524n.
educate 534vb.
teacher 537n.
indication 547n.
reference book 589n.
direct 689vb.
adviser 691n.
theosophy 984n.
guide-book
directory 87n.
guide-book 524n.
guided missile
rocket 276n.
guideless
vulnerable 661adj.
guidon
flag 547n.
guild
business 622n.
corporation 708n.
merchant 794n.
guilder
coinage 797n.
guildhall
mart 796n.
guile
duplicity 541n.
deception 542n.
cunning 698n.
guileful
perfidious 930adj.
guileless
artless 699adj.
honorable 929adj.
innocent 935adj.
guillotine
end 69n.
stop 145n.
shorten 204vb.
killer 362n.
execute 963vb.
means of execution 964n.
guilt
badness 645n.
wrong 914n.
wickedness 934n.
guilt 936n.
lawbreaking 954n.
guilt-feeling
penitence 939n.
guiltless
ignorant 491adj.
virtuous 933adj.
guiltless 935adj.
acquitted 960adj.
guilt-offering
substitute 150n.
guilty
(*see* guilt)
guilty man
offender 904n.
guinea
coinage 797n.
guinea-pig
rodent 365n.
testee 461n.
guisard
actor 594n.
guise
modality 7n.
appearance 445n.
pretext 614n.
way 624n.
conduct 688n.
guitar
harp 414n.
guitarist
instrumentalist 413n.
gulch
gap 201n.
gules
red color 431n.
heraldry 547n.
gulf
entrance 68n.
depth 211n.
cavity 255n.
way in 297n.

gulf 345n.
access 624n.
gull
bird of prey 365n.
credulity 478n.
fool 501n.
befool 542vb.
dupe 544vb.
defraud 788vb.
gullery
nest 192n.
trickery 542n.
gullet
maw 194n.
orifice 263n.
eater 301n.
conduit 351n.
air-pipe 353n.
gullible
misjudging 481n.
credulous 487n.
foolish 499vb.
gullible 544adj.
Gulliver
traveler 268n.
mariner 270n.
gully
gap 210n.
narrowness 206n.
valley 255n.
sharp edge 256n.
conduit 351n.
gulosity
gluttony 947n.
gulp
absorb 299vb.
potion 301n.
eat 301vb.
respiration 352n.
gum
adhesive 47n.
agglutinate 48vb.
viscidity 354n.
resin 357n.
sweet 392n.
gumbo
soup 301n.
semiliquidity 354n.
gummic
resinous 357adj.
gummy
cohesive 48adj.
tough 329adj.
viscid 354adj.
retentive 778adj.
gum on
affix 45vb.
gumption
intelligence 498n.
gumptionless
foolish 499adj.
gumshoe(s)
footwear 228n.
detective 459n.
gun
propellant 287n.
bang 402n.
hunter 619n.
gun 723n.
guna
speech sound 398n.
gunboat
warship 722n.
gun-carriage
war-chariot 274n.
gun 723n.
gun-cotton
propellant 287n.
explosive 723n.
gun-dog
dog 365n.
gun-emplacement
fortification 713n.
gun 723n.
gunfire
loudness 400n.
bombardment 712n.
gun-layer
shooter 287n.
gunlock
tool 630n.
gun 723n.
gunman
shooter 287n.
murderer 362n.
combatant 722n.
robber 789n.
ruffian 904n.
gunmetal
gray 429n.
gunner
shooter 287n.
soldiery 722n.
gunnery
propulsion 287n.
bombardment 712n.
art of war 718n.
arm 723n.
gunning
chase 619n.
gunny
textile 222n.
gun-park
gun 723n.
gunpowder
destroyer 168n.
propellant 287n.
explosive 723n.
gun-rack
arsenal 723n.
gun-room
chamber 194n.
storage 632n.
arsenal 723n.
gun-runner
thief 789n.
gun-shot
short distance 200n.
gunsmith
artisan 686n.
gunstock
fire-arm 723n.
gunwale
edge 234n.
gup
rumor 529n.
fable 543n.
gurge
vortex 315n.
eddy 350n.
gurgle
flow 350vb.
bubble 355vb.
sound faint 401vb.
resound 404vb.
laughter 835n.
gurk
eruct 300vb.
guru
sage 500n.
teacher 537n.
gush
outbreak 176n.
flow out 298vb.
emit 300vb.
ascend 308vb.
flow 350vb.
have feeling 374vb.
overestimation 482n.
diffuseness 570n.
chatter 581n.
gusher
outflow 298n.
climber 308n.
stream 350n.
store 632n.
gushing
feeling 818adj.
impressible 819adj.
gusset
adjunct 40n.
gust
breeze 352n.
taste 386n.
excitable state 822n.
gustation
taste 386n.
gustatory
tasty 386adj.
gustful
savory 390adj.
gustless
tasteless 387adj.
gusto
pleasure 376n.
taste 386n.
feeling 818n.
enjoyment 824n.
gusty
unstable 152adj.
windy 352adj.
gut

destroy 165vb.
tube 263n.
void 300vb.
cook 301vb.
extract 304vb.
gulf 345n.
burn 381vb.
access 624n.
fleece 786vb.
gutless
weak 163adj.
irresolute 601adj.
guts
insides 224n.
vigor 571n.
resolution 599n.
courage 855n.
gutta-percha
elasticity 328n.
gutter
vary 152vb.
furrow 262n.
be agitated 318vb.
drain 351n.
letterpress 587n.
sink 649n.
arena 724n.
vulgar 847adj.
detraction 926n.
gutter-crawl
voyage 269vb.
approach 289vb.
guttering
fitful 142adj.
guttersnipe
low fellow 869n.
guttural
speech sound 398n.
hoarse 407adj.
spoken letter 558n.
vocal 577adj.
gutturalize
rasp 407vb.
guy
tackling 47n.
supporter 218n.
person 371n.
male 372n.
be absurd 497vb.
misinterpret 521vb.
misrepresent 552vb.
laughing-stock 851n.
satirize 851vb.
guzzle
eat 301vb.
gluttonize 947vb.
get drunk 949vb.
gym dress
tunic 228n.
gymkhana
contest 716n.
gymnasium
meeting place 192n.
academy 539n.
arena 724n.
gymnast
athlete 162n.
gymnastics
athletics 162n.
education 534n.
exercise 682n.
contest 716n.
sport 837n.
gynandry
abnormality 84n.
male 372n.
gynarchy
gynocracy 733n.
gyneceum
womankind 373n.
love-nest 887n.
gynecologist
doctor 658n.
gynecology
female 373n.
medical art 658n.
gyniatrics
female 373n.
gynocracy
gynocracy 733n.
gyp
deceive 542vb.
trickster 545n.
domestic 742n.
gypsum
materials 631n.
gypsy
extraneous 59adj.
nonconformist 84n.
wanderer 268n.
diviner 511n.
gyration
rotation 315n.
gyrocompass
sailing aid 269n.
gyron
heraldry 547n.
gyropilot
aeronaut 271n.
directorship 689n.
gyroscope
rotator 315n.
gyrostat
rotator 315n.
gyrostatics
rotation 315n.
gyve
fetter 748n.

H

habeas corpus
transference 272n.
warrant 737n.
legal process 959n.
haberdasher
clothier 228n.
tradesman 794n.
habergeon
armor 713n.
habiliments
clothing 228n.
habit
temperament 5n.
state 7n.
uniformity 16n.
composition 56n.
continuity 71n.
regularity 81n.
recurrence 106n.
tradition 127n.
permanence 144n.
dress 228n.
habit 610n.
vocation 622n.
conduct 688n.
fashion 848n.
habitat
place 185n.
situation 186n.
location 187n.
abode 192n.
habitation
edifice 164n.
abode 192n.
habit-forming
influential 178adj.
habitual 610adj.
habit of mind
affections 817n.
habits of business
assiduity 678n.
habitual
general 79adj.
typical 83adj.
repeated 106adj.
frequent 139adj.
known 490adj.
habitual 610adj.
habituate
make conform 83vb.
break in 369vb.
train 534vb.
habituate 610vb.
make ready 669vb.
habituation
habituation 610n.
habitude
(*see* habit)
habitué
habitué 610n.
social person 882n.
hacienda
house 192n.
farm 370n.
lands 777n.
hack
cut 46vb.
cab 274n.
saddle-horse 273n.
author 589n.

wound 655vb.
worker 686n.
servant 742n.
hackbut
fire-arm 723n.
hackee
rodent 365n.
hackery
carriage 274n.
hackie
driver 268n.
hackle
plumage 259n.
livery 547n.
hackney-carriage
cab 274n.
hackneyed
known 490adj.
aphoristic 496adj.
usual 610adj.
hackneyed saying
maxim 496n.
hack-saw
notch 260n.
had
gullible 544adj.
haddock
table fish 365n.
Hades
death 361n.
the dead 361n.
mythic hell 972n.
hadith
tradition 127n.
non-Biblical scripture 975n.
haft
handle 218n.
tool 630n.
hag
old woman 133n.
sorceress 983n.
haggard
lean 206adj.
deformed 246adj.
fatigued 684adj.
suffering 825adj.
melancholic 834adj.
unsightly 842adj.
haggis
dish 301n.
haggle
make terms 766vb.
bargain 791vb.
be parsimonious 816vb.
Hagiographa
scripture 975n.
hagiography
biography 590n.
praise 923n.
theology 973n.
hagiology
biography 590n.
theology 973n.
hagioscope
window 263n.
view 438n.
church interior 990n.
hag-ridden
spooky 970adj.
bewitched 983adj.
hail
crowd 74n.
wintriness 380n.
assent 488vb.
call 547n.
allocution 583n.
greet 884vb.
show respect 920vb.
applaud 923vb.
hail-fellow-well-met
friendly 880adj.
sociable 882adj.
hailstone
ice 380n.
hair
small thing 33n.
filament 208n.
hair 259n.
hairbreadth escape
danger 661n.
escape 667n.
hair cream
hairwash 843n.
hair-cut, hair-do
hair-dressing 843n.
hairdresser
cleaner 648n.
beautician 843n.
hairiness
roughness 259n.
hairless
hairless 229adj.
hair-net
receptacle 194n.
hair-dressing 843n.
hair-oil
unguent 357n.
scent 396n.
hairwash 843n.
hair on end
nervousness 854n.
hairpin
fastening 47n.
coil 251n.
hair-dressing 843n.
hairpin bend
curve 248n.
hair-raising
frightening 854adj.
hair-restorer
hairwash 843n.
hair's breadth
short distance 200n.
narrowness 206n.
hair shirt
asceticism 945n.
hair space
short distance 200n.
interval 201n.
print-type 587n.
hair-splitting
discrimination 463n.
argument 475n.
sophistry 477n.
hairspring
machine 630n.
hair-style
hair-dressing 843n.
hair-stylist
beautician 843n.
hairwash
cleanser 648n.
hairwash 843n.
hairy
fibrous 208adj.
hairy 259adj.
hajj
land travel 267n.
traveler 268n.
piety 979n.
act of worship 981n.
hajji
pietist 979n.
worshiper 981n.
hake
table fish 365n.
hakim
doctor 658n.
officer 741n.
halberd
spear, ax 723n.
halberdier
soldiery 722n.
halcyon
tranquil 266adj.
peaceful 717adj.
palmy 730adj.
halcyon days
palmy days 730n.
joy 824n.
hale
draw 288vb.
healthy 650adj.
half
part 53n.
incompleteness 55n.
bisection 92n.
half a jiffy
instantaneity 116n.
half-and-half
equal 28adj.
mixed 43adj.
neutral 625adj.
half-and-halfer
moderate 625n.
half-asleep
inattentive 456adj.
sleepy 679adj.
half-awake
abstracted 456adj.

sleepy 679adj.
half-baked
smattering 491adj.
immature 670adj.
unskilled 695adj.
uncompleted 726adj.
half-belief
doubt 486n.
half-blood
hybrid 43n.
nonconformist 84n.
defect 647n.
half-breed
hybrid 43n.
nonconformist 84n.
half-brother
kinsman 11n.
half-caste
hybrid 43n.
half-circle
arc 250n.
half-cock, at
immature 670adj.
half dead
dying 361adj.
half distance
middle 70n.
half-done
incomplete 55adj.
neglected 458adj.
uncompleted 726adj.
half-educated
smattering 491adj.
half-face
laterality 239n.
half-fed
underfed 636adj.
half-finished
incomplete 55adj.
half-frozen
semiliquid 354adj.
half-glimpse
sciolism 491n.
half-hearted
weak 163adj.
unwilling 598adj.
irresolute 601adj.
apathetic 820adj.
indifferent 860adj.
half-hidden
shadowy 419adj.
half-hitch
ligature 47n.
half-hose
legwear 228n.
half in
excluded 57adj.
half-knowledge
sciolism 491n.
half-length
short 204adj.
half-lie
mental dishonesty 543n.
half-light
evening 129n.
half-light 419n.
hue 425n.
half-mast
depress 311vb.
half-masted
lamenting 836adj.
half-measures
incompleteness 55n.
irresolution 601n.
mid-course 625n.
insufficiency 636n.
bungling 695n.
half-melted
semiliquid 354adj.
half-moon
curve 248n.
arc 250n.
moon 321n.
half-nelson
retention 778n.
half out
excluded 57adj.
half-pants
trousers 228n.
half pay
receipt 807n.
halfpenny
coinage 797n.
half-price
cheap 812adj.
half rations
insufficiency 636n.
half-ripe
immature 670adj.
half-shadow
half-light 419n.
half-sight
dim sight 440n.
half-smile
laughter 835n.
half-space
interval 201n.
half-spoken
tacit 523adj.
half-starved
underfed 636adj.
fasting 946adj.
half the battle
chief thing 638n.
half-tide
middle 70n.
mid-course 625n.
half-title
edition 589n.
half-tone
light contrast 417n.
hue 425n.
picture 553n.
edition 589n.
half-truth
mental dishonesty 543n.
half-vision
dim sight 440n.
halfway
middle point 30n.
midway 70adv.
mid-course 625n.
undeviating 625adj.
compromise 770n.
half-wit
fool 501n.
half-witted
unintelligent 499adj.
halibut
table fish 365n.
halitosis
fetor 397n.
hall
edifice 164n.
house 192n.
chamber 194n.
feasting 301n.
access 624n.
hallelujah
rejoicing 835n.
celebration 876n.
hymn 981n.
halliard
tackling 47n.
hall-mark
label 547n.
halloa, halloo
cry 408vb.
pursue 619vb.
hallow
sanctify 979vb.
hallowed
divine 965adj.
hallucination
unsubstantiality 4n.
appearance 445n.
error 495n.
psychopathy 503n.
fantasy 513n.
deception 542n.
hallux
foot 214n.
finger 378n.
halo
circumjacence 230n.
loop 250n.
light 417n.
honors 866n.
haloed
sanctified 979adj.
halt
end 69n.
stop 145n.
crippled 163adj.
quiescence 266n.
move slowly 278vb.
goal 295n.
imperfect 647adj.
be obstructive 702vb.
failure 728n.

halter
halter 47n.
hanger 217n.
loop 250n.
fetter 748n.
means of execution 964n.
halve
sunder 46vb.
bisect 92vb.
apportion 783vb.
halves
portion 783n.
halve the match
be equal 28vb.
halyard
tackling 47n.
ham
housing 192n.
buttocks 238n.
leg 267n.
meat 301n.
dramatic 594adj.
unskilled 695adj.
bungler 697n.
hamadryad
reptile 365n.
vegetability 366n.
hamburger
meat 301n.
ham-handed
clumsy 695adj.
Hamitic
ethnic 11adj.
language type 557n.
hamlet
housing 192n.
hammer
be vigorous 174vb.
pierce 263vb.
hammer 279n.
pulverizer 332n.
be loud 400vb.
strike at 712vb.
hammer and sickle
heraldry 547n.
hammer and tongs
violently 176adv.
knock 279n.
laboriously 682adv.
hammer at
repeat oneself 106vb.
hammer in
affix 45vb.
insert 303vb.
hammer out
efform 243vb.
carry through 725vb.
hammer, under the
saleable 793adj.
hammock
pendant 217n.
bed 218n.
hamper
basket 194n.
impair 655vb.
be difficult 700vb.
hinder 702vb.
restrain 747vb.
hamster
rodent 365n.
hamstring
disable 161vb.
impair 655vb.
hinder 702vb.
hamstrings
leg 267n.
hamstrung
crippled 163adj.
hand
limb 53n.
group 74n.
timekeeper 117n.
long measure 203n.
laterality 239n.
pass 305vb.
person 371n.
feeler, finger 378n.
indicator 547n.
lettering 586n.
instrument 628n.
doer 676n.
worker 686n.
servant 742n.
nippers 778n.
portion 783n.
hand and seal, under
promissory 764adj.
contractual 765adj.
hand, at
early 135adj.
impending 155adj.
on the spot 189adj.
near 200adj.
useful 640adj.
hand back
restore 656vb.
handbill
the press 528n.
handbook
itinerary 267n.
guide-book 524n.
reading matter 589n.
book 589n.
handclasp
friendliness 880n.
sociability 882n.
courteous act 884n.
handcuff
tie 45vb.
fastening 47n.
fetter 747vb.
fetter 748n.
hand down
transfer 272vb.
handfast
conjunct 45adj.
married 894adj.
handful
finite quantity 26n.
bunch 74n.
nonconformist 84n.
fewness 105n.
contents 193n.
hard task 700n.
hand-gallop
gait 265n.
hand, get a
be praised 923vb.
handhold
retention 778n.
handicap
equalize 28vb.
inferiority 35n.
retard 278vb.
inexpedience 643n.
encumbrance 702n.
contest 716n.
handicapped
unintelligent 499adj.
handicraft
business 622n.
hand, in
prepared 669adj.
possessed 773adj.
handiness
instrumentality 628n.
utility 640n.
skill 694n.
hand in glove
accompanying 89adj.
concurrently 181adv.
cooperative 706adj.
hand in hand
conjunct 45n.
with 89adv.
concurrently 181adv.
contiguously 202adv.
in league 708adv.
sociably 882adv.
hand it to
be inferior 35vb.
handiwork
effect 157n.
product 164n.
deed 676n.
handkerchief
cleaning cloth 648n.
handle
opportunity 137n.
operate 173vb.
handle 218n.
strike 279vb.
touch 378vb.
name 561n.
dissert 591vb.
tool 630n.
use 673vb.
work 682vb.

deal with 688vb.
manage 689vb.
trade 791vb.
honors 866n.
title 870n.
handlebar
handle 218n.
hand-made
produced 164adj.
handmaid
instrument 628n.
auxiliary 707n.
handmill
pulverizer 332n.
hand on
transfer 272vb.
hand-out
report 524n.
gift 781n.
hand over
transfer 272vb.
pass 305vb.
relinquish 621vb.
convey 780vb.
give 781vb.
hand over hand
continuously 71adv.
hand-picked
chosen 605adj.
excellent 644adj.
handrail
handle 218n.
supporter 218n.
hand round
provide 633vb.
handrunning
continuously 71adv.
hands
personnel 686n.
handsel
beginning 68n.
security 767n.
gift 781n.
handshake
gesture 547n.
resignation 753n.
friendliness 880n.
sociability 882n.
courteous act 884n.
handsome
liberal 813adj.
beautiful 841adj.
hand, something in
vantage 34n.
handspike
tool 630n.
handspring
overturning 221n.
hand's turn
labor 682n.
hand to
transfer 272vb.
hand to hand
contending 716adj.
hand to hand, from
contiguously 202adv.
in transit 272adv.
hand-to-mouth existence
poverty 801n.
hand-woven
crossed 222adj.
handwriting
writing 586n.
handwriting expert
penman 586n.
handy
little 196adj.
near 200adj.
light 323adj.
instrumental 628adj.
expedient 642adj.
useful 640adj.
skillful 694adj.
wieldy 701adj.
handyman
proficient 696n.
hang
come unstuck 49vb.
pend 136vb.
hang 217vb.
descend 309vb.
kill 362vb.
appearance 445n.
execute 963vb.
hang about
be late 136vb.
be in motion 265vb.
be inactive 679vb.
hangar
stable 192n.
air travel 271n.
hang back
be late 136vb.
be loath 598vb.
avoid 620vb.
be modest 874vb.
hang by a thread
be in danger 661vb.
hangdog look
sullenness 893n.
hanger
hanger 217n.
supporter 218n.
sharp edge 256n.
side-arms 723n.
hanger-on
concomitant 89n.
follower 284n.
auxiliary 707n.
dependent 742n.
toady 879n.
flatterer 925n.
hang fire
pend 136vb.
halt 145vb.
be inert 175vb.
move slowly 278vb.
be loath 598vb.
not act 677vb.
be inactive 679vb.
miscarry 728vb.
hanging judge
tyrant 735n.
hangings
covering 226n.
hangman
killer 362n.
ruffian 904n.
punisher 963n.
hang on
affix 45vb.
go on 146vb.
persevere 600vb.
be subject 745vb.
retain 778vb.
be servile 879vb.
hang one's head
be dejected 834vb.
be humbled 872vb.
hang out
dwell 192vb.
hang over
impend 155vb.
be high 209vb.
jut 254vb.
threaten 900vb.
hangover
sequel 67n.
pain 377n.
intemperance 943n.
crapulence 949n.
hang together
accord 24vb.
unite with 45vb.
cohere 48vb.
concur 181vb.
cooperate 706vb.
hang up
cease 145vb.
be mute 578vb.
hang upon
depend 157vb.
hank
fastening 47n.
bunch 74n.
hanker
desire 859vb.
hanky-panky
deception 542n.
foul play 930n.
Hansard
record 548n.
hansom
cab 274n.
hantle
multitude 104n.
hap
eventuality 154n.
chance 159n., vb.

haphazard
casual 159adj.
indiscriminate 464adj.
designless 618adj.
hapless
unfortunate 731adj.
haply
possibly 469adv.
happen
be 1vb.
happen 154vb.
result 157vb.
chance 159adj.
appear 445vb.
be true 494vb.
happening
(*see* happen)
happen on
discover 484vb.
happiness
(*see* happy)
happy
apt 24adj.
opportune 137adj.
comfortable 376adj.
elegant 575adj.
willing 597adj.
good 615adj.
well-made 694adj.
concordant 710adj.
pacificatory 719adj.
successful 727adj.
happy 824adj.
pleasurable 826adj.
cheerful 833adj.
drunk 949adj.
paradisiac 971adj.
happy ending
good 615n.
happy-go-lucky
unprepared 670adj.
unskillful 695adj.
happy returns
congratulation 886n.
happy thought
idea 451n.
contrivance 623n.
hara-kiri
suicide 362n.
harangue
teach 534vb.
diffuseness 570n.
oration 579n.
dissertation 591n.
harass
fatigue 684vb.
oppress 735vb.
torment 827vb.
harbinger
precursor 66n.
omen 511n.
informant 524n.
messenger 531n.
harbor
goal 295n.
shelter 662n.
hard
painfully 32adv.
strong 162adj.
hard 326adj.
unsavory 391adj.
puzzling 517adj.
imperspicuous 568adj.
laborious 682adj.
difficult 700adj.
hindering 702adj.
severe 735adj.
thick-skinned 820adj.
paining 827adj.
pitiless 906adj.
unjust 914adj.
impenitent 940adj.
intoxicating 949adj.
impious 980adj.
hard at it
laboring 682adj.
hard-bitten
thick-skinned 820adj.
unkind 898adj.
hard-boiled
tough 329adj.
(*see* hard)
hard breathing
fatigue 684n.
hard by
near 200adj.
hard case
ill fortune 731n.
hard core
hardness 326n.
stamina 600n.
chief thing 638n.
hard-drinking
drunken 949adj.
harden
strengthen 162vb.
harden 326vb.
thicken 354vb.
habituate 610vb.
mature 669vb.
be dear 811vb.
make insensitive 820vb.
hardened
(*see* hard, harden)
hardened arteries
blood pressure 651n.
harden one's heart
be inimical 881vb.
be pitiless 906vb.
be impenitent 940vb.
be impious 980vb.
hard-featured
ugly 842adj.
hard feelings
feeling 818n.
enmity 881n.
hard-fought
laborious 682adj.
hard going
difficulty 700n.
hard-headed
intelligent 498adj.
severe 735adj.
hard-hearted
cruel 898adj.
hard-hitting
disapproving 924adj.
hardihood
courage 855n.
insolence 878n.
(*see* hardy)
hard labor
penalty 963n.
hard life
adversity 731n.
hard lines
ill fortune 731n.
severity 735n.
hard-luck story
lament 836n.
hardly
almost 33adv.
slightly 33adv.
seldom 140adv.
with difficulty 700adv.
hard measure
severity 735n.
hard-mouthed
obstinate 602adj.
hardness
stability 153n.
strength 162n.
density 324n.
hardness 326n.
inelegance 576n.
resolution 599n.
obstinacy 602n.
difficulty 700n.
severity 735n.
moral insensibility 820n.
inhumanity 898n.
pitilessness 906n.
wickedness 934n.
impenitence 940n.
hard of hearing
deaf 416adj.
hard on, be
be severe 735vb.
hard-pressed
hasty 680adj.
in difficulties 700adj.
hindered 702adj.
hard run
in difficulties 700adj.
hards
fiber 208n.

hard saying
unintelligibility 517n.
enigma 530n.
hardship
adversity 731n.
annoyance 827n.
hardtack
food 301n.
hard times
adversity 731n.
hard to please
discontented 829adj.
fastidious 862adj.
hard up
poor 801adj.
hardware
produce 164n.
hardness 326n.
hard way, the
difficulty 700n.
hard-won
laborious 682adj.
hard words
imperspicuity 568n.
reproach 924n.
hard-working
industrious 678adj.
laboring 682adj.
hardy
stalwart 162adj.
healthy 650adj.
courageous 855adj.
insolent 878adj.
temperate 942adj.
hare
speeder 277n.
move fast 277vb.
vermin 365n.
coward 856n.
hare-brained
light-minded 456adj.
hare-lip
blemish 845n.
harem
womankind 373n.
love-nest 887n.
hare's foot
cosmetic 843n.
hariolation
divination 511n.
hark
pursue 619vb.
(*see* hearken)
hark back
look back 125vb.
turn back 286vb.
notice 455vb.
regret 830vb.
harl
fiber 208n.
harlequin
changeable thing 152n.
variegation 437n.
entertainer 594n.
harlequinade
stage play 594n.
wit 839n.
harlot
prostitute 952n.
harlotry
unchastity 951n.
social evil 951n.
harm
evil 616n.
be inexpedient 643vb.
harm 645vb.
impairment 655n.
hurt 827vb.
harmful
destructive 165adj.
evil 616adj.
inexpedient 643adj.
harmful 645adj.
insalubrious 653adj.
baneful 659adj.
adverse 731adj.
malevolent 898adj.
wrong 914adj.
harmless
defenseless 161adj.
weak 163adj.
moderate 177adj.
beneficial 644adj.
salubrious 652adj.
safe 660adj.
peaceful 717adj.
humble 872adj.
amiable 884adj.
innocent 935adj.
harmonic
musical note 410n.
harmonica
gong, organ 414n.
harmonic progression
ratio 85n.
harmonics
melody 410n.
harmonious
sweet 392adj.
harmonious 410adj.
friendly 880adj.
(*see* harmony)
harmonist
musician 413n.
harmonium
organ 414n.
harmonize
sing 413vb.
compose music 413vb.
pacify 719vb.
(*see* harmony)
harmony
agreement 24n.
a mixture 43n.
combination 50n.
completeness 54n.
order 60n.
concurrence 181n.
symmetry 245n.
melody 410n.
music 412n.
color 425n.
consensus 488n.
elegance 575n.
concord 710n.
pleasurableness 826n.
harness
affix 45vb.
tackling 47n.
dressing 228n.
start out 296vb.
break in 369vb.
equipment 630n.
make ready 669vb.
armor 713n.
fetter 748n.
harness, in
doing 676adj.
harp
play music 413vb.
harp 414n.
harper
instrumentalist 413n.
harp on
repeat oneself 106vb.
sustain 146vb.
be tedious 838vb.
harpoon
sharp point 256n.
spear 723n.
harpsichord
piano 414n.
harpy
tyrant 735n.
taker 876n.
hell-hag 904n.
demon 970n.
harquebus
fire-arm 723n.
harquebusier
soldiery 722n.
harridan
eyesore 842n.
harrier
bird of prey 365n.
dog 365n.
harrow
farm tool 370n.
cultivate 370vb.
torment 827vb.
frighten 854vb.
harry
attack 712vb.
torment 827vb.
be malevolent 898vb.
harsh

exorbitant 32adj.
vigorous 174adj.
pungent 388adj.
strident 407adj.
discordant 411adj.
florid 425adj.
imperspicuous 568adj.
inelegant 576adj.
harmful 645adj.
oppressive 735adj.
paining 827adj.
ungracious 885adj.
unkind 898adj.
pitiless 906adj.

harshness
roughness 259n.
(*see* harsh)

hart
deer 365n.
male animal 372n.

hartal
strike 145n.

hartshorn
pungency 388n.
tonic 658n.

harum-scarum
disorderly 61adj.
confusedly 61adv.
light-minded 456adj.
rash 857adj.
desperado 857n.

haruspex
diviner 511n.

harvest
great quantity 32n.
increment 36n.
assemblage 74n.
multitude 104n.
autumn 129n.
growth 157n.
product 164n.
abundance 171n.
agriculture 370n.
benefit 615n.
store 632n., vb.
plenty 635n.
earnings 771n.
take 786vb.

harvester
husbandman 370n.

harvest-home
celebration 876n.

has-been
past 125adj.
archaism 127n.
loser 728n.

hash
medley 43n.
confusion 61n.
dish 301n.
be clumsy 695vb.

hashish
poisonous plant 659n.
poison 659n.

haslet
insides 224n.
meat 301n.

hasp
joint 45n.
fastening 47n.

hassock
cushion 218n.
church utensil 990n.

hastate
sharp 256adj.

haste
punctuality 135n.
move fast 277vb.
commotion 318n.
non-preparation 670n.
activity 678n.
haste 680n.
rashness 857n.

hasten
be early 135vb.
cause 156vb.
accelerate 277vb.
incite 612vb.
be busy 678vb.
hasten 680vb.

hasty
brief 114adj.
unwise 499adj.
unprepared 670adj.
hasty 680adj.
excitable 822adj.
rash 857adj.
irascible 892adj.

hat
headgear 228n.

hatband
girdle 47n.

hatbox
box 194n.

hatch
group 74n.
reproduce itself 164vb.
doorway 263n.
breed stock 369vb.
darken 418vb.
imagine 513vb.
fake 541vb.
plan 623vb.
mature 669vb.

hatched
born 360adj.

hatcher
planner 623n.

hatchery
nest 192n.
stock farm 369n.

hatches
lock-up 748n.

hatchet
sharp edge 256n.
ax 723n.

hatching
obscuration 418n.
maturation 669n.

hatchment
obsequies 364n.
heraldry 547n.
monument 548n.

hatchway
doorway 263n.

hate
dislike 861vb.
hatred 888n.
hateful object 888n
resentment 891n.
malevolence 898n.
jealousy 911n.
(*see* hatred)

hateful
not nice 645adj.
unpleasant 827adj.
disliked 861adj.
hateful 888adj.

hatefulness
painfulness 827n.
odium 888n.

hatless
uncovered 229adj.

hatpin
fastening 47n.
hair-dressing 843n.

hatred
prejudice 481n.
dissension 709n.
phobia 854n.
enmity 881n.
hatred 888n.

hatted
dressed 228adj.

hatter
clothier 228n.

hat-trick
triplication 94n.
masterpiece 694n.
success 727n.

hauberk
armor 713n.

haughty
authoritarian 735adj.
noble 868adj.
proud, prideful 871adj.
insolent 878adj.
unsociable 883adj.
despising 922adj.

haul
traction 288n.
work 682vb.
booty 790n.

haulage
transport 272n.

traction 288n.
haulier
carrier 273n.
haul over the coals
reprove 924vb.
haul up
indict 928vb.
haunch
rear 238n.
buttocks 238n.
haunt
focus 76n.
reoccur 106vb.
recur 139vb.
go on 146vb.
district 184n.
locality 187n.
be present 189vb.
abode, home 192n.
dwell 192vb.
appear 445vb.
engross 449vb.
remind 505vb.
be wont 610vb.
torment 827vb.
frighten 854vb.
goblinize 970vb.
bewitch 983vb.
haunted
obsessed 455adj.
remembering 505adj.
nervous 854adj.
spooky 970adj.
bewitched 983adj.
haunter
ghost 970n.
haunting
remembered 505adj.
pleasurable 826adj.
haute couture
fashion 848n.
haute cuisine
savoriness 390n.
haute école
equitation 267n.
hauteur
pride 871n.
have
contain 56vb.
comprise 78vb.
confute 479vb.
understand 516vb.
befool 542vb.
possess 773vb.
be hospitable 882vb.
have a go
essay 617vb.
have a hand in
cooperate 706vb.
participate 775vb.
have a hold on
influence 178vb.
have a mind to
desire 859vb.
have and hold
possess 773vb.
have at
attack 712vb.
strike at 712vb.
have everything
be complete 54vb.
comprise 78vb.
have in mind
be mindful 455vb.
mean 514vb.
intend 617vb.
have it
discover 484vb.
have it all one's way
will 595vb.
do easily 701vb.
win 727vb.
dominate 733vb.
have it coming to one
deserve 915vb.
haven
resting place 266n.
goal 295n.
protection 660n.
shelter 662n.
have-nots
poor man 801n.
lower classes 869n.
have occasion for
require 627vb.
have one's day
pass time 108vb.
triumph 727vb.
prosper 730vb.
have one's head
be free 744vb.
have one's say
affirm 532vb.
have one's turn
come after 65vb.
haver
be loquacious 581vb.
haversack
bag 194n.
haves, the
rich man 800n.
upper class 868n.
have taped
appraise 465vb.
have the makings of
evidence 466vb.
have what it takes
be resolute 599vb.
havildar
army officer 741n.
havoc
disorder 61n.
havoc 165n.
impairment 665n.
spoliation 788n.
haw-haw
speech defect 580n.
hawk
eruct 300vb.
bird of prey 365n.
rasp 407vb.
hunt 619vb.
offer 759vb.
request 761vb.
sell 793vb.
hawker
peddler 794n.
hawk-eyed
seeing 438adj.
hawser
cable 47n.
hay
provender 301n.
grass 366n.
hay-fever
excretion 302n.
ill-health 651n.
hay-fork
shovel 274n.
farm tool 370n.
hayloft
attic 194n.
farm tool 370n.
haymaker
knock 279n.
hayseed
ingenue 699n.
countryman 869n.
haystack
store 632n.
haywire
non-uniform 17adj.
orderless 61adj.
hazard
chance 159n.
gambling 618n.
danger 661n.
pitfall 663n.
obstacle 702n.
hazardous
speculative 618adj.
dangerous 661adj.
haze
cloud 355n.
uncertainty 474n.
oppress 735vb.
torment 827vb.
hazel
brown 430adj.
hazy
cloudy 355adj.
dim 419adj.
opaque 423adj.
ill-seen 444adj.
uncertain 474adj.
puzzling 517adj.
he
male 372n., adj.
children's games

837n.
head
come first 34vb.
come before 64vb.
beginning 68n.
extremity 69n.
classification 77n.
energy 160n.
long measure 203n.
vertex, head 213n.
face 237n.
be in front 237vb.
central 225adj.
strike 279vb.
precede 283vb.
repel 292vb.
bubble 355n.
person 371n.
topic 452n.
intelligence 498n.
image 551n.
picture 553n.
sculpture 554n.
name 561n.
bigwig 638n.
direct 689vb.
director 690n.
trophy 729n.
master 741n.
crapulence 949n.
execute 963vb.
headache
pang 377n.
difficulty 700n.
worry 825n.
head and front
chief thing 638n.
headband
headgear 228n.
head boy
superior 34n.
head-count
numeration 86n.
headdress
headgear 228n.
header
descent 309n.
plunge 313n.
head for
navigate 269vb.
steer for 281vb.
headgear
headgear 228n.
head-hunter
killer 362n.
hunter 619n.
heading
prelude 66n.
beginning 68n.
classification 77n.
precession 283n.
label 547n.
record 548n.
name 561n.
headland
projection 254n.
headless
short 204adj.
headlight, headlamp
radiation 417n.
lamp 420n.
headline
advertisement 528n.
edition 589n.
make important 638vb.
excitant 821n.
(*see* heading)
headlong
violently 176vb.
swiftly 277adv.
hasty 680adj.
rash 857adj.
headman
director 690n.
officer 741n.
headmaster
teacher 537n.
director 690n.
head off
converge 293vb.
dissuade 613vb.
head-on
fore 237adj.
head over heels
completely 54adv.
inverted 221adj.
round and round 315adv.
headphone
hearing aid 415n.
telecommunication 531n.
headpiece
intelligence 498n.
(*see* head)
headquarters
focus 76n.
abode 192n.
plan 623n.
headrest
supporter 218n.
heads
compendium 592n.
headship
magistrature 733n.
headsman
killer 362n.
punisher 963n.
heads or tails
chance 159n.
headstall
fetter 748n.
headstone
supporter 218n.
obsequies 364n.
headstrong
furious 176adj.
willful 602adj.
rash 857adj.
head to foot
longwise 203adv.
head to tail
longwise 203adv.
head-up
vertical 215adj.
head-waters
source 156n.
headway
room 183n.
motion 265n.
water travel 269n.
progression 285n.
headwind
contrariety 14n.
contraposition 240n.
wind 352n.
obstacle 702n.
opposition 704n.
head-work
thought 449n.
heady
strong 162adj.
vigorous 174adj.
pungent 388adj.
exciting 821adj.
intoxicating 949adj.
heal
cure 656vb.
remedy 658vb.
pacify 719vb.
healer
mender 656n.
doctor 658n.
health
vitality 162n.
potion 301n.
goodness 644n.
health 650n.
salubrity 652n.
celebration 876n.
healthless
unhealthy 651adj.
health officer
doctor 658n.
healthy
athletic 162adj.
large 195adj.
(*see* health)
heap
great quantity 32n.
chief part 52n.
accumulation 74n.
multitude 104n.
bulk 195n.
monticle 209n.
not discriminate 464n.
store 632n., vb.

acquisition 771n.
heap on
add 38vb.
hear
hear 415vb.
be mindful 455vb.
inquire 459vb.
judge 480vb.
be informed 524vb.
consent 758vb.
try a case 959vb.
heard
sounding 398adj.
loud 400adj.
known 490adj.
hearer
listener 415n.
allocution 583n.
hearing
sense 374n.
hearing 415n.
listening 415n.
council 691n.
legal trial 959n.
hearing aid
megaphone 400n.
hearing aid 415n.
hearken
hear 415vb.
be willing 597vb.
obey 739vb.
consent 758vb.
hear mass
offer worship 981vb.
hearsay
evidence 466n.
information 524n.
rumor 529n.
hearse
vehicle 274n.
funeral 364n.
heart
essence 1n.
essential part 5n.
middle 70n.
interiority 224n.
centrality 225n.
meat 301n.
life 360n.
spirit 447n.
chief thing 638n.
affections 817n.
courage 855n.
love-token 889n.
darling 890n.
heart-ache
suffering 825n.
dejection 834n.
heart and soul
completely 54adj.
willingly 597adv.
laboriously 682adj.
feelingly 818adv.
heart-breaking
distressing 827adj.
heartbroken
disappointed 509adj.
unhappy 825adj.
heartburn
indigestion 651n.
heartburning
sorrow 825n.
discontent 829n.
regret 830n.
resentment 891n.
jealousy 911n.
heart, by
in memory 505adv.
heart, cockles of the
affections 817n.
heart disease
heart disease 651n.
hearten
invigorate 174vb.
aid 703vb.
animate 821vb.
relieve 831vb.
give courage 855vb.
heartfelt
felt 818adj.
heart-free
impassive 820adj.
hearth
focus 76n.
home 192n.
furnace 383n.
refuge 662n.
hearth and home
family 11n.
hearties
chum 880n.
heartily
willingly 597adv.
feelingly 818adv.
heartiness
(*see* hearty)
heartland
land 344n.
heartless
impassive 820adj.
impenitent 940adj.
heart of grace
hope 852n.
heart of hearts
affections 817n.
heart's blood
essential part 5n.
interiority 224n.
life 360n.
favorite 890n.
heart-sick
melancholic 834adj.
heart-sinking
dejection 834n.
hearts of oak
resolution 599n.
heart-throb
loved one 887n.
heart-to-heart
undisguised 522adj.
heart-warming
pleasant 376adj.
felt 818adj.
pleasurable 826adj.
cheering 833adj.
heart-whole
free 744adj.
impassive 820adj.
indifferent 860adj.
unwedded 895adj.
heartwood
hardness 326n.
wood 366n.
hearty
vigorous 174adj.
healthy 650adj.
felt 818adj.
cheerful 833adj.
ill-bred 847adj.
friendly 880adj.
sociable 882adj.
heat
summer 128n.
dryness 342n.
heat 379n.
contest 716n.
excite 821vb.
excitable state 822n.
libido 859n.
excite love 887vb.
anger 891n.
heater
heater 383n.
heath
desert 172n.
plain 348n.
plant, wood 366n.
heathen
heathen 947n.
idolator 982n.
heathenism
ignorance 491n.
antichristianity 974n.
irreligion 974n.
impiety 980n.
idolatry 982n.
heather
plant 366n.
heave
be periodic 141vb.
carry 273vb
impel 279vb.
propel 287vb.
draw 288n.
vomit 300vb.
oscillate 317vb.
breathe 352vb.

exertion 682n.
show feeling 818vb.
heaven
future state 124n.
heaven 971n.
heaven-born
worshipful 866adj.
heavenly
celestial 321adj.
topping 644adj.
pleasurable 826adj.
divine 965adj.
paradisiac 971adj.
heavenly-minded
pious 979adj.
heavens
influence 178n.
space 183n.
heavens 321n.
heaven-sent
opportune 137adj.
good 615adj.
heave the lead
be deep 211vb.
measure 465vb.
heave to
bring to rest 266vb.
navigate 269vb.
heavily
greatly 32adv.
heaviness
sleepiness 679n.
inactivity 679n.
Heaviside layer
atmosphere 340n.
heavy
substantial 3adj.
unequal 29adj.
great 32adj.
strong 162adj.
inert 175adj.
weighty 322adj.
dense 324adj.
odorous 394adj.
fetid 397adj.
non-resonant 404adj.
unintelligent 499adj.
forceful 571adj.
inelegant 576adj.
bad 645adj.
inactive 679adj.
laborious 682adj.
severe 735adj.
inexcitable 823adj.
melancholic 834adj.
tedious 838adj.
dull 840adj.
heinous 934adj.
heavy-armed
defended 713adj.
heavy-eyed
sleepy 679adj.
heavy father
acting 594n.
tyrant 735n.
heavy-handed
violent 176adj.
tactual 378adj.
clumsy 695adj.
oppressive 735adj.
heavy-laden
full 54adj.
hindered 702adj.
suffering 825adj.
heavy sea
commotion 318n.
wave 350n.
heavy type
punctuation 547n.
print-type 587n.
heavyweight
athlete 162n.
pugilist 722n.
heavy with
impending 155adj.
productive 164adj.
hebdomadal
seasonal 141adj.
Hebe
a beauty 841n.
Olympian god 967n.
hebetude
unintelligence 499n.
Hebraist
antiquarian 125n.
linguist 557n.
Hecate
moon 321n.
sorceress 983n.
hecatomb
hundred 99n.
havoc 165n.
oblation 981n.
heckle
be obstructive 702vb.
torment 827vb.
heckler
dissentient 489n.
hinderer 702n.
hectare
measure 183n.
hectic
heat 379n.
red 431adj.
fervent 818adj.
excited 821adj.
Hector
brave person 855n.
boaster 877n.
hector
be insolent 878vb.
threaten 900vb.
hedge
set off 31vb.
separation 46n.
circumscribe 232vb.
fence 235n.
wood 366n.
screen 421n.
gamble 618vb.
seek safety 660vb.
shelter 662n.
obstacle 702n.
defend 713vb.
be cautious 858vb.
hedgehog
prickle 256n.
hedgehop
be near 200vb.
fly 271vb.
hedge-priest
cleric 986n.
hedonism
pleasure 376n.
philosophy 449n.
enjoyment 824n.
sensualism 944n.
heebie-jeebies
nervousness 854n.
alcoholism 949n.
heed
attention 455n.
carefulness 457n.
observe 768vb.
caution 858n.
heedless
inattentive 456adj.
negligent 458adj.
forgetful 506adj.
heedlessness
rashness 857n.
indifference 860n.
hee-haw
ululation 409n.
heel
extremity 69n.
base, foot 214n.
stand 218n.
be oblique 220vb.
rear 238n.
kick 279vb.
repair 656vb.
cad 938n.
heel and toe
pedestrianism 267n.
heel over
be inverted 221vb.
heel-piece
sequel 67n.
heel-tap
leavings 41n.
dirt 649n.
heft
influence 178n.
bulk 195n.
hefty
whopping 32adj.
stalwart 162adj.
hegemonic

directing 689adj.
hegemony
superiority 34n.
precedence 64n.
influence 178n.
authority 733n.
prestige 866n.
hegira
departure 296n.
heifer
youngling 132n.
cattle 365n.
female animal 373n.
height
degree 27n.
greatness 32n.
superiority 34n.
measure 183n.
size 195n.
height 209n.
high land 209n.
summit 213n.
metrology 465n.
heighten
augment 36vb.
enlarge 197vb.
make higher 209vb.
elevate 310vb.
aggravate 832vb.
heinous
bad 645adj.
heinous 934adj.
heir
survivor 41n.
aftercomer 67n.
descendent 170n.
deputy 755n.
beneficiary 776n.
recipient 782n.
heirdom
possession 773n.
heirloom
dower 778n.
heirs
futurity 124n.
posterity 170n.
heirship
sonship 170n.
acquisition 771n.
possession 773n.
heliacal
celestial 321adj.
helianthus
orange 436n.
Helicon
poetry 593n.
helicopter
aircraft 276n.
heliocentric
central 225adj.
celestial 321adj.
heliograph
signal 547n.
heliography
optics 417n.
helioscope
optical device 442n.
heliotrope
purple 434n., adj.
gem 844n.
heliotype
photography 551n.
printing 555n.
heliport
air travel 271n.
goal 295n.
helium
lifter 310n.
levity 323n.
helix
coil 251n.
circuition 314n.
hell
future state 124n.
depth 211n.
pain 377n.
gaming-house 618n.
bane 659n.
suffering 825n.
hell 972n.
hell-bent
intending 617adj.
rash 857adj.
hell-born
diabolic 969adj.
hell-broth
wickedness 934n.
magic instrument 983n.
hell-cat
violent creature 176n.
hell-hag 904n.
hellebore
poisonous plant 659n.
Hellenist
linguist 557n.
hellenize
transform 147vb.
hell-hag
hell-hag 904n.
monster 938n.
hellish
damnable 645adj.
cruel 898adj.
wicked, heinous 934adj.
diabolic 969adj.
infernal 972adj.
helm
sailing aid 269n.
tool 630n.
directorship 689n.
helmet
headgear 228n.
heraldry 547n.
armor 713n.
helminthagogue
antidote 658n.
helminthology
zoology 367n.
helmsman
navigator 270n.
director 690n.
helot
slave 742n.
helotry
slave 742n.
servitude 745n.
help
concur 181vb.
meal 301vb.
benefit 615vb.
utility 640n.
be expedient 642vb.
do good 644vb.
cleaner 648n.
remedy 658n., vb.
worker 686n.
facilitate 701vb.
aid 703n., vb.
servant 742n.
give 781vb.
helper
auxiliary 707n.
servant 742n.
friend 880n.
benefactor 903n.
helpful
willing 597adj.
cooperative 706adj.
helping
provision 633n.
portion 783n.
helpless
impotent 161adj.
weak 163adj.
vulnerable 661adj.
helpmate
auxiliary 707n.
spouse 894n.
helter-skelter
confusedly 61adv.
swiftly 277adv.
helve
tool 630n.
hem
be contiguous 202vb.
surround 230vb.
edging 234n.
limit 236vb.
flank 239vb.
fold 261n., vb.
decorate 844vb.
hemad
blood 335n.
he-man
athlete 162n.

violent creature 176n.
male 372n.
brave person 855n.
hem and haw
stammer 580vb.
be irresolute 601vb.
hematic
sanguineous 335adj.
hematology
blood 335n.
hematosis
blood 335n.
hemi
fragmentary 53adj.
bisected 92adj.
hemicrania
pang 377n.
hemicycle
arc 250n.
hemiplegia
helplessness 161n.
paralysis 651n.
hemisphere
part 53n.
bisection 92n.
region 184n.
sphere 252n.
dome 253n.
hemistitch
verse form 593n.
hemline
edging 234n.
hemlock
killer 362n.
poisonous plant 659n.
means of execution 964n.
hemoglobin
blood 335n.
hemophilia
hemorrhage 302n.
fluidity 335n.
blood disease 651n.
hemophilic
sanguineous 335adj.
diseased 651adj.
hemorrhage
outflow 298n.
hemorrhage 302n.
hemorrhoids
swelling 253n.
hemostatic
solidifying 324adj.
hemp
fiber 208n.
pungency 388n.
hen
poultry 365n.
female animal 373n.
henbane
poisonous plant 659n.
hen battery
stock farm 369n.
hence
hence 158adv.
henceforth
henceforth 124adv.
henchman
auxiliary 707n.
dependent 742n.
retainer 742n.
hencoop, henhouse
stable 192n.
cattle pen 369n.
hendecasyllable
verse form 593n.
hendiadys
bisection 92n.
henna
orange 436n.
henotheism
deism 973n.
hen party
womankind 373n.
social gathering 882n.
henpeck
bicker 709vb.
henpecked
subjected 745adj.
hepcat
musician 413n.
heptachord
harp 414n.
heptad
over five 99n.
heptagon
angular figure 247n.
her
female 373n.
herald
precursor 66n.
precede 283vb.
omen 511n.
informant 524n.
proclaim 528vb.
messenger 531n.
heraldry 547n.
deputy 755n.
heraldic
heraldic 547adj.
heraldry
heraldry 547n.
herb
potherb 301n.
medicine 658n.
herbaceous
vegetal 366adj.
herbage
grass 366n.
farm 370n.
herbal
vegetal 366adj.
botany 368n.
herbalist
botanist 368n.
doctor 658n.
herbarium
botany 368n.
herbivore
animal 365n.
herbivorous
feeding 301adj.
Herculean
great 32adj.
stalwart 162adj.
huge 195adj.
laborious 682adj.
Herculean task
hard task 700n.
Hercules
athlete 162n.
brave person 855n.
demigod 967n.
herd
group 74n.
cattle 365n.
herdsman 369n.
groom 369vb.
social group 371n.
imprison 747vb.
herd instinct
crowd 74n.
herdsman
herdsman 369n.
here
in place 186adv.
here 189adv.
hereabout
in place 186adv.
nearly 200adv.
hereafter
sequel 67n.
future state 124n.
prospectively 124adv.
destiny 155n.
here and there
here and there 105adv.
somewhere 185adv.
hereditament
estate, lands 777n.
hereditary
genetic 5adj.
inherited 157adj.
filial 170adj.
proprietary 777adj.
heredity
heredity 5n.
recurrence 106n.
reversion 148n.
reproduction 166n.
sonship 170n.
influence 178n.
affections 817n.
herein

inside 224adv.
hereof
concerning 9adv.
heresiarchy
heresy 977n.
heresy
unbelief 486n.
heterodoxy 977n.
heresy 977n.
heresy-hunting
orthodoxism 976n.
orthodox 976adj.
pietism 979n.
here, there and everywhere
widely 183adv.
heretic
nonconformist 84n.
unbeliever 486n.
heretic 977n.
schismatic 978n.
heretical
uncomformable 84adj.
erroneous 495adj.
heterodox 977adj.
heretical 977adj.
schismatical 978adj.
impious 980adj.
heretofore
retrospectively 125adv.
heritable
genetic 5adj.
inherited 157adj.
proprietary 777adj.
not retained 779adj.
transferred 780adj.
due 915adj.
heritage
futurity 124n.
posterity 170n.
possession 773n.
dower 777n.
hermaphrodite
nonconformist 84n.
double 91adj.
eunuch 161n.
hermaphroditism
abnormality 84n.
hermeneutics
hermeneutics 520n.
hermit
nonconformist 84n.
solitary 883n.
celibate 895n.
ascetic 945n.
pietist 979n.
monk 986n.
hermitage
retreat 192n.
refuge 662n.
seclusion 883n.
monastery 986n.
hero
acting 594n.
doer 676n.
brave person 855n.
prodigy 864n.
person of repute 866n.
loved one 887n.
favorite 890n.
good man 937n.
Herodians
non-Christian sect 978n.
heroic
olden 127adj.
descriptive 590adj.
poetic 593adj.
resolute 599adj.
laborious 682adj.
courageous 855adj.
worshipful 866adj.
disinterested 931adj.
heroic age
antiquity 125n.
heroic couplet
prosody 593n.
verse form 593n.
heroics
prowess 855n.
ostentation 875n.
boasting 877n.
heroine
acting 594n.
brave person 855n.
heroism
resolution 599n.
prowess 855n.
courage 855n.
disinterestedness 931n.
heron
bird of prey 365n.
hero-worship
wonder 864n., vb.
love 887n.
praise 923n., vb.
herpes
skin disease 651n.
herpetology
zoology 367n.
Herr
male 372n.
title 870n.
herring
fish food 301n.
table fish 365n.
herringbone
oblique 220adj.
weaving 222n.
pattern 844n.
hesitant
doubting 474adj.
unwilling 598adj.
hesitate
be inactive 679vb.
(*see* hesitation)
hesitation
changeableness 152n.
slowness 278n.
doubt 486n.
speech defect 580n.
unwillingness 598n.
irresolution 601n.
nervousness 854n.
caution 858n.
Hesperides
happiness 824n.
Hesperus
luminary 420n.
hessian
textile 222n.
footwear 228n.
hest
command 737n.
hetaera
kept woman 952n.
heterarchy
governance 733n.
heteroclite
abnormal 84adj.
grammatical 564adj.
heterodoxy
unconformity 84n.
error 495n.
heterodoxy 977n.
heterogeneity
irrelation 10n.
difference 15n.
non-uniformity 17n.
medley 43n.
multiformity 82n.
heteromorphism
non-uniformity 17n.
heteronomy
governance 733n.
heterosexual
correlative 12adj.
hetman
governor 741n.
heuristic
inquiring 459adj.
demonstrating 478adj.
hew
cut 46vb.
shorten 204vb.
efform 243vb.
hexad
over five 99n.
hexagon
angular figure 247n.
hexameter
prosody 593n.
Hexateuch
scripture 975n.
heyday
salad days 130n.
palmy days 730n.
hiatus

interval 201n.
opening 263n.
hibernation
sleep 679n.
Hibernicism
absurdity 497n.
dialect 560n.
ridiculousness 849n.
hiccough
eruct 300vb.
respiration 352n.
drunkenness 949n.
hick
bungler 697n.
countryman 869n.
hidalgo
aristocrat 868n.
hidden
dark 418adj.
invisible 444adj.
unknown 491adj.
unintelligible 517adj.
concealed 525adj.
secluded 883adj.
cabalistic 984adj.
hidden depths
latency 523n.
hidden hand
cause 156n.
influence 178n.
latency 523n.
trouble-maker 663n.
hide
contain 56vb.
measure 183n.
skin 226n.
strike 279vb.
screen 421vb.
be unseen 444vb.
disappear 446vb.
lurk 523vb.
conceal 525vb.
hiding-place 527n.
avoid 620vb.
store 632vb.
safeguard 660vb.
be cowardly 856vb.
be cautious 858vb.
flog 963vb.
hidebound
obstinate 602adj.
restraining 747adj.
hide one's light under a bushel
be modest 874vb.
hideosity
deformity 246n.
eyesore 842n.
hideous
unpleasant 827adj.
ugly 842adj.
frightening 854adj.
hide-out
hiding-place 527n.
seclusion 883n.
hiding
corporal punishment 963n.
hiding-place
concealment 525n.
hiding-place 527n.
hie
move 265vb.
travel 267vb.
move fast 277vb.
hiemal
wintry 129adj.
cold 380adj.
hierarchies
theosophy 984n.
hierarchy
degree 27n.
series 71n.
churchdom 985n.
clergy 986n.
hieratic
written 586adj.
scriptural 975adj.
priestly 985adj.
hierocracy
government 733n.
Churchdom 985n.
hierodule
servant, slave 742n.
prostitute 952n.
hieroglyphic
written 586adj.
hierogyphics
enigma 530n.
symbology 547n.
hierophant
religious teacher 973n.
hieroscopy
theomancy 511n.
higgle
make terms 766vb.
bargain 791vb.
higgledy-piggledy
confusedly 61adv.
higgler
purchaser 792n.
peddler 794n.
high
great 32adj.
high 209adj.
pungent 388adj.
fetid 397adj.
important 638adj.
unclean 649adj.
worshipful 866adj.
noble 868adj.
proud 871adj.
drunk 949adj.
Anglican 976adj.
high and dry
fixed 153adj.
dry 342adj.
safe 660adj.
high and mighty
prideful 871adj.
insolent 878adj.
highball
liquor 301n.
high-binder
murderer 362n.
high-born
noble 868adj.
highboy
cabinet 194n.
highbrow
instructed 490adj.
intellectual 492n.
wise 498adj.
sage 500n.
high-caste
worshipful 866adj.
High Church
Catholicism 976n.
Anglican 976adj.
high-class
genteel 868adj.
high color
redness 431n.
high colored
florid 425adj.
High Command
army officer 741n.
master 741n.
High Commission
commission 751n.
envoy 754n.
High Court
law-court 956n.
high day
festivity 837n.
holy-day 988n.
High Dutch
unmeaningness 515n.
higher critic
theologian 973n.
higher criticism
interpretation 520n.
scripture 975n.
heterodoxy 977n.
highest
supreme 34adj.
high 209adj.
topmost 213adj.
highfalutin
ornate 574adj.
ostentatious 875adj.
boast 877n.
high-fidelity
melodious 410adj.
accurate 494adj.
high-flier
proud man 871n.
high-flown

imaginative 513adj.
rhetorical 574adj.
high-flying
imaginative 513adj.
exaggerated 546adj.
lively 819adj.
high-geared
strong 162adj.
speedy 277adj.
high hand
violence 176n.
high-handed
oppressive 735adj.
proud 871adj.
insolent 878adj.
high-hat
prideful 871adj.
insolent 878adj.
high-hearted
courageous 855adj.
high jinks
revel 837n.
high jump
leap 312n.
capital punishment 963n.
highland
alpine 209adj.
land 344n.
highlander
dweller 191n.
high-level
superior 34adj.
important 638adj.
directing 689adj.
high life
festivity 837n.
upper class 868n.
(*see* high living)
highlight
manifest 522vb.
publish 528vb.
indicate 547vb.
high living
gastronomy 301n.
intemperance 943n.
sensualism 944n.
gluttony 947n.
highly colored
expressive 516adj.
splendid 841adj.
high-mettled
proud 871adj.
high mightiness
prestige 866n.
pride 871n.
high-minded
honorable 929adj.
disinterested 931adj.
highness
sovereign 741n.
high octane
fuel 385n.
high-pitched
strident 407adj.
optimistic 482adj.
rhetorical 574adj.
high-powered
strong 162adj.
high pressure
vigorousness 174n.
weather 340n.
excitation 821n.
high-priced
dear 811adj.
high-priority
important 638adj.
high rank
prestige 866n.
nobility 868n.
high relief, in
salient 254adj.
well-seen 443adj.
highroad
road 624n.
instrument 628n.
high society
beau monde 848n.
upper class 868n.
high-sounding
loud 400adj.
affected 850adj.
ostentatious 875adj.
high-spirited
lively 819adj.
courageous 855adj.
proud 871adj.
high spirits
merriment 833n.
high-stepping
fashionable 848adj.
proud 871adj.
high-strung
sentient 374adj.
lively 819adj.
excitable 822adj.
nervous 854adj.
high tea
meal 301n.
high-tension
strong 162adj.
high tide
high water 209n.
water 339n.
prosperity 730n.
high time
lateness 136n.
occasion 137n.
opportunity 137n.
expedience 642n.
high-toned
defiant 711adj.
insolent 878adj.
high treason
sedition 738n.
perfidy 930n.
high-up
superior 34n.
upper class 868n.
high-water mark
summit 213n.
limit 236n.
gauge 465n.
highway
road 624n.
instrument 628n.
facility 701n.
highwayman
robber 789n.
high words
quarrel 709n.
anger 891n.
hijack
steal 788vb.
hijacker
robber 789n.
hike
walk 267vb.
hiker
pedestrian 268n.
hilarity
merriment 833n.
hill
high land 209n.
acclivity 220n.
ascent 308n.
hillbilly
dweller 191n.
ingenue 699n.
countryman 869n.
hill-dwelling
alpine 209adj.
hillman
dweller 191n.
hillock
monticle 209n.
dome 253n.
hillside
acclivity 220n.
hill-station
abode 192n.
hilltop
high land 209n.
vertex 213n.
hilly
alpine 209adj.
hilt
handle 218n.
himation
robe 228n.
himself
self 80n.
Hinayana
religious faith 973n.
hind
back 238adj.
deer 365n.
female animal 373n.
countryman 869n.

hinder
disable 161vb.
counteract 182vb.
back 238adj.
retard 278vb.
be useless 641vb.
impair 655vb.
hinder 702vb.
resist 715vb.
restrain 747vb.
prohibit 757vb.
(*see* hindrance)
hinderer
hinderer 702n.
opponent 705n.
hindfoot
foot 214n.
Hindi
language 557n.
hindleg
leg 267n.
hindmost
ending 69adj.
back 238adj.
hindquarters
buttocks 238n.
hindrance
derangement 63n.
delay 136n.
stop 145n.
dissuasion 613n.
difficulty 700n.
hindrance 702n.
hinderer 702n.
restraint 747n.
hindsight
intellect 447n.
thought 449n.
remembrance 505n.
Hinduism
religious faith 973n.
Hindustani
language 557n.
hindward
rearward 238adv.
hinge
joint 45n.
fastening 47n.
casual means 156n.
pivot 218n.
rotator 315n.
hinge on
depend 157vb.
be uncertain 474vb.
hinny
hybrid 43n.
hint
similarity 18n.
reminder 505n.
latency 523n.
hint 524n., vb.
indication 547n.
warning 664n.
advice 691n.
command 737vb.
hinterland
district 184n.
rear 238n.
land 344n.
hip
(*see* hips)
hip-bath
vessel 194n.
ablution 648n.
hip flask
vessel 194n.
hippish
insane 503adj.
melancholic 834adj.
hippocampus
rara avis 84n.
hippocras
liquor 301n.
hippocratic
dying 361adj.
medical 658adj.
Hippocratic oath
code of duty 917n.
Hippocrene
poetry 593n.
hippodrome
theater 594n.
arena 724n.
place of amusement 837n.
hippogriff
rara avis 84n.
hippopotamus
giant 195n.
animal 365n.
hips
rear 238n.
buttocks 238n.
hipshot
crippled 163adj.
hircine
animal 365adj.
fetid 397adj.
hire
employ 622vb.
commission 751vb.
lease 784vb.
hire 785vb.
price 809n.
hireling
servant 742n.
venal 930adj.
hire purchase
borrowing 785n.
purchase 792n., vb.
hirer
lender 784n.
purchaser 792n.
hirsute
hairy 259adj.
Hispanicist
linguist 557n.
hispidity
roughness 259n.
hiss
sibilation 406n.
vociferate 408vb.
ululation 409n.
ridicule 851n.
indignity 921n.
despise 922vb.
disapprobation 924n.
hissing and a reproach, an
object of scorn 867n.
despisedness 922n.
histogram
record 548n.
histology
structure 331n.
historian
antiquarian 125n.
chronicler 549n.
author 589n.
narrator 590n.
historic
olden 127adj.
renowned 866adj.
historical
real 1adj.
past 125adj.
certain 473adj.
true 494adj.
descriptive 590adj.
historicity
reality 1n.
truth 494n.
historic tense
preterition 125n.
history
preterition 125n.
remembrance 505n.
record 548n.
narrative 590n.
reading matter 598n.
conduct 688n.
histrionics
exaggeration 546n.
dramaturgy 594n.
acting 594n.
ostentation 875n.
hit
place 187vb.
strike 279vb.
arrive, meet 295vb.
touch 378vb.
be visible 443vb.
discover 484vb.
dramaturgy 594n.
contrivance 623n.
exceller 644n.
success 727n.
favorite 890n.
reproach 924n.

hit and miss
empiricism 461n.
rash 857adj.
hit back
recoil 280vb.
retaliate 714vb.
hitch
tie 45vb.
ligature 47n.
stop 145n.
disappointment 509n.
difficulty 700n.
hitch 702n.
failure 728n.
marry 894vb.
hitch-hike
ride 267vb.
beg 761vb.
hitch up
start out 296vb.
hither
towards 281adv.
hitherto
retrospectively 125adv.
hit it
discover 484vb.
be successful 727vb.
Hitlerism
brute force 735n.
hit off
accord 24vb.
represent 551vb.
hit on
chance 159vb.
discover 484vb.
plan 623vb.
hive
place oneself 187vb.
dwelling 192n.
stock farm 369n.
storage 632n.
activity 678n.
workshop 687n.
hive off
be disjoined 46vb.
be dispersed 75vb.
schismatize 978vb.
hives
formication 378n.
skin disease 651n.
hoar
white 427adj.
gray 429adj.
hoard
store 632n., vb.
safeguard 660vb.
acquire 771vb.
economize 814vb.
be parsimonious 816vb.
hoarder
niggard 816n.
hoar-frost
wintriness 380n.
hoarse
muted 401adj.
non-resonant 405adj.
hoarse 407adj.
vocal 577adj.
voiceless 578adj.
hoarse, make oneself
vociferate 408vb.
hoary
immemorial 127adj.
gray 429adj.
hoax
rumor 529n.
trickery 542n.
fable 543n.
hoaxable
credulous 487adj.
hoaxer
trickster 545n.
hob
stand 218n.
furnace 383n.
countryman 869n.
elf 970n.
Hobbism
brute force 735n.
hobble
tie 45vb.
disable 161vb.
move slowly 278vb.
impair 655vb.
be clumsy 695vb.
hinder 702vb.
fetter 747vb.
fetter 748n.
hobbledehoy
youngster 132n.
hobby
bias 481n.
pursuit 619n.
business 622n.
amusement 837n.
liking 859n.
hobby-horse
vehicle 274n.
hobgoblin
intimidation 854n.
elf 970n.
hobnail
fastening 47n.
countryman 869n.
hobnob
be friendly 880vb.
be sociable 882vb.
hobo
wanderer 268n.
hobo signs
symbology 547n.
Hobson's choice
necessity 596n.
no choice 606n.
compulsion 740n.
hock
disable 161vb.
leg 267n.
wine 301n.
impair 655vb.
give security 767vb.
borrow 785vb.
hockey
ball game 837n.
hocus
trickery 542n.
hocus-pocus
unmeaningness 515n.
sleight 542n.
idolatry 982n.
spell 983n.
hod
plate 194n.
shovel 274n.
hodden
textile 222n.
textural 331adj.
hodman
artisan 686n.
hoe
shovel 274n.
farm tool 370n.
cleaning utensil 648n.
hog
pig 365n.
appropriate 786vb.
be selfish 932vb.
sensualist 944n.
glutton 947n.
hoggish
unclean 649adj.
selfish 932adj.
sensual 944adj.
Hogmanay
anniversary 141n.
hog's back
high land 209n.
hogshead
vat 194n.
metrology 465n.
hogwash
silly talk 515n.
falsehood 541n.
swill 649n.
hoist
verticality 215n.
edge 234n.
lifter 310n.
elevate 310vb.
flag 547n.
hoist sail
navigate 269vb.
hoist with his own petard
retaliate 714vb.
hokum
falsehood 541n.
hold

be 1vb.
fastening 47n.
cohere 48vb.
contain 56vb.
comprise 78vb.
stay 144vb.
cease 145vb.
go on 146vb.
be stable 153vb.
influence 178n.
receptacle 194n.
cellar 194n.
base 214n.
handle 218n.
support 218vb.
opine 485vb.
be true 494vb.
affirm 532vb.
storage 632n.
store 632vb.
preserve 666vb.
wrestling 716n.
restrain 747vb.
lock-up 748n.
possession 773n.
retention 778n.
impress 821vb.

hold a brief for
deputize 755vb.

hold-all
bag 194n.
storage 632n.

hold back
avoid 620vb.
hinder 702vb.
restrain 747vb.

hold cheap
underestimate 483vb.
hold cheap 922vb.

hold classes
teach 534vb.

hold court
hold court 955vb.

hold down
depress 311vb.
function 622vb.
dominate 733vb.
subjugate 745vb.

holder
receptacle 194n.
handle 218n.
storage 632n.
proficient 696n.
possessor 776n.

holdfast
fastening 47n.

hold fast
cohere 48vb.
stand firm 599vb.
retain 778vb.

hold for
opine 485vb.
intend 617vb.

hold forth
teach 534vb.
orate 579vb.

hold good
be 1vb.
stay 144vb.
be proved 478vb.
be true 494vb.

hold hands
caress 889vb.

hold in
circumscribe 232vb.
restrain 747vb.

hold in common
socialize 775vb.

holding
territory 184n.
farm 370n.
lands 777n.

hold in view
see 438vb.
expect 507vb.

hold off
be distant 199vb.
avoid 620vb.
not use 674vb.
parry 713vb.
resist 715vb.

hold office
function 622vb.
direct 689vb.
rule 733vb.

hold on
stay 144vb.
go on 146vb.
progress 285vb.
retain 778vb.

hold one's breath
await 507vb.
wonder 864vb.

hold one's own
be equal 28vb.
parry 713vb.

hold one's tongue
be silent 399vb.
keep secret 525vb.
be mute 578vb.
be taciturn 582vb.

hold out
affirm 532vb.
stand firm 599vb.
oppose 704vb.
resist 715vb.
offer 759vb.
promise 764vb.

hold out for
give terms 766vb.
bargain 791vb.

hold over
put off 136vb.

hold the baby
deputize 755vb.

hold the road
stabilize 153vb.

hold the scales
judge 480vb.

hold tight
retain 778vb.

hold together
accord 24vb.
be true 494vb.
cooperate 706vb.

hold to ransom
overcharge 811vb.

hold under
dominate 733vb.

hold up
put off 136vb.
halt 145vb.
sustain 146vb.
support 218vb.
elevate 310vb.
hinder 702vb.
rob 788vb.

hold water
be proved 478vb.
be true 494vb.

hole
place 185n.
dwelling 192n.
retreat 192n.
receptacle 194n.
gap 201n.
cavity 255n.
orifice 263n.
pierce 263vb.
insert 303vb.
hiding-place 527n.
refuge 662n.

hole-and-corner
stealthy 525adj.

holey
dilapidated 655adj.

holiday
lull 145n.
leisure 681n.
repose 683n.
permit 756n.
amusement 837n.

holiday camp
meeting place 192n.
pleasure-ground 837n.

holiday home
abode 192n.

holiday-maker
traveler 268n.
reveler 837n.

holier than thou
prideful 871adj.
despising 922adj.
disapproving 924adj.
pietistic 979adj.

holiness
(*see* holy)

holism
whole 52n.

holland
textile 222n.
hollow
insubstantial 4adj.
completely 54adv.
empty 190adj.
lowness 210n.
depth 211n.
cavity 255n.
furrow 261n.
opening 263n.
depression 311n.
rare 325adj.
resonant 404adj.
hoarse 407adj.
sophistical 477adj.
hypocritical 541adj.
voiceless 578adj.
ostentatious 875adj.
holly
tree 366n.
Hollywood
cinema 445n.
drama 594n.
holocaust
havoc 165n.
slaughter 362n.
burning 381n.
oblation 981n.
holograph
no imitation 21n.
script 586n.
holophrastic
comprehensive 52adj.
linguistic 557adj.
holster
case 194n.
arsenal 723n.
holy
worshipful 866adj.
virtuous 933adj.
prudish 950adj.
divine, godlike 965adj.
religious 973adj.
scriptural 975adj.
sanctified 979adj.
devotional 981adj.
Holy Communion
Holy Communion 988n.
Christian rite 988n.
holy-day
holy-day 988n.
Holy Ghost
Holy Ghost 965n.
Holy Grail
ritual object 988n.
holy horror
false piety 980n.
Holy Office
ecclesiastical court 956n.
orthodoxism 976n.
ecclesiasticism 985n.
holy of holies
holy place 990n.
holy orders
holy orders 985n.
Christian rite 988n.
Holy See
church office 985n.
Holy Spirit
Holy Ghost 965n.
holy-stone
cleanser 648n.
holy terror
violent creature 176n.
ruffian 904n.
Holy Unction
Christian rite 988n.
holy war
war 718n.
philanthropy 901n.
holy water
ritual object 988n.
Holy Week
holy-day 988n.
homage
submission 721n.
loyalty 739n.
be subject 745vb.
respects 920n.
homager
subject 742n.
homburg
headgear 228n.
home
focus 76n.
native 191adj.
house, home 192n.
near 200adj.
interior 224adj.
resting place 266n.
turn back 286vb.
arrive 295vb.
refuge 662n.
home, at
here 189adv.
inside 224adv.
knowing 490adj.
habituated 610adj.
facilitated 701adj.
free 744adj.
home circle
family 11n.
home-coming
return 286n.
arrival 295n.
homefolks
family 11n.
home ground
focus 76n.
home 192n.
Home Guard
defender 713n.
soldier, army 722n.
home-keeping
quiescent 266adj.
unsociable 883adj.
homeland
territory 184n.
home 192n.
homeless
irrelative 10adj.
alone 88adj.
unstable 152adj.
displaced 188adj.
traveling 267adj.
homeless person
outcaste 883n.
home-life
seclusion 883n.
homely
comfortable 376adj.
dialectical 560adj.
plain 573adj.
pleasurable 826adj.
ugly 842adj.
plebeian 869adj.
home-made
bungled 695adj.
artless 699adj.
homeopath
doctor 658n.
homeopathic
small 33adj.
exiguous 196adj.
medical 658adj.
homeopathy
medical art 658n.
homeostasis
equilibrium 28n.
stability 153n.
homer
metrology 465n.
home rule
government 733n.
independence 744n.
homesickness
suffering 825n.
regret 830n.
melancholy 834n.
desire 859n.
homespun
simple 44adj.
textile 222n.
textural 331adj.
plainness 573n.
artless 699adj.
plebeian 869adj.
homestead
home 192n.
home-stretch
end 69n.
home-thrust
foin 712n.
reproach 924n.
home-truth

truth 494n.
veracity 540n.
censure 924n.
accusation 928n.
homeward-bound
regressive 286adj.
arriving 295adj.
homework
study 536n.
curriculum 536n.
preparation 669n.
homicide
homicide 362n.
homiletics
teaching 534n.
church ministry 985n.
homily
lecture 534n.
oration 579n.
dissertation 591n.
ministration 988n.
hominal
human 371adj.
homing
regressive 286adj.
arriving 295adj.
incoming 297adj.
hominid
mankind 371n.
hominy
corn 366n.
homoeopath
(*see* homeopath)
homoeoteleuton
assimilation 18n.
ornament 574n.
homogeneity
relation 9n.
identity 13n.
uniformity 16n.
similarity 18n.
simpleness 44n.
homogenesis
propagation 164n.
homologate
identify 13vb.
accord 24vb.
homologous
relative 9adj.
uniform 16adj.
equal 28adj.
homomorphism
similarity 18n.
homonym
identity 13n.
word 559n.
homonymous
semantic 514adj.
equivocal 518adj.
homonymy
equivocalness 518n.
homoousian
identical 13adj.
homophene
identity 13n.
word 559n.
homophone
identity 13n.
equivocalness 518n.
word 559n.
homophony
assimilation 18n.
melody 410n.
homo sapiens
mankind 371n.
homosexual
noncomformist 84n.
extramarital 951adj.
homunculus
small animal 33n.
dwarf 196n.
hone
sharpen 256vb.
honest
true 494adj.
genuine 494adj.
veracious 540adj.
plain 573adj.
artless 699adj.
ethical 917adj.
honorable 929adj.
disinterested 931adj.
virtuous 933adj.
honesty
(*see* honest)
honey
viscidity 354n.
sweet 392n.
yellowness 433n.
darling 890n.
honeycomb
cavity 255n.
porosity 263n.
pierce 263vb.
sweet 392n.
storage 632n.
impair 655vb.
honeymoon
concord 710n.
joy 824n.
pleasurableness 826n.
friendship 880n.
be in love 887vb.
wedding 894n.
honeymooners
spouse 894n.
honeypot
focus 76n.
sweet 392n.
honeysuckle
sweet 392n.
honk
loudness 400n.
ululate 409vb.
danger signal 665n.
honky-tonk
tavern 192n.
honor
make important 638vb.
decoration 729n.
promise 764n.
lands 777n.
pay 804vb.
prestige 866n.
dignify 866vb.
title 870n.
celebrate 876vb.
pay respects 884vb.
right 913n.
morals 917n.
do one's duty 917vb.
respect 920n.
probity 929n.
virtue 933n.
purity 950n.
reward 962n., vb.
piety 979n.
sanctify 979vb.
worship 981n., vb.
honorable
honorable 929adj.
honorable intentions
wooing 889n.
honorarium
gift 781n.
reward 962n.
honorary
insubstantial 4adj.
voluntary 597adj.
uncharged 812adj.
honorific
honors 866n.
title 870n.
celebrative 876adj.
honors
victory 727n.
decoration 729n.
honors 866n.
reward 962n.
hooch
liquor 301n.
booty 790n.
hood
covering 226n.
headgear 228n.
screen 421n., vb.
hoodlum
insolent person 878n.
ruffian 904n.
hoodoo
sorcery 983n.
hoodwink
blind 439vb.
deceive 542vb.
hooey
empty talk 515n.
falsehood 541n.
hoof

foot 214n.
dance 837vb.
hoof it
walk 267vb.
leap 312vb.
hoofmark
trace 548n.
hook
coupling 47n.
hanger 217n.
angularity 247n.
sharp edge 256n.
knock 279n.
deflect 282vb.
propel 287vb.
trap 542n.
take 786vb.
hookah
air-pipe 353n.
tobacco 388n.
hook and eye
fastening 47n.
hooker
merchant ship 275n.
hook, line and sinker
all 52n.
completely 54adv.
hook on
affix 45vb.
hook-up
junction 45n.
association 706n.
hooligan
violent creature 176n.
ruffian 904n.
hooliganism
lawlessness 954n.
hoop
bond 47n.
frame 218n.
skirt 228n.
circle 250n.
plaything 837n.
hoop-la
ball game 837n.
hoot
cry 408n., vb.
ululate 409vb.
laugh 835vb.
ridicule 851n.
indignity 921n.
disapprove 924vb.
hooter
timekeeper 117n.
megaphone 400n.
signal 547n.
hop
gait 265n.
land travel 267n.
departure 296n.
leap 312n., vb.
be agitated 318vb.
dancing 837n.
social gathering 882n.
hope
expect 507vb.
motive 612n.
proficient 696n.
cheerfulness 833n.
hope 852n., vb.
desire 859vb.
hope against hope
hope 852vb.
(*see* persevere)
hopeful
youngster 132n.
probable 471adj.
expectant 507adj.
hoper 852n.
promising 852adj.
hopeless
impossible 470adj.
useless 641adj.
unhappy 825adj.
dejected 834adj.
hopeless 853adj.
unpromising 853adj.
impenitent 940adj.
hopelessness
impossibility 470n.
hopelessness 853n.
hopes of, give
predict 511vb.
hop it
decamp 296vb.
hoplite
soldier 722n.
hop, on the
on the move 265adv.
hopper
vat 194n.
ship 275n.
jumper 312n.
hopping mad
angry 891adj.
hops
liquor 301n.
horary
periodic 110adj.
horde
multitude 104n.
party 708n.
army 722n.
rabble 869n.
horizon
distance 199n.
horizontality 216n.
edge 234n.
limit 236n.
view 438n.
horizontality
horizontality 216n.
horme
desire 859n.
hormone
stimulant 174n.
horn
cup 194n.
cone 252n.
protuberance 254n.
sharp point 256n.
structure 331n.
megaphone 400n.
horn 414n.
semitransparency 424n.
weapon 723n.
hornbook
classroom 539n.
textbook 589n.
reading matter 589n.
horned
curved 248adj.
tapering 256adj.
hornet
fly 365n.
shrew 892n.
noxious animal 904n.
hornet's nest
bane 659n.
pitfall 663n.
painfulness 827n.
horn in
intrude 297vb.
encroach 306vb.
hornpipe
dance 837n.
hornswoggle
deceive 542vb.
hornwork
fortification 713n.
horny
hard 326adj.
horny-handed
laboring 682adj.
horologer
timekeeper 117n.
horology
chronometry 117n.
horoscope
looking ahead 124n.
destiny 155n.
astronomy 321n.
prediction 511n.
horrible
not nice 645adj.
unpleasant 827adj.
frightening 854adj.
horribly
extremely 32adv.
horrid
not nice 645adj.
hateful 888adj.
horrific
distressing 827adj.
frightening 854adj.
horrify
displease 827vb.

frighten 854vb.
excite hate 888vb.
horripilation
roughness 259n.
fear 854n.
horror
eyesore 842n.
fear 854n.
dislike 861n.
hell-hag 904n.
monster 938n.
horrors
melancholy 834n.
alcoholism 949n.
horror-struck
fearing 854adj.
hors de combat
impotent 161adj.
useless 641adj.
hors d'oeuvre
dish 301n.
savoriness 390n.
horse
horse 273n.
male animal 372n.
busy person 678n.
cavalry 722n.
horseback
conveyance 267n.
horsecloth
coverlet 226n.
horse-coper
trickster 545n.
horse-dealing
barter 791n.
horse-doctor
animal husbandry 369n.
doctor 658n.
horsehair
hair 258n.
horseman
rider 268n.
cavalry 722n.
horsemanship
equitation 267n.
skill 694n.
horse marine
bungler 697n.
horse-opera
stage play 594n.
horse-play
fight 716n.
ridicule 851n.
horse-power
energy 160n.
horse-racing
gambling 618n.
racing 716n.
horse sense
intelligence 498n.
horse-shoe
curve 248n.
horsewhip
flog 963vb.
scourge 964n.
horsey
equine 273adj.
amused 837adj.
hortative
educational 534adj.
advising 691adj.
hortatory
inducive 612adj.
horticulture
flower 366n.
agriculture 370n.
hortus siccus
botany 368n.
hosanna
rejoicing 835n.
celebration 876n.
applause 923n.
hymn 981n.
hose
legwear 228n.
tube 263n.
water 339n.
irrigation 341n.
conduit 351n.
extinguisher 382n.
cleaning utensil 648n.
hosier
clothier 228n.
hosiery
legwear 228n.
hospice
inn 192n.
hospital 658n.
hospitable
(*see* hospitality)
hospital
hygiene 652n.
hospital 658n.
hospital case
sick person 651n.
hospitality
liberality 813n.
friendliness 880n.
sociability 882n.
benevolence 897n.
hospitalize
doctor 658vb.
host
band 74n.
multitude 104n.
army 722n.
friend 880n.
social person 882n.
the sacrament 988n.
hostage
thing transferred 272n.
prisoner 750n.
security 767n.
hostel
station 187n.
quarters 192n.
hostelry
inn 192n.
hostess
social person 882n.
hostile
counteracting 182adj.
attacking 712adj.
adverse 731adj.
prohibiting 757adj.
disliking 861adj.
enemy 881n.
unsociable 883adj.
(*see* hostility)
hostilities
fight 716n.
belligerency 718n.
hostility
contrariety 14n.
disagreement 25n.
opposition 704n.
dissension 709n.
enmity 881n.
hatred 888n.
disapprobation 924n.
hostler
animal husbandry 369n.
servant 742n.
hosts
great quantity 32n.
hot
violent 176adj.
dry 342adj.
hot 379adj.
pungent 388adj.
musical 412adj.
red 431adj.
fervent 818adj.
excited 821adj.
angry 891adj.
lecherous 951adj.
impure 951adj.
hot air
chatter 381n.
overestimation 482n.
empty talk 515n.
boast 877n.
hotbed
seedbed 156n.
abundance 171n.
heater 383n.
badness 645n.
infection 651n.
hot blood
excitability 822n.
irascibility 892n.
hot-blooded
violent 176adj.
rash 857adj.
hot-box
provisions 301n.

hot-case
heater 383n.
hotchpotch
medley 43n.
confusion 61n.
dish 301n.
hot dog
meat 301n.
hotel
inn 192n.
hotelier
caterer 633n.
hot-foot
hastily 680adv.
hot-gospeler
religionist 979n.
hothead
warm feeling 818n.
desperado 857n.
hot-headed
fervent 818adj.
excitable 822adj.
rash 857adj.
hot-house
extraneous 59adj.
seedbed 156n.
garden 370n.
heater 383n.
hot rod
automobile 274n.
hot seat
means of execution 964n.
Hotspur
violent creature 176n.
brave person 855n.
desperado 857n.
hot stuff
loose woman 952n.
hot-tempered
excitable 822adj.
hot water
heat 379n.
cleanser 648n.
predicament 700n.
painfulness 827n.
hot-water bottle
caldron 194n.
heater 383n.
hough
disable 161vb.
leg 267n.
impair 655vb.
hound
dog 365n.
hunter 619n.
be malevolent 898vb.
defame 926vb.
knave, cad 938n.
hound on
incite 612vb.
hour
juncture 8n.
period 110n.
clock time 117n.
hour angle
uranometry 321n.
hourglass
timekeeper 117n.
contraction 198n.
narrowing 206n.
hour-hand
timekeeper 117n.
indicator 547n.
houri
a beauty 841n.
mythical being 970n.
hourly
while 108adv.
periodic 110adj.
frequent 139adj.
often 139adv.
seasonal 141adj.
periodically 141adv.
house
edifice 164n.
genealogy 169n.
place 187vb.
abode, house 192n.
zodiac 321n.
onlookers 441n.
playgoer 594n.
theater 594n.
corporation 708n.
sovereign 741n.
shop 796n.
brothel 951n.
houseboat
small house 192n.
boat 275n.
housebreaker
incomer 297n.
thief 789n.
offender 904n.
housebreaking
stealing 788n.
housecarl
defender 713n.
soldier 722n.
retainer 742n.
housecoat
informal dress 228n.
house-dog
dog 365n.
warner 664n.
houseful
crowd 74n.
habitancy 191n.
household
family 11n.
group 74n.
habitancy 191n.
home 192n.
known 490adj.
usual 610adj.
householder
resident 191n.
possessor 776n.
household troops
armed force 722n.
household words
plainness 573n.
housekeeper
resident 191n.
caterer 633n.
manager 690n.
retainer 742n.
keeper 749n.
housekeeping
management 689n.
housel
perform ritual 988vb.
houseless
displaced 188adj.
housemaid
domestic 742n.
houseman
resident 191n.
doctor 658n.
domestic 742n.
housemaster
teacher 537n.
manager 690n.
house of cards
weak thing 163n.
brittleness 330n.
House of Commons
parliament 692n.
house of correction
amendment 654n.
prison 748n.
House of God
temple 990n.
House of Lords
parliament 692n.
aristocracy 868n.
house organ
journal 528n.
house party
social gathering 882n.
house-proud
prideful 871adj.
housetop
vertex 213n.
roof 226n.
house-trailer
small house 192n.
house-trained
tasteful 846adj.
well-bred 848adj.
house-warming
social gathering 882n.
housewife
resident 191n.
case 194n.
caterer 633n.
busy person 678n.
manager 690n.
housewifery

management 689n.
housework
labor 682n.
management 689n.
housing
housing 192n.
housings
coverlet 226n.
hovel
small house 192n.
hoveler
boatman 270n.
hover
impend 155vb.
be near 200vb.
be high 209vb.
hang 217vb.
move 265vb.
wander 267vb.
fly 271vb.
move slowly 278vb.
approach 289vb.
be uncertain 474vb.
be irresolute 601vb.
hovercraft
aircraft 276n.
hovering
overhanging 209adj.
hover on the brink
be in danger 661vb.
how
how 624adv.
how come?
why? 158adv.
howdah
seat 218n.
howitzer
gun 723n.
howl
blow 352vb.
feel pain 377vb.
loudness 400n.
cry 408n., vb.
ululate 409vb.
lament 836n.
howler
mistake 495n.
absurdity 497n.
how the land lies
circumstance 8n.
hoy
sailing-ship 275n.
merchant ship 275n.
hoyden
youngster 132n.
hoydenish
infantine 132adj.
artless 699adj.
ill-bred 847adj.
hub
middle 70n.
focus 76n.
centrality 225n.
wheel 250n.
chief thing 638n.
hubble-bubble
tobacco 388n.
hubbub
commotion 318n.
loudness 400n.
quarrel 709n.
hubris
pride 871n.
insolence 878n.
huckster
bargain 791vb.
seller 793n.
peddler 794n.
huddle
confusion 61n.
jumble 63vb.
crowd 74n.
make smaller 198vb.
be near 200vb.
conference 584n.
huddle into
wear 228vb.
Hudibrastic
derisive 881adj.
hue
character 5n.
hue 425n.
hue and cry
chase 619n.
huff
breathe 352vb.
resentment 891n.
huff 891vb.
huffy
irascible 892adj.
hug
cohere 48vb.
make smaller 198vb.
be near 200vb.
surround 230vb.
enclose 235vb.
flank 239vb.
gesture 547n.
retain 778vb.
friendliness 880n.
be hospitable 882vb.
courteous act 884n.
greet 884vb.
caress 889vb.
huge
enormous 32adj.
stalwart 162adj.
huge 195adj.
hugger-mugger
confusion 61n.
stealthy 525adj.
hug oneself
be pleased 824vb.
be content 828vb.
rejoice 835vb.
feel pride 871vb.
be vain 873vb.
boast 877vb.
Huguenot
Protestant 976n.
huissier
law officer 955n.
huke
cloak 228n.
hula-hula
dance 837n.
hulk
ship 275n.
hulking, hulky
whooping 32adj.
unwieldy 195adj.
clumsy 695adj.
graceless 842adj.
hulks
prison 748n.
hull
uncover 229vb.
ship 275n.
hullabaloo
turmoil 61n.
loudness 400n.
cry 408n.
hull down
beyond 199adv.
hum
be many 104vb.
sound faint 401vb.
roll 403n., vb.
shrill 407vb.
resound 404vb.
ululation 409vb.
sing 413vb.
voice 577vb.
activity 678n.
human
animal 365adj.
human 371adj.
benevolent 897adj.
philanthropic 901adj.
frail 934adj.
human being
person 371n.
humane
educational 534adj.
benevolent 897adj.
philanthropic 901adj.
pitying 905adj.
humane scholarship
literature 557n.
humanism
philosophy 449n.
philanthropy 901n.
humanist
linguist 557n.
philanthropist 901n.
humanitarian
philanthropist 901n.
humanitarianism
benevolence 897n.

philanthropy 901n.
humanities
culture 490n.
literature 557n.
humanity
mankind 371n.
lenity 736n.
benevolence 897n.
philanthropy 901n.
pity 905n.
humanize
be lenient 736vb.
be benevolent 897vb.
human nature
mankind 371n.
human race
mankind 371n.
humble
inconsiderable 33adj.
inferior 35adj.
abase 311vb.
unknown 491adj.
disappoint 509vb.
impress 821vb.
plebeian 869adj.
humiliate 872vb.
respectful 920adj.
(*see* humility)
humble oneself
be humble 872vb.
show respect 920vb.
be pious 979vb.
worship 981vb.
humbug
empty talk 515n.
falsehood 541n.
deceive 542vb.
fable 543n.
impostor 545n.
affectation 850n.
humdinger
exceller 644n.
humdrum
plain 573adj.
tedious 838adj.
humectation
moistening 341n.
humic
territorial 344adj.
humid
watery 339adj.
humid 341adj.
humidity
moisture 341n.
humiliation
adversity 731n.
disrepute 867n.
humiliation 872n.
indignity 921n.
contempt 922n.
humility
underestimation 483n.
submission 721n.
humility 872n.
modesty 874adj.
servility 879n.
disinterestedness 931n.
piety 979n.
worship 981n.
humming
multitudinous 104adj.
humming-top
rotator 315n.
organ 414n.
hummock
monticle 209n.
dome 253n.
hummum
heater 383n.
ablution 648n.
humor
temperament 5n.
tendency 179n.
fluid 335n.
whim 604n.
minister to 703vb.
be lenient 736vb.
affections 817n.
please 826vb.
laughter 835n.
amuse 837vb.
wit 839n.
flatter 925vb.
humoresque
musical piece 412n.
humorist
humorist 839n.
humorless
serious 834adj.
dull 840adj.
humorous
funny 849adj.
(*see* humor)
humorsome
capricious 604adj.
sullen 893adj.
hump
monticle 209n.
sphere 252n.
camber 253n.
carry 273vb.
hump bluey
travel 267vb.
humpy
convex 253adj.
humus
soil 344n.
Hun
destroyer 168n.
evildoer 904n.
hunch
intuition 476n.
supposition 512n.
spontaneity 609n.
hunchback
camber 253n.
hunchbacked
deformed 246adj.
blemished 845adj.
hundred
hundred 99n.
district 184n.
hundred per cent
perfect 646adj.
hundredweight
weighment 322n.
hunger
eating 301n.
rapacity 786n.
hunger 859n.
desire 859vb.
hunger-march
deprecation 762n.
hunger-strike
fast 946n.
hungry
hungry 859adj.
fasting 946adj.
gluttonous 947adj.
hunk
piece 53n.
hunkers
buttocks 238n.
hunks
niggard 816n.
hunky
foreigner 59n.
hunky-dory
topping 644adj.
hunt
eject 300vb.
oscillate 317vb.
campanology 412n.
search 459n.
detect 484vb.
chase 619n.
attack 712vb.
be severe 735vb.
be inimical 881vb.
hunter
timekeeper 117n.
thoroughbred 273n.
killer 362n.
hunter 619n.
hunting field
arena 724n.
pleasure-ground 837n.
hunt in pairs
cooperate 706vb.
huntsman
hunter 619n.
hunt with the hounds
do likewise 20vb.
hurdle
bed 218n.
vehicle 274n.
leap 312vb.

obstacle 702n.
hurdler
thoroughbred 273n.
jumper 312n.
hurdles
racing 716n.
hurdy-gurdy
organ 414n.
hurl
propel 287vb.
hurling
propulsion 287n.
ball game 837n.
hurly-burly
commotion 318n.
hurrah
cry 408n., vb.
rejoicing 835n.
hurricane
turmoil 61n.
storm 176n.
gale 352n.
hurried
brief 114adj.
hasty 680adj.
hurry
velocity 277n.
move fast 277vb.
incite 612vb.
activity 678n.
haste 680n.
hurt
weaken 163vb.
pain 377n.
evil 616n.
be inexpedient 643adj.
harm 645vb.
impair 655vb.
hurt 827vb.
resentful 891adj.
huff 891vb.
hurtful
(*see* hurt)
hurtling
speedy 277adj.
husband
male 372n.
store 632vb.
manager 690n.
master 741n.
spouse 894n.
husbandless
unwedded 895adj.
widowed 896adj.
husbandman
accumulator 74n.
producer 167n.
husbandman 370n.
countryman 869n.
husbandry
agriculture 370n.
management 689n.
economy 814n.
hush
assuage 177vb.
quietude 266n.
silence 399n., vb.
make mute 578vb.
hush-hush
occult 523adj.
concealed 525adj.
hush-hush subject
secret 530n.
hush up
keep secret 525vb.
husk
remainder 41n.
skin 226n.
corn 366n.
rubbish 641n.
huskiness
aphony 578n.
husky
stalwart 162adj.
beast of burden 273n.
dog 365n.
hoarse 407adj.
hussar
cavalry 722n.
Hussite
heretic 977n.
hussy
insolent person 878n.
loose woman 952n.
hustings
rostrum 539n.
vote 605n.
arena 724n.
law-court 956n.
hustle
move 265vb.
impel 279vb.
propel 287vb.
activity 678n.
hasten 680vb.
hustle out
eject 300vb.
hustler
speeder 277n.
busy person 678n.
prostitute 952n.
hut
small house 192n.
hutch
stable 192n.
huzza
(*see* hurrah)
hyacinth
blueness 435n.
gem 844n.
hyalescence
transparency 422n.
hybrid
hybrid 43n.
nonconformist 84n.
neology 560n.
hydra
rara avis 84n.
hydragogue
watery 339adj.
hydra-headed
reproductive 166adj.
hydrant
water 339n.
current 350n.
conduit 351n.
extinguisher 382n.
hydrate
add water 339vb.
moisten 341vb.
hydraulics
fluidity 335n.
hydro
hospital 658n.
hydrocele
fluid 335n.
disease 651n.
hydrocephalic
diseased 651adj.
hydrodynamics
science of forces 162n.
fluidity 335n.
hydroelectric
dynamic 160adj.
hydrogen
lifter 310n.
levity 323n.
hydrogenate
gasify 336vb.
hydrogeology
geography 321n.
hydrographer
oceanography 343n.
surveyor 465n.
hydrography
geography 321n.
hygrometry 341n.
oceanography 343n.
hydrokinetics
fluidity 335n.
hydrology
geography 321n.
fluidity 335n.
hygrometry 341n.
hydrolysis
decomposition 51n.
hydromel
sweet 392n.
hydrometer
density 324n.
hygrometry 341n.
hydrometry
fluidity 335n.
hydrophobia
frenzy 503n.
hydroplane
aircraft 276n.
hydroponics

agriculture 370n.
hydrostatics
science of forces 162n.
fluidity 335n.
hydrotherapy
moistening 341n.
therapy 658n.
hydrotic, hydrous
watery 339adj.
hyena
noxious animal 904n.
hyetography
rain 350n.
hygiene
cleansing 648n.
health 650n.
hygiene 652n.
prophylactic 658n.
preservation 666n.
hygienist
sanitarian 652n.
hygiology
hygiene 652n.
hygrometer
weather 340n.
meter 465n.
recording instrument 549n.
hygrometry
hygrometry 341n.
hygroscope
hygrometry 341n.
hyle
substantiality 3n.
matter 319n.
hymeneal
wedding 894n.
matrimonial 894adj.
hymn
vocal music 412n.
poem 593n.
praise 923vb.
hymn 981n.
hymnal
hymnal 988n.
church utensil 990n.
hymnody
hymn 981n.
hymn of hate
hatred 888n.
hymnology
vocal music 412n.
hymn 981n.
hymnal 988n.
hymn-writer
musician 413n.
theologian 973n.
worshiper 981n.
hyp
psychopathy 503n.
hypallage
inversion 221n.
hyperesthesia
sensibility 374n.
hyperbatic
inverted 221adj.
hyperbola
curve 248n.
hyperbole
expansion 197n.
trope 519n.
exaggeration 546n.
ornament 574n.
hyperbolical
exaggerated 546adj.
hyperbolize
exaggerate 546vb.
hyperborean
distant 199adj.
hypercharacterization
pleonasm 570n.
hypercriticism
narrow mind 481n.
discontent 829n.
fastidiousness 862n.
censure 924n.
hyperdulia
cult 981n.
hyperion
particle 33n.
hyperphysical
paranormal 984adj.
hyperphysics
occultism 984n.
hyperpsychological
paranormal 984adj.
hypersonic
speedy 277adj.
hypertension
blood pressure 651n.
hypertrophy
size 195n.
expansion 197n.
hyphen
bond 47n.
punctuation 547n.
hyphenate
join 45vb.
hypnopedagogics
teaching 534n.
therapy 658n.
hypnosis
insensibility 375n.
sleep 679n.
occultism 984n.
hypnotic
lenitive 177adj.
influential 178adj.
insensible 375adj.
inducive 612adj.
remedial 658adj.
somnific 679adj.
psychical 984adj.
hypnotism
insensibility 375n.
occultism 984n.
hypnotist
motivator 612n.
psychic 984n.
hypnotize
influence 178vb.
render insensible 375vb.
convince 485vb.
motivate 612vb.
bewitch 983vb.
practice occultism 984vb.
hypocaust
heater 383n.
hypochondria
psychopathy 503n.
ill-health 651n.
melancholy 834n.
hypochondriac
insane 503adj.
madman 504n.
sick person 651n.
unhealthy 651adj.
moper 834n.
hypocrisy
duplicity 541n.
deception 542n.
flattery 925n.
false piety 980n.
hypocrite
imitator 20n.
deceiver 545n.
slyboots 698n.
affector 850n.
flatterer 925n.
hypogeal
deep 211adj.
hypogeum
depth 211n.
hypomania
mania 503n.
psychopathy 503n.
hypostasis
essence 1n.
substantiality 3n.
substance 3n.
hypostatic
substantial 3adj.
material 319adj.
Hypostatic Union
Trinity 965n.
hypostatize
materialize 319vb.
hypotension
blood pressure 651n.
hypothecation
security 767n.
hypothermal
warm 379adj.
hypothesis
attribution 158n.
opinion 485n.
supposition 512n.
hypothetical
uncertain 474adj.

credible 485adj.
suppositional 512adj.
imaginary 513adj.
hyposometer
altimetry 209n.
hyssop
ritual object 988n.
hysteresis
lateness 136n.
slowness 278n.
hysteria
psychopathy 503n.
hysteric
madman 504n.
hysterical
furious 176adj.
insane 503adj.
capricious 604adj.
fervent 818adj.
excited 821adj.
excitable 822adj.
hysterics
violence 176n.
excitable state 822n.
lamentation 836n.
hysteron proteron
inversion 221n.

I

I
self 80n.
iamb
prosody 593n.
iambic
poetic 593adj.
ianthic
purple 434adj.
ibidem
identically 13adv.
ibis
bird of prey 365n.
Icarus
aeronaut 271n.
ice
desert 172n.
smoothness 258n.
pudding 301n.
ice 380n.
refrigeration 382n.
refrigerator 384n.
sweeten 392vb.
transparency 422n.
preserver 666n.
preserve 666vb.
gem 844n.
ice age
adversity 731n.
Ice Age
era 110n.
iceberg
island 349n.
ice 380n.
unfeeling person 820n.
solitary 883n.
ice-blink
reflection 417n.
ice-box
provisions 301n.
ice 380n.
refrigerator 384n.
ice-cap
ice 380n.
ice-chamber
ice 380n.
ice-chest
refrigerator 384n.
ice-cube
ice 380n.
refrigerator 384n.
iced
cooled 382adj.
preserved 666adj.
ice-field
plain 348n.
ice 380n.
ice-floe
plain 348n.
ice 380n.
ice over
refrigerate 382vb.
ice-pack
refrigerator 384n.
ice-plow
ice 380n.
ice-rink
arena 724n.
ice-sheet
ice 380n.
ice-skate
footwear 228n.
sled 274n.
ice-stream
ice 380n.
ice up
refrigerate 382vb.
ice-yacht
sled 274n.
ice 380n.
ichneumon
rodent 365n.
ichnography
map 551n.
ichor
fluid 335n.
blood 335n.
ichthyology
zoology 367n.
icicle
ice 380n.
unfeeling person 820n.
icing
sweet 392n.
icon
copy 22n.
image 551n.
picture 553n.
ritual object 988n.
iconoclasm
destruction 165n.
iconoclast
destroyer 168n.
violent creature 176n.
evildoer 904n.
religionist 979n.
iconography
representation 551n.
iconolatry
cult 981n.
idolatry 982n.
iconology
theology 973n.
icteric
yellow 433adj.
icterus
yellowness 433n.
ictus
pronunciation 577n.
prosody 593n.
icy
hard 326adj.
cold 380adj.
impassive 820adj.
unsociable 883adj.
id
heredity 5n.
subjectivity 320n.
spirit 447n.
idea
form 243n.
idea 451n.
opinion 485n.
idea'd
imaginative 513adj.
ideal
prototype 23n.
ideational 451adj.
imaginary 513adj.
motive 612n.
perfection 646n.
desired object 859n.
idealism
immateriality 320n.
philosophy 449n.
fantasy 513n.
reformism 654n.
fastidiousness 862n.
philanthropy 901n.
morals 917n.
disinterestedness 931n.
virtues 933n.
idealist
immateriality 320n.
visionary 513n.
reformer 654n.
essayer 671n.
perfectionist 862n.
kind person 897n.
philanthropist 901n.

good man 937n.
idealistic
impossible 470adj.
imaginative 513adj.
improving 654adj.
(*see* idealism)
ideality
thought 449n.
supposition 512n.
ideality 513n.
idealize
imagine 513vb.
overrate 482vb.
ideals
conduct 688n.
philanthropy 901n.
morals 917n.
disinterestedness 931n.
virtues 933n.
ideate
cognize 447vb.
think 449vb.
imagine 513vb.
ideational
ideational 451adj.
idée fixe
positiveness 473n.
prejudgment 481n.
opiniatrety 602n.
identical
identical 13adj.
identification
identity 13n.
assimilation 18n.
comparison 462n.
identification 547n.
identification papers
label 547n.
identify
(*see* identification)
identity
identity 13n.
equivalence 28n.
self 80n.
authenticity 494n.
ideogram
letter 558n.
script 586n.
ideologist
philanthropist 901n.
ides
date 108n.
idiocy
unintelligence 499n.
insanity 503n.
idioglossia
unintelligibility 517n.
language 557n.
neology 560n.
speech defect 580n.
idiolalia
(*see* idioglossia)
idiom
speciality 80n.
connotation 514n.
dialect 560n.
phrase 563n.
speech 579n.
idiomatic
apt 24adj.
special 80adj.
semantic 514adj.
linguistic 557adj.
phraseological 563adj.
stylistic 566adj.
forceful 571adj.
plain 573adj.
elegant 575adj.
idiomorphic
characteristic 5adj.
idioplasm
organism 358n.
idiosyncrasy
temperament 5n.
specialty 80n.
unconformity 84n.
tendency 179n.
style 566n.
idiot
fool 501n.
madman 504n.
idiotic
(*see* idiocy)
idiotism
phrase 563n.
idioverse
circumstance 8n.
whole 52n.
idle
operate 173vb.
move slowly 278vb.
be inattentive 456vb.
useless 641adj.
unused 674adj.
lazy 679adj.
idleness
unproductivity 172n.
inaction 677n.
inactivity 679n.
dutilessness 918n.
idler
slowcoach 278n.
negligence 458n.
slacker 598n.
avoider 620n.
idler 679n.
idol
image 551n.
exceller 644n.
desired object 859n.
person of repute 866n.
loved one 887n.
favorite 890n.
good man 937n.
god 966n.
idol 982n.
idolater
worshiper 981n.
idolater 982n.
idolatrous
approving 923adj.
idolatrous 982adj.
idolatry
love 887n.
praise 923n.
religion 973n.
cult 981n.
idolatry 982n.
idolization
deification 982n.
idolize
love 887vb.
respect 920vb.
praise 923vb.
idolatrize 982vb.
idol-maker
sculptor 556n.
idolater 982n.
idolothyte
idolatry 982n.
idolatrous 982adj.
idol-worship
idolatry 982n.
idoneous
fit 24adj.
idyll
description 590n.
poem 593n.
idyllic
pleasurable 826adj.
if
if 8adv.
provided 468adv.
igloo
dwelling 192n.
igneous
fiery 379adj.
ignis fatuus
insubstantial thing 4n.
glow 417n.
glow-worm 420n.
visual fallacy 440n.
ignite
kindle 381vb.
igniter
lighter 385n.
ignition
burning 381n.
ignoble
discreditable 867adj.
plebeian 869adj.
humble 872adj.
dishonest 930adj.
ignominy
disrepute 867n.
ignoramus
ignoramus 493n.
ignorance
ignorance 491n.
unskillfulness 695n.

I
K

innocence 935n.
ignorant
ignorant 491adj.
foolish 499adj.
inexpectant 508adj.
(*see* ignorance)
ignoratio elenchi
sophism 477n.
ignore
be blind 439n.
be inattentive 456vb.
disregard 458vb.
disbelieve 486vb.
reject 607vb.
not observe 769vb.
make unwelcome 833vb.
be rude 885vb.
not respect 921vb.
ignotum per ignotius
sophism 477n.
iguana
reptile 365n.
ill
evil 616n.
badness 645n.
sick 651adj.
ill-adapted
unapt 25adj.
ill-adjusted
inexact 495adj.
ill-advised
ill-timed 138adj.
unwise 499adj.
inexpedient 643adj.
bungled 695adj.
rash 857adj.
wrong 914adj.
illapse
be turned to 147vb.
ingress 297n.
illaqueate
ensnare 542vb.
ill-breeding
ill-breeding 847n.
discourtesy 885n.
ill-conceived
unwise 499adj.
ill-conditioned
bad, harmful 645adj.
sullen 893adj.
malevolent 898adj.
ill-conducted
bungled 695adj.
ill-considered
(*see* ill-advised)
ill-defined
amorphous 244adj.
ill-seen 444adj.
ill-digested
immature 670adj.
ill-disciplined
disobedient 738adj.
ill-disposed
discontented 829adj.
malevolent 898adj.
ill-done
bungled 695adj.
illegal
prohibited 757adj.
unjust 914adj.
unwarranted 916adj.
dishonest 930adj.
illegal 954adj.
illegality
illegality 954n.
illegibility
unintelligibility 517n.
illegitimacy
sonship 170n.
wrong 914n.
undueness 916n.
bastardy 954n.
illegality 954n.
ill fame
disrepute 867n.
ill-fated
unfortunate 731adj.
ill-favored
ugly 842adj.
ill feeling
dislike 861n.
enmity 881n.
hatred 888n.
ill-formed
unsightly 842adj.
ill fortune
ill fortune 731n.
ill-furnished
unprovided 636adj.
ill-gotten
acquired 771adj.
ill-health
weakness 163n.
ill-health 651n.
ill-humor
resentment 891n.
sullenness 893n.
illiberal
biased 481adj.
parsimonious 816adj.
selfish 932adj.
illiberality
opiniatrety 602n.
(*see* illiberal)
illicit
(*see* illegal)
illimitable
infinite 107adj.
ill-informed
uninstructed 491adj.
mistaken 495adj.
ill-intentioned
malevolent 898adj.
illiterate
uninstructed 491adj.
ignoramus 493n.
ill-judged
indiscriminating 464adj.
(*see* ill-advised)
ill-kept
neglected 458adj.
ill-mannered
(*see* ill-breeding)
ill-matched
disagreeing 25adj.
quarreling 709adj.
ill-natured
malevolent 898adj.
illness
illness 651n.
ill-off
poor 801adj.
illogic
intuition 476n.
sophistry 477n.
folly 499n.
misteaching 535n.
illogical
unthinking 450adj.
illogical 477adj.
biased 481adj.
erroneous 495adj.
unwise 499adj.
illogicality
irrelevance 10n.
discontinuity 72n.
sophism 477n.
unmeaningness 515n.
ill-omened
inopportune 138adj.
cautionary 664adj.
unpromising 853adj.
ill-requited
unthanked 908adj.
ill-seeming
wrong 914adj.
ill-seen
ill-seen 444adj.
ill-spent
wasted 634adj.
profitless 641adj.
ill-starred
inopportune 138adj.
unfortunate 731adj.
ill taste
bad taste 847n.
ill-tempered
sullen 893adj.
ill-timed
ill-timed 138adj.
ill-treat
ill-treat 645vb.
misuse 675vb.
be severe 735vb.
ill-treatment
cruel act 898n.
illude
deceive 542vb.
illuminant
lighter 385n.

luminary 420n.
illuminate
make bright 417vb.
illuminate 420vb.
color 425vb.
interpret 520vb.
manifest 522vb.
paint 553vb.
decorate 844vb.
illuminati
intellectual 492n.
illumination
progression 285n.
light 417n.
lighting 420n.
discovery 484n.
knowledge 490n.
ornamental art 844n.
revelation 975n.
illuminations
fireworks 420n.
spectacle 445n.
celebration 876n.
illuminator
artist 556n.
illumine
educate 534vb.
ill-usage
misuse 675n.
cruel act 898n.
ill-used
suffering 825adj.
illusion
visual fallacy 440n.
appearance 445n.
error 495n.
deception 542n.
sleight 542n.
illusionism
mimicry 20n.
sorcery 983n.
illusionist
conjuror 545n.
illusory
sophistical 477adj.
imaginary 513adj.
deceiving 542adj.
illustrate
(*see* illustration)
illustration
example 83n.
interpretation 520n.
representation 551n.
picture 553n.
edition 589n.
ornamental art 844n.
illustrative
typical 83adj.
expressive 516adj.
illustrator
artist 556n.
illustrious
renowned 866adj.
ill-will
discontent 829n.
enmity 881n.
hatred 888n.
malevolence 898n.
envy 912n.
ill wind
badness 645n.
obstacle 702n.
adversity 731n.
ill-wisher
trouble-maker 663n.
enemy 881n.
ill wishes
malediction 899n.
image
analogue 18n.
copy 22n.
reflection 417n.
appearance 445n.
idea 451n.
ideality 513n.
metaphor 519n.
exhibit 522n.
monument 548n.
image 551n.
sculpture 554n.
idol 982n.
image-building
imagination 513n.
imagery
imagination 513n.
metaphor 519n.
image-worship
cult 981n.
idolatry 982n.
imaginable
possible 469adj.
supposed 512adj.
imaginal
imaginative 513adj.
imaginary
unreal 2adj.
insubstantial 4adj.
supposed 512adj.
imaginary 513adj.
fairylike 970adj.
imagination
thought 449n.
idea 451n.
imagination 513n.
imaginative
unimitative 21adj.
imaginative 513adj.
false 541adj.
descriptive 590adj.
imagine
suppose 512vb.
imagine 513vb.
describe 590vb.
hope 852vb.
imago
vermin 365n.
imam
priest 986n.
imbalance
inequality 29n.
changeableness 152n.
distortion 246n.
imbecile
weak 163adj.
unintelligent 499adj.
foolish 499adj.
fool 501n.
insane 503adj.
inbecility
(*see* imbecile)
imbibe
absorb 299vb.
drink 301vb.
learn 536vb.
imbrication
covering 226n.
imbroglio
medley 43n.
complexity 61n.
predicament 700n.
dissension 709n.
imbrue
infuse 303vb.
drench 341vb.
color 425vb.
imbue
mix 43vb.
pervade 189vb.
infuse 303vb.
drench 341vb.
educate 534vb.
habituate 610vb.
imbued with
believing 485adj.
imitable
imitative 20adj.
imitate
resemble 18vb.
liken 18vb.
imitate 20vb.
fake 541vb.
represent 551vb.
imitated
false 541adj.
imitation
imitation 20n.
substituted 150adj.
sham 542n.
representation 551n.
bad taste 847n.
imitative
stimulating 18adj.
imitative 20adj.
conformable 83adj.
repeated 106adj.
mindless 448adj.
unthinking 450adj.
imitativeness
mimicry 20n.
immaculate
perfect 646adj.
clean 648adj.

honorable 929adj.
innocent 935adj.
pure 950adj.
immanence
intrinsicality 5n.
divine attribute 965n.
immaterial
insubstantial 4adj.
immateriality
insubstantiality 4n.
immateriality 320n.
rarity 325n.
unimportance 639n.
spiritualism 984n.
immature
beginning 68adj.
early 135adj.
unhabituated 611adj.
immaturity
incompleteness 55n.
newness 126n.
youth, nonage 130n.
uintelligence 499n.
imperfection 647n.
non-preparation 670n.
unskillfulness 695n.
non-completion 726n.
immeasurable
infinite 107adj.
immediacy
continuity 71n.
instantaneity 116n.
haste 680n.
immediate
instantaneous 116n.
early 135adj.
impending 155adj.
immedicable
unpromising 853adj.
immemorial
perpetual 115adj.
former 125adj.
immemorial 127adj.
permanent 144adj.
worshipful 866adj.
immemorial usage
tradition 127n.
immense
infinite 107adj.
immensity
greatness 32n.
hugeness 195n.
immeritorious
bad 645adj.
immersed
deep 211adj.
immersion
ingress 297n.
immersion 303n.
plunge 313n.
moistening 341n.
Christian rite 988n.
immigrant
foreigner 59n.
settler 191n.
wanderer 268n.
incomer 297n.
immigration
wandering 267n.
ingress 297n.
imminent
future 124adj.
early 135adj.
impending 155adj.
approaching 289adj.
immiscibility
disjunction 46vb.
non-coherence 49n.
immission
reception 299n.
immitigable
unpromising 853adj.
immixture
mixture 43n.
immobility
permanence 144n.
stability 153n.
inertness 175n.
quiescence 266n.
inaction 677n.
immoderate
violent 176adj.
inelegant 576adj.
immoderately
extremely 32adv.
immoderation
greatness 32n.
exaggeration 546n.
intemperance 943n.
immodest
undisguised 522adj.
immodesty
vanity 783n.
impurity 951n.
immolation
killing 362n.
oblation 981n.
immoral
dishonest 930adj.
immoralism
impiety 980n.
immoralist
wrong 914n.
bad man 938n.
libertine 952n.
impious person 980n.
immortality
wrong 914n.
wickedness 934n.
unchastity 951n.
immortal
existing 1n.
perpetual 115adj.
intellectual 492n.
soldier 722n.
renowned 866adj.
godlike 965adj.
immortality
perpetuity 115n.
famousness 866n.
immortalize
perpetuate 115vb.
honor 866vb.
immortals
armed force 722n.
god 966n.
immovable
firm-set 45adj.
fixed 153adj.
still 266adj.
resolute 599adj.
obstinate 602adj.
immovables
property 777n.
immundity
uncleanness 649n.
immunity
hygiene 652n.
safety 660n.
escape 667n.
freedom 744n.
dueness 915n.
non-liability 919n.
immunization
hygiene 652n.
prophylactic 658n.
protection 660n.
immure
circumscribe 232vb.
enclose 235n.
imprison 747vb.
immutability
permanence 144n.
stability 153n.
divine attribute 965n.
immutable
perpetual 115adj.
antiquated 127adj.
imp
child 132n.
implant 303vb.
cultivate 370vb.
devil 969n.
elf, demon 970n.
sorcerer 983n.
impact
affix, tighten 45vb.
influence 178n.
collision 279n.
insert, implant 303vb.
excitation 821n.
impaction
(*see* impact)
impair
derange 63vb.
disable 161vb.
weaken 163vb.
waste 634vb.
make useless 641vb.
harm 645vb.
impair 655vb.
misuse 675vb.

hinder 702vb.
blemish 845vb.
impairment
incompleteness 55n.
impairment 655n.
impale
kill 362vb.
pierce 263vb.
mark 547vb.
execute 963vb.
impalement
perforation 263n.
impaling
heraldry 547n.
impalpable
minute 196adj.
impanation
the sacrament 988n.
impanel
list 87vb.
imparity
inequality 29n.
impart
inform 524vb.
give 781vb.
impartial
wise 498adj.
neutral 625adj.
impartiality
equality 28n.
moderation 177n.
no choice 606n.
indifference 860n.
justice 913n.
probity 929n.
disinterestedness 931n.
impassable
closed 264adj.
impracticable 470adj.
impasse
closure 264n.
impossibility 470n.
difficulty 700n.
obstacle 702n.
impassibility
insensibility 375n.
moral insensibility 820n.
inexcitability 823n.
impassion
excite 821vb.
impassioned
forceful 571adj.
fervent 818adj.
lively 819adj.
excited 821adj.
impassive
inert 175adj.
unfeeling 375adj.
incurious 454adj.
inattentive 456adj.
indiscriminating 464adj.
non-active 677adj.
inactive 679adj.
impassive 820adj.
inexcitable 823adj.
indifferent 860adj.
unastonished 865adj.
impasto
facing 226n.
art style 553n.
impatience
willingness 597n.
haste 680n.
warm feeling 818n.
excitability 822n.
rashness 857n.
desire 859n.
rudeness 885n.
resentment 891n.
irascibility 892n.
impatient
unwise 499adj.
sensitive 819adj.
impeachment
censure 924n.
detraction 926n.
accusation 928n.
litigation 959n.
impeccable
perfect 646adj.
virtuous 933adj.
innocent 935adj.
impeccancy
perfection 646n.
impecunious
poor 801adj.
impede
hinder 702vb.
impediment
speech defect 580n.
difficulty 700n.
obstacle 702n.
hindrance 702n.
impedimenta
box 194n.
thing transferred 272n.
encumbrance 702n.
property 777n.
impel
move 265vb.
impel 279vb.
propel 287vb.
insert 303vb.
motivate 612vb.
impelling
casual 156adj.
impend
be to come 124vb.
impend 155vb.
await 507vb.
frighten 854vb.
threaten 900vb.
impending
early 135adj.
approaching 289adj.
arriving 295adj.
impenetrable
closed 264adj.
dense 324adj.
latent 523adj.
unintelligent 499adj.
unintelligible 517adj.
difficult 700adj.
thick-skinned 820adj.
impenitence
obstinacy 602n.
impenitence 940n.
imperative
necessary 596adj.
demanding 627adj.
authoritarian 735adj.
commanding 737adj.
compelling 740adj.
obligatory 917adj.
imperator
sovereign 741n.
army officer 741n.
imperceptible
minute 196adj.
slow 278adj.
invisible 444adj.
imperception
moral insensibility 820n.
imperceptive
insensible 375adj.
indiscriminating 464adj.
impercipient
insensible 375adj.
unintelligent 499adj.
imperfect
fragmentary 53adj.
preterit 125adj.
immature 670adj.
uncompleted 726adj.
imperfection
inferiority 35n.
incompleteness 55n.
shortcoming 307n.
badness 645n.
imperfection 647n.
vulnerability 661n.
artlessness 699n.
blemish 845n.
vice 934n.
imperfect tense
course of time 111n.
imperforate
closed 264adj.
imperial
great 32adj.
box 194n.
hair 259n.
ruling 733adj.
imperialism
nation 371n.
governance 733n.
imperil
endanger 661vb.

imperious
authoritative 733adj.
proud 871adj.
insolent 878adj.
imperishable
perpetual 115adj.
unchangeable 153adj.
renowned 866adj.
imperium
superiority 34n.
government 733n.
impermanence
transientness 114n.
changeableness 152n.
impermeable
closed 264adj.
dense 324adj.
screened 421adj.
impermissible
illegal 954adj.
impersonal
general 79adj.
unfeeling 375adj.
impassive 820adj.
indifferent 860adj.
unsociable 883adj.
just 913adj.
disinterested 931adj.
impersonation
representation 551n.
impersonator
imitator 20n.
imperspicuity
unintelligibility 517n.
imperspicuity 568n.
impersuasible
willful 602adj.
impertinence
irrelevance 10n.
sauciness 878n.
rudeness 885n.
impertinent
insolent person 878n.
imperturbability
inexcitability 823n.
non-wonder 865n.
imperturbation
moral insensibility 820n.
impervious
closed 264adj.
dense 324adj.
screened 421adj.
opaque 423adj.
impracticable 470adj.
unbelieving 486adj.
unintelligent 499adj.
obstinate 602adj.
thick-skinned 820adj.
impetiginous
unclean 649adj.
impetrate
entreat 761vb.
impetuosity
vigorousness 174n.
violence 176n.
haste 680n.
excitability 822n.
rashness 857n.
desire 859n.
impetus
spurt 277n.
impulse 279n.
impiety
irreligion 974n.
impiety 980n.
impignorate
give security 767vb.
impinge
collide 279vb.
encroach 306vb.
touch 378vb.
impious
wicked 934adj.
irreligious 974adj.
impious 980adj.
impish
harmful 645adj.
fairylike 970adj.
implacable
resolute 599adj.
obstinate 602adj.
quarreling 709adj.
hating 888adj.
malevolent 898adj.
pitiless 906adj.
revengeful 910adj.
implant
affix 45vb.
implant 303vb.
educate 534vb.
habituate 610vb.
implausibility
unbelief 486n.
implausible
improbable 472adj.
erroneous 495adj.
implead
litigate 959vb.
(*see* indict)
implement
produce 164vb.
instrument 628n.
tool 630n.
do 676vb.
carry out 725vb.
implex
mixed 43n.
implicate
accuse 928vb.
implicated
ingredient 58adj.
implication
relation 9n.
complexity 61n.
meaning 514n.
latency 523n.
implicit
intrinsic 5adj.
meaningful 514adj.
tacit 523adj.
implore
entreat 761vb.
imply
be intrinsic 5vb.
contain 56vb.
accompany 89vb.
conduce 156vb.
evidence 466vb.
make likely 471vb.
mean 514vb.
imply 523vb.
hint 524vb.
indicate 547vb.
impolicy
bungling 695n.
impolite
inelegant 576adj.
ill-bred 847adj.
impertinent 878adj.
discourteous 885adj.
disrespectful 921adj.
impolitic
inexpedient 643adj.
unskillful 695adj.
imponderability
insubstantiality 4n.
immateriality 320n.
levity 323n.
imporous
closed 264adj.
dense 324adj.
import
relation 9n.
add 38vb.
transference 272n.
ingress 297n.
admit 299vb.
insert 303vb.
meaning 514n.
provide 633vb.
importance 638n.
importance
greatness 32n.
superiority 34n.
influence 178n.
materiality 319n.
importance 638n.
prestige 866n.
important
crucial 137adj.
fundamental 156adj.
importation
(*see* import)
imported
extraneous 59adj.
incoming 297adj.
neological 560adj.
importer
transferrer 272n.
carrier 273n.
merchant 794n.

importunate, importunity
(*see* importune)
importune
request 761vb.
torment 827vb.
impose
add 38vb.
place 187vb.
deceive 542vb.
print 587vb.
command 737vb.
compel 740vb.
command respect 920vb.
punish 936vb.
imposing
impressive 821adj.
worshipful 866adj.
imposition
requirement 627n.
bane 659n.
demand 737n.
tax 809n.
injustice 914n.
undueness 916n.
penalty 963n.
impossible
excluded 57adj.
unthought 450adj.
impossible 470adj.
difficult 700adj.
intolerable 827adj.
wonderful 864adj.
impost
tax 809n.
imposter
imitator 20n.
imposter 545n.
bungler 697n.
boaster 877n.
knave 938n.
impostume
ulcer 651n.
imposture
duplicity 541n.
deception 542n.
cunning 698n.
impotence
impotence 161n.
weakness 163n.
unproductivity 172n.
inutility 641n.
failure 728n.
impotent
unimportant 639adj.
non-active 677adj.
impound
imprison 747vb.
improverish
weaken 163vb.
waste 634vb.
make insufficient 636vb.
fleece 786vb.
impoverish 801vb.
impoverishment
deterioration 655n.
poverty 801n.
impracticable
impracticable 470adj.
useless 641adj.
difficult 700adj.
unpromising 853adj.
impractical
irrelevant 10adj.
misjudging 481adj.
imaginative 513adj.
imprecation
entreaty 761n.
malediction 899n.
prayers 981n.
imprecision
generality 79n.
inexactness 495n.
imperspicuity 568n.
impregnable
unyielding 162adj.
invulnerable 660adj.
pure 950adj.
impregnate
mix 43vb.
combine 50vb.
generate 164vb.
make fruitful 171vb.
be present 189vb.
infuse 303vb.
educate 534vb.
impresario
stage manager 594n.
imprescriptible
due 915adj.
impress
effect 157n.
be vigorous 174vb.
motivate 612vb.
take away 786vb.
steal 788vb.
impress 821vb.
delight 826vb.
be wonderful 864vb.
command respect 920vb.
(*see* impression, impress on)
impressibility
liability 180n.
softness 327n.
irresolution 601n.
persuasibility 612n.
moral sensibility 819n.
impression
copy 22n.
influence 178n.
concavity 255n.
sense 374n.
spectacle 445n.
appearance 445n.
idea 451n.
intuition 476n.
opinion 485n.
knowledge 490n.
indication 547n.
label 547n.
printing 555n.
letterpress 587n.
feeling 818n.
excitation 821n.
impressionable
converted 147adj.
unstable 152adj.
sentient 374adj.
receiving 782adj.
impressible 819adj.
excitable 822adj.
impressionism
school of painting 553n.
impressionist
artist 556n.
impressionistic
descriptive 590adj.
impressive
great 32adj.
credible 485adj.
forceful 571adj.
descriptive 590adj.
notable 638adj.
felt 818adj.
impressive 821adj.
(*see* impression)
impressiveness
spectacle 445n.
prestige 866n.
ostentation 875n.
impressment
compulsion 740n.
impress on
cause thought 449vb.
emphasize 532vb.
mark 547vb.
engrave 555vb.
imprest
lending 784n.
imprimatur
assent 488n.
permit 756n.
orthodoxism 976n.
imprimis
initially 68adv.
imprint
make conform 83vb.
concavity 255n.
identification 547n.
label 547n.
letterpress 587n.
imprison
enclose 224vb.
circumscribe 232vb.
close 264vb.
imprison 747vb.
retain 778vb.

punish 963vb.
imprisoned
imprisoned 747adj.
captive 750adj.
imprisonment
detention 747n.
penalty 963n.
improbability
improbability 472n.
unbelief 486n.
inexpectation 508n.
improbable
erroneous 495adj.
wonderful 864adj.
improbation
disapprobation 924n.
improbity
thievishness 788n.
wrong 914n.
improbity 930n.
wickedness 934n.
lawbreaking 954n.
impromptu
instantaneously 116adv.
musical piece 412n.
spontaneity 609n.
non-preparation 670n.
improper
unapt 25adj.
unwise 499adj.
ungrammatical 565adj.
inexpedient 643adj.
not nice 645adj.
vulgar 847adj.
disreputable 867adj.
discreditable 867adj.
wrong 914adj.
undue 916adj.
vicious 934adj.
impropriate
possess 773vb.
convey 780vb.
appropriate 786vb.
impropriator
beneficiary 776n.
impropriety
inaptitude 25n.
solecism 565n.
inelegance 576n.
inexpedience 643n.
bad taste 847n.
wrong 914n.
undueness 916n.
vice 934n.
guilty act 936n.
improve
modify 143vb.
beautify 841vb.
philanthropize 897vb.
(*see* improvement)
improvement
increase 36n.
progression 285n.
benefit 615n.
improvement 654n.
improve on
be superior 34vb.
improver
reformer 654n.
improve the occasion
profit by 137vb.
improvidence
non-preparation 670n.
rashness 857n.
improvident
prodigal 815adj.
improvisation
spontaneity 609n.
contrivance 623n.
non-preparation 670n.
improvise
compose music 413vb.
make ready 699vb.
imprudence
rashness 857n.
impudent
impertinent 878adj.
discourteous 885adj.
impudicity
impurity 951n.
impugn
cause doubt 486vb.
disbelieve 486vb.
negate 533vb.
impulse
energy 160n.
influence 178n.
impulse 279n.
intention 476n.
necessity 596n.
spontaneity 609n.
motive 612n.
feeling 818n.
desire 859n.
impulsion
causation 156n.
propulsion 287n.
motive 612n.
impulsive
intuitive 476adj.
involuntary 596adj.
spontaneous 609adj.
excitable 822adj.
impunity
escape 667n.
non-liability 919n.
acquittal 960n.
impurity
uncleanness 649n.
bad taste 847n.
libido 859n.
wickedness 934n.
sensualism 944n.
impurity 951n.
imputation
attribution 158n.
slur 867n.
accusation 928n.
in
inside 224adv.
inability
impotence 161n.
inutility 641n.
unskillfulness 695n.
hindrance 702n.
inabstinence
intemperance 943n.
inaccessible
removed 199adj.
impracticable 470adj.
inaccuracy
negligence 458n.
indiscrimination 464n.
inexactness 495n.
imperspicuity 568n.
inaction
inertness 175n.
avoidance 620n.
non-use 674n.
inaction 677n.
inactivity 679n.
inactive
powerless 161adj.
insensible 375adj.
apathetic 820adj.
inactivity
delay 136n.
weakness 163n.
unproductivity 172n.
inertness 175n.
quiescence 266n.
negligence 458n.
non-use 674n.
inaction 677n.
inactivity 679n.
leisure 681n.
non-observance 769n.
inexcitability 823n.
inadequacy
inequality 29n.
weakness 163n.
insufficiency 636n.
inutility 641n.
imperfection 647n.
inadequate
powerless 161adj.
deficient 307adj.
unskillful 695adj.
inadjustable
unconformable 84adj.
inadmissible
unapt 25adj.
excluded 57adj.
extraneous 59adj.
inexpedient 643adj.
refused 760adj.
wrong 914adj.
in advance

before 64adj.
inadvertence
inattention 456n.
mistake 495n.
inadvisability
inexpedience 643n.
inalienable
retained 778adj.
due 915adj.
in all
completely 54adv.
inamorata
woman 373n.
loved one 887n.
in and out
to and fro 317adv.
in-and-out system
periodicity 141n.
inane
(*see* inanity)
inanimate
inorganic 359adj.
dead 361adj.
mindless 448adj.
unthinking 450adj.
inactive 679adj.
inanition
helplessness 161n.
weakness 163n.
illness 651n.
inanity
insubstantiality 4n.
insubstantial thing 4n.
emptiness 190n.
incogitance 450n.
unmeaningness 515n.
inutility 641n.
inappeasable
greedy 859adj.
inappetency
indifference 860n.
inapplicability
irrelevance 10n.
inaptitude 25n.
inutility 641n.
inapposite
irrelevant 10adj.
inappreciable
inconsiderable 33adj.
minute 196adj.
unimportant 639adj.
inappreciation
ignorance 491n.
inapprehensible
unintelligible 517adj.
inappropriate
irrelevant 10adj.
unapt 25adj.
misplaced 188adj.
inexpedient 643adj.
undue 916adj.
inaptitude
inaptitude 25n.
inutility 641n.
inexpedience 643n.
inarticulate
voiceless 578adj.
stammering 580adj.
taciturn 582adj.
artless 699adj.
modest 874adj.
inarticulation
aphony 578n.
inartistic
bungled 695adj.
artless 699adj.
graceless 842adj.
inattention
blindness 439n.
inattention 456n.
bungling 695n.
non-observance 769n.
rashness 857n.
inattentive
unthinking 450adj.
negligent 458adj.
inexpectant 508adj.
hasty 680adj.
inaudibility
silence 399n.
faintness 401n.
deafness 416n.
unintelligibility 517n.
inaudible
voiceless 578adj.
inaugural
precursory 66adj.
beginning 68adj.
inaugurate
auspicate 68vb.
cause 156vb.
celebrate 876vb.
inauguration
debut 68n.
fitting out 669n.
mandate 751n.
celebration 876n.
inauspicious
inopportune 138adj.
evil 616adj.
adverse 731adj.
unpromising 853adj.
inbeing
intrinsicality 5n.
inboard
interior 224adj.
inborn
genetic 5adj.
with affections 817adj.
inbred
extrinsic 6adj.
ethnic 11adj.
combined 50adj.
with affections 817adj.
inbreeding
race 11n.
in bulk
collectively 52adv.
incalculable
multitudinous 104adj.
infinite 107adj.
casual 159adj.
incalescence
heat 379n.
incandescence
heat 379n.
light, glow 417n.
incandescent
luminescent 420adj.
incantation
sorcery 983n.
incapable
unapt 25adj.
powerless 161adj.
incapacious
narrow 206adj.
incapacitate
disable 161vb.
incapacity
inaptitude 25n.
impotence 161n.
ignorance 491n.
unintelligence 499n.
unskillfulness 695n.
incarceration
detention 747n.
incarnadine
redden 431vb.
incarnate
genetic 5adj.
alive 360adj.
manifest 522vb.
incarnation
essential part 5n.
combination 50n.
materiality 319n.
representation 551n.
theophany 965n.
revelation 975n.
incautious
unwise 499adj.
spontaneous 609adj.
rash 857adj.
incendiary
destructive 165adj.
violent creature 176n.
violent 176adj.
incendiarism 381n.
motivator 612n.
opponent 705n.
evildoer 904n.
incense
fumigator 385n.
smell 394vb.
inodorousness 395n.
scent 396n.
prophylactic 658n.
honors 866n.
excite hate 888vb.

enrage 891vb.
flattery 925n.
oblation 981n.
ritual object 988n.
incense-breathing
fragrant 396adj.
flattering 925adj.
incensed
angry 891adj.
incentive
impulse 279n.
incentive 612n.
excitant 821n.
reward 962n.
inceptive
beginning 68adj.
causal 156adj.
incessant
continuous 71adj.
repeated 106adj.
perpetual 115adj.
frequent 139adj.
unceasing 146adj.
active 678adj.
incest
illicit love 951n.
inch
small quantity 33n.
short distance 200n.
long measure 203n.
shortness 204n.
move slowly 278vb.
inch by inch
by degrees 27adv.
piecemeal 53adv.
gradatim 278adv.
inchoate
beginning 68adj.
amorphous 244adj.
uncompleted 726adj.
incidence
eventuality 154n.
incident
circumstantial 8adj.
eventuality 154n.
liable 180adj.
incidental
extrinsic 6adj.
irrelevance 10n.
accompanying 89adj.
eventuality 154n.
happening 154adj.
casual 159adj.
liable 180adj.
incidentally
incidentally 137adv.
at random 618adv.
incineration
destruction 165n.
interment 364n.
burning 381n.
incinerator
furnace 383n.
incipient
beginning 68adj.
incircumspection
rashness 857n.
incise
cut 46vb.
groove 262vb.
record 548vb.
engrave 555vb.
wound 655vb.
incision
scission 46n.
furrow 262n.
wound 655n.
incisive
keen 174adj.
assertive 532adj.
forceful 571adj.
incisor
tooth 256n.
incite
cause 156vb.
make violent 176vb.
influence 178vb.
impel 279vb.
incite 612vb.
advise 691vb.
make quarrels 709vb.
excite 821vb.
incivility
ill-breeding 847n.
sauciness 878n.
discourtesy 885n.
incivism
misanthropy 902n.
inclemency
storm 176n.
wintriness 380n.
severity 735n.
pitilessness 906n.
inclination
tendency 179n.
obliquity 220n.
will 595n.
willingness 597n.
choice 605n.
liking 859n.
love 887n.
incline
tend 179vb.
acclivity 220n.
render oblique 220vb.
make curved 248vb.
choose 605vb.
motivate 612vb.
cause desire 859vb.
inclined plane
obliquity 220n.
tool 630n.
include
add 38vb.
join 45vb.
contain 56vb.
comprise 78vb.
possess 773vb.
including
in addition 38adv.
including 78adv.
inclusion
inclusion 78n.
reception 299n.
association 706n.
participation 775n.
inclusiveness
whole 52n.
inclusion 78n.
generality 79n.
incogitance
non-intellect 448n.
incogitance 450n.
inattention 456n.
incognito
unknown 491adj.
disguised 525adj.
anonymous 562adj.
incognizable
unknown 491adj.
unintelligible 517adj.
incognizance
ignorance 491n.
incoherence
non-coherence 49n.
discontinuity 72n.
frenzy 503n.
unmeaningness 515n.
unintelligibility 517n.
incoherent
orderless 61adj.
in column
continuously 71adv.
incombustibility
incombustibility 382n.
income
means 629n.
earnings 771n.
estate 777n.
receipt 807n.
reward 962n.
incomer
incomer 297n.
income tax
tax 809n.
incoming
sequent 65adj.
incoming 297adj.
incommensurable
correlative 10adj.
disagreeing 25adj.
numerical 85adj.
incommode
give pain 377vb.
be inexpedient 643vb.
be difficult 700vb.
hinder 702vb.
incommode 827vb.
incommunicable
inexpressible 517adj.

retained 778adj.
incommunicado
concealed 525adj.
imprisoned 747adj.
incommunicative
reticent 525adj.
taciturn 582adj.
cautious 858adj.
incommutable
unchangeable 153adj.
in company
plural 101adj.
incomparability
dissimilarity 19n.
incomparable
unimitated 21adj.
supreme 34adj.
incompatibility
difference 15n.
disagreement 25n.
enmity 881n.
incompetence
inaptitude 25n.
impotence 161n.
unintelligence 499n.
insufficiency 636n.
unskillfulness 695n.
dutilessness 918n.
illegality 954n.
incompetent
fool 501n.
useless 641adj.
unentitled 916adj.
incomplete
incomplete 55adj.
deficient 307adj.
insufficient 636adj.
imperfect 647adj.
uncompleted 726adj.
incompletely
partly 53adv.
incompletion
imperfection 647n.
incomprehensible
infinite 107adj.
unintelligible 517adj.
incomprehension
ignorance 491n.
incompressible
dense 324adj.
rigid 326adj.
inconceivable
unthought 450adj.
impossible 470adj.
improbable 472adj.
unbelieved 486adj.
unintelligible 517adj.
wonderful 864adj.
inconcinnity
inaptitude 25n.
inelegance 576n.
ugliness 842n.
inconclusive
ill-reasoned 477adj.
incongruent
irrelative 10adj.
different 15adj.
dissimilar 19adj.
unequal 29adj.
incongruity
misfit 25n.
(*see* incongruous)
incongruous
different 15adj.
disagreeing 25adj.
unconformable 84adj.
illogical 477adj.
ungrammatical 565adj.
inconnection
irrelation 10n.
inconsequence
irrelevance 10n.
absurdity 497n.
unimportance 639n.
inconsequential
irrelevant 10adj.
illogical 477adj.
unimportant 639adj.
inconsiderable
inconsiderable 33adj.
unimportant 639adj.
inconsiderate
unthinking 450adj.
inattentive 456adj.
rash 857adj.
discourteous 885adj.
inconsideration
inattention 456n.
spontaneity 609n.
rashness 857n.
inconsistency
unconformity 84n.
changeableness 152n.
(*see* inconsistent)
inconsistent
contrary 14adj.
disagreeing 25adj.
illogical 477adj.
absurd 497adj.
unwise 499adj.
capricious 604adj.
inconsolable
regretting 830adj.
hopeless 853adj.
inconsonant
disagreeing 25adj.
inconspicuous
ill-seen 444adj.
unknown 491adj.
inconstancy
(*see* inconstant)
inconstant
non-uniform 17adj.
fitful 142adj.
changeful 152adj.
light-minded 456adj.
irresolute 601adj.
capricious 604adj.
perfidious 930adj.
incontestable
strong 162adj.
undisputed 473adj.
incontinence
helplessness 161n.
intemperance 943n.
sensualism 944n.
unchastity 951n.
incontinent
impotent 161adj.
intemperate 943adj.
sensual 944adj.
unchaste 951adj.
incontinently
suddenly 135adv.
intemperately 943adv.
incontrovertible
vested 153adj.
undisputed 473adj.
demonstrated 478adj.
inconvenience
inutility 641n.
inexpedience 643n.
difficulty 700n.
hinder 702vb.
obstacle 702n.
suffering 825n.
inconvenient
ill-timed 138adj.
painful 377adj.
inconversable
taciturn 582adj.
unsociable 883adj.
inconvertible
unceasing 146adj.
unchangeable 153adj.
inconvincible
unbelieving 486adj.
incoordination
disorder 61n.
incorporal
immaterial 320adj.
incorporate
join 45vb.
combine 50vb.
comprise 78vb.
absorb 299vb.
material 319adj.
manifest 522vb.
corporate 708adj.
incorporation
(*see* incorporate)
incorporeality
insubstantiality 4n.
immateriality 320n.
rarity 325n.
incorrect
illogical 477adj.
inexact 495adj.

inelegant 576adj.
wrong 914adj.
incorrectness
ill-breeding 847n.
incorrigibility
obstinacy 602n.
impenitence 940n.
incorrigible
obstinate 602adj.
unpromising 853adj.
wicked 934adj.
impenitent 940adj.
incorrupt
honorable 929adj.
innocent 935adj.
incorruptibility
health 650n.
probity 929n.
innocence 935n.
incorruptible
perpetual 115adj.
honorable 929adj.
pure 950adj.
incorruption
perpetuity 115n.
goodness 644n.
health 650n.
innocence 935n.
incrassation
condensation 324n.
thickening 354n.
increase
increase 36n.
growth 157n.
product 164n.
propagation 164n.
expand 197vb.
improvement 654n.
gain 771n.
aggravation 832n.
increate
existing 1adj.
incredible
prodigious 32adj.
unusual 84adj.
impossible 470adj.
improbable 472adj.
unbelieved 486adj.
wonderful 864adj.
incredulity
unbelief 486n.
increment
increment 36n.
addition 38n.
adjunct 40n.
expansion 197n.
benefit 615n.
gain 771n.
increpation
reprimand 924n.
incriminate
blame 924vb.
accuse 928vb.
incubate
generate 164vb.
breed stock 369vb.
mature 669vb.
incubator
seedbed 156n.
incubus
gravity 322n.
encumbrance 702n.
suffering 825n.
demon 970n.
inculcate
educate 334vb.
inculpability
innocence 935n.
inculpation
censure 924n.
accusation 928n.
incumbency
job 622n.
benefice 985n.
church office 985n.
incumbent
resident 191n.
overhanging 209adj.
weighty 322adj.
possessor 776n.
beneficiary 776n.
obligatory 917adj.
cleric 986n.
incunabula
origin 68n.
youth 130n.
edition 589n.
incur
meet with 154vb.
be liable 180vb.
acquire 771vb.
incurable
characteristic 5adj.
deadly 362adj.
impracticable 470adj.
obstinate 602adj.
bad 645adj.
sick 651adj.
unpromising 853adj.
incuriosity
incuriosity 454n.
inattention 456n.
moral insensibility 820n.
indifference 860n.
incursion
ingress 297n.
attack 712n.
incurvation
curvature 248n.
concavity 255n.
incus
ear 415n.
indebtedness
debt 803n.
gratitude 907n.
dueness 915n.
indecent
not nice 645adj.
vulgar 847adj.
disreputable 867adj.
vicious 934adj.
impure 951adj.
indecent assault
rape 951n.
indeciduous
unchangeable 153adj.
indecision
dubiety 474n.
irresolution 601n.
no choice 606n.
indecisive
uncertain 474adj.
irresolute 601adj.
indeclinable
unchangeable 153adj.
indecorum
ill-breeding 847n.
vice 934n.
indeed
positively 32adv.
indefatigability
perseverance 600n.
stamina 600n.
assiduity 678n.
restlessness 678n.
in default of
instead 150adv.
without 190adv.
indefeasible
vested 153adj.
undisputed 473adj.
indefectible
perfect 646adj.
indefensible
defenseless 161adj.
accusable 928adj.
heinous 934adj.
indefinable
unspeakable 32adj.
inexpressible 517adj.
indefinite
general 79adj.
infinite 107adj.
ill-seen 444adj.
imperspicuous 568adj.
indefiniteness
invisibility 444n.
uncertainty 474n.
equivocalness 518n.
indelible
fixed 153adj.
remembered 505adj.
marked 547adj.
indelicacy
bad taste 847n.
impurity 951n.
indelicate
graceless 842adj.
indemnification

compensation 31n.
retaliation 714n.
restitution 787n.
atonement 941n.
indemnify oneself
recoup 31vb.
indemnity
offset 31n.
restitution 787n.
pay 804n.
payment 804n.
forgiveness 909n.
atonement 941n.
indent
crinkle 251vb.
make concave 255vb.
roughen 259vb.
notch 260n., vb.
requirement 627n.
demand 737vb.
contract 765vb.
indentation
gap 201n.
angularity 247n.
convolution 251n.
concavity 255n.
notch 260n.
indenture
compact 765n.
title deed 767n.
independence
irrelation 10n.
non-imitation 21n.
unconformity 84n.
opportunity 137n.
will 595n.
independence 744n.
wealth 800n.
celibacy 895n.
non-liability 919n.
sectarianism 978n.
independent
revolter 738n.
free man 744n.
Independent
sectarist 978n.
sectarian 978adj.
indescribable
unspeakable 32adj.
unusual 84adj.
wonderful 864adj.
indestructible
existing 1adj.
unchangeable 153adj.
in detail
piecemeal 53adv.
severally 80adv.
indeterminacy
chance 159n.
non-design 618n.
indeterminate
causeless 159adj.
uncertain 474adj.
indetermination
(*see* indeterminacy)
indevotion
irreligion 974n.
index
relate 9vb.
class 62vb.
numerical element 85n.
list 87n., vb.
finger 378n.
gauge 465n.
indicator 547n.
record 548n., vb.
edition 589n.
index expurgatorius
prohibition 757n.
disapprobation 924n.
orthodoxism 976n.
ecclesiasticism 985n.
indexterity
unskillfulness 695n.
Indiaman
merchant ship 275n.
indianize
transform 147vb.
Indian red
red pigment 431n.
Indian summer
summer 128n.
autumn 129n.
revival 656n.
india-rubber
elasticity 328n.
indicate
specify 80vb.
point to 281vb.
mean 514vb.
inform 524vb.
(*see* indication)
indication
directory 87n.
evidence 466n.
omen 511n.
manifestation 522n.
hint 524n.
indication 547n.
trace 548n.
warning 664n.
indicative
evidential 466adj.
meaningful 514adj.
disclosing 526adj.
indicating 547adj.
indicator
witness 466n.
indicator 547n.
indict
indict 928vb.
litigate 959vb.
indiction
period 110n.
indictment
accusation 928n.
indifference
incuriosity 454n.
inattention 456n.
negligence 458n.
no choice 606n.
laxity 734n.
non-observance 769n.
moral insensibility 820n.
inexcitability 823n.
indifference 860n.
non-wonder 865n.
justice 913n.
disinterestedness 931n.
indifferent
irrelative 10adj.
moderate 177adj.
neutral 625adj.
not bad 644adj.
bored 838adj.
indifferent 860adj.
indifferentism
irreligion 974n.
indigence
poverty 801n.
indigenous
intrinsic 5adj.
native 191adj.
indigestible
cohesive 48adj.
extraneous 59adj.
tough 329adj.
insalubrious 653adj.
uncooked 670adj.
indigestion
indigestion 651n.
indignation
resentment 891n.
anger 891n.
disapprobation 924n.
indignation meeting
malcontent 829n.
indignity
slur 867n.
rudeness 885n.
scurrility 899n.
indignity 921n.
calumny 926n.
indigo
pigment 425n.
blue pigment 435n.
indirect
oblique 220adj.
deviating 282adj.
evidential 466adj.
occult 523adj.
imperspicuous 568adj.
prolix 570adj.
roundabout 626adj.
dishonest 930adj.
indiscernible
invisible 444adj.
indiscerptible

indivisible 52adj.
one 88adj.
dense 324adj.
indiscipline
anarchy 734n.
disobedience 738n.
dutilessness 918n.
intemperance 943n.
indiscoverable
latent 523adj.
indiscreet
indiscriminating 464adj.
unwise 499adj.
indiscretion
indiscrimination 464n.
information 524n.
disclosure 526n.
bungling 695n.
rashness 857n.
guilty act 936n.
indiscriminate
extensive 32adj.
orderless 61adj.
multiform 82adj.
indiscriminate 464adj.
indiscrimination
generality 79n.
indiscrimination 464n.
misjudgment 481n.
unintelligence 499n.
no choice 606n.
indifference 860n.
indispensable
necessary 596adj.
required 627adj.
important 638adj.
indispose
dissuade 613vb.
indisposed
unwilling 598adj.
sick 651adj.
indisposition
unwillingness 598n.
ill-health 651n.
indisputability
certainty 473n.
needfulness 627n.
indissolubility
density 324n.
indissoluble
tied 45adj.
indivisible 52adj.
one 88adj.
unchangeable 153adj.
indissoluble 324adj.
retentive 778adj.
indistinct
dim 419adj.
ill-seen 444adj.
stammering 580adj.
indistinctness
faintness 401n.
(*see* indistinct)
indistinguishable
identical 13adj.
equivalent 28adj.
invisible 444adj.
indite
compose 56vb.
write 586vb.
individual
irrelative 10adj.
unimitative 21adj.
self 80n.
special 80adj.
unit 88n.
person 371n.
individualism
particularism 80n.
independence 744n.
selfishness 932n.
individualist
egotist 932n.
individuality
speciality 80n.
unconformity 84n.
(*see* individual)
individualize
specify 80vb.
indivisibility
simpleness 44n.
coherence 48n.
whole 52n.
unity 88n.
density 324n.
Indo-Aryan
language type 557n.
indocility
unwillingness 598n.
obstinacy 602n.
indoctrinate
convince 485vb.
teach, educate 534vb.
Indo-European
language type 557n.
indolence
inaction 677n.
sluggishness 679n.
indomitable
unyielding 162adj.
resolute 599adj.
persevering 600adj.
resisting 715adj.
courageous 885adj.
indoor
interior 224adj.
indraft
ingress 297n.
reception 299n.
gulf 345n.
current 350n.
indubitable
undisputed 473adj.
induce
cause 156vb.
influence 178vb.
induce 612vb.
inducement
attraction 291n.
inducement 612n.
offer 759n.
excitation 821n.
reward 962n.
induct
auspicate 68vb.
reason 475vb.
commission 751vb.
celebrate 876vb.
inductance
electricity 160n.
reasoning 475n.
stage play 594n.
holy orders 985n.
inductive
rational 475adj.
indulge
please 826vb.
(*see* indulgence)
indulgence
laxity 734n.
lenity 736n.
permission 756n.
enjoyment 824n.
forgiveness 909n.
intemperance 943n.
sensualism 944n.
gluttony 947n.
indulgent
benevolent 897adj.
indurate
be insensible 375vb.
induration
hardening 326n.
impenitence 940n.
industrial
businesslike 622adj.
industrialism
business 622n.
industrialist
producer 167n.
agent 686n.
industrialization
production 164n.
business 622n.
industrious
vigorous 174adj.
attentive 455adj.
studious 536adj.
persevering 600adj.
businesslike 622adj.
industrious 678adj.
laboring 682adj.
industry
production 164n.
business 622n.
assiduity 678n.
indwelt
occupied 191adj.

inebriate
invigorate 174vb.
drunkard 949n.
inebriate 949vb.
inebriation
drunkenness 949n.
inedible
tough 329adj.
unsavory 391adj.
insalubrious 653adj.
uncooked 670adj.
ineffable
unspeakable 32adj.
inexpressible 517adj.
wonderful 864adj.
divine 965adj.
ineffaceable
with affections 817adj.
(*see* indelible)
ineffective
powerless 161adj.
unproductive 172adj.
feeble 572adj.
useless 641adj.
unsuccessful 728adj.
ineffectual
powerless 161n.
unimportant 639adj.
useless 641adj.
unskillful 695adj.
ineffectuality
ineffectuality 161n.
failure 728n.
inefficacious
powerless 161adj.
inefficacy
inutility 641n.
failure 728n.
inefficiency
impotence 161n.
inutility 641n.
inefficient
powerless 161adj.
useless 641adj.
bad 645adj.
unskillful 695adj.
inelastic
unyielding 162adj.
rigid 326adj.
tough 329adj.
inelasticity
hardness 326n.
inelegant
inelegant 576adj.
clumsy 695adj.
vulgar 847adj.
ineligible
unapt 25adj.
rejected 607adj.
inexpedient 643adj.
ineluctable
certain 473adj.
inept
irrelative 10adj.
irrelevant 10adj.
unapt 25adj.
powerless 161adj.
absurd 497adj.
unwise 499adj.
inexpedient 643adj.
unskillful 695adj.
ineptitude
irrelevance 10n.
(*see* inept)
inequality
difference 15n.
dissimilarity 19n.
disagreement 25n.
inequality 29n.
inequitable
unjust 914adj.
dishonest 930n.
inequity
injustice 914n.
ineradicable
characteristic 5adj.
fixed 153adj.
inerrancy
certainty 473n.
inert
inert 175adj.
quiescent 266adj.
insensible 375adj.
non-active 677adj.
inactive 679adj.
inexcitable 823adj.
inertia
energy 160n.
inertness 175n.
slowness 278n.
inaction 677n.
inactivity 679n.
laxity 734n.
moral insensibility 820n.
indifference 860n.
inescapable
impending 155adj.
necessary 596adj.
obligatory 917adj.
inescutcheon
heraldry 547n.
inessential
insubstantial 4adj.
extrinsic 6adj.
irrelevance 10n.
irrelevant 10adj.
trifle 639adj.
inestimable
valuable 644adj.
of price 811adj.
inevitable
impending 155adj.
certain 473adj.
necessary 596adj.
compelling 740adj.
unpromising 853adj.
inexact
negligent 458adj.
feeble 572adj.
(*see* inexactness)
inexactness
generality 79n.
indiscrimination 464n.
inexactness 495n.
imperspicuity 568n.
inexcitability
inertness 175n.
sluggishness 679n.
moral insensibility 820n.
inexcitability 823n.
indifference 860n.
inexcitable
moderate 177adj.
tranquil 266adj.
inexcusable
wrong 914n.
accusable 928adj.
heinous 934adj.
guilty 936adj.
inexecution
non-completion 726n.
inexhaustible
full 54adj.
multitudinous 104adj.
infinite 107adj.
unceasing 146adj.
plenteous 635adj.
inexist
be intrinsic 5vb.
inexistence
non-existence 2n.
intrinsicality 5n.
absence 190n.
inexorable
certain 473adj.
necessary 596adj.
resolute 599adj.
obstinate 602adj.
severe 735adj.
pitiless 906adj.
inexpectant
vulnerable 661adj.
inexpectation
chance 159n.
improbability 472n.
inexpectation 508n.
non-preparation 670n.
wonder 864n.
inexpedience
inaptitude 25n.
intempestivity 138n.
impossibility 470n.
inutility 641n.
inexpedience 643n.
difficulty 700n.
wrong 914n.
inexpedient

harmful 645adj.
hindering 702adj.
inexpensive
cheap 812adj.
inexperience
desuetude 611n.
unskillfulness 695n.
innocence 935n.
inexperienced
ignorant 491adj.
foolish 499adj.
unhabituated 611adj.
inexpert
ignorant 491adj.
unskilled 695adj.
inexpiable
heinous 934adj.
guilty 936adj.
inexplicability
chance 159n.
unintelligibility 517n.
inexplicable
unusual 84adj.
causeless 159adj.
inexpressible
inexpressible 517adj.
wonderful 864adj.
inexpressibles
breeches 228n.
inexpugnable
invulnerable 660adj.
inextensible
rigid 326adj.
inextension
littleness 196n.
immateriality 320n.
in extenso
wholly 52adv.
completely 54adv.
inextinguishable
unchangeable 153adj.
violent 176adj.
inextricable
tied 45adj.
firm-set 45adj.
cohesive 48adj.
complex 61adj.
impracticable 470adj.
difficult 700adj.
inextricably
inseparably 45adv.
confusedly 61adv.
infallibilism
certainty 473n.
infallibilist
doctrinaire 473n.
infallibility
certainty 473n.
positiveness 473n.
perfection 646n.
infallible
certain 473adj.
accurate 494adj.
veracious 540adj.
successful 727adj.
ecclesiastical 985adj.
infamous
disreputable 867adj.
discreditable 867adj.
dishonest 930adj.
heinous 934adj.
infamy
(*see* infamous)
infancy
beginning 68n.
youth, nonage 130n.
helplessness 161n.
infant
child 132n.
weakling 163n.
descendant 170n.
infanta
sovereign 741n.
infanticide
homicide 362n.
infantile
infantine 132adj.
foolish 499adj.
infantile paralysis
paralysis 651n.
infantilism
unintelligence 499n.
infantine
infantine 132adj.
infantry
pedestrian 268n.
infantry 722n.
infarction
closure 264n.
infatuate
make mad 503vb.
(*see* infatuation)
infatuation
bias 481n.
credulity 487n.
folly 499n.
deception 542n.
opiniatrety 602n.
liking 859n.
love 887n.
infect
infiltrate 297vb.
motivate 612vb.
excite 821vb.
(*see* infection)
infection
mixture 43n.
influence 178n.
transference 272n.
badness 645n.
uncleanness 649n.
infection 651n.
impairment 655n.
poisoning 659n.
infectious
influential 178adj.
transferable 272adj.
harmful 645adj.
unclean 649adj.
diseased 651adj.
infectious 653adj.
dangerous 661adj.
infective
infectious 653adj.
infecundity
unproductivity 172n.
infelicity
bungling 695n.
sorrow 825n.
infer
assume 471vb.
reason 475n.
demonstrate 478vb.
judge 480vb.
mean 514vb.
interpret 520vb.
imply 523vb.
be informed 524vb.
inferable
attributed 158adj.
inference
sequence 65n.
(*see* infer)
inferential
rational 475n.
demonstrating 478adj.
tacit 523adj.
inferior
inconsiderable 33adj.
small 33adj.
inferior 35n., adj.
substituted 150adj.
weakly 163adj.
nonentity 639n.
unimportant 639adj.
bad 645adj.
loser 728n.
mediocre 732adj.
servant 742n.
commoner 869n.
(*see* inferiority)
inferiority
relativeness 9n.
inequality 29n.
inferiority 35n.
lowness 210n.
subjection 745n.
inferiority complex
jealousy 911n.
infernal
deep 211adj.
damnable 645adj.
cruel 898adj.
wicked 934adj.
heinous 934adj.
diabolic 969adj.
infernal 972adj.
infernal machine
bomb 723n.

inferno
turmoil 61n.
hell 972n.
inferred
attributed 158adj.
infertile
impotent 161adj.
infertility
unproductivity 172n.
scarcity 636n.
infest
congregate 74vb.
be many 104vb.
encroach 306vb.
attack 712vb.
incommode 827vb.
infested
full 54adj.
insalubrious 653adj.
infestivity
dullness 840n.
infeudation
giving 781n.
infibulation
joinder 45n.
infidel
unbeliever 486n.
impious person 980n.
profane 980adj.
infidelity
unbelief 486n.
perfidy 930n.
illicit love 951n.
irreligion 974n.
in-fighting
pugilism 716n.
infiltrate
pervade 189vb.
infiltrate 297vb.
infiltration
mixture 43n.
interjacence 231n.
ingress 297n.
passage 305n.
moistening 341n.
sedition 738n.
infinite
absolute 32adj.
multitudinous 104adj.
many 104adj.
infinite 107adj.
infinitesimal
small 33adj.
minute 196adj.
infinitesimal calculus
mathematics 86n.
infinity
greatness 32n.
infinity 107n.
space 183n.
divine attribute 965n.
infinity, to
forever 115adv.
infirm
weakly 163adj.
irresolute 601adj.
unhealthy 651adj.
cowardly 856adj.
infirmary
hospital 658n.
infirmity
weakness 163n.
ill-health 651n.
illness 651n.
vice 934n.
infix
add 38vb.
adjunct 40n.
affix 45vb.
interjection 231n.
implant 303vb.
educate 534vb.
word 559n.
inflame
invigorate 174vb.
make violent 176vb.
heat 381vb.
make bright 417vb.
excite 821vb.
aggravate 832vb.
excite love 887vb.
inflamed
violent 176adj.
diseased 651adj.
inflammability
burning 381n.
excitability 822n.
inflammable
combustible 385adj.
dangerous 661adj.
excitable 822adj.
irascible 892adj.
inflammation
heat 379n.
heating 381n.
ulcer 651n.
painfulness 827n.
inflammatory
violent 176adj.
inflated
ridiculous 849adj.
prideful 871adj.
vain 873adj.
ostentatious 875adj.
inflation
increase 36n.
dilation 197n.
sufflation 352n.
exaggeration 546n.
magniloquence 574n.
finance 597n.
dearness 811n.
inflationary
monetary 797adj.
dear 811adj.
inflect
make curved 248vb.
parse 564vb.
inflected
linguistic 557adj.
inflection
adjunct 40n.
sequel 67n.
extremity 69n.
change 143n.
curvature 248n.
grammar 564n.
pronunciation 577n.
inflexibility
stability 153n.
straightness 249n.
hardness 326n.
resolution 599n.
obstinacy 602n.
severity 735n.
pitilessness 906n.
inflictable
punishable 963adj.
infliction
adversity 731n.
severity 735n.
suffering 825n.
punishment 963n.
inflictive
punitive 963adj.
inflow
ingress 297n.
current 350n.
influence
component 58n.
modify 143vb.
causation 156n.
cause 156n., vb.
effect 157n.
power 160n.
agency 173n.
influence 178n., vb.
tend 179vb.
bias 481vb.
convince 485vb.
teach 534vb.
inducement 612n.
motivate 612vb.
instrumentality 628n.
be important 638vb.
action 676n.
authority 733n.
impress 821vb.
prestige 866n.
sorcery 983n.
influential
great 32adj.
(*see* influence)
influenza
infection 651n.
influx
ingress 297n.
in force
powerful 160adj.

strongly 162adv.
inform
efform 243vb.
inform 524vb.
divulge 526vb.
indicate 547vb.
warn 664vb.
accuse 928vb.
informal
orderless 61adj.
(*see* informality)
informal dress
informal dress 228n.
informality
unconformity 84n.
laxity 734n.
non-observance 769n.
illegality 957n.
informant
witness 466n.
informant 524n.
information
testimony 466n.
knowledge 490n.
erudition 490n.
information 524n.
disclosure 526n.
message 529n.
indication 547n.
warning 664n.
advice 691n.
accusation 928n.
information, piece of
news 529n.
informative
informative 524adj.
disclosing 526adj.
loquacious 581adj.
conversing 584adj.
informatory
informative 524adj.
informed
knowing 490adj.
instructed 490adj.
informed 524adj.
informed circles
informant 524n.
informer
secret service 459n.
witness 466n.
informer 524n.
accuser 928n.
knave 938n.
litigant 959n.
informity
amorphism 244n.
infra
after 65adv.
in front 237adv.
infraction
overstepping 306n.
disobedience 738n.
undueness 916n.
dutilessness 918n.
infra dig
degrading 867adj.
infrangible
cohesive 48adj.
unyielding 162adj.
dense 324adj.
hard 326adj.
tough 329adj.
infrequency
infrequency 140n.
scarcity 636n.
infrequent
discontinuous 72adj.
fitful 142adj.
uncertain 474adj.
infrequently
seldom 140adv.
infringement
unconformity 84n.
overstepping 306n.
opposition 704n.
attack 712n.
disobedience 738n.
non-observance 769n.
undueness 916n.
lawbreaking 954n.
infringer
thief 789n.
usurper 916n.
infundibular
concave 255adj.
tubular 263adj.
infuriate
furious 176adj.
make violent 176vb.
make mad 503vb.
enrage 891vb.
infuse
combine 50vb.
infuse 303vb.
moisten 341vb.
educate 534vb.
infusible
indissoluble 324adj.
infusion
tincture 43n.
potion 301n.
insertion 303n.
solution 337n.
infusoria
animalcule 196n.
ingannation
deception 542n.
ingathering
assemblage 74n.
ingeminate
double 91adj., vb.
repeat 106vb.
ingenerate
genetic 5adj.
ingenious
imaginative 513adj.
planning 623adj.
skillful 694adj.
cunning 698adj.
ingenue
acting 594n.
ingenue 699n.
innocent 935n.
ingenuity
skill 694n.
cunning 698n.
ingenuous
veracious 540adj.
artless 699adj.
honorable 929adj.
trustworthy 929adj.
ingest
absorb 299vb.
eat, drink 301vb.
ingle
furnace 383n.
inglenook
home 192n.
inglorious
unsuccessful 728adj.
unprosperous 731adj.
mediocre 732adj.
inglorious 867adj.
humbled 872adj.
ingot
materials 631n.
bullion 797n.
ingrain
intromit 231vb.
ingrained
genetic 5adj.
combined 50adj.
fixed 153adj.
habitual 610adj.
ingrate
ingratitude 908n.
ingratiate oneself
be servile 879vb.
excite love 887vb.
ingratiating
servile 879adj.
courteous 884adj.
flattering 925adj.
ingratitude
ingratitude 908n.
undueness 916n.
ingredient
adjunct 40n.
part 53n.
component 58n.
contents 193n.
element 319n.
ingress
ingress 297n.
passage 305n.
in-group
group 74n.
self 80n.
ingrown

firm-set 45adj.
interior 224adj.
ingurgitation
reception 299n.
inhabit
dwell 192vb.
possess 773vb.
inhabitant
dweller 191n.
inhale
absorb 299vb.
breathe 352vb.
smoke 388vb.
smell 394vb.
in hand
unfinished 55adj.
stored 632adj.
unused 674adj.
inharmonious
disagreeing 25adj.
strident 407adj.
discordant 411adj.
inhere
be 1vb.
be intrinsic 5vb.
constitute 56vb.
be one of 58vb.
be included 78vb.
belong 773vb.
inherent
ingredient 58adj.
possessed 773adj.
inherit
reproduce 166vb.
inherit 771vb.
inheritable
not retained 779adj.
due 915adj.
inheritance
sequel 67n.
posteriority 120n.
posterity 170n.
acquisition 771n.
dower 777n.
transfer 780n.
receiving 782n.
receipt 807n.
inherited
genetic 5adj.
filial 170adj.
acquired 771adj.
inherited characteristic
heredity 5n.
affections 817n.
inheritor
survivor 41n.
aftercomer 61n.
beneficiary 776n.
recipient 782n.
inhesion
intrinsicality 5n.
inhibition
hindrance 702n.
command 737n.
restraint 747n.
prohibition 757n.
inhibitor
counteraction 182n.
inhospitable
unsociable 883adj.
unkind 898adj.
inhospitality
unsociability 883n.
inhuman
(*see* inhumanity)
inhumane
unkind 898adj.
inhumanity
violence 176n.
severity 735n.
moral insensibility 820n.
inhumanity 898n.
misanthropy 902n.
wickedness 934n.
inhumation
interment 364n.
inimical
contrary 14adj.
disagreeing 25adj.
opposing 704adj.
quarreling 709adj.
disliking 861adj.
inimical 881adj.
hating 888adj.
inimitable
unimitated 21adj.
supreme 34adj.
iniquitous
unjust 914adj.
wrong 914adj.
wicked 934adj.
iniquity
wickedness 934n.
initial
first 68adj.
sign 547vb.
initials 558n.
script 586n.
initiate
initiate 68vb.
cause 156vb.
produce 164vb.
admit 299vb.
train 534vb.
beginner 538n.
initiation
learning 536n.
rite 988n.
initiative
debut 68n.
vigorousness 174n.
willingness 597n.
restlessness 678n.
freedom 744n.
initiator
teacher 537n.
inject
infuse 303vb.
motivate 612vb.
injection
insertion 303n.
moistening 341n.
therapy 658n.
injudicial
illegal 954adj.
injudicious
unwise 499adj.
rash 857adj.
injunction
requirement 627n.
advice 691n.
precept 693n.
command 737n.
prohibition 757n.
legal process 959n.
injure
weaken 163vb.
harm, ill-treat 645vb.
impair 655vb.
oppress 735vb.
hurt 827vb.
blemish 845vb.
be malevolent 898vb.
do wrong 914vb.
injurious
evil 616adj.
harmful 645adj.
insalubrious 653adj.
insolent 878adj.
wrong 914adj.
disrespectful 921adj.
detracting 926adj.
injury
evil 616n.
wound 655n.
misuse 675n.
injustice 914n.
guilty act 936n.
injustice
misjudgment 481n.
misrepresentation 552n.
evil 616n.
injustice 914n.
improbity 930n.
guilty act 936n.
illegality 954n.
ink
black thing 428n.
art equipment 553n.
ink-bottle
stationery 586n.
ink-horn
receptacle 194n.
stationery 586n.
in kind
in exchange 151adv.
inkle

ligature 47n.
inkling
knowledge 490n.
supposition 512n.
hint 524n.
ink-slinging
contention 716n.
inkwell
receptacle 194n.
stationery 586n.
inky
black 428adj.
inlaid
ornamented 844adj.
inland
interior 224adj.
land 344n.
inland sea
lake 346n.
in-laws
family 11n.
inlay
line 227vb.
insert 303vb.
variegate 437vb.
ornamental art 844n.
inlet
entrance 68n.
gap 201n.
cavity 255n.
orifice 263n.
way in 297n.
gulf 345n.
in lieu
instead 150adv.
in line with
conformably 83adv.
inly
inside 224adv.
inmate
resident 191n.
interiority 224n.
in memoriam
in memoriam 364adv.
in memory 505adv.
inmost
(*see* innermost)
inmost being
interiority 224n.
inmost soul
affections 817n.
inn
inn 192n.
inner
included 78adj.
interior 224adj.
inner being
essence 1n.
inner man
insides 224n.
spirit 447n.
affections 817n.
innermost
interior 224adj.
innings
period 110n.
knock 279n.
land 344n.
earnings 771n.
receipt 807n.
innkeeper
caterer 633n.
innocence
helplessness 161n.
ignorance 491n.
artlessness 699n.
benevolence 897n.
probity 929n.
virtue 933n.
innocence 935n.
purity 950n.
acquittal 960n.
innocent
ignoramus 493n.
foolish 499adj.
ninny 501n.
dupe 544n.
gullible 544adj.
beneficial 644adj.
perfect 646adj.
ingenue 699n.
innocent 935n., adj.
good man 937n.
(*see* innocence)
innocuous
moderate 177adj.
beneficial 644adj.
salubrious 652adj.
innocent 935adj.
innominate
anonymous 562adj.
innovation
newness 126n.
change 143n.
innovator
precursor 66n.
innuendo
latency 523n.
hint 524n.
censure 924n.
detraction 926n.
innumerable
multitudinous 104adj.
infinite 107adj.
inobservance
non-observance 769n.
inoculate
implant 303vb.
teach 534vb.
motivate 612vb.
sanitate 652vb.
doctor 658vb.
safeguard 660vb.
inoculation
prophylactic 658n.
inodorousness
inodorousness 395n.
cleansing 648n.
inoffensive
beneficial 644adj.
humble 872adj.
amiable 884adj.
innocent 935adj.
in one piece
whole 52adj.
in one's stride
habitually 610adv.
inoperable
deadly 362adj.
impracticable 470adj.
sick 651adj.
unpromising 853adj.
inoperative
powerless 161adj.
unproductive 172adj.
useless 641adj.
non-active 677adj.
inopportune
unapt 25adj.
inopportune 138adj.
inexpedient 643adj.
inordinacy
undueness 916n.
inordinate
exorbitant 32adj.
exaggerated 546adj.
inorganic
inorganic 359adj.
mindless 448adj.
unthinking 450adj.
inosculation
joinder 45n.
crossing 222n.
convolution 251n.
in particular
specially 80adv.
inpatient
resident 191n.
sick person 651n.
in person
here 189adv.
in pickle
impending 155adj.
in point
typical 83adj.
in preparation
unfinished 55adj.
input
requirement 627n.
inquest
inquest 364n.
inquiry 459n.
legal trial 959n.
inquietude
changeableness 152n.
worry 825n.
inquiline
settler 191n.

inquination
impairment 655n.
inquire
be curious 453vb.
inquire 459vb.
not know 491vb.
study 536vb.
inquirer
inquirer 459n.
experimenter 461n.
hunter 619n.
petitioner 763n.
inquiry
inquiry 459n.
experiment 461n.
dissertation 591n.
legal trial 959n.
inquiry agent
detective 459n.
inquisition
inquiry 459n.
severity 735n.
legal trial 859n.
orthodoxism 976n.
ecclesiasticism 985n.
Inquisition
ecclesiastical court 956n.
inquisitive
inquisitive 453adj.
inquisitor
inquisitor 453n.
questioner 459n.
tyrant 735n.
punisher 963n.
inroad
ingress 297n.
waste 634n.
impairment 655n.
attack 712n.
arrogation 916n.
inrush
ingress 297n.
insalubrious
deadly 362adj.
harmful 645adj.
unclean 649adj.
dangerous 661adj.
insalubrity
infection 651n.
insalubrity 653n.
ins and outs
particulars 80n.
place 185n.
insane
insane 503adj.
(*see* insanity)
insanitary
insalubrious 653adj.
insanity
non-intellect 448n
error 495n.
unintelligence 499n.
insanity 503n.
excitable state 822n.
insatiability
rapacity 786n.
desire 859n.
gluttony 947n.
insatiable
unprovided 636adj.
insatiate
greedy 859adj.
inscape
form 243n.
inscribe
list 87vb.
record 548vb.
write 586vb.
inscriber
commender 923n.
inscribe to
honor 866vb.
inscription
commentary 520n.
indication 547n.
monument 548n.
phrase 563n.
script 586n.
description 590n.
inscrutable
unintelligible 517adj.
impassive 820adj.
inexcitable 823adj.
serious 834adj.
insect
animalcule 196n.
vermin 365n.
cad 938n.
insecticide
killer 362n.
prophylactic 658n.
poison 659n.
insectile
animal 365adj.
insecurity
unreliability 474n.
danger 661n.
vulnerability 661n.
insemination
propagation 164n.
productiveness 171n.
inseminator
producer 167n.
insensate
insensible 375adj.
unwise 499adj.
thick-skinned 820adj.
insensibility
helplessness 161n.
inertness 175n.
insensibility 375n.
indiscrimination 464n.
ignorance 491n.
oblivion 506n.
inaction 677n.
sluggishness 679n.
sleep 679n.
indifference 860n.
non-wonder 865n.
insensible
impassive 820adj.
unkind 898adj.
(*see* insensibility)
insensitive
unsharpened 257adj.
insensible 375adj.
indiscriminating 464adj.
inexact 495adj.
inelegant 576adj.
impassive 820adj.
thick-skinned 820adj.
ill-bred 847adj.
inseparable
firm-set 45adj.
cohesive 48adj.
indivisible 52adj.
concomitant 89n.
near 200adj.
friendly 880adj.
insert
affix 45vb.
load 193vb.
intromit 231vb.
enter 297vb.
inserted
discontinuous 72adj.
insertion
addition 38n.
adjunct 40n.
mixture 43n.
piece 53n.
location 187n.
reception 299n.
insertion 303n.
advertisement 528n.
repair 656n.
inset
insertion 303n.
insert 303vb.
edition 589n.
ornamental art 844n.
inseverable
one 88adj.
inshore
near 200adj.
inside
contents 193n.
interiority 224n.
imprisoned 747adj.
inside job
plot 623n.
inside out
inverted 221adj.
insides
component 58n.
insides 224n.
insidious

occult 523adj.
deceiving 542adj.
evil 616adj.
cunning 698adj.
perfidious 930adj.

insight
intellect 447n.
discrimination 463n.
intuition 476n.
knowledge 490n.
imagination 513n.
interpretation 520n.

insignia
badge 547n.
regalia 743n.

insignificance
smallness 33n.
unimportance 639n.
despisedness 922n.

insignificant
unmeaning 515adj.

insincere
sophistical 477adj.

insincerity
unmeaningness 515n.
duplicity 541n.
deception 542n.
affectation 850n.
ostentation 875n.
flattery 925n.
improbity 930n.

insinuate
intromit 231vb.
imply 523vb.
inform, hint 524vb.

insinuate oneself
infiltrate 297vb.
excite love 887vb.
flatter 925vb.

insinuation
influence 178n.
ingress 297n.
insertion 303n.
censure 924n.
detraction 926n.

insipid
weak 163adj.
tasteless 387adj.
feeble 572adj.
tedious 838adj.
dull 840adj.
unwanted 860adj.

insist
emphasize 532vb.
be resolute 599vb.
be obstinate 602vb.
incite 612vb.
contend 716vb.
compel 740vb.
beg 761vb.

insistence
(*see* insist)

insistent
assertive 532adj.
forceful 571adj.
resolute 599adj.
important 638adj.
requesting 761adj.

in situ
in place 186adv.
here 189adv.

insobriety
drunkenness 949n.

insolation
desiccation 342n.
heat 379n.
heating 381n.

insolence
defiance 711n.
pride 871n.
insolence 878n.
rudeness 885n.

insolent
anarchic 734adj.
authoritarian 735adj.

insoluble
indissoluble 324adj.
impracticable 470adj.
puzzling 517adj.

insolvency
insufficiency 636n.
failure 728n.
non-observance 769n.
poverty 801n.
debt 803n.
insolvency 805n.

insomnia
restlessness 678n.

insomniac
sick person 651n.

insouciance
incuriosity 454n.
negligence 458n.
moral insensibility 820n.
indifference 860n.

insouciant
light-minded 456adj.

inspan
start out 296vb.

inspection
inspection 438n.
attention 455n.
surveillance 457n.
inquirer 459n.
estimate 480n.

inspector
spectator 441n.
inquirer 459n.
estimator 480n.
manager 690n.

inspectorship
magistrature 733n.

inspiration
causation 156n.
influence 178n.
respiration 352n.
intuition 476n.
intelligence 498n.
imagination 513n.
diffuseness 570n.
inducement 612n.
contrivance 623n.
warm feeling 818n.
excitation 821n.
excitable state 822n.
revelation 975n.
piety 979n.

inspirational
intuitive 476adj.
revelational 975adj.

inspire
cheer 833vb.
give courage 855vb.
make pious 979vb.
(*see* inspiration)

inspired
intuitive 476adj.
diffuse 570adj.
forceful 571adj.
induced 612adj.
scriptural 975adj.
revelational 975adj.
pietistic 979adj.

inspiring
cause 156n.
motivator 612n.

inspiring
causal 156adj.
influential 178adj.
exciting 821adj.

inspirit
incite 612vb.
animate 821vb.
cheer 833vb.
give hope 852vb.
give courage 855vb.

inspissation
condensation 324n.
thickening 354n.

in spite of
although 182adv.
nevertheless 468adv.

instability
changeableness 152n.
weakness 163n.
vulnerability 661n.
excitability 822n.

install
auspicate 68vb.
place 187vb.
commission 751vb.
dower 777vb.
dignify 866vb.

installation
location 187n.
workshop 687n.
mandate 751n.
celebration 876n.

holy orders 985n.
installment
part 53n.
incompleteness 55n.
reading matter 589n.
security 767n.
payment 804n.
instance
example 83n.
inducement 612n.
request 761n.
instant
brief span 114n.
instant 116n.
present 121adj.
impending 155adj.
demanding 627adj.
ready-made 669adj.
active 678adj.
requesting 761adj.
instantaneity
transientness 114n.
instantaneity 116n.
present time 121n.
synchronism 123n.
punctuality 135n.
velocity 277n.
instantaneous
instantaneous 116adj.
instant, be
emphasize 532vb.
instantly
transiently 114adv.
instantaneously 116adv.
instate
celebrate 876vb.
in statu pupillari
young 130adj.
subject 745adj.
in statu quo
as before 144adv.
instead
instead 150adv.
instep
foot 214n.
curve 248n.
instigation
inducement 612n.
instigator
instigator 612n.
aider 703n.
instill
infuse 303vb.
educate 534vb.
instilled
extrinsic 6adj.
instinct
tendency 179n.
intellect 447n.
non-intellect 448n.
incogitance 450n.
empiricism 461n.
intuition 476n.
supposition 512n.
habit 610n.
non-design 618n.
instinctive
ill-reasoned 477adj.
educational 534adj.
involuntary 596adj.
spontaneous 609adj.
instincts
affections 817n.
instinct with
possessing 773adj.
with affections 817adj.
institute
auspicate 68vb.
cause 156vb.
produce 164vb.
academy 539n.
corporation 708n.
institution
academy 539n.
practice 610n.
law 953n.
rite 988n.
institutionalism
orthodoxism 976n.
instruct
(*see* instruction)
instruction
culture 490n.
information 524n.
teaching 534n.
advice 691n.
precept 693n.
command 737n.
instructive
influential 178adj.
informative 524adj.
cautionary 664adj.
instructor
teacher, trainer 537n.
instrument
contrivance 623n.
instrument 628n.
means 629n.
tool 630n.
agent 686n.
auxiliary 707n.
slave 742n.
title-deed 767n.
toady 879n.
instrumental
musical 412adj.
musicianly 413adj.
mechanical 628adj.
useful 640adj.
used 673adj.
instrumentalist
instrumentalist 413n.
instrumentality
agency 173n.
instrumentality 628n.
instrumentation
composition 56n.
melody 410n.
insubordination
anarchy 734n.
disobedience 738n.
insubstantial
unreal 2adj.
insubstantial 4adj.
inconsiderable 33adj.
transient 114adj.
powerless 161adj.
weak, flimsy 163adj.
immaterial 320adj.
brittle 330adj.
insufficient 636adj.
insubstantiality
unimportance 639n.
vanity 873n.
insufferable
intolerable 827adj.
disliked 861adj.
insufficiency
inequality 29n.
smallness 33n.
incompleteness 55n.
shortcoming 307n.
requirement 627n.
insufficiency 636n.
imperfection 647n.
non-completion 726n.
insufficient
discontenting 829adj.
(*see* insufficiency)
insufflation
sufflation 352n.
insular
separate 46adj.
alone 88adj.
regional 184adj.
dweller 191n.
insular 349adj.
insularity
irrelation 10n.
disjunction 46n.
island 349n.
narrow mind 481n.
prejudice 481n.
insulate
set apart 46vb.
insulation
protection 660n.
defense 713n.
insulin
drug 658n.
insult
hurt 827n.
ridicule 851n.
slur 867n.
sauciness 878n.
rudeness 885n.
hate 888vb.
scurrility 899n.

indignity 921n.
not respect 921vb.
calumny 926n.
insulting
defiant 711adj.
insuperable
impracticable 470adj.
difficult 700adj.
insupportable
intolerable 827adj.
insurance
calculation of chance 159n.
protection 660n.
promise 764n.
security 767n.
caution 858n.
insure
seek safety 660vb.
prepare 669vb.
give security 767vb.
(*see* ensure)
insurer
consignee 754n.
insurgence
revolt 738n.
insurgent
revolter 738n.
insurmountable
impracticable 470adj.
insurrection
resistance 715n.
revolt 738n.
insurrectional
resisting 715adj.
insurrectionist
revolter 738n.
intact
intact 52adj.
complete 54adj.
undamaged 646adj.
safe 660adj.
preserved 666adj.
intaglio
mold 23n.
concavity 255n.
sculpture 554n.
ornamental art 844n.
intake
size 195n.
ingress 297n.
way in 297n.
reception 299n.
requirement 627n.
waste 634n.
intangibility
insubstantiality 4n.
intangible
minute 196adj.
immaterial 320adj.
integer
whole 52n.
number 85n.
unit 88n.
integral
whole 52adj.
complete 54adj.
numerical element 85n.
integral calculus
mathematics 86n.
integrality
(*see* integral)
integral part
component 58n.
integrant
part 53n.
integrate
make complete 54vb.
integration
combination 50n.
whole 52n.
completeness 54n.
numerical operation 86n.
unity 88n.
association 706n.
integrity
whole 52n.
probity 929n.
virtue 933n.
integument
layer 207n.
skin 226n.
intellect
intellect 447n.
knowledge 490n.
intellectual
mental 447adj.
instructed 490adj.
intellectual 492n.
wise 498adj.
sage 500n.
proficient 696n.
intellectualism
intellect 447n.
intelligence 498n.
intellectualize
cognize 447vb.
meditate 449vb.
intelligence
secret service 459n.
intelligence 498n.
news 529n.
wit 839n.
intelligent
intelligent 498adj.
skillful 694adj.
cunning 698adj.
intelligentsia
intellectual 492n.
intelligibility
simpleness 44n.
sanity 502n.
intelligibility 516n.
intelligible
known 490adj.
semantic 514adj.
intelligible 516adj.
perspicuous 567adj.
intemperance
exaggeration 546n.
festivity 837n.
intemperance 943n.
sensualism 944n.
gluttony 947n.
intemperate
intemperate 943adj.
drunken 949adj.
intempestivity
irrelation 10n.
inaptitude 25n.
derangement 63n.
anachronism 118n.
intempestivity 138n.
inexpedience 643n.
intend
predestine 155vb.
mean 514vb.
will 595vb.
be willing 597vb.
be resolute 599vb.
predetermine 608vb.
intend 617vb.
plan 623vb.
desire 859vb.
intendant
official 690n.
officer 741n.
intended
veracious 540adj.
volitional 595adj.
loved one 887n.
intense
great 32n.
vigorous 174adj.
florid 425adj.
fervent 818adj.
intensification
increase 36n.
stimulation 174n.
aggravation 832n.
intensify
enlarge 197vb.
exaggerate 546vb.
animate 821vb.
aggravate 832vb.
intensity
degree 27n.
greatness 32n.
vigorousness 174n.
hue 425n.
intensive
increasing 36adj.
part of speech 564n.
intent
attentive 455adj.
resolute 599adj.
(*see* intention)

intention
relation 9n.
connotation 514n.
will 595n.
predetermination 608n.
intention 617n.
plan 623n.
aspiration 852n.
prayers 981n.
intentional
volitional 595adj.
intended 617adj.
intentness
atttention 455n.
assiduity 678n.
inter
inter 364vb.
interaction
correlation 12n.
agency 173n.
action 676n.
interbreeding
race 11n.
mixture 43n.
intercalary
intermediate 108adj.
interjacent 231adj.
intercalation
interjection 231n.
insertion 303n.
intercede
interfere 231vb.
patronize 703vb.
mediate 720vb.
worship 981vb.
intercept
interfere 231vb.
converge 293vb.
hear 415adj.
screen 421vb.
be curious 454vb.
obstruct 702vb.
take 786vb.
interceptor
inquisitor 453n.
interceptor 702n.
intercession
aid 703n.
mediation 720n.
deprecation 762n.
divine function 965n.
prayers 981n.
intercessional
redemptive 965adj.
intercessor
intermediary 231n.
mediator 720n.
God the Son 965n.
intercessory
mediatory 720adj.
deprecatory 762adj.
devotional 981adj.
interchange
correlation 12n.
derangement 63n.
substitution 150n.
interchange 151n., vb.
displacement 188n.
inversion 221n.
crossing 222n.
transfer 780n.
barter, trade 791vb.
interchangeability
identity 13n.
equivalence 28n.
intercommunicate
connect 45vb.
intercommunicating
contiguous 202adj.
intercommunication
junction 45n.
bond 47n.
contiguity 202n.
information 524n.
nitercommunion
interlocution 584n.
public worship 981n.
intercommunity
sociality 882n.
interconnection
correlation 12n.
junction 45n.
bond 47n.
intercontinental
interchanged 151adj.
intercontinental ballistic missile
rocket 276n.
missile weapon 723n.
intercostal
interjacent 231adj.
intercourse
junction 45n.
coition 45n.
friendship 880n.
sociality 882n.
intercourse, have
unite with 45vb.
interdepartmental
interchanged 151adj.
interdependence
correlation 12n.
interdict
prohibition 757n.
interdigitation
crossing 222n.
interjacence 230n.
interest
relation 9n.
increment 36n.
extra 40n.
product 164n.
influence 178n.
topic 452n.
curiosity 453n.
attention 455n.
attract notice 455vb.
motivate 612vb.
importance 638n.
aid 703n.
gain 771n.
estate 777n.
interest 803n.
receipt 807n.
impress 821vb.
pleasurableness 826n.
amuse 837vb.
interested
inquisitive 453adj.
obsessed 455adj.
selfish 932adj.
interest oneself in
be active 678vb.
interests
affairs 154n.
business 622n.
interface
partition 231n.
interfere
disagree 25vb.
derange 63vb.
counteract 182vb.
interfere 231vb.
be curious 453vb.
meddle 678vb.
obstruct 702vb.
prohibit 757vb.
interference
radiation 717n.
instrumentality 628n.
(*see* interfere)
interferer
meddler 678n.
hinderer 702n.
interfuse
infiltrate 297vb.
interfusion
mixture 43n.
interglacial
intermediate 108adj.
interim
incompleteness 55n.
interim 108n.
period 110n.
transientness 114n.
lull 145n.
interval 201n.
interior
intrinsic 5adj.
included 78adj.
interiority 224n.
inland 344adj.
art subject 553n.
interiority
essence 1n.
interiority 224n.
latency 523n.
interjacence
centrality 225n.
interjacence 231n.

interject
be obstructive 702vb.
(*see* interjection)
interjection
addition 38n.
discontinuity 72n.
interjection 231n.
insertion 303n.
affirmation 532n.
allocution 583n.
interlace
mix 43vb.
enlace 222vb.
interlard
mix 43vb.
line 227vb.
put between 231vb.
interleave
put between 231vb.
interlineation
adjunct 40n.
interjection 231n.
interlink
enlace 222vb.
interlock
correlate 12vb.
join 45vb.
enlace 222vb.
interlocking
correlative 12adj.
complexity 61n.
interlocution
interrogation 459n.
speech 579n.
interlocution 584n.
interlocutor
questioner 459n.
interlocutor 584n.
interlocutory
conversing 584adj.
interlope
obstruct 702vb.
interloper
intruder 59n.
interjector 231n.
hinderer 702n.
free man 744n.
interloping
extraneous 59adj.
interlude
interim 108n.
lull 145n.
stage play 594n.
interlunar
intermediate 108adj.
intermarriage
mixture 43n.
type of marriage 894n.
intermeddle
meddle 678vb.
mediate 720vb.
intermediary
interjacence 231n.
intermediary 231n.
interjacent 231adj.
messenger 531n.
instrumentality 628n.
mediator 720n.
consignee 754n.
deputizing 755adj.
intermediate
median 30adj.
middle 70adj.
intermediate 108adj.
interjacent 231adj.
undeviating 625adj.
intermedium
bond 47n.
intermediary 231n.
mediator 720n.
interment
immersion 303n.
interment 364n.
intermezzo
adjunct 40n.
musical piece 412n.
intermigration
wandering 267n.
interminable
infinite 107adj.
protracted 113adj.
perpetual 115adj.
long 203adj.
intermingle
mix 43vb.
intermission
discontinuity 72n.
interim 108n.
lull 145n.
dramaturgy 594n.
intermit
be discontinuous 72vb.
be periodic 141vb.
halt 145vb.
intermittent
discontinuous 72adj.
infrequent 140adj.
periodic 141adj.
fitful 142adj.
intermixture
mixture 43n.
intermutation
interchange 151n.
intern
be inside 224vb.
doctor 658n.
imprison 747vb.
internal
intrinsic 5adj.
interior 224adj.
internal organs
insides 224n.
international
correlative 12adj.
comprehensive 52adj.
universal 79adj.
national 371adj.
unpossessed 774adj.
sharing 775adj.
internationalism
generality 79n.
philanthropy 901n.
internationalize
socialize 775vb.
internecine
destructive 165adj.
murderous 362adj.
internee
interiority 224n.
internment
war measures 718n.
detention 747n.
internment camp
prison camp 748n.
internuncio
envoy 754n.
interpellant
interlocutor 584n.
interpellation
interrogation 459n.
question 459n.
allocution 583n.
interpellator
questioner 459n.
interpenetration
interjacence 231n.
ingress 297n.
passage 305n.
interplanetary
extraneous 59adj.
interjacent 231adj.
interplay
correlation 12n.
interchange 151n.
interpolate
put between 231vb.
interpolation
adjunct 40n.
numerical operation 86n.
interjection 231n.
interpolator
interjector 231n.
interport
stable 192n.
interpose
discontinue 72vb.
put between 231vb.
be instrumental 628vb.
meddle 678vb.
obstruct 702vb.
hinder 702vb.
mediate 720vb.
prohibit 757vb.
interpret
account for 158vb.
play music 413vb.
interpret 520vb.
teach 534vb.
facilitate 701vb.

interpretation
answer 460n.
connotation 514n.
intelligibility 516n.
interpretation 520n.
interpreter
interpreter 520n.
interracial
ethnic 11adj.
correlative 12adj.
interregnum
interim 108n.
transientness 114n.
lull 145n.
interval 201n.
anarchy 734n.
interrelation
correlation 12n.
interrex
potentate 741n.
interrogation
interrogation 459n.
interrogation mark
question 459n.
interrogative
inquiring 459adj.
interrogator
questioner 459n.
interrupt
interfere 231vb.
intrude 297vb.
distract 456vb.
interrupter
dissentient 489n.
hinderer 702n.
interruption
derangement 63n.
discontinuity 72n.
intempestivity 138n.
stop 145n.
interval 201n.
interjection 231n.
overactivity 678n.
hindrance 702n.
rudeness 885n.
intersection
joint 45n.
crossing 222n.
passage 305n.
access, road 624n.
interspace
interval 201n.
interiority 224n.
intersperse
mix 43vb.
put between 231vb.
interstate
correlative 12adj.
interstellar
extraneous 59adj.
interjacent 231adj.
cosmic 321n.
interstellar matter
nebula 321n.
interstice
gap 201n.
interstitial
interior 224adj.
interjacent 231adj.
intertexture
crossing 222n.
intertribal
ethnic 11adj.
correlative 12adj.
intertwine
mix 43vb.
tie 45vb.
combine 50vb.
enlace 222vb.
interval
degree 27n.
disjunction 46n.
incompleteness 55n.
discontinuity 72n.
interim 108n.
period 110n.
lull 145n.
interval 201n.
musical note 410n.
dramaturgy 594n.
repose 683n.
intervale
gap 201n.
intervene
discontinue 72vb.
interfere 231vb.
lie between 231vb.
meddle 678vb.
mediate 720vb.
prohibit 757vb.
intervener
hinderer 702n.
litigant 959n.
intervention
interjection 231n.
instrumentality 628n.
hindrance 702n.
war 718n.
mediation 720n.
interview
listening 415n.
exam 459n.
interrogate 459vb.
conference 584n.
interviewer
questioner 459n.
interlocutor 584n.
interwar
intermediate 108adj.
interweave
mix 43vb.
combine 50vb.
compose 56vb.
enlace 222vb.
put between 231vb.
interworking
agency 173n.
interworld
correlative 12adj.
intestate
obliterated 550adj.
intestinal
interior 224adj.
intestine
insides 224n.
drain 351n.
in the light
hindering 702adj.
in the long run
generally 79adv.
at last 113adv.
in the main
wholly 52adv.
in the running
contending 716adj.
in the way
nigh 200adv.
hindering 702adj.
in the wind
happening 154adj.
impending 155adj.
intimacy
relation 9n.
coition 45n.
knowledge 490n.
friendship 880n.
sociability 882n.
intimate
conjunct 45adj.
private 80adj.
interior 224adj.
knowing 490adj.
inform, hint 524vb.
indicate 547vb.
close friend 880n.
intimation
hint 524n.
intimidate
hinder 702vb.
frighten 854vb.
threaten 900vb.
intimidation
dissuasion 613n.
terror tactics 712n.
intimidation 854n.
intimidator
alarmist 854n.
intinction
ritual act 988n.
intolerable
bad 645adj.
intolerable 827adj.
disliked 861adj.
intolerance
uniformity 16n.
exclusion 57n.
weakness 163n.
prejudice 481n.
opiniatrety 602n.
severity 735n.
prohibition 757n.
enmity 881n.

inhumanity 898n.
pitilessness 906n.
orthodoxism 976n.
intonation
sound 398n.
voice 577n.
intone
sing 413vb.
intorsion
convolution 251n.
in toto
completely 54adv.
intoxicant
poison 659n.
intoxicate
invigorate 174vb.
delight 826vb.
intoxicated
drunk 949adj.
intoxicating
strong 162adj.
intoxication
impairment 655n.
excitation 821n.
excitable state 822n.
intemperance 943n.
drunkenness 949n.
intractability
hardness 326n.
obstinacy 602n.
intractable
difficult 700adj.
disobedient 738adj.
intramural
interior 224adj.
intransigence
obstinacy 602n.
intransigent
resolute 599adj.
in transit
convertibly 147adv.
in transit 272adv.
intransmutable
lasting 113adj.
unchangeable 153adj.
intravenous
interior 224adj.
in-tray
receptacle 194n.
compartment 194n.
intrepidity
courage 855n.
intricacy
complexity 61n.
crossing 222n.
convolution 251n.
difficulty 700n.
intricate
tied 45adj.
difficult 700adj.
(*see* intricacy)
intrigant
deceiver 545n.
planner 623n.
libertine 952n.
intrigue
latency 523n.
deceive 542vb.
motivate 612vb.
plot 623n., vb.
overactivity 678n.
be cunning 698vb.
sedition 738n.
impress 821vb.
love affair 887n.
illicit love 951n.
intriguer
planner 623n.
meddler 678n.
slyboots 698n.
intriguing
lovable 887adj.
intrinsic
intrinsic 5adj.
ingredient 58adj.
included 78adj.
interior 224adj.
intrinsicality
essence 1n.
intrinsicality 5n.
relation 9n.
introception
reception 299n.
introduce
add 38vb.
come before 64vb.
initiate 68vb.
intromit 231vb.
precede 283vb.
admit 299vb.
insert 303vb.
befriend 880vb.
greet 884vb.
introduction
prelude 66n.
beginning 68n.
reception 299n.
insertion 303n.
teaching 534n.
friendship 880n.
introductory
precursory 66adj.
beginning 68adj.
prior 119adj.
introit
vocal music 412n.
Holy Communion 988n.
intromission
interjection 231n.
reception 299n.
intromit
insert 303vb.
introspection
inspection 438n.
meditation 449n.
attention 455n.
inquiry 459n.
knowledge 490n.
introspective
thoughtful 449adj.
introversion
inversion 221n.
interiority 224n.
introvert
invert 221vb.
interiority 224n.
introverted
intrinsic 5adj.
intrude
mistime 138vb.
interfere 231vb.
intrude 297vb.
insert 303vb.
encroach 306vb.
meddle 678vb.
obstruct 702vb.
intruder
intruder 59n.
settler 191n.
interjector 231n.
incomer 297n.
intrusion
irrelation 10n.
inaptitude 25n.
(*see* intrude)
intrusive
irrelative 10adj.
extraneous 59adj.
intuition
intellect 447n.
non-intellect 448n.
intuition 476n.
intelligence 498n.
supposition 512n.
conjecture 512n.
spontaneity 609n.
revelation 975n.
intuitive
mindless 448adj.
intuitive 476adj.
intumescence
dilation 197n.
convexity 253n.
in turn
severally 80adv.
by turns 141adv.
inundate
overlie 226vb.
irrigate 341vb.
(*see* inundation)
inundation
havoc 165n.
outflow 298n.
moistening 341n.
waterfall 350n.
redundance 637n.
inurbanity
ill-breeding 847n.
discourtesy 885n.
inure
train 534vb.

habituate 610vb.
make ready 669vb.
inured
unfeeling 375adj.
thick-skinned 820adj.
inurn
inter 364vb.
inutility
ineffectuality 161n.
superfluity 637n.
inutility 641n.
inexpedience 643n.
non-use 674n.
invade
interfere 231vb.
irrupt 297vb.
attack 712vb.
wage war 718vb.
invading
extraneous 59adj.
invaginate
invert 221vb.
intromit 231vb.
invalid
powerless 161adj.
weakling 163n.
illogical 477adj.
useless 641adj.
sick person 651n.
unhealthy 651adj.
unwarranted 916adj.
invalidate
disable 161vb.
weaken 163vb.
confute 479vb.
negate 533vb.
abrogate 752vb.
disentitle 916vb.
invalid chair
pushcart 274n.
invalidism
weakness 163n.
ill-health 651n.
invalidity
impotence 161n.
unmeaningness 515n.
invalid out
not retain 779vb.
invaluable
profitable 640adj.
valuable 644adj.
of price 811adj.
invariability
permanence 144n.
invariable
characteristic 5adj.
identical 13adj.
uniform 16adj.
orderly 60adj.
unchangeable 153adj.
usual 610adj.
tedious 838adj.
invariant
identity 13n.
identical 13adj.
invasion
crowd 74n.
ingress 297n.
attack 712n.
invective
oratory 579n.
scurrility 899n.
reproach 924n.
detraction 926n.
inveigh
curse 899vb.
dispraise 924vb.
inveigle
ensnare 542vb.
tempt 612vb.
invent
initiate 68vb.
imagine 513vb.
fake 541vb.
(*see* invention)
invention
causation 156n.
production 164n.
thought 449n.
idea 451n.
discovery 484n.
falsehood 541n.
untruth, fable 543n.
contrivance 623n.
inventiveness
non-imitation 21n.
productiveness 171n.
thought 449n.
imagination 513n.
cunning 697n.
inventor
precursor 66n.
producer 167n.
inquirer 459n.
detector 484n.
inventorial
accounting 808adj.
inventorize
specify 80vb.
number 86vb.
inventory
all 52n.
arrangement 62n.
class 62vb.
list 87n., vb.
contents 193n.
account 808vb.
inverse
contrariety 14n.
inverted 221adj.
contraposition 240n.
inversion
derangement 63n.
transformation 143n.
reversion 148n.
revolution 149n.
inversion 221n.
contraposition 240n.
trope 519n.
ornament 574n.
invert
demolish 165vb.
invert 221vb.
invertebrate
impotent 161adj.
weak 163adj.
animal 365n.
inverted commas
punctuation 547n.
invest
place 187vb.
surround 230vb.
circumscribe 232vb.
store 632vb.
besiege 712vb.
commission 751vb.
lend 784vb.
speculate 791vb.
expend 806vb.
invested
dressed 228adj.
investigation
inquiry 459n.
police inquiry 459n.
study 536n.
investigator
inquirer 459n.
detective 459n.
invest in
purchase 792vb.
investiture
dressing 228n.
mandate 751n.
investment
dressing 228n.
closure 264n.
(*see* invest)
investor
creditor 802n.
lender 784n.
invest with
give 781vb.
inveteracy
tradition 127n.
habit 610n.
inveterate
lasting 113adj.
immemorial 127adj.
permament 144adj.
vested 153adj.
habitual 610adj.
invidious
unpleasant 827adj.
hateful 888adj.
invigilate
invigilate 457vb.
invigilation
carefulness 457n.
invigilator
keeper 749n.

invigorate
strengthen 162vb.
invigorate 174vb.
vitalize 360vb.
incite 612vb.
refresh 685vb.
animate 821vb.
cheer 833vb.
invigorating
salubrious 652adj.
invincible
unyielding 162adj.
unbeaten 727adj.
inviolable
strong 162adj.
concealed 525adj.
due 915adj.
inviolate
permanent 144adj.
concealed 525adj.
honorable 929adj.
invious
closed 264adj.
difficult 700adj.
invisibility
insubstantiality 4n.
smallness 33n.
invisibility 444n.
disappearance 446n.
latency 523n.
invisible
minute 196adj.
distant 199n.
invisible ink
secrecy 525n.
invitation
reception 299n.
inducement 612n.
command 737n.
offer 759n.
request 761n.
excitation 821n.
courteous act 884n.
invite
delight 826vb.
desire 859vb.
be hospitable 882vb.
invitee
friend 880n.
inviting
accessible 289adj.
pleasurable 826adj.
invocation
allocution 583n.
edition 589n.
entreaty 761n.
praise 923n.
prayers 981n.
sorcery 983n.
invocatory
vocative 583adj.
supplicatory 761adj.
devotional 981adj.
invoice
list 87n.
demand 737vb.
accounts 808n.
price 809n., vb.
invoke
orate 579vb.
speak to 583vb.
entreat 761vb.
desire 859vb.
worship 981vb.
practise sorcery 983vb.
involuntariness
non-design 618n.
involuntary
intuitive 476adj.
unmeant 515adj.
involuntary 596adj.
spontaneous 609adj.
compelling 740adj.
involution
complexity 61n.
numerical operation 86n.
convolution 251n.
involve
be intrinsic 5vb.
contain 56vb.
bedevil 63vb.
comprise 78vb.
conduce 156vb.
evidence 466vb.
make likely 471vb.
mean 514vb.
imply 523vb.
indicate 547vb.
accuse 928vb.
involved
ingredient 58adj.
concurrent 181adj.
intricate 251adj.
imperspicuous 568adj.
involvement
relation 9n.
junction 45n.
complexity 61n.
affairs 154n.
difficulty 700n.
participation 775n.
feeling 818n.
liking 859n.
guilt 936n.
invulnerable
strong 162adj.
invulnerable 660adj.
defended 713adj.
inward
intrinsic 5adj.
interior 224adj.
incoming 297adj.
inward-looking
intrinsic 5adj.
interior 224adj.
inwardly
inside 224adv.
inwardness
intrinsicality 5n.
inwoven
intrinsic 5adj.
inwrought
intrinsic 5adj.
interior 224adj.
iodine
prophylactic 658n.
ion
particle 33n.
element 319n.
ionic
prosody 593n.
ornamental 844adj.
ionosphere
atmosphere 340n.
iota
small quantity 33n.
iotacism
dialect 560n.
prounciation 577n.
IOU
title deed 767n.
ipecac
cathartic 658n.
ipse dixit
certainty 473n.
affirmation 532n.
decree 737n.
ipsissima verba
identity 13n.
accuracy 494n.
ipso facto
actually 1adv.
IQ
intelligence 498n.
irascibility
quarrelsomeness 709n.
excitability 822n.
irascibility 892n.
irascible
violent 176adj.
ungracious 885adj.
sullen 893adj.
(*see* irascibility)
irate
angry 891adj.
ire
anger 891n.
irenic
peaceful 717adj.
pacificatory 719adj.
irenicon
irenics 719n.
irenics
argument 475n.
peace 717n.
irenics 719n.
iridal
variegated 437adj.
iridescence

light 417n.
variegation 437n.
iridescent
mixed 43adj.
iridescent 437adj.
iridization
dim sight 440n.
iris
eye 438n.
irisate
variegate 437vb.
Irish bull
mistake 495n.
absurdity 497n.
ridiculousness 849n.
irk
fatigue 684vb.
be difficult 700vb.
torment 824vb.
bore 838n.
be tedious 838vb.
irksome
(*see* irk)
iron
strength 162vb.
flatten 216vb.
smoother 258n.
food content 301n.
hardness 326n.
rub 333vb.
resolution 599n.
(*see* iron out)
iron age
adversity 731n.
Iron Age
era 110n.
iron boot
instrument of torture 964n.
iron-clad
covered 226adj.
defended 713adj.
(*see* warship)
Iron Cross
badge 547n.
decoration 729n.
iron curtain
exclusion 57n.
partition 231n.
screen 421n.
obstacle 702n.
iron hand
brute force 735n.
iron heel
brute force 735n.
instrument of torture 964n.
ironical
figurative 519adj.
untrue 543adj.
funny 849adj.
affected 850adj.
derisive 851adj.
ironist
humorist 839n.
affector 850n.
iron lung
compartment 194n.
hospital 658n.
ironmonger
tradesman 794n.
iron out
unravel 62vb.
flatten 216vb.
straighten 249vb.
smooth 258vb.
facilitate 701vb.
iron ration
small quantity 33n.
provisions 301n.
provision 633n.
insufficiency 636n.
portion 783n.
fasting 946n.
irons
supporter 218n.
fetter 748n.
pillory 964n.
Ironsides
cavalry 722n.
irons in the fire
business 622n.
activity 678n.
irony
underestimation 483n.
metaphor 519n.
mental dishonesty 543n.
wit 839n.
affectation 850n.
ridicule 851n.
reproach 924n.
irradiation
light 417n.
lighting 420n.
irrational
numerical 85adj.
unthinking 450adj.
illogical 477adj.
unwise 499adj.
irreclaimable
wicked 934adj.
impenitent 940adj.
irreconcilability
irrelation 10n.
contrariety 14n.
disagreement 25n.
revengefulness 910n.
irreconcilable
opponent 705n.
malcontent 829n.
regretting 830adj.
inimical 881adj.
irrecoverable
past 125adj.
lost 772adj.
unpromising 853adj.
irredeemable
bad 645adj.
lost 772adj.
unpromising 853adj.
wicked 934adj.
impenitent 940adj.
irredentism
regret 830n.
desire 859n.
patriotism 901n.
irredentist
regret 830n.
desirer 859n.
patriot 901n.
irreducible
simple 44adj.
unchangeable 153adj.
irrefragable
undisputed 473adj.
demonstrated 478adj.
irrefutable
undisputed 473adj.
demonstrated 478adj.
irregular
multiform 82adj.
distorted 246adj.
neological 560adj.
grammatical 565adj.
soldier 722n.
unsightly 842adj.
wrong 914adj.
extramarital 951adj.
(*see* irregularity)
irregularity
non-uniformity 17n.
inequality 29n.
disorder 61n.
discontinuity 72n.
unconformity 84n.
fitfulness 142n.
changeableness 152n.
solecism 565n.
illegality 954n.
irrelation
irrelation 10n.
dissimilarity 19n.
irrelative
severable 46adj.
irrelevance
insubstantiality 4n.
irrelevance 10n.
inaptitude 25n.
absurdity 497n.
unmeaningness 515n.
unimportance 639n.
irrelevant
misplaced 188adj.
deviating 282adj.
prolix 570adj.
irreligion
unbelief 486n.
irreligion 974n.
impiety 980n.
irreligious
wicked 934adj.

irremediable
bad 645adj.
harmful 645adj.
unpromising 853adj.
irremissible
heinous 934adj.
irremovable
fixed 153adj.
obstinate 602adj.
irreparable
unpromising 853adj.
irreplaceable
important 638adj.
valuable 644adj.
irrepressible
violent 176adj.
willful 602adj.
independent 744adj.
lively 819adj.
cheerful 833adj.
irreproachable
perfect 646adj.
virtuous 933adj.
guiltless 935adj.
irresistible
powerful 160adj.
strong 162adj.
influential 178adj.
demonstrated 478adj.
necessary 596adj.
inducive 612adj.
compelling 740adj.
lovable 887adj.
irresoluble
unchangeable 153adj.
irresolute
weak 163adj.
doubting 474adj.
irresolute 601adj.
choiceless 606adj.
neutral 625adj.
lax 734adj.
nervous 854adj.
irresolution
(*see* irresolute)
irrespective
irrelative 10adj.
irresponsible
changeful 152adj.
irresolute 601adj.
capricious 604adj.
rash 857adj.
dutiless 918adj.
lawless 954adj.
irretrievable
lost 772adj.
irreverence
non-wonder 865n.
disrespect 921n.
impiety 980n.
irreversible
vested 153adj.
unchangeable 153adj.
progressive 285adj.
necessary 596adj.
obstinate 602adj.
unpromising 853adj.
irrevocable
vested 153adj.
impossible 470adj.
certain 473adj.
necessary 596adj.
unpromising 853adj.
irrigable
dry 342n.
irrigate
make fruitful 171vb.
add water 339vb.
irrigate 341vb.
make flow 350vb.
cultivate 370vb.
irrigator
irrigator 341n.
irriguous
drenched 341adj.
irritable
sensitive 819adj.
excitable 822adj.
irascible 892adj.
irritant
excitant 821n.
aggravation 832n.
irritate
make violent 176vb.
give pain 377vb.
itch 378vb.
make quarrels 709vb.
excite 821vb.
torment 827vb.
aggravate 832vb.
make enemies 881vb.
enrage 891vb.
irritation
excitation 821n.
worry 825n.
painfulness 827n.
aggravation 832n.
anger 891n.
resentment 891n.
irrupt
be violent 176vb.
irrupt 297vb.
pass 305vb.
attack 712vb.
irruption
ingress 297n.
attack 712n.
irruptive
incoming 297adj.
isagogics
theology 973n.
Ishmael
outcaste 883n.
isinglass
thickening 354n.
Isis
Egyptian gods 967n.
Islam
religious faith 973n.
Islamite
religionist 970n.
island
region 184n.
island 349n.
seclusion 883n.
islanded
insular 349adj.
secluded 883adj.
islander
dweller 191n.
island 349n.
Islands of the Blest
mythic heaven 971n.
island universe
universe, star 321n.
isle
(*see* island)
islesman
island 349n.
ism
creed 485n.
isobar
weather 340n.
isocheimenal
cold 380adj.
isochronous
chronological 117adj.
synchronous 123adj.
isocracy
government 733n.
isogloss
limit 236n.
isogonic line
outline 233n.
limit 236n.
isolable
alone 88adj.
isolate
set apart 46vb.
be one 88vb.
sanitate 652vb.
seclude 883vb.
isolated
alone 88adj.
insular 349adj.
isolated instance
specialty 80n.
unconformity 84n.
unit 88n.
isolation
irrelation 10n.
disjunction 46n.
unity 88n.
freedom 744n.
seclusion 883n.
isolationism
freedom 744n.
isolationist
free man 744n.
independent 744adj.
solitary 883n.
isolation ward

hospital 658n.
isomorphism
form 243n.
isoperimetric
equal 28adj.
isosceles
symmetrical 245adj.
isothermal layer
atmosphere 340n.
isotonic
harmonious 410adj.
isotropy
equivalence 28n.
issue
kinsman 11n.
subdivision 53n.
eventuality 154n.
effect 157n.
posterity 170n.
outflow 298n.
emerge 298vb.
flow 350vb.
topic 452n.
the press 528n.
publish 528vb.
reading matter 589n.
completion 725n.
coinage 797n.
mint 797vb.
litigation 959n.
issue, at
contending 716adj.
issueless
unproductive 172adj.
issuing in
caused 157adj.
isthmian
narrow 206adj.
land 344n.
isthmus
bond 47n.
contraction 198n.
narrowness 206n.
land 344n.
bridge 624n.
it
identity 13n.
no imitation 21n.
fitness 24n.
authenticity 492n.
Italianate
extraneous 59adj.
italic
letter 558n.
lettering 586n.
written 586adj.
print-type 587n.
italicize
emphasize 532vb.
italics
punctuation 547n.
itch
attraction 291n.
agitation 318n.
formication 378n.
curiosity 453n.
skin disease 651n.
desire 859n.
itching
inquisitive 453adj.
excited 821adj.
itching palm
avarice 816n.
item
in addition 38adv.
extra 40n.
part 53n.
unit 88n.
object 319n.
itemize
specify 80vb.
list 87vb.
items
particulars 80n.
list 87n.
contents 193n.
iterate
repeat 106vb.
iteration
duplication 91n.
vigor 571n.
perseverance 600n.
iterative
repeated 106adj.
itinerant
traveling 267adj.
traveler 268n.
itinerary
itinerary 267n.
guide-book 524n.
way 624n.
itself
self 80n.
ivories
tooth 256n.
piano 414n.
gambling 618n.
ivory
white thing 427n.
dunce 501n.
ivory tower
seclusion 883n.
ivy
plant 366n.
izzat
prestige 866n.

J

jab
knock 279n.
wound 655n.
therapy 658n.
foin 712n.
jab at
essay 671n.
jabber
empty talk 515n.
speak 579vb.
chatter 581n.
jacinth
gem 844n.
jack
lifter 310n.
rotator 315n.
flag 547n.
tool 630n.
jackal
aftercomer 67n.
auxiliary 707n.
dependent 742n.
toady 879n.
noxious animal 904n.
jackanapes
fop 848n.
insolent person 878n.
jackboot
footwear 228n.
tyrant 735n.
jackdaw
bird 365n.
jacket
wrapping 226n.
skin 226n.
tunic 228n.
bookbinding 589n.
jack-in-office
tyrant 735n.
official 690n.
autocrat 741n.
insolent person 878n.
jack-in-the-box
inexpectation 508n.
plaything 837n.
jack-knife
sharp edge 256n.
jack-of-all-trades
proficient 696n.
jack-o'-lantern
glow 417n.
glow-worm 420n.
jackpot
acquisition 771n.
jacks
plaything 837n.
jack up
support 218vb.
elevate 310vb.
Jacobin
opponent 705n.
revolter 738n.
Jacob's ladder
ascent 308n.
Jacob's staff
gauge 465n.
jaconet
textile 222n.
jacquerie
terror tactics 712n.
jactation
boasting 877n.

jactitation
agitation 318n.
affirmation 532n.
boasting 877n.
jaculation
propulsion 287n.
jade
saddle-horse 273n.
greenness 432n.
fatigue 684vb.
be tedious 838vb.
gem 844n.
cause dislike 861vb.
sate 863vb.
bad man 938n.
loose woman 952n.
jadedness
fatigue 684n.
satiety 863n.
jag
notch 260vb.
drunkenness 949n.
jagged
angular 247adj.
rough 259adj.
notched 260adj.
jaggery
sweet 392n.
jaggy
notched 260adj.
jaguar
cat 365n.
jail
jail 748n.
jail-bird
prisoner 750n.
offender 904n.
jailer
janitor 264n.
jailer 749n.
Jainism
religious faith 973n.
jakes
latrine 649n.
jam
join, tighten 45vb.
crowd 74n.
halt 145vb.
close 264vb.
be quiescent 266vb.
sweetmeat 301n.
viscidity 354n.
pulpiness 356n.
condiment 389n.
sweet 392n.
predicament 700n.
obstruct 702vb.
jamb
pillar 218n.
jamboree
amusement 837n.
jammed
firm-set 45adj.
full 54adj.
jammy
viscid 354adj.
jam session
dancing 837n.
jangle
disagree 25vb.
resound 404vb.
rasp 407vb.
discord 411vb.
dissension 709n.
jangling
argument 475n.
janissary
soldier 722n.
janitor
janitor 264n.
servant 742n.
Janus
duality 90n.
tergiversator 603n.
japan
coat 226vb.
resin 357n.
color 425vb.
black pigment 428n.
decorate 844vb.
jape
amuse oneself 837vb.
witticism 839n.
japer
humorist 839n.
jar
differ 15vb.
disagree 25vb.
vessel 194n.
agitation 318n.
give pain 377vb.
rasp 407vb.
discord 411vb.
dissension 709n.
displease 827vb.
cause dislike 861vb.
excite hate 888vb.
jardiniere
vessel, bowl 194n.
jargon
specialty 80n.
absurdity 497n.
unmeaningness 515n.
slang 560n.
jarvey
driver 268n.
Jason
mariner 270n.
jasper
variegate 437vb.
gem 844n.
jaundice
yellowness 433n.
bias 481vb.
indigestion 651n.
jaundiced
biased 481adj.
melancholic 834adj.
sullen 893adj.
jealous 911adj.
jaunt
land travel 267n.
jaunting-car
carriage 274n.
jaunty
cheerful 833adj.
showy 875adj.
impertinent 878adj.
javelin
spear 723n.
missile weapon 723n.
jaw
projection 254n.
be loquacious 581vb.
chatter 581n.
(*see* jaws)
jawbreaker
hardness 326n.
word 559n.
neology 560n.
inelegance 576n.
jaws
maw 194n.
threshold 234n.
orifice 263n.
eater 301n.
jay
dupe 544n.
chatterer 581n.
jaywalker
bungler 697n.
jazz
music 412n.
dance 837n.
jealous
opposing 704adj.
resentful 891adj.
malevolent 898adj.
selfish 932adj.
(*see* jealousy)
jealousy
imitation 20n.
doubt 486n.
quarrelsomeness 709n.
contention 716n.
discontent 829n.
enmity 881n.
love 887n.
hatred 888n.
jealousy 911n.
jeans
trousers 228n.
jeep
automobile 274n.
jeer
ridicule 851vb.
not respect 921vb.
despise 922vb.
jeers
lifter 310n.
Jehovah
the Deity 965n.

Jehovah's Witnesses
sect 978n.
jehu
driver 268n.
speeder 277n.
jejune
lean 206adj.
tasteless 387adj.
feeble 572adj.
underfed 636adj.
Jekyll and Hyde
multiformity 82n.
jell
thicken 354vb.
jellification
condensation 324n.
jelly
sweetmeat 301n.
sweet 392n.
jellyfish
weakling 163n.
fish 365n.
coward 856n.
jemmy
fop 848n.
(*see* jimmy)
jeopardy
danger 661n.
jerboa
jumper 312n.
jeremiad
lament 836n.
censure 924n.
Jeremiah
weeper 836n.
jerk
revolution 149n.
move 265vb.
impulse 279n.
draw 288vb.
leap 312vb.
agitate 318vb.
jerkin
tunic 228n.
jerkiness
non-uniformity 17n.
discontinuity 72n.
fitfulness 142n.
agitation 318n.
restlessness 678n.
jerks, the
spasm 318n.
jeroboam
vessel 194n.
jerry
vessel 194n.
latrine 649n.
jerry-built
flimsy 163adj.
spurious 542adj.
unsafe 661adj.
jersey
textile 222n.
vest 228n.
cattle 365n.
jess
halter 47n.
jesse
church interior 990n.
jest
trifle 639n.
amuse oneself 837vb.
witticism 839n.
jester
fool 501n.
humorist 839n.
jesuitry
sophistry 477n.
falsehood 541n.
Jesuits
monk 986n.
Jesus
God the Son 965n.
jet
energy 160n.
vigorousness 174n.
outbreak 176n.
speeder 277n.
propellant 287n.
outflow 298n.
emit 300vb.
ascend 308vb.
stream 350n.
black thing 428n.
jet propulsion
energy 160n.
propulsion 287n.
jetsam
thing transferred 272n.
derelict 779n.
jettison
eject 300vb.
lighten 323vb.
disuse 674vb.
not retain 779vb.
jetty
stable 192n.
projection 254n.
black 428adj.
shelter 662n.
jeu d'esprit
witticism 839n.
jeunesse dorée
rich man 800n.
beau monde 848n.
jewel
exceller 644n.
a beauty 841n.
gem 844n.
darling 890n.
jeweler
artisan 686n.
jewelry
jewelry 844n.
Jew's harp
harp 414n.
Jezebel
bad man 938n.
loose woman 952n.
jheel
marsh 347n.
jib
prow 237n.
sail 275n.
recoil 280vb.
deviate 282vb.
turn back 286vb.
be unwilling 598vb.
be irresolute 601vb.
avoid 620vb.
refuse 760vb.
resent 891vb.
jibe
change 143vb.
navigate 269vb.
(*see* gibe)
jiffy
instant 116n.
jig
leap 312n.
agitation 318n.
musical piece 412n.
dance 837n.
jiggle
derange 63vb.
agitate 318vb.
jig-saw
combination 50n.
indoor game 837n.
jihad
war 718n.
jilt
disappoint 509vb.
befool 542vb.
deceiver 545n.
tergiversator 603n.
relinquish 621vb.
be dishonest 930vb.
jim-jams
frenzy 503n.
alcoholism 949n.
jimmy
force 176vb.
tool 630n.
jingal
gun 723n.
jingle
resonance 404n.
doggerel 593n.
jingler
poet 593n.
jingoism
bellicosity 718n.
boasting 877n.
jink
be oblique 220vb.
be in motion 265vb.
avoid 620vb.
jinn
demon 970n.
jinrikisha

cab 274n.
jinx
badness 645n.
jitney
cab 274n.
jitterbug
dance 837n., vb.
jitters
agitation 318n.
nervousness 854n.
jive
music 412n.
dance 837n., vb.
jiver
jumper 312n.
job
agency 173n.
job, function 622n.
undertaking 672n.
deed 676n.
labor 682n.
hard task 700n.
stealing 788n.
foul play 930n.
jobation
reprimand 924n.
jobber
trickster 545n.
jobbery
cunning 698n.
improbity 930n.
jobbing
barter 791n.
venal 930adj.
jobless
unused 674adj.
non-active 677adj.
Job's comforter
moper 834n.
hopelessness 853n.
jockey
rider 268n.
speeder 277n.
trickster 545n.
jockeyship
trickery 542n.
jocko
monkey 365n.
jock-strap
supporter 218n.
jocosity
wit 839n.
jocularity
merriment 833n.
wit 839n.
jocund
gay 833adj.
jocundity
pleasurableness 826n.
amusement 837n.
jodhpurs
breeches 228n.
jog
walk 267vb.
impel 279vb.
agitate 318vb.
gesture 547n.
gesticulate 547vb.
joggle
agitate 318vb.
jog on
go on 146vb.
travel 267vb.
progress 285vb.
be middling 732vb.
jog-trot
gait 265n.
pedestrianism 267n.
slowness 278n.
Johnny, Johnnie
person 371n.
male 372n.
fop 848n.
Johnsonese
imperspicuity 568n.
magniloquence 574n.
joie de vivre
cheerfulness 833n.
join
accrue 38vb.
join 45vb.
agglutinate 48vb.
bring together 74vb.
be included 78vb.
gap 201n.
be contiguous 202vb.
approach 289vb.
meet 295vb.
enter 297vb.
patronize 703vb.
join a party 708vb.
marry 894vb.
joinder
joinder 45n.
combination 50n.
assemblage 74n.
joiner
joinder 45n.
artisan 686n.
joinery
efformation 243n.
join in
be active 678vb.
cooperate 706vb.
participate 775vb.
be sociable 882vb.
join issue
argue 475vb.
fight 716vb.
joint
joint 45n.
concurrent 181adj.
angularity 247n.
fold 261n.
meat 301n.
corporate 708adj.
sharing 775adj.
jointly
cooperatively 706adv.
in common 755adv.
jointness
joint possession 775n.
joint, out of
orderless 61adj.
joint-stock
corporate 708adj.
joint possession 775n.
joint-stock company
association 706n.
corporation 708n.
jointure
dower 777n.
join-up
war measures 718n.
joist
beam 218n.
joke
absurdity 497n.
trickery 542n.
trifle 639n.
witticism 839n.
joker
misfit 25n.
nonconformist 84n.
humorist 839n.
joking
gay 833adj.
witty 839adj.
joking apart
affirmatively 532adv.
jollification
revel 837n.
jollity
merriment 833n.
sociability 882n.
jolly
fleshy 195adj.
naval man 270n.
navy man 722n.
gay 833adj.
amused 837adj.
sociable 882adj.
jolly along
cheer 833vb.
jolly boat
boat 275n.
Jolly Roger
flag 547n.
jolt
be rough 259vb.
move slowly 278vb.
impulse 279n.
agitation 318n.
inexpectation 508vb.
joltiness
discontinuity 72n.
(*see* jolt)
Jonah
unlucky person 731n.
moper 834n.
jongleur
musician 413n.

poet 593n.
entertainer 594n.
jorum
bowl 194n.
Joseph
virgin 950n.
Joseph's coat
variegation 437n.
josh
ridicule 851vb.
joss
idol 982n.
joss-house
temple 990n.
joss-stick
fumigator 385n.
scent 396n.
ritual object 988n.
jostle
counteract 182vb.
be near 200vb.
be contiguous 202vb.
impel 279vb.
obstruct 702vb.
fight 716vb.
not respect 921vb.
jot
small quantity 33n.
write 586vb.
trifle 639n.
jot down
record 548vb.
jottings
record 548n.
reading matter 589n.
jounce
agitate 318vb.
journal
chronology 117n.
the press, journal 528n.
record 548n.
biography 590n.
account book 808n.
journalese
neology 560n.
journalism
publicity 528n.
writing 586n.
journalist
publicizer 328n.
chronicler 549n.
author 589n.
journalistic
dialectical 560adj.
journalize
register 548vb.
account 808vb.
journey
travel 267vb.
passage 305n.
journeyman
artisan 686n.
journey's end
resting place 266n.
goal 295n.
joust
contest, duel 716n.
jouster
combatant 722n.
Jove
Olympian god 967n.
joviality
merriment 833n.
amusement 837n.
sociability 882n.
Jovian
planetary 321adj.
jowl
laterality 239n.
joy
pleasure 376n.
joy 824n.
pleasurableness 826n.
cheerfulness 833n.
joyful, joyous
happy 824adj.
gay 833adj.
joyless
unpleasant 827adj.
melancholic 834adj.
joy-ride
land travel 267n.
easy thing 701n.
borrowing 785n.
stealing 788n.
joy-stick
aircraft 276n.
directorship 689n.
jube
church interior 990n.
jubilant
pleased 824adj.
jubilant 833adj.
rejoicing 835adj.
celebrative 876adj.
jubilate
be pleased 824vb.
rejoice 835vb.
celebrate 876vb.
boast 877vb.
jubilation
(*see* jubilate)
jubilee
over twenty 99n.
period 110n.
anniversary 141n.
merriment 833n.
rejoicing 835n.
celebration 876n.
Judaism
religious faith 973n.
Judaizers
church party 978n.
Judas
deceiver 545n.
knave 938n.
Judas kiss
duplicity 541n.
falsehood 541n.
mental dishonesty 543n.
perfidy 930n.
judge
leader 690n.
have taste 846vb.
punisher 936n.
judge 957n.
(*see* judgment)
judge and jury
tribunal 956n.
judgmatic
judicial 480adj.
wise 498adj.
judgment
intellect 447n.
discrimination 463n.
judgment 480n.
opinion 485n.
sagacity 498n.
decree 737n.
legality 953n.
legal trial 959n.
condemnation 961n.
punishment 963n.
judgment day
future state 124n.
tribunal 956n.
judgment seat
tribunal 956n.
judicatory
judicial 480adj.
tribunal 956n.
curial 956adj.
judicature
jurisdiction 955n.
judicial
judicial 480adj.
curial 956adj.
judiciary
jurisdictional 955adj.
judicious
moderate 177adj.
discriminating 463adj.
judicial 480adj.
wise 498adj.
judo
defense 713n.
wrestling 716n.
judoist
combatant 722n.
jug
vessel 194n.
jail 748n.
imprison 947vb.
juggins
ninny 501n.
juggle
modify 143vb.
sleight 542n.

stratagem 698n.
juggler
conjuror 545n.
entertainer 594n.
slyboots 698n.
sorcerer 983n.
jugglery
(*see* juggle)
jugular vein
essential part 5n.
conduit 351n.
life 360n.
juice
fluid 335n.
moisture 341n.
semiliquidity 354n.
juiceless
dry 342n.
juicy
vernal 128adj.
soft 327adj.
fluidal 335adj.
humid 341adj.
semiliquid 354adj.
pulpy 356adj.
savory 390adj.
topping 644adj.
pleasurable 826adj.
impure 951adj.
jujitsu
defense 713n.
wrestling 716n.
jujitsuist
combatant 722n.
jujube
sweet 392n.
juke box
phonograph 414n.
julep
liquor 301n.
sweet 392n.
jumble
medley 43n.
confusion 61n.
jumble 63vb.
deform 244vb.
not discriminate 464vb.
impair 655vb.
jumbo
large 195adj.
jump
interval 201n.
fly 271vb.
spurt 277n.
progression 285n.
ascent 308n.
leap 312n., vb.
agitation 318n.
neglect 458vb.
not expect 508vb.
improvement 654n.
obstacle 702n.
be excited 821vb.
be excitable 822vb.
amuse oneself 837vb.
fear 854vb.
jump a claim
appropriate 786vb.
jump at
be willing 597vb.
pursue 619vb.
consent 758vb.
desire 859vb.
jumper
vest 228n.
apron 228n.
thoroughbred 273n.
jumper 312n.
jump-off
aider 703n.
jump on the bandwagon
do likewise 20vb.
conform 83vb.
apostatize 603vb.
be in fashion 848vb.
be servile 879vb.
jump over
overstep 306vb.
jumps
agitation 318n.
nervousness 854n.
jump the gun
do before 119vb.
be early 135vb.
jump the queue
be disordered 61vb.
come before 64vb.
precede 283vb.
jump to conclusions
prejudge 481vb.
jump to it
be active 678vb.
jumpy
agitated 318adj.
active 678adj.
nervous 854adj.
junction
junction 45n.
bond 47n.
combination 50n.
accompaniment 89n.
continuity 202n.
goal 295n.
access 624n.
road, railroad 624n.
juncutre
juncture 8n.
joint 45n.
present time 121n.
occasion, crisis 137n.
jungle
confusion 61n.
wood 366n.
jungliness
ill-breeding 847n.
jungly
arboreal 366adj.
artless 699adj.
junior
inferior 35n.
subsequent 120adj.
young 130adj.
youngster 132n.
college student 538n.
juniority
youth 130n.
subjection 745n.
junk
sailing-ship 275n.
rubbish 641n.
Junker
aristocrat 868n.
junket
meal 301n.
milk product 301n.
semiliquidity 354n.
revel 837vb.
Juno
Olympian god 967n.
junta
party 708n.
junto
party 708n.
Jupiter
planet 321n.
mythic god 966n.
Olympian god 967n.
juridical
judicial 480adj.
jurisdictional 955adj.
jurisconsult
jurist 958n.
jurisdiction
authority 733n.
law 953n.
jurisdiction 955n.
legal process 959n.
jurisdictional
curial 956adj.
jurisprudence
jurisprudence 953n.
jurisprudential
legal 953adj.
jurisprudential 958adj.
jurist
jurist 958n.
juristic
judicial 480adj.
juror
estimator 480n.
jury 957n.
jury
estimator 480n.
jury 957n.
jury-box
courtroom 956n.
jury mast
substitute 150n.
safeguard 662n.

jus gentium
law 953n.
jussive
commanding 737adj.
just
rational 475adj.
veracious 540adj.
indifferent 860adj.
just 913adj.
honorable 929adj.
disinterested 931adj.
virtuous 933adj.
legal 953adj.
pietist 979n.
just as
synchronously 123adv.
just cause
vindication 927n.
just do
suffice 635vb.
just excuse
vindication 927n.
justice
indifference 860n.
justice 913n.
probity 929n.
disinterestedness 931n.
virtue 933n.
legality 953n.
judge 957n.
reward 962n.
punishment 963n.
justiciable
accusable 928adj.
legal 953adj.
illegal 954adj.
jurisdictional 955adj.
litigated 959adj.
justifiable
just 913adj.
deserving 915adj.
vindicable 927adj.
justification
counter-evidence 467n.
pretext 614n.
dueness 915n.
vindication 927n.
acquittal 960n.
divine function 965n.
sanctity 979n.
justificatory
excusing 614adj.
justify
regularize 62vb.
demonstrate 478vb.
print 587vb.
(*see* justification)
just mention
hint 524vb.
just now
at present 121adv.
newly 126adv.
just out
new 126adj.
just price
equivalence 28n.
just right
sufficient 635adj.
perfect 646adj.
right 913adj.
just so
in order 60adv.
accurate 494adj.
right 913adj.
jut
jut 254vb.
be visible 443vb.
jute
fiber 208n.
textile 222n.
jutting
salient 254adj.
juvenile
young 130adj.
infantine 132adj.
feeble 572adj.
immature 670adj.
juvenilia
reading matter 589n.
juxtapose
connect 45vb.
bring near 200vb.
juxtapose 202vb.
compare 462vb.
juxtaposition
assemblage 74n.

K

ka
identity 13n.
analogue 18n.
spirit 447n.
mythic god 966n.
Kafir
heathen 974n.
kailyard
dialectical 560adj.
kailyard school
style 566n.
kaiser
sovereign 741n.
kaiserism
despotism 733n.
kale
vegetable 301n.
kaleidoscope
medley 43n.
multiformity 82n.
alterer 143n.
changeable thing 152n.
variegation 437n.
optical device 442n.
spectacle 445n.
kaleidoscopic
colored 425adj.
kangaroo
jumper 312n.
marsupial 365n.
kangaroo court
lawlessness 954n.
Kantianism
philosophy 449n.
kaolin
soil 344n.
materials 631n.
kapellmeister
musician 413n.
kapok
fiber 208n.
kaput
destroyed 165adj.
defeated 728adj.
karma
effect 157n.
fate 596n.
Karmayoga
religion 973n.
karmic
fated 596adj.
kayak
rowboat 275n.
kazi
(*see* cadi)
kebab
meat 301n.
keck
vomit 300vb.
keddah
trap 542n.
chase 619n.
lock-up 748n.
kedge
navigate 269vb.
draw 288vb.
safeguard 662n.
keel
stabilizer 153n.
base 214n.
pivot 218n.
ship 275n.
keelhaul
punish 963vb.
keelson
base 214n.
keen
keen 174adj.
sharp 256adj.
inter 364vb.
cold 380adj.
contending 716adj.
felt 818adj.
lament 836n., vb.
witty 839adj.
desiring 859adj.
condolence 905n.
keener
funeral 364n.
weeper 836n.
keen-eyed
seeing 438adj.

keen on
enamored 887adj.
keep
put off 136vb.
stay 144vb.
go on 146vb.
dwelling 192n.
dwell 192vb.
provisions 301n.
look after 457vb.
store 632vb.
provide 633vb.
safeguard 660vb.
refuge 662n.
subvention 703n.
patronize 703vb.
fort 713n.
defend 713vb.
detention 747n.
retain 778vb.
celebrate 876vb.
observe 768vb.
ritualize 988vb.
keep accounts
number 86vb.
account 808vb.
keep alive
vitalize 360vb.
preserve 666vb.
keep an eye
look after 457vb.
safeguard 660vb.
keep at arm's length
repel 292vb.
parry 713vb.
resist 715vb.
keep awake
be active 678vb.
keep away
be absent 190vb.
avoid 620vb.
keep back
keep secret 525vb.
dissuade 613vb.
store 632vb.
retain 778vb.
be parsimonious 816vb.
keep calm
keep calm 823vb.
keep company
accompany 89vb.
be friendly 880vb.
keep count
list 87vb.
keep down
depress 311vb.
subjugate 745vb.
keeper
concomitant 89n.
janitor 264n.
surveillance 457n.
animal husbandry 569n.
protector 660n.
manager 690n.
interceptor 702n.
servant 742n.
keeper 749n.
consignee 754n.
keep faith
observe faith 768vb.
be honorable 929vb.
keep going
go on 146vb.
be in motion 265vb.
keep holy
celebrate 876vb.
sanctify 979vb.
ritualize 988vb.
keep in
surround 230vb.
imprison 747vb.
retain 778vb.
keep in countenance
give courage 855vb.
keeping
residing 192adj.
protection 660n.
tutelary 660adj.
detention 747n.
keep in hand
store 632vb.
not use 674vb.
keep in step
conform 83vb.
synchronize 123vb.
keep in the dark
not know 491vb.
keep secret 525vb.
keep in with
be friendly 880vb.
be sociable 882vb.
keep off
be distant 199vb.
avoid 620vb.
parry 713vb.
keep on
recur 139vb.
go on 146vb.
progress 285vb.
persevere 600vb.
keep oneself to oneself
be fastidious 862vb.
be unsocial 883vb.
keep one's head
be courageous 855vb.
not wonder 865vb.
keep order
order 60vb.
safeguard 660vb.
keep out
exclude 57vb.
obstruct 702vb.
restrain 747vb.
refuse 760vb.
be unsocial 883vb.
keep out of the way
(*see* keep away)
keep pace with
be equal 28vb.
concur 181vb.
keep quiet
be quiescent 266vb.
not act 677vb.
keepsake
reminder 505n.
keep time
time 117vb.
synchronize 123vb.
keep together
accord 24vb.
keep under
(*see* keep down)
keep up
stay 144vb.
sustain 146vb.
go on 146vb.
keep up with
be equal 28vb.
be friendly 880vb.
be sociable 882vb.
keep up with the Joneses
afford 800vb.
keep well
be healthy 650vb.
kef
drug 658n.
keg
vat 194n.
kelpie
demon 970n.
kelson, keelson
base 214n.
ken
view 438n.
see 438vb.
knowledge 490n.
kennel
group 74n.
stable 192n.
furrow 262n.
drain 351n.
imprison 747vb.
lock-up 748n.
kenning
name 561n.
kenosis
humility 872n.
kepi
headgear 228n.
kept woman
kept woman 952n.
kerchief
headgear 228n.
kerf
notch 260n.
kermes
red pigment 431n.
kermis
festivity 837n.

kern
soldier 722n.
countryman 869n.
kernel
essential part 5n.
middle 70n.
focus 76n.
centrality 225n.
chief thing 638n.
kerosine
oil 357n.
fuel 385n.
kersey
textile 222n.
kerseys
trousers 228n.
ketch
sailing-ship 275n.
kettle
caldron 194n.
heater 383n.
kettle drum
drum 414n.
kettle of fish
complexity 61n.
predicament 700n.
kevel
pulverize 332vb.
key
degree 27n.
crucial 137adj.
influential 178adj.
opener 263n.
stopper 264n.
island 349n.
key 410n.
hue 425n.
answer 460n.
discovery 484n.
interpretation 520n.
translation 520n.
instrument 628n.
important 638adj.
safeguard 662n.
key, be in
harmonize 410vb.
keyboard
musical note 410n.
piano 414n.
keyed up
expectant 507adj.
keyhole
orifice 263n.
window 263n.
key man
bigwig 638n.
key moment
crisis 137n.
keynote
prototype 23n.
rule 81n.
musical note 410n.
chief thing 638n.
key of the door
adultness 134n.
keys
badge of rule 743n.
keystone
summit 213n.
supporter 218n.
completion 725n.
keyword
answer 460n.
khaddar, khadi
textile 222n.
khaki
uniform 228n.
brownness 430n.
khan
inn 192n.
sovereign 741n.
nobleman 868n.
khansamah
domestic 742n.
khedive
governor 741n.
khidmatgar
servant 742n.
khilat
decoration 729n.
badge of rule 743n.
kibble
vessel 194n.
pulverize 332vb.
kibbutz
farm 370n.
joint possession 775n.
kibe
hardness 326n.
ulcer 651n.
kibitzer
meddler 678n.
adviser 691n.
kibosh
absurdity 497n.
kick
reversion 148n.
vigorousness 174n.
be violent 176vb.
kick 279vb.
recoil 280n., vb.
propulsion 287n.
gesture 547n.
be loath 598vb.
oppose 704vb.
strike at 712vb.
resist 715vb.
disobey 738vb.
refuse 760vb.
deprecation 762n.
feeling 818n.
joy 824n.
discontent 829n.
kick back
retaliate 714vb.
kick-off
start 68n.
kick one's heels
be inactive 679vb.
kick out
eject 300vb.
kick over the traces
disobey 738vb.
achieve liberty 746vb.
kickshaw
bauble 639n.
kick the beam
be unequal 29vb.
kick upstairs
improvement 654n.
kid
child 132n.
youngling 132n.
skin 226n.
befool 542vb.
kidder
deceiver 545n.
kidding
deception 542n.
kiddy-cart
pushcart 274n.
kid gloves
cleanness 648n.
lenity 736n.
kidnap
ensnare 542vb.
take away 786vb.
steal 788vb.
kidnapper
taker 786n.
thief 789n.
kidney
sort 77n.
insides 224n.
meat 301n.
kief
drug 658n.
Kilkenny cats
quarreler 709n.
kill
destroy, suppress 165vb.
propulsion 287n.
kill 362vb.
trap 542vb.
success, victory 727n.
prohibit 757vb.
execute 963vb.
killer
killer 362n.
murderer 362n.
combatant 722n.
ruffian 904n.
killick
safeguard 662n.
killing
deadly 362adj.
laborious 682adj.
killjoy
dissuasion 613n.
hinderer 702n.
ascetic 944n.

kill the fatted calf
celebrate 876vb.
be hospitable 882vb.
forgive 909vb.
kill the goose that lays the golden eggs
stultify oneself 695vb.
be prodigal 815vb.
kill time
pass time 108vb.
amuse oneself 837vb.
kill with kindness
pet 889vb.
kiln
furnace 383n.
kilogram
weighment 322n.
kilometer
long measure 203n.
kiloton
weighment 322n.
kilowatt
electricity 160n.
kilt
shorten 204vb.
skirt 228n.
fold 261vb.
kimono
informal dress 228n.
kin
kinsman 11n.
breed 77n.
kind
sort 77n.
form 243n.
aiding 703adj.
amiable 884adj.
benevolent 897adj.
disinterested 931adj.
kindergarten
nonage 130n.
school 539n.
kindheartedness
benevolence 897n.
kind, in
correlatively 12adv.
in exchange 151adv.
kindle
cause 156vb.
invigorate 174vb.
make violent 176vb.
be hot 379vb.
kindle 381vb.
make bright 417vb.
feel 818vb.
excite 821vb.
be excitable 822vb.
get angry 891vb.
kindling
burning 381n.
fuel 385n.
exciting 821adj.
kindly
affectionately 887adv.
benevolent 897adj.
benevolently 897adv.
kindness
lenity 736n.
friendliness 880n.
courtesy 884n
love 887n.
benevolence 897n.
disinterestedness 931n.
kindred
relative 9adj.
consanguinity 11n.
kinsman 11n.
akin 11adj.
kind regards
courteous act 884n.
kine
cattle 365n.
kinematics
motion 265n.
kinesipathy
motion 265n.
kinetic
dynamic 160adj.
kinetics
motion 265n.
king
bigwig 638n.
sovereign 741n.
chessman 837n.
aristocrat 868n.
kingcraft
management 689n.
kingdom
territory 184n.
polity 733n.
kingdom come
future state 124n.
heaven 971n.
Kingdom of God
theocracy 965n.
heaven 971n.
kingfisher
bird of prey 365n.
King Kong
monster 938n.
kingly
ruling 733adj.
impressive 821adj.
worshipful 866adj.
noble 868adj.
proud 871adj.
kingmaker
director 690n.
kingpin
fastening 47n.
bigwig 638n.
kingpost
pillar 218n.
King's Counsel
lawyer 958n.
kingship
government 733n.
magistrature 733n.
king-size
size 195n.
large 195adj.
king's messenger
courier 531n.
kink
coil 251n.
eccentricity 503n.
whim 604n.
defect 647n.
kinless
irrelative 10adj.
defenseless 161adj.
kinsfolk
kinsman 11n.
kinship
relation 9n.
consanguinity 11n.
similarity 18n.
parentage 169n.
kinsman
kinsman 11n.
kiosk
pavilion 192n.
shop 796n.
kip
inn 192n.
brothel 951n.
kip down
sleep 679vb.
repose 683vb.
kipper
fish food 301n.
dry 342vb.
season 388vb.
preserve 666vb.
kirk
church 990n.
kirk session
synod 985n.
kirkyard
church exterior 990n.
kirtle
skirt 228n.
kismet
fate 596n.
kiss
be contiguous 202vb.
touch 378vb.
greet 884vb.
caress 889vb.
kissable
personable 841adj.
kiss and be friends
forgive 909vb.
kiss-curl
hair 259n.
kisser
face 237n.
kiss hands
stoop 311vb.
pay respects 884vb.
kiss of peace

ritual act 988n.
Holy Communion 988n.
kiss the book
swear 532vb.
kiss the rod
knuckle under 721vb.
kist
interment 364n.
payment 804n.
kit
accumulation 74n.
sort 77n.
youngling 132n.
basket 194n.
cat 365n.
viol 414n.
equipment 630n.
kitbag
bag 194n.
kitchen
chamber 194n.
cookery 301n.
heater 383n.
workshop 687n.
kitchener
furnace 383n.
kitchen garden
farm 370n.
kitchen-maid
domestic 742n.
kite
airship 276n.
bird of prey 365n.
cleaner 648n.
false money 797n.
noxious animal 904n.
kite-flying
empiricism 461n.
publication 528n.
kithless
alone 88adj.
defenseless 161adj.
kitten
youngling 132n.
reproduce itself 164vb.
cat 365n.
kittenish
infantine 132adj.
gay 833adj.
amused 837adj.
kitty
store 632n.
joint possession 775n.
kiwi
flightless bird 365n.
klaxon
megaphone 400n.
danger signal 665n.
klepht
robber 789n.
kleptomania
mania 503n.
thievishness 788n.
kleptomaniac
madman 504n.
thieving 788adj.
knack
habit 610n.
contrivance 623n.
aptitude 694n.
knacker
killer 362n.
knackers
gong 414n.
knacker's yard
slaughter-house 362n.
knap
break 46vb.
high land 209n.
knapsack
bag 194n.
knave
low fellow 869n.
ruffian 904n.
knave 938n.
knavery
cunning 698n.
improbity 930n.
wickedness 934n.
knavish
(*see* knavery)
knead
efform 243vb.
soften 327vb.
pulverize 332vb.
rub 333vb.
touch 378vb.
knee
joint 45n.
angularity 247n.
leg 267n.
kick 279vb.
knee action
elasticity 328n.
knee-deep
deep 211adj.
shallow 212adj.
knee-high
infantine 132adj.
dwarfish 196adj.
high 209adj.
kneel
stoop 311vb.
knuckle under 721vb.
be servile 879vb.
pay respects 884vb.
show respect 920vb.
be pious 979vb.
worship 981vb.
perform ritual 988vb.
kneeler
cushion 218n.
seat 218n.
church utensil 990n.
kneel to
entreat 761vb.
knees
seat 218n.
knees, one's
respects 920n.
knell
ruin 165n.
decease 361n.
obsequies 364n.
play music 413vb.
signal 547n.
warning 664n.
raise the alarm 665vb.
lament 836n.
condemnation 961n.
(*see* finality)
Knesset
parliament 692n.
knickerbockers
breeches 228n.
knickers
breeches 228n.
underwear 228n.
knick-knack
bauble 639n.
plaything 837n.
finery 844n.
knife
cut 46vb.
sharp edge 256n.
side-arms 723n.
knife and fork
shovel 274n.
knife-edge
narrowness 206n.
sharp edge 256n.
knife-grinder
mender 656n.
artisan 686n.
knife-thrower
thrower 287n.
knife, use the
doctor 658vb.
knight
rider 268n.
combatant 722n.
cavalry 722n.
chessman 837n.
brave person 855n.
person of repute 866n.
dignify 866vb.
nobleman 868n.
philanthropist 901n.
gentleman 929n.
knightage
aristocracy 868n.
knight-errant
crank 504n.
visionary 513n.
defender 713n.
combatant 722n.
brave person 855n.
philanthropist 901n.
knight-errantry

ideality 513n.
rashness 857n.
disinterestedness 931n.
knighthood
prowess 855n.
honors 866n.
title 870n.
knightly
warlike 718adj.
courageous 855adj.
noble 868adj.
courteous 884adj.
honorable 929adj.
disinterested 931adj.
knight's move
obliquity 220n.
deviation 282n.
knit
tie 45vb.
compose 56vb.
weave 222vb.
close 264vb.
knitting
network 222n.
needlework 844n.
knob
hanger 217n.
handle 218n.
sphere 252n.
swelling 253n.
knobbly
rough 259adj.
knobkerrie
club 723n.
missile weapon 723n.
knobs on, with
crescendo 36adv.
in addition 38adv.
knock
knock 279n.
propulsion 287n.
loudness 400n.
bang 402n.
gesture 547n.
knock-about
dramatic 594adj.
ridiculousness 849n.
knock around
wander 267vb.
knock at the door
arrive 295vb.
request 761vb.
knock down
demolish 165vb.
flatten 216vb.
fell 311vb.
knock-down arguments
confutation 479n.
knock-down price
cheapness 812n.
knock down to
sell 793vb.
knocker
hammer 279n.
signal 547n.
defamer 926n.
detractor 926n.
knock into a cocked hat
be superior 34vb.
knock into the head
educate 534vb.
knock-kneed
crippled 163adj.
oblique 220adj.
deformed 246adj.
angular 247adj.
convergent 293adj.
blemished 845adj.
knock off
cease 145vb.
take 786vb.
steal 788vb.
knock out
render insensible 375vb.
defeat 727vb.
knock-out
end 69n.
ruin 165n.
exceller 644n.
victory 727n.
favorite 890n.
knock up
fatigue 684vb.
knoll
monticle 209n.
knot
tie 45vb.
ligature 47n.
complexity 61n.
crowd, band 74n.
long measure 203n.
cross 222vb.
distortion 246n.
loop 250n.
swelling 253n.
solid body 324n.
garden 370n.
difficulty 700n.
party 708n.
trimming 844n.
knotted
crossed 222adj.
rough 259adj.
dense 324adj.
knotty
dense 324adj.
moot 459adj.
difficult 700adj.
knotty point
question 459n.
unintelligibility 517n.
enigma 530n.
knout
scourge 964n.
know
unite with 45vb.
cognize 447vb.
believe 485vb.
know 490vb.
be wise 498vb.
understand 516vb.
be informed 524vb.
befriend 880vb.
knowable
known 490adj.
intelligible 516adj.
know-all
doctrinaire 473n.
intellectual 492n.
wiseacre 500n.
vain person 873n.
know all the answers
dogmatize 473vb.
know 490vb.
be skillful 694vb.
know-how
intelligence 498n.
way 624n.
means 629n.
skill 694n.
knowing
expert 694adj.
cunning 698adj.
knowingly
knowingly 490adv.
purposely 617adj.
knowledge
knowledge 490n.
information 524n.
skill 694n.
knowledgeable
instructed 490adj.
cunning 698adj.
known
remembered 505adj.
usual 610adj.
renowned 866adj.
known as
named 561adj.
know no better
not know 491vb.
be rude 885vb.
know no bounds
be great 32vb.
know-nothing
ignoramus 493n.
know one's place
conform 83vb.
be modest 874vb.
know what's what
discriminate 463vb.
know 490vb.
be wise 498vb.
be expert 694vb.
knuckle
joint 45n.
angularity 247n.
swelling 253n.
knuckle-duster

hammer 279n.
club 723n.
knuckle under
knuckle under 721vb.
knurl
roughen 259vb.
notch 260vb.
knut
fop 848n.
kobold
elf 970n.
kohl
cosmetic 843n.
Koine
language 557n.
dialect 560n.
kolkhoz
assemblage 74n.
farm 370n.
joint possession 775n.
kopje
monticle 209n.
Koran
non-Biblical scripture 975n.
kosher
edible 301adj.
clean 648adj.
ritual 988adj.
koumiss
milk 301n.
kowtow
obeisance 311n.
submission 721n.
be servile 879vb.
courteous act 884n.
show respect 920vb.
kraal
dwelling 192n.
enclosure 235n.
krait
reptile 365n.
kraken
rara avis 84n.
giant 195n.
Kremlin
magistrature 733n.
kris
sharp edge 256n.
side-arms 723n.
Krishna
Hindu god 767n.
theophany 965n.
the Deity 965n.
kroner
coinage 797n.
Kronos
classical gods 976n.
kudos
approbation 923n.
Ku Klux Klan
society 708n.
rioter 738n.
kukri
sharp edge 256n.
side-arms 723n.
kulak
husbandman 370n.
possessor 776n.
kulakism
sedition 738n.
disobedience 738n.
kultur
civilization 654n.
kursaal
place of amusement 837n.
kyanize
preserve 666vb.
kyles
gulf 345n.
kyphosis
deformity 246n.
curvature 248n.

L

laager
defenses 713n.
fort 713n.
labdanum
resin 357n.
labefy
impair 655vb.
label
adjunct 40n.
label 547n.
labial
marginal 234adj.
spoken letter 558n.
vocal 577adj.
(*see* speech sound)
labiated
marginal 234adj.
labiovelar
speech sound 398n.
labor
repeat oneself 106vb.
obstetrics 164n.
emphasize 532vb.
job 622n.
make important 638vb.
action 676n.
labor 682n.
personnel 686n.
hard task 700n.
bore 838n.
laboratory
workshop 687n.
labor camp
compulsion 740n.
labored
inelegant 576adj.
matured 669adj.
laborious 682adj.
laborer
producer 167n.
worker 686n.
servant 742n.
labor exchange
job 622n.
labor force
personnel 686n.
laboring
in difficulties 700adj.
labor in vain
try impossibilities 470vb.
lost labor 641n.
waste effort 641vb.
stultify oneself 695vb.
fail 728vb.
laborious
persevering 600adj.
industrious 678adj.
laboring 682adj.
laborious 682adj.
fatiguing 684adj.
difficult 700adj.
labor of love
voluntary work 597n.
vocation 622n.
undertaking 672n.
gift 781n.
no charge 812n.
labor-saving
leisurely 681adj.
refreshing 685adj.
wieldy 701adj.
economical 814adj.
labor the obvious
be intelligible 516vb.
be superfluous 637vb.
labor under
be in a state 7vb.
be ill 651vb.
be in difficulty 700vb.
Labourite
political party 708n.
labyrinth
complexity 61n.
meandering 251n.
ear 415n.
enigma 530n.
labyrinthine
difficult 700adj.
lac
resin 357n.
lace
mix 43vb.
tie 45vb.
ligature 47n.
network, textile 222n.
transparency 422n.
needlework 844n.
lacerate
rend 46vb.
give pain 377vb.

wound 655vb.
laches
negligence 458n.
non-observance 769n.
dutilessness 918n.
guilty act 936n.
Lachesis
fate 596n.
mythic god 966n.
classical gods 967n.
lachrymose
melancholic 834adj.
lamenting 836adj.
lack
be inferior 35vb.
deficit 55n.
shortcoming 307n.
requirement 627n.
scarcity 636n.
imperfection 647n.
non-completion 726n.
be poor 801vb.
lackadaisical
inactive 679adj.
inexcitable 823adj.
dejected 834adj.
indifferent 860adj.
lackey
dependent 742n.
domestic 742n.
lacking
absent 190adj.
deficient 307adj.
lost 772adj.
not owning 774adj.
lack-luster
weakly 163adj.
dim 419adj.
colorless 426adj.
dejected 834adj.
lack nothing
be complete 54vb.
laconic
concise 569adj.
taciturn 582adj.
lacquer
facing 226n.
resin 357n.
color 425n.
hairwash 843n.
decorate 844vb.
lacrimatory gas
poison 659n.
weapon 723n.
lacrosse
ball game 837n.
lactescence
semitransparency 424n.
whiteness 427n.
lactescent
semiliquid 354adj.
lactic
edible 301adj.
lactose
food content 301n.
lacuna
interval 201n.
concavity 255n.
opening 263n.
lacustrine
lacustrine 346adj.
lad
youngster 132n.
fop 848n.
ladder
disjunction 46n.
bond 47n.
series 71n.
discontinuity 72n.
ascent 308n.
access 624n.
means of escape 667n.
laddering
separation 46n.
lade
fill 54vb.
stow 187vb.
load 193vb.
laden
full 54adj.
ladies' man
lover 887n.
lading
location 187n.
contents 193n.
gravity 322n.
property 777n.
ladle
ladle 194n.
transpose 272vb.
lady
lady 373n.
master 741n.
spouse 894n.
Lady Bountiful
giver 781n.
good giver 813n.
benefactor 903n.
lady in waiting
retainer 742n.
lady-killer
lover 887n.
libertine 952n.
ladylike
female 373adj.
well-bred 848adj.
noble 868adj.
lady-love
loved one 887n.
ladyship
lady 373n.
title 870n.
lag
be inferior 35vb.
be late 136vb.
be behind 238vb.
slowness 278n.
follow 284vb.
fall short 307vb.
be inactive 679vb.
offender 904n.
lager
liquor 301n.
laggard
lateness 136n.
lazy 679adj.
lagoon
gulf 345n.
lake 346n.
laic
layman 987n.
laical 987adj.
laicality
laicality 987n.
laid
born 360adj.
laid paper
stationery 586n.
laid up
sick 651adj.
disused 674adj.
lair
dwelling 192n.
hiding-place 527n.
refuge 662n.
laird
master 741n.
aristocrat 868n.
laisse
verse form 593n.
laisser aller
not act 677vb.
be lax 734vb.
give scope 744vb.
laisser faire
permanence 144n.
sustain 146vb.
negligence 458n.
not act 677vb.
be lax 734vb.
freedom 744n.
laity
laity 987n.
lake
lake 346n.
lake-dwelling
dwelling 192n.
lacustrine 346adj.
lakh
over one hundred 99n.
Lallans
dialect 560n.
lallation
solecism 565n.
pronunciation 577n.
speech defect 580n.
lama
priest 986n.
Lamarckism
biology 358n.
lamasery

monastery 986n.
lamb
youngling 132n.
reproduce itself 164vb.
sheep 365n.
ingenue 699n.
darling 890n.
innocent 935n.
lambdacism
solecism 556n.
speech defect 580n.
lambent
tactual 378adj.
luminous 417adj.
lamblike
inexcitable 823adj.
innocent 935adj.
lambskin
skin 226n.
lame
incomplete 55adj.
disable 161vb.
crippled 163adj.
make useless 641vb.
imperfect 647adj.
impair 655vb.
unskillful 695adj.
hinder 702vb.
lame and impotent conclusion
sophism 477n.
failure 728n.
lame dog
weakling 163n.
unlucky person 731n.
lame duck
weakling 163n.
unlucky person 731n.
non-payer 805n.
lamellar
layered 201adj.
lament
suffer 825vb.
be discontented 829vb.
regret 830vb.
lament 836n., vb.
pity 905vb.
disapprove 924vb.
be penitent 939vb.
lamentable
bad 645adj.
distressing 827adj.
lamentation
obsequies 364n.
lamentation 836n.
penance 941n.
lamented
dead 361adj.
lamia
demon 970n.
sorceress 983n.
lamina
piece 53n.
lamina 207n.
laminable
layered 207adj.
brittle 330adj.
lamination
stratification 207n.
structure 331n.
Lammas
holy-day 988n.
lammergeier
bird of prey 365n.
lamp
lamp 420n.
guide 520n.
signal 547n.
lampadist
contender 716n.
lampadophoria
racing 716n.
lampblack
ash 381n.
black pigment 428n.
lamplighter
lamp 420n.
lampoon
poetize 593vb.
satire 851n.
calumny 926n.
lampooner
humorist 839n.
disapprover 924n.
lamppost
high structure 209n.
tall creature 209n.
stand 218n.
lamp shade
screen 421n.
lampyrine
glow-worm 420n.
luminescent 420adj.
lanate
smooth 258adj.
downy 259adj.
lance
sharp point 256n.
pierce 263vb.
strike at 712vb.
spear 723n.
lance-corporal
army officer 741n.
lanceolate
tapering 256adj.
lancer
soldiery 722n.
cavalry 722n.
lancet
sharp point 256n.
perforator 263n.
lancination
pain 377n.
land
region 184n.
voyage 269vb.
fly 271vb.
aim 281vb.
approach 289vb.
land 295vb.
admit 299vb.
land 344n.
lands 777n.
take 786vb.
landamman
officer 741n.
landau
carriage 274n.
landaulet
automobile 274n.
carriage 274n.
land-bridge
narrowness 206n.
bridge 624n.
landed
territorial 344adj.
proprietary 777adj.
landes
plain 348n.
landfall
arrival 295n.
landholder
owner 776n.
landing
layer 207n.
vertex 213n.
stand 218n.
arrival 295n.
ascent 308n.
descent 309n.
landing-craft
warship 722n.
landing ground
air travel 271n.
arena 724n.
landlady
owner 776n.
land lies, see how the
be tentative 461vb.
land-locked
circumscribed 232adj.
lacustrine 346adj.
landloper
wanderer 268n.
landlord
caterer 633n.
owner 776n.
landlubber
dweller 191n.
mariner 270n.
landmark
spectacle 445n.
signpost 547n.
land-mass
region 184n.
land-mine
bomb 723n.
land on one's feet
be safe 660vb.
landowner
owner 776n.

lands
farm 370n.
lands 777n.
landscape
open space 263n.
spectacle 445n.
art subject 553n.
beauty 841n.
landslide
revolution 149n.
ruin 165n.
acclivity 220n.
descent 309n.
defeat 728n.
landslip
revolution 149n.
landsman
dweller 191n.
land 344n.
lane
street 192n.
route, path 624n.
langouste
fish food 301n.
table fish 365n.
language
language 557n.
dialect 560n.
speech 579n.
languid
feeble 572adj.
(*see* languish, languor)
languish
decrease 37vb.
be weak 163vb.
be ill 651vb.
be inactive 679vb.
be fatigued 684vb.
be dejected 834vb.
be affected 850vb.
court 889vb.
languish for
desire 859vb.
languor
weakness 163n.
inertness 175n.
slowness 278n.
sluggishness 679n.
fatigue 684n.
laniate
wound 655vb.
lank
long 203adj.
lanky
long 203adj.
narrow 206adj.
tall 209adj.
lanolin
unguent 357n.
balm 658n.
cosmetic 843n.
lantern
lamp 420n.
lantern-jawed
lean 206adj.
lanuginous
downy 259adj.
lanyard
cable 47n.
Laodicean
moderate 625n.
apathetic 820adj.
indifferent 860adj.
lap
part 53n.
period 110n.
periodicity 141n.
seat 218n.
dress 228vb.
surround 230vb.
enclose 235vb.
move fast, outstrip 277vb.
drink 301vb.
outdo 306vb.
circuition 314n.
moisten 341vb.
flow 350vb.
sound faint 401vb.
circuit 626n., vb.
refuge 662n.
pet 889vb.
laparotomy
surgery 658n.
lapdog
dog 365n.
lapel
adjunct 40n.
fold 261n.
trimming 844n.
lapidary
funereal 364adj.
engraver 556n.
lapidate
strike 279vb.
kill 362vb.
lapidate 712vb.
not respect 921vb.
execute 963vb.
lapidescence
hardening 326n.
lapis lazuli
blueness 435n.
gem 844n.
lap of luxury
euphoria 376n.
sensualism 944n.
lappet
adjunct 40n.
pendant 217n.
canonicals 989n.
lapse
time 108n.
elapse 111vb.
conversion 147n.
deviation 282n.
descent 309n.
deteriorate 655vb.
relapse 657n., vb.
loss 772n.
be wicked 934vb.
guilty act 936n.
irreligion 974n.
lapsed
past 125adj.
unbelieving 486adj.
irreligious 974adj.
lapse of memory
oblivion 506n.
lapse of time
course of time 111n.
lapsus calami
mistake 495n.
solecism 565n.
lapsus linguae
mistake 495n.
solecism 565n.
lap up
absorb 299vb.
drink 301vb.
appetize 390vb.
larboard
sinistrality 242n.
larceny
stealing 788n.
larch
tree 366n.
lard
meat 301n.
cook 301vb.
fat 357n.
larder
chamber 194n.
provisions 301n.
storage 632n.
larding
beautification 843n.
Lares and Penates
home 192n.
idol 982n.
large
substantial 3adj.
great 32adj.
extensive 183adj.
large 195adj.
large, at
diffusely 570adv.
escaped 667adj.
free 744adj.
large-hearted
liberal 813adj.
benevolent 897adj.
large-scale
large 195adj.
largess
gift 781n.
liberality 813n.
larghetto
slowly 278adv.
adagio 412adv.
largo

slowly 278adv.
adagio 412adv.
lariat
halter 47n.
loop 250n.
lark
climber 308n.
bird 365n.
vocalist 413n.
enjoyment 824n.
revel 837n.
larrikin
ruffian 904n.
larrup
spank 963vb.
larva
youngling 132n.
laryngitis
respiratory disease 651n.
larynx
air-pipe 353n.
voice 577n.
lascar
mariner 270n.
lasciviousness
unchastity 951n.
lash
tie 45vb.
stimulant 174n.
make violent 176vb.
filament 208n.
incite 612vb.
animate 821vb.
exprobate 924vb.
flog 963vb.
scourge 964n.
lasher
ligature 47n.
lashes
eye 438n.
lashings
great quantity 32n.
plenty 635n.
lash out
be violent 176vb.
lass
youngster 132n.
woman 373n.
lassitude
sleepiness 679n.
fatigue 684n.
lasso
halter 47n.
loop 250n.
missile weapon 723n.
last
mold 23n.
ending 69adj.
continue 108vb.
foregoing 125adj.
stay 144vb.
completive 725adj.
last breath
end 69n.
decease 361n.
last ditcher
stamina 600n.
opinionist 602n.
opponent 705n.
malcontent 829n.
lasting
lasting 113adj.
perpetual 115adj.
unchangeable 153adj.
unyielding 162adj.
last lap
end 69n.
arrival 295n.
last legs, on one's
weakened 163adj.
dying 361adj.
dilapidated 655adj.
unprosperous 731adj.
last man in
aftercomer 67n.
last minute
lateness 136n.
crisis 137n.
last-minute
hasty 680adj.
last place
inferiority 35n.
rear 238n.
last post
evening 129n.
valediction 296n.
obsequies 364n.
call 547n.
last resort
necessity 596n.
means 629n.
refuge 662n.
last rites
obsequies 364n.
Christian rite 988n.
last straw
redundance 637n.
encumbrance 702n.
completion 725n.
annoyance 827n.
last things
finality 69n.
last touch
completeness 54n.
completion 725n.
last word
modernism 126n.
answer 460n.
certainty 473n.
fashion 848n.
last words
sequel 67n.
end 69n.
valediction 296n.
latch
join 45vb.
fastening 47n.
latchet
ligature 47n.
late
anachronistic 118adj.
former 125adj.
modern 126adj.
vespertine 129adj.
late 136adj., adv.
ill-timed 138adj.
slow 278adj.
dead 361adj.
negligent 458adj.
unprepared 670adj.
immature 670adj.
late-comer
aftercomer 67n.
posteriority 120n.
lateness 136n.
lateen sail
sail 275n.
latency
inertness 175n.
influence 178n.
invisibility 444n.
latency 523n.
seclusion 883n.
lateness
evening 129n.
lateness 136n.
latent
deceiving 542adj.
(*see* latency)
later
after 65adv.
subsequent 120adj.
not now 122adj.
future 124adj.
behind 284adj.
laterality
laterality 239n.
lateritious
red 431adj.
latest
present 121adj.
latest, the
modernism 126n.
fashion 848n.
lath
lamina 207n.
strip 208n.
materials 631n.
lathe
district 184n.
rotator 315n.
lather
lubricant 334n.
bubble 355n.
clean 648vb.
lathery
white 427adj.
lathi
club 723n.
Latin
language 557n.

Latinist
linguist 557n.
latitancy
concealment 525n.
latitude
range 183n.
region 184n.
breadth 205n.
scope 744n.
latitude and longitude
bearings 186n.
co-ordinate 465n.
latitudinarian
wise 498adj.
free man 744adj.
latitudinarianism
heterodoxy 977n.
latitudinarians
church party 978n.
latration
ululation 409n.
latria
cult 981n.
latrine
fetor 397n.
latrine 649n.
latrociny
stealing 788n.
latten
lamina 207n.
latter
sequent 65adj.
foregoing 125adj.
latter-day
modern 126adj.
latter end
end 69n.
future state 124n.
latterly
newly 126adv.
lattice
space 201vb.
network 222n.
window 263n.
laud
praise 923vb.
worship 981vb.
laudable
approvable 923adj.
laudanum
moderator 177n.
anesthetic 375n.
laudation
praise 923n.
act of worship 981n.
laudator temporis acti
malcontent 829n.
regret 830n.
laudatory
approving 923adj.
Laudianism
Catholicism 976n.
lauds
church service 988n.
laugh
be pleased 824vb.
be cheerful 833vb.
laughter 835n.
ridicule 851n.
hold cheap 922vb.
laughable
absurd 497adj.
foolish 499adj.
amusing 837adj.
ridiculous 849adj.
laugher
laugher 835n.
laughing gas
gas 336n.
anesthetic 375n.
laughing matter
laughter 835n.
laughing-stock
nonconformist 84n.
fool 501n.
laughing-stock 851n.
laugh off
not think 450vb.
laughter
merriment 833n.
laughter 835n.
festivity 837n.
ridicule 851n.
laughter-loving
gay 833adj.
laugh to scorn
defy 711vb.
despise 922vb.
launch
initiate 68vb.
navigate 269vb.
ship, boat 275n.
propel 287vb.
launched
beginning 68adj.
launching
fitting out 669n.
launch into
undertake 672vb.
launch out
be diffuse 570vb.
be loquacious 581vb.
launch out at
attack 712vb.
launder
smooth 258vb.
clean 648vb.
laundress
cleaner 648n.
laundry
chamber 194n.
ablution 648n.
workshop 687n.
laurels
badge 547n.
trophy 729n.
honors 866n.
lava
rock 344n.
ash 381n.
lavation
ablution 648n.
lavatory
chamber 194n.
ablution 648n.
latrine 649n.
lave
drench 341vb.
purify 648vb.
lavender
purple 434n.
scent 396n.
prophylactic 658n.
preserver 666n.
laver
bowl 194n.
ritual object 988n.
lavish
many 104adj.
plenteous 635adj.
superabound 637vb.
give 781vb.
expend 806vb.
liberal 813adj.
prodigal 815adj.
law
rule 81n.
necessity 596n.
habit 610n.
vocation 622n.
precept 693n.
decree 737n.
compulsion 740n.
restraint 747n.
permit 756n.
law 953n.
punisher 963n.
law-abiding
peaceful 717adj.
submitting 721adj.
obedient 739adj.
honorable 929adj.
legal 953adj.
law agent
law agent 958n.
Law and the Prophets, the
scripture 975n.
law, at
in litigation 959adv.
lawbreaker
offender 904n.
impious person 980n.
lawbreaking
riotous 738adj.
non-observant 769adj.
improbity 930n.
heinous 934adj.
lawbreaking 954n., adj.
law, by
duly 915adv.

legally 953adv.
law-court
law-court 956n.
lawful
due 915adj.
legal 953adj.
law-giver
director 690n.
legislation 953n.
lawless
disorderly 61adj.
unconformable 84adj.
anarchic 734adj.
riotous 738adj.
rascally 930adj.
lawless 954adj.
law-maker
director 690n.
law-making
management 689n.
legislation 953n.
lawn
smoothness 258n.
textile 222n.
grassland 348n.
garden 370n.
lawn sleeves
canonicals 989n.
law officer
law officer 955n.
laws
polity 733n.
Laws of the Medes and Persians
permanence 144n.
fixture 153n.
precept 693n.
lawsuit
litigation 959n.
law to oneself, a
unconformable 84adj.
law to oneself, be a
please oneself 734vb.
disobey 738vb.
be insolent 878vb.
lawyer
reasoner 475n.
adviser 691n.
lawyer 958n.
lax
weak 163adj.
feeble 572adj.
frail 934adj.
(*see* laxity)
laxative
cathartic 658n.
laxity
non-coherence 49n.
softness 327n.
negligence 458n.
inexactness 495n.
irresolution 601n.
laxity 734n.
lenity 736n.
non-observance 769n.
indifference 860n.
improbity 930n.
wickedness 934n.
intemperance 943n.
lay
reproduce itself 164vb.
assuage 177vb.
place 187vb.
laminate 207vb.
cover 266vb.
emit 300vb.
vocal music 412n.
ignorant 491n.
gamble 618vb.
unskilled 695adj.
laical 987adj.
lay aboard
irrupt 297vb.
attack 712vb.
lay about one
strike at 712vb.
fight 716vb.
lay aside
exclude 57vb.
be neglectful 458vb.
reject 607vb.
disuse 674vb.
lay at one's feet
offer 759vb.
lay at the door of
attribute 158vb.
accuse 928vb.
lay bare
disclose 526vb.
lay brother
monk 986n.
layman 987n.
lay-by
station 187n.
stable 192n.
lay by
store 632vb.
lay by the heels
arrest 747vb.
lay down
place 187vb.
flatten 216vb.
let fall 311vb.
premise 475vb.
suppose 512vb.
lay down one's office
resign 753vb.
lay down the law
dogmatize 473vb.
affirm 532vb.
rule 733vb.
decree 737vb.
layer
compartment 194n.
layer 207n.
gambler 618n.
layette
clothing 228n.
lay figure
insubstantial thing 4n.
mold 23n.
image 551n.
lay ghosts
practice sorcery 983vb.
lay hands upon
take 786vb.
lay heads together
combine 50vb.
cooperate 706vb.
lay in
eat 301vb.
store 632vb.
lay low
fell 311vb.
strike at 712vb.
layman
ignorance 491n.
bungler 697n.
layman 987n.
lay off
dismiss 300vb.
disuse 674vb.
make inactive 679vb.
not retain 779vb.
lay on
add 38vb.
fight 716vb.
lay oneself open
be liable 180vb.
face danger 661vb.
lay on hands
perform ritual 988vb.
lay open
uncover 229vb.
open 263vb.
manifest 522vb.
disclose 526vb.
lay out
flatten 216vb.
inter 364vb.
plan 623vb.
expend 806vb.
layout
arrangement 62n.
edition 589n.
lay preacher
preacher 537n.
pastor 986n.
church officer 986n.
layman 987n.
lays
poem 593n.
laystall
sink 649n.
lay the dust
clean 648vb.
lay the foundation
auspicate 68vb.
cause 156vb.

prepare 669vb.
lay to
bring to rest 266vb.
navigate 269vb.
lay under contribution
levy 786vb.
claim 915vb.
lay up
store 632vb.
make useless 641vb.
disuse 674vb.
make inactive 679vb.
lay upon
command 737vb.
lay waste
lay waste 165vb.
sterilize 172vb.
lazaret, lazaretto
compartment 194n.
hospital 658n.
laze
move slowly 278vb.
be inactive 679vb.
laziness
negligence 458n.
unwillingness 598n.
sluggishness 679n.
dutilessness 918n.
lazy
(*see* laziness)
lazybones
idler 679n.
lea
shore 344n.
grassland 348n.
leach
liquefy 337vb.
drench 341vb.
purify 648vb.
leachy
porous 263adj.
lead
vantage 34n.
halter 47n.
come before 64vb.
prelude 66n.
initiate 68vb.
accompany 89vb.
do before 119vb.
prevail 178vb.
space 201n.
depth 211n.
sailing aid 269n.
precede 283vb.
diver 313n.
gravity 322n.
gauge 465n.
hint 524n.
print-type 578n.
actor 594n.
motivate 612vb.
provide 633vb.
direct 689vb.
leaded
spaced 201adj.
printed 587adj.
leaden
weighty 322adj.
dim 419adj.
colorless 426adj.
gray 429adj.
inactive 679adj.
tedious 838adj.
leader
superior 34n.
precursor 66n.
article 591n.
motivator 612n.
leader 690n.
master 741n.
leadership
superiority 34n.
precedence 64n.
directorship 689n.
authority 733n.
prestige 866n.
leader-writer
dissertator 591n.
lead evidence
corroborate 466vb.
leading
first 68adj.
influential 178adj.
foremost 283adj.
important 638adj.
directing 689adj.
successful 727adj.
authoritative 733adj.
noteworthy 866adj.
leading article
article 591n.
leading case
precept 693n.
leading light
sage 500n.
bigwig 638n.
person of repute 866n.
leading strings
nonage 130n.
teaching 534n.
subjection 745n.
fetter 748n.
lead, on a
restrained 747adj.
lead one a dance
mislead 495vb.
avoid 620vb.
circuit 626vb.
be difficult 700vb.
lead one's life
behave 688vb.
leads
vertex 213n.
roof 226n.
leadsman
navigator 270n.
lead the dance
influence 178vb.
precede 283vb.
lead to
conduce 156vb.
tend 179vb.
lead up the garden path
deceive 542vb.
lead up to
prepare 669vb.
leaf
adjunct 40n.
lamina 207n.
shelf 218n.
foliage 366n.
edition 589n.
leafless
uncovered 229adj.
leaflet
the press 528n.
league
combination 50n.
concurrence 181n.
long measure 203n.
association 706n.
society 708n.
concord 710n.
compact 765n.
League of Nations
council 692n.
leaguer
attack 712n.
leak
decrement 42n.
gap 201n.
opening 263n.
outflow 298n.
be wet 341vb.
flow 350vb.
disclosure 526n.
waste 634vb.
defect 647n.
be imperfect 647vb.
escape 667vb.
hitch 702n.
non-retention 779n.
leakage
decrease 37n.
loss 772n.
(*see* leak)
leak into
infiltrate 297vb.
leak out
be disclosed 526vb.
leak through
exude 298vb.
leaky
porous 263adj.
disclosing 526adj.
unsafe 661adj.
lean
small 33adj.
weak 163adj.
tend 179vb.
lean 206adj.
be oblique 220vb.

be biased 481vb.
choose 605vb.
underfed 636adj.
desire 859vb.
lean forward
stoop 311vb.
leaning
unequal 29adj.
willingness 597n.
choice 605n.
habit 610n.
liking 859n.
injustice 914n.
leanness
scarcity 636n.
lean on
be supported 218vb.
be subject 745vb.
lean over backward
stoop 311vb.
be willing 597vb.
lean-to
small house 192n.
leap
spurt 277n.
move fast 277vb.
progression 285n.
ascent 308n.
leap 312n., vb.
be agitated 318vb.
flow 350adj.
rejoice 835vb.
dance 837vb.
leap at
pursue 619vb.
leapfrog
overstepping 306n.
fluctuate 317vb.
children's games 837n.
leap in the dark
uncertainty 474n.
gambling 618n.
danger 661n.
rashness 857n.
leaps and bounds
progression 285n.
leap year
regular return 141n.
learn
know 490vb.
memorize 505vb.
understand 516vb.
be informed 524vb.
learn 536vb.
prepare oneself 669vb.
learned
instructed 490adj.
studious 536adj.
literary 557adj.
learner
scholar 492n.
learner 538n.
learning
knowledge 490n.
learning 536n.
preparation 669n.
learn one's lesson
be penitent 939vb.
lease
estate 777n.
transfer 780n.
lease 784vb.
hire 785vb.
leasehold
proprietary 777adj.
lease-holder
resident 191n.
possessor 776n.
leash
halter 47n.
group 74n.
three 93n.
least
small 33adj.
lesser 35adj.
least one can do
dueness 915n.
leather
skin 226n.
strike 279vb.
toughness 329n.
bookbinding 589n.
materials 631n.
cleaning cloth 648n.
spank 963vb.
leatherneck
navy man 722n.
leathery
tough 329adj.
unsavory 391adj.
leave
be disjoined 46vb.
cease 145vb.
recede 290vb.
depart 296vb.
relinquish 621vb.
store 632vb.
leisure 681n.
repose 683n.
facility 701n.
lenity 736n.
permission 756n.
bequeath 780vb.
non-liability 919n.
leave a gap
be absent 190vb.
not suffice 636vb.
leave alone
not act 677vb.
leave behind
be superior 34vb.
outstrip 277vb.
progress 285vb.
outdo 306vb.
leave hanging
not complete 726vb.
leave hold
relinquish 621vb.
not retain 779vb.
leave in the lurch
disregard 458vb.
befool 542vb.
fail in duty 918vb.
leave it open
facilitate 701vb.
leaven
component 58n.
alterer 143n.
convert 147vb.
influence 178n., vb.
enlarge 197vb.
cookery 301n.
lifter 310n.
leaven 323n.
qualify 468vb.
make better 654vb.
leave no corner
fill 54vb.
leave off
cease 145vb.
disuse 674vb.
leave out
subtract 39vb.
set apart 46vb.
exclude 57vb.
misinterpret 521vb.
be taciturn 582vb.
leave-taking
valediction 296n.
leave word
communicate 524vb.
leavings
leavings 41n.
lebensraum
room 183n.
scope 744n.
lecher
libertine 952n.
lechery
unchastity 951n.
lectern
rostrum 539n.
church utensil 990n.
lection
interpretation 520n.
oration 579n.
lectionary
office-book 988n.
lector
cleric 986n.
lecture
lecture 534n.
oration 579n.
allocution 583n.
dissertation 591n.
reprimand 924n.
lecture-hall
classroom 539n.
conference 584n.
lecturer

teacher 537n.
speaker 579n.
academic title 870n.
pastor 986n.
led-captain
dependent 742n.
toady 879n.
ledge
high land 209n.
horizontality 216n.
shelf 218n.
edge 234n.
projection 254n.
ledger
covering 226n.
record 548n.
account book 808n.
lee
laterality 239n.
shelter 662n.
leech
doctor 658n., vb.
bane 659n.
taker 786n.
toady 879n.
leechcraft
medical art 658n.
leek
vegetable 301n.
green 432adj.
heraldry 547n.
leer
look 438n.
gesture 547n.
excite love 887vb.
court 889vb.
lees
leavings 41n.
rubbish 641n.
dirt 649n.
lee shore
pitfall 663n.
leeward
laterality 239n.
leeway
room 183n.
water travel 269n.
deviation 282n.
shortcoming 307n.
scope 744n.
leeway, make up
recoup 31vb.
left
remaining 41adj.
sinistrality 242n.
forgotten 506adj.
political party 708n.
left, be
be left 41vb.
inherit 771vb.
left-handed
sinistral 242adj.
handed 378adj.
clumsy 695adj.
leftish
moderate 177adj.
leftist
political party 708n.
sectional 708adj.
leftovers
leavings 41n.
left wing
sinistrality 242n.
sectional 708adj.
leg
limb 53n.
stand 218n.
leg 267n.
legacy
sequel 67n.
thing transferred 272n.
dower 777n.
gift 781n.
receipt 807n.
legal
possible 469adj.
preceptive 693adj.
just 913adj.
legal 953adj.
legal adviser
adviser 691n.
law agent, jurist 958n.
legal code
law 953n.
legalist
narrow mind 481n.
jurist 958n.
legalize
permit 756vb.
grant claims 915vb.
make legal 953vb.
legal profession
bar 958n.
legal separation
divorce 896n.
legatary
beneficiary 776n.
recipient 782n.
legate
messenger 531n.
army officer 741n.
envoy 754n.
legatee
beneficiary 776n.
recipient 782n.
legation
commission 751n.
envoy 754n.
legend
commentary 520n.
indication 547n.
record 548n.
phrase 563n.
description 590n.
narrative 590n.
(*see* fable)
legendary
imaginary 513adj.
descriptive 590adj.
legerdemain
sleight 542n.
leggings
legwear 228n.
leggy
crural 267adj.
leghorn
headgear 228n.
legibility
intelligibility 516n.
legion
multitude 104n.
army 722n.
legionary
soldier 722n.
legislate
rule 733vb.
decree 737vb.
make legal 953vb.
legislation
management 689n.
precept 693n.
legislation 953n.
legislative
directing 689adj.
legal 953adj.
legislative assembly
parliament 692n.
legislator
director 690n.
councillor 692n.
legislature
legislation 953n.
legist
jurist 958n.
legitimacy
authority 733n.
legality 953n.
legitimate
genuine 494adj.
dramatic 594adj.
just 913adj.
due 915adj.
legal 953adj.
legitimist
auxiliary 707n.
defender 713n.
legitimize
grant claims 915vb.
make legal 953vb.
leg-pull
trickery 542n.
ridicule 851n.
leg-puller
humorist 839n.
legs
conveyance 267n.
leg-show
stage show 594n.
leg to stand on

pretext 614n.
leguminous
vegetal 366adj.
leg-up
progression 285n.
elevation 310n.
aid 703n.
leiotrichous
smooth 258adj.
leisure
opportunity 137n.
leisure 681n.
repose 683n.
resignation 753n.
amusement 837n.
leisured
free 744adj.
leisurely
tardily 136adv.
tranquil 266adj.
slow 278adj.
inactive 679adj.
leisurely 681adj.
reposeful 683adj.
leitmotiv
melody 410n.
musical piece 412n.
topic 452n.
leman
loved one 887n.
kept woman 952n.
lemma
argumentation 475n.
premise 475n.
lemon
sourness 393n.
yellowness 433n.
lemonade
soft drink 301n.
lemures
ghost 970n.
lemurine
animal 365adj.
lend
provide 633vb.
convey 780vb.
give 781vb.
lend 784vb.
credit 802vb.
lend a hand
aid 703vb.
lend color to
make likely 471vb.
lend ear
hear 415vb.
be mindful 455vb.
be willing 597vb.
lender
creditor 802n.
lend-lease
provision 633n.
length
quantity 26n.
greatness 32n.
piece 53n.
measure 183n.
size 195n.
distance 199n.
interval 201n.
length 203n.
textile 222n.
diffuseness 570n.
length and breadth
all 52n.
lengthen
augment 36vb.
continuate 71vb.
spin out 113vb.
enlarge 197vb.
lengthen 203vb.
be diffuse 570vb.
lengthy
great 32adj.
long 203adj.
prolix 570adj.
lenient
moderate 177adj.
lax 734adj.
lenient 736adj.
benevolent 897adj.
lenify
make better 654vb.
assuage 177vb.
Leninism
government 733n.
lenitive
moderator 177n.
lenitive 177adj.
lubricant 334n.
balm 658n.
pacificatory 719adj.
relieving 831adj.
lenity
softness 327n.
(*see* lenient)
lens
convexity 253n.
transparency 422n.
optical device 442n.
Lent
anniversary 141n.
fast 946n.
holy-day 988n.
lenticular
curved 248adj.
convex 253adj.
lentigo
blemish 845n.
lentil
vegetable 301n.
plant 366n.
lentor
slowness 278n.
semiliquidity 354n.
sluggishness 679n.
lentous
viscid 354adj.
leonine
animal 365adj.
beautiful 841adj.
leopard
cat 365n.
maculation 437n.
leopard's spots
fixture 153n.
leotard
tunic 228n.
leper
dirty person 649n.
outcaste 883n.
leprechaun
elf 970n.
leprosy
skin disease 651n.
leprous
unclean 649adj.
lesbianism
abnormality 84n.
illicit love 951n.
lese majesty
sedition 738n.
lesion
wound 655n.
less
less 35adv.
less and less
diminuendo 37adv.
lessee
resident 191n.
possessor 776n.
recipient 782n.
purchaser 792n.
lessen
bate 37vb.
weaken 163vb.
moderate 177vb.
become small 198vb.
lesson
lecture 534n.
study 536n.
warning 664n.
lessor
lender 784n.
let
obstacle 702n.
give scope 44vb.
permit 756vb.
lending 784n.
lease 784vb.
let alone
in addition 38n.
exclusive of 57adv.
avoid 620vb.
not act 677vb.
give scope 744vb.
let blood
void 300vb.
doctor 658vb.
let down

depress 311vb.
disappoint 509vb.
befool 542vb.
humbled 872adj.
let fall
let fall 311vb.
hint 524vb.
divulge 526vb.
let fly
be violent 176vb.
shoot 287vb.
fire at 712vb.
let go
relinquish 621vb.
liberate 746vb.
not retain 779vb.
be indifferent 860vb.
acquit 960vb.
lethal
deadly 362adj.
lethal chamber
means of execution 964n.
lethargy
sluggishness 679n.
moral insensibility 820n.
Lethe
oblivion 506n.
mythic hell 972n.
lethiferous
deadly 362adj.
let in
intromit 231vb.
admit 299vb.
befool 542vb.
let off
be violent 176vb.
shoot 287vb.
acquit 960vb.
let-off
deliverance 668n.
mercy 905n.
acquittal 960n.
let oneself go
please oneself 734vb.
let out
enlarge 197vb.
lengthen 203vb.
emit 300vb.
lease 784vb.
let slip
be neglectful 458vb.
liberate 746vb.
lose 772vb.
letter
message 529n.
indication 547n.
letter 558n., vb.
script 586n.
print-type 587n.
correspondence 588n.
letter-bag
mails 531n.
letter-box
mails 531n.
correspondence 588n.
lettered
instructed 490adj.
literary 557adj.
literal 558adj.
lettering
lettering 586n.
letterpress 587n.
letter of credit
paper money 797n.
credit 802n.
letter of the law
accuracy 494n.
severity 735n.
pitilessness 906n.
legality 953n.
letterpress
letter 558n.
letterpress 587n.
letters
erudition 490n.
literature 557n.
lettering 586n.
correspondence 588n.
letters of fire
publicity 528n.
letters of gold
publicity 528n.
praise 923n.
letters of marque
brigandage 788n.
letters patent
warrant 737n.
permit 756n.
letter-writer
penman 586n.
correspondent 588n.
lettre de cachet
detention 747n.
lettuce
vegetable 301n.
let up
cease 145vb.
let well alone
be cautious 858vb.
leucoderma
whiteness 427n.
skin disease 651n.
blemish 845n.
leucorrhea
hemorrhage 302n.
leucous
white 427adj.
levant
run away 620vb.
defraud 788vb.
not pay 805vb.
levee
assembly 74n.
social gathering 882n.
level
uniformity 16n.
degree 27n.
equality 28n.
serial place 73n.
synchronous 123adj.
demolish 165vb.
near 200adj.
layer 207n.
horizontality 216adj.
angular measure 247n.
smooth 258adj., vb.
aim 281vb.
fell 311vb.
fire at 712vb.
inexcitable 823adj.
level at
aim 281vb.
level crossing
railroad 624n.
level-headedness
sagacity 498n.
caution 858n.
leveler
uniformist 16n.
destroyer 168n.
levelness
uniformity 16n.
lowness 210n.
smoothness 258n.
level off
become small 198vb.
level-pegging
draw 28n.
lever
opportunity 137n.
causal means 156n.
influence 178n.
handle, pivot 218n.
propellant 287n.
extractor 304n.
lifter 310n.
instrument 628n.
tool 630n.
leverage
influence 178n.
tool 630n.
scope 744n.
leveret
vermin 365n.
leviable
priced 809adj.
Leviathan
giant 195n.
fish 365n.
levigate
smooth 258vb.
pulverize 332vb.
rub 333vb.
levin
flash 417n.
luminary 420n.
levirate

type of marriage 894n.
levitation
elevation 310n.
levity 323n.
Levite
priest 986n.
levity
insubstantiality 4n.
levity 323n.
folly 499n.
irresolution 601n.
whim 604n.
merriment 833n.
rashness 857n.
levogyrate
sinistral 242adj.
levy
assemblage 74n.
armed force 722n.
request 671vb.
demand 737n., vb.
acquire 771vb.
levy 786vb.
tax 809n.
claim 915vb.
levy en masse
army 722n.
lewd
impure 951adj.
lecherous 951adj.
lexical
verbal 559adj.
lexicographer
collector 492n.
linguist 557n.
etymology 559n.
lexicographical
linguistic 557adj.
verbal 559adj.
lexicology
etymology 559n.
lexicon
word list 87n.
commentary 520n.
dictionary 559n.
reference book 589n.
indoor game 837n.
lexigraphy
spelling 558n.
word 559n.
writing 586n.
liability
tendency 179n.
liability 180n.
probability 471n.
bias 481n.
vulnerability 661n.
duty 917n.
guilt 936n.
penalty 963n.
liable
subject 745adj.
(*see* liability)
liaison
relation 9n.
bond 47n.
concurrence 181n.
love affair 887n.
illicit love 951n.
liar
liar 545n.
boaster 877n.
knave 938n.
libation(s)
drinking 301n.
drunkenness 949n.
oblation 981n.
libel
calumny 926n.
false charge 928n.
libelant
accuser 928n.
litigant 959n.
libeler
defamer 926n.
accuser 928n.
liberal
plenteous 635adj.
free man 744n.
expending 806adj.
prodigal 815adj.
philanthropic 901adj.
rewarding 962adj.
(*see* liberality)
liberalism
freedom 744n.
disinterestedness 931n.
liberality
giving 781n.
liberality 813n.
benevolence 897n.
disinterestedness 931n.
liberalize
liberate 746vb.
Liberals
political party 708n.
liberate
disjoin 46vb.
disencumber 701vb.
permit 756vb.
liberation
extraction 304vb.
escape 667n.
deliverance 668n.
freedom 744n.
liberation 746n.
non-retention 779n.
acquittal 960n.
libertarianism
freedom 744n.
liberticide
brute force 735n.
libertinage
love-making 887n.
unchastity 951n.
libertine
bad man 938n.
lecherous 951adj.
libertine 952n.
liberty
opportunity 137n.
freedom, scope 744n.
permission 756n.
dueness 915n.
non-liability 919n.
Liberty Hall
scope 744n.
sociability 882n.
libidinous
desiring 859adj.
loving 887adj.
lecherous 951adj.
libido
libido 859n.
love 887n.
librarian
collector 492n.
bookman 589n.
manager 690n.
library
accumulation 74n.
chamber 194n.
erudition 490n.
library 589n.
edition 589n.
collection 632n.
libration
oscillation 317n.
uranometry 321n.
librettist
musician 413n.
poet 593n.
dramatist 594n.
author 589n.
libretto
vocal music 412n.
reading matter 589n.
stage play 594n.
license
laxity, anarchy 734n.
freedom, scope 744n.
give scope 744vb.
liberate 746vb.
commission 751vb.
permit 756n., vb.
dueness 915n.
non-liability 919n.
exempt 919vb.
unchastity 951n.
licensee
consignee 754n.
recipient 782n.
licentious
anarchic 734adj.
free 744adj.
sensual 944adj.
lecherous 951adj.
lawless 954adj.

lichen
plant 366n.
licit
permitted 756adj.
due 915adj.
legal 953adj.
lick
small quantity 33n.
eat 301vb.
moisten 341vb.
touch 378vb.
taste 386vb.
defeat 727vb.
caress 889vb.
lick and a promise
incompleteness 55n.
lickerish
savory 390adj.
lecherous 951adj.
lick into shape
efform 243vb.
educate 534vb.
lick one's lips
enjoy 376vb.
gluttonize 947vb.
lick one's wounds
feel pain 377vb.
be defeated 728vb.
lickspittle
toady 879n.
licorice
sweetmeat 301n.
sweet 392n.
lictor
officer 741n.
lid
covering 226n.
headgear 228n.
stopper 264n.
lido
shore 344n.
arena 724n.
pleasure-ground 837n.
lie
be 1vb.
be in a state 7vb.
be inert 175vb.
be situate 186vb.
be present 189vb.
dwell 192vb.
be horizontal 216vb.
misteach 535vb.
be false 541vb.
deception 542n.
untruth 543n.
be inactive 679vb.
false charge 928n.
be dishonest 930vb.
lie-abed
lateness 136n.
slowcoach 278n.
idler 679n.
lied, lieder
vocal music 412n.
lie-detector
detector 484n.
lie direct
negation 533n.
lie down
be horizontal 216vb.
repose 683vb.
be dejected 834vb.
lie fallow
be unproductive 172vb.
be unprepared 670vb.
not act 677vb.
liege
master 741n.
subject 742n.
liegeman
dependent 742n.
lie in
reproduce itself 164vb.
lie in wait
ambush 527vb.
lie low
disappear 446vb.
be low 210vb.
lurk 523vb.
elude 667vb.
lie off
be distant 199vb.
lie to
be quiescent 266vb.
navigate 269vb.
lieu, in
in return 31adv.
lie under
be liable 180vb.
lieutenancy
degree 27n.
lieutenant
naval man 270n.
aider 703n.
auxiliary 707n.
soldiery 722n.
army officer 741n.
naval officer 741n.
deputy 755n.
lie with
unite with 45vb.
life
existence 1n.
substantiality 3n.
essential part 5n.
time 108n.
period 110n.
affairs 154n.
vitality 162n.
vigorousness 174n.
life 360n.
biography 590n.
vocation 622n.
activity 678n.
life-belt
support 218n.
wrapping 226n.
safeguard 662n.
preserver 666n.
life-blood
essential part 5n.
blood 335n.
life 360n.
lifeboat
boat 275n.
safeguard 662n.
life-buoy
support 218n.
life cycle
regular return 141n.
transition 147n.
life-giving
generative 171adj.
lifeguard
protector 660n.
shelter 662n.
defender 713n.
armed force 722n.
life-jacket
safeguard 662n.
lifeless
inert 175adj.
dead 361adj.
inactive 679adj.
lifelike
lifelike 18adj.
life-line
bond 47n.
safeguard 662n.
lifelong
lasting 113adj.
lifemanship
tactics 688n.
skill 694n.
life peer
councillor 692n.
nobleman 868n.
life-preserver
safeguard 662n.
club 723n.
lifer
offender 904n.
life-saving
deliverance 668n.
life sentence
diuturnity 113n.
life-size
size 195n.
large 195adj.
life-story
biography 590n.
lifetime
period 110n.
diuturnity 113n.
life to come
future state 124n.
life with
accompaniment 89n.

life-work
vocation 622n.
lift
displace 188vb.
conveyance 267n.
transfer 272vb.
carry 273vb.
promote 285vb.
draw 288vb.
ascent 308n.
lifter 310n.
elevate 310vb.
improvement 654n.
aid 703n.
liberate 746vb.
not retain 779vb.
steal 788vb.
relieve 831vb.
lift a finger
do 676vb.
lifter
lifter 310n.
taker 786n.
thief 789n.
ligament
ligature 47n.
retention 778n.
ligature
ligature 47n.
light
insubstantial 4adj.
unequal 29adj.
small 33adj.
morning 128n.
descend 309vb.
light 323adj.
rare 325adj.
soft 327adj.
fire 379n.
kindle 381vb.
lighter 385n.
light 417n.
luminary 420n.
illuminate 420vb.
soft-hued 425adj.
white 427adj.
appearance 445n.
knowledge 490n.
truth 494n.
interpretation 520n.
irresolute 601adj.
trivial 639adj.
easy 701adj.
gay 833adj.
funny 849adj.
rash 857adj.
unchaste 951adj.
revelation 975n.
light and shade
light contrast 417n.
lighten
bate 37vb.
assuage 177vb.
lighten 323vb.
make bright 417vb.
disencumber 701vb.
take away 786vb.
relieve 831vb.
lighter
boat 275n.
lighter 385n.
torch 420n.
lighterage
price 809n.
lighterman
boatman 270n.
lighter-than-air
aviational 276adj.
light-fingered
light 323adj.
tactual 378adj.
thieving 788adj.
light-footed
speedy 277adj.
active 678adj.
light-grasp
range 183n.
optics 417n.
vision 438n.
light hand
lenity 736n.
light-headed
frenzied 503adj.
light-hearted
cheerful 833adj.
lighthouse
sailing aid 269n.
signal light 420n.
signpost 547n.
safeguard 662n.
lighting
lighting 420n.
lightless
unlit 418adj.
lightly
slightly 33adv.
rashly 857adv.
light-minded
changeful 152adj.
light-minded 456adj.
rash 857adj.
lightness
insubstantiality 4n.
weakness 163n.
levity 323n.
rarity 325n.
unchastity 951n.
lightning
electricity 160n.
velocity 277n.
flash 417n.
luminary 420n.
lightning conductor
electricity 160n.
safeguard 662n.
lightning rod
(*see* lightning conductor)
light of nature
empiricism 461n.
intuition 476n.
light on
land 295vb.
(*see* light upon)
light rein
lenity 736n.
light relief
ridiculousness 849n.
lights
knowledge 490n.
intelligence 498n.
light-shift
displacement 188n.
lightship
sailing aid 269n.
ship 275n.
signal light 420n.
signpost 547n.
safeguard 662n.
lights out
obscuration 418n.
call 547n.
light up
make bright 417vb.
illuminate 420vb.
light upon
chance 159vb.
meet 295vb.
acquire 771vb.
light wave
radiation 417n.
light-weight
insubstantial 4adj.
inconsiderable 33adj.
weakling 163n.
light 323adj.
nonentity 639n.
trivial 639adj.
pugilist 722n.
light-well
window 263n.
light year
period 110n.
long measure 203n.
ligneous
wooden 366adj.
lignite
fuel 385n.
lignography
engraving 555n.
likable
desired 859adj.
lovable 887adj.
like
relative 9adj.
similar 18adj.
equal 28adj.
enjoy 376vb.
appetize 390vb.

be pleased 824vb.
desire 859vb.
be friendly 880vb.
love 887vb.
like for like
retaliation 714n.
likelihood
liability 180n.
possibility 469n.
probability 471n.
likely
probable 471adj.
credible 485adj.
true 494adj.
promising 852adj.
like-minded
agreeing 24adj.
assenting 488adj.
liken
relate 9vb.
liken 18vb.
compare 462vb.
figure 519vb.
likeness
similarity 18n.
copy 22n.
equivalence 28n.
comparison 462n.
metaphor 519n.
representation 551n.
like new
restored 656adj.
likes of, the
analogue 18n.
like well
approve 923vb.
likewise
in addition 38adv.
liking
tendency 179n.
liking 859n.
love 887n.
lilac
tree 366n.
purple 434adj.
lilies
heraldry 547n.
lilliputian
dwarf 196n.
lilt
sing 413vb.
be cheerful 833vb.
lily
white thing 427n.
a beauty 841n.
lily-livered
cowardly 856adj.
limature
powder 332n.
friction 333n.
limb
adjunct 40n.
piece, limb 53n.
extremity 69n.
leg 267n.
tree, foliage 366n.
limber
affix 45vb.
war-chariot 274n.
flexible 327adj.
gun 723n.
limber up
prepare oneself 669vb.
limb from limb
apart 46adv.
limbless
fragmentary 53adj.
incomplete 55adj.
limbo
prison 748n.
hell 972n.
lime
adhesive 47n.
tree 366n.
bleacher 426n.
green 432adj.
ensnare 542vb.
take 786vb.
Limehouse
scurrility 899n.
limejuicer
foreigner 59n.
lime-kiln
furnace 383n.
limelight
lighting 420n.
advertisement 528n.
theater 594n.
limelight, in the
manifest 522adj.
publicly 528adv.
on stage 594adv.
limen
threshold 234n.
limerick
doggerel 593n.
witticism 839n.
ridiculousness 849n.
impurity 951n.
limestone
rock 344n.
soil 344n.
liminal
marginal 234adj.
limit
finite quantity 26n.
bate 37vb.
completeness 54n.
extremity 69n.
moderate 177vb.
farness 199n.
edge 234n.
limit 236n., vb.
qualify 468vb.
hinder 702vb.
restriction 747n.
apportionment 783n.
annoyance 827n.
limitary
limited 236adj.
restraining 747adj.
limitation
decrease 37n.
circumscription 232n.
limit 236n.
qualification 468n.
defect 647n.
restriction 747n.
conditions 766n.
limiting factor
limit 236n.
restriction 747n.
limitless
infinite 107adj.
huge 195adj.
limitrophe
near 200adj.
limn
represent 551vb.
paint 553vb.
limousine
automobile 274n.
limp
weak 163adj.
move slowly 278vb.
soft 327adj.
feeble 572adj.
be clumsy 695vb.
miscarry 728vb.
limpet
coherence 48n.
limpid
transparent 422adj.
intelligible 516adj.
perspicuous 567adj.
lin
lake 346n.
linage
letterpress 587n.
linch pin
fastening 47n.
linctus
medicine 658n.
line
race 11n.
cable 47n.
fill 54vb.
sequence 65n.
continuity 71n.
breed 77n.
posteriority 120n.
strengthen 162vb.
genealogy 169n.
sonship 170n.
load 193vb.
line 203n.
narrowness 206n.
fiber 208n.
line 227vb.

put between 231vb.
limit 236n.
groove 262vb.
sailing aid 269n.
train 274n.
direction 281n.
insert 303vb.
indication 547n.
lettering 586n.
correspondence 588n.
vocation 622n.
policy 623n.
way, route 624n.
tactics 688n.
battle 718n.
formation 722n.
merchandise 794n.
lineage
consanguinity 11n.
sequence 65n.
series 71n.
posteriority 120n.
source 156n.
genealogy 169n.
sonship 170n.
nobility 868n.
(*see* linage)
line ahead
line 203n.
lineal
continuous 71adj.
filial 170n.
longitudinal 203adj.
lineament
outline 233n.
form 243n.
feature 445n.
linear
continuous 71adj.
parental 169adj.
longitudinal 203adj.
straight 249adj.
metric 465adj.
painted 553adj.
linear measure
long measure 203n.
metrology 465n.
lined
furrowed 262adj.
line-drawing
picture 553n.
line, in
uniform 16adj.
longwise 203adv.
straight 249adj.
linen
fiber 208n.
textile 222n.
bodywear 228n.
bookbinding 589n.
linen-draper
clothier 228n.
line of communication
route 624n.
line of country
function 622n.
line of sight
direction 281n.
view 438n.
liner
ship 275n.
lines
station 187n.
abode 192n.
form 243n.
feature 445n.
poem 593n.
railroad 624n.
defenses 713n.
penalty 963n.
line up
be in order 60vb.
arrange 62vb.
assemblage 74n.
line with, in
conformably 83adv.
ling
plant 366n.
lingam
genitalia 164n.
idol 982n.
linger
drag on 113vb.
be late 136vb.
lingerer
slowcoach 278n.
lingerie
underwear 228n.
lingo
language 557n.
dialect 560n.
lingua franca
language 557n.
dialect 560n.
lingual
vocal 577adj.
linguist
interpreter 520n.
linguist 557n.
linguistic
semantic 514adj.
linguistic 557adj.
linguistics
linguistics 557n.
etymology 559n.
liniment
unguent 357n.
balm 658n.
lining
contents 193n.
lining 227n.
insertion 303n.
link
relation 9n.
connect 45vb.
bond 47n.
component 58n.
cross 222vb.
intermediary 231n.
torch 420n.
gauge 465n.
linkage
(*see* link)
link-boy
torch 420n.
director 690n.
links
pleasure-ground 837n.
linnet
bird 365n.
linoleum
floor-cover 226n.
linotype
print 587n.
linseed
medicine 658n.
linsey-woolsey
mixed 43adj.
textural 331adj.
linstock
lighter 385n.
lint
wrapping 226n.
lintel
summit 213n.
beam 218n.
doorway 263n.
lion
cat 365n.
heraldry 547n.
bigwig 638n.
brave person 855n.
person of repute 866n.
favorite 890n.
lion-hearted
courageous 855adj.
lion-hunter
toady 879n.
lionize
honor 866vb.
celebrate 876vb.
respect 920vb.
praise 923vb.
lion's share
main part 52n.
redundance 637n.
undueness 916n.
lion-tamer
breeder 369n.
trainer 537n.
lip
edge 234n.
projection 254n.
sauciness 878n.
rudeness 885n.
lip-homage
duplicity 541n.
flattery 925n.
lippitude

dim sight 440n.
lip-read
hear 415vb.
be deaf 416vb.
translate 520vb.
lip-reverence
false piety 980n.
lips
speech 579n.
lipsalve
cosmetic 843n.
flattery 925n.
lipstick
red pigment 421n.
cosmetic 843n.
liquefaction
decomposition 51n.
fluidity 335n.
liquefaction 337n.
heating 381n.
liquescent
fluidal 335adj.
liqueur
liquor 301n.
sweet 392n.
liquid
non-adhesive 49adj.
amorphous 244adj.
liquor 301n.
fluid 335n.
speech sound 398n.
transparent 422adj.
vocal 577adj.
liquidation
destruction 165n.
slaughter 362n.
payment 804n.
liquidator
receiver 782n.
treasurer 798n.
liquidity
fluidity 335n.
means 629n.
funds 797n.
liquid measure
metrology 465n.
liquor
stimulant 174n.
liquor 301n.
lubricate 334vb.
fluid 335n.
add water 339vb.
lira
coinage 797n.
lisp
solecize 565vb.
voice 577vb.
speech defect 580n.
lissome
flexible 327adj.
list
specify 80vb.
number 86vb.
list 87n., vb.
filament 208n.
obliquity 220n.
edging 234n.
register 548vb.
will 595vb.
listen (to)
hear 415vb.
be curious 453vb.
be attentive 455vb.
consult 691vb.
obey 739vb.
consent 758vb.
be pious 979vb.
listened to
influential 178adj.
listener
listener 415n.
witness 466n.
allocution 583n.
listen in
hear 415vb.
listless
weakly 163adj.
incurious 454adj.
inattentive 456adj.
inactive 679adj.
dejected 834adj.
indifferent 860adj.
lists
duel 716n.
arena 724n.
lit
fiery 379adj.
heated 381adj.
luminous 417adj.
litanist
ritualist 988n.
litany
prayers 981n.
office book 988n.
liter
metrology 465n.
literal
imitative 20adj.
narrow-minded 481adj.
accurate 494adj.
semantic 514adj.
interpretive 520adj.
literal 558adj.
verbal 559adj.
observant 768adj.
orthodox 976adj.
literal-minded
narrow-minded 481adj.
accurate 494adj.
literary
instructed 490adj.
literary 557adj.
stylistic 566adj.
literary man
author 589n.
literate
instructed 490adj.
written 586adj.
literati
intellectual 492n.
literature
culture 490n.
erudition 490n.
literature 557n.
writing 586n.
reading matter 589n.
lithe
flexible 327adj.
lithograph
copy 22n.
representation 551n.
engrave 555vb.
print 587vb.
lithology
mineralogy 359n.
litigable
litigated 959adj.
litigant
combatant 722adj.
accuser 928n.
litigant 959n.
litigation
argument 475n.
quarrel 709n.
litigation 959n.
litigious
quarreling 709adj.
litigating 959adj.
litmus paper
testing agent 461n.
litotes
underestimation 483n.
trope 519n.
litter
confusion 61n.
jumble 63vb.
youngling 132n.
posterity 170n.
bed 218n.
vehicle 274n.
rubbish 641n.
litterer
slut 61n.
dirty person 649n.
little
small 33adj.
infantine 132adj.
little 196adj.
short 204adj.
unimportant 639adj.
contemptible 922adj.
little, a
partially 33adv.
little by little
by degrees 27adv.
gradatim 278adv.
little game
stratagem 698n.

little go
exam 459n.
little man
common man 30n.
everyman 79n.
commoner 869n.
littleness
invisibility 444n.
(*see* little)
littoral
edge 234n.
coastal 344adj.
liturgics
ritualism 988n.
liturgiologist
ritualist 988n.
liturgy
ritual 988n.
office book 988n.
Holy Communion 988n.
livable
contenting 828adj.
live
pass time 108vb.
dynamic 160adj.
operative 173adj.
vigorous 174adj.
alive 360adj.
live 360vb.
dramatic 594adj.
active 678adj.
feel 818vb.
live and let live
not act 677vb.
give scope 744vb.
live in the past
retrospect 505vb.
livelihood
vocation 622n.
liveliness
energy 160n.
vitality 162n.
vigorousness 174n.
vigor 571n.
restlessness 678n.
moral sensibility 819n.
cheerfulness 833n.
livelong
lasting 113adj.
lively
imaginative 513adj.
forceful 571adj.
lively 819adj.
excitable 822adj.
sociable 882adj.
(*see* liveliness)
liven
vitalize 360vb.
liver
rara avis 84n.
insides 224n.
meat 301n.
sullenness 893n.
liverish
irascible 892adj.
liverishness
indigestion 651n.
livery
uniform 228n.
hue 425n.
livery 547n.
badge of rule 743n.
transfer 780n.
livery company
corporation 708n.
merchant 794n.
liveryman
free man 744n.
merchant 794n.
livestock
cattle 365n.
live through
continue 108vb.
be restored 656vb.
live wire
electricity 160n.
vigorousness 174n.
busy person 678n.
live with
unite with 45vb.
accompany 89vb.
livid
blackish 428adj.
gray 429adj.
colorless 426adj.
purple 434adj.
blue 435adj.
angry 891adj.
living
benefice 985n.
living being
life 360n.
living death
suffering 825n.
living image
analogue 18n.
living space
room 183n.
scope 744n.
living wage
sufficiency 635n.
lixiviate
liquefy 337vb.
drench 341vb.
purify 648vb.
lixivium
solution 337n.
lizard
reptile 365n.
llama
fiber 208n.
beast of burden 273n.
load
fill 54vb.
bunch 74n.
stow 187vb.
contents 193n.
thing transferred 272n.
gravity 322n.
redundance 637n.
encumbrance 702n.
adversity 731n.
worry 825n.
decorate 844vb.
loads
great quantity 32n.
multitude 104n.
load with
add 38vb.
loaf
cereal 301n.
be inactive 679vb.
loafer
wanderer 268n.
idler 679n.
loafers
footwear 228n.
loam
soil 344n.
loan
subvention 703n.
lending 784n.
borrowing 785n.
credit 802n.
loanee
debtor 803n.
loan-word
neology 560n.
loath
dissenting 489adj.
unwilling 884adj.
disliking 887adj.
loathing
dislike 861n.
enmity 881n.
hatred 888n.
loathsome
unsavory 391n.
not nice 645adj.
unpleasant 827adj.
ugly 842adj.
disliked 861adj.
hateful 888adj.
loaves and fishes
prosperity 730n.
lob
propulsion 287n.
elevate 310vb.
lobby
lobby 194n.
incite 612vb.
access 624n.
lobbyist
motivator 612n.
petitioner 763n.
lobe
pendant 217n.

ear 415n.
lobster
fish food 301n.
table fish 365n.
redness 431n.
local
regional 184adj.
situated 186adj.
native 191n.
tavern 192n.
provincial 192adj.
near 200adj.
local color
accuracy 494n.
painting 553n.
localism
dialect 560n.
locality
district 184n.
region 184n.
place 185n.
locality 187n.
localize
place 187vb.
restrain 747vb.
locate
specify 80vb.
place 187vb.
orientate 281vb.
discover 484vb.
location
situation 186n.
location 187n.
location, on
absent 190adj.
loch
lake 346n.
lock
join 45vb.
fastening 47n.
filament 208n.
hair 259n.
stopper 264n.
close 264vb.
conduit 351n.
access 624n.
safeguard 662n.
fire-arm 723n.
retain 778vb.
lock and key
fastening 47n.
locker box
box 194n.
locket
jewelry 844n.
lockjaw
spasm 318n.
infection 651n.
lock-out
exclusion 57n.
strike 145n.
locksmith
artisan 686n.
lock, stock and barrel
all 52n.
lock up
cover 226vb.
conceal 525vb.
safeguard 660vb.
imprison 747vb.
punish 963vb.
lock-up
lock-up 748n.
loco
crazed 503adj.
locomotion
motion 265n.
locomotive
locomotive 274n.
vehicular 274adj.
locomotor ataxia
helplessness 161n.
locular
cellular 194adj.
loculus
compartment 194n.
locum tenens
substitute 150n.
resident 191n.
doctor 658n.
deputy 755n.
locus
continuity 71n.
locus classicus
example 83n.
locus standi
pretext 614n.
locust
destroyer 168n.
eater 301n.
vermin 365n.
bane 659n.
taker 786n.
noxious animal 904n.
glutton 947n.
locution
word 559n.
phrase 563n.
lode
layer 207n.
store 632n.
lodestar
attraction 291n.
signpost 547n.
incentive 612n.
directorship 689n.
lodestone
traction 288n.
attraction 291n.
incentive 612n.
lodge
place 187vb.
small house 192n.
dwell 192vb.
society 708n.
lodger
resident 191n.
possessor 776n.
lodging(s)
quarters 192n.
lodgment
location 187n.
presence 189n.
loess
leavings 41n.
soil 344n.
loft
attic 194n.
propel 287vb.
elevate 310vb.
lofty
high 209adj.
elevated 310adj.
forceful 571adj.
worshipful 866adj.
proud 871adj.
insolent 878adj.
despising 922adj.
disinterested 931adj.
log
sailing aid 269n.
raft 275n.
fuel 385n.
gauge 465n.
record 548n.
logarithm
numerical element 85n.
mathematics 86n.
log-book
chronology 117n.
record 548n.
loggerheads, at
disagreeing 25adj.
quarreling 709adj.
contending 716adj.
warring 718adj.
loggia
lobby 194n.
logia
narrative 590n.
logic
reasoning 475n.
curriculum 536n.
necessity 596n.
logical
relevant 9adj.
philosophic 449adj.
plausible 471adj.
rational 475adj.
true 494adj.
necessary 596adj.
logical conclusion
conformance 24n.
logicality
relevance 9n.
logic-chopping
discrimination 463n.

argument 475n.
sophistry 477n.
logician
reasoner 475n.
logistics
provision 633n.
fitting out 669n.
art of war 718n.
logography
writing 586n.
logogriph
enigma 530n.
logomachy
argument 475n.
sophistry 477n.
conference 584n.
logometer
counting instrument 86n.
logometric
numerical 85adj.
Logos
word 559n.
God the Son 965n.
log-rolling
interchange 151n.
cooperation 706n.
loin
rear 238n.
loincloth
wrapping 226n.
loincloth 228n.
loins
source 156n.
genitalia 164n.
parentage 169n.
loiter
be late 136vb.
be stealthy 525vb.
be inactive 679vb.
loiterer
slowcoach 278n.
Lok Sabha
parliament 692n.
loll
be horizontal 216vb.
be inactive 679vb.
repose 683vb.
Lollardy
heresy 977n.
lollipop
sweetmeat 301n.
sweet 392n.
lollop
be inactive 679vb.
lolloping
unwieldy 195adj.
lolly
sweetmeat 301n.
dibs 797n.
lone
non-uniform 17adj.
alone 88adj.
unsociable 883adj.
lonely
separate 46adj.
alone 88adj.
empty 190adj.
friendless 883adj.
secluded 883adj.
lone wolf
non-uniformity 17n.
revolter 738n.
solitary 883n.
long
lasting 113adj.
long 203adj.
prolix 570adj.
tedious 838adj.
desire 859vb.
long ago
long ago 113adv.
formerly 125adv.
longanimity
patience 823n.
forgiveness 909n.
long arm
governance 733n.
long-bow
propellant 287n.
missile weapon 723n.
long-cloth
textile 222n.
long clothes
robe 228n.
long clothes, in
infantine 132adj.
long-drawn
long 203adj.
prolix 570adj.
longevity
diuturnity 113n.
age 131n.
life 360n.
health 650n.
long face
dejection 834n.
longhand
writing 586n.
long-headed
intelligent 498adj.
longimetry
long measure 203n.
metrology 465n.
longing
suffering 825n.
regret 830n.
desire 859n.
love 887n.
longinquity
distance 199n.
longitude
length 203n.
long-legged
long 203adj.
narrow 206adj.
tall 209adj.
long-lived
alive 360adj.
long measure
long measure 203n.
long odds
fair chance 159n.
improbability 472n.
long-player
phonograph 414n.
recording instrument 549n.
long-range
distant 199adj.
long rope
scope 744n.
long run
period 110n.
protraction 113n.
long run, in the
in the long run 113adv.
prospectively 124adv.
in the future 155adv.
long-service
lasting 113adj.
longshoreman
boatman 270n.
long-sightedness
foresight 510n.
longsome
long 203adj.
prolix 570adj.
long-standing
lasting 113adj.
immemorial 127adj.
permanent 144adj.
longstop
interceptor 702n.
long-suffering
lenient 736adj.
patience 823n.
mercy 905n.
forgiveness 909n.
long-term
lasting 113adj.
long-winded
protracted 113adj.
prolix 570adj.
loquacious 581adj.
longwise
longwise 203adv.
loo
latrine 649n.
card game 837n.
looby
bungler 697n.
countryman 869n.
look
similarity 18n.
form 243n.
look 438n.
appearance 445n.

mien 445n.
be curious 453vb.
attention 455n.
hint 524n.
look after
look after 457vb.
safeguard 660vb.
look after oneself
be selfish 932vb.
look a gift horse in the mouth
be discontented 829vb.
be cautious 858vb.
be fastidious 862vb.
be ungrateful 908vb.
look ahead
look ahead 124vb.
foresee 510vb.
plan 623vb.
look as if
resemble 18vb.
look askance
dissent 489vb.
dislike 861vb.
disapprove 924vb.
look at
watch 441vb.
look back
look back 125vb.
be late 136vb.
turn back 286vb.
retrospect 505vb.
regret 830vb.
look big
defy 711vb.
be insolent 878vb.
look black
be dark 418vb.
show feeling 818vb.
be angry 891vb.
be sullen 893vb.
disapprove 924vb.
look blue
be disappointed 509vb.
show feeling 818vb.
be discontented 829vb.
be dejected 834vb.
look daggers
be angry 891vb.
threaten 900vb.
disapprove 924vb.
look down on
be proud 871vb.
be insolent 878vb.
not respect 921vb.
despise 922vb.
looker
inquirer 459n.
looker-on
spectator 441n.
look for
inquire 459vb.
search 459vb.
assume 471vb.
expect 507vb.
pursue 619vb.
desire 859vb.
look for trouble
make quarrels 709vb.
look forward
look ahead 124vb.
expect 507vb.
hope 852vb.
look in
be present 189vb.
enter 297vb.
watch 441vb.
visit 882vb.
looking back
reversion 148n.
tergiversation 603n.
looking-glass
mirror 442n.
look in the face
withstand 704vb.
be courageous 855vb.
look into
be attentive 455vb.
look like
resemble 18vb.
look of the thing
appearance 445n.
look of things
circumstance 8n.
look on
be impotent 161vb.
be present 189vb.
watch 441vb.
acquiesce 488vb.
not act 677vb.
look-out
view 438n.
spectator 441n.
surveillance 457n.
expectation 507n.
function 622n.
protector 660n.
warner 664n.
keeper 749n.
worry 825n.
look out
scan 438vb.
invigilate 457vb.
be cautious 858vb.
look over
scan 438vb.
look over one's shoulder
turn back 286vb.
be loath 598vb.
regret 830vb.
look-see
inspection 438n.
look silly
be ridiculous 849vb.
lose repute 867vb.
look the other way
be blind 439vb.
avoid 620vb.
look to
be attentive 455vb.
look after 457vb.
impose a duty 917vb.
look twice
be cautious 858vb.
look up
visit 882vb.
look up and down
be insolent 878vb.
look up to
honor 866vb.
respect 920vb.
loom
be great 32vb.
impend 156vb.
produce 164vb.
handle 218n.
textile 222n.
weave 222vb.
be dim 419vb.
blur 440vb.
be visible 443vb.
endanger 661vb.
workshop 687n.
loon
dunce 501n.
madman 504n.
countryman 869n.
loop
handle 218n.
be curved 248vb.
circuit 626n.
loophole
window 263n.
outlet 298n.
view 438n.
pretext 614n.
contrivance 623n.
defect 647n.
means of escape 667n.
fortification 713n.
loop-line
circuit 626n.
loop the loop
fly 271vb.
circuit 626vb.
loopy
crazed 503adj.
loose
disjoin 46vb.
non-adhesive 49adj.
unstick 49vb.
general 79adj.
unstable 152adj.
pendent 217adj.
deviating 282adj.
ill-reasoned 477adj.
feeble 572adj.
lax 734adj.
free 744adj.

liberate 746vb.
unchaste 951adj.
loose end, at a
leisurely 681adj.
loose ends
negligence 458n.
loose-knit
non-adhesive 49adj.
loose-limbed
flexible 327adj.
loose liver
sensualist 944n.
libertine 952n.
loosen, looseness
(*see* loose)
loose terms
indiscrimination 464n.
loose thread
mistake 495n.
loot
take away 786vb.
rob 788vb.
booty 790n.
looting
spoliation 788n.
lop
subtract 39vb.
cut 46vb.
shorten 204vb.
lope
gait 265n.
pedestrianism 267n.
move fast 277vb.
lopsided
unequal 29adj.
clumsy 695adj.
(*see* oblique)
lopsidedness
distortion 246n.
loquacious
informative 524adj.
loquacity
diffuseness 570n.
speech 579n.
loquacity 581n.
lord
male 372n.
bigwig 638n.
nobleman 868n.
title 870n.
master 741n.
owner 776n.
lord and master, one's
spouse 894n.
lord it
dominate 733vb.
oppress 735vb.
seek repute 866vb.
be proud 871vb.
be insolent 878vb.
lordliness
authority 733n.
lordly
authoritative 733adj.
authoritarian 735adj.
liberal 813adj.
worshipful 866adj.
proud 871adj.
insolent 878adj.
Lord Mayor
officer 741n.
law officer 955n.
Lord Mayor's Show
pageant 875n.
lord of creation
mankind 371n.
Lord of Misrule
anarch 61n.
bungler 697n.
lord of the manor
master 741n.
owner 776n.
lordosis
convexity 253n.
Lord's day
repose 683n.
holy-day 988n.
lordship
magistrature 733n.
lands 777n.
aristocracy 868n.
title 870n.
Lord's Supper
Holy Communion 988n.
Lord's Table
ritual object 988n.
altar 990n.
lore
tradition 127n.
knowledge 490n.
erudition 490n.
learning 536n.
cunning 698n.
Lorelei
rara avis 84n.
vocalist 413n.
mythical being 970n.
lorgnette
eyeglass 442n.
loricated
covered 226adj.
lorn
friendless 883adj.
lorry
carrier 273n.
automobile 274n.
lose
decrease 37vb.
misdate 118vb.
be late 136vb.
misplace 188vb.
be defeated 728vb.
lose 772vb.
lose a chance
lose a chance 138vb.
lose caste
lose repute 867vb.
lose color
be dim 419vb.
lose consciousness
be impotent 161vb.
lose control
be lax 734vb.
lose face
lose repute 867vb.
lose ground
decelerate 278vb.
regress 286vb.
fall short 307vb.
be defeated 728vb.
lose height
descend 309vb.
lose no time
be early 135vb.
hasten 680vb.
lose numbers
decrease 37vb.
lose one's bearings
stray 282vb.
lose one's head
go mad 503vb.
be unskillful 695vb.
lose patience
get angry 891vb.
loser
bungler 697n.
loser 728n.
unlucky person 731n.
laughing-stock 851n.
lose sight of
be blind 439vb.
forget 506vb.
lose the scent
be uncertain 474vb.
lose the thread
be unrelated 10vb.
stray 282vb.
be inattentive 456vb.
be uncertain 474vb.
lose the way
stray 282vb.
lose weight
decrease 37vb.
become small 198vb.
losing
profitless 641adj.
unsuccessful 728adj.
losing business
unproductivity 172n.
losing game
defeat 728n.
losing side
loser 728n.
loss
decrement 42n.
deficit 55n.
ruin 165n.
absence 190n.

outflow 298n.
shortcoming 307n.
waste 634n.
impairment 655n.
failure 728n.
loss 772n.
loss, at a
doubting 474adj.
losses
failure 728n.
loss-making
profitless 641adj.
lost
past 125adj.
destroyed 165adj.
misplayed 188adj.
absent 190adj.
deviating 282adj.
disappearing 446adj.
abstracted 456adj.
doubting 474adj.
unknown 491adj.
concealed 525adj.
lost 772adj.
impenitent 940adj.
condemned 961adj.
lost cause
defeat 728n.
lost labor
lost labor 641n.
lost leader
tergiversator 603n.
lost sheep
bad man 938n.
lost soul
bad man 938n.
lot
state 7n.
finite quantity 26n.
great quantity 32n.
all 52n.
bunch 74n.
multitude 104n.
chance 159n.
territory 184n.
enclosure 235n.
oracle 511n.
fate 596n.
plenty 635n.
participation 775n.
portion 783n.
lothario
lover 887n.
libertine 952n.
lotion
water 339n.
moistening 341n.
cleanser 648n.
balm 658n.
cosmetic 833n.
lottery
chance 159n.
gambling 618n.
lotus-eater
idler 679n.
loud
strident 407adj.
crying 408adj.
florid 425adj.
manifest 522adj.
ornate 574adj.
rhetorical 574adj.
(*see* loudness)
loud-hailer
megaphone 400n.
telecommunication 531n.
loud-mouthed
loud 400adj.
loudness
loudness 400n.
bang 402n.
resonance 404n.
publication 528n.
ill-breeding 847n.
loud pedal
megaphone 400n.
piano 414n.
loud-speaker
megaphone 400n.
hearing aid 415n.
telecommunication 531n.
lough
lake 346n.
lounge
chamber 194n.
be inactive 679vb.
lounger
idler 679n.
lounge suit
dress 228n.
lour
(*see* lower)
louse
vermin 365n.
cad 938n.
lousy
not nice 645adj.
unclean 649adj.
lousy with
full 54adj.
lout
dunce 501n.
bungler 697n.
countryman 869n.
rude person 885n.
ruffian 904n.
loutish
ill-bred 847adj.
plebeian 869adj.
discourteous 885adj.
lovable
pleasurable 826adj.
personable 841adj.
amiable 884adj.
lovable 887adj.
love
zero 103n.
concord 710n.
liking 859n.
desire 859vb.
love 887n., vb.
lover, loved one 887n.
pet, caress 889vb.
darling 890n.
jealousy 911n.
disinterestedness 931n.
divineness 965n.
love affair
love affair 887n.
love all
draw 28n.
love-birds
lovers 887n.
love-child
bastardy 954n.
love-feast
social gathering 882n.
public worship 981n.
love, for
uncharged 812adj.
love, in
enamored 887adj.
love-knot
badge 547n.
trophy 729n.
loveless
indifferent 860adj.
unwanted 860adj.
disliking 861adj.
disliked 861adj.
hated 888adj.
hating 888adj.
love-letter
correspondence 588n.
love-token 889n.
wooing 889n.
lovelock
hair 259n.
lovely
pleasant 376adj.
topping 644adj.
pleasurable 826adj.
a beauty 841n.
beautiful 841adj.
lovable 887adj.
love-making
love-making 887n.
wooing 889n.
love-match
type of marriage 894n.
love-nest
love-nest 887n.
love-philter
stimulant 174n.
love-play
wooing 889n.

lover
desirer 859n.
lover 887n.
loverlike
loving 887adj.
loveseat
seat 218n.
love-sickness
love 887n.
lovesome
personable 841adj.
lovable 887adj.
love-song
vocal music 412n.
poem 593n.
wooing 889n.
love-story
novel 590n.
love to
be wont 610vb.
love-token
indication 547n.
love-token 889n.
loving
careful 457adj.
(*see* love)
loving care
carefulness 457n.
loving cup
cup 194n.
sociability 882n.
loving it
pleased 824adj.
loving-kindness
benevolence 897n.
lovingly
carefully 457adv.
affectionately 887vb.
loving words
endearment 889n.
low
small 33adj.
inferior 35adj.
weak 163adj.
low 210adj.
muted 401adj.
ululate 409vb.
not nice 645adj.
cheap 812adj.
dejected 834adj.
vulgar 847adj.
disreputable 867adj.
plebeian 869adj.
humble 872adj.
rascally 930adj.
low-born
plebeian 869adj.
low-brow
uninstructed 491adj.
ignoramus 493n.
unintelligent 499adj.
low-caste
plebeian 869adj.
Low Church
sectarian 978adj.
low-class
plebeian 869adj.
low company
lower classes 869n.
Low Countries
plain 348n.
lowdown
information 524n.
low-down
plebeian 869adj.
rascally 930adj.
lower
inferior 35adj.
bate 37vb.
impend 155vb.
be low 210vb.
hang 217vb.
depress 311vb.
be dark 418vb.
be dim 419vb.
predict 511vb.
impair 655vb.
pervert 655vb.
warn 664vb.
cheapen 812vb.
vulgarize 847vb.
humiliate 872vb.
threaten 900vb.
not respect 921vb.
hold cheap 922vb.
defame 926vb.
lower case
print-type 587n.
lower classes
inferior 35n.
lower classes 869n.
lower deck
layer 207n.
lower classes 869n.
Lower House
parliament 692n.
lowering
impending 155adj.
cheerless 834adj.
lowermost
undermost 214adj.
lower oneself
demean oneself 867vb.
lower orders
social group 371n.
nonentity 639n.
lower classes 869n.
lower world
hell 972n.
low-geared
slow 278adj.
lowlander
dweller 191n.
lowlands
district 184n.
lowness 210n.
land 344n.
plain 348n.
low-level
inferior 35adj.
unimportant 639adj.
low life
lower classes 869n.
lowliness
humility 872n.
low-lying
low 210adj.
low-necked
uncovered 229adj.
lowness
lowness 210n.
depth 211n.
base 214n.
(*see* low)
low opinion
disapprobation 924n.
low pressure
rarity 325n.
weather 340n.
low-spirited
dejected 834adj.
low water
lowness 210n.
water 339n.
scarcity 636n.
poverty 801n.
loy
shovel 274n.
loyal
conformable 83adj.
patriotic 901adj.
trustworthy 929adj.
(*see* loyalty)
loyalist
conformist 83n.
auxiliary 707n.
defender 713n.
loyalty
willingness 597n.
submission 721n.
loyalty 739n.
service 745n.
observance 768n.
friendship 880n.
love 887n.
duty 917n.
probity 929n.
disinterestedness 931n.
piety 979n.
lozenge
angular figure 247n.
heraldry 547n.
medicine 658n.
lubber
ignoramus 493n.
ninny 501n.
idler 679n.

bungler 697n.
lubberly
unwieldy 195adj.
clumsy 695adj.
ill-bred 847adj.
lubricant
smoother 258n.
lubricant 334n.
lubricate
smooth 258vb.
soften 327vb.
lubricate 334vb.
lubrication
lubrication 334n.
unctuousness 357n.
lubricity
changeableness 152n.
smoothness 258n.
lubrication 334n.
unctuousness 357n.
unchastity 951n.
lucid
undimmed 417adj.
luminous 417adj.
transparent 422adj.
sane 502adj.
intelligible 516adj.
perspicuous 567adj.
lucifer
lighter 385n.
Lucifer
luminary 420n.
Satan 969n.
lucimeter
optical device 442n.
luck
opportunity 137n.
chance 159n.
good 615n.
non-design 618n.
prosperity 730n.
luck-bringer
talisman 983n.
luckless
unfortunate 731adj.
lucky
opportune 137adj.
successful 727adj.
prosperous 730adj.
happy 824adj.
lucky dip
non-uniformity 17n.
confusion 61n.
chance 159n.
lucky dog
made man 730n.
lucrative
gainful 771adj.
lucre
acquisition 771n.
money 797n.
wealth 800n.
lucubration
thought 449n.
Lucullus
gastronomy 301n.
eater 301n.
sensualist 944n.
glutton 947n.
Luddite
rioter 738n.
ludicrous
absurd 497adj.
foolish 499adj.
ridiculous 849adj.
ludo
board game 837n.
luff
navigate 269vb.
lug
handle 218n.
sail 275n.
draw 288vb.
ear 415n.
tool 630n.
luge
sled 274n.
descend 309vb.
luggage
box 194n.
thing transferred 272n.
property 777n.
luggage-van
box 194n.
train 274n.
lugger
sailing-ship 275n.
lug-sail
sail 275n.
traction 288n.
lugubrious
cheerless 834adj.
lukewarm
median 30adj.
warm 379adj.
irresolute 601adj.
neutral 625adj.
apathetic 820adj.
indifferent 860adj.
lull
discontinuity 72n.
delay 136n.
lull 145n.
assuage 177vb.
interval 201n.
quiescence 266n.
bring to rest 266vb.
silence 399n., vb.
befool 542vb.
inactivity 679vb.
make inactive 679vb.
repose 683n.
peace 717n.
tranquilize 823vb.
please 826vb.
relieve 831vb.
flatter 925vb.
lullaby
vocal music 412n.
soporific 679n.
relief 831n.
lulu
a beauty 841n.
lumbago
pang 377n.
lumbar
back 238adj.
lumber
leavings 41n.
confusion 61n.
move slowly 278vb.
fell 311vb.
wood 366n.
rubbish 641n.
be clumsy 695vb.
encumbrance 702n.
lumberjack
forestry 366n.
worker 686n.
lumber-room
chamber 194n.
collection 632n.
luminarist
artist 556n.
luminary
luminary 420n.
sage 500n.
luminescence
glow 417n.
luminescent
luminescent 420adj.
luminosity
light 417n.
luminous
luminescent 420adj.
white 427adj.
intelligible 516adj.
lump
great quantity 32n.
main part 52n.
piece 53n.
bulk 195n.
gravity 322n.
solid body 324n.
bungler 697n.
lumpish
inert 175adj.
unwieldy 195adj.
inactive 679adj.
lump sum
funds 797n.
lump together
combine 50vb.
bring together 74vb.
not discriminate 464vb.
lumpy
rough 259adj.

dense 324adj.
semiliquid 354adj.
lunacy
insanity 503n.
lunar
celestial 321adj.
lunar mansion
zodiac 321n.
lunate
curved 248adj.
celestial 321adj.
lunatic
insane 503adj.
madman 504n.
lunatic asylum
madhouse 503n.
lunation
period 110n.
lunch
meal 301n.
eat 301vb.
lunch-counter
café 192n.
lunette
fort 713n.
lung
space 183n.
plain 348n.
(*see* lungs)
lunge
strike 279vb.
foin 712n.
strike at 712vb.
lungi
dress 228n.
lungs
respiration 352n.
voice 577n.
lunik
satellite 321n.
space-ship 276n.
lunule
curve 248n.
lupine
animal 365adj.
lurch
obliquity 220n.
walk 267vb.
move slowly 278vb.
tumble 309vb.
fluctuation 317n.
be agitated 318vb.
be drunk 949vb.
lurcher
dog 365n.
lure
attraction 291n.
ensnare 542vb.
tempt 612vb.
desired object 859n.
lurid
florid 425adj.
colorless 426adj.
dark 418adj.
impure 951adj.
lurk
be unseen 444vb.
escape notice 456vb.
lurk 523vb.
avoid 620vb.
elude 667vb.
be cautious 858vb.
lurker
hider 527n.
slyboots 698n.
lurking
latent 523adj.
stealthy 525adj.
luscious
savory 390adj.
sweet 392adj.
pleasurable 826adj.
ornamental 844adj.
lush
prolific 171adj.
vigorous 174adj.
vegetal 366adj.
plenteous 635adj.
lushy
tipsy 949adj.
lusory
amusing 837adj.
lust
libido 859n.
desire 859vb.
love 887n.
vice 934n.
unchastity 951n.
luster
light 417n.
lamp 420n.
prestige 866n.
lusterless
colorless 426adj.
lusterware
pottery 381n.
lustful
desiring 859adj.
loving 887adj.
lecherous 951adj.
lustily
vigorously 174adv.
loudly 400adv.
laboriously 682adv.
lustiness
vigorousness 174n.
lustless
weakly 163adj.
lustral
cleansing 648adj.
atoning 941adj.
lustration
cleansing 648n.
penance 941n.
ritual act 988n.
lustrous
luminous 417adj.
noteworthy 866adj.
lustrum
period 110n.
lusty
strong 162adj.
vigorous 174adj.
large, fleshy 195adj.
loud 400adj.
lusus naturae
nonconformist 84n.
lutanist
instrumentalist 413n.
lute
adhesive 47n.
harp 414n.
lutein
yellow pigment 433n.
Lutheranism
Protestantism 976n.
sectarianism 978n.
luxation
separation 46n.
luxuriance
productiveness 171n.
vegetability 366n.
plenty 635n.
redundance 637n.
luxuriant
dense 324n.
luxuriate
enjoy 376vb.
be pleased 824vb.
be intemperate 943vb.
luxurious
ostentatious 875adj.
(*see* luxury)
luxury
extra 40n.
euphoria 376n.
plenty 635n.
superfluity 637n.
prosperity 730n.
wealth 800n.
intemperance 943n.
sensualism 944n.
luxury-loving
sensual 944adj.
luxury price
dearness 811n.
lycanthrope
demon 970n.
lycanthropy
psychotherapy 503n.
lycée
academy 539n.
lych-gate
funeral 364n.
church exterior 990n.
lyddite
explosive 723n.
Lydian
harmonic 410adj.

lye
solution 337n.
cleanser 648n.
lying
erroneous 495adj.
falsehood 541n.
untrue 543adj.
lying-in
obstetrics 164n.
lymph
blood 335n.
fluid 335n.
transparency 422n.
lymphad
galley 275n.
lymphatic
sanguineous 335adj.
watery 339adj.
lynch
disapprove 924vb.
execute 963vb.
lynching
capital punishment 963n.
lynch law
anarchy 734n.
lawlessness 954n.
lynx
cat 365n.
eye 438n.
lynx-eyed
seeing 438adj.
vigilant 457adj.
lyre
harp 414n.
lyric
vocal music 412n.
musicianly 413adj.
poetic 593adj.
lyrical
poetic 593adj.
excited 821adj.
excitable 822adj.
rejoicing 835adj.
approving 923adj.
lyricism
vocal music 412n.
excitable state 822n.
lyric-writer
dramatist 594n.
lyrist
musician 413n.
instrumentalist 413n.
poet 593n.

M

ma'am
lady 373n.
title 870n.
macabre
frightening 854adj.
spooky 970adj.
macadam
road 624n.
building material 631n.
macadamize
smooth 258vb.
macaroni
dish 301n.
fop 848n.
macaronic
absurd 497adj.
poetic 593adj.
macaronics
slang 560n.
doggerel 593n.
macaw
bird 365n.
mace
hammer 279n.
potherb 301n.
condiment 389n.
club 723n.
badge of rule 743n.
mace-bearer
officer 741n.
law officer 955n.
macerate
soften 327vb.
drench 341vb.
maceration
penance 941n.
asceticism 945n.
machete
sharp edge 256n.
side-arms 723n.
Machiavellian
hypocritical 541adj.
planning 623adj.
slyboots 698n.
cunning 698adj.
perfidious 930adj.
Machiavellianism
duplicity 541n.
machicolation
notch 260n.
fortification 713n.
machination
deception 542n.
plot 623n.
stratagem 698n.
machine
source 156n.
produce 164vb.
print 587vb.
fatalist 596n.
instrument 628n.
machine 630n.
slave 742n.
machine-gun
gun 723n.
machine-like
involuntary 596adj.
machine-made
produced 164adj.
machine-minded
mechanical 630adj.
machinery
complexity 61n.
machine 630n.
machinist
stage-hand 594n.
machinist 630n.
artisan 686n.
macilent
lean 206adj.
mackerel
fish food 301n.
table fish 365n.
bawd 952n.
mackerel sky
cloud 355n.
striation 437n.
mackintosh
overcoat 228n.
macrobiotic
lasting 113adj.
macrocosm
generality 79n.
universe 321n.
macrology
pleonasm 570n.
macromolecule
life 360n.
macron
punctuation 547n.
macroscopic
large 195adj.
visible 443adj.
maculate
variegate 437vb.
make unclean 649vb.
blemished 845adj.
maculation
maculation 437n.
blemish 845n.
macule
skin disease 651n.
maculous
mottled 437adj.
mad
insane 503adj.
capricious 604adj.
excited 821adj.
angry 891adj.
mad after
desiring 859adj.
madam
lady 373n.
master 741n.
title 870n.
bawd 952n.
madcap
violent creature 176n.
madman 504n.
excitable 822adj.
desperado 857n.

rash 857adj.
madden
make violent 176vb.
make mad 503vb.
excite love 887vb.
enrage 891vb.
maddening
annoying 827adj.
madder
red pigment 431n.
madefaction
moistening 341n.
Madeira
wine 301n.
made man
made man 730n.
made of
composing 56adj.
made to measure
adjusted 24adj.
made-up
culinary 301adj.
beautified 843adj.
madhouse
confusion 61n.
madhouse 503n.
madly
extremely 32adv.
madman
fool 501n.
madman 504n.
madness
insanity 503n.
excitable state 822n.
love 887n.
Madonna
Madonna 968n.
madrigal
vocal music 412n.
Maecenas
intellectual 492n.
patron 707n.
maelstrom
vortex 315n.
pitfall 663n.
activity 678n.
maenad
madman 504n.
drunkard 949n.
maestoso
adagio 412adv.
orchestra 413n.
Mae West
wrapping 226n.
safeguard 662n.
maffick
rampage 61vb.
rejoice 835vb.
celebrate 876vb.
Mafia
disobedience 738n.
revolter 738n.
magazine
accumulation 74n.
journal 528n.
book 589n.
reading matter 589n.
storage 632n.
arsenal 723n.
fire-arm 723n.
magdalen
penitent 939n.
mage, magian, Magi
sorcerer 983n.
magenta
red color 431n.
maggot
animalcule 196n.
vermin 365n.
ideality 513n.
whim 604n.
maggoty
capricious 604adj.
unclean 649adj.
magic
influence 178n.
sleight 542n.
instrumentality 628n.
thaumaturgy 864n.
wonderful 864adj.
prestige 866n.
fairylike 970adj.
sorcery 983n.
occultism 984n.
magical
magical 983adj.
magic carpet
airship 276n.
speeder 277n.
magic formula
spell 983n.
magician
conjuror 545n.
proficient 696n.
sorcerer 983n.
magic lantern
lamp 420n.
optical device 442n.
plaything 837n.
magic world
fairy 970n.
Maginot Line
defenses 713n.
magisterial
skillful 694adj.
authoritative 733adj.
ruling 733adj.
insolent 878adj.
magistery
powder 332n.
magistracy
magistrature 733n.
jurisdiction 955n.
magistracy 957n.
magistrate
official 690n.
officer 741n.
judge 957n.
magistrature
(*see* magistracy)
magnanimous
disinterested 931adj.
virtuous 933adj.
magnate
aristocrat 868n.
magnet
focus 76n.
traction 288n.
attraction 291n.
incentive 612n.
desired object 859n.
magnetic
dynamic 160adj.
magnetic needle
indicator 547n.
directorship 689n.
magnetic north
compass point 281n.
magnetism
energy 160n.
influence 178n.
traction 288n.
attraction 291n.
inducement 612n.
magnetize
attract 291vb.
Magnificat
hymn 981n.
magnification
increase 36n.
vision 438n.
exaggeration 546n.
(*see* magnify)
magnificent
beauty 841n.
ornamentation 844n.
ostentation 875n.
magnificent
excellent 644adj.
splendid 841adj.
ostentatious 875adj.
magnifico
aristocrat 868n.
magnify
augment 36vb.
enlarge 197vb.
overrate 482vb.
exaggerate 546vb.
make important 638vb.
boast 877vb.
respect 920vb.
praise 923vb.
worship 981vb.
magnifying glass
eyeglass 442n.
magniloquence
exaggeration 546n.

vigor 571n.
magniloquence 574n.
eloquence 579n.
affectation 850n.
ostentation 875n.
magnitude
quantity 26n.
degree 27n.
greatness 32n.
size 195n.
importance 638n.
magnum
vessel 194n.
size 195n.
magnum opus
book 589n.
magpie
bird 365n.
chatterer 581n.
niggard 816n.
magsman
trickster 545n.
defrauder 789n.
maharajah
potentate 741n.
mahatma
sage 500n.
good man 937n.
Mahayana
religious faith 973n.
Mahdi
leader 690n.
Mah-jongg
indoor game 837n.
mahogany
smoothness 258n.
tree 366n.
brownness 430n.
mahout
rider, driver 268n.
maid
domestic 742n.
(*see* maiden)
maiden
first 68adj.
new 126adj.
youngster 132n.
woman 373n.
spinster 895n.
virgin 950n.
instrument of torture 964n.
maidenhood
celibacy 895n.
purity 950n.
maidenly
young 130adj.
female 373adj.
unwedded 895adj.
pure 950adj.
maiden name
name 561n.
maiden over
unproductiveness 172n.
maiden speech
debut 68n.
maid-of-all-work
busy person 678n.
worker 686n.
domestic 742n.
maieutic
inquiring 459adj.
rational 475adj.
instrumental 628adj.
mail
send 272vb.
mails 531n.
correspondence 588n.
safeguard 662n.
armor 713n.
weapon 723n.
mailbag
mails 531n.
mail-clad
defended 713adj.
mail-coach
stage-coach 274n.
mails 531n.
mailed fist
compulsion 740n.
lawlessness 954n.
maim
disable 161vb.
impair 655vb.
maimed
incomplete 55adj.
imperfect 647adj.
main
great 32adj.
supreme 34adj.
tube 263n.
conduit 351n.
main chance
fair chance 159n.
benefit 615n.
chief thing 638n.
gain 771n.
main force
strength 162n.
compulsion 740n.
main, in the
substantially 3adv.
intrinsically 5adv.
materially 638adv.
mainland
land 344n.
mainlander
dweller 191n.
land 344n.
mainly
generally 79adv.
main part
main part 32n.
chief part 52n.
mainpernor
security 767n.
mainprize
security 767n.
mainsail
sail 275n.
mainspring
cause 156n.
motive 612n.
machine 630n.
mainstay
supporter 218n.
chief thing 638n.
refuge 662n.
hope 852n.
main stream
tendency 179n.
maintain
stay 144vb.
sustain 146vb.
operate 173vb.
support 218vb.
believe 485vb.
affirm 532vb.
persevere 600vb.
provide 633vb.
preserve 666vb.
celebrate 876vb.
vindicate 924vb.
maintenance
subvention 703n.
receipt 807n.
(*see* maintain)
maisonette
flat 192n.
maize
cereal 301n.
corn 366n.
majestic
impressive 821adj.
beautiful 841adj.
proud 871adj.
formal 875adj.
godlike 965adj.
(*see* majesty)
majesty
greatness 32n.
superiority 34n.
authority 733n.
sovereign 741n.
prestige 866n.
nobility 868n.
Majlis
parliament 692n.
majolica
pottery 381n.
major
great 32adj.
superior 34adj.
older 131adj.
grown up 134adj.
harmonic 410adj.
important 638adj.

army officer 741n.
majordomo
retainer 742n.
major in
learn 536vb.
majority
main part 32n.
chief part 52n.
greater number 104n.
adultness 134n.
majorize
augment 36vb.
major premise
argumentation 475n.
major suit
skill 694n.
majuscule
letter 558n.
make
character 5n.
composition 56n.
compose 56vb.
constitute 56vb.
sort 77n.
convert 147vb.
cause 156vb.
produce 164vb.
influence 178vb.
efform 243vb.
arrive 295vb.
structure 331n.
flow 350vb.
estimate 480vb.
make better 654vb.
compel 740vb.
gain 771vb.
make acquainted
befriend 880vb.
make a face
dislike 861vb.
disapprove 924vb.
make a leg
show respect 920vb.
make a man of
give courage 855vb.
make amends
compensate 31vb.
atone 941vb.
reward 962vb.
make as if
imitate 20vb.
make available
offer 759vb.
make away with
destroy 165vb.
kill 362vb.
make a whole
be complete 54adj.
make a will
bequeath 780vb.
make-believe
imitate 20vb.
fantasy 513n.
imaginary 513adj.
hypocritical 541adj.
sham 542n.
spurious 542adj.
untrue 543adj.
be untrue 543vb.
make bold
be free 744vb.
be insolent 878vb.
make both ends meet
afford 800vb.
economize 814vb.
make certain
make certain 473vb.
make contact
connect 45vb.
touch 378vb.
make difficulties
be difficult 700vb.
make do with
substitute 150vb.
avail of 673vb.
make eyes
court 889vb.
make for
congregate 74vb.
steer for 281vb.
promote 285vb.
make free with
be free 744vb.
appropriate 786vb.
be insolent 878vb.
make friends
accord 24vb.
make peace 719vb.
make good
compensate 31vb.
make complete 54vb.
corroborate 466vb.
replenish 633vb.
succeed 727vb.
vindicate 927vb.
make hay
prosper 730vb.
make head
progress 285vb.
make head against
withstand 704vb.
triumph 727vb.
make interest for
patronize 703vb.
request 761vb.
make into
convert 147vb.
make it up
make peace 719vb.
forgive 909vb.
make it up to
restitute 787vb.
atone 941vb.
make light of
underestimate 483vb.
do easily 701vb.
be indifferent 860vb.
make love
love 887vb.
caress 889vb.
make merry
rejoice 835vb.
revel 837vb.
ridicule 851vb.
make money
flourish 615vb.
prosper 730vb.
gain 771vb.
get rich 800vb.
make much of
love 887vb.
pet 889vb.
make no bones
be willing 597vb.
make nothing of
not understand 517vb.
do easily 701vb.
make off
run away 620vb.
make off with
steal 788vb.
make one of
augment 36vb.
be included 78vb.
be present 189vb.
join a party 708vb.
make one's bed
choose 605vb.
make oneself scarce
go away 190vb.
run away 620vb.
elude 667vb.
make one's mark
succeed 727vb.
make one's point
affirm 532vb.
make one's way
travel 267vb.
get better 654vb.
prosper 730vb.
make or mar
cause 156vb.
influence 178vb.
make out
see 438vb.
corroborate 466vb.
demonstrate 478vb.
understand 516vb.
decipher 520vb.
plead 614vb.
succeed 727vb.
make-peace
mediator 720n.
maker
cause 156n.
producer 167n.
make sense
be intelligible 516vb.
interpret 520vb.
makeshift
inferior 35adj.

transientness 114n.
substitute 150n.
spontaneous 609adj.
pretext 614n.
instrument 628n.
means 629n.
sufficient 635adj.
imperfection 647n.
unprepared 670adj.
make shift with
avail of 673vb.
make short work of
destroy 165vb.
eat 301vb.
do easily 701vb.
succeed 727vb.
make something of
transform 147vb.
make sure
stabilize 153vb.
make certain 473vb.
be cautious 858vb.
make terms
accord 24vb.
make terms 766vb.
make the best of
(*see* make the most of)
make the grade
succeed 727vb.
make the most of
overrate 482vb.
avail of 673vb.
be ostentatious 875vb.
make the running
outstrip 277vb.
outdo 306vb.
make to measure
adjust 24vb.
make tracks
decamp 296vb.
make trouble
make quarrels 709vb.
cause discontent 829vb.
make up
compensate 31vb.
make complete 54vb.
constitute 56vb.
imagine 513vb.
print 587n.
replenish 633vb.
primp 843vb.
makeup
dissimilarity 19n.
composition 56n.
specialty 80n.
print 587n.
stage-set 594n.
affections 817n.
beautification 843n.
cosmetic 843n.
make up one's mind
be resolute 599vb.
choose 605vb.
make up to
approach 289vb.
flatter 925vb.
make water
excrete 302vb.
make way
navigate 269vb.
progress 285vb.
recede 290vb.
avoid 620vb.
facilitate 701vb.
show respect 920vb.
makeweight
offset 31n.
plenitude 54n.
gravity 322n.
make work
be busy 678vb.
work 682vb.
make worse
aggravate 832vb.
malachite
greenness 432n.
malacology
zoology 367n.
maladjusted
inexact 495adj.
clumsy 695adj.
maladjustment
misfit 25n.
discontent 829n.
maladministration
misuse 675n.
bungling 695n.
malady
disease 651n.
bane 659n.
mala fides
perfidy 930n.
malaise
pain 377n.
evil 616n.
suffering 825n.
malapertness
sauciness 878n.
malapropism
mistake 495n.
inexactness 495n.
absurdity 497n.
neology 560n.
misnomer 562n.
solecism 565n.
ridiculousness 849n.
malaria
malaria 651n.
malarial
infectious 653adj.
malcontent
dissentient 489n.
opponent 705n.
malcontent 829n.
disapprover 924n.
mal du pays
melancholy 834n.
male
vitality 162n.
athletic 162adj.
male 372n., adj.
malediction
discontent 829n.
hatred 888n.
malediction 899n.
detraction 926n.
condemnation 961n.
impiety 980n.
prayers 981n.
maledictory
threatening 900adj.
malefactor
offender 904n.
maleficent
harmful 645adj.
maleficent 898adj.
malevolence
badness 645n.
quarrelsomeness 709n.
enmity 881n.
hatred 888n.
malevolence 898n.
wickedness 934n.
malfeasance
lawbreaking 954n.
malformation
deformity 246n.
malice
joy 824n.
hatred 888n.
resentment 891n.
malevolence 898n.
malice aforethought, with
purposely 617adj.
malicious
harmful 645adj.
hating 888adj.
malevolent 898adj.
malign
harmful 645adj.
adverse 731adj.
shame 867vb.
malevolent 898adj.
defame 926vb.
malignant
harmful 645adj.
hating 888adj.
malevolent 898adj.
sorcerous 983adj.
malignant tumor
carcinosis 651n.
malignity
violence 176n.
badness 645n.
annoyance 827n.
(*see* malevolence)
malinger
dissemble 541vb.
fail in duty 918vb.

malingerer
imposter 545n.
dutilessness 918n.
malison
malediction 899n.
mall
street 192n.
pleasance 192n.
hammer 279n.
mallard
waterfowl 365n.
malleability
conformity 83n.
malleable
conformable 83adj.
unstable 152adj.
flexible 327adj.
impressible 819adj.
mallet
hammer 279n.
malleus
ear 415n.
malnutrition
disease 651n.
malodor
odium 888n.
malodorous
fetid 397adj.
unclean 649adj.
unpleasant 827adj.
dishonest 930adj.
malpractice
guilty act 936n.
lawbreaking 954n.
Malthusianism
deterioration 655n.
maltose
food content 301n.
maltreat
ill-treat 645vb.
misuse 675vb.
torment 827vb.
be malevolent 898vb.
malversation
misuse 675n.
peculation 788n.
prodigality 815n.
foul play 930n.
guilty act 936n.
mamba
reptile 365n.
mamelon
dome 253n.
(*see* monticle)
mamilla
bosom 253n.
Mamluke
militarist 722n.
mamma
maternity 169n.
bosom 253n.
mammal
animal 365n.
mamma's boy
weakling 163n.
mammer
stammer 580vb.
mammiferous
female 373adj.
mammiform
arcuate 253adj.
mammon
money 797n.
wealth 800n.
devil 969n.
mammoth
giant 195n.
animal 365n.
mammy
negro 428n.
protector 660n.
keeper 749n.
man
adult 134n.
mankind 371n.
male 372n.
provide 633vb.
worker 686n.
defend 713vb.
domestic 742n.
dependent 742n.
subject 742n.
chessman 837n.
brave person 855n.
spouse 894n.
mana
power 160n.
influence 178n.
divineness 965n.
manacle
tie 45vb.
fetter 748n.
manage
arrange 62vb.
be able 160vb.
look after 457vb.
motivate 612vb.
undertake 672vb.
do 676vb.
deal with 688vb.
manage 689vb.
be successful 727vb.
rule 733vb.
deputize 755vb.
manageable
wieldy 701adj.
management
management 689n.
director 690n.
manager
stage-manager 594n.
motivator 612n.
doer 676n.
agent 686n.
protector 690n.
director 690n.
manager 690n.
consignee 754n.
managerial
directing 689adj.
mañana
delay 136n.
man and wife
spouse 894n.
man-at-arms
soldier 722n.
man at the wheel
navigator 270n.
mandamus
warrant 737n.
mandarin
fruit 301n.
language 557n.
official 690n.
officer 741n.
mandate
job 622n.
requirement 627n.
precept 693n.
policy 733n.
command 737n.
mandate 751n.
permit 756n.
conditions 766n.
mandatory
preceptive 693adj.
authoritative 733adj.
commanding 737adj.
mandibles
eater 301n.
mandolin
harp 414n.
mandrake, mandragora
medicine 658n.
soporific 679n.
mandrel
rotator 315n.
mandrill
monkey 365n.
manducate
chew 301vb.
mane
hair 259n.
man-eater
killer 362n.
animal 365n.
noxious animal 904n.
manege
equitation 267n.
animal husbandry 369n.
manes
corpse 363n.
ghost 970n.
maneuver
motion 265n.
deed 676n.
tactics 688n.
manage 689vb.
be cunning 698vb.
wage war 718vb.
maneuverability

scope 744n.
maneuverable
wieldy 701adj.
maneuverer
influence 178n.
motivator 612n.
planner 623n.
slyboots 698n.
manful
athletic 162adj.
courageous 855adj.
manfully
resolutely 599adv.
mange
skin disease 651n.
animal disease 651n.
manger
bowl 194n.
mangle
compressor 198n.
flattener 216n.
smoother 258n.
dry 342vb.
wound 655vb.
mangled
incomplete 55adj.
inexact 495adj.
mango
fruit 301n.
mangonel
propellant 287n.
missile weapon 723n.
mangy
hairless 229adj.
unhealthy 651adj.
man-handle
move 265vb.
touch 378vb.
man-hater
misanthrope 902n.
manhole
orifice 263n.
manhood
adultness 134n.
male 372n.
manliness 855n.
man-hours
labor 682n.
mania
bias 481n.
mania 503n.
psychopathy 503n.
warm feeling 818n.
excitable state 822n.
liking 859n.
maniac
madman 504n.
manic
insane 503adj.
manic-depressive
insane 503adj.
madman 504n.
Manichaeism
heresy 977n.
Manichee
heretic 977n.
manicure
surgery 658n.
beautification 843n.
manicured
elegant 575adj.
manicurist
doctor 658n.
beautician 843n.
manifest
list 87n.
open 263adj.
appearing 445adj.
evidence 466vb.
manifest 522adj., vb.
well-known 528adj.
accounts 808n.
manifestation
visibility 443n.
manifestation 522n.
disclosure 526n.
indication 547n.
representation 551n.
manifesto
publication 528n.
manifold
multiform 82adj.
manikin
small animal 33n.
dwarf 196n.
image 551n.
man in the moon
moon 321n.
fantasy 513n.
man in the street
common man 30n.
everyman 79n.
social group 371n.
mediocrity 732n.
commoner 869n.
maniple
formation 722n.
vestments 989n.
manipulate
operate 173vb.
touch 378vb.
fake 541vb.
motivate 612vb.
plot 623vb.
use 673vb.
misuse 675vb.
do 676vb.
deal with 688vb.
manage 689vb.
manipulation
foul play 930n.
(*see* manipulate)
manipulator
influence 178n.
trickster 545n.
motivator 612n.
gambler 618n.
mankind
mankind 371n.
manlike
male 372adj.
manliness
(*see* manly)
manly
grown up 134adj.
manly 162adj.
male 372adj.
beautiful 841adj.
courageous 855adj.
honorable 929adj.
man milliner
fop 848n.
manna
food 301n.
subvention 703n.
gift 781n.
pleasurableness 826n.
manned
occupied 191adj.
mannequin
living model 23n.
mannequin parade
exhibit 522n.
fashion 848n.
manner
sort 77n.
style 566n.
way 624n.
conduct 688n.
mannered
stylistic 566adj.
inelegant 576adj.
ridiculous 849adj.
affected 850adj.
mannerism
speciality 80n.
unconformity 84n.
school of painting 553n.
phrase 563n.
style 566n.
inelegance 576n.
affectation 850n.
airs 873n.
mannerless
discourteous 885adj.
mannerly
courteous 884adj.
manners
practice 610n.
conduct 688n.
good taste 846n.
etiquette 848n.
courtesy 884n.
manners and customs
practice 610n.
mannish
male 372adj.
man of action
doer 676n.
busy person 678n.
man of business

expert 696n.
consignee 754n.
man of honor
person of repute 866n.
gentleman 929n.
man of letters
linguist 557n.
bookman 589n.
man of, make a
do good 644vb.
man of mark
bigwig 638n.
person of repute 866n.
man of prayer
pietist 979n.
worshiper 981n.
man of property
made man 730n.
owner 776n.
man of straw
insubstantial thing 4n.
ineffectuality 161n.
sham 542n.
nonentity 639n.
non-payer 805n.
man of the people
vulgarian 847n.
commoner 869n.
man of the world
expert 696n.
beau monde 848n.
man-of-war
warship 722n.
man-of-war's man
naval man 270n.
navy man 722n.
man on the spot
delegate 754n.
manor
house 192n.
lands 777n.
manorial
agrarian 370adj.
proprietary 777adj.
man-power
band 74n.
power 160n.
means 629n.
personnel 686n.
manqué
deviating 282adj.
unsuccessful 728adj.
mansard roof
roof 226n.
manse
parsonage 986n.
man-servant
domestic 742n.
man's estate
adultness 134n.
mansion
place 185n.
house 192n.
zodiac 321n.
man-size
great 32adj.
large 195adj.
manslaughter
homicide 362n.
mansuetude
courtesy 884n.
manteau
cloak 228n.
mantelet, mantlet
cloak 228n.
armor 713n.
mantelpiece
shelf 218n.
mantic
predicting 511adj.
manticore
rara avis 84n.
mantilla
shawl 228n.
mantle
wrapping 226n.
cloak 228n.
bubble 355vb.
darken 418vb.
lamp 420n.
screen 421n.
redden 431vb.
be modest 874vb.
man, to a
unanimously 488adv.
mantology
divination 311n.
occultism 984n.
mantua
cloak 228n.
manual
series 71n.
handed 378adj.
musical note 410n.
piano, organ 414n.
guide-book 524n.
textbook 589n.
manufacture
production 164n.
produce 164vb.
business 622n.
action 676n.
manufacturer
producer 167n.
agent 686n.
manumission
liberation 746n.
manure
fertilizer 171n.
invigorate 174vb.
agriculture 370n.
patronize 703vb.
manuscript
prototype 23n.
script 586n.
book 589n.
many
many 104adj.
frequent 139adj.
commonalty 869n.
many-colored
multiform 82adj.
colored 425n.
variegated 437adj.
many-headed
multiform 82adj.
many 104adj.
commonalty 869n.
many-sided
multiform 82adj.
plural 101adj.
lateral 239adj.
skillful 694adj.
map
situation 186n.
outline 233n.
face 237n.
itinerary 267n.
gauge 465vb.
guide-book 524n.
map 551n.
represent 551vb.
plan 623n.
maple
tree 366n.
maquis
wood 366n.
soldier 722n.
revolter 738n.
mar
derange 63vb.
modify 143vb.
lay waste 165vb.
influence 178vb.
impair 655vb.
be clumsy 695vb.
hinder 702vb.
marabout
worshiper 981n.
monk 986n.
holy place 990n.
marasmus
contraction 198n.
disease 651n.
dilapidation 655n.
marathon
lasting 113adj.
distance 199n.
racing 716n.
maraud
rob 788vb.
marauder
militarist 722n.
robber 789n.
marble
sphere 252n.
smoothness 258n.
hardness 326n.
rock 344n.
white thing 427n.
variegate 437vb.
sculpture 554n.

building material 631n.
unfeeling person 820n.
marbles
plaything 837n.
marbling
maculation 437n.
bookbinding 589n.
march
region 184n.
limit 236n.
motion, gait 265n.
itinerary 267n.
walk 267vb.
progression 285n.
musical piece 412n.
route 624n.
wage war 718vb.
march against
charge 712vb.
märchen
fable 543n.
marcher
dweller 191n.
pedestrian 268n.
agitator 738n.
marches
limit 236n.
marching
marching 267n.
marchioness
nobleman 868n.
march of time
course of time 111n.
progression 285n.
improvement 654n.
march past
pageant 875n.
march with
be contiguous 202vb.
marconigram
message 529n.
mare
horse 273n.
female animal 373n.
mare's nest
fable 543n.
mare's tail
cloud 355n.
margarine
fat 357n.
margin
remainder 41n.
room 183n.
edge 234n.
letterpress 587n.
edition 589n.
superfluity 637n.
redundance 637n.
scope 744n.
discount 810n.
marginal
inconsiderable 33adj.
marginal 234adj.
economical 814adj.
marginalia
commentary 520n.
record 548n.
reading matter 589n.
margrave
potentate 741n.
nobleman 868n.
mariage de convenance
type of marriage 894n.
marihuana
poison 659n.
marimba
piano, gong 414n.
marina
stable 19n.
shelter 662n.
marinate
immerse 303vb.
preserve 666vb.
marine
seafaring 269adj.
shipping 275n.
marine 275adj.
oceanic 343adj.
navy man 722n.
Marine Corps
navy man 722n.
mariner
mariner 270n.
Mariolatry
Madonna 968n.
marionette(s)
image 551n.
stage-play 594n.
plaything 837n.
marital
matrimonial 894adj.
maritime
seafaring 269adj.
marine 275adj.
oceanic 343adj.
marjoram
potherb 301n.
mark
character 5n.
degree 27n.
serial place 73n.
sort 77n.
specialty 80n.
effect 157n.
feature 445n.
assent 488n.
indication 547n.
mark 547vb.
trace 548n.
script 586n.
select 605vb.
objective 617n.
importance 638n.
wound 655n.
impair 655vb.
coinage 797n.
blemish 845n., vb.
slur 867n.
mark, beside the
irrelevant 10adj.
mark down
underestimate 483vb.
select 605vb.
discount 810vb.
cheapen 812vb.
mark down for
intend 617vb.
markedly
remarkably 32adv.
market
focus 76n.
meeting place 192n.
purchase 792vb.
sell 793vb.
mart 796n.
marketable
trading 791adj.
salable 793adj.
marketer
purchaser 792n.
market garden
farm 370n.
market, in the
offering 759adj.
salable 793adj.
market-place
activity 678n.
arena 724n.
(*see* market)
markings
identification 547n.
mark, of
remarkable 32adj.
notable 638adj.
mark off
gauge 465vb.
mark, off the
deviating 282adj.
astray 282adv.
mark of recognition
courteous act 884n.
mark out
differentiate 15vb.
set apart 46vb.
select 605vb.
dignify 866vb.
marksman
shooter 287n.
hunter 619n.
proficient 696n.
marksmanship
skill 694n.
mark the occasion
celebrate 876vb.
mark the time
play music 413vb.
mark time
pass time 108vb.
time 117vb.

be quiescent 266vb.
await 507vb.
mark, up to the
expert 694adj.
marl
soil 344n.
marmalade
sweetmeat 301n.
condiment 389n.
sweet 392n.
marmoreal
glyptic 554adj.
marmoset
monkey 365n.
marmot
rodent 365n.
idler 679n.
maroon
set apart 46vb.
brown 430adj.
red color 431n.
derelict 779n.
not retain 779vb.
solitary 883n.
marplot
bungler 677n.
hinderer 702n.
evildoer 904n.
marquee
pavilion 192n.
canopy 226n.
marquetry
checker 437n.
marquis
nobleman 868n.
marriage
junction 45n.
combination 50n.
marriage 894n.
marriageable
grown up 134adj.
marriageable 894adj.
marriage adviser
mediator 720n.
marriage-broker
intermediary 231n.
matchmaker 894n.
marriage lines
record 548n.
marriage 894n.
marriage portion
dower 777n.
marriage service
Christian rite 988n.
married man
spouse 894n.
marrow
substance 3n.
essential part 5n.
vitality 162n.
interiority 224n.
centrality 225n.
vegetables 301n.
plant 366n.
marrowless
weak 163adj.
marry
join 45vb.
combine 50vb.
marry, wed 894vb.
marry off
not retain 779vb.
convey 780vb.
marry 894vb.
Mars
planet 321n.
redness 431n.
quarrelsomeness 709n.
war 718n.
mythic god 966n.
Olympian god 967n.
marsh, marshland
desert 172n.
moisture 341n.
marsh 347n.
semiliquidity 354n.
dirt 649n.
marshal
arrange 62vb.
mark 547vb.
auxiliary 707n.
officer 741n.
army officer 741n.
marshaling yard
railroad 624n.
marshiness
softness 327n.
marshmallows
sweetmeat 301n.
marshy
humid 341adj.
marshy 347adj.
pulpy 356adj.
dirty 649adj.
insalubrious 653adj.
marsupial
cellular 194adj.
marsupial 365n.
mart
(*see* market)
martello tower
fort 713n.
marten
skin 226n.
martial
warlike 718adj.
courageous 855adj.
martial law
government 733n.
anarchy 734n.
brute force 735n.
Martian
foreigner 59n.
planetary 321adj.
martin
bird 365n.
martinet
tyrant 735n.
martingale
fetter 748n.
Martinmas
holy-day 988n.
martlet
heraldry 547n.
martyr
kill 362vb.
torment 827vb.
pietist 979n.
martyrdom
death 361n.
killing 362n.
pain 377n.
suffering 825n.
disinterestedness 931n.
capital punishment 963n.
martyr-like
disinterested 931adj.
martyrologist
narrator 590n.
martyrology
list 87n.
death roll 361n.
biography 590n.
martyry
holy place 990n.
marvel
wonder 864n., vb.
marvelous
prodigious 32adj.
excellent 644adj.
pleasurable 826adj.
wonderful 864adj.
Marxism
materiality 319n.
philosophy 449n.
antichristianity 974n.
Marxist
revolutionist 149n.
reformer 654n.
irreligionist 974n.
marzipan
sweetmeat 301n.
sweet 392n.
mascara
cosmetic 843n.
mascot
preserver 666n.
talisman 983n.
masculine
generic 77adj.
manly 162adj.
male 372adj.
grammatical 564adj.
masculinity
male 372n.
mash
medley 43n.
confusion 61n.
soften 327vb.
pulverize 332vb.

semiliquidity 354n.
thicken 354vb.
pulpiness 356n.
be clumsy 695vb.
masher
pulverizer 332n.
fop 848n.
masjid
temple 990n.
mask
covering 226n.
screen 421n., vb.
conceal 525vb.
disguise 527n.
sham 542n.
mental dishonesty 543n.
masked
invisible 444adj.
masochism
abnormality 84n.
mason
efform 243vb.
artisan 686n.
Masonic
sectional 708adj.
masonry
accumulation 74n.
building material 631n.
Masorete
interpreter 520n.
theologian 973n.
Masoretic
scriptural 975adj.
masque
stage play 594n.
drama 594n.
festivity 837n.
masquerade
clothing 228n.
concealment 525n.
sham 542n.
dancing 837n.
masquerader
hider 527n.
imposter 545n.
mass
quantity 26n.
great quantity 32n.
main part 32n.
extensive 32adj.
chief part 52n.
confusion 61n.
accumulation 74n.
crowd 74n.
congregate 74vb.
general 79adj.
greater number 104n.
size, bulk 195n.
matter 319n.
gravity 322n.
solid body 324n.
army 722n.
public worship 981n.
Holy Communion 988n.
massacre
slaughter 362n., vb.
execute 963vb.
massage
soften 327vb.
friction 333n.
touch 378n., vb.
surgery 658n.
beautification 843n.
massed
multitudinous 104adj.
dense 324adj.
masses, the
everyman 79n.
social group 371n.
commonalty 869n.
masseur, masseuse
(*see* massage)
massif
high land 209n.
mass, in a
together 74adv.
massive
great 32adj.
large 195adj.
weighty 322adj.
dense 324adj.
mass-meeting
assembly 74n.
mass-money
oblation 981n.
mass movement
activity 678n.
mass murder
destruction 165n.
cruel act 898n.
capital punishment 963n.
mass-produce
produce 164vb.
mass production
uniformity 16n.
reproduction 166n.
productiveness 171n.
massy
great 32adj.
large 195adj.
material 319adj.
weighty 322adj.
dense 324adj.
mast
high structure 209n.
hanger 217n.
supporter 318n.
frenzied 503adj.
mastaba
tomb 364n.
master
superior 34n.
youngster 132n.
prevail 178vb.
mariner 270n.
sage 500n.
understand 516vb.
learn 536vb.
teacher 537n.
director 690n.
proficient 696n.
victor 727n.
overmaster 727vb.
master 741n.
owner 776n.
title 870n.
theosophy 984n.
masterful
authoritative 733adj.
authoritarian 735adj.
master-key
opener 263n.
masterless
independent 744adj.
unpossessed 774adj.
masterly
perfect 646adj.
skillful 694adj.
successful 727adj.
master-mariner
mariner 270n.
master-mind
intellectual 492n.
sage 500n.
proficient 696n.
master of ceremonies
leader 690n.
reveler 837n.
masterpiece
product 164n.
picture 553n.
exceller 644n.
perfection 646n.
masterpiece 694n.
success 727n.
a beauty 841n.
master-plan
prototype 23n.
plan 623n.
mastership
skill 694n.
magistrature 733n.
master spirit
sage 500n.
bigwig 638n.
proficient 696n.
person of repute 866n.
master-stroke
contrivance 623n.
masterpiece 694n.
success 727n.
mastery
knowledge 490n.
skill 694n.
victory 727n.
rule 733n.
magistrature 733n.

possession 773n.
masthead
high structure 209n.
vertex 213n.
punish 963vb.
mastic
viscidity 354n.
resin 357n.
mastication
eating 301n.
pulpiness 356n.
mastiff
dog 368n.
mastadon
animal 365n.
mat
enlace 222vb.
floor-cover 226n.
semi-transparent 424adj.
soft-hued 425adj.
cleaning cloth 648n.
matador
killer 362n.
combatant 722n.
match
analogue 18n.
resemble 18vb.
accord 24vb.
compeer 28n.
join 45vb.
pair 90vb.
burning 381n.
lighter 385n.
torch 420n.
compare 462vb.
contest, duel 716n.
marriage 894n.
match against
oppose 704vb.
matchbox
small box 194n.
lighter 385n.
matchet
side-arms 723n.
matching
harmonious 410adj.
soft-hued 425adj.
matchless
supreme 34adj.
best 644adj.
matchlock
fire-arm 723n.
match-make
marry 894vb.
match-maker
intermediary 231n.
mediator 720n.
match-maker 894n.
match-stick
weak thing 163n.
match-winner
victor 727n.
match-winning
successful 727adj.
match with
make quarrels 709vb.
matchwood
weak thing 163n.
brittleness 330n.
mate
analogue 18n.
compeer 28n.
unite with 45vb.
combine 50vb.
concomitant 89n.
pair 90vb.
mariner 270n.
personnel 686n.
colleague 707n.
overmaster 727vb.
defeat 728n.
chum 880n.
spouse 894n.
marry, wed 894vb.
maté
soft drink 301n.
mateless
unwedded 895adj.
materfamilias
maternity 169n.
material
real 1adj.
substantiality 3n.
textile 222n.
matter 319n.
materials 631n.
important 638adj.
sensual 944adj.
materialism
materiality 319n.
philosophy 449n.
antichristianity 974n.
impiety 980n.
materialistic
selfish 932adj.
(*see* materialism)
materiality
substantiality 3n.
materiality 319n.
importance 638n.
materialization
manifestation 522n.
materialize
happen 154vb.
materialize 319vb.
be visible 443vb.
appear 445vb.
practice occultism 984vb.
materials
source 156n.
object 319n.
means 629n.
materials 631n.
materia medica
medicine 658n.
maternal
akin 11adj.
parental 169adj.
benevolent 897adj.
maternity
propagation 164n.
maternity 169n.
matey
friendly 880adj.
sociable 882adj.
mathematical
statistical 86adj.
accurate 494adj.
mathematician
computer 86n.
reasoner 475n.
mathematics
mathematics 86n.
matinee
evening 129n.
dramaturgy 594n.
mating
coition 45n.
libido 859n.
matins
morning 128n.
public worship 981n.
church service 988n.
matriarch
family 11n.
maternity 169n.
master 741n.
matriarchy
gynocracy 733n.
matricide
homicide 362n.
matriculate
list 87vb.
matriculation
exam. 459n.
matrilinear
akin 11adj.
parental 169adj.
matrimonial
matrimonial 894adj.
matrimonial agent
match-maker 894n.
matrimony
marriage 894n.
matrix
mold 23n.
print-type 587n.
matron
adult 134n.
maternity 169n.
woman 373n.
nurse 658n.
manager 690n.
spouse 894n.
matronage
womankind 373n.
matronhood
female 373n.
marriage 894n.
matronly

aged 131adj.
grown up 134adj.
parental 169adj.
female 373adj.
matrimonial 894adj.
matron of honor
bridesman 894n.
matronymic
name 561n.
matted
crossed 222adj.
hairy 259adj.
dense 324adj.
dirty 649adj.
matter
substantiality 3n.
matter 319n.
solid body 324n.
semiliquidity 354n.
topic 452n.
meaning 514n.
be important 638vb.
dirt 649n.
ulcer 651n.
matter in hand
undertaking 672n.
matter of course
practice 610n.
non-wonder 865n.
matter of fact
reality 1n.
eventuality 154n.
certainty 473n.
truth 494n.
dullness 840n.
matter-of-fact
narrow-minded 481adj.
prosaic 593adj.
artless 699adj.
matter-of-factness
plainness 573n.
matter of time
course of time 111n.
matters
affairs 154n.
mattery
fluidal 335adj.
toxic 653adj.
matting
network 222n.
floor-cover 226n.
mattock
sharp edge 256n.
mattress
cushion 218n.
maturation
maturation 669n.
(*see* mature)
mature
grow 36vb.
be complete 54vb.
grown up 134adj.
be turned to 147vb.
plan 623vb.
perfect 646vb.
make better 654vb.
mature 669vb.
carry through 725vb.
matured
formed 243adj.
maturing
future 124adj.
maturity
oldness 127n.
adultness 134n.
preparedness 669n.
completion 725n.
matutinal
matinal 128adj.
maudlin
foolish 499adj.
tipsy 949adj.
maul
be violent 176vb.
hammer 279n.
strike 279vb.
ill-treat 645vb.
impair, wound 655vb.
attack 712vb.
dispraise 924vb.
maund
basket 194n.
weighment 322n.
maunder
be foolish 499vb.
be diffuse 570vb.
be loquacious 581vb.
Maundy-money
gift 781n.
Maundy Thursday
holy-day 988n.
mausoleum
edifice 164n.
tomb 364n.
monument 548n.
mauvaise honte
affectation 850n.
modesty 874n.
mauvais quart d'heure
suffering 825n.
reprimand 924n.
mauve
purple 434n.
maverick
cattle 365n.
revolter 738n.
mavis
bird 365n.
vocalist 413n.
mavourneen
darling 890n.
maw
maw 194n.
insides 224n.
eater 301n.
mawkish
feeling 818adj.
maxim
rule 81n.
maxim 496n.
precept 693n.
maximal
crowning 34adj.
maximalism
reformism 654n.
maximalist
reformer 654n.
revolter 738n.
maximize
augment 36vb.
overrate 482vb.
exaggerate 546vb.
maximum
greatness 32n.
crowning 34adj.
plenitude 54n.
size 195n.
summit 213n.
maximus
older 131adj.
may
be possible 469vb.
maya
insubstantiality 4n.
maybe
possibly 469adv.
mayfly
brief span 114n.
fly 365n.
mayonnaise
dish 301n.
mayor
official 690n.
councillor 692n.
officer 741n.
law officer 955n.
mayoralty
magistrature 733n.
jurisdiction 955n.
Mazdaism
religious faith 973n.
maze
complexity 61n.
meandering 251n.
enigma 530n.
difficulty 700n.
mazurka
musical piece 412n.
dance 837n.
mead
liquor 301n.
grassland 348n.
sweet 392n.
meadow
grassland 348n.
farm 370n.
meager
small 33adj.
exiguous 196adj.
lean 206adj.
feeble 572adj.
underfed 636adj.

poor 801adj.
economical 814adj.
fasting 946adj.
meal
meal 301n.
cereal 301n.
powder 332n.
corn 366n.
festivity 837n.
mealies
corn 366n.
mealy-mouthed
hypocritical 541adj.
flattering 925adj.
mean
average 30n.
middle 70n., adj.
interjacent 231adj.
be willing 597vb.
intend 617vb.
unimportant 639adj.
bad 645adj.
parsimonious 816adj.
disreputable 867adj.
plebeian 869adj.
humble 872adj.
servile 879adj.
contemptible 922adj.
rascally 930adj.
selfish 932adj.
(*see* meaning)
meander
meander 251vb.
flow 350vb.
meaning
relation 9n.
meaning 514n.
interpretation 520n.
affirmative 532adj.
indication 547n.
meaningful
meaningful 514adj.
intelligible 516adj.
important 638adj.
meaningless
insubstantial 4adj.
semantic 514adj.
unmeaning 515adj.
designless 618adj.
dull 840adj.
mean-minded
selfish 932adj.
meanness
smallness 33n.
unimportance 639n.
parsimony 816n.
despisedness 922n.
selfishness 932n.
mean nothing
mean nothing 515vb.
means
opportunity 137n.
contrivance 623n.
instrumentality 628n.
means 629n.
estate 777n.
funds 797n.
wealth 800n.
means, by no
in no way 33adv.
mean-spirited
cowardly 856adj.
means test
inquiry 459n.
meant
veracious 540adj.
meantime, meanwhile
while 108adv.
mean well
be benevolent 897vb.
measles
infection 651n.
measly
bad 645adj.
diseased 651adj.
measurable
numerable 86adj.
measure
finite quantity 26n.
graduate 27vb.
comprise 78vb.
counting instrument 86n.
moderation 177n.
measure 183n.
size 195n.
tempo 410n.
tune 412n.
gauge 465n.
mete out 465vb.
estimate 480vb.
prosody 593n.
deed 676n.
portion 783n.
measured
periodic 141adj.
moderate 177adj.
measured 465adj.
sufficient 635adj.
temperate 942adj.
measured by
comparative 27adj.
measure for measure
compensation 31n.
retaliation 714n.
measureless
infinite 107adj.
measurement
measurement 465n.
(*see* measure)
measures
policy 623n.
action 676n.
measure up to
be equal 28vb.
be able 160vb.
suffice 635vb.
meat
meat 301n.
food 301n.
meatiness
substance 3n.
bulk 195n.
meatless day
fast 946n.
holy-day 988n.
meaty
forceful 571adj.
(*see* meatiness)
mecca
focus 76n.
holy place 990n.
mechanic
machinist 630n.
artisan 686n.
mechanical
involuntary 596adj.
mechanical 630adj.
mechanics
means 629n.
mechanics 630n.
mechanism
machine 630n.
mechanization
instrumentality 628n.
medal
badge 547n.
decoration 729n.
jewelry 844n.
honors 866n.
reward 962n.
medalist
proficient 696n.
victor 727n.
medallion
ornamentation 844n.
jewelry 844n.
meddle
derange 63vb.
interfere 231vb.
be curious 453vb.
busy oneself 622vb.
impair 655vb.
meddle 678vb.
be clumsy 695vb.
obstruct 702vb.
mediate 720vb.
meddler
inquisitor 453n.
meddler 678n.
bungler 697n.
hinderer 702n.
meddlesome
inquisitive 453adj.
meddling 678adj.
medial
middle 70adj.
median
quantity 26n.
average 30n.
interjacent 231adj.
mediant

musical note 410n.
mediate
interfere 231vb.
be instrumental 628vb.
pacify 719vb.
mediate 720vb.
mediation
mediation 720n.
deprecation 762n.
mediator
moderator 177n.
intermediary 231n.
speaker 579n.
mediator 720n.
match-maker 894n.
mediatory
pacificatory 719adj.
mediatory 720adj.
redemptive 965adj.
medicable
medical 658adj.
medical
medical 658adj.
medical treatment
therapy 658n.
medicament
medicine 658n.
medicate
cure 656vb.
doctor 658vb.
medicinal
improving 654adj.
remedial 658adj.
medicine
vocation 622n.
cure 656vb.
medicine 658n.
medicine-man
doctor 658n.
sorcerer 983n.
mediety
middle point 30n.
middle 70n.
mediocrity 732n.
medieval
olden 127adj.
medievalism
palaetiology 125n.
mediocre
inconsiderable 33adj.
typical 83adj.
not bad 644adj.
mediocre 732adj.
modest 874adj.
mediocrity
average 30n.
inferiority 35n.
generality 79n.
moderation 177n.
mid-course 625n.
nonentity 639n.
imperfection 647n.
mediocrity 732n.
meditate
meditate 449vb.
inquire 459vb.
intend 617vb.
meditation
meditation 449n.
attention 455n.
piety 979n.
worship, prayers 981n.
mediterranean
middle 70adj.
interjacent 231adj.
medium
average 30n.
middle 70n.
circumjacence 230n.
intermediary 231n.
interjacent 231adj.
pigment 425n.
oracle 511n.
interpreter 520n.
instrumentality 628n.
mediocre 732adj.
psychic 984n.
medlar
fruit 301n.
medley
medley 43n.
confusion 61n.
accumulation 74n.
musical piece 412n.
medullary
soft 327adj.
Medusa
intimidation 854n.
meed
portion 783n.
reward 962n.
meek
submitting 721adj.
obedient 739n.
humble 782adj.
inexcitable 823adj.
patient 823adj.
meerschaum
tobacco 388n.
meet
fit 24adj.
congregate 74vb.
synchronize 123vb.
meet with 154vb.
be near 200vb.
touch 378vb.
discover 484vb.
withstand 704vb.
fight 716vb.
pay 804vb.
(*see* meeting)
meet an obligation
grant claims 915vb.
meet at every turn
be present 189vb.
meet half-way
be willing 597vb.
be half-way 625vb.
pacify 719vb.
compromise 770vb.
meeting
junction 45n.
assembly 74n.
eventuality 154n.
contiguity 202n.
collision 279n.
approach 289n.
approaching 289adj.
convergence 293n.
arrival 295n.
conference 584n.
council 692n.
social gathering 882n.
meeting house
meeting place 192n.
church 990n.
meeting place
focus 76n.
meeting place 192n.
goal 295n.
social round 882n.
meeting-point
junction 45n.
meet one's wishes
consent 758vb.
meet requirements
suffice 635vb.
meet the bill
defray 804vb.
megalith
antiquity 125n.
monument 548n.
megalithic
large 195adj.
megalomania
overestimation 482n.
mania 503n.
megalomaniac
madman 504n.
megaphone
megaphone 400n.
hearing aid 415n.
megascope
optical device 442n.
megatherium
giant 195n.
animal 365n.
megaton
weighment 322n.
megawatt
electricity 160n.
megilp
resin 357n.
megrims
spasm 318n.
animal disease 651n.
melancholy 834n.
meiny
band 74n.
meiosis
underestimation 483n.

meistersinger
poet 593n.
melancholia
psychopathy 503n.
melancholy 834n.
melancholic
insane 503adj.
madman 504n.
melancholic 834adj.
melancholy
bad 645adj.
sorrow 825n.
unhappy 825adj.
discontent 829n.
melancholy 834n.
cheerless 834adj.
melancholic 834adj.
tedium 838n.
sullenness 893n.
mélange
a mixture 43n.
melanism
blackness 428n.
melanoma
carcinosis 651n.
melee
turmoil 61n.
fight 716n.
melic
musical 412adj.
musicianly 413adj.
melioration
improvement 654n.
meliorism
reformism 654n.
mellifluous
sweet 392adj.
melodious 410adj.
elegant 575adj.
mellow
aged 131adj.
be turned to 147vb.
soften 327vb.
soft-hued 425adj.
color 425vb.
get better 654vb.
mature 669vb.
drunk 949adj.
melodeon
organ 414n.
melodic
melodious 410adj.
musical 412adj.
musicianly 413adj.
melodious
pleasant 376adj.
melodious 410adj.
melodist
vocalist 413n.
melodize
harmonize 410vb.
compose music 413vb.
melodrama
stage play 594n.
excitation 821n.
melodramatic
dramatic 594adj.
exciting 821adj.
melody
sweetness 392n.
melody 410n.
tune 412n.
concord 710n.
pleasurableness 826n.
melon
fruit 301n.
plant 366n.
melt
not be 2vb.
decrease 37vb.
come unstuck 49vb.
decompose 51vb.
be dispersed 75vb.
be transient 114vb.
deform 244vb.
liquefy 337vb.
be hot 379vb.
heat 381vb.
sound faint 401vb.
disappear 446vb.
waste 634vb.
weep 836vb.
pity 905vb.
melting
unstable 152adj.
soft 327adj.
fluidal 335adj.
melting mood
lamentation 836n.
pity 905n.
melting point
heat 379n.
melting-pot
mixture 43n.
crucible 147n.
workshop 687n.
melt into
shade off 27vb.
be turned to 147vb.
mem
lady 373n.
title 870n.
member
part, limb 53n.
component 58n.
genitalia 164n.
society 708n.
participator 775n.
member of Parliament
councillor 692n.
membership
inclusion 78n.
association 706n.
participation 775n.
sociality 882n.
membrane
layer 207n.
memento
reminder 505n.
trophy 729n.
memento mori
dejection 834n.
memoir
record 548n.
dissertation 591n.
memoirs
remembrance 505n.
reading matter 589n.
biography 590n.
memorabilia
remembrance 505n.
reading matter 589n.
biography 590n.
memorable
remembered 505adj.
notable 638adj.
memorandum
reminder 505n.
record 548n.
plan 623n.
important matter 638n.
memorial
reminder 505n.
report 524n.
monument 548n.
trophy 729n.
honors 866n.
memorialist
chronicler 549n.
memorialize
request 761vb.
memoriam, in
in memoriam 364adv.
in memory 505adv.
memories
remainder 41n.
memorize
memorize 505vb.
learn 536vb.
memory
thought 449n.
memory 505n.
famousness 866n.
memsahib
lady 373n.
title 870n.
men
mariner 270n.
personnel 686n.
armed force 722n.
menace
predict 511vb.
danger 661n.
warning 664n.
frighten 854vb.
hateful object 888n.
threat 900n.
ménage
habitancy 191n.
management 689n.
menagerie

accumulation 74n.
zoo 369n.
collection 632n.
mend
get healthy 650vb.
rectify 654vb.
repair 656vb.
mendable
restored 656adj.
mendacity
falsehood 541n.
Mendelian
inherited 157adj.
filial 170adj.
mender
reformer 654n.
mender 656n.
mendicancy
request 761n.
poverty 801n.
mendicant
idler 679n.
beggar 763n.
poor man 801n.
monk 986n.
menfolk
male 372n.
menhir
tomb 364n.
monument 548n.
menial
inferior 35n., adj.
worker 686n.
servant 742n.
meninx
head 213n.
intellect 447n.
meniscus
curve 248n.
optical device 442n.
menology
chronometry 117n.
menopause
age 131n.
unproductivity 172n.
mensal
mensal 301adj.
menses
regular return 141n.
hemorrhage 302n.
Mensheviks
political party 708n.
Menshevist
moderate 625n.
mens rea
intention 617n.
menstrual
seasonal 141adj.
menstruum
liquefaction 337n.
mensurable
numerable 86adj.
measured 465adj.
mensuration
measurement 465n.
mental
mental 447adj.
insane 503adj.
mental act
thought 449n.
mental age
present time 121n.
mental balance
wisdom 498n.
sanity 502n.
mental caliber
intelligence 498n.
mental case
madman 504n.
sick person 651n.
mental disease
insanity 503n.
mental dishonesty
mental dishonesty 543n.
mental hospital
madhouse 503n.
hospital 658n.
mental hygiene
sanity 502n.
mentality
intellect 447n.
mental reservation
sophistry 477n.
equivocalness 518n.
concealment 525n.
mental dishonesty 543n.
menticulture
civilization 654n.
mention
referral 9n.
notice 455vb.
information 524n.
speak 579vb.
mentor
sage 500n.
teacher 537n.
adviser 691n.
menu
list 87n.
meal 301n.
meow
ululation 409n.
Mephistopheles
Mephisto 969n.
Mephistophelian
wicked 934adj.
mephitic
fetid 397adj.
toxic 653adj.
mephitis
fetor 397n.
insalubrity 653n.
poison 659n.
meracious
pungent 388adj.
mercantile
trading 791adj.
mercantilism
restriction 747n.
trade 791n.
Mercator's projection
distortion 246n.
map 551n.
mercature
barter 791n.
mercenary
militarist 722n.
servant 742n.
avaricious 816adj.
venal 930adj.
selfish 932adj.
mercer
clothier 228n.
tradesman 794n.
mercerize
be tough 329vb.
mercery
dressing 228n.
merchandise
equipment 630n.
store 632n.
trade 791vb.
sale 793n.
merchandise 795n.
merchant
bargain 791vb.
trade 791vb.
merchant 794n.
merchantman
merchant ship 275n.
merchant navy
shipping 275n.
merchantry
trade 791n.
merciful
lenient 736adj.
benevolent 897adj.
pitying 905adj.
merciless
destructive 165adj.
resolute 599adj.
obstinate 602adj.
severe 735adj.
cruel 898adj.
malevolent 898adj.
pitiless 906adj.
mercurial
changeful 152adj.
unstable 152adj.
moving 265adj.
speedy 277adj.
light-minded 456adj.
irresolute 601adj.
capricious 604adj.
excitable 822adj.
Mercurian
planetary 321adj.
mercury
weather 340n.
Mercury

speeder 277n.
planet 321n.
courier 531n.
Olympian god 967n.
mercy
irenics 719n.
lenity 736n.
benevolence 897n.
mercy 905n.
divine attribute 965n.
mercy-killing
killing 362n.
mercy of, at the
liable 180adj.
subject 745adj.
mercy seat
ritual object 988n.
holy place 990n.
mere
absolute 32adj.
inconsiderable 33adj.
simple 44adj.
limit 236n.
lake 346n.
meretricious
false 541adj.
spurious 542adj.
ornate 574adj.
inelegant 576adj.
ornamented 844adj.
vulgar 847adj.
unchaste 951adj.
meretriciousness
spectacle 445n.
merfolk
mythical being 970n.
merganser
diver 313n.
waterfowl 365n.
merge
be identical 13vb.
mix 43vb.
join 45vb.
combine 50vb.
be one of 58vb.
be included 78vb.
be turned to 147vb.
immerse 303vb.
cooperate 706vb.
join a party 708vb.
merged
included 78adj.
interjacent 231adj.
merger
combination 50n.
association 706n.
meridian
noon 128n.
region 184n.
summit 213n.
meridional
topmost 213adj.
directed 281adj.
merino
fiber 208n.
textile 222n.
merit
importance 638n.
utility 640n.
goodness 644n.
right 913n.
deserve 915vb.
virtues 933n.
meritless
unentitled 916adj.
vicious 934adj.
meritorious
excellent 644adj.
deserving 915adj.
approvable 923adj.
virtuous 933adj.
Merlin
sorcerer 983n.
merlon
fortification 713n.
mermaid
rara avis 84n.
sea nymph 343n.
vocalist 413n.
mythical being 970n.
merman
rara avis 84n.
sea god 343n.
mythical being 970n.
merriment
enjoyment 824n.
merriment 833n.
rejoicing 835n.
amusement 837n.
wit 839n.
merry
drunk 949adj.
(*see* merriment)
merry-andrew
entertainer 594n.
merry-go-round
rotation 315n.
pleasure-ground 837n.
merry-maker
reveler 837n.
merry-making
sociability 882n.
(*see* merriment)
merry men
band 74n.
merrythought
magic instrument 983n.
merwoman
mythical being 970n.
mesa
high land 209n.
plain 348n.
mésalliance
misfit 25n.
type of marriage 894n.
mescal
antidote 658n.
mescaline
drug 658n.
mesh
gap 201n.
space 201vb.
network 222n.
meshes
encumbrance 702n.
mesh with
accord 24vb.
meshwork
network 222n.
mesial
middle 70adj.
mesmeric
influential 178adj.
insensible 375adj.
inducive 612adj.
psychical 984adj.
mesmerism
influence 178n.
occultism 984n.
mesmerist
psychic 984n.
mesmerize
render insensible 375vb.
convince 485vb.
frighten 854vb.
(*see* mesmerism)
mesne lord
owner 776n.
mesne profits
receipt 807n.
mesogastric
central 225adj.
Mesolithic
secular 110adj.
meson
particle 33n.
element 319n.
Mesozoic
secular 110adj.
mess
medley 43n.
confusion 61n.
jumble 63vb.
chamber 194n.
feasting 301n.
eat 301vb.
predicament 700n.
failure 728n.
portion 783n.
message
information 524n.
message 529n.
Messalina
loose woman 952n.
mess can, mess tin
caldron 194n.
messenger

precursor 66n.
traveler 268n.
informant 524n.
messenger 531n.
delegate 754n.
deputy 755n.
messenger boy
courier 531n.
messer
eater 301n.
messiah
leader 690n.
philanthropist 901n.
Messiah
God the Son 965n.
religious teacher 973n.
messianic
redemptive 965adj.
messianism
aspiration 852n.
messing
eating 301n.
mensal 301adj.
mess jacket
tunic 228n.
mess kit
uniform 228n.
messmate
eater 301n.
chum 880n.
messroom
chamber 194n.
messuage
house 192n.
lands 777n.
mess up
make unclean 649vb.
impair 655vb.
messy
orderless 61adj.
amorphous 244adj.
dirty 649adj.
mestizo
hybrid 43n.
nonconformist 84n.
met
assembled 74adj.
synchronous 123adj.
metabolism
transformation 143n.
metacenter
centrality 225n.
metachronism
anachronism 118n.
metachronous
non-contemporary 122adj.
metagalactic
cosmic 321adj.
metage
measurement 465n.
metabenesis
change 143n.
transformation 143n.
metagrammatism
spelling 558n.
metal
hardness 326n.
mineral 359n.
heraldry 547n.
materials 631n.
metaled
covered 226adj.
communicating 624adj.
metallic
strident 407adj.
metallography
mineralogy 359n.
metallurgy
mineralogy 359n.
metamorphic
multiform 82adj.
territorial 344adj.
metamorphism
multiformity 82n.
metamorphosis
multiformity 82n.
transformation 143n.
metaphor
metaphor 519n.
ornament 574n.
metaphorical
compared 462adj.
semantic 514adj.
figurative 519adj.
metaphrase
copy 22n.
translation 520n.
metaphysician
philosopher 449n.
metaphysics
existence 1n.
psychology 447n.
philosophy 449n.
occultism 984n.
metapsychological
paranormal 984adj.
metapsychology
psychology 447n.
metastasis
change 143n.
transference 272n.
metathesis
transformation 143n.
inversion 221n.
transference 272n.
trope 519n.
metayage
joint possession 775n.
métayer
husbandman 370n.
participator 775n.
metazoon
animal 365n.
mete
measure 465vb.
mete out 465vb.
apportion 783vb.
metempsychosis
transformation 143n.
reproduction 166n.
transference 272n.
materiality 319n.
meteor, meteorite
wanderer 268n.
meteor 321n.
luminary 420n.
meteoric
brief 114adj.
speedy 277adj.
celestial 321adj.
luminous 417adj.
meteorological
celestial 321adj.
airy 340adj.
meteorologist
weather 340n.
oracle 511n.
meteorology
weather 340n.
meter
long measure 203n.
meter, gauge 465n.
prosody 593n.
metheglin
sweet 392n.
method
uniformity 16n.
order 60n.
arrangement 62n.
regularity 81n.
campanology 412n.
way 624n.
means 629n.
conduct 688n.
ritual 988n.
methodical
periodical 141adj.
(*see* method)
Methodism
Protestantism 976n.
methodize
regularize 62vb.
plan 623vb.
methodological
rational 475n.
methodology
order 60n.
Methuselah
old man 133n.
metic
foreigner 59n.
settler 191n.
incomer 297n.
meticulosis
strike 145n.
slowness 278n.

meticulous
attentive 455adj.
careful 457adj.
accurate 494adj.
fastidious 862adj.
trustworthy 929adj.
métier
vocation 622n.
skill 694n.
métis
nonconformist 84n.
Metonic cycle
era 110n.
metonymy
substitution 150n.
trope 519n.
metope
interval 201n.
ornamental art 844n.
metoposcopy
hermeneutics 520n.
face 237n.
metric
metric 465adj.
metrical
metric 465adj.
poetic 593adj.
metrics
measurement 465n.
prosody 593n.
metric system
metrology 465n.
metrist
poet 573n.
metro
train 274n.
metrology
metrology 465n.
metronome
timekeeper 117n.
meter 465n.
mteropolis
magistrature 733n.
metropolitan
urban 192adj.
central 225adj.
governor 741n.
ecclesiastical 985adj.
ecclesiarch 986n.
metropolitanate
parish 985n.
church office 985n.
mettle
vigorousness 174n.
resolution 599n.
affections 817n.
courage 855n.
mettlesome
vigorous 174adj.
active 678adj.
lively 819adj.
excitable 822adj.
courageous 855adj.
meum et tuum
property 777n.
mew
doff 229vb.
ululate 409vb.
imprison 747vb.
mewl
cry 408vb.
ululate 409vb.
mews
flat, stable 192n.
mezzanine
compartment 194n.
layer 207n.
theater 594n.
mezzo soprano
vocalist 413n.
mezzotint
light contrast 417n.
hue 425n.
engraving 555n.
M.I.5
secret service 459n.
miasma
gas 336n.
infection 651n.
poison 659n.
miasmal
harmful 645adj.
mica
semitransparency 424n.
micaceous
layered 207adj.
mi-carême
festivity 837n.
Micawber
lateness 136n.
negligence 458n.
Micawberish
hoping 852adj.
Michaelmas
holy-day 988n.
microbe
animalcule 196n.
Microcard
record 548n.
microcosm
miniature 196n.
universe 321n.
microfilm
camera 442n.
record 548n.
micrography
micrology 196n.
writing 586n.
micro-inch
long measure 203n.
microlith
antiquity 125n.
micrology
micrology 196n.
micrometer
micrology 196n.
meter 465n.
micrometer-minded
accurate 494adj.
micrometric
accurate 494adj.
micrometry
measurement 465n.
accuracy 494n.
micron
long measure 203n.
microorganism
animalcule 196n.
microphone
megaphone 400n.
hearing aid 415n.
telecommunication 531n.
microphotography
micrology 196n.
microscope 442n.
camera 442n.
microscope
micrology 196n.
microscope 442n.
microscopic
small 33adj.
minute 196adj.
ill-seen 444adj.
microscopy
micrology 196n.
microspectroscope
micrology 196n.
microspore
powder 332n.
microwave
radiation 417n.
microzoon
animalcule 196n.
micturition
excretion 302n.
mid
middle 70adj.
between 231adv.
Midas
rich man 800n.
Midas touch
prosperity 730n.
wealth 800n.
mid-course
mid-course 625n.
midday
noon 128n.
midden
rubbish 641n.
sink 649n.
midders
obstetrics 164n.
middle
median 30adj.
middle 70n., adj.
interim 108n.
narrowing 206n.

centrality 225n.
interjacent 231adj.
mediocre 732adj.
middle age
age 131n.
Middle Ages
antiquity 125n.
middle class
middle class 30n.
mediocrity 732n.
middle-class
median 30adj.
middle distance
middle point 30n.
middle, in the
centrally 225adv.
middleman
intermediary 231n.
provider 633n.
mediator 720n.
consignee 754n.
tradesman 794n.
middle-of-the-road
neutral 625adj.
middle term
average 30n.
compromise 770n.
middle-weight
pugilist 722n.
middling
median 30adj.
inconsiderable 33adj.
not bad 644adj.
imperfect 647adj.
mediocre 732adj.
middy
naval man 270n.
naval officer 741n.
midge
animalcule 196n.
fly 365n.
midget
small animal 33n.
dwarf 196n.
midinette
woman 373n.
midland
land 344n.
inland 344adj.
midline
middle 70n.
midmost
middle 70adj.
interior 224adj.
central 225adj.
midnight
midnight 129n.
darkness 418n.
midrib
middle 70n.
centrality 225n.
midriff
partition 231n.
midshipman
youngster 132n.
naval man 270n.
naval officer 741n.
midships
middle 70adv.
midst
middle 70n.
centrally 225adv.
between 231adv.
mid-stream
mid-course 625n.
midsummer
summer 128n.
midway
midway 70adv.
midweek
interim 108n.
intermediate 108adj.
midwife
obstetrics 164n.
instrument 628n.
doctor 658n.
auxiliary 707n.
midwifery
obstetrics 164n.
instrumentality 628n.
medical art 658n.
midwinter
winter 129n.
mien
look 438n.
mien 445n.
conduct 688n.
might
greatness 32n.
power 160n.
strength 162n.
be possible 469vb.
might and main
exertion 682n.
might and main, with
strongly 162adv.
violently 176adv.
actively 678adv.
laboriously 682adv.
might have been, the
possibility 469n.
mightiness
(*see* might, mighty)
mighty
great 32adj.
powerful 160adj.
strong 162adj.
influential 178adj.
huge 195adj.
worshipful 866adj.
proud 871adj.
mignon
favorite 890n.
mignonette
green color 432n.
migraine
pang 377n.
migrant
foreigner 59n.
wanderer 268n.
incomer 297n.
egress 298n.
bird 365n.
migration
wandering 267n.
departure 296n.
migratory
traveling 267adj.
mikado
sovereign 741n.
mike
(*see* microphone)
milady
lady 373n.
milch-cow
abundance 171n.
cattle 365n.
store 632n.
mild
moderate 177adj.
warm 379adj.
tasteless 387adj.
lenient 736adj.
inexcitable 823adj.
amiable 884adj.
mildew
destroyer 168n.
bedim 419vb.
dirt 649n.
dilapidation 655n.
impair 655vb.
blight 659n.
mildewed
antiquated 127adj.
mile
long measure 203n.
racing 716n.
mileage
distance 119n.
length 203n.
milepost
signpost 547n.
Milesian
impure 951adj.
milestone
degree 27n.
serial place 73n.
situation 186n.
itinerary 267n.
gauge 465n.
signpost 547n.
miliaria
skin disease 651n.
milieu
circumstance 8n.
relation 9n.
locality 187n.
circumjacence 230n.
militancy

bellicosity 718n.
(*see* militant)
militant
active 678adj.
opposing 704adj.
quarreling 709adj.
defiant 711adj.
attacker 712n.
warlike 718adj.
militarist 722n.
courageous 855adj.
inimical 881adj.
militarism
bellicosity 718n.
brute force 735n.
militarist
militarist 722n.
tyrant 735n.
military
warlike 718adj.
military service
warfare 718n.
militate against
counteract 182vb.
oppose 704vb.
militia
defender 713n.
army 722n.
militiaman
soldier 722n.
milk
moderator 177n.
void 300vb.
milk 301n.
extract 304vb.
waste 334vb.
fluid 335n.
white thing 427n.
provide 633vb.
acquire 771vb.
take 786vb.
milk and honey
prosperity 730n.
milk and water
weak thing 163n.
insipidity 387n.
milk-bar
café 192n.
milk-float
cart 274n.
milkiness
semitransparency 424n.
milkmaid
herdsman 369n.
servant 742n.
milkman
seller 793n.
milk of magnesia
cathartic 658n.
milk-pail
vessel 194n.
milksop
weakling 163n.
ninny 501n.
coward 856n.
innocent 935n.
milk-tooth
brief span 114n.
tooth 256n.
milky
edible 301adj.
semiliquid 354adj.
fatty 357adj.
semitransparent 424adj.
whitish 427adj.
Milky Way
star 321n.
glow 417n.
luminary 420n.
mill
roughen 259vb.
notch 260vb.
pulverizer 332n.
pulverize 332vb.
workshop 687n.
pugilism 716n.
mill around
congregate 74vb.
rotate 315vb.
milldam
lake 346n.
millenarian
improving 654adj.
hoper 852n.
philanthropist 901n.
heretic 977n.
millenarianism
aspiration 852n.
millenary
fifth and over 99adj.
millennial
secular 110adj.
future 124adj.
promising 852adj.
celebrative 876adj.
paradisiac 971adj.
millennium
over one hundred 99n.
period 110n.
future state 124n.
fantasy 513n.
aspiration 852n.
heaven 971n.
miller
pulverizer 332n.
millesimal
multifid 100adj.
millet
cereal 301n.
grass 366n.
milliard
over one hundred 99n.
milliardaire
rich man 800n.
millibar
weather 340n.
millimeter
small quantity 33n.
short distance 200n.
long measure 203n.
milliner
clothier 228n.
millinery
dressing 228n.
milling
edging 234n.
pulverulence 332n.
pugilism 716n.
millionaire
rich man 800n.
million, for the
intelligible 516adj.
easy 701adj.
million, the
social group 371n.
commonalty 869n.
mill-pond
lake 346n.
mill-race
lake 346n.
current 350n.
millstone
gravity 322n.
pulverizer 332n.
encumbrance 702n.
mill-stream
current 350n.
milord
nobleman 868n.
milt
fertilizer 171n.
insides 224n.
mim
affectation 850n.
Mimamsa
philosophy 449n.
mimation
grammar 564n.
mime
mimicry 20n.
imitate 20vb.
gesticulate 547vb.
represent 551vb.
actor 594n.
stage play 594n.
act 594vb.
mimeograph
copy 20vb.
mimesis
imitation 20n.
representation 551n.
mimetic
dramatic 594adj.
mimic
imitate 20vb.

gesticulate 547vb.
represent 551vb.
actor 594n.
satirize 851vb.
mimicry
mimicry 20n.
(*see* mime, mimic)
mimographer
dramatist 594n.
mina
coinage 797n.
minacity
threat 900n.
minaret
high structure 209n.
minatory
cautionary 664adj.
frightening 884adj.
threatening 900adj.
minauderie
affectation 850n.
mince
cut, rend 46vb.
move slowly 278vb.
dish 301n.
pulverize 332vb.
be affected 850vb.
extenuate 927vb.
mincing
affected 850adj.
fastidious 862adj.
mind
be attentive 455vb.
be careful 457vb.
look after 457vb.
intellect, spirit 447n.
opinion 485n.
remember 505vb.
will 595n.
willingness 597n.
intention 617n.
suffer 825vb.
be discontented 829vb.
liking 859n.
dislike 861vb.
resent 891vb.
minded
intending 617adj.
minder
machinist 630n.
mindful
attentive 455adj.
careful 457adj.
remembering 505adj.
mindless
mindless 448adj.
foolish 499adj.
forgetful 506adj.
mind made up
bias 481n.
resolution 599n.
mind one's business
be careful 457vb.
do business 622vb.
mind-reading
psychics 984n.
mind's eye
imagination 513n.
mind, to one's
lovable 887adj.
mine
great quantity 32n.
source 156n.
produce 164vb.
demolish 165vb.
lowness 210n.
depth 211n.
excavation 255n.
tunnel 263n.
extract 304vb.
descend 309vb.
darkness 417n.
trap 542n.
store 632n.
impair 655vb.
workshop 687n.
besiege 712vb.
defenses 713n.
bomb 723n.
acquire 771vb.
take 786vb.
wealth 800n.
mine-field
defenses 713n.
mine host
caterer 633n.
mine-layer
warship 722n.
miner
producer 167n.
excavator 255n.
extractor 304n.
artisan 686n.
soldiery 722n.
mineral
soft drink 301n.
mineral 359n.
unthinking 450adj.
materials 631n.
mineralogy
mineralogy 359n.
minestrone
soup 301n.
mine-sweeper
warship 722n.
mine-thrower
gun 723n.
mingle
mix 43vb.
mingy
insufficient 636adj.
parsimonious 816adj.
miniate
paint 553vb.
miniature
small 33adj.
miniature 196n.
little 196adj.
picture 553n.
miniaturist
artist 556n.
minicar
miniature 196n.
automobile 274n.
minify
bate 37vb.
minikin
small animal 33n.
minim
small quantity 33n.
notation 410n.
metrology 465n.
minimal
small 33adj.
lesser 35adj.
exiguous 196adj.
minimalism
reformism 654n.
minimalist
moderate 625n.
reformer 654n.
minimize
bate 37vb.
misjudge 481vb.
underestimate 483vb.
detract 926vb.
minimum
small quantity 33n.
lesser 35adj.
sufficiency 635n.
minimus
small animal 33n.
young 130adj.
mining
extraction 304n.
descent 309n.
minion
type size 587n.
dependent 742n.
flatterer 925n.
minister
instrument 628n.
agent 686n.
manage 689vb.
official 690n.
envoy 754n.
offer worship 981vb.
pastor 986n.
perform ritual 988vb.
ministerial
instrumental 628adj.
governmental 733adj.
clerical 986adj.
ministering spirit
angel 968n.
ministership
church office 985n.
minister to

miserly
careful 457adj.
parsimonious 816adj.
avaricious 816adj.
misery
evil 616n.
adversity 731n.
sorrow 825n.
dejection 834n.
moper 834n.
bore 838n.
hopelessness 853n.
misestimate
misjudge 481vb.
misexposition
misinterpretation 521n.
misrepresentation 552n.
misfeasance
wrong 914n.
lawbreaking 954n.
misfire
bungling 695n.
miscarry 728vb.
misfit
irrelation 10n.
misfit 25n.
nonconformist 84n.
displacement 188n.
bungler 697n.
misfortune
evil 616n.
misgiving
doubt 486n.
nervousness 854n.
misgovern
be unskillful 695vb.
be lax 734vb.
oppress 735vb.
misguidance
error 495n.
misteaching 535n.
misguided
misjudging 481adj.
mistaken 495adj.
bungled 695adj.
mishandle
ill-treat 645vb.
misuse 675vb.
be unskillful 695vb.
mishap
eventuality 154n.
ill fortune 731n.
mishit
bungling 695n.
mishmash
a mixture 43n.
confusion 61n.
Mishnah
scripture 975n.
misinformation
inexactness 495n.
concealment 525n.
misteaching 535n.
untruth 543n.
misrepresentation 551n.
misinstruction
misteaching 535n.
misinterpret
transform 147vb.
distort 246vb.
misjudge 481vb.
blunder 495vb.
misinterpret 521vb.
be false 541vb.
misjoin
mismatch 25vb.
misjoinder
misfit 25n.
misjudge
mistime 138vb.
not think 450vb.
underestimate 483vb.
be credulous 487vb.
misinterpret 521vb.
misjudgment
misjudgment 481n.
overestimation 482n.
error 495n.
unintelligence 499n.
bungling 695n.
wrong 914n.
injustice 914n.
mislaid
misplaced 188adj.
mislay
derange 63vb.
lose 772vb.
mislead
deflect 282vb.
puzzle 474vb.
sophisticate 477vb.
mislead 495vb.
misteach 535vb.
deceive, befool 542vb.
obstruct 702vb.
mislike
dislike 861vb.
mismanage
be lax 734vb.
(*see* mismanagement)
mismanagement
misuse 675n.
bungling 695n.
dutilessness 918n.
mismanager
bungler 697n.
mismatch
mismatch 25vb.
mismate
mismatch 25vb.
misname
misteach 535vb.
misname 562vb.
misnomer
name 561n.
misnomer 562n.
misnumber
blunder 495vb.
misogamist
enemy 881n.
misanthrope 902n.
misogamy
celibacy 895n.
misogynist
enemy 881n.
celibate 895n.
misanthrope 902n.
disapprover 924n.
misplace
derange 63vb.
misplace 188vb.
misplaced
irrelevant 10adj.
unapt 25adj.
misplacement
unconformity 84n.
displacement 188n.
misprint
mistake 495n.
misprison
contempt 922n.
lawbreaking 954n.
misprison of treason
sedition 738n.
misprize
underestimate 483vb.
not respect 921vb.
hold cheap 922vb.
mispronounce
solecize 565vb.
stammer 580vb.
mispronunciation
solecism 565n.
inelegance 576n.
pronunciation 577n.
misproportion
distortion 246n.
misproportioned
unsightly 842adj.
misquotation
inexactness 495n.
misrepresentation 552n.
misquote
misinterpret 521vb.
be false 541vb.
misread
blunder 495vb.
misinterpret 521vb.
misreckon
err 495vb.
misreckoning
misjudgment 481n.
misreport
inexactness 495n.
misrepresentation 552n.
be false 541vb.

misrepresent
make unlike 19vb.
distort 246vb.
sophisticate 477vb.
misinterpret 521vb.
satirize 851vb.
misrepresentation
misteaching 535vb.
falsehood 541n.
untruth 543n.
misrepresentation 552n.
calumny 926n.
misrule
bungling 695n.
anarchy 734n.
oppress 735vb.
miss
be incomplete 55vb.
youngster 132n.
be late 136vb.
fall short 307vb.
lady 373n.
blunder 495vb.
require 627vb.
be unsatisfied 636vb.
bungling 695n.
fail 728vb.
lose 772vb.
be discontented 829vb.
regret 830vb.
desire 859vb.
title 870n.
loose woman 952n.
missal
scripture 975n.
prayers 981n.
office-book 988n.
missaying
neology 560n.
solecism 565n.
missed
remembered 505adj.
miss, give it a
not act 677vb.
misshape
distort 246vb.
make ugly 842vb.
misshapen
amorphous 244adj.
deformed 246adj.
unsightly 842adj.
missile
missile 287n.
propulsive 287adj.
missing
non-existent 2adj.
incomplete 55adj.
misplaced 188adj.
absent 190adj.
disappearing 446adj.
unknown 491adj.
required 627adj.
lost 772adj.
missing link
incompleteness 55n.
deficit 55n.
discontinuity 72n.
completion 725n.
mission
job 622n.
vocation 622n.
mandate 751n.
envoy 754n.
philanthropy 901n.
church ministry 985n.
missionary
preacher 537n.
philanthropist 901n.
religious teacher 973n.
pastor 986n.
missionary spirit
philanthropy 901n.
pietism 979n.
missioner
pastor 986n.
missionize
convert 147vb.
missive
correspondence 588n.
miss nothing
be attentive 455vb.
miss out
be incomplete 55vb.
exclude 57vb.
misspell
misinterpret 521vb.
solecize 565vb.
misspend
be prodigal 815vb.
misstatement
inexactness 495n.
untruth 543n.
miss the bus
lose a chance 138vb.
miss the point
be insensitive 820vb.
missus
spouse 894n.
mist
insubstantial thing 4n.
moisture 341n.
cloud 355n.
dimness 419n.
obfuscation 421n.
opacity 423n.
blur 440vb.
invisibility 444n.
uncertainty 474n.
mistake
mistake 495n.
misinterpretation 521n.
solecism 565n.
bungling 695n.
failure 728n.
wrong 914n.
mistaken
misjudging 481adj.
mistaught
uninstructed 491adj.
misteach
sophisticate 477vb.
not know 491vb.
mislead 495vb.
misinterpret 521vb.
misteach 535vb.
misrepresent 552vb.
mister
male 372n.
master 741n.
title 870n.
misterm
misname 562vb.
misthrow
bungling 695n.
mistiming
intempestivity 138n.
inexactness 495n.
mistiness
(*see* misty)
mistitle
misname 562vb.
mistral
wind 352n.
mistranslate
blunder 495vb.
misinterpret 521vb.
mistranslated
inexact 495adj.
unmeant 515adj.
misinterpreted 521adj.
mistress
woman 373n.
lady 373n.
master 741n.
owner 776n.
title 870n.
loved one 887n.
kept woman 952n.
mistrust
doubt 486n.
nervousness 854n.
jealousy 911n.
mistrustful
doubting 474adj.
unbelieving 486adj.
misty
insubstantial 4adj.
humid 341adj.
cloudy 355adj.
dim 419adj.
opaque 423adj.
semitransparent 424adj.
ill-seen 444adj.
uncertain 474adj.
puzzling 517adj.
misunderstand

not know 491vb.
err 495vb.
misinterpret 521vb.
misunderstanding
dissension 709n.
misunderstood
mistaken 495adj.
guiltless 935adj.
misusage
misuse 675n.
misuse
force 176vb.
waste 634n., vb.
ill-treat 645vb.
impairment 655n.
misuse 675n., vb.
be unskillful 695vb.
be severe 735vb.
prodigality 815n.
mite
small quantity 33n.
small coin 33n.
child 132n.
animalcule 196n.
vermin 365n.
insufficiency 636n.
miter
badge of rule 743n.
vestments 989n.
mitered
clerical 986adj.
miter-joint
joint 45n.
angularity 247n.
mithridate
antidote 658n.
mitigate
bate 37vb.
moderate 177vb.
qualify 468vb.
make better 654vb.
relieve 831vb.
extenuate 927vb.
mitigatory
qualifying 468adj.
mitraille
ammunition 723n.
mitten
glove 228n.
mix
mix 43vb.
combine 50vb.
jumble 63vb.
modify 143vb.
agitate 318vb.
be sociable 882vb.
mixed bag
non-uniformity 17n.
mixed blessing
inexpedience 643n.
mixer, be a good
be sociable 882vb.
mix in
add 38vb.
mixing-bowl
bowl 194n.
mix it
fight 716vb.
mixolydian
key 410n.
mixture
mixture 43n.
combination 50n.
composition 56n.
imperfection 647n.
medicine 658n.
mixture as before
uniformity 16n.
recurrence 106n.
mix-up
confusion 61n.
mix with
add 38vb.
unite with 45vb.
mizzen
back 238adj.
mizzenmast
poop 238n.
mizzle
rain 350n., vb.
mnemonics 505n.
reminder 505n.
mnemonics 505n.
moa
flightless bird 365n.
moan
blow 352vb.
faintness 401n.
cry 408vb.
be discontented 829vb.
weep 836vb.
moat
fence 235n.
furrow 262n.
conduit 351n.
protection 660n.
obstacle 702n.
defenses 713n.
mob
rampage 61vb.
crowd 74n.
multitude 104n.
be violent 176vb.
charge 712vb.
rabble 869n.
celebrate 876vb.
gratulate 886vb.
caress 889vb.
not respect 921vb.
disapprove 924vb.
mobcap
headgear 228n.
mobility
changeableness 152n.
motion 265n.
moral sensibility 819n.
mobilization
assemblage 74n.
preparation 669n.
war measures 718n.
mobilize
move 265vb.
mob law
government 733n.
anarchy 734n.
lawlessness 954n.
moble
cover 226vb.
mobocracy
government 733n.
moccasin
footwear 228n.
mock
simulating 18adj.
disbelieve 486vb.
spurious 542adj.
befool 542vb.
laugh 835vb.
be witty 839vb.
laughing-stock 851n.
ridicule 851n., vb.
shame 867vb.
not respect 921vb.
despise 922vb.
detract 926vb.
mock-epic
poem 593n.
mocker
imitator 20n.
(*see* mock)
mockery
insubstantial thing 4n.
mimicry 20n.
impiety 980n.
(*see* mock)
mock-heroic
poetic 593adj.
funny 849adj.
derisive 851adj.
mock-modest
depreciating 483adj.
affected 850adj.
mock-up
prototype 23n.
modal
conditionate 7adj.
circumstantial 8adj.
harmonic 410adj.
modality
extrinsicality 6n.
modality 7n.
mode
modality 7n.
key 410n.
practice 610n.
way 624n.
fashion 848n.
model
copy, duplicate 22n.
prototype 23n.
living model 23n.

be example 23vb.
superior 34n.
rule 81n.
example 83n.
miniature 196n.
little 196adj.
efform 243vb.
comparison 462n.
show 522vb.
image 551n.
represent 551vb.
art equipment 553n.
sculpt 554vb.
plan 623n.
paragon 646n.
perfect 646adj.
plaything 837n.
person of repute 866n.
modeler
sculptor 556n.
moderate
median 30adj.
small 33adj.
bate 37vb.
moderate 177adj., vb.
retard 278vb.
qualify 468vb.
moderate 625n.
imperfect 647adj.
restrain 747vb.
cheap 812adj.
tranquilize 823vb.
relieve 831vb.
indifferent 860adj.
modest 874adj.
moderation
counteraction 182n.
softness 327n.
underestimation 483n.
mid-course 625n.
sanation 656n.
irenics 719n.
mediocrity 732n.
inexcitability 823n.
temperance 942n.
(*see* moderate)
moderations
exam. 459n.
moderator
nucleonics 160n.
moderator 177n.
director 690n.
mediator 720n.
church officer 986n.
ecclesiarch 986n.
modern
present 121adj.
modern 126adj.
progressive 285n.
fashionable 848adj.
modernism
modernism 126n.
art 551n.
heterodoxy 977n.
modernity
newness 126n.
modernize
modernize 126vb.
change, modify 143vb.
revolutionize 149vb.
make better 654vb.
restore 656vb.
be in fashion 848vb.
modest
inconsiderable 33adj.
depreciating 483adj.
mediocre 732adj.
inglorious 867adj.
humble 872adj.
disinterested 931adj.
(*see* modesty)
modesty
moderation 177n.
plainness 573n.
artlessness 699n.
nervousness 854n.
modesty 874n.
purity 950n.
modicum
small quantity 33n.
portion 783n.
modifiable
changeable 143adj.
modification
difference 15n.
change 143n.
qualification 468n.
modifier
alterer 143n.
modify
make unlike 19vb.
(*see* modification)
modish
usual 610adj.
fashionable 848adj.
reputable 866adj.
modiste
clothier 228n.
modulate
make unlike 19vb.
adjust 24vb.
modulation
change 143n.
moderation 177n.
key 410n.
module
prototype 23n.
modulus
numerical element 85n.
modus operandi
way 624n.
conduct 688n.
modus vivendi
substitute 150n.
way 624n.
mogul
sovereign 741n.
mohair
fiber 208n.
textile 222n.
Mohammedan
religionist 973n.
Mohawk, Mohock
anarch 61n.
insolent person 878n.
ruffian 904n.
Mohurrum
anniversary 141n.
holy-day 988n.
moider
be inattentive 456vb.
be uncertain 474vb.
moidered
crazed 503adj.
moiety
part 53n.
bisection 92n.
portion 783n.
moil
work 682vb.
moiré
iridescent 437adj.
moist
watery 339adj.
humid 341adj.
moisten
add water 339vb.
moisten 341vb.
moisture
moisture 341n.
moither
(*see* moider)
moke
beast of burden 273n.
animal 365n.
mokes
network 222n.
molar
tooth 256n.
pulverizer 332n.
molasses
sweet 392n.
mold
modality 7n.
mold 23n.
decay 51n.
sort 77n.
convert 147vb.
fertilizer 171n.
form 243n.
efform 243vb.
structure 331n.
soil 344n.
represent 551vb.
sculpt 554vb.
dirt 649n.
blight 659n.
decorate 844vb.
moldable
flexible 327adj.

molded on
imitative 20adj.
molder
decompose 51vb.
be old 127vb.
sculptor 556n.
be unclean 649vb.
deteriorate 655vb.
moldiness
dilapidation 655n.
molding
ornamental art 844n.
mold oneself
do likewise 20vb.
conform 83vb.
mold the figure
cohere 48vb.
mole
projection 254n.
rodent 365n.
gray 429adj.
skin disease 651n.
safeguard 662n.
defenses 713n.
blemish 845n.
molecular
minute 196adj.
molecule
particle 33n.
minuteness 196n.
element 319n.
molehill
minuteness 196n.
monticle 209n.
lowness 210n.
moleskin
textile 222n.
molest
harm 645vb.
be obstructive 702vb.
torment 827vb.
be malevolent 898vb.
moll
woman 373n.
fly 365n.
kept woman 952n.
mollification
moderation 177n.
softness 327n.
pacification 719n.
mollusk
animal 365n.
fish 365n.
mollycoddle
weakling 613n.
ninny 501n.
Moloch
Semitic gods 967n.
molt
doff 229vb.
molten
liquefied 337adj.
fiery 379adj.
heated 381adj.
molten image
idol 982n.
moment
juncture 8n.
small quantity 33n.
date 108n.
brief span 114n.
instant 116n.
occasion 137n.
cause 156n.
importance 638n.
momentariness
instantaneity 116n.
momentary
transient 114adj.
momentous
crucial 137adj.
eventful 154adj.
influential 178adj.
important 638adj.
momentum
impulse 279n.
mommy, mom
maternity 169n.
monachism
monasticism 985n.
monad
existence 1n.
unit 88n.
minuteness 196n.
element 319n.
monandry
type of marriage 894n.
monarch
sovereign 741n.
possessor 776n.
monarchy
government 733n.
monastery
house 192n.
retreat 192n.
monastery 986n.
monastic
unwedded 895adj.
monk 986n.
monasticism
seclusion 883n.
celibacy 895n.
monasticism 985n.
monatomic
alone 88adj.
monetary
monetary 797adj.
monetize
mint 797vb.
money
means 629n.
money 797n.
wealth 800n.
money-bag, money-box
pocket 194n.
storage 632n.
treasury 799n.
money-changer
alterer 143n.
merchant 794n.
moneyer 797n.
money-conscious
economical 814adj.
parsimonious 816adj.
moneyer
merchant 794n.
moneyer 797n.
money for jam
easy thing 701n.
money-grubber
niggard 816n.
egotist 932n.
money-grubbing
acquisition 771n.
(*see* money-grubber)
money-lender
lender 784n.
moneyless
poor 801adj.
money-mad
avaricious 816adj.
money-making
wealth 800n.
money market
finance 797n.
money-saving
economical 814adj.
money-spinner
moneyer 797n.
rich man 800n.
money's worth
price 809n.
monger
seller 793n.
sell 793vb.
tradesman 794n.
Mongolian
ethnic 11adj.
mongolian idiot
madman 504n.
mongoose
rodent 365n.
mongrel
hybrid 43n.
nonconformist 84n.
dog 365n.
rascally 930adj.
monied
moneyed 800adj.
moniker
name 561n.
moniliform
rotund 252adj.
monism
philosophy 449n.
monition
hint 524n.
warning 664n.
monitor
inquire 459vb.

teacher 537n.
warner 664n.
official 690n.
adviser 691n.
warship 722n.
monitorial
cautionary 664adj.
monitorial system
education 534n.
monitory
predicting 511adj.
dissuasive 613adj.
cautionary 664adj.
monk
celibate 895n.
pietist 979n.
monk 986n.
monkey
imitator 20n.
ram 279n.
monkey 365n.
evildoer 904n.
monkey jacket
tunic 228n.
monkey-trick
foolery 497n.
revel 837n.
monkey with
impair 655vb.
monkhood
celibacy 895n.
monasticism 985n.
monkshood
poisonous plant 659n.
monochord
harp 414n.
monochromatic
colored 425adj.
monochrome
achromatism 426n.
painting 553n.
monocle
eyeglass 442n.
monocracy
despotism 733n.
monocular
dim-sighted 440adj.
monocycle
bicycle 274n.
monodrama
stage play 594n.
monody
duet 412n.
monogamy
type of marriage 894n.
monogram
label 847n.
initials 558n.
monograph
dissertation 591n.
monolith
uniformity 16n.
coherence 48n.
unit 88n.
monument 548n.
monolithic
simple 44adj.
indivisible 52adj.
dense 324adj.
(*see* monolith)
monologist
entertainer 594n.
monologue
uniformity 16n.
oration 579n.
soliloquy 585n.
monomachy
duel 716n.
monomania
attention 455n.
prejudgment 481n.
mania 503n.
eccentricity 503n.
opiniatrety 602n.
monomaniac
madman 504n.
monomaniacal
obsessed 455adj.
monomark
label 547n.
monophonic
harmonious 410adj.
monophthongization
speech sound 398n.
Monophysitism
heresy 977n.
monoplane
aircraft 276n.
monopolist
restriction 747n.
egotist 932n.
monopolistic
restraining 747adj.
possessing 773adj.
avaricious 816adj.
selfish 932adj.
monopolize
engross 449vb.
attract attention 455vb.
appropriate 786vb.
be selfish 932vb.
monopoly
exclusion 57n.
corporation 708n.
restriction 747n.
possession 773n.
sale 793n.
avarice 816n.
board game 837n.
monorail
train 274n.
railroad 624n.
monosaccharide
food content 301n.
monostich
conciseness 569n.
monosyllabic
linguistic 557adj.
concise 569adj.
taciturn 582adj.
monosyllable
spoken letter 558n.
word 559n.
monotheism
deism 973n.
Monothelitism
heresy 977n.
monotone
uniformity 16n.
musical note 410n.
painting 553n.
monotonous
equal 28adj.
one 88adj.
permanent 144adj.
feeble 572adj.
monotony
uniformity 16n.
continuity 71n.
recurrence 106n.
tedium 838n.
monotype
breed 77n.
unit 88n.
press 587n.
monseigneur
church title 986n.
monsieur
male 372n.
title 870n.
monsignor
title 870n.
church title 986n.
monsoon
rain 350n.
wind 352n.
monster
violent creature 176n.
giant 195n.
eyesore 842n.
prodigy 864n.
monster 938n.
demon 970n.
monstrance
ritual object 988n.
monstrosity
unconformity 84n.
hugeness 195n.
deformity 246n.
prodigy 864n.
monstrous
exorbitant 32adj.
unusual 84adj.
huge 195adj.
not nice 645adj.
ugly 842adj.
ridiculous 849adj.
wonderful 864adj.
heinous 934adj.

montage
cinema 445n.
Montanism
heresy 977n.
Montessori method
education 534n.
month
period 110n.
monthlies
regular return 141n.
monthly
seasonal 141adj.
periodically 141adv.
journal 328n.
usual 610adj.
monticle
monticle 209n.
monument
antiquity 125n.
edifice 164n.
tomb 364n.
obsequies 364n.
reminder 505n.
signpost 547n.
monument 548n.
trophy 729n.
honors 866n.
monumental
enormous 32adj.
large 195adj.
tall 209adj.
recording 548adj.
monumental mason
obsequies 364n.
sculptor 556n.
moo
ululation 409n.
mooch
be inactive 679vb.
steal 788vb.
mood
temperament 5n.
state 7n.
change 143n.
tendency 179n.
grammar 564n.
conduct 688n.
affections 817n.
moody
fitful 142adj.
melancholic 834adj.
irascible 892adj.
sullen 893adj.
moon
period 110n.
changeable thing 152n.
follower 284n.
circler 314n.
moon 321n.
luminary 420n.
be inattentive 456vb.
be inactive 679vb.
moonbeam
glimmer 419n.
mooncalf
fool 501n.
mooning
abstracted 456adj.
loving 887adj.
moonless
unlit 418adj.
moonlight
moon 321n.
light 417n.
glimmer 419n.
moonlight flit
departure 296n.
moonlit
undimmed 417adj.
moonraker
ninny 501n.
moonrise
ascent 308n.
moonshee
teacher 537n.
moonshine
insubstantial thing 4n.
light 417n.
empty talk 515n.
fable 543n.
pretext 614n.
booty 790n.
moonsif
officer 741n.
judge 957n.
moonstone
gem 844n.
moon-struck
insane 503adj.
moor
tie 45vb.
place 187vb.
navigate 269vb.
arrive 295vb.
(*see* moorland)
moored
fixed 153adj.
quiescent 266adj.
mooring(s)
cable 47n.
station 187n.
moorish
marshy 347adj.
moorland
space 183n.
high land 209n.
marsh 347n.
plain 348n.
moose
deer 365n.
moot
moot 459adj.
uncertain 474adj.
argue 475vb.
propound 512vb.
council 692n.
mooted
topical 452adj.
mooter
reasoner 475n.
moot point
topic 452n.
question 459n.
mop
distortion 246n.
hair 259n.
drier 342n.
cleaning utensil 648n.
mop and mow
distort 246vb.
goblinize 970vb.
mope
be dejected 834vb.
be sullen 893vb.
moped
bicycle 274n.
moper
idler 679n.
moper 834n.
moppet
darling 890n.
mopsy
darling 890n.
kept woman 952n.
mop up
destroy 165vb.
dry 342vb.
clean 648vb.
carry through 725vb.
mopus
visionary 513n.
idler 679n.
dibs 797n.
moraine
leavings 41n.
piece 53n.
thing transferred 272n.
soil 344n.
moral
judgment 480n.
maxim 496n.
commentary 520n.
phrase 563n.
good 615adj.
advising 691adj.
precept 693n.
reputable 866adj.
ethical 917adj.
pure 950adj.
piety 979n.
morale
obedience 739n.
manliness 855n.
virtue 933n.
moralistic
judicial 480adj.
ethical 917adj.
morality
(*see* morals)
moralize

judge 480vb.
teach 534vb.
make better 654vb.
moralizing
advice 691n.
moral rearmament
virtue 933n.
morals
conduct 688n.
right 913n.
morals 917n.
virtue 933n.
purity 950n.
moral turpitude
improbity 930n.
morass
marsh 347n.
moratorium
delay 136n.
lull 145n.
non-payment 805n.
morbidity
badness 645n.
ill-health 651n.
morbiferous
infectious 653adj.
morbific
diseased 651adj.
infectious 653adj.
morbilli
infection 651n.
mordacity
malevolence 898n.
mordancy
(*see* mordant)
mordant
keen 174adj.
pungent 388adj.
pigment 425n.
forceful 571adj.
disapproving 924adj.
mordent
musical note 410n.
musical piece 412n.
more
beyond 34adv.
in addition 38adv.
plural 101adj.
more and more
crescendo 36adv.
more or less
quantitative 26adj.
about 33adv.
nearly 200adv.
moreover
in addition 38adv.
more so
superior 34adj.
crescendo 36adv.
more than enough
plenteous 635adj.
redundance 637n.
more than ever
greatly 32adv.
morganatic
matrimonial 894adj.
morgue
cemetery 364n.
inactivity 679n.
moribund
dying 361adj.
sick 651adj.
morion
headgear 228n.
armor 713n.
Mormon
polygamist 894n.
religionist 973n.
Mormons
sect 978n.
morning
beginning 68n.
period 110n.
morning 128n.
earliness 135n.
morning after
sequel 67n.
posteriority 120n.
morning dress
formal dress 228n.
morocco
skin 226n.
bookbinding 589n.
moron
ignoramus 493n.
fool 501n.
madman 504n.
moronic
mindless 448adj.
unintelligent 499adj.
insane 503adj.
moroseness, morosity
unsociability 883n.
sullenness 893n.
misanthropy 902n.
morpheme
part of speech 564n.
morphia
anesthetic 375n.
drug 658n.
soporific 679n.
morphine
drug 658n.
poison 659n.
morphography
form 243n.
morphology
form 243n.
biology 358n.
zoology 367n.
linguistics 557n.
etymology 559n.
morris dance
dance 837n.
morrow
futurity 124n.
morse
fastening 47n.
Morse
telecommunication 531n.
signal 547n.
morsel
small quantity 33n.
piece 53n.
mouthful 301n.
mortal
ephemeral 114adj.
destructive 165adj.
deadly 362adj.
person 371n.
human 371adj.
tedious 838adj.
mortality
transientness 114n.
death, death roll 361n.
mankind 371n.
mortally
extremely 32adv.
mortal remains
corpse 363n.
mortar
adhesive 47n.
gun 723n.
mortgage
encumbrance 702n.
security 767n.
lending 784n.
borrowing 785n.
debt 803n.
mortgaged
subject 745adj.
mortgagee
possessor 776n.
lender 784n.
creditor 802n.
mortgage, on
pledged 767adj.
mortgagor
owner 776n.
debtor 803n.
mortician
interment 364n.
mortiferous
deadly 362adj.
toxic 653adj.
mortification
decay 51n.
death 361n.
sorrow 825n.
annoyance 827n.
discontent 829n.
regret 830n.
humiliation 872n.
asceticism 945n.
mortify
cause discontent 829vb.
mortise
join 45vb.
receptacle 194n.

intromit 231vb.
mortmain, in
retained 778adj.
Morton's fork
dubiety 474n.
argumentation 475n.
mortuary
death 361n.
interment 364n.
cemetery 364n.
mosaic
non-uniformity 17n.
combination 50n.
checker 437n.
picture 553n.
ornamental art 844n.
Mosaic
religious 973adj.
scriptural 975adj.
mosque
temple, church 990n.
mosquito
fly 365n.
mosquito net
canopy 226n.
moss
marsh 347n.
plant 366n.
greenness 432n.
mossback
laughing-stock 851n.
moss-grown
antiquated 127adj.
dilapidated 655adj.
moss-trooper
soldier 722n.
robber 789n.
mossy
soft 327adj.
vegetal 366adj.
most
great 32adj.
mot
maxim 496n.
witticism 839n.
mote
small thing 33n.
levity 323n.
dirt 649n.
mote in the eye
prejudice 481n.
motel
inn 192n.
motet
hymn 981n.
moth
destroyer 168n.
blight 659n.
mothball
prophylactic 658n.
preserver 666n.
mothballed
disused 674adj.
moth-eaten
antiquated 127adj.
dirty 649adj.
dilapidated 655adj.
mother
kinsman 11n.
maternity 169n.
pet 889vb.
philanthropize 897vb.
church title 986n.
nun 986n.
mother earth
abundance 171n.
mythic god 966n.
mothered
born 360adj.
motherhood
family 11n.
propagation 164n.
maternity 169n.
life 360n.
motherland
territory 184n.
home 192n.
mother-love
love 887n.
motherly
parental 169adj.
loving 887adj.
benevolent 897adj.
mother-of-pearl
variegation 437n.
mother's darling
weakling 163n.
favorite 890n.
Mother's Union
society 708n.
mother superior
ecclesiarch 986n.
nun 986n.
mother tongue
intelligibility 516n.
language 557n.
mother-wit
intelligence 498n.
motif
topic 452n.
pattern 844n.
motility
motion 265n.
motion
displacement 188n.
motion 265n.
cacation 302n.
topic 452n.
gesture 547n.
plan 623n.
activity 678n.
advice 691n.
offer 759n.
request 761n.
motionless
still 266adj.
inactive 679adj.
motion picture
cinema 445n.
motivate
influence 178vb.
motivate 612vb.
cause desire 859vb.
motivation
causation 156n.
motive 612n.
activity 678n.
motivator
motivator 612n.
director 690n.
adviser 691n.
motive
causation 156n.
influence 178n.
moving 265adj.
motive 612n.
motiveless
capricious 604adj.
choiceless 606adj.
designless 618adj.
motive power
energy 160n.
motion 265n.
mot juste
accuracy 494n.
motley
non-uniformity 17n.
mixed 43adj.
multiform 82adj.
variegation 437n.
motor
causal means 156n.
strengthen 162vb.
moving 265adj.
automobile 274n.
machine 630n.
motor car
automobile 274n.
motor cycle
bicycle 274n.
motor cyclist
rider 268n.
motor horn
danger signal 665n.
motoring
land travel 267n.
motorist
driver 268n.
motorman
driver 268n.
motor rally
racing 716n.
motorway
road 624n.
mottle
variegate 437vb.
motto
maxim 496n.
commentary 520n.
indication 547n.
heraldry 547n.

phrase 563n.
moue
distortion 246n.
gesture 547n.
affectation 850n.
mound
bulk 195n.
monticle 209n.
dome 253n.
defenses 713n.
mount
be great 32vb.
grow 36vb.
unite with 45vb.
be high 209vb.
support 218vb.
enclose 235vb.
ride 267vb.
conveyance 267n.
saddle-horse 273n.
start out 296vb.
insert 303vb.
ascend, climb 308vb.
elevate 310vb.
break in 369vb.
prepare 669vb.
mountain
bulk 195n.
high land 209n.
mountaineer
dweller 191n.
traveler 268n.
climber 308n.
climb 308vb.
mountaineering
sport 837n.
mountainous
great 32adj.
large, huge 195adj.
alpine 209adj.
mountebank
impostor 545n.
entertainer 594n.
mount guard
invigilate 457vb.
safeguard 660vb.
mount one's high horse
be proud 871vb.
mount the throne
take authority 733vb.
mourn
inter 364vb.
lament 836vb.
mourner
funeral 364n.
weeper 836n.
mournful
distressing 827adj.
melancholic 834adj.
mournfulness
sorrow 825n.
mourning
funeral dress 228n.
obsequies 364n.
funereal 364adj.
black thing 428n.
lamentation 836n.
mouse
animalcule 196n.
rodent 365n.
testee 461n.
hunt 619vb.
coward 856n.
humility 872n.
mouse-like
humble 872adj.
mouser
cat 365n.
hunter 619n.
mousse
pudding 301n.
pulpiness 356n.
moustache, mustachio
hair 259n.
mousy
colorless 426adj.
gray 429adj.
mouth
entrance 68n.
maw 194n.
threshold 234n.
orifice 263n.
way in 297n.
eater 301n.
gulf 345n.
voice 577vb.
orate 579vb.
mouthful
small quantity 33n.
mouthful 301n.
oration 579n.
mouth-organ
organ 414n.
mouthpiece
orifice 263n.
air-pipe 353n.
flute 414n.
interpreter 520n.
informant 524n.
speaker 579n.
deputy 755n.
mouth-pipe
air-pipe 353n.
mouth-wash
cleanser 648n.
prophylactic 658n.
mouthy
rhetorical 574adj.
moutonné
arcuate 253adj.
movable
moving 265adj.
transferable 272adj.
property 777n.
move
derange 63vb.
debut 68n.
operate 173vb.
displace 188vb.
move 265vb.
transpose 272vb.
move fast 277vb.
propel 287vb.
attract 291vb.
excrete 302vb.
touch 378vb.
propound 512vb.
gesture 547n.
motivate 612vb.
essay 671n.
action, deed 676n.
be active 678vb.
tactics 688n.
advise 691vb.
stratagem 698n.
offer 759vb.
excite 821vb.
moveable
(*see* movable)
move away
recede 290vb.
move in
enter 297vb.
moveless
still 266adj.
movement
transition 147n.
motion 265n.
cacation 302n.
melody 410n.
musical piece 412n.
dramaturgy 594n.
action 676n.
activity 678n.
party, society 708n.
move out
relinquish 621vb.
mover
cause 156n.
producer 167n.
influence 178n.
motivator 612n.
doer 676n.
adviser 691n.
move up
bring near 200vb.
move with the times
modernize 126vb.
change 143vb.
progress 285vb.
movie
cinema 445n.
movie goer
spectator 441n.
moving pavement
transport 272n.
carrier 273n.
conveyor 274n.
moving picture

cinema 445n.
moving staircase
transport 272n.
carrier 273n.
conveyor 274n.
lifter 310n.
mow
cut 46vb.
shorten 204vb.
distortion 246n.
smooth 258vb.
cultivate 370vb.
store 632n., vb.
mow down
demolish 165vb.
slaughter 362vb.
mower
husbandman 370n.
mowing
product 164n.
moxa
burning 381n.
Mr. and Mrs.
spouse 894n.
Mr. Facing-both-ways
tergiversator 603n.
Mrs. Grundy
etiquette 848n.
prude 950n.
Mr. X
unknown thing 491n.
no name 562n.
much
great quantity 32n.
many 104adj.
much ado
activity 678n.
much cry and little wool
overestimation 482n.
disappointment 509n.
boast 877n.
much-married
married 894adj.
muchness, much of a
median 30adj.
imperfect 647adj.
mediocre 732adj.
much obliged
grateful 907adj.
much of, make
make important 638vb.
much the same
similar 18adj.
mucilage
semiliquidity 354n.
mucilaginous
viscid 354adj.
muck
rubbish 641n.
dirt 649n.
muckrake
defame 926vb.
muckraker
reformer 654n.
defamer 926n.
muck up
jumble 63vb.
make unclean 649vb.
impair 655vb.
mucky
dirty 649adj.
mucoid
viscid 354adj.
mucous
viscid 354adj.
mucronate
sharp 256adj.
mucus
fluid 335n.
semiliquidity 354n.
dirt 649n.
mud
moisture 341n.
marsh 347n.
semiliquidity 354n.
dirt 649n.
muddied
opaque 423adj.
muddle
disorder 61n.
confusion 61n.
derange 63vb.
failure 278n.
distract 456vb.
not discriminate 464vb.
predicament 700n.
muddled
ill-reasoned 477adj.
muddle-head
fool 501n.
muddle-headed
ill-reasoned 477adj.
unintelligent 499adj.
muddy
humid 341adj.
marshy 347adj.
semiliquid 354adj.
thicken 354vb.
dim 419adj.
opaque 423adj.
dirty 649adj.
make unclean 649vb.
mudguard
shelter 662n.
mudhopper
ship 275n.
mudlark
dirty person 649n.
low fellow 869n.
mud pack
beautification 843n.
mud-slinging
detraction 926n.
muff
glove 228n.
warm clothes 381n.
be clumsy 695vb.
bungler 697n.
muffetee
glove 228n.
muffin
pastry 301n.
muffle
cover 226vb.
silence 399vb.
mute 401vb.
conceal 525vb.
make mute 578vb.
muffled
muted 401adj.
non-resonant 405adj.
occult 523adj.
voiceless 578adj.
muffled drum
obsequies 364n.
non-resonance 405n.
signal 547n.
muffler
shawl 228n.
warm clothes 381n.
mufti
non-uniformity 17n.
informal dress 228n.
judge 957n.
theologian 973n.
mug
cup 194n.
face 237n.
ninny 501n.
study 536vb.
dupe 544n.
mugger
reptile 365n.
learner 538n.
muggins
ninny 501n.
muggy
sealed off 264adj.
humid 341adj.
mugient
ululant 409adj.
mugwump
tergiversator 603n.
mukhtar
consignee 754n.
law agent 958n.
mukti
liberation 746n.
mulatto
hybrid 43n.
mulberry
purple 434adj.
mulch
covering 226n.
mulct
punish 963vb.
mulctable
punishable 963adj.
mulctuary

punitive 963adj.
mule
hybrid 43n.
nonconformist 84n.
footwear 228n.
animal 365n.
opinionist 602n.
muleteer
driver 268n.
muliebrity
female 373n.
mulish
equine 273adj.
obstinate 602adj.
mull
textile 222n.
projection 254n.
sweeten 392vb.
think 449vb.
be attentive 455vb.
study 536vb.
muller
pulverizer 332n.
mullet
fish food 301n.
table fish 365n.
mulligatawny
soup 301n.
mulligrubs
sullenness 893n.
mullioned
crossed 222adj.
mullock
rubbish 641n.
mulmul
textile 222n.
multicolored
variegated 437adj.
multifarious
irrelative 10adj.
different 15adj.
non-uniform 17adj.
multiform 82adj.
multiferous
multitudinous 104adj.
multifid
fragmentary 53adj.
multifid 100adj.
multiform
different 15adj.
non-uniform 17adj.
mixed 43adj.
multiform 82adj.
changeful 152adj.
multilateral
lateral 239adj.
angulated 247adj.
contractual 765adj.
multilingual
linguistic 557adj.
multimillion
over one hundred 99n.
multitude 104n.
multinomial
many 104adj.
multiparous
prolific 171adj.
multipartite
disjunct 46adj.
multiple
quantity 26n.
numerical element 85n.
plural 101adj.
many 104adj.
multiple personality
spirit 447n.
psychopathy 503n.
multiplex
multiform 82adj.
multiplicand
numerical element 85n.
multiplicate
multiform 82adj.
multiplication
increase 36n.
numerical operation 86n.
propagation 164n.
reproduction 166n.
productiveness 171n.
multiplication sign
punctuation 547n.
multiplication table
counting instrument 86n.
multiplicity
plurality 101n.
multitude 104n.
multiplier
numerical element 85n.
multiply
copy 20vb.
be many 104vb.
(*see* multiplication)
multipurpose
general 79adj.
useful 640adj.
multiracial
mixed 43adj.
multiracial state
medley 43n.
multisection
multisection 100n.
multitude
great quantity 32n.
crowd 74n.
plurality 101n.
multitude 104n.
multitudinous
frequent 139adj.
multum in parvo
compendium 592n.
multure
pulverulence 332n.
mum
voiceless 578adj.
taciturn 582adj.
mum, be
keep secret 525vb.
mumble
chew 301vb.
stammer 580vb.
mumbo-jumbo
god 966n.
idolatry 982n.
spell 983n.
mummer
impostor 545n.
actor 594n.
mummery
foolery 497n.
sham 542n.
festivity 837n.
ostentation 875n.
false piety 980n.
mummify
dry 342vb.
inter 364vb.
preserve 666vb.
mummy
corpse 363n.
mummy-case
interment 364n.
mummy-chamber
tomb 364n.
mummy-cloth
wrapping 226n.
mumpish
melancholic 834adj.
mumps
infection 651n.
mumpsimus
laughing-stock 851n.
munch
chew 301vb.
mundane
selfish 932adj.
irreligious 974adj.
munerary
rewarding 962adj.
mungo
fiber 208n.
municipal
regional 184adj.
municipality
jurisdiction 955n.
municipalize
convey 780vb.
appropriate 786vb.
munificence
liberality 813n.
muniment
record 548n.
defenses 713n.
title-deed 767n.
muniment room
recorder 549n.
munitions

means 629n.
defense 713n.
arm 723n.
munshi
teacher 537n.
mural
picture 553n.
murder
killing 362n.
murder 362vb.
solecize 565vb.
cruel act 898n.
execute 963vb.
murderee
corpse 363n.
murderer
murderer 362n.
murderous
murderous 362adj.
murex
red pigment 431n.
muricate
sharp 256adj.
rough 259adj.
murk
darkness 418n.
dimness 419n.
murky
dense 324adj.
dark 418adj.
opaque 423adj.
cheerless 834adj.
murmur
flow 350vb.
faintness 401n.
danger signal 665n.
deprecation 762n.
discontent 829n.
murmuring
disobedience 738n.
murrain
plague 651n.
animal disease 681n.
murrey
red color 431n.
muscadine
fragrant 396adj.
muscat
fruit 301n.
muscle
ligature 47n.
power 160n.
vitality 162n.
exertion 682n.
muscle-bound
unwieldy 195adj.
rigid 326adj.
muscular
stalwart 162adj.
muse
be inattentive 456vb.
meditate 449vb.
Muses
choir 413n.
literature 557n.
poetry 593n.
lesser god 967n.
musette
flute 414n.
museum
accumulation 74n.
antiquity 125n.
exhibit 522n.
collection 632n.
museum piece
archaism 127n.
exhibit 522n.
exceller 644n.
laughing-stock 851n.
mush
semiliquidity 354n.
pulpiness 356n.
mushroom
upstart 126n.
new 126adj.
high structure 209n.
round 252vb.
vegetable 301n.
plant 366n.
radiation 417n.
poison 659n.
bomb 723n.
mushy
soft 327adj.
semiliquid 354adj.
pulpy 356adj.
music
music 412n.
musical instrument 414n.
musical
melodious 410adj.
musical 412adj.
musicianly 413adj.
stage play 594n.
pleasurable 826adj.
musical appreciation
musical skill 413n.
musical box
phonograph 414n.
musical comedy
vocal music 412n.
stage play 594n.
musical glasses
gong 414n.
musical instrument
musical instrument 414n.
musical notation
notation 410n.
musical note
musical note 410n.
music hall
theater 594n.
place of amusement 837n.
musician
musician 413n.
musicianly
musicianly 413adj.
musicianship
musical skill 413n.
musing
thought 449n.
musk
scent 396n.
musket
fire-arm 723n.
musketeer
shooter 287n.
soldiery 722n.
musketry
propulsion 287n.
bombardment 712n.
art of war 718n.
arm 723n.
musky
fragrant 396adj.
Muslim, Moslem
religionist 973n.
muslin
textile 222n.
semitransparency 424n.
mussel
fish food 301n.
table fish 365n.
mussiness
amorphism 244n.
Mussulman
religionist 973n.
must, a
necessity 596n.
requirement 627n.
mustang
saddle-horse 273n.
mustard
pungency 388n.
condiment 389n.
yellowness 433n.
mustard gas
gas 336n.
poison 659n.
weapon 723n.
mustard plaster
surgical dressing 658n.
mustardseed
minuteness 196n.
mustee
hybrid 43n.
muster
assemblage 74n.
statistics 86n.
number 86vb.
pageant 875n.
muster courage
take courage 855vb.
muster-roll
statistics 86n.

list 87n.
musth, must
lecherous 951adj.
musty
fetid 397adj.
dirty 649adj.
mutability
transientness 114n.
change 143n.
changeableness 152n.
mutation
change 143n.
conversion 147n.
mutatis mutandis
(*see* change)
mute
funeral 364n.
silent 399adj.
silencer 401n.
mute 401vb.
non-resonance 405n.
mute 401vb.
spoken letter 558n.
aphony 578n.
taciturn 582adj.
actor 594n.
weeper 836n.
mutilate
deform 244vb.
make ugly 842vb.
torture 963vb.
mutilated
imperfect 647adj.
mutilation
incompleteness 55n.
impairment 655n.
mutineer
revolter 738n.
schismatic 978n.
mutinous
disobedient 738adj.
dutiless 918adj.
(*see* mutiny)
mutiny
strike 145n.
resist 715vb.
revolt 738n., vb.
dutilessness 918n.
mutism
helplessness 161n.
aphony 578n.
mutt
dog 365n.
(*see* fool)
mutter
blow 352vb.
sound faint 401vb.
cry 408vb.
stammer 580vb.
be sullen 893vb.
threaten 900vb.
muttering
danger signal 665n.
mutton
meat 301n.
mutton-chops
hair 259n.
mutual
correlative 12adj.
interchanged 151adj.
mutual agreement
compact 765n.
mutual assistance
cooperation 706n.
mutual concession
mid-course 625n.
cooperation 706n.
compromise 770n.
mutualism
joint possession 775n.
mutuality
correlation 12n.
interchange 151n.
mutualize
correlate 12vb.
socialize 775vb.
muzhik
husbandman 370n.
possessor 776n.
muzzle
disable 161vb.
projection 254n.
orifice 263n.
stopper 264n.
silence 399vb.
make mute 587vb.
hinder 702vb.
fire-arm 723n.
restrain 747vb.
fetter 748n.
muzzle-loader
fire-arm 723n.
muzzy
tipsy 949adj.
myalgia
rheumatism 651n.
mycology
botany 368n.
my lord
male 372n.
title 870n.
mynheer
title 870n.
myocarditis
heart disease 651n.
myology
structure 331n.
myopia, myosis
dim sight 440n.
myopic
dim-sighted 440adj.
midjudging 481adj.
myriad
over one hundred 99n.
multitude 104n.
myrmidon
soldier 722n.
myrrh
resin 357n.
scent 396n.
myrtle
tree 366n.
greenness 432n.
love emblem 887n.
myself
identity 13n.
self 80n.
subjectivity 320n.
mystagogic
revelational 975adj.
mystagogue
teacher 537n.
leader 690n.
mysteries
religion 973n.
act of worship 981n.
rite 988n.
mysterious
unusual 84adj.
invisible 444adj.
uncertain 474adj.
unknown 491adj.
puzzling 517adj.
occult 523adj.
concealed 525adj.
imperspicuous 568adj.
wonderful 864adj.
cabalistic 984adj.
mystery
invisibility 444n.
unknown thing 491n.
latency 523n.
secrecy 525n.
secret, enigma 530n.
stage play 594n.
business 622n.
rite 988n.
mystery man
latency 523n.
mystic
spectator 441n.
inexpressible 517adj.
occult 523adj.
religious 973adj.
revelational 975adj.
pietist 979n.
worshiper 981n.
devotional 981adj.
occultist 984n.
mystical
divine 968adj.
(*see* mystic)
mysticism
meditation 449n.
latency 523n.
religion 973n.
piety 979n.
occultism 984n.
mystification
sophistry 477n.

unmeaningness 515n.
unintelligibility 517n.
concealment 525n.
misteaching 535n.
mystify
puzzle 474vb.
deceive 542vb.
mystique
prestige 866n.
cult 981n.
myth
fantasy 513n.
fable 543n.
narrative 590n.
mythical, mythic
imaginary 513adj.
theotechnic 966adj.
mythical being
mythical being 970n.
mythological
olden 127adj.
erroneous 495adj.
imaginary 513adj.
untrue 543adj.
descriptive 590adj.
theotechnic 966adj.
mythologist
liar 545n.
narrator 590n.
mythology
tradition 127n.
anthropology 371n.
fable 543n.
narrative 590n.
mythomania
falsehood 541n.

N

nab
ensnare 542vb.
arrest 747vb.
take 786vb.
nabob
rich man 800n.
(*see* nawab)
nacelle
airship 276n.
nacre
variegation 437n.
nadir
inferiority 35n.
extremity 69n.
serial place 73n.
zero 103n.
lowness 210n.
depth 211n.
base 214n.
nag
saddle-horse 273n.
incite 612vb.
bicker 709vb.
animate 821vb.
torment 827vb.
enrage 891vb.
Nagari
letter 558n.
naiad
sea nymph 343n.
nymph 967n.
mythical being 970n.
nail
affix 45vb.
fastening 47n.
long measure 203n.
hanger 217n.
sharp point 256n.
perforator 263n.
pierce 263vb.
tobacco 388n.
tool 630n.
nail-brush
cleansing utensil 648n.
nail-file
smoother 258n.
cosmetic 843n.
nail polish
cosmetic 843n.
nails
hardness 326n.
weapon 723n.
nippers 778n.
naïve
credulous 487adj.
ignorant 491adj.
foolish 499adj.
artless 699adj.
naked
simple 44adj.
uncovered 229adj.
visible 443adj.
undisguised 522adj.
vulnerable 661adj.
nakedness
purity 950n.
name
class 62vb.
auspicate 68vb.
inform 524vb.
indicate 547vb.
word 559n.
name 561n., vb.
commission 751vb.
repute 866n.
accuse 928vb.
name and address
label 547n.
name 561n.
name-board
label 547n.
name-day
special day 876n.
name-giver
nomenclator 561n.
nameless
unconformable 84adj.
anonymous 562adj.
inglorious 867adj.
namely
namely 80adv.
name of, in the
in aid of 703adv.
by authority 733adv.
name-plate
label 547n.
namesake
name 561n.
naming
identification 547n.
nomenclature 561n.
naming 561adj.
nankeen
textile 222n.
nanny
protector 660n.
domestic 742n.
retainer 742n.
keeper 749n.
naos
holy place 990n.
nap
hair 259n.
texture 331n.
sleep 679n., vb.
card game 837n.
napalm
fuel 385n.
bomb 723n.
nape
rear 238n.
napery
cleaning cloth 648n.
Napier's bones
counting instrument 86n.
napiform
rotund 252adj.
napkin
cleaning cloth 648n.
napless
hairless 229adj.
Napoleonic
warlike 718adj.
nappe
descent 309n.
waterfall 350n.
napping
abstracted 456adj.
sleepy 679adj.
nappy
loincloth 228n.
downy 259adj.
drunk 949adj.
narcissism
vanity 873n.
love 887n.
selfishness 932n.
Narcissus
a beauty 841n.
vain person 873n.

narcolepsy
insensibility 375n.
narcosis
helplessness 161n.
insensibility 375n.
narcotic
lenitive 177adj.
anesthetic 375n.
toxic 653adj.
drug 658n.
nard
unguent 357n.
nargileh
tobacco 388n.
nark
informer 524n.
accuser 928n.
narration
remembrance 505n.
information 524n.
description 590n.
narrative
record 548n.
narrative 590n.
narrator
narrator 590n.
narrow
small 33adj.
tighten 45vb.
make smaller 198vb.
narrow 206adj.
narrow-minded 481adj.
restraining 747adj.
prohibit 757vb.
narrow down
simplify 44vb.
converge 293vb.
narrow-mindedness
narrow mind 481n.
narrowness
contraction 198n.
narrowness 206n.
narrows
narrowness 206n.
narrow squeak
escape 667n.
nasal
speech sound 398n.
vocal 577adj.
stammering 580adj.
nasality
stridor 407n.
nasalize
stammer 580vb.
nascent
beginning 68adj.
nastiness
bad taste 847n.
discourtesy 885n.
(*see* nasty)
nasty
inferior 35adj.
unsavory 391adj.
fetid 397adj.
not nice 645adj.
unclean 649adj.
insalubrious 653adj.
unpleasant 827adj.
ugly 842adj.
hateful 888adj.
malevolent 898adj.
threatening 900adj.
impure 951adj.
nasty type
bad man 938n.
natal
first 68adj.
natation
aquatics 269n.
natatorium
ablution 648n.
nation
nation 371n.
national
ethnic 11adj.
regional 184adj.
native 191adj.
national 371adj.
subject 742n.
national dress
livery 547n.
national flag
talisman 983n.
National Guard
defender 713n.
army 722n.
nationalism
particularism 80n.
nation 371n.
patriotism 901n.
nationalist
patriot 901n.
nationalistic
biased 481adj.
patriotic 901adj.
nationality
consanguinity 11n.
subjection 745n.
(*see* nationalism)
nationalization
association 706n.
nationalize
socialize 775vb.
appropriate 786vb.
national service
war measures 718n.
nation-state
nation 371n.
nation-wide
universal 79adj.
native
genetic 5adj.
intrinsic 5adj.
ingredient 58adj.
special 80adj.
native 191n., adj.
social group 371n.
artless 699adj.
native land
home 192n.
native state
undevelopment 670n.
nativity
origin 68n.
date 108n.
propagation 164n.
life 360n.
Nativity
holy-day 988n.
natty
clean 648adj.
personable 841adj.
natural
real 1adj.
substantial 3adj.
lifelike 18adj.
agreeing 24adj.
typical 83adj.
material 319adj.
musical note 410n.
probable 471adj.
true, genuine 494adj.
fool 501n.
madman 504n.
plain 573adj.
elegant 575adj.
descriptive 590adj.
spontaneous 609adj.
usual 610adj.
artless 699adj.
friendly 880adj.
natural bent
aptitude 694n.
natural child
bastardy 954n.
natural history
biology 358n.
naturalist
biology 358n.
naturalistic
representing 551adj.
naturalization
conformity 83n.
conversion 147n.
location 187n.
reception 299n.
habituation 610n.
freedom 744n.
naturalized
native 191adj.
naturally
consequently 157adv.
skillfully 694adv.
rightly 913adv.
naturalness
adaptation 24n.
plainness 573n.
artlessness 699n.
natural selection
biology 358n.

nature
essence 1n.
character 5n.
composition 56n.
tendency 179n.
matter 319n.
truth 494n.
habit 610n.
affections 817n.
nature cure
therapy 658n.
nature god
mythic god 966n.
nature study
biology 358n.
naturism
uncovering 229n.
naught
insubstantiality 4n.
zero 103n.
naughtiness
disobedience 738n.
wickedness 934n.
guilty act 936n.
naughty
unchaste 961adj.
nausea
voidance 300n.
indigestion 651n.
painfulness 827n.
tedium 838n.
dislike 861n.
hatred 888n.
nauseant
cathartic 658n.
nauseate
be unpalatable 391n.
displease 827vb.
cause discontent 829vb.
be tedious 838vb.
cause dislike 861vb.
excite hate 888vb.
nauseated
vomiting 300adj.
nauseous
unsavory 391n.
not nice 645adj.
unclean 649adj.
unpleasant 827adj.
tedious 838adj.
disliked 861adj.
hateful 888adj.
nautch
dance 837vb.
nautch-girl
jumper 312n.
entertainer 594n.
dancing 837n.
nautical
seafaring 269adj.
seamanlike 270adj.
marine 275adj.
nautical almanac
chronology 117n.
guide-book 524n.
naval
seafaring 269adj.
seamanlike 270adj.
marine 275adj.
warlike 718adj.
naval man
naval man 270n.
nave
middle 70n.
centrality 225n.
church interior 990n.
navel
middle 70n.
centrality 225n.
navigable
deep 211adj.
seafaring 269adj.
navigate
navigate 269vb.
orientate 281vb.
navigator
navigator 270n.
aeronaut 271n.
director 690n.
navvy
worker 686n.
navy
shipping 275n.
blue 435adj.
navy 722n.
Navy List
directory 87n.
nawab
potentate 741n.
nobleman 868n.
(*see* nabob)
nay
negation 533n.
refusal 760n.
nay rather
contrarily 14adv.
Nazarene
religionist 973n.
Nazirites
non-Christian sect 978n.
Nazism
brute force 735n.
N.C.O.
army officer 741n.
Neanderthal man
mankind 371n.
neap, neap tide
decrease 37n.
near
akin 11adj.
future 124adj.
early 135adj.
impending 155adj.
near 200adj.
approach 289vb.
parsimonious 816adj.
nearly
almost 33adv.
nearness
similarity 18n.
nearness 200n.
contiguity 202n.
near side
sinistrality 242n.
near-sightedness
dim sight 440n.
near thing
draw 28n.
short distance 200n.
escape 667n.
neat
unmixed 44adj.
orderly 60adj.
cattle 365n.
careful 457adj.
plain 573adj.
concise 569adj.
elegant 575adj.
clean 648adj.
skillful 694adj.
personable 841adj.
intoxicating 949adj.
neaten
arrange, unravel 62vb.
make better 654vb.
beautify 841vb.
neat-fingered
skillful 694adj.
nebula
nebula 321n.
cloud 355n.
nebular
dim 419adj.
celestial 321adj.
nebulosity
(*see* nebulous)
nebulous
celestial 321adj.
cloudy 355adj.
dim 419adj.
puzzling 517adj.
necessaries
requirement 627n.
necessarily
consequently 157adv.
necessarily 596adv.
in need 627adv.
on terms 766adv.
necessary
certain 473adj.
necessary 596adj.
choiceless 606adj.
required 627adj.
important 638adj.
compelling 740adj.
necessary, a
necessity 596n.

requirement 627n.
necessary house
latrine 649n.
necessitarian
fatalist 596n.
necessitarianism
necessity 596n.
necessitate
predestine 155vb.
make certain 473vb.
necessitate 596vb.
require 627vb.
compel 740vb.
necessitous
necessitous 627adj.
poor 801adj.
necessitude
necessity 596n.
necessity
destiny 155n.
cause 156n.
certainty 473n.
necessity 596n.
no choice 606n.
requirement 627n.
needfulness 627n.
compulsion 740n.
poverty 801n.
neck
bond 47n.
contraction 198n.
narrowness 206n.
supporter 218n.
pillar 218n.
conduit 351n.
bridge 624n.
caress 889vb.
neck and crop
completely 54adv.
neck-and-neck
equal 28adj.
synchronous 123adj.
neckband
neckwear 228n.
loop 250n.
neckcloth
neckwear 228n.
necking
endearment 889n.
necklace
neckwear 228n.
loop 250n.
jewelry 844n.
neck of land
land 344n.
neck or nothing
resolutely 599adv.
necrologist
obsequies 364n.
necrologue
obsequies 364n.
necrology
death roll 361n.
biography 590n.
necromancer
conjuror 545n.
sorcerer 983n.
necromancy
sorcery 983n.
necrophilia
abnormality 84n.
necropolis
cemetery 364n.
necropsy
death 361n.
inquest 364n.
necrosis
decay 51n.
nectar
liquor 301n.
savoriness 390n.
sweet 392n.
need
deficit 55n.
shortcoming 307n.
requirement 627n.
scarcity 636n.
adversity 731n.
poverty 801n.
desire 859n.
needful
required 627adj.
needful, the
funds 797n.
need, in
necessitous 627adj.
in need 627adv.
poor 801adj.
neediness
poverty 801n.
needle
sharp point 256n.
prickle 256n.
perforator 263n.
sailing aid 269n.
indicator 547n.
engraving 555n.
directorship 689n.
torment 827vb.
enrage 891vb.
needles
nervousness 854n.
needless
superfluous 637adj.
rash 857adj.
needlewoman
artisan 686n.
needlework
needlework 844n.
needling
therapy 658n.
needy
poor 801adj.
ne'er-do-well
desperado 857n.
vicious 934adj.
bad man 938n.
nefarious
disreputable 867adj.
wrong 914adj.
heinous 934adj.
negate
nullify 2vb.
confute 479vb.
(*see* negation)
negation
contrariety 14n.
counter-evidence 467n.
unbelief 486n.
dissent 489n.
negation 533n.
recantation 603n.
rejection 607n.
opposition 704n.
abrogation 752n.
refusal 760n.
negative
nullify 2vb.
copy 22n.
prototype 23n.
imperfect 647adj.
unsuccessful 728adj.
(*see* negation)
negativeness
non-existence 2n.
negatory
countervailing 467adj.
negative 533adj.
negatron
element 319n.
neglect
disorder 61n.
lose a chance 138vb.
be inattentive 456vb.
negligence 458n.
be loath 598vb.
avoid 620vb.
dilapidation 655n.
non-preparation 670n.
not use 674vb.
inaction 677n.
non-completion 726n.
not observe 769vb.
rashness 857n.
dutilessness 918n.
disrespect 921n.
neglected
undervalued 483adj.
neglectful
negligent 458adj.
apathetic 820adj.
negligee
informal dress 228n.
negligence
negligence 458n.
inexactness 495n.
sluggishness 679n.
laxity 734n.
indifference 860n.
guilty act 936n.

(*see* neglect)
negligent
negligent 458adj.
forgetful 506adj.
clumsy 695adj.
(*see* negligence)
negligible
inconsiderable 33adj.
unimportant 639adj.
negotiable
transferable 272adj.
possible 469adj.
expedient 642adj.
transferred 780adj.
negotiate
accord 24vb.
pass 305vb.
do business 622vb.
cooperate 706vb.
deputize 755vb.
contract 765vb.
make terms 766vb.
bargain 791vb.
negotiation
conference 584n.
mediation 720n.
(*see* negotiate)
negotiator
intermediary 231n.
mediator 720n.
consignee 754n.
envoy 754n.
signatory 765n.
negress
negro 428n.
negrito
ethnic 11adj.
negro 428n.
negro
negro 428n.
negroid
ethnic 11adj.
black 428adj.
negrophobia
prejudice 481n.
phobia 854n.
negus
liquor 301n.
sovereign 741n.
neigh
ululate 409vb.
neighbor
be near 200vb.
friend 880n.
neighborhood
locality 187n.
near place 200n.
circumjacence 230n.
neighborly
aiding 703adj.
sociable 882adj.
neither
neither 606adv.
neither here nor there
irrelevant 10adj.
neither one thing nor the other
nonconformist 84n.
neutral 625adj.
nem con
unanimously 488adv.
Nemesis
trouble-maker 663n.
retaliation 714n.
avenger 910n.
justice 913n.
punishment 963n.
nenia
lament 836n.
Neocene
secular 110adj.
neolalia
neology 560n.
Neolithic
secular 110adj.
neological
modern 126adj.
neological 560adj.
neologism
newness 126n.
neology 560n.
neologist
modernist 126n.
dialect 560n.
neology
neology 560n.
neon
air 340n.
luminescent 420adj.
neonomianism
newness 126n.
abrogation 752n.
neophyte
changed person 147n.
beginner 538n.
pietist 979n.
Neoplatonism
philosophy 449n.
neoteric
modern 126adj.
neoterism
newness 126n.
neology 560n.
nepenthe
drug 658n.
nephalism
sobriety 948n.
nephew
kinsman 11n.
nephology
cloud 355n.
ne plus ultra
superiority 34n.
completeness 54n.
extremity 69n.
farness 199n.
limit 236n.
perfection 646n.
completion 725n.
fashion 848n.
nepotism
injustice 914n.
improbity 930n.
Neptune
mariner 270n.
planet 321n.
sea god 343n.
mythic god 966n.
Olympian god 967n.
Neptunian
planetary 321adj.
Nereid
satellite 321n.
sea nymph 343n.
nymph 967n.
nerve
strengthen 162vb.
courage 855n.
give courage 855vb.
sauciness 878n.
nerveless
impotent 161adj.
weak 163adj.
feeble 572adj.
irresolute 601adj.
nerve-racking
distressing 827adj.
frightening 854adj.
nerves
psychopathy 503n.
excitability 822n.
nervousness 854n.
nervous
impotent 161adj.
weak 163adj.
agitated 318adj.
distracted 456adj.
expectant 507adj.
forceful 571adj.
irresolute 601adj.
avoiding 620adj.
lively 819adj.
excitable 822adj.
nervous 854adj.
cowardly 856adj.
cautious 858adj.
nervous breakdown
helplessness 161n.
psychopathy 503n.
nervous disorder
psychopathy 503n.
nervousness
(*see* nervous)
nervous tic
spasm 318n.
nervy
(*see* nerves)
nescience
ignorance 491n.
nest
group 74n.

focus 76n.
seedbed 156n.
nest 192n.
dwell 192vb.
sit down 311vb.
refuge 662n.
nest-egg
store 632n.
wealth 800n.
nestle
dwell 192vb.
be safe 660vb.
caress 889vb.
nestling
youngling 132n.
bird 365n.
Nestor
old man 133n.
sage 500n.
adviser 691n.
Nestorianism
heresy 977n.
net
remaining 41adj.
bring together 74vb.
receptacle 194n.
network 222n.
enclosure 235n.
trap 542n.
hunt 619vb.
acquire 771vb.
receive 782vb.
take 786vb.
net-ball
ball game 837n.
nether
low 210adj.
nethermost
undermost 241adj.
netherworld
the dead 361n.
hell 972n.
netting
network 222n.
nettle
prickle 256n.
bane 659n.
hurt 827vb.
huff 891vb.
nettlerash
formication 378n.
network
correlation 12n.
gap 201n.
network 222n.
texture 331n.
neuralgia
pang 377n.
neurasthenic
insane 503adj.
neuritis
pang 377n.
neurologist
doctor 658n.
neurology
structure 331n.
neuropath
madman 504n.
sick person 651n.
doctor 658n.
neuropathy
psychopathy 503n.
neurosis
psychopathy 503n.
neurosurgeon
doctor 658n.
neurotic
insane 503adj.
madman 504n.
neuter
generic 77adj.
eunuch 161n.
impotent 161adj.
grammatical 564adj.
neutral
median 30adj.
inert 175adj.
moderate 177adj.
gray 429adj.
choiceless 606adj.
avoiding 620adj.
neutral 625adj.
non-active 677adj.
peaceful 717adj.
mediocre 732adj.
independent 744adj.
cautious 858adj.
indifferent 860adj.
just 913adj.
disinterested 931adj.
neutralization
compensation 31n.
counteraction 182n.
neutralize
disable 161vb.
weaken 163vb.
counteract 182vb.
remedy 658vb.
neutrino
particle 33n.
neutron
particle 33n.
element 319n.
névé
ice 380n.
never
never 109adv.
never-ending
perpetual 115adj.
prolix 570adj.
uncompleted 726adj.
never-failing
successful 727adj.
never-never system
borrowing 785n.
never-resting
industrious 678adj.
never say die
persevere 600vb.
nevertheless
nevertheless 468adv.
never the same
non-uniform 17adj.
changeful 152adj.
new
first 68adj.
new 126adj.
early 135adj.
unknown 491adj.
unhabituated 611adj.
new arrival
intruder 59n.
aftercomer 67n.
posteriority 120n.
arrival 295n.
incomer 297n.
new birth
life 360n.
revival 656n.
sanctity 979n.
newborn
new 126adj.
infantine 132adj.
newborn babe
innocent 935n.
new broom
busy person 678n.
newcomer
intruder 59n.
aftercomer 67n.
incomer 297n.
new deal
apportionment 783n.
New Dealer
reformer 654n.
newel-post
pillar 218n.
newfangled
unusual 84adj.
modern 126adj.
changeable 143adj.
neological 560adj.
fashionable 848adj.
Newgate
prison 748n.
Newgate calendar
biography 590n.
legal trial 959n.
New Jerusalem
Heaven 971n.
holy place 990n.
new leaf
amendment 654n.
new life
revival 656n.
new look
modernism 126n.
newlywed
spouse 894n.
married 894adj.
new man

changed person 147n.
new-model
transform 147vb.
revolutionize 149vb.
rectify 654vb.
newness
non-imitation 21n.
beginning 68n.
newness 126n.
news
topic 452n.
information 524n.
news 529n.
news agent
newsmonger 529n.
news business
the press 528n.
newscast
publication 528n.
publicity 528n.
news 529n.
newsletter
publicity 528n.
the press 528n.
newsman
newsmonger 529n.
chronicler 549n.
newsmonger
inquisitor 453n.
informant 524n.
newsmonger 529n.
newspaper
the press 528n.
newspeak
neology 560n.
newsprint
stationery 586n.
paper 631n.
newsreel
cinema 445n.
publicity 528n.
news 529n.
news value
news 529n.
news vendor
newsmonger 529n.
newsy
informative 524adj.
loquacious 581adj.
newt
frog 365n.
New Testament
scripture 975n.
new version
variant 15n.
New Year
anniversary 141n.
next
sequent 65adj.
subsequent 120adj.
futurity 124n.
contiguously 202adv.
next door
near place 200n.
next friend
deputy 755n.
close friend 880n.
next of kin
kinsman 11n.
next step
progression 285n.
next world
destiny 155n.
the dead 361n.
nexus
bond 47n.
niagara
waterfall 350n.
nib
extremity 69n.
vertex 213n.
sharp point 256n.
stationery 586n.
nibble
mouthful 301n.
eat 301vb.
taste 386vb.
be duped 544vb.
endearment 889n.
nice
pleasant 376adj.
savory 390adj.
careful 457adj.
discriminating 463adj.
accurate 494adj.
not bad 644adj.
clean 648adj.
pleasurable 826adj.
beautiful 841adj.
tasteful 846adj.
fastidious 862adj.
amiable 884adj.
nicety
differentiation 15n.
carefulness 457n.
discrimination 463n.
good taste 846n.
fastidiousness 862n.
niche
place 185n.
compartment 194n.
shelf 218n.
angularity 247n.
cavity 255n.
hiding-place 527n.
honors 866n.
nick
cut 46vb.
notch 260n., vb.
mark 547vb.
wound 655vb.
steal 788vb.
nickel
small coin 33n.
coinage 797n.
nickelodeon
phonograph 414n.
nickname
name 561n.
misnomer 562n.
nick of time
occasion 137n.
opportunity 137n.
nicotine
tobacco 388n.
poison 659n.
nictitation
dim sight 440n.
nidget
coward 856n.
nidification
nest 192n.
nidor
odor 394n.
niece
kinsman 11n.
woman 373n.
niello
black pigment 428n.
niffy
odorous 394adj.
fetid 397adj.
niggard
niggard 816n.
egotist 932n.
niggardly
insufficient 636adj.
parsimoniously 816adv.
selfish 932adj.
nigger
negro 428n.
busy person 678n.
nigger in the woodpile
latency 523n.
hider 527n.
slyboots 698n.
niggler
detractor 926n.
niggling
trivial 639adj.
disapprobation 924n.
nigh
almost 33adv.
nigh 200adv.
night
darkness 418n.
(*see* evening)
night-blindness
blindness 439n.
dim sight 440n.
nightcap
nightwear 228n.
valediction 296n.
potion 301n.
soporific 679n.
night club
place of amusement 837n.
nightfall
evening 129n.

darkness 418n.
nightgown, nightshirt
nightwear 228n.
night-hag
sorceress 983n.
nightingale
bird 365n.
vocalist 413n.
night life
festivity 837n.
night-light
torch 420n.
nightly
vespertine 129adj.
seasonal 141adj.
nightmare
pain 377n.
fantasy 513n.
false alarm 615n.
suffering 825n.
intimidation 854n.
demon 970n.
night-soil
dirt 649n.
night-time
evening 129n.
night-watch
period 110n.
midnight 129n.
armed force 722n.
night-watchman
protector 660n.
keeper 749n.
nigrescence, nigritude
blackness 428n.
nigrosine
black pigment 428n.
nihilism
extinction 2n.
disorder 61n.
anarchy 734n.
sedition 738n.
nihilist
anarch 61n.
destroyer 168n.
revolter 738n.
evildoer 904n.
irreligionist 974n.
nihilistic
violent 176adj.
nihil obstat
permit 756n.
nil
non-existence 2n.
zero 103n.
nil admirari
be insensitive 820vb.
indifference 860n.
non-wonder 865n.
detraction 926n.
nilometer
hygrometry 341n.
meter 465n.
nimble
speedy 277adj.
active 678adj.
nimble-witted
intelligent 498adj.
nimbus
cloud 355n.
light 417n.
honors 866n.
nimiety
redundance 637n.
nincompoop
ninny 501n.
nine days' wonder
insubstantial thing 4n.
brief span 114n.
prodigy 864n.
ninepins
series 71n.
ball game 837n.
nine points of the law
possession 773n.
nineteenth hole
refreshment 685n.
nineteen to the dozen
swiftly 277adv.
ninny
ninny 501n.
ninon
textile 222n.
Niobe
weeper 836n.
nip
make smaller 198vb.
shorten 204vb.
make thin 206vb.
notch 260vb.
move fast 277vb.
potion 301n.
pang 377n.
touch 378vb.
refrigerate 382vb.
blight 659n.
hinder 702vb.
endearment 889n.
nip in the bud
suppress 165vb.
hinder 702vb.
nipper
youngster 132n.
nippers
cross 222n.
extractor 304n.
eyeglass 442n.
tool 630n.
nippers 778n.
nipping
cold 380adj.
nipple
bosom 253n.
nippy
vigorous 174adj.
active 678adj.
servant 742n.
nirvana
extinction 2n.
divineness 965n.
heaven 971n.
nit
animalcule 196n.
vermin 365n.
dirt 649n.
niter
pungency 388n.
nitrogen
air 340n.
nitroglycerin
explosive 723n.
niveous
cold 380adj.
white 427adj.
nix
zero 103n.
nixie
mythical being 970n.
nizam
potentate 741n.
no
no 489adv.
nay 533adv.
refusal 760n.
no account, of
unimportant 639adj.
unrespected 921adj.
contemptible 922adj.
no admission
exclusion 57n.
Noah's Ark
medley 43n.
accumulation 74n.
ship 275n.
cattle pen 369n.
nob
head 213n.
fop 848n.
aristocrat 868n.
no-ball
failure 728n.
nobble
disable 161vb.
impair 655vb.
take 786vb.
steal 788vb.
nobilitate
dignify 866vb.
nobility
superiority 34n.
genealogy 169n.
bigwig 638n.
elite 644n.
beauty 841n.
aristocracy 868n.
probity 929n.
disinterestedness 931n.
virtues 933n.
noble
important 638adj.

coinage 797n.
liberal 813adj.
impressive 821adj.
splendid 841adj.
well-bred 848adj.
worshipful 866adj.
renowned 866adj.
nobleman 868n.
noble 868adj.
proud 871adj.
honorable 929adj.
(*see* nobility)
nobleman
nobleman 868n.
noblesse
aristocracy 868n.
nobody
non-existence 2n.
insubstantiality 4n.
zero 103n.
nobody 190n.
nonentity 639n.
commoner 869n.
nobody's
unpossessed 774adj.
nobody's business
irrelation 10n.
nobody's darling
hateful object 888n.
nobody's fool
sage 500n.
no business
irrelation 10n.
no change
identity 13n.
permanence 144n.
no chicken
aged 131adj.
adult 134n.
no conjuror
dunce 501n.
bungler 697n.
noctambulist
pedestrian 268n.
noctiluca
glimmer 419n.
glow-worm 420n.
noctivagant
vespertine 129adj.
traveling 267adj.
dark 418adj.
nocturnal
vespertine 129adj.
dark 418adj.
black 428adj.
nocturne
musical piece 412n.
picture 553n.
art subject 553n.
nod
obeisance 311n.
oscillate 317vb.
be inattentive 456vb.
be neglectful 458vb.
assent 488n., vb.
hint 524n.
gesture 547n.
sleep 679vb.
be fatigued 684vb.
command 737n., vb.
permit 756vb.
consent 758vb.
courteous act 884n.
respects 920n.
approve 923vb.
nodding
pendent 217adj.
noddle
head 213n.
noddy
ninny 501n.
node
joint 45n.
swelling 253n.
uranometry 321n.
nodosity
swelling 253n.
roughness 259n.
nodular
rough 259adj.
nodule
swelling 253n.
Noel
holy-day 988n.
noes, the
dissentient 489n.
noesis
intellect 447n.
nog
liquor 301n.
noggin
cup 194n.
potion 301n.
no go
shortcoming 307n.
failure 728n.
no good
profitless 641adj.
bad 645adj.
nohow
impossibly 470adv.
no ice, cut
have no repute 867vb.
noise
sound 398n.
loudness 400n.
discord 411n.
proclaim 528vb.
rumor 529n.
indication 547n.
noise abatement
faintness 401n.
noiseless
silent 399adj.
noises off
mimicry 20n.
concomitant 89n.
representation 551n.
dramaturgy 594n.
noisome
fetid 397adj.
bad, harmful 645adj.
unclean 649adj.
baneful 659adj.
noisy
great 32adj.
loud 400adj.
no joke
reality 1n.
important matter 638n.
nolens volens
necessarily 596adv.
by force 740adv.
nolle prosequi
abrogation 752n.
no love lost
dissension 709n.
hatred 888n.
nomad
extraneous 59adj.
nonconformist 84n.
traveling 267adj.
wanderer 268n.
nomadism
wandering 267n.
no-man
eunuch 161n.
no man's land
territory 184n.
emptiness 190n.
intermediary 231n.
battleground 724n.
non-ownership 774n.
nomarch
governor 741n.
no matter
trifle 639n.
nom de guerre
misnomer 562n.
nom de plume
misnomer 562n.
nomenclator
nomenclator 561n.
nomenclature
identification 547n.
linguistics 557n.
nomenclature 561n.
nominal
insubstantial 4adj.
powerless 161adj.
indicating 547adj.
verbal 559adj.
named 561adj.
trivial 639adj.
nominalism
philosophy 449n.
nomination
nomenclature 561n.
choice 605n.
mandate 751n.
nominee

delegate 754n.
consignee 754n.
nomology
jurisprudence 953n.
nomothetic
directing 689adj.
legal 953adj.
non-acceptance
rejection 607n.
refusal 760n.
non-adherence
non-observance 769n.
non-adhesive
non-adhesive 49adj.
smooth 258adj.
non-adjustment
inexactness 495n.
non-admission
exclusion 57n.
disapprobation 924n.
non-adult
immature 670adj.
nonage
nonage 130n.
helplessness 161n.
nonagenarian
old man 133n.
non-aggression
peace 717n.
non-alignment
freedom 744n.
non-appealable
commanding 737adj.
non-appearance
invisibility 444n.
non-approval
rejection 607n.
disapprobation 924n.
non-association
unwillingness 598n.
opposition 704n.
non-attachment
freedom 744n.
non-attendance
absence 190n.
non-belief
unbelief 485n.
non-causal
casual 159adj.
nonce, for the
singly 88adv.
at present 121adv.
opportunely 137adv.
incidentally 137adv.
nonce-word
non-uniformity 17n.
word 559n.
neology 560n.
nonchalance
negligence 458n.
moral insensibility 820n.
inexcitability 823n.
indifference 860n.
non-clergiable
laical 987adj.
non-clerical
laical 987n.
non-combatant
pacifist 717n.
non-commissioned officer
army officer 741n.
non-committal
reticent 525adj.
no choice 606n.
avoiding 620adj.
mid-course 625n.
neutral 625adj.
cautious 858adj.
indifferent 860adj.
non-compliance
dissent 489n.
disobedience 738n.
refusal 760n.
non-observance 769n.
nonconformist
nonconformist 84n.
unconformable 84adj.
deviating 282adj.
dissentient 489n.
free man 744n.
non-observant 769adj.
heterodox 977adj.
schismatic 978n.
nonconformity
difference 15n.
unconformity 84n.
non-observance 769n.
sectarianism 978n.
non-consummation
divorce 896n.
non-cooperation
dissent 489n.
unwillingness 598n.
avoidance 620n.
opposition 704n.
dissension 709n.
resistance 715n.
disobedience 738n.
dutilessness 918n.
non-cooperator
dissentient 489n.
opponent 705n.
non-credal
irreligious 974adj.
nondescript
unconformable 84adj.
non-design
chance 159n.
non-design 618n.
none
zero 103n.
church service 988n.
non-ego
extrinsicality 6n.
non-entitlement
undueness 916n.
nonentity
non-existence 2n.
insubstantial thing 4n.
weakling 163n.
nonentity 639n.
object of scorn 867n.
nones
date 108n.
non-essential
extrinsic 6adj.
irrelevance 10n.
unimportant 639adj.
nonesuch
supreme 34adj.
exceller 644n.
paragon 646n.
none the worse
restored 656n.
non-existence
non-existence 2n.
insubstantiality 4n.
disappearance 446n.
non-extremist
moderate 625n.
nonfeasance
non-observance 769n.
non-friction
smooth 258adj.
non-fulfillment
incompleteness 55n.
shortcoming 307n.
disappointment 509n.
insufficiency 636n.
non-completion 726n.
failure 728n.
non-observance 769n.
non-functional
useless 641adj.
ornamental 844adj.
non-immunity
vulnerability 661n.
non-inflammable
incombustible 382adj.
non-intellectual
mindless 448adj.
non-interference
negligence 458n.
freedom 744n.
non-intervention
avoidance 620n.
peace 717n.
non-involvement
avoidance 620n.
peace 717n.
freedom 744n.
disinterestedness 931n.
nonius
gauge 465n.
non-juror
dissentient 489n.
schismatic 978n.
non-liability

non-liability 919n.
non-mandatory
voluntary 597adj.
non-observance
inattention 456n.
negligence 458n.
non-observance 769n.
non-occupancy
non-ownership 774n.
non-ownership
non-ownership 774n.
non-pacific
quarreling 709adj.
contending 716adj.
nonpareil
type size 587n.
exceller 644n.
paragon 646n.
non-participating
inactive 679adj.
non-partisan
wise 498adj.
independent 744adj.
non-party
assented 488adj.
non-payment
delay 136n.
non-payment 805n.
non-performance
non-completion 726n.
non-observance 769n.
dutilessness 918n.
nonplus
dubiety 474n.
puzzle 474vb.
confute 479vb.
predicament 700n.
be difficult 700vb.
defeat 728n.
non-practicing
unconformable 84adj.
irreligious 974adj.
impious 980adj.
non-professional
ignorant 491adj.
unskilled 695adj.
bungler 697n.
layman 987n.
non-profitmaking
disinterested 931adj.
non-provision
non-preparation 670n.
non-recognition
prohibition 757n.
schism 978n.
non-recovery
loss 772n.
non-recurrent
discontinuous 72adj.
non-residence
absence 190n.
non-resistance
concurrence 181n.
submission 721n.
obedience 739n.
non-satisfaction
insufficiency 636n.
nonsense
absurdity 497n.
connotation 514n.
silly talk 515n.
trifle 639n.
non sequitur
irrelevance 10n.
discontinuity 72n.
sophism 477n.
non-significant
unmeaning 515adj.
non-skid
dry 342adj.
non-smoker
train 274n.
non-standard
abnormal 84adj.
non-starter
slowcoach 278n.
loser 728n.
non-sterile
infectious 653adj.
non-stop
continuous 71adj.
perpetual 115adj.
frequent 139adj.
unceasing 146adj.
vehicular 274adj.
loquacious 581adj.
non-suit
defeat 728n.
condemn 961vb.
non-supporter
disapprover 924n.
non-theological
irreligious 974adj.
non-traditional
modern 126adj.
non-transferable
retained 778adj.
non-transparent
opaque 423adj.
non-U
ill-bred 847adj.
plebeian 869adj.
non-uniform
non-uniform 17adj.
non-uniformity
fitfulness 142n.
changeableness 152n.
non-use
non-use 674n.
non-violence
moderation 177n.
peace 717n.
non-vitaminous
insalubrious 653adj.
non-voter
disapprover 924n.
non-voting
choiceless 606adj.
non-wonder
non-wonder 865n.
noodle
ninny 501n.
nook
place 185n.
compartment 194n.
angularity 247n.
hiding-place 527n.
noology
intellect 447n.
no omission
inclusion 78n.
noon, noonday
noon 128n.
light 417n.
noose
halter 47n.
trap 542n.
means of execution 964n.
no other
identity 13n.
no purpose, to
uselessly 641adv.
unsuccessfully 728vb.
no quarter
pitilessness 906n.
no question
certainly 473adv.
N or M
everyman 79n.
norm
average 30n.
rule 81n.
paragon 646n.
precept 693n.
normal
average 30n.
median 30adj.
typical 83adj.
(*see* normality)
normalcy
regularity 81n.
normality
regularity 81n.
sanity 502n.
right 913n.
normalize
make uniform 16vb.
regularize 62vb.
make conform 83vb.
normal school
training school 539n.
normative
regular 81adj.
formative 243adj.
educational 534adj.
Norns
fate 596n.
mythic god 966n.
north
be high 209vb.
compass point 281n.

northern lights
heavens 321n.
glow 417n.
luminary 420n.
northing
bearings 186n.
North Pole
coldness 380n.
North Star
star 321n.
signpost 547n.
northwester
gale 352n.
no score
zero 103n.
nose
face, prow 237n.
protuberance 254n.
person 371n.
smell 394vb.
detective 459n.
nosebag
bag 194n.
nose-dive
aeronautics 271n.
descent 309n.
plunge 313n.
nosegay
bunch 74n.
fragrance 396n.
ornamentation 844n.
noseless
odorless 394adj.
nose out
be curious 453vb.
nose-ring
jewelry 844n.
nose to tail
continuously 71adv.
nosology
pathology 651n.
nostalgia
suffering 825n.
regret 830n.
melancholy 834n.
desire 859n.
nostology
gerontology 131n.
nostril
orifice 263n.
air-pipe 353n.
odor 394n.
nostrum
contrivance 623n.
remedy 658n.
nosy
inquisitive 453adj.
inquiring 459adj.
Nosy Parker
inquisitor 453n.
meddler 678n.
notability
importance 638n.
bigwig 638n.
famousness 866n.
notable
manifest 522adj.
notable 638adj.
person of repute 866n.
noteworthy 866adj.
notandum
important matter 638n.
not a patch on
inferior 35adj.
not a pin to choose
equivalence 28n.
notarial
jurisprudential 958adj.
notary
recorder 549n.
notary 958n.
not at all
in no way 33adv.
not at home, be
be engaged 138vb.
not at home with
ignorant 491adj.
notation
numerical operation 86n.
notation 410n.
not born yesterday
intelligent 498adj.
cunning 698adj.
notch
degree 27n.
cut 46vb.
gap 201n.
angularity 247n.
make concave 255vb.
notch 260n., vb.
indication 547n.
notched
toothed 256adj.
not cricket
injustice 914n.
not done
unconformable 84adj.
unwonted 611adj.
note
character 5n.
ululation 409n.
musical note 410n.
cognize 447vb.
notice 455vb.
reminder 505n.
indication 547n.
record 548vb.
write 586vb.
correspondence 588n.
compendium 592n.
paper money 797n.
famousness 866n.
notebook
reminder 505n.
record 548n.
stationery 586n.
reference book 589n.
anthology 592n.
note-case
case 194n.
noted
known 490adj.
renowned 866adj.
note of exclamation
wonder 864n.
(*see* punctuation)
note of hand
title-deed 767n.
paper money 797n.
note of interrogation
question 459n.
punctuation 547n.
notepaper
stationery 586n.
paper 631n.
notes
commentary 520n.
record 548n.
noteworthy
special 80adj.
unusual 84adj.
notable 638adj.
wonderful 864adj.
noteworthy 866adj.
nothing
non-existence 2n.
insubstantiality 4n.
zero 103n.
trifle 639n.
nothing doing
without action 677adv.
nothing, for
given 781adj.
unchanged 812adj.
nothing like
best 644adj.
nothing loath
willingly 597adv.
nothingness
insubstantiality 4n.
smallness 33n.
zero 103n.
unimportance 639n.
nothing of, make
not understand 517vb.
nothing to add
completeness 54n.
nothing to do with
irrelative 10adj.
nothing to do with, have
avoid 620vb.
nothing to it
trifle 639n.
easy thing 701n.
notice
period 110n.
see 438vb.

cognize 447vb.
attention 455n.
estimate 480n.
prediction 511n.
information 524n.
article 591n.
warning 664n.
demand 737n.
greet 884vb.
noticeable
remarkable 32adj.
visible 443adj.
manifest 522adj.
notice board
advertisement 528n.
notification
information 524n.
publication 528n.
indication 547n.
notify
predict 511vb.
communicate 524vb.
proclaim 528vb.
warn 664vb.
notion
idea 451n.
supposition 512n.
ideality 513n.
contrivance 623n.
notional
ideational 451adj.
suppositional 512adj.
imaginary 513adj.
not mind
acquiesce 488vb.
be willing 597vb.
be indifferent 860vb.
hold cheap 922vb.
notoriety
knowledge 490n.
publicity 528n.
famousness 866n.
disrepute 867n.
not out
unceasing 146adj.
not there
abstracted 456adj.
not to be thought of
unthought 450adj.
rejected 607adj.
prohibited 757adj.
undue 916adj.
blameworthy 924adj.
notwithstanding
although 182adv.
noumenon
idea 451n.
noun
name 561n.
part of speech 564n.
noun of assembly
assemblage 74n.
nourish
support 218vb.
feed 301vb.
aid 703vb.
nourishing
salubrious 652adj.
nourishment
food 301n.
life 360n.
nous
intelligence 498n.
nouveau riche
upstart 126n.
made man 730n.
rich man 800n.
vulgarian 847n.
commoner 869n.
nova
star 321n.
Novatian
heretic 977n.
novel
dissimilar 19adj.
unimitative 21adj.
new 126adj.
unknown 491adj.
reading matter 589n.
novel 590n.
novelese
neology 560n.
novelist
author 589n.
narrator 590n.
novelty
bauble 639n.
(*see* novel)
novena
period 110n.
church service 988n.
novercal
akin 11adj.
novice
ignoramus 493n.
beginner 538n.
bungler 697n.
ingenue 699n.
monk, nun 986n.
layman 987n.
novitiate
learning 536n.
preparation 669n.
novocaine
anesthetic 375n.
novus homo
intruder 59n.
now
present time 121n.
at present 121adv.
now and then
sometimes 139adv.
fitfully 142adv.
at intervals 201adv.
nowhere
non-existent 2adj.
absent 190adj.
not here 190adv.
no wiser
uninstructed 491adj.
now or never
at present 121adv.
opportunely 137adv.
noxious
harmful 645adj.
insalubrious 653adj.
noyade
slaughter 362n.
terror tactics 712n.
capital punishment 963n.
nozzle
orifice 263n.
air-pipe 353n.
nuance
differentiation 15n.
degree 27n.
small quantity 33n.
discrimination 463n.
nub
essential part 5n.
centrality 225n.
swelling 253n.
chief thing 638n.
nubbly
rough 259adj.
nubile
grown up 134adj.
marriageable 894adj.
nubilous
cloudy 355adj.
opaque 423adj.
nucleal
central 225adj.
nuclear
dynamic 160adj.
central 225adj.
nuclear fission
nucleonics 160n.
nucleate
make smaller 198vb.
centralize 225vb.
be dense 324vb.
nucleonics
nucleonics 160n.
nucleoplasm
organism 358n.
nucleus
middle 70n.
centrality 225n.
element 319n.
solid body 324n.
chief thing 638n.
nude
stripper 229n.
uncovered 229adj.
art subject 553n.
nudge
knock 279n.
hint 524n., vb.
indication 547n.
gesture 547n.

nudism
uncovering 229adj.
nudist
stripper 229n.
sanitarian 652n.
nudity
bareness 229n.
nugacity
folly 499n.
unimportance 639n.
inutility 641n.
nugatory
powerless 161adj.
unimportant 639adj.
useless 641adj.
nugget
bulk 195n.
bullion 797n.
nuisance
evil 616n.
meddler 678n.
annoyance 827n.
null
non-existent 2adj.
insubstantial 4adj.
not one 103adj.
unmeaning 515adj.
null and void
powerless 161adj.
abrogated 752adj.
illegal 954adj.
nullification
revolution 149n.
destruction 165n.
counteraction 182n.
abrogation 752n.
nullifidianism
unbelief 486n.
irreligion 974n.
nullify
nullify 2vb.
set off 31vb.
(*see* nullification)
nulli secundus
supreme 34adj.
nullity
zero 103n.
unmeaningness 515n.
unimportance 639n.
divorce 896n.
numb
impotent 161adj.
inert 175adj.
still 266adj.
insensible 375adj.
apathetic 820adj.
number
quantity 26n.
subdivision 53n.
specify 80vb.
number 85n.
number 86vb.
plurality 101n.
label 547n.
numberless
infinite 107adj.
number one
self 80n.
numbers
great quantity 32n.
multitude 104n.
safety 660n.
gambling game 837n.
number with
number with 78vb.
numbness
(*see* numb)
numdah
coverlet 226n.
floor-cover 226n.
numen
divineness 965n.
numerable
numerable 86adj.
numeral
number 85n.
numeration
numeration 86n.
measurement 465n.
accounts 808n.
numerator
numerical element 85n.
numerical
numerical 85adj.
numerous
many 104adj.
numinous
frightening 854adj.
divine 965adj.
spooky 970adj.
numismatics
money 797n.
numismatist
collector 492n.
nummary
monetary 797adj.
numskull
ignoramus 493n.
dunce 501n.
nun
spinster 895n.
nun 986n.
nunation
grammar 564n.
nuncio
messenger 531n.
envoy 754n.
nuncupation
nomenclature 561n.
nundination
barter 791n.
nunnery
monastery 986n.
nuptial
matrimonial 894adj.
nuptials
wedding 894n.
nurse
look after 457vb.
train 534vb.
teacher 537n.
cure 656vb.
nurse 658n.
doctor 658vb.
safeguard 660vb.
preserve 666vb.
mature 669vb.
manage 689vb.
minister to 703vb.
domestic 742n.
keeper 749n.
pet 889vb.
philanthropize 897vb.
nursemaid
keeper 749n.
nursery
nonage 130n.
child 132n.
seedbed 156n.
abundance 171n.
chamber 194n.
farm 370n.
training school 539n.
workshop 687n.
nurseryman
gardener 370n.
nursery rhyme
doggerel 593n.
nursing
therapy 658n.
nursing home
hospital 658n.
nursling
child 132n.
favorite 890n.
nurture
support 218n.
food 301n.
breed stock 369vb.
educate 534vb.
maturation 669n.
nut
fastening 47n.
head 213n.
fruit 301n.
madman, crank 504n.
nutation
oscillation 317n.
uranometry 321n.
nutmeg
condiment 389n.
nutmeg-grater
pulverizer 332n.
nutriment
food 301n.
nutrition
eating 301n.
food 301n.
nutritional
remedial 658adj.

nutritionist
doctor 658n.
nutritious
nourishing 301adj.
salubrious 652adj.
nuts
crazed 503adj.
benefit 615n.
nutshell
small quantity 33n.
conciseness 569n.
nutty
pungent 388adj.
foolish 499adj.
crazed 503adj.
nux vomica
cathartic 658n.
nuzzle
caress 889vb.
nyctalopia
dim sight 440n.
nylon
fiber 208n.
textile 222n.
nylons
legwear 228n.
nymph
youngster 132n.
woman 373n.
nymph 967n.
mythical being 970n.
nymphet
youngster 132n.
loose woman 952n.
nympholepsy
spell 983n.
nymphomania
abnormality 84n.
mania 503n.
libido 859n.
illicit love 951n.
nymphomaniac
loose woman 952n.
nystagmus
dim sight 440n.

O

oaf
dunce 501n.
bungler 697n.
elf 970n.
oafish
unintelligent 499adj.
oak
strength 162n.
hardness 326n.
tree 366n.
oakum
fiber 208n.
oar
propeller 269n.
boatman 270n.
propellant 278n.
badge 547n.
oarsman
boatman 270n.
oasis
land 344n.
oasthouse
furnace 383n.
oat
flute 414n.
oath
testimony 466n.
oath 532n.
promise 764n.
scurrility 899n.
oath-helper
vindicator 927n.
oatmeal
cereal 301n.
oats
provender, cereal 301n.
corn 366n.
obbligato
concomitant 89n.
obduction
covering 226n.
obduracy
obstinacy 602n.
inhumanity 898n.
impenitence 940n.
obdurate
severe 735adj.
(*see* obduracy)
obeah
sorcery 983n.
talisman 983n.
obedience
willingness 597n.
submission 721n.
obedience 739n.
observance 768n.
servility 879n.
churchdom 985n.
obedient
subject 745adj.
(*see* obedience)
obediental
ecclesiastical 985adj.
obeisance
obeisance 311n.
submission 721n.
courteous act 884n.
ritual act 988n.
obelisk
high structure 209n.
monument 548n.
obelize
mark 547vb.
obelus
punctuation 547n.
obesity
bulk 195n.
dilation 197n.
obey
be inferior 35vb.
conform 83vb.
obey 739vb.
be subject 745vb.
(*see* obedience)
obeyed
influential 178adj.
obfuscation
obscuration 418n.
obfuscation 421n.
concealment 525n.
misteaching 535n.
obi
belt 228n.
bewitch 983vb.
obi-man
sorcerer 983n.
obit
obsequies 364n.
obiter
unrelatedly 10adv.
obiter dictum
irrelevance 10n.
interjection 231n.
obituary
valediction 296n.
death roll 361n.
obsequies 364n.
description 590n.
biography 590n.
object
substantiality 3n.
product 164n.
object 319n.
objective 617n.
eyesore 842n.
(*see* objection)
object-glass
astronomy 321n.
optical device 442n.
objectify
make extrinsic 6vb.
externalize 223vb.
materialize 319vb.
cognize 447vb.
imagine 513vb.
objection
qualification 468n.
doubt 486n.
dissent 489n.
unwillingness 598n.
dissuasion 613n.
hindrance 702n.
resistance 715n.
refusal 760n.
discontent 829n.
disapprobation 924n.
objectionable
inexpedient 643adj.
unpleasant 827adj.
disreputable 867adj.
wrong 914adj.

O P

objective
substantial 3adj.
material 319adj.
true 494adj.
objective 617n.
aspiration 852n.
objectiveness
extrinsicality 6n.
objectivity
substantiality 3n.
extrinsicality 6n.
wisdom 498n.
justice 913n.
object lesson
example 83n.
experiment 461n.
objector
dissentient 489n.
opponent 705n.
litigant 959n.
objet d'art
masterpiece 694n.
ornamentation 844n.
objurgation
reproach 924n.
oblate
worshiper 981n.
oblation
offering 781n.
propitiation 941n.
act of worship 981n.
oblation 981n.
oblationary
receiver 782n.
devotional 981adj.
obligation
necessity 596n.
needfulness 627n.
undertaking 672n.
promise 674n.
debt 803n.
dueness 915n.
duty 917n.
obligatory
necessary 596adj.
commanding 737adj.
compelling 740adj.
conditional 766adj.
obligatory 917adj.
oblige
necessitate 596vb.
require 627vb.
minister to 703vb.
compel 740vb.
be courteous 884vb.
be benevolent 897vb.
impose a duty 917vb.
obliged
fated 596adj.
indebted 803adj.
grateful 907adj.
dutied 917adj.
obligee
moneyer 797n.
obliging
aiding 703adj.
courteous 884adj.
benevolent 897adj.
obligor
debtor 803n.
oblique
oblique 220adj.
angular 247adj.
curved 248adj.
directed 281adj.
deviating 282adj.
dishonest 930adj.
obliquity
obliquity 220n.
deviation 282n.
improbity 930n.
wickedness 934n.
obliterate
forgive 909vb.
(*see* obliteration)
obliteration
extinction 2n.
destruction 165n.
oblivion 506n.
obliteration 550n.
desuetude 611n.
oblivion
extinction 2n.
oblivion 506n.
obliteration 550n.
desuetude 611n.
oblivious
inattentive 456adj.
negligent 458adj.
forgetful 506adj.
oblong
longitudinal 203adj.
obloquy
slur 867n.
detraction 926n.
obmutescence
aphony 578n.
taciturnity 582n.
obnoxious
liable 180adj.
not nice 645adj.
unpleasant 827adj.
hateful 888adj.
oboe
flute 414n.
oboist
instrumentalist 413n.
obol
coinage 797n.
obreption
concealment 525n.
obreptitious
stealthy 525adj.
obscenity
uncleanness 649n.
bad taste 847n.
impurity 951n.
obscurantism
ignorance 491n.
misteaching 535n.
opiniatrety 602n.
obscurantist
ignoramus 493n.
opponent 705n.
obscuration
obscuration 418n.
deterioration 655n.
obscure
bedim 419vb.
blind 439vb.
unknown 491adj.
semantic 514adj.
latent 523adj.
conceal 525vb.
inglorious 867adj.
plebeian 869adj.
obscurity
inferiority 35n.
darkness 418n.
invisibility 444n.
uncertainty 474n.
unintelligibility 517n.
imperspicuity 568n.
nonentity 639n.
difficulty 700n.
disrepute 867n.
obsecration
entreaty 761n.
obsequial
funereal 364adj.
obsequies
valediction 296n.
obsequies 364n.
lamentation 836n.
obsequious
willing 597adj.
obedient 739adj.
servile 879adj.
respectful 920adj.
flattering 925adj.
observability
visibility 443n.
observance
conformity 83n.
attention 455n.
practice 610n.
conduct 688n.
obedience 739n.
observance 768n.
celebration 876n.
rite 988n.
observant
attentive 455adj.
vigilant 457adj.
(*see* observance)
observation
inspection 438n.
idea 451n.
attention 455n.
maxim 496n.

affirmation 532n.
speech 579n.
observation balloon
airship 276n.
view 438n.
air force 722n.
observatory
astronomy 321n.
view 438n.
observe
see, scan 438vb.
watch 441vb.
affirm 532vb.
do 676vb.
observe 768vb.
celebrate 876vb.
ritualize 988vb.
observer
aeronaut 271n.
spectator 441n.
obsess
recur 139vb.
go on 146vb.
engross 449vb.
make mad 503vb.
remind 505vb.
incommode 827vb.
frighten 854vb.
obsession
attention 455n.
positiveness 473n.
bias 481n.
belief 485n.
folly 499n.
eccentricity 503n.
opiniatrety 602n.
obsessive
unceasing 146adj.
habitual 610adj.
obsidian
rock 344n.
obsidional
attacking 712adj.
obsolescence
extinction 2n.
non-use 674n.
obsolete
extinct 2adj.
past 125adj.
antiquated 127adj.
powerless 161adj.
neological 560adj.
useless 641adj.
disused 674adj.
obstacle
counteraction 182n.
impossibility 470n.
inexpedience 643n.
defect 647n.
difficulty 700n.
obstacle 702n.
opposition 705n.
obstetric
productive 164adj.
instrumental 628adj.
medical 658adj.
obstetrics
obstetrics 164n.
medical art 658n.
obstinacy
stability 153n.
inertness 175n.
will 595n.
perseverance 600n.
obstinacy 602n.
opposition 704n.
resistance 715n.
obstinate
unconformable 84adj.
impenitent 940adj.
(*see* obstinacy)
obstreperous
violent 176adj.
loud 400adj.
obstruct
halt 145vb.
stanch 350vb.
screen 421vb.
be difficult 700vb.
obstruct 702vb.
parry 713vb.
resist 715vb.
defeat 727vb.
incommode 827vb.
obstruction
derangement 63n.
delay 136n.
closure 264n.
hindrance 702n.
dutilessness 918n.
obstructionism
disobedience 738n.
obstructionist
hinderer 702n.
opponent 705n.
obstructive
dissenting 489adj.
hindering 702adj.
discontented 829adj.
obstructor
dissentient 489n.
hinderer 702n.
obtain
be 1vb.
be general 79vb.
be wont 610vb.
acquire 771vb.
obtainable
accessible 289adj.
possible 469adj.
obtestation
entreaty 761n.
obtrusion
interjection 231n.
hindrance 702n.
obtrusive
vulgar 847adj.
obtund
blunt 257vb.
obturation
closure 264n.
obtuse
unsharpened 257adj.
insensible 375adj.
indiscriminating 464adj.
unintelligent 499adj.
thick-skinned 820adj.
obverse
fore 237adj.
obvious
well-seen 443adj.
intelligible 516adj.
manifest 522adj.
ocarina
flute 414n.
occasion
juncture 8n.
fitness 24n.
occasion 137n.
eventuality 154n.
reason why 156n.
cause 156vb.
instrumentality 628n.
expedience 642n.
amusement 837n.
celebration 876n.
occasional
present 121adj.
timely 137adj.
infrequent 140adj.
fitful 142adj.
happening 154adj.
uncertain 474adj.
celebrative 876adj.
occasionally
discontinuously 72adv.
sometimes 139adv.
occasion, for the
present 121adj.
incidentally 137adv.
occidental
directed 281adj.
occiput
head 213n.
rear 238n.
occlusion
closure 264n.
hindrance 702n.
occultation
obscuration 418n.
disappearance 446n.
concealment 525n.
occultism
spirit 447n.
latency 523n.
occultism 984n.
occultist
oracle 511n.
sorcerer 983n.
occultist 984n.
occupancy

presence 189n.
possession 773n.
occupant
resident 191n.
possessor 776n.
occupation
presence 189n.
habit 610n.
business, job 622n.
undertaking 672n.
action 676n.
(*see* occupy)
occupational
habitual 610adj.
occupational disease
habit 610n.
occupied, be
be engaged 138vb.
occupier
resident 191n.
possessor 776n.
occupy
fill 54vb.
be present 189vb.
dwell 192vb.
engross 449vb.
attract notice 455vb.
employ 622vb.
be obstructive 702vb.
possess 773vb.
appropriate 786vb.
occur
be 1vb.
happen 154vb.
be present 189vb.
occurrence
eventuality 154n.
appearance 445n.
occur to
dawn upon 449vb.
ocean
region 184n.
depth 211n.
water 339n.
ocean 343n.
ocean-going
seafaring 269adj.
marine 275adj.
oceanic 343adj.
Oceanid
sea nymph 343n.
nymph 967n.
mythical being 970n.
oceanographer
oceanography 343n.
surveyor 465n.
oceanography
geography 321n.
oceanography 343n.
ocher
brown paint 430n.
orange 436n.
ochlocracy
government 733n.
octad
over five 99n.
octagon
angular figure 247n.
octaroon
hybrid 43n.
octave
period 110n.
musical note 410n.
octavo
edition 589n.
octet
over five 99n.
duet 412n.
octogenarian
old man 133n.
octopus
fish 365n.
tyrant 735n.
octroi
tax 809n.
octuple
fifth and over 99adj.
ocular
seeing 438adj.
optical device 442n.
oculist
vision 438n.
eyeglass 442n.
doctor 658n.
od
occultism 984n.
odalisque
slave 742n.
odd
disagreeing 25adj.
unequal 29adj.
remaining 41adj.
unusual 84adj.
numerical 85adj.
crazed 503adj.
ridiculous 849adj.
wonderful 864adj.
wrong 914adj.
oddity
misfit 25n.
unconformity 84n.
eccentricity 503n.
crank 504n.
odd-job man
servant 742n.
odd man out
non-uniformity 17n.
misfit 25n.
nonconformist 84n.
dissentient 489n.
oddment(s)
adjunct, extra 40n.
medley 43n.
odds
difference 15n.
inequality 29n.
vantage 34n.
fair chance 159n.
dissension 709n.
odds and ends
non-uniformity 17n.
leavings 41n.
medley 43n.
piece 53n.
rubbish 641n.
odds, at
quarreling 709adj.
contending 716adj.
odds, by all
probably 471adv.
odds on
fair chance 159n.
approved 923adj.
ode
poem 593n.
Odin
Nordic gods 967n.
odious
unpleasant 827adj.
ugly 842adj.
disreputable 867adj.
hateful 888adj.
odium
disrepute 867n.
odium 888n.
odium theologicum
narrow mind 481n.
pietism 979n.
odontoid
toothed 256adj.
odor
odor 394n.
odor, bad
odium 888n.
odorless
odorless 395adj.
odor of sanctity
virtue 933n.
sanctity 979n.
odorous
odorous 394adj.
odyl
occultism 984n.
oecumenicalism
(*see* ecumenicalism)
Oedipus complex
love 887n.
of course
conformably 83adv.
consequently 157adv.
certainly 473adv.
of course 478adv.
off
apart 46adv.
decomposed 51adj.
ending 69adj.
absent 190adj.
pungent 388adj.
unprovided 636adj.
unpleasant 827adj.
offal
insides 224n.

meat 301n.
rubbish 641n.
dirt 649n.
off and on
by turns 141adj.
changeably 152adv.
at intervals 201adv.
off-beam
astray 282adv.
off-center
irrelevant 10adj.
distant 199n.
deviating 282adj.
off-chance
possibility 469n.
improbability 472n.
off color
colorless 426adj.
imperfect 647adj.
sick 651adj.
off-day
bungling 695n.
failure 728n.
off-drive
propulsion 287n.
off duty
leisure 681n.
offend
displease 827vb.
cause dislike 861vb.
be wicked 934vb.
offended
resentful 891adj.
offender
nonconformist 84n.
prisoner 750n.
offender 904n.
impious person 980n.
offense
annoyance 827n.
resentment 891n.
guilty act 936n.
lawbreaking 954n.
offensive
unsavory 391adj.
fetid 397adj.
inelegant 576adj.
unclean 649adj.
attack 712n.
battle 718n.
unpleasant 827adj.
impertinent 878adj.
ungracious 885adj.
hateful 888adj.
impure 951adj.
offer
opportunity 137n.
affirm 532vb.
will 595vb.
choice 605n.
incentive 612n.
provide 633vb.
essay 671vb.
permit 756vb.
offer 759n., vb.
promise 764n., vb.
make terms 766vb.
give 781vb.
offered
voluntary 597adj.
offering
offer 759n.
offering 781n.
propitiation 941n.
oblation 981n.
offer, on
offering 759adj.
offer satisfaction
atone 941vb.
offertory
offering 781n.
oblation 981n.
offer up
kill 362vb.
give 781vb.
offer worship 981vb.
off form
imperfect 647adj.
off guard
negligent 458adj.
inexpectant 508adj.
off-hand
instantaneously 116adv.
suddenly 135adv.
inattentive 456adj.
negligent 458adj.
spontaneous 609adj.
unreadily 670adv.
impertinent 878adj.
discourteous 885adj.
disrespectful 921adj.
office
agency 173n.
chamber 194n.
job, function 622n.
use 673n.
workshop 687n.
authority 733n.
mandate 796n.
duty 917n.
jurisdiction 955n.
church service 988n.
office-bearer
official 690n.
consignee 754n.
office-book
office-book 988n.
office-boy
courier 531n.
officer 741n.
office, in
authoritative 733adj.
officer
official 690n.
officer 741n.
offices
adjunct 40n.
offices, good
aid 703n.
pacification 719n.
mediation 720n.
kind act 897n.
official
certain 473adj.
genuine 494adj.
usual 610adj.
businesslike 622adj.
directing 689adj.
official 690n.
authoritative 733adj.
governmental 733adj.
officer 741n.
servant 742n.
formal 875adj.
officialese
language 557n.
neology 560n.
officialism
governance 733n.
officiant
worshiper 981n.
officiate
function 622vb.
do 676vb.
offer worship 891vb.
perform ritual 988vb.
officiousness
curiosity 453n.
redundance 637n.
overactivity 678n.
offing
distance 199n.
offish
unsociable 883adj.
off-key
discordant 411adj.
off-load
displace 188vb.
off-peak
small 33adj.
off-pitch
discordant 411adj.
offprint
letterpress 587n.
offscourings
leavings 41n.
dirt 649n.
rabble 869n.
off-season
ill-timed 138adj.
cheap 812adj.
offset
equalization 28n.
offset 31n.
remainder 41n.
counteract 182n.
qualification 468n.
print 587vb.
offshoot
adjunct 40n.
subdivision 53n.

effect 157n.
descendent 170n.
sect 978n.
off-shore
distant 199adj.
offside
unconformable 84adj.
dextral 241adj.
sinistral 242adj.
wrong 914adj.
illegal 954adj.
offspring
kinsman 11n.
effect 157n.
product 164n.
posterity 170n.
off-stage
on stage 594adv.
off-take
decrement 42n.
egress 298n.
off-target
irrelevant 10adj.
mistaken 495adj.
off the peg
ready-made 669adj.
off the rails
unconformable 84adj.
mistaken 495adj.
off the record
private 80adj.
undisguised 522adj.
occult 523adj.
off-white
whitish 427adj.
oflag
prison camp 748n.
often
often 139adv.
ogee
pattern 844n.
ogham
lettering 586n.
oghamic
literal 558adj.
ogive
supporter 218n.
ogle
gaze 438vb.
watch 441vb.
gesture 547n.
desire 859vb.
wooing 889n.
Ogpu
police inquiry 459n.
ogre
giant 195n.
intimidation 854n.
monster 938n.
demon 970n.
ogress
hell-hag 904n.
Ogygian
past 125adj.
ohm
electricity 160n.
metrology 465n.
oil
smoother 258n.
propellant 287n.
soften 327vb.
lubricant 334n.
oil 357n.
fuel 385n.
silencer 401n.
bribe 612vb.
balm 658n.
facilitate 701vb.
primp 843vb.
oil-can
lubricant 334n.
oilcloth
floor-cover 226n.
oiled
smooth 258adj.
unctuous 357adj.
tipsy 949adj.
oil-field
store 632n.
oil-painting
art style 553n.
oils
pigment 425n.
art equipment 553n.
oilskins
overcoat 228n.
oilstone
sharpener 256n.
oil-well
store 632n.
oily
lenitive 177adj.
smooth 258adj.
unctuous 357adj.
hypocritical 541adj.
dirty 649adj.
servile 879adj.
flattering 925adj.
oinomania
alcoholism 949n.
ointment
facing 226n.
lubricant 334n.
unguent 357n.
balm 658n.
OK
in order 60adv.
assent 488n.
okra
vegetable 301n.
old, olden
past 125adj.
olden, antiquated 127adj.
aged 131adj.
weak 163adj.
old age
age 131n.
Oldbuck
antiquarian 125n.
olden days
preterition 125n.
old-fashioned
anachronistic 118adj.
antiquated 127adj.
unwonted 611adj.
old fogy
old man 133n.
fool 501n.
laughing-stock 851n.
old folks
family 11n.
old couple 133n.
Old Glory
flag 547n.
old hand
expert 696n.
old iron
rubbish 641n.
old lag
offender 904n.
old maid
woman 373n.
card game 837n.
spinster 895n.
virgin 950n.
old-maidish
prudish 950adj.
Old Man of the Sea
mariner 270n.
sea god 343n.
encumbrance 702n.
mythical being 970n.
old master
picture 553n.
artist 556n.
Old Moore
chronology 117n.
oracle 511n.
oldness
beginning 68n.
time 108n.
durability 113n.
preterition 125n.
oldness 127n.
age 131n.
old, old story
love affair 887n.
old school
opiniatrety 602n.
habit 610n.
old school tie
livery 547n.
old stager
old man 133n.
actor 594n.
expert 696n.
old story
repetition 106n.
news 529n.
Old Style

chronology 117n.
Old Testament
scripture 975n.
old-timer
archaism 127n.
old man 133n.
old-world
olden 127adj.
courteous 884adj.
oleaginous
unctuous 357adj.
olein
fat 357n.
oleograph
representation 551n.
olericulture
agriculture 370n.
olfactory
odor 394n.
olid
fetid 397adj.
oligarch
master 741n.
oligarchy
government 733n.
olivaceous
green 432adj.
olive
fruit 301n.
greenness 432n.
olive branch
irenics 719n.
olivine
gem 844n.
olla podrida
a mixture 43n.
ologies and isms
science 490n.
olympiad
period 110n.
Olympian
aristocrat 868n.
genteel 868adj.
Olympian god 967n.
paradisiac 971adj.
Olympics
contest 716n.
Olympus
mythic heaven 971n.
ombre
card game 837n.
omega
extremity 69n.
omelet
dish 301n.
omen
precursor 66n.
foresight 510n.
omen 511n.
indication 547n.
warning 664n.
danger signal 665n.
threat 900n.
omentum
obstetrics 164n.
ominate
predict 511vb.
ominous
presageful 511adj.
indicating 547adj.
harmful 645adj.
dangerous 661adj.
cautionary 664adj.
adverse 731adj.
unpromising 853adj.
frightening 854adj.
threatening 900adj.
omission
incompleteness 55n.
exclusion 57n.
negligence 458n.
failure 728n.
non-observance 769n.
guilty act 936n.
omit
be taciturn 582vb.
(*see* omission)
omitted
non-existent 2adj.
absent 190adj.
omneity
whole 52n.
universe 321n.
omnibus
comprehensive 52adj.
bus, stage-coach 274n.
omnibus train
slowcoach 278n.
omnicompetent
powerful 160adj.
omnicompetent state
despotism 733n.
omnifarious
multiform 82adj.
omnific
generative 171adj.
omniformity
multiformity 82n.
omnipotence
power 160n.
divine attribute 965n.
omnipotent
compelling 740adj.
omnipresence
presence 189n.
divine attribute 965n.
omniscience
knowledge 490n.
divine attribute 965n.
omnium gatherum
medley 43n.
confusion 61n.
(*see* assembly)
omnivore
animal 365n.
omnivorous
feeding 301adj.
greedy 859adj.
gluttonous 947adj.
omphalos
middle 70n.
on
concerning 9adv.
impending 154adj.
in place 186adv.
on the spot 189adj.
forward 285adv.
on 310adv.
provisionary 633adj.
on account of
hence 158adv.
on and on
forever 115adv.
on behalf of
in aid of 703adv.
once
singly 88adv.
not now 122adv.
seldom 140adv.
once bitten
warned 664adj.
cautious 858adj.
once for all
finally 69adv.
resolutely 599adv.
once-over
inspection 438n.
once-removed
akin 11adj.
deviating 282adj.
once upon a time
when 108adv.
not now 122adv.
retrospectively 125adv.
oncoming
fore 237adj.
approaching 289adj.
on demand
cash down 804adv.
on-drive
propulsion 287n.
one
simple 44adj.
whole 52adj.
unit 88n.
infrequent 140adj.
person 371n.
one after another
continuously 71adv.
following 284n.
one and only
dissimilar 19adj.
unimitated 21adj.
one 88adj.
one and the same
identical 13adj.
one another
correlation 12n.
one, as
cooperatively 706adv.
one at a time
singly 88adv.

one by one
separately 46adv.
severally 80adv.
singly 88adv.
one consent, with
concurrently 181adv.
unanimously 488adv.
one day
when 108adv.
not now 122adv.
one-dimensional
longitudinal 203adj.
one-eyed
dim-sighted 440adj.
one for the road
valediction 296n.
potion 301n.
one-horse
little 196adj.
trivial 639adj.
one in a million
nonconformist 84n.
exceller 644n.
oneirocritic
interpreter 520n.
oneness
identity 13n.
simpleness 44n.
whole 52n.
unity 88n.
one of
ingredient 58adj.
one of the best
exceller 644n.
favorite 890n.
good man 937n.
one of these days
not now 122adv.
one or two
plurality 101n.
fewness 105n.
one-piece
uniform 16adj.
onerous
difficult 700adj.
hindering 702adj.
annoying 827adj.
(*see* heavy)
one's day
success 727n.
one's despair
bungler 697n.
difficulty 700n.
oneself
identity 13n.
one-sided
biased 481adj.
unjust 914adj.
dishonest 930adj.
one's people
family 11n.
one-step
dance 837n.
one swoop, at
instantaneously 116adv.
one-time
prior 119adj.
former 125adj.
resigning 753adj.
one too many
redundant 637adj.
one-track mind
narrow mind 481n.
one up
superior 34adj.
surpassing 306adj.
one-upmanship
superiority 34n.
tactics 688n.
onion
sphere 252n.
vegetable 301n.
condiment 389n.
onlooker
spectator 441n.
only
inconsiderable 33adj.
slightly 33adv.
one 88adj.
only-begotten
one 88adj.
only pebble on the beach
vain person 873n.
onomasiology
linguistics 557n.
etymology 559n.
onomasticon
name 561n.
onomatology
nomenclature 561n.
on one's own
alone 88adj.
onrush
outbreak 176n.
onset
beginning 68n.
approach 289n.
attack 712n.
on-shore
coastal 344adj.
onslaught
attack 712n.
malediction 899n.
censure 924n.
on tap
provisionary 633adj.
on the go
actively 678adv.
on the make
acquiring 771adj.
selfish 932adj.
on the map, put
make important 638vb.
ontic
existing 1adj.
ontology
existence 1n.
philosophy 449n.
onus
demonstration 478n.
encumbrance 702n.
duty 917n.
guilt 936n.
onward
forward 285adv.
onyx
gem 844n.
oodles
great quantity 32n.
oof
dibs 797n.
ooze
move slowly 278vb.
exude 298vb.
emit 300vb.
moisture 341n.
ocean 343n.
marsh 347n.
flow 350vb.
semiliquidity 354n.
oozing
full 54adj.
oozy
slow 278adj.
outgoing 298adj.
humid 341adj.
marshy 347adj.
flowing 350adj.
opacity
dimness 419n.
opacity 423n.
imperspicuity 568n.
opal
gem 844n.
opalescent, opaline
semitransparent 424adj.
iridescent 437adj.
opaque
(*see* opacity)
open
disjoin, cut 46vb.
come before 64vb.
begin 68vb.
auspicate 68vb.
expand 197vb.
spaced 201n.
broad 205adj.
uncover 229vb.
open 263adj., vb.
air 340n.
champaign 348n.
visible 443adj.
uncertain 474adj.
manifest 522vb.
disclosed 526adj.

veracious 540adj.
vocal 577adj.
artless 699adj.
easy 701adj.
liberate 746vb.
offering 759adj.
trustworthy 929adj.
open air
air 340n.
exteriority 223n.
salubrity 652n.
open an account
trade 791vb.
credit 802vb.
open and shut
demonstrated 478adj.
open-and-shut case
certainty 473n.
open arms
reception 299n.
friendliness 880n.
open country
plain 348n.
open door
way in 297n.
open-eared
auditory 415adj.
open-ended
disjunct 46adj.
non-adhesive 49adj.
pendent 217adj.
opener
opener 263n.
instrument 628n.
open-eyed
vigilant 437adj.
attentive 455adj.
expectant 507adj.
open fire
initiate 68vb.
shoot 287vb.
fire at 712vb.
give battle 718vb.
open hand
liberality 813n.
open-hearted
trustworthy 929adj.
open house
generality 79n.
liberality 813n.
sociability 882n.
opening
prelude 66n.
debut, entrance 68n.
opportunity 137n.
room 183n.
gap 201n.
open space 263n.
way in 297n.
open, in the
externally 223adv.
alfresco 340adv.
open into
connect 45vb.
open letter
generality 79n.
publicity 528n.
deprecation 762n.
censure 924n.
open market
scope 744n.
trade 791n.
mart 796n.
open-mindedness
no choice 606n.
open-mouthed
open 263adj.
expectant 507adj.
greedy 859adj.
wondering 864adj.
open question
uncertainty 474n.
open secret
knowledge 490n.
publicity 528n.
open sesame
answer 460n.
instrument 628n.
spell 983n.
open to
liable 180adj.
vulnerable 661adj.
open to all
easy 701adj.
open up
initiate 68vb.
accelerate 277vb.
manifest 522vb.
disclose 526vb.
open verdict
dubiety 474n.
open work
needlework 844n.
ornamental art 844n.
opera
vocal music 412n.
stage play 594n.
operable
possible 469adj.
restored 656adj.
medical 658adj.
opera glass
telescope 442n.
opera-goer
musician 413n.
playgoer 594n.
opera house
theater 594n.
operate
motivate 612vb.
function 622vb.
use 673vb.
deal with 688vb.
manage 689vb.
speculate 791vb.
(*see* operation)
operatic
musical 412adj.
dramatic 594adj.
operation
agency 173n.
instrumentality 628n.
surgery 658n.
undertaking 672n.
action 676n.
doing 676adj.
labor 682n.
operational
operative 173adj.
warlike 718adj.
operative
powerful 160adj.
operative 173adj.
instrumental 628adj.
worker 686n.
operator
numerical element 85n.
machinist 630n.
doctor 658n.
doer 676n.
agent 686n.
operculum
covering 226n.
operose
laboring 682adj.
laborious 682adj.
difficult 700adj.
ophicleide
horn 414n.
ophidian
animal 365adj.
reptile 365n.
ophthalmia
dim sight 440n.
ophthalmologist
eyeglass 442n.
vision 438n.
doctor 658n.
ophthalmoscope
optical device 442n.
opiate
moderator 177n.
soporific 679n.
opine
opine 485vb.
suppose 512vb.
affirm 532vb.
(*see* opinion)
opiniatrety
positiveness 473n.
narrow mind 481n.
opiniatrety 602n.
opinion
idea 451n.
estimate 480n.
bias 481n.
opinion 485n.
supposition 512n.
repute 866n.
opinionated
positive 473adj.

narrow-minded 481adj.
believing 485adj.
obstinate 602adj.
vain 873adj.
opinionist
doctrinaire 473n.
opinionist 602n.
opium
moderator 177n.
anesthetic 375n.
drug 658n.
poison 659n.
soporific 679n.
opium-eater
idler 679n.
opossum
marsupial 365n.
oppidan
native 191n.
urban 192adj.
oppilation
hindrance 702n.
opponent
dissentient 489n.
opponent 705n.
enemy 881n.
opportune
circumstantial 8adj.
apt 24adj.
opportune 137adj.
expedient 642adj.
opportunism
expedience 642n.
improbity 930n.
opportunist
enterprising 672adj.
egotist 932n.
opportunity
juncture 8n.
present time 121n.
opportunity 137n.
fair chance 159n.
possibility 469n.
expedience 642n.
facility 701n.
scope 744n.
oppose
restrain 747vb.
(*see* opposition)
opposite
correlative 12adj.
contrary 14adj.
difference 15n.
inverted 221adj.
opposite 240adj.
countervailing 467adj.
opposing 704adj.
opposite number
correlation 12n.
compeer 28n.
opposition
disagreement 25n.
counteraction 182n.
contraposition 240n.
qualification 468n.
dissent 489n.
unwillingness 598n.
hindrance 702n.
opposition 704n.
dissension 709n.
resistance 715n.
disobedience 738n.
deprecation 762n.
enmity 881n.
oppress
suppress 165vb.
ill-treat 645vb.
oppress 735vb.
impress 821vb.
torment 827vb.
oppression
severity 735n.
subjection 745n.
dejection 834n.
oppressive
violent 176adj.
warm 379adj.
frightening 854adj.
inimical 881adj.
lawless 954adj.
oppressor
bane 659n.
tyrant 735n.
opprobrious
degrading 867adj.
opprobrium
slur 867n.
oppugnation
opposition 704n.
resistance 715n.
opsimathy
lateness 136n.
learning 536n.
opt
choose 605vb.
optical
luminous 417adj.
seeing 438adj.
optical illusion
insubstantial thing 4n.
visual fallacy 440n.
optician
vision 438n.
eyeglass 442n.
doctor 658n.
optics
optics 417n.
vision 438n.
eye 438n.
optimate
aristocrat 868n.
optimism
overestimation 482n.
exaggeration 546n.
cheerfulness 833n.
hope 852n.
optimistic
optimistic 482adj.
optimum
best 644adj.
option
will 595n.
willingness 597n.
choice 605n.
card game 837n.
optional
volitional 595adj.
voluntary 597adj.
choosing 605adj.
opulent
plenteous 635adj.
rich 800adj.
opus
product 164n.
musical piece 412n.
opuscule
book 589n.
or
orange 436n.
heraldry 547n.
oracle
answer 460n.
certainty 473n.
doctrinaire 473n.
sage 500n.
oracle 511n.
equivocalness 518n.
latency 523n.
adviser 691n.
holy place 990n.
oracular
uncertain 474adj.
aphoristic 496adj.
wise 498adj.
predicting 511adj.
puzzling 517adj.
equivocal 518adj.
imperspicuous 568adj.
oral
vocal 577adj.
speaking 579adj.
orale
vestments 989n.
orange
fruit 301n.
orange 436n., adj.
orangery
wood 366n.
garden 370n.
orangutan
monkey 365n.
orarion
vestments 989n.
orate
be diffuse 570vb.
oration
oration 579n.
allocution 583n.
orator
preacher 537n.

phrasemonger 574n.
speaker 579n.
motivator 612n.

oratorical
figurative 519adj.
rhetorical 574adj.
eloquent 579n.

oratorio
vocal music 412n.

oratorium
temple 990n.

oratory
style 566n.
oratory 579n.
inducement 612n.
church 990n.

orb
region 184n.
circle 250n.
eye 438n.
badge 547n.
regalia 743n.

orbicularity
circularity 250n.
rotundity 252n.

orbit
orbit 250n.
fly 271vb.
passage 305n.
circuition 314n.
circle 314vb.
rotate 315vb.
route 624n.
circuit 626n.

orbital
circuitous 314adj.

orchard
wood 366n.
farm, garden 370n.

orchestra
band 74n.
orchestra 413n.
theater 594n.

orchestral
musical 412adj.

orchestrate
compose 56vb.
arrange 62vb.
harmonize 410vb.
compose music 413vb.

ordain
decree 737vb.
commission 751vb.
make legal 953vb.
ecclesiasticize 985vb.
perform ritual 988vb.

ordained
fated 596adj.
clerical 986adj.

ordeal
experiment 461n.
suffering 825n.
painfulness 827n.

order
relation 9n.
uniformity 16n.
order 60n., vb.
serial place 73n.
regularity 81n.
send 272vb.
meal 301n.
judgment 480n.
badge 547n.
practice 610n.
plan 623vb.
requirement 627n.
precept 693n.
community 708n.
decoration 729n.
command 737n., vb.
demand 737vb.
compel 740vb.
badge of rank 743n.
paper money 797n.
honors 866n.
nobility 868n.
title 870n.
impose a duty 917vb.
legislation 953n.
sect 978n.
ecclesiasticize 985vb.
monk 986n.
ritual, rite 988n.

order, keep
rule 733vb.
restrain 747vb.

orderless
orderless 61adj.
unassembled 75adj.
unconformable 84adj.
amorphous 244adj.
unsightly 842adj.

orderly
orderly 60adj.
regular 81adj.
careful 457adj.
businesslike 622adj.
servant 742n.

order off
dismiss 300vb.

order of the day
affairs 154n.
predetermination 608n.
policy 623n.
command 737n.

order, out of
orderless 61adj.

orders
holy orders 985n.

orders, at one's
obedient 739adj.

orders, in
clerical 986adj.

ordinal
numerical 85adj.
office-book 988n.

ordinance
precept 693n.
command 737n.
legislation 953n.
rite 988n.

ordinand
pietist 979n.
cleric 986n.
layman 987n.

ordinary
median 30adj.
general 79adj.
typical 83adj.
meal 301n.
heraldry 547n.
usual 610adj.
trivial 639adj.
not bad 644adj.
imperfect 647adj.
mediocre 732adj.
unastonishing 865adj.

ordinate and abscissa
metrology 465n.

ordination
mandate 751n.
holy orders 985n.
Christian rite 988n.

ordnance
gun 723n.

ordure
excrement 302n.
dirt 649n.

ore
origin 156n.
materials 631n.

oread
nymph 967n.

oreanthropus
mankind 371n.

orfray
vestments 989n.

organ
organ 414n.
the press 528n.
instrument 628n.
church utensil 990n.

organ-blower
organ 414n.

organdy
textile 222n.

organ-grinder
instrumentalist 413n.

organic
conditionate 7adj.
structural 331adj.
organic 358adj.

organic nature
organism 358n.

organic remains
organism 358n.
corpse 363n.

organism

structure 331n.
life 360n.
organist
instrumentalist 413n.
organization
composition 56n.
order 60n.
arrangement 62n.
production 164n.
structure 331n.
organism 358n.
plan 623n.
corporation 708n.
organizational
arranged 62adj.
structural 331adj.
organic 358adj.
organizer
planner 623n.
organ-loft
organ 414n.
church interior 990n.
organology
structure 331n.
orgasm
spasm 318n.
orgiastic
disorderly 61adj.
violent 176adj.
sensual 944adj.
orgy
feasting 301n.
plenty 635n.
festivity 837n.
intemperance 943n.
sensualism 944n.
oriel
compartment 194n.
angularity 247n.
window 263n.
orient
laterality 239n.
luminous 417adj.
oriental
lateral 239adj.
orientalize
transform 147vb.
orientate
navigate 269vb.
orientation
direction 281n.
orifice
entrance 68n.
gap 201n.
cavity 255n.
orifice 263n.
oriflamme
flag 547n.
origin
origin 68n.
source 156n.
genealogy 169n.
original
intrinsic 5adj.
irrelative 10adj.
prototype 23n.
first 68adj.
nonconformist 84n.
new 126adj.
fundamental 156adj.
script 586n.
unwonted 611adj.
laughing-stock 851n.
jurisdictional 955adj.
(*see* originality)
originality
difference 15n.
dissimilarity 19n.
non-imitation 21n.
specialty 80n.
unconformity 84n.
imagination 513n.
original side
tribunal 956n.
originate
initiate 68vb.
cause 156vb.
produce 164vb.
will 595vb.
originate from
result 157vb.
originative
generative 171adj.
originator
producer 167n.
planner 623n.
Orion
star 321n.
orismology
nomenclature 561n.
orison
entreaty 761n.
prayers 981n.
orle
heraldry 547n.
orlop
base 214n.
orlop deck
layer 207n.
ormolu
sham 542n.
ornamental art 844n.
ornament
ornament 574n., vb.
make better 654vb.
beauty 841n.
beautify 841vb.
ornamentation 844n.
ornamental
useless 641adj.
beautiful 841adj.
ornamental 844adj.
ornamentation
concomitant 89n.
spectacle 445n.
ostentation 875n.
(*see* ornament)
ornate
figurative 519adj.
stylistic 566adj.
ornate 574adj.
splendid 841adj.
affected 850adj.
ornithology
zoology 367n.
orography
geography 321n.
orotund
rhetorical 574adj.
eloquent 579adj.
ostentatious 875adj.
orphan
survivor 41n.
derelict 779n.
deprive 786vb.
vestments 989n.
sadden 834vb.
outcaste 883n.
orphanage
shelter 662n.
orphaned
alone 88adj.
Orphean
musicianly 413adj.
Orphism
religion 973n.
orphrey
orpiment
yellow pigment 433n.
orrery
astronomy 321n.
orris root
scent 396n.
medicine 658n.
orthodox
habitual 610adj.
orthodox 976adj.
pious 979adj.
worshiping 981adj.
ecclesiastical 985adj.
(*see* orthodoxy)
Orthodox Church
the Church 976n.
orthodoxism
orthodoxism 976n.
orthodoxy
generality 79n.
conformity 83n.
certainty 473n.
positiveness 473n.
creed 485n.
orthodox 976n.
orthoepy
etymology 559n.
orthogonal
vertical 215adj.
angulated 247adj.
orthography
spelling 558n.

orthology
accuracy 494n.
orthometry
measurement 465n.
orthopedist
doctor 658n.
orthopedy
therapy 658n.
orthopraxy
therapy 658n.
orthoptic
seeing 438adj.
ortolan
table bird 365n.
orts
rubbish 641n.
oryctology
mineralogy 359n.
zoology 367n.
oscillate
hang 217vb.
deviate 282vb.
oscillate 317vb.
oscillation
correlation 12n.
periodicity 141n.
fitfulness 142n.
reversion 148n.
changeableness 152n.
laterality 239n.
motion 265n.
oscillation 317n.
oscitancy
opening 263n.
sleepiness 679n.
osculation
contiguity 202n.
endearment 889n.
osculatory
ritual object 988n.
osier
ligature 47n.
plant 366n.
osmose, osmosis
ingress 297n.
passage 305n.
osmotic
passing 305adj.
osprey
bird of prey 365n.
trimming 844n.
osseous
hard 326adj.
ossicle
solid body 324n.
ossification
condensation 324n.
hardening 326n.
ossified
antiquated 127adj.
ossuary
interment 364n.
ostensible
appearing 445adj.
plausible 471adj.
manifest 522adj.
ostensible 614adj.
ostensible motive
pretext 614n.
ostentation
manifestation 522n.
publicity 528n.
prodigality 815n.
ornamentation 844n.
affectation 850n.
vanity 873n.
ostentation 875n.
osteology
structure 331n.
osteopath
doctor 658n.
osteopathy
therapy 658n.
ostiary
janitor 264n.
cleric 986n.
ostiole
orifice 263n.
ostracism
exclusion 57n.
unsociability 883n.
disapprobation 924n.
penalty 963n.
ostracize
eject 300vb.
make unwelcome 883vb.
ostrich
flightless bird 365n.
visionary 513n.
other
extrinsicality 6n.
different 15adj.
other half
analogue 18n.
other hand, on the
conversely 467adv.
otherness
difference 15n.
other ranks
inferior 35n.
nonentity 639n.
other self
analogue 18n.
other side
contrariety 14n.
opposition 704n.
enemy 881n.
otherwise
contrarily 14adv.
differently 15adv.
otherworldliness
sanctity 979n.
otherworldly
immaterial 320adj.
psychic 447adj.
imaginative 513adj.
pious 979adj.
magical 983adj.
otiose
unproductive 172adj.
useless 641adj.
inactive 679adj.
otology
ear 415n.
otoscope
hearing aid 415n.
ottoman
seat 218n.
oubliette
hiding-place 527n.
prison 748n.
ouch
fastening 47n.
jewelry 844n.
ought
be due 915vb.
ouija board
spiritualism 984n.
ounce
small quantity 33n.
weighment 322n.
ourselves
self 80n.
mankind 371n.
oust
substitute 150vb.
eject 300vb.
depose 752vb.
deprive 786vb.
ouster
loss of right 916n.
out
absent 190adj.
expanded 197adj.
externally 223adv.
open 263adj.
astray 282adv.
eject 300vb.
dark 418adj.
misjudging 481adj.
mistaken 495adj.
inexact 495adj.
sleepy 679adj.
fatigued 684adj.
dead drunk 949adj.
out-and-out
consummate 32adj.
completely 54adv.
out-argue
argue 475vb.
confute 479vb.
out-at-elbows
uncovered 229adj.
disreputable 867adj.
outback
space 183n.
outbid
outdo 306vb.
bargain 791vb.

outboard
exterior 223adj.
boat 275n.
out-bowed
convex 253adj.
outbreak
disorder 61n.
beginning 68n.
outbreak 176n.
egress 298n.
revolt 738n.
excitable state 822n.
outburst
outbreak 176n.
egress 298n.
excitable state 822n.
outcast
bad man 938n.
heathen 974n.
outcaste
exclude 57vb.
reject 607vb.
commoner 689n.
derelict 779n.
disreputable 867adj.
outcaste 883n.
outclass
be superior 34vb.
outdo 306vb.
defeat 727vb.
outclassed
inferior 35adj.
outcome
eventuality 154n.
effect 157n.
egress 298n.
outcrop
layer 207n.
outcropping
visible 443adj.
appearing 445adj.
outcry
loudness 400n.
cry 408n.
lament 836n.
disapprobation 924n.
outdare
defy 711vb.
be courageous 855vb.
outdistance
be distant 199n.
outstrip 277vb.
progress 285vb.
outdo 306vb.
outdo
be early 135vb.
outdo 306vb.
defeat 727vb.
outdoor
exterior 233adj.
outdoors
salubrity 652n.
outer, outermost
exterior 223adj.
outer darkness
exclusion 57n.
outface
be resolute 599vb.
resist 715vb.
be courageous 855vb.
be insolent 878vb.
outfall
outflow 298n.
outfit
all 52n.
component 58n.
unit 88n.
clothing 228n.
equipment 630n.
party 708n.
outfitter
clothier 228n.
outflank
flank 239vb.
outdo 306vb.
defeat 727vb.
outflow
outflow 298n.
waterfall 350n.
waste 634n.
out for
intending 617adj.
outgate
outlet 298n.
outgeneral
defeat 727vb.
outgo
outdo 306vb.
outgoing
preceding 64adj.
former 125adj.
resigning 753adj.
outgoings
expenditure 806n.
out-group
group 74n.
outgrow
disaccustom 611vb.
outgrown
unwonted 611adj.
outgrowth
growth 157n.
out-Herod Herod
be violent 176vb.
exaggerate 546vb.
outhouse
adjunct 40n.
small house 192n.
chamber 194n.
outing
land travel 267n.
amusement 837n.
outland
district 184n.
outlandish
extraneous 59adj.
unusual 84adj.
ridiculous 849adj.
wonderful 864adj.
outlands
farness 199n.
outlast
continue 108vb.
outlast 113vb.
stay 144vb.
be stable 153vb.
outlaw
exclude 57vb.
nonconformist 84n.
robber 789n.
enemy 881n.
outcaste 883n.
make unwelcome 883vb.
offender 904n.
make illegal 954vb.
condemn 961vb.
outlawry
prohibition 757n.
brigandage 788n.
lawlessness 954n.
condemnation 961n.
outlay
waste 634n.
expenditure 806n.
outlet
orifice 263n.
outlet 298n.
outlier
entrance 68n.
outline
prototype 23n.
incompleteness 55n.
beginning 68n.
circumjacence 230n.
outline 233n., vb.
limit 236n.
form 243n.
appearance 445n.
representation 551n.
map 551n.
picture 553n.
be concise 569vb.
compendium 592n.
plan 623n.
prepare 669vb.
outlive
continue 108vb.
outlast 113vb.
stay 144vb.
outlook
futurity 124n.
destiny 155n.
view 438n.
spectacle 445n.
expectation 507n.
outlying
exterior 223adj.
outmaneuver
be superior 34vb.
navigate 269vb.
outdo 306vb.

deceive 542vb.
defeat 727vb.
outmarch
outstrip 277vb.
outdo 306vb.
outmatch
be superior 34vb.
outmoded
useless 641adj.
outnumber
be many 104vb.
superabound 637vb.
out of
akin 11adj.
caused 157adj.
born 360adj.
out of bounds
too far 199adv.
surpassing 306adj.
prohibited 757adj.
illegal 954adj.
out of character
unapt 25adj.
out of countenance
dejected 834adj.
humbled 872adj.
out of court
wrong 914adj.
out of date
anachronistic 118adj.
antiquated 127adj.
out of doors
exteriority 223n.
externally 223adv.
alfresco 340adv.
air 340n.
out of fashion
antiquated 127adj.
out of favor
unfortunate 731adj.
disliked 861adj.
out of form
clumsy 695adj.
out of joint
unapt 25adj.
impotent 161adj.
evil 616adj.
clumsy 695adj.
out of keeping
unapt 25adj.
unconformable 84adj.
out of line
unconformable 84adj.
out of love
disliking 861adj.
hating 888adj.
out of luck
unfortunate 731adj.
out of mind
forgotten 506adj.
out of one's death
deeply 211adv.
puzzled 517adj..
in difficulties 700adj.
unsuccessful 728adj.
out of order
irrelevant 10adj.
unconformable 84adj.
useless 641adj.
out of place
unconformable 84adj.
misplaced 188adj.
inexpedient 643adj.
out of pocket
losing 772adj.
out of proportion
irrelative 10adj.
out of reach
unimitated 21adj.
too far 199adv.
impracticable 470adj.
out of season
anachronistic 118adj.
scarce 636adj.
out of shape
distorted 246adj.
out of sight
too far 199adv.
invisible 444adj.
out of sorts
sick 651adj.
dejected 834adj.
out of spirits
dejected 834adj.
out of step
non-uniform 17adj.
unapt 25adj.
unconformable 84adj.
out of the ordinary
special 80adj.
out of the question
impossible 470adj.
unadmitted 489adj.
rejected 607adj.
refused 760adj.
unpromising 853adj.
undue 916adj.
out-of-the-way
unusual 84adj.
roundabout 626adj.
out of this world
prodigious 32adj.
dead 361adj.
impossible 470adj.
pleasurable 826adj.
out of work
unused 674adj.
non-active 677adj.
outpace
outstrip 277vb.
outdo 306vb.
out-patient
sick person 651n.
outplay
be superior 34vb.
defeat 727vb.
outpoint
be superior 34vb.
defeat 727vb.
outpost
farness 199n.
front 237n.
outpouring
outflow 298n.
information 524n.
diffuseness 570n.
plenty 635n.
output
production 164n.
outrage
violence 176n.
evil 616n.
ill-treat 645vb.
impairment 655n.
misuse 675n., vb.
shame 867vb.
be insolent 878vb.
huff 891vb.
cruel act 898n.
indignity 921n.
guilty act 936n.
debauch 951vb.
outrageous
exorbitant 32adj.
violent 176adj.
exaggerated 546adj.
insolent 878adj.
cruel 898adj.
disrespectful 921adj.
heinous 934adj.
outrange
be distant 199vb.
outdo 306vb.
outrank
be unequal 29vb.
be superior 34vb.
come before 64vb.
outré
unusual 84adj.
exaggerated 546adj.
ridiculous 849adj.
outreach
be superior 34vb.
be distant 199vb.
deceive 542vb.
outrider
precursor 66n.
outrigger
supporter 218n.
projection 254n.
rowboat 275n.
outright
completely 54adv.
outrival
be superior 34vb.
outdo 306vb.
contend 716vb.
outrun
outstrip 277vb.
outdo 306vb.
outrush
outbreak 176n.

outset
start 68n.
departure 296n.
outshine
be superior 34vb.
defeat 727vb.
outshone
inferior 35adj.
outside
extraneous 59adj.
exteriority 223n.
around 230adv.
appearance 445n.
duplicity 541n.
outside edge
limit 236n.
annoyance 827n.
outsider
misfit 25n.
intruder 59n.
nonconformist 84n.
exteriority 223n.
outcaste 883n.
hateful object 888n.
outsize
unusual 84adj.
huge 195adj.
outskirts
entrance 68n.
farness 199n.
circumjacence 230n.
outsmart
deceive 542vb.
be cunning 698vb.
outspan
arrive 295vb.
outspoken
undisguised 522adj.
assertive 532adj.
veracious 540adj.
artless 699adj.
disrespectful 921adj.
outspread
broad 205adj.
outstanding
remarkable 32adj.
superior 34adj.
remainder 41n.
exterior 223adj.
notable 638adj.
owed 803adj.
outstare
humiliate 872vb.
be insolent 878vb.
outstation
farness 199n.
outstay
outlast 113vb.
outstay one's welcome
intrude 297vb.
be tedious 838vb.
outstretch
be long 203vb.
outstrip
outstrip 277vb.
progress 285vb.
hasten 680vb.
out-talk
be loquacious 581vb.
out to
intending 617adj.
out-tray
receptacle 194n.
compartment 194n.
outturn
production 164n.
outvote
reject 607vb.
outward
extrinsic 6adj.
exterior 223adj.
appearing 445adj.
outward bound
departing 296adj.
outgoing 298adj.
outwear
outlast 113vb.
outweigh
prevail 178vb.
weigh 322vb.
outwit
be superior 34vb.
outdo 306vb.
befool 542vb.
outwork
projection 254n.
fortification 713n.
outworn
antiquated 127adj.
outwrite oneself
be dull 840vb.
ouzel
waterfowl 365n.
oval
arc 250n.
round 250adj.
ovary
genitalia 164n.
ovate
round 250adj.
ovation
trophy 729n.
celebration 876n.
applause 923n.
oven
cookery 301n.
furnace 383n.
oven-ready
culinary 301adj.
ready-made 669adj.
over
beyond 34adv.
superior 34adj.
remaining 41adj.
ending 69adj.
past 125adj.
overact
exaggerate 546vb.
act 594vb.
be unskillful 695vb.
be affected 850vb.
overactivity
overactivity 678n.
over-age
antiquated 127adj.
overall
inclusive 78adj.
longwise 203adv.
apron 228n.
trousers 228n.
overambitious
rash 857adj.
over and above
in addition 38adv.
superfluous 637adj.
over and over
repeatedly 106adv.
overarch
overlie 226vb.
over-attentive
servile 879adj.
overawe
prevail 178vb.
dominate 733vb.
oppress 735vb.
frighten 854vb.
command respect 920vb.
overbalance
be unequal 29vb.
tumble 309vb.
weigh 322vb.
overbear
prevail 178vb.
motivate 612vb.
overbearing
oppressive 735adj.
proud 871adj.
insolence 878n.
overbid
overstep 306vb.
bargain 791vb.
overblown
aged 131adj.
expanded 197adj.
overborne
defeated 728adj.
subjected 745adj.
overbrimming
redundance 637n.
overbuilt
covered 226adj.
overburden
load 193vb.
make heavy 322vb.
ill-treat 645vb.
fatigue 684vb.
overbusy
inquisitive 453adj.
meddling 678adj.
overcall

outdo 306vb.
overcast
cloudy 355adj.
darken 418vb.
shadowy 419adj.
cheerless 834adj.
sullen 893adj.
overcaution
irresolution 601n.
overcharge
exaggerate 546vb.
dearness 811n.
over-clever
intelligent 498adj.
vain 873adj.
overcloud
(*see* overcast)
overcoat
overcoat 228n.
warm clothes 381n.
overcolor
exaggerate 546vb.
overcoloring
misinterpretation 521n.
overcome
prevail 178vb.
overmaster 727vb.
dejected 834adj.
tipsy 949adj.
over-communicative
informative 524adj.
overcompensate
be unequal 29vb.
compensate 31vb.
exaggerate 546vb.
over-compression
imperspicuity 568n.
over-confidence
rashness 857n.
over-confident
optimistic 482adj.
credulous 487adj.
rash 857adj.
over-critical
fastidious 862adj.
disapproving 924adj.
overcrop
waste 634vb.
make insufficient 636vb.
overcrowded
assembled 74adj.
over-curious
inquisitive 453adj.
over-daring
rash 857adj.
over-delicate
prudish 950adj.
overdevelop
enlarge 197vb.
darken 418vb.
blacken 428vb.
overdo
overstep 306vb.
exaggerate 546vb.
superabound 637vb.
overdone
tough 329adj.
overrated 482adj.
absurd 497adj.
exaggerated 546adj.
affected 850adj.
flattering 925adj.
overdose
redundance 637n.
satiety 863n.
overdraft
loss 772n.
debt 803n.
insolvency 805n.
over-dramatize
misrepresent 552vb.
act 594vb.
overdraw
exaggerate 546vb.
misrepresent 552vb.
lose 772vb.
be in debt 803vb.
be prodigal 815vb.
overdrawn
losing 772adj.
indebted 803adj.
overdressed
vulgar 847adj.
overdrive
power 160n.
fatigue 684vb.
overdue
late 136adj.
important 638adj.
owed 803adj.
just 913adj.
overeat
be intemperate 943vb.
gluttonize 947vb.
over-economical
parsimonious 816adj.
over-emphasis
exaggeration 546n.
overemployment
superfluity 637n.
overestimate
overstep 306vb.
misjudge 481vb.
overestimation 482n.
make important 638vb.
praise 923vb.
overestimation
exaggeration 546n.
over-exertion
overactivity 678n.
fatigue 684n.
overexpose
darken 418vb.
over-extension
overactivity 678n.
overfall
waterfall 350n.
wave 350n.
overfamiliar
impertinent 878adj.
overfed
sensual 944adj.
gluttonous 947adj.
overfeed
superabound 637vb.
sate 863vb.
overfill
fill 54vb.
sate 863vb.
overflow
be complete 54vb.
be many 104vb.
irrupt 297vb.
outflow 298n.
encroach 306vb.
moistening 341n.
waterfall 350n.
drain 351n.
have feeling 374vb.
diffuseness 570n.
abound 635vb.
redundance 637n.
overflowing
great 32adj.
full 54adj.
over-fulfill
superabound 637vb.
overfull
redundant 637adj.
overgo
overstep 306vb.
overgrow
hinder 702vb.
overgrown
expanded 197adj.
vegetal 366adj.
overgrowth
expansion 197n.
roughness 259n.
overhang
be to come 124vb.
be high 209vb.
hang 217vb.
jut 254vb.
overlie 226vb.
overhaul
outstrip 277vb.
outdo 306vb.
be attentive 455vb.
search 459vb.
repair 656vb.
overhead
aloft 209adv.
overheads
cost 809n.
overhear
hear 415vb.
be informed 524vb.

overhearing
listening 415n.
over-heated
hot 379adj.
insalubrious 653adj.
excited 821adj.
overhung
salient 254adj.
over-indulgence
laxity 734n.
intemperance 943n.
sensualism 944n.
gluttony 947n.
over-insure
be cautious 858vb.
over-interested
obsessed 455adj.
overjoyed
pleased 824adj.
overland
on land 344adv.
overlap
continuity 71n.
be included 78vb.
be contiguous 202vb.
stratification 207n.
covering 226n.
encroach 306vb.
touch 378vb.
superfluity 637n.
overlarge
huge 195adj.
overlay
laminate 207vb.
overlay 226vb.
kill 362vb.
conceal 525vb.
ornament 574vb.
overleaf
against 240adv.
overlie
hang 217vb.
overlie 226vb.
overload
load 193vb.
make heavy 322vb.
exaggerate 546vb.
ornament 574vb.
redundance 637n.
encumbrance 702n.
overlong
surpassing 306adj.
tedious 838adj.
overlook
be high 209vb.
be inattentive 456vb.
neglect 458vb.
not use 674vb.
be patient 823vb.
forgive 909vb.
bewitch 983vb.
overlord
superior 34n.
master 741n.
overlordship
superiority 34n.
magistrature 733n.
governance 733n.
overly
extremely 32adv.
redundantly 637adv.
overlying
overhanging 209adj.
overlying 226adj.
overmaster
overmaster 727vb.
subjugate 745vb.
overmatch
be strong 162vb.
overmaster 727vb.
over-measure
redundance 637n.
over-mighty
powerful 160adj.
influential 178adj.
oppressive 735adj.
proud 871adj.
lawless 954adj.
over-modesty
underestimation 483n.
prudery 950n.
overmost
topmost 213adj.
overmuch
redundant 637adj.
over-nice
fastidious 862adj.
overnight
instantaneously 116adv.
foregoing 125adj.
over one's head
deeply 211adv.
puzzling 517adj.
overpage
against 240adv.
overpaid
rich 800adj.
unwarranted 916adj.
overpaint
coat 226vb.
make opaque 423vb.
conceal 525vb.
obliterate 550vb.
overpass
be superior 34vb.
overstep 306vb.
overpay
be liberal 813vb.
overpayment
redundance 637n.
undueness 916n.
overpersuade
induce 612vb.
over-piety
pietism 979n.
overplus
remainder 41n.
part 53n.
redundance 637n.
over-populate
superabound 637vb.
over-populated
multitudinous 104adj.
over-population
crowd 74n.
overpower
be strong 162vb.
overmaster 727vb.
overpowering
impressive 821adj.
overpraise
overestimation 482n.
overrate 482vb.
misinterpret 521vb.
exaggerate 546vb.
redundance 637n.
praise 923n., vb.
flatter 925vb.
over-priced
dear 811adj.
overprint
substitute 150vb.
mark 547vb.
obliterate 550vb.
overprize
overrate 482vb.
overproduce
superabound 637vb.
over-proof
unmixed 44adj.
pungent 388adj.
intoxicating 949adj.
overproud
prideful 871adj.
overrate
overrate 482vb.
exaggerate 546vb.
make important 638vb.
overrated
overrated 482adj.
unimportant 639adj.
dear 811adj.
overreach
outdo 306vb.
deceive 542vb.
be cunning 698vb.
over-refinement
fastidiousness 862n.
override
prevail 178vb.
overstep 306vb.
be resolute 599vb.
overmaster 727vb.
dominate 733vb.
oppress 735vb.
overriding
supreme 34adj.
necessary 596adj.
important 638adj.
compelling 740adj.

over-righteous
pietistic 979adj.
over-ripe
aged 131adj.
soft 327adj.
pulpy 356adj.
overrule
dominate 733vb.
abrogate 752vb.
overruling
supreme 34adj.
important 638adj.
authoritative 733adj.
overrun
fill 54vb.
be many 104vb.
encroach 306vb.
attack 712vb.
appropriate 786vb.
over-sanguine
optimistic 482adj.
rash 857adj.
oversea
extraneous 59adj.
removed 199adj.
oversee
manage 689vb.
overseer
manager 690n.
oversell
exaggerate 546vb.
overset
demolish 165vb.
overturning 221n.
depression 311n.
overshadow
be superior 34vb.
be high 209vb.
overlie 226vb.
darken 418vb.
bedim 419vb.
dominate 733vb.
overshoe
footwear 228n.
overshoot
overstep 306vb.
be clumsy 695vb.
oversight
inspection 438n.
inattention 456n.
negligence 458n.
mistake 495n.
management 689n.
oversize
huge 195adj.
overskirt
skirt 228n.
oversleep
lose a chance 138vb.
be neglectful 458vb.
fail in duty 918vb.
oversoul
divineness 965n.
overspecialize
misjudge 481vb.
overspend
be prodigal 815vb.
overspending
waste 634n.
overspill
redundance 637n.
overspread
overlay 226vb.
overstatement
overestimation 482n.
affirmation 532n.
untruth 543n.
exaggeration 546n.
magniloquence 574n.
overstay
overstep 306vb.
overstep
overstep 306vb.
not observe 769vb.
overstock
superabound 637vb.
overstrain
overrate 482vb.
waste 634vb.
fatigue 684vb.
overstress
overrate 482vb.
exaggerate 546vb.
over-strung
sentient 374adj.
lively 819adj.
over-subscribe
superabound 637vb.
over-subtlety
sophistry 477n.
over-sure
rash 857adj.
over-suspicious
unbelieving 486adj.
overt
undisguise 522adj.
overtake
outstrip 277vb.
outdo 306vb.
hasten 680vb.
overtaking
spurt 277n.
approach 289n.
overtask
misuse 675vb.
fatigue 684vb.
impose a duty 917vb.
overtax
misuse 675vb.
fatigue 684vb.
oppress 735vb.
levy 786vb.
overthrow
revolution 149n.
demolish 165vb.
fell 311vb.
confute 479vb.
bungling 695n.
overmaster 727vb.
overthrown
defeated 728adj.
overtime
addition 38n.
extra 40n.
protraction 113n.
exertion 682n.
overtone
musical note 410n.
overtop
be great 32vb.
be superior 34vb.
be high 209vb.
crown 213vb.
overtrick
remainder 41n.
overtrump
overmaster 727vb.
over-trustful
credulous 487adj.
overture
prelude 66n.
approach 289n.
musical piece 412n.
irenics 719n.
offer 759n.
request 761n.
friendship 880n.
overturn
derange 63vb.
revolutionize 149vb.
demolish 165vb.
invert 221vb.
overvalue
misjudge 481vb.
overrate 482vb.
overweening
rash 857adj.
proud 871adj.
vain 873adj.
insolent 878adj.
overweigh
predominate 34vb.
be many 104vb.
prevail 178vb.
motivate 612vb.
overweight
inequality 29n.
unwieldy 195adj.
make heavy 322vb.
exaggerate 546vb.
redundance 637n.
make important 638vb.
overwhelm
fill 54vb.
be many 104vb.
be strong 162vb.
destroy 165vb.
be violent 176vb.
confute 479vb.
superabound 637vb.
attack 712vb.

defeat 727vb.
impress 821vb.
sadden 834vb.
overwhelming
prodigious 32adj.
felt 818adj.
impressive 821adj.
wonderful 864adj.
overwork
waste 634vb.
misuse 675vb.
be busy 678vb.
work 682vb.
fatigue 684vb.
overwriting
lettering 586n.
over-wrought
matured 669adj.
fervent 818adj.
excited 821adj.
affected 850adj.
oviform
rotund 252adj.
ovine
animal 365adj.
oviparous
productive 164adj.
ovoid
round 250adj.
rotund 252adj.
ovule
arc 250n.
owe
be in debt 803vb.
owe nothing to
be unrelated 10vb.
owing
owed 803adj.
due 915adj.
owing to
caused 157adj.
attributed 158adj.
hence 158adv.
owl
bird 365n.
fool 501n.
omen 511n.
owlish
unintelligent 499adj.
own
assent 488vb.
confess 526vb.
possess 773vb.
own accord, of one's
at will 595adv.
own a connection
be akin 11vb.
owner
master 741n.
owner 776n.
ownerless
unpossessed 774adj.
ownership
possession 773n.
own generation, one's
contemporary 123n.
own, on one's
friendless 883adj.
ox
beast of burden 273n.
male animal 372n.
cattle 365n.
Oxford movement
Catholicism 976n.
sect 978n.
oxide
ash 381n.
oxygen
air 340n.
oxygenate
gasify 336vb.
aerify 340vb.
oxymoron
misfit 25n.
oxytone
punctuation 547n.
oyster
fish food 301n.
table fish 365n.
gray 429n.
taciturnity 582n.
ozone
air 340n.
salubrity 652n.

P

pabulum
food 301n.
pace
synchronize 123vb.
long measure 203n.
gait 265n.
walk 267vb.
velocity 277n.
measure 465vb.
pacemaker
leader 690n.
pacer
pedestrian 268n.
thoroughbred 273n.
pace-stick
gauge 465n.
pachyderm
animal 365n.
pachydermatous
unfeeling 375adj.
thick-skinned 820adj.
pacific
inert 175adj.
moderate 177adj.
concordant 710adj.
peaceful 717adj.
pacification
moderation 177n.
pacification 719n.
friendship 880n.
propitiation 941n.
pacificator, pacifier
mediator 720n.
pacificatory
lenitive 177adj.
pacificatory 719adj.
mediatory 720adj.
courteous 884adj.
pacifism
peace 717n.
pacifist
pacifist 717n.
pacify
pacify 719vb.
mediate 720vb.
tranquilize 823vb.
pack
fill 54vb.
group 74n.
stow 187vb.
load 193vb.
line 227vb.
close 264vb.
travel 267vb.
be dense 324vb.
dog 365n.
fake 541vb.
hunter 619n.
store 632vb.
make ready 669vb.
encumbrance 702n.
beautification 843n.
do wrong 914vb.
package
bunch 74n.
inclusion 78n.
unit 88n.
(*see* pack)
pack a jury
predetermine 608vb.
pack a punch
be strong 162vb.
packer
preparer 669n.
worker 686n.
packet
great quantity 32n.
bunch 74n.
small box 194n.
ship 275n.
wealth 800n.
pack-horse
beast of burden 273n.
pack-ice
ice 380n.
packing
location 187n.
contents 193n.
lining 227n.
packing-case
box 194n.
storage 632n.
packthread
fiber 208n.

pact
agreement 24n.
compact 765n.
Pactolus
wealth 800n.
pad
load 193vb.
enlarge 197vb.
foot 214n.
seat 218n.
line 227vb.
saddle-horse 273n.
sound faint 401vb.
be diffuse 570vb.
stationery 586n.
padded
expanded 197adj.
soft 327adj.
pleonastic 570adj.
padded cell
madhouse 503n.
shelter 662n.
padding
increment 36n.
adjunct 40n.
lining 227n.
stopper 264n.
softness 327n.
warm clothes 381n.
pleonasm 570n.
paddle
walk 267vb.
row, swim 269vb.
strike 279vb.
propellant 287n.
be wet 341vb.
spank 963vb.
paddle one's own canoe
be free 744vb.
paddler
pedestrian 268n.
paddle-wheel
propeller 269n.
paddling
acquatics 269n.
paddock
enclosure 235n.
paddy
corn 366n.
anger 891n.
padishah
sovereign 741n.
padlock
fastening 47n.
lock-up 748n.
padnag
saddle-horse 273n.
pad out
augment 36vb.
be diffuse 570vb.
padre
title 870n.
cleric 986n.
paean
rejoicing 835n.
celebration 876n.
thanks 907n.
applause 923n.
hymn 981n.
paedeutics
teaching 534n.
pagan
heathen 974n.
profane 980adj.
idolater 982n.
paganism
religion 973n.
antichristianity 974n.
impiety 980n.
idolatry 982n.
paganize
convert 147vb.
paganize 974vb.
page
part 53n.
courier 531n.
mark 547vb.
edition 589n.
retainer 742n.
bridesman 894n.
pageant, pageantry
spectacle 445n.
pageant 875n.
page-boy
youngster 132n.
servant 742n.
pages
great quantity 32n.
pagination
numeration 86n.
pagoda
high structure 209n.
temple 990n.
paid
subject 745adj.
gainful 771adj.
receiving 782adj.
expended 806adj.
paid for
bought 792adj.
pail
vessel 194n.
pain
pain 377n.
evil 616n.
suffering 825vb.
painfulness 827n.
discontent 829n.
sadden 834vb.
pained
resentful 891adj.
painful
painful 377adj.
laborious 682adj.
paining 827adj.
painfully
carefully 457adv.
pain-killer
anesthetic 375n.
antidote 658n.
relief 831n.
pain-killing
lenitive 177adj.
painless
comfortable 376adj.
easy 701adj.
pleasurable 826adj.
pains
obstetrics 164n.
attention 455n.
carefulness 457n.
exertion 682n.
pains and penalties
penalty 963n.
painstaking
careful 457adj.
assiduity 678n.
exertion 682n.
laborious 682adj.
paint
imitate 20vb.
coat 226vb.
pigment 425n.
imagine 513vb.
sham 542n.
represent 551vb.
paint 553vb.
describe 590vb.
cleanser 648n.
preserve 660vb.
cosmetic 843n.
decorate 844vb.
paintable
painted 553adj.
beautiful 841adj.
paint-box
pigment 425n.
art equipment 553n.
paint brush
art equipment 553n.
painted
florid 425adj.
red 431adj.
false 541adj.
deceiving 542adj.
beautified 843adj.
painter
cable 47n.
artist 556n.
painting
composition 56n.
color 425n.
representation 551n.
picture 553n.
beautification 843n.
ornamental art 844n.
paints
art equipment 553n.
pair
identify 13vb.
analogue 18n.
unite with 45vb.

combine 50vb.
group 74n.
concomitant 89n.
duality 90n.
compare 462vb.
paired
married 894adj.
pairing
coition 45n.
pajamas
informal dress 228n.
nightwear 228n.
pal
colleague 707n.
chum 880n.
palace
house 192n.
magistrature 733n.
parsonage 986n.
paladin
defender 713n.
combatant 722n.
brave person 855n.
philanthropist 901n.
palaetiology
palaetiology 125n.
attribution 158n.
palais de danse
place of amusement 837n.
palanquin
vehicle 274n.
palatable
edible 301adj.
pleasant 376adj.
tasty 386adj.
savory 390adj.
palatal
speech sound 398n.
spoken letter 558n.
palatalize
voice 577vb.
palate
taste 386n.
good taste 846n.
palate-tickling
gastronomy 301n.
palatial
architectural 192adj.
palatinate
territory 184n.
polity 733n.
palaver
empty talk 515n.
speech 579n.
chatter 581n.
conference 584n.
pale
fastening 47n.
exclusion 57n.
weak 163adj.
region 184n.
fence, barrier 235n.
be dim 419vb.
soft-hued 425adj.
colorless 426adj.
loose color 426vb.
whitish 427adj.
disappear 446vb.
heraldry 547n.
unhealthy 651adj.
paleface
foreigner 59n.
paleocrystic
primal 127adj.
paleographer
interpreter 520n
paleography
palaetiology 125n.
hermeneutics 520n.
linguistics 557n.
Paleolithic
secular 110adj.
antiquity 125n.
primal 127adj.
paleontologist
antiquarian 125n.
paleontology
palaetiology 125n.
zoology 367n.
Paleozoic
secular 110adj.
primal 127adj.
palestra
athletics 162n.
academy 539n.
arena 724n.
palestric
contending 716adj.
palette
plate 194n.
art equipment 553n.
palewise
vertical 215adj.
palfrey
saddle-horse 273n.
Pali
language 557n.
palilogy
repetition 106n.
affirmation 532n.
palimpsest
substitute 150n.
script 586n.
book 589n.
palindrome
inversion 221n.
paling
fence 235n.
defenses 713n.
palingenesis
reproduction 166n.
palinode
negation 533n.
poem 593n.
recantation 603n.
palisade
barrier 235n.
protection 660n.
defenses 713n.
palkee
vehicle 274n.
palkee-bearer
bearer 273n.
pall
funeral 364n.
render insensible 375vb.
be unpalatable 391n.
obfuscation 421n.
invisibility 444n.
regalia 743n.
be tedious 838vb.
cause dislike 861vb.
sate 863vb.
vestments 989n.
palladium
protection 660n.
refuge 662n.
talisman 983n.
pall-bearer
funeral 364n.
pallet
bed 218n.
palliate
moderate 177vb.
qualify 468vb.
plead 614vb.
make better 654vb.
remedy 658vb.
relieve 831vb.
extenuate 927vb.
palliative
moderator 177n.
remedial 658adj.
pallid
colorless 426adj.
pallium
robe 228n.
vestments 989n.
pallone
ball game 837n.
pallor
hue 425n.
achromatism 426n.
pally
friendly 880adj.
sociable 882adj.
palm
long measure 203n.
feeler 378n.
touch 378vb.
oracle 511vb.
trophy 729n.
palmate
notched 260adj.
palmer
traveler 268n.
pietist 979n.
worshiper 981n.
palm-greasing
inducement 612n.

palmistry
divination 511n.
occultism 984n.
palm off
deceive 542vb.
palmy days
palmy days 730n.
happiness 824n.
joy 824n.
palomino
horse 273n.
palp
feeler 378n.
touch 378vb.
palpable
substantial 3adj.
material 319adj.
tactual 378adj.
visible 443adj.
manifest 522adj.
palpation
touch 378n.
palpitation
oscillation 317n.
agitation 318n.
feeling 818n.
nervousness 854n.
palpitations
heart disease 651n.
fatigue 684n.
palpus
feeler 378n.
palsied
aged 131adj.
apathetic 820adj.
(*see* palsy)
palsy
helplessness 161n.
unman 161vb.
agitation, spasm 318n.
insensibility 375n.
paralysis 651n.
frighten 854vb.
palter
be false 541vb.
dissemble 541vb.
be irresolute 601vb.
not observe 769vb.
palterer
liar 545n.
paltry
inconsiderable 33adj.
unimportant 639adj.
contemptible 922adj.
rascally 930adj.
selfish 932adj.
paludal
marshy 347adj.
pampas
plain 348n.
pamper
pet 889vb.
be sensual 944vb.
pampered
sensual 944adj.
gluttonous 947adj.
pamphlet
the press 528n.
book 589n.
pamphleteer
argue 475vb.
publicizer 528n.
preacher 537n.
dissertator 591n.
Pan
animality 365n.
vegetability 366n.
musician 413n.
mythic god 966n.
lesser god 967n.
pan
eliminate 44vb.
plate 194n.
face 237n.
scales 322n.
panacea
remedy 658n.
panache
plumage 259n.
trimming 844n.
ostentation 875n.
panama
headgear 228n.
panary
storage 632n.
pancake
horizontality 216n.
aeronautics 271n.
cereal 301n.
pancarditis
heart disease 651n.
pancratiast
athlete 162n.
pandect
dissertation 591n.
compendium 592n.
law 953n.
pandemic
universal 79adj.
plague 651n.
infectious 653adj.
unchaste 951adj.
pandemonium
turmoil 61n.
loudness 400n.
discord 411n.
hell 972n.
pander to
tempt 612vb.
be instrumental 628vb.
provide 633vb.
minister to 703vb.
please 826vb.
be servile 879vb.
flatter 925vb.
cad 938n.
be impure 951vb.
bawd 952n.
pandiculate
expand 197vb.
lengthen 203vb.
pandiculation
opening 263n.
sleepiness 679n.
pane
brittleness 330n.
transparency 422n.
panegyric
overestimation 482n.
praise 923n.
panel
band 74n.
list 87n.
lamina 207n.
partition 231n.
paneled
variegated 437adj.
paneling
lining 227n.
ornamental art 844n.
pang
spasm 318n.
pang 377n.
suffering 825n.
panhandle
beg 761vb.
panhandler
beggar 763n.
low fellow 869n.
panic
fear 854n., vb.
be cowardly 856vb.
panicky
fearing 854adj.
panjandrum
bigwig 638n.
aristocrat 868n.
pannier
basket 194n.
skirt 228n.
pannikin
cup 194n.
panoply
protection 660n.
armor 713n.
panopticon
prison 748n.
panorama
whole 52n.
generality 79n.
open space 263n.
view 438n.
spectacle 445n.
art subject 553n.
pan out
happen 154vb.
result 157vb.
pan-pipes
flute 414n.

pansophy
erudition 490n.
pansy
weakling 163n.
purple 434n.
libertine 952n.
pant
oscillate 317vb.
be agitated 318vb.
breathe 352vb.
be hot 379vb.
be fatigued 684vb.
show feeling 818vb.
desire 859vb.
pantalets
trousers 228n.
Pantaloon
old man 133n.
entertainer 594n.
pantaloons
trousers 228n.
pantechnicon
cart 274n.
pantheism
deism 973n.
pantheist
religionist 971adj.
pantheon
god 966n.
temple 990n.
panther
cat 365n.
panties
underwear 228n.
pantile
roof 226n.
drain 351n.
panting
(*see* pant)
pantisocracy
government 733n.
pantler
provider 633n.
pantologist
scholar 492n.
export 696n.
vain person 873n.
pantomime
mimicry 20n.
gesture 547n.
gesticulate 547vb.
stage play 594n.
act 594vb.
pantophagist
glutton 947n.
pantophagy
eating 301n.
pantry
chamber 194n.
provisions 301n.
storage 632n.
pants
trousers 228n.
underwear 228n.
panurgic
skillful 694adj.
pap
bosom 253n.
food 301n.
semiliquidity 354n.
pulpiness 356n.
insipidity 387n.
trifle 639n.
papacy
churchdom 985n.
church office 985n.
papal
ecclesiastical 985adj.
papal court
ecclesiastical court 956n.
papaya
fruit 301n.
paper
insubstantial 4adj.
weak thing 163n.
thinness 206n.
wrapping 226n.
overlay 226vb.
line 227vb.
white thing 427n.
report 524n.
the press 528n.
stationery 586n.
dissertation 591n.
paper 631n.
title-deed 767n.
paperback
book 589n.
novel 590n.
paperchase
chase 619n.
racing 716n.
paper over
repair 656vb.
paper over the cracks
not suffice 636vb.
be unskillful 695vb.
not complete 726vb.
papers
record 548n.
paper war
argument 475n.
quarrel 709n.
contention 716n.
war 718n.
papery
brittle 330adj.
papier-mâché
pulpiness 356n.
paper 631n.
papilla
bosom 253n.
papist
Catholic 976n.
papistical
popish 976adj.
papistry
Catholicism 976n.
papoose
child 132n.
pappose
downy 259adj.
pappus
hair 259n.
pappy
pulpy 356adj.
paprika
vegetable 301n.
condiment 389n.
papule
swelling 253n.
skin disease 651n.
papyrus
stationery 586n.
par
equivalence 28n.
parable
metaphor 519n.
lecture 534n.
narrative 590n.
parabola
curve 248n.
parabolical
figurative 519adj.
parabolize
figure 519vb.
paracentesis
voidance 300n.
parachronism
anachronism 118n.
different time 122n.
parachute
fly 271vb.
aircraft 276n.
descend 309vb.
safeguard 662n.
parachutist
aeronaut 271n.
Paraclete
Holy Ghost 965n.
parade
assemblage 74n.
street 192n.
marching 267n.
spectacle 445n.
show 522vb.
path 624n.
pageant 875n.
parade ground
meeting place 192n.
arena 724n.
paradigm
prototype 23n.
grammar 564n.
paradisal
pleasurable 826adj.
paradisiac 971adj.
paradise
happiness 824n.
heaven 971n.
parados

defenses 713n.
paradox
contrariety 14n.
misfit 25n.
argumentation 475n.
absurdity 497n.
inexpectation 508n.
unintelligibility 517n.
ridiculousness 849n.
paraffin
oil 357n.
fuel 385n.
paragon
prototype 23n.
exceller 644n.
paragon 646n.
prodigy 864n.
person of repute 866n.
good man 937n.
paragram
equivocalness 518n.
paragraph
subdivision 53n.
punctuation 547n.
phrase 563n.
edition 589n.
parakeet
bird 365n.
paralalia
speech defect 580n.
paraleipsis
negligence 458n.
trope 519n.
parallax
distance 199n.
parallel
correlative 12adj.
analogue 18n.
equal 28adj.
concurrent 181adj.
region 184n.
parallelism 219n.
compare 462vb.
defenses 713n.
parallel course
accompaniment 89n.
parallelepiped
parallelism 219n.
angular figure 247n.
parallelism
similarity 18n.
conformance 24n.
parallelism 219n.
symmetry 245n.
parallelogram
parallelism 219n.
angular figure 247n.
paralogism
sophism 477n.
paralysis
helplessness 161n.
inertness 175n.
insensibility 375n.
paralysis 651n.
hindrance 702n.
paralytic
sick person 651n.
paralyze
disable 161vb.
render insensible 375vb.
prohibit 757vb.
paralyzed
still 266adj.
non-active 677adj.
(*see* paralysis)
Paramatman
divineness 965n.
paramatta
textile 222n.
paramnesia
error 495n.
oblivion 506n.
paramount
supreme 34adj.
authoritative 733adj.
paramountcy
superiority 34n.
importance 638n.
prestige 866n.
paramour
lover 887n.
kept woman 952n.
parang
sharp edge 256n.
side-arms 723n.
paranoia
psychopathy 503n.
paranoiac
madman 504n.
paranormal
paranormal 984adj.
paranymph
auxiliary 707n.
bridesman 894n.
parapet
summit 213n.
fortification 713n.
paraph
label 547n.
sign 547vb.
paraphasia
speech defect 580n.
paraphemia
speech defect 580n.
paraphernalia
medley 43n.
equipment 630n.
property 777n.
paraphrase
imitation 20n.
copy 22n.
intelligibility 516n.
translation 520n.
phrase 563n.
paraphrast
interpreter 520n.
paraphrastic
semantic 514adj.
interpretive 520adj.
paraphrenia
psychopathy 503n.
paraphronesis
frenzy 503n.
paraplegia
paralysis 651n.
parapraxia
inattention 456n.
parapsychology
psychology 447n.
phychics 984n.
parasang
long measure 203n.
paraselene
moon 321n.
parasite
concomitant 89n.
settler 191n.
eater 301n.
vermin 365n.
superfluity 637n.
bane 659n.
idler 679n.
dependent 742n.
beggar 763n.
desirer 859n.
toady 879n.
social person 882n.
flatterer 925n.
parasitic
inferior 35adj.
residing 192adj.
parasitology
pathology 651n.
parasol
shade 226n.
parataxis
grammar 564n.
paratrooper
aeronaut 271n.
armed force 722n.
paratyphoid
infection 651n.
parboil
cook 301vb.
parbuckle
tool 630n.
parcel
sunder 46vb.
piece 53n.
bunch 74n.
apportion 783vb.
parch
dry 342vb.
be hot 379vb.
heat 381vb.
cause desire 859vb.
parchment
stationery 586n.
bookbinding 589n.
pardon

amnesty 506n.
lenity 736n.
liberate 746vb.
forgiveness 909n.
non-liability 919n.
acquittal 960n.
pardonable
vindicable 927adj.
guiltless 935adj.
pardoner
pastor 986n.
pare
shade off 27vb.
bate 37vb.
subtract 39vb.
cut 46vb.
shorten 204vb.
paregoric
remedial 658adj.
parent
kinsman 11n.
precursor 66n.
source 156n.
producer 167n.
parent 169n.
parentage
consanguinity 11n.
source 156n.
attribution 158n.
parentage 169n.
parental
parental 169adj.
parenthesis
irrelevance 10n.
discontinuity 72n.
interjection 231n.
insertion 303n.
punctuation 547n.
parenthood
propagation 164n.
parentage 169n.
life 360n.
par excellence
eminently 34adv.
parget
paving 226n.
coat 226vb.
pargeting
ornamental art 844n.
parhelion
sun 321n.
pariah
nonconformist 84n.
outcaste 883n.
parietal
lateral 239adj.
paring
small thing 33n.
leavings 41n.
piece 53n.
economy 814n.
pari passu
equally 28adv.
synchronously 123adv.
parish
subdivision 53n.
district 184n.
parish 985n.
laity 987n.
parish clerk
church officer 986n.
parishioner
native 191n.
layman 987n.
parish pump
trifle 639n.
parison
ornament 574n.
paritor
law officer 955n.
parity
similarity 18n.
equality 28n.
park
accumulation 74n.
station 187n.
place oneself 187vb.
pleasance 192n.
enclosure 235n.
grassland 348n.
wood 366n.
garden 370n.
pleasure-ground 837n.
parka
tunic 228n.
warm clothes 381n.
parking-meter
timekeeper 117n.
meter 465n.
parking place
station 187n.
Parkinson's law
expansion 197n.
parkway
road 624n.
parlance
style 566n.
speech 579n.
parlementaire
messenger 531n.
irenics 719n.
parley
interlocution 584n.
conference 584n.
consult 691vb.
make terms 766vb.
parliament
parliament 692n.
parliamentarian
councillor 692n.
parliamentary system
vote 605n.
parlor
chamber 194n.
parlor game
indoor game 837n.
parlor-maid
domestic 742n.
parochial
regional 184adj.
provincial 192adj.
narrow-minded 481adj.
ecclesiastical 985adj.
parochialism
narrow mind 481n.
patriotism 901n.
parodist
humorist 839n.
parodos
dramaturgy 594n.
parody
mimicry 20n.
foolery 497n.
misinterpretation 521n.
misrepresentation 552n.
satire 851n.
parole
liberation 746n.
permit 756n.
promise 764n.
parolee
prisoner 750n.
offender 904n.
parole, on
restrained 747adj.
promissory 764adj.
par, on a
equal 28adj.
paronomasia
assimilation 18n.
equivocalness 518n.
trope 519n.
ornament 574n.
paronym
word 559n.
parotitis
infection 651n.
paroxysm
violence 176n.
spasm 318n.
frenzy 503n.
anger 891n.
paroxytone
punctuation 547n.
parquetry
checker 437n.
parricide
homicide 362n.
parrot
imitator 20n.
repeat 106vb.
bird 365n.
chatterer 581n.
parrot cry
conformity 83n.
parrotry
conformity 83n.
parry
repel 292vb.

avoid 620vb.
obstruct 702vb.
parry 713vb.
resist 715vb.
parse
decompose 51vb.
parse 564vb.
parsec
long measure 203n.
parsimonious
careful 457adj.
temporate 942adj.
parsimony
insufficiency 636n.
parsimony 816n.
selfishness 932n.
parsley
potherb 301n.
parsnip
tuber 301n.
parson
cleric 986n.
parsonage
benefice 985n.
parsonage 986n.
part
finite quantity 26n.
adjunct 40n.
disjoin 46vb.
part 53n.
incompleteness 55n.
component 58n.
bisection 92n.
fraction 102n.
open 263vb.
diverge 294vb.
melody 410n.
vocal music 412n.
reading matter 589n.
acting 594n.
function 622n.
portion 783n.
partake
eat 301vb.
partaking
eating 301n.
sharing 775adj.
parterre
garden 370n.
theater 594n.
parthenogenesis
propagation 164n.
Parthian shot
stratagem 698n.
bombardment 712n.
partial
fragmentary 53adj.
incomplete 55adj.
fractional 102adj.
imperfect 647adj.
uncompleted 726adj.
desiring 859adj.
(*see* partiality)
partiality
inequality 29n.
prejudice 481n.
liking 859n.
friendliness 880n.
injustice 914n.
improbity 930n.
partible
severable 46adj.
particeps criminis
colleague 707n.
participant
conjunct 45adj.
participate
be one of 58vb.
be instrumental 628vb.
feel 818vb.
be sociable 882vb.
(*see* participation)
participation
similarity 18n.
activity 678n.
association 706n.
cooperation 706n.
participation 775n.
condolence 905n.
participator
personnel 686n.
colleague 707n.
participator 775n.
beneficiary 776n.
particle
particle 33n.
piece 53n.
element 319n.
part of speech 564n.
particolored
colored 425adj.
variegated 437adj.
particular
part 53n.
special 80adj.
eventuality 154n.
attentive 455adj.
careful 457adj.
discriminating 463adj.
veracious 540adj.
descriptive 590adj.
capricious 604adj.
sensitive 819adj.
fastidious 862adj.
particularism
particularism 80n.
selfishness 932n.
sectarianism 978n.
particularist
egotist 932n.
sectarist 978n.
particularity
(*see* particular)
particularize
differentiate 15vb.
specify 80vb.
be diffuse 570vb.
particularly
eminently 34adv.
particulars
particulars 80n.
description 590n.
parting
separation 46n.
dividing line 92n.
centrality 225n.
partition 231n.
limit 236n.
divergence 294n.
departure 296n.
parti pris
bias 481n.
predetermination 608n.
partisan
patron 707n.
sectional 708adj.
spear 723n.
revolter 738n.
friend 880n.
sectarian 978adj.
partisanship
prejudice 481n.
cooperation 706n.
friendliness 880n.
injustice 914n.
partition
separation 46n.
decomposition 51n.
part 53vb.
exclusion 57n.
dividing line 92n.
partition 231n.
limit 236n.
screen 421n.
obstacle 702n.
apportionment 783n.
partly
partially 33adv.
partly 53adv.
partner
join 45vb.
combine 50vb.
concomitant 89n.
personnel 686n.
cooperate 706vb.
colleague 707n.
participator 775n.
friend 880n.
spouse 894n.
partnership
concurrence 181n.
corporation 708n.
participation 775n.
(*see* partner)
part of speech
word 559n.
part of speech 564n.
partridge
table bird 365n.
parts
genitalia 164n.
region 184n.

locality 187n.
contents 193n.
intellect 447n.
aptitude 694n.
parts, man of
proficient 696n.
parturient
prolific 171adj.
parturition
obstetrics 164n.
part with
not retain 779vb.
give 781vb.
party
group, band 74n.
follower 282n.
person 371n.
prejudice 481n.
assenter 488n.
conference 584n.
association 706n.
party 708n.
signatory 765n.
festivity 837n.
social gathering 882n.
litigant 959n.
sect 978n.
party capital
injustice 914n.
party line
rule 81n.
policy 623n.
tactics 688n.
party man
sectarist 978n.
party-minded
biased 481adj.
sociable 882adj.
sectarian 978adj.
party spirit
prejudice 481n.
dissent 489n.
government 733n.
cheerfulness 833n.
injustice 914n.
sectarianism 978n.
party to
assenting 488adj.
party-wall
dividing line 92n.
partition 231n.
parvenu
upstart 126n.
made man 730n.
rich man 800n.
vulgarian 847n.
commoner 869n.
proud man 871n.
paschal
seasonal 141adj.
ritual 988adj.
pash
love 887n.
pasha
tyrant 735n.
governor 741n.
nobleman 868n.
pashalic
magistrature 733n.
pasilaly
language 557n.
pasquinade
calumny 926n.
pass
circumstance 8n.
be superior 34vb.
entrance 68n.
conform 83vb.
continue 108vb.
elapse 111vb.
be past 125vb.
be turned to 147adj.
eventuality 154n.
gap 201n.
narrowness 206n.
opener 263n.
be in motion 265vb.
transfer 272vb.
ingress 297n.
emit 300vb.
excrete 302vb.
passage 305n.
overstep 306vb.
disappear 446vb.
assent 488n.
sleight 542n.
select 605vb.
access 624n.
suffice 635vb.
be good 644vb.
protection 660n.
predicament 700n.
foin 712n.
success 727n.
permit 756n., vb.
consent 758vb.
change hands 780vb.
endearment 889n.
approve 923vb.
make legal 953vb.
spell 983n.
passable
inconsiderable 33adj.
not bad 644adj.
mediocre 732adj.
contenting 828adj.
personable 841adj.
passage
bond 47n.
part 53n.
entrance 68n.
change 143n.
transition 147n.
street 192n.
lobby 194n.
gap 201n.
doorway 263n.
motion 265n.
land travel 267n.
water travel 269n.
transference 272n.
deviate 282vb.
passage 305n.
musical piece 412n.
anthology 592n.
access 624n.
passant
heraldic 547adj.
pass away
pass away 2vb.
end 69vb.
be transient 114vb.
die, perish 361vb.
disappear 446vb.
pass belief
cause doubt 486vb.
passbook
account book 808n.
pass by
elapse 111vb.
disregard 458vb.
(*see* pass)
pass current
be believed 485vb.
be published 528vb.
be in fashion 848vb.
passé
antiquated 127adj.
aged 131adj.
passed
expert 694adj.
passementerie
trimming 844n.
passenger
thing transferred 272n.
train 274n.
idler 679n.
encumbrance 702n.
passe-partout
opener 263n.
passer-by
spectator 441n.
passerine
animal 365adj.
pass for
resemble 18vb.
passibility
sensibility 374n.
passim
somewhere 185adv.
in place 186adv.
passing
exorbitant 32adj.
excretion 302n.
decease 361n.
passing bell
obsequies 364n.
passing show
fashion 848n.
passing word
hint 524n.
pass into

shade off 27vb.
be turned to 147vb.
passion
violence 176n.
vigor 571n.
affections 817n.
warm feeling 818n.
excitable state 822n.
suffering 825n.
desire 859n.
love 887n.
anger 891n.
passionate
fervent 818adj.
excitable 822adj.
loving 887adj.
irascible 892adj.
passionless
impassive 820adj.
indifferent 860adj.
passive
inert 175adj.
latent 523adj.
peaceful 717adj.
obedient 739adj.
inexcitable 823adj.
passivity
inaction 677n.
(*see* passive)
passman
college student 538n.
pass muster
suffice 635vb.
be good 644vb.
be middling 732vb.
be praised 923vb.
pass off
be past 125vb.
happen 154vb.
pass on
transfer 272vb.
progress 285vb.
communicate 524vb.
pass out
be impotent 161vb.
emerge 298vb.
be drunk 949vb.
pass over
exclude 57vb.
die 361vb.
neglect, disregard 458vb.
be taciturn 582vb.
reject 607vb.
forgive 909vb.
exempt 919vb.
Passover
holy-day 988n.
passport
opener 263n.
credential 466n.
label 547n.
instrument 628n.
protection 660n.
warrant 737n.
permit 756n.
pass round
publish 528vb.
pass sentence
judge 480vb.
pass the buck
transfer 272vb.
be exempt 919vb.
pass the time
be 1vb.
amuse oneself 837vb.
password
opener 263n.
answer 460n.
identification 547n.
instrument 628n.
warfare 718n.
permit 756n.
past
priority 119n.
preterition 125n.
antiquated 127adj.
paste
a mixture 43n.
adhesive 47n.
agglutinate 48vb.
viscidity 354n.
pulpiness 356n.
sham 542n.
finery 844n.
bad taste 847n.
pasteboard
paper 631n.
pastel
pigment 425n.
soft-hued 425adj.
art equipment 553n.
picture 553n.
pastern
foot 214n.
pasteurize
purify 648vb.
sanitate 652vb.
doctor 658vb.
past, have a
have no repute 867vb.
past history
precedence 64n.
past hope
unpromising 853adj.
pastiche, pasticcio
copy 22n.
a mixture 43n.
picture 553n.
art style 553n.
pastille, pastil
inodorousness 395n.
scent 396n.
pastime
business 622n.
pleasurableness 826n.
amusement 837n.
past it
aged 131adj.
weak 163adj.
past master
artisan 686n.
proficient 696n.
pastor
teacher 537n.
pastor 986n.
pastoral
agrarian 370adj.
pleasurable 826adj.
priestly 985adj.
clerical 986adj.
pastorale
musical piece 412n.
pastoral letter
ministration 988n.
pastoral staff
vestments 989n.
pastorate
church ministry 985n.
pastry
pastry 301n.
sweet 392n.
pastry-cook
caterer 633n.
past tense
time 108n.
preterition 125n.
pasture
provender 301n.
graze, feed 301vb.
soil 344n.
grassland 348n.
grass 366n.
stock farm 369n.
farm 370n.
pasty
pastry 301n.
pulpy 356adj.
colorless 426adj.
pat
apt 24adj.
fixed 153adj.
knock 279n.
touch 378n.
please 826vb.
relieve 831vb.
caress 889vb.
patch
adjunct 40n.
join 45vb.
piece 53n.
modify 143vb.
garden 370n.
variegate 437vb.
repair 656n., vb.
dirt 649n.
surgical dressing 658n.
eyesore 842n.

cosmetic 843n.
blemish 845n.
patcher
mender 656n.
patchiness
non-uniformity 17n.
inequality 29n.
maculation 437n.
imperfection 647n.
patchouli
scent 396n.
patch up
repair 656vb.
compromise 770vb.
patchwork
non-uniformity 17n.
discontinuity 72n.
variegation 437n.
needlework 844n.
patchy
inferior 35adj.
mixed 43adj.
discontinuous 72adj.
(*see* patchiness)
pate
head 213n.
patefaction
opening 263n.
patella
plate 194n.
paten
plate 194n.
ritual object 988n.
church utensil 990n.
patent
open 263adj.
manifest 522adj.
permit 756n., vb.
estate 777n.
dueness 915n.
patented
private 80adj.
proprietary 777adj.
patentee
beneficiary 776n.
recipient 782n.
patera
plate 194n.
paterfamilias
parent 169n.
paternal
akin 11adj.
parental 169adj.
benevolent 897adj.
paternalism
governance 733n.
despotism 733n.
paternity
propagation 164n.
parentage 169n.
paternoster
prayers 981n.
pater patriae
benefactor 903n.
path
direction 281n.
way in 297n.
outlet 298n.
passage 305n.
trace 548n.
path 624n.
pathetic
unimportant 639adj.
felt 818adj.
distressing 827adj.
lamenting 836adj.
pathfinder
precursor 66n.
traveler 268n.
pathless
spacious 183adj.
closed 264adj.
difficult 700adj.
pathogen
infection 651n.
pathogenic
diseased 651adj.
infectious 653adj.
pathological
diseased 651adj.
medical 658adj.
pathologist
doctor 658n.
pathology
pathology 651n.
medical art 658n.
pathoneurosis
psychopathy 503n.
pathos
feeling 818n.
excitation 821n.
painfulness 827n.
patience
perseverance 600n.
lenity 736n.
patience 823n.
card game 837n.
caution 858n.
forgiveness 909n.
patient
testee 461n.
sick person 651n.
sufferer 825n.
(*see* patience)
patina
layer 207n.
hue 425n.
greenness 432n.
impairment 655n.
blemish 845n.
ritual object 988n.
patio
place 185n.
patisserie
pastry 301n.
patois
specialty 80n.
dialect 560n.
pat on the back
relieve 831vb.
applause 923n.
patriarch
family 11n.
precursor 66n.
old man 133n.
parent 169n.
master 741n.
governor 741n.
ecclesiarch 986n.
patriarchal
olden 127adj.
primal 127adj.
patriarchate
parish 985n.
church office 985n.
parsonage 986n.
patrician
aristocrat 868n.
genteel 868adj.
patricide
homicide 362n.
patrilinear
akin 11adj.
parental 169adj.
patrimony
acquisition 771n.
possession 773n.
dower 777n.
dueness 915n.
patriot
defender 713n.
patriot 901n.
benefactor 903n.
patriotic
(*see* patriotism)
patriotism
love 887n.
patriotism 901n.
disinterestedness 931n.
patripassianism
heresy 977n.
patristic
scriptural 975adj.
patrol
traverse 267vb.
passage 305n.
circler 314n.
spectator 441n.
safeguard 660vb.
defender 713n.
armed force 722n.
restrain 747vb.
patrol-boat
warship 722n.
patron
supporter 218n.
protector 660n.
aider 703n.
patron 707n.
defender 713n.
master 741n.
purchaser 792n.

friend 880n.
kind person 897n.
benefactor 903n.
commender 923n.
patronage
influence 178n.
protection 660n.
management 689n.
aid 703n.
authority 733n.
security 767n.
purchase 792n.
approbation 923n.
benefice 985n.
patronize
endorse 488vb.
choose 605vb.
patronize 703vb.
defend 713vb.
be proud 871vb.
befriend 880vb.
be benevolent 897vb.
patronizing
prideful 871adj.
patronymic
name 561n.
patten
footwear 228n.
patter
be in motion 265vb.
strike 279vb.
rain 350n., vb.
faintness 401n.
roll 403vb.
empty talk 515n.
language 557n.
slang 560n.
be loquacious 581vb.
patterer
speaker 579n.
entertainer 594n.
pattern
correlation 12n.
uniformity 16n.
prototype 23n.
composition 56n.
arrangement 62n.
rule 81n.
example 83n.
form 243n.
structure 331n.
comparison 462n.
paragon 646n.
pattern 844n.
patternless
non-uniform 17adj.
patty
pastry 301n.
patulous
expanded 197adj.
paucity
smallness 33n.
fewness 105n.
littleness 196n.
scarcity 636n.
Paul Pry
inquisitor 453n.
paunch
maw 194n.
insides 224n.
swelling 253n.
eater 301n.
paunchy
fleshy 195adj.
pauper
poor man 801n.
pauperism
non-ownership 774n.
poverty 801n.
pauperize
impoverish 801vb.
pause
discontinuity 72n.
interim 108n.
period 110n.
delay 136n.
lull 145n.
interval 201n.
quiescence 266n.
notation 410n.
be uncertain 474vb.
doubt 486vb.
not act 677vb.
repose 683n.
pave
laminate 207vb.
overlay 226vb.
smooth 258vb.
prepare 669vb.
pavement
base 214n.
basis 218n.
paving 226n.
smoothness 258n.
road, path 624n.
pave the way
prepare 669vb.
facilitate 701vb.
pavilion
pavilion 192n.
arbor 194n.
canopy 226n.
paving-stone
base 214n.
paving 226n.
road 624n.
pavonian
blue 435adj.
iridescent 437adj.
paw
foot 214n.
strike 279vb.
feeler 378n.
touch 378vb.
nippers 778n.
pawky
witty 839adj.
pawl
fastening 47n.
pawn
inferior 35n.
dupe 544n.
fatalist 596n.
instrument 628n.
nonentity 639n.
slave 742n.
security 767n.
transfer 780n.
borrow 785vb.
chessman 837n.
pawnbroker
lender 784n.
pawnee
treasurer 798n.
creditor 802n.
pawn, in
pledged 767adj.
pawnshop
pawnshop 784n.
pax
ritual object 988n.
pay
coat, overlay 226vb.
incentive 612n.
benefit 615vb.
employ 622vb.
be useful 640vb.
earnings 771n.
be profitable 771vb.
restitute 787vb.
pay 804n., vb.
expend 806vb.
receipt 807n.
reward 962n., vb.
payable
owed 803adj.
due 915adj.
pay attention
be attentive 455vb.
court 889vb.
pay back
compensate 31vb.
pay-day
date 108n.
pay 804n.
payee
recipient 782n.
payer
pay 804n.
pay for
patronize 703vb.
purchase 792vb.
defray 804vb.
paying
profitable 640adj.
gainful 771adj.
payload
contents 193n.
paymaster

treasurer 798n.
pay 804n.
payment
quid pro quo 150n.
incentive 612n.
payment 804n.
expenditure 806n.
pay off
navigate 269vb.
disuse 674vb.
make inactive 679vb.
pay-off
end 69n.
pay 804n.
pay out
lengthen 203vb.
retaliate 714vb.
payroll
list 87n.
personnel 686n.
pea
vegetable 301n.
peace
quietude 266n.
euphoria 376n.
silence 399n.
concord 710n.
peace 717n.
pleasurableness 826n.
peaceable
amiable 884adj.
peaceful
inert 175adj.
moderate 177adj.
tranquil 266adj.
comfortable 376adj.
silent 399adj.
reposeful 683adj.
peaceful 717adj.
submitting 721adj.
obedient 739adj.
inexcitable 823adj.
pleasurable 826adj.
content 828adj.
peace-lover
pacifist 717n.
peacemaker
moderator 177n.
pacifist 717n.
mediator 720n.
peacemaking
pacification 719n.
peace offering
irenics 719n.
offering 781n.
propitiation 941n.
peach
fruit 301n.
redness 431n.
inform 524vb.
divulge 526vb.
a beauty 841n.
accuse 928vb.
peacher
tergiversator 603n.
peachy
downy 259adj.
personable 841adj.
peacock
bird 365n.
blueness 435n.
variegation 437n.
exhibitor 522n.
a beauty 841n.
fop 848n.
vain person 873n.
pea-jacket
tunic 228n.
overcoat 228n.
peak
completeness 54n.
extremity 69n.
high land 209n.
summit 213n.
shade 226n.
headgear 228n.
sharp point 256n.
perfection 646n.
be ill 651vb.
peaky
lean 206adj.
sick 651adj.
peal
loudness 400n.
roll 403n., vb.
resonance 404n.
campanology 412n.
gong 414n.
call 547n.
pean
heraldry 547n.
peanut
fruit 301n.
pear
fruit 301n.
pearl
white thing 427n.
type size 587n.
exceller 644n.
a beauty 841n.
gem 844n.
pearlies
clothing 228n.
pearly
semitransparent 424adj.
soft-hued 425adj.
whitish 427adj.
gray 429adj.
iridescent 437adj.
pearly king
fop 848n.
pear-shaped
curved 248adj.
round 250adj.
rotund 252adj.
peasant
dweller 191n.
husbandman 370n.
possessor 776n.
countryman 869n.
pea-shooter
propellant 287n.
air-pipe 353n.
toy gun 723n.
pea-souper
opacity 423n.
peat
fuel 385n.
pebble
hardness 326n.
soil 344n.
pebble dash
facing 226n.
peccable
imperfect 647adj.
peccadillo
trifle 639n.
vice 934n.
guilty act 936n.
peccant
bad 645adj.
diseased 651adj.
wicked 934adj.
guilty 936adj.
peck
great quantity 32n.
eat 301vb.
metrology 465n.
bicker 709vb.
pecker
eater 301n.
peckish
hungry 859adj.
pectinated
sharp 256adj.
pectoral
vestments 989n.
peculation
peculation 788n.
foul play 930n.
peculator
defrauder 789n.
peculiar
different 15adj.
special 80adj.
unusual 84adj.
crazed 503adj.
peculiarity
temperament 5n.
(*see* peculiar)
Peculiar People
particularism 80n.
sect 978n.
peculium
dower 777n.
pecuniary
monetary 797adj.
pedagogic
educational 534adj.

severe 735adj.
pedagogue
scholar 492n.
teacher 537n.
pedagogy
teaching 534n.
pedal
footed 214adj.
propellant 287n.
play music 413vb.
mute 414n.
tool 630n.
pedant
conformist 83n.
narrow mind 481n.
scholar 492n.
sciolist 493n.
teacher 537n.
opinionist 602n.
tyrant 735n.
affector 850n.
perfectionist 862n.
pedantry
attention 455n.
carefulness 457n.
narrow mind 481n.
erudition 490n.
sciolism 491n.
accuracy 494n.
severity 735n.
pretension 850n.
fastidiousness 862n.
peddle
sell 793vb.
peddler
traveler 268n.
peddler 794n.
peddling
trivial 639adj.
parsimonious 816adj.
pederast
libertine 952n.
pedestal
stand 218n.
pedestrian
pedestrian 268n.
prosaic 593adj.
dull 840adj.
pedestrian crossing
traffic control 305n.
road 624n.
pedestrianism
motion 265n.
pediatrician
doctor 658n.
pediatrics
medical art 658n.
pedicel, pedicle
supporter 218n.
pediculosis
formication 378n.
uncleanness 649n.
pedicure
surgery 658n.
beautification 843n.
pedicurist
beautician 843n.
pedigree
series 71n.
list 87n.
genealogy 169n.
nobility 868n.
pediment
summit 213n.
pedometer
meter 465n.
peduncle
supporter 218n.
peek
(*see* peep)
peel
bate 37vb.
leavings 41n.
disjoin 46vb.
unstick 49vb.
layer 207n.
skin 226n.
uncover, doff 229vb.
rubbish 641n.
peeler
stripper 229n.
protector 660n.
police 955n.
peel-house
fort 713n.
peen
hammer 279n.
peep
look 438n.
gaze, scan 438vb.
be curious 453vb.
inquire 459vb.
peepers
eye 438n.
peephole
window 263n.
view 438n.
Peeping Tom
inquisitor 453n.
peep-show
spectacle 445n.
plaything 837n.
pleasure-ground 837n.
peer
compeer 28n.
scan 438vb.
be dim-sighted 440vb.
inquire 459vb.
councillor 692n.
nobleman 868n.
peerage
honors 866n.
aristocracy 868n.
peerless
supreme 34adj.
best 644adj.
noteworthy 866adj.
peeve
enrage 891vb.
peevish
ungracious 885adj.
irascible 892adj.
sullen 893adj.
peg
fastening 47n.
hanger 217n.
stopper 264n.
potion 301n.
tool 630n.
peg at
persevere 600vb.
peg out
die 361vb.
pegs
leg 267n.
peg-top
cone 252n.
peignoir
informal dress 228n.
cleaning cloth 648n.
peine forte et dure
corporal punishment 963n.
pejorative
depreciating 483adj.
word 559n.
disrespectful 921adj.
detracting 926adj.
Pelagianism
heresy 977n.
pelagic
oceanic 343adj.
pelerine
cloak 228n.
pelf
money 797n.
wealth 800n.
pelisse
robe, cloak 228n.
pellagra
disease 651n.
pellet
sphere 252n.
missile 287n.
ammunition 723n.
pellicle
layer 207n.
skin 226n.
pell-mell
confusedly 61adv.
pellucid
transparent 422adj.
intelligible 516adj.
pelorus
direction 281n.
pelota
sphere 252n.
ball game 837n.
pelt
skin 226n.
move fast 277vb.

strike 279vb.
propel 287vb.
rain 350vb.
lapidate 712vb.

peltast
soldier 722n.

peltry
skin 226n.

pemmican
food 301n.

pen
enclosure 235n.
waterfowl 365n.
female animal 373n.
recording instrument 549n.
art equipment 553n.
stationery 586n.
write 586vb.
imprison 747vb.
lock-up 748n.

penal
prohibiting 757adj.
punitive 963adj.

penal code
precept 693n.
law 953n.
penalty 963n.

penalize
be expedient 643vb.
punish 936vb.
make illegal 954vb.

penal servitude
penalty 963n.

penal settlement
prison camp 748n.

penalty
cost 809n.
penalty 963n.

penance
offset 31n.
penitence 939n.
penance 941n.
asceticism 945n.
punishment 963n.
Christian rite 988n.

Penates
mythic god 966n.
lesser god 967n.

penchant
tendency 179n.
willingness 597n.

pencil
radiation 417n.
recording instrument 549n.
art equipment 553n.
paint 553vb.
stationery 586n.
write 586vb.

pencraft
lettering 586n.

pend
continue 108vb.
pend 136vb.

pendant
analogue 18n.
adjunct 40n.
extremity 69n.
pendant 217n.
flag 547n.
jewelry 844n.
trimming 844n.

pendency
interim 108n.
pendency 217n.

pendent
non-adhesive 49adj.
pendent 217adj.

pendicle
pendant 217n.

pending
while 108adv.

pen-driver
penman 586n.

pendular
oscillating 317adj.

pendulous
non-adhesive 49adj.
pendent 217adj.
oscillating 317adj.

pendulum
timekeeper 117n.
periodicity 141n.
pendant 217n.
oscillation 317n.

peneplain
plain 348n.

penetrable
intelligible 516adj.

penetralia
interiority 224n.
latency 523n.
hiding-place 527n.

penetrate
be general 79vb.
pierce 263vb.
infiltrate 297vb.
pass 305vb.
cause thought 449vb.
be wise 498vb.
understand 516vb.
impress 821vb.

penetrating
incoming 297adj.
pungent 388adj.
intelligent 498adj.
felt 818adj.

penetration
interjacence 231n.
ingress 297n.
passage 305n.
sagacity 498n.

pen-friend
correspondent 588n.
chum 880n.

penguin
flightless bird 365n.

penholder
case 194n.
stationery 586n.

penicillin
plant 366n.
drug 658n.

peninsula
region 184n.
projection 254n.
land 344n.
island 349n.

penis
genitalia 164n.

penitence
regret 830n.
penitence 939n.

penitencer
pastor 986n.

penitent
penitent 939n.
repentant 939adj.
ascetic 945n.

penitent form
penance 941n.
pillory 964n.

penitential
atoning 941adj.

penitentiary
prison 748n.
repentant 939adj.
atoning 941adj.
pastor 986n.

penknife
sharp edge 256n.
stationery 586n.

penman
penman 586n.
moneyer 797n.

penmanship
lettering 586n.

pen name
misnomer 562n.

pennant
flag 547n.

penniless
not owning 774adj.
poor 801adj.

penny
coinage 797n.

penny-a-liner
author 589n.

penny dreadful
novel 590n.

penny-farthing
bicycle 274n.

pennyweight
small quantity 33n.
weighment 322n.

penny-wise
parsimonious 816adj.

penology
punishment 963n.

pensile
pendent 217adj.

pension
quarters 192n.
resignation 753n.
earnings 771n.
pay 804n.
receipt 807n.
reward 962n.
pensioner
dependent 742n.
resignation 753n.
recipient 782n.
pension off
disuse 674vb.
not retain 779vb.
pensive
thoughtful 449adj.
abstracted 456adj.
melancholic 834adj.
penstock
conduit 351n.
pentacle
indication 547n.
pentad
five and over 99n.
pentagon
angular figure 247n.
Pentagon
master 741n.
pentameter
prosody 593n.
Pentateuch
law 953n.
scripture 975n.
pentathlon
contest 716n.
penteconter
galley 275n.
Pentecost
holy-day 988n.
penthouse
small house 192n.
flat 192n.
attic 194n.
penultimate
ending 69adj.
penumbra
cone 252n.
half-light 419n.
penurious
careful 457adj.
poor 801adj.
parsimonious 816adj.
penury
poverty 801n.
pen-wiper
stationery 586n.
peon
courier 531n.
infantry 722n.
servant 742n.
peonin
red pigment 431n.
peony
redness 431n.
people
place oneself 187vb.
habitancy 191n.
native 191n.
dwell 192vb.
nation 371n.
social group 371n.
subject 742n.
commonalty 869n.
laity 987n.
peopled
multitudinous 104adj.
pep
vigorousness 174n.
vigor 571n.
restlessness 678n.
pepastic
cathartic 658n.
peplos
robe 228n.
peplum
robe, skirt 228n.
pepper
pierce 263vb.
vegetable 301n.
pungency 388n.
season 388vb.
condiment 389n.
wound 655vb.
fire at 712vb.
pepper-and-salt
whitish 427adj.
gray 429adj.
checker 437n.
peppercorn
condiment 389n.
cheapness 812n.
peppery
pungent 388adj.
irascible 892adj.
peppy
vigorous 174adj.
forceful 571adj.
inducive 612adj.
pepsin
condensation 324n.
thickening 354n.
pep-talk
stimulant 174n.
inducement 612n.
peptic
remedial 658adj.
per
through 628adv.
peragrate
traverse 267vb.
perambulate
walk, traverse 267vb.
perambulator
pushcart 274n.
percale
textile 222n.
per capita
pro rata 783adv.
perceivable
visible 443adj.
perceive
have feeling 374vb.
cognize 447vb.
detect 484vb.
know 490vb.
per cent
ratio 85n.
percentage
increment 36n.
extra 40n.
part 53n.
ratio 85n.
discount 810n.
percentile
statistical 86adj.
percept
idea 451n.
perceptible
seeing 438adj.
visible 443adj.
perception
vision 438n.
intellect 447n.
idea 451n.
discrimination 463n.
knowledge 490n.
sagacity 498n.
perceptive
sentient 374adj.
mental 447adj.
perceptual
mental 447adj.
perch
place oneself 187vb.
nest 192n.
dwell 192vb.
long measure 203n.
basis 218n.
land 295vb.
descend 309vb.
sit down 311vb.
table fish 365n.
sleep 679vb.
repose 683vb.
percheron
drafthorse 273n.
percipience
intellect 447n.
percolate
infiltrate 297vb.
exude 298vb.
pass 305vb.
irrigate 341vb.
flow 350vb.
purify 648vb.
percolator
caldron 194n.
per contra
conversely 467adv.
percussion
impulse 279n.
orchestra 413n.

musical instrument 414n.
percussion instrument
gong 414n.
perdition
ruin 165n.
defeat 728n.
loss 772n.
peregrination
land travel 267n.
peremptory
assertive 532adj.
authoritative 733adj.
commanding 737adj.
compelling 740adj.
obligatory 917adj.
perennial
continuous 71adj.
lasting 113adj.
unchangeable 153adj.
perennity
perpetuity 115n.
perfect
whole 52adj.
complete 54adj.
regular 81adj.
preterition 125n.
excellent 644adj.
perfect 646adj., vb.
mature 669vb.
carry through 725vb.
(*see* perfection)
perfectibility
imperfection 647n.
improvement 654n.
perfection
summit 213n.
goodness 644n.
perfection 646n.
completion 725n.
beauty 841n.
innocence 935n.
perfectionism
carefulness 457n.
reformism 654n.
essay 671n.
discontent 829n.
fastidiousness 862n.
perfectionist
perfectionist 862n.
perfections
beauty 841n.
virtues 933n.
perfective
completive 725adj.
perfidious
(*see* perfidy)
perfidy
unreliability 474n.
latency 523n.
falsehood 541n.
deception 542n.
untruth 543n.
tergiversation 603n.
non-observance 769n.
dutilessness 918n.
perfidy 930n.
perflation
sufflation 352n.
perforate
pierce 263vb.
pass 305vb.
perforation
perforation 263n.
perforator
perforator 263n.
perforce
by force 740adv.
perform
operate 173vb.
be instrumental 628vb.
be useful 640vb.
do one's duty 917vb.
(*see* performance)
performable
possible 469adj.
performance
effect 157n.
production 164n.
music 412n.
musical skill 413n.
representation 551n.
dramaturgy 594n.
action, deed 676n.
effectuation 725n.
observance 768n.
celebration 876n.
ministration 988n.
performer
musician 413n.
interpreter 520n.
entertainer 594n.
doer 676n.
agent 686n.
perfume
emit 300vb.
odor 394n.
scent 396n.
cosmetic 843n.
perfumed
pleasant 376adj.
perfumery
fragrance 396n.
perfunctory
incomplete 55adj.
deficient 307adj.
negligent 458adj.
unwilling 598adj.
imperfect 647adj.
hasty 680adj.
bungled 695adj.
uncompleted 726adj.
indifferent 860adj.
perfusion
transference 272n.
surgery 658n.
pergola
arbor 194n.
perhaps
possibly 469adv.
peri
a beauty 841n.
fairy 970n.
periapt
talisman 983n.
pericarditis
heart disease 651n.
perichondritis
respiratory disease 651n.
pericope
piece 53n.
pericranium
head 213n.
peridot
gem 844n.
perigee
short distance 200n.
perihelion
short distance 200n.
peril
danger 661n.
perimeter
circumjacence 230n.
outline 233n.
enclosure 235n.
limit 236n.
per incuriam
inadvertently 456vb.
negligently 458adv.
period
part 53n.
composition 56n.
end 69n.
time 108n.
period 110n.
periodicity 141n.
regular return 141n.
limit 236n.
punctuation 547n.
phrase 563n.
periodic
discontinuous 72adj.
regular 81adj.
continuing 108adj.
periodic 110adj.
periodic 141adj.
fitful 142adj.
phraseological 563adj.
periodical
journal 528n.
reading matter 589n.
book 589n.
(*see* periodicity)
periodicity
discontinuity 72n.
recurrence 106n.
frequency 139n.
periodicity 141n.
oscillation 317n.
peripatetic
traveling 267adj.

pedestrian 268n.
Peripatetics
philosopher 449n.
peripeteia
revolution 149n.
eventuality 154n.
inexpectation 508n.
disclosure 526n.
peripheral
irrelevant 10adj.
excluded 57adj.
unimportant 639adj.
periphery
distance 199n.
exteriority 223n.
circumjacence 230n.
outline 233n.
enclosure 235n.
limit 236n.
periphrasis
phrase 563n.
pleonasm 570n.
periplus
water travel 269n.
periscope
optical device 442n.
periscopic
visible 443adj.
perish
decompose 51vb.
be destroyed 165vb.
perish 361vb.
be cold 380vb.
deteriorate 655vb.
perishability
transientness 114n.
perishable
ephemeral 114adj.
dying 361adj.
perispomenon
punctuation 547n.
perissology
pleonasm 570n.
peristaltic
labyrinthine 251adj.
elastic 328adj.
peristyle
series 71n.
pavilion 192n.
periwig
wig 228n.
perjurer
liar 545n.
perjury
falsehood 541n.
untruth 543n.
perks
incentive 612n.
earnings 771n.
gift 781n.
reward 962n.
perk up
be refreshed 685vb.
be cheerful 833vb.
perky
cheerful 833adj.
vain 783adj.
perlustration
inspection 438n.
permanence
durability 113n.
permanence 144n.
continuance 146n.
stability 153n.
perseverance 600n.
preservation 666n.
permanency
job 622n.
permanent
continuing 108adj.
habitual 610adj.
(*see* permanence)
permanent way
railroad 624n.
permeable
porous 263adj.
permeate
prevail 178vb.
(*see* permeation)
permeating
ubiquitous 189adj.
permeation
mixture 43n.
presence 189n.
interiority 224n.
interjacence 231n.
passage 305n.
permed
undulatory 251adj.
per mil
ratio 85n.
permissible
possible 469adj.
permitted 756adj.
approvable 923adj.
legal 953adj.
permission
permission 756n.
permit
credential 466n.
make possible 469vb.
assent 488n., vb.
facilitate 701vb.
be lax 734vb.
be lenient 736vb.
give scope 744vb.
commission 751n.
permit 756n., vb.
consent 758vb.
convey 780vb.
permitted
reputable 866adj.
permutation
numerical operation 86n.
change 143n.
interchange 151n.
pernicious
harmful 645adj.
pernicity
velocity 277n.
pernickety
fastidious 862adj.
perorate
be diffuse 570vb.
peroration
sequel 67n.
end 69n.
oration 579n.
eloquence 579n.
peroxide
pigment 425n.
bleacher 426n.
hairwash 843n.
perpend
meditate 449vb.
notice 455vb.
estimate 480vb.
perpendicular
vertical 215adj.
straight 249adj.
written 586adj.
perpetrate
do 676vb.
be clumsy 695vb.
do wrong 914vb.
perpetrator
doer 676n.
agent 686n.
perpetual
existing 1adj.
frequent 139adj.
(*see* perpetuity)
perpetuate
perpetuate 115vb.
sustain 146vb.
perpetuation
perpetuity 115n.
continuance 146n.
perpetuity
continuity 71n.
infinity 107n.
diuturnity 113n.
permanence 144n.
continuance 146n.
perplex
bedevil 63vb.
distract 456vb.
puzzle 474vb.
incommode 827vb.
perplexity
dubiety 474n.
unintelligibility 517n.
difficulty 700n.
perquisite
earnings 771n.
receipt 807n.
reward 962n.
perquisites
gift 781n.
perquisition
search 459n.

perry
liquor 301n.
per se
singly 88adv.
perse
blue 435adj.
persecute
ill-treat 645vb.
torment 827vb.
be pitiless 906vb.
(*see* persecution)
persecuted
suffering 825adj.
persecution
destruction 165n.
counteraction 182n.
prejudice 481n.
pursuit 619n.
severity 735n.
enmity 881n.
cruel act 898n.
penalty 963n.
orthodoxism 976n.
pietism 979n.
persecutor
opinionist 602n.
tyrant 735n.
punisher 963n.
religionist 979n.
perseverance
continuance 146n.
perseverance 600n.
obstinacy 602n.
persevere
stay 144vb.
stand firm 599vb.
exert oneself 682vb.
persevering
unyielding 162adj.
industrious 678adj.
Persian wheel
extractor 304n.
irrigator 341n.
persienne
shade 226n.
curtain 421n.
persiflage
witticism 839n.
ridicule 851n.
persist
be active 678vb.
persistence
uniformity 16n.
permanence 144n.
continuance 146n.
perseverance 600n.
persistent
lasting 113adj.
unyielding 162adj.
remembered 505adj.
person
substance 3n.
self 80n.
object 319n.
person 371n.
person of repute 866n.
personable
personable 841adj.
personage
person 371n.
bigwig 638n.
persona grata
friend 880n.
favorite 896n.
personal
substantial 3adj.
intrinsic 5adj.
unimitative 21adj.
special, private 80adj.
human 371adj.
possessed 773adj.
proprietary 777adj.
impertinent 878adj.
selfish 932adj.
personal attendance
presence 189n.
personal characteristic
specialty 80n.
personal column
advertisement 528n.
personal considerations
selfishness 932n.
personal effects
property 777n.
personal equation
specialty 80n.
personality
substantiality 3n.
intrinsicality 5n.
specialty, self 80n.
influence 178n.
materiality 319n.
spirit 447n.
bigwig 638n.
affections 817n.
sauciness 878n.
rudeness 885n.
scurrility 899n.
calumny 926n.
personalize
specify 80vb.
personal recognizance
security 767n.
legal process 959n.
personalty
property 777n.
personal world
circumstance 8n.
persona non grata
enemy 881n.
personate
represent 551vb.
act 594vb.
personification
metaphor 519n.
representation 551n.
acting 594n.
personify
materialize 319vb.
manifest 522vb.
personnel
band 74n.
personnel 686n.
means 629n.
perspectival
relative 9adj.
seeing 438adj.
perspective
relativeness 9n.
range 183n.
length 203n.
depth 211n.
convergence 293n.
view 438n.
spectacle 445n.
perspicacious
(*see* perspicacity)
perspicacity
vision 438n.
sagacity 498n.
fastidiousness 862n.
perspicuity
intelligibility 516n.
perspicuity 567n.
elegance 575n.
perspicuous
semantic 514adj.
stylistic 566adj.
perspiration
outflow 298n.
excretion 302n.
perspire
exude 298vb.
emit 300vb.
be wet 341vb.
be hot 379vb.
persuade
convince 485vb.
induce 612vb.
request 761vb.
persuaded
positive 473adj.
believing 485adj.
persuader
motivator 612n.
persuasibility
credulity 487n.
willingness 597n.
persuasibility 612n.
persuasible
impressible 819adj.
persuasion
classification 77n.
influence 178n.
positiveness 473n.
belief, opinion 485n.
teaching 534n.
inducement 612n.
persuasive
influential 178adj.
plausible 471adj.
credible 485adj.

induciive 612adj.
pert
cheerful 833adj.
impertinent 878adj.
discourteous 885adj.
pertain
be related 9vb.
be included 78vb.
belong 773vb.
pertinacity
perseverance 600n.
pertinence
relevance 9n.
fitness 24n.
pertness
sauciness 878n.
rudeness 885n.
perturbation
derangement 63n.
stimulation 174n.
agitation 318n.
excitation 821n.
excitable state 822n.
nervousness 854n.
pertussis
respiratory disease 651n.
peruke
wig 228n.
perusal
study 536n.
pervade
fill 54vb.
be general 79vb.
prevail 178vb.
pervade 189vb.
lie between 231vb.
pass 305vb.
pervasion
mixture 43n.
presence 189n.
interiority 224n.
pervasive
universal 79adj.
ubiquitous 189adj.
perverse
erroneous 495adj.
willful 602adj.
difficult 700adj.
perversion
conversion 147n.
obliquity 220n.
distortion 246n.
misinterpretation 521n.
misteaching 535n.
falsehood 541n.
untruth 543n.
deterioration 665n.
misuse 675n.
impiety 980n.
perversity
(*see* perverse)
pervert
derange 63vb.
nonconformist 84n.
modify 143vb.
changed person 147n.
transform 147vb.
distort 246vb.
mislead 495vb.
harm 645vb.
pervert 655vb.
make wicked 934vb.
cad 938n.
libertine 952n.
(*see* perversion)
pervicacity
obstinacy 602n.
pervious
porous 263adj.
pesky
annoying 827adj.
pessary
surgical dressing 658n.
pessimism
overestimation 482n.
underestimation 483n.
dejection 834n.
hopelessness 853n.
nervousness 854n.
pessimist
loser 728n.
moper 834n.
alarmist 854n.
pest
vermin 365n.
evil 616n.
plague 651n.
bane 659n.
worry 825n.
annoyance 827n.
hateful object 888n.
noxious animal 904n.
pester
recur 139vb.
meddle 678vb.
torment 827vb.
enrage 891vb.
pest-house
insalubrity 653n.
hospital 658n.
pesticide
poison 569n.
pestiferous
infectious 653adj.
pestilence
badness 645n.
plague 651n.
pestilent
infectious 653adj.
baneful 659adj.
pestilential
toxic 653adj.
hateful 888adj.
pestle
hammer 279n.
pulverizer 332n.
pet
animal 365n.
look after 457vb.
chosen 605adj.
be lenient 736vb.
please 826vb.
love 887vb.
pet, caress 889vb.
darling 890n.
anger 891n.
philanthropize 897vb.
petal
flower 366n.
petard
gun 723n.
petard, hoist with one's own
retaliate 714vb.
petasos
headgear 228n.
peter out
end 69vb.
cease 145vb.
Peter's pence
offering 781n.
tax 809n.
petiole
foliage 366n.
petite
little 196adj.
shapely 841adj.
petite amie
kept woman 952n.
petition
remind 505vb.
request 761n., vb.
deprecate 762vb.
litigation 959n.
prayers 981n.
petitionary
devotional 981adj.
petitioner
petitioner 763n.
malcontent 829n.
litigant 959n.
petition-writer
notary 958n.
petitio principii
sophism 477n.
petit-maître
fop 848n.
petit mal
paralysis 651n.
petit point
needlework 844n.
Petrarchan
poetic 593adj.
petrel
bird of prey 365n.
petrifaction
condensation 324n.
hardening 326n.
petrify
be dense 324vb.

harden 326vb.
refrigerate 382vb.
impress 821vb.
frighten 854vb.
be wonderful 864vb.
petroglyph
sculpture 554n.
petrol
propellant 287n.
oil 357n.
fuel 385n.
petroleum
oil 357n.
pétroleur
incendiarism 381n.
petrology
mineralogy 359n.
petronel
pistol 723n.
petticoat
bodywear 228n.
woman 373n.
petticoat government
gynocracy 733n.
pettifog
deceive 542vb.
pettifogger
trickster 545n.
lawyer 958n.
pettifogging
trivial 369adj.
sophistical 477adj.
trickery 542n.
rascally 930adj.
pettiness
(*see* petty)
petting
endearment 889n.
pettish
irascible 892adj.
sullen 893adj.
petty
inconsiderable 33adj.
little 196adj.
unimportant 639adj.
contemptible 922adj.
selfish 932adj.
petty officer
naval officer 741n.
petulance
sauciness 878n.
irascibility 892n.
pew
compartment 194n.
seat 218n.
church interior 990n.
pewter
a mixture 43n.
white thing 427n.
phaeton
carriage 274n.
phalanx
coherence 48n.
multitude 104n.
solid body 324n.
party 708n.
army, formation 722n.
phallic
impure 951adj.
phallus
genitalia 164n.
phantasm
visual fallacy 440n.
appearance 445n.
ghost 970n.
phantasmagoria
medley 43n.
visual fallacy 440n.
spectacle 445n.
phantom
the dead 361n.
visual fallacy 440n.
fantasy 513n.
ghost 970n.
pharaoh
sovereign 741n.
Pharisaic
sectarian 978adj.
pietistic 979adj.
pharisaical
hypocritical 541adj.
pharisaism
duplicity 541n.
false piety 980n.
Pharisees
non-Christian sect 978n.
pharmaceutics
medical art 658n.
pharmacist
druggist 658n.
pharmacology
medical art 658n.
pharmacopoeia
medicine 658n.
pharmacy
hospital 658n.
pharos
sailing aid 269n.
pharyngitis
respiratory disease 651n.
phase
modality 7n.
be identical 13vb.
arrange 62vb.
time 117vb.
synchronize 123vb.
appearance 445n.
phase, in
agreeing 24adj.
pheasant
table bird 365n.
phenomenal
unusual 84adj.
appearing 445adj.
wonderful 864adj.
phenomenalism
philosophy 449n.
phenomenon
eventuality 154n.
appearance 445n.
prodigy 864n.
phial
vessel 194n.
philander
excite love 887vb.
court 889vb.
philanderer
lover 887n.
libertine 952n.
philanthropic
friendly 880adj.
philanthropic 901adj.
virtuous 933adj.
philanthropist
reformer 654n.
kind person 897n.
philanthropist 901n.
good man 937n.
philanthropy
benevolence 897n.
philanthropy 901n.
disinterestedness 931n.
philatelist
collector 492n.
philharmonic
musical 412adj.
philippic
censure 924n.
oration 579n.
philistine
conformist 83n.
ignorance 491n.
artless 699adj.
vulgarian 847n.
commoner 869n.
philistinism
artlessness 699n.
moral insensibility 820n.
bad taste 847n.
philological
semantic 514adj.
philologist
collector 492n.
linguist 557n.
etymology 559n.
philology
linguistics 557n.
etymology 559n.
grammar 564n.
philomath
scholar 492n.
philoprogenitive
productive 164adj.
generative 171adj.
philosophe
intellectual 492n.
philosopheme
argumentation 475n.
philosopher

philosopher 449n.
inquirer 459n.
sage 500n.
philosopher's stone
remedy 658n.
philosophic
philosophic 449adj.
inexcitable 823adj.
patient 823adj.
content 828adj.
philosophize
meditate 449vb.
reason 475vb.
philosophy
intellect 447n.
philosophy 449n.
philter
stimulant 174n.
spell 983n.
magic instrument 983n.
phiz
face 237n.
feature 445n.
phlebitis
blood pressure 651n.
phlebotomy
voidance 300n.
surgery 658n.
phlegm
excrement 302n.
semiliquidity 354n.
sluggishness 679n.
moral insensibility 820n.
phlegmatic
slow 278adj.
viscid 354adj.
non-active 677adj.
impassive 820adj.
indifferent 860adj.
phlegmatism
incuriosity 454n.
phlogiston
heat 379n.
phobia
psychopathy 503n.
phobia 854n.
hatred 888n.
phoenix
rara avis 84n.
reproduction 166n.
paragon 646n.
mythical being 970n.
phoenix-like
restored 656adj.
phonate
sound 398vb.
phone
speech sound 398n.
hearing aid 415n.
spoken letter 558n.
phoneme
spoken letter 558n.
word 559n.
phone-tapper
inquisitor 453n.
phone-tapping
listening 415n.
phonetic
sounding 398adj.
literal 558adj.
vocal 577adj.
phonetician
acoustics 398n.
linguist 557n.
phonetics
acoustics 398n.
phonics
acoustics 398n.
phonogram
speech sound 398n.
writing 586n.
phonograph
sound 398n.
phonograph 414n.
hearing aid 415n.
phonograph record
repetition 106n.
rotator 315n.
phonography
writing 586n.
phonology
acoustics 398n.
etymology 559n.
phony
imitative 20adj.
false 541adj.
spurious 542adj.
untrue 543adj.
phosphorescence
glow 417n.
phosphorescent
luminescent 420adj.
phosphorus
food content 301n.
luminary 420n.
photics
optics 417n.
photo
(*see* photograph)
photoelectric cell
radiation 417n.
photo finish
draw 28n.
short distance 200n.
photogenic
representing 551adj.
beautiful 841adj.
photograph
copy 22n.
photography 551n.
photographer
recorder 549n.
photographic
lifelike 18adj.
accurate 494adj.
representing 551adj.
descriptive 590adj.
photography
optics 417n.
camera 442n.
photography 551n.
photogravure
picture 553n.
printing 555n.
photolithography
printing 555n.
photolysis
decomposition 51n.
photometer
optical device 442n.
photometry
optics 417n.
photomicroscope
microscope 442n.
photon
particle 33n.
element 319n.
radiation 417n.
photoplay
cinema 445n.
photoprint
duplicate 22n.
photography 551n.
picture 553n.
photosphere
sun 321n.
photostat
copy 22n.
recording instrument 549n.
photography 551n.
phototherapy
therapy 658n.
phrase
subdivision 53n.
tune 412n.
word 559n.
phrase 563n.
style 566n.
phrasemonger
phrasemonger 574n.
stylist 575n.
phraseology
phrase 563n.
style 566n.
phratry
family 11n.
phrenetic
frenzied 503adj.
phrenology
hermeneutics 520n.
Phrygian mode
key 410n.
phthiriasis
formication 378n.
uncleanness 649n.
phthisis
phthisis 651n.

phylactery
maxim 496n.
talisman 983n.
phyle
race 11n.
phyletic
ethnic 11adj.
parental 169adj.
phylogeny
genealogy 169n.
biology 358n.
phylum
breed 77n.
physic
cure 656vb.
medicine 658n.
physical
real 1adj.
substantial 3adj.
material 319adj.
sensuous 376adj.
physical culture
civilization 654n.
physical energy
energy 160n.
vigorousness 174n.
physical jerks
education 534n.
physical science
physics 319n.
physical wreck
dilapidation 655n.
physician
doctor 658n.
physics
physics 319n.
physiocrat
economy 814n.
physiognomy
face 237n.
form 243n.
feature 445n.
physiography
geography 321n.
uranometry 321n.
physiology
structure 331n.
biology 358n.
physiotherapy
therapy 658n.
physique
vitality 162n.
structure 331n.
animality 365n.
phytography
biology 358n.
botany 368n.
phytology, phytonomy
botany 368n.
pi
pietistic 979adj.
piacular
atoning 941adj.
piaffer
gait 265n.
equitation 267n.
slowness 278n.
pia mater
head 213n.
pianissimo
faintly 401adv.
adagio 412adv.
pianist
instrumentalist 413n.
piano
slowly 278adv.
muted 401adj.
faintly 401adv.
adagio 412adv.
piano 414n.
dejected 834adj.
pianoforte, pianola
piano 414n.
pibroch
musical piece 412n.
war 718n.
pica
type size 587n.
picador
killer 362n.
combatant 722n.
picaresque
descriptive 590adj.
rascally 930adj.
picaroon
robber 789n.
piccolo
flute 414n.
pice
small coin 33n.
pick
sharp point 256n.
perforator 263n.
extractor 304n.
cultivate 370vb.
choice 605n.
chief thing 638n.
elite 644n.
clean 648vb.
acquire 771vb.
take 786vb.
steal 788vb.
pick a bone with
bicker 709vb.
pick and choose
be capricious 604vb.
select 605vb.
be fastidious 862vb.
picaninny
child 132n.
negro 428n.
pickax
sharp point 256n.
perforator 263n.
extractor 304n.
picked man
proficient 696n.
picker
accumulator 74n.
husbandman 370n.
picker and chooser
perfectionist 862n.
picket
tie 45vb.
circumscribe 232vb.
be obstructive 702vb.
defender 713n.
armed force 722n.
fetter 747vb.
punish 963vb.
picketing
hindrance 702n.
pick holes
dispraise, blame 924vb.
detract 926vb.
pickings
choice 605n.
earnings 771n.
booty 790n.
pickle
state 7n.
circumstance 8n.
drench 341vb.
season 388vb.
store 632vb.
preserver 666n.
predicament 700n.
inebriate 949vb.
pickles
condiment 389n.
pick-me-up
stimulant 174n.
pungency 388n.
tonic 658n.
excitant 821n.
pick off
fire at 712vb.
pick one's steps
be careful 457vb.
pick out
set apart 46vb.
extract 304vb.
see 438vb.
discriminate 463vb.
select 605vb.
pickpocket
thief 789n.
picksome
fastidious 862adj.
pickthank
meddler 678n.
toady 879n.
flatterer 925n.
pick the brains
interrogate 459vb.
pick up
accelerate 277vb.
detect 484vb.
get better 654vb.
arrest 747vb.
acquire 771vb.

pick-up
phonograph 414n.
prostitute 952n.
Pickwickian
absurd 497adj.
funny 849adj.
picnic
meal 301n.
easy thing 701n.
participation 775n.
amusement 837n.
pictogram
letter 558n.
lettering 586n.
pictorial
representing 551adj.
painted 553adj.
picture
composition 56n.
spectacle 445n.
imagine 513vb.
represent 551vb.
picture 553n.
describe 590vb.
a beauty 841n.
picture-book
picture 553n.
picture-frame
art equipment 553n.
picture-gallery
art equipment 553n.
picture, in the
informed 524adj.
picture palace
cinema 445n.
theater 594n.
picturesque
descriptive 590adj.
impressive 821adj.
pleasurable 826adj.
beautiful 841adj.
ornamental 844adj.
picture-writing
symbology 547n.
representation 551n.
writing 586n.
piddle
be inactive 679vb.
excrete 302vb.
pidgin
language 557n.
dialect 560n.
neological 560adj.
pie
small coin 33n.
medley 43n.
pastry 301n.
sweet 392n.
color 425vb.
print-type 587n.
easy thing 701n.
piebald
horse 273n.
pied 437adj.
piece
small thing 33n.
piece 53n.
incompleteness 55n.
unit 88n.
product 164n.
textile 222n.
musical piece 412n.
stage play 594n.
gun 723n.
portion 783n.
chessman 837n.
loose woman 952n.
piece, collector's
(*see* collector's piece)
pièce de résistance
dish 301n.
exceller 644n.
masterpiece 694n.
piecegoods
textile 222n.
piecemeal
piecemeal 53adv.
piece, of a
uniform 16adj.
similar 18adj.
simple 44adj.
piece of cake
easy thing 701n.
piece of one's mind
reprimand 924n.
piece together
join 45vb.
make complete 54vb.
decipher 520vb.
repair 656vb.
piecework
labor 682n.
pie-crust
brittleness 330n.
pastry 301n.
pied
pied 437adj.
Pied Piper
musician 413n.
sorcerer 983n.
pie in the sky
fantasy 513n.
pier
stable 192n.
street 192n.
supporter 218n.
projection 254n.
arena 724n.
pierce
cut 46vb.
pierce 263vb.
pass 305vb.
give pain 377vb.
wound 655vb.
impress 821vb.
piercing
perforation 263n.
cold 380adj.
loud 400adj.
strident 407adj.
felt 818adj.
pier-glass
mirror 442n.
Pierian
poetic 593adj.
pierrette, pierrot
actor 594n.
entertainer 594n.
pietà
art subject 553n.
ritual object 988n.
pietism
pietism 979n.
pietist
affector 850n.
pietist 979n.
piety
religion 973n.
piety 979n.
worship 981n
piffle
silly talk 515n.
piffling
unmeaning 515adj.
trivial 639adj.
pig
pig 365n.
dirty person 649n.
cad 938n.
sensualist 944n.
glutton 947n.
pigeon
bird 365n.
credulity 487n.
dupe 544n.
defraud 788vb.
pigeoncote
stable 192n.
pigeon-hearted
cowardly 856adj.
pigeon-hole
class 62vb.
classification 77n.
put off 136vb.
place 185n.
compartment 194n.
be neglectful 458vb.
pigeon-post
mails 531n.
pigeon's neck
variegation 437n.
pigeon-toed
deformed 246adj.
blemished 845adj.
piggery
stock farm 369n.
piggin
vessel 194n.
piggyback
astride 218adv.
bearing 273adv.

pig-headed
unintelligent 499adj.
obstinate 602adj.
pig in a poke
uncertainty 474n.
gambling 618n.
piglet
youngling 132n.
pig 365n.
pigment
pigment 425n.
pigmentation
hue 425n.
blackness 428n.
pigment-deficiency
achromatism 426n.
pigmy
dwarf 196n.
pignoration
security 767n.
pigpen
stable 192n.
sink 649n.
pigskin
skin 226n.
bookbinding 589n.
pigsticker
side-arms 723n.
pigsticking
chase 619n.
pigsty
cattle pen 369n.
sink 649n.
pigtail
pendant 217n.
rear 238n.
hair 259n.
pig together
congregate 74vb.
pi-jaw
empty talk 515n.
pike
high land 209n.
sharp point 256n.
fish 365n.
road 624n.
soldiery 722n.
spear 723n.
piker
gambler 618n.
pilaster
pillar 218n.
projection 254n.
ornamental art 844n.
pilaf, pilau, pilaff
dish 301n.
pile
fastening 47n.
accumulation 74n.
edifice 164n.
high structure 209n.
pillar 218n.
hair 259n.
texture 331n.
heraldry 547n.
store 632vb.
acquisition 771n.
wealth 800n.
pile-driver
ram, hammer 279n.
pile in
fill 54vb.
start out 296vb.
enter 297vb.
pile on
add 38vb.
piles
swelling 253n.
pile up
bring together 74vb.
exaggerate 546vb.
store 632vb.
superabound 637vb.
acquire 771vb.
pile-up
collision 279n.
pilfer
steal 788vb.
pilferer
thief 789n.
pilgrim
traveler 268n.
pietist 979n.
worshiper 981n.
pilgrimage
land travel 267n.
piety 979n.
pilgrimage, place of
focus 76n.
holy place 990n.
Pilgrim Fathers
settler 191n.
pill
mouthful 301n.
medicine 658n.
punishment 963n.
pillage
rob 788vb.
booty 790n.
pillager
robber 789n.
pillar
fixture 153n.
high structure 209n.
pillar 218n.
monument 548n.
refuge 662n.
person of repute 866n.
seclusion 883n.
Pillars of Hercules
limit 236n.
signpost 547n.
pillars to post, from
in transit 272adv.
irresolutely 601adv.
round about 626adv.
pillbox
headgear 228n.
cylinder 252n.
fort 713n.
pill, coat the
sweeten 392vb.
pillion
seat 218n.
pilliwinks
instrument of torture 964n.
pillory
hanger 217n.
fetter 747vb.
lock-up 748n.
satirize 851vb.
shame 867vb.
dispraise 924vb.
defame 926vb.
accuse 928vb.
penitence 939n.
punish 963vb.
pillory 964n.
pillow
cushion 218n.
support 218vb.
softness 327n.
euphoria 376n.
relief 831n.
pillow-case
covering 226n.
pilose
hairy 259adj.
pilot
aeronaut 271n.
navigate 269vb.
navigator 270n.
direct 689vb.
director 690n.
pilotage, pilotship
navigation 269n.
directorship 689n.
pilot scheme
experiment 461n.
pimento
vegetable 301n.
condiment 389n.
pimp
provider 633n.
cad 938n.
be impure 951vb.
bawd 952n.
pimple
monticle 209n.
lowness 210n.
swelling 253n.
skin disease 651n.
blemish 845n.
pimply
convex 253adj.
pin
join 45vb.
fastening 47n.
sharp point 256n.

perforator 263n.
trifle 639n.
restrain 747vb.
retain 778vb.
jewelry 844n.
pinafore
apron 228n.
pince-nez
eyeglass 442n.
pincer movement
convergence 293n.
attack 712n.
pincers
cross 222n.
extractor 304n.
nippers 778n.
pinch
circumstance 8n.
small quantity 33n.
certain quantity 104n.
crisis 137n.
make smaller 198vb.
make thin 200vb.
notch 260vb.
converge 293vb.
pang 377n.
touch 378vb.
needfulness 627n.
predicament 700n.
adversity 731n.
arrest 747vb.
steal 788vb.
poverty 801n.
economize 814vb.
be parsimonious 816vb.
endearment 889n.
pinch, at a
in need 627adv.
with difficulty 700adv.
pinchbeck
spurious 542adj.
trivial 639adj.
pinch of salt, with a
doubtfully 486adv.
pin-cushion
receptacle 194n.
pin down
place 187vb.
compel 740vb.
pine
tree 366n.
animal disease 651n.
be ill 651vb.
pineapple
fruit 301n.
pine for
desire 859vb.
pine-needle
foliage 366n.
pinery
wood 366n.
garden 370n.
pinfold
enclosure 235n.
cattle pen 369n.
ping
roll 403n.
resonance 404n.
ping-pong
ball game 837n.
pinguescence
unctuousness 357n.
pinguid
fatty 357adj.
pin-head
minuteness 196n.
dunce 501n.
pin-hole
orifice 263n.
pinion
tie 45vb.
plumage 259n.
wing 271n.
fetter 747vb.
pink
moderate 177adj.
notch 260vb.
pierce 263vb.
strike 279vb.
redness 431n.
perfection 646n.
wound 655vb.
pink of condition
health 650n.
pin-money
dower 777n.
money 797n.
receipt 807n.
pinna
ear 415n.
pinnace
boat 275n.
pinnacle
summit 213n.
pinnate
flying 271adj.
pinned down
fixed 153adj.
pin on
affix 45vb.
accuse 928vb.
pinpoint
small thing 33n.
specify 80vb.
place 185n., vb.
minuteness 196n.
orientate 281vb.
pin-prick
trifle 639n.
annoyance 827n.
enrage 891vb.
pins
leg 267n.
conveyance 267n.
pins and needles
formication 378n.
pinscher
dog 365n.
pin-stripe
pattern 844n.
pint
metrology 465n.
pin-table
plaything 837n.
pintle
pivot 218n.
pinto
horse 273n.
pied 437adj.
pint-size
little 196adj.
pinup girl
a beauty 841n.
favorite 890n.
pioneer
come before 64vb.
precursor 66n.
initiate 68vb.
settler 191n.
traveler 268n.
preparer 669n.
undertake 672vb.
direct 689vb.
facilitate 701vb.
soldiery 722n.
pious
believing 485adj.
pious 979adj.
pious fraud
duplicity 541n.
mental dishonesty 543n.
false piety 980n.
pious hope
improbability 472n.
aspiration 852n.
pip
timekeeper 117n.
powder 332n.
signal 547n.
pipe
vat 194n.
cylinder 252n.
tube 263n.
conduit 351n.
blow 352vb.
air-pipe 353n.
tobacco 388n.
stridor 407n.
shrill 407vb.
ululate 409vb.
play music 413vb.
flute 414n.
metrology 465n.
store 632n.
pipe-band
orchestra 413n.
pipeclay
white thing 427n.
practice 610n.
pipe-cleaner

tobacco 388n.
cleaning utensil 648n.
pipe down
cease 145vb.
be quiescent 266vb.
be taciturn 582vb.
pipe-dream
insubstantial thing 4n.
fantasy 513n.
pleasurableness 826n.
aspiration 852n.
pipe-line
tube 263n.
conduit 351n.
store 632n.
provide 633vb.
pipe of peace
peace 717n.
irenics 719n.
piper
instrumentalist 413n.
pipe-rack
tobacco 388n.
pipette
tube 263n.
pipe up
cry 408vb.
speak 579vb.
pip, have the
be sullen 893vb.
piping
edging 234n.
tube 263n.
stridor 407n.
peaceful 717adj.
trimming 844n.
piping times
palmy days 730n.
pipkin
vessel 194n.
pipped
defeated 728adj.
pippin
fruit 301n.
darling 890n.
pips
badge, livery 547n.
badge of rank 743n.
pipsqueak
dwarf 196n.
nonentity 639n.
piquancy
unconformity 84n.
pungency 388n.
vigor 571n.
joy 824n.
piquant
aphoristic 496adj.
exciting 821adj.
impure 951adj.
pique
excite 821vb.
hurt 827vb.
discontent 829n.
resentment 891n.
piracy
brigandage 788n.
pirate
mariner 270n.
militarist 722n.
steal 788vb.
robber 789n.
enemy 881n.
knave 938n.
piratical
thieving 788adj.
pirouette
rotation 315n.
pis aller
substitute 150n.
expedience 642n.
inexpedience 643n.
imperfection 647n.
compromise 770vb.
piscatorial
animal 365adj.
Pisces
zodiac 321n.
pisciculture
animal husbandry 369n.
piscina
lake 346n.
drain 351n.
stock farm 369n.
ritual object 988n.
church utensil 990n.
piss
excrete 302vb.
pistachio nut
fruit 301n.
pistol
kill 362vb.
pistol 723n.
piston
periodicity 141n.
stopper 264n.
pit
depth 211n.
interiority 224n.
cavity 255n.
tunnel 263n.
trap 542n.
playgoer 594n.
pitfall 663n.
stratagem 698n.
blemish 845vb.
pit against
oppose 704vb.
make quarrels 709vb.
pit-a-pat
agitation 318n.
jerkily 318adv.
pitch
adjust 24vb.
degree 27n.
serial place 73n.
territory 184n.
place 185n.
dwell 192vb.
height 209n.
summit 213n.
make vertical 215vb.
coat 266vb.
voyage 269vb.
propel 287vb.
tumble 309vb.
depress 311vb.
oscillate 317vb.
be agitated 318vb.
resin 357n.
sound 398n.
musical note 410n.
black thing 428n.
voice 577n.
arena 734n.
pitcher
vessel 194n.
thrower 287n.
pitchfork
shovel 274n.
propel 287vb.
farm tool 370n.
pitch into
attack 712vb.
fight 716vb.
pitch on
place oneself 187vb.
meet 295vb.
acquire 771vb.
pitch-pipe
flute 414n.
pitchy
resinous 357adj.
dark 418adj.
black 428adj.
piteous
pitiable 905adj.
pitfall
invisibility 444n.
latency 523n.
ambush 527n.
trap 542n.
danger 661n.
pitfall 663n.
stratagem 698n.
pith
substance 3n.
essential part 5n.
vitality 162n.
interiority 224n.
centrality 225n.
pulpiness 356n.
topic 452n.
meaning 514n.
importance 638n.
pithecanthropus
mankind 371n.
pithily
concisely 569vb.
pithless

weak 163adj.
pithy
substantial 3adj.
soft 327adj.
aphoristic 496adj.
meaningful 514adj.
concise 569adj.
compendious 592adj.
pitiable
unimportant 639adj.
bad 645adj.
unhappy 825adj.
distressing 827adj.
pitiable 905adj.
contemptible 922adj.
pitiful
unimportant 639adj.
bad 645adj.
distressing 827adj.
disreputable 867adj.
benevolent 897adj.
pitying 905adj.
pitiable 905adj.
pitilessness
resolution 599n.
severity 735n.
pitilessness 906n.
pittance
finite quantity 26n.
insufficiency 636n.
portion 783n.
receipt 807n.
pitted
rough 259adj.
blemished 845adj.
pittite
playgoer 594n.
pituita
semiliquidity 354n.
pity
lenity 736n.
lamentation 836n.
benevolence 897n.
pity 905n., vb.
pivot
joint 45n.
causal means 156n.
influence 178n.
pivot 218n.
centrality 225n.
chief thing 638n.
pivotal
important 638adj.
pivot on
depend 157vb.
pixie, pixy
elf 970n.
pixilated
crazed 503adj.
placability
benevolence 897n.
mercy 905n.
forgiveness 909n.
placard
exhibit 522n.
advertisement 528n.
placate
pacify 719vb.
place
degree 27n.
order 60n.
arrange 62vb.
serial place 73n.
specify 80vb.
region 184n.
place 185n.
situation 186n.
locality 187n.
abode 192n.
meal 301n.
discover 484vb.
authority 733n.
place after
place after 65vb.
place-hunting
greedy 859adj.
placeman
consignee 754n.
placement, placing
arrangement 62n.
location 187n.
placenta
sequel 67n.
obstetrics 164n.
placet
decree 737n.
place under
number with 78vb.
placidity
inexcitability 823n.
placket
pocket 194n.
plage
shore 344n.
plagiarism
imitation 20n.
copy 22n.
repetition 106n.
stealing 788n.
plagiarist
imitator 20n.
plagiarize
fake 541vb.
borrow 785vb.
plagihedral
oblique 220adj.
plague
recur 139vb.
badness 645n.
plague 651n.
bane, blight 659n.
be difficult 700vb.
adversity 731n.
oppress 735vb.
annoyance 827n.
ruffian 904n.
plague-spot
badness 645n.
sink 649n.
infection 651n.
insalubrity 653n.
plague-stricken
diseased 651adj.
infectious 653adj.
plaguey
evil 616adj.
not nice 645adj.
infectious 653adj.
baneful 659adj.
difficult 700adj.
annoying 827adj.
plaice
fish food 301n.
table fish 365n.
plaid
shawl 228n.
checker 437n.
plain
simple 44adj.
space 183n.
lowness 210n.
horizontality 216n.
open space 263n.
land 344n.
plain 348n.
soft-hued 425adj.
well-seen 443adj.
meaningful 514adj.
intelligible 516adj.
manifest 522adj.
undisguised 522adj.
informative 524adj.
assertive 532adj.
veracious 540adj.
stylistic 566adj.
plain 573adj.
elegant 575adj.
prosaic 593adj.
artless 699adj.
lament 836vb.
tedious 838adj.
ugly 842n.
tasteful 846adj.
plebeian 869adj.
disrespectful 921adj.
temperate 942adj.
ascetic 945adj.
plain-clothes man
detective 459n.
police 955n.
plain dealing
veracity 540n.
plain living
temperance 942n.
asceticism 945n.
plain man
common man 30n.
ingenue 699n.
plainness
simpleness 44n.
unsavoriness 391n.

dullness 840n.
probity 929n.
(*see* plain)
plain sailing
navigation 269n.
easy thing 701n.
plainsman
dweller 191n.
plainsong
vocal music 412n.
plain speaking
intelligibility 516n.
veracity 540n.
plain-spoken
intelligible 516adj.
undisguised 522adj.
informative 524adj.
plaint
cry 408n.
discontent 829n.
lament 836n.
accusation 928n.
plaintiff
malcontent 829n.
accuser 928n.
litigant 959n.
plaintive
lamenting 836adj.
plaintiveness
cry 408n.
plait
tie 45vb.
ligature 47n.
crossing 222n.
weave 222vb.
hair 259n.
fold 261n.
plan
prototype 23n.
arrangement 62n.
predestine 155vb.
cause 156vb.
produce 164vb.
itinerary 267n.
structure 331n.
foresight 510n.
guide-book 524n.
map 551n.
predetermine 608vb.
intention 617n.
plan 623n., vb.
preparation 669n.
undertaking 672n.
tactics 688n.
be cunning 698vb.
planchette
spiritualism 984n.
plane
horizontality 216n.
sharp edge 256n.
smoother 258n.
fly 271vb.
aircraft 276n.
tree 366n.
plane sailing
navigation 269n.
planet, planetoid
rotator 315n.
planet 321n.
planetarium
astronomy 321n.
planetary, planetoidal
planetary 321adj.
planets
fate 596n.
plangency
loudness 400n.
resonance 404n.
lamentation 836n.
plangent
(*see* plangency)
planimeter
meter 465n.
planing
aeronautics 271n.
planisphere
gauge 465n.
plank
lamina 207n.
shelf 218n.
policy 623n.
materials 631n.
planless
orderless 61adj.
designless 618adj.
planner
producer 167n.
theorist 512n.
motivator 612n.
planner 623n.
meddler 678n.
expert 696n.
plan out
plan 623vb.
plant
make fruitful 171vb.
place 187vb.
aim 281vb.
implant 303vb.
cultivate 370vb.
trap 542n.
workshop 687n.
property 777n.
false charge 928n.
plantain
fruit 301n.
plantation
habitancy 191n.
maturation 669n.
(*see* farm)
planted
firm-set 45adj.
arboreal 366adj.
agrarian 370adj.
planter
producer 167n.
settler 191n.
husbandman 370n.
preparer 669n.
plaque
lamina 207n.
honors 866n.
plash
flow 250vb.
sound faint 401vb.
resound 404vb.
sibilation 406n.
plasma
matter 319n.
fluid, blood 335n.
plasmic
formative 243adj.
organic 358adj.
plaster
adhesive 47n.
flatten 216vb.
wrapping 226n.
coat 226vb.
repair 656vb.
surgical dressing 658n.
fire at 712vb.
relieve 831vb.
plastic
unstable 152adj.
formative 243adj.
flexible 327adj.
materials 631n.
impressible 819adj.
plasticine
softness 327n.
sculpture 554n.
plasticity
changeableness 152n.
softness 327n.
moral sensibility 819n.
plastic surgery
surgery 658n.
beautification 843n.
plate
mold 23n.
plate 194n.
lamina 207n.
horizontality 216n.
coat 226vb.
circle 250n.
tooth 256n.
camera 442n.
label 547n.
photography 551n.
picture 553n.
print 587n.
edition 589n.
trophy 729n.
plateau
high land 209n.
horizontality 216n.
vertex 213n.
plain 348n.
plateful
finite quantity 26n.

plate glass
lamina 207n.
transparency 422n.
platelet
blood 335n.
platform
layer 207n.
horizontality 216n.
stand 218n.
publicity 528n.
rostrum 539n.
policy 623n.
railroad 624n.
arena 724n.
platinum
white thing 427n.
yellow 433adj.
bullion 797n.
platitude
unmeaningness 515n.
platitudinous
dull 840adj.
Platonic
pure 950adj.
Platonism
immateriality 320n.
philosophy 449n.
platoon
band 74n.
formation 722n.
platter
plate 194n.
horizontality 216n.
plaudits
rejoicing 835n.
applause 923n.
plausible
plausible 471adj.
sophistical 477adj.
credible 485adj.
hypocritical 541adj.
ostensible 614adj.
promising 852adj.
flattering 925adj.
vindicable 927adj.
plausive
approving 923adj.
play
agency 173n.
operate 173vb.
range 183n.
oscillate 317vb.
flow 350vb.
play music 413vb.
flash 417n.
variegate 437vb.
stage play 594n.
gambling 618n.
action 676n.
easy thing 701n.
parry 713vb.
contend 716vb.
scope 744n.
amusement 837n.
caress 889vb.
play-act
dissemble 541vb.
act 594vb.
be affected 850vb.
play a part
influence 178vb.
dissemble 541vb.
act 594vb.
do 676vb.
play at
be inattentive 456vb.
play back
repeat 106vb.
play-back
phonograph 414n.
play ball
cooperate 706vb.
playbill
list 87n.
playbook
stage play 594n.
playboy
reveler 837n.
play double
be dishonest 930vb.
play down
underestimate 483vb.
player
instrumentalist 413n.
interpreter 520n.
actor 594n.
gambler 618n.
doer 676n.
agent 686n.
player 837n.
play false
tergiversate 603vb.
playful
capricious 604adj.
gay 833adj.
amused 837adj.
witty 839adj.
innocent 935adj.
playgoer
playgoer 594n.
play gooseberry
look after 457vb.
safeguard 660vb.
playground
arena 724n.
pleasure-ground 837n.
playhouse
theater 594n.
place of amusement 837n.
play, in
operative 173adj.
in jest 839adv.
playing field
arena 724n.
pleasure-ground 837n.
play lead
act 594vb.
have repute 866vb.
playmate
colleague 707n.
player 837n.
chum 880n.
play off
use 673vb.
play out
terminate 69vb.
playroom
chamber 194n.
play safe
seek safety 660vb.
be cautious 858vb.
play second fiddle
be inferior 35vb.
obey 739vb.
have no repute 867vb.
be modest 874vb.
playsuit
beachwear 228n.
play the fool
be absurd 497vb.
amuse oneself 837vb.
be rash 857vb.
play the game
behave 688vb.
be honorable 929vb.
play the market
speculate 791vb.
plaything
bauble 639n.
plaything 837n.
playtime
interim 108n.
festivity 837n.
play to the gallery
be affected 850vb.
be ostentatious 875vb.
play tricks
befool 542vb.
be capricious 604vb.
be cunning 698vb.
amuse oneself 837vb.
play up
overrate 482vb.
disobey 738vb.
play upon
operate 173vb.
motivate 612vb.
play upon words
absurdity 497n.
equivocalness 518n.
wit 839n.
play with
distract 456vb.
neglect 458vb.
be expert 694vb.
caress 889vb.
playwright
author 589n.
dramatist 594n.
plea

testimony 466n.
argument 475n.
pretext 614n.
request 761n.
vindication 927n.
litigation 959n.

pleach
weave 222vb.

plead
testify 466vb.
argue 475vb.
plead 614vb.
justify 927vb.
do law 958vb.
litigate 959vb.

pleader
intermediary 231n.
reasoner 475n.
speaker 579n.
motivator 612n.
mediator 720n.
law agent 958n.

pleadings
legal trial 959n.

pleasance
pleasance 192n.
pleasure-ground 837n.

pleasant
pleasant 376adj.
pleasurable 826adj.
amusing 837adj.
witty 839adj.

pleasantry
wit 839n.

please
please 826vb.
content 828vb.
cheer 833vb.
amuse 837vb.

pleased
willing 597adj.

please oneself
will 595vb.
please oneself 734vb.
be free 744vb.

pleasurable
pleasurable 826adj.

pleasure
pleasure 376n.
easy thing 701n.
joy 824n.
amusement 837n.

pleasure-ground
pleasance 192n.
pleasure-ground 837n.

pleasure-loving
sensuous 376adj.
sensual 944adj.

pleasure-seeker
reveler 837n.

pleasure, with
willingly 597adv.

pleat
fold 261n., vb.

plebeian
ill-bred 847adj.
commonalty 869n.
plebeian 869adj.

plebiscite
judgment 480n.
vote 605n.
decree 737n.
legislation 953n.

plectrum
harp 414n.

pledge
thing transferred 272n.
drink 301vb.
oath 532n.
promise 764n., vb.
security 767n.
convey 780vb.
borrow 785vb.
toast 876vb.
duty 917n.

pledgee
treasure 798n.
creditor 802n.

pledget
covering 226n.
stopper 264n.
surgical dressing 658n.

pledgor
debtor 803n.

Pleistocene
secular 110adj.

plenary
complete 54adj.

plenipotentiary
delegate, envoy 754n.

plenitude
greatness 32n.
plenitude 54n.
plenty 635n.

plentiful
great 32adj.
plenteous 635adj.

plenty
great quantity 32n.
productiveness 171n.
store 632n.
plenty 635n.
liberality 635n.
redundance 637n.
prosperity 730n.
wealth 800n.

plenum
substantiality 3n.
materiality 319n.
universe 321n.

pleonasm
pleonasm 570n.

pleonastic
pleonastic 570adj.
superfluous 637adj.

Plesianthropus
mankind 371n.

plesiosaurus
animal 365n.

plethora
redundance 637n.
satiety 863n.

pleura
laterality 239n.

plexure
crossing 222n.

plexus
network 222n.

pliable
flexible 327adj.

pliancy
conformity 83n.
changeableness 152n.
softness 327n.
willingness 597n.
irresolution 601n.
persuasibility 612n.
facility 701n.
obedience 739n.
servility 879n.

pliant
(*see* pliancy)

plication
fold 261n.

pliers
extractor 304n.
tool 630n.
nippers 778n.

plight
state 7n.
circumstance 8n.
adversity 731n.
promise 764n.

plimsoll
footwear 228n.

Plimsoll line
gauge 465n.

plinth
base 214n.
stand 218n.

Pliocene
secular 110adj.

plod
walk 267vb.
move slowly 278vb.
persevere 600vb.
work 682vb.

plonk
crackle 402vb.
non-resonance 405n.

plop
plunge 313vb.
non-resonance 405n.

plosive
speech sound 398n.

plot
combination 50n.
grassland 348n.
garden 370n.
topic 452n.

gauge 465vb.
represent 551vb.
narrative 590n.
dramaturgy 594n.
plot 623n., vb.
prepare 669vb.
stratagem 698n.
compact 765n.

plotter
deceiver 545n.
planner 623n.
slyboots 698n.

plow
cut 46vb.
groove 262vb.
farm tool 370n.
cultivate 370vb.
disapprove 924vb.

plow back
economize 814vb.

plowman
husbandman 370n.
preparer 669n.
countryman 869n.

plow-share
sharp edge 256n.
farm tool 370n.

ploy
job 622n.
stratagem 698n.

pluck
rend 46vb.
insides 224n.
uncover 229vb.
move 265vb.
draw 288vb.
extract 304vb.
agitate 318vb.
cultivate 370vb.
touch 378vb.
deceive 542vb.
resolution 599n.
stamina 600n.
take 786vb.
fleece 786vb.
defraud 788vb.
courage 855n.
disapprove 924vb.

pluck a crow with
bicker 709vb.

plucked
unsuccessful 728adj.

plucking
hair-dressing 843n.

plucky
persevering 600adj.
courageous 855adj.

plug
repeat oneself 106vb.
go on 146vb.
covering 226n.
stopper 264n.
stanch 350vb.
tobacco 388n.
advertise 528vb.
emphasize 532vb.
persevere 600vb.

plug in
connect 45vb.

plug-ugly
low fellow 869n.
ruffian 904n.

plum
over one hundred 99n.
fruit 301n.
redness 431n.
elite 644n.
trophy 729n.
desired object 859n.

plumage
plumage 259n.
wing 271n.
softness 327n.

plumb
positively 32adv.
be deep 211vb.
vertical 215adj.
straight on 249adv.
smooth 258adj.
plunge 313vb.
measure 465vb.

plumbago
lubricant 334n.

plumber
mender 656n.
artisan 686n.

plumbing
conduit 351n.
cleansing 648n.

plumb-line
verticality 215n.

plume
headgear 228n.
plumage 259n.
trimming 844n.

plume oneself
feel pride 871vb.
be vain 873vb.

plummet
depth 211n.
verticality 215n.
sailing aid 269n.
diver 313n.
gravity 322n.

plump
instantaneously 116adv.
fleshy 195adj.
tumble 309vb.
plunge 313vb.
non-resonance 405n.

plump for
choose 605vb.

plumpness
bulk 195n.

plump up
enlarge 197vb.

plunder
acquisition 771n.
take away 786vb.
rob 788vb.
booty 790n.

plunderer
robber 789n.

plunge
decrease 37n., vb.
revolution 149n.
be destroyed 165vb.
be deep 211vb.
motion 265vb.
aquatics 269n.
impel 279vb.
enter 297vb.
immersion 303n., vb.
descent 309n.
depress 311vb.
leap 312vb.
plunge 313n., vb.
fluctuate 317vb.
be agitated 318vb.
drench 341vb.
gambling 618n.
ablution 648n.
be cheap 812vb.
be rash 857vb.
be intemperate 943vb.

plunge into
enter 297vb.
undertake 672vb.

plunger
diver 313n.
gambler 618n.
desperado 857n.

plunging
deep 211adj.

plunk
non-resonance 405n.

pluperfect
preterition 125n.

plural
grammatical 564adj.

pluralist
cleric 986n.

plurality
plurality 101n.
greater number 104n.

plus
difference 15n.
in addition 38adv.

plus fours
breeches 228n.

plush
hair 259n.
softness 327n.
rich 800adj.
ornamental 844adj.

plushy
ostentatious 875adj.

plus sign
punctuation 547n.

Pluto
planet 321n.
conduit 351n.
death 361n.
mythic god 966n.
Olympian god 967n.
plutocracy
government 733n.
wealth 800n.
rich man 800n.
plutocrat
master 741n.
rich man 800n.
plutonian
planetary 321adj.
infernal 972adj.
plutonic
fiery 379adj.
pluvial
humid 341adj.
rainy 350adj.
pluviometer
hygrometry 341n.
ply
be periodic 141vb.
layer 207n.
fold 261n.
voyage 269vb.
busy oneself 622vb.
use 673vb.
do 676vb.
work 682vb.
Plymouth Brethren
sect 978n.
pneuma
spirit 447n.
pneumatic
soft 327adj.
gaseous 336adj.
airy 340adj.
pneumatics
gaseity 336n.
pneumatics 340n.
anemology 352n.
pneumatoscopic
immaterial 320adj.
pneumonia
respiratory disease 651n.
poaceous
vegetal 366adj.
poach
cook 301vb.
encroach 306vb.
steal 788vb.
poached, poachy
rough 259adj.
marshy 347adj.
poacher
thief 789n.
pock
blemish 845vb.
pocked
mottled 437adj.
pocket
classification 77n.
place 185n.
stow 187vb.
pocket 194n.
little 196adj.
opening 263n.
insert 303vb.
battleground 724n.
receive 782vb.
take 786vb.
treasury 799n.
be patient 823n.
pocket borough
electorate 605n.
pocket-money
receipt 807n.
pocket-size
little 196adj.
pock-mark
cavity 255n.
maculation 437n.
skin disease 651n.
pod
receptacle 194n.
skin 226n.
podgy
fleshy 195adj.
podium
seat, stand 218n.
poem
poem 593n.
poet
author 589n.
poet 593n.
poetic
imaginative 513adj.
poetic 593adj.
poetic justice
retaliation 714n.
punishment 963n.
poetics
poetry 593n.
poetry
ideality 513n.
reading matter 589n.
poetry 593n.
pogrom
slaughter 362n.
poignancy
keenness 174n.
pungency 388n.
vigor 571n.
poignant
painful 377adj.
felt 818adj.
point
juncture 8n.
relevance 9n.
degree 27n.
small thing 33n.
extremity 69n.
serial place 73n.
unit 88n.
instant 116n.
keenness 174n.
place 185n.
situation 186n.
minuteness 196n.
projection 254n.
sharpen 256vb.
aim, point to 281vb.
topic 452n.
reasons 475n.
punctuation 547n.
gesticulate 547vb.
mark 547vb.
lettering 586n.
use 673n.
point a moral
teach 534vb.
point at
aim at 617vb.
not respect 921vb.
accuse 928vb.
point at issue
topic 452n.
question 459n.
casus belli 709n.
point, beside the
irrelevant 10adj.
point-blank
toward 281adv.
plainly 573adv.
point-device
regular 83adj.
pointedness
sharpness 256n.
wit 839n.
pointer
dog 365n.
indicator 547n.
pointillism
school of painting 553n.
point, in
apt 24adj.
pointless
insubstantial 4adj.
irrelevant 10adj.
unsharpened 257adj.
prolix 570adj.
useless 641adj.
dull 840adj.
point of difference
specialty 80n.
point of honor
probity 929n.
point of no return
juncture 8n.
limit 236n.
progression 285n.
point of view
situation 186n.
view 438n.
appearance 445n.
idea 451n.
bias 481n.

opinion 485n.
point out
specify 80vb.
orientate 281vb.
attract notice 455vb.
show 522vb.
inform 524vb.
indicate 547vb.
points
vantage 34n.
numeration 86n.
railroad 624n.
points of the compass
laterality 239n.
point to
attribute 158vb.
point to 281vb.
predict 511vb.
mean 514vb.
indicate 547vb.
point-to-point
racing 716n.
point, to the
relevant 9adj.
rational 475adj.
concise 569adj.
poise
equality 28n.
conduct 688n.
inexcitability 823n.
poised
well-bred 848adj.
poison
destroy 165vb.
destroyer 168n.
murder 362vb.
unsavoriness 390n.
be unpalatable 391vb.
motivate 612vb.
make unclean 649vb.
impair 655vb.
poison 659n.
excite hate 888vb.
enrage 891vb.
be malevolent 898vb.
poisoner
murderer 362n.
poisoning 659n.
offender 904n.
poison gas
gas 336n.
poison 659n.
weapon 723n.
poisonous
deadly 362adj.
unsavory 391n.
not nice 645adj.
harmful 645adj.
unclean 649adj.
diseased 651adj.
toxic 653adj.
baneful 659adj.
dangerous 661adj.
paining 827adj.
maleficent 898adj.
intoxicating 949adj.
poison pen
correspondent 588n.
defamer 926n.
poke
make violent 176vb.
pocket 194n.
pierce 263vb.
gesticulate 547vb.
doctor 658vb.
poke at
strike 279vb.
strike at 712vb.
poke fun
be witty 839vb.
ridicule 851vb.
poke out
jut 254vb.
poker
furnace 383n.
card game 837n.
poker-faced
still 266adj.
unintelligible 517adj.
reticent 525adj.
impassive 820adj.
pokerwork
ornamental art 844n.
poking
inquiring 459adj.
poky
restraining 747adj.
graceless 842adj.
polar
ending 69adj.
topmost 213adj.
opposite 240adj.
telluric 321adj.
cold 380adj.
Polaris
star 321n.
signpost 547n.
directorship 689n.
polariscope
optical device 442n.
polarity
polarity 14n.
duality 90n.
tendency 179n.
counteraction 182n.
contraposition 240n.
opposition 704n.
polarization
reflection 417n.
pole
extremity 69n.
measure 183n.
farness 199n.
long measure 203n.
high structure 209n.
summit 213n.
verticality 215n.
pivot 218n.
limit 236n.
gauge 465n.
pole-ax
slaughter 362vb.
ax 723n.
polecat
vermin 365n.
fetor 397n.
polemic
reasoner 475n.
argument 475n.
quarrel 709n.
polemics
argument 475n.
conference 584n.
contention 716n.
poles asunder
contrary 14adj.
different 15adj.
pole star
signpost 547n.
directorship 689n.
pole to pole, from
widely 183adv.
afar 199adv.
police
order 60vb.
protector 660n.
safeguard 660vb.
manage 689vb.
rule 733vb.
restrain 747vb.
police 955n.
police action
war 718n.
police inquiry
police inquiry 459n.
policeman
protector 660n.
police 955n.
police state
despotism 733n.
police station
lock-up 748n.
policy
topic 452n.
sagacity 498n.
policy 623n.
action 676n.
tactics 688n.
cunning 698n.
title-deed 767n.
poliomyelitis
infection 651n.
paralysis 651n.
polis
polity 733n.
polish
facing 226n.
smoothness 258n.
friction 333n.
make bright 417vb.
elegance 575n.
cleanness 648n.

amendment 654n.
beauty 841n.
good taste 846n.
etiquette 848n.
polish off
carry through 725vb.
polite
literary 557adj.
elegant 575adj.
well-bred 848adj.
courteous 884adj.
respectful 920adj.
politic
wise 498adj.
expedient 642adj.
skillful 694adj.
political
governmental 733adj.
political economy
management 689n.
politician
manager 690n.
expert 696n.
political party 708n.
politics
tactics 688n.
polity
government 733n.
polity 733n.
polka
musical piece 412n.
dance 837n.
poll
numeration 86n.
make smaller 198vb.
shorten 204vb.
inquiry 459n.
judgment 480n.
vote 605n., vb.
pollard
make smaller 198vb.
shorten 204vb.
tree 366n.
pollen
genitalia 164n.
powder 332n.
pollex
finger 378n.
pollination
propagation 164n.
pollinator
producer 166vb.
pollinctor
interment 364n.
polliniferous
productive 164adj.
pollinosis
excretion 302n.
pollster
computer 86n.
inquirer 459n.
experimenter 461n.
poll tax
tax 809n.
pollution
uncleanness 649n.
infection 651n.
insalubrity 653n.
impairment 655n.
misuse 675n.
slur 867n.
Pollyanna
cheerfulness 833n.
polo
ball game 837n.
polonaise
musical piece 412n.
dance 837n.
poltergeist
hinderer 702n.
elf, ghost 970n.
poltergeistery
spiritualism 984n.
poltroonery
cowardice 856n.
polyandry
type of marriage 894n.
polychromatic
colored 425adj.
variegated 437adj.
polychrome
multiform 82adj.
variegation 437n.
painting 553n.
polygamy
type of marriage 894n.
polygastric
cellular 194adj.
polygenous
multiform 82adj.
polyglot
interpreter 520n.
linguist 557n.
linguistic 557adj.
polygon
angular figure 247n.
polygraphy
writing 586n.
polygynist
polygamist 894n.
polyhedron
angular figure 247n.
polymath, become a
study 536vb.
polymorphism
multiformity 82n.
polyphony
melody 410n.
polypsychism
multiformity 82n.
polypus
swelling 253n.
polysyllabic
long 203adj.
diffuse 570adj.
polysyllable
speech sound 398n.
spoken letter 558n.
word 559n.
polytechnic
trade school 539n.
polytheism
deism 973n.
pomade, pomatum
unguent 357n.
scent 396n.
cosmetic 843n.
pomander
scent 396n.
pomegranate
fruit 301n.
pomiculture
agriculture 370n.
pommel
handle 218n.
sphere 252n.
pommy
foreigner 59n.
pomp
pride 871n.
ostentation 875n.
pompadour
hair 259n.
hair-dressing 843n.
pom-pom
gun 723n.
trimming 844n.
pomposity
magniloquence 574n.
inelegance 576n.
pride 871n.
ostentation 875n.
pompous
vain 873adj.
(*see* pomposity)
ponce
libertine 952n.
poncho
cloak 228n.
pond
shallowness 212n.
lake 346n.
ponder
meditate 449vb.
estimate 480vb.
ponderability
substantiality 3n.
ponderable
material 319adj.
weighty 322adj.
ponderous
weighty 322adj.
inelegant 576adj.
clumsy 695adj.
pongee
textile 222n.
pongo
soldier 722n.
pongyi

monk 986n.
priest 986n.
poniard
sharp point 256n.
side-arms 723n.
pons asinorum
unintelligibility 517n.
pontiff
priest 986n.
pontifical
positive 473adj.
assertive 532adj.
ecclesiastical 985adj.
vestmental 989adj.
pontificals
vestments 989n.
pontificate
dogmatize 473vb.
be biased 481vb.
affirm 532vb.
church office 985n.
pontoon
bridge 624n.
card game 837n.
pony
over twenty 99n.
pony 273n.
funds 797n.
pony-tail
hair 259n.
hair-dressing 843n.
poodle
dog 365n.
poodlefake
caress 889vb.
pooh-pooh
disregard 458vb.
underestimate 483vb.
hold cheap 922vb.
pool
lake 346n.
store 632vb.
association 706n.
acquisition 771n.
joint possession 775n.
ball game 837n.
pool room
gaming-house 618n.
poop
poop 238n.
poor
weak 163adj.
unproductive 172adj.
feeble 572adj.
necessitous 627adj.
insufficient 636adj.
unimportant 639adj.
bad 645adj.
imperfect 647adj.
unprosperous 731adj.
unfortunate 731adj.
not owning 774adj.
poor 801adj.
unhappy 825adj.
disreputable 867adj.
poor hand
bungler 697n.
poor head
unintelligence 499n.
poorhouse
retreat 192n.
shelter 662n.
poor in spirit
humble 872adj.
poorly
slightly 33adv.
weakly 163adj.
sick 651adj.
poor opinion
disapprobation 924n.
poor quality
inferiority 35n.
poor rate
(*see* poor relief)
poor relation
inferior 35n.
imperfection 647n.
poor relief
subvention 703n.
sociology 901n.
poor white
low fellow 869n.
pop
parent 169n.
jut 254vb.
soft drink 301n.
sound faint 401vb.
give security 767vb.
borrow 785vb.
pope
sovereign 741n.
ecclesiarch 986n.
popedom
churchdom 985n.
popery
Catholicism 976n.
pop-eyed
wondering 864adj.
pop-gun
bang 402n.
toy gun 723n.
plaything 837n.
popinjay
fop 848n.
poplar
tree 366n.
Poplarism
sociology 901n.
poplin
textile 222n.
popliteal
back 238adj.
crural 267adj.
pop out
jut 254vb.
emerge 298vb.
poppet
darling 890n.
popple
crinkle 251vb.
roughen 259vb.
be agitated 318vb.
flow 350vb.
poppy
redness 431n.
soporific 679n.
poppycock
empty talk 515n.
pop-shop
pawnshop 784n.
pop singer
person of repute 866n.
popsy
darling 890n.
pop the question
interrogate 459vb.
request 761vb.
court 889vb.
populace
habitancy 191n.
commonalty 869n.
popular
general 79adj.
native 191adj.
intelligible 516adj.
governmental 733adj.
reputable 866adj.
welcomed 882adj.
approved 923adj.
laical 987adj.
Popular Front
association 706n.
political party 708n.
popularity
repute 866n.
sociability 882n.
lovableness 887n.
approbation 923n.
popularize
be intelligible 516vb.
interpret 520vb.
facilitate 701vb.
vulgarize 847vb.
popular will
government 733n.
populate
be fruitful 171vb.
place oneself 187vb.
dwell 192vb.
appropriate 786vb.
populated
multitudinous 104adj.
population
location 187n.
habitancy 191n.
social group 371n.
populous
assembled 74adj.
multitudinous 104adj.
pop up
reoccur 106vb.
happen 154vb.

chance 159vb.
arrive 295vb.
be visible 443vb.
appear 445vb.
porcelain
pottery 381n.
porch
entrance 68n.
lobby 194n.
threshold 234n.
doorway 263n.
access 624n.
church exterior 990n.
porcine
animal 365adj.
porcupine
prickle 256n.
rodent 365n.
pore
cavity 255n.
orifice 263n.
outlet 298n.
scan 438vb.
be attentive 455vb.
study 536vb.
porism
question 459n.
judgment 480n.
pork
meat 301n.
pork barrel
booty 790n.
treasury 799n.
porker
pig 365n.
pornography
impurity 951n.
porosity
cavity 255n.
porosity 263n.
porpoise
fish 365n.
porridge
cereal 301n.
pulpiness 356n.
porringer
bowl 194n.
port
stable 192n.
sinistrality 242n.
window 263n.
gait 265n.
goal 295n.
wine 301n.
mien 445n.
shelter 662n.
conduct 688n.
portable
little 196adj.
transferable 272adj.
light 323adj.
portage
transport 272n.
portal
threshold 234n.
doorway 263n.
portcullis
barrier 235n.
obstacle 702n.
fort 713n.
portend
predict 511vb.
portent
omen 511n.
prodigy 864n.
portentous
presageful 511adj.
frightening 854adj.
threatening 900adj.
porter
janitor 264n.
bearer 273n.
liquor 301n.
worker 686n.
servant 742n.
porterage
transport 272n.
portfire
lighter 385n.
portfolio
list 87n.
case 194n.
collection 632n.
title-deed 767n.
estate 777n.
jurisdiction 955n.
porthole
window 263n.
portico
entrance 68n.
series 71n.
lobby 194n.
pillar 218n.
temple 990n.
portion
part 53n.
fraction 102n.
meal 301n.
provision 633n.
participation 775n.
dower 777n.
portion 783n.
portionless
poor 801adj.
portly
fleshy 195adj.
portmanteau
box 194n.
storage 632n.
portmanteau word
assemblage 74n.
conciseness 569n.
portolano, portulan
sailing aid 269n.
map 551n.
portrait
copy 22n.
picture 553n.
portraiture
assimilation 18n.
mimicry 20n.
representation 551n.
art style 553n.
portray
paint 553vb.
(*see* portrayal)
portrayal
assimilation 18n.
mimicry 20n.
representation 551n.
description 590n.
pose
imitate 20vb.
be example 23vb.
situation 186n.
interrogate 459vb.
represent 551vb.
conduct 688n.
be affected 850vb.
poser
living model 23n.
question 459n.
enigma 530n.
art equipment 553n.
difficulty 700n.
affector 850n.
poseur
affector 850n.
posh
fashionable 848adj.
posit
premise 475vb.
suppose 512vb.
position
state 7n.
degree 27n.
order 60n.
arrange 62vb.
serial place 73n.
situation 186n.
station 187n.
opinion 485n.
supposition 572n.
job 622n.
prestige 866n.
positive
real 1adj.
copy 22n.
absolute 32adj.
numerical 85adj.
positive 473adj.
narrow-minded 481adj.
believing 485adj.
intelligible 516adj.
forceful 571adj.
obstinate 602adj.
positiveness
affirmation 532n.
positivism
materiality 319n.
philosophy 449n.

positron
particle 33n.
element 319n.
posology
measurement 465n.
medical art 658n.
posse
band 74n.
possess
dwell 192vb.
know 490vb.
make mad 503vb.
inform 524vb.
possess 773vb.
dower 777vb.
excite 821vb.
diabolize 969vb.
possessed
obsessed 455adj.
frenzied 503adj.
possession
territory 184n.
use 673n.
possession 773n.
property 777n.
excitation 821n.
enjoyment 824n.
spell 983n.
possessive
acquiring 771adj.
taking 786n.
avaricious 816adj.
greedy 859adj.
loving 887adj.
jealous 911adj.
selfish 932adj.
possessiveness
exclusion 57n.
(*see* possessive)
possessor
resident 191n.
master 741n.
possessor 776n.
posset
liquor 301n.
possibility
existence 1n.
opportunity 137n.
fair chance 159n.
ability 160n.
liability 180n.
possibility 469n.
probability 471n.
expectation 507n.
supposition 512n.
possible
unreal 2adj.
future 124adj.
accessible 289adj.
possible 469adj.
latent 523adj.
easy 701adj.
(*see* possibility)
post
subsequent 120adj.
situation 186n.
place 187vb.
pillar 218n.
travel 267vb.
transpose 272vb.
send 272vb.
move fast 277vb.
communicate 524vb.
advertise 528vb.
mails 531n.
register 548vb.
correspondence 588n.
job 622n.
hasten 680vb.
commission 751vb.
account 808vb.
shame 867vb.
impose a duty 917vb.
postage
price 809n.
postal
epistolary 588adj.
postal order
paper money 797n.
postbag
correspondence 588n.
postbox
mails 531n.
postboy
driver 268n.
rider 268n.
servant 742n.
postcard
message 529n.
correspondence 588n.
post chaise
stage-coach 274n.
post-Christian
dated 108adj.
subsequent 120adj.
irreligious 974adj.
postdate
misdate 118vb.
posted
informed 524adj.
poster
advertisement 528n.
poste restante
mails 531n.
posterior
sequent 65adj.
subsequent 120adj.
future 124adj.
back, buttocks 238adj.
posterity
survivor 41n.
sequence 65n.
aftercomer 67n.
posteriority 120n.
futurity 124n
posterity 170n.
postern
entrance 68n.
back 238adj.
doorway 263n.
fort 713n.
postexistence
future state 124n.
destiny 155n.
postfix
add 38vb.
adjunct 40n.
part of speech 564n.
posthaste
speeding 277n.
hastily 680adv.
posthumous
subsequent 120adj.
late 136adj.
postilion
driver 268n.
rider 268n.
servant 742n.
posting
location 187n.
transference 272n.
mandate 751n.
postliminious
subsequent 120adj.
late 136adj.
postlude
sequel 67n.
stage play 594n.
postman
bearer 273n.
mails 531n.
postmeridian
vespertine 129adj.
postmortem
death 361n.
post-obit 361adv.
inquest 364n.
in memoriam 364adv.
inquiry 459n.
postnate
subsequent 120adj.
postnatus
posteriority 120n.
post-obit
posteriority 120n.
subsequent 120adj.
post-obit 361adv.
in memoriam 364adv.
post office
transferrer 272n.
mails 531n.
postpone
put off 136vb.
avoid 620vb.
relinquish 621vb.
not complete 726vb.
postponement
unwillingness 598n.
(*see* postpone)
postposition

adjunct 40n.
sequence 65n.
part of speech 564n.
postprandial
subsequent 120adj.
reposeful 683adj.
sociable 882adj.
postscript
adjunct 40n.
sequel 67n.
extremity 69n.
postulant
petitioner 703n.
nun 986n.
layman 987n.
postulate
premise 475n., vb.
axiom 496n.
supposition 512n.
request 761n.
posture
circumstance 8n.
situation 186n.
form 243n.
mien 445n.
conduct 688n.
be affected 850vb.
postwar
dated 108adj.
subsequent 120adj.
peaceful 717adj.
posy
bunch 74n.
ornamentation 844n.
love-token 889n.
pot
vessel 194n.
shorten 204vb.
propulsion 287n.
insert 303vb.
pottery 381n.
abstract 592vb.
preserve 666vb.
trophy 729n.
reward 962n.
potable
edible 301adj.
potation
drinking 301n.
drunkenness 949n.
potato
tuber 301n.
pot-bellied
fleshy 195adj.
expanded 197adj.
rotund 252adj.
convex 253adj.
potboiler
book 589n.
reading matter 589n.
novel 590n.
potboiling
trivial 639adj.
pot-boy
servant 742n.
poteen
liquor 301n.
potency
power 160n.
strength 162n.
utility 640n.
potent
productive 164adj.
generative 171adj.
operative 173adj.
vigorous 174adj.
influential 178n.
intoxicating 949adj.
(*see* potency)
potentate
potentate 741n.
potential
unreal 2adj.
intrinsic 5adj.
quantity 26n.
future 124adj.
energy 160n.
electricity 160n.
(*see* potentiality)
potentiality
existence 1n.
intrinsicality 5n.
ability 160n.
influence 178n.
liability 180n.
possibility 469n.
latency 523n.
pother
turmoil 61n.
excitable state 822n.
pot herb
pot herb 301n.
condiment 389n.
pot-hole
cavity 255n.
orifice 263n.
pot-holing
search 459n.
discovery 484n.
pot-hook
lettering 586n.
pothouse
tavern 192n.
pot-hunter
contender 716n.
player 837n.
potion
potion 301n.
medicine 658n.
pot-luck
chance 159n.
meal 301n.
gambling 618n.
non-preparation 670n.
sociability 882n.
potpourri
medley 43n.
scent 396n.
musical piece 412n.
potsherd
piece 53n.
pot-shot
propulsion 287n.
potted
short 204adj.
compendious 592adj.
preserved 666adj.
tipsy 949adj.
potter
epitomizer 592n.
be inactive 679vb.
artisan 686n.
pottery
brittleness 330n.
pottery 381n.
art 551n.
pottle
vat 194n.
potty
vessel 194n.
crazed 503adj.
pot-valiance
courage 855n.
cowardice 856n.
pot-valiant
drunk 949adj.
pouch
stow 187vb.
pocket 194n.
receive 782vb.
take 786vb.
pouchy
recipient 194n.
expanded 197adj.
pouf
seat 218n.
poulterer
provider 633n.
poultice
pulpiness 356n.
surgical dressing 658n.
relieve 831vb.
poultry
meat 301n.
poultry 365n.
pounce
spurt 277n.
descent 309n.
plunge 313n.
pounce on
surprise 508vb.
attack 712vb.
take 786vb.
pound
enclosure 235n.
strike 279vb.
weighment 322n.
pulverize 332vb.
sound dead 405vb.
lock-up 748n.
coinage 797n.

poundage
discount 810n.
poundal
metrology 465n.
pound of flesh
severity 735n.
interest 803n.
pitilessness 906n.
pour
emit 300vb.
descend 309vb.
let fall 311vb.
be wet 341vb.
flow, rain 350vb.
abound 635vb.
pour down the drain
waste 634vb.
be prodigal 815vb.
pour in
converge 293vb.
irrupt 297vb.
pour out
land 295vb.
flow out 298vb.
void 300vb.
make flow 350vb.
be diffuse 570vb.
give 781vb.
pourparler
conference 584n.
advice 691n.
pout
be convex 253vb.
jut 254vb.
gesture 547n.
sullenness 893n.
poverty
feebleness 572n.
necessity 596n.
needfulness 627n.
scarcity 636n.
dilapidation 655n.
adversity 731n.
non-ownership 774n.
poverty 801n.
asceticism 945n.
poverty-stricken
beggarly 801adj.
powder
overlay 226vb.
smoother 258n.
powder 332n.
pulverize 332vb.
variegate 437n.
medicine 658n.
explosive 723n.
cosmetic 843n.
primp 843vb.
powder and shot
ammunition 723n.
powder-barrel
arsenal 723n.
powder-horn
arsenal 723n.
powder-magazine
pitfall 663n.
arsenal 723n.
powder-monkey
youngster 132n.
navy man 722n.
powder puff
cosmetic 843n.
powder room
beauty parlor 843n.
powdery
brittle 330adj.
powdery 332adj.
dry 342adj.
power
intrinsicality 5n.
greatness 32n.
numerical element 85n.
power 160n.
strength 162n.
operate 173vb.
style 566n.
vigor 571n.
eloquence 579n.
instrumentality 628n.
means 629n.
authority 733n.
brute force 735n.
mandate 751n.
virtue 933n.
power behind the throne
influence 178n.
latency 523n.
authority 733n.
deputy 755n.
power cut
scarcity 636n.
power-dive
spurt 277n.
descent 309n.
plunge 313n.
powered
dynamic 160adj.
mechanical 630adj.
powerful
influential 178adj.
loud 400adj.
(*see* power)
powerless
powerless 161adj.
weak 163adj.
inert 175adj.
unimportant 639adj.
powerlessness
anarchy 734n.
power of attorney
mandate 751n.
power of, in the
subject 745adj.
power of speech
eloquence 579n.
power of the purse
authority 733n.
finance 797n.
power politics
selfishness 932n.
powers of darkness
devil 969n.
powers that be
influence 178n.
master 741n.
power vacuum
impotence 161n.
anarchy 734n.
pow-wow
conference 584n.
pox
skin disease 651n.
venereal disease 651n.
practicable
possible 469adj.
useful 640adj.
expedient 642adj.
practical
operative 173adj.
intelligent 498adj.
instrumental 628adj.
useful 640adj.
expedient 642adj.
used 673adj.
practical ability
skill 694n.
practical demonstration
example 83n.
practical joke
foolery 497n.
trickery 542n.
trifle 639n.
witticism 839n.
ridicule 851n.
practice
continuity 71n.
regularity 81n.
conformity 83n.
numerical operation 86n.
repetition 106n.
permanence 144n.
empiricism 461n.
train 534vb.
learn 536vb.
deception 542n.
practice 610n.
habituate 610vb.
vocation 622n.
plot 623n.
way 624n.
medical art 658n.
preparation 669n.
use 673n.
action 676n.
exercise 682n.
conduct 688n.
cunning 698n.
bombardment 712n.
art of war 718n.

observance 768n.
etiquette 848n.
foul play 930n.
rite 988n.
practiced
knowing 490adj.
expert 694adj.
practice, in
prepared 669adj.
used 673adj.
practicing
religious 973adj.
orthodox 976adj.
pious 979adj.
practitioner
doer 676n.
agent 686n.
expert 696n.
praedial
territorial 344adj.
agrarian 370adj.
proprietary 777adj.
praetorian
defender 713n.
soldier 722n.
pragmatic
useful 640adj.
expedient 642adj.
pragmatism
philosophy 449n.
expedience 642n.
use 763n.
prairie
space 183n.
plain 348n.
prairie-schooner
cart 274n.
praise
honor 866vb.
thanks 907n.
respect 920vb.
praise 923n., vb.
reward 962n.
act of worship 981n.
praiser
commender 923n.
worshiper 981n.
praiseworthy
excellent 644adj.
approvable 923adj.
virtuous 933adj.
pram
push cart 274n.
prance
walk 267vb.
ride 267vb.
leap 311n.
be ostentatious 875vb.
boast 877vb.
prandial
mensal 301adj.
prang
aeronautics 271n.
tumble 309vb.
prank
dress 228vb.
whim 604n.
revel 837n.
beautify 841vb.
primp 843vb.
decorate 844vb.
prankish
capricious 604adj.
amused 837adj.
prate
empty talk 515n.
chatter 581n.
prater
boaster 877n.
prattle
empty talk 515n.
speech 579n.
chatter 581n.
prawn
fish food 301n.
table fish 365n.
praxis
grammar 564n.
action 676n.
pray
entreat 761vb.
desire 859vb.
be pious 979vb.
worship 981vb.
pray aloud
soliloquize 585vb.
prayer
entreaty 761n.
request 761n.
prayers 981n.
prayer-book
scripture 975n.
prayers 981n.
office-book 988n.
church utensil 990n.
prayer-cap
canonicals 989n.
prayerful
supplicatory 761adj.
pious 979adj.
worshiping 981adj.
prayer-house
church 990n.
prayer-meeting
public worship 981n.
prayers
aid 703n.
kind act 897n.
prayers 981n.
prayer-wheel
rotator 315n.
prayers 981n.
ritual object 988n.
pray for
patronize 703vb.
pre-
prior 119adj.
before 119adv.
preach
teach 534vb.
orate 579vb.
preacher
preacher 537n.
speaker 579n.
chatterer 581n.
religionist 979n.
pastor 986n.
preachiness
pietism 979n.
preaching office
church ministry 985n.
preaching order
pastor 986n.
preachment
lecture 543n.
oration 579n.
inducement 612n.
ministration 988n.
preachy
educational 534adj.
pietistic 979adj.
pre-adamite
primal 127adj.
old man 133n.
preamble
come before 64vb.
prelude 66n.
prearrangement
predetermination 608n.
preparation 669n.
prebend
benefice 985n.
prebendery
ecclesiarch 986n.
precarious
ephemeral 114adj.
unreliable 474adj.
unsafe 661adj.
precatory
supplicatory 761adj.
devotional 981adj.
precaution
protection 660n.
security 767n.
precautionary
preparatory 669adj.
precede
come before 64vb.
be before 119vb.
do before 119vb.
precede 283vb.
motivate 612vb.
dlrect 689vb.
precedence
superiority 34n.
precedence 64n.
priority 119n.
seniority 131n.
importance 638n.
prestige 866n.
precedent

non-imitation 21n.
prototype 23n.
precursor 66n.
beginning 68n.
rule 81n.
example 83n.
priority 119n.
guide 520n.
habit 610n.
precept 693n.
precentor
choir 413n.
leader 690n.
church officer 986n.
precept
rule 81n.
maxim 496n.
advice 691n.
precept 693n.
decree 737n.
preceptor
teacher 537n.
precession
priority 119n.
motion 265n.
precession 283n.
uranometry 321n.
precinct
region 184n.
place 185n.
circumjacence 230n.
enclosure 235n.
preciosity
ornament 574n.
affectation 850n.
precious
great 32adj.
ornate 574adj.
valuable 644adj.
of price 811adj.
affected 850adj.
preciousness
ornament 574n.
precious stone
gem 844n.
precipice
high land 209n.
verticality 215n.
acclivity 220n.
descent 309n.
pitfall 663n.
precipitance
non-preparation 670n.
haste 680n.
rashness 857n.
precipitate
leavings 41n.
effect 157n.
speedy 277adj.
propel 287vb.
eject 300vb.
depress 311vb.
let fall 311vb.
solid body 324n.
dirt 649n.
hasten 680vb.
rash 857adj.
precipitated
indissoluble 324adj.
precipitation
velocity 277n.
propulsion 287n.
ejection 300n.
condensation 324n.
precipitous
vertical 215adj.
sloping 220adj.
précis
translation 520n.
compendium 592n.
precise
definite 80adj.
accurate 494adj.
intelligible 516adj.
fastidious 862adj.
formal 875adj.
orthodox 976adj.
pietistic 979adj.
precisian
conformist 83n.
tyrant 735n.
man of taste 846n.
affector 850n.
perfectionist 862n.
religionist 979n.
precision
touch 378n.
accuracy 494n.
intelligibility 516n.
preclude
exclude 57vb.
restrain 747vb.
preclusive
excluding 57adj.
precociously
betimes 131adv.
precocity
anticipation 135n.
non-preparation 670n.
precognition
knowledge 490n.
foresight 510n.
psychics 984n.
preconceive
prejudge 481vb.
preconception
prejudgment 481n.
preconcert
predetermine 608vb.
preconsultation
preparation 669n.
precursive
preceding 64adj.
precursor
precursor 66n.
beginning 68n.
example 83n.
priority 119n.
earliness 135n.
precession 283n.
messenger 531n.
preparer 669n.
guide 690n.
precursory
preceding 64adj.
precursory 66adj.
predicting 511adj.
(*see* precursor)
predacity
rapacity 786n.
predator
taker 786n.
robber 789n.
predatory
oppressive 735adj.
taking 786adj.
thieving 788adj.
predecessor
precursor 66n.
parent 169n.
predeliberation
foresight 510n.
predetermination 608n.
predella
stand 218n.
altar 990n.
predestinarian
fatalist 596n.
predestination
destiny 155n.
fate 596n.
predetermination 608n.
predestine
predestine 155vb.
necessitate 596vb.
motivate 612vb.
intend 617vb.
predetermination
foresight 510n.
will 595n.
necessity 596n.
resolution 599n.
predetermination 608n.
preparation 669n.
predetermine
predestine 155vb.
prejudge 481vb.
predetermine 608vb.
motivate 612vb.
intend 617vb.
plan 623vb.
predicable
affirmative 532adj.
predicament
plight 8n.
circumstance 8n.
classification 77n.
crisis 137n.
danger 661n.

predicament 700n.
adversity 731n.
predicant
pastor 986n.
predicate
attribute 158vb.
predication
argumentation 475n.
affirmation 532n.
predict
expect 507vb.
indicate 547vb.
(*see* prediction)
predictable
future 124adj.
unchangeable 153adj.
prediction
looking ahead 124n.
destiny 155n.
prediction 511n.
warning 664n.
predictive
foreseeing 510adj.
predicting 511adj.
predigested
edible 301adj.
intelligible 516adj.
ready-made 669adj.
predilection
prejudice 481n.
choice 605n.
affections 817n.
liking 859n.
love 887n.
predispose
bias 481vb.
predetermine 608vb.
motivate 612vb.
prepare 669vb.
predisposition
tendency 179n.
willingness 597n.
affections 817n.
predominance
superiority 34n.
power 160n.
influence 178n.
authority 733n.
predominate
prevail 178vb.
motivate 612vb.
overmaster 727vb.
dominate 733vb.
preeminence
superiority 34n.
precedence 64n.
preeminent
authoritative 733adj.
noteworthy 866adj.
preempt
exclude 57vb.
be early 135vb.
acquire 771vb.
possess 773vb.
bargain 791vb.
purchase 792vb.
preen
primp 843vb.
decorate 844vb.
preen oneself
feel pride 871vb.
be vain 873vb.
preexistence
existence 1n.
priority 119n.
prefab
house 192n.
prefabricate
produce 164vb.
preface
prepose 64vb.
come before 64vb.
prelude 66n.
edition 589n.
prefatory
preceding 64adj.
precursory 66adj.
beginning 68adj.
prefect
teacher 537n.
official 690n.
officer 741n.
prefecture
magistrature 733n.
prefer
promote 285vb.
choose 605vb.
desire 859vb.
ecclesiasticize 985vb.
preferable
superior 34adj.
chosen 605adj.
excellent 644adj.
preference
precedence 64n.
will 595n.
choice 605n.
restriction 747n.
preferential treatment
aid 703n.
injustice 914n.
preferment
progression 285n.
improvement 654n.
holy orders 985n.
church office 985n.
prefigure
predict 511vb.
indicate 547vb.
prefigurement
precursor 66n.
omen 511n.
prefix
adjunct 40n.
affix 45vb.
prepose 64vb.
precursor 66n.
front 237n.
spoken letter 558n.
pre-glacial
primal 127adj.
pregnancy
propagation 164n.
pregnant
productive 164adj.
prolific 171adj.
meaningful 514adj.
concise 569adj.
important 638adj.
pregnant with
impending 155adj.
presageful 511adj.
prehensile
taking 786adj.
prehension
retention 778n.
taking 786n.
prehistorian
antiquarian 125n.
prehistoric
past 125adj.
former 125adj.
olden 127adj.
prehistory
antiquity 125n.
unknown thing 491n.
prejudgment
prejudgment 481n.
prejudice
influence 178vb.
tendency 179n.
prejudice, bias 481n.
error 495n.
predetermination 608n.
motivate 612n.
evil 616n.
dislike 861n.
hatred 888n.
injustice 914n.
prejudicial
harmful 645adj.
prelacy
Catholicism 976n.
churchdom 985n.
prelate
ecclesiarch 986n.
prelection
lecture 534n.
oration 579n.
prelector
teacher 537n.
preliminaries
beginning 68n.
preparation 669n.
preliminary
preceding 64adj.
prelude 66n.
precursory 66adj.
preparatory 669adj.
prelims

edition 589n.
prelude
come before 64vb.
prepose 64vb.
prelude 66n.
musical piece 412n.
prelusory
(*see* prelude)
premature
early 135adj.
ill-timed 138adj.
immature 670adj.
unsuccessful 728adj.
prematurity
anticipation 135n.
premeditate
intend 617vb.
premeditation
predetermination 608n.
preparation 669n.
premier
director 690n.
premiere
debut 68n.
dramaturgy 594n.
premier pas
debut 68n.
premiership
directorship 689n.
magistrature 733n.
premise
premise 475n., vb.
supposition 512n.
premises
place 185n.
shop 796n.
premium
interest 803n.
receipt 807n.
premium, at a
dear 811adj.
premium bond
chance 159n.
gambling 618n.
paper money 797n.
premolar
tooth 256n.
premonition
precursor 66n.
foresight 510n.
warning 664n.
prenatal
prior 119adj.
prenomen
name 561n.
prentice
new 126adj.
beginner 538n.
immature 670adj.
prenticeship
learning 536n.
preoccupation
exclusion 57n.
attention 455n.
abstractedness 456n.
obstacle 702n.
preoccupied
obsessed 455adj.
distracted 456adj.
preoccupy
exclude 57vb.
engross 449vb.
possess 773vb.
preoption
choice 605n.
preordain
predestine 155vb.
preordination
fate 596n.
predetermination 608n.
prep
curriculum 536n.
study 536n.
preparation 669n.
preparation
beginning 68n.
looking ahead 124n.
production 164n.
foresight 510n.
study 536n.
provision 633n.
medicine 658n.
preparation 669n.
preparatory
preceding 64adj.
preparatory 669adj.
prepare
arrange 62vb.
train 534vb.
plan 623vb.
prepare 669vb.
prepared
expectant 507adj.
willing 597adj.
prepense
volitional 595adj.
predetermined 608adj.
preponderance
inequality 29n.
superiority 34n.
influence 178n.
authority 733n.
prepose
prepose 64vb.
preposition
adjunct 40n.
precursor 66n.
part of speech 564n.
prepositional
preceding 64adj.
fore 237adj.
grammatical 564adj.
prepossess
bias 481vb.
prepossessing
personable 841adj.
lovable 887adj.
prepossession
prejudice 481n.
preposterous
absurd 497adj.
imaginative 513adj.
exaggerated 546adj.
ridiculous 849adj.
undue 916adj.
preprandial
mensal 301adj.
prepuce
front 237n.
Pre-Raphaelite
antiquarian 125n.
olden 127adj.
artist 556n.
pre-release
priority 119n.
prerequisite
requirement 627n.
required 627adj.
prerogative
vantage 34n.
authority 733n.
freedom 744n.
nobility 868n.
right 913n.
dueness 915n.
presage
predestine 155vb.
omen 511n.
indicate 547vb.
threaten 900vb.
presageful
impending 155adj.
presageful 511adj.
frightening 854n.
presbyter
ecclesiarch 986n.
church officer 986n.
presbyterate
church office 985n.
Presbyterianism
Protestantism 976n.
sectarianism 978n.
churchdom 985n.
presbytery
seniority 131n.
synod 985n.
parish 985n.
churchdom 985n.
parsonage 986n.
church exterior 990n.
prescience
foresight 510n.
prescientific
ignorant 491adj.
prescribe
doctor 658vb.
manage 689vb.
advise 691vb.
decree 737vb.

prescript
  precept 693n.
  decree 737n.
prescription
  tradition 127n.
  habit 610n.
  remedy 658n.
  advice 691n.
  precept 693n.
  decree 737n.
  possession 773n.
  dueness 915n.
prescriptive
  immemorial 127adj.
  permanent 144adj.
  vested 153adj.
  habitual 610adj.
  preceptive 693adj.
  due 915adj.
presence
  existence 1n.
  generality 79n.
  presence 189n.
  arrival 295n.
  appearance 445n.
  mien 445n.
  ghost 970n.
present
  present 121adj.
  synchronous 123adj.
  modern 126adj.
  on the spot 189adj.
  near 200adj.
  show 522vb.
  represent 551vb.
  dramatize 594vb.
  offer 759n., vb.
  gift 781n.
  reward 962vb.
  ecclesiasticize 985vb.
presentable
  personable 841adj.
present arms
  greet 884vb.
  show respect 920vb.
presentation
  spectacle 445n.
  manifestation 522n.
  representation 551n.
  offer 759n.
  giving 781n.
  reward 962n.
  holy orders 985n.
presenter
  speaker 579n.
  actor 594n.
present, for the
  during pleasure 112adv.
  transiently 114adv.
presentiment
  intuition 476n.
  prejudgment 481n.
  foresight 510n.
  prediction 511n.
present of, make a
  cheapen 812vb.
preservation
  permanence 144n.
  protection 660n.
  preservation 666n.
preservative
  preserver 666n.
preserve
  sustain 146vb.
  dry 342vb.
  sweet 392n.
  store 632vb.
  sanitate 652vb.
  safeguard 660vb.
  preserve 660vb.
  retain 778vb.
preserver
  protector 660n.
  preserver 666n.
preside
  direct 689vb.
presidency
  magistrature 733n.
president
  superior 34n.
  director 690n.
  master, officer 741n.
presidium
  council 692n.
press
  crowd 74n.
  cabinet 194n.
  make smaller 198vb.
  flattener 216n.
  be supported 218vb.
  smooth 258vb.
  impel 279n.
  weigh 322vb.
  touch 378vb.
  the press 528n.
  press 587n.
  be resolute 599vb.
  incite 612vb.
  activity 678n.
  advise 691vb.
  compel 740vb.
  offer 759vb.
  request 761vb.
  take away 786vb.
  steal 788vb.
  caress 889vb.
press-cuttings
  record 548n.
press-gang
  compulsion 740n.
  taker 786n.
  police 955n.
pressing
  important 638adj.
press into service
  avail of 673vb.
pressman
  publicizer 528n.
  chronicler 549n.
  printer 587n.
  author 589n.
pressure
  crisis 137n.
  energy 160n.
  vigorousness 174n.
  influence 178n.
  compression 198n.
  impulse 279n.
  gravity 322n.
  touch 378n.
  inducement 612n.
  instrumentality 628n.
  action 676n.
  exertion 682n.
  adversity 731n.
  restriction 747n.
  request 761n.
  endearment 889n.
pressure group
  inducement 612n.
  motivator 612n.
  petitioner 763n.
pressure, under
  hastily 680adv.
  by force 740adj.
presswork
  print 587n.
  letterpress 587n.
prestidigitation
  sleight 542n.
prestidigitator
  conjuror 545n.
prestige
  influence 178n.
  importance 638n.
  authority 733n.
  prestige 866n.
  pride 871n.
  ostentatious 875adj.
presto
  instantaneously 116adv.
  swiftly 277adv.
  adagio 412adv.
presumable
  probable 471adj.
presume
  assume 471vb.
  prejudge 481vb.
  (*see* presumption)
presume on
  avail of 673vb.
presumption
  probability 471n.
  opinion 485n.
  expectation 507n.
  supposition 512n.
  rashness 857n.
  insolence 878n.
  arrogation 916n.
presumptive

evidential 466adj.
probable 471adj.
supposed 512adj.
presumptuous
rash 857adj.
insolent 878adj.
unwarranted 916adj.
presupposition
supposition 512n.
pretend
imagine 513vb.
pretender
impostor 545n.
petitioner 763n.
affector 850n.
boaster 877n.
usurper 916n.
pretendership
arrogation 916n.
pretense
insubstantial thing 4n.
mimicry 20n.
supposition 512n.
duplicity 541n.
sham 542n.
mental dishonesty 543n.
pretext 614n.
pretension 850n.
ostentation 875n.
pretension
pretension 850n.
airs 873n.
ostentation 875n.
pretentious
absurd 499adj.
feeble 572adj.
ornate 574adj.
affected 850adj.
vain 873adj.
ostentatious 875adj.
boastful 877adj.
pretentiousness
affectation 850n.
preterit
preterit 125adj.
preterition
precedence 64n.
preterition 125n.
pretermit
neglect 458vb.
preternatural
abnormal 84adj.
pretext
reason why 156n.
reasons 475n.
sophistry 477n.
mental dishonesty 543n.
pretext 614n.
stratagem 698n.
prettify
beautify 841vb.
primp 843vb.
decorate 844vb.
prettiness
beauty 841n.
pretty
greatly 32adv.
beautiful 841adj.
prettyism
ornamentation 844n.
pretty pass
predicament 700n.
pretty-pretty
ornamentation 844n.
prevail
be 1vb.
be general 79vb.
be able 160vb.
prevail 178vb.
be wont 610vb.
motivate 612vb.
overmaster 727vb.
prevail upon
induce 612vb.
prevalence
existence 1n.
generality 79n.
power 160n.
influence 178n.
prevalent
existing 1adj.
extensive 32adj.
usual 610adj.
(*see* prevalence)
prevaricate
be dishonest 930adj.
prevarication
equivocalness 518n.
falsehood 541n.
prevenience
anticipation 135n.
prevenient
preceding 64adj.
prevenient grace
divine function 965n.
prevent
counteract 182vb.
avoid 620vb.
obstruct 702vb.
prohibit 757vb.
preventable
avoidable 620adj.
prevention
hindrance 702n.
restraint 747n.
preventive
counteraction 182n.
prophylactic 658n.
preserving 666adj.
preventive medicine
hygiene 652n.
medical art 658n.
preservation 666n.
preview
precursor 66n.
priority 119n.
cinema 445n.
foresight 510n.
manifestation 522n.
previous
preceding 64adj.
anachronistic 118adj.
prior 119adj.
early 135adj.
prevision
foresight 510n.
prewar
prior 119adj.
antiquated 127adj.
peaceful 717adj.
prey
objective 617n.
chase 619n.
loser 728n.
unlucky person 731n.
booty 790n.
sufferer 825n.
prey on
eat 301vb.
ill-treat 645vb.
incommode 827vb.
frighten 854vb.
priapism
libido 859n.
price
equivalence 28n.
quid pro quo 150n.
appraise 465vb.
goodness 644n.
price 809n., vb.
penalty 963n.
priceless
valuable 644adj.
of price 811adj.
funny 849adj.
price ring
restriction 747n.
prick
small thing 33n.
cut 46vb.
stimulant 174n.
sharp point 256n.
pierce 263vb.
give pain 377vb.
itch 378vb.
indication 547n.
mark 547vb.
incite 612vb.
wound 655n.
excitant 821n.
prickle
itch 378vb.
prickliness
sharpness 256n.
quarrelsomeness 709n.
moral sensibility 819n.
pride 871n.
irascibility 892n.
prickly

unconformable 84adj.
prickly heat
formication 378n.
prick up one's ears
hear 415vb.
be curious 453vb.
be attentive 455vb.
pride
pride 871n.
vanity 873n.
ostentation 875n.
insolence 878n.
unsociability 883n.
vice 934n.
impiety 980n.
prideful
prideful 871adj.
pride of place
superiority 34n.
precedence 64n.
prie-dieu
seat 218n.
priest
priest 986n.
priestcraft
sorcery 983n.
priestdom
ecclesiasticism 985n.
priesthood
church office 985n.
clergy 986n.
priestly
priestly 985adj.
clerical 986adj.
priest-ridden
pietistic 979adj.
ecclesiastical 985adj.
prig
steal 788vb.
affector 850n.
prude 950n.
priggish
affected 880adj.
prudish 950adj.
priggishness
airs 873n.
prim
serious 834adj.
dull 840adj.
affected 850adj.
fastidious 862adj.
primacy
superiority 34n.
importance 638n.
prestige 866n.
church office 985n.
prima donna
superior 34n.
vocalist 413n.
actor 594n.
bigwig 638n.
proficient 696n.
prima facie
at sight 438n.
evidential 466adj.
probably 471adv.
manifestly 522adv.
primage
extra 40n.
decrement 42n.
primal
primal 127adj.
fundamental 156adj.
primary
intrinsic 5adj.
unimitative 21adj.
simple 44adj.
fundamental 156adj.
star 321n.
educational 534adj.
vote 605n.
important 638adj.
primate
ecclesiarch 986n.
primatial
animal 365adj.
prime
numerical 85adj.
oldness 127n.
morning 128n.
adultness 134n.
early 135adj.
educate 534vb.
important 638adj.
elite 644n.
excellent 644adj.
make ready 669vb.
church service 988n.
prime constituent
essence 1n.
essential part 5n.
prime minister
director 690n.
officer 741n.
prime of life
salad days 130n.
adultness 134n.
primer
beginning 68n.
textbook 589n.
primeval
primal 127adj.
primigenous
primal 127adj.
priming
preparation 669n.
ammunition 723n.
primitive
past 125adj.
primal 127adj.
earliness 135n.
fundamental 156adj.
violent 176adj.
low fellow 869n.
plebeian 869adj.
primness
prudery 950n.
(*see* prim)
primogenital
older 131adj.
filial 170adj.
primogeniture
priority 119n.
oldness 127n.
seniority 131n.
sonship 170n.
primordial
unimitative 21adj.
primal 127adj.
fundamental 156adj.
primp
beautify 841vb.
primp 843vb.
be vain 873adj.
be ostentatious 875vb.
primrose
yellowness 433n.
badge 547n.
primrose path
deterioration 655n.
facility 701n.
wickedness 934n.
primum mobile
cause 156n.
divineness 965n.
primus inter pares
superior 34n.
prince
sovereign 741n.
potentate 741n.
aristocrat 868n.
princely
ruling 733adj.
liberal 813adj.
worshipful 866adj.
noble 868adj.
prince of
paragon 646n.
princess
sovereign 741n.
principal
supreme 34adj.
first 68adj.
teacher 537n.
director 690n.
master 741n.
principality
territory 184n.
polity 733n.
principate
magistrature 733n.
principle
essential part 5n.
rule 81n.
source 156n.
element 319n.
idea 451n.
premise 475n.
opinion 485n.
axiom 496n.
motive 612n.
probity 929n.

principled
virtuous 933adj.
principles
creed 485n.
probity 929n.
prink
beautify 841vb.
primp 843vb.
print
copy 22n., vb.
effect 157n.
publish 528vb.
indication 547n.
record 548vb.
photography 551n.
picture 553n.
printing 555n.
write 586vb.
writing 586n.
letterpress 587n.
pattern 844n.
printable
permitted 756adj.
pure 950adj.
printed
intelligible 516adj.
printer
publicizer 528n.
printer 587n.
print, in
published 528adj.
printing
reproduction 166n.
printing 555n.
print 587n.
printless
obliterated 550adj.
print-type
print-type 587n.
prior
prior 119adj.
older 131adj.
ecclesiarch 986n.
monk 986n.
priorate
church office 985n.
priority
precedence 64n.
time 108n.
priority 119n.
preterition 125n.
seniority 131n.
chief thing 638n.
priory
monastery 986n.
prism
angular figure 247n.
chromatics 425n.
variegation 437n.
optical device 442n.
prismatic
colored 425adj.
variegated 437adj.
prison
enclosure 235n.
prison 748n.
seclusion 883n.
pillory 964n.
prisoner
prisoner 750n.
accused person 928n.
litigant 959n.
prison, in
captive 750adj.
pristine
former 125adj.
privacy
seclusion 883n.
private
inferior 35n.
private 80adj.
concealed 525adj.
soldiery 722n.
possessed 773adj.
commoner 869n.
secluded 883adj.
private enterprise
particularism 80n.
trade 791n.
privateer
warship 722n.
navy man 722n.
robber 789n.
privateering
brigandage 788n.
private parts
genitalia 164n.
privation
loss 772n.
poverty 801n.
privative
taking 786adj.
privilege
vantage 34n.
freedom 744n.
permit 756vb.
right 913n.
dueness 915n.
non-liability 919n.
privities
genitalia 164n.
privity
knowledge 490n.
privy
knowing 490adj.
concealed 525adj.
latrine 649n.
privy purse
receipt 807n.
privy seal
badge of rule 743n.
prize
force 176vb.
monument 548n.
benefit 615n.
objective 617n.
elite 644n.
trophy 729n.
acquisition 771n.
gift 781n.
taking 786n.
booty 790n.
receipt 807n.
desired object 859n.
honor 866vb.
love 887vb.
approve 923vb.
reward 962n.
prize-fight
pugilism 716n.
prize-fighter
contender 716n.
pugilist 722n.
prize-giving
giving 781n.
prizeman
superior 34n.
college student 538n.
proficient 696n.
victor 727n.
prize-money
reward 962n.
prize-winner
superior 34n.
exceller 644n.
proficient 696n.
recipient 782n.
prize-winning
successful 727adj.
pro
deputy 755n.
probabilism
philosophy 449n.
probability 471n.
irreligion 974n.
probability
fair chance 159n.
appearance 445n.
probability 471n.
expectation 507n.
probable
future 124adj.
impending 155adj.
tending 179adj.
probable 471adj.
credible 485adj.
probation
experiment 461n.
demonstration 478n.
essay 671n.
probationary
experimental 461adj.
probationer
beginner 538n.
offender 904n.
probation officer
nurse 658n.
probative
experimental 461adj.
evidential 466adj.
demonstrating 478adj.
probe

depth 211n.
perforator 263n.
inquiry 459n.
experiment 461n.
measure 465vb.
probity
veracity 540n.
right 913n.
morals 917n.
probity 929n.
innocence 935n.
problem
topic 452n.
question 459n.
argumentation 475n.
enigma 530n.
difficulty 700n.
worry 825n.
problematic
moot 459adj.
uncertain 474adj.
proboscis
projection 254n.
feeler 378n.
procacity
rudeness 885n.
procedure
policy 623n.
way 624n.
action 676n.
conduct 688n.
ritual 988n.
proceed
elapse 111vb.
go on 146vb.
travel 267vb.
progress 285vb.
do 676vb.
deal with 688vb.
proceeding
eventuality 154n.
deed 676n.
proceedings
record 548n.
legal process 959n.
proceeds
earnings 771n.
receiving 782n.
receipt 807n.
process
change 143n.
convert 147vb.
production 164n.
agency 173n.
motion 265n.
way 624n.
action 676n.
procession
retinue 67n.
procession 71n.
concomitant 89n.
marching 267n.
pageant 875n.
ritual act 988n.
process-server
law officer 955n.
prochronism
anachronism 118n.
proclaim
proclaim 528vb.
affirm 532vb.
raise the alarm 665vb.
honor 866vb.
proclamation
publication 528n.
call 547n.
proclitic
sequel 67n.
proclivity
tendency 179n.
proconsul
official 690n.
officer 741n.
governor 741n.
deputy 755n.
proconsulate
magistrature 733n.
procrastinate
spin out 113vb.
put off 136vb.
be neglectful 458vb.
not act 677vb.
procreation
propagation 164n.
reproduction 166n.
productiveness 171n.
procreator
parent 169n.
proctor
teacher 537n.
manager 690n.
consignee 754n.
law agent 958n.
proctorship
management 689n.
procumbent
supine 216adj.
procuration
agency 173n.
commission 751n.
procurator
manager 690n.
consignee 754n.
law agent 958n.
procure
cause 156vb.
induce 612vb.
provide 633vb.
acquire 771vb.
be impure 951vb.
procurement
agency 173n.
acquisition 771n.
procurer
provider 633n.
bawd 952n.
procuress
bawd 952n.
prod
stimulant 174n.
impel 279vb.
incentive 612n.
prodigal
wasteful 634adj.
plenteous 635adj.
expending 806adj.
liberal 813adj.
prodigal 815n., adj.
bad man 938n.
intemperate 943adj.
prodigality
prodigality 815n.
rashness 857n.
(*see* prodigal)
prodigal son
prodigal 815n.
bad man 938n.
penitent 939n.
prodigious
prodigious 32adj.
wonderful 864adj.
prodigy
intellectual 492n.
exceller 644n.
paragon 646n.
proficient 696n.
prodigy 864n.
prodition
dutilessness 918n.
perfidy 930n.
prodrome
precursor 66n.
produce
increment 36n.
cause 156vb.
growth 157n.
product 164n.
make fruitful 171vb.
lengthen 203vb.
manifest 522vb.
dramatize 594vb.
provide 633vb.
earnings 771n.
producer
producer 167n.
exhibitor 522n.
stage-manager 594n.
produce results
be expedient 642vb.
producible
shown 522adj.
product
numerical result 85n.
eventuality 154n.
effect 157n.
product 164n.
earnings 771n.
production
composition 56n.

causation 156n.
product 164n.
lengthening 203n.
manifestation 522n.
dramaturgy 594n.
production line
workshop 687n.
productive
prolific 171adj.
profitable 640adj.
gainful 771adj.
rich 800adj.
productivity
production 164n.
productiveness 171n.
diffuseness 570n.
plenty 635n.
proem
prelude 66n.
proemial
preceding 64adj.
beginning 68adj.
proemium
oration 579n.
profanation
misuse 675n.
undueness 916n.
impiety 980n.
profane
unclean 649adj.
impair 655vb.
shame 867vb.
maledicent 899adj.
not respect 921vb.
wicked 934adj.
irreligious 974adj.
profane 980adj.
laical 987adj.
profanity
scurrility 899n.
impiety 980n.
profess
believe 485vb.
teach 534vb.
professing
affirmative 532adj.
pious 979adj.
profession
creed 485n.
assent 488n.
affirmation 532n.
mental dishonesty 543n.
pretext 614n.
pursuit 619n.
vocation 622n.
promise 764n.
ostentation 875n.
duty 917n.
professional
instructed 490adj.
usual 610adj.
businesslike 622adj.
expert 694adj.
expert 696n.
professionalism
skill 694n.
professor
scholar 492n.
teacher 537n.
expert 696n.
academic title 870n.
professoriat
scholar 492n.
teacher 537n.
professorship
lecture 534n.
proffer
offer 759n., vb.
promise 764vb.
proficiency
culture 490n.
skill 694n.
proficient
knowing 490adj.
scholar 492n.
expert 694adj.
proficient 696n.
profile
outline 233n., vb.
laterality 239n.
form 243n.
feature 445n.
picture 553n.
description 590n.
profit
increment 36n.
growth 157n.
incentive 612n.
benefit 615n., vb.
utility 640n.
expedience 642n.
gain 771n., vb.
reward 962n.
profitability
utility 640n.
profitable
prolific 171adj.
good 615adj.
(*see* profit)
profit by
profit by 137vb.
find useful 640vb.
get better 654vb.
use 673vb.
profiteer
made man 730n.
prosper 730vb.
speculate 791vb.
overcharge 811vb.
profit, for
trading 791adj.
profitless
unproductive 172adj.
wasted 634adj.
profitless 641adj.
unsuccessful 728adj.
losing 772adj.
profit-making
trade 791n.
profit-taking
acquisition 771n.
profligacy
wickedness 934n.
profligate
vicious 934adj.
bad man 938n.
lecherous 951adj.
libertine 952n.
profluent
progressive 285adj.
flowing 350adj.
profound
great 32adj.
deep 211adj.
wise 498adj.
inexpressible 517adj.
imperspicuous 568adj.
felt 818adj.
profundity
thought 448n.
(*see* profound)
profuse
diffuse 570adj.
liberal 813adj.
profusion
great quantity 32n.
multitude 104n.
plenty 635n.
redundance 637n.
prodigality 815n.
prog
food 301n.
progenitive
reproductive 166adj.
progenitor
source 156n.
parent 169n.
progeny
posterity 170n.
prognosis
foresight 510n.
prediction 511n.
medical art 658n.
prognostic
foreseeing 510adj.
omen 511n.
cautionary 664adj.
prognostication
foresight 510n.
prediction 511n.
program
list 87n.
prediction 511n.
publication 528n.
policy 623n.
plan 623n., vb.
undertaking 672n.
tactics 688n.
progress
increase 36n.

elapse 111vb.
continuance 146n.
conversion 147n.
motion 265n.
travel 267vb.
progression 285n.
approach 289vb.
pass 305vb.
way 624n.
improvement 654n.
be active 678vb.
success 727n.
progression
series 71n.
ratio 85n.
(*see* progress)
progressism
reformism 654n.
progressive
continuous 71adj.
elapsing 111adj.
vigorous 174n.
progressive 285adj.
reformer 654n.
enterprising 672adj.
prohibit
exclude 57vb.
counteract 182vb.
negate 533vb.
obstruct 702vb.
command 737vb.
restrain 747vb.
prohibit 757vb.
make illegal 954vb.
prohibition
temperance 942n.
(*see* prohibit)
prohibitionist
abstainer 942n.
sober person 948n.
prohibitive
dear 811adj.
project
make extrinsic 6vb.
externalize 223vb.
jut 254vb.
propel 287vb.
emerge 298vb.
be visible 443vb.
represent 551vb.
predetermination 608n.
intention 617n.
plan 623n., vb.
undertaking 672n.
projectile
missile 287n.
ammunition 723n.
projection
extrinsicality 6n.
distortion 246n.
convexity 253n.
projection 254n.
propulsion 287n.
image, map 551n.
projector
thrower 287n.
lamp 420n.
optical device 442n.
cinema 445n.
planner 623n.
prolapse
descend 309vb.
prolation
speech 579n.
prole
(*see* proletarian)
prolegomenon
prelude 66n.
dissertation 591n.
prolepsis
anachronism 118n.
proletarian
vulgarian 847n.
commoner 869n.
plebeian 869adj.
proletarianism
government 733n.
proletariat
lower classes 869n.
commonalty 869n.
proliferate
grow 36vb.
reproduce 164vb.
be fruitful 171vb.
abound 635vb.
prolific
increasing 36adj.
multitudinous 104adj.
productive 164adj.
prolific 171adj.
diffuse 570adj.
profitable 640adj.
prolix
protracted 113adj.
long 203adj.
prolix 570adj.
tedious 838adj.
prolixity
speech 579n.
(*see* prolix)
prolocutor
interpreter 520n.
speaker 579n.
prologize
come before 64vb.
prologue
prelude 66n.
oration 579n.
speaker 579n.
stage play 594n.
actor 594n.
prolong
augment 36vb.
continuate 71vb.
spin out 113vb.
sustain 146vb.
lengthen 203vb.
prolongation
adjunct 40n.
sequence 65n.
delay 136n.
tempo 410n.
(*see* prolong)
prolusion
prelude 66n.
promenade
street 192n.
land travel 267n.
pedestrianism 267n.
path 624n.
pageant 875n.
prominence
superiority 34n.
prominence 254n.
elevation 310n.
light 417n.
importance 638n.
prestige 866n.
prominent
overhanging 209adj.
salient 254adj.
well-seen 443adj.
manifest 522adj.
(*see* prominence)
promiscuity
indiscrimination 464n.
indifference 860n.
unchastity 951n.
promiscuous
mixed 43adj.
orderless 61adj.
designless 618adj.
promise
predict 511vb.
oath 532n.
affirm 532vb.
intention 617n.
undertaking 672n.
be auspicious 730vb.
promise 764n., vb.
compact 765n.
give hope 852vb.
promised land
fantasy 513n.
objective 617n.
aspiration 852n.
promise oneself
expect 507vb.
promising
probable 471adj.
presageful 511adj.
promissory
promissory 764adj.
promissory note
title-deed 767n.
paper money 797n.
promontory
projection 254n.
land 344n.
promote
augment 36vb.

conduce 156vb.
tend 179vb.
concur 181vb.
promote 285vb.
make likely 471vb.
be instrumental 628vb.
find means 629vb.
be useful 640vb.
be expedient 642vb.
make better 654vb.
undertake 672vb.
aid 703vb.
dignify 866vb.
promoter
planner 623n.
patron 707n.
prompt
initiate 68vb.
early 135adj.
influence 178vb.
speedy 277adj.
reminder 505n.
hint 524n., vb.
willing 597adj.
incite 612vb.
active 678adj.
hasty 680adj.
advise 691vb.
promptbook
stage play 594n.
prompter
reminder 505n.
stage-hand 594n.
motivator 612n.
adviser 691n.
auxiliary 707n.
promptitude
punctuality 135n.
velocity 277n.
activity 678n.
promptly
instantaneously 116adv.
promptuary
storage 632n.
promulgate
proclaim 528vb.
decree 737vb.
pronation
supination 216n.
inversion 221n.
prone
supine 216adj.
inverted 221adj.
proneness
tendency 179n.
supination 216n.
prong
sharp point 256n.
pronounce
judge 480vb.
proclaim 528vb.
affirm 532vb.
voice 577vb.
speak 579vb.
pronounced
well-seen 443adj.
manifest 522adj.
vocal 577adj.
pronouncement
judgment 480n.
publication 528n.
pronunciamento
publication 528n.
pronunciation
pronunciation 577n.
proof
duplicate 22n.
unyielding 162adj.
sealed off 264adj.
dry 342adj.
hard 326adj.
unfeeling 375adj.
experiment 461n.
evidence 466n.
certainty 473n.
demonstration 478n.
letterpress 587n.
reading matter 589n.
resolute 599adj.
plan 623n.
amendment 654n.
invulnerable 660adj.
resisting 715adj.
impassive 820adj.
proofread
print 587vb.
rectify 654vb.
prop
bond 47n.
strengthen 162vb.
supporter 218n.
elevate 310vb.
aid 703vb.
propaedeutics
curriculum 534n.
propagable
generative 171adj.
propaganda
argument 475n.
publicity 528n.
teaching 534n.
misteaching 535n.
inducement 612n.
warfare 718n.
propagandist
publicizer 528n.
preacher 537n.
motivator 612n.
propagandize
pervert 655vb.
propagate
generate 164vb.
be fruitful 171vb.
publish 528vb.
proparoxytone
punctuation 547n.
propel
move 265vb.
send 272vb.
propel 287vb.
propellant
propeller 269n.
propellant 287n.
explosive 723n.
propeller
propeller 269n.
aircraft 276n.
propellant 287n.
rotator 317n.
propensity
tendency 179n.
willingness 597n.
liking 859n.
proper
characteristic 5adj.
relevant 9adj.
ingredient 58adj.
special 80adj.
regular 83adj.
expedient 642adj.
possessed 773adj.
personable 841adj.
tasteful 846adj.
well-bred 848adj.
right 913adj.
due 915adj.
virtuous 933adj.
proper fraction
numerical element 85n.
properispomenon
punctuation 547n.
properly
aright 644adv.
proper time
occasion 137n.
opportunity 137n.
expedience 642n.
property
essential part 5n.
ability 160n.
stage-set 594n.
store 632n.
property 777n.
propertyless
not owning 774adj.
prophecy
prediction 511n.
hermeneutics 520n.
revelation 975n.
prophesy
foresee 510vb.
predict 511vb.
prophet
sage 500n.
oracle 511n.
preacher 537n.
veracity 540n.
warner 664n.
religious teacher 973n.

prophylactic
hygiene 652n.
salubrious 652adj.
prophylactic 658n.
preserving 666adj.
hindering 702adj.
prophylaxis
protection 660n.
(*see* prophylactic)
propinquity
consanguinity 11n.
nearness 200n.
propitiate
pacify 719vb.
mediate 720vb.
content 828vb.
ask mercy 905vb.
atone 941vb.
offer worship 981vb.
propitiation
divine function 965n.
(*see* propitiate)
propiatory
redemptive 965adj.
propitious
opportune 137adj.
beneficial 644adj.
aiding 703adj.
palmy 730adj.
promising 852adj.
prop-man
stage-hand 594n.
proponent
reasoner 475n.
proportion
relativeness 9n.
correlation 12n.
fitness 24n.
degree 27n.
part 53n.
order 60n.
ratio 85n.
numerical operation 86n.
symmetry 245n.
elegance 575n.
portion 783n.
proportional, proportionable, proportionate
(*see* proportion)
proportional • representation
vote 605n.
proportions
measure 183n.
size 195n.
proposal
supposition 512n.
intention 617n.
plan 623n.
advice 691n.
offer 759n.
request 761n.
propose
argue 475vb.
propound 512vb.
intend 617vb.
advise 691vb.
patronize 703vb.
court 889vb.
proposer
planner 623n.
patron 707n.
proposition
topic 453n.
argumentation 475n.
supposition 512n.
affirmation 532n.
(*see* proposal)
propound
propound 512vb.
affirm 532vb.
(*see* propose)
proprietary
proprietary 777adj.
proprietor
owner 776n.
proprietorship
possession 773n.
propriety
relevance 9n.
fitness 24n.
elegance 575n.
expedience 642n.
good taste 846n.
etiquette 848n.
right 913n.
purity 950n.
props
stage-set 594n.
propugnant
defending 713adj.
propulsion
energy 160n.
impulse 279n.
propulsion 287n.
ejection 300n.
propylaeum
lobby 194n.
doorway 263n.
temple 990n.
propylon
entrance 68n.
pro rata
pro rata 783adv.
prorogation
delay 136n.
prorogue
put off 136vb.
prosaic
typical 83adj.
unintelligent 499adj.
plain 573adj.
prosaic 593adj.
artless 699adj.
tedious 838adj.
dull 840adj.
pros and cons
reasons 475n.
proscenium
front 237n.
stage-set 594n.
proscribe
command 737vb.
prohibit 757vb.
condemn 961vb.
proscribed
heterodox 977adj.
proscription
command 737n.
prohibition 757n.
malediction 899n.
condemnation 961n.
penalty 963n.
prose
plainness 573n.
be loquacious 581vb.
reading matter 589n.
prose 593n.
prosecute
do 676vb.
prosecution
pursuit 619n.
accusation 928n.
legal trial 959n.
proselyte
changed person 147n.
learner 538n.
tergiversator 603n.
proselytize
convert 147vb.
teach 534vb.
proser
chatterer 581n.
bore 838n.
prose-writer
author 589n.
prose 593n.
prosiness
feebleness 572n.
(*see* prosaic)
prosing
prolix 570adj.
loquacious 581adj.
(*see* prosaic)
prosody
prosody 593n.
prosopography
description 590n.
prosopopoeia
metaphor 519n.
prospect
futurity 124n.
looking ahead 124n.
destiny 155n.
range 183n.
view 438n.
spectacle 445n.
search 459vb.

be tentative 461vb.
probability 471n.
expectation 507n.
prediction 511n.
art subject 553n.
prospective
future 124adj.
prospector
inquirer 459n.
experimenter 461n.
prospectus
list 87n.
prediction 511n.
compendium 592n.
policy 623n.
prosper
progress 285vb.
flourish 615vb.
get better 654vb.
succeed 727vb.
prosper 730vb.
be profitable 771vb.
prosperity
(*see* prosper, prosperous)
prosperous
opportune 137adj.
beneficial 644adj.
prosperous 730adj.
rich 800adj.
happy 824adj.
promising 852adj.
prosthetic
additional 38n.
preceding 64adj.
fore 237adj.
prostitute
pervert 655vb.
debauch 951vb.
prostitute 952n.
prostitution
deterioration 655n.
misuse 675n.
social evil 951n.
prostrate
disable 161vb.
demolish 165vb.
low 210adj.
supine 216adj.
flatten 216vb.
depressed 311adj.
sick 651adj.
fatigue 684vb.
submitting 721adj.
sadden 834vb.
servile 879adj.
respectful 920adj.
prostrate oneself
stoop 311vb.
greet 884vb.
show respect 920vb.
worship 981vb.
perform ritual 988vb.
prostration
(*see* prostrate)
prosy
prolix 570adj.
prosyllogism
argumentation 475n.
protagonist
actor 594n.
proficient 696n.
protean
multiform 82adj.
changeful 152adj.
protect
accompany 89vb.
screen 421vb.
preserve 666vb.
patronize 703vb.
befriend 880vb.
(*see* protection)
protected
non-liable 919n.
protection
surveillance 457n.
protection 660n.
safeguard 662n.
defense 713n.
restriction 747n.
protectionism
restriction 747n.
protective clothing
armor 713n.
protective coloring
disguise 527n.
protective custody
detention 747n.
protectiveness
love 887n.
protector
influence 178n.
protector 660n.
patron 707n.
defender 713n.
master 741n.
keeper 749n.
friend 880n.
libertine 952n.
protectorate
protection 660n.
polity 733n.
protectorship
magistrature 733n.
protégé
dependent 742n.
friend 880n.
protein
food content 301n.
organism 358n.
protest
dissent 489n., vb.
affirm 532vb.
negate 533vb.
unwillingness 598n.
oppose 704vb.
resistance 715n.
revolt 738vb.
refusal 760n.
deprecation 762n.
non-observance 769n.
non-payment 805n.
be discontented 829vb.
disapprobation 924n.
protestant
dissentient 489n.
negative 533adj.
deprecatory 762adj.
protestant 976n.
church party 978n.
protester
agitator 738n.
protest too much
exaggerate 546vb.
protest, under
by force 740adv.
disapprovingly 924adv.
Proteus
multiformity 82n.
changeable thing 152n.
prothalamion
poem 593n.
wedding 894n.
prothesis
precedence 64n.
altar 990n.
proto-
past 125adj.
protocol
practice 610n.
treaty 765n.
etiquette 848n.
formality 875n.
protomartyr
precursor 66n.
proton
particle 33n.
element 319n.
protonotary
recorder 549n.
protoplasm
origin 68n.
matter 319n.
organism 358n.
life 360n.
prototypal
unimitative 21adj.
prototypal 23adj.
prototype
prototype 23n.
idea 451n.
protozoon
animalcule 196n.
animal 365n.
protract
spin out 113n.
put off 136vb.

sustain 146vb.
lengthen 203vb.
be diffuse 570vb.
be obstructive 702vb.
protractor
angular measure 247n.
gauge 465n.
protreptic
inducive 612adj.
protrude
jut 254vb.
protrusion
convexity 253n.
protuberance
convexity 253n.
protuberance 254n.
proud
defiant 711adj.
worshipful 866adj.
proud 871adj.
vain 873adj.
insolent 878adj.
proud flesh
swelling 253n.
prove
happen 154vb.
expand 197vb.
experiment 461vb.
demonstrate 478vb.
be true 494vb.
indicate 547vb.
feel 818vb.
proven
trustworthy 929adj.
provenance
origin 68n.
provender
provender 301n.
provision 633n.
proverb
maxim 496n.
proverbial
known 490adj.
aphoristic 496adj.
proverbialist
preacher 537n.
phrase 563n.
provide
foresee 510vb.
find means 629vb.
store 632vb.
provide 633vb.
make ready 669vb.
permit 756vb.
give 781vb.
provided
if 8adv.
provided 468adv.
providence
foresight 510n.
divineness 965n.
theocracy 965n.
provident
vigilant 457adj.
intelligent 498adj.
foreseeing 510adj.
providential
opportune 137adj.
divine 965adj.
province
classification 77n.
district 184n.
abode 192n.
function 622n.
polity 733n.
parish 985n.
provincial
regional 184adj.
provincial 192adj.
narrow-minded 481adj.
subject 742n.
ill-bred 847adj.
countryman 869n.
plebeian 869adj.
ecclesiastical 985adj.
provincialism
narrow mind 481n.
prejudice 481n.
dialect 560n.
proving ground
testing agent 461n.
provision
accumulation 74n.
foresight 510n.
means 629n.
store 632n.
provision 633n.
fitting out 669n.
subvention 703n.
conditions 766n.
funds 797n.
provisional
circumstantial 8adj.
inferior 35adj.
ephemeral 114adj.
changeable 143adj.
substituted 150adj.
experimental 461adj.
qualifying 468adj.
uncertain 474adj.
preparatory 669adj.
conditional 766adj.
provisionally
conditionally 7adv.
if 8adv.
during pleasure 112adv.
transiently 114adv.
on terms 766adv.
provisionary
provisionary 633adj.
provisions
provisions 301n.
proviso
qualification 468n.
pretext 614n.
conditions 766n.
provisory
conditional 766adj.
provocation
causation 156n.
inducement 612n.
excitation 821n.
annoyance 827n.
sauciness 878n.
resentment 891n.
provocative
defiant 711adj.
impure 951adj.
(*see* provocation, provoke)
provoke
cause 156vb.
incite 612vb.
make quarrels 709vb.
torment 827vb.
be insolent 878vb.
provoking
annoying 827adj.
provost
master 741n.
provost marshal
police 955n.
prow
prow 237n.
prowess
deed 676n.
skill 694n.
success 727n.
prowess 855n.
prowl
wander 267vb.
be stealthy 525vb.
proximate
sequent 65adj.
near 200adj.
proximity
nearness 200n.
contiguity 202n.
proximo
subsequently 120adv.
proxy
substitute 150n.
commission 751n.
consignee 754n.
deputy 755n.
prude
prude 950n.
(*see* prudish)
prudence
thought 449n.
carefulness 457n.
sagacity 498n.
foresight 510n.
economy 814n.
caution 858n.
virtues 933n.
prudent
cowardly 856adj.
prudery

fastidiousness 862n.
modesty 874n.
prudish
severe 735adj.
affected 850adj.
fastidious 862adj.
modest 874adj.
prudish 950adj.
prune
subtract 39vb.
cut 46vb.
shorten 204vb.
fruit 301n.
extract 304vb.
cultivate 370vb.
prunes and prisms
pretension 850n.
pruning-hook
sharp edge 256n.
prurience
curiosity 453n.
desire, libido 859n.
impurity 951n.
Prussianism
bellicosity 718n.
brute force 735n.
pry
inquisitor 453n.
be curious 453vb.
inquire 459vb.
psalm
vocal music 412n.
hymn 981n.
psalm-book
(*see* psalter)
psalmist
musician 413n.
theologian 973n.
worshiper 981n.
psalmodist
worshiper 981n.
psalmody
vocal music 412n.
act of worship 981n.
hymn 981n.
public worship 981n.
psalm-singing
pietistic 979adj.
psalter
vocal music 412n.
scripture 975n.
hymn 981n.
hymnal 988n.
psaltery
harp 414n.
psephism
legislation 953n.
pseudo
simulating 18adj.
imitative 20adj.
spurious 542adj.
pseudologist
liar 545n.
pseudonym
name 561n.
misnomer 562n.
psi
intuition 476n.
psychics 984n.
psittacosis
animal disease 651n.
psyche
subjectivity 320n.
intellect, spirit 447n.
psychiatry
psychology 447n.
insanity 503n.
therapy 658n.
psychic
immaterial 320adj.
psychic 447adj.
psychic 984n.
psychic bid
gambling 618n.
psychic research
spirit 447n.
spiritualism 984n.
psychics 984n.
psychism
immateriality 320n.
occultism 984n.
psychics 984n.
psychoanalysis
psychology 447n.
therapy 658n.
psychobiology
psychology 447n.
psychogenesis
intellect 447n.
psychogram
record 548n.
spiritualism 984n.
psychography
psychology 447n.
description 590n.
spiritualism 984n.
psychological
psychic 447adj.
behaving 688adj.
psychological moment
crisis 137n.
psychologist
psychologist 447n.
psychology
psychology 447n.
conduct 688n.
affections 817n.
psychics 984n.
psychomancy
spirit 447n.
theomancy 511n.
sorcery 983n.
occultism 984n.
spiritualism 984n.
psychometry
psychology 447n.
psychoneurosis
psychopathy 503n.
psychopath
madman 504n.
psychopathologist
psychologist 447n.
doctor 658n.
psychopathology
psychology 447n.
psychopathy
psychopathy 503n.
psychopedics
therapy 658n.
psychopharmacology
medical art 658n.
psychophysicist
psychist 984n.
psychophysics
psychology 447n.
psychophysiology
psychology 447n.
psychosis
psychopathy 503n.
psychotherapy
psychology 447n.
insanity 503n.
therapy 658n.
psychotic
insane 503adj.
madman 504n.
pterodactyl
animal 365n.
ptisan
tonic 658n.
Ptolemaic system
centrality 225n.
world 321n.
pub
tavern 192n.
pub-crawl
drunkenness 949n.
puberty
preparedness 669n.
(*see* adultness)
pubescence
youth 130n.
hair 259n.
public
social group 371n.
national 371adj.
known 490adj.
manifest 522adj.
well-known 528adj.
formal 875adj.
public address system
telecommunication 531n.
publican
caterer 633n.
tyrant 735n.
receiver 782n.
publication
information 524n.
disclosure 526n.
publication 528n.
call 547n.

book 589n.
public convenience
latrine 649n.
public domain
joint possession 775n.
public health officer
sanitarian 652n.
public house
tavern 192n.
publicist
intellectual 492n.
publicizer 528n.
dissertator 591n.
publicity
generality 79n.
knowledge 490n.
manifestation 522n.
publicity 528n.
ostentation 875n.
publicity agent
publicizer 528n.
publicize
(*see* publish)
public opinion
belief 485n.
consensus 488n.
tribunal 956n.
Public Orator
speaker 579n.
public ownership
joint possession 775n.
public purse
treasury 799n.
public relations officer
publicizer 328n.
public sector
apportionment 783n.
trade 791n.
public service
commission 751n.
public spirit
patriotism 901n.
publish
attract notice 455vb.
manifest 522vb.
publish 528vb.
print 587vb.
publisher
publicizer 528n.
bookman 589n.
puce
brown 430adj.
red color 431n.
purple 434adj.
pucelage
nonage 130n.
celibacy 895n.
puck
missile 287n.
Puck
fairy 970n.
elf 970n.
pucker
fold 261n., vb.
puckish
harmful 645adj.
fairylike 970adj.
pudding
pudding 301n.
softness 327n.
semiliquidity 354n.
pulpiness 356n.
sweet 392n.
puddle
shallowness 212n.
agitate 318vb.
lake 346n.
thicken 354vb.
puddled
opaque 423adj.
pudency, pudicity
purity 950n.
pudenda
genitalia 164n.
pudgy
fleshy 195adj.
puerile
trivial 639adj.
puerility
folly 499n.
despisedness 922n.
puerperal
productive 164adj.
puff
dilation 197n.
emit 300vb.
pastry 301n.
breeze 352n.
blow, breathe 352vb.
smoke 388vb.
overrate 482vb.
exaggerate 546vb.
advertisement 528n.
be fatigued 684vb.
boast 877n., vb.
praise 923vb.
puffed-up
prideful 871adj.
vain 873adj.
puffery
exaggeration 546n.
boasting 877n.
puffin
bird of prey 365n.
puffy
unstable 152adj.
fleshy 195adj.
expanded 197adj.
windy 352adj.
pug
foot 214n.
pugilist 722n.
puggaree
headgear 228n.
coil 251n.
pugilism
pugilism 716n.
sport 837n.
pugilist
athlete 162n.
pugilist 722n.
pug-mark
trace 548n.
pugnacious
(*see* pugnacity)
pugnacity
quarrelsomeness 709n.
bellicosity 718n.
irascibility 892n.
puisne
subsequent 120adj.
young 130adj.
puissant
powerful 160adj.
strong 162adj.
authoritative 733adj.
puja
festivity 837n.
holy-day 988n.
puke
vomit 300vb.
pukka
genuine 494adj.
pulchritude
beauty 841n.
pule
cry 408vb.
ululate 409vb.
weep 836vb.
pull
duplicate 22n.
vantage 34n.
influence 178n.
blunt 257vb.
row 269vb.
deflect 282vb.
propel 287vb.
traction 288n.
attraction 291n.
extract 304vb.
touch 378vb.
letterpress 587n.
reading matter 589n.
exertion 682n.
bungling 695n.
pull back
restrain 747vb.
pull down
demolish 165vb.
fell 311vb.
pulled down
weakly 163adj.
pullet
youngling 132n.
poultry 365n.
pulley
wheel 250n.
tool 630n.

Pullman
train 274n.
pull one's leg
be witty 839vb.
ridicule 851vb.
pull one's punches
avoid 620vb.
pull one's weight
influence 178vb.
pull on with
be friendly 880vb.
pull out
lengthen 203vb.
open 263vb.
start out 296vb.
eject 300vb.
extract 304vb.
pull-out
aeronautics 271n.
pullover
vest 228n.
pull-punkah
ventilation 352n.
pull strings
influence 178vb.
be instrumental 628vb.
pull through
be restored 656vb.
pull-through
opener 263n.
cleaning utensil 648n.
cleanser 648n.
cathartic 658n.
pull together
concur 181vb.
pull to pieces
demolish 165vb.
argue 475vb.
detract 926vb.
pullulate
be many 104vb.
reproduce itself 164vb.
be fruitful 171vb.
pullulation
expansion 197n.
pull up
halt 145vb.
come to rest 266vb.
extract 304vb.
elevate 310vb.
indict 928vb.
pull-up
stopping place 145n.
café 192n.
pulmonary
puffing 352adj.
pulp
demolish 165vb.
deform 244vb.
soften 327vb.
thicken 354vb.
pulpiness 356n.
paper 631n.
pulpit
stand 218n.
publicity 528n.
rostrum 539n.
church utensil 990n.
pulpiteer
preacher 537n.
speaker 579n.
religionist 979n.
pastor 986n.
pulpitry
teaching 534n.
oration 579n.
ministration 988n.
pulpy
soft 327adj.
semiliquid 354adj.
pulpy 356adj.
pulsate
be periodic 141vb.
oscillate 317vb.
pulsation
feeling 818n.
(*see* pulse)
pulse
periodicity 141n.
vegetable 301n.
oscillation 317n.
spasm 318n.
plant 366n.
pulverize
break 46vb.
demolish 165vb.
strike 279vb.
soften 327vb.
pulverize 332vb.
pulverizer
pulverizer 332n.
pulverulence
pulverulence 332n.
puma
cat 365n.
pumice stone
cleanser 648n.
pummel
strike 279vb.
fight 716vb.
pump
footwear 228n.
irrigator 341n.
make flow 350vb.
sufflation 352n.
interrogate 459vb.
pump in
provide 633vb.
pumpkin
vegetable 301n.
pump out
make smaller 198vb.
void 300vb.
sufflate 352vb.
pump-room
meeting place 192n.
hospital 658n.
place of amusement 837n.
pump up
enlarge 197vb.
sufflate 352vb.
pun
assimilation 18n.
equivocalness 518n.
word 559n.
witticism 839n.
punch
mold 23n.
vigorousness 174n.
perforator 263n.
pierce 263vb.
drafthorse 273n.
knock 279n.
liquor 301n.
mark 547vb.
printing 555n.
vigor 571n.
Punch and Judy
stage play 594n.
plaything 837n.
punchbowl
bowl 194n.
cavity 255n.
punch-drunk
insensible 375adj.
puncheon
vat 194n.
perforator 263n.
punch in
make concave 255vb.
punchinello
entertainer 594n.
punch out
efform 243vb.
punctilio
etiquette 848n.
formality 875n.
probity 929n.
punctilious
accurate 494adj.
observant 768adj.
well-bred 848adj.
fastidious 862adj.
formal 875adj.
trustworthy 929adj.
punctual
instantaneous 116adj.
synchronous 123adj.
early 135adj.
periodic 141adj.
accurate 494adj.
observant 768adj.
punctuate
discontinue 72vb.
variegate 437vb.
mark 547vb.
parse 564vb.
punctuation
punctuation 547n.
puncture
make smaller 198vb.

perforation 263n.
wound 655n.
hitch 702n.
pundit
sage 500n.
jurist 958n.
pungency
sharpness 256n.
sourness 393n.
vigor 571n.
pungent
keen 174adj.
pungent 388adj.
unsavory 391adj.
odorous 394adj.
fetid 397adj.
forceful 571adj.
felt 818adj.
witty 839adj.
ungracious 885adj.
Punic faith
falsehood 541n.
perfidy 930n.
punish
be severe 735vb.
punish 963vb.
punishable
illegal 954adj.
punishable 963adj.
punisher
avenger 910n.
vindicator 927n.
punisher 963n.
punishing
vigorous 174adj.
fatiguing 684adj.
paining 827adj.
punishment
suffering 825n.
reprimand 924n.
condemnation 961n.
punishment 963n.
punitive
punitive 963adj.
punitive action
retaliation 714n.
punitive expedition
revenge 910n.
punk
lighter 385n.
bad 645adj.
prostitute 952n.
punkah
ventilation 352n.
refrigerator 384n.
punnet
basket 194n.
punster
humorist 839n.
punt
row 269vb.
rowboat 275n.
kick 279vb.
propel 287vb.
gamble 618vb.
punter
boatman 270n.
gambler 618n.
puny
small 33adj.
weak 163adj.
little 196adj.
unimportant 639adj.
pup
reproduce itself 164vb.
(*see* puppy)
pupa
youngling 132n.
pupil
centrality 225n.
eye 438n.
learner 538n.
pupilage
nonage 130n.
helplessness 161n.
learning 536n.
puppet
dwarf 196n.
dupe 544n.
image 551n.
nonentity 639n.
auxiliary 707n.
slave 742n.
puppetry
stage play 594n.
puppy
youngling 132n.
dog 365n.
fop 848n.
insolent person 878n.
puppyism
affectation 850n.
Purana
non-Biblical scripture 975n.
purblind
dim-sighted 440adj.
misjudging 481adj.
purchasable
bought 792adj.
venal 930adj.
purchase
pivot 218n.
requirement 627n.
acquire 771vb.
booty 790n.
purchase 792n., vb.
purchaser
owner 776n.
recipient 782n.
purchaser 792n.
purdah
womankind 373n.
concealment 525n.
seclusion 883n.
(*see* screen)
pure
absolute 32adj.
unmixed 44adj.
whole 52adj.
white 427adj.
genuine 494adj.
elegant 575adj.
excellent 644adj.
perfect 646adj.
clean 648adj.
salubrious 652adj.
tasteful 846adj.
honorable 929adj.
disinterested 931adj.
virtuous 933adj.
innocent 935adj.
pure 950adj.
puree
soup 301n.
pure gold
exceller 644n.
pure gospel
orthodoxy 976n.
purfle
hem 234vb.
purgation
progression 285n.
cleansing 648n.
penance 941n.
purgative
opener 263n.
excretory 302adj.
cleansing 648adj.
cathartic 658n.
purgatorial
paining 827adj.
atoning 941adj.
purgatory
cleansing 648adj.
suffering 825n.
penance 941n.
purge
eliminate 44vb.
slaughter 362n., vb.
purify 648vb.
cathartic 658n.
purification
simplification 44n.
inodorousness 395n.
cleansing 648n.
amendment 654n.
ritual act 988n.
purify
exclude 57vb.
purify 648vb.
sanitate 652vb.
purism
pretension 850n.
purist
stylist 575n.
man of taste 846n.
affector 850n.

perfectionist 862n.
puritan
affector 850n.
disapprover 924n.
prude 950n.
Puritan
sectarist 978n.
religionist 979n.
puritanical
severe 735adj.
serious 834adj.
fastidious 862adj.
ascetic 945adj.
prudish 950adj.
puritanism
(*see* puritan)
Puritans
church party 978n.
purity
simpleness 44n.
elegance 575n.
artlessness 699n.
good taste 846n.
modesty 874n.
celibacy 895n.
probity 929n.
virtue 933n.
innocence 935n.
temperance 942n.
purity 950n.
sanctity 979n.
purl
flow 350vb.
sound faint 401vb.
needlework 844n.
purlieu
district 184n.
circumjacence 230n.
near place 290n.
purloin
steal 788vb.
defraud 788vb.
purple
purple 434n., adj.
purple patch
discontinuity 72n.
ornament 574n.
eloquence 579n.
purport
meaning 514n.
purpose
will 595n.
be resolute 599vb.
intention 617n.
use 673n.
purposeful
resolute 599adj.
intended 617adj.
planning 623adj.
purposeless
capricious 604adj.
designless 618adj.
useless 641adj.
purpose, to the
apt 24adj.
purpure
heraldry 547n.
purr
sound faint 401vb.
ululate 409vb.
be pleased 824vb.
be content 828vb.
pur sang
noble 868adj.
purse
stow 187vb.
pocket 194n.
become small 198vb.
insert 303vb.
funds 797n.
treasury 799n.
purse-bearer
treasurer 798n.
purser
provider 633n.
treasurer 798n.
purse-strings
finance 797n.
treasury 799n.
pursuance
sequence 65n.
following 284n.
pursuit 619n.
pursue
pursue 619vb.
desire 859vb.
court 889vb.
(*see* pursuit)
pursuer
hunter 619n.
pursuit
sequence 65n.
following 284n.
search 459n.
intention 617n.
pursuit 619n.
business 622n.
pursuivant
messenger 531n.
heraldry 547n.
officer 741n.
pursy
fleshy 195adj.
purulent
diseased 651adj.
toxic 653adj.
purvey
feed 301vb.
provide 633vb.
purveyor
caterer 633n.
purview
range 183n.
intention 617n.
pus
fluid 335n.
semiliquidity 354n.
dirt 649n.
ulcer 651n.
push
crisis 137n.
vigorousness 174n.
transpose 272vb.
impulse 279n.
propulsion 287n.
ejection 300n.
gesture 547n.
motivate 612vb.
be active 678vb.
haste 680n.
party 708n.
attack 712n., vb.
push away
repel 292vb.
push-bicycle
bicycle 274n.
push-bike
ride 267vb.
push button
instrument 628n.
push-button
instrumental 628adj.
pushcart
pushcart 274n.
pusher
ram 279n.
propellant 287n.
busy person 678n.
push forward
promote 285vb.
be vain 873vb.
pushful, pushing
vigorous 174adj.
assertive 532adj.
active 678adj.
push off
start out 296vb.
decamp 296vb.
push on
progress 285vb.
push out
eject 300vb.
push-over
victory 727n.
push-pin
fastening 47n.
pusillanimity
cowardice 856n.
puss
cat 365n.
pussy
toxic 653adj.
pussyfoot
be stealthy 525vb.
hinderer 702n.
be cautious 858vb.
disapprover 924n.
abstainer 942n.
ascetic 945n.

sober person 948n.
pustule
skin disease 651n.
put
firm-set 45adj.
place 187vb.
put across
convince 485vb.
put aside
set apart 46vb.
exclude 57vb.
be neglectful 458vb.
put at ease
please 826vb.
putative
attributed 158adj.
credible 485adj.
supposed 512adj.
put away
destroy 165vb.
stow 187vb.
divorce 896vb.
put back
replace 187vb.
turn back 286vb.
restore 656vb.
put by
store 632vb.
put down
destroy 165vb.
suppress 165vb.
kill 362vb.
overmaster 727vb.
pay 804vb.
put down to
attribute 158vb.
put first
make important 638vb.
put forth
expand 197vb.
propound 512vb.
put forward
promote 285vb.
offer 759vb.
put in
number with 78vb.
arrive 295vb.
insert 303vb.
put in the way of
make possible 469vb.
put in words
phrase 563vb.
put off
put off 136vb.
repel 292vb.
distracted 456adj.
be neglectful 458vb.
dissuade 613vb.
cause dislike 861vb.
put on
imitate 20vb.
wear 228vb.
dissemble 541vb.
be affected 850vb.
put one's finger on
place 187vb.
detect 484vb.
put one's foot down
be resolute 599vb.
put one's foot in it
be clumsy 695vb.
put on the map
advertise 528vb.
put on trial
indict 928vb.
put on weight
grow 36vb.
expand 197vb.
put out
derange 63vb.
disable 161vb.
suppress 165vb.
start out 296vb.
eject 300vb.
extinguish 382vb.
distracted 456adj.
communicate 524vb.
publish 528vb.
cause discontent 829vb.
enrage 891vb.
put over
convince 485vb.
put paid to
terminate 69vb.
putrefaction
decay 51n.
death 361n.
fetor 397n.
uncleanness 649n.
putrefy
deteriorate 655vb.
putrid
fetid 397adj.
not nice 645adj.
put right
inform 524vb.
rectify 654vb.
repair 656vb.
be just 913vb.
putsch
revolt 738n.
putt
insert 303vb.
puttees
legwear 228n.
put teeth into
empower 160vb.
put the cart before the horse
invert 221vb.
stultify oneself 695vb.
put the clock back
be unconformable 84vb.
be late 136vb.
put through
do 676vb.
deal with 688vb.
put to
advise 691vb.
put to flight
defeat 724vb.
put together
join 45vb.
combine 50vb.
compose 56vb.
bring together 74vb.
put to it
in difficulties 700adj.
put to music
harmonize 410vb.
compose music 413vb.
put to rights
regularize 62vb.
put to the proof
experiment 461vb.
put to the question
torment 827vb.
putty
adhesive 47n.
put up
replace 187vb.
dwell 192vb.
elevate 310vb.
put-up
predetermined 608adj.
put-up job
duplicity 541n.
predetermination 608n.
false charge 928n.
put upon
ill-treat 645vb.
oppress 735vb.
put up to
incite 612vb.
put up with
acquiesce 488vb.
be patient 823vb.
suffer 825vb.
forgive 909vb.
puzzle
complexity 61n.
distract 456vb.
puzzle 474vb.
mean nothing 515vb.
enigma 530n.
difficulty 700n.
puzzle out
decipher 520vb.
puzzling
imperspicuous 568adj.
pyemia
infection 651n.
pylon
electricity 160n.

high structure 209n.
pyramid
accumulation 74n.
fixture 153n.
edifice 164n.
high structure 209n.
angular figure 247n.
tomb 364n.
pyramidal
tapering 256adj.
pyre
interment 364n.
fire 379n.
pyrexia
heat 379n.
illness 651n.
pyrogenesis
infection 651n.
pyrography
ornamental art 844n.
pyrology
thermometry 379n.
pyromania
incendiarism 381n.
pyrophobia
phobia 854n.
pyrotechnics
fire 379n.
fireworks 420n.
spectacle 445n.
Pyrrhic
dear 811adj.
Pyrrhonism
philosophy 449n.
doubt 486n.
irreligion 974n.
Pythagoreanism
philosophy 449n.
temperance 942n.
python
compressor 198n.
reptile 365n.
pythoness
oracle 511n.
priest 986n.
pyx
small box 194n.
testing agent 461n.
ritual object 988n.

Q

Q-boat
warship 722n.
Q.E.D.
argumentation 475n.
of course 478adv.
quack
ululation 409n.
sciolist 493n.
false 541adj.
impostor 545n.
be loquacious 581vb.
doctor 658n.
unskilled 695adj.
bungler 697n.
affector 850n.
quackery
sciolism 491n.
misteaching 535n.
unskillfulness 695n.
pretension 850n.
quad
meeting place 192n.
quadrable
fourfold 97adj.
quadragesimal
fasting 946adj.
quadrangle
quaternity 96n.
place 185n.
meeting-place 192n.
angular figure 247n.
quadrant
angular measure 247n.
arc 250n.
gauge 465n.
quadrate
four 96adj.
quadratic
four 96adj.
quadrature
quaternity 96n.
angular figure 247n.
quadrennial
seasonal 141adj.
quadrennium
quaternity 96n.
quadri-
four 96adj.
quadrifid
quartered 98adj.
quadriga
carriage 274n.
quadrilateral
four 96adj.
lateral 239adj.
angular figure 247n.
quadrille
dance 837n.
card game 837n.
quadrillion
over one hundred 99n.
quadriplegia
paralysis 651n.
quadrisection
quadrisection 98n.
quadrivium
curriculum 536n.
quadroon
hybrid 43n.
quadruped
horse 273n.
animal 365n.
quadruple
quadruple 97vb.
quadruplication
quadruplication 97n.
quaestor
official 690n.
officer 741n.
treasurer 798n.
quaff
drink 301vb.
revel 837vb.
get drunk 949vb.
quagmire
marsh 347n.
dirt 649n.
pitfall 663n.
difficulty 700n.
quaich
cup 194n.
quail
table bird 365n.
quake 854vb.
be cowardly 856vb.
quaint
beautiful 841adj.
ornamental 844adj.
ridiculous 849adj.
quaintness
ridiculousness 849n.
quake
show feeling 818vb.
quake 854vb.
Quaker
protestant 976n.
sectarist 978n.
qualification
fitness 24n.
ability 160n.
counter-evidence 467n.
qualification 468n.
sufficiency 635n.
aptitude 694n.
success 727n.
conditions 766n.
dueness 915n.
qualified
fit 24adj.
mixed 43adj.
gifted 694adj.
expert 694adj.
qualify
mix 43vb.
modify 143vb.
moderate 177vb.
discriminate 463vb.
qualify 468vb.
doubt 486vb.
dissent 489vb.
qualify for
be expedient 642vb.
qualitative
characteristic 5adj.
qualities

affections 817n.
virtues 933n.
quality
character 5n.
superiority 34n.
sort 77n.
goodness 644n.
nobility 868n.
virtue 933n.
qualm
doubt 486n.
unwillingness 598n.
nervousness 854n.
qualmish
disliking 861adj.
fastidious 862adj.
qualms of conscience
penitence 939n.
quandary
dubiety 474n.
predicament 700n.
quantification
measurement 465n.
quantify
quantify 26vb.
specify 80vb.
measure 465vb.
quantitative
quantitative 26adj.
quantities
great quantity 32n.
quantity
quantity 26n.
degree 27n.
number 85n.
multitude 104n.
quantum
finite quantity 26n.
element 319n.
portion 783n.
quarantine
set apart 46vb.
exclusion 57n.
hygiene 652n.
prophylactic 658n.
protection 660n.
preservation 666n.
detention 747n.
seclusion 883n.
quarrel
disagreement 25n.
quarrel 709n., vb.
contention 716n.
war 718n.
missile weapon 723n.
be discontented 829vb.
enmity 881n.
be angry 891vb.
quarreler
quarreler 709n.
quarrelsome
quarreling 709adj.
contending 716adj.
sullen 893adj.
quarrelsomeness
irascibility 892n.
quarrier
excavator 255n.
extractor 304n.
quarry
source 156n.
excavation 255n.
extract 304vb.
objective 617n.
chase 619n.
store 632n.
workshop 687n.
booty 790n.
quart
metrology 465n.
quarter
sunder 46vb.
part 53n.
quadrisect 98vb.
period 110n.
district 184n.
locality 187n.
place 187vb.
poop 238n.
laterality 239n.
compass point 281n.
weighment 322n.
metrology 465n.
mark 547vb.
lenity 736n.
coinage 797n.
mercy 905n.
quarter-day
date 108n.
regular return 141n.
quarterdeck
vertex 213n.
quarterings
heraldry 547n.
quarterly
journal 528n.
quartermaster
navigator 270n.
provider 633n.
army officer 741n.
quarters
quarters 192n.
quarter-staff
club 723n.
quarter-tone
musical note 410n.
quarter upon
place 187vb.
quartet
quaternity 96n.
duet 412n.
orchestra 413n.
quartic, quartite
four 96adj.
quarto
quadrisection 98n.
edition 589n.
quartz
hardness 326n.
quash
suppress 165vb.
abrogate 752vb.
quasi
similar 18adj.
supposed 512adj.
misnamed 562adj.
quassia
unsavoriness 390n.
quaternal, quaternary
four 96adj.
quaternion
quaternity 96n.
quaternity
quaternity 96n.
quatrain
verse form 593n.
quatrefoil
quaternity 96n.
quaver
be agitated 318vb.
roll 403vb.
notation 410n.
sing 413vb.
stammer 580vb.
quake 854vb.
quay
stable 192n.
edge 234n.
shelter 662n.
quean
woman 373n.
loose woman 952n.
queasy
disliking 861adj.
queen
sovereign 741n.
chessman 837n.
queen it
seek repute 866vb.
be proud 871vb.
be insolent 878vb.
queenly
ruling 733adj.
impressive 821adj.
worshipful 866adj.
noble 868adj.
proud 871adj.
Queen of Hearts
favorite 890n.
Queen's Bench
law court 956n.
Queensberry rules
justice 913n.
Queen's Counsel
lawyer 958n.
Queen's English
language 557n.
Queen's evidence

testimony 466n.
disclosure 526n.
queer
nonconformist 84n.
abnormal 84adj.
crazed 503adj.
sick 651adj.
ridiculous 849adj.
wrong 914adj.
queer fish
laughing-stock 851n.
queerness
eccentricity 503n.
Queer Street
poverty 801n.
quell
suppress 165vb.
moderate 177vb.
hinder 702vb.
overmaster 727vb.
subjugate 745vb.
frighten 854vb.
queller
victor 727n.
quench
suppress 165vb.
extinguish 382vb.
snuff out 418vb.
sate 863vb.
quenchless
violent 176adj.
greedy 859adj.
querimonious
lamenting 836adj.
querist
questioner 459n.
quern
pulverizer 332n.
querulous
lamenting 836adj.
irascible 892adj.
query
question 459n.
uncertainty 474n.
quest
search 459n.
pursuit 619n.
job 622n.
essay 671n.
undertaking 672n.
question
topic 452n.
curiosity 453n.
question 459n.
interrogate 459vb.
uncertainty 474n.
doubt 486n.
negate 533vb.
questionable
moot 459ad.
uncertain 474adj.
unbelieved 486adj.
disreputable 867adj.
dishonest 930adj.
question and answer
interrogation 459n.
answer 460n.
interlocution 584n.
questioner
listener 415n.
inquisitor 453n.
questioner 459n.
questionless
undisputed 473adj.
question list
question 459n.
question mark
question 459n.
uncertainty 474n.
punctuation 547n.
questionnaire
list 87n.
question 459n.
question paper
question 459n.
question time
interrogation 459n.
queue
retinue 67n.
procession 71n.
pendant 217n.
rear 238n.
queue-jumping
precession 283n.
queue up
await 507vb.
quibble
argue 475vb.
sophistry 477n.
absurdity 497n.
equivocalness 518n.
pretext 614n.
quibbler
reasoner 475n.
sophist 477n.
quick
brief 114adj.
speedy 277adj.
alive 360adj.
intelligent 498adj.
willing 597adj.
active 678adj.
skillful 694adj.
moral sensibility 819n.
quick-change
changeful 152adj.
quick-change artist
alterer 143n.
entertainer 594n.
quicken
strengthen 162vb.
invigorate 174vb.
make violent 176vb.
accelerate 277vb.
live 360vb.
animate 821vb.
quicklime
cleanser 648n.
quick march
gait 265n.
marching 267n.
speeding 277n.
quickness
(*see* quick)
quickness of the hand
sleight 542n.
quicksand
marsh 347n.
pitfall 663n.
quicksilver
changeable thing 152n.
vigorousness 174n.
velocity 277n.
quick, to the
on the raw 819adv.
quick-witted
intelligent 498adj.
quid
mouthful 301n.
tobacco 388n.
coinage 797n.
quiddity
essence 1n.
essential part 5n.
quidnunc
inquisitor 453n.
inquirer 459n.
newsmonger 529n.
quid pro quo
offset 31n.
substitute 150n.
interchange 151n.
retaliation 714n.
reward 962n.
quids in
acquiring 771adj.
quiescence
stability 153n.
inertness 175n.
quiescence 266n.
inaction 677n.
inactivity 679n.
peace 717n.
quiescent
apathetic 820adj.
inexcitable 823adj.
quiet
inert 175adj.
moderation 177n.
assuage 177vb.
smooth 258adj.
quietude 266n.
euphoria 376n.
silence 399n.
soft-hued 425adj.
gray 429adj.

inaction 677n.
reposeful 683adj.
peaceful 717adj.
submitting 721adj.
mediocre 732adj.
inexcitable 823adj.
pleasurable 826adj.
modest 874adj.
secluded 883adj.
quieten
bring to rest 266vb.
silence 399vb.
quietism
quietude 266n.
moral insensibility 820n.
inexcitability 823n.
content 828n.
quiet time
worship 981n.
quietude
(*see* quiet)
quietus
end 69n.
death 361n.
killing 362n.
defeat 728n.
quiff
hair 259n.
hair-dressing 843n.
quill
sharp point 256n.
plumage 259n.
stationery 586n.
quill-driver
penman 586n.
quillet
sophistry 477n.
quilt
coverlet 226n.
variegate 437vb.
quinary
fifth and over 99adj.
quincunx
crossing 222n.
quinine
antidote 658n.
prophylactic 658n.
quinquennial
seasonal 141adj.
quinquennium
period 110n.
quinquereme
galley 275n.
warship 722n.
quinquesection
multisection 100n.
quintal
weighment 322n.
quintessence
essential part 5n.
eminence 644n.
perfection 646n.
quintet
duet 412n.
orchestra 413n.
quintuple
fifth and over 99adj.
quip
witticism 839n.
indignity 921n.
quipu
counting instrument 86n.
quire
letterpress 587n.
edition 589n.
paper 631n.
quirk
whim 604n.
witticism 839n.
quirt
scourge 964n.
quisling
tergiversator 603n.
revolter 738n.
knave 938n.
quit
depart 296vb.
relinquish 621vb.
resign 753vb.
fail in duty 918vb.
quitclaim
liberation 746n.
quite
greatly 32adv.
slightly 33adv.
completely 54adv.
quite, not
almost 33adv.
quit of
losing 772adj.
quit-rent
price 809n.
quits
equivalence 28n.
atonement 941n.
quits, be
retaliate 714vb.
quittance
liberation 746n.
title-deed 767n.
payment 804n.
atonement 941n.
quitter
tergiversator 603n.
avoider 620n.
resignation 753n.
coward ,856n.
quiver
accumulation 74n.
case 194n.
oscillate 317vb.
be agitated 318vb.
feel pain 377vb.
be cold 380vb.
storage 632n.
arsenal 723n.
show feeling 818vb.
be excited 821vb.
quake 854vb.
qui vive, on the
vigilant 457adj.
quixotic
imaginative 513adj.
quixotry
ideality 513n.
rashness 857n.
quiz
gaze 438vb.
watch 441vb.
be curious 453vb.
interrogation 459n.
witticism 839n.
ridicule 851n.
quizmaster
reveler 837n.
quizzical
derisive 851adj.
quizzing-glass
eyeglass 442n.
quoin
press 587n.
quoit
circle 250n.
missile 287n.
quoits
ball game 837n.
quondam
former 125adj.
resigning 753adj.
quorum
finite quantity 26n.
electorate 605n.
sufficiency 635n.
quota
finite quantity 26n.
part 53n.
portion 783n.
quotable
relevant 9adj.
repeated 106adj.
pure 950adj.
quotation
referral 9n.
identity 13n.
repetition 106n.
evidence 466n.
exhibit 522n.
anthology 592n.
price 809n.
quotation marks
punctuation 547n.
quote
exemplify 83vb.
(*see* quotation)
quotes
punctuation 547n.
quotidian

seasonal 141adj.
quotient
quantity 26n.
numerical element 85n.
quotum
finite quantity 26n.

R

R.A.
artist 556n.
Ra
Egyptian gods 967n.
rabbet
join 45vb.
rabbi
theologian 973n.
priest 986n.
rabbinic
theological 973adj.
rabbit
abundance 171n.
vermin 365n.
testee 461n.
beginner 538n.
coward 856n.
rabbit's foot
cosmetic 843n.
rabble
crowd 74n.
rabble 869n.
rabble-rouser
leader 690n.
agitator 738n.
excitant 821n.
Rabelaisian
impure 951n.
rabid
frenzied 503adj.
excitable 822adj.
angry 891adj.
rabies
frenzy 503n.
raccoon
rodent 365n.
race
race 11n.
genealogy 169n.
speeding 277n.
outdo 306vb.
current 350n.
pungency 388n.
vocation 622n.
haste 680n.
community 708n.
racing 716n.
racecourse
meeting-place 192n.
speeding 277n.
gaming-house 618n.
racing 716n.
arena 724n.
race-horse
thoroughbred 273n.
speeder 277n.
race prejudice
prejudice 481n.
pride 871n.
racer
thoroughbred 273n.
speeder 277n.
contender 716n.
race-riot
lawlessness 954n.
rachis
rear 238n.
rachitic
deformed 246adj.
racial
ethnic 11adj.
parental 169adj.
human 371adj.
racialism, racism
prejudice 481n.
hatred 888n.
raciness
(see racy)
racing
chase 619n.
racing 716n.
racing driver
speeder 277n.
rack
compartment 194n.
shelf 218n.
distort 246vb.
cloud 355n.
give pain 377vb.
ill-treat 645vb.
purify 648vb.
oppress 735vb.
torment 827vb.
torture 963vb.
instrument of torture 967n.
racket
commotion 318n.
loudness 400n.
discord 411n.
quarrel 709n.
foul play 930n.
racketeer
speculate 791vb.
offender 904n.
be dishonest 930vb.
rackets
ball game 837n.
rackety
loud 400adj.
riotous 738adj.
gay 833adj.
unchaste 951adj.
rack one's brains
think 449vb.
rack-rent
levy 786vb.
overcharge 811vb.
be parsimonious 816vb.
raconteur
narrator 590n.
racy
vigorous 174adj.
tasty 386adj.
savory 390adj.
stylistic 566adj.
forceful 571adj.
lively 819adj.
impure 951adj.
radar
sailing aid 269n.
optical device 442n.
detector 484n.
telecommunication 531n.
indicator 547n.
directorship 689n.
raddle
network 222n.
redden 431vb.
raddled
beautified 843adj.
radially
longwise 203adv.
radian
angular measure 247n.
radiance
light, glow 417n.
beauty 841n.
radiant
divergent 294adj.
luminous 417adj.
radiating 417adj.
luminescent 420adj.
happy 824adj.
cheerful 833adj.
beautiful 841adj.
splendid 841adj.
radiant energy
radiation 417n.
radiant point
centrality 225n.
meteor 321n.
radiate
transfer 272vb.
emit 300vb.
(see radiation)
radiation
dispersion 75n.
divergence 294n.
oscillation 317n.
radiation 417n.
poison 659n.
radiator
ejector 300n.
heater 383n.
radical
intrinsic 5adj.

complete 54adj.
numerical 85adj.
revolutionist 149n.
revolutionary 149adj.
source 156n.
fundamental 156adj.
important 638adj.
reformer 654n.
opponent 705n.
sectional 708adj.
radical change
revolution 149n.
radicalism
reformism 654n.
radication
habituation 610n.
radicle
foliage 366n.
radiesthesia
intuition 476n.
discovery 484n.
divination 511n.
radio
publicity 528n.
telecommunication 531n.
radioactive
dynamic 160adj.
vigorous 174adj.
radiating 417adj.
radioactivity
radiation 417n.
insalubrity 653n.
poison 659n.
radio astronomy
astronomy 321n.
radiogram
gramophone 414n.
hearing aid 415n.
information 524n.
message 529n.
radiograph
photography 551n.
radiolocation
bearings 186n.
discovery 484n.
radiology
optics 417n.
radio mast
high structure 209n.
telecommunication 531n.
radiometer
optical device 442n.
radiometry
optics 417n.
radio-mirror
space-ship 276n.
radiophone
hearing aid 415n.
radioscopy
optics 417n.
radio telescope
astronomy 321n.
radiotherapy
therapy 658n.
radius
range 183n.
line 203n.
breadth 205n.
radix
source 156n.
raff
dirt 649n.
raffia
ligature 47n
fiber 208n.
raffle
chance 159n.
gambling 618n.
raft
space 201vb.
carry 273vb.
raft 275n.
cultivate 370vb.
safeguard 662n.
rafter(s)
beam 218n.
roof 226n.
materials 631n.
rag
book 589n.
torment 827vb.
revel 837n.
be witty 839vb.
ridicule 851vb.
raga
key 410n.
ragamuffin
slut 61n.
low fellow 869n.
ragbag
non-uniformity 17n.
rage
violence 176n.
prevail 178vb.
blow 352vb.
be active 678vb.
excitable state 822n.
fashion 848n.
desire, libido 859n.
anger 891n.
rage against
dispraise 924vb.
ragged
uncovered 229adj.
convoluted 251adj.
undulatory 251adj.
raggedness
non-uniformity 17n.
poverty 801n.
raglan
overcoat 228n.
ragout
a mixture 43n.
rag-picker
poor man 801n.
rags
clothing 228n.
rubbish 641n.
rags, in
dilapidated 655adj.
beggarly 801adj.
rag, tag and bobtail
commonalty 869n.
ragtime
music 412n.
raid
lay waste 165vb.
ingress 297n.
irrupt 299vb.
attack 712n.
taking 786n.
rob 788vb.
raider
attacker 712n.
soldier 722n.
warship 722n.
taker 786n.
robber 789n.
raiding
warfare 718n.
brigandage 788n.
rail
handle 218n.
transport 272n.
carry 273vb.
curse 899vb.
exprobate 924vb.
railer
defamer 926n.
rail in
circumscribe 232vb.
railing
handle 218n.
edge 234n.
fence 235n.
raillery
ridicule 851n.
sauciness 878n.
railroad, railway
railroad 624n.
rails
parallelism 219n.
fence 235n.
railroad 624n.
railway train
train 274n.
raiment
clothing 228n.
rain
descend 309vb.
moisture 341n.
rain 350n., vb.
abound 635vb.
rainbow
curve 248n.
arc 250n.

light 417n.
color 425n.
variegation 437n.
rainbow effect
variegation 437n.
rain-cloud
cloud 355n.
raincoat
overcoat 228n.
rainfall
moisture 341n.
rain 350n.
rain-gauge
hygrometry 341n.
rain 350n.
rainless
dry 342n.
rain or shine
certainly 473adv.
rainproof
dry 342adj.
rainy
humid 341adj.
rainy 350adj.
rainy day
adversity 731n.
raise
augment 36vb.
initiate 68vb.
generate 164vb.
displace 188vb.
make higher 209vb.
make vertical 215vb.
move 265vb.
promote 285vb.
elevate 310vb.
lighten 323vb.
breed stock 369vb.
see 438vb.
improvement 654n.
acquire 771vb.
levy 786vb.
relieve 831vb.
raise Cain
be loud 400vb.
revolt 738vb.
be angry 891vb.
raise one's banner
go to war 718vb.
raise one's glass to
toast 876vb.
raise one's hand
gesticulate 547vb.
vote 605vb.
raise one's hat
greet 884vb.
raise one's voice
vociferate 400vb.
dissent 489vb.
emphasize 532vb.
speak 579vb.
deprecate 762vb.
raiser
producer 167n.
lifter 310n.
raise steam
navigate 269vb.
make ready 669vb.
raise subscriptions
beg 761vb.
raise the alarm
signal 547vb.
raise the alarm 665vb.
frighten 854vb.
raise the bid
bargain 791vb.
overcharge 811vb.
raise the sights
augment 36vb.
aim at 617vb.
raise the subject
initiate 68vb.
raise the wind
borrow 785vb.
raisin
fruit 301n.
raison d'être
reason why 156n.
intention 617n.
raja
potentate 741n.
Rajput
militarist 722n.
aristocrat 868n.
rake
obliquity 220n.
draw 288vb.
extractor 304n.
farm tool 370n.
search 459vb.
cleaning utensil 648n.
fire at 712vb.
bad man 938n.
sensualist 944n.
libertine 952n.
rake in
bring together 74vb.
draw 288vb.
rake-off
decrement 42n.
earnings 771n.
portion 783n.
receipt 807n.
price 809n.
discount 810n.
rake over, rake through
search 459vb.
rake up
retrospect 505vb.
rakish
oblique 220adj.
fashionable 848adj.
lecherous 951adj.
rallentando
tempo 410n.
adagio 412adv.
rally
assemblage 74n.
congregate 74vb.
interchange 151n.
propulsion 287n.
call 547n.
persevere 600vb.
incite 612vb.
get better 645vb.
restore 656vb.
contest 716n.
give battle 718vb.
ridicule 851vb.
give courage 855vb.
rallying cry
call 547n.
danger signal 665n.
rallying point
focus 76n.
rally round
be in order 60vb.
ram
demolish 165vb.
ram 279n.
collide 279vb.
sheep 365n.
male animal 372n.
strike at 712vb.
charge 712vb.
ramble
pedestrianism 267n.
wander 267vb.
stray 282vb.
be insane 503vb.
be diffuse 570vb.
rambler
wanderer 208n.
rambling
irrelevant 10adj.
fitful 142adj.
unstable 152adj.
(*see* ramble)
ram down
fill 54vb.
close 264vb.
be dense 324vb.
ramification
bond 47n.
branch 53n.
bifurcation 92n.
descendent 170n.
sonship 170n.
range 183n.
filament 208n.
divergence 294n.
ramify
angulate 247vb.
(*see* ramification)
rammer
stopper 264n.
ram 279n.
ramp

be vertical 215vb.
obliquity 220n.
ascent 308n.
leap 312vb.
be agitated 318vb.
trickery 542n.
be excited 821vb.
get angry 891vb.
foul play 930n.

rampage
rampage 61vb.
be violent 176vb.
be agitated 318vb.
be loud 400vb.
be active 678vb.
excitable state 822n.
anger 891n.

rampant
furious 176adj.
vertical 215adj.
heraldic 547adj.
lecherous 951adj.

rampart
fortification 713n.
defense 713n.

Ram Raj
palmy days 730n.
happiness 824n.

ramrod
stopper 264n.
ram 279n.
fire-arm 723n.

ramshackle
flimsy 163adj.
dilapidated 655adj.
unsafe 661adj.

ranch
breed stock 369vb.
farm 370n.
lands 777n.

rancher
herdsman 369n.

rancid
decomposed 51adj.
unsavory 391adj.
fetid 397adj.

rancor
enmity 881n.
hatred 888n.
resentment 891n.
malevolence 898n.

rancorous
revengeful 910adj.
(*see* rancor)

random
orderless 61adj.
casual 159adj.
deviating 282adj.
indiscriminate 464adj.
uncertain 474adj.
designless 618adj.
unconfined 744adj.

randomness
discontinuity 72n.

random order
disorder 61n.

random sample
empiricism 461n.

random shot
gambling 618n.

randy
lecherous 951adj.

range
arrange 62vb.
series 71n.
accumulation 74n.
classification 77n.
ability 160n.
range 183n.
distance 199n.
breadth 205n.
layer 207n.
traverse 267vb.
plain 348n.
furnace 383n.
hearing 415n.
visibility 443n.
arena 724n.
scope 744n.
merchandise 795n.

range-finder
direction 281n.
telescope 442n.

range oneself
be in order 60vb.

range oneself with
join a party 708vb.

ranger
wanderer 268n.
keeper 749n.

range together
juxtapose 202vb.

range under, range with
be included 78vb.

ranging
extensive 32adj.
free 744adj.

rangy
narrow 206adj.
tall 209adj.

rani
potentate 741n.

rank
relativeness 9n.
degree 27n.
order 60n.
class 62vb.
series 71n.
serial place 73n.
vegetal 366adj.
unsavory 391adj.
fetid 397adj.
estimate 480vb.
plenteous 635adj.
bad 645adj.
formation 722n.
prestige 866n.
nobility 868n.
heinous 934adj.
impure 951adj.

rank and file
commonalty 869n.

ranker
commoner 869n.

ranking
notable 638adj.
noteworthy 866adj.

rankle
hurt 827vb.

rankling
resentment 891n.

rankness
(*see* rank)

ransack
search 459vb.
rob 788vb.

ransom
equivalence 28n.
restoration 656n.
deliverance 668n.
restitution 787n.
purchase 792vb.
price 809n.
penalty 963n.

ransomed
sanctified 979adj.

ransomer
benefactor 903n.

ransom, hold to
overcharge 811vb.

rant
be absurd 497vb.
empty talk 515n.
exaggeration 546n.
be diffuse 570vb.
magniloquence 574n.
oratory 579n.
act 594vb.
boast 877n.

ranter
chatterer 581n.
boaster 877n.

rap
small coin 33n.
knock 279n.
crackle 402vb.
false money 797n.
corporal punishment 963n.

rapacious
(*see* rapacity)

rapacity
rapacity 786n.
thievishness 788n.
avarice 816n.
desire 859n.
gluttony 947n.

rape

force 176vb.
stealing 788n.
taking 876n.
rape 951n.
debauch 951vb.
raper
libertine 952n.
rapidity
velocity 277n.
rapids
outbreak 176n.
waterfall 350n.
pitfall 663n.
rapid succession
frequency 139n.
rapier
sharp point 256n.
side-arms 723n.
rapine
spoliation 788n.
rap out
voice 577vb.
rap over the knuckles
reprimand 924n.
reprove 924vb.
spank 963vb.
rapparee
robber 789n.
rappee
tobacco 388n.
rapport
relation 9n.
concord 710n.
rapportage
publicity 528n.
rapprochement
concord 710n.
pacification 719n.
friendship 880n.
rapscallion
knave 938n.
rapt
obsessed 455adj.
abstracted 456adj.
impressed 818adj.
rap tables
practice occultism 984vb.
raptorial
taking 786adj.
thieving 788adj.
rapture
excitation 821n.
joy 824n.
love 887n.
rapturous
felt 818adj.
pleased 824adj.
enamored 887adj.
rara avis
rara avis 84n.
infrequency 140n.
rare
superior 34adj.
unusual 84adj.
few 105adj.
infrequent 140adj.
culinary 301adj.
rare 325adj.
airy 340adj.
improbable 472adj.
scarce 636adj.
excellent 644adj.
uncooked 760adj.
of price 811adj.
wonderful 864adj.
raree show
spectacle 445n.
pleasure-ground 837n.
plaything 837n.
rarefaction
rarity 325n.
rarefy
enlarge 197vb.
make smaller 198vb.
make thin 206vb.
rarefy 325vb.
rarely
greatly 32adv.
seldom 140adv.
rareripe
early 135adj.
rarity
levity 323n.
rarity 325n.
paragon 646n.
dearness 811n.
(*see* rare)
rascal
low fellow 869n.
knave 938n.
rascality
improbity 930n.
rascally
cunning 698adj.
disreputable 867adj.
rascally 930adj.
vicious 934adj.
rase
obliterate 550vb.
rash
skin disease 651n.
(*see* rashness)
rasher
piece 53n.
lamina 207n.
meat 301n.
rashness
inattention 456n.
negligence 458n.
indiscrimination 464n.
folly 499n.
non-preparation 670n.
haste 680n.
courage 854n.
rashness 857n.
rashy
diseased 651adj.
rasp
pulverize 332vb.
rub 333vb.
breathe 352vb.
rasp 407vb.
discord 411vb.
raspberry
fruit 301n.
reprimand 924n.
rasping
hoarse 407adj.
rasure
obliteration 550n.
rat
rodent 365n.
inform 524vb.
divulge 526vb.
tergiversator 603n.
apostatize 603vb.
relinquish 621vb.
coward 856n.
noxious animal 904n.
knave 938n.
ratan
(*see* rattan)
rat-a-tat
roll 403n.
rat-catcher
killer 362n.
hunter 619n.
ratchet
tooth 256n.
notch 260n.
rate
quantify 26vb.
degree 27n.
class 62vb.
grade 73vb.
velocity 277n.
appraise 465vb.
estimate 480n.
price 809n., vb.
exprobate 924vb.
rather
slightly 33adv.
optionally 605adv.
ratification
assent 488n.
consent 757n.
compact 765n.
ratificatory
assenting 488adj.
ratifier
signatory 765n.
ratify
stabilize 153vb.
corroborate 466vb.
make certain 473vb.
endorse 488vb.
sign 547vb.
approve 923vb.
make legal 953vb.
rating

naval man 270n.
measurement 465n.
navy man 722n.
tax 809n.
reprimand 924n.
(*see* rate)
ratio
relativeness 9n.
degree 27n.
ratio 85n.
portion 783n.
ratiocination
reasoning 475n.
ration
finite quantity 26n.
provisions 301n.
restrain 747vb.
portion 783n.
rational
numerical 85adj.
mental 447adj.
philosophic 449adj.
plausible 471adj.
rational 475adj.
wise 498adj.
sane 502adj.
rational animal
mankind 371n.
rationale
reason why 156n.
attribution 158n.
motive 612n.
rationalism
philosophy 449n.
reasoning 475n.
antichristianity 974n.
rationalist
reasoner 475n.
interpreter 520n.
irreligionist 974n.
rationalistic
rational 475adj.
irreligious 974adj.
rationalization
arrangement 62n.
sophistry 477n.
plan 623n.
rationalize
reason 475vb.
plan 623vb.
ration book
portion 783n.
rationing
war measures 718n.
restriction 747n.
rations
provisions 633n.
ratline
tackling 47n.
ascent 308n.
rat race
activity 678n.
rattan
club 723n.
ratten
disable 161vb.
ratter
tergiversator 603n.
hunter 619n.
rattle
derange 63vb.
oscillate 317vb.
respiration 352n.
loudness 400n.
crackle 402vb.
roll 403vb.
gong 414n.
distract 456vb.
chatterer 581n.
bauble 639n.
fire at 712n.
frighten 854vb.
rattled
irresolute 601adj.
rattle the saber
boast 877vb.
threaten 900vb.
rattletrap
carriage 274n.
automobile 274n.
ratty
angry 891adj.
irascible 892adj.
raucous
hoarse 407adj.
discordant 411adj.
ravage
havoc 165n.
lay waste 165vb.
impair 655vb.
attack 712vb.
wage war 718vb.
rob 788vb.
ravaged
unsightly 842adj.
rave
overrate 482vb.
be absurd 497vb.
be insane 503vb.
mean nothing 515vb.
be pleased 824vb.
ravel
unravel 62vb.
bedevil 63vb.
enlace 222vb.
raveled
intricate 251adj.
ravelin
fortification 713n.
ravelment
complexity 61n.
raven
eat 301vb.
bird 365n.
black thing 428n.
omen 511n.
be hungry 859vb.
be malevolent 898vb.
ravening
furious 176adj.
ravenous
taking 786adj.
hungry 859adj.
ravenously
gluttonously 947adv.
ravine
gap 201n.
narrowness 206n.
valley 255n.
furrow 262n.
conduit 351n.
raving
excited 821adj.
pleased 824adj.
(*see* rave)
ravish
force 176vb.
take away 786vb.
delight 826vb.
debauch 951vb.
ravisher
libertine 952n.
ravishment
coition 45n.
excitation 821n.
joy 824n.
rape 951n.
raw
incomplete 55adj.
beginning 68adj.
new 126adj.
young 130adj.
uncovered 229adj.
amorphous 244adj.
culinary 301adj.
sentient 374adj.
painful 377adj.
cold 380adj.
unsavory 391adj.
florid 425adj.
ignorant 491adj.
unhabituated 611adj.
imperfect 647adj.
immature 670adj.
uncooked 670adj.
unskilled 695adj.
sensitive 819adj.
excitable 822adj.
raw-boned
lean 206adj.
raw deal
ill fortune 731n.
(*see* injustice)
raw feelings
moral sensibility 819n.
raw material
source 156n.
materials 631n.
undevelopment 670n.
rawness
(*see* raw)

raw, on the
on the raw 819adv.
raw recruit
beginner 538n.
bungler 697n.
ray
divergence 294n.
flash 417n.
radiation 417n.
rayon
fiber 208n.
textile 222n.
raze
demolish 165vb.
fell 311vb.
razor
sharp edge 256n.
razor edge
narrowness 206n.
sharp edge 256n.
danger 661n.
reach
degree 27n.
ability 160n.
distance 199n.
be long 203vb.
straightness 249n.
arrive 295vb.
pass 305vb.
stream 350n.
hearing 415n.
trickery 542n.
suffice 635vb.
governance 733n.
reachless
deep 211adj.
reach-me-down
ready-made 669adj.
reach-me-downs
clothing 228n.
reach out for
take 786vb.
reach to
fill 54vb.
extend 183vb.
be distant 199vb.
be contiguous 202vb.
react
correlate 12vb.
be active 678vb.
(*see* reaction)
react against
dislike 861vb.
reaction
compensation 31n.
reversion 148n.
effect 157n.
counteraction 182n.
recoil 280n.
sense 374n.
answer 460n.
restoration 656n.
retaliation 714n.
deprecation 762n.
feeling 818n.
reactionary
tergiversating 603adj.
opponent 705n.
revolter 738n.
disobedient 738adj.
reactivation
revival 656n.
reactor
nucleonics 160n.
read
gauge 465vb.
interpret 520vb.
decipher 520vb.
study 536vb.
indicate 547vb.
speak 579vb.
readability
intelligibility 516n.
read a lecture
reprove 924vb.
read and re-read
be attentive 455vb.
read between the lines
decipher 520vb.
reader
teacher 537n.
classroom 538n.
literature 557n.
reading matter 589n.
bookman 589n.
academic title 870n.
readership
publicity 528n.
lecture 534n.
readily
instantaneously 116adv.
willingly 597adv.
easily 701adv.
read in
instructed 490adj.
readiness
tendency 179n.
attention 455n.
intelligence 498n.
foresight 510n.
elegance 575n.
willingness 597n.
utility 640n.
preparedness 669n.
completion 725n.
obedience 739n.
reading
measurement 465n.
erudition 490n.
interpretation 520n.
lecture 534n.
study 536n.
reading desk
classroom 539n.
reading glass
eyeglass 442n.
reading in
holy orders 985n.
reading matter
reading matter 589n.
read into
add 38vb.
readjustment
restoration 656n.
read off
gauge 465vb.
read out
speak 579vb.
read the future
foresee 510vb.
divine 511vb.
ready
impending 155adj.
on the spot 189adj.
intelligent 498adj.
expectant 507adj.
elegant 575adj.
loquacious 581adj.
instrumental 628adj.
useful 640adj.
prepared 669adj.
active 678adj.
skillful 694adj.
obedient 739adj.
consenting 758adj.
ready-formed
ready-made 669adj.
ready for more
refreshed 685adj.
ready-made
dressed 228adj.
formed 243adj.
predetermined 608adj.
ready-made 669adj.
ready money
money, funds 797n.
ready reckoner
counting instrument 86n.
ready to
future 124adj.
tending 179adj.
reaffirm
emphasize 532vb.
reagent
testing agent 461n.
real
real 1adj.
substantial 3adj.
numerical 85adj.
material 319adj.
true 494adj.
proprietary 777adj.
real estate
lands 777n.
realism
existence 1n.
mimicry 20n.
philosophy 449n.
accuracy 494n.
veracity 540n.

representation 551n.
school of painting 553n.
description 590n.
realist
materiality 319n.
realistic
lifelike 18adj.
true 494adj.
wise 498adj.
representing 551adj.
descriptive 590adj.
reality
reality 1n.
substantiality 3n.
truth 494n.
chief thing 638n.
realizable
possible 469adj.
intelligible 516adj.
realization
eventuality 154n.
appearance 445n.
discovery 484n.
knowledge 490n.
representation 551n.
acquisition 771n.
feeling 818n.
realize
make extrinsic 6vb.
copy 20vb.
materialize 319vb.
cognize 447vb.
imagine 513vb.
understand 516vb.
be informed 516vb.
carry out 725vb.
sell 793vb.
draw money 797vb.
(*see* realization)
real-life
descriptive 594adj.
really
actually 1adv.
truly 494adv.
realm
territory 184n.
nation 371n.
function 622n.
polity 733n.
real nature
essence 1n.
realness
reality 1n.
authenticity 494n.
realpolitik
tactics 688n.
real presence
the sacrament 988n.
real self
self 80n.
real thing
reality 1n.
identity 13n.
no imitation 21n.
authenticity 494n.
love 887n.
realtor
merchant 794n.
realty
lands 777n.
ream
enlarge 197vb.
open 263vb.
bubble 355vb.
paper 631n.
reamer
perforator 263n.
tobacco 388n.
cleaning utensil 648n.
reams
great quantity 32n.
reanimate
vitalize 360vb.
reanimation
strengthening 162n.
reproduction 166n.
materiality 319n.
revival 656n.
refreshment 685n.
reap
cultivate 370vb.
store 632vb.
acquire 771vb.
take 786vb.
be rewarded 962vb.
reaper
husbandman 370n.
farm tool 370n.
reaping
product 164n.
agriculture 370n.
reaping-hook
sharp edge 256n.
farm tool 370n.
reappear
be visible 443vb.
be restored 656vb.
reappearance
recurrence 106n.
reappoint
restore 656vb.
rear
sequel 67n.
extremity 69n.
generate 164vb.
make vertical 215vb.
rear, buttocks 238n.
back 238adj.
leap 312n.
breed stock 369vb.
educate 534vb.
armed force 722n.
rear admiral
naval man 270n.
naval officer 741n.
rear guard
rear 238n.
defender 713n.
armed force 722n.
rearing
animal husbandry 369n.
rearmost
back 238adj.
rearrange
modify 143vb.
rear rank
rear 238n.
rear up
elevate 310vb.
get angry 891vb.
rearward
rearward 238adv.
reason
reason why 156n.
intellect 447n.
thought 449n.
discriminate 463vb.
reasoning 475n.
sanity 502n.
motive 612n.
reasonability
probability 471n.
reasonable
moderate 177adj.
possible 469adj.
plausible 471adj.
rational 475adj.
credible 485adj.
true 494adj.
wise 498adj.
sane 502adj.
cheap 812adj.
just 913adj.
reasonableness
moderation 177n.
justice 913n.
reasoner
reasoner 475n.
reason ill
reason ill 477vb.
reasoning
reasoning 475n.
reasoning power
intellect 447n.
reasons
reasons 475n.
reason why
reason why 156n.
attribution 158n.
reassemble
congregate 74vb.
restore, repair 656vb.
reassurance
hope 852n.
reassure
give courage 855vb.
reasty
fetid 397adj.
reaver

robber 789n.
reawakening
revival 656n.
rebarbative
disliked 861adj.
rebate
decrement 42n.
discount 810n.
rebec, rebeck
viol 414n.
rebel
nonconformist 84n.
go to war 718vb.
revolter 738n.
revolt 738vb.
fail in duty 918vb.
schismatic 978n.
rebellion
revolution 149n.
revolt 738n.
dutilessness 918n.
lawlessness 954n.
rebellious
unwilling 598adj.
quarreling 709adj.
anarchic 734adj.
disobedient 738adj.
dutiless 918adj.
rebirth
recurrence 106n.
future state 124n.
revival 656n.
sanctity 979n.
reborn
converted 147adj.
restored 656adj.
sanctified 979adj.
rebound
recoil 280n.
elasticity 328n.
rebuff
recoil 280n.
repulsion 292n.
rejection 607n.
hitch 702n.
oppose 704vb.
resistance 715n.
defeat 728n., vb.
adversity 731n.
refusal 760n.
rudeness 885n.
contempt 922n.
rebuild
reproduce 166vb.
restore 656vb.
rebuke
reprimand 924n.
punish 963vb.
rebuked
humbled 872adj.
rebus
enigma 530n.
rebut
(*see* rebuttal)
rebuttal
rejoinder 460n.
counter-evidence 467n.
confutation 479n.
negation 533n.
vindication 927n.
legal trial 959n.
rebutter
rejoinder 460n.
recalcitrance
opposition 704n.
resistance 715n.
refusal 760n.
recalcitrant
nonconformist 84n.
counteracting 182adj.
recoiling 280adj.
unwilling 598adj.
disobedient 738adj.
recall
transference 272n.
remembrance 505n.
retrospect 505vb.
recant 603vb.
restoration 656n.
deposal 752n.
abrogation 752n.
recant
negate 533vb.
be false 541vb.
not retain 779vb.
recantation
recantation 603n.
rejection 607n.
abrogation 752n.
penitence 939n.
recanter
tergiversator 603n.
recapitulate
shorten 204vb.
remind 505vb.
be intelligible 516vb.
describe 590vb.
recapitulation
numeration 86n.
repetition 106n.
compendium 592n.
recapture
retrospect 505vb.
imagine 513vb.
retrieve 656vb.
acquire 771vb.
recast
modify 143vb.
plan 623vb.
rectify 654vb.
recede
decrease 37vb.
revert 148vb.
regress 286vb.
recede 290vb.
receipt
cookery 301n.
contrivance 623n.
remedy 658n.
precept 693n.
title-deed 767n.
earnings 771n.
receive 782vb.
payment 804n.
receipt 807n.
receipt of custom
receiving 782n.
treasury 799n.
receipts
earnings 771n.
receiving 782n.
taking 786n.
receive
meet 295vb.
admit 299vb.
believe 485vb.
receive 782vb.
take 786vb.
be hospitable 882vb.
be rewarded 962vb.
received
usual 610adj.
receiver
vessel 194n.
hearing aid 415n.
telecommunication 531n.
receiver 782n.
recipient 782n.
thief 789n.
treasurer 798n.
receivership
receiving 782n.
recency
newness 126n.
recension
numeration 86n.
amendment 654n.
recent
secular 110adj.
foregoing 125adj.
new 126adj.
receptacle
receptacle 194n.
receptibility
reception 299n.
reception
arrival 295n.
ingress 297n.
reception 299n.
sound 398n.
hearing 415n.
conference 584n.
receiving 782n.
celebration 876n.
social gathering 882n.
approbation 923n.
receptionist
recorder 549n.
receptive

recipient 194adj.
admitting 299adj.
studious 536adj.
willing 597adj.
receiving 782adj.
receptivity
reception 299n.
recess
interim 108n.
lull 145n.
compartment 194n.
angularity 247n.
cavity 255n.
hiding-place 527n.
repose 683n.
recession
decrease 37n.
contraction 198n.
regression 286n.
recession 290n.
departure 296n.
deterioration 655n.
inactivity 679n.
recessional
hymn 981n.
ritual 988adj.
recessive
reverted 148adj.
receding 290adj.
recessive characteristic
specialty 80n.
réchauffé
duplicate 22n.
repetition 106n.
dish 301n.
restoration 656n.
recheck
be careful 457adj.
recherché
unusual 84adj.
excellent 644adj.
fashionable 848adj.
recidivation
return 286n.
tergiversation 603n.
relapse 657n.
recidivism
reversion 148n.
tergiversation 603n.
deterioration 655n.
relapse 657n.
wickedness 934n.
impiety 980n.
recidivist
tergiversator 603n.
offender 904n.
bad man 938n.
impious person 980n.
recipe
cookery 301n.
contrivance 623n.
remedy 658n.
precept 693n.
recipient
receptacle 194n.
recipient 782n.
reciprocal
relative 9adj.
correlative 12adj.
equivalent 28adj.
numerical element 85n.
retaliatory 714adj.
reciprocate
be related 9vb.
correlate 12vb.
be periodic 141vb.
cooperate 706vb.
concord 710vb.
reciprocation
correlation 12n.
interchange 151n.
fluctuation 317n.
retaliation 714n.
reciprocity
correlation 12n.
equalization 28n.
compensation 31n.
interchange 151n.
cooperation 706n.
concord 710n.
recision
subtraction 39n.
recital
repetition 106n.
oration 579n.
description 590n.
recitation
oration 579n.
recitative
vocal music 412n.
recite
number 86vb.
repeat 106vb.
(*see* recital)
reck
be careful 457vb.
reckless
negligent 458adj.
unwise 499adj.
defiant 711adj.
prodigal 815adj.
rash 857adj.
recklessness
indifference 860n.
reckon
expect 507vb.
be cautious 858vb.
(*see* reckoning)
reckon among
number with 78vb.
reckoning
numeration 86n.
measurement 465n.
expectation 507n.
accounts 808n.
accounting 808adj.
price 809n.
punishment 963n.
reckon on
believe 485vb.
reckon to
intend 617vb.
reckon with
pay 804vb.
reckon without one's host
misjudge 481vb.
be rash 857vb.
reclaim
make better 654vb.
restore 656vb.
retrieve 656vb.
demand 737vb.
acquire 771vb.
appropriate 786vb.
claim 915vb.
reclaimed
repentant 939adj.
reclamation
restoration 656n.
recline
be horizontal 216vb.
sit down 311vb.
repose 683vb.
recline on
be supported 218vb.
recluse
solitary 883n.
ascetic 945n.
recognition
assent 488n.
knowledge 490n.
thanks 907n.
dueness 915n.
approbation 923n.
reward 962n.
recognitor
jury 957n.
recognizable
visible 443adj.
intelligible 516adj.
manifest 522adj.
recognizance
security 767n.
legal process 959n.
recognize
identify 13vb.
see 438vb.
notice 455vb.
discover 484vb.
remember 505vb.
understand 516vb.
permit 756vb.
consent 758vb.
greet 884vb.
recognized
influential 178adj.
usual 610adj.
recoil
counteraction 182n.
recoil 280n.

recession 290n.
repulsion 292n.
elasticity 328n.
be loath 598vb.
avoidance 620n.
dislike 861adj.
recoin
reproduce 166vb.
recollection
remembrance 505n.
recommencement
reversion 148n.
recommend
incite 612vb.
patronize 703vb.
befriend 880vb.
recommendation
credential 466n.
advice 691n.
approbation 923n.
recommended
good 615adj.
recommend oneself
be praised 923vb.
recompense
compensation 31n.
retaliation 714n.
reward 962n., vb.
reconcilable
agreeing 24adj.
reconcile
pacify 719vb.
content 828vb.
reconcilement
adaptation 24n.
conformity 83n.
reconciliation
concord 710n.
pacification 719n.
content 828n.
friendship 880n.
forgiveness 909n.
propitiation 941n.
recondite
puzzling 517adj.
concealed 525adj.
reconditioning
repair 656n.
reconnaissance
land travel 267adj.
inspection 438n.
inquiry 459n.
reconnoiter
traverse 267vb.
scan 438vb.
inquire 459vb.
reconsideration
amendment 654n.
reconstitute
restore 656vb.
reconstruction
reproduction 166n.
conjecture 512n.
restoration 656n.
reconversion
reversion 148n.
restoration 656n.
record
enormous 32adj.
superiority 34n.
phonograph 414n.
evidence 466n.
record 548n., vb.
writing 586n.
narrative 590n.
describe 590vb.
best 644adj.
conduct 688n.
title-deed 767n.
record-breaker
exceller 644n.
record-breaking
crowning 34adj.
record clerk
recorder 549n.
recorder
chronologist 117n.
flute 414n.
recorder 549n.
narrator 590n.
judge 957n.
record-holder
superior 34n.
recording
musical piece 412n.
record 548n.
record-keeper
recorder 549n.
record-player
phonograph 414n.
record room
recorder 549n.
records
record 548n.
recount
numeration 86n.
communicate 524vb.
describe 590vb.
recoup
recoup 31vb.
retrieve 656vb.
recoupment
compensation 31n.
acquisition 771n.
taking 786n.
restitution 787n.
recourse
contrivance 623n.
means 629n.
recourse to, have
avail of 673vb.
recover
recoup 31vb.
revert 148vb.
be strong 162vb.
counteract 182vb.
retrieve 656vb.
deliver 668vb.
re-cover
repair 656vb.
recoverable
restored 656adj.
recovered
refreshed 685adj.
recovery
improvement 654n.
sanation 656n.
restoration 656n.
revival 656n.
acquisition 771n.
taking 786n.
restitution 787n.
recreancy
impiety 980n.
recreant
tergiversator 603n.
cowardly 856adj.
knave 938n.
recreation
refreshment 685n.
amusement 837n.
recreational
amusing 837adj.
recriminate
dispraise, blame 924n.
recrimination
dissension 709n.
retaliation 714n.
vindication 927n.
accusation 928n.
recrudescence
relapse 657n.
recruit
augment 36vb.
accrue 38vb.
strengthen 162vb.
invigorate 174vb.
beginner 538n.
employ 622vb.
replenish 633vb.
make better 654vb.
revive 656vb.
refresh 685vb.
aid 703vb.
auxiliary 707n.
soldier 722n.
recruitment
war measures 718n.
relief 831n.
(*see* recruit)
rectangle
angular figure 247n.
rectangular
vertical 215adj.
rectification
compensation 31n.
desiccation 342n.
amendment 654n.
repair 656n.
rectify
regularize 62vb.

modify 143vb.
straighten 249vb.
perfect 646vb.
rectify 654vb.
rectilinear
continuous 71adj.
straight 249adj.
rectitude
straightness 249n.
probity 929n.
virtue 933n.
recto
dextrality 241n.
edition 589n.
rector
director 690n.
pastor, cleric 986n.
church title 986n.
rectorship
church office 985n.
rectory
parsonage 986n.
rectum
insides 224n.
recumbent
low 210adj.
supine 216adj.
oblique 220adj.
recuperate
get healthy 650vb.
recuperation
sanation 656n.
refreshment 685n.
restitution 787n.
recur
recur 139vb.
go on 146vb.
(*see* recurrence)
recurrence
continuity 71n.
recurrence 106n.
periodicity 141n.
reversion 148n.
remembrance 505n.
revival 656n.
relapse 657n.
recur to
avail of 673vb.
recurvature
curvature 248n.
recusancy
dissent 489n.
negation 533n.
refusal 760n.
impenitence 940n.
schism 978n.
recusant
dissentient 489n.
disobedient 738adj.
schismatic 978n.
red
revolutionist 149n.
red color 431n.
reformer 654n.
uncooked 670adj.
sectional 708adj.
revolter 738n.
redaction
amendment 654n.
redactor
bookman 589n.
redan
defenses, fort 713n.
redargution
confutation 479n.
red, be in the
lose 772vb.
be in debt 803vb.
red blood
vitality 162n.
red-blooded
courageous 855adj.
red-brick
regional 184adj.
redcap
bearer 273n.
redcoat
soldier 722n.
Red Cross
doctor 658n.
redden
redden 431vb.
show feeling 818vb.
be humbled 872vb.
get angry 891vb.
rede
advice 691n.
redeem
observe faith 768vb.
pay 804vb.
(*see* redemption)
redeemed
sanctified 979adj.
redeemer
purchaser 792n.
benefactor 903n.
God the Son 965n.
redemption
compensation 31n.
quid pro quo 150n.
restoration 656n.
deliverance 668n.
liberation 746n.
acquisition 771n.
restitution 787n.
purchase 792n.
propitiation 941n.
divine function 965n.
redemptive
redemptive 965adj.
red-eyed
angry 891adj.
red flag
flag 547n.
signal 547n.
danger signal 665n.
red-handed
murderous 362adj.
doing 676adj.
in the act 676adv.
guilty 936adj.
redhead
shrew 892n.
red herring
irrelevance 10n.
unimportance 639n.
hinderer 702n.
red-hot
violent 176adj.
hot 379adj.
fervent 818adj.
red ink
amendment 654n.
redintegration
repair 656n.
red, in the
losing 772adj.
indebted 803adj.
redirect
send 272vb.
rediscovery
reproduction 166n.
redivivus
restored 656adj.
red-letter day
important matter 638n.
amusement 837n.
special day 876n.
red light
dimness 419n.
signal light 420n.
signal 547n.
danger signal 665n.
red-light district
brothel 951n.
redolence
odor 394n.
fragrance 396n.
redone
modernized 126adj.
restored 656adj.
redouble
augment 36vb.
double 91vb.
repeat 106vb.
invigorate 174vb.
enlarge 197vb.
redoubling
frequency 139n.
redoubtable
frightening 854adj.
redound
tend 179vb.
redraft
rectify 654vb.
red rag to a bull
resentment 891n.
redress
restoration 656n.
remedy 658n.

justice 913n.
red-tab
army officer 741n.
red tape
delay 136n.
habit 610n.
red-tapeism
governance 733n.
red-tapist
official 690n.
tyrant 735n.
reduce
decompose 51vb.
do sums 86vb.
render few 105vb.
weaken 163vb.
make smaller 198vb.
abstract 592vb.
overmaster 727vb.
subjugate 745vb.
be temperate 942vb.
starve 946vb.
(*see* reduction)
reduced
lesser 35adj.
reduce to
liken 18vb.
convert 147vb.
reduce to the ranks
abase 311vb.
depose 752vb.
shame 867vb.
punish 963vb.
reducing
dieting 301n.
reductio ad absurdum
argumentation 475n.
confutation 479n.
reduction
diminution 37n.
simplification 44n.
numerical operation 86n.
conversion 147n.
miniature 196n.
contraction 198n.
shortening 204n.
depression 311n.
qualification 468n.
photography 551n.
discount 810n.
redundance
plenitude 54n.
overstepping 306n.
diffuseness 570n.
plenty 635n.
redundance 637n.
cheapness 812n.
satiety 863n.
undueness 916n.
redundant
useless 641adj.
liberal 813adj.
reduplication
imitation 20n.
duplication 91n.
repetition 106n.
reproduction 166n.
reecho
do likewise 20vb.
repeat oneself 106vb.
resound 404vb.
reed
weak thing 163n.
plant 366n.
flute 414n.
stationery 586n.
reedited
modernized 126adj.
reedy
strident 407adj.
reef
retard 278vb.
fold 261vb.
rock 344vb.
island 349n.
pitfall 663n.
reefer
navigator 270n.
tobacco 388n.
reefer-jacket
tunic 228n.
reef knot
ligature 47n.
reek
gas 336n.
vaporize 338vb.
be hot 379vb.
odor 394n.
fetor 397n.
reel
vary 152vb.
be weak 163vb.
leap 312n.
rotate 315vb.
oscillate 317vb.
be agitated 318vb.
musical piece 412n.
show feeling 818vb.
dance 837n.
be drunk 949vb.
reel off
speak 579vb.
be loquacious 581vb.
reembody
combine 50vb.
reenter
acquire 771vb.
possess 773vb.
reentrant
curved 248adj.
reentrant angle
angle 247n.
reentry
return 286n.
ingress 297n.
taking 786n.
reerection
restoration 656n.
reestablishment
restoration 656n.
reeve
affix 45vb.
officer 741n.
reexamination
interrogation 459n.
amendment 654n.
legal trial 959n.
reface
make better 654vb.
repair 656vb.
refashion
revolutionize 149vb.
reproduce 166vb.
rectify 654vb.
refection
meal 301n.
refreshment 685n.
refectory
chamber 194n.
feasting 301n.
refer
indicate 547vb.
consult 691vb.
(*see* refer to)
referable
relative 9adj.
attributed 158adj.
referee
referral 9n.
estimator 480n.
adviser 691n.
mediator 720n.
magistracy 957n.
reference
relation 9n.
referral 9n.
class 62vb.
evidence 466n.
credential 466n.
connotation 514n.
indicate 547vb.
advice 691n.
approbation 923n.
referencer
recorder 549n.
reference system
sorting 62n.
reference to
attribution 158n.
referendary
referral 9n.
estimator 480n.
referendum
judgment 480n.
vote 605n.
referent
referral 9n.
referential
relative 9adj.
referral
referral 9n.

referrible
relative 9adj.
attributed 158adj.
refer to
relate 9vb.
be related 9vb.
be included 78vb.
attribute 158vb.
mean 514vb.
refill
plenitude 54n.
store 632vb.
replenish 633vb.
refine
differentiate 15vb.
rarefy 325vb.
make better 654vb.
purify 648vb.
(*see* refinement)
refined
soft-hued 425adj.
personable 841adj.
tasteful 846adj.
pure 950adj.
refinement
discrimination 463n.
elegance 575n.
civilization 654n.
beauty 841n.
good taste 846n.
fastidiousness 846n.
refiner
cleaner 648n.
refinery
workshop 687n.
refit
repair 656vb.
reflation
dilation 197n.
reflect
correlate 12vb.
resemble 18vb.
imitate 20vb.
retrospect 505vb.
show 522vb.
(*see* reflection)
reflection
analogue 18n.
copy 22n.
repulsion 292n.
resonance 404n.
reflection 417n.
lamp 420n.
visual fallacy 440n.
appearance 445n.
meditation 449n.
idea 451n.
image 551n.
slur 866n.
scurrility 899n.
reproach 924n.
detraction 926n.
reflective
radiating 417adj.
thoughtful 449adj.
reflect on
shame 867vb.
reprove 924vb.
defame 926vb.
reflector
reflection 417n.
lamp 420n.
telescope 442n.
reflex
copy 22n.
recoil 280n.
regressive 286adj.
sense 374n.
involuntary 596adj.
spontaneity 609n.
habituation 610n.
reflex action
necessity 596n.
reflexive
intrinsic 5adj.
reverted 148adj.
reflexively
backward 286adv.
refluent
recoiling 280adj.
regressive 286adj.
reflux
decrease 37n.
recoil 280n.
return 286n.
current, eddy 350n.
refocillation
strengthening 162n.
refreshment 685n.
reforest
restore 656vb.
reforestation
restoration 656n.
reform
modify 143vb.
transform 147vb.
tergiversate 603vb.
amendment 654n.
repair 656vb.
philanthropize 897vb.
justice 913n.
be penitent 939vb.
become pious 979vb.
reformable
improved 654adj.
reformation
conversion 147n.
amendment 654n.
restoration 656n.
Reformation, the
Protestantism 976n.
reformatory
school 539n.
amendment 654n.
improving 654adj.
prison 748n.
reformed
improved 654adj.
right 913adj.
repentant 939adj.
protestant 976adj.
reformer
alterer 143n.
reformer 654n.
religious teacher 973n.
protestant 976n.
reformism
progression 285n.
reformism 654n.
reformist
progressive 285adj.
refoundation
restoration 656n.
refounder
patron 707n.
refraction
deviation 282n.
reflection 417n.
visual fallacy 440n.
refractor
astronomy 321n.
telescope 442n.
refractoriness
unwillingness 589n.
refractory
willful 602adj.
capricious 604adj.
difficult 700adj.
opposing 704adj.
disobedient 738adj.
sullen 983adj.
refrain
repetition 106n.
periodicity 141n.
cease 145vb.
vocal music 412n.
tune 412n.
verse form 593n.
avoid 620vb.
not act 677vb.
be lenient 736vb.
be temperate 942vb.
refresh
invigorate 174vb.
refrigerate 382vb.
make better 654vb.
revive 656vb.
refresher
extra 40n.
tonic 658n.
refreshment 685n.
price 809n.
refresher course
study 536n.
refreshing
lenitive 177adj.
beneficial 644adj.
salubrious 652adj.
refreshment
strengthening 162n.
meal 301n.

pleasure 376n.
repose 683n.
refreshment 685n.
aid 703n.
enjoyment 824n.
pleasurableness 826n.
relief 831n.
amusement 837n.
refrigeration
anesthetic 375n.
refrigeration 382n.
preservation 666n.
refrigerator
provisions 301n.
refrigeration 382n.
refrigerator 384n.
storage 632n.
preserver 666n.
reft of
losing 772adj.
refuel
store 632vb.
replenish 633vb.
refuge
retreat 192n.
resting place 266n.
hiding-place 527n.
protection 660n.
refuge 662n.
fort 713n.
refugee
foreigner 59n.
displacement 188n.
wanderer 268n.
ejection 300n.
escaper 667n.
outcaste 883n.
refulgence
light 417n.
refund
restitution 787n.
refurbish
make better 654vb.
repair 656vb.
refusal
repulsion 292n.
dissent 489n.
negation 533n.
unwillingness 598n.
rejection 607n.
avoidance 620n.
refusal 760n.
deprecation 762n.
non-observance 769n.
disapprobation 924n.
refuse
leavings 41n.
waste 634n.
rubbish 641n.
dirt 649n.
(*see* refusal)
refuse bail
imprison 747vb.
refutable
confuted 479adj.
refutation
counter-evidence 467n.
confutation 479n.
negation 533n.
refutatory
countervailing 467adj.
confuted 479adj.
refuting
answering 460adj.
regain
retrieve 656vb.
acquire 771vb.
regal
ruling 733adj.
impressive 821adj.
worshipful 866adj.
regale
eat 301vb.
pleasure 376n.
refresh 685vb.
delight 826vb.
amuse 837vb.
be hospitable 882vb.
regalia
formal dress 228n.
regalia 743n.
jewelry 844n.
formality 875n.
regality
magistrature 733n.
regard
relation 9n.
look 438n.
attention 455n.
observe 768vb.
repute 866n.
friendliness 880n.
love 887n., vb.
respect 920n., vb.
approbation 923n.
regard as
opine 485vb.
regardful
attentive 455adj.
careful 457adj.
regarding
concerning 9adv.
regardless
irrelative 10adj.
inattentive 456adj.
negligent 458adj.
ignorant 491adj.
apathetic 820adj.
rash 857adj.
regards
courteous act 884n.
respects 920n.
regatta
racing 716n.
(*see* aquatics)
regency
authority 733n.
magistrature 733n.
governance 733n.
commission 751n.
regenerate
repentant 939adj.
sanctify 979vb.
(*see* regeneration)
regeneration
conversion 147n.
reproduction 166n.
revival 656n.
divine function 965n.
regent
potentate 741n.
regicide
homicide 362n.
revolt, revolter 738n.
regime
circumstance 8n.
dieting 301n.
management 689n.
governance 733n.
regimen
dieting 301n.
therapy 658n.
management 689n.
regiment
band 74n.
formation 722n.
dominate 733vb.
subjugate 745vb.
regimentals
uniform 228n.
regimentation
uniformity 16n.
compulsion 740n.
regimented
obedient 739adj.
regimenter
uniformist 16n.
regiment of women
gynocracy 733n.
region
region 184n.
regional
regional 184adj.
provincial 192adj.
region of, in the
about 33adv.
register
be identical 13vb.
accord 24vb.
degree 27n.
class 62vb.
list 87n.
musical note 410n.
notice 455vb.
understand 516vb.
indicate 547vb.
record 548n.
represent 551vb.
account book 808n.
registrar
recorder 549n.
doctor 658n.

registration
registration 548n.
registry
registration 548n.
regnal
ruling 733adj.
regnant
influential 178adj.
ruling 733adj.
regrate
purchase 792vb.
sell 793vb.
regrater
merchant 794n.
regress
decrease 37vb.
regression 286n.
recede 290vb.
fall short 307vb.
relapse 657vb.
regression
change 143n.
reversion 148n.
regression 286n.
deterioration 655n.
regressive
tergiversating 603adj.
regret
helplessness 161n.
disappointment 509n.
be loath 598vb.
sorrow 825n.
be discontented 829vb.
regret 830n., vb.
desire 859n., vb.
dislike 861vb.
disapprove 924vb.
penitence 939n.
regretful
unwilling 598adj.
unhappy 825adj.
regrets
remembered 505adj.
regrettable
regretted 830adj.
regretted
dead 361adj.
remembered 505adj.
regroup
combine 50vb.
reguardant
heraldic 547adj.
regular
equal 28adj.
consummate 32adj.
regular 81adj.
frequent 139adj.
unceasing 146adj.
unchangeable 153adj.
symmetrical 245adj.
accurate 494adj.
soldier 722n.
shapely 841adj.
monk 986n.
regularity
uniformity 16n.
order 60n.
regularity 81n.
periodicity 141n.
permanence 144n.
symmetry 245n.
habit 610n.
regularize
regularize 62vb.
make conform 83vb.
regulate
adjust 24vb.
order 60vb.
regularize 62vb.
regulation
rule 81n.
management 689n.
precept 693n.
legislation 953n.
regulations
command 737n.
regulative
regular 81adj.
regurgitation
regression 286n.
return 286n.
voidance 300n.
eddy 350n.
rehabilitation
restoration 656n.
restitution 787n.
dignification 866n.
vindication 927n.
rehandling
repetition 106n.
rehash
repetition 106n.
translate 520vb.
restoration 656n.
rehearsal
repetition 106n.
remembrance 504n.
description 590n.
dramaturgy 594n.
preparation 669n.
rehearse
experiment 461vb.
Reichstag
parliament 692n.
reign
be 1vb.
date 108n.
influence 178n.
governance 733n.
reign of terror
anarchy 734n.
intimidation 854n.
reign supreme
rule 733vb.
reimburse
restitute 787vb.
pay 804vb.
rein
halter 47n.
moderator 177n.
management 689n.
fetter 748n.
reincarnated
material 319adj.
reincarnation
recurrence 106n.
future state 124n.
transformation 143n.
occultism 984n.
reincarnationism
theosophy 984n.
reindeer
beast of burden 273n.
deer 365n.
reinfection
relapse 657n.
reinforce
augment 36vb.
accrue 38vb.
strengthen 162vb.
enlarge 197vb.
support 218vb.
replenish 633vb.
restore 656vb.
aid 703vb.
defend 713vb.
reinforcement
extra 40n.
auxiliary 707n.
armed force 722n.
rein in
retard 278vb.
restrain 747vb.
reinspire
revive 656vb.
reinstallation
restoration 656n.
reinstate
replace 187vb.
reinstatement
reversion 148n.
restitution 787n.
reinsure
make certain 473vb.
seek safety 660vb.
be cautious 858vb.
reinvest
replace 187vb.
restitute 787vb.
economize 814vb.
reissue
variant 15n.
repetition 106n.
edition 589n.
reiterate
repeat 106vb.
reiterated
persevering 600adj.
reiteration
diffuseness 570n.
vigor 571n.

reject
inferior 35n.
leavings 41n.
be unsatisfied 636vb.
rubbish 641n.
not use 674vb.
oppose 704vb.
dislike 861vb.
object of scorn 867n.
outcaste 883n.
despise 922vb.
disapprove 924vb.
condemn 961vb.
(*see* rejection)
rejection
exclusion 57n.
ejection 300n.
dissent 489n.
negation 533n.
unwillingness 598n.
rejection 607n.
avoidance 620n.
refusal 760n.
non-observance 769n.
rejoice
be pleased 824vb.
delight 826vb.
rejoice 835vb.
revel 837vb.
rejoicing
celebration 876n.
rejoin
congregate 74vb.
meet 295vb.
answer 460vb.
rejoinder
rejoinder 460n.
retaliation 714n.
wit 839n.
vindication 927n.
rejoining
arrival 295n.
rejuvenation
revival 656n.
rekindle
kindle 381vb.
revive 656vb.
animate 821vb.
relapse
reversion 148n.
return 286n.
tergiversation 603n.
deterioration 655n.
relapse 657n., vb.
relate
attribute 158vb.
related
akin 11adj.
near 200adj.
relater
narrator 590n.
relation
circumstance 8n.
relation 9n.
kinsman 11n.
correlation 12n.
fitness 24n.
bond 47n.
description 590n.
relational
relative 9adj.
relationship
relation 9n.
consanguinity 11n.
relative
relative 9adj.
kinsman 11n.
correlative 12adj.
comparative 27adj.
compared 462adj.
relative quantity
degree 27n.
relativism
relativeness 9n.
philosophy 449n.
relativity
relativeness 9n.
philosophy 449n.
relax
bate 37vb.
disjoin 46vb.
decompose 51vb.
pause 145vb.
weaken 163vb.
decelerate 278vb.
soften 327vb.
qualify 468vb.
keep calm 823vb.
relieve 831vb.
be sociable 882vb.
show mercy 905vb.
relaxation
moderation 177n.
repose 683n.
laxity 734n.
liberation 746n.
amusement 837n.
relaxed
non-adhesive 49adj.
tranquil 266adj.
unthinking 450adj.
relay
periodicity 141n.
publish 528vb.
telecommunication 531n.
cooperation 706n.
auxiliary 707n.
release
disjoin 46vb.
transference 272n.
decease 361n.
show 522vb.
deliverance 668n.
give scope 744vb.
liberation 746n.
permit 756vb.
non-retention 779n.
exempt 919vb.
releasee
beneficiary 776n.
recipient 782n.
relegate
displace 188vb.
transpose 272vb.
relegation
transference 272n.
ejection 300n.
relent
be moderate 177vb.
soften 327vb.
show mercy 905vb.
forgive 909vb.
relentless
resolute 599adj.
severe 735adj.
pitiless 906adj.
revengeful 910adj.
impenitent 940adj.
relevance
relevance 9n.
fitness 24n.
meaning 514n.
relevant
rational 475adj.
important 638adj.
reliability
credit 802n.
(*see* reliable)
reliable
unchangeable 153adj.
evidential 466adj.
probable 471adj.
certain 473adj.
credible 485adj.
genuine 494adj.
veracious 540adj.
willing 597adj.
resolute 599adj.
safe 660adj.
observant 768adj.
trustworthy 929adj.
reliance
belief 485n.
expectation 507n.
hope 852n.
relic
antiquity 125n.
archaism 127n.
reminder 505n.
trace 548n.
talisman 983n.
relics
corpse 363n.
ritual object 988n.
relict
survivor 41n.
widowed spouse 896n.
relief
contrariety 14n.

aftercomer 67n.
substitute 150n.
moderation 177n.
displacement 188n.
outline 233n.
form 243n.
relievo 254n.
feature 445n.
sculpture 554n.
sanation 656n.
deliverance 668n.
refreshment 685n.
aid 703n.
deposal 752n.
relief 831n.
ornamental art 844n.
kind act 897n.
relieve
come after 65vb.
assuage 177vb.
remedy 658vb.
aid 703vb.
liberate 746vb.
tranquilize 823vb.
relieve 831vb.
cheer 833vb.
(*see* relief)
relieved
comfortable 376adj.
relieve of
take away 786vb.
convey 870vb.
relievo
relievo 254n.
ornamental art 844n.
religion
religion 973n.
piety 979n.
public worship 981n.
religionism
pietism 979n.
religiosity
pietism 979n.
religious
observant 768adj.
trustworthy 929adj.
honorable 929adj.
divine 965adj.
religious 973adj.
pious 979adj.
monk 986n.
religious mania
mania 503n.
religiousness
piety 979n.
religious truth
orthodoxy 976n.
reline
repair 656vb.
relinquish
cease 145vb.
be irresolute 601vb.
tergiversate 603vb.
relinquish 621vb.
disuse 674vb.
abrogate 752vb.
resign 753vb.
not retain 779vb.
relinquished
empty 190adj.
relinquishment
recession 290n.
temperance 942n.
(*see* relinquish)
reliquary
small box 194n.
ritual object 988n.
relish
pleasure 376n.
taste 386n.
condiment 389n.
savoriness 390n.
feeling 818n.
enjoyment 824n.
pleasurableness 826n.
liking 859n.
relive
be restored 656vb.
reload
replenish 663vb.
reluctance
slowness 278n.
unwillingness 598n.
resistance 715n.
dislike 861n.
reluctant
avoiding 620adj.
reluctantly
unwillingly 598adv.
disapprovingly 924adj.
rely
assume 471vb.
hope 852vb.
rely on
be supported 218vb.
be certain 473vb.
believe 485vb.
take a pledge 764vb.
remade
restored 656adj.
remain
be left 41vb.
continue 108vb.
last 113vb.
stay 144vb.
go on 146vb.
dwell 192vb.
be quiescent 266vb.
remainder
difference 15n.
remainder 41n.
piece 53n.
numerical result 85n.
posteriority 120n.
effect 157n.
book 589n.
superfluity 637n.
dower 777n.
sell 793vb.
remainder, leave a
be unequal 29vb.
remainderman
beneficiary 776n.
remaindership
possession 773n.
remaining
separate 46adj.
remains
remainder 41n.
trace 548n.
reading matter 589n.
remake
reproduce 166vb.
restore 656vb.
remand
put off 136vb.
detention 747n.
remanded
captive 750adj.
accused 928adj.
remand home
school 539n.
remark
notice 455n.
maxim 496n.
affirmation 532n.
affirm 532vb.
speech 579n.
remarkable
remarkable 32adj.
unusual 84adj.
visible 443adj.
notable 638adj.
wonderful 864adj.
noteworthy 866adj.
remarks
estimate 480n.
remarriage
type of marriage 894n.
remedial
lenitive 177adj.
counteracting 182adj.
improving 654adj.
remedial 658adj.
successful 727adj.
relieving 831adj.
remediless
unpromising 853adj.
remedy
moderator 177n.
counteract 182vb.
contrivance 623n.
means 629n.
sanation 656n.
remedy 658n., vb.
be just 913vb.
remember

think 449vb.
be mindful 455vb.
remember 505vb.
remembered
known 490adj.
remembrance
remembrance 505n.
famousness 866n.
celebration 876n.
remembrancer
reminder 505n.
recorder 549n.
adviser 691n.
remembrances
courteous act 884n.
respects 920n.
remigration
return 286n.
arrival 295n.
departure 296n.
remind
remind 505vb.
hint 524vb.
warn 664vb.
reminder
reminder 505n.
record 548n.
monument 548n.
reminiscence
remembrance 505n.
narrative 590n.
reminiscent
remembering 505adj.
remiss
negligent 458adj.
unwilling 598n.
lazy 679adj.
lax 734adj.
remission
lull 145n.
moderation 177n.
forgiveness 909n.
remit
bate 37vb.
halt 145vb.
be moderate 177vb.
send 272vb.
forgive 909vb.
remittance
transference 272n.
funds 797n.
payment 804n.
remittance man
egress 298n.
recipient 782n.
remittent
periodical 141adj.
fitful 142adj.
remitter
transferrer 272n.
remnant
leavings 41n.
fewness 105n.
remodel
revolutionize 149vb.
rectify 654vb.
repair 656vb.
remold
modify 143vb.
rectify 654vb.
remonstrance
dissuasion 613n.
deprecation 762n.
reprimand 924n.
remonstrate
(*see* remonstrance)
remora
coherence 48n.
encumbrance 702n.
remorse
sorrow 825n.
regret 830n.
pity 905n.
penitence 939n.
remorseless
pitiless 906adj.
revengeful 910adj.
remote
irrelevant 10adj.
distant 199adj.
invisible 444adj.
remote control
directorship 689n.
remount
substitute 150n.
war-horse 273n.
removable
excluded 57adj.
removal
subtraction 39n.
separation 46n.
exclusion 57n.
displacement 188n.
farness 199n.
transference 272n.
departure 296n.
extraction 304n.
deposal 752n.
taking 786n.
removal man
displacement 188n.
removal van
cart 274n.
remove
degree 27n.
serial place 73n.
destroy 165vb.
be in motion 265vb.
class 538n.
(*see* removal)
remover
destroyer 168n.
remunerate
be useful 640vb.
remuneration
earnings 771n.
pay 804n.
receipt 807n.
reward 962n.
remunerative
profitable 640adj.
gainful 771adj.
rewarding 962adj.
renaissance
preterition 125n.
revival 656n.
renascent
reproductive 166adj.
restored 656adj.
rend
rend 46vb.
demolish 165vb.
chew 301vb.
force 176vb.
wound 655vb.
hurt 827vb.
detract 926vb.
render
convert 147vb.
coat 226vb.
liquefy 337vb.
play music 413vb.
translate 520vb.
give 781vb.
restitute 787vb.
rendering
translation 520n.
rendezvous
congregate 74vb.
focus 76n.
meet 295vb.
social round 882n.
rendition
submission 721n.
restitution 787n.
renegade
alterer 143n.
changed person 147n.
tergiversator 603n.
avoider 620n.
knave 938n.
renew
make better 654vb.
(*see* renewal)
renewal
duplication 91n.
repetition 106n.
newness 126n.
reproduction 166n.
repair, revival 656n.
refreshment 685n.
renewed
persevering 600adj.
sanctified 979adj.
renitency
counteraction 182n.
hardness 326n.
unwillingness 598n.
resistance 715n.

rennet
condensation 324n.
thickening 354n.
renounce
negate 533vb.
recant 603vb.
relinquish 621vb.
resign 753vb.
refuse 760vb.
not retain 779vb.
renovate
make better 654n.
renovation
newness 126n.
reproduction 166n.
repair 656n.
renovator
mender 656n.
renown
famousness 866n.
honor 866vb.
renowned
known 490adj.
renownless
inglorious 867adj.
rent
disjunction 46n.
gap 201n.
hire 785vb.
purchase 792vb.
price 809n.
rental
price 809n.
rent-collector
receiver 782n.
renter
resident 191n.
possessor 776n.
lender 784n.
purchaser 792n.
rent-free
uncharged 812adj.
rentier
idler 679n.
receiver 782n.
rent-payer
possessor 776n.
rent-roll
estate 777n.
receipt 807n.
rents
flat 192n.
receipt 807n.
renunciation
negation 533n.
recantation 603n.
relinquishment 621n.
laxity 734n.
resignation 753n.
refusal 760n.
non-retention 779n.
seclusion 883n.
non-liability 919n.
temperance 942n.
reoccur
reoccur 106vb.
recur 139vb.
be periodic 141vb.
reopen
begin 68vb.
reorganization
arrangement 62n.
restoration 656n.
reorganize
transform 147vb.
rectify 654vb.
rep
textile 222n.
drama 594n.
repair
adjust 24vb.
amendment 654n.
repair 656n., vb.
repairer
mender 656n.
repair to
travel 267vb.
reparation
compensation 31n.
repair 656n.
restoration 656n.
restitution 787n.
atonement 941n.
repartee
interchange 151n.
answer 460n.
confutation 479n.
interlocution 584n.
witticism 839n.
repartition
apportionment 783n.
repass
pass 305vb.
repast
meal 301n.
repatriation
restitution 787n.
repay
compensate 31vb.
benefit 615vb.
be profitable 771vb.
restitute 787vb.
pay 804vb.
thank 907vb.
reward 962vb.
repayable
owed 803adj.
repay with interest
augment 36vb.
repeal
abrogation 752n.
repeat
do likewise 20vb.
double 91vb.
repetition 106n.
memorize 505vb.
emphasize 532vb.
be diffuse 570vb.
repeated
uniform 16adj.
many 104adj.
frequent 139adj.
tedious 838adj.
repeatedly
persistently 600adv.
repeater
timekeeper 117n.
pistol 723n.
repel
repel 292vb.
be unpalatable 391vb.
dissuade 613vb.
parry 713vb.
resist 715vb.
refuse 760vb.
displease 827vb.
cause dislike 861vb.
make unwelcome 883vb.
excite hate 888vb.
repellent
repellent 292adj.
unpleasant 827adj.
ugly 842adj.
disliked 861adj.
hateful 888adj.
repent
be wise 498vb.
become pious 979vb.
(*see* repentance)
repentance
tergiversation 603n.
amendment 654n.
regret 830n.
penitence 939n.
repercussion
effect 157n.
counteraction 182n.
recoil 280n.
repertoire, repertory
list 87n.
acting 594n.
collection 632n.
store 632n.
merchandise 795n.
repetend
number 85n.
recurrence 106n.
repetition
identity 13n.
mimicry 20n.
repetition 106n.
frequency 139n.
continuance 146n.
reproduction 166n.
perseverance 600n.
repetitious
repeated 106adj.

pleonastic 570adj.
tedious 838adj.
repetitive
uniform 16adj.
continuous 71adj.
pleonastic 570adj.
repetitive job
habituation 610n.
repetitiveness
diffuseness 570n.
rephrase
repeat 106vb.
translate 520vb.
phrase 563vb.
repine
be discontented 829vb.
regret 830vb.
be dejected 834vb.
replace
substitute 150vb.
replace 187vb.
eject 300vb.
restore 656vb.
disuse 674vb.
depose 752vb.
deputize 755vb.
not retain 779vb.
replaceable
superfluous 637adj.
replacement
reversion 148n.
(*see* replace)
replant
replace 187vb.
restore 656vb.
replay
repetition 106n.
replenish
fill 54vb.
store 632vb.
replenish 633vb.
suffice 635vb.
replete
full 54adj.
repletion
sufficiency 635n.
satiety 863n.
replevin
security 767n.
acquisition 771n.
restitution 787n.
replica
copy 22n.
reply
answer 460n., vb.
rejoinder 460n.
vindication 927n.
reply by return
correspond 588vb.
report
loudness 400n.
bang 402n.
report 524n.
communicate 524vb.
divulge 526vb.
publicity 528n.
news 529vb.
record 548n.
correspond 588vb.
describe 590vb.
reported
rumored 529adj.
reported against
accused 928adj.
reported case
legal trial 959n.
reporter
estimator 480n.
informant 524n.
publicizer 528n.
newsmonger 529n.
chronicler 549n.
author 589n.
narrator 590n.
reporting
publicity 528n.
report on
estimate 480vb.
reports
record 548n.
repose
quietude 266n.
inaction 677n.
leisure 681n.
repose 683n., vb.
be refreshed 685vb.
reposeful
tranquil 266adj.
comfortable 376adj.
reposeful 683adj.
pleasurable 826adj.
content 828adj.
repose on
be supported 218vb.
reposition
location 187n.
repoussé
salient 254adj.
reprehend
(*see* reprehension)
reprehension
disapprobation 924n.
reprimand 924n.
censure 924n.
reprehensive
not nice 645adj.
blameworthy 924adj.
heinous 934adj.
guilty 936adj.
represent
be 1vb.
resemble 18vb.
figure 519vb.
affirm 532vb.
describe 590vb.
deputize 755vb.
(*see* representation)
representation
imitation 20n.
copy 22n.
manifestation 522n.
report 524n.
indication 547n.
representation 551n.
drama 594n.
vote 605n.
commission 751n.
rite 988n.
representational
representing 551adj.
descriptive 590adj.
representative
general 79adj.
typical 83adj.
substitute 150n.
agent 686n.
councillor 692n.
mediator 720n.
consignee 754n.
delegate 754n.
representative government
government 733n.
representative selection
example 83n.
representing
interpretive 520adj.
repress
hinder 702vb.
subjugate 745vb.
tranquilize 823vb.
repression
exclusion 57n.
counteraction 182n
avoidance 620n.
restraint 747n.
prohibition 757n.
moral insensibility 820n.
fear 854n.
repressive
avoiding 620adj.
restraining 747adj.
reprieve, reprieval
delay 136n.
escape 667n.
deliverance 668n.
forgiveness 909n.
acquittal 960n.
reprimand
warning 664n.
reprimand 924n.
punishment 963n.
reprint
copy 20vb.
duplicate 22n.
repeat 106vb.
reproduction 166n.

edition 589n.
reprisal
retaliation 714n.
revenge 910n.
penalty 963n.
reprise
decrement 42n.
repetition 106n.
taking 786n.
reproach
slur 867n.
object of scorn 867n.
malediction 899n.
despisedness 922n.
reproach 924n.
accusation 928n.
reproachful
resentful 891adj.
maledicent 899adj.
disapproving 924adj.
reproach oneself
be penitent 939vb.
reprobate
blameworthy 924adj.
exprobate 924vb.
wicked 934adj.
bad man 938n.
impious person 980n.
reprobation
reprimand 924n.
impiety 980n.
reproduce
copy 20vb.
repeat 106vb.
reproduction
analogue 18n.
copy 22n.
increase 36n.
propagation 164n.
reproduction 166n.
representation 551n.
picture 553n.
reproof
dissuasion 613n.
reprove
warn 664vb.
deprecate 762vb.
curse 899vb.
reprove 924vb.
punish 963vb.
reptile
reptile 365n.
animal 365n.
bane 659n.
knave 938n.
reptilian
animal 365adj.
republic
territory 184n.
polity 733n.
republican
governmental 733adj.
commoner 869n.
republicanism
government 733n.
republic of letters
literature 557n.
repudiate
recant 603vb.
(*see* repudiation)
repudiation
dissent 489n.
negation 533n.
rejection 607n.
abrogation 752n.
non-observance 769n.
non-payment 805n.
divorce 896n.
repugnance
contrariety 14n.
unwillingness 598n.
opposition 704n.
resistance 715n.
dislike 861n.
hatred 888n.
repulse
recoil 280n.
repulsion 292n.
rejection 607n.
hitch 702n.
parry 713vb.
resistance 715n.
defeat 728n.
refusal 760n.
repulsion
energy 160n.
repulsion 292n.
dislike 861n.
repulsive
repellent 292adj.
unsavory 391adj.
inelegant 576adj.
ugly 842adj.
disliked 861adj.
hateful 888adj.
reputable
reputable 866adj.
honorable 929adj.
reputation
(*see* repute)
repute
importance 638n.
credit 802n.
repute 866n.
probity 929n.
reputedly
supposedly 512adv.
request
requirement 627n.
demand 737n.
request 761n., vb.
request, by
desirously 859adv.
request stop
stopping place 145n.
requiem
obsequies 364n.
lament 836n.
requiem mass
Christian rite 988n.
require
not suffice 636vb.
demand 737vb.
impose a duty 917vb.
(*see* requirement)
requirement
deficit 55n.
necessity 596n.
requirement 627n.
imperfection 647n.
request 761n.
conditions 766n.
desire 859n.
requisite
necessary 596adj.
requirement 627n.
requisition
requirement 627n.
demand 737n., vb.
request 761n., vb.
taking 786n.
requital
retaliation 714n.
pay 804n.
thanks 907n.
reward 962n.
punishment 963n.
rerebrace
armor 713n.
reredos
altar 990n.
rescind
recant 603vb.
abrogate 752vb.
rescission
abrogation 752n.
rescript
answer 460n.
correspondence 588n.
precept 693n.
decree 737n.
legislation 953n.
rescue
restoration 656n.
safety 660n.
escape 667n.
deliverance 668n.
aid 703n.
defend 713vb.
liberation 746n.
restitution 787n.
vindicate 927vb.
rescuer
preserver 666n.
defender 713n.
benefactor 903n.
research
be curious 453vb.
inquiry 459n.

experiment 461n., vb.
study 536n.
resection
scission 46n.
reseda
green color 432n.
resemblance
similarity 18n.
copy 22n.
resemble
accord 24vb.
appear 445vb.
resent
hate 888vb.
be revengeful 910vb.
(*see* resentment)
resentful
malevolent 898adj.
(*see* resentment)
resentment
discontent 829n.
enmity 881n.
resentment 891n.
jealousy 911n.
reservation
qualification 468n.
doubt 486n.
dissent 489n.
registration 548n.
conditions 766n.
seclusion 883n.
Christian rite 988n.
reserve
aftercomer 67n.
be early 135vb.
put off 136vb.
substitute 150n.
enclosure 235n.
doubt 486n.
concealment 525n.
register 548vb.
taciturnity 582n.
select 605vb.
require 627vb.
store 632vb.
not use 674vb.
modesty 874n.
seclusion 883n.
reserved
reticent 525adj.
required 627adj.
promised 764adj.
possessed 773adj.
retained 778adj.
inexcitable 823adj.
due 915adj.
reserve, in
impending 155adj.
inactively 175adv.
prepared 669adj.
reserves
extra 40n.
means 629n.
provision 633n.
armed force 722n.
funds 797n.
reservist
substitute 150n.
soldier 722n.
reservoir
receptacle 194n.
irrigator 341n.
lake 346n.
storage 632n.
reset
modify 143vb.
replace 187vb.
reshape
modify 143vb.
transform 147vb.
reshuffle
begin 68vb.
reside
be 1vb.
dwell 192vb.
residence
place 185n.
locality 187n.
presence 189n.
abode, house 192n.
resident
resident 191n.
settler 191n.
envoy 754n.
cleric 986n.
resident alien
foreigner 59n.
residual
remainder 41n.
remaining 41adj.
numerical result 85n.
residue, residuum
remainder 41n.
dirt 649n.
resign
disuse 674vb.
not retain 779vb.
(*see* resignation)
resignation
relinquishment 621n.
submission 721n.
resignation 753n.
patience 823n.
content 828n.
humility 872n.
resignee
consignee 754n.
resile
recoil 280vb.
recant 603vb.
resilience
strength 162n.
return 286n.
elasticity 328n.
resilient
cheerful 833adj.
resin
resin 357n.
viol 414n.
resipiscence
penitence 939n.
resist
be loath 598vb.
give battle 718vb.
(*see* resistance)
resistance
energy 160n.
electricity 160n.
counteraction 182n.
hardness 326n.
hindrance 702n.
opposition 704n.
defense 713n.
resistance 715n.
revolt 738n.
refusal 760n.
resistant
dissenting 489adj.
resister
opponent 705n.
resistless
strong 162adj.
necessary 596adj.
res judicata
certainty 473n.
judgment 480n.
resole
repair 656vb.
resolute
unchangeable 153adj.
unyielding 162adj.
resolute 599adj.
completive 725adj.
courageous 855adj.
resolution
decomposition 51n.
conversion 147n.
vigorousness 174n.
melody 410n.
topic 452n.
will 595n.
resolution 599n.
obstinacy 602n.
intention 617n.
plan 623n.
assiduity 678n.
courage 855n.
resolve
liquefy 337vb.
decipher 520vb.
resolution 599n.
predetermination 608n.
resonance
recoil 280n.
oscillation 317n.
loudness 400n.
roll 403n.

resonance 404n.
resonant
rhetorical 574adj.
resorb
absorb 299vb.
resorption
reception 299n.
resort
focus 76n.
convergence 293n.
contrivance 623n.
means 629n.
stratagem 698n.
resort to
congregate 74vb.
be present 189vb.
travel 267vb.
avail of 673vb.
resound
(*see* resonance)
resource
contrivance 623n.
stratagem 698n.
resourceful
prolific 171adj.
imaginative 513adj.
cunning 698adj.
resources
means 629n.
materials 631n.
estate 777n.
wealth 800n.
respect
relation 9n.
appearance 445n.
observe 768vb.
fear 854n.
honor 866vb.
courtesy 884n.
respect 920n., vb.
respectability
mediocrity 732n.
repute 866n.
probity 929n.
respectable
great 32adj.
reputable 866adj.
respected 920adj.
honorable 929adj.
respectful
courteous 884adj.
respectful 920adj.
respective
relative 9adj.
special 80adj.
respectively
severally 80adv.
pro rata 783adv.
respects
courteous act 884n.
respects 920n.
respiration
respiration 352n.
life 360n.
respirator
safeguard 662n.
preserver 666n.
respire
oscillate 317vb.
breathe 352vb.
live 360vb.
be refreshed 685vb.
respite
interim 108n.
delay 136n.
lull 145n.
deliverance 668n.
repose 683n.
acquit 960vb.
resplendent
splendid 841adj.
respond
accord 24vb.
answer 460n., vb.
cooperate 706vb.
concord 710vb.
feel 818vb.
respondent
testee 461n.
interlocutor 584n.
accused person 928n.
litigant 959n.
responder
rejoinder 460n.
response
effect 157n.
sense 374n.
answer 460n.
feeling 818n.
friendliness 880n.
hymn 981n.
responsibility
liability 180n.
directorship 689n.
mandate 751n.
duty 917n.
guilt 936n.
responsible
adult 134adj.
causal 156adj.
liable 180adj.
wise 498adj.
observant 768adj.
indebted 803adj.
cautious 858adj.
dutied 917adj.
trustworthy 929adj.
responsible person
manager 690n.
responsions
exam. 459n.
responsive
sentient 374adj.
answering 460adj.
impressible 819adj.
responsiveness
feeling 818n.
benevolence 897n.
rest
be left 41vb.
be discontinuous 72vb.
stay 144vb.
lull 145n.
cease 145vb.
go on 146vb.
stability 153n.
inertness 175n.
supporter 218n.
quiescence 266n.
death 361n.
euphoria 376n.
pleasure 376n.
silence 399n.
notation 410n.
inaction 677n.
be inactive 679vb.
leisure 681n.
repose 683n., vb.
restart
revert 148vb.
rest, at
free 744adj.
restate
repeat 106vb.
restaurant
café 192n.
cookery 301n.
restaurateur
caterer 633n.
restful
tranquil 266adj.
comfortable 376adj.
reposeful 683adj.
rest home
hospital 658n.
resthouse
inn 192n.
resting
remaining 41adj.
unused 674adj.
resting place
resting place 266n.
goal 295n.
restitution
reversion 148n.
restitution 787n.
payment 804n.
dueness 915n.
vindication 927n.
atonement 941n.
restitutory
compensatory 31adj.
restoring 787adj.
restive
unwilling 598adj.
willful 602adj.
disobedient 738adj.
excited 821adj.
excitable 822adj.

discontented 829adj.
restlessness
changeableness 152n.
motion 265n.
agitation 318n.
restlessness 678n.
disobedience 738n.
excitability 822n.
discontent 829n.
restock
replenish 633vb.
rest on
be supported 218vb.
restoration
equalization 28n.
newness 126n.
reversion 148n.
strengthening 162n.
improvement 654n.
restoration 656n.
deliverance 668n.
refreshment 685n.
restitution 787n.
dueness 915n.
vindication 927n.
penalty 963n.
restorative
stimulant 174n.
salubrious 652adj.
tonic 658n.
refreshing 685adj.
relieving 831adj.
restore
compensate 31vb.
make complete 54vb.
reproduce 166vb.
remedy 658vb.
relieve 831vb.
vindicate 927vb.
(*see* restoration)
restored
whole 52adj.
restorer
reformer 654n.
mender 656n.
restrain
make smaller 198vb.
circumscribe 232vb.
retard 278vb.
dissuade 613vb.
make insufficient 636vb.
hinder 702vb.
retain 778vb.
tranquilize 823vb.
(*see* restraint)
restrained
small 33adj.
restraint
diminution 37n.
moderation 177n.
counteraction 182n.
elegance 575n.
compulsion 740n.
restraint 747n.
prohibition 757n.
temperance 942n.
restrict
make smaller 198vb.
(*see* restriction)
restricted
small 33adj.
restrictedly
partially 33adv.
restriction
circumscription 232n.
limit 236n.
qualification 468n.
hindrance 702n.
restriction 747n.
prohibition 757n.
restringent
restraining 747adj.
result
remainder 41n.
sequel 67n.
end 69n.
ensue 120vb.
eventuality 154n.
effect 157n.
product 164n.
instrumentality 628n.
completion 725n.
resultant
remaining 41adj.
result, no
failure 728n.
results
answer 460n.
resume
be concise 569vb.
abstract 592vb.
(*see* resumption)
résumé
compendium 592n.
resumption
start 68n.
repetition 106n.
reversion 148n.
restoration 656n.
taking 786n.
resurgence
reproduction 166n.
revival 656n.
resurrection
reproduction 166n.
revival 656n.
heaven 971n.
resurrectional
reproductive 166adj.
paradisiac 971adj.
resurrection day
finality 69n.
future state 124n.
revival 656n.
resurrectionist
thief 789n.
resuscitate
reproduce 166vb.
revive 656vb.
animate 821vb.
retable
shelf 218n.
retail
disperse 75vb.
communicate 524vb.
publish 528vb.
trading 791adj.
sell 793vb.
retailer
intermediary 231n.
provider 633n.
seller 793n.
tradesman 794n.
retain
tie 45vb.
stabilize 153vb.
remember 505vb.
understand 516vb.
store 632vb.
preserve 666vb.
restrain 747vb.
refuse 760vb.
possess 773vb.
retain 778vb.
retainer
inferior 35n.
concomitant 89n.
protector 660n.
retainer 742n.
reward 962n.
retake
retrieve 656vb.
retaliate
answer 460vb.
(*see* retaliation)
retaliation
equalization 28n.
compensation 31n.
interchange 151n.
retaliation 714n.
penalty 963n.
retaliative
retaliatory 714adj.
revengeful 910adj.
retard
bate 37vb.
halt 145vb.
retard 278vb.
retardation
delay 136n.
slowness 278n.
hindrance 702n.
restraint 747n.
retarded
unintelligent 499adj.
retarding
counteracting 182adj.
retch

vomit 300vb.
retching
indigestion 651n.
retell
repeat 106vb.
retention
coherence 48n.
memory 505n.
possession 773n.
retention 778n.
retentive
tough 329adj.
retentive 778adj.
greedy 859adj.
retiarius
combatant 722n.
reticence
concealment 525n.
taciturnity 582n.
caution 858n.
reticle
network 222n.
reticular
reticular 222adj.
reticulate
space 201vb.
cross 222vb.
reticulation
network 222n.
convolution 251n.
reticule
bag 194n.
retiform
reticular 222adj.
retina
eye 438n.
retinoscope
optical device 442n.
retinue
retinue 67n.
procession 71n.
band 74n.
rear 238n.
follower 284n.
retainer 742n.
retire
cease 145vb.
be concave 255vb.
be quiescent 266vb.
regress 286vb.
recede 290vb.
depart 296vb.
disappear 446vb.
run away 620vb.
relinquish 621vb.
resign 753vb.
not retain 779vb.
retired
former 125adj.
disused 674adj.
leisurely 681adj.
resigning 753adj.
secluded 833adj.
retirement
regression 286n.
recession 290n.
relinquishment 621n.
leisure 681n.
resignation 753n.
retiring
modest 874adj.
unsociable 883adj.
retold
repeated 106adj.
retort
crucible 147n.
reversion 148n.
interchange 151n.
vessel 194n.
vaporizer 338n.
heater 383n.
answer 460n., vb.
testing agent 461n.
confutation 479n.
retaliation 714n.
witticism 839n.
be insolent 878vb.
retouch
repair 656vb.
retrace
revert 148vb.
retrospect 505vb.
retrace one's steps
repeat oneself 106vb.
turn back 286vb.
retract
recant 603vb.
abrogate 752vb.
resign 753vb.
retractation
non-observance 769n.
(*see* retract)
retractable
drawing 288adj.
retraction
traction 288n.
negation 533n.
recantation 603n.
retractive
drawing 288adj.
retractor
traction 288n.
retral
back 238adj.
retread
repair 656vb.
retreat
decrease 37n.
focus 76n.
reversion 148n.
go away 190vb.
retreat 192n.
be concave 255vb.
marching 267n.
regression 286n.
recession 290n.
meditation 449n.
hiding-place 527n.
call 547n.
avoidance 620n.
refuge 662n.
escape 667n.
defeat 728n.
seclusion 883n.
prayers 981n.
monastery 986n.
retrench
(*see* retrenchment)
retrenchment
diminution 37n.
subtraction 39n.
shortening 204n.
restriction 747n.
economy 814n.
retrial
legal trial 959n.
retribution
retaliation 714n.
punishment 963n.
retrieval
reversion 148n.
restoration 656n.
deliverance 668n.
acquisition 771n.
taking 786n.
retrieve
recoup 31vb.
counteract 182vb.
retrieve 656vb.
retriever
dog 365n.
retro
rearward 238adv.
retroaction
reversion 148n.
counteraction 182n.
recoil 280n.
regression 286n.
retroactive
retrospective 125adj.
reverted 148adj.
recoiling 280adj.
retrocession
reversion 148n.
regression 286n.
recession 290n.
restoration 656n.
retroflexion
reversion 148n.
curvature 248n.
regression 286n.
retrograde
regressive 286adj.
regress 286vb.
deteriorate 655vb.
relapse 657vb.
retrogression
reversion 148n.

regression 286n.
deterioration 655n.
retrospect
look back 125vb.
remembrance 505n.
retrospection
preterition 125n.
thought 449n.
remembrance 505n.
retrospective
retrospective 125adj.
reverted 148adj.
regretting 830adj.
retroussé
short 204adj.
curved 248adj.
retroversion
inversion 221n.
return
recurrence 106n.
be periodic 141vb.
reversion 148n.
product 164n.
inversion 221n.
recoil 280n., vb.
turn round 282vb.
return 286n.
propel 287vb.
arrival 295n.
circuition 314n.
answer 460n.
report 525n.
tergiversation 603n.
vote 605n., vb.
reject 607vb.
benefit 615n.
relapse 657n., vb.
retaliate 714vb.
commission 751vb.
earnings 771n.
restitution 787n.
receipt 807n.
thanks 907n.
reward 962n.
returnable
owed 803adj.
returned
chosen 605adj.
rejected 607adj.
returned prodigal
penitent 939n.
return, in
in return 31adv.
return journey
reversion 148n.
return match
equalization 28n.
repetition 106n.
returns
list 87n.
record 548n.
return ticket
reversion 148n.
reunion
junction 45n.
assembly 74n.
concord 710n.
social gathering 882n.
revalidate
restore 656vb.
revalorization
restoration 656n.
revaluation
improvement 654n.
revamp
modify 143vb.
revanchism
revengefulness 910n.
revanchist
avenger 910n.
reveal
manifest 522vb.
inform 524vb.
disclose 526vb.
publish 528vb.
indicate 547vb.
revealed
scriptural 975adj.
revelational 975adj.
revealing
transparent 422adj.
reveille
call 547n.
revel
enjoy 376vb.
rejoicing 835n.
revel 837n., vb.
celebration 876n.
sociability 882n.
intemperance 943n.
drunkenness 949n.
revelation
appearance 445n.
discovery 484n.
truth 494n.
inexpectation 508n.
prediction 511n.
manifestation 522n.
disclosure 526n.
scripture 975n.
revelation 975n.
reveler
laugher 835n.
reveler 837n.
revenant
ghost 970n.
revendicate
demand 737vb.
claim 915vb.
revenge
equalization 28n.
retaliation 714n.
revenge 910n.
jealousy 911n.
vindicate 927vb.
reward 962n.
punishment 963n.
revengeful
hating 888adj.
resentful 891adj.
malevolent 898adj.
pitiless 906adj.
revengeful 910adj.
revenue
means 629n.
earnings 771n.
estate 777n.
receipt 807n.
reverberate
be loud 400vb.
reverberation
repetition 106n.
recoil 280n.
roll 403n.
resonance 404n.
reverberatory
furnace 383n.
revere
honor 866vb.
love 887vb.
respect 920vb.
be pious 979vb.
worship 981vb.
reverence
obeisance 311n.
respect 920n., vb.
piety 979n.
worship 981vb.
reverence
worshipful 866adj.
title 870n.
sanctified 979adj.
cleric 986n.
reverent
respectful 920adj.
pious 979adj.
worshiping 981adj.
reverie
thought 449n.
abstractedness 456n.
fantasy 513n.
reversal
reversion 148n.
inversion 221n.
inexpectation 508n.
tergiversation 603n.
abrogation 752n.
reverse
contrariety 14n.
revert 148vb.
invert 221vb.
back 238adj.
contraposition 240n.
fold 261n.
retard 278vb.
turn round 282vb.
defeat 728n.
adversity 731n.
abrogate 752vb.

loss 772n.
reverse, in
backwards 286adv.
reversible
regressive 286adj.
reversion
return 286n.
reversion 148n.
revolution 149n.
inversion 221n.
regression 286n.
possession 773n.
dower 777n.
transfer 780n.
restitution 787n.
reversionary
reverted 148adj.
transferred 780adj.
reversioner
beneficiary 776n.
revert
reoccur 106vb.
revert 148vb.
revert to
repeat oneself 106vb.
notice 455vb.
change hands 780vb.
revet
coat 226vb.
revetment
facing 226n.
revictual
replenish 633vb.
review
assemblage 74n.
inspection 438n.
spectacle 445n.
meditate 449vb.
attention 455n.
inquiry 459n.
estimate 480n., vb.
remembrance 505n.
interpretation 520n.
journal 528n.
reading matter 589n.
describe 590vb.
article 591n.
compendium 592n.
rectify 654vb.
pageant 875n.
reviewer
estimator 480n.
interpreter 520n.
bookman 589n.
dissertator 591n.
revile
curse 899vb.
dispraise 924vb.
exprobate 924vb.
be impious 980vb.
reviler
defamer 926n.
revise
modify 143vb.
be attentive 455vb.
letterpress 587n.
reading matter 589n.
plan 623n., vb.
(*see* revision)
reviser
alterer 143n.
author 589n.
reformer 654n.
revision
inspection 438n.
study 536n.
amendment 654n.
revisit
be present 189vb.
revitalize
vitalize 360vb.
revive 656vb.
revival
newness 126n.
strengthening 162n.
reproduction 166n.
improvement 654n.
revival 656n.
relief 831n.
revivalism
public worship 981n.
revivalist
antiquarian 125n.
worshiper 981n.
pastor 986n.
revive
augment 36vb.
repeat 106vb.
revert 148vb.
vitalize 360vb.
get healthy 650vb.
refresh 685vb.
animate 821vb.
(*see* revival)
reviver
tonic 658n.
refreshment 685n.
revocable
possible 469adj.
revocation
transference 272n.
recantation 603n.
abrogation 752n.
revocatory
negative 533adj.
revoke
suppress 165vb.
abrogate 752vb.
prohibit 757vb.
not retain 779vb.
revolt
revolution 149n.
be violent 176vb.
opposition 704n.
resistance 715n.
revolt 738n., vb.
displease 827vb.
cause discontent 829vb.
cause dislike 861vb.
fail in duty 918vb.
lawlessness 954n.
revolter
revolter 738n.
revolting
not nice 645adj.
unpleasant 827adj.
frightening 854adj.
disliked 861adj.
hateful 888adj.
revolution
disorder 61n.
regular return 141n.
change 143n.
reversion 148n.
revolution 149n.
destruction 165n.
outbreak 176n.
rotation 315n.
revolt 738n.
revolutionary
modern 126adj.
revolutionist 149n.
revolutionary 149adj.
violent creature 176n.
reformer 654n.
revolter 738n.
revolutionize
modify 143vb.
revolutionize 149vb.
revolve
be periodic 141vb.
circle 314vb.
rotate 315vb.
meditate 449vb.
revolver
pistol 723n.
revue
spectacle 445n.
stage show 594n.
revulsion
reversion 148n.
recoil 280n.
tergiversation 603n.
rev up
accelerate 277vb.
reward
incentive 612n.
trophy 729n.
acquisition 771n.
gift 781n.
pay 804n., vb.
honors 866n.
thanks 907n.
reward 962vb.
rewarding
gainful 771adj.
rewarding 962adj.
rewardless

unthanked 908adj.
reword
repeat 106vb.
translate 520vb.
phrase 563vb.
rewrite
rectify 654vb.
Reynard
slyboots 698n.
rhabdology
mathematics 86n.
Rhadamanthus
magistracy 957n.
mythic hell 972n.
rhapsode
poet 593n.
rhapsodical
fitful 142adj.
imaginative 513adj.
rhapsodist
crank 504n.
visionary 513n.
poet 593n.
rhapsodize
be absurd 497vb.
rhapsody
discontinuity 72n.
musical piece 412n.
absurdity 497n.
ideality 513n.
rhetoric
curriculum 536n.
vigor 571n.
ornament 574n.
oratory 579n.
ostentation 875n.
rhetorical
exaggerated 546adj.
stylistic 566adj.
rhetorical 574adj.
eloquent 579n.
rhetorical figure
trope 519n.
rhetorician
phrasemonger 574n.
speaker 579n.
rheum
excrement 302n.
fluid 335n.
rheumatic
crippled 163adj.
diseased 657adj.
rheumatism
pang 377n.
rheumatism 651n.
rheumatoid
diseased 651adj.
rheumy
excretory 302adj.
fluidal 335adj.
rhinestone
finery 844n.
rhinitis
respiratory disease 651n.
rhinocerous
animal 365n.
rhinoplasty
surgery 658n.
beautification 843n.
rhinorrhea
respiratory disease 651n.
rhizome
tuber 301n.
Rhodes scholar
college student 538n.
rhododendron
tree 366n.
rhomb
angular figure 247n.
magic instrument 983n.
rhomboid
obliquity 220n.
angular figure 247n.
rhombus
angular figure 247n.
rhubarb
vegetable 301n.
rhumb
compass point 281n.
rhyme
assimilation 18n.
repetition 106n.
poetry 593n.
rhyme royal
prosody 593n.
rhymer, rhymester
poet 593n.
rhyming
harmonious 410adj.
poetic 593adj.
rhyming slang
slang 560n.
rhythm
uniformity 16n.
recurrence 106n.
periodicity 141n.
symmetry 245n.
motion 265n.
tempo 410n.
elegance 575n.
prosody 593n.
rhythmic
continuous 71adj.
(*see* rhythm)
rialto
mart 796n.
rib
spouse 894n.
(*see* ribs)
ribald
vulgar 847adj.
derisive 851adj.
disreputable 867adj.
maledicent 899adj.
impure 951adj.
ribaldry
(*see* ribald)
riband
ligature 47n.
strip 208n.
ribbed
textural 331adj.
ribbon
ligature 47n.
strip 208n.
badge 547n.
monument 548n.
decoration 729n.
trimming 844n.
honors 866n.
ribbon-development
production 164n.
overstepping 306n.
ribbons
halter 47n.
headgear 228n.
fetter 748n.
finery 844n.
ribs
frame 218n.
laterality 239n.
meat 301n.
rib-tickling
witty 839adj.
rice
corn 366n.
rice-paper
brittleness 330n.
stationery 586n.
rich
powerful 160adj.
prolific 171adj.
nourishing 301adj.
fatty 357adj.
tasty 386adj.
savory 390adj.
florid 425adj.
diffuse 570adj.
ornate 574adj.
plenteous 635adj.
valuable 644adj.
rich 800adj.
splendid 841adj.
ornamental 844adj.
funny 849adj.
riches
good 615n.
plenty 635n.
wealth 800n.
richly
greatly 32adv.
richly deserved
due 915adj.
rich uncle
patron 707n.
giver 781n.

good giver 813n.
rich vein
store 632n.
rick
derange 63vb.
bunch 74n.
disable 161vb.
store 632n.
rickets
disease 651n.
rickety
weak 163adj.
flimsy 163adj.
lean 206adj.
deformed 246adj.
diseased 651adj.
ricksha
pushcart, cab 274n.
ricochet
recoil 280n., vb.
rictus
distortion 246n.
rid
eliminate 44vb.
eject 300vb.
deliver 668vb.
liberate 746vb.
riddable
extricable 668adj.
riddance
elimination 44n.
escape 667n.
deliverance 668n.
liberation 746n.
loss 772n.
ridden, be
carry 273vb.
riddle
class 62vb.
porosity 263n.
pierce 263vb.
unintelligibility 517n.
enigma 530n.
cleaning utensil 648n.
purify 648vb.
riddler
questioner 459n.
ride
land travel 267n.
break in 369vb.
path 624n.
ride at anchor
be quiescent 266vb.
ride down
pursue 619vb.
charge 712vb.
ride off
avoid 620vb.
ride out
navigate 269vb.
be safe 660vb.
rider
rider 268n.
thing transferred 272n.
gravity 322n.
cavalry 722n.
ride roughshod
be violent 176vb.
kick 279vb.
oppress 735vb.
be insolent 878vb.
ride to death
repeat oneself 106vb.
ride to hounds
hunt 619vb.
ridge
bond 47n.
narrowness 206n.
high land 209n.
roof 226n.
partition 231n.
ridged
rough 259adj.
ridicule
underestimate 483vb.
disbelieve 486vb.
foolery 497n.
misinterpret 521vb.
befool 542vb.
misrepresentation 552n.
laughter 835n.
wit 839n.
ridicule 851n., vb.
shame 867vb.
rudeness 885n.
contempt 922n.
disapprobation 924n.
detract 926vb.
ridiculous
abnormal 84adj.
absurd 497adj.
foolish 499adj.
amusing 837adj.
ridiculous 849adj.
ridiculousness
ridiculousness 849n.
riding
district 184n.
land travel 267n.
equitation 267n.
sport 837n.
riding-school
arena 724n.
rid of
escaped 667adj.
(*see* rid, riddance)
rifacimento
repetition 106n.
rife
existing 1adj.
rumored 529adj.
rife, be
be 1vb.
prevail 178vb.
rifeness
generality 79n.
riffraff
rabble 869n.
rifle
groove 262vb.
fire-arm 723n.
steal 788vb.
rifleman
shooter 287n.
soldiery 722n.
rifle-range
arena 724n.
rifling
furrow 262n.
rift
disjunction 46n.
gap 201n.
defect 647n.
dissension 709n.
rig
dressing 228n.
carriage 274n.
fake 541vb.
make ready 669vb.
rigadoon
dance 837n.
rigged
marine 275adj.
false 541adj.
prepared 669adj.
rigged out
dressed 228adj.
rigger
trickster 545n.
artisan 686n.
rigging
tackling 47n.
riggish
unchaste 951adj.
right
apt 24adj.
dextrality 241n.
straight 249adj.
true 494adj.
accurate 494adj.
usual 610adj.
expedient 642adj.
repair 656vb.
political party 708n.
estate 777n.
right 913n.
dueness 915n.
probity 929n.
virtuous 933adj.
right about, to the
backwards 286adv.
right about turn
be inverted 221vb.
right and left
widely 183adv.
around 230adv.
sideways 239adv.
right angle

verticality 215n.
angle 247n.
right answer
remedy 658n.
right arm
power 160n.
right ascension
bearings 186n.
uranometry 321n.
right ascension and declension
coordinate 465n.
right belief
orthodoxy 976n.
right, by
duly 915adv.
righteous
just 913adj.
virtuous 933adj.
right form
formality 875n.
rightful
right 913adj.
due 915adj.
right hand
power 160n.
dextrality 241n.
auxiliary 707n.
right-handed
dextral 241adj.
right-hand man
auxiliary 707n.
servant 742n.
deputy 755n.
rightist
political party 708n.
right itself
equalize 28vb.
cure 656vb.
right line
line 203n.
straightness 249n.
rightly served
retaliatory 714adj.
right man
fitness 24n.
expert 696n.
right-minded
wise 498adj.
just 913adj.
virtuous 933adj.
orthodox 976adj.
right mind, in one's
sane 502adj.
restored 656adj.
right mood
willingness 597n.
rightness
truth 494n.
right 913n.
right of way
access 624n.
right people
beau monde 848n.
Right Reverend
title 870n.
church title 986n.
rights
freedom 744n.
right 913n.
right thing
duty 917n.
right time
juncture 8n.
clock time 117n.
opportunity 137n.
occasion 137n.
expedience 642n.
right touch, have the
be skillful 694vb.
right-wing
dextral 241adj.
right-winger
political party 708n.
right wrongs
be just 913vb.
rigid
unconformable 84adj.
unyielding 162adj.
still 266adj.
rigid 326adj.
obstinate 602adj.
severe 735adj.
rigidity
(*see* rigid)
rigmarole
unmeaningness 515n.
diffuseness 570n.
rigor
spasm 318n.
hardness 326n.
coldness 380n.
accuracy 494n.
illness 651n.
severity 735n.
pitilessness 906n.
rigorism
opinatrety 602n.
rigorist
opinionist 602n.
tyrant 735n.
disapprover 924n.
rigorous
severe 735adj.
fastidious 862adj.
pitiless 906adj.
ascetic 945adj.
rig out
dress 228vb.
Rigsdag
parliament 692n.
rig the market
speculate 791vb.
Rigveda
non-Biblical scripture 975n.
rile
make unclean 649vb.
enrage 891vb.
rill
stream 350n.
rim
outline 233n.
edge 234n.
rime
gap 201n.
wintriness 380n.
rimer
perforator 263n.
rimose, rimous
spaced 201adj.
rind
skin 226n.
rinderpest
animal disease 651n.
ring
fastening 47n.
band 74n.
hanger 217n.
circumscription 232n.
outline 233n.
enclosure 235n.
circle 250n.
orifice 263n.
be loud 400vb.
roll 403n.
resonance 404n.
play music 413vb.
communicate 524vb.
message 529n.
obliterate 550vb.
association 706n.
party 708n.
pugilism 716n.
arena 724n.
badge of rule 743n.
restriction 747n.
jewelry 844n.
love-token 889n.
wedding 894n.
ring a bell
be remembered 505vb.
ring a change
play music 413vb.
ring-bolt
fetter 748n.
ring-dove
bird 365n.
ring down the curtain
terminate 69vb.
cease 145vb.
ringed
round 250adj.
ringer
substitute 150n.
impostor 545n.
ring in
initiate 68vb.
time 117vb.
ringing
resonant 404adj.

melodious 410adj.
campanology 412n.
ringleader
motivator 612n.
leader 690n.
agitator 738n.
ringlet
loop 250n.
hair 259n.
ringmaster
leader 690n.
ring off
terminate 69vb.
cease 145vb.
be mute 578vb.
ringside seat
near place 200n.
view 438n.
ring the bell
be successful 727vb.
ring the changes
vary 152vb.
ring the knell
kill 362vb.
ring true
be true 494vb.
ring up
communicate 524vb.
ringworm
skin disease 651n.
rink
arena 724n.
pleasure-ground 837n.
rinse
drench 341vb.
clean 648vb.
hairwash 843n.
rinsings
dirt 649n.
riot
turmoil 61n.
multitude 104n.
abundance 171n.
violence 176n.
plenty 635n.
superabound 637vb.
quarrel 709n.
fight 716n.
revolt 738n.
rejoice 835vb.
lawlessness 954n.
rioter
rioter 738n.
reveler 837n.
riot in
enjoy 376vb.
riotous
violent 176adj.
anarchic 734adj.
riotous 738adj.
excitable 822adj.
jubilant 833adj.
intemperate 943adj.
sensual 944adj.
lawless 954adj.
rip
rend 46vb.
open 263vb.
move fast 277vb.
wave 350n.
wound 654vb.
libertine 952n.
riparian
coastal 344adj.
ripcord
fastening 47n.
ripe
aged 131adj.
pulpy 356adj.
perfect 646adj.
matured 669adj.
ripe experience
wisdom 498n.
ripen
perfect 646vb.
get better 654vb.
mature 669vb.
carry through 725vb.
ripeness
(*see* ripe)
ripening
future 124adj.
young 130adj.
maturation 669n.
ripen into
be turned to 147vb.
riper age
age 131n.
rip-hook
sharp edge 256n.
ripieno
extra 40n.
musician 413n.
riposte
impulse 279n.
answer 460n., vb.
parry 713vb.
retaliation 714n.
rip out
extract 304vb.
ripping
topping 644adj.
ripple
shallowness 212n.
hang 217vb.
convolution 251n.
crinkle 251vb.
furrow 262n.
agitate 318vb.
wave 350n.
sound faint 401vb.
ripple-bed
hospital 658n.
riproaring
loud 400adj.
gay 833adj.
Rip van Winkle
old man 133n.
insensibility 375n.
rise
increase 36n.
beginning 68n.
be high 209vb.
verticality 215n.
acclivity 220n.
progression 285n.
flow out 298vb.
ascent 308n.
lift oneself 310vb.
appear 445vb.
be duped 544vb.
flourish 615vb.
improvement 654n.
go to war 718vb.
succeed 727vb.
prosper 730vb.
revolt 738vb.
gain 771n.
show respect 920vb.
rise above
be superior 34vb.
outdo 306vb.
rise above oneself
be disinterested 931vb.
rise to the occasion
be superior 34vb.
improvise 609vb.
rishi
sage 500n.
religious teacher 973n.
risibility
laughter 835n.
ridiculousness 849n.
rising
future 124adj.
aged 131adj.
powerful 160adj.
influential 178adj.
sloping 220adj.
resistance 715n.
successful 727adj.
prosperous 730adj.
revolt 738n.
dear 811adj.
rising generation
youth 130n.
posterity 170n.
rising ground
high land 209n.
acclivity 220n.
rising man
made man 730n.
rising sun
person of repute 866n.
risk
gambling 618n.
possibility 469n.
danger 661n.
speculate 791vb.
risk it
chance 159vb.

face danger 661vb.
risk-taker
gambler 618n.
brave person 855n.
risk-taking
calculation of chance 159n.
risky
uncertain 474adj.
speculative 618adj.
dangerous 661adj.
impure 951adj.
risotto
dish 301n.
risqué
vulgar 847adj.
disreputable 867adj.
impure 951adj.
rite
practice 610n.
legality 953n.
rite 988n.
ritornello
prelude 66n.
repetition 106n.
ritual
formality 875n.
celebration 876n.
ritual 988n., adj.
(*see* rite)
ritualism
pietism 979n.
ritualism 988n.
ritualistic
formal 875adj.
theological 973adj.
pietistic 979adj.
worshiping 981adj.
devotional 981adj.
ritualistic 988adj.
ritual object
church utensil 990n.
ritzy
rich 800adj.
dear 811adj.
ostentatious 875adj.
rival
compeer 28n.
hinderer 702n.
opponent 705n.
quarreler 709n.
contender 716n.
enemy 881n.
(*see* rivalry)
rivalry
imitation 20n.
opposition 704n.
quarrelsomeness 709n.
contention 716n.
jealousy 911n.
envy 912n.
rive
cut, rend 46vb.
river
stream 350n.
riverbed
cavity 255n.
conduit 351n.
riverine
marginal 234adj.
coastal 344adj.
riverless
dry 342adj.
riverside
edge 234n.
marginal 234adj.
shore 344n.
coastal 344adj.
rivet
affix 45vb.
fastening 47n.
riveter
joinder 45n.
riviera
shore 344n.
pleasure-ground 837n.
rivulet
stream 350n.
rixation
quarrel 709n.
anger 891n.
reproach 924n.
road
street 192n.
transport 272n.
direction 281n.
gulf 345n.
road 624n.
road agent
robber 789n.
roadblock
obstacle 702n.
road-book
itinerary 267n.
road hog
egotist 932n.
road-holding ability
equilibrium 28n.
roadhouse
tavern 192n.
road map
itinerary 267n.
map 551n.
road roller
smoother 258n.
roads
stable 192n.
shelter 662n.
roadside
edge 234n.
marginal 234adj.
accessible 289adj.
roadstead
station 187n.
stable 192n.
goal 295n.
gulf 345n.
shelter 662n.
roadster
automobile 274n.
roadway
road 624n.
roadworthy
transferable 272adj
roam
wander 267vb.
be free 744vb.
roan
horse 273n.
brown 430adj.
pied 437adj.
roar
be violent 176vb.
be agitated 318vb.
blow 352vb.
loudness 400n.
roll 403vb.
vociferate 408vb.
ululate 409vb.
emphasize 532vb.
laugh 835vb.
be angry 891vb.
threaten 900vb.
roaring
furious 176adj.
roaring trade
prosperity 730n.
roast
cook 301vb.
be hot 379vb.
heat 381vb.
ridicule 851vb.
rob
weaken 163vb.
pulpiness 356n.
take away 786vb.
rob 788vb.
impoverish 801vb.
robber
robber 789n.
robbery
stealing 788n.
loss of right 916n.
robe
robe 228n.
dress 228vb.
badge of rule 743n.
canonicals 989n.
Robe, the
bar 958n.
robin
bird 365n.
Robinson Crusoe
solitary 883n.
robot
image 551n.
fatalist 596n.
instrument 628n.
machine 630n.
slave 742n.

rob Peter to pay Paul
substitute 150vb.
robust
stalwart 162adj.
healthy 650adj.
roc
rara avis 84n.
rochet
vestments 989n.
rock
be unequal 29vb.
permanence 144n.
vary 152vb.
fixture 153n.
assuage 177vb.
bring to rest 266vb.
sweetmeat 301n.
oscillate 317vb.
solid body 324n.
hardness 326n.
rock 344n.
sweet 392n.
refuge 662n.
pitfall 663n.
tranquilize 823vb.
gem 844n.
pet 889vb.
rock bottom
base 214n.
basis 218n.
rock-carving
sculpture 554n.
rocker
fluctuation 317n.
rocket
vigorousness 174n.
rocket 276n.
speeder 277n.
missile 287n.
climber 308n.
signal light 420n.
signal 547n.
missile weapon 723n.
reprimand 924n.
rocketry
aeronautics 271n.
rocket 276n.
arm 723n.
rockiness
hardness 326n.
rocking chair
seat 218n.
fluctuation 317n.
rocking horse
plaything 837n.
rock 'n roll
music 412n.
dance 837n., vb.
rocks, on the
endangered 661adj.
grounded 728adj.
rocky
unstable 152adj.
weakly 163adj.
hard 326adj.
territorial 344adj.
rococo
school of painting 553n.
ornamental 844adj.
rod
measure 183n.
long measure 203n.
support 218n.
cylinder 252n.
gauge 465n.
trainer 537n.
incentive 612n.
pistol 723n.
badge of rule 743n.
rod and line
chase 619n.
rodent
rodent 365n.
rodeo
contest 716n.
rodomontade
empty talk 515n.
exaggeration 546n.
magniloquence 574n.
oration 579n.
boast 877n.
roe
fertilizer 171n.
deer 365n.
roebuck
deer 365n.
rogation
request 761n.
prayers 981n.
rogue
trickster 545n.
ruffian 904n.
noxious animal 904n.
knave 938n.
roguery
improbity 930n.
wickedness 934n.
rogues' gallery
record 548n.
rogue's march
ejection 300n.
roguish
gay 833adj.
amused 837adj.
witty 839adj.
roister
rampage 61vb.
revel 837vb.
roisterer
reveler 837n.
Roland for an Oliver, a
retaliation 714n.
role
acting 594n.
function 622n.
roll
piece 53n.
bunch 74n.
list 87n.
make smaller 198vb.
strip 208n.
flatten 216vb.
textile 222n.
wrapping 226n.
coil 251n.
twine 251vb.
cylinder 252n.
smooth 258vb.
go smoothly 258vb.
hair 259n.
fold 261vb.
move 265vb.
travel 267vb.
aeronautics 271n.
tumble 309vb.
rotation 315n.
fluctuation 317n.
flow 350vb.
loudness 400n.
roll 403n., vb.
play music 413vb.
call 547n.
record 548n.
pronunciation 577n.
book 589n.
surgical dressing 658n.
be servile 879vb.
roll call
statistics 86n.
nomenclature 561n.
rolled into one
conjunct 45adj.
one 88adj.
roller
girdle 47n.
ligature 47n.
flattener 216n.
wheel 250n.
cylinder 252n.
smoother 258n.
rotator 315n.
pulverizer 332n.
wave 350n.
roller-bandage
ligature 47n.
rollers
hair-dressing 843n.
rollerskate
sled 274n.
rollick
be cheerful 833vb.
rejoice 835vb.
amuse oneself 837vb.
rollicking
gay 833adj.
roll in
approach 289vb.
irrupt 297vb.
enjoy 376vb.
abound 635vb.

superabound 637vb.
be received 782vb.
rolling
alpine 209adj.
undulatory 251adj.
rotation 315n.
fluctuation 317n.
champaign 348adj.
moneyed 800adj.
rolling country
high land 209n.
rolling in
full 54adj.
rolling pin
flattener 216n.
cylinder 252n.
smoother 258n.
rotator 315n.
rolling stock
train 274n.
rolling stone
wanderer 268n.
roll of honor
list 87n.
roll on
continue 108vb.
elapse 111vb.
go on 146vb.
move 265vb.
roll out
flatten 216vb.
roll up
congregate 74vb.
fold 261vb.
approach 289vb.
converge 293vb.
arrive 295vb.
rotate 315vb.
roly-poly
cylinder 252n.
pudding 301n.
roman
written 586adj.
print-type 587n.
Roman
popish 976adj.
Roman candle
fireworks 420n.
Roman Catholicism
Catholicism 976n.
romance
absurdity 497n.
ideality 513n.
be false 541vb.
fable 543n.
novel 590n.
love affair 887n.
romancer
visionary 513n.
liar 545n.
narrator 590n.
Roman eagle
flag 547n.
Romanesque
ornamental 844adj.
Roman holiday
slaughter 362n.
Romanism
Catholicism 976n.
roman numerals
number 85n.
romantic
visionary 513n.
imaginative 513adj.
descriptive 590adj.
feeling 818adj.
impressible 819adj.
excitable 822adj.
romanticism
fantasy 513n.
school of painting 553n.
romanticist
visionary 513n.
romanticize
imagine 513vb.
Romany
wanderer 268n.
slang 560n.
Rome
focus 76n.
Romeo
lover 887n.
Romish
popish 976adj.
romp
rampage 61vb.
youngster 132n.
be cheerful 833vb.
revel 837n.
caress 889vb.
rompers
breeches 228n.
romping
light-minded 456adj.
rompish
amused 837adj.
rondeau
verse form 593n.
rondo
musical piece 412n.
rood
cross 222n.
ritual object 988n.
rood-screen
church interior 990n.
roof
home 192n.
vertex 213n.
roof 226n.
overlay 226vb.
shelter 662n.
roofless
displaced 188adj.
roof-top
vertex 213n.
roof 226n.
rook
bird 365n.
defraud 788vb.
chessman 837n.
rookery
rest 192n.
room
inclusion 78n.
opportunity 137n.
room 183n.
dwell 192vb.
chamber 194n.
scope 744n.
roomer
resident 191n.
roommate
chum 880n.
rooms
quarters 192n.
roomy
spacious 183adj.
roorback
calumny 926n.
roost
nest 192n.
dwell 192vb.
sit down 311vb.
sleep 679vb.
repose 683vb.
rooster
poultry 365n.
male animal 372n.
root
numerical element 85n.
stabilize 153vb.
source 156n.
place 187n.
base 214n.
tuber 301n.
plant 366n.
vociferate 408vb.
word 559n.
applaud 923vb.
root and branch
completely 54adv.
revolutionary 149adj.
destructive 165adj.
rooted
firm-set 45adj.
immemorial 127adj.
fixed 153adj.
located 187adj.
still 266adj.
habitual 610adj.
rooter
cry 408n.
rootless
irrelative 10adj.
alone 88adj.
transient 114adj.
unstable 152adj.
displaced 188adj.
traveling 267adj.
root out

destroy 165vb.
eject 300vb.
extract 304vb.
rope
tie 45vb.
cable 47n.
line 203n.
fiber 208n.
safeguard 662n.
scope 744n.
fetter 748n.
jewelry 844n.
means of execution 964n.
rope-dancing
skill 694n.
rope of sand
non-coherence 49n.
weak thing 163n.
ropes
arena 924n.
rope's end
scourge 964n.
ropes, know the
be expert 694vb.
ropeway
railroad 624n.
ropework
fiber 208n.
ropy
thick 205adj.
fibrous 208adj.
dense 324adj.
semiliquid 354adj.
bad 645adj.
requelaure
cloak 228n.
rorification
moistening 341n.
rosary
prayers 981n.
office-book 988n.
roscid
humid 341adj.
rose
irrigator 341n.
fragrance 396n.
redness 431n.
heraldry 547n.
a beauty 841n.
roseate
red 431adj.
promising 852adj.
rose-colored
red 431adj.
promising 852adj.
rosemary
potherb 301n.
rosette
badge 547n.
trimming 844n.
rose water
moderator 177n.
scent 396n.
flattery 925n.
rose window
pattern 844n.
church interior 990n.
Rosicrucian
occultist 984n.
rosin
resin 357n.
rosiness
(*see* rosy)
roster
list 87n.
rostrate
angular 247adj.
curved 248adj.
rostrum
stand 218n.
prow 237n.
protuberance 254n.
publicity 528n.
rostrum 539n.
rosy
red 431adj.
healthy 650adj.
palmy 730adj.
personable 841adj.
promising 852adj.
rot
decay 51n.
absurdity 497n.
silly talk 515n.
dirt 649n.
ulcer 651n.
dilapidation 655n.
blight 659n.
rota
list 87n.
regular return 141n.
Rotarian
social person 882n.
rotary
rotary 315adj.
rotation
continuity 71n.
regular return 141n.
revolution 149n.
motion 265n.
circuition 314n.
rotation 315n.
rotator
rotator 315n.
rote, by
in memory 505adv.
rotodyne
aircraft 276n.
rotograph
photography 551n.
picture 553n.
rotor
rotator 315n.
rotten
antiquated 127adj.
weakened 163adj.
bad 645adj.
vicious 934adj.
(*see* rot)
rottenness
unsavoriness 390n.
rotter
cad 938n.
rotund
round 250adj.
rotund 252adj.
convex 253n.
rotunda
pavilion 192n.
roué
bad man 938n.
libertine 952n.
rouge
pigment 425n.
red pigment 431n.
beautify 841n.
cosmetic 843n.
rouge et noir
gambling 618n.
gambling game 837n.
rough
non-uniform 17adj.
incomplete 55adj.
amorphous 244adj.
rough 259adj.
unsavory 390adj.
hoarse 407adj.
hindering 702adj.
oppressive 735adj.
graceless 842adj.
low fellow 869n.
cruel 898adj.
ruffian 904n.
(*see* roughness)
roughage
food content 301n.
rough-and-ready
useful 640adj.
hasty 680adj.
bungled 695adj.
rough-and-tumble
turmoil 61n.
fight 716n.
rough breathing
pronunciation 577n.
rough-cast
facing 226n.
efform 243vb.
roughen 259vb.
plan 623n.
rough copy
undevelopment 670n.
rough diamond
amorphism 244n.
undevelopment 670n.
ingenue 699n.
vulgarian 847n.
good man 937n.
rough draft
incompleteness 55n.
roughen

roughen 259vb.
rough ground
difficulty 700n.
rough guess
conjecture 512n.
rough-hew
efform 243vb.
prepare 669vb.
rough-hewn
incomplete 55adj.
rough 259adj.
immature 670adj.
roughhouse
turmoil 61n.
fight 716n.
roughly
nearly 200adv.
roughneck
low fellow 869n.
bad man 938n.
roughness
discontinuity 72n.
violence 176n.
roughness 259n.
pungency 388n.
unsavoriness 390n.
stridor 407n.
inelegance 575n.
difficulty 700n.
painfulness 827n.
rudeness 885n.
(*see* rough)
rough-rider
rider 268n.
cavalry 722n.
rough side of one's tongue
reproach 924n.
rough sketch
experiment 461n.
rough with the smooth
all 52n.
roulette
gambling 618n.
gambling game 837n.
round
uniformity 16n.
degree 27n.
whole 52n.
continuity 71n.
numerical 85adj.
recurrence 106n.
period 110n.
fleshy 195adj.
efform 243vb.
make curved 248vb.
round 250adj.
rotund 252adj.
unsharpened 257adj.
circle 314vb.
bang 402n.
vocal music 412n.
campanology 412n.
assertive 532adj.
phrase 563vb.
habit 610n.
business 622n.
circuit 626n., vb.
pugilism 716n.
ammunition 723n.
roundabout
exterior 223adj.
circumjacent 230adj.
circle 250n.
deviating 282adj.
circuitous 314adj.
rotator 315n.
prolix 570adj.
road 624n.
roundabout 626adj.
pleasure-ground 837n.
round barrow
dome 253n.
tune 364n.
rounded
low 210adj.
unsharpened 257adj.
smooth 258adj.
shapely 841adj.
rounded period
elegance 575n.
roundel
circle 250n.
badge 547n.
rounders
ball game 837n.
round-eyed
wondering 864adj.
roundhouse
chamber 194n.
lock-up 748n.
rounding off
completion 725n.
roundness
equality 28n.
(*see* round)
round off
equalize 28vb.
round on
attack 712vb.
retaliate 714vb.
blame 924vb.
round-robin
report 524n.
request 761n.
deprecation 762n.
round-shouldered
deformed 246adj.
roundsman
traveler 268n.
circler 314n.
seller 793n.
round-table conference
conference 584n.
round the bend
crazed 503adj.
round the clock
all along 113adv.
round trip
reversion 148n.
land travel 267n.
circuition 314n.
round up
bring together 74vb.
roup
sale 793n.
rouse
invigorate 174vb.
incite 612vb.
excite 821vb.
rouse oneself
be active 678vb.
rousing
vigorous 174adj.
crying 408adj.
rout
retinue 67n.
crowd 74n.
disperse 75vb.
concomitant 89n.
multitude 104n.
commotion 318n.
defeat 728n., vb.
revel 837n.
rabble 869n.
route
itinerary 267n.
direction 281n.
passage 305n.
way, route 624n.
direct 689vb.
route-map
itinerary 267n.
route-march
marching 267n.
routine
uniformity 16n.
order 60n.
regularity 81n.
recurrence 106n.
regular return 141n.
practice 610n.
business 622n.
way 624n.
conduct 688n.
formality 875n.
ritual 988n.
roux
sauce 389n.
rove
wander 267vb.
stray 282vb.
rover
wanderer 268n.
roving
unstable 152adj.
roving commission
uncertainty 474n.
roving eye
unchastity 951n.
row
turmoil 61n.

series 71n.
violence 176n.
housing 192n.
row
(a boat) 269vb.
loudness 400n.
quarrel 709n.
fight 716vb.
rowan
tree 366n.
rowboat
rowboat 275n.
rowdiness
loudness 400n.
rowdy
violent creature 176n.
violent 176adj.
combatant 722n.
ill-bred 847adj.
ruffian 904n.
rowel
sharp point 256n.
rower
boatman 270n.
rowing
aquatics 269n.
traction 288n.
sport 837n.
row in the same boat
accompany 89vb.
cooperate 706vb.
rowlock
pivot 218n.
row of buttons
trifle 639n.
royal
supreme 34adj.
sail 275n.
ruling 733adj.
liberal 813adj.
impressive 821adj.
worshipful 866adj.
noble 868adj.
proud 871adj.
ostentatious 875adj.
Royal Highness
sovereign 741n.
title 870n.
royal road
facility 701n.
royalty
magistrature 733n.
authority 733n.
sovereign 741n.
receipt 807n.
nobility 868n.
rub
be contiguous 202vb.
friction 333n.
give pain 377vb.
touch 378vb.
clean 648vb.
wound 655vb.
difficulty 700n.
hindrance 702n.
adversity 731n.
painfulness 827n.
rub-a-dub
roll 403n.
rubber
elasticity 328n.
friction 333n.
silencer 401n.
contest 716n.
rubberneck
traveler 268n.
scan 438vb.
spectator 441n.
be curious 453vb.
rubbers
footwear 228n.
rubber stamp
assent 488n.
rubber-stamp
conform 83vb.
endorse 488vb.
rubbery
tough 329adj.
rubbing
duplicate 22n.
rubbing noses
friendliness 880n.
rubbish
leavings 41n.
absurdity 497n.
silly talk 515n.
waste 634n.
rubbish 641n.
dirt 649n.
derelict 779n.
rubbish-heap
rubbish 641n.
sink 649n.
rubbishy
unmeaning 515adj.
spurious 542adj.
trivial 639adj.
profitless 641adj.
rubble
piece 53n.
rub down
smooth 258vb.
pulverize 332vb.
groom 369vb.
rube
ingenue 699n.
countryman 869n.
rubella
infection 651n.
rubescence
redness 431n.
Rubicon
limit 236n.
rubicundity
redness 431n.
rubigo
blight 659n.
rub in
emphasize 532vb.
make important
638vb.
ruble
coinage 797n.
rub off
obliterate 550vb.
rub off on
cohere 48vb.
rub one's eyes
wonder 864vb.
rub one's hands
rejoice 835vb.
rub out
eject 300vb.
murder 362vb.
rub 333vb.
obliterate 550vb.
rubric
redness 431n.
label 547n.
precept 693n.
office-book 988n.
rite 988n.
rubricate
redden 431vb.
paint 553vb.
rub shoulders with
be contiguous 202vb.
rub the wrong way
roughen 259n.
make quarrels 709vb.
rub up
make bright 417vb.
ruby
redness 431n.
type size 587n.
exceller 644n.
gem 844n.
ruche
fold 261vb.
ruck
average 30n.
generality 79n.
fold 261vb.
rucksack
bag 194n.
ructation
voidance 300n.
ruction
turmoil 61n.
fight 716n.
rudder
poop 238n.
sailing aid 269n.
aircraft 276n.
tool 630n.
directorship 689n.
rudderless
impotent 161adj.
ruddle
red pigment 431n.

ruddy
florid 425adj.
red 431adj.
healthy 650adj.
personable 841adj.
rude
violent 176adj.
amorphous 244adj.
inelegant 576adj.
immature 670adj.
graceless 842adj.
ill-bred 847adj.
impertinent 878adj.
discourteous 885adj.
disrespectful 921adj.
rude person
rude person 885n.
rudiment
beginning 68n.
source 156n.
rudimental
immature 670adj.
rudimentary
beginning 68adj.
exiguous 196adj.
student-like 538adj.
rue
unsavoriness 390n.
regret 830vb.
be penitent 939vb.
rueful
regretting 830adj.
melancholic 834adj.
ruff
neckwear 228n.
overmaster 727vb.
ruffian
murderer 362n.
low fellow 869n.
ruffian 904n.
bad man 938n.
ruffianism
ill-breeding 847n.
inhumanity 898n.
lawlessness 954n.
ruffianly
ill-bred 847adj.
insolent 878adj.
ruffle
jumble 63vb.
roughen 259vb.
fold 261n., vb.
agitate 318vb.
enrage 891vb.
rufous
red 431adj.
rug
floor-cover 226n.
coverlet 226n.
rugged
stalwart 162adj.
amorphous 244adj.
difficult 700adj.
graceless 842adj.
ungracious 885adj.
ruggedness
non-uniformity 17n.
roughness 259n.
rugger
ball game 837n.
rugosity
roughness 259n.
ruin
antiquity 125n.
oldness 127n.
ruin 165n.
influence 178n.
waste 634vb.
delapidation 655n.
bane 659n.
defeat 728n.
adversity 731n.
loss 772n.
impoverish 801vb.
debauch 951vb.
ruination
ruin 165n.
dilapidation 655n.
impairment 655n.
ruinous
destructive 165adj.
harmful 645adj.
dilapidated 655adj.
adverse 731adj.
ruinous charge
dearness 811n.
rule
prototype 23n.
order 60n.
rule 81n.
prevail 178vb.
line 203n.
horizontality 216n.
judge 480vb.
creed 485n.
maxim 496n.
print-type 587n.
manage 689vb.
precept 693n.
governance 733n.
command 737vb.
conditions 766n.
legislation 953n.
try a case 959vb.
rule of three
numerical operation 86n.
rule of thumb
empiricism 461n.
intuition 476n.
rule out
exclude 57vb.
make impossible 470vb.
ruler
gauge 465n.
club 723n.
potentate 741n.
rulership
magistrature 733n.
rules and regulations
practice 610n.
right 913n.
ruling
judgment 480n.
legal trial 959n.
ruling class
master 741n.
upper class 868n.
ruling passion
opiniatrety 602n.
affections 817n.
rum
unusual 84adj.
liquor 301n.
ridiculous 849adj.
rumba
dance 837n., vb.
rumble
roll 403vb.
fight 716n.
rumble seat
seat 218n.
rumbling
voidance 300n.
rumbustious
disorderly 61adj.
loud 400adj.
riotous 738adj.
excitable 822adj.
ruminant
animal 365adj.
thoughtful 449adj.
rumination
eating 301n.
meditation 449n.
rummage
search 459vb.
rummer
cup 194n.
rummy
unusual 84adj.
card game 837n.
rumor
insubstantial thing 4n.
topic 452n.
publish 528vb.
rumor 529n.
fable 543n.
rump
remainder 41n.
buttocks 238n.
rumple
jumble 63vb.
roughen 259vb.
fold 261n., vb.
agitate 318vb.
rumpus
turmoil 61n.
violence 176n.
quarrel 709n.

fight 716n.
run
be disjoined 46vb.
come unstuck 49vb.
continuity 71n.
series 71n.
discontinuity 72n.
generality 79n.
recurrence 106n.
elapse 111vb.
continuance 146n.
motion 265n.
pedestrianism 267n.
voyage 269vb.
move fast 277vb.
flow out 298vb.
liquefy 337vb.
flow 350vb.
lose color 426vb.
habit 610n.
chase 619n.
run away 620vb.
path 624n.
be active 678vb.
hasten 680vb.
deal with 688vb.
manage 689vb.
steal 788vb.
runabout
automobile 274n.
run after
pursue 619vb.
desire 859vb.
court 889vb.
run against
counteract 182vb.
runagate
tergiversator 603n.
avoider 620n.
coward 856n.
run aground
fixed 153adj.
navigate 269vb.
land 295vb.
fail 728vb.
run amok
lay waste 165vb.
be violent 176vb.
go mad 503vb.
strike at 712vb.
be excitable 822vb.
run at
attack 712vb.
charge 712vb.
run away
decamp 296vb.
run away 620vb.
seek safety 660vb.
escape 667vb.
runaway
wanderer 268n.
speedy 277adj.
tergiversator 603n.
avoider 620n.
escaper 667n.
coward 856n.
run counter
counteract 182vb.
tell against 467vb.
rundle
circle 250n.
coil 251n.
run down
decrease 37vb.
cease 145vb.
weakened 163adj.
approach 289vb.
underestimate 483vb.
pursue 619vb.
make insufficient 636vb.
charge 712vb.
not respect 921vb.
dispraise 924vb.
rune
lettering 586n.
doggerel 593n.
spell 983n.
run for
steer for 281vb.
offer oneself 759vb.
rung
degree 27n.
serial place 73n.
stand 218n.
cylinder 252n.
ascent 308n.
run high
be violent 176vb.
runic
literal 558adj.
written 586adj.
sorcerous 983adj.
run in
begin 68vb.
run in one's head
engross 449vb.
run in pairs
resemble 18vb.
run into
collide 279vb.
runlet
stream 350n.
run low
decrease 37vb.
runnel
furrow 261n.
stream 350n.
conduit 351n.
runner
hanger 217n.
pedestrian 268n.
speeder 277n.
conduit 351n.
courier 531n.
contender 716n.
servant 742n.
thief 789n.
runners
sled 274n.
runner-up
opponent 705n.
contender 716n.
running
continuous 71adj.
running jump
leap 312n.
running knot
ligature 47n.
running sore
outflow 298n.
bane 659n.
loss 772n.
painfulness 827n.
running track
path 624n.
arena 724n.
runny
non-adhesive 49adj.
fluidal 335adj.
liquefied 337adj.
run-off
contest 716n.
run off
void 300vb.
print 587vb.
run off with
take away 786vb.
run of one's teeth
no charge 812n.
run of the mill
average 30n.
generality 79n.
run on
continuate 71vb.
go on 146vb.
progress 285vb.
be loquacious 581vb.
run on savings
expenditure 806n.
run, on the
on the move 265adv.
endangered 661adj.
run out
end 69vb.
cease 145vb.
impel 279vb.
dismiss, void 300vb.
not suffice 636vb.
run over
be complete 54vb.
collide 279vb.
run riot
be violent 176vb.
exaggerate 546vb.
superabound 637vb.
be active 678vb.
be excitable 822vb.
run short
fall short 307vb.
runt
animalcule 196n.

dwarf 196n.
run the gauntlet
face danger 661vb.
defy 711vb.
run through
make uniform 16vb.
consume 165vb.
prevail 178vb.
be present 189vb.
pierce 263vb.
strike 279vb.
exude 298vb.
waste 634vb.
strike at 712vb.
expend 806vb.
be prodigal 815vb.
run to
avail of 673vb.
request 761vb.
run together
accord 24vb.
combine 50vb.
run to seed
aged 131adj.
waste 634vb.
run to waste
waste 634vb.
runty
dwarfish 196adj.
run up an account
be in debt 803vb.
run upon, run on
requirement 627n.
runway
air travel 271n.
run wild
be violent 176vb.
rupee
coinage 797n.
rupture
disagreement 25n.
separation 46n.
rend 46vb.
gap 201n.
wound 655n.
dissension 709n.
rural
regional 184adj.
provincial 192adj.
rural economy
agriculture 370n.
ruralist
dweller 191n.
solitary 883n.
Ruritania
fantasy 513n.
ruse
trickery 542n.
stratagem 698n.
rush
rampage 61vb.
crowd 74n.
vigorousness 174n.
outbreak 176n.
spurt 277n.
commotion 318n.
flow 350vb.
plant 366n.
torch 420n.
trifle 639n.
non-preparation 670n.
be active 678vb.
haste 680n.
attack 712n.
rush at
pursue 619vb.
charge 712vb.
be rash 857vb.
rushed
hasty 680adj.
rush hour
crowd 74n.
rush in, rush into
irrupt 297vb.
be rash 857vb.
rush-light
glimmer 419n.
torch 420n.
rush to conclusions
prejudge 481vb.
rusk
cereal 301n.
russet
brown 430adj.
red 431adj.
Russophile
xenophile 880n.
rust
decay 51n.
oldness 127n.
destroyer 168n.
be unproductive 172vb.
blunt 257vb.
pulverize 332vb.
bedim 419vb.
red color 431n.
desuetude 611n.
dirt 649n.
dilapidation 655n.
blight 659n.
inaction 677n.
inactivity 679n.
blemish 845n.
rustic
dweller 191n.
provincial 192adj.
agrarian 370adj.
ill-bred 847adj.
countryman 869n.
rustication
seclusion 883n.
rusticity
ill-breeding 847n.
rustiness
bluntness 257n.
stridor 407n.
dimness 419n.
unskillfulness 695n.
(*see* rust)
rusting
disused 674adj.
rustle
sound faint 401vb.
sibilation 406n.
hiss 406vb.
steal 788vb.
rustler
thief 789n.
rustle up
make ready 699vb.
rustproof
unyielding 162adj.
rusty
antiquated 127adj.
unsharpened 257adj.
strident 407adj.
dim 419adj.
red 431adj.
unhabituated 611adj.
clumsy 695adj.
(*see* rust, rustiness)
rusy
cunning 698adj.
rut
regularity 81n.
roughness 259n.
furrow 262n.
habit 610n.
libido 859n.
ruth
pity 905n.
ruthless
resolute 599adj.
cruel 898adj.
pitiless 906adj.
ruthlessness
revengefulness 910n.
rutilant
luminous 417adj.
rutting, ruttish
desiring 859adj.
lecherous 951adj.
rutty
rough 259adj.
furrowed 262adj.
rye
cereal 301n.
liquor 301n.
corn 366n.
ryot
husbandman 370n.
possessor 776n.

S

Sabbatarian
ascetic 945n.
religionist 979n.
ritualist 988n.

S T

Sabbatarians
sect 978n.
sabbath
repose 683n.
holy-day 988n.
sabbatical
reposeful 683adj.
Sabellianism
heresy 977n.
saber
kill 362vb.
cavalry 722n.
side-arms 723n.
saber-rattling
intimidation 854n.
threat 900n.
sable
skin 226n.
black 428adj.
heraldry 547n.
sabot
footwear 228n.
sabotage
derangement 63n.
disable 161vb.
destruction 165n.
make useless 641vb.
impairment 655n.
hindrance 702n.
revolt 738n., vb.
dutilessness 918n.
saboteur
destroyer 168n.
hinderer 702n.
rioter 738n.
sabretache
bag 194n.
sabreur
combatant 722n.
sabulosity
pulverulence 332n.
sac
bladder 194n.
saccharine
sweet 392n.
saccharometer
sweetness 392n.
saccular
capsular 194adj.
sacellum
temple 990n.
sacerdotal
priestly 985adj.
clerical 986adj.
sacerdotalism
ecclesiasticism 985n.
sachem
potentate 741n.
sachet
scent 396n.
sack
bag 194n.
dismiss 300n.
wine 301n.
deposal 752n.
spoliation 788n.
sackbut
horn 414n.
sackcloth
textile 222n.
roughness 259n.
asceticism 945n.
sackcloth and ashes
lamentation 836n.
penitence 939n.
penance 941n.
ritual object 988n.
sacker
taker 786n.
robber 789n.
sackful
finite quantity 26n.
sacking
textile 222n.
spoliation 788n.
sacrament
rite 988n.
the sacrament 988n.
sacramental
religious 973adj.
devotional 981adj.
priestly 985adj.
sacramentalist
ritualist 988n.
sacrarium
altar 990n.
holy place 990n.
sacred
worshipful 866adj.
divine 965adj.
religious 973adj.
sanctified 979adj.
devotional 981adj.
sacredness
sanctity 979n.
sacred season
holy-day 988n.
sacred text
scripture 975n.
sacred thread
ritual object 988n.
sacrificatory
atoning 941adj.
devotional 981adj.
sacrifice
decrease 37n.
decrement 42n.
killing 362n.
loser 728n.
offer 759n.
loss 772n.
offering 781n.
cheapen 812vb.
sufferer 825n.
be disinterested 931vb.
propitiation 941n.
be pious 979vb.
oblation 981n.
sacrifice oneself
be willing 597vb.
offer oneself 759vb.
be disinterested 931vb.
sacrificer
giver 781n.
worshiper 981n.
sacrificial
destructive 165adj.
losing 772adj.
giving 781adj.
disinterested 831adj.
atoning 941adj.
devotional 981adj.
ritual 988adj.
sacrificial price
cheapness 812n.
sacrilege
impiety 980n.
sacrilegious
disrespectful 921adj.
profane 980adj.
sacring bell
signal 547n.
ritual object 988n.
sacristan
church officer 986n.
sacristy
church interior 990n.
sacrosanct
worshipful 866adj.
due 915adj.
divine 965adj.
sanctified 979adj.
sad
funereal 364adj.
soft-hued 425adj.
black 428adj.
gray 429adj.
bad 645adj.
unhappy 825adj.
distressing 827adj.
discontented 829adj.
melancholic 834adj.
sadden
hurt 827vb.
sadden 834vb.
sadder and wiser man
penitent 939n.
saddle
affix 45vb.
narrowness 206n.
high land 209n.
seat 218n.
start out 296vb.
meat 301n.
break in 369vb.
saddlebag
bag 194n.
saddlecloth
coverlet 226n.
saddled
prepared 669adj.

saddled with, be
carry 273vb.
saddle-horse
saddle-horse 273n.
saddle with
attribute 158vb.
hinder 702vb.
impose a duty 917vb.
accuse 928vb.
Sadducees
non-Christian sect 978n.
sadhu
pietist 979n.
sadism
abnormality 84n.
inhumanity 898n.
sadist
monster 938n.
sadistic
cruel 898adj.
pitiless 906adj.
sadness
sorrow 825n.
dejection 834n.
sad work
bungling 695n.
safari
land travel 267n.
safe
box 194n.
certain 473adj.
hiding-place 527n.
storage 632n.
safe 660adj.
treasury 799n.
cautious 858adj.
safe bet
certainty 473n.
safe-conduct
opener 263n.
instrument 628n.
protection 660n.
preservation 666n.
permit 756n.
safe conscience, with a
innocently 935adv.
safe-deposit
hiding-place 527n.
storage 632n.
treasury 799n.
safeguard
look after 457vb.
protection 660n.
safeguard 662n.
preserver 666n.
means of escape 667n.
obstacle 702n.
defense 713n.
talisman 983n.
safeguarded
conditional 766adj.
safe hands
protection 660n.
safe-keeping
protection 660n.
preservation 666n.
defense 713n.
safety
bicycle 274n.
safety 660n.
safety belt
safeguard 662n.
safety catch
fastening 47n.
safeguard 662n.
safety first
cowardice 856n.
caution 858n.
safety harness
safeguard 662n.
safety lamp
lamp 420n.
safety match
lighter 385n.
safety pin
fastening 47n.
safety valve
safeguard 662n.
means of escape 667n.
saffron
condiment 389n.
yellowness 433n.
sag
be weak 163vb.
hang 217vb.
be oblique 220vb.
be curved 248vb.
descend 309vb.
be dejected 834vb.
saga
narrative 590n.
sagacious
(*see* sagacity)
sagacity
sagacity 498n.
foresight 510n.
skill 694n.
saga-man
chronicler 549n.
narrator 590n.
sage
potherb 301n.
green color 432n.
wise 498adj.
sage 500n.
teacher 537n.
bigwig 638n.
adviser 691n.
proficient 696n.
sagittal
sharp 256adj.
Sagittarius
zodiac 321n.
sagittary
rara avis 84n.
Sahara
desert 172n.
Saharan
dry 342adj.
sahib
male 372n.
master 741n.
title 870n.
said
preceding 64adj.
prior 119adj.
sail
water travel 269n.
swim 269vb.
ship, sail 275n.
rotator 315n.
navy 722n.
sailboat
sailing-ship 275n.
sailer
sailing-ship 275n.
sailing
aquatics 269n.
sailing master
navigator 270n.
sailing-ship
ship 275n.
sailing-ship 275n.
sail into
fight 716vb.
sailor
mariner 270n.
navy man 722n.
sailorlike, sailorly
seafaring 269adj.
seamanlike 270adj.
expert 694adj.
sain
sanctify 979vb.
perform ritual 988vb.
saint
benefactor 903n.
good man 937n.
angel 968n.
pietist 979n.
ecclesiasticize 985vb.
sainted
dead 361adj.
pious 979adj.
sanctified 979adj.
St. Elmo's fire
fire 379n.
glow 417n.
sainthood
sanctity 979n.
St. John's Ambulance
doctor 658n.
saintly
virtuous 933adj.
angelic 968adj.
pious 979adj.
saint's day
regular return 141n.
special day 876n.
holy-day 988n.

saints, the
church member 976n.
St. Vitus' dance
spasm 318n.
Saivites
non-Christian sect 978n.
sake
liquor 301n.
sake, for one's own
selfishly 932adv.
sake of, for the
in aid of 703adv.
salaam
obeisance 311n.
courteous act 884n.
respects 920n.
salable
not retained 779adj.
salable 793adj.
salable commodity
merchandise 795n.
salacious
(*see* salacity)
salacity
unchastity 951n.
salad
a mixture 43n.
dish 301n.
salad days
salad days 130n.
salamander
rara avis 84n.
reptile 365n.
heater 383n.
noxious animal 904n.
salami
meat 301n.
price 809n.
sal ammoniac
pungency 388n.
salariat
upper class 868n.
salary
incentive 612n.
earnings 771n.
pay 804n.
receipt 807n.
reward 962n.
sale
transfer 780n.
sale 793n.
salebrosity
roughness 259n.
sale price
cheapness 812n.
salesman
speaker 579n.
motivator 612n.
seller 793n.
salesmanship
publicity 528n.
inducement 612n.
sale 793n.
sales talk
inducement 612n.
salient
region 184n.
overhanging 209adj.
convex 253adj.
projection 254n.
salient 254adj.
manifest 522adj.
battleground 724n.
salient point
chief thing 638n.
salina
marsh 347n.
saline
salty 388adj.
saliva
excrement 302n.
lubricant 334n.
fluid 335n.
moisture 341n.
salivary
expulsive 300adj.
salivation
ejection 300n.
excretion 302n.
moisture 341n.
sallet
armor 713n.
sallow
weakly 163adj.
colorless 426adj.
whitish 427adj.
yellow 433adj.
unhealthy 651adj.
sally
emerge 298vb.
attack 712n., vb.
retaliation 714n.
witticism 839n.
sally port
outlet 298n.
fort 713n.
salmagundi
a mixture 43n.
salmi
dish 301n.
salmon
fish food 301n.
table fish 365n.
redness 431n.
salon
assembly 74n.
chamber 194n.
beau monde 848n.
social gathering 882n.
saloon
tavern 192n.
chamber 194n.
automobile 274n.
salsuginous
salty 388adj.
salt
mariner 270n.
pungency 388n.
salty 388adj.
season 388vb.
condiment 389n.
chief thing 638n.
preserve 666vb.
wit 839n.
saltatory
leaping 312adj.
agitated 318adj.
salt away
store 632vb.
salt flat
desert 172n.
marsh 347n.
saltire
cross 222n.
heraldry 547n.
salt lick
provender 301n.
salt of the earth
elite 644n.
benefactor 903n.
good man 937n.
saltpeter
pungency 388n.
explosive 723n.
salty
seafaring 269adj.
salty 388adj.
forceful 571adj.
exciting 821adj.
witty 839adj.
salubrious
healthy 650n.
remedial 658adj.
salubrity
salubrity 652n.
salutary
beneficial 644adj.
salubrious 652adj.
salutation
allocution 583n.
courteous act 884n.
respects 920n.
salute
notice 455vb.
signal 547vb.
speak to 583vb.
courteous act 884n.
congratulation 886n.
endearment 889n.
show respect 920vb.
approve 923vb.
praise 923vb.
salvage
restoration 656vb.
deliverance 668n.
price 809n.
salvager

mender 656n.
salvation
restoration 656n.
preservation 666n.
deliverance 668n.
liberation 746n.
divine function 965n.
Salvation Army
sect 978n.
salvationism
pietism 979n.
salvationist
sectarist 978n.
religionist 979n.
pastor 986n.
salve
lubricant 334n.
unguent 357n.
balm 658n.
salver
plate 194n.
church utensil 990n.
salvo
bang 402n.
qualification 468n.
pretext 614n.
bombardment 712n.
celebration 876n.
sal volatile
tonic 658n.
Samaritan, Good
kind person 897n.
benefactor 903n.
sambo
negro 428n.
same
(*see* sameness)
same age
synchronism 123n.
same mind
consensus 488n.
sameness
identity 13n.
uniformity 16n.
equivalence 28n.
tedium 838n.
same old round
recurrence 106n.
same time
synchronism 123n.
samisen
harp 414n.
samite
textile 222n.
samovar
caldron 194n.
sampan
sailing ship 275n.
sample
prototype 23n.
part 53n.
example 83n.
taste 386vb.
experiment 461vb.
exhibit 522n.
sampler
inquirer 459n.
needlework 844n.
sampling
empiricism 461n.
Samson
athlete 162n.
samurai
militarist 722n.
samvat
era 110n.
sanation
sanation 656n.
sanative
salubrious 652adj.
restorative 656adj.
remedial 658adj.
sanatorium
abode 192n.
hygiene 652n.
hospital 658n.
sanbenito
tunic 228n.
canonicals 989n.
sanctification
(*see* sanctify)
sanctify
dignify 866vb.
celebrate 876vb.
sanctify 979vb.
offer worship 981vb.
idolatrize 982vb.
ecclesiasticize 985vb.
sanctimonious
hypocritical 541adj.
affected 850adj.
prudish 950adj.
pietistic 979adj.
sanctimony
false piety 980n.
sanction
assent 488n.
endorse 488vb.
compulsion 740n.
permission 756n.
commission 756vb.
consent 758n., vb.
approbation 923n.
sanctioned
reputable 866adj.
due 915adj.
sanctions
compulsion 740n.
sanctity
virtue 933n.
divine attribute 965n.
sanctity 979n.
sanctuary
retreat 192n.
reception 299n.
protection 660n.
refuge 662n.
holy place 990n.
church interior 990n.
sanctum
chamber 194n.
refuge 662n.
seclusion 883n.
holy place 990n.
sand
desert 172n.
powder 332n.
drier 342n.
soil 344n.
sandal
footwear 228n.
scent 396n.
sandbag
strike 279vb.
kill 362vb.
club 723n.
scourge 964n.
sandbank
island 349n.
sandcastle
weak thing 163n.
sandglass
timekeeper 117n.
sandhi
speech sound 398n.
sandiness
(*see* sandy)
sandman
sleep 679n.
sandpaper
sharpener 256n.
smoother 258n.
roughness 259n.
pulverizer 332n.
sandstone
rock 344n.
sandstorm
storm 176n.
sandwich
stratification 207n.
put between 231vb.
mouthful 301n.
sandwich board
advertisement 528n.
sandwich man
publicizer 528n.
sandy
powdery 332adj.
dry 342adj.
red 431adj.
yellow 433adj.
sane
wise 498adj.
sane 502adj.
sangfroid
moral insensibility 820n.
inexcitability 823n.
Sangreal

ritual object 988n.
sanguinary
sanguineous 335adj.
murderous 362adj.
bloodshot 431adj.
sanguine
red 431adj.
optimistic 482adj.
expectant 507adj.
hoping 852adj.
Sanhedral
ecclesiastical 985adj.
Sanhedrin
council 692n.
synod 985n.
Sanhedrist
councillor 692n.
sanies
fluid, blood 335n.
sanitarian
sanitarian 652n.
sanitary
healthy 650adj.
salubrious 652adj.
sanitary engineer
cleaner 648n.
sanitary inspector
sanitarian 652n.
doctor 658n.
sanitary precaution
prophylactic 658n.
protection 660n.
sanitation
cleansing 648n.
hygiene 652n.
prophylactic 658n.
protection 660n.
sanity
sagacity 498n.
sanity 502n.
Sankhya
philosophy 449n.
sannyasi
ascetic 945n.
sansculotte
rioter 738n.
poor man 801n.
low fellow 869n.
ruffian 904n.
san serif
print-type 587n.
Sanskritist
antiquarian 125n.
linguist 557n.
Santa Claus
giver 781n.
good giver 813n.
fairy 970n.
santon
monk 986n.
sap
essential part 5n.
disable 161vb.
weaken 163vb.
demolish 165vb.
excavation 255vb.
descend 309vb.
fluid 335n.
moisture 341n.
semiliquidity 354n.
ninny 501n.
impair 655vb.
besiege 712vb.
sapidity
taste 386n.
sapience
wisdom 498n.
sapless
weak 163adj.
dry 342n.
sapling
young plant 132n.
tree 366n.
saponaceous
fatty 357adj.
saporific
tasty 386adj.
sapper
excavator 255n.
soldiery 722n.
sapphire
blueness 435n.
gem 844n.
sappy
vernal 128adj.
young 130adj.
fluidal 335adj.
humid 341adj.
semiliquid 354adj.
pulpy 356adj.
foolish 499adj.
sarcasm
wit 839n.
ridicule 851n.
rudeness 885n.
indignity 921n.
reproach 924n.
calumny 926n.
sarcastic
keen 174adj.
(*see* sarcasm)
sarcenet
textile 222n.
sarcoma
swelling 253n.
sarcophagus
box 194n.
interment 364n.
Sardanapalus
sensualist 944n.
sardine
fish food 301n.
table fish 365n.
sardonic
derisive 851adj.
disapproving 924adj.
sardonyx
gem 844n.
sargasso
plant 366n.
sari
dress 228n.
robe 228n.
sarkstone
gem 844n.
sarong
dress 228n.
sartorial
dressed 228adj.
sash
girdle 47n.
frame 218n.
belt 228n.
loop 250n.
badge 547n.
badge of rank 743n.
sash-window
window 263n.
sassenach
foreigner 59n.
Satan
Satan 969n.
satanic
evil 616adj.
cruel 898adj.
wicked 934adj.
diabolic 969adj.
satanism
diabolism 969n.
antichristianity 974n.
satchel
bag 194n.
sate, satiate
fill 54vb.
superabound 637vb.
make insensitive 820vb.
content 828vb.
be tedious 838vb.
sate 863vb.
sated
disliking 861adj.
sated 863adj.
sateen
textile 222n.
satellitic
concomitant 89n.
space-ship 276n.
follower 284n.
satellite 321n.
auxiliary 707n.
subject 742n.
dependent 742n.
satellite status
subjection 745n.
satellite town
housing 192n.
satellitic
subject 745adj.

satiety
plenitude 54n.
sufficiency 635n.
superfluity 637n.
tedium 838n.
dislike 861n.
satiety 863n.
satin
textile 222n.
smoothness 258n.
satiny
smooth 258adj.
textural 331adj.
satire
exaggeration 546n.
description 590n.
doggerel 593n.
wit 839n.
satire 851n.
reproach 924n.
calumny 926n.
satirical
untrue 543adj.
funny 849adj.
derisive 851adj.
disrespectful 921adj.
satirist
humorist 839n.
disapprover 924n.
detractor 926n.
satirize
(*see* satire)
satisfaction
sufficiency 635n.
observance 768n.
payment 804n.
enjoyment 824n.
content 828n.
atonement 941n.
satisfactory
sufficient 635adj.
not bad 644adj.
contenting 828adj.
satisfy
fill 54vb.
answer 460vb.
demonstrate 478vb.
convince 485vb.
suffice 635vb.
pacify 719vb.
content 828vb.
satisfying
pleasant 376adj.
sufficient 635adj.
satisfy oneself
be certain 473vb.
satrap
governor 741n.
saturate
fill 54vb.
drench 341vb.
saturation
superfluity 637n.
satiety 863n.
saturation point
plenitude 54n.
Saturnalia
turmoil 61n.
festivity 837n.
sensualism 944n.
Saturnalian
disorderly 61adj.
Saturnian
foreigner 59n.
primal 127adj.
planetary 321adj.
innocent 935adj.
Saturnian Age
era 110n.
palmy days 730n.
saturnine
serious 834adj.
ugly 842adj.
satyagraha
resistance 715n.
disobedience 738n.
satyr
libertine 952n.
lesser god 967n.
satyriasis
libido 859n.
satyr play
poem 593n.
sauce
adjunct 40n.
a mixture 43n.
stimulant 174n.
dish 301n.
season 388vb.
sauce 389n.
sauciness 878n.
rudeness 885n.
scurrility 899n.
sauceboat
bowl 194n.
saucebox
insolent person 878n.
saucepan
caldron 194n.
saucer
plate 194n.
cavity 255n.
saucy
defiant 711adj.
impertinent 878adj.
discourteous 885adj.
disrespectful 921adj.
sauna
ablution 648n.
saunter
wander 267vb.
move slowly 278vb.
saurian
animal 365n.
sausage
meat 301n.
sauté
cook 301vb.
sauve qui peut
fear 854n.
savage
violent creature 176n.
violent 176adj.
mankind 371n.
ignorant 491adj.
ill-treat 645vb.
wound 655vb.
immature 670adj.
ingenue 699n.
attack 712vb.
severe 735adj.
excitable 822adj.
vulgarian 847n.
courageous 855adj.
low fellow 869n.
plebeian 869adj.
angry 891adj.
cruel 898adj.
ruffian 904n.
monster 938n.
savageness
unsociability 883n.
savagery
violence 176n.
artlessness 699n.
inhumanity 898n.
savanna
plain 348n.
savant
scholar 492n.
expert 696n.
save
in deduction 39adv.
exclusive of 57adv.
store 632vb.
preserve 666vb.
deliver 668vb.
not use 674vb.
liberate 746vb.
acquire 771vb.
retain 778vb.
economize 814vb.
saved
sanctified 979adj.
save labor
have leisure 681vb.
saving
qualifying 468adj.
saving clause
qualification 468n.
means of escape 667n.
conditions 766n.
saving grace
virtues 933n.
savings
store 632n.
gain 771n.
economy 814n.

savings bank
treasury 799n.
savior
preserver 666n.
benefactor 903n.
savoir faire
skill 694n.
etiquette 848n.
savor
taste 386n., vb.
appetize 390vb.
savoriness
savoriness 390n.
pleasurableness 826n.
savorless
tasteless 387adj.
savor of
resemble 18vb.
savory
dish 301n.
tasty 386adj.
savoriness 390n.
sweet 392n.
saw
cut 46vb.
tooth 256n.
notch 260n.
rasp 407vb.
discord 411vb.
maxim 496n.
sawbones
doctor 658n.
sawbuck
paper money 797n.
sawder
flatter 925vb.
sawdust
leavings 41n.
powder 332n.
saw-edge
roughness 259n.
sawmill
workshop 687n.
sawney
foolish 499adj.
ninny 501n.
saw the air
gesticulate 547vb.
sawyer
artisan 686n.
sax
sharp edge 256n.
side-arms 723n.
Saxonism
inelegance 576n.
saxophone
horn 414n.
saxophonist
instrumentalist 413n.
say
affirm 532vb.
speech 579n.
speak 579vb.
sayable
permitted 756adj.
say after
do likewise 20vb.
repeat 106vb.
sayer
speaker 579n.
saying
maxim 496n.
affirmation 532n.
phrase 563n.
say nothing
be taciturn 582vb.
say of
attribute 158vb.
say office
perform ritual 988vb.
say over
repeat 106vb.
say-so
affirmation 532n.
command 737n.
sayyid
aristocrat 868n.
sbirro
police 955n.
scab
nonconformist 84n.
covering 226n.
overlie 226vb.
tergiversator 603n.
cure 656vb.
revolter 738n.
hateful object 888n.
cad 938n.
scabbard
case 194n.
arsenal 723n.
scabby
layered 207adj.
rough 259adj.
unclean 649adj.
scab over
join 45vb.
cure 656vb.
scabrous
rough 259adj.
impure 951adj.
scads
great quantity 32n.
funds 797n.
scaffold
structure 331n.
means of execution 964n.
scaffolding
frame 218n.
preparation 669n.
scalable
ascending 308adj.
scalar
gradational 27adj.
ascending 308adj.
scalawag, scallywag
bad man 938n.
scald
burning 381n.
wound 655n.
scalding
hot 379adj.
paining 827adj.
scale
relativeness 9n.
degree 27n.
series 71n.
counting instrument 86n.
plate 194n.
layer 207n.
covering, skin 226n.
climb 308vb.
scales 322n.
musical note 410n.
key 410n.
obfuscation 421n.
opacity 423n.
gauge 465n.
scale down
bate 37vb.
render few 105vb.
scale, in
comparative 27adj.
scalene
unequal 29adj.
scales
scales 322n.
gauge 465n.
scale, to
relatively 9adv.
scaliness
stratification 207n.
scallop
edging 234n.
crinkle 251vb.
notch 260n., vb.
fish food 301n.
cook 301vb.
scallywag
(*see* scalawag)
scalp
head 213n.
skin 226n.
uncover 229n.
trophy 729n.
scalpel
sharp edge 256n.
scalplock
hair 259n.
scaly
layered 207adj.
dermal 226adj.
scamble
rend 46vb.
scamp
neglect 458vb.

be loath 598vb.
not complete 726vb.
bad man 938n.
scamper
move fast 277vb.
scampi
fish food 301n.
scamping
negligence 458n.
scampish
rascally 930adj.
scan
scan 438vb.
be attentive 455vb.
inquire 459vb.
know 490vb.
poetize 593vb.
scandal
rumor 529n.
badness 645n.
slur 867n.
wrong 914n.
calumny 926n.
false charge 928n.
wickedness 934n.
scandalize
displease 827vb.
cause dislike 861vb.
be wonderful 864vb.
shame 867vb.
incur blame 924vb.
defame 926vb.
scandalized
disapproving 924adj.
scandalizing
heinous 934adj.
scandalmonger
newsmonger 529n.
defamer 926n.
scandalous
bad 645adj.
discreditable 867adj.
wrong 914adj.
detracting 926adj.
heinous 934adj.
scandent
ascending 308adj.
scansion
prosody 593n.
scansorial
ascending 308adj.
scant
shorten 204vb.
make insufficient 636vb.
restrained 747adj.
(*see* scanty)
scanties
underwear 228n.
scantiness
scarcity 636n.
(*see* scanty)
scantling
prototype 23n.
small quantity 33n.
size 195n.
scanty
small 33adj.
incomplete 55adj.
few 105adj.
exiguous 196adj.
short 204adj.
fasting 946adj.
scapegoat
substitute 150n.
unlucky person 731n.
deputy 755n.
sufferer 825n.
propitiation 941n.
oblation 981n.
scapegrace
desperado 857n.
bad man 938n.
scapular
canonicals 989n.
scar
high land 209n.
rock 344n.
identification 547n.
mark 547vb.
trace 548n.
wound 655n.
trophy 729n.
blemish 845n., vb.
scarab
talisman 983n.
scaramouch
bad man 938n.
scarce
infrequent 140adj.
unproductive 172adj.
deficient 307adj.
scarce 636adj.
of price 811adj.
scarcely
slightly 33adv.
scarcity
scarcity 636n.
poverty 801n.
dearness 811n.
(*see* scarce)
scare
false alarm 665n.
fear 854n.
frighten 854vb.
scarecrow
thinness 206n.
sham 542n.
image 551n.
false alarm 665n.
eyesore 842n.
intimidation 854n.
scaremonger
alarmist 854n.
coward 856n.
scarf
wrapping 226n.
shawl 228n.
neckwear 228n.
vestments 989n.
scarfskin
skin 226n.
scarify
cut 46vb.
notch 260vb.
rub 333vb.
wound 655vb.
scarlatina
infection 651n.
scarlet
red color 431n.
heinous 934adj.
unchaste 951adj.
scarlet fever
infection 651n.
scarlet runner
vegetables 301n.
scarlet woman
loose woman 952n.
Scarlet Woman
Catholicism 976n.
scarp
acclivity 220n.
fortification 713n.
scars
trophy 729n.
scathe
harm 645vb.
impairment 655n.
scatheless
undamaged 646adj.
scathing
paining 827adj.
scatological
impure 951adj.
scatology
uncleanness 649n.
scatter
disjoin 46vb.
be disordered 61vb.
jumble 63vb.
dispersion 75n.
displace 188vb.
diverge 294vb.
let fall 311vb.
disappear 446vb.
waste 634vb.
defeat 727vb.
scatterbrained
light-minded 456adj.
foolish 499adj.
crazed 503adj.
scatterbrains
fool 501n.
scattered
few 105adj.
scattering
non-coherence 49n.
reflection 417n.

(*see* scatter)
scatty
foolish 499adj.
crazed 503adj.
scavenger
cleaner 648n.
dirty person 649n.
scazon
verse form 593n.
scenario
cinema 445n.
reading matter 589n.
narrative 590n.
stage play 594n.
scene
circumjacence 230n.
view 438n.
visibility 443n.
spectacle 445n.
exhibit 522n.
art subject 553n.
stage-set 594n.
arena 724n.
excitable state 822n.
pageant 875n.
scene-painter
artist 556n.
stage-hand 594n.
scenery
beauty 841n.
(*see* scene)
scene-shifter
stage-hand 594n.
scenic
painted 553adj.
dramatic 594adj.
impressive 821adj.
pleasurable 826adj.
beautiful 841adj.
ornamental 844adj.
showy 875adj.
scenic railway
pleasure-ground 837n.
scenograph
map 551n.
scent
emit 300vb.
odor 394n.
smell 394vb.
scent 396n.
detect 484vb.
knowledge 490n.
foresee 510vb.
indication 547n.
trace 548n.
cosmetic 843n.
scent-bottle
scent 396n.
scented darling
fop 848n.
scentless
odorless 395adj.
scent, off the
mistaken 495adj.
scent oneself
primp 843vb.
scent, on the
discovering 484adj.
pursuing 619adj.
scepter
regalia 743n.
schadenfreude
joy 824n.
schedule
list 87n., vb.
plan 623vb.
schematic
orderly 60adj.
arranged 62adj.
planned 623adj.
schematize
regularize 62vb.
plan 623vb.
scheme
prototype 23n.
arrangement 62n.
plan 623n.
plot 623vb.
preparation 669n.
be cunning 698vb.
schemer
slyboots 698n.
scheming
perfidious 930adj.
dishonest 930adj.
(*see* scheme)
scherzo
musical piece 412n.
schism
dissension 709n.
revolt 738n.
schism 978n.
schismatic
dissentient 489n.
dissenting 489adj.
quarreling 709adj.
schismatic 978n.
schismatical
independent 744adj.
schismatical 978adj.
schismatize
schismatize 978vb.
schist
rock 344n.
schistosity
stratification 207n.
schistous
layered 207adj.
schizoid
insane 503adj.
madman 504n.
schizophrenia
psychopathy 503n.
schizophrenic
multiform 82adj.
insane 503adj.
schnapps
liquor 301n.
schnorrer
beggar 763n.
scholar
scholar 492n.
learner 538n.
proficient 696n.
scholarly
instructed 490adj.
educational 534adj.
studious 536adj.
studentlike 538adj.
scholarship
erudition 490n.
learning 536n.
subvention 703n.
reward 962n.
scholastic
reasoner 475n.
intellectual 492n.
educational 534adj.
theologian 973n.
scholasticism
philosophy 449n.
theology 973n.
scholiast
interpreter 520n.
scholium
maxim 496n.
commentary 520n.
school
group 74n.
philosophy 449n.
creed 485n.
educate, train 534vb.
school 539n.
schoolbook
classroom 539n.
textbook 589n.
schoolboy
youngster 132n.
learner 538n.
schooled
instructed 490adj.
schoolfellow
chum 880n.
schoolgirl
youngster 132n.
learner 538n.
schoolgoer
learner 538n.
schooling
teaching 534n.
schoolman
reasoner 475n.
intellectual 492n.
theologian 973n.
schoolmaster, schoolmistress
teacher 537n.

school of painting
school of painting 553n.
schoolroom
chamber 194n.
classroom 539n.
schooner
sailing-ship 275n.
schottische
musical piece 412n.
schrecklichkeit
terror tactics 712n.
sciamachy
foolery 497n.
sciatica
pang 377n.
science
physics 319n.
philosophy 449n.
science 490n.
skill 694n.
scientific
accurate 494adj.
educational 534adj.
well-made 694adj.
expert 694adj.
scientist
intellectual 492n.
scimitar
sharp edge 256n.
side-arms 723n.
scintilla
small quantity 33n.
luminary 420n.
scintillate
shine 417vb.
be wise 498vb.
be witty 839vb.
scintillation
flash 417n.
sciolism
erudition 490n.
sciolism 491n.
sciolist
sciolist 493n.
scion
branch 53n.
young plant 132n.
descendent 170n.
tree 366n.
sciosophy
occultism 984n.
scissile
severable 46adj.
brittle 330adj.
scission
scission 46n.
scissors
cross 222n.
sharp edge 256n.
sclerosis
hardening 326n.
scobs
powder 332n.
scoff
food 301n.
ridicule 851n., vb.
not respect 921vb.
contempt 922n.
detract 926vb.
scoff at
disbelieve 486vb.
scoffer
unbeliever 486n.
humorist 839n.
detractor 926n.
scold
violent creature 176n.
quarreler 709n.
bicker 709vb.
shrew 892n.
cuss 899vb.
exprobate 924vb.
scolding
irascible 892adj.
reprimand 924n.
scold's bridle
pillory 964n.
scoliosis
obliquity 220n.
scollop
(*see* scallop)
sconce
head 213n.
lamp 420n.
penalty 963n.
scone
pastry 301n.
scoop
ladle 194n.
make concave 255vb.
extractor 304n.
information 524n.
news 529n.
acquisition 771n.
scoot
move fast 277vb.
run away 620vb.
scooter
bicycle 274n.
scope
opportunity 137n.
influence 178n.
range 183n.
meaning 514n.
function 622n.
facility 701n.
scope 744n.
scopophilia
curiosity 453n.
impurity 951n.
scorbutic
unclean 649adj.
scorch
move fast 277vb.
dry 342vb.
be hot 379vb.
burn 381vb.
impair 655vb.
wage war 718vb.
scorched earth
havoc 165n.
scorcher
speeder 277n.
heat 379n.
a beauty 841n.
score
degree 27n.
cut, rend 46vb.
composition 56n.
arrangement 62n.
numerical result 85n.
numeration 86n.
list 87n., vb.
over five 99n.
groove 262vb.
notation 410n.
music 412n.
compose music 413vb.
mark 547vb.
register 548vb.
obliterate 550vb.
wound 655vb.
triumph 727vb.
credit 802n.
accounts 808n.
score-board, score-sheet
record 548n.
score off
be superior 34vb.
confute 479vb.
humiliate 872vb.
score of, on the
concerning 9adv.
scores
multitude 104n.
scoria
leavings 41n.
ash 381n.
dirt 649n.
scorify
heat 381vb.
scoring stroke
success 727n.
scorn
underestimate 483vb.
unbelief 486n.
reject 607vb.
shame 867vb.
scurrility 899n.
disrespect 921n.
contempt 922n.
detraction 926n.
scorner
unbeliever 486n.
impious person 980n.
scornful
(*see* scorn)

scorpion
noxious animal 904n.
Scorpius, Scorpio
zodiac 321n.
scot
tax 809n.
scotch
disable 161vb.
notch 260n.
liquor 301n.
wound 655vb.
hinder 702vb.
scotch mist
moisture 341n.
scotch-tape
adhesive 47n.
scot-free
escaped 667adj.
free 744adj.
uncharged 812adj.
non-liable 919adj.
Scotland Yard
police 955n.
scotoma
dim sight 440n.
Scotticism
dialect 560n.
scoundrel
cad 938n.
scoundrelism
improbity 930n.
scour
traverse 267vb.
move fast 277vb.
pass 305vb.
rub 333vb.
search 459vb.
clean 648vb.
scourge
plague 651n.
bane 659n.
adversity 731n.
oppress 735vb.
ruffian 904n.
dispraise 924vb.
flog 963vb.
scourge 964n.
scourge oneself
do penance 941vb.
scourings
leavings 41n.
rubbish 641n.
dirt 649n.
scout
precursor 66n.
traverse 267vb.
scan 438vb.
spectator 441n.
watch 441vb.
inquirer 459n.
reject 607vb.
warner 664n.
domestic 742n.
despise 922vb.
scout signs
symbology 547n.
scowl
distort 246vb.
look 438n.
gesture 547n.
discontent 829n.
rudeness 885n.
hatred 888n.
hate 888vb.
anger 891n.
sullenness 893n.
scowling
serious 834adj.
scrabble
make concave 255vb.
search 459vb.
take 786vb.
indoor game 837n.
scrag, scrag-end
remainder 41n.
meat 301n.
scraggy
exiguous 196adj.
lean 209adj.
scram
decamp 296vb.
run away 620vb.
scramble
confusion 61n.
bedevil 63vb.
cook 301vb.
climb 308vb.
activity 678n.
haste 680n.
fight 716n.
scramble for
take 786vb.
scrap
insubstantiality 4n.
small thing 33n.
piece 53n.
reject 607vb.
disuse 674vb.
fight 716n., vb.
battle 718n.
scrap-album
anthology 592n.
scrap-book
reminder 505n.
record 548n.
scrape
bate 37vb.
subtract 39vb.
make smaller 198vb.
be contiguous 202vb.
uncover 229vb.
blunt 257vb.
stoop 311vb.
pulverize 332vb.
rub 333vb.
touch 378vb.
rasp 407vb.
discord 411vb.
play music 413vb.
foolery 497n.
engrave 555vb.
clean 648vb.
predicament 700n.
economize 814vb.
be parsimonious 816vb.
be servile 879vb.
show respect 920vb.
vice 934n.
guilty act 936n.
scrape acquaintance
befriend 880vb.
be sociable 882vb.
scrape home
win 727vb.
scraper
sharp edge 256n.
cleaning utensil 648n.
niggard 816n.
scrape through
pass 305vb.
scrape together
bring together 74vb.
scrapings
leavings 41n.
scrap of paper
ineffectuality 161n.
unreliability 474n.
perfidy 930n.
scrappy
fragmentary 53adj.
incomplete 55adj.
scraps
leavings 41n.
rubbish 641n.
scratch
inferior 35adj.
cut, rend 46vb.
be violent 176vb.
shallowness 212n.
make concave 255vb.
be rough 259vb.
groove 262vb.
strike 279vb.
friction 333n.
touch, itch 378vb.
faintness 401n.
rasp 407vb.
trace 548n.
misrepresentation 552n.
write 586vb.
tergiversate 603vb.
relinquish 621vb.
trifle 639n.
imperfect 647adj.
wound 655n., vb.
unprepared 670adj.
unskilled 695adj.

fight 716vb.
resign 753vb.
be excitable 822vb.
blemish 845n.
scratchiness
formication 378n.
scratch one's back
flatter 925vb.
scratch out
obliterate 550vb.
scratchy
agitated 318adj.
strident 407adj.
irascible 892adj.
scrawl
unintelligibility 517n.
script 586n.
scrawler
penman 586n.
scrawny
lean 206adj.
scream
feel pain 377vb.
loudness 400n.
cry 408n., vb.
proclaim 528vb.
weep 836vb.
screamer
mistake 495n.
absurdity 497n.
advertisement 528n.
screaming
whopping 32adj.
loud 400adj.
florid 425adj.
vulgar 847adj.
scree
piece 53n.
acclivity 220n.
thing transferred 272n.
screech
stridor 407n.
rasp 407vb.
cry 408vb.
ululation 409vb.
screed
oration 579n.
script 586n.
dissertation 591n.
screen
separation 46n.
exclusion 57n.
canopy 226n.
partition 231n.
porosity 263n.
stopper 264n.
screen 421n., vb.
opacity 423n.
blind 439vb.
cinema 445n.
concealment 525n.
disguise 527n.
pretext 614n.
cleaning utensil 648n.
purify 648vb.
safeguard 660vb.
defense 713n.
screened
dark 418adj.
invisible 444adj.
latent 523adj.
safe 660adj.
secluded 883adj.
screw
affix 47vb.
fastening 45n.
distort 246vb.
coil 251n.
propeller 269n.
saddle-horse 273n.
deflect 282vb.
propellant 287n.
rotator 315n.
earnings 771n.
niggard 816n.
be parsimonious 816vb.
screwball
madman 504n.
crank 504n.
laughing-stock 851n.
screwdriver
extractor 304n.
tool 630n.
screw loose
eccentricity 503n.
screw-thread
coil 251n.
screw up
tighten 45vb.
strengthen 162vb.
make ready 669vb.
screwy
crazed 503adj.
scribal
instructed 490adj.
scribble
unmeaningness 515n.
unintelligibility 517n.
mark 547vb.
lettering 586n.
scribbler
penman 586n.
author 589n.
scribe
imitator 20n.
recorder 549n.
penman 586n.
write 586vb.
theologian 973n.
religionist 979n.
scrim
bookbinding 589n.
scrimmage
quarrel 709n.
fight 716n., vb.
scrimp
shorten 204vb.
underfed 636adj.
niggard 816n.
scrimshanker
avoider 620n.
scrimshaw
sculpture 554n.
scriniary
recorder 549n.
scrip
bag 194n.
title-deed 767n.
paper money 797n.
script
script 586n.
lettering 586n.
reading matter 589n.
stage play 594n.
scriptorium
chamber 194n.
stationery 586n.
scriptural
evidential 466adj.
scriptural 975adj.
orthodox 976adj.
scripturalist
theologian 973n.
scripturality
orthodoxy 976n.
scripture
credential 466n.
scripture 975n.
scriptwriter
penman 586n.
author 589n.
dramatist 594n.
scrivener
penman 586n.
notary 958n.
scrofulous
unclean 649adj.
impure 951adj.
scroll
list 87n.
coil 251n.
rotate 315vb.
lettering 586n.
scrollwork
pattern 844n.
Scrooge
niggard 816n.
scrotum
genitalia 164n.
scrounge
beg 761vb.
take 786vb.
steal 788vb.
scrub
lean 206adj.
rub 333vb.

wood 366n.
clean 648vb.
scrubber
cleaner 648n.
scrubbing-brush
roughness 159n.
cleaning utensil 648n.
scrubby
exiguous 196adj.
arboreal 366adj.
rascally 930adj.
scruff
rear 238n.
scruffy
unimportant 639adj.
not nice 645adj.
unclean 649adj.
beggarly 801adj.
disreputable 867adj.
scrum
crowd 74n.
fight 716n.
scrumptious
topping 644adj.
scrunch
rend 46vb.
chew 301vb.
pulverize 332vb.
rasp 407vb.
scruple
small quantity 33n.
weighment 322n.
doubt 486n., vb.
dissent 489vb.
unwillingness 598n.
scrupulosity
doubt 486n.
pietism 979n.
scrupulous
careful 457adj.
accurate 494adj.
fastidious 862adj.
trustworthy 929adj.
honorable 929adj.
scrutator
spectator 441n.
scrutineer
inquirer 459n.
scrutinize
scan 438vb.
(*see* scrutiny)
scrutiny
attention 455n.
inquiry 459n.
scud
navigate 269vb.
move fast 277vb.
cloud 355n.
scuff
move slowly 278vb.
scuffle
fight 716n., vb.
scull
propeller 269n.
row 269vb.
sculler
boatman 270n.
rowboat 275n.
scullery
chamber 194n.
scullion
cleaner 648n.
domestic 742n.
sculpt
produce 164vb.
efform 243vb.
sculpt 554vb.
sculptor
sculptor 556n.
sculpture
sculpture 554n.
scum
leavings 41n.
layer 207n.
bubble 355n., vb.
rubbish 641n.
purity 648vb.
dirt 649n.
rabble 869n.
scumble
coat 226vb.
make opaque 423vb.
color 425vb.
paint 553vb.
scummy
dirty 649adj.
scupper
suppress 165vb.
drain 351n.
slaughter 362vb.
scurf
leavings 41n.
dirt 649n.
scurfy
unclean 649adj.
scurrility
scurrility 889n.
(*see* scurrilous)
scurrilous
quarreling 709adj.
insolent 878adj.
maledicent 899adj.
disrespectful 921adj.
disapproving 924adj.
detracting 926adj.
scurry
move fast 277vb.
be busy 678vb.
hasten 680vb.
scurvy
underfed 636adj.
disease 651n.
rascally 930adj.
scut
rear 238n.
scutage
quid pro quo 150n.
tax 809n.
scutcheon
(*see* escutcheon)
scutellum
cavity 255n.
scuttle
suppress 165vb.
vessel 194n.
pierce 263vb.
move fast 277vb.
plunge 313vb.
run away 620vb.
haste 680n.
be cowardly 856vb.
fail in duty 918vb.
scythe
cut 46vb.
sharp edge 256n.
farm tool 370n.
sea
ocean 343n.
wave 350n.
blueness 435n.
sea air
salubrity 652n.
sea, at
at sea 343adv.
doubting 474adj.
mistaken 495adj.
seaboard
shore 344n.
sea chest
box 194n.
sea dog
mariner 270n.
expert 696n.
seafarer
mariner 270n.
seafaring
water travel 269n.
seafaring 269adj.
marine 275adj.
sea-god
sea-god 343n.
seagoing
seafaring 269adj.
marine 275adj.
oceanic 343adj.
sea king
mariner 270n.
seal
mold 23n.
close 264vb.
fish 365n.
credential 465n.
make certain 473vb.
endorse 488vb.
label 547n.
carry through 725vb.
badge of rule 743n.
compact 765n.
give security 767vb.

sea lawyer
reasoner 475n.
sealed book
unknown thing 491n.
unintelligibility 517n.
secret 530n.
sealed off
sealed off 264adj.
sealed orders
secret 530n.
sea legs
equilibrium 28n.
sealer
fishing-boat 275n.
sealing wax
adhesive 47n.
sea lord
naval officer 741n.
sealskin
skin 226n.
seal up
conceal 525vb.
imprison 747vb.
seam
joint 45n.
dividing line 92n.
gap 201n.
layer 207n.
seaman
mariner 270n.
seamanlike
seamanlike 270adj.
expert 694adj.
seamanship
navigation 268n.
tactics 688n.
skill 694n.
art of war 718n.
seamark
limit 236n.
sailing aid 269n.
signpost 547n.
seamless
whole 52adj.
seamstress
clothier 228n.
artisan 686n.
séance
manifestation 522n.
council 692n.
spiritualism 984n.
sea nymph
sea nymph 343n.
mythical being 970n.
sea power
navy 722n.
authority 733n.
sear
dry 342vb.
heat 381vb.
make insensitive 820vb.
blemish 845n.
search
search 459n., vb.
pursuit 619n.
undertaking 672n.
searcher
inquisitor 453n.
inquirer 459n.
hunter 619n.
searching
inquisitive 453adj.
oppressive 735adj.
paining 827adj.
searchlight
radiation 417n.
lamp 420n.
search-party
search 459n.
hunter 619n.
search-warrant
search 459n.
legal process 959n.
sea room
room 183n.
scope 744n.
seascape
spectacle 445n.
art subject 553n.
beauty 841n.
sea scout
mariner 270n.
sea serpent
rara avis 84n.
seashore
edge 234n.
shore 344n.
seasick
seafaring 269adj.
vomiting 300adj.
seaside
edge 234n.
shore 344n.
pleasure-ground 837n.
season
time 108n.
period 110n.
regular return 141n.
season 388vb.
appetize 390vb.
habituate 610vb.
preserve 666vb.
mature 669vb.
social round 882n.
seasonable
apt 24adj.
timely 137adj.
seasonal
periodic 110adj.
seasonal 141adj.
celebrative 876adj.
seasoned
expert 694adj.
seasoning
tincture 43n.
stimulant 174n.
condiment 389n.
habituation 610n.
seat
equilibrium 28n.
situation 186n.
station 187n.
house 192n.
seat 218n.
buttocks 238n.
seating
room 183n.
seat of justice
tribunal 956n.
seat oneself
sit down 311vb.
sea trip
water travel 269n.
seawall
safeguard 662n.
obstacle 702n.
seaway
room 183n.
seaweed
plant 366n.
seaworthy
seafaring 269adj.
marine 275adj.
oceanic 343adj.
perfect 646adj.
invulnerable 660adj.
sebaceous
fatty 357adj.
secant
ratio 85n.
secateur
sharp edge 256n.
farm tool 370n.
seccotine
adhesive 47n.
secede
(*see* secession)
secession
dissent 489n.
tergiversation 603n.
relinquishment 621n.
revolt 738n.
dutilessness 918n.
schism 978n.
secessionist
tergiversator 603n.
revolter 738n.
schismatic 978n.
seclude
imprison 747vb.
(*see* seclusion)
secluded
tranquil 266adj.
invisible 444adj.
concealed 525adj.
seclusion
separation 46n.
exclusion 57n.

displacement 188n.
farness 199n.
invisibility 444n.
relinquishment 621n.
seclusion 883n.
monasticism 985n.
second
inferior 35n., adj.
double 91adj., vb.
period 110n.
instant 116n.
angular measure 247n.
melody 410n.
measurement 465n.
endorse 488vb.
patronize 703vb.
secondary
unimportant 639adj.
imperfect 647adj.
second-best
inferior 35adj.
substitute 150n.
imperfect 647adj.
mediocre 732adj.
second birth
revival 656n.
second chance
mercy 905n.
second childhood
age 131n.
folly 499n.
second edition
duplicate 22n.
seconder
assenter 488n.
patron 707n.
second fiddle
inferior 35n.
nonentity 639n.
second-hand
imitative 20adj.
timekeeper 117n.
antiquated 127adj.
used 673adj.
second-in-command
deputy 755n.
second line
auxiliary 707n.
second nature
habit 610n.
second opinion
estimate 480n.
second part
sequel 67n.
second place
sequence 65n.
second-rate
inferior 35adj.
trivial 639adj.
imperfect 647adj.
mediocre 732adj.
second-rater
inferior 35n.
second self
colleague 707n.
second sight
vision 438n.
foresight 510n.
psychics 984n.
second string
inferior 35n.
second thought(s)
sequel 67n.
tergiversation 603n.
amendment 654n.
regret 830n.
caution 858n.
second to none
supreme 34adj.
best 644adj.
secrecy
secrecy 525n.
taciturnity 582n.
caution 858n.
secret
private 80adj.
dark 418adj.
invisible 444adj.
unknown thing 491n.
unintelligibility 517n.
occult 523adj.
information 524n.
secret 530n.
(*see* secrecy)
secretariat
workshop 687n.
management 689n.
magistrature 733n.
jurisdiction 955n.
secret art
occultism 984n.
secretary
cabinet 194n.
recorder 549n.
official 690n.
auxiliary 707n.
servant 742n.
deputy 755n.
secret ballot
vote 605n.
freedom 744n.
secret, be in the
know 490vb.
secrete
emit 300vb.
conceal 525vb.
(*see* secretion)
secretion
ejection 300n.
excretion 302vb.
secretive
reticent 525adj.
cautious 858adj.
secret, no
known 490adj.
secretory
ejector 300n.
expulsive 300adj.
excretory 302adj.
secret service
secret service 459n.
secret society
latency 523n.
society 708n.
rioter 738n.
secret, the
interpretation 520n.
secret weapon
weapon 723n.
threat 900n.
sect
community 708n.
party 708n.
sect 978n.
sectarian
nonconformist 84n.
biased 481adj.
dissentient 489n.
sectional 708adj.
sectarist 978n.
sectarianism
sectarianism 978n.
sectary
dissentient 489n.
auxiliary 707n.
sectarist 978n.
section
scission 46n.
subdivision 53n.
classification 77n.
topic 452n.
formation 722n.
sectional
fragmentary 53adj.
classificatory 77adj.
sectional 708adj.
sectarian 978adj.
sector
subdivision 53n.
arc 250n.
battleground 724n.
secular
secular 110adj.
lasting 113adj.
seasonal 141adj.
irreligious 974adj.
clerical 986adj.
laical 987adj.
secularist
irreligionist 974n.
secularity
laicality 987n.
secularize
depose 752vb.
appropriate 786vb.
paganize 974vb.
laicize 987vb.
secundiness
sequel 67n.

secure
tighten 45vb.
be early 135vb.
believing 485adj.
safeguard 660vb.
promise 764vb.
give security 767vb.
securities
estate 777n.
security
safety 660n.
promise 764n.
security 767n.
paper money 797n.
hope 852n.
dueness 915n.
legal process 959n.
sedan
automobile 274n.
sedan-chair
vehicle 274n.
sedate
inexcitable 823adj.
serious 834adj.
sedation
moderation 177n.
sedative
moderator 177n.
lenitive 177adj.
soporific 679n.
sedentary
quiescent 266adj.
sedge
plant 366n.
sedilia
church interior 990n.
sediment
leavings 41n.
thing transformed 272n.
solid body 324n.
marsh 347n.
semiliquidity 354n.
dirt 649n.
sedimentary
remaining 41adj.
indissoluble 324adj.
sedimentation
condensation 324n.
sedition
disorder 61n.
sedition 738n.
perfidy 930n.
seditionist
revolutionist 149n.
motivator 612n.
revolter 738n.
agitator 738n.
malcontent 829n.
seditious
revolutionary 149adj.
disobedient 738adj.
seduce
induce 612vb.
bribe 612vb.
delight 826vb.
excite love 887vb.
debauch 951vb.
make wicked 934vb.
seducer
deceiver 545n.
motivator 612n.
libertine 952n.
seduction
attraction 291n.
inducement 612n.
(*see* seduce)
seductive
attracting 291adj.
pleasurable 826adj.
lovable 887adj.
sedulity
perseverance 600n.
assiduity 678n.
sedulous
(*see* sedulity)
see
see, scan 438vb.
know 490vb.
understand 516vb.
church office 985n.
seeable
visible 443adj.
seed
class 62vb.
reproduce itself 164vb.
source 156n.
product 164n.
genitalia 164n.
posterity 170n.
fertilizer 171n.
powder 332n.
select 605vb.
seedbed
seedbed 156n.
flower 366n.
garden 370n.
seeded player
proficient 696n.
seediness
(*see* seedy)
seeding
sorting 62n.
seedless
unproductive 172adj.
seedling
young plant 132n.
see double
be dim-sighted 440vb.
be drunk 949vb.
seed pearl
gem 844n.
seedsman
gardener 370n.
seed-time
spring 128n.
seedy
weakly 163adj.
sick 651adj.
dilapidated 655adj.
beggarly 801adj.
see fit
will 595vb.
seeing
vision 438n.
visibility 443n.
see into
inquire 459vb.
see it coming
look ahead 124vb.
foresee 510vb.
not wonder 865vb.
see it through
sustain 146vb.
be resolute 599vb.
carry through 725vb.
seek
be curious 453vb.
search 459vb.
pursue 619vb.
essay 671vb.
request 761vb.
seeker
inquisitor 453n.
inquirer 459n.
hunter 619n.
petitioner 763n.
seem
resemble 18vb.
appear 445vb.
seeming
appearance 445n.
hypocritical 541adj.
ostentatious 875adj.
seemliness
good taste 846n.
right 913n.
seemly
expedient 642adj.
seen
evidential 466adj.
known 490adj.
see nothing
be incurious 454vb.
see off
start out 296vb.
dismiss 300vb.
see out
carry through 725vb.
seep
infiltrate 297vb.
exude 298vb.
be wet 341vb.
seepage
outflow 298n.
seer
spectator 441n.
sage 500n.
oracle 511n.
visionary 513n.
sorcerer 983n.

psychic 984n.
see red
be violent 176vb.
go mad 503vb.
get angry 891vb.
seersucker
textile 222n.
see-saw
correlation 12n.
fluctuation 317n.
to and fro 317adv.
be uncertain 474vb.
be irresolute 601vb.
pleasure-ground 837n.
seethe
cook 301vb.
effervesce 318vb.
be hot 379vb.
hiss 406vb.
be excited 821vb.
see the light
discover 484vb.
become pious 979vb.
seething
excited 821adj.
excitable 822adj.
seething mass
confusion 61n.
see through
be wise 498vb.
understand 516vb.
carry out 725vb.
see to
look after 457vb.
deal with 688vb.
segar
tobacco 388n.
segment
part, piece 53n.
subdivision 53n.
segmentation
scission 46n.
segnitude
sluggishness 679n.
segregate
sanitate 652vb.
exempt 919vb.
(*see* segregation)
segregation
separation 46n.
exclusion 57n.
prejudice 481n.
protection 660n.
seclusion 883n.
seigneur
master 741n.
nobleman 868n.
seigniory
magistrature 733n.
possession 773n.
lands 777n.
seignorial
proprietary 777adj.
seine
network 222n.
enclosure 235n.
seisachtheia
non-payment 805n.
seisin
possession 773n.
seismic
revolutionary 149adj.
violent 176adj.
oscillating 317adj.
important 638adj.
notable 638adj.
seismograph
oscillation 317n.
meter 465n.
recording instrument 549n.
seismology
oscillation 317n.
seize
halt 145vb.
understand 516vb.
take 786vb.
seize on
make important 638vb.
seizure
spasm 318n.
illness 651n.
paralysis 651n.
taking 786n.
loss of right 916n.
sejant
heraldic 547adj.
Sejm
parliament 692n.
sejunction
separation 46n.
seldom
seldom 140adv.
seldom occur
be few 105vb.
select
set apart 46vb.
excellent 644adj.
(*see* selection)
selection
part 53n.
accumulation 74n.
discrimination 463n.
textbook 589n.
anthology 592n.
choice 605n.
selective
separate 46adj.
discriminating 463adj.
choosing 605adj.
selenic
celestial 321adj.
selenography
astronomy 321n.
self
intrinsicality 5n.
identical 13adj.
self 80n.
subjectivity 320n.
spirit 447n.
self-abasement
humility 872n.
self-abnegation
humility 872n.
disinterestedness 931n.
temperance 942n.
self-absorption
selfishness 932n.
self-accusation
penitence 939n.
self-acting
mechanical 630adj.
self-admiration
pride 871n.
vanity 873n.
selfishness 932n.
self-advertisement
boasting 877n.
self-assertion
affirmation 532n.
insolence 878n.
self-assurance
vanity 873n.
insolence 878n.
self-assured
positive 473adj.
assertive 532adj.
self-cancelling
compensatory 31adj.
self-centered
vain 873adj.
self-command
resolution 599n.
inexcitability 823n.
self-complacency
vanity 873n.
self-conceit
pride 871n.
vanity 873n.
self-conceited
narrow-minded 481adj.
self-condemnation
penitence 939n.
self-confidence
positiveness 473n.
courage 855n.
pride 871n.
self-confident
resolute 599adj.
self-congratulation
vanity 873n.
self-conscious
affected 850adj.
nervous 854adj.
self-consciousness
intellect 447n.
self-consideration
selfishness 932n.
self-consistent
uniform 16adj.

true 494adj.
self-contained
complete 54adj.
independent 744adj.
self-control
moderation 177n.
will 595n.
resolution 599n.
restraint 747n.
inexcitability 823n.
disinterestedness 931n.
virtues 933n.
temperance 942n.
self-convicted
repentant 939adj.
condemned 961adj.
self-correcting
compensatory 31adj.
self-deception
credulity 487n.
error 495n.
deception 542n.
self-defense
defense 713n.
vindication 927n.
self-denial
severity 735n.
disinterestedness 931n.
temperance 942n.
asceticism 945n.
act of worship 981n.
self-depreciation
underestimation 483n.
mental dishonesty 543n.
humility 872n.
modesty 874n.
self-determination
will 595n.
independence 744n.
self-devotion
suicide 362n.
resolution 599n.
disinterestedness 931n.
oblation 981n.
self-discipline
temperance 942n.
punishment 963n.
act of worship 981n.
self-display
vanity 873n.
self-distrust
nervousness 854n.
modesty 874n.
self-drive
traveling 267adj.
self-effacement
humility 872n.
modesty 874n.
disinterestedness 931n.
self-employed
businesslike 622adj.
self-esteem
vanity 873n.
self-evident
certain 473adj.
manifest 522adj.
self-evident truth
premise 475n.
axiom 496n.
self-examination
act of worship 981n.
self-exile
seclusion 883n.
self-existence
existence 1n.
self-existent
godlike 965adj.
self-existing
irrelative 10adj.
self-expression
independence 744n.
self-forgetful
disinterested 931adj.
self-glory
boasting 877n.
self-governing
independent 744adj.
governmental 753adj.
self-government
government 733n.
selfhood
self 80n.
subjectivity 320n.
self-importance
vanity 873n.
ostentation 875n.
self-imposed
voluntary 597adj.
self-imposed task
vocation 622n.
self-improvement
learning 536n.
virtue 933n.
self-indulgence
pleasure 376n.
selfishness 932n.
intemperance 943n.
sensualism 944n.
self-interest
selfishness 932n.
selfish
greedy 859adj.
selfish 932adj.
selfishness
parsimony 816n.
selfishness 932n.
self-knowledge
humility 872n.
selfless
disinterested 931adj.
self-love
vanity 873n.
selfishness 932n.
self-made man
victor 727n.
self-mortification
asceticism 945n.
punishment 963n.
self-opinion
opiniatrety 602n.
self-opinionated
positive 473adj.
self-opinioned
narrow-minded 481adj
self-pity
pity 905n.
selfishness 932n.
self-possession
resolution 599n.
inexcitability 823n.
self-praise
pride 871n.
vanity 873n.
praise 923n.
selfishness 932n.
self-preservation
selfishness 931n.
self-protection
protection 660n.
self-raising
light 323adj.
self-reference
intrinsicality 5n.
self-regarding
selfish 932adj.
self-reliance
courage 855n.
self-reliant
resolute 599adj.
self-repression
inexcitability 823n.
self-reproach
regret 830n.
penitence 939n.
self-respecting
proud 871adj.
self-restraint
resolution 599n.
restraint 747n.
inexcitability 823n.
temperance 942n.
self-rule
independence 744n.
self-sacrifice
offering 781n.
disinterestedness 931n.
oblation 981n.
selfsame
identical 13adj.
self-satisfaction
content 828n.
self-satisfied
vain 873adj.
self-seeker
egotist 932n.
self-service
meal 301n.

mensal 301adj.
provision 633n.
provisionary 633adj.
self-slaughter
suicide 362n.
self-sought
desired 859adj.
self-starter
start 68n.
self-styled
misnamed 562adj.
self-sufficiency
completeness 54n.
independence 744n.
wealth 800n.
vanity 873n.
self-support
independence 744n.
self-surrender
disinterestedness 931n.
piety 979n.
self-taught
studious 536adj.
self-torture
asceticism 945n.
self-will
will 595n.
obstinacy 602n.
sell
absurdity 497n.
advertise 528vb.
trickery 542n.
deceive 542vb.
provide 633vb.
sell 793vb.
sell an idea to
convince 485vb.
sell dear
overcharge 811vb.
seller
seller 793n.
peddler 794n.
seller's market
scarcity 636n.
prosperity 730n.
request 761n.
mart 796n.
dearness 811n.
sell for
cost 809vb.
sell oneself
boast 877vb.
sell out
be dishonest 930vb.
sell-out
sale 793n.
selvage
edging 234n.
semanteme
word 559n.
part of speech 564n.
semantic
semantic 514adj.
semantics
meaning 514n.
linguistics 557n.
semaphore
communicate 524vb.
telecommunication 531n.
indicator 547n.
signal 547n., vb.
gesticulate 547vb.
semasiological
semantic 514adj.
literary 557adj.
semasiologist
linguist 557n.
semasiology
meaning 514n.
linguistics 557n.
etymology 559n.
semblance
similarity 18n.
mimicry 20n.
copy 22n.
appearance 445n.
probability 471n.
semeiology
hermeneutics 520n.
indication 547n.
gesture 547n.
semeiotics
indication 547n.
semen
fertilizer 171n.
semester
time 108n.
period 110n.
semi
fragmentary 53adj.
incomplete 55adj.
bisected 92adj.
semibreve
notation 410n.
semicircle
arc 250n.
semicircular
curved 248adj.
semicolon
punctuation 547n.
semidarkness
half-light 419n.
semidetached
non-adhesive 49adj.
semidiameter
breadth 205n.
semieducated
smattering 491adj.
semifinal
contest 716n.
semiliquid
thick 205adj.
semiliquidity
semiliquidity 354n.
semiliterate
smattering 491adj.
semilunar
curved 248adj.
seminal
causal 156adj.
productive 164adj.
generative 171adj.
seminal fluid
genitalia 164n.
seminar
curriculum 536n.
class 538n.
conference 584n.
seminarist
college student 538n.
cleric 986n.
layman 987n.
seminary
academy 539n.
monastery 986n.
semiplosive
speech sound 398n.
semiquaver
notation 410n.
semiskilled
unskilled 695adj.
Semitic
ethnic 11adj.
language type 559n.
semitone
interval 201n.
musical note 410n.
semitransparency
semitransparency 424n.
semitransparent
ill-seen 444adj.
semivowel
speech sound 398n.
spoken letter 558n.
voice 577n.
sempiternity
durability 113n.
perpetuity 115n.
sempstress
(*see* seamstress)
senarius
prosody 593n.
senary
fifth and over 99adj.
senate
seniority 131n.
parliament 692n.
senator
councillor 692n.
master 741n.
aristocrat 868n.
senatorial
aged 131adj.
parliamentary 692adj.
genteel 868adj.
senatus consultum
decree 737n.
send
displace 188vb.
move 265vb.

send 272vb.
emit 300vb.
give 781vb.
excite 821vb.
delight 826vb.
send after
pursue 619vb.
send back
put off 136vb.
send down
bate 37vb.
eject 300vb.
sender
transferrer 272n.
send flying
propel 287vb.
send for
pursue 619vb.
send forth
publish 528vb.
send haywire
bedevil 63vb.
send home
liberate 746vb.
send-off
start 68n.
valediction 296n.
send one's compliments
pay respects 884vb.
gratulate 886vb.
send out
emit 300vb.
commission 751vb.
send packing
repel 292vb.
dismiss 300vb.
send to blazes
be insolent 878vb.
curse 899vb.
send to Coventry
set apart 46vb.
eject 300vb.
make unwelcome 883vb.
send up
augment 36vb.
elevate 310vb.
send word
communicate 521vb.
senescence
age 131n.
senescent
deteriorated 655adj.
seneschal
officer 741n.
retainer 742n.
keeper 749n.
senile decay
insanity 503n.
senility
oldness 127n.
age 131n.
helplessness 161n.
weakness 163n.
folly 499n.
dilapidation 655n.
senior
older 131adj.
old man 133n.
college student 538n.
master 741n.
seniority
superiority 34n.
oldness 127n.
seniority 131n.
authority 733n.
senior service
navy man 722n.
senna
potherb 301n.
sennet
musical note 410n.
call 547n.
sensation
sense 374n.
news 529n.
feeling 818n.
prodigy 864n.
sensational
striking 374adj.
dramatic 594adj.
exciting 821adj.
wonderful 864adj.
showy 875adj.
sensationalism
publicity 528n.
exaggeration 546n.
excitation 821n.
ostentation 875n.
sensationalize
impress 821vb.
be ostentatious 875vb.
sense
sense 374n.
have feeling 374vb.
intellect 447n.
intuit 476vb.
detect 484vb.
intelligence 498n.
meaning 514n.
feeling 818n.
sense datum
element 319n.
senseless
insensible 375adj.
absurd 497adj.
foolish 499adj.
unmeaning 515adj.
sense of duty
duty 917n.
sense of honor
probity 929n.
sense of humor
laughter 835n.
wit 839n.
sense organ
instrument 628n.
sense perception
feeling 818n.
senses
intellect 447n.
sanity 502n.
sensibility
sensibility 374n.
discrimination 463n.
painfulness 827n.
sensible
material 319adj.
sentient 374adj.
rational 475adj.
wise 498adj.
useful 640adj.
feeling 818adj.
impressible 819adj.
sensible of
knowing 490adj.
sensitive
sentient 374adj.
attentive 455adj.
discriminating 463adj.
accurate 494adj.
elegant 575adj.
feeling 818adj.
sensitive 819adj.
excitable 822adj.
sensitiveness
sensibility 374n.
moral sensibility 819n.
sensitive plant
sensibility 374n.
moral sensibility 819n.
sensitivity
sensibility 374n.
discrimination 463n.
accuracy 494n.
persuasibility 612n.
moral sensibility 819n.
sensitize
cause feeling 374vb.
sensorial
feeling 818adj.
sensorium
intellect 447n.
sensory
feeling 818adj.
sensory perception
feeling 818n.
sensory process
sense 374n.
sensual
material 319adj.
sensuous 376adj.
feeling 818adj.
intemperate 943adj.
sensual 944adj.
lecherous 951adj.
sensualism
sensualism 944n.
sensualist
sensualist 944n.

sensuality
materiality 319n.
pleasure 376n.
sensualism 944n.
sensuous
sentient 374adj.
sensuous 376adj.
feeling 818adj.
sentence
period 110n.
judgment 480n.
maxim 496n.
affirmation 532n.
phrase 563n.
condemnation 961n.
penalty 963n.
sentential
phraseological 563adj.
sententious
judicial 480adj.
aphoristic 496adj.
concise 569adj.
forceful 571adj.
sentient
sentient 374adj.
feeling 818adj.
impressible 819adj.
sentience
feeling 818n.
sentiment
opinion 485n.
feeling 818n.
excitation 821n.
love 887n.
sentimental
foolish 499adj.
feeble 572adj.
feeling 818adj.
impressible 819adj.
loving 887adj.
sentimentality
moral sensibility 819n.
love 887n.
sentimental value
lovableness 887n.
sentinel, sentry
janitor 264n.
spectator 441n.
surveillance 457n.
protector 660n.
warner 664n.
defender 713n.
armed force 722n.
keeper 749n.
sentry-box
compartment 194n.
sentry-go
surveillance 457n.
separability
disjunction 46n.
non-coherence 49n.
separable
severable 46adj.
separate
irrelative 10adj.
different 15adj.
separate 46adj.
discontinuous 72adj.
disperse 75vb.
bifurcate 92vb.
open 263vb.
select 605vb.
(*see* separation)
separated brethren
schismatic 978n.
separateness
irrelation 10n.
separation
separation 46n.
decomposition 51n.
unity 88n.
farness 199n.
gap 201n.
divergence 294n.
discrimination 463n.
dissension 709n.
liberation 746n.
seclusion 883n.
divorce 896n.
schism 978n.
sectarianism 978n.
Sephardim
non-Christian sect 978n.
sepia
fish 365n.
brown paint 430n.
seposition
separation 46n.
exclusion 57n.
sepoy
soldier 722n.
sepsis
infection 651n.
sept
race 11n.
breed 77n.
genealogy 169n.
septennium
over five 99n.
septentrional
opposite 240adj.
septet
duet 412n.
septic
not nice 645adj.
unclean 649adj.
toxic 653adj.
dangerous 661adj.
septicemia
infection 651n.
septic tank
latrine 649n.
septuagenarian
over twenty 99n.
Septuagint
scripture 975n.
septum
partition 231n.
sepulcher
tomb 364n.
holy place 990n.
sepulchral
funereal 364adj.
resonant 404adj.
hoarse 407adj.
sepulture
interment 364n.
sequacious
sequent 65adj.
flexible 327adj.
tough 329adj.
sequel
sequel 67n.
end 69n.
posteriority 120n.
effect 157n.
sequela
sequel 67n.
effect 157n.
sequence
relativeness 9n.
order 60n.
sequence 65n.
posteriority 120n.
following 284n.
sequent
continuous 71adj.
caused 157n.
(*see* sequence)
sequester
set apart 46vb.
exclude 57vb.
deprive 786vb.
not pay 805vb.
seclude 883vb.
sequestered
tranquil 266adj.
invisible 444adj.
sequestration
expropriation 786n.
seclusion 883n.
penalty 963n.
sequestrator
taker 786n.
sequin
finery 844n.
sequoia
tall creature 209n.
tree 366n.
serac
ice 380n.
seraglio
womankind 373n.
love-nest 887n.
brothel 951n.
seraph
angel 968n.
seraphic
virtuous 933adj.
angelic 968adj.

pietistic 979adj.
sere
lean 206adj.
dry 342adj.
deteriorated 655adj.
serenade
musical piece 412n.
vocal music 412n.
sing 413vb.
wooing 889n.
serenader
vocalist 413n.
serendipity
chance 159n.
discovery 484n.
serene
transparent 422adj.
(*see* serenity)
serenity
inexcitability 823n.
content 828n.
non-wonder 865n.
serf
husbandman 370n.
slave 742n.
possessor 776n.
countryman 869n.
serfdom
servitude 745n.
serge
textile 222n.
sergeant
soldiery 722n.
army officer 741n.
serial
relative 9adj.
continuous 71adj.
recurrence 106n.
periodic 141adj.
the press 528n.
reading matter 589n.
serialization
sequence 65n.
continuity 71n.
periodicity 141n.
serialize
publish 528vb.
serial order
relativeness 9n.
serial place
degree 27n.
serial place 73n.
seriate
continuous 71adj.
seriatim
in order 60adv.
continuously 71adv.
sericulture
animal husbandry 369n.
series
all 52n.
order 60n.
sequence 65n.
series 71n.
accumulation 74n.
number 85n.
recurrence 106n.
continuance 146n.
following 284n.
library 589n.
edition 589n.
serif
print-type 587n.
seriocomic
funny 849adj.
serious
great 32adj.
attentive 455adj.
wise 498adj.
resolute 599adj.
intending 617adj.
important 638adj.
dangerous 661adj.
serious 834adj.
dull 840adj.
heinous 934adj.
seriously
positively 32adv.
affirmatively 532adv.
resolutely 599adv.
seriousness
vigor 571n.
warm feeling 818n.
(*see* serious)
serjeant
lawyer 958n.
(*see* sergeant)
sermon
lecture 534n.
diffuseness 570n.
oration 579n.
dissertation 591n.
sermonize
be pious 979vb.
serolin
blood 335n.
seroon
bunch 74n.
serosity
fluid, blood 335n.
serous
fluidal 335adj.
sanguineous 335adj.
serpent
serpent 251n.
reptile 365n.
sibilation 406n.
horn 414n.
deceiver 545n.
bane 659n.
slyboots 698n.
noxious animal 904n.
knave 938n.
Satan 969n.
serpentine
snaky 251adj.
wriggle 251vb.
cunning 698adj.
serpigo
skin disease 651n.
serration
sharpness 256n.
roughness 259n.
notch 260n.
serratodentate
notched 260adj.
serried
cohesive 48adj.
assembled 74adj.
dense 324adj.
serrulation
notch 260n.
serum
fluid, blood 335n.
servant
worker 686n.
auxiliary 707n.
servant 742n.
servant-class
plebeian 869adj.
serve
be inferior 35vb.
follow 284vb.
function 622vb.
be instrumental 628vb.
suffice 635vb.
be expedient 642vb.
work 682vb.
serve 742vb.
be subject 745vb.
apportion 783vb.
(*see* service)
server
thrower 287n.
auxiliary 707n.
church officer 986n.
ritualist 988n.
serve rightly
retaliate 714vb.
be just 913vb.
serve up
make ready 669vb.
service
agency 173n.
propulsion 287n.
benefit 615n.
provision 633n.
utility 640n.
revive 656vb.
aid 703n.
obedience 739n.
service 745n.
sale 793n.
kind act 897n.
public worship 981n.
cult 981n.
church service 988n.
(*see* serve)
serviceable
instrumental 628adj.

useful 640adj.
service-book
office-book 988n.
service, in
serving 742adj.
serviceman
soldier 722n.
service road
road 624n.
services
instrumentality 628n.
army 722n.
service stripe
decoration 729n.
servicing
preservation 666n.
servile
conformable 83adj.
inglorious 867adj.
plebeian 869adj.
(*see* servility)
servility
subjection 745n.
servility 879n.
respect 920n.
serving man
domestic 742n.
serving sentence
imprisoned 747adj.
servitor
domestic 742n.
servitude
submission 721n.
servitude 745n.
servomechanics
mechanics 630n.
sesquipedalian
long 203adj.
diffuse 570adj.
ornate 574adj.
sesquipedality
inelegance 576n.
sessile
cohesive 48adj.
session
council 692n.
sessions
law-court 956n.
legal trial 959n.
sestet, sestina
verse form 593n.
set
modality 7n.
uniformity 16n.
decrease 37vb.
firm-set 45adj.
affix 45vb.
all 52n.
component 58n.
series 71n.
accumulation 74n.
band 74n.
sort 77n.
unit 88n.
young plant 132n.
stabilize 153vb.
tend 179vb.
situated 186adj.
place 187vb.
hang 217vb.
form 243n.
sharpen 256vb.
direction 281n.
descend 309vb.
be dense 324vb.
current 350n.
cultivate 370vb.
appearance 445n.
positive 473adj.
print 587vb.
stage-set 594n.
obstinate 602adj.
usual 610adj.
collection 632n.
doctor 658vb.
make ready 669vb.
party 708n.
contest 716n.
command 737vb.
beautify 841vb.
hair-dressing 843n.
decorate 844vb.
set about
begin 68vb.
setaceous
hairy 259adj.
set across
transfer 272vb.
set afloat
stabilize 153vb.
cause 156vb.
set against
dissuade 613vb.
make quarrels 709vb
cause dislike 861vb.
set apart
set apart 46vb.
exclude 57vb.
select 605vb.
exempt 919vb.
set aside
displace 188vb.
negate 533vb.
reject 607vb.
store 632vb.
abrogate 752vb.
set at ease
content 828vb.
set at naught
underestimate 483vb.
reject 607vb.
oppose 704vb.
defy 711vb.
hold cheap 922vb.
setback
disappointment 509n.
deterioration 655n.
adversity 731n.
loss 772n.
set books
curriculum 534n.
set by the ears
make quarrels 709vb.
set-down
humiliation 872n.
set down
record 548vb.
write 586vb.
set down to
attribute 158vb.
set fair
palmy 730adj.
be auspicious 730vb.
set fire
kindle 381vb.
set form
regularity 81n.
set forth
start out 296vb.
set forward
undertake 672n.
set free
deliver 668vb.
give scope 744vb.
liberate 746vb.
set going
initiate 68vb.
move 265vb.
impel 269vb.
dispose of 673vb.
set in
begin 68vb.
stay 144vb.
tend 179vb.
set off
correlate 12vb.
initiate 68vb.
beautify 841vb.
decorate 844vb.
set-off
offset 31n.
set on
incite 612vb.
attack 712vb.
enamored 887adj.
set on edge
roughen 259vb.
give pain 377vb.
displease 827vb.
setose, setous
hairy 259adj.
set out
arrange 62vb.
travel 267vb.
start out 296vb.
show 522vb.
dissert 591vb.
set piece
stage show 594n.
set right
straighten 249vb.
disclose 526vb.

rectify 654vb.
vindicate 927vb.
set sail
voyage 269vb.
navigate 269vb.
start out 296vb.
set-square
gauge 465n.
sett
paving 226n.
settee
seat 218n.
setter
dog 365n.
printer 587n.
set the alarm
time 117vb.
set the fashion
influence 178vb.
motivate 612vb.
be in fashion 848vb.
set the pace
motivate 612vb.
setting
situation 186n.
circumjacence 230n.
musical piece 412n.
view 438n.
spectacle 445n.
print 587n.
stage-set 594n.
hair-dressing 843n.
ornamental art 844n.
setting-up
composition 56n.
settle
arrange 62vb.
terminate 69vb.
be stable 153vb.
prevail 178vb.
place oneself 187vb.
dwell 192vb.
seat 218n.
be quiescent 266vb.
descend 309vb.
make certain 473vb.
judge 480vb.
contract 765vb.
appropriate 786vb.
pay 804vb.
settle accounts
account 808vb.
settled
characteristic 5adj.
ending 69adj.
vested 153adj.
situated 186adj.
located 187adj.
native 191adj.
positive 473adj.
usual 610adj.
settle down
come of age 134vb.
be stable 153vb.
settle for
bargain 791vb.
settle into
be turned to 147vb.
settlement
territory 184n.
location 187n.
station 187n.
habitancy 191n.
compact 765n.
dower 777n.
transfer 780n.
payment 804n.
settler
settler 191n.
incomer 297n.
settlor
giver 781n.
set-to
fight 716n.
set to
begin 68vb.
eat 301vb.
be resolute 599vb.
work 682vb.
set to music
compose music 413vb.
set to rights
repair 656vb.
set toward
approach 289vb.
set up
arrange 62vb.
stabilize 153vb.
cause 156vb.
strengthen 162vb.
place 187vb.
make vertical 215vb.
elevate 310vb.
cure 656vb.
prosperous 730adj.
setup
circumstance 8n.
composition 56n.
structure 331n.
set upon
desiring 859adj.
resolute 899adj.
set watch
invigilate 457vb.
seven deadly sins
vice 934n.
seven-league boots
speeder 277n.
magic instrument 983n.
Seventh-day Adventists
sect 978n.
seventh heaven
happiness 824n.
heaven 971n.
seventy-four
warship 722n.
gun 723n.
sever
subtract 39vb.
disjoin 46vb.
severable
severable 46adj.
brittle 330adj.
several
special 80adj.
plurality 101n.
many 104adj.
severalize
differentiate 15vb.
discriminate 463vb.
severalty
disjunction 46n.
severance
(*see* sever)
severe
exorbitant 32adj.
strong 162adj.
vigorous 174adj.
violent 176adj.
accurate 494adj.
plain 573adj.
severe 735adj.
paining 827adj.
serious 834adj.
fastidious 862adj.
pitiless 906adj.
ascetic 945adj.
severity
severity 735n.
inhumanity 898n.
(*see* severe)
Sèvres china
pottery 381n.
sew
tie 45vb.
sewage
leavings 41n.
swill 649n.
sewer
receptacle 194n.
cavity 255n.
tunnel 263n.
lake 346n.
drain 351n.
fetor 397n.
badness 645n.
cleanser 648n.
sink 649n.
insalubrity 653n.
retainer 742n.
sewerage
cleansing 648n.
dirt 649n.
sewing
bookbinding 589n.
sex
classification 77n.
life 360n.

impurity 951n.
sexagenarian
over twenty 99n.
old man 133n.
sex appeal
pleasurableness 826n.
beauty 841n.
lovableness 887n.
sex-consciousness
unchastity 951n.
sex-crazy, sex-mad
lecherous 951adj.
sex crime
rape 951n.
sexless
impotent 161adj.
sexologist
doctor 658n.
sexology
medical art 658n.
sext
church service 988n.
sextant
angular measure 247n.
arc 250n.
gauge 465n.
sextet
over five 99n.
duet 412n.
sex, the
womankind 373n.
sexton
interment 364n.
servant 742n.
church officer 986n.
sextuple
fifth and over 99adj.
sexual
generic 77adj.
impure 951adj.
sexual abnormality
abnormality 84n.
sexual desire
libido 859n.
sexual intercourse
coition 45n.
sexuality
unchastity 951n.
sexy
impure 951adj.
shabbiness
inferiority 35n.
improbity 930n.
shabby
unimportant 639adj.
dilapidated 655adj.
beggarly 801adj.
parsimonious 816adj.
disreputable 867adj.
rascally 930adj.
shack
small house 192n.
shackle
tie 45vb.
halter 47n.
make insufficient 636vb.
obstacle 702n.
encumbrance 702n.
fetter 748n., vb.
shackled
restrained 747adj.
captive 750adj.
shad
table fish 365n.
shade
insubstantial thing 4n.
differentiate 15vb.
degree 27n.
small quantity 33n.
shade 226n.
corpse 363n.
refrigerate 382vb.
darken 418n.
dimness 419n.
screen 421n.
hue 425n.
qualify 468vb.
conceal 525vb.
paint 553vb.
safeguard 660vb.
refresh 685vb.
defend 713vb.
relieve 831vb.
ghost 970n.
shade of difference
discrimination 463n.
shade off
shade off 27vb.
shade, throw into the
be superior 34vb.
shadiness
darkness 418n.
improbity 930n.
shading off
gradational 27adj.
shadoof
extractor 304n.
irrigator 341n.
shadow
insubstantial thing 4n.
analogue 18n.
imitation 20n.
compeer 28n.
concomitant 89n.
thinness 206n.
follow 284vb.
refrigerate 382vb.
darkness 418n.
dimness 419n.
screen 421vb.
color 425vb.
fantasy 513n.
hunter 619n.
pursue 619vb.
make ugly 842vb.
primp 843vb.
close friend 880n.
shadow-boxing
ideality 513n.
shadow cabinet
futurity 124n.
preparation 669n.
shadow forth
predict 511vb.
represent 551vb.
shadowless
undimmed 417adj.
shadow out
represent 551vb.
shadowy
insubstantial 4adj.
inconsiderable 33adj.
amorphous 244adj.
immaterial 320adj.
dark 418adj.
shadowy 419adj.
invisible 444adj.
uncertain 474adj.
imaginary 513adj.
puzzling 517adj.
shady
cold 380adj.
dark 418adj.
shadowy 419adj.
screened 421adj.
disreputable 867adj.
dishonest 930adj.
lawbreaking 954adj.
shaft
depth 211n.
pillar 218n.
handle 218n.
excavation 255n.
sharp point 256n.
tunnel 263n.
missile 287n.
tool 630n.
missile weapon 723n.
shag
hair 259n.
roughen 259vb.
tobacco 388n.
shaggy
hairy 259adj.
shagreen
skin 226n.
shah
sovereign 741n.
shake
mix 43vb.
come unstuck 49vb.
derange 63vb.
vary 152vb.
weaken 163vb.
force 176vb.
impel 279n.
oscillate 317vb.
brandish 317vb.
be agitated 318vb.
be cold 352vb.

roll 403vb.
musical note 410n.
cause doubt 486vb.
dissuade 613vb.
impair 655vb.
show feeling 818vb.
impress 821vb.
frighten, quake 854vb.
shake-down
bed 218n.
sleep 679n.
shake hands
meet 295vb.
make peace 719vb.
bargain 791vb.
be friendly 880vb.
greet 887vb.
shaken
irresolute 601adj.
deteriorated 655adj.
shake off
unstick 49vb.
eject 300vb.
shake one's head
dissent 489n.
negate 533vb.
disapprove 927vb.
shakes, no great
inconsiderable 33adj.
Shakespearean
poetic 593adj.
shakes, the
agitation 318n.
shake-up
revolution 149n.
shako
headgear 228n.
armor 713n.
shaky
weak 163adj.
flimsy 163adj.
unsafe 661adj.
nervous 854adj.
shale
lamina 207n.
brittleness 330n.
rock 344n.
shalloon
textile 222n.
shallot
vegetable 301n.
shallow
inconsiderable 33adj.
foolish 499adj.
affected 850adj.
(*see* shallowness)
shallowness
shallowness 212n.
inattention 456n.
sciolism 491n.
unintelligence 499n.
scarcity 636n.
unimportance 639n.
shallow pretext
pretext 614n.
shallows
shallowness 212n.
pitfall 663n.
shaly
layered 207adj.
territorial 344adj.
sham
mimicry 20n.
dissemble 541vb.
sham 542n.
spurious 542adj.
mental dishonesty 543n.
stratagem 698n.
shaman
sorcerer 983n.
priest 986n.
shamanism
sorcery 983n.
shamble
move slowly 278vb.
shambles
confusion 61n.
havoc 165n.
slaughter 362n.
slaughter-house 362n.
sink 649n.
shame
disrepute, slur 867n.
shame 867vb.
humiliation 872n.
wrong 914n.
defame 926vb.
improbity 930n.
wickedness 934n.
purity 950n.
shame-faced
modest 874adj.
guilty 936adj.
shameful
evil 616adj.
bad 645adj.
discreditable 867adj.
heinous 934adj.
shamefulness
improbity 930n.
shameless
undisguised 522adj.
thick-skinned 820adj.
vulgar 847adj.
insolent 878adj.
dishonest 930adj.
wicked 934adj.
unchaste 951adj.
shamiana
canopy 226n.
pavilion 192n.
shammer
deceiver 545n.
impostor 545n.
slyboots 698n.
shampoo
friction 333n.
ablution 648n.
surgery 658n.
hairwash 843n.
shamrock
three 93n.
grass 366n.
heraldry 547n.
shandrydan
carriage 274n.
shandy
liquor 301n.
shanghai
ensnare 542vb.
take away 786vb.
steal 788vb.
Shangri-la
fantasy 513n.
shank
stand 218n.
leg 267n.
deflect 282vb.
propel 287vb.
print-type 587n.
shantung
textile 222n.
shanty
small house 192n.
poem 593n.
shape
sort 77n.
make conform 83vb.
convert 147vb.
outline 233n.
form 243n.
efform 243vb.
structure 331n.
feature 445n.
represent 551vb.
plan 623vb.
ghost 970n.
shapeless
non-uniform 17adj.
amorphous 244adj.
unsightly 842adj.
shapely
symmetrical 245adj.
shapely 841adj.
shapen
convert 147vb.
shape well
give hope 852vb.
shard
piece 53n.
share
part 53n.
be one of 58vb.
sharp edge 256n.
mete out 465vb.
participation 775n.
give 781vb.
portion 873n.
be sociable 882vb.
sharecropping

joint possession 775n.
shareholder
owner 776n.
share out
apportion 783vb.
share-pusher
merchant 794n.
sharer
colleague 707n.
participator 775n.
shares
apportionment 783n.
sharing
equal 28adj.
participation 775n.
shark
fish 365n.
lender 784n.
taker 786n.
defrauder 789n.
sharkskin
textile 222n.
sharp
keen 174adj.
violent 176adj.
sharp 256adj.
striking 374adj.
pungent 388adj.
strident 407adj.
musical note 410n.
discordant 411adj.
intelligent 498adj.
deceive 542vb.
cunning 698adj.
felt 818adj.
painful 827adj.
unpleasant 827adj.
witty 839adj.
ungracious 885adj.
irascible 892adj.
sharp-eared
auditory 415adj.
sharpen
invigorate 174vb.
sharpen 256vb.
animate 821vb.
sharpener
sharpener 256n.
sharpen the wits
educate 534vb.
sharper
trickster 545n.
expert 696n.
slyboots 698n.
defrauder 789n.
sharp-eyed
attentive 455adj.
vigilant 457adj.
sharpness
sourness 393n.
vigor 571n.
skill 694n.
(*see* sharp)
sharp point
sharp point 256n.
sharp practice
trickery 542n.
foul play 930n.
sharp-set
hungry 859adj.
sharpshooter
shooter 287n.
attacker 712n.
soldier 722n.
sharp-tempered
irascible 892adj.
sharp-tongued
irascible 892adj.
sharp-witted
intelligent 498adj.
shastra
non-Biblical scripture 975n.
shatter
break 46vb.
demolish 165vb.
be brittle 330vb.
pulverize 332adj.
shattered surface
roughness 259n.
shattering
notable 638adj.
wonderful 864adj.
shatter-proof
unyielding 162adj.
invulnerable 660adj.
shattery
flimsy 163adj.
brittle 330adj.
shave
cut 46vb.
make smaller 198vb.
be near 200vb.
shorten 204vb.
laminate 207vb.
smooth 258vb.
hair-dressing 843n.
shaved, shaven
short 204adj.
hairless 229adj.
clean 648adj.
shaveling
monk 986n.
shaver
youngster 132n.
shavetail
soldiery 722n.
army officer 741n.
Shavian
funny 849adj.
shaving
small thing 33n.
thinness 206n.
lamina 207n.
strip 208n.
hair-dressing 843n.
shaving-mug
bowl 194n.
shavings
leavings 41n.
piece 53n.
rubbish 641n.
shawl
wrapping 226n.
shawl 228n.
shawm
flute 414n.
shay
carriage 274n.
she
female 373n., adj.
sheaf
bunch 74n.
cultivate 370vb.
shear
subtract 39vb.
make smaller 198vb.
shorten 204vb.
distortion 246n.
groom 369vb.
fleece 786vb.
shears
sharp edge 256n.
farm tool 370n.
sheath
receptacle 194n.
case 194n.
layer 207n.
covering 226n.
arsenal 723n.
sheathe
replace 187vb.
cover 226vb.
dress 228vb.
intromit 231vb.
insert 303vb.
sheave
tool 630n.
shebeen
tavern 192n.
shed
decrease 37vb.
unstick 49vb.
small house 192n.
doff 229vb.
emit 300vb.
let fall 311vb.
disaccustom 611vb.
relinquish 621vb.
sheen
light 417n.
reflection 417n.
sheep
imitator 20n.
sheep 365n.
laity 937n.
sheepcote
stable 192n.
sheep-farming
animal husbandry 369n.

sheepfold
stable 192n.
enclosure 235n.
cattle pen 369n.
sheepish
weak 163adj.
animal 365adj.
modest 874adj.
sheep-rot
animal disease 651n.
sheeprun
place 185n.
grassland 348n.
stock farm 369n.
sheep's eyes
desire 859n.
wooing 889n.
sheepshank
ligature 47n.
sheepwalk
stock farm 369n.
sheer
simple 44adj.
verticality 215n.
vertical 215adj.
sloping 220adj.
transparent 422adj.
sheer off
recede 290vb.
deviate 282vb.
sheet
part 53n.
lamina 207n.
coverlet 226n.
robe 228n.
dress 228vb.
lake 346n.
rain 350vb.
the press 528n.
letterpress 587n.
edition 589n.
paper 631n.
sheet anchor
coupling 47n.
safeguard 662n.
hope 852n.
sheet-lightning
luminary 420n.
sheets
tackling 47n.
sheikh
potentate 741n.
nobleman 868n.
sheikhdom
magistrature 733n.
shekel
coinage 797n.
Shekinah
manifestation 522n.
theophany 965n.
shelf
compartment 194n.
shelf 218n.
storage 632n.
shell
mold 23n.
emptiness 190n.
exterior 223n.
covering, skin 226n.
uncover 229vb.
rowboat 275n.
extract 304vb.
hardness 326n.
structure 331n.
horn 414n.
class 538n.
print 587n.
fire at 712vb.
armor 713n.
ammunition 723n.
missile weapon 723n.
seclusion 883n.
shellac
resin 357n.
shellback
mariner 270n.
expert 696n.
shellburst
loudness 400n.
shellcase
ammunition 723n.
shellfish
fish food 301n.
table fish 365n.
shell out
pay 804vb.
shell shock
psychopathy 503n.
illness 651n.
shelter
small house 192n.
dwelling 192n.
stable 192n.
retreat 192n.
dwell 192vb.
resting place 266n.
admit 299vb.
screen 421n., vb.
hiding-place 527n.
safeguard 660vb.
shelter 662n.
defenses 713n.
shelterless
vulnerable 661adj.
shelter under
plead 614vb.
shelty
pony 273n.
shelve
put off 136vb.
be oblique 220vb.
be neglectful 458vb.
avoid 620vb.
relinquish 621vb.
shelving
compartment 194n.
shend
curse 899vb.
exprobate 924vb.
Sheol
death 361n.
hell 972n.
shepherd
bring together 74vb.
herdsman 369n.
groom 369vb.
protector 660n.
direct 689vb.
leader 690n.
servant 742n.
pastor 986n.
shepherdess
herdsman 369n.
sherbet
soft drink 301n.
sherd
piece 53n.
sheriff
protector 660n.
officer 741n.
law officer 955n.
sherry
wine 301n.
shewbread
ritual object 988n.
shibboleth
identification 457n.
call 547n.
shield
covering 226n.
screen 421n., vb.
safeguard 660vb.
shelter 662n.
armor 713n.
defend 713vb.
honors 866n.
shield-bearer
retainer 742n.
shieling
small house 192n.
shift
period 110n.
periodicity 141n.
change 143n., vb.
transition 147n.
vary 152vb.
displacement 188n.
bodywear 228n.
move 265vb.
transpose 272vb.
move fast 277vb.
deflect 282vb.
trickery 542n.
mental dishonesty 543n.
pretext 614n.
contrivance 623n.
labor 682n.
stratagem 698n.
change hands 780vb.
shiftless

impenitent 940adj.
shifty
changeful 152adj.
cunning 698adj.
dishonest 930adj.
Shiites
non-Christian sect 978n.
shillelagh
club 723n.
shilling
coinage 797n.
shilly-shally
be irresolute 601vb.
shimmer
flash 417n.
shimmy
wriggle 251vb.
dance 837n.
shin
leg 267n.
shindy
quarrel 709n.
fight 716n.
shine
smooth 258vb.
light 417n.
shine 417vb.
be visible 443vb.
be wise 498vb.
cleanness 648n.
be skillful 694vb.
be beautiful 841vb.
have repute 866vb.
shine on
patronize 703vb.
be auspicious 730vb.
shingle
shorten 204vb.
laminate 207vb.
roof 226n.
shore 344n.
building material 631n.
hair-dressing 843n.
shingles
skin disease 651n.
shining light
sage 500n.
Shintoism
religious faith 973n.
shiny
smooth 258adj.
luminous 417adj.
clean 648adj.
ship
load 193vb.
send 272vb.
carry 273vb.
ship 275n.
shipload
contents 193n.
shipman
mariner 270n.
shipmate
chum 880n.
shipment
contents 193n.
transport 272n.
thing transferred 272n.
ship-money
tax 809n.
shipper
transferrer 272n.
carrier 273n.
shipping
transport 272n.
shipping 275n.
shipshape
orderly 60adj.
regular 83adj.
marine 275adj.
well-made 694adj.
shipwreck
ruin 165n.
shipwright
artisan 686n.
shipyard
workshop 687n.
shire
district 184n
shiremoot
assembly 74n.
shirk
disregard 458vb.
be loath 598vb.
avoid 620vb.
fail in duty 918vb.
shirker
coward 856n.
shirr
fold 261vb.
shirt
bodywear 228n.
shirt-waist
bodywear 228n.
shirty
angry 891adj.
sullen 893adj.
shive-knife
sharp edge 256n.
shiver
break 46vb.
demolish 165vb.
strip 208n.
oscillate 317vb.
be agitated 318vb.
be brittle 330vb.
be cold 380vb.
quake 854vb.
shivers
agitation 318n.
coldness 380n.
illness 651n.
nervousness 854n.
shoal
group 74n.
shallow 212adj.
pitfall 663n.
shock
bunch 74n.
violence 176n.
collision 279n.
agitation 318n.
inexpectation 508n.
illness 651n.
attack 712n., vb.
excitation 821n.
suffering 825n.
displease 827vb.
cause discontent 829vb.
fear 854n.
cause dislike 861vb.
wonder 864n.
excite hate 888vb.
incur blame 927vb.
shockable
modest 874adj.
innocent 935adj.
prudish 950adj.
shock-absorber
moderator 177n.
shocked
disapproving 924adj.
shocker
novel 590n.
monster 938n.
shock-headed
hairy 259adj.
shocking
whopping 32adj.
unusual 84adj.
not nice 645adj.
distressing 827adj.
ugly 842adj.
frightening 854adj.
wonderful 864adj.
discreditable 867adj.
heinous 934adj.
shock-proof
tough 329adj.
unfeeling 375adj.
shock tactics
attack 712n.
shock treatment
therapy 658n.
shock troops
attacker 712n.
armed force 722n.
shod
dressed 228adj.
shoddy
inferior 35adj.
flimsy 163adj.
fiber 208n.
spurious 542adj.
trivial 639adj.

bad 645adj.
bad taste 847n.
shoe
affix 45vb.
stand 218n.
footwear 228n.
fetter 748n.
shoeblack
cleaner 648n.
shoemaker
clothier 228n.
shoestring, on a
parsimoniously 816adv.
shogun
tyrant 735n.
autocrat 741n.
shoo off
dismiss 300vb.
shoot
branch 53n.
young plant 132n.
descendent 170n.
expand 197vb.
navigate 269vb.
kick 279vb.
shoot 287vb.
pass 305vb.
kill 362vb.
tree 366n.
vegetate 366vb.
give pain 377vb.
radiate 417vb.
photograph 551vb.
fire at 712vb.
execute 963vb.
shoot a line
be ostentatious 875vb.
boast 877vb.
shooter
shooter 287n.
shooting box
small house 192n.
shooting-brake
automobile 274n.
shooting range
arena 724n.
shooting star
meteor 321n.
luminary 420n.
shoot the sun
orientate 281vb.
shoot up
grow 36vb.
jut 254vb.
ascend 308vb.
shop
topic 452n.
workshop 687n.
purchase 792vb.
shop 796n.
shop-assistant
servant 742n.
seller 793n.
shopkeeper
provider 633n.
tradesman 794n.
shop-lifting
stealing 788n.
shopman
seller 793n.
tradesman 794n.
shopper
purchaser 792n.
shopping
purchase 792n.
buying 792adj.
shopping center
emporium 796n.
shopping list
requirement 627n.
shop-soiled
inferior 35adj.
imperfect 647adj.
blemished 845adj.
shop-steward
leader 690n.
delegate 754n.
shop-walker
servant 742n.
seller 793n.
shop-window
transparency 422n.
exhibit 522n.
mart 796n.
shore
region 184n.
edge 234n.
limit 236n.
shore 344n.
shoreless
spacious 183adj.
shore up
support 218vb.
preserve 666vb.
shorn
short 204adj.
clean 648adj.
shorn of
losing 772adj.
short
incomplete 55adj.
brief 114adj.
dwarfish 196adj.
short 204adj.
low 210adj.
deficient 307adj.
brittle 330adj.
concise 569adj.
taciturn 582adj.
compendious 592adj.
scarce 636adj.
poor 801adj.
ungracious 885adj.
irascible 892adj.
shortage
decrement 42n.
deficit 55n.
shortcoming 307n.
shortbread
pastry 301n.
short circuit
electricity 160n.
deviation 282n.
escape 667n.
hitch 702n.
shortcoming
shortcoming 307n.
insufficiency 636n.
imperfection 647n.
non-completion 726n.
non-observance 769n.
vice 934n.
(*see* shortage)
short commons
insufficiency 636n.
fasting 946n.
short cut
short distance 200n.
straightness 249n.
shorten
bate 37vb.
cut 46vb.
shorten 204vb.
abstract 592vb.
shortfall
deficit 55n.
shortcoming 307n.
scarcity 636n.
shorthand
writing 586n.
shorthanded
imperfect 647adj.
shorties
nightwear 228n.
short-lived
ephemeral 114adj.
shortness
smallness 33n.
(*see* short)
short notice, at
suddenly 135adv.
hastily 680adv.
short of
less 35adv.
exclusive of 57adv.
short run
brief span 114n.
shorts
leavings 41n.
trousers 228n.
short-service
brief 114adj.
short shrift
pitilessness 906n.
short-sighted
dim-sighted 440adj.
misjudging 481adj.

unwise 499adj.
short supply
scarcity 636n.
short tempered
irascible 892adj.
short-term
brief 114adj.
short weight
inequality 29n.
shot
mixed 43adj.
missile 287n.
shooter 287n.
insertion 303n.
bang 402n.
iridescent 437adj.
conjecture 512n.
photography 551n.
hunter 619n.
therapy 658n.
missile weapon 723n.
ammunition 723n.
shotgun
fire-arm 723n.
shotgun wedding
type of marriage 894n.
shot in one's locker
means 629n.
shot in the dark
empiricism 461n.
conjecture 512n.
gambling 618n.
shotten
deteriorated 655adj.
shoulder
supporter 218n.
angularity 247n.
camber 253n.
carry 273vb.
impel 279vb.
propel 287vb.
elevate 310vb.
print-type 587n.
shoulder to shoulder
cohesive 48adj.
in league 708adv.
shout
loudness 400n.
vociferate 408vb.
proclaim 528vb.
affirm 532vb.
call 547n.
voice 577vb.
rejoicing 835n.
be rude 885vb.
shout down
affirm 532vb.
make mute 578vb.
be insolent 878vb.
disapprove 924vb.
shouter
boaster 877n.
shout for
applaud 923vb.
shove
move 265vb.
transpose 272vb.
impulse 279n.
propel 287vb.
gesture 547n.
be active 678vb.
shovel
ladle 194n.
transpose 272vb.
shovel 274n.
extractor 304n.
shovel-hat
canonicals 989n.
shove off
impel 279vb.
decamp 296vb.
show
produce 164vb.
be visible 443vb.
spectacle 445n.
appear 445vb.
attract notice 455vb.
evidence 466vb.
demonstrate 478vb.
interpret 520vb.
exhibit 522n.
show 522vb.
duplicity 541n.
deception 542n.
indicate 547vb.
stage play 594n.
dramatize 594vb.
amusement 837n.
pride 871n.
pageant 875n.
showable
shown 522adj.
showboat
ship 275n.
theater 594n.
show business
drama 594n.
show-card
advertisement 528n.
showcase
exhibit 522n.
showdown
disclosure 526n.
shower
propel 287vb.
descend 309vb.
let fall 311vb.
rain 350n., vb.
exhibition 522n.
abound 635vb.
ablution 648n.
shower upon
be liberal 813vb.
showery
rainy 350adj.
show fight
be vigorous 174vb.
defy 711vb.
attack 712vb.
parry 713vb.
take courage 855vb.
show, for
ostentatious 875adj.
show girl
actor 594n.
show in
admit 299vb.
showiness
ostentation 875n.
showing
uncovered 229adj.
visible 443adj.
show-jumper
rider 268n.
show-jumping
equitation 267n.
showman
guide 520n.
exhibitor 522n.
stage-manager 594n.
showmanship
manifestation 522n.
publicity 528n.
show of
probability 471n.
show of hands
vote 605n.
show off
beautify 841vb.
be affected 850vb.
seek repute 866vb.
be proud 871vb.
be vain 873vb.
be ostentatious 875vb.
boast 877vb.
show, on
shown 522adj.
show one's face
be present 189vb.
be plain 522vb.
show one's hand
divulge 526vb.
show one's mind
be plain 522vb.
show out
dismiss 300vb.
showpiece
exhibit 522n.
showplace
exhibit 522n.
show results
be successful 727vb.
showroom
exhibit 522n.
show signs
indicate 547vb.
show the way
come before 64vb.

orientate 281vb.
prepare 669vb.
show through
be inside 224vb.
be transparent 422vb.
appear 445vb.
show up
arrive 295vb.
be visible 443vb.
be plain 522vb.
show 522vb.
disclose 526vb.
satirize 851vb.
shame 867vb.
accuse 928vb.
showy
florid 425adj.
ornate 574adj.
splendid 841adj.
vulgar 847adj.
prideful 871adj.
showy 875adj.
shrapnel
missile weapon 723n.
shred
small thing 33n.
piece 53n.
fraction 102n.
shredded
fragmentary 53adj.
shreds and tatters
poverty 801n.
shreds, in
dilapidated 655adj.
shrew
violent creature 176n.
quarreler 709n.
shrew 892n.
hell-hag 904n.
defamer 926n.
shrewd
knowing 490adj.
intelligent 498adj.
skillful 694adj.
cunning 698adj.
shrewd idea
conjecture 512n.
shrewdly
painfully 32adv.
shrewish
quarreling 709adj.
irascible 892adj.
shriek
feel pain 377vb.
stridor 407n.
cry 408vb.
lament 836n.
weep 836vb.
shrieking
florid 425adj.
shrievalty
jurisdiction 955n.
shrift
forgiveness 909n.
penance 941n.
church ministry 985n.
ministration 988n.
shrill
loud 400adj.
shrill 407vb.
shrimp
dwarf 196n.
animalcule 196n.
fish food 301n.
table fish 365n.
hunt 619vb.
shrine
small box 194n.
ritual object 988n.
temple 990n.
shrink
decrease 37vb.
become small 198vb.
recoil 280vb.
turn back 286vb.
recede 290vb.
avoid 620vb.
deteriorate 655vb.
be nervous 854vb.
be modest 874vb.
shrinkage
decrement 42n.
contraction 198n.
shrink from
dislike 861vb.
hate 888vb.
shrinking
modest 874adj.
shrive
perform ritual 988vb.
shrivel
dry 342vb.
heat 381vb.
deteriorate 655vb.
shriveled
lean 206adj.
shriven
forgiven 909adj.
shroff
merchant 794n.
shroud
tackling 47n.
wrapping 226n.
robe 228n.
dress 228vb.
grave clothes 364n.
conceal 525vb.
safeguard 660vb.
defend 713vb.
shrub
tree 366n.
shrubbery
wood 366n.
shrug
be impotent 161vb.
gesture 547n.
be indifferent 860vb.
shrug away
hold cheap 922vb.
shrunk
dwarfish 196adj.
contracted 198adj.
shuck
skin 226n.
uncover 229vb.
extract 304vb.
shudder
agitation 318n.
be cold 380vb.
quake 854vb.
shudder at
dislike 861vb.
shuffle
mix 43vb.
jumble 63vb.
interchange 151n., vb.
vary 151vb.
gait 265n.
walk 267vb.
move slowly 278vb.
deflect 282vb.
sophistry 477n.
dissemble 541vb.
be irresolute 601vb.
tergiversate 603vb.
dance 837n., vb.
be dishonest 930vb.
shuffler
deceiver 545n.
shun
be stealthy 525vb.
avoid 620vb.
dislike 861vb.
shunt
transpose 272vb.
deflect 282vb.
shunter
driver 268n.
locomotive 274n.
shut
close 264vb.
shut down
cease 145vb.
shut-eye
sleep 679n.
shut in
interior 224adj.
surround 230vb.
close 264vb.
imprison 747vb.
shut out
exclude 57vb.
shutter
covering, shade 226n.
stopper 264n.
darken 418vb.
curtain 421n.
shuttle

periodicity 141n.
weaving 222n.
fluctuation 317n.
shuttlecock
fluctuation 317n.
waverer 601n.
shuttle service
periodicity 141n.
fluctuation 317n.
shuttlewise
correlatively 12adv.
to and fro 317adv.
shut up
cease 145vb.
confute 479vb.
make mute 578vb.
imprison 747vb.
seclude 883vb.
shy
recoil 280vb.
deviate 282vb.
turn back 286vb.
propel 287vb.
unwilling 598adj.
avoid 620vb.
artless 699adj.
lapidate 712vb.
nervous 854adj.
disliking 861adj.
modest 874adj.
unsociable 883adj.
shy at
doubt 486vb.
refuse 760vb.
Shylock
lender 784n.
shy of
incomplete 55adj.
shyster
trickster 545n.
knave 938n.
lawyer 958n.
sialagogue
ejector 300n.
sib
akin 11adj.
sibilation
sibilation 406n.
disapprobation 924n.
sibyl
oracle 511n.
sorceress 983n.
sic
truly 494adv.
siccative
drier 342n.
sick
weakly 163n.
vomiting 300adj.
sick 651adj.
suffering 825adj.
crapulous 949adj.
sickbay
hospital 658n.
sickbed
bed 218n.
illness 651n.
hospital 658n.
sicken
be weak 163vb.
be unpalatable 391vb.
superabound 637vb.
be ill 651vb.
deteriorate 655vb.
displease 827vb.
cause discontent 829vb.
be tedious 838vb.
cause dislike 861vb.
sickener
plenitude 54n.
unsavoriness 391n.
superfluity 637n.
bane 659n.
sickening
unsavory 391n.
not nice 645adj.
discontenting 829adj.
disliked 861adj.
sickening for
sick 651adj.
sickle
angularity 247n.
sharp edge 256n.
farm tool 370n.
sick list
sick person 651n.
sickly
weakly 163adj.
colorless 426adj.
unhealthy 651adj.
sickness
illness 651n.
sick of
bored 838adj.
disliking 861adj.
sated 863adj.
sickroom
hospital 658n.
side
race 11n.
part 53n.
situation 186n.
edge 234n.
laterality 239n.
appearance 445n.
choose 605vb.
party 708n.
pride 871n.
vanity 873n.
ostentation 875n.
side against
oppose 704vb.
side-arms
side-arms 723n.
sideboard
cabinet 194n.
stand 218n.
side by side
with 89adv.
nigh 200adv.
sideways 239adv.
in league 708adv.
sidecar
bicycle 274n.
side-dish
dish 301n.
side-face
laterality 239n.
side-glance
look 438n.
wooing 889n.
side-issue
question 459n.
side-kick
chum 880n.
side-light
lamp 420n.
knowledge 490n.
sideline
edge 234n.
laterality 239n.
sidelong
obliquely 220adv.
lateral 239adj.
sideways 239adv.
side-pressure
obliquity 220n.
inducement 612n.
sidereal
celestial 321adj.
side-saddle
seat 218n.
side-show
trifle 639n.
sideslip
flank 239vb.
aeronautics 271n.
deviation 282n.
be in danger 661vb.
sidesman
church officer 986n.
side-splitting
funny 849adj.
sidestep
be oblique 220vb.
laterality 239n.
deviation 282vb.
avoidance 620n.
side to side
to and fro 317adv.
sidetrack
deflect 282vb.
avoid 620vb.
sidewalk
road 624n.
path 624n.
sideways
obliquely 220adv.

sideways 239adv.
side with
assent 488vb.
patronize 703vb.
siding
laterality 239n.
railroad 624n.
sidle
be oblique 220vb.
flank 239vb.
deviate 282vb.
siege
circumscription 232n.
attack 712n.
siegecraft
art of war 718n.
sienna
brown paint 430n.
sierra
high land 209n.
siesta
sleep 679n.
sieve
sorting 62n.
porosity 263n.
cleaning utensil 648n.
(*see* sift)
sift
eliminate 44vb.
exclude 57vb.
class 62vb.
inquire 459vb.
discriminate 463vb.
select 605vb.
purify 648vb.
sifter
(*see* sieve)
sigh
respiration 352n.
breathe 352vb.
sound faint 401vb.
cry 408n., vb.
suffer 825vb.
be dejected 834vb.
lamentation 836n.
be in love 887vb.
wooing 889n.
sigh for
desire 859vb.
sight
aim 281vb.
arrive 295vb.
vision 438n.
visibility 443n.
spectacle 445n.
detect 484vb.
eyesore 842n.
prodigy 864n.
sightless
blind 439adj.
invisible 444adj.
sightly
personable 841adj.
sight of
great quantity 32n.
multitude 104n.
sight-read
be musical 413vb.
sights
direction 281n.
sight-seeing
inspection 438n.
curiosity 453n.
sightseer
traveler 268n.
spectator 441n.
inquisitor 453n.
sight-testing
vision 438n.
sigla
punctuation 547n.
sigma
sibilation 406n.
sigmatism
sibilation 406n.
dialect 560n.
pronunciation 577n.
sigmoidal
labyrinthine 251adj.
sign
numerical element 85n.
evidence 466n.
endorse 488vb.
omen 511n.
manifestation 522n.
indication 547n.
badge, label 547n.
gesture 547n.
letter 588n.
warning 664n.
command 737n., vb.
contract 765vb.
give security 767vb.
prodigy 864n.
signal
remarkable 32adj.
communicate 524vb.
message 529n.
signal 547n., vb.
railroad 624n.
notable 638adj.
signal box
railroad 624n.
signaling
telecommunication 531n.
signalize
indicate 547vb.
dignify 866vb.
celebrate 876vb.
signal light
signal light 420n.
signation
ritual act 988n.
signatory
witness 466n.
assenter 488n.
signatory 765n.
signature
notation 410n.
assent 488n.
label 547n.
identification 547n.
name 561n.
edition 589n.
compact 765n.
title-deed 767n.
sign-board
label 547n.
signet
badge of rule 743n.
signet ring
jewelry 844n.
significance
meaning 514n.
importance 638n.
significant
evidential 466adj.
presageful 511adj.
signification
connotation 514n.
indication 547n.
signify
specify 80vb.
predict 511vb.
mean 514vb.
inform 524vb.
indicate 547vb.
be important 638vb.
sign language
mimicry 20n.
gesture 547n.
language 557n.
sign-manual
label 547n.
script 586n.
sign off
resign 753vb.
sign on
join a party 708vb.
sign-painter
artist 556n.
signpost
direction 281n.
signpost 547n.
sign-writer
penman 586n.
silage
agriculture 370n.
silence
stop 145n.
disable 161vb.
quietude 266n.
silence 399n., vb.
confute 479vb.
make mute 578vb.
taciturnity 582n.
silencer

silencer 401n.
non-resonance 405n.
silent
lubricated 334adj.
non-resonant 405adj.
reticent 525adj.
voiceless 578adj.
unsociable 883adj.
disapproving 924adj.
(*see* silence)
silent trade
barter 791n.
silenus
vegetability 366n.
lesser god 967n.
silhouette
copy 22n.
outline 233n., vb.
efform 243vb.
darken 418vb.
feature 445n.
picture 553n.
silk
fiber 208n.
textile 222n.
smoothness 258n.
silk gown
lawyer 958n.
silky
smooth 258adj.
soft 327adj.
textural 331adj.
sill
base 214n.
shelf 218n.
projection 254n.
silly
credulous 487adj.
absurd 497adj.
foolish 499adj.
fool 501n.
gullible 544adj.
silly season
absurdity 497n.
silly symphony
foolery 497n.
silly talk
silly talk 315n.
silo
farm tool 370n.
storage 632n.
preserver 666n.
silt
leavings 41n.
fertilizer 171n.
solid body 324n.
soil 344n.
marsh 347n.
semiliquidity 354n.
silty
territorial 344adj.
semiliquid 354adj.
silver
coat 266vb.
color 425vb.
white thing 427n.
money, bullion 797n.
silvered
gray 429adj.
silver lining
hope 852n.
silversmith
artisan 686n.
silver-toned
melodious 410adj.
silver-tongued
melodious 410adj.
eloquent 579adj.
silver wedding
anniversary 141n.
special day 876n.
wedding 894n.
silvery
melodious 410adj.
white 427adj.
gray 429adj.
silviculture
forestry 366n.
agriculture 370n.
simar, simarra
canonicals 989n.
similar
(*see* similarity)
similarity
relativeness 9n.
correlation 12n.
uniformity 16n.
similarity 18n.
copy 22n.
equivalence 28n.
simile
analogue 18n.
comparison 462n.
metaphor 519n.
ornament 574n.
similitude
comparison 462n.
representation 551n.
simmer
cook 301vb.
effervesce 318vb.
resent 891vb.
simmering
excitable 822adj.
simony
sale 793n.
improbity 930n.
simoom
gale 352n.
heat 379n.
simous
deformed 246adj.
simper
smile 835n.
be affected 850vb.
simple
simple 44adj.
credulous 487adj.
ignorant 491adj.
foolish 499adj.
intelligible 516adj.
veracious 540adj.
plain 573adj.
elegant 575adj.
medicine 658n.
artless 699adj.
easy 701adj.
tasteful 846adj.
plebeian 869adj.
simplemindedness
artlessness 699n.
simpleness
simpleness 44n.
unity 88n.
(*see* simple)
Simple Simon
ninny 501n.
dupe 544n.
simpleton
ignoramus 493n.
ninny 501n.
simplicity
(*see* simple, simpleness)
simplification
simplification 44n.
arrangement 62n.
intelligibility 516n.
translation 520n.
facility 701n.
simplify
decompose 51vb.
(*see* simplification)
simulacrum
mimicry 20n.
sham 542n.
pretext 614n.
(*see* image)
simulation
assimilation 18n.
mimicry 20n.
duplicity 541n.
simulator
imitator 20n.
simultaneity
synchronism 123n.
(*see* simultaneous)
simultaneous
accompanying 89adj.
instantaneous 116adj.
simurgh
rara avis 84n.
sin
badness 645n.
disobedience 738n.
wrong 914n.
wickedness 934n.
vice 934n.
be wicked 934vb.

guilty act 936n.
impiety 980n.
Sinanthropus
mankind 371n.
sinapism
surgical dressing 658n.
since
subsequently 120adv.
hence 158adv.
sincere
simple 44adj.
(*see* sincerity)
sincerity
no imitation 21n.
veracity 540n.
artlessness 699n.
feeling 818n.
probity 929n.
piety 979n.
sinciput
head 213n.
sine
ratio 85n.
sinecure
inaction 677n.
leisure 681n.
easy thing 701n.
sinecure, no
activity 678n.
sinecurist
idler 679n.
sine die
never 109adv.
sine qua non
specialty 80n.
concomitant 89n.
requirement 627n.
chief thing 638n.
conditions 766n.
sinews
vitality 162n.
sinews of war
defense 713n.
funds 797n.
sinewy
stalwart 162adj.
sinful
bad 645adj.
wrong 914adj.
heinous 934adj.
wicked 934adj.
guilty 936adj.
impious 980adj.
sing
resound 404vb.
ululate 409vb.
harmonize 410vb.
sing 413vb.
poetize 593vb.
be cheerful 833vb.
rejoice 835vb.
singable
melodious 410adj.
musical 412n.
singe
burn 381vb.
blacken 428vb.
embrown 430vb.
hair-dressing 843n.
singer
vocalist 413n.
singing-bird
bird 365n.
single
simple 44adj.
whole 52adj.
one 88adj.
infrequent 140adj.
independent 744adj.
unwedded 895adj.
single blessedness
celibacy 895n.
single combat
duel 716n.
single entry
accounts 808n.
single file
procession 71n.
line 203n.
single-handed
alone 88adj.
hindered 702adj.
single-hearted
artless 699adj.
trustworthy 929adj.
single-minded
simple 44adj.
obsessed 455adj.
singlemindedness
attention 455n.
resolution 599n.
preseverance 600n.
artlessness 699n.
singleness
unity 88n.
celibacy 895n.
(*see* single)
single out
differentiate 15vb.
set apart 46vb.
single piece
unit 88n.
single state
celibacy 895n.
single-stick
duel 716n.
singlet
bodywear 228n.
singleton
unit 88n.
single voice
consensus 488n.
sing out
vociferate 408vb.
Sing Sing
prison 748n.
sing small
be humble 872vb.
sing-song
uniform 16adj.
repeated 106adj.
discordant 411adj.
music 412n.
social gathering 882n.
singular
grammatical 564adj.
(*see* singularity)
singularity
irrelation 10n.
specialty 80n.
unconformity 84n.
unity 88n.
sinister
sinistrality 242n.
sinistral 242adj.
presageful 511adj.
evil 616adj.
bad 645adj.
harmful 645adj.
adverse 731adj.
frightening 854adj.
dishonest 930adj.
sink
decrease 37vb.
suppress 165vb.
receptacle 194n.
cavity 255n.
descend 309vb.
founder 313vb.
weigh 322vb.
drain 351n.
fetor 397n.
storage 632n.
badness 645n.
sink 649n.
insalubrity 653n.
deteriorate 655vb.
be fatigued 684vb.
defeat 727vb.
fail 728vb.
sinkable
descending 309adj.
sinkage
depth 211n.
descent 309n.
gravity 322n.
sink back
relapse 657vb.
sinker
diver 313n.
gravity 322n.
sink in
infiltrate 297vb.
cause thought 449vb.
sinking fund
finance 797n.
sink into

be turned to 147vb.
sink money
expend 806vb.
sin-laden
wicked 934adj.
sinless
innocent 935adj.
pure 950adj.
sinner
offender 904n.
evildoer 904n.
bad man 938n.
impious person 980n.
sin-offering
substitute 150n.
propitiation 941n.
oblation 981n.
sinologist
linguist 557n.
sinuosity
convolution 251n.
curvature 248n.
sinuous
convoluted 251adj.
sinus
cavity 255n.
sinusitis
respiratory disease 651n.
sip
small quantity 33n.
mouthful 301n.
drink 301vb.
taste 386vb.
siphon
transferrer 272n.
transpose 272vb.
void 300vb.
soft drink 301vb.
extractor 304n.
conduit 351n.
sir
old man 133n.
male 372n.
name 561vb.
master 741n.
dignify 866vb.
title 870n.
be courteous 884vb.
sirdar
potentate 741n.
domestic 742n.
sire
be akin 11vb.
generate 164vb.
parent 169n.
master 741n.
title 870n.
sired
born 360adj.
siren
rara avis 84n.
timekeeper 117n.
attraction 291n.
sea nymph 343n.
megaphone 400n.
vocalist 413n.
signal 547n.
motivator 612n.
warning 664n.
danger signal 665n.
sirene
flute 414n.
siriasis
frenzy 503n.
sirloin
meat 301n.
sirocco
wind 352n.
heat 379n.
sisal
fiber 208n.
sissy
weakling 163n.
coward 856n.
sister
kinsman 11n.
analogue 18n.
nurse 658n.
church title 986n.
nun 986n.
sisterhood
family 11n.
community 708n.
sect 978n.
nun 986n.
sisterly
akin 11adj.
friendly 880adj.
benevolent 897adj.
sistrum
gong 414n.
sit
place oneself 187vb.
wait 136vb.
sit down 311vb.
be inactive 679vb.
sit at the feet of
learn 536vb.
sit down
pause 145vb.
be quiescent 266vb.
sit down 311vb.
repose 683vb.
besiege 712vb.
site
place 185n.
situation 186n.
place 187vb.
sit for
be example 23adj.
represent 551vb.
sit loose to
come unstuck 49vb.
be indifferent 860vb.
sit on
suppress 165vb.
subjugate 745vb.
restrain 747vb.
sit on one's tail
pursue 619vb.
sit on the fence
be uncertain 474vb.
be half-way 625vb.
sit out
carry through 725vb.
sit pretty
be content 828vb.
sitter
living model 23n.
exam. 459n.
testee 461n.
art equipment 553n.
easy thing 701n.
sit tight
be quiescent 266vb.
sitting
maturation 669n.
council 692n.
sitting pretty
successful 727adj.
sitting-room
chamber 194n.
situate
(*see* situation)
situation
circumstance 8n.
degree 27n.
complexity 61n.
affairs 154n.
place 185n.
situation 186n.
station 187n.
direction 281n.
job 625n.
predicament 700n.
situ, in
in place 186adv.
here 189adv.
sit up
be attentive 455vb.
sit up with
look after 457vb.
sit with
confer 584vb.
Siva
Hindu god 967n.
sixes and sevens, at
confusedly 61adv.
six-footer
tall creature 209n.
six of one and half a dozen of the other
equivalence 28n.
no choice 606n.
indifference 860n.
sixpence
coinage 797n.
six-shooter

pistol 723n.
sixth form
class 538n.
sixth sense
sense 374n.
intuition 476n.
occultism 984n.
sizable
large 195adj.
sizar
college student 538n.
recipient 782n.
sizarship
subvention 703n.
receipt 807n.
size
make uniform 16vb.
adjust 24vb.
degree 27n.
greatness 32n.
adhesive 47n.
arrange 62vb.
measure 183n.
size 195n.
viscidity 354n.
importance 638n.
size of it
similarity 18n.
size up
appraise 465vb.
estimate 480vb.
sizing
provisions 301n.
provision 633n.
sizzle
effervesce 318vb.
be hot 379vb.
crackle 402vb.
hiss 406vb.
sjambok
scourge 964n.
skald
poet 593n.
skate
go smoothly 258vb.
be in motion 265vb.
travel 267vb.
carrier 273n.
sled 274n.
table fish 365n.
skater
pedestrian 268n.
skean
side-arms 723n.
skedaddle
move fast 277vb.
decamp 296vb.
run away 620vb.
skein
crossing 222n.
bunch 74n.
skeletal
lean 206adj.
structural 331adj.
skeleton
remainder 41n.
main part 52n.
thinness 206n.
frame 218n.
outline 233n.
structure 331n.
corpse 363n.
compendium 592n.
plan 623n.
skeleton at the feast
moper 834n.
skeleton in the cupboard
secret 530n.
skelp
strike 279vb.
skelter
move fast 277vb.
skeltron
formation 722n.
skeptic
unbeliever 486n.
irreligionist 974n.
skeptical
doubting 474adj.
unbelieving 486adj.
dissenting 489adj.
skepticism
philosophy 449n.
doubt 486n.
irreligion 974n.
skeptophilia
impurity 951n.
skerry
rock 344n.
sketch
copy 22n.
incompleteness 55n.
outline 233n., vb.
efform 243vb.
representation 551n.
picture 553n.
be concise 569vb.
description 590n.
compendium 592n.
plan 623n.
sketcher
artist 556n.
sketchy
incomplete 55adj.
uncompleted 726adj.
skewbald
horse 273n.
pied 437adj.
skewer
fastening 47n.
sharp point 256n.
perforator 263n.
skewness
inequality 29n.
obliquity 220n.
ski
go smoothly 258vb.
travel 267vb.
carrier 273n.
sled 274n.
skiagraphy
darkness 418n.
photography 551n.
skiascope
optical device 442n.
skid
supporter 218n.
go smoothly 258vb.
deviate 282vb.
fetter 748n.
skiddy
smooth 258adj.
skid-proof
dry 342adj.
skier
pedestrian 268n.
skiff
boat 275n.
skiffle-group
orchestra 413n.
ski-lift
ascent 308n.
lifter 310n.
skill
skill 694n.
cunning 698n.
skilled worker
artisan 686n.
expert 696n.
skillet
caldron 194n.
skillful
fit 24adj.
intelligent 498adj.
skillful 694adj.
skill-less
bad 645adj.
unskilled 695adj.
skilly
cereal, soup 301n.
skim
be near 200vb.
be contiguous 202vb.
travel 267vb.
swim 269vb.
move fast 277vb.
select 605vb.
purify 648vb.
skimble-skamble
orderless 61adj.
skimmings
leavings 41n.
skimp
shorten 204vb.
neglect 458vb.
make insufficient 636vb.

be parsimonious 816vb.
skimpy
small 33adj.
short 204adj.
skin
leavings 41n.
rend 46vb.
layer 207n.
shallowness 212n.
exteriority 223n.
skin 226n.
uncover 229vb.
fleece 786vb.
overcharge 811vb.
skin and bone
thinness 206n.
skin-deep
inconsiderable 33adj.
shallow 212adj.
exterior 223adj.
skin disease
skin disease 651n.
skindiving
sport 837n.
skinflint
niggard 816n.
skin-grafting
beautification 843n.
skinny
lean 206adj.
skin over
cure 656vb.
skin-tight
cohesive 48adj.
skip
decamp 296vb.
leap 312n., vb.
neglect 458vb.
study 536vb.
escape 667vb.
not complete 726vb.
rejoice 835vb.
skipper
mariner 270n.
jumper 312n.
skippingly
discontinuously 72adv.
skipping-rope
plaything 837n.
skirl
be loud 400vb.
stridor 407n.
skirmish
fight 716n., vb.
battle 718n.
skirmisher
precursor 66n.
soldier 722n.
skirt
be near 200vb.
base 214n.
pendant 217n.
skirt 228n.
edge 234n.
flank 239vb.
pass 305vb.
circle 314vb.
woman 373n.
circuit 626vb.
skirting
edging 234n.
skirts
entrance 68n.
skit
satire 851n.
calumny 926n.
skitter
swim 269n.
skittish
leaping 312adj.
capricious 604adj.
lively 819adj.
excitable 822adj.
lecherous 951adj.
skittle-alley
place of amusement 837n.
skittle out
defeat 727vb.
skittles
ball game 837n.
skive
cut 46vb.
laminate 207vb.
skiver
sharp point 256n.
skivvy
domestic 742n.
skulduggery
trickery 542n.
improbity 930n.
skulk
wander 267vb.
be stealthy 525vb.
avoid 620vb.
quake 854vb.
be cowardly 856vb.
skulker
hider 527n.
skull
head 213n.
skull and crossbones
heraldry 847n.
intimidation 854n.
skull-cap
headgear 228n.
canonicals 989n.
skunk
vermin 365n.
fetor 397n.
coward 856n.
cad 938n.
sky
space 183n.
height 209n.
summit 213n.
propel 287vb.
elevate 310vb.
heavens 321n.
blueness 435n.
skyey
airy 340adj.
skylark
climb 308vb.
skylarker
reveler 837n.
skylight
window 263n.
sky-line
distance 199n.
edge 234n.
sky-rocket
rocket 276n.
climber 308n.
fireworks 420n.
skysail
sail 275n.
skyscraper
edifice 164n.
house 192n.
high structure 209n.
sky-writing
publicity 528n.
slab
lamina 207n.
horizontality 216n.
shelf 218n.
monument 548n.
slabber
exude 298vb.
exrement 302n.
moisture 341n.
slabby
marshy 347adj.
semiliquid 354adj.
slack
non-adhesive 49adj.
decompose 51vb.
orderless 61adj.
weak 163adj.
slow 278adj.
add water 339vb.
coal 385n.
negligent 458adj.
be loath 598vb.
lazy 679adj.
lax 734adj.
slacken
disjoin 46vb.
unstick 49vb.
moderate 177vb.
decelerate 278vb.
be inactive 679vb.
slackening
decrease 37n.
slacker
insensibility 375n.
be inattentive 456vb.
sleep 679n., vb.

indifference 860n.
slacks
trousers 228n.
slack, take up the
recoup 31vb.
slack water
mid-course 625n.
slag
leavings 41n.
solid body 324n.
ash 381n.
rubbish 641n.
dirt 649n.
slake
decompose 51vb.
assuage 177vb.
add water 339vb.
sate 863vb.
slam
be vigorous 174vb.
close 264vb.
impulse 279n.
strike 279vb.
propel 287vb.
loudness 400n.
bang 402n., vb.
victory 727n.
slander
slur 867n.
scurrility 899n.
censure 924n.
calumny 926n.
false charge 928n.
slanderer
evildoer 904n.
defamer 926n.
accuser 928n.
slang
unintelligibility 517n.
slang 560n.
cuss 899vb.
dispraise 924vb.
slanging match
scurrility 899n.
slangy
linguistic 557adj.
dialectical 560adj.
slant
obliquity 220n.
view 438n.
idea 451n.
bias 481n.
slap
knock 279n.
bang 402n.
endearment 889n.
spank 963vb.
slap-bang
instantaneously 116adv.
slapdash
instantaneously 116adv.
negligent 458adj.
clumsy 695adj.
rash 857adj.
slap-happy
rash 857adj.
slap in the face
refusal 760n.
indignity 921n.
slapstick
dramatic 594adj.
wit 839n.
ridiculousness 849n.
slap-up
rich 800adj.
liberal 813adj.
slash
cut, rend 46vb.
notch 260vb.
cheapen 812vb.
dispraise 924vb.
detract 926vb.
slashing
forceful 571adj.
slat
lamina 207n.
strip 208n.
slate
lamina 207n.
brittleness 330n.
classroom 539n.
stationery 586n.
policy 623n.
building material 631n.
dispraise 924vb.
detract 926vb.
slats
bed 218n.
shade 226n.
slattern
slut 61n.
dirty person 649n.
bungler 697n.
slatternly
orderless 61adj.
clumsy 695adj.
slaty
layered 207adj.
slaughter
slaughter 362n., vb.
be severe 735vb.
cruel act 898n.
slaughter-house
slaughter-house 362n.
slave
instrument 628n.
busy person 678n.
work 682vb.
worker 686n.
minister to 703vb.
slave 742n.
prisoner 750n.
toady 879n.
slave-born
plebeian 869adj.
slave camp
prison camp 748n.
slave-driver
tyrant 735n.
slaver
merchant ship 275n.
exude 298vb.
emit 300vb.
excrement 302n.
tyrant 735n.
merchant 794n.
slave-raid
taking 786n.
slave-raider
thief 789n.
slavery
labor 682n.
servitude 745n.
slave to, a
subject 745adj.
slave-trade
trade 791n.
slave-trader
merchant 794n.
slavey
domestic 742n.
slavish
imitative 20adj.
conformable 83adj.
obedient 739adj.
subjected 745adj.
servile 879adj.
slavishness
submission 721n.
slaw
vegetable 301n.
slay
kill 362vb.
slayer
killer 362n.
sleave
complexity 61n.
crossing 222n.
sleazy
flimsy 163adj.
sled
sled 274n.
sledge
sled 274n.
hammer 279n.
pulverizer 332n.
sleek
smooth 258adj.
prosperous 730adj.
personable 841adj.
sleep
be inert 175vb.
be quiescent 266vb.
insensibility 375n.
be inattentive 456vb.
sleep 679n., vb.

repose 683n., vb.
be fatigued 684vb.
sleeper
railroad 624n.
idler 679n.
sleepiness
(*see* sleepy)
sleep-inducing
somnific 679adj.
sleeping
latent 523n.
inactive 679adj.
abrogated 752adj.
sleeping bag
bag 194n.
sleeping-car
train 274n.
sleeping draft
anesthetic 375n.
soporific 679n.
relief 831n.
sleeping partner
nonentity 639n.
idler 679n.
sleepless
persevering 600adj.
active 678adj.
sleep off
be restored 656vb.
be refreshed 685vb.
be relieved 831vb.
be sober 948vb.
sleep on it
wait 136vb.
meditate 449vb.
sleep-walker
pedestrian 268n.
sleep-walking
sleep 679n.
sleep with
unite with 45vb.
debauch 951vb.
sleepy
quiescent 266adj.
abstracted 456adj.
sleepy 679adj.
fatigued 684adj.
sleepy-head
slowcoach 278n.
idler 679n.
sleet
wintriness 380n.
sleety
cold 380adj.
sleeve
sleeve 228n.
pocket 194n.
trophy 729n.
sleigh
sled 274n.
sleight
visual fallacy 440n.
sleight 542n.
skill 694n.
cunning 698n.
slender
small 33adj.
narrow 206adj.
shapely 841adj.
sleuth
detective 459n.
informer 524n.
slice
cut 46vb.
piece 53n.
lamina 207n.
notch 260vb.
deflect 282vb.
mouthful 301n.
be clumsy 695vb.
portion 783n.
slicer
sharp edge 256n.
slick
smooth 258adj.
skillful 694adj.
slicker
overcoat 228n.
trickster 545n.
slide
fastening 47n.
elapse 111vb.
obliquity 220n.
go smoothly 258vb.
move 265vb.
deviate 282vb.
descend 309vb.
optical device 442n.
photography 551n.
representation 551n.
deteriorate 655vb.
slide back
relapse 657vb.
slide in
intromit 231vb.
slide into
be turned to 147vb.
slide-rule
counting instrument 86n.
gauge 465n.
slight
inconsiderable 33adj.
inferior 35adj.
demolish 165vb.
exiguous 196n.
narrow 206adj.
shallow 212adj.
rare 325adj.
disregard 458vb.
underestimate 483vb.
trivial 639adj.
not observe 769vb.
indignity 921n.
hold cheap 922vb.
detract 926vb.
slim
small 33adj.
make smaller 198vb.
narrow 206adj.
shapely 841adj.
slime
moisture 341n.
marsh 347n.
semiliquidity 354n.
slimy
dirty 649adj.
servile 879adj.
flattering 925adj.
sling
pendant 217n.
hang 217vb.
propel 287vb.
surgical dressing 658n.
lapidate 712vb.
missile weapon 723n.
slinger
shooter 287n.
thrower 287n.
soldiery 722n.
slink
lurk 523vb.
be stealthy 525vb.
be cowardly 856vb.
slink off
decamp 296vb.
run away 620vb.
slinky
narrow 206adj.
slip
come unstuck 49vb.
elapse 111vb.
young plant 132n.
bodywear 228n.
go smoothly 258vb.
descent 309n.
tumble 309vb.
viscidity 354n.
mistake 495n.
solecism 565n.
deteriorate 655vb.
be in danger 661vb.
failure 728n.
slip back
relapse 657vb.
slip into, slip on
wear 228vb.
slip knot
ligature 47n.
slip off
doff 229vb.
slip out
go away 190vb.
slipper
footwear 228n.
spank 963vb.
slippered
comfortable 376adj.

reposeful 683adj.
slipperiness
changeableness 152n.
unreliability 474n.
(*see* slippery)
slippery
non-adhesive 49adj.
transient 114adj.
smooth 258adj.
speedy 277adj.
unctuous 357adj.
uncertain 474adj.
deceiving 542adj.
tergiversating 603adj.
unsafe 661adj.
escaped 667adj.
cunning 698adj.
dishonest 930adj.
slippery slope
danger 661n.
predicament 700n.
slips
workshop 687n.
slipshod
orderless 61adj.
feeble 572adj.
lax 734adj.
slip-stream
wind 352n.
slip through
escape 667vb.
slipway
smoothness 258n.
road 624n.
slit
sunder, rend 46vb.
gap 201n.
furrow 262n.
slither
move 265vb.
slithery
smooth 258adj.
sliver
small thing 33n.
piece 53n.
slob
semiliquidity 354n.
bungler 697n.
slobber
exude 298vb.
emit 300vb.
excrete 302vb.
moisture 341n.
make unclean 649vb.
sloe
black thing 428n.
slog
propel 287vb.
persevere 600vb.
be busy 678vb.
exert oneself 682vb.
slogan
maxim 496n.
call 547n.
warfare 718n.
slogger
busy person 678n.
slogging
industrious 678adj.
sloka
maxim 496n.
prosody 593n.
verse form 593n.
sloop
sailing-ship 275n.
warship 722n.
sloosh
drench 341vb.
slop
flow out 298vb.
let fall 311vb.
moisten 341n.
waste 634vb.
slop-bowl
bowl 194n.
slope
high land 209n.
obliquity 220n.
ascent 308n.
descent 309n.
slope off
run away 620vb.
slopping
full 54adj.
redundant 637adj.
sloppy
orderless 61adj.
feeble 572adj.
feeling 818adj.
slops
weak thing 163n.
clothing 228n.
swill 649n.
slopshop
clothier 228n.
slot
receptacle 194n.
gap 201n.
furrow 262n.
groove 262vb.
orifice 263n.
trace 548n.
sloth
inertness 175n.
sluggishness 679n.
slot-machine
receptacle 194n.
storage 632n.
treasury 799n.
slouch
move slowly 278vb.
be inactive 679vb.
sloucher
slowcoach 278n.
avoider 620n.
idler 679n.
slouching
graceless 842adj.
slough
leavings 41n.
unstick 49vb.
excrement 302n.
marsh 347n.
disaccustom 611vb.
sink 649n.
disuse 674vb.
sloven
slut 61n.
dirty person 649n.
bungler 697n.
slovenly
orderless 61adj.
negligent 458adj.
feeble 572adj.
dirty 649adj.
clumsy 695adj.
slow
protracted 113adj.
anachronistic 118adj.
late 136adj.
inert 175adj.
slow 278adj.
unintelligent 499adj.
unwilling 598adj.
lazy 679adj.
leisurely 681adj.
inexcitable 823adj.
tedious 838adj.
dull 840adj.
slow burn
discontent 829n.
slowcoach
slowcoach 278n.
idler 679n.
slow down
bate 37vb.
come to rest 266vb.
decelerate 278vb.
hinder 702vb.
slow-down
strike 145n.
slowness 278n.
slow-motion
slowness 278n.
slow 278adj.
slowness
caution 858n.
(*see* slow)
sloyd
education 534n.
slub
weave 222vb.
slubber
make unclean 649vb.
be clumsy 695vb.
sludge
leavings 41n.
slue
rotate 315vb.
slug
slowcoach 278n.
move slowly 278vb.

strike 279vb.
vermin 365n.
print-type 587n.
ammunition 723n.
sluggard
slowcoach 278n.
idler 679n.
sluggish
late 136adj.
inert 175adj.
slow 278adj
flowing 350adj.
lazy 679adj.
apathetic 820adj.
dull 840adj.
sluice
outlet 298n.
irrigator 341n.
drench 341vb.
waterfall 350n.
conduit 351n.
clean 648vb.
slum
housing 192n.
sink 649n.
insalubrity 653n.
dilapidation 655n.
poverty 801n.
eyesore 842n.
lower classes 869n.
slumber
quietude 266n.
sleep 679n., vb.
slum-dweller
poor man 801n.
low fellow 869n.
slummer
reformer 654n.
philanthropist 901n.
slumming
sociology 901n.
slummy
unclean 649adj.
dilapidated 655adj.
slump
decrease 37n.
contraction 198n.
regression 286n.
descend 309vb.
deterioration 655n.
inactivity 679n.
adversity 731n.
cheapness 812n.
slur
neglect 458vb.
conceal 525vb.
slur 867n.
censure 924n.
calumny 926n.
extenuate 927vb.
slush
marsh 347n.
semiliquidity 354n.
slut
slut 61n.
loose woman 952n.
sluttish
negligent 458adj.
dirty 649adj.
sly
stealthy 525adj.
false 541adj.
cunning 698adj.
gay 833adj.
witty 839adj.
slyboots
slyboots 698n.
smack
small quantity 33n.
tincture 43n.
sailing ship 275n.
knock 279n.
taste 386n.
crackle 402vb.
spank 963vb.
smacker
paper money 797n.
endearment 889n.
smack of
resemble 18vb.
smack one's lips
enjoy 376vb.
appetize 390vb.
small
small 33adj.
fractional 102adj.
infantine 132adj.
weak 163adj.
little 196adj.
insufficient 636n.
unimportant 639adj.
small arms
fire-arm 723n.
small beer
nonentity 639n.
trifle 639n.
small clothes
breeches 228n.
smaller
lesser 35adj.
contracted 198adj.
small fry
animalcule 196n.
nonentity 639n.
lower classes 869n.
smallholder
husbandman 370n.
small hours
morning 128n.
midnight 129n.
lateness 136n.
smallness
invisibility 444n.
(*see* small)
small number
fewness 105n.
smallpox
skin disease 651n.
smalls
breeches 228n.
small talk
chatter 581n.
chat 584n.
smalt
blue pigment 435n.
smalto
ornamental art 844n.
smarm
flatter 925vb.
smart
speedy 277adj.
pang 377n.
intelligent 498adj.
active 678adj.
suffer 825vb.
witty 839adj.
personable 841adj.
fashionable 848adj.
smart aleck
wiseacre 500n.
smarten
decorate 844vb.
smarting
painful 377adj.
felt 818adj.
discontented 829adj.
resentful 891adj.
smart money
reward 962n.
smart under
feel 818vb.
smarty-boots
vain person 873n.
smash
break 46vb.
demolish 165vb.
force 176vb.
collision 279n.
strike 279vb.
propel 287vb.
wound 655vb.
smash and grab
rob 788vb.
smasher
a beauty 841n.
smash hit
dramaturgy 594n.
exceller 644n.
success 727n.
favorite 890n.
smashing
topping 644adj.
smatterer
sciolist 493n.
smattering
erudition 490n.
sciolism 491n.
smattering 491adj.
smear
overlay 226vb.
bedim 419vb.

make unclean 649vb.
blemish 854n., vb.
shame 867vb.
calumny 926n.
smear campaign
detraction 926n.
smear-word
calumny 926n.
smeddum
powder 332n.
smell
small quantity 33n.
emit 300vb.
odor 394n.
stink 397vb.
trace 548n.
be unclean 649vb.
deteriorate 655vb.
smell a rat
detect 484vb.
doubt 486vb.
smelling bottle
scent 396n.
smelling salts
pungency 388n.
tonic 658n.
smell out
discover 484vb.
smell powder
wage war 718vb.
smelly
odorous 394adj.
fetid 397adj.
smelt
table fish 365n.
heat 381vb.
smile
gesticulate 547vb.
be pleased 824vb.
laughter 835n.
greet 884vb.
smile at
ridicule 851vb.
smile on
patronize 703vb.
be auspicious 730vb.
smiles
cheerfulness 833n.
smiling
content 828adj.
sociable 882adj.
smirch
bedim 419vb.
blacken 428vb.
make unclean 649vb.
defame 926vb.
smirk
laughter 835n.
smile 835vb.
be affected 850vb.
flatter 925vb.
smite
strike 279vb.
kill 302vb.
impress 821vb.
smith
efform 243vb.
artisan 686n.
smithereens
small thing 33n.
smithy
workshop 687n.
smitten
induced 612adj.
enamored 887adj.
smock
bodywear 228n.
fold 261vb.
smocking
needlework 844n.
smog
cloud 355n.
opacity 423n.
poison 659n.
smoke
emit 300vb.
powder 332n.
gas 336n.
vaporize 338vb.
dry 342vb.
ash 381n.
season, smoke 388vb.
odor 394n.
be hot 397vb
bedim 419vb.
screen 421vb.
make opaque 423vb.
blacken 428vb.
blur 440vb.
lurk 523vb.
dirt 649n.
preserve 666vb.
mature 669vb.
smoke-duct
chimney 263n.
smoke out
eject 300vb.
extract 304vb.
hunt 619vb.
smoker
train 274n.
tobacco 388n.
smoke-ring
vortex 315n.
smoke-screen
obfuscation 421n.
opacity 423n.
invisibility 444n.
concealment 525n.
disguise 527n.
defenses 713n.
smoke-signal
telecommunication 531n.
signal 547n.
smoke-stack
chimney 263n.
air-pipe 353n.
smoking room
chamber 194n.
smoking-room story
witticism 839n.
impurity 951n.
smoky
powdery 332adj.
vaporific 338vb.
heated 381adj.
pungent 388adj.
dim 419adj.
opaque 423adj.
black 428adj.
gray 429adj.
dirty 649adj.
smolder
be inert 175vb.
be hot 379vb.
lurk 523vb.
be inactive 679vb.
resent 891vb.
smoldering
sullen 893adj.
smooth
uniform 16adj.
equalize 28vb.
non-adhesive 49adj.
orderly 60adj.
regular 81adj.
make conform 83vb.
lenitive 177adj.
flatten 216vb.
hairless 229adj.
symmetrical 245adj.
smooth 258adj., vb.
tranquil 266adj.
soft 327adj.
rub 333vb.
touch 378vb.
deceiving 542adj.
elegant 575adj.
facilitate 701vb.
relieve 831vb.
courteous 884adj.
flattering 925adj.
smooth-bore
fire-arm 723n.
smooth citizen
slyboots 698n.
smoothing-iron
smoother 258n.
smoothness
texture 331n.
lubrication 334n.
cunning 698n.
(*see* smooth)
smooth out
not discriminate 464vb.
smooth-running
lubricated 334adj.
wieldy 701adj.
smooth-spoken
hypocritical 541adj.
smother

moderate 177vb.
cover 226vb.
close 264vb.
murder 362vb.
conceal 525vb.

smouse
seller 793n.
peddler 794n.

Smriti
tradition 127n.
non-Biblical scripture 975n.

smudge
blacken 428vb.
blur 440vb.
make unclean 649vb.
blemish 845n., vb.

smug
affected 850adj.

smuggle
steal 788vb.

smuggle in
intromit 231vb.

smuggler
free man 744n.
thief 789n.

smugness
happiness 824n.
content 828n.

smut
ash 381n.
dirt 649n.
impurity 951n.

smutch
blacken 428vb.
make unclean 649vb.

snack
meal 301n.
mouthful 301n.

snack-bar
café 192n.

snacks, go
participate 775vb.

snaffle
restraint 747n.
fetter 748n.
take 786vb.
steal 788vb.

snafu
orderless 61adj.

snag
projection 254n.
danger 661n.
pitfall 663n.
difficulty 700n.
hitch 702n.

snaggy
sharp 256adj.

snail
slowcoach 278n.

snake
serpent 251n.
meander 251vb.
reptile 365n.
bane 659n.
slyboots 698n.
noxious animal 904n.
knave 938n.

snake-charmer
sorcerer 983n.

snake in the grass
latency 523n.
deceiver 545n.
trouble-maker 663n.
evildoer 904n.

snaky
snaky 251adj.
cunning 698adj.
dishonest 930adj.

snap
break 46vb.
discontinue 72vb.
close 264vb.
pastry 301n.
be brittle 330vb.
crackle 402vb.
photography 551n.
spontaneous 609adj.
sullenness 893n.

snap of the fingers
unimportance 639n.

snap one's fingers
defy 711vb.
disobey 738vb.
not observe 769vb.
hold cheap 922vb.

snappish
sullen 893adj.
irascible 982adj.

snappy
vigorous 174adj.
speedy 277adj.
aphoristic 496adj.
witty 839adj.
personable 841adj.

snapshot
photography 551n.

snap up
eat 301vb.
take 786vb.

snare
trap 542n.
take 786vb.

snark
rara avis 84n.

snarl
distortion 246n.
distort 246vb.
ululation 409n.
ululate 409vb.
sullenness 893n.
threat 900n.
threaten 900vb.

snarled
complex 61adj.

snatch
pursue 619vb.
take 786vb.

snatcher
taker 786n.

sneak
be stealthy 525vb.
steal 788vb.
coward 856n.
be servile 879vb.
knave 938n.

sneaker
thief 789n.

sneakers
footwear 228n.

sneaking
servile 879adj.
dishonest 930adj.

sneer
be discontented 829vb.
dislike 861vb.
insolence 878n.
not respect 921vb.
contempt 922n.
dispraise 924vb.
detraction 926n.

sneeze
breathe 352vb.
sibilation 406n.

sneezy
puffing 352adj.

snick
cut 46vb.

snicker
laughter 835n.
laugh 835vb.
ridicule 851n.

snickersnee
side-arms 723n.

snide
false money 797n.

sniff
breathe 352vb.
smell 394vb.
detraction 926n.

sniff at
eat 301vb.
dislike 861vb.
despise 922vb.
detract 926vb.

sniffy
puffing 352adj.
despising 922adj.

snifter
potion 301n.

snip
small thing 33n.
cut 46vb.
piece 53n.
clothier 228n.

snipe
table bird 365n.
fire at 712vb.

sniper
shooter 287n.

attacker 712n.
soldier 722n.
snippet
table bird 365n.
snitch
informer 524n.
steal 788vb.
snivel
weep 836vb.
snob
vulgarian 847n.
proud man 871n.
snobbery
etiquette 848n.
pride 871n.
snobbish
biased 481adj.
ill-bred 847adj.
fashionable 848adj.
affected 850adj.
prideful 871adj.
despising 922adj.
Sno-Cat
vehicle 274n.
snood
receptacle 194n.
headgear 228n.
loop 250n.
hair-dressing 843n.
snook
sauciness 878n.
indignity 921n.
snooker
ball game 837n.
snoop
scan 438vb.
spectator 441n.
be curious 453vb.
detective 459n.
informer 524n.
be stealthy 525vb.
snoopy
inquisitive 453adj.
snooty
insolent 878adj.
despising 922adj.
snooze
sleep 679n., vb.
snore
rasp 407vb.
sleep 679vb.
snort
breathe 352vb.
hiss 406vb.
rasp 407vb.
ululate 409vb.
stammer 580vb.
be irascible 892vb.
sullenness 893n.
contempt 922n.
snorter
potion 301n.
snot
dirt 649n.
snotty
naval man 270n.
snout
face 237n.
projection 254n.
snow
snow 380n.
refrigerator 384n.
white thing 427n.
drug 658n.
poison 659n.
snowball
grow 36vb.
continuity 71n.
accumulation 74n.
expand 197vb.
strike 279vb.
missile 287n.
propel 287vb.
snow 380n.
snowballer
thrower 287n.
snowflake
softness 327n.
powder 332n.
snow 380n.
white thing 427n.
snowman
insubstantial thing 4n.
brief span 114n.
snow 380n.
image 551n.
snow-shoe
footwear 228n.
carrier 273n.
sled 274n.
snow-storm
storm 176n.
wintriness 380n.
snow 380n.
snowy
cold 380adj.
white 427adj.
snub
short 204adj.
unsharpened 257adj.
repel 292vb.
humiliate 872vb.
be rude 885vb.
reprimand 924n.
snubby
short 204adj.
snuff
suppress 165vb.
absorb 299vb.
extinguish 382vb.
tobacco 388n.
smell 394vb.
brownness 430n.
snuff-box
small box 194n.
tobacco 388n.
snuffle
breathe 352vb.
hiss 406vb.
stammer 580vb.
snuffy
dirty 649adj.
snug
adjusted 24adj.
dry 342adj.
comfortable 376adj.
warm 379adj.
invulnerable 660adj.
reposeful 683adj.
snuggery
retreat 192n.
small house 192n.
snuggle
caress 889vb.
so
thus 8adv.
hence 158adv.
true 494adj.
soak
fill 54vb.
drink 301vb.
immerse 303vb.
add water 339vb.
drench 341vb.
superabound 637vb.
overcharge 811vb.
drunkard 949n.
soaker
rain 350n.
drunkard 949n.
soak into, soak through
infiltrate 297vb.
pass 305vb.
soak up
absorb 299vb.
dry 342vb.
so-and-so
person 371n.
no name 562n.
soap
softness 327n.
lubricant 334n.
fat 357n.
cleanser 648n.
flatter 925vb.
soap-box
publicity 528n.
rostrum 539n.
soapiness
unctuousness 357n.
soap opera
stage play 594n.
soapy
smooth 258adj.
fatty 357adj.
white 427adj.
servile 879adj.
flattering 925adj.
soar
be high 209vb.

fly 271vb.
ascend 308vb.
be dear 811vb.
soar above
outdo 306vb.
sob
respiration 352n.
rasp 407vb.
cry 408n., vb.
aphony 578n.
stammer 580vb.
lamentation 836vb.
sober
moderate 177adj., vb.
soft-hued 425adj.
wise 498adj.
sane 502adj.
educate 534vb.
plain 573adj.
inexcitable 823adj.
serious 834adj.
deject 834vb.
cautious 858adj.
ascetic 943adj.
sober 948adj.
sobered
repentant 939adj.
soberly
modestly 874adv.
sober-minded
sane 502adj.
inexcitable 823adj.
sobersides
moper 834n.
sober person 948n.
sobriety
moderation 177n.
wisdom 498n.
sanity 502n.
inexcitability 823n.
seriousness 834n.
caution 858n.
temperance 942n.
sobriety 948n.
sob-sister
newsmonger 529n.
author 589n.
excitant 821n.
sob-story
lament 836n.
sobstuff
excitation 821n.
lament 836n.
socage
possession 773n.
so-called
unbelieved 486adj.
supposed 512adj.
spurious 542adj.
untrue 543adj.
named 561adj.
misnamed 562adj.
soccer
ball game 837n.
sociability
cheerfulness 833n.
sociability 882n.
sociable
seat 218n.
carriage 274n.
amiable 884adj.
social
national 371adj.
corporate 708adj.
social gathering 882n.
social circle
sociality 882n.
social class
community 708n.
social climber
vulgarian 847n.
commoner 869n.
social person 882n.
social conscience
philanthropy 901n.
social engineering
sociology 901n.
social evil
social evil 951n.
social gathering
social gathering 882n.
social graces
sociability 882n.
social group
group 74n.
social group 371n.
community 708n.
socialism
government 733n.
joint possession 775n.
sociology 901n.
socialist
political party 708n.
participator 775n.
socialistic
sharing 775adj.
philanthropic 901adj.
Socialists
political party 708n.
socialite
beau monde 848n.
social person 882n.
sociality
sociality 882n.
socialize
socialize 775vb.
convey 780vb.
social planning
sociology 901n.
social register
upper class 868n.
social round
social round 882n.
social science
anthropology 371n.
sociology 901n.
social security
safety 660n.
social service
sociology 901n.
social state
polity 733n.
social success
sociability 882n.
social person 882n.
social worker
reformer 654n.
societal
national 371adj.
society
accompaniment 89n.
social group 371n.
association 706n.
society 708n.
beau monde 848n.
sociality 882n.
Society of Friends
sect 978n.
Socinianism
heresy 977n.
sociologist
reformer 654n.
sociology
anthropology 371n.
reformism 654n.
sociology 901n.
sociopath
madman 504n.
sock
legwear, footwear 228n.
strike 279vb.
socket
place 185n.
receptacle 194n.
cavity 255n.
socle
stand 218n.
Socratic method
interrogation 459n.
sod
soil 344n.
grassland 348n.
grass 366n.
cultivate 370vb.
soda
soft drink 301n.
cleanser 648n.
soda-fountain
café 192n.
sodality
association 706n.
society 708n.
community 708n.
friendship 880n.
soda-water
soft-drink 301n.
water 339n.
sodden
drenched 341adj.
drunken 949adj.

sodomite
libertine 952n.
sodomy
illicit love 951n.
sofa
seat 218n.
soffit
projection 254n.
soft
unstable 152adj.
weak 163adj.
lenitive 177adj.
smooth 258adj.
soft 327adj.
fluidal 335adj.
comfortable 376adj.
silent 399adj.
muted 401adj.
melodious 410adj.
foolish 499adj.
lenient 736adj.
impressible 819adj.
cowardly 856adj.
pitying 905adj.
sober 948adj.
soft drink
soft drink 301n.
soften
soften 327vb.
relieve 831vb.
extenuate 927vb.
(*see* soft)
softened
repentant 939adj.
soft-hued
soft-hued 425adj.
soft impeachment
love affair 887n.
softness
softness 327n.
pulpiness 356n.
irresolution 601n.
laxity 734n.
benevolence 897n.
sensualism 944n.
(*see* soft)
soft nothings
empty talk 515n.
endearment 889n.
soft pedal
silence 399vb.
silencer 401n.
mute 401vb.
sound dead 405vb.
mute 414n.
underestimate 483vb.
extenuate 927vb.
soft sawder
flattery 925n.
soft soap
falsehood 541n.
flattery 925n.
soft-spoken
courteous 884adj.
soft spot
sensibility 374n.
defect 647n.
vulnerability 661n.
moral sensibility 819n.
painfulness 827n.
soft underbelly
vulnerability 661n.
softy
weakling 163n.
ninny 501n.
sogginess
softness 327n.
moisture 341n.
soggy
pulpy 356adj.
soi-disant
untrue 543adj.
named 561adj.
misnamed 562adj.
vain 873adj.
soigné
dressed 228adj.
elegant 575adj.
soil
region 184n.
soil 344n.
make unclean 649vb.
make ugly 842vb.
blemish 845vb.
soiree
social gathering 882n.
sojourn
be present 189vb.
dwell 192vb.
visit 882vb.
sojourner
dweller 191n.
soke
district 184n.
solace
relief 831n.
amuse 837vb.
solar
celestial 321adj.
solarium
heater 383n.
hospital 658n.
solar flare
prominence 254n.
sun 321n.
solar plexus
insides 224n.
solar system
sun 321n.
solatium
extra 40n.
reward 962n.
solder
join 45vb.
adhesive 47n.
soldier
killer 362n.
wage war 718vb.
soldier 722n.
brave person 855n.
soldierly
warlike 718adj.
courageous 855adj.
soldier of fortune
militarist 722n.
soldiery
soldiery 722n.
sold on
believing 485adj.
sole
one 88adj.
foot 214n.
table fish 365n.
repair 656vb.
solecism
mistake 495n.
solecism 565n.
solecistic
abnormal 84adj.
erroneous 495adj.
neological 560adj.
ungrammatical 565adj.
solemn
great 32adj.
affirmative 532adj.
important 638adj.
serious 834adj.
formal 875adj.
devotional 981adj.
ritual 988adj.
solemn affirmation
oath 532n.
solemn declaration
promise 764n.
solemnity
formality 875n.
rite 988n.
(*see* solemn)
solemnization
celebration 876n.
ministration 988n.
solemnize
do 676vb.
celebrate 876vb.
solenoid
magnet 291n.
sol-fa
vocal music 412n.
sing 413vb.
solfatara
furnace 383n.
solfeggio
vocal music 492n.
solferino
red pigment 431n.
solicitant
desirer 859n.
solicitation
inducement 612n.
offer 759n.

request 761n.
solicitor
petitioner 763n.
law agent 958n.
solicitous
careful 457adj.
desiring 859adj.
solicitude
carefulness 457n.
worry 825n.
nervousness 854n.
solid
real 1adj.
substantial 3adj.
firm-set 45adj.
cohesive 48adj.
one 88adj.
unyielding 162adj.
thick 205adj.
material 319adj.
solid body 324n.
dense 324adj.
assenting 488adj.
solidarity
unity 88n.
stability 153n.
cooperation 706n.
association 706n.
concord 710n.
friendship 880n.
solid body
solid body 324n.
solidification
condensation 324n.
refrigeration 382n.
solidify
cohere 48vb.
be dense 324vb.
solidity
substantiality 3n.
completeness 54n.
permanence 144n.
materiality 319n.
density 324n.
opacity 423n.
solid vote
consensus 488n.
soliloquy
soliloquy 585n.
dramaturgy 594n.
solitaire
card game 837n.
gem 844n.
solitary
unconformable 84adj.
alone 88adj.
wanderer 268n.
solitary 883n.
friendless 883adj.
unsociable 883adj.
solitude
unity 88n.
desert 172n.
seclusion 883n.
solmization
notation 410n.
vocal music 412n.
solo
unit 88n.
tune 412n.
soloist
musician 413n.
Solomon
sage 500n.
polygamist 894n.
Solon
sage 500n.
solstice
winter 129n.
solstitial
celestial 321adj.
solubility
mixture 43n.
fluidity 335n.
liquefaction 337n.
soluble
(*see* solubility)
solution
solution 337n.
answer 460n.
discovery 484n.
interpretation 520n.
remedy 658n.
solution of continuity
discontinuity 72n.
solve
decipher 520vb.
solvency
wealth 800n.
solvent
moderator 177n.
liquefaction 337n.
moneyed 800adj.
soma
liquor 301n.
Hindu god 967n.
somatic
material 319adj.
somatics
physics 319n.
somatology
anthropology 371n.
somber
funereal 364adj.
dark 418adj.
soft-hued 425adj.
black 428adj.
gray 429adj.
cheerless 834adj.
some
quantitative 26adj.
partially 33adv.
plurality 101n.
anonymous 562adj.
somebody
substance 3n.
person 371n.
person of repute 866n.
somehow
somehow 158adv.
somehow feel
intuit 476vb.
someone
person 371n.
some place
somewhere 185adv.
some purpose, to
successfully 727adv.
somersault
overturning 221n.
something
substance 3n.
object 319n.
something else
variant 15n.
something for everybody
generality 79n.
something or other
uncertainty 474n.
something over
extra 40n.
redundance 637n.
sometime
former 125adj.
some time or other
not now 122adv.
sometimes
sometimes 139adv.
somewhere
somewhere 185adv.
somewhere else
not here 190adv.
somnambulism
fantasy 513n.
sleep 679n.
somnambulist
pedestrian 268n.
visionary 513n.
somnific
somnific 679adj.
somnipathy
sleep 679n.
somnolence
sleepiness 679n.
son
descendent 170n.
male 372n.
sonant
speech sound 398n.
spoken letter 558adj.
vocal 577adj.
sonantal
sounding 398adj.
sonar
detector 484n.
sonata, sonatina
musical piece 412n.
sone
sound 398n.
metrology 465n.

son et lumière
lighting 420n.
pageant 875n.
song
repetition 106n.
vocal music 412n.
poem 593n.
hymn 981n.
song and dance
loudness 400n.
stage-show 594n.
song-bird
bird 365n.
vocalist 413n.
songbook
vocal music 412n.
song, for a
cheaply 812adv.
songful
musicianly 413adj.
poetic 593adj.
songster
bird 365n.
vocalist 413n.
song-writer
musician 413n.
poet 593n.
sonic
sounding 398adj.
sonic barrier
sound 398n.
sonnet
verse form 593n.
sonneteer
poet 593n.
poetize 593vb.
sonny
darling 890n.
sonometer
acoustics 398n.
sonorant
sounding 398adj.
sonority
sound 398n.
loudness 400n.
resonance 404n.
sonorous
ornate 574adj.
(*see* sonority)
sonship
sequence 65n.
sonship 170n.
sons of Belial
insolent person 878n.
soon
not now 122adv.
prospectively 124adv.
betimes 135adv.
in the future 155adv.
sooner
optionally 605adv.
sooner or later
not now 122adv.
prospectively 124adv.
soot
powder 332n.
ash 381n.
black thing 428n.
dirt 649n.
soothe
assuage 177vb.
remedy 658vb.
make inactive 679vb.
please 826vb.
flatter 925vb.
soothing
deceiving 542adj.
relief 831n.
soothing syrup
moderator 177n.
balm 658n.
relief 831n.
soothsay
divine 511vb.
soothsayer
oracle 511n.
sorcerer 983n.
sooty
dark 418adj.
dim 419adj.
opaque 423adj.
black 428adj.
dirty 649adj.
sop
mouthful 301n.
potion 301n.
moisture 341n.
incentive 612n.
lenity 736n.
sophism
sophism 477n.
sophist
sophist 477n.
intellectual 492n.
sophisticate
mix 43vb.
sophisticate 477vb.
man of taste 846n.
sophistication
mixture 43n.
culture 490n.
impairment 655n.
skill 694n.
good taste 846n.
sophistry
irrelevance 10n.
sophistry 477n.
misteaching 535n.
deception 542n.
wrong 914n.
sophomore
college student 538n.
sophy
sovereign 741n.
soporific
moderator 177n.
anesthetic 375n.
soporific 679n.
relief 831n.
tedious 838adj.
sopping
drenched 341adj.
soppy
foolish 499adj.
ninny 501n.
soprano
vocalist 413n.
sorcerer
diviner 511n.
conjuror 545n.
prodigy 864n.
sorcerer 983n.
occultist 984n.
sorcery
conversion 147n.
thaumaturgy 864n.
sorcery 983n.
occultism 984n.
sordid
avaricious 816adj.
vulgar 847adj.
sordine
silencer 401n.
non-resonance 405n.
mute 414n.
sore
pain 377n.
evil 616n.
bad 645adj.
ulcer 651n.
diseased 651adj.
sensitive 819adj.
painfulness 827n.
discontented 829adj.
resentful 891adj.
sorely
painfully 32adv.
sore point
sensibility 374n.
moral sensibility 819n.
resentment 891n.
sorghum
corn 366n.
sorites
argumentation 475n.
relevance 9n.
sorority
family 11n.
community 708n.
sorrel
horse 273n.
potherb 301n.
brown 430adj.
sorrow
bane 659n.
adversity 731n.
sorrow 825n.
dejection 834n.
lament 836vb.
sorry
unimportant 369adj.

unhappy 825adj.
regretting 830adj.
melancholic 834adj.
repentant 939adj.
sorry sight
painfulness 827n.
sort
class 62vb.
sort 77n.
discriminate 463vb.
sortable
fit 24adj.
sorter
sorting 62n.
mails 531n.
sortes Vergilianae
oracle 511n.
non-design 618n.
sortie
outbreak 176n.
attack 712n.
retaliation 714n.
sortilege
divination 511n.
sorcery 983n.
occultism 984n.
sort out
exclude 57vb.
render few 105vb.
discriminate 463vb.
select 605vb.
sort with
accord 24vb.
S.O.S.
signal 547n.
danger signal 665n.
so-so
moderately 177adv.
imperfect 647adj.
sot
fool 501n.
drunkard 949n.
soteriology
theology 973n.
Sothic cycle
era 110n.
sottish
unintelligent 499adj.
drunken 949adj.
sotto voce
faintly 401adv.
secretly 525adv.
voicelessly 578adv.
sou
small coin 33n.
soubrette
acting 594n.
soufflé
pudding 301n.
sough
lake 346n.
marsh 347n.
drain 351n.
blow, breathe 352n.
sound faint 401vb.
swill 649n.
sought-after
welcomed 882adj.
soul
essence 1n.
essential part 5n.
main part 32n.
interiority 224n.
life 360n.
person 371n.
spirit 447n.
affections 817n.
soulful
feeling 818adj.
soulless
inactive 679adj.
impassive 820adj.
soulmate
spouse 894n.
soul-searching
regret 830n.
honorable 929adj.
soul-stirring
felt 818adj.
exciting 821adj.
sound
regular 83adj.
unyielding 162adj.
depth 211n.
be deep 211vb.
plunge 313vb.
gulf 345vb.
sound 398n., vb.
loudness 400n.
be loud 400adj.
play music 413vb.
inquire 459vb.
interrogate 459vb.
be tentative 461vb.
measure 465vb.
genuine 484adj.
wise 498adj.
access 624n.
valuable 644adj.
beneficial 644adj.
not bad 644adj.
perfect 646adj.
healthy 650adj.
skillful 694adj.
monetary 797adj.
moneyed 800adj.
orthodox 976adj.
sound barrier
sound 398n.
soundbox
phonograph 414n.
sound-detector
detector 484n.
sounding board
gong 414n.
sounding brass
resonance 404n.
unmeaningness 515n.
sounding lead
depth 211n.
soundless
deep 211adj.
still 266adj.
silent 399adj.
sound like
resemble 18vb.
sound mind
sanity 502n.
soundproof
silent 399adj.
non-resonant 405adj.
sound-tape
hearing aid 415n.
sound-track
trace 548n.
soup
soup 301n.
soup-bowl
bowl 194n.
soupçon
small quantity 33n.
tincture 43n.
soup, in the
in difficulties 700adj.
soupspoon
ladle 194n.
soupy
semiliquid 354adj.
sour
unsavory 391adj.
sour 393adj.
unpleasant 827adj.
cause discontent 829vb.
aggravate 832vb.
sullen 893adj.
source
origin 68n.
source 156n.
parentage 169n.
summit 213n.
stream 350n.
informant 524n.
store 632n.
sourdough
experimenter 461n.
sour grapes
impossibility 470n.
pretext 714n.
jealousy 911n.
sourness
malevolence 898n.
(*see* sour)
souse
immerse 303vb.
plunge 313vb.
drench 341vb.
preserve 666vb.
get drunk 949vb.
soutane
tunic 228n.

canonicals 989n.
south
be high 209vb.
compass point 281n.
Southerner, Southron
foreigner 59n.
southing
bearings 186n.
souvenir
reminder 505n.
plaything 837n.
sou'wester
overcoat 228n.
gale 352n.
sovereign
supreme 34adj.
strong 162adj.
remedial 658adj.
successful 727adj.
ruling 733adj.
sovereign 741n.
coinage 797n.
aristocrat 868n.
sovereignty
superiority 34n.
governance 733n.
soviet
council 692n.
sovietism
government 733n.
sow
disperse 75vb.
cause 156vb.
produce 164vb.
let fall 311vb.
pig 365n.
cultivate 370vb.
female animal 373n.
sower
husbandman 370n.
preparer 669n.
sow one's wild oats
revel 837vb.
be wicked 934vb.
be intemperate 943vb.
sow the seed
educate 534vb.
prepare 669vb.
sozzled
tipsy 949adj.
spa
hygiene 652n.
hospital 658n.
space
quantity 26n.
grade 73vb.
time 108n.
opportunity 137n.
space 183n.
room 193n.
size 195n.
distance 199n.
interval 201n.
opening 263n.
air 340n.
storage 632n.
space-dweller
native 191n.
space flight
aeronautics 271n.
space-man
traveler 268n.
aeronaut 271n.
space-ship, space station
space-ship 276n.
satellite 321n.
space-time continuum
universe 321n.
space-traveler
traveler 268n.
aeronaut 271n.
spacious
great 32adj.
spacious 183adj.
large 195adj.
palmy 730adj.
spade
ladle 194n.
make concave 255vb.
transpose 272vb.
shovel 274n.
farm tool 370n.
spaghetti
dish 301n.
spalpeen
bad man 938n.
span
connect 45vb.
bond 47n.
group 74n.
duality 90n.
time 108n.
period 110n.
extend 183vb.
distance 199n.
long measure 203n.
be broad 205vb.
overlie 226vb.
measure 465vb.
bridge 624n.
spandrel
pattern 844n.
church interior 990n.
spangle
variegate 437vb.
finery 844n.
decorate 844vb.
spaniel
dog 365n.
toady 879n.
spank
strike 279vb.
spank 963vb.
spanker
whopper 195n.
sail 275n.
spanner
tool 630n.
spanner in the works
hitch 702n.
spar
hanger 217n.
supporter 218n.
strike 279vb.
bicker 709vb.
pugilism 716n.
spare
additional 38n.
extra 40n.
remaining 41adj.
lean 206adj.
avoid 620vb.
underfed 636adj.
superfluous 637adj.
dispose of 673vb.
not use 674vb.
be lenient 736vb.
not retain 779vb.
give 781vb.
economize 814vb.
relieve 831vb.
show mercy 905vb.
exempt 919vb.
be temperate 942vb.
spare diet
fasting 946n.
spare hours, spare time
opportunity 137n.
leisure 681n.
spare part
extra 40n.
component 58n.
safeguard 662n.
spargefaction
dispersion 75n.
water 339n.
moistening 341n.
sparing
economical 814adj.
parsimonious 816adj.
temperate 942adj.
spark
small quantity 33n.
electricity 160n.
fire 379n.
flash 417n.
luminary 420n.
fop 848n.
lover 887n.
caress 889vb.
sparkle
shine 417vb.
vigor 571n.
cheerfulness 833n.
be witty 839vb.
sparkler
fireworks 420n.
gem 844n.
sparkling
bubbly 355adj.
splendid 841adj.
(*see* sparkle)

spark off
initiate 68vb.
sparring partner
pugilist 722n.
sparrow
bird 365n.
sparse
unassembled 75adj.
few 105adj.
unproductive 172adj.
scarce 636adj.
sparseness, sparsity
insubstantiality 4n.
Spartan
severe 735adj.
abstainer 942n.
temperate 942adj.
ascetic 945adj.
fasting 946adj.
Spartan brevity
conciseness 569n.
spasm
brief span 114n.
fitfulness 142n.
violence 176n.
spasm 318n.
pang 377n.
paralysis 651n.
activity 678n.
feeling 818n.
excitation 821n.
spasmodic
discontinuous 72adj.
unstable 152adj.
(*see* spasm)
spastic
sick person 651n.
spasticity
paralysis 651n.
spat
reproduce itself 164vb.
quarrel 709n.
spate
great quantity 32n.
plenty 635n.
redundance 637n.
spate, in
flowing 350adj.
spatial
spatial 183adj.
spatiotemporal
spatial 183adj.
material 319adj.
spat on
unrespected 921adj.
spats, spatterdashes
legwear 228n.
spatter
disperse 75vb.
emit 300vb.
make unclean 649vb.
defame 926vb.
spatula
shovel 274n.
spavin
animal disease 651n.
spawn
youngling 132n.
reproduce itself 164vb.
posterity 176n.
spawned
born 360adj.
spawning
prolific 171adj.
spay
unman 161vb.
speak
communicate 524vb.
inform 524vb.
divulge 526vb.
signal 547vb.
voice 577vb.
speak 579vb.
speak at
speak to 583vb.
speakeasy
tavern 192n.
speaker
megaphone 400n.
speaker 579n.
master 741n.
speak for
deputize 755vb.
speak for itself
be visible 443vb.
evidence 466vb.
be intelligible 516vb.
be plain 522vb.
speaking of
concerning 9adv.
speaking tube
hearing aid 415n.
speak one's mind
be truthful 540vb.
speak out
be plain 522vb.
speak to
speak to 583vb.
speak up
be loud 400vb.
emphasize 532vb.
speak up for
approve 923vb.
vindicate 927vb.
speak volumes
evidence 466vb.
spear
sharp point 256n.
pierce 263vb.
strike at 712vb.
spear 723n.
spearhead
front 237n.
chief thing 638n.
leader 690n.
attacker 712n.
armed force 722n.
spearman
soldiery 722n.
spearmint
scent 396n.
special
characteristic 5adj.
different 15adj.
unimitative 21adj.
special 80adj.
unconformable 84adj.
special case
non-uniformity 17n.
specialty 80n.
special constable
police 955n.
special correspondent
informant 524n.
newsmonger 529n.
author 589n.
delegate 754n.
special day
special day 876n.
specialism
knowledge 490n.
skill 694n.
specialist
scholar 492n.
doctor 658n.
expert 696n.
specialization
specialty 80n.
specialize
study 536vb.
specialized
instructed 490adj.
expert 694adj.
specially
greatly 32adv.
special pleading
argument 475n.
sophistry 477n.
pretext 614n.
specialty
irrelation 10n.
specialty 80n.
dish 301n.
(*see* special)
specie
coinage 797n.
species
subdivision 53n.
group 74n.
breed 77n.
specific
special 80adj.
means 629n.
remedy 658n.
specification
differentiation 15n.
classification 77n.
particulars 80n.
qualification 468n.
report 524n.
description 590n.

specific gravity
gravity 322n.
density 324n.
specify
class 62vb.
specify 80vb.
indicate 547vb.
name 561vb.
specimen
duplicate 22n.
prototype 23n.
example 83n.
exhibit 522n.
specious
appearing 445adj.
plausible 471adj.
sophistical 477adj.
ostensible 614adj.
splendid 841adj.
affected 850adj.
ostentatious 875adj.
flattering 925adj.
speck, speckle
small thing 33n.
maculation 437n.
variegate 437vb.
blemish 845n.
spectacle
spectacle 445n.
exhibit 522n.
stage show 594n.
beauty 841n.
prodigy 864n.
pageant 875n.
spectacles
eyeglass 442n.
spectacular
well-seen 443adj.
appearing 445n.
showy 875adj.
spectator
presence 189n.
spectator 441n.
specter
visual fallacy 440n.
appearance 445n.
intimidation 854n.
ghost 970n.
specter at the feast, be the
hinder 702vb.
spectral
insubstantial 4adj.
variegated 437adj.
spooky 970adj.
spectrology
optics 417n.
spectroscope
astronomy 321n.
chromatics 425n.
optical device 442n.
spectroscopic
colored 425adj.
spectroscopy
optics 417n.
spectrum
light 417n.
variegation 437n.
color 425n.
speculate
(*see* speculation)
speculation
calculation of chance 159n.
meditation 449n.
empiricism 461n.
conjecture 512n.
gambling 618n.
essay 671n.
undertaking 672n.
trade 791n.
speculative
philosophic 449adj.
thoughtful 449adj.
experimental 461adj.
uncertain 474adj.
suppositional 512adj.
speculative 618adj.
dangerous 661adj.
trading 791adj.
rash 857adj.
speculator
experimenter 461n.
theorist 512n.
gambler 618n.
speculum
mirror 442n.
sped
completed 725adj.
speech
language 557n.
voice 577n.
speech, oration 579n.
allocution 583n.
speech accent
pronunciation 577n.
speech defect
speech defect 580n.
speeches
diffuseness 570n.
speechify
orate 579vb.
speechless
silent 399adj.
voiceless 578adj.
wondering 864adj.
speechless, be
be taciturn 582vb.
speech-making
oratory 579n.
speech sound
speech sound 398n.
speed
motion 265n.
velocity 277n.
facilitate 701vb.
aid 703vb.
speedboat
boat 275n.
speed limit
limit 236n.
speed merchant
speeder 277n.
speedometer
velocity 277n.
meter 465n.
recording instrument 549n.
speed-rate
velocity 277n.
speed-track
path, road 624n.
speed-trap
velocity 277n.
speed-up
spurt 277n.
speed well
succeed 727vb.
speedwriting
writing 586n.
speedy
speedy 277adj.
speer
interrogate 459vb.
speleology
descent 309n.
mineralogy 359n.
search 459n.
discovery 484n.
sport 837n.
spell
period 110n.
influence 178n.
predict 511vb.
mean 514vb.
interpret 520vb.
imply 523vb.
study 536vb.
indicate 547vb.
spell 558vb.
malediction 899n.
spell 983n.
spellbind
orate 579vb.
motivate 612vb.
be wonderful 864vb.
bewitch 983vb.
spellbinder
speaker 579n.
sorcerer 983n.
spellbound
induced 612adj.
wondering 864adj.
bewitched 983adj.
spelling
spelling 558n.
spell out
decipher 520vb.
spelt
corn 366n.
speluncar

concave 255adj.
spencer
overcoat, vest 228n.
spend
emit 300vb.
waste 634vb.
use 673vb.
expend 806vb.
spender
prodigal 815n.
spending spree
prodigality 815n.
spendthrift
prodigal 815n.
intemperate 943adj.
spend time
pass time 108vb.
spent
weakened 163adj.
outgoing 298adj.
fatigued 684adj.
lost 772adj.
expended 806adj.
spent fires
inertness 175n.
sperm
source 156n.
genitalia 164n.
fertilizer 171n.
spermaceti
fat 357n.
spermatic
generative 171adj.
spermatozoa
genitalia 164n.
spew
eject, vomit 300vb.
sphagnum
plant 366n.
sphere
group 74n.
classification 77n.
range 183n.
region 184n.
abode 192n.
sphere 252n.
function 622n.
spherical
round 250adj.
rotund 252adj.
sphericity
rotundity 252n.
convexity 253n.
sphery
rotund 252adj.
celestial 321adj.
spheterize
appropriate 786vb.
sphinx
rara avis 84n.
oracle 511n.
sphinxlike
unintelligible 517adj.
spica
prickle 256n.
spice
small quantity 33n.
tincture 43n.
mix 43vb.
stimulant 174n.
cook 301vb.
season 388vb.
condiment 389n.
appetize 390vb.
preserver 666n.
pleasurableness 826n.
spicery
condiment 389n.
scent 396n.
spicilegium
anthology 592n.
spick and span
clean 648adj.
spicula
prickle 256n.
spiculate
sharpen 256vb.
spicy
tasty 386adj.
pungent 388adj.
savory 390adj.
fragrant 396adj.
exciting 821adj.
impure 951adj.
spider
weaving 222n.
planner 623n.
spiderman
elevation 310n.
spider's web
complexity 61n.
ambush 527n.
spidery
lean 206adj.
spiel
speak 579vb.
spieler
trickster 545n.
speaker 579n.
spiffing
topping 644adj.
spigot
stopper 264n.
spike
disable 161vb.
vertex 213n.
sharp point 256n.
pierce 263vb.
stopper 264n.
defenses 713n.
spikenard
unguent 357n.
spiky
sharp 256adj.
Anglican 976adj.
pietistic 979adj.
spill
filament 208n.
overturning 221n.
flow out 298vb.
emit 300vb.
let fall 311vb.
make flow 350vb.
lighter 385n.
torch 420n.
waste 634vb.
spilled milk
loss 772n.
spill over
overstep 306vb.
spill the beans
divulge 526vb.
spillway
waterfall 350n.
conduit 351n.
spin
weave 222vb.
aeronautics 271n.
rotation 315n.
fake 541vb.
spinach
vegetable 301n.
spinal
supporting 218adj.
central 225adj.
back 238adj.
spin a web
be cunning 698vb.
spin a yarn
be untrue 543vb.
exaggerate 546vb.
describe 590vb.
spindle
pivot 218n.
rotator 315n.
spindle-shaped
tapering 256adj.
spindly
lean 206adj.
spindrift
moisture 341n.
bubble 355n.
spine
supporter 218n.
pillar 218n.
centrality 225n.
rear 238n.
prickle 256n.
spineless
impotent 161adj.
weak 163adj.
spinet
piano 414n.
spinnaker
sail 275n.
spinner
weaving 222n.
rotator 315n.
spinney
wood 366n.

spinning jenny
rotator 315n.
spinning wheel
rotator 315n.
spin of the coin
chance 159n.
spinosity
sharpness 256n.
spin out
continuate 71vb.
spin out 113vb.
be diffuse 570vb.
be loquacious 581vb.
spinster
woman 373n.
spinster 895n.
spinsterhood
celibacy 895n.
spin words
show style 566vb.
spiny
sharp 256adj.
spiracle
orifice 263n.
outlet 298n.
air-pipe 353n.
spiral
coil 251n.
twine 251vb.
ascend 308vb.
tumble 309vb.
rotation 315n.
spirant
speech sound 398n.
spirantal
sounding 398adj.
spire
high structure 209n.
vertex 213n.
summit 213n.
twine 251vb.
sharp point 256n.
ascend 308vb.
church exterior 990n.
spirit
insubstantial thing 4n.
temperament 5n.
vigorousness 174n.
life 360n.
fuel 385n.
spirit 447n.
meaning 514n.
vigor 571n.
cleanser 648n.
restlessness 678n.
affections 817n.
moral sensibility 819n.
courage 855n.
ghost 970n.
spirit away
steal 788vb.
spirit body
spiritualism 984n.
spirited
lively 819adj.
cheerful 833adj.
courageous 855adj.
spiritism
spiritualism 984n.
spirit-laying
sorcery 983n.
spiritless
apathetic 820adj.
inexcitable 823adj.
melancholic 834adj.
cowardly 856adj.
spirit-level
horizontality 216n.
spirit of the age
tendency 179n.
spirit-raising
sorcery 983n.
spirit-rapping
spiritualism 984n.
spirits
liquor 301n.
tonic 658n.
cheerfulness 833n.
spirits, the
the dead 361n.
spiritual
immaterial 320adj.
psychic 447adj.
divine 965adj.
religious 973adj.
pious 979adj.
priestly 985adj.
spiritual adviser
pastor 986n.
spiritual comfort
church ministry 985n.
spiritualism
immateriality 320n.
spirit 447n.
occultism 984n.
spiritualism 984n.
spiritualist
occultist 984n.
spiritualistic
psychic 447adj.
spooky 970adj.
psychical 984adj.
spirituality
immateriality 320n.
virtue 933n.
sanctity 979n.
spiritualize
disembody 320vb.
make pious 979vb.
sanctify 979vb.
spiritual life
sanctity 979n.
spirituous
edible 301adj.
intoxicating 949adj.
spirit-writing
spiritualism 984n.
spirit
flow out 298vb.
(*see* spurt)
spissitude
density 324n.
semiliquidity 354n.
spit
projection 254n.
sharp point 256n.
perforator 263n.
pierce 263vb.
emit, eruct 300vb.
excrement 302n.
rotator 315n.
effervesce 318vb.
hiss 406vb.
be angry 891vb.
be sullen 893vb.
threaten 900vb.
disapprove 924vb.
spit and polish
cleanness 648n.
formality 875n.
spite
quarrelsomeness 709n.
severity 735n.
oppress 735vb.
enmity 881n.
hatred 888n.
resentment 891n.
malevolence 898n.
revengefulness 910n.
envy 912n.
detraction 926n.
spiteful
harmful 645adj.
(*see* spite)
spite of, in
in defiance of 25adv.
although 182adv.
nevertheless 488adv.
with difficulty 700adv.
in opposition 704adv.
spitfire
violent creature 176n.
shrew 892n.
spit of
analogue 18n.
spit on
not respect 921vb.
spit out
eject 300vb.
spittle
excrement 302n.
spittoon
bowl 194n.
spiv
idler 679n.
spivery
improbity 930n.
splanchnology
structure 331n.

splash
small quantity 33n.
water 339n.
moisten 341vb.
lake 346n.
flow 350vb.
sibilation 406n.
color 425n.
advertise 528vb.
make important 638vb.
make unclean 649vb.
ostentation 875n.
splashboard
shelter 662n.
splay
diverge 294vb.
splay-footed
deformed 246adj.
spleen
insides 224n.
discontent 829n.
melancholy 834n.
sullenness 893n.
envy 912n.
spleenful
hating 888adj.
resentful 891adj.
irascible 892adj.
malevolent 898adj.
spleenless
benevolent 897adj.
splendid
luminous 417adj.
excellent 644adj.
liberal 813adj.
pleasurable 826adj.
splendid 841adj.
noteworthy 866adj.
ostentatious 875adj.
splendor
light 417n.
beauty 841n.
prestige 866n.
ostentation 875n.
splenetic
(*see* spleenful)
splice
tie 45vb.
cross 222vb.
intromit 231vb.
repair 656vb.
marry 894vb.
splice-joint
joint 45n.
spline
strip 208n.
splint
supporter 218n.
hardness 326n.
surgical dressing 658n.
splinter
break 46vb.
piece 53n.
be brittle 330vb.
splinter group
dissentient 489n.
party 708n.
revolter 738n.
splintery
brittle 330adj.
split
disjunction 46n.
discontinuity 72n.
bisect 92vb.
gap 201n.
open 263vb.
be brittle 330vb.
inform 524vb.
divulge 526vb.
dissension 709n.
apportion 783vb.
split hairs
discriminate 463vb.
sophisticate 477vb.
be fastidious 862vb.
split personality
psychopathy 503n.
split second
instant 116n.
split the difference
average out 30vb.
splotch
blemish 845n.
splurge
ostentation 875n.
splutter
emit 300vb.
flow 350vb.
hiss 406vb.
stammer 580vb.
haste 680n.
spoil
derange 63vb.
weaken 163vb.
lay waste 165vb.
impair 655vb.
be clumsy 695vb.
hinder 702vb.
trophy 729n.
be lenient 736vb.
rob 788vb.
booty 790n.
make ugly 842vb.
blemish 845vb.
pet 889vb.
spoilage
decrement 42n.
spoiled child
satiety 863n.
favorite 890n.
spoiler
hinderer 702n.
taker 786n.
robber 789n.
evildoer 904n.
spoiling for
willing 597adj.
spoilsport
dissuasion 613n.
meddler 678n.
hinderer 702n.
disapprover 924n.
spoke
line 203n.
divergence 294n.
spoken
linguistic 577adj.
spokeshave
sharp edge 256n.
spokesman
interpreter 520n.
informant 524n.
messenger 531n.
speaker 579n.
agent 686n.
deputy 755n.
spoliation
spoliation 788n.
spondaic
poetic 593adj.
sponge
porosity 263n.
absorb 299vb.
drier 342n.
obliteration 550n.
cleaning utensil 648n.
beg 761vb.
fleece 786vb.
toady 879n.
be servile 879vb.
drunkard 949n.
sponger
idler 679n.
beggar 763n.
toady 879n.
sponging house
prison 748n.
spongy
concave 255adj.
porous 265adj.
rare 325adj.
soft 327adj.
marshy 347adj.
pulpy 356adj.
sponsor
witness 466n.
patronize 703vb.
sponsorship
aid 703n.
security 767n.
spontaneity
spontaneity 609n.
non-design 618n.
non-preparation 670n.
feeling 818n.
spontaneous

intuitive 476adj.
involuntary 596adj.
voluntary 597adj.
artless 699adj.
(*see* spontaneity)
spoof
deceive 542vb.
spoofer
trickster 545n.
spook
ghost 970n.
spoon
ladle 194n.
shovel 274n.
extractor 304n.
caress 889vb.
spoonerism
inversion 221n.
absurdity 497n.
neology 560n.
witticism 839n.
ridiculousness 849n.
spoonfeed
manage 689vb.
be lax 734vb.
be lenient 736vb.
pet 889vb.
spoonfeeding
teaching 534n.
aid 703n.
spoonful
small quantity 33n.
spooning
love-making 887n.
wooing 889n.
spoor
identification 547n.
trace 548n.
sporadic
unassembled 75adj.
infrequent 140adj.
uncertain 474adj.
sporran
skirt 228n.
sport
misfit 25n.
nonconformist 84n.
athletics 162n.
wear 228vb.
show 522vb.
exercise 682n.
contest 716n.
merriment 833n.
sport 837n.
laughing-stock 851n.
prodigy 864n.
be ostentatious 875vb.
gentleman 929n.
good man 937n.
sporting
(*see* sportsmanlike)
sporting chance
fair chance 159n.
probability 471n.
sportive
gay 833adj.
amused 837adj.
amusing 837adj.
witty 839adj.
sportsman
hunter 619n.
player 837n.
gentleman 929n.
sportsmanlike
just 913adj.
honorable 929adj.
sportsmanship
sport 837n.
probity 929n.
sportulary
recipient 782n.
sporty
amused 837adj.
sporule
powder 332n.
spot
small thing 33n.
place 185n.
variegate 437vb.
detect 484vb.
understand 516vb.
defect 647n.
make unclean 649vb.
impair 655vb.
pattern 844n.
blemish 845n.
slur 867n.
spot cash
money 797n.
spot, in a
in difficulties 700adj.
spotless
perfect 646adj.
clean 648adj.
innocent 935adj.
pure 950adj.
spotlight
lighting 420n.
manifest 522vb.
advertisement 528n.
theater 594n.
spot, on the
instantaneously 116adv.
at present 121adv.
on the spot 189adj.
near 200adj.
spots
skin disease 651n.
spotter
spectator 441n.
spotty
mottled 347adj.
diseased 651adj.
blemished 845adj.
spousal
wedding 894n.
spouse
spouse 894n.
spouseless
unwedded 895adj.
spout
orifice 263n.
outlet 298n.
flow 350vb.
conduit 351n.
orate 579vb.
sprachgefühl
linguistics 557n.
style 566n.
sprain
derange 63vb.
disable 161vb.
weaken 163vb.
distort 246vb.
sprat
animalcule 196n.
table fish 365n.
sprawl
be horizontal 216vb.
tumble 309vb.
repose 683vb.
sprawl over
fill 54vb.
be dispersed 75vb.
spray
branch 53n.
disperse 75vb.
vaporizer 338n.
moisture 341n.
irrigator 341n.
bubble 355n.
foliage 366n.
spread
be 1vb.
grow 36vb.
dispersion 75n.
generalize 79vb.
range 183n.
pervade 189vb.
expansion 197n.
flatten 216vb.
overlay 226vb.
progress 285vb.
diverge 294vb.
meal 301n.
advertisement 528n.
publish 528vb.
spread canvas
navigate 269vb.
start out 296vb.
spreadeagle
lengthen 203vb.
diverge 294vb.
punish 963vb.
spreadeagleism
boasting 877n.
spreading
influential 178adj.

spacious 183adj.
prolix 570adj.
spread out
lengthen 203vb.
spread over
fill 54vb.
spread the carpet
celebrate 876vb.
spread the table
make ready 669vb.
spree
revel 837n.
drunkenness 949n.
sprig
branch 53n.
young plant 132n.
foliage 366n.
sprightly
active 678adj.
cheerful 833adj.
spring
period 110n.
spring 128n.
vernal 128adj.
young plant 132n.
source 156n.
energy 160n.
strength 162n.
be weak 163vb.
coil 251n.
spurt 277n.
move fast 277vb.
recoil 280n.
outflow 298n.
lifter 310n.
leap 312n., vb.
elasticity 328n.
be elastic 328vb.
stream 350n.
motive 612n.
machine 630n.
take 786vb.
spring a mine
surprise 508vb.
besiege 712vb.
spring apart
be disjoined 46vb.
spring-balance
scales 322n.
springboard
recoil 280n.
lifter 310n.
fluctuation 317n.
aider 703n.
springbok
jumper 312n.
deer 365n.
spring-clean
clean 648vb.
springe
trap 542n.
springer
supporter 218n.
spring from
result 157vb.
spring-gun
trap 542n.
springing line
obliquity 220n.
springless
rigid 326adj.
tough 329adj.
spring tide
great quantity 32n.
increase 36n.
high water 204n.
current 350n.
springtide, springtime
spring 128n.
salad days 130n.
spring up
become 1vb.
begin 68vb.
happen 154vb.
expand 197vb.
ascend 308vb.
lift oneself 310vb.
leap 312vb.
be visible 443vb.
spring upon
surprise 508vb.
springy
soft 327adj.
elastic 328adj.
sprinkle
small quantity 33n.
mix 43vb.
disperse 75vb.
emit 300vb.
let fall 311vb.
moisten 341vb.
rain 350vb.
variegate 437vb.
sprinkler
irrigator 341n.
extinguisher 382n.
cleaning utensil 648n.
sprint
spurt 277n.
racing 716n.
sprit
projection 245n.
sprite
elf 970n.
sprocket
tooth 256n.
sprout
grow 36vb.
young plant 132n.
reproduce itself 164vb.
descendent 170n.
expand 197vb.
vegetate 366vb.
sprouts
vegetable 301n.
spruce
tree 366n.
clean 648adj., vb.
personable 841adj.
sprung
soft 327adj.
elastic 328adj.
sprung rhythm
prosody 593n.
spry
active 678adj.
cheerful 833adj.
spud
shovel 274n.
tuber 301n.
spume
effervesce 318vb.
bubble 355n., vb.
spumy
bubbly 355adj.
white 427adj.
spunk
vigorousness 174n.
lighter 385n.
courage 855n.
spunkless
cowardly 856adj.
spunky
courageous 855adj.
spur
branch 53n.
stimulant 174n.
high land 209n.
projection 254n.
sharp point 256n.
accelerate 277vb.
impel, kick 279vb.
incentive 612n.
hasten 680vb.
animate 821vb.
spurge
plant 366n.
spurious
false 541adj.
spurious 542adj.
bastard 954adj.
spurn
kick 279vb.
reject 607vb.
despise 922vb.
spur of the moment
spontaneity 609n.
spur of the moment, on the
instantaneously 116adv.
at present 121adv.
incidentally 137adv.
extempore 609adv.
hastily 680adv.
spurs
badge of rank 743n.
honors 866n.

spurt
increase 36n.
brief span 114n.
vigorousness 174n.
outbreak 176n.
accelerate 277vb.
progression 285n.
flow out 298vb.
emit 300vb.
ascend 308vb.
flow 350vb.
activity 678n.
haste 680n.
sputnik
space-ship 276n.
satellite 321n.
sputter
emit 300vb.
be agitated 318vb.
hiss 406vb.
be dim 419vb.
stammer 580vb.
sputum
excrement 302n.
spy
see, scan 438vb.
spectator 441n.
inquisitor 453n.
be curious 453vb.
secret service 459n.
detective 459n.
informer 524n.
warner 664n.
spy-glass
telescope 442n.
spy-mania
inquiry 459n.
phobia 854n.
spy-ring
secret service 459n.
squab
youngling 132n.
fleshy 195adj.
short 204adj.
thick 205adj.
cushion 218n.
bird 365n.
squabble
quarrel 709n.
squad
band 74n.
personnel 686n.
formation 722n.
squadron
band 74n.
shipping 275n.
formation 722n.
air force 722n.
navy 722n.
squalid
unclean 649adj.
beggarly 801adj.
graceless 842adj.
disreputable 867adj.
squall
gale 352n.
cry 408n.
weep 836vb.
squally
windy 352adj.
squalor
uncleanness 649n.
poverty 801n.
ugliness 842n.
squamation
stratification 207n.
squamous
layered 207adj.
dermal 226adj.
squander
consume 165vb.
waste 634vb.
make insufficient 636vb.
misuse 675vb.
lose 772vb.
be prodigal 815vb.
squandermania
prodigality 815n.
square
uniform 16adj.
equal 28adj.
compensate 31vb.
regular 81adj.
make conform 83vb.
do sums 86vb.
quaternity 96n.
quadruple 97vb.
place 185n.
housing 192n.
fleshy 195adj.
verticality 215n.
efform 243vb.
angular figure 247vb.
unsharpened 257adj.
navigate 269vb.
bribe 612vb.
formation 722n.
just 913adj.
honorable 929adj.
square accounts
pay 804vb.
account 808vb.
square accounts with
pay 804vb.
squared
symmetrical 245adj.
square measure
measure 183n.
square peg in a round hole
misfit 25n.
square root
numerical element 85n.
square up to
fight 716vb.
square with
accord 24vb.
squash
suppress 165vb.
flatten 216vb.
strike 279vb.
vegetables 301n.
abase 311vb.
soften 327vb.
marsh 347n.
semiliquidity 354n.
pulpiness 356n.
ball game 837n.
humiliate 872vb.
social gathering 882n.
squashy
soft 327adj.
fluidal 335adj.
humid 341adj.
marshy 347adj.
semiliquid 354adj.
pulpy 356adj.
squat
place oneself 187vb.
dwell 192vb.
dwarfish 196adj.
short 204adj.
thick 205adj.
low 210adj.
encroach 306vb.
sit down 311vb.
possess 773vb.
appropriate 786vb.
squatter
intruder 59n.
resident 191n.
possessor 776n.
usurper 916n.
squaw
woman 373n.
spouse 894n.
squawk
stridor 407n.
ululation 409n.
squeak
sound faint 401vb.
stridor 407n.
cry 408n.
ululation 409n.
deprecation 762n.
discontent 829n.
squeaker
informer 524n.
squeaky
strident 407adj.
squeal
cry 408n.
inform 524vb.
divulge 526vb.
squealer
informer 524n.

tergiversator 603n.
knave 938n.
squeamish
unwilling 598adj.
irresolute 601adj.
sick 651adj.
disliking 861adj.
fastidiousness 862adj.
honorable 929adj.
prudish 950adj.
squeegee
cleaning utensil 648n.
squeeze
copy 22n.
compression 198n.
touch 378vb.
obstruct 702vb.
oppress 735vb.
compel 740vb.
restriction 747n.
levy 786vb.
endearment 889n.
caress 889vb.
squeeze from, squeeze out
extract 304vb.
squeeze in
fill 54vb.
stow 187vb.
squelch
suppress 165vb.
be wet 341vb.
sibilation 406n.
squelchy
soft 327adj.
humid 341adj.
marshy 347n.
semiliquid 354adj.
squib
bang 402n.
the press 528n.
satire 851n.
calumny 926n.
squid
fish 365n.
squiggle
coil 251n.
punctuation 547n.
squilgee
cleaning utensil 648n.
squinny
gaze, scan 438vb.
squint
obliquity 220n.
window 263n.
look 438n.
dim sight 440n.
church interior 990n.
squire
accompany 89vb.
minister to 703vb.
retainer 742n.
serve 742vb.
aristocrat 868n.
be servile 879vb.
lover 887n.
court 889vb.
squirearchy
aristocracy 868n.
squire of dames
fop 848n.
lover 887n.
libertine 952n.
squirm
wriggle 251vb.
feel pain 377vb.
suffer 825vb.
be servile 879vb.
squirrel
rodent 365n.
squirt
emit 300vb.
irrigator 341n.
squirt in
infuse 303vb.
squit
nonentity 639n.
sruti
non-Biblical scripture 975n.
revelation 975n.
stab
pierce 263vb.
kill 362vb.
give pain 377vb.
wound 655n., vb.
therapy 658n.
strike at 712vb.
suffering 825n.
stabilimeter
stabilizer 153n.
stability
equilibrium 28n.
durability 113n.
stability 153n.
stabilize
equalize 28vb.
stabilize 153vb.
stabilizer
stabilizer 153n.
stable
group 74n.
strong 162adj.
stable 192n.
chamber 194n.
horse 273n.
groom 369vb.
inexcitable 823adj.
(*see* stability)
stable-boy
animal husbandry 369n.
servant 742n.
stable-companion
concomitant 89n.
chum 880n.
stack
great quantity 32n.
bunch 74n.
store 632n., vb.
staddle
stand 218n.
stade
long measure 203n.
stadholder
governor 741n.
stadium
meeting place 192n.
racing 716n.
arena 724n.
staff
supporter 218n.
employ 622vb.
personnel 686n.
director 690n.
club 723n.
master 741n.
army officer 741n.
domestic 742n.
badge of rule 743n.
vestments 989n.
staff college
training school 539n.
council 692n.
staff-work
arrangement 62n.
management 689n.
art of war 718n.
stag
deer 365n.
male animal 372n.
gambler 618n.
purchaser 792n.
stage
juncture 8n.
relativeness 9n.
degree 27n.
serial place 73n.
situation 186n.
layer 207n.
stand 218n.
stage-coach 274n.
goal 295n.
show 522vb.
rostrum 539n.
drama, theater 594n.
dramatize 594vb.
arena 724n.
stage-coach
stage-coach 274n.
stage-craft
dramaturgy 594n.
stage-directions
dramaturgy 594n.
stage-door
theater 594n.
stage effect
pageant 875n.
stage-fright

acting 594n.
fear 854n.
stage-manager
stage-manager 594n.
stage-set
spectacle 445n.
stage-set 594n.
stage show
stage show 594n.
stage-struck
dramatic 594adj.
stage trick
pageant 815n.
stage-whisper
voice 577n.
speak low 578vb.
dramaturgy 594n.
stagger
grade 73vb.
vary 152vb.
obliquity 220n.
walk 267vb.
move slowly 278vb.
tumble 309vb.
oscillate 317vb.
be agitated 318vb.
surprise 508vb.
dissuade 613vb.
be fatigued 684vb.
impress 821vb.
be wonderful 864vb.
be drunk 949vb.
staggers
spasm 318n.
animal disease 651n.
stagnant, stagnate
(*see* stagnation)
stagnation
unproductivity 172n.
inertness 175n.
quiescence 266n.
non-use 674n.
inaction 677n.
inactivity 679n.
moral insensibility 820n.
stag-party
male 372n.
social gathering 882n.
stagy
dramatic 594adj.
affected 850adj.
showy 875adj.
staid
wise 498adj.
inexcitable 823adj.
serious 834adj.
stain
tincture 43n.
coat 226vb.
pigment 425n.
decolorize 426vb.
variegate 437vb.
mark 547vb.
trace 548n.
obliteration 550n.
defect 647n.
dirt 649n.
blemish 845n., vb.
slur 867n.
stained glass
screen 421n.
variegation 437n.
church interior 990n.
stainless
clean 648adj.
honorable 929adj.
virtuous 933adj.
innocent 935adj.
stair
degree 27n.
stand 218n.
ascent 308n.
staircase
series 71n.
ascent 308n.
access 624n.
stair-head
vertex 213n.
stake
fastening 47n.
furnace 383n.
gambling 618n.
endanger 661vb.
undertaking 672n.
contend 716vb.
promise 764vb.
security 767n.
property 777n.
portion 783n.
means of execution 964n.
stake a claim
claim 915vb.
stake, at
dangerous 661adj.
stakeboat
departure 296n.
stake-holder
consignee 754n.
stake-money
security 767n.
stake out
limit 236vb.
stakes
contest 716n.
Stakhanovism
assiduity 678n.
overactivity 678n.
Stakhanovite
busy person 678n.
worker 686n.
stalactite
pendant 217n.
stalag
prison camp 748n.
stale
repeated 106adj.
antiquated 127adj.
excrete 302adj.
tasteless 387adj.
fetid 397adj.
feeble 572adj.
insalubrious 653adj.
impair 655vb.
use 673vb.
fatigued 684adj.
cheapen 812vb.
make insensitive 820vb.
tedious 838adj.
dull 840adj.
stalemate
draw 28n.
stop 145n.
obstacle 702n.
parry 713vb.
non-completion 726n.
staleness
(*see* stale)
Stalinism
despotism 733n.
brute force 735n.
stalk
source 156n.
supporter 218n.
cylinder 252n.
gait 265n.
walk 267vb.
foliage 366n.
hunt 619vb.
stalk abroad
be general 79vb.
stalker
hunter 619n.
stalking horse
ambush 527n.
pretext 614n.
stall
put off 136vb.
halt 145n., vb.
stable 192n.
compartment 194n.
seat 218n.
fly 271vb.
theater 594n.
obstruct 702vb.
parry 713vb.
shop 796n.
church interior 990n.
stallion
horse 273n.
male animal 372n.
stall-keeper
peddler 794n.
stalls
onlookers 441n.
stalwart
stalwart 162adj.

fleshy 195adj.
healthy 650adj.
colleague 707n.
stamina
strength 162n.
resolution 599n.
stamina 600n.
courage 855n.
stammer
speech defect 580n.
be clumsy 695vb.
show feeling 818vb.
stamp
character 5n.
modality 7n.
uniformity 16n.
mold 23n.
sort 77n.
make conform 83vb.
form 243n.
make concave 255vb.
gait 265n.
walk 267vb.
knock 279n.
be loud 400vb.
endorse 488vb.
label 547n.
gesticulate 547vb.
picture 553n.
engrave 555vb.
print 587vb.
correspondence 588n.
title-deed 767n.
mint 799vb.
be angry 891vb.
applaud 923vb.
stamp-collector
collector 492n.
stamp down
flatten 216vb.
stampede
defeat 728n.
fear 854n., vb.
frighten 854vb.
stamping ground
home 192n.
stamp on
suppress 165vb.
kick 279vb.
be severe 735vb.
stamp out
suppress 165vb.
extinguish 382vb.
subjugate 745vb.
stance
form 243n.
stanch
close 264vb.
dry 342vb.
stanch 350vb.
repair 656vb.
obstruct 702vb.
restrain 747vb.
(*see* staunch)
stand
be 1vb.
be in a state 7vb.
last 113vb.
pend 136vb.
stay 144vb.
cease 145vb.
be stable 153vb.
be situate 186vb.
place 187vb.
be present 189vb.
meeting place 192n.
be vertical 215vb.
stand 218n.
support 218vb.
be quiescent 266vb.
view 438n.
be proved 478vb.
supposition 512n.
suffice 635n.
difficulty 700n.
opposition 704n.
resistance 715n.
offer oneself 759vb.
give 781vb.
defray 804vb.
be patient 823vb.
stand about
wait 136vb.
stand a chance
be likely 471vb.
standard
uniform 16adj.
prototype 23n.
degree 27n.
median 30adj.
general 79adj.
rule 81n.
typical 83adj.
high structure 209n.
stand 218n.
testing agent 461n.
gauge 465n.
class 538n.
flag 547n.
paragon 646n.
right 913adj.
standard-bearer
soldier 722n.
standardization
uniformity 16n.
standardize
order 60vb.
regularize 62vb.
make conform 83vb.
standards
morals 917n.
stand aside
recede 290vb.
resign 753vb.
stand by
be present 189vb.
be near 200vb.
await 507vb.
not act 677vb.
patronize 703vb.
defend 713vb.
observe faith 768vb.
stand-by
means 629n.
aider 703n.
colleague 707n.
stand down
resign 753vb.
stand for
be 1vb.
steer for 281vb.
mean 514vb.
deputize 755vb.
stand forth
be visible 443vb.
stand-in
substitute 150n.
actor 594n.
deputy 755n.
standing
state 7n.
circumstance 8n.
degree 27n.
serial place 73n.
permanent 144adj.
unceasing 145adj.
fixed 153adj.
vertical 215adj.
prestige 866n.
standing order
rule 81n.
permanence 144n.
practice 610n.
legislation 953n.
standing start
start 68n.
slowness 278n.
standing water
lake 346n.
stand in the corner
do penance 941vb.
stand in the stead of
deputize 755vb.
stand in the way
hinder 702vb.
stand of arms
arsenal 723n.
stand off
be distant 199vb.
recede 290vb.
make inactive 679vb.
not retain 779vb.
standoffish
prideful 871adj.
unsociable 883adj.
stand on
be supported 218vb.
stand on ceremony

show respect 920vb.
stand one in good stead
be useful 640vb.
stand on one's dignity
be proud 871vb.
stand on one's head
be inverted 221vb.
stand out
jut 254vb.
be visible 443vb.
be plain 522vb.
be obstinate 602vb.
resist 715vb.
stand over
pend 136vb.
stand pat
stay 144vb.
be quiescent 266vb.
be obstinate 602vb.
standpipe
current 350n.
conduit 351n.
extinguisher 382n.
standpoint
situation 186n.
view 438n.
supposition 512n.
standstill
stop 145n.
lull 145n.
stand the test
be true 494vb.
be good 644vb.
stand to
be liable 180vb.
be quiescent 266vb.
invigilate 457vb.
stand together
concur 181vb.
stand to reason
be certain 473vb.
be reasonable 475vb.
be proved 478vb.
be plain 522vb.
be right 913vb.
stand trial
stand trial 959vb.
stand up
be vertical 215vb.
lift oneself 310vb.
stand up for
safeguard 660vb.
patronize 703vb.
approve 923vb.
vindicate 927vb.
stand up to
support 218vb.
defy 711vb.
stand well
command respect 920vb.
stang
supporter 218n.
stannary
workshop 687n.
stanza
verse form 593n.
stapes
ear 415n.
staple
fastening 47n.
main part 52n.
source 156n.
hanger 217n.
texture 331n.
important 638adj.
mart 796n.
stapler
perforator 263n.
star
come first 34vb.
diverge 294vb.
star 321n.
be brittle 330vb.
luminary 420n.
guide 520n.
signpost 547n.
punctuation 547n.
actor 594n.
dramatize 594vb.
bigwig 638n.
exceller 644n.
decoration 729n.
badge of rank 743n.
desired object 859n.
honors 866n.
person of repute 866n.
favorite 890n.
starboard
dextrality 241n.
starch
smooth 258vb.
food content 301n.
harden 326vb.
thickening 354n.
clean 648vb.
Star Chamber
council 692n.
law-court 956n.
starchy
rigid 326adj.
semiliquid 354adj.
affected 850adj.
prideful 871adj.
formal 875adj.
star-crossed
unfortunate 731adj.
stardom
prestige 866n.
stare
gaze 438vb.
watch 441vb.
be curious 453vb.
wonder 864vb.
be rude 885vb.
stare one in the face
impend 155vb.
be plain 522vb.
star-gazer
astronomy 321n.
spectator 441n.
inattention 456n.
stark
absolute 32adj.
completely 54adv.
uncovered 229adj.
rigid 326adj.
manifest 522adj.
plain 573adj.
starless
unlit 418adj.
starlight
star 321n.
light 417n.
glimmer 419n.
luminary 420n.
starlit
undimmed 417adj.
starring
noteworthy 866adj.
starry
celestial 321adj.
undimmed 417adj.
starry-eyed
happy 824adj.
hoping 852adj.
stars
influence 178n.
fate 596n.
start
vantage 34n.
be disjoined 46vb.
start 68n.
cause 156vb.
open 263vb.
impel 279vb.
departure 296n.
leap 312vb.
agitation 318n.
inexpectation 508n.
hunt 619vb.
fear 854vb.
start again
revert 148vb.
starter
contender 716n.
starting-point
start 68n.
departure 296n.
premise 475n.
starting-post
departure 296n.
startle
surprise 508vb.
raise the alarm 665vb.
excite 821vb.

frighten 854vb.
be wonderful 864vb.
start out
jut 254vb.
start out 296vb.
star trap
stage-set 594n.
start up
grow 36vb.
initiate 68vb.
happen 154vb.
operate 173vb.
jut 254vb.
star turn
stage show 594n.
starvation
scarcity 636n.
fasting 946n.
starve
weaken 163vb.
make thin 206vb.
be poor 801vb.
be parsimonious 816vb.
be hungry 859vb.
starve 946vb.
starveling
lean 206adj.
underfed 636adj.
poor man 801n.
starving
necessitous 627adj.
statant
heraldic 547n.
state
state 7n.
eventuality 154n.
territory 184n.
situation 186n.
nation 371n.
inform 524vb.
affirm 532vb.
community 708n.
polity 733n.
lands 777n.
formality 875n.
state assistance
subvention 703n.
state control
governance 733n.
statecraft
management 689n.
state enterprise
trade 791n.
statehood
nation 371n.
independence 744n.
stateless person
wanderer 268n.
outcaste 883n.
stately
rhetorical 574adj.
impressive 821adj.
beautiful 841adj.
well-bred 848adj.
worshipful 866adj.
formal 875adj.
proud 871adj.
statement
list 87n.
musical piece 412n.
topic 452n.
testimony 466n.
report 524n.
affirmation 532n.
description 590n.
pretext 614n.
accounts 808adj.
state of affairs
affairs 154n.
state of grace
innocence 935n.
sanctity 979n.
state of, in a
conditionate 7adj.
state of mind
affections 817n.
state of nature
bareness 229n.
state of war
belligerency 718n.
enmity 881n.
state one's terms
bargain 791vb.
state ownership
joint possession 775n.
stateroom
chamber 194n.
state's evidence
testimony 466n.
disclosure 526n.
states-general
parliament 692n.
statesman
sage 500n.
planner 623n.
manager 690n.
statesmanlike
intelligent 498adj.
skillful 694adj.
statesmanship
sagacity 498n.
policy 623n.
tactics 688n.
management 689n.
state-wide
universal 79adj.
static
science of forces 162n.
quiescent 266adj.
statics
gravity 322n.
station
degree 27n.
serial place 73n.
stopping place 145n.
place 185n.
situation 186n.
station 187n.
abode 192n.
railroad 624n.
nobility 868n.
stationary
permanent 144adj.
quiescent 266adj.
non-active 677adj.
inactive 679adj.
stationer
bookman 589n.
stationery
stationery 586n.
stations of the cross
ritual act 988n.
ritual object 988n.
church interior 990n.
station wagon
automobile 274n.
statism
despotism 733n.
governance 733n.
statist
computer 86n.
manager 690n.
statistical
statistical 86adj.
statistician
computer 86n.
accountant 808n.
statistics
statistics 86n.
accuracy 494n.
statuary
sculpture 554n.
sculptor 556n.
ornamental art 844n.
statue
copy 22n.
monument 548n.
image 551n.
sculpture 554n.
honors 866n.
idol 982n.
statuesque
tall 209adj.
glyptic 554adj.
beautiful 841adj.
proud 871adj.
statuette
image 551n.
sculpture 554n.
statu pupillari, in
young 130adj.
studentlike 538adj.
subject 745adj.
stature
height 209n.
status
state 7n.
circumstances 8n.

relativeness 9n.
degree 27n.
serial place 73n.
situation 186n.
prestige 866n.
status quo
equilibrium 28n.
permanence 144n.
reversion 148n.
statute
precept 693n.
legislation 953n.
statutory
preceptive 693adj.
legal 953adj.
staunch
unyielding 162adj.
sealed off 264adj.
resolute 599adj.
friendly 880adj.
trustworthy 929adj.
(*see* stanch)
stave
notation 410n.
vocal music 412n.
verse form 593n.
club 723n.
stave in
make concave 255vb.
pierce 263vb.
depress 311vb.
stave off
obstruct 702vb.
stay
tackling 47n.
continue 108vb.
last 113vb.
delay 136n.
stay 144vb.
cease 145vb.
go on 146vb.
be stable 153vb.
presence 189n.
dwell 192vb.
supporter 218n.
support 218vb.
bring to rest 266vb.
be inactive 679vb.
obstacle 702n.
visit 882vb.
stay-at-home
quiescent 266adj.
solitary 883n.
unsociable 883adj.
stay away
be absent 190vb.
stayer
thoroughbred 273n.
stamina 600n.
staying power
strength 162n.
stamina 600n.
stay order
legal process 959n.
stay outside
be excluded 57vb.
stay put
pend 136vb.
be quiescent 266vb.
stand firm 599vb.
be obstinate 602vb.
stays
compressor 198n.
supporter 218n.
underwear 228n.
stay up
fly 271vb.
stead
utility 640n.
aid 703n., vb.
steadfast
fixed 153adj.
obedient 739adj.
steadfastness
perseverance 600n.
steady
uniform 16adj.
equal 28adj.
orderly 60adj.
regular 81adj.
periodic 141adj.
unceasing 146adj.
unchangeable 153adj.
fixed 153adj.
support 218vb.
still 266adj.
resolute 599adj.
persevering 600adj.
tranquilize 823vb.
courageous 855adj.
lover 887n.
steak
piece 53n.
meat 301n.
steal
copy 20vb.
be stealthy 525vb.
steal 788vb.
steal a march
do before 119vb.
be early 135vb.
outdo 306vb.
deceive 542vb.
be cunning 698vb.
stealing
stealing 788n.
stealth
cunning 698n.
(*see* secrecy)
steal the show
be superior 34vb.
act 594vb.
have repute 866vb.
stealthy
slow 278adj.
muted 401adj.
occult 523adj.
stealthy 525adj.
cunning 698adj.
cautious 858adj.
steal upon
surprise 508vb.
steam
energy 160n.
stimulation 174n.
voyage 269vb.
propellant 287n.
exude 298vb.
emit 300vb.
cook 301vb.
gas 336n.
vaporize 338vb.
water 339n.
be wet 341vb.
bubble 355vb.
heat 379n.
heater 383n.
steam engine
locomotive 274n.
steamer
ship 275n.
steamroller
demolish 165vb.
flattener 216n.
smoother 258n.
locomotive 274n.
steamy
gaseous 336adj.
vaporific 338adj.
cloudy 355adj.
heated 381adj.
stearin
fat 357n.
steatorrhea
indigestion 651n.
steed
horse 273n.
steel
strengthen 162vb.
sharp edge 256n.
hardness 326n.
lighter 385n.
resolution 599n.
make insensitive 820vb.
steel-clad
invulnerable 660adj.
steeled against
impassive 820adj.
steel helmet
armor 713n.
steely
strong 162adj.
hard 326adj.
gray 429adj.
blue 435adj.
resolute 599adj.
cruel 898adj.

steelyard
scales 322n.
workshop 687n.
steep
high land 209n.
high 209adj.
deep 211adj.
vertical 215adj.
sloping 220adj.
immerse 303vb.
ascending 308adj.
soften 327vb.
add water 339vb.
drench 341vb.
exaggerated 546adj.
difficult 700adj.
steeped
pulpy 356adj.
steepen
ascend 308vb.
steeple
high structure 209n.
sharp point 256n.
church exterior 990n.
steeplechase
leap 312vb.
chase 619n.
racing 716n.
steeplechaser
thoroughbred 273n.
jumper 312n.
steeple-house
church 990n.
steeple-jack
climber 308n.
steepness
(*see* steep)
steer
eunuch 161n.
navigate 269vb.
steer for 281vb.
cattle 365n.
male animal 372n.
direct 689vb.
steerage
direction 281n.
directorship 689n.
lower classes 869n.
steerage way
water travel 269n.
steer clear
deviate 282vb.
steer for
steer for 281vb.
pursue 619vb.
steering committee
director 690n.
steersman
navigator 270n.
director 690n.
steersmanship
directorship 689n.
steganography
latency 523n.
secrecy 525n.
writing 586n.
stegophilist
climber 308n.
stein
cup 194n.
stele
obsequies 364n.
stellar
celestial 321adj.
stem
main part 52n.
source 156n.
genealogy 169n.
supporter 218n.
stanch 350vb.
foliage 366n.
word 559n.
withstand 704vb.
stem to stern
longwise 203adv.
stench
fetor 397n.
stencil
duplicate 22n.
paint 553vb.
stenographer
recorder 549n.
stenographer 586n.
stenography
writing 586n.
stenosis
contraction 198n.
stenotypist
stenographer 586n.
stentorian
sounding 398adj.
loud 400adj.
crying 408adj.
step
degree 27n.
serial place 73n.
long measure 203n.
stand 218n.
gait 265n.
walk 267n.
access 624n.
essay 671n.
deed 676n.
stepbrother
kinsman 11n.
step by step
by degrees 27adv.
step-dance
dance 837n.
step down
bate 37vb.
descend 309vb.
stepfather
parent 169n.
step, in
agreeing 24adj.
step-ins
underwear 228n.
step into
possess 773vb.
step into the shoes of
come after 65vb.
substitute 150vb.
inherit 771vb.
step-ladder
ascent 308n.
access 624n.
stepmother
maternity 169n.
stepmotherly
unkind 898adj.
step on it
accelerate 277vb.
step out
move 265vb.
move fast 277vb.
steppe
space 183n.
lowness 210n.
horizontality 216n.
land 344n.
plain 348n.
stepped
oblique 220adj.
stepper
thoroughbred 273n.
stepping-stone
opportunity 137n.
bridge 624n.
instrument 628n.
steps
series 71n.
ascent 308n.
policy 623n.
means 629n.
action 676n.
stepson
family 11n.
step up
augment 36vb.
invigorate 174vb.
accelerate 277vb.
promote 285vb.
stercoraceous
unclean 649adj.
stereobate
basis 218n.
stereometry
geometry 465n.
stereoscope
optical device 442n.
stereoscopic
seeing 438adj.
visible 443adj.
stereotype
uniformity 16n.
copy 22n.
printing 555n.
print 587vb.

stereotyped
  unchangeable 153adj.
  habitual 610adj.
sterile
  impotent 161adj.
  unproductive 172adj.
  profitless 641adj.
  clean 648adj.
  salubrious 652adj.
sterility
  (*see* sterile)
sterilization
  prophylactic 658n.
  (*see* sterilize)
sterilize
  unman 161vb.
  lay waste 165vb.
  sterilize 172vb.
  make useless 641vb.
  purify 648vb.
  sanitate 652vb.
sterling
  genuine 494adj.
  valuable 644adj.
  money 797n.
  monetary 797n.
  virtuous 933adj.
stern
  buttocks 238n.
  poop 238n.
  resolute 599adj.
  severe 735adj.
  serious 834adj.
  angry 891adj.
  sullen 893adj.
  unkind 898adj.
stern-chase
  chase 619n.
stern-chaser
  gun 723n.
sternmost
  rearward 238adv.
sternness
  (*see* stern)
stern rake
  projection 254n.
stern-sheets
  poop 238n.
sternutation
  respiration 352n.
  sibilation 406n.
sternway
  motion 265n.
  water travel 269n.
stern-wheel
  propeller 269n.
stern-wheeler
  ship 275n.
stertorous
  puffing 352adj.
  hoarse 407adj.
stertorousness
  loudness 400n.
stet
  stabilize 153vb.
stethoscope
  hearing aid 415n.
stetson
  headgear 228n.
stevedore
  boatman 270n.
  bearer 273n.
  worker 686n.
stew
  a mixture 43n.
  dish 301n.
  cook 301vb.
  heat 381vb.
  predicament 700n.
  excitable state 822n.
  anger 891n.
  inebriate 949vb.
  brothel 951n.
steward
  provider 633n.
  manager 690n.
  domestic 742n.
  consignee 754n.
  treasurer 798n.
stewardship
  management 689n.
stew-pan
  caldron 194n.
  heater 383n.
stichomythia
  verse form 593n.
stick
  cohere 48vb.
  halt 145vb.
  be contiguous 202vb.
  supporter 218n.
  pierce 263vb.
  transfer 272vb.
  rub 333vb.
  ninny 501n.
  be loath 598vb.
  be in difficulty 700vb.
  club 723n.
  fail 728vb.
  compulsion 740n.
  scourge 964n.
stick at
  doubt 486vb.
stick at nothing
  be resolute 599vb.
  be intemperate 943vb.
sticker
  coherence 48n.
stick fast
  be stable 153vb.
  be quiescent 266vb.
  stand firm 599vb.
stickiness
  (*see* sticky)
sticking plaster
  coherence 48n.
  surgical dressing 658n.
stick-in-the-mud
  permanence 144n.
  opinionist 602n.
  unskilled 695adj.
stick in the throat
  make mute 578vb.
  displease 827vb.
stick into
  insert 303vb.
stick it out
  stand firm 599vb.
  persevere 600vb.
stickjaw
  coherence 48n.
  stopper 264n.
  mouthful 301n.
stickle
  be uncertain 474vb.
  be loath 598vb.
  bargain 791vb.
stickler
  narrow mind 481n.
  opinionist 602n.
  tyrant 735n.
stick on
  affix 45vb.
stick one's neck out
  be rash 857vb.
stick out
  jut 254vb.
  be visible 443vb.
stickpin
  fastening 47n.
sticks
  racing 716n.
stick to
  retain 778vb.
stick to one's guns
  persevere 600vb.
  be obstinate 602vb.
  be courageous 855vb.
stick to one's point
  argue 475n.
stick to rule
  conform 83vb.
stick-up
  stealing 788n.
stick up
  be vertical 215vb.
stick up for
  patronize 703vb.
sticky
  cohesive 48adj.
  tough 329adj.
  viscid 354adj.
  difficult 700adj.
  retentive 778adj.
sticky wicket
  predicament 700n.
stiff
  unyielding 162adj.

crippled 163adj.
still 266adj.
rigid 326adj.
dead 361adj.
corpse 363n.
cadaverous 363adj.
insensible 375adj.
narrow-minded 481adj.
ninny 501n.
imperspicuous 568adj.
obstinate 602adj.
inactive 679adj.
clumsy 695adj.
severe 735adj.
restraining 747adj.
prideful 871adj.
formal 875adj.
affected 880adj.
unsociable 883adj.
dead drunk 949adj.

stiffen
strengthen 162vb.
harden 326vb.

stiffener
supporter 218n.

stiffening
stability 153n.

stiff job
hard task 700n.

stiff-necked
obstinate 602adj.
proud 871adj.

stiffness
(*see* stiff)

stiff upper lip
manliness 855n.

stiff with
full 54adj.

stifle
disable 161vb.
suppress 165vb.
kill 362vb.
be hot 379vb.
heat 381vb.
extinguish 382vb.
silence 399vb.
mute 401vb.
conceal 525vb.
make mute 578vb.
hinder 702vb.
prohibit 757vb.

stigma
label 547n.
slur 867n.
censure 924n.
detraction 926n.
false charge 928n.

stigmata
indication 547n.

stigmatize
mark 547vb.
blemish 845vb.
shame 867vb.
dispraise 924vb.
defame 926vb.
accuse 928vb.

stile
access 624n.
obstacle 702n.

stiletto
sharp point 256n.
perforator 263n.
side-arms 723n.

still
fixed 153adj.
assuage 177vb.
still 266adj.
vaporizer 338n.
watery 339adj.
dead 361adj.
heater 361adj.
silent 399adj.
nevertheless 468adv.
photography 551n.
make mute 578vb.
inactive 679adj.

stillborn
dead 361adj.
unsuccessful 728adj.

still life
art subject 553n.

stillness
(*see* still)

still-room
chamber 194n.
provisions 301n.
storage 632n.

stilly
silent 399adj.

stilt
stand 218n.

stilted
ornate 574adj.
inelegant 576adj.
ridiculous 849adj.
affected 850adj.

stilts
plaything 837n.

stimulant
stimulant 174n.
impulse 279n.
liquor 301n.
incentive 612n.
drug 658n.
refreshment 685n.
excitant 821n.

stimulate
make violent 176vb.
incite 612vb.
cause desire 859vb.
(*see* stimulation)

stimulation
increase 36n.
causation 156n.
strengthening 162n.
agency 173n.
stimulation 174n.
activity 678n.
excitation 821n.

stimulative
remedial 658adj.

stimulus
(*see* stimulant)

sting
sharpness 256n.
pang 377n.
pungency 388n.
wound 655vb.
bane 659n.
overcharge 811vb.
excitant 821n.
suffering 825n.
torment 827vb.
enrage 891vb.

stinginess
insufficiency 636n.
parsimony 816n.

stingo
liquor 301n.

stink
fetor 397n.
uncleanness 649n.
deteriorate 655vb.

stinkard
fetor 397n.

stinker
cad 938n.

stinking
unsavory 391adj.
not nice 645adj.
unpleasant 827adj.
impure 951adj.

stink of
superabound 637vb.

stink-pot
fetor 397n.

stint
finite quantity 26n.
period 110n.
limit 236vb.
make insufficient 636vb.
labor 682n.
be parsimonious 816vb.
portion 873n.

stinted
unprovided 636adj.

stipend
subvention 703n.
reward 962n.

stipendiary
subject 745adj.
recipient 782n.
receiving 782adj.

stipple
variegate 437vb.
paint 553vb.
engrave 555vb.

stipulation
premise 475n.

supposition 512n.
requirement 627n.
conditions 766n.
stir
mix 43vb.
stimulation 174n.
make violent 176vb.
motion 265n.
commotion 318n.
activity 678n.
jail 748n.
excite 821vb.
stirpiculture
animal husbandry 369n.
stirred
impressed 818adj.
stirring
eventful 154adj.
stirrup
supporter 218n.
stirrup cup
valediction 296n.
potion 301n.
stirrup-pump
sufflation 352n.
stir-up
impulse 279n.
stitch
tie 45vb.
component 58n.
pang 377n.
needlework 844n.
stitchery
needlework 844n.
stitch in time
anticipation 135n.
stithy
workshop 687n.
stive
heat 381vb.
stiver
small coin 33n.
stoa
pavilion 192n.
lobby 194n.
pillar 218n.
philosopher 449n.
stoat
vermin 365n.
fetor 397n.
stoccado
foin 712n.
stock
race 11n.
ligature 47n.
accumulation 74n.
typical 83adj.
source 156n.
genealogy 169n.
pillar 218n.
neckwear 228n.
soup 301n.
animal 365n.
tree 366n.
dunce 501n.
usual 610adj.
materials 631n.
store 632n.
provide 633vb.
property 777n.
merchandise 795n.
stockade
enclosure 235n.
barrier 235n.
shelter 662n.
defenses 713n.
stockbroker
consignee 754n.
merchant 794n.
stock exchange
bourse 618n.
mart 796n.
stock-farm
stock-farm 369n.
stock-farmer
producer 167n.
stockholder
participator 775n.
owner 776n.
stockinette
textile 222n.
stockings
legwear 228n.
stock-in-trade
means 629n.
equipment 630n.
store 632n.
property 777n.
merchandise 795n.
stock-jobber
merchant 794n.
stock-list
list 87n.
stockman
herdsman 369n.
stockpile
store 632vb.
stock-room
storage 632n.
stocks
seat 218n.
lock-up 748n.
pillory 964n.
stock saying
maxim 496n.
stocks, on the
unfinished 55adj.
in preparation 669adv.
on the stocks 726adv.
stock-still
still 266adj.
stocky
short 204adj.
stock-yard
enclosure 235n.
stodgy
semiliquid 354adj.
plain 573adj.
tedious 838adj.
dull 840adj.
stoic
unfeeling person 820n.
stoical
impassive 820adj.
patient 823adj.
stoicism
philosophy 449n.
moral insensibility 820n.
patience 823n.
inexcitability 823n.
disinterestedness 931n.
temperance 942n.
stoke
make violent 176vb.
kindle 381vb.
fire 385vb.
stoker
driver 268n.
stole
robe 228n.
shawl 228n.
neckwear 228n.
vestments 989n.
stolen goods
booty 790n.
stolid
unthinking 450adj.
unintelligent 499adj.
inactive 679adj.
impassive 820adj.
stolidity
inertness 175n.
(*see* stolid)
stomach
maw 194n.
insides 224n.
taste 386n.
be willing 597vb.
be patient 823vb.
liking 859n.
forgive 909vb.
stomach-ache
indigestion 651n.
stomacher
bodywear 228n.
stomachic
cellular 194adj.
stomach, turn the
be unpalatable 391n.
stone
uncover 229vb.
missile 287n.
weighment 322n.
solid body 324n.
hardness 326n.
rock 344n.
kill 362vb.
dunce 501n.
sculpture 554n.
engraving 555n.

building material 631n.
lapidate 712vb.
unfeeling person 820n.
gem 844n.
execute 963vb.

Stone Age
era 110n.
antiquity 125n.

stone-cutting
sculpture 554n.

stone's throw
short distance 200n.

stonewall
repel 292vb.
parry 713vb.

stonewalling
protraction 113n.

stoneware
product 164n.

stonework
edifice 164n.
structure 331n.

stoning
capital punishment 963n.

stony
unproductive 172adj.
rough 259adj.
hard 326adj.
territorial 344adj.
insensible 375adj.

stony-hearted
cruel 898adj.

stooge
entertainer 594n.
instrument 628n.
nonentity 639n.
bungler 697n.
auxiliary 707n.
dependent 742n.
laughing-stock 851n.

stooge for
be servile 879vb.

stook
bunch 74n.
cultivate 370vb.

stool
seat 218n.
excrement 302n.
dirt 649n.

stool of repentance
penance 941n.
pillory 964n.

stool-pigeon
informer 524n.
ambush 527n.
trickster 545n.

stoop
be low 210vb.
be oblique 220vb.
descend 309vb.
stoop 311vb.
plunge 313n., vb.
obey 739vb.
demean oneself 867vb.
be humble 872vb.
be servile 879vb.

stooping
respectful 920adj.

stop
end 69n., vb.
stop 145n.
close 264vb.
come to rest 266vb.
goal 295n.
stanch 350vb.
speech sound 398n.
punctuation 547n.
repair 656vb.
doctor 658vb.
be inactive 679vb.
obstacle 702n.
prohibit 757vb.
retention 778n.

stop-cock
stopper 264n.
tool 630n.

stop-gap
substitute 150n.
stopper 264n.

stoplight
signal light 420n.

stop off
arrive 295vb.

stop-over
itinerary 267n.
goal 295n.

stoppage
strike 145n.
closure 264n.
hitch 702n.
non-payment 805n.
discount 810n.

stopper
end 69n.
covering 226n.
stopper 264n.

stopping
discontinuous 72adj.
lining 227n.
surgery 658n.

stopping-place
stopping-place 145n.

stop up
obstruct 702vb.

stopwatch
timekeeper 117n.
recording instrument 549n.

storage
assemblage 74n.
room 183n.
storage 632n.

store
great quantity 32n.
accumulation 74n.
stow 187vb.
store 632n., vb.
provide 633vb.
plenty 635n.
preserve 666vb.
make ready 669vb.
not use 674vb.
acquire 771vb.
retain 778vb.
shop 796n.
treasury 799n.
wealth 800n.

store-house
storage 632n.

store, in
impending 155adj.
possessed 773adj.

storekeeper
provider 633n.
tradesman 794n.

store-room
chamber 194n.
storage 632n.

storied
descriptive 590adj.

stork
obstetrics 164n.
bird of prey 365n.

storm
turmoil 61n.
crowd 74n.
havoc 165n.
storm 176n.
irrupt 297vb.
commotion 318n.
gale 352n.
loudness 400n.
attack 712n., vb.
overmaster 727vb.
take 786vb.
be angry 891vb.

storm against
dispraise 924vb.

storm along
move fast 277vb.

storm-bound
windy 352adj.

storm, by
violently 176adv.

storm in a tea-cup
overestimation 482n.
exaggeration 546n.

storm signal
warning 664n.

storm-tossed
rough 259adj.

storm troops
attacker 712n.
armed force 722n.

stormy
violent 176adj.
windy 352adj.
excitable 822adj.

Storthing
parliament 692n.
story
compartment 194n.
layer 207n.
news 529n.
fable 543n.
narrative 590n.
story-teller
liar 545n.
narrator 590n.
stot
cattle 365n.
male animal 372n.
stoup
cup 194n.
church utensil 990n.
stout
stalwart 162adj.
strong 162adj.
fleshy 195adj.
thick 205adj.
liquor 301n.
courageous 855adj.
stoutness
vitality 162n.
stove
furnace 383n.
stow
stow 187vb.
load 193vb.
store 632vb.
stowage
room 183n.
location 187n.
storage 632n.
stowaway
intruder 59n.
incomer 297n.
hider 527n.
strabismus
dim sight 440n.
straddle
connect 45vb.
be broad 205vb.
overlie 266vb.
walk 267vb.
diverge 294vb.
pass 305vb.
strafe
bombardment 712n.
exprobate 924vb.
punish 963vb.
straggle
be dispersed 75vb.
wander 267vb.
stray 282vb.
straggler
wanderer 268n.
straggling
orderless 61adj.
straight
uniform 16adj.
simple 44adj.
orderly 60adj.
continuous 71adj.
vertical 215adj.
straightness 249n.
undeviating 625adj.
shapely 841adj.
honorable 929adj.
straight-edge
gauge 465n.
straighten
straighten 249vb.
rectify 654vb.
repair 656vb.
straighten out
unravel 62vb.
straight-faced
serious 834adj.
straightforward
directed 281adj.
intelligible 516adj.
undisguised 522adj.
veracious 540adj.
artless 699adj.
trustworthy 929adj.
straightforwardness
facility 701n.
straight on
straight on 249adj.
straight up
vertical 215adj.
strain
race 11n.
tincture 43n.
derange 63vb.
breed 77n.
weaken 163vb.
genealogy 169n.
force 176vb.
distortion 246n.
traction 288n.
exude 288n.
overstep 306vb.
pain 377n.
sound 398n.
be loud 400vb.
be false 541vb.
exaggerate 546vb.
style 566n.
purify 648vb.
essay 671vb.
misuse 675vb.
exertion 682n.
fatigue 684n., vb.
be severe 735vb.
worry 825n.
enmity 881n.
strainer
sorting 62n.
porosity 263n.
cleaning utensil 648n.
strain off
transpose 272vb.
void 300vb.
strains
poem 593n.
strain the sense
misinterpret 521vb.
strait
narrowness 206n.
gulf 345n.
access 624n.
restraining 747adj.
straiten
tighten 45vb.
be narrow 206vb.
imprison 747vb.
straitened
in difficulties 700adj.
poor 801adj.
strait-jacket
compressor 198n.
fetter 748n.
strait-laced
severe 735adj.
prudish 950adj.
straits
poverty 801n.
strait-waistcoat
fetter 748n.
strand
cable 47n.
fiber 208n.
hair 259n.
shore 344n.
stranded
grounded 728adj.
strange
irrelative 10adj.
extraneous 59adj.
unusual 84adj.
unknown 491adj.
ridiculous 849adj.
wonderful 864adj.
stranger
foreigner 59n.
stranger to
ignorant 491adj.
strangle
disable 161vb.
make smaller 198vb.
kill 362vb.
stranglehold
retention 778n.
strangler
murderer 362n.
strangles
respiration 352n.
strangulation
compression 198n.
closure 264n.
capital punishment 963n.
strangury
closure 264n.
strap
tie 45vb.
girdle 47n.
strip 208n.

spank 963vb.
scourge 964n.
straphanger
rider 268n.
strappado
corporal punishment 963n.
strapper
whopper 195n.
strapping
stalwart 162adj.
fleshy 195adj.
stratagem
trickery 542n.
tactics 688n.
stratagem 698n.
strategic
planned 623adj.
warlike 718adj.
strategist
planner 623n.
expert 696n.
slyboots 698n.
strategy
policy 623n.
tactics 688n.
art of war 718n.
stratification
stratification 207n.
structure 331n.
stratiform
layered 207adj.
stratigraphy
stratification 207n.
stratocracy
government 733n.
stratosphere
height 209n.
atmosphere 340n.
stratum
layer 207n.
horizontality 216n.
stratus
cloud 355n.
straw
insubstantial thing 4n.
levity 323n.
corn 366n.
flute 414n.
trifle 639n.
strawberry
fruit 301n.
redness 431n.
strawberry mark
identification 547n.
blemish 845n.
straw-board
wrapping 226n.
bookbinding 589n.
paper 631n.
straw-colored
yellow 433adj.
straw vote
inquiry 459n.
empiricism 461n.
stray
be dispersed 75vb.
unconformable 84adj.
casual 159adj.
wander 267vb.
wanderer 268n.
stray 282vb.
be inattentive 456vb.
err 495vb.
be lost 772vb.
derelict 779n.
be wicked 934vb.
streak
temperament 5n.
tincture 43n.
line 203n.
narrowness 206n.
strip 208n.
move fast 277vb.
flash 417n.
striation 437n.
stream
crowd, group 74n.
classification 77n.
tendency 179n.
hang 217vb.
motion 265n.
be wet 341adj.
stream 350n.
flow, rain 350vb.
class 538n.
abound 635vb.
superabound 637vb.
streamer
advertisement 528n.
flag 547n.
trimming 844n.
streaming
non-adhesive 49adj.
unassembled 75adj.
pendent 217adj.
streamlet
stream 350n.
streamline
smooth 258vb.
rectify 654vb.
streamlined
speedy 277adj.
streamlining
arrangement 62n.
streams
great quantity 32n.
street
locality 187n.
street 192n.
road 624n.
street arab
wanderer 268n.
low fellow 869n.
street artist
entertainer 594n.
streetcar
conveyance 267n.
streetcar 274n.
streetcar lines
regularity 81n.
parallelism 219n.
habit 610n.
railroad 624n.
street-corner
plebeian 869adj.
streets ahead
superior 34adj.
streetwalker
prostitute 952n.
streetwalking
social evil 951n.
strength
power 160n.
strength 162n.
vigorousness 174n.
toughness 329n.
vigor 571n.
stamina 660n.
strengthen
augment 36vb.
accrue 38vb.
strengthen 162vb.
harden 326vb.
corroborate 466vb.
safeguard 660vb.
strengthless
weak 163adj.
strenuous
vigorous 174adj.
persevering 600adj.
industrious 678adj.
laboring 682adj.
streptomycin
drug 658n.
stress
agency 173n.
distortion 246n.
attract notice 455vb.
argue 475vb.
emphasize 532vb.
pronunciation 577n.
prosody 593n.
needfulness 627n.
make important 638vb.
exertion 682n.
difficulty 700n.
stretch
period 110n.
space, range 183n.
enlarge 197vb.
lengthen 203vb.
overstep 306vb.
elasticity 328n.
exaggerate 546vb.
stretchable
flexible 327adj.
stretch a point

be lax 734vb.
be lenient 736vb.
not observe 769vb.
exempt 919vb.
stretched
protracted 113adj.
stretcher
bond 47n.
bed 218n.
footwear 228n.
vehicle 274n.
stretcher-bearer
bearer 273n.
nurse 658n.
stretcher-case
sick person 651n.
stretching
opening 263n.
stretch one's legs
repose 683vb.
stretch, on the
attentive 455adj.
laboring 682adj.
stretch to
be distant 119vb.
be long 203vb.
strew
disperse 75vb.
striate
groove 262vb.
striation
striation 437n.
stricken
unfortunate 731adj.
suffering 825adj.
strict
regular 83adj.
severe 735adj.
restraining 747adj.
obligatory 917adj.
honorable 929adj.
orthodox 976adj.
strictness
severity 735n.
orthodoxism 976n.
stricture
contraction 198n.
narrowing 206n.
reprimand 924n.
censure 924n.
accusation 928n.
stride
gait 265n.
walk 267vb.
progression 285n.
stride, in one's
skillfully 694adv.
stridency
(*see* strident)
strident
loud 400adj.
strident 407adj.
discordant 411adj.
stride, take in one's
be expert 694vb.
do easily 701vb.
stridor
stridor 407n.
stridulate
shrill 407vb.
rasp 407vb.
ululate 409vb.
strife
quarrel 709n.
contention 716n.
strigil
cleaning utensil 648n.
strike
strike 145n.
cease 145vb.
horizontality 216n.
strike 279vb.
rub 333vb.
cause thought 449vb.
discovery 484n.
be inactive 679vb.
be obstructive 702vb.
strike at 712vb.
resistance 715n.
revolt 738n.
impress 821vb.
fail in duty 918vb.
strike a bad patch
have trouble 731vb.
strike a balance
average out 30vb.
strike a light
kindle 381vb.
make bright 417vb.
strike an acquaintance
befriend 880vb.
strike at
strike at 712vb.
strike attitudes
be affected 880vb.
strike-breaker
tergiversator 603n.
strike-breaking
hindrance 702n.
strike hands
contract 765vb.
be friendly 880vb.
greet 884vb.
strike-happy
hindering 702adj.
strike off
exclude 57vb.
eject 300vb.
print 587vb.
strike oil
have luck 730vb.
get rich 800vb.
strike, on
inactive 679adj.
strike one's colors
submit 721vb.
strike out
destroy 165vb.
start out 296vb.
obliterate 550vb.
plan 623vb.
striker
thrower 287n.
revolter 738n.
strike root
be stable 153vb.
prevail 178vb.
place oneself 187vb.
strike sail
retard 278vb.
strike work
cease 145vb.
be obstructive 702vb.
resist 715vb.
revolt 738vb.
striking
well-seen 443adj.
manifest 522adj.
impressive 821adj.
wonderful 864adj.
striking distance
short distance 200n.
striking force
armed force 722n.
string
adjust 24vb.
tie 45vb.
cable 47n.
series 71n.
band 74n.
play music 413vb.
viol 414n.
befool 542vb.
jewelry 844n.
string along with
accompany 89vb.
string band
orchestra 413n.
stringency
severity 735n.
stringent
exorbitant 32adj.
vigorous 174adj.
severe 735adj.
string, on a
obedient 739adj.
string out
disperse 75vb.
lengthen 203vb.
strings
influence 178n.
orchestra 413n.
musical instrument 414n.
conditions 766n.
strings, with
restraining 747adj.
string together
connect 45vb.
string up
execute 963vb.

stringy
fibrous 208adj.
tough 329adj.
strip
subtract 39vb.
disjoin, rend 46vb.
piece 53n.
demolish 165vb.
line 203n.
narrowness 206n.
lamina 207n.
strip 208n.
uncover, doff 229vb.
fleece 786vb.
deprive 786vb.
impoverish 801vb.
stripe
line 203n.
narrowness 206n.
striation 437n.
badge of rank 743n.
pattern 844n.
corporal punishment 963n.
stripling
youngster 132n.
adult 134n.
stripper
stripper 229n.
striptease
uncovering 229n., adj.
strive
essay 671vb.
exert oneself 682vb.
contend 716vb.
stroke
instant 116n.
row 269vb.
knock 279n.
propulsion 287n.
spasm 318n.
rub 333vb.
touch 378n., vb.
punctuation 547n.
lettering 586n.
contrivance 623n.
paralysis 651n.
deed 676n.
direct 689vb.
director 690n.
caress 889vb.
corporal punishment 963n.
stroll
pedestrianism 267n.
stroller
wanderer 268n.
strolling
traveling 267adj.
strong
great 32adj.
unmixed 44adj.
strong 162adj.
violent 176adj.
pungent 388adj.
fetid 397adj.
florid 425adj.
expressive 516adj.
assertive 532adj.
forceful 571adj.
healthy 650adj.
invulnerable 660adj.
fervent 818adj.
intoxicating 949adj.
strong arm
compulsion 740n.
strongarm man
protector 660n.
combatant 722n.
strong-box
treasury 799n.
stronghold
habitancy 191n.
refuge 662n.
fort 713n.
strong in
instructed 490adj.
strong language
vigor 571n.
scurrility 899n.
strongly worded
expressive 516adj.
assertive 532adj.
forceful 571adj.
strong-minded
wise 498adj.
courageous 855adj.
strong point
skill 694n.
fort 713n.
strong-room
storage 632n.
treasury 799n.
strop
sharpener 256n.
strophe
verse form 593n.
strow
disperse 75vb.
struck
impressed 818adj.
structural
supporting 218adj.
structural 331adj.
structure
composition 56n.
arrangement 62n.
edifice 164n.
form 243n.
structure 331n.
pattern 844n.
struggle
be violent 176vb.
move slowly 278vb.
essay 671n., vb.
undertaking 672n.
exertion 682n.
be in difficulty 700vb.
contest 716n.
struggle against
withstand 704vb.
resist 715vb.
struggler
contender 716n.
combatant 722n.
strum
play music 413vb.
mean nothing 515vb.
strummer
instrumentalist 413n.
strumpet
prostitute 952n.
strung
adjusted 24adj.
strung out
long 203adj.
strung up
excited 821adj.
strut
bond 47n.
supporter 218n.
gait 265n.
walk 267vb.
be proud 871vb.
ostentation 875n.
boast 877vb.
strychnine
poison 659n.
stub
unsharpened 257adj.
label 547n.
stubble
leavings 41n.
roughness 259n.
corn 366n.
rubbish 641n.
stubborn
unyielding 162adj.
rigid 326adj.
tough 329adj.
persevering 600adj.
obstinate 602adj.
difficult 700adj.
impenitent 940adj.
stubborn fact
reality 1n.
stubby
short 204adj.
thick 205adj.
unsharpened 257adj.
stub one's toe
collide 279vb.
stub out
extinguish 382vb.
stucco
adhesive 47n.
facing 226n.
coat 226vb.
stuck
firm-set 45adj.
in difficulties 700adj.

stuck on
enamored 887adj.
stuck up
prideful 871adj.
vain 873adj.
stud
fastening 47n.
sharpen 256vb.
roughen 259vb.
horse 273n.
stock-farm 369n.
variegate 437vb.
jewelry 844n.
decorate 844vb.
studded with
multitudinous 104adj.
student
scholar 492n.
learner 538n.
studied
predetermined 608adj.
intended 617adj.
studio
chamber 194n.
art equipment 553n.
workshop 687n.
studious
thoughtful 449adj.
attentive 455adj.
studious 536adj.
industrious 678adj.
study
retreat 192n.
chamber 194n.
musical piece 412n.
scan 438vb.
meditation 449n.
topic 452n.
be attentive 455vb.
inquiry 459n.
study 536n., vb.
classroom 539n.
picture 553n.
dissertation 591n.
habit 610n.
intention 617n.
prepare oneself 669vb.
workshop 687n.
stuff
substantiality 3n.
essential part 5n.
fill 54vb.
strengthen 162vb.
load 193vb.
enlarge 197vb.
textile 222n.
line 227vb.
close 264vb.
matter 319n.
texture 331n.
absurdity 497n.
silly talk 515n.
materials 631n.
rubbish 641n.
merchandise 795n.
sate 863vb.
gluttonize 947vb.
stuff and nonsense
absurdity 497n.
silly talk 515n.
stuffed shirt
insubstantial thing 4n.
vain person 873n.
stuffing
adjunct 40n.
contents 193n.
lining 227n.
stopper 264n.
stuff into
insert 303vb.
stuff up
befool 542vb.
stuffy
sealed off 264adj.
dense 324adj.
fetid 397adj.
warm 397adj.
insalubrious 653adj.
tedious 838adj.
dull 840adj.
stultify
be obstructive 702vb.
stultify oneself
stultify oneself 695vb.
stumble
tumble 309vb.
blunder 495vb.
be clumsy 695vb.
stumble on
chance 159vb.
discover 484vb.
stumbling
clumsy 695adj.
unsuccessful 728adj.
stumbling-block
obstacle 702n.
stump
remainder 41n.
walk 267vb.
leg 267n.
move slowly 278vb.
puzzle 474vb.
orate 579vb.
be difficult 700vb.
stumper
question 459n.
interceptor 702n.
stumps
leg 267n.
stump up
pay 804vb.
stumpy
short 204adj.
deformed 246adj.
stun
strike 279vb.
render insensible 375vb.
be loud 400vb.
deafen 416vb.
surprise 508vb.
impress 821vb.
frighten 854vb.
be wonderful 864vb.
stunning
topping 644adj.
exciting 821adj.
stunt
shorten 204vb.
fly 271vb.
contrivance 623n.
deed 676n.
be expert 694vb.
be vain 873vb.
pageant 875n.
be obstentatious 875vb.
stunted
dwarfish 196adj.
contracted 198adj.
underfed 636adj.
stupa
temple 990n.
stupefaction
wonder 864n.
stupefy
render insensible 375vb.
impress 821vb.
be wonderful 864vb.
stupendous
prodigious 32adj.
huge 195adj.
wonderful 864adj.
stupid
insensible 375adj.
unthinking 450adj.
credulous 487adj.
unintelligent 499adj.
fool 501n.
unskillful 695adj.
dull 840adj.
stupor
insensibility 375n.
sluggishness 679n.
moral insensibility 820n.
wonder 864n.
stupration
rape 951n.
sturdy
stalwart 162adj.
sturgeon
table fish 365n.
stutter
stammer 580vb.
be clumsy 695vb.
show feeling 818vb.
quake 854vb.
be drunk 949vb.

sty
stable 192n.
enclosure 235n.
swelling 253n.
sink 649n.
stygian
dark 418adj.
infernal 972adj.
style
modality 7n.
sort 77n.
chronology 117n.
meaning 514n.
engraving 555n.
name 561n., vb.
style 566n.
elegance 575n.
way 624n.
skill 694n.
beauty 841n.
fashion 848n.
styled
formed 243adj.
stylet
perforator 263n.
side-arms 723n.
stylish
elegant 575adj.
well-made 694adj.
personable 841adj.
fashionable 848adj.
stylist
phrasemonger 574n.
stylist 575n.
stylistic
stylistic 566adj.
stylitism
seclusion 883n.
stylized
formed 243adj.
stylo, stylus
stationery 586n.
stylobate
stand 218n.
stylograph
stationery 586n.
stymie
obstruct 702vb.
styptic
solidifying 324adj.
sour 393adj.
styptic pencil
cosmetic 843n.
Styx
mythic hell 972n.
suasible
induced 612adj.
suasion
influence 178n.
suasive
inducive 612adj.
suave
smooth 258adj.
courteous 884adj.
suavity
courtesy 884n.
sub
inferior 35adj.
substitute 150n.
subaltern
inferior 35n.
army officer 741n.
servant 742n.
subapostolic
scriptural 975adj.
subaqueous
deep 211adj.
subastral
telluric 321adj.
subatom
element 319n.
subbranch
branch 53n.
subclause
subdivision 53n.
subconscious
spirit 447n.
psychic 447adj.
subcontrary
opposite 240adj.
subcutaneous
interior 224adj.
subdivision
scission 46n.
subdivision 53n.
subdivisional
regional 184adj.
subdual
victory 727n.
subduction
subtraction 39n.
subdue
overmaster 727vb.
subjugate 745vb.
restrain 747vb.
subdued
moderate 177adj.
muted 401adj.
dejected 834adj.
subfusc
dark 418adj.
dim 419adj.
subgrade
inferior 35adj.
subgroup
subdivision 53n.
subhead
classification 77n.
subhuman
animal 365adj.
cruel 898adj.
subinfeudate
lease 784vb.
subinspector
police 955n.
subjacent
low 210adj.
deep 211adj.
subject
living model 23n.
prototype 23n.
inferior 35adj.
liable 180adj.
topic 452n.
testee 461n.
overmaster 727vb.
subject 742n.
subject 745adj.
subjugate 745vb.
not owning 774adj.
subjection
inferiority 35n.
subjection 745n.
subjective
intrinsic 5adj.
immaterial 320adj.
misjudging 481adj.
subjectivity
intrinsicality 5n.
subjectivity 320n.
error 495n.
fantasy 513n.
subject matter
topic 452n.
subject to
provided 468adv.
on terms 766adj.
subjoin
add 38vb.
place after 65vb.
insert 303vb.
sub judice
on trial 459adv.
sub judice 480adv.
in litigation 959adv.
subjugate
overmaster 727vb.
subjugate 745vb.
subjugation
brute force 735n.
subjection 745n.
subjugator
victor 727n.
subjunctive
conjunctive 45adj.
sublessee
possessor 776n.
sublet
lease 784vb.
sublieutenant
naval officer 741n.
sublimate
elevate 310vb.
vaporize 338vb.
purify 648vb.
sublimated
pure 950adj.
sublimation
amendment 654n.
(*see* sublimate)
sublime
great 32adj.

elevated 310adj.
vaporize 338vb.
impressive 821adj.
(*see* sublimity)
Sublime Porte
sovereign 741n.
subliminal
psychic 447adj.
sublimity
superiority 34n.
height 209n.
vigor 571n.
eloquence 579n.
beauty 841n.
prestige 866n.
disinterestedness 931n.
divine attribute 965n.
sublineation
punctuation 547n.
sublunary
telluric 321adj.
subman
inferior 35n.
submarine
low 210adj.
deep 211adj.
ship 275n.
diver 313n.
oceanic 343adj.
warship 722n.
submariner
diver 313n.
navy man 722n.
submeaning
connotation 514n.
submediant
musical note 410n.
submerge
suppress 165vb.
immerse 303vb.
plunge 313vb.
drench 341vb.
be unseen 444vb.
obliterate 550vb.
submerged
deep 211adj.
latent 523adj.
submerged tenth
lower classes 869n.
submergence
immersion 303n.
descent 309n.
plunge 313n.
submersible
descending 309adj.
depressed 311adj.
submersion
immersion 303n.
moistening 341n.
subministration
aid 703n.
submission
conformity 83n.
argument 475n.
advice 691n.
submission 721n.
obedience 739n.
subjection 745n.
entreaty 761n.
patience 823n.
content 828n.
humility 872n.
servility 879n.
submissive
willing 597adj.
wieldy 701adj.
peaceful 717adj.
(*see* submission)
submit
acquiesce 488vb.
propound 512vb.
communicate 524vb.
affirm 532vb.
be forced 596vb.
submit 721vb.
be defeated 728vb.
(*see* submission)
submonition
advice 691n.
submultiple
numerical element 85n.
subnormal
inferior 35adj.
abnormal 84adj.
insane 503adj.
subordinate
extrinsic 6adj.
inferior 35n., adj.
dependent 742n.
servant 742n.
subordination
inferiority 35n.
arrangement 62n.
subjection 745n.
suborn
bribe 612vb.
subplot
narrative 590n.
plot 623n.
subpoena
warrant 737n.
command 737vb.
legal process 959n.
subreption
acquisition 771n.
subrogation
substitution 150n.
sub rosa
secretly 525adv.
subscribe
testify 466vb.
sign 547vb.
write 586vb.
join a party 708vb.
contract 765vb.
give security 767vb.
give 781vb.
pay 804vb.
subscriber
assenter 488n.
signatory 765n.
giver 781n.
subscribe to
endorse 488vb.
patronize 703vb.
subscript
adjunct 40n.
sequel 67n.
subscription
offering 781n.
giving 781n.
payment 804n.
subsection
classification 77n.
subsequent
subsequent 120adj.
future 124adj.
late 136adj.
following 284adj.
subserve
concur 181vb.
be instrumental 628vb.
be useful 640vb.
minister to 703vb.
subservience
submission 721n.
(*see* subservient)
subservient
tending 179adj.
instrumental 628adj.
useful 640adj.
aiding 703adj.
subjected 745adj.
servile 879adj.
subside
decrease 37vb.
recede 290vb.
subsidence
quiescence 266n.
descent 309n.
subsidiary
extrinsic 6adj.
inferior 35n., adj.
additional 38adj.
unimportant 639adj.
useful 640adj.
aiding 703adj.
subsidize
aid 703vb.
give 781vb.
subsidy
support 218n.
subvention 703n.
gift 781n.
pay 804n.
subsist
be 1vb.
stay 144vb.
live 360vb.
subsistence
existence 1n.

subsistence level
poverty 801n.
subsoil
interiority 224n.
soil 344n.
subspecies
subdivision 53n.
substance
substance 3n.
essential part 5n.
main part 32n.
interiority 224n.
form 243n.
matter 319n.
structure 331n.
meaning 514n.
materials 631n.
importance 638n.
chief thing 638n.
estate 777n.
wealth 800n.
substandard
inferior 35adj.
abnormal 84adj.
deficient 307adj.
substantial
real 1adj.
substantial 3adj.
great 32adj.
material 319adj.
dense 324adj.
true 494adj.
meaningful 514adj.
substantiate
materialize 319vb.
be true 494vb.
substantive
real 1adj.
intrinsic 5adj.
part of speech 564n.
substitute
inferior 35n.
substitute 150n., vb.
displace 188vb.
imperfection 647n.
disuse 674vb.
deputy 755n.
not retain 779vb.
substitution
deposal 752n.
(*see* substitute)
substitutional
substituted 150adj.
substratum
substance 3n.
layer 207n.
base 214n.
basis 218n.
interiority 224n.
substructure
base 214n.
subsultus
spasm 318n.
subsume
contain 56vb.
class 62vb.
number with 78vb.
subtend
be opposite 240vb.
subterfuge
sophistry 477n.
concealment 525n.
mental dishonesty 543n.
pretext 614n.
stratagem 698n.
subterranean
low 210adj.
deep 211adj.
latent 523adj.
concealed 525adj.
dishonest 930adj.
infernal 972adj.
subtilize
rarify 325vb.
subtle
small 33adj.
rare 325adj.
intelligent 498adj.
cunning 698adj.
subtlety
discrimination 463n.
sophistry 477n.
sagacity 498n.
cunning 698n.
subtonic
musical note 410n.
subtopia
mediocrity 732n.
subtraction
diminution 37n.
subtraction 39n.
separation 46n.
numerical operation 86n.
subtractive
subtracted 39adj.
subtrahend
subtraction 39n.
decrement 42n.
numerical element 85n.
suburb
district 184n.
housing 192n.
suburban
regional 184adj.
urban 192adj.
circumjacent 230adj.
tedious 838adj.
vulgar 847adj.
plebeian 869adj.
suburbanite
dweller 191n.
native 191n.
suburbanize
urbanize 192vb.
suburbia
habitancy 191n.
mediocrity 732n.
(*see* suburb)
suburbs
entrance 68n.
circumjacence 230n.
subvention
support 218n.
provision 633n.
subvention 703n.
gift 781n.
pay 804n.
subversion
disorder 61n.
revolution 149n.
destruction 165n.
overturning 221n.
depression 311n.
sedition 738n.
subversive
revolutionary 149adj.
disobedient 738adj.
subvert
revolutionize 149vb.
demolish 165vb.
tell against 467vb.
impair 655vb.
subway
excavation 255n.
tunnel 263n.
train 274n.
railroad 624n.
succedaneum
substitute 150n.
succeed
come after 65vb.
run on 71vb.
substitute 150vb.
follow 284vb.
flourish 615vb.
be expedient 642vb.
succeed 727vb.
prosper 730vb.
possess 773vb.
succentor
church officer 986n.
succès d'estime
prestige 866n.
succès fou
success 727n.
success
success 727n.
successful
completive 725adj.
successful 727adj.
prosperous 730adj.
succession
sequence 65n.
series 71n.
continuity 71n.
recurrence 106n.
posteriority 120n.
successive
continuous 71adj.

periodic 141adj.
(*see* succession)
successless
unsuccessful 728adj.
successor
survivor 41n.
aftercomer 67n.
posteriority 120n.
beneficiary 776n.
recipient 782n.
successorship
futurity 124n.
succinct
concise 569adj.
succor
remedy 658n., vb.
aid 703n., vb.
succotash
cereal 301n.
succuba
demon 970n.
sorceress 983n.
succubus
demon 970n.
sorcerer 983n.
succulent
edible 301adj.
pulpy 356adj.
savory 390adj.
succumb
die 361vb.
be induced 612vb.
be fatigued 684vb.
knuckle under 721vb.
be defeated 728vb.
succussion
agitation 318n.
such
conditionate 7adj.
anonymous 562adj.
such a one
person 371n.
such as
similar 18adj.
suck
absorb 299vb.
drink 301vb.
extract 304vb.
be wet 341vb.
hiss 406vb.
suck dry
waste 634vb.
fleece 786vb.
sucked orange
rubbish 641n.
sucker
young plant 132n.
orifice 263n.
tree, plant 366n.
credulity 487n.
dupe 544n.
sucker for
desirer 859n.
suckling
child 132n.
suck out
void 300vb.
suck the brains
interrogate 459vb.
suck up to
minister to 703vb.
flatter 925vb.
sucrose
sweet 392n.
suction
energy 160n.
reception 299n.
sudary
cleaning cloth 648n.
sudatorium
heater 383n.
ablution 648n.
sudden
brief 114adj.
instantaneous 116adj.
early 135adj.
unexpected 508adj.
spontaneous 609adj.
sudorific
excretory 302adj.
hot 379adj.
suds
bubble 355n.
sue
request, entreat 761vb.
be in love 887vb.
court 889vb.
claim 915vb.
indict 928vb.
litigate 959vb.
suet
fat 357n.
Sufee
(*see* Sufi)
suffer
meet with 154vb.
carry 273vb.
feel pain 377vb.
be ill 651vb.
permit 756vb.
feel 818vb.
be patient 823vb.
suffer 825vb.
sufferance
lenity 736n.
permission 756n.
patience 823n.
suffering 825n.
sufferer
sick person 651n.
unlucky person 731n.
sufferer 825n.
suffering
pain 377n.
evil 616n.
adversity 731n.
feeling 818n., vb.
suffering 825n., adj.
painfulness 827n.
suffice
be equal 28vb.
be able 160vb.
suffice 635vb.
be expedient 642vb.
be middling 732vb.
sate 863vb.
sufficiency
completeness 54n.
sufficiency 635n.
completion 725n.
sufficient
not bad 644adj.
contenting 828adj.
(*see* sufficiency)
sufficing
provisionary 633adj.
suffix
add 38vb.
adjunct 40n.
affix 45vb.
place after 65vb.
sequel 67n.
word 559n.
part of speech 564n.
suffixion
joinder 45n.
sufflation
dilation 197n.
sufflation 352n.
suffocate
suppress 165vb.
kill 362vb.
superabound 637vb.
suffocating
deadly 362adj.
warm 379adj.
fetid 397adj.
suffocation
killing 362n.
suffragan
ecclesiarch 986n.
suffrage
affirmation 532n.
vote 605n.
aid 703n.
prayers 981n.
suffragette
rioter 738n.
suffragettism
vote 605n.
gynocracy 733n.
suffusion
mixture 43n.
feeling 818n.
Sufi
sectarist 978n.
pietist 979n.
worshiper 981n.
monk 986n.
Sufism
religion 973n.

sugar
food content 301n.
sweet 392n.
sugar-candy
sweet 392n.
sugar-daddy
lover 887n.
sugared
sweet 392adj.
deceiving 542adj.
sugarless
unsavory 391adj.
sour 393adj.
sugar the pill
sweeten 392vb.
deceive 542vb.
tempt 612vb.
sugary
pleasant 376adj.
sweet 392adj.
pleasurable 826adj.
suggest
evidence 466vb.
propound 512vb.
imply 523vb.
indicate 547vb.
represent 551vb.
incite 612vb.
offer 759vb.
(*see* suggestion)
suggester
motivator 612n.
suggestibility
persuasibility 612n.
suggestible
sentient 374adj.
irresolute 601adj.
excitable 822adj.
suggestio falsi
falsehood 541n.
mental dishonesty 543n.
suggestion
small quantity 33n.
influence 178n.
reminder 505n.
hint 524n.
plan 623n.
advice 691n.
(*see* suggest)
request 761n.
suggest itself
dawn upon 449vb.
suggestive
evidential 466adj.
suppositional 512adj.
meaningful 514adj.
tacit 523adj.
indicating 547adj.
descriptive 590adj.
inducive 612adj.
exciting 821adj.
impure 951adj.
suicidal
destructive 165adj.
murderous 362adj.
rash 857adj.
suicidal tendency
dejection 834n.
suicide
suicide 362n.
sui generis
special 80adj.
unconformable 84adj.
suit
uniformity 16n.
accord 24vb.
sort 77n.
dress 228n.
request 761n.
beautify 841vb.
wooing 889n.
accusation 928n.
litigation 959n.
suitable
relevant 9adj.
fit 24adj.
expedient 642adj.
marriageable 894adj.
right 913adj.
suit and service
service 745n.
suitcase
box 194n.
suite
retinue 67n.
series 71n.
procession 71n.
concomitant 89n.
flat 192n.
follower 284n.
musical piece 412n.
retainer 742n.
suiting
textile 222n.
dress 228n.
suitor
petitioner 763n.
lover 887n.
litigant 959n.
suit the action to the word
gesticulate 547vb.
sulcus
furrow 262n.
sulfur
fumigator 385n.
sulfureous
fetid 397adj.
sulfurous
angry 891adj.
maledicent 899adj.
sulk
be discontented 829vb.
be dejected 834vb.
be rude 885vb.
be sullen 893vb.
sulker
rude person 885n.
sulks
unwillingness 598n.
discontent 829n.
resentment 891n.
sullenness 893n.
sulky
carriage 274n.
unwilling 598adj.
quarreling 709adj.
discontented 829adj.
melancholic 834adj.
sullen 893adj.
sullage
marsh 347n.
semiliquidity 354n.
ash 381n.
sullen
black 428adj.
unwilling 598adj.
discontented 829adj.
serious 834adj.
ugly 842adj.
unsociable 883adj.
ungracious 885adj.
angry 891adj.
sullen 893adj.
malevolent 898adj.
sully
make unclean 649vb.
shame 867vb.
defame 926vb.
sulpha drug
drug 658n.
sultan
sovereign 741n.
sultanate
magistrature 733n.
polity 733n.
sultry
warm 379adj.
sullen 893adj.
sum
add 38vb.
whole, all 52n.
numerical result 85n.
numeration 86n.
meaning 514n.
funds 797n.
sumless
infinite 107adj.
summarize
be concise 569vb.
abstract 592vb.
summary
brief 114adj.
early 135adj.
concise 569adj.
description 590n.
compendium 592n.
lawless 954adj.
summation

addition 38n.
numeration 86n.
summer
pass time 108vb.
period 110n.
summer 128n.
beam 218n.
heat 379n.
palmy days 730n.
visit 882vb.
summerhouse
arbor 194n.
summery
summery 128adj.
warm 379adj.
summing up
estimate 480n.
legal trial 959n.
summit
completeness 54n.
extremity 69n.
serial place 73n.
height 209n.
summit 213n.
limit 236n.
conference 584n.
perfection 646n.
council 692n.
summitry
conference 584n.
summon
command 737vb.
desire 859vb.
indict 928vb.
litigate 959vb.
summoned
assembled 74adj.
summoner
messenger 531n.
law officer 955n.
summons
publication 528n.
call 547n.
command 737n.
warrant 737n.
desire 859n.
accusation 928n.
law 953n.
legal process 959n.
summon up
retrospect 505vb.
excite 821vb.
summum bonum
good 615n.
happiness 824n.
sumner
church officer 986n.
sum of things
universe 321n.
sump
receptacle 194n.
lake 346n.
storage 632n.
sink 649n.
sumpter-mule
beast of burden 273n.
sumptuary
monetary 797adj.
sumptuary law
prohibition 757n.
economy 814n.
sumptuous
ostentatious 875adj.
sum up
shorten 204vb.
judge, estimate 480vb.
be concise 569vb.
abstract 592vb.
try a case 959vb.
sun
sun 321n.
dry 342vb.
heat 379n., vb.
light 417n.
luminary 420n.
sun-bathe
be hot 379vb.
sun-blind
canopy 226n.
curtain 421n.
sun-bonnet
shade 226n.
headgear 228n.
sunburn
burning 381n.
brownness 430n.
sundae
pudding 301n.
Sunday
holy-day 988n.
Sunday best
clothing 228n.
finery 844n.
sun-deck
hospital 658n.
sunder
sunder 46vb.
decompose 51vb.
disperse 75vb.
sundial
timekeeper 117n.
sundown
evening 129n.
obscuration 418n.
sundowner
wanderer 268n.
sun-dried
dry 342n.
sun-dry
preserve 666vb.
sundry
many 104adj.
sung
renowned 866adj.
sun-glasses
screen 421n.
safeguard 662n.
sun-helmet
shade 226n.
screen 421n.
safeguard 662n.
sun-lamp
hospital 658n.
beautification 863n.
sunless
unlit 418adj.
sunlight
sun 321n.
heater 383n.
light 417n.
Sunni
sectarian 978adj.
Sunnite
sectarist 978n.
sunny
tranquil 266adj.
dry 342adj.
warm 379adj.
undimmed 417adj.
pleasurable 826adj.
cheerful 833adj.
sunny side
pleasurableness 826n.
sun oneself
be hot 379vb.
sunproof
screened 421adj.
sunrise
morning 128n.
ascent 308n.
sunscreen
shade 226n.
screen 421n.
sunset
evening 129n.
glow 417n.
obscuration 418n.
sunshade
shade 226n.
screen 421n.
sunshine
salubrity 652n.
palmy days 730n.
sunshiny
warm 379adj.
undimmed 417adj.
sunspot
sun 321n.
maculation 437n.
blemish 845n.
sunstroke
frenzy 503n.
sun-tan
brownness 430n.
sun-tanned
blackish 428adj.
sun-trap
pavilion 192n.

heater 383n.
sun-up
morning 128n.
sun-worshiper
sanitarian 652n.
idolater 982n.
sup
potion 301n.
eat, drink 301vb.
taste 386vb.
super
superior 34adj.
topmost 213adj.
actor 594n.
topping 644adj.
superable
possible 469adj.
superabundance
great quantity 32n.
productiveness 171n.
plenty 635n.
redundance 637n.
superabundant
many 104adj.
superaddition
addition 38n.
superannuated
antiquated 127adj.
superannuation
age 131n.
non-use 674n.
(*see* resignation)
superb
excellent 644adj.
splendid 841adj.
ostentatious 875adj.
supercharged
dynamic 160adj.
supercilious
prideful 871adj.
insolent 878adj.
disrespectful 921adj.
despising 922adj.
superego
subjectivity 320n.
spirit 447n.
supereminence
goodness 644n.
prestige 866n.
supererogation
superfluity 637n.
supererogatory
additional 38adj.
superfecundation
propagation 164n.
superfetation
productiveness 171n.
superficial
insubstantial 4adj.
inconsiderable 33adj.
incomplete 55adj.
spatial 183adj.
shallow 212adj.
exterior 223adj.
immaterial 320adj.
inattentive 456adj.
negligent 458adj.
smattering 491adj.
foolish 499adj.
hasty 680adj.
bungled 695adj.
uncompleted 726adj.
superfluity
great quantity 32n.
extra 40n.
superfluity 637n.
superfluous
remaining 41adj.
superfluous 637adj.
superfluousness
inutility 641n.
supergiant
star 321n.
superheating
heating 381n.
superhuman
divine 965adj.
superimpose
add 38vb.
cover 226vb.
superimposed
overhanging 209adj.
superintendence
management 689n.
superintendency
magistrature 733n.
superintendent
manager 690n.
superior
superior 34n., adj.
prideful 871adj.
monk 986n.
ecclesiarch 986n.
(*see* superiority)
superiority
superiority 34n.
precedence 64n.
seniority 131n.
goodness 644n.
contempt 922n.
superlative
supreme 34adj.
grammatical 564adj.
excellent 644adj.
superman
superior 34n.
bigwig 638n.
exceller 644n.
paragon 646n.
supermarket
emporium 796n.
shop 796n.
supernal
high 209adj.
immaterial 320adj.
paradisiac 971adj.
supernatural
extraneous 59adj.
abnormal 84adj.
divine 965adj.
spooky 970adj.
magical 983adj.
paranormal 984adj.
supernaturalism
occultism 984n.
supernova
star 321n.
supernumerary
additional 38n.
extra 40n.
actor 594adj.
superfluous 637adj.
superposition
addition 38n.
covering 226n.
superscription
label 547n.
script 586n.
supersede
substitute 150vb.
displace 188vb.
eject 300vb.
disuse 674vb.
depose 752vb.
not retain 779vb.
punish 963vb.
supersensory
immaterial 320adj.
supersession
(*see* supersede)
supersonic
speedy 277adj.
superstition
credulity 487n.
ignorance 491n.
error 495n.
heterodoxy 977n.
idolatry 982n.
superstitious
misjudging 481adj.
(*see* superstition)
superstratum
exteriority 223n.
superstructure
completion 725n.
supertax
tax 809n.
supertonic
musical note 410n.
supervene
be extrinsic 6vb.
accrue 38vb.
ensue 120vb.
happen 154vb.
supervenient
extrinsic 6adj.
supervention
addition 38n.
posterity 120n.

supervise
manage 689vb.
supervisor
manager 690n.
supervisory
directing 689adj.
supine
impotent 161adj.
low 210adj.
supine 216adj.
inverted 221adj.
quiescent 266adj.
inactive 679adj.
apathetic 820adj.
indifferent 860adj.
supineness
submission 721n.
supper
meal 301n.
supperless
hungry 859adj.
fasting 946adj.
supplant
come after 65vb.
substitute 150vb.
eject 300vb.
supple
flexible 327adj.
tergiversating 603adj.
servile 879adj.
dishonest 930adj.
supplement
increment 36n.
augment 36vb.
adjunct 40n.
make complete 54vb.
sequel 67n.
enlarge 197vb.
price 809n.
supplemental
additional 38adj.
suppleness
softness 327n.
skill 694n.
cunning 698n.
(*see* supple)
suppliant
supplicatory 761adj.
petitioner 763n.
worshiper 981n.
supplication
entreaty 761n.
prayers 981n.
supplier
provider 633n.
supplies
means 629n.
provision 633n.
subvention 703n.
merchandise 795n.
supply
make complete 54vb.
find means 629vb.
store 632n.
provide 633vb.
support
sustain 146vb.
strengthen 162vb.
support 218n., vb.
carry 273vb.
corroborate 466vb.
endorse 488vb.
choose 605vb.
instrumentality 628n.
suffice 635vb.
safeguard 660vb.
preservation 666n.
aid 703n., vb.
auxiliary 707n.
be patient 823vb.
friendship 880n.
approve 923vb.
vindicate 927vb.
supportance
feeling 818n.
patience 823n.
supporter
receptacle 194n.
supporter 218n.
heraldry 547n.
patron 707n.
supporting
undermost 214adj.
evidential 466adj.
supporting role
inferiority 35n.
acting 594n.
supposable
supposed 512adj.
supposal
supposition 512n.
suppose
assume 471vb.
opine 485vb.
not know 491vb.
suppose 512vb.
supposing
if 8adv.
provided 468adj.
suppositional 512adj.
supposition
topic 452n.
(*see* suppose)
suppositional
mental 447adj.
uncertain 474adj.
credible 485adj.
suppositional 512adj.
imaginary 513adj.
supposititious
supposed 512adj.
suppository
surgical dressing 658n.
suppress
suppress 165vb.
counteract 182vb.
misinterpret 521vb.
obliterate 550vb.
make mute 578vb.
overmaster 727vb.
suppression
exclusion 57n.
destruction 165n.
depression 311n.
concealment 525n.
severity 735n.
restraint 747n.
abrogation 752n.
prohibition 757n.
suppressio veri
falsehood 541n.
mental dishonesty 543n.
suppressive
avoiding 620adj.
suppurate
be ill 651vb.
deteriorate 655vb.
suppurating
fetid 397adj.
toxic 653adj.
suppuration
infection 651n.
impairment 655n.
supputation
numeration 86n.
supra
before 64adv.
retrospectively 125adv.
supramundane
divine 965adj.
supremacy
importance 638n.
governance 733n.
(*see* supreme)
supreme
great 32adj.
supreme 34adj.
topmost 213adj.
important 638adj.
Supreme Being
the Deity 965n.
supreme control
directorship 689n.
governance 733n.
supreme court
law-court 956n.
Supreme Pontiff
ecclesiarch 986n.
surcease
cessation 145n.
surcharge
account 808vb.
price 809n.
surcingle
girdle 47n.
surd
number 85n.

speech sound 398n.
voiceless 578adj.
sure
certain 473adj.
believing 485adj.
expectant 507adj.
safe 660adj.
trustworthy 929adj.
sure-fire
successful 727adj.
sure-footed
vigilant 457adj.
skillful 694adj.
successful 727adj.
sure thing
certainty 473n.
easy thing 701n.
surety
safety 660n.
security 767n.
legal process 959n.
suretyship
security 767n.
surf
wave 350n.
bubble 355n.
surface
space 183n.
measure 183n.
shallowness 212n.
exteriority 223n.
navigate 269vb.
emerge 298vb.
ascend 308vb.
be light 323vb.
texture 331n.
be visible 443vb.
road 624n.
surf-bathing
sport 837n.
surf-board
swim 269vb.
surfeit
superfluity 637n.
satiety 863n.
surf-riding
aquatics 269n.
sport 837n.
surge
increase 36n.
congregate 74vb.
flow out 298vb.
vortex 315n.
eddy 350n.
flow 350vb.
sibilation 406n.
be active 678vb.
surgeon
doctor 658n.
surgery
surgery 658n.
hospital 658n.
surgical
medical 658adj.
surly
ungracious 885adj.
surmise
opinion 485n.
foresee 510vb.
conjecture 512n.
surmount
be high 209vb.
crown 213vb.
overstep 306vb.
climb 308vb.
triumph 727vb.
surmountable
possible 469adj.
surname
name 561n., vb.
surpass
be superior 34vb.
outdo 306vb.
surpassing
great 32adj.
supreme 34adj.
excellent 644adj.
surplice
vestments 989n.
surplus
remainder 41n.
part 53n.
superfluity 637n.
surprise
inexpectation 508n.
pitfall 663n.
non-preparation 670n.
attack 712n., vb.
wonder 864n.
surprising
unusual 84adj.
unexpected 508adj.
wonderful 864adj.
surrealism
school of painting 553n.
surrealist
artist 556n.
surrebutter
rejoinder 460n.
surrender
relinquish 621vb.
non-use 674n.
submission 721n.
resignation 753n.
surreptitious
stealthy 525adj.
surrey
carriage 274n.
surrogate
deputy 755n.
surrogation
substitution 150n.
surround
surround 230vb.
circumscribe 232vb.
outline 233n.
enclosure 235n.
close 264vb.
circuit 626vb.
surroundings
locality 187n.
circumjacence 230n.
surtax
tax 809n.
surveillance
surveillance 457n.
management 689n.
survey
inspection 438n.
inquiry 459n.
measure 465vb.
estimate 480n., vb.
dissertation 591n.
surveying
measurement 465n.
surveyor
surveyor 465n.
survival
existence 1n.
remainder 41n.
durability 113n.
life 360n.
survival of the fittest
biology 358n.
contention 716n.
survive
be left 41vb.
continue 108vb.
outlast 113vb.
stay 144vb.
live 360vb.
be restored 656vb.
escape 667vb.
win 727vb.
survivor
survivor 41n.
aftercomer 67n.
escaper 667n.
susceptibility
liability 180n.
sensibility 374n.
persuasibility 612n.
vulnerability 661n.
moral sensibility 819n.
love 887n.
susceptible
impressible 819adj.
excitable 822adj.
suspect
be uncertain 474vb.
opine 485vb.
unbelieved 486adj.
doubt 486vb.
not know 491vb.
be nervous 854vb.
offender 904n.
be jealous 911vb.
wrong 914adj.

accused person 928n.
suspend
put off 136vb.
halt 145vb.
hang 217vb.
abrogate 752vb.
depose 752vb.
punish 963vb.
suspended animation
inactivity 679n.
suspender
fastening 47n.
hanger 217n.
supporter 218n.
underwear 228n.
suspense
lull 145n.
dubiety 474n.
expectation 507n.
suspension
pendency 217n.
softness 327n.
elasticity 328n.
tempo 410n.
non-use 674n.
inaction 677n.
abrogation 752n.
suspensory
surgical dressing 658n.
suspicion
doubt 486n.
conjecture 512n.
hint 524n.
suspicious
unbelieved 486adj.
unbelieving 486adj.
nervous 854adj.
cautious 858adj.
jealous 911adj.
sustain
continue 108vb.
sustain 146vb.
strengthen 162vb.
support 218vb.
feed 301vb.
corroborate 466vb.
persevere 600vb.
aid 703vb.
sustained
frequent 139adj.
unceasing 146adj.
sustenance
support 218n.
food 301n.
provisions 301n.
susurration
faintness 401n.
sutler
provider 633n.
peddler 794n.
sutra
maxim 496n.
non-Biblical scripture 975n.
suttee
suicide 362n.
burning 381n.
disinterestedness 931n.
oblation 981n.
sutural
conjunct 45adj.
suture
joinder 45n.
dividing line 92n.
suzerain
superior 34n.
sovereign 741n.
suzerainty
governance 733n.
svelte
narrow 206adj.
shapely 841adj.
swab
drier 342n.
cleaning utensil 648n.
surgical dressing 658n.
bungler 697n.
navy man 722n.
swaddle
tie 45vb.
dress 228vb.
restrain 747vb.
swaddling clothes
clothing 228n.
swadeshi
native 191adj.
swag
bag 194n.
hang 217n.
obliquity 220n.
be curved 248vb.
oscillate 317vb.
booty 790n.
swag-bellied
expanded 197adj.
swagger
gait 265n.
be proud 871vb.
ostentation 875n.
boasting 877n.
be insolent 878vb.
swagman
wanderer 268n.
swain
male 372n.
countryman 869n.
lover 887n.
swallow
speeder 277n.
absorb 299vb.
mouthful 301n.
eat 301vb.
bird 365n.
be credulous 487vb.
be patient 823vb.
swallow up
destroy 165vb.
consume 165vb.
waste 634vb.
swallow whole
not discriminate 464vb.
believe 485vb.
be credulous 487vb.
swami
sage 500n.
swamp
fill 54vb.
be many 104vb.
destroy 165vb.
drench 341vb.
marsh 347n.
defeat 722vb.
swampy
marshy 347adj.
swan
waterfowl 365n.
a beauty 841n.
swank
fashionable 848adj.
be affected 850vb.
pride 871n.
vanity 873n.
ostentation 875n.
boaster 877n.
swanker
proud man 871n.
swanky
fashionable 848adj.
swannery
nest 192n.
cattle pen 369n.
swansdown
textile 222n.
smoothness 258n.
swanskin
textile 222n.
swansong
end 69n.
decease 361n.
lament 836n.
swap
interchange 151n., vb.
barter 791n.
sward
grassland 348n.
swarm
grow 36vb.
crowd 74n.
congregate 74vb.
be many 104vb.
be fruitful 171vb.
abound 635vb.
swarm in
irrupt 297vb.
swarm over

be present 189vb.
swarm up
climb 308vb.
swarthy
dark 418adj.
blackish 428adj.
swash
moisten 341vb.
flow 350vb.
swashbuckler
combatant 722n.
insolent person 878n.
swastika
cross 222n.
heraldry 547n.
talisman 983n.
swat
strike 279vb.
swath
bunch 74n.
trace 548n.
swathe
tie 45vb.
dress 228vb.
fold 261vb.
cover 266vb.
sway
be periodic 141vb.
vary 152vb.
power 160n.
be weak 163vb.
influence 178n., vb.
hang 217vb.
oscillate 317vb.
be agitated 318vb.
be uncertain 474vb.
be irresolute 601vb.
motivate 612vb.
manage 689vb.
governance 733n.
swear
testify 466vb.
swear 532vb.
promise 764vb.
take a pledge 764vb.
cuss 899vb.
be impious 980vb.
swear by
be certain 473vb.
believe 485vb.
praise 923vb.
swearer
signatory 765n.
impious person 980n.
swear off
negate 533vb.
recant 603vb.
relinquish 621vb.
swear-word
word 559n.
scurrility 899n.
sweat
exude 298vb.
emit 300vb.
excrete 302vb.
be wet 341vb.
be hot 379vb.
labor 682n.
sweated labor
slave 742n.
sweater
vest 228n.
sweat-rag
cleaning cloth 648n.
swede
tuber 301n.
sweeny
animal disease 651n.
sweep
range 183n.
curvature 248n.
traverse 267vb.
propeller 269n.
move fast 277vb.
propellant 287n.
touch 378vb.
inspection 438n.
scan 438vb.
clean 648vb.
dirty person 649n.
sweep away
void 300vb.
sweeper
cleaner 648n.
domestic 742n.
sweeping
comprehensive 52adj.
inclusive 78adj.
general 79adj.
sweepings
leavings 41n.
rubbish 641n.
dirt 649n.
sweepstake
chance 159n.
gambling 618n.
sweet
mouthful 301n.
pudding 301n.
pleasant 376adj.
savory 390adj.
sweet 392n., adj.
melodious 410adj.
pleasurable 826adj.
beautiful 841adj.
amiable 884adj.
lovable 887adj.
benevolent 897adj.
sweetbread
meat 301n.
sweeten
assuage 177vb.
appetize 390vb.
sweeten 392vb.
purify 648vb.
sweetener
gift 781n.
sweetheart
loved one 887n.
lover 887n.
darling 890n.
sweeting, sweetie
darling 890n.
sweetmeat
sweetmeat 301n.
sweet 392n.
sweetness
fragrance 396n.
(*see* sweet)
sweet on
enamored 887adj.
sweet potato
tuber 301n.
flute 414n.
sweet will
will 595n.
whim 604n.
swell
grow 36vb.
add 38vb.
expand 197vb.
be convex 253vb.
wave 350n.
flow 350vb.
loudness 400n.
aristocrat 868n.
fop 848n.
be insolent 878vb.
swelled head
proud man 871n.
vanity 873n.
swelling
monticle 209n.
swelling 253n.
convex 253adj.
loud 400adj.
exaggerated 546adj.
rhetorical 574adj.
skin disease 651n.
wound 655n.
prideful 871adj.
swell the ranks
accrue 38vb.
be included 78vb.
swell up
jut 254vb.
swelter
be hot 379vb.
swerve
be oblique 220n.
deviation 282n.
recede 290vb.
tergiversate 603vb.
swift
speedy 277adj.
bird 365n.
swiftness
velocity 277n.
swig

drink 301vb.
get drunk 949vb.
swill
drink 301vb.
swill 649n.
get drunk 949vb.
swim
swim 269vb.
be light 323vb.
be dim-sighted 440vb.
swim in
enjoy 376vb.
abound 635vb.
swimming
aquatics 269n.
swimming bath
lake 346n.
ablution 648n.
swimmingly
easily 701adv.
successfully 727adv.
prosperously 730adv.
swimsuit
beachwear 228n.
aquatics 269n.
swim with the stream
conform 83vb.
aquatics 269n.
do easily 701vb.
swindle
deceive 542vb.
peculation 788n.
not pay 805vb.
be dishonest 930vb.
swindler
trickster 545n.
defrauder 789n.
swine
pig 365n.
knave, cad 938n.
sensualist 944n.
swing
periodicity 141n.
reversion 148n.
revolution 149n.
vary 152vb.
range 183n.
hang 217vb.
deviate 282vb.
oscillate 317vb.
music 412n.
scope 744n.
pleasure-ground 837n.
be punished 963vb.
swing back
recoil 280vb.
swingeing
whopping 32adj.
swing the lead
be false 541vb.
swinish
sensual 944adj.
swipe
knock 279n.
propulsion 287n.
extractor 304n.
irrigator 341n.
foin 712n.
steal 788vb.
swipes
liquor 301n.
swirl
vortex 315n.
eddy 350n.
swish
faintness 401n.
sibilation 406n.
fashionable 848adj.
switch
revolution 149n.
interchange 151vb.
hair 259n.
move 265vb.
transpose 272vb.
deflect 282vb.
diverge 294vb.
apostatize 603vb.
instrument 628n.
tool 630n.
club 723n.
hair-dressing 843n.
scourge 964n.
switchback
obliquity 220n.
undulatory 251adj.
vehicle 274n.
musical piece 412n.
pleasure-ground 837n.
switchboard
focus 76n.
switch off
terminate 69vb.
cease 145vb.
snuff out 418vb.
switch on
initiate 68vb.
operate 173vb.
swivel
rotator 315n.
gun 723n.
swivel-eye
dim sight 440n.
swizz
absurdity 497n.
trickery 542n.
fable 543n.
swollen
increasing 36adj.
expanded 197adj.
convex 253adj.
rhetorical 574adj.
diseased 651adj.
prideful 871adj.
swoon
be impotent 161vb.
weakness 163n.
fatigue 684n.
(*see* insensibility)
swoop
spurt 277n.
descend 309vb.
plunge 313n.
swoosh
sibilation 406n.
sword
destroyer 168n.
sharp edge 256n.
bane 659n.
combatant 722n.
side-arms 723n.
badge of rank 743n.
sword of Damocles
danger 661n.
intimidation 854n.
threat 900n.
sword-play
duel 716n.
swordsman
contender 716n.
combatant 722n.
sworn
affirmative 532adj.
obedient 739adj.
contractual 765adj.
dutied 917adj.
swot
study 536vb.
learner 538n.
Sybarite
sensualist 944n.
syce
domestic 742n.
servant 742n.
sycophancy
servility 879n.
flattery 925n.
false charge 928n.
sycophant
toady 879n.
flatterer 925n.
accuser 928n.
litigant 959n.
syllabary
letter 558n.
syllabic
literal 558adj.
syllabification
decomposition 51n.
syllable
speech sound 398n.
spoken letter 558n.
spell 558vb.
word 559n.
phrase 563vb.
voice 577n., vb.
speak 579vb.
syllabub
ornament 574n.

eloquence 579n.
syllabus
list 87n.
compendium 592n.
syllogism
relevance 9n.
argumentation 475n.
sylph
fairy 970n.
sylph-like
narrow 206adj.
fairylike 970adj.
sylvan
arboreal 366adj.
symbiosis
life 360n.
cooperation 706n.
symbiotic
agreeing 24adj.
conjunct 45adj.
cooperative 706adj.
symbol
insubstantial thing 4n.
number 85n.
metaphor 519n.
indication 547n.
badge 547n.
image 551n.
symbolic
insubstantial 4adj.
occult 523adj.
indicating 547adj.
representing 551adj.
trivial 639adj.
ritual 988adj.
symbolics
creed 485n.
theology 973n.
symbolism
(*see* symbol, symbolic)
symbolization
symbology 547n.
(*see* symbolize)
symbolize
mean 514vb.
figure 519vb.
interpret 520vb.
manifest 522vb.
imply 523vb.
indicate 547vb.
represent 551vb.
symbolography
symbology 547n.
symbology
symbology 547n.
symmetry
relativeness 9n.
correlation 12n.
uniformity 16n.
equality 28n.
symmetry 245n.
elegance 575n.
beauty 841n.
sympathetic
agreeing 24adj.
(*see* sympathy)
sympathize
(*see* sympathy)
sympathizer
patron 707n.
collaborator 707n.
participator 775n.
kind person 897n.
sympathy
bond 47n.
attraction 291n.
assent 488n.
imagination 513n.
aid 703n.
cooperation 706n.
concord 710n.
participation 775n.
feeling 818n.
liking 859n.
friendliness 880n.
love 887n.
benevolence 897n.
condolence 905n.
pity 905n.
symphonic
harmonious 410adj.
musical 412adj.
musicianly 413adj.
symphony
musical piece 412n.
symphysis
junction 45n.
combination 50n.
symposiarch
leader 690n.
reveller 837n.
symposiast
interlocutor 584n.
symposium
argument 475n.
interlocution 584n.
conference 584n.
festivity 837n.
social gathering 882n.
symptom
concomitant 89n.
evidence 466n.
omen 511n.
hint 524n.
indication 547n.
warning 664n.
symptomatic
accompanying 89adj.
visible 443adj.
evidential 466adj.
indicating 547adj.
cautionary 664adj.
symptomatology
hermeneutics 520n.
indication 547n.
synagogue
church 990n.
synchronism
synchronism 123n.
synchronization
adaptation 24n.
combination 50n.
arrangement 62n.
synchronism 123n.
synchronize
be in order 60vb.
accompany 89vb.
time 117vb.
be now 121vb.
synchronize 123vb.
synchronous
agreeing 24adj.
combined 50adj.
synchronous 123adj.
synchysis
inversion 221n.
synclinal
sloping 220adj.
syncopation
tempo 410n.
music 412n.
syncopator
musician 713n.
syncope
helplessness 161n.
contraction 198n.
shortness 204n.
tempo 410n.
conciseness 569n.
fatigue 684n.
syncretism
mixture 43n.
combination 50n.
syndic
officer 741n.
syndicalism
government 733n.
syndicalist
political party 708n.
corporate 708adj.
syndicate
corporation 708n.
synecdoche
trope 519n.
syneisaktism
type of marriage 894n.
celibacy 895n.
synergism
concurrence 181n.
sanctity 979n.
synergistic effect
increase 36n.
synergy
concurrence 181n.
cooperation 706n.
synesthesia
sense 374n.
syngamy

mixture 43n.
junction 45n.
syngenesis
reproduction 166n.
synod
council 692n.
synod 985n.
synodal
parliamentary 692adj.
synodic
ecclesiastical 985adj.
synodical period
regular return 141n.
synoecism
association 706n.
synonym
identity 13n.
equivalence 28n.
substitute 150n.
connotation 514n.
word 559n.
name 561n.
synonymity
(*see* synonym)
synonymous
semantic 514adj.
interpretive 520adj.
synonymy
equivocalness 518n.
synopsis
combination 50n.
whole 52n.
arrangement 62n.
generality 79n.
list 87n.
compendium 592n.
synoptical
inclusive 78adj.
Synoptic Gospels
scripture 975n.
synovia
lubricant 334n.
syntagm
arrangement 62n.
syntax
relation 9n.
composition 56n.
arrangement 62n.
assemblage 74n.
grammar 564n.
synthesis
junction 45n.
combination 50n.
argumentation 475n.
synthesize
compose 56vb.
synthetic
simulating 18adj.
imitative 20adj.
rational 475n.
untrue 543adj.
syntony
agreement 24n.
synchronism 123n.
syphilis
venereal disease 651n.
syringe
extractor 304n.
irrigator 341n.
moisten 341vb.
syrinx
flute 414n.
syrup
soft drink 301n.
viscidity 354n.
sweet 392n.
syssitia
participation 775n.
systaltic
contracted 198adj.
elastic 328adj.
system
order 60n.
arrangement 62n.
regularity 81n.
creed 485n.
habit 610n.
plan 623n.
systematic
regular 81adj.
philosophic 449adj.
rational 475adj.
businesslike 622adj.
(*see* system)
systematic knowledge
science 490n.
systematic thought
philosophy 449n.
systematize
order 60vb.
regularize 62vb.
make conform 83vb.
plan 623vb.
systole and diastole
fluctuation 317n.
syzygy
contiguity 202n.

T

tab
adjunct 40n.
label 547n.
mark 547vb.
badge of rank 743n.
tabard
tunic 228n.
tabby
cat 365n.
mottled 437adj.
interlocutor 584n.
tabefaction
contraction 198n.
tabernacle
dwelling 192n.
ritual object 988n.
temple, church 990n.
tabid
contracted 198adj.
lean 206adj.
diseased 651adj.
table
arrangement 62n.
list 87n.
put off 136vb.
lamina, layer 207n.
horizontality 216n.
stand, shelf 218n.
eating, meal 301n.
register 548vb.
stationery 586n.
tableau
spectacle 445n.
picture 553n.
stage show 594n.
pageant 875n.
table bird
table bird 365n.
table d'hôte
meal 301n.
table fish
table fish 365n.
tableland
high land 209n.
vertex 213n.
horizontality 216n.
plain 348n.
table manners
eating 301n.
table-napkin
cleaning cloth 648n.
table of contents
list 87n.
tablespoon
ladle 194n.
tablet
lamina 207n.
mouthful 301n.
monument 548n.
stationery 586n.
table-talk
chat 584n.
table-tapping
spiritualism 984n.
table-water
soft drink 301n.
tabloid
the press 528n.
medicine 658n.
taboo
exclusion 57n.
prohibition 757n.
bewitch 983vb.
tabor
drum 414n.
taboret
seat 218n.
drum 414n.
tabular

arranged 62adj.
layered 207adj.
tabula rasa
revolution 149n.
ignorance 491n.
obliteration 550n.
tabulate
class 62vb.
list 87vb.
register 548vb.
Tachism
school of painting 553n.
tachometer
velocity 277n.
tachygraph
stenographer 586n.
tacit
tacit 523adj.
Tacitean
concise 569adj.
taciturn
reticent 525adj.
voiceless 578adj.
taciturn 582adj.
unsociable 883adj.
tack
tie 45vb.
fastening 47n.
change 143vb.
sharp point 256n.
navigate 269vb.
direction 281n.
deviate 282vb.
food 301n.
tergiversate 603vb.
route 624n.
tackle
tackling 47n.
begin 68vb.
equipment 630n.
essay 671n., vb.
undertake 672vb.
do 676vb.
tack on
add 38vb.
tacky
viscid 354adj.
tact
touch 378n.
discrimination 463n.
sagacity 498n.
style 566n.
management 689n.
skill 694n.
good taste 846n.
tactful
wise 498adj.
discriminating 643adj.
tactical
(*see* tactics)
tactician
motivator 612n.
planner 623n.
expert 696n.
slyboots 698n.
tactics
motion 265n.
policy 623n.
way 624n.
deed 676n.
tactics 688n.
skill 694n.
cunning 698n.
art of war 718n.
tactile
tactual 378adj.
tactless
unfeeling 375adj.
indiscriminating 464adj.
foolish 499adj.
clumsy 695adj.
ill-bred 847adj.
discourteous 885adj.
tactual
tactual 378adj.
tadpole
youngling 132n.
frog 365n.
taenia
girdle 47n.
taffeta
textile 222n.
taffrail
fence 235n.
taffy
native 191n.
falsehood 541n.
flattery 925n.
tag
adjunct 40n.
connect 45vb.
sequel 67n.
extremity 69n.
pendant 217n.
sharp point 256n.
label 547n.
mark 547vb.
tag after
follow 284vb.
tag on
add 38vb.
taiga
marsh 347n.
wood 366n.
tail
adjunct 40n.
sequel 67n.
retinue 67n.
extremity 69n.
concomitant 89n.
pendant 217n.
rear 238n.
follow 284vb.
pursue 619vb.
nonentity 639n.
bungler 697n.
tailless
subtracted 39adj.
tail-light
lamp 420n.
tail off
decrease 37vb.
tailor
adjust 24vb.
clothier 228n.
efform 243vb.
artisan 686n.
tailored
adjusted 24adj.
dressed 228adj.
tailor's dummy
mold 23n.
frame 218n.
image 551n.
fop 848n.
tailor's goose
smoother 258n.
tail-piece
sequel 67n.
rear 238n.
tails
formal dress 228n.
tailwind
propellant 287n.
wind 352n.
aid 703n.
taint
infiltrate 297vb.
fetor 397n.
badness 645n.
defect 647n.
uncleanness 649n.
infection 651n.
impair 655vb.
slur 867n.
take
contain 56vb.
bring together 74vb.
comprise 78vb.
admit 299vb.
opine 485vb.
know 490vb.
suppose 512vb.
photograph 551vb.
require 627vb.
be ill 651vb.
overmaster 727vb.
subjugate 745vb.
arrest 747vb.
acquire 771vb.
receive 782vb.
take 786vb.
be patient 823vb.
delight 826vb.
bewitch 983vb.
take aback
navigate 269vb.

surprise 508vb.
take a back seat
be inferior 35vb.
have no repute 867vb.
be modest 874vb.
be disinterested 931vb.
take a chance
face danger 661vb.
essay 671vb.
take action
do 676vb.
take advantage of
use 673vb.
be skillful 694vb.
take after
resemble 18vb.
take alarm
fear 854vb.
take amiss
be discontented 829vb.
resent 891vb.
take apart
sunder 46vb.
take aside
speak to 583vb.
take away
subtract 39vb.
take away 786vb.
take back
recoup 31vb.
revert 148vb.
recant 603vb.
acquire 771vb.
take 786vb.
take breath
pause 145vb.
be quiescent 266vb.
take care of
be mindful 455vb.
look after 457vb.
preserve 666vb.
take command
take authority 733vb.
take cover
be stealthy 525vb.
take down
depress 311vb.
record 548vb.
write 586vb.
ridicule 851vb.
humiliate 872vb.
take effect
operate 173vb.
be successful 727vb.
take exception
resent 891vb.
take for granted
assume 471vb.
premise 475vb.
believe 485vb.
be credulous 487vb.
suppose 512vb.
not wonder 865vb.
be ungrateful 908vb.
take heart of grace
be content 828vb.
be cheerful 833vb.
hope 852vb.
take courage 855vb.
take heed
be warned 664vb.
take hold
cohere 48vb.
prevail 178vb.
be wont 610vb.
take 786vb.
take ill
be discontented 829vb.
resent 891vb.
take in
comprise 78vb.
make smaller 198vb.
shorten 204vb.
admit 299vb.
scan 438vb.
understand 516vb.
befool 542vb.
take in each other's washing
interchange 151vb.
cooperate 706vb.
take in hand
train 534vb.
undertake 672vb.
take into account
number with 78vb.
discriminate 463vb.
take in vain
misuse 675vb.
take it
knuckle under 721vb.
take it easy
move slowly 278vb.
repose 683vb.
do easily 701vb.
take it or leave it
be neutral 606vb.
take it out of
be malevolent 898vb.
take its course
go on 146vb.
happen 154vb.
take liberties
oppress 735vb.
be free 744vb.
taken bad
sick 651adj.
taken up with
obsessed 455adj.
taken with
enamored 887adj.
take off
doff 229vb.
fly 271vb.
start out 296vb.
act 594vb.
discount 810vb.
satirize 851vb.
take offense
be inimical 881vb.
resent 891vb.
take on
admit 299vb.
employ 622vb.
essay 671vb.
undertake 672vb.
do 676vb.
attack 712vb.
contend, fight 716vb.
be discontented 829vb.
incur a duty 917vb.
take orders
take orders 986vb.
take out
extract 304vb.
obliterate 550vb.
take over
come after 65vb.
take authority 733vb.
appropriate 786vb.
take-over
transference 272n.
take-over bid
offer 759n.
purchase 792n.
take place
be 1vb.
happen 154vb.
taker
possessor 776n.
recipient 782n.
taker 786n.
purchaser 792n.
take root
be stable 153vb.
prevail 178vb.
place oneself 187vb.
be wont 610vb.
take shape
become 1vb.
take sides
be biased 481vb.
choose 605vb.
join a party 708vb.
take silk
do law 958vb.
take steps
do 676vb.
take stock
number 86vb.
scan 438vb.
estimate 480vb.
account 808vb.
take the bit between one's teeth
will 595vb.
be obstinate 602vb.

disobey 738vb.
take the bull by the horns
be resolute 599vb.
be courageous 855vb.
take the count
be defeated 728vb.
take the lead
initiate 68vb.
be in front 237vb.
precede 283vb.
be important 638vb.
have repute 866vb.
take the place of
substitute 150vb.
take the veil
live single 895vb.
take orders 986vb.
take the wind out of one's sails
disable 161vb.
navigate 269vb.
abase 311vb.
hinder 702vb.
take time
be late, wait 136vb.
have leisure 681vb.
be cautious 858vb.
take time by the forelock
be early 135vb.
profit by 137vb.
take to
desire 859vb.
be in love 887vb.
take to oneself
appropriate 786vb.
take up
elevate 310vb.
undertake 672vb.
receive 782vb.
befriend 880vb.
take up the cudgels for
patronize 703vb.
defend 713vb.
taking
infectious 653adj.
anger 891n.
takings
increment 36n.
earnings 771n.
booty 790n.
receipt 807n.
talaria
wing 271n.
talbotype
photography 551n.
talcum powder
cosmetic 843n.
tale
numeration 86n.
fable 543n.
narrative 590n.
novel 590n.
tale-bearer
informer 524n.
talent
intelligence 498n.
aptitude 694n.
coinage 797n.
talent scout
inquirer 459n.
tale of woe
sorrow 825n.
lament 836n.
talipes
deformity 246n.
talisman
preserver 666n.
talisman 983n.
talismanic
magical 983adj.
talk
empty talk 515n.
inform 524vb.
rumor 529n.
oration 579n.
speak 579vb.
be loquacious 581vb.
allocution 583n.
chat 584n.
talk about
publish 528vb.
defame 926vb.
talkative
speaking 579adj.
loquacious 581adj.
talk big
be vain 873vb.
boast 877vb.
be insolent 878vb.
threaten 900vb.
talk down
be loquacious 581vb.
talked of
renowned 866adj.
talker
speaker 579n.
chatterer 581n.
interlocutor 584n.
talkie
cinema 445n.
talking
informative 524adj.
talking to
reprimand 924n.
talk it over
confer 584vb.
talk of
publish 528vb.
talk of the town
rumor 529n.
famousness 866n.
talk out
spin out 113vb.
be obstructive 702vb.
talk over
induce 612vb.
talks
conference 584n.
talk to
speak to 583vb.
talk to oneself
soliloquize 585vb.
tall
great 32adj.
whopping 32adj.
tall 209adj.
exaggerated 546adj.
tallage
tax 809n.
tallboy
cabinet 194n.
tallies
counting instrument 86n.
tallith
shawl 228n.
neckwear 228n.
canonicals 989n.
tall order
fable 543n.
undertaking 672n.
hard task 700n.
tallow
fat 357n.
tallow-faced
colorless 726adj.
tall story
news 529n.
fable 543n.
tall talk
insubstantial thing 4n.
boast 877n.
tally
conform 83vb.
numerical result 85n.
numeration 86n.
list 87n.
label 547n.
record 548n.
credit 802n.
debt 803n.
accounts 808n.
tally-clerk
recorder 549n.
tally-ho
stage-coach 274n.
chase 619n.
tallyman
lender 784n.
tradesman 794n.
talma
cloak 228n.
Talmud
scripture 975n.
talmudist
theologian 973n.

talon
foot 214n.
sharp point 256n.
finger 378n.
nippers 778n.
talus
acclivity 220n.
tambourine
drum 414n.
tame
inert 175adj.
moderate 177vb.
break in 369vb.
train 534vb.
feeble 572adj.
habituate 610vb.
subjugate 745vb.
inexcitable 823adj.
servile 879adj.
tameless
furious 176adj.
cruel 898adj.
Tammany
improbity 930n.
tam-o'-shanter
headgear 228n.
tamp
ram 279n.
close 264vb.
tamper
derange 63vb.
impair 655vb.
meddle 678vb.
tamper
modify 143vb.
bribe 612vb.
tampion, tompion
covering 226n.
stopper 264n.
tampon
covering 226n.
stopper 264n.
surgical dressing 658n.
tan
strike 279vb.
be tough 329vb.
burning 381n.
brown 430adj.
spank 963vb.
tandem
duality 90n.
bicycle 274n.
tang
projection 254n.
taste 386n.
pungency 388n.
tangency
contiguity 202n.
tangent
ratio 85n.
convergence 293n.
tangential
contiguous 202adj.
convergent 293adj.
tangerine
fruit 301n.
tangible
substantial 3adj.
material 319adj.
tactual 378adj.
true 494adj.
tangle
medley 43n.
complexity 61n.
bedevil 63vb.
enlace 222vb.
hinder 702vb.
tangled
tied 45adj.
dense 324adj.
imperspicuous 568adj.
tango
dance 837n., vb.
tanist
beneficiary 776n.
tank
vat 194n.
war-chariot 274n.
lake 346n.
storage 632n.
cavalry 722n.
tankard
cup 194n.
tanker
automobile 274n.
locomotive 274n.
merchant ship 275n.
tanner
coinage 797n.
tantalize
fall short 307vb.
make impossible 470vb.
disappoint 509vb.
tempt 612vb.
excite 821vb.
cause desire 859vb.
tantamount
equivalent 28adj.
semantic 514adj.
tantara
roll 403n.
tantrum
excitable state 822n.
anger 891n.
Taoism
religious faith 973n.
tap
tube 263n.
pierce 263vb.
stopper 264n.
transferrer 272n.
strike 279vb.
outlet 298n.
void 300vb.
extract 304vb.
water 339n.
make flow 350vb.
conduit 351n.
touch 378vb.
bang 402n.
play music 413vb.
hear 415vb.
store 632n.
provide 633vb.
acquire 771vb.
take 786vb.
endearment 889n.
tap-dance
dance 837n., vb.
tape
cable 47n.
line 203n.
strip 208n.
appraise 465vb.
taped
measured 465adj.
tape-machine
recording instrument 549n.
tape-measure
counting instrument 86n.
gauge 465n.
taper
shade off 27vb.
make smaller 198vb.
shorten 204vb.
be narrow 206vb.
be sharp 256vb.
converge 293vb.
lighter 385n.
torch 420n.
tape-recorder
recording instrument 549n.
tapering
tapering 256adj.
(*see* taper)
taper off
decrease 37vb.
tapestry
textile 222n.
covering 226n.
art 551n.
picture 553n.
needlework 844n.
decorate 844vb.
tapeworm
narrowness 206n.
thinness 206n.
tapinosis
humility 872n.
tap, on
on the spot 189adj.
provisionary 633adj.
enough 635adv.
useful 640adj.
tap out

signal 547vb.
tapping
extraction 304vb.
tap-room
tavern 192n.
chamber 194n.
taproot
source 156n.
taps
obsequies 364n.
call 547n.
tapster
servant 742n.
tap the line
hear 415vb.
be curious 453vb.
tar
coat 226vb.
mariner 270n.
resin 357n.
black thing 428n.
taradiddle
untruth 543n.
tar and feather
punish 963vb.
tarantella
music 412n.
dance 837n.
tarantism
spasm 318n.
tarboosh, tarbush
headgear 228n.
tardy
late 136adj.
slow 278adj.
lazy 679adj.
tare
decrement 42n.
discount 810n.
tares
rubbish 641n.
target
limit 236n.
direction 281n.
objective 617n.
armor 713n.
targeteer
soldiery 722n.
Targum
commentary 520n.
scripture 975n.
tariff
list 87n.
restriction 747n.
price, tax 809n.
tariff wall
exclusion 57n.
restriction 747n.
tarmac
paving 226n.
smoothness 258n.
air travel 271n.
road 624n.
building material 631n.
tarn
lake 346n.
tarnish
decolorize 426vb.
make unclean 649vb.
blemish 845n.
shame 867vb.
defame 926vb.
tarpaulin
canopy 226n.
tarry
drag on 113vb.
be late 136vb.
stay 144vb.
be quiescent 266vb.
move slowly 278vb.
resinous 357adj.
be inactive 679vb.
tarry for
expect 507vb.
tart
pastry 301n.
pungent 388adj.
sweet 392n.
sour 393adj.
ungracious 885adj.
irascible 892adj.
sullen 893adj.
prostitute 952n.
tartan
checker 437n.
livery 547n.
tartar
sourness 393n.
dirt 649n.
Tartar
destroyer 168n.
shrew 892n.
Tartar, catch a
stultify oneself 695vb.
Tartarean
dark 418adj.
cruel 898adj.
infernal 972adj.
tartuffish
hypocritical 541adj.
tarty
unchaste 951adj.
tasimeter
meter 465n.
task
finite quantity 26n.
job 622n.
undertaking 672n.
deed 676n.
labor 682n.
fatigue 684vb.
hard task 700n.
oppress 735vb.
portion 783n.
duty 917n.
penalty 963n.
task force
armed force 722n.
taskmaster
tyrant 735n.
tassel
pendant 217n.
trimming 844n.
taste
eat 301n.
sense 374n.
pleasure 376n.
taste 386n., vb.
discrimination 463n.
elegance 575n.
choice 605n.
feeling 818n.
good taste 846vb.
taste-buds
taste 386n.
tasteful
elegant 575adj.
personable 841adj.
tasteful 846adj.
taste good
appetize 390vb.
tasteless
weak 163adj.
feeble 572adj.
inelegant 576adj.
vulgar 847adj.
tastelessness
insipidity 387n.
indiscrimination 464n.
bad taste 847n.
tasty
edible 301adj.
pleasant 376adj.
tasty 386adj.
savory 390adj.
pleasurable 826adj.
tatterdemalion
slut 61n.
low fellow 869n.
tattered
beggarly 801adj.
tatters
piece 53n.
clothing 228n.
tatters, in
dilapidated 655adj.
tatting
needlework 844n.
tattle
be loquacious 581vb.
chat 584n.
tattler
informer 524n.
newsmonger 529n.
chatterer 581n.
interlocutor 584n.
tattoo
pierce 263vb.
roll 403n., vb.
play music 413vb.

color 425vb.
variegate 437vb.
call 547n.
mark 547vb.
beautify 841vb.
pageant 875n.
celebration 876n.
tattooer
beautician 843n.
tattooing
ornamental art 844n.
tatty
dilapidated 655adj.
beggarly 801adj.
tau
cross 222n.
taunt
be insolent 878vb.
enrage 891vb.
indignity 921n.
reproach 924n.
calumny 926n.
accusation 928n.
taurine
animal 365adj.
tauromachy
duel 716n.
Taurus
zodiac 321n.
taut
tied 45adj.
rigid 326adj.
tauten
tighten 45vb.
make smaller 198vb.
harden 326vb.
tautologize
be diffuse 570vb.
tautologous
identical 13adj.
tautology
repetition 106n.
pleonasm 570n.
superfluity 637n.
redundance 637n.
tavern
tavern 192n.
tawdry
trivial 639adj.
vulgar 847adj.
tawny
brown 430adj.
red 431adj.
yellow 433adj.
tax
bane 659n.
fatigue 684vb.
oppress 735vb.
demand 737n., vb.
levy 786vb.
tax 809n., vb.
impose a duty 917vb.
taxable
priced 809adj.
taxation
tax 809n.
tax-collector
receiver 782n.
tax-farmer
receiver 782n.
tax-free
uncharged 812adj.
non-liable 919adj.
taxi
move 265vb.
drive 267vb.
fly 271vb.
cab 274n.
taxidermy
zoology 367n.
taxi-driver
carrier 273n.
taximan
driver 268n.
tax on
dearness 811n.
taxonomy
arrangement 62n.
tax with
accuse 928vb.
tea
meal 301n.
soft drink 301n.
tea-caddy
small box 194n.
teach
break in 369vb.
convince 485vb.
show 522vb.
inform 524vb.
educate 534vb.
habituate 610vb.
teachable
intelligible 516adj.
studious 536adj.
willing 597adj.
teachableness
persuasibility 612n.
teacher
scholar 492n.
sage 500n.
interpreter 520n.
teacher 537n.
adviser 691n.
expert 696n.
teacher's pet
favorite 890n.
tea-chest
box 194n.
teaching
teaching 534n.
preparation 669n.
teach one his place
humiliate 872vb.
teacup
cup 194n.
tea-drinker
sober person 948n.
tea-garden
farm 370n.
teahouse
café 192n.
teak
hardness 326n.
tree 366n.
teal
waterfowl 365n.
tea leaves
oracle 511n.
team
group, band 74n.
party 708n.
team-captain
director 690n.
team-mate
collaborator 707n.
team-race
cooperation 706n.
racing 716n.
team spirit
cooperation 706n.
concord 710n.
teamster
driver 268n.
leader 690n.
team up with
join a party 708vb.
teamwork
cooperation 706n.
tea-party
social gathering 882n.
teapot
caldron 194n.
teapoy
stand 218n.
tear
rend 46vb.
be violent 176vb.
gap 201n.
blunt 257vb.
groove 262vb.
move fast 277vb.
ill-treat 645vb.
wound 655vb.
lamentation 836n.
tearable
severable 46adj.
flimsy 163adj.
tear down
demolish 165vb.
fell 311vb.
tear-drop
moisture 341n.
lamentation 836n.
tearful
crying 408adj.
unhappy 825adj.
melancholic 834adj.
lamenting 836adj.
tear gas

poison 659n.
weapon 723n.
tear-jerking
distressing 827adj.
tearless
pitiless 906adj.
tea room
café 192n.
tear out
extract 304vb.
tear strips off
reprove 924vb.
tear to pieces
detract 926vb.
tear up
demolish 165vb.
abrogate 752vb.
tease
tempt 612vb.
excite 821vb.
delight 826vb.
torment 827vb.
be witty 839vb.
cause desire 859vb.
enrage 891vb.
be malevolent 898vb.
teaser
enigma 530n.
difficulty 700n.
worry 825n.
humorist 839n.
tea-set
cup 194n.
teashop
café 192n.
teaspoon
ladle 194n.
teat
bladder 194n.
bosom 253n.
tea-table
stand 218n.
technical
regular 83adj.
trivial 639adj.
well-made 694adj.
technical expression
neology 560n.
technicality
unimportance 639n.
trifle 639n.
precept 693n.
technical knowledge
skill 694n.
technical language
specialty 80n.
technical term
neology 560n.
name 561n.
technician
artisan 686n.
expert 696n.
technicology
mechanics 630n.
technique
way 624n.
means 629n.
skill 694n.
technocracy
government 733n.
technology
science 490n.
mechanics 630n.
skill 694n.
tectonic
structural 331adj.
tectonic
production 164n.
structure 331n.
Teddy-boy
youngster 132n.
fop 848n.
low fellow 869n.
ruffian 904n.
Te Deum
rejoicing 835n.
celebration 876n.
thanks 907n.
hymn 981n.
tedious
long 203adj.
prolix 570adj.
feeble 572adj.
fatiguing 684adj.
tedious 838adj.
dull 840adj.
tedium
tedium 838n.
satiety 863n.
(*see* tedious)
teed up
prepared 669adj.
teem
be many 104vb.
reproduce itself 164vb.
be fruitful 171vb.
abound 635vb.
teen-age
youth 130n.
young 130adj.
teen-ager
youngster 132n.
teeter
oscillate 317vb.
be agitated 318vb.
be irresolute 601vb.
teeth
vigorousness 174n.
eater 301n.
pulverizer 332n.
weapon 723n.
nippers 778n.
teething troubles
beginning 68n.
youth 130n.
learning 536n.
difficulty 700n.
teeth of, in the
with difficulty 700adv.
in opposition 704adv.
teetotal
temperate 942adj.
sober 948adj.
teetotaler
abstainer 942n.
sober person 948n.
teetotalism
temperance 942n.
sobriety 948n.
teetotum
rotator 315n.
plaything 837n.
tee up
make ready 669vb.
tegular
overlying 226adj.
tegument
skin 226n.
tegumentary
dermal 226adj.
teichopsia
dim sight 440n.
teinscope
optical device 442n.
telamon
pillar 218n.
telautograph
recording instrument 549n.
telearchics
directorship 689n.
telecast
publish 528vb.
telecommunication
telecommunication 531n.
telegnosis
psychics 984n.
telegony
genealogy 169n.
influence 178n.
telegram
information 524n.
message 529n.
telegraph
velocity 277n.
communicate 524vb.
telecommunication 531n.
signal 547n.
telegraph boy
courier 531n.
telegraphese
conciseness 569n.
telegraphic
speedy 277adj.
concise 569adj.
telekinesis
spiritualism 984n.
telemechanics
mechanics 630n.

teleology
intention 617n.
telepath
psychic 984n.
telepathy
sense 374n.
thought 449n.
intuition 476n.
psychics 984n.
telephone
hearing aid 415n.
communication 531n.
telephoto lens
camera 442n.
optical device 442n.
teleplasm
spiritualism 984n.
teleprinter
telecommunication 531n.
recording instrument 549n.
telergy
psychics 984n.
telescope
shorten 204vb.
astronomy 321n.
telescope 442n.
detector 484n.
be concise 569vb.
telescopic
distant 199adj.
astronomic 321adj.
visible 443adj.
telespectroscope
optical device 442n.
telesthesia
psychics 984n.
televiewer
spectator 441n.
telecommunication 531n.
televise
communicate 524vb.
publish 528vb.
television
spectacle 445n.
telecommunication 531n.
tell
number 86vb.
influence 178vb.
monticle 209n.
inform 524vb.
divulge 526vb.
indicate 547vb.
describe 590vb.
be important 638vb.
be successful 727vb.
command 737vb.
tell against
tell against 467vb.
tell another story
tell against 467vb.
teller
computer 86n.
informant 524n.
treasurer 798n.
tell fortunes
divine 511vb.
telling
influential 178adj.
evidential 466adj.
expressive 516adj.
instrumental 628adj.
important 638adj.
impressive 821adj.
tell of
evidence 466vb.
mean 514vb.
tell off
command 737vb.
reprove 924vb.
tell-tale
witness 466n.
informer 524n.
disclosing 526adj.
indicating 547adj.
tergiversator 603adj.
tellurian
native 191adj.
telluric 321adj.
mankind 371n.
human 371adj.
telluric
telluric 321adj.
telpher line
railroad 624n.
temenos
enclosure 235n.
holy place 990n.
temerarious
rash 857adj.
temerity
rashness 857n.
temper
temperament 5n.
state 7n.
mix 43vb.
composition 56n.
strength 162n.
strengthen 162vb.
moderate 177vb.
hardness 326n.
harden 326vb.
soften 327vb.
be tough 329vb.
qualify 468vb.
mature 669vb.
affections 817n.
anger 891n.
tempera
pigment 425n.
art equipment 553n.
temperament
temperament 5n.
state 7n.
composition 56n.
caprice 604n.
affections 817n.
sensibility 819n.
excitability 822n.
irascibility 892n.
sullenness 893n.
temperamental
capricious 604adj.
lively 819adj.
excitable 822adj.
temperance
moderation 177n.
avoidance 620n.
restraint 747n.
virtues 933n.
temperance 942n.
asceticism 945n.
temperate
moderate 177adj.
warm 379adj.
cold 380adj.
restrained 747adj.
sober 948adj.
(*see* temperance)
temperature
heat 379n.
illness 651n.
tempered
strong 162adj.
moderate 177adj.
hard 326adj.
tempest
storm 176n.
commotion 318n.
tempestivity
occasion 137n.
tempestuous
disorderly 61adj.
violent 176adj.
speedy 277adj.
windy 352adj.
excitable 822adj.
angry 891adj.
Templars
monk 986n.
temple
laterality 239n.
temple 990n.
temple state
polity 733n.
tempo
tendency 179n.
motion 265n.
velocity 277n.
tempo 410n.
temporal
transient 114adj.
chronological 117adj.
laical 987adj.
temporality
property 777n.
benefice 985n.
laicality 987n.

temporary
ephemeral 114adj.
substituted 150adj.
uncertain 474adj.
temporary accommodation
lending 784n.
temporize
spin out 113vb.
put off 136vb.
temporizing
cunning 698adj.
tempt
influence 178vb.
attract 291vb.
tempt 612vb.
cause desire 859vb.
make wicked 934vb.
temptation
attraction 291n.
inducement 612n.
desired object 859n.
tempter
motivator 612n.
Satan 969n.
tempt fortune
gamble 618vb.
tempting
savory 390adj.
tempt providence
be rash 857vb.
temptress
loose woman 952n.
temulence
drunkenness 949n.
tenable
rational 475adj.
credible 485adj.
invulnerable 660adj.
tenacious
cohesive 48adj.
tough 329adj.
resolute 599adj.
preserving 600adj.
obstinate 602adj.
tenacity
retention 778n.
(*see* tenacious)
tenaculum
nippers 778n.
tenancy
possession 773n.
tenant
resident 191n.
dwell 192vb.
possessor 776n.
tenantless
empty 190adj.
Ten Commandments
fixture 153n.
precept 693n.
code of duty 917n.
law 953n.
revelation 975n.
tend
conduce 156vb.
tend 179vb.
groom 369vb.
look after 457vb.
doctor 658vb.
serve 742vb.
tendency
ability 160n.
tendency 179n.
direction 281n.
probability 471n.
bias 481n.
willingness 597n.
aptitude 694n.
affections 817n.
liking 859n.
tendentious
tending 179adj.
intended 617adj.
tender
ship 275n.
follower 284n.
soft-hued 425adj.
look after 457vb.
careful 457adj.
diseased 651adj.
warship 722n.
offer 759n., vb.
honor 866vb.
pet 889vb.
pitying 905adj.
respect 920vb.
(*see* tenderness)
tender age
youth 130n.
tenderer
petitioner 763n.
tenderfoot
beginner 538n.
tenderize
soften 327vb.
tenderly
carefully 457adv.
tender mercies
severity 735n.
tenderness
weakness 163n.
softness 327n.
sensibility 374n.
pain 377n.
lenity 736n.
moral sensibility 819n.
painfulness 827n.
love 887n.
benevolence 897n.
tender spot
vulnerability 661n.
moral sensibility 819n.
tending
liable 180adj.
possible 469adj.
tendon
ligature 47n.
tendril
ligature 47n.
filament 208n.
coil 251n.
plant 366n.
Tenebrae
church service 988n.
tenebrosity
darkness 418n.
tenement
housing 192n.
estate 777n.
tenet
creed 485n.
precept 693n.
tenfold
fifth and over 99adj.
tenné
orange 436adj.
heraldry 547n.
tenner
funds 797n.
tennis
ball game 837n.
tennis court
horizontality 216n.
pleasure-ground 837n.
tennis player
player 837n.
tenor
modality 7n.
degree 27n.
tendency 179n.
direction 281n.
vocalist 413n.
meaning 514n.
tense
time 108n.
rigid 326adj.
expectant 507adj.
grammar 564n.
fervent 818adj.
feeling 818adj.
excited 821adj.
excitable 822adj.
tensile
elastic 328adj.
tension
energy 160n.
strength 162n.
lengthening 203n.
excitation 821n.
worry 825n.
discontent 829n.
tent
dwelling 192n.
pavilion 192n.
canopy 226n.
hospital 658n.
surgical dressing 658n.

tentacle
nippers 778n.
tentative
slow 278adj.
inquiring 459adj.
experimental 461adj.
clumsy 695adj.
cautious 858adj.
tentativeness
empiricism 461n.
tent-dweller
dweller 191n.
tenterhook
hanger 217n.
tenterhooks, on
expectant 507adj.
tenuity
insubstantiality 4n.
smallness 33n.
thinness 206n.
rarity 325n.
tenuous
(*see* tenuity)
tenure
time 108n.
possession 773n.
estate 777n.
tepee
dwelling 192n.
tepefaction
heating 381n.
tepid
warm 379adj.
teraphim
home 192n.
idol 982n.
teratical
unusual 84adj.
teratogenesis
abnormality 84n.
propagation 164n.
deformity 246n.
teratology
magniloquence 574n.
thaumaturgy 864n.
boasting 877n.
terce
morning 128n.
church service 988n.
tergiversate
turn back 286vb.
tergiversate 603vb.
fail in duty 918vb.
tergiversating
changeful 152adj.
irresolute 601adj.
tergiversation
change 143n.
reversion 148n.
unreliability 474n.
tergiversation 603n.
cowardice 856n.
perfidy 930n.
term
end 69n.
serial place 73n.
date 108n.
period 110n.
limit 236n.
word 559n.
name 561n., vb.
termagant
violent creature 176n.
shrew 892n.
terminal
extremity 69n.
ending 69adj.
stopping place 145n.
distant 199adj.
limit 236n.
goal 295n.
terminate
terminate 69vb.
cease 145vb.
termination
end 69n.
effect 157n.
completion 725n.
terminator
limit 236n.
terminology
etymology 559n.
nomenclature 561n.
phrase 563n.
terminus
extremity 69n.
stopping place 145n.
limit 236n.
itinerary 267n.
goal 295n.
completion 725n.
termite
vermin 365n.
termless
infinite 107adj.
term of art
neology 560n.
name 561n.
terms
conditions 766n.
terms of reference
function 622n.
ternary
treble 94adj.
ternion
three 93n.
terrace
housing 192n.
horizontality 216n.
terra-cotta
pottery 381n.
terra firma
basis 218n.
goal 295n.
land 344n.
terrain
space 183n.
region 184n.
land 344n.
arena 724n.
terrapin
reptile 365n.
terraqueous
telluric 321adj.
terrarium
zoo 369n.
terrene
telluric 321adj.
territorial 344adj.
terrestrial
native 191n.
telluric 321adj.
terret
fastening 47n.
circle 250n.
terrible
frightening 854adj.
terrier
list 87n.
dog 365n.
terrific
prodigious 32adj.
excellent 644adj.
terrify
frighten 854vb.
terrigenous
native 191adj.
territorial 344adj.
territorial
regional 184adj.
territorial 344adj.
soldier 722n.
territory
territory 184n.
land 344n.
polity 733n.
lands 777n.
terror
violent creature 176n.
bane 659n.
fear 854n.
intimidation 854n.
ruffian 904n.
bad man 938n.
terrorism
violence 176n.
sedition 738n.
intimidation 854n.
terrorist
opponent 705n.
revolter 738n.
alarmist 854n.
terrorize
dissuade 613vb.
oppress 735vb.
frighten 854vb.
terror tactics
terror tactics 712n.
terse
short 204adj.
aphoristic 496adj.

terseness
conciseness 569n.
tertian
seasonal 141adj.
tertiary
three 93adj.
secular 110adj.
tertius gaudens
beneficiary 776n.
terza rima
verse form 593n.
tessellation
checker 437n.
tessera
label 547n.
test
exam. 459n.
inquire 459vb.
experiment 461n., vb.
essay 671vb.
hard task 700n.
testable
experimental 461adj.
demonstrated 478adj.
testament
testimony 466n.
title-deed 767n.
testamentary
proprietary 777adj.
testamentary disposition
transfer 780n.
testator
transferrer 272n.
giver 781n.
test case
prototype 23n.
experiment 461n.
litigation 959n.
test-driver
experimenter 461n.
tested
certain 473adj.
excellent 644adj.
approved 923adj.
trustworthy 929adj.
testee
respondent 460n.
testee 461n.
tester
bed 218n.
inquirer 459n.
experimenter 461n.
testicle
genitalia 164n.
testifier
informant 524n.
testify
testify 466vb.
affirm 532vb.
indicate 547vb.
testimonial
credential 466n.
reminder 505n.
monument 548n.
approbation 923n.
testimony
testimony 466n.
affirmation 532n.
testing agent
testing agent 461n.
test-pilot
experimenter 461n.
test-tube
crucible 147n.
vessel 194n.
testing agent 461n.
testudo
armor 713n.
testy
ungracious 885adj.
irascible 892adj.
tetanus
spasm 318n.
infection 651n.
tetchy
irascible 892adj.
tête-a-tête
interlocution 584n.
social gathering 882n.
tether
tie 45vb.
halter 47n.
place 187vb.
obstacle 702n.
fetter 747vb.
fetter 748n.
tetractys, tetrad
quaternity 96n.
tetragon
angular figure 247n.
tetragrammaton
the Deity 265n.
tetralogy
poem 593n.
stage play 594n.
tetrameter
prosody 593n.
tetrarch
potentate 741n.
Teutonism
dialect 560n.
text
prototype 23n.
piece 53n.
topic 452n.
maxim 496n.
meaning 514n.
reading matter 589n.
precept 693n.
textbook
classroom 539n.
reading matter 589n.
dissertation 591n.
compendium 592n.
textile
textile 222n.
texture 331n.
materials 631n.
textual
scriptural 975adj.
orthodox 976adj.
textual criticism
interpretation 520n.
textualist
theologian 973n.
textural
textural 331adj.
texture
weaving 222n.
texture 331n.
pattern 844n.
thakur
potentate 741n.
master 741n.
idol 982n.
thalassic
oceanic 343adj.
thallophyte
plant 366n.
thane
nobleman 868n.
thank
gratulate 886vb.
thank 907vb.
grant claims 915vb.
praise 923vb.
reward 962vb.
thankful
content 828adj.
grateful 907adj.
approving 923adj.
thankfulness
gratitude 907n.
thankless
profitless 641adj.
unpleasant 827adj.
unthanked 908adj.
thanklessness
ingratitude 908n.
thank-offering
offering 781n.
thanks 907n.
oblation 981n.
thanksgiving
rejoicing 835n.
celebration 876n.
thanks 907n.
act of worship 981n.
thanks to
hence 158adv.
in aid of 703adv.
thatch
roof 226n.
repair 656vb.
thatcher
mender 656n.
artisan 686n.
thatness
reality 1n.
thaumatology
thaumaturgy 864n.
thaumatrope

optical device 442n.
thaumaturge
prodigy 864n.
thaumaturgic
wonderful 864adj.
sorcerous 983adj.
thaumaturgy
thaumaturgy 864n.
sorcery 983n.
thaw
come unstuck 49vb.
liquefaction 337n.
liquefy 337vb.
marsh 347n.
semiliquidity 354n.
be hot 379vb.
heat 381vb.
thearchy
government 733n.
theater
region 184n.
meeting place 192n.
view 438n.
cinema 445n.
classroom 539n.
theater 594n.
arena 724n.
place of amusement 837n.
theatergoer
spectator 441n.
playgoer 594n.
theaterland
district 184n.
theater-minded
dramatic 594adj.
theater sister
nurse 658n.
theatricality
dramaturgy 594n.
acting 594n.
affectation 850n.
ostentation 875n.
theatricals
dramaturgy 594n.
thé dansant
dancing 837n.
social gathering 882n.
theft
acquisition 771n.
stealing 788n.
theism
deism 973n.
piety 979n.
theist
religionist 973n.
thelytoky
propagation 164n.
"them"
master 741n.
thematic
interjacent 231adj.
theme
melody 410n.
musical piece 412n.
topic 452n.
dissertation 591n.
thence
hence 158adv.
theocracy
government 733n.
theocracy 965n.
churchdom 985n.
theodicy
theology 973n.
theodolite
angular measure 247n.
gauge 465n.
theogony
genealogy 169n.
god 966n.
theolatry
religion 973n.
theologian
reasoner 475n.
theologian 973n.
theology
theology 973n.
theomancy
theomancy 511n.
theomorphic
godlike 965adj.
theotechnic 966adj.
theopathy
piety 979n.
theophany
appearance 445n.
manifestation 522n.
theophany 965n.
revelation 975n.
theophoric
named 561adj.
theopneust
revelation 975n.
theorbo
harp 414n.
theorem
topic 452n.
argumentation 475n.
axiom 496n.
supposition 512n.
theoretical
mental 447adj.
suppositional 512adj.
theorist
theorist 512n.
theorize
account for 158vb.
suppose 512vb.
theory
attribution 158n.
idea 451n.
opinion 485n.
supposition 512n.
theosophist
occultist 984n.
theosophy
religion 973n.
theosophy 984n.
theotechny
god 966n.
Theotokos
Madonna 968n.
therapeutics
medical art 658n.
therapy 658n.
therapy
therapy 658n.
there
in place 186adv.
here 189adv.
thereabouts
about 33adv.
nearly 200adv.
thereafter, thereupon
subsequently 120adv.
there and back
reversion 148n.
therefore
hence 158adv.
therein
inside 224adv.
theriac
antidote 658n.
therianthropic
animal 365adj.
theriomorphic
animal 365adj.
idolatrous 982adj.
theriomorphic deity
Egyptian gods 967n.
therm
thermometry 379n.
thermae
heater 383n.
ablution 648n.
hygiene 652n.
hospital 658n.
thermantidote
ventilation 352n.
thermod
occultism 984n.
thermodynamics
science of forces 162n.
thermometry 379n.
thermograph
thermometry 379n.
thermology
thermometry 379n.
thermometer
thermometry 379n.
meter 465n.
thermometry
thermometry 379n.
thermonuclear fission
dynamic 160adj.
thermonuclear fission
nucleonics 160n.
thermopile
thermometry 379n.
thermoplastic

flexible 327adj.
thermoscope
thermometry 379n.
thermos flask
preserver 666n.
thermostat
thermometry 379n.
thesaurus
word list 87n.
dictionary 559n.
collection 632n.
treasury 799n.
thesis
topic 452n.
argument 475n.
supposition 512n.
dissertation 591n.
prosody 593n.
theurgy
sorcery 983n.
they
group 74n.
thick
great 32adj.
middle 70n.
assembled 74adj.
multitudinous 104adj.
thick 205adj.
dense 324adj.
semiliquid 354adj.
cloudy 355adj.
dim 419adj.
opaque 423adj.
stammering 580adj.
friendly 880adj.
thick-coming
frequent 139adj.
thicken
grow 36vb.
expand 197vb.
be broad 205vb.
be dense 324vb.
thicken 354vb.
make opaque 423vb.
thickener
condensation 324n.
thickening 354n.
thicket
wood 366n.
thickhead
dunce 501n.
thick, in the
midway 70adv.
thickness
quantity 26n.
thickness 205n.
layer 207n.
density 324n.
metrology 465n.
(*see* thick)
thick of things
middle 70n.
activity 678n.
thick on the ground
multitudinous 104adj.
thick-ribbed
strong 162adj.
thickset
stalwart 162adj.
short 204adj.
thick 205adj.
dense 324adj.
thick-skinned
unfeeling 375adj.
thick-skinned 820adj.
thick speech
speech defect 580n.
thick-witted
unintelligent 499adj.
thief
thief 789n.
knave 938n.
thieve
steal 788vb.
thievery
thievishness 788n.
thigh
leg 267n.
thill
tool 630n.
thimble
armor 713n.
thimbleful
small quantity 33n.
thimblerig
sleight 542n.
thimblerigger
trickster 545n.
thin
insubstantial 4adj.
decrease 37vb.
few 105adj.
weaken 163vb.
exiguous 196adj.
make smaller 198vb.
lean 206adj.
shallow 211adj.
hairless 229adj.
rarefy 325vb.
transparent 422adj.
feeble 572adj.
underfed 636adj.
insufficient 636adj.
fasting 946adj.
thin air
insubstantial thing 4n.
thin end of the wedge
start 68n.
stratagem 698n.
thing
substance 3n.
product 164n.
object 319n.
thing of the past
archaism 127n.
things
clothing 228n.
property 777n.
thingummybob
no name 562n.
thin ice, on
endangered 661adj.
think
think 449vb.
opine 485vb.
suppose 512vb.
imagine 513vb.
thinkable
possible 469adj.
think about
meditate 449vb.
think again
tergiversate 603vb.
be penitent 939vb.
think ahead
plan 623vb.
think alike
cooperate 706vb.
think aloud
soliloquize 585vb.
think back
retrospect 505vb.
think better of it
tergiversate 603vb.
seek safety 660vb.
be nervous 854vb.
thinker
philosopher 449n.
inquirer 459n.
sage 500n.
theorist 512n.
thinking
wise 498adj.
thinking-cap
thought 449n.
think nothing of
be inattentive 456vb.
hold cheap 922vb.
think of
initiate 68vb.
be mindful 455vb.
think twice
be cautious 858vb.
think up
produce 164vb.
imagine 513vb.
plan 623vb.
think well of
respect 920vb.
approve 923vb.
thinness
smallness 33n.
thinness 206n.
levity 323n.
(*see* thin)
thinning
dieting 301n.
hair-dressing 843n.
thin on the ground
few 105adj.

thin out
be dispersed 75vb.
extract 304vb.
cultivate 370vb.
thin red line
armed force 722n.
thin-skinned
sentient 374adj.
sensitive 819adj.
irascible 892adj.
thin time, have a
feel pain 377vb.
suffer 825vb.
third
treble 94adj.
trisection 95n.
musical note 410n.
third degree
interrogation 459n.
police inquiry 459n.
corporal punishment 963n.
third estate
commonalty 869n.
thirst
dryness 342n.
be hot 379vb.
desire, hunger 859n.
thirsty
dry 342n.
hot 379adj.
hungry 859adj.
drunken 949adj.
Thirty-nine Articles
theology 973n.
orthodoxy 976n.
this or that
no name 562n.
anonymous 562adj.
thistle
prickle 256n.
plant 366n.
heraldry 547n.
thistledown
hair 259n.
levity 323n.
thither
toward 281adv.
thole-pin
pivot 218n.
Thomism
philosophy 449n.
theology 973n.
thong
ligature 47n.
scourge 964n.
thorax
bosom 253n.
thorn
prickle 256n.
plant 366n.
thorn in the flesh
badness 645n.
bane 659n.
painfulness 827n.
thorny
sharp 256adj.
difficult 700adj.
thorough
consummate 32adj.
complete 54adj.
careful 457adj.
resolute 599adj.
laboring 682adj.
completive 725adj.
thoroughbred
unmixed 44adj.
thoroughbred 273n.
well-bred 848adj.
aristocrat 868n.
thoroughfare
open space 263n.
passing along 305n.
road 624n.
thoroughgoing
(*see* thorough)
thoroughness
(*see* thorough)
though
in return 31adv.
thought
small quantity 33n.
velocity 277n.
intellect 447n.
thought 449n.
idea 451n.
attention 455n.
opinion 485n.
supposition 512n.
worry 825n.
thoughtful
thoughtful 449adj.
attentive 455adj.
careful 457adj.
wise 498adj.
disinterested 931adj.
thoughtless
unthinking 450adj.
inattentive 456adj.
negligent 458adj.
unwise 499adj.
unprepared 670adj.
unskillful 695adj.
rash 857adj.
thought-provoking
topical 452adj.
suppositional 512adj.
thought-reading
psychics 984n.
thousand and one
many 104adj.
thrall
slave 742n.
thralldom
servitude 745n.
detention 747n.
thrash
strike 279vb.
defeat 727vb.
flog 963vb.
thread
small thing 33n.
connect 45vb.
cable 47n.
ligature 47n.
arrange 62vb.
series 71n.
continuate 71vb.
weak thing 163n.
line 203n.
narrowness 206n.
fiber 208n.
pass 305vb.
threadbare
hairless 229adj.
uncovered 229adj.
dirty 649adj.
beggarly 801adj.
threat
intention 617n.
danger 661n.
warning 664n.
defiance 711n.
intimidation 854n.
insolence 878n.
threat 900n.
threaten
be to come 124vb.
impend 155vb.
predict 511vb.
dissuade 613vb.
warn 664vb.
boast 877vb.
threaten 900vb.
three
three 93n.
three-card trick
sleight 542n.
three cheers
rejoicing 835n.
three-dimensional
spatial 183adj.
formed 243adj.
metric 465adj.
threefold
treble 94adj.
three-line whip
command 737n.
Three Musketeers
close friend 880n.
threepenny bit
coinage 797n.
three-point landing
air travel 271n.
three R's, the
curriculum 534n.
threesome
three 93n.
thremmatology
animal husbandry 369n.
threnody

vocal music 412n.
lament 836n.
thresh
strike 279vb.
cultivate 370vb.
thresh about
be agitated 318vb.
thresher
husbandman 370n.
farm tool 370n.
threshold
entrance 68n.
stand 218n.
threshold 234n.
limit 236n.
doorway 263n.
threshold, at the
nigh 200adv.
thrice
trebly 94adv.
thrift
gain 771n.
economy 814n.
thriftless
prodigal 815adj.
rash 857adj.
thrifty
careful 457adj.
economical 814adj.
thrill
pang 377n.
itch 378vb.
feeling 818n.
excitation 821n.
excitable state 822n.
joy 824n.
please 826vb.
thriller
novel 590n.
thrilling
agitated 318adj.
thrill-loving
excitable 822adj.
thrill-seeker
reveler 837n.
sensualist 944n.
thrive
be vigorous 174vb.
flourish 615vb.
be active 678vb.
prosper 730vb.
throat
orifice 263n.
conduit 351n.
air-pipe 353n.
throaty
hoarse 407adj.
diseased 651adj.
throb
be periodic 141vb.
oscillate 317vb.
spasm 318n.
give pain 377vb.
show feeling 818vb.
throe
obstetrics 164n.
spasm 318n.
pang 377n.
throes
violence 176n.
thrombophlebitis
blood pressure 651n.
thrombosis
solid body 324n.
blood 335n.
blood pressure 651n.
throne
seat 218n.
regalia 743n.
tribunal 956n.
throne, on the
ruling 733adj.
throne-room
chamber 194n.
thrones
angel 968n.
throng
crowd 74n.
multitude 104n.
throng in
irrupt 297vb.
throttle
disable 161vb.
close 264vb.
retard 278vb.
through
until now 121adv.
vehicular 274adj.
toward 281adv.
communicating 624adj.
through 628adv.
by means of 629adv.
throughout
throughout 54adv.
while 108adv.
widely 183adj.
throughput
production 164n.
transference 272n.
throughway
road 624n.
through with, be
climax 725vb.
throw
move 265vb.
impulse 279n.
propel 287vb.
gambling 618n.
exertion 682n.
throw a party
be hospitable 882vb.
throw away
eject 300vb.
act 594vb.
reject 607vb.
waste 634vb.
disuse 674vb.
misuse 675vb.
be prodigal 815vb.
throw-back
recurrence 106n.
reversion 148n.
deterioration 655n.
relapse 657n.
throw back to
reproduce 166vb.
throw bricks
disapprove 924vb.
throw cold water
dissuade 613vb.
hinder 702vb.
deject 834vb.
throw down
demolish 165vb.
fell 311vb.
throw dust in the eyes
blind 439vb.
deceive 542vb.
thrower
thrower 287n.
throw fits
be agitated 318vb.
be excitable 822vb.
throw-in
propulsion 287n.
throw in one's hand
relinquish 621vb.
resign 753vb.
throw in one's teeth
defy 711vb.
accuse 928vb.
throw in the shade
humiliate 872vb.
throw light on
make bright 417vb.
interpret 520vb.
throw mud
disapprove 924vb.
defame 926vb.
thrown
grounded 728adj.
throw off the mask
disclose 526vb.
throw off the scent
puzzle 474vb.
avoid 620vb.
throw off the yoke
revolt 738vb.
achieve liberty 746vb.
throw one's weight about
be vigorous 174vb.
throw open
open 263vb.
admit 299vb.
manifest 522vb.
throw out
eject 300vb.
throw-out
rubbish 641n.
throw over

tergiversate 603vb.
relinquish 621vb.
throw overboard
bate 37vb.
eject 300vb.
lighten 323vb.
disuse 674vb.
throw-stick
missile weapon 723n.
throw stones
not respect 921vb.
disapprove 924vb.
throw up
eject 300vb.
vomit 300vb.
elevate 310vb.
submit 721vb.
resign 753vb.
thrum
filament 208n.
edging 234n.
play music 413vb.
thrummer
instrumentalist 413n.
thrush
bird 365n.
vocalist 413n.
animal disease 651n.
thrust
energy 160n.
vigorousness 174n.
influence 178n.
distortion 246n.
spurt 277n.
impulse 279n.
propellant 287n.
foin 712n.
thruster
busy person 678n.
thrustful
vigorous 174adj.
impelling 279adj.
assertive 532adj.
active 678adj.
thrust in
interfere 231vb.
thud
sound faint 401vb.
non-resonance 405n.
thug
murderer 362n.
robber 789n.
ruffian 904n.
bad man 938n.
thuggee
homicide 362n.
stealing 788n.
thumb-impression
trace 548n.
thumb index
directory 87n.
indication 547n.
thumb-nail
small 33adj.
compendium 592n.
thumbscrew
torture 963vb.
instrument of torture 964n.
thumbs down
condemnation 961n.
thumbs up
approbation 923n.
acquittal 960n.
thump
strike 279vb.
non-resonance 405n.
thumper
whopper 195n.
thumping
whopping 32adj.
large 195adj.
thunder
storm 176n.
loudness 400n.
proclaim 528vb.
emphasize 532vb.
be angry 891vb.
malediction 899n.
threaten 900vb.
thunderbolt
missile weapon 723n.
thunderbox
vessel 194n.
latrine 649n.
thunder-clap
loudness 400n.
inexpectation 508n.
thunderous
loud 400adj.
approving 923adj.
thunderstorm
commotion 318n.
gale 352n.
thunderstruck
inexpectant 508adj.
wondering 864adj.
thurible
scent 396n.
ritual object 988n.
thurifer
church officer 986n.
ritualist 988n.
thurify
be fragrant 396vb.
perform ritual 988vb.
thus
thus 8n.
hence 158adv.
thwack
strike 279vb.
thwart
oblique 220adj.
across 222adv.
disappoint 509vb.
be obstructive 702vb.
oppose 704vb.
adverse 731adj.
incommode 827vb.
thwarted
impotent 161adj.
disappointed 509adj.
defeated 728adj.
thyme
potherb 301n.
scent 396n.
thyrotoxic
active 678adj.
thyrsus
badge of rule 743n.
tiara
headgear 228n.
regalia 743n.
jewelry 844n.
vestments 989n.
tibia
leg 267n.
tic
spasm 318n.
paralysis 651n.
tick
instant 116n.
animalcule 196n.
oscillate 317vb.
sound faint 401vb.
roll 403vb.
mark 547vb.
credit 802n.
ticker-tape
recording instrument 549n.
ticket
list 87n.
opener 263n.
ingress 297n.
credential 466n.
label 547n.
electorate 605n.
policy 623n.
permit 756n.
ticket-holder
incomer 297n.
ticket-of-leave man
prisoner 750n.
offender 904n.
tickle
strike 279vb.
itch 378vb.
tempt 612vb.
delight 826vb.
amuse 837vb.
endearment 889n.
tickler
incentive 612n.
tickle the palm
bribe 612vb.
pay 804vb.
ticklish
sentient 374adj.
unreliable 474adj.
unsafe 661adj.
difficult 700adj.

tick off
number 86vb.
mark 547vb.
register 548vb.
reprove 924vb.
tick over
operate 173vb.
move slowly 278vb.
tick-tock
roll 403n.
tidal
periodic 141adj.
unstable 152adj.
flowing 350adj.
tidal wave
outbreak 176n.
wave 350n.
tidbit
mouthful 301n.
savoriness 390n.
news 529n.
elite 644n.
pleasurableness 826n.
tiddlywinks
indoor game 837n.
tide
increase 36n.
time 108n.
periodicity 141n.
progression 285n.
ocean 343n.
current 350n.
plenty 635n.
tide-mark
limit 236n.
gauge 465n.
signpost 547n.
tide over
pass time 108vb.
put off 136vb.
navigate 269vb.
triumph 727vb.
tideway
current 350n.
conduit 351n.
tidiness
carefulness 457n.
tidings
news 529n.
tidy
orderly 60adj.
arrange 62vb.
bag 194n.
careful 457n.
clean 841adj.
tie
draw 28n.
be equal 28vb.
tie 45vb.
bond 47n.
neckwear 228n.
obstaçle 702n.
restrain 747vb.
fetter 747vb.
duty 917n.
tie-beam
bond 47n.
beam 218n.
tie down
compel 740vb.
give terms 766vb.
tie-pin
fastening 47n.
jewelry 844n.
tier
series 71n.
layer 207n.
tierce
vat 194n.
(*see* terce)
ties of blood
consanguinity 11n.
tie-up
relation 9n.
association 706n.
tie up with
connect 45vb.
tiff
bicker 709vb.
tiffin
meal 301n.
tigella
foliage 366n.
tiger
violent creature 176n.
cat 365n.
striation 437n.
domestic 742n.
brave person 855n.
noxious animal 904n.
tigerish
furious 176adj.
cruel 898adj.
tight
adjusted 24adj.
firm-set 45adj.
cohesive 48adj.
full 54adj.
sealed off 264adj.
rigid 326adj.
dry 342adj.
invulnerable 660adj.
prepared 669adj.
retentive 778adj.
parsimonious 816adj.
tipsy 949adj.
tight corner
predicament 700n.
tight-drawn
narrow 206adj.
tighten
tighten 45vb.
make smaller 198vb.
close 264vb.
harden 326vb.
restrain 747vb.
tightener
compressor 198n.
tight-fisted
parsimonious 816adj.
tight-lipped
reticent 525adj.
taciturn 582adj.
tight-rope walker
equilibrium 28n.
tight-rope walking
skill 694n.
tights
coherence 48n.
legwear 228n.
tightwad
niggard 816n.
tigroid
animal 365adj.
tilde
punctuation 547n.
tile
lamina 207n.
roof 226n.
headgear 228n.
pottery 381n.
variegate 437vb.
building material 631n.
plaything 837n.
till
while 108adv.
box 194n.
cultivate 370vb.
storage 632n.
treasury 799n.
tillage
agriculture 370n.
maturation 669n.
tiller
handle 218n.
sailing aid 269n.
husbandman 370n.
directorship 689n.
tilt
obliquity 220n.
be inverted 221vb.
canopy 226n.
descent 309n.
attack 712n.
contest, duel 716n.
tilt at
pursue 619vb.
charge 712vb.
dispraise 924vb.
tilter
combatant 722n.
tilth
agriculture 370n.
tilt-yard
arena 724n.
timber
wood 366n.
materials 631n.
timbre
sound 398n.
voice 577n.

timbrel
drum 414n.
time
finality 69n.
time 108n.
era 110n.
time 117vb.
tempo 410n.
time after time
repeatedly 106adv.
time, all the
while 108adv.
time, a long
diuturnity 113n.
time and motion study
economy 814n.
time and place
situation 186n.
time being
present time 121n.
time-bound
transient 114adj.
time-chart
chronology 117n.
timed
adjusted 24adj.
synchronous 123adj.
time-fuse
timekeeper 117n.
time-honored
immemorial 127adj.
worshipful 866adj.
respected 920adj.
time, in
in time 111adv.
concurrently 123adv.
early 135adj.
betimes 135adv.
timely 137adj.
in the future 155adv.
timekeeper
timekeeper 117n.
meter 465n.
recording instrument 549n.
timeless
perpetual 115adj.
godlike 965adj.
timelessness
neverness 109n.
time limit
limit 236n.
conditions 766n.
timely
apt 24adj.
chronological 117adj.
early 135adj.
timely 137adj.
expedient 642adj.
time of day
period 110n.
clock time 117n.
time off
lull 145n.
leisure 681n.
time of, in the
when 108adv.
time of life
date 108n.
age 131n.
timeous
timely 137adj.
timepiece
timekeeper 117n.
time-saving
economy 814n.
timescale
gauge 465n.
time-server
tergiversator 603n.
egotist 932n.
time-serving
tergiversating 603adj.
expedience 642n.
cunning 698adj.
servility 879n.
perfidious 930adj.
rascally 930adj.
selfish 932adj.
time's forelock
opportunity 137n.
time-signal
timekeeper 117n.
signal 547n.
times, the
present time 121n.
time-switch
timekeeper 117n.
meter 465n.
timetable
directory 87n.
chronology 117n.
itinerary 267n.
guide-book 524n.
reference book 589n.
time up
finality 69n.
time was
formerly 125adv.
retrospectively 125adv.
time-wasting
protracted 113adj.
timid
irresolute 601adj.
nervous 854adj.
cowardly 856adj.
cautious 858adj.
modest 874adj.
timidity, timidness
(*see* timid)
timing
chronometry 117n.
periodicity 141n.
tempo 410n.
discrimination 463n.
timocracy
rich man 800n.
(*see* government)
timorous
nervous 854adj.
cowardly 856adj.
timpani
drum 414n.
timpanist
instrumentalist 413n.
tin
small box 194n.
preserve 666vb.
dibs 797n.
tinct
color 425vb.
tincture
small quantity 33n.
tincture 43n.
color 425n.
tinder
lighter 385n.
tine
sharp point 256n.
tinge
small quantity 33n.
tincture 43n.
mix 43vb.
hue 425n.
qualification 468n.
tingle
feel pain 377vb.
formication 378n.
feel 818vb.
be excited 821vb.
tin god
autocrat 741n.
tin hat
armor 713n.
tinker
waste effort 641vb.
impair 655vb.
mender 656n.
repair 656vb.
meddle 678vb.
artisan 686n.
be unskillful 695vb.
bungler 697n.
be cunning 698vb.
not complete 726vb.
tinkering
insufficiency 636n.
tinker's damn
trifle 639n.
tinkle
sound faint 401vb.
resonance 404n.
melodious 410adj.
tinkling cymbal
resonance 404n.
unmeaningness 515n.
tinned
preserved 666adj.
tinnitus
roll 403n.

resonance 404n.
tinny
strident 407adj.
tin-opener
opener 263n.
tin-pan alley
music 412n.
tinsel
flash 417n.
sham 542n.
inelegance 576n.
bauble 639n.
finery 844n.
bad taste 847n.
ostentation 875n.
tint
hue 425n.
paint 553vb.
tintack
fastening 47n.
tinting
hairwash 843n.
tintinnabulation
resonance 404n.
gong 414n.
tintometer
chromatics 425n.
tin whistle
flute 414n.
tiny
small 33adj.
child 132n.
little 196adj.
tip
extra 40n.
prepose 64vb.
extremity 69n.
vertex 213n.
obliquity 220n.
invert 221vb.
cover 226vb.
edge 234n.
depress 311vb.
hint 524n.
bribe 612vb.
advice 691n.
thank 907vb.
reward 962n., vb.
tip-and-run
escape 667adj.
tip-off
hint 524n.
tip of one's tongue, have on the
forget 506vb.
tipper
giver 781n.
tippet
pendant 217n.
cloak 228n.
vestments 989n.
tipple
drink 301vb.
get drunk 949vb.
tipstaff
law officer 955n.
tipster
diviner 511n.
informant 524n.
gambler 618n.
tipsy
oblique 220adj.
tipsy 949adj.
tip the scale
be unequal 29vb.
predominate 34vb.
weigh 322vb.
tip the wink
hint 524vb.
command 737vb.
permit 756vb.
tiptilted
curved 248adj.
tiptoe
atop 213adv.
be stealthy 525vb.
tip-top
supreme 34adj.
topmost 213adj.
best 644adj.
tirade
exaggeration 546n.
diffuseness 570n.
oration 579n.
censure 924n.
tire
dress 228vb.
outline 233n.
edge 234n.
wheel 250n.
fatigue 684vb.
incommode 827vb.
be tedious 838vb.
tired
sleepy 679adj.
tireless
unyielding 162adj.
industrious 678adj.
active 678adj.
tirelessness
perseverance 600n.
tiresome
fatiguing 684adj.
annoying 827adj.
tedious 838adj.
tirewoman
clothier 228n.
tisane
tonic 658n.
tissue
textile 222n.
texture 331n.
life 360n.
cleaning cloth 648n.
tissue paper
weak thing 163n.
thinness 206n.
paper 631n.
tit
animalcule 196n.
saddle-horse 273n.
pony 273n.
bird 365n.
Titan
athlete 162n.
sun 321n.
satellite 321n.
classical gods 967n.
titanic
stalwart 162adj.
huge 195adj.
tit for tat
equalization 28n.
interchange 151n.
retaliation 714n.
tithe
part 53n.
trifle 639n.
tax 809n.
benefice 985n.
tithing
district 184n.
titillate
itch 378vb.
delight 826vb.
amuse 837vb.
cause desire 859vb.
titivate
make better 654vb.
beautify 841vb.
decorate 844vb.
title
label 547n.
name 561n., vb.
book 589n.
decoration 729n.
estate 777n.
honors 866n.
title 870n.
dueness 915n.
titled
named 561adj.
worshipful 866adj.
noble 868adj.
title-deed
title-deed 767n.
dueness 915n.
title-holder
exceller 644n.
titleless
inglorious 867adj.
plebeian 869adj.
title-page
beginning 68n.
edition 589n.
Titoism
unconformity 84n.
titter
laughter 835n.
tittle

small quantity 33n.
trifle 639n.
tittle-tattle
rumor 529n.
chatter 581n.
chat 584n.
tittup
ride 267vb.
titubancy
drunkenness 949n.
titubation
descent 309n.
titular
verbal 559adj.
named 561adj.
tmesis
inversion 221n.
toad
frog 365n.
eyesore 842n.
toady 879n.
toadstool
plant 366n.
toady
toady 879n.
be servile 879vb.
toady to
flatter 925vb.
to a man
generally 79adv.
to and fro
by turns 141adv.
in exchange 151adv.
to and fro 317adv.
to-and-fro movement
periodicity 141n.
toast
cereal, potion 301n.
drink 301vb.
heat 381vb.
a beauty 841n.
toast 876vb.
congratulation 886n.
favorite 890n.
show respect 920vb.
applaud 923vb.
toasted
brown 430adj.
toaster
heater 383n.
toast-master
nomenclator 561n.
reveler 883n.
to a T
truly 494adv.
tobacco
tobacco 388n.
tobacconist
tobacco 388n.
tobacco-pipe
air-pipe 353n.
tobacco 388n.
to be
future 124adj.
toboggan
sled 274n.
descend 309vb.
to boot
in addition 38adv.
toby-jug
vessel 194n.
toccata, toccatina
musical piece 412n.
to come
future 124adj.
impending 155adj.
tocsin
gong 414n.
danger signal 665n.
today
present time 121n.
toddle
be in motion 265vb.
walk 267vb.
move slowly 278vb.
toddler
child 132n.
pedestrian 268n.
toddy
liquor 301n.
toddy-shop
tavern 192n.
to-do
turmoil 61n.
activity 678n.
toe
extremity 69n.
base, foot 214n.
toe in
converge 293vb.
toe-nail
foot 214n.
toes, on one's
actively 678adv.
toe the line
conform 83vb.
acquiesce 488vb.
obey 739vb.
toff
fop 848n.
toffee
coherence 48n.
sweetmeat 301n.
sweet 392n.
toft
home 192n.
toga
tunic 228n.
badge of rule 743n.
toga virilis
adultness 134n.
together
in addition 38adv.
together 74adv.
with 89adv.
toggery, togs
clothing 228n.
finery 844n.
toggle pin
fastening 47n.
toil
labor 682n.
toil and trouble
exertion 682n.
toiler
worker 686n.
toilet
dressing 228n.
latrine 649n.
beautification 843n.
toiletry
cosmetic 843n.
toilette
dressing 228n.
toilsome
laborious 682adj.
difficult 700adj.
toilworn
fatigued 684adj.
token
insubstantial thing 4n.
reminder 505n.
indication 547n.
badge 547n.
trivial 639adj.
security 767n.
gift 781n.
tolerable
inconsiderable 33adj.
not bad 644adj.
imperfect 647adj.
mediocre 732adj.
contenting 828adj.
tolerance
strength 162n.
limit 236n.
wisdom 498n.
permission 756n.
patience 823n.
benevolence 897n.
tolerant
(*see* tolerance, toleration)
tolerate
acquiesce 488vb.
not act 677vb.
consent 758vb.
forgive 909vb.
(*see* toleration)
tolerated house
brothel 951n.
toleration
laxity 734n.
lenity 736n.
permission 756n.
patience 823n.
to let
offering 759adj.
toll
addition 38n.
roll 403vb.
play music 413vb.

raise the alarm 665vb.
levy 786vb.
tax 809n.
tollbooth
mart 796n.
toll the knell
inter 364vb.
lament 836vb.
tomahawk
sharp edge 256n.
ax 723n.
tomato
vegetable 301n.
tomb
resting place 266n.
tomb 364n.
concealment 525n.
monument 548n.
tombola
chance 159n.
gambling 618n.
tomboy
youngster 132n.
tombstone
obsequies 364n.
Tom, Dick and Harry
everyman 79n.
commonalty 869n.
tome
book 589n.
tomentose
downy 259adj.
tomfoolery
foolery 497n.
wit 839n.
ostentation 875n.
tommyrot
silly talk 515n.
tomorrow
futurity 124n.
Tom Thumb
dwarf 196n.
Tom Tiddler's ground
territory 184n.
tom-tom
drum 414n.
ton
weighment 322n.
fashion 848n.
tonal
harmonic 410adj.
linguistic 557adj.
vocal 577adj.
tonality
melody 410n.
musical note 410n.
light contrast 417n.
tone
strength 162n.
tendency 179n.
sound 398n.
musical note 410n.
hue 425n.
painting 553n.
style 566n.
voice 577n.
speech 579n.
conduct 688n.
affections 817n.
tone-deaf
deaf 416adj.
indiscriminating 464adj.
artless 699adj.
tone down
moderate 177vb.
darken 418vb.
decolorize 426vb.
misrepresent 552vb.
tone in with
accord 24vb.
toneless
discordant 411adj.
colorless 426adj.
tone up
make better 654vb.
tonga
carriage 274n.
tongs
furnace 383n.
nippers 778n.
hair-dressing 843n.
tongue
projection 254n.
feeler 378n.
taste 386n.
language 557n.
voice 577n.
speech 579n.
exprobate 927vb.
tongue in cheek
falsehood 541n.
deception 542n.
mental dishonesty 543n.
tongue-in-cheek
affected 850adj.
flattering 925adj.
tongue-lashing
reprimand 924n.
tongueless
silent 399adj.
voiceless 578adj.
tongue-scraper
cleaning utensil 648n.
tongue-tied
voiceless 578adj.
stammering 580adj.
taciturn 582adj.
tongue-wagging
loquacious 581adj.
tonic
stimulant 174n.
musical note 410n.
incentive 612n.
salubrious 652adj.
tonic 658n.
remedial 658adj.
excitant 821n.
cheering 833adj.
tonic accent
pronunciation 577n.
tonic effect
strengthening 162n.
stimulation 174n.
tonic solfa
notation 410n.
tonnage
size 195n.
tonnage and poundage
tax 809n.
tonsilitis
respiratory disease 651n.
tonsure
bareness 229n.
ecclesiasticize 985vb.
canonicals 989n.
tonsured
monastic 986adj.
tontine
gambling 618n.
receipt 807n.
tony
fashionable 848adj.
too
in addition 38adv.
tool
dupe 544n.
fatalist 596n.
contrivance 623n.
instrument 628n.
means 629n.
tool 630n.
agent 686n.
decorate 844vb.
toady 879n.
tooling
bookbinding 589n.
tool of, make a
use 673vb.
tool-using
mechanical 630adj.
too much
great quantity 32n.
redundance 637n.
redundantly 637adv.
intemperance 743n.
tedious 838adj.
satiety 863n.
too much for, be
be superior 34vb.
to order
specially 80adv.
toot, tootle
loudness 400n.
resound 404vb.
play music 413n.
danger signal 665n.
tooth
notch 260n., vb.
taste 386n.

tooth and nail
violently 176adv.
laboriously 682adv.
toothbrush
hair 259n.
cleaning utensil 648n.
tooth-drawer
doctor 658n.
tooth for a tooth
interchange 151n.
revenge 910n.
toothiness
roughness 259n.
toothless
aged 131adj.
unsharpened 257adj.
toothpaste
cleanser 648n.
prophylactic 658n.
toothpick
extractor 304n.
cleaning utensil 648n.
toothsome
savory 390adj.
toothy
toothed 256adj.
top
superiority 34n.
fill 54vb.
prepose 64vb.
extremity 69n.
summit 213n.
covering 226n.
limit 236vb.
stopper 264n.
climb 308vb.
rotator 315n.
bubble 355n.
perfection 646n.
completion 724n.
plaything 837n.
top and lop
cultivate 370vb.
topaz
yellowness 433n.
gem 844n.
top drawer
elite 644n.
top-drawer
genteel 868adj.
top-dress
make fruitful 171vb.
overlay 226vb.
tope
drink 301vb.
wood 366n.
get drunk 949vb.
temple 990n.
toper
drunkard 949n.
top-flight
notable 638adj.
top-hamper
inequality 29n.
vertex 213n.
top-heavy
unequal 29adj.
inverted 221adj.
unsafe 661adj.
clumsy 695adj.
Tophet
hell 972n.
top-hole
topping 644adj.
tophus
solid body 324n.
topiarism
ornamental art 844n.
topiarist
gardener 370n.
topiary
horticultural 370adj.
ornamental 844adj.
topic
topic 452n.
supposition 512n.
meaning 514n.
topical
present 121adj.
modern 126adj.
situated 186adj.
topical 452adj.
topicality
present time 121n.
modernism 126n.
topknot
hair 259n.
top-level
superior 34adj.
directing 689adj.
top-liner
favorite 890n.
topmast
high structure 209n.
vertex 213n.
topmost
supreme 34adj.
high 209adj.
topmost 213adj.
top-notch
topping 644adj.
topographer
surveyor 465n.
topography
situation 186n.
guide-book 524n.
top, on
superior 34adj.
aloft 209adv.
atop 213adv.
successful 727adj.
toponymy
nomenclature 561n.
top people
superior 34n.
bigwig 638n.
elite 644n.
topper
headgear 228n.
topping
topping 644adj.
topple down
tumble 309vb.
topple over
be inverted 221vb.
top-rank
notable 638adj.
top-sawyer
superior 34n.
proficient 696n.
top-secret
concealed 525adj.
important 638adj.
topside
vertex 213n.
topsoil
soil 344n.
tops, the
exceller 644n.
favorite 890n.
good man 937n.
topsy-turvy
contrarily 14adv.
orderless 61adj.
inverted 221adj.
top to toe
longwise 203adv.
top up
fill 54vb.
store 632vb.
replenish 633vb.
toque
headgear 228n.
tor
high land 209n.
Torah
scripture 975n.
torch
lamp, torch 420n.
lighter 385n.
torch-bearer
torch 420n.
preparer 669n.
director 690n.
toreador
killer 362n.
combatant 722n.
toreutic
glyptic 554adj.
toreutics
ornamental art 844n.
torii
church exterior 990n.
torment
pain 377n.
harm 645vb.
bane 659n.
oppress 735vb.
suffering 825n.

torment 827vb.
enrage 891vb.
torture 963vb.
tormentor
stage set 594n.
torn
disjunct 46adj.
tornado
turmoil 61n.
vortex 315n.
gale 352n.
torpedo
suppress 165vb.
destroyer 168n.
fish 365n.
fire at 712vb.
bomb 723n.
torpedo-boat
warship 722n.
torpescence
sluggishness 679n.
torpid
inert 175adj.
inactive 679adj.
apathetic 820adj.
inexcitable 823adj.
torpids
racing 716n.
torpor
helplessness 161n.
weakness 163n.
(*see* torpid)
torque
loop 250n.
jewelry 844n.
torrefy
heat 381vb.
torrent
velocity 277n.
stream 350n.
torrential
violent 176adj.
torrid
hot, warm 379adj.
torse
heraldry 547n.
torsion
convolution 251n.
torso
chief part 52n.
piece 53n.
incompleteness 55n.
image 551n.
sculpture 554n.
tort
wrong 914n.
guilty act 936n.
lawbreaking 954n.
tortfeasor
offender 904n.
tortility
convolution 251n.
tortious
wrong 914adj.
illegal 954adj.
tortoise
slowcoach 278n.
reptile 365n.
armor 713n.
tortoise-shell
covering 226n.
variegation 437n.
tortuous
convoluted 251adj.
sophistical 477adj.
dishonest 930adj.
torture
violence 176n.
distort 246vb.
give pain 377vb.
interrogate 459vb.
ill-treat 645vb.
oppress 735vb.
compel 740vb.
suffering 825n.
torment 827vb.
make ugly 842vb.
cruel act 898n.
corporal punishment 963n.
torture 963vb.
torture-chamber
lock-up 748n.
tortured
figurative 519adj.
torturer
punisher 963n.
torus
swelling 253n.
torvity
sullenness 893n.
Tory
sectional 708adj.
tosh
silly talk 515n.
to spare
superfluous 637adj.
toss
jumble 63vb.
propel 287vb.
oscillate 317vb.
agitation 318n.
toss about
be agitated 318vb.
tossing
seafaring 269adj.
toss one's head
be proud 871vb.
despise 922vb.
toss up
chance 159n.
elevate 310vb.
uncertainty 474n.
tot
potion 301n.
pungency 388n.
acquire 771vb.
take 786vb.
steal 788vb.
total
quantity 26n.
addition 38n.
all 52n.
complete 54adj.
inclusive 78adj.
numerical result 85n.
number 86vb.
total abstainer
abstainer 942n.
sober person 948n.
totalitarianism
despotism 733n.
brute force 735n.
totality
whole 52n.
completeness 54n.
totalizator
counting instrument 86n.
gaming house 618n.
total situation
circumstance 8n.
tote
counting instrument 86n.
carry 273vb.
gaming house 618n.
totem
idol 982n.
totem group
race 11n.
totemist
idolater 982n.
to the eye
apparently 445adv.
to the point
important 638adj.
to the quick
to the quick 374adv.
totient
numerical element 85n.
totter
come unstuck 49vb.
be weak 163vb.
move slowly 278vb.
tumble 309vb.
oscillate 317vb.
be agitated 318vb.
tottering
unstable 152adj.
weak 163adj.
deteriorated 655adj.
unsafe 661adj.
tottings
booty 790n.
tot up to
number 86vb.
touch

be related 9vb.
be equal 28vb.
small quantity 33n.
tincture 43n.
derange 63vb.
operate 173vb.
be situate 186vb.
be contiguous 202vb.
limit 236n.
softness 327n.
texture 331n.
touch 378n., vb.
campanology 412n.
musical skill 413n.
empiricism 461n.
discrimination 463n.
gesture 547n.
use 673vb.
meddle 678vb.
skill 694n.
borrow 785vb.
feeling 818n.
excite 821vb.
touchable
tactual 378adj.
touch and go
unstable 152adj.
unreliable 474adj.
unsafe 661adj.
touch depth
be inferior 35vb.
be deep 211vb.
touch down
air travel 271n.
arrival 295n.
touch down
descend 309vb.
touched
crazed 503adj.
impressed 818adj.
touched up
false 541adj.
touch-hole
orifice 263n.
burning 381n.
furnace 383n.
touching
distressing 827adj.
touch-line
limit 236n.
touch off
initiate 68vb.
kindle 381vb.
touch on
relate 9vb.
notice 455vb.
touch-paper
burning 381n.
touchstone
testing agent 461n.
touch up
color 425vb.
paint 553vb.
make better 654vb.
repair 656vb.
touchwood
lighter 385n.
touchy
sensitive 819adj.
irascible 892adj.
tough
strong 162adj.
violent creature 176n.
hard 326adj.
tough 329adj.
unsavory 391adj.
uncooked 670adj.
difficult 700adj.
thick-skinned 820adj.
courageous 855adj.
unkind 898adj.
ruffian 904n.
pitiless 906adj.
toughen
be tough 329vb.
make insensitive 820vb.
toughness
obstinacy 602n.
(*see* tough)
toupee
wig 228n.
hair 259n.
tour
travel 267vb.
circuition 314n.
tour de force
deed 676n.
masterpiece 694n.
tourer
automobile 274n.
tourism
land travel 267adj.
sport 837n.
tourist
traveler 268n.
spectator 441n.
reveler 837n.
tourist-class
cheap 812adj.
tourmaline
gem 844n.
tournament, tourney
contest, duel 716n.
pageant 875n.
tourniquet
ligature 47n.
compressor 198n.
stopper 264n.
surgical dressing 658n.
tournure
skirt 228n.
outline 233n.
tousle
jumble 63vb.
roughen 259vb.
tousled
orderless 61adj.
unsightly 842adj.
tout
request 761vb.
petitioner 763n.
seller 793n.
commender 923n.
tout ensemble
all 52n.
tovarich
title 870n.
tow
fiber 208n.
navigate 269vb.
traction 288n.
towardly
wieldy 701adj.
towards
towards 281adv.
towel
drier 342n.
cleaning cloth 648n.
toweling
textile 222n.
tower
edifice 164n.
house 192n.
be great 32vb.
be large 195vb.
high structure 209n.
be high 209vb.
ascend 308vb.
refuge 662n.
fort 713n.
prison 748n.
church exterior 990n.
towering
high 209adj.
tower of silence
cemetery 364n.
tomb 364n.
tower of strength
athlete 162n.
influence 178n.
protection 660n.
refuge 662n.
tower over
be superior 34vb.
influence 178vb.
tow-headed
whitish 427adj.
to wit
namely 80adv.
tow-line, tow-rope
cable 47n.
traction 288n.
town
district 184n.
abode, housing 192n.
beau monde 848n.

town-crier
megaphone 400n.
cry 408n.
publicizer 528n.
town-dweller
dweller 191n.
townee, townsman
native 191n.
town hall
meeting place 192n.
town-plan
urbanize 192vb.
township
district 184n.
townspeople
habitancy 191n.
towny
urban 192adj.
tow-path
path 624n.
toxemia
infection 651n.
poisoning 659n.
toxic
harmful 645adj.
unclean 649adj.
toxic 653adj.
baneful 659adj.
dangerous 661adj.
toxicity
infection 651n.
poison 659n.
toxicology
poison 659n.
toxin
poison 659n.
toxophilite
shooter 287n.
player 837n.
toy
little 196adj.
bauble 639n.
trivial 639adj.
plaything 837n.
amuse oneself 837vb.
excite love 887vb.
caress 889vb.
toy gun
toy gun 723n.
trace
copy 20vb.
small quantity 33n.
remainder 41n.
effect 157n.
outline 233n., vb.
detect 484vb.
identification 547n.
trace 548n.
decorate 844vb.
traceable
attributed 158adj.
trace back
look back 125vb.
retrospect 505vb.
tracery
network 222n.
curve 248n.
pattern 844n.
ornamental art 844n.
traces
coupling 47n.
fetter 748n.
trace to
attribute 158vb.
trace upon
mark 547vb.
trachea
air-pipe 353n.
tracheitis
respiratory disease 651n.
tracing
imitation 20n.
copy 22n.
representation 551n.
track
continuity 71n.
water travel 269n.
direction 281n.
follow 284vb.
identification 547n.
trace 548n.
pursue 619vb.
path, railroad 624n.
racing 716n.
arena 724n.
track down
detect 484vb.
tracker
concomitant 89n.
hunter 619n.
trackless
spacious 183adj.
difficult 700adj.
track, off the
mistaken 495adj.
track, on the
discovering 484adj.
tract
region 184n.
land 344n.
reading matter 589n.
dissertation 591n.
tractability
willingness 597n.
persuasibility 612n.
tractable
wieldy 701adj.
tractarian
dissertator 591n.
Anglican 976adj.
Tractarians
church party 978n.
tractate
reading matter 589n.
dissertation 591n.
tractile
drawing 288adj.
flexible 327adj.
traction
transport 272n.
traction 288n.
tractive
dynamic 160adj.
tractor
carrier 273n.
vehicle 274n.
traction 288n.
farm tool 370n.
trade
interchange 151vb.
transference 272n.
vocation 622n.
business 622n.
transfer 780n.
trade 791n., vb.
sell 793vb.
trade fair
mart 796n.
trade-mark
identification 547n.
label 547n.
trade organ
journal 528n.
trader
merchant ship 275n.
merchant 794n.
tradesman
provider 633n.
artisan 686n.
tradesman 794n.
trade union
society 708n.
trade wind
wind 352n.
trading center
emporium 796n.
tradition
tradition 127n.
permanence 144n.
information 524n.
narrative 590n.
habit 610n.
theology 973n.
traditional
conformable 83n.
immemorial 127adj.
descriptive 590adj.
habitual 610adj.
orthodox 976adj.
traditionalism
conformity 83n.
traditionalist
the orthodox 976n.
traditionary
habitual 610adj.
traduce
transform 147vb.
misinterpret 521vb.

misrepresent 552vb.
defame 926vb.
traducianism
heredity 5n.
traffic
motion 265n.
conveyance 267n.
passing along 305n.
trade 791n., vb.
trafficator
signal light 420n.
indicator 547n.
traffic control
traffic control 305n.
traffic cop
protector 660n.
police 955n.
traffic engineering
traffic control 305n.
trafficker
merchant 794n.
trafficky
communicating 624adj.
traffic lane
route 624n.
traffic light
timekeeper 117n.
signal light 420n.
signal 547n.
traffic rules
traffiic control 305n.
tragacanth
resin 357n.
tragedian
actor 594n.
tragedy
stage play 594n.
evil 616n.
deterioration 655n.
tragic
dramatic 594adj.
distressing 827adj.
tragicomic
dramatic 594adj.
funny 849adj.
trail
continuity 71n.
be dispersed 75vb.
be long 203vb.
hang 217vb.
be behind 238vb.
wander 267vb.
move slowly 278vb.
follow 284vb.
draw 288vb.
odor 394n.
identification 547n.
trace 548n.
pursue 619vb.
path 624n.
trailer
retinue 67n.
example 83n.
small house 192n.
carriage 274n.
follower 284n.
traction 288n.
cinema 445n.
hunter 619n.
trail one's coat
make quarrels 709vb.
defy 711vb.
trail, on the
discovering 484adj.
pursuing 619adj.
train
adjunct 40n.
retinue 67n.
procession 71n.
make conform 83adj.
concomitant 89n.
pendant 217n.
rear 238n.
train 274n.
follower 284n.
break in 369vb.
train 534vb.
learn 536vb.
habituate 610vb.
make ready 669vb.
retainer 742n.
train-bearer
retainer 742n.
bridesman 894n.
train-driver
carrier 273n.
trained
expert 694adj.
trainee
beginner 538n.
trainer
breeder 369n.
trainer 537n.
preparer 669n.
director 690n.
training
exercise 682n.
training, in
athletic 162adj.
training school
training school 539n.
train one's sights
aim 281vb.
aim at 617vb.
train-sick
vomiting 300adj.
traipse
wander 267vb.
dirty person 649n.
trait
temperament 5n.
specialty 80n.
feature 445n.
affections 817n.
traitor
deceiver 545n.
tergiversator 603n.
revolter 738n.
enemy 881n.
evildoer 904n.
dutilessness 918n.
knave 938n.
trajection
transference 272n.
trajectory
route 624n.
tralatition
metaphor 519n.
tralineate
deviate 282vb.
trammel
obstacle 702n.
hinder 702vb.
fetter 747vb.
fetter 748n.
tramontane
extraneous 59adj.
tramp
gait 265n.
walk 267vb.
wanderer 268n.
voyage 269vb.
merchant ship 275n.
move slowly 278vb.
idler 679n.
beggar 763n.
low fellow 869n.
bad man 938n.
tramper
pedestrian 268n.
trample
flatten 216vb.
kick 279vb.
fell 311vb.
oppress 735vb.
trample on
ill-treat 645vb.
oppress 735vb.
subjugate 745vb.
be insolent 878vb.
despise 922vb.
trample out
suppress 165vb.
trampoline
lifter 310n.
trance
quiescence 266n.
insensibility 375n.
fantasy 513n.
sleep 679n.
tranced
insensible 375adj.
imaginative 513adj.
bewitched 983adj.
tranquil
tranquil 266adj.
reposeful 683adj.
peaceful 717adj.

impassive 820adj.
inexcitable 823adj.
pleasurable 826adj.
tranquilize
assuage 177vb.
pacify 719vb.
tranquilize 823vb.
tranquilizer
moderator 177n.
drug 658n.
tranquillity
content 828n.
non-wonder 865n.
(*see* tranquil)
transact
do business 622vb.
deal with 688vb.
transaction(s)
eventuality 154n.
affairs 154n.
record 548n.
deed 676n.
trade 791n.
transalpine
removed 199adj.
transatlantic
removed 199adj.
transcend
be great 32vb.
be good 644vb.
(*see* transcendence)
transcedence
extrinsicality 6n.
non-imitation 21n.
superiority 34n.
overstepping 306n.
perfection 646n.
divine attribute 965n.
transcendental
inexpressible 517adj.
divine 965adj.
cabalistic 984adj.
transcendentalism
philosophy 449n.
occultism 984n.
transcribe
copy 20vb.
translate 520vb.
write 586vb.
transcriber
penman 586n.
transcript
copy 22n.
script 586n.
transcription
transformation 143n.
transference 272n.
musical piece 412n.
script 586n.
transcursion
passage 305n.
overstepping 306n.
transduction
transference 272n.
transect
bisect 92vb.
be oblique 220vb.
transection
crossing 222n.
transept
church interior 990n.
transfer
duplicate 22n.
disjoin 46vb.
change 143n.
transition 147n.
substitution 150n.
displace 188vb.
move 265vb.
transference 272n.
carry 273vb.
picture 553n.
deposal 752n.
non-retention 779n.
convey 780vb.
giving 781vb.
transferable
transferable 272adj.
transferee
recipient 782n.
purchaser 792n.
transference
transference 272n.
passage 305n.
metaphor 519n.
(*see* transfer)
transferor
seller 793n.
transferrer
transferrer 272n.
transfiguration
transformation 143n.
conversion 147n.
improvement 654n.
beautification 843n.
theophany 965n.
transfix
pierce 263vb.
transfixed
fixed 153adj.
transformation
transformation 143n.
conversion 147n.
improvement 654n.
beautification 843n.
transformation scene
stage show 594n.
thaumaturgy 864n.
pageant 875n.
transfuse
infuse 303vb.
(*see* transfusion)
transfusion
mixture 43n.
transference 272n.
surgery 658vb.
transgress
disobey 738vb.
(*see* transgression)
transgression
overstepping 306n.
non-observance 769n.
wrong 914n.
wickedness 934n.
guilty act 936n.
lawbreaking 954n.
transgressive
non-observant 769adj.
transhipment
displacement 188n.
transport 272n.
transience
(*see* transient)
transient
elapsing 111adj.
transient 114adj.
unstable 152adj.
short 204adj.
uncertain 474adj.
transientness
instantaneity 116n.
transilience
revolution 149n.
passage 305n.
overstepping 306n.
transillumination
transparency 422n.
transit
transition 147n.
motion 265n.
passage 305n.
transit circle
angular measure 247n.
transit, in
on foot 267adv.
via 624adv.
transition
change 143n.
transformation 143n.
transition 147n.
transference 272n.
passage 305n.
transitional
changeable 143adj.
converted 147adj.
moving 265adj.
passing 305adj.
transitory
transient 114adj.
translate
displace 188vb.
ecclesiasticize 985vb.
(*see* translation)
translation
imitation 20n.
copy 22n.
change 143n.
transference 272n.

translation 520n.
translationese
language 557n.
translative
interpretive 520adj.
translator
interpreter 520n.
transliteration
imitation 20n.
transference 272n.
translation 520n.
translocation
displacement 188n.
transference 272n.
translucent
undimmed 417adj.
transparent 422adj.
semitransparent 424adj.
transmigration
transformation 143n.
transition 147n.
wandering 267n.
transference 272n.
transmigration of souls
reproduction 166n.
transference 272n.
transmissible
transferable 272adj.
transmission
transference 272n.
passage 305n.
transfer 780n.
transmit
transfer 272vb.
send 272vb.
communicate 524vb.
transmitter
transferrer 272n.
telecommunication 531n.
transmogrification
transformation 143n.
transmutation
transformation 143n.
conversion 147n.
transmute
modify 143vb.
transoceanic
removed 199adj.
transom
supporter 218n.
beam 218n.
cross 222n.
window 263n.
transonic
speedy 277adj.
transparency
thinness 206n.
transparency 422n.
photography 551n.
transparent
insubstantial 4adj.
undimmed 417adj.
transparent 422adj.
intelligible 516adj.
disclosing 526adj.
perspicuous 567adj.
artless 699adj.
transpire
emerge, exude 298vb.
vaporize 338vb.
be plain 522vb.
be disclosed 526vb.
transplant
implant 303vb.
cultivate 370vb.
transplantation
transference 272n.
transport
displace 188vb.
move 265vb.
transport 272n.
carry 273vb.
vehicle 274n.
ship 275n.
warm feeling 818n.
delight 826vb.
punish 963vb.
transportable
transferable 272adj.
transportation
penalty 963n.
transporter
carrier 273n.
transpose
interchange 151vb.
invert 221vb.
move 265vb.
transpose 272vb.
compose music 413vb.
transposition
(*see* transpose)
transubstantiate
modify 143vb.
transubstantiation
transformation 143n.
the sacrament 988n.
transude
exude 298vb.
transume
transpose 272vb.
transumption
transference 272n.
transvaluation
estimate 480n.
transverse
oblique 220adj.
crossed 222adj.
transversion
crossing 222n.
transvestism
abnormality 84n.
tranter
carrier 273n.
trap
receptacle 194n.
orifice 263n.
close 264vb.
carriage 274n.
detect 484vb.
surprise 508vb.
trap 542n.
ensnare 542vb.
stage-set 594n.
danger 661n.
pitfall 663n.
defenses 713n.
imprison 747vb.
take 786vb.
trapan
(*see* trepan)
trapdoor
doorway 263n.
trap 542n.
pitfall 663n.
trapezist
entertainer 594n.
trapper
killer 362n.
hunter 619n.
trappings
adjunct 40n.
coverlet 226n.
dressing 228n.
equipment 630n.
Trappist
monk 986n.
traps
clothing 228n.
property 777n.
trash
bauble 639n.
nonentity 639n.
rubbish 641n.
restrain 747vb.
loose woman 952n.
trash can
vessel 194n.
trash-cord
halter 47n.
trashy
unmeaning 515adj.
feeble 572adj.
trivial 639adj.
traulism
speech defect 580n.
trauma
disease 651n.
wound 655n.
traumatic
surgical dressing 658n.
travail
obstetrics 164n.
labor 682n.
adversity 731n.
trave
beam 218n.

frame 218n.
travel
motion 265n.
land travel 267n.
move fast 277vb.
traveler
traveler 268n.
seller 793n.
traveler's check
paper money 797n.
traveler's tale
fable 543n.
exaggeration 546n.
travelogue
oration 579n.
description 590n.
travel-stained
traveling 267adj.
travel with
assent 488vb.
traverse
counteract 182vb.
beam 218n.
traverse 267vb.
pass 305vb.
tell against 467vb.
negate 533vb.
be obstructive 702vb.
oppose 704vb.
defenses 713n.
travesty
mimicry 20n.
copy 22n.
misinterpretation 521n.
misrepresentation 552n.
laughing-stock 851n.
satire 851n.
travolator
transport 272n.
carrier 273n.
conveyor 274n.
trawl
receptacle 194n.
network 222n.
enclosure 235n.
draw 288vb.
be tentative 461vb.
hunt 619vb.
trawler
mariner 270n.
fishing-boat 275n.
hunter 619n.
tray
receptacle 194n.
plate 194n.
treacherous
uncertain 474adj.
occult 523adj.
false 541adj.
deceiving 542adj.
unsafe 661adj.
malevolent 898adj.
dutiless 918adj.
perfidious 930adj.
treachery
latency 523n.
tergiversation 603n.
perfidy 930n.
treacle
viscidity 354n.
sweet 392n.
treacly
viscid 354adj.
feeling 818adj.
tread
degree 27n.
stand 218n.
gait 265n.
walk 267vb.
ascent 308n.
trace 548n.
access 624n.
use 673vb.
tread down
oppress 735vb.
treadmill
uniformity 16n.
labor 682n.
bore 838n.
instrument of torture 964n.
tread on
kick 279vb.
ill-treat 645vb.
subjugate 745vb.
tread on one's toes
make quarrels 709vb.
tread on the heels
come after 65vb.
be near 200vb.
follow 284vb.
tread water
swim 269vb.
treason
sedition 738n.
perfidy 930n.
treasonable
perfidious 930adj.
treasure
store 632n., vb.
exceller 644n.
safeguard 660vb.
preserve 666vb.
acquisition 771n.
funds 797n.
a beauty 841n.
honor 866vb.
love 887vb.
pet 889vb.
darling 890n.
treasure chest
treasury 799n.
treasure-house
storage 632n.
treasury 799n.
treasure-hunt
search 459n.
treasurer
provider 633n.
consignee 754n.
treasurer 798n.
accountant 808n.
treasure-trove
discovery 484n.
benefit 615n.
acquisition 771n.
treasury
accumulation 74n.
anthology 592n.
storage 632n.
treasurer 798n.
treasury 799n.
treasury note
title-deed 767n.
paper money 797n.
treat
modify 143vb.
pleasure 376n.
dissert 591vb.
remedy, doctor 658vb.
behave 688vb.
contract 765vb.
make terms 766vb.
give 781vb.
enjoyment 824vb.
pleasurableness 826n.
amusement 837n.
treat as
substitute 150vb.
treat as one
identify 13vb.
treat as one's own
appropriate 786vb.
treatise
dissertation 591n.
treat like dirt
subjugate 745vb.
hold cheap 922vb.
treatment
change 143n.
agency 173n.
way 624n.
therapy 658n.
use 673n.
conduct 688n.
treaty
conference 584n.
treaty 765n.
treaty, in
agreeing 24adj.
treaty-maker
signatory 765n.
treaty-making
conference 584n.
conditions 766n.
treble
treble 94vb.

stridor 407n.
treble clef
notation 410n.
trebuchet
pillory 964n.
tree
dwelling 192n.
tree 366n.
treenail
fastening 47n.
tree-top
vertex 213n.
foliage 366n.
trefoil
three 93n.
grass 366n.
trek
land travel 267n.
trekker
traveler 268n.
trellis
network 222n.
tremble
vary 152vb.
be weak 163vb.
be agitated 318vb.
sound faint 401vb.
roll 403vb.
show feeling 818vb.
be excited 821vb.
quake 854vb.
tremble in the balance
pend 136vb.
be uncertain 474vb.
be in danger 661vb.
tremendous
frightening 854adj.
tremendously
extremely 32adv.
tremolo
roll 403n.
musical note 410n.
adagio 412adv.
tremor
outbreak 176n.
oscillation 317n.
agitation 318n.
paralysis 651n.
danger signal 665n.
feeling 818n.
nervousness 854n.
tremulous
agitated 318adj.
irresolute 601adj.
nervous 854adj.
trench
gap 201n.
fence 235n.
excavation 255n.
furrow 262n.
conduit 351n.
refuge 662n.
defenses 713n.
trenchancy
vigor 571n.
trenchant
keen 174n.
assertive 532adj.
concise 569adj.
forceful 571adj.
disapproving 924adj.
trencher
plate 194n.
lamina 207n.
trencherman
eater 301n.
glutton 947n.
trenches
battleground 724n.
trench upon
be near 200vb.
encroach 306vb.
trend
continuity 71n.
ability 160n.
tendency 179n.
liability 180n.
point to 281vb.
approach 289n.
intention 617n.
liking 859n.
trepan
perforator 263n.
pierce 263vb.
ensnare 542vb.
doctor 658vb.
trephine
doctor 658vb.
trepidation
agitation 318n.
excitable state 822n.
fear 854n.
trespass
interfere 231vb.
intrude 279vb.
encroach 306n.
disobey 738vb.
wrong 914n.
be undue 916vb.
be wicked 934vb.
guilty act 936n.
lawbreaking 954n.
trespasser
possessor 776n.
offender 904n.
usurper 916n.
trespassing
extraneous 59adj.
tresses
hair 259n.
trestle
frame 218n.
trews
trousers 228n.
trey
three 93n.
tri
three 93adj.
triable
legal 953adj.
illegal 954adj.
triad
three 93n.
Trinity 965n.
trial
inquiry 459n.
experiment 461n.
pursuit 619n.
bane 659n.
preparation 669n.
essay 671n.
difficulty 700n.
contest 716n.
suffering 825n.
legal trial 959n.
trial and error
empiricism 461n.
triality
triality 93n.
trialogue
interlocution 584n.
triangle
three 93n.
angular figure 247n.
gong 414n.
instrument of torture 964n.
triangle of forces
science of forces 162n.
triangular
angulated 247adj.
triangulation
measurement 465n.
tribal
ethnic 11adj.
native 191n.
national 371n.
tribalism
race 11n.
social group 371n.
government 733n.
tribe
race 11n.
group 74n.
breed 77n.
multitude 104n.
genealogy 169n.
community 708n.
tribesman
kinsman 11n.
tribrach
prosody 593n.
tribulation
difficulty 700n.
suffering 825n.
painfulness 827n.
tribunal

council 692n.
jurisdiction 955n.
tribunal 956n.
tribunate
magistrature 733n.
tribune
rostrum 539n.
tributary
stream 350n.
subject 745adj.
giver 781n.
giving 781adj.
tribute
service 745n.
gift 781n.
offering 781n.
receiving 782n.
payment 804n.
tax 809n.
thanks 907n.
dueness 915n.
reward 962n.
oblation 981n.
tributes
praise 923n.
tricar
automobile 274n.
trice
instant 116n.
draw 288vb.
trice up
tie, tighten 45vb.
trichology
hair-dressing 843n.
trichotomy
trisection 95n.
trichroism
variegation 437n.
trick
trickery 542n.
befool 542vb.
habit 610n.
contrivance 623n.
labor 694n.
means of escape 667n.
stratagem 698n.
affectation 850n.
foul play 930n.
trickery
trickery 542n.
trickle
small quantity 33n.
fewness 105n.
move slowly 278vb.
flow out 298vb.
be wet 341vb.
flow 350vb.
trifle 639n.
trick of, have the
be skillful 694vb.
trick out
decorate 844vb.
trick-rider
rider 268n.
tricks of the trade
trickery 542n.
stratagem 698n.
trickster
trickster 545n.
slyboots 698n.
knave 938n.
tricksy
cunning 698adj.
gay 833adj.
tricky
deceiving 542adj.
cunning 698adj.
dishonest 930adj.
tricolor
striation 437n.
variegated 437adj.
flag 547n.
tricorne
headgear 228n.
tricycle
bicycle 274n.
trident
three 93n.
authority 733n.
Tridentine decrees
orthodoxy 976n.
tridimensional
three 93adj.
tried
certain 473adj.
matured 669adj.
expert 694adj.
approved 923adj.
trustworthy 929adj.
triennial
seasonal 141adj.
flower 366n.
triennium
three 93n.
trier
stamina 600n.
essayer 671n.
contender 716n.
trierarch
director 690n.
naval officer 741n.
trifid
trifid 95adj.
trifle
insubstantial thing 4n.
pudding 301n.
be inattentive 456vb.
neglect 458vb.
trifle 639n.
amuse oneself 837vb.
caress 889vb.
trifler
fool 501n.
nonentity 639n.
trifle with
befool 542vb.
not respect 921vb.
hold cheap 922vb.
trifling
inconsiderable 33adj.
wit 839n.
triforium
church interior 990n.
triform
three 93adj.
trigger
handle 218n.
tool 630n.
fire-arm 723n.
trigger-happy
rash 857adj.
irascible 892adj.
trigger off
cause 156vb.
triglyph
furrow 262n.
ornamental art 844n.
trigon
angular figure 247n.
trigonometry
mathematics 86n.
angular measure 247n.
measurement 465n.
trilateral
three 93adj.
lateral 239adj.
angulated 247adj.
trilby
headgear 228n.
trilithon
supporter 218n.
trill
flow 350vb.
roll 403n., vb.
musical note 410n.
sing 413vb.
pronunciation 577n.
voice 577vb.
trillion
over one hundred 99n.
trilogy
three 93n.
poem 593n.
stage play 594n.
trim
state 7n.
adjust 24vb.
equalize 28vb.
cut 46vb.
orderly 60adj.
conform 83vb.
make smaller 198vb.
shorten 204vb.
dress 228n.
form 243n.
dissemble 541vb.

be elegant 575vb.
tergiversate 603vb.
clean 648vb.
make ready 669vb.
personable 841adj.
hair-dressing 843n.
decorate 844vb.
trimester
three 93n.
period 110n.
trimeter
prosody 593n.
trimmer
deceiver 545n.
tergiversator 603n.
trimming
edging 234n.
trimming 844n.
reprimand 924n.
trimmings
adjunct 40n.
leavings 41n.
Trimurti
triality 93n.
Hindu god 967n.
trinacrian
three 93adj.
trinal
three 93adj.
trine
three 93n.
Trinitarianism
orthodoxy 976n.
trinity
triality 93n.
Trinity 965n.
trinket
bauble 639n.
plaything 837n.
finery 844n.
trinomial
three 93adj.
trio
three 93n.
duet 412n.
triolet
verse form 593n.
trip
be in motion 265vb.
land travel 267n.
walk 267vb.
collide 279vb.
tumble 309vb.
elevate 310vb.
fell 311vb.
leap 312vb.
mistake 495n.
blunder 495vb.
ensnare 542vb.
be clumsy 695vb.
hinder 702vb.
failure 728n.
dance 837vb.
tripartite
trifid 95adj.
tripe
insides 224n.
silly talk 515n.
triphthong
speech sound 398n.
spoken letter 558n.
voice 577n.
triple
augment 36vb.
treble 94vb.
triple crown
badge of rule 743n.
vestments 989n.
triples
campanology 412n.
triplet
three 93n.
verse form 593n.
triplex
treble 94adj.
triplication
triplication 94n.
tripod
stand 218n.
oracle 511n.
tripos
exam. 459n.
tripper
traveler 268n.
hinderer 702n.
reveler 837n.
tripping
elegant 575adj.
active 678adj.
trippingly
swiftly 277adv.
by leaps and bounds 312adv.
triptych
three 93n.
picture 553n.
trip-wire
trap 542n.
obstacle 702n.
defenses 713n.
trireme
galley 275n.
warship 722n.
trisection
trisection 95n.
trisulcate
trifid 95adj.
furrowed 262adj.
trite
known 490adj.
aphoristic 496adj.
unmeaning 515adj.
usual 610adj.
dull 840adj.
triturate
break 46vb.
pulverize 332vb.
triumph
procession 71n.
victory 727n.
triumph 727vb.
trophy 729n.
subjugate 745vb.
rejoice 835vb.
celebration 876n.
boast 877vb.
triumphal
celebrative 876adj.
gratulatory 886adj.
triumphant
successful 727adj.
jubilant 833adj.
celebrative 876adj.
boastful 877adj.
triumphator
victor 727n.
triumph over
humiliate 872vb.
triumvirate
government 733n.
triune
three 93adj.
trivet
supporter 218n.
stand 218n.
furnace 383n.
trivial
unmeaning 315adj.
trivial 639adj.
trivium
curriculum 534n.
troat
ululate 409vb.
trocar
perforator 263n.
trochee
prosody 593n.
trochilics
rotation 315n.
trodden
flat 216adj.
usual 610adj.
troglodyte
dweller 191n.
solitary 883n.
Trojan
busy person 678n.
Trojan horse
ambush 527n.
trap 542n.
stratagem 698n.
enemy 881n.
perfidy 930n.
troll
rotate 315vb.
demon 970n.
trolley
pushcart 274n.
tram 274n.

trollop
prostitute 952n.
trombone
horn 414n.
troop
band 74n.
congregate 74vb.
be many 104vb.
formation 722n.
troop-carrier
air-force 722n.
trooper
cavalry 722n.
warship 722n.
trooping the color
pageant 875n.
troops
armed force 722n.
troopship
warship 722n.
trope
trope 519n.
ornament 574n.
trophy
reminder 505n.
badge 547n.
monument 548n.
trophy 729n.
gift 781n.
booty 790n.
honors 866n.
reward 962n.
tropical
hot 379adj.
figurative 519adj.
rhetorical 574adj.
tropopause
atmosphere 340n.
troposphere
atmosphere 340n.
trot
gait 265n.
pedestrianism 267n.
ride 267vb.
move fast 277vb.
troth
belief 485n.
promise 764n.
trot out
repeat 106vb.
manifest 522vb.
speak 579vb.
trotter
foot 214n.
thoroughbred 273n.
trottoir
road 624n.
troubadour
musician 413n.
vocalist 413n.
poet 593n.
trouble
turmoil 61n.
derange 63vb.
attention 455n.
evil 616n.
exertion 682n.
difficulty 700n.
adversity 731n.
worry 825n.
incommode 827vb.
troubled
agitated 318adj.
dejected 834adj.
trouble-maker
bane 659n.
trouble-maker 663n.
agitator 738n.
trouble, no
easy thing 701n.
trouble one for
request 761vb.
trouble oneself
exert oneself 682vb.
trouble-shooter
mediator 720n.
troublesome
laborious 682adj.
annoying 827adj.
trouble spot
pitfall 663n.
troublous
violent 176adj.
evil 616adj.
trough
vessel 194n.
bowl 194n.
cavity 255n.
furrow 262n.
conduit 351n.
trounce
strike 279vb.
defeat 727vb.
reprove 924vb.
spank 963vb.
trouncer
punisher 963n.
troupe
band 74n.
actor 594n.
party 708n.
trouper
actor 594n.
trousered
male 372adj.
trouser-press
flattener 216n.
trousers
trousers 228n.
trousseau
clothing 228n.
store 632n.
trout
fish food 301n.
table fish 365n.
trover
discovery 484n.
acquisition 771n.
trow
fishing-boat 275n.
opine 485vb.
trowel
ladle 194n.
sharp edge 256n.
shovel 274n.
farm tool 370n.
troy weight
weighment 322n.
truancy
absence 190n.
escape 667n.
dutilessness 918n.
truant
avoider 620n.
escaper 667n.
(*see* truancy)
truce
delay 136n.
lull 145n.
interval 201n.
quiescence 266n.
peace 717n.
pacification 719n.
trucial
pacificatory 719adj.
truck
vertex 213n.
train 274n.
automobile 274n.
carrier 273n.
pushcart 274n.
barter 791n.
truckle
wheel 250n.
be servile 879vb.
flatter 925vb.
truckman
driver 268n.
truculence
rudeness 885n.
malevolence 898n.
trudge
travel, walk 267vb.
move slowly 278vb.
true
symmetrical 245adj.
straight 249adj.
true, accurate 494adj.
observant 768adj.
patriotic 901adj.
right 913adj.
trustworthy 929adj.
pious 979adj.
true bill
accusation 928n.
true-blue
conformable 83adj.
obedient 739adj.
patriotic 901adj.

trustworthy 929adj.
true-bred
genuine 494adj.
true faith
orthodoxy 976n.
true saying
maxim 496n.
true to life
lifelike 18adj.
true to type
typical 83adj.
truffle
tuber 301n.
vegetable 301n.
plant 366n.
trug
basket 194n.
vessel 194n.
truism
maxim, axiom 496n.
unmeaningness 515n.
trull
loose woman 952n.
truly
positively 32adv.
truly 494adv.
as promised 764adv.
trump
be superior 34vb.
contrivance 623n.
instrument 628n.
means 629n.
masterpiece 694n.
overmaster 727vb.
gentleman 929n.
good man 937n.
trumped-up
unattested 467adj.
deceiving 542adj.
untrue 543adj.
trumpery
unmeaning 515adj.
bauble 639n.
trivial 639adj.
trumpet
megaphone 400n.
resound 404n.
stridor 407n.
play music 413vb.
horn 414n.
proclaim 528vb.
messenger 531n.
call 547n.
be ostentatious 875vb.
boast 877vb.
trumpet-call
danger signal 665n.
command 737n.
trumpeter
instrumentalist 413n.
trump up
fake 541vb.
truncate
shorten 204vb.
deform 244vb.
truncated
incomplete 55adj.
trunnion
club 723n.
badge of rule 743n.
trundle
move 265vb.
propel 287vb.
rotate 315vb.
trunk
chief part 52n.
part, piece 53n.
incompleteness 55n.
source 156n.
box 194n.
supporter 218n.
cylinder 252n.
tree 366n.
communicating 624adj.
trunk road
road 624n.
trunks
legwear 228n.
beachwear 228n.
trunnion
pivot 218n.
truss
tie 45vb.
bunch 74n.
supporter 218n.
trust
thing transferred 272n.
belief 485n.
expectation 507n.
association 706n.
corporation 708n.
mandate 751n.
credit 802n.
hope 852n., vb.
piety 979n.
trustee
consignee 754n.
possessor 776n.
recipient 782n.
treasurer 798n.
trusteeship
commission 751n.
trustful
believing 485adj.
credulous 487adj.
trust in
be certain 473vb.
trustiness
probity 929n.
trust with
commission 751vb.
trustworthy
credible 485adj.
genuine 494adj.
veracious 540adj.
safe 660adj.
observant 786adj.
reputable 866adj.
trustworthy 929adj.
trusty
trustworthy 929adj.
truth
demonstration 478n.
truth 494n.
maxim 496n.
probity 929n.
orthodoxy 976n.
truth-claim
affirmation 532n.
truthful
true 494adj.
veracious 540adj.
trustworthy 929adj.
truthfulness
veracity 540n.
probity 929n.
try
taste 386vb.
inquire 459vb.
experiment 461vb.
judge 480vb.
be willing 597vb.
persevere 600vb.
tempt 612vb.
essay 671n., vb.
avail of 673vb.
exert oneself 682vb.
torment 827vb.
be tedious 838vb.
try conclusions with
quarrel 709vb.
contend 716vb.
trying
fatiguing 684adj.
annoying 827adj.
try it on
deceive 542vb.
try one's luck
be tentative 461vb.
gamble 618vb.
try-out
experiment 461n.
tryst
focus 76n.
T-square
horizontality 216n.
gauge 465n.
tsunami
high water 209n.
wave 350n.
tub
vat, vessel 194n.
ship 275n.
ablution 648n.
tuba
horn 414n.

tubby
fleshy 195adj.
thick 205adj.
tube
cylinder 252n.
tube 263n.
conduit 351n.
(*see* subway)
tuber
tuber 301n.
tuberculosis
phthisis 651n.
tuberous
convex 253adj.
tub-thumper
speaker 579n.
agitator 738n.
tub-thumping
oration 579n.
tubular
rotund 252adj.
tubular 263adj.
tuck
fold 261n., vb.
food 301n.
side-arms 723n.
tucker
apron 228n.
tucket
loudness 400n.
publication 528n.
tuck in
place 187vb.
load 193vb.
eat 301vb.
tuck up
place 187vb.
shorten 204vb.
tuff
rock 344n.
ash 381n.
tuft
bunch 74n.
hair 259n.
tuft-hunter
toady 879n.
tufty
hairy 259adj.
tug
move 265vb.
boat 275n.
traction 288n.
attraction 291n.
extraction 304n.
exertion 682n.
tugboat
traction 288n.
tug-of-war
traction 288n.
opposition 704n.
contest 716n.
tuition
teaching 534n.
tulle
textile 222n.
tumble
jumble 63vb.
tumble 309vb.
oscillate 317vb.
debauch 951vb.
tumble-down
flimsy 163adj.
descending 309adj.
dilapidated 655adj.
tumbler
athlete 162n.
cup 194n.
entertainer 594n.
tumbril
cart 274n.
vehicle 274n.
means of execution 964n.
tumefaction
dilation 197n.
tumescence
dilation 197n.
convexity 253n.
tumescent, tumid
rhetorical 574adj:
tummy
maw 194n.
insides 224n.
tummy ache
indigestion 651n.
tumor
dilation 197n.
carcinosis 651n.
tumult
turmoil 61n.
commotion 318n.
loudness 400n.
discord 411n.
activity 678n.
revolt 738n.
tumultuary
violent 176adj.
riotous 738adj.
tumultuous
disorderly 61adj.
violent 176adj.
loud 400adj.
tumulus
tomb 364n.
tun
vat 194n.
bulk 195n.
drunkard 949n.
tunable
melodious 410adj.
tundra
plain 348n.
tune
adjust 24vb.
synchronize 123vb.
sound 398n.
harmonize 410vb.
tune 412n.
play music 413vb.
make ready 669vb.
tuneful
pleasant 376adj.
melodious 410adj.
poetic 593adj.
tune in
hear 415vb.
tuneless
discordant 411adj.
tune up
harmonize 410vb.
make ready 669vb.
tunic
tunic 228n.
tunicle
vestments 989n.
tuning fork
prototype 23n.
gong 414n.
tunnage
size 195n.
tunnel
excavation 255n.
tunnel 263n.
pierce 263vb.
descend 309vb.
bridge 624n.
railroad 624n.
tup
unite with 45vb.
sheep 365n.
male animal 372n.
tu quoque
rejoinder 460n.
tu quoque argument
counter-evidence 467n.
confutation 479n.
accusation 928n.
turban
headgear 228n.
coil 251n.
turbid
opaque 423adj.
dirty 649adj.
turbinate
coiled 251adj.
rotary 315adj.
turbination
rotation 315n.
turbine
causal means 156n.
turbo-jet
aircraft 276n.
turbo-prop
aircraft 276n.
turbot
fish food 301n.
table fish 365n.
turbulence
turmoil 61n.

violence 176n.
roughness 259n.
commotion 318n.
excitability 822n.
tureen
bowl 194n.
turf
piece 53n.
soil 344n.
grassland 348n.
grass 366n.
fuel 385n.
gambling 618n.
racing 716n.
arena 724n.
turf out
eject 300vb.
turfy
soft 327adj.
vegetal 366adj.
turgescent
expanded 197adj.
turgid
expanded 197adj.
convex 253adj.
rhetorical 574adj.
inelegant 576adj.
redundant 637adj.
ostentatious 875adj.
turgidity
bulk 195n.
(*see* turgid)
turkey
table bird 365n.
turkey cock
proud man 871n.
Turkish bath
heater 383n.
ablution 648n.
Turkish delight
sweetmeat 301n.
sweet 392n.
turmeric
condiment 389n.
turmoil
turmoil 61n.
havoc 165n.
violence, storm 176n.
commotion 318n.
activity 678n.
anarchy 734n.
revolt 738n.
turn
period 110n.
periodicity 141n.
change 143n., vb.
reversion 148n.
tendency 179n.
efform 243vb.
curvature 248n.
make round 250n.
blunt 257vb.
fold 261vb.
land travel 267n.
deviate 282vb.
circuition 314n.
rotation 315n.
be sour 393vb.
inexpectation 508n.
interpretation 520n.
stage show 594n.
circuit 626vb.
aptitude 694n.
parry 713vb.
dislike 861n.
turn a blind eye
disregard 458vb.
be patient 823vb.
turn about
revert 148vb.
turnabout
tergiversator 603n.
turn adrift
eject 300vb.
turn against
tergiversate 603vb.
turn and turn about
correlatively 12adv.
turn aside
avoid 620vb.
turn away
regress 286vb.
dismiss 300vb.
be loath 598vb.
refuse 760vb.
turncoat
changed person 147n.
deceiver 545n.
waverer 601n.
tergiversator 603n.
turn color
show feeling 818vb.
turn down
invert 221vb.
bedim 419vb.
refuse 760vb.
turned-up
curved 248adj.
turner
artisan 686n.
turn in
sleep 679vb.
turning
unstable 152adj.
labyrinthine 251adj.
circuition 314n.
turning point
juncture 8n.
degree 27n.
crisis 137n.
reversion 148n.
summit 213n.
limit 236n.
return 286n.
important matter 638n.
turn into
convert 147vb.
translate 520vb.
turnip
tuber 301n.
turnkey
janitor 264n.
jailer 749n.
turn nasty
be angry 891vb.
turn off
dismiss 300vb.
kill 362vb.
execute 963vb.
turn of the tide
reversion 148n.
summit 213n.
inversion 221n.
return 286n.
turn on
depend 157vb.
operate 173vb.
turn out
become 1vb.
happen 154vb.
result 157vb.
eject 300vb.
search 459vb.
make unwelcome 883vb.
turn-out
dressing 228n.
carriage 274n.
pageant 875n.
turn over
be inverted 221vb.
make curved 248vb.
fold 261vb.
transfer 272vb.
meditate 449vb.
search 459vb.
do business 791vb.
sell 793vb.
turnover
pastry 301n.
earnings 771n.
receipt 807n.
reward 962n.
turn over a new leaf
change 143vb.
tergiversate 603vb.
be penitent 939vb.
turnpike
road 624n.
obstacle 702n.
turn State's evidence
inform 524vb.
confess 526vb.
accuse 928vb.
turns, by
by turns 141adv.

in exchange 151adv.
turnscrew
tool 630n.
turnspit
domestic 742n.
turnstile
barrier 235n.
recording instrument 549n.
access 624n.
obstacle 702n.
treasury 799n.
turntable
rotator 315n.
turn tail
regress 286vb.
run away 620vb.
be cowardly 856vb.
turn the corner
change 143vb.
get better 654vb.
turn the other cheek
be patient 823vb.
be humble 872vb.
forgive 909vb.
turn the scale
predominate 34vb.
modify 143vb.
cause 156vb.
influence 178vb.
tell against 467vb.
dominate 733vb.
turn the screw
compel 740vb.
turn the tables
be contrary 14vb.
invert 221vb.
tell against 467vb.
retaliate 714vb.
turn to
be turned to 147vb.
speak to 583vb.
busy oneself 622vb.
seek refuge 662vb.
turn to account
use 673vb.
turn turtle
be inverted 221vb.
navigate 269vb.
turn-up
fold 261n.
turn up
happen 151vb.
chance 159vb.
be present 189vb.
arrive 295vb.
be visible 443vb.
turn up one's nose
be fastidious 862vb.
despise 922vb.
turn up trumps
be successful 727vb.
be auspicious 730vb.
be honorable 929vb.
turpitude
disrepute 867n.
improbity 930n.
wickedness 934n.
turquoise
blueness 435n.
gem 844n.
turret
high structure 209n.
fort 713n.
turtle
reptile 365n.
savoriness 390n.
turtle-dove
bird 365n.
love-emblem 887n.
turtle-doves
lovers 887n.
tusk, tush
tooth 256n.
tusker
animal 365n.
pig 365n.
tusky
toothed 256adj.
tussah
fiber 208n.
textile 222n.
tussle
contention 716n.
tussler
contender 716n.
combatant 722n.
tussock
monticle 209n.
tutelage
teaching 534n.
learning 536n.
protection 660n.
subjection 745n.
tutelary
tutelary 660adj.
defending 713adj.
tutelary genius
patron 707n.
tutor
teach 534vb.
teacher 537n.
protector 660n.
manager 690n.
servant 742n.
domestic 742n.
keeper 749n.
tutorial
teaching 534n.
educational 534adj.
tut-tut
deprecation 762n.
tutu
skirt 228n.
tu-whit-tu-whoo
ululation 409n.
tuxedo
tunic 228n.
informal dress 228n.
tuyere
heater 383n.
twaddle
absurdity 497n.
silly talk 515n.
be loquacious 581vb.
twain
duality 90n.
twang
taste 386n.
pungency 388n.
sound 398n.
stridor 407n.
play music 413vb.
speech defect 580n.
tweak
give pain 377vb.
touch 378vb.
tweed
textile 222n.
Tweedledum and Tweedledee
identity 13n.
duality 90n.
tweeds
clothing 228n.
tweeny
domestic 742n.
tweet
ululate 409vb.
tweezers
extractor 304n.
tool 630n.
nippers 778n.
twelfth man
substitute 150n.
twelve-mile limit
territory 184n.
twelvemonth
period 110n.
twelve o'clock
noon 128n.
Twelve Tables
precept 693n.
code of duty 917n.
law 953n.
twerp
cad 938n.
twice
twice 91adv.
twice-born, the
upper class 868n.
twice-told
repeated 106adj.
twice-told tale
diffuseness 570n.
bore 838n.
twiddle
touch 378vb.
twiddle one's thumbs

be inactive 679vb.
twig
branch 53n.
young plant 132n.
foliage 366n.
know 490vb.
understand 516vb.
twilight
evening 129n.
light 417n.
half-light 419n.
deterioration 655n.
twilight sleep
obstetrics 164n.
insensibility 375n.
twill
weave 222vb.
fold 261vb.
twilled
textural 331adj.
twin
kinsman 11n.
identity 13n.
analogue 18n.
accord 24vb.
compeer 28n.
concomitant 89n.
dual 90adj.
double 91vb.
contemporary 123n.
twine
tie 45vb.
fiber 208n.
enlace 222vb.
distort 246vb.
make curved 248vb.
convolution 251n.
twine 251vb.
deviate 282vb.
twine round
cohere 48vb.
surround 230vb.
twinge
pang 377n.
suffering 825n.
twinkle
instantaneity 116n.
vary 152vb.
agitation 318n.
flash 417n.
laughter 835n.
twin-screw
propeller 269n.
twirl
twine 251vb.
rotate 315vb.
twist
tie 45vb.
complexity 61n.
derange 63vb.
modify 143vb.
bag 194n.
fiber 208n.
obliquity 220n.
enlace 222vb.
deform 244vb.
distortion 246n.
coil 251n.
twine 251vb.
deviate 282vb.
tobacco 388n.
bias 481vb.
eccentricity 503n.
misinterpret 521vb.
misrepresentation 552n.
defect 647n.
pervert 655vb.
make ugly 842vb.
twister
trickster 545n.
knave 938n.
twistiness
improbity 930n.
twisting
labyrinthine 251adj.
twists and turns
meandering 251n.
twit
be witty 839vb.
ridicule 851vb.
not respect 921vb.
dispraise 924vb.
accuse 928vb.
twitch
move 265vb.
draw 288vb.
spasm 318n.
feel pain 377vb.
touch 378vb.
gesture 547n.
twitter
agitation 318n.
ululation 409n.
sing 413vb.
two
duality 90n.
two-a-penny
trivial 639adj.
two-dimensional
spatial 183adj.
two-edged
double 91adj.
equivocal 518adj.
two-faced
hypocritical 541adj.
two-fisted
courageous 855adj.
two-fold
double 91adj.
two minds, be in
be uncertain 474vb.
two minds, of
irresolute 601adj.
two of a kind
analogue 18n.
two or three
plurality 101n.
fewness 105n.
two peas
analogue 18n.
two-piece
dress 228n.
twosome
duality 90n.
two-step
dance 837n.
two strings to one's bow
means 629n.
two voices
contrariety 14n.
disagreement 25n.
two voices, speak with
be equivocal 518vb.
two-way
correlative 12adj.
interchanged 151adj.
two-way stretch
underwear 228n.
two-wheeler
carriage 274n.
tycoon
autocrat 741n.
tyke
dog 365n.
tympanum
summit 213n.
ear 415n.
church exterior 990n.
type
character 5n.
uniformity 16n.
analogue 18n.
copy 20vb.
prototype 23n.
example 83n.
form 243n.
person 371n.
omen 511n.
metaphor 519n.
indication 547n.
image 551n.
letter 558n.
write 586vb.
print-type 587n.
type-cutter
printer 587n.
type-face
form 243n.
print-type 587n.
type-foundry
press 587n.
type, in
printed 587adj.
type matter
print-type 587n.
typescript
script 586n.
book 589n.
typesetting
print 587n.

typewriter
stenographer 586n.
typhoid
infection 651n.
typhoon
gale 352n.
typhus
infection 651n.
typical
uniform 16adj.
similar 18adj.
general 79adj.
special 80adj.
regular 81adj.
typical 83adj.
figurative 519adj.
indicating 547adj.
typify
resemble 18vb.
predict 511vb.
mean 514vb.
figure 519vb.
interpret 520vb.
manifest 522vb.
indicate 547vb.
represent 551vb.
typist
stenographer 586n.
typographer
engraver 556n.
printer 587n.
typographical
printed 587adj.
typography
composition 56n.
form 243n.
print 587n.
typology
theology 973n.
tyrannical
violent 176adj.
cruel 898adj.
lawless 954adj.
(*see* tyranny)
tyrannicide
homicide 362n.
revolter 738n.
tyrannize
be violent 176vb.
influence 178vb.
ill-treat 645vb.
meddle 678vb.
rule 733vb.
oppress 735vb.
be malevolent 898vb.
tyrannous
oppressive 735adj.
tyranny
influence 178n.
badness 645n.
despotism 733n.
brute force 735n.
insolence 878n.
arrogation 916n.
tyrant
violent creature 176n.
bane 659n.
tyrant 735n.
autocrat 741n.
tyro
beginner 538n.
tzigane
wanderer 268n.

U

U
well bred 848adj.
genteel 868adj.
uberty
productiveness 171n.
ubiety
presence 189n.
ubiquitous
universal 79adj.
ubiquitous 189adj.
ubiquity
space 183n.
(*see* ubiquitous)
U-boat
warship 722n.
udder
bladder 194n.
bosom 253n.
udometer
hygrometry 341n.
uglify
impair 655vb.
make ugly 842vb.
ugly
deformed 246adj.
inelegant 576n.
dangerous 661adj.
unpleasant 827adj.
ugly 842adj.
sullen 893adj.
ugly customer
trouble-maker 663n.
low fellow 869n.
ruffian 904n.
ugly duckling
nonconformist 84n.
eyesore 842n.
uhlan
cavalry 722n.
uitlander
foreigner 59n.
incomer 297n.
ukase
decree 737n.
ukelele
harp 414n.
ulcer
ulcer 651n.
wound 655n.
bane 659n.
painfulness 827n.
ulceration
ulcer 651n.
impairment 655n.
painfulness 827n.
ulcerous
diseased 651adj.
uliginal
marshy 347adj.
ullage
deficit 55n.
ulna
limb 53n.
ulnar
brachial 53adj.
ulterior
extraneous 59adj.
future 124adj.
distant 199adj.
ultimate
ending 69adj.
distant 199adj.
ultimately
prospectively 124adv.
late 136adv.
eventually 154adv.
ultimate point
extremity 69n.
ultima Thule
extremity 69n.
farness 199n.
limit 236n.
ultimatum
period 110n.
limit 236n.
intention 617n.
requirement 627n.
warning 664n.
demand 737n.
conditions 766n.
ultimo
before 119adv.
formerly 125adv.
ultimogeniture
posteriority 120n.
ultra
extremely 32adv.
ultraconservative
obstinate 602adj.
ultracrepidarian
inquisitor 453n.
meddler 678n.
ultracrepidarianism
overactivity 678n.
ultraist
opponent 705n.
ultramarine
blue pigment 435n.
ultramicroscopic
small 33adj.
minute 196adj.
ultramodern
modern 126adj.
ultramontane

extraneous 59adj.
ecclesiastical 985adj.
ultramontanism
Catholicism 976n.
ultramontanist
Catholic 976n.
popish 976adj.
ultramontanists
church party 978n.
ultra vires
unwarranted 916adj.
ululate
ululate 409vb.
ululation
ululation 409n.
lamentation 836n.
Ulysses
traveler 268n.
umbelliferous
broad 205adj.
umber
brown paint 430n.
umbilical
central 225adj.
umbilical cord
bond 47n.
obstetrics 164n.
umbilicus
middle 70n.
centrality 225n.
umbra
darkness 418n.
umbrage
foliage 366n.
screen 421n.
resentment 891n.
umbrageous
dark 418adj.
shadowy 419adj.
screened 421adj.
umbrella
shade 226n.
protection 660n.
shelter 662n.
umiak
rowboat 275n.
umlaut
speech sound 398n.
punctuation 547n.
umpirage
judgment 480n.
mediation 720n.
umpire
estimator 480n.
mediator 720n.
mediate 720vb.
magistracy 957n.
unabashed
unfearing 855adj.
proud 871adj.
insolent 878adj.
unable
powerless 161adj.
useless 641adj.
unskillful 695adj.
unabolished
intact 52adj.
unabridged
intact 52adj.
long 203adj.
unaccented
muted 410adj.
unacceptable
unpleasant 827adj.
unacclimatized
extraneous 59adj.
unaccommodating
hindering 702adj.
annoying 827adj.
discourteous 885adj.
unaccompanied
alone 88adj.
unaccomplished
unskillful 695adj.
uncompleted 726adj.
unaccountable
unusual 84adj.
changeful 152adj.
causeless 159adj.
wonderful 864adj.
non-liable 919n.
lawless 954adj.
unaccustomed
unusual 84adj.
unhabituated 611adj.
clumsy 695adj.
unachievable
impracticable 470adj.
unacknowledged
unadmitted 489adj.
unthanked 908adj.
unacquaintance
ignorance 491n.
unadaptable
rigid 326adj.
useless 641adj.
unskillful 695adj.
unadmired
unrespected 921adj.
unadmiring
incurious 454adj.
unastonished 865adj.
disapproving 924adj.
unadmitted
unadmitted 489n.
unadorned
intelligible 516adj.
plain 573adj.
artless 699adj.
unadulterated
unmixed 44adj.
whole 52adj.
genuine 494adj.
pure 950adj.
unadventurous
quiescent 266adj.
cautious 858adj.
unadvisable
inexpedient 643adj.
unaesthetic
graceless 842adj.
unaffected
simple 44adj.
intact 52adj.
permanent 144adj.
veracious 540adj.
elegant 575adj.
artless 699adj.
impassive 820adj.
non-liable 919adj.
unaffectedness
plainness 573n.
unaffectionate
unkind 898adj.
unafraid
unfearing 855adj.
unaggressive
inert 175adj.
peaceful 717adj.
unaging
perpetual 115adj.
unagreed
disagreeing 25adj.
unaided
hindered 702adj.
unaimed
indiscriminate 464ac
unalike
dissimilar 19adj.
unalloyed
unmixed 44adj.
unalluring
unwanted 860adj.
unaltered
identical 13adj.
permanent 144adj.
unchangeable 153adj
unambiguity
certainty 473n.
connotation 514n.
intelligibility 516n.
unambiguous
positive 473adj.
veracious 540adj.
perspicuous 567adj.
unambitious
apathetic 820adj.
inexcitable 823adj.
indifferent 860adj.
inglorious 867adj.
modest 874adj.
un-American
extraneous 59adj.
unamiable
unkind 898adj.
unamused
bored 838adj.
disapproving 924adj.
unamusing
tedious 838adj.
dull 840adj.
unanimity

agreement 24n.
consensus 488n.
cooperation 706n.
concord 710n.
unanimous
(*see* unanimity)
unannounced
unexpected 508adj.
unanswerable
demonstrated 478adj.
completive 725adj.
non-liable 919adj.
unapologizing
impenitent 940adj.
unappalled
unfearing 855adj.
unappareled
uncovered 229adj.
unapparent
invisible 444adj.
unappeasable
violent 176adj.
obstinate 602adj.
revengeful 910adj.
unappetizing
unsavory 391adj.
unappreciated
undervalued 483adj.
unapprehended
unknown 491adj.
unapprehensive
unfearing 855adj.
unapproachable
supreme 34adj.
infinite 107adj.
removed 199adj.
impracticable 470adj.
prideful 871adj.
unappropriated
unpossessed 774adj.
not retained 779adj.
unapproved
disapproved 924adj.
unapt
unapt 25adj.
inexpedient 643adj.
unskillful 695adj.
unarmed
defenseless 161adj.
peaceful 717adj.
unarmored
vulnerable 661adj.
unaroused
inert 175adj.
quiescent 266adj.
inactive 679adj.
apathetic 820adj.
unastonished 865adj.
unarranged
orderless 61adj.
unprepared 670adj.
unartificial
artless 699adj.
unascertained
uncertified 474adj.
unashamed
impenitent 940adj.
unasked
voluntary 597adj.
unwedded 895adj.
unaspiring
indifferent 860adj.
inglorious 867adj.
unassailable
invulnerable 660adj.
pure 950adj.
unassembled
unassembled 75adj.
unassenting
involuntary 596adj.
unassimilated
separate 46adj.
extraneous 59adj.
unsociable 883adj.
unassociated
separate 46adj.
unassuming
plain 573adj.
artless 699adj.
humble 872adj.
modest 874adj.
unassured
doubting 474adj.
unastonished
unastonished 865adj.
unatoned
unrepented 940adj.
unattached
separate 46adj.
independent 744adj.
unattempted
avoidable 620adj.
unattended
neglected 458adj.
unattested
unattested 467adj.
uncertified 474adj.
unattracted
indifferent 860adj.
unattractive
unpleasant 827adj.
unwanted 860adj.
unauthentic
uncertified 474adj.
erroneous 495adj.
unauthoritative
uncertified 474adj.
unauthorized
powerless 161adj.
anarchic 734adj.
wrong 914adj.
unwarranted 916adj.
heterodox 977adj.
unavailable
absent 190adj.
impracticable 470adj.
scarce 636adj.
unavoidable
certain 473adj.
necessary 596adj.
compelling 740adj.
obligatory 917adj.
unaware
ignorant 491adj.
inexpectant 508adj.
unawed
unfearing 855adj.
unastonished 865adj.
impious 980adj.
unbacked
unhabituated 611adj.
unbaked
uncooked 670adj.
unbalance
inequality 29n.
derange 63vb.
unbalanced
unwise 499adj.
crazed 503adj.
owed 803adj.
unballasted
unequal 29adj.
unbaptized
heathenish 974adj.
unbar
deliver 668vb.
liberate 746vb.
unbated
sharp 256adj.
unbearable
exorbitant 32adj.
intolerable 827adj.
unbeatable
unyielding 162adj.
unbeaten 727adj.
unbeaten
new 126adj.
persevering 600adj.
unused 674adj.
unbeaten 727adj.
unbecoming
graceless 842adj.
discreditable 867adj.
unbegotten
unborn 2adj.
unbeholden
ungrateful 908adj.
unbeknown
unknown 491adj.
unbelief
unbelief 486n.
irreligion 974n.
unbelievable
unbelieved 486adj.
wonderful 864adj.
unbeliever
unbeliever 486n.
irreligionist 974n.
impious person 980n.
unbelted
reposeful 683adj.
unbend

straighten 249vb.
soften 327vb.
repose 683vb.
be humble 872vb.
be sociable 882vb.
show mercy 905vb.
forgive 909vb.
unbending
rigid 326adj.
narrow-minded 481adj.
resolute 599adj.
obstinate 602adj.
restraining 747adj.
prideful 871adj.
unsociable 883adj.
unbiased
symmetrical 245adj.
judicial 480adj.
wise 498adj.
free 744adj.
just 913adj.
unbiblical
heterodox 977adj.
unbiddable
disobedient 738adj.
unbidden
voluntary 597adj.
unwanted 860adj.
unbigoted
wise 498adj.
unbind
disjoin 46vb.
deliver 668vb.
be lax 734vb.
liberate 746vb.
not retain 779vb.
unbleached
whitish 427adj.
unblemished
perfect 646adj.
beautiful 841adj.
innocent 935adj.
unblessed
unprosperous 731adj.
unfortunate 731adj.
cursed 899adj.
heathenish 974adj.
profane 980adj.
unblessed with
not owning 774adj.
unblinking
still 266adj.
unblown
immature 670adj.
unblunted
sharp 256adj.
unblurred
well-seen 443adj.
unblushing
thick-skinned 820adj.
proud 871adj.
insolent 878adj.
impenitent 940adj.
unchaste 951adj.
unbolt
liberate 746vb.
unborn
unborn 2adj.
immature 670adj.
unborn, the
aftercomer 67n.
unbosom oneself
divulge 526vb.
unbound
unconfined 744adj.
liberated 746adj.
non-liable 919n.
unbounded
infinite 107adj.
unbowed
vertical 215adj.
unbreakable
unyielding 162adj.
dense 324adj.
hard 326adj.
tough 329adj.
invulnerable 660adj.
unbreeched
infantine 132adj.
unbribable
honorable 929adj.
unbridgeable
impracticable 470adj.
unintelligible 517adj.
unbridle
disjoin 46vb.
unbridled
violent 176adj.
anarchic 734adj.
free 744adj.
unconfined 744adj.
unbriefed
uninstructed 491adj.
unbroken
uniform 16adj.
intact 52adj.
complete 54adj.
continuous 71adj.
smooth 258adj.
tranquil 266adj.
unhabituated 611adj.
unbroken front
coherence 48n.
unbrotherly
unkind 898adj.
unburden
disencumber 701vb.
relieve 831vb.
unburnished
dim 419adj.
unbury
exhume 364vb.
unbusinesslike
unskillful 695adj.
unbutton
disjoin 46vb.
doff 229vb.
unbuttoned
reposeful 683adj.
sociable 882adj.
uncage
liberate 746vb.
uncalculating
unwise 499adj.
rash 857adj.
uncalled for
voluntary 597adj.
superfluous 637adj.
useless 641adj.
undue 916adj.
uncanny
spooky 970adj.
magical 983adj.
uncanonical
non-observant 769adj.
uncap
doff 229vb.
greet 884vb.
uncared for
neglected 458adj.
unwanted 860adj.
hated 888adj.
uncaring
negligent 458adj.
lax 734adj.
indifferent 860adj.
uncase
doff 229vb.
uncatholic
heterodox 977adj.
uncaught
free 744adj.
unwedded 895adj.
uncaused
causeless 159adj.
unceasing
perpetual 115adj.
frequent 139adj.
permanent 144adj.
unceasing 146adj.
persevering 600adj.
uncensored
intact 52adj.
impure 951adj.
uncensorious
approving 923adj.
unceremonious
discourteous 885adj.
uncertain
fitful 142adj.
changeful 152adj.
unstable 152adj.
casual 159adj.
moot 459adj.
unattested 467adj.
improbable 472adj.
uncertain 474adj.
irresolute 601adj.
capricious 604adj.
speculative 618adj.

uncertainty
doubt 486n.
ignorance 491n.
equivocalness 518n.
gambling 618n.
(*see* uncertain)
uncertified
uncertified 474adj.
unchain
disjoin 46vb.
liberate 746vb.
unchallengeable
undisputed 473adj.
invulnerable 660adj.
just 813adj.
due 915adj.
unchangeability
permanence 144n.
unchangeable
lasting 113adj.
unchangeable 153adj.
obstinate 602adj.
unchanging
characteristic 5adj.
identical 13adj.
uniform 16adj.
perpetual 115adj.
permanent 144adj.
unchangeable 153adj.
trustworthy 929adj.
godlike 965adj.
unchaperoned
alone 88adj.
unchargeable
cheap 812adj.
uncharged
uncharged 812adj.
uncharitable
parsimonious 816adj.
unkind 898adj.
selfish 932adj.
uncharted
unknown 491adj.
unchartered
unentitled 916adj.
unwarranted 916adj.
illegal 954adj.
unchaste
inelegant 576adj.
intemperate 943adj.
unchaste 951adj.
unchastened
impenitent 940adj.
unchecked
uncertified 474adj.
unconfined 744adj.
uncheckered
permanent 144adj.
unchivalrous
discourteous 885adj.
dishonest 930adj.
unchosen
rejected 607adj.
disliked 861adj.
hated 888adj.
unchurch
perform ritual 988vb.
uncial
letter 558n.
written 586adj.
uncircumcised
heathenish 974adj.
uncircumscribed
spacious 183adj.
uncircumspect
negligent 458adj.
rash 857adj.
uncivic
misanthropic 902adj.
uncivil
ill-bred 847adj.
discourteous 885adj.
impertinent 878adj.
uncivilized
ignorant 491adj.
immature 670adj.
artless 699adj.
ill-bred 847adj.
plebeian 869adj.
unclad
uncovered 229adj.
unclaimable
unwarranted 916adj.
unclaimed
free 744adj.
unpossessed 774adj.
not retained 779adj.
unclarified
opaque 423adj.
unclasp
disjoin 46vb.
unclassical
inelegant 576adj.
unclassifiable
irrelative 10adj.
unconformable 84adj.
unclassified
mixed 43adj.
orderless 61adj.
uncertain 474adj.
unknown 491adj.
uncle
kinsman 11n.
lender 784n.
unclean
unclean 649adj.
uncleaned
opaque 423adj.
uncleanliness
insalubrity 653n.
uncleanly
unclean 649adj.
uncleanness
impurity 951n.
(*see* unclean)
unclean spirit
devil 969n.
unclear
ill-seen 444adj.
imperspicuous 568adj.
unclench
open 263vb.
relinquish 621vb.
not retain 779vb.
unclerical
laical 987adj.
unclinch
be disjoined 46vb.
relinquish 621vb.
liberate 746vb.
not retain 779vb.
unclipped
intact 52adj.
uncloak
uncover 229vb.
disclose 526vb.
unclose
open 263vb.
disclose 526vb.
unclot
liquefy 337vb.
make flow 350vb.
unclothe
uncover 229vb.
unclotted
fluidal 335adj.
unclouded
undimmed 417adj.
well-seen 443adj.
unclubbable
unsociable 883adj.
uncoil
unravel 62vb.
lengthen 203vb.
straighten 249vb.
recoil 280vb.
evolve 316vb.
uncollected
disjunct 46adj.
uncolored
unmixed 44adj.
colorless 426adj.
genuine 494adj.
plain 573adj.
uncombed
orderless 61adj.
uncombined
unmixed 44adj.
non-adhesive 49adj.
decomposed 51adj.
uncomely
ugly 842adj.
uncomfortable
painful 377adj.
suffering 825adj.
unpleasant 827adj.
uncomforted
discontented 829adj.
uncomforting
cheerless 834adj.
uncommendable

inexpedient 643adj.
blameworthy 924adj.
uncommitted
neutral 625adj.
independent 744adj.
uncommon
remarkable 32adj.
special 80adj.
infrequent 140adj.
elegant 575adj.
uncommunicated
retained 778adj.
uncompelled
independent 744adj.
uncompensated
unequal 29adj.
uncomplaining
patient 823adj.
content 828adj.
approving 923adj.
uncompleted
uncompleted 726adj.
uncomplicated
simple 44adj.
artless 699adj.
easy 701adj.
uncomplimentary
ungracious 885adj.
disrespectful 921adj.
disapproving 924adj.
uncompounded
unmixed 44adj.
uncompromising
resolute 599adj.
obstinate 602adj.
severe 735adj.
unconcealed
manifest 522adj.
unconceived
unborn 2adj.
unconcentrated
light-minded 456adj.
unconcern
incuriosity 454n.
inattention 456n.
moral insensibility 820n.
indifference 860n.
unconcerned
irrelative 10adj.
unfearing 855adj.
(*see* unconcern)
unconditional
unconditional 744adj.
permitted 756adj.
obligatory 917adj.
unconfident
doubting 474adj.
unconfined
facilitated 701adj.
unconfined 744adj.
non-liable 919adj.
unconfirmed
uncertified 474adj.
heathenish 974adj.
unconformable
irrelative 10adj.
unimitative 21adj.
disagreeing 25adj.
unconformable 84adj.
unconformity
non-uniformity 17n.
extraneousness 59n.
specialty 80n.
unconformity 84n.
independence 744n.
non-observance 769n.
(*see* unconformable)
unconfused
orderly 60adj.
unconfuted
demonstrated 478adj.
uncongealed
fluid 335adj.
liquefied 337adj.
uncongenial
irrelative 10adj.
disagreeing 25adj.
cheerless 834adj.
unconnected
irrelative 10adj.
unconquerable
unyielding 162adj.
persevering 600adj.
resisting 715adj.
unbeaten 727adj.
independent 744adj.
unconscionable
exorbitant 32adj.
unconscious
impotent 161adj.
insensible 375adj.
ignorant 491adj.
foolish 499adj.
involuntary 596adj.
inactive 679adj.
sleepy 679adj.
impassive 820adj.
unconscious, the
spirit 447n.
unconsecrated
heathenish 974adj.
profane 980adj.
laical 987adj.
unconsidered
unthought 450adj.
neglected 458adj.
unconsoled
discontented 829adj.
unconstitutional
unwarranted 916adj.
illegal 954adj.
unconsumed
remaining 41adj.
unused 674adj.
uncontaminated
perfect 646adj.
uncontested
undisputed 473adj.
uncontradicted
assented 488n.
uncontrasting
uniform 16adj.
uncontrite
impenitent 940adj.
uncontrollable
violent 176adj.
frenzied 503adj.
willful 602adj.
fervent 818adj.
excited 821adj.
excitable 822adj.
uncontrolled
hasty 680adj.
anarchic 734adj.
independent 744adj.
intemperate 943adj.
uncontroversial
undisputed 473adj.
assented 488adj.
unconventional
unconformable 84adj.
unwonted 611adj.
free 744adj.
heterodox 977adj.
unconventionality
unconformity 84n.
unconversant
unskilled 695adj.
unconverted
unconformable 84adj.
dissenting 489adj.
unused 674adj.
impenitent 940adj.
heathenish 974adj.
unconvinced
dissenting 489adj.
unconvincing
improbable 472adj.
uncooked
uncooked 670adj.
uncooperative
unwilling 598adj.
hindering 702adj.
dutiless 918adj.
uncoordinated
orderless 61adj.
uncopied
unimitated 21adj.
uncordial
unkind 898adj.
uncork
open 263vb.
liberate 746vb.
uncorrected
inexact 495adj.
uncorroborated
unattested 467adj.
uncertified 474adj.
uncorrupted
disinterested 931adj.

innocent 935adj.
pure 950adj.
uncostly
cheap 812adj.
uncounted
many 104adj.
uncouple
disjoin 46vb.
uncourtly
ill-bred 847adj.
discourteous 885adj.
uncouth
inelegant 576adj.
artless 699adj.
graceless 842adj.
ill-bred 847adj.
plebeian 869adj.
uncovenanted
unexpected 508adj.
uncover
doff 229vb.
open 263vb.
manifest 522vb.
disclose 526vb.
greet 884vb.
uncovered
vulnerable 661adj.
uncracked
perfect 646adj.
uncrease
unravel 62vb.
smooth 258vb.
uncreated
existing 1adj.
unborn 2adj.
uncritical
indiscriminating 464adj.
approving 923adj.
uncrown
unthrone 734vb.
depose 752vb.
disentitle 916vb.
uncrowned king
influence 178n.
unction
lubrication 334n.
unguent 357n.
warm feeling 818n.
pietism 979n.
unctuous
unctuous 357adj.
flattering 925adj.
uncultivated
unproductive 172adj.
uninstructed 491adj.
ill-bred 847adj.
uncultured
uninstructed 491adj.
artless 699adj.
ill-bred 847adj.
plebeian 869adj.
uncurbed
unconfined 744adj.
uncured
uncooked 670adj.
uncurl
straighten 249vb.
evolve 316vb.
uncurrent
unwonted 611adj.
useless 641adj.
uncurtain
disclose 526vb.
uncustomary
unusual 84n.
uncut
intact 52adj.
immature 670adj.
undamaged
intact 52adj.
undamaged 646adj.
undashed
unfearing 855adj.
undated
anachronistic 118adj.
undaughterly
disobedient 738adj.
unkind 898adj.
dutiless 918adj.
undaunted
resolute 599adj.
persevering 600adj.
unfearing 855adj.
undazzled
wise 498adj.
unastonished 865adj.
undecayed
preserved 666adj.
undeceive
inform 524vb.
disclose 526vb.
displease 827vb.
undeceived
regretting 830adj.
undecided
moot 459adj.
doubting 474adj.
uncertain 474adj.
irresolute 601adj.
undecipherable
unintelligible 517adj.
undeclared
tacit 523adj.
undecorated
inglorious 867adj.
undedicate
paganize 974vb.
laicize 987vb.
undedicated
profane 980adj.
undefaced
shapely 841adj.
undefeated
resisting 715adj.
unbeaten 727adj.
undefiled
innocent 935adj.
pure 950adj.
undefined
amorphous 244adj.
shadowy 419adj.
ill-seen 444adj.
indiscriminate 464adj.
uncertain 474adj.
godlike 965adj.
undeformed
shapely 841adj.
undemanding
easy 701adj.
lax 734adj.
lenient 736adj.
inexcitable 823adj.
undemocratic
unequal 29adj.
authoritarian 735adj.
prideful 871adj.
insolent 878adj.
undemonstrated
uncertified 474adj.
undemonstrative
impassive 820adj.
undeniable
undisputed 473adj.
demonstrated 478adj.
credal 485adj.
undenominational
general 79adj.
undependable
uncertain 474adj.
dishonest 930adj.
undeplored
hated 888adj.
undepraved
honorable 929adj.
under
concerning 9adv.
inferior 35adj.
in place 186adv.
low 210adj.
under 210adv.
subject 745adj.
under a cloud
unprosperous 731adj.
underact
act 594vb.
be unskillful 695vb.
under-age
young 130adj.
under arms
warring 718adj.
under arrest
imprisoned 747adj.
captive 750adj.
underbelly
lowness 210n.
insides 224n.
underbid
bargain 791vb.
underbodice
underwear 228n.

underbred
ill-bred 847adj.
under canvas
under way 269adv.
undercapitalized
unprovided 636adj.
undercarriage
frame 218n.
aircraft 276n.
undercharge
account 808vb.
cheapen 812vb.
underclothed
uncovered 229adj.
underclothes
underwear 228n.
under consideration
in mind 449adv.
in question 452adv.
planned 623adj.
under construction
in preparation 669adv.
on the stocks 726adv.
under control
orderly 60adj.
obedient 739adj.
restrained 747adj.
under cover
covered 226adj.
latent 523adj.
concealed 525adj.
under shelter 660adv.
undercover agent
secret service 459n.
under cover of
deceptively 542adv.
undercurrent
cause 156n.
current 350n.
latency 523n.
undercut
meat 301n.
sell 793vb.
cheapen 812vb.
underdeveloped
incomplete 55adj.
immature 670adj.
under discipline
obedient 739adj.
restrained 747adj.
under discussion
in question 452adv.
underdog
inferior 35n.
loser 728n.
unlucky person 731n.
underdone
uncooked 670adj.
uncompleted 726adj.
underdressed
uncovered 229adj.
vulgar 847adj.
underemployment
superfluity 637n.
inaction 677n.
underestimate
misjudge 481vb.
underestimate 483vb.
err 495vb.
misinterpret 521vb.
not respect 921vb.
detract 926vb.
underestimation
untruth 543n.
(*see* underestimate)
underexposure
achromatism 426n.
photography 551n.
underfed
lean 206adj.
necessitous 627adj.
underfed 636adj.
unhealthy 651adj.
hungry 859adj.
fasting 946adj.
underfeed
make thin 206vb.
underfoot
low 210adj.
subjected 745adj.
underframe
supporter 218n.
undergo
meet with 154vb.
feel 818vb.
suffer 825vb.
undergraduate
college student 538adj.
immature 670adj.
underground
low 210adj.
deep 211adj.
tunnel 263n.
train 274n.
buried 364adj.
concealed 525adj.
hiding-place 527n.
revolter 738n.
underground activities
sedition 738n.
undergrowth
roughness 259n.
wood 366n.
underhand
occult 523adj.
stealthy 525adj.
dishonest 930adj.
underheated
insalubrious 653adj.
underhung
salient 254adj.
under-insurance
rashness 857n.
underived
unimitative 21adj.
underlayer
layer 207n.
base 214n.
underlie
be low 210vb.
lurk 523vb.
underline
strengthen 162vb.
attract notice 455vb.
emphasize 532vb.
mark 547vb.
make important 638vb.
underlinen
underwear 228n.
underling
inferior 35n.
nonentity 639n.
servant 742n.
commoner 869n.
underlining
punctuation 547n.
underlying
undermost 214adj.
latent 523adj.
underman
render few 105vb.
undermanned
unprovided 636adj.
imperfect 647adj.
undermine
disable 161vb.
weaken 163vb.
demolish 165vb.
make concave 255vb.
descend 309vb.
tell against 467vb.
plot 623vb.
impair 655vb.
be cunning 698vb.
hinder 702vb.
undermining
overturning 221n.
undermost
base 214adj.
underneath
under 210adv.
undernourished
underfed 636adj.
unhealthy 651adj.
underpaid
cheap 812adj.
unwarranted 916adj.
underpants
underwear 228n.
underpass
tunnel 263n.
passage 305n.
traffic control 305n.
bridge 624n.
underpay
be undue 916vb.
underpin
support 218vb.
underplot

plot 623n.
underpopulation
fewness 105n.
underpraise
misinterpret 521vb.
underprice
underestimate 483vb.
underpriced
undervalued 483adj.
cheap 812adj.
underprivileged
unentitled 916adj.
underprivileged, the
poor man 801n.
lower classes 869n.
underproduction
decrease 37n.
under proof
tasteless 387adj.
underprop
support 218vb.
underrate
underestimate 483vb.
cheapen 812vb.
not respect 921vb.
hold cheap 922vb.
underripe
immature 670adj.
underscore
mark 547vb.
undersea
deep 211adj.
oceanic 343adj.
undersell
cheapen 812vb.
undershot
salient 254adj.
underside
lowness 210n.
undersign
sign 547n.
undersigned, the
signatory 765n.
undersized
small 33adj.
dwarfish 196adj.
lean 206adj.
underskirt
underwear 228n.
undersong
vocal music 412n.
latency 523n.
understaff
render few 105vb.
understaffed
unprovided 636adj.
understand
cognize 447vb.
be certain 473vb.
know 490vb.
be wise 498vb.
understand 516vb.
imply 523vb.
be informed 524vb.
be benevolent 897vb.
understandable
intelligible 516adj.
understand by
interpret 520vb.
understanding
agreement 24n.
intellect 447n.
intelligence 498n.
imagination 513n.
concord 710n.
pacification 719n.
compact 765n.
pity 905n.
understand one another
cooperate 706vb.
understatement
underestimation 483n.
untruth 543n.
understood
tacit 523adj.
usual 610adj.
understrapper
inferior 35n.
nonentity 639n.
servant 742n.
understudy
substitute 150n.
actor 594n.
act 594vb.
deputy 755n.
undersurface
lowness 210n.
undertake
begin 68vb.
essay 671vb.
undertake 672vb.
promise 764vb.
contract 765vb.
undertaker
interment 364n.
gambler 618n.
essayer 671n.
doer 676n.
undertaking
undertaking 672n.
promise 764n.
under the sun
existing 1adj.
widely 183adv.
under the sun 321adv.
undertone
faintness 401n.
musical note 410n.
latency 523n.
undertow
current 350n.
pitfall 663n.
undervaluation
diminution 37n.
misjudgment 481n.
underestimation 483n.
disrespect 921n.
undervalue
hold cheap 922vb.
(*see* undervaluation)
undervitaminized
underfed 636adj.
unhealthy 651adj.
underwater
deep 211adj.
oceanic 343adj.
underwear
underwear 228n.
underweight
inequality 29n.
inferior 35adj.
light 323adj.
spurious 542adj.
underwood
wood 366n.
underworld
depth 211n.
the dead 361n.
lower classes 869n.
offender 904n.
wickedness 934n.
hell 972n.
underwrite
promise 764vb.
contract 765vb.
give security 767vb.
underwriter
consignee 754n.
underwriting
calculation of chance 159n.
security 767n.
undeserved
unwarranted 916adj.
undeserving
unentitled 916adj.
wicked 934adj.
undesigned
causeless 159adj.
unintentional 618adj.
undesigning
artless 699adj.
undesirability
inexpedience 643n.
undesirable
trouble-maker 663n.
unpleasant 827adj.
unwanted 860adj.
disliked 861adj.
bad man 938n.
undestroyed
existing 1adj.
intact 52adj.
permanent 144adj.
undetected
latent 523adj.
undetermined
general 79adj.
causeless 159adj.
moot 459adj.

uncertain 474adj.
choiceless 606adj.
undeveloped
incomplete 55adj.
unintelligent 499adj.
latent 523adj.
imperfect 647adj.
immature 670adj.
unskilled 695adj.
undevelopment
undevelopment 670n.
non-completion 726n.
undeviating
uniform 16adj.
unchangeable 153adj.
straight 249adj.
directed 281adj.
accurate 494adj.
undeviating 625adj.
indifferent 860adj.
orthodox 976adj.
undevout
irreligious 974adj.
impious 980adj.
undifferentiated
uniform 16adj.
simple 44adj.
indiscriminate 464adj.
undigested
extraneous 59adj.
immature 670adj.
uncooked 670adj.
undignified
vulgar 847adj.
undiluted
unmixed 44adj.
undiminished
absolute 32adj.
intact 52adj.
strong 162adj.
undamaged 646adj.
undimmed
undimmed 417adj.
undine
sea nymph 343n.
mythical being 970n.
undirected
deviating 282adj.
indiscriminate 464adj.
designless 618adj.
undiscerning
blind 439adj.
inattentive 456adj.
indiscriminating 464adj.
unwise 499adj.
undisciplined
disorderly 61adj.
capricious 604adj.
disobedient 738adj.
intemperate 943adj.
undisclosed
occult 523adj.
concealed 525adj.
undiscouraged
persevering 600adj.
hoping 852adj.
undiscoverable
unborn 2adj.
unknown 491adj.
unintelligible 517adj.
latent 523adj.
undisguised
well-seen 443adj.
undisguised 522adj.
veracious 540adj.
artless 699adj.
undismayed
unfearing 655adj.
undisposed of
unused 674adj.
possessed 773adj.
retained 778adj.
undisputed
undisputed 473adj.
undistinguished
indiscriminate 464adj.
mediocre 732adj.
undistorted
symmetrical 245adj.
straight 249adj.
true 494adj.
veracious 540adj.
undistracted
attentive 455adj.
undisturbed
tranquil 266adj.
undiversified
uniform 16adj.
undivided
intact 52adj.
complete 54adj.
undividedness
unity 88n.
undivulged
tacit 523adj.
undo
disjoin 46vb.
revert 148vb.
destroy 165vb.
counteract 182vb.
doff 229vb.
make useless 641vb.
abrogate 752vb.
undoing
ruin 165n.
undomesticated
unhabituated 611adj.
undone
neglected 458adj.
uncompleted 726adj.
unprosperous 731adj.
hopeless 853adj.
undoubted
undisputed 473adj.
undoubting
positive 473adj.
believing 485adj.
undrained
humid 341adj.
marshy 347adj.
insalubrious 653adj.
undramatic
feeble 572adj.
plain 573adj.
undreamed
unthought 450adj.
undress
informal dress 228n.
uncover 229vb.
undressed
uncovered 229adj.
unsavory 391adj.
unequipped 670adj.
uncooked 670adj.
undrilled
unprepared 670adj.
undrinkable
unsavory 391adj.
insalubrious 653adj.
undue
undue 916adj.
undueness
overstepping 306n.
inexpedience 643n.
undueness 916n.
undulate
be periodic 141vb.
(*see* undulation)
undulation
convolution 251n.
oscillation 317n.
wave 350n.
undulatory
periodic 141adj.
undulatory 251adj.
undutiful
dutiless 918adj.
undying
existing 1adj.
perpetual 115adj.
unceasing 146adj.
unchangeable 153adj.
remembered 505adj.
unearned
unwarranted 916adj.
unearned increment
benefit 615n.
unearth
eject 300vb.
exhume 364vb.
discover 484vb.
unearthly
immaterial 320adj.
divine 965adj.
spooky 970adj.
uneasiness
worry 825n.
discontent 829n.
nervousness 854n.
uneasy

nervous 854adj.
uneatable
unsavory 391adj.
uneconomic
wasteful 634adj.
prodigal 815adj.
unedifying
misteaching 535adj.
discreditable 867adj.
vicious 934adj.
unedited
intact 52adj.
tacit 523adj.
uneducated
uninstructed 491adj.
unelevated
feeble 572adj.
unembarrassed
well-bred 848adj.
unembroidered
veracious 540adj.
unemotional
impassive 820adj.
unemphatic
tranquil 266adj.
muted 401adj.
feeble 572adj.
plain 573adj.
inexcitable 823adj.
unemployable
useless 641adj.
unused 674adj.
unemployment
superfluity 637n.
non-use 674n.
inaction 677n.
inactivity 679n.
adversity 731n.
unempowered
powerless 161adj.
unentitled 916adj.
unending
perpetual 115adj.
unendurable
intolerable 827adj.
unenjoyable
tedious 838adj.
unenlightened
ignorant 491adj.
unwise 499adj.
unentailed
non-liable 919adj.
unenterprising
cautious 858adj.
unentertaining
tedious 838adj.
dull 840adj.
unenthusiastic
unwilling 598adj.
apathetic 820adj.
inexcitable 823adj.
unentitled
unentitled 916adj.
unenvious
content 828adj.
benevolent 897adj.
disinterested 931adj.
unequal
dissimilar 19adj.
unequal 29adj.
inferior 35adj.
unequaled
supreme 34adj.
best 644adj.
unequal to
insufficient 636adj.
unequipped
unequipped 670adj.
unequivocal
absolute 32adj.
positive 473adj.
intelligible 516adj.
unerring
certain 473adj.
accurate 494adj.
successful 727adj.
innocent 935adj.
unescorted
alone 88adj.
vulnerable 661adj.
unethical
dishonest 930adj.
uneven
non-uniform 17adj.
unequal 29adj.
discontinuous 72adj.
fitful 142adj.
rough 259adj.
imperfect 647adj.
unjust 914adj.
uneventful
tranquil 266adj.
trivial 639adj.
unevolved
unreal 2adj.
unexaggerated
genuine 494adj.
unexamined
neglected 458adj.
unexampled
unusual 84n.
unexpected 508adj.
unexceptionable
not bad 644adj.
guiltless 935adj.
unexceptional
regular 81adj.
unexciting
lenitive 177adj.
feeble 572adj.
tedious 838adj.
unexecuted
uncompleted 726adj.
unexempt from
liable 180adj.
unexercised
powerless 161adj.
unprepared 670adj.
unused 674adj.
unexhausted
unyielding 162adj.
unexpected
unexpected 508adj.
puzzling 517adj.
capricious 604adj.
wonderful 864adj.
unexpended
remaining 41adj.
stored 632adj.
unexpired
remaining 41adj.
unexplained
causeless 159adj.
uncertain 474adj.
unknown 491adj.
puzzling 517adj.
latent 523adj.
unexplored
neglected 458adj.
unknown 491adj.
latent 523adj.
secluded 883adj.
unexposed
latent 523adj.
safe 660adj.
unexpressed
tacit 523adj.
unexpurgated
intact 52adj.
impure 951adj.
unextinguished
violent 176adj.
fiery 379adj.
unextreme
moderate 177adj.
neutral 625adj.
unfactual
erroneous 495adj.
unfading
lasting 113adj.
perpetual 115adj.
colored 425adj.
renowned 866adj.
unfailing
permanent 144adj.
unceasing 146adj.
persevering 600adj.
liberal 813adj.
unfair
false 541adj.
unjust 914adj.
dishonest 930adj.
unfaith
unbelief 486n.
perfidy 930n.
unfaithful
changeful 152adj.
unbelieving 486adj.
irresolute 601adj.
non-observant 769adj.
inimical 881adj.
perfidious 930adj.

extramarital 951adj.
unfallen
innocent 935adj.
pure 950adj.
unfaltering
persevering 600adj.
unfamiliar
unusual 84adj.
unknown 491adj.
unhabituated 611adj.
secluded 883adj.
unfamiliarity
ignorance 491n.
unfashionable
unconformable 84adj.
unwonted 611adj.
ill-bred 847adj.
plebeian 869adj.
unfashioned
amorphous 244adj.
immature 670adj.
unfastened
separate 46adj.
unfastidious
unclean 649adj.
vulgar 847adj.
dishonest 930adj.
unfathered
negative 533adj.
unfathomable
infinite 107adj.
deep 211adj.
unintelligible 517adj.
unfavorable
inopportune 138adj.
hindering 702adj.
opposing 704adj.
adverse 731adj.
disapproving 924adj.
unfavored
unprosperous 731adj.
unfearing
unfearing 855adj.
unfeasible
impracticable 470adj.
unfed
underfed 636adj.
fasting 946adj.
unfeeling
unfeeling 375adj.
impassive 820adj.
unkind 898adj.
pure 950adj.
impious 980adj.
unfeigned
veracious 540adj.
unfeminine
male 372adj.
ill-bred 847adj.
unfetter
disencumber 701vb.
liberate 746vb.
unfilial
disobedient 738adj.
unkind 898adj.
dutiless 918adj.
unfilled
unprovided 636adj.
hungry 859adj.
unfilling
discontenting 829adj.
unfinished
fragmentary 53adj.
unfinished 55adj.
inelegant 576adj.
imperfect 647adj.
immature 670adj.
uncompleted 726adj.
unfit
unapt 25adj.
disable 161vb.
useless 641adj.
unskillful 695adj.
wrong 914adj.
unfitness
inexpedience 643n.
non-preparation 670n.
(*see* unfit)
unfitting
inexpedient 643adj.
undue 916adj.
unfix
displace 188vb.
unfixed
unstable 152adj.
light-minded 456adj.
irresolute 601adj.
unflagging
unyielding 162adj.
persevering 600adj.
industrious 678adj.
unflappable
inexcitable 823adj.
unflattered
wise 498adj.
discontented 829adj.
unflattering
true 494adj.
ungracious 885adj.
maledicent 899adj.
disrespectful 921adj.
disapproving 924adj.
detracting 926adj.
unflavored
unmixed 44adj.
tasteless 387adj.
unflawed
perfect 646adj.
unfledged
new 126adj.
young 130adj.
infantine 132adj.
uncovered 229adj.
immature 670adj.
unfleshed
new 126adj.
unflinching
resolute 599adj.
courageous 855adj.
unfold
become 1vb.
result 157vb.
produce 164vb.
lengthen 203vb.
uncover 229vb.
straighten 249vb.
open 263vb.
evolve 316vb.
interpret 520vb.
disclose 526vb.
unforbidden
permitted 756adj.
unforced
voluntary 597adj.
independent 744adj.
unforeseeable
causeless 159adj.
improbable 472adj.
uncertain 474adj.
unexpected 508adj.
unforeseeing
unwise 499adj.
rash 857adj.
unforeseen
unexpected 508adj.
unforfeited
retained 778adj.
unforgettable
remembered 505adj.
notable 638adj.
unforgetting
revengeful 910adj.
unforgivable
wrong 914adj.
accusable 928adj.
heinous 934adj.
guilty 936adj.
unforgiving
severe 735adj.
unkind 898adj.
malevolent 898adj.
pitiless 906adj.
revengeful 910adj.
unformed
amorphous 244adj.
immature 670adj.
unforthcoming
avoiding 620adj.
impassive 820adj.
unsociable 883adj.
unkind 898adj.
unfortified
unmixed 44adj.
defenseless 161adj.
weak 163adj.
vulnerable 661adj.
unfortunate
inopportune 138adj.
unfortunate 731adj.
unhappy 825adj.
annoying 827adj.

unforward
unskillful 695adj.
unfound
unequipped 670adj.
unfounded
unreal 2adj.
insubstantial 4adj.
illogical 477adj.
erroneous 495adj.
unfranchised
subject 745adj.
unentitled 916adj.
unfraternal
unkind 898adj.
unfree
serving 742adj.
subject 745adj.
unfreeze
liquefy 337vb.
unfreezing
non-retention 779n.
unfresh
bad 645adj.
insalubrious 653adj.
unfriended
defenseless 161adj.
friendless 883adj.
unfriendliness
unsociability 883n.
(*see* unfriendly)
unfriendly
opposing 704adj.
disliking 861adj.
inimical 881adj.
ungracious 885adj.
unkind 898adj.
unfrock
depose 752vb.
deprive 786vb.
disentitle 916vb.
punish 963vb.
perform ritual 988vb.
unfrozen
warm 379adj.
unfrugal
intemperate 943adj.
unfruitful
unproductive 172adj.
unfunny
serious 834adj.
tedious 838adj.
dull 840adj.
unfurl
lengthen 203vb.
straighten 249vb.
evolve 316vb.
manifest 522vb.
disclose 526vb.
unfurnished
unprovided 636adj.
unequipped 670adj.
ungainly
clumsy 695adj.
graceless 842adj.
ungallant
discourteous 885adj.
ungenerous
parsimonious 816adj.
unkind 898adj.
selfish 932adj.
ungenial
insalubrious 653adj.
ungenteel
ill-bred 847adj.
ungentle
violent 176adj.
oppressive 735adj.
ungracious 885adj.
ungentlemanly
ill-bred 847adj.
discourteous 885adj.
dishonest 930adj.
un-get-at-able
removed 199adj.
ungifted
unintelligent 499adj.
unskillful 695adj.
ungodly
irreligious 974adj.
ungovernable
violent 176adj.
willful 602adj.
disobedient 738adj.
independent 744adj.
lawless 954adj.
ungoverned
anarchic 734adj.
independent 744adj.
ungraceful
inelegant 576adj.
clumsy 695adj.
graceless 842adj.
ungracious
ungracious 885adj.
ungrammatical
ungrammatical 565adj.
ungrateful
forgetful 506adj.
ungrateful 908adj.
ungratified
refused 760adj.
discontented 829adj.
ungreedy
temperate 942adj.
ungrounded
illogical 477adj.
erroneous 495adj.
ungrown
immature 670adj.
ungrudging
liberal 813adj.
disinterested 931adj.
unguaranteed
uncertified 474adj.
unguarded
neglected 458adj.
spontaneous 609adj.
vulnerable 661adj.
unprepared 670adj.
unguent
lubricant 334n.
unguent 357n.
cosmetic 843n.
unguessed
unexpected 508adj.
latent 523adj.
unguided
deviating 282adj.
designless 618adj.
ungulate
footed 214adj.
unhabituated
unhabituated 611adj.
unhackneyed
unimitated 21adj.
new 126adj.
unwonted 611adj.
unhallowed
unclean 649adj.
heathenish 974adj.
profane 980adj.
unhand
liberate 746vb.
not retain 779vb.
unhandled
unused 674adj.
unhandseled
new 126adj.
unprepared 670adj.
unhandy
clumsy 695adj.
unhappy
inopportune 138adj.
inexpedient 643adj.
bungled 695adj.
unfortunate 731adj.
unhappy 825adj.
discontented 829adj.
dejected 834adj.
nervous 854adj.
unharmed
healthy 650adj.
safe 660adj.
unharness
disjoin 46vb.
arrive 295vb.
liberate 746vb.
unhatched
immature 670adj.
unhealthy
deadly 362adj.
inexpedient 643adj.
harmful 645adj.
unhealthy 651adj.
insalubrious 653adj.
dangerous 661adj.

unheard
silent 399adj.
unknown 491adj.
inglorious 867adj.
modest 874adj.
unheard of
new 126adj.
impossible 470adj.
improbable 472adj.
wonderful 864adj.
unhearing
insensible 375adj.
deaf 416adj.
inattentive 456adj.
impassive 820adj.
unheated
cold 380adj.
unheeding
inattentive 456adj.
unheld
unpossessed 774adj.
unhelpful
unwilling 598adj.
inexpedient 643adj.
hindering 702adj.
unkind 898adj.
unheralded
unexpected 508adj.
unheroic
irresolute 601adj.
cowardly 856adj.
inglorious 867adj.
unhinge
derange 63vb.
disable 161vb.
make mad 503vb.
unhistorical
erroneous 495adj.
unhitch
disjoin 46vb.
unholy
heathenish 974adj.
profane 980adj.
laical 987adj.
unhook
disjoin 46vb.
unhopeful
dejected 834adj.
hopeless 853adj.
unhorsed
grounded 728adj.
unhoused
displaced 188adj.
unhousetrained
ill-bred 847adj.
unhurried
tranquil 266adj.
slow 278adj.
leisurely 681adj.
inexcitable 823adj.
unhurt
undamaged 646adj.
unhygienic
insalubrious 653adj.
unicameral
one 88adj.
parliamentary 692adj.
unicorn
rara avis 84n.
heraldry 547n.
unicycle
bicycle 274n.
unideal
existing 1adj.
true 494adj.
unidealistic
selfish 932adj.
unidentifiable
unconformable 84adj.
unidentified
irrelative 10adj.
unknown 491adj.
unidiomatic
unapt 25adj.
abnormal 84adj.
unmeaning 515adj.
neological 560adj.
unification
simplification 44n.
combination 50n.
unity 88n.
association 706n.
uniform
dress, uniform 228n.
livery 547n.
badge of rank 743n.
(*see* uniformity)
uniformed
dressed 228adj.
uniformist
uniformist 16n.
uniformity
identity 13n.
uniformity 16n.
order 60n.
continuity 71n.
regularity 81n.
unify
join 45vb.
combine 50vb.
(*see* unification)
unilateral
irrelative 10adj.
one 88adj.
independent 744adj.
unimaginable
unusual 84adj.
impossible 470adj.
improbable 472adj.
unbelieved 486adj.
wonderful 864adj.
unimaginative
imitative 20adj.
unthinking 450adj.
indiscriminating 464adj.
narrow-minded 481adj.
unintelligent 499adj.
plain 573adj.
thick-skinned 820adj.
impassive 820adj.
dull 840adj.
unastonished 865adj.
unimitated
unimitated 21adj.
special 80adj.
unimitative
unimitative 21adj.
unimpaired
intact 52adj.
unimpassioned
apathetic 820adj.
unimpeachable
undisputed 473adj.
true 494adj.
just 913adj.
due 915adj.
approvable 923adj.
guiltless 935adj.
unimportance
irrelevance 10n.
unimportance 639n.
unimportant
inconsiderable 33adj.
humble 872adj.
(*see* unimportance)
unimposing
modest 874adj.
unimpressed
indifferent 860adj.
unastonished 865adj.
disapproving 924adj.
unimpressionable
impassive 820adj.
uninfluenced
obstinate 602adj.
free 744adj.
independent 744adj.
uninfluential
unimportant 639adj.
uninformed
amorphous 244adj.
uninstructed 491adj.
inexpectant 508adj.
uninhabitable
empty 190adj.
uninhabited
secluded 883adj.
uninitiated
ignorant 491adj.
unskilled 695adj.
uninquisitive
incurious 454adj.
uninspired
feeble 572adj.
plain 573adj.
apathetic 820adj.
tedious 838adj.

uninstructed
uninstructed 491adj.
unprepared 670adj.
unintellectual
mindless 448adj.
unthinking 450adj.
unintelligent 499adj.
unwise 499adj.
unintelligent
unthinking 450adj.
unintelligent 499adj.
unintelligibility
unintelligibility 517n.
imperspicuity 568n.
difficulty 700n.
unintended
causeless 159adj.
unmeant 515adj.
involuntary 596adj.
unintentional 618adj.
unintentional
involuntary 596adj.
spontaneous 609adj.
unintentional 618adj.
uninterest
incuriosity 454n.
uninterested
incurious 454adj.
choiceless 606adj.
inactive 679adj.
apathetic 820adj.
bored 838adj.
indifferent 860adj.
uninteresting
tedious 838adj.
dull 840adj.
uninterrupted
continuous 71adj.
perpetual 115adj.
unceasing 146adj.
uninventive
imitative 20adj.
mindless 448adj.
unthinking 450adj.
uninvited
disobedient 738adj.
unwanted 860adj.
friendless 883adj.
uninvited guest
intruder 59n.
uninviting
unpleasant 827adj.
uninvolved
irrelative 10adj.
incurious 454adj.
intelligible 516adj.
independent 744adj.
indifferent 860adj.
disinterested 931adj.
union
agreement 24n.
junction 45n.
coition 45n.
coherence 48n.
combination 50n.
unity 88n.
concurrence 181n.
association 706n.
society 708n.
marriage 894n.
Union Jack
flag 547n.
unique
non-uniform 17adj.
dissimilar 19adj.
unimitated 21adj.
special 80adj.
unconformable 84adj.
one 88adj.
valuable 644adj.
unirritable
inexcitable 823adj.
unirritating
lenitive 177adj.
unison
uniformity 16n.
agreement 24n.
melody 410n.
concord 710n.
unit
whole 52n.
group 74n.
unit 88n.
person 371n.
formation 722n.
unitarianism
philosophy 449n.
heresy 977n.
Unitarians
sect 978n.
unitary
one 88adj.
unite
join 45vb.
combine 50vb.
bring together 74vb.
be one 88vb.
concur 181vb.
converge 293vb.
cooperate 706vb.
united
agreeing 24adj.
cohesive 48adj.
concordant 710adj.
married 894adj.
united front
association 706n.
unity
identity 13n.
uniformity 16n.
simpleness 44n.
completeness 54n.
unity 88n.
association 706n.
concord 710n.
divine attribute 965n.
universal
extensive 32adj.
comprehensive 52adj.
universal 79adj.
one 88adj.
ubiquitous 189adj.
cosmic 321adj.
universal aunt
servant 742n.
universality
generality 79n.
indiscrimination 464n.
(*see* universal)
universalize
generalize 79vb.
universals
premise 475n.
universe
substantiality 3n.
great quantity 32n.
whole 52n.
universe 321n.
university
academy 539n.
univocal
one 88adj.
certain 473adj.
semantic 514adj.
unjealous
content 828adj.
disinterested 931adj.
unjust
bad 645adj.
oppressive 735adj.
unjust 914adj.
dishonest 930adj.
wicked 934adj.
unjustifiable
unjust 914adj.
unwarranted 916adj.
blameworthy 924adj.
accusable 928adj.
heinous 934adj.
guilty 936adj.
unkempt
orderless 61adj.
rough 259adj.
neglected 458adj.
dirty 649adj.
unkind
harmful 645adj.
unkind 898adj.
unknowable
unknown 491adj.
unintelligible 517adj.
unknown
new 126adj.
unknown 491adj.
disguised 525adj.
anonymous 562adj.
secluded 883adj.
unknown quantity
unknown thing 491n.

secret 530n.
unlace
doff 229vb.
unladylike
ill-bred 847adj.
unlamented
hated 888adj.
disapproved 924adj.
unlatch
disjoin 46vb.
open 263vb.
unlaughing
serious 834adj.
unlawful
prohibited 757adj.
non-observant 769adj.
extramarital 951adj.
illegal 954adj.
unlearn
not know 491vb.
forget 506vb.
unlearned
uninstructed 491adj.
artless 699adj.
unleash
liberate 746vb.
unleavened
ritual 988adj.
unlegalized
unwarranted 916adj.
unlegislated
illegal 954adj.
unless
if 8adv.
provided 468adj.
unlettered
uninstructed 491adj.
unlicensed
unwarranted 916adj.
unlicked
immature 670adj.
unlicked cub
youngster 132n.
amorphism 244n.
undevelopment 670n.
vulgarian 847n.
rude person 885n.
unlikable
not nice 645adj.
unlike
different 15adj.
dissimilar 19adj.
unlikely
improbable 472adj.
unlikeness
non-imitation 21n.
unlimited
absolute 32adj.
infinite 107adj.
unconditional 744adj.
unlit
unlit 418adj.
invisible 444adj.
unliterary
dialectical 560adj.
unlively
inexcitable 823adj.
serious 834adj.
dull 840adj.
unload
displace 188vb.
transpose 272vb.
void 300vb.
extract 304vb.
disencumber 701vb.
sell 793vb.
unlock
disjoin 46vb.
open 263vb.
liberate 746vb.
unlooked for
unexpected 508adj.
undue 916adj.
unloose
disjoin 46vb.
deliver 668vb.
liberate 746vb.
unlovely
ugly 842adj.
disliked 861adj.
unlucky
inopportune 138adj.
evil 616adj.
unsuccessful 728adj.
unfortunate 731adj.
unmade
unborn 2adj.
amorphous 244adj.
unmake
revert 148vb.
destroy 165vb.
abrogate 752vb.
unmalleable
unconformable 84adj.
rigid 326adj.
unman
unman 161vb.
sterilize 172vb.
frighten 854vb.
unmanageable
willful 602adj.
clumsy 695adj.
difficult 700adj.
unmanifested
latent 523adj.
unmanly
female 373adj.
cowardly 856adj.
dishonest 930adj.
unmannerly
discourteous 885adj.
unmarred
undamaged 646adj.
unmarried
unwedded 895adj.
unmarry
divorce 896vb.
unmartial
cowardly 856adj.
unmask
disclose 526vb.
unmasterful
lax 734adj.
unmatched
dissimilar 19adj.
unimitated 21adj.
best 644adj.
unwedded 895adj.
unmeaning
absurd 497adj.
semantic 514adj.
unmeaning 515adj.
designless 618adj.
unimportant 639adj.
unmeaningness
unintelligibility 517n.
equivocalness 518n.
unmeant
unmeant 515adj.
unintentional 618adj.
unmeasured
indiscriminate 464adj.
plenteous 635adj.
simple 44adj.
continuous 71adj.
unmediated
intemperate 943adj.
unmeditated
spontaneous 609adj.
unmeet
undue 916adj.
unmelting
pitiless 906adj.
unmentionable
unusual 84adj.
inexpressible 517adj.
prohibited 757adj.
discreditable 867adj.
impure 951adj.
unmentioned
tacit 523adj.
inglorious 867adj.
unmerciful
pitiless 906adj.
unmerited
unwarranted 916adj.
unmeritorious
unentitled 916adj.
wicked 934adj.
unmilitary
peaceful 717adj.
unmindful
inattentive 456adj.
negligent 458adj.
ungrateful 908adj.
unmingled
unmixed 44adj.
unmissed
neglected 458adj.

unwanted 860adj.
hated 888adj.
unmistakable
visible 443adj.
certain 473adj.
intelligible 516adj.
manifest 522adj.
unmitigated
consummate 32adj.
complete 54adj.
violent 176adj.
unmixed
absolute 32adj.
unmixed 44adj.
whole 52adj.
unmodified
unmixed 44adj.
permanent 144adj.
unmoor
be disjoined 46vb.
navigate 269vb.
start out 296vb.
unmotivated
causeless 159adj.
spontaneous 609adj.
unmotorable
impracticable 470adj.
unmourned
hated 888adj.
unmoved
quiescent 266adj.
obstinate 602adj.
apathetic 820adj.
indifferent 860adj.
unastonished 865adj.
unkind 898adj.
pitiless 906adj.
unmusical
discordant 411adj.
deaf 416adj.
unmuzzle
liberate 746vb.
unnamed
unknown 490adj.
concealed 525adj.
anonymous 562adj.
unnatural
disagreeing 25adj.
extraneous 59adj.
abnormal 84adj.
impossible 470adj.
inelegant 576adj.
affected 850adj.
unkind, cruel 898adj.
unnavigable
shallow 212adj.
impracticable 470adj.
difficult 700adj.
unnecessary
wasteful 634adj.
superfluous 637adj.
unimportant 639adj.
useless 641adj.
unused 674adj.
unnerve
unman 161vb.
weaken 163vb.
deject 834vb.
frighten 854vb.
unnoticeable
inconsiderable 33adj.
slow 278adj.
invisible 444adj.
unnoticed
neglected 458adj.
inglorious 867adj.
unnourishing
insufficient 636adj.
unnumbered
many 104adj.
infinite 107adj.
unobjectionable
not bad 644adj.
mediocre 732adj.
contenting 828adj.
vindicable 927adj.
guiltless 935adj.
unobliged
ungrateful 908adj.
unobservant
inattentive 456adj.
unobstructed
open 263adj.
accessible 289adj.
facilitated 701adj.
unconfined 744adj.
unobtainable
impracticable 470adj.
scarce 636adj.
unobtrusive
modest 874adj.
unoccupied
empty 190adj.
unthinking 450adj.
non-active 677adj.
inactive 679adj.
leisurely 681adj.
unpossessed 774adj.
unoffending
humble 872adj.
unofficial
uncertified 474adj.
independent 744adj.
illegal 954adj.
unopened
closed 264adj.
unopposed
assented 488adj.
unorganized
orderless 61adj.
inorganic 359adj.
unprepared 670adj.
lax 734adj.
unoriginal
imitative 20adj.
caused 157adj.
mindless 448adj.
usual 610adj.
dull 840adj.
unorthodoxy
unconformity 84n.
error 495n.
heterodoxy 977n.
unowned
unpossessed 774adj.
unpack
uncover 229vb.
void 300vb.
extract 304vb.
unpacking
displacement 188n.
transference 272n.
unpaid
voluntary 597adj.
owed 803adj.
uncharged 812adj.
unpalatable
unsavory 391adj.
unpleasant 827adj.
unpampered
temperate 942adj.
ascetic 945adj.
unparalleled
unusual 84adj.
best 644adj.
unpardonable
wrong 914adj.
accusable 928adj.
heinous 934adj.
guilty 936adj.
unparliamentary
maledicent 899adj.
unpartnered
unwedded 895adj.
unpatriotic
misanthropic 902adj.
selfish 932adj.
unpeaceful
contending 716adj.
unperceived
neglected 458adj.
unknown 491adj.
unperceptive
unintelligent 499adj.
unperjured
veracious 540adj.
trustworthy 929adj.
unphilosophical
unwise 499adj.
unpick
disjoin 46vb.
unpigmented
colorless 426adj.
unpin
unstick 49vb.
unpitied
disapproved 924adj.

unplaced
unsuccessful 728adj.
defeated 728adj.
unplanned
bungled 695adj.
unpleasant
painful 377adj.
unsavory 391adj.
fetid 397adj.
unpleasant 827adj.
discourteous 885adj.
threatening 900adj.
unpleasantness
dissension 709n.
suffering 825n.
painfulness 827n.
discourtesy 885n.
unpleasing
unpleasant 827adj.
unplumbed
deep 211adj.
unknown 491adj.
unpoetical
plain 573adj.
prosaic 593adj.
artless 699adj.
unpointed
unsharpened 257adj.
unpolished
rough 259adj.
dim 419adj.
inelegant 576adj.
dirty 649adj.
immature 670adj.
artless 699adj.
plebeian 869adj.
unpopular
unpleasant 827adj.
disliked 861adj.
disreputable 867adj.
friendless 883adj.
hated 888adj.
unpopularity
odium 888n.
disapprobation 924n.
unpossessive
disinterested 931n.
unpractical
useless 641adj.
unskillful 695adj.
unpracticed
unwonted 611adj.
unprepared 670adj.
clumsy 695adj.
unpraised
disapproved 924adj.
unprecedented
dissimilar 19adj.
first 68adj.
new 126adj.
infrequent 140adj.
unknown 491adj.
unexpected 508adj.
unwonted 611adj.
wonderful 864adj.
unpredictable
non-uniform 17adj.
fitful 142adj.
changeful 152adj.
causeless 159adj.
uncertain 474adj.
unintelligible 517adj.
capricious 604adj.
unprejudiced
wise 498adj.
undamaged 646adj.
free 744adj.
just 913adj.
unpremeditated
involuntary 596adj.
spontaneous 609adj.
unintentional 618adj.
unprepared
negligent 458adj.
inexpectant 508adj.
spontaneous 609adj.
unprepared 670adj.
uncooked 670adj.
hasty 680adj.
unskilled 695adj.
unprepossessing
ugly 842adj.
unpresentable
ill-bred 847adj.
unpretending
artless 699adj.
modest 874adj.
unpretentious
veracious 540adj.
plain 573adj.
humble 872adj.
modest 874adj.
unpriestly
laical 987adj.
unprincipled
dishonest 930adj.
wicked 934adj.
unprintable
prohibited 757adj.
impure 951adj.
unprivileged
subject 745adj.
unentitled 916adj.
unprized
undervalued 483adj.
unprocurable
absent 190adj.
scarce 636adj.
unproductive
impotent 161adj.
unproductive 172adj.
profitless 641adj.
unproductivity
unproductivity 172n.
unprofessional
non-observant 769adj.
unprofitable
unproductive 172adj.
profitless 641adj.
inexpedient 643adj.
losing 772adj.
unprogressive
permanent 144adj.
quiescent 266adj.
deteriorated 655adj.
non-active 677adj.
unpromising
unpromising 853adj.
unprompted
voluntary 597adj.
spontaneous 609adj.
unpronounceable
inexpressible 517adj.
unpronounced
tacit 523adj.
unpropitious
inopportune 138adj.
opposing 704adj.
unpromising 853adj.
unprosperous
unprosperous 731adj.
unprotected
vulnerable 661adj.
unprotesting
humble 872adj.
unproved
unattested 467adj.
uncertified 474adj.
ill-reasoned 477adj.
unprovided
unprovided 636adj.
poor 801adj.
unprovoked
spontaneous 609adj.
unwanted 860adj.
unpublished
tacit 523adj.
unpunctual
anachronistic 118adj.
late 136adj.
ill-timed 138adj.
fitful 142adj.
unpunishable
non-liable 919n.
unpunished
forgiven 909adj.
acquitted 960adj.
unpurposed
unintentional 618adj.
unqualified
unmixed 44adj.
complete 54adj.
positive 473adj.
useless 641adj.
unequipped 670adj.
unskilled 695adj.
unentitled 916adj.
(*see* unconditional)
unquenchable

unyielding 162adj.
greedy 859adj.
unquenched
violent 176adj.
fiery 379adj.
unquestionable
undisputed 473adj.
assertive 532adj.
unquestioning
believing 485adj.
unquiet
moving 265adj.
agitated 318adj.
reslessness 678n.
excitable 822adj.
worry 825n.
unquotable
impure 951adj.
unratified
uncertified 474adj.
unravel
simplify 44vb.
unravel 62vb.
straighten 249vb.
extract 304vb.
evolve 316vb.
decipher 520vb.
disencumber 701vb.
liberate 746vb.
unreached
deficient 307adj.
unread
uninstructed 491adj.
tedious 838adj.
unreadable
unintelligible 517adj.
tedious 838adj.
dull 840adj.
unreadiness
incompleteness 55n.
lateness 136n.
non-preparation 670n.
unready
(*see* unreadiness)
unreal
unreal 2adj.
erroneous 495adj.
imaginary 513adj.
unrealistic
impossible 470adj.
misjudging 481adj.
erroneous 495adj.
unreality
immateriality 320n.
error 495n.
unrealized
unreal 2adj.
unknown 491adj.
uncompleted 726adj.
unreason
irrelevance 10n.
non-intellect 448n.
intuition 476n.
folly 499n.
unmeaningness 515n.
wrong 914n.
unreasonable
impossible 470adj.
illogical 477adj.
biased 481adj.
unwise 499adj.
capricious 604adj.
wrong 914adj.
unreasoned
illogical 477adj.
unreasoning
mindless 448adj.
biased 481adj.
unwise 499adj.
unreclaimed
impenitent 940adj.
unrecognizable
converted 147adj.
invisible 444adj.
unintelligible 517adj.
disguised 525adj.
unrecognized
unknown 491adj.
unreconciled
unwilling 598adj.
inimical 881adj.
impenitent 940adj.
unredeemed
wicked 934adj.
unrefined
indiscriminating 464adj.
inelegant 576adj.
unclean 649adj.
artless 699adj.
ill-bred 847adj.
unreflecting
unthinking 450adj.
incurious 454adj.
inattentive 456adj.
unreformed
impenitent 940adj.
unrefreshed
fatigued 684adj.
unrefuted
demonstrated 478adj.
unregarded
neglected 458adj.
unrespected 921adj.
unregenerate
impious 980adj.
unregretted
hated 888adj.
disapproved 924adj.
unrepented 940adj.
unregretting
impenitent 940adj.
unrehearsed
spontaneous 609adj.
unprepared 670adj.
unrelated
irrelative 10adj.
dissimilar 19adj.
unrelenting
pitiless 906adj.
revengeful 910adj.
impenitent 940adj.
unreliability
tergiversation 603n.
(*see* unreliable)
unreliable
changeful 152adj.
unreliable 474adj.
unbelieved 486adj.
irresolute 601adj.
capricious 604adj.
unsafe 661adj.
dutiless 918adj.
flattering 925adj.
dishonest 930adj.
unrelieved
uniform 16adj.
discontented 829adj.
aggravated 832adj.
cheerless 834adj.
unrelished
disliked 861adj.
unremarked
neglected 458adj.
inglorious 867adj.
unremembered
forgotten 506adj.
unremitting
continuous 71adj.
unceasing 146adj.
persevering 600adj.
unrenowned
inglorious 867adj.
unrepealable
permanent 144adj.
unrepeated
one 88adj.
unrepentant
impenitent 940adj.
unrepining
content 828adj.
cheerful 833adj.
unrepresentative
abnormal 84adj.
unrepresented
absent 190adj.
unrepressed
violent 176adj.
unrequited
unthanked 908adj.
unresentful
forgiving 909adj.
unreserved
undisguised 522adj.
veracious 540adj.
artless 699adj.
free 744adj.
unresigned

resentful 891adj.
unresisting
inactive 679adj.
peaceful 717adj.
submitting 721adj.
obedient 739adj.
unresolved
puzzling 517adj.
irresolute 601adj.
choiceless 606adj.
unrespected
unrespected 921adj.
unresponsive
impassive 820adj.
indifferent 860adj.
unkind 898adj.
pitiless 906adj.
unrest
changeableness 152n.
motion 265n.
discontent 829n.
unrestrained
facilitated 701adj.
unconfined 744adj.
unrestraint
inelegance 576n.
intemperance 943n.
unrestricted
absolute 32adj.
unconditional 744adj.
unrevised
inexact 495adj.
unrewarded
profitless 641adj.
unthanked 908adj.
unrewarding
profitless 641adj.
unrhythmical
fitful 142adj.
unriddle
decipher 520vb.
unrighteous
wrong 914adj.
wicked 934adj.
unrightful
wrong 914adj.
unrigorous
inexact 495adj.
unripe
incomplete 55adj.
new 126adj.
young 130adj.
sour 393adj.
unhabituated 611adj.
imperfect 647adj.
immature 670adj.
unskilled 695adj.
uncompleted 726adj.
unrivaled
supreme 34adj.
unroll
lengthen 203vb.
straighten 249vb.
evolve 316vb.
manifest 522vb.
disclose 526vb.
unromantic
true 494adj.
inexcitable 823adj.
unroof
demolish 165vb.
uncover 229vb.
unroot
extract 304vb.
unruffled
orderly 60adj.
smooth 258adj.
tranquil 266adj.
impassive 820adj.
inexcitable 823adj.
unruly
violent 176adj.
willful 602adj.
anarchic 734adj.
disobedient 738adj.
riotous 738adj.
unsaddle
depose 752vb.
(*see* unseat)
unsafe
unsafe 661adj.
unsaid
tacit 523adj.
unsalable
profitless 641adj.
cheap 812adj.
unsanctified
heathenish 974adj.
profane 980adj.
unsanctioned
unwarranted 916adj.
heterodox 977adj.
unsated
greedy 859adj.
envious 912adj.
unsatisfactory
disappointing 509adj.
insufficient 636adj.
inexpedient 643adj.
bad 645adj.
unpleasant 827adj.
discontenting 829adj.
disapproved 924adj.
unsatisfied
unprovided 636adj.
discontented 829adj.
greedy 859adj.
envious 912adj.
unsatisfying
disappointing 509adj.
unsavory
unsavory 391adj.
unpleasant 827adj.
disliked 861adj.
unsay
recant 603vb.
unscathed
undamaged 646adj.
unscented
odorless 395adj.
unschematic
orderless 61adj.
unschismatical
orthodox 976adj.
unscholarly
uninstructed 491adj.
unschooled
uninstructed 491adj.
unscientific
impossible 470adj.
illogical 477adj.
ignorant 491adj.
erroneous 495adj.
unscramble
simplify 44vb.
decompose 51vb.
unravel 62vb.
unscriptural
erroneous 495adj.
heterodox 977adj.
unscrupulous
dishonest 930adj.
wicked 934adj.
unseal
disclose 526vb.
unsearchable
unintelligible 517adj.
unseasonable
unapt 25adj.
ill-timed 138adj.
unseasoned
unhabituated 611adj.
unseat
unstick 49vb.
derange 63vb.
displace 188vb.
unthrone 734vb.
depose 752vb.
unsectarian
general 79adj.
unseeing
insensible 375adj.
blind 439adj.
inattentive 456adj.
misjudging 481adj.
ignorant 491adj.
unwise 499adj.
impassive 820adj.
unseemliness
bad taste 847n.
unseemly
inexpedient 643adj.
unsightly 842adj.
wrong 914n.
undue 916adj.
vicious 934adj.
unseen
invisible 444adj.
unknown 491adj.

latent 523adj.
modest 874adj.
inglorious 876adj.
secluded 883adj.
unselective
indiscriminating 464adj.
unself-controlled
intemperate 943adj.
unselfishness
benevolence 897n.
disinterestedness 931n.
virtues 933n.
unsensational
plain 573adj.
unsentimental
impassive 820adj.
inexcitable 823adj.
unseparable
cohesive 48adj.
unserious
witty 839adj.
unserviceable
useless 641adj.
unsettle
derange 63vb.
unsettled
transient 114adj.
unstable 152adj.
displaced 188adj.
unsettlement
irresolution 601n.
unseverable
firm-set 45adj.
unsexed
impotent 161adj.
unshackle
disencumber 701vb.
liberate 746vb.
unshakable
firm-set 45adj.
certain 473adj.
credal 485adj.
resolute 599adj.
retentive 778adj.
unfearing 855adj.
unshapely
amorphous 244adj.
unsightly 842adj.
unshapen
amorphous 244adj.
unshared
possessed 773adj.
unsharpened
unsharpened 257adj.
unshaven
hairy 259adj.
unsheathe
uncover 229vb.
manifest 522vb.
unshielded
vulnerable 661adj.
unshifting
unceasing 146adj.
unship
displace 188vb.
void 300vb.
unshocked
impassive 820adj.
unshod
uncovered 229adj.
unshorn
intact 52adj.
hairy 259adj.
unshrinking
resolute 599adj.
courageous 855adj.
unshriven
impenitent 940adj.
unshroud
disclose 526vb.
unsightly
unsightly 842adj.
unsigned
uncertified 474adj.
anonymous 562adj.
unsinkable
light 323adj.
unskillful
unhabituated 611adj.
unskillful 695adj.
unsleeping
persevering 600adj.
industrious 678adj.
unsmart
ill-bred 847adj.
unsmiling
serious 834adj.
ungracious 885adj.
sullen 893adj.
unsociable
unconformable 84adj.
alone 88adj.
independent 744adj.
unsociable 883adj.
discourteous 885adj.
sullen 893adj.
unsociality
misanthropy 902n.
unsold
possessed 773adj.
retained 778adj.
unsolvable
impracticable 470adj.
puzzling 517adj.
unsophisticated
genuine 494adj.
artless 699adj.
ill-bred 847adj.
unsorted
mixed 43adj.
disorderly 61adj.
indiscriminate 464adj.
unsought
voluntary 597adj.
avoidable 620adj.
unsound
illogical 477adj.
erroneous 495adj.
bad 645adj.
imperfect 647adj.
unhealthy 651adj.
insalubrious 653adj.
unskilled 695adj.
unsounded
deep 211adj.
silent 399adj.
unsound mind
insanity 503n.
unsoundness
vulnerability 661n.
non-retention 779n.
unsown
unproductive 172adj.
unsparing
plenteous 635adj.
oppressive 735adj.
severe 735adj.
liberal 813adj.
disinterested 931adj.
intemperate 943adj.
unspeakable
unspeakable 32adj.
inexpressible 517adj.
wonderful 864adj.
unspecified
general 79adj.
unspent
remaining 41adj.
unused 674adj.
unspiced
tasteless 387adj.
unspirited
feeble 572adj.
apathetic 820adj.
inexcitable 823adj.
unspiritual
material 319adj.
sensual 944adj.
irreligious 974adj.
unspoiled
not bad 644adj.
undamaged 646adj.
unspoken
silent 399adj.
unknown 491adj.
tacit 523adj.
unsportsmanlike
unjust 914adj.
unspotted
perfect 646adj.
innocent 935adj.
unsprung
tough 329adj.
unstable
unstable 152adj.
weak 163adj.

irresolute 601adj.
capricious 604adj.
unsafe 661adj.
excitable 822adj.
unstable personality
madman 504n.
unstaffed
empty 190adj.
unstaid
changeful 152adj.
excitable 822adj.
unstained
perfect 646adj.
honorable 929adj.
unstatutory
illegal 945adj.
unsteadiness
weakness 163n.
agitation 318n.
unreliability 474n.
unsteady
fitful 142adj.
unstable 152adj.
unsafe 661adj.
unsterilized
infectious 653adj.
unstick
unstick 49vb.
unstinting
liberal 813adj.
unstitch
disjoin 46vb.
unstop
open 263vb.
liberate 746vb.
unstrained
friendly 880adj.
unstressed
muted 401adj.
unstretchable
unyielding 162adj.
unstrict
lax 734adj.
unstring
disjoin 46vb.
disable 161vb.
soften 327vb.
discord 411vb.
unstudied
neglected 458adj.
unprepared 670adj.
unsubdued
resisting 715adj.
unbeaten 727adj.
unsubstantiated
erroneous 495adj.
unsuccessful
profitless 641adj.
unskillful 695adj.
unsuccessful 728adj.
unprosperous 731adj.
unsuccessive
discontinuous 72adj.
unsuitability
inutility 641n.
inexpedience 643n.
wrong 914n.
unsuitable
unapt 25adj.
unsullied
clean 648adj.
honorable 929adj.
unsung
tacit 523adj.
inglorious 867adj.
unsure
uncertain 474adj.
unsafe 661adj.
unsurpassed
supreme 34adj.
perfect 646adj.
unsusceptible
impassive 820adj.
unsuspected
latent 523adj.
unsuspecting
believing 485adj.
credulous 487adj.
inexpectant 508adj.
unsuspicious
artless 699adj.
honorable 929adj.
unswerving
straight 249adj.
directed 281adj.
undeviating 625adj.
indifferent 860adj.
just 913adj.
orthodox 976adj.
unsympathetic
opposing 704adj.
disliking 861adj.
disliked 861adj.
inimical 881adj.
unkind 898adj.
pitiless 906adj.
selfish 932adj.
unsystematic
non-uniform 17adj.
orderless 61adj.
fitful 142adj.
untalented
unintelligent 499adj.
unskillful 695adj.
untamable
cruel 898adj.
untamed
unhabituated 611adj.
avoiding 620adj.
warlike 718adj.
disobedient 738adj.
cruel 898adj.
untangle
unravel 62vb.
untaught
uninstructed 491adj.
spontaneous 609adj.
unprepared 670adj.
unskilled 695adj.
untaxed
uncharged 812adj.
unteach
educate 534vb.
misteach 534vb.
unteachable
unwise 499adj.
obstinate 602adj.
untearable
tough 329adj.
untempered
weak 163adj.
untempted
indifferent 860adj.
untenable
defenseless 161adj.
illogical 477adj.
unbelieved 486adj.
untenanted
empty 190adj.
unpossessed 774adj.
untended
neglected 458adj.
untender
unkind 898adj.
untested
new 126adj.
uncertified 474adj.
unknown 491adj.
unthanked
unthanked 908adj.
unthankfulness
ingratitude 908n.
unthawed
indissoluble 324adj.
cold 380adj.
unthinkability
impossibility 470n.
unthinking
unthinking 450adj.
incurious 454adj.
inattentive 456adj.
unwise 499adj.
involuntary 596adj.
unthorough
incomplete 55adj.
inattentive 456adj.
negligent 458adj.
uncompleted 726adj.
unthought
unthought 450adj.
unthreatening
safe 660adj.
unthrifty
unprepared 670adj.
prodigal 815adj.
unthrone
unthrone 734vb.
deprive 786vb.
disentitle 916vb.

(*see* depose)
untidy
non-uniform 17adj.
orderless 61adj.
jumble 63vb.
agitate 318vb.
negligent 458adj.
dirty 649adj.
make unclean 649vb.
untie
disjoin 46vb.
doff 229vb.
deliver 668vb.
disencumber 701vb.
not retain 779vb.
until
while 108adv.
untilled
unproductive 172adj.
unprepared 670adj.
until now
until now 121adv.
untimeliness
anachronism 118n.
(*see* untimely)
untimely
irrelative 10adj.
unapt 25adj.
ill-timed 138adj.
inexpedient 643adj.
untinged
unmixed 44adj.
untiring
persevering 600adj.
untitled
plebeian 896adj.
untold
many 104adj.
infinite 107adj.
tacit 523adj.
untouchable
prohibited 757adj.
derelict 779n.
(*see* outcaste)
untouched
intact 52adj.
clean 648adj.
unused 674adj.
apathetic 820adj.
non-liable 919adj.
pure 950adj.
untoward
contrary 14adj.
inopportune 138adj.
ill-timed 138adj.
inexpedient 643adj.
adverse 731adj.
annoying 827adj.
untraceable
lost 772adj.
untraditional
modern 126adj.
unwonted 611adj.
untrained
uninstructed 491adj.
unhabituated 611adj.
imperfect 647adj.
unprepared 670adj.
immature 670adj.
unskilled 695adj.
untrammeled
facilitated 701adj.
unconfined 744adj.
untranslatable
inexpressible 517adj.
untraveled
quiescent 266adj.
untried
new 126adj.
moot 459adj.
uncertified 474adj.
unknown 491adj.
unused 674adj.
untrodden
new 126adj.
closed 264adj.
unused 674adj.
untroubled
moderate 177adj.
content 828adj.
untrue
erroneous 495adj.
false 541adj.
deceiving 542adj.
untrue 543adj.
wrong 914adj.
perfidious 930adj.
untrustworthy
unreliable 474adj.
unsafe 661adj.
dishonest 930adj.
untruth
falsehood 541n.
untruth 543n.
untruthfulness
error 495n.
falsehood 541n.
improbity 930n.
untune
discord 411adj.
untuneful
discordant 411adj.
untutored
uninstructed 491adj.
unprepared 670adj.
artless 699adj.
untypical
dissimilar 19adj.
abnormal 84adj.
unused
unwonted 611adj.
unused 674adj.
clumsy 695adj.
unusual
unusual 84adj.
infrequent 140adj.
ridiculous 849adj.
wonderful 864adj.
unutilized
unused 674adj.
unutterable
unspeakable 32adj.
inexpressible 517adj.
wonderful 864adj.
unvalued
unwanted 860adj.
hated 888adj.
unvaried
unceasing 146adj.
(*see* uniform)
unvarnished
genuine 494adj.
veracious 540adj.
plain 573adj.
artless 699adj.
unveil
uncover 229vb.
be plain 522vb.
disclose 526vb.
unveiling
debut 68n.
unventilated
sealed off 264adj.
fetid 397adj.
insalubrious 653adj.
unverified
uncertified 474adj.
suppositional 512adj.
unversed
ignorant 491adj.
unskilled 695adj.
unversified
prosaic 593adj.
unviable
impracticable 470adj.
unvirtuous
wicked 934adj.
unchaste 951adj.
unvisited
secluded 883adj.
unvocal
voiceless 578adj.
unvoiced
tacit 523adj.
voiceless 578adj.
unwanted
rejected 607adj.
superfluous 637adj.
useless 641adj.
unused 674adj.
unpossessed 774adj.
cheap 812adj.
unwanted 860adj.
disliked 861adj.
unwarlike
peaceful 717adj.
inexcitable 823adj.
cowardly 856adj.

unwarrantable
illegal 954adj.
unwarranted
uncertified 474adj.
illogical 477adj.
wrong 914adj.
unwarranted 916adj.
unwary
negligent 458adj.
rash 857adj.
unwashed
opaque 423adj.
dirty 649adj.
unwavering
unchangeable 153adj.
persevering 600adj.
unwearied
persevering 600adj.
industrious 678adj.
unweave
unravel 62vb.
unwedded
independent 744adj.
unwedded 895adj.
unwelcome
unpleasant 827adj.
unwanted 860adj.
hateful 888adj.
unwelcoming
unsociable 883adj.
unwell
sick 651adj.
unwept
hated 888adj.
unwholesome
harmful 645adj.
insalubrious 653adj.
unwieldy
unequal 29adj.
unwieldy 195adj.
weighty 322adj.
clumsy 695adj.
difficult 700adj.
graceless 842adj.
unwilled
involuntary 596adj.
unwilling
dissenting 489n.
involuntary 596adj.
unwilling 598adj.
avoiding 620adj.
refusing 760adj.
unwind
evolve 316vb.
unwinking
still 266adj.
unwisdom
folly 499n.
unwise
unwise 499adj.
inexpedient 643adj.
rash 857adj.
unwish
abrogate 752vb.
regret 830vb.
unwished
unwanted 860adj.
disliked 861adj.
unwitnessed
uncertified 474adj.
unwitting
ignorant 491adj.
involuntary 596adj.
unwomanly
manly 162adj.
male 372adj.
unwonted
unusual 84adj.
unwonted 611adj.
unwooed
unwedded 895adj.
unworkable
powerless 161adj.
impracticable 470adj.
useless 641adj.
unworldly
honorable 929adj.
innocent 935adj.
pious 979adj.
unworn
unyielding 162adj.
unworried
tranquil 266adj.
inexcitable 823adj.
content 828adj.
unworthy
inferior 35adj.
bad 645adj.
discreditable 867adj.
unentitled 916adj.
dishonest 930adj.
vicious 934adj.
unwrap
uncover 229vb.
extract 304vb.
unwrinkled
young 130adj.
flat 216adj.
smooth 258adj.
unwritten
tacit 523adj.
obliterated 550adj.
unwrought
immature 670adj.
unyielding
unyielding 162adj.
rigid 326adj.
tough 329adj.
resolute 599adj.
obstinate 602adj.
difficult 700adj.
resisting 715adj.
restraining 747adj.
unyoke
liberate 746vb.
up
aloft 209adv.
vertically 215adv.
up 308adv.
bubbly 355adj.
acquiring 771adj.
up against it
in difficulties 700adj.
unprosperous 731adj.
up-and-coming
active 678adj.
prosperous 730adj.
up and doing
operative 173adj.
doing 676adj.
up and down
by turns 141adv.
to and fro 317adv.
up-and-down
undulatory 251adj.
up and up
crescendo 36adv.
up and up, on the
well 615adv.
successful 727adj.
prosperous 730adj.
Upanishad
non-Biblical scripture 975n.
upbraid
exprobate 927vb.
upbringing
teaching 534n.
up-country
regional 184adj.
interior 224adj.
updraught
ascent 308n.
up-end
make vertical 215vb.
upgrade
make better 654vb.
dignify 866vb.
upgrowth
expansion 197n.
ascent 308n.
upheaval
disorder 61n.
revolution 149n.
havoc 165n.
elevation 310n.
uphill
sloping 220adj.
ascending 308adj.
laborious 682adj.
difficult 700adj.
uphold
sustain 146vb.
support 218vb.
corroborate 466vb.
upholder
assenter 488n.
upholstered
rich 800adj.

upholstery
lining 227n.
equipment 630n.
up in
expert 694adj.
up in arms
active 678adj.
quarreling 709adj.
attacking 712adj.
warring 718adj.
riotous 738adj.
upkeep
support 218n.
preservation 666n.
subvention 703n.
upland
space 183n.
high land 209n.
plain 348n.
uplift
displace 188vb.
support 218n.
move 265n.
elevation 310n.
improvement 654n.
delight 826vb.
make pious 979vb.
uplifted
high 209adj.
up one's street
fit 24adj.
up on, to be
predominate 34vb.
upper
superior 34adj.
upper case
print-type 587n.
upper class
upper class 868n.
upper crust
beau monde 848n.
upper class 868n.
uppercut
knock 279n.
upper hand
vantage 34n.
victory 727n.
Upper House
parliament 692n.
upper limit
finite quantity 26n.
limit 236n.
uppermost
supreme 34adj.
topmost 213adj.
topical 452adj.
important 638adj.
upper ten
elite 644n.
beau monde 848n.
upper class 868n.
uppish
ill-bred 847adj.
prideful 871adj.
upraise, uprear
elevate 310vb.
upright
vertical 215adj.
just 913adj.
honorable 929adj.
virtuous 933adj.
uprightness
equilibrium 28n.
(*see* upright)
uprise
ascent 308n.
uprising
elevation 310n.
revolt 738n.
uproar
turmoil 61n.
violence 176n.
loudness 400n.
fight 716n.
uproarious
violent 176adj.
loud 400adj.
excitable 822adj.
gay 833adj.
uproot
revolutionize 149vb.
destroy 165vb.
displace 188vb.
eject 300vb.
extract 304vb.
uprush
increase 36n.
spurt 277n.
ascent 308n.
redundance 637n.
ups and downs
fluctuation 317n.
upset
derange 63vb.
revolution 149n.
demolish 165vb.
overturning 221n.
depression 311n.
distract 456vb.
hinder 702vb.
revolt 738vb.
impress 821vb.
incommode 827vb.
cause discontent 829vb.
cause dislike 861vb.
enrage 891vb.
upshot
eventuality 154n.
effect 157n.
judgment 480n.
completion 725n.
upside down
contrarily 14adv.
orderless 61adj.
inverted 221adj.
upstage
stage set 594n.
prideful 871adj.
insolent 878adj.
upstairs
aloft 209adv.
up 308adv.
upstanding
vertical 215adj.
elevated 310adj.
upstart
intruder 59n.
upstart 126n.
progression 285n.
made man 730n.
commoner 869n.
insolent person 878n.
up sticks
decamp 296vb.
upstream
toward 281adv.
upsurge
increase 36n.
ascent 308n.
redundance 637n.
upswing
elevation 310n.
improvement 654n.
up to
while 108adv.
powerful 160adj.
up-to-date
present 121adj.
modern 126adj.
progressive 285adj.
up to every trick, be
be expert 694vb.
up to the ears
completely 54adv.
up to the hilt
completely 54adv.
up to the mark
sufficient 635adj.
not bad 644adj.
up-to-the-minute
(*see* up-to-date)
uptown
afar 199adv.
uptrend
elevation 310n.
improvement 654n.
upturn
invert 221vb.
upwards
aloft 209adv.
upwards of
beyond 34adv.
plural 101adj.
upwind
directed 281adj.
uraeus
regalia 743n.
uranium

materials 631n.
uranometry
uranometry 321n.
Uranus
planet 321n.
classical gods 967n.
urban
regional 184adj.
urban 192adj.
urbane
well-bred 848adj.
sociable 882adj.
courteous 884adj.
urbanity
(*see* urbane)
urbanize
urbanize 192vb.
urchin
youngster 132n.
dwarf 196n.
elf 970n.
urge
influence 176vb.
accelerate 277vb.
impel 279vb.
propound 512vb.
affirm 532vb.
be resolute 599vb.
incite 612vb.
hasten 680vb.
advise 691vb.
compel 740vb.
request 761vb.
animate 821vb.
urgency
inducement 612n.
needfulness 627n.
importance 638n.
haste 680n.
request 761n.
urgent
strong 162adj.
resolute 599adj.
demanding 627adj.
important 638adj.
hasty 680adj.
compelling 740adj.
requesting 761adj.
urgent, be
emphasize 532vb.
urinal
latrine 649n.
urination
excretion 302n.
urine
excrement 302n.
urn
vessel 194n.
interment 364n.
pottery 381n.
ursine
animal 365adj.
urticaria
formication 378n.
skin disease 651n.
urticate
itch 378vb.
urtication
formication 378n.
antidote 658n.
usable
useful 640adj.
used 673adj.
usage
connotation 514n.
habit 610n.
use 673n.
use
operate 173vb.
habit 610n.
instrumentality 628n.
importance 638n.
utility 640n.
use 673n., vb.
action 676n.
possess 773vb.
used to
habituated 610adj.
used up
impotent 161adj.
disused 674adj.
use force
force 176vb.
use for, have no
not use 674vb.
not respect 921vb.
despise 922vb.
useful
operative 173adj.
instrumental 628adj.
useful 640adj.
expedient 642adj.
beneficial 644adj.
used 673adj.
aiding 703adj.
useless
absurd 497adj.
superfluous 637adj.
trivial 639adj.
useless 641adj.
inexpedient 643adj.
bad 645adj.
unused 674adj.
uselessness
ineffectuality 161n.
unimportance 639n.
(*see* useless)
user
habit 610n.
(*see* operator)
use up
disable 161vb.
waste 634vb.
dispose of 673vb.
expend 806vb.
usher
accompany 89vb.
teacher 537n.
stage-hand 594n.
greet 884vb.
bridesman 894n.
usherette
stage-hand 594n.
usher in
come before 64vb.
initiate 68vb.
precede 283vb.
admit 299vb.
predict 511vb.
usual
general 79adj.
regular 81adj.
usual 610adj.
trivial 639adj.
dull 840adj.
fashionable 848adj.
unastonishing 865adj.
usufruct
use 673n.
enjoyment 824n.
usurer
lender 784n.
niggard 816n.
usurious
lending 784adj.
avaricious 816adj.
usurp
encroach 306vb.
take authority 733vb.
unthrone 734vb.
appropriate 786vb.
(*see* usurpation)
usurpation
arrogation 918n.
lawlessness 954n.
usurper
imposter 545n.
taker 786n.
usurper 916n.
usury
lending 784n.
interest 803n.
utensil
tool 630n.
uterine
akin 11adj.
uterus
genitalia 164n.
insides 224n.
utilitarian
useful 640adj.
philanthropist 901n.
utilitarianism
philosophy 449n.
good 615n.
utility 640n.
expedience 642n.
benevolence 897n.
philanthropy 901n.
morals 917n.

utility
benefit 615n.
instrumentality 629n.
utility 640n.
use 673n.
utilization
utility 640n.
use 673n.
uti possedetis
as before 144adv.
possession 773n.
utmost
limit 236n.
utopia
fantasy 513n.
aspiration 852n.
utopian
visionary 513n.
reformer 654n.
philanthropist 901n.
utricle
bladder 194n.
utter
consummate 32adj.
complete 54adj.
disperse 75vb.
divulge 526vb.
publish 528vb.
voice 577vb.
speak 579vb.
mint 797vb.
utterance
cry 408n.
voice 577n.
speech 579n.
uttermost
limit 236n.
U-turn
reversion 148n.
curve 248n.
return 286n.
circuition 314n.
U-valley
valley 255n.
uxoriousness
love 887n.

V

V1, V2
weapon 723n.
bomb 723n.
vacancy
insubstantiality 4n.
emptiness 190n.
job 622n.
unimportance 639n.
(*see* vacant)
vacant
unthinking 450adj.
unintelligent 499adj.
unprovided 636adj.
unpossessed 774adj.
secluded 883adj.
(*see* vacancy)
vacate
displace 188vb.
be absent 190vb.
go away 190vb.
relinquish 621vb.
abrogate 752vb.
resign 753vb.
vacation
leisure 681n.
repose 683n.
vaccinate
doctor 658vb.
safeguard 660vb.
vaccination
hygiene 652n.
prophylactic 658n.
vaccinia
skin disease 651n.
vacillate
be capricious 604vb.
(*see* vacillation)
vacillating
tergiversating 603adj.
vacillation
changeableness 152n.
fluctuation 317n.
dubiety 474n.
irresolution 601n.
vacuity, vacuous
(*see* vacancy, vacant)
vacuum
non-existence 2n.
emptiness 190n.
rarity 325n.
vacuum cleaner
cleaning utensil 648n.
vade mecum
guide-book 524n.
vagabond
traveling 267adj.
wanderer 268n.
low fellow 869n.
outcaste 883n.
knave 938n.
vagabondage
wandering 267n.
vagary
foolery 497n.
ideality 513n.
whim 604n.
vagina
genitalia 164n.
vaginal
productive 164adj.
vagrancy
wandering 267n.
deviation 282n.
vagrant
unstable 152adj.
wanderer 268n.
deviating 282adj.
vague
insubstantial 4adj.
general 79adj.
amorphous 244adj.
shadowy 419adj.
ill-seen 444adj.
uncertain 474adj.
uninstructed 491adj.
equivocal 518adj.
imperspicuous 568adj.
vagueness
indiscrimination 464n.
concealment 525n.
(*see* vague)
vain
insubstantial 4adj.
useless 641adj.
unsuccessful 728adj.
prideful 871adj.
vain 873adj.
vainglorious
(*see* vainglory)
vainglory
pride 871n.
vanity 873n.
boasting 877n.
vain, in
wasted 634adj.
profitless 641adj.
unsuccessfully 728vb.
vair
skin 226n.
heraldry 547n.
Vaishnavism
religious faith 973n.
valance
edging 234n.
trimming 844n.
vale
valley 255n.
valediction
valediction 296n.
valedictory
valediction 296n.
departing 296adj.
oration 579n.
valentine
correspondence 588n.
love-token 889n.
valet
clothier 228n.
clean 648vb.
revive 656vb.
preserve 666vb.
minister to 703vb.
domestic 742n.
serve 742vb.
valetudinarian
sick person 651n.
unhealthy 651adj.
valgus
deformity 246n.
Valhalla

mythic heaven 971n.
valiant
courageous 855adj.
valid
strong 162adj.
genuine 494adj.
affirmative 532adj.
useful 640adj.
validate
stabilize 153vb.
corroborate 466vb.
grant claims 915vb.
make legal 953vb.
validation
certainty 473n.
assent 488n.
validity
authenticity 494n.
legality 953n.
valise
box 194n.
Valkyrie
soldier 722n.
mythical being 970n.
valley
lowness 210n.
depth 211n.
valley 255n.
plain 348n.
conduit 351n.
vallum
fence 235n.
fortification 713n.
valor
courage 855n.
valorize
tax 809vb.
valuable
great 32adj.
good 615adj.
important 638adj.
profitable 640adj.
valuable 644adj.
of price 811adj.
valuables
estate 777n.
valuation
degree 27n.
measurement 465n.
estimate 480n.
value
equivalence 28n.
quid pro quo 150n.
appraise 465vb.
estimate 480vb.
importance 638n.
utility 640n.
goodness 644n.
account 808vb.
price, tax 809vb.
have taste 846vb.
honor 866vb.
love 887vb.
respect 920vb.
approve 923vb.
valueless
trivial 639adj.
profitless 641adj.
cheap 812adj.
valuer
appraiser 465n.
estimator 480n.
valuta
finance 797n.
valve
stopper 264n.
conduit 351n.
vambrace
armor 713n.
vamoose
decamp 296vb.
vamp
modify 143vb.
play music 413vb.
improvise 609vb.
repair 656vb.
lover 887n.
excite love 887vb.
vampire
taker 786n.
lover 887n.
offender 904n.
noxious animal 904n.
glutton 947n.
demon 970n.
sorceress 983n.
vampirish
fairylike 970adj.
vampirism
rapacity 786n.
van
beginning 68n.
front 237n.
cart 274n.
precession 283n.
purify 648vb.
armed force 722n.
Vandal
destroyer 168n.
vulgarian 847n.
low fellow 869n.
evildoer 904n.
vandalism
destruction 165n.
violence 176n.
bad taste 847n.
inhumanity 898n.
vane
changeable thing 152n.
weather 340n.
vanguard
precursor 66n.
front 237n.
armed force 722n.
vanilla
scent 396n.
vanish
not be 2vb.
be transient 114vb.
go away 190vb.
disappear 446vb.
be stealthy 525vb.
vanishing cream
cosmetic 843n.
vanishing point
smallness 33n.
minuteness 196n.
disappearance 446n.
vanishment
invisibility 444n.
disappearance 446n.
vanity
insubstantiality 4n.
ineffectuality 161n.
folly 499n.
unimportance 639n.
inutility 641n.
affectation 850n.
pride 871n.
vanity 873n.
boasting 877n.
vanity bag
bag 194n.
vanity fair
fashion 848n.
vanity 873n.
vanquish
overmaster 727vb.
vantage
vantage 34n.
power 160n.
tactics 688n.
success 727n.
vantage ground
influence 178n.
vanward
in front 237adv.
vapid
tasteless 387adj.
feeble 572adj.
vapor
insubstantial thing 4n.
emit 300vb.
gas 336n.
cloud 355n.
fantasy 513n.
mean nothing 515vb.
boast 877vb.
vaporific
gaseous 336adj.
vaporific 338adj.
vaporimeter
vaporizer 338n.
vaporing
foolish 499adj.
diffuseness 570n.
vaporish
melancholic 834adj.
vaporization

vaporization 338n.
dryness 342n.
disappearance 446n.
vaporize
lighten 323vb.
gasify 336vb.
vaporize 338vb.
dry 342vb.
vaporizer
vaporizer 338n.
vaporous
insubstantial 4adj.
gaseous 336adj.
vaporific 338adj.
cloudy 355adj.
opaque 423adj.
imaginary 513adj.
vapors
melancholy 834n.
variability
non-uniformity 17n.
inequality 29n.
multiformity 82n.
fitfulness 142n.
change 143n.
changeableness 152n.
unreliability 474n.
caprice 604n.
variable
number 85n.
star 321n.
irresolute 601adj.
excitable 822adj.
(*see* variability)
variance
disagreement 25n.
dissension 709n.
variance, at
opposing 704adj.
inimical 881adj.
variant
variant 15n.
variation
contrariety 14n.
difference 15n.
dissimilarity 19n.
numerical operation 86n.
change 143n.
musical piece 412n.
varicella
infection 651n.
varicose
expanded 197adj.
variegation
disagreement 25n.
inequality 29n.
mixture 43n.
discontinuity 72n.
changeableness 152n.
variegation 437n.
ornamental art 844n.
variety
difference 15n.
non-uniformity 17n.
dissimilarity 19n.
mixture 43n.
sort 77n.
multiformity 82n.
nonconformist 84n.
stage show 594n.
variola
infection 651n.
various
(*see* variety)
varlet
low fellow 869n.
knave 938n.
varletry
rabble 869n.
varnish
facing 226n.
smooth 258vb.
resin 357n.
color 425vb.
sophisticate 477vb.
conceal 525vb.
cant 541vb.
sham 542n.
art equipment 553n.
cleanser 648n.
decorate 844vb.
ostentation 875n.
extenuate 927vb.
Varuna
sea god 343n.
mythic god 966n.
Hindu god 967n.
vary
differ 15vb.
change 143vb.
vary 152vb.
be capricious 604vb.
vary as
be related 9vb.
correlate 12vb.
vascular
capsular 194adj.
tubular 263adj.
vasculum
case 194n.
vase
vessel 194n.
vaseline
unguent 357n.
balm 658n.
hairwash 843n.
vassal
subject 742n.
subject 745adj.
vassalage
subjection 745n.
service 745n.
vassalize
subjugate 745vb.
vast
enormous 32adj.
spacious 183adj.
huge 195adj.
vastness
greatness 32n.
hugeness 195n.
vat
vat 194n.
Vatican
church office 985n.
parsonage 986n.
vaticination
divination 511n.
vaudeville
stage show 594n.
place of amusement 837n.
vault
cellar 194n.
curve 248n.
dome 253n.
leap 312n., vb.
tomb 364n.
hiding place 527n.
storage 632n.
church interior 990n.
vaulted
curved 248adj.
concave 255adj.
vaunt
boast 877n., vb.
Vauxhall
pleasure-ground 837n.
V.C.
courage 855n.
brave person 855n.
vection
transport 272n.
vector
quantity 26n.
carrier 273n.
infection 651n.
Veda
non-Biblical scripture 975n.
Vedanta
philosophy 449n.
Vedantism
religious faith 973n.
vedette
armed force 722n.
Vedic
olden 127adj.
religious 973adj.
scriptural 975adj.
veer
change 143vb.
vary 152vb.
navigate 269vb.
deviate 282vb.
veer away
recede 290vb.
veer round
turn back 286vb.
vegetability
vegetability 366n.

non-intellect 448n.
vegetable
vegetable 301n.
vegetal 366adj.
mindless 448adj.
unthinking 450adj.
vegetable physiology
botany 368n.
vegetal
vegetal 366adj.
vegetarian
eater 301n.
feeding 301adj.
abstainer 942n.
ascetic 945n.
vegetarianism
temperance 942n.
vegetate
be 1vb.
pass time 108vb.
be inert 175vb.
be quiescent 266vb.
vegetate 366vb.
be inactive 679vb.
be insensitive 820vb.
vegetation
vegetability 366n.
(*see* vegetate)
vegetative
vegetal 366adj.
apathetic 820adj.
vehemence
vigorousness 174n.
violence 176n.
affirmation 532n.
vigor 571n.
restlessness 678n.
warm feeling 818n.
excitability 822n.
vehement
(*see* vehemence)
vehicle
conveyance 267n.
transport 272n.
vehicle 274n.
vehicular
vehicular 274adj.
veil
shade 226n.
cloak 228n.
darken 418vb.
screen 421n., vb.
invisibility 444n.
conceal 525vb.
disguise 527n.
vocation 622n.
veil, take the
be unsocial 883vb.
live single 895vb.
take orders 986vb.
vein
temperament 5n.
tendency 179n.
filament 208n.
tube 263n.
conduit 351n.
variegate 437n.
style 566n.
diffuseness 570n.
store 632n.
affections 817n.
veld
space 183n.
plain 348n.
velleity
will 595n.
vellicate
agitate 318vb.
touch 378vb.
vellum
stationery 586n.
bookbinding 589n.
velocimeter
velocity 277n.
velocipede
bicycle 274n.
velocity
motion 265n.
velocity 277n.
velour
textile 222n.
hair 259n.
velum
taste 386n.
velure
smoothness 258n.
velvet
textile 222n.
smoothness 258n.
hair 259n.
softness 327n.
euphoria 376n.
palmy days 730n.
velvet glove
lenity 736n.
velvety
smooth 258adj.
downy 259adj.
soft 327adj.
venal
avaricious 816adj.
venal 930adj.
selfish 932adj.
vend
sell 793vb.
vendee
owner 776n.
recipient 782n.
purchaser 792n.
vendetta
quarrel 709n.
enmity 881n.
revenge 910n.
vendible
salable 793adj.
merchandise 795n.
Vendidad
non-Biblical scripture 975n.
vendor
seller 793n.
veneer
laminate 207vb.
shallowness 212n.
facing 226n.
coat 226vb.
disguise 527n.
ostentation 875n.
veneering
ornamental art 844n.
venenation
impairment 655n.
poisoning 659n.
venerable
great 32adj.
immemorial 127adj.
aged 131adj.
respected 920adj.
veneration
respect 920n.
piety 979n.
worship 981n.
venereal
diseased 651adj.
Venerean
planetary 321adj.
venereal ulcer
venereal disease 651n.
venery
unchastity 951n.
venesection
voidance 300n.
surgery 658n.
vengeance
revenge 910n.
vengeance, with a
completely 54adv.
violently 176adv.
venial
trivial 639adj.
forgiven 909adj.
vindicable 927adj.
guiltless 935adj.
venison
meat 301n.
savoriness 390n.
venom
poison 659n.
malevolence 898n.
venomous
harmful 645adj.
toxic 653adj.
baneful 659adj.
inimical 881adj.
malevolent 898adj.
vent
orifice 263n.
outlet 298n.
void 300vb.
air-pipe 353n.
divulge 526vb.
means of escape

667n.
sale 792n.
venter
maw 194n.
ventiduct
ventilation 352n.
air-pipe 353n.
ventilate
aerify 340vb.
divulge 526vb.
publish 528vb.
dissert 591vb.
purify 648vb.
refresh 685vb.
sanitate 852vb.
(*see* ventilation)
ventilation
ventilation 352n.
refrigeration 382n.
(*see* ventilate)
ventilator
air 340n.
ventilation 352n.
air-pipe 353n.
refrigerator 384n.
ventosity
respiration 352n.
wind 352n.
ventral
cellular 194adj.
ventricle
compartment 194n.
ventricular
cellular 194adj.
ventriloquism
mimicry 20n.
deception 542n.
sleight 542n.
voice 577n.
ventriloquist
imitator 20n.
conjuror 545n.
entertainer 594n.
venture
be tentative 461vb.
gambling 618n.
danger 661n.
essay 671n., vb.
undertaking 672n.
property 777n.
trade 791n.
speculate 791vb.
be courageous 855vb.
venture, at a
at random 618adj.
venturesome
experimental 461adj.
speculative 618adj.
dangerous 661adj.
enterprising 672adj.
courageous 855adj.
rash 857adj.
venue
focus 76n.
locality 187n.
venule
filament 208n.
Venus
planet 321n.
woman 373n.
luminary 420n.
a beauty 841n.
love god 887n.
mythic god 966n.
Olympian god 967n.
veracious
(*see* veracity)
veracity
veracity 540n.
artlessness 699n.
probity 929n.
veranda
lobby 194n.
verb
part of speech 564n.
verbal
semantic 514adj.
informative 524adj.
verbal 559adj.
grammatical 564adj.
speaking 579adj.
verbatim
imitatively 20adv.
verbally 559adv.
verbiage
empty talk 515n.
word 559n.
imperspicuity 568n.
diffuseness 570n.
verbosity
word 559n.
diffuseness 570n.
loquacity 581n.
verdant
vegetal 366adj.
green 432adj.
verderer
forestry 366n.
judge 957n.
verdict
judgment 480n.
legal trial 959n.
verdigris
greenness 432n.
poison 659n.
verdure
grass 366n.
greenness 432n.
verecundity
modesty 874n.
verge
extremity 69n.
tend 179vb.
nearness 200n.
edge 234n.
limit 236n.
point to 281vb.
verge on
approach 289vb.
verger
church officer 986n.
veridical
veracious 540adj.
verifiable
experimental 461adj.
evidential 466adj.
certain 473adj.
verification
experiment 461n.
demonstration 478n.
assent 488n.
verified
known 490adj.
veracious 540adj.
verify
corroborate 466vb.
make certain 473vb.
discover 484vb.
give security 767vb.
(*see* verification)
verisimilitude
probability 471n.
truth 494n.
accuracy 494n.
veracity 540n.
veritable
true 494adj.
verity
truth 494n.
verjuice
sourness 393n.
vermicular
labyrinthine 251adj.
animal 365adj.
vermifuge
antidote 658n.
vermilion
red pigment 431n.
vermin
vermin 365n.
dirt 649n.
rabble 869n.
knave, cad 938n.
verminous
insalubrious 653adj.
vernacular
native 191adj.
language 557n.
dialect 560n.
plainness 573n.
vernal
new 126adj.
vernal 128adj.
young 130adj.
vernier
gauge 465n.
vernier scale
micrology 196n.
verruca
skin disease 651n.
verrucose

convex 253adj.
versatile
multiform 82adj.
changeful 152adj.
tergiversating 603adj.
useful 640adj.
skillful 694adj.
verse
subdivision 53n.
vocal music 412n.
poetry 593n.
versed in
knowing 490adj.
expert 694adj.
verse-filler
pleonasm 570n.
versicle
verse form 593n.
versicolor
iridescent 437adj.
versification
poetry 593n.
versify
poetize 593vb.
version
specialty 80n.
transformation 143n.
translation 528n.
vers libre
verse form 593n.
verso
rear 238n.
edition 589n.
verst
long measure 203n.
versus
toward 281adv.
in opposition 704adj.
vert
green color 432n.
heraldry 547n.
vertebrae
pillar 218n.
vertebral
central 225adj.
back 238adj.
vertebrate
animal 365n.
vertex
extremity 69n.
vertex 213n.
vertical
vertical 215adj.
verticil
coil 251n.
verticity
rotation 315n.
vertiginous
high 209adj.
rotary 315adj.
crazed 503adj.
vertigo
rotation 315n.
frenzy 503n.
indigestion 651n.
verve
vigorousness 174n.
vigor 571n.
moral sensibility 819n.
vervel
fastening 47n.
circle 250n.
very
greatly 32adv.
Very light
signal light 420n.
very one, the
identity 13n.
very same, the
identity 13n.
very thing, the
no imitation 21n.
fitness 24n.
authenticity 494n.
vesicant
surgical dressing 658n.
vesicle
bladder 194n.
skin 226n.
sphere 252n.
swelling 253n.
skin disease 651n.
vesicular
capsular 194adj.
convex 253adj.
vesper
luminary 420n.
vespers
evening 129n.
church service 988n.
vespiary
crowd 74n.
vessel
vessel 194n.
ship 275n.
pottery 381n.
vest
bodywear 228n.
vest 228n.
belong 773vb.
give 781vb.
make legal 953vb.
vestal
spinster 895n.
virgin 950n.
pure 950adj.
priest 986n.
vested
vested 153adj.
located 187adj.
due 915adj.
vested interest
estate 777n.
right 913n.
dueness 915n.
vestiary
vestimental 989adj.
vestibule
entrance 68n.
lobby 194n.
theater 594n.
access 624n.
vestige
remainder 41n.
trace 548n.
vestigial
remaining 41adj.
recorded 548adj.
vestmentary
vestmental 989adj.
vestments
clothing 228n.
uniform 228n.
vestments 989n.
vestry
council 692n.
synod 985n.
church interior 990n.
vestryman
church officer 986n.
vesture
dressing 228n.
vet
animal husbandry 369n.
be attentive 455vb.
estimate 480vb.
doctor 658n.
vetch
plant 366n.
veteran
old man 133n.
matured 669adj.
expert 694adj.
expert 696n.
warlike 718adj.
soldier 722n.
veterinary medicine
medical art 658n.
veterinary surgeon
animal husbandry 369n.
doctor 658n.
veto
restraint 747n.
prohibition 757n.
vex
(*see* vexation)
vexation
difficulty 700n.
sorrow 825n.
annoyance 827n.
anger 981n.
vexatious
annoying 827adj.
litigating 959adj.
vexillary
soldier 722n.
army officer 741n.
via

toward 281adv.
via 624adv.
viability
life 360n.
possibility 469n.
viaduct
crossing 222n.
bridge 624n.
vial
vessel 194n.
via media
mid-course 625n.
viands
food 301n.
viaticum
Christian rite 988n.
the sacrament 988n.
vibrancy
oscillation 317n.
vibrant
vigorous 174adj.
resonant 404adj.
vibrate
vary 152vb.
oscillate 317vb.
roll 403vb.
resound 404vb.
show feeling 818vb.
vibration
oscillation 317n.
agitation 318n.
resonance 404n.
vibratory
changeful 152adj.
oscillating 317adj.
vibroscope
oscillation 317n.
vicar
deputy 755n.
church title 986n.
pastor 986n.
vicarage
parsonage 986n.
vicarial
clerical 986adj.
vicariate
church office 985n.
vicarious
substituted 150adj.
commissioned 751adj.
vice
badness 645n.
bane 659n.
deputy 755n.
nippers 778n.
wrong 914n.
vice 934n.
vice-chancellor
director 690n.
officer 741n.
deputy 755n.
viceroy
governor 741n.
deputy 755n.
vice versa
correlatively 12adv.
contrarily 14adv.
in exchange 151adv.
inversely 221adv.
against 240adv.
vicinity
nearness 200n.
circumjacence 230n.
vicious
furious 176adj.
evil 616adj.
disobedient 738adj.
malevolent 898adj.
wrong 914adj.
vicious 934adj.
vicious circle
obstacle 702n.
vicissitude
changeable thing 152n.
vicissitudes
affairs 154n.
victim
weakling 163n.
corpse 363n.
dupe 544n.
chase 619n.
loser 728n.
unlucky person 731n.
booty 790n.
sufferer 825n.
laughing-stock 851n.
oblation 981n.
victimize
befool 542vb.
ill-treat 645vb.
oppress 735vb.
rob 788vb.
be malevolent 898vb.
avenge 910vb.
punish 963vb.
victor
victor 727n.
victoria
carriage 274n.
Victoria Cross
badge 547n.
decoration 729n.
(*see* V.C.)
Victorian
antiquated 127adj.
prudish 950adj.
victorious
superior 34adj.
successful 727adj.
victory
superiority 34n.
victory 727n.
victrola
phonograph 414n.
victual
food 301n.
feed 301vb.
provide 633vb.
victualler
provider 633n.
vicuna
fiber 208n.
textile 222n.
videlicet
namely 80adv.
vidual
widowed 896adj.
viduity
widowhood 896n.
vie
be good 644vb.
contend 716vb.
view
range 183n.
open space 263n.
view 438n.
watch 441vb.
spectacle 445n.
appearance 445n.
idea 451n.
estimate 480vb.
opinion 485n.
manifestation 522n.
art subject 553n.
intention 617n.
beauty 841n.
viewable
visible 443adj.
viewer
spectator 441n.
viewership
onlookers 441n.
publicity 528n.
view-finder
telescope 442n.
view halloo
loudness 400n.
cry 408n.
view, in
impending 155adj.
at sight 438adv.
visible 443adj.
expected 507adj.
viewless
invisible 444adj.
view, on
visibly 443adv.
appearing 445adj.
apparently 445adv.
viewpoint
view 438n.
opinion 485n.
viewy
believing 485adj.
vigil
precursor 66n.
period 110n.
priority 119n.
carefulness 457n.
church service 988n.
vigilance
sagacity 498n.

restlessness 678n.
vigilant
attentive 455adj.
vigilant 457adj.
expectant 507adj.
tutelary 660adj.
prepared 669adj.
vigils
prayers 981n.
vignette
picture 553n.
description 590n.
vigor
energy 160n.
vitality 162n.
vigorousness 174n.
affirmation 532n.
vigor 571n.
resolution 599n.
restlessness 678n.
warm feeling 818n.
moral sensibility 819n.
vigorous
great 32adj.
(*see* vigor)
Viking
mariner 270n.
robber 789n.
vile
unimportant 639adj.
bad 645adj.
cowardly 856adj.
rascally 930adj.
heinous 934adj.
vilification
scurrility 899n.
detraction 926n.
vilify
shame 867vb.
dispraise 924vb.
defame 926vb.
villa
house 192n.
villadom
housing 190n.
habitancy 191n.
mediocrity 732n.
village
district 184n.
housing 192n.
village green
focus 76n.
meeting place 192n.
pleasure-ground 837n.
villager
dweller 191n.
villain
evildoer 904n.
knave 938n.
villainous
bad 645adj.
ugly 842adj.
rascally 930adj.
vicious 934adj.
villainy
improbity 930n.
wickedness 934n.
villein
slave 742n.
possessor 776n.
countryman 869n.
villenage
servitude 745n.
villosity
roughness 259n.
villous
hairy 259adj.
vim
vigorousness 174n.
vigor 571n.
vinaigrette
scent 396n.
vinculum
bond 47n.
vindicable
vindicable 927adj.
vindicate
demonstrate 478vb.
claim 915vb.
vindicate 927vb.
vindication
liberation 746n.
avenger 910n.
vindication 927n.
vindicator 927n.
acquittal 960n.
punisher 963n.
vindictive
hating 888adj.
resentful 891adj.
pitiless 906adj.
revengeful 910adj.
vine
plant 366n.
vinegar
sourness 393n.
painfulness 827n.
vinegary
sour 393adj.
irascible 892adj.
sullen 893adj.
vinery
farm 370n.
vineyard
farm 370n.
viniculture
agriculture 370n.
vinous
intoxicating 949adj.
drunken 949adj.
vintage
assemblage 74n.
date 108n.
product 164n.
agriculture 370n.
tasty 386adj.
savory 390adj.
store 632n.
goodness 644n.
excellent 644adj.
earnings 771n.
vintner
provider 633n.
violate
be unconformable 84vb.
force 176vb.
ill-treat 645vb.
disobey 738vb.
be undue 916vb.
fail in duty 918vb.
debauch 951vb.
be illegal 954vb.
(*see* violation)
violation
coition 45n.
rape 951n.
violator
usurper 916n.
libertine 952n.
impious person 980n.
violence
disorder 61n.
derangement 63n.
havoc 165n.
vigorousness 174n.
violence 176n.
misuse 675n.
cruel act 898n.
violent
revolutionary 149adj.
violent 176adj.
assertive 532adj.
harmful 645adj.
hasty 680n.
oppressive 735adj.
fervent 818adj.
excited 821adj.
excitable 822adj.
lawless 954adj.
violet
fragrance 396n.
purple 434n.
blueness 435n.
humility 872n.
modesty 844n.
violin, viola
viol 414n.
violinist
instrumentalist 413n.
V.I.P.
person 371n.
bigwig 638n.
viper
reptile 365n.
sibilation 406n.
bane 659n.
noxious animal 904n.
knave 938n.
viraginity
abnormality 84n.

male 372n.
virago
athlete 162n.
violent creature 176n.
woman 373n.
shrew 892n.
virelay
verse form 593n.
virgin
new 126adj.
woman 373n.
unknown 491adj.
unwedded 895adj.
virgin 950n.
virginal
young 130adj.
unwedded 895adj.
virtuous 933adj.
pure 950adj.
virginals
piano 414n.
virginibus puerisque
pure 950adj.
virginity
unproductivity 172n.
celibacy 895n.
purity 950n.
virgin soil
unknown thing 491n.
undevelopment 670n.
Virgo
zodiac 321n.
viridescent
green 432adj.
virile
athlete 162adj.
male 372adj.
virilism
abnormality 84n.
virility
adultness 134n.
vitality 162n.
virology
medical art 658n.
virtu
good taste 846n.
virtual
intrinsic 5adj.
powerful 160adj.
possible 469adj.
virtue
essential part 5n.
ability 160n.
utility 640n.
goodness 644n.
conduct 688n.
manliness 855n.
nobility 868n.
modesty 874n.
morals 917n.
virtue 933n.
purity 950n.
virtuosity
musical skill 413n.
skill 694n.
good taste 846n.
virtuoso
musician 413n.
proficient 696n.
virtuous
virtuous 933adj.
pure 950adj.
pietistic 979adj.
virulence
keenness 174n.
badness 645n.
poison 659n.
rudeness 885n.
resentment 891n.
malevolence 898n.
virus
animalcule 196n.
infection 651n.
poison 659n.
visa
credential 465n.
assent 488n.
permit 756n.
visage
face 237n.
feature 445n.
vis-à-vis
in front 237adv.
against 240adv.
carriage 274n.
viscera
insides 224n.
visceral
interior 224adj.
viscid
thick 205adj.
viscid 354adj.
viscidity
viscidity 354n.
semiliquidity 354n.
vis conservatrix
preservation 666n.
viscount
nobleman 868n.
viscous
cohesive 48adj.
visibility
substantiality 3n.
visibility 443n.
appearance 445n.
visible
impending 155adj.
visible 443adj.
intelligible 516adj.
manifest 522adj.
disclosed 526adj.
vis inertiae
energy 160n.
counteraction 182n.
vision
insubstantial thing 4n.
vision 438n.
visual fallacy 440n.
appearance 445n.
spectacle 445n.
fantasy 513n.
manifestation 522n.
a beauty 841n.
aspiration 852n.
visionary
unreal 2adj.
insubstantial 4adj.
seeing 438adj.
spectator 441n.
impossible 470adj.
misjudging 481adj.
erroneous 495adj.
visionary 513n.
imaginative 513adj.
imaginary 513adj.
hoper 852n.
philanthropist 901n.
worshiper 981adj.
visionless
blind 439adj.
visit
presence 189n.
dwell 192vb.
travel 267vb.
arrive 295vb.
enter 297vb.
be severe 735vb.
social round 882n.
visit 882vb.
punish 963vb.
goblinize 970vb.
visitant
wanderer 268n.
arrival 295n.
visitation
inquiry 459n.
bane 659n.
adversity 731n.
severity 735n.
suffering 825n.
punishment 963n.
visiting card
label 547n.
visiting terms
social round 882n.
visitor
resident 191n.
arrival 295n.
incomer 297n.
inquirer 459n.
social person 882n.
visor
shade 226n.
screen 421n.
disguise 527n.
armor 713n.
vista
open space 263n.
view 438n.
spectacle 445n.
visual

seeing 438adj.
visual aid
classroom 539n.
visualize
see 438vb.
imagine 513vb.
vital
alive 360adj.
required 627adj.
cheerful 833adj.
vital concern
important matter 638n.
vitalism
biology 358n.
vitality
vitality 162n.
life 360n.
vigor 570n.
health 650n.
restlessness 678n.
cheerfulness 833n.
vitalize
vitalize 360vb.
vitalness
needfulness 627n.
vital role
influence 178n.
vital spark
life 360n.
vital statistics
statistics 86n.
beauty 841n.
vitamin
tonic 658n.
vitaminize
feed 301vb.
vitaminous
nourishing 301adj.
vitamins
food content 301n.
dieting 301n.
vitiate
impair, pervert 655vb.
be clumsy 695vb.
vitiated
diseased 651adj.
vicious 934adj.
vitiation
deterioration 655n.
wickedness 934n.
viticulture
agriculture 370n.
vitreosity
transparency 422n.
vitreous
hard 326adj.
transparent 422adj.
vitrify
harden 326vb.
vitriol
burning 381n.
poison 659n.
vitriolic
paining 827adj.
maledicent 899adj.
vituperation
oratory 579n.
scurrility 899n.
reproach 924n.
vituperator
defamer 926n.
viva
exam. 459n.
vivacious
feeling 818adj.
lively 819adj.
(*see* vivacity)
vivacity
vigor 571n.
restlessness 678n.
moral sensibility 819n.
cheerfulness 833n.
vivandière
peddler 794n.
vivarium
stock farm 639n.
vivid
lifelike 18adj.
vigorous 174adj.
striking 374adj.
luminous 417adj.
florid 425adj.
expressive 516adj.
representing 551adj.
forceful 571adj.
descriptive 590adj.
vivify
strengthen 162vb.
vitalize 360vb.
animate 821vb.
viviparous
productive 164adj.
vivisect
give pain 377vb.
experiment 461vb.
vivisection
killing 362n.
pain 377n.
vivisector
inquirer 459n.
experimenter 461n.
vixen
vermin 365n.
female animal 373n.
shrew 892n.
vixenish
animal 365adj.
irascible 892adj.
sullen 893adj.
viz.
namely 80adv.
vizier
official 690n.
officer 741n.
vocable
speech sound 398n.
word 559n.
vocabulary
list 87n.
dictionary 559n.
style 566n.
vocal
sounding 398adj.
musical 412adj.
vocal 577adj.
speaking 579n.
vocal chords
voice 577n.
vocalic
literal 558adj.
vocal 577adj.
vocalism
vocal music 412n.
vocalist
vocalist 413n.
vocalize
sing 413vb.
voice 577vb.
vocation
call 547n.
motive 612n.
pursuit 619n.
vocation 622n.
duty 917n.
church ministry 985n.
vocational
businesslike 622adj.
vocative
vocative 583adj.
devotional 981adj.
vociferation
loudness 400n.
cry 408n.
voice 577n.
vogue
practice 610n.
fashion 848n.
repute 866n.
vogue-word
word 559n.
neology 560n.
voice
publish 528vb.
affirmation 532n.
grammar 564n.
voice 577n., vb.
speak 579vb.
vote 605n.
voiced
sounding 398adj.
literal 558adj.
vocal 577adj.
voiceless
voiceless 578adj.
taciturn 582adj.
voicelessness
aphony 578n.
void
insubstantiality 4n.

space 183n.
emptiness 190n.
gap 201n.
void 300vb.
rarefy 325vb.
abrogate 752vb.
voidance
voidance 300n.
voile
textile 222n.
volatile
transient 114adj.
light 323adj.
gaseous 336adj.
vaporific 338adj.
light-minded 456adj.
capricious 604adj.
excitable 822adj.
volatilize
lighten 323vb.
rarefy 325vb.
vaporize 338vb.
volcanic
violent 176adj.
outgoing 298adj.
fiery 379adj.
excitable 822adj.
volcano
outbreak 176n.
cavity 255n.
chimney 263n.
ejector 300n.
fire 379n.
furnace 383n.
pitfall 663n.
volition
will 595n.
volitional
volitional 595adj.
volley
crowd 74n.
strike 279vb.
shoot 287vb.
bang 402n.
bombardment 712n.
fire at 712vb.
volley-ball
ball game 837n.
volt, voltage
electricity 160n.
volte-face
return 286n.
tergiversation 603n.
perfidy 930n.
volubility
speech 579n.
loquacity 581n.
volume
quantity 26n.
subdivision 53n.
inclusion 78n.
space, measure 183n.
size 195n.
metrology 465n.
book 589n.
volumetric
spatial 183adj.
metric 465adj.
voluminous
great 32adj.
recipient 194adj.
large 195adj.
voluntarism
philosophy 449n.
will 595n.
voluntary
prelude 66n.
musical piece 412n.
volitional 595adj.
voluntary 597adj.
volunteer
volunteer 597n.
be willing 597vb.
undertake 672vb.
worker 686n.
soldier 722n.
offer oneself 759vb.
voluptuary
sensualist 944n.
voluptuous
sensuous 376adj.
pleasurable 826adj.
sensual 944adj.
lecherous 951adj.
volutation
rotation 315n.
volute
coil 251n.
vomit
voidance 300n.
vomit 300vb.
dislike 861vb.
vomiting
indigestion 651n.
vomitory
orifice 263n.
doorway 263n.
remedial 658adj.
voodoo
sorcery 983n.
voracious
taking 786adj.
greedy 859adj.
gluttonous 947adj.
voracity
eating 301n.
desire 859n.
gluttony 947n.
vortex
coil 251n.
vortex 315n.
commotion 318n.
eddy 350n.
pitfall 663n.
vortical
rotary 315adj.
votary
patron 707n.
desirer 859n.
lover 887n.
pietist 979n.
worshiper 981n.
vote
judge 480vb.
affirmation 532n.
vote 605n., vb.
decree 737n.
commission 751vb.
credit 802n., vb.
vote against, vote down
oppose 704vb.
vote-catcher
motivator 612n.
vote-catching
choosing 605adj.
flattering 925adj.
voted
assented 488adj.
legal 953adj.
vote for
endorse 488vb.
vote 605vb.
patronize 703vb.
voteless
choiceless 606adj.
unentitled 916adj.
voter
estimator 480n.
electorate 605n.
patron 707n.
free man 744n.
voters' list
electorate 605n.
votes for women
vote 605n.
gynocracy 733n.
vote-snatcher
motivator 612n.
vote-snatching
choosing 605adj.
flattering 925adj.
voting list
list 87n.
electorate 605n.
voting paper
electorate 605n.
votive
promissory 764adj.
giving 781adj.
devotional 981adj.
votive offering
oblation 981n.
voucher
credential 466n.
record 548n.
title-deed 767n.
receipt 807n.
vouch for
testify 466vb.
promise 764vb.
vouchsafe

permit 756vb.
consent 758vb.
give 781vb.
vow
affirm 532vb.
promise 764n., vb.
offering 781n.
offer worship 981vb.
vowed
dutied 917adj.
vowel
speech sound 398n.
spoken letter 558n.
voice 577n.
vox populi
consensus 488n.
vote 605n.
government 733n.
tribunal 956n.
voyage
water travel 267n.
passage 305n.
voyager
traveler 268n.
voyeur
libertine 952n.
voyeurism
curiosity 453n.
impurity 951n.
vriddhi
speech sound 398n.
vulcanize
harden 326vb.
be tough 329adj.
heat 381vb.
vulgar
inferior 35adj.
general 79adj.
indiscriminating 464adj.
linguistic 557adj.
feeble 572adj.
inelegant 576adj.
not nice 645adj.
artless 699adj.
graceless 842adj.
vulgar 847adj.
disreputable 867adj.
plebeian 869adj.
showy 875adj.
maledicent 899adj.
vicious 934adj.
impure 951adj.
vulgarian
upstart 126n.
vulgarian 847n.
commoner 869n.
vulgarism
slang 560n.
inelegance 576n.
bad taste 847n.
vulgarity
(*see* vulgar)
vulgarize
impair 655vb.
use 673vb.
facilitate 701vb.
cheapen 812vb.
vulgarize 847vb.
not respect 921vb.
vulgate
interpretation 520n.
Vulgate
scripture 975n.
vulnerable 661adj.
defenseless 161adj.
liable 180adj.
imperfect 647adj.
vulnerable 661adj.
unprepared 670adj.
accusable 928adj.
frail 934adj.
vulpine
animal 365adj.
cunning 698adj.
vulture
eater 301n.
bird 365n.
cleaner 648n.
tyrant 735n.
taker 786n.
noxious animal 904n.
glutton 947n.
vulva
genitalia 164n.

W

wacky
crazed 503adj.
wad
load 193vb.
line 227vb.
stopper 264n.
close 264vb.
ammunition 723n.
wadding
contents 193n.
lining 227n.
stopper 264n.
softness 327n.
warm clothes 381n.
waddle
gait 265n.
walk 267vb.
move slowly 278vb.
oscillate 317vb.
wade
walk 267vb.
swim 269vb.
be wet 341vb.
wader
pedestrian 268n.
waders
legwear 228n.
footwear 228n.
wade through
study 536vb.
exert oneself 682vb.
wadi
cavity 255n.
stream 350n.
conduit 351n.
wads
great quantity 32n.
funds 797n.
wafer
adhesive 47n.
lamina 207n.
pastry 301n.
the sacrament 988n.
waffle
cereal 301n.
mean nothing 515vb.
be loquacious 581vb.
waft
transport 272n.
transfer 272vb.
carry 273vb.
blow 352vb.
waftage
transport 272n.
wag
brandish 317vb.
oscillate 317vb.
be agitated 318vb.
gesticulate 547vb.
humorist 839n.
wage
employ 622vb.
wage war 718vb.
earnings 771n.
(*see* wages)
wage-bill
cost 809n.
wage-earner
worker 686n.
recipient 782n.
wager
gambling 618n.
contest 716n.
wages
pay 804n.
receipt 807n.
cost 809n.
reward 962n.
waggish
gay 833adj.
amused 837adj.
witty 839adj.
funny 849adj.
waggle
brandish 317vb.
agitate 318vb.
gesticulate 547vb.
wagon
cart 274n.
wagonage
transport 272n.
wagoner

driver 268n.
carrier 273n.
wag one's finger
reprove 924vb.
wag one's tongue
speak 579vb.
wagonette
carriage 274n.
wagon-lit
train 274n.
waif
wanderer 268n.
derelict 779n.
outcaste 883n.
wail
cry 408vb.
ululate 409vb.
be discontented 829vb.
lamentation 836n.
wain
cart 274n.
wainscot
base 214n.
lining 227n.
wainwright
artisan 686n.
waist
narrowing 206n.
centrality 225n.
bodywear 228n.
waistband
girdle 47n.
belt 228n.
loop 250n.
waistcoat
vest 228n.
waistline
narrowing 206n.
centrality 225n.
wait
pass time 108vb.
protraction 113n.
wait 136vb.
pause 145vb.
be quiescent 266vb.
await 507vb.
not act 677vb.
be inactive 679vb.
wait and see
wait 136vb.
be tentative 461vb.
not act 677vb.
wait-and-see policy
caution 858n.
waiter
concomitant 89n.
spectator 441n.
servant 742n.
waiting list
list 87n.
record 548n.
hoper 852n.
waiting room
inn 192n.
lobby 194n.
waiting woman
domestic 742n.
wait on
accompany 89vb.
result 157vb.
follow 284vb.
minister to 703vb.
visit 882vb.
waits
choir 413n.
wait upon
obey 739vb.
serve 742vb.
waive
put off 136vb.
be neutral 606vb.
relinquish 621vb.
not use 674vb.
resign 753vb.
refuse 760vb.
not retain 779vb.
waiver
rejection 607n.
relinquishment 621n.
non-use 674n.
resignation 753n.
loss of right 916n.
wake
remainder 41n.
retinue 67n.
continuity 71n.
effect 157n.
rear 238n.
furrow 261n.
water travel 269n.
follower 284n.
eddy 350n.
obsequies 364n.
trace 548n.
be active 678n.
excite 821vb.
lament 836n.
festivity 837n.
condolence 905n.
wakeful
attentive 455adj.
vigilant 457adj.
active 678adj.
wake up
have feeling 374vb.
walk
pleasance 192n.
gait 265n.
pedestrianism 267n.
walk 267vb.
move slowly 278vb.
vocation 622n.
path 624n.
conduct 688n.
goblinize 970vb.
walker
traveler 268n.
pedestrian 268n.
ghost 970n.
walkie-talkie
hearing aid 415n.
telecommunication 531n.
walking encyclopedia
scholar 492n.
expert 696n.
walking out
love-making 887n.
walking-stick
supporter 218n.
walk of life
state 7n.
vocation 622n.
conduct 688n.
walk on
act 594vb.
walk-out
strike 145n.
departure 296n.
egress 298n.
dissent 489n.
opposition 704n.
walk out with
accompany 89vb.
court 889vb.
walk-over
easy thing 701n.
victory 727n.
walkup
flat 192n.
wall
separation 46n.
exclusion 57n.
verticality 215n.
supporter 218n.
circumjacence 230n.
partition 231n.
fence 235n.
solid body 324n.
screen 421n.
fortification 713n.
means of execution 964n.
wallet
case 194n.
treasury 799n.
wall-eye
dim sight 440n.
wallflower
rejection 607n.
indifference 860n.
wallop
potion 301n.
spank 963vb.
wallow
be low 210vb.
voyage 269vb.
plunge 313vb.

rotate 315vb.
fluctuate 317vb.
be agitated 318vb.
weigh 322vb.
be wet 341vb.
marsh 347n.
swill 649n.
be unclean 649vb.
be intemperate 943vb.
wallower
dirty person 649n.
sensualist 944n.
wallow in
enjoy 376vb.
abound 635vb.
superabound 637vb.
wallpaper
covering 226n.
lining 227n.
Wall Street
mart 796n.
walnut
fruit 301n.
tree 366n.
brownness 430n.
waltz
rotation 315n.
musical piece 412n.
dance 837n., vb.
wampum
coinage 797n.
wan
dim 419adj.
colorless 426adj.
melancholic 834adj.
unsightly 842adj.
wand
badge of rule 743n.
magic instrument 983n.
wander
be unrelated 10vb.
be dispersed 75vb.
wander 267vb.
be inattentive 456vb.
be insane 503vb.
be diffuse 570vb.
be free 744vb.
wanderer
displacement 188n.
wanderer 268n.
idler 679n.
wandering
unstable 152adj.
deviation 282n.
unconfined 744adj.
(*see* wander)
wanderlust
wandering 267n.
wane
decrease 37n., vb.
become small 198vb.
be dim 419vb.
waste 634vb.
deteriorate 655vb.
wangle
trickery 542n.
contrivance 623n.
foul play 930n.
want
deficit 55n.
shortcoming 307n.
requirement 627n.
scarcity 636n.
be unsatisfied 636vb.
imperfection 647n.
adversity 731n.
request 761n.
poverty 801n.
desire 859n., vb.
want back
regret 830vb.
wanted
absent 190adj.
required 627adj.
wanting
incomplete 55adj.
absent 190adj.
deficient 307adj.
unintelligent 499adj.
insane 503adj.
lost 722adj.
wanton
changeful 152adj.
capricious 604adj.
free 744adj.
amuse oneself 837vb.
revel 837vb.
rash 857adj.
caress 889vb.
unchaste 951adj.
loose woman 952n.
wapentake
district 184n.
wappenschaw
assemblage 74n.
pageant 875n.
war
slaughter 362n.
dissension 709n.
war 718n.
be inimical 881vb.
warble
ululate 409vb.
sing 413vb.
warbler
vocalist 413n.
war-chariot
war-chariot 274n.
war correspondent
author 589n.
delegate 754n.
warcraft
art of war 718n.
war-cry
call 547n.
danger signal 665n.
defiance 711n.
ward
subdivision 53n.
youth 130n.
district 184n.
hospital 658n.
protection 660n.
refuge 662n.
fort 713n.
dependent 742n.
detention 747n.
mandate 751n.
warden
janitor 264n.
protector 660n.
manager 690n.
officer 741n.
keeper 749n.
wardenship
protection 660n.
warder
jailer 749n.
ward off
parry 713vb.
wardrobe
cabinet 194n.
clothing 228n.
wardroom
chamber 194n.
wardship
nonage 130n.
protection 660n.
subjection 745n.
ware
product 164n.
property 777n.
merchandise 795n.
warehouse
storage 632n.
emporium 796n.
warfare
warfare 718n.
(*see* war)
war footing
war measures 718n.
war-god
war 718n.
mythic god 966n.
warhead
ammunition 723n.
explosive 723n.
war-horse
war-horse 273n.
cavalry 722n.
wariness
attention 455n.
carefulness 457n.
caution 858n.
warlike
violent 176adj.
warlike 718adj.
courageous 855adj.

warlike habits
bellicosity 718n.
warlock
sorcerer 983n.
war-lord
militarist 722n.
army officer 741n.
warm
summery 128adj.
near 200adj.
comfortable 376adj.
warm 379adj.
warm clothes 381n.
heat 381vb.
red 431adj.
forceful 571adj.
laborious 682adj.
rich 800adj.
fervent 818adj.
excite 821vb.
cheer 833vb.
friendly 880adj.
sociable 882adj.
excite love 887vb.
angry 891adj.
irascible 892adj.
warmed-up
repeated 106adj.
heated 381adj.
war memorial
trophy 729n.
warm-heartedness
benevolence 897n.
warming pan
caldron 194n.
heater 383n.
war-monger
militarist 722n.
war-mongering
contending 716adj.
warmth
heat 379n.
hue 425n.
redness 431n.
vigor 571n.
excitable state 822n.
friendliness 880n.
anger 891n.
warm the heart
cheer 833vb.
warm to
feel 818vb.
desire 859vb.
befriend 880vb.
be in love 887vb.
warm up
start out 296vb.
heat 381vb.
make ready 669vb.
show feeling 818vb.
warn
predict 511vb.
hint 524vb.
dissuade 613vb.
warn 664vb.
advise 691vb.
defy 711vb.
frighten 854vb.
reprove 924vb.
warned
expectant 507adj.
warned 664adj.
prepared 669adj.
warning
precursor 66n.
period 110n.
prediction 511n.
omen 511n.
warning 664n.
intimidation 854n.
(*see* warn)
warning light
signal light 420n.
signal 547n.
warning notice
demand 737n.
warn off
exclude 57vb.
prohibit 757vb.
war of words
quarrel 709n.
contention 716n.
warp
break 46vb.
modify 143vb.
force 176vb.
obliquity 220n.
weaving 222n.
deform 244vb.
distortion 246n.
draw 288vb.
bias 481n., vb.
impair 655vb.
warpaint
pigment 425n.
cosmetic 843n.
warp and weft
texture 331n.
warpath
warfare 718n.
warpath, on the
attacking 712adj.
warped
distorted 246adj.
biased 481adj.
imperfect 647adj.
warplane
air force 722n.
war policy
bellicosity 718n.
warrant
credential 466n.
make certain 473vb.
affirmation 532n.
safeguard 660vb.
precept 693n.
warrant 737n.
mandate 751n.
permit 756n., vb.
promise 764n., vb.
security 767n.
paper money 797n.
justify 927vb.
legal process 959n.
warranty
credential 466n.
permission 756n.
promise 764n.
security 767n.
warren
abundance 171n.
dwelling 192n.
excavation 255n.
warrior
combatant 722n.
soldier 722n.
warship
warship 722n.
wars, in the
unprosperous 731adj.
wart
swelling 253n.
skin disease 651n.
blemish 845n.
wartime
belligerency 718n.
war-weary
peaceful 717adj.
wary
nervous 854adj.
cautious 858adj.
wash
facing 226n.
moisten 341vb.
lake 346n.
marsh 347n.
eddy, wave 350n.
pigment 425n.
whiten 427vb.
trace 548n.
suffice 635n.
be expedient 642vb.
ablution 648n.
clean 648vb.
balm 658n.
wash and brush up
refreshment 695n.
beautification 843n.
washed out
colorless 426adj.
fatigued 684adj.
washed up
fatigued 684adj.
washer
lining 227n.
interjection 231n.
circle 250n.
washerwoman
cleaner 648n.

wash-house
ablution 648n.
washing board
cleaning utensil 648n.
wash-leather
cleaning cloth 648n.
wash off
obliterate 550vb.
wash one's hands
avoid 603vb.
be exempt 919vb.
disapprove 924vb.
wash out
decolorize 426vb.
obliterate 550vb.
wash-out
failure 728n.
washroom
ablution 648n.
washy
unmeaning 515adj.
(*see* wishy-washy)
wasp
noxious animal 904n.
waspish
furious 176adj.
irascible 892adj.
wasp-waist
contraction 198n.
narrowing 206n.
wassail
festivity 837n.
get drunk 949vb.
wastage
decrement 42n.
waste 634n.
loss 772n.
waste
decrease 37n.
leavings 41n.
decompose 51vb.
lay waste 165vb.
desert 172n.
space 183n.
emptiness 190n.
become small 198vb.
outflow 298n.
waste 634n., vb.
make insufficient 636vb.
rubbish 641n.
impair 655vb.
use 673n., vb.
misuse 675n., vb.
loss 772n.
expend 806vb.
prodigality 815n.
intemperance 943n.
waste away
be ill 651vb.
wasted
lean 206adj.
lost 772adj.
waste effort
waste effort 641vb.
wasteful
destructive 165adj.
wasteful 634adj.
profitless 641adj.
prodigal 815adj.
intemperate 943adj.
waste of breath
lost labor 641n.
waste of time
unproductivity 172n.
lost labor 641n.
waste paper
ineffectuality 161n.
rubbish 641n.
waste-pipe
drain 351n.
waste product
dirt 649n.
waster
negligence 458n.
prodigal 815n.
bad man 938n.
waste time
pass time 108vb.
drag on 113vb.
lose a chance 138vb.
be inactive 679vb.
wastrel
bad man 938n.
watch
period 110n.
timekeeper 117n.
scan 438vb.
spectator 441n.
watch 441vb.
attention 455n.
be attentive 455vb.
invigilate 457vb.
warner 664n.
be active 678vb.
defend 713vb.
keeper 749n.
police 955n.
watch and ward
protection 660n.
watch-chain
jewelry 844n.
watch-dog
protector 660n.
warner 664n.
keeper 749n.
watcher
spectator 441n.
protector 660n.
watchet
blueness 435n.
watch-fire
fire 379n.
signal 547n.
watchful
attentive 455adj.
vigilant 457adj.
intelligent 498adj.
tutelary 660adj.
active 678adj.
observant 768adj.
cautious 858adj.
watch-glass
plate 194n.
transparency 422n.
optical device 442n.
watch-hand
indicator 547n.
watchmaker
timekeeper 117n.
artisan 686n.
watchman
janitor 264n.
spectator 441n.
protector 660n.
keeper 749n.
watch over
safeguard 660vb.
watch-tower
high structure 209n.
view 438n.
watchword
call 547n.
identification 547n.
warfare 718n.
water
bate 37vb.
mix 43vb.
weak thing 163n.
weaken 163vb.
make fruitful 171vb.
drink, soft drink 301n.
excrement 302n.
fluid 335n.
water 339n.
add water 339vb.
irrigate 341vb.
make flow 350vb.
groom 369vb.
cultivate 370vb.
extinguisher 382n.
insipidity 387n.
transparency 422n.
provide 633vb.
cleanser 648n.
water at the mouth
exude 298vb.
be hungry 859vb.
gluttonize 947vb.
waterborne
seafaring 269adj.
water bottle
vessel 194n.
water cart
water 339n.
cleaning utensil 648n.

water channel
conduit 351n.
water closet
latrine 649n.
watercolor
pigment 425n.
picture 553n.
art equipment 553n.
watercourse
stream 350n.
conduit 351n.
watercress
potherb 301n.
water diviner
inquirer 459n.
diviner 511n.
psychic 984n.
water down
weaken 163vb.
add water 339vb.
water drinker
ascetic 945n.
sober person 948n.
waterer
irrigator 341n.
waterfall
outflow 298n.
descent 309n.
waterfall 350n.
water filter
cleaning utensil 648n.
waterfowl
waterfowl 365n.
waterfront
edge 234n.
water gate
conduit 351n.
water hole
lake 346n.
watering can
vessel 194n.
irrigator 341n.
watering cart
water 339n.
irrigator 341n.
watering place
abode 192n.
hospital 658n.
water jump
gap 201n.
obstacle 702n.
waterless
dry 342n.
water level
layer 207n.
horizontality 216n.
waterline
edge 234n.
waterlog
drench 341vb.
waterlogged
impotent 161adj.
marshy 347adj.
semiliquid 354adj.
unsafe 661adj.
hindered 702adj.
waterloo
ruin 165n.
defeat 728n.
waterman
boatman 270n.
watermark
gauge 465n.
label 547n.
pattern 844n.
water pipe
conduit 351n.
water pistol
irrigator 341n.
toy gun 723n.
plaything 837n.
water polo
ball game 837n.
sport 837n.
waterproof
unyielding 162adj.
coat 226vb.
overcoat 228n.
sealed off 264adj.
dry 342adj.
invulnerable 660adj.
preserve 666vb.
resisting 715adj.
watershed
summit 213n.
partition 231n.
water spirit
mythical being 970n.
water sports
acquatics 268n.
waterspout
vortex 315n.
conduit 351n.
water supply
provision 633n.
water system
cleansing 648n.
water table
layer 207n.
horizontality 216n.
watertight
dry 342adj.
water travel
water travel 269n.
water vapor
gas 336n.
water 339n.
water wagon, on the
sober 948adj.
waterway
stream 350n.
water wings
bladder 194n.
watery
non-adhesive 49adj.
weak 163adj.
excretory 302adj.
fluidal 335adj.
watery 339adj.
humid 341adj.
tasteless 387adj.
watt
electricity 160n.
metrology 465n.
wattle
network 222n.
wave
hang 217vb.
make curved 248vb.
convolution 251n.
hair 259n.
be in motion 265vb.
elevate 310vb.
brandish 317vb.
agitate 318vb.
wave 350n.
show 522vb.
gesticulate 547vb.
hair-dressing 843n.
greet 884vb.
wave a wand
practice sorcery 983vb.
wave by
signal 547vb.
wavelength
long measure 203n.
oscillation 317n.
radiation 417n.
wave on
signal 547vb.
waver
come unstuck 49vb.
vary 152vb.
be uncertain 474vb.
doubt 486vb.
be irresolute 601vb.
waverer
waverer 601n.
waviness
convolution 251n.
wave 350n.
waving
pendent 217adj.
wavy
curved 248adj.
undulatory 251adj.
furrowed 262adj.
wax
grow 36vb.
be turned to 147vb.
expand 197vb.
smooth 258vb.
harden 326vb.
softness 327n.

lubricant 334n.
viscidity 354n.
fat 357n.
sculpture 554n.
cleanser 648n.
anger 891n.
wax and wane
change 143vb.
waxen
fatty 357adj.
whitish 427adj.
wax figure
mold 23n.
image 551n.
waxwork
image 551n.
sculpture 554n.
waxworks
collection 632n.
waxy
soft 327adj.
fatty 357adj.
angry 891adj.
way
state 7n.
degree 27n.
room 183n.
itinerary 267n.
water travel 269n.
direction 281n.
progression 285n.
way in 297n.
habit 610n.
way 624n.
means 629n.
fashion 848n.
ritual 988n.
way, by the
en passant 305adv.
wayfarer
traveler 268n.
way in
entrance 68n.
doorway 263n.
way in 297n.
waylay
ambush 527vb.
ensnare 542vb.
be cunning 698vb.
waymark
signpost 547n.
way of life
conduct 688n.
way of the world
fashion 848n.
way, on the
on the move 265adj.
in transit 272adv.
towards 281adv.
forward 285adv.
way out
outlet 298n.
contrivance 623n.
route 624n.
means of escape 667n.
deliverance 668n.
way out, on the
deteriorated 655adj.
ways and means
means 629n.
wayside
edge 234adj.
accessible 289adj.
way, under
forward 285adv.
wayward
changeful 152adj.
willful 602adj.
capricious 604adj.
disobedient 738adj.
way with
management 689n.
wayworn
traveling 267adj.
fatigued 684adj.
wayzgoose
amusement 837n.
wazir
officer 741n.
wazirate
magistrature 733n.
W.C.
latrine 649n.
we
self 80n.
weak
small 33adj.
mixed 43adj.
ephemeral 114adj.
powerless 161adj.
weak 163adj.
moderate 177adj.
little 196adj.
watery 339adj.
muted 401adj.
unintelligent 499adj.
feeble 572adj.
insufficient 636adj.
unimportant 639adj.
unsafe 661adj.
lax 734adj.
pitying 905adj.
frail 934adj.
weak case
sophism 477n.
weaken
bate 37vb.
mix 43vb.
impair 65vb.
modify 143vb.
disable 161vb.
weaken 163vb.
moderate 177vb.
rarefy 325vb.
add water 339vb.
qualify 468vb.
weak in the head
insane 503adj.
weak-kneed
irresolute 601adj.
submitting 721adj.
lax 734adj.
weakling
weakling 163n.
sick person 651n.
unlucky person 731n.
coward 856n.
weakly
weakly 163adj.
weak-minded
irresolute 601adj.
cowardly 856adj.
weakness
impotence 161n.
tendency 179n.
liability 180n.
irresolution 601n.
insufficiency 636n.
imperfection 647n.
defect 647n.
ill-health 651n.
bane 659n.
vulnerability 661n.
liking 859n.
vice 934n.
weak-willed
irresolute 601adj.
lax 734adj.
weal
trace 548n.
good 615n.
prosperity 730n.
blemish 845n.
weald
plain 348n.
wood 366n.
wealth
abundance 171n.
means 629n.
plenty 634n.
estate 777n.
money 797n.
wealth 800n.
wealthy
rich 800adj.
weaned
unhabituated 611adj.
wean from
convince 485vb.
disaccustom 611vb.
dissuade 613vb.
weanling
child 132n.
weapon
contrivance 623n.
instrument 628n.
tool 630n.
protection 660n.
defense 713n.

weapon 723n.
weaponless
defenseless 161adj.
wear
decompose 51vb.
last 113vb.
clothing 228n.
wear 228vb.
show 522vb.
use 673n., vb.
fatigue 684n., vb.
wear and tear
decrease 37n.
decay 51n.
waste 634n.
dilapidation 655n.
weariness
sleepiness 679n.
fatigue 684n.
dejection 834n.
tedium 838n.
wearing
bedecked 844adj.
wearisome
laborious 682adj.
fatiguing 684adj.
annoying 827adj.
tedious 838adj.
wear off
disappear 446vb.
be unused 611vb.
wear on
elapse 111vb.
wear out
waste 634vb.
deteriorate 655vb.
impair 655vb.
fatigue 684vb.
be tedious 838vb.
wear ship
navigate 269vb.
deflect 282vb.
wear the breeches
influence 178vb.
dominate 733vb.
wear thin
be weak 163vb.
be brittle 330vb.
wear well
last 113vb.
be healthy 650vb.
weary
weakened 163adj.
laborious 682adj.
fatigue 684vb.
incommode 827vb.
bored 838adj.
sate 863vb.
weasand
maw 194n.
orifice 263n.
air-pipe 353n.
weasel
vehicle 274n.
vermin 365n.
weather
storm 176n.
navigate 269vb.
pulverize 332vb.
weather 340n.
wind 352n.
color 425vb.
deteriorate 655vb.
mature 669vb.
weather balloon
airship 276n.
weather-beaten
weakened 163adj.
dilapidated 655adj.
weather-bound
restrained 747adj.
weathercock
changeable thing 152n.
pneumatics 340n.
anemology 352n.
indicator 547n.
waverer 601n.
tergiversator 603n.
weathered
soft-hued 425adj.
matured 669adj.
weather eye
carefulness 457n.
weather gauge
navigation 269n.
weatherproof
unyielding 162adj.
invulnerable 660adj.
weather side
contrariety 14n.
laterality 239n.
weather the storm
be stable 153vb.
be restored 656vb.
be safe 660vb.
escape 667vb.
triumph 727vb.
weather-vane
pneumatics 340n.
weather 340n.
anemology 352n.
weather-wise
airy 340adj.
foreseeing 510adj.
predicting 511adj.
weave
arrangement 62n.
produce 164vb.
textile 222n.
weave 222vb.
pass 305vb.
texture 331n.
pattern 844n.
weaver
weaving 222n.
web
complexity 61n.
filament 208n.
network 222n.
texture 331n.
plot 623n.
stratagem 698n.
webbing
network 222n.
webby
reticular 222adj.
web-footed
deformed 246adj.
blemished 845adj.
wed
combine 50vb.
wed 894vb.
wedded to
believing 485adj.
obstinate 602adj.
habituated 610adj.
wedding
wedding 894n.
wedding garment
ritual object 988n.
wedding ring
jewelry 844n.
love token 889n.
ritual object 988n.
wedge
affix 45vb.
piece 53n.
supporter 218n.
interjection 231n.
angular figure 247n.
sharp edge 256n.
stopper 264n.
tool 630n.
wedge apart
sunder 46vb.
wedged
firm-set 45adj.
wedge in
intromit 231vb.
wedlock
junction 45n.
marriage 894n.
weed
eliminate 44vb.
exclude 57vb.
render few 105vb.
plant 366n.
cultivate 370vb.
tobacco 388n.
purify 648vb.
make better 654vb.
weeding
displacement 188n.
weed out
bate 37vb.
eject 300vb.
weeds
clothing 228n.
rubbish 641n.
weedy
lean 206adj.

vegetal 366adj.
week
period 110n.
weekday
period 110n.
week-end
pass time 108vb.
regular return 141n.
visit 882vb.
weekly
seasonal 141adj.
journal 528n.
reading matter 589n.
week of Sundays, a
diuturnity 113n.
weep
flow out 298vb.
be wet 341vb.
be dejected 834vb.
weep 836vb.
weeper
funeral 364n.
weeper 836n.
weepers
formal dress 228n.
badge 547n.
weep for
be sensitive 819vb.
pity 905vb.
weeping
pendent 217adj.
weeping and wailing
obsequies 364n.
lamentation 836n.
weepy
unhappy 825adj.
weevil
vermin 365n.
weft
weaving 222n.
weigh
equalize 28vb.
influence 178vb.
load 193vb.
weigh 322vb.
meditate 449vb.
discriminate 463vb.
mete out 465vb.
estimate 480vb.
motivate 612vb.
be important 638vb.
oppress 735vb.
weigh anchor
navigate 269vb.
start out 296vb.
weigh-bridge
scales 322n.
weighed against
compensatory 31adj.
weighing-machine
scales 322n.
weighment
weighment 322n.
weigh one's words
be truthful 540vb.
weight
substantiality 3n.
quantity 26n.
power 160n.
influence 178n.
size, bulk 195n.
materiality 319n.
gravity, scales 322n.
make heavy 322vb.
vigor 571n.
importance 638n.
encumbrance 702n.
weighted
distorted 246adj.
unjust 914adj.
weighting
compensation 31n.
weightless
small 33adj.
light 323adj.
weight of numbers
greater number 104n.
weights
weighment 322n.
metrology 465n.
weights and measures
metrology 465n.
weighty
substantial 3adj.
great 32adj.
strong 162adj.
influential 178adj.
material 319adj.
weighty 322adj.
evidential 466adj.
forceful 571adj.
instrumental 628adj.
important 638adj.
weir
waterfall 350n.
conduit 351n.
obstacle 702n.
weird
fate 596n.
frightening 854adj.
wonderful 864adj.
spooky 970adj.
welcome
meet 295vb.
reception 299n.
pleasant 376adj.
assent 488vb.
pleasurable 826adj.
desired 859adj.
celebration 876n.
friendliness 880n.
sociability 882n.
courteous act 884n.
congratulation 886n.
show respect 920vb.
applaud 923vb.
weld
join 45vb.
agglutinate 48vb.
heat 381vb.
yellow pigment 433n.
welder
joinder 45n.
welfare
good 615n.
prosperity 730n.
welfare state
shelter 662n.
polity 733n.
sociology 901n.
welfare work
sociology 901n.
welkin
heavens 321n.
air 340n.
well
greatly 32adv.
receeptacle 194n.
lowness 210n.
depth 211n.
flow out 298vb.
stream 350n.
well 615adv.
store 632n.
aright 644adv.
healthy 650adj.
skillfully 694adv.
well-advised
wise 498adj.
well-affected
friendly 880adj.
well-aimed
apt 24adj.
accurate 494adj.
well-behaved
obedient 739adj.
amiable 884adj.
well-being
euphoria 376n.
good 615n.
health 650n.
salubrity 652n.
prosperity 730n.
wealth 800n.
happiness 824n.
well-born
worshipful 866adj.
noble 868adj.
well-bred
tasteful 846adj.
well-bred 848adj.
genteel 868adj.
well-built
strong 162adj.
well-cut
adjusted 24adj.
well-defended
safe 660adj.
well-directed
relevant 9adj.
well-disposed

aiding 703adj.
innocent 935adj.
well-done
excellent 644adj.
well-made 694adj.
well-drawn
descriptive 590adj.
well-dressed
personable 841adj.
fashionable 848adj.
well-drilled
orderly 60adj.
Wellerism
witticism 839n.
well-favored
beautiful 841adj.
well-feathered
rich 800adj.
well-fed
fleshy 195adj.
feeding 301adj.
well-fought
contending 716adj.
well-founded
vested 153adj.
plausible 471adj.
certain 473adj.
true 494adj.
well-grown
large 195adj.
fleshy 195adj.
well-head
source 156n.
summit 213n.
well-inclined
approving 923adj.
well-intentioned
aiding 703adj.
friendly 880adj.
benevolent 897adj.
virtuous 933adj.
innocent 935adj.
well-judged
wise 498adj.
well-kept
safe 660adj.
preserved 666adj.
well-knit
cohesive 48adj.
stalwart 162adj.
well-known
well-known 528adj.
renowned 866adj.
well-laid
cunning 698adj.
well-lined
full 54adj.
well made 694adj.
well-made 694adj.
beautiful 841adj.
well-mannered
well-bred 848adj.
courteous 884adj.
well-meaning
friendly 880adj.
well-meant
aiding 703adj.
benevolent 897adj.
well-off
prosperous 730adj.
rich 800adj.
well over
flow out 298vb.
superabound 637vb.
well-pitched
melodious 410adj.
accurate 494adj.
well-read
instructed 490adj.
studious 536adj.
well-regulated
orderly 60adj.
well-rounded
phraseological 563adj.
well-spent
successful 727adj.
well-spent life
virtue 933n.
well-spoken
speaking 579adj.
well-bred 848adj.
well-spring
source 156n.
well-stocked
filled 635adj.
well-thumbed
used 673adj.
well-timed
timely 137adj.
expedient 642adj.
well-to-do
prosperous 730adj.
rich 800adj.
well-trodden
used 673adj.
well-turned
elegant 575adj.
shapely 841adj.
well up in
expert 694adj.
well-wisher
patron 707n.
friend 880n.
kind person 897n.
well with
friendly 880adj.
well-worn
usual 610adj.
dilapidated 655adj.
used 673adj.
welsh
decamp 296vb.
run away 620vb.
elude 667vb.
defraud 788vb.
not pay 805vb.
welsher
avoider 620n.
defrauder 789n.
non-payer 805n.
welt
edge 234n.
trace 548n.
spank 963vb.
welter
confusion 61n.
plunge 313vb.
rotate 315vb.
be wet 341vb.
welter-weight
pugilist 722n.
weltschmerz
suffering 825n.
melancholy 834n.
pity 905n.
wen
swelling 253n.
letter 558n.
blemish 845n.
wench
youngster 132n.
woman 373n.
be impure 951vb.
loose woman 952n.
wenching
unchastity 951n.
wend
move 265vb.
travel 267vb.
werewolf
demon 970n.
wergild
irenics 719n.
atonement 941n.
Wesleyanism
Protestantism 976n.
west
laterality 239n.
compass point 281n.
West End
district 184n.
beau monde 848n.
westerly
lateral 239adj.
western
lateral 239adj.
directed 281adj.
novel 590n.
stage play 594n.
Westerner
foreigner 59n.
West Point
training school 539n.
westward
lateral 239adj.
wet
excrete 302vb.
watery 339adj.
moisture 341n.
rainy 350adj.
foolish 499adj.
ninny 501n.

intemperate 943adj.
wet blanket
moderator 177n.
dissuasion 613n.
hinderer 702n.
moper 834n.
bore 838n.
wet bob
boatman 270n.
wet-eyed
unhappy 825adj.
lamenting 836adj.
wether
sheep 365n.
wet-nurse
provider 633n.
patronize 703vb.
keeper 749n.
wet plate
camera 442n.
wetted
incombustible 382adj.
wetting
moistening 341n.
whack
strike 279vb.
fatigue 684vb.
portion 783n.
spank 963vb.
whack at
essay 671n.
whacked
defeated 728adj.
whacking
whopping 32adj.
large 195adj.
whale
giant 195n.
fish 365n.
hunt 619vb.
whalebone
compressor 198n.
supporter 218n.
underwear 228n.
hardness 326n.
elasticity 328n.
fetter 748n.
whaler
mariner 270n.
fishing boat 275n.
hunter 619n.
wham
strike 279vb.
wharf
stable 192n.
edge 234n.
storage 632n.
workshop 687n.
emporium 796n.
wharfage
price 809n.
what for?
inquiringly 459adv.
what-have-you
no name 562n.
what it is about
topic 452n.
what it will fetch
price 809n.
what might be
possibility 469n.
what one is worth
estate 777n.
what's to come
destiny 155n.
what the doctor ordered
salubrious 652adj.
what the soldier said
evidence 466n.
wheal
swelling 253n.
wheat
cereal 301n.
corn 366n.
wheaten
edible 301adj.
wheat pit
mart 796n.
wheedle
tempt 612vb.
induce 612vb.
pet 889vb.
flatter 925vb.
wheedler
motivator 612n.
flatterer 925n.
wheel
wheel 250n.
move 265vb.
sailing aid 269n.
turn round 282vb.
circle 314vb.
rotate 315vb.
tool 629n.
directorship 689n.
instrument of torture 964n.
wheel about, wheel round
be inverted 221vb.
turn round 282vb.
turn back 286vb.
circle 314vb.
tergiversate 603vb.
wheelbarrow
pushcart 274n.
wheel-chair
pushcart 274n.
wheeled
vehicular 274adj.
wheeled traffic
conveyance 267n.
vehicle 274n.
wheelman
rider 268n.
navigator 270n.
wheel of fortune
changeable thing 152n.
chance 159n.
non-design 618n.
wheels within wheels
complexity 61n.
machine 630n.
wheelwright
artisan 686n.
wheeze
respiration 352n.
breathe 352vb.
hiss 406vb.
idea 451n.
hint 524n.
contrivance 623n.
wheezy
puffing 352adj.
sibilant 406adj.
whelk
swelling 253n.
fish food 301n.
table fish 365n.
whelm
drench 341vb.
whelp
youngling 132n.
reproduce itself 164vb.
dog 365n.
bad man 938n.
when
while, when 108adj.
when and where
situation 186n.
whence
hence 158adv.
why 158adv.
where
here 189adv.
whereabouts
situation 186n.
wherein
inside 224adv.
where it hurts most
on the raw 819adv.
where the shoe pinches
difficulty 700n.
moral sensibility 819n.
painfulness 827n.
wherever
widely 183adv.
wherewith
by means of 629adv.
wherewithal
means 629n.
funds 797n.
wherret
torment 827vb.
wherry
boat 275n.
wherryman
boatman 270n.
whet
sharpen 256vb.
animate 821vb.

cause desire 859vb.
whetstone
sharpener 256n.
whetted
sharp 256adj.
whey
milk product 301n.
fluid 335n.
whey-faced
colorless 426adj.
whiff
breeze 352n.
breathe 352vb.
odor 394n.
indication 547n.
whiffling
unstable 152adj.
trivial 639adj.
whiffy
odorous 394adj.
fetid 397adj.
Whigs
political party 708n.
while
while 108adv.
interim 108n.
synchronously 123adv.
while, a
time 108n.
while away
pass time 108vb.
be inactive 679vb.
have leisure 681vb.
amuse oneself 837vb.
whilom
prior 119adj.
former 125adj.
formerly 125adv.
whim
foolery 497n.
ideality 513n.
whim 604n.
liking 859n.
whimper
cry 408vb.
weep 836vb.
whimsical
multiform 82adj.
uncertain 474adj.
misjudging 481adj.
crazed 503adj.
unexpected 508n.
imaginative 513adj.
irresolute 601adj.
capricious 604adj.
witty 839adj.
ridiculous 849adj.
whimsy
foolery 497n.
ideality 513n.
whim 604n.
liking 859n.
whine
shrill 407vb.
cry 408n., vb.
ululate 409vb.
discord 411vb.
be discontented 829vb.
lamentation 836vb.
be servile 879vb.
whinny
ululation 409n.
whinyard
side-arms 923n.
whip
accumulator 74n.
make violent 176vb.
driver 268n.
strike 279vb.
cook 301vb.
agitate 318vb.
break in 369vb.
incentive 612n.
hunter 619n.
manager 689n.
defeat 727vb.
oppress 735vb.
command 737n.
officer 741n.
excitant 821n.
flog 963vb.
scourge 964n.
whipcord
fiber 208n.
whip hand
vantage 34n.
victory 727n.
governance 733n.
whip in
bring together 74vb.
whip out
extract 304vb.
whipped
light 323adj.
whipper
punisher 963n.
whipper-in
hunter 619n.
whippersnapper
youngster 132n.
nonentity 639n.
whippet
small animal 33n.
animalcule 196n.
dog 365n.
whipping-boy
substitute 150n.
propitiation 941n.
whipping post
pillory 964n.
whipping top
plaything 837n.
whipping up
excitation 821n.
whippy
flexible 327adj.
whir
rotate 315vb.
be agitated 318vb.
faintness 401n.
roll 403n., vb.
resound 404vb.
ululate 409vb.
whirl
rotate 315vb.
be agitated 318vb.
activity 678n.
excitable state 822n.
festivity 837n.
whirligig
rotator 315n.
whirling
speedy 277adj.
whirlpool
vortex 315n.
commotion 318n.
eddy 350n.
pitfall 663n.
whirlwind
turmoil 61n.
vortex 315n.
commotion 318n.
gale 352n.
whisk
move fast 277vb.
cook 301vb.
agitate 318vb.
cleansing utensil 648n.
clean 648vb.
whisker
filament 208n.
feeler 378n.
whiskers
hair 259n.
whisket
basket 194n.
whiskey
liquor 301n.
whisper
sound faint 401vb.
imply 523vb.
hint 524n., vb.
voice 577n., vb.
speak low 578vb.
speak 579vb.
detraction 926n.
whisperer
detraction 926n.
whist
silent 399adj.
card game 837n.
whistle
blow 352vb.
megaphone 400n.
be loud 400vb.
hiss 406vb.
stridor 407n.
cry 408vb.
ululate 409vb.
play music 413vb.

sing 413vb.
flute 414n.
signal 547n.
be cheerful 833vb.
wonder 864n., vb.
applaud 923vb.
disapprobation 924n.
whistle for
beg 761vb.
desire 859vb.
whistle-stop
stopping-place 145n.
whit
small quantity 33n.
trifle 639n.
white
colorless 426adj.
white 427adj.
eye 438n.
clean 648adj.
honorable 929adj.
virtuous 933adj.
innocent 935adj.
pure 950adj.
white ant
vermin 365n.
white caps
wave 350n.
white-collar worker
worker 686n.
whited sepulcher
sham 542n.
deceiver 545n.
white dwarf
star 321n.
white elephant
bane 659n.
encumbrance 702n.
dearness 811n.
white ensign
flag 547n.
white feather
cowardice 856n.
white flag
flag 547n.
irenics 719n.
white goods
merchandise 795n.
white hairs
age 131n.
Whitehall
workshop 687n.
magistrature 733n.
master 741n.
white hope
proficient 696n.
white horses
wave 350n.
White House
house 192n.
magistrature 733n.
white lead
whiting 427n.
white lie
equivocalness 518n.
concealment 525n.
mental dishonesty 543n.
stratagem 698n.
white line
traffic control 305n.
indicator 547n.
white-livered
cowardly 856adj.
white magic
sorcery 983n.
white man
gentleman 929n.
good man 937n.
whiten
color 425vb.
lose color 426vb.
whiten 427vb.
show feeling 818vb.
whiteness
light 417n.
whiteness 427n.
cleanness 648n.
white sheet
penance 941n.
pillory 964n.
canonicals 989n.
white-skinned
white 427adj.
white slave
prostitute 952n.
white slaver
bawd 952n.
white slave traffic
social evil 951n.
white trash
lower classes 869n.
whitewash
facing 226n.
coat 226vb.
pigment 425n.
whiting 427n.
sophisticate 477vb.
overrate 483vb.
sham 542n.
cleanser 648n.
preserve 666vb.
insolvency 805n.
extenuate 927vb.
acquit 960vb.
whither
toward 281adv.
whiting
table fish 365n.
whiting 427n.
cleanser 648n.
Whitsuntide
holy-day 988n.
whittle
shade off 27vb.
bate 37vb.
subtract 39vb.
cut 46vb.
make smaller 198vb.
laminate 207vb.
sharp edge 256n.
whiz
move fast 277vb.
hiss 406vb.
whiz-bang
missile weapon 723n.
whodunit
novel 590n.
whole
finite quantity 26n.
simple 44adj.
whole 52n., adj.
completeness 54n.
generality 79n.
universal 79adj.
numerical 85adj.
undamaged 646adj.
preserved 666adj.
whole-blooded
unmixed 44adj.
whole faith
orthodoxy 976n.
whole-hearted
simple 44adj.
resolute 599adj.
whole-heartedness
assiduity 678n.
whole hog
completeness 54n.
actively 678adv.
whole-hogging
extensive 32adj.
consummate 32adj.
complete 54adj.
resolute 599adj.
completive 725adj.
wholeness
whole 52n.
completeness 54n.
unity 88n.
whole, on the
on an average 30adv.
wholesale
extensive 32adj.
comprehensive 52adj.
complete 54adj.
inclusive 78adj.
indiscriminate 464adj.
plenteous 635adj.
trading 791adj.
sell 793vb.
wholesaler
seller 793n.
merchant 794n.
whole skin
health 650n.
wholesome
nourishing 301adj.
beneficial 644adj.
healthy 650adj.
salubrious 652adj.
whoop

cry 408n., vb.
pursue 619vb.
be cheerful 833vb.
rejoice 835vb.
whoopee
revel 837n.
whooping cough
respiration 352n.
respiratory disease 651n.
whopper
whopper 195n.
untruth 543n.
whopping
whopping 32adj.
large 195adj.
whore
be impure 951vb.
prostitute 952n.
whoredom
unchastity 951n.
social evil 951n.
whoremonger
libertine 952n.
whorish
unchaste 951adj.
whorl
weaving 222n.
coil 251n.
rotator 315n.
whosoever
everyman 79n.
why
why? 158adv.
why and wherefore, the
reason why 156n.
wick
filament 208n.
lighter 385n.
torch 420n.
wicked
evil 616adj.
bad 645adj.
difficult 700adj.
wrong 914adj.
dishonest 930adj.
wicked 934adj.
guilty 936adj.
impenitent 940adj.
lawbreaking 954adj.
irreligious 974adj.
impious 980adj.
wicked fairy
sorceress 983n.
Wicked One
Satan 969n.
wickerwork
basket 194n.
network 222n.
wicket
doorway 263n.
wicket-keeper
interceptor 702n.
defender 713n.
wickiup
dwelling 192n.
widdershins
toward 281adv.
round and round 315adv.
wide
great 32adj.
inclusive 78adj.
spacious 183adj.
distant 199n.
broad 205adj.
deviating 282adj.
mistaken 495adj.
wideawake
headgear 228n.
attentive 455adj.
vigilant 457adj.
wide berth
scope 744n.
wide berth, give a
avoid 620vb.
wide circulation
publicity 528n.
wide currency
publicity 528n.
widen
augment 36vb.
generalize 79vb.
enlarge 197vb.
be broad 205vb.
widening
disjunction 46n.
widen the breach
make quarrels 709vb.
wide of
beyond 199adv.
widespread
extensive 32adj.
comprehensive 52adj.
unassembled 75adj.
universal 79adj.
spacious 183adj.
expanded 197adj.
usual 610adj.
widgeon, wigeon
waterfowl 365n.
widow
survivor 41n.
deprive 786vb.
widowed spouse 896n.
widower
survivor 41n.
widowed spouse 896n.
widowhood
widowhood 896n.
widow's weeds
formal dress 228n.
badge 547n.
lamentation 836n.
width
quantity 26n.
size 195n.
breadth 205n.
wield
operate 173vb.
touch 378vb.
use 673vb.
wieldy
wieldy 701adj.
wiener
meat 301n.
wife
woman 373n.
spouse 894n.
wifehood
marriage 894n.
wifeless
unwedded 895adj.
widowed 896adj.
wifely
loving 887adj.
matrimonial 894adj.
wig
wig 228n.
hair 259n.
hair-dressing 843n.
reprove 924vb.
wigging
reprimand 924n.
wiggle
oscillate 317vb.
wigwam
dwelling 192n.
wild
disorderly 61adj.
desert 172n.
furious 176adj.
space 183n.
plain 348n.
light-minded 456adj.
inexact 495n.
absurd 497adj.
foolish 499adj.
frenzied 503adj.
avoiding 620adj.
unskillful 695adj.
artless 699adj.
disobedient 738adj.
riotous 738adj.
excited 821adj.
gay 833adj.
unsightly 842adj.
rash 857adj.
unsociable 883adj.
angry 891adj.
cruel 898adj.
unchaste 951adj.
wild about
enamored 887adj.
wild beast
violent creature 176n.
noxious animal 904n.
wildcat
cat 365n.
rash 857adj.
independent 744adj.
wilderness

confusion 61n.
havoc 165n.
desert 172n.
space 183n.
land 344n.
wild-goose chase
whim 604n.
lost labor 641n.
bungling 695n.
wildness
(*see* wild)
wild oats, sow one's
come of age 134vb.
be wicked 934vb.
be intemperate 943vb.
wile
trickery 542n.
stratagem 698n.
will
sequel 67n.
will 595n., vb.
be willing 597vb.
resolution 599n.
predetermination 608n.
be free 744vb.
title-deed 767n.
bequeath 780vb.
desire 859n.
will and pleasure
will 595n.
command 737n.
willful
volitional 595adj.
willful 602adj.
capricious 604adj.
rash 857adj.
willies
nervousness 854n.
willing
volitional 595adj.
willing 597adj.
resolute 599adj.
active 678adj.
obedient 739adj.
cheerful 833adj.
willingness
assent 488n.
persuasibility 612n.
cooperation 706n.
consent 758n.
desire 859n.
(*see* will, willing)
will of heaven
fate 596n.
will of one's own, have a
be free 744vb.
will-o'-the-wisp
insubstantial thing 4n.
glow 417n.
glow-worm 420n.
visual fallacy 440n.
deception 542n.
incentive 612n.
willow
tree 366n.
lamentation 836n.
willow pattern
pottery 381n.
willowy
narrow 206adj.
shapely 841adj.
will-power
will 595n.
resolution 599n.
willy-nilly
necessarily 596adv.
wilt
be weak 163vb.
deteriorate 655vb.
knuckle under 721vb.
be dejected 834vb.
wily
intelligent 498adj.
deceiving 542adj.
cunning 698adj.
wimple
headgear 228n.
win
superiority 34n.
victory 727n.
win 727vb.
acquire, gain 771vb.
appropriate 786vb.
wince
recoil 280vb.
feel pain 377vb.
show feeling 818vb.
suffer 825vb.
quake 854vb.
winch
lifter 310n.
wind
insubstantial thing 4n.
disable 161vb.
velocity 277n.
voidance 300n.
circle 314vb.
rotate 315vb.
gas 336n.
flow 350vb.
wind 352n.
smell 394vb.
play music 413vb.
detect 484vb.
empty talk 515n.
indigestion 651n.
fatigue 684vb.
hurt 827vb.
windage
room 183n.
windbag
sufflation 352n.
chatterer 581n.
wind-bound
hindered 702adj.
restrained 747adj.
windbreak
wood 366n.
screen 421n.
shelter 662n.
wind-cheater
overcoat 228n.
wind-cone
anemology 352n.
winded
panting 684adj.
winder
handle 218n.
rotator 315n.
windfall
benefit 615n.
non-design 618n.
acquisition 771n.
gift 781n.
receiving 782n.
wind-gauge
velocity 277n.
anemology 352n.
wind in
draw 288vb.
windiness
rarity 325n.
gaseity 336n.
wind, respiration 352n.
winding
complex 61adj.
meandering 251n.
convoluted 251adj.
deviating 282adj.
flowing 350adj.
dishonest 930adj.
winding sheet
wrapping 226n.
robe 228n.
grave clothes 364n.
wind-jammer
sailing-ship 275n.
windlass
traction 288n.
lifter 310n.
windless
tranquil 266adj.
windmill
rotator 315n.
window
window 263n.
brittleness 330n.
air-pipe 353n.
transparency 422n.
window-dressing
duplicity 541n.
ostentation 875n.
windowed
perforated 263adj.
windowless
opaque 423adj.

insalubrious 653adj.
window-seat
seat 218n.
window-shopper
inquisitor 453n.
purchaser 792n.
window-sill
shelf 218n.
windpipe
respiration 352n.
air-pipe 353n.
wind-rose
anemology 352n.
windrow
series 71n.
windshield
screen 421n.
shelter 662n.
windshield wiper
cleaning utensil 648n.
wind-sock
anemology 352n.
indicator 847n.
windswept
orderless 61adj.
windy 352adj.
wind the clock
time 117vb.
wind the horn
play music 413vb.
wind-tunnel
anemology 352n.
testing agent 461n.
wind up
terminate 69vb.
strengthen 162vb.
operate 173vb.
invigorate 174vb.
draw 288vb.
elevate 310vb.
make ready 669vb.
sell 793vb.
fear 854n.
wind-up
finality 69n.
windward
laterality 239n.
wind-way
air-pipe 353n.
windy
unmeaning 315adj.
gaseous 336adj.
airy 340adj.
windy 352adj.
diffuse 570adj.
loquacious 581adj.
trivial 639adj.
nervous 854adj.
ostentatious 875adj.
wine
wine 301n.
drink 301vb.
redness 431n.
wine-bibbing
drinking 301n.
drunkenness 949n.
wine cellar
tavern 192n.
wine-cooler
refrigerator 384n.
wineglass
cup 194n.
wine-grower
husbandman 370n.
wine-merchant
provider 633n.
wine of life
sensualism 944n.
winepress
farm tool 370n.
wineskin
vessel 194n.
drunkard 949n.
wing
adjunct 40n.
part, limb 53n.
laterality 239n.
plumage 259n.
wing 271n.
fly 271vb.
move fast 277vb.
wound 655vb.
shelter 662n.
hinder 702vb.
armed force 722n.
air force 722n.
wing-feather
wing 271n.
wing, on the
on the move 265adv.
in flight 271adv.
wings
aircraft 276n.
livery 547n.
stage-set 594n.
wink
look 438vb.
be blind 439vb.
be dim-sighted 440vb.
hint 524n., vb.
indication 547n.
gesture 547n.
command 737vb.
excite love 887vb.
approve 923n.
wink at
disregard 458vb.
permit 756vb.
forgive 909vb.
(*see* connive)
winking
vision 438n.
winkle
fish food 301n.
taking 786n.
winkle out
extract 304vb.
winner
superior 34n.
exceller 644n.
victor 727n.
recipient 782n.
winning
acquiring 771adj.
pleasurable 826adj.
amiable 884adj.
lovable 887adj.
winning hit
success 727n.
winning position
vantage 34n.
winning-post
limit 236n.
objective 617n.
winnings
gain 771n.
receiving 782n.
taking 786n.
booty 790n.
receipt 807n.
winning ways
inducement 612n.
lovableness 887n.
winnow
eliminate 44vb.
exclude 57vb.
aerify 340vb.
cultivate 370vb.
inquire 459vb.
discriminate 463vb.
select 605vb.
purify 648vb.
winnowing fan
farm tool 370n.
win one's spurs
succeed 727vb.
be courageous 855vb.
have repute 866vb.
win over
convince 485vb.
induce 612vb.
pacify 719vb.
winsome
personable 841adj.
lovable 887adj.
winter
pass time 108vb.
period 110n.
winter 129n.
wintriness 380n.
adversity 731n.
visit 882vb.
winterized
heated 381adj.
win the race
outstrip 277vb.
win to
arrive 295vb.
wintriness
winter 129n.
storm 176n.

wintriness 380n.
wintry
wintry 129adj.
black 428adj.
winy
intoxicating 949adj.
wipe
dry 342vb.
touch 378vb.
clean 648vb.
wipe off
obliterate 550vb.
wipe off old scores
pay 804vb.
wipe one's feet on
subjugate 745vb.
wipe out
nullify 2vb.
bate 37vb.
destroy 165vb.
slaughter 362vb.
obliterate 550vb.
defeat 727vb.
wipe out a score
retaliate 714vb.
wipe out one's offense
atone 941vb.
wipe up
dry 342vb.
clean 648vb.
carry through 725vb.
wire
cable 47n.
narrowness 206n.
filament 208n.
information 524n.
communicate 524vb.
message 529n.
telecommunication 531n.
wire-draw
lengthen 203vb.
make thin 206vb.
wire-drawn
long 230adj.
narrow 206adj.
fibrous 208adj.
wireless
telecommunication 531n.
wire-puller
influence 178n.
latency 523n.
motivator 612n.
director 690n.
slyboots 698n.
wire-pulling
plot 623n.
(*see* wire-puller)
wires
influence 178n.
wiry
stalwart 162adj.
fibrous 208adj.
wisdom
thought 449n.
erudition 490n.
wisdom 498n.
caution 858n.
wise
knowing 490adj.
wise 498adj.
foreseeing 510adj.
way 624n.
expedient 642adj.
skillful 694adj.
cunning 698adj.
cautious 858adj.
wiseacre
doctrinaire 473n.
sciolist 493n.
wiseacre 500n.
wise after the event
ill-timed 138adj.
wisecrack
witticism 839n.
wise man
sage 500n.
adviser 691n.
consignee 754n.
sorcerer 983n.
wiser, no
uninstructed 491adj.
wish
will 595n., vb.
desire 859n., vb.
desired object 859n.
curse 899vb.
wishbone
magic instrument 983n.
wishful
ill-reasoned 477adj.
desiring 859adj.
wish-fulfilment
content 828n.
wishful thinking
meditation 449n.
credulity 487n.
fantasy 513n.
desire 859n.
wishing well
magic instrument 983n.
wish one joy
gratulate 886vb.
wish undone
regret 830vb.
dislike 861vb.
be penitent 939vb.
wish-wash
silly talk 515n.
wish well
be benevolent 897vb.
wishy-washy
weak 163adj.
tasteless 387adj.
feeble 572adj.
wisp
insubstantial thing 4n.
piece 53n.
bunch 74n.
filament 208n.
wispy
fragmentary 53adj.
flimsy 163adj.
hairy 259adj.
wistful
desiring 859adj.
wit
know 490vb.
intelligence 498n.
wit 839n.
humorist 839n.
witch
old woman 133n.
a beauty 841n.
eyesore 842n.
hell-hag 904n.
fairy 970n.
sorceress 983n.
witchcraft
power 160n.
sorcery 983n.
witch-doctor
doctor 658n.
sorcerer 983n.
priest 986n.
witchery
inducement 612n.
pleasurableness 826n.
sorcery 983n.
witch-hunt
inquiry, search 459n.
pursuit 619n.
defame 926vb.
witch-hunting
orthodox 976adj.
pietism 979adj.
witching
magical 983adj.
witching time
midnight 129n.
darkness 418n.
witenagemot
parliament 692n.
with
in addition 38adv.
conjointly 45adv.
ligature 47n.
with 89adv.
by means of 629adv.
with a vengeance
extremely 32adv.
crescendo 36adv.
in addition 38adv.
with care
carefully 457adv.
with child
productive 164adj.

withdraw
decrease 37vb.
subtract 39vb.
cease 145vb.
revert 148vb.
go away 190vb.
regress 286vb.
recede 290vb.
depart 296vb.
extract 304vb.
dissent 489vb.
tergiversate 603vb.
recant 603vb.
run away 620vb.
relinquish 621vb.
disuse 674vb.
submit 721vb.
resign 753vb.
not retain 779vb.
take 786vb.
demonetize 797vb.
schismatize 978vb.
withdrawal
disjunction 46n.
escape 667n.
non-use 674n.
opposition 753n.
seclusion 883n.
(*see* withdraw)
withdrawn
shadowy 419adj.
reticent 525adj.
taciturn 582adj.
withdraw permission
prohibit 757vb.
wither
be old 127vb.
become small 198vb.
kill 362vb.
deteriorate 655vb.
make ugly 842vb.
withered
weakened 163adj.
lean 206adj.
dry 342adj.
(*see* wither)
withering
baneful 659adj.
oppressive 735adj.
disapproving 924adj.
withers
angularity 247n.
camber 253n.
with hindsight
retrospective 125adj.
withhold
put off 136vb.
keep secret 525vb.
restrain 747vb.
refuse 760vb.
retain 778vb.
be parsimonious 816vb.
within
inside 224adv.
within an ace of
almost 33adv.
nearly 200adv.
within bounds
partially 33adv.
moderately 177adv.
temperate 942adj.
within call
nigh 200adv.
within one's means
cheap 812adj.
within reach
on the spot 189adj.
accessible 289adj.
possibly 469adv.
easy 701adj.
with interest
in addition 38adv.
within the range of
liable 180adj.
without
if 8adv.
subtracted 39adj.
in deduction 39adv.
unconformably 84adv.
without 190adv.
around 230adv.
losing 772adj.
not owning 774adj.
without a hitch
easily 701adv.
without a leg to stand on
powerless 161adj.
condemned 961adj.
without alternative
choiceless 606adj.
without asking
willingly 597adv.
without, be
fall short 307vb.
without comparison
supreme 34adj.
without complaints
content 828adj.
without contrast
uniform 16adj.
without control
intemperately 943adv.
without credit
unthanked 908adj.
without distinction
identically 13adv.
rightly 913adv.
without end
infinite 107adj.
perpetual 115adj.
without exception
uniformly 16adv.
generally 79adv.
without excuse
accusable 928adj.
guilty 936adj.
without fail
certainly 473adv.
without fight
cowardly 856adj.
without issue
unproductive 172adj.
without loss
undamaged 646adj.
without notice
instantaneously 116adv.
suddenly 135adv.
unexpectedly 508adv.
without number
infinite 107adj.
without omission
inclusive 78adj.
without rights
unentitled 916adj.
without spot
perfect 646adj.
without strings
unconditional 744adj.
without warning
instantaneously 116adv.
unexpected 508adj.
unexpectedly 508adv.
withstand
counteract 182vb.
withstand 704vb.
parry 713vb.
resist 715vb.
be inimical 881vb.
with the stream
easy 701adj.
with the years
in time 111adv.
withy
ligature 47n.
with young
productive 164adj.
witless
foolish 499adj.
witling
wiseacre 500n.
fool 501n.
witness
be present 189vb.
see 438vb.
spectator 441n.
watch 441vb.
testimony 466n.
witness 466n.
reminder 505n.
informant 524n.
label 547n.
sign 547vb.
signatory 765n.
witness-box

courtroom 956n.
wits
intellect 447n.
intelligence 498n.
wit's end, at one's
doubting 474adj.
ignorant 491adj.
in difficulties 700adj.
witticism
witticism 839n.
ridiculousness 849n.
ridicule 851n.
wittingly
purposely 617adv.
wittol
cuckold 952n.
witty
aphoristic 496adj.
forceful 571adj.
gay 833adj.
witty 839adj.
derisive 851adj.
sociable 882adj.
wive
wed 894vb.
wizard
sage 500n.
topping 644adj.
skillful 694adj.
proficient 696n.
sorcerer 983n.
wizardry
skill 694n.
sorcery 983n.
wizened
dwarfish 196adj.
contracted 198adj.
lean 206adj.
woad
pigment 425n.
blue pigment 435n.
wobble
change 143vb.
vary 152vb.
move slowly 278vb.
deviate 282vb.
oscillate 317vb.
be irresolute 601vb.
wobbler
waverer 601n.
wobbly
weak 163adj.
(*see* wobble)
Woden
Nordic gods 967n.
woe
evil 616n.
bane 659n.
sorrow 825n.
woeful
bad 645adj.
suffering 825adj.
distressing 827adj.
melancholic 834adj.
lamenting 836adj.
wog
foreigner 59n.
wold
high land 209n.
plain 348n.
wood 366n.
wolf
violent creature 176n.
eat 301vb.
dog 365n.
taker 786n.
noxious animal 904n.
gluttonize 947vb.
wolf at the door
pitfall 663n.
poverty 801n.
wolf in sheep's clothing
hider 527n.
sham 542n.
impostor 545n.
bungler 697n.
wolfish
feeding 301adj.
animal 365adj.
taking 786adj.
cruel 898adj.
gluttonous 947adj.
wolf-whistle
stridor 407n.
wonder 864n.
woman
adult 134n.
woman 373n.
spouse 894n.
woman-chaser
libertine 952n.
woman-crazy
lecherous 951adj.
woman-hater
misanthrope 902n.
womanhood
adultness 134n.
female 373n.
womanish
weak 163n.
female 373adj.
cowardly 856adj.
womankind
mankind 371n.
womankind 373n.
womanize
be impure 951vb.
womanizer
libertine 952n.
womanly
grownup 134adj.
female 373adj.
womb
seedbed 156n.
genitalia 164n.
parentage 169n.
insides 224n.
wombat
marsupial 365n.
women and children
encumbrance 702n.
womenfolk
womankind 373n.
women's army
women's army 722n.
women's quarters
womankind 373n.
women's rule
gynocracy 733n.
wonder
be uncertain 474vb.
not know 491vb.
inexpectation 508n.
not understand 517vb.
exceller 644n.
wonder 864n., vb.
prodigy 864n.
respect 920n., vb.
wonderful
impossible 47adj.
excellent 644adj.
pleasurable 826adj.
wonderful 864adj.
noteworthy 866adj.
worshipful 866adj.
wondering
puzzled 517adj.
wondering 864adj.
wonderland
fantasy 513n.
pleasure-ground 837n.
prodigy 864n.
wonderman
superior 34n.
bigwig 638n.
exceller 644n.
paragon 646n.
prodigy 864n.
wonder-working
thaumaturgy 864n.
sorcery 983n.
wondrous
wonderful 864adj.
wonky
oblique 220adj.
wont
habit 610n.
use 673n.
woo
pursue 619vb.
request 761vb.
desire 859vb.
be in love 887vb.
court 889vb.
wood
sphere 252n.
missile 287n.
hardness 326n.

wood 366n.
wooden 366adj.
heater 383n.
fuel 385n.
plaything 837n.
woodbine
tobacco 388n.
wood-carving
sculpture 554n.
woodcock
table bird 365n.
fool 501n.
woodcut
picture 553n.
engraving 555n.
woodcutter
forestry 366n.
worker 686n.
wooded
arboreal 366adj.
wooden
wooden 366adj.
impassive 820adj.
wood-engraving
engraving 555n.
woodenhead
dunce 501n.
wooden horse
instrument of torture 964n.
woodenness
obstinacy 602n.
moral insensibility 820n.
wood for the trees, not see the
reason ill 477vb.
woodland
wood 366n.
woodman
dweller 191n.
forestry 366n.
woodnote
ululation 409n.
woodpecker
bird 365n.
wood-pulp
pulpiness 356n.
paper 631n.
wood-wind
orchestra 413n.
musical instrument 414n.
flute 414n.
woodwork
structure 331n.
ornamental art 844n.
woodworker
artisan 686n.
woodworm
vermin 365n.
woody
arboreal 366adj.
wooer
concomitant 89n.
petitioner 763n.
desirer 859n.
lover 887n.
wooing
love-making 887n.
wooing 889n.
caressing 889adj.
wool
fiber 208n.
textile 222n.
woolclip
growth 157n.
woolens
clothing 228n.
warm clothes 381n.
woolfell
skin 226n.
wool-gathering
abstracted 456adj.
wool-grower
breeder 369n.
woollies
underwear 228n.
warm clothes 381n.
woolly
undulatory 251adj.
smooth 258adj.
hairy, fleecy 259adj.
ill-reasoned 477adj.
woolly-headed
ill-reasoned 477adj.
woolpack
cloud 355n.
woolsack
seat 218n.
badge of rule 743n.
tribunal 956n.
woomera
missile weapon 723n.
woomerang
missile weapon 723n.
woozy
tipsy 949adj.
word
testimony 466n.
maxim 496n.
information 524n.
hint 524n.
news, message 529n.
oath 532n.
call 547n.
word 559n.
phrase 563n.
speech 579n.
warning 664n.
command 737n.
promise 764n.
Word
God the Son 965n.
word and a blow
contention 716n.
irascibility 892n.
wordbook
dictionary 559n.
word-fence
sophistry 477n.
wit 839n.
word-for-word
imitatively 20adv.
interpretive 520adj.
word, in a
concisely 569adv.
wordiness
word 559n.
diffuseness 570n.
loquacity 581n.
wording
phrase 563n.
word in the ear
hint 524n.
allocution 583n.
wordless
voiceless 578adj.
wondering 864adj.
word list
word list 87n.
dictionary 559n.
Word of God
scripture 975n.
word of honor
promise 764n.
word of mouth
tradition 127n.
message 529n.
speech 579n.
word order
grammar 564n.
word-painting
imagination 513n.
description 590n.
word-play
equivocalness 518n.
trope 519n.
neology 560n.
wit 839n.
words
phrase 563n.
reading matter 589n.
quarrel 709n.
contention 716n.
word-spinner
phrasemonger 574n.
speaker 579n.
word-spinning
style 566n.
diffuseness 570n.
eloquence 579n.
wordstock
dictionary 559n.
word to the wise
hint 524n.
wordy
verbal 559adj.
prolix 570adj.

work
product 164n.
agency 173n.
operate 173vb.
effervesce 318vb.
structure 331n.
musical piece 412n.
book 589n.
stage play 594n.
persevere 600vb.
business 622n.
function 622vb.
busy oneself 622vb.
be instrumental 628vb.
suffice 635vb.
be useful 640vb.
be expedient 642vb.
action 676n.
be busy 678vb.
labor 682n.
fatigue 684vb.
be successful 727vb.
use 763vb.
ornamental art 844n.
workable
powerful 160adj.
operative 173adj.
possible 469adj.
expedient 642adj.
workaday
plain 573adj.
businesslike 622adj.
work against
counteract 182vb.
be inexpedient 643vb.
oppose 704vb.
work-basket
basket 194n.
worked
variegated 437adj.
ornamented 844adj.
worked up
matured 669adj.
angry 891adj.
worker
producer 167n.
doer 676n.
busy person 678n.
worker 686n.
slave 742n.
workhouse
retreat 192n.
workshop 687n.
work in
intromit 231vb.
working arrangement
substitute 150n.
working capital
means 629n.
working-class
plebeian 869adj.
working classes
social group 371n.
personnel 686n.
working day
period 110n.
job 622n.
labor 682n.
working life
labor 682n.
working model
image 551n.
working order, in
prepared 669adj.
workings
structure 331n.
working to rule
slowness 278n.
working toward
tending 179adj.
workman
doer 676n.
worker 686n.
commoner 869n.
workmanlike
industrious 678adj.
well-made 694adj.
workmanship
production 164n.
deed 676n.
(*see* skill)
work of art
composition 56n.
a beauty 841n.
work of supererogation
extra 40n.
voluntary work 597n.
redundance 637n.
work on
use 673vb.
excite 821vb.
(*see* work upon)
work one's way up
climb 308vb.
succeed 727vb.
prosper 730vb.
work out
do sums 86vb.
result 157vb.
decipher 520vb.
plan 623vb.
mature 669vb.
carry through 725vb.
work-out
exercise 682n.
work over
pass 305vb.
think 449vb.
work-party
band 74n.
inquiry 459n.
workpeople
personnel 686n.
workroom
chamber 194n.
workshop 687n.
works
component 58n.
structure 331n.
machine 630n.
workshop 687n.
workshop
activity 678n.
workshop 687n.
shop 796n.
work-shy
lazy 679adj.
work together
cooperate 706vb.
work up
influence 178vb.
use 673vb.
excite 821vb.
work up into
efform 243vb.
work upon
operate 173vb.
influence 178vb.
motivate 612vb.
world
substantiality 3n.
great quantity 32n.
whole 52n.
comprehensive 52adj.
multitude 104n.
affairs 154n.
space 183n.
materiality 319n.
world 321n.
telluric 321adj.
mankind 371n.
sociality 882n.
world-beater
superior 34n.
victor 727n.
world-hater
misanthrope 902n.
world, in the
laical 987adj.
worldling
egotist 932n.
irreligionist 974n.
impious person 980n.
worldly
material 319adj.
telluric 321adj.
selfish 932adj.
irreligious 974adj.
worldly wisdom
skill 694n.
caution 858n.
selfishness 932n.
world of nature
substantiality 3n.
matter 319n.
world's end
extremity 69n.
farness 199n.

world-shaking
revolutionary 149adj.
world-shattering
influential 178adj.
important 638adj.
world-stuff
substantiality 3n.
world to come
destiny 155n.
world-weary
bored 838adj.
world-wide
extensive 32adj.
comprehensive 52adj.
inclusive 78adj.
universal 79adj.
spacious 183adj.
ubiquitous 189adj.
telluric 321adj.
worm
destroyer 168n.
animalcule 196n.
coil, serpent 251n.
wriggle 251vb.
reptile 365n.
blight 659n.
noxious animal 904n.
cad 938n.
worm-eaten
dilapidated 655adj.
worm in
intromit 231vb.
worm into
enter 297vb.
worm out
discover 484vb.
wormwood
unsavoriness 391n.
sourness 393n.
badness 645n.
bane 659n.
wormy
animal 365adj.
worn
weakened 163adj.
lean 206adj.
shown 522adj.
dilapidated 655adj.
used 673adj.
fatigued 684adj.
unsightly 842adj.
worn out
impotent 161adj.
useless 641adj.
deteriorated 655adj.
dilapidated 655adj.
worried
in difficulties 700adj.
worry
chew 301vb.
agitate 318vb.
thought 449n.
carefulness 457n.
expectation 507n.
evil 616n.
bane 659n.
adversity 731n.
impress 821vb.
worry 825n.
suffer 825vb.
annoyance 827n.
incommode 827vb.
dejection 834n.
nervousness 854n.
worse
deteriorated 655adj.
worse and worse
aggravatedly 832adv.
worse for
deteriorated 655adj.
worse for wear
weakened 163adj.
dilapidated 655adj.
worsen
impair 655vb.
deteriorate 655vb.
aggravate 832vb.
worship
honor 866vb.
love 887n., vb.
respect 920n., vb.
piety 979n.
worship 981n., vb.
idolatry 982n.
deification 982n.
worshiper
desirer 859n.
church member 976n.
pietist 979n.
worshiper 981n.
idolater 982n.
worshipful
great 32adj.
worshipful 866adj.
respected 920adj.
godlike 965adj.
sanctified 979adj.
devotional 981adj.
worship, place of
temple 990n.
worst
be superior 34vb.
defeat 727vb.
worsted
fiber 208n.
textile 222n.
defeated 728adj.
worst intentions
malevolence 898n.
worst, the
ill fortune 731n.
wort
plant 366n.
worth
equivalent 28adj.
quid pro quo 150n.
utility 640n.
goodness 644n.
price 809n.
virtues 933n.
worth, be
cost 809vb.
worth considering
important 638adj.
worth its weight in gold
valuable 644adj.
worthless
trivial 639adj.
profitless 641adj.
bad 645adj.
deteriorated 655adj.
contemptible 922adj.
vicious 934adj.
worth nothing
cheap 812adj.
worth, of
of price 811adj.
worth the money
cheap 812adj.
worth-while
good 615adj.
important 638adj.
profitable 640adj.
expedient 642adj.
beneficial 644adj.
approvable 923adj.
worthy
excellent 644adj.
person of repute 866n.
reputable 866adj.
deserving 915adj.
approvable 923adj.
virtuous 933adj.
Wotan
Nordic gods 967n.
would-be
misnamed 562adj.
willing 597adj.
intending 617adj.
hoping 852adj.
desiring 859adj.
ostentatious 875adj.
unwarranted 916adj.
wound
cut 46vb.
weaken 163vb.
strike 279vb.
pain 377n.
ill-treat 645vb.
wound 655n., vb.
hinder 702vb.
hurt 827vb.
huff 891vb.
wounds
trophy 729n.
woven
correlative 12adj.

crossed 222adj.
textural 331adj.
wove paper
stationery 586n.
wowser
sectarist 978n.
religionist 979n.
wrack
ruin 615n.
plant 366n.
wraith
visual fallacy 440n.
ghost 970n.
wraith-like
lean 206adj.
spooky 970adj.
wrangle
disagreement 25n.
argue 475vb.
dissent 489vb.
quarrel 709n.
bicker 709vb.
wrangler
computer 86n.
reasoner 475n.
opponent 705n.
quarreler 709n.
combatant 722n.
wrap
tie 45vb.
cover 226vb.
dress 228vb.
enclose 235vb.
warm clothes 381n.
wrap-around
circumjacence 230n.
wrapped up in
obsessed 455adj.
wrapped up in oneself
selfish 932adj.
wrapper
receptacle 194n.
wrapping 226n.
shawl 228n.
enclosure 235n.
warm clothes 381n.
wrapping
receptacle 194n.
wrapping 226n.
wrap up
dress 228vb.
be hot 379vb.
wrath
hatred 888n.
anger 891n.
wreak one's malice
ill-treat 645vb.
wreak one's spite
be malevolent 898vb.
wreak vengeance
be severe 735vb.
avenge 910vb.
wreath
crossing 222n.
loop 250n.
badge, heraldry 547n.
objective 617n.
trophy 729n.
ornamentation 844n.
honors 866n.
wreathe
enlace 222vb.
twine 251vb.
decorate 844vb.
celebrate 876vb.
pay respects 884vb.
wreathe around
surround 230vb.
wreck
remainder 41n.
destroy 165vb.
dilapidation 655n.
impair 655vb.
defeat 728n.
debauch 951vb.
wreckage
remainder 41n.
ruin 165n.
wrecker
destroyer 168n.
trouble-maker 663n.
rioter 738n.
robber 789n.
evildoer 904n.
wrecking activities
destruction 165n.
revolt 738n.
wren
bird 365n.
wrench
disjoin 46vb.
disable 161vb.
be vigorous 174vb.
violence 176n.
force 176vb.
impulse 279n.
draw 288vb.
extraction 304n.
extractor 304n.
misinterpret 521vb.
tool 630n.
nippers 778n.
wrest
distort 246vb.
misinterpret 521vb.
wrestle
withstand 704vb.
wrestling 716n.
contend 716vb.
wrestler
athlete 162n.
combatant 722n.
wretch
unlucky person 731n.
sufferer 825n.
knave 938n.
wretched
unimportant 639adj.
bad, not nice 645adj.
unfortunate 731adj.
unhappy 825adj.
melancholic 834adj.
rascally 930adj.
wriggle
wriggle 251vb.
be cunning 698vb.
be excited 821vb.
suffer 825vb.
wriggle out of
plead 614vb.
fail in duty 918vb.
wring
extract 304vb.
give pain 377vb.
clean 648vb.
levy 786vb.
wringer
smoother 258n.
drier 342n.
wring one's hand
greet 884vb.
wring one's hands
be impotent 161vb.
lament 836vb.
wring out
dry 342vb.
wring the neck of
kill 362vb.
wrinkle
grow old 131vb.
become small 198vb.
angulate 247vb.
convolution 251n.
crinkle 251vb.
roughen 259vb.
fold 261n., vb.
groove 262vb.
idea 451n.
hint 524n.
trickery 542n.
impair 655vb.
stratagem 698n.
wrinkled
unsightly 842adj.
wrinkle the nose
despise 922vb.
wrist
joint 45n.
wristband
sleeve 228n.
wristlet
jewelry 844n.
wristwatch
timekeeper 117n.
writ
precept 693n.
warrant 737n.
mandate 751n.
security 767n.

law 953n.
legal process 959n.
write
communicate 524vb.
mark 547vb.
record 548vb.
write 586vb.
describe 590vb.
write back
answer 460vb.
write down
record 548vb.
write 586vb.
account 808vb.
write-down
article 591n.
write off
relinquish 621vb.
disuse 674vb.
writer
recorder 549n.
penman 586n.
author 589n.
dissertator 591n.
writership
writing 586n.
writer to the signet
law agent 958n.
write to
correspond 588vb.
be sociable 882vb.
write up
dissert 591vb.
account 808vb.
praise 923vb.
write-up
publicity 528n.
article 591n.
writhe
vary 152vb.
distort 246vb.
wriggle 251vb.
leap 312vb.
be agitated 318vb.
feel pain 377vb.
be excited 821vb.
suffer 825vb.
writing
composition 56n.
production 164n.
writing 586n.
writing materials
stationery 586n.
writing on the wall
warning 664n.
danger signal 665n.
threat 900n.
writing room
chamber 194n.
stationery 586n.
writings
writing 586n.
reading matter 589n.
written
informative 524adj.
literary 557adj.
written 586adj.
written character
letter 558n.
written constitution
permanence 144n.
fixture 153n.
law 953n.
wrong
unapt 25adj.
erroneous 495n.
evil 616n., adj.
amiss 616adv.
inexpedient 643adj.
ill-treat 645vb.
oppress 735vb.
wrong 914n., adj.
do wrong 914vb.
unwarranted 916adj.
foul play 930n.
dishonest 930adj.
wickedness 934n.
heinous 934adj.
lawbreaking 954n.
wrong address
irrelation 10n.
irrelevant 10adj.
wrongdoer
evildoer 904n.
wrongdoing
wickedness 934n.
lawbreaking 954n.
wrongful
bad 645adj.
wrong 914adj.
illegal 954adj.
wrong-headed
misjudging 481adj.
erroneous 495n.
unintelligent 499adj.
wrong 914adj.
wrongheadedness
obstinacy 602n.
wrong idea
error 495n.
wrong side
contrariety 14n.
rear 238n.
wrong side out
reversibly 148adv.
inverted 221adj.
wrong time
intempestivity 138n.
wrong 'un
bad man 938n.
wrought
matured 669adj.
wrought out
completed 725adj.
wrought up
excited 821adj.
angry 891adj.
wrought work
ornamental art 844n.
wry
oblique 220adj.
distorted 246adj.
Wycliffism
heresy 977n.
wynd
street 192n.
road 624n.
wyvern
rara avis 84n.

X

x
number 85n.
xanthin
yellow pigment 433n.
Xanthippe
shrew 892n.
xanthoma
yellowness 433n.
xebec
sailing ship 275n.
xenophile
xenophile 880n.
xenophobe
enemy 881n.
xenophobia
prejudice 481n.
phobia 854n.
dislike 861n.
hatred 888n.
xeroma
skin disease 651n.
xerophagy
fasting 946n.
xerophilous
dry 342adj.
X-ray
radiation 417n.
inquire 459vb.
photography 551n.
X-shaped
crossed 222adj.
xylography
engraving 555n.
xyloid
wooden 366adj.
xylophone
piano 414n.
gong 414n.

Y

yacht
go to sea 269vb.
sailing-ship 275n.
amuse oneself 837vb.
yachter, yachtsman

boatman 270n.
yachting
water travel 269n.
aquatics 269n.
sport 837n.
yahoo
low fellow 869n.
Yajurveda
non-Biblical scripture 975n.
yak
cattle 365n.
Yaksha
mythical being 970n.
yale
heraldry 547n.
Yale lock
fastening 47n.
yam
tuber 301n.
yammer
cry 408vb.
weep 836vb.
yank
draw 288vb.
Yankee
native 191n.
yap
cry 408vb.
ululation 409n.
Yarborough
ill fortune 731n.
yard
place 185n.
long measure 203n.
supporter 218n.
enclosure 235n.
open space 263n.
workshop 687n.
yard-arm
supporter 218n.
yardstick
counting instrument 86n.
testing agent 461n.
gauge 465n.
yarn
fiber 208n.
news 529n.
fable 543n.
exaggeration 546n.
be diffuse 570vb.
narrative 590n.
yarner
liar 545n.
narrator 590n.
yashmak
cloak 228n.
yataghan
side-arms 723n.
yaw
vary 152vb.
navigate 269vb.
deviate 282vb.
yawl
sailing-ship 275n.
ululate 409vb.
yawn
opening 263n.
sleep 679vb.
be fatigued 684vb.
yawning
deep 211adj.
open 263adj.
sleepy 679adj.
yawning gulf
gap 201n.
yawp
stridor 407n.
cry 408vb.
ululate 409vb.
yaws
skin disease 651n.
yea
assent 488n.
yea and nay
changeableness 152n.
yean
reproduce itself 164vb.
year
date 108n.
period 110n.
contemporary 123n.
year in year out
repeatedly 106adv.
yearling
youngling 132n.
cattle 365n.
yearly
seasonal 141adj.
periodically 141adv.
yearn
be dejected 834vb.
desire 859vb.
yearning
desire 859n.
love 887n.
yearn over
pity 905vb.
year, regnal
date 108n.
years
time 108n.
diuturnity 113n.
age 131n.
years of discretion
adultness 134n.
years, riper
adultness 134n.
yeast
lifter 310n.
leaven 323n.
bubble 355n.
yeasty
light 323adj.
bubbly 355adj.
yegg, yeggman
thief 789n.
yell
feel pain 377vb.
cry 408n., vb.
rejoicing 833n.
weep 836vb.
yeller
cry 408n.
yellow
color 425vb.
yellow 433adj.
gild 433vb.
unhealthy 651adj.
cowardly 856adj.
rascally 930adj.
yellow-eyed
jealous 911adj.
yellow fever
yellowness 433n.
infection 651n.
yellow flag
flag 547n.
danger signal 665n.
yellow peril
trouble-maker 663n.
yellow press
the press 528n.
bad taste 847n.
yellow streak
cowardice 856n.
yelp
stridor 407n.
ululation 409n.
yen
coinage 797n.
desire 859n.
yeoman
male 372n.
husbandman 370n.
soldier 722n.
cavalry 722n.
possessor 776n.
countryman 869n.
yeomanly
courageous 855adj.
yeomanry
habitancy 191n.
soldier 722n.
army, cavalry 722n.
yerk
impel 279vb.
yes
assent 488n.
yes-man
imitator 20n.
assenter 488n.
toady 879n.
flatterer 925n.
yesterday
preterition 125n.
formerly 125adv.

yet
while 108adv.
before 119adv.
retrospectively 125adv.
nevertheless 468adv.
yeti
animal 365n.
mythical being 970n.
yet to come
unborn 2adj.
future 124adj.
yew
tree 366n.
yield
be inferior 35vb.
conform 83vb.
be weak 163vb.
product 164n.
reproduce itself 164vb.
soften 327vb.
acquiesce 488vb.
be irresolute 601vb.
be induced 612vb.
relinquish 621vb.
provide 633vb.
submit 721vb.
obey 739vb.
consent 758vb.
be profitable 771vb.
not retain 779vb.
give 781vb.
yielding
unstable 152adj.
wieldy 701adj.
(*see* yield)
yield up
restore 656vb.
yodel
sing 413vb.
Yoga
philosophy 449n.
asceticism 945n.
religion 973n.
yogi
sage 500n.
ascetic 945n.
yogism
occultism 984n.
yogurt, yoghurt
milk product 301n.
yoick, yoicks
cry 408n.
yoke
affix 45vb.
coupling 47n.
duality 90n.
pair 90vb.
hanger 217n.
supporter 218n.
break in 369vb.
servitude 745n.
fetter 748n.
yoked
combined 50adj.
yoke-fellow
concomitant 89n.
collaborator 707n.
yokel
native 191n.
countryman 869n.
yonder
distant 199adj.
afar 199adv.
yoni
genitalia 164n.
idol 982n.
yorker
propulsion 287n.
young
new 126adj.
vernal 128adj.
young 130adj.
infantine 132adj.
strong 162adj.
weak 163adj.
product 164n.
posterity 170n.
immature 670adj.
young blood
youth 130n.
younger
subsequent 120adj.
young 130adj.
Young Guard
armed force 722n.
youngling
youngling 132n.
young man
lover 887n.
youngster
youngster 132n.
your honor
title 870n.
yourself
self 80n.
youth
beginning 68n.
newness 126n.
youth 130n.
youngster 132n.
adult 134n.
youthful
young 130adj.
strong 162adj.
yo-yo
rotator 315n.
plaything 837n.
yuletide
festivity 837n.
holy-day 988n.

Z

zamindar
owner 776n.
zamindari
lands 777n.
zamorin
potentate 741n.
zany
laughing-stock 851n.
Zarathustrianism
religious faith 973n.
zareba
barrier 235n.
enclosure 235n.
shelter 662n.
fort 713n.
zeal
keenness 174n.
willingness 597n.
resolution 599n.
warm feeling 818n.
desire 859n.
zealot
doctrinaire 473n.
narrow mind 481n.
opinionist 602n.
busy person 678n.
religionist 979n.
zealotry
opiniatry 602n.
zealous
willing 597adj.
active 678adj.
fervent 818adj.
zebra
animal 365n.
striation 437n.
zebra crossing
road 624n.
refuge 662n.
traffic control 305n.
zeitgeist
tendency 179n.
zemstvo
council 692n.
zenana
womankind 373n.
love-nest 887n.
Zend-Avesta
non-Biblical scripture 975n.
zenith
superiority 34n.
summit 213n.
zenithal
topmost 213adj.
zephyr
vest 228n.
breeze 352n.
zeppelin
airship 276n.
air force 722n.
zero
insubstantiality 4n.
quantity 26n.

smallness 33n.
zero 103n.
coldness 380n.
zero hour
start 68n.
date 108n.
departure 269n.
zest
vigorousness 174n.
enjoyment 824n.
liking 859n.
zetetic
inquiring 459adj.
Zeus
mythic god 966n.
Olympian god 967n.
ziggurat
high structure 209n.
temple 990n.
zigzag
obliquity 220n.
be oblique 220vb.
angularity 247n.
angular 247adj.
angulate 247vb.
meandering 251n.
meander 251vb.
deviation 282n.
deviating 282adj.
deviate 282vb.
to and fro 317adv.
circuit 626vb.
pattern 844n.
zincography
engraving 555n.
zingy
topping 644adj.
Zion
focus 76n.
heaven 971n.
holy place 990n.
Zionism
patriotism 901n.
zip
spurt 277n.
move fast 277vb.
zipper
fastening 47n.
zippy
speedy 277adj.
zircon
gem 844n.
zither
harp 414n.
zodiac
circle 250n.
zodiac 321n.
zodiacal
celestial 321adj.
zodiacal light
heavens 321n.
glow 417n.
luminary 420n.
Zoilism
detraction 926n.
zollverein
association 706n.
society 708n.
treaty 765n.
zombi
corpse 363n.
ghost 970n.
zone
disjunction 46n.
set apart 46vb.
girdle 47n.
region 184n.
layer 208n.
belt 228n.
outline 233n.
enclosure 235n.
loop 250n.
land 344n.
apportion 783vb.
zoo
medley 43n.
dwelling 192n.
zoo 369n.
collection 632n.
zoography
zoology 367n.
zoohygiantics
animal husbandry 369n.
zoolatry
idolatry 982n.
zoological
biological 358adj.
animal 365adj.
zoological 367adj.
zoology
biology 358n.
zoology 367n.
zoom
move fast 277vb.
ascend 308vb.
zoomorphic
animal 365adj.
zoomorphism
animality 365n.
idolatry 982n.
zoonomy
zoology 367n.
zoophyte
animal 365n.
zoot-suiter
low fellow 869n.
Zoroaster
religious teacher 973n.
Zoroastrianism
religious faith 973n.
Zwinglianism
Protestantism 976n.
zymogen
leaven 323n.
zymotic
light 323adj.
infectious 653adj.